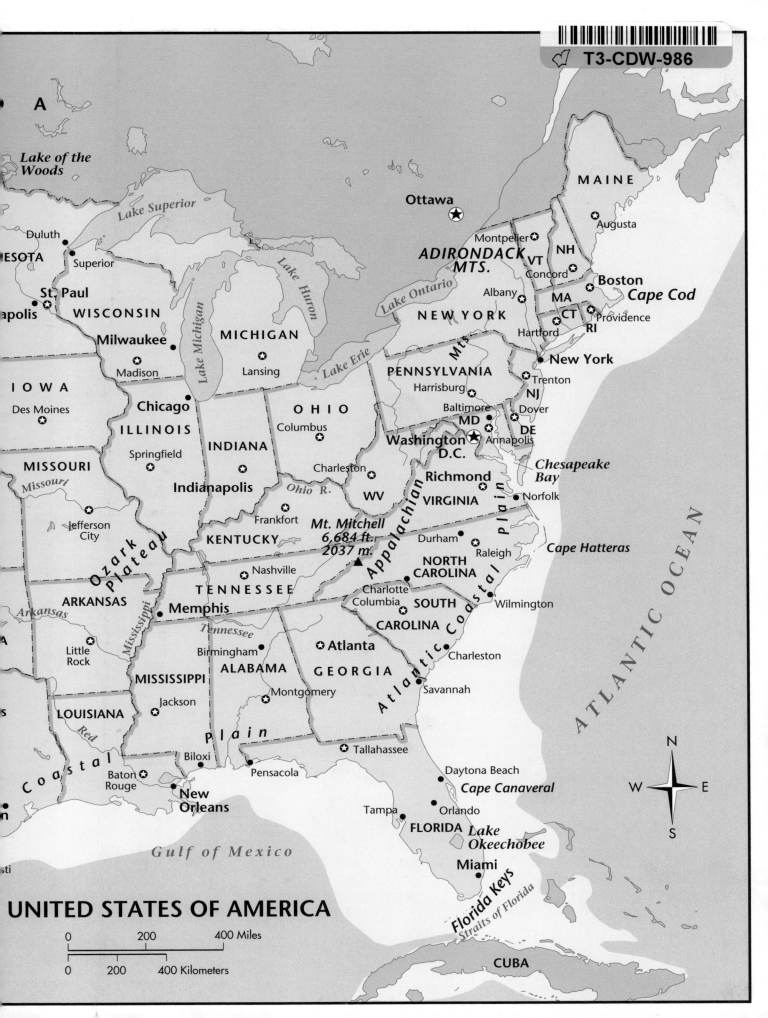

UNITED STATES OF AMERICA

Lake of the Woods

Lake Superior

A

Ottawa

MAINE

Augusta

Montpelier · NH

ADIRONDACK MTS. · VT

Concord

Duluth

Superior

Lake Huron

Lake Michigan

Lake Ontario

Albany

Boston · Cape Cod

MA

Providence

CT

RI

St. Paul

apolis

WISCONSIN

Milwaukee

Madison

MICHIGAN

Lansing

Lake Erie

NEW YORK

Mts.

Hartford

New York

PENNSYLVANIA

Trenton

Harrisburg

NJ

IOWA

Des Moines

Chicago

ILLINOIS

Springfield

INDIANA

Indianapolis

OHIO

Columbus

Charleston

Baltimore

Dover

MD

Washington D.C.

Annapolis

DE

Chesapeake Bay

MISSOURI

Missouri

Jefferson City

Frankfort

KENTUCKY

Nashville

WV

Richmond

VIRGINIA

Norfolk

Appalachian

Mt. Mitchell 6,684 ft. 2037 m.

Durham

Raleigh

NORTH CAROLINA

Cape Hatteras

Ozark Plateau

ARKANSAS

Arkansas

Little Rock

Memphis

Mississippi

TENNESSEE

Tennessee

Charlotte

Columbia

SOUTH CAROLINA

Charleston

Wilmington

Atlantic Coastal Plain

Birmingham

Atlanta

GEORGIA

ATLANTIC OCEAN

ALABAMA

MISSISSIPPI

Jackson

Montgomery

Savannah

LOUISIANA

Red

Coastal

Plain

Biloxi

Pensacola

Tallahassee

Baton Rouge

New Orleans

Daytona Beach

Cape Canaveral

Tampa

Orlando

FLORIDA

Lake Okeechobee

Gulf of Mexico

Miami

Florida Keys

Straits of Florida

CUBA

N
W · E
S

UNITED STATES OF AMERICA

0   200   400 Miles

0   200   400 Kilometers

WORLDMARK
ENCYCLOPEDIA
OF THE STATES

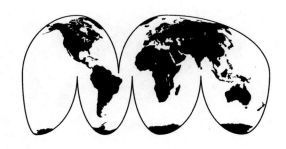

ISSN 1531-1627

WORLDMARK
ENCYCLOPEDIA
OF THE STATES

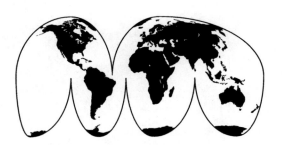

GALE®

THOMSON

™

GALE

Detroit • New York • San Diego • San Francisco • Cleveland • New Haven, Conn. • Waterville, Maine • London • Munich

Worldmark Encyclopedia of the States, Sixth Edition
Timothy L. Gall, Editor in Chief

Project Editor
Mary Rose Bonk

Editorial
Jolen Marya Gedridge

Permissions
Mari Masalin-Cooper

Imaging and Multimedia
Christine O'Bryan

Product Design
Cynthia Baldwin

Manufacturing
Rhonda Williams

ISBN 0-7876-7338-2
ISSN 1531-1627

This title is also available as an e-book
ISBN 0-7876-7774-4
Contact your Gale sales representative for ordering information.

Printed in the United States of America
10 9 8 7 6 5 4 3 2 1

CONTENTS

v

EDITORIAL STAFF

Editor in Chief: Timothy L. Gall

Senior Editors: Jeneen M. Hobby, Jennie B. Watson

Associate Editors: Karen Ellicott, Susan Bevan Gall,
James Henry, Paulette Kurzer, Daniel M. Lucas, Maura E. Malone,
Michael A. Parris, Seth E. Rosenberg, Susan Stern, Jeanne Marie Stumpf,
Rosalie Wieder, Daiva Ziedonis

Cartography: University of Akron Laboratory for Cartographic and Spatial Analysis:
Joseph W. Stoll, Supervisor; Scott Raypholtz; Mike Meyer

CONTRIBUTORS

TO THE FIRST EDITION

ALLEN, HAROLD B. Emeritus Professor of English and Linguistics, University of Minnesota (Minneapolis–St. Paul). LANGUAGES.

BASSETT, T. D. SEYMOUR. Former University Archivist, University of Vermont (Burlington). VERMONT.

BENSON, MAXINE. Curator of Document Resources, Colorado Historical Society. COLORADO.

BROWN, RICHARD D. Professor of History, University of Connecticut (Storrs). MASSACHUSETTS.

CASHIN, EDWARD J. Professor of History, Augusta College. GEORGIA.

CHANNING, STEVEN A. Professor of History, University of Kentucky (Lexington). KENTUCKY.

CLARK, CHARLES E. Professor of History, University of New Hampshire (Durham). MAINE.

COGSWELL, PHILIP, JR. Forum Editor, *The Oregonian.* OREGON.

CONLEY, PATRICK T. Professor of History and Law, Providence College. RHODE ISLAND.

CORLEW, ROBERT E. Dean, School of Liberal Arts, Middle Tennessee State University (Murfreesboro). TENNESSEE.

CREIGH, DOROTHY WEYER. Author and historian; member, Nebraska State Board of Education. NEBRASKA.

CUNNINGHAM, JOHN T. Author and historian. NEW JERSEY.

FISHER, PERRY. Director, Columbia Historical Society. DISTRICT OF COLUMBIA.

FRANTZ, JOE B. Professor of History, University of Texas (Austin). TEXAS.

GOODELL, LELE. Member, Editorial Board, *Hawaiian Journal of History.* HAWAII (in part).

GOODRICH, JAMES W. Associate Director, State Historical Society of Missouri. MISSOURI.

HAMILTON, VIRGINIA. Professor of History, University of Alabama (Birmingham). ALABAMA.

HAVIGHURST, WALTER. Research Professor of English Emeritus, Miami University (Oxford). OHIO.

HINTON, HARWOOD P. Editor, *Arizona and the West,* University of Arizona (Tucson). ARIZONA.

HOOGENBOOM, ARI. Professor of History, Brooklyn College of the City University of New York. PENNSYLVANIA.

HOOVER, HERBERT T. Professor of History, University of South Dakota (Vermillion). SOUTH DAKOTA.

HUNT, WILLIAM R. Historian; former Professor of History, University of Alaska. ALASKA.

JENSEN, DWIGHT. Author and historian. IDAHO.

JENSEN, RICHARD J. Professor of History, University of Illinois (Chicago). ILLINOIS.

LARSON, ROBERT W. Professor of History, University of Northern Colorado (Greeley). NEW MEXICO.

MAPP, ALF J., JR. Author, lecturer, and historian; Professor of English, Creative Writing, and Journalism, Old Dominion University (Norfolk). VIRGINIA.

MAY, GEORGE S. Professor of History, Eastern Michigan University (Ypsilanti). MICHIGAN.

MEYER, GLADYS. Professor emeritus, Columbia University. ETHNIC GROUPS.

MOODY, ERIC N. Historian, Nevada Historical Society. NEVADA.

MUNROE, JOHN A. H. Rodney Sharp Professor of History, University of Delaware. DELAWARE.

MURPHY, MARIAM. Associate Editor, *Utah Historical Quarterly.* UTAH.

O'BRIEN, KATHLEEN ANN. Project Director, Upper Midwest Women's History Center for Teachers. MINNESOTA.

PADOVER, SAUL K. Distinguished Service Professor Emeritus, Graduate Faculty, New School (New York City). UNITED STATES OF AMERICA.

PECKHAM, HOWARD H. Professor emeritus, University of Michigan. INDIANA.

PRYOR, NANCY. Research consultant and librarian, Washington State Library. WASHINGTON.

RAWLS, JAMES J. Instructor of History, Diablo Valley College (Pleasant Hill). CALIFORNIA.

RICE, OTIS K. Professor of History, West Virginia Institute of Technology (Montgomery). WEST VIRGINIA.

RICHMOND, ROBERT W. Assistant Executive Director, Kansas State Historical Society. KANSAS.

RIGHTER, ROBERT W. Assistant Professor of History, University of Wyoming (Laramie). WYOMING.

ROTH, DAVID M. Director, Center for Connecticut Studies, Eastern Connecticut State College (Willimantic). CONNECTICUT.

SCHEFFER, BARBARA MOORE. Feature Writer. OKLAHOMA (in part).

SCHEFFER, WALTER F. Regents' Professor of Political Science and Director, Graduate Program in Public Administration, University of Oklahoma (Norman). OKLAHOMA (in part).

SCHMITT, ROBERT C. Hawaii State Statistician. HAWAII (in part).

SCUDIERE, PAUL J. Senior Historian, New York State Education Department. NEW YORK.

SKATES, JOHN RAY. Professor of History, University of Southern Mississippi (Hattiesburg). MISSISSIPPI.

SMITH, DOUG. Writer, *Arkansas Gazette* (Little Rock). ARKANSAS.

STOUDEMIRE, ROBERT H. Professor of State and Local Government and Senior Research Associate, Bureau of Governmental Research, University of South Carolina (Columbia). SOUTH CAROLINA.

SULLIVAN, LARRY E. Librarian, New York Historical Society. MARYLAND.

TAYLOR, JOE GRAY. Professor of History, McNeese State University (Lake Charles). LOUISIANA.

TEBEAU, CHARLTON W. Emeritus Professor of History, University of Miami. FLORIDA.

THOMPSON, WILLIAM FLETCHER. Director of Research, State Historical Society of Wisconsin. WISCONSIN.

VIVO, PAQUITA. Author and consultant. PUERTO RICO.

WALL, JOSEPH FRAZIER. Professor of History, Grinnell College. IOWA.

WALLACE, R. STUART. Assistant Director/Editor, New Hampshire Historical Society. NEW HAMPSHIRE.

WATSON, HARRY L. Assistant Professor of History, University of North Carolina (Chapel Hill). NORTH CAROLINA.

WEAVER, KENNETH L. Associate Professor of Political Science, Montana State University (Bozeman). MONTANA.

WILKINS, ROBERT P. Professor of History, University of North Dakota (Grand Forks). NORTH DAKOTA.

WOODS, BOB. Editor, *Sierra Club Wildlife Involvement News.* FLORA AND FAUNA.

PREFACE

In 1980, editor and publisher Moshe Y. Sachs set out to create the *Worldmark Encyclopedia of the Nations,* a new kind of reference work that would view every nation of the world as if through a "world mirror" and not from the perspective of any one country or group of countries. In 1981, a companion volume, the *Worldmark Encyclopedia of the States,* was introduced. It was selected as an "Outstanding Reference Source" by the Reference Sources Committee of the American Library Association, Reference and Adult Services Division. The Gale Group now offers a revised and updated sixth edition of the *Worldmark Encyclopedia of the States.*

The fitness of the United States of America as a subject for encyclopedic study is plain. No discussion of world politics, economics, culture, technology, or military affairs would be complete without an intensive examination of the American achievement. What is not so obvious is why the editors chose to present this work as an encyclopedia of the *states* rather than of the United States. In so doing, they emphasize the fact that the United States is a federal union of separate states with divergent histories, traditions, resources, laws, and economic interests.

Every state, large or small, is treated in an individual chapter, within a framework of 50 standard subject headings; generally, the more populous the state, the longer the article. The District of Columbia and the Commonwealth of Puerto Rico each have their own chapters, and two additional articles describe in summary the other Caribbean and Pacific dependencies. The concluding chapter is an overview of the nation as a whole. Supplementing this textual material are tables of conversions and abbreviations, a glossary, and more than 50 black-and-white maps prepared especially for this encyclopedia.

Publication of this encyclopedia was a collective effort that enlisted the talents of scholars, government agencies, editor-writers, artists, cartographers, typesetters, proofreaders, and many others. Perhaps only those involved in the production of reference books fully appreciate how complex that endeavor can be. Readers customarily expect that a reference book will be correct in every particular; and yet, by the time it has been on the shelves for a few months, a conscientious editor may already have a long list of improvements and corrections to be made in a subsequent edition. We invite you, the reader, to add your suggestions to our list.

Send comments to:

Worldmark Encyclopedia of the States
The Gale Group
27500 Drake Road
Farmington Hills, MI 48331

The Editors

NOTES

GENERAL NOTE: In producing the sixth edition of *Worldmark Encyclopedia of the States,* the editors were aided by the wealth of information now available from state governments on the World Wide Web. The information included in this volume from postings by state agencies was supplemented by data from the Census Bureau, the Bureau of Economic Analysis, the National Center for Education Statistics, the Bureau of Justice Statistics, the Department of Energy, the National Science Board, the National Center for Health Statistics, the Federal Highway Administration, the Department of Defense, the Department of Veterans Affairs, the Department of the Interior, the Federal Deposit Insurance Corporation, and a wide variety of additional federal agencies and offices. This state and federal information was indispensable to *Worldmark* editors in revising state articles. Space does not permit listing of the hundreds of additional documents from private sources which were consulted for each state's entry. Listed below are notable sources of data which were used in revising a majority of entries.

MAPS: The maps of the states were produced by the University of Akron Laboratory for Cartographic and Spatial Analysis under the direction of Joseph W. Stoll. The maps originated from the United States Geological Survey 1:2,000,000 Digital Line Graphs (DLG). Additional sources used to determine and verify the positioning of text and symbols include 1990 United States Census Data, USGS 1:500,000 Topographic State Maps, brochures and maps from the state visitor bureaus, and the *Rand McNally United States Road Atlas.* For definitions of abbreviations used on the maps please refer to the section entitled "Abbreviations and Acronyms" appearing on page 859 of this volume.

WEIGHTS AND MEASURES: Recognizing the trend toward use of the metric system throughout the United States, the text provides metric equivalents for customary measures of length and area, and both Fahrenheit and Centigrade expressions for temperature. Production figures are expressed exclusively in the prevailing customary units.

LOCATION, SIZE, AND EXTENT: The lengths of interstate boundary segments and the total lengths of state boundaries appear in roman type when derived from official government sources; italic type indicates data derived from other sources. Discrepancies in the boundary lengths of neighboring states as specified by official sources arise from divergent methodologies of measurement.

FLORA AND FAUNA: Discussions of endangered species are based on the *List of Endangered and Threatened Wildlife and Plants* maintained by the Fish and Wildlife Service of the US Department of the Interior, and on data supplied by the states.

POPULATION: Population figures are from data released by the US Census Bureau's Population Estimates Program as of June 2002. These data can be found at http://eire.census.gov/popest/estimates.php together with a wide variety of additional economic and demographic data collected by the US Department of Commerce and other related federal agencies. Tables of counties, county seats, county areas, and estimates of county populations as of July 2002 accompany the articles on the 14 most populous states; the editors regret that space limitations prevented the publication of such a table for each state. Because of rounding of numbers, county areas in these tables may not equal the total.

LANGUAGES: Examples of lexical and pronunciation patterns cited in the text are meant to suggest the historic development of principal linguistic features and should not be taken as a comprehensive statement of current usage. Data on languages spoken in the home were obtained from "Languages Spoken at Home: 2000" issued online at http://factfinder.census.gov by the US Census Bureau.

TRANSPORTATION: Transportation statistics were compiled from the *Transportation Profile* for each of the states and the District of Columbia published by the Bureau of Transportation Statistics, US Department of Transportation.

JUDICIAL SYSTEM: *Uniform Crime Reports for the United States,* published annually by the Federal Bureau of Investigation and embodying the FBI Crime Index (tabulations of offenses known to the police), was the principal source for the crime statistics cited in the text.

ARMED FORCES: The number of veterans of US military service are as reported by Census 2000. Additional data came from the *State Summary* reports prepared by the Office of Public Affairs, Media Relations, Department of Veterans Affairs issued in 2002 and 2003.

INCOME: Data on income was extracted in part from *State BEARFACTS 2000–2001* published online at http://www.bea.gov/bea/regional/bearfacts by the Bureau of Economic Analysis of the US Department of Commerce.

LABOR: Statistics on the labor force and union membership were obtained from Bureau of Labor Statistics, United States Department of Labor and are available online at http://www.bls.gov.

ENERGY AND POWER: Data for proved reserves and production of fossil fuels were derived from publications of the American Gas Association, American Petroleum Institute, National Coal Association, and US Department of Energy. Data on nuclear power facilities were obtained from the Nuclear Information and Resource Service and from state sources.

INSURANCE: The principal statistical sources for information on insurance were annual publications of the Insurance Information Institute and the American Council of Life Insurance.

PUBLIC FINANCE: Tables of state government revenues and expenditures were obtained from *2002 State Government Tax Collections* and *State Government Finances: 2001* issued by the US Census Bureau and available online at http://www.census.gov/govs/www/statetax02.html and http://www.census.gov/govs.state. Additional information came from the official web sites of the individual states.

HEALTH: The principal statistical sources for hospitals and medical personnel were annual publications of the American Dental Association, American Hospital Association, and American Medical Association.

LIBRARIES AND MUSEUMS: In most cases, library and museum names are listed in the *American Library Directory* by R. R. Bowker, and the *Official Museum Directory,* compiled by the National Register Publishing Co. in cooperation with the American Association of Museums.

PRESS: Circulation data follow the 2002 *Editor & Publisher International Yearbook*.

FAMOUS PERSONS: Entries are current through July 2003. Where a person described in one state is known to have been born in another, the state of birth follows the personal name, in parentheses.

BIBLIOGRAPHY: Bibliographies are intended as a guide to landmark works on each state for further research and not as a listing of sources in preparing the articles. Such listings would have far exceeded space limitations.

GUIDE TO STATE ARTICLES

All information contained within a state article is uniformly keyed by means of small superior numerals to the left of the subject headings. A heading such as "Population," for example, carries the same key numeral (6) in every article. Thus, to find information about the population of Alabama, consult the table of contents for the page number where the Alabama article begins and look for section 6 thereunder.

Introductory matter for each state includes: Origin of state name
Nickname
Capital
Date and order of statehood
Song
Motto
Flag
Official seal
Symbols (animal, tree, flower, etc.)
Legal holidays
Time zone

FLAG COLOR SYMBOLS

 Yellow   Red   Green   Blue   Orange   Brown   White   Black

SUBJECT HEADINGS IN NUMERICAL ORDER

1	Location, size, and extent	27	Mining
2	Topography	28	Energy and power
3	Climate	29	Industry
4	Flora and fauna	30	Commerce
5	Environmental protection	31	Consumer protection
6	Population	32	Banking
7	Ethnic groups	33	Insurance
8	Languages	34	Securities
9	Religions	35	Public finance
10	Transportation	36	Taxation
11	History	37	Economic policy
12	State government	38	Health
13	Political parties	39	Social welfare
14	Local government	40	Housing
15	State services	41	Education
16	Judicial system	42	Arts
17	Armed forces	43	Libraries and museums
18	Migration	44	Communications
19	Intergovernmental cooperation	45	Press
20	Economy	46	Organizations
21	Income	47	Tourism, travel, and recreation
22	Labor	48	Sports
23	Agriculture	49	Famous persons
24	Animal husbandry	50	Bibliography
25	Fishing		
26	Forestry		

SUBJECT HEADINGS IN ALPHABETICAL ORDER

Agriculture	23	Intergovernmental cooperation	19
Animal husbandry	24	Judicial system	16
Armed forces	17	Labor	22
Arts	42	Languages	8
Banking	32	Libraries and museums	43
Bibliography	50	Local government	14
Climate	3	Location, size, and extent	1
Commerce	30	Migration	18
Communications	44	Mining	27
Consumer protection	31	Organizations	46
Economic policy	37	Political parties	13
Economy	20	Population	6
Education	41	Press	45
Energy and power	28	Public finance	35
Environmental protection	5	Religions	9
Ethnic groups	7	Securities	34
Famous persons	49	Social welfare	39
Fishing	25	Sports	48
Flora and fauna	4	State government	12
Forestry	26	State services	15
Health	38	Taxation	36
History	11	Topography	2
Housing	40	Tourism, travel, and recreation	47
Income	21	Transportation	10
Industry	29		
Insurance	33		

EXPLANATION OF SYMBOLS

A fiscal split year is indicated by a stroke (e.g. 1994/95).
A dollar sign ($) stands for US$ unless otherwise indicated.
Note that 1 billion = 1,000 million = 10^9.
The use of a small dash (e.g., 1990–94) normally signifies the full period of calendar years covered (including the end year indicated).

CONVERSION TABLES*

LENGTH

1 centimeter ....0.3937 inch
1 centimeter .... 0.03280833 foot
1 meter (100 centimeters).........................3.280833 feet
1 meter..1.093611 US yards
1 kilometer (1,000 meters) ....0.62137 statute mile
1 kilometer................................0.539957 nautical mile
1 inch.......................................2.540005 centimeters
1 foot (12 inches) ....30.4801 centimeters
1 US yard (3 feet) ....0.914402 meter
1 statute mile (5,280 feet; 1,760 yards) .... 1.609347 kilometers
1 British mile ....1.609344 kilometers
1 nautical mile (1.1508 statute miles
or 6,076.10333 feet) .... 1.852 kilometers
1 British nautical mile (6,080 feet) .... 1.85319 kilometers

AREA

1 sq centimeter .... 0.154999 sq inch
1 sq meter (10,000 sq centimeters) ....10.76387 sq feet
1 sq meter...1.1959585 sq yards
1 hectare (10,000 sq meters) ....2.47104 acres
1 sq kilometer (100 hectares) ....0.386101 sq mile
1 sq inch...................................6.451626 sq centimeters
1 sq foot (144 sq inches) ....0.092903 sq meter
1 sq yard (9 sq feet) ....0.836131 sq meter
1 acre (4,840 sq yards) .... 0.404687 hectare
1 sq mile (640 acres) ....2.589998 sq kilometers

VOLUME

1 cubic centimeter ....0.061023 cubic inch
1 cubic meter
(1,000,000 cubic centimeters) ....35.31445 cubic feet
1 cubic meter............................1.307943 cubic yards
1 cubic inch.........................16.387162 cubic centimeters
1 cubic foot (1,728 cubic inches)............0.028317 cubic meter
1 cubic yard (27 cubic feet) ....0.764559 cubic meter

LIQUID MEASURE

1 liter .... 0.8799 imperial quart
1 liter .... 1.05671 US quarts
1 hectoliter ....21.9975 imperial gallons
1 hectoliter .... 26.4178 US gallons
1 imperial quart ....1.136491 liters
1 US quart .... 0.946333 liter
1 imperial gallon ....0.04546 hectoliter
1 US gallon...........................0.037853 hectoliter

WEIGHT

1 kilogram (1,000 grams)............................35.27396 avoirdupois ounces
1 kilogram.................................32.15074 troy ounces
1 kilogram..........................2.204622 avoirdupois pounds
1 quintal (100 kg) ....220.4622 avoirdupois pounds
1 quintal....................................1.9684125 hundredweights
1 metric ton (1,000 kg) ....1.102311 short tons

1 metric ton .... 0.984206 long ton
1 avoirdupois ounce .... 0.0283495 kilogram
1 troy ounce .... 0.0311035 kilogram
1 avoirdupois pound .... 0.453592 kilogram
1 avoirdupois pound .... 0.00453592 quintal
1 hundred weight (cwt., 112 lb) .... 0.50802 quintal
1 short ton (2,000 lb) .... 0.907185 metric ton
1 long ton (2,240 lb) .... 1.016047 metric tons

ELECTRIC ENERGY

1 horsepower (hp) .... 0.7457 kilowatt
1 kilowatt (kw) ....1.34102 horsepower

TEMPERATURE

Celsius (C) ....Fahrenheit–32 x 5/9
Fahrenheit (F) .... 9/5 Celsius + 32

BUSHELS

	LB	METRIC TON	BUSHELS PER METRIC TON
Barley (US)	48	0.021772	45.931
(UK)	50	0.022680	44.092
Corn (UK, US)	56	0.025401	39.368
Linseed (UK)	52	0.023587	42.396
(Australia, US)	56	0.025401	39.368
Oats (US)	32	0.014515	68.894
(Canada)	34	0.015422	64.842
Potatoes (UK, US)	60	0.027216	36.743
Rice (Australia)	42	0.019051	52.491
(US)	45	0.020412	48.991
Rye (UK, US)	56	0.025401	39.368
(Australia)	60	0.027216	36.743
Soybeans (US)	60	0.027216	36.743
Wheat (UK, US)	60	0.027216	36.743

BAGS OF COFFEE

	LB	KG	BAGS PER METRIC TON
Brazil, Columbia Mexico, Venezuela	132.28	60	16.667
El Salvador	152.12	69	14.493
Haiti	185.63	84.2	11.876

BALES OF COTTON

	LB	METRIC TON	BALES PER METRIC TON
India	392	0.177808	5.624
Brazil	397	0.180000	5.555
US (net)	480	0.217724	4.593
US (gross)	500	0.226796	4.409

PETROLEUM

One barrel = 42 US gallons = 34.97 imperial gallons = 158.99 liters = 0.15899 cubic meter (or 1 cubic meter = 6.2898 barrels).

*Includes units of measure cited in the text, as well as certain other units employed in parts of the English-speaking world.

ALABAMA

State of Alabama

ORIGIN OF STATE NAME: Probably after the Alabama Indian tribe. **NICKNAME:** The Heart of Dixie. **CAPITAL:** Montgomery. **ENTERED UNION:** 14 December 1819 (22nd). **SONG:** "Alabama." **MOTTO:** *Aldemus jura nostra defendere* (We dare defend our rights). **COAT OF ARMS:** Two eagles, symbolizing courage, support a shield bearing the emblems of the five governments (France, England, Spain, Confederacy, US) that have held sovereignty over Alabama. Above the shield is a sailing vessel modeled upon the ships of the first French settlers of Alabama; beneath the shield is the state motto. **FLAG:** Crimson cross of St. Andrew on a square white field. **OFFICIAL SEAL:** Map of Alabama, including names of major rivers and neighboring states, surrounded by the words "Alabama Great Seal." **BIRD:** Yellowhammer. **FISH:** Tarpon. **FLOWER:** Camellia. **TREE:** Southern (longleaf) pine. **GEM:** Star blue quartz. **STONE:** Marble. **MINERAL:** Hematite. **LEGAL HOLIDAYS:** New Year's Day, 1 January; Birthdays of Robert E. Lee and Martin Luther King, Jr., 3rd Monday in January; George Washington's/Thomas Jefferson's Birthdays, 3rd Monday in February; Mardi Gras, February or March; Confederate Memorial Day, 4th Monday in April; Jefferson Davis's Birthday, 1st Monday in June; Independence Day, 4 July; Labor Day, 1st Monday in September; Columbus Day, 2nd Monday in October; Veterans Day, 11 November; Thanksgiving Day, 4th Thursday in November; Christmas Day, 25 December. **TIME:** 6 AM CST = noon GMT.

¹LOCATION, SIZE, AND EXTENT

Located in the eastern south-central US, Alabama ranks 29th in size among the 50 states.

The total area of Alabama is 51,705 sq mi (133,915 sq km), of which land constitutes 50,767 sq mi (131,486 sq km) and inland water 938 sq mi (2,429 sq km). Alabama extends roughly 200 mi (320 km) E-W; the maximum N-S extension is 300 mi (480 km). Alabama is bordered on the N by Tennessee; on the E by Georgia (with part of the line formed by the Chattahoochee River); on the S by Florida (with part of the line defined by the Perdido River) and the Gulf of Mexico; and on the W by Mississippi (with the northernmost part of the line passing through the Tennessee River).

Dauphin Island, in the Gulf of Mexico, is the largest offshore island. The total boundary length of Alabama is 1,044 mi (1,680 km). The state's geographic center is in Chilton County, 12 mi (19 km) SW of Clanton.

²TOPOGRAPHY

Alabama is divided into four major physiographic regions: the Gulf Coastal Plain, Piedmont Plateau, Ridge and Valley section, and Appalachian (or Cumberland) Plateau. The physical characteristics of each province have significantly affected settlement and industrial development patterns within the state.

The coastal plain, comprising the southern half of Alabama, consists primarily of lowlands and low ridges. Included within the coastal plain is the Black Belt—historically, the center of cotton production and plantation slavery in Alabama—an area of rich, chalky soil that stretches across the entire width of central Alabama. Just to the north, the piedmont of east-central Alabama contains rolling hills and valleys. Alabama's highest elevation, Cheaha Mountain, 2,405 ft (733 m) above sea level, is located at the northern edge of this region. North and west of the piedmont is a series of parallel ridges and valleys running in a northeast-southwest direction. Mountain ranges in this area include the Red, Shades, Oak, Lookout, and other noteworthy southern extensions of the Appalachian chain; elevations of 1,200 ft (366 m) are found

as far south as Birmingham. The Appalachian Plateau covers most of northwestern Alabama, with a portion of the Highland Rim in the extreme north near the Tennessee border. The floodplain of the Tennessee River cuts a wide swath across both these northern regions.

The largest lake wholly within Alabama is Guntersville Lake, covering about 108 sq mi (280 sq km) and formed during the development of the Tennessee River region by the Tennessee Valley Authority (TVA). The TVA lakes—also including Wheeler, Pickwick, and Wilson—are all long and narrow, fanning outward along a line that runs from the northeast corner of the state westward to Florence.

The longest rivers are the Alabama, extending from the mid-central region to the Mobile River for a distance of about 160 mi (260 km); the Tennessee, which flows across northern Alabama for about the same distance; and the Tombigbee, which flows south from north-central Alabama for some 150 mi (240 km). The Alabama and Tombigbee rivers, which come together to form the Mobile River, and the Tensaw River flow into Mobile Bay, an arm of the Gulf of Mexico.

About 450 million years ago, Alabama was covered by a warm, shallow sea. Over millions of years, heavy rains washed gravel, sand, and clay from higher elevations onto the rock floor of the sea to help form the foundation of modern Alabama. The skeletons and shells of sea animals, composed of limy material from rocks that had been worn away by water, settled into great thicknesses of limestone and dolomite. Numerous caves and sinkholes formed as water slowly eroded the limestone subsurface of northern Alabama. Archaeologists believe that Russell Cave, in northeastern Alabama, was the earliest site of human habitation in the southeastern US. Other major caves in northern Alabama are Manitou and Sequoyah; near Childersburg is DeSoto Caverns, a huge onyx cave once considered a sacred place by Creek Indians.

Wheeler Dam on the Tennessee River is now a national historic monument. Other major dams include Guntersville, Martin, Millers Ferry, Jordan, Mitchell, and Holt.

[3] CLIMATE

Alabama's three climatic divisions are the lower coastal plain, largely subtropical and strongly influenced by the Gulf of Mexico; the northern plateau, marked by occasional snowfall in winter; and the Black Belt and upper coastal plain, lying between the two extremes. Among the major population centers, Birmingham has an annual mean temperature of 62°F (17°C), with a normal July daily maximum of 90°F (32°C) and a normal January daily minimum of 34°F (1°C). Montgomery has an annual mean of 65°F (18°C), with a normal July daily maximum of 91°F (33°C) and a normal January daily minimum of 37°F (3°C). The mean in Mobile is 67°F (19°C), with a normal July daily maximum of 91°F (33°C) and a normal January daily minimum of 41°F (51°C). The record low temperature for the state is –27°F (–33°C), registered at New Market, in the northeastern corner, on 30 January 1966; the all-time high is 112°F (44°C), registered at Centerville, in the state's midsection, on 5 September 1925. Mobile, one of the rainiest cities in the United States, recorded an average precipitation of 66.3 in (168 cm) a year between 1971 and 2000.

[4] FLORA AND FAUNA

Alabama was once covered by vast forests of pine, which still form the largest proportion of the state's forest growth. Alabama also has an abundance of poplar, cypress, hickory, oak, and various gum trees. Red cedar grows throughout the state; southern white cedar is found in the southwest, hemlock in the north. Other native trees include hackberry, ash, and holly, with species of palmetto and palm in the Gulf Coast region. There are more than 150 shrubs, mountain laurel and rhododendron among them. Cultivated plants include wisteria and camellia, the state flower.

In a state where large herds of bison, elk, bear, and deer once roamed, only the white-tailed deer remains abundant. Other mammals still found are the Florida panther, bobcat, beaver, muskrat, and most species of weasel. The fairly common raccoon, opossum, rabbit, squirrel, and red and gray foxes are also native, while nutria and armadillo have been introduced to the state. Alabama's birds include golden and bald eagles, osprey and various other hawks, yellowhammer or flicker (the state bird), and black and white warblers; game birds include quail, duck, wild turkey, and goose. Freshwater fish such as bream, shad, bass, and sucker are common. Along the Gulf Coast there are seasonal runs of tarpon (the state fish), pompano, redfish, and bonito.

Ninety-seven animals, fish, and birds (including the Alabama beach mouse, gray bat, Alabama red-belly turtle, finback and humback whales, bald eagle, and wood stork), and eighteen plant species were listed as endangered as of August 2003 by the US Fish and Wildlife Service.

[5] ENVIRONMENTAL PROTECTION

Under the 1982 Alabama Environmental Management Act, the Alabama Environmental Management Commission was created and the Alabama Department of Environmental Management (ADEM) was established. The ADEM absorbed several commissions, programs, and agencies that had been responsible for Alabama's environment.

The Environmental Commission, whose seven members are appointed to six-year terms by the governor and approved by the Alabama Senate, is charged with managing the state's land, air, and water resources. The ADEM administers all major federal environmental groups including the Clean Air Act, Safe Drinking Water Act, and solid and hazardous waste laws. The most active environmental groups in the state are the Alabama Environmental Council, Sierra Club, League of Women Voters, Alabama Audubon Council, and Alabama Rivers Alliance.

Major concerns of environmentalists in the state are the improvement of land-use planning and the protection of groundwater. Another issue is the transportation, storage, and disposal of hazardous wastes. In 2003, the Environmental Protection Agency's database listed 258 hazardous waste sites in Alabama, 13 of which were on the National Priorities List. One of the nation's five largest commercial hazardous waste sites is in Emelle, in Sumter County. Alabama's solid waste stream is 4.500 tons a year (1.10 tons per capita). There are 108 municipal land fills and 8 curbside recycling programs in the state. Air quality is generally satisfactory. In 2001, Alabama received $54,490,000 in federal grants from the EPA; EPA expenditures for procurement contracts in Alabama that year amounted to $1,978,000.

[6] POPULATION

Alabama ranked 23rd in population among the 50 states with an estimated total of 4,486,508 in 2002, an increase of 0.9% since 2000. Between 1990 and 2000, Alabama's population grew from 4,040,587 to 4,447,100, an increase of 10.1%. The population is projected to reach 4,631,000 by 2005 and 5,200,000 by 2025.

In 2000 the median age was 35.8%. Persons under 18 years old accounted for 25.3% of the population, while 13% were age 65 or older.

Alabama experienced its greatest population growth between 1810 and 1820, following the defeat of the Creek Nation by General Andrew Jackson and his troops. Population in what is now Alabama boomed from 9,046 in 1810 to 127,901 in 1820, as migrants from older states on the eastern seaboard poured into the territory formerly occupied by the Creek Indians. Thousands of farmers, hoping to find fertile land or to become wealthy cotton planters, brought their families and often their slaves into the young state, more than doubling Alabama's population between 1820 and 1830. By 1860, Alabama had almost 1,000,000 residents, nearly one-half of whom were black slaves. The Civil War brought Alabama's population growth almost to a standstill, largely because of heavy losses on the battlefield. The total population gain between 1860 and 1870 was only about 30,000 whereas between 1870 and 1970, Alabama's population rose 150,000–300,000 every decade. During the 1980s the population increased 148,000.

In 2000, Alabama had a population density of 87.6 persons per sq mi. First in size among Alabama's metropolitan areas comes greater Birmingham, which had an estimated 915,000 residents in July 1999. Other major metropolitan areas were greater Mobile, 535,472; greater Montgomery, 322,441; and greater Huntsville, 343,418. The city of Birmingham proper was Alabama's largest city, with an estimated 239,416 residents in 2002; Montgomery had 201,425, and Mobile had 194,862.

[7] ETHNIC GROUPS

Alabama's population is largely divided between whites of English and Scotch-Irish descent, and blacks descended from African slaves. The 2000 census counted about 22,430 Indians (up from 17,000 in 1990), or 0.5% of the total population, mostly of Creek or Cherokee descent. Creek Indians are centered around the small community of Poarch in southern Alabama; most of the Cherokee live in the northeastern part of the state, where the Cherokee reservation had 12,294 residents as of 2000.

The black population of Alabama in 2000 numbered 1,155,930, or about 26% of the total population. As before the Civil War, rural blacks are most heavily represented in the Black Belt of central Alabama.

In 2000, the Asian population totaled 31,346, or less than 1% of the total, and Pacific Islanders numbered 1,409; in the same year, the population of Hispanic or Latino descent totaled 75,830, up from 43,000 in 1990, an increase from 1% to 1.7% of the total population within the decade. In 2000, Alabama had

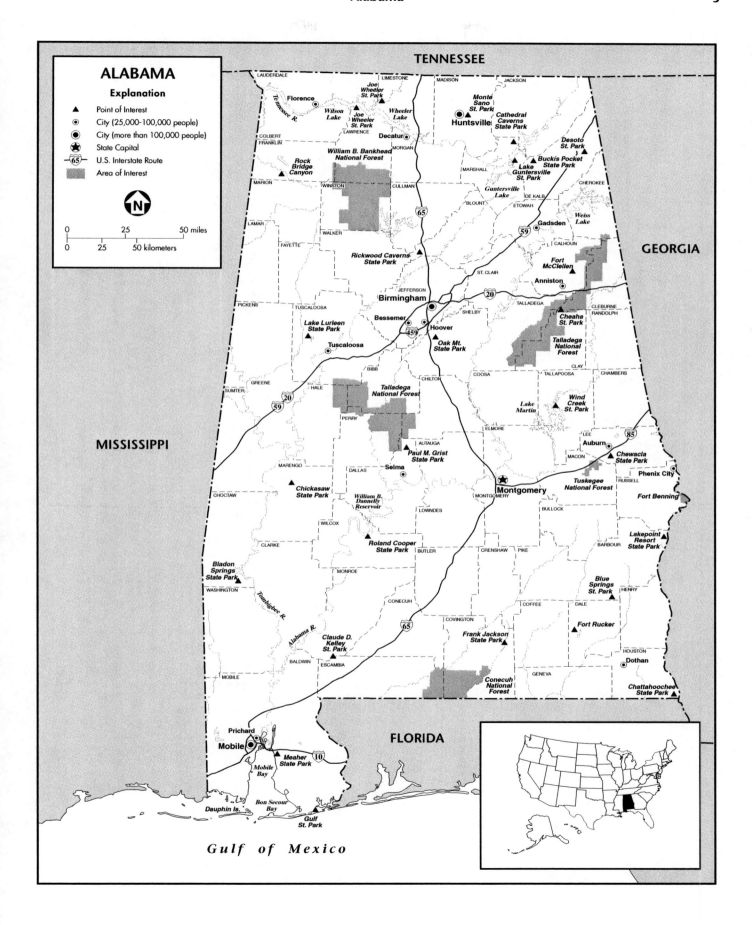

ALABAMA

Explanation

▲ Point of Interest
⊙ City (25,000-100,000 people)
◉ City (more than 100,000 people)
★ State Capital
—65— U.S. Interstate Route
▨ Area of Interest

N

0 · · 25 · · 50 miles
0 · · 25 · · 50 kilometers

TENNESSEE

LAUDERDALE · LIMESTONE · MADISON · JACKSON

Florence
Tennessee R.
Wilson Lake
Joe Wheeler St. Park
Wheeler Lake

Monte Sano St. Park
Huntsville
Cathedral Caverns State Park

COLBERT · FRANKLIN

Joe Wheeler St. Park
LAWRENCE
Decatur
MORGAN

Rock Bridge Canyon

William B. Bankhead National Forest

MARION

WINSTON · CULLMAN

Desoto St. Park
Buck's Pocket State Park
Lake Guntersville St. Park

MARSHALL

Guntersville Lake
DE KALB

CHEROKEE

GEORGIA

LAMAR

FAYETTE

WALKER

BLOUNT
ETOWAH

Gadsden
59

Weiss Lake

CALHOUN

Rickwood Caverns State Park

Fort McClellen

Anniston

PICKENS

TUSCALOOSA

JEFFERSON

Birmingham

ST. CLAIR

20

TALLADEGA

CLEBURNE
RANDOLPH

Bessemer
Hoover
SHELBY
459

Cheaha St. Park

Lake Lurleen State Park

Tuscaloosa

Oak Mt. State Park

Talladega National Forest

GREENE

HALE
BIBB

CHILTON

COOSA

CLAY

CHAMBERS

SUMTER

Talladega National Forest

PERRY

AUTAUGA

ELMORE

Lake Martin

Wind Creek St. Park

LEE

Auburn
85

MISSISSIPPI

MARENGO

DALLAS

Paul M. Grist State Park

Selma

Chewacla State Park

Phenix City

RUSSELL

Chickasaw State Park

William B. Dannelly Reservoir

MONTGOMERY

Montgomery

Tuskegee National Forest

MACON

Fort Benning

CHOCTAW

CLARKE

WILCOX

Roland Cooper State Park

BUTLER

CRENSHAW

PIKE

BARBOUR

Lakepoint Resort State Park

Bladon Springs State Park

WASHINGTON

Tombigbee R.

MONROE

CONECUH

Blue Springs St. Park

HENRY

Alabama R.

Claude D. Kelley St. Park

65

COVINGTON

COFFEE

DALE

Fort Rucker

BALDWIN

ESCAMBIA

Frank Jackson State Park

HOUSTON

Dothan

MOBILE

Conecuh National Forest

GENEVA

Chattahoochee State Park

FLORIDA

Prichard
Mobile
Meaher State Park
10

Mobile Bay

Dauphin Is.
Bon Secour Bay
Gulf St. Park

Gulf of Mexico

6,900 Asian Indians (up from 3,686 in 1990), 4,116 Koreans, and 6,337 Chinese (up from 3,529 in 1990). All told, the foreign born numbered 87,772 (2% of the state's population) in 2000, up from 1% ten years earlier. Among persons reporting a single ancestry group, the leaders were Irish, 343,254 (down from 617,065 in 1990), and English, 344,735 (down from 479,499 in 1990).

Alabama's Cajuns, of uncertain racial origin (Anglo-Saxon, French, Spanish, Choctaw, Apache, and African elements may all be represented), are ethnically unrelated to the Cajuns of Louisiana. Thought to number around 10,000, they live primarily in the pine woods area of upper Mobile and lower Washington counties. Many Alabama Cajuns suffer from poverty, poor health, and malnutrition.

[8]LANGUAGES

Four Indian tribes—the Creek, Chickasaw, Choctaw, and Cherokee—occupied the four quarters of Alabama as white settlement began, but by treaty agreement they were moved westward between 1814 and 1835, leaving behind such place-names as Alabama, Talladega, Mobile, and Tuscaloosa.

Alabama English is predominantly Southern, with a transition zone between it and a smaller area into which South Midland speech was taken across the border from Tennessee. Some features common to both dialects occur throughout the state, such as *croker sack* (burlap bag), *batter cakes* (made of cornmeal), *harp* (harmonica), and *snap beans*. In the major Southern speech region are found the decreasing loss of final /r/, the /boyd/ pronunciation of *bird*, *soft peach* (freestone), *press peach* (clingstone), *mosquito hawk* (dragonfly), *fire dogs* (andirons), and *gopher* (burrowing turtle). In the northern third of the state are found South Midland *arm* and *barb* rhyming with *form* and *orb*, *redworm* (earthworm), *peckerwood* (woodpecker), *snake doctor and snake feeder* (dragonfly), *tow sack* (burlap bag), *plum peach* (clingstone), *French harp* (harmonica), and *dog irons* (andirons).

Alabama has experienced only minor foreign immigration, and in 2000, 96.1% of all residents five years old or older spoke only English at home, a slight decrease over the 97.1% recorded in 1990.

The following table gives selected statistics from the 2000 census for language spoken at home by persons five years old and over. The category "African languages" includes Amharic, Ibo, Twi, Yoruba, Bantu, Swahili, and Somali.

LANGUAGE	NUMBER	PERCENT
Population 5 years and over	**4,152,278**	**100.0**
Speak only English	3,989,795	96.1
Speak a language other than English	162,483	3.9
Speak a language other than English	**162,483**	**3.9**
Spanish or Spanish Creole	89,729	2.2
German	14,905	0.4
French (incl. Patois, Cajun)	13,656	0.3
Chinese	5,271	0.1
Vietnamese	4,561	0.1
Korean	4,029	0.1
Arabic	2,620	0.1
African languages	2,306	0.1
Japanese	2,201	0.1
Italian	2,158	0.1

[9]RELIGIONS

Although predominantly Baptist today, Alabama was officially Roman Catholic throughout most of the 18th century, under French and Spanish rule. A century passed between the building of the first Catholic Church in 1702 and the earliest sustained efforts by Protestant evangelists. The first Baptist church in the state, the Flint River Church in Madison County, was organized in 1808; the following year, the Old Zion Methodist Church was founded in the Tombigbee area.

During the second decade of the 19th century, settlers from the southeastern states brought the influence of the Great Revival to Alabama, along with the various Methodist, Presbyterian, and Baptist sects that had developed in its wake. The first black church in Alabama probably dates from 1820. As in other southern states, black slaves who had previously attended the churches of their masters formed their own churches after the Civil War. One of the earliest of these, the Little Zion Methodist Church, was established in 1867 in Mobile. Most freed blacks became Baptists, however.

The vast majority of congregations in the state belong in the category of Evangelical Protestants. As of 2000, the Southern Baptist Convention was still the fastest growing and the largest denomination within the state, with 1,380,121 adherents and 3,148 congregations, representing an increase of 83 congregations since 1990. The United Methodist Church claimed 327,734 adherents with 1,416 congregations, a decrease of 56 congregations since 1990. The Church of Christ was the 3rd-largest denomination with 119,049 adherents and 895 congregations. Roman Catholics in Alabama numbered 150,647 and there were an estimated 9,100 Jews. About 45.2% of the population were not counted as members of any religious organization.

[10]TRANSPORTATION

The first rail line in the state—the Tuscumbia Railroad, chartered in 1830—made its first run, 44 mi (71 km) around the Muscle Shoals from Tuscumbia to Decatur, on 15 December 1834. By 1852, however, Alabama had only 165 mi (266 km) of track, less than most other southern states. Further development awaited the end of the Civil War. Birmingham, as planned by John T. Milner, chief engineer of the South and North Railroad, was founded in 1871 as a railroad intersection in the midst of Alabama's booming mining country; it subsequently became the state's main rail center, followed by Mobile. As of the end of 2000, Alabama had 3,687 total rail mi (5,933 km) of track. There were five class I railroads operating in the state, accounting for 3,149 rail mi (5,067 km). Coal is the major commodity sent by rail—29% of all rail tonnage originating from and 49% of all rail tonnage terminating within the state was coal in 1998. An Amtrak passenger rail connected Birmingham, Anniston, and Tuscaloosa with Washington and New Orleans. Other passenger service included a route connecting Montgomery and Mobile with Birmingham and New Orleans.

In settlement days the principal roads into Alabama were the Federal Road, formerly a Creek horse path, from Georgia and South Carolina; and the Natchez Trace, bought by the federal government (1801) from the Choctaw and Chickasaw, leading from Kentucky and Tennessee. Throughout most of the 19th century, road building was in the hands of private companies. Only after the establishment of a state highway department in 1911 and the securing of federal aid for rural road building in 1916 did Alabama begin to develop modern road systems.

As of 2000 there were 94,311 mi (151,778 km) of public streets, roads, and highways. In the same year, the state had 1,961,806 registered automobiles, 1,989,567 trucks, and 8,766 buses. There were 3,521,444 licensed drivers in 2000. Most of the major interstate highways in Alabama intersect at Birmingham: I-65, running from the north to Montgomery and Mobile; and I-59 from the northeast and I-20 from the east, which, after merging at Birmingham, run southwestward to Tuscaloosa and into Mississippi. Route I-85 connects Montgomery with Atlanta; and I-10 connects Mobile with New Orleans and Tallahassee, Florida.

The coming of the steamboat to Alabama waters, beginning in 1818, stimulated settlement in the Black Belt; however, the high price of shipping cotton by water contributed to the eventual displacement of the steamboat by the railroad. Thanks to the Tennessee Valley Authority, the Tennessee River has been transformed since the 1930s into a year-round navigable waterway, with three locks and dams in Alabama. The 234-mi (377-km), $2-billion Tennessee-Tombigbee project, which opened in 1985, provided a new barge route, partly through Alabama, from the Midwest to the Gulf of Mexico, for which the US Army Corps of Engineers cut a 39-mi (63-km) canal and built 10 locks and dams. This was not only the largest civilian engineering project in the US during the early 1980s but also by far the largest earth-moving project in US history, displacing more earth than was moved to build the Panama Canal.

The Alabama-Coosa and Black Warrior-Tombigbee systems also have been made navigable by locks and dams: river barges carry bulk cargoes. There are 1,270 mi (2,043 km) of navigable inland water and 50 mi (80 km) of Gulf coast. The only deepwater port is Mobile, with a large ocean-going trade; total tonnage in 2000 was 54.2 million tons. The Alabama State Docks also operates a system of 10 inland docks; and there are several privately run inland docks.

In 2000, Alabama had 102 public-use airports, of which six were for commercial service with 2,500 or more passengers enplaned. Mobile, on the Gulf of Mexico, is Alabama's only international port. The largest and busiest facility is Birmingham International Airport.

11 HISTORY

The region now known as Alabama has been inhabited for some 9,000–10,000 years. The earliest evidence of human habitation, charcoal from an ancient campfire at Russell Cave in northeastern Alabama, is about 9,000 years old. These early peoples, probably descended from humans who crossed from Asia to North America via the Bering Strait, moved from caves and open campsites to permanent villages about AD 1000. Some of their descendants, popularly called Mound Builders, erected huge earthen temple mounds and simple huts along Alabama's rivers, beginning around 1100. Moundville (near Tuscaloosa), one of the most important Mound Builder sites in the southeastern US, includes 20 "platform mounds" for Indian buildings, dating from 1200 to 1500. When the first Europeans arrived, Alabama was inhabited by Indians, half of them either Creek or members of smaller groups living within the Creek confederacy. The Creeks resided in central and eastern Alabama; Cherokee Indians inhabited northeastern Alabama, the Chickasaws lived in the northwest, and the Choctaws settled in the southwest.

During the 16th century, five Spanish expeditions entered Mobile Bay or explored the region now called Alabama. The most extensive was that of Hernando de Soto, whose army marched from the Tennessee Valley to the Mobile Delta in 1540. In 1702, two French naval officers—Pierre Le Moyne, Sieur d'Iberville; and Jean Baptiste Le Moyne, Sieur de Bienville—established Ft. Louis de la Mobile, the first permanent European settlement in present-day Alabama. Mobile remained in French hands until 1763, when it was turned over to the British under the terms of the Treaty of Paris. Because a British garrison held Mobile during the American Revolution, that city was captured in 1780 by the forces of Spain, an ally of the rebellious American colonists. In 1803, the United States claimed the city as part of the Louisiana Purchase, but in vain. Spanish control of Mobile lasted until the city was again seized during the War of 1812, this time by American troops in 1813. West Florida, including Mobile, was the only territory added to the US as a result of that war.

At the start of the 19th century, Indians still held most of present-day Alabama. War broke out in 1813 between American settlers and a Creek faction known as the Red Sticks, who were determined to resist white encroachment. After General Andrew Jackson and his Tennessee militia crushed the Red Sticks in 1814 at the Battle of Horseshoe Bend in central Alabama, he forced the Creek to sign a treaty ceding some 40,000 sq mi (103,600 sq km) of land to the US, thereby opening about three-fourths of the present state to white settlement. By 1839, nearly all Alabama Indians had been removed to Indian Territory.

From 1814 onward, pioneers, caught up by what was called "Alabama fever," poured out of the Carolinas, Virginia, Georgia, Tennessee, and Kentucky into what Andrew Jackson called "the best unsettled country in America." Wealthy migrants came in covered wagons, bringing their slaves, cattle, and hogs. But the great majority of pioneers were ambitious farmers who moved to the newly opened area in hopes of acquiring fertile land on which to grow cotton. Cotton's profitability had increased enormously with the invention of the cotton gin. In 1817, Alabama became a territory; on 2 August 1819, a state constitution was adopted; and on the following 14 December, Alabama was admitted to statehood. Alabama, then as now, was sparsely populated. In 1819, its residents comprised 1.3% of the US population. That percentage had grown to only 2% in 1980.

During the antebellum era, 95% of white Alabamians lived and worked in rural areas, primarily as farmers. Although "Cotton was king" in 19th-century Alabama, farmers also grew corn, sorghum, oats, and vegetables, as well as razorback hogs and cattle. By 1860, 80% of Alabama farmers owned the land they tilled. Only about 33% of all white Alabamians were slaveowners. Whereas in 1820 there were 85,451 whites and 41,879 slaves, by 1860 the number of slaves had increased to 435,080, constituting 45% of the state population. Large planters (owners of 50 slaves or more) made up less than 1% of Alabama's white population in 1860. However, they owned 28% of the state's total wealth and occupied 25% of the seats in the legislature. Although the preponderance of the wealth and the population in Alabama was located in the north, the success of Black Belt plantation owners at forging coalitions with industrialists enabled planters to dominate state politics both before and after the Civil War. The planters led the secessionist movement, and most other farmers, fearing the consequences of an end to slavery, eventually followed suit. However, 2,500 white Alabamians served in the Union Army, and an estimated 8,000–10,000 others acted as Union scouts, deserted Confederate units, or hid from conscription agents.

Alabama seceded from the Union in January 1861 and shortly thereafter joined the Confederate States of America. The Confederacy was organized in Alabama's senate chamber in Montgomery, and Jefferson Davis was inaugurated president on the steps of the capitol. Montgomery served as capital of the Confederacy until May, when the seat of government was moved to Richmond, VA.

Remote from major theaters of war, Alabama experienced only occasional Union raids during the first three years of the conflict. In the summer of 1864, however, Confederate and Union ships fought a major naval engagement in Mobile Bay, which ended in surrender by the outnumbered southern forces. During the Confederacy's dying days in the spring of 1865, federal troops swept through Tuscaloosa, Selma, and Montgomery. Their major goal, Selma, one of the Confederacy's main industrial centers, was left almost as heavily devastated as Richmond or Atlanta. Estimates of the number of Alabamians killed in the Civil War range from 25,000 upward.

During Reconstruction, Alabama was under military rule until it was readmitted to the Union in 1868. For the next six years, Republicans held most top political positions in the state. With the help of the Ku Klux Klan, Democrats regained political control of the state in November 1874.

Cotton remained the foundation of the Alabama economy in the late 19th and early 20th centuries. However, with the abolition of slavery it was now raised by sharecroppers—white and black landless farmers who paid for the land they rented from planters with the cotton they harvested. Alabama also attempted to create a "New South" in which agriculture would be balanced by industry. In the 1880s and 1890s, at least 20 Alabama towns were touted as ironworking centers. Birmingham, founded in 1871, became the New South's leading industrial center. Its promoters invested in pig iron furnaces, coal mines, steel plants, and real estate. Small companies merged with bigger ones, which were taken over, in turn, by giant corporations. In 1907, Birmingham's Tennessee Coal, Iron, and Railroad Co. was purchased by the nation's largest steelmaker, US Steel.

Another major Alabama enterprise was cotton milling. By 1900, 9,000 men, women, and children were employed in Alabama mills; most of these white workers were farm folk who had lost their land after the Civil War because of mounting debts and low cotton prices. Wages in mills were so low that entire families had to work hours as long as those they had endured as farmers.

The rise in the rate of farm tenancy produced a corresponding increase in social and political unrest. Discontented farmers and factory workers allied during the 1890s in the Populist Party in an attempt to overthrow the Bourbon Democrats who had dominated Alabama politics for two decades. Although a number of Populists were elected to the Alabama legislature, no Populist candidate succeeded in winning the governorship, primarily because Democrats manipulated the black vote to their own advantage. In 1901, Alabama adopted a new state constitution containing numerous restrictions on voting, supposedly to end vote manipulation and restore honest elections. The tangible result of these new rules was to disenfranchise almost all Alabama black voters and thousands of poor whites. For example, the total of blacks registered in 14 counties fell from 78,311 in 1900 to 1,081 in 1903. As recently as 1941, fewer than 25% of Alabama adults were registered voters. In 1960, no blacks voted in Lowndes or Wilcox counties, 80% and 78% black, respectively.

As one of the poorest states in the country, Alabama benefited disproportionately from the New Deal. Yet, like other southern states, Alabama viewed the expansion of the national government's role with mixed feelings. Alabamians embraced federal aid, even lobbying for military bases, while seeing federal power as a threat to the "Southern way of life" that included racial segregation.

During the 1950s and 1960s, national attention focused on civil rights demonstrations in Alabama, including the Montgomery bus boycott of 1955, the Birmingham and University of Alabama demonstrations of 1963, and the voting rights march from Selma to Montgomery in 1965. The primary antagonists were Dr. Martin Luther King, Jr., head of the Southern Christian Leadership Conference; and Governor George C. Wallace, an opponent of integration. These black protests and the sometimes violent reactions to them, such as the 1963 bombing of a church in Birmingham in which four young black girls—Denise McNair, Cynthia Wesley, Carole Rosamond Robertson, and Addie Mae Collins—were killed, helped influence the US Congress to pass the Civil Rights Act of 1964 and the Voting Rights Act of 1965. Four former Ku Klux Klansmen were suspects of the church bombing: Robert E. Chambliss, Bobby Frank Cherry, Herman Frank Cash, and Thomas E. Blanton, Jr. In 1977, Robert Chambliss was convicted of the murders, and was sentenced to a life term. He died in prison in 1985. Suspect

Herman Cash died in 1994, without having been charged of the crime. Blanton and Cherry were indicted on four counts each of first-degree and reckless murder in 2000. Cherry was subsequently ruled mentally incompetent to stand trial, but Blanton was convicted of four counts of first-degree murder in 2001, and sentenced to four life terms. Cherry was later deemed competent to stand trial, and in 2002, he was convicted and sentenced to an automatic life term in prison.

Once the most tightly segregated city in the nation, Birmingham has become thoroughly integrated in public facilities, and in 1979 the city elected its first black mayor, Richard Arrington. The civil rights era brought other momentous changes to Alabama. Hundreds of thousands of black voters are now an important force in state politics. Blacks attend school, colleges, and universities of their choice and enjoy equal access to all public facilities. On the whole, new racial attitudes among most whites have contributed to a vast improvement in the climate of race relations since 1960. Indeed, a significant amount of black support contributed to Wallace's election to a fourth term as governor in 1982. When he died in September 1998 he was given a full state funeral and his family received condolences from black leaders. In 1984 there were 314 black elected officials, including 25 mayors, 19 lawmakers in the Alabama state legislature, and an associate justice of the state supreme court. In 1990, 704 blacks held elective office.

In many respects Alabama has resisted change more successfully than any other state in the deep South. The state's tax system remains the most regressive in the country. In 1982, the state legislature passed a law prohibiting taxation of land owned by timber companies at market value (timber comprises the state's largest industry). Alabama does not use property taxes to fund schools; instead, public education revenue is derived principally from state income tax (52.9% in 2000) and sales tax (33.5% in 2000). In the late 1990s the state worked to increase teachers' salaries and bring other measures in line with national education statistics. Alabama has had one of the highest infant mortality rates in the nation (it ranked 3rd-highest in 1996), owing in part to widespread poverty. Though Alabama's poverty rate steadily declined during the last decades of the 1900s, it remained among the nation's poorer states. In 1969, 25.4% of Alabamians lived below federal poverty levels. By 1989 the figure dropped to 18.3% and in 1998 it decreased to an estimated 15%, the 13th highest rate in the nation.

A strange turn of events in 1986 resulted in the election of the first Republican governor since Reconstruction. The Democratic candidate, State Attorney General Charles Graddick, was stripped of his party's nomination by a federal panel because of crossover Republican voting in the Democratic primary. His replacement, Lieutenant Governor Bill Baxley, lost the election to a little-known pro-business Republican and former Baptist preacher, Guy Hunt. Hunt was reelected in 1990 but was confronted early in his second term with accusations of financial misdeeds, including personal use of official resources and mismanagement of public funds. In 1992 Hunt was indicted on 13 separate felony counts. The following year, he was found guilty of fraud and conspiracy charges and forced to resign the governorship, becoming the fourth governor in the nation's history to be convicted of criminal charges while in office.

In 1995–96 Alabama was one of five southern states in which a string of fires were set at predominantly black churches. Early in 1996, Attorney General Janet Reno announced that the federal government planned to investigate the fires.

In 1999, Alabama received the 2nd-largest surplus in the history of the state; the $57 million budget surplus was credited to tight controls over agency spending. In 2003, the state had a $675 million budget deficit, and Governor Bob Riley proposed a $1.3 billion tax increase raising individual and corporate taxes by

$461 million and local and state property taxes by $465 million. Voters were to decide the fate of Riley's proposal in a referendum held in September 2003.

[12] STATE GOVERNMENT

Alabama has had six constitutions, the most recent one dating from 1901. By January 2003 that document had been amended 743 times. In 2002 amid calls for a constitutional convention, voters approved a constitutional amendment providing that no constitution could be adopted without voter approval. Governor Robert Riley, elected in 2002, appointed a constitutional commission to prepare recommendations on reforms in 2003.

Alabama's bicameral legislature consists of a 35-seat senate and a 105-seat house of representatives, all of whose members are elected at the same time for four-year terms. Legislative sessions are held each year, convening in early January in general election years, in late April in years following general election years, and in early February all other years. Session length is limited to 30 legislative days in 105 calendar days. Only the governor may call special sessions, which are limited to 12 legislative days in 30 calendar days. Senators must be at least 25 years old; representatives, 21. Legislators must have resided in the state for at least three years before election and in the district at least one year. Under federal pressure, the legislature in 1983 approved a reapportionment plan, effective in 1986, that was expected to increase black representation. In 2002 Alabama's legislators received a per diem salary of $10 during regular sessions; each member is also paid $32.50 per diem for the performance of his or her duties as a member of any authorized interim legislative committee or subcommittee. Legislators in 2002 received living expenses in the amount of $2,280 per month plus $50 per day for three days per week that the legislature actually meets. Legislators' terms of office begin on the day after election and expire on the day after election four years later.

State elected officials are the governor and lieutenant-governor (separately elected), secretary of state, attorney general, treasurer, auditor, commissioner of agriculture and industries, and three members of the Public Service Commission. The governor, who serves for four years, must be at least 30 years old and must have been a US citizen for ten years and a citizen of the state for seven. The governor is limited to a maximum of two consecutive terms. As of 2002 Alabama's governor earned a salary of $101,432, and was entitled to reimbursement of travel expenses up to $40 per day for travel within Alabama, and for total actual expenses outside the state.

A bill becomes a law when it is passed by at least a majority of a quorum of both houses and is either signed by the governor or left unsigned for six days (Sundays excluded) while the legislature is in session, or passed over the governor's veto by a majority of the elected members of each house. A bill must pass both houses in the same form. The governor may pocket veto a measure submitted fewer than five days before adjournment by not signing it within ten days after adjournment. The governor has the power to approve or disapprove any particular item of an appropriation bill without vetoing the entire bill. Vetoed items are returned to the legislature while the remainder of the bill becomes law.

The submission of a constitutional amendment to the electorate requires the approval of three-fifths of the membership of each house, but such amendments can also be adopted by constitutional convention. Amendments are ratified by a majority vote of the electorate.

Voters in Alabama must be US citizens, state and county citizens, and at least 18 years old. Restrictions apply to convicted felons and those declared mentally incompetent by the court.

[13] POLITICAL PARTIES

The major political parties in Alabama are the Democratic and Republican parties, each affiliated with the national party organization. The Republicans are weak below the federal-office level.

Pre-Civil War political divisions in the state reflected those elsewhere in the South. Small and subsistence farmers, especially in the northern hill country and pine forest areas, tended to be Jacksonian Democrats, while the planters of the Black Belt and the river valleys often voted Whig. After a period of Radical Republican rule during Reconstruction, the Bourbon Democrats, whose party then served largely the interests of wealthy property owners, business people, and white supremacists, ran the state for the rest of the century, despite a challenge in the 1890s by the Populist Party.

On two occasions, 1948 and 1964, the Alabama Democratic Party bolted the national Democratic ticket, each time because of disagreement over civil rights. Barry Goldwater in 1964 was the first Republican presidential candidate in the 20th century to carry Alabama. In 1968, George Wallace carried Alabama overwhelmingly on the American Independent Party slate.

In the 2000 presidential elections, 57% of the vote went to Republican George W. Bush; 42% to Democrat Al Gore; and 1% to Green Party candidate Ralph Nader. In 2002 there were 2,356,423 registered voters; there is no party registration. The state had nine electoral votes in the 2000 presidential election. US Senator Richard Shelby was reelected as a Democrat in 1992, but switched his affiliation to Republican on 9 November 1994, the day after the Republicans swept into power in the Senate. He was reelected in 1998. In 1996 Democratic Senator Howell Heflin retired, and his seat was won by Republican Jeff B. Sessions. Sessions was reelected in 2002. Alabama's delegation of US Representatives following the 2002 elections consisted of two Democrats and five Republicans.

During the 20th century, the Democratic Party commanded virtually every statewide office, major and minor. Democrat James Folsom was elected Lieutenant Governor in 1990 and became governor in April of 1993 when Governor Guy Hunt was convicted of illegally using money from his inauguration for personal expenses. Folsom lost his election bid for governor to Fob James, Jr., in 1994. James had served as governor of the state from 1979–83 as a Democrat, but he switched party affiliations for the 1994 election and upset Folsom in a narrow victory. In the 1998 election Democrat Don Siegelman was elected to the governor's office. In 2002, Republican Bob Riley was elected governor, after serving six years in the US House of Representatives. The Alabama legislature in mid-2003 consisted of 25 Democrats and 10 Republicans in the senate and 63 Democrats and 42 Republicans in the house.

[14] LOCAL GOVERNMENT

In 2002 Alabama had 67 counties, 451 municipalities, 128 public school districts, and 525 special districts. Counties are governed by county commissions, usually consisting of three to seven commissioners, elected by district. Other county officials include a judges of probate, clerk, tax assessor and collector, sheriff, and superintendent of education. Elections for municipal officers are held every four years.

Today, mayor-council is the most common form of municipal government. But until the late 1970s, the predominant form of municipal government, especially in the larger cities, was the commission, whose members are elected either at-large or by district. Partly in response to court orders requiring district elections in order to permit the election of more black officials, after the 1970s there was a trend toward the mayor-council form, although the US Supreme Court ruled in May 1980 that Mobile may elect its public officials at-large.

An alteration in local government had a significant effect on the racial climate in Birmingham during the 1960s, when the Young Men's Business Club led a movement to change to the mayor-council system, in order to oust a commission (including Eugene "Bull" Connor as public safety commissioner) that for nearly a decade had reacted negatively to every black demand. After a narrow vote in favor of the change, a moderate was elected mayor in April 1963, but the former commissioners then contested the initial vote that had changed the system. At the height of Birmingham's racial troubles, both the former commissioners and the newly elected council claimed to govern Birmingham, but neither did so effectively. When peace came, it was as the result of an unofficial meeting held between local black leaders and 77 of the city's most influential whites, with federal officials serving as mediators. Although the council, like the commissioners, publicly opposed these negotiations, once they were over and the council's election confirmed, the new moderate leadership permitted peaceful racial accommodation to go forward. In addition to the mayor-council and commission forms of administration, some municipalities employ city managers.

15STATE SERVICES

To address the continuing threat of terrorism and to work with the federal Department of Homeland Security (created in 2002 following the terrorist attacks of 11 September 2001), homeland security in Alabama in 2003 operated under the authority of executive order; the adjutant general was designated as the state homeland security advisor.

Alabama's Ethics Commission administers the state's ethics law, makes financial disclosure records available to the public, and receives monthly reports from lobbyists. Educational services are administered primarily by the Department of Education and the Alabama Commission on Higher Education. The Alabama Public Library Service supports and promotes the development of public libraries. The Department of Aeronautics, Highway Department, and Public Service Commission (PSC) administer transportation services; the PSC supervises, regulates, and controls all transportation companies doing business in the state. Drivers' licenses are issued by the Department of Public Safety.

Health and welfare services are offered primarily through the Department of Public Health, Department of Mental Health, Department of Veterans Affairs, the Commission on Aging, Department of Youth Services, and Department of Pensions and Security. Planning for the state's future health-care needs is carried out by the Health Planning and Development Agency.

Public protection services are administered by the Military Department, Board of Corrections, Alabama Law Enforcement Planning Agency, and Department of Public Safety, among other agencies. Numerous government bodies offer resource protection services: the Department of Conservation and Natural Resources, Department of Environmental Management, Alabama Forestry

Alabama Presidential Vote by Political Parties, 1948–2000

YEAR	ELECTORAL VOTE	ALABAMA WINNER	DEMOCRAT	REPUBLICAN	STATES' RIGHTS DEMOCRAT	PROHIBITION	PROGRESSIVE
1948	11	Thurmond (SRD)	—	40,930	171,443	1,026	1,522
1952	11	Stevenson (D)	275,075	149,231	—	1,814	—
1956	11	Stevenson (D)	279,542	195,694	UNPLEDGED 20,323	—	—
1960	11	*Kennedy (D)	318,303	236,110	NAT'L STATES' RIGHTS 4,367	—	—
1964	10	Goldwater (R)	—	479,085	UNPLEDGED DEMOCRAT 210,782	—	—
1968	10	Wallace AI)	195,918	146,591	AMERICAN IND. 687,664	AM. IND. DEMOCRAT 3,814	10,518
1972	9	*Nixon (R)	256,923	728,701	AMERICAN 11,928	8,559	—
1976	9	*Carter (D)	659,170	504,070	AMERICAN IND. 9,198	6,669	COMMUNIST 1,954
1980	9	*Reagan (R)	636,730	654,192	—	—	—
1984	9	*Reagan (R)	551,899	872,849	LIBERTARIAN 9,504	—	—
1988	9	*Bush (R)	549,506	815,576	8,460	3,311	
1992	9	Bush (R)	690,080	804,283	5,737	2,161	IND.(PEROT) 183,109
1996	9	Dole (R)	662,165	769,044	5,290	—	92,149
2000	9	*Bush, G. W. (R)	692,611	941,173	5,893	IND. (BUCHANAN) 6,351	IND.(NADER) 18,323

*Won US presidential election.

Commission, Oil and Gas Board, Surface Mining Reclamation Commission, and Alabama State Soil and Water Conservation Committee.

16JUDICIAL SYSTEM

The high court of Alabama is the supreme court, consisting of a chief justice and eight associate justices, all elected for staggered six-year terms. It issues opinions on constitutional issues, and hears cases appealed from the lower courts. The court of civil appeals has exclusive appellate jurisdiction in all suits involving sums up to $10,000; its three judges are elected for six-year terms, and the one who has served the longest is the presiding judge. The five judges of the court of criminal appeals are also elected for six-year terms; they choose the presiding judge by majority vote.

Circuit courts, which encompassed 131 judgeships in 1999, have exclusive original jurisdiction over civil actions involving sums of more than $5,000, and over criminal prosecutions involving felony offenses. They also have original jurisdiction, concurrent with the district courts, in all civil matters exceeding $500. They have appellate jurisdiction over most cases from district and municipal courts. A new system of district courts replaced county and juvenile courts as of January 1977, staffed by judges who serve six-year terms. Municipal court judges are appointed by the municipality.

As of June 2001, 27,286 prisoners were held in 31 state and federal prisons in Alabama, an increase of 5.8% over the previous year. Alabama had an incarceration rate of 592 per 100,000 population. In 1976, US District Court Judge Frank M. Johnson, Jr., ruled that conditions in Alabama prisons inflicted "cruel and unusual punishment" upon inmates, spurring the process of prison reform.

Alabama had an FBI Crime Index rate in 2001 of 4,319.4 crimes per 100,000 population, including a total of 19,582 violent crimes and 173,253 property crimes in that year. Alabama has a death penalty and has executed 162 persons since 1930. There were 27 executions in the state between 1977 and 2003. In 2003, there were 193 persons under sentence of death.

An Alabama case that became internationally notorious was that of the nine "Scottsboro boys," eight of whom were sentenced to death and one to life imprisonment in 1931 for the alleged rape of two white girls, one of whom later recanted her charges. After multiple appeals and reversals, five indictments were subsequently dropped; of the four remaining defendants, all sentenced to lengthy jail terms, three were paroled and one escaped to Michigan, which refused extradition.

17ARMED FORCES

The US Department of Defense had 11,354 active military personnel in Alabama in 2002. The major installation in terms of expenditures was the US Army's Redstone Arsenal at Huntsville. Redstone is the center of the Army's missile and rocket programs and contains the George C. Marshall Space Flight Center of the National Aeronautics and Space Administration, which directs all private contractors for the space program. Among the spacecraft developed there were the Redstone rocket, which launched the first US astronaut; Explorer I, the first US earth-orbiting satellite; and the Saturn rocket, which boosted the Apollo missions to the moon. Other installations include Ft. Rucker (near Enterprise); the Anniston Army Depot; Maxwell Air Force Base (Montgomery), site of the US Air University, Air War Colleges, and national headquarters for the Civil Air Patrol; and Gunter Air Force Base (also in Montgomery). During 2001, Alabama firms received defense contract awards totaling over $3.4 billion.

There were 447,397 veterans of US military service in Alabama as of 2000, of whom 73,515 served in World War II; 55,278 in the Korean conflict; 126,847 during the Vietnam era; and 60,227 during 1990–2000 (including the Persian Gulf War). For the fiscal year 2002, total Veterans Affairs expenditures amounted to $1.0 billion. As of June 2000, the Alabama Department of Public Safety employed 628 full-time sworn officers.

18MIGRATION

After 1814, Alabama was the mecca of a great migratory wave, mainly of whites of English and Scotch-Irish descent (some with their black slaves) from Virginia, Georgia, and the Carolinas. Since the Civil War, migration to Alabama has been slight. Many blacks left Alabama from World War I (1914–18) through the 1960s to seek employment in the East and Midwest, and the proportion of blacks in Alabama's population fell from 35% in 1940 to 26% in 1998, where it remained through mid-2002. Overall, Alabama may have lost as many as 944,000 residents through migration between 1940 and 1970, but enjoyed a net gain from migration of over 143,000 between 1970 and 1990, and an additional 114,000 in domestic and 13,000 in international migration between 1990 and 1998. In the period 1995–2000, 326,212 people moved into the state and 300,389 moved out, for a net gain of 25,823, 3,031 of whom were age 65 or over.

19INTERGOVERNMENTAL COOPERATION

Among the interstate compacts and commissions in which Alabama participates are the Gulf States Marine Fisheries Commission, Interstate Mining Compact Commission, Interstate Oil and Gas Compact, Southeastern Forest Fire Protection Compact, Southern Growth Policies Board, Southern Regional Education Board, Historic Chattahoochee Compact, and the Tennessee-Tombigbee Waterway Development Authority. In 1997, the state began two new water resources projects: the Alabama-Coosa-Tallapoosa (ACT) River Basin Compact between Alabama and Georgia, and the Apalachicola-Chattahoochee-Flint (ACF) River Basin Compact between Alabama, Florida, and Georgia. The Office of State Planning and Federal Programs coordinates planning efforts by all levels of government. During fiscal year 2001, Alabama received federal grants amounting to $5.3 billion.

20ECONOMY

Cotton dominated Alabama's economy from the mid-19th century to the 1870s, when large-scale industrialization began. The coal, iron, and steel industries were the first to develop, followed by other resource industries such as textiles, clothing, paper, and wood products. Although Alabama's prosperity has increased, particularly in recent decades, the state still lags in wage rates and per capita income. One factor that has hindered the growth of the state's economy is declining investment in resource industries owned by large corporations outside the state. Between 1974 and 1983, manufacturing grew at little more than half the rate of all state goods and services. Industries such as primary metals, once the backbone of Alabama's economy, were clearly losing importance. The 1980–82 recession hit the state economy harder than the nation as a whole: 39,000 jobs were lost in manufacturing alone, and real output in manufacturing fell by 10.5%. Recovery began in mid-1980s, and in the economic expansion during the 1990s. Alabama job growth averaged close to 2% a year. However, at the end of the decade, Alabama entered recession earlier than most of the nation. State payrolls began to decline in mid-2000, over six months before the national recession in the first quarter of 2001. The annual growth in the gross state product, at about 5% in 1998 and 1999, fell to 3.6% in 2000, and then to 1.8% in 2001. In 2002, the state economy had still not recovered, as layoffs replaced job creation at a record annual pace of more than 1%. Manufacturing job losses were most severe in non-metropolitan counties, and in the textile and apparel industries which is concentrated in Florence and counties to the south. By contrast, the transportation industry continued to grow, with a new Hyundai plant to opening in Montgomery.

In 2001, Alabama's gross state product was $121.5 billion, 16% from the public sector. The main contributions were from general services ($22 billion, up 26% from 1997), manufacturing ($21.6 billion, down 0.6% from 1997), wholesale and retail trade ($20.4 billion, up 17%); government ($19.3 billion, up 17.5%); financial services, including insurance and real estate ($18 billion, up 22%), and transportation and public utilities ($10.3 billion, up 13.7% from 1997. In the first quarter 2002, personal bankruptcies continued to rise, as they had throughout 2001, correlated with a rise in the foreclosure rate from less than 1.5% to almost 2.4%.

[21]INCOME

According to the Bureau of Economic Analysis, in 2001, Alabama had a per capita personal income (PCPI) of $24,477 which ranked 44th in the United States (including the District of Columbia) and was 80% of the national average, $30,413. The 2001 PCPI reflected an increase of 3.3% from 2000 compared to the national change of 2.2%. In 2001, Alabama had a total personal income (TPI) of $109,387,677,000 which ranked 24th in the United States and accounted for 1.3% of the national total. The 2001 TPI reflected an increase of 3.7% from 2000 compared to the national change of 3.3%.

Earnings of persons employed in Alabama increased from $72,251,982,000 in 2000 to $74,544,566,000 in 2001, an increase of 3.2%. The largest industries in 2001 were services, 24.8% of earnings; state and local government, 13.6%; and durable goods manufacturing, 10.2%. Of the industries that accounted for at least 5% of earnings in 2001, the slowest growing from 2000 to 2001 was durable goods manufacturing, which decreased 4.1%; the fastest was services, which increased 5.8%.

According to data released by the US Census Bureau, in 2000, the median household income was $33,105 compared to the national average of $42,148. In 2001, the median income for a family of four was $54,594 compared to the national average of $63,278. For the period 1999 to 2001, the average poverty rate was 14.8% which placed it 44th among the 50 states and the District of Columbia ranked lowest to highest.

[22]LABOR

According to Bureau of Labor Statistics (BLS) provisional estimates, in July 2003 the seasonally adjusted civilian labor force in Alabama numbered 2,153,300, with approximately 121,800 workers unemployed, yielding an unemployment rate of 5.7%, compared to the national average of 6.2% for the same period. Since the beginning of the BLS data series in 1978, the highest unemployment rate recorded was 15.6% in December 1982. The historical low was 4.1% in August 1998. In 2001, an estimated 5.2% of the labor force was employed in construction; 17.8% in manufacturing; 5.5% in transportation, communications, and public utilities; 20.1% in trade; 5.8% in finance, insurance, and real estate; 22.5% in services; 14.8% in government; and 2.0% in agriculture.

In 1871, James Thomas Rapier, a black Alabamian who would later serve a term as a US representative from the state, organized the first black labor union in the South, the short-lived Labor Union of Alabama. The Knights of Labor began organizing in the state in 1882. A serious obstacle to unionization and collective bargaining was the convict leasing system, which was not ended officially until 1923, and in practice, not until five years later. In 1888, the Tennessee Coal, Iron, and Railroad Co. (later taken over by US Steel) was granted an exclusive 10-year contract to use the labor of all state convicts, paying the state $9–18 per person per month.

Child labor was also exploited. Alabama had limited a child's working day to eight hours in 1887, but a Massachusetts company that was building a large mill in the state secured the repeal of that law in 1895. A weaker measure passed 12 years later limited the child's workweek to 60 hours and set the minimum working age at 12.

The US Department of Labor reported that in 2002, 157,000 of Alabama's 1,761,000 employed wage and salary workers were members of unions. This represented 8.9% of those so employed, down from 9.4% in 2001. The national average is 13.2%. In all, 185,000 workers (10.5%) were represented by unions. In addition to union members, this category includes workers who report no union affiliation but whose jobs are covered by a union contract. Alabama is one of 22 states with a right-to-work law. Unions were especially strong in the northern industrial cities and in Mobile.

[23]AGRICULTURE

Alabama ranked 23rd among the 50 states in farm marketing in 2001, with $3.5 billion, of which only $705 million came from crops.

There was considerable diversity in Alabama's earliest agriculture. By the mid-19th century, however, cotton had taken over, and production of other crops dropped so much that corn and other staples, even work animals, were often imported. In 1860, cotton was grown in every county, and one-crop agriculture had already worn out much of Alabama's farmland.

Diversification began early in the 20th century, a trend accelerated by the destructive effects of the boll weevil on cotton growing. In 2002, only 590,000 acres (238,800 hectares) were planted in cotton, compared to 3,500,000 acres (1,400,000 hectares) in 1930. As of 2002 there were some 47,000 farms in Alabama, occupying approximately 8.9 million acres (3.6 million hectares), or roughly 30% of the state's land area. Soybeans and livestock are raised in the Black Belt; peanuts in the southeast; vegetables, livestock, and timber in the southwest; and cotton and soybeans in the Tennessee River Valley.

In 2002, Alabama ranked 3rd in the US in production of peanuts, with 379,250,000 lb (172,024,000 kg), worth about $63,714,000. Other crops included soybeans, 3,720,000 bushels, $19,902,000; corn for fresh market, 102,000 hundredweight (4,630,000 kg), $1,734,000; wheat, 2,400,000 bushels, $6,960,000; tomatoes for fresh market, 322,000 hundredweight (14,605,000 kg), $7,438,000; sweet potatoes, 624,000 hundredweight (28,304,000 kg), $11,400,000; and pecans, 7,000,000 lb (3,175,500 kg), $4,039,000. The 2002 cotton crop of 575,000 bales was valued at $117,300,000.

[24]ANIMAL HUSBANDRY

The principal livestock-raising regions of Alabama are the far north, the southwest, and the Black Belt, where the lime soil provides excellent pasturage. In 2001 Alabama produced an estimated 493.2 million lb (223.7 million kg) of cattle and calves, valued at $362 million, and an estimated 65.5 million lb (29.7 million kg) of hogs, valued at $28.2 million. There were 1,370,000 cattle and an estimated 165,000 hogs and pigs on Alabama farms and ranches in 2002. According to preliminary figures, 21,000 milk cows yielded 300 million lb (136 million kg) of milk in 2001.

Alabama is a leading producer of chickens, broilers, and eggs. In broiler production, the state was surpassed only by Georgia and Arkansas in 2001, with an estimated 5.1 billion lb (2.3 billion kg), valued at $2 billion. That year, Alabama ranked fifth in chicken production, with over 64.8 million lb (29.4 million kg), worth $4.6 million. Egg production totaled 2.4 billion, worth $265.4 million.

25 FISHING

Alabama's commercial fish catch was 30,081,000 lb (13,644,000 kg), worth $46,985,000, in 1998. The principal fishing port is Bayou La Batre, which brought in about 23,600,000 lb (10,620,000 kg), worth $36,400,000, 11th-highest by value in the nation. Catfish farming is of growing importance. As of January 1999, there were 246 catfish farms (down from 370 in 1990) covering 21,016 acres (9,534 hectares) of water surface, with an average farm size of about 85 acres (34 hectares). In early 2000, Alabama growers had an inventory of 54.2 million stocker-size and 55.4 million fingerling/fry catfish. There were 84 processing and 55 wholesaling plants, with a combined total of about 2,300 employees in 1997. There were 499,132 sport fishing licenses issued by Alabama in 1998. Fish farms distributed 1.7 million bass and 159,000 catfish to Alabama waters in 1998.

26 FORESTRY

Forestland in Alabama, predominantly pine, covering 22,987,000 acres (9,302,000 hectares), was over 3% of the nation's total in 2002. Nearly all of that was classified as commercial timberland, and 21,696,000 of it privately owned. Four national forests covered a gross acreage of 1,288,000 acres (521,250 hectares) in 2001. Production of softwood and hardwood lumber totaled 2.55 billion board feet in 2002 (sixth in the US).

Alabama has a program in place, called TREASURE Forest, to recognize and certify sustainable forestry management on private lands. This program has already certified over 1.57 million acres (635,000 hectares).

27 MINING

In 2001, Alabama's nonfuel mineral industry mined and processed an estimated $938 million of mineral commodities (about 2.5% of the US total), according to statistics related by the US Geological Survey. This was a decrease of about 1% from the value reported by the state's 155 mineral producers in 2000. Value increased for cement, clay, sand, gravel, and stone, the mineral commodities used in construction.

According to preliminary figures, in 2001 Alabama produced 4.4 million metric tons of portland cement valued at $344 million, 2.3 billion metric tons of clay worth $28.6 million, 58.1million metric tons of construction sand and gravel valued at $58.1 million, and 50.5 million metric tons of crushed stone worth $318 million. Portland cement, crushed stone, lime, and construction sand and gravel accounted for 94% of the total nonfuel mineral value in 2001.

The state ranked 16th nationally in total mineral production, and remained 2nd in kaolin, 3rd in lime, common clays, and bentonite, and 4th in iron oxide pigments. Alabama was also among the top five masonry-producing states.

28 ENERGY AND POWER

Electrical generating plants in Alabama had a total installed capacity (utility and nonutility) of 22.7 million kW in 1999, and total production was 120.9 billion kWh in the same year. About half of the capacity and production came from private sources (the Alabama Power Company and Alabama Electric Cooperative), with most of the remainder attributable to the Tennessee Valley Authority, which also owned three of the state's five nuclear reactors, three at Brown's Ferry and two at the Joseph M. Farley plant.

Significant petroleum finds in southern Alabama date from the early 1950s. The 2002 output was 24,000 barrels per day; proved reserves as of 31 December 2001 totaled 42 million barrels. During 2002, marketed gas production was 356 billion cu ft (10.1 billion cu m) of natural gas; proved reserves in 2001 totaled 3,915 billion cu ft (110.8 billion cu m). Coal production, which began in the 19th century, was 19,324,000 tons in 2000, down from 23,013,000 tons in 1998, of which all was bituminous and about 75% was surface mined. Coal reserves in 2001 totaled 352 million tons. In 2000 Alabama's total per capita energy consumption was 443 million Btu (111.6 million kcal), ranking it ninth among the states.

29 INDUSTRY

Alabama's industrial boom, which began in the 1870s with the exploitation of the coal and iron fields in the north, quickly transformed Birmingham into the leading industrial city in the South, producing pig iron more cheaply than its American and English competitors. An important stimulus to manufacturing in the north was the development of ports and power plants along the Tennessee River. Although Birmingham remains highly dependent on steel, the state's industry has diversified considerably since World War II (1939–45).

By the late 1970s, the older smokestack industries were clearly in decline, but Birmingham received a boost in 1984 when US Steel announced it would spend $1.3 billion to make its Fairfield plant the newest fully integrated steel mill in the nation. In 1997, Mercedes Benz began manufacturing its sport utility vehicle at a new facility in Vance.

As of 1999, the principal employers among industry groups were food and kindred products, textile mill products, apparel and other textile products, primary metal industries, industrial machinery and equipment, electronic equipment, and transportation equipment. Electrical machinery, computer equipment, and transportation equipment in Alabama are typically exported to Canada, Mexico, and Germany. The value of manufacturing shipments in 1997 equaled $69.7 billion, with a 31.9% growth from 1992. Alabama was found directly in the middle of states ranked by growth in manufacturing. Mineral industries grew at a much slower rate (5.9%), on par with the US as a whole. Construction, on the other hand, grew at a rate of 65.4% from 1992 to 1997, to $12.6 billion of business done during 1997.

Earnings of persons employed in Alabama increased from $63.8 billion in 1997 to $66.9 billion in 1998, an increase of 4.9%. The largest industries in 1998 were services, 23.2% of earnings; state and local government, 12.5%; and durable goods manufacturing, 12.1%. Of the industries that accounted for at least 5% of earnings in 1998, the slowest growing from 1997 to 1998 was transportation and public utilities (6.6% of earnings in 1998), which increased 2.7%; the fastest was finance, insurance, and real estate (5.7% of earnings in 1998), which increased 7.7%.

30 COMMERCE

According to the 1997 Census of Wholesale Trade, Alabama had 7,476 wholesale trade establishments (5.8% higher than in 1992), with sales of $43.3 billion. Retail establishments numbered 25,586 with sales of $37.6 billion.

The leading types of retail businesses by number of establishments were eating and drinking places (5,900), food stores (3,200), and miscellaneous retail (4,500). Alcoholic beverages, except for beer, are sold in ABC (Alcoholic Beverage Control) stores, run by the state. Prohibition is by local option; 26 of the 67 counties were dry in 1994, but some dry counties had wet cities.

Exporters located in Alabama exported $6.4 billion in merchandise during 1998.

31CONSUMER PROTECTION

The Office of Consumer Affairs, established in 1972, was transferred to the Office of the Attorney General in 1979. The major duties of the office are to enforce the Deceptive Trade Practices Act and other criminal laws to combat consumer fraud; and to offer programs in consumer education. In response to a myriad of inquiries, complaints, and fraudulent schemes, recent attorneys general have expanded the Division's role in their administrations, and it has become one of the most effective arms of the Attorney General's law enforcement efforts.

The Office of Consumer Affairs also acts as a mediator or negotiator in response to approximately 3,000 consumer complaints received each year, three-quarters of which are registered by residents over age 65. In this capacity, the Attorney General undertakes to assist the complaining consumer and the business or person complained against in resolving the dispute. These complaints are submitted to the Attorney General in writing and made available to the business for a response. If a business or person fails to respond to the Attorney General's request for cooperation in addressing the problem, the Attorney General possesses subpoena power to compel these persons to appear at his or her office for this purpose.

32BANKING

As of 2002, Alabama's 121 insured banks had assets of $19.57 billion. There were no insured savings institutions in 2002. By the end of 1995, the Resolution Trust Corporation had resolved 11 Alabama savings and loan institutions which had $4.0 billion in assets and $3.3 billion in deposits through 498,000 accounts.

The economic downturn that began in 2001 affected Alabama before the nation as a whole. The deterioration of the economy, in terms of job losses, for example, did not however affect the banking industry in the same way. Community banks (those with assets under $1 billion) headquartered in Alabama registered strong performance from 2001 to 2002, as net income rose 15%, propelled by improvements in net interest margins (NIMs) (the difference between the lower rates offered to savers and the higher rates charged on loans). During that period, the Federal Reserve cut interest rates a number of times, which increased banks' profitability. As well, the state saw a shift in loan portfolios to higher yielding commercial real estate (CRE) loans. At the end of September 2002, CRE loans accounted for 16% of assets. Personal bankruptcy filings increased throughout the state in 2001/02, however.

33INSURANCE

In 2001 there were 6 million ordinary life insurance policies in force with a total value of $155.7 billion; total value for all categories of life insurance (ordinary, group, industrial, and credit) was $239.2 billion. Death benefits paid that year totaled $752.7 million. As of 2003, there were 24 property and casualty and 14 life and health insurance companies incorporated or organized in the state.

Property and casualty insurers wrote premiums amounting to $4.85 billion in 2001. That year, there were 37,545 flood insurance policies in force in the state, with a total value of $4.5 million. There were also 3,738 beach and windstorm insurance policies against hurricane and other windstorm damage in force, with a total value of $336.8 million.

34SECURITIES

Alabama has no securities exchanges. The state has approximately 377 securities brokers and dealers industries, with over 2,800 agents. There are 74 registered businesses that provide securities investment advice services. A total of 37 NASDAQ companies are headquartered in Alabama, and six companies incorporated in Alabama are listed on the NYSE; including

Medical Assurance, Inc., Alabama Power Co., Minolta-QMS, Inc., Russell Corp., Energen Corp., and Colonial Properties Trust.

35PUBLIC FINANCE

The Division of the Budget within the Department of Finance prepares and administers the state budget, which the governor submits to the legislature for amendment and approval. The fiscal year runs from 1 October through 30 September (one of only four states in which the fiscal year does not begin in July).

A total of $9.04 billion from the General Fund and Earmarked Funds was appropriated for 2003, including $3.3 billion for the Medicaid, $1.57 billion for transportation, and $1.06 billion for Human Resources. The Educational Trust Fund appropriated approximately $8.34 billion to education for the same year.

The following table from the US Census Bureau contains information on revenues, expenditures, indebtedness, and cash/securities for 2001.

	($000)	PERCENT	PER CAPITA
Population (thousands, 2001)	4,469	(X)	(X)
Total Revenue	17,859,899	100.00	3,996.40
General revenue	15,731,646	88.08	3,520.17
Utility revenue	–	–	–
Liquor store revenue	155,329	0.89	34.76
Insurance trust revenue	1,972,924	11.29	441.47
Exhibit: Salaries and wages	2,587,494	15.48	578.99
Total expenditure	16,718,151	100.00	3,740.92
General expenditure	15,055,914	90.06	3,368.97
Education	6,385,451	38.19	1,428.83
Public welfare	3,776,253	22.59	844.99
Hospitals	1,074,849	6.43	240.51
Health	644,288	3.85	144.17
Highways	1,163,889	6.96	260.44
Police protection	124,884	0.75	27.94
Correction	303,759	1.82	67.97
Natural resources	205,794	1.23	46.05
Parks and recreation	15,956	0.10	3.57
Government administration	380,880	2.28	85.23
Interest on general debt	267,537	1.60	59.87
Other and unallocable	712,374	4.26	159.40
Utility expenditure	–	–	–
Liquor store expenditure	156,389	0.94	34.99
Insurance trust expenditure	1,505,848	9.01	336.95
Debt at end of fiscal year	5,577,158	100.00	1,247.97
Cash and security holdings	28,094,479	100.00	6,286.52

36TAXATION

Per capita tax revenues of all state and local governments ($2,234) were less than those of every other state except New Hampshire and Tennessee, and per capita state receipts from property taxes ($43.49) were the lowest in the country.

As of 2002, the personal income tax ranged from 2% to 5%, with $2000 basic individual deductible and $300 for each child. A family of four becomes liable for income tax at $4,600 annual income, the lowest in the country. A reduction in the personal deduction from $2,000 to $1,500 for 2003 lowers the threshold further to $3,600. The tax on corporate net income was 5% for most enterprises, and 6.5% for financial institutions. The state also imposes a sales tax of 4%; localities may charge up to an additional 3%. Prescription drugs are tax-exempt, but food and non-prescription drugs are taxable. The General Fund draws on 36 tax sources, the leading ones in 2002 being the insurance company premium tax, interest on state deposits, interest earnings, corporate taxes, oil and gas production taxes, the cigarette tax, the ad valorum (property) tax, and profits from the alcohol control board. The Educational Trust Fund draws on 12 tax sources, the most important being the personal income tax, sales taxes, utility taxes, and use taxes.

Alabama's tax rates are according to those set in its 1901 Constitution, and in 2002, analysts estimated than sizeable portions of Alabama's potential tax base remained untaxed including half of sales revenues (most services being untaxed), 52% of personal income, and 88% of property value. Taxes are complex, with sales taxes imposed according to four schedules, one for general merchandise, and three separate ones for manufactures, cars, and vending machine products. State collections in 2002 were approximately $6.88 billion ($1,533 per capita), including $3.38 billion from general and selective sales taxes, $2.9 billion from individual income tax, $322,636 from corporate taxes, and $195,132 from property taxes. Revenue shortfalls obliged the Alabama legislature to make cuts of $19.9 million in the enacted 2001/02 budget, and of a reported $14.8 million in the enacted budget of 2002/03. In both years, Alabama was one of a record 37 states making such downward adjustments. Alabama exempted only debt service, federal court-ordered payments, and its Youth Services Operations from budget cuts.

The following table from the US Census Bureau provides a summary of taxes collected by the state in 2002.

	($000)	PER CAPITA
Total Taxes	6,878,923	1,533.25
Property taxes	195,132	43.49
Sales and gross receipts	3,383,068	754.05
General sales and gross receipts	1,748,235	389.66
Selective sales taxes	1,634,833	364.39
Alcoholic beverage	129,876	28.95
Amusements	125	0.03
Insurance Premiums	219,773	48.99
Motor fuels	511,927	114.1
Pari-mutuels	3,594	0.8
Public utilities	540,541	120.48
Tobacco products	63,782	14.22
Other selective sales	165,215	36.82
Licenses	394,973	88.04
Alcoholic beverages	2,424	0.54
Amusements	(X)	(X)
Corporation	72,080	16.07
Hunting and fishing	15,178	3.38
Motor vehicle	183,299	40.86
Motor vehicle operators	12,888	2.87
Public utility	10,148	2.26
Occupation and business, NEC	98,943	22.05
Other	13	0
Other taxes	2,905,750	647.66
Individual income	2,399,852	534.9
Corporation net income	322,636	71.91
Death and gift	82,970	18.49
Documentary and stock transfer	34,625	7.72
Severance	65,667	14.64
Other	(X)	(X)

37 ECONOMIC POLICY

Alabama seeks to attract out-of-state business by means of tax incentives and plant-building assistance. The Alabama Development Office (ADO) plans for economic growth through industrial development. It also extends loans, issues bonds, and offers other forms of financing to growing companies, to firms that create permanent jobs, and to small businesses. The International Trade Division of the ADO provides a variety of service to help Alabama companies export, and in 2002 sponsored trade mission to Mexico and Costa Rica. In 1987 The Alabama Enterprise Zone Program was passed. As of 2003, 27 Enterprise Zones had been authorized across the state in areas considered to have depressed economies, each zone offering packages of local tax and nontax incentives to encourage business to local in the area. The Alabama Industrial Development Training Institute, within the Department of Education, provides job training especially designed to suit the needs of high technology industries. Alabama offers zero-interest loans and grants to rural economic development projects. In an effort to attract new industries or help existing companies grow, the state helps counties and municipalities pay for site improvements, and assists communities in financing infrastructures such as water and sewer lines or access roads. The Alabama Commerce Commission promotes legislation that protects and nurtures the Alabaman economy, including infrastructural projects on the state's roads, bridges and docks. In 2000, the Alabama Commission on Environmental Initiatives was created by executive order charged with setting a program for improving the environmental quality of the state. In 2002, a Brownfields Redevelopment Program was introduced.

38 HEALTH

Alabama's infant death rate for the 12 months ending December 2000—9.4 per 1,000 live births—was one of the highest in the US. The abortion rate stood at 14 per 1,000 women in 1999.

The state's overall death rate in 2000—1,027.0 deaths per 100,000 population—included a death rate from heart disease of 305.5 per 100,000, compared to the national rate of 258.2. Alabama also ranked above the national rate in death rates from cancer, cerebrovascular diseases, accidents, traffic fatalities, and suicide. Smoking prevalence was 25.3% of adults age 18 and older in 2000. The rate of death from lung disease for 2000 was 72.5 per 100,000 people. The mortality rate from HIV infection was 4.6 per 100,000 population, lower than the national average of 5.3 per 100,000 population for 2000. There had been 6,706 documented AIDS cases reported through 2001.

Alabama had 107 community hospitals in 2001; there were 16,627 beds and 684,923 admissions. Hospital personnel included 17,216 registered nurses. Alabama had 218 physicians per 100,000 population in 2000. The average per capita expense to hospitals in the state for care in 2001 was $1,269. Federal government grants to cover the Medicare and Medicaid services in 2001 totaled $2.1 billion; 695,195 enrollees received Medicare benefits that year. At least 13.1% of Alabama's adult population was uninsured in 2002.

39 SOCIAL WELFARE

In 2001, the average weekly unemployment benefit was $163.57. Average monthly participation in the food stamp program in FY2002 comprised 443,547 persons (173,295 households). The average monthly benefit was $78.42, and the sum total of benefits paid in FY2002 was $417,376,930.

With the enactment of the Personal Responsibility and Work Opportunity Reconciliation Act of 1996, the US government has changed the form and regulations for many of its social welfare programs. Most significantly, it replaces Aid to Families with Dependent Children (AFDC), an open-ended entitlement program, with Temporary Assistance for Needy Families (TANF), a limited system of assistance funded largely through federal block grants. The reform act also impacts the food stamp program, the Supplemental Security Income program, and the child nutrition program. The law took effect on 1 July 1997 and provided $16.38 billion in block grants for fiscal years 1997–2002. The grants were to be divided among the states based on an equation involving the numbers of former AFDC recipients in each state. Reauthorization of the 1996 social welfare legislation, scheduled for 2002, was delayed, and the original law had been extended three times as of July 2003, with the most recent extension running through September 2003. Alabama's TANF program is called the Family Assistance Program (FA). In June 2000 the state had 55,168 welfare recipients. State expenditures on the TANF program in FY2002 totaled $38,686,168.

In December 2001, Social Security benefits were paid to 841,730 Alabamians. This number included 465,860 retired workers, 103,210 widows and widowers, 129,880 disabled workers, 51,080 spouses, and 91,700 children. Social Security beneficiaries represented 18.8% of the total state population and 92.7% of the state's population age 65 and older. Retired workers (excluding persons with special benefits) received an average monthly payment of $827; widows and widowers, $743; disabled workers, $784; and spouses, $411. Payments for children of retired workers averaged $398 per month; children of deceased workers, $541; and children of disabled workers, $230.

Federal Supplemental Security Income payments in December 2001 went to 161,521 Alabama residents, averaging $343 a month.

40HOUSING

In 2002, there were an estimated 2,014,536 housing units in Alabama, of which 1,729,893 were occupied. In the same year, about 72.5% of all housing units were owner-occupied. About 68.7% of all housing units were detached, single-family homes; 14.7% were mobile homes. It was estimated that about 81,014 households across the state were without telephone service, 4,505 lacked complete plumbing facilities, and 6,525 lacked complete kitchen facilities.

Approximately 18,403 new privately owned units were authorized the same year. The median home value was $93,917. The median monthly housing cost for mortgage owners was $892 while the cost for renters was $488. During 2002, the Alabama state program received over $50.6 million in aid from the US Department of Housing and Urban Development (HUD), including $31.6 million in HUD community development block grants.

The Fairhope Single Tax Corp., near Point Clear, was founded in 1893 by Iowans seeking to put into practice the economic theories of Henry George. Incorporated under Alabama law in 1904, this oldest and largest of US single-tax experiments continues to lease land in return for the payment of a rent (the "single tax") based on the land's valuation; the combined rents are used to pay taxes and to provide and improve community services.

41EDUCATION

In 2000, 75.3% of Alabamians age 25 and older were high school graduates. Some 19% had obtained a bachelor's degree or higher.

The total enrollment for fall 1999 in Alabama's public schools stood at 740,732. Of these, 538,687 attended schools from kindergarten through grade eight, and 202,045 attended high school. Minority students made up approximately 42% of the total enrollment in public elementary and secondary schools in 2001. Total enrollment was estimated at 726,259 in fall 2000 and was expected to reach 768,000 by fall 2005. Enrollment in nonpublic schools in fall 2001 was 73,352. Expenditures for public education in 2000/01 were estimated at $4,334,139.

As of fall 2000, there were 243,275 students enrolled in college or graduate school. In the same year Alabama had 76 degree-granting institutions. The largest state universities are Auburn University and the three University of Alabama campuses, including Birmingham, Huntsville, and the main campus in Tuscaloosa. Tuskegee University, founded as a normal and industrial school in 1881 under the leadership of Booker T. Washington, has become one of the nation's most famous black colleges. Minority students comprised 27.8% of total postsecondary enrollment as of 1997.

42ARTS

The Alabama State Council on the Arts, established by the legislature in 1966, provides aid to local nonprofit arts organizations; there were 62 local arts councils in 2003. The Alabama Humanities Foundation was established in 1974. In 2000, the National Endowment for the Humanities awarded grants totaling $759,034 to 15 Alabama organizations. In 2003, the National Endowment for the Arts awarded grants totaling $871,400 to Alabama arts organizations. The grants supported the efforts of about 125,000 artists and more than 400 arts associations.

A community arts development and residency program is financed by a state income tax check-off and private contributions. The Alabama Center for Traditional Culture, established in 1990, works in conjunction with the State Council to promote and preserve local arts and culture. The Alabama Jazz and Blues Federation, also established in 1990, has been very active in offering monthly jam sessions for artists, an annual summer festival, and several concerts throughout the year.

The Alabama Shakespeare Festival State Theater performs in Montgomery. Over one million people have attended the festival. The Birmingham Festival of Arts was founded in 1951 and the city's Alabama School of Fine Arts has been state-supported since 1971. Huntsville, Montgomery, and Tuscaloosa have symphony orchestras.

Sacred Harp a cappella "sings" of old hymn tunes are held regularly. The Tennessee Valley Old Time Fiddlers Convention takes place in October at Athens State College. Every June, the annual Hank Williams Memorial Celebration is held near the country singer's birthplace at the Olive West Community. There are opera groups in Huntsville and Mobile.

43LIBRARIES AND MUSEUMS

As of 2000, Alabama had 20 county and multi-county regional library systems. Alabama's 206,000 public libraries had a combined total of 8,600,000 volumes in 2000, when the total circulation was 15,340,000. The University of Alabama had 1,896,687 volumes; the Birmingham Public Library had 19 branches and 973,936 volumes. The Alabama Department of Archives and History Library, at Montgomery, had 260,000 volumes and several special collections on Alabama history and government. Collections on aviation and space exploration in Alabama's libraries, particularly its military libraries, may be the most extensive in the US outside of Washington, D.C. In 1997 the Alabama Public Library Service and its regional library for the blind and physically handicapped had over 480,000 books, videos, and audio tapes, including more than 25,000 books in Braille. Memorabilia of Wernher von Braun are in the library at the Alabama Space and Rocket Center at Huntsville; the Redstone Arsenal's Scientific Information Center holds over 227,000 volumes and 1,800,000 technical reports. Total income for the public library system in 2003 was $64,927,000; including $908,978 in federal grants and $4,479,963 in state grants. State libraries spent 64.2% of that income on staff, and $15.1 on collections.

Alabama had 81 museums in 2000. The most important art museum is the Birmingham Museum of Art. Other museums include the George Washington Carver Museum at Tuskegee Institute, the Women's Army Corps Museum and Military Police Corps Museum at Ft. McClellan, the US Army Aviation Museum at Ft. Rucker, the Pike Pioneer Museum at Troy, the Museum of the City of Mobile, and the Montgomery Museum of Fine Arts. Also in Montgomery are Old Alabama Town and the F. Scott and Zelda Fitzgerald home. Russell Cave National Monument has an archaeological exhibit. In Florence is the W.C. Handy Home; at Tuscumbia, Helen Keller's birthplace, Ivy Green.

44COMMUNICATIONS

In 2001, 93.0% of Alabama's occupied housing units had telephones.

During 2003, Alabama had 95 major operating radio stations (20 AM, 75 FM) and 22 major television stations. In 2000, 69%

of television households in the Birmingham area subscribed to cable television. A total of 44,371 Internet domain names had been registered in Alabama by 2000.

45 PRESS

The earliest newspaper in Alabama, the short-lived *Mobile Centinel* (sic), made its first appearance on 23 May 1811. The oldest newspaper still in existence in the state is the *Mobile Register*, founded in 1813.

As of 2002 Alabama had 20 morning dailies; 4 evening dailies; and 20 Sunday papers. The following table shows the leading dailies with their 2002 circulations:

AREA	NAME	DAILY	SUNDAY
Birmingham	*News** (m,S)	145,760	186,269
	Post–Herald (m)	154,249	
Huntsville	*Times**(m,S)	56,540	77,664
Mobile	*Register**(m,S)	95,975	113,433
Montgomery	*Advertiser* (m,S)	51,023	63,857
Tuscaloosa	*News* (m,S)	37,319	38,498

*Owned by the Alabama Group of Advance Publications

46 ORGANIZATIONS

In 2003, there were over 1,800 organizations within the state. National organizations with headquarters in Alabama include Civitan International (Birmingham); the National Speleological Society (Huntsville); Klanwatch; and the Southern Poverty Law Center, both located in Montgomery. The last-named is one of the major civil rights organizations active in Alabama, along with the Southern Christian Leadership Conference (SCLC) and the National Association for the Advancement of Colored People (NAACP). Two branches of the Ku Klux Klan are also active in Alabama.

State cultural organizations include the Alabama Historical Association and Alabama Preservation Alliance, both in Montgomery.

47 TOURISM, TRAVEL, AND RECREATION

In 2000, about 18 million people visited the State of Alabama, spending about $6.1 billion (a 7% increase from 1999). With a statewide impact of 137,000 jobs and about 3% of GSP, tourism is an important industry for Alabama. About 73% of all tourists choose destinations in one of six counties: Baldwin, Jefferson, Madison, Mobile, Montgomery and Tuscaloosa.

A top tourist attraction is the Alabama Space and Rocket Center at Huntsville, home of the US Space Camp. Other attractions include many antebellum houses and plantations: Magnolia Grove (a state shrine) at Greensboro; Gaineswood and Bluff Hall at Demopolis; Arlington in Birmingham; Oakleigh at Mobile; Sturdivant Hall at Selma; Shorter Mansion at Eufaula; and the first White House of the confederacy at Montgomery.

The celebration of Mardi Gras in Mobile, which began in 1704, predates that in New Orleans and now occupies several days before Ash Wednesday. Gulf beaches are a popular attraction and Point Clear, across the bay from Mobile, has been a fashionable resort, especially for southerners, since the 1840s. The state fair is held at Birmingham every October.

During 2000, Baldwin and Jefferson counties were the biggest tourist beneficiaries; home to Alabama's four national park sites, which include Tuskegee Institute National Historic Site and Russell Cave National Monument, an almost continuous archaeological record of human habitation from at least 7000 BC to about AD 1650. Tannehill Historical State Park features ante- and postbellum dwellings, a restored iron furnace over a century old, and a museum of iron and steel.

The Alabama Deep Sea Fishing Rodeo at Dauphin Island also attracts thousands of visitors. Alabama's Robert Trent Jones Golf Trail is a major tourist attraction, with seven championship courses located from Huntsville to Mobile.

48 SPORTS

Alabama is home to a number of professional teams in various sports. The National Basketball Developmental League (NBDL) is an affiliate with the NBA and has teams in Mobile and Huntsville. The Birmingham Power is a member of the National Womens Basketball League (NWBL) and the Birmingham Steeldogs are an Arena League2 football squad. The Birmingham Steel Magnolias are a professional women's football team. There are minor league baseball clubs at Birmingham, Mobile, and Huntsville, and minor league hockey teams at Birmingham, Huntsville, and Mobile. Two major professional stock car races, the DieHard 500 and the Winston 500, in April and October, respectively, are held at Alabama International Motor Speedway in Talladega. Dog racing was legalized in Mobile in 1971. Four of the major hunting-dog competitions in the US are held annually in the state.

Football reigns supreme among collegiate sports. The University of Alabama finished number one in 1961,1964, 1965 (against Michigan State), 1978 (against USC), 1979, and 1992 and is a perennial top-ten entry. Competing in the Southeastern Conference, Alabama's Crimson Tide won the Sugar Bowl in 1962, 1964, 1967, 1978, 1979, 1980, and 1993; the Orange Bowl in 1943, 1953, 1963, and 1966; the Cotton Bowl in 1942 and 1981; the Sun Bowl in 1983 and 1988; the Gator Bowl in 1993; the Florida Citrus Bowl in 1995; and the Outback Bowl in 1997. They also captured the 2001 Independence Bowl. The Crimson Tide have won a total of 12 national championships and 21 SEC titles. Auburn University, which also competes in the Southeastern Conference, won the Sugar Bowl in 1984; the Florida Citrus Bowl in 1982 and 1987; the Gator Bowl in 1954, 1971, and 1972; the Peach Bowl in 1990; the Hall of Fame Bowl in 1990; and the Sun Bowl in 1968. The Tigers have won 14 bowl games and have produced two Heisman trophy winners (Pat Sullivan and Bo Jackson). The Blue-Gray game, an all-star contest, is held at Montgomery on Christmas Day, and the Senior Bowl game is played in Mobile in January. Additionally, Alabama-Huntsville won NCAA Division II hockey championships in 1996, 1997, and 1998.

Boat races include the annual Dauphin Island Race, the largest one-day sailing race in the United States. The Alabama Sports Hall of Fame is located at Birmingham.

There are several famous athletes who were born in Alabama. Among the most notable are Willie Mays, Hank Aaron, Jesse Owens, and Bo Jackson.

49 FAMOUS ALABAMIANS

William Rufus De Vane King (b.North Carolina, 1786–1853) served as a US senator from Alabama and as minister to France before being elected US vice president in 1852 on the Democratic ticket with Franklin Pierce; he died six weeks after taking the oath of office. Three Alabamians who served as associate justices of the US Supreme Court were John McKinley (b.Virginia, 1780–1852), John A. Campbell (b.Georgia, 1811–89), and Hugo L. Black (1886–1971). Campbell resigned from the court in 1861, later becoming assistant secretary of war for the Confederacy; Black, a US senator from 1927 to 1937, served one of the longest terms (1937–71) in the history of the court and is regarded as one of its most eminent justices.

Among the most colorful figures in antebellum Alabama was William Lowndes Yancey (b.Georgia, 1814–63), a fiery orator who was a militant proponent of slavery, states' rights, and eventually secession. During the early 20th century, a number of Alabamians became influential in national politics. Among them were US senators John Hollis Bankhead (1842–1920) and John

Hollis Bankhead, Jr. (1872–1946); the latter's brother, William B. Bankhead (1874–1940), who became speaker of the US House of Representatives in 1936; and US Senator Oscar W. Underwood (b.Kentucky, 1862–1929), a leading contender for the Democratic presidential nomination in 1912 and 1924. Other prominent US senators from Alabama have included (Joseph) Lister Hill (1894–1984) and John Sparkman (1899–1985), who was the Democratic vice-presidential nominee in 1952. Alabama's most widely known political figure is George Corley Wallace (1919–98), who served as governor in 1963–67 and 1971–79, and was elected to a fourth term in 1982. Wallace, an outspoken opponent of racial desegregation in the 1960s, was a candidate for the Democratic presidential nomination in 1964; four years later, as the presidential nominee of the American Independent Party, he carried five states. While campaigning in Maryland's Democratic presidential primary on 15 May 1972, Wallace was shot and paralyzed from the waist down by a would-be assassin. In 1976, Wallace made his fourth and final unsuccessful bid for the presidency.

Civil rights leader Martin Luther King, Jr. (b.Georgia, 1929–68), winner of the Nobel Peace Prize in 1964, first came to national prominence as leader of the Montgomery bus boycott of 1955; he also led demonstrations at Birmingham in 1963 and at Selma in 1965. His widow, Coretta Scott King (b.1927) is a native Alabamian. Federal judge Frank M. Johnson, Jr. (1918–99), has made several landmark rulings in civil rights cases.

Helen Keller (1880–1968), deaf and blind as the result of a childhood illness, was the first such multihandicapped person to earn a college degree; she later became a world-famous author and lecturer. Another world figure, black educator Booker T. Washington (b.Virginia, 1856–1915), built Alabama's Tuskegee Institute from a school where young blacks were taught building, farming, cooking, brickmaking, dressmaking, and other trades into an internationally known agricultural research center. Tuskegee's most famous faculty member was George Washington Carver (b.Missouri, 1864–1943), who discovered some 300 different peanut products, 118 new ways to use sweet potatoes, and numerous other crop varieties and applications. Among Alabama's leaders in medicine was Dr. William Crawford Gorgas (1854–1920), head of sanitation in Panama during the construction of the Panama Canal; he later served as US surgeon general. Brought to the US after World War II (1939–45), the internationally known scientist Wernher von Braun (b.Germany, 1912–77) came to Alabama in 1950 to direct the US missile program.

Two Alabama writers, (Nelle) Harper Lee (b.1926) and Edward Osborne Wilson (b.1929), have won Pulitzer Prizes. Famous musicians from Alabama include blues composer and performer W(illiam) C(hristopher) Handy (1873–1958), singer Nat "King" Cole (1917–65), and singer-songwriter Hank Williams (1923–53). Alabama's most widely known actress was Tallulah Bankhead (1903–68), the daughter of William B. Bankhead.

Among Alabama's sports figures are track and field star Jesse Owens (James Cleveland Owens, 1913–80), winner of four gold medals at the 1936 Olympic Games in Berlin; boxer Joe Louis (Joseph Louis Barrow, 1914–81), world heavyweight champion from 1937 to 1949; and baseball stars Leroy Robert "Satchel" Paige (1906?–82), Willie Mays (b.1931), and (Louis) Henry Aaron (b.1934), all-time US home-run leader.

[50]BIBLIOGRAPHY

Barnard, William D. *Dixiecrats and Democrats: Alabama Politics, 1942–1950.* University, Ala.: University of Alabama Press, 1974.

Carmer, Carl Lamson. *Stars Fell on Alabama.* Tuscaloosa: University of Alabama Press, 2000.

Carter, Dan T. *Scottsboro. A Tragedy of the American South.* Baton Rouge: Louisiana State University Press, 1969.

Lamar, Jay and Jeanie Thompson, eds. *The Remembered Gate: Memoirs by Alabama Writers.* Tuscaloosa: University of Alabama Press, 2002.

Lofton, J. Mack. *Voices from Alabama: A Twentieth-Century Mosaic.* Tuscaloosa: University of Alabama Press, 1993.

Marks, Henry S., and Marsha Marks. *Alabama Past Leaders.* Huntsville, Ala.: Strode, 1981.

Martin, David L. *Alabama's State and Local Government.* University, Ala.: University of Alabama Press, 1985.

Permaloff, Anne. *Political Power in Alabama: The More Things Change—.* Athens: University of Georgia Press, 1995.

Rogers, William Warren, and Robert David Ward. *August Reckoning: Jack Turner and Racism in Post-Civil War Alabama.* Baton Rouge: Louisiana State University Press, 1973.

Rosengarten, Theodore. *All God's Dangers: The Life of Nate Shaw.* New York: Knopf, 1974.

Van De Veer Hamilton, Virginia. *Hugo Black: The Alabama Years.* Baton Rouge: Louisiana State University Press, 1972.

ALASKA

State of Alaska

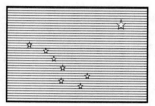

ORIGIN OF STATE NAME: From the Aleut word *alyeska*, meaning "great land." **NICKNAME:** The Last Frontier; also, the Land of the Midnight Sun. **CAPITAL:** Juneau. **ENTERED UNION:** 3 January 1959 (49th). **SONG:** "Alaska's Flag." **MOTTO:** North to the Future. **FLAG:** On a blue field, eight gold stars form the Big Dipper and the North Star. **OFFICIAL SEAL:** In the inner circle symbols of mining, agriculture, and commerce are depicted against a background of mountains and the northern lights. In the outer circle are a fur seal, a salmon, and the words "The Seal of the State of Alaska." **BIRD:** Willow ptarmigan. **FISH:** King salmon. **FLOWER:** Wild forget-me-not. **TREE:** Sitka spruce. **GEM:** Jade. **MINERAL:** Gold. **SPORT:** Dogteam racing (mushing). **LEGAL HOLIDAYS:** New Year's Day, 1 January; Birthday of Martin Luther King, Jr., 3rd Monday in January; Lincoln's Birthday, 12 February; Washington's Birthday, 3rd Monday in February; Seward's Day, last Monday in March; Memorial Day, last Monday in May; Independence Day, 4 July; Labor Day, 1st Monday in September; Alaska Day, 18 October; Veterans Day, 11 November; Thanksgiving Day, 4th Thursday in November; Christmas Day, 25 December. **TIME:** noon GMT = 3 AM Alaska Standard Time, 2 AM Hawaii-Aleutian Standard Time.

¹LOCATION, SIZE, AND EXTENT

Situated at the northwest corner of the North American continent, Alaska is separated by Canadian territory from the coterminous 48 states. Alaska is the largest of the 50 states, with a total area of 591,004 sq mi (1,530,699 sq km). Land takes up 570,833 sq mi (1,478,456 sq km) and inland water 20,171 sq mi (52,243 sq km). Alaska is more than twice the size of Texas, the next-largest state, and occupies 16% of the total US land area; the E-W extension is 2,261 mi (3,639 km); the maximum N-S extension is 1,420 mi (2,285 km).

Alaska is bounded on the N by the Arctic Ocean and Beaufort Sea; on the E by Canada's Yukon Territory and province of British Columbia; on the S by the Gulf of Alaska, Pacific Ocean, and Bering Sea; and on the W by the Bering Sea, Bering Strait, Chukchi Sea, and Arctic Ocean.

Alaska's many offshore islands include St. Lawrence, St. Matthew, Nunivak, and the Pribilof group in the Bering Sea; Kodiak Island in the Gulf of Alaska; the Aleutian Islands in the Pacific; and some 1,100 islands constituting the Alexander Archipelago, extending SE along the Alaska panhandle.

The total boundary length of Alaska is 8,187 mi (13,176 km), including a general coastline of 6,640 mi (10,686 km); the tidal shoreline extends 33,904 mi (54,563 km). Alaska's geographic center is about 60 mi (97 km) NW of Mt. McKinley. The northern-most point in the US—Point Barrow, at 71°23′ 30″N, 156°28′ 30″W—lies within the state of Alaska, as does the western-most point—Cape Wrangell on Attu Island in the Aleutians, at 52°55′ 30″N, 172°28′ E. Little Diomede Island, belonging to Alaska, is less than 2 mi (3 km) from Big Diomede Island, belonging to Russia.

²TOPOGRAPHY

Topography varies sharply among the six distinct regions of Alaska. In the southeast is a narrow coastal panhandle cut off from the main Alaskan landmass by the St. Elias Range. This region, featuring numerous mountain peaks of 10,000 ft (3,000 m) in elevation, is paralleled by the Alexander Archipelago. South-central Alaska, which covers a 700-mi (1,100-km) area along the Gulf of Alaska, includes the Kenai Peninsula and Cook Inlet, a great arm of the Pacific penetrating some 200 mi (320

km) to Anchorage. The southwestern region includes the Alaska Peninsula, filled with lightly wooded, rugged peaks; and the 1,700-mi (2,700-km) sweep of the Aleutian islands, barren masses of volcanic origin. Western Alaska extends from Bristol Bay to the Seward Peninsula, an immense tundra dotted with lakes and containing the deltas of the Yukon and Kuskokwim rivers, the longest in the state at 1,900 mi (3,058 km) and 680 mi (1,094 km), respectively. Interior Alaska extends north of the Alaska Range and south of the Brooks Range, including most of the drainage of the Yukon and its major tributaries, the Tanana and Porcupine rivers. The Arctic region extends from Kotzebue, north of the Seward Peninsula, east to Canada. From the northern slopes of the Brooks Range, the elevation falls to the Arctic Ocean.

The 11 highest mountains in the US—including the highest in North America, Mt. McKinley (20,320 ft/6,198 m), located in the Alaska Range—are in the state, which also contains half the world's glaciers; the largest, Malaspina, covers more area than the entire state of Rhode Island. Ice fields cover 4% of the state. Alaska has more than three million lakes larger than 20 acres (eight hectares), and more than one-fourth of all the inland water wholly within the US lies inside the state's borders. The largest lake is Iliamna, occupying about 1,000 sq mi (2,600 sq km).

The most powerful earthquake in US recorded history, measuring 8.5 on the Richter scale, struck the Anchorage region on 27 March 1964, resulting in 114 deaths and $500 million in property damage in Alaska and along the US west coast.

³CLIMATE

Americans, who called Alaska "Seward's icebox" when it was first purchased from the Russians, were unaware of the variety of climatic conditions within its six topographic regions. Although minimum daily winter temperatures in the Arctic region and in the Brooks Range average –20°F (–29°C) and the ground at Point Barrow is frozen permanently to 1,330 ft (405 m), summer maximum daily temperatures in the Alaskan lowlands average above 60°F (16°C) and have been known to exceed 90°F (32°C). The southeastern region is moderate, ranging from a daily average of 30°F (–1°C) in January to 56°F (13°C) in July; the south-central zone has a similar summer range, but winters are somewhat harsher, especially in the interior. The Aleutian Islands have chilly, damp winters and rainy, foggy weather for most of the year; western Alaska is also rainy and cool. The all-time high for the state was 100°F (38°C), recorded at Ft. Yukon on 27 June 1915; the reading of –79.8°F (–62°C), registered at Prospect Creek Camp in the northwestern part of the state on 23 January 1971, is the lowest temperature ever officially recorded in the US.

Juneau received an annual average precipitation of 58.3 in (148 cm), with 98.5 in (250 cm) of snowfall recorded at the airport there each year. The entire southeastern region of Alaska has a wide range of microclimates with varying levels of precipitation; Juneau's metropolitan area precipitation ranges from 40 in (102 cm) to over 100 in (254 cm) per year.

⁴FLORA AND FAUNA

Life zones in Alaska range from grasslands, mountains, and tundra to thick forests, in which Sitka spruce (the state tree), western hemlock, tamarack, white birch, and western red cedar predominate. Various hardy plants and wild flowers spring up during the short growing season on the semiarid tundra plains. Species of poppy and gentian are endangered.

Mammals abound amid the wilderness. Great herds of caribou migrate across some northern areas of the state. Moose move within ranges they establish, but do not migrate seasonally or move in herds as do caribou. Reindeer were introduced to Alaska as herd animals for Alaska Natives, and there are no free-ranging herds in the state. Kodiak, polar, black, and grizzly bears, Dall sheep, and an abundance of small mammals are also found. The sea otter and musk ox have been successfully reintroduced. Round Island, along the north shore of Bristol Bay, has the world's largest walrus rookery. North America's largest population of bald eagles nest in Alaska, and whales migrate annually to the icy bays. Pristine lakes and streams are famous for trout and salmon fishing. In all, 386 species of birds, 430 fishes, 105 mammals, 7 amphibians, and 3 reptiles have been found in the state.

Seven species listed as endangered by the US Fish and Wildlife Service as of August 2003 included the Eskimo curlew, short-tailed albatross, leatherback sea turtle, steller sea-lion, and bowhead, finback, and humpback whales. Three species listed as threatened included the spectacled eider, Steller's aider, and Steller sea-lion. Numerous species considered endangered in the conterminous US remain common in Alaska.

⁵ENVIRONMENTAL PROTECTION

In 1997, Alaska's number one environmental health problem was the unsafe water and sanitation facilities in over 135 of Alaska's communities—mostly Alaska Native villages. The people of these communities must carry their water from streams or watering points to their homes; people must use "honey buckets" or privies for disposal of human waste; and solid waste lagoons are usually a collection of human waste, trash, and junk, infested with flies and other carriers of disease. The government of Alaska, under then-governor Tony Knowles, established a goal of "putting the honey bucket in museums" by the year 2005. To accomplish this goal, in 1993 Knowles established the "Rural Sanitation Task Force" to guide the effort and has committed approximately $40 million per year in state and federal funds to finance new water, sewer, and solid waste facilities.

A tremendous backlog of contaminated sites from World War II (1939–45) military installations exists, and some of these sites many years later were discovered to be the source of contamination of groundwater, drinking water, and fisheries habitat. The Environmental Protection Agency's database listed 86 hazardous waste sites, six of which were on the National Priorities List, in Alaska in 2003. Sites have been identified and prioritized and an aggressive state/federal cleanup effort is underway. Two former pulp mill sites in southeast Alaska are also the subject of major cleanup efforts. In 2001, Alaska received $85,248,000 in federal grants from the EPA; EPA expenditures for procurement contracts in Alaska that year amounted to $788,000.

The 1989 Exxon Valdez oil spill highlighted the need for better prevention and response abilities. Since then these capabilities have been increased through stronger laws and more clearly defined roles among all the various governments and communities and greatly enhanced state regulatory agency capabilities. State-of-the-art tugs are now escorting tankers in Prince William Sound; these tankers are constantly monitored to ensure that they stay on course, and their crews have been increased to ensure redundancy of critical positions.

Oil development on the North Slope and in Cook Inlet, mining throughout the state, and timber harvesting largely in the southern regions continue to be areas of focus for environmental protection, as do winter violations of air quality standards for carbon monoxide in Anchorage and Fairbanks.

⁶POPULATION

Alaska, with a land area one-fifth the size of the conterminous US, ranked 47th in population in 2002 with an estimated total of 643,786, an increase of 2.7% since 2000. Between 1990 and 2000, Alaska's population grew from 550,043 to 626,932, or 14%.

Population projections for 2005 reach 700,000, and the state is projected to have a population of 885,000 by 2025. Regions of settlement and development constitute less than 1% of Alaska's total land area. The population density was 1.1 persons per sq mi in 2000, making Alaska the nation's most sparsely settled state.

Historically, population shifts in Alaska have directly reflected economic and political changes. The Alaska gold rush of the 1890s resulted in a population boom from 32,052 in 1890 to 63,592 a decade later; by the 1920s, however, when mining had declined, Alaska's population had decreased to 55,036. The region's importance to US national defense during the 1940s led to a rise in population from 72,524 to 128,643 during that decade. Oil development, especially the construction of the Alaska pipeline, brought a 78% population increase between 1960 and 1980. Almost all of this gain was from migration.

The state's population is much younger than that of the nation as a whole. The median age was 32.4 in 2000, compared with the national average of 35.3, and only 5.7% of all Alaskans were 65 years of age or older—by far the lowest such percentage in any state—while 30.4% were under 18 years old (compared with the national average of 25.7). Alaska is one of the few states where men outnumber women; as of 2000 men accounted for 51.7% of Alaskan residents.

About half of Alaska's residents live in and around Anchorage, whose population was estimated at 268,983 in 2002. The 2001 estimated populations of other leading metropolitan areas were Fairbanks, 83,694, and Juneau, 30,558. Less than a quarter of the population lives in Western Alaska.

⁷ETHNIC GROUPS

In 2000 Native Americans accounted for 15.6% of Alaska's population—the highest percentage of any state. Indians—primarily Athabaskan (14,520) and Tlingit-Haida (14,825)—living in southeastern Alaska (Alaska Panhandle) numbered around 29,345 in 2000. There are also small numbers of Tsimshian living in this area. Eskimos (45,919) and Aleuts (11,941), the other native peoples, live mostly in scattered villages to the north and northwest. Taken together, Alaska Natives were estimated in 2000 to number about 98,043, up from 86,000 (16%) in 1996. The Native Claims Settlement Act of 1971 gave 13 native corporations nearly $1 billion in compensation for

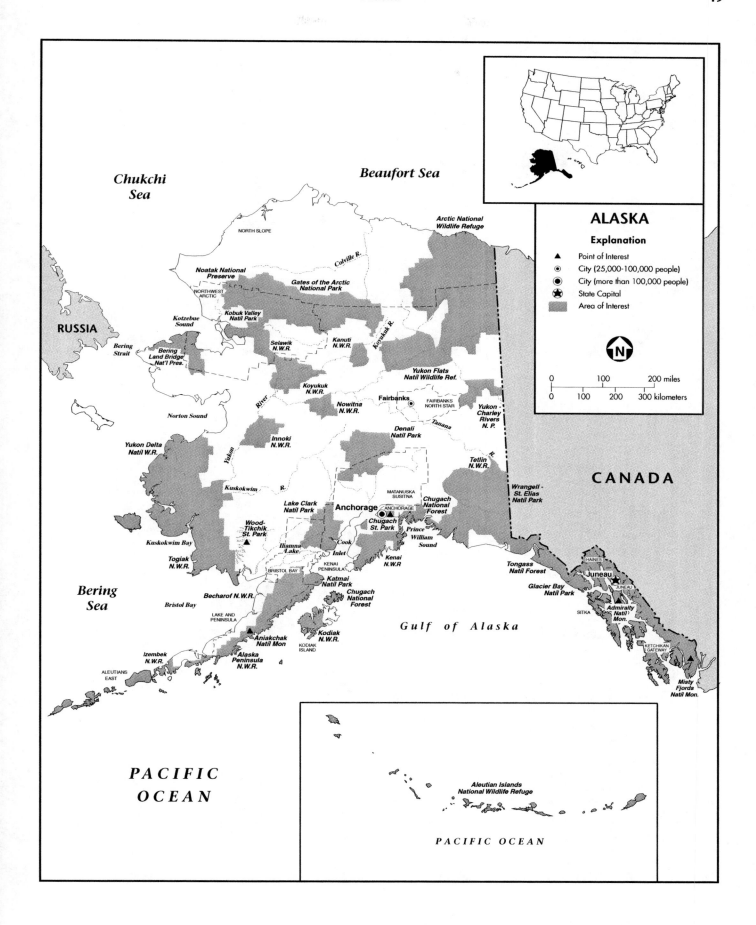

ALASKA

Explanation

▲ Point of Interest

⊙ City (25,000-100,000 people)

◉ City (more than 100,000 people)

★ State Capital

Area of Interest

exploration, mining, and drilling rights, and awarded them royalties on oil and the rights to nearly 12% of Alaska's land area.

In 2000, the black population was 21,787, or 3.5% of the total population, down slightly from 22,000 in 1990. Among those of Asian origin in 2000 were 12,712 Filipinos, 1,414 Japanese, and 4,573 Koreans; in the same year, the total Asian population was 25,116 and Pacific Islanders numbered 3,309. In 2000, of Alaska's total population, about 25,852 individuals were of Hispanic or Latino origin, with 13,334 of those claiming Mexican ancestry (up from 6,888 in 1990). Foreign-born persons numbered 37,170, or 5.9% of the population (up from 4.4% in 1990).

8LANGUAGES

From the Tlingit, Haida, and Tsimshian groups of lower Alaska almost no language influence has been felt, save for *hooch* (from Tlingit hoochino); but some native words have escaped into general usage, notably Eskimo *mukluk* and Aleut *parka*. Native place-names abound: Skagway and Ketchikan (Tlingit), Kodiak and Katmai (Eskimo), and Alaska and Akutan (Aleut).

In 2000, 85.7% of the population five years old and older was reported to speak only English in the home, a decrease over 87.9% recorded in 1990.

The following table gives selected statistics from the 2000 census for language spoken at home by persons five years old and over. The category "Other Native North American languages" includes Apache, Cherokee, Choctaw, Dakota, Keres, Pima, and Yupik. The category "Other Pacific Island languages" includes Chamorro, Hawaiian, Ilocano, Indonesian, and Samoan.

LANGUAGE	NUMBER	PERCENT
Population 5 years and over	**579,740**	**100.0**
Speak only English	496,982	85.7
Speak a language other than English	82,758	14.3
Speak a language other than English	**82,758**	**14.3**
Other Native North American languages	30,121	5.2
Spanish or Spanish Creole	16,674	2.9
Tagalog	8,934	1.5
Korean	4,369	0.8
German	3,574	0.6
Russian	2,952	0.5
Other Pacific Island languages	2,591	0.4
French (incl. Patois, Cajun)	2,197	0.4
Japanese	1,392	0.2
Chinese	1,295	0.2

9RELIGIONS

The largest religious organization in the state is the Roman Catholic Church, which had 54,359 and 102 congregations in 2000. Southern Baptists constituted the largest Protestant denomination, with 22,959 adherents and 68 congregations.

Many Aleuts were converted to the Russian Orthodox religion during the 18th century, and small Russian Orthodox congregations are still active on the Aleutian Islands, in Kodiak and southeastern Alaska, and along the Yukon River. The Orthodox Church in America—Territorial Dioceses had 20,000 adherents and 46 congregations in 2000.

Other major groups were the Latter-Day Saints (Mormons), 19,019 adherents; Assembly of God, 11,638; Independent, Non-Charismatic Churches, 7,600; and Episcopalians, 6,693. There were about 3,525 Jews and 1,381 Muslims. About 65.7% of the population were not counted as members of any religious organization.

10TRANSPORTATION

The first rail transportation networks in Alaska were constructed to serve mining interests. The 110-mile-long (177-km-long) White Pass and Yukon Railway (WP&YRR), originally constructed during the Klondike Gold Rush and completed in 1900, constituted the key link between tidewater at Skagway, the Yukon River, and the gold fields. Today, this line runs as a summer-only tourist attraction and provides service between Skagway and Fraser, British Columbia. Shortly after the turn of the century, the Guggenheims financed the construction of the Copper River & Northwestern Railway, which connected Cordova and McCarthy to service the Kennicott Copper Mining Company.

Regular passenger and freight railroad service began in 1923, when the Alaska Railroad began operation. The Alaska Railroad links communities between Whittier, Seward, Anchorage, and Fairbanks. This railroad of 482 route mi (776 km) is not connected to any other North American line (although rail-barge service provides access to the rest of the US rail network). The Alaska Railroad was federally operated until 1985 when it was bought by the state government for $22.3 million. The railroad carries volumes of coal from Healy north to Fairbanks (600,000 tons/year) and south to Seward for export (800,000 tons/year). The railroad also carries large volumes of gravel to Anchorage (more than two million tons from Palmer in the mid-1990s) and petroleum products (more than one million tons from Mapco's North Pole refinery) to Anchorage and various military bases in the area. The railroad is increasing summer passenger travel, often by hauling dome/dining rail cars owned by tour companies.

The Alaska Highway, which extends 1,523 mi (2,451 km) from Dawson Creek, British Columbia, to Fairbanks, is the only total road link with the rest of the US. In-state roads are few and far between: although Fairbanks, Anchorage, and Seward are linked, Juneau, the state capital, has no road link. In total, 12,823 mi (20,636 km) of roads were in use in 2000, including more than 1,800 mi (2,896 km) of roads in national parks and forests. During the same year, the state had 623,222 registered vehicles and 465,256 licensed drivers. The largest public transit system, that of Anchorage, accommodated over three million unlinked passenger trips annually in the mid-1990s.

The Alaska Marine Highway System (AMHS) provides year-round scheduled ferry service to over 30 communities throughout southeast and southwest Alaska. Service extends from Bellingham, Washington, and Prince Rupert, British Columbia. This ferry system extends over 3,500 route mi (5,632 km) and connects communities with each other, with regional centers, and with the continental road system.

Water transport in Alaska is dominated by Valdez, which annually ships about 100 million tons of crude petroleum from the Trans-Alaska Pipeline Terminal. Kenai/Nikishka is the state's 2nd-largest freight-handling port and also has petroleum as its principal commodity. Anchorage is the state's largest general cargo port with over three million tons per year.

Air travel is the primary means of intrastate transportation, with regional carriers serving remote communities. The state operates 386 airports, including two major international airports in Anchorage and Juneau. In addition, there are 205 privately-owned airports in the state. Anchorage International Airport (AIA) is a major refueling stop for international freight airplanes and is a freight hub for Federal Express and United Parcel Service.

11HISTORY

At some time between 10,000 and 40,000 years ago, the ancestors of all of America's aboriginal peoples trekked over a land bridge that connected northeastern Siberia with north-western America. These early hunter-gatherers dispersed, eventually becoming three distinct groups: Aleut, Eskimo, and Indian.

Ages passed before overseas voyagers rediscovered Alaska. Separate Russian parties led by Aleksei Chirikov and Vitas Bering (who had sailed in 1728 through the strait that now bears his name) landed in Alaska in 1741. Within a few years, the discoverers were followed by the exploiters, who hunted the region's fur-bearing animals. In 1784, the first permanent Russian settlement was established on Kodiak Island: 15 years later, the Russian American Company was granted a monopoly over the region. Its manager, Aleksandr Baranov, established Sitka as the company's headquarters. In 1802, the Tlingit Indians captured Sitka, but two years later lost the town and the war with the Russian colonizers. Fluctuations in the fur trade, depletion of the sea otter, and the Russians' inability to make their settlements self-sustaining limited their development of the region. Increasingly, the czarist government viewed the colonies as a drain on the treasury. In 1867, as a result of the persistence of Secretary of State William H. Seward, a devoted American expansionist, Russia agreed to sell its American territories to the US for $7,200,000. From 1867 until the first Organic Act of 1884, which provided for a federally appointed governor, Alaska was administered first by the US Army, then by the US Customs Service.

The pace of economic development quickened after the discovery of gold in 1880 at Juneau. Prospectors began moving into the eastern interior after this success, leading to gold strikes on Forty Mile River in 1886 and at Circle in 1893. But it was the major strike in Canada's Klondike region in 1896 that sparked a mass stampede to the Yukon Valley and other regions of Alaska, including the Arctic. The gold rush led to the establishment of permanent towns in the interior for the first time.

Subsequent development of the fishing and timber industries increased Alaska's prosperity and prospects, although the region suffered from a lack of transportation facilities. A significant achievement came in 1914, when construction started on the Alaska Railroad connecting Seward, a new town with an ice-free port, with Anchorage and Fairbanks. Politically there were advances as well. In 1906, Alaskans were allowed to elect a nonvoting delegate to Congress for the first time. Congress granted territorial status to the region in 1912, and the first statehood bill was introduced in Congress four years later.

Mineral production declined sharply after 1914. Population declined too, and conditions remained depressed through the 1920s, although gold mining was helped by a rise in gold prices in 1934. World War II (1939–45) provided the next great economic impetus for Alaska; the Aleutian campaign that followed the Japanese invasion of the islands, though not as pivotal as the combat in other areas of the Pacific, did show American policymakers that Alaska's geography was in itself an important resource. Thus the spurt of federal construction and movement of military personnel continued even after the war ended, this time directed at the Soviet Union—only 40 mi (64 km) across the Bering Strait—rather than Japan.

The US government built the Alaska Highway and many other facilities, including docks, airfields, and an extension of the Alaska Railroad. Population soared as thousands of civilian workers and military personnel moved to the territory. The newcomers added impetus to a new movement for statehood, and the Alaska Statehood Act was adopted by Congress in June 1958 and ratified by Alaska voters that August. On 3 January 1959, President Dwight Eisenhower signed the proclamation that made Alaska the 49th state.

In 1971, the Native Claims Settlement Act provided an extensive grant to the state's natives but also precipitated a long federal-state controversy over land allocations. A major oil field was discovered in 1968, and in 1974, over the opposition of many environmentalists, construction began on the 789-mi (1,270-km) Trans-Alaska Pipeline from Prudhoe Bay to Valdez. The oil that began flowing through the pipeline in 1977 made Alaska almost immediately one of the nation's leading energy producers.

Alaska's extraordinary oil wealth enabled it to embark on a heavy program of state services and to abolish the state income tax. However, state spending failed to stimulate the private sector to the degree expected. Further, the state's dependence on oil—82% of its revenue came from oil industry taxes and royalties—became a disadvantage when overproduction in the Middle East drove the price of oil down from $36 a barrel at the peak of Alaska's oil boom in 1980–81 to $13.50 a barrel in 1988. In 1986, the state's revenues had declined by two-thirds. Alaska lost 20,000 jobs between 1985 and 1989. The economy's collapse forced 10,000 properties into foreclosure in those years. At the same time, the state rapidly depleted its oil reserves. In 1981, the Interior Department estimated that 83 billion barrels of undiscovered oil existed. By 1989, that estimate had dropped to 49 barrels.

On 24 March 1989, the *Exxon Valdez*, a 987-ft (300-m) oil tanker, hit a reef and ran aground. The tanker spilled 11 million gallons of crude oil. The oil eventually contaminated 1,285 mi (2,068 km) of shoreline, fouling Prince William Sound and its wildlife sanctuary, the Gulf of Alaska, and the Alaska Peninsula. In the settlement of the largest environmental suit in US history brought by the state and federal governments, Exxon was fined $1.025 billion in civil and criminal penalties. By 1992, Exxon had spent some $2 billion cleaning up Prince William Sound and paid another $300 million in compensation for losses. Ten years after the spill, a $100-million response system was in place to prevent future disasters and every tanker that departed the Valdez terminal in Prince William Sound was escorted by tugboats.

In the early 1990s, oil production in Prudhoe Bay was declining, a development that forced Governor Tony Knowles to implement cutbacks in state spending and brought a renewal of proposals to open areas of the nearly 20-million-acre (8,097,000-hectare) Arctic National Wildlife Refuge (ANWR) to commercial development. A Congressional bill introduced in October 1999 by Alaskan Senator Frank Murkowski and backed by the state's other Congressmen, would allow oil and gas, tourism, and residential development in the refuge, which is often called "America's Serengeti" for its wealth and diversity of wildlife. As the Republican-dominated Congress considered the bill in 2000 and after, conservationists rallied against it. In November 2002, Murkowski was elected governor of Alaska, and continued his support for oil drilling in ANWR. In March 2003, the US Senate voted 52–48 to reject a proposal to add Arctic oil drilling to the US budget. On 10 April 2003, however, the US House of Representatives voted in favor of drilling in ANWR. Nonetheless, on 11 April, the full Congress adopted a budget resolution that was clear of any instruction to authorizing committees to begin Arctic drilling.

12 STATE GOVERNMENT

Under Alaska's first and only constitution—adopted in 1956, effective since the time of statehood and amended 28 times by January 2003—the house of representatives consists of 40 members elected for two-year terms; the senate has 20 members elected for staggered four-year terms. The minimum age is 21 for a representative, 25 for a senator; legislators must have resided in the state for at least three years before election and in the district at least one year. Annual legislative sessions begin in January and are limited to 120 calendar days. Special sessions, limited to 30 calendar days, may be called by a two-thirds vote of the members. As of 2002, legislators' salaries were $24,012. Legislators receive reimbursement for living expenses at the rate of $161 per day.

Alaska's executive branch, modeled after New Jersey's, features a strong governor who appoints all cabinet officers (except the commissioner of education) and judges subject to legislative confirmation. The lieutenant governor (elected jointly with the governor) is the only other elected executive. The governor must be at least 30 years old, and must have been a US citizen for seven years and an Alaska resident for seven years. The term of office is four years, and the governor is limited to two consecutive terms. The qualifications for the lieutenant governor are the same as for the governor. As of November 2002, the governor's salary was $83,280.

After a bill has been passed by the legislature, it becomes law if signed by the governor; if left unsigned for 15 days (Sundays excluded) while the legislature is in session, or for 20 days after it has adjourned; or if passed by a two-thirds vote of the elected members of the combined houses over a gubernatorial veto (to override a veto of an appropriations bill requires a three-fourths vote). Constitutional amendments require a two-thirds vote of the legislature and ratification by the electorate. Voters must be 18 years old (within 90 days of registration), US citizens, and not registered to vote in another state. Restrictions apply to convicted felons and those declared mentally incompetent by the court.

Between 1993 and 1995, the Constitutional Revision Task Force studied alternatives to existing methods of revising the state constitution, recommending the appointment of a permanent advisory commission to submit proposals to the state legislature. In 2002 voters rejected a proposal that called for a constitutional convention.

13POLITICAL PARTIES

When Congress debated the statehood question in the 1950s, it was assumed that Alaska would be solidly Democratic, but this expectation has not been borne out; as of 2002 there were 462,388 registered voters, of which only nearly 16% were Democratic, while 25% were Republican and 59% were unaffiliated or members of other parties.

In 1990, a member of the Alaskan Independent party, Walter J. Hickel, was elected governor. Democrat Tony Knowles won the governorship in the November 1994 election and was reelected in 1998. Two Republicans, Frank Murkowski and Ted Stevens, were reelected to the US Senate in 1998 and 2002, respectively. Murkowski was elected Alaska's governor in 2002; he appointed his daughter Lisa to the US Senate to fill his vacancy when he assumed the office of governor.

In 2002 Alaska's US Representative, Republican Don Young, was reelected. In presidential elections since 1968, Alaskans have voted Republican nine consecutive times. Alaskans gave George W. Bush 59% of the vote in 2000, while Al Gore received 28% and Green Party candidate Ralph Nader garnered 10%. The state had three electoral votes in the 2000 presidential election. Alaska's state legislature in 2002 consisted of six Democrats and 14 Republicans in the senate, and 13 Democrats and 27 Republicans in the house. Twelve women held statewide elected office in 2002.

Alaska Presidential Vote by Major Political Parties, 1960–2000

YEAR	ELECTORAL VOTE	ALASKA WINNER	DEMOCRAT	REPUBLICAN
1960	3	Nixon (R)	29,809	30,953
1964	3	*Johnson (D)	44,329	22,930
1968	3	*Nixon (R)	35,411	37,600
1972	3	*Nixon (R)	32,967	55,349
1976	3	Ford (R)	44,058	71,555
1980	3	*Reagan (R)	41,842	86,112
1984	3	*Reagan (R)	62,007	138,377
1988	3	*Bush (R)	72,584	119,251
1992**	3	Bush (R)	78,294	102,000
1996***	3	Dole (R)	80,380	122,746
2000	3	*Bush, G. W. (R)	79,004	167,398

*Won US presidential election.
**Independent candidate Ross Perot received 73,481 votes.
***Independent candidate Ross Perot received 26,333 votes.

14LOCAL GOVERNMENT

Alaska is divided into 149 municipalities, ranging from the geographically small Bristol Bay (519 sq mi or 1,344 sq km) to the expansive North Slope (87,860 sq mi or 227,557 sq mi). In 2002, there were 12 counties in the state. Most municipalities were governed by elected mayors and councils, and more than 100 village councils. Juneau, Sitka, and Anchorage, Alaska's three unified municipalities, have consolidated city and borough functions. There are 43 public school systems in Alaska. The state has 14 special districts.

In 1971 land claims were settled, returning 44 million acres of federal land to Alaska's native population. Through the US Bureau of Indian Affairs, native communities receive varying levels of assistance including help in setting up villages in accordance with governing laws.

15STATE SERVICES

To address the continuing threat of terrorism and to work with the federal Department of Homeland Security (created in 2002 following the terrorist attacks of 11 September 2001), homeland security in Alaska in 2003 operated under the authority of the governor; the adjutant general was designated as the state homeland security advisor.

By law, Alaska's government may contain no more than 20 administrative departments. As of 2002 departments in Alaska were: Administration, Commerce and Economic Development, Community and Regional Affairs, Education, Environmental Conservation, Fish and Game, Health and Social Services, Labor, Law, Military Affairs, Natural Resources, Public Safety, Revenue, and Transportation and Public Facilities. In addition, the state has an ombudsman with limited powers to investigate citizen complaints against state agencies.

16JUDICIAL SYSTEM

The supreme court, consisting of a chief justice and 4 associate justices, hears appeals for civil matters from the 15 superior courts, whose 40 judges are organized among the four state judicial districts, and for criminal matters from the 3-member court of appeals. The superior court has original jurisdiction in all civil and criminal matters, and it hears appeals from the district court. The lowest court is the district court, of which there are 56 in four districts. All judges are appointed by the governor from nominations made by the Judicial Council, but are thereafter subject to voter approval; supreme court justices serve terms of ten years; court of appeals and superior court judges, eight years; and district judges, four years.

As of June 2001, 4,197 prisoners were held in 20 state and federal prisons in Alaska, an increase of 4.3% from the previous year. Alaska had an incarceration rate of 336 per 100,000 population.

In 2001, the crime rate was 4,236.2 crimes per 100,000 population, including a total of 3,735 violent crimes and 23,160 property crimes in that year. Alaska has no capital punishment statute.

17ARMED FORCES

A huge buildup of military personnel occurred after World War II (1939–45), as the Cold War with the Soviet Union led the US to establish the Distant Early Warning (DEW) System, Ballistic Missile Early Warning System, and Joint Surveillance System in the area. Later years saw a cutback in personnel, however, from a high of 40,214 in 1962 to 15,906 in 2002, 9,136 of them in the Air Force. Anchorage is the home of both the largest Army base, Fort Richardson, and the largest Air Force base, Elmendorf. In the Aleutians are several Navy facilities and the Shemya Air Force Base. Alaska firms received defense contracts worth $836 million in 2001.

There were 71,552 veterans of US military service in Alaska as of 2000, of whom 5,288 served in World War II; 4,448 in the Korean conflict; 26,148 during the Vietnam era; and 15,320 during 1990–2000 (including the Persian Gulf War). Expenditures on veterans amounted to $196 million in 2002.

The Alaska State Troopers provide police protection throughout the state, except in the larger cities, where municipal police forces have jurisdiction. As of June 2000, the Alaska State Troopers employed 232 full-time sworn officers.

[18] MIGRATION

The earliest immigrants to North America, more than 10,000 years ago, likely came to Alaska via a land bridge across what is now the Bering Strait. The Russian fur traders who arrived during the 1700s found Aleuts, Eskimos, and Indians already established there. Despite more than a century of Russian sovereignty over the area, however, few Russians came, and those that did returned to the mother country with the purchase of Alaska by the US in 1867. Virtually all other migration to Alaska has been from the continental US—first during the gold rush of the late 19th century and most recently during the oil boom of the 1970s. Between 1970 and 1983, Alaska's net gain from migration was 78,000, but Alaska suffered net losses in domestic migration of over 37,500 from 1985 to 1990, and 21,000 between 1990 and 1998.

Mobility is a way of life in Alaska. Urbanization increased with migration during the 1980s; the urban population increased from 64.5% in 1980 to 67.5% of the total population in 1990. In the 1990s, migration added 17,000 people to the state. In 1998, Alaska admitted 1,008 immigrants. Between 1995 and 1998, the population increased 2.1%. In the period 1995–2000, 95,562 people moved into the state and 126,060, for a net loss of 30,498 people.

[19] INTERGOVERNMENTAL COOPERATION

Alaska participates with Washington, Oregon, and California in the Pacific States Marine Fisheries Commission. Alaska also belongs to other western regional agreements covering energy, corrections, radioactive waste, and education. The most important federal–state effort, the Joint Federal-State Land Use Planning Commission, was involved with the Alaska lands controversy throughout the 1970s. The Interstate Oil and Gas Compact was enacted in 1980. In 1990, Alaska also joined the Western States/British Columbia Oil Spill Tax Force. Federal grants to Alaska amounted to $2.3 billion in fiscal year 2001.

[20] ECONOMY

When Alaska gained statehood in 1959, its economy was almost totally dependent on the US government. Fisheries, limited mining (mostly gold and gravel), and some lumber production made up the balance. That all changed with development of the petroleum industry during the 1970s. Construction of the Trans–Alaska Pipeline brought a massive infusion of money and people into the state. Construction, trade, and services boomed—only to decline when the pipeline was completed.

In the mid-1980s, the economy was dependent on government spending, especially by the state, and on the oil industry, which by 1984 supplied 85% of state revenues. The collapse of the oil prices in the mid-1980s hit Alaska hard. Employment dropped 9.4% between 1986 and 1988. By 1990, a recovery was underway. Accumulated gains in employment, while small, more than compensated for the losses of a few years before.

One area of growth in the 1980s and early 1990s was the Alaska groundfish industry. Commercial fishing is one of the bulwarks of the Alaska economy. The seafood industry had wholesale values of more than $3 billion in 1990, and Alaska's fishery accounts for 50% of the total annual US catch. The volume of Alaska groundfish catches rose from 69 million lb (31.3 million kg) in 1980 to 4.8 billion lb (2.2 billion kg) in 1990. Employment in seafood harvesting grew from 45,000 in 1980 to 54,000 in 1991, although the boom has slowed somewhat since.

Retrenchment of oil and gas companies reduced mining jobs by 11% in 1992. Log exports began to decline in 1990 and were expected to drop 50% by 1997 as the supply of timber shrank. In 1993, the state sued the federal government for violating the Statehood Act. The act had entitled Alaska to 90% of the revenues from mineral leasing on federal lands. Since passage of the Act, however, half of the federal lands had been withdrawn from mineral leasing. Job creation rates, which ranged from 2% to 4% in the early 1990s, rose and fell from nearly 3% to less than 1% for the rest of the decade roughly in line with the rise and fall in North Slope oil prices, which hit troughs in 1994 and 1999 (during which the oil price hit a low of $12.73 a barrel). Gross state product fell 7.2% in 1998, but then increased 3.6% in 1998 and then soared 10.1% in 2000. In 2000, Alaska oil revenues still accounted for almost 85% of total state revenues, although low oil prices and production during the late 1990s threatened to lower this percentage. The tourism industry attracted over 1.1 million visitors in 2000, and contrary to national trends, continued to expand into 2002. The number of inbound cruise ship visitors, for example, increased 14% from summer 2001 to summer 2002. Other important industries include timber, mining (including gold, coal, silver, and zinc), and agriculture. The national recession of 2001 reduced gross state product growth to 1.6% and slowed employment growth to less than 1% in early 2002, again in line with sharply falling oil prices. Loan delinquency increased, with the median past-due loan ratio rising from 1.52 % to 1.62% from September 2001 to September 2002. From 1997 to 2002 increased environmental regulations and foreign competition from, particularly, Chile and Norway, contributed to a decline in employment in the traditional seafood packing industry of more than 15%. On the other hand, employment in both state and local government, and in the hotels and lodging industry increased by almost 15%. Employment in the oil and gas extraction sector increased by about 5% 1997 to 2002, while employment with the federal government decreased almost 3%. In 2003, rising oil prices, reflecting political instability in Iraq and Venezuela and other factors, were expected to benefit the Alaskan economy

In 2001, Alaska's gross state product was $28.6 billion, with 19.5% accounted for by the public sector, the 2nd-highest percent among the states (after Hawaii), and well above the state average of 12%. Both mining and government contributed about $5.6 billion to gross state product in 2001, but for mining this represented a 19% decrease from 1997 and for government a 10.8% increase over the same period. Public utilities and transportation contributed $4.6 billion, up 15% from 1997. Both general services, contributing $3.96 billion, and the finance, insurance and real estate sector, contributing $3.2 billion, increased about 29% 1997 to 2001. Other important sectors included retail trade, at $1.9 billion (up 12% from 1997) and construction, at $1.4 billion (up 24% from 1997). The manufacturing sector contributed $1.06 billion, down 5% from 1997.

[21] INCOME

According to the Bureau of Economic Analysis, in 2001, Alaska had a per capita personal income (PCPI) of $31,027 which ranked 15th in the United States (including the District of Columbia) and was 102% of the national average, $30,413. The 2001 PCPI reflected an increase of 3.6% from 2000 compared to the national change of 2.2%. In 2001, Alaska had a total personal income (TPI) of $19,659,927,000 which ranked 48th in the United States and accounted for 0.2% of the national total.

The 2001 TPI reflected an increase of 4.5% from 2000 compared to the national change of 3.3%.

Earnings of persons employed in Alaska increased from $14,182,106,000 in 2000 to $14,953,370,000 in 2001, an increase of 5.4%. The largest industries in 2001 were services, 22.3% of earnings; state and local government, 16.8%; and transportation and public utilities, 10.4%. Of the industries that accounted for at least 5% of earnings in 2001, the slowest growing from 2000 to 2001 was federal civilian government (7.8% of earnings in 2001), which increased 1.0%; the fastest was mining (7.6% of earnings in 2001), which increased 14.4%.

According to data released by the US Census Bureau, in 2000, the median household income was $50,746 compared to the national average of $42,148. In 2001, the median income for a family of four was $71,395 compared to the national average of $63,278. For the period 1999 to 2001, the average poverty rate was 7.9% which placed it 7th among the 50 states and the District of Columbia ranked lowest to highest.

22LABOR

According to Bureau of Labor Statistics (BLS) provisional estimates, in July 2003 the seasonally adjusted civilian labor force in Alaska numbered 345,000, with approximately 27,100 workers unemployed, yielding an unemployment rate of 7.9%, compared to the national average of 6.2% for the same period. Since the beginning of the BLS data series in 1978, the highest unemployment rate recorded was 11.6% in August 1986. The historical low was 5.6% in November 1998. It is estimated that in 2001, 5.8% of the labor force was employed in construction; 2.9% in manufacturing; 8.8% in transportation, communications, and public utilities; 17.0% in trade; 2.9% in finance, insurance, and real estate; 23.4% in services; 26.2% in government; and 0.8% in agriculture.

The US Department of Labor reported that in 2002, 64,000 of Alaska's 262,000 employed wage and salary workers were members of unions. This represented 24.3% of those so employed, up from 21.7% in 2001. The national average is 13.2%. Alaska is one of only four states with a union membership rate over 20%. In all, 70,000 workers (26.7%) were represented by unions. In addition to union members, this category includes workers who report no union affiliation but whose jobs are covered by a union contract. The International Brotherhood of Teamsters is especially strong in the state, covering a range of workers from truck drivers to school administrators.

23AGRICULTURE

A short but intense growing season provides good potential for Alaska commercial agriculture, although the expense of getting agricultural products to market is a limiting factor. International export opportunities are being developed. Alaska's 590 farms covered 920,000 acres (372,324 hectares) in 2002. Hay, potatoes, lettuce, cabbage, carrots, beef, pork, dairy products, and greenhouse and nursery items are common commodities produced. In 2002, hay production was 26,000 tons, valued at $5,590,000; potatoes, 154,000 hundredweight (6,985,200 kg), $3,065,000; and barley for grain, 158,000 tons, $561,000 The leading farming regions of Alaska are the Matanuska Valley, northeast of Anchorage, and Delta Junction, north of Fairbanks.

24ANIMAL HUSBANDRY

Dairy and livestock products account for about two-thirds of Alaska's agricultural receipts. In 2001, an estimated 14.4 million lb (6.5 million kg) of milk were produced. Milk cows numbered 900 in 2000. Meat and poultry production is negligible by national standards.

25FISHING

Alaska was the leading fishing state in terms of earnings and in the total weight of catch in 1998. The salmon catch, the staple of the industry, amounted to 626.1 million lb (284 million kg) of fish valued at $242.7 million in 1998. The distribution of Alaska salmon landings by species that year was sockeye, 20%; pink, 53%; chum, 20%; coho, 5%; and chinook, 2%. Concerns of possible exhaustion of wild pollock stocks have resulted in a reduction in the total allowable catch for pollock. Crab, a major export item, had recently declined in availability; the sablefish harvest, however, was over 33.5 million lb (15.1 million kg) in 1998, accounting for 77% of the US sablefish catch in 1998. In all, Alaska's commercial catch in 1998 totaled over 4.8 billion lb (2.2 billion kg, down from the record high of 5.9 billion lb, or 2.7 billion kg, in 1993), valued at $951.5 million—providing 53% of the total commercial landing volume (and 30% of total value) of the US. In that year, Dutch Harbor– Unalaska ranked 1st and Kodiak 3rd among US fishing ports for both quantity (597.1 million lb/270.8 million kg, 357.6 million lb/ 162.2 million kg) and value ($110 million, $78.7 million). Alaska had 414 processing and wholesale plants with an average of about 7,988 employees during 1997, as well as a commercial fishing fleet of 16,442 boats and vessels that year.

Anglers are attracted by Alaska's abundant stocks of salmon and trout. There were 399,680 sport anglers licensed in Alaska in 1998.

26FORESTRY

In 2002, Alaska's forested area was 126,869,000 acres (51,343,000 hectares), far more than any other state. However, the area of harvestable timberland was only 11,865,000 acres (4,801,000 hectares). Some 18,887,000 acres (7,644,000 hectares) of forestland were privately held in 2002. Alaska contains the nation's largest national forests, Tongass in the southeast (17.4 million acres—seven million hectares) and Chugach along the Gulf Coast (6.9 million acres—2.8 million hectares).

Timber companies harvest logs from the two national forests with the majority from the Tongass National Forest. The timber is made available for harvest through a competitive bidding process.

27MINING

The US Geological Survey estimated the 2001 value for Alaska nonfuel mineral production at $1.1 billion, about 5% less than the amount reported in 2000. Metallic minerals accounted for 90% of Alaska's total nonfuel mineral production in 2001, much of it provided by production of zinc, lead, and silver at the Red Dog Mine in the northwestern part of the state and by gold production at Fort Knox Mine near Fairbanks. The reduction in value between 2000 and 2001 reflected a drop in both the production and the price of zinc. The $105 million Mill Optimization Project at the Red Dog Mine was completed in early 2001. Red Dog is among the largest producers of zinc in the world. Production at the mine was expected to increase by around 8% in 2002.

According to preliminary figures, in 2001 Alaska produced 1.5 million metric tons of crushed stone, valued at $7.9 million; 16,500 kg of gold, $148 million; and 14 million metric tons of sand and gravel, $71.8 million. The state ranked 13th nationally in the value of nonfuel mineral production and accounted for about 3% of the national total produced. Its ranking among the states for specific minerals was: zinc (1st), lead and silver (2nd), and gold (4th).

The number of placer gold mines and the amount of gold mined there continued the decline begun in 1997. Low global prices for metals hampered the ability of producers to raise capital for exploration.

The Alaska Department of Natural Resources (DNR) presents reclamation awards to mining firms for exemplary work in returning disturbed ground to useful condition as required by state law.

28ENERGY AND POWER

As of 2002, Alaskan production of crude oil was 17% of the nation's total, and, at 984,000 barrels per day, 2nd only to that of Texas. The Trans-Alaska Pipeline runs 789 mi (1,270 km) from the North Slope oil fields to the port of Valdez on the southern coast. Most of Alaska's energy products are produced and refined locally. The state's six refineries have a combined crude distillation capacity of 357,000 barrels per day. Proved reserves as of 2001 totaled 4.85 billion barrels, or about 22% of national reserves.

Marketed natural gas production in 2002 was 464.7 billion cu ft (13.2 billion cu m). In 2001, proved reserves were 8.8 trillion cu ft (0.25 trillion cu m). Total electric power production (utility and nonutility) was over 5.8 billion kWh in 1999; total installed capacity was over 2 million kW, and almost all generating facilities were government owned. Alaska has no nuclear power plants.

Alaska also had proved coal reserves totaling 6.5 billion tons in 1996 (more recent figures have been withheld to avoid disclosure of company data). Production of coal in 2000 was 1,641,000 tons, from a single mine at Healy. In 2000 Alaska ranked first among the states in per capita energy consumption, with a total of 944 million Btu (237.9 million kcal).

29INDUSTRY

Alaska's small but growing manufacturing sector is centered on petroleum refining and the processing of lumber and food products, especially seafood.

Of Alaska's ten top employers, five are engaged in the petroleum industry: ARCO Alaska, VECO, BP Exploration, Alyeska Pipeline Service, and Alaska Petroleum Contractors. Other principal employers among industry groups are food and kindred products, lumber and wood products, and printing and publishing. Manufacturing shipments valued at $3,760 million in 1997 placed Alaska 49th among the 50 states in terms of manufacturing growth, at the low rate of 3.6% from 1992, and fourth to last in terms of value added. Shipments from mineral industries reached over $10 billion for 1997, putting the state 2nd only to Louisiana and Texas (primarily from the oil and gas industries). Growth for the mineral industry, however, was average.

The following table provides the number of persons employed, the annual payroll, and the total number of establishments for the major industries within the state.

Earnings of persons employed in Alaska increased from $12.6 billion in 1997 to $13 billion in 1998, an increase of 3.6%. The largest industries in 1998 were services, 21.3% of earnings; state and local government, 17.8%; and transportation and public utilities, 10.4%. Of the industries that accounted for at least 5% of earnings in 1998, the slowest growing from 1997 to 1998 was military (5.2% of earnings in 1998), which decreased 1.1%; the fastest was transportation and public utilities, which increased 8.1%.

30COMMERCE

Alaska had 951 wholesale trade establishments in 1997, according to the Census of Wholesale Trade, with growth in number of 4.7% since 1992. That year, the Census of Retail Trade counted 4,090 retail establishments in the state, with $6.6 billion in sales. More than 71% of all retail sales were in the Anchorage metropolitan area. Eating and drinking places accounted for one-third of all establishments; followed by food stores, 10%; and automotive dealers, 10%. General merchandise stores sold a total of $978 million in goods, while food stores sold $1,434 million.

During 1998, Alaskan exporters sold $2 billion of merchandise. Many of Alaska's resource products, including the salmon and crab catch, pass through the Seattle customs district. By federal law, Alaskan petroleum cannot be exported to other countries, a provision many Alaskans would like to see repealed. One-third of Alaska's manufactured goods were exported to other countries, the highest ratio of all the states, with paper and food products being the leading items. Alaska was the leading fish-exporting state and the largest exporter of salmon.

31CONSUMER PROTECTION

The Alaska Department of Law's Consumer Protection Unit, which falls under the Office of the Attorney General, provides consumers with information, investigates business and trade practices, and enforces statutes prohibiting unfair, false, misleading or deceptive acts and practices.

32BANKING

As of 2002, Alaska had 8 insured banks, with total assets amounting to $7.1 billion. There was also one state-chartered mutual savings bank (Mt. McKinley).

Alaska's state-chartered banks are under the regulatory authority of the Department of Community and Economic Development's Division of Banking, Securities, and Corporations; including Denali State Bank and Northrim Bank. As of 2003, approximately 18.72% of all bank assets in Alaska were held in state-chartered institutions. In addition to the state-chartered banks in 2003, there were four nationally chartered commercial banks, one federal chartered savings bank, and 13 federal credit unions. The nationally chartered banks are under the regulatory authority of the Office of the Comptroller of the Currency. National banks are regulated by the Office of Thrift Supervision; including Key Bank, First National Bank, and Wells Fargo Bank.

Lower interest rates in 2001/02 increased net interest margins (NIMs) (the difference between the lower rates offered to savers and the higher rates charged on loans) favorably when compared to national medians. Overall earnings performance for insured banks in Alaska increased. As of September 2002, about one-third of the assets held by insured banks headquartered in Alaska were in securities.

33INSURANCE

In 2001 there were 193,000 ordinary life insurance policies in force with a total value of $20.8 billion; total value for all categories of life insurance (ordinary, group, industrial, and credit) was $31.0 billion. Death benefits paid that year totaled $77.3 million. As of 2003, there were no life insurance companies based on Alaska, but seven property and casualty insurance companies domiciled there.

Property and casualty insurers wrote premiums amounting to $910 million in 1998. That year, there were 2,458 flood insurance policies in force in the state, with a total value of $325,568.

The insurance industry is regulated by the Department of Commerce and Economic Development's Division of Insurance.

34SECURITIES

There are no securities exchanges in Alaska. Alaska has 89 securities brokers and dealers industries, with over 500 agents. There are also 19 investment advisor firms registered to provide services within the state. Three NASDAQ companies are headquartered in Alaska.

The Alaska Securities Act of 1959 serves as the foundation for the regulation of the sale of securities through a triple-tiered system of registration for brokers and dealers, as well as through anti-fraud provisions.

[35]PUBLIC FINANCE

Alaska's annual budget is prepared by the Division of Budget and Management within the Office of the Governor, and is submitted by the governor to the legislature for amendment and approval. The fiscal year runs from 1 July through 30 June.

The 2003 budget authorized $7.39 billion in expenditures, including $4.4 billion under the Operating Budget (which includes the state's main education, public safety, health and social services and natural resource management programs); $1.19 billion under the Capital Budget (three-fourths of which is made up of federal funds for highway, airport, sewer, water, and sanitation projects); and $406 million (5%) for debt servicing and supplemental appropriations. Also included, and unique to Alaska, was $1.38 billion authorized for the operations of the state's Permanent Fund (PF), including $690 million for dividend payments to Alaskans, and $693 to inflation-proof the principal in the PF. The PF, operative since 1982, is funded from the state's windfall in oil lease fees connected with the Alaska oil pipeline, and as protection against the time when revenues from the oil sector will decrease. In 2003, the PF capital base was at $21 billion.

The following table from the US Census Bureau contains information on revenues, expenditures, indebtedness, and cash/securities for 2001.

	($000)	PERCENT	PER CAPITA
Population (thousands, 2001)	634	(X)	(X)
Total Revenue	6,185,917	100.00	9,756.97
General revenue	6,043,307	97.69	9,532.03
Utility revenue	25,257	0.41	39.84
Liquor store revenue	–	–	–
Insurance trust revenue	117,353	1.90	185.10
Exhibit: Salaries and wages	1,042,670	11.52	1,644.59
Total expenditure	9,047,480	100.00	14,270.47
General expenditure	8,389,078	92.72	13,231.98
Education	1,443,738	15.96	2,277.19
Public welfare	1,022,604	11.30	1,612.94
Hospitals	18,734	0.21	29.55
Health	162,273	1.79	255.95
Highways	649,746	7.18	1,024.84
Police protection	64,035	0.71	101.00
Correction	172,610	1.91	272.26
Natural resources	254,906	2.82	402.06
Parks and recreation	9,648	0.11	15.22
Government administration	356,908	3.94	562.95
Interest on general debt	263,801	2.92	416.09
Other and unallocable	3,970,075	43.88	6,261.95
Utility expenditure	59,285	0.66	93.51
Liquor store expenditure	–	–	–
Insurance trust expenditure	599,117	6.62	944.98
Debt at end of fiscal year	4,507,108	100.00	7,109.00
Cash and security holdings	43,846,219	100.00	69,158.07

[36]TAXATION

The large sums generated by the sale of oil leases and by oil and gas royalties make Alaska's tax structure highly atypical, and its revenues dependent upon the market price of fuels. To smooth out fluctuations due to oil price changes, the Constitutional Budget Reserve Fund was set up. There is no state sales tax or personal income tax in Alaska, but some localities impose a sales tax, as well as a property tax. The corporate tax rate in 2000 ranged from 1% on the first $10,000 of taxable income to 9.4% on amounts over $90,000. Selective sales taxes (excises) are imposed on tobacco products, motor fuels, insurance premiums, alcoholic beverages, public utilities and amusements. The state

property tax excludes the first $150, 000 for owners over 65. Only 25 of Alaska's 161 municipalities collect local property taxes. There is no death tax, and Alaska's estate tax is tied to the federal tax exemption for state estate taxes, and is therefore scheduled to be phase out in tandem with the exemption by 2007. Other taxes include various license and franchise fees, but there is no fee for vehicle operating licenses. There are also no documentary and stock transfer taxes. The most unique feature about Alaska's state taxes is that over half ($552 million in 2002 amounting to 50.6% of total state tax collections) come from severance taxes, a very minor source of revenue in most states. Alaska is the only state that has neither a state sales tax nor a state personal income tax. Corporate income taxes make an unusually high contribution, amounting to almost 25% in 2002. Excise taxes accounted for 13%, license fees for 6.8% and property taxes for 4.5%. In all, Alaska has the lowest combined state and local tax burden in the country, 5.5% of income in 2003, compared to the national average of 9.7%.

The following table from the US Census Bureau provides a summary of taxes collected by the state in 2002.

	($000)	PER CAPITA
Total Taxes	1,089,504	1,692.34
Property taxes	49,652	77.13
Sales and gross receipts	142,050	220.65
General sales and gross receipts	(X)	(X)
Selective sales taxes	142,050	220.65
Alcoholic beverage	12,889	20.02
Amusements	2,537	3.94
Insurance Premiums	37,323	57.97
Motor fuels	40,352	62.68
Pari-mutuels	(X)	(X)
Public utilities	3,139	4.88
Tobacco products	45,810	71.16
Other selective sales	(X)	(X)
Licenses	74,119	115.13
Alcoholic beverages	1,523	2.37
Amusements	1	0
Corporation	1,281	1.99
Hunting and fishing	20,351	31.61
Motor vehicle	37,304	57.94
Motor vehicle operators	(X)	(X)
Public utility	232	0.36
Occupation and business, NEC	11,137	17.3
Other	2,290	3.56
Other taxes	823,683	1,279.44
Individual income	(X)	(X)
Corporation net income	269,273	418.26
Death and gift	3,117	4.84
Documentary and stock transfer	(X)	(X)
Severance	551,293	856.33
Other	(X)	(X)

[37]ECONOMIC POLICY

The Alaska Industrial Development and Energy Authority (AIDEA), a public corporation of the state created, provides long-term financing for capital investments and loans for most commercial and industrial activities, including manufacturing, small business, tourism, mining, commercial fishing, and other enterprises. In 1985 its mission was extended to provide financing for infrastructural projects to support private enterprise in Alaska. In 2002, a prominent example of the latter was the Delong Mountain Transportation System, a 52-mile rail system built to support the Red Dog lead and zinc mine. In 2000, economic development projects included the Gateway Alaska project that undertook reconstruction of the Ted Stevens Anchorage International Airport and surrounding roads. The Diamond Center Hotel in south Anchorage, begun in 2000 and completed in 2002, and to be operated by the Seldovia Native Association (SNA) and to feature native art, was financed with the help of the AIDEA. Under the AIDEA's Conduit Revenue

Bond Program, designed to facilitate access to the state bond market, Hope Community Resources in 2002 was able to borrow to expand its facilities for providing services for the developmentally disabled. In 1999 the Rural Development Initiative Fund, created in 1992 to help small businesses not eligible for traditional commercial finance, was transferred to the AIDEA where, in 2002, it was being restructured to improve finance options for small business. The AIDEA also has oversight over the Alaska Energy Authority which was created in 1976 and which has responsibility for two major programs, the Alaska Rural Energy Plan and the Statewide Energy Plan. The rural population poses a challenge to economic development of the state, which the state government has begun to address by broadening the utilities infrastructure and by subsidizing energy costs. For the ten years 1992 to 2002, the AIDEA claimed credit for helping to create 3,400 permanent jobs and 3,700 temporary jobs, and for helping to mobilize about $222 million for business finance. The Alaska Science and Technology Foundation (ASTF), created in 1988, has as its mission the improvement of the state economy through investments in science and technology. Due to state budget problems, an original appropriation of $10.5 million for the ASTF was reduced to $5.8 for FY2003. The state imposes no taxes on income, sales, gross receipts or inventories. It offers an investment tax credit for the development of gas-processing projects and for the mining of minerals and other natural deposits, except oil and gas.

38HEALTH

Alaska's infant mortality rate was 6.8 per 1,000 live births for the year ending with December 2000. The abortion ratio was 15 per 1,000 women in 1966.

Alaska's overall death rate of 468.4 per 100,000 population in 2000 was slightly more than half the US rate, but the death rate from accidents (55.1 per 100,000) was one of the highest in the US and higher than the national rate. The suicide rate of 22.0—the highest in the country—was over twice the national rate of 10.7. The commercial fishing industry has one of the highest occupational fatality rates in Alaska; during the early 1990s the annual occupational fatality rate for the fishing industry was 200 per 100,000 workers. The fatality rate for the shellfish industry was 530 per 100,000 in that period. Among Alaskan adults age 18 and older, 25% were current smokers in 2000. The death rate of 27.3 per 100,000 for cerebrovascular diseases was significantly lower than the national rate of 60.9, due to the relative youth of the state's population. Deaths due to heart disease were also much lower (97.6 per 100,000 population) than the US average of 258.2. The HIV incidence rate was 13.03 per 100,000 in 1995. There had been 495 AIDS cases reported through 2001.

Alaska's 19 hospitals in 2001 had 1,442 beds and 49,065 admissions; hospital personnel included 1,983 registered nurses in 2001. The average daily expense to Alaskan hospitals per inpatient day amounted to $1,447 in 2001. Alaska had only 194 physicians per 100,000 population in 2000, as compared to the national average of 288.

In 2002, 15.7% of the Alaskan population was uninsured. Federal government grants to cover the Medicare and Medicaid services in 2001 totaled $436 million; 43,815 enrollees received Medicare benefits that year. Alaska's Pioneer Homes, operated by the state's Department of Administration, are residential facilities for Alaskans over 65 (with at least one year of residency in the state) that offer five levels of care from independent living to full medical care, including Alzheimer's units. As of 1997, a total of 600 residents were being served at six locations.

39SOCIAL WELFARE

In 2001, the average weekly unemployment benefit was $193.68. Average monthly participation in the food stamp program in FY2002 comprised 46,165 persons (16,138 households). The average monthly benefit was $107.32, and the sum total of benefits paid in FY2002 was $59,454,787.

With the enactment of the Personal Responsibility and Work Opportunity Reconciliation Act of 1996, the US government has changed the form and regulations for many of its social welfare programs. Most significantly, it replaces Aid to Families with Dependent Children (AFDC), an open-ended entitlement program, with Temporary Assistance for Needy Families (TANF), a limited system of assistance funded largely through federal block grants. The reform act also impacts the food stamp program, the Supplemental Security Income program, and the child nutrition program. The law took effect on 1 July 1997 and provided $16.38 billion in block grants for fiscal years 1997–2002. The grants are to be divided among the states based on an equation involving the numbers of former AFDC recipients in each state.

Reauthorization of the 1996 social welfare legislation, scheduled for 2002, was delayed, and the original law had been extended three times as of July 2003, with the most recent extension running through September 2003. Alaska's TANF program is called the Alaska Temporary Assistance Program (ATAP). In June 2000 the state had 24,389 welfare recipients. State expenditures on the TANF program in FY2002 totaled $44,320,973.

In December 2001, Social Security benefits were paid to 56,940 Alaskans. This number included 32,750 retired workers, 4,970 widows and widowers, 7,860 disabled workers, 2,820 spouses, and 8,540 children. Social Security beneficiaries represented 8.9% of the total state population and 93.9% of the state's population age 65 and older. Retired workers (excluding persons with special benefits) received an average monthly payment of $848; widows and widowers, $759; disabled workers, $796; and spouses, $398. Payments for children of retired workers averaged $367 per month; children of deceased workers, $550; and children of disabled workers, $224.

Federal Supplemental Security Income payments in December 2001 went to 9,123 Alaska residents, averaging $359 a month.

In 1979, Alaska became the first state to withdraw its government workers from the Social Security system.

40HOUSING

Despite the severe winters, housing designs in Alaska do not differ notably from those in other states. Builders do usually provide thicker insulation in walls and ceilings, but the high costs of construction have not encouraged more energy-efficient adaptation to the environment. In 1980, the state legislature passed several measures to encourage energy conservation in housing and in public buildings. In native villages, traditional dwellings like the half-buried huts of the Aleuts and others have long since given way to conventional, low-standard housing. In point of fact, Alaska's Eskimos never built snow houses, as did those of Canada; in the Eskimo language, the word igloo refers to any dwelling.

In 2002, there were an estimated 265,377 housing units, 64.2% of which were owner-occupied. About 59.4% of all units were single-family, detached dwellings. It was estimated that about 4,796 units statewide were without telephone service while 7,094 lacked complete plumbing facilities and 4,782 lacked complete kitchen facilities.

From 1970 to 1978, 43,009 building permits were issued, as construction boomed during the years of pipeline building. In 2002, the state authorized 3,003 new privately owned housing units. The median home value was $162,526. The median monthly cost for mortgage owners was $1,363 while the median monthly rental cost was $761. During 2002, the Alaska state program received $6.4 million in aid from the US Department of

Housing and Urban Development, including $3.2 million in community development block grants.

The Alaska State Housing Authority acts as an agent for federal and local governments in securing financial aid for construction and management of low-rent and moderate-cost homes.

[41]EDUCATION

As of 2000, 88.3% of the population 25 years or older had completed high school. Some 24.7% had obtained a bachelor's degree or higher.

Enrollment in public schools was 134,391 in the fall of 1999. Of these, 95,601 attended schools from kindergarten through grade eight, and 38,790 attended high school. Minority students made up approximately 40% of the total enrollment in public elementary and secondary schools in 2001. Total enrollment was estimated at 135,869 in fall 2000 and expected to reach 137,000 by fall 2005. Private school enrollment was 6,172 in fall 2001. Expenditures for public education in 2000/01 were estimated at $1,226,966.

The University of Alaska is the state's leading higher-educational institution. The main campus, established in 1917, is at Fairbanks; satellite campuses are located in Anchorage and Juneau. Private institutions include Sheldon Jackson College, Alaska Bible College (a theological seminary), and Alaska Pacific University. The University of Alaska's Rural Education Division has a network of education centers and offers 90 correspondence courses in 22 fields of study. As of fall 2000, there were 32,303 students enrolled in college or graduate school. In the same year Alaska had nine degree-granting institutions. In 1997, minority students comprised 21.7% of total postsecondary enrollment.

[42]ARTS

The Council on the Arts, founded in 1966, sponsors tours by performing artists, supports artists' residences in the schools, aids local arts projects, and purchases the works of living Alaskans for display in state buildings. In 2000, the National Endowment for the Humanities awarded grants totaling $1,001,864 to 11 Alaska organizations. In 2003, the National Endowment for the Arts awarded grants totaling $789,200 to Alaska arts organizations. The funds were used for arts education and assistance for the nearly 90,000 artists who contributed to Alaska's art programs. Alaska is also a member state of the regional Western States Arts Federation.

By 1996, there were about 250 arts-related associations in Alaska and about 32 local art groups. Fairbanks, Juneau, and Anchorage have symphony orchestras and Anchorage has a civic opera. The Alaska Repertory Theater tours the state. The annual Alaska Folk Festival in Juneau (est. 1975) is one of the largest cultural/musical festivals in the state, drawing over 10,000 people each year.

[43]LIBRARIES AND MUSEUMS

Alaska's 15 public systems had an estimated combined book stock of 2,224,000 and a circulation of 3,664,000 in 2000; facilities were located in seven boroughs and in most larger towns. Anchorage had the largest public library system, with five branches and 554,686 volumes in 1998. Also notable are the State Library in Juneau and the library of the University of Alaska at Fairbanks (with 954,510 and 60,000 volumes, respectively). Total income for the public library system in 2000 was $24,458,000; including $782,656 in state grants.

Alaska had 44 museums in 2000. The Alaska State Museum in Juneau offers an impressive collection of native crafts and Alaskan artifacts. Sitka National Historical Park features Indian and Russian items, and the nearby Museum of Sheldon Jackson College holds important native collections. Noteworthy historical and archaeological sites include the Totem Heritage Center in Ketchikan. Anchorage has the Anchorage Museum of History and Art and the Alaska Zoo.

[44]COMMUNICATIONS

Considering the vast distances traveled and the number of small, scattered communities, the US mail is a bargain for Alaskans. In 2001, 94.7% of the state's residences had telephones. There were 41 major radio stations (12 AM, 29 FM) in 2003, along with 15 television stations. Prime Cable of Alaska is the state's major cable carrier. A total of 13,558 Internet domain names had been registered in Alaska by the year 2000.

[45]PRESS

Alaska's most widely read newspaper, among its seven dailies and five Sunday papers, is the *Anchorage Daily News*. Below are the leading newspapers with their circulations.

Anchorage Daily News	(m) 69,979	(S) 85,943
Fairbanks Daily News-Miner	(m) 16,654	(S) 21,832

There are about 30 publishers in Alaska, including the University of Alaska Press, Denali Press, Alaska Geographic, Rainforest Publishers, and Inside Passage Press. *Alaska Business Monthly, Alaska* magazine, and *Alaska Outdoors* are popular statewide magazines.

[46]ORGANIZATIONS

In 2003, there were at least 590 associations represented in the state. There are no major national organizations based in Alaska. The largest statewide organization, the Alaska Federation of Natives, with headquarters in Anchorage, represents the state's Eskimos, Aleuts, and Indians. The Maniilaq Association, based in Kotzebue, is another tribal organization serving native Eskimos.

Environmental groups include the Alaska Conservation Alliance, the Alaska Conservation Foundation, the Alaska Geographic Society, and the Alaska Wildlife Alliance. Arts and culture are represented in part by the Alaska Historical Society.

[47]TOURISM, TRAVEL, AND RECREATION

With thousands of miles of unspoiled scenery and hundreds of mountains and lakes, Alaska has vast tourist potential. In fact, tourism has become the 2nd-largest private-sector employer in the state. Alaska's tourism industry is estimated at over $1 billion per year. The industry, directly and indirectly, generates an annual average of 30,700 jobs and $640 million in payroll (not including employment on cruise ships). In 2000, about 52,000 visitors came from overseas.

Cruise travel along the Gulf of Alaska is one of the fastest growing sectors in the tourist trade. Sportsfishing and outdoor adventure opportunities have also become popular. Millions of visitors travel to the state's national parks, preserves, historical parks, and monuments, which totaled 52.9 million acres (21.7 million hectares) in 1999. Denali State Park is home to Mt. McKinley, the highest peak in North America. Another popular tourist destination is Glacier Bay National Monument.

[48]SPORTS

There are no major league professional sports teams in Alaska, but there is a minor league hockey team in Anchorage. In addition, college hockey teams, such as University of Alaska-Fairbanks, are involved at the NCAA Division I level. Sports in Alaska generally revolve around the outdoors, including skiing, fishing, hiking, mountain biking, and camping. Perhaps the biggest sporting event in the state is the Iditarod Trail Sled Dog Race, covering 1,159 mi (1,865 km) from Anchorage to Nome. The race is held in March, and both men and women compete. With a $50,000 purse, it is the most lucrative sled dog race in the world.

Other annual sporting events include the Great Alaska Shootout, in which college basketball teams from around the country compete in Anchorage in November, and the World Eskimo–Indian Olympics in Fairbanks in July.

49 FAMOUS ALASKANS

Alaskan's best-known federal officeholder was Ernest Gruening (b.New York, 1887–1974), a territorial governor from 1939 to 1953 and US senator from 1959 to 1969. Alaska's other original US senator was E. L. "Bob" Bartlett (1904–68). Walter Hickel (b.Kansas, 1919), the first Alaskan to serve in the US cabinet, left the governorship in 1969 to become secretary of the interior. Among historical figures, Vitus Bering (b.Denmark, 1680–1741), a seaman in Russian service who commanded the discovery expedition in 1741, and Aleksandr Baranov (b.Russia, 1746–1819), the first governor of Russian America, are outstanding. Secretary of State William H. Seward (b.New York, 1801–72), who was instrumental in the 1867 purchase of Alaska, ranks as the state's "founding father," although he never visited the region.

Sheldon Jackson (b.New York, 1834–1909), a Presbyterian missionary, introduced the reindeer to the region and founded Alaska's first college in Sitka. Carl Ben Eielson (1897–1929), a famed bush pilot, is a folk hero. Benny Benson (1913–72), born at Chignik, designed the state flag at the age of 13.

50 BIBLIOGRAPHY

Alaska, State of. *The Alaska Economy*. Vol. 7. Juneau: Department of Commerce and Economic Development, Division of the Economic Enterprises, 1979.

Alaska, State of. *Alaska Blue Book 1983*. Juneau: Department of Education, Division of State Libraries and Museums, 1983.

Brooks, Alfred Hulse. *Blazing Alaska's Trails*. Fairbanks: University of Alaska Press, 1972.

Gruening, Ernest. *State of Alaska*. New York: Random House, 1968.

Haycox, Stephen W., and Mary Childers Mangusso, ed. *An Alaska Anthology: Interpreting the Past*. Seattle: University of Washington Press, 1996.

———. Frigid Embrace: *Politics, Economics, and the Environment in Alaska*. Corvallis: Oregon State University Press, 2002.

Hedin, Robert, and Gary Holthaus (eds.). *The Great Land: Reflections on Alaska*. Tucson: University of Arizona Press, 1994.

Hunt, William R. *Alaska: A Bicentennial History*. New York: Norton, 1976.

Hunt, William R. *North of 53°: The Wild Days of the Alaska-Yukon Mining Frontier*. New York: Macmillan, 1974.

Jenkins, Peter. *Looking for Alaska*. New York : St. Martin's Press, 2001.

Kizzia, Tom. *The Wake of the Unseen Object: Among the Native Cultures of Bush Alaska*. New York: Henry Holt, 1992.

Kollin, Susan. *Nature's State: Imagining Alaska as the Last Frontier*. Chapel Hill: University of North Carolina Press, 2001.

McBeath, Gerald A. *Alaska Politics & Government*. Lincoln: University of Nebraska Press, 1994.

McPhee, John. *Coming into the Country*. New York: Farrar, Straus & Giroux, 1977.

Ryan, Alan, ed. *The Reader's Companion to Alaska*. San Diego, Calif.: Harcourt Brace, 1997.

ARIZONA

State of Arizona

ORIGIN OF STATE NAME: Probably from the Pima or Papago Indian word *arizonac,* meaning "place of small springs." **NICKNAME:** The Grand Canyon State. **CAPITAL:** Phoenix. **ENTERED UNION:** 14 February 1912 (48th). **SONGS:** "Arizona March Song" and "Arizona." **MOTTO:** *Ditat Deus* (God enriches). **FLAG:** A copper-colored five-pointed star symbolic of the state's copper resources rises from a blue field; six yellow and seven red segments radiating from the star cover the upper half. **OFFICIAL SEAL:** Depicted on a shield are symbols of the state's economy and natural resources, including mountains, a rising sun, and a dam and reservoir in the background; irrigated farms and orchards in the middle distance; and a quartz mill, a miner, and cattle in the foreground; as well as the state motto. The words "Great Seal of the State of Arizona 1912" surround the shield. **BIRD:** Cactus wren. **FLOWER:** Blossom of the saguaro cactus. **TREE:** Palo verde. **OFFICIAL NECKWEAR:** Bola tie. **LEGAL HOLIDAYS:** New Year's Day, 1 January; Birthday of Martin Luther King, Jr., 3rd Monday in January; Lincoln's Birthday, 1st Monday in February; Washington's Birthday, 3rd Monday in February; Memorial Day, last Monday in May; Independence Day, 4 July; Labor Day, 1st Monday in September; Columbus Day, 2nd Monday in October; Veterans Day, 11 November; Thanksgiving Day, 4th Thursday in November; Christmas Day, 25 December. **TIME:** 5 AM MST = noon GMT.

¹LOCATION, SIZE, AND EXTENT

Located in the Rocky Mountains region of the southwestern US, Arizona ranks 6th in size among the 50 states.

The total area of Arizona is 114,000 sq mi (295,260 sq km), of which land takes up 113,508 sq mi (293,986 sq km) and inland water 492 sq mi (1,274 sq km). Arizona extends about 340 mi (547 km) E-W; the state's maximum N-S extension is 395 mi (636 km).

Arizona is bordered on the N by Utah and on the Eby New Mexico (with the two borders joined at Four Corners, the only point in the US common to four states); on the S by the Mexican state of Sonora; and on the W by the Mexican state of Baja California Norte, California, and Nevada (with most of the line formed by the Colorado River). The total boundary length of Arizona is 1,478 mi (2,379 km). The state's geographic center is in Yavapai County, 55 mi (89 km) ESE of Prescott.

²TOPOGRAPHY

Arizona is a state of extraordinary topographic diversity and beauty. The Colorado Plateau, which covers two-fifths of the state in the north, is an arid upland region characterized by deep canyons, notably the Grand Canyon, a vast gorge more than 200 mi (320 km) long, up to 18 mi (29 km) wide, and more than 1 mi (1.6 km) deep. Also within this region are the Painted Desert and Petrified Forest, as well as Humphreys Peak, the highest point in the state, at 12,633 ft (3,853 m).

The Mogollon Rim separates the northern plateau from a central region of alternating basins and ranges with a general northwest–southeast direction. Ranges in the Mexican Highlands in the southeast include the Chiricahua, Dos Cabezas, and Pinaleno mountains. The Sonora Desert, in the southwest, contains the lowest point in the state, 70 ft (21 m) above sea level, on the Colorado River near Yuma.

The Colorado is the state's major river, flowing southwest from Glen Canyon Dam on the Utah border through the Grand Canyon and westward to Hoover Dam, then turning south to form the border with Nevada and California. Tributaries of the Colorado include the Little Colorado and Gila rivers. Arizona has few natural lakes, but there are several large artificial lakes formed by dams for flood control, irrigation, and power development. These include Lake Mead (shared with Nevada), formed by Hoover Dam; Lake Powell (shared with Utah); Lake Mohave and Lake Havasu (shared with California), formed by David Dam and Parker Dam, respectively; Roosevelt Lake, formed by Theodore Roosevelt Dam; and the San Carlos Lake, created by Coolidge Dam.

³CLIMATE

Arizona has a dry climate, with little rainfall. Temperatures vary greatly from place to place, season to season, and day to night. Average daily temperatures at Yuma, in the southwestern desert range from 43° to 67°F (6° to 19°C) in January, and from 81° to 106°F (27° to 41°C) in July. At Flagstaff, in the interior uplands, average daily January temperatures range from 14° to 41°F (–10° to 5°C), and average daily July temperatures range from 50° to 81°F (10° to 27°C). The maximum recorded temperature was 128°F (53°C), registered at Lake Havasu City on 29 June 1994; the minimum, –40°F (–40°C), was set at Hawley Lake on 7 January 1971.

The highest elevations of the state, running diagonally from the southeast to the northwest, receive between 25 and 30 in (63 to 76 cm) of precipitation a year, and the rest, for the most part, between 7 and 20 in (18 to 51 cm). Average annual precipitation at Phoenix (1971–2000) was 8.3 in (21 cm). The driest area is the extreme southwest, which receives less than 3 in (8 cm) a year. Snow, sometimes as much as 100 in (254 cm), falls on the highest peaks each winter but is rare in the southern and western lowlands.

The greatest amount of sunshine is registered in the southwest, with the proportion decreasing progressively toward the northeast; overall, the state receives more than 80% of possible sunshine, among the highest in the US, and Phoenix's 86% is higher than that of any other major US city.

⁴FLORA AND FAUNA

Generally categorized as desert, Arizona's terrain also includes mesa and mountains; consequently, the state has a wide diversity of vegetation. The desert is known for many varieties of cacti, from the saguaro, whose blossom is the state flower, to the cholla and widely utilized yucca. Desert flowers include the night-blooming cereus; among medicinal desert flora is the jojoba, also harvested for its oil-bearing seeds. Below the tree line (about 12,000 ft, or 3,658 m) the mountains are well timbered with varieties of spruce, fir, juniper, ponderosa pine, oak, and piñon. Rare plants, some of them endangered or threatened, include various cacti of commercial or souvenir value.

Arizona's fauna range from desert species of lizards and snakes to the deer, elk, and antelope of the northern highlands. Mountain lion, jaguar, coyote, and black and brown bears are found in the state, along with the badger, black-tailed jackrabbit, and gray fox. Small mammals include various cottontails, mice, and squirrels; prairie dog towns dot the northern regions. Rattlesnakes are abundant, and the desert is rife with reptiles such as the collared lizard and chuckwalla. Native birds include the thick-billed parrot, white pelican, and cactus wren (the state bird).

Forty-one animal species and 19 plant species were listed as endangered or threatened as of August 2003 by the US Fish and Wildlife Service. Arizona counts the desert tortoise and lesser long-nosed bat among its threatened wildlife. Officially listed as endangered or threatened in 2003 were the southern bald eagle, masked bobwhite (quail), Sonoran pronghorn, ocelot, jaguar, black-footed ferret, four species of chub, two species of gray wolf, woundfin, Apache trout, Gila topminnow, Gila trout, and southwestern willow flycatcher.

⁵ENVIRONMENTAL PROTECTION

Aside from Phoenix, whose air quality is poorer than that of most other US cities, Arizona has long been noted for its clear air, open lands, and beautiful forests. The main environmental concern of the state is to protect these resources in the face of growing population, tourism, and industry.

State agencies with responsibility for the environment include the State Land Department, which oversees natural resource conservation and land management; the Game and Fish Commission, which administers state wildlife laws; the Department of Health Services, which supervises sewage disposal, water treatment, hazardous and solid waste treatment, and air pollution prevention programs; and the Department of Water Resources, formed in 1980, which is concerned with the development, management, use, and conservation of water. The Department of Water Resources created five zones to monitor water use by about 80% of the population (using about 75% of the state's water). The Rural Arizona Watershed Alliance, representing the remaining 20% of its population who reside in the rural areas making up 85% of Arizona's land mass, has been funded by the legislature since 1999/2000 to undertake statewide planning for water resource use and allocation.

Legislation enacted in 1980 attempts to apportion water use among cities, mining, and agriculture, the last of which, through irrigation, accounts for the largest share of the state's annual water consumption. Less than 1% of Arizona's land is wetlands. In 2003, the Environmental Protection Agency's database listed 167 hazardous waste sites in Arizona, nine of which were on the National Priorities List. In 2001, Arizona received $60,402,000 in federal grants from the EPA; EPA expenditures for procurement contracts in Arizona that year amounted to $202,000.

⁶POPULATION

Arizona's population growth rate has been one of the nation's highest for two decades.

The state ranked 19th in population in the US with an estimated total of 5,456,453 in 2002, an increase of 6.4 % since 2000. Between 1990 and 2000, Arizona's population grew from 3,665,228 to 5,130,632, the 5th-largest increase and 2nd-largest percentage gain (40%) among the 50 states. The population is projected to reach 6.4 million by 2025.

Despite its rapid population growth, the state still had a population density of only 45.2 persons per sq mi in 2000. The median age was 34.2. Arizonans 65 years of age or older comprised 13% of the population in 2000, while persons under 18 years old accounted for 26.6%.

Three out of four Arizonans live in urban areas. The largest metropolitan areas are Phoenix-Mesa, with a 1999 estimated population of 3,013,696, and Tucson, with an estimated 803,618. The largest cities proper are Glendale, with a 2002 estimated population of 230,564; Scottsdale, 215,779; and Tempe, 159,508. More than half the state's population resides in Maricopa County, which includes every leading city except Tucson. Phoenix was the nation's sixth-largest city in 2002.

⁷ETHNIC GROUPS

Arizona has by far the nation's greatest expanse of Indian lands: the state's 22 reservations have a combined area of 19.1 million acres (7.7 million hectares)—26% of the total state area. In 2000, Arizona had the nation's 3rd-highest Indian population, 255,879, or 5% of the state total population.

The largest single American Indian nation, the Navaho, with a population of 104,565 in 2000, is located primarily in the northeastern part of the state. The Navaho reservation, covering 14,221 sq mi (36,832 sq km) within Arizona, extends into Utah and New Mexico and comprises desert, mesa, and mountain terrain. Herders by tradition, the people are also famous for their crafts. The reservation's total Indian population in 2000 was 173,631, up 21% from 143,405 in 1990. Especially since 1965, the Navaho have been active in economic development; reservation resources in uranium and coal have been leased to outside corporations, and loans from the US Department of Commerce have made possible roads, telephones, and other improvements. There are at least 12 and perhaps 17 other tribes (depending on definition). After the Navaho, the leading tribes are the Papago in the south, Apache in the east, and Hopi in the northeast. The Hopi reservation had a population of 6,946 in 2000.

The southern part of Arizona has most of the state's largest ethnic majority, a Hispanic and Latino population estimated at 1,295,617 in 2000, or 25.3% of the total population (up from the 1990 figure of 668,000, or 18% of the population). There are some old, long-settled Spanish villages, but the bulk of Hispanics (1,065,578) are of Mexican origin. Raul Castro, a Mexican-American, served as governor in 1975–77. There were an estimated 158,873 blacks as of 2000. Filipinos, Chinese, Japanese, and other Asians made up 1.8% of the population.

⁸LANGUAGES

With the possible exception of the Navaho word *hogan* (earth-and-timber dwelling), the linguistic influence of Arizona's Papago, Pima, Apache, Navaho, and Hopi tribes is almost totally limited to some place-names: Arizona itself, Yuma, Havasu, Tucson, and Oraibi. Indian loan-words spreading from Arizona derive from the Nahuatl speech of the Mexican Aztecs—for example, *coyote, chili, mesquite,* and *tamale.* Spanish, dominant in some sections, has given English *mustang, ranch, stampede, rodeo, marijuana, bonanza, canyon, mesa, patio,* and *fiesta.*

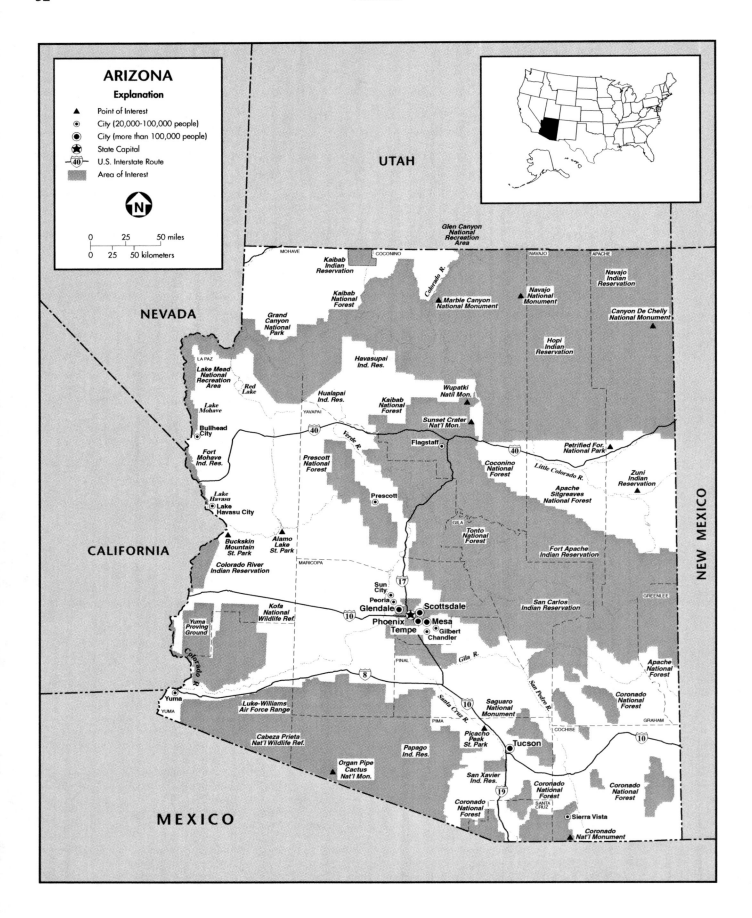

ARIZONA
Explanation
▲ Point of Interest
⊙ City (20,000-100,000 people)
◉ City (more than 100,000 people)
★ State Capital
40 U.S. Interstate Route
   Area of Interest

N

0   25   50 miles
0   25   50 kilometers

UTAH

NEVADA

CALIFORNIA

MEXICO

NEW MEXICO

MOHAVE

COCONINO

NAVAJO

APACHE

Glen Canyon
National
Recreation
Area

Kaibab
Indian
Reservation

Kaibab
National
Forest

Colorado R.

▲ Marble Canyon
National Monument

Navajo
National
Monument ▲

Navajo
Indian
Reservation

Canyon De Chelly
National Monument ▲

Grand
Canyon
National
Park

Havasupai
Ind. Res.

Hopi
Indian
Reservation

LA PAZ

Lake Mead
National
Recreation
Area

Red
Lake

Hualapai
Ind. Res.

Kaibab
National
Forest

Wupatki
Natil Mon. ▲

Lake
Mohave

YAVAPAI

Sunset Crater
Nat'l Mon. ▲

Bullhead
City ⊙

40

Verde R.

Flagstaff ⊙

40

Petrified For.
National Park ▲

Zuni
Indian
Reservation ▲

Fort
Mohave
Ind. Res.

Prescott
National
Forest

Coconino
National
Forest

Little Colorado R.

Lake
Havasu

Prescott ⊙

Apache
Sitgreaves
National Forest

Lake
Havasu City ●

GILA

Buckskin
Mountain
St. Park ▲

Alamo
Lake
St. Park ▲

Tonto
National
Forest

Fort Apache
Indian Reservation

Colorado River
Indian Reservation

MARICOPA

Kofa
National
Wildlife Ref.

Sun
City ⊙

17

San Carlos
Indian Reservation

GREENLEE

10

Peoria ⊙
Glendale ◉
Phoenix ★
Tempe ◉

Scottsdale ◉
Mesa ◉
Gilbert ⊙
Chandler ⊙

Yuma Proving
Ground

Colorado R.

PINAL

Gila R.

Apache
National
Forest

8

Luke-Williams
Air Force Range

YUMA

Yuma ⊙

10

Santa Cruz R.

San Pedro R.

Saguaro
National
Monument

Coronado
National
Forest

GRAHAM

Cabeza Prieta
Nat'l Wildlife Ref.

PIMA

Papago
Ind. Res.

Picacho
Peak
St. Park ▲

10

Tucson ◉

COCHISE

Organ Pipe
Cactus
Nat'l Mon. ▲

San Xavier
Ind. Res.

19

Coronado
National
Forest

Coronado
National
Forest

MEXICO

Coronado
National
Forest

SANTA
CRUZ

Sierra Vista ⊙

Coronado
Nat'l Monument ▲

English in the state represents a blend of North Midland and South Midland dialects without clear regional differences, although new meanings developed in the north and east for meadow and in the southern strip for swale as terms for flat mountain valleys. The recent population surge from eastern states has produced an urban blend with a strong Northern flavor. In 2000, 3,523,487 Arizonans—74.1% of all residents five years old and older—spoke only English at home, a decrease over the 79.2% reported in 1990.

The following table gives selected statistics from the 2000 census for language spoken at home by persons five years old and over. The category "Other Native North American languages" includes Apache, Cherokee, Choctaw, Dakota, Keres, Pima, and Yupik.

LANGUAGE	NUMBER	PERCENT
Population 5 years and over	4,752,724	100.0
Speak only English	3,523,487	74.1
Speak a language other than English	1,229,237	25.9
Speak a language other than English	1,229,237	25.9
Spanish or Spanish Creole	927,395	19.5
Navajo	89,951	1.9
Other Native North American languages	30,109	0.6
German	25,103	0.5
Chinese	17,111	0.4
French (incl. Patois, Cajun)	15,663	0.3
Tagalog	10,049	0.2
Vietnamese	9,999	0.2
Italian	8,992	0.2
Korean	7,689	0.2

[9] RELIGIONS

The first religions of Arizona were the sacred beliefs and practices of the Indians. Catholic missionaries began converting Arizona Indians (Franciscans among the Hopi, and Jesuits among the Pima) to the Christian faith in the late 17th century. By the late 18th century, the Franciscans were the main missionary force, and the Roman Catholic Church was firmly established. In 2000, the state had 974,883 Catholics in 267 congregations.

The Church of Jesus Christ of Latter-day Saints (Mormons) constitutes the 2nd-largest Christian denomination with 251,974 adherents in 643 congregations. Mormons were among the state's earliest Anglo settlers. Other major Christian denominations include the Southern Baptist Convention, 138,516 adherents; Assemblies of God, 82,802; and the United Methodist Church, 53,232.

In 2000, Arizona's estimated Jewish population was 81,675. There were about 11,857 Muslims. There were also about 25 Buddhist and 9 Hindu congregations.

[10] TRANSPORTATION

Until the last decade of the 19th century, the principal reason for the development of transportation in Arizona was to open routes to California. The most famous early road was El Camino de Diablo (The Devil's Highway), opened by the missionary Eusebio Kino in 1699. The first wagon road across Arizona was the Gila Trail (Cooke's Wagon Road), opened in 1846 as a southern route to California: Beale's Road was inaugurated in 1857. Also in 1857, the first stagecoach began operations. Until the coming of the railroads in the 1880s, however, the bulk of territorial commerce was by water transport on the Colorado River. Railroad construction reached its peak in the 1920s and declined rapidly thereafter.

Railroad trackage totaled 1,909 rail mi (3,072 km) in 2000, with ten railroads operating in the state. The state's two Class I railroads, Burlington Northern Santa Fe and Union Pacific, controlled about two-thirds of Arizona's total rail miles. In 1998, the top rail tonnage commodities originating from within the state included metallic ores and glass and stone. That year, over

half the rail tonnage terminating within the state was coal/coke. Amtrak provides limited passenger service through Flagstaff, Kingman, and other cities in the north, and through Tucson, Phoenix, and Yuma on the southern route.

In 2000, the state had 55,195 mi (88,827 km) of public streets and roads, of which 36,989 mi (59,528 km) were classified as rural and 18,206 mi (29,299 km) as urban. Interstate highways in Arizona totaled 1,168 mi (1,879 km). Of the 3,794,538 motor vehicles registered in 2000, there were 2,163,141 automobiles, 1,626,803 trucks, and 4,594 buses. There were 3,433,995 licensed drivers in 2000.

Arizona had 195 airports and 104 heliports in 2002. The leading air terminal was Phoenix Sky Harbor International Airport; Tucson International Airport ranked second.

[11] HISTORY

Evidence of a human presence in Arizona dates back more than 12,000 years. The first Arizonans—the offshoot of migrations across the Bering Strait—were large-game hunters: their remains have been found in the San Pedro Valley in the southeastern part of the state. By AD 500, their descendants had acquired a rudimentary agriculture from what is now Mexico and divided into several cultures. The Basket Makers (Anasazi) flourished in the northeastern part of the state; the Mogollon hunted and foraged in the eastern mountains; the Hokoham, highly sophisticated irrigators, built canals and villages in the central and southern valleys: and the Hakataya, a less-advanced river people, lived south and west of the Grand Canyon. For reasons unknown—a devastating drought is the most likely explanation—these cultures were in decay and the population much reduced by the 14th century. Two centuries later, when the first Europeans arrived, most of the natives were living in simple shelters in fertile river valleys, dependent on hunting, gathering, and small-scale farming for subsistence. These Arizona Indians belonged to three linguistic families: Uto-Aztecan (Hopi, Paiute, Chemehuevi, Pima-Papago), Yuman (Yuma, Mohave, Cocopa, Maricopa, Yavapai, Walapai, Havasupai), and Athapaskan (Navaho-Apache). The Hopi were the oldest group, their roots reaching back to the Anasazi; the youngest were the Navaho-Apache, migrants from the Plains, who were not considered separate tribes until the early 18th century.

The Spanish presence in Arizona involved exploration, missionary work, and settlement. Between 1539 and 1605, four expeditions crossed the land, penetrating both the upland plateau and the lower desert in ill-fated attempts to find great riches. In their footsteps came Franciscans from the Rio Grande to work among the Hopi; and Jesuits from the south, led by Eusebio Kino in 1692, to proselytize among the Pima. Within a few years, Kino had established a major mission station at San Xavier del Bac, near present-day Tucson. In 1736, a rich silver discovery near the Pima village of Arizona, about 20 mi (32 km) southwest of present-day Nogales, drew Spanish prospectors and settlers northward. To control the restless Pima, Spain in 1752 placed a military outpost, or presidio, at Tubac on the Santa Cruz River north of Nogales. This was the first major European settlement in Arizona. The garrison was moved north to the new fort at Tucson, also on the Santa Cruz, in 1776. During these years, the Spaniards gave little attention to the Santa Cruz settlements, administered as part of the Mexican province of Sonora, regarding them merely as way stations for colonizing expeditions traveling overland to the highly desirable lands of California. The end of the 18th century and the beginning of the 19th were periods of relative peace on the frontier; mines were developed and ranches begun. Spaniards removed hostile Apache bands onto reservations and made an effort to open a road to Santa Fe.

When Mexico revolted against Spain in 1810, the Arizona settlements were little affected. Mexican authorities did not take control at Arizpe, the Sonoran capital, until 1823. Troubled times followed, characterized by economic stagnation, political chaos, and renewed war with the Apache. Sonora was divided into *partidos* (counties), and the towns on the Santa Cruz were designated as a separate partido, with the county seat at Tubac. The area north of the Gila River, inhabited only by Indians, was vaguely claimed by New Mexico. With the outbreak of the Mexican War in 1846, two US armies marched across the region: Col. Stephen W. Kearny followed the Gila across Arizona from New Mexico to California, and Lt. Col. Philip Cooke led a Mormon battalion westward through Tucson to California. The California gold rush of 1849 saw thousands of Americans pass along the Gila toward the new El Dorado. In 1850, most of present-day Arizona became part of the new US Territory of New Mexico; the southern strip was added by the Gadsden Purchase in 1853.

Three years later, the Sonora Exploring and Mining Co. organized a large party, led by Charles D. Poston, to open silver mines around Tubac. A boom followed, with Tubac becoming the largest settlement in the valley; the first newspaper, the Weekly Arizonian, was launched there in 1859. The great desire of California for transportation links with the rest of the Union prompted the federal government to chart roads and railroad routes across Arizona, erect forts there to protect Anglo travelers from the Indians, and open overland mail service. Dissatisfied with their representation at Santa Fe, the territorial capital, Arizona settlers joined those in southern New Mexico in 1860 in an abortive effort to create a new territorial entity. The outbreak of the Civil War in 1861 saw the declaration of Arizona as Confederate territory and abandonment of the region by the Union troops. A small Confederate force entered Arizona in 1862 but was driven out by a volunteer Union army from California. On 24 February 1863, President Abraham Lincoln signed into law a measure creating the new Territory of Arizona. Prescott became the capital in 1864, Tucson in 1867, Prescott again in 1877, and finally Phoenix in 1889.

During the early years of territorial status, the development of rich gold mines along the lower Colorado River and in the interior mountains attracted both people and capital to Arizona, as did the discovery of silver bonanzas in Tombstone and other districts in the late 1870s. Additional military posts were constructed to protect mines, towns, and travelers. This activity, in turn, provided the basis for a fledgling cattle industry and irrigated farming. Phoenix, established in 1868, grew steadily as an agricultural center. The Southern Pacific Railroad, laying track eastward from California, reached Tucson in 1880, and the Atlantic and Pacific (later acquired by the Santa Fe), stretching west from Albuquerque through Flagstaff, opened service to California in 1883. By 1890, copper had replaced silver as the principal mineral extracted in Arizona. In the Phoenix area, large canal companies began wrestling with the problem of supplying water for commercial agriculture. This problem was resolved in 1917 with the opening of the Salt River Valley Project, a federal reclamation program that provided enormous agricultural potential.

As a creature of the Congress, Arizona Territory was presided over by a succession of governors, principally Republicans, appointed in Washington. In reaction, the populace was predominantly Democratic. Within the territory, a merchant-capitalist class, with strong ties to California, dominated local and territorial politics until it was replaced with a mining-railroad group whose influence continued well into the 20th century. A move for separate statehood began in the 1880s but did not receive serious attention in Congress for another two decades. In 1910, after Congress passed an enabling act that allowed Arizona to apply for statehood, a convention met at Phoenix and drafted a state constitution. On 14 February 1912, Arizona entered the Union as the 48th state.

During the first half of the 20th century, Arizona shook off its frontier past. World War I (1914–18) spurred the expansion of the copper industry, intensive agriculture, and livestock production. Goodyear Tire and Rubber established large farms in the Salt River Valley to raise pima cotton. The war boom also generated high prices, land speculation, and labor unrest; at Bisbee and Jerome, local authorities forcibly deported more than 1,000 striking miners during the summer of 1917. The 1920s brought depression: banks closed, mines shut down, and agricultural production declined. To revive the economy, local boosters pushed highway construction, tourism, and the resort business. Arizona also shared in the general distress caused by the Great Depression of the 1930s and received large amounts of federal aid for relief and recovery. A copper tariff encouraged the mining industry, additional irrigation projects were started, and public works were begun on Indian reservations, in parks and forests, and at education institutions. Prosperity returned during World War II (1939–45) as camps for military training, prisoners of war, and displaced Japanese-Americans were built throughout the state. Meat, cotton, and copper markets flourished, and the construction of processing and assembly plants suggested a new direction for the state's economy.

Arizona emerged from World War II as a modern state. War industries spawned an expanding peacetime manufacturing boom that soon provided the principal source of income, followed by tourism, agriculture, and mining. During the 1950s, the political scene changed. Arizona Republicans captured the governorship, gained votes in the legislature, won congressional seats, and brought a viable two-party system to the state. The rise of Barry Goldwater of Phoenix to national prominence further encouraged Republican influence. Meanwhile, air conditioning changed lifestyles, prompting a significant migration to the state.

But prosperity did not reach into all sectors. While the state ranked as only the 19th poorest in the nation in 1990 (with a poverty rate of 13.7%), by 1998, it ranked 6th poorest, with a poverty rate of 16.6%.

For many years Arizona had seen its water diverted to California. In 1985, however, the state acted to bring water from the Colorado River to its own citizens by building the Central Arizona Project (CAP). The CAP was a $3 billion network of canals, tunnels, dams and pumping stations which had the capacity to bring 2.8 million acre-feet of water a year from the Colorado River to Arizona's desert lands, cities, and farms. By 1994, however, many considered the project to be a failure, as little demand existed for the water it supplied. Farmers concluded that water-intensive crops such as cotton were not profitable, and Arizona residents complained that the water provided by the CAP was dirty and undrinkable.

Arizona politics in recent years has been rocked by the discovery of corruption in high places. In 1988, Governor Evan Mecham was impeached on two charges of official misconduct. In 1989, Senators John McCain and Dennis DeConcini were indicted for interceding in 1987 with federal bank regulators on behalf of Lincoln Savings and Loan Association. Lincoln's president, Charles Keating, Jr., had contributed large sums to the Senators' reelection campaigns. In 1990, Peter MacDonald, the leader of the Navajo Nation, was convicted in the Navajo Tribal Court of soliciting $400,000 in bribes and kickbacks from corporations and individuals who sought to conduct business with the tribe in the 1970s and 1980s. A year later, seven members of the Arizona state legislature were charged with bribery, money laundering, and filing false election claims as the result of a sting operation. The legislators were videotaped accepting thousands of dollars from a man posing as a gaming consultant in return for agreeing to legalize casino gambling.

Arizona Presidential Vote by Political Party, 1948–2000

YEAR	ELECTORAL VOTE	ARIZONA WINNER	DEMOCRAT	REPUBLICAN	PROGRESSIVE
1948	4	*Truman (D)	95,251	77,597	3,310
1952	4	*Eisenhower (R)	108,528	152,042	—
1956	4	*Eisenhower (R)	112,880	176,990	—
1960	4	Nixon (R)	176,781	221,241	—
1964	5	Goldwater (R)	237,753	242,535	—
					AMERICAN IND.
1968	5	*Nixon (R)	170,514	266,721	46,573
					AMERICAN
1972	6	*Nixon (R)	198,540	402,812	21,208
1976	6	Ford (R)	295,602	418,642	7,647
1980	6	*Reagan (R)	246,843	529,688	18,784
1984	7	*Reagan (R)	333,854	681,416	10,585
1988	7	*Bush (R)	454,029	702,541	13,351
					IND. (PEROT)
1992	8	Bush (R)	543,086	572,086	353,741
1996	8	*Clinton (D)	653,288	622,073	112,072
					GREEN
2000	8	*Bush, G. W. (R)	685,341	781,652	45,645

*Won US presidential election.

The most recent in Arizona's series of political scandals was the investigation and 1996 indictment of Governor Fife Symington on 23 counts of fraud and extortion in connection with his business ventures before he became governor in 1991, and his filing of personal bankruptcy. The case went to trial in May 1997. Convicted of fraud, Symington was replaced by Secretary of State Jane Hull, also a Republican. In 1998 gubernatorial elections, Hull was elected in her own right. Janet Napolitano was elected governor in 2002. In 2003, the Arizona Supreme Court decided to individually review the death sentences of 27 inmates by judges rather than juries, which was a practice deemed unconstitutional by the US Supreme Cout.

12STATE GOVERNMENT

The current constitution of Arizona, drafted in 1910 at the height of the Progressive era, contained reform provisions that were very advanced for the time; initiative, referendum, workers' compensation, short terms for elected officials, suffrage for women, and the barring of trusts and monopolies from the state. The constitution was adopted in 1911 and had been amended 133 times January 2003.

Legislative authority is vested in a 30-member senate and a 60-member house of representatives. Legislative sessions are annual, begin in January, and must adjourn no later than the Saturday of the week during which the 100th day of the session falls. Special sessions, which are not limited in duration, may be called by petition of two-thirds the membership of each house. All senators and representatives serve two-year terms and are chosen at the general election in November of each even-numbered year. A legislator must be a US citizen, at least 25 years old, and must have been an Arizona resident for at least three years and a member of their district for at least a year. The legislative salary in 2002 was $24,000.

Chief executive officials elected statewide include the governor, secretary of state (the designated successor to the governor, as there is not lieutenant governor), treasurer, attorney general, and superintendent of public instruction, all of whom serve 4-year terms. The governor is limited to a maximum of two consecutive terms. The three members of the Corporation Commission, which regulates public services and utilities, are elected for staggered six-year terms, and the state mine inspector is elected for two years. Candidates for executive office must have been US citizens for at least ten years, must be at least 25 years old, and

must have been a citizen of Arizona for at least five years. In 2002 the governor's salary was $95,000.

Bills may originate in either house of the legislature and must be passed by both houses and approved by the governor in order to become law. A two-thirds vote of the elected members in each house is necessary to override the governor's veto. If the governor fails to sign or veto a bill, it becomes law after five days (Sundays excluded) or ten days after the legislature has adjourned. Under the initiative procedure, legislation and proposed constitutional amendments can be placed on the ballot by petition. The petition must be signed by 15% of total votes cast for all candidates for governor at the last election. Constitutional amendments proposed in the legislature are ratified by a majority vote of the electorate.

In order to vote in Arizona, a person must be 18 years old, a US citizen, and must have been a resident of the state for at least 29 days prior to the next election. Restrictions apply to convicted felons and those declared mentally incapacitated by the court.

13POLITICAL PARTIES

Of Arizona's 17 territorial governors, all federally appointed, 14 were Republicans and three Democrats. Statehood meant a prolonged period of Democratic dominance. From 1912 through 1950, the state had nine Democratic and three Republican governors; during that period, Republicans held the statehouse for only six years.

Republican Party fortunes improved dramatically after 1950, largely because of the rise to state and national prominence of a conservative Republican, Barry Goldwater, first elected to the US Senate in 1952. From 1951 to 1994, eight Republican governors occupied the state house for 26 years, and five Democratic governors for 18 years. Several Arizona Republicans were appointed to high office during the Nixon years, and in 1973, another Republican, John J. Rhodes, became minority leader in the US House of Representatives. Democrat and former governor Bruce Babbitt was named Secretary of the Interior for the Clinton administration in 1992.

In 1996 Bill Clinton ended 40 years of Republican presidential victories in Arizona, becoming the first Democratic winner since 1952, with 47% of the vote to Bob Dole's 44% and 8% for Independent Ross Perot. In 2000, the pendulum swung back to the Republican side, with George W. Bush winning 51% of the vote to Al Gore's 45% and 3% for Green Party candidate Ralph Nader. In 2002 there were 2,229,180 registered voters; 38% were

Democratic, 43% Republican, and 19% unaffiliated or members of other parties in 2001. The state had eight electoral votes in the 2000 presidential election.

Democrat Dennis DeConcini won reelection to the US Senate in 1988; he retired in 1994, and his seat was won by Republican Jon Kyl. Republican John McCain was reelected senator in 1992 and again in 1998; McCain ran for the presidency in 2000 but dropped his bid. Following the November 1994 election, Arizona's delegation of US Representatives went from three Democrats and three Republicans to one Democrat and five Republicans; in the 108th Congress (2003–04), Arizona's congressional delegation had increased, and there were six Republicans and two Democrats in the House. Arizonans elected a Democrat, Janet Napolitano, as governor in 2002; she was the first female governor to be elected back-to-back behind another female governor, Jane Dee Hull. In 2003, Arizona's state legislature consisted of 17 Republicans and 13 Democrats in the senate, and 39 Republicans, 20 Democrats, and one independent in the state house. In 2003 there were 25 women serving in the state legislature.

14LOCAL GOVERNMENT

Each of Arizona's 15 counties has a sheriff, county attorney, county recorder, treasurer, assessor, superintendent of schools, and three or five supervisors, each elected to a four-year term. Counties act as agents of the state.

Other local governmental units are cities, charter cities, and towns (communities with populations under 3,000). Towns generally follow the council-mayor form of government. All of Arizona's largest cities are charter cities. In all, there were 638 local government units in 2002, of which 87 were municipal governments. There were 305 special districts. As of 2002, the state had 245 school systems.

Each of the 21 Indian reservations in Arizona has a tribal council or board with members elected by the people.

15STATE SERVICES

To address the continuing threat of terrorism and to work with the federal Department of Homeland Security (created in 2002 following the terrorist attacks of 11 September 2001), homeland security in Arizona in 2003 operated under the authority of the governor; the state homeland security advisor was a director appointed by the governor.

The Arizona Department of Education regulates the school system. The Arizona Board of Regents governs the state's three public universities. A commission for postsecondary education provides students with financial aid, and school information. The Department of Transportation administers the state's highway and air-transport systems, among other functions. The Banking Department supervises the financial institutions and enterprises of the state.

The Department of Health Services operates programs for environmental health, behavioral health (including alcohol abuse, drug abuse, and mental-illness treatment facilities), and family health services. The National Guard falls under the jurisdiction of the Department of Emergency and Military Affairs, while prisons and rehabilitation programs are administered by the State Department of Corrections and the Board of Pardons and Paroles. The Department of Public Safety oversees the state highway patrol.

Natural resources are the responsibility of several agencies, including the Game and Fish Commission, Department of Mines and Mineral Resources, Oil and Gas Conservation Commission, Parks Board, and Department of Water Resources. The Department of Economic Security handles employment services and public-assistance programs.

16JUDICIAL SYSTEM

The supreme court is the highest court in Arizona and has administrative responsibility over all other courts in the state. The five supreme court justices, appointed by the governor for staggered six-year terms, choose a chief justice and vice-chief justice to preside over the court.

The court of appeals, established in 1964, is organized in two geographical divisions which together have 22 judges. Appeals court judges are appointed for terms of six years.

The superior court is the general trial court of the state, and there must be at least one superior court judge in every Arizona county. In 1999 there were 136 superior court judges, plus 2 part-time judges, in the state's 15 counties. In counties with populations over 150,000, superior court judges are appointed by the governor; they hold office for terms ending 60 days following the next regular general election after expiration of a two-year term. Those seeking retention run at the next general election on a nonpartisan ballot. In counties with populations of under 150,000, superior court judges are elected by nonpartisan ballot to four-year terms.

Counties are divided into precincts, each of which has a justice court. Every incorporated city and town has a police court. The jurisdiction of justice courts and police courts is limited to minor civil and criminal cases. Local judges are elected for terms of four years.

According to the FBI Crime Index of 1998, Arizona had a crime rate of 6,077.4 per 100,000 population, including a total of 28,675 violent crimes and 293,874 property crimes in that year. As of June 2001, federal and state institutions held 27,136 prisoners, an increase of 3.2% over the previous year. Arizona had an incarceration rate of 478 per 100,000 population.

In 2003, 124 prisoners were under sentence of death. Arizona has executed 22 prisoners since 1976.

17ARMED FORCES

In 2002, 22,448 active-duty federal military personnel were stationed at nine military installations in Arizona. Major military installations include the Army's Fort Huachuca at Sierra Vista; the Air Force's Williams base near Phoenix, and the Luke and Davis-Monthan bases, near Phoenix and Tucson, respectively; and the Marine Corps' Yuma Air Station. Defense Department expenditures in Arizona were approximately $8.9 billion in 2002, $6.6 billion for contracts and about $2.1 billion for payroll.

There were 562,916 veterans of US military service in Arizona as of 2000, of whom 115,615 served in World War II; 71,943 in the Korean conflict; 150,138 during the Vietnam era; and 66,563 during 1990–2000 (including the Persian Gulf War). On 10 September 1992, Nathan E. Cook, the last veteran of the Spanish-American War (1898–1902), died in Phoenix at the age of 106. Veterans' benefits totaled $1.0 billion in 2002.

As of June 2000, the Arizona Department of Public Safety employed 1,050 full-time sworn officers.

18MIGRATION

Arizona's first migrants were the ancient peoples who came from Asia across the Bering Strait more than 12,000 years ago. Hispanic settlers began arriving in the late 17th century. Anglo migration, especially from the South, became significant as the US developed westward to California, and increased at an even faster rate with the building of the railroads during the 1880s. Migration has accelerated since World War II (1939–45), and Arizona showed a net gain of 519,000 in domestic and 96,000 in international migration from 1990 to 1998. Mexico is the main source of foreign immigrants. In the 1980s, half of Arizona's total population increase was from migration; about 530,000 persons moved there during that time. By 1998, Arizona's Hispanic population numbered 963,000; those of Hispanic origin numbered 1,034,000. In 1998, 6,211 immigrants from foreign countries arrived in Arizona, of these 3,209 were from Mexico. Arizona's total population increased 27.4% between 1990 and 1998. In the period 1995–2000, 796,420 people moved into the state and 480,272 moved out, for a net gain of 316,148, 53,241 of whom were age 65 or over.

[19]INTERGOVERNMENTAL COOPERATION

Arizona is a signatory to a boundary agreement with California (1963) and Nevada; and to such interstate accords as the Colorado River Compact, Desert Pacific Economic Region Compact, Interstate Compact for Juveniles, Interstate Oil and Gas Compact, Upper Colorado River Basin Compact, Western Interstate Commission for Higher Education, Wildlife Violator Compact, and Western Interstate corrections, nuclear, and education compacts.

The most important federal project in the state has been the Central Arizona Project, approved by Congress in 1968 and designed to divert water from the Colorado River to the Phoenix and Tucson areas for agriculture, energy, and other purposes. Federal grants totaled $5.2 billion in fiscal year 2001.

[20]ECONOMY

Mining and cattle-raising were the principal economic activities in Arizona during the territorial period. With the introduction of irrigation in the early 1900s, farming assumed a greater importance. Improvements in transportation later in the 20th century led to the development of manufacturing and tourism. sector.

Arizona's economy compiled an impressive growth record during the 1970s and early 1980s. Between 1973 and 1983, the state population increased by 39% (4th in the US); nonfarm wage and salary employment grew by 49% (5th in the United States); and total personal income by 218% (6th in the United States). Over-expansion brought a slowdown in the late 1980s, with vacancy rates reaching record levels in the late 1980s and early 1990s. In the national recession of 1991, the Arizona's annual job creation rate dropped from 3% to zero. However, economic recovery in the 1990s was rapid. Arizona's annual job creation rate rose to a peak of about 8% in 1994 and continued above 4% until the national recession of 2001. The state gross product grew at an average annual rate of 8.75% in 1998 and 1999, and at 6.1% in 2000. However, the growth rate fell to 4.7% in 2001. Job growth was negative in 2001, and only 0.2% in 2002. In addition to substantial layoffs in the manufacturing, transportation and utilities, and finance, insurance, and real estate sectors, the state budget crunch prompted scheduled layoffs in the government for fiscal 2004. Total assets in Arizona's financial institutions, which had grown from $38.8 billion in September 1998 to $65.3 billion by September 2001 (+68.3%), fell to $46.8 billion (-28.3%) as of September 2002. Vacancy rates of 12% (in Tucson) to 22% (in Phoenix) in late 2002, though below previous highs except for hotels, exceeded national averages.

In 2001, state gross product totaled $160.7 billion, 12.6% from the public sector. The biggest contributions to state gross product came from general services ($34.5 billion, up 36.8% from 1997), financial services, including insurance and real estate ($31.4 billion, up 33.6% from 1997); manufacturing ($21.7 billion, up 20% from 1997 but including a 4.4% decline in the electronics sector); and government ($20.3 billion, up 32% from 1997).

[21]INCOME

According to the Bureau of Economic Analysis, in 2001, Arizona had a per capita personal income (PCPI) of $25,878 which ranked 38th in the United States (including the District of Columbia) and was 85% of the national average, $30,413. The 2001 PCPI reflected an increase of 2.0% from 2000 compared to the national change of 2.2%. In 2001, Arizona had a total personal income (TPI) of $137,331,072,000 which ranked 23rd in the United States and accounted for 1.6% of the national total. The 2001 TPI reflected an increase of 4.8% from 2000 compared to the national change of 3.3%.

Earnings of persons employed in Arizona increased from $93,526,642,000 in 2000 to $97,001,206,000 in 2001, an increase of 3.7%. The largest industries in 2001 were services, 29.3% of earnings; state and local government, 11.9%; and retail trade, 10.4%. Of the industries that accounted for at least 5% of earnings in 2001, the slowest growing from 2000 to 2001 was durable goods manufacturing (9.9% of earnings in 2001), which decreased 3.3%; the fastest was state and local government, which increased 16.7%.

According to data released by the US Census Bureau, in 2000, the median household income was $41,456 compared to the national average of $42,148. In 2001, the median income for a family of four was $56,067 compared to the national average of $63,278. For the period 1999 to 2001, the average poverty rate was 12.9% which placed it 37th among the 50 states and the District of Columbia ranked lowest to highest.

[22]LABOR

According to Bureau of Labor Statistics (BLS) provisional estimates, in July 2003 the seasonally adjusted civilian labor force in Arizona numbered 2,674,200, with approximately 163,800 workers unemployed, yielding an unemployment rate of 6.1%, compared to the national average of 6.2% for the same period. Since the beginning of the BLS data series in 1978, the highest unemployment rate recorded was 11.7% in February 1983. The historical low was 3.7% in January 2001. In 2001, an estimated 7.8% of the labor force was employed in construction; 9.5% in manufacturing; 5.4% in transportation, communications, and public utilities; 20.2% in trade; 7.5% in finance, insurance, and real estate; 22.6% in services; 16.4% in government; and 2.6% in agriculture.

Organized labor has a long history in Arizona. A local of the Western Federation of Miners was founded in 1896, and labor was a powerful force at the constitutional convention in 1910. Nevertheless, the state's work force is much less organized than that of the nation as a whole. The US Department of Labor reported that in 2002, 120,000 of Arizona's 2,184,000 employed wage and salary workers were members of unions. This represented 5.5% of those so employed, down from 5.9% in 2001. The national average is 13.2%. In all, 144,000 workers (6.6%) were represented by unions. In addition to union members, this category includes workers who report no union affiliation but whose jobs are covered by a union contract. Arizona is one of 22 states with a right-to-work law.

[23]AGRICULTURE

Arizona's agricultural output (including livestock products) was valued at $2.5 billion in 2001 (29th in the US). Cash receipts from crops alone amounted to $1.4 billion.

In 2002 there were about 7,300 farms covering 26.5 million acres (10.7 million hectares), or about 39% of the state's total area, but only 1,961,000 acres (389,000 hectares), or 1.3% of the state, were actually farmed for crops. Arizona's farmed cropland is intensely cultivated and highly productive. In 2002, Arizona was 2nd among all states in cotton yield per acre (1,262 lb per acre). About 95% of all farmland is dependent on irrigation provided by dams and water projects.

Cotton is the leading cash crop in Arizona. In 2002 the state produced 560,000 bales of Upland cotton on 215,000 acres (87,000 hectares), with a total value of $131,443,000. Arizona also produced 16,000 bales of American-Pima cotton on 4,900 acres (1,980 hectares) valued at $6,359,000. Vegetables, especially head lettuce, accounted for a value of $705,701,000 in 2001. Hay is also an important item; total hay production was 2,034,000 tons in 2002, for a value of $202,289,000. Other crops are wheat, sorghum, barley, grapes, and citrus fruits.

24ANIMAL HUSBANDRY

The total inventory of cattle and calves was an estimated 820,000 in 2003, with a value of $623 million. In 2003, the state had an estimated 131,000 sheep and lambs. In 2002, the state had 143,000 hogs and pigs valued at $10.9 million.

A total of 2.9 billion lb (1.3 billion kg) of milk was produced in 2001.

25FISHING

Arizona has no commercial fishing. The state's lakes and mountain streams lure the state's 458,098 licensed anglers and are an increasingly important tourist attraction. In 1995/96, over 217,700 lb (98,750 kg) of live fish and 3 million fish eggs were distributed within the state by federal authorities.

26FORESTRY

The lumber industry in Arizona began during the 19th century, when the building of the transcontinental railroad created a demand for railroad ties. Production of lumber from Arizona's forests remained strong until the 1990s, during which the primary emphasis shifted to conservation and recreation. Lumber production in 2002 was 62 million board feet.

The main forest regions stretch from the northwest to the southeast, through the center of the state. Altogether, in 2002 there were 19,427,000 acres (7,862,000 hectares) of forestland in Arizona, over 25% of the state's area and 2.6% of the US total forestland. Commercial timberland accounted for only 3,527,000 acres (1,427,000 hectares). National forests covered 11,890,609 acres (4,812,129 hectares) as of 2001. Lumber production remains an important emphasis on the Kaibab, Coconino, and Apache-Sitgreaves National Forests, and on the Hualapai, Navajo, Ft. Apache, and San Carlos Apache Indian Reservations.

27MINING

Arizona ranked fourth in nonfuel mineral production value in 2001, thanks to the state's copper industry. According to US Geological Survey estimates, nonfuel mineral production in Arizona during 2001was valued at $2.17 billion, down 14% from 2000. Copper represented 68% of the nonfuel mineral production value in 2001. Construction sand and gravel was the state's 2nd-leading nonfuel mineral, followed by portland cement, molybdenum concentrates, and crushed stone. According to preliminary figures, production and values in 2001 for principal minerals are as follows: copper, 875,000 metric tons ($1.5 billion); sand and gravel, 56.6 million metric tons ($294 million); and crushed stone, 7 million metric tons ($43.3 million). In 2000 silver production was 132 metric tons ($21.2 million), and gold production in 1999 was 786 kg ($7 million).

Arizona continued to lead the country in copper production in 2001, a rank it has held for more than 80 years. The state accounted for almost two-thirds of all copper mined and produced in the US. Arizona also ranked 1st in production of molybdenum; 2nd in gemstones; 3rd in perlite; 4th in construction sand and gravel, silver, and zeolites; 5th in pumice and pumicite; 6th in iron oxide; 7th in bentonite; and 8th in dimension stone.

Population growth and freeway construction projects in metropolitan Phoenix have contributed to Arizona's ranking as the nation's fourth-largest producer of sand and gravel.

28ENERGY AND POWER

In 1999, Arizona produced 84 billion kWh of electric power (utility and nonutility); total installed capacity in the same year was 15.3 million kW. The state had 33 power plants, of which 14 were hydroelectric, accounting for 17% of power output. Electric energy retail sales in the state were 57.7 billion kWh; the surplus production was exported to other states, primarily California. The Palo Verde nuclear plant in Maricopa County, which generated electricity for 4 million customers, had the largest combined capacity of any nuclear power facility in the US.

Arizona's fossil-fuel potential remains largely undeveloped, though oil and natural-gas exploration began in the 1980s. In 2002, the state marketed 301 billion cu ft (8.5 billion cu m) of natural gas. Coal production in 2000 was 13,111,000 metric tons, all of it from two surface mines. In 2000 Arizona's total per capital energy consumption was 237 million Btu (59.7 million kcal), ranking it 50th among the states.

Energy resource development in the state is encouraged by the Department of Mines and Mineral Resources, Oil and Gas Conservation Commission, and Department of Water Resources.

29INDUSTRY

Manufacturing, which has grown rapidly since World War II (1939–45), became the state's leading economic activity in the 1970s. Factors contributing to this growth included a favorable tax structure, available labor, plentiful electric power, and low land costs. The major manufacturing centers are the Phoenix and Tucson areas. Principal manufacturing industries include nonelectrical machinery, electrical and electronic equipment (computers, semiconductors, communication equipment), aircraft equipment, food products, and printing and publishing. Military equipment accounts for much of the output. The total value added by manufacturing in 1997 amounted to an estimated $44 billion. Principal manufacturers of electronic and technology-intensive equipment in Arizona include: Motorola, Allied Signal Aerospace, Honeywell, Hughes Missile Systems Co., and Intel. Intel expanded its operations in Arizona with the construction of a $1.3 billion plant in 1994. While high-tech manufacturing actually declined in Arizona in 1998 and early 1999 in part because of the Asian financial crisis, the 62% of the state's low-tech manufacturing improved. The manufacturing and construction employment growth rates shrank from 1994 to 1999.

Earnings of persons employed in Arizona increased from $72 billion in 1997 to $79 billion in 1998, an increase of 10%. The largest industries in 1998 were services, 28.9% of earnings; state and local government, 11.2%; and durable goods manufacturing, 11.2%. Of the industries that accounted for at least 5% of earnings in 1998, the slowest growing from 1997 to 1998 was state and local government, which increased 4.9%; the fastest was wholesale trade (6.4% of earnings in 1998), which increased 11.8%.

30COMMERCE

Arizona had 7,708 wholesale trade establishments in 1997, according to the Census of Wholesale Trade; with sales of $49.5 billion, and the 2nd-fastest sales growth rate in the country (77%) over a five-year period. Most wholesale establishments were concentrated in Maricopa and Pima Counties. Retail trade was conducted by 23,469 establishments in 1997, with sales of $44.9 billion, and the fourth highest growth rate (53%). Automotive dealers accounted for 11% of establishments; food stores, 9%; and eating and drinking places, 32%. Food stores sold a total of $8.8 billion in 1997, while general merchandise stores sold $5.3 billion. In 1998, exports from Arizona amounted to $11.4 billion.

31CONSUMER PROTECTION
The Arizona Attorney General has primary enforcement powers regarding consumer protection. The Consumer Fraud Act gives the Attorney General the authority to combat consumer fraud.

32BANKING
As of 2002, there were 45 insured banks in Arizona. Total assets of insured banks were $46.8 billion. Arizona has a high percentage of new banking institutions—as of 2002, 11 were less than 3 years old, and 26 were less than 9 years old. Due to the fact that many of the state's banks are young and asset-sensitive, their earnings were weak as of late 2002, due in part to narrower net interest margins (NIMs) (the difference between the lower rates offered to savers and the higher rates charged on loans). The state's median annualized return on average assets (ROA) ratio (the measure of earnings in relation to all resources) compared unfavorably to the national median in 2002.

The banking industry in Arizona is regulated by the Department of Banking. Nationally chartered institutions do not come under the jurisdiction of the Arizona Department of Banking, including Bank of America, Bank One, Wells Fargo Bank, Desert Schools Federal Credit Union, and Arizona Federal Credit Union.

33INSURANCE
In 2001 there were 4.6 million ordinary life insurance policies in force with a total value of $151.2 billion; total value for all categories of life insurance (ordinary, group, industrial, and credit) was $234.5 billion. Death benefits paid that year totaled $670.6 million. As of 2003, there were 54 property and casualty and 328 life and health insurance companies incorporated or organized in the state.

Property and casualty insurers wrote premiums amounting to $5.69 billion in 2001. That year, there were 27,389 flood insurance policies in force in the state, with a total value of $3.9 million.

The Department of Insurance regulates the state's insurance industry and examines and licenses agents and brokers.

34SECURITIES
Arizona has the Arizona Stock Exchange, formed in 1990. The exchange is an electronic call market which trades equity securities, including many Arizona-based companies. AZX conducts single-price auctions, of NYSE, NASDAQ, and AMEX securities, in what is often called "Dutch Auctions." In 1997, securities transactions were conducted by approximately 832 broker-dealer companies with 6,905 employees. There are 158 investment advisory organizations in Arizona. A total of 68 NASDAQ companies are headquartered in Arizona, and nine NASDAQ market makers. Four companies incorporated in Arizona are listed on the NYSE; including CSK Auto Corp., Pinnacle West Capital Corp., Simula, Inc., and Unisource Energy Corp.

35PUBLIC FINANCE
The governor's budgets are prepared in the Office of Strategic Planning and Budgeting (OSPB). During the 1990's, Arizona moved from an annual to a biennial budget format. Agency requests are submitted to the OSPB by September 1, and agency hearings are held in November and December. The governor's budget is submitted in January, and the legislature is expected to pass the budget in the period January to April.

In 1998, a depressed economy resulted from the Asian crisis and the Russian devaluation, forcing growth in Arizona to drop below 4% for the first time since 1992. In 1999, the economic picture was looking much brighter: the governor of Arizona recommended adjustments to the biennial budget pursuant to

increases in revenue attributed to high sales levels and corporate tax collections. General fund revenues for 1999 exceeded projections by almost $100 million, most of which was slated for educational improvements in the state. The governor was also able to reduce tax rates in 2002 for corporations, but not for individuals. However, the recession in 2001 brought a budget crisis in 2002. Medicaid expenditures grew 38.6% in 2001/02 (and by 26.4% in 2002/03, the largest percent increases among the states), exceeding appropriations by $62 million, while revenues came in below projections. A total of $671.2 million was cut from the 2001/02 after it was enacted. Measures taken to close the budget gap in the General Fund included fee increases, layoffs, across-the-board budget cuts, reduced local aid, program reorganizations, infusions from the state's rainy day fund and from other funds. Despite an 8.1% decrease in General Fund appropriations for 2002/03, cuts amounting to $393.6 million were made in state's budget after it was enacted. The budget deficit for 2002/03 was estimated at $500 million (about 8% of the total budget), and for 2003/04 projected at $1 billion (about 15.8%), despite constitutional provisions that require the governor to submit, legislature to pass, and the governor to sign, a balanced budget. Fiscal year 2001 ended with a balance of $409 million, including $373 million in the state's stabilization (rainy day) fund. Fiscal 2002, ended with a balance of $66 million, $65 million in the stabilization fund, and 2002/03 was estimated to end with a $61 million balance, but with the rainy day fund emptied. Fiscal year 2004 was projected to end with a total balance of $2 million, with nothing in the rainy day fund.

The following table from the US Census Bureau contains information on revenues, expenditures, indebtedness, and cash/securities for 2001.

	($000)	PERCENT	PER CAPITA
Population (thousands, 2001)	5,307	(X)	(X)
Total Revenue	15,488,897	100.00	2,918.58
General revenue	15,165,637	97.91	2,857.67
Utility revenue	20,734	0.13	3.91
Liquor store revenue	–	–	–
Insurance trust revenue	302,526	1.95	57.01
Exhibit: Salaries and wages	2,680,834	15.64	505.15
Total expenditure	17,143,148	100.00	3,230.29
General expenditure	15,528,201	90.58	2,925.98
Education	5,689,018	33.19	1,071.98
Public welfare	3,222,661	18.80	607.25
Hospitals	84,634	0.49	15.95
Health	954,431	5.57	179.84
Highways	1,584,079	9.24	298.49
Police protection	161,140	0.94	30.36
Correction	760,323	4.44	143.27
Natural resources	175,688	1.02	33.10
Parks and recreation	57,828	0.34	10.90
Government administration	501,859	2.93	94.57
Interest on general debt	192,049	1.12	36.19
Other and unallocable	2,144,491	12.51	404.09
Utility expenditure	25,168	0.15	4.74
Liquor store expenditure	–	–	–
Insurance trust expenditure	1,589,779	9.27	299.56
Debt at end of fiscal year	3,710,911	100.00	699.25
Cash and security holdings	37,541,254	100.00	7,073.91

36TAXATION
Approximately half (50.6% in 2002) of state tax revenues are raised by the Arizona's general sales tax, and approximately a quarter (24.6% in 2002) by the state's personal income tax. The state general sales tax rate is 5.6% (with exemptions for food and prescription drugs), and localities can impose up to 3% additional sales tax producing a maximum 8.6%. The personal income tax has five brackets ranging from 2.87% (up to $10,000 taxable income) to 5% (above $150,000). Selective income taxes (excises) accounted for 12.6% of state tax collections in 2002,

and cover motor fuels, tobacco products, insurance premiums, alcoholic beverages, public utilities, pari-mutuels, and amusements. Arizona's corporate income tax is a flat 6.968% on net income, and in 2002 accounted for 4% of state tax collections. Various license and franchise fees accounted for 3.2% of state collections in 2002, and death and gift taxes, a little less than 1%. In 2003, Arizona ranked 14th among the states in total state and local tax burden, which amounted to 9.9% of personal income, a little above the national average of 9.7%.

State tax receipts for the general fund in 1999 came to slightly more than $5.6 billion, compared to $8.48 billion in 2002.

The following table from the US Census Bureau provides a summary of taxes collected by the state in 2002.

	($000)	PER CAPITA
Total Taxes	8,477,001	1,553.57
Property taxes	329,245	60.34
Sales and gross receipts	5,358,307	982.01
General sales and gross receipts	4,289,778	786.18
Selective sales taxes	1,068,529	195.83
Alcoholic beverage	52,641	9.65
Amusements	630	0.12
Insurance Premiums	198,770	36.43
Motor fuels	624,655	114.48
Pari-mutuels	732	0.13
Public utilities	29,347	5.38
Tobacco products	161,754	29.64
Other selective sales	(X)	(X)
Licenses	270,631	49.6
Alcoholic beverages	3,906	0.72
Amusements	22	0
Corporation	8,418	1.54
Hunting and fishing	20,345	3.73
Motor vehicle	152,442	27.94
Motor vehicle operators	14,712	2.7
Public utility	(X)	(X)
Occupation and business, NEC	62,201	11.4
Other	8,585	1.57
Other taxes	2,518,818	461.62
Individual income	2,090,645	383.15
Corporation net income	346,280	63.46
Death and gift	81,893	15.01
Documentary and stock transfer	(X)	(X)
Severance	(X)	(X)
Other	(X)	(X)

37ECONOMIC POLICY

The Department of Commerce has primary responsibility for attracting business and industry to Arizona, aiding existing business and industry, and assisting companies engaged in international trade. Its programs emphasize job opportunities, energy conservation, support of small businesses, and development of the film industry. The Commerce and Economic Development Commission (CEDC), a six-member agency chaired by the Director of the Department of Commerce, was established in 1989 as the state economic policy and planning board. Its budget is provided by two scratch games in the Arizona lottery, which amounted to about $4.5 million for FY2002 and the first three quarters of FY 2003. Of these limited funds, 43% went to a study and marketing campaign on increasing Arizona's economic diversity; 33% to support federal loan guarantees for the troubled America West airline; 21% to local development projects, including those encouraging tourism, as matching funds for federal grants; and 3% to a job training program in advanced technology. Other economic development programs supported at least in part by the state in 2003 included the Arizona Enterprise Zone (EZ) Program, which offers tax reductions and exemptions for investment in areas where poverty and/or unemployment are high; the Military Reuse Zone (MRZ) program, established 1992, which offers incentives for investments to retool military installations for civilian use (the first MRZ was Williams Air

force Base which became Williams Gateway Airport, and the latest, the US Naval Air Facility in Goodyear which became the Phoenix/Goodyear Airport in December 2002); the Tucson Empowerment Zone Tax Incentive Plan, a $17 billion tax incentive program designed after Tucson won designation by the federal government as an empowerment zone; the Arizona Job Training Program, which designs job training programs; the Economic Strengths Program (ESP), which provides grants for road construction; the Waste Reduction Assistance (WRA), which, in 2003, had $700,000 to support waste reduction programs; the Waste Reduction Initiative Through Education (WRITE), which, in 2003, had $250,000 to support education programs on waste reduction; the Private Activity Bonds (PAB) Program, which replaced in 1986, the Industrial Development Bond Program, and which offers finance in favorable terms for the construction of industrial and manufacturing facilities, student loans, housing, private utility projects and some municipal project; the Lease Excise Tax Program, which offers tax abatements to businesses that lease, rather than own, city property; and the IT Training Tax Credit, which was offered in 2002 for training up to 20 employees in information technology (IT) skills. As of 2003, the state had also designated seven Foreign Trade Zones (FTZs) that were accorded treatment as territory outside of the state's tax jurisdiction. Other tax incentives offered by Arizona include a 10% Pollution Control Tax credit on real and personal property used to control pollution; a schedule of tax credits for research and development expenditures; and accelerated depreciation for capital investments.

38HEALTH

Arizona's infant mortality for the year ending with December 2000 was 6.7 per 1,000 live births. There were 10,765 legal abortions in 1999, a ratio of 11 per 1,000 women. Arizona's overall death rate (829.5 per 100,000 population) was below the US norm in 2000 and was especially low for heart disease and cardiovascular diseases. Deaths from accidents (47.6 per 100,000) and suicide (16.1 per 100,000) were above the national rates, however. Among adults age 18 and older in Arizona, 18.6% were current smokers in 2000. Serious public-health problems include multidrug-resistant tuberculosis and San Joaquin Valley fever (coccidioidomycosis), especially among older adults. There had been 540 AIDS cases reported through 2001, and 158 HIV deaths in 2000.

In 2001, there were 61 community hospitals, with 10,732 beds. Hospital personnel included 12,328 registered nurses. The state had 230 physicians per 100,000 people in 2000. In that same year, the average expense to a hospital for care provided per inpatient day was $939.50. Federal government grants to cover the Medicare and Medicaid services in 2001 totaled $1.9 billion; 690,628 enrollees received Medicare benefits that year. At least 17.9% of the adult population was uninsured in 2002, the 2nd-highest percentage in the nation.

39SOCIAL WELFARE

In 2001, the average weekly unemployment benefit was $171.48. Average monthly participation in the food stamp program in FY2002 comprised 378,722 persons (143,826 households). The average monthly benefit was $84.91, and the sum total of benefits paid in FY2002 was $385,908,411.

With the enactment of the Personal Responsibility and Work Opportunity Reconciliation Act of 1996, the US government has changed the form and regulations for many of its social welfare programs. Most significantly, it replaces Aid to Families with Dependent Children (AFDC), an open-ended entitlement program, with Temporary Assistance for Needy Families (TANF), a limited system of assistance funded largely through federal block grants. The reform act also impacts the food stamp

program, the Supplemental Security Income program, and the child nutrition program. The law took effect on 1 July 1997 and provided $16.38 billion in block grants for fiscal years 1997–2002. The grants are to be divided among the states based on an equation involving the numbers of former AFDC recipients in each state.

Reauthorization of the 1996 social welfare legislation, scheduled for 2002, was delayed, and the original law had been extended three times as of July 2003, with the most recent extension running through September 2003. Arizona's TANF program is called EMPOWER (Employing and Moving People Off Welfare and Encouraging Responsibility). In June 2000 the state had 82,851 welfare recipients. State expenditures on the TANF program in FY2002 totaled $81,525,366.

In December 2001, Social Security benefits were paid to 813,180 Arizona residents. This number included 531,200 retired workers, 76,060 widows and widowers, 91,190 disabled workers, 52,210 spouses, and 62,520 children. Social Security beneficiaries represented 15.4% of the total state population and 85.1% of the state's population age 65 and older. Retired workers (excluding persons with special benefits) received an average monthly payment of $888; widows and widowers, $847; disabled workers, $845; and spouses, $444. Payments for children of retired workers averaged $397 per month; children of deceased workers, $550; and children of disabled workers, $237.

Federal Supplemental Security Income payments in December 2001 went to 84,796 Arizona residents, averaging $375 a month.

[40]HOUSING

In 2002, an estimated 2,328,720 units of year-round housing were in Arizona, of which 2,014,316 were occupied. In the same year, 68.6% of all housing units were owner-occupied. About 58.5% of all units were single-family detached homes; about 14% were mobile homes. It was estimated that about 88,015 units statewide were without telephone service, 14,369 lacked complete plumbing facilities, and 15,199 lacked complete kitchen facilities.

From 1980 to 1990, the housing boom in Arizona caused the number of housing units to increase by 55%; about 38% of all housing structures in Arizona were built in the 1980s, and only 3.2% were built before 1940. During 2002, the Arizona state program received $19.1 million in aid from the US Department of Housing and Urban Development, including nearly $11.3 million in community development block grants. The median value of a home was $136,434. The median monthly cost for mortgage owners was $1,105; the median cost monthly cost for renters was $659. Approximately 66,31 new units were authorized in 2002.

[41]EDUCATION

In 2000, 81% of Arizonans 25 years old and over were high school graduates. Some 23.5% had obtained a bachelor's degree or higher.

The first public school in the state opened in 1871 at Tucson, with 1 teacher and 138 students. In the fall of 1999, total enrollment in public schools was 852,612. Of these, 623,561 attended schools from kindergarten through grade eight, and 229,051 attended high school. Minority students made up approximately 49% of the total enrollment in public elementary and secondary schools in 2001. Total enrollment was estimated at 856,984 in fall 2000 and expected to reach 995,000 by fall 2005. Enrollment in nonpublic schools in fall 2001 was 44,060. Expenditures for public education in 2000/01 were estimated at $4.257,374.

As of fall 2000, there were 331,099 students enrolled in college or graduate school. In the same year Arizona had 75 degree-granting institutions. In 1997, minority students comprised 26.7% of total postsecondary enrollment. The leading public higher educational institutions, the University of Arizona at Tucson and Arizona State University (originally named the Arizona Territorial Normal School) at Tempe, were both established in 1885. The American Graduate School of International Management, a private institution, is located in Glendale.

[42]ARTS

The Arizona Commission on the Arts was established as a permanent state agency in 1967. The Arizona Humanities Council was established in 1973. In 2003, the National Endowment for the Arts (NEA) awarded grants totaling $924,600 to Arizona art organizations. In 2000, the National Endowment for the Humanities (NEH) awarded grants totaling $1,611,571 to 12 organizations. State arts programs are also supported by the Arizona Arts Endowment Fund (also called Arizona ArtShare), which was established in 1996. Arizona is also a member state of the Western States Art Federation. Contributions from the state to arts-related institutions have reached over 85,000 artists. Arts education programs have been provided for 77,600 children. In 1996, Arizona's arts associations numbered 350.

Arizona has traditionally been a center for Indian folk arts and crafts. The Arizona State Museum (Tucson), Colorado River Indian Tribes Museum (Parker), Heard Museum of Anthropology and Primitive Art (Phoenix), Mohave Museum of History and Arts (Kingman), Navaho Tribal Museum (Window Rock), and Pueblo Grande Museum (Phoenix) all display Indian creations, both historic and contemporary. Modern Arizona artists are featured at the Tucson Museum of Art and the Yuma Art Center.

Musical and dramatic performances are presented in Phoenix, Tucson, Scottsdale, and other major cities. There are two major orchestras, the Phoenix Symphony and the Tucson Symphony Orchestra. The Arizona Opera Company and the Arizona Theatre Company perform in both Tucson and Phoenix. Ballet Arizona is based in Phoenix. The annual Grand Canyon Music Festival (est. 1984) features the finest in both classical and folk music.

[43]LIBRARIES AND MUSEUMS

In 2000, Arizona's 15 different public library systems had a combined book stock of 8,723,000 volumes, and total circulation was 30,790,000. There were a total of 39,000 public libraries in the state. Principal public libraries include the Phoenix Public Library and the State Library and Department of Archives in Phoenix, and the Arizona Historical Society Library in Tucson. The largest university libraries are located at the University of Arizona and Arizona State University. Total income for the public library system amounted to $110,803,000 in 2000; including $997,227 in federal grants and $443,312 in state grants.

Arizona has more than 120 museums and historic sites. Attractions in Tucson include the Arizona State Museum, University of Arizona Museum of Art, Arizona Historical Society, Arizona-Sonora Desert Museum, Flandreau Planetarium, and Gene C. Reid Zoological Park. Phoenix has the Heard Museum (anthropology and primitive art), Arizona Mineral Resources Museum, Phoenix Art Museum, Phoenix Zoo, Pueblo Grande Museum, and Desert Botanical Garden. The Museum of Northern Arizona and Lowell Observatory are in Flagstaff. Kitt Peak National Observatory is in Tucson.

Archaeological and historical sites include the cliff dwellings at the Canyon de Chelly, Casa Grande Ruins, Montezuma Castle, Tonto, and Tuzigoot national monuments; the town of Tombstone, the site of the famous O. K. Corral gunfight in the early 1880s; and the restored mission church at Tumacacori National Monument and San Xavier del Bac Church near Tucson.

44COMMUNICATIONS

Over 93.5% of housing units had telephones in 2001. There were 66 major radio stations broadcasting in Arizona in 2003 (21 AM and 45 FM). The state also had 14 major television stations in 2000. In that same year, 59% of Phoenix's 1,390,750 television households received cable. A total of 131,164 Internet domain names had been registered in Arizona by the year 2000.

45PRESS

The *Weekly Arizonian*, started in 1859, was the first newspaper in the state. The *Daily Arizona Miner*, the state's first daily, was founded at Prescott in 1866. In 2001, *The Arizona Republic* was the 15th largest newspaper in the country, based on daily circulation rates. As of 2002 there were 7 morning dailies and 9 evening dailies; 11 dailies had Sunday editions. The following table shows 2002 circulations for leading dailies:

AREA	NAME	DAILY	SUNDAY
Phoenix	*Arizona Republic* (m,S)	451,288	554,482
Tucson	*Citizen* (e)	37,034	
	Arizona Daily Star (m,S)	96,671	164,746

Among the most notable magazines and periodicals published in Arizona were *Phoenix Magazine, Phoenix Living*, and *Arizona Living*, devoted to the local and regional life-style; *American West*, dedicated to the Western heritage; *Arizona and the West*, published quarterly by the University of Arizona Library in Tucson; and Arizona Highways, a beautifully illustrated monthly published by the Department of Transportation in Phoenix.

46ORGANIZATIONS

In 2003, there were over 2,000 regional, national, and international organizations within the state. Among the organizations headquartered in Arizona are the National Foundation for Asthma (Tucson), the Pianists Foundation of America (Tucson), the National Indian Athletic Association (Mesa), the American Federation of Jazz Societies (Phoenix), the American Bicycle Association (Chandler), the Kampground Owners Association (Phoenix), the American Federation of Astrologers (Tempe), the American Rock Art Research Association (Tucson), the American Science Fiction Association (Scottsdale), the Muscular Dystrophy Association (Tucson), the Southwest Parks and Monuments Association (Globe), the Make-A-Wish Foundation of America (Phoenix), Safari Club International (Tucson), United States Handball Association (Tucson), and Up With People (Tucson). National collector clubs located in Arizona are the Lionel Collectors Club of America (Tucson) and the Fisher-Price Collector's Club (Mesa).

The National Native American Cooperative in Tucson serves local and national members who strive to preserve and promote interest in native arts and cultures. The Desert Botanical Garden in Phoenix presents tours of the gardens and a museum as well as offering seminars on the flora of arid lands. Offices for the Messianic Jewish Movement International are based in Chandler.

47TOURISM, TRAVEL, AND RECREATION

Tourism and travel is a leading industry in Arizona. In 2000, tourism and travel accounted for more than $13.76 billion in direct sales. There were about 26.73 million domestic visitors and 899,000 from overseas. More than 380,900 people were directly and indirectly employed in the tourism industry the same year.

There are 22 national parks and monuments located entirely within Arizona. By far the most popular is Grand Canyon National Park. Petrified Forest National Park and Saguaro National Monument are also popular national parks. There are also 14 state parks that regularly attract over 1 million visitors per year.

Arizona offers excellent camping on both public and private land, and there are many farm vacation sites and dude ranches,

particularly in the Tucson and Wickenburg areas. Popular for sightseeing and shopping are the state's Indian reservations, particularly those of the Navaho and Hopi. Boating and fishing on Lake Mead, Lake Powell, Lake Mohave, Lake Havasu, the Colorado River, and the Salt River lakes are also attractions. The red rock country of Sedona is a popular destination. There are also a number of resorts and spas across the state. Biosphere 2 in Oracle is another popular tourist attraction.

48SPORTS

There are five major league professional teams in Arizona, all in Phoenix: the Cardinals of the National Football League, the Suns of the National Basketball Association, the Coyotes of the National Hockey League, the Mercury of the Women's National Basketball Association, and the Diamondbacks of the National League in baseball. The Diamondbacks captured the World Series in 2001. There is a minor league hockey team, also in Phoenix. Several Major League Baseball teams hold spring training in Arizona, and there is a minor league team in Tucson, as well as several rookie league teams throughout the state. There is horse racing at Turf Paradise in Phoenix, and dog racing at Phoenix, Tucson, and Yuma. Auto racing is held at Manzanita Raceway and International Raceway, in Phoenix. Phoenix International Raceway also hosts a NASCAR Winston Cup event in early November. Both Phoenix and Tucson have hosted tournaments on the Professional Golfers Association's nationwide tour.

The first organized rodeo that awarded prizes and charged admission was held in Prescott on 4 July 1988, and rodeos continue to be held throughout the state.

Both Arizona State and the University of Arizona joined the Pacific 10 Conference in 1978. The Sun Devils won the Rose Bowl in their first appearance in 1987, and also appeared in 1997. The Wildcats captured NCAA Division I baseball championships in 1975, 1980, and 1986, and the NCAA Division I men's basketball championship in 1997. The Sun Devils won the championship in 1981. College football's Fiesta Bowl is held annually at Sun Devil Stadium in Tempe, the home stadium for the Arizona State football team.

Other annual sporting events include the Thunderbird Balloon Classic in Scottsdale in November.

49FAMOUS ARIZONIANS

Although Arizona entered the Union relatively late (1912), many of it citizens have achieved national prominence, especially since World War II (1939–45). William H. Rehnquist (b.Wisconsin, 1924) was appointed associate justice of the US Supreme Court in 1971 and chief justice in 1986; in 1981 Sandra Day O'Connor (b.Texas, 1930) became the first woman to serve on the Supreme Court. Arizona natives who became federal officeholders include Lewis Douglas (1894–1974), a representative who served as director of the budget in 1933–34 and ambassador to the Court of St. James's from 1947 to 1950; Stewart L. Udall (b.1920), secretary of the interior, 1961–69; and Richard B. Kleindienst (1923–2000), attorney general, 1972–73, who resigned during the Watergate scandal. Another native son was Carl T. Hayden (1877–1972), who served in the US House of Representatives from statehood in 1912 until 1927 and in the US Senate from 1927 to 1969, thereby setting a record for congressional tenure. Barry Goldwater (1909–98), son of a pioneer family, was elected to the US Senate in 1952, won the Republican presidential nomination in 1964, and returned to the Senate in 1968. His Republican colleague, John J. Rhodes (b.Kansas, 1916–2003), served in the US House of Representatives for 30 years and was House minority leader from 1973 to 1980. Raul H. Castro (b.Mexico, 1916), a native of Sonora, came to the US in 1926, was naturalized, served as Arizona governor from 1975 to 1977, and has held several ambassadorships to Latin America. Morris

K. Udall (1922–98), first elected to the US House of Representatives in 1960, contended for the Democratic presidential nomination in 1976.

Prominent state officeholders include General John C. Frémont (b.Georgia, 1813–90), who was territorial governor of Arizona from 1878 to 1883, and George W. P. Hunt (1859–1934), who presided over the state constitutional convention in 1910 and was elected governor seven times during the early decades of statehood. Eusebio Kino (b.Italy, 1645?–1711) was a pioneer Jesuit who introduced missions and European civilization to Arizona. Also important to the state's history and development were Charles D. Poston (1825–1902), who in the late 1850s promoted settlement and separate territorial status for Arizona; Chiricahua Apache leaders Cochise (1812?–74) and Geronimo (1829–1909), who, resisting the forced resettlement of their people by the US government, launched a series of raids that occupied the Army in the Southwest for over two decades; Wyatt Earp (b.Illinois, 1848–1929), legendary lawman of Tombstone during the early 1880s; John C. Greenway (1872–1926), copper magnate and town builder who was a nominee on the Democratic ticket in 1924 for US vice president; and Frank Luke, Jr. (1897–1918), a World War I flying ace who was the first American airman to receive the Medal of Honor.

Distinguished professional people associated with Arizona have included James Douglas (b.Canada, 1837–1918), metallurgist and developer of the Bisbee copper district; Percival Lowell (b.Massachusetts, 1855–1916), who built the Lowell Observatory in Flagstaff; and Andrew Ellicott Douglass (b.Vermont, 1867–1962), astronomer, university president, and inventor of dendrochronology, the science of dating events and environmental variations through the study of tree rings and aged wood. Cesar Chavez (1927–93) was president of the United Farm Workers of America.

Writers whose names have been associated with Arizona include novelist Harold Bell Wright (b.New York, 1872–1944), who lived for an extended period in Tucson; Zane Grey (b.Ohio, 1875–1939), who wrote many of his Western adventure stories in his summer home near Payson; and Joseph Wood Krutch (b.Tennessee, 1893–1970), an essayist and naturalist who spent his last two decades in Arizona. Well-known performing artists from Arizona include singers Marty Robbins (1925–1970), and Linda Ronstadt (b.1946). Joan Ganz Cooney (b.1929), president of the Children's Television Workshop, was one of the creators of the award-winning children's program, *Sesame Street*.

50BIBLIOGRAPHY

Alampi, Gary, ed. *Gale State Rankings Reporter*. Detroit: Gale Research, Inc., 1994.

Arizona: Its People and Resources. 2nd rev. ed., rev. Tucson: University of Arizona Press, 1972.

Arizona Yearbook, 1979–80: A Guide to Government in Arizona. Yuma: Arizona Informational Press, 1979.

Barnes, Will C. *Arizona Place Names*. Revised by Byrd H. Granger. Tucson: University of Arizona Press, 1960.

Bischoff, Matt C. *Touring Arizona Hot Springs*. Helena, Mont.: Falcon, 1999.

Comeaux, Malcolm. *Arizona: A Geography*. Boulder, Colo.: Westview Press, 1981.

Council of State Governments. *The Book of the States, 1994–1995 Edition*. Vol. 30. Lexington, Ky.: The Council of State Governments, 1994.

Faulk, Odie B. *Arizona: A Short History*. Norman: University of Oklahoma Press, 1970.

FDIC, Division of Research and Statistics. *Statistics on Banking: A Statistical Profile of the United States Banking Industry*. Washington, D.C.: Federal Deposit Insurance Corporation, 1993.

Federal Writers' Project. *Arizona: The Grand Canyon State*. 1940. Reprint, New York: Hastings House, 1968.

Fireman, Bert M. *Arizona: Historic Land*. New York: Knopf, 1982.

Goldwater, Barry. *Arizona*. New York: Random House, 1978.

Johnson, James W. *Arizona Politicians: The Noble and the Notorious*. Tucson: University of Arizona Press, 2002.

Kessell, John L. *Spain in the Southwest: A Narrative History of Colonial New Mexico, Arizona, Texas, and California*. Norman: University of Oklahoma Press, 2002.

Lamar, Howard R. *The Far Southwest, 1846–1912: A Territorial History*. New Haven, Conn.: Yale University Press, 1966.

Powell, Lawrence C. *Arizona: A Bicentennial History*. New York: Norton, 1976.

Schmittroth, Linda, and Mary Kay Rosteck, ed. *Cities of the United States*. 2nd ed. Detroit: Gale Research, Inc., 1994.

Sheridan, Thomas E. *Arizona: A History*. Tucson: University of Arizona Press, 1995.

Trimble, Marshall. *Arizona 2000: A Yearbook for the Millennium*. Flagstaff, Ariz.: Northland Pub., 1999.

University of Arizona Library. *The Arizona Index: A Subject Index to Periodical Articles about the State*. Boston: Hall Library, 1978.

US Department of Education, National Center for Education Statistics. Office of Educational Research and Improvement. *Digest of Education Statistics, 1993*. Washington, D.C.: US Government Printing Office, 1993.

US Department of the Interior, US Fish and Wildlife Service. *Endangered and Threatened Species Recovery Program*. Washington, D.C.: US Government Printing Office, 1990.

Walker, Henry P., and Don Bufkin. *Historical Atlas of Arizona*. 2nd ed. Norman: University of Oklahoma Press, 1986.

ARKANSAS

State of Arkansas

ORIGIN OF STATE NAME: French derivation of *Akansas* or *Arkansas,* a name given to the Quapaw Indians by other tribes. **NICKNAME:** The Natural State. **CAPITAL:** Little Rock. **ENTERED THE UNION:** 15 June 1836 (25th). **SONG:** "Arkansas." **MOTTO:** *Regnat populus* (The people rule). **COAT OF ARMS:** In front of an American eagle is a shield displaying a steamboat, plow, beehive, and sheaf of wheat, symbols of Arkansas's industrial and agricultural wealth. The angel of mercy, the goddess of liberty encircled by 13 stars, and the sword of justice surround the eagle, which holds in its talons an olive branch and three arrows and in its beak a banner bearing the state motto. **FLAG:** On a red field, 25 stars on a blue band border a white diamond containing the word "Arkansas" and four blue stars. **OFFICIAL SEAL:** Coat of arms surrounded by the words "Great Seal of the State of Arkansas." **BIRD:** Mockingbird. **INSECT:** Honeybee. **FLOWER:** Apple blossom. **TREE:** Pine. **GEM:** Diamond. **LEGAL HOLIDAYS:** New Year's Day, 1 January; Robert E. Lee's birthday, 19 January; Birthday of Martin Luther King, Jr., 3rd Monday in January; George Washington's Birthday, 3rd Monday in February; Memorial Day, last Monday in May; Independence Day, 4 July; Labor Day, 1st Monday in September; Veterans Day, 11 November; Thanksgiving Day, 4th Thursday in November; Christmas Eve, 24 December; Christmas Day, 25 December. **TIME:** 6 AM CST = noon GMT.

¹LOCATION, SIZE, AND EXTENT

Located in the western south-central US, Arkansas ranks 27th in size among the 50 states.

The total area of Arkansas is 53,187 sq mi (137,754 sq km), of which land takes up 52,078 sq mi (134,882 sq km); and inland water, 1,109 sq mi (2,872 sq km). Arkansas extends about 275 mi (443 km) E-W and 240 mi (386 km) N-S.

Arkansas is bordered on the N by Missouri; on the E by Missouri, Tennessee, and Mississippi (with part of the line passing through the St. Francis and Mississippi rivers); on the S by Louisiana; on the SW by Texas (with part of the line formed by the Red River), and on the W by Oklahoma. The total boundary length of Arkansas is 1,168 mi (1,880 km). The state's geographic center is in Pulaski County, 12 mi (19 km) NW of Little Rock.

²TOPOGRAPHY

The Boston Mountains (an extension of the Ozark Plateau, sometimes called the Ozark Mountains) in the northwest and the Ouachita Mountains in the west-central region not only constitute Arkansas's major uplands but also are the only mountain chains between the Appalachians and the Rockies. Aside from the wide valley of the Arkansas River, which separates the two chains, the Arkansas lowlands belong to two physiographic regions: the Mississippi Alluvial Plain and the Gulf Coastal Plain. The highest elevation in Arkansas, at 2,753 ft (840 m), is Magazine Mountain, standing north of the Ouachitas in the Arkansas River Valley. The state's lowest point, at 55 feet (17 meters), is on the Ouachita River in south-central Arkansas.

Arkansas's largest lake is the artificial Lake Ouachita, covering 63 sq mi (163 sq km); Lake Chicot, in southeastern Arkansas, and oxbow of the Mississippi River, is the state's largest natural lake, with a length of 18 mi (29 km). Bull Shoals Lake, occupying 71 sq mi (184 sq km), is shared with Missouri. Principal rivers include the Mississippi, forming most of the eastern boundary; the Arkansas, beginning in Colorado and flowing 1,450 mi (2,334 km) through Kansas and Oklahoma and across central Arkansas to the Mississippi; and the Red, White, Ouachita, and

St. Francis rivers, all of which likewise drain south and southeast into the Mississippi. Numerous springs are found in Arkansas, of which the best known are Mammoth Springs, near the Missouri border, one of the largest in the world, with a flow rate averaging nine million gal (34 million l) an hour, and Hot Springs in the Ouachitas.

Crowley's Ridge, a unique strip of hills formed by sedimentary deposits and windblown sand, lies west of and parallel to the St. Francis River for about 180 mi (290 km). The ridge is rich in fossils and has an unusual diversity of plant life.

³CLIMATE

Arkansas has a temperate climate, warmer and more humid in the southern lowlands than in the mountainous regions. At Little Rock, the normal daily temperature ranges from 40°F (4°C) in January to 81°F (27°C) in July. A record low of –29°F (–34°C) was set on 13 February 1905 at the Pond weather station, and a record high of 120°F (49°C) was recorded on 10 August 1936 at the Ozark station.

Average yearly precipitation is approximately 45 in (114 cm) in the mountainous areas and greater in the lowlands; Little Rock received an annual average (1971–2000) of 50.9 in (129.2 cm), with an average relative humidity ranging from 84% at 7 AM to 57% at 1 PM. Snowfall in the capital averages 5.2 in (13.2 cm) a year.

⁴FLORA AND FAUNA

Arkansas has at least 2,600 native plants, and there are many naturalized exotic species. Cypresses, water oak, hickory, and ash grow in the Mississippi Valley, while the St. Francis Valley is home to the rare cork tree. Crowley's Ridge is thick with tulip trees and beeches. A forest belt of oak, hickory, and pine stretches across south-central and southwestern Arkansas, including the Ozark and Ouachita mountains. The Mexican juniper is common along the White River's banks. The state has at least 26 native varieties of orchid; the passion flower is so abundant that it was once considered for designation as the state flower, but the apple blossom was finally chosen instead.

Arkansas's native animals include 15 varieties of bat and 3 each of rabbit and squirrel. Common throughout the state are mink, armadillo, white-tailed deer, and eastern chipmunk. Black bear roam the swamp and mountain regions. Among 300 native birds are such game birds as the eastern wild turkey, mourning dove, and bobwhite quail. Among local fish are catfish, gar, and the unusual paddle fish. Arkansas counts 20 frog and toad species, 23 varieties of salamander, and 36 kinds of snake.

Twenty three animal species were listed as endangered or threatened as of April 2003 by the US Fish and Wildlife Service. The Arkansas Game and Fish Commission lists the leopard darter and fat pocketbook pearly mussel as threatened species. The bald eagle is listed as endangered, along with the Indiana and gray bats, cave crayfish, pink mucket, several species of mussel, pallid sturgeon, least tern, and red-cockaded woodpecker. Among six endangered or threatened plants listed in 2003 are the Missouri bladderpod, pondberry, eastern prairie fringed orchid, and running buffalo clover. In 1983, Arkansas established the Non-Game Preservation Committee to promote sound management, conservation, and public awareness of the state's non-game animals and native plants.

5ENVIRONMENTAL PROTECTION

In 1949, the Arkansas General Assembly created the Arkansas Pollution Control Commission. This legislation was amended in later years to be known as the Arkansas Water and Air Pollution Control Act. Under an extensive reorganization of state government in 1971, the Arkansas Department of Pollution Control and Ecology (ADPC&E) was created as a cabinet-level agency and the Commission was renamed the Arkansas Pollution Control and Ecology Commission. Although the terms are frequently confused or used interchangeably by persons not connected with either governmental unit, the Commission and the Department are two separate, but related, entities. The Commission, with guidance from the governor and the Arkansas General Assembly, determines the environmental policies for the state, and the Department employees are responsible for implementing those policies. In 1996, the Arkansas General Assembly voted to change the name of the Department to the Arkansas Department of Environmental Quality (ADEQ) on 31 March 1999. The initial authority to regulate water and air sources has been expanded to open-cut mining, solid waste, hazardous waste, recycling, and underground storage tanks. In 2001, an ADEQ focus on recycling waste oil resulted in a 91% increase in the amount of waste oil recycled, from 21,189 tons in 2000 to 41,500 tons in 2001. In 2002, ADEQ turned its attention to recycling of wood waste.

In 1987, the state adopted some of the first "ecoregion" water quality standards in the nation. These standards recognize the distinct physical, chemical, and biological properties of the six geographical regions of the state and establish separate water quality standards within each region.

The US Environmental Protection Agency (EPA) has delegated responsibility for its clean-air programs to the ADPC&E. These programs include New Source Performance Standards (NSPS), National Emission Standards for Hazardous Air Pollutants (NESHAPS), Prevention of Significant Deterioration (PSD), and State Implementation Plan (SIP).

Citizens' groups actively involved with environmental issues include: the Arkansas Native Plant Society, Arkansas Audubon Society, Arkansas Canoe Club, Arkansas Herpetological Society, Arkansas Wildlife Federation, Audubon Society of Central Arkansas, League of Women Voters, Ozark Society, Sierra Club—Arkansas Chapter, and National Water Center. The Arkansas Environmental Federation presents industry's viewpoints on environmental issues.

The Buffalo River, designated as a national river, flows through northern Arkansas. One of the wildest areas in the state is the 113,000-acre (46,000-hectare) White River Refuge, which contains more than 100 small lakes. The Arkansas Natural Heritage Commission was established in 1975 for, among other purposes, the preservation of rivers and natural areas and to serve as a source of information on plant and animal species of Arkansas.

In 2003, the Environmental Protection Agency's database listed 78 hazardous waste sites, 12 of which were on the National Priorities List, in Arkansas. In 2001, Arkansas received $36,262,000 in federal grants from the EPA.

6POPULATION

Arkansas ranked 33rd in population in the US with an estimated total of 2,710,079 in 2002, an increase of 1.4% since 2000. Between 1990 and 2000, Arkansas's population grew from 2,350,725 to 2,673,400, an increase of 13.7%. The population is projected to reach 2,750,000 by 2005 and 3.1 million by 2025. The average population density in 2000 was 51.3 per sq mi.

As of 2000, 14% of the population was age 65 or over (compared with a national average of 12.4%), partially reflecting the large number of retirees who settled in the state during the early 1980s. The median age was 36, and 25.4% of the population was under 18 years old.

The largest city in Arkansas is Little Rock, which had a 2002 estimated population of 184,055. The Little Rock–North Little Rock metropolitan area had an estimated 559,074 residents in 1999. Other major cities with large populations include Ft. Smith, North Little Rock, Pine Bluff, and Fayetteville.

7ETHNIC GROUPS

Arkansas's population is predominantly white, composed mainly of descendants of immigrants from the British Isles. The largest minority group consists of black Americans, estimated at 418,950 in 2000, or 15.7% of the population. The American Indian population was estimated at 17,808 in 2000. About 86,866 Arkansans, or 3.2% of the total population, were of Hispanic or Latino origin, nearly double the 1990 figure of 44,000 (1.9%). In 2000 the Asian population was estimated at 20,220, and Pacific Islanders numbered 1,668. The 2000 census listed 3,974 Vietnamese (up from 1,788 in 1990), 3,126 Chinese (1,575 in 1990), 2,489 Filipinos, 3,104 Asian Indians (1,202 in 1990), and 1,036 Japanese. The foreign-born population numbered 73,690, or 2.8% of all Arkansas residents, up from 24,867, or 1%, in 1990.

8LANGUAGES

A few place-names—such as Arkansas itself, Choctaw, Caddo, and Ouachita—attest to the onetime presence of American Indians in the Territory of Arkansas, mostly members of the Caddoan tribe, with the Cherokee the most influential.

Arkansas English is essentially a blend of Southern and South Midland speech, with South Midland dominating the mountainous northwest; and Southern, the southeastern agricultural areas. Common in the east and south are *redworm* (earthworm) and *mosquito hawk* (dragonfly). In the northwest appear south Midland *whirlygig* (merry-go-round) and *sallet* (garden greens).

In 2000, 2,368,450 Arkansans—95% of the residents five years old or older—spoke only English at home, a decrease over the 97.2% recorded in 1990.

The following table gives selected statistics from the 2000 census for language spoken at home by persons five years old and

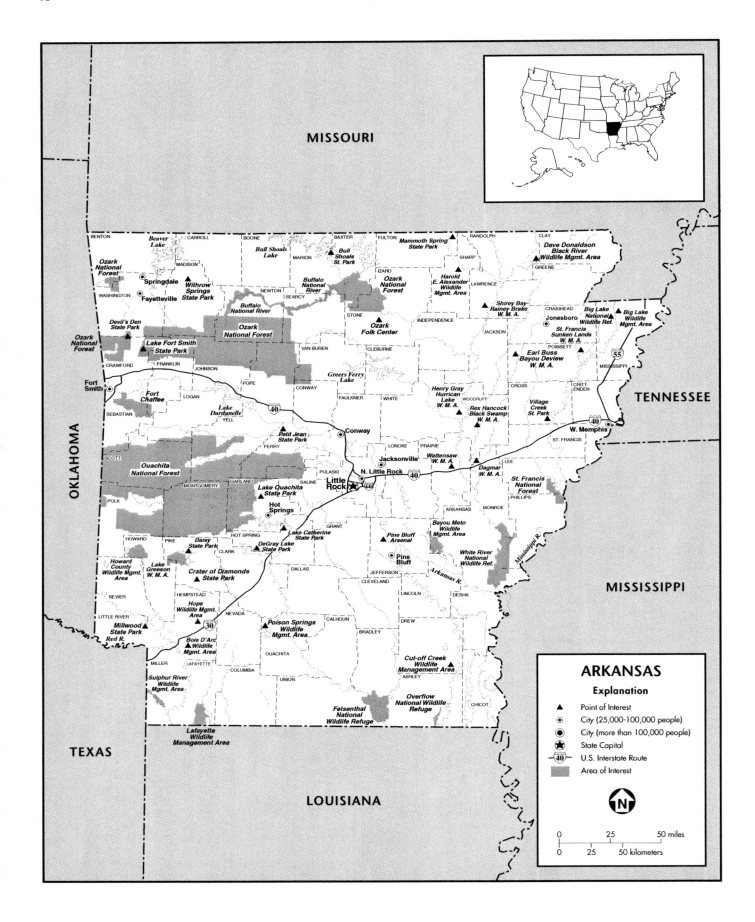

over. The category "Other Pacific Island languages" includes Chamorro, Hawaiian, Ilocano, Indonesian, and Samoan.

LANGUAGE	NUMBER	PERCENT
Population 5 years and over	2,492,205	100.0
Speak only English	2,368,450	95.0
Speak a language other than English	123,755	5.0
Speak a language other than English	123,755	5.0
Spanish or Spanish Creole	82,465	3.3
German	7,444	0.3
French (incl. Patois, Cajun)	7,312	0.3
Vietnamese	3,467	0.1
Chinese	2,529	0.1
Laotian	2,502	0.1
Tagalog	1,627	0.1
Korean	1,250	0.1
Japanese	1,193	0.0
Other Pacific Island languages	1,185	0.0
Italian	1,106	0.0

9 RELIGIONS

Although French Roman Catholic priests had worked as missionaries among the Indians since the early 18th century, the state's first mission was founded among the Cherokee by a Congregationalist, Cephas Washburn, in 1820. When the Cherokee were removed to Indian Territory (present-day Oklahoma), the mission moved there as well, remaining active through the Civil War. William Patterson may have been the first Methodist to preach in Arkansas, around 1800, in the area of Little Prairie: the first Methodist circuit, that of Spring River, was organized in 1815. The first Baptist church was likely that of the Salem congregation, begun in 1818 near what is now Pochahontas.

The vast majority of religious adherents in the state belong to Evangelical Protestant congregations. The largest denomination is the Southern Baptist Convention, which had 685,301adherents in 1,372 congregations in 2000. The American Baptist Association had 115,916 adherents and 570 congregations and the Baptist Missionary Association of America had 87,244 adherents and 359 congregations. The Churches of Christ claimed 86,342 adherents in 754 congregations.

The leading mainline Protestant group in 2000 was the United Methodist Church, with 179,383 adherents in 747 congregations. The Roman Catholic population of Arkansas was 115,967 with 130 congregations. The estimated Jewish population was 1,600.

10 TRANSPORTATION

Although railroad construction began in the 1850s, not until after the Civil War (1861–65) were any lines completed. The most important railroad—the St. Louis, Iron Mountain, and Southern line—reached Little Rock in 1872 and was subsequently acquired by financier Jay Gould, who added the Little Rock and Ft. Smith line to it in 1882. By 1890, the state had about 2,200 mi (3,500 km) of track; in 1974, trackage totaled 3,559 mi (5,728 km). As of 2000, Arkansas was served by three major railroads and had 3,674 rail mi (5,912 km) of track. In 1998, nonmetallic minerals accounted for 32% of the rail tonnage originating within the state, and coal made up 53% of the rail tonnage terminating within Arkansas. Amtrak passenger trains serviced Little Rock, Walnut Ridge, Malvern, Arkadelphia, and Texarkana en route from St. Louis to Dallas.

Intensive road building began in the 1920s, following the establishment of the State Highway Commission and the inauguration of a gasoline tax. By 2000, Arkansas had 97,600 mi (157,071 km) of public roads, streets, and highways. During the same year, 951,243 automobiles and 882,266 trucks were registered in Arkansas, and there were 1,947,867 licensed drivers.

Beginning in the 1820s, steamboats replaced keelboats and flatboats on Arkansas rivers. Steamboat transportation reached its peak during 1870–90 until supplanted by the railroads that were opened during the same two decades. Development of the Arkansas River, completed during the early 1970s, made the waterway commercially navigable all the way to Tulsa.

In 2002, Arkansas had 212 airports and 79 heliports. The principal airport in the state is Adams Field at Little Rock.

11 HISTORY

Evidence of human occupation of Arkansas reaches back to about 10,000 BC. The bluff dwellers of the Ozark Plateau were among the first human beings to live in what is now Arkansas, making their homes in caves and beneath overhanging rock cliffs along the banks of the upper White River. Farther south are the remains of another primitive people, the Mound Builders. The most significant of the Stone Age monuments they left are those of the Toltec group in Lonoke County, some 25 mi (40 km) southeast of Little Rock. Eventually, both ancient peoples vanished, for reasons that remain unclear.

Foremost among the Indian tribes in Arkansas were the Quapaw (meaning "downstream people" or "South Wind people"), agriculturists who had migrated to southern Arkansas in the early 16th century; the Caddo, fighters from Texas, who claimed the western region between the Red and Arkansas rivers; the warlike Osage, who hunted north of the Arkansas River and in present-day Missouri; and the Choctaw. Another prominent tribe, the Cherokee, arrived in the early 19th century, after federal and state authorities had taken their land east of the Mississippi and driven them westward. Nearly all these Indians had been expelled to what is now Oklahoma by the time Arkansas became a state.

The first Europeans to set foot in Arkansas were Spaniards, led by Hernando de Soto. They crossed the Mississippi River, probably near present-day Helena, in the spring of 1541, roamed the land for a year or so, and then returned to the mighty river, where De Soto was buried in 1542. More than 100 years later, in 1673, a small band of Frenchmen led by Jacques Marquette, a Jesuit missionary, and Louis Jolliet, a fur trader and explorer, ended their voyage down the Mississippi at the mouth of the Arkansas River and returned north after being advised by friendly Indians that hostile tribes lay to the south. Nine years later, Robert Cavelier, Sieur de la Salle, led an expedition from Canada down the Mississippi to the Gulf of Mexico, stopping at Indian villages in Arkansas along the way and, on 9 April 1682, claiming all the Mississippi Valley for his king, Louis XIV.

Henri de Tonti, who had been second in command to La Salle, came back to Arkansas in 1686 to claim a land grant at the confluence of the Arkansas and White rivers, a few miles inland from the Mississippi. He left six men there; the log house they built was the beginning of Arkansas Post, the first permanent white settlement in the lower Mississippi Valley. Though tiny and isolated, Arkansas Post upheld the French claim to the Mississippi Valley until 1762, when France ceded the territory to Spain. Restored to France in 1800, the territory was sold to the US in the Louisiana Purchase of 1803. White settlers soon began arriving in Arkansas, and in 1806, the Louisiana territorial legislature created the District of Arkansas as a separate entity. When the Louisiana Purchase was further subdivided, Arkansas became part of the Missouri Territory. In 1819, Arkansas gained territorial status in its own right, and its boundaries were fixed by Congress. The territorial capital was moved from Arkansas Post to Little Rock in 1821. By 1835, Arkansas Territory had a population of 52,240, including 9,838 slaves. It was admitted to the Union in 1836 as a slave state, paired with the free state of Michigan in accordance with the Missouri Compromise.

Increasing numbers of slaves were brought into the largely agricultural state as the cultivation of cotton spread. Arkansas, like the rest of the South, was headed for secession, although it waited to commit itself until the Civil War (1861–65) had begun. There was considerable Union sentiment in the state, especially in the hilly northern and western counties, which lacked the large plantations and the slaves of southern and eastern Arkansas. But the pro-Union sympathies crumbled after Confederate guns fired on Ft. Sumter, SC, and the secession convention was held at Little Rock on 6 May 1861. The final vote to leave the Union was 69–1: the lone holdout was Isaac Murphy of Madison County, who became the first Unionist Democrat governor at the end of the war.

The largest Civil War battle fought in Arkansas, and one of the most significant battles of the war west of the Mississippi, was at Pea Ridge, in the northwest corner of the state. After three days of fighting, the Union forces retreated, and then the Confederate forces relinquished the field. By September 1863, the Union Army had taken Little Rock, and the Confederate capital was moved to Washington, in Hempstead County, until the conclusion of hostilities in 1865. Like virtually all white southerners, Arkansas's white majority hated the postwar Reconstruction government and repudiated it thoroughly at the first opportunity. Reconstruction officially ended in 1874, when the reenfranchised white Democratic majority adopted a new state constitution, throwing out the carpetbagger constitution of 1868. The most colorful figure in postwar Arkansas was federal judge Isaac C. Parker, known as the Hanging Judge. From his court at Ft. Smith, he had sole jurisdiction over Indian Territory, which had become a gathering place for the nation's worst cutthroats. Parker and his deputy marshals fought them relentlessly. From 1875 through 1896, the judge hanged 79 men on his Ft. Smith gallows. The struggle was not one-sided: 65 of Parker's deputy marshals were killed.

Industrialization, urbanization, and modernization did not come to Arkansas until after the depression of the 1930s. Following World War II (1939–45), the state became the first in the South to integrate its public colleges and universities. Little Rock's school board decided in 1954 to comply with the US Supreme Court's desegregation decision. Nevertheless, in September 1957, Governor Orval E. Faubus called out the National Guard to block the integration of Central High School at Little Rock. US President Dwight D. Eisenhower enforced a federal court order to integrate the school by sending in federal troops. The 1957 crisis brought years of notoriety to Arkansas, as Faubus, then in his second term, was elected to a third term and then to three more.

By the end of the Faubus administration, the public mood had changed, and the contrast between Faubus and his successor could not have been greater. Winthrop Rockefeller, millionaire scion of a famous family, moved to Arkansas from New York in the early 1950s, established himself as a gentleman rancher, and devoted himself to luring industry into his adopted state and building a Republican Party organization in one of the most staunchly Democratic states in the Union. Elected governor in 1966, Rockefeller thus became the first Republican to capture the Arkansas statehouse since Reconstruction. The specific accomplishments of his two terms were relatively few—he and the Democratic-controlled legislature warred incessantly—but he helped immeasurably in bringing a new image and a new spirit to the state.

Rockefeller's successors have continued the progressive approach he took. Governor Bill Clinton, who became United States President in 1992, introduced a number of reforms. These included investment tax credits to help corporations modernize their facilities and thereby to create jobs. Clinton also signed a "bare bones" health insurance law which dropped state requirements for some of the more costly coverages and thus made health insurance affordable for small businesses. He increased expenditures for education and passed legislation requiring competency tests for teachers. But Clinton, like other governors before him, remained hampered in his efforts to improve Arkansas's economy and standard of living by the state constitutional requirement that any increase in the state income tax obtain approval of two-thirds of the legislature. Arkansas continued to rank among the poorest states in the nation, with a per capita income in 1990 of only $14,000 (46th among the states). By 1998, its ranking had improved, with 14.8% of its people living below poverty level, making it the 12th poorest state in the nation.

In 1994, a federal special prosecutor began to investigate the actions of several members of Little Rock's Rose law firm, in which First Lady Hillary Rodham Clinton had been a partner, in connection with the failed Whitewater real estate venture. Governor Jim Guy Tucker resigned from office in July 1996 after

Arkansas Presidential Vote by Political Parties, 1948–2000

YEAR	ELECTORAL VOTE	ARKANSAS WINNER	DEMOCRAT	REPUBLICAN	STATES' RIGHTS DEMOCRAT
1948	9	*Truman (D)	149,659	50,959	40,068
1952	8	Stevenson (D)	226,300	177,155	—
					CONSTITUTION
1956	8	Stevenson (D)	213,277	186,287	7,008
					NAT'L STATES' RIGHTS
1960	8	*Kennedy (D)	215,049	184,508	28,952
1964	6	*Johnson (D)	314,197	243,264	2,965
					AMERICAN IND.
1968	6	Wallace (AI)	188,228	190,759	240,982
					AMERICAN
1972	6	*Nixon (R)	199,892	448,541	2,887
1976	6	*Carter (D)	498,604	267,903	—
					LIBERTARIAN
1980	6	*Reagan (R)	398,041	403,164	8,970
1984	6	*Reagan (R)	388,646	534,774	2,2221
1988	6	*Bush (R)	349,237	466,578	3,297
					IND. (Perot)
1992	6	*Clinton (D)	505,823	337,324	99,132
1996	6	*Clinton (D)	475,171	325,416	69,884
					GREEN
2000	6	*Bush, G. W. (R)	422,768	472,940	13,421

* Won US presidential election.

his conviction on fraud and conspiracy charges stemming from his bank dealings. In March 2000, independent counsel Robert Ray began filing final reports detailing the six-year investigation into Whitewater, and that September, he issued a report finding that neither President Clinton nor First Lady Hillary Clinton knowingly participated in any criminal conduct. Susan McDougal, with her husband a controlling partner in the Whitewater land deal, found guilty of fraud in 1996, was pardoned by President Clinton in January 2001, just before he left office.

While the state was rocked by political scandal in the 1990s, it also coped with tragic school shootings. On 24 March 1998, two students (ages 11 and 13) went on a rampage in a Jonesboro school, killing four students and one teacher, and wounding ten others. Another shooting occurred in the small community of Prairie Grove on 11 May 2000, when a seventh-grade student left school in a rage and later engaged in an exchange of gunfire with an officer nearby; both were injured. While the nation wrestled with the problem of violence in its schools and the issue of gun control, for Arkansas residents it was a problem that was too close to home.

12STATE GOVERNMENT

Arkansas's fifth constitution, enacted in 1874, has survived several efforts to replace it with a more modern charter. In November 1980, voters turned down yet another proposed new constitution. In May 1995, the Governor's Task Force for a New Constitution was appointed in anticipation of a proposed 1996 constitutional convention. However, in December 1995, a referendum authorizing the convention was defeated by the voters. The constitution had been amended 89 times by the end of 2002.

Arkansas's bicameral legislature, the general assembly, consists of a 35-member senate and a 100-member house of representatives. Regular legislative sessions are held in odd-numbered years, begin in January, and are limited to 60 calendar days. Senators serve four-year terms and must be at least 25 years old; representatives serve for two years and must be at least 21. Each legislator must be a US citizen and have resided for at least two years in the state and one year in the county or district prior to election. Legislators' salaries in 2002 were $12,796 per biennial session.

The executive officers elected statewide are the governor, lieutenant governor, secretary of state, treasurer, auditor, and attorney general, all of whom serve four-year terms. The governor is limited to a maximum of two consecutive elected terms. The governor and lieutenant governor, who run separately, must be US citizens, must be at least 30 years old, and must have resided in Arkansas for seven years. In 2002 the governor's salary was $71,738

A bill passed by a majority in both houses of the legislature becomes law if signed by the governor, if passed over his veto by a majority of all elected members of each house, or if neither signed nor returned by the governor within four days (Sundays excepted) when the legislature is in session or 20 days (Sundays included) after session adjournment. Under an initiative procedure, 8% of those who voted for governor in the last election may propose a law, and 10% of the voters (for governor at the last election) may initiate a constitutional amendment; initiative petitions must be filed at least four months before the general election in order to be voted upon at that time. A referendum on any measure passed by the general assembly or any item of an appropriations bill or other measure may be petitioned by 6% of the voters; referendum petitions must be filed within 90 days of the session in which the act in question was passed. A successful referendum measure may be repealed by a two-thirds vote of all elected members of the general assembly.

Constitutional amendments may also be proposed by the general assembly (and approved by a majority vote of both houses) or by constitutional convention. Proposed amendments must be ratified by a majority of voters.

To vote in Arkansas, one must be a US citizen, at least 18 years old, a state resident, and not able to claim the right to vote in another jurisdiction. Restrictions apply to convicted felons.

13POLITICAL PARTIES

The principal political groups in Arkansas are the Democratic Party and the Republican Party, each affiliated with the national party organizations.

Before the Civil War (1861–65), politics in Arkansas were fraught with violence. Republicans ruled during Reconstruction, which officially ended in Arkansas after the constitution of 1874 had been adopted by the new Democratic majority. During the election of 1872, the Liberal Republicans, nicknamed Brindletails, opposed the Radical Republicans, or Minstrels. After the Minstrel candidate, Elisha Baxter, was elected, he proved so independent a governor that some of the party leaders who had supported him attempted to oust him through a court order in April 1874, declaring his defeated opponent, Joseph Brooks, the winner. Supported by a militia of about 300 blacks under white command, Brooks took over the statehouse; Baxter, bolstered by his own 300-man black army, set up his headquarters three blocks away. The so-called Brooks-Baxter War finally ended with President Ulysses S. Grant's proclamation of Baxter as the lawful governor. Baxter did not seek reelection-instead Augustus H. Garland was elected, the first of a long series of Bourbon Democrats who were to rule the state well into the 20th century.

After Reconstruction, blacks in Arkansas continued to vote and to be elected to public office; under what became known as the fusion principle, black Republican and white Democratic leaders in the plantation belt often agreed not to oppose each other's candidates. Segregation in public places was still outlawed, and Little Rock was perhaps the most integrated city in the South. During the 1890s, however, as in the rest of the South, Democrats began to pass laws imposing segregation and disfranchising blacks as well as poor whites. In 1906, the Democrats instituted a nominating primary for whites only.

On the rocky path to progressive government, Arkansans elected several governors who stand out as progressive: George Donaghey (1909–13), Charles Brush (1917–21), Thomas McRae (1921–25), Carl Bailey (1935–39) and Sidney McMath (1948–53). Although elected to the governorship as a progressive in 1954, McMath's protégé Orval Faubus took a segregationist stand in 1957. In subsequent years, poor whites tended to support Faubus, while blacks and more affluent whites opposed him. Faubus's successor, progressive Republican Winthrop Rockefeller, was strongly supported by blacks. Rockefeller was followed by three more progressives, all Democrats: Dale Bumpers, David Pryor, and—after Bumpers and Pryor had graduated to the US Senate—Bill Clinton. In a major upset, Clinton was defeated in 1980 by Republican Frank White, but he recaptured the statehouse in 1982 and won reelection in 1984, 1986, and 1990. Clinton ran for and won the presidency in 1992 with a plurality of 53% in Arkansas. Clinton won presidential reelection in 1996, gaining 54% of the vote, against 37% for Republican challenger Bob Dole and 8% for Independent Ross Perot. In the 2000 presidential election, George W. Bush won 51% of the vote to Al Gore's 45% and 2% for Green Party candidate Ralph Nader. In 2002 there were 1,616,895 registered voters; there is no party registration in the state. The state had six electoral votes in the 2000 presidential election.

On 8 November 1994, Democratic governor Jim Guy Tucker was one of the few of his party nationwide to resist a Republican challenge. However, in 1996 Tucker was forced to resign following his conviction on charges related to the Whitewater prosecution, and the governorship was assumed by Lieutenant Governor Mike Huckabee. Huckabee was elected in his own right in 1998 and reelected in 2002.

In 1996 the vacated US Senate seat of Democrat David Pryor was won by US Representative Tim Hutchinson, a Republican. Hutchinson was the first Republican ever to be popularly elected to the US Senate from Arkansas. In 1998 Democrat Blanche Lincoln was voted into office, only the second woman in Arkansas history to be elected to the Senate. Democrat Mark Pryor, son of David Pryor, was elected to the US Senate in 2002. Arkansas's US Representatives following the 2002 elections included one Republican and three Democrats. In mid-2003, the state legislature had 27 Democrats and 8 Republicans in the senate, and 70 Democrats and 30 Republicans in the house. In early 2003 there were 22 women serving in the state legislature.

14LOCAL GOVERNMENT

There are 75 counties in Arkansas, 10 of them with 2 county seats. Each county is governed by a quorum court, consisting of 9–15 justices of the peace, elected for two-year terms; the county judge, who presides, does not vote but has veto power, which may be overridden by a three-fifths vote of the total membership. Elected county officials, who serve two-year terms, include the sheriff, assessor, coroner, treasurer, and county supervisor. In 2002, Arkansas had 499 municipalities, administered under the mayor-council or city-manager form of government. There were 704 special districts and 310 public school districts.

15STATE SERVICES

To address the continuing threat of terrorism and to work with the federal Department of Homeland Security (created in 2002 following the terrorist attacks of 11 September 2001), homeland security in Arkansas in 2003 operated under the authority of the governor; the emergency management director was designated as the state homeland security advisor.

Educational services in Arkansas are administered primarily by the Department of Education and the Department of Higher Education. The State Highway and Transportation Department has primary responsibility for roads, rails, and public transit; the offices of motor vehicle registration and driver services are in the Department of Finance and Administration The Department of Information Systems governs the state's computer links, while the Department of Parks and Tourism encourages visitors.

Health and welfare services are under the jurisdiction of the Department of Health and the Department of Human Services. Public protection is provided primarily through the Department of Public Safety—which includes the Office of Emergency Services, State Police, National Guard, and Civil Air Patrol—and the Department of Correction, which operates three prisons and three work-release centers. The Public Service Commission, within the Department of Commerce, regulates utilities in the state. Housing services are provided through the Housing Development Agency and the Department of Local Services, whose Division of Manpower offers employment and training programs.

16JUDICIAL SYSTEM

Arkansas's highest court is the supreme court, consisting of a chief justice and six associate justices, elected for staggered eight-year terms. An appeals court of 12 judges, also elected for eight-year terms, was established in 1978.

Arkansas's courts of original jurisdiction are the circuit courts (law) and the chancery courts (equity), of which there are 24 circuits each. In 1999, there were 30 circuit court judges serving four-year terms and 33 chancery probate court judges serving six-year terms; an additional 43 judges were serving both circuit and

chancery courts. Courts of limited jurisdiction include justice of the peace, county, municipal, and police courts, and courts of common pleas.

Arkansas had an FBI Crime Index rate of 4.132.2 per 100,000 population in 2001. The state's once notorious prisons, which had been under federal jurisdiction for more than a decade, were returned in 1978 to state authority, subject to monitoring by an independent ombudsman. By then, the decaying system of the 1960s had been almost entirely replaced by modern facilities. As of June 2001 there were 12,332 prisoners in state and federal correctional institutions, a 6.7% increase over the previous year. The incarceration rate stood at 455 per 100,000 inhabitants. Arkansas has a death penalty and has executed 24 prisoners since 1977. There were 42 persons under sentence of death in 2003.

17ARMED FORCES

As of 2002, there were five military installations in Arkansas, the principal ones being Little Rock Air Force Base and the Army's Pine Bluff Arsenal. Military personnel in the state numbered 4,855 in 2002. Firms in the state received $382 million in defense contract awards in 2001.

There were 281,714 veterans of US military service in Arkansas as of 2000, of whom 53,716 served in World War II; 32,910 in the Korean conflict; 79,453 during the Vietnam era; and 33,386 during 1990–2000 (including the Persian Gulf War). Arkansas veterans received $885 million in benefits in 2002. In 2000, the Arkansas State Police had 559 full-time sworn officers.

18MIGRATION

Near the end of the 18th century, Indians from east of the Mississippi, displaced by white settlement, entered the area now known as Arkansas. However, as the availability of cheap land in Louisiana Territory drew more and more white settlers—in particular, veterans of the War of 1812, who had been promised 160-acre (65-hectare) tracts—the Indians were pressured to cross the border from Arkansas to present-day Oklahoma.

After the end of the Mexican War, thousands of Arkansans immigrated to Texas, and others were attracted to California in 1849 by the gold rush. Because of a law passed in 1859 requiring free blacks to leave the state by the end of the year or risk being enslaved, Arkansas's population of free blacks dropped from 682 in 1858 to 144 in 1860. During Reconstruction, the state government encouraged immigration by both blacks and whites. Literature sent out by the Office of State Lands and Migration, under the tenure of William H. Grey, a black leader, described the state as a new Africa. Railroads, seeking buyers for the lands they had acquired through government grants, were especially active in encouraging immigration after Reconstruction. Later immigrants included Italians and, in the early 1900s, Germans.

During the Depression era (1930s) and thereafter, Arkansas lost a substantial proportion of its farm population, and many blacks left the state for the industrial cities of the Midwest and the east and west coasts. The net loss from migration totaled 919,000 between 1940 and 1970. Between 1970 and 1980, however, the state gained 180,000 residents through migration, as the Ozarks became one of the fastest-growing rural areas in the US. The state experienced a small net decline of 2,000 in migration between 1980 and 1983. Net migration from 1985 to 1990 amounted to a gain of nearly 36,600. Between 1990 and 1998, there were net gains of 106,000 in domestic migration and 9,000 in international migration. In 1998, Arkansas admitted 914 immigrants. Between 1990 and 1998, the state's overall population increased by 8%. In the period 1995–2000, 252,100 people moved into the state and 209,984 moved out, for a net gain of 42,116, 2,496 of whom were age 65 or over.

[19]INTERGOVERNMENTAL COOPERATION

Among the many interstate agreements in which Arkansas participates are the Arkansas River Basin Compact of 1970 (with Oklahoma), Arkansas-Mississippi Great River Bridge Construction Compact, Bi-State Criminal Justice Center Compact, Central Interstate Low-Level Radioactive Waste Compact, Interstate Mining Compact Commission, Interstate Oil and Gas Compact, Red River Compact, South Central Interstate Forest Fire Protection Compact, Southern Growth Policies Board, Southern Regional Education Board, and Southern States Energy Board. There are boundary agreements with Mississippi, Missouri, and Tennessee. In 2001, Arkansas received federal grants totaling $3.4 billion.

[20]ECONOMY

During the 19th century, Arkansas's economic growth was hindered by credit problems. When the state's two central banks, the Arkansas State Bank and the Real Estate Bank, failed during the 1840s, the government defaulted on bonds issued by the latter and amended the constitution to prohibit all banking in Arkansas. Although banking was restored after the Civil War (1861–65), the state defaulted on its obligations once more in 1877, this time following a decision by the Arkansas supreme court that $10 million worth of railroad bonds issued during Reconstruction were unconstitutional. Not until 1917 did New York banks again accept Arkansas securities.

Cotton dominated Arkansas's agricultural economy until well into the 20th century, when rice, soybeans, poultry, and fish farming diversified the output. Coal mining began in the 1870s, bauxite mining near the turn of the century, and oil extraction in the 1920s; lumbering developed in the last quarter of the 19th century, reached its peak about 1909, and then declined until the 1920s, when reforestation started. Industrialization was limited, however, and resources were generally shipped out of state for processing. Not until the 1950s did Arkansas enjoy significant success in attracting industry, thanks in large part to the efforts of Winthrop Rockefeller. Although the Little Rock integration crisis of 1957 was a severe setback to industrial growth in its own Pulaski County the following year, development resumed during the following decades.

By the 1990s, Arkansas's principal industries had become manufacturing, dominated by lumber and wood products companies; agriculture; forestry; and tourism. Fifty-seven Fortune 500 parent firms are found in Arkansas, including Wal-Mart Stores, Tyson Foods, Dillard Department Stores, Beverly Enterprises, and Alltel. Other important corporations include Jacuzzi, Riceland Foods, Maybelline, Whirlpool, International Paper, American Greetings, and Georgia Pacific. Stephens Inc., in Little Rock, is the largest off-Wall Street investment firm in the country. Growth in state gross product rose to 6% in 1999, but fell to 2.8% in 2000 and 1.7% in 2001. Contributing to Arkansas's gross state product of $67.9 billion in 2001 were manufacturing, $13 billion (down 9.9% from its peak in 1999); general services, $11.5 billion (up 28.7% from 1997); and government, $8.9 billion (up 22% from 1997). In 2001, Arkansas ranked 34th among the states in total gross state product, 48th in per capita income ($22,887) and 4th in personal bankruptcy filings.

[21]INCOME

According to the Bureau of Economic Analysis, in 2001, Arkansas had a per capita personal income (PCPI) of $22,750 which ranked 50th in the United States (including the District of Columbia) and was 75% of the national average, $30,413. The 2001 PCPI reflected an increase of 3.4% from 2000 compared to the national change of 2.2%. In 2001, Arkansas had a total personal income (TPI) of $61,303,612,000 which ranked 34th in the United States and accounted for 0.7% of the national total. The 2001 TPI reflected an increase of 4.0% from 2000 compared to the national change of 3.3%.

Earnings of persons employed in Arkansas increased from $40,566,152,000 in 2000 to $41,727,223,000 in 2001, an increase of 2.9%. The largest industries in 2001 were services, 22.7% of earnings; state and local government, 12.9%; and retail trade, 11.4%. Of the industries that accounted for at least 5% of earnings in 2001, the slowest growing from 2000 to 2001 was durable goods manufacturing (10.8% of earnings in 2001), which decreased 5.3%; the fastest was state and local government, which increased 6.7%.

According to data released by the US Census Bureau, in 2000, the median household income was $30,293 compared to the national average of $42,148. In 2001, the median income for a family of four was $47,838 compared to the national average of $63,278. For the period 1999 to 2001, the average poverty rate was 16.3% which placed it 48th among the 50 states and the District of Columbia ranked lowest to highest.

[22]LABOR

According to Bureau of Labor Statistics (BLS) provisional estimates, in July 2003 the seasonally adjusted civilian labor force in Arkansas numbered 1,303,700, with approximately 71,100 workers unemployed, yielding an unemployment rate of 5.5%, compared to the national average of 6.2% for the same period. Since the beginning of the BLS data series in 1978, the highest unemployment rate recorded was 10.5% in February 1983. The historical low was 4.2% in November 1999. In 2001, an estimated 4.4% of the labor force was employed in construction; 16.9% in manufacturing; 5.6% in transportation, communications, and public utilities; 20.2% in trade; 4.8% in finance, insurance, and real estate; 20.6% in services; 16.3% in government; and 3.3% in agriculture.

Chartered in 1865, the Little Rock Typographical Union, consisting of *Arkansas Gazette* employees, was the first labor union in the state. The United Mine Workers was established in the Ft. Smith area by 1898; six years later, the UMW led in the founding of the Arkansas Federation of Labor. Between 1904 and World War I (1914–18), a series of progressive labor laws was enacted, including a minimum wage, restrictions on child labor, and prohibitions against blacklisting and payment of wages in scrip. Union strength waned after the war, however, and the labor movement is not a powerful force in the state today.

The US Department of Labor reported that in 2002, 63,000 of Arkansas's 1,064,000 employed wage and salary workers were members of unions. This represented 5.9% of those so employed, up from 6.3% in 2001. The national average is 13.2%. In all, 73,000 workers (6.8%) were represented by unions. In addition to union members, this category includes workers who report no union affiliation but whose jobs are covered by a union contract. Arkansas is one of 22 states with a right-to-work law.

[23]AGRICULTURE

Farm marketings in Arkansas were over $5.13 billion in 2001 (13th in the US), with crops and livestock accounting for about 32% and 68%, respectively. The state is the nation's leading producer of rice and is among the leaders in cotton, soybeans, and grain sorghum.

Cotton was first grown in the state about 1800, along the river valleys. Confined mainly to slaveholding plantations before the Civil War (1861–65), cotton farming became more widespread in the postwar period, expanding into the hill country of the northwest and eventually into the deforested areas of the northeast, which proved to be some of the most fertile farmland in the nation. As elsewhere in the postbellum South, sharecropping by tenant farmers predominated well into the 20th century, until mechanization and diversification gradually brought an end to the system. Rice was first grown commercially in the early 1900s; by 1920, Arkansas had emerged as a poultry and soybean producer.

During 2002, Arkansas produced 96,480,000 bushels of soybeans, valued at $545,112,000; 38,640,000 bushels of wheat, worth $112,056,000; 3,595,000 tons of hay, worth $198,835,000; and 17,710 bushels of sorghum for grain, valued at $43,637,000. The rice harvest in 2002 was 96,752,000 hundredweight (4,388,574,000 kg), worth $348,307,000. The cotton crop in 2002, 1,650,000 bales, was worth $332,640,000.

24ANIMAL HUSBANDRY

Poultry farms are found throughout Arkansas, but especially in the northern and western regions. Broiler production accounts for about 40% of the state's agricultural receipts. Arkansas was the 2nd-highest broiler-producing state in the US in 2001 (after Georgia); 5.7 billion lb (2.6 billion kg) of broilers were valued at $2.2 billion.

In 2001 it was estimated that Arkansas produced 3.4 billion eggs. In 2001 Arkansas produced 472 million lb (214 million kg) of turkey valued at $189 million. Arkansas sold 97.3 million lb (44 million kg) of chickens valued at $7.8 million.

The dairy yield of the state's 35,000 milk cows in 2001 was 432 million lb (196 million kg) of milk. In 2003 Arkansas had an estimated 1.85 million cattle and calves valued at $1.15 billion. In 2002 Arkansas had an estimated 305,000 hogs and pigs valued at $20.7 million.

25FISHING

Aquaculture is of greater economic importance to Arkansas than is traditional commercial fishing. As of 1999, the state ranked 1st in the US in minnow farming, and 2nd only to Mississippi in catfish farming. As of 1 January 1999, there were 152 catfish operations covering 28,978 acres (13,144 hectares) of water surface, with 128.5 million stocker-size and 185 million fingerling/fry catfish. Some producers rotate fish crops with row crops, periodically draining their fish ponds and planting grains in the rich and well-fertilized soil. Arkansas had 575,130 licensed anglers in 1998.

26FORESTRY

Forestland comprised 18,771,000 acres (7,596,000 hectares), more than 50% of the state's total land area, in 2002. Of that total, 18,373,000 acres (7,435,000 hectares) were commercial timberland. The southwest and central plains, the state's timber belt, constitute one of the most concentrated sources of yellow pine in the US. Lumber production in 2002 totaled 2.6 billion board feet, fifth in the US. Two national forests in Arkansas covered a total of 3,540,000 acres (1,432,638 hectares) in 2001.

27MINING

The US Geological Survey estimate of the value of mineral production in Arkansas in 2001 was $491 million, an increase of about 1% from the final figure reported by the state's more than 200 mineral producers for 2000.

According to preliminary figures, 33 million metric tons of crushed stone were produced in 2001 (valued at $165 million), as well as 10.7 million metric tons of construction sand and gravel with a value of $53.8 million.

Arkansas continues to be the leading bromine-producing state, accounting for most US production. After bromine, crushed stone was Arkansas's leading nonfuel mineral, with 33% of the state's nonfuel mineral value. In 3rd place is cement (both portland and masonry). Arkansas also ranked 6th in gemstones in 2001, with a value of $675,000.

28ENERGY AND POWER

Although Arkansas possesses substantial and varied energy resources—petroleum, natural gas, coal, and water—the state was slow to develop them. As late as 1935, only 1% of Arkansas farms had electric power. The struggle that began during the 1930s over whether Arkansas's rivers would be publicly developed for the production of electricity (in the manner of the Tennessee Valley Authority) was won by the advocates of private power development. As of 1999, Arkansas power plants had a combined capacity (utility and nonutility) of 9.68 million kW, of which about three-fourths was privately owned; production totaled 46.6 billion kWh. As of 2001, two reactor units were operating at Arkansas Nuclear One, the state's only nuclear power plant.

During 2002, 20,000 barrels per day of crude petroleum were produced. At the beginning of 2001, proved reserves were 43 million barrels. Production of natural gas was 166.8 billion cu ft (4.7 billion cu m) in 2001, with 1.62 trillion cu ft (0.05 trillion cu m) of reserves remaining. About 12,000 tons of bituminous coal were mined in 2000. In 2000 Arkansas's total per capita energy consumption was 406 million Btu (102.3 million kcal), ranking it 13th among the states.

29INDUSTRY

Manufacturing in Arkansas is diverse, ranging from blue jeans to bicycles, though resource industries such as rice processing and woodworking still play a major role.

Earnings of persons employed in Arkansas increased from $35 billion in 1997 to $37 billion in 1998, an increase of 5.1%. The largest industries in 1998 were services, 21.3% of earnings; durable goods manufacturing, 12.5%; and state and local government, 11.7%. Of the industries that accounted for at least 5% of earnings in 1998, the slowest growing from 1997 to 1998 was construction (5.8% of earnings in 1998), which increased 3.5%; the fastest was retail trade (11.0% of earnings in 1998), which increased 7.4%.

30COMMERCE

In 1997, Arkansas had a total of 4,463 wholesale establishments, with sales of over $29 billion, and the fourth fastest sales growth rate in the country. There were a total of 15,980 retail establishments in 1997, with sales of $22 billion (18th in the US in terms of growth in sales). The leading retail categories for type of enterprise were automotive dealers, 17%; food stores, 12%; and automotive dealers and gasoline service stations, 23%. Food store sales totaled $3.6 billion, while general merchandise sales totaled approximately $3 billion. During 1997, exports of goods from the state were valued at $2.3 billion, at a rank of 34th in the nation.

31CONSUMER PROTECTION

Under the mandate of Consumer Protection Act of 1971, the Consumer Protection Division of the Office of the Attorney General has principal responsibility for consumer affairs. The CPD serves as a central coordinating agency for individual consumer complaints, conducts investigations, acts as an advocate and mediator in resolving complaints, and prosecutes civil cases on behalf of Arkansas citizens.

32BANKING

In 1836, the first year of statehood, the legislature created the Arkansas State Bank; and the Real Estate Bank, which was intended to promote the plantation system. Fraud, mismanagement, and the consequences of the financial panic of 1837 ruined both banks and led to the passage in 1846 of a constitutional amendment prohibiting the incorporation of any lending institution in Arkansas. Money grew scarce, with credit being rendered largely by suppliers and brokers to farmers and planters until after the Civil War (1861–65), when the prohibition was removed.

Arkansas had 178 insured banks in 2002. At the end of 2002, the state's insured banks had $34.7 billion in assets.

As of the early 1980s, Arkansas's usury law imposed a 10% ceiling on interest rates (one of the most rigid in the US); which the US Supreme Court upheld in 1981. The rise of the federal rate above that limit, beginning in mid-1979, caused a considerable outflow of capital from Arkansas. The Arkansas Usury Law was changed in December 1992 with the Interest Rate Control Amendment, which set the maximum interest rate on general loans at 5% above the Federal Reserve Discount Rate. The Arkansas Supreme Court interpreted the amendment to mean that the rate on consumer loans would be 5% above the discount rate, up to 17%. Although many institutions offered higher interest rates anyway, the ability to do so was formalized in the Financial Modernization Act of 1999. Opposition to usury came primarily from religious factions and labor unions, but low levels of investment during the 1990s motivated the Arkansas government to change the law.

Arkansas experienced weak economic conditions in 2001/02, and rising debt levels, slow income growth, and job losses contributed to a rise in personal bankruptcy filings. Arkansas ranked fourth in the nation in number of bankruptcy filings in 2002. Asset quality among Arkansas' insured banks remained a problem, with higher past-due loan levels. Median net interest margins (NIMs) (the difference between the lower rates offered to savers and the higher rates charged on loans) for Arkansas' insured institutions improved, however, due to the wide spread between short- and long-term interest rates.

33INSURANCE

In 2001 there were 1.7 million ordinary life insurance policies in force with a total value of $67.7 billion; total value for all categories of life insurance (ordinary, group, industrial, and credit) was $111.2 billion. Death benefits paid that year totaled $380.5 million. As of 2003, there were 12 property and casualty and 41 life and health insurance companies incorporated or organized in the state.

Property and casualty insurers wrote premiums amounting to $2.86 billion in 2001. That year, there were 13,816 flood insurance policies in force in the state, with a total value of $1,030,497.

34SECURITIES

There are no securities exchanges in Arkansas, but the state has a total of 329 companies operating in financial markets, with 2,758 employees. Investment advisor organizations number twenty-nine. There are 19 NASDAQ companies with their headquarters in Arkansas, one NASDAQ market maker, and four Arkansas-incorporated companies on the NYSE; including Fairfield Communities, Inc., Southwestern Energy Corp., Tyson Foods, Inc., and Webb (Del) Corp.

35PUBLIC FINANCE

Under the 1874 constitution, state expenditures may not exceed revenues. The mechanism adopted each biennium to prevent deficit spending is a Revenue Stabilization Act. This Act provides the funding for state appropriations by assigning levels of funding priority to the appropriations. All appropriations in a higher level must be fully funded before any appropriations in a lower level are funded. In the event of insufficient revenues to fund appropriations, each agency reduces its appropriations, to correspond to the general revenues allocated to the agency.

Total general revenue available for distribution in 2001 was forecast at $3.3 billion. Major funding areas in 2000 and 2001 in

order of importance were: public primary and secondary schools (47%), human services (20%), higher learning institutions (16%), and general government (10%). Revenues for these projects came primarily from income taxes and sales taxes (94%). These figures represent an increase of over 10% on public schools since 1997.

The following table from the US Census Bureau contains information on revenues, expenditures, indebtedness, and cash/securities for 2001.

	($000)	PERCENT	PER CAPITA
Population (thousands, 2001)	2,695	(X)	(X)
Total Revenue	10,330,394	100.00	3,833.17
General revenue	9,804,136	94.91	3,637.90
Utility revenue	–	–	–
Liquor store revenue	–	–	–
Insurance trust revenue	526,258	5.09	195.27
Exhibit: Salaries and wages	1,785,329	16.85	662.46
Total expenditure	10,597,097	100.00	3,932.13
General expenditure	9,848,226	92.93	3,654.26
Education	4,149,058	39.15	1,539.54
Public welfare	2,215,168	20.90	821.95
Hospitals	353,476	3.34	131.16
Health	298,356	2.82	110.71
Highways	939,390	8.86	348.57
Police protection	77,425	0.73	28.73
Correction	290,520	2.74	107.80
Natural resources	215,001	2.03	79.78
Parks and recreation	75,162	0.71	27.89
Government administration	389,227	3.67	144.43
Interest on general debt	124,873	1.18	46.34
Other and unallocable	720,570	6.80	267.37
Utility expenditure	–	–	–
Liquor store expenditure	–	–	–
Insurance trust expenditure	748,871	7.07	277.87
Debt at end of fiscal year	2,841,828	100.00	1,054.48
Cash and security holdings	17,839,949	100.00	6,619.65

36TAXATION

In 2000, the state income tax ranged from 0% to 6%; the corporate income tax ranged from 1% on the first $3,000 to 6.5% on amounts over $100,000. Corporate taxpayers with a net income of $100,000 or greater pay a flat rate of 6.5%. The state sales tax is 4.625%. The state also imposes severance taxes on oil, natural gas, and other natural resources, along with levies on liquor, gasoline, and cigarettes. City and county property taxes in Arkansas are among the lowest in the nation.

Total tax revenues for 2001 were forecast at approximately $3.3 billion, including $1.8 billion from individual income, and $1.4 billion from the sales tax. The severance and corporate franchise taxes were repealed in 1999, causing a drop in revenue from 1998.

The following table from the US Census Bureau provides a summary of taxes collected by the state in 2002.

	($000)	PER CAPITA
Total Taxes	5,034,109	1,857.55
Property taxes	486,895	179.66
Sales and gross receipts	2,589,256	955.42
General sales and gross receipts	1,918,140	707.78
Selective sales taxes	671,116	247.64
Alcoholic beverage	30,739	11.34
Amusements	(X)	(X)
Insurance Premiums	80,386	29.66
Motor fuels	415,050	153.15
Pari-mutuels	4,032	1.49
Public utilities	(X)	(X)
Tobacco products	93,073	34.34
Other selective sales	47,836	17.65
Licenses	234,931	86.69
Alcoholic beverages	1,579	0.58
Amusements	1,924	0.71
Corporation	7,983	2.95

	($000)	PER CAPITA
Licenses	234,931	86.69
Hunting and fishing	21,294	7.86
Motor vehicle	97,453	35.96
Motor vehicle operators	13,205	4.87
Public utility	10,311	3.8
Occupation and business, NEC	76,838	28.35
Other	4,344	1.6
Other taxes	1,723,027	635.78
Individual income	1,488,250	549.15
Corporation net income	161,021	59.42
Death and gift	35,697	13.17
Documentary and stock transfer	19,086	7.04
Severance	13,217	4.88
Other	5,756	2.12

37ECONOMIC POLICY

First as chairman of the Arkansas Industrial Development Commission and later as governor of the state from 1967–71, Winthrop Rockefeller succeeded in attracting substantial and diverse new industries to Arkansas. In 1979, Governor Bill Clinton formed the Department of Economic Development from the former Arkansas Industrial Development Commission for the purpose of stimulating the growth of small business and finding new export markets. The Arkansas Development Finance Authority was created in 1985 in order to support small-scale economic development of new businesses, mortgages, education, and health care. The Economic Development Commission offers such incentives to new businesses as an Enterprise Zone Program, income tax credit, sales and use tax refunds, amongst others. In 2003, the legislature passed the Consolidated Incentive Act which combined six previous economic development incentive programs into one package, plus added some additional incentives for investment and regional development. The six programs consolidated in the Act were the Enterprise Zone program (Advantage Arkansas), which provides incentives for investments in areas with high poverty and/or unemployment); the Economic Investment Tax Credit program (InvestArk Program); the Economic Development Incentives Act (CreateRebate); the Arkansas Economic Development Act (AEDA), which offers tax reductions for investments of at least $5 million dollars creating at least 100 new permanent jobs; plus incentive programs for improvements in energy technology and biotechnology. By the act, companies would be allowed to sell tax credits earned in order to realize the benefits earlier. The act seeks to promote regional development by rewarding counties which enter into binding compacts with each other to further economic development.

38HEALTH

The infant death rate for the year ending December 2000 was 8.4 per 1,000 live births. There were 5,755 legal abortions performed in 1999, when the state's abortion ratio was 11 per 1,000 women. In 2000, Arkansas's death rate, 1,095.2 per 100,000 population, was well above the national rate of 873.1, and the incidence of cerebrovascular disease was 87.5 per 100,000 population. Death rates from heart disease, cancer, accidents, and motor vehicle accidents also exceeded the national rates. The number of AIDS cases reported through 2001 totaled 3,177. The HIV death rate in Arkansas (2.9 per 100,000 population) was much lower than the national average of 5.3 per 100,000 population in 2000. Of adults age 18 years and older, 25.2% were current smokers in 2000.

Arkansas's 83 hospitals had 9,535 beds and recorded 371,080 admissions in 2001. Hospital expenses for services provided in 2001 were $1,207.2 per inpatient day. In 2000, the state had 208 physicians per 100,000 population and a total of 10,093 full-time registered nurses. Federal government grants to cover the Medicare and Medicaid services in 2001 totaled $1.4 billion;

441,863 enrollees received Medicare benefits that year. At least 16.1% of the adult population was uninsured in 2002, the ninth-highest percentage in the nation.

39SOCIAL WELFARE

In 2001, the average weekly unemployment benefit was $219.56. Average monthly participation in the food stamp program in FY2002 comprised 283,909 persons (113,238 households). The average monthly benefit was $77.65, and the sum total of benefits paid in FY2002 was $264,534,345.

With the enactment of the Personal Responsibility and Work Opportunity Reconciliation Act of 1996, the US government has changed the form and regulations for many of its social welfare programs. Most significantly, it replaces Aid to Families with Dependent Children (AFDC), an open-ended entitlement program, with Temporary Assistance for Needy Families (TANF), a limited system of assistance funded largely through federal block grants. The reform act also impacts the food stamp program, the Supplemental Security Income program, and the child nutrition program. The law took effect on 1 July 1997 and provided $16.38 billion in block grants for fiscal years 1997–2002. The grants are to be divided among the states based on an equation involving the numbers of former AFDC recipients in each state.

Reauthorization of the 1996 social welfare legislation, scheduled for 2002, was delayed, and the original law had been extended three times as of July 2003, with the most recent extension running through September 2003. Arkansas's TANF program is called Transitional Employment Assistance (TEA). In June 2000 the state had 28,113 welfare recipients. State expenditures on the TANF program in FY2002 totaled $22,546,419.

In December 2001, Social Security benefits were paid to 520,680 Arkansas residents. This number included 298,680 retired workers, 61,000 widows and widowers, 79,640 disabled workers, 30,800 spouses, and 50,560 children. Social Security beneficiaries represented 19.6% of the total state population and 93.2% of the state's population age 65 and older. Retired workers (excluding persons with special benefits) received an average monthly payment of $805; widows and widowers, $723; disabled workers, $766; and spouses, $393. Payments for children of retired workers averaged $390 per month; children of deceased workers, $522; and children of disabled workers, $226.

Federal Supplemental Security Income payments in December 2001went to 85,088 Arkansas residents, averaging $325 a month.

40HOUSING

In 2002, there were an estimated 1,202,028 housing units in Arkansas, of which 1,062,677 were occupied. In the same year, 67.9% of all housing units were owner-occupied. About 70% of all units were single-family, detached homes; 13% were mobile homes. The average household size was 2.48 people. It was estimated that about 60,790 units were without telephone service, 4,494 lacked complete plumbing facilities, and 7,389 lacked complete kitchen facilities. Though most units relied on gas and electricity for heating fuels, about 43,236 households used wood for a primary heating source.

The Department of Housing and Urban Development awarded $39.6 million in grants to the Arkansas state program in 2002, including $24.9 million in community development block grants. About 12,436 new housing units were authorized in 2002. The median home value was $79,043. The median monthly cost for mortgage owners was $772 while the monthly cost for renters was at a median of $497.

[41]EDUCATION

In 2000, 75.3% of all Arkansans 25 years of age and older were high school graduates. Only 16.7% had completed four or more years of college, up only 0.2% from 1990 statistics.

In some ways, Little Rock was an unlikely site for the major confrontation over school integration that occurred in 1957. The school board had already announced its voluntary compliance with the Supreme Court's desegregation decision, and during Governor Faubus's first term (1955–56), several public schools in the state had been peaceably integrated. Nevertheless, on 5 September 1957, Faubus, claiming that violence was likely, ordered the National Guard to seize Central High School to prevent the entry of nine black students. When a mob did appear following the withdrawal of the National Guardsmen in response to a federal court order later that month, President Dwight Eisenhower dispatched federal troops to Little Rock, and they patrolled the school grounds until the end of the 1958 spring semester. Although Faubus's stand encouraged politicians in other southern states to resist desegregation, in Arkansas integration proceeded at a moderate pace. By 1980, Central High School had a nearly equal balance of black and white students, and the state's school system was one of the most integrated in the South.

Public school enrollment in fall 1999 totaled 451,034. Of these, 317,714 attended schools from kindergarten through grade eight, and 133,320 attended high school. Minority students made up approximately 29% of the total enrollment in public elementary and secondary schools in 2001. Total enrollment was estimated at 448,018 in fall 2000 and expected to reach 465,000 by fall 2005. Expenditures for public education in 2000/01 were estimated at $2,360,599. Enrollment in nonpublic schools in fall 2001 was 26,424.

As of fall 2000, there were 128,063 students enrolled in college or graduate school. In the same year Arkansas had 47 degree-granting institutions. In 1997 minority students comprised 19.3% of total postsecondaryenrollment. The largest institution of higher education in the state is the University of Arkansas at Fayetteville (established in 1871). The state university system also has campuses at Fort Smith, Little Rock, Monticello, and Pine Bluff and a medical school. Student aid is provided by the State Scholarship Program within the Department of Higher Education, by the Arkansas Student Loan Guarantee Foundation, and by the Arkansas Rural Endowment Fund, Inc.

[42]ARTS

The Arkansas Arts Council was established in 1971 as one of six agencies of the Department of Arkansas Heritage. Major funding comes from the State and the National Endowment for the Arts. In 2003, the National Endowment for the Arts awarded grants totaling $574,300 to Arkansas arts organizations. In 2000, the National Endowment for the Humanities awarded grants totaling $500,597 to 5 organizations. Arkansas is also affiliated with the regional Mid-America Arts Alliance. Funding for the arts has reached over 71,000 artists and over 66,000 schoolchildren who have participated in arts education programs. There are over 50 arts-related associations in Arkansas and several local groups.

Little Rock is the home of the Arkansas Symphony Orchestra, the Arkansas Festival Ballet, the Arkansas Repertory Theater, and the Arkansas Arts Center, which holds art exhibits and classes, and children's theater performances. The Shakespeare Festival of Arkansas is staged at the Center Stage Theater in Little Rock.

The best-known center for traditional arts and crafts is the Ozark Folk Center at Mountain View; every evening from late spring through October, folk music of the Ozarks may be heard. The Arkansas Folk Festival is held there during two weekends in April, and the Family Harvest Festival for three weeks in October. Lyon College at Batesville sponsors two-week summer workshops in Ozark crafts, music, and folklore in association with the center.

The Grand Prairie Festival of Arts is held at Stuttgart in September.

[43]LIBRARIES AND MUSEUMS

During 2000, Arkansas had 35 library systems, including 11 single-county systems, 18 multi-county systems, and six city public libraries. That year, the state's 43,000 public libraries held a total of 5,408,000 volumes and circulation amounted to 10,240,000. Important collections include those of the University of Arkansas at Fayetteville (1,556,572 volumes), Arkansas State University at Jonesboro (544,326), the Central Arkansas Library System of Little Rock (528,982), and the News Library of the Arkansas Gazette, also in Little Rock. The total income of the public library system was $38,531,000 in 2000. Arkansas received no federal grants, but state grants came to 4,816,375. The state spent 59.3% of this income on staff, and 17.7% on collections.

There were 78 museums in 2000 and a number of historic sites. Principal museums include the Arkansas Arts Center and the Museum of Science and History, both at Little Rock; the Arkansas State University Museum at Jonesboro; and the University of Arkansas Museum at Fayetteville, specializing in archaeology, anthropology, and the sciences. Also of interest are the Stuttgart Agricultural Museum; the Arkansas Post County Museum at Gillett, whose artifacts are housed in re-created plantation buildings; Hampson Museum State Park, near Wilson, which has one of the largest collections of Mound Builder artifacts in the US; the Mid-American Museum at Hot Springs, which has visitor-participation exhibits; and the Saunders Memorial Museum at Berryville, with an extensive collection of firearms.

Civil War battle sites include the Pea Ridge National Military Park, the Prairie Grove Battlefield State Park, and the Arkansas Post National Memorial. The Ft. Smith National Historic Site includes buildings and museums from the days when the town was a military outpost on the border of Indian Territory.

[44]COMMUNICATIONS

In 2001, 91.4% of the state's occupied housing units had telephones, the lowest rate in the nation. There were 63 major radio stations (7AM, 56FM) and 17 major television stations in 2003. A total of 23,195 Internet domain names had been registered in Arkansas by the year 2000.

[45]PRESS

The first newspaper in Arkansas, the *Arkansas Gazette*, established at Arkansas Post in 1819 by William E. Woodruff, ceased publication in 1991. In 2002, there were 15 morning dailies, 13 evening papers, and 16 Sunday papers. In 1992, Little Rock's two major dailies, the *Arkansas Democrat* and the *Democrat Gazette*, merged. The following table shows the 2002 circulations of the leading dailies:

AREA	NAME	DAILY	SUNDAY
Ft. Smith	*Southwest Times Record*(m, S)	42,201	44,444
Little Rock	*Arkansas Democrat-Gazette* (m, S)	182,609	282,795
Jonesboro	*Jonesboro Sun* (m, S)	25,560	30,220
Springdale-Rogers	*Morning News*(m, S)	36,295	37,718

[46]ORGANIZATIONS

In 2003, there were over 1,000 regional, national, and international organizations within the state. Among the national organizations with headquarters in Arkansas are the American Crossbow Association in Huntsville; the American Fish Farmers Federation in Lonoke; and the Ozark Society, the American Parquet Association, the Federation of American Hospitals, and the Civil War Round Table Associates, all located in Little Rock.

There is an active chapter of the Knights of the Ku Klux Klan in Harrison.

ACORN, the Association of Community Organizations for Reform Now, was founded in Little Rock in 1970 and has since spread to some 20 other states and has become one of the most influential citizens' lobbies in the US.

⁴⁷TOURISM, TRAVEL, AND RECREATION

Leading attractions in Arkansas are the mineral waters and recreational facilities at Hot Springs, Eureka Springs, Mammoth Spring, and Heber Springs. The Crater of Diamonds, near Murfreesboro, is the only known public source of natural diamonds in North America. For a fee, visitors may hunt for diamonds and keep any they find; more than 100,000 diamonds have been found in the area since 1906, of which the two largest are the 40.42-carat Uncle Sam and the 34.25-carat Star of Murfreesboro. The World's Championship Duck Calling Contest is held at the beginning of the winter duck season in Stuttgart.

In support of the industry, the Arkansas Tourism Development Act of 1999 provides incentives for qualified new or expanding tourism facilities and attractions. The program applies to cultural or historical sites; recreational or entertainment facilities; natural, theme, and amusement parks; plays and musicals; and gardens. To qualify, the project must cost more than $500,000 and have a positive effect on the state. The state has 14 tourist information centers. In 2002, the state had about 19.9 million visitors with travel expenditures reaching over $3.9 billion dollars (a 2.8% increase from 2000).

⁴⁸SPORTS

Arkansas has no major league professional sports teams but has a minor league baseball team, the Travelers, and two minor league hockey teams, the RiverBlades and GlacierCats. Oaklawn Park in Hot Springs has a 62-day thoroughbred-racing season each spring, and dog races are held in West Memphis from April through November. Several major rodeos take place in summer and fall, including the Rodeo of the Ozarks in Springdale in early July.

The University of Arkansas has competed in the Southeastern Conference since 1990, when it ended its 76-year affiliation with the Southwest Conference. The Razorback football team won the Cotton Bowl in 1947, 1965, 1976, and 2000; the Orange Bowl in 1978; the Sugar Bowl in 1969; and the Bluebonnet Bowl in 1982. The men's basketball team won the NCAA Division I basketball championship in 1994; won or shared the Southwest Conference championship in 1977, 1978, 1979, 1981, and 1982; and won the Southeastern Conference in 1994 and 2000.

⁴⁹FAMOUS ARKANSANS

Arkansas has produced one president of the United States, William Jefferson Clinton (b.1946). Clinton, a Democrat, defeated President George Bush in the 1992 presidential election and was reelected in 1996. Hillary Rodham Clinton (b.Illinois, 1947), the wife of the former president, was elected as the US Senator for New York in 2000. Arkansas has yet to produce a vice president or a Supreme Court justice, although one Arkansan came close to reaching both offices: US Senator Joseph T. Robinson (1872–1937) was the Democratic nominee for vice president in 1928, on the ticket with Al Smith; later, he was Senate majority leader under President Franklin D. Roosevelt. At the time of his death, Robinson was leading the fight for Roosevelt's bill to expand the Supreme Court's membership and had reportedly been promised a seat on the court if the bill passed. Robinson's colleague, Hattie W. Caraway (b.Tennessee, 1878–1950), was the first woman elected to the US Senate, serving from 1931 to 1945.

After World War II (1939–45), Arkansas's congressional delegation included three men of considerable power and fame: Senator John L. McClellan (1896–1977), investigator of organized labor and organized crime and champion of the Arkansas River navigation project; Senator J. William Fulbright (b.Missouri, 1905–95), chairman of the Senate Foreign Relations Committee; and Representative Wilbur D. Mills (1909–92), chairman of the House Ways and Means Committee until scandal ended his political career in the mid-1970s.

Other federal officeholders include Brooks Hays (1898–1981), former congressman and special assistant to Presidents John F. Kennedy and Lyndon B. Johnson, as well as president of the Southern Baptist Convention, the nation's largest Protestant denomination; and Frank Pace, Jr. (1912–88), secretary of the Army during the Truman administration.

General Douglas MacArthur (1880–1964), supreme commander of Allied forces in the Pacific during World War II, supervised the occupation of Japan and was supreme commander of UN troops in Korea until relieved of his command in April 1951 by President Truman.

Orval E. Faubus (1910–94) served six terms as governor (a record), drew international attention during the 1957 integration crisis at Little Rock Central High School, and headed the most powerful political machine in Arkansas history. Winthrop Rockefeller (b.New York, 1917–73) was Faubus's most prominent successor. At the time of his election in 1978, Bill Clinton was the nation's youngest governor.

Prominent business leaders include the Stephens brothers, W. R. "Witt" (1907–91) and Jackson T. (b.1923), whose Stephens, Inc., investment firm in Little Rock is the largest off Wall Street; and Kemmons Wilson (b.1913), founder of Holiday Inns.

Other distinguished Arkansans are Edward Durrell Stone (1902–78), renowned architect; C. Vann Woodward (1908–99), Sterling Professor Emeritus of History at Yale University; and the Right Reverend John M. Allin (1921–98), who served as bishop of the Episcopal Church of the United States. John H. Johnson (b.1918), publisher of the nation's leading black-oriented magazines—*Ebony, Jet,* and others—is an Arkansan, as is Helen Gurley Brown (b.1922), former editor of *Cosmopolitan.*

Harry S. Ashmore (b.South Carolina, 1916–98) won a Pulitzer Prize for his *Arkansas Gazette* editorials calling for peaceful integration of the schools during the 1957 crisis; the *Gazette* itself won a Pulitzer for meritorious public service that year. Paul Greenberg (b.Louisiana, 1937), of the *Pine Bluff Commercial,* is another Pulitzer Prize-winning journalist. John Gould Fletcher (1886–1950) was a Pulitzer Prize-winning poet. Other Arkansas writers include Dee Brown (b.Louisiana, 1908–2002), Maya Angelou (b.Missouri, 1928), Charles Portis (b.1933), and Eldridge Cleaver (1935–98).

Arkansas planter Colonel Sanford C. Faulkner (1803–74) is credited with having written the well-known fiddle tune "The Arkansas Traveler" and its accompanying dialogue. Perhaps the best-known country music performers from Arkansas are Johnny Cash (1932–2003) and Glen Campbell (b.1938). Film stars Dick Powell (1904–63) and Alan Ladd (1913–64) were also Arkansans.

Notable Arkansas sports personalities include Jerome Herman "Dizzy" Dean (1911–74) and Bill Dickey (1907–93), both members of the Baseball Hall of Fame; Brooks Robinson (b.1937), considered by some the best-fielding third baseman in baseball history; and star pass-catcher Lance Alworth (b.Mississippi, 1940), a University of Arkansas All-American and member of the Professional Football Hall of Fame.

⁵⁰BIBLIOGRAPHY

Alampi, Gary, ed. *Gale State Rankings Reporter.* Detroit: Gale Research, Inc., 1994.

Angelou, Maya. *I Know Why the Caged Bird Sings*. New York: Bantam, 1971.

Arkansas, University of. Industrial Research and Extension Center. *Arkansas State and County Economic Data*. Little Rock: University of Arkansas, 1984.

Council of State Governments. *The Book of the States, 1994–1995 Edition*. Vol. 30. Lexington, Ky.: The Council of State Governments, 1994.

FDIC, Division of Research and Statistics. *Statistics on Banking: A Statistical Profile of the United States Banking Industry*. Washington, D.C.: Federal Deposit Insurance Corporation, 1993.

Federal Writers' Project. *Arkansas: A Guide to the State*. 1941. Reprint, New York: Somerset, n.d.

Fletcher, John Gould. *Arkansas*. Fayetteville: University of Arkansas Press, 1989.

Gatewood, Willard B., and Jeannie Whayne, ed. *The Arkansas Delta: Land of Paradox*. Fayetteville: University of Arkansas Press, 1993.

Hamilton, Nigel. *Bill Clinton: An American Journey*. New York: Random House, 2003.

Lankford, George E., ed. *Bearing Witness: Memories of Arkansas Slavery Narratives from the 1930s WPA Collections*. Fayetteville: University of Arkansas Press, 2003.

McDougal, Jim and Curtis Wilkie. *Arkansas Mischief: the Birth of a National Scandal*. New York: Henry Holt, 1998.

Paulson, Alan C. *Roadside History of Arkansas*. Missoula, Mont.: Mountain Press Pub., 1998.

Polakow, Amy. *Daisy Bates: Civil Rights Crusader*. North Haven, Conn.: Linnet Books, 2003.

Ross, Margaret. *Arkansas Gazette: The Early Years, 1819–66*. Little Rock: Arkansas Gazette Foundation, 1969.

Schmittroth, Linda, and Mary Kay Rosteck, ed. *Cities of the United States*. 2nd ed. Detroit: Gale Research, Inc., 1994.

Streb, Matthew J. *The New Electoral Politics of Race*. Tuscaloosa: University of Alabama Press, 2002.

Taylor, Orville, W. *Negro Slavery in Arkansas*. Durham, N.C.: Duke University Press, 1958.

US Department of the Interior, US Fish and Wildlife Service. *Endangered and Threatened Species Recovery Program*. Washington, D.C.: US Government Printing Office, 1990.

Whayne, Jeannie M. *A New Plantation South: Land, Labor, and Federal Favor in Twentieth-Century Arkansas*. Charlottesville: University Press of Virginia, 1996.

Williams, C. Filed. *A Documentary History of Arkansas*. Fayetteville: University of Arkansas Press, 1983.

Woodruff, Nan Elizabeth. *American Congo: The African American Freedom Struggle in the Delta*. Cambridge, Mass.: Harvard University Press, 2003.

CALIFORNIA REPUBLIC

CALIFORNIA

State of California

ORIGIN OF STATE NAME: Probably from the mythical island California in a 16th-century romance by Garci Ordóñez de Montalvo. **NICKNAME:** The Golden State. **CAPITAL:** Sacramento. **ENTERED UNION:** 9 September 1850 (31st). **SONG:** "I Love You, California." **MOTTO:** *Eureka* (I have found it). **FLAG:** The flag consists of a white field with a red star at upper left and a red stripe and the words "California Republic" across the bottom; in the center, a brown grizzly bear stands on a patch of green grass. **OFFICIAL SEAL:** In the foreground is the goddess Minerva; a grizzly bear stands in front of her shield. The scene also shows the Sierra Nevada, San Francisco Bay, a miner, a sheaf of wheat, and a cluster of grapes, all representing California's resources. The state motto and 31 stars are displayed at the top. The words "The Great Seal of the State of California" surround the whole. **COLORS:** Yale blue and golden yellow. **ANIMAL:** California grizzly bear (extinct). **BIRD:** California valley quail. **FISH:** South Fork golden trout. **MARINE MAMMAL:** California gray whale. **REPTILE:** California desert tortoise. **INSECT:** California dog-face butterfly (flying pansy). **FLOWER:** Golden poppy. **TREE:** California redwood. **ROCK:** Serpentine. **MINERAL:** Native gold. **FOSSIL:** California saber-toothed cat. **LEGAL HOLIDAYS:** New Year's Day, 1 January; Birthday of Martin Luther King, Jr., 3rd Monday in January; Lincoln's Birthday, 12 February; Presidents' Day, 3rd Monday in February; Memorial Day, last Monday in May; Independence Day, 4 July; Labor Day, 1st Monday in September; Admission Day, 9 September; Columbus Day, 2nd Monday in October; Veterans Day, 11 November, Thanksgiving Day, 4th Thursday in November; Christmas Day, 25 December. **TIME:** 4 AM PST = noon GMT.

¹LOCATION, SIZE, AND EXTENT

Situated on the Pacific coast of the southwestern US, California is the nation's 3rd-largest state (after Alaska and Texas).

The total area of California is 158,706 sq mi (411,048 sq km), of which land takes up 156,299 sq mi (404,814 sq km) and inland water 2,407 sq mi (6,234 sq km). California extends about 350 mi (560 km) E-W; its maximum N-S extension is 780 mi (1,260 km).

California is bordered on the N by Oregon; on the E by Nevada; on the SE by Arizona (separated by the Colorado River); on the S by the Mexican state of Baja California Norte; and on the W by the Pacific Ocean.

The eight Santa Barbara islands lie from 20 to 60 mi (32–97 km) off California's southwestern coast; the small islands and islets of the Farallon group are about 30 mi (48 km) W of San Francisco Bay. The total boundary length of the state is 2,050 mi (3,299 km), including a general coastline of 840 mi (1,352 km); the tidal shoreline totals 3,427 mi (5,515 km). California's geographic center is in Madera County, 38 mi (61 km) E of the city of Madera.

²TOPOGRAPHY

California is the only state in the US with an extensive seacoast, high mountains, and deserts. The extreme diversity of the state's landforms is best illustrated by the fact that Mt. Whitney (14,494 ft/4,419 m), the highest point in the contiguous US, is situated no more than 80 mi (129 km) from the lowest point in the entire country, Death Valley (282 ft/86 m, below sea level). The mean elevation of the state is about 2,900 ft (885 m).

California's principal geographic regions are the Sierra Nevada in the east, the Coast Ranges in the west, the Central Valley between them, and the Mojave and Colorado deserts in the southeast. The mountain-walled Central Valley, more than 400 mi (640 km) long and about 50 mi (80 km) wide, is probably the

state's most unusual topographic feature. It is drained in the north by the Sacramento River, about 320 mi (515 km) long, and in the south by the San Joaquin River, about 350 mi (560 km). The main channels of the two rivers meet at and empty into the northern arm of San Francisco Bay, flowing through the only significant break in the Coast Ranges, a mountain system that extends more than 1,200 mi (1,900 km) alongside the Pacific. Lesser ranges, including the Siskiyou Mountains in the north and the Tehachapi Mountains in the south, link the two major ranges and constitute the Central Valley's upper and lower limits.

California has 41 mountains exceeding 10,000 ft (3,050 m). After Mt. Whitney, the highest peaks in the state are Mt. Williamson, in the Sierra Nevada, at 14,375 ft (4,382 m) and Mt. Shasta (14,162 ft/4,317 m), an extinct volcano in the Cascades, the northern extension of the Sierra Nevada. Lassen Peak (10,457 ft/3,187 m), also in the Cascades, is a dormant volcano.

Beautiful Yosemite Valley, a narrow gorge in the middle of the High Sierra, is the activity center of Yosemite National Park. The Coast Ranges, with numerous forested spurs and ridges enclosing dozens of longitudinal valleys, vary in height from about 2,000 to 7,000 ft (600–2,100 m).

Melted snow from the Sierra Nevada feeds the state's principal rivers, the Sacramento and San Joaquin. The Coast Ranges are drained by the Klamath, Eel, Russian, Salinas, and other rivers. In the south, most rivers are dry creek beds except during the spring flood season; they either dry up from evaporation in the hot summer sun or disappear beneath the surface, like Death Valley's Amargosa River. The Salton Sea, in the Imperial Valley of the southeast, is the state's largest lake, occupying 374 sq mi (969 sq km). This saline sink was created accidentally in the early 1900s when Colorado River water, via an irrigation canal, flooded a natural depression 235 ft (72 m) below sea level in the Imperial Valley. Lake Tahoe, in the Sierra Nevada at the angle of the California-Nevada border, covers 192 sq mi (497 sq km).

The California coast is indented by two magnificent natural harbors, San Francisco Bay and San Diego Bay, and two smaller bays, Monterey and Humboldt. Two groups of islands lie off the California shore: the Santa Barbara Islands, situated west of Los Angeles and San Diego; and the rocky Farallon Islands, off San Francisco.

The Sierra Nevada and Coast Ranges were formed more than 100 million years ago by the uplifting of the earth's crust. The Central Valley and the Great Basin, including the Mojave Desert and Death Valley, were created by sinkage of the earth's crust; inland seas once filled these depressions but evaporated over eons of time. Subsequent volcanic activity, erosion of land, and movement of glaciers until the last Ice Age subsided some 10,000 years ago and gradually shaped the present topography of California. The San Andreas Fault, extending from north of San Francisco Bay for more than 600 mi (970 km) southeast to the Mojave Desert, is a major active earthquake zone and was responsible for the great San Francisco earthquake of 1906. Damage from that earthquake amounted to $24 million, with an additional $350–500 in fire losses (total losses would amount to about $6 billion in current dollars). More recently, the 1994 earthquake in Northridge caused damage estimated at $13–20 billion, making it the costliest earthquake in US history.

Because water is scarce in the southern part of the state and because an adequate water supply is essential both for agriculture and for industry, more than 1,000 dams and reservoirs have been built in California. By 1993, there were 1,336 reservoirs in the state. Popular reservoirs for recreation are located along the tributaries of the Sacramento and San Joaquin rivers. Clair Lake Eagle, also known as Trinity Lake, is located on the Trinity River. The reservoir has a surface area of 16,400 acres (6,640 ha). Lake Shasta, located on the Sacramento River, has a surface area of 15,800 acres (6,397 ha). Lake Berryessa, located on Putah Creek, has a surface area of 19,250 acres (7,794 ha). Lake New Melones, located on the Stanislaus River, has a surface area of 12,500 acres (5,061 ha). The San Luis Reservoir, fed by the California Aqueduct, has a surface area of 12,500 acres (5,061 ha). Don Pedro Lake, located on the Toulumme River, has a surface area of 13,000 acres (5,263 ha).

³CLIMATE

Like its topography, California's climate is varied and tends toward extremes. Generally there are two seasons—a long, dry summer, with low humidity and cool evenings, and a mild, rainy winter—except in the high mountains, where four seasons prevail and snow lasts from November to April. The one climatic constant for the state is summer drought.

California has four main climatic regions. Mild summers and winters prevail in central coastal areas, where temperatures are more equable than virtually anywhere else in the US; in the area between San Francisco and Monterey, for example, the difference between average summer and winter temperatures is seldom more than 10°F (6°C). During the summer there are heavy fogs in San Francisco and all along the coast. Mountainous regions are characterized by milder summers and colder winters, with markedly low temperatures at high elevations. The Central Valley has hot summers and cool winters, while the Imperial Valley is marked by very hot, dry summers, with temperatures frequently exceeding 100°F (38°C).

Average annual temperatures for the state range from 47°F (8°C) in the Sierra Nevada to 73°F (23°C) in the Imperial Valley. The highest temperature ever recorded in the US was 134° (57°C), registered in Death Valley on 10 July 1913. Death Valley has the hottest average summer temperature in the Western Hemisphere, at 98°F (37°C). The state's lowest temperature was –45°F (–43°C), recorded on 20 January 1937 at Boca, near the Nevada border.

Among the major population centers, Los Angeles has an average annual temperature of 63°F (17°C), with an average January minimum of 48°F (9°C) and an average July maximum of 75°F (24°C). San Francisco has an annual average of 57°F (14°C), with a January average minimum of 42°F (6°C) and a July average maximum of 72°F (22°C). The annual average in San Diego is 64°F (18°C), the January average minimum 49°F (9°C), and the July average maximum 76°F (24°C). Sacramento's annual average temperature is 61°F (16°C), with January minimums averaging 38°F (3°C) and July maximums of 93°F (34°C).

Annual precipitation varies from only 2 in (5 cm) in the Imperial Valley to 68 in (173 cm) at Blue Canyon, near Lake Tahoe. San Francisco had an average annual precipitation (1971–2000) of 20 in (51 cm), Sacramento 17.9 in (45.5 cm), Los Angeles 13.2 in (33.5 cm), and San Diego 10.8 in (27.4 cm). The largest one-month snowfall ever recorded in the US—390 in (991 cm)—fell in Alpine County in January 1911. Snow averages between 300 and 400 in (760 to 1,020 cm) annually in the high elevations of the Sierra Nevada, but is rare in the coastal lowlands.

Sacramento has the greatest percentage (73%) of possible annual sunshine among the state's largest cities; Los Angeles has 72% and San Francisco 71%. San Francisco is the windiest, with an average annual wind speed of 11 mph (18 km/hr). Tropical rainstorms occur often in California during the winter.

⁴FLORA AND FAUNA

Of the 48 conterminous states, California embraces the greatest diversity of climate and terrain. The state's six life zones are the lower Sonoran (desert); upper Sonoran (foothill regions and some coastal lands); transition (coastal areas and moist northeastern counties); and the Canadian, Hudsonian, and Arctic zones, comprising California's highest elevations.

Plant life in the arid climate of the lower Sonoran zone features a diversity of native cactus, mesquite, and paloverde. The Joshua tree (Yucca brevifolia) is found in the Mojave Desert. Flowering plants include the dwarf desert poppy and a variety of asters. Fremont cottonwood and valley oak grow in the Central Valley. The upper Sonoran zone includes the unique chaparral belt, characterized by forests of small shrubs, stunted trees, and herbaceous plants. Nemophila, mint, phacelia, viola, and the golden poppy (Eschscholtzia californica)—the state flower—also flourish in this zone, along with the lupine, more species of which occur here than anywhere else in the world.

The transition zone includes most of the state's forests, with such magnificent specimens as the redwood (Sequoia sempervirens) and "big tree" or giant sequoia (Sequoia gigantea), among the oldest living things on earth (some are said to have lived at least 4,000 years). Tanbark oak, California laurel, sugar pine, madrona, broad-leaved maple, and Douglas fir are also common. Forest floors are carpeted with swordfern, alumroot, barrenwort, and trillium, and there are thickets of huckleberry, azalea, elder, and wild currant. Characteristic wild flowers include varieties of mariposa, tulip, and tiger and leopard lilies.

The high elevations of the Canadian zone are abundant with Jeffrey pine, red fir, and lodgepole pine. Brushy areas are covered with dwarf manzanita and ceanothus; the unique Sierra puffball is also found here. Just below timberline, in the Hudsonian zone, grow the whitebark, foxtail, and silver pines. At approximately 10,500 ft (3,200 m) begins the Arctic zone, a treeless region whose flora includes a number of wild flowers, including Sierra primrose, yellow columbine, alpine buttercup, and alpine shooting star.

Common plants introduced into California include the eucalyptus, acacia, pepper tree, geranium, and Scotch broom. Among the numerous species found in California that are federally classified as endangered are the Contra Costa

California

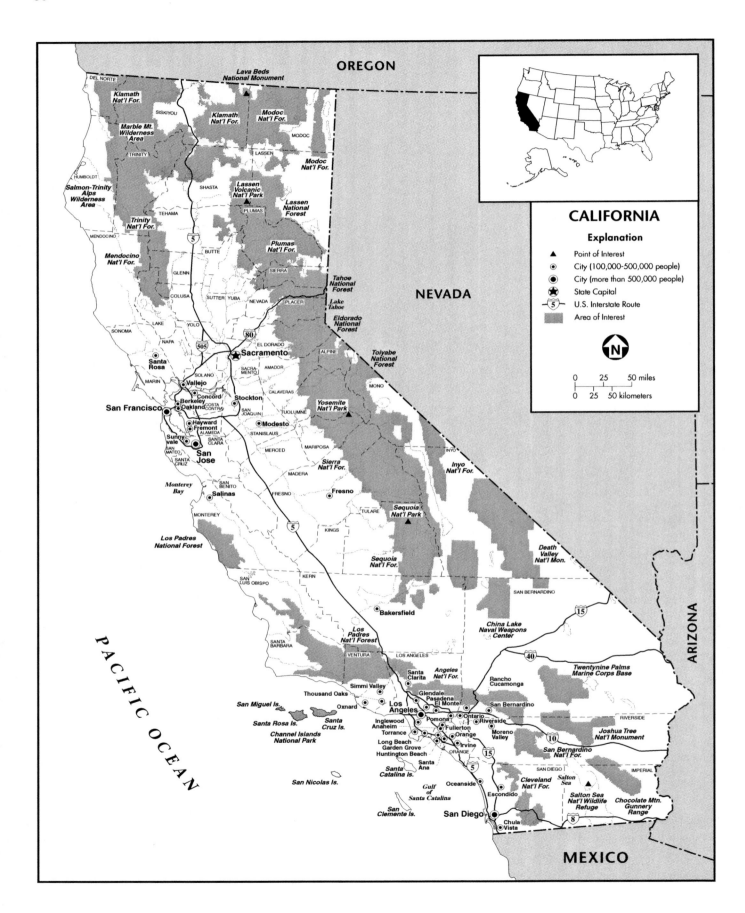

OREGON

Lava Beds
National Monument

DEL NORTE

Klamath
Nat'l For.

SISKIYOU

Klamath
Nat'l For.

Modoc
Nat'l For.

Marble Mt.
Wilderness
Area

TRINITY

MODOC

LASSEN

Modoc
Nat'l For.

HUMBOLDT

SHASTA

Salmon-Trinity
Alps Wilderness
Area

TEHAMA

Lassen
Volcanic
Nat'l Park

Lassen
National
Forest

PLUMAS

Trinity
Nat'l For.

BUTTE

MENDOCINO

Plumas
Nat'l For.

Mendocino
Nat'l For.

GLENN

SIERRA

COLUSA

Tahoe
National
Forest

NEVADA

LAKE

SUTTER

YUBA

PLACER

Lake
Tahoe

SONOMA

NAPA

YOLO

Eldorado
National
Forest

Santa
Rosa

MARIN

SOLANO

SACRA-
MENTO

Sacramento

EL DORADO

ALPINE

Toiyabe
National
Forest

NEVADA

Vallejo

AMADOR

Concord
Berkeley
Oakland

Stockton

CALAVERAS

San Francisco

COSTA
CONTRA

SAN
JOAQUIN

TUOLUMNE

MONO

Hayward
Fremont

ALAMEDA

Yosemite
Nat'l Park

Sunny-
vale

SANTA
CLARA

STANISLAUS

Modesto

San Jose

SAN
MATEO

SANTA
CRUZ

MERCED

MARIPOSA

Monterey
Bay

SAN
BENITO

Salinas

MADERA

Sierra
Nat'l For.

Inyo
Nat'l For.

MONTEREY

FRESNO

Fresno

INYO

Los Padres
National Forest

TULARE

Sequoia
Nat'l Park

KINGS

Sequoia
Nat'l For.

Death
Valley
Nat'l Mon.

SAN
LUIS
OBISPO

KERN

SAN BERNARDINO

Bakersfield

China Lake
Naval Weapons
Center

SANTA
BARBARA

Los
Padres
Nat'l Forest

Santa
Clarita

Angeles
Nat'l For.

Twentynine Palms
Marine Corps Base

VENTURA

LOS ANGELES

Rancho
Cucamonga

Simi Valley

Glendale
Pasadena
El Monte

San Bernardino

Thousand Oaks

Oxnard

Los
Angeles

Pomona
Ontario
Riverside

Inglewood
Anaheim
Torrance

Fullerton
Orange

Moreno
Valley

Long Beach
Garden Grove
Huntington Beach

Irvine

RIVERSIDE

San Miguel Is.

Santa Rosa Is.

Santa
Cruz Is.

Channel Islands
National Park

ORANGE

San Bernardino
Nat'l For.

Joshua Tree
Nat'l Monument

Santa
Ana

Cleveland
Nat'l For.

Salton
Sea

Santa
Catalina Is.

San Nicolas Is.

Oceanside

Escondido

Salton Sea
Nat'l Wildlife
Refuge

SAN DIEGO

IMPERIAL

Chocolate Mtn.
Gunnery
Range

Gulf
of
Santa Catalina

San
Clemente Is.

San Diego

Chula
Vista

MEXICO

PACIFIC OCEAN

ARIZONA

CALIFORNIA

Explanation

▲ Point of Interest

⊙ City (100,000-500,000 people)

◉ City (more than 500,000 people)

★ State Capital

—⑤— U.S. Interstate Route

▨ Area of Interest

Ⓝ

0   25   50 miles

0   25   50 kilometers

wallflower, Antioch Dunes evening primrose, Solano Grass, San Clemente Island larkspur, salt marsh bird's beak, McDonald's rock-cress, and Santa Barbara Island Liveforever. Eighty-five plant species were listed as threatened or endangered as of December 1997.

Mammals found in the deserts of the lower Sonoran zone include the jackrabbit, kangaroo rat, squirrel, and opossum. The Texas night owl, roadrunner, cactus wren, and various species of hawk are common birds, and the sidewinder, desert tortoise, and horned toad represent the area's reptilian life. The upper Sonoran zone is home to such mammals as the antelope, brown-footed woodrat, and ring-tailed cat. Birds distinctive to this zone are the California thrasher, bush tit, and California condor.

Animal life is abundant amid the forests of the transition zone. Colombian black-tailed deer, black bear, gray fox, cougar, bobcat, and Roosevelt elk are found. Garter snakes and rattlesnakes are common, as are such amphibians as the water-puppy and redwood salamander. The kingfisher, chickadee, towhee, and hummingbird represent the bird life of this region.

Mammals of the Canadian zone include the mountain weasel, snowshoe hare, Sierra chickaree, and several species of chipmunk. Conspicuous birds include the blue-fronted jay, Sierra hermit thrush, water ouzel, and Townsend solitaire. Birds become scarcer as one ascends to the Hudsonian zone, and the wolverine is now regarded as rare. Only one bird is native to the high Arctic region—the Sierra rosy finch—but others often visit, including the hummingbird and Clark nutcracker. Principal mammals of this region are also visitors from other zones; the Sierra coney and white-tailed jackrabbit make their homes here. The bighorn sheep also lives in this mountainous terrain; as of April 2003, the bighorn sheep was listed as endangered by the US Fish and Wildlife Service. Among fauna found throughout several zones are the mule deer, coyote, mountain lion, red-shafted flicker, and several species of hawk and sparrow.

Aquatic life in California is abundant, from the state's mountain lakes and streams to the rocky Pacific coastline. Many trout species are found, among them rainbow, golden, and Tahoe; migratory species of salmon are also common. Deep-sea life forms include sea bass, yellowfin tuna, barracuda, and several types of whale. Native to the cliffs of northern California are seals, sea lions, and many types of shorebirds, including several migratory species.

The Resources Agency of California's Department of Fish and Game is especially active in listing and providing protection for rare, threatened, and endangered fauna. Joint efforts by state and federal wildlife agencies have established an ambitious—if somewhat controversial—recovery program to revitalize the dwindling population of the majestic condor, the largest bird native to the US.

As of April 2003, 118 California animals were on the federal endangered list; 181 plants were listed as endangered or threatened. Endangered animals include the San Joaquin kit fox, Point Arena mountain beaver, Pacific pocket mouse, salt marsh harvest mouse, Morro Bay kangaroo rat (and five other species of kangaroo rat), Amargosa vole, California least tern, California condor, San Clemente loggerhead shrike, San Clemente sage sparrow, San Francisco garter snake, five species of salamander, three species of chub, and two species of pupfish. Eleven butterflies listed as endangered and two as threatened on the federal list are California species. Among threatened animals are the coastal California gnatcatcher, Paiute cutthroat trout, southern sea otter, and northern spotted owl. California has a total of 290,821 acres (117,6791 ha) of National Wildlife Refuges.

5ENVIRONMENTAL PROTECTION

Efforts to preserve natural wilderness areas in California go back at least to 1890, when the US Congress created three national parks in the Sierra Nevada: Sequoia, Grant (now part of Kings Canyon), and Yosemite. Three years later, some 4 million acres (1.6 million hectares) of the Sierra Nevada were set aside in national forests. In 1892, naturalist John Muir and other wilderness lovers founded the Sierra Club which, with other private groups of conservationists, has been influential in saving the Muir Woods and other stands of redwoods from the lumbermen's axes. Over the next century, numerous other natural areas were designated national parklands. Among the most recent were Death Valley National Park (1994), Joshua Tree National Park (1994), and "Rosie the Riveter" World War II Home Front National Historical Park (2000).

California's primary resource problem is water: the southern two-thirds of the state account for about 75% of annual water consumption but only 30% of the supply. Water has been diverted from the Sierra Nevada snow runoff and from the Colorado River to the cities and dry areas largely by means of aqueducts, some 700 mi (1,100 km) of which have been constructed in federal and state undertakings. In 1960, California embarked on one of the largest public works programs ever undertaken in the United States when voters approved a bond issue to construct the California Water Project, designed to deliver 1.4 trillion gallons of water annually to central and southern California for residential, industrial, and agricultural use. Other purposes of the project were to provide flood control, generate electric power, and create recreation areas.

Maintaining adequate water resources continued to be a problem in the 1990s. As the result of a US Supreme Court decision, southern California lost close to 20% of its water supply in December 1985, when a portion of the water it had been permitted to draw from the Colorado River was diverted to Arizona. In 1982, California voters turned down a proposal to build a canal that would have delivered water that flows into San Francisco Bay to southern California; no other plans to cope with the impending shortage were approved at that time. In December 1994 the state and federal governments joined together to form the Bay Delta Accord, intended to restore the environmentally threatened San Francisco Bay area through a combination of better conservation efforts and public and private investment. In November 1996 voters approved a bond issue valued at nearly $1 billion to implement the Accord.

Air pollution has been a serious problem since July 1943, when heavy smog enveloped Los Angeles for the first time; smog conditions in October 1954 forced the closing of the city's airport and harbor. Smog is caused by an atmospheric inversion of cold air that traps unburned hydrocarbons at ground level; perhaps two-thirds of the smog particles are created by automobile exhaust emissions. In 1960, the state legislature passed the first automobile antismog law in the nation, requiring that all cars be equipped with antismog exhaust devices within three years. (Federal laws controlling exhaust emissions on new cars came into effect in the 1970s.) The city's smog problem has since been reduced to manageable proportions, but pollution problems from atmospheric inversions still persist there and in other California cities. Nonetheless there is reason for optimism—in 1996, for example, Southern California had the best air quality ever measured in the post–World War II era. A key factor was introduction of a reformulated gasoline touted as the cleanest-burning in the world—which reduced polluting emissions by 15% when put into use in 1996. The state inspection-and-maintenance program is also being reformed and updated, focusing on the small number of cars linked to as much as 50% of vehicular pollution in the state.

In early 1995, the Environmental Protection Agency (EPA) approved a California ozone-reduction plan that ordered car manufacturers to design and produce cars that will be 50% to 84% cleaner than the ones sold in 1990. In 1998 new regulations were introduced to give tax credits to Californians who drove very low emission vehicles. In 2001 regulators proposed offering credits for use of a shared fleet of vehicles. California's plan that 10% of the 2003 cars offered for sale would be zero emission vehicles (ZEV) was not realized.

State land-reclamation programs have been important in providing new agricultural land and controlling flood damage. One of the earliest such programs, begun shortly before 1900, reclaimed 500,000 acres (200,000 hectares) by means of a network of dams, dikes, and canals in the swampy delta lying within the fork of the Sacramento and San Joaquin rivers. In 1887, a state law created irrigation districts in the southeastern region; the Imperial Valley was thus transformed from a waterless, sandy basin into some of the most productive agricultural land in the United States.

Flood control was one of the main purposes of the $2.6 billion Feather River Project in the Central Valley, completed during the 1970s. Ironically, in the western portion of the Central Valley, farmland is now threatened by irrigation water tainted by concentrated salts and other soil minerals, for which current drainage systems are inadequate. One drainage system, the San Luis Drain, originally intended to carry the water to San Francisco Bay, was stopped short of completion and goes only as far as the Kesterson National Wildlife Refuge, where, according to the US Fish and Wildlife Service, the tainted water has caused birth defects in birds.

In the 1980s, the state legislature enacted stringent controls on toxic waste. California has also been a leader in recycling waste products—for example, using acid waste from metal-processing plants as a soil additive in citrus orchards. In 2003, the Environmental Protection Agency's database listed 903 hazardous waste sites, 96 of which were on the National Priorities List, in California.

The California Department of Water Resources is responsible for maintaining adequate groundwater levels, enforcing water-quality standards, and controlling floodwaters. The state Department of Conservation has overall responsibility for conservation and protection of the state's soil, mineral, petroleum, geothermal, and marine resources. The California Coastal Commission, created in 1972, is designated by federal law to review projects that effect California's coastline, including offshore oil leasing, which has become a source of concern in recent years. In 2001, California received $320,783,000 in federal grants from the EPA; EPA expenditures for procurement contracts in California that year amounted to $41,087,000.

⁶POPULATION

About 12% of all Americans live in California, which ranked first in population among the 50 states in 2002 with an estimated total of 35,116,033, an increase of 3.7% since 2000. California replaced New York as the decennial census leader in 1970, with a total of 19,971,069 residents, and has lengthened its lead ever since. Between 1990 and 2000, California's population grew from 29,760,021 to 33,871,648, an increase of 13.8%. The population is projected to reach 49.3 million by 2025. Los Angeles is the second most populous city in the US, and Los Angeles County ranks first in population among all US counties.

In 2000 the median age was 33.3. Persons under 18 years old accounted for 27.3% of the population while only 10.6% were age 65 or older, lower than the national average of 12.4%

When Europeans first arrived in California, at least 300,000 Indians lived in the area. By 1845, the Indian population had been reduced to about 150,000. Although Spanish missions and settlements were well established in California by the late 18th century, the white population numbered only about 7,000 until the late 1840s. The Gold Rush brought at least 85,000 adventurers to the San Francisco Bay area by 1850, however, and the state's population increased rapidly thereafter. California's population grew to 379,994 by 1860 and had passed the one million mark within 30 years. Starting in 1890, the number of state residents just about doubled every two decades until the 1970s, when the population increased by 18.5%, down from the 27.1% increase of the 1960s. However, the total growth rate during the 1980s was 25.7%, reflecting a population increase of over 6 million.

More than 90% of California's residents live in metropolitan areas. The population density in 2000 was 217.2 persons per sq mi, up from 190.8 per sq mi in 1990. Densities in urban areas were much higher—7,873 per sq mi in Los Angeles and 16,632 per sq mi in San Francisco—the country's second most densely populated city, surpassed only by New York City. In 2000, only 10.6% of all Californians were over 65, lower than the national average of 12.7%.

The majority of Californians live in urban areas; 65% reside in metropolitan San Francisco and Los Angeles. Between 1997 and 2002 the largest population growth occurred mainly in the Central Valley and foothill counties, and in Riverside and San Bernardino Counties in Southern California. The five counties of Los Angeles, Orange, Riverside, San Bernardino, and San Diego accounted for 55% of California's total population in 2002, and 52% of the total increase in population since 1997. The city of Los Angeles had an estimated 2002 population of 3,798,981; San Diego, 1,259,532; San Jose, 894,943; San Francisco, 776,733; Long Beach, 472,412; Fresno, 445,227; Sacramento, 435,245; Oakland, 402,777; Santa Ana, 343,413; and Anaheim, 332,642. The first four all placed among the nation's 15 most populous cities in 2002.

Los Angeles, which expanded irregularly and lacks a central business district, nearly quadrupled its population from 319,000 in 1910 to 1,240,000 in 1930, and then doubled it to 2,479,000 by 1960. A major component of the city's population growth was the upsurge in the number of blacks after World War II, especially between 1960 and 1970, when the number of blacks increased from 335,000 to 504,000, many of them crowded into the deteriorating Watts section.

In 1999, the Los Angeles–Riverside–Orange County urban complex, with a total estimated population of 16,036,587, was the second most populous metropolitan area in the US (after that of New York). Other estimates for that year include the San Francisco–Oakland–San Jose area, 6,873,645; metropolitan San Diego, 2,820,844; and metropolitan Sacramento, 1,741,002.

⁷ETHNIC GROUPS

In 2000, California's foreign-born population numbered 8,864,255, or 26% of the state's total population, the largest percentage among the 50 states. Nearly one-third of all foreign-born persons in the US live in California. Latin Americans account for about half of foreign-born Californians, while Asians account for another third. As of 2002, nearly four-fifths of foreign-born Californians lived in the metropolitan areas of Los Angeles (5.1 million) and San Francisco (1.9 million).

The westward movement of American settlers in the third quarter of the 19th century, followed by German, Irish, North Italian, and Italian Swiss immigrants, overshadowed but did not obliterate California's Spanish heritage. In 2000, 10,966,556 (32.4%) of the state's residents were of Hispanic or Latino origin, up from 7,688,000 (25.8%) in 1990, and more than the total for any other state. The census of 2000 recorded that the majority—

California Counties, County Seats, and County Areas and Populations

COUNTY	COUNTY SEAT	LAND AREA (SQ MI)	POPULATION (2002 EST.)	COUNTY	COUNTY SEAT	LAND AREA (SQ MI)	POPULATION (2002 EST.)
Alameda	Oakland	735	1,472,310	Orange	Santa Ana	798	2,938,507
Alpine	Markleeville	739	1,200	Placer	Auburn	1,416	278,509
Amador	Jackson	589	36,657	Plumas	Quincy	2,573	20,890
Butte	Oroville	1,646	209,203	Riverside	Riverside	7,214	1,699,112
Calaveras	San Andreas	1,021	42,978	Sacramento	Sacramento	971	1,305,082
Colusa	Colusa	1,153	19,312	San Benito	Hollister	1,388	55,938
Contra Costa	Martinez	730	992,358	San Bernardino	San Bernardino	20,064	1,816,072
Del Norte	Crescent City	1,007	27,482	San Diego	San Diego	4,212	2,906,660
El Dorado	Placerville	1,715	165,744	San Francisco	San Francisco*	46	764,049
Fresno	Fresno	5,978	834,632	San Joaquin	Stockton	1,415	614,302
Glenn	Willows	1,319	26,623	San Luis Obispo	San Luis Obispo	3,308	253,408
Humboldt	Eureka	3,579	127,159	San Mateo	Redwood City	447	703,202
Imperial	El Centro	4,173	146,248	Santa Barbara	Santa Barbara	2,748	403,084
Inyo	Independence	10,223	18,214	Santa Clara	San Jose	1,293	1,683,505
Kern	Bakersfield	8,130	694,059	Santa Cruz	Santa Cruz	446	253,814
Kings	Hanford	1,392	135,043	Shasta	Redding	3,786	171,799
Lake	Lakeport	1,262	61,9970	Sierra	Downieville	959	3,552
Lassen	Susanville	4,553	34,007	Siskiyou	Yreka	6,281	44,103
Los Angeles	Los Angeles	4,070	9,806,577	Solano	Fairfield	834	411,072
Madera	Madera	2,145	130,265	Sonoma	Santa Rosa	1,604	468,386
Marin	San Rafael	523	247,581	Stanislaus	Modesto	1,506	482,440
Mariposa	Mariposa	1,456	17,195	Sutter	Yuba City	602	82,580
Mendocino	Ukiah	3,512	87,240	Tehama	Red Bluff	2,953	57,472
Merced	Merced	1,944	225,398	Trinity	Weaverville	3,190	13,174
Modoc	Alturas	4,064	9,289	Tulare	Visalia	4,808	381,772
Mono	Bridgeport	3,019	13,117	Tuolumne	Sonora	2,234	55,850
Monterey	Salinas	3,303	413,408	Ventura	Ventura	1,862	783,920
Napa	Napa	744	130,268	Yolo	Woodland	1,014	180,856
Nevada	Nevada City	960	95,047	Yuba	Marysville	640	62,339
				TOTALS		156,299	35,116,033

*The city and county of San Francisco are coterminous.

8,455,926, up from 5,322,170 in 1990—were Mexican-Americans; there were also 140,570 Puerto Ricans and 72,286 Cubans. After World War II, the Hispanic communities of Los Angeles, San Diego, and other southern California cities developed strong political organizations. Increasing numbers of Mexican-Americans have won local, state, and federal elective office, though their potential remains unrealized.

In 2000 California had the largest Asian population of any state—3,697,513 (up from 2,846,000 in 1990), or 10.9% of the state's total population (the 2nd-highest percentage in the nation). In the same year there were 116,961 Pacific Islanders (including more native Hawaiians than in any state except Hawaii). Chinese workers were first brought to California between 1849 and 1882, when the Chinese Exclusion Act was passed by Congress. In 2000 the Chinese constituted the largest group among California's Asian population, numbering 980,642, or 2.9% of the population. The nation's oldest and largest Chinatown is in San Francisco. Although Chinese-Americans, as they prospered, moved to suburban areas, the seats of the powerful nationwide and worldwide merchant and clan associations are in that city. Los Angeles also has a Chinese district.

The Japanese, spread throughout the western seaboard states, were engaged mainly in agriculture, along with fishing and small business, until their removal and internment during World War II. After the war, some continued in market gardening and other family agriculture, but most, deprived of their landholdings, entered urban occupations, including the professions; many dispersed to other regions of the country. In 2000 there were 288,854 Japanese in California, down from 353,251 in 1990.

After the Chinese, the most populous Asian group in California in 2000 was the Filipino community, with 918,678, or 2.7% of the total state population. In 2000 California also had

345,882 Koreans, 447,032 Vietnamese (up from 242,946 in 1990), 314,819 Asian Indians (up from 112,560), 55,456 Laotians, 20,571 native Hawaiians (down from 43,418 in 1990), 37,498 Samoans, and 20,918 Guamanians.

American Indians and Alaska natives numbered around 333,346 in 2000 (up from 242,000 in 1990), the greatest number of any state in the country. The figure for American Indians includes Indians native to California and many others coaxed to resettle there under a policy that sought to terminate tribal status. Along with the remaining indigenous tribes in California, there is also a large urban Indian population, especially in Los Angeles, which has more Indians than any other US city. Many of the urban Indians were unprepared for the new kind of life and unable to earn an adequate living; militant Indians have made dramatic, but on the whole unsuccessful, protests aimed at bettering their condition.

Black Americans constitute a smaller proportion of California's population than of the nation's as a whole: less than 7% in 2000. Nevertheless, California still had the fifth-largest black population, numbering 2,263,882. Considerable migration of blacks took place during World War II, when defense industries on the West Coast offered new opportunities.

8LANGUAGES

The speakers of Russian, Spanish, and English who first came to what is now California found an amazing diversity of Indian cultures, ranging from the Wiyot in the north to the Yokuts in the Central Valley and the Diegueño in the south, and of Indian languages, representing four great language families—Athapaskan, Penutian, Kokan-Siouan, and Aztec. Yet, except for place names such as Shasta, Napa, and Yuba, they have not lent any of their words to California speech.

As in much of the West, California English is a composite of the eastern dialects and subdialects brought by the continuing westward migration from the eastern states, first for gold and timber, then for farming, for diversified manufacture, for Hollywood, and for retirement. The interior valley is Midland-oriented with such retained terms as *piece* (a between-meals lunch), *quarter till, barn lot* (barnyard), *dog irons* (andirons), and *snake feder and snake doctor* (dragonfly), but generally, in both northern and southern California, Northern dominates the mixture of North Midland and South Midland speech in the same communities. Northern *sick to the stomach*, for example, dominates Midland *sick at* and *sick in*, with a 46% frequency; Northern *angleworm* has 53% frequency, as compared with 21% for Midland *fishworm*; and Northern *string beans* has 80% frequency, as compared with 17% North Midland *green beans* and South Midland and Southern *snap beans*. Northern *comforter* was used by 94% of the informants interviewed in a state survey; Midland *comfort* by only 21%. Dominant is Northern /krik/ as the pronunciation of *creek*, but Midland *bucket* has a greater frequency than Northern *pail*, and the Midland /greezy/ for *greasy* is scattered throughout the state. Similarly, the distinction between the /wh/ in *wheel* and the /w/ of *weal* is lost in the use of simple /w/ in both words, and *cot* and *caught* sound alike, as do caller and collar.

There are some regional differences. San Francisco, for instance has *sody* or *soda water* for a soft drink; there the large sandwich is a *grinder*, while in Sacramento it is either a *poor Joe* or a *submarine*. Notable is the appearance of *chesterfield* (meaning sofa or davenport), found in the Bay region and from San Jose to Sacramento; this sense is common in Canada but now found nowhere else in the US. Boonville, a village about 100 mi (160 km) north of San Francisco, is notorious for "Boontling," a local dialect contrived in the mid-19th century by Scotch-Irish settlers who wanted privacy and freedom from obscenities in their conversation. Now declining in use, Boontling has about 1,000 vocabulary replacements of usual English words, together with some unusual pronunciations and euphemisms.

As the nation's major motion picture, radio, and television entertainment center, Los Angeles has influenced English throughout the nation—even the world—by making English speakers of many dialects audible and visible and by making known new terms and new meanings. It has thus been instrumental in reducing dialectal extremes and in developing increased language awareness.

California's large foreign-language populations have posed major educational problems. In 1974, a landmark San Francisco case, *Lau v. Nichols*, brought a decision from the US Supreme Court that children who do not know English should not thereby be handicapped in school, but should receive instruction in their native tongue while learning English. California's Chacon-Moscone law required native-language instruction, but the law expired in 1987. In 1997, a federal judge ruled against an injunction that had blocked English immersion classes in Orange County. The ruling ended the bilingual education program in the school district and opened the possibility for a statewide vote in June 1998 to decide if non-English-speaking students will be permitted to learn English upon entering public schools. On 2 June 1998 California voters enacted Proposition 227, which called for students to be taught English by being submerged in English language classrooms.

In 2000, 19,014,873 Californians—or 60.5% of the population five years old or over—reported speaking only English at home, down from 68.5% in 1990.

The following table gives selected statistics from the 2000 census for language spoken at home by persons five years old and over.

LANGUAGE	NUMBER	PERCENT
Population 5 years and over	**31,416,629**	**100.0**
Speak only English	19,014,873	60.5
Speak a language other than English	12,401,756	39.5
Speak a language other than English	**12,401,756**	**39.5**
Spanish or Spanish Creole	8,105,505	25.8
Chinese	815,386	2.6
Tagalog	626,399	2.0
Vietnamese	407,119	1.3
Korean	298,076	0.9
Armenian	155,237	0.5
Japanese	154,633	0.5
Persian	154,321	0.5
German	141,671	0.5
French (incl. Patois, Cajun)	135,067	0.4
Russian	118,382	0.4

9 RELIGIONS

The first Roman Catholics in California were Spanish friars, who established 21 Franciscan missions from San Diego to Sonoma between 1769 and 1823. After an independent Mexican government began to secularize the missions in 1833, the Indian population at the missions declined from about 25,000 to only about 7,000 in 1840. With the American acquisition of California in 1848, the Catholic Church was reorganized to include the archdiocese of San Francisco.

Protestant ministers accompanied migrant miners during the gold rush, founding 32 churches in San Francisco by 1855. These early Protestants included Baptists, Congregationalists, Methodists, Presbyterians, and Episcopalians; a group of Mormons had arrived by ship via Cape Horn in 1846. The Midwesterners who began arriving in large numbers in the 1880s were mostly Protestants who settled in southern California. By 1900, the number of known Christians in the state totaled 674,000, out of a population of nearly 1,500,000.

Small Jewish communities were established throughout California by 1861 and, in 1880, the Jewish population was estimated at 18,580.

The mainstream religions did not satisfy everybody's needs, however, and in the early 20th century, many dissident sects sprang up, including such organizations as Firebrands for Jesus, the Psychosomatic Institute, the Mystical Order of Melchizedek, the Infinite Science Church, and Nothing Impossible, among many others.

Perhaps the best-known founder of a new religion was Canadian-born Aimee Semple McPherson, who preached her Foursquare Gospel during the 1920s at the Angelus Temple in Los Angeles, won a large radio audience and thousands of converts, and established 240 branches of her church throughout the state before her death in 1944. She was typical of the many charismatic preachers of new doctrines who gave—and still give—California its exotic religious flavor. Since World War II, religions such as Zen Buddhism and Scientology have won enthusiastic followings, along with various cults devoted to self-discovery and self-actualization.

Nevertheless, the large majority of religious adherents in California continue to follow traditional faiths. In 2000, there were 10,079,310 Roman Catholics in 1,315 congregations. The next largest religion is Judaism with 994,000 adherents in 425 congregations. The Latter-day Saints follow with 529,575 adherents in 1,316 congregations. The largest Protestant churches include Southern Baptist, 471,119; Assembly of God, 310,522; Presbyterian Church USA, 229,918; and the United Methodist Church, 228,844. In 2000, there were 489 Buddhist, 131, Hindu, and 163 Muslim congregations in the state. About 53.9% of the population were not counted as members of any religious organization.

The Church of Scientology in Los Angeles, established in 1954 by the religions founder L. Ron Hubbard, is religions largest facility and also serves as a training center for leaders. The Crystal Cathedral opened in 1980 in Garden Grove, California, is the home base for the international Crystal Cathedral Ministries and the internationally televised *Hour of Power*. Dr. Robert H. Schuller, a minister of the Reformed Church in America presides over a congregation of over 10,000 members.

[10] TRANSPORTATION

California has—and for decades has had—more motor vehicles than any other state, and ranked second only to Texas in interstate highway mileage in 2000. An intricate 8,300-mi (13,400-km) network of urban interstate highways, expressways, and freeways is one of the engineering wonders of the modern world—but the traffic congestion in the state's major cities during rush hours may well be the worst in the country. In 2000, California had a total of 168,076 mi (270,492 km) of public roads, streets, and highways.

In pioneer days, the chief modes of transportation were sailing ships and horse-drawn wagons; passage by sea from New York took three months, and the overland route from Missouri was a six-week journey. The gold rush spurred development of more rapid transport. The state's first railroad, completed in 1856, was a 25-mi (40-km) line from Sacramento northeast to Folsom, in the mining country. The Central Pacific–Union Pacific transcontinental railroad, finished 13 years later, was financed in part by several Sacramento business leaders, including Leland Stanford, who became governor of the state in 1861, the same year he assumed the presidency of the Central Pacific. Railroad construction crews, mostly imported Chinese laborers, started from Sacramento and dug and blasted the route through the solid granite of the Sierra Nevada and then across the Nevada desert, linking up with the Union Pacific at Promontory, Utah, on 10 May 1869. Stanford himself helped to drive the golden spike that marked the historic occasion. The Southern Pacific completed a line from Sacramento to Los Angeles in 1876 and another to Texas the following year. Other railroads took much longer to build; the coastal railroad from San Francisco to Los Angeles was not completed until 1901, and another line to Eureka was not finished until 1914. The railroads dominated transportation in the state until motor vehicles came into widespread use in the 1920s.

As of 2000, California had 7,710 rail mi (12,408 km) of track, with Class I track constituting 75%; Class I railroads operating within the state in 2000 included Burlington Northern and Santa Fe Railway and Union Pacific. Amtrak passenger trains connect the state's major population centers with an average of 38 inter-city trains and an additional 170 commuter trains every day.

Urban transit began in San Francisco in 1861 with horse-drawn streetcars. Cable-car service was introduced in 1873; a few cable cars are still in use, mainly for the tourist trade. The 71-mi (114-km) Bay Area Rapid Transit System (BART) was completed in the 1970s despite many mechanical problems and costly delays. BART connects San Francisco with Oakland by high-speed, computerized subway trains via a 3.6-mi (5.8-km) tunnel under San Francisco Bay and runs north-south along the San Francisco peninsula.

Public transit in the Los Angeles metropolitan area was provided by electric trolleys beginning in 1887. By the early 1930s, the Los Angeles Railway carried 70% of the city's transit passengers, and in 1945 its trolleys transported 109 million passengers. Competition from buses—which provided greater mobility, but aggravated the city's smog and congestion problems—forced the trolleys to end service in 1961. During the late 1980s, plans were developed for a commuter rail transportation system in the Southern California region. In 1992, the first three lines of the Metrolink system began operation. By 1995, six Metrolink lines were serving the counties of Los Angeles, Orange, Riverside, San Bernardino, and Ventura.

California's extensive highway system had its beginning in the mid-19th century, when stagecoaches began hauling freight to the mining camps from San Francisco, Sacramento, and San Jose. In the early 1850s, two stagecoach lines, Adams and Wells Fargo, expanded their routes and began to carry passengers; by 1860, some 250 stagecoach companies were operating in the state. The decline of stagecoach service corresponded with the rise of the railroads. In 1910, at a time when only 36,000 motor vehicles were registered in the state, the California Highway Commission was established. Among its first acts was the issuance of $18 million in bonds for road construction, and the state's first paved highway was constructed in 1912. The number of automobiles surged to 604,000 by 1920; by 1929, about 1 of every 11 cars in the US belonged to a Californian. Ironically, in view of the state's subsequent traffic problems, the initial effect of the automobile was to disperse the population to outlying areas, thus reducing traffic congestion in the cities.

The Pasadena Freeway, the first modern expressway in California, opened in 1941. During the 1960s and 1970s, the state built a complex toll-free highway network linking most cities of more than 5,000 population, tying in with the federal highway system, and costing more than $10 billion. Local, state, and federal authorities combined spent over $9.3 billion on California highways in 1997, nearly $2 billion of that amount for maintenance. Also in 1997, federal aid to California from the Federal Highway Administration fund totaled about $2 billion.

By providing easy access to beach and mountain recreation areas, the new freeways—in combination with the favorable climate and low price of gasoline—further encouraged the use of the automobile and led to massive traffic tie-ups, contributed to the decline of public transit, and worsened the coastal cities' air-pollution problems. Los Angeles County claims more automobiles, more miles of streets, and more intersections than any other city in the US. The greatest inducement to automobile travel in and out of San Francisco was the completion in 1936 of the 8-mi (13-km) San Francisco–Oakland Bay Bridge. The following year saw the opening of the magnificent Golden Gate Bridge, which at 4,200 ft (1,280 m) was the world's longest suspension bridge until New York's Verrazano–Narrows Bridge opened to traffic in 1964.

In 2000, California had 168,076 mi (270,492 km) of public roads. Included in this total were 83,428 mi (134,264 km) of roads classified as rural and 84,648 mi (136,227 km) classified as urban. Also in 2000, the state registered 28,146,424 motor vehicles, first in the nation—including 17,321,413 automobiles, 10,329,198 trucks, and 47,312 buses. California also leads the nation in private and commercial motorcycle registrations, at 448,501. There were 21,243,939 California drivers' licenses in force in 2000.

The large natural harbors of San Francisco and San Diego monopolized the state's maritime trade until 1912 when Los Angeles began developing port facilities at San Pedro by building a breakwater that eventually totaled 8 mi (13 km) in length. In 1924, Los Angeles surpassed San Francisco in shipping tonnage handled and became one of the busiest ports on the Pacific coast. In 2000, the port at Long Beach handled 70.1 million tons of cargo. The port at Los Angeles handled 48.2 million tons in 2000. Other main ports and their 2000 cargo quantities include Richmond, 19.5 million tons; Oakland, 12.2 million tons; and San Diego, with 3.7 million tons.

In 2002, California had nearly 935 aircraft facilities, including 539 airports, 383 heliports, 11 seaplane bases, and 2 stolports. California's most active air terminal—and one of the nation's most active—is Los Angeles International Airport, which handled enplaned 32,167,896 passengers in 2000. Also among the nation's 20 busiest air traffic control towers in 2000 were those at San Diego, Oakland, San Jose, Sacramento, Santa Ana, and San Francisco.

11HISTORY

The region now known as California has been populated for at least 10,000 years, and possibly far longer. Estimates of the prehistoric Indian population have varied widely, but it is clear that California was one of the most densely populated areas north of Mexico. On the eve of European discovery, at least 300,000 Indians lived there. This large population was divided into no fewer than 105 separate tribes or nations speaking at least 100 different languages and dialects, about 70% of which were as mutually unintelligible as English and Chinese. No area of comparable size in North America, and perhaps the world, contained a greater variety of native languages and cultures than did aboriginal California.

In general, the California tribes depended for their subsistence on hunting, fishing, and gathering the abundant natural food resources. Only in a few instances, notably along the Colorado River, did the Indians engage in agriculture. Reflecting the mild climate of the area, their housing and dress were often minimal. The basic unit of political organization was the village community, consisting of several small villages, or the family unit. For the most part, these Indians were sedentary people: they occupied village sites for generations, and only rarely warred with their neighbors.

European contact with California began early in the Age of Discovery, and was a product of the two great overseas enterprises of 16th-century Europe: the search for a western passage to the East and the drive to control the riches of the New World. In 1533, Hernán Cortés, Spanish conqueror of the Aztecs, sent a naval expedition northward along the western coast of Mexico in search of new wealth. The expedition led to the discovery of Baja California (now part of Mexico), mistakenly described by the pilot of the voyage, Fortún Jiménez, as an island. Two years later, Cortés established a settlement on the peninsula at present-day La Paz, but because Baja California seemed barren of any wealth, the project was soon abandoned. The only remaining interest in California was the search for the western mouth of the transcontinental canal—a mythical waterway the Spanish called the Strait of Anian. In 1542, Juan Rodriquez Cabrillo led a voyage of exploration up the western coast in a futile search for the strait. On 28 September, Cabrillo landed at the bay now known as San Diego, thus becoming the first European discoverer of Alta (or Upper) California.

European interest in the Californias waned in the succeeding decades, and California remained for generations beyond the periphery of European activity in the New World. Subsequent contact was limited to occasional landfalls by Manila galleons, such as those of Pedro de Unamuno (1587) and Sebastián Cermeno (1595), and the tentative explorations of Sebastián Vizcaino in 1602–3.

Spanish interest in California revived during the late 18th century, largely because Spain's imperial rivals were becoming increasingly aggressive. For strategic and defensive reasons, Spain decided to establish permanent settlements in the north. In 1769, José de Gálvez, visitor-general in New Spain, selected the president of the Franciscan missions in Baja California, Father Junípero Serra, to lead a group of missionaries on an expedition to Alta California. Accompanying Serra was a Spanish military force under Gaspar de Portolá. This Portolá-Serra expedition marks the beginning of permanent European settlement in California. Over the next half-century, the 21 missions established by the Franciscans along the Pacific coast from San Diego to San Francisco formed the core of Hispanic California. Among the prominent missions were San Diego de Alcalá

(founded in 1769), San Francisco de Asis (1776), Santa Barbara (1786), and San José (1797). During most of the Spanish period, Mission San Carlos Borromeo (1770), at Carmel, was the ecclesiastical headquarters of the province, serving as the residence of the president-general of the Alta California missions.

These missions were more than just religious institutions. The principal concern of the missionaries was to convert the Indians to Christianity—a successful enterprise, if the nearly 88,000 baptisms performed during the mission period are any measure. The Franciscans also sought to bring about a rapid and thorough cultural transformation. The Indians were taught to perform a wide variety of new tasks: making bricks, tiles, pottery, shoes, saddles, wine, candles, and soap; herding horses, cattle, sheep, and goats; and planting, irrigating, and harvesting. In addition to transforming the way of life of the California Indians, the missions also reduced their number by at least 35,000. About 60% of this decline was due to the introduction of new diseases, especially those of the nonepidemic and venereal type.

Spain also established several military and civilian settlements in California. The four military outposts, or presidios, at San Diego (1769), Monterey (1770), San Francisco (1776), and Santa Barbara (1783) served to discourage foreign influence in the region and to contain Indian resistance. The presidio at Monterey also served as the political capital, headquarters for the provincial governors appointed in Mexico City. The first civilian settlement, or pueblo, was established at San José de Guadalupe in 1777, with 14 families from the Monterey and San Francisco presidios. The pueblo settlers, granted supplies and land by the government, were expected to provide the nearby presidios with their surplus agricultural products. The second pueblo was founded at Los Angeles (1781), and a third, Branciforte, was established near present-day Santa Cruz in 1797.

During the 40 years following the establishment of the Los Angeles pueblo, Spain did little to strengthen its outposts in Alta California. The province remained sparsely populated and isolated from other centers of Hispanic civilization. During these years, the Spanish-speaking population of 600 grew nearly fivefold, but this expansion was almost entirely due to natural increase rather than immigration.

Spanish control of California ended with the successful conclusion of the Mexican Revolution in 1821. For the next quarter-century, California was a province of the independent nation of Mexico. Although California gained a measure of self-rule with the establishment of a provincial legislature, the real authority still remained with the governor appointed in Mexico City. The most important issues in Mexican California were the secularization of the missions, the replacement of the Franciscans with parish or "secular" clergy, and the redistribution of the vast lands and herds the missions controlled. Following the secularization proclamation of Governor José Figueroa in 1834, the Mexican government authorized more than 600 rancho grants in California to Mexican citizens. The legal limit of an individual grant was 11 square leagues (about 76 sq mi, 197 sq km), but many large landholding families managed to obtain multiple grants.

The rancho economy, like that of the missions, was based on the cultivation of grain and the raising of huge herds of cattle. The rancheros traded hides and tallow for manufactured goods from foreign traders along the coast. As at the missions, herding, slaughtering, hide tanning, tallow rendering, and all the manual tasks were performed by Indian laborers. By 1845, on the eve of American acquisition, the non-Indian population of the region stood at about 7,000.

During the Mexican period, California attracted a considerable minority of immigrants from the US. Americans first came to California in the late 18th century in pursuit of the sea otter, a marine mammal whose luxurious pelts were gathered in

California waters and shipped to China for sale. Later, the hide and tallow trade attracted Yankee entrepreneurs, many of whom became resident agents for American commercial firms. Beginning in 1826, with the arrival overland of Jedediah Strong Smith's party of beaver trappers, the interior of California also began to attract a growing number of Americans. The first organized group to cross the continent for the purpose of settlement in California was the Bidwell-Bartleson party of 1841. Subsequent groups of overland pioneers included the ill-fated Donner party of 1846, whose members, stranded by a snowstorm near the Sierra Nevada summit, resorted to cannibalism so that 47 of the 87 travelers could survive.

Official American efforts to acquire California began during the presidency of Andrew Jackson in the 1830s, but it was not until the administration of James K. Polk that such efforts were successful. Following the American declaration of war against Mexico on 13 May 1846, US naval forces, under command of Commodores John D. Sloat and Robert F. Stockton, launched an assault along the Pacific coast, while a troop of soldiers under Stephen W. Kearny crossed overland. On 13 January 1847, the Mexican forces in California surrendered. More than a year later, after protracted fighting in central Mexico, a treaty of peace was signed at Guadalupe-Hidalgo on 2 February 1848. Under the terms of the treaty, Mexico ceded California and other territories to the US in exchange for $15 million and the assumption by the US of some $3 million in claims by Mexican citizens.

Just nine days before the treaty was signed, James Wilson Marshall discovered gold along the American River in California. The news of the gold discovery, on 24 January 1848, soon spread around the globe, and a massive rush of people poured into the region. By the end of 1848, about 6,000 miners had obtained $10 million worth of gold. During 1849, production was two or three times as large, but the proceeds were spread among more than 40,000 miners. In 1852, the peak year of production, about $80 million in gold was mined in the state, and during the century following its discovery, the total output of California gold amounted to nearly $2 billion.

California's census population quadrupled during the 1850s, reaching nearly 380,000 by 1860, and continued to grow at a rate twice that of the nation as a whole in the 1860s and 1870s. The new population of California was remarkably diverse. The 1850 census found that nearly a quarter of all Californians were foreign-born, while only a tenth of the national population had been born abroad. In succeeding decades, the percentage of foreign-born Californians increased, rising to just under 40% during the 1860s.

One of the most serious problems facing California in the early years of the gold rush was the absence of adequate government. Miners organized more than 500 "mining districts" to regulate their affairs; in San Francisco and other cities, "vigilance committees" were formed to combat widespread robbery and arson. The US Congress, deadlocked over the slavery controversy, failed to provide any form of legal government for California from the end of the Mexican War until its admission as a state in the fall of 1850. Taking matters into their own hands, 48 delegates gathered at a constitutional convention in Monterey in September 1849 to draft a fundamental law for the state. The completed constitution contained several unique features, but most of its provisions were based on the constitutions of Iowa and New York. To the surprise of many, the convention decided by unanimous vote to exclude slavery from the state. After considerable debate, the delegates also established the present boundaries of California. Adopted on 10 October, the constitution was ratified by the voters on 13 November 1849; at the same time, Californians elected their first state officials. California soon petitioned Congress for admission as a state, having bypassed the preliminary territorial stage, and was admitted after southern objections to the creation of another free state were overcome by adoption of the stringent new Fugitive Slave Law. On 9 September 1850, President Millard Fillmore signed the admission bill, and California became the 31st state to enter the union.

The early years of statehood were marked by racial discrimination and considerable ethnic conflict. Indian and white hostilities were intense; the Indian population declined from an estimated 150,000 in 1845 to less than 30,000 by 1870. In 1850, the state legislature enacted a foreign miners' license tax, aimed at eliminating competition from Mexican and other Latin American miners. The Chinese, who replaced the Mexicans as the state's largest foreign minority, soon became the target of a new round of discrimination. By 1852, 25,000 Chinese were in California, representing about a tenth of the state's population. The legislature enacted new taxes aimed at Chinese miners, and passed an immigration tax (soon declared unconstitutional) on Chinese immigrants.

Controversy also centered on the status of the Mexican ranchos, those vast estates created by the Mexican government that totaled more than 13 million acres (5 million hectares) by 1850. The Treaty of Guadalupe-Hidalgo had promised that property belonging to Mexicans in the ceded territories would be "inviolably protected." Nevertheless, in the early years of statehood, thousands of squatters took up residence on the rancho lands. Ultimately, about three-fourths of the original Mexican grants were confirmed by federal commissions and courts; however, the average length of time required for confirmation was 17 years. During the lengthy legal process, many of the grantees either sold parts of their grants to speculators or assigned portions to their attorneys for legal fees. By the time title was confirmed, the original grantees were often bankrupt and benefited little from the decision.

Despite the population boom during the gold rush, California remained isolated from the rest of the country until completion of the transcontinental railroad in 1869. Under terms of the Pacific Railroad Act of 1862, the Central Pacific was authorized by Congress to receive long-term federal loans and grants of land, about 12,500 acres per mi (3,100 hectares per km) of track, to build the western link of the road. The directors of the California corporation—Leland Stanford, Collis P. Huntington, Charles Crocker, and Mark Hopkins, who became known as the Big Four—exercised enormous power in the affairs of the state. Following completion of the Central Pacific, the Big Four constructed additional lines within California, as well as a second transcontinental line, the Southern Pacific, providing service from southern California to New Orleans.

To a degree unmatched anywhere in the nation, the Big Four established a monopoly of transportation in California and the Far West. Eventually the Southern Pacific, as the entire system came to be known after 1884, received from the federal government a total of 11,588,000 acres (4,690,000 hectares), making it the largest private landowner in the state. Opponents of the railroad charged that it had established not only a transportation monopoly but also a corrupt political machine and a "land monopoly" in California. Farmers in the San Joaquin Valley became involved in a protracted land dispute with the Southern Pacific, a controversy that culminated in a bloody episode in 1880, known as the Battle of Mussel Slough, in which seven men were killed. This incident, later dramatized by novelist Frank Norris in The Octopus (1901), threw into sharp relief the hostility between many Californians and the state's largest corporation.

In the late 19th century, California's economy became more diversified. The early dependence on gold and silver mining was overcome through the development of large-scale irrigation projects and the expansion of commercial agriculture. Southern

California soon was producing more than two-thirds of the nation's orange crop, and more than 90% of its lemons. The population of southern California boomed in the 1880s, fueled by the success of the new citrus industry, an influx of invalids seeking a warmer climate, and a railroad rate war between the Southern Pacific and the newly completed Santa Fe. For a time, the tariff from Kansas City to Los Angeles fell to a dollar a ticket. Real estate sales in Los Angeles County alone exceeded $200 million in 1887.

During the early 20th century, California's population growth became increasingly urban. Between 1900 and 1920, the population of the San Francisco Bay area doubled, while residents of metropolitan Los Angeles increased fivefold. On 18 April 1906, San Francisco's progress was interrupted by the most devastating earthquake ever to strike California. The quake and the fires that raged for three days killed at least 452 people, razed the city's business section, and destroyed some 28,000 buildings. The survivors immediately set to work to rebuild the city, and completed about 20,000 new buildings within three years.

By 1920, the populations of the two urban areas were roughly equal, about 1 million each. As their population grew, the need for additional water supplies became critical, and both cities became involved in bitter "water fights" with other state interests. Around 1900, San Francisco proposed the damming of the Tuolumne River at the Hetch Hetchy Valley to form a reservoir for the city's water system. Conservationist John Muir and the Sierra Club objected strongly to the proposal, arguing that the Hetch Hetchy was as important a natural landmark as neighboring Yosemite Valley. The conservationists lost the battle, and the valley was flooded. (The dam there is named for Michael O'Shaughnessy, San Francisco's city engineer from 1912 to 1932 and the builder of many of California's water systems.) When Los Angeles began its search for new water supplies, it soon became embroiled in a long controversy over access to the waters of the Owens River. The city constructed a 250-mi (400-km) aqueduct that eventually siphoned off nearly the entire flow of the river, thus jeopardizing the agricultural development of Owens Valley. Residents of the valley dramatized their objection to the project by dynamiting sections of the completed aqueduct.

Important movements for political reform began simultaneously in San Francisco and Los Angeles in the early 20th century. Corruption in the administration of San Francisco Mayor Eugene Schmitz led to a wide-ranging public investigation and to a series of trials of political and business leaders. Meanwhile, in Los Angeles, a coalition of reformers persuaded the city to adopt a new charter with progressive features such as initiative, referendum, and recall. Progressive Republican Hiram Johnson won the governorship in 1910, and reformers gained control of both houses of the state legislature in 1911. Subsequent reform legislation established effective regulation of the railroads and other public utilities, greater governmental efficiency, female suffrage, closer regulation of public morality, and workers' compensation.

During the first half of the 20th century, California's population growth far outpaced that of the nation as a whole. The state's climate, natural beauty, and romantic reputation continued to attract many, but new economic opportunities were probably most important. In the early 1920s, major discoveries of oil were made in the Los Angeles Basin, and for several years during the decade, California ranked 1st among the states in production of crude oil. The population of Los Angeles County more than doubled during the decade, rising to 2,208,492 by 1930. Spurred by the availability and low price of petroleum products and by an ever expanding system of public roadways, Los Angeles also became the most thoroughly motorized and automobile-conscious city in the world. By 1925, Los Angeles

had one automobile for every three persons—more than twice the national average.

Even during the 1930s, when California shared in the nationwide economic depression, hundreds of thousands of refugees streamed into the state from the dust bowl of the southern Great Plains. The film industry, which offered at least the illusion of prosperity to millions of Americans, continued to prosper during the depression. By 1940 there were more movie theaters in the US than banks, and the films they showed were almost all California products.

Politics in the Golden State in the 1930s spawned splinter movements like the Townsend Plan and the "Ham'n' Eggs" Plan, both of which advocated cash payments for the elderly. In 1934, Socialist author Upton Sinclair won the Democratic gubernatorial nomination with a plan called End Poverty In California (EPIC), but he lost the general election to the Republican incumbent, Frank Merriam.

During World War II, the enormous expansion of military installations, shipyards, and aircraft plants attracted millions of new residents to California. The war years also saw an increase in the size and importance of ethnic minorities. By 1942, only Mexico City had a larger urban Mexican population than Los Angeles. During the war, more than 93,000 Japanese-Americans in California—most of whom were US citizens and American-born—were interned in "relocation centers" throughout the Far West.

California continued to grow rapidly during the postwar period, as agricultural, aerospace, and service industries provided new economic opportunities. Politics in the state were influenced by international tensions, and the California legislature expanded the activities of its Fact-Finding Committee on Un-American Activities. The University of California became embroiled in a loyalty-oath controversy, culminating in the dismissal in 1950 of 32 professors who refused to sign an anti-communist pledge. Blacklisting became common in the film industry. The early 1950s saw the rise to the US vice presidency of Richard Nixon, whose early campaigns capitalized on fears of communist subversion.

In 1958 Congress decided that some Native American tribes could no longer be considered as such; the move denied these groups, 38 of them in California, federal benefits. More than 40 years later, one group, the Miwok, sought to regain official status. Calling themselves the Federated Indians of the Graton Rancheria, the 360 remaining members aimed to restore their culture and heritage. Promising a no-gambling policy, the federation was recognized in 1999 by the US House of Representatives, which said it was righting a wrong. If the bill were approved by the Senate, the tribe was to receive health, education, and economic benefits. They could also reclaim tribal lands in northern California, as long as there were no adverse claims to the property.

At the beginning of 1963, California (according to census estimates) became the nation's most populous state; its population continued to increase at a rate of 1,000 net migrants a day through the middle of the decade. By 1970, however, California's growth rate had slowed considerably. During the 1960s, the state was beset by a number of serious problems that apparently discouraged would-be immigrants. Economic opportunity gave way to recessions and high unemployment. Such rapid-growth industries as aerospace experienced a rapid decline in the late 1960s and early 1970s. Pollution of air and water called into question the quality of the California environment. The traditional romantic image of California was overshadowed by reports of mass murders, bizarre religious cults, extremist social and political movements, and racial and campus unrest. Nevertheless, the state's population has continued to grow. According to government figures, California had a population of 31.6 million in 1995, making it the most populous state in the nation. By 2000 its population was estimated at 33.8 million, and officials believed the state would retain its status of most populated through the year 2025.

The political importance of California's preeminence in population can be measured in the size of its congressional delegation and electoral votes. Defeated in his quest for the presidency in 1960, former vice president Nixon in 1968 became the first native Californian to win election to the nation's highest office. Both Ronald Reagan, governor of the state from 1967 to 1975, and Edmund G. Brown, Jr., elected governor in 1974 and reelected in 1978, were active candidates for the US presidency in 1980. Reagan was the Republican presidential winner that year and in 1984.

Assisted by the Reagan administration's military build-up, which invested billions of dollars into California manufacturers of bombers, missiles, and spacecraft as well as into its military bases, the California economy rebounded in the early and mid-1980s, bringing increases in total output, personal income, and employment which surpassed the national average. By the late 1980s and early 1990s, however, a recession and cuts in military spending, combined with existing burdens of expensive commercial and residential real estate, strict environmental regulations, and the effects of a savings and loan scandal, produced a dramatic economic decline. In 1992, the state's unemployment rate climbed to 10.1%. Jobs in the California aerospace and manufacturing sector dropped by 24%. For the first time in the state's history, substantial numbers of Californians migrated—over a million left between 1991 and 1994. Although such factors as air pollution, traffic congestion, and earthquakes were cited as reasons for this exodus, research has shown that most left in search of better job opportunities.

California's economic woes were matched by civil disorders. In 1991, an onlooker released a seven-minute videotape showing a group of police officers beating Rodney King, a black motorist, with nightsticks. The driver had pulled over after giving chase. In a jury trial which took place in a mostly white suburb northwest of Los Angeles, four police officers who had been charged with unnecessary brutality were acquitted. The verdict set off riots in South Central Los Angeles, killing 60 people and causing an estimated one billion dollars in property damage.

In the late 1980s and early 1990s California was also hit by two severe earthquakes. The first, which struck the San Francisco area in 1989, measured 7.1 on the Richter scale. The quake caused the collapse of buildings, bridges, and roadways, including the upper level of Interstate Highway 880 in Oakland and a 30-ft section of the Bay Bridge. As many as 270 people were killed and 100,000 houses were damaged. The quake caused $5–7 billion worth of property damage. In 1994, an earthquake measuring 6.7 on the Richter scale occurred 20 mi northwest of downtown Los Angeles. Three major overpasses ruptured and 680,000 people were left without electricity. The quake produced $13–20 million in property damage.

In 1994, anger over illegal immigration led to passage of Proposition 187, which would bar illegal aliens from welfare, education, and nonemergency health services. The measure was approved by a 59% to 41% margin. Passage of the measure prompted immediate challenges in the courts by the opposition. The following year, Governor Pete Wilson signed an executive order limiting the application of affirmative action in hiring and contracting by the state. He also approved the elimination of affirmative action in university admissions, a policy implemented by the Board of Regents and effective as of January 1997. After most of Proposition 187 was ruled unconstitutional in US district court, in 1999 Governor Gray Davis agreed to end the legal battle over the controversial measure. The only part that survived was a provision strengthening the penalties for manufacture and use of

false documents to conceal illegal immigrant status. While the governor said he was reluctant to go against the will of the majority of voters, civil rights groups had successfully challenged most of the language in the proposition. Further, by the time Davis agreed to stop defending the measure, federal laws had accomplished much of the intent of Proposition 187. All states were by then required to deny welfare benefits and all health benefits (except emergency care) to anyone who could not verify their presence in the US was legal.

In November 1996, the California Civil Rights Initiative (Proposition 209) passed with 55% of the vote, banning the use of racial and sex-based preferences in state-run affirmative action programs. Three weeks later, a federal judge blocked the enforcement of the initiative, claiming that it might be unconstitutional. In April 1997, however, a federal appeals court upheld the constitutionality of Proposition 209.

In mid-2000 Governor Gray Davis signed the state's $99.4-billion budget, which included a $1.35-billion education reform program. The state's goals for its school system included recruiting 300,000 new teachers by 2010, retaining and rewarding good teachers, placing computers and Internet connections in classrooms, and raising student achievement by awarding state-funded college scholarships to top students. The package was considered one of the most comprehensive education reform plans in the nation.

Some observers believed California's biggest struggle in the 21st century would be over water. In 2000, California and six other states were on the verge of a historic agreement that would give Southern California a 15-year deadline to cut its use of the Colorado River. Municipalities began discussing ways to turn waste water into drinking water. In June Governor Gray Davis, Secretary of the Interior Bruce Babbitt, and Senator Dianne Feinstein announced the CALFED Bay-Delta Program, calling it an "unprecedented effort" between state and federal governments, local agencies, the public, and private businesses to build a framework for managing water. Highlights of the plan included multimillion dollar investments in ecosystem restoration projects, projects to increase water storage capacity, loan and grant programs for agricultural and urban water use efficiency, water recycling capitol improvement projects, and improving water supply reliability through integration of storage, conveyance, water use efficiency, water quality, and water transfer programs.

Beginning in 2000, California experienced an energy crisis that saw electricity prices spike to their highest levels in 2001. Prices went from $12 per megawatt hour in 1998 to $200 in December 2000 and $250 in January 2001, and at times a megawatt hour cost $1000. A series of rolling blackouts in various areas occurred during 2001. California subsequently signed $40 billion in long-term power contracts, which were seen as assuring the state's power supply at reasonable rates, but after the crisis, when electricity rates fell, they proved to be very costly. Governor Davis pledged to fight the energy companies accused of profiting from the crisis, including the Enron Corporation, and in March 2003, the Federal Energy Regulatory Commission issued a ruling that companies would have to pay $3.3 billion in refunds for gaming the state's energy markets. California claimed it was owed $9 billion in refunds.

Gray Davis was reelected governor in 2002, but by 2003, his popularity ratings had dropped dramatically, due in part to the state's $38 billion budget deficit and the 2000–01 energy crisis, and a gubernatorial recall election was approved for 7 October 2003. Voters were to be asked if they wanted to oust Governor Davis or not, and if so, who his successor would be. One hundred thirty-five candidates were certified as candidates in the election, including Hollywood movie star and political novice Arnold Schwarzenegger. Lieutenant Governor Cruz Bustamante, although indicating Davis should stay in office, was running in the election in order to give voters the choice of voting for a strong Democratic candidate. To remain in office, Davis needed to secure at least 50% of the vote. If Davis were to be recalled, the candidate with the most votes would replace him.

12STATE GOVERNMENT

The first state constitution, adopted in 1849, outlawed slavery and was unique in granting property rights to married women in their own name. A new constitution, drafted in 1878 and ratified the following year, sought to curb legislative abuses—even going so far as to make lobbying a felony—and provided for a more equitable system of taxation, stricter regulation of the railroads, and an eight-hour workday. Of the 152 delegates to the 1878 constitutional convention, only two were natives of California, and 35 were foreign-born; no Spanish-speaking persons or Indians were included. This second constitution, as amended, is the basic document of state government today.

In April 1994 the California Constitutional Revision Commission was appointed to make recommendations to the governor and legislature for constitutional revisions affecting budget process, governmental structure, local government duties, and other areas. The Commission made its final report in 1996, on schedule. Through 2002 the California constitution had been amended 507 times.

The California legislature consists of a 40-member senate and an 80-member assembly. Senators are elected to four-year terms, half of them every two years, and assembly members are elected to two-year terms. As a result of a 1972 constitutional amendment, the legislature meets in a continuous two-year session, thus eliminating the need to reintroduce or reprint bills proposed in the first year of the biennium. Each session begins with an organizational meeting on the first Monday in December of even-numbered years; then, following a brief recess, the legislature reconvenes on the first Monday in January (of the odd-numbered year) and continues in session until November 30 of the next even-numbered year. Special sessions may be called by the governor to consider certain specific matters. Members of the senate and assembly must be over 18 years old, and have been US citizens and residents of the state for at least three years and residents of the districts they represent for at least one year prior to election. Legislative salaries in 2002 were $99,000 annually, unchanged from 1999.

Bills, which may be introduced by either house, are referred to committees, and must be read before each house three times. Legislation must be approved by an absolute majority vote of each house, except for appropriations bills, certain urgent measures, and proposed constitutional amendments, which require a two-thirds vote for passage. Gubernatorial vetoes may be overridden by two-thirds vote of the elected members in both houses. In the 1973/74 session, the legislature overrode a veto for the first time since 1946, but overrides have since become more common.

Constitutional amendments and proposed legislation may also be placed on the ballot through the initiative procedure. For a constitutional amendment, petitions must be signed by at least 8% of the number of voters who took part in the last gubernatorial election; for statutory measures, 5%. In each case, a simple majority vote at the next general election is required for passage.

Officials elected statewide include the governor and lieutenant governor (who run separately), secretary of state, attorney general, controller, treasurer, and superintendent of public instruction. Each serves a four-year term, without limitation. As chief executive officer of the state, the governor is responsible for the state's policies and programs, appoints department heads and members of state boards and commissions, serves as commander in chief of the California National Guard, may declare states of emergency, and may grant executive clemency to convicted criminals. In general, if the governor fails to sign or veto a bill within 12 days (excluding Saturdays, Sundays, and holidays), it becomes law. Candidates for governor must be at least 18 years old, a five-year citizen of the United States, and a five-year resident of California. The governor is limited to a maximum of two consecutive terms. The governor's annual salary in 2002 was $175,000.

The lieutenant governor acts as president of the senate and may assume the duties of the governor in case of the latter's death, resignation, impeachment, inability to discharge the duties of the office, or absence from the state. To vote in California, one must be a US citizen, at least 18 years old, and have been a resident of the state. Restrictions apply to convicted felons and those declared mentally incompetent by the court.

13POLITICAL PARTIES

As the state with the largest number of US representatives (52 in 2000) and electoral votes (54 in 2000), California plays a key role in national and presidential politics. In 2002 there were 15,303,469 registered voters; 44% were Democratic, 35% Republican, and 21% unaffiliated or members of other parties.

In 1851, the year after California entered the Union, the state Democratic Party was organized. But the party soon split into a pro-South faction, led by US Senator William Gwin, and a pro-North wing, headed by David Broderick. A political leader in San Francisco, Broderick became a US senator in 1857 but was killed in a duel by a Gwin stalwart two years later. This violent factionalism helped switch Democratic votes to the new Republican Party in the election of 1860, giving California's four electoral votes to Abraham Lincoln. This defeat, followed by the Civil War, demolished Senator Gwin's Democratic faction, and he fled to exile in Mexico.

The Republican party itself split into liberal and conservative wings in the early 1900s. Progressive Republicans formed the Lincoln-Roosevelt League to espouse political reforms, and succeeded in nominating and electing Hiram Johnson as governor on the Republican ticket in 1910. The following year, the legislature approved 23 constitutional amendments, including the initiative, referendum, recall, and other reform measures. Johnson won reelection on a Progressive Party line in 1915. After Johnson's election to the US Senate in 1916, Republicans (both liberal and conservative) controlled the state house uninterruptedly for 22 years, from 1917 to 1939. Democratic fortunes sank so low that in 1924 the party's presidential candidate, John W. Davis, got only 8% of the state's votes, leading humorist Will Rogers to quip, "I don't belong to any organized political party-I am a California Democrat." An important factor in the Progressive Republicans' success was the cross-filing system, in effect from 1913 to 1959, which blurred party lines by permitting candidates to appear on the primary ballots of several parties. This favored such Republican moderates as Earl Warren, who won an unprecedented three terms as governor-in 1946, he won both Republican and Democratic party primaries-before being elevated to US chief justice in 1953.

Political third parties have had remarkable success in California since the secretive anti-foreign, anti-Catholic Native American Party-called the Know-Nothings because party members were instructed to say they "knew nothing" when asked what they stood for-elected one of their leaders, J. Neely Johnson, as governor in 1855. The Workingmen's Party of California, as much anti-Chinese as it was anti-monopolist and pro-labor, managed to elect about one-third of the delegates to the 1878 constitutional convention. The most impressive third-party triumph came in 1912, when the Progressive Party's presidential candidate, Theodore Roosevelt, and vice-presidential nominee, Governor Hiram Johnson, defeated both the Republican and Democratic candidates among state voters. The Socialist Party also attracted support in the early 20th century. In 1910, more than 12% of the vote went to the Socialist candidate for governor, J. Stitt Wilson. Two years later, Socialist congressional nominees in the state won 18% of the vote, and a Socialist assemblyman was elected from Los Angeles. In 1914, two Socialist assemblymen and one state senator were elected. During the depression year of 1934, the Socialist Party leader and author Upton Sinclair won the Democratic nomination for governor on his End Poverty In California program and received nearly a million votes while losing to Republican Frank Merriam. Nonparty political movements have also won followings: several southern California congressmen were members of the ultraconservative John Birch Society during the 1960s, and in 1980 the Grand Dragon of the Ku Klux Klan won the Democratic Party nomination for a US House seat. Even when they lost decisively, third parties have won enough votes to affect the outcome of elections. In 1968, for example, George Wallace's American Independent Party received 487,270 votes, while Republican presidential candidate Richard Nixon topped Democrat Hubert Humphrey by only 223,346. In 1992, Ross Perot picked up 20.6% of the vote. In 2000, Green Party candidate Ralph Nader won 4% of the vote, or 405,722 votes.

Even with a historic advantage in voter registration, however, the Democrats managed to carry California in presidential elections only three times between 1948 and 1992, and to elect only two governors—Edmund G. "Pat" Brown (in 1958 and 1962) and his son, Edmund G. "Jerry" Brown, Jr. (in 1974 and 1978)—during the same period. Three times Californians gave their electoral votes to a California Republican, Richard Nixon, though they turned down his bid for governor in 1962. They elected one former film actor, Republican George Murphy, as US senator in 1964, and another, Republican Ronald Reagan, as governor in 1966 and 1970 and as president in 1980 and 1984. Democratic nominee Bill Clinton garnered 51% of the popular vote in 1996, while Republican Bob Dole received 38% and Independent Ross Perot picked up just under 7%. In the 2000 presidential election, Democrat Al Gore carried the state with 54% of the vote to George W. Bush's 42%. In November 1998 Democrat Gray Davis, formerly lieutenant governor, was elected to be the state's 37th governor by 58% of voters. He won reelection in 2002, but by fall 2003, he was facing a recall vote on his governorship.

Both US senators in 2003 were women: Democrat Barbara Boxer, who won reelection to a second term in 1998; and Dianne Feinstein, elected in 1992 to replace Senator Pete Wilson (who was elected governor in 1990) and reelected in 1994 to serve her first full (6-year) term. She was reelected once again in 2000 with 56% of the vote. California's delegation of US Representatives to the 108th Congress (2003–04) consisted of 33 Democrats and 20 Republicans (an increase of one congressional seat over the 2000 election). Democrat Nancy Pelosi was elected House Minority Leader in 2003. After 2002 elections, the Democrats kept control of the state senate (26–14) and house (48–32).

Minority groups of all types are represented in California politics. In mid-2003, there were 31 women, 24 Latino members, and six black members in the state legislature. Two of the most prominent black elected officials include Los Angeles Mayor Thomas Bradley, who served from 1973–90, and San Francisco Mayor Willie L. Brown, Jr., who began his first term in 1996 and won reelection in 1999. Organized groups of avowed homosexuals began to play an important political role in San Francisco during the 1970s.

¹⁴LOCAL GOVERNMENT

As of 2002, California had 57 counties and 1,047 public school districts. The Department of Education worked steadily throughout the 1900s to reorganize, reducing the number of districts from a high of 3,579 in 1932 to just over 1,000 in 1967. In 2002 there were 2,830 special districts and 475 municipal governments.

County government is administered by an elected board of supervisors, which also exercises jurisdiction over unincorporated towns within the county. Government operations are administered by several elected officials, the number varying according to the population of the county. Most counties have a district attorney, assessor, treasurer-tax collector, superintendent of schools, sheriff, and coroner. Larger counties may also have an

California Presidential Vote by Political Parties, 1948–2000

YEAR	ELECTORAL VOTE	CALIFORNIA WINNER	DEMOCRAT	REPUBLICAN	STATES' RIGHTS	PROGRESSIVE	SOCIALIST	PROHIBITION
1948	25	*Truman (D)	1,913,134	1,895,269	1,228	190,381	3,459	16,926
					CONSTITUTION		SOC. LABOR	
1952	32	*Eisenhower (R)	2,197,548	2,897,310	3,504	24,692	273	16,117
1956	32	*Eisenhower (R)	2,420,135	3,027,668	6,087		300	11,119
1960	32	Nixon (R)	3,224,099	3,259,722			1,051	21,706
1964	40	*Johnson (D)	4,171,877	2,879,108			489	
					AMERICAN IND.		PEACE & FREEDOM	
1968	40	*Nixon (R)	3,244,318	3,467,664	487,270		27,707	
						AMERICAN	PEOPLE'S	LIBERTARIAN
1972	45	*Nixon (R)	3,475,847	4,602,096		232,554	55,167	980
					COMMUNIST			
1976	45	Ford (R)	3,742,284	3,882,244	51,096	12,766	41,731	56,388
						CITIZENS	PEACE & FREEDOM	
1980	45	*Reagan (R)	3,039,532	4,444,044		9,687	60,059	17,797
1984	47	*Reagan (R)	3,922,519	5,467,009	39,265	NEW ALLIANCE	26,297	49,951
1988	47	*Bush (R)	4,702,233	5,054,917	27,818	31,181		70,105
						IND. (Perot)		
1992	54	*Clinton (D)	5,121,325	3,630,574	12,711	2,296,006	18,597	48,139
							GREEN (Nader)	
1996	54	*Clinton (D)	5,119,835	3,828,380		697,847	237,016	73,600
					REFORM			
2000	54	Gore (D)	5,861,293	4,567,429	44,987		418,707	45,520

*Won US presidential election.

elected planning director, public defender, public works director, purchasing agent, and social welfare services director.

Municipalities are governed under the mayor-council, council-manager, or commission system. Most large cities are run by councils of from 5 to 15 members, elected to four-year terms, the councils being responsible for taxes, public improvements, and the budget. An elected mayor supervises city departments and appoints most city officials. Other elected officials usually include the city attorney, treasurer, and assessor. Los Angeles and San Francisco have the mayor-council form of government, but in San Francisco, the city and county governments are consolidated under an elected board of supervisors, and the mayor appoints a manager who has substantial authority. San Diego and San Jose each have an elected mayor and city manager chosen by an elected city council.

The state's direct primary law had a salutary effect on local politics by helping end the power of political machines in the large cities. In 1910, Los Angeles voters adopted the nonpartisan primary and overthrew the corrupt rule of Mayor A. C. Harper in favor of reformer George Alexander. At the same time, voters were revolting against bossism and corruption in San Francisco, Sacramento, Oakland, and other cities.

15STATE SERVICES

To address the continuing threat of terrorism and to work with the federal Department of Homeland Security (created in 2002 following the terrorist attacks of 11 September 2001), homeland security in California in 2003 operated under the authority of the governor and state statute; a special advisor was appointed to oversee the state's homeland security activities, which included enhanced highway patrol operations and the California Anti-Terrorism Information Center.

In accordance with the Political Reform Act of 1974, the Fair Political Practices Commission investigates political campaign irregularities, regulates lobbyists, and enforces full disclosure of political contributions and public officials' assets and income.

Educational services are provided by the Department of Education, which administers the public school system. The department, which is headed by the superintendent of public instruction, also regulates special schools for blind, deaf, and disabled children. The University of California system is governed by a board of regents headed by the governor.

Transportation services are under the direction of the Department of Transportation (CALTRANS), which oversees mass transit lines, highways, and airports. Intrastate rate regulation of pipelines, railroads, buses, trucks, airlines, and waterborne transportation is the responsibility of the Public Utilities Commission, which also regulates gas, electric, telephone, water, sewer, and steam-heat utilities. The Department of Motor Vehicles licenses drivers, road vehicles, automotive dealers, and boats.

Health and welfare services are provided by many state departments, most of which are part of the Health and Welfare Agency. The Department of Health Services provides health care for several millions of persons through the state's Medi-Cal program. The department's public health services include controlling infectious disease, conducting cancer research, safeguarding water quality, and protecting the public from unsafe food and drugs. The department also has licensing responsibility for hospitals, clinics, and nursing homes. Care for the mentally ill is provided through the Department of Mental Health by means of state hospitals and community outpatient clinics. Disabled people receive counseling, vocational training, and other aid through the Department of Rehabilitation. Needy families receive income maintenance aid and food stamps from the Department of Social Services. Senior citizens can get help from the Department of Aging, which allocates federal funds for the elderly. The Commission on the Status of Women reports to the legislature on women's educational and employment needs, and on statutes or practices that infringe on their rights. The Youth Authority, charged with the rehabilitation of juvenile offenders, operates training schools and conservation camps. The Department of Alcohol and Drug Programs coordinates prevention and treatment activities.

Public protection services are provided by the Military Department, which includes the Army and Air National Guard and the California Cadet Corps, and by the Youth and Adult Correctional Agency, which maintains institutions and programs to control and treat convicted felons and narcotics addicts. The California Highway Patrol has its own separate department within the Business, Transportation and Housing Agency. This agency also includes the Department of Housing and Community Development. The State and Consumer Services Agency has jurisdiction over the Department of Consumer Affairs, the Department of Veterans Affairs, and several other state departments. A state innovation was the establishment in 1974 of the Seismic Safety Commission to plan public safety programs in connection with California's continuing earthquake problem.

Programs for the preservation and development of natural resources are centralized in the Resources Agency. State parks and recreation areas are administered by the Department of Parks and Recreation. California's vital water needs are the responsibility of the Department of Water Resources. In 1975, as a result of a national oil shortage, the state established the Energy Resources Conservation and Development Commission to develop contingency plans for dealing with fuel shortages, to forecast the state's energy needs, and to coordinate programs for energy conservation. The California Conservation Corps provides employment opportunities for young people in conservation work.

The Department of Industrial Relations has divisions dealing with fair employment practices, occupational safety and health standards, and workers' compensation. The Employment Development Department provides unemployment and disability benefits and operates job-training and work-incentive programs. The Department of Information Technology supports high-tech development in California, and the Environmental Protection Agency guards the natural environment.

16JUDICIAL SYSTEM

California has a complex judicial system and a very large correctional system.

The state's highest court is the supreme court, which may review appellate court decisions and superior court cases involving the death penalty. The high court has a chief justice and six associate justices, all of whom serve 12-year terms; justices are appointed by the governor, confirmed or disapproved by the Commission on Judicial Appointments (headed by the chief justice), and then submitted to the voters for ratification. The chief justice also chairs the Judicial Council, which seeks to expedite judicial business and to equalize judges' caseloads.

Courts of appeal, organized in six appellate districts, review decisions of superior courts and, in certain cases, of municipal and justice courts. There were 93 district appeals court judgeships in 1999. All district court judges are appointed by the governor, reviewed by the Commission on Judicial Appointments, and subject to popular election for 12-year terms.

Superior courts in each of the 58 county seats have original jurisdiction in felony, juvenile, probate, and domestic relations cases, as well as in civil cases involving more than $15,000. They also handle some tax and misdemeanor cases and appeals from lower courts. Municipal courts, located in judicial districts with populations of more than 40,000, hear misdemeanors (except those involving juveniles) and civil cases involving $15,000 or less. In districts with less than 40,000 population, justice courts have jurisdiction similar to that of municipal courts. All trial court judges are elected to six-year terms.

As of June 2001 there were 163,965 prisoners in state and federal prisons in California, a decrease of 0.3% from the previous year. The State Department of Corrections maintains 32 state prisons and 38 minimum custody facilities located in wilderness areas where inmates are trained as wildland firefighters.

According to the FBI, California's crime rate in 2001 was 3,902.9 crimes per 100,000 population, including a total of 212,855 violent crimes and 1,133,702 property crimes in that year. In 1965, California became the first state to institute a victim compensation program.

California's death penalty statute received its most serious challenge after the 1948 conviction of Carl Chessman on a charge of forcible rape. Chessman served 12 years on death row at San Quentin, got eight stays of execution, and wrote a best seller about his ordeal. Despite highly publicized attempts to overturn capital punishment and save Chessman's life, the legislature refused to act, and he was executed in 1960. The death penalty was carried out 292 times in California from 1930 to 1977, but only ten times between 1977 and 2003. California had 624 persons under sentence of death in 2003, more than any other state in the nation.

17ARMED FORCES

California leads the 50 states in defense contracts received, numbers of National Guardsmen and military veterans, veterans' benefit payments, and funding for police forces.

In 2002, the US Department of Defense had 123,9548 active-duty military personnel and 58,076 civilian personnel in California. Army military personnel totaled 7,932; the Navy (including Marines), 96,047; and the Air Force, 19,969 Army bases are located at Oakland and San Francisco, and naval facilities in the San Diego area. There are weapons stations at Concord and Seal Beach, and supply depots at Oakland and San Pedro. The Marine Corps training base, Camp Pendleton, is at Oceanside. The Air Force operates three main bases—McClellan AFB at Sacramento, Travis AFB at Fairfield, and Norton AFB at San Bernardino—and numerous smaller installations. In 2001, California companies were awarded $19.9 billion in defense contracts, more than two times the total for Texas and nearly 15% of the US total. Defense Department expenditures in California were approximately $36.5 billion in 2002, $23.8 billion for contracts and about $12.3 billion for payroll

There were 2,569,340 veterans of US military service in California as of 2000, of whom 504,010 served in World War II; 301,034 in the Korean conflict; 754,682 during the Vietnam era; and 278,003 during 1990–2000 (including the Persian Gulf War). Veterans' benefits paid to Californians in 2002 exceeded $4.4 billion.

California's military forces consist of the Army and Air National Guard, the naval and state military reserve (militia), and the California Cadet Corps. In 2000, the California Highway Patrol employed 6,678 full-time sworn officers.

18MIGRATION

A majority of Californians today are migrants from other states. The first great wave of migration, beginning in 1848, brought at least 85,000 prospectors by 1850. Perhaps 20,000 of them were foreign-born, mostly from Europe, Canada, Mexico, and South America, as well as a few from the Hawaiian Islands and China. Many thousands of Chinese were brought in during the latter half of the 19th century to work on farms and railroads. When Chinese immigration was banned by the US Congress in 1882, Japanese migration provided farm labor. These ambitious

workers soon opened shops in the cities and bought land for small farms. By 1940, about 94,000 Japanese lived in California. During the depression of the 1930s, approximately 350,000 migrants came to California, most of them looking for work. Many thousands of people came there during World War II to take jobs in the burgeoning war industries; after the war, some 300,000 discharged servicemen settled in the state. All told, between 1940 and 1990 California registered a net gain from migration of 12,426,000, representing well over half of its population growth during that period.

In the 1990s California registered net losses in domestic migration, peaking with a loss of 444,186 in 1993–94. Altogether net losses in domestic migration between 1990 and 1998 totaled 2,082,000 people. During the same period, net gains in international migration totaled 2,019,000. As of 1996, nearly 22% of all foreign immigrants in the US were living in California, a higher proportion than in any other state. Although the 1970s brought an influx of refugees from Indochina, and, somewhat later, from Central America, the bulk of post-war foreign immigration has come from neighboring Mexico. At first, Mexicans—as many as 750,000 a year—were imported legally to supply seasonal labor for California growers. Later, hundreds of thousands—perhaps even millions—of illegal Mexican immigrants crossed the border in search of jobs and then, unless they were caught and forcibly repatriated, stayed on. Counting these state residents for census purposes is extremely difficult, since many of them are unwilling to declare themselves for fear of being identified and deported. As of 1990, California's foreign-born population was reported at 8,055,000, or 25% of the state's total. As of 1994, the number of undocumented immigrants was estimated at between 1,321 and 1,784—the highest number of any state and close to 40% of the total number thought to be residing in the US. As of 1998, California was the intended residence of 170,126 foreign immigrants (more than any other state and 26% of the US total that year), of these 62,113 were from Mexico.

Intrastate migration has followed two general patterns: rural to urban until the mid-20th century, and urban to suburban thereafter. In particular, the percentage of blacks increased in Los Angeles, San Francisco, and San Diego between 1960 and 1970 as black people settled or remained in the cities while whites moved into the surrounding suburbs. In the 1970s and 1980s, the percentage of blacks in Los Angeles and San Francisco decreased slightly; in San Diego, the percentage of blacks increased from 8.9% to 9.4%. By 1997, blacks represented 8.3% of the Los Angeles metropolitan population, 8.8% of the San Francisco metropolitan population, and only 6.4% of the San Diego metropolitan population, a 3% decrease from the 1980s. California's net gain from migration during 1970–80 amounted to about 1,573,000. In the 1980s, migration accounted for 54% of the net population increase, with about 2,940,000 new residents. Between 1990 and 1998, the state's overall population increased by 9.7%. In the period 1995–2000, 1,448,964 people moved into the state and 2,204,500 moved out, for a net loss of 755,536.

19INTERGOVERNMENTAL COOPERATION

The Colorado River Board of California represents the state's interests in negotiations with the federal government and other states over utilization of Colorado River water and power resources. California also is a member of the Colorado River Crime Enforcement Compact, California-Nevada Compact for Jurisdiction on Interstate Waters, the Klamath River Compact Commission (with Oregon), and the Tahoe Regional Planning Agency (with Nevada). Regional agreements signed by the state include the Pacific States Marine Fisheries Commission, Western Interstate Commission for Higher Education, Western Interstate

Corrections Compact, and Western Interstate Energy Compact. The Arizona-California boundary accord dates from 1963. California also is a member of the Commission of the Californias, along with the State of Baja California Norte and the territory of Baja California Sur, both in Mexico. During the 2001 fiscal year, federal grants to California exceeded $39.7 billion, the most received by any state.

20 ECONOMY

California leads the 50 states in economic output and total personal income. In the 1960s, when it became the nation's most populous state, California also surpassed Iowa in agricultural production and New York in value added by manufacturing.

The gold rush of the mid-19th century made mining (which employed more people than any other industry in the state until 1870) the principal economic activity and gave impetus to agriculture and manufacturing. Many unsuccessful miners took up farming or went to work for the big cattle ranches and wheat growers. In the 1870s, California became the most important cattle-raising state and the 2nd-leading wheat producer. Agriculture soon expanded into truck farming and citrus production, while new manufacturing industries began to produce ships, metal products, lumber, leather, cloth, refined sugar, flour, and other processed foods. Manufacturing outstripped both mining and agriculture to produce goods valued at $258 million by 1900, and 10 times that by 1925. Thanks to a rapidly growing work force, industrial output continued to expand during and after both world wars, while massive irrigation projects enabled farmers to make full use of the state's rich soil and favorable climate.

By the late 1970s, one of every four California workers was employed in high-technology industry. California has long ranked 1st among the states in defense procurement, and in 1997, defense contracts awarded to southern California firms surpassed the combined totals of New York and Texas.

From its beginnings in the late 18th century, California's wine industry has grown to encompass some 500 wineries. In 1981, they accounted for about 90% of total US production. By 1985, California had surpassed Chicago to rank 2nd in advertising among the states.

A highly diversified economy made California less vulnerable to the national recession of the early 1980s than most other states. During the first half of the 1980s, the state generally outperformed the national economy. In 1984, California enjoyed an estimated increase of 12.1% in personal income and a 6.1% increase in nonagricultural employment, and reduced the unemployment rate from 9.7% to an estimated 7.8%. The boom was short-lived, however. Cuts in the military budget in the late 1980s, a decline in Japanese investment, and the national recession in the early 1990s had a devastating impact on the state, particularly on southern California. Unemployment in 1992 rose to 9.1%, up from 5.1% in 1989. The aerospace and construction industries suffered disproportionately. Employment in aerospace declined 22.3% between May of 1990 and September of 1992; construction lost 20% of its jobs in the same period.

Stock market growth in the high-technology sector led California's growth during the late 1990s. The gross state product in 1997 was approximately one trillion. Annual growth rates in 1998 and 1999 averaged 7.75 in 1998 and 1999, and soared to 9.6% in 2000. The national recession of 2002, however, brought the growth rate down to 2.2%. While employment in southern California continued to expand, the San Francisco Bay area, severely impacted by the decline in the high-tech manufacturing and software sectors, the bursting of the dot.com bubble on the stock market, and the collapse of the venture capital market, experienced its worst recession in 50 years. In 2002, recovery remained elusive, and in 2003, the state faced a projected $38 billion budget deficit that was the main issue in an unprecedented campaign to the recall the governor.

Total gross state product in 2001 was $1.36 trillion in 2001, 11.2% from the public sector. The main contributions to gross state product were general services ($326 billion, up 36% from 1997); financial services, including insurance and real estate ($317.5 billion, up 37% from 1997); manufacturing ($163.8 billion, up 11.2% from 1997, but down 12.4% from its peak in 2000); government ($152 billion, up 27.7% from 1997); and transportation and public utilities ($92.4 billion, up 25% from 1997). California continued to have the highest gross state product among the 50 states, accounting for 13.4% of the total.

21 INCOME

According to the Bureau of Economic Analysis, in 2001, California had a per capita personal income (PCPI) of $32,655 which ranked 11th in the United States (including the District of Columbia) and was 107% of the national average, $30,413. The 2001 PCPI reflected an increase of 0.9% from 2000 compared to the national change of 2.2%. In 2001, California had a total personal income (TPI) of $1,129,868,238,000 which ranked 1st in the United States and accounted for 13% of the national total. The 2001 TPI reflected an increase of 2.7% from 2000 compared to the national change of 3.3%.

Earnings of persons employed in California increased from $818,770,591,000 in 2000 to $830,828,637,000 in 2001, an increase of 1.5%. The largest industries in 2001 were services, 33.0% of earnings; state and local government, 12.2%; and durable goods manufacturing, 9.7%. Of the industries that accounted for at least 5% of earnings in 2001, the slowest growing from 2000 to 2001 was durable goods manufacturing, which decreased 14.9%; the fastest was state and local government, which increased 10.6%.

According to data released by the US Census Bureau, in 2000, the median household income was $46,802 compared to the national average of $42,148. In 2001, the median income for a family of four was $63,761 compared to the national average of $63,278. For the period 1999 to 2001, the average poverty rate was 13.1% which placed it 39th among the 50 states and the District of Columbia ranked lowest to highest.

22 LABOR

California has the largest work force in the nation and the greatest number of employed workers. During the 1970s, California's work force also grew at a higher annual rate than that of any other state. According to Bureau of Labor Statistics (BLS) provisional estimates, in July 2003 the seasonally adjusted civilian labor force in California numbered 17,635,700, with approximately 1,166,500 workers unemployed, yielding an unemployment rate of 6.6%, compared to the national average of 6.2% for the same period. Since the beginning of the BLS data series in 1980, the highest unemployment rate recorded was 11.0% in February 1983. The historical low was 4.7% in February 2001. It is estimated that in 2001, 5.4% of the labor force was employed in construction; 13.0% in manufacturing; 5.2% in transportation, communications, and public utilities; 18.6% in trade; 5.4% in finance, insurance, and real estate; 26.0% in services; 14.0% in government; and 2.7% in agriculture.

The unemployment rate during the 1970s and early 1980s ranged from the 1973 low of 7% to a high of 9.9% in 1975 and 1982. From 1967 to 1976, an average of 226,000 Californians entered the labor market each year, but the economy generated only about 175,000 jobs annually, so unemployment rose steadily.

The labor movement in California was discredited by acts of violence during its early years. On 1 October 1910, a bomb explosion at a *Los Angeles Times* plant killed 21 workers, resulting in the conviction and imprisonment of two labor organizers a year later. Another bomb explosion, this one killing 10 persons in San Francisco on 22 July 1916, led to the conviction of two radical union leaders, Thomas Mooney and Warren Billings. The death penalty for Mooney was later commuted to life imprisonment (the same sentence Billings had received), and after evidence had been developed attesting to his innocence, he was pardoned in 1939. These violent incidents led to the state's Criminal Syndicalism Law of 1919, which forbade "labor violence" and curtailed militant labor activity for more than a decade.

Unionism revived during the depression of the 1930s. In 1934, the killing of two union picketers by San Francisco police during a strike by the International Longshoremen's Association led to a three-day general strike that paralyzed the city, and the union eventually won the demand for its own hiring halls. In Los Angeles, unions in such industries as automobiles, aircraft, rubber, and oil refining obtained bargaining rights, higher wages, and fringe benefits during and after World War II. In 1958, the California Labor Federation was organized, and labor unions have since increased both their membership and their benefits.

The US Department of Labor reported that in 2002, 2,454,000 of California's 13,983,000 employed wage and salary workers were members of unions. This represented 17.5% of those so employed, up from 16.2% in 2001. The national average is 13.2%. In all, 2,639,000 workers (18.9%) were represented by unions. In addition to union members, this category includes workers who report no union affiliation but whose jobs are covered by a union contract.

Of all working groups, migrant farm workers have been the most difficult to organize because their work is seasonal and because they are largely members of minority groups, mostly Mexicans, with few skills and limited job opportunities. During the 1960s, a Mexican-American "stoop" laborer named Cesar Chavez established the National Farm Workers Association (later the United Farm Workers Organizing Committee, now the United Farm Workers of America), which, after a long struggle, won bargaining rights from grape, lettuce, and berry growers in the San Joaquin Valley. Chavez's group was helped by a secondary boycott against these California farm products at some grocery stores throughout the US. When his union was threatened by the rival Teamsters Union in the early 1970s, Chavez got help from the AFL-CIO and from Governor Brown, who in 1975 pushed through the state legislature a law mandating free elections for agricultural workers to determine which union they wanted to represent them. The United Farm Workers and Teamsters formally settled their jurisdictional dispute in 1977.

23AGRICULTURE

California has led the United States in agriculture for nearly 50 years with a diverse economy of over 250 crop and livestock commodities. With only 4% of the nation's farms and 3% of the nation's farm acreage, the state accounts for over 13% of US gross cash farm receipts. Famous for its specialty crops, California produces virtually all (99% or more) of the following crops grown commercially in the US: almonds, artichokes, avocados, clovers, dates, figs, kiwifruit, olives, persimmons, pistachios, prunes, raisins, and English walnuts. California's total cash farm receipts for 2001 amounted to $25.9 billion.

Agriculture has always thrived in California. The Spanish missions and Mexican ranchos were farming centers until the mid-19th century, when large ranches and farms began to produce cattle, grain, and cotton for the national market. Wheat was a major commodity by the 1870s, when the citrus industry was established and single-family farms in the fertile Central Valley and smaller valleys started to grow large quantities of

fruits and vegetables. European settlers planted vineyards on the slopes of the Sonoma and Napa valleys, beginning California's wine industry, which today produces over 90% of US domestic wines. Around 1900, intensive irrigation transformed the dry, sandy Imperial Valley in southeastern California into a garden of abundance for specialty crops. Since World War II, corporate farming, or agribusiness, has largely replaced small single-family farms. Today, the state grows approximately 55% of all fruits and vegetables marketed in the US.

In 2002, California devoted nearly one-third (27.7 million acres/ 11.2 million hectares) of its 100 million acres (40.4 million hectares) to agricultural production with 84,000 farms comprising 27.7 million acres (11.2 million hectares. One-fourth of all farmland represents crop growth, and currently 10% of all cropland uses irrigation.

Irrigation is essential for farming in California. Agriculture consumes 28% of the state's annual water supply. A major irrigation system was implemented, including the Colorado River Project, which irrigated 500,000 acres (200,000 hectares) in the Imperial Valley in 1913; the Central Valley Project, completed by 1960, which harnessed the runoff of the Sacramento River; and the Feather River Project, also in the Central Valley, which was finished during the 1970s. Largest of all is the California Water Project, begun in 1960 and completed in 1973. During 1983, this project delivered 1.3 million acre-feet of water.

On 16 June 1980, the US Supreme Court ended 13 years of litigation by ruling that federally subsidized irrigation water in the Imperial Valley could not be limited to family farms of fewer than 160 acres (56 hectares) but must be made available to all farms regardless of size; the ruling represented a major victory for agribusiness interests.

The leading crops in 2002 (by value) included greenhouse and nursery products, grapes, and lettuce. These three commodities accounted for 37% of the state's crop receipts that year. Other important crops include cotton, almonds, hay, tomatoes, flowers and foliage, strawberries, oranges, rice, broccoli, walnuts, carrots, celery, and cantaloupe.

California was the top agricultural exporter in the US with $7.7 billion in 1997. Leading agricultural exports in 1998 included vegetables ($1.9 billion), fruits ($1.7 billion), and tree nuts ($1.1 billion). Japan accounts for more than 25% of all California agricultural exports, and the entire Pacific Rim accounts for more than half its total exports. Export markets hold the greatest potential for expanding sales of California agriculture products.

24ANIMAL HUSBANDRY

California is a leading producer of livestock and dairy products.

In 2003 there were an estimated 5.3 million cattle and calves valued at $4.9 billion. There were 135,000 hogs and pigs on California farms and ranches in 2002, valued at $12.4 million. In 2001 California produced 51.6 million lb (23.4 million kg) of sheep and lambs for a gross income of $53.7 million.

In 2001 California was the leading milk producer among the 50 states with 33.25 billion lb (15.1 billion kg) of milk produced. Milk cows, raised mainly in the southern interior, totaled 1.59 million head in the same year.

California ranked fifth among the 50 states in egg production in 2001, with an output of 6 billion eggs. In 2001, California produced 450.7 million lb (204.4 million kg) of turkey, which was valued at $211.8 million.

25FISHING

The Pacific whaling industry, with its chief port at San Francisco, was important to the California economy in the 19th century, and commercial fishing is still central to the food-processing industry. In 1998, California ranked 6th in the US in commercial fishing, with a catch of 336.1 million lb (152.4 million kg); the value of the catch, $110.7 million, ranked 8th and only accounted for 3.5% of the national value. Los Angeles ranked 10th among fishing ports in 1998, with landings totaling 145.3 million lb (65.9 million kg).

In 1997, the California fishing fleet numbered 7,121 vessels. In 1998, principal commercial species included squid, dungeness crab, 10.6 million lb (4.8 million kg); shrimp, 3.2 million lb (1.4 million kg); salmon, 2.1 million lb (0.9 million kg); sablefish, 3.2 million lb (1.4 million kg); and jack mackerel. California accounted for 54% of US landings of jack mackerel in 1998.

Deep-sea fishing is a popular sport. World records for giant sea bass, California halibut, white catfish, and sturgeon have been set in California. Fish farms distributed over 57.5 million salmon and 15.1 million trout and 48.5 million trout eggs within the state in 1998. There were 2,261,823 anglers licensed in the state in 1998. Sport fishing off the coast of California involved an estimated 1,098,000 coastal residents, 65,000 inland Californians, and 198,000 persons from other states in 1998. In 1998, marine recreational anglers caught an estimated 12 million fish along the Pacific coast of California, with Pacific mackerel and kelp bass the principal species.

26 FORESTRY

California has more forests than any other state except Alaska. Forested lands in 2002 covered 40,233,000 acres (16,282,000 hectares).

Forests are concentrated in the northwestern part of the state and in the eastern Sierra Nevada. Commercial forestland in private hands was estimated at 17,781,000 acres (7,196,000 hectares) in 2002; an additional 18,515,000 acres (7,493,000 hectares) were US Forest Service lands, and 2,208,000 acres (893,600 hectares) were regulated by the Bureau of Land Management. In 2002, lumber production totaled 2.9 billion board feet (fourth in the US), mostly such softwoods as fir, pine, cedar, and redwood.

About half of the state's forests are protected as national forests and state parks or recreational areas. Although stands of coast redwood trees have been preserved in national and state parks since the late 19th century, only about 46% of the original 2 million acres (800,000 hectares) of redwoods between Monterey Bay and southern Oregon remain.

Reforestation of public lands is supervised by the National Forest Service and the California Department of Forestry. In 1924–25, more than 1.5 million redwood and Douglas fir seedlings were planted in the northwestern corner of the state. During the 1930s, the Civilian Conservation Corps replanted trees along many mountain trails, and the California Conservation Corps performed reforestation work in the 1970s.

As of 2003, there were 18 national forests in California. The total area within their boundaries in California amounted to 24,430,000 acres (9,886,821 hectares), of which 85% was National Forest System land.

27 MINING

According to data compiled by the US Geological Survey, California was the leading state in the nation in the value of nonfuel minerals produced during 2001, accounting for more than 8% of the US total. The value of the nonfuel mineral commodities produced in the state during the year was estimated to be $3.25 billion, a decrease of less than 1% from 2000. Industrial minerals accounted for 95% of the nonfuel mineral production value, with the rest supplied by gold and silver. California remained the only state to produce boron minerals (1.1 million metric tons, valued at $557 million) and led the nation in production of construction sand and gravel (148 million metric tons, valued at $953 million), accounting for over 13% of

all US production and more than 17% of total US value. Construction sand and gravel was also California's leading nonfuel mineral, accounting for more than 29% of the state nonfuel mineral production value. Cement (portland and masonry) was the 2nd-leading nonfuel mineral (10.8 million metric tons, worth $818 million), followed by boron minerals and crushed stone. Together these four exercised the most influence on California's nonfuel mineral industry.

California retained 1st place in production of construction sand and gravel and diatomite and rose to 1st place in masonry cement; it was 2nd among the three states that produced soda ash, and in production of pumice, pumicite, pyrophyllite, and feldspar; 3rd in gemstones; 4th in fire clays; and 5th in magnesium compounds and perlite.

More than 20 industrial minerals are produced in California. Portland cement was the most valuable commodity produced, followed in order by construction sand and gravel, boron, gold, and crushed stone (61 million metric tons, worth $393 million). Gold accounts for more than 95% of metal production value; in 2001, the state produced 15,200 kg, valued at $137 million.

In 2001 California had about 1,000 mines actively producing nonfuel minerals, which employed about 9,300 people. At the beginning of 2002 the Division of Mines and Geology was renamed the California Geological Survey (CGS). The CGS grants mining permits. Among the programs it oversees are Mineral Resources and Mineral Hazards Mapping, Seismic Hazards Mapping, and Timber Harvest Enforcement and Watershed Restoration. Siting and permitting of mining operations throughout California often generate local controversies. The leading issues involve intense land use competition and wide-ranging environmental concerns, along with the typical noise, dust, and truck-traffic issues in populated areas.

28 ENERGY AND POWER

In 1999, petroleum supplied an estimated 1% of the state's electric power production, natural gas 47%, coal 1%, nuclear power 17%, hydroelectric power 21%, and other sources about 13%. California ranks 3rd among the 50 states in crude oil reserves and fourth in crude oil production. California utilities own and operate coal-fired power plants across the southwest. This electricity shows up as "imports" in federal accounting. California utilities buy electricity from out-of-state suppliers if it is less expensive than in-state operation. Installed electric capacity (utility and nonutility) was 53.2 million kW in 1999. In the same year, total electrical output was 191.6 billion kWh.

Originally ordered by the Pacific Gas and Electric Co. in 1966, the Diablo Canyon nuclear power plant near San Luis Obispo has been a source of controversy ever since 1971, when an earthquake fault line was discovered offshore, 2.5 mi (4 km) from the plant. After years of delays and demonstrations by environmental groups, the first unit of the plant began operation in November 1984, the second reactor in 1985, for a total of four reactors at two plants operating in the state, with a net capacity of over 4,500 MW. (The other plant is the San Onofre facility near San Clemente.)

In 1999, retail sales of electric power in the state totaled 221 billion kWh, of which roughly 30% went to commercial businesses, 33% to home consumers, and 27% to industries. In part because of the mild California climate and the state's aggressive 20-year effort to improve energy efficiency, utility bills are lower than in many other states. In 2000, per capita energy consumption in California was 252 million Btu (63.5 million kcal), or 46th among the states.

Crude oil was discovered in Humboldt and Ventura counties as early as the 1860s with the first year of commercial production occurring in 1876. It was not until the 1920s, however, that large oil strikes were made at Huntington Beach, near Los Angeles, and at Santa Fe Springs and Signal Hill, near Long Beach. These fields added vast pools of crude oil to the state's reserves, which were further augmented in the 1930s by the discovery of large offshore oil deposits in the Long Beach area.

The state's attempts to retain rights to tideland oil reserves as far as 30 mi (48 km) offshore were denied by the US Supreme Court in 1965; state claims were thus restricted to Monterey Bay and other submerged deposits within a 3-mi (5-km) offshore limit. In 1994, however, California banned any further oil drilling in state offshore waters because of environmental concerns, high operating costs, and resource limitations. In 1998, state and federal offshore resources accounted for 21% and 19% of state oil and gas production, respectively. The state's largest oil companies include Chevron, with headquarters in San Francisco, and Los Angeles–based Atlantic Richfield.

California's proved oil reserves as of 31 December 2001 were estimated at more than 3.6 billion barrels, 16% of the US total and 3rd behind Alaska and Texas. Petroleum production in 2002 totaled 707,000 barrels per day, 12% of the US total. Marketed production totaled 360.6 billion cu ft (10.2 billion cu m) in 2002; proved reserves were nearly 2.7 trillion cu ft (0.08 trillion cu m) in 2001. In 2001 there were 1,244 active natural gas wells in the state.

California has been a leader in developing solar and geothermal power as alternatives to fossil fuels. As of the end of 1998, geothermal, wind, and solar energy electric generation amounted to 5.1 billion kWh, or nearly 4.4% of the total electric generation for the state. About 73% of the geothermal, wind, and solar electric capacity nationally comes from California.

29INDUSTRY

California is the nation's leading industrial state, ranking 1st in almost every general manufacturing category: number of establishments, number of employees, total payroll, value added by manufacture, value of shipments, and new capital spending. Specifically, California ranks among the leaders in machinery, fabricated metals, agricultural products, food processing, computers, aerospace technology, and many other industries.

With its shipyards, foundries, flour mills, and workshops, San Francisco was the state's first manufacturing center. The number of manufacturing establishments in California nearly doubled between 1899 and 1914, and the value of manufactures increased almost tenfold from 1990 to 1925. New factories for transportation equipment, primary metal products, chemicals and food products sprang up in the state during and after World War II. Second to New York State in industrial output for many years, California finally surpassed that state in most manufacturing categories in the 1972 Census of Manufacturers.

California's industrial workforce is mainly located in the two major manufacturing centers: almost three-fourths work in either the Los Angeles–Long Beach–Orange County area or the San Francisco–Oakland–San Jose area. Although the state workforce has a wide diversity of talents and products, the majority produces food, electronic and other electrical equipment, transportation equipment, apparel, and fabricated and industrial machinery.

Computers and aerospace manufacturers stand out among California's largest publicly owned corporations. Hewlett-Packard, Sun Microsystems, Tandem Computers, Varian Associates, and Silicon Graphics are leading names of the Silicon Valley (Santa Clara County) area just south of San Francisco. Southern California's manufacturing leaders are Rockwell International, Lockheed, Northrop, and Computers Sciences.

Leading manufacturers on the list of California private companies are Levi Strauss, Del Monte, Sunkist Growers, and Ernest and Julio Gallo Winery, showing the continuing strength that the Golden State has historically maintained in apparel and food production and processing. Apparel manufacturers employed over 144,000 people in 1999. Over $50 billion of food products is shipped annually.

The aerospace industry in California accounts for $28 billion in sales annually, employs about 117,000, and takes up a 20% share of the nation's total aerospace employment.

In 1999, California's motion picture industry, based primarily in Los Angeles, had receipts of at least $28 billion. In 1999, the film and TV production industry generated an annual payroll of $13.4 billion and pays $14.6 billion to suppliers while providing jobs to 475,000 Californians.

The tourism industry in California brings in over $60 billion in sales annually, and provides jobs for nearly 700,000 Californians.

Earnings of persons employed in California increased from $627 billion in 1997 to $677 billion in 1998, an increase of 7.9%. The largest industries in 1998 were services, 32.4% of earnings; state and local government, 11.4%; and durable goods manufacturing, 11.1%. Of the industries that accounted for at least 5% of earnings in 1998, the slowest growing from 1997 to 1998 was state and local government, which increased 5.5%; the fastest was durable goods manufacturing, which increased 10.9%.

30COMMERCE

California's wholesale trade in 1997 was $71 billion from 63,528 establishments. Of the total sales of durable goods in that year, electronic equipment made up 28%; industrial machinery, 26%; and instruments, 14%. Of the nondurable goods, groceries and related products accounted for more than 26%; printing and publishing, 21%; and chemicals, 16%.

The state's 1997 retail sales amounted to $91 billion. Of total 1997 types of establishments, food stores accounted for 11%; automobile dealers and service stations, 11%; and eating and drinking places, 33%. Food sales for 1997 totaled $47 billion, while general merchandise sales totaled $24 billion. Retail sales in the Los Angeles–Riverside–Orange County area totaled $107.6 billion, 48% of the state total and 5.7% of the US total. San Francisco–Oakland–San Jose accounted for 23.4% of the state's retail sales in 1992, and 2.8% of US retail sales.

Foreign trade is important to the California economy. In 1998, goods exported from California were valued at an estimated $116 billion. The Los Angeles metropolitan area handled $64 billion in exports during 1998. About 16% of the nation's exports were distributed from California in 1998. Imports totaled $209 billion. California's major markets are Japan, Canada, South Korea, Mexico, the European Community, and the industrializing countries of East Asia.

Leading exports include data-processing equipment, electrical tubes and transistors, scientific equipment, measuring instruments, optical equipment, and aircraft parts and spacecraft. California's leading agricultural export is cotton.

California's customs districts are the ports of Los Angeles, San Francisco, and San Diego. San Francisco and San Jose have been designated as federal foreign-trade zones, where imported goods may be stored duty-free for reshipment abroad, or customs duties avoided until the goods are actually marketed in the US.

31CONSUMER PROTECTION

Numerous California state and local government agencies protect, promote, and serve the interests of consumers.

The California Department of Consumer Affairs comprises 40 entities (9 bureaus, 1 programs, 24 boards, 3 committees, 1 commission, 1 office, and 1 task force) that license more than 2.3 million Californians in more than 230 occupations and professions. These entities establish minimum qualifications and levels of competency for licensure; license, register, or certify practitioners; investigate complaints; and discipline violators.

The California Department of Consumer Affairs also administers the Consumer Affairs Act (consumer information, education, complaints, and advocacy), the Arbitration Certification Program (auto warranty dispute resolution), and the Dispute Resolution Programs Act (funding of local dispute resolution programs). It helps carry out the Small Claims Act by publishing materials for those who administer and use the Small Claims Court, and by training small claims advisors and attorneys who serve as judges.

Other state agencies that serve consumers include the Department of Fair Employment and Housing (unlawful employment and housing discrimination), the Department of Real Estate (licensing of real estate brokers and sales agents), the Department of Corporations (licensing of personal finance companies, and a new service dedicated to combat investment fraud on the internet), and the Department of Insurance (licensing and conduct of insurance companies).

Consumers are also assisted by a variety of state and local law enforcement agencies that enforce the state's laws on false and deceptive advertising, unfair and deceptive trade practices, unfair competition, and other laws. These agencies include the California Attorney General, the District Attorneys of most counties, the City Attorneys of San Francisco, Los Angeles, and San Diego counties, and county consumer affairs departments.

32BANKING

In 1848, California's first financial institution—the Miners' Bank—was founded in San Francisco. Especially since 1904, when A. P. Giannini founded the Bank of Italy, now known as the Bank of America, California banks have pioneered in branch banking for families and small businesses. Today, California is among the leading states in branch banking, savings and loan associations, and credit union operations.

In 2002, there were 328 insured banks in California. As of September 2002, insured banks in California had total assets of $839 billion. Although net interest margins (NIMs) (the difference between the lower rates offered to savers and the higher rates charged on loans) for California's insured institutions declined in 2001/02, the state's median return on average assets (ROA) ratio (the measure of earnings in relation to all resources) increased, due in part to improved overhead efficiencies and gains in securities.

Until 30 June 1997, the State Banking Department administered laws and regulations governing state-chartered banks, foreign banks, trust companies, issuers of payment instruments, issuers of travelers' checks, and transmitters of money abroad. On 1 July 1997 a new department began supervising all of California's depository institutions. The Department of Financial Institutions now supervises over 700 commercial banks, credit unions, industrial loan companies, savings and loans, and other licensees formerly supervised by the State Banking Department.

33INSURANCE

Insurance companies provide a major source of California's investment capital by means of premium payments collected from policyholders. Life insurance companies also invest heavily in real estate; in 2001, life insurance firms owned $5,101.7 billion in real estate, and held an estimated $41.8 billion in mortgage debt on California properties.

In 2001 there were 10.3 million ordinary life insurance policies in force with a total value of $1,188 billion; total value for all categories of life insurance (ordinary, group, industrial, and credit) was $1,870 billion. Death benefits paid that year totaled $4.4 billion.

In 2003 there were 33 life and health and 159 property and casualty companies domiciled in California. Property and casualty insurers wrote premiums amounting to $44.09 billion in 2001. That year, there were 322,698 flood insurance policies in force in the state, with a total value of $50.3 million. Also in 2001, there were $543.1 million in direct premiums in earthquake insurance written, representing 53% of the US total.

34SECURITIES

California's Pacific Stock Exchange (PSE), the largest securities market in the US outside New York City and the 3rd-largest stock options marketplace in the world, is an association of some 500 member brokers who provide an auction market for the stocks, options, and bonds of national and local corporations. The exchange, which the only one in America to operate two trading floors (in Los Angeles and San Francisco), traces its roots to the San Francisco Stock and Bond Exchange formed in 1882. In 1957, the Los Angeles Oil Exchange merged with the Pacific Stock Exchange. Between 1957 and 1983, the volume of shares traded increased 30-fold, to more than one billion. Nearly 2,500 stocks, bonds, and other securities, and options on 800 underlying stocks and indexes, are traded on the PSE. Because of the time difference between the east and west coasts, the PSE begins trading at 6:30 AM PST and stays open until 1:30 PM PST, a half hour after the New York exchanges have closed.

There are 7,017 securities dealers' operations in California (the largest number of all states), with a total of 74,536 employees. Over 1,582 investment advisory organizations operate in the state. California is home to 939 NASDAQ company headquarters, 52 NASDAQ market makers, 107 AMEX corporation headquarters (16.5% of the nation's total), and 82 NYSE California-incorporated companies. The top ten NYSE companies in order of revenue size are: Hewlett-Packard, The Walt Disney Co., PG&E Corp., Caterpillar, The Gap, Tenet Healthcare Corp., Edison International, Northrop Grumman Corp., Solectron Corp., and Seagate Technology.

35PUBLIC FINANCE

California has the largest state budget in the nation, and in 2003 it was facing the country's largest projected state deficit in both absolute ($38.2 billion) and relative (almost 50% of the state's budget) terms. (The budget deficit was the main issue in the recall vote to remove the governor, also unprecedented, scheduled for October 2003.) Most analysts would agree on three major contributors to California's budget debacle: voter initiatives that rigidly limited the state's ability to raise taxes while establishing equally rigid expenditure mandates; the highly progressive income tax schedule, with the country's highest threshold for taxable income ($35,000 for a family of four; and the impact of the collapse of the dot.com boom, resulting in taxes on capital gains and stock options fall from $18 billion in 2000 to $8 billion in 2001. The shortfalls in projected revenue in the face of the economic downturn in 2001, and continued sluggishness into 2002 and 2003, rapidly snowballed into an overwhelming deficit.

The Governor's Budget is prepared by the Department of Finance (DOF) and presented by the governor to the legislature for approval. The state's fiscal year begins 1 July and ends 30 June. The Governor's Budget is the result of a process that begins more than one year before the budget becomes law. When presented to the legislature by 10 January of each year, the Governor's Budget incorporates revenue and expenditure estimates based upon the most current information available through late December. The DOF proposes adjustments to the Governor's Budget through "Finance Letters" in March. These adjustments are to update proposals made in January or to submit any new proposal of significant importance that has arisen since the fall process. By 14 May, the DOF submits revised expenditure and revenue estimates for both the current and budget years to the legislature. This revision, known as the May Revision, incorporates changes in enrollment, caseload, and population estimates. The constitution requires that the governor submit a balanced budget and it is a statutory requirement that the governor sign a balanced budget. The legislature is supposed to adopt a budget by June 15, but California law requires a two-thirds supermajority to pass the budget. A 2003/04 budget was not adopted until 29 July 2003. The governor signed it into law 2 August 2003.

The 2000/01 budget forecast total general fund revenue of over $68 billion from taxes, or an increase of 4.7% from 1999/00. These increases occurred despite a general fund tax relief program, partly because of tobacco company litigation that brought in over $500 million in 1999/00. Strong employment growth and increased income also contributed to the growth in revenues. California entered 2001/02 with a balance of $9.4 billion with revenues of $71.4 billion; Total resources of $80.8 billion were available for general fund expenditures of about $78 billion. In 2002/03, however, as total revenues fell $5.4 billion below forecasts, the general fund went from a beginning balance of over $2.35 billion to a deficit of –$2.13 billion, which include $1.4 billion held in an emergency reserve fund plus $1.4 billion transferred from the Special Fund for Economic Uncertainties, California's rainy day fund. Cuts made in expenditures made after the 2002/03 budget had been enacted totaled nearly $1.9 billion, and many general fund costs were shifted to other funds, loans, debt restructuring, and transfers. In 2003/04, the hole in the general fund deepened to –$4.45 billion.

The California State Budget for 2003/04 calls for general fund expenditures to fall to $71.1 billion from $78.1 billion in 2001/02. The $38.2 billion budget gap is to be met by expenditure cuts and savings (44.6%), fund shifts (11.1%); increased revenues from increases in the cigarette tax, vehicle license fee, and various court fees; loans and borrowing (5.9%); and deficit financing (27.1%). General Fund expenditures include 41.2% for K-12 education, 32.9% for health and human services, 12.2% for higher education, and 7.9% for corrections.

The following table from the US Census Bureau contains information on revenues, expenditures, indebtedness, and cash/securities for 2001.

	($000)	PERCENT	PER CAPITA
Population (thousands, 2001)	34,600	(X)	(X)
Total Revenue	176,080,892	100.00	5,089.04
General revenue	148,976,786	85.31	4,305.69
Utility revenue	1,772,519	1.01	51.23
Liquor store revenue	–	–	–
Insurance trust revenue	25,331,587	14.51	732.13
Exhibit: Salaries and wages	17,936,089	10.52	518.38
Total expenditure	170,470,259	100.00	4,926.89
General expenditure	145,582,238	85.40	4,207.58
Education	54,115,884	31.75	1,564.04
Public welfare	37,251,330	21.85	1,076.63
Hospitals	4,121,426	2.42	119.12
Health	6,522,891	3.83	188.52
Highways	6,339,813	3.72	183.23
Police protection	1,324,682	0.78	38.29
Correction	5,313,697	3.12	153.58
Natural resources	2,702,532	1.59	78.11
Parks and recreation	561,500	0.33	16.23
Government administration	5,961,869	3.50	172.31
Interest on general debt	2,758,540	1.62	79.73
Other and unallocable	18,608,074	10.92	537.81
Utility expenditure	7,918,662	4.65	228.86
Liquor store expenditure	–	–	–
Insurance trust expenditure	16,969,359	9.95	490.44
Debt at end of fiscal year	62,343,083	100.00	1,801.82
Cash and security holdings	324,515,571	100.00	9,379.06

36 TAXATION

In the mid-1970s, Californians were paying more in taxes than residents of any other state. On a per capita basis, California ranked 3rd among the 50 states in state and local taxation in 1977, but this heavy tax burden was reduced by the passage in 1978 of Proposition 13. By 1982, California ranked 5th in per capita state and local taxes. The state ranked 12th in federal tax burden per capita in 1990. In 2003, California ranked 8th, with combined state and local taxes amounting to 10.6% of income.

The state's progressive income tax rates range from 0% to 9.3% on net taxable income. The state corporate income tax on general corporations is 8.84% of net income from California sources; a minimum franchise tax of $800 is applied to all firms except banks and financial corporations, whose net income is taxed at rates 2% above the general corporation rate.

The state sales tax is 6% on retail sales (excepting food for home consumption, prescription medicines, gas, water, electricity, and certain other exempt products); 5.0% represented the basic state rate, and .50% was designated for localities. Localities derive most of their revenue from property taxes, which were limited in 1978 by Proposition 13 to 1% of market value, with annual increases in the tax not to exceed 2%. Other state taxes include inheritance and gift taxes, insurance tax, motor vehicle fees, cigarette tax, and an alcoholic beverage tax. In 2002, state taxes collected totaled $77.75 billion, of which 42.5% was from income taxes, 30.6% from the general sales tax, 30.6% from selective sales taxes, 7.3% from license fees, 6.85% from corporate taxes, 2.5% from state property taxes, and 1.2% from inheritance and gift taxes.

The following table from the US Census Bureau provides a summary of taxes collected by the state in 2002.

	($000)	PER CAPITA
Total Taxes	77,755,376	2,214.24
Property taxes	1,951,507	55.57
Sales and gross receipts	30,702,048	874.3
General sales and gross receipts	23,816,406	678.22
Selective sales taxes	6,885,642	196.08
Alcoholic beverage	292,627	8.33
Amusements	(X)	(X)
Insurance Premiums	1,596,002	45.45
Motor fuels	3,295,903	93.86
Pari-mutuels	44,622	1.27
Public utilities	482,696	13.75
Tobacco products	1,102,807	31.4
Other selective sales	70,985	2.02
Licenses	5,693,058	162.12
Alcoholic beverages	36,680	1.04
Amusements	4,355	0.12
Corporation	47,982	1.37
Hunting and fishing	74,037	2.11
Motor vehicle	1,740,434	49.56
Motor vehicle operators	151,342	4.31
Public utility	75,064	2.14
Occupation and business, NEC	3,551,204	101.13
Other	11,960	0.34
Other taxes	39,408,763	1,122.24
Individual income	33,046,665	941.07
Corporation net income	5,333,036	151.87
Death and gift	1,000,493	28.49
Documentary and stock transfer	(X)	(X)
Severance	28,569	0.81
Other	(X)	(X)

37 ECONOMIC POLICY

The California Trade and Commerce Agency was created by Governor Pete Wilson as a cabinet-level agency that consolidated the former Department of Commerce, the World Trade Commission, and the state's overseas offices. In 2001, under Governor Gray Davis, it became the Technology, Trade and Commerce Agency (TTCA) The TTCA is the state's lead agency for promoting economic development, job creation, and business retention. The agency oversees all state economic development efforts, international commerce, and tourism. Some of the array of agencies coordinated by the TTCA include the California Infrastructure and Economic Development Bank (I-Bank), which helps local governments and businesses secure capital for infrastructural and non-profit projects; the California Export Finance Office (CEFO), which provides loan guarantees to financial institutions lending to small and medium-sized California exporters; the Small Business Loan Guarantee Program (SBLGP); and the California Financing Coordination Committee (CFCC) which consists of state and federal agencies that work together to coordinate and streamline infrastructure financing in local communities.

In fulfilling its mission to improve California's business climate, the agency works closely with domestic and international businesses, economic development corporations, chambers of commerce, regional visitor and convention bureaus, and the various permit-issuing state and municipal government agencies.

The International Trade and Investment Division is headquarters for California's international offices and the Offices of Foreign Investment, Export Finance, and Export Development. The Agency also houses the Tourism Division, and the Economic Development Division, which includes the Offices of Business Development, Small Business, Strategic Technology, Permit Assistance, Major Corporate Projects, and the California Film Commission.

California offers a broad array of state economic development incentives, including a business assistance program, including guidance through regulatory and permitting processes. California also has a statewide network of small business development centers. California has an enterprise zone program with 39 zones offering various tax credits, deductions, and exemptions. The zones focus on rural and economically distressed areas.

There are ten foreign trade zones in the state, and an Office of Foreign Investment with incentives to attract foreign companies. In 2003, the legislature voted to stop funding for the states 12 foreign trade office, which had received $6 million in 2002, amid the state's budget crisis and questions about the trade offices' claims to have generated $44 million in business for state enterprises. The foreign trade office established in Yerevan, Armenia in 2002 remained open because it was financed by the Armenian community.

Among the development projects being pursued in 2003 was the STAR (State Theatrical Arts Resources) program begun in 2001 as a continuation of the successful "Film California First" program of 2000. The STAR program seeks to support California's $33 billion filmmaking industry, and in April 2003 the government announced the completion of eight distinctive filming locations. In January 2003, the Governor introduced a "Build California" program aimed at expediting the construction of schools, housing, roads, and other infrastructural projects as a means of reviving the state economy. In January 2002, the TTCA gave its support to a national campaign called Back on Track America which aimed at helping small businesses through the country's economic turndown. In January 2003, the government announced that outstanding loans under the SBLGP, created in 1999, had surpassed $200 million. Through the Goldstrike partnership, the Office of Strategic Technology supports the growth of high technology in California. The conversion of former military bases to new manufacturing and commercial sites is also a priority of the state government. Among the development projects announced in 2003 was $10 million in low-cost state financing, arranged through the I-Bank, for Sacramento County to be used for the economic development of the former McClennan and Mather air force bases.

[38] HEALTH

California's infant death rate for the 12 months ending with 2000 was 5.4 per 1,000 live births, well below the US norm of 7.3. California's abortion rate of 39 per 1,000 women was the highest among the states, with a total of 280,180 abortions performed.

California registered 229,551 deaths in 2000, but with a death rate of 682.5 per 100,000 population still ranked below the national death rate of 873.1. California also ranked below the national death rates for HIV, diabetes, Alzheimer's disease, heart diseases, cerebrovascular diseases, pulmonary diseases, accidents, traffic fatalities, and suicide. In 2000 17.2% of the population age 18 and older were smokers. California had recorded 123,819 AIDS cases through 2001, second only to New York. The HIV death rate in California (4.4 per 100,000 population) was lower than the national HIV death rate of 5.3 per 100,000 population in 2000.

As of 1995, there were 70 psychiatric hospitals, including three institutions for the mentally retarded. In recent years, an increasing number of patients have been treated through community mental health programs rather than in state hospitals.

In 2001, California's 384 community hospitals had 73,291 beds and reported 3,332,839 admissions. In the same year, hospital personnel included 85,961 full-time registered nurses and 10,387 full-time licensed practical nurses. In 2000, there were 281 physicians per 100,000 population. The average expense per inpatient day for a hospital in the state amounted to $1,146.60.

Medi-Cal is a statewide program that pays for the medical care of persons who otherwise could not afford it. California has also been a leader in developing new forms of health care, including the health maintenance organization (HMO), which provides preventive care, diagnosis, and treatment for which the patient pays a fixed annual premium. Federal government grants to cover the Medicare and Medicaid services in 2001 totaled $13.9 billion; 3,954,996 enrollees received Medicare benefits that year. A large portion of California's population, 19.5%, remained uninsured in 2002.

[39] SOCIAL WELFARE

In 2001, the average weekly unemployment benefit was $176.30. Average monthly participation in the food stamp program in FY2002 comprised 1,710,306 persons (647,661 households). The average monthly benefit was $83.10, and the sum total of benefits paid in FY2002 was $1,705,424,019.

With the enactment of the Personal Responsibility and Work Opportunity Reconciliation Act of 1996, the US government has changed the form and regulations for many of its social welfare programs. Most significantly, it replaces Aid to Families with Dependent Children (AFDC), an open-ended entitlement program, with Temporary Assistance for Needy Families (TANF), a limited system of assistance funded largely through federal block grants. The reform act also impacts the food stamp program, the Supplemental Security Income program, and the child nutrition program. The law took effect on 1 July 1997 and provided $16.38 billion in block grants for fiscal years 1997–2002. The grants are to be divided among the states based on an equation involving the numbers of former AFDC recipients in each state.

Reauthorization of the 1996 social welfare legislation, scheduled for 2002, was delayed, and the original law had been extended three times as of July 2003, with the most recent extension running through September 2003. California's TANF program is called CALWORKS (California Work Opportunity and Responsibility to Kids). In June 2000 the state had 1,272,468 welfare recipients. State expenditures on the TANF program in FY2002 totaled $2,225,511,540.

In December 2001, Social Security benefits were paid to 4,247,470 California residents. This number included 2,743,610 retired workers, 421,540 widows and widowers, 451,530 disabled workers, 295,460 spouses, and 335,330 children. Social Security beneficiaries represented 12.3% of the total state population and 85.7% of the state's population age 65 and older. Retired workers (excluding persons with special benefits) received an average monthly payment of $882; widows and widowers, $851; disabled workers, $828; and spouses, $432. Payments for children of retired workers averaged $402 per month; children of deceased workers, $577; and children of disabled workers, $246.

Federal Supplemental Security Income payments in December 2001 went to 1,106,294 Californians, averaging $500 a month.

40HOUSING

California had long led the United States both in the number of housing units built annually and in the value of their construction, but by 1982 it was overtaken by Texas in both categories and by Florida in the former. However, California still ranks first in the number of housing units, with 12,507,767 in 2002.

The earliest homes in southern California were Spanish colonial structures renowned for their simplicity and harmony with the landscape. These houses were one-story high and rectangular in plan, with outside verandas supported by wooden posts; their thick adobe walls were covered with whitewashed mud plaster. In the north, the early homes were usually two stories high, with thick adobe walls on the ground floor, balconies at the front and back, and tile roofing. Some adobe houses dating from the 1830s still stand in coastal cities and towns, particularly Monterey.

During the 1850s, jerry-built houses of wood, brick, and stone sprang up in the mining towns, and it was not until the 1870s that more substantial homes, in the Spanish mission style, were built in large numbers in the cities. About 1900, the California bungalow, with overhanging eaves and low windows, began to sweep the state and then the nation. The fusion of Spanish adobe structures and traditional American wooden construction appeared in the 1930s, and "California style" houses gained great popularity throughout the West. Adapted from the functional international style of Frank Lloyd Wright and other innovative architects, modern domestic designs, emphasizing split-level surfaces and open interiors, won enthusiastic acceptance in California. Wright's finest California homes include the Freeman house in Los Angeles and the Millard house in Pasadena. One of Wright's disciples, Viennese-born Richard Neutra, was especially influential in adapting modern design principles to California's economy and climate.

Between 1960 and 1990, some 6.3 million houses and apartments were built in the state, comprising more than 56% of California housing stock. Housing construction boomed at record rates during the 1970s but slowed down at the beginning of the 1980s because rising building costs and high mortgage interest rates made it difficult for people of moderate means to enter the housing market. The total number of housing units in the state increased by 53% during 1940–50; 52%, 1950–60; 28% 1960–70; 33%, 1970–80; and 20%, 1980–90.

Of the state's estimated 12,507,767 housing units in 2002, 11,705,477 were occupied; about 57% were owner-occupied. About 56.5% of all units were single-family, detached homes; about 11% of dwellings were in buildings with 20 or more units. It was estimated that about 198,166 units were without telephone service, 63,034 lacked complete plumbing facilities, and 110,062 lacked complete kitchen facilities. While most homes used gas or electricity as a heating fuel, about 263,583 households relied on wood and about 4,742 employed solar heating. California ranked second in the nation for highest home values in 2002 when the median value of a one-family home was $275,526. The median monthly cost for mortgage owners was about $1,592 while the cost for renters was at a median of about $840. The average household had 2.93 people.

California housing policies have claimed national attention on several occasions. In 1964, state voters approved Proposition 14, a measure repealing the Fair Housing Act and forbidding any future restrictions on the individual's right to sell, lease, or rent to anyone of his own choosing. The measure was later declared unconstitutional by state and federal courts. In March 1980, a Los Angeles city ordinance banned rental discrimination on the basis of age. A municipal court judge had previously ruled it was illegal for a landlord to refuse to rent an apartment to a couple simply because they had children. Ordinances banning age discrimination had previously been enacted in the cities of San Francisco, Berkeley, and Davis, and in Santa Monica and Santa Clara counties. During 2002, the US Department of Housing and Urban Development awarded over $107.6 million in community development aid to California state programs. About 159,573 new units were authorized in 2002.

41EDUCATION

The history of public education in California goes back at least to the 1790s, when the governor of the Spanish colony assigned retired soldiers to open one-room schools at the Franciscan mission settlements of San Jose, Santa Barbara, San Francisco, San Diego, and Monterey. Most of these schools, and others opened during the next three decades, were short-lived, however. During the 1830s, a few more schools were established for Spanish children, including girls, who were taught needlework. Easterners and Midwesterners who came to California in the 1840s laid the foundation for the state's present school system. The first American school was opened in an old stable at the Santa Clara mission in 1846, and the following year a schoolroom was established in the Monterey customhouse. San Francisco's first school was founded in April 1848 by a Yale graduate, Thomas Douglass, but six weeks later, caught up in Gold Rush fever, he dropped his books and headed for the mines. Two years after this inauspicious beginning, the San Francisco city council passed an ordinance providing for the first free public school system in California. Although the first public high school was opened in San Francisco in 1856, the California legislature did not provide for state financial support of secondary schools until 1903.

The state's first colleges, Santa Clara College (now the University of Santa Clara), founded by Jesuits, and California Wesleyan (now the University of the Pacific), located in Stockton, both opened in 1851. A year later, the Young Ladies' Seminary (now Mills College) was founded at Benicia. The nucleus of what later became the University of California was established at Oakland in 1853 and moved to nearby Berkeley in 1873. Subsequent landmarks in education were the founding of the University of Southern California (USC) at Los Angeles in 1880 and of Stanford University in 1885, the opening of the first state junior colleges in 1917, and the establishment in 1927 of the Department of Education, which supervised the vast expansion of the California school system in the years following.

California ranks first among the states in enrollment in public schools and in institutions of higher learning. In 2000, 76.8% of Californians age 25 and older were high school graduates. Some 26.6% had obtained a bachelor's degree or higher.

The total enrollment for fall 1999 in California's public schools stood at 6,038,589. Of these, 4,336,687 attended schools from kindergarten through grade eight, and 1,701,902 attended high school. Minority students made up approximately 63% of the total enrollment in public elementary and secondary schools in 2001. Total enrollment was estimated at 6,239,539 in fall

2000 and expected to reach 6,357,000 by fall 2005. Enrollment in nonpublic schools in fall 2001 was 619,067. Expenditures for public education in 2000/01 were estimated at $39,026,563.

As of fall 2000, there were 2,556,598 students enrolled in institutions of higher education. In the same year California had 419 degree-granting institutions. In 1997, minority students comprised 49.3% of total postsecondary enrollment. The University of California has its main campus at Berkeley and branches at Davis, Irvine, Los Angeles (UCLA), Merced, Riverside, San Diego, San Francisco, Santa Barbara, and Santa Cruz. The Hastings College of Law is also part of the UC system. The California state college and university system is not be confused with the University of California. California's 23 state universities include those at Los Angeles, Sacramento, San Diego, San Francisco, and San Jose; locations of state colleges include Bakersfield, San Bernardino, and Stanislaus. Privately endowed institutions with the largest student enrollments are the University of Southern California (USC) and Stanford University. Other independent institutions are Occidental College in Los Angeles, Mills College at Oakland, Whittier College, the Claremont consortium of colleges (including Harvey Mudd College, Pomona College, and Claremont McKenna College), and the California Institute of Technology at Pasadena. California has 16 Roman Catholic colleges and universities, including Loyola Marymount University of Los Angeles.

The California Student Aid Commission administers the California Guaranteed Student Loan Program and the State Graduate Fellowship Program. All recipients must have been California residents for at least 12 months.

42 ARTS

The arts have always thrived in California—at first in the Franciscan chapels with their religious paintings and church music, later in the art galleries, gas-lit theaters, and opera houses of San Francisco and Los Angeles, and today in seaside artists' colonies, regional theaters, numerous concert halls, and, not least, in the motion picture studios of Hollywood.

In the mid-19th century, many artists came from the East to paint western landscapes, and some stayed on in California. The San Francisco Institute of Arts was founded in 1874; the E. B. Crocker Art Gallery was established in Sacramento in 1884; and the Monterey-Carmel artists' colony sprang up in the early years of the 20th century. Other art colonies developed later in Los Angeles, Santa Barbara, Laguna Beach, San Diego, and La Jolla. Notable art museums and galleries include the Los Angeles County Museum of Art (founded in 1910), Huntington Library, Art Gallery and Botanical Gardens at San Marino (1919), San Francisco Museum of Modern Art (1921), Norton Simon Museum of Art at Pasadena (1924), and San Diego Museum of Art (1925).

The theater arrived in California as early as 1846 in the form of stage shows at a Monterey amusecment hall. The first theater building was opened in 1849 in Sacramento by the Eagle Theater Co. Driven out of Sacramento by floods, the company soon found refuge in San Francisco; by 1853, that city had seven theaters. During the late 19th century, many famous performers, including dancer Isadora Duncan and actress Maude Adams, began their stage careers in California. Today, California theater groups with national reputations include the American Conservatory Theater of San Francisco, Berkeley Repertory Theater, Mark Taper Forum in Los Angeles, and Old Globe Theater of San Diego.

The motion picture industry did not begin in Hollywood—the first commercial films were made in New York City and New Jersey in the 1890s—but within a few decades this Los Angeles suburb had become synonymous with the new art form. California became a haven for independent producers escaping an East Coast monopoly on patents related to filmmaking. (If patent infringements were discovered, the producer could avoid a lawsuit by crossing the border into Mexico.) In 1908, an independent producer, William Selig, completed in Los Angeles a film he had begun in Chicago, The Count of Monte Cristo, which is now recognized as the first commercial film produced in California. He and other moviemakers opened studios in Los Angeles, Santa Monica, Glendale, and— finally—Hollywood, where the sunshine was abundant, land was cheap, and the workforce plentiful. These independent producers developed the full-length motion picture and the star system, utilizing the talents of popular actors like Mary Pickford, Douglas Fairbanks, and Charlie Chaplin again and again. In 1915, D. W. Griffith produced the classic "silent" The Birth of a Nation, which was both a popular and an artistic success. Motion picture theaters sprang up all over the country, and an avalanche of motion pictures was produced in Hollywood by such increasingly powerful studios as Warner Brothers, Fox, and Metro-Goldwyn-Mayer. Hollywood became the motion picture capital of the world. By 1923, film production accounted for one-fifth of the state's annual manufacturing value; in 1930, the film industry was one of the 10 largest in the US.

Hollywood flourished by using the latest technical innovations and by adapting itself to the times. Sound motion pictures achieved a breakthrough in 1927 with The Jazz Singer, starring Al Jolson; color films appeared within a few years; and Walt Disney originated the feature-length animated cartoon with Snow White and the Seven Dwarfs (1937). Whereas most industries suffered drastically from the depression of the 1930s, Hollywood prospered by providing, for the most part, escapist entertainment on a lavish scale. The 1930s saw the baroque spectacles of Busby Berkeley, the inspired lunacy of the Marx Brothers, and the romantic historical drama Gone with the Wind (1939). During World War II, Hollywood offered its vast audience patriotic themes and pro-Allied propaganda.

In the postwar period, the motion picture industry fell on hard times because of competition from television, but it recovered fairly quickly by selling its old films to television and producing new ones specifically for home viewing. In the 1960s, Hollywood replaced New York City as the main center for the production of television programs. Fewer motion pictures were made, and those that were produced were longer and more expensive, including such top box-office attractions as The Sound of Music (1965), Star Wars (1977), E.T.—The Extra-Terrestrial (1982), Jurassic Park (1993), Independence Day (1996), Titanic (1997), Armageddon (1998), and The Matrix Reloaded (2003). No longer are stars held under exclusive contracts, and the power of the major studios has waned as the role of independent filmmakers like Francis Ford Coppola, Steven Spielberg, and George Lucas has assumed increased importance.

Among the many composers who came to Hollywood to write film music were Irving Berlin, George Gershwin, Kurt Weill, George Antheil, Ferde Grofe, Erich Korngold, and John Williams; such musical luminaries as Igor Stravinsky and Arnold Schoenberg were longtime residents of the state. Symphonic music is well established. In addition to the renowned Los Angeles Philharmonic, whose permanent conductors have included Zubin Mehta and Carlo Maria Giulini, there are the San Francisco Symphony and other professional symphonic orchestras in Oakland and San Jose. Some 180 semiprofessional or amateur orchestras have been organized in other communities. Resident opera companies perform regularly in San Francisco and San Diego. Annual musical events include the Sacramento and Monterey jazz festivals and summer concerts at the Hollywood Bowl.

California has also played a major role in the evolution of popular music since the 1960s. The "surf sound" of the Beach Boys dominated California pop music in the mid-1960s. By 1967, the "acid rock" of bands like the Grateful Dead, Jefferson Airplane (later Jefferson Starship), and the Doors had started to gain national recognition—and that year the heralded "summer of love" in San Francisco attracted young people from throughout the country. It was at the Monterey International Pop Festival, also in 1967, that Jimi Hendrix began his rise to stardom. During the 1970s, California was strongly identified with a group of resident singer-songwriters, including Neil Young, Joni Mitchell, Randy Newman, Jackson Browne, and Warren Zevon, who brought a new sophistication to rock lyrics. Los Angeles is a main center of the popular music industry, with numerous recording studios and branch offices of the leading record companies. Los Angeles-based Motown Industries, the largest black-owned company in the US, is a major force in popular music.

California has nurtured generations of writers, many of whom moved there from other states. In 1864, Mark Twain, a Missourian, came to California as a newspaperman. Four years later, New York–born Bret Harte published his earliest short stories, many set in mining camps, in San Francisco's *Overland Monthly*. The writer perhaps most strongly associated with California is Nobel Prize–winner John Steinbeck, a Salinas native. Hollywood's film industry has long been a magnet for writers, and San Francisco in the 1950s was the gathering place for a group, later known as the Beats (or "Beat Generation"), that included Jack Kerouac and Allen Ginsberg. The City Lights Bookshop, owned by poet Lawrence Ferlinghetti, was the site of readings by Beat poets during this period.

In 2003, the California Arts Council and other arts organizations received grants totaling $8,429,100 from the National Endowment for the Arts. In 2000, California organizations received $6.89 million from the National Endowment for the Humanities. The California Arts Council also used state financial resources to promote arts organizations. The California Council for the Humanities has offices in San Diego, San Francisco, and Los Angeles. California is also a member state of the regional Western States Arts Federation. A California law, effective 1 January 1977, is the first in the nation to provide living artists with royalties on the profitable resale of their work.

43 LIBRARIES AND MUSEUMS

As of 2000, California had 171 public library jurisdictions and 52 public library systems with 179,000 public libraries that held a total of 66,193,000 volumes or 1.9 volumes per capita, with a circulation of 165,950,000. California has three of the largest public library systems in the nation, along with some of the country's finest private collections. The Los Angeles Public Library System had 5,811,492 volumes in 1998; the San Francisco Public Library, 2,137,618; and the San Diego Public Library, 2,670,375. Public library income came to $830,267,000 in 2000, including $5,811,169 in federal grants and $70,572,695 in state grants. While California's public libraries had the 2nd-largest income of all states, spending per capita was mediocre.

Outstanding among academic libraries is the University of California's library at Berkeley, with its Bancroft collection of western Americana. Stanford's Hoover Institution has a notable collection of research materials on the Russian Revolution, World War I, and worldwide relief efforts thereafter. Numerous rare books, manuscripts, and documents are held in the Huntington Library in San Marino.

California has nearly 576 museums and over 50 public gardens. Outstanding museums include the California Museum of Science and Industry, Los Angeles County Museum of Art, and Natural History Museum, all in Los Angeles; the San Francisco Museum of Modern Art, Fine Arts Museums of San Francisco, and Asian Art Museum of San Francisco; the San Diego Museum of Man; the California State Indian Museum in Sacramento; the

Norton Simon Museum in Pasadena; and the J. Paul Getty Museum at Malibu. Among historic sites are Sutter's Mill, northeast of Sacramento, where gold was discovered in 1848, and a restoration of the Mission of San Diego de Alcala, where in 1769 the first of California's Franciscan missions was established. San Diego has an excellent zoo, and San Francisco's Strybing Arboretum and Botanical Gardens has beautiful displays of Asian, Mediterranean, and California flora.

44 COMMUNICATIONS

Mail service in California, begun in 1851 by means of mule-drawn wagons, was soon taken over by stagecoach companies. The need for speedier delivery led to the founding in April 1860 of the Pony Express, which operated between San Francisco and Missouri. On the western end, relays of couriers picked up mail in San Francisco, carried it by boat to Sacramento, and then conveyed it on horseback to St. Joseph, Missouri, a hazardous journey of nearly 2,000 mi (3,200 km) within 10 days. The Pony Express functioned for only 16 months, however, before competition from the first transcontinental telegraph line (between San Francisco and New York) put it out of business; telegraph service between San Francisco and Los Angeles had begun a year earlier.

California has more telephones than any other state. In 2001, 97.0% of the state's occupied housing units had telephones.

The state's first radio broadcasting station, KQW in San Jose, began broadcasting speech and music on an experimental basis in 1912. California stations pioneered in program development with the earliest audience-participation show (1922) and the first "soap opera," One Man's Family (1932). When motion picture stars began doubling as radio performers in the 1930s, Hollywood emerged as a center of radio network broadcasting. Similarly, Hollywood's abundant acting talent, experienced film crews, and superior production facilities enabled it to become the principal production center for television programs from the 1950s onward.

California ranks 1st in the US in the number of commercial television stations, and 2nd only to Texas in radio stations. In 2003 there were 268 FM and 86 AM major radio stations and 68 major television stations. In 1999, Los Angeles alone had 3,392,820 cable television households (65% of television-owning households); second only to the New York City area. The Sacramento-Stockton-Modesto area had 64% cable penetration of 1,19,820 television households. The San Francisco-Oakland-San Jose area had cable in 72% of its TV-owning homes. San Diego had cable in 83% of its television-viewing households.

A total of 1,511,571 Internet domain names had been registered in California by the year 2000; the most of any state.

45 PRESS

In 2002 there were 67 morning dailies and 26 evening dailies; 60 newspapers had Sunday editions. The following table shows California's leading newspapers, with their 2002 circulations:

AREA	NAME	DAILY	SUNDAY
Fresno	*Bee* (m,S)	157,820	188,093
Long Beach	*Press-Telegram* (m,S)	95,659	109,203
Los Angeles	*Times* (m,S)	944,303	1,369,066
	Investor's Business Daily(m)	281,173	
	Daily News(m,S)	178,156	200,167
	La Opinion(Spanish, m,S)	127,576	77,907
Oakland	*Tribune* (m,S)	68,962	65,320
Orange County– Santa Ana	*Register* (m,S)	324,056	378,934
Riverside	*Press-Enterprise* (m,S)	168,765	176,968
Sacramento	*Bee* (m,S)	285,863	344,791
San Diego	*Union Tribune* (m,S)	351,762	433,495
San Francisco	*Chronicle* (a,S)	512,042	523,096
	Examiner (e,S)	107,129	552,400
San Jose	*Mercury-News* (m,S)	268,621	301,649

Investor's Business Daily has nationwide circulation. In 2001, The *Los Angeles Times* was the 4th-largest daily newspaper in the country, based on circulation rates. It ranked 2nd in the nation for Sunday circulation the same year. The San Francisco *Chronicle* had the 11th-largest daily circulation and the 17th-largest Sunday circulation in 2001. San Francisco has long been the heart of the influential Hearst newspaper chain.

In August 1846, the state's first newspaper, the *Californian,*, printed (on cigarette paper—the only paper available) the news of the U.S. declaration of war on Mexico. The *Californian* moved to San Francisco in 1847 to compete with a new weekly, the *California Star.* When gold was discovered, both papers failed to mention the fact and both soon went out of business as their readers headed for the hills. On the whole, however, the influx of gold seekers was good for the newspaper business. In 1848, the *Californian* and the *Star* were resurrected and merged into the *Alta Californian,* which two years later became the state's first daily newspaper; among subsequent contributors were Mark Twain and Bret Harte. Four years later there were 57 newspapers and periodicals in the state.

The oldest continuously published newspapers in California are the *Sacramento Bee* (founded in 1857), San Francisco's *Examiner* (1865) and *Chronicle* (1868), and the *Los Angeles Times* (1881). *Times* owner and editor Harrison Gray Otis quickly made his newspaper preeminent in Los Angeles—a tradition continued by his son-in-law, Henry Chandler, and by the Otis-Chandler family today. Of all California's dailies, the *Times* is the only one with a depth of international and national coverage to rival the major east coast papers. In 1887, young William Randolph Hearst took over his father's *San Francisco Daily Examiner* and introduced human interest items and sensational news stories to attract readers. The *Examiner* became the nucleus of the Hearst national newspaper chain, which later included the *News-Call Bulletin* and *Herald Examiner* in Los Angeles. The *Bulletin,* like many other newspapers in the state, ceased publication in the decades following World War II because of rising costs and increased competition for readers and advertisers.

California has more book publishers—about 225—than any state except New York. Among the many magazines published in the state are *Architectural Digest, Bon Appetit, Motor Trend, PC World, Runner's World,* and *Sierra.*

46ORGANIZATIONS

Californians belong to thousands of nonprofit societies and organizations, many of which have their national headquarters in the state. In 2003, there were over 12,000 regional, national, and international organizations within the state.

National service organizations operating out of California include the National Assistance League and the Braille Institute of America, both in Los Angeles, and Knights of the Round Table International, Pasadena. Cultural and educational groups headquartered in the state are the American Aviation Historical Society, Garden Grove; American Battleships Association, San Diego; and American Society of Zoologists, Thousand Oaks.

Environmental and scientific organizations include the Sierra Club, Friends of the Earth, and Save-the-Redwoods League, all with headquarters in San Francisco; Animal Protection Institute of America, Sacramento; Geothermal Resources Council, Davis; and Seismological Society of America, Berkeley.

Among entertainment-oriented organizations centered in the state are the Academy of Motion Picture Arts and Sciences and the Academy of Television Arts and Sciences, both in Beverly Hills; Directors Guild of America and Writers Guild of America (West), both in Los Angeles; Screen Actors Guild and American Society of Cinematographers, both in Hollywood; and the National Academy of Recording Arts and Sciences, Burbank.

Other commercial and professional groups are the Institute of Mathematical Statistics, San Carlos; Manufacturers' Agents National Association, Irvine; National Association of Civil Service Employees, San Diego; and Pacific Area Travel Association, San Francisco.

The many national sports groups with California headquarters include the Association of Professional Ball Players of America (baseball), Garden Grove; US Hang Gliding Association, Los Angeles; National Hot Rod Association, North Hollywood; Professional Karate Association, Beverly Hills; United States Youth Soccer Association, Castro Valley; Soaring Society of America, Santa Monica; International Softball Congress, Anaheim Hills; American Surfing Association, Huntington Beach; and US Swimming Association, Fresno.

There are numerous state, regional, and local organizations dedicated to arts and culture. These include the California Arts Council, California Council for the Humanities, and the California Hispanic Cultural Society. There are also a number of regional conservation, environmental, and agricultural organizations. California also hosts the National Investigations Committee on UFOs, Van Nuys.

47TOURISM, TRAVEL, AND RECREATION

California has been the number one travel destination in the United States for a number of years. In 2002, tourism was the state's 3rd-largest employer and, with travel expenditures of over $75 billion per year, the tourist industry is the fifth-largest contributor to GSP. In support of the industry, the state adopted the California Tourism Marketing Act in 1995. This marketing referendum of California businesses established the California Travel and Tourism Commission (CTTC) and a statewide marketing fund derived from mandatory assessments. The California Tourism Program, a joint venture between the CTTC and the California Division of Tourism, has succeeded so well that it is being look to as a model program by other states. From 1998-2002, the state saw increased visitor spending of $8.7 billion dollars and created 120,833 new tourism-related jobs.

In 2002, the state hosted about 318 domestic travelers and 8 million international visitors. Overseas visitors that year (about 4.5 million) were primarily from Japan, the United Kingdom, South Korea, Germany, and France. Nearly 3 million travelers were from Mexico and about 870,000 were from Canada. In 2002, it was estimated that 1,030,000 people are employed in the tourism industry. There are 11 Official California Welcome Centers within the state. There are also five international travel trade offices (in Brazil, Australia, Germany, Japan, and the United Kingdom.

While the state's mild, sunny climate and varied scenery of seacoast, mountains, and desert lure many visitors, the San Francisco and Los Angeles metropolitan areas offer the most popular tourist attractions. San Francisco's Fisherman's Wharf, Chinatown, and Ghirardelli Square are popular for shopping and dining; tourists also frequent the city's unique cable cars, splendid museums, Opera House, and Golden Gate Bridge. The Golden Gate National Recreation Area, comprising 68 sq mi (176 sq km) on both sides of the entrance to San Francisco Bay, includes Fort Point in the Presidio park, Alcatraz Island (formerly a federal prison) in the bay, the National Maritime Museum with seven historic ships, and the Muir Woods, located 17 mi (27 km) north of the city. South of the city, the rugged coastal scenery of the Monterey peninsula attracts many visitors; to the northeast, the wineries of the Sonoma and Napa valleys offer their wares for sampling and sale.

The Los Angeles area has the state's principal tourist attractions: the Disneyland amusement center at Anaheim, and Hollywood, which features visits to motion picture and television studios and sightseeing tours of film stars' homes in Beverly Hills.

One of Hollywood's most popular spots is Mann's (formerly Grauman's) Chinese Theater, where the impressions of famous movie stars' hands and feet (and sometimes paws or hooves) are embedded in concrete. The New Year's Day Tournament of Roses at Pasadena is an annual tradition. Southwest of Hollywood, the Santa Monica Mountain National Recreation Area was created by Congress in 1978 as the country's largest urban park, covering 150,000 acres (61,000 hectares). The Queen Mary ocean liner, docked at Long Beach, is now a marine-oceanographic exposition center and hotel-convention complex.

The rest of the state offers numerous tourist attractions, including some of the largest and most beautiful national parks in the US. In the north are Redwood National Park and Lassen Volcanic National Park. In east-central California, situated in the Sierra Nevada, are Yosemite National Park, towering Mt. Whitney in Sequoia National Park, and Lake Tahoe on the Nevada border. About 80 mi (129 km) east of Mt. Whitney is Death Valley. Among the popular tourist destinations in southern California are the zoo and Museum of Man in San Diego's Balboa Park and the Mission San Juan Capistrano, to which, according to tradition, the swallows return each spring. The San Simeon mansion and estate of the late William Randolph Hearst are now state historical monuments.

48 SPORTS

There are at least 35 professional sports teams in California, considerably more than in any other state. California has everything from baseball to hockey to soccer to women's basketball. The Major League Baseball teams are the Los Angeles Dodgers, the San Francisco Giants, the San Diego Padres, the Oakland Athletics, and the Anaheim Angels. The Oakland Raiders, the San Francisco 49ers, and the San Diego Chargers play in the National Football League. In basketball the Los Angeles Lakers, the Los Angeles Clippers, the Golden State Warriors, and the Sacramento Kings play in the National Basketball Association. The Los Angeles Sparks and Sacramento Monarchs are in the Women's NBA. The Los Angeles Kings, the Anaheim Mighty Ducks, and the San Jose Sharks are members of the National Hockey League. The Los Angeles Galaxy and San Jose Earthquakes play in Major League Soccer.

Since moving from Brooklyn, NY, in 1959, the Dodgers have won the National League Pennant 10 times, going on to win the World Series in 1959, 1963, 1965, 1981, and 1988. The Athletics won the American League Pennant six times, going on to win the World Series in 1972, 1973, 1974, and 1980. The Giants, who moved from New York City in 1959, won the National League Pennant in 1962, 1989, and 2002, losing all three World Series. The Padres won the National League Pennant in 1984 and lost the World Series. They returned to the World Series after claiming the National League Pennant in 1999, but lost again. The Anaheim Angels (formerly the California Angels) won the 2002 World Series.

The Lakers won the NBA Championship in 1972, 1980, 1982, 1985, 1987, 1988, and from 2000 through 2002. The Warriors won the Championship in 1975. The Los Angeles Rams, who moved to St. Louis in 1996, played in NFL title games in 1949, 1950, 1951, 1955, 1974, 1975, 1976, 1978, and 1978. They won in 1951, and lost the Super Bowl in 1980. The Raiders won the Super Bowl three times: twice from Oakland, in 1977 and 1981, and once from Los Angeles, in 1984. The Raiders returned to Oakland in 1996. They were defeated by the Tampa Bay Buccaneers in the 2003 Super Bowl. The 49ers were the 1980s' most successful NFL team, winning the Super Bowl in 1982, 1985, 1989, 1990, and 1995. The Kings became the first California hockey team to make it to the Stanley Cup Finals in 1993, but they lost to the Montreal Canadiens.

Another popular professional sport is horse racing at such well-known tracks as Santa Anita and Hollywood Park. Because of the equitable climate, there is racing virtually the whole year round. An auto racing track was built in Fontana and now hosts a NASCAR Winston Cup event in April. The track at Sears Point Raceway hosts a NASCAR Winston Cup event in June.

California's teams have fielded powerhouses in collegiate sports. The University of Southern California's baseball team won five consecutive national championships between 1970 and 1974. Its football team was number one in the nation in 1928, 1931, 1932, 1962, 1967, and 1972, and was a co-national champion in 1974 and 1978. USC has won the Rose Bowl 20 times, most recently in 1996. The UCLA basketball team won 10 NCAA titles, while the Bruins football team won Rose Bowls in 1966, 1976, 1983, 1984, and 1986. Additionally, Stanford has won five Rose Bowl titles, and California, two. Stanford also won the NCAA men's basketball championship in 1942, and women's championships in 1990 and 1992. Cal won the men's title in 1959. All four schools compete in the PAC-10 Conference.

Among the famous athletes who were born in California are Joe DiMaggio, Venus and Serena Williams, Mark McGwire, and Jeff Gordon.

49 FAMOUS CALIFORNIANS

Richard Milhous Nixon (1913–94) is the only native-born Californian ever elected to the presidency. Following naval service in World War II, he was elected to the US House of Representatives in 1946, then to the US Senate in 1950. He served as vice president during the Eisenhower administration (1953–61) but failed, by a narrow margin, to be elected president as the Republican candidate in 1960. Returning to his home state, Nixon ran for the California governorship in 1962 but was defeated. The next year he moved his home and political base to New York, from which he launched his successful campaign for the presidency in 1968. As the nation's 37th president, Nixon withdrew US forces from Vietnam while intensifying the US bombing of Indochina, established diplomatic relations with China, and followed a policy of détente with the Soviet Union. In 1972, he scored a resounding reelection victory, but within a year his administration was beset by the Watergate scandal. On 9 August 1974, after the House Judiciary Committee had voted articles of impeachment, Nixon became the first president ever to resign the office.

The nation's 31st president, Herbert Hoover (b.Iowa, 1874–1964), moved to California as a young man. There he studied engineering at Stanford University and graduated with its first class (1895) before beginning the public career that culminated in his election to the presidency on the Republican ticket in 1928. Former film actor Ronald Reagan (b.Illinois, 1911) served two terms as state governor (1967–75) before becoming president in 1981. He was elected to a second presidential term in 1984.

In 1953, Earl Warren (1891–1974) became the first Californian to serve as US chief justice (1953–69). Warren, a native of Los Angeles, was elected three times to the California governorship and served in that office (1943–53) longer than any other person. Following his appointment to the US Supreme Court by President Eisenhower, Warren was instrumental in securing the unanimous decision in *Brown v. Board of Education of Topeka* (1954) that racial segregation was unconstitutional under the 14th Amendment. Other cases decided by the Warren court dealt with defendants' rights, legislative reapportionment, and First Amendment freedoms.

Before the appointment of Earl Warren, California had been represented on the Supreme Court continuously from 1863 to 1926. Stephen J. Field (b.Connecticut, 1816–99) came to California during the gold rush, practiced law, and served as chief justice of the state supreme court from 1859 to 1863. Following his appointment to the highest court by President Lincoln, Field served what was at that time the longest term in the court's history (1863–97). Joseph McKenna (b.Pennsylvania, 1843–1926) was appointed to the Supreme Court to replace Field upon his retirement. McKenna, who moved with his family to California in 1855, became US attorney general in 1897 and was then elevated by President McKinley to associate justice (1898–1925).

Californians have also held important positions in the executive branch of the federal government. Longtime California resident Victor H. Metcalf (b.New York, 1853–1936) served as Theodore Roosevelt's secretary of commerce and labor. Franklin K. Lane (b.Canada, 1864–1921) was Woodrow Wilson's secretary of the interior, and Ray Lyman Wilbur (b.Iowa, 1875–1949) occupied the same post in the Hoover administration. Californians were especially numerous in the cabinet of Richard Nixon. Los Angeles executive James D. Hodgson (b.Minnesota, 1915) was secretary of labor; former state lieutenant governor Robert H. Finch (b.Arizona, 1925–95) and San Francisco native Caspar W. Weinberger (b.1917) both served terms as secretary of health, education, and welfare; and Claude S. Brinegar (b.1926) was secretary of transportation. Weinberger and Brinegar stayed on at their respective posts in the Ford administration; Weinberger later served as secretary of defense under Ronald Reagan. An important figure in several national administrations, San Francisco-born John A. McCone (1902–91) was chairman of the Atomic Energy Commission (1958–60) and director of the Central Intelligence Agency (1961–65).

John Charles Frémont (b.Georgia, 1813–90) led several expeditions to the West, briefly served as civil governor of California before statehood, became one of California's first two US senators (serving only until 1851), and ran unsuccessfully as the Republican Party's first presidential candidate in 1856. Other prominent US senators from the state have included Hiram Johnson (1866–1945), who also served as governor from 1911 to 1917; William F. Knowland (1908–74); and, more recently, former college president and semanticist Samuel Ichiye Hayakawa (b.Canada, 1906–92) and former state controller Alan Cranston (1914–2001). Governors of the state since World War II include Reagan, Edmund G. "Pat" Brown (1905–96), 4th-generation Californian Edmund G. "Jerry" Brown, Jr. (b.1938), and George Deukmejian (b.New York, 1928). Other prominent state officeholders are Rose Elizabeth Bird (b.Arizona, 1936–99), the first woman to be appointed chief justice of the state supreme court, and Wilson Riles (b.Louisiana, 1917–99), superintendent of public instruction, the first black Californian elected to a state constitutional office. Prominent among mayors are Thomas Bradley (b.Texas, 1917–98) of Los Angeles, Pete Wilson (b.Illinois, 1933) of San Diego, Dianne Feinstein (b.1933) of San Francisco, and Janet Gray Hayes (b.Indiana, 1926) of San Jose.

Californians have won Nobel Prizes in five separate categories. Linus Pauling (b.Oregon, 1901–94), professor at the California Institute of Technology (1927–64) and at Stanford (1969–74), won the Nobel Prize for chemistry in 1954 and the Nobel Peace Prize in 1962. Other winners of the Nobel Prize in chemistry are University of California (Berkeley) professors William Francis Giauque (b.Canada, 1895–1982), in 1949; Edwin M. McMillan (1907–91) and Glenn T. Seaborg (b.Michigan, 1912–99), who shared the prize in 1951; and Stanford Professor Henry Taube (b.Canada, 1915), in 1983. Members of the Berkeley faculty who have won the Nobel Prize for physics include Ernest Orlando Lawrence (b.South Dakota, 1901–58), in 1939; Emilio Segré (b.Italy, 1905–89) and Owen Chamberlain (b.1920), who shared the prize in 1959; and Luis W. Alvarez (1911–88), in 1968. Stanford professor William Shockley (b.England, 1910–89) shared the physics prize with two others in 1956; William A. Fowler (b.Pennsylvania, 1911–95), professor at the California

Institute of Technology, won the prize in 1983. The only native-born Californian to win the Nobel Prize for literature was novelist John Steinbeck (1902–68), in 1962. Gerald Debreu (b.France, 1921), professor at the University of California at Berkeley, won the 1983 prize for economics.

Other prominent California scientists are world-famed horticulturist Luther Burbank (b.Massachusetts, 1849–1926) and nuclear physicist Edward Teller (b.Hungary, 1908–2003). Naturalist John Muir (b.Scotland, 1838–1914) fought for the establishment of Yosemite National Park. Influential California educators include college presidents David Starr Jordan (b.New York, 1851–1931) of Stanford, and Robert Gordon Sproul (1891–1975) and Clark Kerr (b.Pennsylvania, 1911) of the University of California.

Major figures in the California labor movement were anti-Chinese agitator Denis Kearney (b.Ireland, 1847–1907); radical organizer Thomas Mooney (b.Illinois, 1882–1942); and Harry Bridges (b.Australia, 1901–90), leader of the San Francisco general strike of 1934. The best-known contemporary labor leader in California is Cesar Chavez (b.Arizona, 1927–93).

The variety of California's economic opportunities is reflected in the diversity of its business leadership. Prominent in the development of California railroads were the men known as the Big Four: Charles Crocker (b.New York, 1822–88), Mark Hopkins (b.New York, 1813–78), Collis P. Huntington (b.Connecticut, 1821–1900), and Leland Stanford (b.New York, 1824–93). California's long-standing dominance in the aerospace industry is a product of the efforts of such native Californians as John Northrop (1895–1981) and self-taught aviator Allen Lockheed (1889–1969), along with Glenn L. Martin (b.Iowa, 1886–1955); the San Diego firm headed by Claude T. Ryan (b.Kansas, 1898–1982), built the monoplane, *Spirit of St. Louis*, flown by Charles Lindbergh across the Atlantic in 1927. Among the state's banking and financial leaders was San Jose native Amadeo Peter Giannini (1870–1949), founder of the Bank of America. Important figures in the development of California agriculture include Edwin T. Earl (1856–1919), developer of the first ventilator-refrigerator railroad car, and Mark J. Fontana (b.Italy, 1849–1922), whose California Packing Corp., under the brand name of Del Monte, became the largest seller of canned fruit in the US. Leaders of the state's world-famous wine and grape-growing industry include immigrants Ágostan Haraszthy de Mokcsa (b.Hungary, 1812?–69), Charles Krug (b.Prussia, 1830–94), and Paul Masson (b.France, 1859–1940), as well as two Modesto natives, Ernest (b.1910) and Julio (1911–93) Gallo. It was at the mill of John Sutter (b.Baden, 1803–80) that gold was discovered in 1848.

Leading figures among the state's newspaper editors and publishers were William Randolph Hearst (1863–1951), whose publishing empire began with the *San Francisco Examiner*, and Harrison Gray Otis (b.Ohio, 1837–1917), longtime owner and publisher of the *Los Angeles Times*. Pioneers of the state's electronics industry include David Packard (b.Colorado, 1912–96) and William R. Hewlett (b.Michigan, 1913); Stephen Wozniak (b.1950) and Steven Jobs (b.1955) were cofounders of Apple Computer. Other prominent business leaders include clothier Levi Strauss (b.Germany, 1830–1902), paper producer Anthony Zellerbach (b.Germany, 1832–1911), cosmetics manufacturer Max Factor (b.Poland, 1877–1938), and construction and manufacturing magnate Henry J. Kaiser (b.New York, 1882–1967).

California has been home to a great many creative artists. Native California writers include John Steinbeck, adventure writer Jack London (1876–1916), novelist and dramatist William Saroyan (1908–81), and novelist-essayist Joan Didion (b.1934). One California-born writer whose life and works were divorced from his place of birth was Robert Frost (1874–1963), a native of

San Francisco. Many other writers who were residents but not natives of the state have made important contributions to literature. Included in this category are Mark Twain (Samuel Langhorne Clemens, b.Missouri, 1835–1910); local colorist Bret Harte (b.New York, 1836–1902); author-journalist Ambrose Bierce (b.Ohio, 1842–1914); novelists Frank Norris (b.Illinois, 1870–1902), Mary Austin (b.Illinois, 1868–1934), and Aldous Huxley (b.England, 1894–1963); novelist-playwright Christopher Isherwood (b.England, 1904–86); and poets Robinson Jeffers (b.Pennsylvania, 1887–1962) and Lawrence Ferlinghetti (b.New York, 1920). California has been the home of several masters of detective fiction, including Raymond Chandler (b.Illinois, 1888–1959), Dashiell Hammett (b.Connecticut, 1894–1961), Erle Stanley Gardner (b.Massachusetts, 1889–1970), creator of Perry Mason, and Ross Macdonald (1915–83). Producer-playwright David Belasco (1853–1931) was born in San Francisco.

Important composers who have lived and worked in California include natives Henry Cowell (1897–1965) and John Cage (1912–92), and immigrants Arnold Schoenberg (b.Austria, 1874–1951), Ernest Bloch (b.Switzerland, 1880–1959), and Igor Stravinsky (b.Russia, 1882–1971). Immigrant painters include landscape artists Albert Bierstadt (b.Germany, 1830–1902) and William Keith (b.Scotland, 1839–1911), as well as abstract painter Hans Hofmann (b.Germany, 1880–1966). Contemporary artists working in California include Berkeley-born Elmer Bischoff (b.1916–91), Wayne Thiebaud (b.Arizona, 1920), and Richard Diebenkorn (b.Oregon, 1922–93). San Francisco native Ansel Adams (1902–84) is the best known of a long line of California photographers that includes Edward Curtis (b.Wisconsin, 1868–1952), famed for his portraits of American Indians, and Dorothea Lange (b.New Jersey, 1895–1965), chronicler of the 1930s migration to California.

Many of the world's finest performing artists have also been Californians: Violinist Ruggiero Ricci (b.1918) was born in San Francisco, while fellow virtuosos Yehudi Menuhin (b.New York, 1916–99) and Isaac Stern (b.Russia, 1920–2001) were both reared in the state. Another master violinist, Jascha Heifetz (b.Russia, 1901–84), made his home in Beverly Hills. California jazz musicians include Dave Brubeck (b.1920) and Los Angeles-reared Stan Kenton (b.Kansas, 1912–79).

Among the many popular musicians who live and record in the state are California natives David Crosby (b.1941), Randy Newman (b.1943), and Beach Boys Brian (b.1942) and Carl (1946–98) Wilson.

The list of talented and beloved film actors associated with Hollywood is enormous. Native Californians on the screen include child actress Shirley Temple (Mrs. Charles A. Black, b.1928) and such greats as Gregory Peck (b.1916) and Marilyn Monroe (Norma Jean Baker, 1926–62). Other longtime residents of the state include Douglas Fairbanks (b.Colorado, 1883–1939), Mary Pickford (Gladys Marie Smith, b.Canada, 1894–1979), Harry Lillis "Bing" Crosby (b.Washington, 1904–77), Cary Grant (Archibald Leach, b.England, 1904–86), John Wayne (Marion Michael Morrison, b.Iowa, 1907–79), Bette Davis (b.Massachusetts, 1908–89), and Clark Gable (b.Ohio, 1901–60). Other actors born in California include Clint Eastwood (b.1930), Robert Duvall (b.1931), Robert Redford (b.1937), Kevin Costner (b.1955), and Dustin Lee Hoffman (b.1937).

Hollywood has also been the center for such pioneer film producers and directors as D. W. Griffith (David Lewelyn Wark Griffith, b.Kentucky, 1875–1948), Cecil B. DeMille (b.Massachusetts, 1881–1959), Samuel Goldwyn (b.Poland, 1882–1974), Frank Capra (b.Italy, 1897–1991), and master animator Walt Disney (b.Illinois, 1901–66).

California-born athletes have excelled in every professional sport. A representative sampling includes Baseball Hall of Famers Joe Cronin (1906–1984), Vernon "Lefty" Gomez (1908–89), and Joe DiMaggio (1914–99), along with tennis greats John Donald "Don" Budge (1915–2000), Richard A. "Pancho" Gonzales (1928–95), Maureen "Little Mo" Connelly (1934–69), and Billie Jean (Moffitt) King (b.1943); Gene Littler (b.1930) in golf, Frank Gifford (b.1930) and Orenthal James "O. J." Simpson (b.1947) in football, Mark Spitz (b.1950) in swimming, and Bill Walton (b.1952) in basketball. Robert B. "Bob" Mathias (b.1930) won the gold medal in the decathlon at the 1948 and 1952 Olympic Games.

50 BIBLIOGRAPHY

Bean, Walton, and James J. Rawls. *California: An Interpretive History.* 4th ed. N.Y.: McGraw-Hill, 1982.

Caughey, John W. *California: A Remarkable State's Life-History.* 4th ed. Englewood Cliffs, N.J.: Prentice-Hall, 1982.

Dawson, Robert and Gray Brechin. *Farewell, Promised Land: Waking from the California Dream.* Berkeley, Calif.: University of California Press, 1999.

Finson, Bruce, ed. *Discovering California.* San Francisco: California Academy of Sciences, 1983.

Hart, James D. *A Companion to California.* Rev. ed. Berkeley: University of California Press, 1987.

Hesse, Georgia I. *California and the West 1985.* Robert C. Fisher, ed. New York: NAL, 1984.

Hohm, Charles F., ed. *California's Social Problems.* New York: Longman, in collaboration with the California Sociological Association, 1997.

Holliday, J. S. *The World Rushed In: The California Gold Rush Experience.* Norman: University of Oklahoma Press, 2002.

Kahrl, William L. *Water and Power: The Conflict over Los Angeles's Water Supply in the Owens Valley.* Berkeley: University of California Press, 1982.

Kessell, John L. *Spain in the Southwest: A Narrative History of Colonial New Mexico, Arizona, Texas, and California.* Norman: University of Oklahoma Press, 2002.

McCarthy, Kevin F. and Georges Vernez. *Immigration in a Changing Economy: California's Experience.* Santa Monica, Calif.: Rand, 1997.

Martin, Stoddard. *California Writers: Jack London, John Steinbeck, the Tough Guys.* N.Y.: St. Martin's Press, 1984.

May, Kirse Granat. *Golden State, Golden Youth: The California Image in Popular Culture, 1955–1966.* Chapel Hill: University of North Carolina Press, 2002.

Miller, Crane S., and Richard S. Hysolp. *California: The Geography of Diversity.* Palo Alto, Calif.: Mayfield, 1983.

Muir, John. *Mountains of California.* New York: Penguin, 1985.

Starr, Kevin. *The Dream Endures: California Enters the 1940s.* New York: Oxford University Press, 1997.

———. *Inventing the Dream: California Through the Progressive Era.* New York: Oxford University Press, 1985.

Williams, James C. *Energy and the Making of Modern California.* Akron, Ohio: University of Akron Press, 1997.

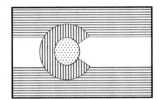

COLORADO

State of Colorado

ORIGIN OF STATE NAME: From the Spanish word *colorado,* meaning red or reddish brown. **NICKNAME:** The Centennial State. **CAPITAL:** Denver. **ENTERED UNION:** 1 August 1876 (38th). **SONG:** "Where the Columbines Grow." **MOTTO:** *Nil sine numine* (Nothing without providence). **COAT OF ARMS:** The upper portion of a heraldic shield shows three snow-capped mountains surrounded by clouds; the lower portion has a miner's pick and shovel, crossed. Above the shield are an eye of God and a Roman fasces, symbolizing the republican form of government; the state motto is below. **FLAG:** Superimposed on three equal horizontal hands of blue, white, and blue is a large red "C" encircling a golden disk. **OFFICIAL SEAL:** The coat of arms surrounded by the words "State of Colorado 1876." **ANIMAL:** Rocky Mountain bighorn sheep. **BIRD:** Lark bunting. **FLOWER:** Columbine. **TREE:** Blue spruce. **GEM:** Aquamarine. **FOSSIL:** Stegasaurus. **LEGAL HOLIDAYS:** New Year's Day, 1 January; Birthday of Martin Luther King, Jr., 3rd Monday in January; Lincoln's Birthday, 12 February; Washington's Birthday, 3rd Monday in February; Memorial Day, last Monday in May; Independence Day, 4 July; Colorado Day, 1st Monday in August; Labor Day, 1st Monday in September; Columbus Day, 2nd Monday in October; Election Day, 1st Tuesday after 1st Monday in November in even-numbered years; Thanksgiving Day, 4th Thursday in November; Christmas Day, 25 December. **TIME:** 5 AM MST = noon GMT.

¹LOCATION, SIZE, AND EXTENT

Located in the Rocky Mountain region of the US, Colorado ranks eighth in size among the 50 states.

The state's total area is 104,091 sq mi (269,596 sq km), of which 103,595 sq mi (268,311 sq km) consists of land and 496 sq mi (1,285 sq km) comprise inland water. Shaped in an almost perfect rectangle, Colorado extends 387 mi (623 km) E–W and 276 mi (444 km) N–S.

Colorado is bordered on the N by Wyoming and Nebraska; on the E by Nebraska and Kansas; on the S by Oklahoma and New Mexico; and on the W by Utah (with the New Mexico and Utah borders meeting at Four Corners). The total length of Colorado's boundaries is 1,307 mi (2,103 km). The state's geographic center lies in Park County, 30 mi (48 km) NW of Pikes Peak.

²TOPOGRAPHY

With a mean average elevation of 6,800 ft (2,074 m), Colorado is the nation's highest state. Dominating the state are the Rocky Mountains. Colorado has 54 peaks 14,000 ft (4,300 m) or higher, including Elbert, the highest in the Rockies at 14,433 ft (4,402 m), and Pikes Peak, at 14,110 ft (4,301 m), one of the state's leading tourist attractions.

The entire eastern third of the state is part of the western Great Plains, a high plateau that rises gradually to the foothills of the Rockies. Colorado's lowest point, 3,350 ft (1,022 m), on the Arkansas River, is located in this plateau region. Running in a ragged north–south line, slightly west of the state's geographic center, is the Continental Divide, which separates the Rockies into the Eastern and Western slopes. The Eastern Slope Front (Rampart) Range runs south from the Wyoming border and just west of Colorado Springs. Also on the Eastern Slope are the Park, Mosquito, Medicine Bow, and Laramie mountains. Western Slope ranges include the Sawatch, Gore, Elk, Elkhead, and William Fork mountains. South of the Front Range, crossing into New Mexico, is the Sangre de Cristo Range, separated from the San Juan Mountains to its west by the broad San Luis Valley. Several glaciers, including Arapahoe, St. Mary's, Andrews, and Taylor,

are located on peaks at or near the Continental Divide. Colorado's western region is mostly mesa country—broad, flat plateaus accented by deep ravines and gorges, with many subterranean caves. Running northwest from the San Juans are the Uncompahgre Plateau, Grand Mesa, Roan Plateau, the Flat Tops, and Danforth Hills. The Yampa and Green gorges are located in the northwestern corner of the state.

Blue Mesa Reservoir in Gunnison County is Colorado's largest lake. Six major river systems originate in Colorado: the Colorado River, which runs southwest from the Rockies to Utah; the South Platte, northeast to Nebraska; the North Platte, north to Wyoming; the Rio Grande, south to New Mexico; and the Arkansas and Republican, east to Kansas. Dams on these rivers provide irrigation for the state's farmland and water supplies for cities and towns. Eighteen hot springs are still active in Colorado; the largest is at Pagosa Springs.

³CLIMATE

Abundant sunshine and low humidity typify Colorado's highland continental climate. Winters are generally cold and snowy, especially in the higher elevations of the Rocky Mountains. Summers are characterized by warm, dry days and cool nights.

The average annual temperature statewide ranges from 54°F (12°C) at Lamar and at John Martin Dam to about 32°F (0°C) at the top of the Continental Divide; differences in elevation account for significant local variations on any given day. Denver's annual average is 50°F (10°C); normal temperatures range from 16° to 43°F (–9° to 6°C) in January and from 59° to 88°F (15° to 31°C) in July. Bennett recorded the highest temperature in Colorado, 118°F (48°C), on 11 July 1888; the record low was –61°F (–52°C), in Moffat County on 1 February 1985.

Annual precipitation ranges from a low of 7 in (18 cm) in Alamosa to a high of 25 in (64 cm) in Crested Butte, with Denver receiving about 15.8 in (40 cm) during 1971–2000. Denver's snowfall averages 60.3 in (153.2 cm) yearly. The average snowfall at Cubres in the southern mountains is nearly 300 in (762 cm); less than 30 mi (48 km) away at Manassa, snowfall is less than 25 in (64 cm). On 14–15 April 1921, Silver Lake had 76 in (193 cm) of snowfall, the highest amount ever recorded in North America during a 24-hour period.

⁴FLORA AND FAUNA

Colorado's great range in elevation and temperature contributes to a variety of vegetation, distributed among five zones: plains, foothills, montane, subalpine, and alpine. The plains teem with grasses and as many as 500 types of wildflowers. Arid regions contain two dozen varieties of cacti. Foothills are matted with berry shrubs, lichens, lilies, and orchids, while fragile wild flowers, shrubs, and conifers thrive in the montane zone. Aspen and Engelmann spruce are found up to the timberline. As of 2003, 13 plant species were listed as threatened or endangered, including three species of cacti, two species of milk-vetch, Penland beardtongue, and Colorado butterfly plant.

Colorado has counted as many as 747 non-game wildlife species and 113 sport-game species. Principal big-game species are the elk, mountain lion, Rocky Mountain bighorn sheep (the state animal), antelope, black bear, and white-tailed and mule deers; the mountain goat and the moose—introduced in 1948 and 1975, respectively—are the only non-native big-game quarry. The lark bunting is the state bird; blue grouse and mourning doves are numerous, and 28 duck species have been sighted. Colorado has about 100 sport-fish species. Scores of lakes and rivers contain bullhead, kokanee salmon, and a diversity of trout. Rare Colorado fauna include the golden trout, white pelican, and wood frog. Nineteen animal species were listed as endangered or threatened by the US Fish and Wildlife Service in 2003. The Mexican spotted owl and bald eagle are among threatened species. The razorback sucker, gray wolf, whooping crane, black-footed ferret, southwestern willow flycatcher, and bonytail chub are among endangered species.

⁵ENVIRONMENTAL PROTECTION

The Department of Natural Resources and the Department of Health share responsibility of state environmental programs. The first efforts to protect Colorado's natural resources were the result of federal initiatives. On 16 October 1891, US president Benjamin Harrison set aside the White River Plateau as the first forest reserve in the state. Eleven years later, President Theodore Roosevelt incorporated six areas in the Rockies as national forests. By 1906, 11 national forests covering about one-fourth of the state had been created. Mesa Verde National Park, founded in 1906, and Rocky Mountain National Park (1915) were placed under the direct control of the National Park Service. In 1978, Colorado became the first state in the US to encourage taxpayers to allocate part of their state income tax refunds to wildlife conservation. In addition, a state lottery was approved in the late 1980s, with proceeds approved for Great Outdoors Colorado (GOCO) to be used for parks improvement and wildlife and resource management.

Air pollution, water supply problems, and hazardous wastes head the list of Colorado's current environmental concerns. The Air Quality Control Commission, within the Department of Health, has primary responsibility for air pollution control. Because of high levels of carbon monoxide, nitrogen dioxide, and particulates in metropolitan Denver, Colorado Springs, Pueblo, and other cities, a motor vehicle emissions inspection system was inaugurated in January 1982 for gasoline-powered vehicles and in January 1985 for diesel-powered vehicles. The high altitudes of Colorado almost double auto emissions compared to auto emissions at sea level. The high level of particulates in the air is because of frequent temperature inversions along Colorado's Front Range. The state has launched an aggressive campaign to improve air quality. Cars must use oxygenated fuels, and pass tough vehicle emissions controls, and driving is discouraged on high pollution days.

Formal efforts to ensure the state's water supply date from the Newlands Reclamation Act of 1902, a federal program designed to promote irrigation projects in the semiarid plains areas; its first effort, the Uncompahgre Valley Project, reclaimed 146,000 acres (59,000 hectares) in Montrose and Delta counties. One of the largest undertakings, the Colorado–Big Thompson Project, started in the 1930s, diverts a huge amount of water from the Western to the Eastern Slope. Colorado's efforts to obtain water rights to the Vermejo River in the Rockies were halted in 1984 by the US Supreme Court, which ruled that New Mexico would retain these rights. Some 98% of Colorado's drinking water complies with federal and state standards. The Colorado Department of Health works with local officials to ensure federal standards for drinking water are met. Isolated aquifers are generally in good condition in Colorado, though a few are contaminated. Colorado's groundwater quality is generally high.

Colorado's rapid population growth during the 1970s and early 1980s taxed an already low water table, especially in the Denver metropolitan area. The Department of Natural Resources' Water Conservation Board and Division of Water Resources are responsible for addressing this and other water-related problems.

The Department of Health has primary responsibility for hazardous waste management. From 1984 until the mid-1990s, the department, along with federal agencies, undertook the cleanup of nearly 7,000 contaminated sites in Grand Junction and other parts of Mesa County; these sites—homes and properties—were contaminated during the 1950s and 1960s by radioactive mill tailings that had been used as building material and that were not considered hazardous at the time. (It is now known that the low-level radiation emitted by the mill tailings can cause cancer and genetic damage.) In the fall of 1984, Aspen was placed on the federal Environmental Protection Agency's (EPA) list of dangerous waste sites because potentially hazardous levels of cadmium, lead, and zinc were found in Aspen's streets, buildings, and water. Cadmium, lead, and zinc mill tailings had been used as filling material during the construction of the popular resort. Also in the mid-1980s, Rocky Flats, a former plutonium production site near Golden, was closed and a major cleanup was begun; by 2003 all plutonium and uranium had been removed. During 2004 and 2005 the buildings at Rocky Flats were scheduled to be demolished. Rocky Flats National Wildlife Refuge was planned for the site when the demolition was complete. (The site had been the focus of many protests during the 1970s, and has been a major newsmaker since the start of the cleanup. In 2003, the Environmental Protection Agency's database listed 202 hazardous waste sites in Colorado, 15 of which were on the National Priorities List. Some 1.5% of the state's land is covered with wetlands, a 50% decrease over the last two centuries. In 2001, Colorado received $49,955,000 in federal grants from the EPA; EPA expenditures for procurement contracts in Colorado that year amounted to $25,479,000.

⁶POPULATION

Colorado ranked 22nd in population in the US with an estimated total of 4,506,542 in 2002, an increase of 4.8% since 2000. Between 1990 and 2000, Colorado's population grew from 3,294,394 to 4,301,261, an increase of 30.6%, the 3rd-largest percentage increase in the country for this period (exceeded only by Nevada and Arizona), and the 8th-largest gain in population size. The population is projected to reach 5.2 million by 2025.

Colorado rose from 30th in population in 1970 to 28th in 1980, and 26th in 1990, with a 14% increase during the 1980s. The population density in 2000 was 41.5 per sq mi. The estimated median age in 2000 was 34.3 years, 9.7% of the

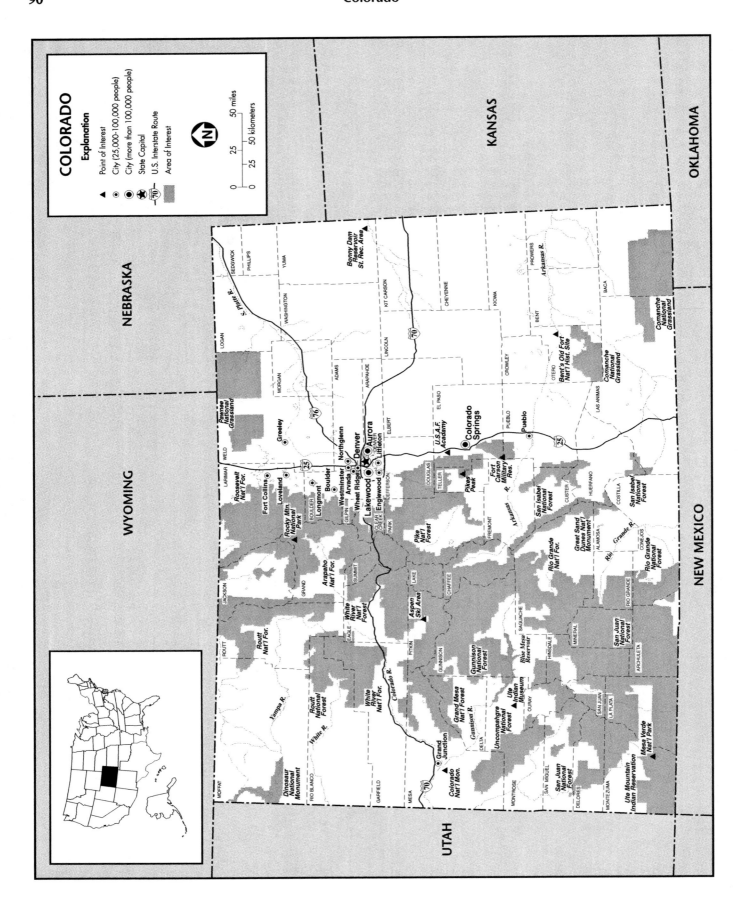

COLORADO

Explanation

Point of Interest
City (25,000–100,000 people)
City (more than 100,000 people)
State Capital
U.S. Interstate Route
Area of Interest

50 miles
50 kilometers
0 25 50

N

NEBRASKA

WYOMING

KANSAS

OKLAHOMA

UTAH

NEW MEXICO

LOGAN
SEDGWICK
PHILLIPS
YUMA
WASHINGTON
KIT CARSON
CHEYENNE
KIOWA
PROWERS
BENT
BACA
LAS ANIMAS
OTERO
CROWLEY
LINCOLN
ADAMS
ARAPAHOE
ELBERT
EL PASO
PUEBLO
MORGAN
WELD
LARIMER
BOULDER
GILPIN
CLEAR CREEK
JEFFERSON
DOUGLAS
TELLER
FREMONT
CUSTER
HUERFANO
COSTILLA
PARK
LAKE
CHAFFEE
SAGUACHE
ALAMOSA
CONEJOS
RIO GRANDE
MINERAL
ARCHULETA
HINSDALE
GUNNISON
PITKIN
EAGLE
SUMMIT
GRAND
JACKSON
ROUTT
RIO BLANCO
GARFIELD
MESA
DELTA
MONTROSE
SAN MIGUEL
DOLORES
MONTEZUMA
LA PLATA
SAN JUAN
OURAY
MOFFAT

S. Platte R.
Bonny Dam Reservoir St. Rec. Area
Arkansas R.
Comanche National Grassland
Comanche National Grassland
Bent's Old Fort Nat'l Hist. Site
Pawnee National Grassland
Greeley
Fort Collins
Loveland
Longmont
Boulder
Roosevelt Nat'l For.
Northglenn
Denver
Aurora
Littleton
Westminster
Arvada
Wheat Ridge
Lakewood
Englewood
U.S.A.F. Academy
Colorado Springs
Pueblo
Fort Carson Military Res.
Pikes Peak
Rocky Mtn. National Park
Arapaho Nat'l For.
Pike Nat'l Forest
San Isabel National Forest
San Isabel National Forest
Great Sand Dunes Nat'l Monument
Rio Grande Nat'l For.
Rio Grande National Forest
Rio Grande R.
White River Nat'l Forest
Routt Nat'l For.
Aspen Ski Area
Blue Mesa Reservoir
Gunnison National Forest
San Juan National Forest
Yampa R.
White R.
Routt National Forest
White River Nat'l For.
Colorado R.
Grand Mesa Nat'l Forest
Gunnison R.
Uncompahgre National Forest
Ute Indian Museum
San Juan National Forest
Mesa Verde Nat'l Park
Ute Mountain Indian Reservation
Dinosaur National Monument
Grand Junction
Colorado Nat'l Mon.

population was over 65, and persons under 18 years old accounted for 25.6% of the population.

Denver is the state's largest city and was, in 2002, the 26th largest US city. Its estimated 2002 population was 560,415, but its metropolitan area (including Boulder and Greeley) exceeded 2,417,908 or more than half the state's population in 1999. Other major cities, with their estimated 2002 population figures, are Colorado Springs, 371,182; Aurora, 286,028; Lakewood, 143,754; Fort Collins, 124,665; Westminster, 103,599; and Pueblo, 103,411.

7ETHNIC GROUPS

Once the sole inhabitants of the state, American Indians in 2000 numbered 44,241, up from 28,000 in 1990. The black population is also small, 165,063, or 3.8% in 2000; the percentage for Denver, however, was considerably higher (11.1% in 2000). Of far greater importance to the state's history, culture, and economy are its Hispanic and Latino residents, of whom there were 735,601 in 2000 (17.1%), up from 424,000 (under 13%) in 1990. Among residents of Denver, 31.7% were Hispanic or Latino in 2000. Of over 95,213 Asians (2.2%), up from 60,000 in 1990, 11,571 were Japanese (down from 15,198 in 1990); 16,395 Korean (up from 12,490 in 1990); 15,457 Vietnamese (more than double the 1990 total of 6,679); 15,658 Chinese (up from 9,117 in 1990); and 8,941 Filipino. The population of Pacific Islanders was estimated at 4,621 in 2000. In all, 369,903 residents, or 8.6% of the state population, were foreign born in 2000.

8LANGUAGES

The first whites to visit Colorado found Arapaho, Kiowa, Comanche, and Cheyenne Indians roaming the plains and often fighting the Ute in the mountains. Despite this diverse heritage, Indian place-names are not numerous: Pagosa Springs, Uncompahgre, Kiowa, and Arapahoe.

Colorado English is a mixture of the Northern and Midland dialects, in proportions varying according to settlement patterns. Homesteading New Englanders in the northeast spread *sick to the stomach, pail,* and *comforter* (tied and filled bedcover), which in the northwest and the southern half are Midland *sick at the stomach, bucket,* and *comfort.* South Midland *butter beans* and *snap beans* appear in the eastern agricultural strip. Denver has *slat fence,* and *Heinz dog* (mongrel). In the southern half of the state, the large Spanish population has bred many loanwords such as *arroyo* (small canyon or gulley) and *penco* (pet lamb).

In 2000, 3,402,266 Coloradans—84.9% of the residents five years old and older—spoke only English at home, down from 89.5% in 1990. The following table gives selected statistics from the 2000 census for language spoken at home by persons five years old and over.

LANGUAGE	NUMBER	PERCENT
Population 5 years and over	4,006,285	100.0
Speak only English	3,402,266	84.9
Speak a language other than English	604,019	15.1
Speak a language other than English	604,019	15.1
Spanish or Spanish Creole	421,670	10.5
German	30,824	0.8
French (incl. Patois, Cajun)	18,045	0.5
Vietnamese	12,499	0.3
Korean	12,045	0.3
Chinese	11,333	0.3
Russian	10,737	0.3
Japanese	6,605	0.2
Italian	5,703	0.1
Polish	5,064	0.1
Tagalog	5,013	0.1
Arabic	4,998	0.1

9RELIGIONS

The Spanish explorers who laid claim to (but did not settle in) Colorado were Roman Catholic, but the first American settlers were mostly Methodists, Lutherans, and Episcopalians. Some evangelical groups sought to proselytize the early mining camps during the mid-19th century.

Roman Catholics comprise the single largest religious group in the state, with 752,505 adherents in 298 congregations in 2000. The United Methodist Church, which was the 2nd-largest Protestant denomination in 1990, slipped down to 4th in 2000 with 77,286 adherents in 222 congregations. The 2nd-largest group is the Latter-day Saints with 92,326 adherents in 243 congregations, followed by the Southern Baptist Convention with 85,083 adherents in 243 congregations.

There were about 72,000 adherents in the Jewish community in 2000. The same year, there were about 72 Buddhist, 7 Hindu, and 12 Muslim congregations in the state. About 60.5% of the population were not counted as members of any religious organization.

The World Evangelical Fellowship and the Focus on the Family are both headquartered in Colorado Springs.

10TRANSPORTATION

As the hub of the Rocky Mountain states, Colorado maintains extensive road and rail systems.

Because of its difficult mountain terrain, Colorado was bypassed by the first transcontinental railroads. In 1870, however, the Denver Pacific built a line from Denver to the Union Pacific's cross-country route at Cheyenne, Wyoming. Several intrastate lines were built during the 1870s, connecting Denver with the mining towns. In particular, the Denver and Rio Grande built many narrow-gauge lines through the mountains. Denver finally became part of a main transcontinental line in 1934. As of 2000, there were 3,515 rail mi (5,656 km) of track in the state, utilized by 12 railroads. This included two Class I railroads (which by definition carry more than $250 million a year in freight revenue). AMTRAK trains in Colorado had an annual ridership of nearly 250,000 persons in the mid-1990s.

Colorado has an extensive network of roads, including 29 mountain passes. As of 2000 there were 85,409 mi (137,452 km) of roadway in Colorado: 70,946 mi (114,176 km) classified as rural and 14,463 mi (23,275 km) as urban. The major state roads are Interstate 70, US 40, and US 50 crossing the state from east to west, and Interstate 25 running north–south along the Front Range of the Rocky Mountains between Raton Pass and Cheyenne, Wyoming. Interstate 76 connects Denver on a northeasterly diagonal with Nebraska's I-80 to Omaha.

Of the 3,724,309 motor vehicles registered in 2000, 1,920,757 were automobiles; 1,699,469 were trucks; and 5,786 were buses. There were 3,107,258 licensed drivers that year.

A total of 91 public-use airfields served the state in 2002. Denver International Airport (DIA) replaced the former Stapleton International Airport in 1994 as the state's largest and busiest. In 2000, DIA handled 18,382,940 enplanements. In 2003, Centennial Airport ranked as the 2nd-busiest general aviation airport in the nation and one of the 25 busiest airports of any kind.

11HISTORY

A hunting people lived in eastern Colorado at least 20,000 years ago, but little is known about them. The Basket Makers, who came to southwestern Colorado after 100 BC, grew corn and squash and lived in pit houses. By AD 800 there were Pueblo tribes who practiced advanced forms of agriculture and pottery making. From the 11th through the 13th centuries (when they migrated southward), the Pueblo Indians constructed elaborate apartment-like dwellings in the cliffs of the Colorado canyons and planted their crops both on the mesa tops and in the surrounding valleys.

In the 1500s, when Spanish conquistadors arrived in the Southwest, northeastern Colorado was dominated by the Cheyenne and Arapaho, allied against the Comanche and Kiowa to the south. These plains-dwellers also warred with the mountain-dwelling Ute Indians, who were divided into the Capote, Moache, and Wiminuche in the southwest; the Yampa, Grand River, and Uintah in the northwest; and the Tabeguache and Uncompahgre along the Gunnison River.

The exact date of the first Spanish entry into the region now called Colorado is undetermined; the explorer Juan de Onate is believed to have traveled into the southeastern area in 1601. More than a century later, in 1706, Juan de Uribarri claimed southeastern Colorado for Spain, joining it with New Mexico. Meanwhile, French traders did little to stake out their claim to the Colorado region, which included most of the area east of the Rocky Mountains. In 1763, France formally ceded the Louisiana Territory to Spain, which returned it to the French in 1801. Two years later, as part of the Louisiana Purchase, Colorado east of the Rockies became US land; the rest of Colorado still belonged to Spain.

Formal boundaries had never been demarcated between the lands of French Louisiana and Spanish New Mexico. In 1806, the US government sent out a group led by Lt. Zebulon M. Pike to explore this southwestern border. Pike's group reached Pueblo on 23 November 1806 and then attempted without success to scale the peak that now bears his name. Not until 1819 did the US and Spain agree to establish the boundary along the Arkansas River and then northward along the Continental Divide. The following year, Maj. Stephen Long explored this new border, and Dr. Edwin James made the first known ascent of Pikes Peak.

Eastern Colorado remained a wilderness for the next few decades, although traders and scouts like Charles and William Bent, Kit Carson, and Jim Bridger did venture into the largely uncharted and inhospitable land, establishing friendly relations with the Indians. It was in 1840 at Bent's Fort, the area's major trading center, that the four major eastern tribes ended their warfare and struck an alliance, a bond that lasted through their later struggle against the white settlers and US government. Between 1842 and 1853, John C. Frémont led five expeditions into the region, the first three for the US government. In 1842, he traveled along the South Platte River; on the next two trips, he crossed the Rockies. In his fourth expedition, he and a few of his party barely survived severe winter conditions. Finally, in 1853, Frémont led an expedition over a route traveled by Capt. John Gunnison earlier that year through the San Luis Valley over Cochetopa Pass and along the Gunnison River. The 1853 trips were made five years after western and southern Colorado had come into US possession through the Mexican War.

The magnet that drew many Americans to Colorado was the greatly exaggerated report of a gold strike in Cherry Creek (present-day Denver) in July 1858. Within a year, thousands of prospectors had crossed the plains to seek their fortune. Many were disappointed and headed back east, but those who stayed benefited from a second strike at North Clear Creek, some 40 mi (64 km) to the west. The subsequent boom led to the founding of such mining towns as Central City, Tarryall, Golden, Blackhawk, Boulder, Nevadaville, Colorado City, and Gold Hill. By 1860, the population exceeded 30,000. A bill to organize a territory called Colorado, along the lines of the state's present-day boundaries, was passed by the US Congress on 28 February 1861. Colorado City, Golden, and Denver served at various times as the territorial capital until 1867 when Denver was selected as the permanent site. Colorado sided with the Union during the Civil War, though some settlers fought for the Confederacy. Union troops from Colorado helped defeat a contingent led by Confederate Gen. Henry H. Sibley at La Glorieta Pass in New Mexico in 1862.

The 1860s also saw the most serious conflict between Indians and white settlers in Colorado history. Cheyenne and Arapaho chiefs had ceded most of their tribal holdings to the US government in 1861. Sent to a reservation in the Arkansas Valley, these nomadic tribes were expected to farm the land. Unsuccessful at farming, the Indians rebelled against the poor rations supplied them by the US government and sought to resume a nomadic lifestyle, hunting buffalo, raiding towns, and attacking travelers along the Overland and Sante Fe trails. Col. John Chivington was placed in charge of controlling the Indian unrest in the summer of 1864 as Territorial Governor John Evans departed for Washington, DC, leaving the situation in the hands of the military. On 29 November of that year, Chivington led his forces to Sand Creek, on the reservation's northeastern border, where they brutally massacred perhaps 200 Indian men, women, and children who thought they were under the protection of US military forces at nearby Ft. Lyon. Five more years of warfare followed, with the Indians finally defeated at Beecher Island (1868) and Summit Spring (1869). By 1874, most Plains Indians were removed to reservations in what is now Oklahoma. After gold and silver were discovered in areas belonging to the Ute in 1873, they too were forced off the land. By 1880, a series of treaties limited the Ute to a small reservation in the barren mesa country.

The first bill to admit Colorado to statehood was vetoed in 1866 by President Andrew Johnson, who at that time was in the midst of an impeachment fight and feared the entry of two more Republicans into the US Senate. Colorado finally entered the Union as the 38th state on 1 August 1876 less than a month after the nation's 100th birthday during the presidency of Ulysses S. Grant.

In the early years of statehood, silver strikes at Leadville and Aspen brought settlers and money into Colorado. Rail lines, smelters, and refineries were built, and large coalfields were opened up. The High Plains attracted new farmers, and another new industry, tourism, emerged. As early as the 1860s, resorts had opened near some of the state's mineral springs. By the mid-1870s, scenic canyons and towns became accessible by train. One of the first major spas, Colorado Springs, recorded 25,000 tourists in 1878, and by the mid-1880s, Denver was accommodating up to 200,000 visitors a year. Colorado's boom years ended with a depression during the early 1890s. Overproduction of silver coupled with the US government's decision to adopt a gold standard in 1893 wiped out the silver market, causing the closing of mines, banks, and some businesses. Coinciding with this economic disaster was a drought that led to the abandonment of many farms. A more positive development was a gold find at Cripple Creek in 1891.

By the dawn of the 20th century, farmers were returning to the land and making better use of it. Immigrants from Germany and Russia began to grow sugar beets in the Colorado, Arkansas, and South Platte river valleys. Huge reclamation projects brought water to semiarid cropland, and dry-land farming techniques also helped increase yields. The development of the automobile and good roads opened up more of the mountain areas, bringing a big boom in tourism by the 1920s.

Following World War I, the agricultural and mining sectors fell into depression. From 1920 to 1940, statewide employment declined, and the population growth rate lagged behind that of the US as a whole. World War II (1939–45) brought military training camps, airfields, and jobs to the state. Colorado also became the site of several major POW camps as well as relocation centers for Japanese Americans (Nisei), especially the northeastern and southeastern areas of the state. After the war, the expansion of federal facilities in Colorado led to new employment opportunities. The placement of both the North American Air Defense Command and the US Air Force Academy in Colorado Springs helped stimulate the growth of defense, federal research, and aerospace-related industries in the state. As these and other industries grew, so too did Colorado's population and income: between 1960 and 1983, the state's population growth rate was more than twice that of the nation as a whole; and between 1970 and 1983, Colorado moved from eighteenth to ninth rank among the states in personal income per capita. The construction of the Air Force Space Operations Center at Colorado Springs, announced in 1983, also contributed Colorado's economic and population growth.

In the 1970s and early 1980s, Colorado experienced a boom in its oil, mining, and electronics industries. Prosperity attracted immigrants from other states, and for about a decade Colorado's population increased at an average of 3% a year. The economy began to shrink, however, in the mid-1980s with the drop in oil prices and the closing of mines, culminating in a full-scale recession by 1987. The economy rebounded by the early 1990s, spurred by an educated workforce and the low cost of doing business in the state. Industry in the state became more diverse, now including oil and gas, telecommunications, retail, and, very importantly, high technology. In 1998 the state ranked ninth nationally in per capita personal income, and by 1999 its unemployment rate, just 2.9%, was among the lowest in the country. Due to the 2001 economic recession in the United States and its aftermath, the Colorado unemployment rate stood at 5.8% in May 2003, below the national average of 6.1% but still causing difficulties for the Colorado economy.

On 20 April 1999, the affluent Denver suburb of Littleton made headlines around the world after two teenaged gunmen entered Columbine High School and went on a shooting rampage, killing 12 students and one teacher before turning their guns on themselves. Several others were injured. The tragic event escalated the national debate on gun control and reopened the discussion about what effect media violence has on the nation's youth.

Major challenges facing Colorado in the 1990s and into the 2000s included industrial pollution of its air and water, overcrowding on the Rockies eastern slope (home to four-fifths of its population), and water shortages. By spring 2000 one issue emerged that encompassed many of the problems Coloradans faced: the practice of open-pit gold mining. Gaping holes, forged by explosives and chemicals, had been created by mining companies across western states since 1980. According to environmentalists and other concerned citizens, the cost-efficient method for extracting the precious metal from stone had come at a price: cyanide, used to dissolve gold in the mines, leached into streams and rivers; and mishaps occurred, including the accidental cyanide release that contaminated 17 mi (27 km) of Colorado's Alamosa River in the early 1990s, the costliest mining disaster in US history. Banning open-pit mining had gained wide public support in the months preceding the 2000 election, when organizers hoped to place the initiative on the ballot. Although about 72% of Colorado voters were thought to be in agreement with the ban, the initiative failed to make the ballot in November 2000.

Colorado was among the western states ravaged by wildfires the summer of 2000, the worst fire season since 1988. In 2001, 2002 and 2003, wildfires broke out in the west once again. In the summer of 2002, wildfires burned over 7.1 million acres of public and private land. Twelve western states, including Colorado, were the victims of severe wildfires that burned 2.7 million acres as of September 2003.

[12]STATE GOVERNMENT

Colorado's state constitution, ratified on 1 July 1876, is a complex and extremely detailed document specifying the duties and structure of state and local government. Despite numerous amendments (143 by January 2003) and revisions, some anachronistic legislation has remained on the books. In 2002 voters approved several constitutional reforms, including a campaign finance reform measure.

The general assembly, which meets annually from the 2nd Wednesday of January into May (for a maximum of 120 calendar days), consists of a 35-member senate and 65-member house of representatives. The legislature may call special sessions by request of two-thirds of the members of each house. The governor may also call a special session of the legislature. Members of the legislature must be US citizens, at least 25 years old, and have lived in their district for at least one year. The legislative salary in 2002 was $30,000, unchanged from 1999.

The executive branch is headed by the governor, who submits the budget and legislative programs to the general assembly, and appoints judges, department heads, boards, and commissions. The governor, who is limited to serving two consecutive terms, must be a US citizen, at least 30 years old, and have been a resident of the state for two years or more. Elected with the governor is the lieutenant governor, who assumes the governor's duties in the governor's absence. Other elective officers include the secretary of state, attorney general, and treasurer, all of whom serve four-year terms. In 2002 the governor's salary was $90,000, unchanged from 1999.

Bills may originate in either house of the general assembly and become law when passed by majority vote of each house and signed by the governor; a bill may also become law if the governor fails to act on it within 10 days after receiving it (or within 30 days after the legislature has adjourned). A two-thirds vote of the elected members in each house is needed to override a gubernatorial veto.

The state constitution may be amended in several ways. An amendment may be introduced in the legislature, passed by a two-thirds majority in both houses, and submitted to the voters for approval. Alternatively, an initiative amendment, signed by a number of eligible voters equaling at least 5% of the number of votes cast for secretary of state in the previous election and then published in every county, may be filed no later than four months before the general election. If approved by the voters, it then becomes law.

Any US citizen 18 or older who is a resident of a Colorado county 30 days prior to an election may register to vote. Prisoners may not vote.

[13]POLITICAL PARTIES

The Democratic and Republican parties are the major political organizations in Colorado. Although both parties were in existence when Colorado achieved statehood, the Republicans controlled most statewide offices prior to 1900. Since then, the parties have been more evenly balanced. Of the 2,490,088 registered voters in 2002, 30% were estimated to be Democratic, 36% Republican, and 33% unaffiliated or members of other parties. In 2000, 51% of all Coloradan voters cast their ballots for Republican George W. Bush; Democrat Al Gore won 42% of the vote; Green Party candidate Ralph Nader won 5% of the vote. The state had eight electoral votes in the 2000 presidential election.

Following the election in November 2002, the state had two Republican US senators, and five Republican and two Democratic US representatives. Ben Nighthorse Campbell was elected US senator in 1992 as a Democrat. The only Native American in Congress, Campbell switched parties in March 1995. When he successfully ran for reelection in 1998, it was as a

Republican. Another Republican, Wayne Allard, was elected to the Senate in 1996 and reelected in 2002.

In 2003 the Republicans controlled the state senate (18 Republicans to 17 Democrats) and the state house (37 Republicans to 28 Democrats). Colorado's governor, Republican Bill Owens, was elected in 1998, succeeding Democrat Roy Romer, who had been in office for the maximum two terms. Owens was the first Republican elected to the governor's office in 28 years, and he was reelected in 2002. In 2003, Colorado had the 2nd-highest representation of women in its state legislature, with 34% (Washington was first with 36.7%).

[14]LOCAL GOVERNMENT

As of 2002 there were 62 counties and 182 public school districts. That year there were 270 municipal governments, cities, and towns; and 1,414 special districts. The administrative and policymaking body in each county is the board of county commissioners, whose three to five members (dependent on population) are elected to staggered, usually four-year, terms. Other county officials include the county clerk, treasurer, assessor, sheriff, coroner, superintendent of schools, surveyor, and attorney.

Statutory cities are those whose structure is defined by the state constitution. Power is delegated by the general assembly to either a council-manager or mayor-council form of government. Colorado municipalities have increasingly opted for home rule, taking control of local functions from the state government. Towns, which generally have fewer than 2,000 residents, are governed by a mayor and a board of trustees. The major source of revenue for both cities and towns is the property tax.

Denver, Colorado's capital and largest city, is run by a mayor and city council; a city auditor, independently elected, serves as a check on the mayor.

[15]STATE SERVICES

To address the continuing threat of terrorism and to work with the federal Department of Homeland Security (created in 2002 following the terrorist attacks of 11 September 2001), homeland security in Colorado in 2003 operated under the authority of state statute; the public safety director was designated as the state homeland security advisor.

The Department of Education, under the direction of the State Board of Education, supervises and makes policy decisions for all public elementary and secondary schools. The State Board is made up of seven elected representatives from the state's congressional districts, plus the Commissioner of Education, who is hired by the State Board. The Board of Regents of the University of Colorado governs the operations of that institution as well as its affiliates, the Colorado University Hospital, Children's Diagnostic Center, Psychiatric Hospital, and schools of medicine, nursing, and dentistry. All other state-run colleges, as well as the Colorado Historical Society, Council on the Arts and Humanities, and Advanced Technology Institute, are under the jurisdiction of the Department of Higher Education.

The Department of Transportation builds, operates, and maintains state roads. The Department of Social Services administers welfare, medical assistance, rehabilitation, and senior-citizens programs. Human resource planning and development are under the Department of Labor and Employment, and health conditions are monitored by the Department of Health and Environment. The Department of Institutions oversees mental health, youth services, and developmental disabilities programs. The state's correctional facilities are administered by the Department of Corrections.

All programs concerned with the protection and control of Colorado's natural resources are the responsibility of the Department of Natural Resources. Other state agencies include the Department of Agriculture, Department of Military Affairs, Department of Regulatory Agencies, Department of Public Safety, and Department of Law.

Colorado Presidential Vote by Political Parties, 1948–2000

YEAR	ELECTORAL VOTE	COLORADO WINNER	DEMOCRAT	REPUBLICAN	PROGRESSIVE	SOCIALIST	SOC. LABOR
1948	6	*Truman (D)	267,288	239,714	6,115	1,678	—
						CONSTITUTION	
1952	6	*Eisenhower (R)	245,504	379,782	1,919	2,181	—
1956	6	*Eisenhower (R)	263,997	394,479	—	759	3,308
						SOC. WORKERS	
1960	6	Nixon (R)	330,629	402,242	—	563	2,803
1964	6	*Johnson (D)	476,024	296,767	—	2,537	—
					AMERICAN IND.		
1968	6	*Nixon (R)	335,174	409,345	60,813	235	3,016
					AMERICAN		
1972	7	*Nixon (R)	329,980	597,189	17,269	666	4,361
							LIBERTARIAN
1976	7	Ford (R)	460,801	584,278	397	1,122	5,338
					STATESMAN	CITIZENS	
1980	7	*Reagan (R)	368,009	652,264	1,180	5,614	25,744
1984	8	Reagan (R)	454,975	821,817	NEW ALLIANCE	—	11,257
1988	8	*Bush (R)	621,453	728,177	2,491	—	15,482
					IND. (PEROT)		
1992	8	*Clinton (D)	629,681	562,850	366,010	1,608	8,669
						GREEN (NADER)	
1996	8	Dole (R)	671,152	691,848	99,629	25,070	12,392
					FREEDOM (BUCHANAN)		
2000		*Bush, G. W. (R)	738,227	883,748	10,465	91,434	12,799

* Won US presidential election.

16JUDICIAL SYSTEM

The supreme court, the highest court in Colorado, consists of seven justices elected on a nonpartisan ballot. The number of justices may be increased to nine upon request of the court and concurrence of two-thirds of the members of the General Assembly. The justices select a chief justice, who also serves as the supervisor of all Colorado courts. The next highest court, the court of appeals, consists of 16 judges, and is confined to civil matters. The 22 district courts have original jurisdiction in civil, criminal, juvenile, mental health, domestic relations, and probate cases, except in Denver, where probate and mental health matters are heard by the probate court and all juvenile matters by the juvenile court.

All judges in state courts are appointed to two-year terms by the governor from a list of names recommended by a judicial nominating commission. The appointees must then be elected by the voters: supreme court justices for 10-year terms, appeals court judges for eight years, and district court judges for six.

County courts hear minor civil disputes and misdemeanors. Appeals from the Denver county courts are heard in Denver's superior court. Municipal courts throughout the state handle violations of municipal ordinances. Colorado's FBI Crime Index crime rate in 2001 was 4,218.9 per 100,000 people, including a total of 15,492 violent crimes and 170,887 property crimes in that year.

As of June 2001, there were 17,122 prisoners held in state and federal facilities, an increase of 4.9% over the previous year. The state's incarceration rate stood at 338 per 100,000 inhabitants. Colorado has a death penalty and has executed 48 persons since 1930, only one of whom was put to death between 1977 and 2003. There were no prisoners under sentence of death as of 2003.

17ARMED FORCES

As of 2002, 60,752 personnel, of whom 10,183 were civilians, were stationed at the nine military facilities in the state. The largest Army base is Ft. Carson in Colorado Springs, headquarters of the 4th Infantry Division. At the Army's Rocky Mountain Arsenal near Denver, chemical weapons have been produced and stored. Colorado Springs is the site of the US Air Force Academy. Peterson Air Force Base is also located in Colorado Springs, as is the North American Air Defense Command (NORAD). Defense contracts awarded in 2001 totaled nearly $2.3 billion.

There were 446,385 veterans of US military service in Colorado as of 2000, of whom 64,101 served in World War II; 44,532 in the Korean conflict; 142,958 during the Vietnam era; and 67,184 during 1990–2000 (including the Persian Gulf War). Veterans benefits paid in the state in 2002 were $1 billion.

In 2000, the Colorado State Police employed 654 full-time sworn officers.

18MIGRATION

The discovery of gold in 1858 brought an avalanche of prospectors. Some of these migrants later moved westward into the Rockies and Colorado River canyons. In 1873, another gold strike brought settlers into the Ute territory, eventually driving the Indians into a small reservation in the southwestern corner of the state. During the late 19th and early 20th centuries, the sparsely populated eastern plains were settled by farmers from Kansas and Nebraska and by immigrants from Scandinavia, Germany, and Russia. Five years of drought, from 1933 to 1938, helped drive many rural Coloradoans off the land into the cities or westward to California.

Since the end of World War II, net migration into the state has been substantial, amounting to over 880,000 between 1950 and 1990. Between 1990 and 1998, Colorado had net gains of 359,000 in domestic migration and 58,000 in international migration. In 1998, 6,513 foreign immigrants were admitted to the state. Growth has been evident in both urban and rural areas, but the largest increase has been in the Denver metropolitan area, where by 1997 14.3% of the total population were of Hispanic origin. A number of migrant workers, mostly Mexican Americans, work seasonally in the western orchards and fields. In the 1980s, migration accounted for 27% of the net population increase, with some 117,000 persons, even though there was a net loss from migration every year from 1986 to 1990. In 1990, native Coloradoans made up 43.3% of the population. Between 1990 and 1998, Colorado's overall population increased 20.5%. In the period 1995–2000, 643,820 people moved into the state and 481,187 moved out, for a net gain of 162,633.

19INTERGOVERNMENTAL COOPERATION

Among the most important interstate agreements for Coloradoans are those governing water resources. Colorado participates with New Mexico in the Animas–La Plata Project, Costilla Creek, and La Plata River compacts; with Kansas in the Arkansas River Compact of 1949; and with Nebraska in the South Platte River Compact. The Cumbres and Toltec Scenic Railroad Compact supports the tourism industry. Multistate compacts allocate water from the Colorado and Republican rivers and the Rio Grande. Colorado also is a signatory to such regional agreements as the Interstate Oil and Gas Compact and the Western Interstate Energy Compact.

The Western Interstate Commission for Higher Education has its headquarters in Boulder, and the National Conference of State Legislatures has its headquarters in Denver. Federal grants to Colorado totaled over $3.9 billion in 2001.

20ECONOMY

During the late 1880s, Colorado was the nation's leading silver producer and an important source of gold. With its abundant reserves of coal, natural gas, and other minerals—and the economic potential of its vast oil-shale deposits—Colorado remains a major mining state, although the mineral industry's share of the state economy has declined throughout this century. Agriculture, primarily livestock, retains its historic importance.

Trade, services, government, and manufacturing were responsible for more than 75% of new jobs created between 1975 and 1985. From 1972 to 2000, Colorado's employment in advanced technology grew from 39,000 to 125,000 employees. A driving force behind Colorado's economy is the US government, which employs over 93,000 civilian and military personnel in the state. Mining and construction suffered the greatest losses of employment between 1982 and 1992. Mining jobs declined 53% in that decade, and construction jobs dropped 29%. Employment in services, in contrast, rose 36% in those years, and jobs in finance, insurance and real estate increased by 15%. Tourism has also expanded rapidly in all areas of the state. Colorado's economy recovered strongly in the 1990s. By 1997 Colorado's gross state product was nearly $130 billion. By 2000, it had grown nearly 31%, with annual growth rates of 7.9% in 1998, 8.9% in 1999, and 11.2% in 2000. In the national recession of 2001, growth slowed abruptly to 2.6% as manufacturing fell 10.2% from the year before, leaving only a net gain of 1.5% in the sector from 1997 to 2001. Recovery remained elusive in 2002, as the state posted its first annual decline in employment since 1986.

In 2001, Colorado's gross state product stood at $173.8 billion, the 21st highest among the states. The public sector accounted for 11.8% of the total, close to the state average. The main contributors to gross state product were general services ($41.9 billion, up 31% since 1997); financial services ($31.8 billion, up 45.2% from 1997), government ($20.5 billion, up

21% from 1997); transportation and utilities ($19.3 billion, up 30%); and manufacturing ($15 billion). Conventional foreclosure rates, which had reached 3.25% in the recession of the early 1990s, and then fallen to less than 1% by the mid-1990s, ticked up to about 1.25% in 2002.

21INCOME

According to the Bureau of Economic Analysis, in 2001, Colorado had a per capita personal income (PCPI) of $33,455 which ranked 8th in the United States (including the District of Columbia) and was 110% of the national average, $30,413. The 2001 PCPI reflected an increase of 1.2% from 2000 compared to the national change of 2.2%. In 2001, Colorado had a total personal income (TPI) of $148,238,613,000 which ranked 21st in the United States and accounted for 1.7% of the national total. The 2001 TPI reflected an increase of 3.6% from 2000 compared to the national change of 3.3%.

Earnings of persons employed in Colorado increased from $111,210,509,000 in 2000 to $114,684,737,000 in 2001, an increase of 3.1%. The largest industries in 2001 were services, 30.3% of earnings; state and local government, 10.1%; and transportation and public utilities, 10.0%. Of the industries that accounted for at least 5% of earnings in 2001, the slowest growing from 2000 to 2001 was transportation and public utilities, which decreased 3.7%; the fastest was state and local government, which increased 8.7%.

According to data released by the US Census Bureau, in 2000, the median household income was $48,506 compared to the national average of $42,148. In 2001, the median income for a family of four was $67,634 compared to the national average of $63,278. For the period 1999 to 2001, the average poverty rate was 9.0% which placed it 13th among the 50 states and the District of Columbia ranked lowest to highest.

22LABOR

According to Bureau of Labor Statistics (BLS) provisional estimates, in July 2003 the seasonally adjusted civilian labor force in Colorado numbered 2,477,800, with approximately 141,700 workers unemployed, yielding an unemployment rate of 5.7%, compared to the national average of 6.2% for the same period. Since the beginning of the BLS data series in 1978, the highest unemployment rate recorded was 8.8% in October 1982. The historical low was 2.6% in January 2001. In 2001, an estimated 7.0% of the labor force was employed in construction; 10.2% in manufacturing; 7.0% in transportation, communications, and public utilities; 19.6% in trade; 6.3% in finance, insurance, and real estate; 26.9% in services; 12.7% in government; and 2.0% in agriculture.

Colorado's labor history has been marked by major disturbances in the mining industry. From 1881 to 1886, the Knights of Labor led at least 35 strikes in the mines; during the 1890s, the Western Federation of Miners struck hard-rock mines in Telluride and Cripple Creek. The United Mine Workers, who came into the state in 1899, shut down operations at numerous mines in 1900 and 1903. Violence was common in these disputes. In one well-known episode, after striking miners and their families set up a tent colony at Ludlow, near Trinidad, the governor called out the militia; in the ensuing conflict, on 20 April 1914, the miners' tents were burned, killing two women and 11 children, an event that touched off a rebellion in the whole area. Federal troops restored order in June, and the strike ended with promises of improved labor conditions. In 1917, the state legislature created the Colorado Industrial Commission, whose purpose is to investigate all labor disputes.

The US Department of Labor reported that in 2002, 157,000 of Colorado's 1,999,000 employed wage and salary workers were members of unions. This represented 7.8% of those so employed, down from 8.7% in 2001. The national average is 13.2%. In all, 180,000 workers (9.0%) were represented by unions. In addition to union members, this category includes workers who report no union affiliation but whose jobs are covered by a union contract.

23AGRICULTURE

Colorado ranked 16th among the 50 states in agricultural income in 2001, with $4.73 billion, of which more than $1.36 billion came from crops.

As of 2002 there were 30,000 farms and ranches covering about 31.3 million acres (12.7 million hectares); the average farm (including ranches) was 1,091 acres (442 hectares). The major crop-growing areas are the east and east-central plains for sugar beets, beans, potatoes, and grains; the Arkansas Valley for grains and peaches; and the Western Slope for grains and fruits.

Colorado ranked seventh in the US in production of dry edible beans in 2002, with 1,519,000 hundredweight; seventh in sugar beets, with 794,000 tons; fifth in barley, with 7.2 million bushels. Colorado is also a leading producer of wheat, with 38.7 million bushels. Other field crops include corn, hay, and sorghum. In 2002, Colorado produced 469,500 tons of fresh market vegetables, 20 million lb (9.1 million kg) of commercial apples, and 19 million lb (8.6 million kg) of peaches. About 3 tons (3,048 kg) of tart cherries were harvested in 2002. Colorado is also a major grower of roses.

24ANIMAL HUSBANDRY

A leading sheep-producing state, Colorado is also a major area for cattle and other livestock.

From 1858 to about 1890, cattle drives were a common sight in Colorado, as a few cattle barons had their Texas longhorns graze on public-domain lands along the eastern plains and Western Slope. This era came to an end when farmers in these regions fenced in their lands, and the better-quality shorthorns and Herefords took over the market. Today, huge tracts of pasture-land are leased from the federal government by both cattle and sheep ranchers, with cattle mostly confined to the eastern plains and sheep to the western part of the state.

Preliminary estimates of the number of cattle and calves for 2003 was 2,650,000 with an estimated total value at $2.04 billion. Colorado had an estimated 790,000 hogs and pigs in 2002 with an estimated total value at $58.5 million. In 2001 Colorado produced 75.8 million lb (34.4 million kg) of sheep and lambs at a gross income of $81.5 million. Colorado was estimated to have produced an estimated 3.07 million lb (1.39 million kg) of shorn wool in 2001.

Other livestock products in 2001 included chickens, at an estimated 6.1 million lb (2.77 million kg), and milk, estimated at 1.97 billion lb (0.89 billion kg). In the same year, the state produced an estimated 946 million eggs.

25FISHING

There is virtually no commercial fishing in Colorado. The many warm-water lakes lure the state's 769,846 licensed sport anglers with perch, black bass, and trout, while walleyes are abundant in mountain streams. In 1998, 18 fish farms distributed 10 million trout for restoration or conservation purposes.

26FORESTRY

Approximately 21,637,000 acres (8,756,494 hectares) of forested lands were located in Colorado as of 2002. In spite of this wood resource, however, commercial forestry is not a major element of the state's economy. Lumber production in 2002 was 135 million board feet. In Colorado, forestry emphasis occurs in diverse areas: traditional forest management and stewardship; urban and community forestry; resource protection (from wildfire, insects, and disease); and tree planting and care. As of 2003 Colorado had 13 national forests; gross national forest acreage as of 2001 was 16,015,000 acres (6,481,271 hectares).

27 MINING

According to US Geological Survey estimates, the value of 2001 nonfuel mineral production was about $577 million, down 2% from 2000. Industrial minerals, especially construction gravel, portland cement, and crushed stone, accounted for about 82% of the state's nonfuel mineral production.

According to preliminary figures, in 2001 Colorado ranked 2nd in the nation in production of molybdenum and 3rd in soda ash. The state ranked 22nd among the 50 states in total nonfuel mineral production value, with 1.5% of the national total. In 2001, Colorado mined 39.5 million metric tons of sand and gravel ($197 million), 13.5 million metric tons of crushed stone ($87.7 million), 35,000 tons of lime ($2.1 million), and 296,000,000 metric tons of clay ($2 million).

28 ENERGY AND POWER

An abundant supply of coal, oil, and natural gas makes Colorado a major energy-producing state.

During 1999, 39.5 billion kWh of electricity (utility and nonutility) were generated in Colorado, about 83% of that in coal-fired plants; total installed capacity was 8 million kW.

Petroleum production in 2002 was 49,000 barrels per day (11th highest in the nation); proved reserves were 196 million barrels (12th highest). Natural gas marketed production in 2002 was 605.3 billion cu ft (17.1 billion cu m); in 2001 reserves were nearly 12.5 trillion cu ft (0.35 trillion cu m).

Colorado's coal output, which reached a peak of some 19 million short tons in 1981, had declined during the 1980s, but rose back to 29.1 million metric tons in 2000. In 2000 Colorado's total per capita energy consumption was 279 million Btu (70.3 million kcal), ranking it 41st among the states.

Colorado holds the major portion of the nation's proved oil shale reserves. Because of its ample sunshine and wind, Colorado is also well suited to renewable energy development. Among the many energy-related facilities in the state is the National Renewable Energy Laboratory in Golden.

29 INDUSTRY

Colorado is the main manufacturing center of the Rocky Mountain states; value of shipments by manufacturers in 1997 was $42 billion, growing by a five-year total of 43% since 1992. The major sectors for value of shipments by manufacturers were food, printing and publishing, industrial machinery and equipment, and electronic equipment. Mineral shipments amounted to $3.5 billion, growing at only 4.8% since 1992, while the construction business pulled in over $19 billion, with the 3rd-largest growth rate in the country for that field (78.6%). The construction sector was expected to cool in 2000.

High-technology research and manufacturing grew substantially in Colorado during the 1980s and 1990s. Advanced technology exports were 61% of all exports in 2000. Storage Technology in Louisville is the largest high-tech company with headquarters in the state, but many large out-of-state companies—including Apple Computer, IBM, Hewlett-Packard, Eastman Kodak, Digital Equipment, Ball Aerospace, Martin-Lockheed Corporation, MCI Telecommunications, TCI Cable, and Cobe Laboratories—have divisions there. There are three Fortune 500 companies headquartered in Colorado: US West, Tele-Communications, and Cyprus Amax Minerals.

Earnings of persons employed in Colorado increased from $81.8 billion in 1997 to $90.2 billion in 1998, an increase of

10.3%. The largest industries in 1998 were services, 29.3% of earnings; state and local government, 10.2%; and retail trade, 9.8%. Of the industries that accounted for at least 5% of earnings in 1998, the slowest growing from 1997 to 1998 was state and local government, which increased 5.7%; the fastest was wholesale trade (6.1% of earnings in 1998), which increased 11.2%.

30 COMMERCE

Colorado is the leading wholesale and retail distribution center for the Rocky Mountain states. In 1997 there were 8,532 wholesale establishments, with sales of $63 billion. Retail sales in 1997 totaled $42 billion from 26,130 establishments. Colorado ranked eighth in the growth of retail sales between 1992 and 1997, and sixteenth in the growth of wholesale revenues. Major retail sectors by type of establishment included food stores, 7.3%; automotive dealers and service stations, 12%; and eating and drinking places, 31%. Food sales brought in $7 billion, while general merchandise sales were recorded at $5 billion. Colorado's foreign exports in 1998 included nearly $5.2 billion in goods.

31 CONSUMER PROTECTION

Colorado Attorney General's Consumer Protection Office is responsible for enforcing the state consumer protection laws including the Colorado Consumer Protection Act, the Unfair Trade Practices Act, the Fair Debt Collection Practices Act, the Uniform Consumer Credit Code, the Credit Services Organization Act and the Rental Purchase Agreement Act. Other applicable legislation includes the Motor Vehicle Repair Act, the Lemon Law, the Unsolicited Merchandise Act, the Charitable Solicitations Act, and the Colorado Statutes Concerning Pyramid Schemes. The office also represents the interests of consumers, small business, and agriculture before the Public Utilities Commission in matters involving electric, gas, and telephone utility services.

32 BANKING

In 2002, Colorado had 181 insured banks, with assets of $50 billion. Most of these institutions were concentrated in metropolitan Denver, the leading banking center between Kansas City and the Pacific. Colorado credit unions and savings and loans are regulated by the Division of Financial Services, under the Department of Regulatory Agencies (DORA). Chartered commercial banks are regulated by the Division of Banking.

Although Colorado experienced negative economic conditions in 2001/02 (including a rate of job losses that exceeded that of the nation), insured institutions headquartered in the state performed well. The average return on assets (ROA) ratio (the measure of earnings in relation to all resources) was among the highest level in a decade, in part due to the low cost of funds.

33 INSURANCE

In 2001 there were 1.8 million ordinary life insurance policies in force with a total value of $174.9 billion; total value for all categories of life insurance (ordinary, group, industrial, and credit) was $278.8 billion. Death benefits paid that year totaled $614.2 million.

As of 2003, 35 property and casualty insurance companies and 14 life and health insurance companies were domiciled in Colorado. Property and liability insurers wrote premiums amounting to about $6.7 billion in 2001. That year, there were 14,631 flood insurance policies in force in the state, with a total value of $2.1 million.

34SECURITIES

There are no stock or commodity exchanges in Colorado. There are 1,310 securities dealer industries in Colorado, with 12,264 employees. A total of 417 companies offer investment services. Colorado is home to 146 NASDAQ companies, 20 AMEX companies, and four NYSE-listed Colorado-incorporated companies; including Barrett Resources Corp., Graphics Packaging International Corporation, Scott's Liquid Gold, and Transmedia.

35PUBLIC FINANCE

The governor's Office of State Planning and Budgeting has lead responsibility for preparing the annual budget, which is presented to the General Assembly on 1 November. The legislature is expected to adopt the budget in May for the fiscal year, which runs from 1 July to 30 June. The constitution requires that the budget be balanced as submitted, as passed, and as signed into law. These requirements are part of the Colorado Taxpayer's Bill of Rights (TABOR), the name for a set of amendments adopted in 1992. The TABOR limits increases in per capita spending to the inflation rate and mandates the immediate refund to the taxpayers of any surplus unless they vote to allocate those funds to the state. The voters may also vote for tax increases beyond the inflation rate, which they did for school spending in 2001. Colorado taxpayers received rebates totaling $3.2 billion under the TABOR provisions over six consecutive years (1997–2002). From 1991 to 2002, combined state and local taxes in Colorado declined from 9.8% of income to 9.2% of income (from 25th-highest to 32nd-highest in the country). Ironically, in the sharp decline in state revenues in 2002 and 2003 stemming from the country's economic slowdown, the rebates owed (over $900 million for 2001) became part a major contributor to the state's budget crisis.

The budget deficit in 2002/03 was $558 million and was estimated at $900 million for 2003/04. The relative size of these deficits—9.2% of the state budget and 13.4% of the state budget—reflects the rigidities of the Colorado state tax system under the TABOR.

General Fund revenues totaled $6.72 billion in 2001, but then dropped by 12.6%, to $5.87 billion in 2002, and by a further 3.4%, to $5.67 billion, in 2003. In 2002 cuts made in the budget after it had been passed totaled $554 million, and in 2003, in spite of reduced appropriations, $621.5 million. Methods used to reduce General Fund spending included across-the-board cuts (although K-12 programs and special education programs were exempted), hiring freezes, construction freezes, transfers from other funds ($816.7 million in 2002 and $559.6 million in 2003), and some furloughs in the judiciary department. In the General Fund budget for 2004, available resources were projected at $5.95 billion, after diversion of revenues of $272 million to help replenish the State Education Fund and the Old Coloradoans Program.

For 2003/04 appropriations for the General Fund totaled $5.58 billion (down from General Fund expenditures of $6.69 billion the previous year)is for education, including higher education; 29.5% for health care, human services and public health, and 9.4% for corrections and public safety. There is also a Cash Fund derived mainly from fees, like tuition charges. Under the TABOR, fees are not limited to cost-of-living increases, but the total Cash Fund is limited to 27.5% of the General Fund, so for 2003-4 Cash Funds appropriations totaled about $1.52 billion. There is a third, larger fund not subject to the TABOR revenue cap called the Cash Fund Exempt in which was appropriated $3.17 billion. The fourth fund in Colorado's total appropriations is for federal funds, at $3.12 billion for 2003/04, bring total appropriations to $13.92 billion.

The following table from the US Census Bureau contains information on revenues, expenditures, indebtedness, and cash/securities for 2001.

	($000)	PERCENT	PER CAPITA
Population (thousands, 2001)	4,431	(X)	(X)
Total Revenue	19,774,425	100.00	4,462.75
General revenue	13,868,004	70.13	3,129.77
Utility revenue	–	–	–
Liquor store revenue	–	–	–
Insurance trust revenue	5,906,421	29.87	1,332.98
Exhibit: Salaries and wages	2,471,751	15.76	557.83
Total expenditure	15,685,926	100.00	3,540.04
General expenditure	13,702,406	87.35	3,092.40
Education	5,287,541	33.71	1,193.31
Public welfare	3,312,898	21.12	747.66
Hospitals	157,390	1.00	35.52
Health	309,353	1.97	69.82
Highways	1,342,195	8.56	302.91
Police protection	95,073	0.61	21.46
Correction	704,421	4.49	158.98
Natural resources	233,924	1.49	52.79
Parks and recreation	64,377	0.41	14.53
Government administration	393,523	2.51	88.81
Interest on general debt	319,612	2.04	72.13
Other and unallocable	1,482,099	9.45	334.48
Utility expenditure	7,834	0.05	1.77
Liquor store expenditure	–	–	–
Insurance trust expenditure	1,975,686	12.60	445.88
Debt at end of fiscal year	4,917,187	100.00	1,109.72
Cash and security holdings	36,841,428	100.00	8,314.47

36TAXATION

In 2003, individual income in Colorado was taxed at a flat rate of 4.63% of federal taxable income. The corporate income tax rate is also a flat 4.63%. The Taxpayer's Bill of Rights (TABOR) limits the state's revenue growth to the sum of inflation plus population growth in the previous calendar year. It also mandates an immediate rebate of any surplus tax money collected. As part of the rebate process, the individual and corporate income tax rates were reduced from 5% to 4.75% as of 1 January 1999, and then to 4.63% as of 1 January 2000. The formula for taxable corporate income takes into consideration both total profits and those derived solely from state sources. By 2003, Colorado had also reduced its general sales tax from 5% in 1999 to 2.9% in 2001. Food and prescription drugs are exempt from the general sales tax. Colorado municipalities are also allowed to levy sales and use taxes, with a top rate reduced to 6.9% (from 7%) in 2001. There are also state excise taxes on tobacco products, alcoholic beverages, pari-mutuel racing, motor fuels, insurance premiums, public utilities, and other selected goods, as well as various license fees. The state inheritance tax is set equal to the federal tax credit for such taxes, and so is set to be phased out by 2007 in tandem with the phasing out of the federal inheritance tax absent any countervailing action by the Colorado legislature. Estimated revenue losses from the phasing out of the state inheritance tax are $14.3 million in 2002/03, $35.7 million in 2003/04, and $73.7 million in 2006/07. Colorado also imposes severance taxes on extractive operations with rates varying according to the substance, as well an Oil and Gas Conservation levy (at 0.11% as of March 2002). Property taxes are the major source of revenue for local governments.

State tax collections in Colorado in 2002 totaled $6.923 billion in 2002, down from $7.57 billion (-8.5%) in 2001. Of the total, 50% came from individual income taxes, 27.5% from the general sales tax, 13.5% from selective sales taxes, 4% from license fees, and 3% from the corporate income tax.

The following table from the US Census Bureau provides a summary of taxes collected by the state in 2002.

	($000)	PER CAPITA
Total Taxes	**6,923,171**	**1,536.25**
Property taxes	(X)	(X)
Sales and gross receipts	2,834,580	628.99
General sales and gross receipts	1,901,972	422.05
Selective sales taxes	932,608	206.95
Alcoholic beverage	30,028	6.66
Amusements	95,176	21.12
Insurance Premiums	158,199	35.1
Motor fuels	569,079	126.28
Pari-mutuels	5,750	1.28
Public utilities	8,132	1.8
Tobacco products	66,244	14.7
Other selective sales	(X)	(X)
Licenses	278,018	61.69
Alcoholic beverages	4,753	1.05
Amusements	1,422	0.32
Corporation	6,838	1.52
Hunting and fishing	57,297	12.71
Motor vehicle	151,444	33.61
Motor vehicle operators	16,639	3.69
Public utility	(X)	(X)
Occupation and business, NEC	39,122	8.68
Other	503	0.11
Other taxes	3,810,573	845.56
Individual income	3,475,760	771.27
Corporation net income	205,217	45.54
Death and gift	72,199	16.02
Documentary and stock transfer	(X)	(X)
Severance	57,130	12.68
Other	267	0.06

[37] ECONOMIC POLICY

The Colorado Office of Economic Development and International Trade (OED&IT) implements the state government's economic plans. In 2000, the Governor's Office of Innovation and Technology (OIT) was established, and Colorado's first Secretary of Technology was appointed. Colorado's economic programs are aimed at encouraging new industry, helping existing companies expand and compete, and providing assistance to small businesses and to farmers. Economic development in rural areas is a priority. It offers real estate loans to help companies purchase or expand existing buildings or to construct new buildings. It assists employers with training programs for newly created and existing jobs. Colorado seeks to aid small businesses by contributing to lenders' reserve funds for small commercial and agricultural loans, by extending to small businesses loans with fixed interest rates, by giving grants to small technology-based firms for research and development projects, and by offering capital loans and credit to small export/import companies. The state operates a network of Small Business Development Centers (SBDCs), the latest established in Centennial in June 2003. The SBDCs offer Leading Edge courses to train business people and people seeking to start business in entrepreneurial behaviors, covering such topics as strategic planning, marketing research, marketing, an cash-flow analysis. Several local economic development organizations in Colorado received Excellence in Economic Development Awards from the US Department of Commerce in 2003. The state offers a variety of loan programs for economic development and manages a number of loan programs for farmers and agricultural producers. A limited program of grants are earmarked for agriculture feasibility studies, technology, and defense conversion programs.

[38] HEALTH

Colorado's infant mortality rate was 6.2 per 1,000 live births in 2000. There were 5,017 legal abortions in 1999. Colorado's death rate from all causes in 2000 was 659.7 per 100,000 population, as compared to the national rate of 873.1. Specific death rates for heart disease, cancer, and cerebrovascular diseases were far below the US norm while those for accidents were slightly higher. The mortality rate from heart disease was one of the lowest in the country at 149.5 per 100,000 people. The suicide rate of 14.8 per 100,000 was considerably higher than the US rate of 10.7 in 2000. In the same year, the death rate due to HIV infection was 2.2 per 100,000 population, lower than the US average of 5.3 that year. There were 7,381 AIDS cases reported through 2001.

In 2001, Colorado's 66 community hospitals had 9,442 beds and reported 413,605 admissions. Hospital personnel included 12,230 full-time registered nurses and 964 full-time licensed practical nurses. The state had 263 physicians per 100,000 population in 2000. In 2001, the average cost per inpatient day to community hospitals providing services in Colorado was $1,120.20. The state's only medical school is the University of Colorado Medical Center in Denver.

Federal government grants to cover the Medicare and Medicaid services in 2001 totaled $1.2 billion; 475,616 enrollees received Medicare benefits that year. The percentage of uninsured adults in Colorado in 2002 was 15.6%.

[39] SOCIAL WELFARE

In 2001, the average weekly unemployment benefit was $291.72. Average monthly participation in the food stamp program in FY2002 comprised 178,490 persons (78,902 households). The average monthly benefit was $77.24, and the sum total of benefits paid in FY2002 was $165,442,169.

With the enactment of the Personal Responsibility and Work Opportunity Reconciliation Act of 1996, the US government has changed the form and regulations for many of its social welfare programs. Most significantly, it replaces Aid to Families with Dependent Children (AFDC), an open-ended entitlement program, with Temporary Assistance for Needy Families (TANF), a limited system of assistance funded largely through federal block grants. The reform act also impacts the food stamp program, the Supplemental Security Income program, and the child nutrition program. The law took effect on 1 July 1997 and provided $16.38 billion in block grants for fiscal years 1997–2002. The grants are to be divided among the states based on an equation involving the numbers of former AFDC recipients in each state.

Reauthorization of the 1996 social welfare legislation, scheduled for 2002, was delayed, and the original law had been extended three times as of July 2003, with the most recent extension running through September 2003. Colorado's TANF program is called Colorado Works. In June 2000 the state had 27,699 welfare recipients. State expenditures on the TANF program in FY2002 totaled $92,692,595.

In December 2001, Social Security benefits were paid to 542,320 Colorado residents. This number included 341,280 retired workers, 57,070 widows and widowers, 62,540 disabled workers, 38,380 spouses, and 42,940 children. Social Security beneficiaries represented 12.2% of the total state population and 91.7% of the state's population age 65 and older. Retired workers (excluding persons with special benefits) received an average monthly payment of $852; widows and widowers, $830; disabled workers, $808; and spouses, $433. Payments for children of retired workers averaged $450 per month; children of deceased workers, $588; and children of disabled workers, $245.

Federal Supplemental Security Income payments in December 2001 went to 53,466 Colorado residents, averaging $356 a month.

[40] HOUSING

In 2002, there were an estimated 1,929,092 housing units in the state, of which 1,804,111 units were occupied; 68% were owner-occupied. About 63.6% of all units were single-family, detached homes. It was estimated that about 47,124 units were without telephone service, 5,500 lacked complete plumbing facilities, and 8,163 lacked complete kitchen facilities. Though most homes employed gas and electricity as heating fuel, about 1,620 units were equipped for solar power heating. The average household size was 2.4 people.

In 2002, 47,871 new privately-owned housing units were authorized. Colorado received over $53 million in aid from the US Department of Housing and Urban Development. The Denver-Boulder area is Colorado's primary region of housing growth. The median home value was $199,039. The median monthly cost for mortgage owners was $1,333 while the cost for renters was at a median of $730 per month.

41EDUCATION

Colorado residents are better educated than the average American. As of 2000, 32.7% of the adult population of Colorado had completed four or more years of college; 86.9% of all adult Coloradans were high school graduates.

In fall 1999, Colorado's public elementary and secondary schools had 708,109 pupils. Of these, 506,568 attended schools from kindergarten through grade eight, and 201,541 attended high school. Minority students made up approximately 33% of the total enrollment in public elementary and secondary schools in 2001. Total enrollment was estimated at 724,508 in fall 2000 and expected to reach 738,000 by fall 2005. Enrollment in nonpublic schools in fall 2001 was 52,142. Expenditures for public education in 2000/01 were estimated at $4,408,670.

As of fall 2000, there were 282,832 students enrolled in institutions of higher education. In the same year Colorado had 74 degree-granting institutions. In 1997, minority students comprised 18.6% of total postsecondary enrollment. The oldest state school is the Colorado School of Mines, founded in Golden in 1869. Although chartered in 1861, the University of Colorado did not open until 1876; its Boulder campus is now the largest in the state. Colorado State University was founded at Ft. Collins in 1870. The University of Denver was chartered in 1864 as the Colorado Seminary of the Methodist Episcopal Church. Colorado is also the home of the United States Air Force Academy.

42ARTS

In 2003, the Colorado Council on the Arts (est. 1967) and other arts organizations received grants totaling $2,256,700 from the National Endowment for the Arts. The Colorado Endowment for the Humanities was established in 1974. In 2000, $942,670 was granted to state organizations from the National Endowment for the Humanities. The Council on the Arts is affiliated with the regional Western States Art Federation. The State of Colorado also provides a sizeable share of the total for the support of the artists. In 1988, arts organizations in Denver successfully supported a proposal to contribute 0.1% of the area's sales tax to the development of the arts. Colorado's arts programs include the contributions of well over 100,000 artists. Arts education programs are presented to over 11,000 schoolchildren. In 2003, there were over 80 local arts organizations in the state.

From its earliest days of statehood, Colorado has been receptive to the arts. Such showplaces as the Tabor Opera House in Leadville and the Tabor Grand Opera House in Denver were among the most elaborate buildings in the Old West. Newer centers are Denver's Boettcher Concert Hall, which opened in 1978 as the home of the Denver Symphony, and the adjacent Helen G. Bonfils Theater Complex, which opened in 1980 and houses a repertory theater company.

Other artistic organizations include the Colorado Springs Symphony and Colorado Opera Festival of Colorado Springs; the Central City Opera House Association, which sponsors a summer opera season in this old mining town; and the Four Corners Opera Association in Durango. The amphitheater in Red Rocks Park near Denver, formed by red sandstone rocks, provides a natural and acoustically excellent concert area.

Aspen FilmFest, founded in 1979, offers several festivals throughout the year promoting interest in independent filmmaking. The annual Moondance International Film Festival for independent filmmakers has been considered to be one of the most important film festivals in the country. The Aspen Music Festival and School, founded in 1949, is an annual internationally renowned classical music festival that offers over 200 events and educational opportunities throughout the summer.

43LIBRARIES AND MUSEUMS

In 2000, the state's 113,000 public libraries held nearly 10,863,000 volumes and circulated more than 39,130,000. The largest system was the Denver Public Library with 1,882,487 volumes in 27 branches. The leading academic library is at the University of Colorado at Boulder, with over 2.8 million volumes. Total public library income came to $158,704,000 in 2000; including federal grants worth $317,408 and state grants worth $2,697,968. The libraries spent 62.4% of this income on staff, and 16.3% on the collections.

Colorado has more than 174 museums and historic sites. One of the most prominent museums in the West is the Denver Art Museum, with its large collection of American Indian, South Seas, and Oriental art. Another major art museum is the Colorado Springs Fine Arts Center, specializing in southwestern and western American art.

Other notable museums include the Denver Museum of Natural History, University of Colorado Museum in Boulder, Western Museum of Mining and Industry in Colorado Springs, and the Colorado Ski Museum–Ski Hall of Fame in Vail. Museums specializing in state history include the Colorado Heritage Center of the Colorado Historical Society in Denver, Ute Indian Museum in Montrose, Ft. Carson Museum of the Army in the West, Bent's Old Fort National Historic Site in La Junta, Georgetown–Silver Plume Historic District, Healy House–Dexter Cabin and Tabor Opera House Museum in Leadville, and Ft. Vasquez in Platteville.

44COMMUNICATIONS

Colorado's first mail and freight service was provided in 1859 by the Leavenworth and Pikes Peak Express. Over 97.4% of the state's occupied housing units had telephones as of 2001. Of the 80 major radio stations in operation in 2003, 23 were AM and 57 FM. The Denver area had cable in 61% of its 1,268,230 television-owning households. A total of 109,775 Internet domain names were registered in Colorado by 2000.

45PRESS

As of 2002, there were 20 morning dailies, 9 afternoon dailies, and 15 Sunday papers. The leading newspapers are as follows:

AREA	NAME	DAILY	SUNDAY
Denver	Rocky Mountain News(m, S)	309,938	801,315
	Denver Post(m, S)	305,929	801,315
Colorado Springs	Gazette (m, S)	101,274	119,671

46ORGANIZATIONS

In 2003, there were over 2,600 regional, national, and international organizations within the state.

Among the environmental associations located in the state are the National Environmental Health Association and the American Humane Association, both in Denver. The International Association of Meteorology and Atmospheric

Physics and the American Solar Energy Society are in Boulder. Among the many professional and trade groups in the state are the Geological Society of America in Boulder; National Cattlemen's Association in Englewood; and the American School Food Service Association, American Sheep Producers Council, College Press Service, and National Livestock Producers Association, all in Denver.

Colorado Springs is the home of several important sports organizations, including the US Olympic Committee, Amateur Basketball Association of the USA, Amateur Hockey Association of the US, Professional Rodeo Cowboys Association, and the US Ski Association. The Sports Car Club of America is in Englewood.

State arts and cultural organizations include the Colorado Artists Guild, the Colorado Historical Society, and Young Audiences of Colorado.

[47] TOURISM, TRAVEL, AND RECREATION

Tourism is making a comeback in the state as a result of improved funding and attention to the industry. A major slump for the industry began in 1993, when voters discontinued the state tourism tax. This resulted in a loss of $2.3 billion dollars per year and a 33% decrease in Colorado's market share. The legislature reinstated funding of $6 million in 1999 and in 2000 the Colorado Tourism Office (CTO) was established as a branch of the office of Economic Development and International Trade. The new CTO is led by a 13-member board of directors representing various segments of the industry.

In 2000, tourism was the 2nd-largest industry in the state, with travel spending reaching $8 billion. The state had over 24 million visitors. Tourism accounts for over 200,000 jobs within the state.

Scenery, history, and skiing combine to make Colorado a prime tourist Mecca. Vail is the most popular ski resort center, followed by Keystone and Steamboat. Skiing aside, the state's most popular attraction is the US Air Force Academy near Colorado Springs. Nearby are Pikes Peak, the Garden of the Gods (featuring unusual red sandstone formations), and Manitou Springs, a resort center. Besides its many museums, parks, and rebuilt Larimer Square district, Denver's main attraction is the US Mint.

All nine national forests in Colorado are open for camping, as are the state's two national parks: Rocky Mountain, encompassing 265,000 acres (107,000 hectares) in the Front Range; and Mesa Verde, 52,000 acres (21,000 hectares) of mesas and canyons in the southwest.

Other attractions include the fossil beds at Dinosaur National Monument, Indian cliff dwellings at Mesa Verde, Black Canyon of the Gunnison, Colorado National Monument at Fruita, Curecanti National Recreation Area, Florissant Fossil Beds, Great Sand Dunes, Hovenweep National Monument, Durango-Silverton steam train, and white-water rafting on the Colorado, Green, and Yampa rivers.

[48] SPORTS

There are four major league professional sports teams in Colorado, all in Denver: the Broncos of the National Football League, the Nuggets of the National Basketball Association, the Avalanche of the National Hockey League, and the Colorado Rockies of Major League Baseball. The Broncos won the American Football Conference Championship in 1978, 1987, 1988, and 1990, losing each year in the Super Bowl. They won back-to-back Super Bowl titles in 1998 and 1999. The Avalanche, who moved to Denver from Quebec after the 1995 season, won the Stanley Cup in 1996. The Colorado Springs Sky Sox compete in the Pacific Coast division of minor league baseball, and the Colorado Gold Kings compete in the West Coast Hockey League.

Colorado is home to some of the world's finest alpine skiing resorts, such as Vail, Aspen, and Steamboat Springs.

The Buffaloes of the University of Colorado produced some excellent football teams in the late 1980s and early 1990s, and they were named National Champions in 1990 (with Georgia Tech). Colorado won the Orange Bowl in 1957 and 1991, the Fiesta Bowl in 1995, and the Cotton Bowl in 1996. The Buffaloes have won or shared five Big Eight titles, the last one in 1991. Since the conference expanded to the Big Twelve, the Buffaloes have won the title once, in 2001.

Jack Dempsey, the famous heavyweight boxer of the 1920s, was born in Manassa, Colorado, and was appropriately named the "Manassa Mauler."

[49] FAMOUS COLORADANS

Ft. Collins was the birthplace of Byron R. White (1917–2002), who as an associate justice of the US Supreme Court beginning in 1962, had been the state's most prominent federal officeholder. Colorado's first US senator, Henry M. Teller (b.New York, 1830–1914), also served as secretary of the interior. Gary Hart (b.Kansas, 1937) was a senator and a presidential candidate in 1984 and 1988.

Charles Bent (b.Virginia, 1799–1847), a fur trapper and an early settler in Colorado, built a famous fort and trading post near present-day La Junta. Early explorers of the Colorado region include Zebulon Pike (b.New Jersey, 1779–1813) and Stephen Long (b.New Hampshire, 1784–1864). John Evans (1814–97) was Colorado's second territorial governor and founder of the present-day University of Denver. Ouray (1820–83) was a Ute chief who ruled at the time when mining districts were being opened. Silver magnate Horace Austin Warner Tabor (b.Vermont, 1830–99) served as mayor of Leadville and lieutenant governor of the state, spent money on lavish buildings in Leadville and Denver, but lost most of his fortune before his death. The story of Tabor and his second wife Elizabeth McCourt Doe Tabor (1862–1935), is portrayed in Douglas Moore's opera *The Ballad of Baby Doe* (1956). Willard F. Libby (1909–80), winner of the Nobel Prize for chemistry in 1960, and Edward L. Tatum (1909–75), co-winner of the 1958 Nobel Prize for physiology or medicine, were born in Colorado. Among the performers born in the state were actors Lon Chaney (1883–1930) and Douglas Fairbanks (1883–1939), and band leader Paul Whiteman (1891–1967). Singer John Denver (Henry John Deutschendorf, Jr., b.New Mexico, 1943–97) was closely associated with Colorado and lived in Aspen until his death in a plane crash.

Colorado's most famous sports personality is Jack Dempsey (1895–1983), born in Manassa and nicknamed the "Manassa Mauler," who held the world heavyweight boxing crown from 1919–26.

[50] BIBLIOGRAPHY

Abbott, Carl. *Colorado: A History of the Centennial State*. 3rd ed. Boulder: Colorado Associated University Press, 1994.

Athearn, Robert G. *The Coloradans*. Albuquerque: University of New Mexico Press, 1982.

Aylesworth, Thomas G. *The Southwest: Colorado, New Mexico, Texas*. Chicago: Chelsea House Publishers, 1996.

Babb, Sanora. *An Owl on Every Post*. New York: McCall, 1970.

Baggs, Mae Lacy. *Colorado, the Queen Jewel of the Rockies—A Description of its Climate and of its Mountains, Rivers, Forests and Valleys*. Denver: The Page Company, 1918.

Casewit, Curtis W. *Colorado*. New York: Viking, 1973.

Cronin, Thomas E. *Colorado Politics & Government: Governing the Centennial State*. Lincoln, Nebr.: University of Nebraska Press, 1993.

Federal Writers' Project. *Colorado: A Guide to the Highest State*. Reprint. New York: Somerset, 1987 (orig. 1941).

Harris, Katherine. *Long Vistas: Women and Families on Colorado Homesteads.* Niwot, Colo.: University of Colorado Press, 1993.

Litvak, Dianna. *Colorado.* Santa Fe, N.M.: John Muir Pub., 1999.

Mahoney, Paul F., Thomas J. Noel, and Richard E. Stevens. *Historical Atlas of Colorado.* Norman, Okla.: University of Oklahoma Press, 1994.

Noel, Thomas J. and John Fielder. *Colorado, 1870–2000, Revisited: The History Behind the Images.* Englewood, Colo.: Westcliffe, 2001.

Reyher, Ken. *High Country Cowboys: A History of Ranching in Western Colorado.* Montrose, Colo.: Western Reflections, 2002.

Sprague, Marshall. *Colorado: A Bicentennial History.* New York: Norton, 1976.

Ubbelohde, Carol, Maxine Benson, and Duane A. Smith. *A Colorado History.* 5th ed. Boulder: Pruett, 1982.

Walton, Roger A. *Colorado: A Practical Guide to Its Government and People.* Ft. Collins, Colo.: Publishers Consultants, 1976.

Wyckoff, William. *Creating Colorado: the Making of a Western American Landscape, 1860–1940.* New Haven, Conn.: Yale University Press, 1999.

CONNECTICUT

State of Connecticut

ORIGIN OF STATE NAME: From the Mahican word *quinnehtukqut,* meaning "beside the long tidal river." **NICKNAME:** The Constitution State (official in 1959); also, the Nutmeg State. **CAPITAL:** Hartford. **ENTERED UNION:** 9 January 1788 (5th). **SONG:** "Yankee Doodle." **MOTTO:** *Qui transtulit sustinet* (He who transplanted still sustains). **COAT OF ARMS:** On a rococo shield, three grape vines, supported and bearing fruit, stand against a white field. Beneath the shield is a streamer bearing the state motto. **FLAG:** The coat of arms appears on a blue field. **OFFICIAL SEAL:** The three grape vines and motto of the arms surrounded by the words *Sigillum reipublicae Connecticutensis* (Seal of the State of Connecticut). **ANIMAL:** Sperm whale. **BIRD:** American robin. **INSECT:** European praying mantis. **FLOWER:** Mountain laurel. **TREE:** White oak. **MINERAL:** Garnet. **SHIP:** *USS Nautilus.* **LEGAL HOLIDAYS:** New Year's Day, 1 January; Birthday of Martin Luther King, Jr., 3rd Monday in January; Lincoln's Birthday, 12 February; Washington's Birthday, 3rd Monday in February; Good Friday, March or April; Memorial Day, last Monday in May; Independence Day, 4 July; Labor Day, 1st Monday in September; Columbus Day, 2nd Monday in October; Veterans Day, 11 November; Thanksgiving Day, 4th Thursday in November; Christmas Day, 25 December. **TIME:** 7 AM EST = noon GMT.

¹LOCATION, SIZE, AND EXTENT

Located in New England in the northeastern US, Connecticut ranks 48th in size among the 50 states.

The state's area, 5,018 sq mi (12,997 sq km), consists of 4,872 sq mi (12,619 sq km) of land and 146 sq mi (378 sq km) of inland water. Connecticut has an average length of 90 mi (145 km) E–W, and an average width of 55 mi (89 km) N–S.

Connecticut is bordered on the N by Massachusetts; on the E by Massachusetts and Rhode Island (with part of the line formed by the Pawcatuck River); on the S by New York (with the line passing through Long Island Sound); and on the W by New York. On the SW border, a short panhandle of Connecticut territory juts toward New York City. The state's geographic center is East Berlin in Hartford County. Connecticut has a boundary length of 328 mi (528 km) and a shoreline of 253 mi (407 km).

²TOPOGRAPHY

Connecticut is divided into four main geographic regions. The Connecticut and Quinnipiac river valleys form the Central Lowlands, which bisect the state in a north–south direction. The Eastern Highlands range from 500 ft (150 m) to 1,100 ft (335 m) near the Massachusetts border and from 200 ft (60 m) to 500 ft (150 m) in the southeast. Elevations in the Western Highlands, an extension of the Green Mountains, range from 200 ft (60 m) in the south to more than 2,000 ft (600 m) in the northwest; within this region, near the Massachusetts border, stands Mt. Frissell, the highest point in the state at 2,380 ft (726 m). The Coastal Lowlands, about 100 mi (160 km) long and generally 2–3 mi (3–5 km) wide, consist of rocky peninsulas, shallow bays, sand and gravel beaches, salt meadows, and good harbors at Bridgeport, New Haven, New London, Mystic, and Stonington.

Connecticut has more than 6,000 lakes and ponds. The two largest bodies of water—both artificial—are Lake Candlewood, covering about 5,000 acres (2,000 ha), and Barkhamsted Reservoir, a major source of water for the Hartford area. The main river is the Connecticut, New England's longest river at 407 mi (655 km), of which 69 mi (111 km) lie within Connecticut; this waterway, which is navigable as far north as Hartford by

means of a 15-ft (5-m) channel, divides the state roughly in half before emptying into Long Island Sound. Other principal rivers include the Thames, Housatonic, and Naugatuck.

Connecticut's bedrock geology and topography are the product of a number of forces: uplift and depression, erosion and deposit, faulting and buckling, lava flows, and glaciation. About 180 million years ago, the lowlands along the eastern border sank more than 10,000 ft (3,000 m); the resultant trough or fault extends from northern Massachusetts to New Haven Harbor and varies in width from about 20 mi (32 km) to approximately 4 mi (6 km). During the Ice Ages, the melting Wisconsin glacier created lakes, waterfalls, and sand plains, leaving thin glaciated topsoil and land strewn with rocks and boulders.

³CLIMATE

Connecticut has a generally temperate climate, with mild winters and warm summers. The January mean temperature is 27°F (–3°C) and the July mean is 70°F (21°C). Coastal areas have warmer winters and cooler summers than the interior. Norfolk, in the northwest, has a January mean temperature of 22°F (–6°C) and a July mean of 66°F (19°C), while Bridgeport, on the shore, has a mean of 30°F (–1°C) in January and of 71°F (22°C) in July. The highest recorded temperature in Connecticut was 106°F (41°C) in Danbury on 15 July 1995; the lowest, –32°F (–36°C) in Falls Village on 16 February 1943. The annual rainfall (1971–2000) was 46.2 in (117 cm), evenly distributed throughout the year. The state receives some 25 to 60 in (64 to 150 cm) of snow each year, with heaviest snowfall in the northwest.

Weather annals reveal a remarkable range and variety of climatic phenomena. Severe droughts were experienced in 1749, 1762, 1929–33, the early 1940s, 1948–50, and 1956–57. The worst recent drought, which occurred in 1963–66, resulted in a severe forest-fire hazard, damage to crops, and rationing of water. Downtown Hartford was inundated by a flood in March 1936. On 21 September 1938, a hurricane struck west of New Haven and followed the Connecticut Valley northward, causing 85 deaths and property losses of more than $125 million. Severe flooding occurred in 1955 and again in 1982. In the latter year, property damage exceeded $266 million.

⁴FLORA AND FAUNA

Connecticut has an impressive diversity of vegetation zones. Along the shore of Long Island Sound are tidal marshes with salt grasses, glasswort, purple gerardia, and seas lavender. On slopes fringing the marshes are black grass, switch grass, marsh elder, and sea myrtle.

The swamp areas contain various ferns, abundant cattails, cranberry, tussock sedge, skunk cabbage, sweet pepperbush, spicebush, and false hellebore. The state's hillsides and uplands support a variety of flowers and plants, including mountain laurel (the state flower), pink azalea, trailing arbutus, Solomon's seal, and Queen Anne's lace. Only two plant species were listed as threatened or endangered as of August 2003: the small whorled pogonia (threatened) and the sandplain gerardia (endangered).

The first Englishmen arriving in Connecticut in the 1630s found a land teeming with wildlife. Roaming the forests and meadows were black bear, white-tailed deer, red and gray foxes, timber wolf, cougar, panther, raccoon, and enough rattlesnakes to pose a serious danger. The impact of human settlement on Connecticut wildlife has been profound, however. Only the smaller mammals—the woodchuck, gray squirrel, cottontail, eastern chipmunk, porcupine, raccoon, and striped skunk—remain common. Snakes remain plentiful but are mostly harmless, except for the northern copperhead and timber rattlesnake. Freshwater fish are abundant, and aquatic life in Long Island Sound even more so. Common birds include the robin (the state bird), blue jay, song sparrow, wood thrush, and many species of waterfowl; visible in winter are the junco, pine grosbeak, snowy owl, and winter wren.

Seventeen animal species were listed as threatened or endangered by the US Fish and Wildlife Service in August 2003. Among these were five kinds of sea turtles, the bald eagle, the roseate tern, two species of whale, and the gray wolf.

⁵ENVIRONMENTAL PROTECTION

The Department of Environmental Protection, established in 1971, is responsible for protecting natural resources and controlling water, air, and land pollution.

Its fiscal 1997 estimated expenditures for all programs from all sources will be approximately $90,400,000. State funds of $37,500,000 total less than 1% of the overall state budget.

Since the Connecticut Clean Water Act was passed in 1967, upgrading of sewage treatment plants, correction of combined sewer overflows, and improved treatment, at and sewage treatment tie-ins, by industrial facilities have resulted in significant water quality improvement in many state rivers. In 1997, about 75% of the state's 900 mi (1,448 km) of major streams meet federal "swimmable-fishable" standards. The Connecticut Clean Water Fund was created in 1986 to provide grants and low interest loans to municipalities to finance more than $1 billion in municipal sewerage infrastructure improvements over 20 years. Connecticut was the first state in the country to adopt, in 1980, a comprehensive statewide groundwater quality management system.

In 1994 the governors of Connecticut and New York formally adopted a comprehensive plan to manage Long Island Sound, an "estuary of national significance."

The Tidal Wetlands Act (1969) and the Inland Wetlands and Watercourses Act (1972) put the state in the forefront in wetland protection. In 1997 the DEP estimates permitted tidal wetland losses at less than one acre per year and inland wetland losses at about 630 acres per year. Two thousand or more acres of wetlands and watercourses have been restored.

For five of six criteria for air pollutants (lead, carbon monoxide, particulates, nitrogen dioxide, sulfur dioxide), Connecticut has virtually eliminated violations of health-based federal standards, and levels of these pollutants continue to decrease. The state exceeds the national standard for ozone but has reduced the number of days the standard is exceeded each year by 60% since the early 1970s. Vehicle-related emissions of ozone precursors have been reduced by almost 50%, and the state is working closely with other northeastern and mid-Atlantic states on regional ozone reduction.

In 1986 the state adopted a hazardous air pollutant regulation that covers over 850 substances. Permitting and enforcement processes and voluntary reductions have resulted in at least a 68% reduction in toxins emitted to the air.

In 1987 Connecticut adopted statewide mandatory recycling. As of 1997 the state has achieved a recycling rate of 23%, with its goal 40% recycling by the year 2000.

Since 1986, five regional resource recovery facilities have begun operation, while dozens of landfills closed as they became full or federal regulations prohibited continued operation. The combination of resource recovery, recycling, and reduction of waste by consumers has resulted in landfilled garbage declining from 1,400 pounds per capita in 1986 to about 300 in 1996. In 2003, the Environmental Protection Agency's database listed 424 hazardous waste sites, 15 of which were on the National Priorities List, in Connecticut.

Connecticut DEP has been a pioneer in efforts to restore anadromous fish runs and extirpated species such as wild turkeys and fishers and to document and preserve habitats for numerous plant and animal species. In 2001, Connecticut received $49,969,000 in federal grants from the EPA; EPA expenditures for procurement contracts in Connecticut that year amounted to $1,711,000.

⁶POPULATION

Connecticut ranked 29th in population in the US with an estimated total of 3,460,503 in 2002, an increase of 1.6% since 2000. Between 1990 and 2000, Connecticut's population grew from 3,287,116 to 3,405,565, an increase of 3.6%. The population is projected to reach 3.7 million by 2025.

The state had a population gain of 5.8% (about 180,000 residents) for the entire decade of the 1980s, compared with a US population growth of 9.7%. One sign of the population lag was that in 1990 Connecticut had the 11th lowest birthrate in the US, 14.5 live births per 1,000 population.

In 2000, Connecticut had the fourth-highest population density of all 50 states: 702.9 persons per sq mi, up from 678.5 persons per sq mi in 1990. The median age of residents in 2000 was 37.4; 13.8% were age 65 or older, while 24.7% were under 18 years old.

Major cities, with 2002 population estimates, are Bridgeport, 140,104; Hartford, 124,558; New Haven, 124,176; Stamford, 119,850; and Waterbury, 107,883. The three largest cities each had a slight net growth in population between 1990 and 2002, helping to reverse their losses during the 1960s and 1970s due to an exodus to the suburbs, which had increased rapidly in population. For example, Bloomfield, to the north of Hartford, gained in population from 5,700 in 1950 to 19,023 in 1984; and Trumbell, near Bridgeport, increased from 8,641 in 1950 to 33,285 in 1984.

⁷ETHNIC GROUPS

Connecticut has large populations of second-generation European descent. The biggest groups came from Italy, Ireland, Poland, and Quebec, Canada. Most of these immigrants clustered in the cities of New Haven, Hartford, Bridgeport, and New London. The number of Roman Catholic newcomers drew the

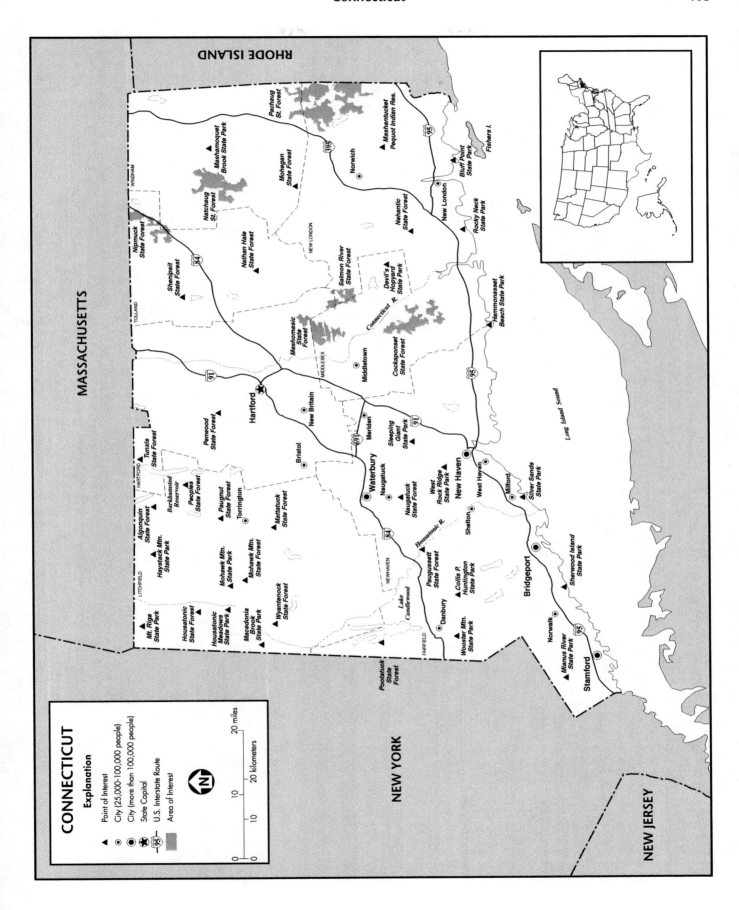

hostility of many native-born Connecticuters, particularly during the decade 1910–20, when state officials deported 59 "dangerous aliens" on scant evidence of radicalism and Ku Klux Klan chapters enrolled some 20,000 members.

Since 1950, ethnic groups of non-Yankee ancestry have exercised leadership roles in all facets of Connecticut life, especially in politics. Connecticut elected a Jewish governor in 1954, and its four subsequent governors were of Irish or Italian ancestry. A wave of newcomers to the state during and after World War II consisted chiefly of blacks and Hispanics seeking employment opportunities. In 2000, the black population numbered 309,843, about 9.1% of the state total. According to the 2000 federal census, there were also about 320,323 residents of Hispanic or Latino origin, or 9.4% of the state's total population (up from 213,000 in 1990), of whom 194,443 were Puerto Ricans (more than double the 1990 total of 93,608). In 2000, Connecticut had 9,639 American Indians, up from 7,000 in 1990, 82,313 Asians, and 1,366 Pacific Islanders. About 369,967 Connecticut residents, or 10.9% of the population, were foreign born in 2000, up from 279,000 (8.5%) in 1990.

8 LANGUAGES

Connecticut English is basically that of the Northern dialect, but features of the eastern New England subdialect occur east of the Connecticut River. In the east, *half* and *calf* have the vowel of father: *box* is /bawks/ and *cart* is /kaht/; *yolk* is /yelk/; *care* and *chair* have the vowel of cat; and many speakers have the intrusive / r/, as in *swaller it* (swallow it). In the western half, *creek* is /krik/ ; *cherry* may be /chirry/; *on* has the vowel of *father*; an /r/ is heard after a vowel, as in *cart*. Along the Connecticut river, *butcher* is / boocher/, and *tomorrow* is pronounced /tomawro/. Along the coast, the wind may be *breezing on*, and a *creek* is a saltwater inlet. The sycamore is *buttonball*, one is *sick to his stomach*, gutters are *eavestroughs*, a lunch between meals is a *bite*, and in the northwest, an earthworm is an *angledog*.

In 2000, 2,600,601 Connecticuters (81.7% of the resident population five years old and older, down from 84.8% in 1990) spoke only English at home.

The following table gives selected statistics from the 2000 census for language spoken at home by persons five years old and over. The category "Other Indo-European languages" includes Albanian, Gaelic, Lithuanian, and Rumanian.

LANGUAGE	NUMBER	PERCENT
Population 5 years and over	**3,184,514**	**100.0**
Speak only English	2,600,601	81.7
Speak a language other than English	583,913	18.3
Speak a language other than English	**583,913**	**18.3**
Spanish or Spanish Creole	268,044	8.4
Italian	50,891	1.6
French (incl. Patois, Cajun)	42,947	1.3
Polish	38,492	1.2
Portuguese or Portuguese Creole	30,667	1.0
Chinese	15,782	0.5
German	14,310	0.4
Other Indo-European languages	11,978	0.4
Greek	9,445	0.3
Russian	8,807	0.3
French Creole	7,856	0.2
Vietnamese	6,598	0.2

9 RELIGIONS

Connecticut's religious development began in the 1630s with the designation of the Congregational Church as the colony's "established church." The Puritan fathers enacted laws decreeing church attendance on Sundays and other appointed days, and requiring all residents to contribute to the financial maintenance of local Congregational ministers. Educational patterns, business practices, social conduct, and sexual activities were all comprehensively controlled in accordance with Puritan principles. "Blue Laws" provided penalties for offenses against God's word, such as profanation of the Sabbath and swearing, and capital punishment was mandated for adultery, sodomy, bestiality, lesbianism, harlotry, rape, and incest.

Connecticut authorities harassed and often persecuted such non-Congregationalists as Quakers, Baptists, and Anglicans. However, the church was weakened during the 18th century by increasing numbers of dissenters from the Congregational order. A coalition of dissenters disestablished the church by the Connecticut constitution of 1818. The final blow to Congregational domination came in the late 19th and early 20th centuries, with the arrival of many Roman Catholic immigrants.

Since World War I, Roman Catholics have been the most numerous religious group in the state. As of 2000, there were 1,372,562 Roman Catholics in 411 congregations. Mainline Protestants represent the 2nd-largest category of churches and include the United Church of Christ with 124,770 adherents in 253 congregations, the Episcopal Church with 73,550 adherents in 186 congregations, and the United Methodist Church with 51,183 adherents in 133 congregations. The estimated number of Jewish adherents was 108,280 and Muslims numbered about 29,647. About 42.1% of the population were not counted as members of any religious organization.

10 TRANSPORTATION

Because of both the state's traditional conservatism and the opposition by turnpike and steamboat companies, rail service did not fully develop until the 1840s. Hartford and New Haven were connected in 1839, and in 1850 that line was extended to Northampton, MA. In the 1840s and the 1850s, a network of lines connected Hartford with eastern Connecticut communities. Railroad expansion peaked during the 1890s when total trackage reached 1,636 mi (2,633 km). The giant in Connecticut railroading from the 1870s until its second and final collapse in 1961 was the New York, New Haven, and Hartford Railroad.

In the late 1960s, the Interstate Commerce Commission required that the assets of the bankrupt New York, New Haven, and Hartford Railroad be included into the Penn Central Transportation Company, which was formed by the merger of the New York Central and Pennsylvania Railroads. In 1970, Penn Central went bankrupt. In 1976, Penn Central's profitable assets were merged with the profitable assets of other northeast bankrupt railroads to form the Consolidated Rail Corporation (Conrail). As of 1997, Conrail had divested itself of most of its services in Connecticut, which is now served by eight regional and short-line railroads. As of 2000, there were approximately 743 mi (1,195 km) of railroad in Connecticut.

In October of 1970 the Connecticut Department of Transportation (CDOT) and the Metropolitan Transportation Authority of New York (MTA) entered an agreement (effective 1 January 1971) with the Trustees of Penn Central to oversee the operation of the New Haven Line Commuter Rail Service between New Haven and Grand Central Terminal in New York City and to jointly fund the operating deficit. In 1976 Conrail succeeded Penn Central as the operator of the New Haven Line and operated it until the end of 1982 when CDOT and MTA decided to operate the New Haven Line themselves.

On 1 January 1983, the Metro-North Railroad, which had been created as a subsidiary of the MTA, took over the operations of the New Haven Line in New York. CDOT and MTA continue to jointly oversee the operations of the New Haven Line service and fund the operating deficit. The costs of New Haven Line capital projects in Connecticut are funded by Connecticut, and the costs of capital projects in New York are funded by MTA. CDOT and MTA share the capital costs of rolling stock rehabilitation and acquisition. In 1985, CDOT purchased from Penn Central the Connecticut portion of the New Haven Line's main line and the three branch lines in Connecticut, including the right of way and support facilities.

On an average weekday, nearly 900 trains serve over 250,000 Metro-North customers from Connecticut and New York. In the mid-l990s, the on-time performance of New Haven Line trains ranged between 94.5% and 96.2%.

In 1990 CDOT contracted with Amtrak to operate the Shore Line East Commuter Rail Service between Old Saybrook and New Haven. Following a period of free service between 29 May and 29 June 1990, weekday only revenue service was implemented on 2 July 1990. In February of 1996, Shore Line East service was extended to New London. CDOT oversees the operation and provides the rolling stock, maintenance facilities, and funding necessary to cover the operating deficit. On an average weekday, 18 revenue trains serve about 600 customers. In the mid-l990s, the on-time performance of Shore Line East trains ranged between 90.0% and 96.3%.

Since 1971, Amtrak has provided inter-city passenger service to Connecticut on the Northeast Corridor main line (Boston–New Haven–New York City–Philadelphia–Washington, DC) and on the Springfield Line (New Haven–Hartford–Springfield). In 1996, Amtrak served 927,805 customers at 12 Connecticut stations.

Local bus systems provide intra-city transportation. These services are generally subsidized by the state and, in some instances, by the Federal Transit Administration. Inter-city bus service (not subsidized by the state or the federal government) is provided in over 30 municipalities by some 30 companies.

Connecticut has an extensive system of expressways, state highways, and local roads, aggregating 20,845 mi (33,546 km) in 2000; over 99% of the roads are either paved or hard-surfaced. Major highways include I-95, the John Davis Lodge Turnpike, which crosses the entire length of the state near the shore; I-91, linking New Haven and Springfield, MA; and I-84 from the Massachusetts Turnpike southwestward through Hartford, Waterbury, and Danbury to New York State. Over the past two decades, Connecticut has embarked on an ambitious infrastructure renewal program. Almost $2.2 billion has been expended to rehabilitate or replace over 1,866 of the 3,820 bridges that the state maintains. Approximately $927 million was used to resurface an average of 475 two-lane miles of state highway per year.

As of 2000 there were 2,009,190 automobiles, 833,730 trucks, and 10,529 buses registered in the state. Connecticut had 2,652,593 licensed drivers during the same year.

Presently, most of Connecticut's waterborne traffic is handled through the two major ports of New Haven and Bridgeport, which collectively handled approximately 15 million tons of cargo in 2000. The New London State Pier, which underwent reconstruction in the mid-1990s, unloaded its first post-renovation ship in March 1998 with Logistec Connecticut, Inc. in charge of operations.

In 2002, there were 151 civil and joint-use air facilities in Connecticut including 55 airports, 90 heliports, 1 stolport, and 5 seaplane bases. Connecticut's principal air terminal is Bradley International Airport in Windsor Locks, located 14 mi (23 km) north of Hartford. Bradley had a total of 3,651,943 enplanements in 2000.

11 HISTORY

The first people known to have lived in the area now called Connecticut were American Indians, whose forebears may have come to New England as many as 10,000 years ago. By the early 17th century, Connecticut had between 6,000 and 7,000 Indians organized into 16 tribes, all members of the lose Algonquian Confederation. The most warlike of these tribes were the Pequot,

who apparently had migrated not long before from the Hudson River region to escape the Mohawk and had settled along the Connecticut coast. There was also a heavy concentration of Indian groups in the Connecticut River Valley, but fear of Mohawk hunting parties kept them from occupying most of western and northwestern Connecticut.

Because of their fear of the Pequot along the shore and of the Mohawk to the west, most of Connecticut's Indians sought the friendship of English newcomers in the 1630s. The Indians sold land to the English and provided instruction in New World agricultural, hunting, and fishing techniques. The impact of English settlers on Connecticut's friendly Indians was devastating, however. The Indians lost their land, were made dependents in their own territory, and were decimated by such European imports as smallpox and measles. The Pequot, who sought to expel the English from Connecticut by a series of attacks in 1636–37, were defeated during the Pequot War by a Connecticut-Massachusetts force, aided by a renegade Pequot named Uncas. By the 1770s, Connecticut's Indian population was less than 1,500.

The first recorded European penetration of Connecticut was in 1614 by the Dutch mariner Adriaen Block, who sailed from Long Island Sound up the Connecticut River, probably as far as the Enfield Rapids. The Dutch established two forts on the Connecticut River, but they were completely dislodged by the English in 1654.

The early English settlers were part of a great migration of some 20,000 English Puritans who crossed the treacherous Atlantic to New England between 1630 and 1642. The Puritans declared that salvation could be achieved only by returning to the simplicity of the early Christian Church and the truth of God as revealed in the Bible. They sailed to America in order to establish a new society that could serve as a model for the rest of Christendom. Attracted by the lushness of the Connecticut River Valley, the Puritans established settlements at Windsor (1633), Wethersfield (1634), and Hartford (1636). In 1639, these three communities joined together to form the Connecticut Colony, choosing to be governed by the Fundamental Orders, a relatively democratic framework for which the Reverend Thomas Hooker was largely responsible. (According to some historians, the Fundamental Orders comprised the world's first written constitution, hence the state nickname, adopted in 1959.) A separate Puritan colony was planted at New Haven in 1638 under the leadership of John Davenport, a Puritan minister, and Theophilus Eaton, a successful merchant.

In 1662, the Colony of Connecticut secured legal recognition by England. Governor John Winthrop, Jr., persuaded King Charles II to grant a charter that recognized Connecticut's existing framework of government and established its north and south boundaries as Massachusetts and Long Island Sound and its east and west borders as Narragansett Bay and the Pacific Ocean. In 1665, New Haven reluctantly became part of the colony because of economic difficulties and feat of incorporation into Anglican New York.

Connecticut had acrimonious boundary disputes with Massachusetts, Rhode Island, New York, and Pennsylvania. The most serious disagreement was with New York, which claimed the entire area from Delaware Bay to the Connecticut River. The issue was resolved in 1683 when the boundary was set 20 mi (32 km) east of and parallel to the Hudson River, although it was not until 1881 that Connecticut, New York, and Congress established the exact line.

Connecticut functioned throughout the colonial period much like an independent republic. It was the only American colony that generally did not follow English practice in its legislative proceedings, nor did it adopt a substantial amount of English common and statute law for its legal code. Connecticut's autonomy was threatened in 1687 when Sir Edmund Andros, appointed by King James II as the governor of the Dominion of New England, arrived in Hartford to demand surrender of the 1662 charter. Connecticut leaders protected the colony's autonomy by hiding the charter in an oak tree, which subsequently became a landmark known as the Charter Oak.

With its Puritan roots and historic autonomy, Connecticut was a Patriot stronghold during the American Revolution. Tories numbered no more than 7% of the adult male population 2,000 to 2,500 out of a total of 38,000 males. Connecticut sent some 3,600 men to Massachusetts at the outbreak of fighting at Lexington and Concord in April 1775. Jonathan Trumbull, who served as governor from 1769 to 1784, was the only colonial governor in office in 1775 who supported the Patriots. He served throughout the Revolutionary War, during which Connecticut troops participated in most of the significant battles. Connecticut's privateers captured more than 500 British merchant vessels, and its small but potent fleet captured at least 40 enemy ships. Connecticut also produced arms and gunpowder for state and Continental forces, thus beginning an arms-making tradition that would lead to the state's unofficial designation as the "arsenal of the nation." It was also called the Provisions State, in large part because of the crucial supplies of foodstuffs it sent to General George Washington throughout the war. The state's most famous Revolutionary War figure was Nathan Hale, executed as a spy by the British in New York City in 1776.

On 9 January 1788, Connecticut became the 5th state to ratify the Constitution. Strongly Federalist during the 1790s, Connecticut ardently disagreed with the foreign policy of presidents Thomas Jefferson and James Madison, opposed the War of 1812, and even refused to allow its militia to leave the state. Connecticut's ire over the war was exacerbated by the failure of the government to offer significant help when the British attacked Essex and Stonington in the spring and summer of 1814. The politically vulnerable Federalists were defeated in 1817 by the Toleration Party. This coalition of Republicans and non-Congregationalists headed the drive for the new state constitution (1818) that disestablished the Congregational Church, a Federalist stronghold.

Long before the Civil War, Connecticut was stoutly antislavery. In the early years of independence, the general assembly enacted legislation providing that every black born after 1 March 1784 would be free at age 25. Connecticut had a number of antislavery and abolition societies whose members routed escaped slaves to Canada via the Underground Railroad. The state's pro-Union sentiment was reflected in the enormous support given to the Union war effort; some 55,000 Connecticut men served in the Civil War, suffering more than 20,000 casualties. Arms manufacturers such as Colt and Winchester produced desperately needed rifles and revolvers, and the state's textile, brass, and rubber firms turned out uniforms buttons, ponchos, blankets, and boots for Union troops.

The contributions by Connecticut industries to the war effort signaled the state's emergence as a manufacturing giant. Its industrial development was facilitated by abundant waterpower, the growth of capital held by banks and insurance companies, a sophisticated transportation network, and, most important, the technological and marketing expertise of the people. The first American hat factory was established in Danbury in 1780, and the nation's brass industry had its roots in Naugatuck Valley between 1806 and 1809. Connecticut clocks became known throughout the world. Micah Rugg organized the first nut and bolt factory in Marion in 1840; Elias Howe invented the first practical sewing machine in Hartford in 1843. Perhaps the most important figure in the development of Connecticut manufacturing was Eli Whitney, best known for inventing the cotton gin (1793).

Seventy-five years after Whitney's death, Connecticut was a leader in the production of hats, typewriters, electrical fixtures, machine tools, and hardware. The state's textile industry ranked 6th in the nation in 1900, with an annual output of $50 million. By 1904, Connecticut's firearms industry was producing four-fifths of the ammunition and more than one-fourth of the total value of all firearms manufactured by nongovernment factories in the US. These great strides in manufacturing transformed Connecticut from a rural, agrarian society in the early 1800s to an increasingly urban state.

The state's contribution to the Allied forces in World War I (1914–18) more than equaled its Civil War effort. Four Liberty Loan drives raised $437 million, more than the contribution from any other state. About 66,000 Connecticuters served in the armed forces, and the state's manufacturers produced 450,000 Enfield rifles, 45,000 Browning automatic rifles, 2 million bayonets, and much other war materiel. By 1917–18, four-fifths of Connecticut's industry was involved in defense production.

The prosperity sparked by World War I continued, for the most part, until 1929. During the 1920s, Connecticuters enjoyed a rising standard of living, as the state became a national leader in the production of specialty parts for the aviation, automotive, and electric power industries. However, from 1919 to 1929, Connecticut lost 14 of its 47 cotton mills to southern states.

The stock market crash of 1929 and the subsequent depression of the 1930s hit highly industrialized Connecticut hard. By the spring of 1932, the state's unemployed totaled 150,000, and cities such as Bridgeport fell deeply in debt. The economic reversal led to significant political change: the ousting of a business-oriented Republican administration, which had long dominated the state, by a revitalized Democratic Party under the leadership of Governor Wilbur L. Cross (1931–39). During his tenure, Connecticut reorganized its state government, improved facilities in state hospitals and penal institutions, and tightened state regulations of business.

Connecticut was pulled out of the unemployment doldrums in 1939 when the state's factories were once again stimulated by defense contracts. The value of World War II (1939–45) contracts placed in Connecticut was $8 billion by May 1945, and industrial employment increased from 350,000 in 1939 to 550,000 by late 1944. Connecticut's factories turned out submarines, Navy Corsair fighter aircraft, helicopters, 80% of all ball bearings manufactured in the US, and many thousands of small arms. Approximately 220,000 Connecticut men and women served in the US armed forces.

Since 1945, Connecticut has seen substantial population growth, economic diversification with a greater proportion of service industries, the expansion of middle-class suburbs, and an influx of black and Hispanic migrants to the major cities. Urban renewal projects in Hartford and New Haven have resulted in expanded office and recreational facilities, but not much desperately needed new housing. A major challenge facing Connecticut in the 1980s was once again how to effect the social and economic integration of this incoming wave of people and industries. Providing greater economic opportunities for people living in its cities remained a challenge for Connecticut into 2003.

Connecticut became the nation's wealthiest state during the 1980s, achieving the highest per capita income in 1986, a position still held in 1992 when its residents' per capita income of $26,797 was 35% above the average for the United States. The state's prosperity came in part from the expansion of the military budget, as 70% of Connecticut's manufacturing sector was defense related. The end of the cold war, however, brought cuts in military spending which reduced the value of defense related contracts in Connecticut from $6 billion in 1989 to $4.2 billion in 1990. By 1992, manufacturing jobs had declined by 25% while jobs in such service industries as retail, finance, insurance and real estate increased by 23%. The total number of jobs, however, dropped by 10% during the period. Tax relief measures were taken to make manufacturing more competitive in the state. In the mid-1990s, Connecticut's economy was on the upswing, fueled in part by the recovering banking industry, and its employment outlook improved.

In the 1980s and through the 1990s, Connecticut witnessed an increasing contrast between the standard of living enjoyed by urban and suburban residents, blacks and whites, and the wealthy and the poor. In 1992, the median family income in many of the state's suburbs was nearly twice that of families living in urban areas. Governor Lowel Weicker's administration imposed a personal income tax (designed to address the inequities of the sales tax system) and implemented a program to modify state funding formulas so that urban communities received a larger share. The state also launched an effort to improve the quality of public education in relatively poor cities, to bring it in alignment with suburban schools.

While per-capita income levels remained high in the state through the rest of the decade, poverty increased. According to government figures, in 1998 Connecticut still ranked first in the nation in per capita personal income ($37,700), but the state's poverty rate, just 6% (the lowest in the nation) in 1990, had climbed to 9.2% by 1998. While the state remained divided economically, it also was divided racially. Minority (black and Hispanic) populations were centered in urban Bridgeport, Hartford, and New Haven; smaller cities and suburbs remained predominately white.

Like many states across the nation, Connecticut faced a multi-million dollar budget deficit in 2003. Its legislature was considering a transportation package in 2003 that would increase a number of motor vehicle registration and licensing fees to raise an additional $20 million for 2004. Connecticut adopted a stringent welfare reform law under Governor John G. Rowland's tenure, limiting benefits to 21 months. A new death penalty law was passed for the state, as was a law requiring communities to be notified when sex offenders are released from prison. Connecticut in 2003 was looking to attract further business investment to the state.

12 STATE GOVERNMENT

Connecticut has been governed by four basic documents: the Fundamental Orders of 1639; the Charter of the Colony of Connecticut of 1662; the constitution of 1818 (which remained in effect until 1964, when a federal district court, acting on the basis of the US Supreme Court's "one person, one vote" ruling, ordered Connecticut to reapportion and redistrict its legislature); and the constitution of 1965. This last document adjusted representation to conform with population and provided for mandatory reapportionment every 10 years. The 1965 constitution had been amended 29 times by January 2003.

The state legislature is the general assembly, consisting of a 36-member senate and 151-member house of representatives. Regular legislative sessions are held each year, beginning in January in odd-numbered years (when sessions must end no later than in June) and in February in even-numbered years (when sessions must end no later than in May). A majority of legislators may call for special session. Legislators, who must be 18 years old, residents of their districts, and qualified voters in Connecticut, are elected to both houses for two-year terms from single-member districts of substantially equal populations. The legislative salary in 2002 was $28,000.

Elected members of the executive branch are the governor and lieutenant governor (who run jointly and must each be at least 30 years of age), secretary of state, treasurer, comptroller, and attorney general. All are elected for four-year terms and may be reelected. The governor, generally with the advice and consent of

the general assembly, selects the heads of state departments, commissions, and offices. In 2002 the governor's salary was $150,000.

A bill becomes law when approved by both houses of the general assembly and signed by the governor. If the governor fails to sign it within five days when the legislature is in session, or within 15 days after it has adjourned, the measure also becomes law. A bill vetoed by the governor may be overridden by a two-thirds vote of the elected members of each house.

A constitutional amendment may be passed in a single legislative session if approved by three-fourths of the total membership of each house. If approved in one session by a majority but by less than three-fourths, the proposed amendments requires approval by majority vote in the next legislative session following a general election. After passage by the legislature, the amendment must be ratified by the voters in the next even-year general election in order to become part of the state constitution.

To vote in state elections, a person must be a US citizen, at least 18 years old, a state resident, and a resident in the town where he or she will vote. Restrictions apply to convicted felons.

13 POLITICAL PARTIES

Connecticut's major political groups during the first half of the 19th century were successively the Federalist Party, the Democratic-Republican coalition, the Democrats, and the Whigs. The political scene also included a number of minor political parties—the Anti-Masonic, Free Soil, Temperance, and Native American (Know-Nothing) parties—of which the Know-Nothings were the most successful, holding the governorship from 1855 to 1857. The Whig Party collapsed during the controversy over slavery in the 1850s, when the Republican Party emerged as the principal opposition to the Democrats.

From the 1850s to the present, the Democratic and Republican parties have dominated Connecticut politics. The Republicans held power in most of the years between the Civil War and the 1920s. Republican hegemony ended in 1930, when the Democrats elected Wilbur L. Cross as governor. Cross greatly strengthened the Connecticut Democratic Party by supporting organized labor and providing social legislation for the aged and the needy. The success of the increasingly liberal Democrats in the 1930s prodded Connecticut Republicans to become more forward-looking, and the two parties were fairly evenly matched between 1938 and 1954. Connecticut's Democrats have held power in most years since the mid-1950s.

Republican presidential candidates carried Connecticut for five successive elections starting in 1972 and ending with the victory of Democrat Bill Clinton in 1992. In the 1996 election, Clinton again carried the state. In the 2000 presidential election, Democrat Al Gore took the state with 56% of the vote to Republican George W. Bush's 39%. Green Party candidate Ralph Nader won 4% of the vote. In 2002 there were 1,847,247 registered voters; 36% were Democratic, 24% Republican, and 40% unaffiliated or members of other parties in 1998. The state had eight electoral votes in the 2000 presidential election.

In 2003 Democrats controlled the state senate, 21–15, and formed a majority in the state house (94 Democrats to 57 Republicans). Following the 2002 elections, Connecticut's delegation of US Representatives consisted of two Democrats and three Republicans (Connecticut lost a congressional seat in 2002). Both of Connecticut's US senators are Democrats: Christopher Dodd, reelected in 1998 for his fourth consecutive term; and Joseph Lieberman, elected to his third term in 2000. Democratic presidential candidate Al Gore chose Lieberman as his running mate in the 2000 presidential election. In 2003, Connecticut ranked eighth among the 50 states in the percentage of women state legislators, at 29.4%.

In 1994 Republican John G. Rowland was elected governor on a platform that included a promise to repeal the state income tax; he was reelected in 1998 and 2002. US Representative Gary Franks, the first black member of the US House of Representatives from Connecticut and the first black House Republican in 55 years, was unseated in 1996, in his bid for a fourth term. In 1998 he made an unsuccessful run for US Senate, against incumbent (Democrat) Christopher Dodd.

¹⁴LOCAL GOVERNMENT

As of 2002, Connecticut had 30 municipalities, 149 township governments, 17 public school districts, and 384 special districts. Counties in Connecticut have been geographical subdivisions without governmental functions since county government was abolished in 1960.

Connecticut's cities generally use the council-manager or mayor-council forms of government. The council-manager system provides for an elected council that determines policy, enacts local legislation, and appoints the city manager. The mayor-council system employs an elected chief executive with extensive appointment power and control over administrative agencies.

In most towns, an elected, three-member board of selectmen heads the administrative branch. The town meeting, in which all registered voters may participate, is usually the legislative body. Boroughs are generally governed by an elected warden, and borough meetings exercise major legislative functions.

¹⁵STATE SERVICES

To address the continuing threat of terrorism and to work with the federal Department of Homeland Security (created in 2002 following the terrorist attacks of 11 September 2001), homeland security in Connecticut in 2003 operated under the authority of the governor; the deputy commissioner for protective services was designated as the state homeland security advisor.

The Department of Education administers special programs for the educationally disadvantaged, the emotionally and physically disabled, and non-English-speaking students. The Department of Transportation operates state-owned airports, oversees bus system operations, and provides for snow removal from state highways and roads. The Department of Social Services has a variety of social programs for state residents, including special services for the physically disabled. The Department of Children and Youth Services investigates cases of child abuse and administers programs dealing with child protection, adoption, juvenile corrections and rehabilitation, and prevention of delinquency. The Department on Aging has state and regional ombudsmen to handle problems involving nursing homes. Among programs sponsored by the Health Services Department are ones that help people to stop smoking, increase their nutritional awareness, and improve their dental health. The Labor Department provides a full range of services to the unemployed, to job seekers, and to disadvantaged workers. Other departments deal with consumer protection, economic development, environmental protection, housing, mental retardation, information technology, and public safety.

¹⁶JUDICIAL SYSTEM

Connecticut's judicial system has undergone significant streamlining in recent years, with the abolition of municipal courts (1961), the circuit court (1974), the court of common pleas (1978), and the juvenile court (1978), and the creation of an appellate court (1983). Currently, the Connecticut judicial system consists of the supreme court, appellate court, superior court, and probate courts.

The supreme court comprises the chief justice, five associate justices, and two senior associate justices. The high court hears cases on appeal, primarily from the appellate court but also from the superior court in certain special instances, including the review of a death sentence, reapportionment, election disputes, invalidation of a state statute, or censure of a probate judge. Justices of the supreme court, as well as appellate and superior court judges, are nominated by the governor and appointed by the general assembly for eight-year terms.

The superior court, the sole general trial court, has the authority to hear all legal controversies except those over which the probate courts have exclusive jurisdiction. The superior court sits in 12 state judicial districts and is divided into trial divisions for civil, criminal, and family cases. As of 1999, there were 167 superior court trial judges.

Connecticut Presidential Vote by Political Parties, 1948–2000

YEAR	ELECTORAL VOTE	CONNECTICUT WINNER	DEMOCRAT	REPUBLICAN	PROGRESSIVE	SOCIALIST
1948	8	Dewey (R)	423,297	437,754	13,713	6,964
1952	8	*Eisenhower (R)	481,649	611,012	1,466	2,244
1956	8	*Eisenhower (R)	405,079	711,837	—	—
1960	8	*Kennedy (D)	657,055	565,813	—	—
1964	8	*Johnson (D)	826,269	390,996	—	—
					AMERICAN IND.	
1968	8	Humphrey (D)	621,561	556,721	76,660	—
						AMERICAN
1972	8	*Nixon (R)	555,498	810,763	—	17,239
						US LABOR
1976	8	Ford (R)	647,895	719,261	7,101	1,789
					LIBERTARIAN	CITIZENS
1980	8	*Reagan (R)	541,732	677,210	8,570	6,130
					CONN-ALLIANCE	COMMUNIST
1984	8	*Reagan (R)	569,597	890,877	1,274	4,826
					LIBERTARIAN	NEW ALLIANCE
1988	8	*Bush (R)	676,584	750,241	14,071	2,491
						IND. (PEROT)
1992	8	*Clinton (D)	682,318	578,313	5,391	348,771
1996	8	*Clinton (D)	735,740	483,109	5,788	139,523
					GREEN	REFORM
2000	8	Gore (D)	816,015	561,094	64,452	4,731

* Won US presidential election.

Connecticut has 132 probate courts. These operate on a fee basis, with judges receiving their compensation from fees paid for services rendered by the court. Each probate district has one probate judge, elected for a four-year term.

Connecticut had an inmate population of 18,875 as of June 2001, an increase of 1.4% over the previous year. The state's incarceration rate stood at 384 per 100,000 population. State law provides for the death penalty (by electrocution). There were 21 executions performed between 1930 and 2003, with seven persons were under sentence of death in 2003. The total crime rate in 2001 was 3,117.9 per 100,000 inhabitants, including a total of 11,492 violent crimes and 95,299 property crimes in that year.

[17]ARMED FORCES

In 2002, there were 4,239 active-duty military personnel stationed in Connecticut. The principal military installation in the state is the US Navy submarine base at Groton. Across the Thames River in New London is one of the nation's four service academies—the US Coast Guard Academy. Founded in 1876 and located at its present site since 1932, this institution offers a four-year curriculum leading to a BS degree and a commission as ensign in the Coast Guard.

In fiscal year 2001, the value of defense contracts was $4.2 billion, and defense payroll amounted to $581 million.

There were 310,069 veterans of US military service in Connecticut as of 2000, of whom 75,822 served in World War II; 42,918 in the Korean conflict; 87,712 during the Vietnam era; and 21,180 during 1990–2000 (including the Persian Gulf War). Veterans' benefits in fiscal year 2002 totaled $485million.

In 2000, the Connecticut State Police employed 1,135 full-time sworn officers.

[18]MIGRATION

Connecticut has experienced four principal migrations: the arrival of European immigrants in the 17th century, the out-migration of many settlers to other states beginning in the 18th century, renewed European immigration in the late 19th century, and the intrastate migration of city dwellers to the suburbs since 1945.

Although the first English settlers found an abundance of fertile farmland in the Connecticut Valley, later newcomers were not so fortunate. It is estimated that in 1800, when Connecticut's population was 250,000, nearly three times that many people had moved away from the state, principally to Vermont, western New York, Ohio, and other Midwestern states.

The influx of European immigrants increased the number of foreign-born in the state from 38,518 in 1850 to about 800,000 by World War I. After World War II, the rush of middle-class whites (many from neighboring states) to Connecticut suburbs, propelled in part by the "baby boom" that followed the war, was accompanied by the flow of minority groups to the cities. All told, Connecticut had a net increase from migration of 561,000 between 1940 and 1970, followed by a net loss of 113,000 from 1970 to 1990. Between 1990 and 1998, the state had a net loss of 217,000 residents in domestic migration, and a net gain of 68,000 in international migration. In 1998, Connecticut admitted 7,780 foreign immigrants. Between 1990 and 1998, the state's overall population decreased by 0.4%. In the period 1995–2000, 260,823 people moved into the state and 325,433 moved out, for a net loss of 64,610.

[19]INTERGOVERNMENTAL COOPERATION

Among the regional interstate agreements to which Connecticut belongs are the Atlantic States Marine Fisheries Commission, Connecticut River Atlantic Salmon Commission, Connecticut Valley Flood Control Commission, Interstate Compact for Juveniles, Interstate Sanitation Commission (with New York and New Jersey), New England Board of Higher Education, New England Interstate Water Pollution Control Commission, and the Northeastern Forest Fire Protection Compact. Boundary agreements are in effect with Massachusetts, New York, and Rhode Island. In fiscal year 2001, federal grants to Connecticut were almost $4.4 billion.

[20]ECONOMY

Connecticut has had a strong economy since the early 19th century when the state, unable to support its population by farming, turned to a variety of nonagricultural pursuits. Shipbuilding and whaling were major industries; in the 1840s and 1850s. New London ranked behind only New Bedford and Nantucket, Massachusetts, among US whaling ports. Connecticut has been a leader of the insurance industry since the 1790s.

Because defense production has traditionally been important to the state, the economy fluctuates with the rise and fall of international tensions. Connecticut's unemployment rate stood at 8.7% in 1949, dropped to 3.5% in 1951 during the Korean conflict, and rose sharply after the war to 8.3% in 1958. From 1966 to 1968, during the Vietnam war, unemployment averaged between 3.1% and 3.7%, but the rate subsequently rose to 9.5% in 1976. In 1984, in the midst of the Reagan administration's military build-up, Connecticut's unemployment rate dropped below 5%, becoming the lowest in the country. Connecticut lessened its dependence on the defense sector somewhat by attracting nonmilitary domestic and international firms to the state during the 1980s and 1990s. In 1984, more than 250 international companies employed more than 30,000 Connecticut workers. Connecticut was a leader in the manufacture of aircraft engines and parts, bearings, hardware, submarines, helicopters, typewriters, electronic instrumentation, electrical equipment, guns and ammunition, and optical instruments. Despite its dependence on military contracts, between 1984 and 1991 manufacturing employment declined 22.4%, while nonmanufacturing jobs rose by 11.6%. Nevertheless, the state was hard hit by cuts in military spending in the late 1980s and early 1990s. In 1991, defense related prime contract awards had dropped 37.7% from the 1990 level. Pratt and Whitney, the jet engine maker, and General Dynamics' Electric Boat division, manufacturer of submarines, announced in 1992 that they would lay off a total of 16,400 workers over the following six years. In 1992, an estimated 70% of manufacturing was defense related, either through direct federal contracts, subcontracts with other companies, or in the manufacturing of basic metals used for weaponry. In 1993, unemployment stood at 7.3%. During the prosperous 1990s, unemployment fell steadily, and had reached 3% by 1999, although the ratio of manufacturing jobs continued to decline (overall, from nearly 50% in 1950 to 20% in 1999). Gross state product grew at annual rates of 5.7% in 1998, and 4.4% in 1999, and then soared to 8.7% in 2000. The national recession of 2001, growth slowed abruptly to 2.6%, as unemployment began to rise again. The downturn continued into 2002, as unemployment rose from 3.5% in June to 4.4% November 2002.

In 2001, Connecticut had the 22nd largest gross state product among the states, totaling $166.2 billion. Only 9% of the total was from the public sector, the 2nd-smallest proportion among the states (after Delaware, and tied with Massachusetts). The main contributors to the gross state product in 2001 were financial services, including insurance and real estate ($51.5 billion); general services ($35.7 billion); manufacturing ($24.3 billion), government ($15 billion); and transportation and utilities ($9.8 billion). While the service sectors had grown sharply since 1997 (financial services up 35.8%, general services up 20.4%, government up 27.5%, and transportation utilities up

17.3%), the output of Connecticut's manufacturing sector was only 5.5% above the output in 1997.

21 INCOME

According to the Bureau of Economic Analysis, in 2001, Connecticut had a per capita personal income (PCPI) of $42,377 which ranked 1st in the United States (including the District of Columbia) and was 139% of the national average, $30,413. The 2001 PCPI reflected an increase of 2.2% from 2000 compared to the national change of 2.2%. In 2001, Connecticut had a total personal income (TPI) of $145,547,796,000 which ranked 22nd in the United States and accounted for 1.7% of the national total. The 2001 TPI reflected an increase of 2.9% from 2000 compared to the national change of 3.3%.

Earnings of persons employed in Connecticut increased from $98,862,948,000 in 2000 to $101,700,116,000 in 2001, an increase of 2.9%. The largest industries in 2001 were services, 29.1% of earnings; finance, insurance, and real estate, 16.3%; and durable goods manufacturing, 11.8%. Of the industries that accounted for at least 5% of earnings in 2001, the slowest growing from 2000 to 2001 was durable goods manufacturing, which decreased 3.9%; the fastest was state and local government (10.5% of earnings in 2001), which increased 14.2%.

According to data released by the US Census Bureau, in 2000, the median household income was $50,360 compared to the national average of $42,148. In 2001, the median income for a family of four was $82,517 compared to the national average of $63,278. For the period 1999 to 2001, the average poverty rate was 7.4% which placed it 4th among the 50 states and the District of Columbia ranked lowest to highest.

22 LABOR

According to Bureau of Labor Statistics (BLS) provisional estimates, in July 2003 the seasonally adjusted civilian labor force in Connecticut numbered 1,786,200, with approximately 92,300 workers unemployed, yielding an unemployment rate of 5.2%, compared to the national average of 6.2% for the same period. Since the beginning of the BLS data series in 1978, the highest unemployment rate recorded was 8.2% in February 1992. The historical low was 2.1% in August 2000. In 2001, 4.0% of the labor force was employed in construction; 14.8% in manufacturing; 4.4% in transportation, communications, and public utilities; 17.5% in trade; 8.4% in finance, insurance, and real estate; 29.4% in services; 13.0% in government; and 1.3% in agriculture.

During the early 20th century, Connecticut was consistently anti-union and was one of the leading open-shop states in the northeastern US. But great strides were made by organized labor in the 1930s with the support of New Deal legislation recognizing union bargaining rights. All workforce services—recruiting, training, workplace regulation, labor market information, and unemployment insurance—are offered through a statewide partnership of Connecticut's Department of Labor, Regional Workforce Development Boards, and state and community organizations.

The US Department of Labor reported that in 2002, 257,000 of Connecticut's 1,534,000 employed wage and salary workers were members of unions. This represented 16.7% of those so employed, up from 15.8% in 2001. The national average is 13.2%. In all, 273,000 workers (17.8%) were represented by unions. In addition to union members, this category includes workers who report no union affiliation but whose jobs are covered by a union contract.

23 AGRICULTURE

Agriculture is no longer of much economic importance in Connecticut. The number of farms declined from 22,241 in 1945 to 3,900 in 2002, covering a total of 360,000 acres (145,700 hectares).

Cash receipts from crop sales in 2001 were $299 million. Tobacco production was 3,148,000 lb. (1,428,000 kg) in 2002. Other principal crops are hay, silage, potatoes, sweet corn, tomatoes, apples, and peaches.

24 ANIMAL HUSBANDRY

There were an estimated 56,000 cattle and calves on Connecticut farms in 2003. Their estimated value was $56.6 million. In 2002 there were an estimated 3,800 hogs and pigs, valued at $350,000. During 2001, Connecticut dairy farmers produced an estimated 456 million lb (206.8 million kg) of milk. Also during 2001, poultry farmers produced an estimated 8.5 million lb. (3.9 million kg) of chicken and received $122,000 for 108,000 lb (49,000 kg) of turkey. Connecticut produced an estimated 883,000 eggs in 2001 at an estimated value of $41.8 million.

25 FISHING

Commercial fishing does not play a major role in the economy. In 1998, the value of commercial landings was $34.4 million for a catch of 17,625,00 lb (7,994,000 kg) of edible finfish and shellfish.

During 1995–96, programs to restore the Atlantic salmon and trout populations continued on the Connecticut River. Streams also were surveyed that year to update the trout stocking program. Connecticut had nearly 173,052 sport fishing license holders in 1998.

26 FORESTRY

By the early 20th century, the forests that covered 95% of Connecticut in the 1630s were generally destroyed. Woodland recovery has been stimulated since the 1930s by an energetic reforestation program. Of the state's 1,859,000 acres (752,337 hectares) of forestland in 2002, more than half was wooded with new growth.

State forests covered some 168,000 acres (67,990 hectares) in 2002.

27 MINING

The value of nonfuel mineral production in Connecticut in 2001 was estimated by the US Geological Survey to be nearly $104 million. Crushed stone (7 million metric tons, worth $60.9 million) and construction sand and gravel (7.2 million metric tons, valued at $42.7 million), the state's two leading mineral commodities, accounted for nearly all the value. Other commodities produced included clays, industrial sand, and dimension stone. Production of construction sand and gravel was up 23% from 2000, and its value was up 44% from 1999. Crushed stone production (predominantly Jurassic-age basalt, which is commonly called traprock) increased by 8% from the output in 2000. Crushed stone value also rose by almost 14% over the same period. In October 1995, a new law came into effect allowing towns to protect traprock ridges within their borders from development, including quarrying.

Demand for virtually all of the state's mineral output is dependent on a healthy construction industry, the main consumer of aggregates.

28 ENERGY AND POWER

Two of the four Northeast Heating Oil Reserves established by Congress in 2000 are located in Connecticut; their combined capacities total 850 thousand barrels. In 2000 Connecticut's total per capita energy consumption was 253 million Btu (63.8 million kcal), ranking it 45th among the states.

Production of electricity (utility and nonutility) was 28.8 billion kWh in 1999; total installed capacity was 7.1 million kW.

The use of coal to generate electric power declined from 85% of the total fuel used in 1965 to 9% in 1999 because of the increased utilization of nuclear energy and oil. As of 2001, Connecticut had two nuclear reactors at Millstone (216,300 kW).

Having no petroleum or gas resources of its own, Connecticut must rely primarily on imported oil from Saudi Arabia, Venezuela, Nigeria, and other countries. Most of the natural gas used in Connecticut is piped in from Texas and Louisiana.

[29]INDUSTRY

Connecticut is one of the most industrialized states, and it has recently diversified toward a broader economic portfolio. Six diverse industry clusters drive the state's economy: aerospace and advanced manufacturing; communications, information, and education; financial services; health and biomedical; business services; and tourism and entertainment. The state's value of shipments of manufactured goods totaled $49 billion in 1997. The mineral industry was negligible, and shrinking, while the construction industry posted sales of approximately $7 billion.

Leading industrial and service corporations with headquarters in Connecticut include General Electric, United Technologies, GTE, Xerox, American Brands, Champion International, Union Carbide, Dun & Bradstreet, Deloitte and Touche, Pitney Bowes, Northeast Utilities, Praxair, and Ultramar. In 1997, 22 Connecticut-based companies appeared on Fortune magazine's list of the 500 biggest industrial companies in the US.

Earnings of persons employed in Connecticut increased from $81 billion in 1997 to $86.1 billion in 1998, an increase of 6.2%. The largest industries in 1998 were services, 30.2% of earnings; durable goods manufacturing, 14.5%; and finance, insurance, and real estate, 13.1%. Of the industries that accounted for at least 5% of earnings in 1998, the slowest growing from 1997 to 1998 was state and local government (9.2% of earnings in 1998), which increased 2.8%; the fastest was wholesale trade (6.7% of earnings in 1998), which increased 11.5%.

[30]COMMERCE

Considering its small size, Connecticut is a busy commercial state. In 1997, Connecticut had 6,091 wholesale establishments. Retail sales in 1997 totaled $36 billion, from 20,606 establishments. Of total retail establishments in 1997, food stores accounted for 10%; automotive dealers and service stations, 12%; and restaurants and taverns, 29%. Food sales amounted to $6.4 billion while general merchandise sales came to $2.9 billion in 1997. The estimated value of Connecticut's goods exported abroad was $7.3 billion in 1998. Shipments of transport equipment, nonelectrical machinery, electric and electronic equipment, and instruments accounted for most of the state's foreign sales. Tobacco is the major agricultural export. Foreign exports go primarily to Canada and France.

[31]CONSUMER PROTECTION

Since 1959, the Connecticut Department of Consumer Protection has been protecting consumers from injury by product use or merchandising deceit. The department conducts regular inspections of wholesale and retail food establishments, drug-related establishments, liquor retailers, bedding and upholstery dealers and manufacturers, and commercial establishments that use weighing and measuring devices. The department conducts investigations into alleged fraudulent activities, provides information and referral services to consumers, and responds to their complaints. It also licenses most professional and occupational trades and registers home improvement contractors. The Lemon Law Arbitration program and consumer guarantee funds in the areas of home improvement, real estate, and health clubs have returned millions of dollars to aggrieved consumers.

[32]BANKING

The first banks in Connecticut were established in Hartford, New Haven, Middletown, Bridgeport, Norwich, and New London between 1792 and 1805. By 1850, the state had 54 commercial and 15 savings banks. As of late 2002, Connecticut had 66 insured institutions. Assets of the state's insured banks amounted to $53 billion in 2002.

At the start of 1995 there were 59 (FDIC-insured) savings institutions, with combined assets of $38.8 billion. The Resolution Trust Corporation resolved eight Connecticut savings institutions by the end of 1995 at a cost of $191 million.

Banking operations are regulated by the state Department of Banking. The National Graam-Leach-Bliley Financial Modernization Act of 1999, which allowed the conglomeration of banking, securities, and insurance services, was badly received by the Connecticut Banking Commissioner. The over weighted savings sector in Connecticut discriminates against the movement of capital in securities markets.

Connecticut has a large percentage of thrifts and residential lenders. Two-thirds of insured institutions in the state are savings institutions. Residential real estate loans comprise 57% of the average loan portfolio in Connecticut. In 2001/02, there was an increase in consumer and commercial real estate loan delinquencies. As of the end of 2002, Connecticut had eight institutions under three years old, or 12% of all institutions.

[33]INSURANCE

Connecticut's preeminence in the insurance field and Hartford's title as "insurance capital" of the nation date from the late 18th century, when state businessmen agreed to bear a portion of a shipowner's financial risks in return for a share of the profits. Marine insurance companies were established in Hartford and major port cities between 1797 and 1805. The state's first insurance company had been formed in Norwich in 1795 to provide fire insurance. The nation's oldest fire insurance firm is Hartford Fire Insurance, active since 1810. Subsequently, Connecticut companies have been leaders in life, accident, casualty, automobile, and multiple-line insurance. The insurance industry is regulated by the state department of insurance.

In 2001 there were 1.8 million ordinary life insurance policies in force with a total value of $194.1 billion; total value for all categories of life insurance (ordinary, group, industrial, and credit) was $337.2 billion. Death benefits paid that year totaled $914.7 million. That year, there were 29,482 flood insurance policies in force in the state, with a total value of $4.5 million.

In 2003 there were 73 property and casualty and 32 life and health insurance companies domiciled in Connecticut. In 2001, property and casualty insurers wrote premiums totaling $5.5 billion.

[34]SECURITIES

There are no securities or commodities exchanges in Connecticut. Securities broker-dealers organizations within the state number 1,310, with 12,166 employees. There are also 358 investment advisory firms. The state is headquarters to 106 NASDAQ companies, 16 NASDAQ market makers, 21 AMEX companies, and 12 NYSE listed companies that were incorporated in Connecticut. The top five according to revenues are AETNA, Stanley Works, Hubbell Corp., MBIA, and The United Illuminating Co.

[35]PUBLIC FINANCE

In 1991, the state of Connecticut underwent a massive restructuring of its revenue stream, the cornerstone of which was the introduction of a personal income tax. The sales tax rate was dropped from 8% to 6% and the corporate tax rate from 13.8% to 11.5%. As part of the same reform package, the state instituted a rainy day fund (the Budget Reserve Fund) with a size set at 5% of net General Fund appropriations, and also enacted a statutory spending cap, which was reinforced by a constitutional expenditure cap when approved by the electorate in November 1992. The constitutional cap requires a balanced budget and limits appropriations in all state funds to the growth in the consumer price index for the most recent 12 months or the five-year average growth in personal income, whichever is greater. The 1991 legislature also revised the debt limit statute. The current law limits authorized plus outstanding bonds payable from the general fund to not more than 1.6 times estimated general fund net tax revenues.

By the close of 1995/96, which finished with a surplus in excess of $160 million, the state had experienced five consecutive year-end surpluses, allowing it to set aside roughly $240,000 in its Budget Reserve Fund. In 1995, the legislature began a series of tax reductions. By 2002, the Budget Reserve Fund contained nearly $600 million. Individual income taxes were reduced by the addition of a second, lower (3%), bracket, to Connecticut's income tax schedule applicable to the first $10,000 of taxable income. A seven-year phase out of the state's inheritance tax rate was scheduled (although in the budget crisis that began with revenue shortfalls in 2001/02 the final phase-out was extended to 2005), and the corporate income tax was slated for reduction to 7.5% by 2000.

The state budget is prepared biennially by the Budget and Financial Management Division of the Office of Policy and Management and submitted by the governor to the General Assembly for consideration. In odd-numbered years, the governor transmits a budget document setting forth his financial program for the ensuing biennium with a separate budget for each of the two fiscal years in the biennium. In the even-numbered years, the governor transmits a report on the status of the budget enacted in the previous year and recommendations for adjustments and revisions. The budgets are submitted to the legislature in February, and the legislature is supposed to adopt a biennium budget in May or June before the beginning of the fiscal year 1 July. In 2003, the Democrat-controlled legislature adopted two budgets that were vetoed by Republican governor, the second veto coming on 13 June 2003. For the first time since 1991, Connecticut entered the new fiscal year without an enacted budget. Throughout July, the governor issued one-week and two-week executive orders calling for the continued funding of essential state services, but on 29 July 2003, the governor issued a 48-week executive order.

Tax revenues in Connecticut, the wealthiest state in the country, were affected by the collapse of the stock market that began in 2001 as capital gains earnings plummeted. The constitution requires that the legislature adopt, and that the governor sign, a balanced budget, but this could not prevent a deficit of more than $800 million in 2001/02 as revenue fell 9.5%. To be able to pass a balanced budget in 2001/03, the legislature emptied the Budget Reserve Fund (an automatic transfer of $594.7 million); cut $92.9 million from the enacted 2001/02 budget; raised cigarette taxes (from $0.50 to $1.11 per pack) and diesel fuel taxes; deferred or eliminated a number of increased exemptions, tax credits and tax holidays; extended the phase-out of gift taxes and of taxes on computer and data-processing services; and issued short-term five year notes to cover the rest of the gap. In 2002/03 strategies to reduce the budget gap entailed across-the-board percentage cuts; reduced local aid; a one-year, 10% surcharge on corporate profits; fee increases; personnel layoffs and early retirements; and program reorganizations. Over $192 million in expenditure cuts were made after the budget was enacted. A 6% tax on newspaper sales was imposed on 1 April 2003, only to be repealed in the budget passed in August 2003. More significantly, the personal income

tax rates were raised in April 2003 (to 3.5% from 3% and 5% from $0.5%) effective for the 2003 tax year. The deficit in 2002/03 reached $495.5 million (4.1% of the state budget), and was projected at $1–1.2 billion (8.6% to 10.3% of the state budget) for 2003/04. Deficit-reduction measures enacted in 2003, besides the income tax increase, included a reduction in the maximum property tax credit for homeowners; elimination of cash payments to single adults on general assistance; an extension of the surcharge on corporate profits; and a contingent six-month reinstatement of the inheritance tax on estates valued at over $1 million should the state not receive an anticipated $250 million in federal funds in 2004.

The governor's budget for 2003/04 proposed General Fund appropriations totaling $12.477 billion, with 29.6% for human services; 21.9% for education; 9.7% for health care and hospitals; 8.5% for government operations and regulation; and 0.6% for conservation and development. Over one-fifth (20.5%) was appropriated for a "nonfunctional" category that included debt service (9.4%), employee fringe benefits, and other miscellaneous accounts. In the governor's recommended appropriations for 2004/05 totaling over $13 billion, debt servicing increased to 10.2%, with the nonfunctional category as a whole increasing to 21.9%. Under the functional categories, 29.3% is allocated to human services, 21.2% to education, 9.6% to health and hospitals, 9.1% to corrections, 8.3% to government operations and regulation, and 0.6% to conservation and development.

The following table from the US Census Bureau contains information on revenues, expenditures, indebtedness, and cash/securities for 2001.

	($000)	PERCENT	PER CAPITA
Population (thousands, 2001)	3,435	(X)	(X)
Total Revenue	17,750,445	100.00	5,167.52
General revenue	16,283,522	91.74	4,740.47
Utility revenue	22,960	0.13	6.68
Liquor store revenue	–	–	–
Insurance trust revenue	1,443,963	8.13	420.37
Exhibit: Salaries and wages	3,081,329	16.94	897.04
Total expenditure	18,189,210	100.00	5,295.26
General expenditure	16,098,051	88.50	4,686.48
Education	4,231,198	23.26	1,231.79
Public welfare	3,498,701	19.24	1,018.54
Hospitals	1,130,604	6.22	329.14
Health	549,848	3.02	160.07
Highways	758,246	4.17	220.74
Police protection	156,543	0.86	45.57
Correction	604,890	3.33	176.10
Natural resources	116,961	0.64	34.05
Parks and recreation	119,578	0.66	34.81
Government administration	821,912	4.52	239.28
Interest on general debt	1,106,324	6.08	322.07
Other and unallocable	3,003,246	16.51	874.31
Utility expenditure	242,592	1.33	70.62
Liquor store expenditure	–	–	–
Insurance trust expenditure	1,848,567	10.16	538.16
Debt at end of fiscal year	19,027,060	100.00	5,539.17
Cash and security holdings	29,311,523	100.00	8,533.19

³⁶TAXATION

Connecticut's principal taxes are a general state sales and use tax of 6%, a two-bracket personal income tax of 3.5% and 5% (as of April 2003), and flat-rate corporate income tax of 7.5%. There are also state excise taxes on gasoline (25 cents per gallon), other motor fuels, cigarettes ($1.11 a pack, with Connecticut being one of seven states to more than double this tax in 2002), other tobacco products, alcoholic beverages, amusements, insurance premiums, pari-mutuels, public utilities, and other selected goods. After having been scheduled in 1995 to be phased out by 2001, Connecticut's inheritance tax is now scheduled to be phased out by 2005. There are also various state license fees and stamp taxes. All property taxes are local, whereas there are no local sales taxes in Connecticut. In 2001/02, state taxes totaled $9.03 billion, 40.8% from the individual income taxes, 33.7% from the general sales tax, 16.3% from selective sales taxes, 4.4% from license fees, 1.76% from inheritance and gift taxes, 1.65% from corporate taxes, and 1.3% from stamp taxes.

In 2003, combined state and local taxes in Connecticut amounted to 10.9% of income, the fifth highest in the country. In 1990, before the introduction of the state income tax, combined state and local taxes were 9.4% of income, placing Connecticut 33rd among US states. The highest combined totals were in 1997 and 1998, both 11.1% of income, when Connecticut ranked 7th among US states in terms of the state and local tax burden.

The following table from the US Census Bureau provides a summary of taxes collected by the state in 2002.

	($000)	PER CAPITA
Total Taxes	9,032,787	2,610.25
Property taxes	(X)	(X)
Sales and gross receipts	4,516,123	1,305.05
General sales and gross receipts	3,043,971	879.63
Selective sales taxes	1,472,152	425.42
Alcoholic beverage	41,619	12.03
Amusements	365,010	105.48
Insurance Premiums	207,445	59.95
Motor fuels	424,669	122.72
Pari-mutuels	7,339	2.12
Public utilities	166,580	48.14
Tobacco products	158,348	45.76
Other selective sales	101,142	29.23
Licenses	404,522	116.9
Alcoholic beverages	5,874	1.7
Amusements	67	0.02
Corporation	17,006	4.91
Hunting and fishing	2,583	0.75
Motor vehicle	240,604	69.53
Motor vehicle operators	33,803	9.77
Public utility	300	0.09
Occupation and business, NEC	100,361	29
Other	3,924	1.13
Other taxes	4,112,142	1,188.31
Individual income	3,685,244	1,064.94
Corporation net income	149,454	43.19
Death and gift	159,819	46.18
Documentary and stock transfer	117,625	33.99
Severance	(X)	(X)
Other	(X)	(X)

37ECONOMIC POLICY

Connecticut's economic development program are overseen by its Department of Economic and Community Development (DECD). An important task is administering federal grants made through the Community Development Block Grant (CDBG) program operating since 1974. Connecticut was the first state to establish Enterprise Zones (EZs), starting with six EZ's in 1982 and up to 17 in 2003. EZ's are areas with high rates of unemployment, poverty and/or public assistance that are granted stimulus packages of tax reductions and exemptions. In 1994, the state established the Community Economic Development Fund (CEDF) to help revitalize distressed neighborhoods by providing greater access to capital for small business and community development organizations. The CEDF provides loans, grants and technical assistance with the aim of supporting job creation and retention and community planning efforts. The state offers low-interest loans and grants for capital expenditures, machinery, land, building, training, and recruiting. In April 2003, the CEDF awarded its first grant to faith-based organization—a grant to the Philips Metropolitan Church for planning consultants for a proposed new office building. Connecticut offers tax credits and abatements for machinery and equipment. Connecticut

Innovations is the state's technology development corporation. The Connecticut Economic Resource Center, Inc., coordinates business-to-business marketing and recruitment on behalf of the state. Business recruitment missions have been sent to Europe and Japan to stimulate the state's export program. In 1998, the Governor's Council on Economic Compositeness and Technology was established composed of a collection of CEO's, industry representatives, educators, labor leaders, state commissioners, and legislators. The Governor's Council adopted an Industry Cluster approach to economic development, and has since identified six clusters for particular attention in Connecticut: Tourism (already a separate office), BioScience (since 1998); Aerospace; Software and Information Technology; and Metals Manufacturing (all identified in 1999); and the Maritime Industry (2001). . In 2002, Connecticut became the first state to establish an Office of BioScience, located within the DECD. Industry Cluster program, administered by the DECD, is regularly monitored by the Governor's Council to assess progress within the clusters. In 2003, Connecticut's Industry Cluster Program was given an award for Excellence in Economic Development by the US Commerce Department because of, particularly, the private/public partnerships at the heart of the approach.

38HEALTH

The infant mortality rate in 2000 was 6.6 per 1,000 live births, below the national rate of 7.3. There were 12,958 legal abortions in 1999, averaging 19 per 1,000 women. Death rates for chronic pulmonary diseases, chronic liver disease and cirrhosis, accidents and adverse effects, motor vehicle accidents, homicide, and suicide were below their respective national rates in 1998. However, the death rate for heart diseases (272.7 per 100,000 population) rose above the national rate (258.2 per 100,000) in 2000. Some 20% of the population age 18 and older were smokers, and deaths from lung disease occurred at a rate of 63.2 per 100,000 population in 2000. HIV-related deaths occurred at a rate of 6.1 per 100,000 in 2000, slightly above the US rate of 5.3 in the same year. A total of 12,148 AIDS cases had been reported through 2001.

In 2001, Connecticut's 35 community hospitals had 8,041 beds and reported 360,007 admissions. In the same year, there were 45,744 total personnel working in Connecticut hospitals, of whom 10,252 were full-time registered nurses and 522 were full-time licensed practical nurses. Connecticut had 385 physicians per 100,000 population in 2000. Outstanding medical schools are those of Yale University and the University of Connecticut.

Hospital expenses in 2001 averaged $1,377.60 per day. Federal government grants to cover the Medicare and Medicaid services in 2001 totaled $1.7 billion; 516,359 enrollees received Medicare benefits that year. Most people in Connecticut are insured; 10.2% of the population went without insurance in 2002.

39SOCIAL WELFARE

In 2001, the average weekly unemployment benefit was $271.08. Average monthly participation in the food stamp program in FY2002 comprised 168,591 persons (87,963 households). The average monthly benefit was $72.07, and the sum total of benefits paid in FY2002 was $145,797,723.

With the enactment of the Personal Responsibility and Work Opportunity Reconciliation Act of 1996, the US government has changed the form and regulations for many of its social welfare programs. Most significantly, it replaces Aid to Families with Dependent Children (AFDC), an open-ended entitlement program, with Temporary Assistance for Needy Families (TANF), a limited system of assistance funded largely through federal block grants. The reform act also impacts the food stamp

program, the Supplemental Security Income program, and the child nutrition program. The law took effect on 1 July 1997 and provided $16.38 billion in block grants for fiscal years 1997–2002. The grants are to be divided among the states based on an equation involving the numbers of former AFDC recipients in each state.

Reauthorization of the 1996 social welfare legislation, scheduled for 2002, was delayed, and the original law had been extended three times as of July 2003, with the most recent extension running through September 2003. Connecticut's TANF program is called JOBS FIRST. In June 2000 the state had 63,589 welfare recipients. State expenditures on the TANF program in FY2002 totaled $169,160,545.

In December 2001, Social Security benefits were paid to 581,180 Connecticut residents. This number included 405,620 retired workers, 51,300 widows and widowers, 55,180 disabled workers, 27,700 spouses, and 40,380 children. Social Security beneficiaries represented 16.9% of the total state population and 94.8% of the state's population age 65 and older. Retired workers (excluding persons with special benefits) received an average monthly payment of $959; widows and widowers, $912; disabled workers, $841; and spouses, $499. Payments for children of retired workers averaged $492 per month; children of deceased workers, $634; and children of disabled workers, $247.

Federal Supplemental Security Income payments n December 2001 went to 49,586 Connecticut residents, averaging $376 a month.

40 HOUSING

In 2002, there were 1,402,643 housing units in Connecticut, 1,305,518 of which were occupied; 69% were owner-occupied. About 59.6% of all units were single-family, detached homes. It was estimated that about 16,499 units were without telephone service, 2,998 lacked complete plumbing facilities, and 2,995 lacked complete kitchen facilities. Most households (49%) relied on fuel oil (such as kerosene) for heating. The average household size was 2.57 people. New privately owned housing units authorized in 2002 numbered 9,731.

As of 2002, the median value of a one-family home was

41 EDUCATION

Believing that the Bible was the only true source of God's truths, Connecticut's Puritan founders viewed literacy as a theological necessity. A law code in 1650 required a town of 50 families to hire a schoolmaster to teach reading and writing, and a town of 100 families to operate a school to prepare students for college. Despite such legislation, many communities in colonial Connecticut did not provide sufficient funding to operate first-rate schools. Public education was greatly strengthened in the 19th century by the work of Henry Barnard, who advocated free public schools, state supervision of common schools, and the establishment of schools for teacher training. By the late 1860s and early 1870s, all of Connecticut's public elementary and high schools were tuition free. In 1865, the Board of Education was established.

A characteristic of public-school financing in Connecticut has been high reliance on local support for education. Differences among towns in their wealth bases and taxation were compounded by the mechanism used to distribute a majority of state funds for public education—the flat-grant-per-pupil formula. After the Connecticut supreme court in Horton v. Meskill (1978) declared this funding mechanism to be unconstitutional, the general assembly in 1979 replaced it with an equity-based model in order to reduce the disparity among towns in expenses per pupil.

In 2000, 84% of Connecticut residents age 25 and older were high school graduates. Some 31.4% had obtained a bachelor's

degree or higher. As of fall 1999, Connecticut's public schools had a total enrollment of 553,993 students. Of these, 403,913 attended schools from kindergarten through grade eight, and 150,080 attended high school. Minority students made up approximately 30% of the total enrollment in public elementary and secondary schools in 2001. Total enrollment was estimated at 562,138 in fall 2000 but expected to drop to 541,000 by fall 2005. Expenditures for public education in 2000/01 were estimated at $5,697,000. Enrollment in nonpublic schools in fall 2001 was 70,058. The state's private preparatory schools include Choate Rosemary Hall (Wallingford), Taft (Waltertown), Westminster (Simsbury), Loomis Chaffee (Windsor), and Miss Porter's (Farmington).

Fall enrollment in college or graduate school was 204,212 in 2000. In the same year Connecticut had 46 degree-granting institutions. In 1997 minority students comprised 18.3% of total postsecondary enrollment. Public institutions of higher education include the University of Connecticut at Storrs; four divisions of the Connecticut State University, at New Britain, New Haven, Danbury, and Willimantic; 12 regional community colleges; and five state technical colleges. Connecticut also has 23 private four-year colleges and universities. Among the oldest institutions are Yale, founded in 1701 and settled in New Haven between 1717 and 1719; Trinity College (1823) in Hartford; and Wesleyan University (1831) in Middletown. Other private institutions include the University of Hartford, University of Bridgeport, Fairfield University, and Connecticut College in New London.

42 ARTS

The Connecticut Commission on the Arts, established in 1965, has 20 members appointed by the general assembly and 5 by the governor. It administers a state art collection and establishes policies for an art bank program. The Commission also partners with the New England Foundation for the Arts. The Connecticut Humanities Council was established in 1974 and has since distributed over $12 million to more than 900 nonprofit organizations statewide. In 2003, Connecticut arts organizations received grants totaling $1,232,000 from the National Endowment for the Arts. In 2000, $1,437,928 was granted to 16 projects through the National Endowment for the Humanities. State funds are also vital to both organizations.

In the 1990s, the state's arts programs had a total audience attendance of over 18 million people per year, and the number of participating artists totaled over 80,000. Connecticut's arts education programs were offered to 23,100 schoolchildren. There were approximately 900 arts associations in the state and 65 local arts groups.

Art museums in Connecticut include the Wadsworth Athenaeum in Hartford, the oldest (1842) free public art museum in the US; the Yale University Art Gallery and the Yale Center for British Art in New Haven; the New Britain Museum of American Art; and the Lyman Allyn Museum of Connecticut College in New London. The visual arts are easily accessible through numerous other art museums, galleries, and more than 150 annual arts shows and festivals.

The theater is vibrant in contemporary Connecticut, which has numerous dinner theaters, at least l00 community theater groups, and many college and university theater groups. Professional theaters include the American Shakespeare Festival Theater in Stratford, the Long Wharf Theater and the Yale Repertory Theater in New Haven, the Hartford Stage Company, and the Eugene O'Neill Memorial Theater Center in Waterford.

The state's foremost metropolitan orchestras are the Hartford and New Haven symphonies. Professional opera is presented by the Stanford State Opera and by the Connecticut Opera in Hartford. Prominent dance groups include the Connecticut

Dance Company in New Haven, the Hartford Ballet Company, and the Pilobolus Dance Theater in the town of Washington.

The annual International Festival of Arts and Ideas in New Haven has grown steadily since its inception in 1996 and now presents over 300 events throughout the month of June. The Sunken Garden Poetry Festival, presented every summer at the Hill Stead Museum in Farmington, reportedly draws about 1,500 to 3,000 people per reading event.

43 LIBRARIES AND MUSEUMS

As of 2000, Connecticut's 194,000 public libraries held 14,238,000 volumes and had a combined circulation of 27,948,000. The leading public library is the Connecticut State Library (Hartford), which houses about 1,015,463 bound volumes and over 2,451 periodicals as well as the official state historical museum. Connecticut's most distinguished academic collection is the Yale University library system (over nine million volumes), headed by the Sterling Memorial Library and the Beinecke Rare Book and Manuscript Library. Special depositories include the Hartford Seminary Foundation's impressive material on Christian-Muslim relations; the Connecticut Historical Society's especially strong collection of materials pertaining to state history and New England genealogy; the Trinity College Library's collection of church documents; the Indian Museum in Old Mystic; the maritime history collections in the Submarine Library at the US Navy submarine base in Groton; and the G. W. Blunt White Library at Mystic Seaport. Total income for the public library system amounted to $137,326,000 in 2000, including $961,282 in federal grants and $2,197,216 in state grants. Libraries spent 68.8% of their income on staff, and 13.8% on collections.

Connecticut has more than 162 museums, in addition to its historic sites. The Peabody Museum of Natural History at Yale includes an impressive dinosaur hall. Botanical gardens include Harkness Memorial State Park in Waterford, Elizabeth Park in West Hartford, and Hamilton Park Rose Garden in Waterbury. Connecticut's historical sites include the Henry Whitfield House in Guilford (1639), said to be the oldest stone house in the US; the Webb House in Wethersfield, where George Washington met with the Comte de Rochambeau in 1781 to plan military strategy against the British; Noah Webster's birthplace in West Hartford; and the Jonathan Trumbull House in Lebanon.

44 COMMUNICATIONS

As of 2001, 96.8% of the state's occupied housing units had telephones.

In 2003, Connecticut had 18 AM and 33 FM major radio stations, and 5 major network television stations. There were educational television stations in Bridgeport, Hartford, and Norwich. In addition, the Hartford and New Haven metropolitan area had the highest cable penetration rate of any urban area, at 88%. A total of 109,775 domain names were registered in Connecticut by 2000.

45 PRESS

The *Hartford Courant*, founded in 1764, is generally considered to be the oldest US newspaper in continuous publication. The leading Connecticut dailies in 2002 were the *Hartford Courant*, with an average morning circulation of 198,651 (Sundays, 291,111), and the *New Haven Register*, with an average morning circulation of 100,108 (Sundays, 100,273). Statewide, in 2002 there were 13 morning newspapers, 4 evening newspapers, and 13 Sunday newspapers.

Leading periodicals are *American Scientist, Greenwich Magazine, Connecticut Magazine, Fine Woodworking, Golf Digest,* and *Tennis*.

46 ORGANIZATIONS

In 2003, there were at least 2,061 regional, national, and international organizations within the state.

National organizations with headquarters in Connecticut included the Knights of Columbus (New Haven), the American Institute for Foreign Study (Greenwich), Junior Achievement (Stanford), the International Association of Approved Basketball Officials (West Hartford), Keep America Beautiful (Stamford), and Save the Children Federation (Westport). The Academic Council on the United Nations System is housed at Yale University in New Haven.

State arts and educational organizations include the Connecticut Children's Musical Theatre, the Connecticut Educational Media Association, and the Connecticut Historical Commission

47 TOURISM, TRAVEL, AND RECREATION

Tourism has become an increasingly important part of the economy in recent decades for a state that promotes itself as "full of surprises. " The state invests over $2.5 million each year to market tourism products. Tourist spending reached about $9.9 billion in 2001. The same year tourism accounted for about 6% of the GSP and 13.35% of employment across the state.

Popular tourist attractions include the Mystic Seaport restoration and its aquarium, the Mark Twain House and state capitol in Hartford, the American Clock and Watch Museum in Bristol, the Lock Museum of America in Terryville, and the Yale campus in New Haven. Outstanding events are the Harvard–Yale regatta held each June on the Thames River in New London, and about 50 fairs held in Guilford and other towns between June and October.

48 SPORTS

The Connecticut Sun became the state's first major league team when it joined the WNBA in 2003. The team was formerly the Orlando Miracle. Connecticut's only other major league professional team, the Hartford Whalers of the National Hockey League, moved to North Carolina following the 1996–97 season and became the Carolina Hurricanes. The New England Seawolves are members of the Arena Football League. New Haven has a minor league baseball franchise, the Ravens, as do Norwich and New Britain. There are also minor league hockey and basketball teams in the state. Auto racing takes place at Lime Rock Race Track, which is located in Salisbury.

The state licenses off-track betting facilities for horse racing (not actually held in the state) and pari-mutuel operations for greyhound racing and jai alai.

Connecticut schools, colleges, and universities provide amateur athletic competitions, highlighted by Ivy League football games on autumn Saturdays at the Yale Bowl in New Haven. While Yale has won 13 Ivy League football titles, the University of Connecticut has become a force in men's and women's basketball. The Huskies' women's team won the NCAA championship in 1995 and 2000, and back-to-back titles in 2002 and 2003. They have also advanced to two other Final Four tournaments. The men's team won the National Invitational Tournament in 1988 and has made 37 NCAA Tournament appearances and won the national championship in 1999. Other annual sporting events include the US Eastern Ski Jumping Championships in Salisbury in February and the Greater Hartford Open Golf Tournament in Cromwell in June and July.

49 FAMOUS CONNECTICUTERS

Although Connecticut cannot claim any US president or vice president as a native son, John Moran Bailey (1904–75), chairman of the state Democratic Party (1946–75) and of the national party (1961–68), played a key role in presidential politics as a supporter of John F. Kennedy's successful 1960 campaign.

Two Connecticut natives have served as chief justice of the US: Oliver Ellsworth (1745–1807) and Morrison R. Waite (1816–88). Associate justices include Henry Baldwin (1780–1844), William Strong (1808–95), and Stephen J. Field (1816–99). Other prominent federal officeholders were Oliver Wolcott (1760–1833), secretary of the treasury; Gideon Welles (1802–78), secretary of the navy; Dean Acheson (1893–1971), secretary of state; and Abraham A. Ribicoff (1910–98), secretary of health, education, and welfare. An influential US senator was Orville H. Platt (1827–1905), known for his authorship of the Platt Amendment (1901), making Cuba a virtual protectorate of the United States. Also well known are Connecticut senator Ribicoff (served 1963–81) and former governor Lowell P. Weicker, Jr. (b.France, 1931 and served 1991–95), the latter first brought to national attention while a US Senator by his work during the Watergate hearings in 1973.

Notable colonial and state governors include John Winthrop, Jr. (b.England, 1606–76), Jonathan Trumbull (1710–85), William A. Buckingham (1804–75), Simeon Eben Baldwin (1840–1927), Marcus Holcomb (1844–1932),Wilbur L. Cross (1862–1948), Chester Bowles (1901–86), Ribicoff, and Ella Tambussi Grasso (1919–81), elected in 1974 and reelected in 1978 but forced to resign for health reasons at the end of 1980 (Grasso was the first woman governor in the US who did not succeed her husband in the post).

In addition to Winthrop, the founding fathers of Connecticut were Thomas Hooker (b.England, 1586–1647), who was deeply involved in establishing and developing Connecticut Colony, and Theophilus Eaton (b.England, 1590–1658) and John Davenport (b.England, 1597–1670), cofounders and leaders of the strict Puritan colony of New Haven. Other famous historical figures are Israel Putnam (b.Massachusetts, 1718–90), Continental Army major general at the Battle of Bunker Hill, who supposedly admonished his troops not to fire "until you see the whites of their eyes"; diplomat Silas Deane (1737–89); and Benedict Arnold (1741–1801), known for his treasonous activity in the Revolutionary War but also remembered for his courage and skill at Ft. Ticonderoga and Saratoga. Roger Sherman (b.Massachusetts, 1721–93), a signatory to the Articles of Association, Declaration of Independence (1776), Articles of Confederation (1777), Peace of Paris (1783), and the US Constitution (1787), was the only person to sign all these documents; at the Constitutional Convention, he proposed the "Connecticut Compromise," calling for a dual system of congressional representation. Connecticut's most revered Revolutionary War figure was Nathan Hale (1755–76), the Yale graduate who was executed for spying behind British lines. Radical abolitionist John Brown (1800–1859) was born in Torrington.

Connecticuters prominent in US cultural development include painter John Trumbull (1756–1843), son of Governor Trumbull, known for his canvases commemorating the American Revolution. Joel Barlow (1754–1812) was a poet and diplomat in the early national period. Lexicographer Noah Webster (1758–1843) compiled the *American Dictionary of the English Language* (1828). Frederick Law Olmsted (1822–1903), the first American landscape architect, planned New York City's Central Park. Harriet Beecher Stowe (1811–96) wrote one of the most widely read books in history, *Uncle Tom's Cabin* (1852). Mark Twain (Samuel L. Clemens, b.Missouri, 1835–1910) was living in Hartford when he wrote *The Adventures of Tom Sawyer* (1876), *The Adventures of Huckleberry Finn* (1885), and *A Connecticut Yankee in King Arthur's Court* (1889). Charles Ives (1874–1954), one of the nation's most distinguished composers, used his successful insurance business to finance his musical career and to help other musicians. Eugene O'Neill (b.New York, 1888–1953), the playwright who won the Nobel Prize for literature in 1936, spent summers in New London during his early years. A seminal voice in modern poetry, Wallace Stevens (b.Pennsylvania, 1879–1955), wrote the great body of his work while employed as a Hartford insurance executive. James Merrill (b.New York, 1926–95), a poet whose works have won the National Book Award (1967), Bollingen Prize (1973), and numerous other honors, lived in Stonington.

Native Connecticuters important in the field of education include Eleazar Wheelock (1711–79), William Samuel Johnson (1727–1819), Emma Willard (1787–1870), and Henry Barnard (1811–1900). Shapers of US history include Jonathan Edwards (1703–58), a Congregationalist minister who sparked the 18th-century religious revival known as the Great Awakening; Samuel Seabury (1729–96), the first Episcopal bishop in the US; Horace Bushnell (1802–76), said to be the father of the Sunday school; Lyman Beecher (1775–1863), a controversial figure in 19th-century American Protestantism who condemned slavery, intemperance, Roman Catholicism, and religious intolerance with equal fervor; and his son Henry Ward Beecher (1813–87), also a religious leader and abolitionist.

Among the premier inventors born in Connecticut were Abel Buel (1742–1824), who designed the first American submarine; Eli Whitney (1765–1825), inventor of the cotton gin and a pioneer in manufacturing; Charles Goodyear (1800–60), who devised a process for the vulcanization of rubber; Samuel Colt (1814–62), inventor of the six-shooter; Frank Sprague (1857–1934), who designed the first major electric trolley system in the US; and Edwin H. Land (1909–91), inventor of the Polaroid Land Camera. The Nobel Prize in physiology or medicine was won by three Connecticuters: Edward Kendall (1886–1972) in 1949, John Enders (1897–1985) in 1954, and Barbara McClintock (1902–92) in 1983.

Other prominent Americans born in Connecticut include clock manufacturer Seth Thomas (1785–1859), circus impresario Phineas Taylor "P. T." Barnum (1810–91), jeweler Charles Lewis Tiffany (1812–1902), financier John Pierpont Morgan (1837–1913), pediatrician Benjamin Spock (1903–98), cartoonist Al Capp (1909–79), soprano Eileen Farrell (b.1920), and consumer advocate Ralph Nader (b.1934). Leading actors and actresses are Ed Begley (1901–70), Katherine Hepburn (1909–2003), Rosalind Russell (1911–76), and Robert Mitchum (1917–97).

Walter Camp (1859–1925), athletic director of Yale University who helped formulate the rules of US football, was a native of Connecticut.

50 BIBLIOGRAPHY

Anderson, Ruth O.M. *From Yankee to American: Connecticut, 1865–1914.* Chester, Conn.: Pequot Press, 1975.

Bachman, Ben. *Upstream: A Voyage on the Connecticut River.* Boston: Houghton Mifflin, 1985.

Bingham, Harold J. *History of Connecticut.* 4 vols. New York: Lewis, 1962.

Bixby, William. *Connecticut: A New Guide.* New York: Scribner, 1974.

Boyle, Joseph Lee. *Fire Cake and Water: the Connecticut Infantry at the Valley Forge Encampment.* Baltimore, Md.: Clearfield, 1999.

Bushman, Richard L. *From Puritan to Yankee: Character and the Social Order in Connecticut, 1690–1765.* Cambridge, Mass.: Harvard University Press, 1967.

Connecticut, State of. Secretary of State. *Register and Manual 1984.* Hartford, 1984.

Dayton, Cornelia Hughes. *Women Before the Bar: Gender, Law, and Society in Connecticut, 1839–1789.* Chapel Hill, N.C.: University of North Carolina Press, 1995.

Dugger, Elizabeth L. *Adventure Guide to Massachusetts & Western Connecticut*. Edison, N.J.: Hunter, 1999.

Hamblen, Charles P. *Connecticut Yankees at Gettysburg*. Kent, Ohio: Kent State University Press, 1993.

Janick, Herbet F. *A Diverse People: Connecticut, 1914 to the Present*. Chester, Conn.: Pequot Press, 1975.

Lee, W. Storrs. *The Yankee of Connecticut*. New York: Holt, 1957.

Morse, Jarvis Means, *A Neglected Period of Connecticut's History: 1818–1850*. New Haven, Conn.: Yale University Press, 1933.

Niven, John. *Connecticut for the Union: The Role of the State in the Civil War*. New Haven: Yale University Press, 1965.

Oberg, Michael Leroy. *Uncas: First of the Mohegans*. Ithaca, N.Y.: Cornell University Press, 2003.

Peirce, Neal R. *The New England States: People, Politics, and Power in the Six New England States*. New York: Norton, 1976.

Rose, Gary L. *Connecticut Politics at the Crossroads*. Lanham, Md.: University Press of America, 1992.

Roth David, M., and Freeman Myer. *From Revolution to Constitution: Connecticut, 1763–1818*. Chester, Conn.: Pequot Press, 1975.

Siskind, Janet. *Rum and Axes: The Rise of a Connecticut Merchant Family, 1795–1850*. Ithaca, N.Y.: Cornell University Press, 2002.

Stuart, Patricia. *Units of Local Government in Connecticut*. Storrs: Institute of Public Service. University of Connecticut, 1979.

Taylor, Robert J. *Colonial Connecticut*. Milkwood, N.Y.: KTO Press, 1979.

Trecker, Janice Law. *Preachers, Rebels, and Traders: Connecticut, 1818–1865*. Chester, Conn.: Pequot Press, 1975.

Van Dusen, Albert E. *Connecticut*. New York: Random House, 1961.

———. *Puritans Against the Wilderness: Connecticut to 1763*. Chester, Conn.: Pequot Press, 1975.

Warren, William L. *Connecticut Art and Architecture: Looking Backwards Two Hundred Years*. Hartford: American Revolution Bicentennial Commission of Connecticut, 1976.

Wetherell, W. D., ed. *This American River: Five Centuries of Writing about the Connecticut*. Hanover, N.H.: University Press of New England, 2002.

Whipple, Chandler. *The Indian in Connecticut*. Stockbridge, Mass.: Berkshire Traveler Press, 1972.

Zeichner, Oscar. *Connecticut's Years of Controversy, 1775–1776*. Chapel Hill: University of North Carolina Press, 1949.

DECEMBER 7, 1787

DELAWARE

State of Delaware

ORIGIN OF STATE NAME: Named for Thomas West, Baron De La Warr, colonial governor of Virginia; the name was first applied to the bay. **NICKNAMES:** The First State; also, the Diamond State. **CAPITAL:** Dover. **ENTERED UNION:** 7 December 1787 (1st). **SONG:** "Our Delaware." **COLORS:** Colonial blue and buff. **MOTTO:** Liberty and Independence. **COAT OF ARMS:** A farmer and a rifleman flank a shield that bears symbols of the state's agricultural resources—a sheaf of wheat, an ear of corn, and a cow. Above is a ship in full sail; below, a banner with the state motto. **FLAG:** Colonial blue with the coat of arms on a buff-colored diamond; below the diamond is the date of statehood. **OFFICIAL SEAL:** The coat of arms surrounded by the words "Great Seal of the State of Delaware 1793, 1847, 1907." The three dates represent the years in which the seal was revised. **BIRD:** Blue hen chicken. **FISH:** Sea trout. **INSECT:** Ladybug. **FLOWER:** Peach blossom. **TREE:** American holly. **ROCK:** Sillimanite. **LEGAL HOLIDAYS:** New Year's Day, 1 January; Birthday of Martin Luther King, Jr., 3rd Monday in January; Lincoln's Birthday, 1st Monday in February; Washington's Birthday, 3rd Monday in February; Good Friday, March or April; Memorial Day, last Monday in May; Independence Day, 4 July; Labor Day, 1st Monday in September; Columbus Day, 2nd Monday in October; Veterans Day, 11 November; General Election Day, 1st Tuesday after the 1st Monday in November in even-numbered years; Thanksgiving Day, 4th Thursday in November; Christmas Day, 25 December. **TIME:** 7 AM EST = noon GMT.

¹LOCATION, SIZE, AND EXTENT

Located on the eastern seaboard of the US, Delaware ranks 49th in size among the 50 states. The state's total area is 2,044 sq mi (5,295 sq km), of which land takes up 1,932 sq mi (5,005 sq km) and inland water 112 sq mi (290 sq km). Delaware extends 35 mi (56 km) E-W at its widest; its maximum N-S extension is 96 mi (154 km).

Delaware is bordered on the N by Pennsylvania; on the E by New Jersey (with the line passing through the Delaware River into Delaware Bay) and the Atlantic Ocean; and on the S and W by Maryland.

The boundary length of Delaware, including a general coastline of 28 mi (45 km), totals 200 mi (322 km). The tidal shoreline is 381 mi (613 km). The state's geographic center is in Kent County, 11 mi (18 km) S of Dover.

²TOPOGRAPHY

Delaware lies entirely within the Atlantic Coastal Plain except for its northern tip, above the Christina River, which is part of the Piedmont Plateau. The state's highest elevation is 448 ft (137 m) on Ebright Road, near Centerville, New Castle County. The rolling hills and pastures of the north give way to marshy regions in the south (notably Cypress Swamp), with sandy beaches along the coast. Delaware's mean elevation, 60 ft (18 m), is the lowest in the US.

Of all Delaware's rivers, only the Nanticoke, Choptank, and Pocomoke flow westward into Chesapeake Bay. The remainder—including the Christina, Appoquinimink, Leipsic, St. Jones, Murderkill, Mispillion, Broadkill, and Indian—flow into Delaware Bay. There are dozens of inland freshwater lakes and ponds.

³CLIMATE

Delaware's climate is temperate and humid. The normal daily mean temperature in Wilmington is 54°F (12°C), ranging from 31°F (–1°C) in January to 76°F (24°C) in July. Both the record low and the record high temperatures for the state were established at Millsboro: –17°F (–27°C) on 17 January 1893 and 110°F (43°C) on 21 July 1930. The average annual precipitation (1971–2000) was 42.8 in (108.7 cm) during 1971–2000; about 21 in (53 cm) of snow falls each year. Wilmington's average share of sunshine is 55%—one of the lowest percentages among leading US cities.

⁴FLORA AND FAUNA

Delaware's mixture of northern and southern flora reflects its geographical position. Common trees include black walnut, hickory, sweetgum, and tulip poplar. Shadbush and sassafras are found chiefly in southern Delaware. Five plant species were listed as threatened or endangered as of August 2003 1997.

Mammals native to the state include the white-tailed deer, red and gray foxes, eastern gray squirrel, muskrat, raccoon, woodcock, and common cottontail. The quail, robin, wood thrush, cardinal, and eastern meadowlark are representative birds, while various waterfowl, especially Canada geese, are common. Fifteen animal species were considered threatened or endangered by the US Fish and Wildlife Service as of August 2003. Among these are the bald eagle, puma, five species of sea turtle, three species of whale, and the Delmarva Peninsula fox squirrel.

⁵ENVIRONMENTAL PROTECTION

The Coastal Zone Act of 1971 outlaws new industry "incompatible with the protection of the natural environment" of shore areas, but in 1979 the act was amended to permit offshore oil drilling and the construction of coastal oil facilities. The traffic of oil tankers into the Delaware Bay represents an environmental hazard.

In 1982, Delaware enacted a bottle law requiring deposits on most soda and beer bottles; deposits for aluminum cans were made mandatory in 1984. In that year, Delaware became the first state to administer the national hazardous waste program at the state level. The state's municipal governments have constructed three municipal land fills to handle the solid waste produced by the state's 670,000 residents. In 2003, the Environmental

Protection Agency's database listed 64 hazardous waste sites, 15 of which were on the National Priorities List, in Delaware.

State environmental protection agencies include the Department of natural resources and Environmental Control, Coastal Zone Industrial Control Board, and Council on Soil and Water Conservation. In 2001, Delaware received $26,356,000 in federal grants from the EPA; EPA expenditures for procurement contracts in Delaware that year amounted to $3,153,000.

6POPULATION

Delaware ranked 44th in population in the US with an estimated total of 807,385 in 2002, an increase of 3% since 2000. Between 1990 and 2000, Delaware's population grew from 666,168 to 783,600, an increase of 17.6%. The population is projected to reach 861,000 by 2025.

In 2000, the population density was 401.1 people per square mile, the seventh-highest among the 50 states. The median age in 2000 was 36; 13% were age 65 or over, while 24.8% were under 18 years of age.

The largest cities in 2000 were Wilmington, with an estimated population of 72,664, and Dover, the capital, with 32,135.

7ETHNIC GROUPS

Black Americans constitute Delaware's largest racial minority, numbering 150,666 in 2000 and comprising about 19.2% of the population. As of 2000, approximately 37,277 reidents, or 4.8% of the total population (up from 16,000, or 2.4% in 1990), were of Hispanic origin.

Delaware's 44,898 foreign born made up 5.7% of the state's population in 2000 (more than double the total of 22,275, or 3.3%, in 1990). The United Kingdom, Germany, India, Italy, and Canada were the leading places of origin.

8LANGUAGES

English in Delaware is basically North Midland, with Philadelphia features in Wilmington and the northern portion. In the north, one *wants off* a bus, lowers *curtains* rather than blinds, pronounces *wharf* without /h/, and says /noo/ and /doo/ for *new* and *due* and /krik/ for *creek*. In 2000, 662,845 Delawareans—90.5% of the resident population five years of age or older—spoke only English at home.

The following table gives selected statistics from the 2000 census for language spoken at home by persons five years old and over. The category "African languages" includes Amharic, Ibo, Twi, Yoruba, Bantu, Swahili, and Somali. The category "Other Asian languages" includes Dravidian languages, Malayalam, Telugu, Tamil, and Turkish. The category "Other West Germanic languages" includes Dutch, Pennsylvania Dutch, and Afrikaans.

LANGUAGE	NUMBER	PERCENT
Population 5 years and over	732,378	100.0
Speak only English	662,845	90.5
Speak a language other than English	69,533	9.5
Speak a language other than English	69,533	9.5
Spanish or Spanish Creole	34,690	4.7
French (incl. Patois, Cajun)	4,041	0.6
Chinese	3,579	0.5
German	3,420	0.5
Italian	2,860	0.4
Polish	2,036	0.3
Korean	1,598	0.2
African languages	1,289	0.2
Tagalog	1,284	0.2
Other Asian languages	1,280	0.2
Other West Germanic languages	1,245	0.2
French Creole	1,199	0.2
Other Indic languages	1,186	0.2

9RELIGIONS

The earliest permanent European settlers in Delaware were Swedish and Finnish Lutherans and Dutch Calvinists. English Quakers, Scotch-Irish Presbyterians, and Welsh Baptists arrived in the 18th century, though Anglicization was the predominant trend. The Great Awakening, America's first religious revival, began on 30 October 1739 at Lewes with the arrival of George Whitefield, an Anglican preacher involved in the movement that would later become the Methodist Church. The Methodist Church was the largest denomination in Delaware by the early 19th century. Subsequent immigration brought Lutherans from Germany; Roman Catholics from Ireland, Germany, Italy, and Poland; and Jews from Germany, Poland, and Russia. Most of the Catholic and Jewish immigrants settled in cities, Wilmington in particular.

From 1990–2000, the Catholic Church gained 35,399 new members, enough to outnumber the previously dominant mainline Protestants. There were 151,740 Catholics in about 46 congregations in 2000. The United Methodist Church had 59,471 adherents in 162 congregations, Episcopalians numbered 12,993 in 35 congregations, and the Presbyterian Church USA claimed 14,880 adherents in about 37 congregations. There were about 13,500 adherents to Judaism. About 59.4% of the population were not counted as members of any religious organization.

10TRANSPORTATION

The New Castle and Frenchtown Railroad, a portage route, was built in 1832; the state's first passenger line—the Philadelphia, Wilmington, and Baltimore Railroad—opened six years later. As of 2000, there were 281 rail mi (452 km) of track. In 1998, Delaware's six railroads carried nearly 14.1 million tons of freight—54% of the rail tonnage originating from within the state were chemicals. Consolidated Rail and CSX are Delaware's main freight carriers. In the mid-1990s, Amtrak operated approximately 70 daily trains through Delaware and served both Newark and Wilmington. The Delaware Authority for Regional Transit (DART) provides state-subsidized bus service.

In 2000, the state had 5,779 mi (9,300 km) of public highways, roads, and streets. In the same year, there were 641,426 registered vehicles and 556,688 licensed drivers. Delaware's first modern highway—and the first dual highway in the US—running about 100 mi (160 km) from Wilmington to the southern border, was financed by industrialist T. Coleman du Pont between 1911 and 1924. The twin spans of the Delaware Memorial Bridge connect Delaware highways to those in New Jersey; The Delaware Turnpike section of the John F. Kennedy Memorial Highway links the bridge system with Maryland. The Lewes–Cape May Ferry provides auto and passenger service between southern Delaware and New Jersey.

In 2000, New Castle, Delaware's chief port, handled 8.7 million tons of goods, followed by Wilmington, with a tonnage of 5.2 million tons that year. The Delaware River is the conduit for much of the oil brought by tanker to the US east coast.

Delaware had 45 airfields (29 airport, 15 heliports, 1 seaplane base) in 2002, of which Greater Wilmington Airport was the largest and busiest.

11HISTORY

Delaware was inhabited nearly 10,000 years ago, and a succession of various cultures occupied the area until the first European contact. At that time, the Leni-Lenape (Delaware) Indians occupied northern Delaware, while several tribes, including the Nanticoke and Assateague, inhabited southern Delaware. The Dutch in 1631 were the first Europeans to settle in what is now Delaware, but their little colony (at Lewes) was destroyed by Indians. Permanent settlements were made by the

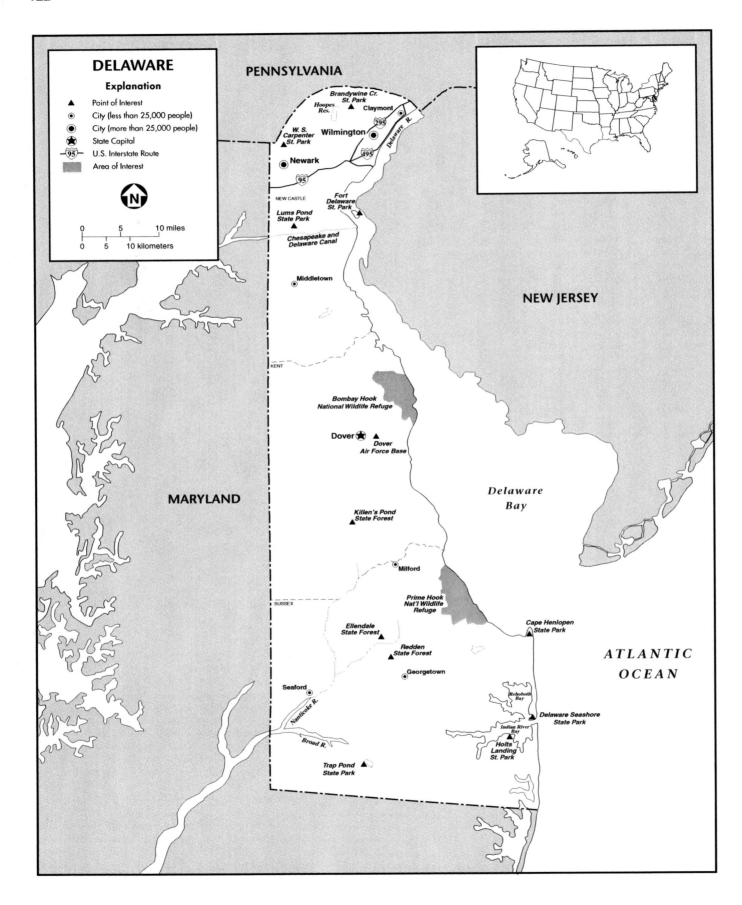

DELAWARE

Explanation

▲ Point of Interest
⊙ City (less than 25,000 people)
◉ City (more than 25,000 people)
★ State Capital
95 U.S. Interstate Route
Area of Interest

N

0   5   10 miles
0   5   10 kilometers

PENNSYLVANIA

Brandywine Cr. St. Park
Hoopes Res.
Claymont
W. S. Carpenter St. Park
Wilmington
Delaware R.
Newark
295
495
95
NEW CASTLE
Fort Delaware St. Park
Lums Pond State Park
Chesapeake and Delaware Canal
Middletown

NEW JERSEY

KENT

Bombay Hook National Wildlife Refuge

Dover ★ ▲
Dover Air Force Base

Delaware Bay

MARYLAND

Killen's Pond State Forest

Milford

Prime Hook Nat'l Wildlife Refuge

SUSSEX

Ellendale State Forest

Redden State Forest

Georgetown

Seaford
Nanticoke R.

Broad R.

Trap Pond State Park

Cape Henlopen State Park

ATLANTIC OCEAN

Rehoboth Bay

Delaware Seashore State Park

Indian River Bay

Holts Landing St. Park

Swedes in 1638 (at Wilmington, under the leadership of a Dutchman, Peter Minuit) and by the Dutch in 1651 (at New Castle). The Dutch conquered the Swedes in 1655, and the English conquered the Dutch in 1664. Eighteen years later, the area was ceded by the duke of York (later King James II), its first English proprietor, to William Penn. Penn allowed Delaware an elected assembly in 1704, but the colony was still subject to him and to his deputy governor in Philadelphia; ties to the Penn family and Pennsylvania were not severed until 1776. Boundary quarrels disturbed relations with Maryland until Charles Mason and Jeremiah Dixon surveyed the western boundary of Delaware (and the Maryland-Pennsylvania boundary) during the period 1763–68. By this time, virtually all the Indians had been driven out of the territory.

In September 1777, during the War for Independence, British soldiers marched through northern Delaware, skirmishing with some of Washington's troops at Cooch's Bridge, near Newark, and seizing Wilmington, which they occupied for a month. In later campaigns, Delaware troops with the Continental Army fought so well that they gained the nickname "Blue Hen's Chicken," after a famous breed of fighting gamecocks. On 7 December 1787, Delaware became the first state to ratify the federal Constitution. Although Delaware had not abolished slavery, it remained loyal to the Union during the Civil War. By that time, it was the one slave state in which a clear majority of blacks (about 92%) were already free. However, white Delawareans generally resented the Reconstruction policies adopted by Congress after the Civil War, and by manipulation of registration laws denied blacks the franchise until 1890.

The key event in the state's economic history was the completion of a railroad between Philadelphia and Baltimore through Wilmington in 1838, encouraging the industrialization of northern Delaware. Wilmington grew so rapidly that by 1900 it encompassed 41% of the state's population; by mid-century the city was home to roughly half the state's population. Considerable foreign immigration contributed to this growth, largely from the British Isles (especially Ireland) and Germany in the mid-19th century and from Italy, Poland, and Russia in the early 20th century.

Flour and textile mills, shipyards, carriage factories, iron foundries, and morocco leather plants were Wilmington's leading enterprises for much of the 19th century. By the early 1900s however, E. I. du Pont de Nemours and Co., founded near Wilmington in 1802 as a gunpowder manufacturer, made the city famous as a center for the chemical industry. Du Pont remained the state's largest employer in the 1990s.

During the same period, Delaware's agricultural income rose. Peaches and truck crops flourished in the 19th century, along with corn and wheat; poultry, sorghum, and soybeans became major sources of agricultural income in the 20th century. Sussex County, home to much of the state's farming, had become the fastest-growing county in Delaware by the mid-1990s. The beach areas of rural Sussex had attracted resort-goers and retirees. Tourism was expected to be aided by the construction of a north-south expressway that will cut travel time to the state's southern beach communities.

During the 1950s, Delaware's population grew by an unprecedented 40%. The growth was greatest around Dover, site of the East Coast's largest air base, and on the outskirts of Wilmington. Wilmington itself lost population after 1945 because of the proliferation of suburban housing developments, offices, and factories, including two automobile assembly plants and an oil refinery. Although many neighborhood schools became racially integrated during the 1950s, massive busing was instituted by court order in 1978 to achieve a racial balance in schools throughout northern Delaware.

The 1980s ushered in a period of dramatic economic improvement. According to state sources, Delaware was one of only two states to improve its financial strength during the recession that plagued the early part of the decade. In 1988, Delaware enjoyed an unemployment rate of 3.3%, the 2nd-lowest in the country. The state's revenues grew at an average of 7.7% in the early 1980s, even while it successively cut the personal income tax. Some of Delaware's prosperity came from a 1981 state law that raised usury limits and lowered taxes for large financial institutions. More than 30 banks established themselves in Delaware, including Chase Manhattan Bank and Manufacturers Hanover.

The state also succeeded in using its simplified incorporation procedures to attract both US and foreign companies, bringing in an estimated $1 million in incorporation fees from Asian companies alone in the late 1980s. By the mid-1990s, the state was the registered home of roughly half the Fortune 500 companies and hundreds of thousands of smaller corporations; however, for most, their presence in the state was strictly on paper. The state sustained a low rate of unemployment into the 1990s; in 1999 it was 3.5%, still below the national average. A year earlier the state ranked sixth in the nation for per capita income ($29,932).

While business fared well in Delaware, the state lagged behind in social welfare indicators in the mid-1990s. Delaware's rates of teenage pregnancy and infant mortality were among the highest in the country while its welfare benefits were lower than those of any other mid-Atlantic state with the exception of West Virginia. Other problems in the 1990s included housing shortages, urban sprawl, and pollution.

Ruth Ann Minner, elected Delaware's first woman governor in 2001, was once a receptionist in the governor's office before winning the position herself. In her 2003 State of the State address, she targeted issues such as pollution, industrial cleanups, and toughening campaign finance laws. In September 2003, Delaware was launching a prisoner reentry program, designed to help former inmates successfully reenter society instead of committing further crimes and returning to prison. The three-year pilot program was financed with a $2 million federal grant and was to save the state millions of dollars a year and reduce crime.

12 STATE GOVERNMENT

Delaware has had four state constitutions, adopted in 1776, 1792, 1831, and 1897. Under the 1897 document, as amended (136 times by January 2003), the legislative branch is the general assembly, consisting of a 21-member senate and a 41-member house of representatives. Annual legislative sessions begin in January and must conclude by 30 June. The presiding officers of both houses may issue a joint call for a special session, which is not limited in length. Senators are elected for four years, representatives for two. Members of the house must be at least 24 years old; senators must be 27. All legislators must have been residents of the state for three years and must have lived in their district for one year prior to election. Legislators earned $33,400 annually in 2002.

Delaware's elected executives are the governor and lieutenant governor (separately elected), treasurer, attorney general, and comptroller. All serve four-year terms. The governor, who may be reelected only once, must be at least 30 years old and must have been a US citizen for 12 years and a state resident for six years before taking office. In 2002 the governor's salary was $114,000. The legislature may override a gubernatorial veto by a three-fifths vote of the elected members of each house. A bill that the governor fails to sign or veto becomes law after 10 days (Sundays excluded) when the legislature is in session. An amendment to the state constitution must be approved by a two-thirds vote in each house of the general assembly in two successive sessions with an election intervening; Delaware is the only state in which amendments need not be ratified by the voters.

Voters in Delaware must be US citizens, at least 18 years old, and permanent state residents. Restrictions apply to convicted felons and those declared mentally incompetent by the court.

13 POLITICAL PARTIES

The Democrats were firmly entrenched in Delaware for three decades after the Civil War; a subsequent period of Republican dominance lasted until the depression of the 1930s. Since then, the two parties have been relatively evenly matched.

In 2002 there were 522,768 registered voters; 42% were Democratic, 36% Republican, and 23% unaffiliated or members of other parties in 1998. In the 2000 election, Democrat Al Gore won the state with 55% of the vote, to Republican George W. Bush's 42%. Green Party candidate Ralph Nader won 3% of the vote. The state had three electoral votes in the 2000 presidential election. Democratic Senator Joseph Biden was the ranking member of the Senate Foreign Relations Committee in 2003. Democrat Tom Carper was elected Delaware's junior Senator in 2000, after having served two terms as state governor, and five terms in the US House of Representatives. Former two-term governor and Republican Michael Castle was reelected Delaware's House Representative in 2002.

Democratic Governor Ruth Ann Minner, elected in 2001, was the first woman to serve in a leadership position in Delaware's House of Representatives, the state's first female lieutenant governor and first female governor. In 2003, Republicans controlled the state house (29–12), and Democrats controlled the state senate (13–8).

Delaware Presidential Vote by Major Political Parties, 1948–2000

YEAR	ELECTORAL VOTE	DELAWARE WINNER	DEMOCRAT	REPUBLICAN
1948	3	Dewey (R)	67,813	69,588
1952	3	*Eisenhower (R)	83,315	90,059
1956	3	*Eisenhower (R)	79,421	98,057
1960	3	*Kennedy (D)	99,590	96,373
1964	3	*Johnson (D)	122,704	78,078
1968	3	*Nixon (R)	89,194	96,714
1972	3	*Nixon (R)	92,283	140,357
1976	3	*Carter (D)	122,596	109,831
1980	3	*Reagan (R)	105,700	111,185
1984	3	*Reagan (R)	101,656	152,190
1988	3	*Bush (R)	108,647	139,639
1992**	3	*Clinton(D)	126,054	102,313
1996**	3	*Clinton(D)	140,355	99,062
2000	3	Gore (D)	180,068	137,288

* Won US presidential election.

**Independent Ross Perot received 59,213 votes in 1992 and 28,719 votes in 1996.

14 LOCAL GOVERNMENT

As of 2002, Delaware was divided into three counties. In New Castle, voters elect a county executive and a county council; in Sussex, the members of the elective county council choose a county administrator, who supervises the executive departments of the county government. Kent operates under an elected levy court, which sets tax rates and runs the county according to regulations spelled out by the assembly. Most of Delaware's 57 municipalities elect a mayor and council. In 2002 Delaware had 19 public school districts and 260 special districts. Because of the state's small geographic size, local government in Delaware tends to be weaker than that in other states; here the state operates many programs that elsewhere are found at the local level.

15 STATE SERVICES

To address the continuing threat of terrorism and to work with the federal Department of Homeland Security (created in 2002 following the terrorist attacks of 11 September 2001), homeland security in Delaware in 2003 operated under the authority of the governor; a homeland security director was appointed to oversee programs related to homeland security.

Public education is supervised by the Department of Education. Highways are the responsibility of the Department of Transportation, while medical care, mental health facilities, drug- and alcohol-abuse programs, and help for the aging fall within the jurisdiction of the Department of Health and Social Services. Public protection services are provided primarily through the Department of Public Safety and Department of Correction. The Department of Labor has divisions covering employment services, vocational rehabilitation, unemployment insurance, and equal employment opportunity. The Economic Development Office supports the economic interests of the state. Other services include those of the Department of Services to Children, Youth and Their Families and the Department of Community Affairs. The environment is protected by the Department of Natural Resources and Environmental Control.

16 JUDICIAL SYSTEM

Delaware's highest court is the supreme court, composed of a chief justice and four associate justices, all appointed by the governor and confirmed by the senate for 12-year terms, as are all state judges. Other state courts include the court of chancery, comprising a chancellor and two vice-chancellors, and the superior court, which has a president judge and 16 associate judges. There are also judges on the Court of Common Pleas in Wilmington.

Delaware was the last state to abolish the whipping post. During the 1900–42 period, 1,604 prisoners (22% of the state's prison population) were beaten with a cat-o'-nine-tails. The whipping post, nicknamed "Red Hannah," was used for the last time in 1952 but was not formally abolished until 1972. The death penalty is authorized in Delaware, with lethal injection as the method of execution. Delaware has executed 25 persons since 1930, thirteen of whom were put to death between 1977 and 2003. In 2003 there were 19 persons under sentence of death. In 2001, Delaware had a total crime rate of 4,052.8 per 100,000 population, including a total of 4,868 violent crimes and 27,399 property crimes in that year. As of June 2001, there were 7,122 inmates held in state and federal correctional facilities, an increase of 1.1% over the previous year. The state's incarceration rate stood at 505 per 100,000 inhabitants.

17 ARMED FORCES

Delaware's main defense facility is the military airlift wing at Dover Air Force Base. Active-duty military personnel stationed in Delaware in 2002 totaled 3,899. Department of Defense contracts awarded the state in 2001 totaled $84 million. There were 84,289 veterans of US military service in Delaware as of 2000, of whom 15,403 served in World War II; 10,416 in the Korean conflict; 23,680 during the Vietnam era; and 9,967 during 1990–2000 (including the Persian Gulf War). Veterans' benefits totaled $142 million in 2002. In 2000, the Delaware state police employed 580 full-time sworn officers.

18 MIGRATION

Delaware has attracted immigrants from a variety of foreign countries: Sweden, Finland, and the Netherlands in the early days; England, Scotland, and Ireland during the later colonial period; and Italy, Poland, and Russia, among other countries, during the first 130 years of statehood. The 1960s and 1970s saw the migration of Puerto Ricans to Wilmington. Delaware enjoyed a net gain from migration of 122,000 persons between 1940 and 1970. Between 1970 and 1990, however, there was a net migration of only about 25,000. Net domestic migration between 1990 and 1998 totaled 29,000 while net international migration totaled 8,000. In 1998, Delaware admitted 1,063 foreign immigrants. Between 1990 and 1998, the state's overall population increased 11.6%. In the period 1995–2000, 101,461people moved into the state and 84,078 moved out, for a net gain of 17,383, 2,679 of whom were age 65 or over.

[19]INTERGOVERNMENTAL COOPERATION

Among the interstate agreements to which Delaware subscribes are the Delaware River and Bay Authority Compact, Delaware River Basin Commission, Atlantic States Marine Fisheries Commission, Interstate Compact for Juveniles, Mid-Atlantic Fishery Management Council, and Southern Regional Education Board. The Delmarva Advisory Council, representing Delaware, Maryland, and Viriginia, works with local organizations on the Delmarva Peninsula to develop and implement economic improvement programs. Federal grants to Delaware were $892 million in fiscal year 2001, least among all the states.

[20]ECONOMY

Since the 1930s, and particularly since the mid-1970s, Delaware has been one of the nation's most prosperous states. It was one of the few states that whose economic growth rate actually increased during the national recession of 200, accelerating from 4.5% in 1998 to 6.1% in 1999 to 7.3% in 2000, and to 8.75% in 2001. Although manufacturing—preeminently the chemical and automotive industries—has historically been the main contributor to the state's economy, its contribution to gross state product shrunk from 16.5% in 1997 to 12.9% in 2001, compared to a 43% contribution from the finance, insurance and real estate sector and 15.3% from general services (hotels, auto repair, personal, health, legal, educational, recreational, etc). The largest employers in the manufacturing sector, the chemical and automobile manufacturing industries, experienced negative growth coming into the 21st century, output from motor vehicles and equipment manufacturing falling 34% 1999 to 2001, and the output from chemicals and allied products manufacturing showing a net decline of 2.6% 1997 to 2001. By contrast, financial services grew 43% during this period, and general services grew 36.4%. Job creation in manufacturing, which was at a positive 2% year-on-year rate in 1999, turned negative (to net layoffs) by the beginning of 2000 and continued at negative rates throughout 2001 and 2002. Job creation in the finance, insurance and real estate (FIRE) sector continued at year-on-year rates of 2% to 3%, but then turned sharply negative in 2002, reaching –4% by the end of the year. Office space vacancy in Wilmington reached 15% in the fourth quarter 2002, but this was below the national average of 16.5%. Positive factors that augur well for a relatively rapid economic recovery in Delaware are continued moderate housing costs that make Delaware more attractive than neighboring states with higher costs, and a related above-average 17% gain in population 1991 to 2001 (the national average-was 13%) that largely reflected the movement of businesses to Delaware's relatively low-cost business environment.

Delaware's gross state product in 2001 was $40.5 billion, up 29.6% from 1997, only 8.5% of which was attributable to the public sector, the lowest percent among the states. The major contributors to gross state product in 2001were financial services ($17.5 billion); general services ($6.2 billion); manufacturing ($5.2 billion); wholesale and retail trade ($4.3 billion), government ($3.4 billion); and transportation and public utilities ($1.9 billion).

[21]INCOME

According to the Bureau of Economic Analysis, in 2001, Delaware had a per capita personal income (PCPI) of $32,166 which ranked 13th in the United States (including the District of Columbia) and was 106% of the national average, $30,413. The 2001 PCPI reflected an increase of 3.5% from 2000 compared to the national change of 2.2%. In 2001, Delaware had a total personal income (TPI) of $25,623,568,000 which ranked 44th in the United States and accounted for 0.3% of the national total. The 2001 TPI reflected an increase of 4.8% from 2000 compared to the national change of 3.3%.

Earnings of persons employed in Delaware increased from $19,088,028,000 in 2000 to $19,959,326,000 in 2001, an increase of 4.6%. The largest industries in 2001 were services, 26.2% of earnings; finance, insurance, and real estate, 17.0%; and nondurable goods manufacturing, 14.1%. Of the industries that accounted for at least 5% of earnings in 2001, the slowest growing from 2000 to 2001 was nondurable goods manufacturing, which increased 1.8%; the fastest was finance, insurance, and real estate, which increased 10.4%.

According to data released by the US Census Bureau, in 2000, the median household income was $50,154 compared to the national average of $42,148. In 2001, the median income for a family of four was $73,301 compared to the national average of $63,278. For the period 1999 to 2001, the average poverty rate was 8.5% which placed it 11th among the 50 states and the District of Columbia ranked lowest to highest.

[22]LABOR

According to Bureau of Labor Statistics (BLS) provisional estimates, in July 2003 the seasonally adjusted civilian labor force in Delaware numbered 419,400, with approximately 17,000 workers unemployed, yielding an unemployment rate of 4.1%, compared to the national average of 6.2% for the same period. Since the beginning of the BLS data series in 1978, the highest unemployment rate recorded was 9.1% in January 1982. The historical low was 2.9% in May 1988. In 2001, an estimated 6.3% of the labor force was employed in construction; 13.3% in manufacturing; 4.9% in transportation, communications, and public utilities; 17.4% in trade; 11.4% in finance, insurance, and real estate; 27.3% in services; 12.9% in government; and 1.9% in agriculture.

The US Department of Labor reported that in 2002, 41,000 of Delaware's 369,000 employed wage and salary workers were members of unions. This represented 11.1% of those so employed, down from 12.1% in 2001 and from 13.6% in 1998. The national average is 13.2%. In all, 45,000 workers (12.1%) were represented by unions. In addition to union members, this category includes workers who report no union affiliation but whose jobs are covered by a union contract.

[23]AGRICULTURE

Though small by national standards, Delaware's agriculture is efficient and productive. In 2001, Delaware's total farm marketings were $848 million, and its income from crops was $186 million.

Tobacco was a leading crop in the early colonial era but was soon succeeded by corn and wheat. Peaches were a mainstay during the mid-19th century, until the orchards were devastated by "the yellows," a tree disease. Today, the major field crops are corn, soybeans, barley, wheat, melons, potatoes, mushrooms, lima beans, and green peas. Production in 2002 included corn for grain, 13,900,000 bushels, valued at $39,500,000; soybeans, 4,625,000 bushels, $26,360,000; wheat, 4,060,000 bushels, $4,060,000; and barley, 1,932,000 bushels, $2,705,000.

[24]ANIMAL HUSBANDRY

In 2001 an estimated 9,000 milk cows produced 151 million lb of milk (68.5 million kg). Also during 2001 an estimated 1.5 billion lb (680 million kg) of broilers were produced and valued at an estimated $597.9 million. Broilers account for the majority of Delaware's farm receipts. Delaware produced an estimated 369 million eggs valued at around $20.8 million in 2001.

[25]FISHING

Fishing, once an important industry in Delaware, has declined in recent decades. The total commercial landings in 1998 were 7,898,000 lb, worth $5,882,000. Clams, plentiful until the mid-1970s, are in short supply because of overharvesting. Delaware issued 24,903 sport fishing licenses in 1998.

[26]FORESTRY

In 2002 Delaware had approximately 383,000 acres (155,000 hectares) of forestland, of which approximately 92% was classified as private forestland. Nonindustrial private landowners owned 85% of Delaware's forests while approximately 8% was publicly owned, and 7% was owned by the forest industry.

Southern Delaware contains many loblolly pine forests as well as the northernmost stand of bald cypress. Northern Delaware contains more hardwoods, such as oak and yellow poplar. Other common species are gum, maple, and American holly, which is Delaware's state tree. Delaware has approximately 32,000 acres (12,950 hectares) of state forests, which are managed on a multiple-use basis and are open to the public.

[27]MINING

The value of nonfuel mineral production in Delaware in 2001 was about $13.1 million, according to estimated data compiled by the US Geological Survey. However, this figure reflects only the state's production of construction sand and gravel (2.42 million metric tons). Production data for Delaware's other significant nonfuel mineral, magnesium compounds produced for use in chemical and pharmaceutical manufacturing, was withheld to protect company proprietary data. Delaware ranked fourth nationally in production of magnesium compounds and was one of only five states that produced them in the US. They are extracted from seawater close to the mouth of the Delaware Bay near Lewes and, with aluminum hydroxides, are used in the manufacture of antacid products.

[28]ENERGY AND POWER

Installed electric capacity (utility and nonutility) totaled 2.45 million kW in 1999; production of electric power reached 6.9 billion kWh in the same year. Most of the power is supplied by coal- and oil-fired plants. Delaware has no nuclear reactors, nor does it have any fossil fuel resources. In 2000 Delaware's total per capita energy consumption was 386 million Btu (97.3 million kcal), ranking it 17th among the states.

[29]INDUSTRY

From its agricultural beginnings, Delaware has developed into an important industrial state. There are a total of three fortune 500 companies headquartered in Delaware. The incorporation industry employs about 1,000 people and brings in about one-quarter of the state budget in taxes and fees. Wilmington is called the "Chemical Capital of the World," largely because of E. I. du Pont de Nemours and Co., a chemical industry giant originally founded as a powder mill in 1802. As of 1999 the company was the 16th largest US industrial corporation, with sales of $28 billion. The Chrysler Corp. is another leading employer. Notable Delaware manufactures, in addition to chemicals and transportation equipment, include apparel, processed meats and vegetables, paper, printing and publishing, scientific instruments, and plastic products.

Earnings of persons employed in Delaware increased from $15.7 billion in 1997 to $16.9 billion in 1998, an increase of 7.9%. The largest industries in 1998 were services, 23.1% of earnings; nondurable goods manufacturing, 21.0%; and finance, insurance, and real estate, 13.8%. Of the industries that accounted for at least 5% of earnings in 1998, the slowest growing from 1997 to 1998 was nondurable goods manufacturing, which increased 1.6%; the fastest was finance, insurance, and real estate, which increased 15.3%.

[30]COMMERCE

Wholesale trade in Delaware totaled $13 billion, conducted by 1,118 establishments in 1997. Retail sales totaled $8.6 billion, conducted by 5,040 establishments. The leading types of retail enterprises were food stores, 10%; automotive dealers, 12%; and eating and drinking places, 28%. Food sales totaled $1.3 billion, and general merchandise sales totaled one billion in 1997. In 1998, Delaware exported $2.2 billion worth of products to foreign markets.

[31]CONSUMER PROTECTION

The Consumer Protection Unit of the Attorney General's Office is responsible for enforcing state consumer protection laws. It investigates consumer complaints; mediates resolution, when appropriate; and takes enforcement, when warranted. It also provides consumer education programs.

[32]BANKING

At the end of 2002, there were 37 insured banks in Delaware. Delaware was home to six of the nation's 41 insured credit card banks in 2002, including three of the nation's five largest. These credit card banks manage or hold one-third of total credit card loans nationally. Total assets as of September 2002 for Delaware's 37 insured institutions were $186 billion. Banking is Delaware's most profitable industry: 12% of jobs and 36% of the gross state product are represented by the finance insurance and real estate (FIRE) sectors. Since 2001, however, FIRE employment declined steadily (as of 2003). As of late 2002, the median past-due loan rate increased, due to an increase in multifamily and construction loan delinquency rates, weakening credit quality among the state's insured institutions. The median net interest margin (NIM) (the difference between the lower rates offered to savers and the higher rates charged on loans) in 2002 was above the level in 2001, but as long-term interest rates reached historic lows, and short-term interest rates declined to a lesser extent, asset yields and funding costs declined.

[33]INSURANCE

In 2001 there were 518,000 ordinary life insurance policies in force with a total value of $36 billion; total value for all categories of life insurance (ordinary, group, industrial, and credit) was $86.1 billion. Death benefits paid that year totaled $221.5 million. As of 2003, there were 87 property and casualty and 46 life and health insurance companies incorporated or organized in the state. In 2001, property and casualty insurers wrote premiums totaling $1.5 billion. That year, there were 16,810 flood insurance policies in force in the state, with a total value of $2.4 million.

[34]SECURITIES

Delaware has no securities exchanges. There are over 487 broker and dealer firms in the state, with over 2,500 employees. A total of 39 registered investment advisory organizations operate in Delaware. The state is home to nine NASDAQ companies, and is the incorporator of over 910 NYSE listed companies (the most of all states). The top five companies in 2000 according to revenue are; GM, Wal-Mart, Ford, Citigroup, and Boeing.

³⁵PUBLIC FINANCE

The Budget Director has lead responsibility for preparing Delaware's annual executive budget for submission to the legislature in January, which is expected to adopt a budget by 30 June for the fiscal year, which begins 1 July. There are both constitutional and statutory requirements that the governor submit, the legislature adopt, and the governor sign, a balanced budget.

The general fund budget for 2002/03 totaled $2.39 billion, a 3.9% increase over the budget for 2001/02, and included a 2% increase for state employees. In June 2003, Delaware's revenue estimating council (the Delaware Economic and Financial Advisory Council or DEFAC) increased its estimates for 2001/02 and 2002/03 by $49 million, eliminating the need for a proposed hike in the cigarette tax. The budget crunch that afflicted most states in 2002 and 2003 was relatively mild in Delaware. Businesses incorporate in Delaware but most do not actually operate there, so while the recession and collapse of the stock market affected capital gains income elsewhere it mainly affected incorporation fees in Delaware. Even bankrupt companies are likely to maintain the incorporation status, although many did disappear without a trace and without paying their fees in 2001–03. Shortfalls in expected revenues led to cuts in Delaware's budgets after they were enacted—$23.8 million in 2002 and $44.1 million in 2003, mainly through across-the-board percentage cuts which exempted only debt service. The rainy day fund (the Budget Reserve Account), which requires a three-fifths vote of the legislature to activate, was not tapped, however, and there were no tax increases.

The general fund budget for 2003/04 was proposed at $2.432 billion, 1.6% above 2002/03. Appropriations included 41.5% for public and higher education, 30.7% for health, social services, and services for children and youth, 7.8% for corrections, 3.8% for safety and homeland security, and 16.2% for judicial and other operating expenses. Sources of revenues included business taxes (combination of corporate fees, business gross receipts taxes, franchise taxes, and the corporate income tax totaling 36.4%); personal income tax (29.4%); lottery earnings (9%); and abandoned corporate property turned over to the state (5%).

The following table from the US Census Bureau contains information on revenues, expenditures, indebtedness, and cash/securities for 2001.

	($000)	PERCENT	PER CAPITA
Population (thousands, 2001)	797	(X)	(X)
Total Revenue	5,114,008	100.00	6,416.57
General revenue	4,459,029	87.19	5,594.77
Utility revenue	9,400	0.18	11.79
Insurance trust revenue	645,579	12.62	810.01
Exhibit: Salaries and wages	1,027,032	23.82	1,288.62
Total expenditure	4,311,551	100.00	5,409.73
General expenditure	3,952,326	91.67	4,959.00
Education	1,368,755	31.75	1,717.38
Public welfare	608,127	14.10	763.02
Hospitals	66,546	1.54	83.50
Health	242,769	5.63	304.60
Highways	341,003	7.91	427.86
Police protection	66,259	1.54	83.14
Correction	247,987	5.75	311.15
Natural resources	81,047	1.88	101.69
Parks and recreation	52,842	1.23	66.30
Government administration	326,708	7.58	409.92
Interest on general debt	188,722	4.38	236.79
Other and unallocable	361,561	8.39	453.65
Utility expenditure	67,711	1.57	84.96
Insurance trust expenditure	291,514	6.76	365.76
Debt at end of fiscal year	3,888,567	100.00	4,879.01
Cash and security holdings	11,286,551	100.00	14,161.29

³⁶TAXATION

Delaware is the country's corporate tax haven, with over half of its publicly held corporations registered there, including 58% of the Fortune 500. Corporations are attracted by Delaware's exemption from taxation of the subsidiaries of holding companies (so the holding-company headquarters are located in Delaware and the operating subsidiaries generally elsewhere). Financial institutions are attracted by its absence of usury limits. The fees paid by hundreds of thousands companies allow it to be one of five states with no sales tax. Combined state and local taxes in 2003 amounted to 7.3% of income, the 3rd smallest percentage in the US, ahead of only New Hampshire and Alaska. In Delaware's state tax revenues come primarily from levies on personal and corporate income, inheritance and estates, motor fuels, cigarettes, state lottery, and alcoholic beverages.

Delaware's individual income tax is a seven-bracket progressive schedule ranging from 2.2% to 5.55% for income under $60,000 and 5.95% for income over that amount. Personal exemptions are in the form of $110 tax credits per adult and per child. There is no general sales tax, but selective sales taxes (excises) are imposed on gasoline (23 cents per gallon) and other motor fuels, cigarettes (24 cents a pack) and other tobacco products, alcoholic beverages, amusements, insurance premiums, pari-mutuels, public utilities, and other selected items. The corporate income tax is a flat tax of 8.7%. As part of their business and occupational license fees, businesses are assessed a gross receipts tax ranging from 0.096% to 1.92%, with the highest rate applied to rentals. Except for rentals, license fees also include an annual flat fee (generally $75 per business establishment) and monthly exclusions from the gross receipts tax ($1million for manufacturers and $50,000 for most services). The annual franchise tax ranges from a minimum of $35 to a maximum of $165,000, calculated either according to the number of authorized shares in the company (the minimum applying to companies with 3,000 or fewer shares) or according to the assumed par value of capital (the minimum applying to assumed par values of less than $140,000, and the maximum reached at a par value of $660 million). As is true for most states, Delaware's estate tax is set equal to the federal exemption from the payment of the federal death tax for the payment of state death taxes (estate taxes), and is, therefore, scheduled to be phased out by 2007 in tandem with the phase-out of the federal tax credit, absent countervailing action by the state. Revenue losses from the phase-out of Delaware's estate tax are estimated at $7.6 million in 2003, $16.3 million in 2004, and $34.7 million in 2007. Delaware has repealed its gift tax. Other taxes include various state license fees, a lodging tax, a realty transfer tax and local property taxes.

In 2003, state tax collections totaled $2.174 billion, or $2,692 per capita, including 36% from licenses, 33% from individual income taxes, 14.8% from selective sales taxes, 11.5% from corporate income taxes, and 1.9% from death and gift taxes.

The following table from the US Census Bureau provides a summary of taxes collected by the state in 2002.

	($000)	PER CAPITA
Total Taxes	2,173,600	2,692.15
Property taxes	(X)	(X)
Sales and gross receipts	322,835	399.85
General sales and gross receipts	(X)	(X)
Selective sales taxes	322,835	399.85
Alcoholic beverage	11,739	14.54
Amusements	(X)	(X)
Insurance Premiums	76,178	94.35
Motor fuels	107,713	133.41
Pari-mutuels	198	0.25
Public utilities	30,477	37.75
Tobacco products	27,652	34.25
Other selective sales	68,878	85.31

	($000)	PER CAPITA
Licenses (continued)		
Alcoholic beverages	627	0.78
Amusements	373	0.46
Corporation	533,528	660.81
Hunting and fishing	931	1.15
Motor vehicle	31,850	39.45
Motor vehicle operators	200	0.25
Public utility	3,442	4.26
Occupation and business, NEC	185,591	229.87
Other	23,830	29.52
Other taxes	1,070,393	1,325.75
Individual income	716,647	887.61
Corporation net income	251,643	311.68
Death and gift	41,342	51.2
Documentary and stock transfer	60,192	74.55
Severance	(X)	(X)
Other	569	0.7

37 ECONOMIC POLICY

Legislation passed in 1899 permits companies to be incorporated and chartered in Delaware even if they do no business in the state and hold their stockholders' meetings elsewhere. Another incentive to chartering in Delaware is the state's court of chancery, which has extensive experience in dealing with corporate problems.

The Delaware Economic Development Office (DEDO) seeks to create jobs by helping existing businesses to grow and by encouraging out-of-state companies to relocate to Delaware. The Development Office offers a variety of financing programs for small businesses, including assistance with land acquisition, loans and tax credits for capital investments, and state grants to match federal awards for research and development. The Delaware Innovation Fund is a private, non-profit public/private initiative to assist companies with pre-startup seed money, with long-term loans for establishing patents, business plans, and to begin commercialization ($10,000–$150,000). In the year 2000, the Delaware Economic Development Office Director, and several Delaware lawmakers led a trade mission to Taiwan, establishing a Delaware-Taiwan trade office. In 2003, DEDO was one of 70 organizations participating in bioscience "hotbed" campaign, a concerted effort by a group made up of government development agencies, pharmaceutical and bioscience companies, research institutes, universities, and non-profits to attract capital, personnel and resources to develop a life sciences cluster. Delaware, Maryland, Virginia and Washington DC are recognized as forming a major life sciences hub, dubbed the BioCapital hub by the industry.

38 HEALTH

Infant mortality for 2000 was 9.2 per 1,000 live births. With an overall death rate of 902 per 100,000 residents (higher than the national average), Delaware had lower death rates than the nation as a whole for heart diseases, cerebrovascular diseases, motor vehicle accidents, and suicide, but higher death rates for accidents, chronic liver and pulmonary diseases. Many of Delaware's residents 18 years of age and older (approximately 23%) were smokers in 2000. In 2000, the HIV-related death rate (8.9 per 100,000 population) was much higher than the US rate (5.3 per 100,000 population); 2,827 AIDS cases had been reported through 2001.

Delaware's five community hospitals had 83,047 admissions and 1,853 beds in 2001. There were 2,820 full-time registered nurses and 210 full-time licensed practical nurses in 2001 and 261 physicians per 100,000 population in that same year. The average expense of a community hospital for care was $1,317.60 per inpatient day.

Federal government grants to cover the Medicare and Medicaid services in 2001 totaled $332 million; 113,967 enrollees received Medicare benefits that year. At least 9.2% of the population was uninsured in 2002.

39 SOCIAL WELFARE

Delaware does not have a history of expansive social programs. A survey made in 1938 found that the state, which then ranked fourth nationally in per capita income, spent little more than the poorest southern states on public assistance. By 1991, however, the state ranked 25th in terms of public aid recipients as a percentage of population.

In 2001, the average weekly unemployment benefit was $218.38. Average monthly participation in the food stamp program in FY2002 comprised 39,628 persons (16,483 households). The average monthly benefit was $82.63, and the sum total of benefits paid in FY2002 was $39,293,407.

With the enactment of the Personal Responsibility and Work Opportunity Reconciliation Act of 1996, the US government has changed the form and regulations for many of its social welfare programs. Most significantly, it replaces Aid to Families with Dependent Children (AFDC), an open-ended entitlement program, with Temporary Assistance for Needy Families (TANF), a limited system of assistance funded largely through federal block grants. The reform act also impacts the food stamp program, the Supplemental Security Income program, and the child nutrition program. The law took effect on 1 July 1997 and provided $16.38 billion in block grants for fiscal years 1997–2002. The grants are to be divided among the states based on an equation involving the numbers of former AFDC recipients in each state.

Reauthorization of the 1996 social welfare legislation, scheduled for 2002, was delayed, and the original law had been extended three times as of July 2003, with the most recent extension running through September 2003. Delaware's TANF program is called ABC (A Better Chance). In June 2000 the state had 17,262 welfare recipients. State expenditures on the TANF program in FY2002 totaled $25,966,885.

In December 2001, Social Security benefits were paid to 137,170 Delaware residents. This number included 89,140 retired workers, 13,710 widows and widowers, 16,010 disabled workers, 7,520 spouses, and 10,790 children. Social Security beneficiaries represented 16.9% of the total state population and 92.9% of the state's population age 65 and older. Retired workers (excluding persons with special benefits) received an average monthly payment of $913; widows and widowers, $882; disabled workers, $843; and spouses, $473. Payments for children of retired workers averaged $423 per month; children of deceased workers, $611; and children of disabled workers, $258.

Federal Supplemental Security Income payments in December 2001 went to 12,197 Delaware residents, averaging $362 a month.

40 HOUSING

In 2002, there were approximately 352,031 housing units in Delaware, of which 306,205 were occupied; 73.4% were owner-occupied. About 55.9% of all units were single-family, detached homes. It was estimated that about 5,382 units lacked telephone service, 768 lacked complete plumbing facilities, and 638 lacked complete kitchen facilities. Most homes are heated by gas or electricity. The average household size was 2.55 people.

In 2002, there were 6,331 new privately owned housing units authorized for construction. The same year, Delaware received over $14 million in community planning and development aid from the US Department of Housing and Urban Development. The median home value was $145,004. The median monthly cost for mortgage owners was $1,149 while renters paid a median of $679 per month.

41 EDUCATION

The development of public support and financing for an adequate public educational system was the handiwork of progressive industrialist Pierre S. du Pont, who undertook the project in 1919. Today's schools compare favorably with those of neighboring states. Approximately 82.6% of adult Delawareans were high school graduates in 2000; 25% had obtained a bachelor's degree or higher.

In fall 1999, 112,836 students were enrolled in public elementary and secondary schools. Of these, 80,274 attended schools from kindergarten through grade eight, and 32,562 attended high school. Minority students made up approximately 40% of the total enrollment in public elementary and secondary schools in 2001. Total enrollment was estimated at 114,424 in fall 2000 and expected to remain the same in fall 2005. Enrollment in nonpublic schools in fall 2001 was 22,779.

As of fall 2000, there were 51,407 students enrolled in institutions of higher education. In the same year Delaware had 10 degree-granting institutions. In 1997, minority students comprised 20.4% of total postsecondary enrollment. Delaware has two public four-year institutions: the University of Delaware (Newark) and Delaware State College (Dover). Alternatives to these institutions include Widener University and the Delaware Technical and Community College, which has four campuses. There are three independent colleges: Goldey-Beacom College (Wilmington), Wesley College (Dover), and Wilmington College.

42 ARTS

The Delaware Division of the Arts (DDOA) is a branch of the Delaware Department of State, which administers arts-related grants and programs. The Delaware State Arts Council serves as the advisory board for the DDOA. In 2003, Delaware arts organizations received $610,400 of grant money from the National Endowment for the Arts. The Delaware Humanities Forum, an independent, non-profit organization was established in 1973 to sponsor programs and distribute grants to organizations promoting the understanding and appreciation of the humanities. In 2000, the National Endowment for the Humanities award three grants totaling $641,612 for state programs. In 1998, the state's arts programs attracted audiences numbering over 1.62 million, including 397,000 visitors from out of state. The same year, at least 136,000 children and youth were involved in the arts through classes and workshops.

Wilmington has a local symphony orchestra, opera society, and drama league. The Playhouse, located in the Du Pont Building in Wilmington, shows first-run Broadway plays. The restored Grand Opera House in Wilmington, Delaware's Center for the Performing Arts, is the home of the Delaware Symphony and the Delaware Opera Guild as well as host to performances of popular music and ballet.

43 LIBRARIES AND MUSEUMS

Delaware had three public library systems in 2000, with 1,445,000 books and other materials and a circulation of 4,196,000. The University of Delaware's Hugh M. Morris Library, with 2,259,121 volumes, is the largest academic library in the state. Other distinguished libraries include the Eleutherian Mills Historical Library, the Winterthur Library, and the Historical Society of Delaware Library (Wilmington). The Delaware Library Information connects all types of libraries through a statewide computer/telecommunication system. Total public library income came to $14,513,000 in 2000, including $101,591 in federal grants and $2,017,307 in state grants.

Notable among the state's 27 museums and numerous historical sites are the Hagley Museum and Delaware Art Museum, both in Wilmington, where the Historical Society of Delaware maintains a museum in the Old Town Hall. The Henry Francis du Pont Winterthur Museum features a collection of American antiques and decorative arts. The Brandywine Zoo, adjacent to Rockford Park, is popular with Wilmington's children. The Delaware State Museum is in Dover.

44 COMMUNICATIONS

In 2001, about 95.7% of Delaware's housing units had telephones. The state had 5 AM and 9 FM major radio stations and three television stations in 2003, with one public television station based in Seaford. Philadelphia and Baltimore commercial television stations are within range. A total of 19,351 Internet domain names were registered in Delaware by 2000.

45 PRESS

The *Wilmington Morning News* and the *Wilmington Evening Journal* merged with the *News Journal* in 1989. The *News Journal* has a daily (afternoon) circulation of 121,480 (141,471 on Sunday), as of 2002. In the state's capital is the *Delaware State News* with a daily and Sunday circulation averaging at about 18,753, as of 2002. Statewide, there were two morning, one evening, and two Sunday papers in 2002. Smaller publications include the *Dover Post* and the *Delaware Coast Press*. Magazines include *Delaware Today*.

46 ORGANIZATIONS

In 2003, there were about 408 regional, national, and international organizations within the state.

Among national organizations headquartered in Delaware are the International Reading Association, the Jean Piaget Society, and the American Philosophical Association, all located in Newark. State arts and educational organizations include the Delaware Academy of Medicine and the Historical Society of Delaware.

47 TOURISM, TRAVEL, AND RECREATION

Delaware's travel and recreation industry is second only to manufacturing in economic importance. But the Delaware Tourism Office continues to work on ways to improve the industry within the state. In 2001, the state launched a new brand campaign entitled, "Delaware: It's Good to be First," which plays upon the state's claim as the first of the original 13 states to ratify the Constitution. In 2001, there were about 12 million visitors to the state. About 36% were day-trip travelers from surrounding states. Shopping (with no sales tax) and the state's beaches are the most popular attractions.

Rehoboth Beach on the Atlantic Coast bills itself as the "Nation's Summer Capital" because of the many federal officials and foreign diplomats who summer there. Events are the Delaware Kite Festival at Cape Henlopen State Park (east of Lewes) every Good Friday, Old Dover Days during the first weekend in May, and Delaware Day ceremonies (7 December, commemorating the day in 1787 when the state ratified the Constitution) throughout the state. Fort Delaware is a popular historic site. Fishing, clamming, crabbing, boating, and swimming are the main recreational attractions.

48 SPORTS

Delaware has two major horse-racing tracks: Harrington, which has harness racing, and Dover Downs, which also has a track for auto racing. The MBNA Platinum 500 stock car race is held in June and the MBNA.com 400 is run in September. Thoroughbred races are held at Delaware Park in Wilmington. Wilmington has a minor league baseball team, the Blue Rocks, in the Carolina League. Additionally, the Fightin' Blue Hens of the University of Delaware field teams in a large number of both men's and women's sports.

[49]FAMOUS DELAWAREANS

Three Delawareans have served as US secretary of state: Louis McLane (1786–1857), John M. Clayton (1796–1856), and Thomas F. Bayard (1828–98). Two Delawareans have been judges on the Permanent Court of International Justice at The Hague: George Gray (1840–1925) and John Bassett Moore (1860–1947). James A. Bayard (b.Pennsylvania, 1767–1815), a US senator from Delaware from 1805 to 1813, was chosen to negotiate peace terms for ending the War of 1812 with the British.

John Dickinson (b.Maryland, 1732–1808), the "Penman of the Revolution," and Caesar Rodney (1728–84), wartime chief executive of Delaware, were notable figures of the Revolutionary era. George Read (b.Maryland, 1733–98) and Thomas McKean (b.Pennsylvania, 1734–1817) were, with Rodney, signers for Delaware of the Declaration of Independence. Naval officers of note include Thomas Macdonough (1783–1825) in the War of 1812 and Samuel F. du Pont (b.New Jersey, 1803–65) in the Civil War.

Morgan Edwards (b.England, 1722–95), Baptist minister and historian, was a founder of Brown University. Richard Allen (b.Pennsylvania, 1760–1831) and Peter Spencer (1779–1843) established separate denominations of African Methodists. Welfare worker Emily P. Bissell (1861–1948) popularized the Christmas seal in the US, and Florence Bayard Hilles (1865–1954) was president of the National Woman's Party.

Among scientists and engineers were Oliver Evans (1755–1819), inventor of a high-pressure steam engine; Edward Robinson Squibb (1819–1900), physician and pharmaceuticals manufacturer; Wallace H. Carothers (b.Iowa, 1896–1937), developer of nylon at Du Pont; and Daniel Nathans (1928–99), who shared the Nobel Prize in medicine in 1978 for his research on molecular genetics. Eleuthère I. du Pont (b.France, 1771–1834) founded the company that bears his name; Pierre S. du Pont (1870–1954) was architect of its modern growth.

Delaware authors include Robert Montgomery Bird (1806–54), playwright; Hezekiah Niles (b.Pennsylvania, 1777–1839), journalist; Christopher Ward (1868–1944), historian; Henry Seidel Canby (1878–1961), critic; and novelist Anne Parrish (b.Colorado, 1888–1957). Howard Pyle (1853–1911) was known as a writer, teacher, and artist-illustrator.

[50]BIBLIOGRAPHY

Blashfield, Jean F. *Delaware*. New York: Children's Press, 2000.

Boyer, William W. *Governing Delaware: Policy Problems in the First State*. Newark: University of Delaware Press, 2000.

Colbert, Judy. *Maryland and Delaware: Off the Beaten Path*. Old Saybrook, Conn.: Globe Pequot Press, 1999.

Essah, Patience. *A House Divided: Slavery and Emancipation in Delaware, 1638–1865*. Charlottesville, Va.: University Press of Virginia, 1996.

Federal Writers Project. *Delaware: A Guide to the First State*. Reprint. New York: Somerset, 1955 (orig. 1938).

Hoffecker. Carol E. *Delaware: A Bicentennial History*. New York: Norton, 1977.

Mosley, Leonard. *Blood Relations: The Rise and Fall of Du Ponts of Delaware*. New York: Atheneum, 1980.

Munroe, John A. *Colonial Delaware: A History*. Millwood, N.Y.: KTO Press, 1978.

———. *History of Delaware*. 4th ed. Newark: University of Delaware Press, 2001.

Vessels, Jane. *Delaware: Small Wonder*. New York: Abrams, 1984.

FLORIDA

State of Florida

ORIGIN OF STATE NAME: Named in 1513 by Juan Ponce de León, who landed during *Pascua Florida*, the Easter festival of flowers. **NICKNAME:** The Sunshine State. **CAPITAL:** Tallahassee. **ENTERED UNION:** 3 March 1845 (27th). **SONG:** "Old Folks at Home" (also known as "The Swannee River"). **MOTTO:** In God We Trust. **FLAG:** The state seal appears in the center of a white field, with four red bars extending from the seal to each corner; the flag is fringed on three sides. **OFFICIAL SEAL:** In the background, the sun's rays shine over a distant highland; in the foreground are a sabal palmetto palm, a steamboat, and an Indian woman scattering flowers on the ground. The words "Great Seal of the State of Florida" and the state motto surround the whole. **ANIMAL:** Florida panther. **MARINE MAMMALS:** Manatee, dolphin (saltwater). **BIRD:** Mockingbird. **FISH:** Largemouth bass (freshwater), Atlantic sailfish (saltwater). **FLOWER:** Orange blossom. **TREE:** Sabal palmetto palm. **GEM:** Moonstone. **STONE:** Agatized coral. **SHELL:** Horse conch. **BEVERAGE:** Orange juice. **LEGAL HOLIDAYS:** New Year's Day, 1 January; Robert E. Lee's Birthday, 19 January; Birthday of Martin Luther King, Jr., 3rd Monday in January; Lincoln's Birthday, 12 February; Susan B. Anthony's Birthday, 15 February; Washington's Birthday, 3rd Monday in February; Shrove Tuesday, February or March; Good Friday, March or April; Pascua Florida Day, 2 April; Confederate Memorial Day, 26 April; Memorial Day, last Monday in May; Jefferson Davis's Birthday, 3 June; Independence Day, 4 July; Labor Day, 1st Monday in September; Columbus Day and Farmers' Day, 2nd Monday in October; General Election Day, 1st Tuesday after the 1st Monday in November in even-numbered years; Veterans Day, 11 November; Thanksgiving Day, 4th Thursday in November; Christmas Day, 25 December. **TIME:** 7 AM EST = noon GMT; 6 AM CST = noon GMT.

¹LOCATION, SIZE, AND EXTENT

Located in the extreme southeastern US, Florida is the 2nd-largest state (after Georgia) east of the Mississippi River, and ranks 22nd in size among the 50 states.

The total area of Florida is 58,664 sq mi (151,939 sq km), of which land takes up 54,153 sq mi (140,256 sq km) and inland water 4,511 sq mi (11,683 sq km). Florida extends 361 mi (581 km) E–W; its maximum N–S extension is 447 mi (719 km). The state comprises a peninsula surrounded by ocean on three sides, with a panhandle of land in the NW.

Florida is bordered on the N by Alabama and Georgia (with the line in the NE formed by the St. Marys River); on the E by the Atlantic Ocean; on the S by the Straits of Florida; and on the W by the Gulf of Mexico and Alabama (separated by the Perdido River).

Offshore islands include the Florida Keys, extending form the state's southern tip into the Gulf of Mexico. The total boundary length of Florida is 1,799 mi (2,895 km). The state's geographic center is in Hernando County, 12 mi (19 km) NNW of Brooksville.

²TOPOGRAPHY

Florida is a huge plateau, much of it barely above sea level. The highest point in the state is believed to be a hilltop in the panhandle, 345 ft (105 m) above sea level, near the city of Lakewood, in Walton County. No point in the state is more than 70 mi (113 km) from saltwater.

Most of the panhandle region is gently rolling country, much like that of southern Georgia and Alabama, except that large swampy areas cut in from the Gulf coast. Peninsular Florida, which contains extensive swampland, has a relatively elevated central spine of rolling country, dotted with lakes and springs. Its east coast is shielded from the Atlantic by a string of sandbars. The west coast is cut by numerous bays and inlets, and near its

southern tip are the Ten Thousand Islands, a mass of mostly tiny mangrove-covered islets. Southwest of the peninsula lies Key West, which, at 24°33' N, is the southernmost point of the US mainland.

Almost all the southeastern peninsula and the entire southern end are covered by the Everglades, the world's largest sawgrass swamp, with an area of approximately 5,000 sq mi (13,000 sq km). The Everglades is, in a sense, a huge river, in which water flows south–southwest from Lake Okeechobee to Florida Bay. No point in the Everglades is more than 7 ft (2 m) above sea level. Its surface is largely submerged during the rainy season—April to November—and becomes a muddy expanse in the dry months. Slight elevations, known as hammocks, support clumps of cypress and the only remaining stand of mahogany in the continental US. To the west and north of the Everglades is Big Cypress Swamp, covering about 2,400 sq mi (6,200 sq km), which contains far less surface water.

Lake Okeechobee, in south-central Florida, is the largest of the state's approximately 30,000 lakes, ponds, and sinks. With a surface area of about 700 sq mi (1,800 sq km), it is the fourth-largest natural lake located entirely within the US. Like all of Florida's lakes, it is extremely shallow, having a maximum depth of 15 ft (5 m), and was formed through the action of groundwater and rainfall in dissolving portions of the thick limestone layer that underlies Florida's sandy soil. The state's numerous underground streams and caverns were created in a similar manner. Because of the high water table, most of the caverns are filled, but some spectacular examples thick with stalactites can be seen in Florida Caverns State Park, near Marianna. More than 200 natural springs send up some seven billion gallons of groundwater per day through cracks in the limestone. Silver Springs, near Ocala in north-central Florida, has the largest average flow of all inland springs, 823 cu ft (23 cu m) per second.

Florida has more than 1,700 rivers, streams, and creeks. The longest river is the St. Johns, which empties into the Atlantic 19 mi (42 km) east of Jacksonville: estimates of its length range from 273 to 318 mi (439 to 512 km), an exact figure being elusive because of the swampy nature of the headwaters. Other major rivers are the Suwannee, which flows south from Georgia for 177 mi (285 km) through Florida and empties into the Gulf of Mexico; and the Apalachicola, formed by the Flint and Chattahoochee rivers at the Florida-Georgia border, and flowing southward across the panhandle for 94 mi (151 km) to the Gulf. Jim Woodruff Lock and Dam is located on the Apalachicola about 1,000 ft (300 m) below the confluence of the two feeder rivers. Completed in 1957, the dam created Lake Seminole, most of which is in Georgia.

More than 4,500 islands ring the mainland. Best known are the Florida Keys, of which Key Largo—about 29 mi (47 km) long and less than 2 mi (3 km) wide—is the largest. Key West—less than 4 mi (6 km) long and 2 mi (3 km) wide—a popular resort, is the westernmost.

For much of the geological history of the US, Florida was under water. During this time, the shells of countless millions of sea animals decayed to form the thick layers of limestone that now blanket the state. The peninsula rose above sea level perhaps 20 million years ago. Even then, the southern portion remained largely submerged, until the buildup of coral and sand around its rim blocked out the sea, leaving dense marine vegetation to decay and form the peaty soil of the present-day Everglades.

³CLIMATE

A mild, sunny climate is one of Florida's most important natural resources, making it a major tourist center and a retirement home for millions of transplanted northerners. Average annual temperatures range from 65° to 70°F (18° to 21°C) in the north, and from 74° to 77°F (23° to 25°C) in the southern peninsula and on the Keys. At Jacksonville, the average annual temperature is 68°F (20°C); the average low is 57°F (14°C), the average high 79°F (26°C). At Miami, the annual average is 76°F (24°C), with a low of 69°F (21°C) and a high of 83°F (28°C). Key West has the highest annual average temperature in the US, at 78.2°F (25.7°C). The record high temperature, 109°F (43°C), was registered at Monticello on 29 June 1931; the record low, –2°F (–19°C), at Tallahassee on 13 February 1899.

Florida's proximity to the Atlantic and the Gulf of Mexico, and the state's many inland lakes and ponds, together account for the high humidity and generally abundant rainfall, although precipitation can vary greatly from year to year and serious droughts have occurred. At Jacksonville, the average annual precipitation (1971–2000) was 52.3 in (132.8 cm), with an average of 116 days of precipitation a year. At Miami during the same period, precipitation averaged 58.5 in (148.6 cm), with 130 rainy days a year. Rainfall is unevenly distributed throughout the year, more than half generally occurring from June through September; periods of extremely heavy rainfall are common. The highest 24-hour total ever recorded in the US, 38.7 in (98.3 cm), fell at Yankeetown, west of Ocala on the Gulf coast, on 5–6 September 1950. Despite the high annual precipitation rate, the state also receives abundant sunshine—61% of the maximum possible at Jacksonville, and 68% at Miami. Snow is virtually unheard of in southern Florida but does fall on rare occasions in the panhandle and the northern peninsula.

Winds are generally from the east and southeast in the southern peninsula; in northern Florida, winds blow from the north in winter, bringing cold snaps, and from the south in summer. Average wind velocities are 7.9 mph (12.7 km/hr) at Jacksonville and 9.2 mph (14.8 km/hr) at Miami. Florida's long

coastline makes it highly vulnerable to hurricanes and tropical storms, which may approach from either the Atlantic or the Gulf coast, bringing winds of up to 150 mph (240 km/hr). Hurricane Donna, which struck the state 9–10 September 1960, and until 1992 was considered the most destructive in Florida's history, caused an estimated $300 million in damage. On 23–24 August 1992, Hurricane Andrew caused over $10 billion in damage in Florida, making it the most costly insured disaster in US history. In addition to hurricanes and tropical storms, tornadoes and waterspouts are not uncommon in Florida.

⁴FLORA AND FAUNA

Generally, Florida has seven floral zones: flatwoods, scrublands, grassy swamps, savannas, salt marshes, hardwood forests (hammocks), and pinelands. Flatwoods consist of open forests and an abundance of flowers, including more than 60 varieties of orchid. Small sand pines are common in the scrublands; other trees here are the saw palmetto, blackjack, and water oak. The savannas of central Florida support water lettuce, American lotus, and water hyacinth. North Florida's flora includes longleaf and other pines, oaks, and cypresses; one giant seminole cypress is thought to be 3,500 years old. The state is known for its wide variety of palms, but only 15 are native, and more than 100 have been introduced; common types include royal and coconut. Although pine has the most commercial importance, dense mangrove thickets grow along the lower coastal regions, and northern hardwood forests include varieties of rattan, magnolia, and oak. Numerous rare plants have been introduced, among them bougainvillea and oleander. All species of cacti and orchids are regarded as threatened, as are most types of ferns and palms. Endangered and threatened species, numbering 54 as of August 2003, include the key tree-cactus, Chapman rhododendron, Harper's beauty, fragrant prickly-apple, two species of pawpaw, four species of ming, and Florida torreya.

Florida once claimed more than 80 land mammals. The white-tailed deer, wild hog, and gray fox can still be found in the wild; such small mammals as the raccoon, eastern gray and fox squirrels, and cottontail and swamp rabbits remain common. Florida's bird population includes many resident and migratory species. The mockingbird was named the state bird in 1927; among game birds are the bobwhite quail, wild turkey, and at least 30 duck species. Several varieties of heron are found, as well as coastal birds such as gulls, pelicans, and frigates. The Arctic tern stops in Florida during its remarkable annual migration between the North and South poles.

Common Florida reptiles are the diamondback rattler and various water snakes. Turtle species include mud, green, and loggerhead, and various lizards abound. More than 300 native butterflies have been identified. The peninsula is famous for its marine life: scores of freshwater and saltwater fish, rays, shrimps, live coral reefs, and marine worms.

All of Florida's lands have been declared sanctuaries for the bald eagle, of which Florida has about 350 pair (2nd only to Alaska among the 50 states). The state's unusually long list of threatened and endangered wildlife (57 species) as of August 2003 included the American crocodile, shortnose sturgeon, six species of sea turtle, red-cockaded woodpecker, Florida panther, key deer, West Indian (Florida) manatee, six species of mouse, Key Largo woodrat, Everglade snail kite, two species of sparrow, Atlantic salt marsh snake, eastern indigo snake, Okaloosa darter, Stock Island tree snail, and Schaus swallowtail butterfly.

⁵ENVIRONMENTAL PROTECTION

Throughout the 20th century, a rapidly growing population, the expansion of agriculture, and the exploitation of such resources as timber and minerals have put severe pressure on Florida's natural environment.

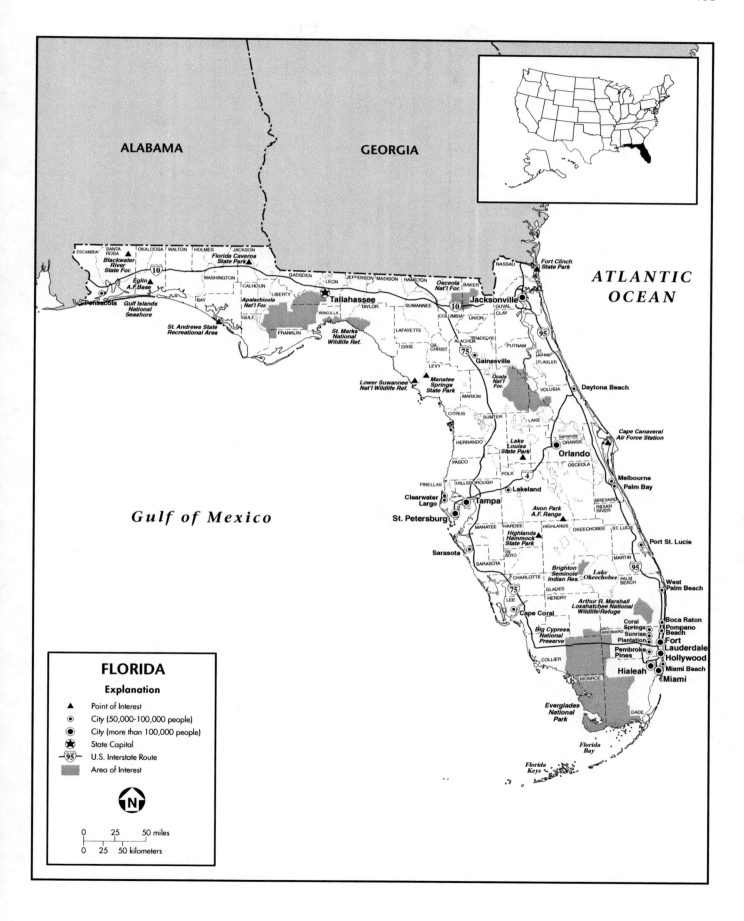

ALABAMA

GEORGIA

ATLANTIC
OCEAN

ESCAMBIA
SANTA ROSA
OKALOOSA
WALTON
HOLMES
JACKSON
Blackwater River State For.
Florida Caverns State Park
Eglin A.F. Base
Pensacola
Gulf Islands National Seashore
St. Andrews State Recreational Area
WASHINGTON
CALHOUN
BAY
GULF
FRANKLIN
Apalachicola Nat'l For.
GADSDEN
LIBERTY
LEON
Tallahassee
WAKULLA
St. Marks National Wildlife Ref.
JEFFERSON
MADISON
HAMILTON
TAYLOR
SUWANNEE
LAFAYETTE
DIXIE
GIL CHRIST
Osceola Nat'l For.
BAKER
COLUMBIA
UNION
BRADFORD
ALACHUA
Jacksonville
DUVAL
CLAY
NASSAU
Fort Clinch State Park
ST. JOHNS
PUTNAM
FLAGLER
Lower Suwannee Nat'l Wildlife Ref.
Manatee Springs State Park
LEVY
Gainesville
MARION
Ocala Nat'l For.
VOLUSIA
Daytona Beach
CITRUS
SUMTER
LAKE
HERNANDO
Lake Louisa State Park
Seminole
ORANGE
Orlando
Cape Canaveral Air Force Station
PASCO
OSCEOLA
POLK
PINELLAS
HILLSBOROUGH
Lakeland
Melbourne
Palm Bay
BREVARD
Clearwater
Largo
Tampa
St. Petersburg
Avon Park A.F. Range
INDIAN RIVER
MANATEE
HARDEE
HIGHLANDS
Highlands Hammock State Park
ST. LUCIE
Port St. Lucie
Sarasota
SARASOTA
DE SOTO
OKEECHOBEE
MARTIN
Brighton Seminole Indian Res.
Lake Okeechobee
PALM BEACH
West Palm Beach
CHARLOTTE
GLADES
LEE
HENDRY
Arthur R. Marshall Loxahatchee National Wildlife Refuge
Boca Raton
Pompano Beach
Cape Coral
Coral Springs
Sunrise
Plantation
Fort Lauderdale
Big Cypress National Preserve
BROWARD
Pembroke Pines
Hollywood
COLLIER
Hialeah
Miami Beach
Miami
MONROE
DADE
Everglades National Park
Florida Bay
Florida Keys

Gulf of Mexico

FLORIDA

Explanation

▲ Point of Interest
◉ City (50,000-100,000 people)
◉ City (more than 100,000 people)
★ State Capital
—95— U.S. Interstate Route
░ Area of Interest

N

0   25   50 miles
0   25   50 kilometers

The state agency principally responsible for safeguarding the environment is the Department of Environmental Protection (DEP), created in 1993 by the merger of the Departments of Natural Resources and Environmental Regulation. Its duties include implementing state pollution control laws and improving water-resource management. The Department oversees and coordinates the activities of the state's five water-management districts, which have planning and regulatory responsibilities. The Department also protects the state's coastal and marine resources. Its Division of State Lands acquires environmentally endangered tracts of land in what has been called the nation's largest environmental land-buying program. More than 1.2 million acres of environmentally important lands have been purchased. The Department also administers state parks and wilderness lands.

The Department of Agriculture and Consumer Services' Division of Forestry manages four state forests plus the Talquin State Lands. The Game and Fresh Water Fish Commission manages nature preserves and regulates hunting and fishing.

Growth, contamination of groundwater, and control of stormwater (non-point sources) are the state's most serious environmental problems. Groundwater supplies 90% of the drinking water in the state, as well as 8.2% of industry's needs and 53% of agricultural uses. Groundwater, surface water, and soil contamination have been found across the state. Among the major contaminants were the pesticides ethylene dibromide (EDB) (2,300 wells statewide) and other chemicals (about 1,000 additional wells). The state's program to clean groundwater contaminated by leaking underground storage tanks is one of the nation's largest and pioneered the pattern followed by many other states. Florida's groundwater quality standards are among the most stringent in the nation.

Contamination of groundwater is not the state's only water problem. The steadily increasing demand for water for both residential and farm use has reduced the subterranean runoff of fresh water into the Atlantic and the Gulf of Mexico. As a result, saltwater from these bodies has begun seeping into the layers of porous limestone that hold Florida's reserves of fresh water. This problem has been aggravated in some areas by the cutting of numerous inlets by developers of coastal property.

The DEP and South Florida Water Management District are undertaking, with various federal agencies, a massive restoration program for the Kissimmee River, Lake Okeechobee, the Everglades, and Florida Bay. This undertaking resulted from the settlement of a lawsuit brought by the federal government. The restoration effort includes: rechannelization of the Kissimmee River canal to restore its floodplains and prevent water pollution from entering Lake Okeechobee; other measures to reduce suficants in the lake caused by agricultural operations around its edges; creation of large stormwater treatment areas within the Everglades to treat nutrient-rich agricultural waters that are upsetting the ecological balance of the Everglades; and hydrological corrections to improve water delivery to the Everglades and Florida Bay.

In 1960, the only undersea park in the US, the John Pennekamp Coral Reef State Park, was established in a 75-sq-mi (194-sq-km) sector off the Atlantic coast of Key Largo, in an effort to protect a portion of the beautiful reefs, rich in tropical fish and other marine life, that adjoin the Keys. Untreated sewage from the Miami area, runoff water polluted by pesticides and other chemicals, dredging associated with coastal development, and the removal of countless pieces of live coral by growing numbers of tourists and souvenir dealers have severely damaged large areas of the reefs. However, most of the Keys is now a National Marine Sanctuary and efforts are being made to improve water quality.

In 2003, the Environmental Protection Agency's database listed 598 hazardous waste sites, 51 of which were on the National Priorities List, in Florida. In 2001, Florida received $117,565,000 in federal grants from the EPA; EPA expenditures for procurement contracts in Florida that year amounted to $2,150,000.

6POPULATION

Florida, the most populous state in the southeastern US, is also one of the fastest growing of the 50 states. In 1960, it was the 10th most populous state; by 1980, it ranked 7th with a population of 9,746,324; and by 1990, it ranked 4th, with a population of 12,937,926. Between 1990 and 2000, Florida had the 3rd-largest population gain among the states, surpassed only by California and Texas. In that decade, Florida's population grew from 12,937,926 to 15,982,378, an increase of 23.5% (also one of the largest percentage gains in the country). In 2002, Florida had the 4th-largest population of all 50 states, with an estimated total of 16,713,149, a 4.6% increase since 2000. By 2025 Florida is expected to be the 3rd most populous state, with a population of 20.7 million.

The first US census to include Florida, in 1830, recorded a total population of only 34,730. By 1860, on the eve of the Civil War, the population had more than quadrupled, to 140,424 people; about 80% of them lived in the state's northern rim, where cotton and sugarcane plantations flourished. Newcomers migrating southward in the late 19th century through the early 1920s sharply increased the state's population; the 1930 census was the first in which the state passed the million mark. Migration from other states, especially of retirees, caused a population explosion in the post-World War II period, with much of the increase occurring along the south Atlantic coast. From 1950 to 1960, Florida's population increased 79%—the fastest rate of all the states. From 1960 to 1970, the growth rate was 37%; from 1970 to 1980, 44%; from 1980 to 1990, 33%; and from 1990 to 1998, 15.3%.

In 2000, the average population density was 296.4 per sq mi, the eighth highest in the nation. The median age of the population was 38.7. Nearly 22.8% of the population was under age 18 while over 17.6% of was 65 years of age or older, the highest such percentage of all the states and nearly 50% above the US average.

The most populous city in Florida is Jacksonville, the 14th-largest city in the US in 2002. Its population in that year was estimated at 762,461. Miami is Florida's 2nd-largest city, with an estimated 2002 population of 374,791. The Miami-Ft. Lauderdale metropolitan area, the state's largest metropolitan region, had an estimated 3,711,102 residents in 1999; the Jacksonville metropolitan area's population was 1,056,332. Florida's 2nd-largest metropolitan area was Tampa-St. Petersburg-Clearwater, with an estimated 2,278,169 residents; the city of Tampa had an estimated 315,140 people in 2002, and St. Petersburg had 248,546. Ft. Lauderdale had an estimated population of 158,194 in 2002. Tallahassee, the state capital, had a population of 155,171.

7ETHNIC GROUPS

Florida's population consists mainly of whites of northern European stock, blacks, and Hispanics. European immigrants came primarily from Germany and the United Kingdom. Germans were particularly important in the development of the citrus fruit industry. Since World War II, the development of southern Florida as a haven for retired northerners has added new population elements to the state, a trend augmented by the presence of numerous military bases.

Florida's foreign-born population numbered 2,670,828 in 2000, or 16.7% of the state total—the fourth-highest percentage of foreign born in the nation. The largest group of first- and second-generation residents are Cubans, who represented 5.2%

of Florida's population in 2000. There were 2,682,715 Hispanics and Latinos in 2000, including 833,120 Cubans (more than 100,000 of whom arrived on Florida shores as refugees in 1980), 482,027 Puerto Ricans, and 363,925 Mexicans.

The nonwhite population, as reported in 2000, was 3,517,349, or 12% of the total state population. Black-white relations in the 20th century were tense. There were race riots following World War I, and the Ku Klux Klan was openly active until World War II. One of the worst race riots in US history devastated black areas of Miami in the spring of 1980. The black population was estimated at 2,335,505 as of 2000, the fourth-largest in the nation.

Florida's indigenous inhabitants resisted encroachment from settlers longer and more militantly than tribes in other seaboard states. The leaders in resistance were the Seminole, most of whom by the 1850s had been killed or removed to other states, had fled to the Florida swamplands, or had been assimilated as small farmers. No peace treaty was signed with the Seminole until 1934, following the Indian Reorganization Act that attempted to establish tribal integrity and self-government for Indian nations. In 1939, the Native American population was reported as only 600, but the 2000 census reported a figure of 53,541 Native Americans. The difference is too large to be explained by natural increase, and there is no evidence of marked in-migration; presumably, then, it reflects a growing consciousness of Indian identity. There are seven Indian reservations: five for the Seminole—Big Cypress, Hollywood, Brighton, Immokalee, and Tampa, and two for the Miccosuckee—one on the Tamiami Trail and one north of Alligator Alley near Big Cypress.

As of 2000 Florida had an Asian population of 266,256 (eighth largest in the nation), or 1.7% of the total state population. The number of Pacific Islanders was estimated at 8,625. In 2000 there were 54,310 Filipinos, 46,368 Chinese, 70,740 Asian Indians (up from 22,240 in 1990), 33,190 Vietnamese (up from 14,586 in 1990), 10,897 Japanese, 19,139 Koreans, and 2,131 native Hawaiians.

[8]LANGUAGES

Spanish and English settlers found what is now Florida inhabited by Indians recently separated from the Muskogean Creeks, who, with the addition of escaped black slaves and remnants of the Apalachee Indians of the panhandle, later became known as the Seminole Indians. Although the bulk of the Seminole were removed to Indian Territory in the 1840s, enough remained to provide the basis of the present population. Florida has such Indian place-names as Okeechobee, Apalachicola, Kissimmee, Sarasota, Pensacola, and Hialeah.

The rapid population change that has occurred in Florida since World War II makes accurate statements about the language difficult. Massive migration from the North Central and North Atlantic areas, including a large number of speakers of Yiddish, has materially affected the previously rather uniform Southern speech of much of the state. Borrowing from the Spanish of the expanding number of Cubans and Puerto Ricans in the Miami area has had a further effect.

Representative words in the Southern speech of most native-born Floridians are *light bread* (white bread), *pallet* (temporary bed on the floor), *fairing off* (clearing up), *serenade* (shivaree),

Florida Counties, County Seats, and County Areas and Populations

COUNTY	COUNTY SEAT	LAND AREA (SQ MI)	POPULATION (2002 EST.)	COUNTY	COUNTY SEAT	LAND AREA (SQ MI)	POPULATION (2002 EST.)
Alachua	Gainesville	901	222,254	Lake	Tavares	954	233,835
Baker	MacClenny	585	22,793	Lee	Ft. Myers	803	475,639
Bay	Panama City	758	151,901	Leon	Tallahassee	676	243,995
Bradford	Starke	293	26,297	Levy	Bronson	1,100	35,953
Brevard	Titusville	995	495,576	Liberty	Bristol	837	6,902
Broward	Ft. Lauderdale	1,211	1,709,118	Madison	Madison	710	18,309
Calhoun	Blountstown	568	12,567	Manatee	Bradenton	747	280,511
Charlotte	Punta Gorda	690	148,678	Marion	Ocala	1,610	272,553
Citrus	Inverness	629	123,685	Martin	Stuart	555	132,218
Clay	Green Cove Springs	592	152,093	Monroe	Key West	1,034	79,330
Collier	East Naples	1,994	276,691	Nassau	Fernandina Beach	649	60,558
Columbia	Lake City	796	58,028	Okaloosa	Crestview	936	175,708
Dade	Miami	1,955	2,332,599	Okeechobee	Okeechobee	770	36,906
De Soto	Arcadia	636	32,819	Orange	Orlando	910	946,484
Dixie	Cross City	701	14,063	Osceola	Kissimmee	1,350	190,187
Duval	Jacksonville	776	806,120	Palm Beach	West Palm Beach	1,993	1,190,390
Escambia	Pensacola	660	297,272	Pasco	Dade City	738	371,245
Flagler	Bunnell	491	57,377	Pinellas	Clearwater	280	926,716
Franklin	Apalachicola	545	10,069	Polk	Bartow	1,823	498,721
Gadsden	Quincy	518	45,279	Putnam	Palatka	733	71,016
Gilchrist	Trenton	354	14,720	St. Johns	St. Augustine	617	136,038
Glades	Moore Haven	763	10,786	St. Lucie	Ft. Pierce	581	205,420
Gulf	Port St. Joe	559	14,789	Santa Rosa	Milton	1,024	127,212
Hamilton	Jasper	517	13,710	Sarasota	Sarasota	573	339,625
Hardee	Wauchula	637	27,333	Seminole	Sanford	298	381,686
Hendry	La Belle	1,163	36,891	Sumter	Bushnell	561	57,517
Hernando	Brooksville	1.163	138,470	Suwannee	Live Oak	690	36,121
Highlands	Sebring	1,029	89,952	Taylor	Perry	1,058	19,339
Hillsborough	Tampa	1,053	1,053,864	Union	Lake Butler	246	13,877
Holmes	Bonifay	488	18,628	Volusia	DeLand	1,113	459,435
Indian River	Vero Beach	497	118,007	Wakulla	Crawfordville	601	24,900
Jackson	Marianna	942	46,408	Walton	De Funiak Springs	1,066	43,843
Jefferson	Monticello	609	13,695	Washington	Chipley	590	21,419
Lafayette	Mayo	545	7,009				
				TOTALS		54,153	16,713,149

tote (carry), *snap beans* (green beans); *mosquito hawk* (dragonfly), *crocus sack* (burlap bag), *pullybone* (wishbone), and *comforter* (tied and filled bedcover), especially in south Florida. Largely limited to the northern half of the state are *pinder* (peanut), *croker sack* instead of crocus sack, *fire dogs* (andirons); also, in the Tampa Bay area, *comfort* (tied and filled bedcover), and, in the panhandle, *whirlygig* (merry-go-round). Some north-Florida terms are clearly imported from Georgia: *mutton corn* (green corn), *light-wood* (kindling), and *co-wench!* (a call to cows).

In 2000, 11,569,739 Floridians—76.9% of the resident population five years old and older—spoke only English at home, down from 82.7% in 1990.

The following table gives selected statistics from the 2000 census for language spoken at home by persons five years old and over. The category "Other Indo-European languages" includes Albanian, Gaelic, Lithuanian, and Rumanian.

LANGUAGE	NUMBER	PERCENT
Population 5 years and over	15,043,603	100.0
Speak only English	11,569,739	76.9
Speak a language other than English	3,473,864	23.1
Speak a language other than English	3,473,864	23.1
Spanish or Spanish Creole	2,476,528	16.5
French Creole	208,487	1.4
French (incl. Patois, Cajun)	129,118	0.9
German	89,656	0.6
Italian	67,257	0.4
Portuguese or Portuguese Creole	55,014	0.4
Tagalog	38,442	0.3
Chinese	35,071	0.2
Arabic	32,418	0.2
Vietnamese	30,962	0.2
Polish	24,850	0.2
Greek	23,041	0.2
Russian	19,729	0.1
Other Indo-European languages	18,473	0.1
Yiddish	18,225	0.1
Korean	16,702	0.1
Hebrew	15,360	0.1

[9] RELIGIONS

Dominican and Franciscan friars, intent on converting the Indians, arrived with the Spanish conquistadors and settlers in the 1500s, and for some 200 years Florida's white population was overwhelmingly Catholic. Protestant colonists from Britain arrived in the late 1700s, and significant influx of Protestant settlers from the southern United States followed in the early 1800s. Sephardic Jews from the Carolinas also moved into Florida around this time, although the largest influx of Jews has occurred during the 20th century.

The Catholic Church was the largest religious organization in 2000 with 2,596,148 adherents in about 527 congregations. The next largest group was the Southern Baptist Convention with 1,292,097 adherents in 2,054 congregations. Judaism claimed 628,485 adherents. Other Protestant denominations follow with the United Methodist Church, 458,623 adherents; the Assemblies of God, 189,387; Presbyterian Church USA, 157,751; and Episcopalians, 152,526. About 58.9% of the population were not counted as members of any religious organization.

[10] TRANSPORTATION

Railroad building in the 19th century opened southern Florida to tourism and commerce. During the 20th century, long-distance passenger trains and, more recently, planes and automobiles have brought millions of visitors to the state each year.

The first operating railway in Florida was the St. Joseph Railroad, which inaugurated service on an 8-mi (13-km) track between St. Joseph Bay and Lake Wimico on 14 April 1836—using mules to pull the train. The railroad soon put into operation the state's first steam locomotive on 5 September 1836. By the time the Civil War broke out, railroads connected most of northern Florida's major towns, but the rapid expansion of the state's railroad system—and with it the development of southern Florida—awaited two late-19th-century entrepreneurs, Henry B. Plant and Henry M. Flagler. Plant's South Florida Railroad extended service to Tampa in 1884. Flagler consolidated a number of small lines in the 1880s into the Florida East Coast Railway with service as far south as Daytona. He then extended service down the Atlantic coast, reaching Palm Beach in 1894, Miami in 1896, and, after construction of an extensive series of bridges, Key West in 1912. The "overseas" railway down the Keys was abandoned in 1935 after a hurricane severely damaged the line.

In 2000, there was a total of 2,957 rail mi (4,758 km) of track in Florida, operated by 15 railroads. In the same year, Florida-originated rail tonnage of nonmetallic minerals (43.8 million tons), accounting for 64% of the total tonnage originated within the state. CSX Transportation and Norfolk Southern were the state's operating Class I railroads in 2000, with about 1,895 route mi (3,049 km) of Class I track between them. As of 1997, Amtrak provided passenger rail service to 29 Florida stations; ridership exceeded one million.

On 7 June 1979, construction began on a surface rail system for Miami and surrounding areas of Dade County. The first stage of this $1.1-billion mass transit system (known as Metrorail), a 20.5-mi (33-km) line serving Hialeah, Miami International Airport, downtown Miami, and areas to the south, was opened on 20 May 1984.

In 2000, Florida had 116,649 mi (187,728 km) of public roads. Of this total, 67,422 mi (108,505 km) were rural, and 49,227 mi (79,223 km) were urban. The Florida Turnpike's 265-mi (426-km) main section extends from Wildwood in north-central Florida to Ft. Pierce on the Atlantic coast and then south to Miami; a 50-mi (80-km) extension runs between Miramar and Homestead. The Overseas Highway down the Keys, including the famous Seven Mile Bridge (which is actually 35,716 feet, or 10,886 meters—6.8 mi—in length), is part of the state highway system. In 1983, 37 of the 44 bridges connecting the Florida Keys were replaced at a cost of $189 million.

Florida had 23,562,020 registered motor vehicles in 2000. As of 2000, 12,853,428 people held active Florida drivers' licenses.

Inland waterways in Florida include the southernmost section of the Atlantic Intracoastal Waterway and the easternmost section of the Gulf Intracoastal Waterway, encompassing approximately 1,200 navigable miles (1,931 km); federally maintained coastal channels for commercial vessels and pleasure craft. Construction began on 27 February 1964 on a barge canal across northern Florida to connect the two intracoastal systems; however, work was ordered stopped by President Richard Nixon on 19 January 1971 because of the threat the canal posed to flora and fauna in the surrounding area.

Florida has several commercially important ports. By far the largest in terms of gross tonnage is Tampa, which handled over 46.5 million tons of cargo in 2000, ranking it the 17th-busiest port in the US. Other major ports and their 2000 tonnage handled include Port Everglades in Ft. Lauderdale, 22.5 million; Jacksonville, 19.7; Port Manatee, 4.3 million; Miami, 8.6 million; Panama City, 2.6 million; Port Canaveral, 4.2 million; and Palm Beach, 3 million.

In addition to civil aviation activity, Florida has more than 20 military airfields. During the mid-1990s, over 47,000,000 passengers took off annually from Florida's 19 commercial service airports. There were 112 public airports in 2002. Florida's busiest airport is Miami International, with a total of 16,489,341 enplanements in 2000. Other major airports in the state include

Orlando International, Tampa International, and Ft. Lauderdale-Hollywood International.

[11] HISTORY

Indians entered Florida from the north 10,000 to 12,000 years ago, and had reached the end of the peninsula by 1400 BC. As they grew in number, the Indians developed more complex economic and social organization. In northeastern Florida and nearby Georgia, they apparently invented pottery independently about 2000 BC, some 800 years earlier than any other Indian group in North America.

In north Florida, an agricultural and hunting economy organized around village life was typical by this time. South of Tampa Bay and Cape Canaveral, Indians lived mostly along the coast and relied heavily on wild plants and on a large variety of aquatic and land animals for meat. The southern groups did not practice agriculture until about 450 BC, when they began to plant corn in villages around Lake Okeechobee.

As they spread over Florida and adjusted to widely different local conditions, the Indians fell into six main divisions, with numerous subgroups and distinctive cultural traits. When Europeans arrived in the early 16th century, they found nearly 100,000 Indians: 25,000 Apalachee around Tallahassee; 40,000 Timucua in the northeast; on Tampa Bay, 7,000 Tocobaga; on the southwest coast and around Lake Okeechobee, 20,000 Calusa; on the lower southeast coast, 5,000 Tequesta; and in the Jupiter area, 2,000 Ais and Jeaga.

The Spanish who began arriving in the 16th century found the Indians in upper Florida to be relatively tractable, but those in the lower peninsula remained uniformly hostile and resisted to the last. The Spaniards sought to convert the Indians to Christianity and settle them around missions to grow food, to supply labor, and to help defend the province. By 1674, 70 Franciscan friars were working in dozens of missions and stations in a line running west from St. Augustine and north along the sea island coast to Carolina.

The impact of the Europeans on the Indian population was, on the whole, disastrous. Indians died of European-introduced diseases, were killed in wars with whites or with other Indians, or moved away. Raids from South Carolina by the Creeks, abetted by the British, between 1702 and 1708 completely destroyed the missions. When the Spanish departed Florida in 1763, the remaining 300 of the original 100,000 Indians left with them.

As early as 1750, however, small groups of Creek tribes from Georgia and Alabama had begun to move into the north Florida area vacated by the first Indian groups. Called Seminole, the Creek word for runaway or refugee, these Indians did not then constitute a tribe and had no common government or leadership until resistance to white plans to resettle them brought them together. They numbered only 5,000 when Florida became part of the US.

Pressures on the US president and Congress to remove the Seminole intensified after runaway black slaves began seeking refuge with the Indians. In 1823, the Seminole accepted a reservation north of Lake Okeechobee. Nine years later, an Indian delegation signed a document pledging the Seminole to move within three years to lands in present-day Oklahoma. The Indians' subsequent resistance to removal resulted in the longest and most costly of Indian wars, the Seminole War of 1835–42. The warfare and the Indians' subsequent forced migration left fewer than 300 Seminole in Florida.

The history of the twice-repeated annihilation of Florida Indians is, at the same time, the history of white settlers' rise to power. After Christopher Columbus reached the New World at Hispaniola in 1492, the Caribbean islands became the base for wider searches, one of which brought Juan Ponce de León to Florida. Sailing from Puerto Rico in search of the fabled island of Bimini, he sighted Florida on 27 March 1513 and reached the coast a week later. Ponce de León claimed the land for Spain and named it La Florida, for Pascua Florida, the Easter festival of flowers; sailing southward around Florida, he may have traveled as far as Apalachicola, on the shore of the panhandle. In 1521, he returned to found a colony at Charlotte Harbor, on the lower Gulf coast, but the Indians fought the settlers. After Ponce was seriously wounded, the expedition sailed for Cuba, where he died the same year.

Other Spaniards seeking treasure and lands to govern came after Ponce. Pánfilo de Narváez arrived in 1528, landing near Tampa Bay and marching inland and northward to Tallahassee. Hernando de Sota, a rich and famous associate of Francisco Pizarro in the conquest of Peru, found many men eager to try the same with him in Florida. Appointed governor of Cuba and *adelantado* (loosely, conqueror) of Florida, he followed the route of Narváez to Tallahassee in 1539, finding some food but no promise of wealth. In 1559, Spain sought to establish a settlement on Pensacola Bay, but it was abandoned at the end of two years.

In 1562, Jean Ribault, with a small expedition of French Huguenots, arrived at the St. Johns River, east of present-day Jacksonville, and claimed Florida for France. Another group of French Huguenot settlers built Ft. Caroline, 5 mi (8 km) upriver, two years later. In the summer of 1565, Ribault brought in naval reinforcements, prepared to defend the French claim against the Spaniards, who had sent Pedro Menéndez de Avilés to find and oust the intruders. Menéndez selected St. Augustine as a base, landing on 28 August, and with the aid of a storm withstood the French effort to destroy him. He then marched overland to take Ft. Caroline by surprise, killing most of the occupants and later captured Ribault and his shipwrecked men, most of whom he slaughtered. St. Augustine, the first permanent European settlement in the US, served primarily, under Spanish rule, as a military outpost, maintained to protect the wealth of New Spain. The Spanish established a settlement at Pensacola in 1698, but it too remained only a small frontier garrison town. In 1763, when Spain ceded Florida to England in exchange for Cuba, about 3,000 Spaniards departed from St. Augusta and 800 from Pensacola, leaving Florida to the Seminole.

British Florida reached from the Atlantic to the Mississippi River and became two colonies, East and West Florida. Settlers established farms and plantations, traded with the Indians, and moved steadily toward economic and political self-sufficiency. These settlers did not join the American Revolution, but Florida was affected by the war nonetheless, as thousands of Loyalists poured into East Florida. In 1781, Spain attacked and captured Pensacola. Two years later, Britain ceded both Floridas back to Spain, whereupon most of the Loyalists left for the West Indies.

The second Spanish era was only nominally Spanish. English influence remained strong, and US penetration increased. Florida west of the Perdido River was taken over by the US in 1810, as part of the Louisiana Purchase (1803). Meanwhile, renegade whites, runaway slaves, pirates, and political adventures operated almost at will.

Present-day Florida was ceded to the US in 1821, in settlement of $5 million in claims by US citizens against the Spanish government. At this time, General Andrew Jackson who three years earlier had led a punitive expedition against the Seminole and their British allies came back to Florida as military governor. His main tasks were to receive the territory for the US and to set up a civilian administration, which took office in 1822. William P. DuVal of Kentucky was named territorial governor, and a legislative council was subsequently elected. The new council met first in Pensacola and in St. Augustine, and then, in 1824, in the newly selected capital of Tallahassee, located in the wilderness of north-central Florida, from which the Indians had just been removed. Middle Florida, as it was called, rapidly became an area of slaveowning cotton plantations and was for several decades the fastest-growing part of the territory. The war to remove the Seminole halted the advance of frontier settlement, however, and the Panic of 1837 bankrupted the territorial government and the three banks whose notes it had guaranteed. Floridians drew up a state constitution at St. Joseph in 1838–39 but, being proslavery, had to wait until 1845 to enter the Union paired with the free state of Iowa.

In 1861, Florida, with only 140,000 people, about 40% of them blacks (mostly slaves), only 400 mi (644 km) of railroad, and no manufacturing, seceded from the Union and joined the Confederacy. Some 15,000 whites (one-third of whom died) served in the Confederate army, and 1,200 whites and almost as many blacks joined the Union army. Bitterness and some violence accompanied the Republican Reconstruction government in 1868–76. The conservative Bourbon Democrats then governed for the rest of the century. They encouraged railroad building and other forms of business, and they kept taxes low by limiting government services. Cotton production never recovered to prewar levels, but cattle raising, citrus and vegetable cultivation, forestry, phosphate mining, and, by late in the century, a growing tourist industry took up the slack.

The Spanish-American War in 1898, during which Tampa became the port of embarkation for an expedition to Cuba, stimulated the economy and advertised the state nationwide, not always favorably. Naval activity at Key West and Pensacola became feverish. Lakeland, Miami, Jacksonville, and Fernandina were briefly the sites of training camps.

In 1904, Napoleon Bonaparte Broward was elected governor on a moderately populist platform, which included a program to drain the Everglades lands which the state had received under the Swamp and Overflowed Lands Act of 1850. Drainage did lower water levels, and settlements grew around Lake Okeechobee, developments whose full environmental impact was recognized only much later. By the time Broward took office, Jacksonville had become the state's largest city, with Pensacola and Tampa not far behind, and Key West had dropped from first to fourth. During World War I, more than 42,030 Floridians were in uniform.

Boom, bust, and depression characterized the 1920s. Feverish land speculation brought hundreds of thousands of people to Florida in the first half of the decade. Cresting in 1925, the boom was already over in 1926, when a devastating hurricane struck Miami, burying all hope of recovery. Yet population jumped by more than 50% during the decade, and Miami rose from 4th to 2nd place among Florida cities. Florida's choice of Republican Herbert Hoover over Al Smith in the 1928 presidential election reflected the Protestant and prohibitionist attitudes of most of the state voters at that time.

The 1930s were marked first by economic depression, then by recovery, new enterprise, and rapidly growing government activity. Bank and business failures, as well as defaults on city and county bond issues and on mortgage payments, produced growing economic distress. The state joined the federal government in assuming responsibility for relief and recovery. The legalization of parimutuel betting in 1931 created a new industry and a new tax source. The state's first paper mill opened in the same year, revolutionizing the forest industry. Private universities in Miami, Tampa, and Jacksonville were started during the Depression years.

The 1940s opened with recovery and optimism, arising from the stimulus of production for World War II, production that began well before the actual entry of the US into the war. New army and navy installations and training programs brought business growth. After 1941, Florida seemed to become a vast military training school. The number of army and navy airfield flying schools increased from five to 45. Tourist facilities in all

major cities became barracks, mess halls, and classrooms, with 70,000 rooms in Miami Beach alone being used to house troops in 1942. Families of thousands of trainees visited the state. Florida was on the eve of another boom.

First discovered but nearly last to be developed, Florida reached a rank of 27th in population only in 1940. Migration brought Florida's ranking to fourth in 1990, increasing its population to more than 12.8 million people. In 1986, Florida absorbed 1,000 arrivals a day. Until the early 1980s, many of those migrants were 65 years of age or over, swelling the proportion of senior citizens in Florida to 50% above the national average. In the mid-1980s, however, the preponderance of newcomers was somewhat younger, 25 to 44 years old. With an influx of younger residents, of family-rearing age, schools became overcrowded by the 1990s.

Newcomers came in search of opportunities provided by Florida's growing and diversifying economy. Whereas the state once depended on the three industries (tourism, citrus, and construction) for its survival, military spending increased the presence of high tech, banking, and service industries. In 1990, only 10% of Florida workers held jobs in the manufacturing industry, in contrast to 19% of the labor force nationwide.

The management of growth in Florida dominated state politics through the second half of the century and promised to remain at the fore at least through the early 2000s. The state's low taxes combined with its rapid population growth to overburden the infrastructure. Roads, water supply, and sewer systems were pushed beyond capacity by the 1990s, posing real environmental threats. Development, both residential and commercial, eroded the state's natural beauty.

Efforts to reapportion Florida's 23 congressional districts and the state legislature's 40 senate and 120 house seats were complicated by battles between blacks (holding steady at 14% of the population in 1999) and Hispanics over the number and character of minority districts. The absence of black state congressmen or senators, and the paucity of black officials at the state and local levels provoked demands for the creation of "safe districts" for blacks that thereby ensure their representation. Likewise Hispanics, whose numbers grew from 8.8% of the state population in 1980 to 14% by 1999, called for Hispanic districts. However, in the 1990s, Florida's third congressional district, which had a majority of black voters, was declared unconstitutional and ordered redrawn by the US Supreme Court.

Racial and ethnic relations were another central issue. Tensions between blacks and Hispanics led to violence in 1989 when a Hispanic police officer shot and killed a black motorcyclist who was speeding and driving erratically. Riots broke out in the predominantly black Overton section of Miami and continued for three days.

Miami was again the site of rioting in late April 2000, as some Cuban-Americans took to the streets to protest the federal government's handling of the custody case of six-year-old Cuban refugee Elian Gonzalez. The child was the center of an international debacle after he was rescued offshore in November 1999; a fisherman found the boy clinging to a raft after the boat in which he and his mother escaped Cuba had capsized. His mother dead, Miami relatives claimed and cared for the boy while federal officials, including the US Attorney General, the Immigration and Naturalization Service, and several courts, grappled with the problem of returning him to his Cuban father. The incident, which ended when the boy arrived back in Havana, remained a point of protest for Miami's Cuban-American community, among whom the prevailing sentiment was that, for political reasons, the child should have remained in the states.

The state's crime level received nationwide attention in the early 1990s when a series of incidents claimed the lives of several foreign tourists. For most of the decade Florida held the unwelcome distinction of leading the nation in violent crime. Numbers began to decline, and in 1998, the rate of violent crime per 100,000 residents dropped below 1,000 (to 939), according to the FBI. (That year New Mexico recorded 955 violent crimes per 100,000 residents, making it the most violent state in the nation.)

Tropical storms and hurricanes periodically strike Florida. In August 1992, Hurricane Andrew caused $26.5 billion in damages in south Florida, primarily in and around Homestead. In October 1995, Hurricane Opal wrought an estimated $3 billion in damage in the Panhandle, destroying marinas and shipyards. In the late 1990s wildfires plagued the state. Fires during the summer of 1998 burned 500,000 acres and caused $400 million in damage. In spring 1999, flames ravaged 90,000 acres of the Everglades, where dry sawgrass caught fire and winds fueled the blaze. Stricken by drought, fires charred hundreds of thousands more acres the summer of 2000, with Volusia County, near Daytona, particularly hard hit.

In December 1998 Floridians mourned the death of Governor Lawton Chiles; the Democrat first rose to prominence in 1970 when he made a 1,000-mi (1,600-km) trek through the state as he successfully campaigned for the US Senate, earning him the nickname "Walkin' Lawton."

Florida became the center of national and international attention in the 7 November 2000 US presidential election. The race between Democratic Vice-President Al Gore and Republican challenger George W. Bush was extremely close, and on election night, Florida's 25 electoral college votes became the ones that would decide the election. In the early morning hours of 8 November, Gore called Bush to concede the election, but he subsequently retracted his concession when it became apparent that the vote was in question. Because the vote was so close, Florida's election officials began a mandatory recount In addition to the automatic recount, an investigation was launched into voting irregularities denying rights to minority voters.

Democrats requested hand recounts in four counties, but Bush called for an order banning them. The Florida Supreme Court intervened in the certification process run by the Florida Secretary of State, permitting hand recounts in Broward and Palm Beach counties and blocking certification until an appeal by Gore was heard. The United States 11th Circuit Court of Appeals refused Bush's request that it stop the hand recounts, and Miami-Dade county officials began a manual recount. Bush's lead was gradually reduced from the 537 votes certified on 26 November to 154 by adding votes from partial recounts in Miami-Dade and Palm Beach counties. When the Florida Supreme Court ordered a manual recount of 43,432 "under votes" from as many as 62 counties, the Bush campaign appealed to the United States Supreme Court to stop any vote recounts in Florida. On 9 December 2000, the US Supreme Court, divided 5–4, stepped in to order a stay of the Florida Supreme Court-ordered manual recounts, and on 12 December, it decided, in Bush v. Gore, that the Florida Supreme Court had erred in its decision to order manual vote recounts. On 13 December, Gore conceded the election to Bush, who became the nation's 43rd president when the electoral college votes cast on 18 December 2000 were tallied, including Florida's 25 votes.

12STATE GOVERNMENT

Florida's first constitutional convention, which met from December 1838 to January 1839, drew up the document under which the state entered the Union in 1845. A second constitutional convention, meeting in 1861, adopted the ordinance of secession that joined Florida to the Confederacy. After the war, a new constitution was promulgated in 1865, but not until still another document was drawn up and ratified by the state—the Fourteenth Amendment to the US Constitution—was

Florida readmitted to statehood in 1868. A fifth constitution was framed in 1885 and adopted the following year; extensively revised in 1968, this is the document under which the state is now governed. In 1998 Florida voters approved extensive revisions to the constitution; in 2002, voters approved a death penalty amendment, adding the death penalty to the constitution. In addition, in 2002 Florida voters approved several amendments: one requires the state to offer pre-kindergarten for four-year-olds by 2005; another, to reduce class size in schools by 2010; another animal rights measure protects pregnant pigs from unnecessary confinement; and another prohibits smoking in certain work environments. Overall the constitution had been amended 96 times by January 2003.

The 1968 constitutional revision instituted annual (rather than biennial) regular sessions of the legislature, which consists of a 40-member senate and a 120-member house of representatives. Sessions begin the Tuesday after the first Monday of March and are limited to 60 calendar days. The legislature may also call special sessions, by joint call of the presiding officers of both houses. Senators serve four-year terms, with half the senate being elected every two years; representatives serve two-year terms. All legislators must be at least 21 years old, must have been residents of Florida for at least two years, and must be registered voters and residents of the district. The maximum length of a regular legislative session is 60 calendar days, unless it is extended by a three-fifths vote of each house. Special sessions may be called by the governor or by joint action of the presiding officers of the two houses (the president of the senate and speaker of the house of representatives). In addition, a special session may be convened by a three-fifths vote of all legislators, the poll being conducted by mail by the secretary of state upon a written request from at least 20% of the members. The legislative salary in 2002 was $27,900.

The governor is elected for a four-year term; a two-term limit is in effect. The lieutenant governor is elected on the same ticket as the governor. An amendment adopted by voters in 1998, which took effect in 2002, merged the cabinet offices of treasurer and comptroller into one chief financial office. The other cabinet members will be the attorney general and agriculture commissioner; the amendment eliminated the offices of secretary of state and education commissioner from the cabinet. State officials must be at least 30 years old, US citizens, and registered voters, and must have been residents of Florida for at least seven years. In 2002 the governor's salary was $120,171.

Passage of legislation requires a majority vote of those present and voting in both houses. A bill passed by the legislature becomes law if it is signed by the governor; should the governor take no action on it, it becomes law seven days after receipt if the legislature is still in session, or 15 days after presentation to the governor if the legislature has adjourned. The governor may veto legislation and, in general appropriations bills, may veto individual items. Gubernatorial vetoes may be overridden by a two-thirds vote of the elected legislators in each house.

Amendments to the constitution may originate in three ways: by a joint resolution of the legislature passed by a three-fifths majority of the membership of each house; by action of a constitutional revision commission which, under the constitution, must be periodically convened; or by initiative petition (signed by 8% of the total votes cast in the state in the last election for presidential electors), which may call for a constitutional convention. A proposed amendment becomes part of the constitution if it receives a majority vote in a statewide election.

To vote in state elections, a person must be at least 18 years old, a US citizen, and a resident in the county of registration. Restrictions apply to those judged by the court as mentally incapacitated.

13 POLITICAL PARTIES

The Democratic and Republican parties are Florida's two principal political organizations. The former is the descendant of one of the state's first two political parties, the Jeffersonian Republican Democrats; this party, along with the Florida Whig Party, was organized shortly before statehood.

Florida's Republican Party was organized after the Civil War and dominated state politics until 1876, when the Democrats won control of the statehouse. Aided from 1889 to 1937 by a poll tax, which effectively disfranchised most of the state's then predominantly Republican black voters, the Democrats won every gubernatorial election but one from 1876 through 1962; the Prohibition Party candidate was victorious in 1916.

By the time Republican Claude R. Kirk, Jr., won the governorship in 1966, Florida had already become, for national elections, a two-party state, although Democrats retained a sizable advantage in party registration. Beginning in the 1950s, many registered Democrats became "presidential Republicans," crossing party lines to give the state's electoral votes to Dwight D. Eisenhower in 1952 and 1956 and to Richard M. Nixon in 1960.

A presidential preference primary, in which crossover voting is not permitted, is held on the 2nd Tuesday in March of presidential election years. Because it occurs so early in the campaign season, this primary is closely watched as an indicator of candidates' strength. Primaries to select state and local candidates are held in early September, with crossover voting again prohibited; runoff elections are held on the Tuesday five weeks before the general election.

In 2002 there were 9,302,360 registered voters; 45% were Democratic, 40% Republican, and 15% unaffiliated or members of other parties in 1998. In addition to the Democratic and Republican parties, organized groups include the Greens, Reform, and Libertarian parties. Minor parties running candidates for statewide office can qualify by obtaining petition signatures from 3% of the state's voters.

In the 1996 presidential election, Florida backed a Democrat for the first time in 20 years, giving 48% of the vote to Bill Clinton; 42% to Republican Bob Dole; and 9% to Independent Ross Perot. In the 2000 presidential election, a mere 275 votes separated Republican candidate George W. Bush from Democrat Al Gore as of 13 December 2000, when the US Supreme Court ruled a controversial hand recount of the Florida vote be stopped.

George Bush won Florida's 25 electoral votes, and became president.

Former US Senator Lawton Chiles (Democrat) was elected governor in 1990 and reelected in 1994. In 1998 Florida voters elected Republican Jeb Bush to the gubernatorial spot; he was reelected in 2002. Connie Mack, Republican, was reelected to a second US Senate term in 1994, but decided not to seek a third term in 2000. Democrat Bill Nelson was elected to the Senate in 2000. Democratic Senator Robert Graham was reelected in 1998. Graham gave up his bid for reelection to the Senate in 2004 due to the fact that he was running for president in 2003.

Florida's US House delegation following the 2002 elections had 18 Republicans and seven Democrats. The state senate in mid-2003 was comprised of 14 Democrats and 26 Republicans, and the state house had 81 Republicans and 39 Democrats.

14 LOCAL GOVERNMENT

In 2002, Florida had 66 counties, 404 municipalities, and 95 public school districts.

Generally, legislative authority within each county is vested in a five-member elected board of county commissioners, which also has administrative authority over county departments, except those headed by independently elected officials. In counties without charters, these elected officials usually include a sheriff, tax collector, property appraiser, supervisor of elections, and clerk of the circuit court. County charters may provide for a greater or lesser number of elected officials, and for a professional county administrator (city manager). Before 1968 there was state legislation that restricted county government operations; most of these laws have now been repealed. Counties may generally enact any law not inconsistent with state law. However, the taxing power of county and other local governments is severely limited.

Municipalities are normally incorporated and chartered by an act of the state legislature. Except where a county charter specifies otherwise, municipal ordinances override county laws. Municipal governments may provide a full range of local services. But as populations rapidly expand beyond municipal boundaries, many of these governments have found they lack the jurisdiction to deal adequately with area problems. Annexations of surrounding territory are permissible but difficult under state law. Some municipal governments have reached agreements with

Florida Presidential Vote by Political Parties, 1948–2000

YEAR	ELECTORAL VOTE	FLORIDA WINNER	DEMOCRAT	REPUBLICAN	STATES' RIGHTS DEMOCRAT	PROGRESSIVE
1948	8	*Truman (D)	281,988	194,280	89,755	11,620
1952	10	*Eisenhower (R)	444,950	544,036		
1956	10	*Eisenhower (R)	480,371	643,849		
1960	10	Nixon (R)	748,700	795,476		
1964	14	*Johnson (D)	948,540	905,941		
					AMERICAN IND.	
1968	14	*Nixon (R)	676,794	886,804	624,207	
1972	17	*Nixon (R)	718,117	1,857,759		
					AMERICAN	
1976	17	*Carter (D)	1,636,000	1,469,531	21,325	
						LIBERTARIAN
1980	17	*Reagan (R)	1,417,637	2,043,006		30,457
1984	21	*Reagan (R)	1,448,816	2,730,350		744
					NEW ALLIANCE	
1988	21	*Bush	1,656,701	2,618,885	6,665	19,796
					IND. (PEROT)	
1992	25	Bush (R)	2,072,798	2,173,310	1,053,067	15,079
1996	25	*Clinton (D)	2,546,870	2,244,536	483,870	23,965
					GREEN	
2000**	25	*Bush, G. W. (R)	2,912,253	2,912,790	97,488	16,415

*Won US presidential election. **Reform candidate Pat Buchanan received 17,484 votes.

county or other local governments for consolidation of overlapping or redundant services or for provision of service by one local government to another on a contract basis. Complete consolidation of a municipal and a county government is authorized by the state constitution, requiring state legislation and voter approval in the area affected. Jacksonville and Duval County succeeded in consolidating by 1985.

The problem of overlapping and uncoordinated service is most serious in the case of the state's 626 special districts (as of 2002). These districts, established by state law and approval of the affected voters, provide a specified service in a defined geographic area. An urban area may have dozens of special districts. State legislation in the 1970s attempted to deal with this problem by permitting counties to set up their own special-purpose districts, whose operations could be coordinated by the county government.

Regional planning councils resulted from the need to cope with problems of greater than local concern. These councils deal with such issues as land management, resource management, and economic development.

15 STATE SERVICES

To address the continuing threat of terrorism and to work with the federal Department of Homeland Security (created in 2002 following the terrorist attacks of 11 September 2001), homeland security in Florida in 2003 operated under state statute; the public safety commissioner, designated as the state homeland security advisor, oversaw programs in training and law enforcement.

A "Sunshine" amendment to the constitution and a statutory code of ethics require financial disclosure by elected officials and top-level public employees; the code prohibits actions by officials and employees that would constitute a conflict of interest. The Commission on Ethics, established in 1974, is empowered to investigate complaints of breach of public trust or violation of the code of ethics. In addition, an auditor general appointed by the legislature conducts financial and performance audits of state agencies.

Educational services are provided by the State Department of Education, which sets overall policy and adopts comprehensive objectives for public education, operates the state university and community college systems, and issues bonds (as authorized by the state constitution) to finance capital projects. The Department of Transportation is responsible for developing long-range transportation plans and for construction and maintenance of the state highway system. The Department of Highway Safety and Motor Vehicles licenses drivers, regulates the registration and sale of motor vehicles, and administers the Florida Highway Patrol.

Health and welfare services are the responsibility primarily of the Department of Health and Rehabilitative Services. In 1994, this department operated 16 major institutions and 71 other facilities, including mental hospitals, institutions for the mentally retarded, alcoholic treatment centers, and training schools for juvenile delinquents. In addition, the department administers such social welfare programs as Medicaid, aid to families with dependent children, food stamps, home health care, and foster care and adoption. It is also responsible for disease prevention and for assisting localities in performing health services.

The Department of Corrections maintains approximately 50 major correctional institutions. The Corrections Commission reviews the state's correctional efforts, recommends policies, and evaluates the implementation of approved policies. The Department of Law Enforcement is responsible for maintaining public order and enforcing the state criminal code; enforcement activities emphasize combating organized crime, vice, and racketeering. The state's Army and Air National Guard are under the jurisdiction of the Department of Military Affairs. The Florida Highway Patrol, within the Department of Highway Safety and Motor Vehicles, is the only statewide uniformed police force.

The Housing Finance Agency, created in 1980, encourages the investment of private capital in residential housing through the use of public financing. The Northwest Florida Regional Housing Authority provides housing for low-income and other residents of that area. The Florida Housing Advisory Council assists the Department of Community Affairs in carrying out its duties related to housing. The Division of Local Resource Management is designated as the state's housing and urban development agency.

The Department of Labor and Employment Security enforces legislation protecting the state's workers (including child labor and industrial safety laws) and administers the federally funded workers' compensation and unemployment insurance programs and the State Employment Service, whose offices provide employment counseling and assist in job placement. Included in the department are the Division of Employment and Training and the Division of Employment Security. The Department of Administration includes the Division of Personnel, Office of Career Service and State Retirement Commissions, Florida Commission on Human Relations, and Division of Veterans Affairs.

The Department of State manages state historic sites, archives, museums, libraries, and fine arts centers. Enterprise Florida supports new business starts in the state, and the Technology Office encourages high-tech industry.

16 JUDICIAL SYSTEM

The state's highest court is the supreme court, a panel of seven justices that sits in Tallahassee; every two years, the presiding justices elect one of their number as chief justice. All justices are appointed to six-year terms by the governor upon the recommendation of a judicial nominating commission. They may seek further six-year terms in a yes-no vote in a general election; if the incumbent justice does not receive a majority of "yes" votes, the governor appoints another person to fill the vacancy from the recommended list of qualified candidates.

The supreme court has appellate jurisdiction only. The state constitution, as amended, prescribes certain types of cases in which an appeal must be heard, including those in which the death penalty has been ordered and those in which a lower appellate court has invalidated a state law or a provision of the state constitution. The court also hears appeals of state agency decisions on utility rates and may, at its discretion, hear appeals in many other types of cases.

Below the supreme court are five district courts of appeal, which sit in Tallahassee, Lakeland, Miami, West Palm Beach, and Daytona Beach. There are 61 district court judges; the method of their selection and retention in office is the same as for supreme court justices. District courts hear appeals of lower court decisions and may review the actions of executive agencies. District court decisions are usually final, since most requests for supreme court review are denied.

The state's principal trial courts are its 20 circuit courts, which have original jurisdiction in many types of cases, including civil suits involving more than $5,000, felony cases, and all cases involving juveniles. Circuit courts may also hear appeals from county courts if no constitutional question is involved. Circuit court judges are elected for six-year terms and must have been members of the Florida bar for at least five years before election. There were 468 circuit court judges in 1999.

Each of Florida's 67 counties has a county court with original jurisdiction in misdemeanor cases, civil disputes involving $5,000 or less, and traffic-violation cases. County court judges are elected for four-year terms and must be members of the bar only in counties with populations of 40,000 or more.

In 2001, the total crime rate was 5,569.7 per 100,000 population, including a total of 130,713 violent crimes and 782,517 property crimes in that year. As of June 2001, a total of 72,007 persons were serving prison sentences in state and federal institutions run by Florida's correctional authorities, an increase of 1.1% over the previous year. The state's incarceration rate stood at 439 per 100,000 inhabitants. Florida has a capital punishment statute, which was upheld by the US Supreme Court in 1976. Between 1977 and 2003, 56 people were executed. In 2003 Florida had 381 persons under sentence of death, the 3rd-largest number after California and Texas.

17ARMED FORCES

In 2002, there were 55,815 active-duty military personnel in Florida. Military and civilian personnel were stationed at facilities in Pensacola, Orlando, Jacksonville, and at Eglin AFB. In October 1979, the Key West Naval Air Station was made the headquarters of a new Caribbean Joint Task Force, established to coordinate US military activities in the Caribbean. The state had 25,147 active-duty Air Force personnel in 2002 the largest Air Force bases were Eglin, in Valparaiso; MacDill, near Tampa; and Tyndall, west of Tallahassee. The US Air Force Missile Test Center at Cape Canaveral (called Cape Kennedy from 1963 to 1973) has been the launching site for most US space flights, including all manned flights. US Department of Defense procurement contracts in Florida in 2001 totaled $6.7 billion.

There were 1,875,597 veterans of US military service in Florida as of 2000, of whom 461,291 served in World War II; 242,777 in the Korean conflict; 444,997 during the Vietnam era; and 201,065 during 1990–2000 (including the Persian Gulf War). US Veterans Administration spending in Florida in 2002 totaled $3.4 billion.

In 2000, the Florida Highway Patrol employed 1,658 full-time sworn officers.

18MIGRATION

Florida is populated mostly by migrants. In 1990, only 30.5% of all state residents were Florida-born, compared with 61.8% for the US as a whole. Only Nevada had a lower proportion of native residents. Migration from other states accounted for more than 85% of Florida's population increase in the 1970s. From 1985 to 1990, net migration gains added another 1,461,550 new residents. Between 1990 and 1998, net domestic migration added 1,035,000 while international migration added 553,000. Florida's overall population increased 15.3% during that same period.

The early European immigrants to Florida—first the Spanish, then the English—never populated the state in significant numbers. Immigration from southern states began even before the US acquisition of Florida and accelerated thereafter. In the 20th century, US immigrants to Florida came, for the most part, from the Northeast and Midwest, their motivation to escape harsh northern winters. A large proportion of migrants have been retirees and other senior citizens. Between 1970 and 1980, the number of Floridians 65 or over increased by 70%, compared with a 44% increase for the US population as a whole. By 1998, 18.3% of the Florida populace was age 65 or older. In the period 1995–2000, 1,860,772 people moved into the state and 1,253,749 moved out, for a net gain of 607,023 of whom 149,440 were age 65 or over.

Since the 1960s, Florida has also experienced large-scale migration from the Caribbean and parts of Latin America. Although the state has had a significant Cuban population since the second half of the 19th century, the number of immigrants surged after the Cuban revolution of 1959. From December 1965

to April 1973, an airlift agreed to by the Cuban and US governments landed a quarter of a million Cubans in Miami. Another period of large-scale immigration from Cuba, beginning in April 1980, brought more than 100,000 Cubans into Florida harbors. At the same time, Haitian "boat people" were arriving in Florida in significant numbers—often reaching the southern peninsula packed in barely seaworthy small craft. The number of ethnic Haitians in Florida was reported at 105,495 in 1990. By 1990, a reported 541,011 ethnic Cubans were living in southern Florida, mostly in and around Miami, where the Cuban section had become known as "Little Havana." The US government classified some of them as illegal aliens, fleeing extreme poverty in their native country, but the immigrants claimed to be political refugees and sued to halt deportation proceedings against them. In 1996, a reported 2,186,000 Floridians (15%) were foreign-born. In 1998, 59,965 foreign immigrants were admitted into Florida, the 3rd-highest total of any state, accounting for over 9% of all foreign immigration that year. Of that total, 14,265 were from Cuba; 6,613 from Haiti; and 4,795 from Jamaica. As of 1998, Florida's Hispanic population numbered 2,080,000; those of Hispanic origin numbered 2,243,000.

19INTERGOVERNMENTAL COOPERATION

In 1953, Florida became a signatory to the Alabama-Florida Boundary Compact. Among the interstate regional compacts in which Florida participates are the Apalachicola-Chattahoochee-Flint River Basin Compact, Southern Regional Education Board, Southern States Energy Board, Southeastern Forest Fire Protection Compact, Atlantic States Marine Fisheries Commission, and Gulf States Marine Fisheries Commission. Federal grants to Florida in 2001 totaled over $13.6 billion.

20ECONOMY

Farming and the lumbering and naval stores industries, all concentrated in northern Florida, were early mainstays of the economy. In the late 19th century, the extension of the railroads down the peninsula opened up an area previously populated only by Indians; given the favorable climate, central and southern Florida soon became major agricultural areas. Tourism, aggressively promoted by the early railroad builders, became a major industry after World War I and remains so today.

Tourists and winter residents with second homes in Florida contribute billions of dollars annually to the state economy and make retailing and construction particularly important economic sectors. However, this dependence on discretionary spending by visitors and part-time dwellers also makes the economy—and especially the housing industry—highly vulnerable to recession.

The arms build-up during the Reagan administration helped to expand Florida's aerospace and electronics industries. Even in 1991, after the reduction of the national military budget, Florida ranked seventh nationally in the value of Department of Defense contracts awarded. Florida ranked fourth in the nation in defense electronics manufacturing employment in 1999.

The state's economy—particularly that of the Miami area—has also benefited from an influx of Latin American investment funds. Miami is said to have one of the largest underground economies in the US, a reference both to the sizable inflow of cash from illicit drug trafficking and to the large numbers of Latin American immigrants working for low, unreported cash wages. Florida's population increased by 16% between 1990 and 1999, due primarily to migration. Strong annual economic growth rates in the late 1990s (averaging 6.6% 1998 to 2000) were only moderated to 4.2% in the national recession of 2001. Growth continued damped in 2002, reflecting, particularly, a slowdown in Florida's tourist industry, but remained above the national average. By July 2002, the state was experiencing positive, if small (less than 1%), job growth. As was true in much of the country, the share of manufacturing in Florida's economy decreased in both absolute and relative terms coming into the 21st century. From a peak of $31 billion in 1999, output from the manufacturing sector declined 6.3% by 2001. As a share of the Florida economy, manufacturing declined from 7.7% in 1997 to 5.9% in 2001. By contrast, the financial services and trade sectors (wholesale and retail) each grew by more than 27% 1997 to 2001, and general services (including hotels and tourist services) grew 36.9% during this period.

Florida's gross state product in 2001 totaled $491.5 billion (fourth largest in the nation), of which the public sector contributed 12.2%). The major contributors to the state's gross output in 2001 were general services ($125.9 billion); financial services ($108.5 billion); trade ($$83.4 billion); transportation and public utilities ($39.4 billion), manufacturing ($29 billion) and construction ($27 billion).

21 INCOME

According to the Bureau of Economic Analysis, in 2001, Florida had a per capita personal income (PCPI) of $29,048 which ranked 22nd in the United States (including the District of Columbia) and was 96% of the national average, $30,413. The 2001 PCPI reflected an increase of 2.4% from 2000 compared to the national change of 2.2%. In 2001, Florida had a total personal income (TPI) of $475,606,702,000 which ranked 4th in the United States and accounted for 5.5% of the national total. The 2001 TPI reflected an increase of 4.5% from 2000 compared to the national change of 3.3%.

Earnings of persons employed in Florida increased from $284,163,202,000 in 2000 to $296,484,468,000 in 2001, an increase of 4.3%. The largest industries in 2001 were services, 35.0% of earnings; state and local government, 11.8%; and retail trade, 11.0%. Of the industries that accounted for at least 5% of earnings in 2001, the slowest growing from 2000 to 2001 was wholesale trade (6.4% of earnings in 2001), which increased 0.8%; the fastest was construction (6.3% of earnings in 2001), which increased 7.1%.

According to data released by the US Census Bureau, in 2000, the median household income was $37,998 compared to the national average of $42,148. In 2001, the median income for a family of four was $56,824 compared to the national average of $63,278. For the period 1999 to 2001, the average poverty rate was 12.0% which placed it 31 among the 50 states and the District of Columbia ranked lowest to highest.

22 LABOR

According to Bureau of Labor Statistics (BLS) provisional estimates, in July 2003 the seasonally adjusted civilian labor force in Florida numbered 8,068,400, with approximately 430,100 workers unemployed, yielding an unemployment rate of 5.3%, compared to the national average of 6.2% for the same period. Since the beginning of the BLS data series in 1978, the highest unemployment rate recorded was 9.7% in March 1983. The historical low was 3.5% in July 2000. It is estimated that in 2001, 7.1% of the labor force was employed in construction; 8.1% in manufacturing; 5.6% in transportation, communications, and public utilities; 22.7% in trade; 7.1% in finance, insurance, and real estate; 28.7% in services; 12.2% in government; and 2.4% in agriculture. As in the United States generally, unemployment was higher among non-whites and teenagers than among white adults—and highest among black teenagers.

In 1998, about 62% of the state's civilian population, age 16 or older, were in the labor force, compared with 67.1% for the United States as a whole. The major reason for the difference is the extremely low participation rate for Floridians 65 or older, reflecting the fact that many people migrate to the state for their retirement years.

The US Department of Labor reported that in 2002, 380,000 of Florida's 6,697,000 employed wage and salary workers were members of unions. This represented 5.7% of those so employed, down from 6.3% in 2001. The national average is 13.2%. In all, 507,000 workers (7.6%) were represented by unions. In addition to union members, this category includes workers who report no union affiliation but whose jobs are covered by a union contract. Florida is one of 22 states with a right-to-work law.

23 AGRICULTURE

Florida's most important agricultural products, and the ones for which it is most famous, are its citrus fruits. Florida continues to supply the vast majority of orange juice consumed in the US. Florida produced nearly 80% of the nation's oranges and 79% of its grapefruits in 2002. It is also an important producer of other fruits, vegetables, and sugarcane.

The total value of Florida's crops in 2001 exceeded $4.9 billion, 4th highest among the 50 states. Total farm marketings, including livestock marketings and products, exceeded $6.4 billion in 2001 (9th in the US). There were about 44,000 farms covering some 10.2 million acres (4.13 million hectares) in 2002; the total represented nearly 30% of the state's entire land area.

The orange was introduced to Florida by Spanish settlers around 1570. Oranges had become an important commercial crop by the early 1800s, when the grapefruit was introduced. In 1886, orange production for the first time exceeded one million boxes (one box equals 90 lb/41 kg). Much of this production came from groves along the northern Atlantic coast and the St. Johns River, which offered easy access to maritime shipping routes north. The expansion of the railroads and severe freezes in the 1890s encouraged the citrus industry to move farther south. Polk, St. Lucie, Indian River, Hendry, and Hardee counties in central Florida are the largest producers of citrus fruits.

The orange crop totaled 230,000,000 90-lb (41-kg) boxes in the 2001/2002 season. The grapefruit crop was 46,700,000 85-lb (39-kg) boxes; tangerines, 6,600,000 95-lb (43-kg) boxes; and tangelos and temple oranges, 3,700,000 90-lb (41-kg) boxes. There are about 50 processing plants in Florida where citrus fruits are processed into canned or chilled juice, frozen or pasteurized concentrate, or canned fruit sections. Production of frozen concentrate orange juice totaled 235.9 million gallons in 2000. Stock feed made from peel, pulp, and seeds is an important by-product of the citrus-processing industry; annual production is nearly one million tons. Other citrus by-products are citrus molasses, D-limonene, alcohol, wines, preserves, and citrus seed oil.

Florida is the country's 2nd-leading producer of vegetables. Vegetable farming is concentrated in central and southern Florida, especially in the area south of Lake Okeechobee, where drainage of the Everglades left exceptionally rich soil. In 1998, Florida farmers harvested 14,400,000 hundredweight of tomatoes; they sold 9,295,000 hundredweight of potatoes. Florida's tomato and vegetable growers, who had at one time enjoyed a near-monopoly of the US winter vegetable market, began in the 1990s to face increasing competition from Mexican growers, whose lower-priced produce had captured about half the market by 1995. About two-thirds of all farm laborers are hired hands.

Florida's major field crop is sugarcane (mostly grown near Lake Okeechobee), which enjoyed a sizable production increase in the 1960s and 1970s, following the cutoff of imports from Cuba. In 2002, Florida's sugarcane production was 17,606,000 tons. Florida's 2nd-largest field crop is peanuts (197,800,000 lb/ 89,720,000 kg in 2002), followed by cotton, hay, corn, tobacco, soybeans, and wheat. Florida leads the nation in the production of watermelons.

24ANIMAL HUSBANDRY

Florida is an important cattle-raising state. The Kissimmee Plain, north of Lake Okeechobee, is the largest grazing area. In 2003, Florida had an estimated 1.8 million cattle and calves valued at an estimated $1.17 billion. During 2002, Florida had an estimated 35,000 hogs and pigs valued at around $2.59 million. An estimated 2.7 billion eggs were produced in 2001, worth $122.3 million. Florida had an estimated 153,000 milk cows in 2001 that produced around 2.4 billion lb (1.1 billion kg) of milk. Also during 2001, Florida poultry farmers produced 634.2 million lb (287.7 million kg) of broilers, valued at $253.7 million.

25FISHING

Florida's extensive shoreline and numerous inland waterways make sport fishing a major recreational activity. Commercial fishing is also economically important.

In 1998, Florida's commercial fish catch was 114,440,000 lb (51,910,000 kg), worth $188,560,000. That year, 76% of the volume and 79% of the value came from fishing in the Gulf of Mexico; the remainder was from Atlantic waters. The most important commercial species of shellfish are shrimp, spiny lobster, and crabs. Landings of spiny lobster in 1998 totaled 5.2 million lb (2.4 million kg) with a value of $19.4 million, accounting for 89% of the volume and 80% of the value for the US spiny lobster catch that year. Gulf coast shrimp landings totaled 25.2 million lb (11.4 million kg) in 1998. Valuable finfish species include grouper, swordfish, and snapper. Florida's commercial fishing fleet had 9,805 boats and vessels in 1997. In 1997, Florida had 28 Atlantic and 460 Gulf coast processing and wholesale plants employing on average 816 and 5,337 employees, respectively.

Both freshwater and saltwater fishing are important sports. Tarpon, sailfish, and redfish are some of the major saltwater sport species; largemouth bass, panfish, sunfish, catfish, and perch are leading freshwater sport fish. Florida had 1,044,603 sport fishing license holders in 1998 (coastal marine fishing does not require a license).

26FORESTRY

About 47% of Florida's land area—16,285,000 acres (6,590,000 hectares)—was forested in 2002, when the state had about 2.2% of all forested land in the US. A total of 4,016,000 acres (1,625,000 hectares) was owned by the forest industry. The most common tree is the pine, which occurs throughout the state but is most abundant in the north.

Florida's logging industry is concentrated in the northern part of the state. The most important forestry product is pulpwood for paper manufacturing. Lumber production in 2002 was 888 million board feet, mostly softwoods.

Four national forests—Apalachicola, Ocala, Osceola, and Choctawhatchee—covering 1,434,000 acres (580,034 hectares) are located in Florida. State forests covered 1,403,000 acres (567,794 hectares) in 2002. Three of the main activities of state forests are forest management, outdoor recreation, and wildlife management.

Virtually all of Florida's natural forest had been cleared by the mid-20th century; the forests existing today are thus almost entirely the result of reforestation. Since 1928, more than 5.6 billion seedlings have been planted in the state.

27MINING

According to the US Geological Survey, Florida's estimated nonfuel mineral production in 2001 was valued at nearly $1.75 billion (fifth among the states and about 4.5% of the US total). This was a decrease of about 4% from the amount reported in 2000. The phosphate industry usually has the greatest impact on the state's nonfuel mineral economy, and exports of phosphate fertilizers are important to the industry's vitality. The decrease in value in 2001 resulted from lower export sales and prices due to the opening of new phosphoric acid and diammonium phosphate (DAP) plants in Asia. The largest foreign consumers of Florida phosphate are China, India, and the countries of Eastern Europe and the former Soviet Union. Rising phosphate production has led to increased employment in the sector.

Florida leads the nation in phosphate rock, masonry cement, and peat output and ranks among the top three states in crushed stone and masonry cement production. It is also the only state producing rutile concentrates and staurolite. Phosphate rock is the leading mineral commodity in terms of value. Phosphate rock, crushed stone, portland and masonry cement, and construction sand and gravel, together with ilmenite and rutile, accounted for about 94% of the state's nonfuel mineral value in 2001. The state continued as the world's leader in phosphate rock production and led the nation in heavy-mineral output. Florida supplies 25% of the world's and 75% of the nation's phosphate, and five times as much as the next leading state. Crushed stone (90 million metric tons produced, value of $494 million) was the 2nd-leading mineral commodity. Ranking 3rd was Portland cement (4 million metric tons, $305 million). Sand, gravel, and clays rounded out the top five commodities in terms of reportable value.

28ENERGY AND POWER

In 2000, a total of 4 quadrillion Btu (1 quadrillion kcal) of energy was consumed in Florida, ranking it eighth among the 50 states in total energy consumption, and 47th in per capita energy consumption, which was 247 million Btu (62.2 million kcal). The major source of energy consumed is petroleum, which accounted for 47.8% in 1998. Although Florida produces some oil and natural gas, it is a net importer of energy resources. Its mild climate and abundant sunshine offer great potential for solar energy development, but this potential has not been extensively exploited.

In 1999, Florida had an installed electric energy generating capacity (utility and nonutility) of 40,940 MW; net generation was 196.9 billion kWh. In 1999, 20% of electricity produced came from residual fuel oil, 36% from coal, 17% from nuclear, and 23% from natural gas; hydroelectricity and distillate fuels totaled less than 4%. Nuclear generating capacity increased by 27% in August 1983, when the 830,000-kW St. Lucie 2 facility, operated by the Florida Power and Light Co., south of Ft. Pierce, began commercial operation. Also owned by Florida Power and Light are St. Lucie 1, with a capacity of 830,000 kW, and Turkey Point Units 3 and 4, each with a capacity of 693,000 kW, located in Dade County. Florida Power Corp. operates the state's other nuclear power plant, the 830,000-kW Crystal River 3 facility, on the northern Gulf coast.

In 2002, the state produced 10,000 barrels per day of crude oil; proved reserves as of 31 December 2001 were 75 million barrels. Natural gas marketed production in 2002 was 3,343 million cu ft (94.6 million cu m); proved reserves were 84 billion cu ft (2.4 billion cu m) in 2001.

29INDUSTRY

Florida is not a center of heavy industry, and many of its manufacturing activities are related to agriculture and exploitation of natural resources. Leading industries include food processing, electric and electronic equipment, transportation equipment, and chemicals. The value of manufacturing shipments in 1997 totaled $82 billion for the state. Florida's major industrial categories, in terms of value of shipments, were electronic equipment, 15.2%; printing and publishing, 11.8%; food, 11.4%; and chemicals and allied products, 9.1%.

From 1980 to 1990, manufacturing grew by 14.4% in Florida, while declining 6% nationwide. The share of manufacturing to

GSP declined marginally from 10.7% in 1977 to 7.6% in 1997. Florida ranks 2nd only to California in both employment and number of firms engaged in the manufacture of guided missiles and space vehicles; 10% of all US aircraft engines and engine parts are manufactured in Florida. Nearly 20% of the nation's boat manufacturers are located in the state. Electric components are primarily manufactured in three east coast counties (Brevard, Palm Beach, and Broward), where about half of the state's electronic component workers reside, Since the perfection of the laser by Martin-Marietta in Orlando in the 1950s, the greater Orlando area has grown to have the 3rd-highest concentration of electro-optics and laser manufacturers in the US.

The cigar-making industry, traditionally important in Florida, has declined considerably with changes in taste and the cutoff of tobacco imports from Cuba. In the late 1930s, the Tampa area alone had well over 100 cigar factories, employing some 10,000 people. The 1987 Census of Manufactures found just 35 plants statewide. In 1997, cigar manufacturer Havatampa Inc. sold up to $25 million in cigars in the US and abroad.

Manufacturing is currently concentrated in and around Florida's largest cities, such as Miami, Tampa–St. Petersburg, Ft. Lauderdale–Hollywood, and Orlando. Dade and Broward counties (Greater Miami), Hillsborough County (Tampa), Pinellas County (St. Petersburg), Duval County (Jacksonville), Orange County (Orlando), and Palm Beach County account for almost two-thirds of all manufacturing employment.

In 2000, there were 14 Fortune 500 companies headquartered in Florida, including Autonation, Tech Data, Winn-Dixie Stores, Publix Super Markets, Office Depot, CHS Electronics, FPL Group, Ryder System, Florida Progress, Harris, Darden Restaurants, Interim Services, Lennar, and Budget Group.

Earnings of persons employed in Florida increased from $229.7 billion in 1997 to $248.3 billion in 1998, an increase of 8.1%. The largest industries in 1998 were services, 33.6% of earnings; retail trade, 11.6%; and state and local government, 11.5%. Of the industries that accounted for at least 5% of earnings in 1998, the slowest growing from 1997 to 1998 was durable goods manufacturing (5.6% of earnings in 1998), which increased 4.7%; the fastest was finance, insurance, and real estate (9.2% of earnings in 1998), which increased 8.4%.

30COMMERCE

Wholesale trade in 1997 totaled $195 billion, conducted by 34,936 establishments. The state ranked 3rd in retail employment, with 5.9% of the US total. The fashionable shops lining Palm Beach's Worth Avenue make it one of the nation's most famous shopping streets.

In 1997 retail sales totaled $159 billion, conducted by 89,744 establishments. At least 27% of all retail establishments were restaurants, cafeterias, bars, and similar businesses—a reflection, in part, of the importance of the travel business in Florida's economy. Food stores accounted for 11% of establishments; and automotive dealers and service stations, 13%. Food sales amounted to $26 billion in 1997, and general merchandise sales came to $20 billion.

The value of all exports sent from Florida was over $28 billion in 1999, ranked 7th in the nation and accounting for 4% of all US exports. Duty-free goods for reshipment abroad pass through Port Everglades, Miami, Orlando, Jacksonville, Tampa, and Panama City—free-trade zones established to bring international commerce to the state. Exports, including machinery, medical instruments, fertilizers, and knit apparel; went primarily to Brazil ($5.8 billion), Venezuela ($2.6 billion), the Dominican Republic ($2.2 billion), Argentina ($2 billion), and Colombia ($1.8 billion) in 1999. Imports, including motor vehicles, apparel, aircraft and spacecraft, and machinery; came primarily (in order of importance) from Japan, Germany, Brazil, Costa Rica, and the Dominican Republic.

Florida is believed to be the principal entry point for marijuana, cocaine, and other illicit drugs being smuggled into the US from Latin America.

31CONSUMER PROTECTION

The Division of Consumer Services, a division of the Department of Agriculture and Consumer Services, is the state's clearinghouse for consumer complaints and information and performs the initial review under the Motor Vehicle Warranty Enforcement Act—the so-called "Lemon Law." The division also regulates ballroom dance studios, charitable organizations, health studios, motor vehicle repair shops, pawnshops, sellers of travel, sellers of business opportunities, and telemarketers, and maintains the state's No Sales Solicitation Calls list. The Florida Consumers' Council advises the commissioner of agriculture on consumer issues.

The public counsel to the Public Service Commission (PSC), appointed by a joint committee of the legislature, represents the public interest in commission hearings on utility rates and other regulations. The public counsel can also seek judicial review of PSC rulings, and may appear before other state and federal bodies on the public's behalf in utility and transportation matters.

The Department of Business and Professional Regulation oversees pari-mutuel betting; land sales; the operations of condominiums, cooperative apartments, hotels, and restaurants; professions and professional boards; real estate; certified public accounting; and the regulation and licensing of alcoholic beverage and tobacco sales.

In 1983, the state legislature enacted the Motor Vehicle Warranty Enforcement Act, which forces automobile dealers to replace new cars or refund the purchase price if the cars are in constant need of repairs.

32BANKING

The Florida Department of Financial Services, Division of Banking, has regulatory and supervisory authority over state-chartered financial institutions in Florida, including commercial banks and nondeposit trust companies, credit unions, savings associations, offices of foreign banks operating in Florida, and money transmitters. The Florida Department of Financial Services also has regulatory and supervisory authority over mortgage brokers and mortgage lenders, consumer finance companies, motor vehicle sales finance companies, commercial and consumer debt collection agencies, cemeteries, and abandoned property.

As of late 2002, there were 231 insured banks in Florida. Assets of Florida's banks as of September 2002 totaled $39 billion.

International banking grew in Florida during the late 1970s and early 1980s with the establishment of the Edge Act banks in Miami. Located close to Central and South America, with a bilingual population, Florida (and especially Miami) has become a Latin America banking center. Many banks in Miami have headquarters outside Florida and engage exclusively in international banking. At the end of 1999, there were a total of 102 international banking offices in Florida, including state-licensed international bank agencies, foreign representative offices, and administrative offices, with assets of over $44 billion in 1999. The largest of these included Barclays, Lloyds, and Dresdner banks. The largest Edge Act banks included HSBC, Citibank, and Banco Santander Central Hispano International.

Economic growth in Florida, though moderate in 2002, was above the national average, and performance of banks headquartered in Florida improved. Florida's banks experienced higher net interest margins (NIMs) (the difference between the lower rates offered to savers and the higher rates charged on loans) and increased profitability. Community bank loan portfolios grew 22% as of the year ending September 2002; the majority of the increase occurred in commercial real estate (CRE) loans.

33INSURANCE

In 2001 there were 7.9 million ordinary life insurance policies in force with a total value of $561.6 billion; total value for all categories of life insurance (ordinary, group, industrial, and credit) was $864.5 billion. Death benefits paid that year totaled $2.81 Billion. In 2003, 25 life and health insurance companies and 105 property and casualty insurance companies were domiciled in Florida.

In 2001, property and casualty insurers wrote premiums totaling $23.4 billion. That year, Florida ranked first in the nation in flood insurance, with 1.8 million flood insurance policies in force, with a total value of $249.4 million.

The insurance industry is regulated by the state's Department of Insurance.

34SECURITIES

No securities exchanges are located in Florida, but there 3,401 brokers and dealers businesses in the state. A large portion of the industry's total employment is concentrated in the three Gold Coast counties—Dade, Broward, and Palm Beach, totaling 33,293. Investment advisory organizations total 536 (fourth largest amount in the nation). Florida has the headquarters of 251 NASDAQ companies, 28 NASDAQ market makers (fourth most in the nation), 42 AMEX companies (with 6.5% of the nation's total), and 32 incorporations of NYSE listed companies. Major companies include, in order of importance, Winn-Dixie Stores, Office Depot, Entergy, FPL Group, and Ryder System.

35PUBLIC FINANCE

The Office of Planning and Budget of the governor's office prepares and submits to the legislature the budget for each fiscal year, which runs from 1 July to 30 June. The largest expenditure items are education, health and social concerns, general government, and transportation. By prohibiting borrowing to finance operating expenses, Florida's constitution requires a balanced budget.

The issuance of state bonds is overseen by the State Board of Administration, which consists of the governor, the state treasurer, and the comptroller. Three principal types of bonds are issued. The first consists of bonds backed by the "full faith and credit" of the state and payable from general revenue. Issuance of such bonds generally requires voter approval. The second type consists of revenue bonds, payable from income derived from the capital project financed, for example, from bridge or highway tolls. The third type consists of bonds payable from a constitutionally specified source, for example, higher education bonds backed by the state gross receipts tax, or elementary and secondary education bonds backed by the motor vehicle license tax.

In 2000, the state administration enacted the largest tax cut in the state's history ($1.24 billion) involving an 11% reduction in the school property tax back to 1989 levels, a reductions in taxes on intangibles, a one-time 0.5% reduction in employers' payments to the unemployment compensation fund, a one-time $50 rebate on electricity billings, and an extension of the state's obligation to pay interest on tax refunds. In November 2000 Florida voters passed an amendment to the state constitution requiring construction of a high speed railway to begin not later than November 2003, and the voters approved constitutional amendments that mandated the state provide high-quality voluntary pre-kindergarten for all four-year olds by 2005, and

that class sizes be reduced to prescribed limits by 2010 with the first reductions in 2003. Florida was projected to finish 2002/03 with a positive general fund balance of $140 million and about $960 million in its rainy day fund, but on 15 November 2002 the state reduced its revenue estimate by $7 million for the current year, and by $234 million for 2003/04. Also in 2002, the government raised the state's gasoline tax from 4 cents a gallon to 13.9 cents a gallon. Revenue shortfalls, together with mandated spending to implement the recent constitutional amendments, led to an estimated deficit for 2003/04 of $2 billion to $2.5 billion (about 10% of the state budget).

In 2002/03 expenditures from the general fund totaled $21.081 billion, 51.2% allocated to education, 25.5% to health and human services, 13.5% to public safety, 5% for government operations and the courts, 1.6% for economic development, and 0.75% for natural resources and the environment. The general fund accounted for only 36% of state administered funds, with over half (51.3%) coming from dedicated trust funds, of which Florida has over 400. In the recommended appropriations in the governor's budget for 2003/04, general fund expenditures were increased 3% to $21.7 billion (35% of total state administered expenditures), 51.5% for education, 25.9% for health and human services, 13.8% for public safety, 6.1% for government operations and the courts, 2.4% for economic opportunities, and 1.5% natural resources and the environment.

The following table from the US Census Bureau contains information on revenues, expenditures, indebtedness, and cash/securities for 2001.

	($000)	PERCENT	PER CAPITA
Population (thousands, 2001)	16,373	(X)	(X)
Total Revenue	46,370,565	100.00	2,832.14
General revenue	44,197,759	95.31	2,699.43
Utility revenue	6,566	0.01	0.40
Liquor store revenue	–	–	–
Insurance trust revenue	2,166,240	4.67	132.31
Exhibit: Salaries and wages	8,438,503	16.79	515.39
Total expenditure	50,264,767	100.00	3,069.98
General expenditure	46,595,398	92.70	2,845.87
Education	15,849,719	31.53	968.04
Public welfare	10,894,948	21.68	665.42
Hospitals	218,976	0.44	13.37
Health	2,566,357	5.11	156.74
Highways	4,615,902	9.18	281.92
Police protection	398,715	0.79	24.35
Correction	2,248,117	4.47	137.31
Natural resources	1,551,244	3.09	94.74
Parks and recreation	173,936	0.35	10.62
Government administration	1,934,279	3.85	118.14
Interest on general debt	1,061,867	2.11	64.85
Other and unallocable	5,081,338	10.11	310.35
Utility expenditure	49,118	0.10	3.00
Liquor store expenditure	–	–	–
Insurance trust expenditure	3,620,251	7.20	221.11
Debt at end of fiscal year	18,613,380	100.00	1,136.83
Cash and security holdings	103,313,635	100.00	6,310.00

36TAXATION

Florida's constitution prohibits a personal income tax, and the 6% sales and use tax provides over half of state revenue. Over half of Florida's non-federal revenue is collected at the local level, however, most through local property taxes, but there are also some local sales taxes, ranging up to 1.5%. The state sales tax applies to most retail items (but excludes groceries, medicines, and certain other items), as well as to car and hotel room rentals and theater admissions. The use tax is levied on wholesale items brought into Florida for sale. Various selective sales taxes (excises) are imposed, including the gasoline tax, which was raised in 2002. The state corporate income tax is a flat 5.5% on net income, over $5,000 with an alternative minimum tax (AMT) of 3.3%. The state estate tax is set equal to the state tax exemption from the federal estate tax, and thus is scheduled to be phased out by 2007 in tandem with the phase out of the federal tax credit absent any countervailing action by the Florida government. Estimated state losses from the phase-out of its estate tax are -$153.2 million in 2003, -$361.6 million in 2004, and -$930.3 million in 2007. Other taxes include state property taxes, an oil, gas and sulfur production tax, a solid minerals severance tax and state license fees.

In 2002, state revenues in Florida totaled $24.8 billion, of which 58% came from the general sales tax, 18% from selective sales taxes, 7.6% from documentary and stock transfer taxes, 6.2% from license fees and 4.9% from corporate income taxes.

The following table from the US Census Bureau provides a summary of taxes collected by the state in 2002.

	($000)	PER CAPITA
Total Taxes	24,815,964	1,484.82
Property taxes	427,626	25.59
Sales and gross receipts	18,920,191	1,132.05
General sales and gross receipts	14,408,709	862.12
Selective sales taxes	4,511,482	269.94
Alcoholic beverage	547,682	32.77
Amusements	(X)	(X)
Insurance Premiums	414,369	24.79
Motor fuels	1,808,863	108.23
Pari-mutuels	29,822	1.78
Public utilities	769,480	46.04
Tobacco products	466,464	27.91
Other selective sales	474,802	28.41
Licenses	1,556,806	93.15
Alcoholic beverages	30,607	1.83
Amusements	4,697	0.28
Corporation	128,147	7.67
Hunting and fishing	12,926	0.77
Motor vehicle	940,387	56.27
Motor vehicle operators	121,316	7.26
Public utility	30,503	1.83
Occupation and business, NEC	281,803	16.86
Other	6,420	0.38
Other taxes	3,911,341	234.03
Individual income	(X)	(X)
Corporation net income	1,218,864	72.93
Death and gift	751,611	44.97
Documentary and stock transfer	1,900,752	113.73
Severance	40,114	2.4
Other	(X)	(X)

37ECONOMIC POLICY

In the late 1990s, Florida intensified its efforts to attract high-tech, high-wage industries such as silicon technologies and aviation/aerospace industries. Florida became the first state in the nation to close its Department of Commerce. All of the state's economic development and international trade strategies are now handled through a partnership of business and government, Enterprise Florida. This new approach calls for collaboration among leaders in government, business, and academia. Enterprise Florida and its regional and local partner organizations provide a statewide network of business assistance resources in the areas of capital acquisition, technology commercialization, manufacturing competitiveness, training, minority and rural business development, incentives, site selection, permitting, and trade development. Through buying blocks of discounting tickets, arranging for bargain airfares, setting up meeting with local business people, and providing a distinctive Florida booth, Enterprise Florida lowers the cost of attending trade shows for Florida exporters. Promoting Florida exports has been a major concern of recent economic policy. As of mid-2002, Governor Jeb Bush had personally led trade missions to Argentina, Brazil, Chile, Israel, Mexico and the UK. The International Trade and Business Development unit of Enterprise Florida is based in

Miami with six field offices in the state and 14 international offices, including ones in Frankfurt, Germany; London, England; Taipei, Republic of China; Toronto, Canada; Seoul, South Korea; Mexico City, Mexico; Tokyo, Japan; and Sao Paolo, Brazil. Florida has 14 deep-water commercial seaports; 5 barge ports; 9 major shallow-water ports; 4 river ports; and 16 customs ports of entry. As of 2003, 20 Free Trade Zones (FTZs) had been designated, all located at or near seaports and international airports. Value added in the FTZs is not subject to US customs duties unless processed goods are imported for sale in the domestic market.

38HEALTH

Reflecting the age distribution of the state's population, Florida has a relatively low birthrate and a high death rate. Florida's live birthrate was 13.2 per 1,000 population in 2001. The state's 2000 infant mortality rate was 7 per 1,000 live births. Some 83,971 legal abortions were performed in Florida in 1999, averaging 28 abortions per 1,000 women.

Florida's 2000 death rate, 1,072.2 per 100,000 population, was the fifth highest of all the states and well above the national rate of 873.1, due in part to the state's considerable geriatric population. A better measure is the age-adjusted death rate. For 2000, the age-adjusted death rate for Florida was 828.8 per 100,000 persons, substantially below the national rate of 872. In 2000, Florida exceeded the national rate in deaths from heart disease, cerebrovascular disease, accidents, and suicide. Of the residents 18 years of age and older 23.2% were smokers in 2000. In the same year, the HIV-related death rate was 11.7 per 100,000 population. AIDS cases numbering 85,324 had been reported through 2001.

In 2001, Florida had 202 community hospitals with 216,509 full-time equivalent personnel. In the same year, the total number of beds available was 51,762; admissions totaled 2,207,147. There were 55,402 full-time registered nurses and 7,003 full-time licensed practical nurses in 2001 and 280 physicians per 100,000 population in 2000.

In 2001, the preliminary average cost per inpatient day was $1,248.80. Federal government grants to cover the Medicare and Medicaid services in 2001 totaled $5.4 billion; 2,838,345 enrollees received Medicare benefits that year. At least 17.5% of the population was uninsured in 2002.

39SOCIAL WELFARE

In 2001, the average weekly unemployment benefit was $221.39. Average monthly participation in the food stamp program in FY2002 comprised 985,130 persons (472,697 households). The average monthly benefit was $74.31, and the sum total of benefits paid in FY2002 was $878,454,831.

With the enactment of the Personal Responsibility and Work Opportunity Reconciliation Act of 1996, the US government has changed the form and regulations for many of its social welfare programs. Most significantly, it replaces Aid to Families with Dependent Children (AFDC), an open-ended entitlement program, with Temporary Assistance for Needy Families (TANF), a limited system of assistance funded largely through federal block grants. The reform act also impacts the food stamp program, the Supplemental Security Income program, and the child nutrition program. The law took effect on 1 July 1997 and provided $16.38 billion in block grants for fiscal years 1997–2002. The grants are to be divided among the states based on an equation involving the numbers of former AFDC recipients in each state. Reauthorization of the 1996 social welfare legislation, scheduled for 2002, was delayed, and the original law had been extended three times as of July 2003, with the most recent extension running through September 2003. Florida's TANF program is called the Welfare Transition Program. In June 2000 the state had 135,903 welfare recipients. State expenditures on the TANF program in FY2002 totaled $368,880,050.

In December 2001, Social Security benefits were paid to 3,235,390 Floridians. This number included 2,193,890 retired workers, 306,820 widows and widowers, 321,540 disabled workers, 190,710 spouses, and 222,430 children. Social Security beneficiaries represented 19.8% of the total state population and 85.3% of the state's population age 65 and older. Retired workers (excluding persons with special benefits) received an average monthly payment of $870; widows and widowers, $846; disabled workers, $818; and spouses, $439. Payments for children of retired workers averaged $405 per month; children of deceased workers, $558; and children of disabled workers, $242.

Federal Supplemental Security Income payments in December 2001 went to 386,334 Florida residents, averaging $367 a month.

40 HOUSING

Florida's housing market fluctuated widely in the 1970s and early 1980s. During the mid-1970s recession, home buying dropped off markedly, and much newly completed housing could not be sold. By late in the decade, however, the unused housing stock had been depleted, and a new building boom was under way. The number of housing units in Florida increased 73.2% between 1970 and 1980, but only by 39.4% between 1980 and 1990. In 1990, 35% of all housing units had been built in the previous decade; only 3.7% were built before 1940.

In 2002, there were an estimated 7,624,378 housing units in Florida, ranking the state fourth in the nation for total number of housing units (after California, Texas, and New York). About 6,568,733 of the units were occupied; 70.4% were owner-occupied. About 52.5% of all units were single-family, detached homes; 11.8% were in buildings with 20 units or more; and about 11% were mobile homes. It was estimated that about 222,508 units were without telephone service, 27,078 lacked complete plumbing facilities, and 38,126 lacked complete kitchen facilities. About 76% of all units relied on electricity for heating; about 2,189 units were equipped for solar power heating. The average household size was 2.48 people.

In 2002, 185,431 new privately owned housing units were authorized for construction. Multifamily housing ranges from beachfront luxury high rises along the Gold Coast to dilapidated residential hotels in the South Beach section of Miami Beach. In 2002, the median value of one-family homes was $128,120. The median monthly cost for mortgage owners was $1,091 while renters paid a median of $702 per month. Florida received over $280.6 million in community planning and development aid from the US Department of Housing and Urban Development in 2002.

The Division of Florida Land Sales and Condominiums, within the Department of Business Regulation, registers all sellers of subdivided land and oversees the advertising and selling of land, condominiums, and cooperatives. A major controversy involving condominiums in the early 1970s centered on "rec leases." Until the practice was outlawed in mid-decade, condominium developers often retained ownership of such recreational facilities as the swimming pool, clubhouse, and tennis courts, requiring apartment purchasers to pay rent for their use. The rents were generally set quite low at the time of sale, but raised sharply soon after.

41 EDUCATION

In the 1970s, Florida was an innovator in several areas of education, including competency testing, expansion of community colleges, and school finance reform. Further advances were made in 1983 and 1984, when the state increased taxes to help fund education, raised teachers' salaries, initiated the nation's strictest high school graduation requirements, and reformed the curriculum.

Student achievement in reading, writing, and mathematics is measured by national norm-referenced tests selected at the district level, and by the High School Competency Test (HSCT), measuring communication and math skills of 11th-grade students. In 2000, 79.9% of Floridians 25 years of age or older were high school graduates; 22.3% had four or more years of college.

The total enrollment for fall 1999 in Florida's public schools stood at 2,381,396. Of these, 1,725,493 attended schools from kindergarten through grade eight, and 655,903 attended high school. Minority students made up approximately 47% of the total enrollment in public elementary and secondary schools in 2001. Total enrollment was estimated at 2,434,403 in fall 2000 and expected to reach 2,441,000 by fall 2005. Enrollment in nonpublic schools in fall 2001 was 290,872. Expenditures for public education in 2000/01 were estimated at $14,562,376.

As of fall 2000, there were 886,825,259 students enrolled in college or graduate school. In the same year Florida had 164 degree-granting institutions. In 1997, minority students comprised 33.9% of total postsecondary enrollment. Florida has nine state universities, the largest being the University of Florida (Gainesville). Also part of the state university system are special university centers, such as the University of Florida's Institute of Food and Agricultural Science, which provide advanced and graduate courses. The State University System also offers instruction at strategic sites away from the regular campuses. In 1972, Florida completed a community college system that put a public two-year college within commuting distance of virtually every resident. As a result, the state has 28 community colleges. Of Florida's 83 private four-year institutions of higher education, by far the largest is the University of Miami (Coral Gables).

The policy-making body for the state university system is the Board of Regents; the chancellor is the system's chief administrative officer. Florida's school finance law, the Florida Education Finance Act of 1973, establishes a funding formula aimed at equalizing both per-pupil spending statewide and the property tax burdens of residents of different school districts.

42 ARTS

Florida is home to a vibrant and diverse cultural community. Florida ranks near the top nationally in state funding for culture and the arts. Cultural organizations thrive in virtually every county and include museums, galleries, symphonies, dance and opera companies, and literary organizations. Offerings range from the Miami Book Fair International at one end of the state, to the widely renowned Jacksonville Jazz Festival, to the Naval Aviation Museum in Pensacola at the other end. According to the 1990 US Census, Florida ranked fourth nationally in the number of individual artists living and working in the state. Key West has long been a gathering place for creative artists, ranging from John James Audubon and Winslow Homer to Ernest Hemingway and Tennessee Williams.

Regional and metropolitan symphony orchestras include the Florida Philharmonic Orchestra (Fort Lauderdale), Florida Orchestra (Tampa), Jacksonville Symphony, and the Florida West Coast Symphony (Sarasota). Opera companies include the Florida Grand Opera (Miami) and the Sarasota Opera. The four state theater companies are the Caldwell Theatre Company (Boca Raton), Hippodrome State Theatre (Gainesville), Coconut Grove Playhouse (Miami), and the Asolo Theatre Company (Sarasota). The annual Florida International Festival (FIF), established in 1966, features world-renowned artists in music and dance. The London Symphony Orchestra, which has a summer residency in Daytona Beach, provides an annual concert series for the FIF and the city.

Florida is also home to premier museums and performing arts halls, such as the John and Mable Ringling Museum of Art (Sarasota), the Norton Gallery (West Palm Beach), the Miami Art Museum, Orlando Museum of Art, Philharmonic Center for the Arts (Naples), Tampa Bay Performing Arts Center, and the Kravis Center for the Performing Arts (West Palm Beach).

Truly unique cultural institutions also located in Florida include Fairchild Tropical Garden (Miami), the Atlantic Center for the Arts (New Smyrna Beach), and Bok Tower Gardens (Lake Wales), which has a working carillon.

The State of Florida's Division of Cultural Affairs (DCA) was established in 1969. The Florida Arts Council (previously the Fine Arts Council of Florida) serves in an advisory capacity to the DCA. The DCA has a partnership with the Southern Arts Federation. The DCA also coordinates a touring program, a public art program that acquires artwork for new state buildings, an arts license plate program, and the Florida Artists Hall of Fame, which includes such luminaries as Zora Neale Hurston, Ernest Hemingway, Ray Charles, Marjorie Kinnan Rawlings, and Robert Rauschenberg. In 2003, Florida arts organizations received grant awards from the National Endowment of the Arts that totaled $1,334,900.

The Florida Humanities Council, established in 1971, sponsors about 300 free programs per year throughout the state. In 2000, the National Endowment for the Humanities supported 33 Florida based programs with grants totaling $1,697,758. In 1997, it was estimated that attendance at arts and cultural events reached about 80 million people.

43 LIBRARIES AND MUSEUMS

Florida had nine multi-county library systems and 40 county systems in 2000. Circulation totaled 75,708,000. The largest public library systems are those of Miami–Dade County (3,886,852 volumes in 1999) and Jacksonville (2,351,104 volumes). The State Library in Tallahassee housed 661,849 volumes; the State Library also distributes federal aid to local libraries and provides other assistance. Total public library income totaled $355,388,000 in 2000. Federal aid to Florida public libraries totaled $3.6 million; state aid to public libraries was $33.1 million. The largest university library in the state is that of the University of Florida, with holdings of more than 3.4 million volumes in 1999. Other major university libraries are those of the University of Miami and Florida State University (2.2 million each).

Florida has about 278 museums, galleries, and historical sites, as well as numerous public gardens. One of the best-known museums is the John and Mabel Ringling Museum of Art (Sarasota), a state owned facility which houses the collection of the late circus entrepreneur, featuring Italian and North European Renaissance paintings. Also in Sarasota are the Ringling Museum of the Circus and the Circus Hall of Fame, and Ca'd'Zan, the Ringling mansion. The estates and homes of a number of prominent former Florida residents are now open as museums. The Villa Vizcaya Museum and Gardens in Miami, originally the estate of International Harvester founder James R. Deering, displays his collection of 15th–18th-century antiques. Railroad developer Henry Morrison Flagler's home in Palm Beach is now a museum in his name. The Society of the Four Arts is also in Palm Beach. On Key West, Ernest Hemingway's home is also a museum. The John James Audubon house in Key West and Thomas Edison's house in Ft. Myers are two of Florida's other great homes.

The Metrozoo-Miami, with an average annual attendance of 650,000, and the Jacksonville Zoological park, 522,000, are among the state's leading zoos. Both Busch Gardens (Tampa) and Sea World of Florida (Orlando) report average annual attendances of over 3,000,000.

The largest historic restoration in Florida is in St. Augustine, where several blocks of the downtown area have been restored to their 18th-century likeness under the auspices of the Historic St. Augustine Preservation Board, a state agency. Castillo de San Marcos, the 17th-century Spanish fort at St. Augustine, is now a national monument under the jurisdiction of the National Park Service and is open to the public. Other Florida cities having historic preservation boards are Pensacola, Tallahassee, and Tampa.

44 COMMUNICATIONS

As of 2001, 93.2% of the state's occupied housing units had telephones.

Florida's first radio station was WFAW (later WQAM) in Miami, which went on the air in 1920. In 2003, the state had 73 major AM stations and 124 major FM radio stations. Miami was also the site of the state's first television station, WTVJ, which began broadcasting on 27 January 1949.

Film and television production in Florida is a billion-dollar per year industry with over 5,000 production companies providing more than 100,000 jobs. There were 62 major TV stations in Florida in 2003. In 1999, the Tampa-St. Petersburg-Sarasota area had 1,485,980 television households, 74% of which had cable. The Orlando-Daytona Beach-Melbourne area had a 77% penetration rate for cable in television-owning households. At West Palm Beach-Fort Pierce, 85% of television households had cable. The Miami-Fort Lauderdale area had 1,441,570 television households, with a 73% penetration rate for cable. A total of 471,645 Internet domain names were registered in Florida by 2000, the fourth most of any state.

45 PRESS

The *East Florida Gazette,* published in St. Augustine in 1783–84, was Florida's earliest newspaper. The oldest paper still publishing is the *Jacksonville Times-Union* (now *Florida Times-Union*), which first appeared in February 1883.

In 2002, the state had 40 morning papers, 3 evening papers, and 38 Sunday papers. The leading English-language dailies and their circulations in 2002 were:

AREA	NAME	DAILY	SUNDAY
Ft. Lauderdale	*Sun-Sentinel*(m,S)	251,886	363,063
Jacksonville	*Florida Times-Union*(m,S)	172,239	231,627
Miami	*Herald*(m,S)	317,690	426,058
Orlando	*Sentinel*(all day,S)	254,956	375,768
St. Petersburg	*Times*(m,S)	331,903	414,195
Sarasota	*Herald-Tribune*(m,S)	106,077	133,092
Tampa	*Tribune*(m,S)	212,983	297,317
West Palm Beach	*Palm Beach Post*(m,S)	171,572	212,641

Spanish language newspapers include *Diario Las Americas* and *El Nuevo Herald*, both published in Miami with circulations under 100,000. The most widely read periodical published in Florida is the sensationalist *National Enquirer*. There were 30 book publishers in Florida in 1997, including Academic Press and University Presses of Florida.

46 ORGANIZATIONS

In 2003, there were over 5,000 regional, national, and international organizations within the state. Commercial, trade, and professional organizations based in Florida include the American Accounting Association (Sarasota), American Welding Society (Miami), American Electroplaters' Society (Winter Park), Florida Citrus Mutual (Lakeland), the International Songwriters Guild (Orlando), and Florida Fruit and Vegetable Association (Orlando).

Sports groups include the National Association for Stock Car Auto Racing, better known as NASCAR (Daytona Beach), American Surfing Association (Lake Worth), American Water Ski

Association (Winter Haven), International Game Fish Association (Ft. Lauderdale), the International Softball Association (Plant City), and International Swimming Hall of Fame (Ft. Lauderdale).

The Academy of Arts and Sciences of the Americas and the National Foundation for Advancement in the Arts are located in Miami. State and regional organizations for the arts include the Florida Cultural Alliance, the Florida Keys Council of the Arts, and the Jazz Society of Pensacola. State organizations for the environment include the Florida Wildlife Federation and Friends of the Everglades.

Among other organizations with headquarters in Florida are the American Sunbathing Association, formerly the International Nudist Conference (Kissimmee), the American Automobile Association (Heathrow), and the National Head Start Association (Bradenton).

47 TOURISM, TRAVEL, AND RECREATION

Tourism is a mainstay of the state's economy. Most of Florida's tourists are from elsewhere in the US although Miami attracts large numbers of affluent Latin American travelers, lured at least in part by the Latin flavor the large Cuban community has given the city. In 2002, there were about 75.5 million visitors to the state, a figure that represents a 10% increase in domestic visitors (from 2001), but a 4% decrease in overseas travelers.

Supporting the industry is VISIT FLORIDA, a public and private partnership organization established in 1996 in cooperation with the Florida Commission on Tourism. A portion of the funding for the organization comes from the state's $2.05 per day rental car surcharge. Most funding comes from the private sector.

Over 839,000 Floridians work directly in tourist- and recreation-related businesses, and the state ranks 2nd in the nation in the number of travel and tourism employees. In 1999, the state had 4,717 hotels and motels. More than half of all hotels were located in Dade County, where hotels and other tourist accommodations stretch for miles along Collins Avenue in Miami Beach, in the heart of the state's tourist industry.

Florida's biggest tourist attractions are its sun, sand, and surf. According to the state's Department of Commerce, leisure-time activity is the principal reason why more than four-fifths of auto travelers enter the state. Major tourist attractions include Walt Disney World, Universal Orlando, and Sea World Orlando. Other major attractions are the Kennedy Space Center at Cape Canaveral and the St. Augustine historic district.

Nine parks and other facilities in Florida operated by the National Park Service draw millions of visitors annually, inducing Biscayne National Park and Everglades National Park. The most popular destination is the Gulf Islands National Seashore, located near Pensacola, followed by the Canaveral National Seashore. Approximately 110 facilities are operated by the Division of Recreation and Parks of the state's Department of Natural Resources. These facilities include 28 state parks, 28 state recreation areas, and 18 state historical sites. Fishing and boating are major recreational activities at these sites.

In the 1970s and early 1980s, the Miami Beach tourist hotels faced increasing competition from Caribbean and Latin American resorts. The city's business community, seeking to boost tourism, strongly backed a 1978 statewide referendum to authorize casino gambling along part of Collins Avenue in Miami Beach and Hollywood; however, the proposal was defeated by a wide margin. In a local advisory referendum in March 1980, Miami Beach voters approved development in South Beach of an $850 million, 250-acre (100-hectare) complex that included hotels and a convention center. Off-track betting, horse racing (four thoroughbred racetracks and one harness racetrack), dog racing (18 greyhound tracks), jai alai (nine frontons), and bingo are all legalized and operative forms of gaming.

48 SPORTS

Florida has nine major league professional sports teams: the Miami Dolphins, Tampa Bay Buccaneers, and Jacksonville Jaguars of the National Football League; the Miami Heat and the Orlando Magic of the National Basketball Association; the Tampa Bay Lightning and the Florida Panthers of the National Hockey League; and the Florida Marlins and the Tampa Bay Devil Rays of Major League Baseball. Two WNBA teams and two Major League Soccer teams folded or relocated in 2002. Of the football teams, the Dolphins have been by far the most successful, winning the Super Bowl in 1973 (following the NFL's only undefeated season) and 1974, and appearing in three other Super Bowls (in 1972, 1983, and 1985). The Tampa Bay Buccaneers captured a Super Bowl title in 2003, their first ever since joining the NFL in the 1970s. Many Major League Baseball teams have their spring training camps in Florida and play exhibition games (in the "Grapefruit League") in the spring.

Several tournaments on both the men's and women's professional golf tours are played in Florida. In auto racing, the Daytona 500 is a top race on the NASCAR Winston Cup circuit, and the Pennzoil 400 is run at the Homestead-Miami Speedway, while the 24 Hours of Daytona is one of the top sports car races in the world. Three of the major collegiate football bowl games are played in the state: the Orange Bowl in Miami, the Gator Bowl in Jacksonville, and the Florida Citrus Bowl in Orlando.

In collegiate sports, football dominates. The University of Florida, Florida State, and the University of Miami all emerged as nationally ranked powerhouses in the 1980s and 1990s. Miami won the Orange Bowl in 1946, 1984, 1988, 1989, and 1992, the Sugar Bowl in 1990, the Gator Bowl in 2000, and the Cotton Bowl in 1991. The Hurricanes were named national champions in 1983, 1987, 1989, 1991, and 2001. Florida State won the Orange Bowl in 1993, 1994, and 1996, the Sugar Bowl in 1989, 1998, and 2000, and the Cotton Bowl in 1992. The Seminoles were named national champions in 1993 and 1999. The University of Florida won the Orange Bowl in 1967 and 1999, the Gator Bowl in 1984 and 1993, the Florida Citrus Bowl in 1998, the Sugar Bowl in 1994, and defeated Florida State in the 1997 Sugar Bowl to win the national championship.

Other annual sporting events include rodeos in Arcadia and Kissimmee and the Pepsi 400 Auto Race in Daytona Beach. Emmitt Smith, Steve Carlton, Chris Evert, and Tracy McGrady were all born in the Sunshine State.

49 FAMOUS FLORIDIANS

The first Floridian to serve in a presidential cabinet was Alan S. Boyd (b.1922), named the first secretary of transportation (1967–69) by President Lyndon Johnson. Florida also produced one of the major US military figures of World War II, General Joseph Warren Stilwell (1883–1946), dubbed "Vinegar Joe" for his strongly stated opinions. Graduated from West Point in 1904, he served in France during World War I. First posted to China in the 1920s, he became chief of staff to General Chiang Kai-shek and commander of US forces in the China-Burma-India theater during World War II. He was promoted to full general in 1944 but forced to leave China because of his criticism of the Chiang Kai-shek regime. Janet Reno (b.1938), Attorney General of the United States in the Clinton administration, was born in Miami.

David Levy Yulee (b.St. Thomas, 1810–86) came to Florida in 1824 and, after serving in the US House of Representatives, was appointed one of the state's first two US senators in 1845, thereby becoming the first Jew to sit in the Senate. He resigned in 1861 to serve in the Confederate Congress. Yulee built the first cross-state railroad, from Fernandina to Cedar Key, in the late 1860s. Ruth

Bryan Owen Rohde (b.Illinois, 1885–1954), a longtime Miami resident and member of the US House of Representatives (1929–33), in 1933 became the first woman to head a US diplomatic office abroad when she was named minister to Denmark.

Prominent governors of Florida include Richard Keith Call (b.Virginia, 1792–1862), who came to Florida with General Andrew Jackson in 1821 and remained to become governor of the territory in 1826–39 and 1841–44. In the summer of 1836, Call commanded the US campaign against the Seminole. Although a southerner and a slaveholder, he steadfastly opposed secession. Napoleon Bonaparte Broward (1857–1910) was, before becoming governor, a ship's pilot and owner of St. Johns River boats. He used one of these, *The Three Friends*, a powerful seagoing tug, to run guns and ammunition to Cuban rebels in 1896. As governor (1905–9), he was noted for a populist program that included railroad regulation, direct elections, state college reorganization and coordination, and drainage of the Everglades under state auspices. As governor in 1955–61, Thomas LeRoy Collins (1909–91), met the desegregation issue by advocating moderation and respect for the law, helping the state avoid violent confrontations. He served as chairman of both the southern and national governors' conferences, and he was named by President Johnson as the first director of the Community Relations Service under the 1964 Civil Rights Act.

Military figures who have played a major role in Florida's history include the Spanish conquistadors Juan Ponce de León (c.1460–1521), the European discoverer of Florida, and Pedro Menéndez de Avilés (1519–74), founder of the first permanent settlement, St. Augustine. Andrew Jackson (b.South Carolina, 1767–1845), a consistent advocate of US seizure of Florida, led military expeditions into the territory in 1814 and 1818 and, after US acquisition, served briefly in 1821 as Florida's military governor before leaving for Tennessee. During the Seminole War of 1835–42, one of the leading military tacticians was Osceola (c.1800–1838), who, although neither born a chief nor elected to that position, rose to the leadership of the badly divided Seminole by force of character and personality. He rallied them to fierce resistance to removal, making skillful use of guerrilla tactics. Captured under a flag of truce in 1837, he was imprisoned; already broken in health, he died in Fort Moultrie in Charleston harbor. During the Civil War, General Edmund Kirby Smith (1824–93), a native of St. Augustine who graduated from West Point in 1845, served as commander (1863–65) of Confederate forces west of the Mississippi River. He surrendered the last of the southern forces at Galveston, Texas, on 26 May 1865.

Among the late-19th-century entrepreneurs who played significant roles in Florida's development, perhaps the most important was Henry Morrison Flagler (b.New York, 1830–1913). Flagler made a fortune in Ohio as an associate of John D. Rockefeller in the Standard Oil Co. and did not even visit Florida until he was in his fifties. However, in the 1880s he began to acquire and build railroads down the length of Florida's east coast and to develop tourist hotels at various points, including St. Augustine, Palm Beach, and Miami, helping to create one of the state's major present-day industries. Henry Bradley Plant (b.Connecticut, 1819–99) did for Florida's west coast what Flagler did for the east. Plant extended railroad service to Tampa in 1884, built a huge tourist hotel there, developed the port facilities, and established steamship lines.

Among Floridians prominent in science was Dr. John F. Gorrie (b.South Carolina, 1802–55), who migrated to Apalachicola in 1833 and became a socially and politically prominent physician, specializing in the treatment of fevers. He blew air over ice brought in by ship from the north to cool the air in sickrooms, and he independently developed a machine to manufacture ice, only to have two others beat him to the patent office by days.

The noted labor and civil rights leader A. Philip Randolph (1889–1979) was a native of Crescent City. Mary McLeod Bethune (b.South Carolina, 1875–1955) was an advisor to President Franklin D. Roosevelt on minority affairs, became the first president (1935) of the National Council of Negro Women, and was a consultant at the 1945 San Francisco Conference that founded the UN. A prominent black educator, she opened a school for girls at Daytona Beach in 1904. The school merged with Cookman Institute in 1923 to become Bethune-Cookman College, which she headed until 1942 and again in 1946–47.

Prominent Florida authors include James Weldon Johnson (1871–1938), perhaps best known for his 1912 novel *Autobiography of an Ex-Colored Man*. He was also the first black to be admitted to the Florida bar (1897) and was a founder and secretary of the NAACP. Marjory Stoneman Douglas (b.Minnesota, 1890–1998), who came to Miami in 1915, was the author of several works reflecting her concern for the environment, including *The Everglades: River of Grass* (first published in 1947), *Hurricane* (1958), and *Florida: The Long Frontier* (1967). Marjorie Kinnan Rawlings (b.Washington, D.C., 1895–1953) came to Florida in 1928 to do creative writing. After her first novel, *South Moon Under* (1933), came the Pulitzer Prize–winning *The Yearling* (1938), the poignant story of a 12-year-old boy on the Florida frontier in the 1870s. Zora Neale Hurston (1901–60), born in poverty in the all-Negro town of Eatonville and a graduate of Barnard College, spent four years collecting folklore, which she published in *Mules and Men* (1935) and *Tell My Horse* (1938).

Entertainers born in Florida include Sidney Poitier (b.1927), Charles Eugene "Pat" Boone (b.1934), Faye Dunaway (b.1941), and Ben Vereen (b.1946).

Florida's most famous sports figure is Chris Evert Lloyd (Christine Marie Evert, b.1953), who became a dominant force in women's tennis in the mid-1970s. After turning pro in 1973, she won the Wimbledon singles title in 1974, 1976, and 1981, and the US Open from 1975 to 1978 and in 1980 and 1982. She retired from tennis in 1990.

50 BIBLIOGRAPHY

Baptist, Edward E. *Creating an Old South: Middle Florida's Plantation Frontier Before the Civil War.* Chapel Hill: University of North Carolina Press, 2002.

Bennett, Charles E. *Florida's French Revolution, 1793–1795.* Gainesville: University Presses of Florida, 1981.

Danese, Tracy E. *Claude Pepper and Ed Ball: Politics, Purpose, and Power.* Gainesville: University Press of Florida, 2000.

Daver, Manning J., ed. *Florida Politics and Government.* 2nd ed. Gainesville: University Presses of Florida, 1984.

Douglas, Marjory Stoneman. *The Everglades: River of Grass.* Rev. ed. Miami: Banyan, 1978.

Federal Writers' Project. *Florida: A Guide to the Southernmost State.* Reprint. New York: Somerset, 1981 (orig. 1939).

Gannon, Michael, ed. *The New History of Florida.* Gainesville, Fla.: University Presses of Florida, 1996.

Groene, Janet and Gordon Groene. *Florida Guide.* Cold Spring Harbor, N.Y.: Open Road Publishing, 2000.

Hanna, Kathryn T. Abbey. *Florida: Land of Change.* Chapel Hill: University of North Carolina Press, 1948.

Jahoda, Gloria. *Florida: A Bicentennial History.* New York: Norton, 1976.

Johns, John E. *Florida During the Civil War.* Gainesville: University Presses of Florida, 1963.

Lyon, Eugene. *The Enterprise of Florida: Pedro Menèndez de Avilès and the Spanish Conquest of 1565–68.* Gainesville: University Presses of Florida, 1976.

MacDonald, John D. *Condominium*. Philadelphia: Lippincott, 1977.

Mahon, John K. *The Second Seminole War*. Gainesville: University Presses of Florida, 1967.

Patrick, Rembert W. *Florida Under Five Flags*. Gainesville: University Presses of Florida, 1960.

Rawlings, Marjorie Kinnan. *The Yearling*. New York: Scribner, 1938.

Shofner, Jerrell M. *Nor Is It Over Yet: Florida in the Era of Reconstruction, 1863–77*. Gainesville: University Presses of Florida, 1974.

Smiley, Nixon. *Knights of the Fourth Estate: The Story of the Miami Herald*. Miami: Seeman, 1974.

———. *Yesterday's Florida*. Miami: Seeman, 1974.

Tebeau, Charlton. *A History of Florida*. Coral Gables: University of Miami Press, 1981 (orig. 1971).

Thulesius, Olav. *Harriet Beecher Stowe in Florida, 1867 to 1884*. Jefferson, N.C.: McFarland, 2001.

Wright J. Leitch, Jr. *Florida in the American Revolution*. Gainesville: University Presses of Florida, 1975.

GEORGIA

State of Georgia

ORIGIN OF STATE NAME: Named for King George II of England in 1732. **NICKNAME:** The Empire State of the South; also, the Peach State. **CAPITAL:** Atlanta. **ENTERED UNION:** 2 January 1788 (4th). **SONG:** "Georgia on My Mind." **MOTTO:** Wisdom, Justice and Moderation. **COAT OF ARMS:** Three columns support an arch inscribed with the word "Constitution"; intertwined among the columns is a banner bearing the state motto. Right of center stands a soldier with a drawn sword, representing the aid of the military in defending the Constitution. Surrounding the whole are the words "State of Georgia 1776." **FLAG:** Three red-and-white stripes and the state coat of arms in the upper left corner on a field of blue. **OFFICIAL SEAL:** OBVERSE: same as the coat of arms. REVERSE: a sailing vessel and a smaller boat are offshore; on land, a man and horse plow a field, and sheep graze in the background. The scene is surrounded by the words "Agriculture and Commerce 1776." **BIRD:** Brown thrasher. **FISH:** Largemouth bass. **INSECT:** Honeybee. **FLOWER:** Cherokee rose. **WILDFLOWER:** Azalea. **TREE:** Live oak. **GEM:** Quartz. **FOSSIL:** Shark tooth. **LEGAL HOLIDAYS:** New Year's Day, 1 January; Robert E. Lee's Birthday, 19 January; Birthday of Martin Luther King, Jr., 3rd Monday in January; Washington's Birthday, 3rd Monday in February; Confederate Memorial Day, 26 April; National Memorial Day, last Monday in May; Jefferson Davis's Birthday, 3 June; Independence Day, 4 July; Labor Day, 1st Monday in September; Columbus Day, 2nd Monday in October; Veterans Day, 11 November; Thanksgiving Day, 4th Thursday in November; Christmas Day, 25 December. **TIME:** 7 AM EST = noon GMT.

¹LOCATION, SIZE, AND EXTENT

Located in the southeastern US, Georgia is the largest state east of the Mississippi River, and ranks 21st in size among the 50 states.

The total area of Georgia is 58,910 sq mi (152,576 sq km), of which land comprises 58,056 sq mi (150,365 sq km) and inland water 854 sq mi (2,211 sq km). Georgia extends 254 mi (409 km) E–W; the maximum N–S extension is 320 mi (515 km).

Georgia is bordered on the N by Tennessee and North Carolina; on the E by South Carolina (with the line formed by the Chattooga, Tugaloo, and Savannah rivers) and by the Atlantic Ocean; on the S by Florida (with the line in the SE defined by the St. Marys River); and on the W by Alabama (separated in the SW by the Chattahoochee River). The state's geographic center is located in Twiggs County, 18 mi (29 km) SW of Macon.

The Sea Islands extend the length of the Georgia coast. The state's total boundary length is 1,039 mi (1,672 km).

²TOPOGRAPHY

Northern Georgia is mountainous, the central region is characterized by the rolling hills of the Piedmont Plateau, and southern Georgia is a nearly flat coastal plain.

The Blue Ridge Mountains tumble to an end in northern Georgia, where Brasstown Bald, at 4,784 ft (1,459 m), is the highest point in the state. The piedmont slopes slowly to the fall line, descending from about 2,000 ft (610 m) to 300 ft (90 m) above sea level. Stone Mountain, where a Confederate memorial is carved into a mass of solid granite 1,686 ft (514 m) high, is the region's most famous landmark.

The piedmont region ends in a ridge of sand hills running across the state from Augusta to Columbus. The residue of an ancient ocean was caught in the vast shallow basin on the Florida border, known as the Okefenokee Swamp, which filled with fresh water over the centuries. The coastal plain, thinly populated except for towns at the mouths of inland rivers, ends in marshlands along the Atlantic Ocean. Lying offshore are the Sea Islands, called the Golden Isles of Georgia, the most important of

which are, from north to south, Tybee, Ossabaw, St. Catherines, Sapelo, St. Simons, Sea Island, Jekyll, and Cumberland.

Two great rivers rise in the northeast: the Savannah, which forms part of the border with South Carolina, and the Chattahoochee, which flows across the state to become the western boundary. The Flint joins the Chattahoochee at the southwestern corner of Georgia to form the Apalachicola, which flows through Florida into the Gulf of Mexico. The two largest rivers of central Georgia, the Ocmulgee and Oconee, flow together to form the Altamaha, which then flows eastward to the Atlantic. Perhaps the best-known Georgia river, though smaller than any of the above, is the Suwannee, flowing southwest through the Okefenokee Swamp, across Florida, and into the Gulf of Mexico, and famous for its evocation by Stephen Foster in the song "Old Folks at Home." Huge lakes created by dams on the Savannah River are Clark Hill Reservoir and Hartwell Lake; artificial lakes on the Chattahoochee River include Lake Seminole, Walter F. George Reservoir, Lake Harding, West Point Reservoir, and Lake Sidney Lanier.

³CLIMATE

The Chattahoochee River divides Georgia into separate climatic regions. The mountain region to the northwest is colder than the rest of Georgia, averaging 39°F (4°C) in January and 78°F (26°C) in July. The state experiences mild winters, ranging from a January average of 44°F (7°C) in the piedmont to 54°F (12°C) on the coast. Summers are hot in the piedmont and on the coast, with July temperatures averaging 80°F (27°C) or above. The record high is 113°F (45°C) at Greenville on 27 May 1978; the record low is –17°F (–27°C), registered in Floyd County on 27 January 1940.

Humidity is high, ranging from 82% in the morning to 56% in the afternoon in Atlanta. Rainfall varies considerably from year to year, but averages 50 in (127 cm) annually in the lowlands, increasing to 75 in (191 cm) in the mountains; snow falls occasionally in the interior. Tornadoes are an annual threat in mountain areas, and Georgia beaches are exposed to hurricane tides.

The growing season is approximately 185 days in the mountains and a generous 300 days in southern Georgia.

4FLORA AND FAUNA

Georgia has some 250 species of trees, 90% of which are of commercial importance. White and scrub pines, chestnut, northern red oak, and buckeye cover the mountain zone, while loblolly and shortleaf (yellow) pines and whiteback maple are found throughout the piedmont. Pecan trees grow densely in southern Georgia, and white oak and cypress are plentiful in the eastern part of the state. Trees found throughout the state include red cedar, scaly-bark and white hickories, red maple, sycamore, yellow poplar, sassafras, sweet and black gums, and various dogwoods and magnolias. Common flowering shrubs include yellow jasmine, flowering quince, and mountain laurel. Spanish moss grows abundantly on the coast and around the streams and swamps of the entire coastal plain. Kudzu vines, originally from Asia, are ubiquitous.

The state lists 58 protected plants, of which 23—including hairty rattleweed, Alabama leather flower, smooth coneflower, two species of quillwort, pondberry, Canby's dropwort, harperella, fringed campion, and two specied of trillium—are endangered.

Prominent among Georgia fauna is the white-tailed (Virginia) deer, found in some 50 counties. Other common mammals are the black bear, muskrat, raccoon opossum, mink, common cottontail, and three species of squirrel—fox, gray, and flying. No fewer than 160 birds species breed in Georgia, among them the mockingbird, brown thrasher (the state bird), and numerous sparrows; the Okefenokee Swamp is home to the sandhill piper, snowy egret, and white ibis. The bobwhite quail is the most popular game bird. There are 79 species of reptile, including such poisonous snakes as the rattler, copperhead, and cottonmouth moccasin. The state's 63 amphibian species consist mainly of various salamanders, frogs, and toads. The most popular freshwater game fish are trout, bream, bass, and catfish, all but the last of which are produced in state hatcheries for restocking. Dolphins, porpoises, shrimp, oysters, and blue crabs are found off the Georgia coast.

Forty-three animal species were considered endangered or threatened by the US Fish and Wildlife Service as of August 2003. Among these are the bald eagle, eastern indigo snake, West Indian manatee, four species of moccasinshell, five species of turtle, wood stork, three species of whale, red-cockaded woodpecker, and shortnose sturgeon.

5ENVIRONMENTAL PROTECTION

In the early 1970s, environmentalists pointed to the fact that the Savannah River had been polluted by industrial waste and that an estimated 58% of Georgia's citizens lived in districts lacking adequate sewage treatment facilities. In 1972, at the prodding of Governor Jimmy Carter, the general assembly created the Environmental Protection Division (EPD) within the Department of Natural Resources (DNR). This agency administers 21 state environmental laws, most of them passed during the 1970s: the Water Quality Control Act, the Safe Drinking Water Act, the Groundwater Use Act, the Surface Water Allocation Act, the Air Quality Act, the Safe Dams Act, the Asbestos Safety Act, the Vehicle Inspection and Maintenance Act, the Hazardous Site Response Act, the Comprehensive Solid Waste Management Act, the Scrap Tire Amendment, the Underground Storage Tank Act, the Hazardous Waste Management Act, the Sedimentation and Erosion Control Act, the River Basin Management Plans, The Water Well Standards Act, the Oil and Hazardous Materials Spill Act, the Georgia Environmental Policy Act, the Surface Mining

Act, and the Oil and Gas and the Deep Drilling Act. The EPD issues all the environmental permits, with the exception of those required by the Marshlands Protection and Shore Assistance Acts, which are enforced by the Coastal Resources Division of the DNR. Georgia's greatest environmental problems are an increasingly scarce water supply, nonpoint source water pollution, and hazardous waste sites. In 2003, the Environmental Protection Agency's database listed 408 hazardous waste sites, 14 of which were on the National Priorities List, in Georgia. As of 1997 the state had 7.7 million acres of wetlands. In 2001, Georgia received $66,447,000 in federal grants from the Environmental Protection Agency; EPA expenditures for procurement contracts in Georgia that year amounted to $24,113,000.

6POPULATION

Georgia ranked 10th in population in the US with an estimated total of 8,560,310 in 2002, an increase of 4.6% since 2000. Between 1990 and 2000, Georgia's population grew from 6,478,453 to 8,186,453, an increase of 26.4% and the fourth-largest population gain among the 50 states for this period. The population is projected to reach 9.9 million by 2025. The population density was 141.4 per sq mi in 2000.

During the first half of the 18th century, restrictive government policies discouraged settlement. In 1752, when Georgia became a royal colony, the population numbered only 3,500, of whom 500 were blacks. Growth was rapid thereafter, and by 1773 there were 33,000 people, almost half of them black. The American Revolution brought free land and an influx of settlers, so that by 1800 the population has swelled to 162,686. Georgia passed the million mark by 1860, the two million mark by 1900, and by 1960, the population had doubled again. Georgia's population increased 19% between 1980 and 1990.

In 2000, the median age was 33.4, up from 26.7 in 1990. Over 26.5% of the population was under the age of 18 in 1998 while 9.6% were age 65 or older.

There has always been a strained relationship between rural and urban Georgians, and the state's political system long favored the rural population. Since before the American Revolution, the city people have called the country folk "crackers," a term that implies a lack of good manners and which may derive from the fact that these pioneers drove their cattle before them with whips.

The state's three largest cities in 2002 were Atlanta, with an estimated population of 424,868; Columbus, 185,948; and Savannah, 127,691. The Atlanta metropolitan area had an estimated population of 3,857,097 in 1999.

7ETHNIC GROUPS

Georgia has been fundamentally a white/black state, with minimal ethnic diversity. Most Georgians are of English or Scotch-Irish descent. The number of Georgians who were foreign born rose dramatically between 1990 and 2000, from 173,126 (or 2.6% of the population) to 577,273 (7.1%). The 1990 figure was, in turn, a considerable increase over the 1980 total of 91,480 foreign-born Georgians and the 1970 figure of 33,000.

Between 1970 and 2000, the number of Georgians from Asia or the Pacific Islands increased from 8,838 in 1970 to 24,461 in 1980, to 76,000 in 1990, to an estimated 177,416 in 2000 (173,170 Asians and 4,246 Pacific Islanders). In 2000, Asian Indians were the largest group, with a population of 46,132, followed by Vietnamese (29,016, up from 6,284 in 1990), Koreans (28,745), and Chinese (27,446).

Georgia's black population declined from a high of 47% of the total population in 1880 to about 26% in 1970, when there were 1,187,149 blacks. Black citizens accounted for 27% of the total population and numbered 1,747,000 in 1990. In 2000, the black population was estimated at 2,349,542, or 28.7% of the state

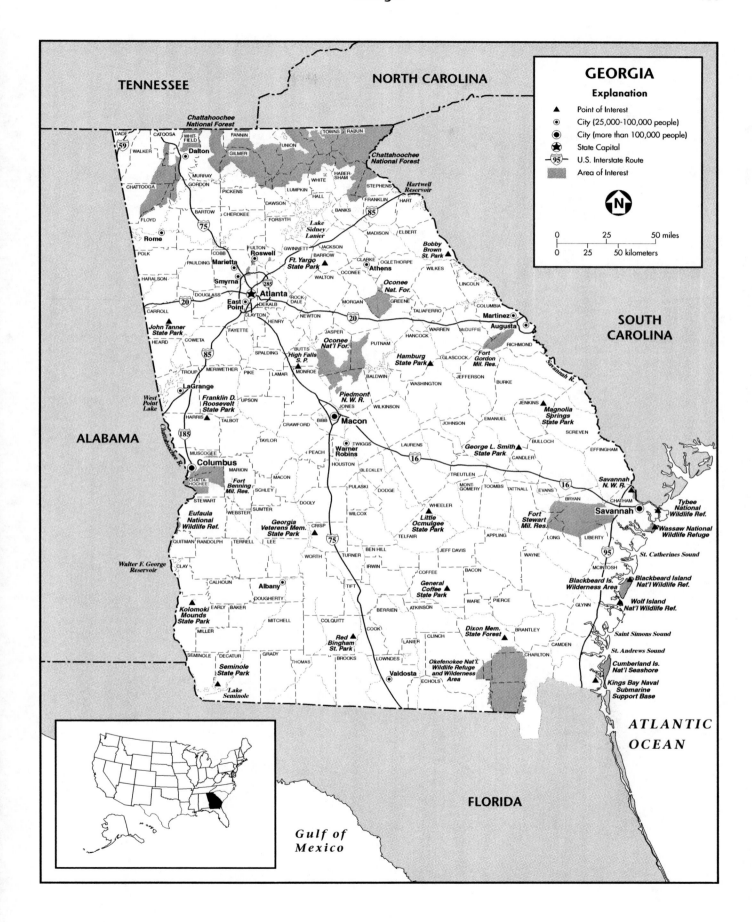

GEORGIA

Explanation

▲ Point of Interest
⊙ City (25,000-100,000 people)
◉ City (more than 100,000 people)
✪ State Capital
🛡95 U.S. Interstate Route
▨ Area of Interest

N

0   25   50 miles
0   25   50 kilometers

TENNESSEE

NORTH CAROLINA

Chattahoochee
National Forest

DADE
CATOOSA
WHIT-
FIELD
WALKER
FANNIN
TOWNS RABUN
Dalton
MURRAY
GILMER
UNION
Chattahoochee
National Forest
CHATTOOGA
GORDON
PICKENS
LUMPKIN
WHITE
HABER-
SHAM
STEPHENS
Hartwell
Reservoir
FLOYD
BARTOW
CHEROKEE
DAWSON
FORSYTH
HALL
BANKS
FRANKLIN
HART
85
Rome
POLK
Lake
Sidney
Lanier
GWINNETT
JACKSON
MADISON
ELBERT
Bobby
Brown
St. Park
COBB
FULTON
Roswell
Ft. Yargo
State Park
BARROW
CLARKE
OGLETHORPE
WILKES
PAULDING
Marietta
Athens
OCONEE
LINCOLN
HARALSON
Smyrna
285
WALTON
Oconee
Nat. For.
COLUMBIA
Atlanta
East
Point
DEKALB
ROCK
DALE
GREENE
TALIAFERRO
Martinez
Augusta
20
DOUGLAS
CLAYTON
NEWTON
MORGAN
20
CARROLL
John Tanner
State Park
FAYETTE
HENRY
JASPER
WARREN
McDUFFIE
RICHMOND
SOUTH
CAROLINA
HEARD
COWETA
Oconee
Nat'l For.
PUTNAM
HANCOCK
GLASCOCK
Fort
Gordon
Mil. Res.
85
SPALDING
High Falls
S.P.
BUTTS
Hamburg
State Park
BURKE
MERIWETHER
PIKE
LAMAR
MONROE
BALDWIN
WASHINGTON
JEFFERSON
LaGrange
TROUP
Franklin D.
Roosevelt
State Park
UPSON
JONES
WILKINSON
JENKINS
Magnolia
Springs
State Park
West
Point
Lake
HARRIS
TALBOT
CRAWFORD
BIBB
Macon
JOHNSON
EMANUEL
SCREVEN
185
MUSCOGEE
Columbus
TAYLOR
PEACH
Warner
Robins
TWIGGS
HOUSTON
LAURENS
George L. Smith
State Park
BULLOCH
EFFINGHAM
CHATTA-
HOOCHEE
Fort Benning
Mil. Res.
MARION
MACON
16
Savannah
N. W. R.
STEWART
SCHLEY
DOOLY
PULASKI
DODGE
TREUTLEN
MONT-
GOMERY
TOOMBS
TATTNALL
EVANS
CANDLER
16
CHATHAM
Savannah
Tybee
National
Wildlife Ref.
Eufaula
National
Wildlife Ref.
WEBSTER
SUMTER
Georgia
Veterens Mem.
State Park
CRISP
WILCOX
WHEELER
Fort
Stewart
Mil. Res.
BRYAN
LIBERTY
Wassaw National
Wildlife Refuge
QUITMAN
RANDOLPH
TERRELL
LEE
75
Little
Ocmulgee
State Park
APPLING
LONG
St. Catherines Sound
Walter F. George
Reservoir
CLAY
CALHOUN
DOUGHERTY
WORTH
TURNER
BEN HILL
IRWIN
TELFAIR
JEFF DAVIS
WAYNE
McINTOSH
95
Blackbeard Is.
Wilderness Area
Blackbeard Island
Nat'l Wildlife Ref.
Albany
General
Coffee
State Park
COFFEE
BACON
PIERCE
GLYNN
Wolf Island
Nat'l Wildlife Ref.
Kolomoki
Mounds
State Park
EARLY
BAKER
MITCHELL
COLQUITT
BERRIEN
ATKINSON
WARE
Saint Simons Sound
MILLER
COOK
LANIER
CLINCH
BRANTLEY
St. Andrews Sound
Red
Bingham
St. Park
Dixon Mem.
State Forest
CHARLTON
CAMDEN
Cumberland Is.
Nat'l Seashore
SEMINOLE
DECATUR
GRADY
THOMAS
BROOKS
LOWNDES
Okefenokee Nat'l
Wildlife Refuge
and Wilderness
Area
Kings Bay Naval
Submarine
Support Base
Seminole
State Park
Lake
Seminole
Valdosta
ECHOLS

ALABAMA

Chattahoochee R.

ATLANTIC
OCEAN

FLORIDA

Gulf of
Mexico

Georgia Counties, County Seats, and County Areas and Populations

COUNTY	COUNTY SEAT	LAND AREA (SQ MI)	POPULATION (2002 EST.)	COUNTY	COUNTY SEAT	LAND AREA (SQ MI)	POPULATION (2002 EST.)
Appling	Baxley	510	17,650	Jenkins	Millen	353	8,647
Atkinson	Pearson	344	7,712	Johnson	Wrightsville	307	8,676
Bacon	Alma	286	10,055	Jones	Gray	394	24,492
Baker	Newton	347	4,025	Lamar	Barnesville	186	16,442
Baldwin	Milledgeville	258	44,787	Lanier	Lakeland	194	7,216
Banks	Homer	234	15,123	Laurens	Dublin	816	45,890
Barrow	Winder	163	51,016	Lee	Leesburg	358	27,382
Bartow	Cartersville	456	82,607	Liberty	Hinesville	517	61,749
Ben Hill	Fitzerald	254	17,450	Lincoln	Lincolnton	196	8,459
Berrien	Nashville	456	16,285	Long	Ludowici	402	10,761
Bibb	Macon	253	154,824	Loundes	Valdosta	507	93,658
Bleckley	Cochran	219	11,855	Lumpkin	Dahlonega	287	22,665
Brantley	Nahunta	444	15,060	Macon	Oglethorpe	404	14,062
Brooks	Quitman	491	16,428	Madison	Danielsville	285	26,717
Bryan	Pembroke	441	25,256	Marion	Buena Vista	366	7,238
Bulloch	Statesboro	678	57,307	McDuffie	Thomson	256	21,438
Burke	Waynesboro	833	22,794	McIntosh	Darien	425	11,150
Butts	Jackson	187	21,346	Meriwether	Greenville	506	22,623
Calhoun	Morgan	284	6,395	Miller	Colquitt	284	6,400
Camden	Woodbine	649	44,702	Mitchell	Camilla	512	23,974
Candler	Metter	248	9,764	Monroe	Forsyth	397	22,675
Carroll	Carrollton	502	94,907	Montgomery	Mt. Vernon	244	8,397
Catoosa	Ringgold	163	56,341	Morgan	Madison	349	16,301
Charlton	Folkston	780	10,533	Murray	Chatsworth	345	38,544
Chatham	Savannah	444	233,702	Muscogee	Columbus	218	185,948
Chattahoochee	Cusseta	250	15,440	Newton	Covington	277	71,594
Chattooga	Summerville	314	26,161	Oconee	Watkinsville	186	27,264
Cherokee	Canton	424	159,295	Oglethorpe	Lexington	442	13,176
Clarke	Athens	122	103,881	Paulding	Dallas	312	94,184
Clay	Ft. Gaines	197	3,392	Peach	Ft. Valley	151	24,224
Clayton	Jonesboro	148	252,733	Pickens	Jasper	232	25,619
Clinch	Homerville	821	6,904	Pierce	Blackshear	344	15,982
Cobb	Marietta	343	651,485	Pike	Zebulon	219	14,599
Coffee	Douglas	602	38,298	Polk	Cedartown	312	39,444
Colquitt	Moultrie	556	42,802	Pulaski	Hawkinsville	249	9,716
Columbia	Appling	290	94,958	Putman	Eatonton	344	19,390
Cook	Adel	232	16,122	Quitman	Georgetown	146	2,621
Coweta	Newman	444	97,771	Rabun	Clayton	370	15,521
Crawford	Knoxville	328	12,509	Randolph	Cuthbert	431	7,451
Crisp	Cordele	275	22,018	Richmond	Augusta	326	197,842
Dade	Trenton	176	16,615	Rockdale	Conyers	132	73,558
Dawson	Dawsonville	210	17,538	Schley	Ellaville	169	3,975
Decatur	Bainbridge	586	28,243	Screven	Sylvania	655	15,201
DeKalb	Decatur	270	676,996	Seminole	Donalsonville	225	9,310
Dodge	Eastman	504	19,047	Spalding	Griffin	199	59,410
Dooly	Vienna	397	11,505	Stephens	Toccoa	177	25,712
Dougherty	Albany	330	95,875	Stewart	Lumpkin	452	5,040
Douglas	Douglasville	203	98,650	Sumter	Americus	488	33,247
Early	Blakely	516	12,172	Talbot	Talbotton	395	6,713
Echols	Statenville	420	3,842	Taliaferro	Crawfordville	196	1,977
Effingham	Springfield	482	40,832	Tattnall	Reidsville	484	22,560
Elbert	Elberton	367	20,667	Taylor	Butler	382	8,913
Emanuel	Swainsboro	688	22,099	Telfair	MacRae	444	11,780
Evans	Claxton	186	11,095	Terrell	Dawson	337	10,871
Fannin	Blue Ridge	384	20,986	Thomas	Thomasville	551	42,976
Fayette	Fayetteville	199	96,611	Tift	Tifton	268	39,338
Floyd	Rome	519	92,606	Toombs	Lyons	371	26,388
Forsyth	Cumming	226	116,924	Towns	Hiawassee	165	9,768
Franklin	Carnesville	264	20,778	Treutlen	Soperton	202	6,837
Fulton	Atlanta*	534	825,431	Troup	La Grange	415	59,767
Gilmer	Ellijay	427	25,203	Turner	Ashburn	289	9,691
Glascock	Gibson	144	2,598	Twiggs	Jeffersonville	362	10,545
Glynn	Brunswick	412	69,036	Union	Blairsville	320	18,275
Gordon	Calhoun	355	46,531	Upson	Thomaston	326	27,773
Grady	Cairo	459	23,838	Walker	La Fayette	446	61,949
Greene	Greensboro	390	15,101	Walton	Monroe	330	67,069
Gwinnett	Lawrenceville	435	650,771	Ware	Waycross	970	35,558
Habersham	Clarkesville	278	37,979	Warren	Warrenton	286	6,211
Hall	Gainesville	379	152,235	Washington	Sandersville	683	20,803
Hancock	Sparta	469	10,026	Wayne	Jesup	647	27,062
Haralson	Buchanan	283	26,755	Webster	Perston	210	2,315
Harris	Hamilton	464	25,092	Wheeler	Alamo	299	6,183
Hart	Hartwell	230	23,249	White	Cleveland	242	21,904
Heard	Franklin	292	11,340	Whitefield	Dalton	291	87,037
Henry	McDonough	321	139,699	Wilcox	Abbeville	382	8,529
Houston	Perry	380	116,768	Wilkes	Washington	470	10,734
Irwin	Ocilla	362	9,945	Wilkinson	Irwinton	451	10,357
Jackson	Jefferson	342	45,374	Worth	Sylvester	575	21,767
Jasper	Monticello	371	12,283				
Jeff Davis	Hazlehurst	335	12,910		TOTALS	58,056	8,560,310
Jefferson	Louisville	529	17,138				

*Atlanta city limits extend into DeKalb County

total, and the 3rd-largest black population among the 50 states. Atlanta, which had 255,689 black residents (61.4%) in 2000, has been a significant center for the development of black leadership, especially at Atlanta University. With its long-established black elite, Atlanta has also been a locus for large black-owned business enterprises. There are elected and appointed blacks in the state government, and in 1973, Atlanta elected its first black mayor, Maynard Jackson. By 1984 there were 13 black mayors, including Andrew J. Young of Atlanta.

The American Indian population in Georgia was estimated to be 21,737 in 2000. The great Cherokee nation and other related tribes had been effectively removed from the state 150 years earlier. About 5.3% of the population (435,227 people) were of Hispanic or Latino origin as of 2000.

[8]LANGUAGES

The first Europeans entering what is now Georgia found it occupied almost entirely by Creek Indians of the Muskogean branch of Hokan-Siouan stock. Removed by treaty to Indian Territory after their uprising in 1813, the Creek left behind only such places-names as Chattahoochee, Chattooga, and Okefenokee. Except for the South Midland speech of the extreme northern up-country, Georgia English is typically Southern. Loss of /r/ after a vowel in the same syllable is common. The diphthong /ai/ as in *right* is so simplified that Northern speakers hear the word as rat. *Can't* rhymes with *paint*, and *borrow, forest, foreign,* and *orange* all have the /ah/ vowel as in *father*. However, a highly unusual variety of regional differences, most of them in long vowels and diphthongs, makes a strong contrast between northern up-country and southern low-country speech. In such words as care and stairs, for example, many up-country speakers have a vowel like that in *cat*, while many low-country speakers have a vowel like in *pane*.

In general, northern Georgia *snake doctor* contrasts with southern Georgia *mosquito hawk* (dragonfly), *goobers* with *pinders* (peanuts), *French harp* with *harmonica, plum peach* with *press peach* (both clingstone peaches), *nicker* with *whicker* for a horse's neigh, and *sallet* with *salad*. In Atlanta a big sandwich is a *poorboy*; in Savannah, a peach pit is a *kernel*.

A distinctive variety of black English, called Gullah, is spoken in the islands off the Georgia and South Carolina coast, to which Creole-speaking slaves escaped from the mainland during the 17th and 18th centuries. Characteristic grammatical features include lack of inflection in the personal pronoun, the invariant form of the *be* verb, and the absence of the final *s* in the third person singular of the present tense. Many of the private personal names stem directly from West African languages.

In 2000, 6,843,038 Georgians—90.1% of the population five years old and older—spoke only English at home, down from 95.2% in 1990.

The following table gives selected statistics from the 2000 census for language spoken at home by persons five years old and over. The category "African languages" includes Amharic, Ibo, Twi, Yoruba, Bantu, Swahili, and Somali. The category "Other Indic languages" includes Bengali, Marathi, Punjabi, and Romany. The category "Other Asian languages" includes Dravidian languages, Malayalam, Telugu, Tamil, and Turkish.

LANGUAGE	NUMBER	PERCENT
Population 5 years and over	7,594,476	100.0
Speak only English	6,843,038	90.1
Speak a language other than English	751,438	9.9
Speak a language other than English	751,438	9.9
Spanish or Spanish Creole	426,115	5.6
French (incl. Patois, Cajun)	43,428	0.6
German	32,777	0.4
Vietnamese	27,671	0.4
Korean	25,814	0.3
African languages	24,752	0.3

LANGUAGE	NUMBER	PERCENT
Speak a language other than English (continued)		
Chinese	23,812	0.3
Gujarathi	11,133	0.1
Other Indic languages	9,473	0.1
Other Asian languages	8,673	0.1
Arabic	8,557	0.1
Japanese	8,257	0.1
Hindi	7,596	0.1
Tagalog	7,308	0.1
Russian	7,175	0.1
Urdu	7,109	0.1

[9]RELIGIONS

The Church of England was the established church in colonial Georgia. During this period, European Protestants were encouraged to immigrate and German Lutherans and Moravians took advantage of the opportunity. Roman Catholics were barred and Jews were not welcomed, but persons of both denominations came anyway. In the mid-18th century, George Whitefield, called the Great Itinerant, helped touch off the Great Awakening, the religious revival out of which came the Methodist and Baptist denominations. Daniel Marshall, the first "separate" Baptist in Georgia, established a church near Kiokee Creek in 1772. Some 16 years later, James Asbury formed the first Methodist Conference in Georgia.

The American Revolution resulted in the lessening of the authority of Anglicanism and a great increase in the number of Baptists, Methodists, and Presbyterians. During the 19th century, fundamentalist sects were especially strong among blacks. Roman Catholics from Maryland, Ireland, and Hispaniola formed a numerically small but important element in the cities, and Jewish citizens were active in the leadership of Savannah and Augusta. Catholics and Jews enjoyed general acceptance from the early 1800s until the first two decades of the 20th century, when they became the targets of political demagogues, notably Thomas E. Watson.

In 2000, most of the religious adherents in the state were Evangelical Protestants with the Southern Baptist Convention claiming 1,719,484 adherents in about 3,233 congregations. Mainline Protestants included 570,674 United Methodists, 105,774 USA Presbyterians, and 71,950 Episcopalians. Catholic adherents numbered about 374,185. Judaism claimed about 93,500 adherents and there were about 38,882 Muslims. Only 16 Buddhist and 15 Hindu congregations were reported, without membership numbers. About 55.2% of the population were not counted as members of any religious organization.

[10]TRANSPORTATION

Georgia's location between the Appalachian Mountains and the Atlantic Ocean makes it the link between the eastern seaboard and the Gulf states. In the 18th century, Carolina fur traders crossed the Savannah River at the site of Augusta and followed trails to the Mississippi River. Pioneer farmers soon followed the same trails and used the many river tributaries to send their produce to Savannah, Georgia's first great depot. Beginning in 1816, steamboats plied the inland rivers, but they never replaced the older shallow-drafted Petersburg boats, propelled by poles.

From the 1830s onward, businessmen in the eastern cities of Savannah, Augusta, and Brunswick built railroads west to maintain their commerce. The two principal lines, the Georgia and the Central of Georgia, were required by law to make connection with a state-owned line, the Western and Atlantic, at the new town of Atlanta, which thus became in 1847 the link between Georgia and the Ohio Valley. By the Civil War, Georgia, with more miles of rail than any other Deep South state, was a vital link between the eastern and western sectors of the Confederacy. After the war, the railroads contributed to urban growth as towns sprang up along their routes. Trackage increased from 4,532 mi (7,294 km) in 1890 to 7,591 mi (12,217 km) in 1920. But with competition from motor carriers, total trackage had declined to 4,897 rail mi (7,880 km) by 2000. In the same year, CSX and Norfolk Southern were the only Class I railroads operating within the state. In the mid-1990s, Amtrak operated five long-distance trains through the state, with east-west routes through Atlanta, and north-south routes through Savannah. In 1979, Atlanta inaugurated the first mass-transit system in the state, including the South's first subway.

Georgia's old intracoastal waterway carries about one million tons of shipping annually and is also used by pleasure craft and fishing vessels. Savannah's modern port facilities handled 22.3 million tons of cargo in 2000; the coastal cities of Brunswick and St. Mary's also have deepwater docks.

In the 1920s, Georgia became the gateway to Florida for motorists. Today, I-75 is the main route from Atlanta to Florida, and I-20 is the major east-west highway; both cross at Atlanta with I-85, which proceeds southeast from South Carolina to Alabama. I-95 stretches along the coast from South Carolina through Savannah to Jacksonville, Florida. During the 1980s, Atlanta invested $1.4 billion in a freeway expansion program that permitted capacity to double. In 2000, Georgia had 114,727 mi (184,635 km) of public roads, 7,321,013 registered motor vehicles, and 5,550,176 licensed drivers. In 2002, there were 219 private and 106 public airports in Georgia. Hartsfield International Airport in Atlanta is the hub of air traffic in the Southeast and in March 2000 topped Chicago's O'Hare for title of world's busiest airport.

11 HISTORY

The history of what is now Georgia was influenced by two great prehistoric events: first, the upheaval that produced the mountains of the north, and second, the overflow of an ancient ocean that covered and flattened much of the rest of the state. Human beings have inhabited Georgia for at least 12,000 years. The first nomadic hunters were replaced by shellfish eaters who lived along the rivers. Farming communities later grew up at these sites, reaching their height in the Master Farmer culture about AD 800. These Native Americans left impressive mounds at Ocmulgee, near Macon, and at Etowah, north of Atlanta.

During the colonial period, the most important Indian tribes were the Creek, who lived along the central and western rivers, and the Cherokee, who lived in the mountains. By clever diplomacy, the Creek were able to maintain their position as the fulcrum of power between the English on the one hand and the French and Spanish on the other. With the ascendancy of the English and the achievement of statehood, however, the Creek lost their leverage and were expelled from Georgia in 1826. The Cherokee sought to adopt the white man's ways in their effort to avoid expulsion or annihilation. Thanks to their remarkable linguist Sequoyah, they learned to write their own language, later running their own newspaper, the *Cherokee Phoenix*, and their own schools. Some even owned slaves. Unfortunately for the Cherokee, gold was discovered on their lands; the Georgia state legislature confiscated their territory and outlawed the system of self-government the Cherokee had developed during the 1820s. Despite a ruling by the US Supreme Court, handed down by Chief Justice John Marshall, that Georgia had acted illegally, federal and state authorities expelled the Cherokee between 1832 and 1838. Thousands died on the march to Indian Territory (Oklahoma), known ever since as the Trail of Tears.

Georgia's first European explorer was Hernando de Soto of Spain, who in 1540 crossed the region looking for the fabled Seven Cities of Gold. French Huguenots under Jean Ribault claimed the Georgia coast in 1562 but were driven out by the Spanish captain Pedro Menéndez Avilés in 1564, who by 1586

had established the mission of Santa Catalina de Gaule on St. Catherines Island. (The ruins of this mission—the oldest European settlement in Georgia—were discovered by archaeologists in 1982.) By 1700, Jesuit and Franciscan missionaries had established an entire chain of missions along the Sea Islands and on the lower Chattahoochee.

From Charles Town, in Carolina colony, the English challenged Spain for control of the region, and by 1702 they had forced the Spaniards back to St. Augustine, Florida. In 1732, after the English had become convinced of the desirability of locating a buffer between the valuable rice-growing colony of Carolina and Indian-held lands to the south and west, King George II granted a charter to a group called the Trustees for Establishing the Colony of Georgia in America. The best known of the trustees was the soldier-politician and philanthropist James Edward Oglethorpe. His original intention was to send debtors from English prisons to Georgia, but Parliament refused to support the idea. Instead, Georgia was to be a place where the industrious poor would produce those things England needed, such as silk and wine, and would guard the frontier. Rum and slavery were expressly prohibited.

Oglethorpe and the first settlers landed at Yamacraw Bluff on 12 February 1733 and were given a friendly reception by a small band of Yamacraw Indians and their chief, Tomochichi. Oglethorpe is best remembered for laying out the town of Savannah in a unique design, featuring numerous plazas that still delight tourists today; however, as a military man, his main interest was defending the colony against the Spanish. After war was declared in 1739, Oglethorpe conducted an unsuccessful siege of St. Augustine. The Spaniards counterattacked at Oglethorpe's fortified town of Frederica on St. Simons Island in July 1742 but were repulsed in a confused encounter known as the Battle of Bloody Marsh, which ended Spanish threats to the British colonies. Soon afterward, Oglethorpe returned permanently to England.

The trustees' restrictions on rum and slavery were gradually removed, and in 1752, control over Georgia reverted to Parliament. Georgia thus became a royal colony, its society, like that of Carolina, shaped by the planting of rice, indigo, and cotton. After the French and Indian War, settlers began to pour into the Georgia backcountry above Augusta. Because these back-country pioneers depended on the royal government for protection against the Indians, they were reluctant to join the protests by Savannah merchants against new British mercantile regulations. When war came, however, the backcountry seized the opportunity to wrest political control of the new state away from Savannah.

Georgians spent the first three years of the Revolutionary War in annual attempts to invade Florida, each of them unsuccessful. The British turned their attention to Georgia late in 1778, reestablishing control of the state as far as Briar Creek, midway between Savannah and Augusta. After a combined French and American force failed to retake Savannah in October 1779, the city was used by the British as a base from which to recapture Charleston, in present-day South Carolina, and to extend their control further inland. For a year, most of Georgia was under British rule, and there was talk of making the restoration permanent in the peace settlement. However, Augusta was retaken in June 1781, and independent government was restored. A year later, the British were forced out of Savannah.

With Augusta as the new capital of Georgia, a period of rapid expansion began. Georgia ratified the US Constitution on 2 January 1788, the 4th state to do so. The invention of the cotton gin by Eli Whitney in 1793 made cotton cultivation profitable in the lands east of the Oconee River, relinquished by the Creek Indians under the Treaty of New York three years earlier. A mania for land speculation was climaxed by the mid-1790s

Yazoo Fraud, in which the state legislature sold 50 million acres (20 million hectares), later the states of Alabama and Mississippi, to land companies of which many of the legislators were members.

Georgia surrendered its lands west of the Chattahoochee River to the federal government in 1802. As the Indians were removed to the west, the lands they had occupied were disposed of by successive lotteries. The settlement of the cotton lands brought prosperity to Georgia, a fact that influenced Georgians to prefer the Union rather than secession during the constitutional crises of 1833 and 1850, when South Carolina was prepared to secede.

After South Carolina did secede in 1860, Georgia also withdrew from the Union and joined the Confederate States of America. Union troops occupied the Sea Islands during 1862. Confederate forces defeated the Union Army's advance into northern Georgia at Chickamauga in 1863, but in 1864, troops under General William Tecumseh Sherman moved relentlessly upon Atlanta, capturing it in September. In November, Sherman began his famous "march to the sea," in which his 60,000 troops cut a swath of destruction 60 mi (97 km) wide. Sherman presented Savannah as a Christmas present to President Abraham Lincoln.

After ratifying the 14th and 15th amendments, Georgia was readmitted to the Union on 15 July 1870. Commercial interests were strong in antebellum Georgia, but their political power was balanced by that of the great planters. After the Democrats recovered control of the state in 1871, business interests dominated politics. Discontented farmers supported an Independent Party in the 1870s and 1880s, and then the Populist Party in the 1890s. Democratic Representative Thomas E. Watson, who declared himself a Populist during the early 1890s, was defeated three times in congressional races by the party he had deserted. Watson subsequently fomented anti-black, anti-Jewish, and anti-Catholic sentiment in order to control a bloc of rural votes with which he dominated state politics for 10 years. In 1920, Watson finally was elected to the US Senate, but he died in 1922. Rebecca L. Felton was appointed to succeed him, thus becoming the first woman to serve in the US Senate, although she was replaced after one day.

Franklin D. Roosevelt learned the problems of Georgia farmers firsthand when he made Warm Springs his second home in 1942. However, his efforts to introduce the New Deal to Georgia after he became president in 1933 were blocked by Governor Eugene Talmadge, who advertised himself as a "real dirt farmer." It was not until the administration of Eurith D. Rivers (1937–41) that progressive social legislation was enacted. Governor Ellis Arnall gained national attention for his forward-looking administration (1943–47), which revised the outdated 1877 state constitution and gave the vote to 18-year-olds. Georgia treated the nation to the spectacle of three governors at once when Eugene Talmadge was elected for a fourth time in 1946 but died before assuming office. His son Herman was then elected by the legislature, but the new lieutenant governor, M. E. Thompson, also claimed the office, and Arnall refused to step aside until the issue was resolved. The courts finally decided in favor of Thompson.

The Supreme Court order to desegregate public schools in 1954 provided Georgia politicians with an emotional issue they exploited to the hilt. A blow was dealt to old-style politics in 1962, however, when the US Supreme Court declared the county-unit system unconstitutional. Under this system, state officers and members of Congress had been selected by county units instead of by popular vote since 1911; the new ruling made city voters as important as those in rural areas. During the 1960s, Atlanta was the home base for the civil rights efforts of Martin Luther King, Jr., though his campaign to end racial discrimination in Georgia focused most notably on the town of Albany. Federal civil-rights legislation in 1964 and 1965 changed the state's political climate

by guaranteeing the vote to black citizens. A black man, Julian Bond, was elected to the state legislature in 1965; in 1973, Maynard Jackson was elected major of Atlanta, thus becoming the first black mayor of a large southern city. For decades the belief that defense of segregation was a prerequisite for state elective office cost white southerners any chance they might have had for national leadership. Governor Jimmy Carter's unequivocal renunciation of racism in his inaugural speech in 1971 thus marked a turning point in Georgia politics and was a key factor in his election to the presidency in 1976.

Another African American, former US Ambassador to the United Nations Andrew Young, succeeded Jackson as mayor of Atlanta in 1981, when that city—and the state—was experiencing an economic boom. The prosperity of Atlanta in the 1970s and 1980s stemmed largely from its service-based economy, which was centered on such industries as the airlines, telecommunications, distribution, and insurance. The decline of service industries in the early 1990s, however, pulled Atlanta and the state of Georgia as a whole into a recession. That decline was epitomized by the 1991 collapse of one of the two airlines that used Atlanta as its hub, Eastern Airlines, which cost Atlanta 10,000 jobs. While Atlanta's economic expansion produced a more mature economy, it also raised the price of labor. Nevertheless, as the decade progressed, the state's economy rebounded, fueled in part by the science and technology sector. By 1900 Georgia had emerged as "a leading light" in the South in building a strong research and technology infrastructure. Both 1996 and 1999 were record years for job growth. The state's unemployment rate was 4% in 1999, slightly lower than the national rate. While the economy boomed, there were changes on the horizon: in 2000 major employers Lockheed Martin, Coca-Cola, and BellSouth announced combined layoffs of more than 15,000 Georgia workers. Still, some analysts predicted the state economy could weather such fluctuations.

In 1996 Atlanta hosted the 26th Summer Olympic Games, which marked the 100th anniversary of the modern games. The event was marred by the July 27 explosion of a homemade pipe bomb in Centennial Olympic Park, killing one person and injuring dozens of others.

In July 1994 record flooding over a 10-day period caused 31 deaths and millions of dollars in damage in central and southwest Georgia. But in the summer of 2000, Georgians had a decidedly different problem. The state was parched by drought. Some areas had received less rain in the previous 25 months than at any time in recorded weather history. Peanut and cotton farmers in the southern part of the state struggled to irrigate fields. The residents of greater Atlanta, where nearly 100,000 people are added each year, felt the effects as well. Increased demand combined with drought conditions to require authorities to restrict outdoor watering in the 15-county Atlanta region. But the situation promised to reach beyond prevailing weather conditions and preservation measures: officials estimated that, based on current growth rates, by 2020 the region's demand for water would increase by 50%. Meanwhile Georgia's governor worked with the governors of neighboring Alabama and Florida to reach a voluntary agreement on how to share water from rivers the states share.

Governor Sonny Purdue outlined problems Georgia faced in his 2003 State of the State Address, including a weak economy (following the US recession that began in 2001), declining tax revenues, and poor SAT scores. To address the last topic, Purdue stressed the need for higher education standards. In 2003, the Georgia Board of Regents approved raising tuition by as much as 15% at the state's public colleges and universities to compensate for state budget cuts. Georgia's $460 million HOPE Scholarship program, funded by the state lottery, covers all tuition, mandatory fees, and book costs for all Georgia residents attending a state school and maintaining a B average.

12STATE GOVERNMENT

Georgia's first constitution, adopted in 1777, was considered one of the most democratic in the new nation. Power was concentrated in a unicameral legislature; a senate was added in 1789. The Civil War period brought a flurry of constitution-making in 1861, 1865, and 1868. When the Democrats displaced the Republicans after Reconstruction, they felt obliged to replace the constitution of 1868 with a rigidly restrictive one. This document, adopted in 1877, modified by numerous amendments, and revised in 1945 and 1976, continued to govern the state until July 1983, when a new constitution, ratified in 1982, took effect. There were 61 amendments by January 2003.

The legislature, called the general assembly, consists of a 56-seat senate and a 180-seat house of representatives; all the legislators serve two-year terms. The legislature convenes on the 2nd Monday in January and stays in session for 40 legislative days. Recesses called during a session may considerably extend its length. Special sessions may be called by petition of three-fifths of the members of each house. During the 1960s and 1970s, the legislature engaged in a series of attempts to redistrict itself to provide equal representation based on population; it was finally redistricted in 1981 on the basis of 1980 census results. House members must be at least 21 years old and senators, at least 25. All legislators must be US citizens, must have lived in the state for two years, and have been a resident in their district for at least one year. Legislators received a salary of $16,200 in 2002.

Elected executives include the governor, lieutenant governor, secretary of state, attorney general, state school superintendent, commissioner of agriculture, commissioner of labor, and five public service commissioners. Each serves a four-year term. The governor is limited to a maximum of two consecutive terms. To be eligible for office, the governor and lieutenant governor, who are elected separately, must be at least 30 years old and have been US citizens for 15 years and Georgia citizens for six years preceding the election. In 2002 the governor's salary was $127,303.

To become law, a bill must be passed by both houses of the legislature and approved by the governor or passed over the executive veto by a two-thirds vote of the elected members of both houses. All revenue measures originate in the house, but the

senate can propose, or concur in, amendments to these bills. Amendments to the constitution may be proposed by two-thirds votes of the elected members of each chamber and must then be ratified by a majority of the popular vote. If the governor does not sign or veto a bill, it becomes law after six days when the legislature is in session or after 40 days after the legislature has adjourned.

To be eligible to vote in state elections, a person must be at least 18 years old, a US citizen, and a resident in the county of registration. Restrictions apply to convicted felons and those declared mentally incompetent by the court.

13POLITICAL PARTIES

The first political group to emerge in the state was the Federalist Party, but it was tainted by association with the Yazoo Fraud of the 1790s. The reform party at this time was the Democratic-Republican Party, headed in Georgia by James Jackson (whose followers included many former Federalists), William Crawford, and George Troup. During the presidency of Andrew Jackson (1829–37), one wing, headed by John Clark, supported the president and called itself the Union Party. The other faction, led by Troup, defended South Carolina's right to nullify laws and called itself the States' Rights Party. Subsequently the Union Party affiliated with the Democrats, and the States' Rights Party merged with the Whigs. When the national Whig Party collapsed, many Georgia Whigs joined the Native American (Know-Nothing) Party. During Reconstruction, the Republican Party captured the governor's office, but Republican hopes died when federal troops were withdrawn from the state in 1870.

Georgia voted solidly Democratic between 1870 and 1960, despite challenges from the Independent Party in the 1880s and the Populists in the 1890s. Georgia cast its electoral votes for the Democratic presidential candidate in every election until 1964, when Republican Barry Goldwater won the state. Four years later, George C. Wallace of the American Independent Party received Georgia's 12 electoral votes. Republican Richard Nixon carried the state in 1972, as the Republicans also became a viable party at the local level. In 1976, Georgia's native son Jimmy Carter returned the state to the Democratic camp in presidential balloting. Another native Georgian and former Georgia governor, Lester Maddox, was the American Independent candidate in 1976.

Georgia Presidential Vote by Political Parties, 1948–2000

YEAR	ELECTORAL VOTE	GEORGIA WINNER	DEMOCRAT	REPUBLICAN	STATES' RIGHTS DEMOCRAT	PROGRESSIVE	
1948	12	*Truman (D)	254,646	76,691	85,136	1,636	
1952	12	Stevenson (D)	456,823	198,961			
1956	12	Stevenson (D)	444,6878	222,778			
1960	12	*Kennedy (D)	458,638	274,472			
1964	12	Goldwater (R)	522,163	616,584			
1968	12	Wallace (AI)	334,440	380,111	535,550		
1972	12	*Nixon (R)	289,529	881,490			Write-In
1976	12	*Carter (D)	979,409	483,743		1,1681	1,071
					LIBERTARIAN		
1980	12	Carter (D)	890,955	654,168	15,627		
1984	12	*Reagan (R)	706,628	1,068,722	1521		
					NEW ALL.		
1988	12	*Bush (R)	714,792	1,081,331	8,435	5,099	
					IND. (Perot)		
1992	13	*Clinton (D)	1,008,966	995,252	7,110	309,657	
1996	13	Dole (R)	1,053,849	1,080,843	17,870	146,337	
					IND. (Buchanan)		(Nader)
2000	13	*Bush, G. W. (R)	1,116,230	1,419,720	36,332	10,926	13,432

* Won US presidential election.

Republican George W. Bush won 55% of the vote, and Democrat Al Gore won 43% in the 2000 presidential election. In 1996, four-term US Democratic Senator Sam Nunn vacated his seat, which was won by Democrat Max Cleland, a Vietnam War veteran and triple amputee who had formerly headed the Veterans Administration. Georgia's other senator, Republican Paul Coverdell, was elected in a special runoff election in 1992 and reelected in 1998. Coverdell died of a stroke in July 2000; former governor Zell Miller (Democrat) was appointed to succeed him. Miller was elected in November 2000 to serve the remaining four years of the term, but in 2003, he announced he would not run for reelection to the Senate in 2004. Republican Saxby Chambliss was elected Senator in 2002.

After the 1994 elections, Georgia congressman Newt Gingrich became the first Republican to hold the position of Speaker of the House of Representatives in 40 years. He resigned from Congress in 1999.

In 1998 Georgians elected Democrat Roy Barnes governor, who replaced outgoing (two-term) Democratic Governor Zell Miller. Long-time Democrat Sonny Purdue changed party affiliations in 1998 to the Republican Party, and won election as governor in 2002. He became the first Republican governor elected since Reconstruction in Georgia. Following the 2002 elections, Georgia's delegation to the House comprised eight Republicans and five Democrats. At the state level there were 30 Republicans and 26 Democrats in the state senate; and 106 Democrats, 73 Republicans, and one independent in the state house in mid-2003. In 2002 there were 3,715,263 registered voters; there is no party registration in the state.

[14]LOCAL GOVERNMENT

The history of county government in Georgia is a long one. In 1758, colonial Georgia was divided into eight parishes, the earliest political districts represented in the royal assembly. By the constitution of 1777, the parishes were transformed into counties, and as settlement gradually expanded, the number of counties grew. The Georgia constitution of 1877 granted counties from one to three seats in the house of representatives, depending on population. This county-unit system was used in counting votes for elected state and congressional offices until 1962, when it was ruled unconstitutional by the US Supreme Court. Originally administered by judges of county courts, today Georgia counties are administered by the commission system. In 1965, the legislature passed a home-rule law permitting local governments to amend their own charters. As of 2002 Georgia had 156 counties.

The traditional and most common form of municipal government is the mayor-council form. But city managers are employed by some communities, and a few make use of the commission system. During the 1970s there were efforts to merge some of the larger cities with their counties. However, most county voters showed an unwillingness to be burdened with city problems.

In 2002, Georgia had 531 municipal governments, 180 public school districts, and 581 special districts.

[15]STATE SERVICES

To address the continuing threat of terrorism and to work with the federal Department of Homeland Security (created in 2002 following the terrorist attacks of 11 September 2001), homeland security in Georgia in 2003 operated under the authority of the governor; the public safety director was designated as the state homeland security advisor.

The State Ethics Commission is charged with providing procedures for public disclosure of all state and local campaign contributions and expenditures.

Educational services are provided by the Board of Education, which exercises jurisdiction over all public schools, including teacher certification and curriculum approval. The superintendent of schools is the board's executive officer. The public colleges are operated by the Board of Regents of the University System of Georgia, whose chief administrator is the chancellor. Air, water, road, and rail services are administered by the Department of Transportation.

The Reorganization Act of 1972 made the Department of Human Resources a catch-all agency for health, rehabilitation, and social-welfare programs. The department offers special services to the mentally ill, drug abusers and alcoholics, neglected and abused children and adults, juvenile offenders, the handicapped, the aged, and the poor.

Public protection services are rendered through the Department of Public Safety. Responsibility for natural-resource protection is lodged with the Department of Natural Resources, into which 33 separate agencies were consolidated in 1972. The Environmental Protection Division is charged with maintaining air, land, and water quality standards; the Game and Fish Division manages wildlife resources; and the Parks and Historic Sites Division administers state parks, recreational areas, and historic sites. Labor services are provided by the Department of Labor, which oversees workers' compensation programs.

[16]JUDICIAL SYSTEM

Georgia's highest court is the supreme court, created in 1845 and consisting of a chief justice, presiding justice (who exercises the duties of chief justice in his absence), and five associate justices. They are elected by the people to staggered six-year terms in nonpartisan elections.

Georgia's general trial courts are the superior courts, which have exclusive jurisdiction in cases of divorce and land title, and in felony cases. As of 1999 there were 175 superior court judges, all of them elected for four-year terms in nonpartisan elections. Cases from local courts can be carried to the court of appeals, consisting of 10 judges elected for staggered six-year terms in nonpartisan elections. Each county has a probate court; there are also separate juvenile courts. Most judges of the county and city courts are appointed by the governor with the consent of the senate.

The prison population in Georgia numbered 45,363 as of June 2001, an increase of 4.0% over the previous year. The state's incarceration rate stood at 540 per 100,000 population. Between 1930 and 2003, Georgia executed 388 persons, 2nd only to Texas. However, in 2003 there were only two executions in Georgia. Executions are carried out by electrocution. As of 2003, 117 people were under sentence of death.

According to the FBI Crime Index, the crime rate per 100,000 inhabitants for 2001 was 4,646.3, including a total of 41,671 violent crimes and 347,872 property crimes in that year.

[17]ARMED FORCES

In 2002 there were 64,392 active-duty military personnel stationed in Georgia. Major facilities include Dobbins Air Force Base, Ft. Gillem, Ft. McPherson, and the Atlanta Naval Air Station, all located in the Atlanta area; Ft. Stewart and Hunter Army Airfield near Savannah; Ft. Gordon at Augusta; Moody Air Force Base at Macon; Ft. Benning, a major Army training installation at Columbus; Robins Air Force Base, between Columbus and Macon; and a Navy Supply School in Athens. In 2001, Georgia firms received defense contracts worth $6.0 billion.

There were 768,675 veterans of US military service in Georgia as of 2000, of whom 97,796 served in World War II; 73,642 in the Korean conflict; 232,891 during the Vietnam era; and 133,149 during 1990–2000 (including the Persian Gulf War). In all, 77,000 Georgians fought and 1,503 died in World War I, and 320,000 served and 6,754 were killed in World War II. In 2002, Georgia veterans received benefits amounting to $1.6 billion.

In 2000, the Georgia State Police employed 786 full-time sworn officers. The Georgia Bureau of Investigation, part of the Department of Public Safety, operates the Georgia Crime Laboratory, one of the oldest and largest in the US.

[18]MIGRATION

During the colonial period, the chief source of immigrants to Georgia was England; other important national groups were Germans, Scots, and Scotch-Irish. The number of African slaves increased from 1,000 in 1752 to nearly 20,000 in 1776. After the Revolution, a large number of Virginians came to Georgia, as well as lesser numbers of French refugees from Hispaniola and immigrants from Ireland and Germany. Following the Civil War, there was some immigration from Italy, Russia, and Greece. The greatest population shifts during the 20th century have been from country to town and, after World War I, of black Georgians to northern cities. Georgia suffered a net loss through migration of 502,000 from 1940 to 1960, but enjoyed a net gain of 329,000 during 1970–80 and about 500,000 during 1980–90. From 1985 to 1990, Georgia's net gain through migration was greater than that of any other state except California and Florida. There were net gains of 598,000 in domestic migration and 90,000 in international migration between 1990 and 1998. From 1980 to 1990, the proportion of native-born residents in Georgia fell from 71% to 64.5%. In 1998 Georgia admitted 10,445 immigrants from foreign countries. Between 1990 and 1998, the state's overall population increased 18%. In the period 1995–2000, 965,558 people moved into the state and 624,853 moved out, for a net gain of 340,705, 13,926 of whom were age 65 or over.

[19]INTERGOVERNMENTAL COOPERATION

Multistate agreements in which Georgia participates include the Alabama-Coosa-Tallapoosa River Basin Compact, Appalachian Regional Commission, Atlantic States Marine Fisheries Commission, Historic Chattahoochee Compact, Interstate Rail Passenger Network Compact, Apalachicola-Chattahoochee-Flint River Basin Compact, Southern Regional Education Board, Southeastern Forest Fire Protection Compact, Southern Growth Policies Board, and Southern States Energy Board. In 2001, federal aid to Georgia totaled $7.9 billion.

[20]ECONOMY

According to the original plans of Georgia's founders, its people were to be sober spinners of silk. The reality was far different, however; during the period of royally appointed governors, Georgia became a replica of Carolina, a plantation province producing rice, indigo, and cotton. After the Revolution, the invention of the cotton gin established the plantation system even more firmly by making cotton planting profitable in the piedmont. Meanwhile, deerskins and other furs and lumber were produced in the backcountry; rice remained an important staple along the coast; turnpikes, canals, and railroads were built; and textile manufacturing became increasingly important, especially in Athens and Augusta.

At the end of the Civil War, the state's economy was in ruins, and tenancy and sharecropping were common. Manufacturing, especially of textiles, was promoted by "New South" spokesmen like Henry Grady of Atlanta and Patrick Walsh of Augusta. Atlanta, whose nascent industries included production of a thick sweet syrup called Coca-Cola, symbolized the New South idea—then as now. Farmers did not experience the benefits of progress, however. Many of them flocked to the mills while others joined the Populist Party in an effort to air their grievances. To the planters' relief, cotton prices rose from the turn of the century

through World War I. Meanwhile, Georgians lost control of their railroads and industries to northern corporations. During the 1920s, the boll weevil wrecked the cotton crops, and farmers resumed their flight to the cities. Not until the late 1930s did Georgia accept Social Security, unemployment compensation, and other relief measures.

Georgia's economy underwent drastic changes as a result of World War II. Many northern industries moved to Georgia to take advantage of low wages and low taxes, conditions that meant low benefits for Georgians. The raising of poultry and livestock became more important than crop cultivation, and manufacturing replaced agriculture as the chief source of income. In 1997, less than 1% of the employed labor force was working in agriculture; 32% were service workers; 22% retail salespeople; and 19% were manufacturers. Georgia is a leader in the making of paper products, tufted textile products, processed chickens, naval stores, lumber, and transportation equipment.

Textile manufacturing, Georgia's oldest industry, remains its single most important industrial source of income until 1999 when output from food processing exceeded it. From 1997 to 2001, annual textile output declined 8.4% whereas output from food processing increased 12.1%. Other manufacturing sectors were also increasing, so that from 1997 to 2000, there was an overall 16% increase in Georgia's manufacturing output. More than half of the gain was lost, however, in the national recession in 2001, as manufacturing output fell 8.3% in one year, reducing the net gain since 1997 to 6.4%. By contrast, output from general services increased nearly 40% 1997 to 2001, and from financial services (including insurance and real estate) increased almost 32%. Output from other service areas—wholesale and retail trade, transportation and public utilities, and government—all increased more than 25% 1997 to 2001. The national recession of 2000, however, impacted Georgia's economy worse than most, as its strong annual growth rates at the end of the 20th century (8.2% in 1998, 8.5% in 1999 and 6.7% in 2000) dropped abruptly to 1.5% in 2001. The state lost more than 133,000 jobs from January 2001 to October 2002. Layoffs in the fourth quarter of 2002 amounted to a 2.2% increase over the fourth quarter of 2001, the worst performance in the country.

Georgia's gross state product in 2001 was 10th in the nation at $299.9 billion, to which general services contributed $61.1 billion; financial services, $49 billion; trade, $55.1 billion; government, $37.2 billion, transportation and public utilities, $33.4 billion, and manufacturing, $43.5 billion. The public sector constituted 12.4% of gross state product.

[21]INCOME

According to the Bureau of Economic Analysis, in 2001, Georgia had a per capita personal income (PCPI) of $28,523 which ranked 27th in the United States (including the District of Columbia) and was 94% of the national average, $30,413. The 2001 PCPI reflected an increase of 1.5% from 2000 compared to the national change of 2.2%. In 2001, Georgia had a total personal income (TPI) of $239,753,556,000 which ranked 11th in the United States and accounted for 2.8% of the national total. The 2001 TPI reflected an increase of 3.6% from 2000 compared to the national change of 3.3%.

Earnings of persons employed in Georgia increased from $177,874,724,000 in 2000 to $183,090,588,000 in 2001, an increase of 2.9%. The largest industries in 2001 were services, 27.9% of earnings; transportation and public utilities, 10.6%; and state and local government, 10.3%. Of the industries that accounted for at least 5% of earnings in 2001, the slowest growing from 2000 to 2001 was durable goods manufacturing (6.2% of earnings in 2001), which decreased 5.3%; the fastest was state and local government, which increased 6.9%.

According to data released by the US Census Bureau, in 2000, the median household income was $42,887 compared to the national average of $42,148. In 2001, the median income for a family of four was $59,497 compared to the national average of $63,278. For the period 1999 to 2001, the average poverty rate was 12.6% which placed it 34th among the 50 states and the District of Columbia ranked lowest to highest.

22LABOR

According to Bureau of Labor Statistics (BLS) provisional estimates, in July 2003 the seasonally adjusted civilian labor force in Georgia numbered 4,386,400, with approximately 218,400 workers unemployed, yielding an unemployment rate of 5.0%, compared to the national average of 6.2% for the same period. Since the beginning of the BLS data series in 1978, the highest unemployment rate recorded was 8.5% in December 1982. The historical low was 3.5% in March 2001. In 2001, an estimated 6.1% of the labor force was employed in construction; 15.1% in manufacturing; 8.9% in transportation, communications, and public utilities; 19.2% in trade; 5.4% in finance, insurance, and real estate; 25.2% in services; 12.7% in government; and 1.7% in agriculture.

The most remarkable change in the labor force since World War II has been the rising proportion of employed women, whose share increased from less than 28% in 1940 to an estimated 60.4% in 1998.

The trend during the 1970s, 1980s, and 1990s was toward increased employment in trade and service industries and toward multiple job holding. Employment in agriculture, the leading industry prior to World War II, continued its long-term decline. One indication of declining employment was the decrease in farm population, which went from 515,000 in 1960 to 228,000 in 1970 to 121,000 in 1980 and 73,647 in 1990. Georgia's farm employment in 1996 totaled about 42,000. The mining, construction, and manufacturing industries registered employment increases but declined in importance relative to such sectors as trade and services.

Georgia is not considered to be a unionized state. Among state laws strictly regulating union activity is a right-to-work law enacted in 1947. In that year, union members in Georgia numbered 256,800.

In 1962, the Georgia legislature denied state employees the right to strike. Strikes in Georgia tend to occur less frequently than in most heavily industrialized states. One of the earliest state labor laws was an 1889 act requiring employers to provide seats for females to use when resting. A child-labor law adopted in 1906 prohibited the employment of children under 10 years of age in manufacturing. A general workers' compensation law was enacted in 1920.

The US Department of Labor reported that in 2002, 218,000 of Georgia's 3,643,000 employed wage and salary workers were members of unions. This represented 6.0% of those so employed, down from 7.1% in 2001. The national average is 13.2%. In all, 256,000 workers (7.0%) were represented by unions. In addition to union members, this category includes workers who report no union affiliation but whose jobs are covered by a union contract.

23AGRICULTURE

In 2001, Georgia's farm marketings totaled $5.5 billion (11th in the US). Georgia ranked first in the production of peanuts and pecans, harvesting 25% of all the pecans grown in the US in 2001 and 40% of the peanuts.

Cotton, first planted near Savannah in 1734, was the mainstay of Georgia's economy through the early 20th century, and the state's plantations also grew corn, rice, tobacco, wheat, and sweet potatoes. World War I stimulated the cultivation of peanuts along with other crops. By the 1930s, tobacco and peanuts were challenging cotton for agricultural supremacy, and Georgia had also become an important producer of peaches, a product for which the "peach state" is still widely known. In fact in 2002, Georgia produced 110 million pounds of peaches.

After 1940, farm mechanization and consolidation were rapid. The number of tractors increased from 10,000 in 1940 to 85,000 by 1955. In 1940, 6 out of 10 farms were tenant-operated; by the mid-1960s, this proportion had decreased to fewer than 1 in 6. The number of farms declined from 226,000 in 1945 to 50,000 in 2002, when the average farm size was 226 acres (91 hectares). Georgia's farmland area of 11 million acres (4.6 million hectares) represents roughly 30% of its land area.

Sales of potted flowering plants produced in Georgia amounted to nearly $9 million in 2001.

24ANIMAL HUSBANDRY

In 2003, Georgia had an estimated 1.3 million cattle and calves valued at around $774 million, and an estimated 345,000 hogs and pigs in 2002 valued at around $21.7 million. Cows kept for milk production numbered an estimated 86,000 in 2001, when Georgia dairies produced around 1.4 billion lb (0.64 billion kg) of milk. In the same year poultry farmers sold an estimated 6.2 billion lb (2.8 billion kg) of broilers, more than any other state, with a value of $2.43 billion. The total egg production was 5.11 billion in 2001, valued at $367.9 million.

25FISHING

Georgia's total commercial catch of fish and shellfish in 1998 was 13,017,000 lb, valued at $23,737,000—a volume representing only 0.1% of the national catch. Commercial fishing in Georgia involves more shellfish—mainly shrimp and crabs—than finfish, the most important of which are caught in the nets of shrimp trawlers. Leading finfish are snappers, groupers, tilefish, and porgy.

In brisk mountain streams and sluggish swamps, anglers catch bass, catfish, jackfish, bluegill, crappie, perch, and trout. In 1998, over 4.8 million bass were distributed within the state. Georgia issued 622,027 sport fishing licenses in 1998.

26FORESTRY

Georgia, which occupies 1.6% of the total US land area, has nearly 3.3% of the nation's forestland and nearly 5% of the nation's commercial forests. In 2002 Georgia's forest area totaled 24,405,000 acres (9,877,000 hectares), of which 23,802,000 acres (9,633,000 hectares) are commercial forest.

Forests cover about two-thirds of the state's land area. The most densely wooded counties are in the piedmont hills and northern mountains. Ware and Charlton counties in southeastern Georgia, containing the Okefenokee Swamp, are almost entirely forested. In 2002, about 90% of Georgia's forestland was privately owned.

The chief products of Georgia's timber industry are pine lumber and pine panels for the building industry, hardwood lumber for the furniture industry, and pulp for the paper and box industry. In 2002, Georgia produced over 3.04 billion board feet of lumber (3rd in the US), of which 87% was softwood (pine).

The chief recreational forest areas are in the Chattahoochee-Oconee National Forest, consisting of two main tracts in the northern and central part of the state. Georgia has 1,856,000 acres (751,123 hectares) of National Forest System lands, 99% of which are within the boundaries of the two major tracts.

27MINING

Statistics released by the US Geological Survey indicated that the estimated value of nonfuel minerals produced in Georgia in 2001 was $1.61 billion, a marginal increase over the value in 2000.

The state ranked seventh nationally in value of nonfuel mineral production.

According to preliminary figures, in 2001 Georgia produced about 24% of all clay output in the US. Kaolin clay was Georgia's foremost nonfuel mineral commodity, accounting for 54% of the total nonfuel mineral value in 2001, while crushed stone represented about 29%. Other minerals increasing in value included portland cement, fuller's earth, crushed stone, and industrial sand and gravel.

The state once again in 2001 was the national leader in the quantity of kaolin, fuller's earth, and iron oxide pigments. Georgia also ranked 2nd in barite (used by the chemical and the industrial filler and pigments industries), 4th in common clays and feldspar, 5th in dimension stone, and 9th in masonry cement. Blue-gray granite, known as "Elberton granite," is the mainstay of the industry—the granite is commonly used for road curbing in the northeastern US. Overall, the estimated quantity of dimension stone produced was 74 million metric tons valued at $11 million in 2001. Output of crushed stone, Georgia's 2nd-leading mineral commodity, was 76 million metric tons valued at $463 million.

28ENERGY AND POWER

Georgia is an energy-dependent state which produces only a small proportion of its energy needs, most of it through hydroelectric power. There are no commercially recoverable petroleum or natural gas reserves, and the state's coal deposits are of no more than marginal importance. Georgia does have large amounts of timberland, however, and it has been estimated that 20–40% of the state's energy demands could be met by using wood that is currently wasted. The state's southern location and favorable weather conditions also make solar power an increasingly attractive energy alternative. Georgia's extensive river system also offers the potential for further hydroelectric development.

In 2000 Georgia's total per capita energy consumption was 338 million Btu (85.2 million kcal), ranking it 28th among the 50 states.

In 1999, Georgia produced 117.7 billion kWh of electricity (utility and nonutility) and had a total installed capacity of 25 million kW. As of 2001 the Georgia Power Co. operated two atomic reactors at the Edwin I Hatch power plant near Baxley, with a combined capacity of 1,726,000 kW, and two more reactors, with a combined capacity of 2,297,000 kW, at the Vogtle plant at Waynesboro. All utilities are regulated by the Georgia Public Service Commission, which must approve their rates.

Exploration for oil is currently in progress off the coast, but the state's offshore oil resources are expected to be slight.

29INDUSTRY

Georgia had 9,804 manufacturing firms in 1997. The total value of shipments was $127 billion in that year. Important products included textiles, clothing, aircraft, soft drinks, paper, paints and varnishes, bricks and tiles, glassware, and ceramics.

Georgia was primarily an agrarian state before the Civil War, but afterward the cities developed a strong industrial base by taking advantage of abundant waterpower to operate factories. Textiles have long been dominant, but new industries have also been developed. Charles H. Herty, a chemist at the University of Georgia, discovered a new method of extracting turpentine which worked so well that Georgia led the nation in producing turpentine, tar, rosin, and pitch by 1982. Herty also perfected an economical way of making newsprint from southern pines, which was adopted by Georgia's paper mills. With the onset of World War II, meat-processing plants were built at rail centers, and fertilizer plants and cottonseed mills were expanded.

The state's—and Atlanta's—most famous product was created in 1886 when druggist John S. Pemberton developed a formula which he sold to Asa Griggs Candler, who in 1892 formed the Coca-Cola Co. In 1919, the Candlers sold the company to a syndicate headed by Ernest Woodruff, whose son Robert made "Coke" into the world's most widely known commercial product. The transport equipment, chemical, food-processing, apparel, and forest-products industries today rival textiles in economic importance.

Georgia's heavily forested northern region is dominated by carpet mills, especially around Dalton. In the piedmont plateau, manufacturing is highly diversified, with textiles and transportation equipment the most significant.

In 1997, 13 of the nation's 500 largest industrial corporations listed by Fortune magazine had headquarters in Georgia.

Earnings of persons employed in Georgia increased from $139.9 billion in 1997 to $151.7 billion in 1998, an increase of 8.4%. The largest industries in 1998 were services, 26.0% of earnings; state and local government, 10.0%; and transportation and public utilities, 9.5%. Of the industries that accounted for at least 5% of earnings in 1998, the slowest growing from 1997 to 1998 was nondurable goods manufacturing (8.9% of earnings in 1998), which increased 4.7%; the fastest was finance, insurance, and real estate (7.3% of earnings in 1998), which increased 10.3%.

30COMMERCE

Georgia's wholesale establishments numbered 16,132 in 1997, with sales of $170 billion (a 49% increase). The state ranked 8th in growth of wholesale trade; and 7th in growth of retail trade from 1992 to 1997, with retail sales totaling $74 billion (a 48% increase). Retail sales in the Atlanta area accounted for about half of the state's total. The largest categories of establishments were automotive dealers, 14%; food stores, 11%; and eating and drinking places, 27%. Food sales in 1997 totaled $13 billion, while merchandise sales totaled $10 billion. Georgia exported goods worth $13 billion in 1998. Savannah is Georgia's most important export center.

31CONSUMER PROTECTION

Georgia's basic consumer protection law is the Fair Business Practices Act of 1975, which forbids representing products as having official approval when they do not, outlaws advertising without the intention of supplying a reasonable number of the items advertised, and empowers the administrator of the law to investigate and resolve complaints and seek penalties for unfair practices. The administrator heads the Office of Consumer Affairs, which now also administers laws that regulate charitable solicitation, offers to sell or buy business opportunities, buying services or clubs, and telemarketing.

A comprehensive "Lemon Law" was passed in 1990. In 1997, a number of changes were made in Georgia's basic consumer protection laws. The Consumer's Utility Counsel became a division of the Office of Consumer Affairs; the Counsel represents the interests of consumers and small businesses before the Georgia Public Service Commission. Telemarketing, internet, and home remodeling/home repair fraud became criminal offenses under the jurisdiction of the Office of Consumer Affairs, with maximum sentences of up to 10 years. Multilevel marketing is now covered along with business opportunities. A Consumer Insurance Advocate represents citizens before the Georgia Commissioner of Insurance, the courts, and federal administrative agencies that speak on behalf of consumers with regard to insurance, such as insurance rate increases or the denial of health care services. The Office of Consumer Education attempts to create a more informed marketplace, so that consumers can protect themselves against fraud.

³²BANKING

The state's first bank was the branch of the Bank of the US established at Savannah in 1802. Eight years later, the Georgia legislature chartered the Bank of Augusta and the Planters' Bank of Savannah, with the state holding one-sixth of the stock of each bank. The state also subscribed two-thirds of the stock of the Bank of the State of Georgia, which opened branches throughout the region. To furnish small, long-term agricultural loans, the state in 1828 established the Central Bank of Georgia, but this institution collapsed in 1856 because the state kept dipping into its reserves. After the Civil War, the lack of capital and the high cost of credit forced farmers to borrow from merchants under the lien system. By 1900 there were 200 banks in Georgia; with an improvement in cotton prices, their number increased to nearly 800 by World War I. During the agricultural depression of the 1920s, about half these banks failed, and the number has remained relatively stable since 1940. Georgia banking practices came under national scrutiny in 1979, when Bert Lance, President Carter's former budget director and the former president of the National Bank of Georgia, was indicted on 33 counts of bank fraud. The federal government dropped its case after Lance was acquitted on nine of the charges, and most of the rest were dismissed.

By September 2002, there were 307 insured banks in Georgia with total assets of over $43.8 billion. At the end of 2002, there were 77 state-chartered credit unions. There is one state-chartered trust company, Reliance Trust Company. The Georgia Department of Banking and Finance regulates banks, credit unions, and trust companies chartered by the state.

At the end of 2002, Georgia's economy was weaker than that of the rest of the nation, with employment down 2.2% from the previous year, the worst performance in the country. Nonetheless, banks with headquarters in Georgia performed well that year, in part due to higher net interest margins (NIMs) (the difference between the lower rates offered to savers and the higher rates charged on loans). Community bank loan portfolios grew by 17%, particularly in the area of commercial real estate (CRE) loans.

³³INSURANCE

In 2001 there were 5.6 million ordinary life insurance policies in force with a total value of $333.2 billion; total value for all categories of life insurance (ordinary, group, industrial, and credit) was $547.2 billion. Death benefits paid that year totaled $1.6 million. In 2003 there were 21 life and health insurance companies and 39 property and casualty insurance companies domiciled in Georgia. In 2001, property and casualty insurers wrote premiums totaling $9.8 billion. That year, there were 64,498 flood insurance policies in force in the state, at a total value of $10.2 million.

³⁴SECURITIES

There are no stock or commodity exchanges in Georgia. Securities brokers and dealers organizations number 1,184, with 10,218 employees. Some 266 securities investment advisory businesses are registered. Georgia is headquarters to 127 NASDAQ companies, six NASDAQ market makers, and 33 Georgia-incorporated NYSE listed companies; including (the top five in order of revenue value) BellSouth, Georgia-Pacific, AFLAC, Genuine Parts, Co., and Sun Trust Banks.

³⁵PUBLIC FINANCE

Since the Georgia constitution forbids the state to spend more than it takes in from all sources, the governor attempts to reconcile the budget requests of the state department heads with the revenue predicted by economists for the coming fiscal year. The governor's Office of Planning and Budget prepares the budget, which is then presented to the general assembly at the beginning of each year's session. The assembly may decide to change the revenue estimate, but it usually goes along with the governor's forecast. The fiscal year begins on 1 July, and the first question for the assembly when it convenes the following January is whether to raise or lower the current year's budget estimate. If the revenues are better than expected, the legislators enact a supplemental budget; if the income is below expectations, cuts can be made.

Revenue for 2001 was forecast at $13.4 billion, but in fact reached $15.3 billion. Expenditures of $15.4 billion from appropriations of $14.4 billion left the state with an ending balance of $2.6 billion, which allowed the legislature to increase the funding in the Revenue Shortfall Reserve (Georgia's rainy day fund). In fiscal 2002, revenue shortfalls led the legislature to cut $783 million from the budget after it was enacted and mandate across-the-board cuts for government agencies of about 2.5%. In 2003, $482.1 million was cut from the budget after it was enacted mainly through a 5% across-the-board cut which exempted only direct instruction, which was required to make only 2% reductions. Drawings from the rainy day fund were made in both fiscal years. Effective fiscal 2004 (1 July 2003), the state increased its taxes on tobacco products and on alcoholic beverages and wine. Appropriations of state funds for 2004 totaled $16.17 billion, including $15.3 billion of general funds, $692 million of lottery funds (allocated to school readiness and student finance programs) and $175 million in tobacco settlement funds (allocated mainly to health programs). The largest appropriations from the General Fund were $5.93 billion for the State Board of Education, $1.6 billion for the Department of Community Health, $1.46 billion for the Board of Regents of the university system, $1.38 billion for the Department of Human Resources, $789 million for general obligation bonds, and $689 million for the Department of Transportation.

The following table from the US Census Bureau contains information on revenues, expenditures, indebtedness, and cash/securities for 2001.

	AMOUNT	PERCENT	PER CAPITA
Population (thousands, 2001)	8,406	(X)	(X)
Total Revenue	25,250,019	100.00	3,003.81
General revenue	25,411,417	100.64	3,023.01
Utility revenue	–	–	–
Liquor store revenue	–	–	–
Insurance trust revenue	–161,398	–0.64	–19.20
Exhibit: Salaries and wages	3,818,178	13.70	454.22
Total expenditure	27,860,155	100.00	3,314.32
General expenditure	25,662,423	92.11	3,052.87
Education	11,522,189	41.36	1,370.71
Public welfare	6,346,391	22.78	754.98
Hospitals	745,701	2.68	88.71
Health	931,213	3.34	110.78
Highways	1,724,297	6.19	205.13
Police protection	270,669	0.97	32.20
Correction	1,006,301	3.61	119.71
Natural resources	493,577	1.77	58.72
Parks and recreation	141,548	0.51	16.84
Government administration	586,178	2.10	69.73
Interest on general debt	437,654	1.57	52.06
Other and unallocable	1,456,705	5.23	173.29
Utility expenditure	516	–	0.06
Liquor store expenditure	–	–	–
Insurance trust expenditure	2,197,216	7.89	261.39
Debt at end of fiscal year	7,520,051	100.00	894.61
Cash and security holdings	60,969,590	100.00	7,253.10

³⁶TAXATION

Georgia was the last of the 13 original colonies to tax its citizens, but today its state tax structure is among the broadest in the US. The first comprehensive state tax was provided by the Property

Tax Act of 1852, which allocated 50% of the tax to the counties; as of 1994, less than 1% of property taxes went to the state. Motor vehicle license fees began in 1910; motor fuel has been taxed since 1921, tobacco since 1923. In 1929, Georgia began taxing incomes; a withholding tax on incomes has been required since 1960.

In 1951, Georgia enacted what at that time was the most all-inclusive sales tax in the US; this 4% tax is now the state's 2nd-largest source of revenue. Basic foods and prescription drugs are exempt. State law allows counties to charge an additional 1% local-option sales tax and to use the money to roll back property taxes. Local sales and use taxes range from 1% to 3%. Almost half of Georgia's taxes (48.1% in 2000) are collected at the local level. The state personal income tax schedule has 6 brackets ranging from 1% to 6%. The lowest rate applies up to $750 of taxable income, and the highest to taxable income above $7000. The basic corporate tax rate is 6%. Other state taxes include selective sales taxes (excises) on tobacco products, alcoholic beverages, motor fuels and insurance premiums, and various license fees. The state estate state is tied to the federal tax exemption for state death taxes, and is therefore scheduled to be phased out by 2007 in tandem with the federal estate tax credit absent some countervailing action by the Georgia government to preserve it. Revenue losses to Georgia from the phasing out of its estate tax are estimated at -$24 million in 2003, -$56million in 2004 and -$129 million in 2007. In 2002 death and gift taxes accounted for 0.89% of state revenue. The state property tax accounted for 0.3%.

State tax collection in Georgia totaled $13.77 billion in 2002, 47.1% from the individual income tax, 35% from the state sales tax, 8.6% from selective sales taxes, 4.1% from the corporate income tax. In 2003, combined state and local taxes amounted to 9.9% of income, the 15th highest in the country.

The following table from the US Census Bureau provides a summary of taxes collected by the state in 2002.

	($000)	PER CAPITA
Total Taxes	13,772,147	1,608.84
Property taxes	54,089	6.32
Sales and gross receipts	6,017,563	702.96
General sales and gross receipts	4,833,521	564.64
Selective sales taxes	1,184,042	138.32
Alcoholic beverage	144,022	16.82
Amusements	(X)	(X)
Insurance Premiums	296,175	34.6
Motor fuels	649,746	75.9
Pari-mutuels	(X)	(X)
Public utilities	(X)	(X)
Tobacco products	94,099	10.99
Other selective sales	(X)	(X)
Licenses	494,227	57.73
Alcoholic beverages	1,892	0.22
Amusements	(X)	(X)
Corporation	41,137	4.81
Hunting and fishing	22,786	2.66
Motor vehicle	268,428	31.36
Motor vehicle operators	24,484	2.86
Public utility	(X)	(X)
Occupation and business, NEC	92,738	10.83
Other	42,762	5
Other taxes	7,206,268	841.82
Individual income	6,487,638	757.87
Corporation net income	568,080	66.36
Death and gift	123,034	14.37
Documentary and stock transfer	(X)	(X)
Severance	(X)	(X)
Other	27,516	3.21

37ECONOMIC POLICY

Since the time of journalist Henry Grady (1851–89), spokesman for the New South, Georgia has courted industry. Corporate taxes have traditionally been low, wages also low, and unions weak. Georgia's main attractions for new businesses are a favorable location for air, highway, and rail transport, a mild climate, a rapidly expanding economy, tax incentives and competitive wage scales, and an abundance of recreational facilities. During the 1990s, Georgia governors aggressively sought out domestic and foreign investors, and German, Japanese, and South American corporations were lured to the state. The state offers loans to businesses unable to obtain conventional financing, provides venture capital to start-up companies, and extends loans to small businesses and to companies in rural areas.

The Georgia Department of Industry, Trade and Tourism (GDITT) is the lead agency for promoting economic development in the state, tasked with recruiting businesses, trade partners, and tourists. The GDITT was established in law in 1949 as the Department of Commerce (replacing the Agricultural and Industrial Development Board), and then renamed in 1989. In 2003, the GDITT had 201 employees, deployed in the state at 11 service delivery locations and in 13 foreign countries. The GDITT is overseen by a board of 20 members appointed by the Governor. The main operational units are Trade, Economic Development, Tourism and Film, Video and Music. In 2003, the creation of jobs was its stated major goal. The state funds city and county development plans, aids recreational projects, promotes research and development, and supports industrial training programs.

38HEALTH

Georgia's public health facilities developed only after the turn of the century. The Ellis Health Law of 1914 placed the responsibility for public health with the counties, but by 1936 only 36 of the state's 159 counties had full-time health departments. Not until after federal funds became available during the 1940s was malaria, one of the oldest afflictions in Georgia, brought under control through the eradication of mosquito breeding places. Federal funds also enabled every county to receive public health nursing services and X-ray clinics.

Georgia's birthrate declined to a record low of 15.9 per 1,000 population in 1976; the 2000 birthrate was 16.5. Fetal abortions have increased dramatically since 1973, when abortion laws were changed. There were 33,095 legal abortions performed in Georgia in 1999, for a rate of 18 per 1,000 women. Georgia's infant mortality rate in 2000 was 8.5 per 1,000 live births. Heart disease, cancer, and cerebrovascular disease were leading causes of death. Of the population age 18 and older, 23.6% were classified as smokers in 2000. In the same year, the HIV-related death rate was 9.4 per 100,000 population. AIDS cases numbering 24,559 had been reported through 2001.

In 1998, there were 147 community hospitals in Georgia, which had a total of 903,663 admissions. The number of hospital beds increased from 9,673 in 1950 to 24,113 beds in 2001. Georgia had 28,326 full-time registered nurses and 4,502 full-time licensed practical nurses in 2001 and 225 physicians per 100,000 population in 2001. The average expense of community hospitals for care in 2001 was $1,173.7 per inpatient day.

Federal government grants to cover the Medicare and Medicaid services in 2001 totaled $3.2 billion; 932,965 enrollees received Medicare benefits that year. At least 16.6% of Georgia's adult population was uninsured in 2002.

The Medical College of Georgia, established at Augusta in 1828, is one of the oldest medical schools in the US and the center of medical research in the state. The Federal Centers for Disease Control (CDC) were established in Atlanta in 1973.

39SOCIAL WELFARE

As a responsibility of state government, social welfare came late to Georgia. The state waited two years before agreeing to participate in the federal Social Security system in 1937. Eighteen years later, Georgia was distributing only $62 million to the aged, blind, and disabled, and to families with dependent children. By 1970, the amount had risen to $150 million, but the state still lagged far behind the national average.

In 2001, the average weekly unemployment benefit was $228.90. Average monthly participation in the food stamp program in FY2002 comprised 645,633 persons (263,076 households). The average monthly benefit was $80.19, and the sum total of benefits paid in FY2002 was $621,290,583.

With the enactment of the Personal Responsibility and Work Opportunity Reconciliation Act of 1996, the US government has changed the form and regulations for many of its social welfare programs. Most significantly, it replaces Aid to Families with Dependent Children (AFDC), an open-ended entitlement program, with Temporary Assistance for Needy Families (TANF), a limited system of assistance funded largely through federal block grants. The reform act also impacts the food stamp program, the Supplemental Security Income program, and the child nutrition program. The law took effect on 1 July 1997 and provided $16.38 billion in block grants for fiscal years 1997–2002. The grants are to be divided among the states based on an equation involving the numbers of former AFDC recipients in each state.

Reauthorization of the 1996 social welfare legislation, scheduled for 2002, was delayed, and the original law had been extended three times as of July 2003, with the most recent extension running through September 2003. In June 2000 the state had 135,381 welfare recipients. State expenditures on the TANF program in FY2002 totaled $175,261,929.

In December 2001, Social Security benefits were paid to 1,125,190 Georgians. This number included 661,970 retired workers, 122,360 widows and widowers, 164,730 disabled workers, 571960 spouses, and 118,940 children. Social Security beneficiaries represented 13.4% of the total state population and 91.4% of the state's population age 65 and older. Retired workers (excluding persons with special benefits) received an average monthly payment of $844; widows and widowers, $752; disabled workers, $794; and spouses, $425. Payments for children of retired workers averaged $420 per month; children of deceased workers, $547; and children of disabled workers, $241.

Federal Supplemental Security Income payments in December 2001 went to 198,063 Georgia residents, averaging $338 a month.

40HOUSING

Post-World War II housing developments provided Georgia families with modern, affordable dwellings. The home-loan guarantee programs of the Federal Housing Administration and the Veterans Administration made modest down payments, low interest rates, and long-term financing the norm in Georgia. The result was a vast increase in both the number of houses constructed and the percentage of families owning their own homes.

Between 1940 and 1970, the number of housing units in the state doubled to 1,470,754. In 1940, only 3 in 10 Georgia homes were owner-occupied; by 1990, nearly 6 in 10 were. In 1970, 13% of all Georgians were still living in units that lacked full plumbing; in 1990, the number decreased to 1.1%.

In 2002, there were an estimated 3,487,088 housing units in Georgia, of which 3,078,258 were occupied; 67.9% were owner-occupied. About 64.9% of all units were single-family, detached homes; about 12% were mobile homes. The average household size was 2.7 people. It was estimated that about 137,503 units were without telephone service, 14,408 lacked complete plumbing facilities, and 16,281 lacked complete kitchen facilities. Most household relied on gas and electricity for heating.

In 2002, 97,523 privately owned housing units were authorized for construction. The median value of a one-family home was about $131,221. The median monthly cost for mortgage owners was $1,125 while renters paid a median of $664 per month. During 2002, Georgia received over $137.5 million in community planning and development aid from the US Department of Housing and Urban Development.

41EDUCATION

During the colonial period, education was in the hands of private schoolmasters. Georgia's first constitution called for the establishment of a school in each county. The oldest school in the state is Richmond Academy (Augusta), founded in 1788. The nation's oldest chartered public university, the University of Georgia, dates from 1784. Public education was inadequately funded, however, until the inauguration of the 3% sales tax in 1951, now 4%. By 1960, rural one-teacher schools had disappeared, and children were riding buses to consolidated schools. In the 1953/54 school year, Georgia spent $190 per white student and $132 per black student. In 1999/2000, expenditures per student amounted to $6,046. Expenditures for public education in 2000/01 were estimated at $9,359,589.

Georgia has a comprehensive pre-kindergarten program for four-year-olds, the "HOPE" (Helping Outstanding Pupils Educationally) scholarship program, and special programs administered by the Georgia Department of Technical and Adult Education. In 2000, 78.6% of the population age 25 or older had a high school diploma; 24.3% had obtained a bachelor's degree or higher. The state offers full-day kindergarten statewide, and preschool for all four-year-olds. Every school has a satellite dish for long-distance learning, and computers are being provided to every school, with extensive technology services, both instructional and administrative. The Board of Regents of the state university system also increased its requirements for students starting college after 1988.

The total enrollment for fall 1999 in Georgia's public schools stood at 1,422,762. Of these, 1,044,030 attended schools from kindergarten through grade eight, and 378,732 attended high school. Minority students made up approximately 46% of the total enrollment in public elementary and secondary schools in 2001. Total enrollment was estimated at 1,444,937 in fall 2000 and expected to reach 1,527,000 by fall 2005. Enrollment in nonpublic schools in fall 2001 was 116,407. Additionally, instructional services are provided for hearing- and sight-impaired students at three state schools: Atlanta Area School for the Deaf, Georgia Academy for the Blind, and Georgia School for the Deaf.

As of fall 2000, there were 436,555 students enrolled in college or graduate school. In the same year Georgia had 125 degree-granting institutions. In 1997, minority students comprised 31.6% of total postsecondary enrollment. Thirty-four public colleges are components of the University System of Georgia; the largest of these is the University of Georgia (Athens). The largest private university is Emory (Atlanta). A scholarship program was established in 1978 for minority students seeking graduate and professional degrees.

42ARTS

During the 20th century, Atlanta replaced Savannah as the major arts center of Georgia, while Athens, the seat of the University of Georgia, has continued to share in the cultural life of the university. The state has eight major art museums, as well as numerous private galleries; especially notable is the High Museum of Art in Atlanta, dedicated in 1983. The Atlanta Memorial Arts Center was dedicated in 1968 to the 100 members of the association who lost their lives in a plane crash. The Atlanta Art Association exhibits the work of contemporary

Georgia artists; Georgia's Art Bus Program delivers art exhibits to Georgia communities, mostly in rural areas, for three-week periods.

The theater has enjoyed popular support since the first professional resident theater troupe began performing in Augusta in 1790. Atlanta has a resident theater, and there are community theaters in some 30 cities and counties. Georgia has actively cultivated the film-making industry, and as of the late 1990s an increasing number of films for cinema and television were being produced in the state.

Georgia has at least 11 symphony orchestras, ranging from the Atlanta Symphony to community and college ensembles throughout the state. Atlanta and Augusta have professional ballet touring companies, Augusta has a professional opera company, and choral groups and opera societies perform in all major cities. Macon has become a major recording center, especially for popular music. The north Georgia mountain communities retain their traditional folk music.

The Georgia Council for the Arts was founded in 1965. Major ongoing programs of the Council include the Georgia Folklife Program (est. 1987), the Grassroots Arts Program (est. 1993), and the State Capitol Gallery (est. 1991), which features exhibits from the State Art Collection of over 600 works of art from Georgian artists. In 2003, the National Endowment for the Arts contributed $2,395,900 to Georgia's arts programs. Arts organizations in the state receiving federal funding include Summer Atlanta Jazz Series, the Chamber Music Rural Residencies, the Augusta Opera, and the Center for Puppetry Arts, Inc. The Georgia Humanities Council was founded in 1971. In 2000, the National Endowment got the Humanities contributed $2,779,467 to 20 state programs. Georgia's arts education programs are offered to about 21,600 students. There are over 200 arts associations in Georgia along with an estimated 30 local arts groups.

43LIBRARIES AND MUSEUMS

In 2000, the Georgia public library system included 33 regional and 24 county systems, each operating under its own board. The holdings of all public libraries totaled 14,869,000 materials in 2000, and the combined circulation was 34,458,000 materials. The University of Georgia had by far the largest academic collection, including over three million books in addition to government documents, microfilms, and periodicals. Emory University, in Atlanta, has the largest private academic library, with about 1,520,921 bound volumes. The total income of the public libraries came to $143,396,000 in 2000, including $1,003,772 in federal grants and $26,384,864 in state grants.

Georgia has at least 179 museums, including the Telfair Academy of Arts and Sciences in Savannah, the Georgia State Museum of Science and Industry in Atlanta, the Columbus Museum of Arts and Sciences, and Augusta-Richmond County Museum in Augusta. Atlanta's Cyclorama depicts the 1864 Battle of Atlanta. The Crawford W. Long Medical Museum in Jefferson is a memorial to Dr. Long, a pioneer in the use of anesthetics. A museum devoted to gold mining is located at Dahlonega.

Georgia abounds in historic sites, 100 of which were selected for acquisition in 1972 by the Georgia Heritage Trust Commission. Sites administered by the National Park Service include the Chickamauga and Chattanooga National Military Park, Kennesaw National Battlefield Park, Ft. Pulaski National Monument, and Andersonville National Monument near Americus, all associated with the Civil War, as well as the Ft. Frederica National Monument, an 18th-century English barracks on St. Simons Island. Also of historic interest are Factors Wharf in Savannah, the Hay House in Macon, and Franklin D. Roosevelt's "Little White House" at Warm Springs. The Martin Luther King, Jr., National Historic Site was established in Atlanta

in 1980. Also in Atlanta are President Jimmy Carter's library, museum, and conference center complex. The state's most important archaeological sites are the Etowah Mounds at Carterville, the Kolomoki Mounds at Blakely, and the Ocmulgee Indian village near Macon.

44COMMUNICATIONS

Airmail service was introduced to Georgia about 1930, and since then the quantity of mail has increased enormously.

As of 2001, 93.2% of Georgian residences had telephones.

In 2003, Georgia had 106 major radio stations, 24 AM and 82 FM. There were 37 major television stations in the same year. Atlanta had 1,774,720 television-owning households in 1999, 70% of which received cable.

On 1 June 1980, Atlanta businessman Ted Turner inaugurated the independent Cable News Network (CNN), which made round-the-clock news coverage available to 4,100 cable television systems throughout the US. By 1985, CNN was available to 32.3 million households in the US through 7,731 cable television systems and was broadcast to 22 other countries. By the late 1980s, CNN had become well known worldwide. In addition, Turner broadcasts CNN Headline News. A total of 183,093 Internet domain names were registered in Georgia by the year 2000.

45PRESS

Georgia's first newspaper was the *Georgia Gazette*, published by James Johnston from 1763 until 1776. When royal rule was temporarily restored in Savannah, Johnston published the Royal Georgia Gazette; when peace came, he changed the name again, this time to the *Gazette of the State of Georgia*. After the state capital was moved to Augusta in 1785, Greensburg Hughes, a Charleston printer, began publishing the *Augusta Gazette*. Today's *Augusta Chronicle* traces its origin to this paper and claims the honor of being the oldest newspaper in the state. In 1817, the *Savannah Gazette* became the state's first daily. After the Indian linguist Sequoyah gave the Cherokee a written language, Elias Boudinot gave them a newspaper, the *Cherokee Phoenix*, in 1828. Georgia authorities suppressed the paper in 1835 and Boudinot joined his tribe's tragic migration westward.

After the Civil War, Henry Grady made the *Atlanta Constitution* the most famous newspaper in the state, with his "New South" campaign. Joel Chandler Harris's stories of Uncle Remus appeared in the *Constitution*, as did the weekly letters of humorist Charles Henry Smith, writing under the pseudonym of Bill Arp. In 1958, Ralph E. McGill, editor and later publisher of the *Constitution*, won a Pulitzer Prize for his editorial opposition to racial intolerance. In 2001, the *Constitution*, the Atlanta *Journal* merged to form the *Journal-Constitution*, owned by Cox Newspapers.

As of 2002, Georgia had 27 morning dailies, 6 evening dailies, and 28 Sunday newspapers. The following table shows leading daily newspapers with their 2002 estimated circulations:

AREA	NAME	DAILY	SUNDAY
Atlanta	*Journal-Constitution* (m,S)	396,464	640,292
Augusta	*Chronicle* (m,S)	69,022	95,724
Columbus	*Ledger-Enquirer* (m,S)	47,174	61,483
Macon	*Telegraph* (m,S)	63,553	88,276
Savannah	*Morning News* (m,S)	60,666	74,475

Periodicals published in Georgia in 2002 included *Golf World*, *Atlanta Weekly*, *Savannah*, *Industrial Engineering*, *Robotics World*, and *Southern Accents*. Among the nation's better-known scholarly presses is the University of Georgia Press, which publishes the *Georgia Review*.

46 ORGANIZATIONS

In 2003, there were over 2,600 regional, national, and international organizations within the state. National organizations headquartered in Georgia include the National Association of College Deans, Registrars, and Admissions Officers, located in Albany, and the Association of Information and Dissemination Centers, the American Risk and Insurance Association, and the American Business Law Association, located in Athens.

Many organizations are headquartered in Atlanta, including the Industrial Development Research Council, the Southern Association of Colleges and Schools, the Southern Education Foundation, the Southern Regional Council, the Southern Christian Leadership Conference, the American Rheumatism Association, the Arthritis Foundation, the American Academy of Psychotherapists, the Federation of Southern Cooperatives, the International Association of Financial Planning, the National Association of Market Developers, and the Textile Quality Control Association.

The Georgia Peanut Commission, Georgia Peanut Producers Association, and the Peanut Advisory Board promote the interests of growers for this popular crop. The Georgia Wildlife Federation addresses issues concerning the environment and conservation.

State and regional organizations that promote the arts, culture, and education include the Blue Ridge Mountains Arts Association, the Georgia Writers Association, and Young Georgia Writers, the Institute for the Study of American Cultures, and the National Indian Festival Association.

47 TOURISM, TRAVEL, AND RECREATION

In 2002, over 42 million travelers spent $23.9 billion on visits to Georgia. The Atlanta Metro Region received the most visitor expenditures, about 60%. More than 207,000 jobs are supported by the tourism industry in Georgia.

Major tourist attractions include national forests, national parks, state parks, and historic areas. Other places of interest include the impressive hotels and convention facilities of downtown Atlanta; the Okefenokee Swamp in southern Georgia; Stone Mountain near Atlanta; former President Jimmy Carter's home in Plains; the birthplace, church, and gravesite of Martin Luther King, Jr., in Atlanta; and the historic squares and riverfront of Savannah.

The varied attractions of the Golden Isles include fashionable Sea Island; primitive Cumberland Island, now a national seashore; and Jekyll Island, owned by the state and leased to motel operators and to private citizens for beach homes. Since 1978, the state, under its Heritage Trust Program, has acquired Ossabaw and Sapelo islands and strictly regulates public access to these wildlife sanctuaries.

Georgia has long been a hunters' paradise. Waynesboro calls itself the "bird dog capital of the world," and Thomasville in South Georgia is a Mecca for quail hunters.

48 SPORTS

There are four major league professional sports teams in Georgia, all in Atlanta. Turner Field and the Georgia Dome, main venues for the 1996 Summer Olympic Games hosted by the city, serve as the home field for two professional teams: baseball's Atlanta Braves, for whom Henry Aaron hit many of his record 755 home runs, and the Atlanta Falcons of the National Football League. The Philips Arena houses the Atlanta Hawks of the National Basketball Association and the Atlanta Thrashers of the National Hockey League. The Atlanta Braves won the National League Pennant in 1991, 1992, 1995, 1996, and 1999. The Braves went on to win their only World Series championship since moving to Atlanta, defeating the Cleveland Indians in 1995. The Braves lost the Series to the New York Yankees in 1996 and 1999, and to the Toronto Blue Jays in 1991 and 1992.

The Cracker Barrel Old Country Store 500 and the NAPA 500 are two of the NASCAR Winston Cup auto races. They are both held at Atlanta Motor Speedway. The Masters, the most publicized golf tournament in the world, has been played at the Augusta National Golf Club since 1934. The Atlanta Golf Classic is also listed on the professional golfers' tour.

Football and basketball dominate college sports. The University of Georgia Bulldogs, who play in the Southeastern Conference, were named National Champions in football in 1980 and advanced to the Final Four in basketball in 1983. Georgia Tech's Yellow Jackets of the Atlantic Coast Conference are a perennial basketball power. The Peach Bowl has been an annual postseason football game in Atlanta since 1968.

Professional fishing, sponsored by the Bass Anglers Sportsman's Society, is one of the fastest-growing sports in the state. Another popular summer pastime is rafting. Massive raft races on the Chattahoochee at Atlanta and Columbus, and on the Savannah River at Augusta, draw many spectators and participants.

Atlanta hosted the 1996 Summer Olympic Games at a cost of more than $1 billion.

Jackie Robinson, who broke baseball's color barrier in 1947, and Ty Cobb, nicknamed the "Georgia Peach," were both born in Georgia.

49 FAMOUS GEORGIANS

James Earl "Jimmy" Carter (b.1924), born in Plains, was the first Georgian to serve as president of the US. He was governor of the state (1971–75) before being elected to the White House in 1976. In 2002, he was the recipient of the Nobel Peace Prize. Georgia has not contributed any US vice presidents; Alexander H. Stephens (1812–83) was vice president of the Confederacy during the Civil War.

Georgians who served on the US Supreme Court include James M. Wayne (1790–1867), John A. Campbell (1811–89), and Joseph R. Lamar (1857–1916). Supreme Court Justice Clarence Thomas, appointed to the court during the Bush administration, was born in Savannah on 23 June 1948. Several Georgians have served with distinction at the cabinet level: William H. Crawford (b.Virginia, 1772–1834), Howell Cobb (1815–68), and William G. McAdoo (1863–1941) as secretaries of the treasury; John M. Berrien (b.New Jersey, 1781–1856) as attorney general; John Forsyth (1781–1841) and Dean Rusk (1909–94) as secretaries of state; George Crawford (1798–1872) as secretary of war; and Hoke Smith (b.North Carolina, 1855–1931) as secretary of the interior.

A leader in the US Senate before the Civil War was Robert Toombs (1810–85). Notable US senators in recent years were Walter F. George (1878–1957), Richard B. Russell (1897–1971), Herman Talmadge (1913–2002), and Sam Nunn (b.1938). Carl Vinson (1883–1981) was chairman of the House Armed Services Committee.

Many Georgians found fame in the ranks of the military. Confederate General Joseph Wheeler (1836–1906) became a major general in the US Army during the Spanish-American War. Other Civil War generals included W. H. T. Walker (1816–64), Thomas R. R. Cobb (1823–62), who also codified Georgia's laws, and John B. Gordon (1832–1904), later a US senator and governor of the state. Gordon, Alfred Colquitt (1824–94), and wartime governor Joseph E. Brown (b.South Carolina, 1821–94) were known as the "Bourbon triumvirate" for their domination of the state's Democratic Party from 1870 to 1890. Generals Courtney H. Hodge (1887–1966) and Lucius D. Clay (1897–1978) played important roles in Europe during and after World War II.

Sir James Wright (b.South Carolina 1714–85) was Georgia's most important colonial governor. Signers of the Declaration of Independence for Georgia were George Walton (b.Virginia, 1741–1804), Button Gwinnett (b.England, 1735–77), and Lyman Hall (b.Connecticut, 1724–90). Signers of the US Constitution were William Few (b.Maryland, 1748–1828) and Abraham Baldwin (b.Connecticut, 1754–1807). Revolutionary War hero James Jackson (b.England, 1757–1806) organized the Democratic-Republican Party (today's Democratic Party) in Georgia.

The first Georgians, the Indians, produced many heroes. Tomochichi (c.1664–1739) was the Yamacraw chief who welcomed Oglethorpe and the first Georgians. Alexander McGillivray (c.1759–93), a Creek chief who was the son of a Scottish fur trader, signed a treaty with George Washington in a further attempt to protect the Creek lands. Osceola (1800–1838) led his Seminole into the Florida swamps rather than move west. Sequoyah (b.Tennessee, 1773–1843) framed an alphabet for the Cherokee, and John Ross (Coowescoowe, b.Tennessee, 1790–1866) was the first president of the Cherokee republic.

Among influential Georgian educators were Josiah Meigs (b.Connecticut, 1757–1822), the first president of the University of Georgia, and Milton Antony (1784–1839), who established the Medical College of Georgia in Augusta in 1828. Crawford W. Long (1815–78) was one of the first doctors to use ether successfully in surgical operations. Paul F. Eve (1806–77) was a leading teacher of surgery in the South, and Joseph Jones (1833–96) pioneered in the study of the causes of malaria.

Distinguished black Georgians include churchmen Henry M. Turner (b.South Carolina, 1834–1915) and Charles T. Walker (1858–1921), educators Lucy Laney (1854–1933) and John Hope (1868–1936), and civil-rights activists William Edward Burghardt DuBois (b.Massachusetts, 1968–1963) and Walter F. White(1893–1955). One of the best-known Georgians was Martin Luther King, Jr. (1929–68), born in Atlanta, leader of the March on Washington in 1963, and winner of the Nobel Peace Prize in 1964 for his leadership in the campaign for civil rights; he was assassinated in Memphis, Tenn., while organizing support for striking sanitation workers. Black Muslim leader Elijah Muhammad (Elijah Poole, 1897–1975) was also a Georgian. Other prominent black leaders include Atlanta mayor and former UN ambassador Andrew Young (b.Louisiana, 1932), former Atlanta Mayor Maynard Jackson (b.Texas, 1938), and Georgia Senator Julian Bond (b.Tennessee, 1940).

Famous Georgia authors include Sidney Lanier (1842–81), Joel Chandler Harris (1848–1908), Lillian Smith (1857–1966), Conrad Aiken (1889–1973), Erskine Caldwell (1902–87), Caroline Miller (1903–92), Frank Yerby (1916–91) Carson McCullers (1917–67), James Dickey (1923–97), and Flannery O'Connor (1925–64). Also notable is Margaret Mitchell (1900–49), whose Pulitzer Prize–winning *Gone with the Wind* (1936) typifies Georgia to many readers.

Entertainment celebrities include songwriter Johnny Mercer (1909–76); actors Charles Coburn (1877–1961) and Oliver Hardy (1877–1961); singers and musicians Harry James (1916–83), Ray Charles (Ray Charles Robinson, b.1930), James Brown (b.1933), Little Richard (Richard Penniman, b.1935), Jerry Reed (b.1937), Gladys Knight (b.1944), and Brenda Lee (b.1944); and actors Melvyn Douglas (1901–81), Sterling Holloway (1905–92), Ossie Davis (b.1917), Barbara Cook (b.1927), Jane Withers (b.1927), Joanne Woodward (b.1930), and Burt Reynolds (b.1936).

Major sports figures include baseball's "Georgia peach," Tyrus Raymond "Ty" Cobb (1886–1961); Jack Roosevelt "Jackie" Robinson (1919–72), the first black to be inducted into the Baseball Hall of Fame; and Robert Tyre "Bobby" Jones (1902–71), winner of the "grand slam" of four major golf tournaments in 1930.

Robert E. "Ted" Turner (b.Ohio, 1939), an Atlanta businessman-broadcaster, owns the Atlanta Hawks and the Atlanta Braves and skippered the *Courageous* to victory in the America's Cup yacht races in 1977. Architect John C. Portman, Jr. (b.South Carolina, 1924), was the developer of Atlanta's Peachtree Center.

50BIBLIOGRAPHY

Bartley, Numan V. *From Thurmond to Wallace: Political Tendencies in Georgia, 1948–68.* Baltimore: John Hopkins University Press, 1970.

Brown, R. Harold. *The Greening of Georgia: The Improvement of the Environment in the Twentieth Century.* Macon, Ga.: Mercer University Press, 2002.

Coleman, Kenneth, et al. *A History of Georgia.* 2nd ed. Athens: University of Georgia Press, 1991.

Grady, Henry W. *The New South.* Savannah, Ga.: Beehive Press, 1971.

Grant, L. Donald. *The Way It Was in the South: The Black Experience in Georgia.* Secaucus, N.J.: Carol Publishing Group, 1993.

Hepburn, Lawrence R. *The Georgia History Book.* Athens: University of Georgia Institute of Government, 1982.

Inscoe, John C., ed. *Georgia in Black and White: Explorations in the Race Relations of a Southern State, 1865–1950.* Athens: University of Georgia Press, 1994.

King, Coretta Scott. *My Life with Martin Luther King.* Rev. ed. New York: H. Holt, 1993.

Lane, Mills. *The People of Georgia: An Illustrated History.* 2nd ed. Savannah: Library of Georgia, 1992.

Lockley, Timothy James. *Lines in the Sand: Race and Class in Lowcountry Georgia, 1750–1860.* Athens: University of Georgia Press, 2001.

Maguire, Jane. *On Shares: Ed Brown's Story.* New York: Norton, 1976.

Malone, Henry. *Cherokees of the Old South.* Athens: University of Georgia Press, 1956.

McAuliffe, Emily. *Georgia Facts and Symbols.* Mankato, Minn.: Hilltop Books, 1999.

Miles, Jim. *To the Sea: A History and Tour Guide of the War in the West, Sherman's March Across Georgia and Through the Carolinas, 1864–1865.* Nashville, Tenn.: Cumberland House, 2002.

Olmstead, Marty. *Hidden Georgia.* Berkeley, CA: Ulysses Press, 2000.

Pearson, Hugh. *Under the Knife: How a Wealthy Negro Surgeon Wielded Power in the Jim Crow South.* New York: Free Press, 2000.

Reidy, Joseph P. *From Slavery to Agrarian Capitalism in the Cotton Plantation South: Central Georgia, 1800–1880.* Chapel Hill: University of North Carolina Press, 1992.

Saye, Albert B. *Georgia History and Government.* Austin: Steck Vaughn, 1973.

Woodward, C. Vann. *Tom Watson: Agrarian Rebel.* New York: Oxford Press, 1970 (orig. 1938).

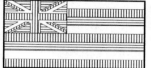

HAWAII

State of Hawaii

ORIGIN OF STATE NAME: Unknown. The name may stem from Hawaii Loa, traditional discoverer of the islands, or from Hawaiki, the traditional Polynesian homeland. **NICKNAME:** The Aloha State. **CAPITAL:** Honolulu. **ENTERED UNION:** 21 August 1959 (50th). **SONG:** "Hawaii Ponoi." **MOTTO:** *Ua mau ke ea o ka aina i ka pono* (The life of the land is perpetuated in righteousness). **COAT OF ARMS:** The heraldic shield of the Hawaiian kingdom is flanked by the figures of Kamehameha I, who united the islands, and Liberty, holding the Hawaiian flag. Below the shield is a phoenix surrounded by taro leaves, banana foliage, and sprays of maidenhair fern. **FLAG:** Eight horizontal stripes, alternately white, red, and blue, represent the major islands, with the British Union Jack (reflecting the years that the islands were under British protection) in the upper left-hand corner. **OFFICIAL SEAL:** Same as coat of arms, with the words "State of Hawaii 1959" above and the state motto below. **BIRD:** Nene (Hawaiian goose). **FLOWER:** Pua aloalo (yellow hibiscus). **TREE:** Kukue tree (candlenut). **ISLAND EMBLEMS:** Each of the eight major islands has its own color and emblem. **HAWAII:** red; lehua (ohia blossom). **KALHOOLAWE:** gray; hinahina (beach heliotrope). **KAUAI:** purple; mokihana (fruit capsule of the *Pelea anisata*). **LANAI:** orange; kaunaoa (*Cuscuta sandwichiana*). **MAUI:** pink; lokelani (pink cottage rose). **MOLOKAI:** green; kukui (candlenut) blossom. **NIIHAU:** white; white pupu shell. **OAHU:** yellow; ilima (*Sida fallax*). **LEGAL HOLIDAYS:** New Year's Day, 1 January; Birthday of Martin Luther King, Jr., 3rd Monday in January; Presidents' Day, 3rd Monday in February; Kuhio Day, 26 March; Good Friday, March or April; Memorial Day, last Monday in May; Kamehameha Day, 11 June; Independence Day, 4 July; Admission Day, 3rd Friday in August; Labor Day, 1st Monday in September; Discoverers Day, 2nd Monday in October; Election Day, 1st Tuesday after 1st Monday in November; Veterans Day, 11 November; Thanksgiving Day, 4th Thursday in November; Christmas Day, 25 December. **TIME:** 2 AM Hawaii-Aleutian Standard Time = noon GMT.

¹LOCATION, SIZE, AND EXTENT

The State of Hawaii is an island group situated in the northern Pacific Ocean, about 2,400 mi (3,900 km) WSW of San Francisco. The smallest of the five Pacific states, Hawaii ranks 47th in size among the 50 states.

The 132 Hawaiian Islands have a total area of 6,470 sq mi (16,758 sq km), including 6,425 sq mi (16,641 sq km) of land and only 45 sq mi (117 sq km) of inland water. The island chain extends over 1,576 mi (2,536 km) N-S and 1,425 mi (2,293 km) E-W. The largest island, Hawaii (known locally as the "Big Island") extends 76 mi (122 km) E-W and 93 mi (150 km) N-S; Oahu, the most populous island, extends 44 mi (71 km) E-W and 30 mi (48 km) N-S.

The eight largest islands of the Hawaiian group are Hawaii (4,035 sq mi—10,451 sq km), Maui (734 sq mi—1,901 sq km), Oahu (617 sq mi—1,598 sq km), Kauai (558 sq mi—1,445 sq km), Molokai (264 sq mi—684 sq km), Lanai (141 sq mi—365 sq km), Niihau (73 sq mi—189 sq km), and Kahoolawe (45 sq mi—117 sq km). The general coastline of the island chain is 750 mi (1,207 km); the tidal shoreline totals 1,052 mi (1,693 km). The state's geographic center is off Maui, at 20°15'n, 156°20'w.

²TOPOGRAPHY

The 8 major and 124 minor islands that make up the State of Hawaii were formed by volcanic eruptions. Mauna Loa, on the island of Hawaii, is the world's largest active volcano, at a height of 13,675 ft (4,168 m). Kilauea, on the eastern slope of Mauna Loa, is the world's largest active volcanic crater: beginning on 24 May 1969, it spewed forth 242 million cu yards (185 million cu m) of lava, spreading over an area of 19.3 sq mi (50 sq km). The longest volcanic eruption in Hawaii lasted 867 days. Further indications of Hawaii's continuing geological activity are the 14

earthquakes, each with a magnitude of 5 or more on the Richter scale, that shook the islands from 1969 to 1979; one quake, at Puna, on Hawaii in 1975, reached a magnitude of 7.2.

Hawaii, Maui, Kauai, and Molokai are the most mountainous islands. The highest peak in the state is Puu Wekiu (13,796 ft/ 4,208 m), on Hawaii; the largest natural lake, Halulu (182 acres/ 74 ha), Niihau; the largest artificial lake, Waiia Reservoir (422 acres/171 ha), Kauai; and the longest rivers, Kaukonahua Stream (33 mi/53 km) in the north on Oahu and Wailuku River (32 mi/ 51 km) on Hawaii. While much of the Pacific Ocean surrounding the state is up to 20,000 ft (6,100 m) deep, Oahu, Molokai, Lanai, and Maui stand on a submarine bank at a depth of less than 2,400 ft (730 m).

³CLIMATE

Hawaii has a tropical climate cooled by trade winds. Normal daily temperatures in Honolulu average 72°F (22°C) in February and 78°F (26°C) in August; the average wind speed is a breezy 11.3 mph (18.2 km/hr). The record high for the state is 100°F (38°C), set at Pahala on 27 April 1931, and the record low is 12°F (–11°C), set at Mauna Kea Observatory on 17 May 1979.

Rainfall is extremely variable, with far more precipitation on the windward (northeastern) than on the leeward side of the islands. Mt. Waialeale, Kauai, is reputedly the rainiest place on earth, with a mean annual total of 486 in (1,234 cm). Kukui, Maui, holds the US record for the most precipitation in one year—739 in (1,878 cm) in 1982. Average annual precipitation in Honolulu (1971–2000) was 18.3 in (46.5 cm). In the driest areas—on upper mountain slopes and in island interiors, as in central Maui—the average annual rainfall is less than 10 in (25 cm). Snow falls at the summits of Mauna Loa, Mauna Kea, and

171

Haleakala—the highest mountains. The highest tidal wave (tsunami) in the state's history reached 56 ft (17 m).

4FLORA AND FAUNA

Formed over many centuries by volcanic activity, Hawaii's topography—and therefore its flora and fauna—have been subject to constant and rapid change. Relatively few indigenous trees remain; most of the exotic trees and fruit plants have been introduced since the early 19th century. Of 2,200 species and subspecies of flora, more than half are endangered, threatened, or extinct. As of August 2003, 273 plant species were listed as endangered or threatened by the US Fish and Wildlife Service.

The only land mammal native to the islands is the Hawaiian hoary bat, now endangered; there are no indigenous snakes. The endangered humpback whale migrates to Hawaiian waters in winter; other marine animals abound. Among the 44 animal species listed as endangered or threatened as of August 2003 were four species of sea turtle and humpback whale. Among threatened birds are several varieties of honeycreeper, short-tailed albatross, Hawaiian coot, and the Hawaiian goose (nene). The nene (the state bird), once close to extinction, now numbers in the hundreds and is on the increase. Animals considered endangered by the state but not on the federal list include the Hawaiian storm petrel, Hawaiian owl, Maui 'amakihi (Loxops virens wilsoni), and 'i'iwi (Vestiaria coccinea).

5ENVIRONMENTAL PROTECTION

Environmental protection responsibilities are vested in the Department of Land and Natural Resources and in the Environmental Management Division of the Department of Health. The Hawaii Environmental Policy Act of 1974 established environmental policies and guidelines for state agencies. Also enacted in 1974 was the Environmental Impact Statement Law, which mandated environmental assessments for all state and county projects and some private projects. Noise pollution requirements for the state are among the strictest in the US, and air and water purity levels are well within federal standards.

The federal Environmental Protection Agency (EPA) banned the use of ethylene dibromide (EDB), a pesticide used in the state's pineapple fields, after high levels of the chemical were found in wells on the island of Oahu in 1983. In 2003, the Environmental Protection Agency's database listed 87 hazardous waste sites, 3 of which were on the National Priorities List, in Hawaii. In 2001, Hawaii received $25,730,000 in federal grants from the EPA.

6POPULATION

Hawaii ranked 42nd in population in the US with an estimated total of 1,244,898 in 2002, an increase of 2.8% since 2000. Between 1990 and 2000, Hawaii's population grew from 1,108,229 to 1,211,537, an increase of 9.3%. The population is projected to reach 1,342,000 by 2005 and 1.8 million by 2025. Almost four-fifths of the population lives on Oahu, primarily in the greater Honolulu metropolitan area. Population density was 188.6 people per sq mi in 2000.

In 2000 the median age was 36.2. Persons under 18 years old accounted for 24.4% of the population while 13.3% were age 65 or older.

By far the largest city is Honolulu, with an estimated 2002 population of 378,155. The greater metropolitan Honolulu area had an estimated 864,571 residents in 1999. The city of Honolulu is coextensive with Honolulu County.

7ETHNIC GROUPS

Hawaii has the nation's highest percentage of Asian residents— 41.6% in 2000, when its Asian population numbered 503,868. In the same year, Pacific Islanders numbered 113,539 (including 80,137 native Hawaiians), 22,003 were black, and 3,535 were American Indians or Alaska natives. About 87,699, or 7.2% of the total population, were Hispanic or Latino in 2000. Foreign-born residents numbered 212,229 in 2000, or 17.5% of the total state population—the 5th-highest percentage of foreign born among the 50 states.

Of Hawaii's Asian residents in 2000, 201,764 were Japanese, 170,635 were Filipino, 56,600 were Chinese, and 23,637 were Korean. The earliest Asian immigrants, the Chinese, were superseded in number in 1900 by the Japanese, who have since become a significant factor in state politics. The influx of Filipinos and other Pacific island peoples was largely a 20th-century phenomenon. In recent decades, ethnic Hawaiians have been increasingly intent on preserving their cultural identity.

8LANGUAGES

Although massive immigration from Asia and the US mainland since the mid-19th century has effectively diluted the native population, the Hawaiian lexical legacy in English is conspicuous. Newcomers soon add to their vocabulary *aloha* (love, good-bye), *haole* (white foreigner), *malihini* (newcomer), *lanai* (porch), *tapa* (bark cloth), *mahimahi* (a kind of fish), *ukulele, muumuu,* and the common directional terms *mauka* (toward the mountains) and *makai* (toward the sea), customarily used instead of "north," "east," "west," and "south." Native place-names are numerous— Waikiki, Hawaii, Honolulu, Mauna Kea, and Molokai for example.

Most native-born residents of Hawaiian ancestry speak one of several varieties of Hawaiian pidgin, a lingua franca incorporating elements of Hawaiian, English, and other Asian and Pacific languages. In 2000, 73.4 % (down from 75.2% in 1990) of Hawaiians five years old or older spoke only English at home.

The following table gives selected statistics from the 2000 census for language spoken at home by persons five years old and over. The category "Other Pacific Island languages" includes Chamorro, Hawaiian, Ilocano, Indonesian, and Samoan. The category "Other Indo-European languages" includes Albanian, Gaelic, Lithuanian, and Rumanian.

LANGUAGE	NUMBER	PERCENT
Population 5 years and over	**1,134,351**	**100.0**
Speak only English	832,226	73.4
Speak a language other than English	302,125	26.6
Speak a language other than English	**302,125**	**26.6**
Other Pacific Island languages	90,111	7.9
Tagalog	60,967	5.4
Japanese	56,225	5.0
Chinese	29,363	2.6
Spanish or Spanish Creole	18,820	1.7
Korean	18,337	1.6
Vietnamese	8,270	0.7
German	3,986	0.4
French (incl. Patois, Cajun)	3,310	0.3
Laotian	1,920	0.2
Thai	1,496	0.1
Other Indo-European languages	1,288	0.1
Portuguese or Portuguese Creole	1,238	0.1

9RELIGIONS

Congregationalist missionaries arrived in 1820 and Roman Catholics in 1827. Subsequent migration brought Mormons and Methodists. Anglican representatives were invited by King Kamehameha IV in 1862. Confucianism, Taoism, and Buddhism arrived with the Chinese during the 1850s; by the turn of the century, Shinto and five forms of Mahayana Buddhism were being practiced by Japanese immigrants.

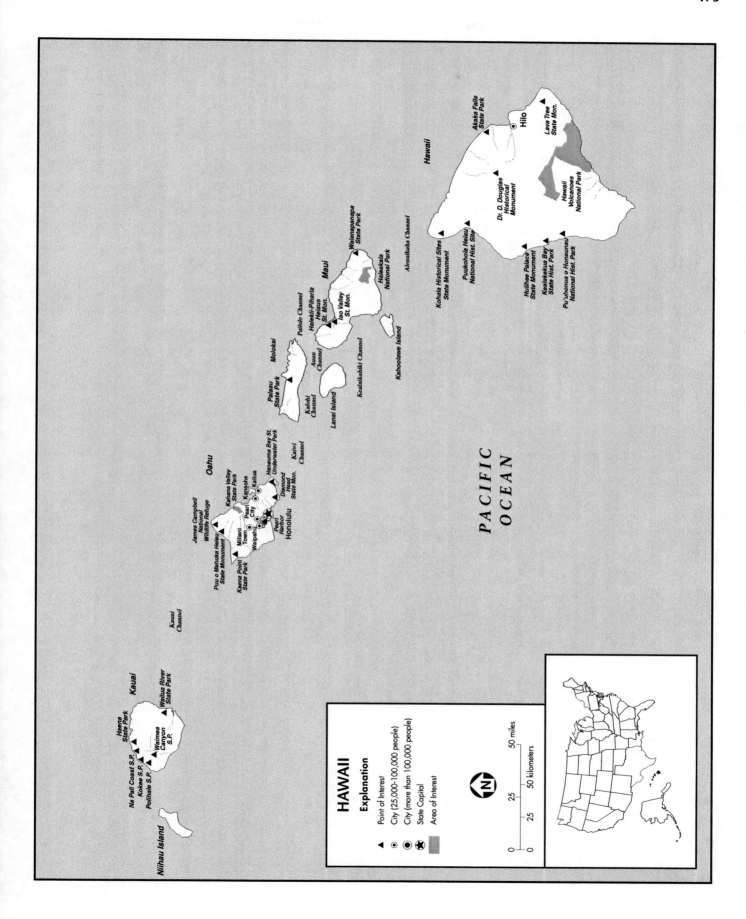

Akaka Falls State Park

Hilo

Lava Tree State Mon.

Hawaii

Dr. D. Douglas Historical Monument

Hawaii Volcanoes National Park

Kohala Historical Sites State Monument

Puukohola Heiau National Hist. Site

Hulihee Palace State Monument

Kealakekua Bay State Hist. Park

Pu'uhonua o Honaunau National Hist. Park

Waianapanapa State Park

Maui

Halekii-Pihaia Heiaus St. Mon.

Iao Valley St. Mon.

Haleakala National Park

Pailoho Channel

Alenuihaha Channel

Kahoolawe Island

Molokai

Palaau State Park

Auau Channel

Kahohi Channel

Lanai Island

Kealaikahiki Channel

PACIFIC OCEAN

Oahu

Kahana Valley State Park

James Campbell National Wildlife Refuge

Kailua

Kaneohe

Hanauma Bay St. Underwater Park

Diamond Head State Mon.

Mililani Town

Pearl City

Waipahu

Pearl Harbor

Honolulu

Kaiwi Channel

Puu o Mahuka Heiau State Monument

Kaena Point State Park

Kauai Channel

Kauai

Haena State Park

Wailua River State Park

Na Pali Coast S.P.

Kokee S.P.

Polihale S.P.

Waimea Canyon S.P.

Niihau Island

HAWAII
Explanation

Point of Interest
City (25,000-100,000 people)
City (more than 100,000 people)
State Capital
Area of Interest

N

0   25   50 miles

0   25   50 kilometers

In 2000, the largest religious group was the Catholic Church, with 240,813 adherents in 95 congregations. The Latter-day Saints followed with 42,758 adherents in 112 congregations. Other major groups include the United Church of Christ, 22,856 adherents; Assemblies of God, 21,754; and the Southern Baptist Convention, 20,901. In 2000, the Jewish population was at about 7,000. There were 73 Buddhist, 1 Muslim, and 8 Hindu congregations reported without specific membership numbers. About 63.8% of the population were not counted as members of any religious organization.

10 TRANSPORTATION

Hawaii has only two railroads: the nonprofit Hawaiian Railway Society, with 6.5 mi (10.5 km) of track on Oahu, and the commercial-recreational Lahaina, Kaanapali & Pacific on Maui, with 6 mi (10 km) of track. The islands of Oahu, Hawaii, Maui, and Kauai have public bus systems. In 2000, Hawaii's 769,383 licensed drivers traversed 4,281 mi (6,889 km) of roads and streets, of which 2,177 mi (3,503 km) were considered rural, and 2,104 mi (3,386 km) urban. There were 459,515 passenger cars registered in 2000, along with 273,735 trucks and 4,301 buses.

Hawaii's busiest port is Honolulu, with 15.8 million tons of cargo handled in 2000. Other major Hawaiian ports and their 2000 tonnage handled include Barbers Point, Oahu, 7.1 million; Hilo, 1.7 million; and Kahului, Maui, 3.5 million.

Most scheduled interisland passenger traffic and most transpacific travel is by air. The state has 31 airports and 16 heliports. The busiest air terminal, Honolulu International Airport, had a total of 11,174,701 enplanements in 2000.

11 HISTORY

Hawaii's earliest inhabitants were Polynesians who came to the islands in double-hulled canoes between 1,000 and 1,400 years ago, either from Southeast Asia or from the Marquesas in the South Pacific. The Western world learned of the islands in 1778, when an English navigator, Captain James Cook, sighted Oahu; he named the entire archipelago the Sandwich Islands after his patron, John Montagu, 4th Earl of Sandwich. At that time, each island was ruled by a hereditary chief under a caste system called *kapu*. Subsequent contact with European sailors and traders exposed the Polynesians to smallpox, venereal disease, liquor, firearms, and Western technology—and fatally weakened the kapu system. Within 40 years of Cook's arrival, one of the island chiefs, Kamehameha (whose birth date, designated as 11 June, is still celebrated as a state holiday), had consolidated his power on Hawaii, conquered Maui and Oahu, and established a royal dynasty in what became known as the Kingdom of Hawaii.

The death of Kamehameha I in 1819 preceded by a year the arrival of Protestant missionaries. One of the first to come was the Reverend Hiram Bingham, who, as pastor in Honolulu, was instrumental in converting Hawaiians to Christianity. Even before Bingham arrive, however, Liholiho, successor to the throne under the title of Kamehameha II, had begun to do away with the kapu system. After the king's death from measles while on a state trip to England in 1824, another son of Kamehameha I, Kauikeaouli, was proclaimed King Kamehameha III. His reign saw the establishment of public schools, the first newspapers, the first sugar plantation, a bicameral legislature, and the establishment of Honolulu as the kingdom's capital city. Hawaii's first written constitution was promulgated in 1840, and in 1848 a land reform called the Great Mahele abolished the feudal land system and legitimized private landholdings, in the process fostering the expansion of sugar plantations. The power behind the throne during this period was Dr. Gerrit P. Judd, a medical missionary who served as finance minister and interpreter for Kamehameha III.

Diplomatic maneuverings during the 1840s and 1850s secured recognition of the kingdom from the US, Britain, and France. As the American presence on the islands increased, however, so did pressure for US annexation—a movement opposed by Alexander Liholiho, who ruled as Kamehameha IV after his father's death in 1854. His brief reign and that of his brother Lot (Kamehameha V) witnessed the arrival of Chinese contract laborers and of the first Japanese immigrants, along with the continued growth of Hawaii as an international port of call (especially for whalers) and of the increasing influence of American sugar planters. Lot's death in 1872 left no direct descendant of Kamehameha, and the legislature elected a new king, whose death only a year later required yet another election. The consequent crowning of Kalakaua, known as the Merry Monarch, inaugurated a stormy decade during which his imperial schemes clashed with the power of the legislature and the interests of the planters. The most significant event of Kalakaua's unstable reign was the signing of a treaty with the US in 1876, guaranteeing Hawaii an American sugar market. The treaty was renewed in 1887 with a clause leasing Pearl Harbor to the US.

Kalakaua died during a visit to San Francisco in 1891 and was succeeded by his sister, Liliuokalani, the last Hawaiian monarch. Two years later, after further political wrangling, she was deposed in an American-led revolution that produced a provisional government under the leadership of Sanford B. Dole. The new regime immediately requested annexation by the US, but the treaty providing for it bogged down in the Senate, and died after the inauguration of President Grover Cleveland, an opponent of expansionism. The provisional government then drafted a new constitution and on 4 July 1894 proclaimed the Republic of Hawaii, with Dole as president. The Spanish-American War, which fanned expansionist feelings in the US and pointed up the nation's strategic interests in the Pacific, gave proponents of annexation the opportunity they had been seeking. The formal transfer of sovereignty took place on 12 August 1898, and Dole became Hawaii's first territorial governor when the act authorizing the annexation became effective in June 1900.

Notable in the territorial period were a steady US military buildup, the creation of a pineapple canning industry by James D. Dole (the governor's cousin), the growth of tourism (spurred in 1936 by the inauguration of commercial air service), and a rising desire for statehood, especially after passage of the Sugar Act of 1934, which lowered the quota on sugar imports from Hawaii. The Japanese attack on Pearl Harbor on 7 December 1941, crippling the US Pacific fleet and causing some 4,000 casualties, quickly turned Hawaii into an armed camp, under martial law. The record of bravery compiled by Nisei of the 442nd Regiment on the European front did much, on the other hand, to allay the mistrust that some mainlanders felt about the loyalties of Hawaiians of Japanese ancestry. Hawaii also bore a disproportionate burden during the Korean conflict, suffering more casualties per capita than any of the 48 states.

Hawaiians pressed for statehood after World War II, but Congress was reluctant, partly because of racial antipathy and partly because of fears that Hawaii's powerful International Longshoremen's and Warehousemen's Union was Communist-controlled. The House of Representatives passed a statehood bill in 1947, but the Senate refused. Not until 1959, after Alaska became the 49th state, did Congress vote to let Hawaii enter the Union. President Eisenhower signed the bill on 18 March, and the question was then put to the Hawaiian electorate, who voted for statehood on 27 June 1959 by a margin of about 17 to 1. Hawaii became the 50th state on 21 August 1959.

Defense, tourism, and food processing have been mainstays of Hawaii's economy, with the state playing an increasingly important role as an economic, educational, and cultural bridge between the US and the nations of Asia and the Pacific. In the

1990s Hawaiians faced the challenge of preserving the natural beauty of their environment while accommodating a growing population (especially on Oahu) and a thriving tourist industry. In May 2000 President Clinton issued orders to federal agencies to expand their coastline protection programs, including those protecting Hawaii's coral reefs.

A prominent political issue in recent years has been the achievement of some form of sovereignty by native Hawaiians. Control of an estimated two million acres of land are also at stake. In 1996 a majority of the islands' roughly 200,000 descendants of indigenous Hawaiians voted to establish some form of self-government. In August 1998, the 100th anniversary of the US annexation of Hawaii, protesters marched in Washington, D.C., demanding their full sovereignty from the US government. In July 2000 the movement got some backing in a rights bill introduced in Congress by Hawaiian Senator Daniel Akaka. The bill asked that native Hawaiians be allowed to form their own government and have status similar to that of American Indians.

Hawaii's tourism industry was negatively affected by the 2001 recession, the 11 September 2001 terrorist attacks on the US, and the 2003 Iraq war. Hawaii's tourism business by April 2003 declined by about one-third since the start of the war with Iraq on 19 March 2003. That year, the Hawaii legislature was debating a non-binding resolution condemning portions of the 2001 USA Patriot Act and the 2002 Homeland Security Act (which include sweeping new federal powers to combat terrorism) and calling on state and local officials to avoid any actions that threatened the civil rights of any of Hawaii's residents. Hawaii would have been the first state to go on record against the Patriot and Homeland Security Acts.

12 STATE GOVERNMENT

The constitution of the state of Hawaii was written by the constitutional convention of 1950, ratified by the people of the Territory of Hawaii that year, and then amended by the 1959 plebiscite on the statehood question. By January 2003, it had been amended 100 times.

There is a bicameral legislature of 25 senators elected from eight senatorial districts for four-year terms, and 51 representatives elected for two-year terms. The legislature meets annually on the 3rd Wednesday in January; the session is limited to 60 legislative days, but a two-thirds petition by the membership secures an extension (limited to 15 days). Special sessions, each limited to 30 legislative days, may be called by petition of two-thirds of the members of each house. To be eligible to serve as a legislator, a person must have attained the age of majority (18), be an American citizen, have been a resident of the state for at least three years, and be a qualified voter of his district. The legislative salary in 2002 was $32,000, unchanged from 1999.

The governor and lieutenant governor are jointly elected for concurrent four-year terms and must be of the same political party. They are the only elected officers of the executive branch, except for the 13 members of the Board of Education, who also serve four-year terms. The governor, who may be reelected only once, must be at least 30 years old and must have resided in the state for five years. In 2002 the governor's salary was $94,780, unchanged from 1999.

The legislature can override the governor's veto by a two-thirds vote of the elected members of both houses. If the governor neither signs nor vetoes a bill, it becomes law after 10 days (excepting Saturdays, Sundays, and holidays) when the legislature is in session or after 45 days (excepting Saturdays, Sundays, and holidays) after the legislature has adjourned.

A constitutional amendment may be proposed by the legislature with a two-thirds vote in each house in one session or a majority vote in each house in two sessions. It must then be approved by a majority of the voters during elections.

Voters in Hawaii must be US citizens at least 18 years old; there is no minimum residency requirement. Restrictions apply to convicted felons and those declared mentally incompetent by the court.

13 POLITICAL PARTIES

Both Republicans and Democrats established party organizations early in the 20th century when Hawaii was still a territory. Before statehood, the Republican Party dominated the political scene; since the 1960s, however, Hawaii was solidly Democratic.

Democrat Al Gore won 56% of the vote in the presidential election in 2000, while Republican George W. Bush garnered 38%, and Green Party candidate Ralph Nader took 6%. Democrat Daniel K Inouye first won election to the US Senate in 1962, he was reelected in 1968, 1974, 1980, 1986, 1992, and 1998. Democratic Senator Daniel K. Akaka, first appointed in 1990 and elected to a full term in 1994, was reelected in 2000. In 2002 there were 676,242 registered voters; there is no party registration in the state. The state had four electoral votes in the 2000 presidential election.

Hawaii Presidential Vote by Major Political Parties, 1960–2000

YEAR	ELECTORAL VOTE	HAWAII WINNER	DEMOCRAT	REPUBLICAN
1960	3	*Kennedy (D)	92,410	92,295
1964	4	*Johnson (D)	163,249	44,022
1968	4	Humphrey (D)	141,324	91,425
1972	4	*Nixon (R)	101,433	168,933
1976	4	*Carter (D)	147,375	140,003
1980	4	Carter (D)	135,879	130,112
1984	4	*Reagan (R)	147,154	185,050
1988	4	Dukakis (D)	192,364	158,625
1992**	4	*Clinton (D)	179,310	136,822
1996**	4	*Clinton (D)	205,012	113,943
2000***	4	Gore (D)	205,286	137,845

*Won US presidential election.
**Independent candidate Ross Perot received 53,003 votes in 1992 and 27,358 votes in 1996.
***Green Party candidate Ralph Nader received 21,623 votes in 2000.

14 LOCAL GOVERNMENT

The state is divided into five principal counties: Hawaii, including the island of Hawaii; Maui, embracing the islands of Maui, Kahoolawe, Lanai, and Molokai; Honolulu, coextensive with the city of Honolulu and covering all of Oahu and the northwestern Hawaiian Islands, from Nihoa to Kure Atoll; Kauai, including the islands of Kauai and Niihau; and Kalawao on Molokai, with a population of 134 in 2001. Kalawao is represented in the state legislature as part of Maui County.

Because there are no further forms of local government, the counties provide some services traditionally performed in other states by cities, towns, and villages, notably fire and police protection, refuse collection, and street maintenance and lighting. On the other hand, the state government provides many functions normally performed by counties on the mainland. Each principal county has an elected council and a mayor.

In 2002 the state had fifteen special districts and one public school system.

15 STATE SERVICES

To address the continuing threat of terrorism and to work with the federal Department of Homeland Security (created in 2002 following the terrorist attacks of 11 September 2001), homeland security in Hawaii in 2003 operated under the authority of the governor; the adjutant general was designated as the state homeland security advisor.

Hawaii's first ombudsman, empowered to investigate complaints by the public about any officer or employee of state or county government, took office in 1969. The State Ethics Commission, a legislative agency, implements requirements for financial disclosure by state officials and investigates alleged conflicts of interest and other breaches of ethics.

The Department of Education is headed by an elected Board of Education. It operates hundreds of schools in the state, including several for the physically and mentally disabled. It also administers the statewide public library system, regulates private schools, and certifies teachers. The Board of Regents of the University of Hawaii oversees the state's higher educational institutions. Highways, airports, harbors, and other facilities are the concern of the Department of Transportation.

The Department of Health operates over 10 public hospitals, the Kalaupapa leper colony, and various programs for the mentally ill, the mentally retarded, and alcoholics. Civil defense and the Air and Army national guards are under the jurisdiction of the Department of Defense. The Department of Land and Natural Resources focuses on the environment.

The Corrections Division of the Department of Social Services and Housing operates the state prison system, along with programs for juvenile offenders. Also within this department are divisions of public welfare and vocational rehabilitation, as well as the Hawaii Housing Authority. The Executive Office on Aging works with state and county departments to coordinate programs for senior citizens. Unemployment insurance, occupational safety and health laws, and workers' compensation programs are run by the Department of Labor and Industrial Relations.

[16]JUDICIAL SYSTEM

The supreme court, the highest in the state, consists of a chief justice and four associate justices, all of them appointed by the governor with the advice and consent of the senate. All serve 10-year terms, up to the mandatory retirement age of 70.

The state is divided into four judicial circuits with 27 circuit court judges and 4 intermediate appellate court judges, also appointed by the governor with the advice and consent of the senate to 10-year terms. Circuit courts are the main trial courts, having jurisdiction in most civil and criminal cases. District courts, whose judges are appointed by the chief justice with the advice and consent of the senate to 6-year terms, function as inferior courts within each judicial circuit; district court judges may also preside over family court proceedings. Hawaii also has a land court and a tax appeal court.

According to the FBI Crime Index, Hawaii's crime rate in 2001 totaled 5,386.1 per 100,000 inhabitants, including a total of 3,117 violent crimes and 62,830 property crimes in that year. There were 5,412 inmates held in correctional institutions as of June 2001, an increase of 7.1% from the previous year. Hawaii does not have a death penalty.

[17]ARMED FORCES

Hawaii is the nerve center of US defense activities in the Pacific. CINCPAC (Commander-in-Chief Pacific), headquartered at Camp H. M. Smith in Honolulu, directs the US Pacific Command, largest of the six US unified commands and responsible for all US military forces in the Pacific and Indian oceans and southern Asia. Military prime contract awards in the fiscal year 2001totaled $1.3 billion.

As of 2002, Hawaii was home base for 62,597 Department of Defense military and civilian personnel on 7 military installations and properties. The US Navy and Marines accounted for 24,899 personnel; the Army, 26,990; and the Air Force, 9,641. Pearl Harbor is home port for 40 ships. The major Army bases, all on Oahu, are Schofield Barracks, Ft. Shafter, and Ft. DeRussy; Air Force bases include Hickam and Wheeler. Military reservations occupy nearly one-fourth of Oahu's land area.

There were 120,587 veterans of US military service in Hawaii as of 2000, of whom 19,844 served in World War II; 13,132 in the Korean conflict; 35,738 during the Vietnam era; and 18,312 during 1990–2000 (including the Persian Gulf War). Veterans' benefits totaled $245 million in fiscal year 2002.

[18]MIGRATION

The US mainland and Asia have been the main sources of immigrants to Hawaii since the early 19th century. Immigration remains a major source of population growth: between 1950 and 1980, Hawaii's net gain from migration was 91,000, and between 1980 and 1983, 15,000. In the 1980s, migration accounted for 23% of the net increase in population.

Since the early 1970s, about 40,000 mainland Americans have come each year to live in Hawaii. More than half are military personnel and their dependents, on temporary residence during their term of military service. From 1985 to 1990, Hawaii suffered a net loss from migration within the US, but experienced an overall net gain in migration due to immigration from abroad. Between 1990 and 1998, the net loss from domestic migration was 80,000. During the same period there was a net gain of 51,000 from international migration. In 1998, 5,465 foreign immigrants arrived in Hawaii. Between 1990 and 1998, the state's overall population increased 7.6%. In the period 1995–2000, 125,160 people moved into the state and 201,293 moved out, for a net loss of 76,133, of whom about 44,192 moved to California.

[19]INTERGOVERNMENTAL COOPERATION

Among the interstate accords in which Hawaii participates are the Western Interstate Corrections Compact and the Western Interstate Commission for Higher Education. Federal grants were estimated at $1.5 billion in fiscal year 2001.

[20]ECONOMY

Tourism remains Hawaii's leading employer, revenue producer, and growth sector. However, agricultural diversification (including the cultivation of flowers and nursery products, papaya, and macadamia nuts), aquaculture, manganese nodule mining, and film and television production have broadened the state's economic base. The public sector has a greater presence in Hawaii's economy than in any other state, accounting for 21.5% of gross state product in 2001, compared to the state average of 12%. Economic growth was relatively sluggish in Hawaii at the end of the 20th century, accelerating only from 2.2% in 1998 to 3.3% in 1999 to 4.6% in 2000. The national recession of 2001 and the after-effects of 9/11 helped reduce the annual growth rate to 2.8% in 2001, mainly through the impact on tourism. By the third quarter of 2002, however, hotel revenue in Hawaii was showing an increase over 2001, in contrast to hotel revenues in other parts of the country. Payroll employment, after declining sharply in 2001, was also showing increases.

Hawaii's gross state product in 2001 was 39th in the nation at $43.7 billion, to which financial services contributed $10.1 billion; general services (including tourism), $10 billion; government, $9.4 billion; trade, $6.5 billion; transportation and public utilities, $4.1 billion, and manufacturing, $1.2 billion. -

[21]INCOME

According to the Bureau of Economic Analysis, in 2001, Hawaii had a per capita personal income (PCPI) of $29,034 which ranked 23rd in the United States (including the District of Columbia) and was 95% of the national average, $30,413. The 2001 PCPI reflected an increase of 2.4% from 2000 compared to the national change of 2.2%. In 2001, Hawaii had a total personal income (TPI) of $35,625,115,000 which ranked 40th in the United States and accounted for 0.4% of the national total. The 2001 TPI reflected an increase of 3.6% from 2000 compared to the national change of 3.3%.

Earnings of persons employed in Hawaii increased from $24,837,274,000 in 2000 to $25,698,409,000 in 2001, an increase of 3.5%. The largest industries in 2001 were services, 29.9% of earnings; state and local government, 11.9%; and retail trade, 11.3%. Of the industries that accounted for at least 5% of earnings in 2001, the slowest growing from 2000 to 2001 was federal civilian government (7.7% of earnings in 2001), which increased 0.9%; the fastest was military (10.0% of earnings in 2001), which increased 7.0%.

According to data released by the US Census Bureau, in 2000, the median household income was $48,026 compared to the national average of $42,148. In 2001, the median income for a family of four was $66,014 compared to the national average of $63,278. For the period 1999 to 2001, the average poverty rate was 10.4% which placed it 27th among the 50 states and the District of Columbia ranked lowest to highest.

[22]LABOR

According to Bureau of Labor Statistics (BLS) provisional estimates, in July 2003 the seasonally adjusted civilian labor force in Hawaii numbered 609,100, with approximately 24,600 workers unemployed, yielding an unemployment rate of 4.0%, compared to the national average of 6.2% for the same period. Since the beginning of the BLS data series in 1978, the highest unemployment rate recorded was 7.8% in September 1978. The historical low was 2.3% in July 1989. In 2001, an estimated 5.1% of the labor force was employed in construction; 3.1% in manufacturing; 7.8% in transportation, communications, and public utilities; 21.6% in trade; 5.9% in finance, insurance, and real estate; 27.8% in services; 17.7% in government; and 3.2% in agriculture.

Unionization was slow to develop in Hawaii. After World War II, however, the International Longshoremen's and Warehousemen's Union (ILWU) organized workers in the sugar and pineapple industries and then on the docks. The Teamsters Union is also well established.

The US Department of Labor reported that in 2002, 120,000 of Hawaii's 492,000 employed wage and salary workers were members of unions. This represented 24.4% of those so employed, up from 23.7% in 2001 but down from 26.5% in 1998. The national average is 13.2%. Hawaii is one of only four states with a union membership rate over 20%. In all, 125,000 workers (25.4%) were represented by unions. In addition to union members, this category includes workers who report no union affiliation but whose jobs are covered by a union contract.

[23]AGRICULTURE

Export crops—especially sugar cane and pineapple—dominate Hawaiian agriculture, which had farm receipts exceeding $511 million in 2001.

The islands of Hawaii (Maui, Molokai, Oahu, and Kauai) are the only places in the US where coffee is grown commercially; production in 2002/2003 totaled 8.5 million lb (3.86 million kg). Another tropical product, papaya, has also become a substantial export crop, with 45.5 million lb (20.6 million kg) produced in 2002, valued at $11.8 million, as well as macadamia nuts and tropical flowers. Taro (coco yam) used for making poi, is also grown; production in 2001 was 6.1 million lb (2.8 million kg), valued at $3,290,000. Banana production in 2002 was 19 million lb (8.6 million kg), valued at $7.9 million.

[24]ANIMAL HUSBANDRY

Hawaii had an estimated 150,000 cattle and calves worth $84 million in 2003. In 2002, the estimated number of hogs and pigs was 24,000, worth $3.4 million. Poultry farms produced an estimated 129 million eggs in 2001, worth $9.6 million. Most of the eggs were for domestic consumption, making eggs one of the very few farm commodities in which the state is close to self-sufficient. Most of the state's cattle farms are in Hawaii and Maui counties.

[25]FISHING

Although expanding, Hawaii's commercial catch remains surprisingly small—36.4 million pounds, worth $62 million, in 1998. The most valuable commercial species are swordfish and bigeye tuna. There were 2,493 commercial fishing vessels in 1997. Sport fishing is extremely popular, with bass, bluegill, tuna, and marlin among the most sought-after varieties by the state's 6,693 sport fishing license holders in 1998.

[26]FORESTRY

As of 2002, Hawaii had 1,748,000 acres (707,940 hectares) of forestland and water reserves, with 700,000 acres (283,500 hectares) classified as commercial timberland, most of it located on the island of Hawaii. The majority of the locally grown wood is used in the manufacture of furniture, flooring, and craft items. As the sugar industry downsizes, there is an initiative to expand the forest industry by planting trees on lands formerly planted in sugar cane.

[27]MINING

The value of Hawaii's nonfuel mineral production in 2001 was estimated to be $70 million, a 24% decrease from 2000. Crushed stone, construction sand and gravel, and portland cement were the principal mineral commodities produced, with values of $51.9 million, $6.97 million, and $10.2 million, respectively. Small amounts of masonry cement ($600,000) and gemstone production were also reported. The overall decrease in value in 2001 was mostly related to decreases in the values of portland cement and crushed stone. Portland cement production has declined since the record high of 522,000 metric tons in 1992, valued at $54 million.

Mineral production in Hawaii is mainly for local construction usage. The rapid growth in construction throughout the state slowed somewhat in 1991, but government policy aimed at expanding the housing industry and at raising public construction levels offset the anticipated drop in private construction, resulting in a modest increase in mineral production. However, production of crushed stone and portland cement are now only about half the size they were in 1992.

[28]ENERGY AND POWER

Devoid of indigenous fossil fuels and nuclear installations, Hawaii depends on imported petroleum for about 78% of its energy needs; coal, hydroelectric power, natural gas, windmills, geothermal energy, and sugar cane wastes contribute the rest. In 1999, Hawaii's electric production from hydro was 1.1%, coal was 14.2%, and methane was 0.5%. In 2000 Hawaii's total per capita energy consumption was 218 million Btu (54.9 million kcal), ranking it 51st among the 50 states.

Installed capacity (utility and nonutility) reached 2.32 million kW in 1999; total generation was 10.5 billion kWh. All of Hawaii's electric power plants are privately owned.

[29]INDUSTRY

Food and food products account for about one-third of the total annual value of shipments by manufacturers, including sugar and pineapples. Other major industries are clothing; stone, clay, and glass products; fabricated metals; and shipbuilding.

Hawaii's publicly held corporations include Amfac, involved in food processing, merchandising, and land development; and Castle & Cooke, which owns the Dole and Bumble Bee food product lines. Other corporations are Dillingham, which is involved in maritime industries and land development, and Brewer (owned by IU International), which produces 20% of the state's sugar and more than half the world's macadamia nuts.

Earnings of persons employed in Hawaii increased from $22.8 billion in 1997 to $23.3 billion in 1998, an increase of 1.9%. The largest industries in 1998 were services, 30.6% of earnings; retail trade, 12.3%; and state and local government, 12.2%. Of the industries that accounted for at least 5% of earnings in 1998, the slowest growing from 1997 to 1998 was construction (6.4% of earnings in 1998), which decreased 5.7%; the fastest was federal civilian government (6.0% of earnings in 1998), which increased 9.2%.

30COMMERCE

In 1997, Hawaii's revenues from 2,106 wholesale trade establishments amounted to $7.7 billion. A total of 7,722 retail establishments had sales totaling $13 billion in 1997. Retail sales totaled $15.7 billion in 1998. The leading shopping centers, all on Oahu, are the Ala Moana Center, Pearlridge Center, and Kahala Mall. Food stores, automotive dealers and service centers, and eating and drinking establishments accounted for 11%, 7.5%, and 34% of store genre, respectively. Food sales and merchandise sales totaled $2.3 billion each in 1997.

Hawaii's central position in the Pacific ensures a sizable flow of goods through the Honolulu Customs District. Exports exceeded $276 million. Hawaii's major trading partners are Japan for exports; and Japan, Singapore and Indonesia for imports. Hawaii's Trade Zone no. 9 is one of the most successful trade programs in the US. In 1998, the zone was used by 279 businesses, handling $2.1 billion worth of merchandise, and providing 6,370 jobs.

31CONSUMER PROTECTION

Hawaii's Office of Consumer Protection, a division of the Department of Commerce and Consumer Affairs, enforces the state's consumer protection laws and provides information regarding landlord-tenant matters. It was created in 1969 to protect the interests of consumers and legitimate businesses, by investigating consumer complaints alleging unfair or deceptive trade practices, in a broad range of areas, including advertising, refunds, motor vehicle rentals, door-to-door sales, and credit practices.

32BANKING

In 2002, Hawaii had nine insured banks, including four state-chartered banks, one foreign bank branch, three credit unions, and one interstate branch, with combined assets of $29.8 billion. Between 1991 and 2002, the number of separately-chartered insured banks decreased from 27 to 9, due to mergers. Hawaii's financial system is protected by the Department of Commerce and Consumer Affairs, with the Division of Financial Institutions.

During 2001 and 2002, the state's insured institutions improved their performance, due in part to increased net interest margins (NIMs) (the difference between the lower rates offered to savers and the higher rates charged on loans) coming from declining interest rates.

33INSURANCE

In 2001 there were 564,000 ordinary life insurance policies in force with a total value of $47.9 billion; total value for all categories of life insurance (ordinary, group, industrial, and credit) was $71.3 billion. Death benefits paid that year totaled $156.9 million.

There were 5 life and health insurance and 33 property and casualty insurance companies headquartered in the state, as well as others authorized to do business in Hawaii in 2003. In 2001, property and casualty insurers wrote premiums totaling $1.45 billion. That year, there were 41,493 flood insurance policies in force in the state, with a total value of $5.14 million.

34SECURITIES

The Honolulu Stock Exchange, established in 1898, discontinued trading on 30 December 1977. However, there are approximately 170 securities dealers' establishments, with 1,552 employees. Investment advisory organizations number 40. Seven NASDAQ companies are headquartered in Hawaii, as well as four Hawaii-incorporated NYSE-listed companies: Castle & Cooke, Inc., Hawaiian Electricity Industry Inc., Dole Food Co., and Pacific Century Financial Corp.

35PUBLIC FINANCE

Development and implementation of Hawaii's biennial budget are the responsibility of the Department of Budget and Finance. The fiscal year runs from 1 July through 30 June.

Beginning in 2000, reductions in state taxes were scheduled through 2006, including cuts in the general excise tax, a cut in the services tax for out-of-state end usage, and incentives for high-technology business in Hawaii. From 1995 to 2000, the number of high-technology companies in Hawaii more than doubled from 300 to 629.

In 2002/03 Hawaii experienced a budget deficit amounting to 4.6% of the state budget. Cuts totaling $20 million were made in the 2002/03 budget after it was passed. The state's beginning balance in 2003/04 was only $8 million, though not counting $53 million in its Emergency and Budget Reserve Fund (Hawaii's rainy day fund). Revenues for 2004 were projected at $3.817 billion and expenditures at $3.816 billion (including an allocation of $10 million to the rainy day fund, which receives 40% of its funds from the tobacco taxes, which were raised in 2002) with an expected ending balance of $9 million, not counting $63 million in the rainy day fund. The following table from the US Census Bureau contains information on revenues, expenditures, indebtedness, and cash/securities for 2001.

	AMOUNT	PERCENT	PER CAPITA
Population (thousands, 2001)	1,227	(X)	(X)
Total Revenue	6,591,146	100.00	5,371.76
General revenue	6,045,188	91.72	4,926.80
Utility revenue	–	–	–
Liquor store revenue	–	–	–
Insurance trust revenue	545,958	8.28	444.95
Exhibit: Salaries and wages	1,825,898	26.88	1,488.10
Total expenditure	6,792,058	100.00	5,535.50
General expenditure	6,144,750	90.47	5,007.95
Education	2,192,291	32.28	1,786.71
Public welfare	1,038,087	15.28	846.04
Hospitals	170,918	2.52	139.30
Health	391,234	5.76	318.85
Highways	232,544	3.42	189.52
Police protection	8,471	0.12	6.90
Correction	148,607	2.19	121.11
Natural resources	91,313	1.34	74.42
Parks and recreation	46,238	0.68	37.68
Government administration	328,096	4.83	267.40
Interest on general debt	318,436	4.69	259.52
Other and unallocable	1,178,515	17.35	960.48
Utility expenditure	–	–	–
Liquor store expenditure	–	–	–
Insurance trust expenditure	647,308	9.53	527.55
Debt at end of fiscal year	5,300,649	100.00	4,320.01
Cash and security holdings	13,478,165	100.00	10,984.65

36TAXATION

Hawaii's per capita tax burden is one of the highest in the US. In 2003, its combined state and local taxes totaled 10.7% of income, the 6th highest in the country. Hawaii has, however, been in the process of reducing the rates on its 8-bracket personal income tax schedule, and in 2002 it reduced all 8 rates. The bottom rate was lowered from 1.5% to 1.4%, and the top rate from 8.5% to 8.25%. Personal and child exemptions are $1040 per person. The lowest rate applies up to $2000 of taxable income, and the highest to taxable income above $40,000. Capital gains are taxed at 4%, down from a maximum of 7.25%. The corporate income tax is 4.4% on taxable income up to $25,000, 5.4% on taxable income over $25,000 but not over $100,000 less $250, and 6.4% on taxable income over $100,000 less $1,250. The state general sales tax rate is 4% with exemptions for prescription drugs. There is a broad-based general use tax of 0.5% on wholesaling and manufacturing activities. There are no local sales taxes, whereas all property taxes are local taxes. Most of Hawaii's taxes (79.4% in 2000) are collected at the state level. There are also selective sales taxes (excises). In 2002 Hawaii raised its tax on cigarettes from $1 to $1.20 a pack. There are other excise on motor fuels, liquor, insurance premiums, public utilities and other selected goods. The state estate tax is tied to the federal exemption for state death taxes and is therefore set to be phased out in tandem with the federal estate tax credit by 2007 absent any action by Hawaii's government to preserve the state assessment. Revenue losses from the phasing out of Hawaii's estate tax are estimated at -$9 million in 2002/03, -$14.1 million in 2003/04 and -$24.2 million in 2007. Death and gift taxes accounted for 0.48% of state collections in 2002. Other state taxes include various license fees and stamp taxes.

Total state tax collection in Hawaii came to $3.4 billion in 2002, 47% from the general sales tax, 32.5% from personal income taxes, 14.7% from excises, 3.2% from license fees, and 1.54% from the corporate income tax.

The following table from the US Census Bureau provides a summary of taxes collected by the state in 2002.

	($000)	PER CAPITA
Total Taxes	3,420,671	2,747.75
Property taxes	(X)	(X)
Sales and gross receipts	2,117,948	1,701.30
General sales and gross receipts	1,612,333	1,295.15
Selective sales taxes	505,615	406.15
Alcoholic beverage	39,090	31.4
Amusements	(X)	(X)
Insurance Premiums	70,059	56.28
Motor fuels	78,088	62.73
Pari-mutuels	(X)	(X)
Public utilities	93,405	75.03
Tobacco products	65,546	52.65
Other selective sales	159,427	128.06
Licenses	111,801	89.81
Alcoholic beverages	(X)	(X)
Amusements	(X)	(X)
Corporation	2,303	1.85
Hunting and fishing	328	0.26
Motor vehicle	79,462	63.83
Motor vehicle operators	313	0.25
Public utility	11,126	8.94
Occupation and business, NEC	17,214	13.83
Other	1,055	0.85
Other taxes	1,190,922	956.64
Individual income	1,111,590	892.92
Corporation net income	52,640	42.28
Death and gift	16,624	13.35
Documentary and stock transfer	10,068	8.09
Severance	(X)	(X)
Other	(X)	(X)

37ECONOMIC POLICY

Business activity in Hawaii is limited by physical factors: land for development is scarce, living costs are relatively high, heavy industry is environmentally inappropriate, and there are few land based mineral operations. On the other hand, Hawaii is well placed as a trading and communications center, and Hawaii's roles as a defense outpost and tourist haven remain vital. The Department of Business, Economic Development and Tourism (DBEDT) is the lead agency for economic development and planning. The Office of Planning, a separate agency attached to the DBEDT, has specific responsibility for the continuous process of long-range strategic planning. In 2003, on-going projects in the Office of Planning included a task force on "Recapturing the Magic of Waikiki," a case study in keeping resort areas vital and attractive; implementing the EPA-funded Brownfields Cleanup Revolving Loan Fund program; mapping the islands' agricultural subdivisions; implementing a state Smart Growth strategy, including conducting stakeholder and public information meetings to increase awareness of Smart Growth principles and practices. The Aloha Tower Development Corporation (ATDC), formed in 1981 to develop the area around the historic landmark in downtown Honolulu, is another separate agency attached to the DBEDT. The Aloha Tower Marketplace, completed in 1994, was its first major project. ATDC seeks to attract private investors to both strengthen the international economic base of the community and to enhance the beautification of the waterfront. The area has been included in an Enterprise Zone (EZ), making business tenants eligible for tax incentives. In 2003, Hawaii has 19 designated EZs, which are areas with high rates of unemployment, poverty and/or public assistance. Another separate agency attached to the DBEDT is the High Technology Development Corporation (HTDC), established in 1982. Other separate agencies coordinated by the DBED include the Hawaii Tourist Authority, the Natural Energy of Hawaii Authority, the Hawaii Community Development Authority, the Land Use Commission, and the Housing and Community Development Corporation. The DBEDT administers the state's Foreign Trade Zone (FTZ) program, established under a grant issued to Hawaii by the federal Foreign-Trade Zones Board in 1965. As of 2003, 13 sites on the islands of Oahu, Maui and Hawaii had received FTZ designations, and, of these, three general-purpose and four special-purpose, zones were active. For FY 2001 it was reported that 301 firms from 33 countries had taken advantage of the customs-exemptions and enhanced facilities offered in the FTZs. Other divisions within the DBEDT include the Business Development and Marketing Division; the Research and Economic Analysis Division; and the Energy, Resources and Technology Division.

38HEALTH

Hawaii's infant mortality rate was 8.1 per 1,000 live births in 2000. In 1999, a total of 4,404 abortions were performed, at a rate of 18 per 1,000 women. Death rates from heart diseases, cerebrovascular diseases, accidents, and suicide were all below their respective national rates in 2000. The HIV-related death rate in Hawaii was also less than the overall US rate (2.3 vs. 5.3 per 100,000) in 2000. Through 2001, 2,569 AIDS cases had been reported Smoking prevalence was 19.7% among Hawaiians age 18 and older in 2000.

In 2001, Hawaii had 23 community hospitals, which together provided 3,235 beds and had a total of 108,252 admissions. There were 3,430 full-time registered nurses and 487 full-time licensed practical nurses in 2001 and 300 physicians per 100,000 population in 2000. The average expense for hospital care provided in 2001 totaled $1,296.30 per inpatient day.

Hawaii comes the closest of any state to providing universal health care coverage as the result of a 1974 law that requires employers to provide health insurance for full-time workers and a state insurance plan for low-income, part-time workers and Medicaid recipients. Federal government grants to cover the Medicare and Medicaid services in 2001 totaled $347 million; 168,296 enrollees received Medicare benefits that year. Only 9.6% of Hawaiian adults were uninsured in 2002.

39 SOCIAL WELFARE

In 2001, the average weekly unemployment benefit was $297.97. Average monthly participation in the food stamp program in FY2002 comprised 106,370 persons (50,981 households). The average monthly benefit was $118.90, and the sum total of benefits paid in FY2002 was $151,768,769.

With the enactment of the Personal Responsibility and Work Opportunity Reconciliation Act of 1996, the US government has changed the form and regulations for many of its social welfare programs. Most significantly, it replaces Aid to Families with Dependent Children (AFDC), an open-ended entitlement program, with Temporary Assistance for Needy Families (TANF), a limited system of assistance funded largely through federal block grants. The reform act also impacts the food stamp program, the Supplemental Security Income program, and the child nutrition program. The law took effect on 1 July 1997 and provided $16.38 billion in block grants for fiscal years 1997–2002. The grants are to be divided among the states based on an equation involving the numbers of former AFDC recipients in each state.

Reauthorization of the 1996 social welfare legislation, scheduled for 2002, was delayed, and the original law had been extended three times as of July 2003, with the most recent extension running through September 2003. Hawaii's TANF program has no separate state name. In June 2000 the state had 42,824 welfare recipients. State expenditures on the TANF program in FY2002 totaled $29,944,710.

In December 2001, Social Security benefits were paid to 188,920 Hawaiians. This number included 134,410 retired workers, 16,140 widows and widowers, 14,630 disabled workers, 10,140 spouses, and 13,600 children. Social Security beneficiaries represented 15.3% of the total state population and 87.9% of the state's population age 65 and older. Retired workers (excluding persons with special benefits) received an average monthly payment of $864; widows and widowers, $701; disabled workers, $795; and spouses, $409. Payments for children of retired workers averaged $409 per month; children of deceased workers, $575; and children of disabled workers, $249.

Federal Supplemental Security Income payments in December 2001 went to 21,303 Hawaii residents, averaging $412 a month.

40 HOUSING

Although statehood set off a building surge in Hawaii, housing remained in short supply throughout the 1970s and early 1980s. In 2002 there were an estimated 470,000 housing units, 415,579 of which were occupied. Only 56.1% were owner-occupied, ranking the state at 49th out of 51 (the 50 states and the District of Columbia) in the number of homeowners. About 50.9% of all units were single-family, detached homes; 20.3% were within buildings of 20 or more units. Most units relied on electricity for heating but about 5,375 units were equipped for solar power. It was estimated that 12,652 units were lacking telephone service, 3,151 lacked complete plumbing facilities, and 5,282 lacked complete kitchen facilities. The average household size was 2.9 people.

In 2002, 5,902 privately owned housing units were authorized for construction. Median home value was at $291,576, the highest in the nation. The median monthly cost for mortgage owners was $1,691 while renters paid a median of $832 per month. During fiscal year 2002, Hawaii received over $27.3

million in community planning and development aid from the US Department of Housing and Urban Development.

41 EDUCATION

Education has developed rapidly in Hawaii: 84.6% of all state residents 25 years of age or older had completed high school in 2000; 26.2% had completed four or more years of college.

Hawaii is the only state to have a single, unified public school system. It was founded in 1840. Total enrollment for fall 1999 stood at 185,860. Of these, 133,250 attended schools from kindergarten through grade eight, and 52,610 attended high school. In 2001 Asian/Pacific Islander students made up approximately 72.3% of the total enrollment in public elementary and secondary schools; white students accounted for 20.3%; Hispanics for 4.5%; blacks 2.4%; and the remaining 0.4% were designated as other. Total enrollment was estimated at 184,360 in fall 2000 and expected to reach 217,000 by fall 2005. Enrollment in nonpublic schools in fall 2001 was 32,193. Expenditures for public education in 2000/01 were estimated at $1,178,281.

As of fall 2000, there were 79,748 students enrolled in college or graduate school. In the same year Hawaii had 21 degree-granting institutions. In 1997, minority students comprised 72.8% of total postsecondary enrollment. The University of Hawaii maintains three campuses—Manoa (by far the largest), Hilo, and West Oahu. There are also three private colleges—Brigham Young University–Hawaii Campus, Chaminade University of Honolulu, and Hawaii Pacific College—and six community colleges.

42 ARTS

The Hawaii State Foundation on Culture and the Arts (SFCA) was founded in 1965. Ongoing programs include the Folk Arts Program (est. 1983) and the Hawaii State Art Museum, which opened in 2002 to feature artworks from the State Art Collection of the SFCA. In 2003, Hawaiian arts organizations received $1,005,300 in grants from the National Endowment for the Arts. The Hawaii Council for the Humanities was established in 1972 and has since granted over $4 million for over 500 projects in the state. In 2000, the state received six grants totaling $937,597from the National Endowment for the Humanities.

The Neal Blaisdell Center in Honolulu has a 2,100-seat theater and concert hall, an 8,400-seat arena, and display rooms. Other performance facilities in Honolulu are the John F. Kennedy Theater at the University of Hawaii, the Waikiki Shell for outdoor concerts, and the Hawaii Opera Theater, which presents three operas each season. The Honolulu Symphony Orchestra performs both on Oahu and on the neighboring islands. Other Oahu cultural institutions are the Honolulu Community Theater, Honolulu Theater for Youth, Windward Theater Guild, and Polynesian Cultural Center.

The annual Cherry Blossom Festival includes a number of Japanese cultural events presented from January through March, mostly on Oahu. The Honolulu Festival, established in 1994 as a forum to encourage cultural cooperation and understanding, presents a number of art exhibits and musical performances. Though fairly new, the Honolulu Festival has grown rapidly, with an attendance of over 300,000 in 2002. The Aloha Festivals, which began in 1946, now consist of over 300 events taking place on six islands throughout the months of August and September to celebrate the music, dance, and history of the various cultures represented in the state.

43 LIBRARIES AND MUSEUMS

The Hawaii State Public Library System (HSPLS) operates as one coordinated system, with a combined book collection of 3,194,000 and total circulation of 6,948,000 in 2000. During the same year, the University of Hawaii library system in Honolulu had approximately 3 million volumes. Total income of the HSPLS came to $22,789,000 in 2000, including $865,982 in federal grants.

Hawaii has 42 major museums and cultural attractions. Among the most popular sites are the National Memorial Cemetery of the Pacific, USS Arizona Memorial at Pearl Harbor, Polynesian Cultural Center, Sea Life Park, Bernice P. Bishop Museum (specializing in Polynesian ethnology and natural history), and Honolulu Academy of Arts. Outside Oahu, the Kilauea Visitor Center (Hawaii Volcanoes National Park) and Kokee Natural History Museum (Kauai) attract the most visitors.

44COMMUNICATIONS

Commercial inter-island wireless service began in 1901, and radiotelephone service to the mainland was established in 1931. In 2001, 96.9% of Hawaii's occupied housing units had telephones. Hawaii had 14 major AM radio stations and 21 major FM stations as of 2003, as well as 10 major television stations. A total of 27,025 Internet domain names were registered in Hawaii by the year 2000.

45PRESS

In 2002, Hawaii had six daily newspapers: the *Honolulu Advertiser* (152,098 daily, 173,336 Sundays), *Honolulu Star-Bulletin* (64,305 daily, 64,344 Sunday), *Hawaii Tribune-Herald* (19,359 daily, 23,193 Sundays), *Maui News* (20,376 daily, 25,694 Sundays), *West Hawaii Today* (11,400 daily, 15,199 Sundays), and *The Garden Island* (8,066 daily, 9,281 Sundays).

46ORGANIZATIONS

In 2003, there were over 600 regional, national, and international organizations within the state.

The leading organization headquartered in Honolulu is the East–West Center, a vehicle of scientific and cultural exchange. Other educational organizations of national and international interest include the International Tsunami Information Center, the Pacific Whale Foundation, and the Meteoritical Society.

State organizations promoting local and regional arts and culture include the Historic Hawaii Foundation, the Native Hawaiian Culture and Arts Program, and the Polynesian Cultural Center. State environmental concerns are supported through the Conservation Council for Hawaii and the Hawaii Agriculture Research Center, which focuses on the local sugarcane industry.

47TOURISM, TRAVEL, AND RECREATION

Jet air service has fueled the Hawaii travel boom in recent decades. In 2002, there were about 6.4 million visitor arrivals to the islands, with travel expenditures at about $10.3 billion dollars. A majority of visitors are from other US states. The largest international market (1.5 million visitors) is Japan. Travel and tourism employment was recorded at 134,300 in 1999.

Visitors come for scuba diving, snorkeling, swimming, fishing, and sailing; for the hula, luau, lei, and other distinctive island pleasures; for the tropical climate and magnificent scenic beauty; and for a remarkable variety of recreational facilities, including 7 national parks and historic sites, 74 state parks, 626 county parks, 17 public golf courses, and 1,600 recognized surfing sites.

48SPORTS

Hawaii has no major league professional sports teams. Since 1982, the Aloha Bowl, a major college football postseason game played on Christmas Day, has been played in Aloha Stadium in Honolulu, as is the Hula Bowl, a postseason all-star game in January for college players. The Pro Bowl (the National Football League's all-star game) is also played in Honolulu, on the weekend following the Super Bowl. Surfing is an extremely popular sport in Hawaii, as it is the home of the Banzai Pipeline, north of Oahu. Here, the yearly Duke Kahanamoku and Makaha surfing meets take place. Hawaii is also the site of an annual Professional Golfers' Association tournament and the world-famous Ironman Triathlon competition. The Transpac Yacht Race is held biennially from California to Honolulu. Kona is the site of the International Billfish Tournament, and the Hawaii Big Game Fishing Club holds statewide tournaments each year. Football, baseball, and basketball are the leading collegiate sports. The University of Hawaii Rainbow Warriors produce the most well-known collegiate teams.

49FAMOUS HAWAIIANS

Hawaii's best-known federal officeholder is Daniel K. Inouye (b.1924), a US senator since 1962 and the first person of Japanese ancestry ever elected to Congress. Inouye, who lost an arm in World War II, came to national prominence during the Senate Watergate investigation of 1973, when he was a member of the Select Committee on Presidential Campaign Activities. George R. Ariyoshi (b.1926), who was elected governor of Hawaii in 1974, was the first Japanese-American to serve as chief executive of a state. Patsy Takemoto Mink (1927–2002) was the first Asian American woman and the first Hawaiian woman elected to Congress.

Commanding figures in Hawaiian history are King Kamehameha I (1758?–1819), who unified the islands through conquest, and Kamehameha III (Kauikeaouli, 1813–54), who transformed Hawaii into a constitutional monarchy. Two missionaries who shaped Hawaiian life and politics were Hiram Bingham (b.Vermont, 1789–1869) and Gerrit Parmele Judd (b.New York, 1803–73). Sanford B. Dole (1844–1926) and Lorrin Andrews Thurston (1858–1931) were leaders of the revolutionary movement that overthrew Queen Liliuokalani (1838–1917), established a republic, and secured annexation by the United States. Dole was the republic's first president and the territory's first governor. Another prominent historical figure is Bernice Pauahi Bishop (1831–88), of the Kamehameha line, who married an American banker and left her fortune to endow the Kamehameha Schools in Honolulu; the Bishop Museum was founded by her husband in her memory. Honolulu-born Luther Halsey Gulick (1865–1918), along with his wife, Charlotte Vetter Gulick (b.Ohio, 1865–1928), founded the Camp Fire Girls.

Don Ho (b.1930) is a prominent Hawaiian-born entertainer; singer-actress Bette Midler (b.1945) was also born in Hawaii. Duke Kahanamoku (1889–1968) held the Olympic 100-meter free-style swimming record for almost 20 years.

50BIBLIOGRAPHY

Coffman, Tom. *Nation Within: the Story of America's Annexation of the Nation of Hawaii*. Kaneohe, Hawaii: Tom Coffman/EPICenter, 1998.

Eyre, David L. *By Wind, by Wave: An Introduction to Hawaii's Natural History*. Honolulu: Bess Press, 2000.

Fuchs, Lawrence H. *Hawaii Pono: A Social History*. San Diego: Harcourt Brace Jovanovich, 1984.

Haas, Michael, ed. *Multicultural Hawaii: the Fabric of a Multiethnic Society*. New York: Garland Pub., 1998.

Hawaii, State of. Department of Planning and Economic Development. *The State of Hawaii Data Book 1984—A Statistical Abstract*. Honolulu, 1985.

Kuykendall, Ralph S., and A. Grove Day. *Hawaii: A History—From Polynesian Kingdom to American State*. Rev. ed. Englewood Cliffs, N.J.: Prentice-Hall, 1961.

Moore, Susanna. *I Myself Have Seen It: The Myth of Hawaii.* Washington, D.C.: National Geographic, 2003.

Mykkänen, Juri. *Inventing Politics: A New Political Anthropology of the Hawaiian Kingdom.* Honolulu: University of Hawaii Press, 2003.

Pratt, Richard C., and Zachary A. Smith, eds. *Politics and Public Policy in Hawaii.* Albany: State University of New York Press, 1992.

Spickard, Paul, Joanne L. Rondilla, and Debbie Hippolite Wright, eds. *Pacific Diaspora: Island Peoples in the United States and Across the Pacific.* Honolulu: University of Hawaii Press, 2002.

Trask, Haunani-Kay. From *A Native Daughter: Colonialism and Sovereignty in Hawaii.* Monroe, Me.: Common Courage, 1993.

Wooden, Wayne S. *Return to Paradise: Continuity and Change in Hawaii.* Lanham, Md.: University Press of America, 1995.

IDAHO

State of Idaho

ORIGIN OF STATE NAME: Apparently coined by a lobbyist-politician, George M. Willing, who claimed the word came from an Indian term meaning "gem of the mountains." **NICKNAME:** The Gem State. **CAPITAL:** Boise. **ENTERED UNION:** 3 July 1890 (43rd). **SONG:** "Here We Have Idaho." **MOTTO:** *Esto perpetua* (Let it be perpetual). **FLAG:** On a blue field with gilt fringe, the state seal appears in the center with the words "State of Idaho" on a red band below. **OFFICIAL SEAL:** With cornucopias at their feet, a female figure (holding the scales of justice in one hand and a pike supporting a liberty cap in the other) and a miner (with pick and shovel) stand on either side of a shield depicting mountains, rivers, forests, and a farm; the shield rests on a sheaf of grain and is surmounted by the head of a stag, above whose antlers is a scroll with the state motto. The words "Great Seal of the State of Idaho" surround the whole. **BIRD:** Mountain bluebird. **HORSE:** Appaloosa. **FLOWER:** Syringa. **TREE:** Western white pine. **GEM:** Star garnet. **LEGAL HOLIDAYS:** New Year's Day, 1 January; Birthday of Martin Luther King, Jr., 3rd Monday in January; Washington's Birthday, 3rd Monday in February; Memorial Day, last Monday in May; Independence Day, 4 July; Labor Day, 1st Monday in September; Columbus Day, 2nd Monday in October; Veterans Day, 11 November; Thanksgiving Day, 4th Thursday in November; Christmas Day, 25 December. **TIME:** 5 AM MST = noon GMT; 4 AM PST = noon GMT.

¹LOCATION, SIZE, AND EXTENT

Situated in the northwestern US, Idaho is the smallest of the eight Rocky Mountain states and 13th in size among the 50 states.

The total area of Idaho is 83,564 sq mi (216,431 sq km), of which land comprises 82,412 sq mi (213,447 sq km) and inland water 1,152 sq mi (2,984 sq km). With a shape described variously as a hatchet, a snub-nosed pistol, and a pork chop, Idaho extends a maximum of 305 mi (491 km) E-W and 479 mi (771 km) N-S.

Idaho is bordered on the N by the Canadian province of British Columbia; on the NE by Montana; on the E by Wyoming; on the S by Utah and Nevada; and on the W by Oregon and Washington (with part of the line formed by the Snake River). The total boundary length of Idaho is 1,787 mi (2,876 km). The state's geographic center is in Custer County, SW of Challis.

²TOPOGRAPHY

Idaho is extremely mountainous. Its northern two-thirds consists of a mountain massif broken only by valleys carved by rivers and streams, and by two prairies: the Big Camas Prairie around Grangeville and the Palouse Country around Moscow. The Snake River Plain extends E-W across Idaho from Yellowstone National Park to the Boise area, curving around the southern end of the mountain mass. A verdant high-mountain area encroaches into the southeastern corner; the rest of Idaho's southern edge consists mostly of low, dry mountains. Among the most important ranges are the Bitterroot (forming the border with Montana), Clearwater (the largest range), Salmon River, Sawtooth, Lost River, and Lemhi mountains. More than 40 peaks rise above 10,000 ft (3,000 m), of which the highest is Mt. Borah, at 12,662 ft (3,862 m), in the Lost River Range. Idaho's lowest point is 710 ft (217 m) near Lewiston, where the Snake River leaves the Idaho border and enters Washington.

The largest lakes are Pend Oreille (180 sq mi/466 sq km), Coeur d'Alene, and Priest in the panhandle, and Bear on the Utah border. The Snake River—one of the longest in the US, extending 1,038 mi (1,671 km) across Wyoming, Idaho, and Washington—dominates the southern part of the state. The Salmon River—the

"River of No Return," a salmon-spawning stream that flows through wilderness of extraordinary beauty—separates northern from southern Idaho. The Clearwater, Kootenai, Bear, Boise, and Payette are other major rivers. There are ice caves near Shoshone and American Falls, and a large scenic cave near Montpelier. Near Arco is an expanse of lava, craters, and caves called the Craters of the Moon, another scenic attraction. At Hell's Canyon in the northernmost part of Adams County, the Snake River cuts the deepest gorge in North America, 7,913 ft (2,412 m) deep.

³CLIMATE

The four seasons are distinct in all parts of Idaho, but not simultaneous. Spring comes earlier and winter later to Boise and Lewiston, which are protected from severe weather by nearby mountains and call themselves "banana belts." Eastern Idaho has a more continental climate, with more extreme temperatures; climatic conditions there and elsewhere vary with the elevation. Mean temperatures in Boise range from 29°F (–2°C) in January to 74°F (23°C) in July. The record low, –60°F (–51°C), was set at Island Park Dam on 16 January 1943; the record high, 118°F (48°C), at Orofino on 28 July 1934. The corresponding extremes for Boise are –23°F (–31°C) and 111°F (44°C).

Humidity is low throughout the state. Precipitation in southern Idaho averages 13 in (33 cm) per year; in the north, over 30 in (76 cm). Average annual precipitation (1971–2000) at Boise was 12.2 in (31 cm), with more than 21 in (53 cm) of snow. Much greater accumulations of snow are experienced in the mountains.

⁴FLORA AND FAUNA

With 10 life zones extending from prairie to mountaintop, Idaho has some 3,000 native plants. Characteristic evergreens are Douglas fir and western white pine (the state tree); oak/mountain mahogany, juniper/piñon, ponderosa pine, and spruce/fir constitute the other main forest types. Syringa is the state flower. MacFarlanes four-o'clock, water howellia, Spalding's catchfly, and Ute ladies-tresses were the state's four threatened plant species as of August 2003.

Classified as game mammals are the elk, moose, white-tailed and mule deer, pronghorn antelope, bighorn sheep, mountain goat, black bear, mountain lion, cottontail, and pigmy rabbit. Several varieties of pheasant, partridge, quail, and grouse are the main game birds, and there are numerous trout, salmon, bass, and whitefish species in Idaho's lakes and streams. Rare animal species include the wolverine, kit fox, and pika. The grizzly bear and bald eagle are listed as threatened, while the woodland caribou, gray (timber) wolf, American peregrine falcon, and whooping crane are endangered. A total of 20 animal species were listed as threatened or endangered as of August 2003, including the woodland caribou, whooping crane, and three species of salmon. There were six national wildlife refuges covering 133,456 acres (54,009 ha) in the mid-1990s.

5ENVIRONMENTAL PROTECTION

The environmental protection movement in Idaho dates from 1897, when President Grover Cleveland established the Bitterroot Forest Preserve, encompassing much of the northern region. In the early 1930s, the US Forest Service set aside some 3 million acres (1.2 million hectares) of Idaho's roadless forestland as primitive areas. The Taylor Grazing Act of 1934 regulated grazing on public lands, providing for the first time some relief from the overgrazing that had transformed much of Idaho's grassland into sagebrush desert. Thirty years later, Idaho Senator Frank Church was floor sponsor for the bill creating the National Wilderness System, which now contains most of the primitive areas set aside earlier. Many miles of Idaho streams are now in the Wild and Scenic Rivers System, another congressional accomplishment in which Senator Church played a leading role. In 1970, Governor Cecil Andrus (later, US secretary of the interior) was elected partly on a platform of environmental protection. On 17 January 2001 the site near Jerome of a World War II camp where Japanese Americans were interned became Minidoka Internment National Monument; the National Park Service began planning for visitor facilities there in 2002.

The Department of Health and Welfare's Division of Environment is responsible for enforcing environmental standards. Air quality improved greatly between 1978 and 1997, following the passage of federal regulations strengthening the Clean Air Act. Vehicle emissions were responsible for high carbon monoxide levels in the Boise area in the late 1970s and 1980s. Emissions have dropped to the point that no carbon monoxide violations have occurred for several years.

Water quality is generally good. Most of the existing problems stem from runoff from agricultural lands. Water quality is rated as only fair in the Upper Snake River Basin and in the Southwest Basin around Boise, and as poor in the Bear River Basin, partly because of municipal effluents from Soda Springs and Preston. The state has 386,000 acres of wetlands. The Idaho Department of Fish and Game has implemented plans to acquire privately owned wetlands deemed to be in danger. The plan runs from 1991 to 2005.

Since 1953, nuclear waste has been buried at the Idaho National Engineering Laboratory west of Idaho Falls or discharged in liquid form into the underground aquifer; some isotopes are migrating toward the boundaries of the site. Tailings from a former uranium-ore milling operation near Lowman are a potential health hazard. A top-priority site for hazardous-waste cleanup is Bunker Hill Mining at Smelterville; two sites in Pocatello are also considered candidates for cleanup. In 2003, the Environmental Protection Agency's database listed 87 hazardous waste sites, 6 of which were on the National Priorities List, in Idaho. In 2001, Idaho received $32,577,000 in federal grants from the EPA; EPA expenditures for procurement contracts in Idaho that year amounted to $100,000.

6POPULATION

Idaho ranked 39th in population in the US with an estimated total of 1,341,131 in 2002, an increase of 3.6% since 2000. Between 1990 and 2000, Idaho's population grew from 1,006,749 to 1,293,953, an increase of 28.5%—the 5th-largest percentage gain among the 50 states for this period. The population is projected to reach 1,480,000 by 2005 and 1.7 million by 2025. Population density in 2000 was 15.6 persons per sq mi.

The median age was 33.2 in 2000. Nearly 28.5% of the population were under age 18 while 11.3% were age 65 or older. Although no part of Idaho except Boise is genuinely urban, even Boise does not have a large central city. Boise's estimated 2002 population was 189,847; Boise's metropolitan area (Ada County) had an estimated 1999 population of 407,844. Other major cities with large populations include Pocatello, Idaho Falls, Nampa, Lewiston, and Twin Falls.

7ETHNIC GROUPS

The 2000 census included 17,645 American Indians. There are five reservations; the most extensive is that of the Nez Perce' in northern Idaho, with a total population of 17,959 in 2000.

There is a very small population of black Americans (5,456 in 2000) and a larger number of Asians (11,889 in 2000), 2,642 of them Japanese. In 2000 there were 101,690 persons of Hispanic origin, and a very visible Basque community in the Boise area, with an organization devoted to preserving their language and culture.

The foreign born (64,080) accounted for about 5% of Idaho's population in 2000, up from 28,905 (2.8%) in 1990.

8LANGUAGES

In the general word stock, only a few place-names, such as Nampa, Pocatello, and Benewah, reflect the presence of Idaho Indians. In Idaho, English reflects a merger of Northern and North Midland features, with certain Northern pronunciations marking the panhandle. In 2000, 90.7% of the people five years old or older spoke only English in the home, down from 93% in 1990. The number of persons speaking other languages at home included the following:

The following table gives selected statistics from the 2000 census for language spoken at home by persons five years old and over. The category "Other Native North American languages" includes Apache, Cherokee, Choctaw, Dakota, Keres, Pima, and Yupik.

LANGUAGE	NUMBER	PERCENT
Population 5 years and over	1,196,793	100.0
Speak only English	1,084,914	90.7
Speak a language other than English	111,879	9.3
Speak a language other than English	111,879	9.3
Spanish or Spanish Creole	80,241	6.7
German	5,666	0.5
French (incl. Patois, Cajun)	3,345	0.3
Other Native North American languages	2,020	0.2
Serbo-Croatian	1,694	0.1
Japanese	1,651	0.1
Chinese	1,456	0.1
Portuguese or Portuguese Creole	1,374	0.1
Vietnamese	1,213	0.1
Tagalog	1,119	0.1
Russian	1,113	0.1
Italian	1,106	0.1

9RELIGIONS

Roman Catholic and Presbyterian missionaries first came to Idaho between 1820 and 1840. The Church of Jesus Christ of Latter-Day Saints (Mormon) has been the leading religion in Idaho since 1860; with about a quarter of the population, the

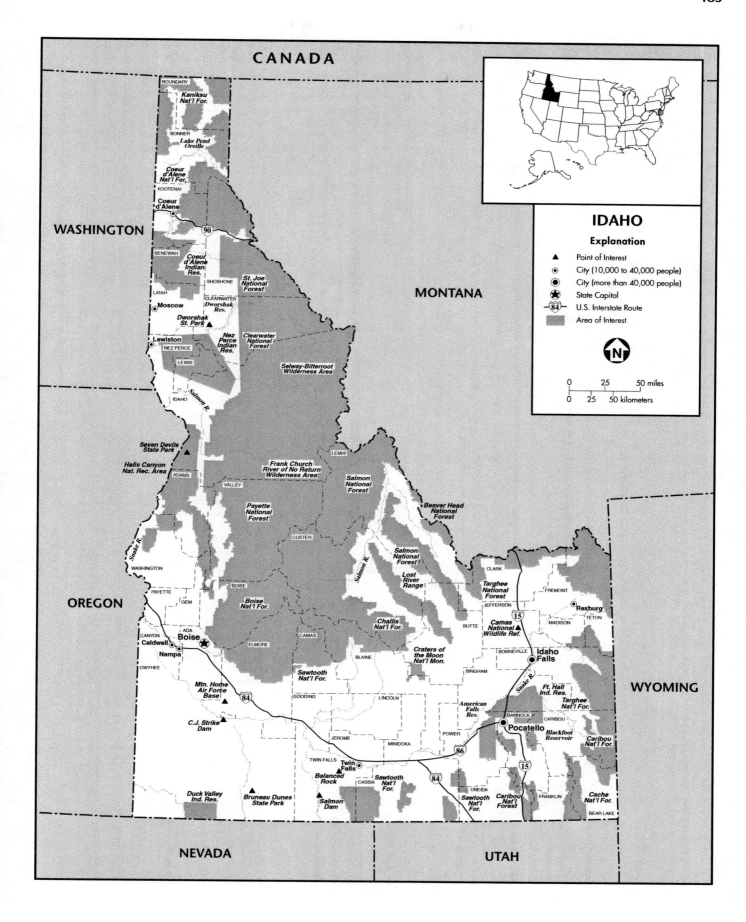

CANADA

WASHINGTON

MONTANA

OREGON

WYOMING

NEVADA

UTAH

IDAHO

Explanation

▲ Point of Interest

⊙ City (10,000 to 40,000 people)

◉ City (more than 40,000 people)

★ State Capital

—84— U.S. Interstate Route

▨ Area of Interest

0   25   50 miles

0   25   50 kilometers

BOUNDARY

Kaniksu
Nat'l For.

BONNER

Lake Pend
Oreille

Coeur
d'Alene
Nat'l For.

KOOTENAI

Coeur
d'Alene

90

BENEWAH

Coeur
d'Alene
Indian
Res.

SHOSHONE

St. Joe
National
Forest

LATAH

Moscow

CLEARWATER

Dworshak
Res.

Dworshak
St. Park

Clearwater
National
Forest

Lewiston

NEZ PERCE

Nez
Perce
Indian
Res.

Selway-Bitterroot
Wilderness Area

LEWIS

IDAHO

Salmon R.

Seven Devils
State Park

Hells Canyon
Nat. Rec. Area

ADAMS

LEMHI

Frank Church
River of No Return
Wilderness Area

Salmon
National
Forest

VALLEY

Payette
National
Forest

Beaver Head
National
Forest

CUSTER

Salmon R.

Salmon
National
Forest

Lost
River
Range

CLARK

Targhee
National
Forest

FREMONT

BOISE

JEFFERSON

Rexburg

TETON

Boise
Nat'l For.

MADISON

Challis
Nat'l. For.

BUTTE

Camas
National
Wildlife Ref.

OREGON

Snake R.

WASHINGTON

PAYETTE

GEM

ADA

Boise

CANYON

Caldwell

Nampa

OWYHEE

ELMORE

CAMAS

Craters of
the Moon
Nat'l Mon.

BLAINE

BONNEVILLE

Idaho
Falls

Snake R.

Mtn. Home
Air Force
Base

84

Sawtooth
Nat'l For.

GOODING

LINCOLN

BINGHAM

American
Falls
Res.

Ft. Hall
Ind. Res.

Targhee
Nat'l For.

WYOMING

C.J. Strike
Dam

JEROME

MINIDOKA

POWER

BANNOCK

Pocatello

CARIBOU

Blackfoot
Reservoir

Caribou
Nat'l For.

86

TWIN FALLS

Twin
Falls

Balanced
Rock

CASSIA

Sawtooth
Nat'l.
For.

15

Duck Valley
Ind. Res.

Bruneau Dunes
State Park

Salmon
Dam

Sawtooth
Nat'l
For.

ONEIDA

Caribou
Nat'l
Forest

FRANKLIN

Cache
Nat'l For.

BEAR LAKE

84

number of Mormons in Idaho is 2nd only to that in Utah. Catholicism predominates north of Boise.

According to 2000 estimates, Idaho has about 311,425 Mormons, 18,745 adherents in the Assemblies of God, and 17,683 United Methodists. There were 130,847 Roman Catholics and an estimated 1,050 Jews.

10 TRANSPORTATION

In 2000, Idaho had 46,456 mi (74,763 km) of public roads and streets, some 95% of them rural. The major east–west highways are I-90, I-84 (formerly I-80N), and US 12; US 95, Idaho 55, US 93, and I-15 are among the most traveled north–south routes. Idaho had 1,219,851 registered vehicles—including 515,266 automobiles, 658,747 trucks, and 2,409 buses—in 2000, when there were 883,546 licensed drivers. Boise, Pocatello, and Idaho Falls have mass transit systems—which are bus lines.

There were 1,758 rail mi (2,829 km) used by the nine railroads operating within the state in 2000. Among the two Class I railroads, the Union Pacific Railroad serves southern Idaho, and the Burlington Northern crosses the panhandle. Amtrak provides limited passenger service to Pocatello, Boise, Shoshone, Nampa, and Sandpoint on two Chicago–Seattle trains. The modern airport at Boise is the state's busiest. In 2002, there were a total of 195 airports, 36 heliports, 5 seaplane bases, and 1 stolport. Other transport facilities are 6,100 mi (9,800 km) of pipeline, carrying virtually all the natural gas and most of the gasoline consumed in Idaho, and a Snake River port at Lewiston that links Idaho, Montana, and the Dakotas with the Pacific via 464 mi (747 km) of navigable waterways in Washington State.

11 HISTORY

Human beings came to the land now known as Idaho about 15,000 years ago. Until 1805, only Indians and their ancestors had ever lived in the area, eking out a bare living from seeds and roots, insects, small animals, and what fishing and big-game hunting they could manage. At the time of white penetration, Shoshone and Northern Paiute lived in the south, as well as two linked tribal families, the Salishan and Shapwailutan (including the Nez Percé, who greeted the Lewis and Clark expedition when it entered Idaho in 1805; it was their food and canoes that helped these explorers reach the Columbia River and the Pacific).

Fur trappers—notably David Thompson, Andrew Henry, and Donald Mackenzie—followed within a few years. Missionaries came later; Henry Harmon Spalding founded a mission among the Nez Percé in 1836. The Oregon Trail opened in 1842, but for two decades, people merely crossed Idaho over it; virtually no one settled. In 1860, 14 years after Idaho had officially become US land through the Oregon Treaty with the United Kingdom, Mormons from Utah established Franklin, Idaho's first permanent settlement, and began farming. Gold was discovered that summer in northern Idaho; a gold rush, lasting several years, led directly to the organizing of Idaho Territory on 10 July 1863.

Boise became the capital of Idaho in 1864, and the following decade saw the inauguration of telegraph service, the linking of Franklin with the transcontinental railway, and the birth of the territory's first daily newspaper. Idaho's population nearly doubled between 1870 and 1880, and the pressure of white settlement impinging on Indian hunting and fishing grounds touched off a series of wars in the late 1870s. The most famous of those was the Nez Percé War, culminating in Chief Joseph's surrender in Montana on 5 October 1877 and in the subsequent confinement of Idaho Indians to reservations.

Lead and silver were discovered in south-central Idaho in 1880 and in the panhandle in 1884, touching off yet another stampede of would-be miners. With a population of 88,548 in 1890, Idaho was eligible to enter the Union, becoming the 43rd state on 3 July. Statehood came to Idaho at a time of turmoil, when Mormons and non-Mormons were contending for political influence, the Populist Party was challenging the established political organizations, and violent labor disputes were sweeping the mining districts. In 1907, in a case that grew out of the labor conflict, William "Big Bill" Haywood (defended by Clarence Darrow) was acquitted on charges that he conspired to assassinate former Idaho Governor Frank Steunenberg, murdered on 30 December 1905.

From 1895 onward, federal land and irrigation projects fostered rapid economic growth. The modern timber industry began in 1906 with the completion of one of the nation's largest sawmills at Potlatch. By World War I, agriculture was a leading enterprise; however, a farm depression of the 1920s lasted up to the Great Depression of the 1930s and ended only with the onset of World War II. After the war, an agro-industrial base was established, with fertilizers and potato processing leading the way. Idaho has also developed a thriving tourist industry, with large numbers of vacationers visiting the Sun Valley ski resort and the state's other scenic areas. Population expansion and the push for economic growth have collided with a new interest in the environment, creating controversies over land-use planning, mineral development, and water supply and dam construction. In April 2000 the National Wildlife Federation urged President Clinton to designate the Owyhee Canyonlands, a 1.8-million acre scenic area in southwest Idaho, a national monument. The efforts to persuade Clinton failed, and environmentalists, ranchers, and off-road vehicle riders in 2003 were coming together to agree on a conservation plan suitable to all.

Idaho celebrated its 100th year of statehood in 1990, at the same time ushering in a decade in which the major environmental issue was nuclear waste contamination. The matter was highlighted by wildfires that raged in western states during the summer of 2000. One blaze charred the grounds of the Idaho National Engineering and Environmental Lab, a nuclear research and waste storage facility. Thirty thousand acres were burned before the fire was brought under control. But environmentalists, concerned citizens, and many Idaho lawmakers remained concerned that such storage facilities are vulnerable to natural disaster and pose a serious threat.

In 2001, 2002 and 2003, wildfires broke out in the west once again. In the summer of 2002, wildfires burned over 7.1 million acres of public and private land in the US, most of it in the west. Twelve western states, including Idaho, were the victims of severe wildfires that burned 2.7 million acres as of September 2003.

12 STATE GOVERNMENT

Idaho's 1889 constitution, amended 117 times as of January 2003, continues to govern the state today. The bicameral legislature, consisting of a 35-seat senate and a 70-member house of representatives, meets annually beginning the Monday closest to 9 January. There is no constitutional limit on the length of the session. Special sessions may only be summoned by the governor and are limited to 20 days. Legislators must be US citizens, at least 18 years old, qualified voters, and residents of their district for at least a year. All legislators serve two-year terms. In 2002 the legislative salary was $15,646.

The executive branch is headed by seven elected officials: the governor and lieutenant governor (who run separately), secretary of state, attorney general, controller, treasurer, and superintendent of public instruction. All serve four-year terms. The governor is limited to a maximum of two consecutive terms. The governor, who must be a US citizen, at least 30 years old, and must have been a state resident for at least two years prior to election, can sign or veto a bill. Vetoes may be overridden by a two-thirds vote of the elected members in each house. If the governor neither signs nor vetoes a bill, it becomes law after five days when the legislature is in session and after 10 days when the legislature has adjourned. In 2002 the governor's salary was $98,500.

The state constitution may be amended with the consent of two-thirds of each house and a majority of the voters at the next general election. Provisions for initiative, referendum, and recall were added by amendment to the state constitution in 1912 but not implemented by the legislature until 1933. The initiative procedure was employed in 1974 to pass the Sunshine Act, mandating registration by lobbyists and campaign financing disclosures by candidates for public office. An Idaho voter must be at least 18 years old, a US citizen, and a resident of the county and state for at least 30 days prior to election day. Restrictions apply to convicted felons.

13POLITICAL PARTIES

Idahoans have usually voted Republican in presidential elections, but sometimes elect Democrats to Congress or the statehouse. The state has become increasingly Republican in the 21st century, however. The dominant Republican in the 20th century was US Senator William E. Borah, an isolationist-progressive who opposed US entry into the League of Nations but advocated world disarmament and supported prohibition, the graduated income tax, and some New Deal reforms; as chairman of the Senate Foreign Relations Committee from 1924 to 1940, he was one of the most influential legislators in the nation.

One measure of the conservatism of Idaho voters in the 1960s and 1970s was the showing by George Wallace's American Independent Party in 1968 (12.6% of the total vote) and his American Party in 1972 (9.3%, the highest of any state). In 2000 Republican George W. Bush received 69% of the vote, while Democrat Al Gore won 28% and Reform Party candidate Patrick Buchanan captured 2%. In 2002 there were 679,535 registered voters; there is no party registration in the state. The state had four electoral votes in the 2000 presidential election.

A Democrat, Cecil Andrus, served four terms as governor, retiring in 1994. In winning the governor's office in November 1994, Republican Phil Batt ended 24 years of Democratic control of that office. He was succeeded by another Republican, Dirk Kempthorne, following the 1998 election; Kempthorne was reelected in 2002. In mid-2003, the state legislature had 28 Republicans and seven Democrats in the senate, and 54 Republicans and 16 Democrats in the house. In 2002 elections, Idaho voters again elected two Republicans to represent them in the US House. Its US senators, Larry Craig, reelected in 2002, and Mike Crapo, elected in 1998, are also Republicans.

Idaho Presidential Vote by Major Political Parties, 1948–2000

YEAR	ELECTORAL VOTE	IDAHO WINNER	DEMOCRAT	REPUBLICAN
1948	4	*Truman (D)	107,370	101,514
1952	4	*Eisenhower (R)	395,081	180,707
1956	4	*Eisenhower (R)	105,868	166,979
1960	4	Nixon (R)	138,853	161,597
1964	4	*Johnson (D)	148,920	143,557
1968	4	*Nixon (R)	389,273	165,369
1972	4	*Nixon (R)	380,826	199,384
1976	4	Ford (R)	126,549	204,151
1980	4	*Reagan (R)	110,192	290,699
1984	4	*Reagan (R)	108,510	297,523
1988	4	*Bush (R)	147,272	253,881
1992**	4	Bush (R)	137,013	202,645
1996**	4	Dole (R)	165,443	256,595
2000	4	*Bush, G. W. (R)	138,637	336,937

* Won US presidential election.

** Independent candidate Ross Perot received 130,395 votes in 1992 and 62,518 votes in 1996.

14LOCAL GOVERNMENT

As of 2002, Idaho had 44 counties, 200 municipal governments, 116 public school districts, and 798 special districts or authorities. Most counties elect three commissioners and other officers, usually including an assessor, treasurer, coroner, and sheriff. Nearly all cities have an elected mayor and council of 4 to 6 members. School districts have elected board members.

15STATE SERVICES

To address the continuing threat of terrorism and to work with the federal Department of Homeland Security (created in 2002 following the terrorist attacks of 11 September 2001), homeland security in Idaho in 2003 operated under the authority of state statue; the adjutant general was designated as the state homeland security advisor.

Executive agencies concerned with education are the State Board of Education and the Department of Education. Under the heading of human resources are the Departments of Health and Welfare, Employment, Correction, and Law Enforcement, which includes the Idaho State Police. Under the general rubric of natural resources come the Department of Lands, Water Resources, Fish and Game, and Parks and Recreation. Self-governing agencies (7 commodity commissions and 15 professional licensing and regulating boards and commissions) and the Departments of Agriculture, Finance, Insurance, Labor and Industrial Services, and Transportation oversee economic development and regulation. Within the Executive Office of the Governor are a number of funds, divisions, boards, commissions, and other bodies The Office of Spaceport Development lobbies for a launch site in Idaho, and the Information Technology Resource Management Council supports high-tech endeavors in the state.

16JUDICIAL SYSTEM

Idaho's highest court, the supreme court, consists of five justices, each elected at large on a nonpartisan ballot, to a six-year term; the justice with the shortest remaining term automatically becomes chief justice. There is a three-member court of appeals. The district court, with 37 judges in 1999, is the main trial court in civil and criminal matters, while magistrates' courts handle traffic, misdemeanor, and minor civil cases and preliminary hearings in felony cases. Like supreme court justices, appeals court justices and district court judges are elected by nonpartisan ballot, for six years and four years, respectively. Magistrates are appointed by a commission and run for four-year terms in the first general election succeeding the 18-month period followed appointment.

Idaho's crime rates are low in almost every category. The total rate in 2001 was 3,133.4 per 100,000 inhabitants, including a total of 3,211 violent crimes and 38,181 property crimes in that year. The state permits execution by lethal injection and since 1930 has executed 4 persons, only one of whom was put to death since 1977. In 2003 there were 21 persons under sentence of death. As of June 2001, there were 5,688 inmates in state and federal prisons, an increase of 4.1% over the previous year. The state's incarceration rate stood at 431 per 100,000 inhabitants.

17ARMED FORCES

Mountain Home Air Force Base is located about 50 mi (80 km) southeast of Boise. In 2002, 4,251 active-duty military personnel and 1,472 civilian personnel were stationed in Idaho. Defense contract awards to Idaho firms in fiscal year 2001 totaled $147 million. Idaho casualties in recent US wars include 1,419 in World War II, 132 in Korea, and 187 in Vietnam. There were 136,584 veterans of US military service in Idaho as of 2000, of whom 24,358 served in World War II; 15,054 in the Korean conflict; 39,851 during the Vietnam era; and 20,340 during

1990–2000 (including the Persian Gulf War). Benefits paid to Idaho veterans totaled $240 million in fiscal year 2002.

In 2000, the Idaho State Police employed 292 full-time sworn officers.

[18]MIGRATION

Idaho's first white immigrants came from Utah, California, and Oregon in the early 1860s. By the end of the Civil War, the chief sources of immigrants were the southern and border states. Homesteaders from the Midwest, Utah, and Scandinavia arrived at the end of the 19th century.

Since 1960, immigrants have come largely from California. Idaho suffered a net loss from migration of 109,000 persons between 1940 and 1970, but had a net gain of 110,000 persons in the 1970s. During the 1980s, Idaho had a net loss of 28,000 persons from migration. Between 1990 and 1998, the state had net gains of 129,000 in domestic migration, and 15,000 in international migration. In 1998, 1,504 immigrants from foreign countries arrived in Idaho. The state's overall population increased 22% between 1990 and 1998, making it one of the fastest growing states in the US, superseded only by Nevada and Arizona for the same time period. In the period 1995–2000, 182,929 people moved into the state and 149,082 moved out, for a net gain of 33,847, most of whom came from California.

[19]INTERGOVERNMENTAL COOPERATION

Idaho participates with Utah and Wyoming in the Bear River Compact; with Oregon, Washington, and Alaska in the Pacific States Marine Fisheries Commission; with Wyoming in the Snake River Compact; with Washington, Oregon, Montana in the Northwest Power and Conservation Council; and in the Western Interstate Commission for Higher Education, Western Interstate Energy Council, Western States Water Council, and in numerous other interstate compacts. Federal grants in fiscal year 2001 amounted to $1.5 billion.

[20]ECONOMY

Fur trapping was Idaho's earliest industry. Agriculture and mining began around 1860, with agriculture dominating since the 1870s. Timber became important after 1900, tourism and manufacturing—especially food processing and forest products—after 1945. Currently, agriculture, mining, forest products, and food processing are Idaho's largest industries.

The Idaho economy prospered in the 1970s. Machinery and transportation equipment manufacturing grew 20% between 1970 and 1980, and services expanded 7.5%. The early 1980s, in contrast, brought a national recession in which Idaho lost 8% of its employment base. Recovery required a restructuring of Idaho's mining, forest products, and agricultural industries that resulted in the laying off of large numbers of employees. Other industries posted significant gains in employment in the 1980s. Chemical manufacturing employment grew 36% in the early and mid-1980s, and jobs in the paper industry increased 30%. Travel and tourism employment rose 35% between 1982 and 1991, and high-tech jobs increased 50% between 1986 and 1990. Disputes with the federal government over the management of federal lands remained central to discussion of Idaho's economic policy, as the federal government owns 60% of Idaho's public land. The disputes center on such matters as grazing fees, costs of water from government projects, species protection, and mining regulations. The electronics industry continued to grow during the 1990s, as evidenced by expansions announced by Hewlett Packard, Micron, and Zilog. Construction employment also increased. Other manufacturing sectors were also increasing, so that from 1997 to 2000, there was an overall 37% increase in Idaho's manufacturing output, and an increase in its relative share of total state output from 20.2% to 22.1%. More than half of the gain was lost, however, in the national recession in 2001,

as manufacturing output fell 19.4% in one year, reducing the net gain since 1997 to 10.3%, and manufacturing's share in the state economy to a new low of 17.8%. The recession and continued slowdown severely impacted Idaho's economy, as strong annual growth rates at the end of the 20th century—5.6% in 1998, 11.4% in 1999 and 6.3% in 2000—abruptly fell to 0.4% in 2001. The highest rate of job loss was in the construction sector, where employment fell 11% from December 2001 to December 2002. Over the same period, employment in manufacturing fell 4% and about 4,500 high-paid high-tech sector jobs were lost. Idaho's economy was also afflicted in 2002 by drought conditions that reduced grazing land and threatened the state's potato crop. Idaho farmers were also hurt by historically low milk prices that in 2002, that continued into 2003.

Idaho's gross state product in 2001 was 44th largest among the states at $36.9 billion, to which general services contributed $6.6 billion; manufacturing,$6.57 billion; trade, $6.2 billion; government, $5.2 billion, financial services, $4.5 billion, transportation and public utilities, $2.9 billion, and construction, $2.6 billion. The public sector constituted 14.1% of gross state product.

[21]INCOME

According to the Bureau of Economic Analysis, in 2001, Idaho had a per capita personal income (PCPI) of $24,506 which ranked 43rd in the United States (including the District of Columbia) and was 81% of the national average, $30,413. The 2001 PCPI reflected an increase of 2.2% from 2000 compared to the national change of 2.2%. In 2001, Idaho had a total personal income (TPI) of $32,362,804,000 which ranked 42nd in the United States and accounted for 0.4% of the national total. The 2001 TPI reflected an increase of 3.8% from 2000 compared to the national change of 3.3%.

Earnings of persons employed in Idaho increased from $22,190,551,000 in 2000 to $22,773,259,000 in 2001, an increase of 2.6%. The largest industries in 2001 were services, 24.2% of earnings; state and local government, 13.2%; and durable goods manufacturing, 11.5%. Of the industries that accounted for at least 5% of earnings in 2001, the slowest growing from 2000 to 2001 was durable goods manufacturing, which decreased 19.1%; the fastest was construction (8.3% of earnings in 2001), which increased 8.9%.

According to data released by the US Census Bureau, in 2000, the median household income was $37,462 compared to the national average of $42,148. In 2001, the median income for a family of four was $51,098 compared to the national average of $63,278. For the period 1999 to 2001, the average poverty rate was 12.7% which placed it 35 among the 50 states and the District of Columbia ranked lowest to highest.

[22]LABOR

According to Bureau of Labor Statistics (BLS) provisional estimates, in July 2003 the seasonally adjusted civilian labor force in Idaho numbered 688,900, with approximately 38,700 workers unemployed, yielding an unemployment rate of 5.6%, compared to the national average of 6.2% for the same period. Since the beginning of the BLS data series in 1978, the highest unemployment rate recorded was 11.4% in January 1983. The historical low was 4.4% in January 2001. In 2001, an estimated 6.8% of the labor force was employed in construction; 11.8% in manufacturing; 4.5% in transportation, communications, and public utilities; 20.9% in trade; 4.3% in finance, insurance, and real estate; 19.5% in services; 16.1% in government; and 6.5% in agriculture.

Idaho was a pioneer in establishing the eight-hour day and in outlawing yellow-dog contracts. In 1958, Idaho voters rejected right-to-work legislation; Governor John Evans vetoed similar legislation in 1982; in 1986, Idaho became one of 22 states with a right-to-work law when voters approved the law.

The US Department of Labor reported that in 2002, 39,000 of Idaho's 547,000 employed wage and salary workers were members of unions. This represented 7.1% of those so employed, down slightly from 7.5% in 2001. The national average is 13.2%. In all, 48,000 workers (8.9%) were represented by unions. In addition to union members, this category includes workers who report no union affiliation but whose jobs are covered by a union contract.

23AGRICULTURE

Receipts from farm marketings totaled $3.8 billion in 2001 (21st in the US); farm industry income was about $1.8 billion. As of 2002, Idaho led the US in potato production; was 2nd in sugar beets and barley; 3rd in hops, peppermint oil; and 4th in spearmint oil.

Development of the russet potato in the 1920s gave Idaho its most famous crop. In 2002, the state produced 133,385,000 hundredweight of potatoes (29% of the US total); some 90% were grown on about 110,000 acres (45,000 hectares) of irrigated land on the Snake River plain. About three-fourths of the crop is processed into frozen french fries, instant mashed potatoes, and other products. Other leading crops were hay, 5,608,000 tons, valued at $534,688,000; wheat, 87,660,000 bushels, $339,628,000; barley, 53,960,000 bushels, $164,578,000; and sugar beets, 5,040,000 tons, $187,758,000.

As of 2002, Idaho had 11.9 million acres (5.4 million hectares) in farms, roughly 22% of the state's land area; an estimated 24,000 farms, (including ranches) averaged about 490 acres (198 hectares). Almost 3.5 million acres (1.4 hectares) of land were irrigated.

24ANIMAL HUSBANDRY

In 2003, there were an estimated 2 million cattle and calves worth around $1.76 billion. In 2002, Idaho had an estimated 22,000 hogs and pigs worth around $1.6 million. Idaho had an estimated 366,000 dairy cows, which produced 7.76 billion lb (3.5 million kg)of milk in 2001. In the same year, Idaho produced an estimated 1.46 million lb (0.662 million kg) of chicken that sold for $29,000, and the state produced an estimated 251 million eggs worth $12.3 million. Also during 2001, the state produced an estimated 26.1 million lb of sheep and lambs, which grossed $14.8 million for Idaho farmers. Shorn wool production in 2001 totaled an estimated 2.1 million lb (0.95 million kg).

25FISHING

In 1998, there were some 422,873 licensed sport fishermen catching trout along with salmon, steelhead, bass, and 32 other game-fish species. Idaho is a leading producer of farm-raised trout. Idaho fish farms distributed 25.9 million trout and 3.3 million salmon in 1998.

26FORESTRY

As of 2002, Idaho forests covered 21,646,000 acres (8,860,000 hectares), or about 40% of the state's land area, with 16,824,000 acres (6,809,000 hectares) classified as commercial timberland. Of the total forest area in 2002, the federal government controlled 79%; state government, 5%; and private owners, 16%. National forest system lands in Idaho totaled 21,653,000 acres (8,763,000 hectares) in 2001. Idaho forests are used increasingly for ski areas, hunting, and other recreation, as well as for timber and pulp. Total lumber production was 1.73 billion board feet (9th in the US) in 2002, almost all softwoods.

27MINING

The estimated value of nonfuel mineral production for Idaho in 2001 was $346 million, a decrease of more than 3% from 2000.

Phosphate rock and construction sand and gravel, silver, portland cement, crushed stone, molybdenum concentrates, and lead were the leading minerals that year, when Idaho ranked 35th nationally. In 2001, Idaho was the only state to produce antimony ore; first of three garnet-producing states; 2nd in phosphate rock; 3rd in silver and lead; 4th in molybdenum and pumice;and 6th in feldspar and zinc. Of 12 gold-producing states, Idaho ranked 9th in 2001. In the same year, the state's production of sand and gravel for construction was 17.2 million metric tons valued at $55.5 million, and output of crushed stone was 4.8 million metric tons ($20.8 million).

Low commodity prices continued to depress Idaho's mining industry in 2001, especially the metals sector. Mining employment declined 16.6% from the previous year, to 2,022 persons. The famous Sunshine Mine, first mined in 1884, was closed down in February 2001. Idaho's Coeur d'Alene District is one of the world's major silver-mining regions.

28ENERGY AND POWER

Installed electrical capacity (utility and nonutility) was 3.02 million kW in 1999; total production (entirely hydroelectric) was 14.4 billion kWh. About half of Idaho's irrigation depends on electric pumping, and electrical energy consumption regularly exceeds the state's supply. Large dams used to generate electricity include the Dworshak on the north fork of the Clearwater, the Anderson Ranch on the south fork of the Boise, and the Brownlee on the Snake at the Oregon border.

Idaho's large size, widespread and relatively rural population, and lack of public transportation foster reliance on motor vehicles and imported petroleum products. Natural gas is also imported. Hot water from thermal springs is used to heat buildings in Boise. In 2000 Idaho's total per capita energy consumption was 395 million Btu (99.5 million kcal), ranking it 15th among the 50 states.

29INDUSTRY

Resource industries—food processing, chemical manufacturing, and lumber production—form the backbone of manufacturing in Idaho. Value added by manufacture increased from $1.4 billion in 1977 to $16 billion in 1995. In 1997, the value of shipments by major industries was $18 billion, reflecting the 6th-fastest growth rate in the previous five years for the nation (66.5%).

Nonelectrical machinery increased by over 500% in value added between 1977 and 1983; during this period, many northern California computer companies, including Hewlett Packard, opened or expanded plants in Idaho. Other major manufacturers of electronic equipment include Micron Technology (Boise), Advanced Input Devices (Coeur d'Alene), Gould Electronics (Pocatello), and Zilog (Nampa).

Ore-Ida Foods is a leading potato processor, and J. R. Simplot engages in food processing and fertilizer production. Boise Cascade (with headquarters at Boise), Potlatch, and Louisiana-Pacific dominate the wood-products industry. Morrison-Knudsen, a diversified engineering and construction company that also has forest-products interests, has its headquarters in Boise.

Earnings of persons employed in Idaho increased from $17.7 billion in 1997 to $18.9 billion in 1998, an increase of 7.1%. The largest industries in 1998 were services, 22.9% of earnings; durable goods manufacturing, 12.2%; and state and local government, 12.1%. Of the industries that accounted for at least 5% of earnings in 1998, the slowest growing from 1997 to 1998 was durable goods manufacturing, which increased 4.0%; the fastest was services, which increased 8.1%.

30COMMERCE

In 1997 Idaho's wholesale establishments registered nearly $11 billion in sales. Retail sales in 1997 totaled $12 billion (with the

6th-highest growth rate in the state for the previous five years, at about 50%), with automotive dealers and service stations accounting for 15% of retail establishments; food stores, 9%; and eating and drinking places, 30%. Food sales totaled $2.4 billion, while merchandise sales totaled $1.4 billion, in 1997. Boise is the headquarters of the Albertson's supermarket chain, a major retailer. About two-thirds of Idaho's wheat crop and a substantial amount of its fertilizer, peas, lentils, beans, potatoes, and barley are exported abroad. Natural gas and sulfate are imported from Canada in significant quantities. Foreign exports of goods from Idaho were valued at $1.5 billion in 1998 (43rd in the US). The Department of Commerce organized two trade missions in 1999, to China and Mexico, worth a potential total of $15 million in trade agreements.

31 CONSUMER PROTECTION

The Idaho attorney general's office is responsible for investigating consumer complaints and enforcing most consumer laws. The Department of Finance administers the Idaho Credit Code and resolves consumer credit complaints under that law. The legislature has enacted Idaho's consumer protection, telephone solicitation, and pay-per-telephone call acts for purposes of protecting both consumers and businesses against unfair or deceptive acts in trade and commerce, and to provide efficient and economical procedures to secure such protection. The Idaho Consumer Protection Unit seeks to fulfill this charge through education, mediation, and enforcement efforts. In 1990, the Idaho Consumer Protection Act was modernized, and in 1992 the Telephone Solicitation and Pay-Per-Telephone Call Acts were passed, as well as the Charitable Solicitation Act in 1993.

32 BANKING

As of 2002, 20 insured banks had $4.1 billion in assets. The 1997 Idaho Savings Bank Act permitted state-chartered savings banks in Idaho, repealing the Savings and Loan Act. The Idaho Department of Finance's Financial Institutions Bureau regulates and supervises Idaho's state-chartered commercial banks, savings banks, credit unions, trust companies, and bank holding companies. The personal bankruptcy rate increased by 5.4% during the year ending September 2002, 20% higher than the national average. Idaho's insured institutions increased their profitability during 2001/02, as the median return on average assets (ROA) ratio (the measure of earnings in relation to all resources) rose, although by a lower percentage than that of nationwide insured institutions. The fact that 45% of all Idaho-based insured banks are under nine years old adversely affected Idaho's banking performance compared with that of the nation.

33 INSURANCE

In 2001 there were 476,000 ordinary life insurance policies in force with a total value of $37.1 billion; total value for all categories of life insurance (ordinary, group, industrial, and credit) was $60.9 billion. Death benefits paid that year totaled $172.4 million. In 2003, 12 property and casualty and 6 life and health insurance companies had home offices in Idaho. In 2001, property and casualty insurers wrote premiums totaling $1.3 billion. That year, there were 5,154 flood insurance policies in force in the state, with a total value of $805,677.

34 SECURITIES

Although Idaho has no stock exchanges, there are nevertheless 193 broker/dealer firms, with over 500 employees. Investment advisor firms number 23, providing advice to Idaho residents relating to securities investments. Idaho is also the headquarters for nine NASDAQ companies, one NASDAQ market maker, and two Idaho-incorporated NYSE listed corporations: Coeur d'Alene Mines Corp., and Micron Technology, Inc.

35 PUBLIC FINANCE

Idaho's annual budget, prepared by the Division of Financial Management, is submitted by the governor to the legislature for amendment and approval. The fiscal year runs from 1 July to 30 June. The state constitution requires that the legislature pass a balanced budget, and the governor, as the chief budget officer, has regularly assured that expenditures do not exceed revenues. This became more difficult as revenues, which grew 5.2% and 4.2% in 2000 and 2001, respectively, fell in 2002 to $1.7 billion from $1.99 billion in 2001, and then remained weak, at $1.77 billion, in 2003. The beginning balance for the general fund in 2000/01 was $285 million. By 2003/04, the beginning balance had dropped to 0, and according to the projected budget for the General Fund, will only be $1 million in 2004/05 including $36 million in Idaho's Budget Stabilization Fund. Also included is additional revenue from a hike in the state sales tax rate from 5% to 6.5% effective 1 May 2003 (generating increased revenues estimated at $18.2 million in 2002/03, and $240.3 million in 2003/04) and an increase in the cigarette tax from 28¢ to 62¢ a pack for 2003/04 (generating an estimated additional $28.7 million in revenues) In 2002, cuts in planned expenditures made after the budget had been passed by the legislature totaled $64.1 million, with no budget sectors exempt from cuts. Budget cuts made after the 2002/03 budget had been passed totaled $19.5 million, including a 1.1% reduction in state Medicaid funding (which, counting just state spending, grew 11.1% in 2001/02 and 11.4% in 2002/03, and is projected to grow 3.2% in 2003/04), plus 3.5% cuts across most other state agencies, exempting only most education budgets (although Idaho State University is reported to have set aside 4.5% of its 2002/03 budget which was already 10% lower than the year before).

General fund revenues are projected to grow 4.1% in 2003/04, to $1.85 billion, still below 2000/01 levels. In 2002/03, estimated general fund expenditures were $1.95 billion. Of total expenditures, 64.7% was allocated to education, 19% to health and human services; 9.2% to corrections and public safety, 3.8% for general government operations, 2% for natural resources, and 1% for economic development.

The following table from the US Census Bureau contains information on revenues, expenditures, indebtedness, and cash/securities for 2001.

	($000)	PERCENT	PER CAPITA
Population (thousands, 2001)	1,321	(X)	(X)
Total Revenue	5,286,097	100.00	4,001.59
General revenue	4,558,746	86.24	3,450.98
Utility revenue	–	–	–
Liquor store revenue	61,344	1.16	46.44
Insurance trust revenue	666,007	12.60	504.17
Exhibit: Salaries and wages	800,901	16.17	606.28
Total expenditure	4,951,659	100.00	3,748.42
General expenditure	4,426,471	89.39	3,350.85
Education	1,768,837	35.72	1,339.01
Public welfare	922,920	18.64	698.65
Hospitals	43,079	0.87	32.61
Health	103,705	2.09	78.50
Highways	501,659	10.13	379.76
Police protection	42,569	0.86	32.22
Correction	159,142	3.21	120.47
Natural resources	148,907	3.01	112.72
Parks and recreation	31,885	0.64	24.14
Government administration	205,387	4.15	155.48
Interest on general debt	140,233	2.83	106.16
Other and unallocable	358,148	7.23	271.12
Utility expenditure	–	–	–
Liquor store expenditure	47,953	0.97	36.30
Insurance trust expenditure	477,235	9.64	361.27
Debt at end of fiscal year	2,341,978	100.00	1,772.88
Cash and security holdings	11,467,894	100.00	8,681.22

36TAXATION

In 2001, with the budget still showing a surplus of $350 million, the legislature cut income tax rates for both individuals and corporations. The revised progressive personal income tax schedule has eight bands, bands ranging from 1.6% (down from 1.9%) for taxable income up to $1,085 (up from $1,000) to 7.8% (down from 8.1%) on taxable income over $21,730 (up from $20,000). For a family of four, standard deductions total $14,900. Idaho's flat tax on corporate income was lowered from 8% to 7.6%, with a minimum tax of $20, and a $10 charge on each tax return. The legislature raised the general sales tax rate temporarily from 5% to 6.5% from 1 May 2003 to 20 June 2005. Prescription drugs are exempted from the sales tax. Groceries are not exempted, but the state extends a grocery tax credit, which was raised by $5 a person beginning in 2003/04 (at an estimated cost in lost revenue of $5.5 million). The state also levies selective sales taxes (excises) on alcoholic beverages (the state controls all sales), cigarettes (increased to 62¢ per pack in 2003/04) and tobacco products, motor fuels, insurance premiums, hotel/motel rooms and campgrounds, and electric utilities. Idaho's estate tax, which is set equal the federal estate tax credit, is scheduled to be gradually eliminated in tandem with the elimination of the federal estate tax by 2007 absent positive action by the Idaho government to prevent it. The revenue loss from the phasing out of the state estate tax is estimated at $2 million a year in 2002/03, 2003/04, and 2006/07. Idaho has no gift tax. Ores produced are subject to a severance tax, and oil and gas to production taxes. Other state taxes include various kinds of license fees. There is no state property tax. Local property taxes are the only major source of local revenue, averaging 1.7% in urban areas, and 1.2% for rural areas. In 2003, a Property Tax Reduction program (administered by the state but according to information from county assessors) offered reduced assessments for older and/or disabled people with 2002 incomes below $21,290.

Total state government tax collections in 2002 were $2.271 billion, equaling $1,693 per capita. Individual income taxes accounted for 37%; the general sales tax for 26.1%; excise taxes for 10.5%; license fees for 9.8%; corporate income taxes for 3.3%; estate taxes for 0.42%; and severance taxes 0.16%.

In 2003, total state and local taxes in Idaho as a percent of income were reported as 10.2%, the 11th highest in the US.

The following table from the US Census Bureau provides a summary of taxes collected by the state in 2002.

	($000)	PER CAPITA
Total Taxes	2,271,075	1,693.40
Property taxes	(X)	(X)
Sales and gross receipts	1,116,372	832.41
General sales and gross receipts	795,384	593.07
Selective sales taxes	320,988	239.34
Alcoholic beverage	6,212	4.63
Amusements	(X)	(X)
Insurance Premiums	65,989	49.2
Motor fuels	213,778	159.4
Pari-mutuels	(X)	(X)
Public utilities	1,795	1.34
Tobacco products	28,392	21.17
Other selective sales	4,822	3.6
Licenses	222,264	165.73
Alcoholic beverages	1,255	0.94
Amusements	343	0.26
Corporation	1,315	0.98
Hunting and fishing	29,612	22.08
Motor vehicle	111,221	82.93
Motor vehicle operators	5,547	4.14
Public utility	28,956	21.59
Occupation and business, NEC	41,355	30.84
Other	2,660	1.98
Other taxes	932,439	695.26

	($000)	PER CAPITA
Individual income	842,375	628.11
Corporation net income	76,769	57.24
Death and gift	9,645	7.19
Documentary and stock transfer	(X)	(X)
Severance	3,650	2.72
Other	(X)	(X)

37ECONOMIC POLICY

The Idaho Department of Commerce coordinates economic development initiatives in the state which are carried out by various departments and executive councils. The International Business Division of the Department of Commerce has as its mission the identification of opportunities for Idaho products in international markets, and helping Idaho companies capitalize on these. In 2003, the division was maintaining fully staffed trade offices in Guadalajara, Taipei, and Washington, DC, and representative offices in Shanghais and Seoul. The Division of Economic and Community Affairs, within the office of the governor, seeks to widen markets for Idaho products and goods and services, encourage film production in the state, attract new business and industry to Idaho, expand and enhance existing enterprises, and promote the state travel industry. A report issued in 2001 by the Governor's Science and Technology Advisory Council laid out a blueprint for Idaho to become a leader in the New Economy. Incentives for investment include conservative state fiscal policies and a pro-business regulatory climate. Idaho offers industrial revenue bonds to assist companies with the financing of land, buildings, and equipment used in manufacturing. The state extends loans to businesses seeking to start up or expand and for energy conservation improvements. To help distressed areas, there are matching grants for economic development as well as training in strategic planning and economic diversification techniques. Cities and counties may also apply for community development block grants. State support in 2003 included funds for job training issued to companies through the Department of Labor, and awards of tourist promotion funds to 35 tourist committees, chambers of commerce and other non-profits through the Idaho Travel Council (an eight-member private sector advisory board appointed by the Governor).

38HEALTH

Idaho's infant mortality rate was 7.5 per 1,000 live births in 2000, above the national rate of 6.9. There were 1,580 legal abortions in Idaho in 1999, with 3 abortions performed per 1,000 women. The overall death rate was 751.1 per 100,000 inhabitants in 2000. Death rates for accidents and adverse effects, motor vehicle accidents, and suicide were above the respective national rates in 2000. Death rates for heart disease and cerebrovascular diseases were below their corresponding national rates in the same year. However, deaths by homicide ranked lowest along with Massachusetts, 1.9 (2.0 age-adjusted). A high birth rate and low death rate are reflected in Idaho's younger-than-average population. Of the population age 18 and older, 22.4% were classified as smokers in 2000. In the same year, there were 10 HIV-related deaths in Idaho. AIDS cases numbering 517 had been reported through 2001.

In all, 40 community hospitals had 3,439 licensed beds and 122,510 admissions in 2001. Community hospital personnel included 3,371 full-time registered nurses and 624 full-time licensed practical nurses. There were 178 physicians per 100,000 population in 2000, significantly less than the national average of 288. The average expense to hospitals for care provided in 2001 was $994.70 per inpatient day.

Federal government grants to cover the Medicare and Medicaid services in 2001 totaled $530 million; 168,550 enrollees received Medicare benefits that year. At least 16% of adults were uninsured in 2002.

39SOCIAL WELFARE

In 2001, the average weekly unemployment benefit was $220.83. Average monthly participation in the food stamp program in FY2002 comprised 69,998 persons (28,006 households). The average monthly benefit was $73.83, and the sum total of benefits paid in FY2002 was $62,014,314.

With the enactment of the Personal Responsibility and Work Opportunity Reconciliation Act of 1996, the US government has changed the form and regulations for many of its social welfare programs. Most significantly, it replaces Aid to Families with Dependent Children (AFDC), an open-ended entitlement program, with Temporary Assistance for Needy Families (TANF), a limited system of assistance funded largely through federal block grants. The reform act also impacts the food stamp program, the Supplemental Security Income program, and the child nutrition program. The law took effect on 1 July 1997 and provided $16.38 billion in block grants for fiscal years 1997–2002. The grants are to be divided among the states based on an equation involving the numbers of former AFDC recipients in each state.

Reauthorization of the 1996 social welfare legislation, scheduled for 2002, was delayed, and the original law had been extended three times as of July 2003, with the most recent extension running through September 2003. Idaho's TANF program is called Temporary Assistance for Families in Idaho. In June 2000 the state had 1,382 welfare recipients. State expenditures on the TANF program in FY2002 totaled $12,973,401.

In December 2001, Social Security benefits were paid to 199,640 Idaho residents. This number included 128,350 retired workers, 19,890 widows and widowers, 21,490 disabled workers, 14,270 spouses, and 15,640 children. Social Security beneficiaries represented 15.2% of the total state population and 96.1% of the state's population age 65 and older. Retired workers (excluding persons with special benefits) received an average monthly payment of $854; widows and widowers, $834; disabled workers, $801; and spouses, $436. Payments for children of retired workers averaged $456 per month; children of deceased workers, $562; and children of disabled workers, $223.

Federal Supplemental Security Income payments in December 2001 went to 18,840 Idaho residents, averaging $351 a month.

40HOUSING

In 2002, there were an estimated 552,117 housing units within the state, 489,032 of which were occupied. About 74.6% of all units were owner-occupied, placing the state as 2nd in the nation in home ownership. About 69.5% of all units were single-family, detached homes; 13% were mobile homes. Most units relied on utility gas and electricity for heating. It was estimated that 12,600 units were without telephone service, 4,102 lacked complete plumbing facilities, and 4,900 lacked complete kitchen facilities. The average household size was 2.68 people.

In 2002, 13,488 privately owned housing units were authorized for construction. Median home value was at $115,744. The median monthly cost for mortgage owners was about $972 while renters paid a median of $529 per month. During fiscal year 2002, Idaho received nearly $18.5 million in community planning and development aid from the US Department of Housing and Urban Development.

41EDUCATION

Idaho's state and local per-pupil expenditure on education, $5,275 in 1999/2000, is one of the lowest among the states. Nevertheless, as of 2000, 84.7% of Idahoans over 25 were high school graduates, well above the national average of 80.4%, and 21.7% had obtained a bachelor's degree or higher.

The total enrollment for fall 1999 in Idaho's public schools stood at 245,331. Of these, 168,822 attended schools from kindergarten through grade eight, and 76,509 attended high school. Minority students made up approximately 14% of the total enrollment in public elementary and secondary schools in 2001. Total enrollment was estimated at 245,650 in fall 2000 and expected to reach 280,000 by fall 2005. Enrollment in nonpublic schools in fall 2001 was 10,209. Expenditures for public education in 2000/01 were estimated at $1,323,127.

As of fall 2000, there were 77,392 students enrolled in college or graduate school. In the same year Idaho had 14 degree-granting institutions. In 1997, minority students comprised 6.5% of total postsecondary enrollment. The leading public higher educational institutions are the University of Idaho at Moscow; Idaho State University (Pocatello); Boise State University; and Lewis-Clark State College in Lewiston. There are three public community colleges and five private institutions. The State Board of Education offers scholarships to graduates of accredited Idaho high schools.

42ARTS

The Idaho Commission on the Arts, founded in 1966, offers grants to support both creative and performing artists. It has also cut records of folk music, mounted a folk art exhibit, and prepared a slide-tape series on Idaho folk life and folk art. In 2003, the Idaho Commission on the Arts and other Idaho arts organizations received grants totaling $700,400 from the National Endowment for the Arts. The Commission is also a partner with the regional Western States Arts Federation. The Idaho Humanities Council was established in 1973. In 2000, the state received $492,997 in the form of eight grants from the National Endowment for the Humanities. Idaho's arts education programs are offered to about 9,000 schoolchildren. Idaho has about 55 arts associations and 26 local art groups.

The Boise Philharmonic is Idaho's leading professional orchestra; other symphony orchestras are in Coeur d'Alene, Moscow, Pocatello, and Twin Falls. Boise and Moscow have seasonal theaters. The annual summer Idaho Shakespeare Festival, in Boise, presents a series of plays in its outdoor Festival Amphitheater and Reserve.

43LIBRARIES AND MUSEUMS

Idaho's 52 public library systems had a combined book stock of nearly 3,506,000 volumes in 2000 and a total circulation of more than 8,263,000. The largest public library system was the Boise Public Library and Information Center, with about 340,800 volumes; the leading academic library, at the University of Idaho (Moscow), had 1,064,707 volumes. Total public library income was $23,811,000 in 2000.

The state also has 31 museums, notably the Boise Art Museum, Idaho State Historical Museum (Boise), and the Idaho Museum of Natural History (Pocatello). The University of Idaho Arboretum is at Moscow, and there is a zoo at Boise and an animal park in Idaho Falls. Major historical sites include Cataldo Mission near Kellogg, Spalding Mission near Lapwai, and Nez Percé National Historical Park in north-central Idaho.

44COMMUNICATIONS

As of 2001, 94.1% of Idaho's occupied housing units had telephones. Idaho's first radio station, built by a Boise high school teacher and his students, began transmitting in 1921, was licensed in 1922, and six years later was sold and given the initials KIDO—the same call letters later assigned to Idaho's first permanent television station, which began broadcasting in 1953 and subsequently became KTVB. As of 2003, the state had 44 major operating radio stations (9 AM, 65 FM), and 13 major television stations. Several large cable systems serviced the state in

2000; and a total of 21,563 Internet domain names were registered in the state in the same year.

45PRESS

Idaho, site of the first printing press in the Northwest, had 12 daily newspapers in 2002 (10 morning and 2 evening), and 8 Sunday papers. The most widely read newspaper was the *Idaho Statesman*, published in Boise, with a circulation of 65,294 daily and 87, Sundays in 2001. Caxton Printers, founded in 1902, is the state's leading publishing house. Leading magazines from the state are *Idaho*magazine and the industry trade magazines, *Spudman* and *Sugar*.

46ORGANIZATIONS

In 2003, there were over 729 regional, national, and international organizations within the state.

Among the few national organizations with headquarters in Idaho are the Food Industries Suppliers Association (Caldwell) and the Appaloosa Horse Club (Moscow). One of the largest state business associations is the Idaho Potato Commission, a department of the state dedicated to research and promotion of the potato growers' industry.

Educational organizations on the national level include the National Center for Constitutional Studies. State educational and cultural organizations include the Idaho Falls Arts Council and the Idaho Humanities Council, as well as a number of county historical societies.

47TOURISM, TRAVEL, AND RECREATION

In 1999-2000, Idaho hosted over 63 million travelers. Tourists come to Idaho primarily for outdoor recreation—river trips, skiing, camping, hunting, fishing, and hiking. There are 19 ski resorts, of which by far the most famous is Sun Valley, which opened in 1936. Boise is the most popular destination within the state.

Tourist attractions include two national parks, the Craters of the Moon National Monument and the Nez Perc National Historical Park, and the Hell's Canyon and Sawtooth national recreational areas. A sliver of Yellowstone National Park is in Idaho. Portions of the Lewis and Clark Trail and the Oregon Trail lie within the state as well.

48SPORTS

Idaho has no major league professional team, although the San Diego Padres have a farm team in Idaho Falls. Idaho also has a team in the Continental Basketball Association and the West Coast Hockey League. In college sports, the Idaho State Bengals and the University of Idaho Vandals play Division I basketball and Division I-A football in the Big Sky and Big West Conferences, respectively. Boise State University is the largest university in the Big West Conference, with a football team in Division I. Most county seats hold pari-mutuel quarter-horse racing a few days a year, and Boise's racing season (including thoroughbreds) runs three days a week for five months. World chariot racing championships have been held at Pocatello, as are the National Circuit Rodeo Finals. Polo was one of Boise's leading sports from 1910 through the 1940s. Idaho cowboys have won numerous riding, roping, and steer-wrestling championships. Skiing is very popular throughout the state, and there is a world-class resort at Sun Valley. Golf is also quite popular. Harmon Killebrew, Hall of Fame baseball player, and Picabo Street, Olympic gold medalist, were born in Idaho.

49FAMOUS IDAHOANS

Leading federal officeholders born in Idaho include Ezra Taft Benson (1899–1994), secretary of agriculture from 1953 to 1961 and president of the Church of Jesus Christ of Latter-Day Saints; and Cecil D. Andrus (b.Oregon, 1931), governor of Idaho from 1971 to 1977 and 1987 to 1995, and secretary of the interior from 1977 to 1981. Maverick Republican William E. Borah (b.Illinois, 1865–1940) served in the US Senate from 1907 until his death. Frank Church (1924–84) entered the US Senate in 1957 and became chairman of the Senate Foreign Relations Committee in 1979; he was defeated in his bid for a fifth term in 1980. Important state officeholders were the nation's first Jewish governor, Moses Alexander (b.Germany, 1853–1932), and New Deal governor C. Ben Ross (1876–1946).

Author Vardis Fisher (1895–1968) was born and spent most of his life in Idaho, which was also the birthplace of poet Ezra Pound (1885–1972). Nobel Prize–winning novelist Ernest Hemingway (b.Illinois, 1899–1961) is buried at Ketchum. Gutzon Borglum (1871–1941), the sculptor who carved the Mt. Rushmore National Memorial in South Dakota, was an Idaho native. Idaho is the only state in the US with an official seal designed by a woman, Emma Edwards Green (b.California, 1856–1942).

Baseball slugger Harmon Killebrew (b.1936) and football star Jerry Kramer (b.1936) are Idaho's leading sports personalities.

50BIBLIOGRAPHY

Arrington, Leonard J. *History of Idaho*. Moscow, Idaho: University of Idaho Press, 1994.

Blew, Mary Clearman, ed. *Written on Water: Essays on Idaho Rivers*. Moscow: University of Idaho Press, 2001.

Domitz, Gary, and Leonard Hitchcock, eds. *Idaho History: A Bibliography*. Centennial ed. Pocatello, Idaho: Idaho State University Press, 1991.

Federal Writers' Project. *Idaho: A Guide in Word and Picture*. Reprint. New York: Somerset, n.d. (orig. 1937).

Johnston, Terry C. *Lay the Mountains Low: the Flight of the Nez Perce from Idaho and the Battle of the Big Hole, August 9-10, 1877*. New York: St. Martin's Press, 2000.

Peavey, Diane Josephy. *Bitterbrush Country: Living on the Edge of the Land*. Golden, Colo.: Fulcrum, 2001.

Spence, Clark C. *For Wood River or Bust: Idaho's Silver Boom of the 1880s*. Moscow, Idaho: University of Idaho Press; Boise, Idaho: Idaho State Historical Society, 1999.

ILLINOIS

ILLINOIS

State of Illinois

ORIGIN OF STATE NAME: French derivative of *Iliniwek*, meaning "tribe of superior men," an Indian group formerly in the region. **NICKNAME:** The Prairie State. **SLOGAN:** Land of Lincoln. **CAPITAL:** Springfield. **ENTERED UNION:** 3 December 1818 (21st). **SONG:** "Illinois." **MOTTO:** State Sovereignty–National Union. **FLAG:** The inner portion of the state seal and the word "Illinois" on a white field. **OFFICIAL SEAL:** An American eagle perched on a boulder holds in its beak a banner bearing the state motto; below the eagle is a shield resting on an olive branch. Also depicted are the prairie, the sun rising over a distant eastern horizon, and, on the boulder, the dates 1818 and 1868, the years of the seal's introduction and revision, respectively. The words "Seal of the State of Illinois Aug. 26th 1818" surround the whole. **ANIMAL:** White-tailed deer. **BIRD:** Cardinal. **FISH:** Bluegill. **INSECT:** Monarch butterfly. **FLOWER:** Native violet. **TREE:** White oak. **MINERAL:** Fluorite. **LEGAL HOLIDAYS:** New Year's Day, 1 January; Birthday of Martin Luther King, Jr., 3rd Monday in January; Lincoln's Birthday, 12 February; George Washington's Birthday, 3rd Monday in February; Memorial Day, last Monday in May; Independence Day, 4 July; Labor Day, 1st Monday in September; Columbus Day, 2nd Monday in October; Election Day, 1st Tuesday after the 1st Monday in November in even-numbered years; Veterans Day, 11 November; Thanksgiving Day, 4th Thursday in November; Christmas Day, 25 December. **TIME:** 6 AM CST = noon GMT.

¹LOCATION, SIZE, AND EXTENT

Situated in the eastern north-central US, Illinois ranks 24th in size among the 50 states. Its area totals 56,345 sq mi (145,934 sq km), of which land comprises 55,645 sq mi (144,120 sq km) and inland water 700 sq mi (1,814 sq km). Illinois extends 211 mi (340 km) E-W; its maximum N-S extension is 381 mi (613 km).

Illinois is bounded on the N by Wisconsin; on the E by Lake Michigan and Indiana (with the line in the SE defined by the Wabash River); on the extreme SE and S by Kentucky (with the line passing through the Ohio River); and on the W by Missouri and Iowa (with the entire boundary formed by the Mississippi River).

The state's boundaries total 1,297 mi (2,088 km). The geographic center of Illinois is in Logan County, 28 mi (45 km) NE of Springfield.

²TOPOGRAPHY

Illinois is flat. Lying wholly within the Central Plains, the state exhibits a natural topographic monotony relieved mainly by hills in the northwest (an extension of Wisconsin's Driftless Area) and throughout the southern third of the state, on the fringes of the Ozark Plateau. The highest natural point, Charles Mound, tucked into the far northwest corner, is only 1,235 ft (377 m) above sea level—far lower than Chicago's towering skyscrapers. The low point, at the extreme southern tip along the Mississippi River, is 279 ft (85 m) above sea level. The average elevation is about 600 ft (183 m).

Although some 2,000 rivers and streams totaling 9,000 mi (14,500 km) crisscross the land, pioneers in central Illinois confronted very poor drainage. The installation of elaborate and expensive networks of ditches and tiled drains was necessary before commercial agriculture became feasible. Most of the 2,000 lakes of 6 acres (2.4 ha) or more were created by dams. The most important rivers are the Wabash and the Ohio, forming the southeastern and southern border; the Mississippi, forming the western border; and the Illinois, flowing northeast–southwest across the central region and meeting the Mississippi at Grafton,

just northwest of the junction between the Mississippi and the Missouri rivers. The artificial Lake Carlyle (41 sq mi/106 sq km) is the largest body of inland water. Illinois also has jurisdiction over 1,526 sq mi (3,952 sq km) of Lake Michigan.

³CLIMATE

Illinois has a temperate climate, with cold, snowy winters and hot, wet summers—ideal weather for corn and hogs. The seasons are sharply differentiated: mean winter temperatures are 22°F (–6°C) in the north and 37°F (3°C) in the south; mean summer temperatures are 70°F (21°C) in the north and 77°F (25°C) in the south. The record high, 117°F (47°C), was set at East St. Louis on 14 July 1954; the record low, –36°F (–37.8°C), was registered at Congerville on 5 January 1999.

The average farm sees rain one day in three, for a total of 36 in (91 cm) of precipitation a year. An annual snowfall of 37 in (94 cm) is normal for northern Illinois, decreasing to 24 in (61 cm) or less in the central and southern regions. Chicago's record 90 in (229 cm) of snow in the winter of 1978–79 created monumental transportation problems, enormous personal hardship, and even a small political upheaval when incumbent Mayor Michael Bilandic lost a primary election to Jane Byrne in February 1979 partly because of his administration's slowness in snow removal.

Chicago is nicknamed the "Windy City" because in the 1800s New York journalists labeled Chicagoans as "the windy citizenry out west" and called some Chicago leaders "loudmouth and windy"—not because of fierce winds. In fact, the average wind speed, 10.4 mph (16.7 km/hr), is lower than that of Boston, Honolulu, Cleveland, and 16 other major US cities. The flat plains of Illinois are favorable to tornado activity.

⁴FLORA AND FAUNA

Urbanization and commercial development have taken their toll on the plant and animal resources of Illinois. Northern and central Illinois once supported typical prairie flora, but nearly all the land has been given over to crops, roads, and suburban lawns. About 90% of the oak and hickory forests that once were common in the north have been cut down for fuel and lumber. In the forests that do remain, mostly in the south, typical trees are black oak, sugar maple, box elder, slippery elm, beech, shagbark hickory, white ash, sycamore, black walnut, sweet gum, cottonwood, black willow, and jack pine. Characteristic wildflowers are the Chase aster, French's shooting star, lupine, primrose violet, purple trillium, small fringed gentian, and yellow fringed orchid. The leafy prairie-clover was listed as endangered in 2003; small-whorled pogonia, lakeside daisy, prairie bush-clover, and eastern prairie fringed orchid are among seven threatened plant species that year.

Before 1800, wildlife was abundant on the prairies, but the bison, elk, bear, and wolves that once roamed freely have long since vanished. The white-tailed deer (the state animal) disappeared in 1910 but was successfully reintroduced in 1933 by the Department of Conservation. Among the state's fur-bearing mammals are opossum, raccoon, mink, red and gray foxes, and muskrat. More than 350 birds have been identified, with such game birds as ruffed grouse, wild turkey, and bobwhite quail especially prized. Other indigenous birds are the cardinal (the state bird), horned lark, blue jay, purple martin, black-capped chickadee, tufted titmouse, bluebird, cedar waxwing, great crested flycatcher, and yellow-shafted flicker. Mallard and black ducks are common, and several subspecies of Canada goose are also found. The state claims 17 types of native turtle, 46 kinds of snake, 19 varieties of salamander, and 21 types of frog and toad. Heavy industrial and sewage pollution have eliminated most native fish, except for the durable carp and catfish. Coho salmon were introduced into Lake Michigan in the 1960s, thus reviving sport fishing.

In 1973, the Department of Conservation established an endangered and threatened species protection program. In 2003, the US Fish and Wildlife Service listed 19 Illinois animal species as endangered or threatened. Included among threatened animals are the bald eagle and gray wolf. Endangered species include the piping plover, pallid sturgeon, Hine's emerald dragonfly, Higgins' eye pearly mussel, and the least tern.

5ENVIRONMENTAL PROTECTION

The history of conservation efforts in Illinois falls into three stages. From 1850 to the 1930s, city and state parks were established and the beauty of Chicago's lakefront was successfully preserved. During the next stage, in the 1930s, federal intervention through the Civilian Conservation Corps and other agencies focused on upgrading park facilities and, most important, on reversing the severe erosion of soils, particularly in the hilly southern areas. Soil conservation laws took effect in 1937, and within a year the first soil conservation district was formed. By 1970, 98 districts, covering 44% of the state's farmland, promoted conservation cropping systems, contour plowing, and drainage.

The third stage of environmentalism began in the late 1960s, when Attorney General William J. Scott assumed the leadership of an antipollution campaign; he won suits against steel mills, sanitary districts, and utility companies, and secured passage of clean air and water legislation. The Illinois Environmental Protection Act of 1970 created the Pollution Control Board to set standards and conduct enforcement proceedings, and the Environmental Protection Agency (EPA) to establish a comprehensive program for protecting environmental quality. In 1980, the Department of Nuclear Safety was established. The federal EPA has also helped upgrade water and air quality in Illinois.

The years since the enactment of specific environmental laws and regulations have seen a noticeable improvement in environmental quality. Dirty air has become less prevalent. The Illinois EPA maintains more than 200 air-monitoring stations to measure different types of pollutants. Many of these stations are in the Chicago area. The agency also conducts about 2,500 facility inspections each year to verify compliance with air regulations. Since Illinois formerly produced about 6 million tons of hazardous wastes annually, the state agency tried to pinpoint and clean up abandoned hazardous waste sites. In 1984, Illinois began a three-year, $20 million program to eliminate the 22 worst sites and to evaluate nearly 1,000 other potential hazardous waste sites. Thanks to that program, over 60 sites were cleaned up by the mid-1990s. Progress has been made toward the voluntary cleanup of contaminated sites. In 1997, the Illinois General Assembly enacted a law developing a state underground storage tank program, and by May of that year over 14,800 releases from underground storage tanks have been reported, 5,800 of which have completed remediation under the new initiative. In 2003, the Environmental Protection Agency's database listed 455 hazardous waste sites, 39 of which were on the National Priorities List, in Illinois. In 2001, Illinois received $173,495,000 in federal grants from the EPA; EPA expenditures for procurement contracts in Illinois that year amounted to $17,833,000.

6POPULATION

Illinois ranked 5th in population in the US with an estimated total of 12,600,620 in 2002, an increase of 1.5% since 2000. Between 1990 and 2000, Illinois's population grew from 11,430,602 to 12,419,293, an increase of 8.6%. The population is projected to reach 13.4 million by 2025. Illinois ceded its 3rd-place ranking to California by 1950, and 4th place to Texas during the 1960s. In 2000, population density was 223.4 per sq mi, the 10th-highest in the US.

The population of Illinois was only 12,282 in 1810. Ten years later, the new state had 55,211 residents. The most rapid period of growth came in the mid-19th century, when heavy immigration made Illinois one of the fastest-growing areas in the world. Between 1820 and 1860, the state's population doubled every 10 years. The rate of increase slowed somewhat after 1900, especially during the 1930s, although the population more than doubled between 1900 and 1960. Population growth was very slow in the 1970s, about 0.3% a year; the rate of growth from 1980 to 1990 was a tiny 0.04%. However, a rebound occurred in the 1990s. The age distribution of the state's population in 2000 closely mirrored the national pattern, with 26.1% under age 18 and 12.1% aged 65 or older.

The rapid rise of Chicago meant that a large proportion of the state's population was concentrated in cities from a relatively early date. Thus, by 1895, 50% of Illinoisans lived in urban areas, whereas the entire country reached that point only in 1920. By 1990, 83% of the population lived in metropolitan areas, compared with 75.2% nationally. With an estimated population of 8,885,919 in 1999, Greater Chicago was the 3rd-largest metropolitan area in the nation, and alone accounted for over 70% of the total state population. The state's other major metropolitan areas, with their estimated 1999 populations, were Peoria, 346,480, and Rockford, 358,640. The largest city proper in 2002 was Chicago, with an estimated 2,886,251 residents, followed by Aurora, 156,974; Rockford, 151,068; Naperville, 135,389; Joliet, 118,423; Peoria, 112,670; and Springfield, 111,834.

7ETHNIC GROUPS

The Indian population of Illinois had disappeared by 1832 as a result of warfare and emigration. By 2000, however, Indian migration from Wisconsin, Minnesota, and elsewhere had brought the Native American population to 31,006, concentrated in Chicago.

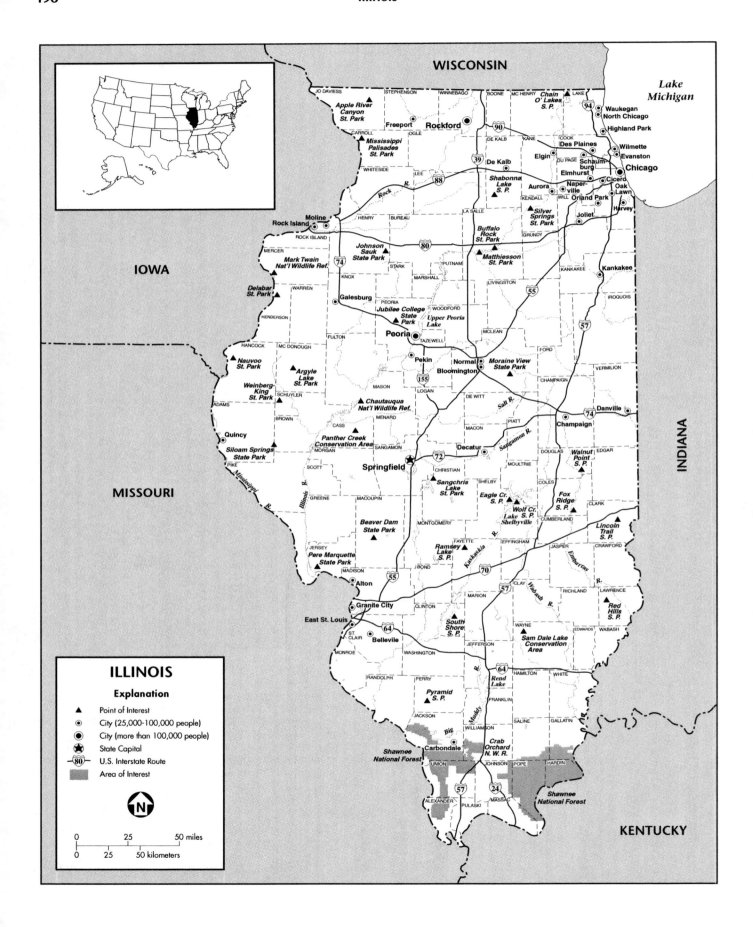

Illinois Counties, County Seats, and County Areas and Populations

COUNTY	COUNTY SEAT	LAND AREA (SQ MI)	POPULATION (2002 EST.)	COUNTY	COUNTY SEAT	LAND AREA (SQ MI)	POPULATION (2002 EST.)
Adams	Quincy	852	67,631	Livingston	Pontiac	1,046	39,596
Alexander	Cairo	236	9,469	Logan	Lincoln	619	30,692
Bond	Greenville	377	17,929	Macon	Decatur	581	112,013
Boone	Belvidere	282	44,620	Macoupin	Carlinville	865	48,636
Brown	Mt. Sterling	306	6,871	Madison	Edwardsville	728	261,409
Bureau	Princeton	869	35,239	Marion	Salem	573	41,036
Calhoun	Hardin	250	5,052	Marshall	Lacon	388	13,031
Carroll	Mt. Carroll	444	16,348	Mason	Havana	536	15,924
Cass	Virginia	374	13,665	Massac	Metropolis	241	15,021
Champaign	Urbana	998	183,159	McDonough	Macomb	590	32,653
Christian	Taylorville	710	35,215	McHenry	Woodstock	606	277,710
Clark	Marshall	506	16,942	McLean	Bloomington	1,185	154,453
Clay	Louisville	469	14,168	Menard	Petersburg	315	12,571
Clinton	Carlyle	472	35,855	Mercer	Aledo	559	16,910
Coles	Charleston	509	52,538	Monroe	Waterloo	388	29,058
Cook	Chicago	958	5,377,507	Montgomery	Hillsboro	705	30,528
Crawford	Robinson	446	20,151	Morgan	Jacksonville	568	36,173
Cumberland	Toledo	346	11,084	Moultrie	Sullivan	325	14,310
DeKalb	Sycamore	634	91,561	Ogle	Oregon	759	52,129
DeWitt	Clinton	397	16,547	Peoria	Peoria	621	182,362
Douglas	Tuscola	417	19,996	Perry	Pinckneyville	443	22,869
DuPage	Wheaton	337	924,589	Piatt	Monticello	439	16,295
Edgar	Paris	623	19,264	Pike	Pittsfield	830	17,079
Edwards	Albion	223	6,781	Pope	Golconda	374	4,284
Effingham	Effingham	478	34,275	Pulaski	Mound City	203	7,159
Fayette	Vandalia	709	21,629	Putnam	Hennepin	160	6,132
Ford	Paxton	486	14,192	Randolph	Chester	583	33,641
Franklin	Benton	414	39,134	Richland	Olney	360	15,934
Fulton	Lewistown	871	37,772	Rock Island	Rock Island	423	148,171
Gallatin	Shawneetown	325	6,191	Saline	Harrisburg	385	26,080
Greene	Carrollton	543	14,511	Sangamon	Springfield	866	190,630
Grundy	Morris	423	38,839	Schuyler	Rushville	436	7,028
Hamilton	McLeansboro	436	8,422	Scott	Winchester	251	5,477
Hancock	Carthage	796	19,726	Shelby	Shelbyville	747	22,558
Hardin	Elizabethtown	181	4,775	Stark	Toulon	288	6,226
Henderson	Oquawka	373	8,147	St. Clair	Belleville	672	257,904
Henry	Cambridge	824	50,614	Stephenson	Freeport	564	48,092
Iroquois	Watseka	1,118	30,944	Tazewell	Pekin	650	128,107
Jackson	Murphysboro	590	59,631	Union	Jonesboro	414	18,157
Jasper	Newton	496	10,011	Vermillion	Danville	900	83,142
Jefferson	Mt. Vernon	570	40,286	Wabash	Mt. Carmel	224	12,605
Jersey	Jerseyville	373	21,858	Warren	Monmouth	543	18,235
Jo Daviess	Galena	603	22,390	Washington	Nashville	563	15,159
Johnson	Vienna	346	13,130	Wayne	Fairfield	715	16,997
Kane	Geneva	524	443,041	White	Carmi	497	15,096
Kankakee	Kankakee	679	104,657	Whiteside	Morrison	682	60,354
Kendall	Yorkville	322	61,222	Will	Joliet	844	559,861
Knox	Galesburg	720	55,056	Williamson	Marion	427	61,713
Lake	Waukegan	454	674,850	Winnebago	Rockford	516	282,627
La Salle	Ottawa	1,139	111,975	Woodford	Eureka	527	36,100
Lawrence	Lawrenceville	374	15,207				
Lee	Dixon	725	36,027	TOTALS		55,651	12,600,620

French settlers brought in black slaves from the Caribbean in the mid-18th century; in 1752, one-third of the small non-Indian population was black. Slavery was slowly abolished in the early 19th century. For decades, however, few blacks entered the state, except to flee slavery in neighboring Kentucky and Missouri. Freed slaves did come to Illinois during the Civil War, concentrating in the state's southern tip and in Chicago. By 1900, 109,000 blacks lived in Illinois. Most held menial jobs in the cities or eked out a precarious existence on small farms in the far south. Large-scale black migration, mainly to Chicago, began during World War I. By 1940, Illinois had a black population of 387,000; extensive wartime and postwar migration brought the total in 2000 to 1,876,875, of whom more than half lived within the city of Chicago, which was close to 40% black. Smaller numbers of black Illinoisans lived in Peoria, Rockford, and certain Chicago suburbs.

The Hispanic population did not become significant until the 1960s. In 2000, the number Hispanics and Latinos was 1,530,262, living chiefly in Chicago. There were 1,144,390 persons of Mexican origin (up from 557,536 in 1990), 157,851 Puerto Ricans, and 18,438 Cubans; most of the remainder came from other Caribbean and Latin American countries. The Hispanic or Latino population represented 12.3% of the total state population.

In 2000 there were 76,725 Chinese in Illinois, 20,379 Japanese, 86,298 Filipinos, 51,453 Koreans, and 19,101 Vietnamese (up from 8,550 in 1990). The total Asian population was estimated at 423,603, placing Illinois 5th among the 50 states and the District of Columbia in number of Asian residents. Pacific Islanders numbered 4,610.

Members of non-British European ethnic groups are prevalent in all the state's major cities and in many farming areas. In 2000, 1,529,058 persons were foreign born (12.3% of the total population), including 389,928 Europeans, 359,812 Asians, 731,397 from Latin American countries, 26,158 Africans, and 2,553 from Oceanic countries. The most common ancestries of Illinois residents were German, Irish, Polish, English, and Italian. There were also significant numbers of Scandinavians, Irish, Lithuanians, Serbs, Eastern European Jews, Ukrainians, Slovaks, Hungarians, Czechs, Greeks, and Dutch. Except for the widely dispersed Germans, most of these ethnic groups lived in and around Chicago.

Most ethnic groups in Illinois maintain their own newspapers, clubs, festivals, and houses of worship. These reminders of their cultural heritage are now largely symbolic for the European ethnics, who have become highly assimilated into a "melting pot" society. Such was not always the case, however. In 1889, the legislature attempted to curtail foreign-language schools, causing a sharp political reaction among German Lutherans, German Catholics, and some Scandinavians. The upshot was the election of a German-born Democrat, John Peter Altgeld, as governor in 1892. During World War I, anti-German sentiment was intense in the state, despite the manifest American loyalty of the large German element, then about 25% of the state's population. The Germans responded by rapidly abandoning the use of their language and dissolving most of their newspapers and clubs. At about the same time, the US government, educators, social workers, and business firms sponsored extensive "Americanization" programs directed at the large numbers of recent arrivals from Poland, Italy, and elsewhere. The public schools especially played a major role in the assimilation process, as did the Catholic parochial schools, which sought to protect the immigrants' religious but not their ethnic identities.

8 LANGUAGES

A number of place-names—Illinois itself, Chicago, Peoria, Kankakee, and Ottawa—attest to the early presence of various Algonkian-speaking tribes, such as the Kickapoo, Sauk, and Fox, and particularly those of the Illinois Federation, the remnants of which moved west of the Mississippi River after the Black Hawk War of 1832.

Nineteenth-century western migration patterns determined the rather complex distribution of regional language features. Excepting the Chicago metropolitan area and the extreme northwestern corner of Illinois, the northern quarter of the state is dominated by Northern speech. An even greater frequency of Northern features appears in the northeastern quadrant; in this region, speakers get *sick to the stomach, catch cold* (take cold), use *dove* as the past tense of dive, pronounce *hog, fog, frog, crop,* and *college* with the vowel /ah/, and sound a clear /h/ in *whine, wheel,* and *wheat.*

Settlement from Pennsylvania and Ohio led to a mix of Northern and North Midland speech in central Illinois, with such dominating Northern features as *white bread, pail, greasy* with an /s/ sound, and *creek* rhyming with *stick.* Here appear Midland *fishworm* (earthworm), *firebug* (firefly), *wait on* (wait for), *dived* as the past tense of dive, *quarter til four* (3:45), and *sick at one's stomach* (but sick on the stomach in German communities near East St. Louis).

Migration from South Midland areas in Indiana and Kentucky affected basic speech in the southern third of Illinois, known as Egypt. Here especially occur South Midland and Southern *pullybone* (wishbone), *dog irons* (andirons), *light bread* (white bread), and, in extreme southern countries, *loaf bread, snakedoctor* (dragonfly), *redworm* (earthworm), *ground squirrel*

(chipmunk), *plum peach* (clingstone peach), *to have a crow to pick* (to have a bone to pick) with someone, and the pronunciations of *coop* with the vowel of *put* and of *greasy* with a /z/ sound. Such speech is found also in the northwestern corner around Galena, where Kentucky miners who came to work in the lead mines brought such pronunciations as bulge with the vowel of *put,* soot with the vowel of *but,* and /yelk/ for *yolk.*

Metropolitan Chicago has experienced such complex in-migration that, although it still has a basic Northern/Midland mix, elements of almost all varieties of English appear somewhere. The influx since World War II of speakers of black English, a Southern dialect, and of nonstandard Appalachian English has aggravated language problems in the schools. Foreign-language schools were common in the 1880s and 1890s, but by 1920 all instruction was in English. The policy of monolingual education came into question in the 1970s, when the state legislature mandated bilingual classes for immigrant children, especially Spanish speakers.

In Chicago, rough-and-tumble politics has created a new meaning for *clout; prairie* means a vacant lot, *porch* includes the meaning of *stoop,* and *cornbread* has been generalized to include the meanings of *corn pone* and *hush puppies.* A fuel and food stop on the Illinois tollway system is an *oasis.*

In 2000, English was spoken at home by 80.8% of all state residents five years of age and older, down from 85.8% in 1990.

The following table gives selected statistics from the 2000 census for language spoken at home by persons five years old and over. The category "Other Indo-European languages" includes Albanian, Gaelic, Lithuanian, and Rumanian. The category "Other Slavic languages" includes Czech, Slovak, and Ukrainian. The category "Other Asian languages" includes Dravidian languages, Malayalam, Telugu, Tamil, and Turkish. The category "Other Indic languages" includes Bengali, Marathi, Punjabi, and Romany.

LANGUAGE	NUMBER	PERCENT
Population 5 years and over	11,547,505	100.0
Speak only English	9,326,786	80.8
Speak a language other than English	2,220,719	19.2
Speak a language other than English	2,220,719	19.2
Spanish or Spanish Creole	1,253,676	10.9
Polish	185,749	1.6
Chinese	65,251	0.6
German	63,366	0.5
Tagalog	62,367	0.5
Italian	51,975	0.5
Korean	43,712	0.4
French (incl. Patois, Cajun)	40,812	0.4
Greek	40,581	0.4
Russian	38,053	0.3
Arabic	35,397	0.3
Other Indo-European languages	32,806	0.3
Urdu	32,420	0.3
Serbo-Croatian	29,631	0.3
Gujarathi	28,725	0.2
Other Slavic languages	27,772	0.2
Other Asian languages	26,745	0.2
Hindi	18,734	0.2
Other Indic languages	17,632	0.2
Vietnamese	16,487	0.1
Other and unspecified languages	15,885	0.1
Japanese	15,481	0.1
African languages	15,379	0.1

9 RELIGIONS

Before 1830, little religion of any sort was practiced on the Illinois frontier. Energetic Protestant missionaries set out to evangelize this un-Christian population and they largely succeeded. By 1890, 36% of the adults in Illinois were affiliated with evangelical denominations—chiefly Methodist, Disciples of

Christ, Baptist, Congregationalist, and Presbyterian—while 35%, mostly immigrants, belonged to liturgical denominations (chiefly Roman Catholic, Lutheran, and Episcopal). The remaining adults acknowledged no particular denomination.

Illinois has had episodes of religious bigotry: at Carthage in 1844 the Mormon founder Joseph Smith was killed by a mob, and strong but brief waves of anti-Catholicism developed in the 1850s (the "Know-Nothing" movement) and 1920s (the Ku Klux Klan). Robert Green Ingersoll, a self-proclaimed agnostic, was appointed attorney general of Illinois in 1867–69, but his identity as an agnostic prevented him from ever being elected into politics. Nevertheless, tolerance of religious diversity has been the norm for most of the state's history.

In 2000, the largest religious institution was the Roman Catholic Church, with 3,874,933 adherents in 1,225 congregations. The largest Protestant denomination was the United Methodist Church, with 365,182 adherents, followed by the Southern Baptist Convention with 305,838 adherents. Other major Protestant groups include the Evangelical Lutheran Church in America with 279,724 adherents and the Lutheran Church—Missouri Synod with 278,008 adherents. The Jewish population was estimated at 270,000 in 2000 and the Muslim community had about 125,203 adherents. There are over 11,000 Mennonites throughout the state. About 44.7% of the population were not counted as members of any religious organization.

10 TRANSPORTATION

The fact that Illinois is intersected by several long-distance transportation routes has been of central importance in the state's economic development for a century and a half. East access by way of the major rivers and the Great Lakes system facilitated extensive migration to Illinois even before the coming of the railroads in the 1850s. Most of the nation's rail lines converge on Illinois, and Chicago and St. Louis (especially East St. Louis) have been the two main US railroad centers since the late 19th century. Interstate highways, notably the main east-west routes, also cross the state, and Chicago's central location in the United States has made it a major transfer point for airline connections.

After several false starts in the 1830s and 1840s, the state's railroad system was begun in the 1850s. The Illinois Central aided by the first federal land grants, opened up the prairie lands in the years before the Civil War. By 1890, about 10,000 mi (16,000 km) of track crisscrossed the state, placing 90% of all Illinois farms no more than 5 mi (8 km) from a rail line. The railroads stimulated not only farming but also coal mining, and in the process created tens of thousands of jobs in track and bridge construction, maintenance, traffic operations, and the manufacture of cars, rails, and other railroad equipment.

The rise of automobile and truck traffic in the 1920s and 1930s dealt the railroads a serious blow, but their utter ruin was staved off by complex mergers that incorporated bankrupt or threatened lines into ever-larger systems. By 1974, the state had 10,607 mi (17,070 km) of track, 2nd only to Texas. Shedding their unprofitable passenger business in the 1970s (except for important commuter lines around Chicago that were taken over by public agencies), the railroads concentrated on long-distance freight traffic. The bankruptcy of the Penn Central, Rock Island, and Milwaukee Road systems during the 1970s impelled some companies, notably the Illinois Central Gulf and the Chicago & North Western, to shift their attention to real estate and manufacturing. Abandoned railroad tracks and right-of-ways were reverting to the private sector in the 1990s and being developed into public bicycle trails, walking paths, and greenways to take advantage of the scenic beauty of the state. There were 41 railroad companies operating 10,159 route mi (16,349 km) of track within the state in 2000. Chicago is the hub of Amtrak's passenger service, which operated approximately 20 train routes through Illinois in 1996. Total ridership through the state's 35 stations amounted to 2,526,721 that year.

Mass transit is of special importance to Chicago, where subways, buses, and commuter railroads are essential to daily movement. The transit systems were built privately but eventually were acquired by the city and regional transportation authorities. Ridership declines every year, as fewer people work in the central city and as more people choose the privacy and convenience of travel by automobile. Federal aid to mass transit, beginning in 1964, and state aid, initiated in 1971, have only partly stemmed the decline. Outside Chicago, transit service is available in some of the older, larger cities.

The road system of Illinois was inadequate until the 1920s, when an elaborate program to build local and trunk highways first received heavy state aid. In 2000, 138,372 mi (222,688 km) of public roadway served 9,168,095 registered vehicles—including 5,953,984 automobiles and 3,000,302 trucks—operated by 7,961,046 licensed drivers. The main east–west routes are I-90, I-88, I-80, I-74, I-72, I-70, and I-64. I-94 links Chicago with Milwaukee to the north and Indiana to the east, while I-57 and I-55 connect Chicago with the south and southwest (St. Louis), respectively.

Barge traffic along the Mississippi, Ohio, and Illinois rivers remains important, especially for the shipment of grain. The Port of Chicago no longer harbors the sailing ships that brought lumber, merchandise, and people to a fast-growing city. However, the port is still the largest on the Great Lakes, handling 23.9 million tons of cargo in 2000, mostly grain and iron ore. Midway Airport in Chicago became the world's busiest after World War II but was superseded by O'Hare Airport, which opened in the late 1950s. O'Hare lost its title as busiest airport in the world in March 2000 when it was superseded by Atlanta's Hartsfield International. With 612 airports and 253 heliports in 2002, Illinois is also an important center for general aviation.

11 HISTORY

Different tribes of paleo-Indians lived in Illinois as long ago as 8000 BC. By 2000 BC, the cultivation of plants and use of ceramics were known to village dwellers; the first pottery appeared during the Woodland phase, a millennium later. Between 500 BC and AD 500, skilled Hopewellian craftsmen practiced a limited agriculture, developed an elaborate social structure, and constructed burial mounds. Huge mounds, which still exist, were built along the major rivers by the Middle Mississippian culture, about AD 900.

It is not known why the early native civilizations died out, but by the time white explorers arrived in the 17th century, the state was inhabited by seminomadic Algonkian-speaking tribes. The Kickapoo, Sauk, and Fox lived in the north, while the shores of Lake Michigan were populated by the Potawatomi, Ottawa, and Ojibwa. The Kaskaskia, Illinois (Iliniwek), and Peoria tribes roamed across the central prairies, and the Cahokia and Tamoroa lived in the south. Constant warfare with tribes from neighboring areas, plus disease and alcohol introduced by white fur traders and settlers, combined to decimate the Native American population. Warfare with the whites led to a series of treaties, the last in 1832, that removed all of the Indians to lands across the Mississippi.

French missionaries and fur traders from Quebec explored the rivers of Illinois in the late 17th century. Father Jacques Marquette and trader Louis Jolliet were the first to reach the area now known as the state of Illinois in 1673, when they descended the Mississippi as far as the Arkansas River and then returned by way of the Illinois River. The first permanent settlement was a mission built by French priests at Cahokia, near present-day St. Louis, in 1699. It was followed by more southerly settlements at Kaskaskia in 1703 and Ft. Chartres in 1719. In 1765, pursuant to the Treaty of Paris (1763) that ended the French and Indian War, the British took control of the Illinois country, but they established no settlements of their own. Most of the French settlers were Loyalists during the American Revolution. However, they put up no resistance when Virginia troops, led by George Rogers Clark, captured the small British forts at Cahokia and Kaskaskia in 1778. Virginia governed its new territory in desultory fashion, and most of the French villagers fled to Missouri. In 1784, Virginia relinquished its claim to Illinois, which three years later became part of the newly organized Northwest Territory. In 1800, Illinois was included in the Indiana Territory. Nine years later the Illinois Territory, including the present state of Wisconsin, was created; Kaskaskia became the territorial capital, and Ninian Edwards was appointed territorial governor by President James Madison. A territorial legislature was formed in 1812. During the War of 1812, British and Indian forces combined in a last attempt to push back American expansion into the Illinois country, and much fighting took place in the area. On 3 December 1818, Illinois was formally admitted to the Union as the 21st state. The capital was moved to Vandalia in 1820 and to Springfield in 1839.

Apart from a few thousand nomadic Indians and the remaining French settlers and their slaves, Illinois was largely uninhabited before 1815; two years after statehood, the population barely exceeded 55,000. The withdrawal of British influence after the War of 1812 and the final defeat of the Indian tribes in the Black Hawk War of 1832 opened the fertile prairies to settlers from the south, especially Kentucky. The federal government owned most of the land, and its land offices did a fast business on easy terms. Before the 1830s, most of the pioneers were concerned with acquiring land titles and pursuing subsistence agriculture, supplemented by hunting and fishing. An effort in 1824 to call a constitutional convention to legalize slavery failed because of a widespread fear that rich slaveholders would seize the best land, squeezing out the poor yeoman farmers. Ambitious efforts in the 1830s to promote rapid economic development led to fiscal disaster. Three state banks failed; a lavish program of building roads, canals, and railroads totally collapsed, leaving a heavy state debt that was not paid off until 1880. Despite these setbacks, the steady influx of land-hungry poor people and the arrival after 1840 of energetic Yankee entrepreneurs, all attracted by the rich soil and excellent water routes, guaranteed rapid growth.

Although Illinois gradually eliminated French slavery and even served as a conduit to Canada for slaves escaping from the South, the state was deeply divided over the slavery issue and remained unfriendly territory for blacks and their defenders. The abolitionist leader Elijah P. Lovejoy was killed in Alton in 1837, and as late as 1853 the state passed legislation providing that free blacks entering Illinois could be sold into slavery. In 1856, however, the new Republican Party nominated and Illinois voters elected a governor, William H. Bissell, on a reform program that included support for school construction, commercial and industrial expansion, and abolition of slavery. During the Civil War, Illinois sent half its young men to the battlefield and supplied the Union armies with huge amounts of food, feed, and horses. The strong-handed wartime administration of Republican Governor Richard Yates guaranteed full support for the policies of Abraham Lincoln, who had been prominent in Illinois political life since the 1840s and had been nominated for the presidency in 1860 at a Republican convention held in Chicago. Democratic dissenters were suppressed, sometimes by force, leaving a legacy of bitter feuds that troubled the "Egypt" section (the southern third of the state) for decades thereafter.

Economic and population growth quickened after 1865, as exemplified by the phenomenal rise of Chicago to become the principal city of the Midwest. Responding to opportunities presented by the coming of the railroads, boosters in hundreds of small towns and cities built banks, grain elevators, retail shops, small factories, ornate courthouses, and plain schools, in an abundance of civic pride. The Democrats sought the support of the working class and small farmers, assuming an attitude of hostility toward banks, high railroad freight rates, protective tariffs, and antiunion employers, but they failed to impose any significant restraints on business expansion. They were more successful, however, in opposing prohibition and other "paternalistic" methods of social control demanded by reformers such as Frances Willard, a leader in the Women's Christian Temperance Union, and the Prohibition Party. In Chicago and other cities the Democrats were less concerned with social reform than with building lucrative political machines on the backs of the poor Irish, Polish, and Czech Catholic immigrants, who kept arriving in large numbers. Statewide, Illinois retained a highly competitive two-party system, even as the excitement and high voter turnouts characteristic of 19th-century elections faded rapidly in the early 20th century.

During the second half of the 19th century, Illinois was a center of the American labor movement. Workers joined the Knights of Labor in the 1870s and 1880s and fought for child-labor laws and the eight-hour day. Union organizing led to several spectacular incidents, including the Haymarket riot in 1886 and the violent Pullman strike in 1894, suppressed by federal troops at the behest of President Grover Cleveland. A coalition of Germans, labor, and small farmers elected John Peter Altgeld to the governorship in 1892. After 1900, Illinois became a center of the Progressive movement, led by Jane Addams and Republican Governor Frank Lowden. Lowden reorganized the state government in 1917 by placing experts in powerful positions in state and municipal administrations.

After the great fire of 1871 destroyed Chicago's downtown section (but not its main residential or industrial areas), the city's wealthy elite dedicated itself to rebuilding Chicago and making it one of the great metropolises of the world. Immense steel mills, meat-packing plants, and factories sprang up, and growth was spectacular in the merchandising, banking, and transportation fields. Their fortunes made, Chicago's business leaders began building cultural institutions in the 1890s that were designed to rival the best in the world: the Chicago Symphony, the Art Institute, and the Field Museum of Natural History. The World's Columbian Exposition of 1893 was a significant international exhibition of the nation's technological achievements, and it focused worldwide attention on what was by then the 2nd-largest American city. A literary renaissance, stimulated by the new realism that characterized Chicago's newspapers, flourished for a decade or two before World War I, but the city was recognized chiefly for its contributions in science, architecture, and (in the 1920s) jazz.

The first three decades of the 20th century witnessed almost unbroken prosperity in all sections except Egypt, the downstate region where poor soil and the decline of the coal industry produced widespread poverty. The slums of Chicago were poor, too, because most of the hundreds of thousands of new immigrants arrived virtually penniless. After 1920, however, large-scale immigration ended, and the immigrants' steady upward mobility, based on savings and education, became apparent. During the prohibition era, a vast organized crime empire rose to prominence, giving Chicago and Joliet a reputation for gangsterism, violence, and corruption; the most notorious gangster was Al Capone. Money, whether legally or illegally acquired, mesmerized Illinois in the 1920s as never before—and never since.

The Great Depression of the 1930s affected the state unevenly, with agriculture hit first and recovering first. Industries began shutting down in 1930 and did not fully recover until massive military contracts during World War II restored full prosperity. The very fact of massive depression brought discredit to the pro-business Republican regime that had run the state with few exceptions since 1856. Blacks, white ethnics, factory workers, and the undereducated, all of whom suffered heavily during the early years of the Depression, responded enthusiastically to Franklin Roosevelt's New Deal. They elected Henry Horner, a Democrat, to the governorship in 1932, reelected him in 1936, and flocked to the new industrial unions of the Congress of Industrial Organizations, founded in 1938.

World War II and its aftermath brought prosperity, as well as new anxiety about national security in a nuclear age. The chilling events of the 1960s and 1970s—assassinations, the Vietnam war, the race riots, and the violence that accompanied the 1968 Democratic National Convention in Chicago—helped reshape many people's attitudes in Illinois. The problems attendant on heavy industrialization, particularly air and water pollution and urban decay, began to be addressed for the first time. This transformation was perhaps best exemplified in Chicago, where voters elected Jane Byrne the city's first woman mayor in 1979 and chose Harold Washington as its first black mayor in 1983.

The economy of Illinois, like those of other Rust Belt states, suffered a severe recession in the early 1980s. By the end of the decade, the economy had begun to rebound, but many industrial jobs were permanently lost, as industries sought to improve efficiency and productivity through automation. In 1990, the unemployment rate in Illinois was 7.2%, in contrast to the national average of 5.2%. Into the 1990s, industrial losses slowed while the service industries and the newer high-tech industries, which had gained a foothold in the greater Chicago area, became more dominant. By 1998, as the US experienced the longest sustained economic boom in its history, many in Illinois felt the prosperity. The state ranked 8th highest in the nation for per capita income and by 1999 Illinois' unemployment rate was 4.3%, in line with the national average. The poverty rate also fell during the decade, from 11.9% in 1989 to 10.1% a decade later.

Chicago's infrastructure has suffered several problems in recent years. In 1992 there was a rupture in the 60-mi (96-km) maze of tunnels that lies beneath downtown. Water from the Chicago River flooded basements and sub-basements in the city's central Loop district with as much as 30 feet of water, forcing the temporary closure of many downtown buildings and businesses, including the Chicago Board of Trade, City Hall, and Marshall Fields department store. In mid-August 1999 the downtown area was without power when a substation failed. About 2,300 Commonwealth Edison customers in the Loop, including skyscrapers, numerous businesses, and university buildings, were without electricity. Again buildings were forced to close, sending thousands of workers home early. Later that month ComEd suffered another high-profile outage when power was lost at the city's popular Field Museum, forcing its closure. In 2000 barge and other commercial boat operators on the Chicago River complained that the increase in recreational boater traffic on the waterway posed a serious danger to safety.

In June 2000 a panel of experts convening for a legislative history roundtable in Springfield concluded that the state's 1980 cutback amendment, which reduced the size of the Illinois General Assembly by one-third, had been a detriment to state government for two decades. The 1980 amendment ended Illinois' system of three-member house districts; experts argued that the old system had encouraged Republicans and Democrats to work together and that the new, one-member house district system resulted in "a higher degree of partisanship and bitterness."

Meanwhile, the state was embroiled in a bribe-for-licenses scandal involving Governor George Ryan. It was alleged that truck-driver licenses were issued in exchange for campaign contributions (from trucking companies) when Ryan was secretary of state. Indictments had been handed down to some state officials, but the governor insisted he knew nothing about the contributions and said if the accusations proved to be true, the money would be contributed to charities. Ryan left after one term in office due to the scandal, to be succeeded by Rod Blagojevich.

In 2003, the state had a $5 billion budget deficit, and was experiencing the worst recession in two decades. In 2002, Illinois lost 23,000 manufacturing jobs. In his State of the State Address, Governor Blagojevich targeted four areas in need of attention: jobs, schools, health care, and crime. In June 2003, the Illinois legislature passed a $10 billion budget allowing for increased school spending. The budget also called for increasing casino taxes and eliminating tax exemptions for trucking, chemical, insurance, and other industries.

12 STATE GOVERNMENT

Illinois has had four constitutions. The first, written in 1818, was a short document modeled on those of New York, Kentucky, and Ohio. An attempt to rewrite the charter to allow slavery failed in a bitterly contested referendum in 1824. A new constitution in 1848 democratized government by providing for the popular election of judges. A third constitution, enacted in 1870, lasted a century; its unique feature was a voting system for the lower house of the state legislature that virtually guaranteed minority party representation in each electoral district. Important amendments in 1884 and 1904, respectively, gave the governor an item veto over appropriation bills and provided a measure of home rule for Chicago. In 1970, a fourth constitution streamlined state offices somewhat, improved accounting procedures, reformed the state tax system, and gave the state, rather than local governments, the major responsibility for financing education. The state bill of rights was expanded to include provisions banning discrimination in housing and employment and recognizing women's rights. An elected judiciary and the state's unique representational system were retained.

Under the 1970 constitution, as amended 11 times as of January 2003, the upper house of the general assembly consists of a senate of 59 members, who are elected on a two-year cycle to four-year terms. Until 1980, the lower house, the house of representatives, consisted of 177 members, with three representatives elected for two-year terms from each district. Each voter was empowered to cast three ballots for representatives, giving one vote to each of three candidates, one and a half votes to each of two, or all three to one candidate; each party never nominated more than two candidates in any single district. In November 1980, however, Illinois voters chose to reduce the size of house membership to 118 (2 representatives from each district) and to eliminate the proportional system. Annual legislative sessions, which are not limited in length, begin in January. A joint call by the presiding officers in both houses may secure a special session, also of unlimited duration. Legislators must be US citizens, at least 21 years old, and residents of their district for at least two years prior to election. The legislative salary was $55,788 in 2002.

The executive officers elected statewide are the governor and lieutenant governor (who are run jointly), secretary of state, treasurer, comptroller, and attorney general. Each serves a four-year term and is eligible for reelection. An important revision of appointive offices in 1917 made most agency heads responsible to the governor. In the 1970s, the governor's office expanded its control over the budget and the higher education complex, further augmenting an already strong executive position. The governor must be a US citizen, at least 25 years old, and must have been a state resident for three years prior to election. In 2002 the governor's salary was $150,691.

Bills passed by both houses of the legislature become law if signed by the governor, if left unsigned for 60 days (whether or not the legislature is in session), or if vetoed by the governor but passed again by three-fifths of the elected members of each house. Constitutional amendments require a three-fifths vote by the legislature for placement on the ballot. Amendments may also be initiated by petition of 8% of the total votes cast in the prior gubernatorial election. Either a simple majority of those voting in the election or three-fifths of those voting on the amendment is sufficient for ratification.

Qualified voters must be US citizens at least 18 years old and not able to claim the right to vote elsewhere. There is a 30-day precinct residency requirement. Jailed felons may not vote.

13 POLITICAL PARTIES

The Republican and Democratic parties have been the only major political groups in Illinois since the 1850s. Illinois is a closely balanced state, with a slight Republican predominance from 1860 to 1930 giving way in seesaw fashion to a highly competitive situation statewide. In Chicago and Cook County, an equally balanced division before 1930 gave way to heavy Democratic predominance forged during the New Deal.

The Democrats, organized by patronage-hungry followers of President Andrew Jackson in the 1830s, dominated state politics to the mid-1850s. They appealed to subsistence farmers, former Southerners, and poor Catholic immigrants. Though they advocated minimal government intervention, Democratic officials were eager for the patronage and inside deals available in a fast-growing state. Their outstanding leader, Stephen Douglas, became a major national figure in the 1850s, but never lost touch with his base of support. After Douglas died in 1861, many Illinois Democrats began to oppose the conduct of the Civil War and became stigmatized as "Copperheads." The success of the Republican war policies left the Democrats in confusion in the late 1860s and early 1870s. Negative attitudes toward blacks, banks, railroads, and prohibition kept a large minority of Illinoisans in the Democratic fold, while the influx of Catholic immigrants replenished the party's voter base. However, the administration of Governor Altgeld (1893–97), coinciding with a deep depression and labor unrest, split the party, and only one other Democrat held the governorship between 1852 and 1932.

The intraparty balance between Chicago and downstate changed with the rise of the powerful Cook County Democratic organization in the 1930s. Built by Mayor Anton Cermak and continued from 1955 to 1976 by six-term Mayor Richard J. Daley, the Chicago Democratic machine totally controlled the city, dominated the state party, and exerted enormous power at the national level. However, the machine lost its clout with the election in 1979 of independent Democrat Jane Byrne as Chicago's first woman mayor, and again in 1983 when Harold Washington became its first black mayor. Although Richard Daley's son, also named Richard Daley, won the mayoralty in 1989, the machine has never recovered the power it once enjoyed. Richard Daley was elected to his fifth consecutive term as mayor in 2003.

The Republican Party, born amid the political chaos of the 1850s, brought together most former Whigs and some Democrats who favored industrialization and opposed slavery. Abraham Lincoln, aided by many talented lieutenants, forged a coalition of commercial farmers, businessmen, evangelical Protestants, skilled craftsmen, professionals, and later, patronage holders and army veterans. Ridiculing the Democrats' alleged parochialism, the GOP called for vigorous prosecution of the Civil War and Reconstruction and for an active policy of promoting economic growth by encouraging railroads and raising tariffs. However, such moralistic crusades as the fight for prohibition frequently alienated large voting blocs (especially the Germans) from the Republicans.

In the early 20th century, Republican politicians built their own ward machines in Chicago and succumbed to corruption. William "Big Bill" Thompson, Chicago's Republican mayor in the 1910s and 1920s, openly allied himself with the gangster Al Capone. Moralistic Republicans, who were strongest in the smaller towns, struggled to regain control of their party. They succeeded in the 1930s, when the Republican political machines in Chicago collapsed or switched their allegiance to the Democrats.

Since then, the Republicans have become uniformly a party of the middle and upper-middle classes, hostile to machine politics, welfare, and high taxes, but favorable to business, education, and environmental protection. Although the GOP has a stronger formal organization in Illinois than in most other states, its

Illinois Presidential Vote by Political Parties, 1948–2000

YEAR	ELECTORAL VOTE	ILLINOIS WINNER	DEMOCRAT	REPUBLICAN	SOCIALIST LABOR	PROHIBITION	COMMUNIST	SOCIALIST
1948	28	*Truman (D)	1,994,715	1,961,103	3,118	11,959	—	11,522
1952	27	*Eisenhower (R)	2,013,920	2,457,327	9,363	—	—	—
1956	27	*Eisenhower (R)	1,775,682	2,623,327	8,342	—	—	—
1960	27	*Kennedy (D)	2,377,846	2,368,988	10,560	—	—	—
1964	26	*Johnson (D)	2,796,833	1,905,946	—	—	—	—
						AMERICAN IND.		
1968	26	*Nixon (R)	2,039,814	2,174,774	13,878	390,958	—	—
						AMERICAN		
1972	26	*Nixon (R)	1,913,472	2,788,179	12,344	2,471	4,541	—
						LIBERTARIAN		SOC. WORKERS
1976	26	Ford (R)	2,271,295	2,364,269	2,422	8,057	9,250	3,615
					CITIZENS			
1980	26	*Reagan (R)	1,981,413	2,358,094	10,692	38,939	9,711	1,302
1984	24	*Reagan (R)	2,086,499	2,707,103	2,716	10,086	—	—
1988	24	*Bush (R)	2,215,940	2,310,939	10,276	14,944	—	—
					NEW ALLIANCE		IND. (Perot)	POPULIST
1992	22	*Clinton (D)	2,453,350	1,734,096	5,267	9,218	840,515	3,577
1996	22	*Clinton (D)	2,341,744	1,587,021	-	22,548	346,408	—
					GREEN		(Buchanan)	
2000	22	Gore (D)	2,589,026	2,019,421	103,759	11,623	16,106	—

* Won US presidential election.

leading candidates have exuded an aura of independence. Republican James R. Thompson, elected to the governorship in 1976 and reelected in 1978 and 1982, served in that office longer than any other. Thompson was followed by Republican Jim Edgar in 1990. In November 1998 Illinois voters elected Republican George H. Ryan for governor, but his administration was dogged by controversy surrounding licensing of truck drivers when Ryan served as secretary of state, and he served only one term. Democrat Rod R. Blagojevich was elected governor in 2002.

The Whigs usually ran a close second to the Democrats from 1832 to 1852. Taken over in the 1840s by a group of professional organizers under Lincoln's leadership, the Whigs simply vanished after their crushing defeat in 1852. Notable among the smaller parties was the Native American ("Know-Nothing") Party, which controlled Chicago briefly in the 1850s. The Prohibitionists, Greenbackers, Union Labor, and Populist parties were weak forces in late-19th-century Illinois. The Socialist Party, strongest among coal miners and central European immigrants, grew to a minor force in the early 20th century and elected the mayor of Rockford for many years.

Illinois provided two important leaders of the national GOP in the 1860s—Abraham Lincoln and Ulysses S. Grant. The only major-party presidential nominee from the state between 1872 and 1976, however, was Governor Adlai Stevenson, the unsuccessful Democratic candidate in 1952 and 1956. In 1980, three native-born Illinoisans pursued the Republican Party nomination. The first, US Representative Philip Crane, was the earliest to declare his candidacy but failed in the primaries. The second, US Representative John Anderson, dropped out of the GOP primaries to pursue an independent candidacy, ultimately winning more than 6% of the popular vote nationally and in Illinois, but no electoral votes. The third, Ronald Reagan, a native of Tampico, won both the Republican nomination and the November election, becoming the 40th president of the US; he was elected by a heavy majority of Illinois voters in 1980 and reelected in 1984.

In the 2000 presidential election, Democrat Al Gore won 55% of the vote, Republican George W. Bush received 43%, and Green Party candidate Ralph Nader garnered 2%. In 2002 there were 7,043,557 registered voters; there is no party registration. The state had 22 electoral votes in the 2000 presidential election.

In 1996 Democratic Senator Richard J. Durbin won the race to succeed retiring US Senator Paul Simon; Durbin was reelected in 2002. Republican Peter G. Fitzgerald was elected to the US Senate in 1998. In the 1994 elections, the once powerful chairman of the US House Ways and Means Committee, Dan Rostenkowski, was defeated by a relative unknown, Michael P. Flanagan. Rostenkowski, an 18-term Chicago Democrat, had been indicted on corruption charges, a fact that did not go unnoticed by an electorate already in an anti-incumbent mood. In the 2002 elections, Illinois voters sent ten Republicans and nine Democrats to the US House of Representatives. In mid-2003 there were 32 Republicans, 26 Democrats, and one independent in the state senate, and 66 Democrats and 52 Republicans in the state house. Illinois elected its first black female senator, Carol Moseley Braun, in 1992. In 2003, Braun was a candidate for the presidency.

14LOCAL GOVERNMENT
Illinois has more units of local government (most with property-taxing power) than any other state. In 2002 there were 102 counties, 1,291 municipalities, 1,431 townships, 934 public school districts, and 3,145 special districts.

County government in Illinois dates from 1778, when Virginia, claiming authority over the territory, established the earliest counties. Today the major county offices are elective: county board chairman, county clerk (chief administrative officer), clerk of the circuit court, sheriff, state's attorney, treasurer, coroner, and superintendent of schools. Cook County, which encompasses all of Chicago and many of its suburbs, controls hospital and welfare programs in Chicago, thus spreading the cost over both the city's own tax base and that of the more affluent suburbs. The New England township system was made optional by the state's 1848 constitution, and eventually 85 counties, including Cook County, adopted the idea. Townships, which elect administrators and local judges, also handle tax collection.

Chicago is governed by an elected mayor, clerk, treasurer, and city council composed of 50 aldermen. The mayor's power has been closely tied with the city's Democratic Party organization. Independent candidates get elected to the city council from time to time, but the Democratic machine generally staffs the city with its members.

Larger municipalities are administered by an elected mayor and council members; most smaller communities are administered by nonpartisan city managers though some have elected mayors.

15STATE SERVICES
To address the continuing threat of terrorism and to work with the federal Department of Homeland Security (created in 2002 following the terrorist attacks of 11 September 2001), homeland security in Illinois in 2003 operated under the authority of the governor; a new position, homeland security director, was created to coordinate homeland security activities in the state.

Officials responsible to the governor of Illinois and the members of Congress, as well as to the mayor of Chicago, actively provide ombudsman service, although there is no state office by that name. Illinois has a board of ethics, but the US attorney's office in Chicago has far more potent weapons at its disposal: many top political leaders were indicted and convicted in the 1970s, including federal judge and former Governor Otto Kerner and, in 1980, Attorney General William Scott. The Office of the Inspector General is assigned with the task of preventing, detecting, and eliminating fraud, waste, abuse, misconduct, and mismanagement in the programs administered by the Illinois Department of Public Aid.

Educational services provided by the Illinois Office of Education include teacher certification and placement, curriculum development, educational assessment and evaluation, and programs for the disadvantaged, gifted, handicapped, and ethnic and racial minorities. The Board of Higher Education and the Illinois Community College Board oversee postsecondary education. The Department of Transportation handles highways, traffic safety, and airports.

Among state agencies offering health and welfare services are the Department of Children and Family Services, which focuses on foster care, the deaf, the blind, and the handicapped; and the Department of Public Aid, which supervises Medicaid, food stamps, and general welfare programs. The Illinois Planning Council on Developmental Disabilities operates homes and outpatient centers for the retarded and the mentally ill. Established in 1973, the Department on Aging provides nutritional and field services. The Board of Vocational Rehabilitation operates programs to retrain the disabled, while the Department of Veterans' Affairs administers bonus and scholarship programs and maintains four veterans' homes with nursing facilities, including one with an Alzheimer's Unit, and at least three with 300 or more beds.

State responsibility for public protection is divided among several agencies: the Office of the Attorney General, Department of Corrections (prisons and parole), Department of Law Enforcement (including the State Police and Bureau of Investigation), Dangerous Drugs Commission, and Military and

Naval Department. Resource protection is supervised by the Department of Natural Resources, which oversees fish hatcheries, state parks, nature reserves, game preserves, and forest fire protection. The Department of Mines and Minerals handles mine safety and land reclamation programs. The Department of Labor mediates disputes and handles unemployment compensation. The Department of Human Rights, founded in 1980, seeks to ensure equal employment, housing, and credit opportunities.

[16] JUDICIAL SYSTEM

The state's highest court is the supreme court, consisting of seven justices elected by judicial districts for 10-year terms; the justices elect one of their number as chief justice for three years. The supreme court has appellate jurisdiction generally, but has original jurisdiction in cases relating to revenue, mandamus, and habeas corpus. The chief justice, assisted by an administrative director, has administrative and supervisory authority over all other courts. The appellate court is divided into five districts; appellate judges, also elected for 10-year terms, hear appeals from the 22 circuit courts, which handle civil and criminal cases. Circuit judges are elected for 6-year terms. Repeated efforts to remove the state's judgeships from partisan politics have failed in the face of strong party opposition.

The penal system, under the general supervision of the Department of Corrections (established in 1970), includes large prisons at Joliet (1860), Pontiac (1871), Menard (1878), and Stateville (1919), near Joliet, plus juvenile facilities and an active parole division. The Cook County House of Corrections is highly active, as are federal facilities in Chicago and Marion. As of June 2001, Illinois had 45,629 prisoners, an increase of 1.4% over the previous year. The state's incarceration rate stood at 370 per 100,000 in population. Prisoner unrest, demands for legal rights, gang activity, and low guard morale continue to be serious problems in the state's penal institutions.

Illinois has a reputation for lawlessness, born of the gang warfare in Chicago during the prohibition era. In the 19th century, southern Illinois was ravaged by numerous bands of outlaws, and one county still carries the nickname "Bloody Williamson" because of its history of murders, massacres, and assassinations. In 2001, the total crime index stood at 4,097.8 per 100,000 inhabitants. This number included 636.9 violent crimes and 3,460.8 property crimes per 100,000 population statewide. Since 1977, Illinois has executed 12 people. In 2003, seven prisoners were under sentence of death.

[17] ARMED FORCES

The most important military installations in Illinois are the Great Lakes Naval Training Center near Chicago and Scott Air Force Base near Belleville. Total active-duty military personnel numbered 25,036 in 2002. Illinois firms received defense contract awards amounting to $1.7 billion in 2001.

About one million Illinoisans served in World War II, of whom 30,000 were killed. There were 1,003,572 veterans of US military service in Illinois as of 2000, of whom 217,908 served in World War II; 133,155 in the Korean conflict; 289,637 during the Vietnam era; and 97,386 during 1990–2000 (including the Persian Gulf War). Veterans' benefits reached $1.6 billion in 2002.

In 2000, the Illinois State Police employed 2,089 full-time officers.

[18] MIGRATION

Apart from the small French settlements along the Mississippi River that were formed in the 18th century, most early white migration into Illinois came from the South, as poor young farm families trekked overland to southern Illinois from Kentucky,

Tennessee, and the Carolinas between 1800 and 1840. After 1830, migration from Indiana, Ohio, and Pennsylvania filled the central portion of the state, while New Englanders and New Yorkers came to the northern portion.

Immigration from Europe became significant in the 1840s and continued in a heavy stream for about 80 years. Before 1890, most of the new arrivals came from Germany, Ireland, Britain, and Scandinavia. These groups continued to arrive after 1890, but they were soon outnumbered by heavy immigration from southern and eastern Europe. The opening of prairie farms, the burgeoning of towns and small cities, and the explosive growth of Chicago created a continuous demand for unskilled and semiskilled labor. Concern for the welfare of these newcomers led to the establishment of Hull House (1889) by Jane Addams in Chicago. Hull House served as a social center, shelter, and advocate for immigrants. Launching the settlement movement in America, its activities helped popularize the concept of cultural pluralism. The University of Chicago was one of the first major universities to concern itself with urban ecology and with the tendency to "ghettoize" culturally and economically disadvantaged populations.

The outbreak of World War I interrupted the flow of European immigrants but also increased the economy's demand for unskilled labor. The migration of blacks from states south of Illinois—especially from Arkansas, Tennessee, Louisiana, Mississippi, and Alabama—played an important role in meeting the demand for labor during both world wars. After World War II, the further collapse of the cotton labor market drove hundreds of thousands more blacks to Chicago and other northern cities.

In contrast to the pattern of foreign and black migration to Illinois was the continued westward search by native-born whites for new farmland, a phenomenon that produced a net outflow by this group from 1870 to 1920. After World War II, native whites again left the state in large numbers, with southern California as a favorite mecca. After 1970 for the first time, more blacks began leaving than entering Illinois.

The major intrastate migration pattern has been from farms to towns. Apart from blacks, who migrated considerable distances from farms in the South, most ex-farmers moved only 10–30 mi (16–48 km) to the nearest town or city.

During the 1970s the state lost 649,000 persons in net migration, for an annual rate of 0.5%. From 1980 to 1983, the net loss from migration totaled 212,000, or 0.6% annually. From 1985 to 1990, the net loss from migration came to 139,360. Between 1990 and 1998, there was a net loss of 516,000 persons from domestic migration and a net gain of 337,000 from international migration. In 1998, 33,163 immigrants from foreign countries arrived in Illinois, the 6th-highest number for any state and over 5% of all foreign immigration to the US for that year. The greatest number of foreign-born residents that year came from Mexico, totaling 10,127. In 1998, the Illinois Hispanic population numbered 1,145,000 while those of Hispanic origin numbered 1,224,000. Between 1990 and 1998, the state's overall population increased 5.4%. In the period 1995–2000, 665,122 people moved into the state and 1,007,738 moved out, for a net loss of 342,616.

[19] INTERGOVERNMENTAL COOPERATION

Illinois participates in many interstate compacts, including such regional accords and commissions as the Bi-State Development Agency Compact (with Missouri), Great Lakes Commission, Wabash Valley Compact, Ohio River Basin Commission, and Ohio River Valley Water Sanitation Commission. In 1985, Illinois and seven other states formed the Great Lakes Charter to protect the lakes' water supply. Federal grants to Illinois totaled almost $11.9 billion in 2001.

20 ECONOMY

The economic development of Illinois falls into four periods: the frontier economy, up to 1860; the industrial transition, 1860–1900; industrial maturity, 1900–1950; and the transition to a service economy, 1950 to the present.

In the first phase, subsistence agriculture was dominant; the cost of transportation was high, cities were small and few, and cash markets for farm products hardly existed. The main activity was settling and clearing the land. A rudimentary market economy developed at the end of the period, with real estate and land speculation the most lucrative activities.

The industrial transition began about 1860, stimulated by the construction of the railroad network, which opened up distant markets for farm products and rural markets for manufactured items. The Civil War stimulated the rapid growth of cash farming, commercial and financial institutions, and the first important factories. The last quarter of the 19th century saw the closing of the agricultural frontier in Illinois and the rapid growth of commercial towns and industrial cities, especially Chicago.

Industrial maturity was reached in the early 20th century. Large factories grew, and small ones proliferated. Chicago's steel industry, actually centered in Gary, Indiana, became 2nd in size only to Pittsburgh's, while the state took a commanding lead in food production, agricultural implement manufacture, and agricultural finance. The depression of the 1930s stifled growth in the state and severely damaged the coal industry, but with the heavy industrial and food demands created by World War II, the state recovered its economic health.

Since 1950, the importance of manufacturing has declined, but a very strong shift into services—government, medicine, education, law, finance, and business—has underpinned the state's economic vigor.

Severe competition from Japan wreaked havoc in the state's steel, television, and automotive industries during the 1980s, while Illinois's high-wage, high-cost business climate encouraged the migration of factories to the southern states. Meat-packing, once the most famous industry in Illinois, dwindled after the closing of the Chicago stockyards in 1972. Chicago remained the nation's chief merchandising center during the early 1980s, and an influx of huge international banks boosted the city's financial strength.

In the 1990s Illinois's major industries included primary and secondary metals; industrial and farm equipment; electric equipment and appliances; electronic components; food processing; and printing equipment. Output from the state's manufacturing sector continued to grow in absolute terms until 1999, after which a small 0.5% contraction in 2000 (more than compensated for by annual overall growth rates averaging over 5.2% 1998 to 2000), was followed by sharp 5% contraction in the national recession of 2001. As a percent of total output, manufacturing fell from 17.8% in 1997 to 14.4% in 2001. By contrast, financial services increased 31.5%, and general services, almost 28%, over this time period. In the period 2001 and 2002, Illinois's diverse economy closely mirrored national trends. The biggest job losses were in manufacturing, totaling approximately 64,000 in the two-year period, compared to 35,700 job lost in general services, 24,700 in trade and 12,700 in transportation and utilities. The annual decline in jobs had moderated to 1.3% by September 2002 (from 1.6% in December 2001).

Illinois's gross state product in 2001 was 5th largest among the states at $475.5 billion, to which general services contributed $108.1 billion; financial services, $105.1 billion, trade, $76.2 billion; manufacturing,$68.3 billion; government, $48.5billion, transportation and public utilities, $40.4 billion, and construction, $23.6 billion. The public sector constituted 10.2% of gross state product, below the state average of 12%

21 INCOME

According to the Bureau of Economic Analysis, in 2001, Illinois had a per capita personal income (PCPI) of $32,990 which ranked 10th in the United States (including the District of Columbia) and was 108% of the national average, $30,413. The 2001 PCPI reflected an increase of 2.1% from 2000 compared to the national change of 2.2%. In 2001, Illinois had a total personal income (TPI) of $413,043,768,000 which ranked 5th in the United States and accounted for 4.8% of the national total. The 2001 TPI reflected an increase of 2.8% from 2000 compared to the national change of 3.3%.

Earnings of persons employed in Illinois increased from $294,112,615,000 in 2000 to $300,146,441,000 in 2001, an increase of 2.1%. The largest industries in 2001 were services, 30.2% of earnings; finance, insurance, and real estate, 10.8%; and state and local government, 10.7%. Of the industries that accounted for at least 5% of earnings in 2001, the slowest growing from 2000 to 2001 was durable goods manufacturing (9.7% of earnings in 2001), which decreased 5.2%; the fastest was state and local government, which

According to data released by the US Census Bureau, in 2000, the median household income was $46,435 compared to the national average of $42,148. In 2001, the median income for a family of four was $66,507 compared to the national average of $63,278. For the period 1999 to 2001, the average poverty rate was 10.2% which placed it 22nd among the 50 states and the District of Columbia ranked lowest to highest.

22 LABOR

According to Bureau of Labor Statistics (BLS) provisional estimates, in July 2003 the seasonally adjusted civilian labor force in Illinois numbered 6,431,500, with approximately 415,200 workers unemployed, yielding an unemployment rate of 6.5%, compared to the national average of 6.2% for the same period. Since the beginning of the BLS data series in 1978, the highest unemployment rate recorded was 12.9% in December 1982. The historical low was 4.1% in April 2000. In 2001, an estimated 5.4% of the labor force was employed in construction; 16.5% in manufacturing; 7.1% in transportation, communications, and public utilities; 18.4% in trade; 6.5% in finance, insurance, and real estate; 27.2% in services; 12.0% in government; and 1.6% in agriculture.

The first labor organizations sprang up among German tailors, teamsters, and carpenters in Chicago in the 1850s, and among British and German coal miners after the Civil War. The period of industrialization after the Civil War saw many strikes, especially in coal mining and construction, many of them spontaneous rather than union-related. The Knights of Labor organized extensively in Chicago, Peoria, and Springfield in the 1870s and 1880s, reaching a membership of 52,000 by 1886. However, in the aftermath of the Haymarket Riot—at which a dynamite blast at a labor rally killed seven policemen and four civilians—the Knights faded rapidly. More durable was the Chicago Federation of Labor, formed in 1877 and eventually absorbed by the American Federation of Labor (AFL). Strongest in the highly skilled construction, transportation, mining, and printing industries, the federation stood aside from the 1894 Pullman strike, led by industrial union organizer Eugene V. Debs, a bitter struggle broken by federal troops over the protest of Governor Altgeld.

Labor unions are powerful in Chicago but relatively weak downstate. The major unions are the International Brotherhood of Teamsters, the United Steelworkers of America, the International Association of Machinists, the United Automobile Workers, the United Brotherhood of Carpenters, and the American Federation of State, County, and Municipal Employees.

The Illinois Education Association, though not strictly a labor union, has become one of the state's most militant employee organizations, often calling strikes and constituting the most active lobby in the state. In 1983, a new law granted all public employees except police and firemen the right to strike.

The US Department of Labor reported that in 2002, 1,066,000 of Illinois's 5,450,000 employed wage and salary workers were members of unions. This represented 19.6% of those so employed, up from 18.1% in 2001 but down slightly from 20% in 1998. The national average is 13.2%. Illinois ranked 3rd in the nation in the largest number of union members. In all, 1,122,000 workers (20.6%) were represented by unions. In addition to union members, this category includes workers who report no union affiliation but whose jobs are covered by a union contract.

[23]AGRICULTURE

Total agricultural income in 2001 reached $7.5 billion in Illinois, 8th in the nation. Crops accounted for nearly 76% of the value of farm marketings, with corn and soybeans the leading cash commodities.

Prior to 1860, agriculture was the dominant occupation, and food for home consumption was the leading product. Enormous effort was devoted to breaking the thick prairie soil in the northern two-thirds of the state. Fences and barns were erected, and in the 1870s and 1880s the drainage of low-lying areas in central Illinois was a major concern. Commercial agriculture was made possible by the extension of the railroad network in the 1860s and 1870s. Corn, wheat, hogs, cattle, and horses were the state's main products in the 19th century. Since then, wheat and poultry have declined greatly in significance, while soybeans and, to a lesser extent, dairy products and vegetables have played an increasingly important role. The mechanization and electrification of agriculture, beginning about 1910, proceeded at an unmatched pace in Illinois. Strong interest in scientific farming, including the use of hybrid corn, sophisticated animal-breeding techniques, and chemical fertilizers, has also fostered a steady, remarkable growth in agricultural productivity.

The number of farms reached a peak at 264,000 in 1900 and began declining rapidly after World War II, down to 76,000 in 2002. Total acreage in farming was 27.7 million acres (11.2 million hectares) in 2002, down from 32.8 million acres (13.3 million hectares) in 1990. The average farm size has more than doubled from 124 acres (50 hectares) in 1900 to 352 acres (142 hectares) in 1998. The farm population, which averaged 1.2 million persons from 1880 to 1900, declined to 314,000 in 1980; by then, moreover, about half the people who lived on farms commuted to work in stores, shops, and offices.

The major agricultural region is the corn belt, covering all of central and about half of northern Illinois. Among the 50 states, Illinois ranked 2nd only to Iowa in production of corn and soybeans in 2002.

Agriculture is big business in the state, though very few farms are owned by corporations (except "family corporations," a tax device). The financial investment in agriculture is enormous, largely because of the accelerating cost of land. The value of land quadrupled during the 1970s to an average of $2,013 per acre in 1980, fell to $1,536 per acre by 1992, but rose to $2,210 by 1997, and $2,640 by 2002.

[24]ANIMAL HUSBANDRY

Livestock is raised almost everywhere in Illinois, but production is concentrated especially in the west-central region. In 2003, Illinois farms had an estimated 1.36 million cattle and calves worth around $966 million. Illinois farms had an estimated 4.05 million hogs and pigs in 2002, worth around $287.6 million. The dairy belt covers part of northern Illinois. Milk production in 2001 totaled and estimated 2 billion lb (0.9 billion kg). During 2001, Illinois poultry farmers sold an estimated 6.4 million lb (2.9 million kg) of chicken. An estimated 888 million eggs were produced in 2001, worth around $35.96 million.

[25]FISHING

Commercial fishing is insignificant in Illinois: only 98,000 lb of fish, valued at $98,000, made up the commercial catch in 1998, down from 405,000 lb and $566,000 in 1994. Sport fishing is of modest importance in southern Illinois and in Lake Michigan. Some 450 lakes and ponds and 200 streams and rivers are open to the public. In 1998, over 422,873 sport anglers were licensed in Illinois.

[26]FORESTRY

Forestland covering 4,331,000 acres (1,753,000 hectares) comprises about 10% of the state's land area. Forests in the northern two-thirds of the state are predominately located in the northwestern part of the state and along major rivers and streams. The majority of Illinois's forests are located in the southern one-third of the state. Some 4,087,000 acres (1,654,000 hectares) are classified as commercial forests and are 90% privately owned. As of 2003 Illinois had two national forests, with a total National Forest System acreage of 857,000 acres (347,000 hectares). In 2002, lumber production totaled 130 million board feet.

[27]MINING

The value of nonfuel mineral production for Illinois in 2001 was estimated to be $911 million, a marginal decrease from 2000. Increased sales of crushed stone, portland cement, and fuller's earth accounted for nearly all the increase in value.

Illinois was the nation's leading producer of industrial sand and gravel (4.43 million metric tons, worth $71.6 million) and tripoli, 4th in fuller's earth, 5th in production of crushed stone (78 million metric tons, worth $417 million) and peat, 9th in lime, and 10th in portland cement (2.94 million metric tons, worth $224 million). It was also a significant producer of construction sand and gravel (29.5 million metric tons, worth $130 million). Nationally, the state continued to rank 17th in nonfuel mineral production value in 2001.

Crushed stone, the state's leading nonfuel mineral commodity, accounted for about 47% of Illinois's nonfuel mineral value in 2001, followed by portland cement, which accounted for nearly 25%, and construction sand and gravel, 14%. Demand for construction aggregate increased significantly in 2001 as a result of projects undertaken by Illinois FIRST, a $12 billion five-year construction program authorized in 1999. Demand for high-quality aggregates grew thanks to the Illinois Coal Revival Initiative.

Until 1997, Illinois was the only state with reported fluorspar production. A combination of increased competition from foreign imports and a decrease in the use of chlorofluorocarbons (because of environmental concerns) has been mostly responsible for the decline in domestic production. Fluorspar had been mined commercially in Hardin County since 1870, and in 1996 the last two operating fluorspar mines in the US were closed (making it difficult to obtain fluorite, the state mineral).

[28]ENERGY AND POWER

Illinois is one of the nation's leading energy producers and consumers. Electric power production (utility and nonutility) totaled 163.6 billion kWh (5th in the US) in 1999; total installed capacity was 34.3 million kW, nearly all of it privately owned. In 2000 Illinois's total per capita energy consumption was 356 million Btu (89.7 million kcal), ranking it 22nd among the 50 states. Commonwealth Edison and Northern Illinois Light and Power are the largest suppliers. Coal-fired plants account for about 45% of the state's power production; nuclear power is also important, particularly for the generation of electricity in the Chicago area. The state's five operating nuclear power plants in 2001 (with 11 reactors) were all owned by Commonwealth Edison.

In 2000, Illinois ranked 3rd nationally in liquefied natural gas consumption, with 2.3 million gal (8.7 million l) per day delivered to over 3.7 million customers. People's Gas, a diversified energy conglomerate based in Chicago, is the largest firm. Marketed gas production in 2001 was 185 million cu ft (5.23 million cu m). Petroleum production, though steadily declining, totaled 33,000 barrels per day in 2002; reserves were 92 million barrels in 2001.

Illinois ranked 7th in the US in coal production in 1998, with 39.7 million tons; production declined to 33.4 tons in 1999. Recoverable reserves were estimated at 819 million tons in 2001. Coal is abundant throughout the state, with the largest mines in the south and central regions. Coal mining reached its peak in the 1920s, but suffered thereafter from high pricing policies, the depression of the 1930s, and the environmental restrictions against burning high-sulfur coal in the 1970s. In 1998 there were 24 productive coal mines—8 surface (strip) mines and 16 underground mines.

29INDUSTRY

Manufacturing in Illinois, concentrated in but not limited to Chicago, has always been diverse. Before 1860s, small gristmills, bakeries, and blacksmith shops handled what little manufacturing was done. Industry tripled in size in the 1860s, doubled in the 1870s, and doubled again in the 1880s, until manufacturing employment leveled off at 10–12% of the population. Value added by manufacture grew at a compound annual rate of 8.1% between 1860 and 1900, and at a rate of 6.3% until 1929.

In 1997, the value of shipments by manufacturers totaled $205 billion. Major industrial items that Illinois produced in 1999 included construction machinery, farm equipment, cellular phones, electrical house wares, commercial printing, metal coatings, appliances and containers, various industrial machinery, and cooking products.

By far the leading industrial center is Chicago, followed by Rockford, the East St. Louis area, Rock Island and Moline in the Quad Cities region, and Peoria.

As of 1997, there were 39 Fortune 500 companies headquartered in Illinois (the 3rd most in the nation), including some of the world's "100 best managed companies": Abbott Laboratories, Amaco, BP, Baxter International, Caterpillar, Deere & Co., Illinois Tool Works, Morton International, Motorola, and Sarah Lee.

Earnings of persons employed in Illinois increased from $247.9 billion in 1997 to $263.4 billion in 1998, an increase of 6.2%. The largest industries in 1998 were services, 28.6% of earnings; durable goods manufacturing, 12.0%; and finance, insurance, and real estate, 9.9%. Of the industries that accounted for at least 5% of earnings in 1998, the slowest growing from 1997 to 1998 was state and local government (9.8% of earnings in 1998), which increased 4.6%; the fastest was finance, insurance, and real estate, which increased 9.0%.

30COMMERCE

Chicago is the leading wholesaling center of the Midwest. In 1997, the state's 24,757 wholesale establishments had sales of $285 billion. Chicago is an especially important trade center for furniture, house wares, and apparel. The state's 65,254 retail

stores recorded sales of $112 billion in 1997. The principal retail store groups were automotive dealers, 12%; food stores, 10%; and eating and drinking places, 33%. Leading Illinois-based retailing companies in 1999 were Sears Roebuck, Household International, McDonald's, and Walgreen.

Illinois ranked 6th among the states in exports with estimated exports of $29 billion in 1998. Export growth was led by industrial machinery and computers with peripheral equipment.

31CONSUMER PROTECTION

Statewide, the Office of the Attorney General is the most active protector of consumers with its Consumer Protection Division, handling 28,000 complaints a year. Within the Consumer Protection Division are the Franchise Bureau, Health Care Bureau, Charitable Trusts Bureau, and Consumer Fraud Bureau. The Department of Insurance also has a Consumer Division. The Department of Human Rights was established in 1979 to protect individuals in regard to employment, public accommodations, and other areas. Nearly half of all claims involve motor vehicle or home repair fraud in the state of Illinois.

32BANKING

Banking was highly controversial in 19th-century Illinois. Modernizers stressed the need for adequate venture capital and money supplies, but traditionalist farmers feared they would be impoverished by an artificial "money monster." Efforts to create a state bank floundered in confusion, while the dubious character of most private banknotes inspired the state to ban private banks altogether. The major breakthrough came during the Civil War, when federal laws encouraged the establishment of strong national banks in all the larger cities, and Chicago quickly became the financial center of the Midwest. Apart from the 1920s and early 1930s, when numerous neighborhood and small-town banks folded, the banking system has flourished. The Bureau of Banks and Trust Companies at the Office of Banks and Real Estate regulates state chartered banks and trust companies.

Illinois had the greatest number of banks in the nation in 2002. There were 791 insured banks in Illinois, 502 of them state-chartered, an unusually large number attributable to regulations restricting branch banking. From 1870 until the 1970, even the largest banks were allowed only one office. Branching without limitation was available in 1993. As of September 2002, insured banks held $535.7 billion in assets. By 1995, the Resolution Trust Corporation (RTC) had assisted 49 Illinois institutions out of insolvency, at a cost of $1.5 billion.

As of the end of 2002, Illinois' largest banks were experiencing an increase in profitability, as median annualized return on assets (ROA) ratio (the measure of earnings in relation to all resources) rose due to lower funding costs. Net interest margins (NIMs) (the difference between the lower rates offered to savers and the higher rates charged on loans) for Illinois' community banks (less than $1 billion in assets) increased.

33INSURANCE

Illinois is a major center of the insurance industry. In 2001 there were 7.7 million ordinary life insurance policies in force with a total value of $503.1 billion; total value for all categories of life insurance (ordinary, group, industrial, and credit) was $879.5 billion. Death benefits paid that year totaled $2.45 billion. In 2003, 83 life and health insurance and 204 property and casualty insurance companies were domiciled in Illinois. In 2001, property and casualty insurers wrote premiums totaling $16.3 billion. That year, there were 45,199 flood insurance policies in force in the state, with a total value of $4.7 million.

Illinois fire and casualty companies are among the US leaders. State Farm is based in Bloomington, and Allstate, a subsidiary of

Sears, Roebuck is in Chicago. Blue Cross–Blue Shield, the nation's largest hospital and medical insurance program, is headquartered in Chicago.

34SECURITIES

Chicago, home of the Midwest Stock Exchange and the Cincinnati Stock Exchange, ranks 2nd only to New York as a center for securities trading. There are 3,539 broker and dealer firms in Illinois with 44,172 employees. Some 509 securities investment advisor firms are registered to do business in the state (5th most in the nation). Illinois is headquarters to 179 NASDAQ companies, 22 NASDAQ market makers, 21 AMEX-listed corporations, and 24 Illinois-incorporated NYSE corporations. The top five according to revenues are: Motorola, Walgreens, Abbott Labs, Aon Corp., and Unicom.

The most intensive trading in Chicago takes place on the three major commodity exchanges. The Chicago Board of Trade has set agricultural prices for the world since 1848, especially in soybeans, corn, and wheat. The Chicago Mercantile Exchange specializes in pork bellies (bacon), live cattle, potatoes, and eggs; since 1972, it has also provided a market for world currency futures. The Mid-America Commodity Exchange, the smallest of the three, has a colorful ancestry dating from 1868. It features small-lot futures contracts on soybeans, silver, corn, wheat, and live hogs.

35PUBLIC FINANCE

Among the larger states, Illinois is known for its low taxes and conservative fiscal policy. The Bureau of the Budget, under the governor's control, has major responsibility for the state's overall fiscal program, negotiating annually with key legislators, cabinet officers, and outside pressure groups. The governor then submits the budget to the legislature for amendment and approval. The fiscal year runs from 1 July to 30 June.

The Illinois State Budget for 2001 funded total appropriations of $46.5 billion, including $22.2 billion in general funds appropriations. Illinois started running a deficit in 2000/01. Spending increases (particularly for Medicare, Employee Group Health Insurance, pensions, and K-12 maintenance) outpaced revenue increases, and revenue declines outpaced spending reductions for 2001/02 and 2002/03. In 2001/02, cuts totaling $500 million were made in the budget after it was passed, and in 2002/03, reductions after passage totaled $202 million. The state's deficit was only $200 million (less than 1% of the state budget) in 2002/03, but was projected at 11.4% for the state budget for 2003/04. Strategies used to reduce the budget gap in 2002/03 included across-the-board cuts (exempting only the State Board of Education), early retirement of some government employees, and the governor's executive order restricting hiring, travel and equipment purchases. The expenditures fell 2.9% relative to 2001/02.

Appropriations from the General Fund totaled $22.298 billion in 2002/03, 39% for education, 23% for public aid, 22% for human and health services, 7% for public protection and justice, and 9% for general operations and other functions. General funds constituted 42% of the states total revenues of $52.564 billion in 2002/03, the other portions being accounted for by Highway Trust Funds (12%), other special state trust funds (21%), federal trust funds (11%), the general obligation bonds fund (10%), and other funds (4%).

The following table from the US Census Bureau contains information on revenues, expenditures, indebtedness, and cash/securities for 2001.

	($000)	PERCENT	PER CAPITA
Population (thousands, 2001)	12,520	(X)	(X)
Total Revenue	47,348,197	100.00	3,781.80
General revenue	40,226,623	84.96	3,212.99
Utility revenue	–	–	–
Liquor store revenue	–	–	–
Insurance trust revenue	7,121,574	15.04	568.82
Exhibit: Salaries and wages	5,329,754	11.80	425.70
Total expenditure	45,170,257	100.00	3,607.85
General expenditure	40,244,967	89.10	3,214.45
Education	12,930,797	28.63	1,032.81
Public welfare	10,629,912	23.53	849.03
Hospitals	881,347	1.95	70.40
Health	2,331,657	5.16	186.23
Highways	3,226,467	7.14	257.71
Police protection	390,950	0.87	31.23
Correction	1,390,834	3.08	111.09
Natural resources	441,727	0.98	35.28
Parks and recreation	290,245	0.64	23.18
Government administration	1,231,059	2.73	98.33
Interest on general debt	1,986,825	4.40	158.69
Other and unallocable	4,513,147	9.99	360.48
Utility expenditure	–	–	–
Liquor store expenditure	–	–	–
Insurance trust expenditure	4,925,290	10.90	393.39
Debt at end of fiscal year	30,247,654	100.00	2,415.95
Cash and security holdings	89,509,545	100.00	7,149.32

36TAXATION

Illinoisans have fiercely resisted the imposition of new and higher taxes. The levying of the first 1% sales tax in 1933 to finance relief programs was bitterly resented, and the inauguration of a state personal income tax in 1970 led to the defeat of Governor Richard Ogilvie in his 1972 reelection campaign.

The state personal income tax is a flat 3%, with personal and child exemptions set at $2000. In 1998, the state abolished the local personal property tax and replaced it with a 2.5% addition to the state's 4.8% corporate income tax, bringing the total corporate tax rate to 7.3%. The proceeds from the 2.5% personal property replacement portion of the corporate tax are distributed to local taxing units. Illinois' general sales and use tax rate is 6.25%. There is a reduced rate of 1% on food and medicines. Local sales taxes range from 0% to 3%. The state imposes a full set of excise taxes, on tobacco products, motor fuels, amusements, pari-mutuels, public utilities, insurance premiums, and other selected items. In the budget crunch of 2001/02, Illinois was one of 20 states to raise the tax on a pack of cigarettes, in its case from $0.58 to $0.98 cents. Most property taxes are collected at the local level, where almost half of non-federal taxes (46.8% in 2000) are collected. Illinois' estate tax is tied to the federal exemption for state death taxes, and is therefore set to be phased out in tandem with the phasing out of the federal estate tax, unless the state takes positive action to establish an independent estate tax. Illinois' revenue losses from the phasing out of its estate tax are estimated at -$150 million for 2002/03, -$250 million for 2003/04, and -$400 million for 2006/07. Death and gift taxes accounted for 1.5% of state collections in 2002. Other state taxes include various license fees and a 4% timber fee that goes to the Department of Conservation.

Total state tax collections in Illinois in 2002 were $22.46 billion, of which 30.9% was generated by the state income tax, 28.5% by the state general sales and use tax, 20.5% by state excise taxes, 9.2% by the corporate income tax (which includes the personal property replacement tax), and 8.5% from license fees. In 2003, combined state and local taxes amounted to 9.4% of income, the 30th highest rate in the country.

The following table from the US Census Bureau provides a summary of taxes collected by the state in 2002.

	($000)	PER CAPITA
Total Taxes	22,460,190	1,782.47
Property taxes	56,823	4.51
Sales and gross receipts	11,083,466	879.6
General sales and gross receipts	6,419,156	509.43
Selective sales taxes	4,664,310	370.17
Alcoholic beverage	140,854	11.18
Amusements	591,080	46.91
Insurance Premiums	285,051	22.62
Motor fuels	1,373,522	109
Pari-mutuels	12,598	1
Public utilities	1,509,883	119.83
Tobacco products	464,447	36.86
Other selective sales	286,875	22.77
Licenses	1,914,257	151.92
Alcoholic beverages	4,120	0.33
Amusements	2,207	0.18
Corporation	165,304	13.12
Hunting and fishing	25,424	2.02
Motor vehicle	1,342,077	106.51
Motor vehicle operators	72,086	5.72
Public utility	(X)	(X)
Occupation and business, NEC	298,661	23.7
Other	4,378	0.35
Other taxes	9,405,644	746.44
Individual income	6,951,265	551.66
Corporation net income	2,061,540	163.61
Death and gift	328,729	26.09
Documentary and stock transfer	63,851	5.07
Severance	259	0.02
Other	(X)	(X)

37 ECONOMIC POLICY

The state's policy toward economic development has engendered political controversy since the 1830s. Before the Civil War, the Democrats in power usually tried to slow, though not reverse, the tide of rapid industrial and commercial growth. The Republican ascendancy between the 1850s and the 1930s (with a few brief interruptions) produced a generally favorable business climate, which in turn fostered rapid economic growth. The manufacturing sector eroded slowly in the 1960s and 1970s, as incentives and tax credits for new industry were kept at a modest level. In 1989, however, the state began to aggressively encourage companies undergoing modernization or commercializing new technologies by enacting the Technology Advancement and Development Act, which invests in companies developing advanced technologies for commercial purposes.

In 2003, the lead government agency coordinating economic development programs was the Department of Commerce and Economic Opportunity (DCEO), previously called the Department of Commerce and Community Affairs. The name change indicated a shift in emphasis towards inclusion ("no community left behind") in the economic downturn that followed the prosperous 1990s; a shift, for instance, from primary emphasis on keeping up with the latest digital technology (as in the government's Science and Technology Initiative of 2000 that included "technology challenge" business and educational grants, and research funding) to a concern, also, with bridging the "digital divide." The Illinois Department of Human Services (DHS) was given managerial control of the Team Illinois initiative announced in July 2003, which featured the pooling of resources of virtually every state agency, including the DCEO, to address the needs of the state's poorest communities. The goal of Team Illinois was to work with residents, elected officials, local business leaders, and community stakeholders to help build needed infrastructure. The creation of public-private partnerships and the empowerment of community stakeholders were to be central parts of the approach. Hopkins Park in Pembroke Township, a rural community in Kankakee County, was the first

of four communities scheduled to receive Team Illinois assistance. Infrastructural improvements underway included road repair, a new Technology Learning Center, public-private partnerships to build affordable housing; the removal and clean-up of tire dumps (by the Illinois EPA), and health screenings and immunizations (by the Department of Public Health). The DCEO role was to work with the Kankakee Community College and the local Workforce Investment Board to form a consortium of employers to develop customized training to meet their hiring needs. Employers who had joined the consortium included Aventis, Armstrong, Bunge, Momence Packaging/Johnsville Sausage, Rohm & Haas, Micro Links, Roehl Transportation Falcon Transportation, Kmart, and Reynolds Food Packaging. Internationally, the DCEO's role is that of the "sales department for Illinois." It maintains trade and investment offices in Washington (DC), Toronto, Budapest, Mexico City, Tokyo, Warsaw, Johannesburg, Brussels, and Hong Kong. The promotion of jobs, tourism, minority-owned enterprises, and foreign markets for Illinois products is the department's major responsibility. The assistance by the DCEO includes equity capital and low interest loans for small businesses; low-interest financing to communities undergoing infrastructure improvements which help create or retain jobs; tax-exempt bonds for companies expanding or renovating their physical plant; and grants for employee training and retraining. The

38 HEALTH

In 2000, infant mortality was 8.5 per 1,000 live births. Nationally, Illinois ranked 8th in infant mortality in 2000; the national rate was 6.9. Although the infant mortality rate fell from 21.5 in 1970 to 13.9 in 1981 to 10.7 in 1991, it did not decline as rapidly as elsewhere. Since the late 1960s, Illinois has had a slightly higher infant mortality rate than the rest of the country; the 1993–94 rate was the 5th highest among the states while the 1996 rate ranked 9th highest. The number of legal abortions performed in 1999 was 45,924, down from 72,000 in 1977.

Illinois's death rate, 875.1 per 100,000 residents, was slightly higher than the national rate of 873.1 in 2000. At that time Illinois also ranked above the national averages in deaths due to heart disease and cerebrovascular disease, but below the averages in accidents and adverse effects and suicide. Major public health problems in the 1980s included rapidly increasing rates of venereal disease and drug abuse. Alcoholism has always been a major problem in Illinois. The state also has a high proportion of residents receiving psychiatric care. In 1995, there were 35.3 breast cancer deaths per 100,000 women, 4th-highest among the states. In 2000, 22.3% of the adults 18 years of age and older in Illinois were smokers. The rate of HIV-related deaths stood at 3.9 per 100,000 population, slightly below the national average of 5.3 in 2000. There were 26,319 AIDS cases reported through 2001.

Hospitals abound in Illinois, with Chicago serving as a diagnostic and treatment center for patients throughout the Midwest. With 192 community facilities (many quite large) and 36,834 beds, Illinois hospitals recorded 1,559,357 admissions in 2001. In the same year, total full-time personnel numbered 190,746, including 44,900 full-time registered nurses and 3,339 full-time licensed practical nurses. In 2000, the state had 285 physicians per 100,000 population. The average expense to hospitals for care provided in 2001 was $1,446.50 per inpatient day.

Federal government grants to cover the Medicare and Medicaid services in 2001 totaled $4.4 billion; 1,639,986 enrollees received Medicare benefits that year. At least 13.6% of adult residents had no insurance in 2002.

³⁹SOCIAL WELFARE

Prior to the 1930s, social welfare programs were the province of county government and private agencies. Asylums, particularly poor farms, were built in most counties following the Civil War; they provided custodial care for orphans, the very old, the helpless, sick, and itinerant "tramps." Most people who needed help, however, turned to relatives, neighbors, or church agencies. The local and private agencies were overwhelmed by the severe depression of the 1930s, forcing first the state and then the federal government to intervene. Social welfare programs are implemented by county agencies but funded by local and state taxes and federal aid. In the early 1990s, the annual outlays for the five largest welfare programs in Illinois totaled more than $2 billion, or $421.05 per capita, in state government expenditures.

In 2001, the average weekly unemployment benefit was $265.40. Average monthly participation in the food stamp program in FY2002 comprised 886,344 persons (392,909 households). The average monthly benefit was $86.81, and the sum total of benefits paid in FY2002 was $923,305,728.

With the enactment of the Personal Responsibility and Work Opportunity Reconciliation Act of 1996, the US government has changed the form and regulations for many of its social welfare programs. Most significantly, it replaces Aid to Families with Dependent Children (AFDC), an open-ended entitlement program, with Temporary Assistance for Needy Families (TANF), a limited system of assistance funded largely through federal block grants. The reform act also impacts the food stamp program, the Supplemental Security Income program, and the child nutrition program. The law took effect on 1 July 1997 and provided $16.38 billion in block grants for fiscal years 1997–2002. The grants are to be divided among the states based on an equation involving the numbers of former AFDC recipients in each state.

Reauthorization of the 1996 social welfare legislation, scheduled for 2002, was delayed, and the original law had been extended three times as of July 2003, with the most recent extension running through September 2003. Illinois's TANF program has no separate state name. In June 2000 the state had 259,242 welfare recipients. State expenditures on the TANF program in FY2002 totaled $426,774,903.

In December 2001, Social Security benefits were paid to 1,845,500 Illinois residents. This number included 1,201,790 retired workers, 207,560 widows and widowers, 179,850 disabled workers, 107,430 spouses, and 148,870 children. Social Security beneficiaries represented 14.8% of the total state population and 91.7% of the state's population age 65 and older. Retired workers (excluding persons with special benefits) received an average monthly payment of $915; widows and widowers, $882; disabled workers, $842; and spouses, $466. Payments for children of retired workers averaged $449 per month; children of deceased workers, $600; and children of disabled workers, $250.

Federal Supplemental Security Income payments in December 2001 went to 249,004 Illinois residents, averaging $401 a month.

⁴⁰HOUSING

Flimsy cabins and shacks provided rude shelter for many Illinoisans in pioneer days. Later, the balloon-frame house, much cheaper to build than traditional structures, became a trademark of the Prairie State. After a third of Chicago's wooden houses burned in 1871, the city moved to enforce more stringent building codes. The city's predominant dwelling then became the three- or five-story brick apartment house. Great mansions were built in elite areas of Chicago (first Prairie Avenue, later the Gold Coast), and high-rise lakefront luxury apartments first became popular in the 1920s. In the 1970s, Chicago pioneered the conversion of luxury apartment buildings to condominiums, which numbered 242,653 (5.4% of all housing units) in 1990.

In 2002 there were an estimated 4,981,258 housing units in Illinois, of which 4,627,667 were occupied; 67.6% were owner-occupied. About 57.6% of all units were single-family, detached homes. Most units rely on utility gas for heating. It was estimated that 199,427 units were without telephone service, 20,546 lacked complete plumbing facilities, and 22,999 lacked complete kitchen facilities. The average household size was 2.65 people.

In 2002, 60,971 new privately owned units were authorized for construction. The median home value was $147,353. The median monthly cost for mortgage owners was $1,284, while renters paid a median of $665 per month. During 2002, Illinois received over $312.3 million in community planning and development aid from the US Department of Housing and Urban Development.

⁴¹EDUCATION

In 1854, Ninian Edwards became the first superintendent of public education. His first and most difficult task was to convince pioneer parents that a formal education was a necessary item in the lives of their children. By the mid-1870s, education in Illinois had become a going enterprise. Edwards helped create an outstanding public school system, although the city of Chicago was hard pressed to construct enough school buildings to serve the growing numbers of students until foreign immigration subsided in the 1920s. The dedication of these educators continued to improve the quality of education, but it was not until the development of a good highway system and state funding for the transporting of students, that rural Illinois was to see the demise of one-room schoolhouses. In one decade, 1944–54, state-mandated school consolidation/reorganization reduced the number of school districts from 11,955 to 2,607.

Illinois tends to have slightly higher literacy levels than the national averages. In 2000, 81.4% of the Illinois adult population held high school diplomas, with 26.1% continuing their education and earning a bachelor's degree or higher.

Total public school enrollment for fall 1999 stood at 2,,027,600. Of these, 1,462,234 attended schools from kindergarten through grade eight, and 565,366 attended high school. Minority students made up approximately 41% of the total enrollment in public elementary and secondary schools in 2001. Total enrollment was estimated at 2,048,197 in fall 2000 and expected to reach 2,251,000 by fall 2005.

Nonpublic schools, dominated by Chicago's extensive Roman Catholic school system, have shown a slight decrease since the early 1980s. Enrollment in nonpublic schools in fall 2001 was 299,081, down from 320,880 in 1995/96. Rising tuition fees, caused in part by higher salaries for lay teachers and a drop in the number of teaching sisters, threatened the parochial schools. High-tuition private schools continue to flourish in Chicago, however.

As of fall 2000, there were 810,038 students enrolled in college or graduate school. In the same year Illinois had 181 degree-granting institutions. In 1997, minority students comprised 29.2% of total postsecondary enrollment. Public universities enroll about one-quarter of the Illinois college student population. The University of Illinois system has both the largest and smallest public university campuses. The University of Illinois at Springfield was formerly Sangamon State University. Champaign-Urbana is the state's most populous campus. Nearly half of all Illinois college students attend one of the state's 48 public community colleges. Private institutions enroll the remaining quarter of Illinois college students. Private-sector institutions are broken down into two broad categories—not-for-profit and proprietary. There are 103 independent, not-for-profit colleges and universities.

Illinois education is financed through a combination of state, local, and federal funds. In 1999/2000, the estimated mean expenditure per student was $5,856; the average United States expenditure was $6,356. Expenditures for public education in 2000/01 were estimated at $7,668,000.

42ARTS

Chicago emerged in the late 19th century as the leading arts center of the Midwest, and it continues to hold this premier position. The major downstate facilities include the Krannert Center at the University of Illinois (Champaign-Urbana) and the Lakeview Center in Peoria.

Architecture is the outstanding art form in Illinois, and Chicago—where the first skyscrapers were built in the 1880s—has been a mecca for modern commercial and residential architects ever since the fire of 1871. The Art Institute of Chicago, incorporated in 1879, is the leading art museum in the state. Although its holdings, largely donated by wealthy Chicagoans, cover all the major periods, its French Impressionist collection is especially noteworthy. An example of bold contemporary architecture is the $172-million State of Illinois Center in Chicago, which opened in 1985.

Theater groups abound—there were 116 theatrical producers in 1982—notably in Chicago, where the Second City comedy troupe and the Steppenwolf Theatre are located; the city's best playwrights and performers, however, often gravitate to Broadway in New York or Hollywood. Film production was an important industry in Illinois before 1920, when operations shifted to the sunnier climate and more opulent production facilities of southern California. By the early 1980s, however, the Illinois Film Office had staged an impressive comeback, and television films and motion pictures were being routinely shot in the state.

The Chicago Symphony Orchestra, organized by Theodore Thomas in 1891, quickly acquired world stature; its permanent conductors have included Frederick Stock, Fritz Reiner, Sir George Solti, who regularly took the symphony on triumphant European tours, and Daniel Barenboim (since 1991). German immigrants founded many musical societies in Chicago in the late 19th century, when the city also became a major center of musical education. Opera flourished in Chicago in the early 20th century, collapsed during the early 1930s, but was reborn through the founding of the Lyric Opera in 1954. Chicago's most original musical contribution was jazz, imported from the South by black musicians in the 1920s. Such jazz greats as King Oliver, Louis Armstrong, Jelly Roll Morton, Benny Goodman, and Gene Krupa all worked or learned their craft in the speakeasies and jazz houses of the city's South Side. More recently, Chicago became the center of an urban blues movement, using electric rather than acoustic guitars and influenced by jazz.

The seamy side of Chicago has fascinated writers throughout the 20th century. Among well-known American novels set in Chicago are two muckraking works, Frank Norris's *The Pit* (1903) and Upton Sinclair's *The Jungle* (1906), as well as James T. Farrell's *Studs Lonigan* (1935) and Saul Bellow's *The Adventures of Augie March* (1953). Famous American plays associated with Chicago are *The Front Page* (1928), by Ben Hecht and Charles MacArthur, and *A Raisin in the Sun* (1959), by Lorraine Hansberry.

The Illinois Arts Council was founded in 1965. In 2003, state organizations received $3,405,300 in grant money from the National Endowment for the Arts. The Illinois Humanities Council, founded in 1974, offers ongoing programs that include a lecture/presentation series program called the Heartland Chautauqua and The Odyssey Project, which offer free college-level courses in the humanities to individuals with incomes below the poverty level. In 2000, the National Endowment for the Humanities sponsored 61 grants for state programs, with a total contribution of $7,277,182. A humanities fellowship of $210,000 was awarded to the American Institute of Indian Studies in Chicago in 2003. The state's arts education programs are offered to over 850,000 schoolchildren. There are over 2,200 arts associations in Illinois and over 80 local associations. There are a number of local arts fairs and festivals held annually throughout the state.

43LIBRARIES AND MUSEUMS

Libraries and library science are particularly strong in Illinois. In 2000 there were 12 public library systems, which had a combined book stock of 41 million and circulation of over 83 million. The facilities in Peoria, Oak Park, Evanston, Rockford, and Quincy are noteworthy; and the Chicago Public Library system (with 6,490,452 volumes) operates 89 branch libraries, and the Illinois Regional Library for the Blind and Physically Handicapped. The outstanding libraries of the University of Illinois (Champaign-Urbana) and the University of Chicago (with over 8,000,000 and 6,419,936 volumes respectively) constitute the state's leading research facilities, and the University of Illinois has a famous library school. Principal historical collections are at the Newberry Library in Chicago, the Illinois State Historical Society in Springfield, and the Chicago Historical Society. Public library income for 2000 was $481,279,000; including $1,687,674 in federal grants and $36,577,204 in state grants.

Illinois has 277 museums and historic sites. Chicago's Field Museum of Natural History, with an annual attendance of over 1.2 million, has sponsored numerous worldwide expeditions in the course of acquiring some 13 million anthropological, zoological, botanical, and geological specimens. The Museum of Science and Industry, near the University of Chicago, attracts two million visitors a year, mostly children, to see its exhibits of industrial technology. Also noteworthy are the Adler Planetarium, Shedd Aquarium, and the Oriental Institute Museum of the University of Chicago. The Brookfield Zoo, near Chicago, opened in 1934; smaller zoos can be found in Chicago's Lincoln Park and in Peoria, Elgin, and other cities.

Just about every town has one or more historic sites authenticated by the state. The most popular is New Salem, near Springfield, where Abraham Lincoln lived from 1831 to 1837. Its reconstruction, begun by press magnate William Randolph Hearst in 1906, includes one original cabin and numerous replicas. The most important archaeological sites are the Dixon Mounds, 40 mi (64 km) south of Peoria, and the Koster Excavation in Calhoun County, north of St. Louis, Mo.

44COMMUNICATIONS

Illinois has an extensive communications system. The state's households with telephones numbered about 93.7% of all households in 2001.

Illinois had 38 major AM and 128 major FM commercial radio stations in 2003, when 31 major television stations served the state. The Chicago area has the 3rd largest number of television households of all metropolitan areas (3,204,710), with cable in 65%.

In 1979, WGN-TV in Chicago became a "superstation," with sports programs, movies, and advertising. Although the three major networks own stations in Chicago, they originate very little programming from the city. However, as a major advertising center, Chicago produces many commercials and industrial films. Most educational broadcasting in Illinois comes from state universities and the Chicago public and Catholic school systems.

A total of 259,713 Internet domain names were registered in the state in the year 2000.

45PRESS

The state's first newspaper, the *Illinois Herald*, was begun in Kaskaskia in 1814. From the 1830s through the end of the 19th century, small-town weeklies exerted powerful political influence. After 1900, however, publishers discovered that they needed large circulations to appeal to advertisers, so they toned down their partisanship and began adding a broad range of features to attract a wider audience.

The most popular magazines published in Chicago are *Playboy* and *Ebony*. Many specialized trade and membership magazines, such as the *Lion* and the *Rotarian*, are published in Chicago, which is also the printing and circulation center for many magazines edited in New York. The popular *Cricket Magazine* for children is published in LaSalle-Peru.

As of 2002, Illinois had 25 morning newspapers (including all-day papers), 42 evening dailies, and 30 Sunday papers. The Illinois editions of St. Louis newspapers are also widely read. The Chicago *Tribune* was the 7th-largest daily and 4th-largest Sunday newspaper nationwide in 2001, based on circulation figures. The following table shows the state's leading dailies with their 2002 estimated circulations:

AREA	NAME	DAILY	SUNDAY
Chicago	*Sun-Times* (m,S)	480,920	393,196
	Tribune (m,S)	675,847	1,010,704
Peoria	*Journal Star* (all day,S)	67,446	90,213
Rockford	*Register Star* (m,S)	69,210	80,550
Springfield	*State Journal–Register*(m,S)	58,519	67,680

46ORGANIZATIONS

Before the Civil War, Yankee-dominated towns and cities in northern Illinois sponsored lyceums, debating circles, women's clubs, temperance groups, and antislavery societies. During the 20th century, Chicago's size and central location attracted the headquarters of numerous national organizations, though far fewer than New York or, more recently, Washington, D.C.

In 2003, there were about 5,437 regional, national, and international organizations within the state. Major national service and fraternal bodies with headquarters in Chicago or nearby suburbs include the Benevolent and Protective Order of Elks of the USA, Lions Clubs International, Loyal Order of Moose, and Rotary International.

Chicago has long been a center for professional organizations, among them the most powerful single US medical group, the American Medical Association, founded in 1847, and the American Hospital Association, begun in 1898. Other major groups include associations of surgeons, dentists, veterinarians, osteopaths, and dietitians, as well as the Blue Cross and Blue Shield Association and the National Easter Seal Society.

The American Bar Association has its headquarters in Chicago, as do several smaller legal groups, including the American Judicature Society and the Commercial Law League of America. Librarians also have a base in Chicago: the American Library Association, the Society of American Archivists, and the associations of law and medical librarians are all headquartered in the city. The National Parent–Teacher Association is the only major national educational group. The Illinois State Historical Society promotes the study of state history.

A variety of trade organizations, such as the American Marketing Association, are based in Chicago, though many have moved to Washington, D.C. The American Farm Bureau Federation operates out of Park Ridge. The National Women's Christian Temperance Union, one of the most important of all US pressure groups in the 19th century, has its headquarters in Evanston. The World Bocce Association is based in Elmhurst.

47TOURISM, TRAVEL, AND RECREATION

The tourist industry is of special importance to Chicago, which has become the nation's leading convention center. Business travel accounts for about 36% of all state travel. In 2002, there were about 83.3 million domestic visitors to the state. Despite declines

in overseas travel, Illinois was the 6th most popular US state for overseas visitors in 2002, with 1,071,000 travelers. The same year, Chicago was the 9th most popular US city for overseas visitors. Tourism and travel expenditures contributed about $22 billion dollars to the state economy. Over 300,000 people were employed in the industry.

Chicago's chief tourist attractions are its museums, restaurants, and shops. Chicago also boasts one of the world's tallest buildings, the Sears Tower, 110 stories and 1,454 feet (443 meters) high. There are 42 state parks, 4 state forests, 36,659 campsites, and 25 state recreation places. The Lincoln Home National Historic Site in Springfield was one of the state's most popular tourist attractions. Swimming, bicycling, hiking, camping, horseback riding, fishing, and motorboating are the most popular recreational activities. Even more popular than hunting is wildlife observation, an activity that engages millions of Illinoisans annually.

48SPORTS

Illinois has six major league professional sports teams, all of which play in Chicago: the Cubs and the White Sox of Major League Baseball, the Bears of the National Football League, the Bulls of the National Basketball Association, the Fire of Major League Soccer, and the Blackhawks of the National Hockey League.

The Cubs last won a World Series in 1908, the White Sox in 1917. The Bears won the Super Bowl in 1986. The Bulls established a remarkable basketball dynasty fueled by the play of Michael Jordan, perhaps the best athlete in the history of basketball, winning NBA championships in 1991, 1992, 1993, 1996, 1997, and 1998. They were the first basketball team to win three consecutive championships since the Boston Celtics set the probably unbreakable record of eight consecutive titles from 1959 to 1966. The Bulls' string of titles has ended, however, as Jordan retired in 1999 and the title-winning team has been dismantled. The Blackhawks won the Stanley Cup in 1934, 1938, and 1961. The state also has minor league baseball, basketball, and hockey.

The White Sox built a new ballpark, Comiskey Park, which opened in 1993. The Cubs play their home games at Wrigley Field, perhaps one of the most venerable parks because of its ivy-covered outfield walls. Horse racing is very popular in the state, with pari-mutuel betting allowed. The Golden Glove Boxing Tournament is held annually in February in Chicago.

In collegiate sports the emphasis is on basketball and football. The University of Illinois and Northwestern compete in the Big Ten Conference. Illinois won the Rose Bowl in 1947, 1952, and 1964, and was named national champion in 1923. In a remarkable revival of its football program, Northwestern won its first Big Ten title in 46 years in 1995. The Wildcats played in the Rose Bowl for the first time since 1949, when they recorded their only victory in the New Year's Day game. Southern Illinois won the National Invitational Tournament in basketball in 1967. The DePaul Blue Demons of Conference USA consistently rank high among college basketball teams.

49FAMOUS ILLINOISANS

Abraham Lincoln (b.Kentucky, 1809–65), 16th president of the US, is the outstanding figure in Illinois history, having lived and built his political career in the state between 1830 and 1861. The only Illinois native to be elected president is Ronald Reagan (b.1911), who left the state after graduating from Eureka College to pursue his film and political careers in California. Ulysses S. Grant (b.Ohio, 1822–85), the nation's 18th president, lived in Galena on the eve of the Civil War. Adlai E. Stevenson (b.Kentucky, 1835–1914), founder of a political dynasty, served as US vice president from 1893 to 1897, but was defeated for the same office in 1900. His grandson, also named Adlai E. Stevenson (b.California, 1900–65), served as governor of Illinois from 1949 to 1953, was the Democratic presidential nominee in 1952 and 1956, and ended his career as US ambassador to the United Nations. Charles Gates Dawes (b.Ohio, 1865–1951), a Chicago financier, served as vice president from 1925 to 1929 and shared the 1925 Nobel Peace Prize for the Dawes Plan to reorganize German finances. William Jennings Bryan (1860–1925), a leader of the free-silver and Populist movements, was the Democratic presidential nominee in 1896, 1900, and 1908.

US Supreme Court justices associated with Illinois include David Davis (b.Maryland, 1815–86); John M. Harlan (1899–1971); Chicago-born Arthur Goldberg (1908–90), who also served as secretary of labor and succeeded Stevenson as UN ambassador; Harry A. Blackmun (1908–97); and John Paul Stevens (b.1920). Melville Fuller (b.Maine, 1833–1910) served as chief justice from 1888 to 1910.

Many other politicians who played important roles on the national scene drew their support from the people of Illinois. They include Stephen Douglas (b.Vermont, 1813–61), senator from 1847 to 1861, Democratic Party leader, 1860 presidential candidate, but equally famous as Lincoln's opponent in a series of debates on slavery in 1858; Lyman Trumbull (b.Connecticut, 1813–96), senator from 1855 to 1873, who helped secure passage of the 13th and 14th amendments to the US Constitution; Joseph "Uncle Joe" Cannon (b.North Carolina, 1836–1926), Republican congressman from Danville for half a century and autocratic speaker of the House from 1903 to 1911; Henry Rainey (1860–1934), Democratic speaker of the House during 1933–34, Everett McKinley Dirksen (1896–1969), senator and colorful Republican leader during the 1950s and 1960s; Charles H. Percy (b.Florida, 1919), Republican senator from 1967 to 1985; John B. Anderson (b.1922), Republican congressman for 20 years and an independent presidential candidate in 1980; and Robert H. Michel (b.1923), House Republican leader in the 1980s.

Among noteworthy governors of the state, in addition to Stevenson, were Richard Yates (b.Kentucky, 1815–73), who maintained Illinois's loyalty to the Union during the Civil War; John Peter Altgeld (b.Germany, 1847–1902), governor from 1893 to 1897; and Republican-Progressive leader Frank Lowden (b.Minnesota, 1861–1943). Richard J. Daley (1902–76) was Democratic boss and mayor of Chicago from 1955 to 1976. Jane Byrne (b.1934), a Daley protégé, became mayor in 1979; she was succeeded in 1983 by Harold Washington (1922–87), the city's first black mayor. Richard Michael Daley (b.1942), son of Richard Daley, also became mayor.

Phyllis Schlafly (b.Missouri, 1924) of Alton became nationally known as an antifeminist conservative crusader during the 1970s. An outstanding Illinoisan was Jane Addams (1860–1935), founder of Hull House (1889), author, reformer, prohibitionist, feminist, and tireless worker for world peace; in 1931, she shared the Nobel Peace Prize. Winners of the Nobel Prize in physics include Albert Michelson (b.Germany, 1852–1931), Robert Millikan (1868–1953), Arthur Holly Compton (b.Ohio, 1892–1962), Enrico Fermi (b.Italy, 1901–54), John Bardeen (b.Wisconsin, 1908–91), John R. Schrieffer (b.1931), and James W. Cronin (b.1931). Chemistry prizes went to Robert Mulliken (b.Massachusetts, 1896–1986), Wendell Stanley (b.Indiana, 1904–71), Willard Libby (b.Colorado, 1908–80), and Stanford Moore (1913–82). Nobel Prizes in physiology or medicine were won by Charles Huggins (b.Canada, 1901–97), George Beadle (b.Nebraska 1903–89), and Robert W. Holley (1922–93). A Nobel award in literature went to Saul Bellow (b.Canada, 1915), and the economics prize was given to Milton Friedman (b.New York, 1912), leader of the so-called Chicago school of

economists, and to Theodore Schultz (b.South Dakota, 1902–98) in 1979.

Some of the most influential Illinoisans have been religious leaders; many of them also exercised social and political influence. Notable are Methodist circuit rider Peter Cartwright (b.Virginia, 1785–1872); Dwight Moody (b.Massachusetts, 1837–99), leading force in the National Women's Christian Temperance Union and the feminist cause; Mother Frances Xavier Cabrini (b.Italy, 1850–1917), the first American to be canonized; Bishop Fulton J. Sheen (1895–1979), influential spokesman for the Roman Catholic Church; Elijah Muhammad (Elijah Poole, b.Georgia, 1897–1975), leader of the Black Muslim movement; and Jesse Jackson (b.North Carolina, 1941), civil rights leader and one of the most prominent black spokesmen of the 1980s and 1990s.

Outstanding business and professional leaders who lived in Illinois include John Deere (b.Vermont, 1804–86), industrialist and inventor of the steel plow; Cyrus Hall McCormick (b.Virginia, 1809–84), inventor of the reaping machine; Nathan Davis (1817–1904), the "father of the American Medical Association"; railroad car inventor George Pullman (b.New York 1831–97); meat-packer Philip Armour (b.New York, 1832–1901); merchant Marshall Field (b.Massachusetts, 1834–1906); merchant Aaron Montgomery Ward (b.New Jersey, 1843–1913); sporting-goods manufacturer Albert G. Spalding (1850–1915); breakfast-food manufacturer Charles W. Post (1854–1911); William Rainey Harper (b.Ohio, 1856–1906), first president of the University of Chicago; lawyer Clarence Darrow (b.Ohio, 1857–1938); public utilities magnate Samuel Insull (b.England, 1859–1938); Julius Rosenwald (1862–1932), philanthropist and executive of Sears, Roebuck; advertising executive Albert Lasker (b.Texas, 1880–1952); and *Chicago Tribune* publisher Robert R. McCormick (1880–1955). Thomas R. Cech (b.1937) was a recipient of the 1989 Nobel prize for chemistry. Jerome Friedman (b.1930), 1990 co-recipient of the Nobel Prize for physics, in Chicago. Harry M. Markowitz (b.1927) won the Nobel prize for economics in 1990. Michael Bishop (b.1936) was a recipient of the 1989 Nobel Prize for physiology or medicine.

Artists who worked for significant periods in Illinois (usually in Chicago) include architects William Le Baron Jenney (b.Massachusetts, 1832–1907), Dankmar Adler (b.Germany, 1844–1900), Daniel H. Burnham (b.New York, 1846–1912), John Wellborn Root (b.Georgia, 1850–91), Louis Sullivan (b.Massachusetts, 1856–1924), Frank Lloyd Wright (b.Wisconsin, 1869–1959), and Ludwig Mies van der Rohe (b.Germany, 1886–1969). Important writers include humorist Finley Peter Dunne (1867–1936), creator of the fictional saloonkeeper-philosopher Mr. Dooley; and novelists Hamlin Garland (b.Wisconsin, 1860–1940), Edgar Rice Burroughs (1875–1950), John Dos Passos (1896–1970), Ernest Hemingway (1899–1961), and James Farrell (1904–79). Poets include Harriet Monroe (1860–1936); Edgar Lee Masters (b.Kansas, 1869–1950); biographer-poet Carl Sandburg (1878–1967); Nicholas Vachel Lindsay (1879–1931); Archibald MacLeish (1892–1982), also librarian of Congress and assistant secretary of state; and Gwendolyn Brooks (b.Kansas, 1917–2000), the first black woman to win a Pulitzer Prize. Robert Butler (b.1945) was the 1993 winner of the Pulitzer Prize for fiction. Performing artists connected with the state include opera stars Mary Garden (b.Scotland, 1877–1967) and Sherrill Milnes (b.1935); clarinetist Benny Goodman (1909–86); pop singers Mel Torme (1925–99) and Grace Slick (b.1939); jazz musician Miles Davis (b.1926–91); showmen Gower Champion (1921–80) and Robert Louis "Bob" Fosse (b.1927–87); comedians Jack Benny (Benjamin Kubelsky, 1894–1974), Harvey Korman (b.1927), Bob Newhart (b.1929), and Richard Pryor (b.1940); and a long list of stage and screen stars, including Gloria Swanson (1899–1983), Ralph Bellamy (b.1904–91), Robert Young (1907–98), Karl Malden (Malden Sekulovich, b.1913), William Holden (1918–81), Jason Robards, Jr. (1922–2000), Charlton Heston (b.1922), Rock Hudson (Roy Fitzgerald, 1925–85), Donald O'Connor (b.1925), Bruce Dern (b.1936), and Raquel Welch (Raquel Tejeda, b.1942). Dominant figures in the Illinois sports world include Ernest "Ernie" Banks (b.Texas, 1931) of the Chicago Cubs; Robert "Bobby" Hull (b.Canada, 1939) of the Chicago Black Hawks; owner George Halas (1895–83) and running backs Harold Edward "Red" Grange (b.Pennsylvania, 1903–91), Gale Sayers (b.Kansas, 1943), and Walter Payton (b.Mississippi, 1954–1999) of the Chicago Bears; and collegiate football coach Amos Alonzo Stagg (b.New Jersey, 1862–1965).

⁵⁰BIBLIOGRAPHY

Carrier, Lois. *Illinois: Crossroads of a Continent*. Urbana: University of Illinois Press, 1993.

Gove, Samuel Kimball. *Illinois Politics & Government: The Expanding Metropolitan Frontier*. Lincoln: University of Nebraska, 1996.

Hendricks, Wanda A. *Gender, Race, and Politics in the Midwest: Black Club Women in Illinois*. Bloomington: Indiana University Press, 1998.

Illinois, State of. Department of Commerce and Community Affairs. *Illinois Data Book*, Springfield. 1994.

Jensen, Richard J. *Illinois: A Bicentennial History*. New York: Norton, 1978.

Leonard, Gerald. *The Invention of Party Politics: Federalism, Popular Sovereignty, and Constitutional Development in Jacksonian Illinois*. Chapel Hill: University of North Carolina Press, 2002.

Meyer, Douglas K. *Making the Heartland Quilt: A Geographical History of Settlement and Migration in Early-Nineteenth-Century Illinois*. Carbondale: Southern Illinois University Press, 2000.

Petterchak, Janice A., ed. *Illinois History: An Annotated Bibliography*. Westport, Conn.: Greenwood, 1995.

Simeone, James. *Democracy and Slavery in Frontier Illinois: The Bottomland Republic*. DeKalb: Northern Illinois University Press, 2000.

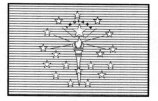

INDIANA

State of Indiana

ORIGIN OF STATE NAME: Named "land of Indians" for the many Indian tribes that formerly lived in the state. **NICKNAME:** The Hoosier State. **CAPITAL:** Indianapolis. **ENTERED UNION:** 11 December 1816 (19th). **SONG:** "On the Banks of the Wabash, Far Away." **MOTTO:** The Crossroads of America. **FLAG:** A flaming torch representing liberty is surrounded by 19 gold stars against a blue background. The word "Indiana" is above the flame. **OFFICIAL SEAL:** In a pioneer setting, a farmer fells a tree while a buffalo flees from the forest and across the prairie; in the background, the sun sets over distant hills. The words "Seal of the State of Indiana 1816" surround the scene. **BIRD:** Cardinal. **FLOWER:** Peony. **TREE:** Tulip poplar. **STONE:** Indiana limestone. **POEM:** "Indiana." **LEGAL HOLIDAYS:** New Year's Day, 1 January; Birthday of Martin Luther King, Jr., 3rd Monday in January; Lincoln's Birthday, 12 February; Washington's Birthday, 3rd Monday in February; Good Friday, March or April; Primary Election Day, 1st Tuesday after 1st Monday in May in even-numbered years; Memorial Day, last Monday in May; Independence Day, 4 July; Labor Day, 1st Monday in September; Columbus Day, 2nd Monday in October; Election Day, 1st Tuesday after 1st Monday in November in even-numbered years; Veterans Day, 11 November; Thanksgiving Day, 4th Thursday in November; Christmas Day, 25 December. **TIME:** 7 AM EST = noon GMT; 6 AM CST = noon GMT.

¹LOCATION, SIZE, AND EXTENT

Situated in the eastern north-central US, Indiana is the smallest of the 12 midwestern states and ranks 38th in size among the 50 states.

Indiana's total area is 36,185 sq mi (93,720 sq km), of which land takes up 35,932 (93,064 sq km) and water the remaining 253 sq mi (656 sq km). Shaped somewhat like a vertical quadrangle, with irregular borders on the S and W, the state extends about 160 mi (257 km) E-W and about 280 mi (451 km) N-S.

Indiana is bordered on the N by Michigan (with part of the line passing through Lake Michigan); on the E by Ohio; on the SE and S by Kentucky (the entire line formed by the north bank of the Ohio River); and on the W by Illinois (with the line in the SW demarcated by the Wabash River). The total boundary length of Indiana is 1,696 mi (2,729 km).

Indiana's geographical center is located in Boone County, 14 mi (23 km) NNW of Indianapolis.

²TOPOGRAPHY

Indiana has two principal types of terrain: slightly rolling land in the northern half of the state and rugged hills in the southern, extending to the Ohio River. The highest point in the state, a hill in Franklin Township (Wayne County), is 1,257 ft (383 m) above sea level; the lowest point, on the Ohio River, is 320 ft (98 m). The richest soil is in the north-central region, where the retreating glacier during the last Ice Age enriched the soil, scooped out lakes, and cut passageways for rivers.

Four-fifths of the state's land is drained by the Wabash River, which flows westward across the north-central region and turns southward to empty into the Ohio, and by its tributaries, the White, Eel, Mississinewa, and Tippecanoe rivers. The northern region is drained by the Maumee River, which flows into Lake Erie at Toledo, Ohio, and by the Kankakee River, which joins the Illinois River in Illinois. In the southwest, the two White River forks empty into the Wabash, and in the southeast, the Whitewater River flows into the Ohio.

In addition to Lake Michigan on the northwestern border, there are more than 400 lakes in the northern part of the state. The largest lakes include Wawasee, Maxinkuckee, Freeman, and Shafer. There are mineral springs at French Lick and West Baden in Orange County, and two large caves at Wyandotte and Marengo in adjoining Crawford County.

The underlying rock strata found in Indiana were formed from sediments deposited during the Paleozoic era, when the land was submerged. About 400 million years ago, the first uplift of land, the Cincinnati arch, divided the Indiana region into two basins, a small one in the north and a large one in the southwest. The land was steadily elevated and at one time formed a lush swamp, which dried up some 200 million years ago when the climate cooled. During the Ice Ages, about five-sixths of the land lay under ice some 2,000 ft (600 m) thick. The retreat of the glacier more than 10,000 years ago left excellent topsoil and drainage conditions in Indiana.

³CLIMATE

Temperatures vary from the extreme north to the extreme south of the state; the annual mean temperature is 49°F–58°F (9°C–12°C) in the north and 57°F (14°C) in the south. The annual mean for Indianapolis is 52°F (11°C). Although Indiana sometimes has temperatures below 0°F (–18°C) during the winter, the average temperatures in January range between 17°F (–8°C) and 35°F (2°C). Average temperatures during July vary from 63°F (17°C) to 88°F (31°C). The record high for the state was 116°F (47°C) set on 14 July 1936 at Collegeville; the record low was –36°F (–38°C) on 19 January 1994 at New Whiteland.

The growing season averages 155 days in the north and 185 days in the south. Rainfall is distributed fairly evenly throughout the year, although drought sometimes occurs in the southern region. The average annual precipitation in the state is 40 in (102 cm), ranging from about 35 in (89 cm) near Lake Michigan to 45 in (114 cm) along the Ohio River; during 1971–2000, Indianapolis had an average of 41 in (104 cm) per year. The annual snowfall in Indiana averages less than 22 in (56 cm).

Average wind speed in the state is 8 mph (13 km/hr), but gales sometimes occur along the shores of Lake Michigan, and there are occasional tornadoes in the interior.

⁴FLORA AND FAUNA

Because the state has a relatively uniform climate, plant species are distributed fairly generally throughout Indiana. There are 124 native tree species, including 17 varieties of oak, as well as black walnut, sycamore, and tulip tree (yellow poplar), the state tree. Fruit trees—apple, cherry, peach, and pear—are common. Local indigenous species—now reduced because of industrialization and urbanization—are the persimmon, black gum, and southern cypress along the Ohio River; tamarack and bog willow in the northern marsh; and white pine, sassafras, and pawpaw near Lake Michigan. American elderberry and bittersweet are common shrubs, while various jack-in-the-pulpits and spring beauties are among the indigenous wild flowers. The peony is the state flower. As of August 2003, Mead's milkweed and Pitcher's thistle were considered threatened and Short's goldenrod and running buffalo clover were considered endangered.

Although the presence of wolves and coyotes has been reported occasionally, the red fox is Indiana's only common carnivorous mammal. Other native mammals are the common cottontail, muskrat, raccoon, opossum, and several types of squirrel. Many waterfowl and marsh birds, including the black duck and great blue heron, inhabit northern Indiana, while the field sparrow, yellow warbler, and red-headed woodpecker nest in central Indiana. Various catfish, pike, bass, and sunfish are native to state waters.

The US Fish and Wildlife Service listed 25 Indiana animal species as threatened or endangered as of August 2003. Among these are the bald eagle, Indiana and gray bats, gray wolf, piping plover, and two species of butterfly.

⁵ENVIRONMENTAL PROTECTION

During the 19th century, early settlers cut down much of Indiana's forests for farms, leaving the land vulnerable to soil erosion and flood damage, particularly in the southern part of the state. In 1919, the legislature created the State Department of Conservation (which in 1965 became the Department of Natural Resources) to reclaim worn-out soil, prevent further erosion, and control pollution of rivers and streams. In 1986 the Indiana Department of Environmental Management was initiated as a watchdog over the environmental laws and regulations designated to preserving the environmental well being of the state. Still, almost 85% of Indiana's original wetlands have been lost and, in 1997, it was estimated that the state continues to lose 1–3% of its remaining wetlands per year.

The Department of Natural Resources regulates the use of Indiana's lands, waters, forests, and wildlife resources. Specifically, the department manages land subject to flooding, preserves natural rivers and streams, grants mining permits and regulates strip-mining, plugs and repairs faulty/abandoned oil and gas wells, administers existing state parks and preserves and buys land for new ones, regulates hunting and fishing, and examines any damage to fish and wildlife by investigating industrial accidents. Also, the department is responsible for preventing soil erosion and flood damage, and for conserving and disposing of water in the state's watersheds.

The Indiana Department of Environmental Management (IDEM) seeks to protect public health through the implementation and management of various environmental programs. The focus of the environmental programs is to protect Indiana's air, land and water resources, since the proper management of these resources contribute to the health and well being of the citizens of Indiana. Prior to April 1986, these environmental programs were under the auspices of the State Board of Health (ISBH).

In addition to IDEM and the Department of Natural Resources the following boards exist to aid in environmental involvement: Air Pollution Control Board, Water Pollution Control Board, Pollution Prevention Control Board, and the Solid Waste Management Board.

In 1990, Indiana lawmakers passed landmark legislation that created an Office of Pollution Prevention and Technical Assistance within IDEM. OPPTA's long-term goal is to ensure that all Indiana industries use pollution prevention techniques as the preferred method for reducing waste and protecting the environment. This policy, along with programs that encourage reuse and recycling and discourage landfilling and incineration, will help conserve natural resources.

In March 1990, Indiana's Water Pollution Control Board adopted some of the strictest water quality standards in the nation. The standards set criteria for more than 90 chemicals and designated almost all water bodies for protection of aquatic life and recreational use. These standards will help improve and protect the quality of water in Indiana's lakes, rivers, and streams.

IDEM devotes much attention to identifying, cleaning up, and remediating all forms of toxic contamination. On 31 January 1986 the agency gained federal delegation for the Resource Conservation and Recovery Act (RCRA), which governs the generation, storage, treatment, transport, and disposal of all hazardous waste. Beyond RCRA, IDEM encourages companies to examine their production cycles and to adopt processes that won't create hazardous waste. The Department of Environmental Management offers technical assistance for the installation of pollution prevention equipment and encourages consumers to rethink their use and disposal of hazardous household goods and chemicals. When that waste is not properly handled and disposed of, expensive remediation is often required. In 2003, the Environmental Protection Agency's database listed 210 hazardous waste sites, 28 of which were on the National Priorities List, in Indiana.

Since IDEM was established in 1986, enforcement activity has increased fivefold. This is due, in part, to its unified Office of Enforcement, which consolidated enforcement staff who had been working separately in offices for air, solid waste, hazardous waste, and water. A key strategy in enforcement actions is to encourage violators to adopt pollution prevention practices or restore environmental damage as part of their penalty.

Some of the state's most serious environmental challenges lie in Lake and Porter counties in Northwest Indiana. A century of spills, emissions and discharges to the environment there require comprehensive, regionally coordinated programs. In 1991, IDEM opened a regional office in Gary to act as a liaison with local officials, concerned citizens, and industry. This office is helping drive the development of a comprehensive remediation plan, including the involvement of concerned citizens through the Citizen's Advisory for the Remediation of the Environment (CARE) committee. The Northwest Indiana Remedial Action Plan (RAP) is a three-phased program designed especially for the Grand Calumet River and the Indiana Harbor Ship Canal. Both waterways are heavily contaminated and, if left in their current state, would certainly degrade the waters of Lake Michigan, the primary source of drinking water for the Northwest Indiana area.

The RAP is a direct result of treaties of the International Joint Commission, a coalition formed to protect the waters between the United States and Canada.

IDEM now offers expertise and approval for voluntary cleanup plans. When a voluntary cleanup is completed properly, IDEM will issue a certificate of completion, and the governor will provide a covenant not to sue for further action involving the

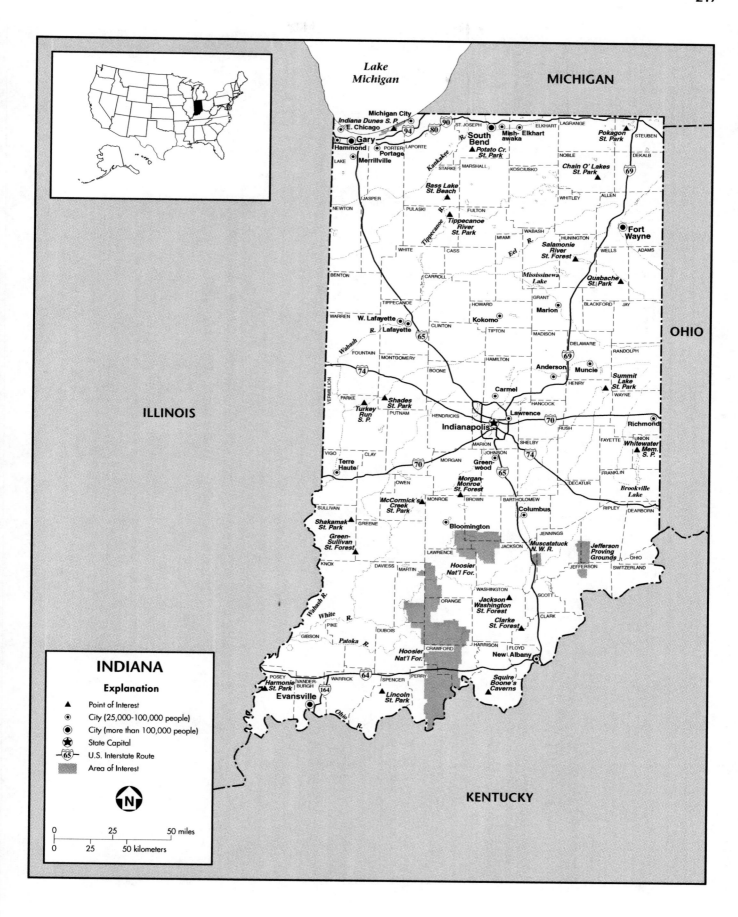

INDIANA

Explanation

▲   Point of Interest

◉   City (25,000-100,000 people)

◉   City (more than 100,000 people)

★   State Capital

🛣65   U.S. Interstate Route

▨   Area of Interest

0   25   50 miles

0   25   50 kilometers

damage revealed to IDEM. This innovative program has led to many cleanups at virtually no cost to Indiana citizens. In 2001, Indiana received $75,183,000 in federal grants from the Environmental Protection Agency; EPA expenditures for procurement contracts in Indiana that year amounted to $4,009,000.

⁶POPULATION

Indiana ranked 14th in population in the US with an estimated total of 6,159,068 in 2002, an increase of 1.3% since 2000. Between 1990 and 2000, Indiana's population grew from 5,544,159 to 6,080,485, an increase of 9.7%. The population is projected to reach 6,215,000 by 2005 and 6.5 million by 2025. The population density in 2000 was 169.5 persons per sq mi.

In 2000 the median age was 35.2. Persons under 18 years old accounted for 25.9% of the population while 12.4% were age 65 or older.

Although the French founded the first European settlement in Indiana in 1717, the census population was no more than 5,641 in 1800, when the Indiana Territory was established. Settlers flocked to the state during the territorial period, and the population rose to 24,520 by 1810. After Indiana became a state in 1816, its population grew even more rapidly, reaching 147,178 in 1820 and 988,416 in 1850. At the outbreak of the Civil War, Indiana had 1,350,428 inhabitants and ranked 5th in population among the states.

Indiana was relatively untouched by the great waves of European immigration that swept the US from 1860 to 1880. In 1880, when the state's population was 1,978,301, Indiana had fewer foreign-born residents (about 7% of its population) than any other northern state. Indiana doubled its 1900 population to 5,193,669 by the time of the 1970 census.

Indianapolis, the capital and largest city, expanded its boundaries in 1970 to coincide with those of Marion County, thereby increasing its area to 388 sq mi (1,005 sq km) and its

Indiana Counties, County Seats, and County Areas and Populations

COUNTY	COUNTY SEAT	LAND AREA (SQ MI)	POPULATION (2002 EST.)	COUNTY	COUNTY SEAT	LAND AREA (SQ MI)	POPULATION (2002 EST.)
Adams	Decatur	340	33,500	Madison	Anderson	453	132,068
Allen	Fort Wayne	659	337,512	Marion	Indianapolis	396	863,429
Bartholomew	Columbus	409	71,636	Marshall	Plymouth	444	45,735
Benton	Fowler	407	9,207	Martin	Shoals	339	10,370
Blackford	Hardford City	166	13,804	Miami	Peru	369	36,199
Boone	Lebanon	424	48,277	Monroe	Bloomington	385	121,229
Brown	Nashville	312	15,211	Montgomery	Crawfordsville	505	37,957
Carroll	Delphi	372	20,226	Morgan	Martinsville	409	67,791
Cass	Logansport	414	40,752	Newton	Kentland	401	14,360
Clark	Jeffersonville	376	98,198	Noble	Albion	413	47,209
Clay	Brazil	360	26,357	Ohio	Rising Sun	87	5,804
Clinton	Frankfort	405	33,972	Orange	Paoli	408	19,433
Crawford	English	307	11,076	Owen	Spencer	386	22,541
Davies	Washington	432	29,851	Parke	Rockville	444	17,262
Dearborn	Lawrenceburg	307	47,333	Perry	Cannelton	481	18,827
Decatur	Greensburg	373	24,515	Pike	Petersburg	341	12,908
Dekalb	Auburn	364	40,525	Porter	Valparaiso	419	150,403
Delaware	Muncie	392	118,197	Posey	Mt.vernon	410	26,990
Dubois	Jasper	429	40,015	Pulaski	Winamac	435	13,731
Elkhart	Goshen	466	186,465	Putnam	Greencastle	482	36,440
Fayette	Connersville	215	25,249	Randolph	Winchester	454	27,191
Floyd	New Albany	150	71,633	Ripley	Versailles	447	27,525
Fountain	Covington	398	17,700	Rush	Rushville	408	17,918
Franklin	Brookville	385	22,585	St. Joseph	South Bend	459	267,120
Fulton	Rochester	369	20,728	Scott	Scottsburg	192	23,334
Gibson	Princeton	490	32,590	Shelby	Shelbyville	412	43,674
Grant	Marion	415	72,189	Spencer	Rockport	400	20,353
Greene	Bloomfield	546	33,155	Starke	Knox	309	22,832
Hamilton	Noblesville	398	205,610	Steuben	Angola	308	33,429
Hancock	Greenfield	307	58,343	Sullivan	Sullivan	452	21,825
Harrison	Corydon	486	35,244	Switzerland	Vevay	224	9,410
Hendricks	Danville	409	114,301	Tippecanoe	Lafayette	502	152,001
Henry	New Castle	395	47,983	Tipton	Tipton	261	16,534
Howard	Kokomo	293	84,838	Union	Liberty	163	7,440
Huntington	Huntington	366	38,243	Vanderburgh	Evansville	236	171,744
Jackson	Brownstown	514	41,557	Vermillion	Newport	260	16,499
Jasper	Rensselaer	561	30,815	Vigo	Terre Haute	405	105,078
Jay	Portland	384	21,630	Wabash	Wabash	398	34,655
Jefferson	Madison	363	32,113	Warren	Williamsport	366	8,747
Jennings	Vernon	378	28,192	Warrick	Boonville	391	53,624
Johnson	Franklin	321	121,604	Washington	Salem	516	27,618
Knox	Vincennes	520	38,531	Wayne	Richmond	404	70,547
Kosciusko	Warsaw	540	74,794	Wells	Bluffton	370	27,796
Lagrange	Lagrange	380	35,410	White	Monticello	506	24,985
Lake	Crown Point	501	487,016	Whitley	Columbia City	336	31,339
Laporte	Laporte	600	110,384				
Lawrence	Bedford	452	46,097	Totals		35,932	6,159,068

population by some 50% (the city and county limits also include four self-governing communities). The estimated population was 783,612 in 2002, and the Indianapolis metropolitan area had an estimated population of 1,536,665 in 1999. Other cities with 2002 populations estimated at more than 100,000 were Fort Wayne, 210,070; Evansville, 119,081; South Bend, 106,558; and Gary, 100,945. All of these cities suffered population declines in the 1970s, 1980s, and 1990s.

[7] ETHNIC GROUPS

Originally an agricultural state, Indiana was settled by Native Americans moving west, by a small group of French Creoles, and by European immigrant farmers. Although railroad building and industrialization attracted other immigrant groups—notably the Irish, Hungarians, Italians, Poles, Croats, Slovaks, and Syrians—foreign immigration to Indiana declined sharply in the 20th century, although there was a rebound in the final decade. As of 2000, foreign-born Hoosiers numbered 186,534 (3% of the total state population), nearly double the figure of 94,263 in 1990.

Restrictions on foreign immigration and the availability of jobs spurred the migration of black Americans to Indiana after World War I; by 2000, the state had 510,034 blacks, representing about 8.4% of the total population. Approximately one-fifth of all Indiana blacks live in the industrial city of Gary.

In 2000, approximately 3.5% (214,536) of Indiana's population was of Hispanic or Latino origin, up sharply from 1.8% (99,000) in 1990. The Asian population was estimated at 59,126 in 2000, including 14,685 Asian Indians (up from 6,093 in 1990), 12,531 Chinese (6,128 in 1990), 6,674 Filipinos, 7,502 Koreans, 5,065 Japanese, and 4,843 Vietnamese (2,420 in 1990). Pacific Islanders numbered 2,005.

The natives of early-19th-century Indiana came from a variety of Algonkian-speaking tribes, including Delaware, Shawnee, and Potawatomi. By 1846, however, all Indian lands in the state had been seized or ceded, and most Indians had been removed. In 2000, there were 15,815 Native Americans.

[8] LANGUAGES

Several Algonkian Indian tribes, including some from the east, met the white settlers who arrived in Indiana in the early 1800s. The heritage of the Delaware, Potawatomi, Miami, and other groups survives in many place-names, from Kokomo to Nappanee, Muncie, and Shipshewana.

Except for the dialect mixture in the industrial northwest corner and for the Northern-dialect fringe of counties along the Michigan border, Indiana speech is essentially that of the South Midland pioneers from south of the Ohio River, with a transition zone toward North Midland north of Indianapolis. Between the Ohio River and Indianapolis, South Midland speakers use evening for late afternoon, eat *clabber cheese* instead of cottage cheese, are wary of *frogstools* rather than toadstools, once held that *toadfrogs* and not plain toads caused warts, eat *goobers* instead of peanuts at a ball game, and may therefore be *sick at the stomach*. In the same region, some Hoosiers use a few Midland words that also occur north of Indianapolis, such as *rock fence* (stone wall), *French harp* (harmonica), *mud dauber* (wasp), *shucks* (leaves on an ear of corn), and perhaps even some expanding North Midland words, such as *run* (a small stream), *teetertotter* (seesaw), and *fishworm*. North of Indianapolis, speakers with a Midland Pennsylvania background wish on the *pullybone* of a chicken, may use a *trestle* (sawhorse), and are likely to get their hands *greezy* rather than *greasy*. Such was the Hoosier talk of James Whitcomb Riley.

In 2000, 93.5% of all Hoosiers five years old and older spoke only English at home, down from 95.2% in 1990.

The following table gives selected statistics from the 2000 census for language spoken at home by persons five years old and over. The category "Other West Germanic languages" includes Dutch, Pennsylvania Dutch, and Afrikaans. The category "Other Slavic languages" includes Czech, Slovak, and Ukrainian.

LANGUAGE	NUMBER	PERCENT
Population 5 years and over	5,657,818	100.0
Speak only English	5,295,736	93.6
Speak a language other than English	362,082	6.4
Speak a language other than English	362,082	6.4
Spanish or Spanish Creole	185,576	3.3
German	44,142	0.8
French (incl. Patois, Cajun)	18,065	0.3
Other West Germanic languages	15,706	0.3
Chinese	9,912	0.2
Polish	7,831	0.1
Serbo-Croatian	5,843	0.1
Japanese	5,339	0.1
Arabic	5,338	0.1
Other Slavic languages	5,129	0.1
Korean	5,032	0.1
Italian	4,798	0.1
Vietnamese	4,746	0.1
Greek	4,233	0.1
Tagalog	4,016	0.1

[9] RELIGIONS

The first branch of Christianity to gain a foothold in Indiana was Roman Catholicism, introduced by the French settlers in the early 18th century. The first Protestant church was founded near Charlestown by Baptists from Kentucky in 1798. Three years later, a Methodist church was organized at Springville; in 1806, Presbyterians established a church near Vincennes; and the following year, Quakers built their first meetinghouse at Richmond. The Disciples of Christ, Lutherans, the United Brethren, Mennonites, and Jews were among the later 19th-century arrivals.

A dissident religious sect, the Shakers, established a short-lived community in Sullivan County in 1808. In 1815, some German separatists, led by George Rapp, founded a community called the Harmonie Society, which flourished briefly. Rapp moved his followers to Pennsylvania and sold the town to a Scottish social reformer, Robert Owen, in 1825. Owen renamed the town New Harmony and tried to establish a nonreligious utopia there, but the experiment failed after three years. A group of religious dissidents founded the Pentecostal Church of God at Beaver Dam in 1881; the world headquarters of the church, which had 101,921 adherents nationwide in 2000, is now at Anderson. The Youth for Christ movement started in Indianapolis in 1943.

In 2000, the Roman Catholic Church was the largest single denomination with about 836,009 adherents in 462 congregations. The largest Protestant denominations were the United Methodist Church (with 288,308 adherents in 1,286 congregations), the Church of Christ (205,408 adherents), the Southern Baptist Convention (124,452), the American Baptist Church (115,101), and the Lutheran Church—Missouri Synod (111,522). The estimated Jewish population of the state in 2000 was 18,000, down from 20,314 members in 1990. The Muslim community had about 11,000 members in 2000. There were also over 17,000 Mennonites and over 19,000 members of Amish communities statewide. About 57% of the population (over 3.4 million people) were not counted as members of any religious organization.

[10] TRANSPORTATION

Indiana's central location in the US and its position between Lake Michigan to the north and the Ohio River to the south gave the state its motto, "The Crossroads of America." Historically, the state took advantage of its strategic location by digging canals to connect Indiana rivers and by building roads and railroads to provide farmers access to national markets.

The success of the state's first railroad, completed in 1847 between Madison and Indianapolis, led to a tenfold increase in track mileage during the 1850s, and more railroad expansion took place after the Civil War. In 2000, there were 42 railroads operating on 4,685 rail mi (7,539 km) of track; Class I railroads operated 3,418 route mi (5,500 km) of track in Indiana. About 62% of the rail freight terminating within the state in 1998 was coal. Regularly scheduled Amtrak passenger trains served Indianapolis, Fort Wayne, Hammond/Whiting, South Bend, and 10 other stations in the state. Indianapolis and other major cities have public transit systems subsidized heavily by the state and federal governments. The South Shore commuter railroad connects South Bend, Gary, and East Chicago with Chicago, Illinois.

The east–west National Road (US 40) reached Indiana in 1827, and the north–south Michigan road (US 421) was built in the late 1830s. In 2000, there were 93,607 mi (150,645 km) of public roads, of which 73,664 mi (118,550 km) were considered rural. In 2001, motor vehicle registrations totaled 5,752,405. There were 3,857,139 licensed drivers in 2001. Several of the nation's largest moving companies have their headquarters in Indiana.

Water transportation has been important from the earliest years of European settlement. The Wabash and Erie Canal, constructed in the 1830s from Fort Wayne east to Toledo, Ohio, and southwest to Lafayette, was vital to the state's market economy. In 1836, the state legislature earmarked $10 million for an ambitious network of canals, but excessive construction costs and the financial panic of 1837 caused the state to go virtually bankrupt and default on its bonds. Nevertheless, the Wabash canal was extended to Terre Haute and Evansville by the early 1850s.

The transport of freight via Lake Michigan and the Ohio River helped to spark Indiana's industrial development. A deepwater port on Lake Michigan, which became operational in 1970, provided access to world markets via the St. Lawrence Seaway. Indiana Harbor handled 16.1 million tons of goods in 2002, and the tonnage at the port of Gary was nearly 9.7 million.

In 2000, there were 516 public and private airports in the state. Indianapolis International Airport is the state's busiest airport, with 3,629,716 passengers enplaned in 2000.

11 HISTORY

When the first human beings inhabited Indiana is not known. Hundreds of sites used by primitive hunters, fishermen, and food gatherers before 1000 BC have been found in Indiana. Burial mounds of the Woodland culture (1000 BC to AD 900), when the bow and arrow appeared, have been located across the state. The next culture, called Mississippian and dating about AD 900 to 1500, is marked by gardens, ceramics, tools, weapons, trade, and social organization. It is well illustrated by remains of an extensive village on the north side of the Ohio River near Newburgh. The unidentified inhabitants are believed to have come up from the south about 1300, for reasons not known, and to have migrated back before 1500, again for unknown reasons.

The next Indian invaders, and the first to be seen by white men, were the Miami and Potawatomi tribes that drifted down the west side of Lake Michigan and turned across the northern sector of what is now Indiana after the middle of the 17th century. The Kickapoo and Wea tribes pushed into upper Indiana from northern Illinois. The southern two-thirds of the present state was a vast hunting ground, without villages.

The first European penetration was made in the 1670s by the French explorers Father Jacques Marquette and René-Robert Cavelier, Sieur de la Salle. After the founding of Detroit in 1701, the Maumee-Wabash river route to the lower Ohio was discovered. At the portage between the two rivers, Jean Baptiste Bissot, Sieur de Vincennes, lived at Kekionga, the principal village of the Miami and the present site of Fort Wayne. The first French fort was built farther down the Wabash among the Wea, near modern Lafayette, in 1717. Three years later, Fort Miami was erected. Vincennes's son constructed another fort on the Wabash in 1732, at the site of the town later named for him.

English traders venturing down the Ohio River disputed the French trade monopoly, and as a result of the French and Indian War, French Canada was given up to the British in 1760. Indians under Chief Pontiac captured the two forts in northern Indiana, and the area was not securely in English hands until 1765. The pre-Revolutionary turbulence in the Atlantic seaboard colonies was hardly felt in Indiana, although the region did not escape the Revolutionary War itself. Colonel George Rogers Clark, acting for Virginia, captured Vincennes from a British garrison early in 1779 after a heroic march. Two years later, a detachment of 108 Pennsylvanians, passing down the Ohio to reinforce Clark, was surprised by a force of French Canadians and Indians under Mohawk Captain Joseph Brant; most of the Pennsylvanians were killed during the battle or after capture.

Following the Revolutionary War, the area northwest of the Ohio River was granted to the new nation; known as the Northwest Territory, it included present-day Indiana, Ohio, Illinois, Michigan, Wisconsin, and part of Minnesota. The first US settlement in Indiana was made in 1784 on land opposite Louisville, Ky., granted to Clark's veterans by Virginia. (The new town, called Clarksville, still exists.) Americans also moved into Vincennes. Government was established by the Continental Congress under the Northwest Ordinance of 1787. Again, Indiana unrest endangered all settlements north of the Ohio, and the small US army, with headquarters at Cincinnati, met defeat at what is now Fort Wayne in 1790 and disaster in neighboring Ohio in 1791. General Anthony Wayne was put in command of an enlarged army and defeated the Indians in 1794 at Fallen Timbers (near Toledo, Ohio). British meddling was ended by Jay's treaty later the same year. Wayne then built a new fort—named for him—among the Miami.

In 1800, as Ohio prepared to enter the Union, the rest of the Northwest Territory was set off and called Indiana Territory, with its capital at Vincennes. There Elihu Stout established a newspaper, the Indiana Gazette, in 1804. After Michigan Territory was detached in 1805, and Illinois Territory in 1809, Indiana assumed its present boundaries. The federal census counted 24,520 people in Indiana in 1810, including a new Swiss colony on the Ohio, where settlers planted vineyards and made wine.

William Henry Harrison was appointed first governor and, with a secretary and three appointed judges, constituted the government of Indiana Territory. Under the Northwest Ordinance, when the population reached 5,000 adult males, it was allowed to elect an assembly and nominate candidates for an upper house. When the population totaled 60,000—as it did in 1815—the voters were allowed to write a state constitution and to apply for admission to the Union. A short constitution excluding slavery and recommending public schools was adopted and Indiana became the 19th state on 11 December 1816.

Meanwhile, Indiana had seen Governor Harrison lead US troops up the Wabash in 1811 and beat off an Indian attack at Tippecanoe. The War of 1812 took Harrison away from Indiana, and battles were fought in other theaters. Hoosiers suffered Indian raids, and two forts were besieged for a few days. After the war, new settlers began pouring into the state from the upper South and in fewer numbers from Ohio, Pennsylvania, New York, and New England. A group of German Pietists under George Rapp settled Harmonie on the lower Wabash in 1815 and stayed 10 years before selling out to Robert Owen, a visionary with utopian dreams that failed at the village he renamed New

Harmony. In 1816, Tom Lincoln brought his family from Kentucky, and his son Abe grew up in southern Indiana from age 7 to 21.

Unlike most other states, Indiana was settled from south to north. The inhabitants were called Hoosiers; the origin of the word is obscure, but the term may have come from an Anglo-Saxon word for hill dwellers. Central and northern Indiana were opened up as land was purchased from the Indians. The Potawatomi were forced to go west in 1838, and the Miami left in 1846. Commerce flowed south to the Ohio River in the form of corn, hogs, whiskey, and timber. Indianapolis was laid out as a planned city and centrally located capital in 1820, but 30 years passed before its population caught up to the size of Madison and New Albany on the Ohio.

An overambitious program of internal improvements (canals and roads) in the 1830s plunged the state into debts it could not pay. Railroads, privately financed, began to tie Indiana commercially with the East. The Irish came to dig canals and lay the rails, and Germans, many of them Catholics, came to do woodworking and farming. Levi Coffin, a Quaker who moved to Fountain City in 1826, opened a different kind of road, the Underground Railroad, to help escaping slaves from the South.

A new constitution in 1851 showed Jacksonian preferences for more elective offices, shorter terms, a one-term governorship, limited biennial legislative sessions, county government, obligatory common schools, and severe limits on state debt. But this constitution also prohibited blacks from entering the state.

Hoosiers showed considerable sympathy with the South in the 1850s, and there was considerable "copperhead" activity in the early 1860s. Nevertheless, Indiana remained staunchly in the Union under Governor Oliver P. Morton, sending some 200,000 soldiers to the Civil War. The state suffered no battles, but General John Hunt Morgan's Confederate cavalry raided the southeastern sector of Indiana in July 1863.

After the Civil War, small local industries expanded rapidly. The first nonfarm enterprises were gristmills, sawmills, meat-packing plants, distilleries and breweries, leatherworking shops, furniture factories, and steamboat and carriage makers. Wagons made by Studebaker in South Bend won fame during the war, as did Van Camp's canned pork and beans from Indianapolis. Discovery of natural gas in several northeastern counties in 1886, and the resultant low fuel prices, spurred the growth of glass factories. Elwood Haynes of Kokomo designed a one-cylinder horseless carriage in 1894 and drove it. As America became infatuated with the new autos, 375 Indiana factories started turning them out. A racetrack for testing cars was built outside Indianapolis in 1908, and the famous 500-mi (805-km) race on Memorial Day weekend began in 1911. Five years earlier, US Steel had constructed a steel plant at the south end of Lake Michigan. The town built by the company to house the workers was called Gary, and it grew rapidly with the help of the company and the onset of World War I. Oil refineries were developed in the same area, known as the Calumet region.

Of the millions of immigrants who flocked to the US from 1870 to 1914, very few settled in Indiana. The percentage of foreign-born residents declined from 9% in 1860 to 7% in 1880, all of them from northern Europe and over half from Germany. By 1920, the percentage was down to 5%, although some workers from southern and eastern Europe had gravitated to the industries of the Calumet.

Although many Hoosiers of German and Irish descent favored neutrality when World War I began, Indiana industries eventually boomed with war orders, and public sympathy swung heavily toward the Allies. Indiana furnished 118,000 men and women to the armed forces and suffered the loss of 3,370—a much smaller participation than in the Civil War, from a population more than twice the size.

After 1920, only about a dozen makes of cars were still being manufactured in Indiana, and those factories steadily lost out to the Big Three car makers in Detroit. The exception was Studebaker in South Bend, which grew to more than 23,000 employees during World War II. The company finally closed its doors in 1965. Auto parts continued to be a big business, however, along with steelmaking and oil refining in the Calumet region. Elsewhere there was manufacturing of machinery, farm implements, railway cars, furniture, and pharmaceuticals. Meat-packing, coal mining, and limestone quarrying continued to be important. With increasing industrialization, cities grew, particularly in the northern half of the state, and the number of farms diminished. The balance of rural and urban population, about even in 1920, tilted in favor of urban dwellers.

World War II had a greater impact on Indiana than did World War I. Most factories converted to production of war materials; 300 held defense orders in 1942. Du Pont built a huge powder plant near Charlestown. The slack in employment was taken up, women went into factories, more rural families moved to cities, and military training facilities were created. The enormous Jefferson Proving Ground tested ammunition and parachutes.

After the war, many locally small industries were taken over by national corporations, and their plants were expanded. By 1984, the largest employer in Indiana was General Motors, with 47,800 employees in six cities. Inland Steel, with 18,500 workers, was 2nd, followed by US Steel with 13,800 workers. Although the state's population in the mid-1980s was about two-thirds urban and one-third rural, agriculture retained much of its importance.

Nostalgia for an older, simpler, rural way of life pervades much Hoosier thinking. The shoreline area of industrial Gary notwithstanding (although it, too, was the subject of cleanups during the 1990s), Indiana stands high in conservation, owing to the vision of Richard Lieber, a state official who from 1933 to 1944 promoted the preservation of land for state parks and recreational areas as well as for state and federal forests.

The percentage of registered voters in Indiana who participate in elections generally exceeded the national average by a wide margin. The evenness of strength between the two major political parties during much of its history has frequently made Indiana a swing state, eagerly courted by Democrats and Republicans alike. In 1967, Democrat Richard Hatcher became one of the nation's first blacks to serve as head of a major city when he was elected mayor of Gary. In 1988 Indiana native son J. Danforth Quayle, then a US senator, was elected vice president of the United States on the Republican ticket with George Bush.

The state legislature was dominated by rural interests until reapportionment in 1966 gave urban counties more representation. Biennial sessions were then changed to annual, although they are still limited in duration. The direct primary for nomination of governor, lieutenant governor, and US senator was mandated in 1975.

In the early 1980s, Indiana, along with the other manufacturing-intensive states, suffered a recession, which was compounded by declining farm prices and high operating costs for farmers. Later in the decade the state's economy improved with the expansion of service industries, which continued through the 1990s. While the state's unemployment rate of 3% in 1999 was below the national average, median income and per capita income levels ranked in the mid-ranges nationally, owing in part to the state's agricultural and manufacturing character. Indiana's business leaders remained concerned in 2000 that Indiana had not attracted enough high-tech companies and that the state's economy was too reliant on the "old economy" manufacturing sector, causing many to worry about the consequences of a downturn. At the same time the Indianapolis area lost several high-profile corporate headquarters.

Educational reform based on increased funding played a prominent role in Indiana public policy in the 1990s. In early 2000 the state was the first in the nation to pass a so-called Ten Commandments law; the legislation allowed the Ten Commandments to be displayed in classrooms, where it would be taught as a historical document.

In October 1999, for the first time in its 183-year history, the state named a black man, Justice Robert D. Rucker, to the Indiana Supreme Court. Governor Frank O'Bannon's appointment won praises from the legal community.

As of January 2003, Indiana had a $300 million budget deficit—like more than half of the 50 states that year that had budget shortfalls. In the struggle to come up with a two-year budget, Republican legislators squared off against Democratic Governor O'Bannon on issues such as funding Medicaid and education.

12 STATE GOVERNMENT

The first state constitution took effect when Indiana became a state in 1816. Reportedly written by convention delegates beneath a huge elm tree in Corydon, the first state capital, the brief document prohibited slavery and recommended a free public school system, including a state university.

This constitution did not allow for amendment, however, and a new constitution that did so was adopted in 1851. The second constitution authorized more elective state officials, gave greater responsibility to county governments, and prohibited the state from going into debt (except under rare circumstances). It also established biennial rather than annual sessions of the state legislature, a provision not repealed until 1971. With amendments (43 as of January 2003), the second constitution is still in effect today.

The Indiana general assembly consists of a 50-member senate elected to four-year terms, with half the senators elected every two years, and a 100-member house of representatives elected to two-year terms. Legislators now meet in annual sessions, beginning the 2nd Monday of January and lasting no longer than 61 legislative days during odd-numbered years (or not past April 30) and no longer than 30 legislative days in even-numbered years (or not past March 15). A member of the general assembly must be a US citizen and have been a resident of Indiana for at least two years and a resident of their district for at least one year. A senator must be at least 25 years old, a representative at least 21 years old. Senators and representatives are paid the same base salary and allowances; legislative leaders receive additional compensation. The legislative salary was $11,600 in 2002, unchanged from 1999.

The state's chief executive is the governor, elected to a 4-year term and eligible for reelection, although ineligible to serve more than eight years in a 12-year period. A governor must be at least 30 years old, a US citizen for at least five years, and a state resident for five years prior to election. Only the governor may call special sessions of the legislature (limited to 30 legislative days or 40 calendar days). The governor may veto bills passed by the legislature, but his veto can be overridden by a majority vote of the elected members in each house. If a bill is left unsigned for seven days (whether or not the legislature is in session), it becomes law. In 2002 the governor's salary was $95,000.

Indiana's other top elected officials are the lieutenant governor, secretary of state, treasurer, auditor, attorney general, and superintendent of public instruction. Each is elected to a four-year term. The lieutenant governor, elected jointly with the governor, is constitutionally empowered to preside over the state senate and to act as governor if the office should become vacant or the incumbent is unable to discharge his duties.

Legislation may be introduced in either house of the general assembly, although bills for raising revenue must originate in the house of representatives. A bill approved by both houses goes to the governor for signing into law; if the governor declines to sign it within seven days, the bill becomes law, but if the governor vetoes it, majorities of at least 26 votes in the senate and 51 votes in the house are required to override the veto. Should the governor veto a bill after the end of a legislative session, it must be returned to the legislature when that body reconvenes.

A proposed amendment to the state constitution must be approved by a majority vote in two successive legislative sessions and be submitted to the voters for approval or rejection at the next general election.

In order to vote in Indiana, a person must be a US citizen, be at least 18 years old, and have been a resident of the voting precinct for 30 days before the next election. Those jailed for criminal convictions may not vote.

13 POLITICAL PARTIES

The Democratic Party has been one of the two major political parties since Indiana became a state in 1816, as has the Republican Party since its inception in 1854. In that year, Hoosiers voted for Democrat James Buchanan for president, but in 1860, the voters supported Republican Abraham Lincoln. After voting Republican in four successive presidential elections, Indiana voted Democratic in 1876 and became a swing state. More recently, a Republican trend has been evident: the state voted Republican in 11 out of 12 presidential elections between 1940 and 1984.

Third-party movements have rarely succeeded in Indiana. Native son Eugene Debs, the Socialist Party leader who was personally popular in Indiana, received only 36,931 votes in the state in 1912, while garnering more than 900,000 votes nationally. Even in 1932, during the Great Depression, Socialist candidate Norman Thomas won only 21,388 votes in Indiana. The most successful third-party movement in recent decades was George Wallace's American Independent Party, which took 243,108 votes (11.5% of the Indiana total) in 1968. In each of the four presidential elections of the 1970s and early 1980s, minority party candidates together received only 1.1% or less of the votes cast.

In 2000, Indiana gave 57% of the vote to Republican George W. Bush, and 41% to Democrat Al Gore. In 1996, Democrat Frank L. O'Bannon was voted in to succeed two-term Democratic governor Evan Bayh; O'Bannon was reelected in 2000. However, O'Bannon suffered a massive stroke in September 2003, and Lieutenant Governor Joseph E. Kernan assumed the role of acting governor while O'Bannon remained in a coma. Republican Richard Lugar won election to his fifth term in the US Senate in 2000. The other Senate seat, which again went to the Republicans in the 1992 election, was surrendered to the Democrats in 1998 when Evan Bayh was voted in.

Indiana's delegation to the US House of Representatives following the 2002 elections included three Democrats and six Republicans. In mid-2003 the state senate had 32 Republicans and 18 Democrats. The state house was narrowly controlled by the Democrats, with 51 representatives to the Republican Party's 49. In 2002 there were 4,008,902 registered voters; there is no party registration in the state. The state had 12 electoral votes in the 2000 presidential election.

14 LOCAL GOVERNMENT

In 1816, when Indians controlled central and northern Indiana, the state had only 15 counties. By 1824, the number of counties had grown to 49. All but one of Indiana's 91 counties were established by 1851. The last county—Newton, in the state's northwest corner—was created in 1859.

Counties in Indiana have traditionally provided law enforcement in rural areas, operated county courts and institutions, maintained county roads, administered public welfare programs, and collected taxes. Under a home-rule law enacted by the state in 1980, they also have "all the power they need for the effective operation of government as to local affairs," or, in effect, all powers not specifically reserved by the state. In 1984, counties were given the power to impose local income taxes.

The county's business is conducted by a board of county commissioners, consisting of three members elected to four-year terms. Nine officials also elected to four-year terms exercise executive functions: the county auditor, treasurer, recorder, clerk, surveyor, sheriff, prosecuting attorney, coroner, and assessor. The county's appointed officials include the county superintendent of schools, highway supervisor, highway engineer, extension agent, attorney, and physician. An elected seven-member county council exercises taxing power and acts as a check on the Board of county commissioners. The major exception to this general pattern is Marion County, which in 1970 was consolidated with the city of Indianapolis and is governed by an elected mayor and council.

Townships (1,008 in 2002) provide assistance for the poor and assess taxable property. Each township is administered by a trustee elected to a four-year term. In a few townships, the trustee oversees township schools, but most public schools are run by community school corporations.

Indiana's municipal governments (567 in 2002) are governed by elected city councils. City officials, including the mayor and city clerk, are generally elected for four-year terms. Indianapolis and Marion County were consolidated in 1969.

In 2002 Indiana had 294 public school districts and 1,125 special districts.

15STATE SERVICES

To address the continuing threat of terrorism and to work with the federal Department of Homeland Security (created in 2002 following the terrorist attacks of 11 September 2001), homeland security in Indiana in 2003 operated under state statute; a new position, terrorism council director, was created to oversee homeland security in the state.

In 1974, Indiana's state legislature created the State Ethics and Conflicts of Interest Commission to formulate and regulate a code of ethics for state officials. The commissioner investigates reported cases of misconduct or violations of the code of ethics by any state official or employee. After holding hearings, the commission reports violations to the governor and makes its findings public. Top-level state officials and heads of state departments must provide statements of their financial interests to the commission.

In 1977, the state established an Interdepartmental board for the coordination of human service programs. Members include the chief administrative officers of state agencies for senior citizens and community services, mental health, health, corrections, and public welfare. The Family and Social Services Administration provides assistance to persons and families requiring help from one of these agencies and monitors federal service programs in the state. The Indiana Office of Social Services Fiscal Office administers programs for the board. An executive assistant to the governor serves as chairperson of the board, which also includes the director of the state budget agency.

Educational services are provided by the Department of Education, the Indiana Educational Services Foundation, and the Commission for Postsecondary Proprietary Education, which accredits private vocational, technical, and trade schools in the state. A public counselor, appointed by the governor, represents the public at hearings of the Public Service Commission, which regulates public transportation agencies and public utilities. Health services are supplied by the state board of health, department of mental health, and emergency medical services commission. Disabled citizens are assisted by the Indiana Rehabilitation Services Agency. The Civil Rights Commission enforces state antidiscrimination laws.

16JUDICIAL SYSTEM

The Indiana supreme court consists of five justices who are appointed by the governor from names submitted by a nonpartisan judicial nominating committee. To qualify for selection, a nominee must have practiced law in the state for at least 10 years or have served as judge of a lower court for at least 5 years. A justice serves for 2 years and then is subject to

Indiana Presidential Vote by Political Parties, 1948–2000

YEAR	ELECTORAL VOTES	INDIANA WINNER	DEMOCRAT	REPUBLICAN	PROGRESSIVE	PROHIBITION
1948	13	Dewey (R)	807,833	821,079	9,649	14,711
1952	13	*Eisenhower (R)	801,530	1,136,259	1,222	15,335
1956	13	*Eisenhower (R)	783,908	1,182,811	—	6,554
1960	13	*Nixon (R)	952,358	1,175,120	—	6,746
1964	13	*Johnson (D)	1,170,848	911,118	—	8,266
					AMERICAN IND.	
1968	13	*Nixon (R)	806,659	1,067,885	243,108	4,616
					PEOPLE'S	SOC. WORKERS
1972	13	*Nixon (R)	708,568	1,405,154	4,544	5,575
					AMERICAN	
1976	13	Ford (R)	1,014,714	1,185,958	14,048	5,695
					CITIZENS	LIBERTARIAN
1980	13	*Reagan (R)	844,197	1,255,656	4,852	19,627
1984	12	*Reagan (R)	841,481	1,377,230	—	6,741
					NEW ALLIANCE	
1988	12	*Bush (R)	860,643	1,297,763	10,215	—
					Ind. (Perot)	
1992	12	Bush (R)	848,420	989,375	455,934	7,936
1996	12	Dole (R)	887,424	1,006,693	224,299	15,632
					(Buchanan)	
2000**	12	*Bush, G. W. (R)	901,980	1,245,836	16,959	15,530

*Won US presidential election. **Write-in candidate Ralph Nader received 18,531 votes in 2000.

approval by referendum in the general election; if approved by the voters, the justice serves a 10-year term before again being subject to referendum. The chief justice of the Indiana supreme court is chosen by the nominating commission and serves a 5-year term.

The state court of appeals consists of 15 justices; they serve 10-year terms. The court exercises appellate jurisdiction under rules set by the state supreme court. Both the clerk and the reporter for the state's high courts are chosen in statewide elections for 4-year terms.

Superior courts, probate courts, and circuit courts all function as general trial courts and are presided over by 279 judges who serve terms of six years. When the justice of the peace system in the counties was abolished by the state legislature in 1976, small-claims dockets (civil cases involving up to $1,500) were added to circuit and county courts.

Indiana had a prison population of 20,576 as of June 2001, an increase of 3.5% over the previous year. The state's incarceration rate stood at 336 per 100,000 inhabitants. For 2001, the FBI Crime Index reported a total crime rate of 3,831.4 per 100,000 people statewide. This included a total of 22,734 violent crimes and 211,548 crimes against property in that year. Indiana has a death penalty and has executed 11 inmates since 1977. There were 41 persons under sentence of death in 2003.

[17]ARMED FORCES

US defense installations in Indiana had 1,041 active duty military personnel in 2002. Army installations include the Jefferson Proving Ground. Grissom Air Force Base, which had been the state's only Air Force base, was closed in 1994. The navy operates a weapons support center at Crane and an avionics center at Indianapolis. Within the state $1.8 billion in prime defense contracts were awarded in fiscal year 2001.

Indiana supported the Union during the Civil War; about 200,000 Hoosiers served in Northern armies, and some 24,400 died while in service. During World War I, a Hoosier reportedly was the first American soldier to fire a shot, and the first American soldier killed was from Indiana; in all, about 118,000 Indiana citizens served and 3,370 lost their lives. In World War II, about 338,000 Hoosiers served in the armed forces and some 10,000 died in line of duty. There were 590,476 veterans of US military service in Indiana as of 2000, of whom 110,729 served in World War II; 74,559 in the Korean conflict; 176,218 during the Vietnam era; and 59,009 during 1990–2000 (including the Persian Gulf War). After World War II, the state paid a bonus to veterans for the first time; in fiscal year 2002, veterans' benefits in Indiana totaled $775 million.

In 2000, the Indiana State Police employed 1,278 full-time sworn officers.

[18]MIGRATION

Indiana's early settlers were predominantly northern Europeans who migrated from eastern and southern states. The influx of immigrants to the US in the late 19th and early 20th centuries had little impact on Indiana. In 1860, only 9% of the state's population was foreign-born, mostly Germans and Irish. The percentage was only 5.6% in 1900 and had further declined to 5.2% by 1920, and to just 1.7% by 1990. The principal migratory pattern since 1920 has been within the state, from the farms to the cities.

In 1860, more than 91% of the population lived in rural areas; the percentage fell to 67% in 1900, 50% in 1920, and 40% in 1960. In 1990, 65% of the population was urban, and only 35% was rural.

Since World War II, Indiana has lost population through a growing migratory movement to other states, mostly to Florida and the Southwest. From 1960 to 1970, Indiana suffered a net loss of about 16,000 persons through migration, and from 1970 to 1983, a net total of 340,000 left the state. From 1985 to 1990, however, there was a net gain in migration of over 35,000, 90% of whom came from abroad. Between 1990 and 1998, the state had a net gain of 76,000 persons through domestic migration and a net gain of 25,000 in international migration. In 1998, 3,981 foreign immigrants arrived in Indiana. Between 1990 and 1998, the state's overall population increased 6.4%. In the period 1995–2000, 451,397 people moved into the state and 429,772 moved out, for a net gain of 21,625, many of whom came from Illinois.

[19]INTERGOVERNMENTAL COOPERATION

Indiana's Commission on Interstate Cooperation promotes cooperation with other states and with the federal government. It acts largely through the Council of State Governments. Indiana is a member of such interstate regulatory bodies as the Great Lakes Commission, the Interstate Mining Compact Commission, the Midwest Interstate Low-Level Radioactive Waste Compact Commission, the Ohio River Basin Commission, and the Ohio River Valley Water Sanitation Commission.

The Indiana-Kentucky Boundary Compact was signed by Indiana in 1943 and received congressional approval the same year. In 1985, Indiana joined seven other states in signing a Great Lakes Charter, aimed at further protecting the lakes' resources. Federal grants to Indiana totaled over $5.8 billion in fiscal year 2001.

[20]ECONOMY

Indiana is both a leading agricultural and industrial state. The economy was almost entirely agricultural until after the Civil War. By 1900, rapid industrial development had tripled the number of factories in the state to 18,000, employing a total of 156,000 workers. During that period, the mechanization of agriculture resulted in the doubling of the number of farms to a peak of 220,000 in 1900.

Metals and other manufacturing industries surged during and after World War I, lagged during the Great Depression of the 1930s, then surged again during and after World War II. Between 1940 and 1950, the number of wage earners in the state nearly doubled. Job opportunities brought in many workers from other states and encouraged the growth of labor unions.

The state's industrial development in Indianapolis, Gary, and other cities has been based on its plentiful natural resources—coal, natural gas, timber, stone, and clay—and on good transportation facilities. The northwestern corner of the state is the site of one of the world's greatest concentrations of heavy industry, especially steel. Indiana produced 24% of the nation's steel in 1999, the most of any state. Until the end of the 20th century, the manufacturing sector continued to grow in absolute terms (15% between 1997 and 2000), and continued to account for about 30% of the Indiana's total output. In the national recession of 2001, however, manufacturing output fell 9.2%, and manufacturing fell to 27.2 of total output. The Indiana economy experienced 8.1% growth in 1998, which moderated to 2.9% in 1999 and 4.7% in 2000, and then plunged to 0.1% in 2001. Job creation, which had averaged over 2% a quarter since 1993, became negative (layoffs exceeding job creation) by the second half of 2001, and remained negative throughout 2002. Although the unemployment rate remained below the national average, Indiana had the highest foreclosure rate on conventional family mortgages among the states in 2002.

Indiana's gross state product in 2001 was 16th largest among the states at $189.9 billion, to which manufacturing contributed $51.6 billion; general services, $34.3 billion; trade, $29.3 billion; financial services, $27.2 billion, government, $20.1 billion, transportation and public utilities, $14.4 billion, and construction, $10 billion. The public sector constituted 10.6% of gross state product.

21INCOME

According to the Bureau of Economic Analysis, in 2001, Indiana had a per capita personal income (PCPI) of $27,522 which ranked 32nd in the United States (including the District of Columbia) and was 90% of the national average, $30,413. The 2001 PCPI reflected an increase of 1.9% from 2000 compared to the national change of 2.2%. In 2001, Indiana had a total personal income (TPI) of $168,621,697,000 which ranked 16th in the United States and accounted for 1.9% of the national total. The 2001 TPI reflected an increase of 2.5% from 2000 compared to the national change of 3.3%.

Earnings of persons employed in Indiana increased from $116,581,259,000 in 2000 to $117,622,957,000 in 2001, an increase of 0.9%. The largest industries in 2001 were services, 23.7% of earnings; durable goods manufacturing, 19.2%; and state and local government, 11.4%. Of the industries that accounted for at least 5% of earnings in 2001, the slowest growing from 2000 to 2001 was durable goods manufacturing, which decreased 7.8%; the fastest was state and local government, which increased 5.6%.

According to data released by the US Census Bureau, in 2000, the median household income was $39,717 compared to the national average of $42,148. In 2001, the median income for a family of four was $63,573 compared to the national average of $63,278. For the period 1999 to 2001, the average poverty rate was 7.9% which placed it 8th among the 50 states and the District of Columbia ranked lowest to highest.

22LABOR

According to Bureau of Labor Statistics (BLS) provisional estimates, in July 2003 the seasonally adjusted civilian labor force in Indiana numbered 3,222,900, with approximately 172,200 workers unemployed, yielding an unemployment rate of 5.3%, compared to the national average of 6.2% for the same period. Since the beginning of the BLS data series in 1978, the highest unemployment rate recorded was 12.7% in November 1982. The historical low was 2.8% in September 2000. In 2001, an estimated 5.4% of the labor force was employed in construction; 22.5% in manufacturing; 5.1% in transportation, communications, and public utilities; 19.1% in trade; 5.4% in finance, insurance, and real estate; 22.9% in services; 11.7% in government; and 2.4% in agriculture. Unemployment rates are usually higher than the state average around Terre Haute and Gary and lower than the state average in the Bloomington area.

Most industrial workers live in Indianapolis and the Calumet area of northwestern Indiana. The AFL first attempted to organize workers at the US Steel Company's plant in Gary in 1919, but a strike to get union recognition failed. Other strikes by Indiana coal miners and railway workers in 1922 had limited success. By 1936, however, the CIO had won bargaining rights and the 40-hour workweek from US Steel, and union organization spread to other industries throughout the state.

The US Department of Labor reported that in 2002, 376,000 of Indiana's 2,826,000 employed wage and salary workers were members of unions. This represented 13.3% of those so employed, down from 14.3% in 2001 and from 16.2% in 1998. The national average is 13.2%. In all, 411,000 workers (14.5%) were represented by unions. The majority of the workers belonged to unions affiliated with the AFL-CIO. In addition to union members, this category includes workers who report no union affiliation but whose jobs are covered by a union contract. Indiana is one of 22 states with a right-to-work law, although the law only applies to school employees.

23AGRICULTURE

Agriculture in Indiana is a large and diverse industry that plays a vital role in the economic stability of Indiana, with 63,000 farms containing 15,400,000 acres (6,230,000 hectares) of farmland. In 2001, cash receipts from the sale of all commodities (crops and livestock) reached $5.1 billion. In the same year, Indiana ranked 14th in the United States in cash receipts from the sale of all commodities; crop sales amounted to $3.2 billion; and livestock sales totaled $1.8 billion.

Over 80% of Indiana's farm operators live on the farm, while more than 51% of farmers have a principal occupation other than farming. The average age for Indiana farmers is 51 years old and the average farm size is 236 acres (96 hectares).

Corn and soybeans are Indiana's two main crops. In 2002 the state produced 631,620,000 bushels of corn for grain, ranking 5th in the US. Indiana also grew 235,750,000 bushels of soybeans, the 4th most in the nation. Other principal field crops, based upon 2002 crop statistics, include spearmint, 84,000 lbs.; peppermint 414,000 lbs.; and cantaloupes 540,000 cwt.

24ANIMAL HUSBANDRY

Indiana dairy farmers produced an estimated 2.6 billion lbs (1.2 billion kg) of milk from 153,000 milk cows in 2001. The state's poultry farmers sold an estimated 34 million lbs (15.4 million kg) of chicken and an estimated 399 million lbs of turkey during 2001.

Indiana had an estimated 860,000 cattle and calves worth around $619.2 million in 2003.

25FISHING

Fishing is not of commercial importance in Indiana; in 1997, only 158,000 lbs of fish valued at $327,000 were landed. Fishing for bass, pike, perch, catfish, and trout is a popular sport with Indiana anglers. In 1998, there were some 643,741 sport fishing licenses issued by the state.

26FORESTRY

About 20% of Indiana's total land area was forested in 2002. Indiana has 4,501,000 acres (1,822,000 hectares) of forestland, of which 96%, or 4,342,000 acres (1,757,000 hectares), is considered commercial timberland. Some 75% of the commercial forestland is located in the southern half of Indiana, where oak, hickory, beech, maple, yellow poplar, and ash predominate in the uplands. Soft maple, sweetgum, pin oak, cottonwood, sycamore, and river birch are the most common species found in wetlands and drainage corridors.

Indiana's wood-using industries manufacture everything from the "crinkle" center lining in cardboard boxes to the finest furniture in the world. Other wood products include pallets, desks, fancy face veneer, millwork, flooring, mobile homes, and recreational vehicle components. In 2002, Indiana produced 324 million board feet of lumber. Indiana has always been noted for the quality of its hardwood forests and the trees it produces.

27MINING

The estimated value of nonfuel mineral production in Indiana in 2001 was about $718 million, up more than 3% from 2000. Increased values of crushed stone and portland and masonry cement were responsible for most of the increase, aided by a record $737 million in highway construction projects completed by the state's department of transportation.

Nationally, Indiana ranked 20th in value of nonfuel mineral production. In 2001, Indiana ranked 1st in dimension stone, 4th in peat, in the top five in masonry cement, 8th in gypsum, and was a significant producer of portland cement, crushed stone, construction sand and gravel, and common clays.

The state's top two mineral commodities were crushed stone (estimated 2001 output 56 million metric tons, valued at $264 million) and cement (portland cement production was an estimated 2.86 million metric tons, valued at $195 million).

28ENERGY AND POWER

Indiana is largely dependent on fossil fuels for its energy supplies. In recent years, petroleum has become an important power source for automobiles, home heating, and electricity. Nevertheless, coal has continued to be the state's major source of power, meeting about half of Indiana's energy needs.

In 2000 Indiana's total per capita energy consumption was 457 million Btu (115.2 million kcal), ranking it 8th among the 50 states.

The state has no nuclear power plants. In 1984, construction of the planned Marble Hill nuclear power plant on the Ohio River near Madison was permanently suspended by the Public Service Co. of Indiana because of escalating construction costs; total cost estimates had risen from $1.4 billion during the planning stage in 1973 to more than $7 billion.

Electric power produced in Indiana in 1999 (utility and nonutility) totaled 121.6 billion kWh; total installed capacity was 22 million kW, 87% of it provided by coal-fired plants. Privately owned power plants account for nearly all of Indiana's production and installed capacity. The major electric utilities were Northern Indiana Public Service Co., Indiana and Michigan Electric Co., Public Service Co. of Indiana, Indianapolis Power and Light Co., and Southern Indiana Gas and Electric Co.

At the end of 2001, Indiana's estimated proved reserves of petroleum totaled 12 million barrels, and production of crude petroleum totaled 5,000 barrels per day in 2002.

In 1998 there were 3 underground coal mines and 38 strip mines active in the state. Indiana's coal production in 2000 was estimated at 28 million tons of coal. Recoverable reserves totaled 397 million tons in 2000.

29INDUSTRY

The industrialization of Indiana that began in the Civil War era was spurred by technological advances in processing agricultural products, manufacturing farm equipment, and improving transportation facilities. Meat-packing plants, textile mills, furniture factories, and wagon works—including Studebaker wagons—were soon followed by metal foundries, machine shops, farm implement plants, and a myriad of other durable-goods plants.

New industries included a pharmaceutical house started in Indianapolis in 1876 by a druggist named Eli Lilly, and several automobile-manufacturing shops established in South Bend and other cities by 1900. In 1906, the US Steel Co. laid out the new town of Gary for steelworkers and their families.

In 1997, the estimated total value of shipments by manufacturers in Indiana was $143 billion. Indiana is a leading producer of compact disks, elevators, recreational vehicles, mobile homes, refrigerators and freezers, storage batteries, small motors and generators, mobile homes, household furniture, burial caskets, and musical instruments. Most manufacturing plants are located in and around Indianapolis and in the Calumet region. As of 1997, there were six Fortune 500 companies headquartered in Indiana.

Earnings of persons employed in Indiana increased from $99,781,241,000 in 1997 to $106,049,254,000 in 1998, an increase of 6.3%. The largest industries in 1998 were durable goods manufacturing, 22.3% of earnings; services, 21.6%; and state and local government, 9.9%. Of the industries that accounted for at least 5% of earnings in 1998, the slowest growing from 1997 to 1998 was state and local government, which increased 2.7%; the fastest was finance, insurance, and real estate (5.8% of earnings in 1998), which increased 8.2%.

30COMMERCE

There were a total of 10,612 wholesale establishments in Indiana during 1997, with $70 billion in sales. Principal goods traded included food and related products, machinery, equipment, and supplies, farm product raw materials, petroleum and petroleum products, and electrical goods.

Retail establishments in 1997 had sales of $59 billion, from 34,398 establishments. Indiana ranked 16th in the nation in growth of retail sales. Automotive dealers accounted for 15% of establishments; food stores, 8.3%; and eating and drinking places, 30%. Food sales and merchandise sales totaled $7.9 billion each in 1997.

Indiana ranked 16th among the 50 states in exports during 1998, when its goods shipped abroad were valued at $12 billion. Major farm exports are soybeans; feed grains; wheat; meat (including poultry) and meat products; fats, oils, and greases; and hides and skins. Principal nonfarm exports include transportation equipment, electric and electronic equipment, nonelectric machinery, primary metals products, chemicals and allied products, food and kindred products, and fabricated metal products.

31CONSUMER PROTECTION

The Division of Consumer Protection of the Office of the Attorney General, created in 1971, is empowered to investigate consumer complaints, initiate and prosecute civil actions, and warn consumers about deceptive sales practices. There is also a Utility Regulatory Commission that regulates the business of public utilities, including rates and environmental compliance plans.

In 1980, the first criminal prosecution of an American corporation because of alleged product defects was brought against the Ford Motor Co. at Winamac. A jury found the company not guilty of reckless homicide in a rear-end collision involving a Pinto automobile in which three young women were killed.

32BANKING

The large-scale mechanization of agriculture in Indiana after 1850 encouraged the growth of banks to lend money to farmers to buy farm machinery, using their land as collateral. The financial panic of 1893 caused most banks in the state to suspend operations, and the depression of the 1930s caused banks to foreclose many farm mortgages and dozens of banks to fail. The nation's subsequent economic recovery, together with the federal reorganization of the banking system, helped Indiana banks to share in the state's prosperity during and after World War II.

In September 2002 there were 214 insured banks in the state, of which 122 were state-chartered. The total assets of insured banks amounted to $118 billion. Twenty of Indiana's insured institutions were less than nine years old as of 2002.

Indiana's bankruptcy levels are relatively high and growing. Indiana's community banks (those with less than $1 billion in assets) saw an increase in profitability in 2002, however, due to improved net interest margins (NIMs) (the difference between the lower rates offered to savers and the higher rates charged on loans). The largest institutions (with assets over $1 billion) realized improved performance as well, with lower delinquencies compared with 2001.

The Department of Financial Institutions regulates the operations of Indiana-chartered banks, savings and loan associations, and credit unions, and monitors observance of a Uniform Consumer Credit Code. The department is headed by a seven-member board, each board member serves a four-year term and no more than four members may be of the same political party. A full-time director, also appointed by the governor to a four-year term, is the department's chief executive and administrative officer.

33INSURANCE

In 2001 there were 3.7 million ordinary life insurance policies in force with a total value of $198.2 billion; total value for all categories of life insurance (ordinary, group, industrial, and credit) was $339.8 billion. Death benefits paid that year totaled $1.1 billion. As of 2003 there were 79 state-licensed property and casualty and 49 life and health insurance companies with home offices in Indiana.

In 2001, property and casualty insurers wrote premiums totaling $7.8 billion. That year, there were 25,609 flood insurance policies in force in the state, with a total value of $2.2 million.

The Department of Insurance licenses insurance carriers and agents in Indiana, and it enforces regulations governing the issuance of policies.

34SECURITIES

There are no securities exchanges in Indiana. There are 761 securities brokers and dealers organizations in Indiana, with over 5,000 employees. Investment advisor firms number 139 for the state. Laws governing the trading and sale of corporate securities are administered by the secretary of state, who also regulates franchise sales and corporate takeover attempts. There are 75 NASDAQ companies headquartered in Indiana, two NASDAQ market makers, and 18 Indiana-incorporated NYSE traded companies: major corporations include Lilly (Eli) & Co., Bindley Western Industries, Conseco, Lincoln National Corporation, and Cummins Engine Co.

35PUBLIC FINANCE

The State Budget Agency acts as watchdog over state financial affairs. The agency prepares the budget for the governor and presents it to the general assembly. The budget director, appointed by the governor, serves with four legislators (two from each house) on the state budget committee, which helps to prepare the budget. The state budget agency receives appropriations requests from the heads of state offices, estimates anticipated revenues for the biennium, and administers the budget. The fiscal year runs from 1 July to 30 June of the following year. Budgets are prepared for the biennium beginning and ending in odd-numbered years.

In the economic recession of 2001, and the slowdowns of 2002 and 2003, Indiana faced serious revenue shortfalls. In 2001/02, cuts totaling $468.7 million were made in the budget mid-term, and in 2002/03, cuts totaling $671.5 million were made after the budget's adoption. In 2001/02, strategies used to deal with the budget gap included tax increases, fee increases, across-the-board cuts and drawings from the state's rainy day fund. (the Counter Cyclical Revenue Fund). In 2003, furloughs, early retirement of government employees, reduced local aid, and the administrative transfer of funds were added to across-the-board cuts and drawings from the rainy day fund. Indiana's budget deficit was about 3% of the state budget in 2002/03, and projected at 8.8% for 2003/04. Revenues for the general fund were projected at $10.481 billion for 2004, while expenditures were projected at $11.292 billion, the difference to be made up by drawings on the rainy day fund and administrative transfers. Of funds appropriated, the major part is for education (36%), health and human services (30%), and transportation (11%).

The following table from the US Census Bureau contains information on revenues, expenditures, indebtedness, and cash/securities for 2001.

	($000)	PERCENT	PER CAPITA
Population (thousands, 2001)	6,127	(X)	(X)
Total Revenue	20,766,968	100.00	3,389.42
General revenue	19,737,963	95.04	3,221.47
Utility revenue	–	–	–
Liquor store revenue	–	–	–
Insurance trust revenue	1,029,005	4.96	167.95
Exhibit: Salaries and wages	2,903,705	13.45	473.92
Total expenditure	21,583,665	100.00	3,522.71
General expenditure	20,255,231	93.85	3,305.90
Education	8,160,202	37.81	1,331.84
Public welfare	4,346,855	20.14	709.46
Hospitals	256,527	1.19	41.87
Health	529,616	2.45	86.44
Highways	2,149,143	9.96	350.77
Police protection	240,440	1.11	39.24
Correction	613,036	2.84	100.05
Natural resources	228,565	1.06	37.30
Parks and recreation	77,747	0.36	12.69
Government administration	599,004	2.78	97.76
Interest on general debt	408,037	1.89	66.60
Other and unallocable	2,646,059	12.26	431.87
Utility expenditure	–	–	–
Liquor store expenditure	–	–	–
Insurance trust expenditure	1,328,434	6.15	216.82
Debt at end of fiscal year	8,517,915	100.00	1,390.23
Cash and security holdings	33,417,332	100.00	5,454.11

36TAXATION

The first state property tax in Indiana was levied in 1852 to support public schools.

In 1923, a state gasoline tax of 2 cents per gallon was introduced. (It ranged from 11.1 cents to 14 cents in 1984, depending on average prices in a specified month) In 2003 the gasoline tax was 15 cents a gallon. In 2002, Indiana was one of 20 states to increase its tax on a pack of cigarettes, and its increase, from 15.5 cents to 55.5 cents, was the biggest percent increase in the group. Indiana imposes a full set of excise taxes—on tobacco products, alcoholic beverages, motor fuels, pari-mutuels, public utilities, amusements, and other selected items.

In 1933, Indiana instituted the personal income tax, which was the major source of state revenue until 1963, when a 2% retail sales tax was enacted. In 1973, the state sales tax was doubled to 4% and optional local income taxes of up to 1% were initiated, while local property taxes were reduced by at least 20% to ease the tax burden on property owners. In 1983, the state sales tax was raised to 5%, and in 2002, Indiana raised the rate to 6%, one of two states to increase its general sales rate that year. Local option sales taxes, however, have been abolished. The state's personal income tax is a flat 3.4% of adjusted gross income with personal and child exemptions of $1000 each. The corporate tax rate was increased from 3.4% to 8.5% in 2003, which was the rate being applied only to financial institutions. The state estate tax, with a maximum rate of 15%, is established in Indiana law independently of the federal exemption for state death taxes, and therefore is unaffected by the phasing out of the federal estate tax credit by 2007. Indiana's inheritance tax ranges from 1% to 10% of fair market value of property transferred ate death. State death and gift taxes accounted for 1.4% of state collections in 2002. Other taxes include various state license fees and 1% petroleum production tax.

In fiscal 2002, state tax collections totaled $6.159 billion, 38% generated by the state sales and use tax, 35.4% by the state personal income tax, 15.4% by state excise taxes, 6.6% by the state corporate income tax, and 3% from license fees. Combined state and local taxes, of which the state portion is about 56.6% (2000 est.), amount to 9.7% of income, with Indiana ranking 22nd in terms of state and local tax burden in 2003.

The following table from the US Census Bureau provides a summary of taxes collected by the state in 2002.

	($000)	PER CAPITA
Total Taxes	9,994,595	1,622.74
Property taxes	4,115	0.67
Sales and gross receipts	5,339,464	866.93
General sales and gross receipts	3,798,490	616.73
Selective sales taxes	1,540,974	250.2
Alcoholic beverage	34,473	5.6
Amusements	516,293	83.83
Insurance Premiums	178,569	28.99
Motor fuels	665,619	108.07
Pari-mutuels	3,529	0.57
Public utilities	4,885	0.79
Tobacco products	123,215	20.01
Other selective sales	14,391	2.34
Licenses	299,723	48.66
Alcoholic beverages	8,690	1.41
Amusements	5,595	0.91
Corporation	5,562	0.9
Hunting and fishing	24,063	3.91
Motor vehicle	197,937	32.14
Motor vehicle operators	(X)	(X)
Public utility	(X)	(X)
Occupation and business, NEC	56,260	9.13
Other	1,616	0.26
Other taxes	4,351,293	706.49
Individual income	3,540,819	574.9
Corporation net income	667,162	108.32
Death and gift	142,732	23.17
Documentary and stock transfer	(X)	(X)
Severance	580	0.09
Other	(X)	(X)

[37]ECONOMIC POLICY

The state's early economic policy was to provide farmers with access to markets by improving transportation facilities. During the Civil War era, Indiana encouraged industrial growth. In modern times, the state has financed extensive highway construction, developed deepwater ports on Lake Michigan and the Ohio River, and worked to foster industrial growth and develop its tourist industry. Tax incentives to business included a phase out, by 1994, of the "intangibles" tax on stocks, bonds, and notes.

In the 1990s, the state government focused on a series of economic development initiatives. These included programs offering job training and retraining, the promotion of new businesses and tourism, the development of infrastructure, and the provision of investment capital for start-up companies—as well as programs providing additional tax incentives. The Department of Commerce, which has sole responsibility for economic development, solicits new businesses to locate in Indiana, promotes sales of exports abroad, plans the development of energy resources, continues to foster the expansion of agriculture, and helps minority-group owners of small businesses. The department's Industrial Development Fund makes loans to municipalities for the purchasing or leasing of property for industrial development. In the 2000 budget, the General Assembly provided $50 million for Governor O'Bannon's 21st Century Research and Technology Fund to stimulate high-technology development.

[38]HEALTH

Mortality rates and infant death rates are above the national average in Indiana. In 2000, the overall mortality rate stood at 928.1 per 100,000 inhabitants, as compared to the national average of 873.1. In 2000, the infant mortality rate was 7.8 per 1,000 live births, as compared with the national average of 6.9. Also, in 1999, 12,109 legal abortions were performed in the state; the legal abortion ratio was 9 per 1,000 women.

The principal causes of death, with rates of death 936.4 per 100,000 population in 2000, were heart disease, 271.2 (274.0 age-adjusted); cerebrovascular diseases, 71.1 (71.9 age-adjusted); accidents and adverse effects, 35.8 (35.8 age-adjusted); motor vehicle injuries 15.4 (15.3 age-adjusted); and suicide, 11.4 (11.4 age-adjusted). Of the population age 18 and older, 27.0% were classified as smokers in 2000. The rate of HIV-related deaths stood at 2.0 per 100,000 population, below the national average of 5.3 in 2000. There were 6,515 AIDS cases reported through 2001.

In 1994, the Indiana State Department of Health identified public health priorities that will be used to develop agency-wide integrated work plans and evaluate the effectiveness of disease intervention and prevention strategies. These priorities included chronic disease (breast and lung cancer, coronary heart disease, diabetes); communicable disease (HIV and STDs, vaccine preventable diseases, emerging conditions); environmental disease (foodborne and waterborne diseases, lead exposure, oral health); infant mortality (infant mortality and high-risk pregnancy); and injury (intentional and unintentional).

Indiana's 110 community hospitals had 718,369 admissions and 19,036 beds in 2001. There were 21,468 full-time registered nurses and 3,160 full-time licensed practical nurses in 2001 and 219 physicians per 100,000 population in 2000. The average expense of a community hospital for care was $1,381.30 per inpatient day in 2001.

Federal government grants to cover the Medicare and Medicaid services in 2001 totaled $2.7 billion; 858,150 enrollees received Medicare benefits that year. At least 11.8% of the population was uninsured in 2002.

[39]SOCIAL WELFARE

In 2001, the average weekly unemployment benefit was $242.36. Average monthly participation in the food stamp program in FY2002 comprised 410,884 persons (171,329 households). The average monthly benefit was $82.76, and the sum total of benefits paid in FY2002 was $408,077,163.

With the enactment of the Personal Responsibility and Work Opportunity Reconciliation Act of 1996, the US government has changed the form and regulations for many of its social welfare programs. Most significantly, it replaces Aid to Families with Dependent Children (AFDC), an open-ended entitlement program, with Temporary Assistance for Needy Families (TANF), a limited system of assistance funded largely through federal block grants. The reform act also impacts the food stamp program, the Supplemental Security Income program, and the child nutrition program. The law took effect on 1 July 1997 and provided $16.38 billion in block grants for fiscal years 1997–2002. The grants are to be divided among the states based on an equation involving the numbers of former AFDC recipients in each state.

Reauthorization of the 1996 social welfare legislation, scheduled for 2002, was delayed, and the original law had been extended three times as of July 2003, with the most recent extension running through September 2003. The employment services section of Indiana's TANF program is called IMPACT (Indiana Manpower Placement and Comprehensive Training). In June 2000 the state had 95,665 welfare recipients. State expenditures on the TANF program in FY2002 totaled $72,602,171.

In December 2001, Social Security benefits were paid to 1,000,050 Indiana residents. This number included 635,280 retired workers, 111,110 widows and widowers, 112,660 disabled workers, 58,160 spouses, and 82,840 children. Social Security beneficiaries represented 16.5% of the total state population and 95.8% of the state's population age 65 and older. Retired workers (excluding persons with special benefits) received an average monthly payment of $915; widows and widowers, $873; disabled workers, $824; and spouses, $466. Payments for children of retired workers averaged $467 per month; children of deceased workers, $608; and children of disabled workers, $235.

Federal Supplemental Security Income payments in December 2001 went to 89,118 Indiana residents, averaging $367 a month.

40 HOUSING

In 2002, the state had an estimated 2,615,750 housing units, 2,345,780 of which were occupied; 71.8% were owner-occupied. About 21% of all units were built before 1939. About 70.5% of all units are single-family, detached homes. Most units relied on utility gas and electricity for heating, but about 1,167 units were equipped for solar power. It was estimated that 125,077 unites lacked telephone service, 8,813 lacked complete plumbing facilities, and 12,863 lacked complete kitchen facilities. The average household size was 2.55 people.

In 2002, 39,596 privately owned housing units were authorized for construction. The median home value was $100,762. The median monthly cost for mortgage owners was $928. Renters paid a median of $545 per month. During fiscal year 2002, Indiana received over $113.8 million in community planning and development aid from the US Department of Housing and Urban Development.

41 EDUCATION

Although the 1816 constitution recommended establishment of public schools, the state legislature did not provide funds for education. The constitution of 1851 more specifically outlined the state's responsibility to support a system of free public schools. Development was rapid following passage of this document; more than 2,700 schoolhouses were built in the state from 1852 to 1857, and an adult literacy rate of nearly 90% was achieved by 1860. The illiteracy rate was reduced to 5.2% for the adult population in 1900, to 1.7% in 1950, and to only 0.7% in 1970, when Indiana ranked 14th among the 50 states. In 2000, 82.1% of those aged 25 years and over were high school graduates, and 19.4% had completed four or more years of college.

The total enrollment for fall 1999 in Indiana's public schools stood at 988,702. Of these, 699,221 attended schools from kindergarten through grade eight, and 289,481 attended high school. Minority students made up approximately 17% of the total enrollment in public elementary and secondary schools in 2001. Total enrollment was estimated at 988,963 in fall 2000 and expected to reach 1,029,000 by fall 2005. In 1999/2000, Indiana spent nearly $6.6 billion on public schools, for an average expenditure of $6,658 per student. Expenditures for public education in 2000/01 were estimated at $7,668,000. Enrollment in nonpublic schools in fall 2001 was 105,533.

As of fall 2000, there were 352,687 students enrolled in college or graduate school. In the same year Indiana had 98 degree-granting institutions. In 1997, minority students comprised 11.5% of total postsecondary enrollment. Indiana University, the state's largest institution of higher education, was founded in 1820. It is one of the largest state universities in the US, with a total of nine campuses. The Bloomington campus has a nationally recognized music program. Other major state universities include Purdue University (Lafayette), Ball State University (Muncie), and Indiana State University (Terre Haute). Well-known private universities in the state include Notre Dame (at South Bend) and Butler (Indianapolis). Small private colleges and universities include DePauw (Greencastle), Earlham (Richmond), Hanover (Hanover), and Wabash (Crawfordsville).

42 ARTS

The earliest center for artists in Indiana was the Art Association of Indianapolis, founded in 1883. It managed the John Herron Art Institute, consisting of a museum and art school (1906–08).

Around 1900, art colonies sprang up in Richmond, Muncie, South Bend, and Nashville. Indianapolis remains the state's cultural center, especially after the opening in the late 1960s of the Lilly Pavilion of the Decorative Arts; the Krannert Pavilion, which houses the paintings originally in the Herron Museum; the Clowes Art Pavilion; and the Grace Showalter Pavilion of the Performing Arts (all collectively known as the Indianapolis Museum of Art). Since 1969, the Indiana Arts Commission has taken art—and artists—into many Indiana communities; the commission also sponsors biennial awards to artists in the state. Indiana has over 450 arts associations.

The state's first resident theater company established itself in Indianapolis in 1840, and the first theater building, the Metropolitan, was opened there in 1858. Ten years later, the Academy of Music was founded as the center for dramatic activities in Indianapolis. In 1875, the Grand Opera House opened there, and the following year it was joined by the English Opera House, where touring performers such as Sarah Bernhardt, Edwin Booth, and Ethel Barrymore held the stage. Amateur theater has been popular since the founding in 1915 of the nation's oldest amateur drama group, the Little Theater Society, which later became the Civic Theater of Indianapolis.

Music has flourished in Indiana. Connersville reportedly was the first American city to establish a high school band, while Richmond claims the first high school symphony orchestra. The Indianapolis Symphony Orchestra was founded in 1930. There are 23 other symphony orchestras in the state. Indianapolis Opera was founded in 1975. The Arthur Jordan College of Music is part of Butler University in Indianapolis, and the music program at Indiana University's Bloomington campus has a national reputation, especially its string department, which has attracted some of the world's most renowned musicians to its faculty. The annual Indiana Fiddlers' Gathering, founded in 1973, is a three-day festival featuring the bluegrass, swing fiddle, string band, and Celtic and other ethnic music.

In 2003, the Indiana Arts Commission and other Indiana arts organizations received grants totaling $845,500 from the National Endowment for the Arts. The Indiana Humanities Council sponsors programs that include Habits of the Heart, a youth volunteer leadership development program, and History Alive, an educational program featuring live portrayals of famous historical figures. In 2000, the National Endowment for the Humanities supported 61 programs in the state with grants totaling $1,512,452. Indiana's arts programs have a total audience of over 86 million people. The number of contributing artists is nearly 200,000.The Indiana Arts Commission also received funds from state and regional programs.

43 LIBRARIES AND MUSEUMS

The state constitution of 1816 provided for the establishment of public libraries. A majority of Indiana cities opened such libraries but neglected to provide adequate financing. Semiprivate libraries did better: workingmen's libraries were set up by a bequest at New Harmony and 14 other towns. After the state legislature provided for township school libraries in 1852, more than two-thirds of the townships established them, and the public library system has thrived ever since. In 2000 there were 24 public library systems, and every county received some form of library service. In total, there were 239,000 public libraries in Indiana. Total income was $224,581,000. Federal grants-in-aid to all public libraries totaled $1,347,486; state grants, $19,089,385. The largest book collections are at public libraries in Indianapolis, Fort Wayne, Gary, Evansville, Merrillville, and Hammond; the total book stock of all Indiana public libraries was 21,730,000 volumes in 2000, and circulation was 57,133,000.

The Indiana State Library has a strong collection of documents about Indiana's history and a large genealogical collection. The Indiana University Library has special collections on American literature and history and an extensive collection of rare books; the University of Notre Dame has a noteworthy collection on medieval history; and Purdue University Libraries contain outstanding industrial and agricultural collections, as well as voluminous materials on Indiana history.

Private libraries and museums include those maintained by historical societies in Indianapolis, Fort Wayne, and South Bend. Also of note are the General Lew Wallace Study museum in Crawfordsville and the Elwood Haynes Museum of early technology in Kokomo. In all, Indiana had 179 museums in 2000 registered with the American Association of Museums. Many county historical societies maintain smaller museums, such as the Wayne County Historical Museum.

Indiana's historic sites of most interest to visitors are the Lincoln Boyhood National Memorial near Gentryville, the Levi Coffin Home (one of the Underground Railroad stops) in Fountain City, the Benjamin Harrison Memorial Home and the James Whitcomb Riley Home in Indianapolis, and the Grouseland Home of William Henry Harrison in Vincennes. Among several archaeological sites are two large mound groups: one at Mounds State Park near Anderson, which dates from about ad 800–900, and a reconstructed village site at Angel Mounds, Newburgh, which dates from 1300–1500.

44COMMUNICATIONS

About 95.0% of all households had telephone service in 2001. The state's first radio station was licensed in 1922 at Purdue University, Lafayette. Indiana had 20 major AM, 123 major FM radio stations, and 30 television stations as of 2003. Powerful radio and television transmissions from Chicago and Cincinnati also blanket the state. In 2000, the Indianapolis area had 963,320 television households, 65% of which received cable. A total of 73,696 Internet domain names were registered in the state in 2000.

45PRESS

The first newspaper in Indiana was published at Vincennes in 1804 and a second pioneer weekly appeared at Madison nine years later. By 1830, newspapers were also being published in Terre Haute, Indianapolis, and 11 other towns; the following year, the state's oldest surviving newspaper, the *Richmond Palladium*, began publication. Most pioneer newspapers were highly political and engaged in acrimonious feuds; in 1836, for example, the *Indianapolis Journal* referred to the editors of the rival *Democrat* as "the Lying, Hireling Scoundrels." By the time of the Civil War, Indiana had 154 weeklies and 13 dailies.

The last third of the 19th century brought a sharp increase in both the number and the quality of newspapers. Two newspapers which later became the state's largest in circulation, the *Indianapolis News* and the *Star*, began publishing in 1869 and 1903, respectively. In 1941 there were 294 weekly and 98 daily newspapers in Indiana; the number declined after World War II because of fierce competition for readers and advertising dollars, rising operating costs, and other financial difficulties.

In 2002, the state had 23 morning dailies and 45 evening dailies; Sunday papers numbered 23. In 2002, the Indianapolis morning *Star* had a daily circulation of 252,349 (Sunday circulation, 367,294)and the Gary *Post-Tribune's* circulation averaged 63,746 daily and 68,269 on Sundays.

A number of magazines are published in Indiana, including *Children's Digest* and *The Saturday Evening Post*.

Indiana is noted for its literary productivity. The list of authors claimed by Indiana up to 1966 showed a total of 3,600. Examination of the 10 best-selling novels each year from 1900 to 1940 (allowing 10 points to the top best-seller, down to 1 point for the 10th best-selling book) showed Indiana with a score of 213 points, exceeded only by New York's 218.

Many Hoosier authors were first published by Indiana's major book publisher, Bobbs-Merrill. Indiana University Press is an important publisher of scholarly books.

46ORGANIZATIONS

In 2003, there were about 3,059 regional, national, and international organizations within the state. National organizations with headquarters in the state include the American Camping Association, located in Martinsville, and the Amateur Athletic Union of the US, the American Legion, the US Gymnastics Federation, and Kiwanis International and Circle K International, all in Indianapolis. National sports and hobby associations based in Indiana include the Academy of Model Aeronautics, the United States Auto Club, the United States Rowing Association, and USA Gymnastics. Professional and educational organizations include the American Theatre Critics Association and Bands of America.

Philanthropic foundations headquartered in Indiana include the Eugene V. Debs Foundation (Terre Haute) and the Irwin Sweeny-Miller Foundation (Columbus).

The Indiana Arts Commission is the primary state organization for promoting study and appreciation for the arts. There are numerous local arts organizations and many county historical societies. The Quilters Hall of Fame is located in Marion.

47TOURISM, TRAVEL, AND RECREATION

Tourism is of moderate economic importance to Indiana and continues to grow. In 2001, there were about 57.7 million visitors to the state with travel expenditures at about $6.7 billion. The industry supports about 113,000 full time jobs.

About 70% of visitors participate in outdoor activities. Summer resorts are located in the north, along Lake Michigan and in Steuben and Kosciusko counties, where there are nearly 200 lakes. Popular tourist sites include the reconstructed village of New Harmony, site of famous communal living experiments in the early 19th century; the Indianapolis Motor Speedway and Museum; and the George Rogers Clark National Historic Park at Vincennes.

Indiana has 23 state parks, comprising 59,292 acres (21,800 hectares). The largest state park is Brown County (15,543 acres/ 16,290 hectares), near Nashville. There are 15 state fish and wildlife preserves, totaling about 75,200 acres (30,400 hectares). The largest are Pigeon River, near Howe, and Willow Slough, at Morocco. Game animals during the hunting season include deer, squirrel, and rabbit; ruffed grouse, quail, ducks, geese, and partridge are the main game birds.

In addition to the Indiana State Museum there are 15 state memorials, including the Wilbur Wright State Memorial at his birthplace near Millville, the Ernie Pyle birthplace near Dana, and the old state capitol at Corydon. Among the natural attractions are the Indiana Dunes National Lakeshore on Lake Michigan (12,534 acres/5,072 hectares); the state's largest waterfall, Cataract Falls, near Cloverdale; and the largest underground cavern, at Wyandotte.

48SPORTS

Indiana is represented in professional sports by the Indiana Pacers of the National Basketball Association, by the Indiana Fever of the Women's National Basketball Association, and by the National Football League's Colts, who moved to Indianapolis from Baltimore in 1984. There are also several minor league baseball, basketball, and hockey teams in the state.

The state's biggest annual sports event is the Indianapolis 500, which has been held at the Indianapolis Motor Speedway on

Memorial Day or the Sunday before every year since 1911 (except for the war years 1917 and 1942–45). The race is now part of a three-day Indiana festival held over Memorial Day weekend that attracts crowds of over 300,000 spectators, the largest crowd for any sporting event anywhere in the world.

The state's most popular amateur sport is basketball. The high school boys' basketball tournament culminates on the last Saturday in March, when the four finalists play afternoon and evening games to determine the winner. A tournament for girls' basketball teams began in 1976. Basketball is also popular at the college level: Indiana University won the NCAA Division I basketball championship in 1940, 1953, 1976, 1981, and 1987, and the National Invitational Tournament (NIT) in 1979; Purdue University won the NIT title in 1974; and Indiana State, led by state basketball legend Larry Bird, advanced to the NCAA finals in 1979. Evansville College won the NCAA Division II championships in 1959–60, 1964–65, and 1971.

Collegiate football in Indiana has a colorful tradition stretching back to at least 1913, when Knute Rockne of Notre Dame unleashed the forward pass as a potent football weapon. Notre Dame, which competes as an independent, was recognized as National Champions in 1946–47, 1949, 1966, 1973 (with Alabama), 1977, and 1988. The Fighting Irish won the following string of bowl games: the Orange Bowl in 1975 and 1990, and the Cotton Bowl in 1971, 1978, 1979, 1993, and 1994, the Sugar Bowl in 1973 and 1992, and the Fiesta Bowl in 1989. Indiana and Purdue compete in the Big Ten. Purdue won the Rose Bowl in 1967. Indiana State is part of the Missouri Valley Conference.

The Little 500, a 50-mi (80-km) bicycle race, is held each spring at Indiana University's Bloomington campus. The RCA Championships are held annually in Indianapolis.

Other annual sporting events include the National Muzzle-loading Rifle Association Championship Shoot which is held in Friendship in September, and the Sugar Creek canoe race, which is held in Crawfordsville in April.

⁴⁹FAMOUS INDIANANS

Indiana has contributed one US president and four vice presidents to the nation. Benjamin Harrison (b.Ohio, 1833–1901), the 23rd president, was a Republican who served one term (1889–93) and then returned to Indianapolis, where his home is now a national historic landmark. Three vice presidents were Indiana residents: Thomas Hendricks (b.Ohio, 1819–85), who served only eight months under President Cleveland and died in office; Schuyler Colfax (b.New York, 1823–85), who served under President Grant; and Charles Fairbanks (b.Ohio, 1852–1918), who served under Theodore Roosevelt. Two vice presidents were native sons: Thomas Marshall (1854–1925), who served two four-year terms with President Wilson and J(ames) Danforth Quayle of Indianapolis (b.1947), President George Bush's running mate in the 1988 presidential election. Marshall, remembered for his wit, originated the remark, "What this country needs is a good five-cent cigar."

Other Indiana-born political figures include Eugene V. Debs (1855–1926), Socialist Party candidate for president five times, and Wendell L. Willkie (1892–1944), the Republican candidate in 1940.

A dozen native and adoptive Hoosiers have held cabinet posts. Hugh McCulloch (b.Maine, 1808–95) was twice secretary of the treasury, in 1865–69 and 1884–85. Walter Q. Gresham (b.England, 1832–95) was successively postmaster general, secretary of the treasury, and secretary of state. John W. Foster (1836–1917) was an editor and diplomat before service as secretary of state under President Benjamin Harrison. Two other postmasters general came from Indiana: Harry S. New (1858–1937) and Will H. Hays (1879–1954). Hays resigned to become president of the Motion Picture Producers and Distributors

(1922–45), and enforced its moral code in Hollywood films through what became widely known as the Hays Office. Two Hoosiers served as secretary of the interior: Caleb B. Smith (b.Massachusetts, 1808–64) and John P. Usher (b.New York, 1816–89). Richard W. Thompson (b.Virginia, 1809–1900) was secretary of the Navy. William H. H. Miller (b.New York, 1840–1917) was attorney general. Two native sons and Purdue University alumni have been secretaries of agriculture: Claude R. Wickard (1873–1967) and Earl Butz (b.1909). Paul V. McNutt (1891–1955) was a governor of Indiana, high commissioner to the Philippines, and director of the Federal Security Administration.

Only one Hoosier, Sherman Minton (1890–1965), has served on the US Supreme Court. Ambrose Burnside (1824–81) and Lew Wallace (1827–1905) were Union generals during the Civil War; Wallace later wrote popular historical novels. Oliver P. Morton (1823–77) was a strong and meddlesome governor during the war, and a leader of the radical Republicans during the postwar Reconstruction. Colonel Richard Owen (b.England, 1810–90) commanded Camp Morton (Indianapolis) for Confederate prisoners; after the war, some of his grateful prisoners contributed to place a bust of Owen in the Indiana statehouse. Rear Admiral Norman Scott (1889–1942) distinguished himself at Guadalcanal during World War II. Nearly 70 Hoosiers have won the Medal of Honor.

Dr. Hermann J. Muller (b.New York, 1890–1967), of Indiana University, won the Nobel Prize in physiology or medicine in 1946 for proving that radiation can produce mutation in genes. Harold C. Urey (1893–1981) won the Nobel Prize in chemistry in 1934, and Wendell Stanley (1904–71) won it in 1946. The Nobel Prize in economics was awarded to Paul Samuelson (b.1915) in 1970. The Pulitzer Prize in biography was awarded in 1920 to Albert J. Beveridge (b.Ohio, 1862–1927) for his *Life of John Marshall.* Beveridge also served in the US Senate. Booth Tarkington (1869–1946) won the Pulitzer Prize for fiction in 1918 and 1921. A. B. Guthrie (1901–91) won it for fiction in 1950. The Pulitzer Prize in history went to R. C. Buley (1893–1968) in 1951 for *The Old Northwest.*

Aviation pioneer Wilbur Wright (1867–1912) was born in Millville. Other figures in the public eye were chemist Harvey W. Wiley (1844–1930), who was responsible for the Food and Drug Act of 1906; Emil Schram (1893–1897), president of the New York Stock Exchange from 1931 to 1951; and Alfred C. Kinsey (b.New Jersey, 1894–1956), who investigated human sexual behavior and issued the two famous "Kinsey reports" in 1948 and 1953.

Indiana claims such humorists as George Ade (1866–1944), Frank McKinney "Kin" Hubbard (b.Ohio, 1868–1930), and Don Herold (1889–1966). Historians Charles (1874–1948) and Mary (1876–1958) Beard, Claude Bowers (1878–1958), and Glenn Tucker (1892–1976) were Hoosiers. Maurice Thompson (1844–1901) and George Barr McCutcheon (1866–1928) excelled in historical romances. The best-known poets were James Whitcomb Riley (1849–1916) and William Vaughn Moody (1869–1910). Juvenile writer Annie Fellows Johnston (1863–1931) produced the "Little Colonel" series.

Other Indiana novelists include Edward Eggleston (1837–1902), Meredith Nicholson (1866–1947), David Graham Phillips (1868–1911) Gene Stratton Porter (1868–1924), Theodore Dreiser (1871–1945), Lloyd C. Douglas (1877–1951), Rex Stout (1886–1975), William E. Wilson (b.1906), Jessamyn West (1907–84), and Kurt Vonnegut (b.1922). Well-known journalists were news analyst Elmer Davis (1890–1958), war correspondent Ernie Pyle (1900–45), and columnist Janet Flanner (1892–1978), "Genet" of *The New Yorker.*

Among the few noted painters Indiana has produced are Theodore C. Steele (1847–1928), William M. Chase (1851–

1927), J. Ottis Adams (1851–1927), Otto Stark (1859–1926), Wayman Adams (1883–1959), Clifton Wheeler (1883–1953), Marie Goth (1887–1975), C. Curry Bohm (1894–1971), and Floyd Hopper (b.1909).

Composers of Indiana origin have worked mainly in popular music: Paul Dresser (1857–1906), Cole Porter (1893–1964), and Howard Hoagland "Hoagy" Carmichael (1899–1981). Howard Hawks (1896–1977) was a renowned film director. Entertainers from Indiana include actor and dancer Clifton Webb (Webb Hollenbeck, 1896–1966); orchestra leader Phil Harris (1904–95); comedians Ole Olsen (1892–1963), Richard "Red" Skelton (1913–97), and Herb Shriner (b.Ohio, 1918–70); actresses Marjorie Main (1890–1975) and Carole Lombard (Jane Peters, 1908–42); and singer Michael Jackson (b.1958).

Hoosier sports heroes include Knute Rockne (b.Norway, 1888–1931), famed as a football player and coach at Notre Dame. Star professionals who played high school basketball in Indiana include Oscar Robertson (b.Tennessee, 1938) and Larry Bird (b.1956), who at Indiana State University in 1978/79 was honored as college basketball's player of the year.

[50]BIBLIOGRAPHY

Banta, R. E. *Indiana Authors and Their Books, 1816–1916.* Crawfordville, Ind.: Wabash College, 1949.

———. *The Wabash.* New York: Farrar & Rinehart, 1950.

Barnhart, John D., and Donald F. Carmony. *Indiana from Frontier to Industrial Commonwealth.* 4 vols. New York: Lewis Historical Publishing, 1954.

Barnhart, John D., and Dorothy L. Riker. *Indiana to 1816: The Colonial Period.* Indianapolis: Indiana Historical Society, 1971.

Boomhower, Ray E. and Jacob Piatt Dunn, Jr.: *A Life in History and Politics, 1855-1924.* Indianapolis: Indiana Historical Society, 1997.

Buley, R. C. *The Old Northwest: Pioneer Period, 1815–1840.* Indianapolis: Indiana Historical Society, 1950.

Carter, Jared, and Darryl Jones. *Indiana.* Portland, Ore.: Graphic Arts Center Publishing Co., 1984.

Cayton, Andrew R.L. *Frontier Indiana.* Bloomington: Indiana University Press, 1996.

Dorson, Ron. *The Indy Five Hundred.* New York: Norton, 1974.

Federal Writers' Project. *Indiana: A Guide to the Hoosier State.* Reprint. New York: Somerset, n.d. (orig. 1941).

Gisler, Margaret. *Fun with the Family in Indiana: Hundreds of Ideas for Day Trips with the Kids.* Guilford, Conn.: Globe Pequot Press, 2000.

Indiana State Chamber of Commerce. *Here Is Your Indiana Government.* Indianapolis, 1983.

Latta, William C. *Outline History of Indiana Agriculture.* Lafayette: Purdue University and Indiana County Agricultural Agents Association, 1938.

Leibowitz, Irving. *My Indiana.* Englewood Cliffs, N.J.: Prentice-Hall, 1964.

Lilly, Eli. *Prehistoric Antiquities of Indiana.* Indianapolis: Indiana Historical Society, 1937.

Lindley, Harlow, ed. *Indiana as Seen by Early Travelers.* Indianapolis: Indiana Historical Commission, 1916.

Martin, John Bartlow. *Indiana: An Interpretation.* New York: Knopf, 1947.

McAuliffe, Bill. *Indiana Facts and Symbols.* New York: Hilltop Books, 1999.

McCord, Shirley S., ed. *Travel Accounts of Indiana, 1679–1961.* Indianapolis: Indiana Historical Bureau, 1970.

Nicholson, Meredith. *The Hoosiers.* New York: Macmillan, 1900.

Nolan, Jeanette C. *Hoosier City: The Story of Indianapolis.* New York: Messner, 1943.

Peat, Wilbur D. *Pioneer Painters of Indiana.* Indianapolis: Art Association of Indianapolis, 1954.

Ritchie, Ingrid and Sheila Suess Kennedy, eds. *To Market, to Market: Reinventing Indianapolis.* Lanham, Md.: University Press of America, 2001.

Shumaker, Arthur W. *A History of Indiana Literature.* Indianapolis: Indiana Historical Society, 1962.

Starr, George W. *Industrial Development of Indiana.* Bloomington: Indiana University Press, 1937.

Thompson, Donald E. *Indiana Authors and Their Books, 1916–66.* Crawfordsville, Ind.: Wabash College, 1974.

Thornbrough, Emma Lou. *Indiana Blacks in the Twentieth Century.* Bloomington: Indiana University Press, 2000.

IOWA

State of Iowa

ORIGIN OF STATE NAME: Named for Iowa Indians of the Siouan family. **NICKNAME:** The Hawkeye State. **CAPITAL:** Des Moines. **ENTERED UNION:** 28 December 1846 (29th). **SONG:** "The Song of Iowa." **MOTTO:** Our Liberties We Prize and Our Rights We Will Maintain. **FLAG:** There are three vertical stripes of blue, white, and red; in the center a spreading eagle holds in its beak a blue ribbon with the state motto. **OFFICIAL SEAL:** A sheaf and field of standing wheat and farm utensils represent agriculture; a lead furnace and a pile of pig lead are to the right. In the center stands a citizen-soldier holding a US flag with a liberty cap atop the staff in one hand and a rifle in the other. Behind him is the Mississippi River with the steamer *Iowa* and mountains; above him an eagle holds the state motto. Surrounding this scene are the words "The Great Seal of the State of Iowa" against a gold background. **BIRD:** Eastern goldfinch. **FLOWER:** Wild rose. **TREE:** Oak. **STONE:** Geode. **LEGAL HOLIDAYS:** New Year's Day, 1 January; Birthday of Martin Luther King, Jr., 3rd Monday in January; Lincoln's Birthday, 12 February; Washington's Birthday, 3rd Monday in February; Memorial Day, last Monday in May; Independence Day, 4 July; Labor Day, 1st Monday in September; Veterans Day, 11 November; Thanksgiving Day, 4th Thursday in November; Christmas Day, 25 December. **TIME:** 6 AM CST = noon GMT.

¹LOCATION, SIZE, AND EXTENT

Located in the western north-central US, Iowa is the smallest of the midwestern states situated W of the Mississippi River, and ranks 25th in size among the 50 states.

The total area of Iowa is 56,275 sq mi (145,752 sq km), of which land takes up 55,965 sq mi (144,949 sq km) and inland water 310 sq mi (803 sq km). The state extends 324 mi (521 km) E–W; its maximum extension N–S is 210 mi (338 km).

Iowa is bordered on the N by Minnesota; on the E by Wisconsin and Illinois (with the line formed by the Mississippi River); on the S by Missouri (with the extreme southeastern line defined by the Des Moines River); and on the W by Nebraska and South Dakota (with the line demarcated by the Missouri River and a tributary, the Big Sioux).

The total boundary length of Iowa is 1,151 mi (1,853 km). The state's geographic center is in Story County near Ames.

²TOPOGRAPHY

The topography of Iowa consists of a gently rolling plain that slopes from the highest point of 1,670 ft (509 m) in the northwest to the lowest point of 480 ft (146 m) in the southeast at the mouth of the Des Moines River. About two-thirds of the state lies between 800 ft (244 m) and 1,400 ft (427 m) above sea level; the mean elevation of land is 1,100 ft (336 m).

Supremely well suited for agriculture, Iowa has the richest and deepest topsoil in the US and an excellent watershed. Approximately two-thirds of the state's area is drained by the Mississippi River, which forms the entire eastern boundary, and its tributaries. The western part of the state is drained by the Missouri River and its tributaries. Iowa has 13 natural lakes. The largest are Spirit Lake (9 mi/14 km long) and West Okoboji Lake (6 mi/10 km long), both near the state's northwest border.

The Iowa glacial plain was formed by five different glaciers. The last glacier, which covered about one-fifth of the state's area, retreated from the north-central region some 10,000 years ago, leaving the topsoil as its legacy. Glacial drift formed the small lakes in the north. The oldest rock outcropping, located in the state's northwest corner, is about 1 billion years old.

³CLIMATE

Iowa lies in the humid continental zone and generally has hot summers, cold winters, and wet springs.

Temperatures vary widely during the year, with an annual average of 49°F (9°C). The state averages 166 days of full sunshine and 199 cloudy or partly cloudy days. Des Moines, in the central part of the state, has a normal daily maximum temperature of 86°F (30°C) in July and a normal daily minimum of 10°F (–4°C) in January. The record low temperature for the state is –47°F (– 44°C), established at Washta on 12 January 1912 and recorded again on Elkader on 3 February 1996; the record high is 118°F (48°C), registered at Keokuk on 20 July 1934. Annual precipitation averaged 34.7 in (88 cm) at Des Moines (1971–2000); statewide, snowfall averages 30 in (76 cm) annually and relative humidity averages 72%.

⁴FLORA AND FAUNA

Although most of Iowa is under cultivation, such unusual wild specimens as bunchberry and bearberry can be found in the northeast, where the loess soil supports tumblegrass, western beard-tongue, and prickly pear cactus. Other notable plants are pink lady's slipper and twinleaf in the eastern woodlands, arrowgrass in the northwest, and erect dryflower and royal and cinnamon ferns in sandy regions. More than 80 native plants can no longer be found, and at least 35 others are confined to a single location. The federal government classified five plant species as threatened as of August 2003. Among these are the northern wild monkshood and the eastern and western prairie fringed orchids.

Common Iowa mammals include red and gray foxes, raccoon, opossum, woodchuck, muskrat, common cottontail, gray fox, and flying squirrel. The bobolink and purple martin have flyways over the state; the cardinal, rose-breasted grosbeak, and eastern goldfinch (the state bird) nest there. Game fish include rainbow trout, smallmouth bass, and walleye; in all, Iowa has 140 native fish species.

Rare animals include the pygmy shrew, ermine, black-billed cuckoo, and crystal darter. Listed as threatened or endangered by the federal government in August 2003 were nine species, including the Indiana bat, bald eagle, Higgins' eye pearlymussel, piping plover, Iowa Pleistocene snail, pallid sturgeon, gray wolf, and least tern.

5ENVIRONMENTAL PROTECTION

Because this traditionally agricultural state's most valuable resource has been its topsoil, Iowa's conservation measures beginning in the 1930s were directed toward preventing soil erosion and preserving watershed runoff. In the 1980s and 1990s, Iowans were particularly concerned with improving air quality, preventing chemical pollution, and preserving water supplies. In 1997, wetlands covered 12% of Iowa. The Wetlands Reserve Program of the 1990 Food, Agriculture, Conservation and Trade Act was created to reclaim some of the state's lost wetlands.

On 1 July 1983, the Department of Water, Air and Waste Management came into operation, with responsibility for environmental functions formerly exercised by separate state agencies. Functions of the new department include regulating operation of the state's 2,900 public water supply systems, overseeing nearly 1,200 municipal and industrial wastewater treatment plants, inspecting dams, and establishing chemical and bacterial standards to protect the quality of lakes. The department also enforces laws prohibiting open dumping of solid wastes, regulates the construction and operation of 140 solid waste disposal projects, and monitors the handling of hazardous wastes. It also establishes standards for air quality and regulates the emission of air pollutants from more than 600 industries and utilities.

In 2003, Iowa had 172 hazardous waste sites listed in the Environmental Protection Agency's database, 13 of which were on the National Priorities List. In 2001, Iowa received $52,181,000 in federal grants from the Environmental Protection Agency; EPA expenditures for procurement contracts in Iowa that year amounted to $7,000.

6POPULATION

Iowa ranked 30th in population in the US with an estimated total of 2,936,760 in 2002, an increase of 0.4% since 2000. Between 1990 and 2000, Iowa's population grew from 2,776,755 to 2,926,324, an increase of 5.4%. The population is projected to reach 2,941,000 by 2005 and 3 million by 2025. The population density in 2000 was 52.4 persons per sq mi.

Iowa's population growth was rapid during the early years of settlement. When the first pioneers arrived in the early 19th century, an estimated 8,000 Indians were living within the state's present boundaries. From 1832 to 1840, the number of white settlers increased from fewer than 50 to 43,112. The population had almost doubled to more than 80,000 by the time Iowa became a state in 1846. The great influx of European immigrants who came via other states during the 1840s and 1850s caused the new state's population to soar to 674,913 at the 1860 census. By the end of the next decade, the population had reached nearly 1,200,000; by 1900, it had surpassed 2,200,000. The state's population growth leveled off in the 20th century.

In 2000, the median age in Iowa was 36.6. Just over 25.1% of the populace were under age 18 while 14.9% were age 65 or older, one of the highest concentrations of elderly in all of the states.

In 2002, the largest cities with populations of 100,000 or more were Des Moines, 198,076, and Cedar Rapids, 122,514. Other large cities include Davenport, Sioux City, Waterloo, Dubuque, and Iowa City. In 1999, the Des Moines metropolitan area had 443,496 residents; the Davenport metropolitan area had 358,842 residents that year.

7ETHNIC GROUPS

In 2000, there were 61,853 black Americans, 8,989 American Indians, and 82,473 Hispanics and Latinos living in Iowa.

In 2000, among Iowans of European descent, there were 1,046,153 Germans (35.7% of the state total); 395,905 Irish (13.5%); and 277,487 English (9.5%). The foreign-born population numbered 91,085 (3.1%), more than double the total of 43,316 in 1990. Primary countries of origin included Germany, Mexico, Laos, Canada, Korea, and Vietnam.

8LANGUAGES

A few Indian place-names are the legacy of early Siouan Iowa Indians and the westward-moving Algonkian Sauk and Fox tribes who pushed them out: Iowa, Ottumwa, Keokuk, Sioux City, Oskaloosa, Decorah.

Iowa English reflects the three major migration streams: Northern in that half of the state above Des Moines and North Midland in the southern half, with a slight South Midland trace in the extreme southeastern corner. Although some Midland features extend into upper Iowa, rather sharp contrasts exist between the two halves. In pronunciation, Northern features contrast directly with Midland: /hyumor/ with /yumor/, /ah/ in *on* and *fog* with /aw/, the vowel of *but* in *bulge* with the vowel of *put*, and /too/ with /tyoo/ for *two*. Northern words also contrast with Midland words: *crab* with *crawdad*, *corn on the cob* with *roasting ears*, *quarter to* with *quarter till*, *barnyard* with *barn lot*, and *gopher* with *ground squirrel*.

In 2000, 94.2% of all Iowans aged five or more spoke only English at home, down from 96.1% in 1990.

The following table gives selected statistics from the 2000 census for language spoken at home by persons five years old and over. The category "Other West Germanic languages" includes Dutch, Pennsylvania Dutch, and Afrikaans. The category "African languages" includes Amharic, Ibo, Twi, Yoruba, Bantu, Swahili, and Somali. The category "Scandinavian languages" includes Danish, Norwegian, and Swedish.

LANGUAGE	NUMBER	PERCENT
Population 5 years and over	2,738,499	100.0
Speak only English	2,578,477	94.2
Speak a language other than English	160,022	5.8
Speak a language other than English	160,022	5.8
Spanish or Spanish Creole	79,491	2.9
German	17,262	0.6
French (incl. Patois, Cajun)	7,476	0.3
Serbo-Croatian	6,452	0.2
Vietnamese	6,182	0.2
Chinese	5,191	0.2
Laotian	3,939	0.1
Other West Germanic languages	3,552	0.1
Korean	2,493	0.1
Scandinavian languages	2,385	0.1
Russian	2,233	0.1
African languages	2,137	0.1
Arabic	2,053	0.1

9RELIGIONS

The first church building in Iowa was constructed by Methodists in Dubuque in 1834; a Roman Catholic church was built in Dubuque the following year. By 1860, the largest religious sects were the Methodists, Presbyterians, Catholics, Baptists, and Congregationalists. Other religious groups who came to Iowa during the 19th century included Lutherans, Dutch Reformers, Quakers, Mennonites, Jews, and the Community of True Inspiration, or Amana Society, which founded seven communal villages.

Mainline Protestantism is predominant in the state even though the largest single Protestant denomination is the Evangelical Free Church of America, which had about 268,211

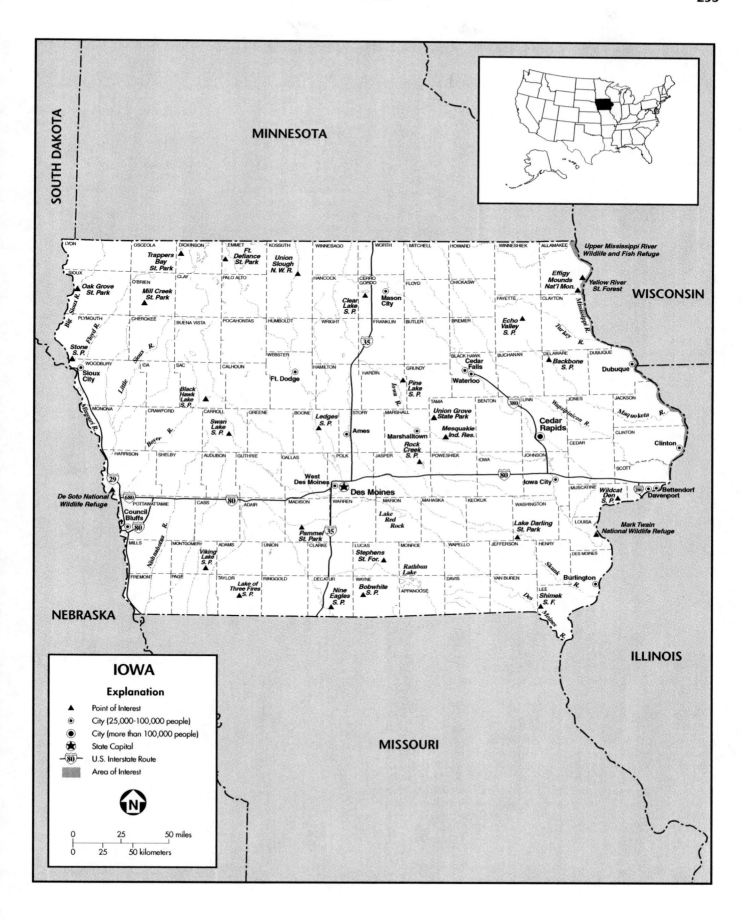

SOUTH DAKOTA

WISCONSIN

NEBRASKA

ILLINOIS

MISSOURI

Upper Mississippi River
Wildlife and Fish Refuge

IOWA

Explanation

▲ Point of Interest

⊙ City (25,000-100,000 people)

◉ City (more than 100,000 people)

★ State Capital

─80─ U.S. Interstate Route

▨ Area of Interest

0   25   50 miles

0   25   50 kilometers

LYON OSCEOLA DICKINSON EMMET KOSSUTH WINNEBAGO WORTH MITCHELL HOWARD WINNESHIEK ALLAMAKEE

Trappers Bay St. Park Ft. Defiance St. Park Union Slough N.W.R.

SIOUX O'BRIEN CLAY PALO ALTO HANCOCK CERRO GORDO FLOYD CHICKASW FAYETTE CLAYTON

Oak Grove St. Park Mill Creek St. Park Clean Lake S.P. Mason City Echo Valley S.P.

Effigy Mounds Nat'l Mon. Yellow River St. Forest

PLYMOUTH CHEROKEE BUENA VISTA POCAHONTAS HUMBOLDT WRIGHT FRANKLIN BUTLER BREMER DELAWARE DUBUQUE

Stone S.P. WOODBURY IDA SAC CALHOUN WEBSTER HAMILTON HARDIN GRUNDY BLACK HAWK BUCHANAN Backbone S.P.

Sioux City Ft. Dodge Cedar Falls Waterloo Dubuque

MONONA CRAWFORD CARROLL GREENE BOONE STORY MARSHALL TAMA BENTON LINN JONES JACKSON

Black Hawk Lake S.P. Swan Lake S.P. Ledges S.P. Pine Lake S.P. Union Grove State Park Mesquakie Ind. Res. Cedar Rapids

HARRISON SHELBY AUDUBON GUTHRIE DALLAS POLK JASPER POWESHIEK IOWA JOHNSON CEDAR CLINTON Clinton

Ames Marshalltown Rock Creek S.P.

West Des Moines Des Moines Iowa City SCOTT MUSCATINE

Council Bluffs POTTAWATTAMIE CASS ADAIR MADISON WARREN MARION MAHASKA KEOKUK WASHINGTON Wildcat Den S.P. Bettendorf Davenport

MILLS MONTGOMERY ADAMS UNION CLARKE LUCAS MONROE WAPELLO JEFFERSON HENRY LOUISA

Pammel St. Park Lake Red Rock Lake Darling St. Park Mark Twain National Wildlife Refuge

Viking Lake S.P. Stephens St. For. Rathbun Lake DES MOINES

FREMONT PAGE TAYLOR RINGGOLD DECATUR WAYNE APPANOOSE DAVIS VAN BUREN LEE Burlington

Lake of Three Fires S.P. Nine Eagles S.P. Bobwhite S.P. Shimek S.F.

De Soto National Wildlife Refuge

Big Sioux R. Floyd R. Little Sioux R. Boyer R. Nishnabotna R. Missouri R. Iowa R. Wapsipinicon R. Maquoketa R. Turkey R. Mississippi R. Skunk R. Des Moines R.

35 380 80 29 680 61

members in 2000. Other major Protestant denominations include the United Methodist Church (with 248,211 adherents), the Lutheran Church—Missouri Synod (120,075 adherents), the Presbyterian Church USA (69,974 adherents), and the United Church of Christ (49,205 adherents). Roman Catholic church membership was about 558,092 in 2000. The Jewish community had about 6,400 members. Muslims numbered about 4,717. Nearly 41.5% (over 1.2 million) of the state population were not counted as members of any religious organization.

10 TRANSPORTATION

The early settlers came to Iowa by way of the Ohio and Mississippi rivers and the Great Lakes, then traveled overland on trails via wagon and stagecoach. The need of Iowa farmers to haul their products to market over long distances prompted the development of the railroads, particularly during the 1880s. River traffic still plays a vital role in the state's transport.

In 2000, Iowa had 4,389 mi (7,063 km) of track, including 2,431 route miles (3,912 km) of Class I track operated by three railroads. Amtrak operates the long-distance California Zephyr (Chicago to Oakland, Calif.) and Southwest Chief (Chicago to Los Angeles, Calif.), serving six major stations in Iowa.

Iowa had 113,377 mi (182,462 km) of public roadway in 2000, including 103,513 rural mi (166,588 km) and 9,864 urban mi (15,874 km). In 2000, there were 3,232,894 registered vehicles in the state, including 1,751,690 automobiles, 1,346,310 trucks, and 8,223 buses, with 1,952,508 licensed drivers.

Iowa is bordered by two great navigable rivers, the Mississippi and the Missouri. They provided excellent transport facilities for the early settlers via keelboats and paddle-wheel steamers. Today, rivers remain an important part of Iowa's intermodal transportation system. In 1996, nearly 43 million tons of cargo moved on the Mississippi past Davenport, including over 26 million tons of grain. Important terminal ports on the Mississippi are Dubuque and Davenport; and on the Missouri, Sioux City and Council Bluffs. These rivers provide shippers a gateway to an extensive inland waterway system that has access to ports in St. Paul, Chicago, Pittsburgh, Houston, and New Orleans. Most docks in Iowa are privately owned, and all are privately operated.

Iowa's busiest airfield is Des Moines Municipal Airport, which handled 845,290 enplaned passengers in 2000.

11 HISTORY

The fertile land now known as the State of Iowa was first visited by primitive hunting bands of the Paleo-Indian period some 12,000 years ago. The first permanent settlers of the land were the Woodland Indians, who built villages in the forested areas along the Mississippi River, introduced agriculture, and left behind only their animal-shaped burial mounds.

Not until June 1673 did the first known white men come to the territory. When Louis Jolliet, accompanied by five French voyageurs and a Jesuit priest, Jacques Marquette, stopped briefly in Iowa on his voyage down the Mississippi, the region was uninhabited except for the Sioux in the west and a few outposts of Illinois and Iowa Indians in the east. Iowa was part of the vast, vaguely defined Louisiana Territory that extended from the Gulf of Mexico to the Canadian border and was ruled by the French until title was transferred to Spain in 1762. Napoleon took the territory back in 1800 and then promptly sold all of Louisiana Territory to the amazed American envoys who had come to Paris seeking only the purchase of New Orleans and the mouth of the Mississippi. After Iowa had thus come under US control in 1803, the Lewis and Clark expedition worked its way up the Missouri River to explore the land that President Thomas Jefferson had purchased so cheaply. Iowa looked as empty as it had to Jolliet 130 years earlier. The only white man who had come to explore its riches before the American annexation was an enterprising former French trapper, Julien Dubuque. Soon after the American Revolution, he had obtained from the Fox Indians the sole right to work the lead mines west of the Mississippi, and for 20 years Dubuque was the only white settler in Iowa.

The first wave of migrants into Iowa were the Winnebago, Sauk, and Fox, driven there by the US Army, which was clearing Wisconsin and Illinois of their Indian populations to make way for white farmers. Although President Andrew Jackson had intended that Louisiana Territory lying north of Missouri should forever be Indian land, the occupation of Iowa by the Indians was brief. Following the abortive attempt by an aging Sauk chieftain, Black Hawk, to win his lands in Illinois, the Sauk and Fox were driven westward in 1832 and forced to cede their lands in eastern Iowa to the incoming white settlers.

Placed under the territorial jurisdiction of Michigan in 1834, and then two years later under the newly created Territory of Wisconsin, Iowa became a separate territory in 1838. The first territorial governor, Robert Lucas, extended county boundaries and local government westward, planned for a new capital city to be located on the Iowa River, resisted Missouri's attempt to encroach on Iowa territory, and began planning for statehood by drawing boundary lines that included not only the present State of Iowa but also southern Minnesota up to present-day Minneapolis.

Because a new state seeking admission to the Union at that time could expect favorable action from Congress only if accompanied by a slave state, Iowa was designed to come into the Union with Florida as its slaveholding counterpart. A serious dispute over how large the state would be delayed Iowa's admission into the Union until 28 December 1846, but by the delay the people of Iowa got what they wanted—all the land between the Mississippi and Missouri rivers—even though they had to abandon Lucas's northern claim.

The settlement of Iowa was rapidly accomplished. With one-fourth of the nation's fertile topsoil located within its borders, Iowa was a powerful magnet that drew farmers by the thousands from Indiana, Ohio, and Tennessee, and even from faraway Virginia, the Carolinas, New York, and New England. Except for German and Irish immigrants along the eastern border and later Scandinavian immigrants during the 1870s and 1880s, Iowa was settled primarily by Anglo-American stock. The settlers were overwhelmingly Protestant in religion and remarkably homogeneous in ethnic and cultural backgrounds. Although New Englanders made up only 5% of Iowa's early population, they had a cultural influence that far exceeded their numbers. Many small Iowa towns—with their large frame houses, elm-lined streets, and Congregational churches—looked like New England villages faithfully replicated on the prairie.

Fiercely proud of its claim to be the first free state created out of the Louisiana Purchase, Iowa was an important center of abolitionist sentiment throughout the 1850s. The Underground Railroad for fugitive slaves from the South ran across the southern portion of Iowa to the Mississippi River. Radical abolitionist John Brown spent the winters of 1857 and 1859 in the small Quaker village of Springdale, preparing for his attack on the US arsenal at Harpers Ferry, in western Virginia.

Although the Democrats had a slight edge over their Whig opposition in the early years of statehood, a majority of Iowa voters in 1856 supported the new Republican Party and, for the most part, did so in succeeding years. A Republican legislative majority in 1857 scrapped the state's first constitution, which had been written by Jacksonian Democrats 12 years earlier. The new document moved the state capital from Iowa City westward to Des Moines, but it provided that the state university would remain forever in Iowa City.

When the Civil War came, Iowa overwhelmingly supported the Union cause. Iowans fought not only for their ideals, the abolition of slavery and the preservation of the Union, but also for the very practical objective of keeping open the Mississippi River, the main artery for transport of agricultural products.

In the decades following the Civil War, Iowans on the national scene, most notably US Senators James Harlan and his successor William B. Allison belonged to the conservative Republican camp, but they frequently faced liberal Republican and Populist opposition inside the state. The railroad had been lavishly welcomed by Iowans in the 1850s; by the 1870s, Iowa farmers were desperately trying to free themselves from the stranglehold of the rail lines. The National Grange was powerful enough in Iowa to put through the legislature the so-called Granger laws to regulate the railroads. At the turn of the century, as the aging Allison's hold on the state weakened, Iowa became a center for Republican progressivism.

Following World War I, the conservatives regained control of the Republican Party. They remained in control until, during the 1960s, new liberal leadership was forced on the party because of the debacle of Barry Goldwater's 1964 presidential campaign, controversy over US involvement in Vietnam, and effective opposition from a revitalized Democratic Party led by Harold Hughes. After Hughes gave up the governorship in 1969 to become a US senator, Republicans once more dominated the executive branch, but Democrats gained control of the state legislature and made strong inroads at the top levels of state government.

Iowa's economy suffered in the 1980s from a combination of high debt, high interest rates, numerous droughts, and low crop prices. Businesses left the state or automated, shrinking their work forces. The population dropped by 7.9%. By the 1990s the companies that had survived were in a much stronger position and diversification efforts in both the agricultural and manufacturing sectors had ushered in a period of cautious prosperity. The number of jobs in the service sector grew by 10%, and the state's unemployment rate in 1992 was 4.7%, substantially lower than the national average. By 1999 it had dropped to 2.5%, the lowest rate in the nation. In Iowa, as elsewhere in the Midwest, high-tech and service industries continued to pull workers away from farming—and away from the state, causing many to worry about a disappearing way of life. While the governor worked with state officials to entice young Iowans who had fled the state to return home, farming promised to be a hard sell for even the best marketers, as many of the state's agricultural producers eked by. By 2003, the US economy was slowly recovering from its 2001 recession, and Iowa was also feeling the effects. In July 2003, Iowa's unemployment rate was 4.6%, however, below the national average of 6.2%.

A debilitating drought hit Iowa in 1988, reducing corn and soybean harvests to their lowest levels in 14 years and prompting Governor Terry Branstad to declare a statewide emergency. In 1993, unusually heavy spring and summer rains produced record floods along the Mississippi River by mid-July. Countless levees, or earthen berms designed to raise the height of river banks, collapsed or were overrun. The entire state of Iowa was declared a disaster area. Altogether, it was estimated that 40 million acres of farmland were severely damaged and 500,000 acres permanently ruined. Agricultural woes continued to plague the state later in the decade. In 1999 Governor Tom Vilsack declared that Iowa was in a farm crisis, warning that problems plaguing the state's agricultural economy would soon affect urban and suburban areas. With the state's farmers getting record low prices for corn, soybeans, cattle, and hogs, producers were struggling to pay their loans.

In 1999 Governor Vilsack proposed one of the most dramatic increases in environmental spending in the state's recent history, asking for $10.5 million in new spending to improve the quality of Iowa's rivers and streams. He said the money was necessary to clean the state's waterways and boost recreation.

In 2001, the state took steps to allow refugees from other countries, including Afghanistan, to locate in small Iowa towns. Governor Vilsack during the early 2000s had established a record for promoting education, by signing into law over $200 million in new bills aimed at reducing class sizes. In 2003, he aimed to further improve education, health care, and the environment. Iowa House and Senate Republican leaders created an "Iowa Values Fund," a $503 economic development program, also supported by Vilsack.

12 STATE GOVERNMENT

Iowa has had two state constitutions. The constitution of 1857 replaced the original constitution of 1846 and with 52 amendments as of January 2003 (three of which were later nullified by the state supreme court), is still in effect.

The state legislature, or general assembly, consists of a 50-member senate and a 100-member house of representatives. Senators serve four-year terms, with half the members elected every two years. Representatives are elected to two-year terms. The legislature convenes each year on the 2nd Monday in January. Length of session is indirectly limited by the legislators' salary. Special sessions may only be called by the governor and length is not limited. Each house may introduce or amend legislation, with a simple majority vote required for passage. Proposed amendments must be approved by a majority vote in two sessions of the legislature before it is sent to voters for ratification. The governor's veto of a bill may be overridden by a two-thirds vote of the elected members in both houses. Unless vetoed, a bill becomes law after three days when the legislature is in session. Legislators must be US citizens and must have resided in the state for a year and in the district for at least 60 days prior to election; a representative must be at least 21 years old, and a senator 25. The legislative salary was $20,758 in 2002, unchanged from 1999.

The state's elected executives are the governor, lieutenant governor, secretary of state, treasurer, attorney general, and secretary of agriculture, all serving four-year terms. The governor and lieutenant governor, elected jointly, must be US citizens, at least 30 years old, and must have been resident of the state for at least two years. In 2002 the governor's salary was $104,482.

To vote in Iowa, a person must be a US citizen, at least 18 years old, a state resident, and not able to claim the right to vote elsewhere. Restrictions apply to those convicted of certain crimes and to those judged by the court as mentally incompetent to vote.

13 POLITICAL PARTIES

For 70 years following the Civil War, a majority of Iowa voters supported the Republicans over the Democrats in nearly all state and national elections. During the Great Depression of the 1930s, Iowa briefly turned to the Democrats, supporting Franklin D. Roosevelt in two presidential elections. But from 1940 through 1992, the majority of Iowans voted Republican in 10 of 12 presidential elections. Republicans won 34 of the 42 gubernatorial elections from 1900 through 1990 and controlled both houses of the state legislature for 112 of the 130 years from 1855 to 1984.

In the 1960s, Iowa showed signs of a Democratic upsurge. Harold Hughes, a liberal Democrat, revitalized the party in Iowa and was elected governor for three two-year terms before moving on to the US Senate. During the post-Watergate period of the mid-1970s, Democrats captured both US Senate seats, five of the six congressional seats, and both houses of the Iowa legislature.

By the early and mid-1990s, a balance had reasserted itself. In 2000, Iowa gave Democrat Al Gore 49% of the vote, while Republican George W. Bush received 48%, and Green Party candidate Ralph Nader picked up 2%. In 2002 there were 1,966,459 registered voters. In 1998, 32% of registered voters were Democratic, 33% Republican, and 35% unaffiliated or members of other parties. The state had seven electoral votes in the 2000 presidential election.

Republican Terry Branstad won election to a fourth term as governor in 1994. But in the 1998 election he was succeeded by Democrat Tom Vilsack, who won reelection in 2002. As of 2003, a Democrat and a Republican both served in the US Senate— Republican Charles Grassley, who won election to a fourth term in 1998, and Democrat Tom Harkin, who won reelection in 2002. In the 2002 elections, Iowans sent four Republicans and one Democrat to represent them in the US House. In mid-2003, there were 29 Republicans and 21 Democrats in the state senate, and 54 Republicans and 46 Democrats in the state house.

Iowa's presidential caucuses are held in January of presidential campaign years, earlier than any other state, thus giving Iowans a degree of influence in national politics.

14LOCAL GOVERNMENT

The state's 99 counties are governed by boards of supervisors. In general, county officials, including auditor, treasurer, recorder, and sheriff, are elected to four-year terms. They enforce state laws, collect taxes, supervise welfare activities, and manage roads and bridges.

Local government was exercised by 948 municipal units in 2002. The mayor-council system functioned in the great majority of these municipalities, though some of the larger cities employ the council-manager or commission system. Iowa's towns and cities derive their local powers from the state constitution, but the power to tax is authorized by the state general assembly. In 2002 there were 386 public school districts and 542 special districts.

15STATE SERVICES

To address the continuing threat of terrorism and to work with the federal Department of Homeland Security (created in 2002 following the terrorist attacks of 11 September 2001), homeland security in Iowa in 2003 operated under state statute; the emergency management director was designated as the state homeland security advisor.

The Department of Education is responsible for educational services in Iowa. It assists local school boards in supplying special educational programs and administers local education agencies.

Transportation services are directed by the Department of Transportation, which is responsible for the safe and efficient operation of highways, motor vehicles, airports, railroads, public transit, and river transportation. The department's motor vehicle division licenses drivers, road vehicles, and car dealers. Other departments include those for corrections, cultural affairs, economic development, human services, justice, and revenue and finance. Iowa 2010 and IowAccess provide Internet gateways to the state.

Health and welfare services are provided by the Department of Public Health, the Iowa Mental Health Authority, and the Department of Social Services. Public protection is the responsibility of the Departments of Public Defense and of Public Safety. Housing programs are supported by the Iowa Housing Finance Authority.

16JUDICIAL SYSTEM

The Iowa supreme court consists of seven justices who are appointed by the governor and confirmed to eight-year terms by judicial elections held after they have served on the bench for at least one year. Judges may stand for reelection before their terms expire. The justices select one of their number as chief justice. The court exercises appellate jurisdiction in civil and criminal cases, supervises the trial courts, and prescribes rules of civil and appellate procedure. The supreme court transfers certain cases to the court of appeals, a six-member appellate court that began reviewing civil and criminal cases in 1977, and may review its decisions. Judges on the court of appeals are appointed and confirmed to six-year terms in the same manner as supreme court justices; they elect one of their members as chief judge.

The state is divided into eight judicial districts, each with a chief judge appointed to a two-year term by the chief justice of the supreme court. District court judges are appointed to six-year terms by the governor from nominations submitted by district nominating commissions. Appointees must stand for election after they have served as judges for at least one year.

Iowa Presidential Vote by Political Parties, 1948–2000

YEAR	ELECTORAL VOTE	IOWA WINNER	DEMOCRAT	REPUBLICAN	PROGRESSIVE	PROHIBITION	SOCIALIST LABOR
1948	10	*Truman (D)	522,380	494,018	12,125	3,382	4,274
1952	10	*Eisenhower (R)	451,513	808,906	5,085	2,882	—
							CONSTITUTION
1956	10	*Eisenhower (R)	501,858	729,187	—	—	3,202
1960	10	Nixon (R)	550,565	722,381	—	—	—
1964	9	*Johnson (D)	733,030	449,148		1,902	—
					SOC. WORKERS	AMERICAN IND.	
1968	9	*Nixon (R)	476,699	619,106	3,377	66,422	—
						AMERICAN	PEACE AND FREEDOM
1972	8	*Nixon (R)	496,206	706,207	—	22,056	1,332
							LIBERTARIAN
1976	8	Ford (R)	619,931	632,863	—	3,040	1,452
					CITIZENS		
1980	8	*Reagan (R)	508,672	676,026	2,191	NA	12,324
1984	8	*Reagan (R)	605,620	703,088	—	—	—
1988	8	Dukakis (D)	670,557	545,355	755	540	2,494
					IND. (Perot)		
1992	7	*Clinton (D)	586,353	504,891	253,468	3,079	1,177
1996	7	*Clinton (D)	620,258	492,644	105,159	-	2,315
					REFORM	GREEN	
2000	7	Gore (D)	638,517	634,373	5,731	29,374	3,209

* Won US presidential election.

As of June 2001 there were 8,101 prisoners in federal and state institutions, an increase of 6.0% from the previous year. The state's incarceration rate stood at 277 per 100,000 inhabitants. Iowa's total crime rate in 2001 was 3,301.2 per 100,000 population, including a total of 7,865 violent crimes and 88,634 crimes against property in that year.

Iowa does not have a death penalty.

[17]ARMED FORCES

In 2002, 447 active-duty military personnel were stationed in Iowa: 274 were in the US Army, 126 in the Navy and Marines, and 47 in the Air Force. Iowa firms received defense contract awards amounting to $503 million in 2001

There were 292,020 veterans of US military service in Iowa as of 2000, of whom 63,292 served in World War II; 42,299 in the Korean conflict; 87,496 during the Vietnam era; and 26,382 during 1990–2000 (including the Persian Gulf War). The federal government expended $515 million for veterans' benefits in Iowa during fiscal year 2002.

In 2000, the Iowa Department of Public Safety employed 455 full-time sworn officers.

[18]MIGRATION

Iowa was opened, organized, and settled by a generation of native migrants from other states. According to the first federal census of Iowa in 1850, 31% of the total population of 192,214 came from nearby midwestern states (Illinois, Wisconsin, Indiana, Michigan, and Ohio), 14% from the five southern border states, and 13% from the Middle Atlantic states.

Another 10% of the state's 1850 population consisted of immigrants from northern Europe. The largest group were Germans who had fled military conscription; the next largest group had sought to escape the hardships of potato famine in Ireland or of agricultural and technological displacement in Scotland, England, and Wales. They were joined in the 1850s by Dutch immigrants seeking religious liberty, and in the 1860s and 1870s by Norwegians and Swedes. During and immediately after the Civil War, some former slaves fled the South for Iowa, and more blacks settled in Iowa cities after 1900.

But many of the migrants who came to Iowa did not stay long. Some Iowans left to join the gold rush, and others settled lands in the West. Migration out of the state has continued to this day as retired Iowans seeking warmer climates have moved to California and other southwestern states; from 1970 through 1990, Iowa's net loss through migration amounted to over 266,000.

An important migratory trend within the state has been from the farm to the city. Although Iowa has remained a major agricultural state, the urban population surpassed the rural population by 1960 and increased to over 60.6% of the total population by 1990. Between 1990 and 1998, Iowa had a net loss of 13,000 in domestic migration and a net gain of 19,000 in international migration. In 1998, 1,655 foreign immigrants arrived in the state. Between 1990 and 1998, Iowa's overall population increased by 3.1%. In the period 1995–2000, 214,841 people moved into the state and 247,853 moved out, for a net loss of 33,012, about 28,695 of whom moved to Illinois.

[19]INTERGOVERNMENTAL COOPERATION

Iowa is a signatory to the Midwest Interstate Low-Level Radioactive Waste Compact Commission, the Iowa-Missouri and Iowa-Nebraska boundary compacts, and a number of other major interstate compacts and agreements. Federal grants to the Iowa state government amounted to over $3 billion in fiscal year 2001.

[20]ECONOMY

Iowa's economy is based on agriculture. Although the value of the state's manufactures exceeds the value of its farm production, manufacturing is basically farm-centered. The major industries are food processing and the manufacture of agriculture-related products, such as farm machinery.

Periodic recessions—and especially the Great Depression of the 1930s—have afflicted Iowa farmers and adversely affected the state's entire economy. But technological progress in agriculture and the proliferation of manufacturing industries have enabled Iowans to enjoy general prosperity since World War II. Because the state's population is scattered, the growth of light manufacturing has extended to hundreds of towns and cities.

In the late 1970s, the state's major economic problem was inflation, which boosted the cost of farm equipment and fertilizers. In the early 1980s, high interest rates and falling land prices created serious economic difficulties for farmers and contributed to the continuing decline of the farm population. By 1992, the state had recovered, but annual growth rates remained comparatively low. At the end of the 20th century, growth rates accelerated somewhat (from 1.7% in 1998 to 3% in 1999 to 4.8% in 2000), but then fell to 1.4% in the national recession of 2001. The recession's impact on Indiana's unemployment rate was relatively mild, as the increase peaked at 4.4% in January 2002, and then fell to 3.9% by the end of the year. From 1997 to 2001, manufacturing output decreased almost every year in both absolute and relative terms, declining 5.7% in absolute terms across these five years, and, as a share of total state output, from about 25% in 1997 to 21% of the total in 200.1. During the same period, output from general services increased 28.6%, from financial services, 24.4%; from the transportation and utilities sector, 23.7%, and from the government sector, 21.6%. Performance in Iowa's agricultural sector was positive in 2002 largely because Iowa escaped the drought that was hampering output in other states and the prices received by Iowa farmers.

Iowa's gross state product in 2001 was 30th largest among the states at $90.9 billion, to which manufacturing contributed $19.1 billion; general services$16.2 billion; financial services, $14.6 billion; trade, $14.5 billion; government, 21.6% and transportation and public utilities, $7.6 billion. The public sector constituted 12.4% of gross state product in 2001.

[21]INCOME

According to the Bureau of Economic Analysis, in 2001, Iowa had a per capita personal income (PCPI) of $27,225 which ranked 34th in the United States (including the District of Columbia) and was 90% of the national average, $30,413. The 2001 PCPI reflected an increase of 2.6% from 2000 compared to the national change of 2.2%. In 2001, Iowa had a total personal income (TPI) of $79,822,447,000 which ranked 30th in the United States and accounted for 0.9% of the national total. The 2001 TPI reflected an increase of 2.7% from 2000 compared to the national change of 3.3%.

Earnings of persons employed in Iowa increased from $54,045,705,000 in 2000 to $54,994,332,000 in 2001, an increase of 1.8%. The largest industries in 2001 were services, 24.1% of earnings; state and local government, 14.1%; and durable goods manufacturing, 11.9%. Of the industries that accounted for at least 5% of earnings in 2001, the slowest growing from 2000 to 2001 was durable goods manufacturing, which decreased 2.9%; the fastest was state and local government, which increased 6.4%.

According to data released by the US Census Bureau, in 2000, the median household income was $42,993 compared to the national average of $42,148. In 2001, the median income for a family of four was $61,656 compared to the national average of

$63,278. For the period 1999 to 2001, the average poverty rate was 7.7% which placed it 5th among the 50 states and the District of Columbia ranked lowest to highest.

22LABOR

Since 1950, Iowa has consistently ranked above the national average in employment of its work force. Iowa's unemployment rate of 4.6% for July 2003 was below the overall US rate of 6.2%. According to Bureau of Labor Statistics (BLS) provisional estimates, in July 2003 the seasonally adjusted civilian labor force in Iowa numbered 1,644,200, with approximately 74,900 workers unemployed. Since the beginning of the BLS data series in 1978, the highest unemployment rate recorded was 8.9% in January 1983. The historical low was 2.3% in November 1999. It is estimated that in 2001, 4.4% of the labor force was employed in construction; 17.6% in manufacturing; 4.8% in transportation, communications, and public utilities; 18.9% in trade; 6.7% in finance, insurance, and real estate; 20.8% in services; 14.4% in government; and 5.2% in agriculture.

The labor movement generally has not been strong in Iowa, and labor unions have had little success in organizing farm laborers. The Knights of Labor, consisting mostly of miners and railroad workers, was organized in Iowa in 1876 and enrolled 25,000 members by 1885. But the Knights practically disappeared after 1893, when the American Federation of Labor (AFL) established itself in the state among miners and other workers. The Congress of Industrial Organizations (CIO) succeeded in organizing workers in public utilities, meat packing, and light industries in 1937. After 1955, when the AFL and CIO merged, the power and influence of labor unions increased in the state.

Iowa did not forbid the employment of women in dangerous occupations or prohibit the employment of children under 14 years of age in factories, shops, or mines until the early 1900s.

The US Department of Labor reported that in 2002, 155,000 of Iowa's 1,395,000 employed wage and salary workers were members of unions. This represented 11.1% of those so employed, down from 12.8% in 2001. The national average is 13.2%. In all, 190,000 workers (13.6%) were represented by unions. In addition to union members, this category includes workers who report no union affiliation but whose jobs are covered by a union contract. Iowa is one of 22 states with a right-to-work law; the Iowa law was enacted in 1947.

23AGRICULTURE

Iowa recorded a (realized) gross farm income of $11.5 billion in 2001, the 3rd highest in the US. Nearly half of all cash receipts from marketing came from the sale of livestock and meat products; about one-fifth derived from the sale of feed grains. In 2002, Iowa ranked 1st in output of corn for grain and soybeans and third for oats.

The early settlers planted wheat. Iowa ranked 2nd in wheat production by 1870, but as the wheat belt moved farther west, the state's farmers turned to raising corn to feed their cattle and hogs. Two important 20th-century developments were the introduction in the 1920s of hybrid corn and the utilization on a massive scale during World War II of soybeans as a feed grain. Significant postwar trends included the rapid mechanization of farming and the decline of the farm population.

In 2002, Iowa had 92,500 farms, with an average size of 340 acres (138 hectares) per farm. This total represents a decrease of 48,000 farms since 1970, although the amount of land being farmed has only declined 0.7% to 32,600,000 acres (13,200,000 hectares) over the same period.

Nearly all of Iowa's land is tillable, and nearly than nine-tenths of it is given to farmland. Corn is grown practically everywhere;

wheat is raised in the southern half of the state and in counties bordering the Mississippi and Missouri rivers.

In 2002, production of corn for grain totaled 6.27 billion bushels, valued at $4.418 billion; soybeans, 494.9 million bushels, $2.67 billion; oats, 13.3 million bushels, making Iowa the 3rd largest producer in the US; and hay, 5.64 million tons.

24ANIMAL HUSBANDRY

Iowa had an estimated 3.6 million cattle and calves in 2003, worth around $2.6 billion. In 2002, Iowa was ranked 1st among the 50 states in the number of hogs and pigs with 15.3 million, worth around $1.15 billion.

Pigs, calves, lambs, and chickens are raised throughout the state, particularly in the Mississippi and Missouri river valleys, where good pasture and water are plentiful. Iowa farmers are leaders in applying modern livestock breeding methods to produce lean hogs, tender corn-fed cattle, and larger-breasted chickens and turkeys.

In 2001, Iowa farmers produced an estimated 30.6 million lb (13.9 million kg) of sheep and lambs, which grossed a total of around $23.7 million. Also during 2001, Iowa farmers produced 216.6 million lb (98.2 million kg) of turkeys, worth $75.8 million. In the same year an estimated 8.7 billion eggs were produced, worth around $282 million.

Iowa dairy farmers produced 3.8 billion lb (1.7 million kg) of milk from 210,000 dairy cows in 2001.

25FISHING

Fishing has little commercial importance in Iowa. Game fishing in the rivers and lakes is a popular sport—there were 408,805 sport fishermen licensed in the state in 1998. Fish farms distributed over 1 million trout and 862,000 walleye within the state in 1998.

26FORESTRY

Lumber and woodworking were important to the early settlers, but the industry has since declined in commercial importance. In 2002, Iowa had 2.05 million acres (830,000 hectares) of forestland, which represents 5.7% of the state's land area. This was a 31% increase in forest area when compared to the 1974 survey's 1.6 million acres. The state's lumber industry produced 77 million board feet of lumber in 2002.

27MINING

The value of nonfuel mineral production in Iowa was estimated at $487 million in 2001, a decrease of about 3% from 2000. Estimated values in 2001 in specific categories included crushed stone ($204 million), construction sand and gravel ($59.4 million), and cement, crude gypsum, lime, and peat combined ($223 million). Combined values of crushed stone, portland cement, and construction sand and gravel, Iowa's leading nonfuel minerals, accounted for about 95% of the total mineral value produced in 2001. In 2001 Iowa ranked 2nd in production of crude gypsum and was a significant producer of crushed stone (38 million metric tons), portland cement, and construction sand and gravel (13.3 million metric tons). That year, Iowa ranked 31st nationally in nonfuel mineral value and 10th in the production of portland cement.

28ENERGY AND POWER

Although Iowa's fossil fuel resources are extremely limited, the state's energy supply has been adequate. In 2000, Iowa consumed 372 million Btu (93.7 million kcal) per capita, to rank 19th among the states.

The state's production of electricity (utility and nonutility) totaled 38.8 billion kWh in 1999; total installed capacity was 9 million kW. Coal-fired plants supplied 85% of generated power and nuclear power plants 9%, with the remainder coming from gas, hydroelectric power, and other sources. Iowa has one single-unit nuclear plant, the Duane Arnold plant in Palo.

Extensive coalfields in southeastern Iowa were first mined in 1840. The boomtown of Buxton, in Monroe County, mined sufficient coal in 1901 to support a population of 6,000 people, of whom 5,500 were transplanted southern blacks, but the mines closed in 1918 and Buxton became a ghost town. The state's annual bituminous coal production reached nearly 9 million tons in 1917–18. Coal output in 1994 was only 46,000 tons; recoverable coal reserves totaled 1.1 billion tons in 2001.

29 INDUSTRY

Because Iowa was primarily a farm state, the first industries were food processing and the manufacture of farm implements. These industries have retained a key role in the economy, with over 100,000 farms operating in the state in 2000. In recent years, Iowa has also added a variety of other manufactures—including pens, washing machines, and even mobile homes.

The estimated total value of shipments by manufacturers was $64 billion in 1997. More than 120 of Fortune magazine's "Top 500" industrial corporations have plants in Iowa, including Caterpillar Tractor, General Motors, Mobil, General Electric, General Foods, Procter & Gamble, and US Steel. Iowa is the nations top producer of beef (4%), pork (24%), corn, soybeans, and grains.

Earnings of persons employed in Iowa increased from $47.4 billion in 1997 to $49.1 billion in 1998, an increase of 3.7%. The largest industries in 1998 were services, 21.6% of earnings; durable goods manufacturing, 13.1%; and state and local government, 12.5%. Of the industries that accounted for at least 5% of earnings in 1998, the slowest growing from 1997 to 1998 was farm (6.7% of earnings in 1998), which decreased 1.7%; the fastest was durable goods manufacturing, which increased 8.7%.

30 COMMERCE

Wholesale establishments numbered 6,755 in 1997, with sales of $38 billion. The most valuable categories of goods traded were agricultural raw materials, durable goods, groceries and related products, and farm supplies.

Retail sales totaled $26 billion in 1997, conducted by 19,647 establishments. Of the total number of establishments, automotive dealers accounted for 16%; food stores, 9%; and eating and drinking places, 30%. Food sales contributed $5.5 billion, and general merchandise sales added $3.9 billion to total retail sales.

The leading exported commodities are feed grains and products, soybeans and soybean products, and meats and meat products. Diversity has been rising with the addition of industrial machinery, instruments and measurement devices, electronics, specialized transportation equipment, and chemicals and pharmaceuticals. Total exports from Iowa increased by 22%, 11%, and 13% in the years 1995 to 1997, with a 3% decline in 1998 due to the Asian crisis, strong harvests worldwide, and a strong US dollar. Exports of goods from Iowa in 1998 had an estimated value of $4.9 billion.

31 CONSUMER PROTECTION

Iowa has laws prohibiting fraud and misrepresentation in sales and advertising and harassment in debt collecting, in addition to others. There is a cooling-off period of three days for door-to-door purchases. The Iowa Attorney General's Consumer Protection Division deals with consumer fraud complaints, educates the public about such schemes, and litigates cases of consumer fraud. The Iowa Consumer Fraud Act is the primary piece of legislation enforced by the Consumer Protection Division.

32 BANKING

As of September 2002, Iowa had 435 insured banks, of which 363 were state-chartered; total insured bank assets amounted to $53 billion. The Division of Banking supervises and regulates the state's chartered banks, loan companies, and mortgage bankers/brokers. Throughout the 1990s and into the early 2000s, community banks in Iowa (those with under $1 billion in assets) saw a decline in net interest margins (NIMs) (the difference between the lower rates offered to savers and the higher rates charged on loans), due in part to increased loan and funding competition. To combat a decline in core deposits, Iowa community banks have increasingly relied upon large time deposits or borrowing (especially Federal Home Loan Bank advances) to support their assets.

33 INSURANCE

In 2001 there were 1.96 million ordinary life insurance policies in force with a total value of $116.9 billion; total value for all categories of life insurance (ordinary, group, industrial, and credit) was $175.9 billion. Death benefits paid that year totaled $508.9 million. In 2003, Iowa had 33 life and health and 59 property and casualty insurance companies. In 2001, property and casualty insurers wrote premiums totaling $3.3 billion. That year, there were 10,101 flood insurance policies in force in the state, with a total value of $873,469. The commissioner of insurance, appointed by the governor, supervises all insurance business transacted in the state.

34 SECURITIES

There are no securities exchanges in Iowa. Securities are sold through 589 brokers and dealers, involving over 2,500 employees. Investment advisory organizations in the state total 99. Iowa is home to 39 NASDAQ corporations, and eight Iowa-incorporated NYSE-listed companies. The top five in terms of revenue are: Gateway, Hon Industries, Meredith, Bandag, Inc., and AmerUs Life Holdings.

35 PUBLIC FINANCE

The public budget is prepared by the Department of Management with the governor's approval and is adopted or revised by the general assembly. Each budget is prepared for the biennium of the upcoming fiscal year and the one following; the fiscal year runs from 1 July to 30 June.

The governor's 2001 budget recommendations outlined recommendations to bring expenditures into line with revenues by 2002, including a $10 million appropriations reduction, and measures to divert capital into more long-term, preventative projects including education, preventative health care, and environmental management. General fund receipts were forecast at almost $5.3 billion for 2001, but in that year of recession, revenues were only $4.648 billion, a 12.3% shortfall. The government filled the gap with drawings from the state's Economic Emergency Fund. In 2001/02, general fund revenues fell further, to $4.463 billion ($4.9 billion had been projected in the budget), which the government met by transfers from the Economic Emergency Fund and the Cash Reserve Fund, one-time transfers from some other funds, and a mid-term lowering of the revenue estimated to $4.3 billion. A total of $246.2 million was cut from the 2001/02 budget after it was passed, exempting only Medicare and public safety. In 2002/03, revenues reached $4.5 billion, allowing the state to end with a $1 million balance and $229 million in the state's rainy day fund. Projected general fund receipts for 2003/04 were $4.526 billion, still well below what had been expected in 2000 going into 2001, but with reduced expenditures (projected at $4.599 billion for 2004) and various fund transfers and tax adjustments, the state appeared to have avoided a major budget crisis.

The following table from the US Census Bureau contains information on revenues, expenditures, indebtedness, and cash/securities for 2001.

	($000)	PERCENT	PER CAPITA
Population (thousands, 2001)	2,932	(X)	(X)
Total Revenue	10,255,453	100.00	3,497.77
General revenue	10,329,425	100.72	3,523.00
Utility revenue	–	–	–
Liquor store revenue	112,227	1.09	38.28
Insurance trust revenue	–186,199	–1.82	–63.51
Exhibit: Salaries and wages	2,588,195	21.09	882.74
Total expenditure	12,271,461	100.00	4,185.36
General expenditure	11,198,506	91.26	3,819.41
Education	4,397,048	35.83	1,499.68
Public welfare	2,593,005	21.13	884.38
Hospitals	726,692	5.92	247.85
Health	223,521	1.82	76.23
Highways	1,331,514	10.85	454.13
Police protection	84,809	0.69	28.93
Correction	291,914	2.38	99.56
Natural resources	291,401	2.37	99.39
Parks and recreation	26,741	0.22	9.12
Government administration	461,390	3.76	157.36
Interest on general debt	133,784	1.09	45.63
Other and unallocable	636,687	5.19	217.15
Utility expenditure	–	–	–
Liquor store expenditure	78,529	0.64	26.78
Insurance trust expenditure	994,426	8.10	339.16
Debt at end of fiscal year	2,542,400	100.00	867.12
Cash and security holdings	23,064,143	100.00	7,866.35

36TAXATION

Iowa's personal income tax schedule has nine brackets, and in 2002 there were reductions in all nine, the lowest bracket lowered from 0.4% to 0.36%, and the highest from 9.98% to 8.98%. Federal personal income taxes are deductible from the state taxes. Iowa's corporate income tax has four brackets, ranging from 6% on the first $25,000 of net income to 12% on amounts over $250,000. 50% of federal corporate taxes paid are deductible. Iowa's retail sales tax is 5%, with exemptions for basic foods and prescription drugs. Some local governments have local-option sales taxes of up to 2%. There are also state excise taxes on motor fuels, tobacco products, amusements, pari-mutuels, insurance premiums, and other selected items. The state directly controls alcohol sales. Iowa's estate tax, with maximum rate of 15%, is independent of the federal tax credit for state estate taxes, and is unaffected by the latter's scheduled phase-out by 2007. Iowa's inheritance tax ranges from 1% to 15% depending on both the amount of the inheritance and the relationship to the recipient. State gift and death taxes accounted for 1.6% of state tax collections in 2002. Other state taxes include license fees and stamp taxes. Property taxes are all local. Localities collect over 40% of the taxes in Iowa.

Total state tax collections in Iowa came to just over $5 billion in 2002, 35.3% generated by the state income tax, 34.9% by the state sales tax, 15.8% by state excise taxes, 10.4% by state license fees, and 1.7% by the state corporate income tax. Combined state and local taxes in Iowa amounted to about 9.5% of income in 2003, placing the state in the middle (26th) in terms of tax burden.

The following table from the US Census Bureau provides a summary of taxes collected by the state in 2002.

	($000)	PER CAPITA
Total Taxes	5,006,251	1,704.69
Property taxes	(X)	(X)
Sales and gross receipts	2,538,484	864.38
General sales and gross receipts	1,747,016	594.88
Selective sales taxes	791,468	269.5
Alcoholic beverage	12,508	4.26
Amusements	202,485	68.95
Insurance Premiums	135,582	46.17
Motor fuels	343,147	116.85
Pari-mutuels	3,266	1.11
Public utilities	(X)	(X)
Tobacco products	94,480	32.17
Other selective sales	(X)	(X)
Licenses	519,787	176.99
Alcoholic beverages	8,756	2.98
Amusements	5,863	2
Corporation	32,494	11.06
Hunting and fishing	20,177	6.87
Motor vehicle	363,652	123.83
Motor vehicle operators	8,087	2.75
Public utility	8,316	2.83
Occupation and business, NEC	70,338	23.95
Other	2,104	0.72
Other taxes	1,947,980	663.31
Individual income	1,769,347	602.48
Corporation net income	88,310	30.07
Death and gift	79,507	27.07
Documentary and stock transfer	10,816	3.68
Severance	(X)	(X)
Other	(X)	(X)

37ECONOMIC POLICY

Since World War II, the state government has attracted new manufacturing industries to Iowa by granting tax incentives and by encouraging a favorable business climate. The Iowa Department of Economic (IDED) coordinates economic development activity in the state. It helps local communities diversify their economies, assists companies already in the state, and helps exporters to sell their products abroad. In the 1990s, the Iowa state government stressed such development goals as agricultural diversification, increased small-business support, creation of high-tech jobs, and expansion of tourism. In 2003, the Iowa Values Fund Board was allotted $9 million to help businesses with start up, expansion, modernization, business attraction, business retention, and marketing. Another initiative was the Venture Network of Iowa (VNI), which, among other activities, facilitated bi-monthly networking meetings of Iowa entrepreneurs, investors, and business advisors. Event sponsored by the IDED in 2003 included an Iowa Venture Capital Conference, and Farm, Food and the Future Conference (focused on marketing Iowa farm products). The state also offers financial assistance programs to businesses for programs to retain or create jobs, capital investment, to utilize agricultural commodities, to establish or expand minority and women-owned enterprises, to support low income and disabled entrepreneurs, to build or improve a community's infrastructure (railroads, roads, etc.), and to foster construction of new industrial facilities.

38HEALTH

Infant mortality for the 12 months ending December 2000 was 6.5 per 1,000 live births, below the national average of 6.9. In 1999, 6,106 legal abortions were performed, a rate of 10 per 1,000 women. The overall death rate was 975.2 per 100,000 population in 2000 higher than the US average of 873.1. Rates for the leading causes of death, heart disease and cerebrovascular disease, were higher than the national averages. The smoking prevalence was 23.3% of all Iowans ages 18 and older. The rate of HIV-related deaths stood at 0.8 per 100,000 population, well below the national average of 5.3 in 2000. There were 1,402 AIDS cases reported through 2001.

Iowa's 116 community hospitals had 370,885 admissions and 11,811 beds in 2001. There were 12,029 full-time registered nurses and 1,310 full-time licensed practical nurses in 2001 and 199 physicians per 100,000 population in 2000. The average expense of a community hospital for care was $1,437.60 per inpatient day in 2001.

Federal government grants to cover the Medicare and Medicaid services in 2001 totaled $1.1 billion; 478,063 enrollees received Medicare benefits that year. Only 7.5% of the population were uninsured in 2002.

39SOCIAL WELFARE

In 2001, the average weekly unemployment benefit was $247.49. Average monthly participation in the food stamp program in FY2002 comprised 140,729 persons (60,549 households). The average monthly benefit was $76.25, and the sum total of benefits paid in FY2002 was $128,762,369.

With the enactment of the Personal Responsibility and Work Opportunity Reconciliation Act of 1996, the US government has changed the form and regulations for many of its social welfare programs. Most significantly, it replaces Aid to Families with Dependent Children (AFDC), an open-ended entitlement program, with Temporary Assistance for Needy Families (TANF), a limited system of assistance funded largely through federal block grants. The reform act also impacts the food stamp program, the Supplemental Security Income program, and the child nutrition program. The law took effect on 1 July 1997 and provided $16.38 billion in block grants for fiscal years 1997–2002. The grants are to be divided among the states based on an equation involving the numbers of former AFDC recipients in each state.

Reauthorization of the 1996 social welfare legislation, scheduled for 2002, was delayed, and the original law had been extended three times as of July 2003, with the most recent extension running through September 2003. Iowa's TANF program is called the Family Investment Program (FIP). In June 2000 the state had 52,293 welfare recipients. State expenditures on the TANF program in FY2002 totaled $53,812,500.

In December 2001, Social Security benefits were paid to 541,280 Iowa residents. This number included 352,450 retired workers, 64,690 widows and widowers, 50,560 disabled workers, 39,250 spouses, and 34,330 children. Social Security beneficiaries represented 18.6% of the total state population and 96.2% of the state's population age 65 and older. Retired workers (excluding persons with special benefits) received an average monthly payment of $874; widows and widowers, $848; disabled workers, $788; and spouses, $447. Payments for children of retired workers averaged $456 per month; children of deceased workers, $588; and children of disabled workers, $243.

Federal Supplemental Security Income payments in December 2001 went to 40,716 Iowa residents, averaging $339 a month.

40HOUSING

In 2002, Iowa ranked 6th in the nation in the number of housing units that are family owned and occupied. There were 1,257,184 housing units in Iowa, of which 1,145,564 were occupied; 72.7% were owner-occupied. About 74% of all units were single-family, detached homes. About 32.9% of all units were built in 1939 or earlier. Most households relied on utility gas and electricity for heating. It was estimated that 29,729 lacked telephone service, 5,452 lacked complete plumbing facilities, and 7,137 lacked complete kitchen facilities. Average household size was 2.57 people.

In 2002, 14,789 privately owned housing units were authorized for construction. Median home value was $88,176

(one of the six lowest values in the nation). The median monthly cost for mortgage owners was $879. Renters paid a median of $498 per month. During fiscal year 2002, Iowa received over $66.7 million in community planning and development aid from the US Department of Housing and Urban Development.

41EDUCATION

In 2000, 86.1% of Iowans age 25 and older were high school graduates; 21.2% had obtained a bachelor's degree or higher.

The total enrollment for fall 1999 in Iowa's public schools stood at 497,301. Of these, 335,919 attended schools from kindergarten through grade eight, and 161,382 attended high school. Minority students made up approximately 10% of the total enrollment in public elementary and secondary schools in 2001. Total enrollment was estimated at 497,301 in fall 2000 but expected to drop to 481,000 by fall 2005. Iowa spent $5,919 per pupil in public schools in 1999/2000. Expenditures for public education in 2000/01 were estimated at $3,335,337. Enrollment in nonpublic schools in fall 2001was 49,565.

As of fall 2000, there were 187,306 students enrolled in institutions of higher education. In the same year Iowa had 64 degree-granting institutions. In 1997, minority students comprised 7.4% of total postsecondary enrollment. Iowa has three state universities, 35 private colleges, and 23 vocational schools and area community colleges. Since the public community college system began offering vocational and technical training in 1960, total enrollment has increased rapidly, and the number of different career programs has grown. Iowa's small liberal arts colleges and universities include Briar Cliff College, Sioux City; Coe College, Cedar Rapids; Cornell College, Mt. Vernon; Drake University, Des Moines; Grinnell College, Grinnell; Iowa Wesleyan College, Mt. Pleasant; Loras College, Dubuque; and Luther College, Decorah.

42ARTS

Beginning with the public lecture movement in the late 19th century and the Chautauqua shows in the early 20th century, cultural activities have gradually spread throughout the state. Today there is an opera company in Des Moines, and there are art galleries, little theater groups, symphony orchestras, and ballet companies in the major cities and college towns. The University of Iowa receives funding from the NEA to support the development of its music and theater activities.

The Des Moines Arts Center is a leading exhibition gallery for native painters and sculptors. The Des Moines Arts Festival, established in 1998, has drawn an attendance of nearly 800,000 people each year. The 2002 ArtFair SourceBook ranked it as the 6th Best Fine Arts Festival in the nation. There are regional theater groups in Des Moines, Davenport, and Sioux City. The Writers' Workshop at the University of Iowa has an international reputation.

The Iowa Arts Council (IAC) was established as a state agency in 1967. In 1986, the IAC became a division of the Department of Cultural Affairs, which also includes the State Historical Society of Iowa. In 2003, state organizations received $639,700 in grants from the National Endowment for the Arts. Humanities Iowa, founded in 1971, sponsors over $1.5 million of programs each year. In 2000, the National Endowment for the Humanities sponsored 17 programs with grants totaling $1,388,137. The state also contributes to the efforts of the Arts Council and Humanities Iowa, and private sources provide additional funding. Iowa's arts programs have a total audience of nearly seven million people. There are over 36,000 contributing artists for the programs. The state offers arts education to about 120,000 schoolchildren. There are over 800 art associations in Iowa.

43 LIBRARIES AND MUSEUMS

Beginning with the founding in 1873 of the state's first tax-supported library at Independence, Iowa's public library system has grown to include seven regional and three county public library systems with total book holdings of 11,595,000 volumes, and a circulation of 25,217,000 in 2000. Among the principal libraries in Iowa are the State Library in Des Moines, the State Historical Society Library in Iowa City, the libraries of the University of Iowa (also in Iowa City), and the Iowa State University Library in Ames. Total income for Iowa public libraries was $70,422,000 in 2000.

Iowa had 134 museums and zoological parks in 2000. The Herbert Hoover National Historical Site, in West Branch, houses the birthplace and grave of the 31st US president and a library and museum with papers and memorabilia. Other historic sites include the grave of French explorer Julien Dubuque, near the city named for him; the girlhood home at Charles City of suffragist Carrie Chapman Catt; and the seven communal villages of the Amana colonies.

44 COMMUNICATIONS

The first post office in Iowa was established at Augusta in 1836. Mail service developed slowly with the spread of population, and rural free delivery of mail did not begin until 1897.

The first telegraph line was built between Burlington and Bloomington (now Muscatine) in 1848. Telegraph service throughout the state is provided by Western Union. In 2001, about 97.2% of all occupied housing units had telephones.

Among the first educational radio broadcasting stations in the US was one established in 1919 at the State University in Iowa City and another in 1921 at Iowa State University in Ames. The first commercial radio station west of the Mississippi, WDC at Davenport, began broadcasting in 1921. In 2003 there were 112 major radio stations, including 38 AM stations and 74 FM stations. In the same year, Iowa had a total of 21 network television stations.

A total of 34,789 Internet domain names were registered in the state in 2000.

45 PRESS

Iowa's first newspaper, the *Dubuque Visitor*, was founded in 1836 but lasted only a year. The following year, the *Fort Madison Patriot* and the *Burlington Territorial Gazette* were established; the latter paper, now the *Hawk Eye*, is the oldest newspaper in the state. In 1860, the *Iowa State Register* was founded. As the *Des Moines Register and Tribune*, it grew to be the state's largest newspaper. The *Tribune* ceased publication in 1982; the *Register* remains preeminent, with a morning circulation of 152,402 and a Sunday circulation of 244,132 as of 2001. Major newspapers and their estimated circulations at 2001–2002 are listed as follows:

AREA	NAME	DAILY	SUNDAY
Cedar Rapids	Gazette	65,954	79,385
Des Moines	Register	152,402	244,132
Dubuque	Telegraph Herald	28,737	33,975
Sioux City	Journal	46,064	44,640
Waterloo	Courier	44,181	51,769

Overall, Iowa had 37 dailies (21 evening, 16 morning) and 12 Sunday papers in 2002. Also published in Iowa were over 100 periodicals, among them *Better Homes and Gardens* and *Successful Farming, Midwest Today*, and *The Iowan*.

46 ORGANIZATIONS

In 2003, there were about 1,845 regional, national, and international organizations within the state. Among the organizations headquartered in Iowa are the National Farmers Organization (Corning), the American College Testing Program (Iowa City), the National Meals on Wheels Foundation (Iowa City), the National Collegiate Honors Council (Ames), and the Antique Airplane Association (Ottumwa). State educational and cultural organizations include the Iowa Arts Council, the Iowa Historic Preservation Alliance, and the State Historical Society of Iowa.

47 TOURISM, TRAVEL, AND RECREATION

The Mississippi and Missouri rivers offer popular water sports facilities for both out-of-state visitors and resident vacationers. Iowa's "Little Switzerland" region in the northeast, with its high bluffs of woodland overlooking the Mississippi, is popular for hiking and camping. Notable tourist attractions in the area include the Effigy Mounds National Monument (near Marquette), which has hundreds of prehistoric Indian mounds and village sites, and the Buffalo Ranch (at Fayette), with its herd of live buffalo. Tourist sites in the central part of the state include the state capitol and the Herbert Hoover National Historic Site, with its Presidential Library and Museum.

Iowa has about 85,000 acres (34,400 hectares) of lakes and reservoirs and 19,000 mi (30,600 km) of fishing streams. There are 52 state parks, covering 33,811 acres, and 7 state forests, covering 25,000 acres (10,000 hectares); these and other state recreational areas attract numerous visitors every year.

In 2002, there were about 17.1 million visitors to the state. This showed an increase from 15.9 million in 2001, but a decline from a five-year peak of 18.4 million in 1999. Travel generated expenditures of about $4.3 billion in 2002. In 2001, there were over 61,000 travel-related jobs in the state.

48 SPORTS

Iowa has no NBA, NFL, NHL or MLB teams, but are proud of their Iowa Barnstormers in the Arena Football League. The team has advanced to two Arena Bowls in the league's short existence. Minor league baseball and basketball teams make their home in Des Moines, Cedar Rapids, Clinton, Sioux City, Burlington, and the Quad Cities. High school and college basketball and football teams draw thousands of spectators, particularly to the state high school basketball tournament at Des Moines in March. Large crowds also fill stadiums and fieldhouses for the University of Iowa games in Iowa City and Iowa State University games in Ames. In intercollegiate competition, the University of Iowa Hawkeyes belong to the Big Ten Conference. They have a legendary wrestling program that has won the NCAA Championship 20 times. Iowa went to the Rose Bowl in 1957, 1959, 1982, 1986, and 1991, winning in 1957 and 1959. The Iowa State University Cyclones are in the Big Twelve Conference. A popular track-and-field meet for college athletes is the Drake Relays, held every April in Des Moines. Horse racing is popular at state and county fairgrounds, as is stock car racing at small-town tracks. The *Register's* Annual Great Bicycle Ride Across Iowa is held each July. There are rodeos in Sidney and Fort Madison, and the National Balloon Classic is held in Indianola.

49 FAMOUS IOWANS

Iowa was the birthplace of Herbert Clark Hoover (1874–1964), the first US president born west of the Mississippi. Although he was orphaned and left the state for Oregon at the age of 10, he always claimed Iowa as his home. His long and distinguished career included various relief missions in Europe, service as US secretary of commerce (1921–29), and one term in the White House (1929–33). Hoover was buried in West Branch, the town of his birth. Iowa has also produced one US vice president, Henry A. Wallace (1888–1965), who served in that office during Franklin D. Roosevelt's third term (1941–45). Wallace also was secretary of agriculture (1933–41) and of commerce (1945–47);

he ran unsuccessfully as the Progressive Party's presidential candidate in 1948.

Two Kentucky-born members of the US Supreme Court were residents of Iowa prior to their appointments: Samuel F. Miller (1816–90) and Wiley B. Rutledge (1894–1949). Iowans who served in presidential cabinets as secretary of the interior were James Harlan (b.Illinois, 1820–99), Samuel J. Kirkwood (b.Maryland, 1813–94), Richard Ballinger (1858–1922), and Ray Lyman Wilbur (1875–1949). Ray Wilbur's brother Curtis (1867–1954) was secretary of the Navy, and James W. Good (1866–1929) was secretary of war. Appropriately enough, Iowans have dominated the post of secretary of agriculture in this century. They included, in addition to Wallace, James "Tama Jim" Wilson (b.Scotland, 1835–1920), who served in that post for 16 years and set a record for longevity in a single cabinet office; Henry C. Wallace (b.Illinois, 1866–1924), the father of the vice president; and Edwin T. Meredith (1876–1928). Harry L. Hopkins (1890–1946) was Franklin D. Roosevelt's closest adviser in all policy matters, foreign and domestic, and served in a variety of key New Deal posts. Prominent US senators from Iowa have included James W. Grimes (b.New Hampshire, 1816–72), whose vote, given from a hospital stretcher, saved President Andrew Johnson from being convicted of impeachment charges in 1868; earlier, Grimes had been governor of the state when its 1857 constitution was adopted. William Boyd Allison (b.Ohio, 1829–1908) was the powerful chairman of the Senate Appropriations Committee for nearly 30 years.

Among Iowa's most influential governors were the first territorial governor, Robert Lucas (b.Virginia, 1781–1853); Cyrus C. Carpenter (b.Pennsylvania, 1829–98); William Larrabee (b.Connecticut, 1832–1912); Horace Boies (b.New York, 1827–1923); and, in recent times, Harold Hughes (1922–96) and Robert D. Ray (b.1928).

Iowa has produced a large number of radical dissenters and social reformers. Abolitionists, strong in Iowa before the Civil War, included James W. Grimes, Josiah B. Grinnell (b.Vermont, 1821–91), and Asa Turner (b.Massachusetts, 1799–1885). George D. Herron (b.Indiana, 1862–1925) made Iowa a center of the Social Gospel movement before helping to found the Socialist Party. William "Billy" Sunday (1862–1935) was an evangelist with a large following among rural Americans. James B. Weaver (b.Ohio, 1833–1912) ran for the presidency on the Greenback-Labor ticket in 1880 and as a Populist in 1892. John L. Lewis (1880–1969), head of the United Mine Workers, founded the Congress of Industrial Organizations (CIO).

Iowa can claim two winners of the Nobel Peace Prize: religious leader John R. Mott (b.New York, 1865–1955) and agronomist and plant geneticist Norman E. Borlaug (b.1914). Three other distinguished scientists who lived in Iowa were George Washington Carver (b.Missouri 1864–1943), Lee De Forest (1873–1961), and James Van Allen (b.1914). George H. Gallup (1904–84), a public-opinion analyst, originated the Gallup Polls.

Iowa writers of note include Hamlin Garland (b.Wisconsin, 1860–1940), Octave Thanet (Alice French, b.Massachusetts, 1850–1934), Bess Streeter Aldrich (1881–1954), Carl Van Vechten (1880–1964), James Norman Hall (1887–1951), Thomas Beer (1889–1940), Ruth Suckow (1892–1960), Phillip D. Strong (1899–1957), MacKinlay Kantor (1904–77), Wallace Stegner (1909–93), and Richard P. Bissell (1913–77). Iowa's poets include Paul H. Engle (1908–91), who directed the University of Iowa's famed Writers' Workshop, and James S. Hearst (1900–83). Two Iowa playwrights, Susan Glaspell (1882–1948) and her husband, George Cram Cook (1873–1924), were instrumental in founding influential theater groups.

Iowans who have contributed to America's musical heritage include popular composer Meredith Willson (1902–84), jazz musician Leon "Bix" Beiderbecke (1903–31), and bandleader Glenn Miller (1904–44). Iowa's artists of note include Grant Wood (1892–1942), whose *American Gothic* is one of America's best-known paintings, and printmaker Mauricio Lasansky (b.Argentina, 1914).

Iowa's contributions to the field of popular entertainment include William F. "Buffalo Bill" Cody (1846–1917); circus impresario Charles Ringling (1863–1926) and his four brothers; the reigning American beauty of the late 19th century, Lillian Russell (Helen Louise Leonard, 1860–1922); and one of America's best-loved movie actors John Wayne (Marion Michael Morrison, 1907–79). Johnny Carson (b.1925), host of the Tonight Show for many years, was born in Corning. Iowa sports figures of note are baseball Hall of Famers Adrian C. "Cap" Anson (1851–1922) and Robert "Bob" Feller (b.1918) and football All-American Nile Kinnick (1918–44).

50 BIBLIOGRAPHY

Bogue, Allen G. *From Prairie to Cornbelt*. Chicago: University of Chicago Press, 1963.

Conard, Rebecca. *Benjamin Shambaugh and the Intellectual Foundations of Public History*. Iowa City: University of Iowa Press, 2002.

Federal Writers' Project. *Iowa: A Guide to the Hawkeye State*. Reprint. New York: Somerset, n.d. (orig. 1938).

Gue, Benjamin F. *History of Iowa*. 4 vols. New York: Century History Co., 1903.

Hamilton, Carl. *In No Time at All*. Ames: Iowa State University Press, 1974.

Iowa Development Commission. *1985 Statistical Profile of Iowa*. Des Moines, 1985.

Landau, Diana. *Iowa: The Spirit of America*. New York: Harry N. Abrams, 1998.

Morain, Thomas J., ed. *Family Reunion: Essays on Iowa*. Ames: Iowa State University Press, 1995.

Offenburger, Chuck. *Ah, You Iowans!: At Home, At Work, At Play, At War*. Ames: Iowa State University Press, 1992.

Riley, Glenda, ed. *Prairie Voices: Iowa's Pioneering Women*. Ames: Iowa State University Press, 1996.

Ross, Earle D. *Iowa Agriculture*. Iowa City: State Historical Society, 1951.

Sage, Leland. *A History of Iowa*. Ames: Iowa State University Press, 1974.

Schwieder, Dorothy, ed. *Patterns and Perspectives in Iowa History*. Ames: Iowa State University Press, 1973.

Swierenga, Robert P. *Pioneers and Profits*. Ames: Iowa State University Press, 1968.

Wall, Joseph Frazier. *Iowa: A Bicentennial History*. New York: Norton, 1978.

Warren, Wilson J. *Struggling with "Iowa's Pride": Labor Relations, Unionism, and Politics in the Rural Midwest Since 1877*. Iowa City: University of Iowa Press, 2000.

Winebrenner, Hugh. *Iowa Precinct Caucuses: The Making of a Media Event*. Ames: Iowa State University Press, 1998.

KANSAS

State of Kansas

ORIGIN OF STATE NAME: Named for the Kansa (or Kaw) Indians, the "people of the south wind." **NICKNAME:** The Sunflower State; also, the Jayhawker State. **CAPITAL:** Topeka. **ENTERED UNION:** 29 January 1861 (34th). **SONG:** "Home on the Range." **MARCH:** "The Kansas March." **MOTTO:** *Ad astra per aspera* (To the stars through difficulties). **FLAG:** The flag consists of a dark blue field with the state seal in the center; a sunflower on a bar of twisted gold and blue is above the seal, the word "Kansas" is below it. **OFFICIAL SEAL:** A sun rising over mountains in the background symbolizes the east; commerce is represented by a river and a steamboat. In the foreground, agriculture, the basis of the state's prosperity, is represented by a settler's cabin and a man plowing a field; beyond this is a wagon train heading west and a herd of buffalo fleeing from two Indians. Around the top is the state motto above a cluster of 34 stars; the circle is surrounded by the words "Great Seal of the State of Kansas, January 29, 1861." **ANIMAL:** American buffalo. **BIRD:** Western meadowlark. **INSECT:** Honeybee. **REPTILE:** Ornate box turtle. **FLOWER:** Wild native sunflower. **TREE:** Cottonwood. **LEGAL HOLIDAYS:** New Year's Day, 1 January; Birthday of Martin Luther King, Jr., 3rd Monday in January; Lincoln's Birthday, 12 February; Washington's Birthday, 3rd Monday in February; Memorial Day, last Monday in May; Independence Day, 4 July; Labor Day, 1st Monday in September; Columbus Day, 2nd Monday in October; Veterans Day, 11 November; Thanksgiving Day, 4th Thursday in November; Christmas Day, 25 December. **TIME:** 6 AM CST = noon GMT; 5 AM MST = noon GMT.

¹LOCATION, SIZE, AND EXTENT

Located in the western north-central US, Kansas is the 2nd-largest midwestern state (following Minnesota) and ranks 14th among the 50 states.

The total area of Kansas is 82,277 sq mi (213,097 sq km), of which 81,778 sq mi (211,805 sq km) are land, and the remaining 499 sq mi (1,292 sq km) inland water. Shaped like a rectangle except for an irregular corner in the NE, the state has a maximum extension E-W of about 411 mi (661 km) and an extreme N-S distance of about 208 mi (335 km).

Kansas is bounded on the N by Nebraska, on the E by Missouri (with the line in the NE following the Missouri River), on the S by Oklahoma, and on the W by Colorado, with a total boundary length of 1,219 mi (1,962 km). The geographic center of Kansas is in Barton County, 15 mi (24 km) NE of Great Bend.

²TOPOGRAPHY

Although the popular image of the state is one of unending flatlands, Kansas has a diverse topography. Three main land regions define the state. The eastern third consists of the Osage Plains, Flint Hills, Dissected Till Plains, and Arkansas River Lowlands. The central third comprises the Smoky Hills (which include the Dakota sandstone formations, Greenhorn limestone formations, and chalk deposits) to the north and several lowland regions to the south. To the west are the Great Plains proper, divided into the Dissected High Plains and the High Plains. Kansas generally slopes eastward from a maximum elevation of 4,039 ft (1,232 m) at Mt. Sunflower (a mountain in name only) on the Colorado border to 679 ft (207 m) by the Verdigris River at the Oklahoma border. More than 50,000 streams run through the state, and there are hundreds of artificial lakes. Major rivers include the Missouri, which defines the state's northeastern boundary; the Arkansas, which runs through Wichita; and the Kansas (Kaw), which runs through Topeka and joins the Missouri at Kansas City.

The geographic center of the 48 contiguous states is located in Smith County, in north-central Kansas, at 39°50'N and 98°35'W. Forty miles (64 km) south of this point, in Osborne County at 39°13'27"N and 98°32'31"W, is the North American geodetic datum, the controlling point for all land surveys in the US, Canada, and Mexico. Extensive beds of prehistoric ocean fossils lie in the chalk beds of two western counties, Logan and Gove.

³CLIMATE

Kansas's continental climate is highly changeable. The average mean temperature is 55°F (13°C). The record high is 121°F (149°C), recorded near Alton on 24 July 1936, and the record low, –40°F (–40°C), was registered at Lebanon on 13 February 1905. The normal annual precipitation ranges from slightly more than 40 in (101.6 cm) in the southeast to as little as 16 in (40.6 cm) in the west; in Wichita, average annual precipitation (1971–2000) was 30.4 in (77.2 cm). The overall annual precipitation for the state averages 27 in (68.6 cm), although years of drought have not been uncommon. About 70–77% of the precipitation falls between 1 April and 30 September. The annual mean snowfall ranges from about 36 in (91.4 cm) in the extreme northwest to less than 11 in (27.9 cm) in the far southeast. Tornadoes are a regular fact of life in Kansas. Dodge City is said to be the windiest city in the US, with an average wind speed of 14 mph (23 kph).

⁴FLORA AND FAUNA

Native grasses, consisting of 60 different groups subdivided into 194 species, cover one-third of Kansas, which is much overgrazed. Bluestem—both big and little—which grows in most parts of the state, has the greatest forage value. Other grasses include buffalo grass, blue and hairy gramas, and alkali sacaton. One native conifer, eastern red cedar, is found generally throughout the state. Hackberry, black walnut, and sycamore grow in the east while box elder and cottonwood predominate in western Kansas. There are no native pines. The wild native sunflower, the state flower, is found throughout the state. Other characteristic wildflowers include wild daisy, ivy-leaved morning glory, and smallflower verbena. The western prairie fringed orchid and Mead's milkweed, listed as threatened species by the US Fish and Wildlife Service in August 2003, are protected under federal statutes.

Kansas's indigenous mammals include the common cottontail, black-tailed jackrabbit, black-tailed prairie dog, muskrat, opossum, and raccoon; the white-tailed deer is the state's only big-game animal. There are 12 native species of bat, 2 varieties of shrew and mole, and 3 types of pocket gopher. The western meadowlark is the state bird. Kansas has the largest flock of prairie chickens remaining on the North American continent. The US Fish and Wildlife Service named 123 Kansas animal species as threatened or endangered in 2003. Among these are the Indiana and gray bats, bald eagle, whooping crane, Eskimo curlew, and black-footed ferret.

5 ENVIRONMENTAL PROTECTION

No environmental problem is more crucial for Kansas than water quality, and its protection remains a primary focus of the state's environmental efforts, which include active regulatory and remedial programs for both surface and groundwater sources. Maintenance of air quality is also a primary effort, and the state works actively with the business community to promote pollution prevention.

Strip mining for coal is decreasing in southeast Kansas, and the restoration of resources damaged by previous activities is ongoing.

The state has sufficient capacity for handling solid waste, although the total number of solid waste facilities has decreased in recent years. In 2003, Kansas had 307 hazardous waste sites listed in the Environmental Protection Agency's database, 10 of which were on the National Priorities List. In 2001, Kansas received $38,968,000 in federal grants from the Environmental Protection Agency; EPA expenditures for procurement contracts in Kansas that year amounted to $26,710,000.

6 POPULATION

Kansas ranked 32nd in population in the US with an estimated total of 2,715,884 in 2002, an increase of 1% since 2000. Between 1990 and 2000, Kansas's population grew from 2,477,574 to 2,688,418, an increase of 8.5%. The population is projected to reach 2,761,000 by 2005 and 3.1 million by 2025. The population density in 2000 was 32.9 persons per sq mi.

When it was admitted to the Union in 1861, Kansas's population was 107,206. During the decade that followed, the population grew by 240%, more than 10 times the US growth rate. Steady growth continued through the 1930s, but in the 1940s the population declined by 4%. Since then, the population has risen, though at a slower pace than the national average.

In 2000, the median age for Kansans was 35.2; 26.5% of the population was below the age of 18 while 13.3% were 65 or older.

Whereas the populations of Wichita and Topeka grew 8.6% and 1.0% respectively, the population of Kansas City dropped 7.1% during the 1980s. Estimates for 2002 showed about 355,126 residents for Wichita, 158,430 for Overland Park, and 146,987 for Kansas City. The Kansas City metropolitan area had an estimated population of 1,755,899 in 1996; the Wichita metropolitan area had an estimated 548,714 residents.

7 ETHNIC GROUPS

White settlers began to pour into Kansas in 1854, dispersing the 36 Indian tribes living there and precipitating a struggle over the legal status of slavery. Remnants of six of the original tribes still

make their homes in the state. Some Indians live on three reservations covering 30,000 acres (12,140 hectares); others live and work elsewhere, returning to the reservations several times a year for celebrations and observances. There were 24,936 Indians in Kansas as of 2000.

Black Americans in Kansas numbered 154,198, or 5.7% of the population, in 2000, when the state also had 188,252 Hispanics and Latinos. The 2000 census recorded 46,806 Asian residents, the largest group being 11,623 Vietnamese (up from 6,001 in 1990), followed by 8,153 Asian Indians and 7,624 Chinese. There were also sizable communities of Laotians and Cambodians.

The foreign born numbered 80,271 (2% of the population) in 2000, the most common lands of origin being Mexico, Germany, and Vietnam. Among persons who reported descent from a single ancestry group, the leading nationalities were German (914,955), English (391,542), and Irish (424,133).

8 LANGUAGES

Plains Indians of the Macro-Siouan group originally populated what is now Kansas; their speech echoes in such place-names as Kansas, Wichita, Topeka, Chetopa, and Ogallah.

Regional features of Kansas speech are almost entirely those of the Northern and North Midland dialects, reflecting the migration into Kansas in the 1850s of settlers from the East. Kansans typically use *fish(ing) worms* as bait, play as children on a *teetertotter*, see a *snakefeeder* (dragonfly) over a /krik/ (creek), make *white bread* sandwiches, carry water in a *pail*, and may designate the time 2:45 as a *quarter to*, or *of*, or *till* three.

The migration by southerners in the mid-19th century is evidenced in southeastern Kansas by such South Midland terms as *pullybone* (wishbone) and *light bread* (white bread); the expression *wait on* (wait for) extends farther westward.

In 2000, 2,281,705 Kansans—91.3% of the residents five years old or older (down from 94.3% in 1990)—spoke only English at home.

The following table gives selected statistics from the 2000 census for language spoken at home by persons five years old and over.

LANGUAGE	NUMBER	PERCENT
Population 5 years and over	**2,500,360**	**100.0**
Speak only English	2,281,705	91.3
Speak a language other than English	218,655	8.7
Speak a language other than English	**218,655**	**8.7**
Spanish or Spanish Creole	137,247	5.5
German	16,821	0.7
Vietnamese	10,393	0.4
French (incl. Patois, Cajun)	6,591	0.3
Chinese	6,473	0.3
Korean	3,666	0.1
Laotian	3,147	0.1
Arabic	2,834	0.1
Tagalog	2,237	0.1
Russian	1,994	0.1

9 RELIGIONS

Protestant missions played an important role in early Kansas history. Isaac McCoy, a Baptist minister, was instrumental in founding the Shawnee Baptist Mission in Johnson County in 1831. Later Baptist, Methodist, Quaker, Presbyterian, and Jesuit missions became popular stopover points for pioneers traveling along the Oregon and Santa Fe trails. Mennonites were drawn to the state by a law passed in 1874 allowing exemptions from military service on religious grounds. Religious freedom is specifically granted in the Kansas constitution, and a wide variety of religious groups is represented in the state.

The leading Protestant denominations in 2000 were the United Methodist Church, with 206,187 adherents; the Southern

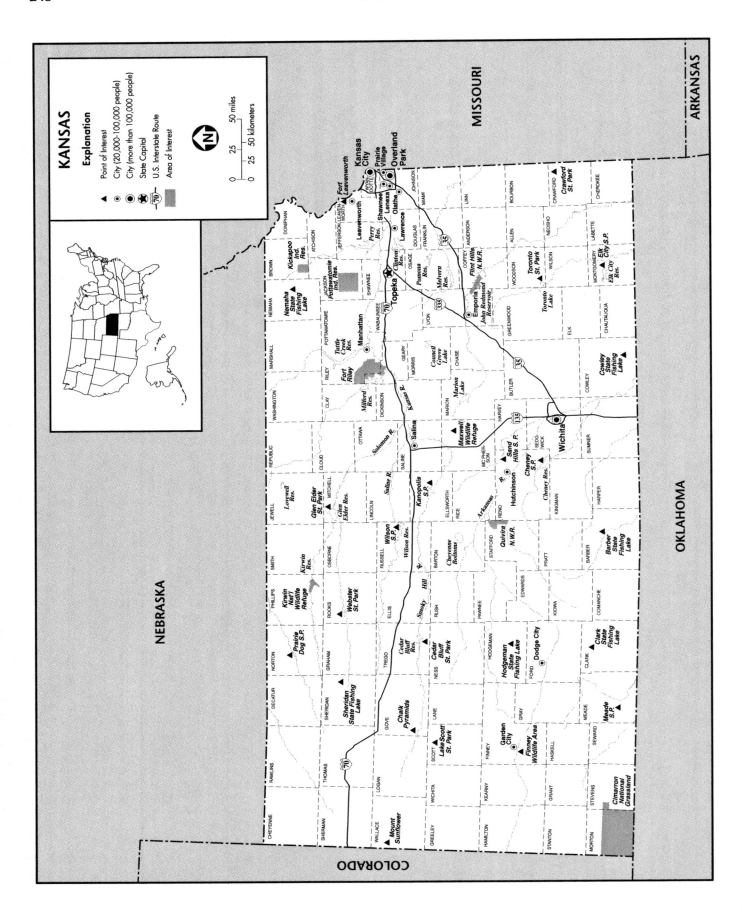

KANSAS

Explanation

▲ Point of Interest
⊙ City (20,000-100,000 people)
◉ City (more than 100,000 people)
✪ State Capital
70 U.S. Interstate Route
▒ Area of Interest

50 miles
25   50 kilometers
0   25   50

NEBRASKA

COLORADO

MISSOURI

OKLAHOMA

ARKANSAS

Baptist Convention, 101,696 adherents; the American Baptist Church, 64,312; the Lutheran Church—Missouri Synod, 62,712; and the Christian Church (Disciples of Christ), 56,908. Roman Catholics constitute the largest single religious group in the state, with 405,844 adherents in 2000. The estimated Jewish population in 2000 was 14,500, which represents an increase of over 5,000 adherents since 1990. There were over 18,000 Mennonites throughout the state and about 3,470 Muslims. About 50.6% of the population (or over 1.3 million people) were not counted as members of any religious organization.

10 TRANSPORTATION

In the heartland of the nation, Kansas is at the crossroads of US road and railway systems. In 2001, Kansas had 25,638 bridges (3rd in the nation behind Texas and Ohio). In 2000, the state had 134,582 mi (216,588 km) of public roads, of which 124,375 mi (200,162 km) were rural, and 10,207 mi (16,426 km) were urban. There were 826,441 automobiles, 1,465,830 trucks, and 3,864 buses registered in Kansas in 2000.

In the late 1800s, the two major railroads, the Kansas Pacific (now the Union Pacific) and the Santa Fe (now the Burlington Northern-Santa Fe) acquired more than 10 million acres (4 million hectares) of land in the state and then advertised for immigrants to come and buy it. By 1872, the railroads stretched across the state, creating in their path the towns of Ellsworth, Newton, Caldwell, Wichita, and Dodge City. One of the first "cow towns" was Abilene, the terminal point for all cattle shipped to the East.

In 2000, the state had 6,859 route mi (11,038 km) of railroad track. That same year, 13.6 million tons of farm products accounted for 57% of the freight originating in the state. An Amtrak passenger train crosses Kansas en route from Chicago to Los Angeles. Total ridership through the state in 1996 was 32,944.

In 2002, the state had 370 airports. The busiest airport is Kansas City International, with 5,903,296 people enplaned in 2000. Approximately two-thirds of all business and private aircraft in the United States are built in Kansas.

River barges move bulk commodities along the Missouri River. The chief river ports are Atchison, Leavenworth, Lansing, and Kansas City.

11 HISTORY

Present-day Kansas was first inhabited by Paleo-Indians approximately 10,000 years ago. They were followed by several prehistoric cultures, forerunners of the Plains tribes—the Wichita, Pawnee, Kansa, and Osage—that were living or hunting in Kansas when the earliest Europeans arrived. These tribes were buffalo hunters who also farmed and lived in small permanent communities. Around 1800, they were joined on the Central Plains by the nomadic Cheyenne, Arapaho, Comanche, and Kiowa.

The first European, explorer Francisco Coronado, entered Kansas in 1541, searching for riches in the fabled land of Quivira. He found no gold but was impressed by the land's fertility. A second Spanish expedition to the Plains was led by Juan de Onate in 1601. Between 1682 and 1739, French explorers established trading contacts with the Indians. France ceded its claims to the area to Spain in 1762, but received it back from Spain in 1800.

Most of Kansas was sold to the US by France as part of the Louisiana Purchase of 1803. (The extreme southwestern corner was gained after the Mexican War.) Lewis and Clark examined the country along the Missouri River in 1804, and expeditions under the command of Zebulon Pike (1806) and Stephen Long (1819) traversed the land from east to west. Pike and Long were not impressed with the territory's dry soil, the latter calling the area "unfit for civilization, and of course uninhabitable by a people depending on agriculture for their subsistence."

Largely because of these negative reports, early settlement of Kansas was sparse, limited to a few thousand eastern Indians who were removed from their lands and relocated in what is now eastern Kansas. Included were such once-powerful tribes as the Shawnee, Delaware, Ojibwa, Wyandot, Ottawa, and Potawatomi. They were joined by a number of Christian missionaries seeking to transform the Indians into Christian farmers.

William Becknell opened the Santa Fe Trail to wagon traffic in 1822, and for 50 years that route, two-thirds of which lay in Kansas, was of commercial importance to the West. During the 1840s and 1850s, thousands of migrants crossed northeastern Kansas on the California-Oregon Trail. In 1827, Ft. Leavenworth was established, followed by Ft. Scott (1842) and Ft. Riley (1853). Today, Ft. Leavenworth and Ft. Riley are still the two largest military installations in the state.

Kansas Territory was created by the Kansas-Nebraska Act (30 May 1854), with its western boundary set at the Rocky Mountains. Almost immediately, disputes arose as to whether Kansas would enter the Union as a free or slave state. Both free-staters and proslavery settlers were brought in, and a succession of governors tried to bring order out of the chaos arising from the two groups' differences. Free-staters established an extralegal government at Topeka following the establishment of a territorial capital at Lecompton.

Because of several violent incidents, the territory became known as Bleeding Kansas. One of the most memorable attacks came in May 1856, when the town of Lawrence was sacked by proslavery forces. John Brown, an abolitionist who had recently arrived from upstate New York, retaliated by murdering five proslavery settlers. Guerrilla skirmishes continued for the next few years along the Kansas-Missouri border. The final act of violence was the Marais des Cygnes massacre in 1858, which resulted in the death of several free-staters. In all, about 50 people were killed in the territorial period—not an extraordinary number for a frontier community.

After several attempts to write a constitution acceptable to both anti- and proslavery groups, the final document was drafted in 1859. Kansas entered the Union on 29 January 1861 as a free state. Topeka was named the capital, and the western boundary was moved to its present location.

Although Kansas lay west of the major Civil War action, more than two-thirds of its adult males served in the Union Army and gave it the highest military death rate among the northern states. Kansas units saw action in the South and West, most notably at Wilson's Creek, Cane Hill, Prairie Grove, and Chickamauga. The only full-scale battle fought in Kansas was at Mine Creek in 1864, at the end of General Sterling Price's unsuccessful Confederate campaign in the West. The most tragic incident on Kansas soil came on 21 August 1863, when Confederate guerrilla William C. Quantrill raided Lawrence, killing at least 150 persons and burning the town.

Following the Civil War, settlement expanded in Kansas, particularly in the central part of the state. White settlers encroached on the hunting grounds of the Plains tribes, and the Indians retaliated with attacks on white settlements. Treaty councils were held, the largest at Medicine Lodge in 1867, but not until 1878 did conflict cease between Indians and whites. Most of the Indians were eventually removed to the Indian Territory in what is now Oklahoma. Also during this period, buffalo, slaughtered for food and hides, all but disappeared from the state.

By 1872, both the Union Pacific and the Santa Fe railroads had crossed Kansas, and other lines were under construction. Rail expansion brought more settlers, who established new communities. It also led to the great Texas cattle drives that meant prosperity to a number of Kansas towns—including Abilene, Ellsworth, Wichita, Caldwell, and Dodge City—from 1867 to 1885. This was when Bat Masterson, Wyatt Earp, Doc Holliday, and Wild Bill Hickok reigned in Dodge City and Abilene—the now romantic era of the Old West.

A strain of hard winter wheat that proved particularly well suited to the state's soil was brought to Kansas in the 1870s by Russian Mennonites fleeing czarist rule, and Plains agriculture was thereby transformed. There were also political changes: the state adopted limited female suffrage in 1887. Prohibition, made part of the state constitution in 1880, was a source of controversy until its repeal in 1948.

Significant changes in agriculture, industry, transportation, and communications came after 1900. Mechanization became commonplace in farming, and vast areas were opened to wheat production, particularly during World War I. Some automobile manufacturing took place, and the movement for "good roads" began. The so-called agrarian revolt of the late 19th century, characterized politically by populism, evolved into the Progressive movement of the early 1900s, which focused attention on control of monopolies, public health, labor legislation, and more representative politics. Much of the Progressive leadership came from Kansas; Kansan newspaper editor and national Progressive leader William Allen White devoted considerable energy to Theodore Roosevelt's Bull Moose campaign in 1912.

Kansas suffered through the Great Depression of the 1930s. The state's western region, part of the Dust Bowl, was hardest hit. Improved weather conditions and the demands of World War II revived Kansas agriculture in the 1940s. The World War II era also saw the development of industry, especially in transportation. Wichita had been a major center of the aircraft industry in the 1920s and 1930s, and its plants became vital to the US war effort. Other heavy industry grew, and mineral production—oil, natural gas, salt, coal, and gypsum—expanded greatly. In 1952, a native Kansan, Dwight D. Eisenhower, was elected to the first of two terms as president of the United States. Two years later, Topeka became the focal point of a landmark in US history—the US Supreme Court ruling in the Brown v. Board of Education case that banned racial segregation in the nation's schools.

After World War II, Kansas grew increasingly urban. Agriculture became highly commercialized and the state became home to dozens of large companies that process and market farm products and supply materials to crop producers. Livestock production, especially in closely controlled feedlots, is a major enterprise. Kansas farmers were hit hard by the recession of the 1980s. Agricultural banks failed and many farms were lost, their owners forced into bankruptcy. As part of a solution, the state government worked to expand international exports of Kansas products, securing, for example, a trade agreement with the St. Petersburg region of Russia in 1993. The late 1980s and early 1990s also saw dramatic extremes of weather. Kansas received less than 25% of its normal average rainfall in 1988. Topsoil erosion damaged 865,000 acres (354,650 hectares) and drought drove up commodity prices and depleted grain stocks. From April through September of 1993, Kansas experienced the worst floods of the century. Some 13,500 people evacuated their homes, and the floods caused $574 million dollars worth of damage.

In the 1990s, in response to the economic problems created by severe weather and to a slowdown in industrial growth, the state government implemented a number of measures, including block grants to cities, to bolster economic development. Amidst the sustained economic boom of the late-1990s, Kansas generally prospered. Unemployment dropped to just 3%, more than one point below the national average, in 1999. The state's poverty rate declined in the period between 1989 (when it was 11.5%) and 1998, when it was 9.6%. But with farmers and ranchers still struggling in 1999, a bipartisan group of rural legislators came together to introduce a plan to address what was by then perceived as a crisis in the state's agricultural economy. Their nine-point plan aimed to shore up the farming sector by restraining the anticompetitive market forces they believed threatened family farmers.

In 1996, native son and US Senate majority leader Robert Dole won the Republican presidential nomination but was defeated by Democratic incumbent Bill Clinton, although Dole carried his home state with 54% of the vote to Clinton's 36%.

In 1999 the Kansas Board of Education voted 6–4 to adopt standards that downplayed the importance of evolution and omitted the Big Bang theory of the universe's origin from the curriculum. Though the standards were not mandatory, they drew national attention, with critics declaiming the standards as "backward-looking." In 2000 elections, the state's voters ousted three of the four board members who had approved the standards and who were up for reelection. New members promised the board would moderate its views. Earlier in the year Wichita school district voters made state history when they approved, by a margin of 2–1, Kansas' largest-ever school bond issue, $284.5 million.

The Kansas economy was improving in 2003, after the 2001 US recession. Unemployment in Kansas stood at 5% in July 2003, down from 5.2% a year prior. The national unemployment rate in July 2003 was 6.2%. In 2003, Kansas had a $230 million budget deficit for 2004, and Governor Kathleen Sebelius that April was calling for bond sales, expanded gambling, and more rapid tax collection to cover the shortfall. Her plans were met with opposition from the Republican-controlled legislature, however. In her 2003 State of the State Address, Sebelius focused on education, health care, transportation, and the economy. She also set forth plans to streamline state government and encourage citizen involvement in local communities.

12 STATE GOVERNMENT

The form of Kansas's constitution was a matter of great national concern, for the question of whether Kansas would be a free or slave state was in doubt throughout the 1850s. After three draft constitutions failed to win popular support or congressional approval, a fourth version, banning slavery, was drafted in July 1859 and ratified by Kansas voters that October. Signed by President James Buchanan on 29 January 1861, this constitution (with 92 subsequent amendments as of 2002, one of which was subsequently nullified by the state supreme court) has governed Kansas to the present day.

The Kansas legislature consists of a 40-member senate and a 125-member house of representatives. Senators serve four-year terms and house members serve for two years; elections are held in even-numbered years. Legislative sessions, which begin the 2nd Monday of January each year, are limited to 90 calendar days in even-numbered years but are unlimited in odd-numbered years. Legislators may call a special session by petition to the governor of two-thirds the membership of each house. Length of special sessions is not limited. Legislators must be at least 18 years old, residents of their districts, and qualified voters. In 2002 legislators received a per diem salary of $78.75 during regular sessions.

Constitutional amendments are proposed by the legislature, where they must be approved by two-thirds of the members before being sent to the voters for ratification. A maximum of five proposed amendments may be submitted to the state's voters at any one time.

Officials elected statewide are the governor and lieutenant governor (elected jointly), secretary of state, attorney general, treasurer, and commissioner of insurance. Members of the state Board of Education are elected by districts. All elected state officials serve four-year terms. The governor cannot serve more than two consecutive terms. Every office in the executive branch is controlled by either the governor or another elected official. There are no formal age, citizenship, or residency provisions for a gubernatorial candidate's qualifications for office. In 2002, the governor's salary was $95,446.

A bill becomes law when it has been approved by 21 senators and 63 representatives and signed by the governor. A veto can be overridden by two-thirds of the elected members of both houses. If the governor neither vetoes nor signs a bill, it becomes law after 10 days (whether or not the legislature is in session).

To vote in the state, a person must be a US citizen, 18 years old at the time of the election, a resident of Kansas, and not able to claim the right to vote elsewhere. Restrictions apply to those convicted of certain crimes and to those judged by the court as mentally incompetent to vote.

13POLITICAL PARTIES

Kansas was dominated by the Republican Party for the first three decades of statehood (1860s–80s). Although the Republicans remain the dominant force in state politics, the Democrats controlled the governorship in the early 2000s.

The Republican Party of early Kansas espoused the abolitionist ideals of the New England settlers who sought to ban slavery from the state. After the Civil War, the railroads played a major role in Republican politics and won favorable tax advantages from the elected officials. The party's ranks swelled with the arrival of immigrants from Scandinavia and Germany, who tended to side with the party's by then strongly conservative beliefs.

The Republicans' hold over state life was shaken by the Populist revolt toward the end of the 19th century. The high point of Populist Party power came in 1892, when the insurgents won all the statewide elective offices and also took control of the senate. When electoral irregularities denied them control of the house, they temporarily seized the house chambers. The two parties then set up separate houses of representatives, the Populists meeting one day and the Republicans the next. This continued for six weeks, until the Kansas supreme court ruled that the Republicans constituted the rightful legal body. After a Republican sweep in 1894, the Populists returned to office in 1896, but the party declined rapidly thereafter.

The Democrats rose to power in the state as a result of the split between the conservative and progressive wings of the Republican Party in 1912. Nevertheless, the Democrats were very much a minority party until after World War II. They held the governorship for 18 of the 28 years between 1957 and 1985; the most recent Democratic governor was Kathleen Sebelius, elected in 2002. Republicans have regularly controlled the legislature. In 2002 there were 1,615,699 registered voters. In 1998, 29% of registered voters were Democratic, 45% Republican, and 26% unaffiliated or members of other parties.

In 1988 and 1992, Kansans voted for George Bush in the presidential elections. In the 1996 election, native Kansan Bob Dole won 54% of the vote; Clinton received 36%; and Independent Ross Perot garnered 9%. In the 2000 election, Republican George W. Bush won 58% of the vote to Democrat Al Gore's 37%. Independent Ralph Nader won 3% of the vote. The state had six electoral votes in the 2000 presidential election.

Bob Dole, first elected to the US Senate in 1968 and elected Senate majority leader in 1984, reclaimed the post of majority leader when the Republicans gained control of the Senate in the elections of 1994. In a surprise move in May 1996, Dole announced his retirement from the Senate to concentrate on his presidential campaign. In November, the race to fill his remaining term was won by Republican Sam Brownback. Completing the term, Brownback won his first full term in November 1998. Kansas's other Republican senator, Nancy Landon Kassebaum, also vacated her seat in 1996; it was won by Republican Congressman Pat Roberts, who was reelected in 2002. In the 2002 elections, Kansas voters sent three Republicans and one Democrat to the US House. In the state legislature in mid-2003, there were 30 Republicans and 10 Democrats in the senate and 80 Republicans and 45 Democrats in the state house.

14LOCAL GOVERNMENT

As of 2002, Kansas had 104 counties, 627 municipalities, 1,299 townships, 324 public school districts, and 1,533 special districts. The total number of local government bodies was 3,887 in 2002. By law, no county can be less than 432 sq mi (1,119 sq km).

Each county government is headed by elected county commissioners. Other county officials include the county clerk, treasurer, register of deeds, attorney, sheriff, clerk of district

Kansas Presidential Vote by Political Parties, 1948–2000

YEAR	ELECTORAL VOTE	KANSAS WINNER	DEMOCRAT	REPUBLICAN	PROGRESSIVE	SOCIALIST	PROHIBITION
1948	8	Dewey (R)	351,902	423,039	4,603	2,807	6,468
1952	8	*Eisenhower (R)	273,296	616,302	6,038	530	6,038
1956	8	*Eisenhower (R)	296,317	566,878	—	—	3,048
1960	8	Nixon (R)	363,213	561,474	—	—	4,138
1964	7	*Johnson (D)	464,028	386,579		1,901	5,393
					AMERICAN IND.		
1968	7	*Nixon (R)	302,996	478,674	88,921		2,192
1972	7	*Nixon (R)	270,287	619,812	21,808		4,188
						LIBERTARIAN	
1976	7	Ford (R)	430,421	502,752	4,724	3,242	1,403
1980	7	*Reagan (R)	326,150	566,812	7,555	14,470	—
1984	7	*Reagan (R)	333,149	677,296	—	3,329	—
1988	7	*Bush (R)	422,636	554,049	3,806	12,553	—
					IND. (Perot)		
1992	6	Bush (R)	390,434	449,951	312,358	4,314	—
1996	6	Dole (R)	387,659	583,245	92,639	4,557	
					(Nader		REFORM)
2000	6	*Bush, G. W. (R)	399,276	622,332	36,086	4,525	7,370

* Won US presidential election.

court, and appraiser. Most cities are run by mayor-council systems.

15STATE SERVICES

To address the continuing threat of terrorism and to work with the federal Department of Homeland Security (created in 2002 following the terrorist attacks of 11 September 2001), homeland security in Kansas in 2003 operated under the authority of the governor; the adjutant general was designated as the state homeland security advisor.

All education services, including community colleges, are handled by the state Board of Education; the state university system lies within the jurisdiction of the Board of Regents. The Department of Human Resources administers employment and worker benefit programs; the Department of Economic Development operates housing and business planning programs. Social, vocational, and children's and youth programs are run by the Department of Social and Rehabilitation Services; the Department of Health and Environment supervises health, environment, and laboratory services. Other departments focus on agriculture, commerce and housing, corrections, revenue, transportation, wildlife and parks, aging, and information resources.

A "Sunset Law" automatically abolishes specified state agencies at certain times unless they receive renewed statutory authority.

16JUDICIAL SYSTEM

The supreme court, the highest court in the state, is composed of a chief justice and six other justices. All justices are appointed by the governor but after one year must run for election at the next general election. They then are elected for six-year terms. In case of rejection by the voters, the vacancy is filled by appointment. An intermediate-level court of appeals consists of a chief judge and six other judges appointed by the governor; like supreme court justices, they must be elected to full terms, in this case for four years.

In January 1977, probate, juvenile, and county courts, as well as magistrate courts of countywide jurisdiction, were replaced by district courts. The 31 district courts are presided over by 156 district and associate district judges and 69 district magistrate judges. Kansas has a death penalty and has executed two persons since 1977. There were 38 prisoners were under sentence of death as of 2003.

The Department of Corrections administers the state correctional system. Kansas had a prison population of 8,543 as of June 2001, a decrease of 2.7% from the previous year. The state's incarceration rate stood at 317 per 100,000. A federal prison is located at Leavenworth. Kansas's crime rate was 4,321.4 per 100,000 inhabitants in 2001, including a total of 10,909 violent crimes and 105,537 crimes against property in that year.

17ARMED FORCES

The US Army's 1st Infantry Division, known as the Big Red One, is located at Ft. Riley in Junction City. The Army's Command and General Staff College is housed at Ft. Leavenworth; McConnell Air Force Base is located in Wichita. A total of 16,659 military personnel were stationed in Kansas in 1997. In 2001, $930 million in defense contracts was awarded to state firms, up from $762 million in 1995–96 and down from $2.4 billion in 1983–84.

There were 267,452 veterans of US military service in Kansas as of 2000, of whom 54,431 served in World War II; 31,692 in the Korean conflict; 79,493 during the Vietnam era; and 33,051 during 1990–2000 (including the Persian Gulf War). During fiscal year 2002, $538 million was spent on veterans' benefits.

In 2000, the Kansas Highway Patrol employed 457 full-time sworn officers.

18MIGRATION

By the 1770s, Kansas was inhabited by a few thousand Indians, mainly from five tribes: the Kansa (Kaw) and the Osage, both of whom had migrated from the east, the Pawnee from the north, and the Wichita and Comanche, who had come from the southwest. In 1825, the US government signed a treaty with the Kansa and Osage that allowed eastern Indians to settle in the state.

The first wave of white migration came during the 1850s with the arrival of New England abolitionists who settled in Lawrence, Topeka, and Manhattan. They were followed by a much larger wave of emigrants from the eastern Missouri and the upper Mississippi Valley, drawn by the lure of wide-open spaces and abundant economic opportunity.

The population swelled as a result of the Homestead Act of 1862, which offered land to anyone who would improve it and live on it for five years. The railroads promoted the virtues of Kansas overseas and helped sponsor immigrant settlers. By 1870, 11% of the population was European. More than 30,000 blacks, mostly from the South, arrived during 1878–80. Crop failures caused by drought in the late 1890s led to extensive out-migration from the western half of the state. Another period of out-migration occurred in the early 1930s, when massive dust storms drove people off the land. Steady migration from farms to cities has been a feature of Kansas since the early 20th century, with urban population surpassing farm population after World War II. From 1980 to 1990, the urban population increased from 66.7% to 69.1% of the state's total. Also from 1980 to 1990, Kansas had a net loss of 63,411 from migration. Only 10 of Kansas's 105 counties recorded a net gain from migration in the 1980s. Between 1990 and 1998, the state had a net loss of 13,000 in domestic migration and a gain of 24,000 in international migration. In 1998, 3,184 foreign immigrants arrived in the state. Between 1990 and 1998, Kansas's overall population increased 6.1%. In the period 1995–2000, 276,786 people moved into the state and 284,587 moved out, for a net loss of 7,792, with most migration occurring to and from Missouri.

19INTERGOVERNMENTAL COOPERATION

Kansas is a member of the Arkansas River Compact of 1949, Arkansas River Compact of 1965, Central Interstate Low-Level Radioactive Waste Compact, Kansas-Nebraska Big Blue River Compact, Kansas City Area Transportation Authority, Kansas-Missouri Boundary Compact and Culture District Compact, Missouri River Toll Bridge Compact, Republican River Compact, and other interstate bodies. The Interstate Cooperation Commission assists state officials and employees in maintaining contact with governmental units in other states. In fiscal year 2001, Kansas received over $2.7 billion in federal grants.

20ECONOMY

Although wheat production has long been the mainstay of the Kansas economy, efforts to bring other industries into the state began as early as the 1870s, when the railroads linked Kansas to eastern markets. By 2000, agricultural products and meat-packing industries were rivaled by the large aircraft industry centered in Wichita. Four Kansas companies, all located in Wichita, manufacture 70% of the world's general aviation aircraft. The Kansas City metropolitan area is a center of automobile production and printing. Metal fabrication, printing, and mineral products industries predominate in the nine southeastern counties. Kansas continues to lead all states in wheat production. The national recession of 2001 had a relatively mild impact on the Kansas economy. The annual economic growth rate, which had averaged 5% 1998 to 2000, dipped to 3.2% in 2001. Net job creation, though sharply slowed by layoffs in 2001 and 2002, including several rounds of layoffs in the Wichita aircraft manufacturing industry, remained positive, in contrast to the nation as whole in which job creation turned to net layoffs in the second half of 2001 and stayed negative throughout 2002. In December 2002, however, unemployment in Kansas was at the relatively high level of 4.6%. The farm sector was also afflicted by drought conditions, which persisted into the winter of 2002–2003. In 2002, on a year-on-year basis, wheat production was down 19%, corn production down 26%, and soybean production down 29%. Kansas's rural population continues its long-term decline as people migrate to urban areas seeking better employment opportunities. Since 1970, 67 of the state's 105 counties have lost population, and in 19 of these the rate of decrease accelerated during the 1990s. From 1997 to 2001, Kansas farm output experienced a net decrease of 34.5%, from $2.7 billion to $1.8 billion.

Kansas's gross state product in 2001 was 44th largest among the states at $87.2 billion, to which general services contributed $15.5 billion; trade, $15.1 billion, manufacturing, $14.1 billion; government, $12 billion, financial services, $11.7 billion, and transportation and public utilities, $11.1 billion. The public sector constituted 13.8% of gross state product in 2001.

21INCOME
According to the Bureau of Economic Analysis, in 2001, Kansas had a per capita personal income (PCPI) of $28,432 which ranked 29th in the United States (including the District of Columbia) and was 93% of the national average, $30,413. The 2001 PCPI reflected an increase of 3.6% from 2000 compared to the national change of 2.2%. In 2001, Kansas had a total personal income (TPI) of $76,828,166,000 which ranked 31st in the United States and accounted for 0.9% of the national total. The 2001 TPI reflected an increase of 4.0% from 2000 compared to the national change of 3.3%.

Earnings of persons employed in Kansas increased from $52,101,857,000 in 2000 to $53,851,852,000 in 2001, an increase of 3.4%. The largest industries in 2001 were services, 24.0% of earnings; state and local government, 12.7%; and durable goods manufacturing, 11.0%. Of the industries that accounted for at least 5% of earnings in 2001, the slowest growing from 2000 to 2001 was transportation and public utilities (9.5% of earnings in 2001), which decreased 0.6%; the fastest was state and local government, which increased 6.9%.

According to data released by the US Census Bureau, in 2000, the median household income was $37,705 compared to the national average of $42,148. In 2001, the median income for a family of four was $61,686 compared to the national average of $63,278. For the period 1999 to 2001, the average poverty rate was 10.1% which placed it 21st among the 50 states and the District of Columbia ranked lowest to highest.

22LABOR
According to Bureau of Labor Statistics (BLS) provisional estimates, in July 2003 the seasonally adjusted civilian labor force in Kansas numbered 1,477,800, with approximately 74,500 workers unemployed, yielding an unemployment rate of 5.0%, compared to the national average of 6.2% for the same period. Since the beginning of the BLS data series in 1978, the highest unemployment rate recorded was 7.5% in August 1982. The historical low was 2.7% in June 1978. In 2001, an estimated 4.8% of the labor force was employed in construction; 13.1% in manufacturing; 6.6% in transportation, communications, and public utilities; 18.7% in trade; 6.1% in finance, insurance, and real estate; 24.0% in services; 17.0% in government; and 3.6% in agriculture.

The US Department of Labor reported that in 2002, 99,000 of Kansas's 1,217,000 employed wage and salary workers were members of unions. This represented 8.2% of those so employed, down from 9.3% in 2001. The national average is 13.2%. In all, 120,000 workers (9.9%) were represented by unions. In addition to union members, this category includes workers who report no union affiliation but whose jobs are covered by a union contract. Kansas is one of 22 states with a right-to-work law.

23AGRICULTURE
Known as the Wheat State and the breadbasket of the nation, Kansas typically produces more wheat than any other state. It ranked 5th in total farm income in 2001, with cash receipts of $8.1 billion.

Because of fluctuating prices, Kansas farmers have always risked economic disaster. During the 1920s, depressed farm prices forced many new farmers out of business. By World War II, Kansas farmers were prospering again, as record prices coincided with record yields. Since then, improved technology has favored corporate farms at the expense of small landholders. Between 1940 and 2002, the number of farms declined from 159,000 to 63,000, while the average size of farms more than doubled (to 730 acres/ 296 hectares). Income from crops in 2001 totaled $2.6 billion.

Other leading crops are alfalfa, hay, oats, barley, popcorn, rye, dry edible beans, corn and sorghums for silage, wild hay, red clover, and sugar beets.

24ANIMAL HUSBANDRY
In 2001, Kansas dairy farmers had an estimated 93,000 milk cows that produced 1.61 billion lb (0.73 billion kg) of milk. Also during 2001 Kansas poultry farmers sold an estimated 2.2 million lb (1 million kg) of chicken, and produced 434 million eggs worth around $13.6 million.

In 2003, Kansas farmers had an estimated 6.35 million cattle and calves worth $4.25 billion (2nd in the US). Kansas farmers had an estimated 1.53 million hogs and pigs worth around $99.5 million in 2002. An estimated 8.2 million lb (3.7 million kg) of sheep and lambs were produced by Kansas farmers in 2001 and sold for $5.1 million.

25FISHING
There is little commercial fishing in Kansas. Sport fishermen can find bass, crappie, catfish, perch, and pike in the state's reservoirs and artificial lakes. In 1998, there were 329,115 fishing licenses issued by the state. The Kansas Department of Wildlife and Parks' objectives for fisheries include provision of 11.7 million angler trips annually on Kansas reservoirs, lakes, streams, and private waters, while maintaining the quantity and quality of the catch.

26FORESTRY
Kansas was at one time so barren of trees that early settlers were offered 160 acres (65 hectares) free if they would plant trees on their land. This program was rarely implemented, however, and today much of Kansas is still treeless.

Kansas has 1,545,000 acres (625,000 hectares) of forestland, 2.9% of the total state area. There are 1,491,000 acres (491,000 hectares) of commercial timberland, of which 96% are privately owned.

27MINING
The value of nonfuel mineral production in Kansas was estimated at $640 million in 2001, up about 2% from 2000. Grade-A helium, portland cement, salt, and crushed stone were the leading nonfuel mineral commodities, accounting for 26%, 23%, 19%, and 17%, respectively, of the total nonfuel mineral production

value in 2001. Kansas continued to rank 1st of 2 states producing crude helium (45 million cu m, valued at $48.7 million). The state also ranked 1st of 4 states producing grade-A helium (85 million cu m, valued at $169 million) and5th in salt production (3.1 million metric tons, $121 million). Production of portland cement was 1.8 million metric tons, valued at $144 million, and crushed stone was 21.4 million metric tons, valued at $107 million.

28ENERGY AND POWER

The state ranked 18th in energy consumption per capita, with 385 million Btu (97 million kcal) in 2000.

In 1999, Kansas had an installed electrical generating capacity (utility and nonutility) of 10.1 million kW. Total electrical output was 42.1 billion kWh, 53% coal-fired. The state has one single-unit nuclear plant, the Wolf Creek plant in Burlington.

In 2000, Kansas was the nation's 8th-leading oil producer. Output in 2002 totaled 90,000 barrels of crude petroleum per day. There were proved reserves of 216 million barrels at the end of 2001.

Natural gas marketed production was 450.8 billion cu ft (12.8 billion cu m) in 2002. Proved reserves in 2001 totaled 5,101 billion cu ft (144.4 billion cu m). About 45% of total consumption went for industrial purposes, 26% for residential use, 19% for commercial applications, and 10% for utilities.

Two surface mines produced 201,000 tons of bituminous coal in 2000. Demonstrated coal reserves were estimated at 975 million tons in 1998.

29INDUSTRY

Industries are concentrated in Douglas, Johnson, Sedgwick, Shawnee, and Wyandotte counties. The estimated value of shipments for all state manufacturing totaled $49 billion in 1997.

Kansas is a world leader in aviation, claiming a large share of both US and world production and sales of commercial aircraft. Wichita is the home of Boeing, Cessna, Learjet, and Raytheon, which combined manufactured approximately 70% of the world's general aviation aircraft and $3.47 billion in sales. The aviation sector employees 19% of the manufacturing sector workforce.

Other major businesses in Kansas include, in order of full-time employee numbers: Sprint, IBP, Burlington Northern Santa Fe Corp., GM, Western Resources, Southwestern Bell, Via Christi Medical Services, and Allied Signal. Many of the major companies in Kansas pack meat.

Earnings of persons employed in Kansas increased from $44.5 billion in 1997 to $47.4 billion in 1998, an increase of 6.5%. The largest industries in 1998 were services, 23.2% of earnings; durable goods manufacturing, 12.2%; and state and local government, 12.0%. Of the industries that accounted for at least 5% of earnings in 1998, the slowest growing from 1997 to 1998 was state and local government, which increased 2.0%; the fastest was durable goods manufacturing, which increased 10.8%.

30COMMERCE

Domestically, Kansas is not a major commercial state. In 1997, Kansas had a total of 5,965 wholesale establishments with sales of $44 billion. The retail sales of 16,629 stores totaled $23 billion. Automotive dealers and service stations accounted for 15% of all retail establishments; food stores, 9%; and eating and drinking places, 29%. Food sales totaled $4.2 billion, while general merchandise sales reached $3.5 billion. In both agricultural and manufactured exports, Kansas plays an important role in US foreign trade. Exports of goods from Kansas totaled $4 billion in 1998. Exports were $4.8 billion in 1999,

increasing at a rate five times the national rate. Most exports went to Japan, Canada, Mexico, and the UK.

31CONSUMER PROTECTION

The Attorney General's Consumer Protection Division enforces the Kansas Consumer Protection Act, which protects consumers against fraud and false advertising. The Consumer Credit Commissioner is responsible for administering the state's investment and common credit codes.

32BANKING

Kansas's 384 insured banks had assets of $50 billion in 2002. Records of all banks and trust companies in the state are examined once a year either by the state bank commissioner, the Office of Comptroller of Currency, the Federal Deposit Insurance Corporation, or by a federal reserve bank. The state savings and loan commissioner's office was merged into the state bank commissioner's office in 1993.

Drought conditions in Kansas as of 2002 were severe, and farm banks in areas of prolonged drought saw higher loan delinquency rates than banks elsewhere. From 2000–02, many insured institutions in Kansas's larger metropolitan areas relied more heavily on commercial real estate (CRE) loans; CRE markets were weak in 2002.

33INSURANCE

In 2001 there were 1.6 million ordinary life insurance policies in force with a total value of $105.7 billion; total value for all categories of life insurance (ordinary, group, industrial, and credit) was $171.6 billion. Death benefits paid that year totaled $478.4 million. In 2003, 14 life and health and 32 property and casualty insurance companies were headquartered in Kansas. In 2001, property and casualty insurers wrote premiums totaling $3.4 billion. That year, there were 10,535 flood insurance policies in force in the state, with a total value of $964,126.

34SECURITIES

There are no stock exchanges in Kansas. There are approximately 559 brokers and dealers with 2,920 employees, and 109 investment advisory firms registered to do business in the state. Kansas holds the headquarters of 30 NASDAQ companies, one NASDAQ market maker, and six NYSE-listed companies: Sprint, CEC Entertainment, Emple Distribution Electronics Co., Fleming Co., Inc., Kinder Morgan, and Western Resources.

35PUBLIC FINANCE

The state budget is prepared by the Division of the Budget and is submitted by the governor to the legislature for approval. The fiscal year runs from 1 July to 30 June. Generally, according to state law, no Kansas governmental unit may issue revenue bonds to finance current activities—these must operate on a cash basis. Bonds may be issued for such capital improvements as roads and buildings.

In 2002/03, general fund revenues totaled $4.44 billion, accounting for 46.6% of all receipts by the state. General fund expenditures went to education (67.8%), human resources (19.7%), public safety (7.4%), general government (4.4%), and agriculture and natural resources (0.7%). Shortfalls in revenue in 2001/02 and 2002/03 led to cuts in programs serving young mothers, the poor and the elderly. The deficit in 2003 was reported at 5.8% of the state budget, and the projected deficit for 2003/04 was 15.7% of the budget.

The following table from the US Census Bureau contains information on revenues, expenditures, indebtedness, and cash/securities for 2001.

	($000)	PERCENT	PER CAPITA
Population (thousands, 2001)	2,702	(X)	(X)
Total Revenue	8,713,237	100.00	3,224.74
General revenue	9,026,660	103.60	3,340.73
Utility revenue	–	–	–
Liquor store revenue	–	–	–
Insurance trust revenue	–313,423	–3.60	–116.00
Exhibit: Salaries and wages	1,503,000	14.74	556.25
Total expenditure	10,196,910	100.00	3,773.84
General expenditure	9,405,968	92.24	3,481.11
Education	4,014,202	39.37	1,485.64
Public welfare	1,643,119	16.11	608.11
Hospitals	102,742	1.01	38.02
Health	469,867	4.61	173.90
Highways	1,228,570	12.05	454.69
Police protection	53,358	0.52	19.75
Correction	336,495	3.30	124.54
Natural resources	158,159	1.55	58.53
Parks and recreation	4,848	0.05	1.79
Government administration	630,540	6.18	233.36
Interest on general debt	119,934	1.18	44.39
Other and unallocable	644,134	6.32	238.39
Utility expenditure	–	–	–
Liquor store expenditure	–	–	–
Insurance trust expenditure	790,942	7.76	292.72
Debt at end of fiscal year	2,183,859	100.00	808.24
Cash and security holdings	12,416,169	100.00	4,595.18

	($000)	PER CAPITA
Total Taxes	4,808,361	1,770.46
Property taxes	54,576	20.1
Sales and gross receipts	2,432,146	895.53
General sales and gross receipts	1,799,485	662.58
Selective sales taxes	632,661	232.95
Alcoholic beverage	81,834	30.13
Amusements	681	0.25
Insurance Premiums	96,894	35.68
Motor fuels	376,241	138.53
Pari-mutuels	3,812	1.4
Public utilities	856	0.32
Tobacco products	52,342	19.27
Other selective sales	20,001	7.36
Licenses	229,968	84.68
Alcoholic beverages	2,281	0.84
Amusements	209	0.08
Corporation	28,576	10.52
Hunting and fishing	17,423	6.42
Motor vehicle	141,794	52.21
Motor vehicle operators	11,878	4.37
Public utility	3,730	1.37
Occupation and business, NEC	21,495	7.91
Other	2,582	0.95
Other taxes	2,091,671	770.16
Individual income	1,854,848	682.96
Corporation net income	121,931	44.9
Death and gift	48,082	17.7
Documentary and stock transfer	(X)	(X)
Severance	66,810	24.6
Other	(X)	(X)

36 TAXATION

The state individual income tax schedule has three brackets, 3.5%, 6.25% and 6.45%. The corporate tax rate is 4.0% with a 3.35% surtax on Kansas taxable income in excess of $50,000, for a total high rate of 7.35%. A statewide 2% sales tax was adopted in 1937. In June 1992, the rate was raised to 4.9%. Cities and counties could vote to adopt an additional 1% local sales tax. For special projects, counties could also assess an additional 1% local sales tax. In January 2003, the state sales tax rate was at 5.3% but scheduled to decrease to 5.2% effective 1 July 2003. Prescription drugs are exempted from the sales tax. Local-option sales taxes can range up to 3%. The state also collects a full set of excise taxes—on motor fuels, insurance premiums, alcoholic beverages, tobacco products, amusements, pari-mutuels, public utilities and other selected items.

In 2002 Kansas was one of 20 states to raise its cigarette tax, and one of seven to more than double it: from 24 cents a pack to 70 cents a pack. Kansas has its own estate tax (maximum rate 15%), which is thus not affected by the scheduled phasing out of the federal estate tax credit by 2007. The Kansas inheritance tax is 10% on amounts up to $100,000 and 15% on amounts above $200,000. Gift and death taxes accounted for about 1% of the state's tax collections in 2002. Other taxes include various license fees, a state property tax, severance taxes for oil and coal, and an Oil and Gas Conservation tax. Property taxes are mainly collected at the local level and are the largest source of income for local governments. Almost half of non-federal tax collections (43.5% in 2000) are collected at the local level in Kansas.

Total state tax collections in Kansas came to $4.808 billion in 2002, 38.5% generated by the state income tax, 37.4% by the state sales tax, 13.2% by state excise taxes, 4.78% by state license fees, and 2.5% by the state corporate income tax. Combined state and local taxes in Kansas amounted to about 9.8% of income in 2003, placing the state 20th in the country in terms of state and local tax burden.

The following table from the US Census Bureau provides a summary of taxes collected by the state in 2002.

37 ECONOMIC POLICY

The first state commission to promote industrial development was formed in 1939. In 1986, this commission was reorganized into the Kansas Department of Commerce, and in 1992 it became the Department of Commerce and Housing. The department now consists of five divisions: Small Business Development, Community Development, Travel, Tourism, and Film Services, Business Development, and Trade Development. In 2000, the KDOC&H recommended investments in the fields of: aviation, plastics, value-added agriculture, call centers, administrative service centers, and wholesale, packaging, and distribution. Events sponsored by KDOC&H in 2003 included training in downtown revitalization, conferences on finding new markets though international trade and, for leaders, facilitating international business, and workshops on applying for Community Development Block Grants (CDBGs).

Kansas has a duty-free foreign trade zone and provides tax-exempt bonds to help finance business and industry. Specific tax incentives include job expansion and investment tax credits; tax exemptions or moratoriums on land, capital improvements, and specific machinery; and certain corporate income tax exemptions.

38 HEALTH

The infant mortality rate in 2000 was 6.8 per 1,000 live births. Kansans reported 12,395 legal abortions in the same year, averaging 22 per 1,000 women. The overall death rate was 927.2 per 100,000 population in 2000 higher than the US average of 873.1. Heart disease, the leading cause of death in the state, occurred at a rate of 260.0 per 100,000 inhabitants in 2000, above the national average of 258.2. Topeka, a major US center for psychiatric treatment, is home to the world-famous Menninger Clinic. The smoking prevalence was 21.1% of all Kansans ages 18 and older. The rate of HIV-related deaths stood at 1.0 per 100,000 population, well below the national average of 5.3 in 2000. There were 2,465 AIDS cases reported through 2001.

Kansas's 133 community hospitals had 322,067 admissions and 11,211 beds in 2001. There were 8,925 full-time registered nurses and 1,356 full-time licensed practical nurses in 2001 and 234 physicians per 100,000 population in 2000. The average expense of a community hospital for care was $1,219.30 per inpatient day in 2001.

Federal government grants to cover the Medicare and Medicaid services in 2001 totaled $1.0 billion; 391,076 enrollees received Medicare benefits that year. At least 11.4% of the population was uninsured in 2002.

The University of Kansas has the state's only medical and pharmacology schools. The university's Mid-America Cancer Center and Radiation Therapy Center are the major cancer research and treatment facilities in the state. The Menninger Foundation has a research and treatment center for mental health.

39SOCIAL WELFARE

Public assistance and social programs are coordinated through the Department of Human Resources and the Department of Social and Rehabilitation Services. In 2001, the average weekly unemployment benefit was $258.25. Average monthly participation in the food stamp program in FY2002 comprised 140,403 persons (62,896 households). The average monthly benefit was $67.23, and the sum total of benefits paid in FY2002 was $113,271,938.

With the enactment of the Personal Responsibility and Work Opportunity Reconciliation Act of 1996, the US government has changed the form and regulations for many of its social welfare programs. Most significantly, it replaces Aid to Families with Dependent Children (AFDC), an open-ended entitlement program, with Temporary Assistance for Needy Families (TANF), a limited system of assistance funded largely through federal block grants. The reform act also impacts the food stamp program, the Supplemental Security Income program, and the child nutrition program. The law took effect on 1 July 1997 and provided $16.38 billion in block grants for fiscal years 1997–2002. The grants are to be divided among the states based on an equation involving the numbers of former AFDC recipients in each state.

Reauthorization of the 1996 social welfare legislation, scheduled for 2002, was delayed, and the original law had been extended three times as of July 2003, with the most recent extension running through September 2003. Kansas's TANF program is called Kansas Works. In June 2000 the state had 36,557 welfare recipients. State expenditures on the TANF program in FY2002 totaled $62,335,582.

In December 2001, Social Security benefits were paid to 440,620 Kansas residents. This number included 286,590 retired workers, 49,220 widows and widowers, 43,730 disabled workers, 28,370 spouses, and 32,710 children. Social Security beneficiaries represented 16.4% of the total state population and 93.7% of the state's population age 65 and older. Retired workers (excluding persons with special benefits) received an average monthly payment of $896; widows and widowers, $873; disabled workers, $793; and spouses, $460. Payments for children of retired workers averaged $451 per month; children of deceased workers, $581; and children of disabled workers, $235.

Federal Supplemental Security Income payments in December 2001 went to 36,600 Kansas residents, averaging $353 a month.

40HOUSING

Kansas has relatively old housing stock. According to a 2002 survey, about 22% of all housing units were built in 1939 or earlier and 49.6% were built between 1940 and 1979. The overwhelming majority (73%) were one-unit, detached structures and 69.6% were owner-occupied. The total number of housing units in 2002 was 1,159,276, of which 1,056,896 were occupied. Most units relied on utility gas and electricity for heating. It was estimated that 38,968 units lacked telephone service, 2,971 lacked complete plumbing facilities, and 3,733 lacked complete kitchen facilities. The average household size was 2.49 people.

In 2002, 12,983 privately owned units were authorized for construction. The median home value was $94,005. The median monthly cost for mortgage owners was $988. Renters paid a median of $545 per month. During 2002, Kansas received over $46.3 million in aid community planning and development aid from the US Department of Housing and Urban Development.

41EDUCATION

Kansans exceed the national averages for educational attainment. In 2000, 86% of those age 25 and older were high school graduates, and 25.8% had obtained a bachelor's degree or higher.

In 1954, Kansas was the focal point of a US Supreme Court decision that had enormous implications for US public education. The court ruled, in Brown v. Board of Education of Topeka, that Topeka's "separate but equal" elementary schools for black and white students were inherently unequal, and it ordered the school system to integrate.

Total public school enrollment for fall 1999 stood at 472,188. Of these, 325,818 attended schools from kindergarten through grade eight, and 146,370 attended high school. Minority students made up approximately 22% of the total enrollment in public elementary and secondary schools in 2001. Total enrollment was estimated at 469,747 in fall 2000 and drop to 462,000 by fall 2005. During 1999/2000, Kansas spent $6,112 per pupil in public school education. Expenditures for public education in 2000/01 were estimated at $3,189,301. Enrollment in nonpublic schools in fall 2001 was 43,113.

As of fall 2000, there were 176,453 students enrolled in institutions of higher education. In the same year Kansas had 59 degree-granting institutions. In 1997, minority students comprised 13.8% of total postsecondary enrollment. There are 6 state universities, 23 two-year community colleges, 5 private two-year colleges, 17 church-affiliated universities and four-year colleges, 12 vocational-technical schools, and 4 technical colleges (4 community colleges have vocational-technical divisions). In addition, Kansas has a state technical institute, a municipal university (Washburn University, Topeka), and an American Indian university. Kansas State University was the nation's first land-grant university. Washburn University and the University of Kansas have the state's two law schools. The oldest higher-education institution in Kansas is Highland Community College, which was chartered in 1857. The oldest four-year institution is Baker University, a United Methodist institution, which received its charter just three days after Highland's was issued. The Kansas Board of Regents offers scholarships and tuition grants to needy Kansas students.

42ARTS

The Kansas Arts Commission is a state arts agency governed by a 12-member panel of commissioners appointed for four-year rotating terms by the governor. The commission's annual budget is made up of funds appropriated by the Kansas legislature and grants awarded to the agency by the National Endowment for the Arts (NEA). In 2003, the Kansas Arts Commission and other Kansas arts organizations received grants totaling $677,300 from the National Endowment for the Arts. The Arts Commission is also in partnership with the regional Mid-America Arts Alliance. The Kansas Humanities Council, founded in 1972, sponsors programs involving over 500,000 people each year. In 2000, the state received $913,929 in grants from the National Endowment for the Humanities.

The largest and most active arts organizations in the state is the Wichita Symphony Orchestra, established in 1944. The Topeka

Performing Arts Center presents concerts and shows of a variety of music. Topeka also hosts a symphony and a ballet company.

43 LIBRARIES AND MUSEUMS

The Dwight D. Eisenhower Library in Abilene houses the collection of papers and memorabilia from the 34th president; there is also a museum. The Menninger Foundation Museum and Archives in Topeka maintains various collections pertaining to psychiatry. The Kansas State Historical Society Library (Topeka) contains the state's archives. Volumes of books and documents on the Old West are found in the Cultural Heritage and Arts Center Library in Dodge City. Kansas had 35 public library systems in 2000, with 10,207,000 volumes and a circulation of 20,808,000. Total public library income was $70,936,000 in 2000; including $1,844,236 in state grants.

Almost 188 museums, historical societies, and art galleries were scattered across the state in 2000. The Dyche Museum of Natural History at the University of Kansas, Lawrence, draws many visitors. The Kansas State Historical Society maintains an extensive collection of ethnological and archaeological materials in Topeka.

Among the art museums are the Mulvane Art Center in Topeka, the Helen Foresman Spencer Museum of Art at the University of Kansas, and the Wichita Art Museum. The Dalton Museum in Coffeyville displays memorabilia from the famed Dalton family of desperadoes. La Crosse is the home of the Barbed Wire Museum, displaying more than 500 varieties of barbed wire. The Emmett Kelly Historical Museum in Sedan honors the world-famous clown born there. The US Cavalry Museum is on the grounds of Ft. Riley. The Sedgwick County Zoo in Wichita and the Topeka Zoo are the largest of seven zoological gardens in Kansas.

The entire town of Nicodemus, where many blacks settled after the Civil War, was made a national historic landmark in 1975. The chalk formations of Monument Rocks in western Kansas constitute the state's only national natural landmark. Ft. Scott and Ft. Larned are national historic parks.

44 COMMUNICATIONS

About 95.4% of all households had telephone service in 2001.

The state had 15 major AM and 55 major FM radio stations, 13 major commercial television stations, and 4 public television stations in 2003. In 2000, Kansas had registered a total of 42,009 Internet domain names.

45 PRESS

Starting with the *Shawnee Sun*, a Shawnee-language newspaper founded by missionary Jotham Meeker in 1833, the press has played an important role in Kansas history. The most famous Kansas newspaperman was William Allen White, whose *Emporia Gazette* was a leading voice of progressive Republicanism around the turn of the century. Earlier, John J. Ingalls launched his political career by editing the *Atchison Freedom's Champion*. Captain Henry King came from Illinois to found the *State Record* and *Daily Capital* in Topeka.

In 2002, Kansas had 44 daily newspapers and 14 Sunday papers. Leading newspapers and their circulations in 2001–2002 were as follows:

AREA	NAME	DAILY	SUNDAY
Topeka	*Capital–Journal* (m,S)	55,466	63,157
Wichita	*Eagle* (m,S)	85,882	149,451

The *Kansas City* (Missouri) *Star* (259,612 daily; 377,765 Sundays) is widely read in the Kansas as well as in the Missouri part of the metropolitan area.

46 ORGANIZATIONS

In 2003, there were about 1,595 regional, national, and international organizations within the state. Among the organizations headquartered in Kansas are the National Collegiate Athletic Association (NCAA) and the Junior College Athletic Association, the American Association for Public Opinion Research, American Institute of Baking, American Medical Society for Sports Medicine, Council for Learning Disabilities, International Association for Jazz Education, and Lefthanders International.

State and regional cultural and educational organizations include the Association of Community Arts Agencies of Kansas and the Kansas State Historical Society, as well as a number of county historical societies and regional arts groups.

47 TOURISM, TRAVEL, AND RECREATION

In 2000, travel expenditures within the state had an economic impact of about $3.7 billion dollars, including the support of about 57,000 travel-related jobs.

Kansas has 23 state parks, 2 national historic sites, 24 federal reservoirs, 48 state fishing lakes, more than 100 privately owned campsites, and more than 304,000 acres (123,000 hectares) of public hunting and game management lands. The two major national historic sites are Ft. Larned and Ft. Scott, both 19th century army bases on the Indian frontier. In 2002, the top five parks (based on number of visitors) were Hillsdale State Park (1.6 million), El Dorado State Park (1 million), Clinton Lake, Perry Lake, and Tuttle Creek Lake.

The most popular tourist attraction, with over 2.4 million visitors in 2002, is Cabela's (Kansas City), a 190,000 square-foot showroom and shopping center featuring a mule deer museum, a 65,000 gallon aquarium, a gun library, and Yukon base camp grill. The next ranking visitor sites in 2002 were Harrah's Prairie Band Casino (Mayetta), the Kansas City Speedway, Sedgwick County Zoo (Wichita), Woodlands Race Tracks (Kansas City), New Theatre Restaurant (Overland Park), Exploration Place (Wichita) and the Kansas Cosmosphere and Space Center (Hutchinson).

Topeka features a number of tourist attractions, including the state capitol, state historical museum, and Menninger Foundation. Dodge City offers a reproduction of Old Front Street as it was when the town was the "cowboy capital of the world." Historic Wichita Cowtown is another frontier-town reproduction. In Hanover stands the only remaining original and unaltered Pony Express station. A recreated "Little House on the Prairie," near the childhood home of Laura Ingalls Wilder, is 13 mi (21 km) southwest of Independence. The Eisenhower Center in Abilene contains the 34th president's family home, library, and museum. The state fair is held in Hutchinson.

48 SPORTS

There are no major professional sports teams in Kansas. The minor league Wichita Wranglers play in the Double-A Texas League. There are also minor league hockey teams in Wichita and Topeka. During spring, summer, and early fall, horses are raced at Eureka Downs. The national Greyhound Association Meet is held in Abilene.

The University of Kansas and Kansas State both play collegiate football in the Big Twelve Conference. Kansas went to the Orange Bowl in 1948 and 1969, losing both times. The Jayhawks won the Aloha Bowl in 1992 and 1995. Kansas State played in the Cotton Bowl in 1996 and 1997, winning in 1996, and they won the Fiesta Bowl in 1998. In basketball, Kansas won the NCAA Championship in 1952 and 1988 and has appeared in 10 Final Fours. The National Junior College Basketball Tournament is held in Hutchinson each March. The Kansas Relays take place at Lawrence in April. The Flint Hills Rodeo in Strong City is one of many rodeos held statewide.

A US sporting event unique to Kansas is the International Pancake Race, held in Liberal each Shrove Tuesday. Women wearing housedresses, aprons, and scarves run along an S-shaped course carrying skillets and flipping pancakes as they go.

Hall of Fame pitcher Walter Johnson was born in Humboldt, NFL great Barry Sanders in Wichita, and basketball legend Adolph Rupp in Halstead.

49 FAMOUS KANSANS

Kansas claims only one US president and one US vice president. Dwight D. Eisenhower (b.Texas, 1890–1969) was elected the 34th president in 1952 and reelected in 1956; he had served as the supreme commander of Allied Forces in World War II. He is buried in Abilene, his boyhood home. Charles Curtis (1860–1936) was vice president during the Hoover administration.

Two Kansans have been associate justices of the US Supreme Court: David J. Brewer (1837–1910) and Charles E. Whittaker (1901–73). Other federal officeholders from Kansas include William Jardine (1879–1955), secretary of agriculture; Harry Woodring (1890–1967), secretary of war; and Georgia Neese Clark Gray (1900–95), treasurer of the US. Prominent US senators include Edmund G. Ross (1826–1907), who cast a crucial acquittal vote at the impeachment trial of Andrew Johnson; John J. Ingalls (1833–1900), who was also a noted literary figure; Joseph L. Bristow (1861–1944), a leader in the Progressive movement; Arthur Caper (1865–1951), a former publisher and governor; Robert Dole (b.1923), who was the Republican candidate for vice president in 1976, twice served as Senate majority leader and was his party's presidential candidate in 1996; and Nancy Landon Kassebaum (b.1932), elected to the US Senate in 1978. Among the state's important US representatives were Jeremiah Simpson (1842–1905), a leading Populist, and Clifford R. Hope (1893–1970), important in the farm bloc. Gary Hart, a senator and a presidential candidate in 1984 and 1988, was born in Ottawa, Kansas, on 28 November 1936.

Notable Kansas governors include George W. Glick (1827–1911); Walter R. Stubbs (1858–1929); Alfred M. Landon (1887–1984), who ran for US president on the Republican ticket in 1936; and Frank Carlson (1893–1984). Other prominent political figures were David L. Payne (1836–84), who helped open Oklahoma to settlement; Carry Nation (1846–1911), the colorful prohibitionist; and Frederick Funston (1865–1917), hero of the Philippine campaign of 1898 and a leader of San Francisco's recovery after the 1906 earthquake and fire.

Earl Sutherland (1915–74) won the Nobel Prize in 1971 for physiology or medicine. Other leaders in medicine and science include Samuel J. Crumbine (1862–1954), a public health pioneer; the doctors Menninger—C. F. (1862–1953), William (1899–1966), and Karl (1893–1990)—who established the Menninger Foundation, a leading center for mental health; Arthur Hertzler (1870–1946), a surgeon and author; and Clyde Tombaugh (1906–97), who discovered the planet Pluto.

Kansas also had several pioneers in aviation including Clyde Cessna (1880–1954), Glenn Martin (1886–1955), Walter Beech (1891–1950), Amelia Earhart (1898–1937), and Lloyd Stearman (1898–1975). Cyrus K. Holliday (1826–1900) founded the Santa Fe railroad; William Coleman (1870–1957) was an innovator in lighting; and Walter Chrysler (1875–1940) was a prominent automotive developer.

Most famous of Kansas writers was William Allen White (1868–1944), whose son William L. White (1900–73) also had a distinguished literary career; Damon Runyon (1884–1946) was a popular journalist and storyteller. Novelists include Edgar Watson Howe (1853–1937), Margaret Hill McCarter (1860–1938), Dorothy Canfield Fisher (1879–1958), Paul Wellman (1898–1966), and Frederic Wakeman (b.1909). Gordon Parks (b.1912) has made his mark in literature, photography, and music. William Inge (1913–73) was a prize-winning playwright who contributed to the Broadway stage. Notable painters are Sven Birger Sandzen (1871–1954), John Noble (1874–1934), and John Steuart Curry (1897–1946). Sculptors include Robert M. Gage (1892–1981), Bruce Moore (1905–80), and Bernard Frazier (1906–76). Among composers and conductors are Thurlow Lieurance (b.Iowa 1878–1963), Joseph Maddy (1891–1966), and Kirke L. Mechem (b.1926). Jazz great Charlie "Bird" Parker (Charles Christopher Parker, Jr., 1920–55) was born in Kansas City.

Stage and screen notables include Fred Stone (1873–1959), Joseph "Buster" Keaton (1895–1966), Milburn Stone (1904–80), Charles "Buddy" Rogers (1904–99), Vivian Vance (1912–79), Edward Asner (b.1929), and Shirley Knight (b.1937). The clown Emmett Kelly (1898–1979) was a Kansan. Operatic performers include Marion Talley (1906–83) and Kathleen Kersting (1909–65).

Glenn Cunningham (1909–88) and Jim Ryun (b.1947) both set running records for the mile. Also prominent in sports history were James Naismith (1861–1939), the inventor of basketball; baseball pitcher Walter Johnson (1887–1946); and Gale Sayers (b.1943), a football running back.

50 BIBLIOGRAPHY

Bair, Julene. *One Degree West: Reflections of a Plainsdaughter.* Minneapolis: Mid-List Press, 2000.

Boyer, Richard O. *The Legend of John Brown.* New York: Knopf, 1973.

Davis, Kenneth S. *Kansas: A Bicentennial History.* New York: Norton, 1976.

——. *Soldier of Democracy: A Biography of Dwight Eisenhower.* New York: Doubleday, 1945. 1952.

Frederickson, H. George, ed. *Public Policy and the Two States of Kansas.* Lawrence, Kans.: University Press of Kansas, 1992.

Howes, Charles C. *This Place Called Kansas.* Norman: University of Oklahoma Press, 1984.

Kansas, University of. Center for Public Affairs. *Kansas Statistical Abstract 1983–84.* 19th ed. Lawrence, 1984.

Napier, Rita, ed. *Kansas and the West: New Perspectives.* Lawrence: University Press of Kansas, 2003.

Peak, Kenneth J. *Kansas Temperance: Much Ado About Booze, 1870–1920.* Manhattan, Kan.: Sunflower University Press, 2000.

Richmond, Robert W. *Kansas, A Land of Contrasts.* Wheeling, Ill.: Harland Davidson, 1999.

Shortridge, James R. *Peopling the Plains: Who Settled Where in Frontier Kansas.* Lawrence, Kans.: University Press of Kansas, 1995.

Socolofsky, Homer, and Huber Self. *Historical Atlas of Kansas.* Norman: University of Oklahoma Press, 1972.

——, and Virgil W. Dean. *Kansas History: An Annotated Bibliography.* New York: Greenwood, 1992.

KENTUCKY

Commonwealth of Kentucky

ORIGIN OF STATE NAME: Derived from the Wyandot Indian word *Kah-ten-tah-teh* (land of tomorrow). **NICKNAME:** The Bluegrass State. **CAPITAL:** Frankfort. **ENTERED UNION:** 1 June 1792 (15th). **SONG:** "My Old Kentucky Home." **MOTTO:** United We Stand, Divided We Fall. **FLAG:** A simplified version of the state seal on a blue field. **OFFICIAL SEAL:** In the center, two men exchange greetings; above and below them is the state motto. On the periphery are two sprigs of goldenrod and the words "Commonwealth of Kentucky." **COLORS:** Blue and gold. **BIRD:** Cardinal. **WILD ANIMAL:** Gray squirrel. **FISH:** Bass. **FLOWER:** Goldenrod. **TREE:** Tulip poplar. **FOSSIL:** Brachiopod. **LEGAL HOLIDAYS:** New Year's Day, 1 January, plus one extra day; Birthday of Martin Luther King, Jr., 3rd Monday in January; Washington's Birthday, 3rd Monday in February; Good Friday, March or April, half-day holiday; Memorial Day, last Monday in May; Independence Day, 4 July; Labor Day, 1st Monday in September; Thanksgiving Day, 4th Thursday in November, plus one extra day; Christmas Day, 25 December, plus one extra day. **TIME:** 7 AM EST = noon GMT; 6 AM CST = noon GMT.

¹LOCATION, SIZE, AND EXTENT

Located in the eastern south-central US, the Commonwealth of Kentucky is the smallest of the eight south-central states and ranks 37th in size among the 50 states.

The total area of Kentucky is 40,409 sq mi (104,659 sq km), of which land makes up 39,669 sq mi (102,743 sq km) and inland water 740 sq mi (1,917 sq km). Kentucky extends about 350 mi (563 km) E-W; its maximum N-S extension is about 175 mi (282 km).

Kentucky is bordered on the N by Illinois, Indiana, and Ohio (with the line roughly following the north bank of the Ohio River); on the NE by West Virginia (with the line formed by the Big Sandy and Tug Fork rivers); on the SE by Virginia; on the S by Tennessee; and on the W by Missouri (separated by the Mississippi River). Because of a double bend in the Mississippi River, about 10 sq mi (26 sq km) of SW Kentucky is separated from the rest of the state by a narrow strip of Missouri.

After 15 years of litigation, Kentucky in 1981 accepted a US Supreme Court decision giving Ohio and Indiana control of at least 100 feet (30 meters) of the Ohio River from the northern shore. This in effect returned Kentucky's border to what it was in 1792, when Kentucky entered the Union.

The total boundary length of Kentucky is 1,290 mi (2,076 km). The state's geographic center is in Marion County, 3 mi (5 km) nw of Lebanon.

²TOPOGRAPHY

The eastern quarter of the state is dominated by the Cumberland Plateau, on the western border of the Appalachians. At its western edge, the plateau meets the uplands of the Lexington Plain (known as the Bluegrass region) to the north and the hilly Pennyroyal to the south. These two regions, which together make up nearly half the state's area, are separated by a narrow curving plain known as the Knobs because of the shapes of its eroded hills. The most level area of the state consists of the western coalfields bounded by the Pennyroyal to the east and the Ohio River to the north. In the far west are the coastal plains of the Mississippi River; this region is commonly known as the Purchase, having been purchased from the Chickasaw Indians.

The highest point in Kentucky is Black Mountain on the southeastern boundary in Harlan County, at 4,139 ft (2,162 m). The lowest point is 257 ft (78 m), along the Mississippi River in Fulton County. The state's mean altitude is 750 ft (229 m).

The only large lakes in Kentucky are artificial. The biggest is Cumberland Lake (79 sq mi/205 sq km); Kentucky Lake, Lake Barkley, and Dale Hollow Lake straddle the border with Tennessee.

Including the Ohio and Mississippi rivers on its borders and the tributaries of the Ohio, Kentucky claims at least 3,000 mi (4,800 km) of navigable rivers—sometimes said to have more water than any other state except Alaska. Among the most important of Kentucky's rivers are the Kentucky, 259 mi (417 km); the Cumberland, partly in Tennessee; the Tennessee, also in Tennessee and Alabama; and the Big Sandy, Green, Licking, and Tradewater rivers. All, except for a portion of the Cumberland, flow northwest into the Ohio and thence to the Mississippi. Completion in 1985 of the Tennessee-Tombigbee Waterway, linking the Tennessee and Tombigbee rivers in Alabama, gave Kentucky's Appalachian coalfields direct water access to the Gulf of Mexico for the first time.

Drainage through porous limestone rock has honeycombed much of the Pennyroyal with underground passages, the best known of which is Mammoth Cave, now a national park. The Cumberland Falls, 92 ft (28 m) high and 100 ft (30 m) wide, are located in Whitely County.

³CLIMATE

Kentucky has a moderate, relatively humid climate, with abundant rainfall.

The southern and lowland regions are slightly warmer than the uplands. In Louisville, the normal monthly mean temperature ranges from 33°F (1°C) in January to 76°F (24°C) in July. The record high for the state was 114°F (46°C), registered in Greensburg on 28 July 1930; the record low, −37°F (−40°C), in Shelbyville on 19 January 1994.

Average daily relative humidity in Louisville ranges from 58% to 81%. The average annual precipitation at Louisville (1971–2000) was 44.5 in (113 cm); snowfall totals about 18 in (46 cm) a year.

[4]FLORA AND FAUNA

Kentucky's forests are mostly of the oak/hickory variety, with some beech/maple stands. Four species of magnolia are found, and the tulip poplar, eastern hemlock, and eastern white pine are also common; the distinctive "knees" of the cypress may be seen along riverbanks. Kentucky's famed bluegrass is said to be actually blue only in May when dwarf iris and wild columbine are in bloom. Rare plants include the swamp loosestrife and showy gentian. In 2003, the US Fish and Wildlife Service listed 9 Kentucky plant species as threatened or endangered, including Braun's rock-cress, Cumberland sandwort, running buffalo clover, and Short's goldenrod.

Game mammals include the raccoon, muskrat, opossum, mink, gray and red foxes, and beaver; the eastern chipmunk and flying squirrel are common small mammals. At least 300 bird species have been recorded, of which 200 are common. Blackbirds are a serious pest, with some roosts numbering 5–6 million; more desirable avian natives include the cardinal (the state bird), robin, and brown thrasher, while eagles are winter visitors. More than 100 types of fish have been identified.

Rare animal species include the swamp rabbit, black bear, raven (Corvus corax), and mud darter. Among the 38 animal species listed as threatened or endangered in Kentucky as of 2003 are three species of bat (Indiana, Virginia big-eared, and gray), bald eagle, puma, piping plover, Kentucky cave shrimp, and three species of pearlymussel.

[5]ENVIRONMENTAL PROTECTION

The National Resources and Environmental Protection Cabinet, with broad responsibility, includes the departments of Natural Resources, Environmental Protection, and Surface Mining Reclamation and Enforcement, as well as the Kentucky Nature Preserves Commission. The Environmental Quality Commission, created in 1972 to serve as a watchdog over environmental concerns, is a citizen's group of seven members appointed by the governor.

The most serious environmental concern in Kentucky is repairing and minimizing damage to land and water from strip-mining. Efforts to deal with such damage are relatively recent. The state has had a strip-mining law since 1966, but the first comprehensive attempts at control did not begin until the passage in 1977 of the Federal Surface Mining Control and Reclamation Act.

Also active in environmental matters is the Department of Environmental Protection, consisting of four divisions. The Division of Water administers the state's Safe Drinking Water and Clean Water acts and regulation of sewage disposal. The Division of Waste Management oversees solid waste disposal systems in the state. The Air Pollution Control Division monitors industrial discharges into the air and other forms of air pollution. Most air pollution has declined since the 1970s, with lead air concentrations down by 97% since 1970. A special division is concerned with Maxey Flats, a closed nuclear waste disposal facility in Fleming County, where leakage of radioactive materials was discovered.

There are 15 major dams in Kentucky, and more than 900 other dams. Flooding is a chronic problem in southeastern Kentucky, where strip-mining has exacerbated soil erosion.

In 2003, Kentucky had 149 hazardous waste sites, 14 of which were on the National Priorities List, listed in the Environmental Protection Agency's database. In 2001, Kentucky received $42,703,000 in federal grants from the Environmental Protection Agency; EPA expenditures for procurement contracts in Kentucky that year amounted to $8,793,000.

[6]POPULATION

Kentucky ranked 26th in population in the US with an estimated total of 4,092,891 in 2002, an increase of 1.3% since 2000. Between 1990 and 2000, Kentucky's population grew from 3,685,296 to 4,041,769, an increase of 9.7%. The population is projected to reach 4.3 million by 2025. The population density in 2000 was 101.7 persons per sq mi.

In 2000 the median age was 35.9. Persons under 18 years old accounted for 24.6% of the population while 12.5% were age 65 or older.

During the early decades of settlement, population grew rapidly, from a few hundred in 1780 to 564,317 in 1820, by which time Kentucky was the 6th most populous state. By 1900, however, when the population was 2,147,174, growth had slowed considerably. For most of the 20th century, Kentucky's growth rate was significantly slower than the national average.

As of 2002, Lexington had replaced Louisville as the state's largest city. Lexington-Fayette had an estimated population of 263,618, compared with 251,399 for Louisville. Owensboro, with over 50,000 residents, was the state's 3rd most populous city. The population of the Louisville (Ky.-Ind.) metropolitan area was estimated at 1,005,849 in 1999; the Lexington metropolitan area had 455,617, up from 435,736 in 1995.

[7]ETHNIC GROUPS

Though a slave state, Kentucky never depended on a plantation economy. In 1830, almost 25% of the population was black. After the Civil War, a lack of jobs and migration to the industrial cities of the Midwest in the 1890s may have accounted for a dwindling black population. In 2000 the black population of Kentucky was relatively low at 295,994 (7.3%). Kentucky was a center of the American (or Know-Nothing) Party, a pre–Civil War movement whose majority were staunchly anti-immigration and anti-Catholic. With relatively little opportunity for industrial employment, Kentucky attracted small numbers of foreign immigrants in the 19th and 20th centuries. The state had 80,271 foreign-born residents in 2000 (2% of the total population), up from 34,119 in 1990. Among persons reporting a single ancestry in the 2000 census, a total of 391,542 claimed English descent, 514,955 German, 424,133 Irish, and 66,147 French.

In 2000, the Asian population was estimated at 29,744, and the Native American population was estimated at 8,616. The 2000 census reported 3,818 Koreans, 6,771 Asian Indians (up from 2,367 in 1990), 3,683 Japanese, 3,596 Vietnamese (up from 1,340 in 1990), and 5,397 Chinese (up from 3,137). In 2000, a total of 59,939 (1.5%) state residents were Hispanic or Latino, up from 33,000 (0.8%) in 1990, with 31,385 reporting Mexican ancestry and 6,469 Puerto Rican ancestry. Pacific Islanders numbered 1,460.

[8]LANGUAGES

Kentucky was a fought-over hunting ground for Ohio Shawnee, Carolina Cherokee, and Mississippi Chickasaw Indians. Place-names from this heritage include Etowah (Cherokee) and Paducah (Chickasaw).

Speech patterns in the state generally reflect the first settlers' Virginia and Kentucky backgrounds. South Midland features are best preserved in the mountains, but some common to Midland and Southern are widespread.

Other regional features are typically both South Midland and Southern. After a vowel, the /r/ may be weak or missing. *Coop* has the vowel of *put,* but *root* rhymes with *boot.* In southern Kentucky, earthworms are *redworms,* a burlap bag a *tow sack* or the Southern *grass sack,* and green beans *snap beans.* A young man may *carry,* not escort, his girlfriend to a party. Subregional terms appear in abundance. In the east, kindling is *pine,* a seesaw

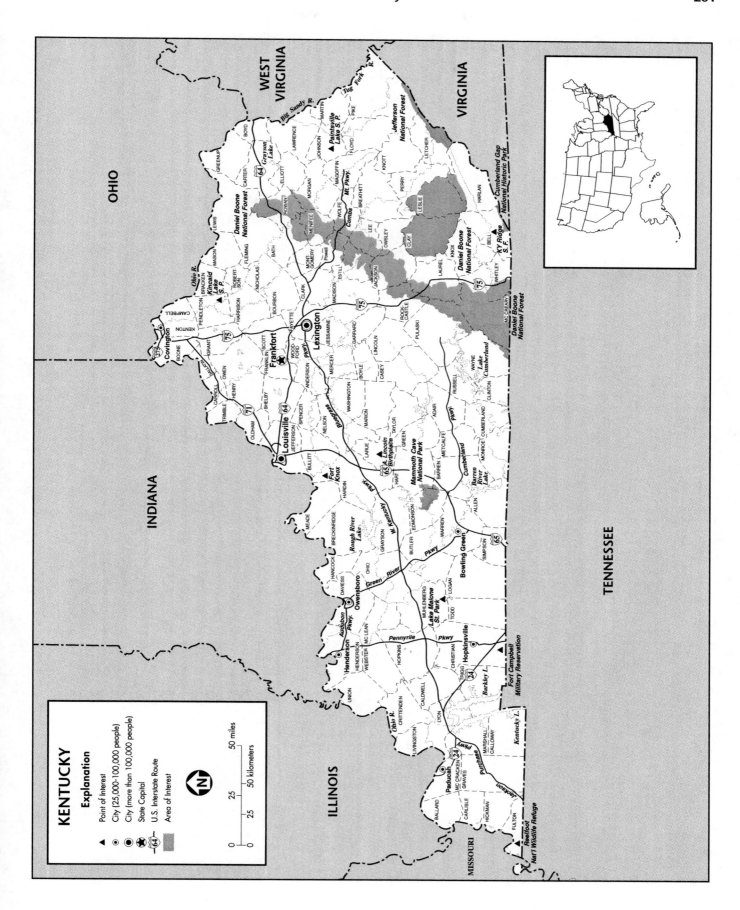

is a *ridyhorse*, and the freestone peach is an *openstone peach*. In central Kentucky, a moth is a *candlefly*.

In 2000, 96.1% of all residents five years old and older spoke only English at home, down from 97.5% in 1990.

The following table gives selected statistics from the 2000 census for language spoken at home by persons five years old and over. The category "Other West Germanic languages" includes Dutch, Pennsylvania Dutch, and Afrikaans.

LANGUAGE	NUMBER	PERCENT
Population 5 years and over	3,776,230	100.0
Speak only English	3,627,757	96.1
Speak a language other than English	148,473	3.9
Speak a language other than English	148,473	3.9
Spanish or Spanish Creole	70,061	1.9
German	17,898	0.5
French (incl. Patois, Cajun)	12,499	0.3
Chinese	4,608	0.1
Japanese	3,777	0.1
Korean	3,730	0.1
Other West Germanic languages	3,616	0.1
Arabic	3,165	0.1
Serbo-Croatian	3,070	0.1
Vietnamese	3,018	0.1
Russian	2,162	0.1
Tagalog	2,070	0.1

[9] RELIGIONS

Throughout its history, Kentucky has been predominantly Protestant. A group of New Light Baptists who, in conflict with established churches in Virginia, immigrated to Kentucky under the leadership of Lewis Craig, built the first church in the state in 1781, near Lancaster. The first Methodist Church was established near Danville in 1783; within a year, Roman Catholics had also built a church, and a presbytery of 12 churches had been organized. There were 42 churches in Kentucky by the time of statehood, with a total membership of 3,095.

Beginning in the last few years of the 18th century, the Great Revival sparked a new religious fervor among Kentuckians, a development that brought the Baptists and Methodists many new members. The revival, which had begun among the Presbyterians, led to a schism in that sect. Presbyterian minister Barton W. Stone organized what turned out to be the era's largest frontier revival meeting, at Cane Ridge (near Paris), in August 1801. Differences over doctrine led Stone and his followers to withdraw from the Synod of Kentucky in 1803, and they formed their own church, called simply "Christian." The group later formed an alliance with the sect now known as the Christian Church (Disciples of Christ).

As of 2000, Evangelical Protestantism was predominant with the single largest denomination within the state being the Southern Baptists Convention with 979,994 adherents. The next largest Protestant denominations are the United Methodist Church with 208,720 adherents and the Christian Churches and Churches of Christ with 106,638 adherents. The Roman Catholic Church has about 406,021 members. There were an estimated 11,350 Jews in Kentucky in 2000 and about 4,696 Muslims. Over 1.8 million people (46.6% of the population) were not counted as members of any religious organization in the 2000 survey.

[10] TRANSPORTATION

Statewide transportation developed slowly in Kentucky. Although freight and passengers were carried by river and later by rail during the 19th century, mountains and lack of good roads made land travel in eastern Kentucky so arduous that the region was for a long time effectively isolated from the rest of the state.

The first railroad in Kentucky, the Lexington and Ohio, opened on 15 August 1832 with a 26-mi (42-km) route from Lexington to Frankfort. Not until 1851 did the railroad reach the Ohio River. In November 1859, Louisville was connected with Nashville, Tennessee, by the Louisville and Nashville Railroad; heavily used by the Union, it was well maintained during the Civil War. Railroad construction increased greatly after the conflict ended. By 1900, Kentucky had three times the track mileage it had had in 1870. As of 2000, Kentucky had 2,962 rail mi (4,766 km), of which about 80% was Class I track. Also in 2000, there were five Class I railroads operating in the state. In the same year, 86% of the rail tonnage originating within Kentucky was coal. Rail service to the state, nearly all of which was freight, was provided by 16 railroads. There are four Amtrak stations in Kentucky.

The trails of Indians and buffalo became the first roads in Kentucky. Throughout the 19th century, counties called on their citizens to maintain some roads although maintenance was haphazard. The best roads were the toll roads. This system came to an end as a result of the "tollgate war" of the late 19th and early 20th centuries—a rebellion in which masked Kentuckians, demanding free roads, raided tollgates and assaulted their keepers. Not until 1909, however, was a constitutional prohibition against the spending of state funds on highways abolished. In 1912, a state highway commission was created, and by 1920, roads had improved considerably. In 2000, Kentucky had 79,267 mi (127,567 km) of public roads and 2,694,469 licensed drivers. In the same year, 1,673,926 automobiles, 1,139,543 trucks, and 12,934 buses were registered in the state.

Until displaced by the railroads in the late 1800s, the Ohio River and its tributaries, along with the Mississippi, were Kentucky's primary commercial routes for trade with the South and the West. The Kentucky Port and River Development Commission was created by the legislature in 1966 to promote river transportation. Louisville, on the Ohio River, is the chief port. In 2000, traffic through the port totaled 8.8 million tons, up from a 1982 low of only 5.7 million tons. Paducah is the outlet port for traffic on the Tennessee River.

In 2002 there were 141 airports and 57 heliports in Kentucky. The largest of these is Cincinnati/Northern Kentucky International Airport, with 11,223,966 people enplaned in 2000.

[11] HISTORY

Six distinctive Indian cultures inhabited the region now known as Kentucky. The earliest nomadic hunters occupied the land for several thousand years, and were followed by the seminomadic Woodland and Adena cultures (1000 BC–AD 1000). Remains of the Mississippian and Fort Ancient peoples (AD 1000–1650) indicate that they were farmers and hunters who often dwelled in stockaded villages, subsisting on plentiful game and fish supplemented by crops of beans, corn, and squash.

No Indian nations resided in central and eastern Kentucky when these areas were first explored by British-American surveyors Thomas Walker and Christopher Gist in 1750 and 1751. The dominant Shawnee and Cherokee tribes utilized the region as a hunting ground, returning to homes in the neighboring territories of Ohio and Tennessee. Early descriptions of Kentucky generated considerable excitement about the fertile land and abundant wildlife. The elimination of French influence after the French and Indian War intensified pressures to open the region to American settlement—pressures that were initially thwarted by Britain's Proclamation of 1763, barring such western migration until Native American interests could be protected. This artificial barrier proved impossible to maintain, however, and the first permanent white settlement in Kentucky was finally established at Harrodstown (now Harrodsburg) in 1774 by a group of settlers from Virginia and Pennsylvania.

The most ambitious settlement scheme involved the Transylvania Land Company, a creation of North Carolina speculator Richard Henderson, assisted by the famed woodsman Daniel Boone. Henderson purchased a huge tract of land in central Kentucky from the Cherokee and established Fort Boonesborough. The first political meeting by whites in Kentucky, held at Fort Boonesborough on 23 May 1775, provided for rule by the Transylvania proprietors and a representative assembly. Henderson then sought approval for creation of a 14th colony, but the plan was blocked by Virginians determined to claim Kentucky as a possession of the Old Dominion. On 1 December 1776, the new state of Virginia incorporated its new County of Kentucky.

Kentucky's image soon changed from "western Eden" to "dark and bloody ground," as it became the scene of frequent clashes between Ohio-based Indians and the growing number of white settlements dotting the central Bluegrass region. Nevertheless, immigrants continued to come westward, down the Ohio River and through the Cumberland Gap. Kentucky became the principal conduit for migration into the Mississippi Valley. By the late 1780s, settlements were gaining in population, wealth, and maturity, and it was obvious that Kentucky could not long remain under the proprietorship of distant Virginia. Virginia yielded permission for the drafting of a Kentucky state constitution, and in June 1792, Kentucky entered the Union as the 15th state.

Over the next several decades, Kentucky prospered because of its diverse agricultural and processing industries. Although there were 225,483 slaves in the state in 1860, Kentucky was spared the evils of one-crop plantation agriculture. Nevertheless, its economy was tightly linked to the lower South's, a tie facilitated by the completion in 1829 of a canal around the Ohio River falls at Louisville. Hemp was one such connection; the plant was the principal source of rope and bagging used to bind cotton bales. Kentucky was also a major supplier of hogs, mules, workhorses, prepared meats, salt, flour, and corn for the plantation markets of the South. The state became a center for breeding and racing fine thoroughbred horses, an industry that thrives today on Bluegrass horse farms as virtually the state symbol. More important was the growing and processing of tobacco, an enterprise accounting for half the agricultural income of Kentucky farmers by 1860. Finally, whiskey began to be produced in vast quantities by the 1820s, culminating in the standardization of a fine, aged amber-red brew known throughout the world as bourbon, after Bourbon County.

Despite this economic development, several social and cultural problems disturbed the state. Much of the agricultural productivity came from farms employing slave labor, while the less affluent majority of white families often dwelled on less fertile upland farms. Efforts were repeatedly made to consider the slavery question. Leaders such as Henry Clay, Reverend Robert J. Breckinridge, and the fiery antislavery advocate Cassius Marcellus Clay urged an end to the "peculiar institution." Because of racial phobias and hostility to "Yankee meddling," the appeal was rejected. During the Civil War, Kentuckians were forced to choose sides between the Union, led in the north by Kentucky native Abraham Lincoln, and the Confederacy, led in the South by Kentucky native Jefferson Davis.

Although the state legislature finally opted for the Union side, approximately 30,000 men went south to Confederate service, while up to 100,000—including nearly 24,000 black soldiers—served in the Union army. For four years the state was torn with conflict over the collapse of slavery and wracked with guerrilla warfare and partisan feuds. Vigilantism and abuse of black people continued into the turbulent Reconstruction period, until legislative changes in the early 1870s began to restrain Ku Klux Klan violence and bring increased civil rights to black people.

The decades to 1900 saw other progress. Aided by liberal tax exemptions, railroad construction increased threefold, and development of timber and coal reserves began in eastern Kentucky. Industrial employment and productivity increased by more than 200%, drawing rural folk into the growing cities of Louisville and Lexington. In 1900, Kentucky ranked 1st among southern states in per capita income.

An economic and political crisis was developing, however, that would send shock waves across the state. Farmers, especially western Kentucky "dark leaf" tobacco farmers, were feeling the brunt of a prolonged price depression. The major national farm protest movements—the Grange, the Farmers' Alliance, and the Populist Party—all found support here, for by 1900 a third of all Kentucky farmers were landless tenants, and the size of the average family farm had fallen below 10 acres (40 hectares). Calls for currency inflation, reform of corporate monopolies, and improved rights for industrial workers reached a climax in the gubernatorial election of 1899. Republican William S. Taylor narrowly defeated the more reform-minded Democrat William Goebel and was sworn into office. Democrats, claiming electoral fraud, instituted a recount. On 30 January 1900, Goebel, a state senator, was shot while approaching the capitol; as he lingered near death, the legislature, controlled by Democrats, declared him governor. Goebel died immediately thereafter, and his lieutenant governor, J. C. W. Beckham, was administered the oath of office. Further bloodshed was averted, the courts upheld the Goebel-Beckham election, and "Governor" Taylor fled the state.

Goebel's assassination weighed heavily, however. The state was polarized, outside investment plummeted, and Kentucky fell into a prolonged economic and moral depression. By 1940, the state ranked last among the 48 states in per capita income and was burdened by an image of clan feuding and homicide, poverty, and provincial courthouse politics. The Great Depression hit the state hard, though an end to Prohibition revived the dormant whiskey industry.

Kentucky changed greatly after World War II. Between 1945 and 1980, the farm population decreased by 76% and the number of farms by 53%. In later decades, after tobacco was revealed to be a public health hazard, many farmers turned to raising other crops. Although Kentucky remained relatively poor, positive change was evident even in rural communities—the result of better roads, education, and government programs. The state's poverty rate fell steadily over the decades, from 22.9% in 1969 to 13.5% in 1998, when it ranked as the 18th poorest state in the nation (a great improvement from earlier in the century). In 2000 Governor Paul Patton announced a $53-million plan to develop the high-tech sector of the state's economy.

In response to lawsuits by a coalition of school districts, Kentucky's supreme court ruled in 1990 that the state's public education system was unconstitutional and ordered the legislature to design a new system of school funding and administration. In response, the Kentucky Education Reform Act was passed that year and implemented over the next five years. But more questions regarding the constitutionality of school programs, or prospective programs, lay ahead. By 2000 legislators were considering a proposal that would allow the Ten Commandments to be displayed in classrooms, alongside other historical documents. The proposal was part of a larger movement that urged officials to allow public schools to teach the role of religion in American history and culture. At the same time, many Kentuckians supported the return of prayer to schools. By 2003, federal judges had ordered the Ten Commandments be removed from school classrooms and courthouses in several Kentucky counties, ruling that the postings of the commandments had violated the separation between church and state.

The Paducah Gaseous Diffusion Plant was a point of concern for state environmentalists in 2000. Senior Kentucky environmental officials complained that the US Department of Energy (DOE) had used security clearances to prevent state environmental inspectors from getting full access to the plant, which enriches uranium for nuclear-reactor fuel. The plant was also the site of a massive clean-up effort in 2000, as DOE officials crushed drums that once contained uranium. Critics charged that the drums had been left in the open for decades and rain water had washed radioactivity into the environment.

[12]STATE GOVERNMENT

Kentucky's current and fourth constitution was adopted on 28 September 1891. By January 2003, it had been amended 40 times. Earlier constitutions were adopted in 1792, 1799, and 1850.

The state legislature, called the general assembly, consists of the house of representatives, which has 100 members elected for two-year terms, and the senate, with 38 members elected for staggered four-year terms. A constitutional amendment approved by the voters in November 1979 provided for the election of legislators in even-numbered years, a change scheduled for completion by November 1988. The assembly meets in regular sessions of no more than 60 legislative days, beginning Tuesday after the first Monday in January of each even-numbered year. Only the governor may call special sessions, which are not limited in length. Except for revenue-raising measures, which must be introduced in the house of representatives, either chamber may introduce or amend a bill. Most bills may be passed by voting majorities equal to at least two-fifths of the membership of each house. Measures requiring an absolute majority in each house include those that appropriate money or create a debt, summon a constitutional convention, or enact emergency measures to take effect immediately. A majority of the members of each house is required to override the governor's veto. If the governor neither vetoes nor signs a bill, it becomes law after 10 days, whether or not the legislature is in session.

A member of the senate must have been a resident of Kentucky for six years preceding election, a representative for two. A senator must be at least 30 and a representative at least 24. Legislators must have been residents in their districts for at least a year prior to election. The constitutional limit of $12,000 for salaries of public officials, which is thought to apply to legislators, has been interpreted by the courts in terms of 1949 dollars and thus may be increased considerably—and has been. In

2002 most legislators in Kentucky probably received less than $14,000 per year based on per diem in-session salaries of $163.56.

The elected executive officers of Kentucky are the governor and lieutenant governor (elected jointly), secretary of state, attorney general, treasurer, auditor of public accounts, and commissioner of agriculture. All serve four-year terms, and a recent constitutional amendment allows a second term for those offices. The governor and lieutenant governor must be at least 30 years old, US citizens, and citizens and residents of Kentucky for six years. As of 2002 the governor's salary was $103,018.

A three-fifths majority of each house plus a voting majority of the electorate must approve any proposed constitutional amendment. Before a constitutional convention may be called, two regular sessions of the general assembly must approve it, and the call must be ratified at the polls by a majority voting on the proposal and equal to at last one-fourth the number of voters who cast ballots in the last general election.

To vote in Kentucky, one must be a US citizen, be at least 18 years old, have been a resident in the county for at least 28 days prior to election day, and not able to claim the right to vote elsewhere. Restrictions apply to convicted felons and those declared mentally incompetent by the court.

[13]POLITICAL PARTIES

A rift was created in Kentucky politics by the presidential election of 1824, which had to be determined in the US House of Representatives because neither John Quincy Adams nor Andrew Jackson won a majority of the Electoral College. Representative Henry Clay voted for Adams, despite orders by the Kentucky general assembly to support Jackson, thereby splitting the state into two factions: supporters of Clay, who became Whigs, and supporters of Jackson, who became Democrats. The Whigs dominated Kentucky politics until Clay's death in 1852, after which, as the Whigs divided over slavery, most Kentuckians turned first to the Native American (or Know-Nothing) Party and then to the Democrats. Regional divisions in party affiliation during the Civil War era, according to sympathy with the South and slavery (Democrats) or with the Union and abolition (Republicans), have persisted in the state's voting patterns. In general, the poorer mountain areas tend to vote Republican,

Kentucky Presidential Vote by Political Parties, 1948–2000

YEAR	ELECTORAL VOTE	KENTUCKY WINNER	DEMOCRAT	REPUBLICAN	STATES' RIGHTS DEMOCRAT	PROHIBITION	PROGRESSIVE	SOCIALIST
1948	11	*Truman (D)	466,756	341,210	10,411	1,245	1,567	1,284
1952	10	Stevenson (D)	495,729	495,029	—	1,161	—	—
1956	10	*Eisenhower (R)	476,453	572,192	—	2,145	—	—
1960	10	Nixon (R)	521,855	602,607	—	—	—	—
					STATES' RIGHTS			
1964	9	*Johnson (D)	669,659	372,977	3,469	—	—	—
					AMERICAN IND.			SOC. WORKERS
1968	9	*Nixon (R)	397,541	462,411	193,098	—	—	2,843
						AMERICAN	PEOPLE'S	
1972	9	*Nixon (R)	371,159	676,446	—	17,627	1,118	—
1976	9	*Carter (D)	615,717	531,852	2,328	8,308	—	—
						LIBERTARIAN		CITIZENS
1980	9	*Reagan (R)	617,417	635,274	—	—	5,531	1,304
1984	9	*Reagan (R)	539,539	821,702	—	—	1,776	599
1988	9	*Bush (R)	580,368	734,281	4,994	1,256	2,118	—
					IND. (Perot)			
1992	8	*Clinton (D)	665,104	617,178	203,944	430	4,513	989
1996	8	*Clinton (D)	636,614	623,283	120,396	—	4,009	—
						REFORM		GREEN
2000	8	*Bush, G. W. (R)	638,898	872,492		4,173	2,896	23,192

*Won US presidential election.

while the more affluent lowlanders in the Bluegrass and Pennyroyal tend to vote Democratic.

Republican presidential candidate George W. Bush won the state by a large margin in 2000—57% to Democrat Al Gore's 41%. Green Party candidate Ralph Nader won 2% of the vote. In 2002 there were 2,649,084 registered voters. In 1998, 61% of registered voters were Democratic, 32% Republican, and 7% unaffiliated or members of other parties. The state had eight electoral votes in the 2000 presidential election.

In 1983, Martha Layne Collins, a Democrat, defeated Republican candidate Jim Bunning to become Kentucky's first woman governor. Democrat Paul E. Patton was elected governor in 1995 and reelected in 1999. Before the November 2003 elections, Republicans held 22 seats in the state senate, Republicans 16; the Democrats dominated the house of representatives, with 65 seats to the Republicans' 35. At the national level, Kentucky was represented by Republican Senator Mitch McConnell, reelected in 2002; and first-term Republican Senator Jim Bunning, elected in 1998. Kentucky voters elected five Republicans and one Democrat to the US House in 2002.

14LOCAL GOVERNMENT

The form of Kentucky's county government is of English origin. The chief governing body is the fiscal court, consisting of the county judge and district magistrates or commissioners. Other elected officials are the sheriff, jailer, attorney, and court clerk. All are elected for four-year terms. As of 2002, the state had 119 counties.

In 2002, Kentucky had 424 municipalities. Cities are assigned by the state's general assembly to six classes, based on population. The two largest cities, categorized as first-class, are Louisville and Lexington. The mayor or other chief executive officer in the top three classes must be elected; in the bottom classes, the executive may be either elected by the people or appointed by a city council or commission. Mayors serve four-year terms; members of city legislative boards, also provided for in the state constitution, are generally elected for terms of two years.

Other units of local government in Kentucky include special districts (720 in 2002), such as districts for sewer and flood control and area-development districts for regional planning. The state had 176 public school districts in 2002.

15STATE SERVICES

To address the continuing threat of terrorism and to work with the federal Department of Homeland Security (created in 2002 following the terrorist attacks of 11 September 2001), homeland security in Kentucky in 2003 operated under the authority of the governor; the adjutant general was designated as the state homeland security advisor.

An ombudsman in the Cabinet for Human Resources receives citizens' complaints concerning services offered by that agency. The Financial Disclosure Review Board was established in 1975 to review the financial status of constitutional officers and government management personnel in order to prevent conflicts of interest.

Educational services are provided through the Department of Education. The Council on Postsecondary Education oversees the state-supported colleges, universities, and technical schools. The Human Rights Commission and the Commission on Women are administered by the governor's office. Rehabilitation services, including the Eastern Kentucky Comprehensive Rehabilitation Center, are under the jurisdiction of the Department of Education. Transportation services are administered by the Transportation Cabinet. Health, welfare, and other human services are provided primarily by the Health Services, Families, and Children Cabinet. Among the agencies that provide public

protection services are the Department of Military Affairs, the Public Protection and Regulation Cabinet, and the Consumer Protection Division of the Department of Law. Corrections and parole were transferred in 1981 from the Department of Justice to the Corrections Cabinet. The Department of State Police is part of the Justice Cabinet.

Housing rights for members of minority groups are provided by the Commission on Human Rights. The Department of Economic Development oversees industrial and community development programs within the Commerce Cabinet. Also assisting in community development are programs within the Department of Local Government, which was organized as an independent agency of the office of the governor in 1982.

Natural resource protection services are provided by the separate departments of Natural Resources, Environmental Protection, and Surface Mining Reclamation and Enforcement, all within the Natural Resources and Environmental Protection Cabinet. The Kentucky state park system is administered by the Department of Parks in the Tourism Cabinet, which also includes the Department of Travel Development, Kentucky Horse Park, and the Department of Fish and Wildlife Resources. The Energy Cabinet, created in 1978, is within the Department of Energy Research and Development.

Labor services are administered by the Labor Cabinet; its areas of concern include labor-management relations, occupational safety and health, and occupational injury and disease compensation. Other cabinets include those for finance and administration, personnel, revenue, and workforce development.

16JUDICIAL SYSTEM

In accordance with a constitutional amendment approved in 1975 and fully implemented in 1978, judicial power in Kentucky is vested in a unified court of justice. The highest court is the supreme court, consisting of a chief justice and six associate justices. It has appellate jurisdiction and also bears responsibility for the budget and administration of the entire system. Justices are elected from seven supreme court districts for terms of eight years; they elect one of their number to serve for the remaining term as chief justice.

The court of appeals consists of 14 judges, 2 elected from each supreme court district. The court divides itself into panels of at least 3 judges that may sit anywhere in the state. The judges also serve eight-year terms and elect one of their number to serve a four-year term as chief judge.

Circuit courts, with original and appellate jurisdiction, are held in each county. There are 56 judicial circuits. Circuit court judges are elected for terms of eight years. In 1999, there were 108 circuit court judges. In circuits with more than one judge, the judges elect one of their number as chief judge for a two-year term. Under the revised judicial system, district courts, which have limited and original jurisdiction, replaced various local and county courts. There is no mandatory retirement age.

In June 2001 there were 15,400 prisoners in Kentucky, a decrease of 0.3% from the previous year. The state's incarceration rate stood at 369 per 100,000 inhabitants. The Department of Corrections maintains 12 correctional institutions, including a career development center, a forestry camp, and two farm centers. There are also 3 private minimum-custody prisons. In 1980, the department entered into a consent decree to eliminate overcrowding and provide more humane conditions at the state reformatory and penitentiary. Death by electrocution is the only method of execution. The state has executed 105 people since 1930, only two of whom were put to death since 1977. In 2003, 38 prisoners were under sentence of death.

In the past, Kentucky had a reputation for lawlessness. In 1890, more homicides were reported in Kentucky than in any other state except New York; blood feuds among Kentucky families were notorious throughout the country. In recent years, however, crime rates have diminished to a comparatively low level. The total crime rate in 2001 was 2,938.1 crimes per 100,000 population, including a total of 10,448 violent crimes and 109,001 crimes against property in that year.

[17]ARMED FORCES

The US Department of Defense had 59,696 personnel in Kentucky in 2002, including 34,081 active-duty military and 8,348 civilians. US Army installations in the state include Ft. Knox (site of the US gold depository) near Louisville, and Ft. Campbell (partly in Tennessee). Kentucky received $1.2 billion in prime federal defense contracts in 2001.

There were 380,618 veterans of US military service in Kentucky as of 2000, of whom 68,404 served in World War II; 47,069 in the Korean conflict; 114,213 during the Vietnam era; and 45,366 during 1990–2000 (including the Persian Gulf War). Kentucky veterans received more than $785 million in benefits during 2002.

In 2000, the Kentucky State Police employed 937 full-time sworn officers.

[18]MIGRATION

During the frontier period, Kentucky first attracted settlers from eastern states, especially Virginia and North Carolina. Prominent among early foreign immigrants were people of English and Scotch-Irish ancestry, who tended to settle in the Kentucky highlands, which resembled their Old World homelands.

Kentucky's black population increased rapidly during the first 40 years of statehood. By the 1830s, however, slavery had become less profitable in the state, and many Kentucky owners either moved to the Deep South or sold their slaves to new owners in that region. During the 1850s, nearly 16% of Kentucky's slave population—more than 43,000 blacks—were sold or moved from the state. A tiny percentage of Kentucky's blacks, probably fewer than 200, immigrated to Liberia under the auspices of the Kentucky Colonization Society.

The waves of European immigration that inundated many states during the late 19th century left Kentucky virtually untouched. In 1890, Kentucky's population was nearly 98% native-born. At that time, there were more than 284,000 blacks in the state—a number that was to fall precipitously until the 1950s because of migration to industrial cities in the Midwest.

Until the early 1970s there was a considerable out-migration of whites, especially from eastern Kentucky to industrial areas of Ohio, Indiana, and other nearby states. The state's net loss to migration from 1960 to 1970 totaled 153,000 persons. This tide of out-migration was temporarily reversed during the 1970s, with Kentucky recording a net migration gain of 131,000 persons. From 1980 to 1990, net loss to migration totaled about 22,000. Between 1990 and 1998, Kentucky had net gains of 90,000 in domestic migration and 14,000 in international migration. In 1998, 2,017 foreign immigrants arrived in the state. Between 1990 and 1998, Kentucky's overall population increased 6.8%. In the period 1995–2000, 318,579 people moved into the state and 284,452 moved out, for a net gain of 34,127, many of whom came from Ohio.

[19]INTERGOVERNMENTAL COOPERATION

Among the many interstate regional commissions in which Kentucky participates are the Breaks Interstate Park Compact with Virginia, Appalachian Regional Commission, Interstate Mining Compact Commission, Interstate Oil and Gas Compact, Southern Growth Policies Board, Ohio Iver Basin Commission, Ohio River Valley Water Sanitation Commission, Southeastern Forest Fire Protection Compact, Southern Regional Energy Board, Southern States Energy Board, and Tennessee-Tombigbee

Waterway Development Authority. Kentucky also participates in the Tennessee Valley Authority. The Council of State Governments, founded in 1925 to foster interstate cooperation, has its headquarters in Lexington. In 2001, Kentucky received $5.1 billion in federal grants.

[20]ECONOMY

Between statehood and the Civil War, Kentucky was one of the preeminent agricultural states, partly because of good access to river transportation down the Ohio and the Mississippi to southern markets. Coal mining had become an important part of the economy by the late 19th century. Although agriculture is still important in Kentucky, manufacturing has grown rapidly since World War II and was, by the mid-1980s, the most important sector of the economy as a source of both employment and personal income. Kentucky leads the nation in the production of bituminous coal and whiskey (distilling half of the nation's total in 1996), and ranks 2nd in tobacco output.

In contrast to the generally prosperous Bluegrass area and the growing industrial cities, eastern Kentucky, highly dependent on coal mining, has long been one of the poorest regions in the US. Beginning in the early 1960s, both the state and federal governments undertook programs to combat poverty in Appalachian Kentucky. Personal income is much lower, and unemployment higher, than in the rest of the state. In 1997, 38 of the 49 Appalachian counties received Local Government Economic Development Fund (LGEDF) aid from the coal severance tax. The Kentucky Rural Development Act, covering all 49 Appalachian counties, gives liberal tax incentives to new manufacturing start-ups in those areas that have had higher unemployment rates than the state during the previous five years, or a have current rate that is at least twice the state average. During the 1990s, declines in Kentucky's traditional sectors— tobacco, textiles, apparel and coal mining—was compensated for by job growth in motor vehicle manufacturing, fabricated metals, appliances and other durable goods. The establishment of a major UPS hub in Kentucky plus growth in agricultural research and commercialization activity helped further the state's economic transformation. Manufactures reached more than 27.5% of gross state product by 1998, when overall growth reached 6%. Growth in 1999 and 2000 averaged 4.35%, and then dropped to 2.6% in 2001 in the context of the national recession an slowdown. Manufacturing output, which had grown 10.6% from 1997 to 2000, fell 1.9% in 2001, and to 25.2% as a percent of total state output. In 2002, job losses in manufacturing slowed while employment in service-producing sectors strengthened. Kentucky was one of only five states where employment grew more than 1% in 2002.

Kentucky's gross state product in 2001 was 26th largest among the states at $120.3 billion, to which manufacturing contributed $30.3 billion; general services, $20.1 billion; trade, $18.3 billion; government, $16.6 billion, financial services, $14.2 billion; transportation and public utilities, $9.9 billion; and construction $5.6 billion. The public sector constituted 13.8% of gross state product in 2001.

[21]INCOME

According to the Bureau of Economic Analysis, in 2001, Kentucky had a per capita personal income (PCPI) of $24,878 which ranked 41st in the United States (including the District of Columbia) and was 82% of the national average, $30,413. The 2001 PCPI reflected an increase of 2.6% from 2000 compared to the national change of 2.2%. In 2001, Kentucky had a total personal income (TPI) of $101,222,546,000 which ranked 26th in the United States and accounted for 1.2% of the national total. The 2001 TPI reflected an increase of 3.1% from 2000 compared to the national change of 3.3%.

Earnings of persons employed in Kentucky increased from $68,851,883,000 in 2000 to $70,491,141,000 in 2001, an increase of 2.4%. The largest industries in 2001 were services, 23.4% of earnings; state and local government, 12.9%; and durable goods manufacturing, 12.5%. Of the industries that accounted for at least 5% of earnings in 2001, the slowest growing from 2000 to 2001 was durable goods manufacturing, which decreased 2.5%; the fastest was state and local government, which increased 7.4%.

According to data released by the US Census Bureau, in 2000, the median household income was $37,186 compared to the national average of $42,148. In 2001, the median income for a family of four was $54,319 compared to the national average of $63,278. For the period 1999 to 2001, the average poverty rate was 12.4% which placed it 32nd among the 50 states and the District of Columbia ranked lowest to highest.

[22]LABOR

According to Bureau of Labor Statistics (BLS) provisional estimates, in July 2003 the seasonally adjusted civilian labor force in Kentucky numbered 1,997,000, with approximately 121,800 workers unemployed, yielding an unemployment rate of 6.1%, compared to the national average of 6.2% for the same period. Since the beginning of the BLS data series in 1978, the highest unemployment rate recorded was 12.6% in December 1982. The historical low was 3.8% in April 2000. In 2001, an estimated 4.6% of the labor force was employed in construction; 14.7% in manufacturing; 6.0% in transportation, communications, and public utilities; 19.5% in trade; 4.4% in finance, insurance, and real estate; 23.7% in services; 15.8% in government; and 3.2% in agriculture.

Although a small number of trade unions existed in Kentucky before the 1850s, it was not until after the Civil War that substantial unionization took place. During the 1930s, there were long, violent struggles between the United Mine Workers (UMW) and the mine owners of eastern Kentucky. The UMW won bargaining rights in 1938, but after World War II the displacement of workers because of mechanization, a drastic drop in the demand for coal, and evidence of mismanagement and corruption within the UMW served to undercut the union's position. Following the announcement by the UMW in 1962 that its five hospitals would be sold or closed, unemployed mine workers began protracted picketing of nonunion mines. Episodes of violence accompanied the movement, which succeeded in closing the mines but not in keeping them closed. The protests dissipated when public works jobs were provided for unemployed fathers among the miners, beginning in late 1973. Increased demand for coal in the 1970s led to a substantial increase in jobs for miners, and the UMW, under different leaders, began a new drive to organize the Cumberland Plateau.

The US Department of Labor reported that in 2002, 164,000 of Kentucky's 1,639,000 employed wage and salary workers were members of unions. This represented 10.0% of those so employed, down from 11.3% in 2001 and from 13.1% in 1998. The national average is 13.2%. In all, 184,000 workers (11.2%) were represented by unions. In addition to union members, this category includes workers who report no union affiliation but whose jobs are covered by a union contract.

[23]AGRICULTURE

With cash receipts totaling $3.5 billion—$1.3 million from crops and $2.2 billion from livestock—Kentucky ranked 21st among the 50 states in farm marketings in 2001.

Kentucky tobacco, first marketed in New Orleans in 1787, quickly became the state's most important crop. Kentucky ranked 1st among tobacco-producing states until it gave way to North Carolina in 1929. Corn has long been one of the state's most important crops, not only for livestock feed but also as a major ingredient in the distilling of whiskey. Although hemp is no longer an important crop in Kentucky, its early significance to Kentucky farmers, as articulated in Congress by Henry Clay, was partly responsible for the establishment by the US of a protective tariff system. From 1849 to 1870, the state produced nearly all the hemp grown in the US.

In 2002 there were approximately 88,000 farms in Kentucky, with an average size of 154 acres (63 hectares). In 1990, almost half of Kentucky's population was considered rural, and nearly one fourth of the state's population owes its living to agriculture. In 2002 Kentucky farms produced some 226,430,000 lb of tobacco, the 2nd most in the nation. Leading field crops in 2002 included corn for grain, 106,000,000; soybeans, 40,950,000; wheat, 18,020,000; sorghum, 825,000; and barley, 512,000. Farmers also harvested 5,520,000 tons of hay, including 900,000 tons of alfalfa.

[24]ANIMAL HUSBANDRY

Since early settlement days, livestock raising has been an important part of Kentucky's economy. The Bluegrass region, which offers excellent pasturage and drinking water, has become renowned as a center for horse breeding, including thoroughbreds, quarter horses, American saddle horses, Arabians, and standardbreds. In 1998, sales of horses accounted for 20% of Kentucky's farm receipts.

In 2003, Kentucky had an estimated 2.43 million cattle and calves worth $1.53 billion. In 2002, Kentucky farmers had an estimated 370,000 hogs and pigs, worth around $19.98 million. Kentucky produced an estimated 1.66 billion lb (0.75 billion kg) of milk from 128,000 dairy cows in 2001.

[25]FISHING

Fishing is of little commercial importance in Kentucky. In 1998, Kentucky had 543,706 fishing license holders.

[26]FORESTRY

In 2002 there were 12,684,000 acres (5,133,000 hectares) of forested land in Kentucky—50% of the state's land area. Over 90% of the forestland is classified as commercially viable for timber production.

The most heavily forested areas are in the river valleys of eastern Kentucky, in the Appalachians. In 2002, Kentucky produced 691 million board feet of lumber, nearly all of it in hardwoods. The Division of Forestry of the Department of Natural Resources manages approximately 30,000 acres (12,300 hectares) of state-owned forestland and operates two forest tree nurseries producing 7–9 million seedling trees a year.

There are two national forests—the Daniel Boone and the Jefferson on Kentucky's eastern border—enclosing two national wilderness areas. These two national forests had a combined area of 1,415,306 acres (572,774 hectares) in 1999. Gross acreage of all Kentucky lands in the National Forest System was 2,210,000 acres (894,400 hectares) in 2001. National parks in the state include the Mammoth Cave National Park and the Cumberland Gap National Historical Park on Kentucky's eastern border.

[27]MINING

The estimated value of nonfuel mineral production in Kentucky in 2001 was about $531 million, up nearly 6% from the 2000 level. Nationally, Kentucky's position was 29th in nonfuel value.

According to preliminary figures, crushed stone accounted for nearly 60% ($316 million) of Kentucky's nonfuel mineral production value in 2001, followed by lime and portland cement (total value of $531 million when combined with ball clays). Nationally, the state ranked 3rd in ball clays, 4th in lime, and 8th in common clay. The state's mines also produce significant quantities of construction sand and gravel, masonry cement, and common clays.

28ENERGY AND POWER

In 1999, Kentucky had 29 electric generating plants. Total installed capacity (utility and nonutility) was 16.5 million kW in the same year, and 93.1 billion kWh of power were produced. Southern Kentucky shares in the power produced by the Tennessee Valley Authority, which supports a coal-fired steam electric plant in Kentucky at Paducah.

Most of Kentucky's coal came from the western fields of the interior coal basin until late in the 19th century, when the lower-sulfur Cumberland Plateau coal reserves of the Appalachian region were discovered. In 2000, eastern Kentucky produced an estimated 104,901,000 tons of coal, and western Kentucky 25,787,000. Kentucky, with 482 active mines in 1998, has more mines than any other state. All coal mined is bituminous. Much of the mining in Kentucky is done by out-of-state companies; a number of oil companies have acquired coal companies as a hedge against declining petroleum resources. Recoverable coal reserves as of 2001 were estimated at 258 million tons in western Kentucky and 829 million tons in eastern Kentucky.

In 2002, Kentucky produced 7,000 barrels per day of crude petroleum; the state was estimated to have about 17 million barrels of proved oil reserves in 2001. The oil industry was centered in Henderson County. In 2001, Kentucky marketed 81.7 billion cu ft (2.3 billion cu m) of natural gas. As of the beginning of 2001, the state was estimated to have proved reserves totaling 1,860 billion cu ft (52.68 billion cu m) of natural gas. In 2000 Kentucky's total per capita energy consumption was 462 million Btu (116.4 million kcal), ranking it 7th among the 50 states.

Oil shale is found in a band stretching from Lawrence County in the northeast through Madison and Washington counties in central Kentucky to Jefferson County in the north-central region.

29INDUSTRY

Although primarily an agricultural state during the 19th century, Kentucky was a leading supplier of manufactures to the South before the Civil War. Kentucky ranked 10th among the 50 states for growth in manufacturing between 1992 and 1997 with shipments of manufactured goods valued at $88 billion in 1997. Manufacturing activities are largely concentrated in Louisville and Jefferson County and other cities bordering the Ohio River. Kentucky is the leading producer of American whiskey. It also is the nation's fourth largest producer of trucks in assembly plants at Louisville as well as the nation's 5th-largest producer of automobiles at Bowling Green and Georgetown.

In 1997, Kentucky was the headquarters for several Fortune 500 companies, including: Lexmark International, KFC Corp., Ashland, Humana, Providian, LG&E Energy, and Vencor. Top manufacturers by employment include GE, Ford, Toyota, Lexmark, Johnson Controls, Technotrim, and Trim Masters. In 1998, Kentucky was home to the UPS "Hub 2000" project, which invested nearly one billion dollars in the creation of the largest warehousing/distribution project of the year. The project tied for the largest job creation in the country that year, and came 3rd in capital investment and new space created.

Earnings of persons employed in Kentucky increased from $57.9 billion in 1997 to $61.2 billion in 1998, an increase of 5.6%. The largest industries in 1998 were services, 22.5% of earnings; durable goods manufacturing, 13.4%; and state and local government, 11.5%. Of the industries that accounted for at least 5% of earnings in 1998, the slowest growing from 1997 to 1998 was nondurable goods manufacturing (8.6% of earnings in 1998), which increased 4.3%; the fastest was construction (6.0% of earnings in 1998), which increased 8.7%.

30COMMERCE

In 1997, Kentucky had 6,215 wholesale establishments, with a total income of $40 billion. Retail sales totaled $34 billion in 1997. Retail establishments included food stores (12%), automotive dealers and service stations (17%), and restaurants and taverns (25%). Food sales totaled $6.2 billion in 1997, and general merchandise sales totaled $5.6 billion. The KFC Corp., which owns and franchises Kentucky Fried Chicken restaurants, has its headquarters in Louisville, as does Papa John's, a pizza restaurant chain. Kentucky's exports to foreign countries in 1998 totaled $8 billion. Over $9.6 billion in goods were exported in 1999, with $3.5 billion in transportation equipment, $1.5 billion in industrial machinery, and $1.2 billion in chemicals. Most exports went to Canada, the UK, France, Japan, and Mexico.

31CONSUMER PROTECTION

The Consumer Protection Division of the Attorney General's Office was created in 1972 to assist consumers with disputes in the marketplace through the mediation of consumer complaints; the litigation of violators of the Consumer Protection Act; and the education of consumers. The mediation branch handles consumer complaints.

32BANKING

Kentucky had 248 insured banks, 171 of them state-chartered, as of 2002. Total assets stood at $55 billion. Ninety-three percent of the state's insured banks are community institutions (with assets under $1 billion). Real estate accounts for the largest proportion of loan portfolios of community banks headquartered in Kentucky. The median return on assets (ROA) ratio (the measure of earnings in relation to all resources) and net interest margin (NIM) (the difference between the lower rates offered to savers and the higher rates charged on loans) increased in 2002 for Kentucky's banks, demonstrating they weathered the recession relatively well.

33INSURANCE

In 2001, Kentuckians held some 2.6 million life insurance policies, with a total value of $109.7 billion; total value for all categories of life insurance (ordinary, group, industrial, and credit) was $185.9 billion. Death benefits paid that year totaled $570.1 million. As of 2003, there were 10 property and casualty and 11 life and health insurance companies incorporated or organized in the state. In 2001, there were 19,762 flood insurance policies in force in the state, with a total value of $1.7 million.

34SECURITIES

There are no securities exchanges in Kentucky. There are 379 securities brokers and dealers organizations (with over 2,500 employees), and 59 investment advisory organizations registered to conduct business in the state. NASDAQ companies headquartered in Kentucky number 35, NASDAQ market makers in the state only one, and Kentucky-incorporated NYSE-listed companies, six. These companies are: Ashland, Inc., Brown-Foreman Corp., Dollar General Corp., CG&E Energy Corp., NS Group Inc., and Ventas.

35PUBLIC FINANCE

The Kentucky biennial state budget is prepared by the Governor's Office for Policy and Management late in each odd-numbered year and submitted by the governor to the general assembly for approval. The fiscal year runs from July 1 to June 30.

Revenues for Kentucky's general fund were projected at $7 billion for 2002, but the actual figure was only $6.560 billion. Most state services (with the exception of roads) are paid for from the general fund. Cuts in general fund expenditures totaling

$231.5 million were made in 2002 after the budget had been enacted, exempting only elementary and secondary education. In 2002/03, the budget deficit totaled about $220 million, and the projected deficit for 2003/04 was $360 million, about 5.1% of the state general fund budget. The legislature could not agree on either expenditure cuts or tax increases, and left it to the governor to make the adjustments. General fund revenue was increased by allocations from the Tobacco Settlement funds ($133 million in 2001/02, $127 million in 2002/03 $110 million in 2003/04). Other adjustments were made by transfers to the general fund from other funds.

In 2002, 80% of general fund expenditures went to three areas: education, Medicaid, and the criminal justice system. The rest of the government accounted for the other 20%, including social services (8.37%), general government (3.28%), finance and administration (3.11%), revenue (1.26%), natural resources and environmental protection (0.95%), workforce development (0.75%) and public protection (0.73%). Revenues for 2003/04 were projected at $7.2 billion, with adjustments mainly from fund transfers bringing total resources to $7.6 billion to cover projected expenditures of $7.42 billion.

The following table from the US Census Bureau contains information on revenues, expenditures, indebtedness, and cash/securities for 2001.

	($000)	PERCENT	PER CAPITA
Population (thousands, 2001)	4,069	(X)	(X)
Total Revenue	18,550,297	100.00	4,558.93
General revenue	15,175,617	81.81	3,729.57
Utility revenue	–	–	–
Liquor store revenue	–	–	–
Insurance trust revenue	3,374,680	18.19	829.36
Exhibit: Salaries and wages	2,929,488	16.90	719.95
Total expenditure	17,330,724	100.00	4,259.21
General expenditure	15,635,933	90.22	3,842.70
Education	5,731,782	33.07	1,408.65
Public welfare	4,378,159	25.26	1,075.98
Hospitals	490,685	2.83	120.59
Health	493,424	2.85	121.26
Highways	1,699,061	9.80	417.56
Police protection	192,738	1.11	47.37
Correction	460,919	2.66	113.28
Natural resources	314,499	1.81	77.29
Parks and recreation	154,561	0.89	37.99
Government administration	550,301	3.18	135.24
Interest on general debt	453,723	2.62	111.51
Other and unallocable	716,081	4.13	175.98
Utility expenditure	–	–	–
Liquor store expenditure	–	–	–
Insurance trust expenditure	1,694,791	9.78	416.51
Debt at end of fiscal year	8,347,565	100.00	2,051.50
Cash and security holdings	34,511,889	100.00	8,481.66

36TAXATION

Kentucky's personal income tax is a five-bracket schedule ranging from 2% on the first $3,000 of taxable income to 6% on the amount over $8,000. Personal and child exemptions are in the form of $20 tax credits. Corporate income is taxed according to a five-bracket schedule ranging from 4% to 8.25%, with the lowest rate applied to net income up to $25,000 and the highest to net income above $250,000. Kentucky also levies a 6% sales and use tax, exempting food and drugs and with no additional local sales taxes permitted. State excise taxes are collected on motor fuels, alcoholic beverages, cigarettes (3 cents on each pack which, after Virginia, is the lowest in the country), pari-mutuels, insurance premiums, amusements, and other selected items. Personal property taxes include a car tax. Kentucky imposes an oil production tax (4.5% of market value), a coal severance tax (4.5% of gross value), and a natural resources severance tax (4.5% of gross value less transportation costs). Kentucky's estate

tax (maximum rate 16%) is tied to the federal exemption for state death taxes, and is therefore set to be phased out in tandem with the phasing out of the federal estate tax credit by 2007, unless the state takes positive action to establish an independent estate tax. Kentucky's revenue losses from the phasing out of its estate tax are estimated at -$11.3 million for 2002/03, -$2.4 million for 2003/04 and -$55.8 million for 2006/07. Kentucky's inheritance tax exempts close (Class A) relatives. Death and gift taxes accounted for 1% of state collections in 2002. Other taxes include various license fees and stamp taxes.

Total state tax collections in Kentucky in 2002 were $7.974 billion, of which 33.5% was generated by the state income tax, 29% by the state general sales and use tax, 17.9% by state excise taxes, 6.76% by state license fees, 5.4% by state property taxes, and 3.79% by the state corporate income tax. In 2003, combined state and local taxes amounted to 9.4% of income, the 31st highest rate in the country.

The following table from the US Census Bureau provides a summary of taxes collected by the state in 2002.

	($000)	PER CAPITA
Total Taxes	7,974,690	1,948.42
Property taxes	437,804	106.97
Sales and gross receipts	3,741,084	914.04
General sales and gross receipts	2,312,224	564.94
Selective sales taxes	1,428,860	349.11
Alcoholic beverage	72,545	17.72
Amusements	260	0.06
Insurance Premiums	258,313	63.11
Motor fuels	461,333	112.72
Pari-mutuels	17,774	4.34
Public utilities	(X)	(X)
Tobacco products	16,828	4.11
Other selective sales	601,807	147.04
Licenses	539,206	131.74
Alcoholic beverages	5,283	1.29
Amusements	3,158	0.77
Corporation	180,805	44.18
Hunting and fishing	21,631	5.29
Motor vehicle	190,299	46.5
Motor vehicle operators	11,934	2.92
Public utility	6,842	1.67
Occupation and business, NEC	115,584	28.24
Other	3,670	0.9
Other taxes	3,256,596	795.67
Individual income	2,678,330	654.39
Corporation net income	302,129	73.82
Death and gift	85,410	20.87
Documentary and stock transfer	3,311	0.81
Severance	187,416	45.79
Other	(X)	(X)

37ECONOMIC POLICY

The Kentucky Cabinet for Economic Development seeks to encourage businesses to locate in Kentucky and to expand through its job creation program. Various available programs offer companies tax credits totaling as much as 100% of their investment. Low interest loans and bonds also are available. Additional incentives are available to qualified businesses for locating in one of Kentucky's enterprise zones, Appalachian counties, or in Kentucky's federal empowerment zone, one of only three in the nation. Incentives also are available for tourist attractions that locate in Kentucky. Regional industrial parks are currently being developed to provide available, accessible, and marketable land in areas where an abundant labor force is available. The Kentucky Economic Development Finance Authority (KEDFA) was established within the Cabinet for Economic Development to further the state's economic goals through financial assistance and tax credit programs. Tax credit programs offered in 2003 included those under the Bluegrass State Skills Corporation Skills Training Investment Act; the

Kentucky Rural Economic Development Act (to support manufacturing enterprises in rural areas); the Kentucky Jobs Act (for the expansion of service and technology related projects); the Kentucky Industrial Development Act (for new and expanding manufacturing projects); the Kentucky Economic Opportunity Zone Program (for certified Opportunity Zones); and the Kentucky Investment Fund Act (for approved venture capital investments). Other incentives were offered under programs for Enterprise Zones, Industrial Revenue Bonds, the Commonwealth Small Business Development Corporation, the Kentucky Tourism Development Act, and the Local Government Economic Development Fund.

38 HEALTH

In 2000, Kentucky's overall death rate was 991.2 per 100,000 inhabitants, significantly higher than the national average of 873.1. The infant mortality rate was 7.2 per 1,000 live births for 2000. In 1999, 5,469 legal abortions were performed in Kentucky, for a ratio of 6 per 1,000 women. In 2000, Kentucky ranked higher than the national averages in death rates from heart diseases, 299.5 per 100,000 residents; cerebrovascular diseases, 63.2; accidents and adverse effects 5 43.6; motor vehicle accidents, 20.9; and suicide, 68.1. The smoking prevalence was 30.1% of all Kentuckians ages 18 and older. There were 1.6 HIV-related deaths per 100,000 population in 2000. According to the Centers for Disease Control, there were 3,675 AIDS cases reported through 2001. Black lung (pneumoconiosis) has been recognized as a serious work-related illness among coal miners.

Kentucky's 103 community hospitals had 594,899 admissions and 15,001 beds in 2001. There were 15,507 full-time registered nurses and 2,693 full-time licensed practical nurses in 2001 and 230 physicians per 100,000 population in 2000. The average expense of a community hospital for care was $1,409.90 per inpatient day in 2001.

Federal government grants to cover the Medicare and Medicaid services in 2001 totaled $2.4 billion; 629,709 enrollees received Medicare benefits that year. At least 12.3% of the population was uninsured in 2002.

39 SOCIAL WELFARE

In 2001, the average weekly unemployment benefit was $234.33. Average monthly participation in the food stamp program in FY2002 comprised 450,102 persons (187,471 households). The average monthly benefit was $75.93, and the sum total of benefits paid in FY2002 was $410,097,309.

With the enactment of the Personal Responsibility and Work Opportunity Reconciliation Act of 1996, the US government has changed the form and regulations for many of its social welfare programs. Most significantly, it replaces Aid to Families with Dependent Children (AFDC), an open-ended entitlement program, with Temporary Assistance for Needy Families (TANF), a limited system of assistance funded largely through federal block grants. The reform act also impacts the food stamp program, the Supplemental Security Income program, and the child nutrition program. The law took effect on 1 July 1997 and provided $16.38 billion in block grants for fiscal years 1997–2002. The grants are to be divided among the states based on an equation involving the numbers of former AFDC recipients in each state.

Reauthorization of the 1996 social welfare legislation, scheduled for 2002, was delayed, and the original law had been extended three times as of July 2003, with the most recent extension running through September 2003. Kentucky's TANF program is called the Kentucky Transition Assistance Program (K-TAP). In June 2000 the state had 85,696 welfare recipients. State expenditures on the TANF program in FY2002 totaled $71,913,100.

In December 2001, Social Security benefits were paid to 746,330 Kentucky residents. This number included 389,330 retired workers, 96,520 widows and widowers, 130,230 disabled workers, 53,380 spouses, and 76,870 children. Social Security beneficiaries represented 18.4% of the total state population and 92.9% of the state's population age 65 and older. Retired workers (excluding persons with special benefits) received an average monthly payment of $821; widows and widowers, $738; disabled workers, $805; and spouses, $390. Payments for children of retired workers averaged $384 per month; children of deceased workers, $546; and children of disabled workers, $235.

Federal Supplemental Security Income payments in December 2001 went to 175,925 Kentucky residents, averaging $364 a month.

40 HOUSING

In 2002, Kentucky had 1,796,900 housing units, 1,599,319 of which were occupied. About 70.8% were owner-occupied. About 66.2% of all units were single-family, detached homes; 14.6% were mobile homes. Though most units relied on utility gas or electricity for heating, about 13,182 units used coke or coal and 41,392 relied on wood. It was estimated that 83,268 units lacked telephone service, 10,116 lacked complete plumbing facilities, and 7,810 lacked complete kitchen facilities. The average household size was 2.49 people.

In 2002, 19,459 privately owned units were authorized for construction. The median home value was $98,132. The median monthly cost for mortgage owners was $870. Renters paid a median of $480 per month. During 2002, Kentucky received $87.2 million in community planning and development aid from the US Department of Housing and Urban Development.

41 EDUCATION

Kentucky was relatively slow to establish and support its public education system and has consistently ranked below the national average in per capita spending on education and in the educational attainments of its citizens. In 2000, only 74.1% of all adults had completed four years of high school, well below the national average of 80.4%; only 17.1% had completed four or more years of college, below the national average of 24.4%. Expenditures per pupil on education by state and local governments totaled $5,876 in 1999/2000, below the national average of $6,356. Expenditures for public education in 2000/01 were estimated at $4,256,345.

The total enrollment for fall 1999 in Kentucky's public schools stood at 648,607. Of these, 458,607 attended schools from kindergarten through grade eight, and 189,573 attended high school. Minority students made up approximately 12% of the total enrollment in public elementary and secondary schools in 2001. Total enrollment was estimated at 623,231 in fall 2000 but is expected to rise again to 651,000 by fall 2005. Enrollment in nonpublic schools in fall 2001 was 75,084.

As of fall 2000, there were 182,051 students enrolled in institutions of higher education. In the same year Kentucky had 69 degree-granting institutions. In 1997, minority students comprised 9.7% of total postsecondary enrollment. Kentucky's higher education facilities include 26 colleges and universities, 3 junior colleges, and 14 community colleges. The University of Kentucky, established in 1865 at Lexington, is the state's largest public institution. The University of Louisville (1798) is also state supported. Loans and grants to Kentucky students are provided by the Kentucky Higher Education Assistance Authority.

In 1990 the Kentucky Education Reform Act established SEEK (Support Education Excellence in Kentucky). SEEK is a program that balances the available education dollars among poor and wealthy counties.

42ARTS

The Actors Theater of Louisville holds a yearly festival of new American plays. The city also has a resident ballet company. The Louisville Orchestra has recorded numerous works by contemporary composers. The Kentucky Arts Council (KAC), a division of the Kentucky Department of the Arts within the Commerce Cabinet, is authorized to promote the arts through such programs as Arts in Education and the State Arts Resources Program. Other ongoing programs include the Craft Marketing Program, which promotes the state's craft industry, and the Folklife Program, a partnership with the Kentucky Historical Society. The Arts Kentucky is a statewide membership organization for artists, performers, craftspeople, and community arts groups.

The Kentucky Center for the Arts in Louisville, dedicated in 1983, serves as home to the Louisville Orchestra (est. 1937), the Louisville Ballet (est. 1952), and the Kentucky Opera. Bluegrass, a form of country music performed on fiddle and banjo and played at a rapid tempo, is named after the style pioneered by Kentuckian Bill Monroe and his Blue Grass Boys.

The Kentucky Arts Council was formed in 1965. In 2003, the KAC and other arts organizations received $1,333,900 in grants from the National Endowment for the Arts. KAC also receives funding from the state to develop its arts education programs. Kentucky Chautauqua, an ongoing program of the Kentucky Humanities Council, sponsors impersonations of ten historical characters from Kentucky's past who travel across the state for presentations. In 2000, the state received $978,862 in grant money from the National Endowment for the Humanities. The state offers arts education to about 23,100 schoolchildren. Kentucky has over 200 arts associations and over 50 local arts associations.

43LIBRARIES AND MUSEUMS

In 2000 there were 13 public library systems, and 93 bookmobiles in Kentucky, with a total of 7,856,000 volumes and a circulation of over 20 million. The regional library system included university libraries and the state library at Frankfort, as well as city and county libraries. The Kentucky Historical Society in Frankfort also maintains a research library of more than 85,000 volumes. Total library income came to $72,818,000 in 2000, including $582,554 in federal grants. Libraries spent 55.7% of income on staff members, and 16.9% on collections.

The state has more than 107 museums. Art museums include the University of Kentucky Art Museum and the Headley-Whitney Museum in Lexington, the Allen R. Hite Art Institute at the University of Louisville, and the J. B. Speed Art Museum, also in Louisville. Among Kentucky's equine museums are the International Museum of the Horse and the American Horse Museum, both in Lexington, and the Kentucky Derby Museum in Louisville. The John James Audubon Museum is located in Audubon State Park at Henderson.

Leading historical sites include Abraham Lincoln's birthplace at Hodgenville and the Mary Todd Lincoln and Henry Clay homes in Lexington. The Kentucky Historical Society in Frankfort operates three museums and supports a mobile museum system that brings exhibits on Kentucky history to schools, parks, and local gatherings, and aids over 400 local historical organizations.

44COMMUNICATIONS

Only 93.7% of all occupied housing units in the state had a telephone in 2001.

In 1922, Kentucky's first radio broadcasting station, WHAS, was established. By 2003, there were 73 major radio stations, 73 AM and 58 FM. That year there were 29 major television broadcasting stations, with 17 public broadcasting stations.

There were 576,850 television households, 65% of which received cable. By 2000, Kentucky had registered a total of 39,264 Internet domain names.

45PRESS

In 2002, Kentucky had 23 daily newspapers (9 morning, 14 evening), and 14 Sunday papers. The following table shows the leading Kentucky newspapers with their approximate 2002 circulations:

AREA	NAME	DAILY	SUNDAY
Lexington	*Herald–Leader* (m,S)	107,670	124,468
Louisville	*Courier–Journal* (m,S)	222,332	284,820

Magazines include *Kentucky Living* and *Kentucky Monthly*.

46ORGANIZATIONS

In 2003, there were about 1,750 regional, national, and international organizations within the state. Notable organizations with headquarters in Kentucky include the Thoroughbred Club of America, the United States Polo Association, the Jockeys' Guild, and the Burley Tobacco Growers Cooperative Association (all in Lexington); the Burley Auction Warehouse Association (Mt. Sterling); the National Softball Association in Nicholasville; and the Association of Dark Leaf Tobacco Dealers and Exporters, Sons of the American Revolution, and the American Saddlebred Horse Association (all in Louisville).

The Council of State Governments in Lexington is a cosponsor of the National Crime Prevention Institute and the National Emergency Management Association (both are also in Lexington). The National Police Officers Association of America is based in Louisville.

The American Quilter's Society is located in Paducah. State organizations for local arts and culture include the Filson Club, the Kentucky Guild of Artists and Craftsmen, and the Ohio Valley Art League.

47TOURISM, TRAVEL, AND RECREATION

In 2002, the economic impact of tourism within the state reached about $9.1 billion dollars, including the support of over 164,000 travel-related jobs. This represented a 5.2% increase in travel expenditures over 2001. The increase has been attributed, in part, to the impact of the Kentucky Tourism Development Act of 1996, which provides incentives for new or expanding tourist-related businesses.

One of the state's top tourist attractions is Mammoth Cave National Park, which contains an estimated 150 mi (241 km) of underground passages. Other units of the national park system in Kentucky include a re-creation of Abraham Lincoln's birthplace in Hodgenville and Cumberland Gap National Historical Park, which extends into Tennessee and Virginia.

The state operates 15 resort parks (13 of them year round). The state also operates 15 recreational parks and 9 shrines. Breaks Interstate Park, on the Kentucky-Virginia border, is noted for the Russell Fork River Canyon, which is 1,600 feet (488 meters) deep; the park is supported equally by the two states.

In 1979, the Kentucky Horse Park opened in Lexington. The Kentucky State Fair is held every August at Louisville.

48SPORTS

There are no major league professional sports teams in Kentucky. There is a minor league baseball team in Louisville that plays in the Triple-A International League. There are also two minor league hockey teams in Kentucky that play in the American Hockey League.

The first known horse race in Kentucky was held in 1783. The annual Kentucky Derby, first run on 17 May 1875, has become the single most famous event in US thoroughbred racing. Held on the first Saturday in May at Churchill Downs in Louisville, the Derby is one of three races for three-year-olds constituting the Triple Crown. Keeneland Race Course in Lexington is the site of the Blue Grass Stakes and other major thoroughbred races. The Kentucky Futurity, an annual highlight of the harness racing season, is usually held on the first Friday in October at the Red Mile in Lexington.

Rivaling horse racing as a spectator sport is collegiate basketball. The University of Kentucky Wildcats, who play in the Southeastern Conference, won NCAA Division I basketball championships in 1948–49, 1951, 1958, 1978, 1996, and 1998, and the National Invitation Tournament in 1946 and 1976. The University of Louisville Cardinals, who play in Conference USA, captured the NCAA crown in 1980 and 1986, and won an NIT title in 1956. Kentucky Wesleyan, at Owensboro, was the NCAA Division II titleholder in 1966, 1968–69, 1973, 1987, 1990, 1999, and 2001.

[49]FAMOUS KENTUCKIANS

Kentucky has been the birthplace of one US president, four US vice presidents, the only president of the Confederacy, and several important jurists, statesmen, writers, artists, and sports figures.

Abraham Lincoln (1809–65) the 16th president of the US, was born in Hodgenville, Hardin (now Larue) County, and spent his developing years in Indiana and Illinois. Elected as the first Republican president in 1860 and reelected in 1864, Lincoln reflected his Kentucky roots in his opposition to secession and the expansion of slavery, and in his conciliatory attitude toward the defeated southern states. His wife, Mary Todd Lincoln (1818–82), was a native of Lexington.

Kentucky-born US vice presidents have all been Democrats. Richard M. Johnson (1780–1850) was elected by the Senate after a deadlock in the Electoral College; John C. Breckinridge (1821–75) in 1857 became the youngest man ever to hold the office; Adlai E. Stevenson (1835–1914) served in Grover Cleveland's second administration. The best-known vice president was Alben W. Barkley (1877–1956), who, before his election with President Harry S Truman in 1948, was a US senator and longtime Senate majority leader.

Frederick M. Vinson (1890–1953) was the only Kentuckian to serve as chief justice of the US. Noteworthy associate justices were John Marshall Harlan (1833–1911), famous for his dissent from the segregationist *Plessy v. Ferguson* decision (1896), and Louis B. Brandeis (1856–1941), the first Jew to serve on the Supreme Court and a champion of social reform.

Henry Clay (b.Virginia, 1777–1852) came to Lexington in 1797 and went on to serve as speaker of the US House of Representatives, secretary of state, and US senator; he was also a three-time presidential candidate. Other important federal officeholders from Kentucky include attorneys general John Breckinridge (b.Virginia, 1760–1806) and John J. Crittenden (1787–1863), who also served with distinction as US senator; treasury secretaries Benjamin H. Bristow (1830–96) and John G. Carlisle (1835–1910); and US senator John Sherman Cooper (1901–91). Zachary Taylor (1784–1850), 12th US president, spent much of his adult life in Kentucky and is buried there.

Among noteworthy state officeholders, Isaac Shelby (b.Maryland 1750–1826) was a leader in the movement for statehood and the first governor of Kentucky. William Goebel (1856–1900) was the only US governor assassinated in office. Albert B. ("Happy") Chandler (1898–1991), twice governor, also served as US senator and as commissioner of baseball.

A figure prominently associated with frontier Kentucky is the explorer and surveyor Daniel Boone (b.Pennsylvania, 1734–1820). Other frontiersmen include Kit Carson (1809–68) and Roy Bean (1825?–1903). During the Civil War, Lincoln's principal adversary was another native Kentuckian, Jefferson Davis (1808–89). Davis moved south as a boy to a Mississippi plantation home, subsequently serving as US senator from Mississippi, US secretary of war, and president of the Confederate States of America.

Other personalities of significance include James G. Birney (1792–1857) and Cassius Marcellus Clay (1810–1903), both major antislavery spokesmen. Clay's daughter Laura (1849–1941) and Madeline Breckinridge (1872–1920) were important contributors to the women's suffrage movement. Henry Watterson (1840–1921) founded and edited the *Louisville Courier-Journal* and was a major adviser to the Democratic Party. Carry Nation (1846–1911) was a leader of the temperance movement. During the 1920s, Kentuckian John T. Scopes (1900–70) gained fame as the defendant in the "monkey trial" in Dayton, Tenn.; Scopes was prosecuted for teaching Darwin's theory of evolution. Whitney M. Young (1921–71), a prominent black leader, served as head of the National Urban League.

Thomas Hunt Morgan (1866–1945), honored for his work in heredity and genetics, was a Nobel Prize winner. Journalists born in Kentucky include Irvin S. Cobb (1876–1944), who was also a humorist and playwright, and Arthur Krock (1887–1974), a winner of four Pulitzer Prizes. Notable businessmen include Harland Sanders (b.Indiana, 1890–1980), founder of Kentucky Fried Chicken restaurants.

Kentucky has produced several distinguished creative artists. These include painters Matthew Jouett (1787–1827), Frank Duveneck (1848–1919), and Paul Sawyer (1865–1917); folk song collector John Jacob Niles (1891–1980); and novelists Harriette Arnow (1908–86) and Wendell Berry (b.1934). Robert Penn Warren (1905–89), a novelist, poet, and critic, won the Pulitzer Prize three times and was the first author to win the award in both the fiction and poetry categories.

Among Kentuckians well recognized in the performing arts are film innovator D. W. Griffith (David Lewelyn Wark Griffith, 1875–1948), Academy Award–winning actress Patricia Neal (b.1926), and country music singer Loretta Lynn (b.1932). Kentucky's sports figures include basketball coach Adolph Rupp (b.Kansas, 1901–77), shortstop Harold ("Pee Wee") Reese (1919–99), football great Paul Hornung (b.1935), and world heavyweight boxing champions Jimmy Ellis (b.1940) and Muhammad Ali (Cassius Clay, b.1942).

[50]BIBLIOGRAPHY

Alvey, R. Gerald. *Kentucky Bluegrass Country*. Jackson: University Press of Mississippi, 1992.

Bryant, Ron D. *Kentucky History: An Annotated Bibliography*. Westport, Conn.: Greenwood Press, 2000.

Buck, Pem Davidson. *Worked to the Bone: Race, Class, Power, and Privilege in Kentucky*. New York: Monthly Review Press, 2001.

Burns, David M. *Gateway: Dr. Thomas Walker and the Opening of Kentucky*. Middlesboro, Ky.: Bell County Historical Society, 2000.

Channing, Steven A. *Kentucky: A Bicentennial History*. New York: Norton, 1977.

Clark, Thomas Dionysius. *The Kentucky*. Lexington: University Press of Kentucky, 1992.

Fuller, Paul E. *Laura Clay and the Woman's Rights Movement*. Lexington: University Press of Kentucky, 1975.

Harrison, Lowell Hayes, and James C. Klotter. *A New History of Kentucky*. Lexington: University Press of Kentucky, 1997.

Hollingsworth, Kent. *The Kentucky Thoroughbred*. Lexington: University Press of Kentucky, 1985.

Kentucky Cabinet for Economic Development. Division of Research. *1997 Kentucky Deskbook of Economic Statistics*. Frankfort, 1997.

Kleber, John E., ed. *The Kentucky Encyclopedia.* Lexington: University Press of Kentucky, 1992.

Kozar, Richard. *Daniel Boone and the Exploration of the Frontier.* Philadelphia: Chelsea House Publishers, 1999.

Lofaro, Michael A. *Daniel Boone: An American Life.* Lexington: University Press of Kentucky, 2003.

Miller, Penny M. *Kentucky Politics & Government: Do We Stand United?* Lincoln: University of Nebraska Press, 1994.

Rennick, Robert M. *Kentucky Place Names.* Lexington: University Press of Kentucky, 1984.

Williams, Rob, comp. *A Citizen's Guide to the Kentucky Constitution.* Rev. ed. Frankfort, Ky.: Legislative Research Commission, 1995.

LOUISIANA

State of Louisiana

ORIGIN OF STATE NAME: Named in 1682 for France's King Louis XIV. **NICKNAME:** The Pelican State. **CAPITAL:** Baton Rouge. **ENTERED UNION:** 30 April 1812 (18th). **SONGS:** "Give Me Louisiana" and "You are My Sunshine." **MOTTO:** Union, Justice, and Confidence. **COLORS:** Gold, white, and blue. **FLAG:** On a blue field, a white pelican feeds her three young, symbolizing the state providing for its citizens; the state motto is inscribed on a white ribbon. **OFFICIAL SEAL:** A pelican, with its head turned to the left, sits in a nest with three young. Around the inner circle are inscribed "Union," "Justice," and under the nest, "Confidence." **BIRD:** Eastern brown pelican. **CRUSTACEAN:** Crawfish. **DOG:** Catahoula leopard. **FLOWER:** Magnolia. **WILDFLOWER:** Louisiana iris. **TREE:** Bald cypress. **GEM:** Agate. **FOSSIL:** Petrified palmwood. **INSECT:** Honeybee. **LEGAL HOLIDAYS:** New Year's Day, 1 January; Battle of New Orleans Day, 8 January; Birthday of Martin Luther King, Jr., 3rd Monday in January; Robert E. Lee's Birthday, 19 January; Washington's Birthday, 3rd Monday in February; Good Friday, March or April; National Memorial Day, last Monday in May; Confederate Memorial Day and Jefferson Davis's Birthday, 3 June; Independence Day, 4 July; Huey Long's Birthday, 30 August, by proclamation of the governor; Labor Day, 1st Monday in September; Columbus Day, 2nd Monday in October; All Saints' Day, 1 November; Veterans Day, 11 November; Thanksgiving Day, 4th Thursday in November; Christmas Day, 25 December. Legal holidays in New Orleans, Jefferson, St. Bernard, St. Charles, and East Baton Rouge parishes also include Mardi Gras, February or March. **TIME:** 6 AM CST = noon GMT.

¹LOCATION, SIZE, AND EXTENT

Situated in the western south-central US, Louisiana ranks 31st in size among the 50 states. The total area of Louisiana is 47,751 sq mi (123,675 sq km), including 44,521 sq mi (115,309 sq km) of land and 3,230 sq mi (8,366 sq km) of inland water. The state extends 237 mi (381 km) E-W; its maximum N-S extension is 236 mi (380 km). Louisiana is shaped roughly like a boot, with the heel in the SW corner and the toe at the extreme SE.

Louisiana is bordered on the N by Arkansas; on the E by Mississippi (with part of the line formed by the Mississippi River and part, in the extreme SE, by the Pearl River); on the S by the Gulf of Mexico; and on the W by Texas (with part of the line passing through the Sabine River and Toledo Bend Reservoir). The state's geographic center is in Avoyelles Parish, 3 mi (5 km) SE of Marksville. The total boundary length of Louisiana is 1,486 mi (2,391 km). Louisiana's total tidal shoreline is 7,721 mi (12,426 km).

²TOPOGRAPHY

Louisiana lies wholly within the Gulf Coastal Plain. Alluvial lands, chiefly of the Red and Mississippi rivers, occupy the north-central third of the state. East and west of this alluvial plain are the upland districts, characterized by rolling hills sloping gently toward the coast. The coastal-delta section, in the southernmost portion of the state, consists of the Mississippi Delta and the coastal lowlands. The highest elevation in the state is Driskill Mountain at 535 ft (163 m), in Bienville Parish; the lowest, 8 ft (2 m) below sea level, in New Orleans.

Louisiana has the most wetlands of all the states, about 11,000 sq mi (28,000 sq km) of floodplains and 7,800 sq mi (20,200 sq km) of coastal swamps, marshes, and estuarine waters. The largest lake, actually a coastal lagoon, is Lake Pontchartrain, with an area of more than 620 sq mi (1,600 sq km). Toledo Bend Reservoir, an artificial lake along the Louisiana-Texas border, has an area of 284 sq mi (736 sq km). The most important rivers are the Mississippi, Red, Pearl, Atchafalaya, and Sabine. Most drainage takes place through swamps between the bayous, which serve as outlets for overflowing rivers and streams. Louisiana has nearly 2,500 coastal islands covering some 2,000 sq mi (5,000 sq km).

³CLIMATE

Louisiana has a relatively constant semitropical climate. Rainfall and humidity decrease, and daily temperature variations increase, with distance from the Gulf of Mexico. The normal daily temperature in New Orleans is 68°F (20°C), ranging from 52°F (11°C) in January to 82°F (28°C) in July. The all-time high temperature is 114°F (46°C), recorded at Plain Dealing on 10 August 1936; the all-time low, –16°F (–27°C), was set at Minden on 13 February 1899. New Orleans has sunshine 60% of the time, and the average annual rainfall (1971–2000) was 64.2 in (163 cm). Snow falls occasionally in the north, but rarely in the south.

Prevailing winds are from the south or southeast. During the summer and fall, tropical storms and hurricanes frequently batter the state, especially along the coast. Tropical Storm Allison (June 2001) caused severe flooding in coastal regions. Among the most severe hurricanes in recent decades were Audrey, which entered Cameron Parish on 28 June 1957, causing 400–500 deaths and property damage of $150 million; Betsy, which entered the coast near Grand Isle on 9 September 1965, causing 58 deaths and damages of $1.2 billion; and Andrew, which landed on 25 August 1992 after devastating southern Florida two days earlier.

⁴FLORA AND FAUNA

Forests in Louisiana consist of four major types: shortleaf pine uplands, slash and longleaf pine flats and hills, hardwood forests in alluvial basins, and cypress and tupelo swamps. Important commercial trees also include beech, eastern red cedar, and black walnut. Among the state's wildflowers are the ground orchid and several hyacinths; two species (Louisiana quillwort and American chaffseed) were listed as endangered in 2003. Spanish moss (actually a member of the pineapple family) grows profusely in the southern regions but is rare in the north.

Louisiana's varied habitats—tidal marshes, swamps woodlands, and prairies—offer a diversity of fauna. Deer, squirrel, rabbit, and bear are hunted as game, while muskrat, nutria, mink, opossum, bobcat, and skunk are commercially significant furbearers. Prized game birds include quail, turkey, woodcock, and various waterfowl, of which the mottled duck and wood duck are native. Coastal beaches are inhabited by sea turtles, and whales may be seen offshore. Freshwater fish include bass, crappie, and bream; red and white crawfishes are the leading commercial crustaceans. Threatened animal species include five species (green, hawksbill, Kemp's ridlly, leatherback, and loggerhead) of sea turtle. Twenty-three Louisiana animal species were on the US Fish and Wildlife Service's threatened and endangered species list for 2003. Among those listed are the Louisiana black bear, bald eagle, Alabama heelsplitter, and red-cockaded woodpecker.

5ENVIRONMENTAL PROTECTION

Louisiana's earliest and most pressing environmental problem was the chronic danger of flooding by the Mississippi River. In April and May 1927, the worst flood in the state's history inundated more than 1,300,000 acres (526,000 hectares) of agricultural land, left 300,000 people homeless, and would have swept away much of New Orleans had levees below the city not been dynamited. The following year, the US Congress funded construction of a system of floodways and spillways to divert water from the Mississippi when necessary. These flood control measures and dredging for oil and gas exploration created another environmental problem—the slowing of the natural flow of silt into the wetlands. As a result, salt water from the Gulf of Mexico has seeped into the wetlands.

In 1984, Louisiana consolidated much of its environmental protection efforts into a new state agency—The Department of Environmental Quality (DEQ). Among its responsibilities are maintenance of air and water quality, solid-waste management, hazardous waste disposal, and control of radioactive materials. According to the Louisiana Environmental Action Plan (LEAP to 2000 Project), toxic air pollution, industrial and municipal wastewater discharges, and coastal wetland loss head the list of state residents' environmental concerns. Louisiana's problem in protecting its wetlands differs from that of most other states in that its wetlands are more than wildlife refuges—they are central to the state's agriculture and fishing industries. Assessment of the environmental impact of various industries on the wetlands has been conducted under the Coastal Zone Management Plan of the Department of Natural Resources.

The two largest wildlife refuges in the state are the Rockefeller Wildlife Refuge, comprising 84,000 acres (34,000 hectares) in Cameron and Vermilion parishes, and the Marsh Island Refuge, 82,000 acres (33,000 hectares) of marshland in Iberia Parish. Both are managed by the Department of Wildlife and Fisheries. Louisiana's coastal marshes represent almost 40% of such lands in the country.

With approximately 100 major chemical and petrochemical manufacturing and refining facilities located in Louisiana, many DEQ programs deal with the regulation of hazardous waste generation, management and disposal, and chemical releases to the air and water. Trends in air monitoring have, for example, continued to show decreases in criteria pollutants. In 1993, Louisiana became one of the first states in the nation to receive federal approval for stringent new solid waste landfill regulations, and the department has developed a Statewide Solid Waste Management Plan which encourages waste reduction. In

2003, Louisiana had 155 hazardous waste sites, 13 of which were included on the National Priorities List, included in the Environmental Protection Agency's database. Of the total river miles in the state impacted by pollution, 69% of the pollution is due to nonpoint sources such as agricultural and urban runoff. Efforts by DEQ to curb nonpoint source pollution have included the support and cooperation of the agricultural community and other state and federal agencies.

Among the most active citizen's groups on environmental issues are the League of Women Voters, the Sierra Club (Delta Chapter), and the Louisiana Environmental Action Network (LEAN). Curbside recycling programs exist 28 parishes. In 1996, wetlands, which once covered more than half the state, accounted for about one-third of Louisiana's land. In 2001, Louisiana received $68,112,000 in federal grants from the Environmental Protection Agency; EPA expenditures for procurement contracts in Louisiana that year amounted to $69,000.

6POPULATION

Louisiana ranked 24th in population in the US with an estimated total of 4,482,646 in 2002, an increase of 48% since 2000. Between 1990 and 2000, Louisiana's population grew from 4,219,973 to 4,468,976, an increase of 5.9%. The population is projected to reach 4,535,000 by 2005 and 5.1 million by 2025.

At the time of the 1980 census, Louisiana ranked 19th among the 50 states, with a population of 4,203,972, representing an increase of more than 15% since 1970. However, by 1990 the population was 4,219,973, representing only a 0.3% gain, and ranking had slipped to 21st. The population density in 2000 was 102.6 persons per sq mi.

In 2000 the median age was 34. Persons under 18 years old accounted for 27.3% of the population while 11.6% were age 65 or older.

New Orleans is the largest city, with an estimated 2002 population of 473,681, followed by Baton Rouge, 225,702; and Shreveport, 199,033. Baton Rouge, the capital, had grown with exceptional speed since 1940, when its population was 34,719; however, since 1980, the population has been decreasing. Among the state's largest metropolitan areas were New Orleans, with an estimated 1,305,479 in 1999, and Baton Rouge, with 578,946.

7ETHNIC GROUPS

Louisiana, most notably the Delta region, is an enclave of ethnic heterogeneity in the South. At the end of World War II, the established population of the Delta, according to descent, included blacks, French, Spanish (among them Central and South Americans and Islenos, Spanish-speaking migrants from the Canary Islands), Filipinos, Italians, Chinese, American Indians, and numerous other groups.

Blacks made up about 32.5% of the population in 2000 (the 2nd-highest percentage among the 50 states), and were estimated to number 1,451,944. They include descendants of "free people of color," some of whom were craftsmen and rural property owners before the Civil War (a few were slaveholding plantation owners). Many of these, of mixed blood, are referred to locally as "colored Creoles" and have constituted a black elite in both urban and rural Louisiana. The black population of New Orleans constituted 67.3% of the city's residents in 2000; New Orleans elected its first black mayor, Ernest N. "Dutch" Morial, in 1977.

Two groups that have been highly identified with the culture of Louisiana are Creoles and Acadians (also called Cajuns). Both descend primarily from early French immigrants to the state, but the Cajuns trace their origins from the mainly rural people exiled from Acadia (Nova Scotia) in the 1740s, while the Creoles tend to be city people from France and, to a lesser extent, from Nova Scotia or Hispaniola. (The term "Creole" also applies to the relatively few early Spanish settlers and their descendants.)

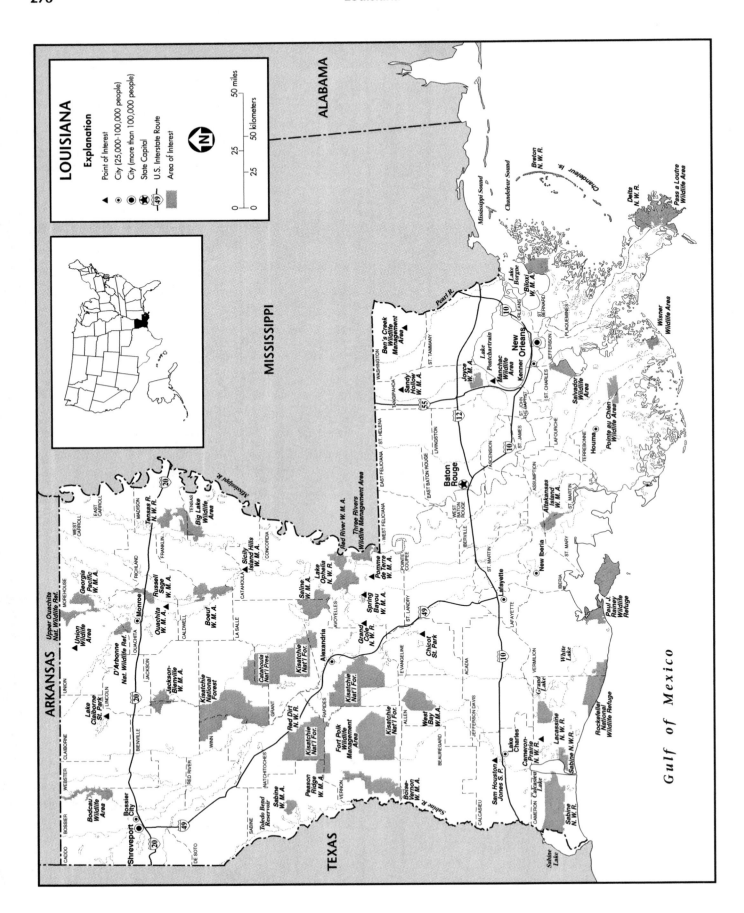

LOUISIANA

Explanation

▲ Point of Interest
⊙ City (25,000-100,000 people)
◉ City (more than 100,000 people)
✪ State Capital
49 U.S. Interstate Route
Area of Interest

50 miles
50 kilometers

ALABAMA

MISSISSIPPI

ARKANSAS

TEXAS

Gulf of Mexico

Although Acadians have intermingled with Spaniards and Germans, they still speak a French patois and retain a distinctive culture and cuisine. In 2000, 179,739 residents claimed Acadian/Cajun ancestry. In 2000, 107,738, or 2.4% of the population, were Hispanic or Latino.

At the time of the 2000 census, 115,885 Louisianians (2.6% of the population) were foreign born. France, Germany, Ireland, and the United Kingdom provided Louisiana with the largest ancestry groups. As of 2000, there were 25,477 American Indians in Louisiana, along with 54,758 and Asians, including 24,358 Vietnamese. Pacific Islanders numbered 1,240.

8LANGUAGES

White settlers in Louisiana found several Indian tribes of the Caddoan confederacy, from at least five different language groups. In 1990, about 495 Louisiana residents spoke an American Indian language at home. Place-names from this heritage include Coushatta, Natchitoches, and Ouachita.

Louisiana English is predominantly Southern. Notable features of the state's speech patterns are *pen* and *pin* as sound-alikes and, in New Orleans, the so-called Brooklyn pronunciation of *bird* as /boyd/. A pecan sugar candy is well known as *praline*.

In 2000, 3,771,003 Louisiana residents—90.8% of the population five years old and older (up from 89.9% in 1990)—spoke only English at home.

Unique to Louisiana is a large enclave, west of New Orleans, where a variety of French called Acadian (Cajun) is the first language. From it, and from early colonial French, English has taken such words as pirogue (dugout canoe), armoire (wardrobe), boudin (blood sausage), and lagniappe (extra gift).

The following table gives selected statistics from the 2000 census for language spoken at home by persons five years old and over. The category "African languages" includes Amharic, Ibo, Twi, Yoruba, Bantu, Swahili, and Somali.

LANGUAGE	NUMBER	PERCENT
Population 5 years and over	4,153,367	100.0
Speak only English	3,771,003	90.8
Speak a language other than English	382,364	9.2
Speak a language other than English	382,364	9.2
French (incl. Patois, Cajun)	194,314	4.7
Spanish or Spanish Creole	105,189	2.5
Vietnamese	23,326	0.6
German	8,047	0.2
Chinese	5,731	0.1
Arabic	5,489	0.1
French Creole	4,470	0.1
Italian	3,730	0.1
Tagalog	3,335	0.1
Korean	2,402	0.1
African languages	2,278	0.1

9RELIGIONS

Spanish missionaries brought Roman Catholicism to Louisiana in the early 16th century, and many of them were killed in their attempts to convert the Indians. During the early days, the most active religious orders were the Jesuits, Capuchins, and Ursuline nuns. Until the Louisiana Purchase, the public practice of any but the Catholic religion was prohibited, and Jews were entirely banned.

Joseph Willis, a mulatto preacher who conducted prayer meetings at what is now Lafayette in 1804, organized the first Baptist church west of the Mississippi, at Bayou Chicot in 1812. In the Opelousas region, in 1806, the first Methodist church in the state was organized. The first Episcopal church was established in New Orleans in 1805, a Methodist church in 1813, a Presbyterian church in 1817, a synagogue in 1828, and a Baptist church in 1834. After the Civil War, blacks withdrew from white-dominated churches to form their own religious groups, mainly Baptist and Methodist.

As of 2000, the Roman Catholic Church was the largest Christian denomination, with 1,382,603 church members. The leading Protestant denominations were the Southern Baptist Convention, 768,587; the United Methodist Church, 160,153; Assemblies of God, 49,041; and the Episcopal Church, 33,653. There were about 16,500 Jews residing in Louisiana in 2000, a majority of them in New Orleans. The Muslim community had about 13,050 members. Voodoo, in some cases blended with Christian ritual, is more widespread in Louisiana than anywhere else in the United States, although the present number of practitioners is impossible to ascertain. Over 1.8 million people (about 41.2% of the population) did not claim any religious affiliation in the 2000 survey.

10TRANSPORTATION

New Orleans is a major center of domestic and international freight traffic. In volume of domestic and foreign cargo handled, however, the Port of South Louisiana, which stretches 54 miles along the Mississippi River, is the largest tonnage port in the Western Hemisphere and 3rd in the world. Although Louisiana's roads remained poor until the 1930s, the state was one of the nation's major rail centers by the end of the 19th century, and New Orleans was one of the first cities to develop a mass transit system.

Several short-run railroads were built in Louisiana during the 1830s. The first of these, and the first rail line west of the Alleghenies, was the Pontchartrain Railroad, which opened, using horse-drawn vehicles, on 23 April 1831. New Orleans was connected with New York before the Civil War, with Chicago by 1873, and with California in 1883 via a line that subsequently became part of the Southern Pacific. Railroads soon rivaled the Mississippi River in the movement of goods to and from New Orleans. There were six Class I line-haul railroads in Louisiana in 2000, and total railroad mileage was 3,192 route mi (5,137 km), of which about 90% was Class I track. That same year, originated tonnage of petroleum products transported by rail totaled more than 57 million tons, and chemicals totaled more than 16 million tons. Amtrak provides passenger links with Los Angeles, Chicago, and New York and carries passengers from nine stations through the state. The New Orleans and Carrollton Railroads, a horse-drawn trolley system, began service in 1835; 59 years later, electric trolleys came into use.

Louisiana's first road-building boom began after Huey Long entered the statehouse. When Long took office in 1928, the state had no more than 300 mi (480 km) of paved roads; by 1931 there were 1,583 mi (2,548 km). At the end of 2000, Louisiana had a total of 60,900 mi (98,009 km) of public roads, over 75% of them rural. Also in 2000, 1,964,694 automobiles and 1,570,804 trucks were registered in the state, and 2,759,120 drivers' licenses were in force.

Early in the nation's history, the Mississippi River emerged as the principal route for north–south traffic, and New Orleans soon became the South's main port. The advent of the steamboat in 1812 solved the problem of upstream navigation, which previously had required three or four months for a distance that could be covered downstream in 15 days. (Barges moved by towboats eventually supplanted steamboats as cargo carriers.) An important breakthrough in international transportation was the deepening of the channel at the mouth of the Mississippi by means of jetties, the first of which were completed in 1879. The port of New Orleans is served by more than 100 steamship lines, 20 common carrier lines, and about 100 contract carrier barge lines. The Louisiana Offshore Oil Port (LOOP), the first deepwater oil port in the US, was opened in 1981. Located south of New Orleans in the Gulf of Mexico, the supertanker facility has a designed capacity of 1,400,000 barrels of oil a day. Large ports include Baton Rouge, with a tonnage of over 65.6 million tons in 2000; New Orleans, with 90.8 million tons; and the Port of Plaquemines, with 59.9 million tons. The Port of South Louisiana, handling 217.8 million tons in 2000, is the US's busiest port.

In 2002, Louisiana had 232 private and public airfields. The busiest was the Louis Armstrong New Orleans International Airport. Louisiana also had 229 heliports and 17 seaplane bases.

11HISTORY

The region now known as Louisiana is largely the creation of the Mississippi River; the process of land building still goes on in the Atchafalaya Basin and below New Orleans on the Mississippi Delta. Louisiana was never densely inhabited in prehistoric times, and at no time, probably, did as many as 15,000 Indians live inside the present boundaries of the state. The main relic of prehistoric inhabitants is the great earthwork at Poverty Point, near Marksville, but other Indian mounds are to be found in alluvial and coastal regions.

When white exploration and settlement of North America began, various tribes of Caddo Indians inhabited northwestern Louisiana, and small Tunican-speaking groups lived in the northeast. In the southwest were a number of rather primitive people of the Atakapa group; in south-central Louisiana, the Chitimacha ranged through the marshes and lowlands. Various small Muskogean tribes, related to the Choctaw, lived east of the Mississippi in the "Florida parishes," so called because they were once part of Spanish West Florida. The Natchez Indians, whose main villages were in present-day Mississippi near the city that still bears their name, fought with the French settlers in Louisiana's early history but were exterminated in the process.

Several Spanish explorers sailed along the coast of Louisiana, but Hernando de Soto was probably the first to penetrate the state's present boundaries, in 1541. Almost a century and a half passed before Robert Cavelier, Sieur de la Salle, departing from Canada, reached the mouth of the Mississippi on 9 April 1682, named the land there Louisiana in honor of King Louis XIV, and claimed it for France. La Salle's later attempt at a permanent settlement failed, but in 1699 an expedition headed by Pierre le Moyne, Sieur d'Iberville, made a settlement on Biloxi Bay. In 1714, Louis Juchereau de St. Denis established Natchitoches, the first permanent European settlement in Louisiana; Iberville's brother, the Sieur de Bienville, established New Orleans four years later.

Louisiana did not thrive economically under French rule, either as a royal colony or, from 1712 to 1731, under the proprietorship first of Antoine Crozat and then of John Law's Company of the Indies. On the other hand, French culture was firmly implanted there, and non-French settlers, especially Germans from Switzerland and the Rhineland, were quickly Gallicized. In 1762, on the verge of losing the rest of its North American empire to Great Britain in the French and Indian War, France ceded Louisiana to Spain. Governed by Spaniards, the colony was much more prosperous, although it was a burden on the Spanish treasury. New settlers—Americans, Spaniards, Canary Islanders, and, above all, Acadian refugees from Nova Scotia—added to the population. By 1800 there were about 50,000 inhabitants, a considerable number of them black slaves imported from Africa and the West Indies. The availability of slave labor, Eli Whitney's invention of the cotton gin, and Étienne de Boré's development of a granulation process for making cane sugar set the stage for future prosperity, though not under Spanish auspices. In 1800, by the secret Treaty of San Ildefonso, Napoleon forced the feeble Spanish government to return Louisiana to France. Three years later, having failed to reestablish French rule and slavery in Haiti,

Napoleon sold Louisiana to the US to keep it from falling into the hands of Great Britain.

President Thomas Jefferson concluded what was probably the best real estate deal in history, purchasing 800,000 sq mi (2,100,000 sq km) for $15,000,000 and thus more than doubling the size of the US at a cost of about 3 cents per acre. He made William C. C. Claiborne the governor of the huge new acquisition. The next year, that part of the purchase south of 33°N was separated from the remainder and designated the Territory of Orleans. The people of the territory then began the process of learning self-government, something with which they had had no experience under France and Spain. After the census of 1810 showed that the population had risen to 76,556, the people were authorized by Congress to draw up a state constitution. The constitutional convention met under the presidency of Julian Poydras in a coffeehouse in New Orleans and adopted, with a few changes, the constitution then in effect in Kentucky. In the meantime, in 1810, a revolt against Spain had taken place in West Florida. When the proposed Louisiana constitution reached Washington, Congress added that part of West Florida between the Mississippi and Pearl rivers to the new state, which entered the Union on 30 April 1812.

The key event in the Americanization of Louisiana was the campaign for New Orleans in December 1814 and January 1815, actually fought after the War of 1812 had ended. A force of British veterans under General Sir Edward Pakenham sailed into Lake Borgne and established itself below New Orleans at Chalmette. There they were met by detachments of Creoles, Acadians, blacks, and even Jean Lafitte's pirates, all from Louisiana, as well as Tennesseans, Kentuckians, and Choctaw Indians, with the whole army under the command of Andrew Jackson. After several preliminary battles, the British were bloodily defeated when they launched an all-out assault on Jackson's line.

From 1815 to 1861, Louisiana was one of the most prosperous states in the South, producing sugar and cotton on its rich alluvial lands and grazing hogs and cattle in the wooded hills of the north and on the prairies of the southwest. Yeoman farmers and New Orleans workers far outnumbered the wealthy planters but the planters, whose slaves made up almost half the population, dominated Louisiana politically and economically. When the secession crisis came in 1861, the planters led Louisiana into the Confederacy and, after four bloody years, to total defeat. The state suffered crippling economic losses during the Civil War, but the greatest loss was the lives of tens of thousands of young white men who died in defense of the South, and of thousands of blacks who died seeking and fighting for freedom. Louisiana did not fully recover from this disaster until the mid-20th century.

After the Civil War, radical Republican governments elected by black voters ruled the state, but declining support from the North and fierce resistance from Louisiana whites brought the Reconstruction period to an end. Black people and their few white allies lost control of state government, and most of the former slaves became laborers on sugar plantations or sharecroppers in the cotton fields. There, as the years passed, they were joined by more and more landless whites. In 1898, blacks were disfranchised almost entirely by a new state constitution drawn up primarily for that purpose. This constitution also significantly reduced the number of poorer whites who voted in Louisiana elections.

The vast majority of Louisiana whites—whether hill farmers, Cajuns along the southern rivers and bayous, lumbermen in the yellow pine forests, or workers in New Orleans—were little better off than the black or white sharecroppers. Many economic changes had taken place: rice had become a staple crop on the southwestern prairies, and an oil boom had begun after the turn of the century. But just as before the Civil War, large landowners—combined with New Orleans bankers, businessmen, and politicians—dominated state government, effectively blocking political and social reform. The Populist movement, which succeeded in effecting some change in other southern states, was crushed in Louisiana.

Not until 1928, with the election of Huey P. Long as governor, did the winds of change strike Louisiana; having been so long delayed, they blew with gale force. The years from 1928 through 1960 could well be called the Long Era: three Longs—Huey, who was assassinated in 1935; his brother Earl, who served as governor three times; and Huey's son Russell, who became a powerful US senator—dominated state politics for most of the period. From a backward agricultural state, Louisiana evolved into one of the world's major petrochemical-manufacturing centers. Offshore drilling sent clusters of oil wells 60 mi (97 km) out into the Gulf. The pine lands were reforested, and soybeans provided a new source of income. What had been one of the most parsimonious states became one of the most liberal in welfare spending, care for the aged, highway building, and education. The state could afford these expanding programs because of ever-increasing revenues from oil and gas.

In the mid-1980s, a drop in world oil prices rocked Louisiana's economy, hurting the oil exploration and service industries and raising the state's unemployment rate in 1986 to 13%, the highest in the nation. For most of the 1990s, in spite of an increase in service-sector and high-tech jobs, Louisiana had more people living in poverty than any other state. Louisiana had for decades been among the nation's poorest; the percentage of residents living in poverty in 1998 was 19.1%, making it the 2nd-poorest state in the nation. In 1999 it was reported that Louisiana also ranked 2nd-lowest in the nation for its care of children; the report took into account such factors as infant mortality rates, teen pregnancy rates, and children who lived in poverty or lacked health care. Other problems confronting the state at the turn of the century included racial tensions, disposing of toxic wastes from the petrochemical industry, depletion of oil and gas resources, and the ongoing struggle to institute good government.

The announcement in February 1985 by Russell B. Long, senator since 1948, that he would not seek reelection, and the indictment of former Governor Edwin W. Edwards by a federal grand jury on conspiracy charges during the same month, caused turmoil in Louisiana's political arena. Edwards was defeated in 1987 by Buddy Roemer, a young, well-educated Republican who promised to clean up government. In 1989, racial tensions surfaced when white supremacist David Duke, running as a Republican, narrowly won a seat in the Louisiana state legislature. Duke later ran unsuccessfully for the US Senate and for governor, but his runs for office had raised concerns about the level of frustration of many white voters. In 1995 gubernatorial candidate Murphy "Mike" Foster, Republican, promised more Roemer-like reforms. As he faced reelection four years later, some analysts said the Bayou State had made progress in building a trustworthy and responsive government. Nevertheless, Foster was criticized for favoring the oil industry and being soft on big gambling. He still managed to win another term, claiming 64% of the vote.

In 1999, Governor Murphy J. (Mike) Foster became the first Republican governor in Louisiana history to be reelected. He offered the New Orleans Saints professional football team $186.5 million in subsidies in 2002 to keep the team from moving out of the state. Foster maintained the football team had a salutary effect on Louisiana's economy.

12STATE GOVERNMENT
Louisiana has had 11 constitutions (more than any other state), the most recent of which was enacted in 1974. By January 2003 it had been amended 113 times. The state legislature consists of a 39-member senate and a 105-member house of representatives. The legislature meets annually, beginning the last Monday in March. In 2002, voters approved a change in the legislative session from odd-numbered years to even-numbered years. Following this change, the even-numbered year session is limited to 60 legislative days in 85 calendar days; the odd-numbered year session is limited to 30 legislative days in 45 calendar days. Special sessions may be called by a majority petition of each house, with length limited to 30 calendar days. All legislators are elected for concurrent four-year terms; they must be at least 18 years old, qualified voters, and have resided in the state for two years and in their districts for at least one year preceding election. The legislative salary in 2002 was $16,800.

Statewide elected executive officials include the governor and lieutenant governor (separately elected), secretary of state, attorney general, treasurer, superintendent of education, commissioner of agriculture, commissioner of insurance, and commissioner of elections. All are elected for four-year terms. The governor must be a qualified elector, be at least 25 years old, and have been a US and Louisiana citizen for five years preceding election; after two full consecutive terms, a governor may not run for reelection. The same eligibility requirements apply to the lieutenant governor, except that there is no limit on succession to the latter office. In 2002 the governor's salary was $95,000, unchanged from 1999. Other executive agencies are the State Board of Elementary and Secondary Education, whose eight elected members and three appointed members serve four-year terms, and the Public Service Commission, whose five members serve for six years.

To become law, a bill must receive majority votes in both the senate and the house and be signed by the governor, be left unsigned (for 10 days when the legislature is in session or for 20 days following the legislature's adjournment) but not vetoed by the governor, or be passed again by two-thirds votes of elected members of both houses over the governor's veto. Appropriation bills must originate in the house but may be amended by the senate. The governor has an item veto on appropriation bills. Constitutional amendments require approval by two-thirds of the elected members of each house and ratification by a majority of the people voting on it at the next general election.

Voters in Louisiana must be US citizens, 18 years old, and state residents. Restrictions apply to convicted felons and those declared mentally incompetent by the court.

13POLITICAL PARTIES
The major political organizations are the Democratic Party and the Republican Party, each affiliated with the national party. However, differences in culture and economic interests have made Louisiana's politics extremely complex. Immediately following statehood, the primary political alignment was according to ethnic background, Anglo or Latin. By the 1830s, however, Louisiana politics reflected the national division of Jacksonian Democrats and National Republicans, who were by mid-decade replaced by the Whigs. By and large, the Whigs were favored by the Anglo-Americans while the Democrats were favored by those of French and Spanish descent. When the Whig Party fell apart over slavery, many former Whigs supported the Native American (Know-Nothing) Party.

Louisiana was one of the three southern states whose disputed electoral votes put Republican Rutherford B. Hayes in the White House in 1877, in return for his agreement to withdraw federal troops from the South, thus putting an end to Reconstruction. The ensuing period of Bourbon Democratic dominance in Louisiana, a time of reaction and racism in politics (though a few blacks continued to hold office), lasted until the early 1890s, when worsening economic conditions inspired Populists and Republicans to challenge Democratic rule. The attempt failed largely because Democratic landowners were able to control the ballots of their black sharecroppers and "vote" them Democrats. The recognition that it was the black vote, however well-controlled, that held the balance in Louisiana politics impelled the Democrats to seek its elimination as an electoral factor. The constitution of 1898 imposed a poll tax, a property requirement, a literacy test, and other measures that succeeded in reducing the number of registered black voters from 130,000 at the beginning of 1897 to 5,320 in March 1900 and 1,342 by 1904. White registration also declined, from 164,000 in 1897 to 92,000 in 1904, because the new constitutional requirements tended to disfranchise poor whites as well as blacks.

Between 1900 and 1920, the New Orleans Ring, or Choctaw Club, was the dominant power in state politics. Growing political discontent led 5,261 Louisianians (6.6% of those voting) to cast their ballots for the Socialist presidential candidate in 1912. A few Socialists won local office that year in Winn Parish, a center of Populist activity in the 1890s and the birthplace of Huey Long in 1893.

During his relatively brief career as a member of the Railroad Commission, governor, and US senator, Long committed government resources to public service to an extent without precedent in the state. He also succeeded in substituting for the traditional Democratic Party organization a state machine geared primarily toward loyalty to himself and, after his assassination in 1935, to the Long family name, which kept its hold on the voters despite a series of scandals that publicized the corruption of his associates. When blacks began voting in increasing numbers during the 1940s, they tended to favor Democratic candidates from the Long camp. The Longs repaid their loyalty: when race became a bitterly divisive issue in the late 1940s and 1950s—Louisiana gave its presidential vote to the States' Rights "Dixiecrat" candidate in 1948—the Longs supported the national Democratic ticket.

The 1960s and 1970s saw a resurgence of the Republican Party and the election in 1979 of David C. Treen, the state's first Republican governor since Reconstruction. Treen was succeeded by Democrat Edwin Edwards in 1983, Democrat Charles Roemer in 1987, and Edwin Edwards again in 1991. In 1995, Louisiana elected another Republican governor—Murphy J. "Mike" Foster, who was reelected in 1999. Foster was unable to run for reelection in November 2003, due to term limits. In 2002 there were 2,810,069 registered voters. In 1998, 62% of registered voters were Democratic, 21% Republican, and 16% unaffiliated or members of other parties.

In 2003, both US senators from Louisiana—John Breux (reelected in 1998) and Mary L. Landrieu (elected 1996 to replaced retiring Senator J. Bennett Johnston, Jr. and reelected in 2002)—were Democrats. Landrieu is the daughter of former New Orleans mayor Moon Landrieu. Following the 2002 elections Louisiana's delegation of US representatives consisted of three Democrats and four Republicans. In mid-2003, 26 of the state senators were Democrats and 13 were Republicans; 70 of the state representatives were Democrats and 35 were Republicans.

In 2000, Louisianians gave Republican George W. Bush 53% of the vote in the presidential election, while Democrat Al Gore received 45%. The state had nine electoral votes in the 2000 presidential election.

14LOCAL GOVERNMENT

The ecclesiastical districts, called parishes, into which Louisiana was divided in the late 17th century remain the primary political divisions in the state, serving functions similar to those of counties in other states.

In 2002 there were 60 parishes, most of them governed by police jury (governing board). Juries range from 3 to 15 elected members. Other parish officials are the sheriff, clerk of court, assessor, and coroner. Each parish elects a school board whose members generally serve six-year terms; all other officers serve four-year terms. In 2002 there were 66 public school districts in the state.

As of 2002, Louisiana also had 302 municipal governments. Municipalities are classed by the state (based on population) as village, town, or city. Municipal officials include the mayor, chief of police, and council or board of aldermen. In 2002 Louisiana had 45 special districts, established by the legislature.

Louisiana Presidential Vote by Political Parties, 1948–2000

YEAR	ELECTORAL VOTE	LOUISIANA WINNER	DEMOCRAT	REPUBLICAN	STATES' RIGHTS DEMOCRAT	PROGRESSIVE	AMERICAN INDEPENDENT
1948	10	Thurmond (SRD)	136,344	72,657	204,290	3,035	—
1952	10	Stevenson (D)	345,027	306,925	—	—	—
					UNPLEDGED		
1956	10	*Eisenhower (R)	243,977	329,047	44,520	—	—
					NAT'L. STATES' RIGHTS		
1960	10	*Kennedy (D)	407,339	230,980	169,572	—	—
1964	10	Goldwater (R)	387,068	509,225	—	—	—
1968	10	Wallace (AI)	309,615	257,535	—	—	530,300
					AMERICAN	SOC. WORKERS	
1972	10	*Nixon (R)	298,142	686,852	44,127	12,169	—
					LIBERTARIAN	COMMUNIST	
1976	10	*Carter (D)	661,365	587,446	3,325	7,417	10,058
						CITIZENS	
1980	10	*Reagan (R)	708,453	792,853	8,240	1,584	10,333
1984	10	*Reagan (R)	651,586	1,037,299	1,876	9,502	—
						POPULIST	N ALLIANCE
1988	10	*Bush (R)	717,460	883,702	4,115	18,612	2,355
						IND. (PEROT)	AMERICA FIRST
1992	9	*Clinton (D)	815,971	733,386	3,155	211,478	18,545
1996	9	*Clinton (D)	927,837	712,586	7,499	123,293	—
						GREEN	REFORM
2000	9	*Bush, G. W. (R)	792,344	927,871	2,951	20,473	14,356

* Won US presidential election.

15 STATE SERVICES

To address the continuing threat of terrorism and to work with the federal Department of Homeland Security (created in 2002 following the terrorist attacks of 11 September 2001), homeland security in Louisiana in 2003 operated under the authority of executive order; the adjutant general was designated as the state homeland security advisor.

Louisiana's ethics laws are administered by the Commission on Ethics for Public Employees and the Board of Ethics for Elected Officials, both under the Department of Civil Service. Departments focus on labor, natural resources, revenue, elections and registration, environmental quality, justice, social services, state civil service, and wildlife and fisheries.

Educational services are provided through the Department of Education, which has jurisdiction over elementary, secondary, higher, and vocational-technical instruction, as well as the state schools for the visually impaired, hearing-impaired, and other handicapped children. Highways, waterways, airports, and mass transit are the province of the Department of Transportation and Development. Environmental affairs, conservation, forestry, and mineral resources are the responsibility of the Department of Natural Resources. The Motor Vehicle Office, Fire Protection Office, Emergency Preparedness Office, and Alcoholic Beverage Control Office are all within the Department of Public Safety.

Health and welfare services are administered mainly through the Department of Health and Hospitals (DHH), which provides welfare services under the Office of Family Security, services for the blind and vocational rehabilitation through the Department of Social Services Office of Rehabilitation Services, and special training for the mentally handicapped under the Office for Citizens with Developmental Disabilities/DHH. The Head Start program for preschool age children is administered by the Department of Education. Such programs as supplemental food and summer youth recreation are administered by the Department of Social Services, which also helps develop and administer housing and urban renewal programs.

16 JUDICIAL SYSTEM

Louisiana's legal system is the only one in the US to be based on civil or Roman law, specifically the Code Napoléon of France. Under Louisiana state law, cases may be decided by judicial interpretation of the statutes, without reference to prior court cases, whereas in other states and in the federal courts the common law prevails, and decisions are generally based on previous judicial interpretations and findings. In actual practice, Louisiana laws no longer differ radically from US common law, and most Louisiana lawyers and judges now cite previous cases in their arguments and rulings.

The highest court in Louisiana is the supreme court, with appellate jurisdiction. It consists of a chief justice who is chosen by seniority of service, and 7 associate justices, all of them elected from 6 supreme court districts (the first district has 2 judges) for staggered 10-year terms. There are 5 appellate circuits in the state, each divided into 3 districts; the 5 circuits are served by 54 judges, all of them elected for overlapping 10-year terms. Each of the state's district courts serves at least 1 parish and has at least 1 district judge, elected for a 6-year term; there are 222 district judges. District courts have original jurisdiction in criminal and civil cases. City courts are the principal courts of limited jurisdiction.

Louisiana may have been the first state to institute a system of leasing convict labor; large numbers of convicts were leased, especially after the Civil War, until the practice was discontinued in the early 1900s. The abuses entailed in this system may be suggested by the fact that, of 700 convicts leased in 1882, 149 died in service. As of June 2001, 35,494 prisoners were in Louisiana's state and federal prisons, an increase of 2.2% over the previous year. The state's incarceration rate stood at 795 per 100,000 inhabitants.

According to the FBI in 2001, Louisiana had a crime index total of 5,338.1 per 100,000, including a total of 30,678 violent crimes and 207,693 crimes against property in that year. Louisiana has a death penalty law; 27 people were executed between 1977 and 2003, and 96 were under sentence of death in 2003. Judges may impose sentences of hard labor.

17 ARMED FORCES

In 2002, there were 16,541 active-duty military personnel stationed in Louisiana. There was one major army installation in the state, Ft. Polk at Leesville; an Air Force base at Barksdale near Bossier City; and a naval air station and support station in the vicinity of New Orleans. During fiscal year 2001, Louisiana firms received defense contracts totaling $1.4 billion.

There were 392,486 veterans of US military service in Louisiana as of 2000, of whom 71,894 served in World War II; 43,980 in the Korean conflict; 114,470 during the Vietnam era; and 53,843 during 1990–2000 (including the Persian Gulf War). Veterans' benefits during fiscal year 2002 amounted to $860 million.

In 2000, the Louisiana State Police employed 934 full-time sworn officers.

18 MIGRATION

Louisiana was settled by an unusually diverse assortment of immigrants. The Company of the Indies, which administered Louisiana from 1717 until 1731, at first began importing French convicts, vagrants, and prostitutes because of the difficulty of finding willing colonists. Next the company turned to struggling farmers in Germany and Switzerland, who proved to be more suitable and productive settlers. The importation of slaves from Africa and the West Indies began early in the 18th century.

Attracted by generous land grants, perhaps 10,000 Acadians, or Cajuns—people of French descent who had been exiled from Nova Scotia (Acadia) during the 1740s—migrated to Louisiana after the French and Indian War. They settled in the area of Lafayette and Breaux Bridge and along Bayou Lafourche and the Mississippi River. Probably the second-largest group to migrate in the late 18th century came from the British colonies and, after the Revolution, from the US. Between 1800 and 1870, Americans settled the area north of the Red River. Small groups of Canary Islanders and Spaniards from Malaga also settled in the south, and in 1791, a number of French people fled to Louisiana during the slave insurrection on Hispaniola.

During the 1840s and 1850s, masses of Irish and German immigrants came to New Orleans. In the late 1880s, a large number of Midwestern farmers migrated to the prairies of southwestern Louisiana to become rice farmers. Louisiana did not immediately begin losing much of its black population after the Civil War. In fact, the number of blacks who migrated to Louisiana from the poorer southeastern states during the postwar years may have equaled the number of blacks who migrated before the war or were brought into the state as slaves. In 1879, however, "Kansas fever" struck blacks from the cotton country of Louisiana and Mississippi, and many of them migrated to the Wheat State; however, many later returned to their home states.

Beginning in World War II, large numbers of both black and white farm workers left Louisiana and migrated north and west. During the 1960s, the state had a net out-migration of 15% of its black population, but the trend had slowed somewhat by 1975.

Recent migration within the state has been from north to south, and from rural to urban areas, especially to Shreveport, Baton Rouge, and the suburbs of New Orleans. From 1980 to 1990, however, the state's urban population fell from 68.6% to 68.1% Overall, Louisiana suffered a net loss from migration of about 368,000 from 1940 to 1990. Between 1990 and 1998, the state had a net loss of 117,000 in domestic migration and a net gain of 25,000 in international migration. In 1998, 2,193 foreign immigrants arrived in Louisiana. Between 1990 and 1998, the state's overall population increased 3.5%. In the period 1995–2000, 253,520 people moved into the state and 329,279 moved out, for a net loss of 75,759, many of whom moved to Texas.

[19]INTERGOVERNMENTAL COOPERATION

Among the interstate and regional efforts in which Louisiana participates are the Central Interstate Low-Level Radioactive Waste Compact, Interstate Oil and Gas Compact, Interstate Compact for Juveniles, Gulf States Marine Fisheries Commission, Red River Compact, Sabine River Compact, Tangipahoa River Waterway Compact, South Central Interstate Forest Fire Protection Compact, Southern Growth Policies Board, Southern Dairy Compact, Southern Rapid Rail Transit Compact, Southern States Energy Board, and Southern Regional Education Board. Federal grants to Louisiana during fiscal year 2001 amounted to over $6.1 billion.

[20]ECONOMY

Before the Civil War, when Louisiana was one of the most prosperous of southern states, its economy depended primarily on two then-profitable crops—cotton and sugar—and on its position as the anchor of the nation's principal north–south trade route. But the upheaval and destruction wrought by the war, combined with severe flood damage to cotton crops, falling cotton prices, and the removal of the federal bounty on sugar, left the economy stagnant through the end of the 19th century, although New Orleans retained its commercial importance as an exporter of cotton and grain.

With the addition of two major crops, rice and soybeans, the rebirth of the timber industry as a result of reforestation, the demand for pine for paper pulp, and most dramatically, the rise of the petrochemical industry, Louisiana's economy has regained much of its former vitality. Today, Louisiana ranks 2nd only to Texas in the value of its mineral products. As of 1997, the value of mineral production (including fossil fuels) was $27 billion, accounting for about 18% of the value of mineral production in the US.

Louisiana is primarily an industrial state, but its industries are to a large degree based on its natural resources, principally oil, natural gas, water, and timber. A booming oil industry fueled an expansion in the Louisiana economy during the 1970s. That expansion ended in the early 1980s, when the price of oil dropped from $37 a barrel in 1981 to $15 a barrel in 1986. Employment in oil and gas extraction dropped from 100,000 to 55,000. Energy-related industries such as barge building, machinery manufacturing, and rig/platform production also suffered. At the same time that oil prices dropped, natural gas prices rose, forcing a contraction in the chemical industry which uses large quantities of natural gas. Chemicals were also hurt by a leap in the exchange value of the dollar in the mid-1980s, as Louisiana exports 25% of its chemical production. A subsequent drop in the dollar's exchange value in the late 1980s and early 1990s enabled the chemical industry not only to rebound but to expand. A higher dollar in the late 1990s once again reversed the chemical industry's growth. In an attempt to offset losses in employment, Louisiana built several riverboat casinos and a land-based casino in 1995 which added about 7,000 jobs. Falling oil prices helped produce a mild recession in 1998 (-0.8% fall in Louisiana's gross state product), but their recovery helped produce robust growth rates of 9.3% and 16.7%. Growth fell abruptly to 2.6% in the national recession and slowdown of 2001. The oil and gas extraction sector, however, continued to grow in both absolute and relative terms. From the trough of $13.3 billion in 1998, when oil and gas output amounted to only 10.9% of gross state product, annual oil and gas output rose 109.3% to nearly $28 billion by 2001, accounting for 18.8% of gross state product. Growth in output from both financial services and general services was about 22% in the period 1997 to 2001, and growth in government output was just under 20% for this period. Output from manufacturing, by contrast, decreased 16.2% 1997 to 2001, falling from 16.8% of gross state product to 11.7%. During the national recession in 2001, employment gains continued in health services, lodging establishments, state services, and in the transportation and public utilities sector. Louisiana's employment levels slowed during the second half of 2002, the largest employment declines occurring in manufacturing, construction, transportation and public utilities, and in financial services.

Louisiana's gross state product in 2001 was 24th largest among the states at $148.7 billion, to which mining contributed $28.1 billion (99.3% from oil and gas extraction); general services, $25.0 billion; trade, $20.4 billion; financial services, $19.6 billion; both government and manufacturing, $17.4 billion; transportation and public utilities, $12.9 billion; and construction $6.5 billion. The public sector constituted 11.8% of gross state product in 2001.

[21]INCOME

According to the Bureau of Economic Analysis, in 2001, Louisiana had a per capita personal income (PCPI) of $24,454 which ranked 45th in the United States (including the District of Columbia) and was 80% of the national average, $30,413. The 2001 PCPI reflected an increase of 5.5% from 2000 compared to the national change of 2.2%. In 2001, Louisiana had a total personal income (TPI) of $109,317,405,000 which ranked 25th in the United States and accounted for 1.3% of the national total. The 2001 TPI reflected an increase of 5.5% from 2000 compared to the national change of 3.3%.

Earnings of persons employed in Louisiana increased from $71,550,764,000 in 2000 to $74,526,989,000 in 2001, an increase of 4.2%. The largest industries in 2001 were services, 27.2% of earnings; state and local government, 14.6%; and retail trade, 9.1%. Of the industries that accounted for at least 5% of earnings in 2001, the slowest growing from 2000 to 2001 was construction (7.2% of earnings in 2001), which decreased 1.2%; the fastest was mining (5.0% of earnings in 2001), which increased 13.2%.

According to data released by the US Census Bureau, in 2000, the median household income was $30,219 compared to the national average of $42,148. In 2001, the median income for a family of four was $51,234 compared to the national average of $63,278. For the period 1999 to 2001, the average poverty rate was 17.5% which placed it 50th among the 50 states and the District of Columbia ranked lowest to highest.

[22]LABOR

According to Bureau of Labor Statistics (BLS) provisional estimates, in July 2003 the seasonally adjusted civilian labor force in Louisiana numbered 2,041,200, with approximately 150,700 workers unemployed, yielding an unemployment rate of 7.4%, compared to the national average of 6.2% for the same period. Since the beginning of the BLS data series in 1978, the highest unemployment rate recorded was 13.6% in September 1986. The historical low was 4.7% in December 1999. It is estimated that in 2001, 6.8% of the labor force was employed in construction; 8.6% in manufacturing; 6.1% in transportation, communications, and public utilities; 20.2% in trade; 4.9% in finance, insurance, and real estate; 24.9% in services; 16.9% in government; and 1.8% in agriculture.

During the antebellum period, Louisiana had both the largest slave market in the US—New Orleans—and the largest slave revolt in the nation's history, in St. Charles and St. John the Baptist parishes in January 1811. New Orleans also had a relatively large free black population, and many of the slaves in the city were skilled workers, some of whom were able to earn their freedom by outside employment. Major efforts to organize Louisiana workers began after the Civil War. There were strikes in the cane fields in the early 1880s, and in the mid-1880s, the Knights of Labor began to organize the cane workers. The strike they called in 1886 was ended by hired strikebreakers, who killed at least 30 blacks. Back in New Orleans, the Knights of Labor led a general strike in 1892. The Brotherhood of Timber Workers began organizing in 1910 but had little to show for their efforts except the scars of violent conflict with the lumber-mill owners.

A right-to-work law was passed in 1976, partly as a result of violent conflict between an AFL-CIO building trades union and an independent union over whose workers would build a petrochemical plant near Lake Charles. In 1979, a police strike began in New Orleans on the eve of Mardi Gras, causing the cancellation of most of the parades, but it collapsed the following month.

The US Department of Labor reported that in 2002, 134,000 of Louisiana's 1,649,000 employed wage and salary workers were members of unions. This represented 8.1% of those so employed, up from 7.6% in 2001 but down from 10% in 1998. The national average is 13.2%. In all, 170,000 workers (10.3%) were represented by unions. In addition to union members, this category includes workers who report no union affiliation but whose jobs are covered by a union contract. Louisiana is one of 22 states with a right-to-work law.

23 AGRICULTURE

With a farm income of $1.82 billion in 2001—61% from crops—Louisiana ranked 33rd among the 50 states. Nearly every crop grown in North America can be raised somewhere in Louisiana. In the south are strawberries, oranges, sweet potatoes, and truck crops; in the southeast, sugarcane; and in the southwest, rice and soybeans. Soybeans—which were introduced into Louisiana after World War I—are also raised in the cotton-growing area of the northeast and in a diagonal belt running east-northwest along the Red River. Oats, alfalfa, corn, potatoes, and peaches are among the other crops grown in the north.

As of 2002, there were an estimated 29,000 farms covering 8.1 million acres (3.3 million hectares) with an average farm size of 290 acres (117 hectares). Louisiana ranked 2nd in the US in sugar cane production. Cash receipts for the sugar crop in 2001 amounted to $368,900,000 for 14,355,000 tons. Louisiana ranked 3rd in the value of its rice production in 2002, $114,660,000 for 29,400,000 hundredweight (a unit of measure equal to 100 lb); and 7th for upland cotton in 2002, $147,960,000 for 750,000 bales.

24 ANIMAL HUSBANDRY

In the mid-19th century, before rice production began there, southwestern Louisiana was a major cattle-raising area. Today, cattle are raised mainly in the southeast (between the Mississippi and Pearl rivers), in the north-central region, and in the west.

In 2003, there were an estimated 860,000 cattle and calves worth $550 million. In 2002, Louisiana had an estimated 20,000 hogs and pigs worth around $1.5 million. Dairy farmers had an estimated 54,000 milk cows, which produced 632 million lb (286.7 million kg) of milk in 2001. Also during 2001, poultry farmers produced an estimated 7.5 million lb (3.4 million kg) of chicken, which sold for $447,000, and an estimated 480 million eggs worth around $31.7 million.

25 FISHING

In 1998, Louisiana was 2nd behind only Alaska in the size of its commercial landings, with more than 1.1 billion lb, and ranked 2nd by value of catch at $291.9 million. Empire-Venice was 3rd highest of all US ports in 1998 with a catch of 328 million lb. The ports of Cameron and Intercoastal City ranked 6th and 7th respectively, together accounting for another 464.1 million lb. The most important species caught in Louisiana are shrimp, menhaden, and oysters. In 1998, shrimp landings amounted to 96,200,000 lb, 34.6% of the US total.

Louisiana produces most of the US crawfish harvest. With demand far exceeding the natural supply, crawfish farming began about 1959. In 1998, nearly 500 crawfish farms covered some 100,000 acres (40,500 hectares), with sales of $9.1 million. Spring water levels of the state's Atchafalaya Basin cause the wild crawfish harvest to vary from year to year. The rapid increase in imports of low-priced frozen crawfish meat from China between 1992 and 1995 greatly concerned the Louisiana crawfish industry. Catfish are also cultivated in Louisiana, on 98 farms covering some 13,728 acres (6,221 hectares) in January 1999, with a 2000 inventory of about 36.6 million fingerlings and 32.4 million stocker-sized catfish. Cash receipts from aquacultural sales were $53.2 million in 1998.

Louisiana had 627,204 sport fishing license holders in 1998. More than 37,000 lb of shellfish were distributed within the state for restoration or conservation purposes in 1998.

26 FORESTRY

As of 2002, there were 13,812,000 acres (5,590,000 hectares) of forestland in Louisiana, representing almost half the state's land area and 2% of all US forests. The principal forest types are loblolly and shortleaf pine in the northwest, longleaf and slash pine in the south, and hardwood in a wide area along the Mississippi River. More than 99% of Louisiana's forests—some 13,722,000 acres (5,553,000 hectares) in 2002—are commercial timberland, over 90% of it privately owned. Lumber production totaled 1.3 billion board feet in 2002.

Louisiana has one national forest, Kisatchie, with a gross area of 1,022,373 acres (413,754 hectares) within its boundaries; gross acreage of National Forest System lands in the state was 2,210,000 acres (894,400 hectares) in 2001. Near the boundaries of Kisatchie's Evangeline Unit is the Alexander State Forest, established in 1923.

27 MINING

The US Geological Survey's 2001 estimate of Louisiana's nonfuel mineral value totaled $274 million, 16% below the figure reported by the state's mineral producers in 2000, and much less than the record $584 million produced in 1980. The leading mineral commodity, accounting for roughly half of all nonfuel mineral production in 2001, was salt (14.5 million metric tons, valued at $142 million). Louisiana is the leading state in salt and sulfur production. Salt brine is produced in Ascension, Assumption, Calcasieu, Iberville, and Lafourche parishes. Rock salt is produced in Iberia and St. Mary parishes. Production of construction sand and gravel in 2001 was an estimated 17.4 million metric tons, valued at $91.3 million.

As of 2001, sulfur production was no longer included in the figures for nonfuel mineral production. All sulfur production came from a mine 17 mi (28 km) off the Louisiana coast that was closed in August 2000. The closure of the sulfur mine plus a $69 million drop in the value of salt accounted for nearly all of the overall decline in nonfuel mineral production for the year. The state's national ranking in mineral value decreased two positions to 37th in 2001.

28 ENERGY AND POWER

In 2000 Louisiana's total per capita energy consumption was 887 million Btu (223.5 million kcal), ranking it 2nd among the 50 states.

In 1999, power plants in Louisiana had a total installed capacity (utility and nonutility) of 20.2million kW. In the same year, total electrical generation was 90.1 billion kWh. As of 2001, Louisiana had two nuclear power plants: Waterford 3 in St. Charles Parish (capacity, 1,091,000 kW), which received a low-power operating license on 18 December 1984, and River Bend I in West Feliciana Parish (980,000 kW), which began commercial operation in December 1985.

Oil and gas production has expanded greatly since World War II, but production reached its peak in the early 1970s and proved reserves are declining. Louisiana produced 256,000 barrels per day of crude oil during 2002, the 4th-highest total among the 50 states and about 5% of the US total. At the end of 2001, remaining proven reserves of oil in Louisiana amounted to 564 million barrels, 3% of the US total and 5th among the 50 states.

Marketed production of natural gas in 2001 was 1,537 billion cu ft (43.5 billion cu m), leaving proven reserves of 9.81 trillion cu ft (0.28 trillion cu m). There were 16,350 producing gas wells in 2001, down from 18,399 in 1998. Energy conservation plans in Louisiana call for development of untapped energy sources, such as the state's lignite and geothermal reserves.

29 INDUSTRY

The Standard Oil Refinery (now owned by Exxon) that is today the largest in North America began operations in Louisiana in 1909, the same year construction started on the state's first long-distance oil pipeline. Since then, a huge and still-growing petrochemical industry has become a dominant force in the state's economy. Other expanding industries are wood products and, especially since World War II, shipbuilding.

In 1997, the total value of shipments of manufactured goods was $81 billion. The principal industrial regions extend along the Mississippi River from north of Baton Rouge to New Orleans, and also include the Monroe, Shreveport, Morgan City, and Lake Charles areas.

Earnings of persons employed in Louisiana increased from $64 billion in 1997 to $67.7 billion in 1998, an increase of 5.8%. The largest industries in 1998 were services, 27.2% of earnings; state and local government, 13.1%; and retail trade, 9.4%. Of the industries that accounted for at least 5% of earnings in 1998, the slowest growing from 1997 to 1998 was nondurable goods manufacturing (8.1% of earnings in 1998), which increased 2.7%; the fastest was mining (5.2% of earnings in 1998), which increased 15.1%.

30 COMMERCE

Louisiana had 7,497 wholesale establishments in 1997, with sales of $49 billion. Retail trade amounted to $37 billion in 1997, conducted by 23,558 establishments. The leading number of retail establishments were food stores, with 15% of total stores; automotive dealers, 14%; and eating and drinking places, 26%. Food sales came to $7.3 billion in 1997, and general merchandise sales came to approximately $6 billion. Total exports amounted to $17 billion in 1998, with Louisiana ranking 9th in the nation in terms of export sales value.

31 CONSUMER PROTECTION

The Consumer Protection Section, Department of Justice, investigates and mediates consumer complaints, takes action against companies allegedly engaging in unfair business practices,

distributes consumer publications, and registers multi-level marketing, telemarketing, and charitable organizations. It does not handle the areas of insurance, banking, or utilities.

32 BANKING

As of September 2002, Louisiana had 174 insured banks with assets totaling $48 billion.

Louisiana state-chartered banks are regulated by the Office of Financial Institutions under the Department of Economic Development. Nationally chartered banks are regulated by the Office of the Comptroller of the Currency.

A favorable interest rate climate in 2002 improved earnings for Louisiana's insured institutions. Nonetheless, the narrowing of the spread between short-term and long-term interest rates at the end of 2002 was projected to have detrimental effects on the net interest margin (NIM) (the difference between the lower rates offered to savers and the higher rates charged on loans), causing earning asset yields to decline.

33 INSURANCE

In 2001 there were 4.7 million ordinary life insurance policies in force with a total value of $145.9 billion; total value for all categories of life insurance (ordinary, group, industrial, and credit) was $186.5 billion. Death benefits paid that year totaled $223.1 million.

There were 65 life and health and 35 property and casualty insurance companies domiciled in the state at the end of 2000. In 2001, property and casualty insurers wrote premiums totaling $5.6 billion. That year, there were 363,469 flood insurance policies in force in the state, with a total value of $43.2 million.

The Department of Insurance administers Louisiana's laws governing the industry.

34 SECURITIES

There are no securities or commodities exchanges in Louisiana. Louisiana has 592 brokers agencies, with 3,418 employees; and 80 investment advisory organizations. Louisiana is home to the headquarters of 26 NASDAQ companies, two NASDAQ market makers, and six Louisiana-incorporated NYSE-listed companies: Hibernia Corp., Murphy Oil Corp., Piccadilly Cafeterias, Inc., Ruby Tuesday, Inc., Shaw Group, Inc., and Southdown Inc.

35 PUBLIC FINANCE

The budget is prepared by the state executive budget director and submitted annually by the governor to the legislature for amendment and approval. The fiscal year runs from 1 July through 30 June.

The governor of Louisiana declared that declining revenues in 2000 would result in a fiscal deficit for the following year unless budget cuts were implemented. These pessimistic forecasts, and corresponding adjustments in expenditures, left the Louisiana state budget in better shape than those of most states after the recession of 2001. Actual revenues in 2000/01 were $6.53 billion, and these declined to $6.48 billion in 2001/02, and were still down, at $6.5 billion, in 2002/03, but these were above official forecasts. Only in 2003, were extra steps taken—drawings on the state's rainy day fund, and $18 million in cuts after the budget was enacted, mainly through targeted executive orders—to close a budget gap. Expenditures from the general fund totaled $6.636 billion in 2002/03, of which 53.5% was targeted for education, 20.6% for human resources, 15.25% for general government, 6.9% for public safety, and 3.35% for other functions including economic development, the infrastructure, and the environment and natural resources.

The following table from the US Census Bureau contains information on revenues, expenditures, indebtedness, and cash/securities for 2001.

	($000)	PERCENT	PER CAPITA
Population (thousands, 2001)	4,470	(X)	(X)
Total Revenue	17,811,457	100.00	3,984.67
General revenue	16,810,432	94.38	3,760.72
Utility revenue	3,462	0.02	0.77
Liquor store revenue	–	–	–
Insurance trust revenue	997,563	5.60	223.17
Exhibit: Salaries and wages	3,784,170	23.06	846.57
Total expenditure	16,410,263	100.00	3,671.20
General expenditure	14,470,179	88.18	3,237.18
Education	5,516,218	33.61	1,234.05
Public welfare	2,801,250	17.07	626.68
Hospitals	1,341,034	8.17	300.01
Health	471,732	2.87	105.53
Highways	925,891	5.64	207.13
Police protection	240,529	1.47	53.81
Correction	581,057	3.54	129.99
Natural resources	353,123	2.15	79.00
Parks and recreation	224,202	1.37	50.16
Government administration	464,339	2.83	103.88
Interest on general debt	454,790	2.77	101.74
Other and unallocable	1,096,014	6.68	245.19
Utility expenditure	3,964	0.02	0.89
Liquor store expenditure	–	–	–
Insurance trust expenditure	1,936,120	11.80	433.14
Debt at end of fiscal year	7,977,398	100.00	1,784.65
Cash and security holdings	36,099,591	100.00	8,075.97

36TAXATION

For most of the state's history, Louisianans paid little in taxes. Despite increases in taxation and expenditures since the late 1920s, when Huey Long introduced the graduated income tax, Louisiana's state tax burden per capita was typically well below the national average. In 2003, however, Louisiana ranked closer to the middle, at 28th in terms combined state and local taxes as a percent of income, which was at 9.5%.

Louisiana's individual income tax has three brackets ranging from 2% to 6%. The corporate income tax has five brackets ranging from 4% on the first $25,000 up to 8% on net income over $200,000. Federal taxes paid are deductible from state liabilities for both individual and corporate income taxes. The state's sales and use tax is levied at 4%. Effective 1 January 2003 (and due to a voter-approved constitutional amendment) the sales tax on food for home consumption, electricity, natural gas and water was reduced to 2%, and then eliminated altogether as of 1 July 2003. Prescription drugs are also exempted from the state sales tax. Parishes and municipalities may impose additional sales taxes up to combined rates of 6.7%, though some localities impose not additional sales taxes. The state imposes a full range of selective sales taxes including excises on motor fuels, tobacco products, soft drinks, alcoholic beverages, amusements, pari-mutuels, public utilities, insurance premiums, and other selected items. The cigarette tax was raised from 24 cents a pack to 36 cents a pack in 2002. Louisiana has natural resources severance taxes whose rates vary according to the resource. There is also an oil field site restoration fee. Louisiana's estate tax is tied to the federal tax credit for state death taxes, and is therefore slated to be phased out in tandem with the federal estate tax credit by 2007 absent any positive action by the Louisiana government to preserve it. Louisiana's revenue losses from the phasing out of its estate tax are estimated at $5.4 million in 2003, $11.5 million in 2004, and $24 million in 2007. Louisiana inheritance tax was scheduled to be abolished as of 1 July 2003. In 2002, 0.9% of state tax revenues came from gift and death taxes. Other state taxes include various license fees. The Louisiana Stadium and Exposition District, and the New Orleans Exhibition Hall Authority impose a tax on hotel and motel room occupancy in the greater New Orleans area. In addition, local taxing authorities may impose a tax on hotel and motel room occupancy. Taxes on beer and chain stores contribute to local revenues, as does the property tax. In 2002, 41.6% of non-federal tax revenue was collected locally.

Total state tax collections in Louisiana in 2002 came to $7.346 billion, of which 31.7% was generated by the state general sales and use tax, 25.4% by state excise taxes, 24.2% by the state income tax, 7% by state license fees, 6.7% by state severance taxes, and 3.6% by the state corporate income tax.

The following table from the US Census Bureau provides a summary of taxes collected by the state in 2002.

	($000)	PER CAPITA
Total Taxes	**7,345,994**	**1,638.76**
Property taxes	33,079	7.38
Sales and gross receipts	4,191,609	935.07
General sales and gross receipts	2,326,873	519.08
Selective sales taxes	1,864,736	415.99
Alcoholic beverage	51,360	11.46
Amusements	497,022	110.88
Insurance Premiums	287,750	64.19
Motor fuels	558,892	124.68
Pari-mutuels	6,100	1.36
Public utilities	7,549	1.68
Tobacco products	128,521	28.67
Other selective sales	327,542	73.07
Licenses	514,724	114.83
Alcoholic beverages	(X)	(X)
Amusements	(X)	(X)
Corporation	264,684	59.05
Hunting and fishing	32,925	7.34
Motor vehicle	114,461	25.53
Motor vehicle operators	10,752	2.4
Public utility	2,819	0.63
Occupation and business, NEC	85,798	19.14
Other	3,285	0.73
Other taxes	2,606,582	581.48
Individual income	1,779,506	396.98
Corporation net income	264,419	58.99
Death and gift	68,995	15.39
Documentary and stock transfer	(X)	(X)
Severance	493,662	110.13
Other	(X)	(X)

37ECONOMIC POLICY

The Office of Commerce and Industry in the Department of Economic Development seeks to encourage investment and create jobs in the state and to expand the markets for Louisiana products. Financial assistance services for industrial development include state and local tax incentives and state "Enterprise Zone" legislation. The Louisiana Small Business Equity Corporation and the Louisiana Minority Business Development Authority offer financial assistance. Since 1999, the Louisiana Economic Development Council has been preparing annual reports and action plans with a view to the implementation of the state's Master Plan for Economic Development dubbed Vision 2020. The three main goals of Vision 2020 are to, by 2020, recreate Louisiana as a place where all citizens are engaged in the pursuit of knowledge; create an economy driven by technology-intensive industries, and rank among the top 10 states in standard of living indicators. Successes in 2002 were reported in providing economic development incentives, and developing infrastructure for biosciences, information technology, research and development and education.

38HEALTH

Louisiana's infant mortality rate in 2000 was 9.2 per 1,000 live births, considerably higher than the national rate of 6.9. Major causes of infant deaths include birth trauma, disorders relating to abnormal gestation, intrauterine hypoxia, and birth asphyxia. Other leading causes of infant death were congenital anomalies and pneumonia. In 1999, 12,008 legal abortions were performed in Louisiana, averaging 12 per 1,000 women.

Like the infant mortality rate, the overall death rate, 940.3 per 100,000 population, was significantly higher than the national rate of 873.1. Death rates from heart disease (265.8 per 100,000), malignant neoplasms (214.9 per 100,000), accidents and adverse effects (45.9 per 100,000), and motor vehicle accidents (23.2 per 100,000) for the entire population of Louisiana were also above national rates. Of the population age 18 and older, 24.1% were classified as smokers in 2000. The rate of HIV-related deaths stood at 8.8 per 100,000 population, below the national average of 5.3 in 2000. There were 13,475 AIDS cases reported through 2001.

Louisiana's 125 community hospitals had 682,586 admissions and 17,975 beds in 2001. There were 17,584 full-time registered nurses and 3,730 full-time licensed practical nurses in 2001 and 268 physicians per 100,000 population in 2000. The average expense of a community hospital for care was $1,395.60 per inpatient day in 2001.

Federal government grants to cover the Medicare and Medicaid services in 2001 totaled $3.0 billion; 605,395 enrollees received Medicare benefits that year. At least 19.3% of the population was uninsured in 2002.

39 SOCIAL WELFARE

During the governorships of Huey and Earl Long, Louisiana developed a relatively progressive welfare system. In 2001, the average weekly unemployment benefit was $192.39. Average monthly participation in the food stamp program in FY2002 comprised 588,458 persons (224,450 households). The average monthly benefit was $83.14, and the sum total of benefits paid in FY2002 was $587,074,354.

With the enactment of the Personal Responsibility and Work Opportunity Reconciliation Act of 1996, the US government has changed the form and regulations for many of its social welfare programs. Most significantly, it replaces Aid to Families with Dependent Children (AFDC), an open-ended entitlement program, with Temporary Assistance for Needy Families (TANF), a limited system of assistance funded largely through federal block grants. The reform act also impacts the food stamp program, the Supplemental Security Income program, and the child nutrition program. The law took effect on 1 July 1997 and provided $16.38 billion in block grants for fiscal years 1997–2002. The grants are to be divided among the states based on an equation involving the numbers of former AFDC recipients in each state.

Reauthorization of the 1996 social welfare legislation, scheduled for 2002, was delayed, and the original law had been extended three times as of July 2003, with the most recent extension running through September 2003. Louisiana's TANF cash assistance program is called the Family Independent Temporary Assistance Program (FITAP), and the work program is called FIND Work (Family Independence Work Program). In June 2000 the state had 79,745 welfare recipients. State expenditures on the TANF program in FY2002 totaled $39,659,847.

In December 2001, Social Security benefits were paid to 716,220 Louisiana residents. This number included 365,420 retired workers, 108,590 widows and widowers, 92,530 disabled workers, 61,410 spouses, and 88,270 children. Social Security beneficiaries represented 16% of the total state population and 90.6% of the state's population age 65 and older. Retired workers (excluding persons with special benefits) received an average monthly payment of $810; widows and widowers, $753; disabled workers, $816; and spouses, $401. Payments for children of retired workers averaged $369 per month; children of deceased workers, $520; and children of disabled workers, $226.

Federal Supplemental Security Income payments in December 2001 went to 166,181 Louisiana residents, averaging $360 a month.

40 HOUSING

The Indians of Louisiana built huts with walls made of clay kneaded with Spanish moss and covered with cypress bark or palmetto leaves. The earliest European settlers used split cypress boards filled with clay and moss; a few early 18th-century houses with clay and moss walls remain in the Natchitoches area. Examples of later architectural styles also survive, including buildings constructed of bricks between heavy cypress posts, covered with plaster; houses in the raised cottage style, supported by brick piers and usually including a wide gallery and colonettes; the Creole dwellings of the Vieux Carre in New Orleans, built of brick and characterized by balconies and French windows; and urban and plantation houses from the Greek Revival period of antebellum Louisiana.

In 2002, Louisiana had 1,880,122 housing units, of which 1,664,877 were occupied. About 70.8% were owner-occupied. An estimated 63.8% of all units were single-family, detached homes. Nearly 41% of all housing units were built between 1970 and 1989. Most units relied on utility gas or electricity for heating. It was estimated that 76,124 units lacked telephone service, 5,134 lacked complete plumbing facilities, and 4,691 lacked complete kitchen facilities. The average household size was 2.61 people.

In 2002, 18,425 privately owned units were authorized for construction. The median home value was $94,786. The median monthly most for mortgage owners was $879. Renters paid a median of $495 per month. During fiscal year 2002, Louisiana received over $125.9 million in community planning and development aid from the US Department of Housing and Urban Development.

41 EDUCATION

Most education in Louisiana was provided through private (often parochial) schools until Reconstruction. Not until Huey Long's administration, when spending for education increased greatly and free textbooks were supplied, did education become a high priority of the state. As of 2000, still only 74.8% of adult Louisianians had completed high school, and 18.7% had completed four or more years of college.

Integration of New Orleans public schools began in 1960; two years later, the archbishop of New Orleans required that all Catholic schools under his jurisdiction be desegregated. However, it took a federal court order in 1966 to bring about integration in public schools throughout the state. By 1980, 36% of minority students in Louisiana were in schools with less than 50% minority enrollment, and 25% were in schools with 99–100% minority enrollment.

The total enrollment for fall 1999 in Louisiana's public schools stood at 756,579. Of these, 548,019 attended schools from kindergarten through grade eight, and 208,560 attended high school. Minority students made up approximately 50% of the total enrollment in public elementary and secondary schools. Total enrollment was estimated at 743,089 in fall 2000 but was expected to drop to 757,000 by fall 2005. For the 1999/2000 school year, expenditure per pupil was estimated at $5,441. Expenditures for public education in 2000/01 were estimated at $4,445,592. Enrollment in nonpublic schools in fall 2001 was 138,135.

As of fall 2000, there were 258,000 students enrolled in college or graduate school. In the same year Louisiana had 85 degree-granting institutions. In 1997, minority students comprised 33.1% of total postsecondary enrollment. In addition to 53 vocational-technical schools, there are 34 institutions of higher education in Louisiana, of which 22 are public and 12 private. The center of the state university system is Louisiana State University (LSU), founded at Baton Rouge; LSU also has campuses at Alexandria, Eunice, and Shreveport, and includes the University of New Orleans. Tulane University, founded in New Orleans in 1834, is one of the most distinguished private universities in the South, as is Loyola University, also in New Orleans. Southern University Agricultural and Mechanical System at Baton Rouge (1881) is one of the largest predominantly black universities in the country; other campuses are in New Orleans and Shreveport. Another mainly black institution is Grambling State University (1901).

The Governor's Special Commission on Education Services administers state loan, grant, and scholarship programs. The state Council for the Development of French in Louisiana (CODOFIL) organizes student exchanges with Quebec, Belgium, and France and aids Louisianians studying French abroad.

42ARTS

New Orleans has long been one of the most important centers of artistic activity in the South. The earliest theaters were French, and the first of these was started by refugees from Hispaniola, who put on the city's first professional theatrical performance in 1791. The American Theater, which opened in 1824, attracted many of the finest actors in America, as did the nationally famous St. Charles. Showboats traveled the Mississippi and other waterways, bringing dramas, musicals, and minstrel shows to river towns and plantations as early as the 1840s, with their heyday being the 1870s and 1880s.

Principal theaters included the New Orleans Theater of the Performing Arts, the Saenger Theater in New Orleans (one of the "grand old theaters"), Le Petit Theatre du Vieux Carre, and the Tulane Theater. Junebug Productions is a black touring company based in New Orleans. Louisiana State University (LSU) at Baton Rouge has theaters for both opera and drama. Baton Rouge, Shreveport, Monroe, Lake Charles, and Hammond are among the cities with little theaters, and Baton Rouge, Lafayette, and Lake Charles have ballet companies. There are symphony orchestras in most of the larger cities, the Louisiana Philharmonic Orchestra being the best known.

It is probably in music that Louisiana has made its most distinctive contributions to culture. Jazz was born in New Orleans around 1900; among its sources was the music played by brass bands at carnivals and at Negro funerals, and its immediate precursor was the highly syncopated music known as ragtime. Early jazz in the New Orleans style is called Dixieland; Louis Armstrong pioneered the transformation of jazz from the Dixieland ensemble style to a medium for solo improvisation. Traditional Dixieland may still be heard in New Orleans at Preservation Hall, Dixieland Hall, and the New Orleans Jazz Club. Equally distinctive is Cajun music, dominated by the sound of the fiddle and accordion. The French Acadian Music Festival, held in Abbeville, takes place in April.

Visual arts in the state continue to flourish, especially in New Orleans, where the New Orleans Museum of Southern Art opened in 1998.

The Louisiana Division of the Arts (LDOA; est. 1977), the largest arts grantmaker in the state, is an agency of the state Office of Cultural Development, Department of Culture, Recreation and Tourism. Arts projects are funded in every parish (county) in the state through the LDOA Decentralized Arts Funding Program. In 2003, Louisiana arts organizations received grants totaling $1,073,000 from the National Endowment for the Arts.

The Louisiana Endowment for the Humanities was established in 1971. Ongoing programs include Relic: Readings in Literature and Culture and Prime Time Family Reading Time, an annual program presented through local libraries. In 2000, the National Endowment for the Humanities awarded 13 grants totaling $927,518 to state organizations.

43LIBRARIES AND MUSEUMS

Louisiana's 64 parishes were served by 65,000 public libraries in 2000. That year, the public library system held 10,608,000 volumes and had a total circulation of 17,791,000. The New Orleans Public Library, with 14 branches and 739,473 books, features a special collection on jazz and folk music, and the Tulane University Library (1,765,000 volumes) has special collections on jazz and Louisiana history. Among the libraries with special black-studies collections are those of Grambling State University, Southern University Agricultural and Mechanical System at Baton Rouge, Xavier University of Louisiana at New Orleans, and the Amistad Collection at Tulane University. The library of Northwestern State University at Natchitoches has special collections on Louisiana history, folklore, Indians, botany, and oral history. Total public library income came to $112,091,000 in 2000; including $112,100 in federal funds and $6,837,551 in state funds.

As of 2000, Louisiana had 89 museums and historic sites, as well as more than 27 art collections. Leading art museums are the New Orleans Museum of Art, the Lampe Gallery in New Orleans, and the R. W. Norton Art Gallery at Shreveport. The art museum of the Louisiana Arts and Science Center at Baton Rouge is located in the renovated Old Illinois Central Railroad Station. The oldest and largest museum in the state is the Louisiana State Museum, an eight-building historic complex in the Vieux Carre. There is a military museum in Beauregard House at Chalmette National Historical Park, on the site of the Battle of New Orleans, and a Confederate Museum in New Orleans. The Bayou Folk Museum at Cloutierville is in the restored home of author Kate Chopin; the Longfellow-Evangeline State Commemorative Area has a historical museum on its site. Among the state's scientific museums are the Lafayette Natural History Museum, Planetarium, and Nature Station, and the Museum of Natural Science in Baton Rouge. Audubon Park and Zoological Gardens are in New Orleans. The "Louisiana and Lower Mississippi Valley Collection" at LSU is an extensive collection of Louisiana history, photographs, and manuscripts.

44COMMUNICATIONS

The second rural free delivery route in the US, and the first in Louisiana, was established on 1 November 1896 at Thibodaux. As of 2001, 94.5% of Louisiana's occupied housing units had telephones.

In 2003, the state had 92 major radio broadcasting stations (14 AM and 78 FM) as well as 32 television stations. That year in New Orleans, there were 629,820 television households, 76% of which had cable TV.

By the year 2000, a total of 46,786 Internet domain names had been registered in Louisiana.

45PRESS

At one time, New Orleans had as many as 9 daily newspapers (4 English, 3 French, 1 Italian, and 1 German), but by 1997 there was only 1, the *Times-Picayune*. In 2002, Louisiana had a total of 13 morning dailies, 13 evening dailies, and 21 Sunday papers. The following table shows the principal dailies with their approximate 2002 circulations:

AREA	NAME	DAILY	SUNDAY
Baton Rouge	*Advocate* (m,S)	90,285	129,740
New Orleans	*Times-Picayune*	254,897	285,425
Shreveport	*Times* (m,S)	66,298	81,876

Two influential literary magazines originated in the state. The *Southern Review* was founded at Louisiana State University in the 1930s by Robert Penn Warren and Cleanth Brooks. The *Tulane Drama Review,* founded in 1955, moved to New York University in 1967 but is still known by its original acronym, TDR.

46 ORGANIZATIONS

In 2003, there were about 1,586 regional, national, and international organizations within the state. Among business or professional organizations with headquarters in Louisiana are the Federated Pecan Growers' Associations of the US and the Louisiana Historical Association, currently in Lafayette; the National Rice Growers Association at Jennings; and the Federal Court Clerks Association and the Southern Forest Products Association, both in New Orleans. Blue Key, a national honor society, has its headquarters in Metairie. The American Bone Marrow Donor Registry is based in Mandeville.

State and local organization for the arts include the Acadiana Arts Council, the Louisiana Division of the Arts, the Louisiana Preservation Alliance, the New Orleans Jazz Club, the North Central Louisiana Arts Council, and the Northeast Louisiana Arts Council.

Civil rights groups represented in the state include the National Association for the Advancement of Colored People (NAACP) and the Urban League. Especially active during the 1970s were the local branches of the American Civil Liberties Union, the Louisiana Coalition on Jails and Prisons, and its legal arm, the Southern Prisoners Defense Council, and the Fishermen's and Concerned Citizens Association of Plaquemines Parish, which organized a campaign against the continued domination of the parish by the descendants of Leander Perez, a racist judge who wielded power there for 50 years until his death in 1969.

The Invisible Empire, Knights of the Ku Klux Klan, is headquartered in Denham Springs.

47 TOURISM, TRAVEL, AND RECREATION

In 2000, there were about 15.4 million visitors to the state of Louisiana. Initial reports for 2001 estimated a total travel-related economic impact of $9 billion, including support for 124,200 jobs. The two most popular activities for tourists are shopping and gambling.

New Orleans is one of the major tourist attractions in the US. Known for its fine restaurants, serving such distinctive fare as gumbo, jambalaya, crawfish, and beignets, along with an elaborate French-inspired haute cuisine, New Orleans also offers jazz clubs, the graceful buildings of the French Quarter, and a lavish carnival called Mardi Gras ("Fat Tuesday"). Beginning on the Wednesday before Shrove Tuesday, parades and balls staged by private organizations called krewes are held almost nightly. In other towns, people celebrate Mardi Gras in their own, no less uproarious, manner.

Among the many other annual events that attract visitors to the state are the blessing of the shrimp fleet at the Louisiana Shrimp and Petroleum Festival in Morgan City on Labor Day weekend and the blessing of the cane fields during the Louisiana Sugar Cane Festival at New Iberia in September. October offers the International Rice Festival (including the Frog Derby) at Crowley, Louisiana Cotton Festival at Ville Platte (with a medieval jousting tournament), the Louisiana Yambilee Festival at Opelousas, and the Louisiana State Fair at Shreveport. Attractions of the Natchitoches Christmas Festival include 170,000 Christmas lights and spectacular fireworks displays.

Louisiana's 34 state parks and recreation sites total 39,000 acres (15,800 hectares).

48 SPORTS

Louisiana has two major league professional sports teams: the Saints of the National Football League and the Hornets of the National Basketball Association. The Hornets were formerly located in Charlotte. Both the Saints and Hornets are located in New Orleans. The Super Bowl has been held in New Orleans six times: in 1978, 1981, 1986, 1990, 1997, and 2002. It has been played in the Louisiana Superdome, the largest indoor arena in the United States.

New Orleans also has a minor league baseball team, the Zephyrs, of the Triple-A Pacific Coast League. In Shreveport, the Captains compete in the Double-A Texas League. There are several other minor league baseball and hockey teams scattered throughout the state.

During the 1850s, New Orleans was the horse-racing center of the US, and racing is still popular in the state. The principal tracks are the Louisiana Jockey Club at the Fair Grounds in New Orleans, and Evangeline Downs at Lafayette. Gambling has long been widespread in Louisiana, particularly in the steamboat days, when races along the Mississippi drew huge wagers.

From the 1880s to World War I, New Orleans was the nation's boxing capital, and in 1893, the city was the site of the longest bout in boxing history, between Andy Bowen and Jack Burke, lasting 7 hours and 19 minutes—110 rounds—and ending in a draw. The TPC of Louisiana at Fairfield is a newly constructed championship-level golf course that will become the home of the PGA's HP Classic beginning in 2005.

In 1935, Tulane University inaugurated the Sugar Bowl (which they won that year for the first and only time), an annual New Year's Day event and one of the most prestigious bowl games in college football. Louisiana State University (LSU) won the Sugar Bowl in 1959, 1965, and 1968. They were named National Champions in 1958. The LSU Tigers baseball team won the College World Series in 1991, 1993, 1996, and 1997. The LSU Tigers have had a number of famous basketball alumni, including "Pistol" Pete Maravich and Shaquille O'Neal.

Professional sports heroes Terry Bradshaw, Bill Russell, and Marshall Faulk all were born within the state's borders.

49 FAMOUS LOUISIANIANS

Zachary Taylor (b.Virginia, 1784–1850) is the only US president to whom Louisiana can lay claim. Taylor, a professional soldier who made his reputation as an Indian fighter and in the Mexican War, owned a large plantation north of Baton Rouge, which was his residence before his election to the presidency in 1848. Edward Douglass White (1845–1921) served first as associate justice of the US Supreme Court and then as chief justice.

Most other Louisianians who have held national office won more fame as state or confederate officials. John Slidell (b.New York, 1793–1871), an antebellum political leader, also played an important role in Confederate diplomacy. Judah P. Benjamin (b.West Indies, 1811–84), of Jewish lineage, was a US senator before the Civil War; during the conflict he held three posts in the Confederate cabinet, after which he went to England and became a leading barrister. Henry Watkins Allen (b.Virginia, 1820–66) was elected governor of Confederate Louisiana in 1864, after he had been maimed in battle; perhaps the best administrator in the South, he installed a system of near-socialism in Louisiana as the fortunes of the Confederacy waned. During and after the Civil War, many Louisianians won prominence as military leaders. Leonidas Polk (b.North Carolina, 1806–64), the state's first Episcopal bishop, became a lieutenant general in the Confederate Army and died in the Atlanta campaign. Zachary Taylor's son Richard (b.Kentucky, 1826–79), a sugar planter who also became a Confederate lieutenant general, is noted for his defeat of Nathaniel P. Bank's Union forces in the Red River campaign of 1864. Pierre Gustave Toutant Beauregard (1818–93) attained the rank of full general in the Confederate Army and later served as director of the Louisiana state lottery, one of the state's major sources of revenue at that time. In the modern era, General Claire

Chennault (b.Texas 1893–1958) commanded the famous "Flying Tigers" and then the US 14th Air Force in China during World War II.

Throughout the 20th century, the Longs have been the first family of Louisiana politics. Without question, the most important state officeholder in Louisiana history was Huey P. Long (1893–1935), a latter-day Populist who was elected to the governorship in 1928 and inaugurated a period of social and economic reform. In the process, he made himself very nearly an absolute dictator within Louisiana. After his election to the US Senate, the "King Fish" became a national figure, challenging Franklin D. Roosevelt's New Deal with his "Share the Wealth" plan and flamboyant oratory. Huey's brother Earl K. Long (1895–1960) served three times as governor. Huey's son, US Senator Russell B. Long (1918–2003), was chairman of the Finance Committee—and, consequently, one of the most powerful men in Congress—from 1965 to 1980.

Also prominent in Louisiana history were Robert Cavelier, Sieur de la Salle (b.France, 1643–87), who was the first to claim the region for the French crown; Pierre le Moyne, Sieur d'Iberville (b.Canada, 1661–1706), who commanded the expedition that first established permanent settlements in the lands La Salle had claimed; his brother, Jean Baptiste le Moyne, Sieur de Bienville (b.Canada, 1680–1768), governor of the struggling colony and founder of New Orleans; and Bernardo de Galvez (b.Spain, 1746–86), who, as governor of Spanish Louisiana during the last years of the American Revolution, conquered British-held Florida in a series of brilliant campaigns. William Charles Coles Claiborne (b.Virginia, 1775–1817) was the last territorial and first state governor of Louisiana. The state's first Republican governor, Henry Clay Warmoth (b.Illinois, 1842–1932), came there as a Union officer before the end of the Civil War and was sworn in at age 26. Jean Étienne de Boré (b.France, 1741–1820) laid the foundation of the Louisiana sugar industry by developing a process for granulating sugar from cane; Norbert Rillieux (birthplace unknown, 1806–94), a free black man, developed the much more efficient vacuum pan process of refining sugar.

Andrew Victor Schally (b.Poland, 1926), a biochemist on the faculty of the Tulane University School of Medicine, shared the Nobel Prize for medicine in 1977 for his research on hormones. Among other distinguished Louisiana professionals have been historian T. Harry Williams (1909–79), who won the Pulitzer Prize for his biography of Huey Long; architect Henry Hobson Richardson (1838–86); and four doctors of medicine: public health pioneer Joseph Jones (b.Georgia, 1833–96), surgical innovator Rudolph Matas (1860–1957), surgeon and medical editor Alton V. Ochsner (b.South Dakota, 1896–1981), and heart specialist Michael De Bakey (b.1908).

Louisiana's important writers include George Washington Cable (1844–1925), an early advocate of racial justice; Kate O'Flaherty Chopin (b.Missouri, 1851–1904); playwright and memoirist Lillian Hellman (1905–84); and novelists Walker Percy (b.Alabama 1916–1990); Truman Capote (1924–84); Ernest Gaines (b.1933), author of *The Autobiography of Miss Jane Pittman*; Shirley Ann Grau (b.1929); and John Kennedy Toole (1937–69), the last two being winners of the Pulitzer Prize.

Louisiana has produced two important composers, Ernest Guiraud (1837–92) and Louis Gottschalk (1829–69). Jelly Roll Morton (Ferdinand Joseph La Menthe, 1885–1941), Pete Fountain (b.1930), and Sidney Bechet (1897–1959) were important jazz musicians, and Louis "Satchmo" Armstrong (1900–1971) was one of the most prolific jazz innovators and popular performers in the nation. The distinctive rhythms of pianist and singer Professor Longhair (Henry Byrd, 1918–80) were an important influence on popular music. Other prominent Louisianians in music are gospel singer Mahalia Jackson (1911–72), pianist-singer-songwriter Antoine "Fats" Domino (b.1928), and pop singer Jerry Lee Lewis (b.1935).

Louisiana baseball heroes include Hall of Famer Melvin Thomas "Mel" Ott (1909–58) and pitcher Ron Guidry (b.1950). Terry Bradshaw (b.1948), a native of Shreveport, quarterbacked the Super Bowl champion Pittsburgh Steelers during the 1970s. Player-coach William F. "Bill" Russell (b.1934) led the Boston Celtics to 10 National Basketball Association championships between 1956 and 1969. Chess master Paul Morphy (1837–84) was born in New Orleans.

50 BIBLIOGRAPHY

Ayres, Thomas. *Dark and Bloody Ground: The Battle of Mansfield and the Forgotten Civil War in Louisiana.* Dallas: Taylor, 2001.

Bell, Caryn Cossé. *Revolution, Romanticism, and the Afro-Creole Protest Tradition in Louisiana, 1718–1868.* Baton Rouge: Louisiana State University Press, 1997.

Fairclough, Adam. *Race & Democracy: The Civil Rights Struggle in Louisiana, 1915–1972.* Athens: University of Georgia Press, 1995.

Hair, William Ivy. *Bourbonism and Agrarian Protest in Louisiana,1877–1900.* Baton Rouge: Louisiana State University Press, 1965.

Jackson, Joy. *New Orleans in the Gilded Age: Politics and Urban Progress, 1880–96.* Baton Rouge: Louisiana State University Press, 1969.

Klier, Betje Black. *Pavie in the Borderlands: The Journey of Théodore Pavie to Louisiana and Texas, 1829–1830.* Baton Rouge: Louisiana State University Press, 2000.

Louisiana, State of. Secretary of State. *Roster of Officials, 1997.* Baton Rouge, 1997.

Louisiana Almanac, 1997–98. Gretna, La.: Pelican Publishing Co., 1997.

McAuliffe, Emily. *Louisiana Facts and Symbols.* Mankato, Minn.: Hilltop Books, 1999.

Schafer, Judith Kelleher. *Slavery, the Civil Law, and the Supreme Court of Louisiana.* Baton Rouge: Louisiana State University Press, 1994.

Shugg, Roger W. *Origins of Class Struggle in Louisiana: A Social History of White Farmers and Laborers During Slavery and After, 1840–75.* Baton Rouge: Louisiana State University Press, 1968 (orig. 1939).

Taylor, Joe Gray. *Louisiana: A Bicentennial History.* New York: Norton, 1976.

———. *Louisiana Reconstructed, 1863–77.* Baton Rouge: Louisiana State University Press, 1974.

Tregle, Joseph George. *Louisiana in the Age of Jackson: A Clash of Cultures and Personalities.* Baton Rouge: Louisiana State University Press, 1999.

Williams, T. Harry. *Huey Long,* New York: Random House, 1981.

Winters, John D. *The Civil War in Louisiana.* Baton Rouge: Louisiana State University Press, 1979.

MAINE

State of Maine

ORIGIN OF STATE NAME: Either from the French for a historical district of France or from the early use of "main" to distinguish coast from islands. **NICKNAME:** The Pine Tree State. **CAPITAL:** Augusta. **ENTERED UNION:** 15 March 1820 (23rd). **SONG:** "State of Maine Song." **MOTTO:** *Dirigo* ("I direct" or "I lead"). **COAT OF ARMS:** A farmer and sailor support a shield on which are depicted a pine tree, a moose, and water. Under the shield is the name of the state; above it, the state motto and the North Star. **FLAG:** The coat of arms on a blue field, with a yellow fringed border surrounding three sides. **OFFICIAL SEAL:** Same as the coat of arms. **ANIMAL:** Moose. **BIRD:** Chickadee. **FISH:** Landlocked salmon. **INSECT:** Honeybee. **FLOWER:** White pine cone and tassel. **TREE:** white pine. **MINERAL:** Tourmaline. **STATE HERB:** Wintergreen. **LEGAL HOLIDAYS:** New Year's Day, 1 January; Birthday of Martin Luther King, Jr., 3rd Monday in January; Washington's Birthday, 3rd Monday in February; Patriots' Day, 3rd Monday in April; Memorial Day, last Monday in May; Independence Day, 4 July; Labor Day, 1st Monday in September; Columbus Day, 2nd Monday in October; Veterans Day, 11 November; Thanksgiving Day, 4th Thursday in November and day following; Christmas Day, 25 December. **TIME:** 7 AM EST = noon GMT.

¹LOCATION, SIZE, AND EXTENT

Situated in the extreme northeastern corner of the US, Maine is the nation's most easterly state, the largest in New England, and 39th in size among the 50 states.

The total area of Maine is 33,265 sq mi (86,156 sq km), including 30,995 sq mi (80,277 sq km) of land and 2,270 sq mi (5,879 sq km) of inland water. Maine extends 207 mi (333 km) E-W; the maximum N-S extension is 322 mi (518 km).

Maine is bordered on the N by the Canadian provinces of Quebec (with the line passing through the St. Francis River) and New Brunswick (with the boundary formed by the St. John River); on the E by New Brunswick (with the lower eastern boundary formed by the Chiputneticook Lakes and the St. Croix River); on the SE and S by the Atlantic Ocean; and on the W by New Hampshire (with the line passing through the Piscataqua and Salmon Falls rivers in the SW) and Quebec.

Hundreds of islands dot Maine's coast. The largest is Mt. Desert Island; others include Deer Isle, Vinalhaven, and Isle au Haut. The total boundary length of Maine is 883 mi (1,421 km).

The state's geographic center is in Piscataquis County, 18 mi (29 km) N of Dover-Foxcroft. The easternmost point of the US is West Quoddy Head, at 66°57'w.

²TOPOGRAPHY

Maine is divided into four main regions: coastal lowlands, piedmont, mountains, and uplands.

The narrow coastal lowlands extend, on average, 10–20 mi (16–32 km) inland from the irregular coastline, but occasionally disappear altogether, as at Mt. Desert Island and on the western shore of Penobscot Bay. Mt. Cadillac on Mt. Desert Island rises abruptly to 1,532 ft (467 m), the highest elevation on the Atlantic coast north of Rio de Janeiro, Brazil. The transitional hilly belt, or piedmont, broadens from about 30 mi (48 km) wide in the southwestern part of the state to about 80 mi (129 km) in the northeast.

Maine's mountain region, the Longfellow range, is at the northeastern end of the Appalachian Mountain system. This zone, extending into Maine from the western border for about

150 mi (250 km) and averaging about 50 mi (80 km) wide, contains nine peaks over 4,000 ft (1,200 m), including Mt. Katahdin, which at 5,267 ft (1,606 m) is the highest point in the state. The summit of Katahdin marks the northern terminus of the 2,000-mi (3,200-km) Appalachian Trail. Maine's uplands form a high, relatively flat plateau extending northward beyond the mountains and sloping downward toward the north and east. The eastern part of this zone is the Aroostook potato-farming region; the western part is heavily forested.

Of Maine's more than 2,200 lakes and ponds, the largest are Moosehead Lake, 117 sq mi (303 sq km), and Sebago Lake, 13 mi (21 km) by 10 mi (16 km). Of the more than 5,000 rivers and streams, the Penobscot, Androscoggin, Kennebec, and Saco rivers drain historically and commercially important valleys. The longest river in Maine is the St. John, but it runs for most of its length in the Canadian province of New Brunswick.

³CLIMATE

Maine has three climatic regions: the northern interior zone, comprising roughly the northern half of the state, between Quebec and New Brunswick; the southern interior zone; and the coastal zone. The northern zone is both drier and cooler in all four seasons than either of the other zones, while the coastal zone is more moderate in temperature year-round than the other two.

The annual mean temperature in the northern zone is about 40°F (5°C); in the southern interior zone, 44°F (7°C); and in the coastal zone, 46°F (8°C). Record temperatures for the state are –48°F (–44°C), registered at Van Buren on 19 January 1925, and 105°F (41°C) at North Bridgton on 10 July 1911. The mean annual precipitation increases from 40.2 in (102 cm) in the north to 41.5 in (105 cm) in the southern interior and 45.7 in (116 cm) on the coast. Average annual precipitation at Portland (1971–2000) was 45.8 in (116 cm). Average annual snowfall is 78 in (198 cm).

⁴FLORA AND FAUNA

Maine's forests are largely softwoods, chiefly red and white spruces, balsam fir (Abies balsamea), eastern hemlock, and white and red pine. Important hardwoods include beech, yellow and white birches, sugar and red maples, white oak, black willow, black and white ashes, and American elm, which has fallen victim in recent years to Dutch elm disease. Maine is home to most of the flowers and shrubs common to the north temperate zone, including an important commercial resource, the low-bush blueberry. Maine has 17 rare orchid species, of which one is considered threatened. Two species, the small whorled pogonia and the eastern prairie fringed orchid, were classified as threatened as of 2003; the furbish lousewart was classified as endangered that year.

About 30,000 white-tailed deer are killed by hunters in Maine each year, but the herd does not appear to diminish. Moose hunting was banned in Maine in 1935; however, in 1980, 700 moose-hunting permits were issued for a six-day season, and moose hunting has continued despite attempts by some residents to ban the practice. Other common forest animals include the bobcat, beaver, muskrat, river otter, mink, fisher, raccoon, red fox, and snowshoe hare. The woodchuck is a conspicuous inhabitant of pastures, meadows, cornfields, and vegetable gardens. Seals, porpoises, and occasionally finback whales are found in coastal waters, along with virtually every variety of North Atlantic fish and shellfish, including the famous Maine lobster. Coastal waterfowl include the osprey, herring and great black-backed gulls, great and double-crested cormorants, and various duck species. Matinicus Rock, a small uninhabited island about 20 mi (32 km) off the coast near the entrance to Penobscot Bay, is the only known North American nesting site of the common puffin, or sea parrot.

Eleven Maine animal species were classified as threatened or endangered by the US Fish and Wildlife Service in 2003, including the bald eagle, piping plover, Atlantic Gulf of Maine salmon, two species of whale, and leatherback sea turtle.

5ENVIRONMENTAL PROTECTION

The Department of Environmental Protection administers laws regulating the development of large residential, commercial, and industrial sites; the protection and improvement of air and water quality; the prevention and cleanup of oil spills; the control of hazardous wastes; the licensing of oil terminals; the protection of state-significant natural resources (including wetlands, rivers, streams and brooks, and fragile mountain areas); and mining. The Land Use Regulation Commission, established in 1969, extends the principles of town planning and zoning to Maine's 411 unorganized townships, 313 "plantations," and numerous coastal islands that have no local government and might otherwise be subject to ecologically unsound development. In 2003, Maine had 59 hazardous waste sites listed in the Environmental Protection Agency's database, 12 of which were on the National Priorities List. In 2001, Maine received $33,811,000 in federal grants from the Environmental Protection Agency; EPA expenditures for procurement contracts in Maine that year amounted to $69,000.

6POPULATION

Maine ranked 40th in population in the US with an estimated total of 1,294,464 in 2002, an increase of 1.5% since 2000. Between 1990 and 2000, Maine's population grew from 1,227,928 to 1,274,923, an increase of 3.8%. The population is projected to reach 1.4 million by 2025. The population density in 2000 was 41.3 persons per sq mi.

In 2000 the median age was 38.6. Persons under 18 years old accounted for 23.6% of the population while 14.4% were age 65 or older.

The area that now comprises the state of Maine was sparsely settled throughout the colonial period. At statehood, Maine had 298,335 residents. The population doubled by 1860, but then grew slowly until the 1970s, when its growth rate outstripped the nation's.

More than half the population lives on less than one-seventh of the land, within 25 mi (40 km) of the Atlantic coast, and almost half of the state is virtually uninhabited. Although almost half of Maine's population is classified as urban; much of the urban population lives in towns and small cities. The state's major cities, all with populations under 100,000, are Portland, Bangor, and Lewiston-Auburn.

7ETHNIC GROUPS

Maine's population is primarily Yankee, both in its English and Scotch-Irish origins and in its retention of many of the values and folkways of rural New England. The largest minority group consists of French-Canadians. Among those reporting at least one specific ancestry group in 2000, 274,423 claimed English ancestry; 181,663 French (not counting 110,344 who claimed Canadian or French-Canadian); and 192,901 Irish. There were 36,691 foreign-born residents. The population of Hispanics and Latinos in 2000 was 9,360, less than 1% of the state total.

The most notable ethnic issue in Maine during the 1970s was the legal battle of the Penobscot and Passamaquoddy Indians—living on two reservations covering 27,546 acres (11,148 hectares)—to recover 12,500,000 acres (5,059,000 hectares) of treaty lands. A compromise settlement in 1980 awarded them $81.5 million, two-thirds of which went into a fund enabling the Indians to purchase 300,000 acres (121,000 hectares) of timberland. In 1995, Maine's American Indian population included the following groups living on or near reservations (with population estimates): the Penobscot Tribe (1,206); the Aristook Band of Micmac (1,155); Pleasant Point (878); the Passamaquoddy (722); and the Houlton Band of Maliseets (331). The Indian population as a whole was reported as 7,098 in 2000.

As of 2000, Maine had 6,760 black residents and 9,111 Asians, including 2,034 Chinese, 1,159 Filipinos, and 1,021 Asian Indians. Pacific Islanders numbered 382.

8LANGUAGES

Descendants of the Passamaquoddy and Penobscot Indians of the Algonkian family who inhabited Maine at the time that European settlers arrived still lived there in the mid-1980s. Algonkian place-names abound: Saco, Millinocket, Wiscasset, Kennebec, Skowhegan.

Maine English is celebrated as typical Yankee speech. Final /r/ is absent, a vowel sound between /ah/ and the /a/ in cat appears in car and garden, aunt and calf. Coat and home have a vowel that to outsiders sounds like the vowel in cut. Maple syrup comes from rock or sugar maple trees in a sap or sugar orchard; cottage cheese is curd cheese; and pancakes are fritters.

In 2000, 92.2% of Maine residents five years old or older reported speaking only English in the home, up from 90.8% in 1990.

The decline of parochial schools and a great increase in the number of young persons attending college have begun to erode the linguistic and cultural separateness that marks the history of the Franco-American experience in Maine.

The following table gives selected statistics from the 2000 census for language spoken at home by persons five years old and over. The category "Other Native North American languages" includes Apache, Cherokee, Choctaw, Dakota, Keres, Pima, and Yupik. The category "Other Indo-European languages" includes Albanian, Gaelic, Lithuanian, and Rumanian. The category "Scandinavian languages" includes Danish, Norwegian, and Swedish.

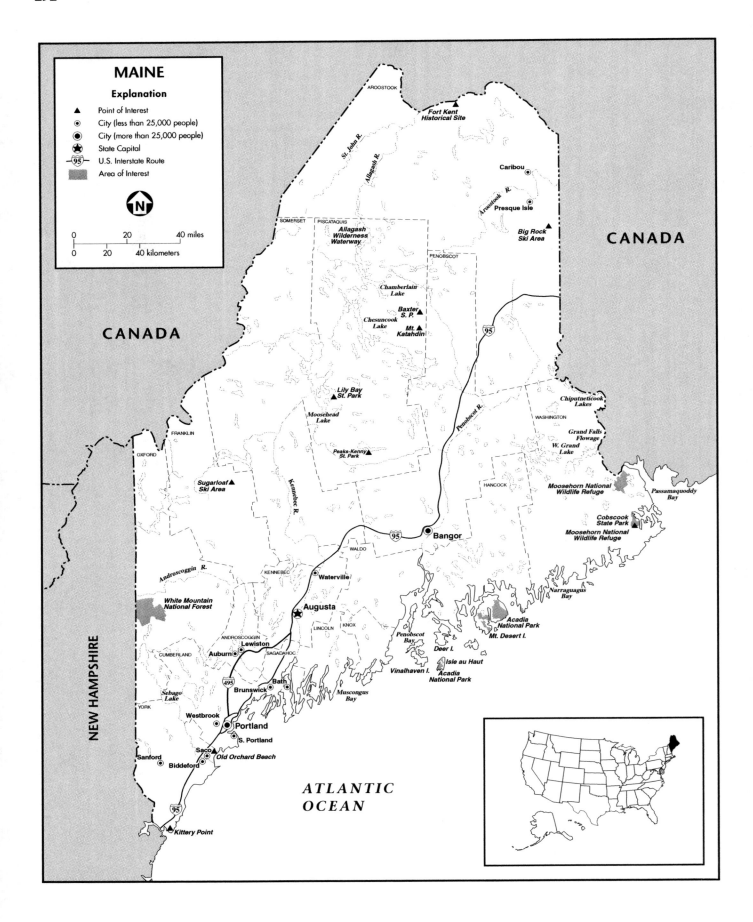

MAINE

Explanation

▲   Point of Interest

⊙   City (less than 25,000 people)

◉   City (more than 25,000 people)

★   State Capital

95   U.S. Interstate Route

▨   Area of Interest

0   20   40 miles

0   20   40 kilometers

CANADA

CANADA

NEW HAMPSHIRE

AROOSTOOK

Fort Kent Historical Site

St. John R.

Allagash R.

Caribou

Aroostook R.

Presque Isle

Big Rock Ski Area

SOMERSET

PISCATAQUIS

PENOBSCOT

Allagash Wilderness Waterway

Chamberlain Lake

Baxter S.P.

Chesuncook Lake

Mt. Katahdin

95

FRANKLIN

Lily Bay St. Park

Moosehead Lake

Penobscot R.

Chiputneticook Lakes

WASHINGTON

Grand Falls Flowage

W. Grand Lake

OXFORD

Peaks-Kenny St. Park

Passamaquoddy Bay

Sugarloaf Ski Area

HANCOCK

Moosehorn National Wildlife Refuge

Cobscook State Park

Moosehorn National Wildlife Refuge

Androscoggin R.

KENNEBEC

Waterville

White Mountain National Forest

95

Bangor

WALDO

Narraguagus Bay

Kennebec R.

Augusta

LINCOLN

KNOX

Penobscot Bay

Acadia National Park

Mt. Desert I.

ANDROSCOGGIN

Lewiston

SAGADAHOC

Auburn

Deer I.

Isle au Haut

CUMBERLAND

495

Brunswick

Bath

Vinalhaven I.

Acadia National Park

Sebago Lake

YORK

Muscongus Bay

Westbrook

Portland

S. Portland

Sanford

Saco

Old Orchard Beach

Biddeford

ATLANTIC OCEAN

95

Kittery Point

LANGUAGE	NUMBER	PERCENT
Population 5 years and over	1,204,164	100.0
Speak only English	1,110,198	92.2
Speak a language other than English	93,966	7.8
Speak a language other than English	93,966	7.8
French (incl. Patois, Cajun)	63,640	5.3
Spanish or Spanish Creole	9,611	0.8
German	4,006	0.3
Italian	1,476	0.1
Chinese	1,259	0.1
Other Native North American languages	1,182	0.1
Mon-Khmer, Cambodian	1,084	0.1
Vietnamese	911	0.1
Russian	896	0.1
Other Indo-European languages	785	0.1
Scandinavian languages	779	0.1
Tagalog	771	0.1
Greek	767	0.1

[9] RELIGIONS

Maine had about 283,024 Roman Catholics and an estimated 8,290 Jews in 2000. The leading Protestant denominations were the United Methodist Church, with 31,689 adherents; the United Church of Christ, 29,122; and the American Baptists USA, 26,259. The Muslim community had about 800 members. Over 800,000 people (about 63.6% of the population) were not counted as members of any religious organization.

[10] TRANSPORTATION

Railroad development in Maine, which reached its peak in 1924, has declined rapidly since World War II, and passenger service has been dropped altogether. Although Maine had no Class I railroads in 2000, nine regional and local railroads operated on 1,202 rail mi (1,934 km) of track.

About three-quarters of all communities and about half the population depend entirely on highway trucking for the overland transportation of freight. In 2000, Maine had 22,670 mi (36,483 km) of public roads. There were 1,052,995 registered motor vehicles and 920,235 licensed drivers in the same year. The Maine Turnpike and I-95, which coincide between Portland and Kittery, are the major highways.

River traffic has been central to the lumber industry; only since World War II has trucking replaced seasonal log drives downstream from timberlands to the mills, a practice that is now outlawed for environmental reasons. Maine has 10 established seaports, with Portland and Searsport being the main depots for overseas shipping. In 2000, Portland harbor handled 29.3 million tons, and Searsport handled 1.4 million tons. Crude oil, fuel oil, and gasoline were the chief commodities. Portland International Jetport is the largest and most active airport in Maine.

[11] HISTORY

The first inhabitants of Maine—dating from 3000 to 1000 BC—are known to archaeologists as the Red Paint People because of the red ocher that has been found in their graves. This Paleolithic group had evidently disappeared long before the arrival of the Algonkian-speaking Abnaki (meaning "living at the sunrise"), or Wabanaki. Just at the time of European settlement, an intertribal war and a disastrous epidemic of smallpox swept away many of the Abnaki, some of whom had begun peaceful contacts with the English. After that, most Indian contacts with Europeans were with the French.

The first documented visit by a European to the Maine coast was that of Giovanni da Verrazano during his voyage of 1524, but one may infer from the record that the Abnaki he met there had encountered white men before. Sometime around 1600, English expeditions began fishing the Gulf of Maine regularly. The first recorded attempts to found permanent colonies, by the French on an island in the St. Croix River in 1604 and by the English at Sagadahoc in 1607, both failed. By 1630, however, there were permanent English settlements on several islands and at nearly a dozen spots along the coast.

The first grant of Maine lands was to Sir Ferdinando Gorges from the Council from New England, a joint-stock company that received and made royal grants of New England territory and which Gorges himself dominated. He and Captain John Mason received the territory between the Merrimack River (in present-day New Hampshire and Massachusetts) and the Kennebec River in 1622. Seven years later, the two grantees divided their land at the Piscataqua River, and Gorges became sole proprietor of the "Province of Maine." The source of the name is not quite clear. It seems likely that some connection with the historical French province of the same name was intended, but the name was also used to distinguish the mainland from the islands.

Sir Ferdinando's various schemes for governing the territory and promoting a feudal-style settlement never worked. A few years after his death in 1647, the government of the Massachusetts Bay Colony began absorbing the small Maine settlements. Massachusetts purchased the title to Maine from the Gorges heirs in 1677, and Maine became a district of Massachusetts with the issuance of a new royal charter in 1691. During the first hundred years of settlement, Maine's economy was based entirely on fishing, trading, and exploitation of the forests. The origin of the Maine shipbuilding industry, the early settlement of the interior parts of southern Maine, and the beginning of subsistence farming all date from about the time that New England's supply center of white-pine masts for the Royal Navy moved from Portsmouth, N.H., to Falmouth (now the city of Portland).

The first naval encounter of the Revolutionary War occurred in Machias Bay, when, on 12 June 1775, angry colonials captured the British armed schooner *Margaretta*. On 8 October 1775, a British naval squadron shelled and set fire to Falmouth. Wartime Maine was the scene of two anti-British campaigns, both of which ended in failure: an expedition through the Maine woods in the fall of 1775 intended to drive the British out of Quebec, and a disastrous 1779 expedition in which a Massachusetts amphibious force, failing to dislodge British troops at Castine, scuttled many of its own ships near the mouth of the Penobscot River.

The idea of separation from Massachusetts began surfacing as early as 1785, but popular pressure for such a movement did not mount until the War of 1812. The overwhelming vote for statehood in an 1819 referendum was a victory for William King, who would become the first governor, and his fellow Jeffersonian Democratic-Republicans. Admission of Maine as a free state was joined with the admission of Missouri as a slave state in the Missouri Compromise of 1820.

Textile mills and shoe factories came to Maine between 1830 and 1860 as part of the industrialization of Massachusetts. After the Civil War, the revolution in papermaking that substituted wood pulp for rags brought a vigorous new industry to Maine. By 1900, Maine was one of the leading papermaking states in the US, and the industry continues to dominate the state today. Shipbuilding joined paper manufacturing as a leading employer in the state, enjoying a boom in government contracts in the 1980s.

In 1972, the Penobscot and Passamaquoddy Indians filed a land claims suit against the federal government for property that amounted to the northern two-thirds of Maine, claiming that a 1794 treaty, under which the Passamaquoddy handed over most of its land while receiving nothing in exchange, had not been ratified by Congress, and therefore violated the Indian Non-Intercourse Act of 1790. The Government settled the suit in 1980 by paying the tribes $81.5 million, which was allocated to purchase commercial and industrial properties in Maine.

The rise of tourism and the often conflicting concerns for economic development and environmental protection have been key issues in the state since the 1940s. Tourism grew substantially in the 1980s and through the 1990s, especially in coastal areas, where an influx of residents changed the character of many seaside towns. Former seasonal resorts were converted to year-round communities, posing new challenges for growth management. The state's environmental concerns included sewage treatment, deforestation, overfishing, and hazardous waste disposal.

Maine's economy turned in its best performance in more than a decade in 1999, with strong job growth, continued increases in retail sales, and significant improvement in nearly all other indicators. The state's income growth topped the national average from 1998 to 1999, finishing among the five fastest growing states. According to government figures, income growth in Maine, which still had the lowest per capita income in New England, was fueled by higher wages in services, construction, finance, insurance, and real estate. At the same time, there were concerns that the gain in income was the result of Maine workers holding down more than one job in order to make ends meet. Analysts also warned that the hot state economy could be threatened by a shortage of workers, since the state's population was not growing at a commensurate rate.

Maine's economy suffered with that of the nation's in the early 2000s, coming on the back of a recession in 2001. By 2003, Maine had a $24 million budget deficit. Governor John Baldacci had plans to implement a large-scale healthcare program for state employees, open it to private employers, and pay for it without increased taxes. A citizen initiative set for referendum in November 2003 was to mandate a large increase in state assistance to local school systems.

12 STATE GOVERNMENT

The Maine constitution, based on that of Massachusetts but incorporating a number of more democratic features, was adopted in 1819 and amended 169 times by January 2003. The state constitution may be amended by a two-thirds vote of the legislature and a majority vote at the next general election.

The bicameral legislature, consisting of a 35-member senate and a 151-member house of representatives, convenes biennially (in even-numbered years) in joint session to elect the secretary of state, attorney general, state treasurer, and auditor. Legislative sessions begin in December of the general election year and run into June of the following (odd-numbered year); the second session begins in January of the next even-numbered year, runs into April, and is limited to consideration of budgetary matters, legislation in the governor's call, emergency legislation, and legislation referred to committees for study. The presiding officers of each house may jointly call for a special session as long as they have the support of a majority of members of each political party in each house. All legislators, who serve two-year terms, must have been US citizens for at least five years, residents of the state for at least two years, and have lived in their district at least three months prior to election. The minimum age for representatives is 21, for senators it is 25. The legislative salary in 2002 was $10,815 for the first year and $7,725 for the second.

The governor, who serves a four-year term and is limited to two consecutive terms, is the only official elected statewide. (Rules of succession dictate that should the governor become incapacitated, he or she would be succeeded by the president of the state senate.) A gubernatorial veto may be overridden by a two-thirds vote of members present and voting in each legislative chamber. An unsigned bill that is not vetoed becomes law after 10 days when the legislature is in session. The governor must be at least 30 years old, a citizen of the US for at least 15 years, and a state resident for five years. In 2002 the governor's salary was $70,000, unchanged from 1999.

To vote in Maine, one must be a US citizen and at least 18 years old; there is no minimum residency requirement. Those under guardianship because of mental illness may not vote.

13 POLITICAL PARTIES

Maine's two major political parties are the Democratic and the Republican, each affiliated with the national party. An independent candidate, James B. Longley, beat the candidates of both major parties in the gubernatorial election of 1974.

During the early decades of statehood, Jeffersonian and Jacksonian Democrats remained in power quite consistently. In 1854, however, reformers rallied around the new Republican Party, which dominated Maine politics for the next hundred years. Maine's strong Republican tradition continued into the middle and late 1950s, when Margaret Chase Smith distinguished herself in the US Senate as a leader of national importance. The rise of Democrat Edmund S. Muskie, elected governor in 1954 and 1956 and to the first of four terms in the US Senate in 1960, signaled a change in Maine's political complexion. Muskie appealed personally to many traditionally Republican voters, but his party's resurgence was also the result of demographic changes, especially an increase in the proportion of French-Canadian voters.

In the November 1994 elections, Independent Angus King was voted into the executive office, and Maine became the only state in the nation with an Independent governor. King was reelected in 1998. In 2002, Democrat John Baldacci was elected governor. In 1994 Republican Olympia Snowe won the US Senate seat vacated by retiring Democrat George J. Mitchell (she was reelected in 2000); in 1996 Republican Susan E. Collins won the seat left vacant by retiring three-term senator William S. Cohen, also a Republican (Collins was reelected in 2002). In the 2000 presidential elections Democrat Al Gore won 49% of the presidential vote, Republican George W. Bush received 44%, and Green Party candidate Ralph Nader won 6%. In 2002 elections, Maine Democrats retained control of both US House seats. Also in 2002 there were 912,092 registered voters. In 1998, 32% of registered voters were Democratic, 29% Republican, and 39% unaffiliated or members of other parties. Before the November 2003 elections, the state house of representatives had 80 Democrats, 67 Republicans, and four independents, while the state senate had 18 Democrats and 17 Republicans. The state had four electoral votes in the 2000 presidential election.

Maine Presidential Vote by Major Political Parties, 1948–2000

YEAR	ELECTORAL VOTE	MAINE WINNER	DEMOCRAT	REPUBLICAN
1948	5	Dewey (R)	111,916	150,234
1952	5	*Eisenhower (R)	118,806	232,353
1956	5	*Eisenhower (R)	102,468	249,238
1960	5	*Eisenhower (R)	102,468	249,238
1960	5	Nixon (R)	181,159	240,608
1964	4	*Johnson (D)	262,264	118,701
1968	4	Humphrey (D)	217,312	169,254
1972	4	*Nixon (R)	160,584	256,458
1976	4	Ford (R)	232,279	236,320
1980	4	*Reagan (R)	220,974	238,522
1984	4	*Reagan (R)	214,515	336,500
1988	4	*Bush (R)	243,569	307,131
1992**	4	*Clinton (D)	263,420	206,504
1996**	4	*Clinton (D)	312,788	186,378
2000	4	Gore (D)	319,951	286,616

*Won US presidential election.

**Independent candidate Ross Perot received 206,820 votes in 1992 and 85,970 votes in 1996.

14LOCAL GOVERNMENT

The principal units of local government in 2002 were the 22 cities and 467 townships. There were 99 public school districts and 222 special districts that year. As is customary in New England, the basic instrument of town government is the annual town meeting, with an elective board of selectmen supervising town affairs between meetings; some of the larger towns employ full-time town managers. Maine's 16 counties (2002) function primarily as judicial districts.

15STATE SERVICES

To address the continuing threat of terrorism and to work with the federal Department of Homeland Security (created in 2002 following the terrorist attacks of 11 September 2001), homeland security in Maine in 2003 operated under the authority of the governor; the adjutant general was designated as the state homeland security advisor.

The State Board of Education and Department of Educational and Cultural Services supervise the public education system. The Department of Transportation, established in 1972, includes divisions responsible for aviation and railroads, a bureau to maintain highways and bridges, the Maine Port Authority, the State Ferry Advisory Board, and the Maine Aeronautical Advisory Board.

Various agencies responsible for health and social welfare were combined into the Department of Human Services in 1975. The Maine State Housing Authority, established in 1969, provides construction loans and technical assistance and conducts surveys of the state's housing needs. The Commission on Governmental Ethics and Election Practices, an advisory and investigative body, was created in 1975 to serve as a watchdog over the legislature. Other organizations include the departments of agriculture, corrections, professional and financial legislation, and labor; and the bureaus of motor vehicles and parks and lands.

16JUDICIAL SYSTEM

The highest state court is the supreme judicial court, with a chief justice and six associate justices appointed by the governor, with the consent of the legislature, for seven-year terms (as are all other state judges). The supreme judicial court has statewide appellate jurisdiction in all civil and criminal matters. The 16-member superior court, which has original jurisdiction in cases involving trial by jury and also hears some appeals, holds court sessions in all 16 counties. The district courts hear non-felony criminal cases and small claims and juvenile cases, and have concurrent jurisdiction with the superior court in divorce and civil cases involving less than $30,000. A probate court judge is elected in each county.

Maine's crime rate in 2001 was 2,688.2 per 100,000 persons, including a total of 1,434 violent crimes and 33,154 crimes against property in that year. There were 1,693 state and federal prisoners in June 2001, or 126 per 100,000, a decrease of 1.3% from the previous year. Maine has not had a death penalty since 1887. The state does provide for life without parole.

17ARMED FORCES

The largest US military installation in Maine is the Naval Air Station at Brunswick, home of a wing of anti-submarine patrol squadrons. Defense Department personnel in Maine totaled 2,689 active military and 5,791 civilians in 2002. State firms received $496 million in defense contracts in 2001. The largest recipient, General Dynamics, a division of which builds warships, is the state's largest private employer.

There were 154,590 veterans of US military service in Maine as of 2000, of whom 29,317 served in World War II; 19,794 in the Korean conflict; 46,434 during the Vietnam era; and 14,326 during 1990–2000 (including the Persian Gulf War). A total of $393 million in veterans' benefits were paid in 2002.

In 2000, the Maine State Police employed 325 full-time sworn officers.

18MIGRATION

Throughout the colonial, Revolutionary, and early national periods, Maine's population grew primarily by immigration from elsewhere in New England. About 1830, after agriculture in the state had passed its peak, Maine farmers and woodsmen began moving west. Europeans and French Canadians came to the state, but not in sufficient numbers to offset this steady emigration.

Net losses from migration have continued through most of this century. Between 1940 and 1970, for example, the net loss was 163,000. However, there was a net gain of about 80,000 from 1970 to 1990. From 1980 to 1990, Maine's urban population declined from 47.5% to 44.6% of the state's total. Between 1990 and 1998, the state had a net loss of 15,000 in domestic migration and a net gain of 3,000 in international migration. In 1998, Maine admitted 709 foreign immigrants. Between 1990 and 1998, the State's overall population increased 1.3%. In the period 1995–2000, 107,999 people moved into the state and 104,259 moved out, for a net gain of 3,640, 1,650 of whom were age 65 or over.

19INTERGOVERNMENTAL COOPERATION

Regional agreements in which Maine participates include the Maine-New Hampshire School Compact, which authorizes interstate public school districts. Maine also takes part in the Atlantic States Marine Fisheries Commission, Interstate Compact for Juveniles, Northeastern Forest Fire Protection Compact; and the New England Interstate Water Pollution Control, Corrections Control, Board of Higher Education, and Radiological Health Protection compacts. In 2001, Maine received over $1.9 billion in federal grants.

20ECONOMY

Maine's greatest economic strengths, as they have been since the beginning of European settlement, are its forests and waters, yielding wood products, water power, fisheries, and ocean commerce. Today, the largest industry by far is paper manufacturing, for which both forests and water power are essential. However, since the 1980s manufacturing employment has dropped; and especially since 1992, services sector and trading sector employment has risen.

Maine's greatest current economic weakness is its limited access to the national transportation network that links major production and manufacturing centers with large metropolitan markets. On the other hand, this relative isolation, combined with the state's traditional natural assets, has contributed to Maine's attractiveness as a place for tourism and recreation. It also meant that the national recession in 2001 largely bypassed Maine's economy because of its limited involvement in the growth fields of information technology and equity venture capitalism. Annual growth in Maine's gross state product, which at 5.9% in both 1998 and 1999, and rising to 6.4% in 2000, did moderate to 3.2% in 2001, but employment had returned to peak levels reached before the recession by mid-2002. Tax revenue shortfalls were also less than other New England states, all more affected by the abrupt decline in capital gains income.

Maine's gross state product in 2001 was 8th smallest among the states at $37.4 billion, to which general services contributed $7.9 billion; financial services, $7.2 billion; trade, $6.7 billion; manufacturing, $5.2 billion; government, $5.4 billion, and transportation and public utilities, $2.5 billion. Output from general services increased 35.2% across the period 1997 to 2001, whereas output from government services, trade and financial services all increased 24% to 25%. Output from manufacturing increased 13.5% from 1997 to 2000, but then fell 8.5% in 2001, reducing the five-year gain to 3.2%. As a percent of total output, manufactures fell from 16.6% in 1997 to 14% in 2001. The public sector constituted a relatively high 14.4% of gross state product in 2001.

21INCOME

According to the Bureau of Economic Analysis, in 2001, Maine had a per capita personal income (PCPI) of $26,853 which ranked 35th in the United States (including the District of Columbia) and was 88% of the national average, $30,413. The 2001 PCPI reflected an increase of 4.4% from 2000 compared to the national change of 2.2%. In 2001, Maine had a total personal income (TPI) of $34,491,316,000 which ranked 41st in the United States and accounted for 0.4% of the national total. The 2001 TPI reflected an increase of 4.9% from 2000 compared to the national change of 3.3%.

Earnings of persons employed in Maine increased from $22,012,300,000 in 2000 to $22,966,978,000 in 2001, an increase of 4.3%. The largest industries in 2001 were services, 29.1% of earnings; state and local government, 13.0%; and retail trade, 11.8%. Of the industries that accounted for at least 5% of earnings in 2001, the slowest growing from 2000 to 2001 was nondurable goods manufacturing (7.1% of earnings in 2001), which decreased 4.8%; the fastest was finance, insurance, and real estate (7.0% of earnings in 2001), which increased 7.2%.

According to data released by the US Census Bureau, in 2000, the median household income was $41,597 compared to the national average of $42,148. In 2001, the median income for a family of four was $58,425 compared to the national average of $63,278. For the period 1999 to 2001, the average poverty rate was 10.3% which placed it 25th among the 50 states and the District of Columbia ranked lowest to highest.

22LABOR

According to Bureau of Labor Statistics (BLS) provisional estimates, in July 2003 the seasonally adjusted civilian labor force in Maine numbered 692,800, with approximately 34,000 workers unemployed, yielding an unemployment rate of 4.9%, compared to the national average of 6.2% for the same period. Since the beginning of the BLS data series in 1978, the highest unemployment rate recorded was 9.9% in February 1983. The historical low was 3.3% in January 2001. In 2001, an estimated 5.6% of the labor force was employed in construction; 12.3% in manufacturing; 4.2% in transportation, communications, and public utilities; 20.3% in trade; 5.6% in finance, insurance, and real estate; 26.2% in services; 13.5% in government; and 1.8% in agriculture.

The US Department of Labor reported that in 2002, 75,000 of Maine's 582,000 employed wage and salary workers were members of unions. This represented 12.9% of those so employed, unchanged from 2001 but down from 14.3% in 1998. In all, 88,000 workers (15.1%) were represented by unions. In addition to union members, this category includes workers who report no union affiliation but whose jobs are covered by a union contract.

23AGRICULTURE

Maine's gross farm income in 2001 was $485 million (43rd in the US). There were 6,700 farms in 2002, with an estimated 1,260,000 acres (510,000 hectares) of land.

Maine's agriculture and food processing industries contribute over $1 billion annually to the state's economy. Maine produces more food crops for human consumption than any other New England state. Maine ranks first in the world in the production of blueberries, producing over 25% of the total blueberry crop and over 50% of the world's wild blueberries. Maine is also home to the largest bio-agricultural firm in the world, which produces breeding stock for the broiler industry worldwide. In New England, Maine ranks 1st in potato production and 2nd in the production of milk and apples. Nationally, Maine ranks 3rd in maple syrup and 8th in potatoes with 16,960,000 hundredweight. The greenhouse/nursery and wild blueberry sectors have also shown steady growth in total sales since 1990. Cranberry production has recently enjoyed a resurgence in Maine; 70 acres (28 hectares) were brought into production in the late 1990s through a $1.4 million capital investment.

24ANIMAL HUSBANDRY

In 2003, Maine had an estimated 93,000 cattle and calves worth around $91.1 million. Dairy farmers had an estimated 38,000 milk cows, which produced 654 million lb (296.7 million kg) of milk in 2001. Poultry farmers sold an estimated 8.8 million lb (4 million kg) of chickens in the same year. South-central Maine is the leading poultry region.

25FISHING

Fishing has been important to the economy of Maine since its settlement. In 1998, 183.9 million lb of finfish and shellfish worth $216.4 million were landed at Maine ports, ranking the state 10th and 3rd in the nation, respectively. Rockland and Portland accounted for 39 million lb and 46.5 million lb, respectively, of the state's landings in 1998. The most valuable Maine fishery product is the lobster. In 1995, Maine led in landings of American lobster for the 17th consecutive year, with 46.9 million lb, valued at $136.6 million. Flounder, halibut, scallops, and shrimp are also caught. Maine also was the leading state in soft clams, with 2.4 million lb (shelled basis) in 1998. The state sought during the late 1970s and early 1980s to conserve and restore Atlantic salmon stocks in Maine's inland waterways. In 1998, fish farms distributed over 449,000 salmon within the state for restoration or conservation. The fishing fleet had 7,561 boats and vessels in 1997. Average employment in 277 processing and wholesaling plants was 3,284 in 1997.

26FORESTRY

Maine's 17.7 million acres (7.2 million hectares) of forest in 2002 contained over 3.6 billion trees and covered 90% of the state's land area, the largest percentage for any state in the US. About 16,952,000 acres (6,860,000 hectares) are classified as commercial timberland, over 96% of it privately owned, and half of that by a dozen large paper companies and land managing corporations. Principal commercial hardwood include ash, hard maple, white and yellow birch, beech, and oak; commercially significant softwoods include white pine, hemlock, cedar, spruce, and fir. Total lumber production in 2002 was 988 million board feet, of which 89% was softwood.

27MINING

The value of nonfuel mineral production in Maine in 2001 was estimated to be $91 million, representing a decrease of about 5% from 2000. The mining and production of construction materials accounted for the vast majority of the state's nonfuel mineral production. Construction sand and gravel alone accounted for more than 64% of total nonfuel mineral value. According to preliminary figures, leading mineral commodities, in terms of value, were construction sand and gravel (9.6 million metric tons, $37.9 million) and crushed stone (3.4 million metric tons, $20.2 million). The combined value of cement, peat, dimension stone, and granite was $32.5 million. Other mineral commodities produced included clay and gemstones.

28ENERGY AND POWER

For more than three centuries, Maine has been exploiting its enormous waterpower potential. In recent decades, however, waterpower has been surpassed in importance by oil-fired steam plants and, most recently, by nuclear power. In referendums in 1980 and 1982, voters decided that the Maine Yankee Atomic Power Company station in Wiscasset, Maine's only nuclear power plant, should remain open and that future nuclear power development should be allowed. For 25 years, the plant was the state's most important producer of electricity; in 1994 it accounted for 74% of power generation. However, due to economic and regulatory concerns, its owners closed the plant in 1997. As of 2003 the plant was being dismantled and the site restored for other uses.

Installed generating capacity (utility and nonutility) in 1999 totaled 2,956,000 kW. Power production in 1999 totaled 13 billion kWh. Oil-fired steam units accounted for 37% of electric power generation in 1999, and hydroelectric units for 29%.

All fuel oil and coal must be imported; natural gas, piped into the southwest corner of the state, is available in Portland and the Lewiston-Auburn area. In 2000 Maine's total per capita energy consumption was 440 million Btu (110.9 million kcal), ranking it 10th among the 50 states.

29INDUSTRY

Manufacturing in Maine has always been dependent upon the forests. From the lath century through much of the 19th, the staples of Maine industry were shipbuilding and lumber; today they are papermaking and wood products, but footwear, textiles and apparel, shipbuilding, and electronic components and accessories are also important items.

Maine has the largest paper-production capacity of any state in the nation. There are large paper mills and pulp mills in more than a dozen towns and cities; the top ten pulp and paper companies, in order of number of employees in 1998 include: Sappi Fine Paper North America, Bowater Great Northern Paper, Mead Paper Division, International Paper, Champion International Corporation, Fraser Paper, Inc., Georgia-Pacific Corp., Fort James Corp., Wausau-Mosinee Paper Corp., and Madison Paper Industries. Wood-related industries—paper, lumber, wood products—account for about half of the value of manufacturers shipments.

Estimated value of manufacturers' shipments in 1997 exceeded $15 billion. In 1997, Maine was the headquarters for two Fortune 500 companies: UNUM and Hannaford Bros.

Earnings of persons employed in Maine increased from $18.5 billion in 1997 to $19.6 billion in 1998, an increase of 5.9%. The largest industries in 1998 were services, 27.3% of earnings; retail trade, 12.0%; and state and local government, 11.8%. Of the industries that accounted for at least 5% of earnings in 1998, the slowest growing from 1997 to 1998 was construction (6.5% of earnings in 1998), which increased 2.6%; the fastest was finance, insurance, and real estate (6.5% of earnings in 1998), which increased 10.0%.

30COMMERCE

In 1997, Maine had 2,084 wholesale establishments with $8 billion in sales. Retail sales totaled $13 billion in 1997, from 9,528 establishments. Food stores accounted for 15% of establishments; automotive dealers, 14%; and eating and drinking places, 27%. Earnings from food sales came to $2.6 billion, while sales of general merchandise came to $1.2 billion.

Maine has shipping facilities located in Portland, Searsport, and Eastport. Exports from Maine totaled $1.8 billion in 1998. Exports reached over $2 billion in 1999. Maine's largest trading partners are Canada, Singapore, Malaysia, Japan, and the UK.

The biggest export items in order of importance were electronics and electrical equipment, paper and allied products, and lumber and wood products.

31CONSUMER PROTECTION

The Public Protection Unit of the Attorney General's Office protects consumers through enforcement of a wide variety of laws including Maine's Unfair Trade Practices Act. The office also provides a consumer mediation service which uses volunteer mediators to resolve disputes between businesses and consumers.

The Office of Consumer Credit Regulation was established in 1974 to protect state residents from unjust and misleading consumer credit practices, particularly in relation to the federal Truth-in-Lending Act. The agency also administers state laws regulating collection agencies, credit reporting agencies, mortgage companies, loan brokers, rent-to-own companies, pawn brokers, money order issuers, check cashers, and money transmitters.

32BANKING

In 2002, Maine had 39 insured banks, with assets of $35 billion. Nine of the insured banks were state-chartered. Sixty-two percent of insured institutions in Maine are savings institutions. Residential real estate loans make up about 54% of the average loan portfolio in the state.

33INSURANCE

In 2001 there were 586,000 ordinary life insurance policies in force with a total value of $36.2 billion; total value for all categories of life insurance (ordinary, group, industrial, and credit) was $72.8 billion. Death benefits paid that year totaled $178.9 million. Three life and health and 14 property and casualty insurance companies were domiciled in Maine in 2000. In 2001, property and casualty insurers wrote premiums totaling $1.4 billion. That year, there were 6,955 flood insurance policies in force in the state, with a total value of $871,502.

34SECURITIES

There are 178 broker-dealer firms with over 1,000 employees in Maine; 59 investment advisors are licensed as well. The state holds the headquarters of 11 NASDAQ companies, one NASDAQ market maker; and has incorporated six NYSE-listed corporations: Bangur Hydro-Electric, CMP Group Fairchild Semiconductor, Idacorp, Inc, Ptlatch, and Zemex.

35PUBLIC FINANCE

Maine's biennial budget is prepared by the Bureau of the Budget, within the Department of Administrative and Financial Services, and submitted by the governor to the Legislature for consideration. The fiscal year extends from 1 July to 30 June.

Maine was not considered among the states with a serious budget crisis in 2002 and 2003, although it experienced some shortfalls. In 2001/02, cuts of $16.4 million were made in the budget after its enactment, and in 2002/03, post-enactment cuts reached $183.7 million. In both years, drawings were made on the Maine Rainy Day Fund, a statewide hiring freeze declared, and programs such as Medicaid and Nursing Facilities were reprojected. For 2003/04, the Rainy Day Fund was at zero. Revenue projections for the general fund in 2003/04 totaled $2.575 billion, and expenditures $2.597 billion, the difference to be made up by transfers from the Highway Fund and the Tobacco Settlement fund. Appropriations from the general fund for the biennium 2004/05 by function were K-12 education (34.4%), Medicaid (20.1%), higher education (8.9%), Corrections (4.3%), public assistance (1.3%), transportation (0.1%, with most spending through the Highway Fund and other, including general operations (30.9%). These proportions were insignificantly different from the allocations for 2002/03.

The following table from the US Census Bureau contains information on revenues, expenditures, indebtedness, and cash/securities for 2001.

	($000)	PERCENT	PER CAPITA
Population (thousands, 2001)	1,284	(X)	(X)
Total Revenue	5,207,414	100.00	4,055.62
General revenue	5,399,812	103.69	4,205.46
Utility revenue	–	–	–
Liquor store revenue	79,839	1.53	62.18
Insurance trust revenue	−272,237	−5.23	−212.02
Exhibit: Salaries and wages	728,362	12.69	567.26
Total expenditure	5,737,911	100.00	4,468.78
General expenditure	5,212,248	90.84	4,059.38
Education	1,393,318	24.28	1,085.14
Public welfare	1,674,173	29.18	1,303.87
Hospitals	42,739	0.74	33.29
Health	317,168	5.53	247.02
Highways	446,756	7.79	347.94
Police protection	51,765	0.90	40.32
Correction	94,514	1.65	73.61
Natural resources	142,762	2.49	111.19
Parks and recreation	9,895	0.17	7.71
Government administration	264,681	4.61	206.14
Interest on general debt	238,396	4.15	185.67
Other and unallocable	536,081	9.34	417.51
Utility expenditure	–	–	–
Liquor store expenditure	55,002	0.96	42.84
Insurance trust expenditure	470,661	8.20	366.56
Debt at end of fiscal year	4,210,901	100.00	3,279.52
Cash and security holdings	11,774,616	100.00	9,170.26

36TAXATION

Maine has the highest state and local tax burden measured as a percent of income (2003, 12.2%). The individual income tax has four brackets ranging from 2% for taxable income up to $4,200 to 8.5% for taxable income over $16,700, with intermediate rates of 4.5% and 7%. The corporate income tax, also with four brackets, ranges from 3.5% of the first $25,000 of net income to 8.93% of net income in excess of $250,000. The state sales tax is 5% on most goods, although basic foods and medicines are exempted. No local sales taxes are permitted. There are also excise taxes on motor fuels, tobacco products, alcoholic beverages (the state controls all sales), insurance premiums, public utilities and pari-mutuels. Maine's estate tax is tied to the federal exemption for state death taxes, and is therefore set to be phased out by 2007 in tandem with the phasing out of the federal estate tax credit, unless the state takes positive action to establish an independent estate tax. Maine's revenue losses from the phasing out of its estate tax are estimated at -$3.6 million for 2002/03, -$16.2 million for 2003/04 and -$32.3 million for 2006/07. Death and gift taxes accounted for 0.9% of state tax collections in 2002. The state also collects various license fees and stamp taxes. Counties do not assess taxes, but they do make levies on municipalities and unorganized territories to meet county budgets. A relatively low 36% of total non-federal taxes are raised at local levels, with 64% raised at the state level.

Total state tax collections in Maine in 2002 amounted to $2.627 billion, of which 40.8% was generated by the state income tax, 31.8% by the state general sales and use tax, 15.3% by state excise taxes, 5.66% by state license fees, 2.9% by the state corporate income tax, and 1.8% by state property taxes.

The following table from the US Census Bureau provides a summary of taxes collected by the state in 2002.

	($000)	PER CAPITA
Total Taxes	2,626,830	2,029.28
Property taxes	48,136	37.19
Sales and gross receipts	1,237,259	955.81
General sales and gross receipts	836,134	645.93
Selective sales taxes	401,125	309.88
Alcoholic beverage	42,891	33.13
Amusements	(X)	(X)
Insurance Premiums	60,376	46.64
Motor fuels	191,694	148.09
Pari-mutuels	4,857	3.75
Public utilities	7,225	5.58
Tobacco products	94,082	72.68
Other selective sales	(X)	(X)
Licenses	148,737	114.9
Alcoholic beverages	4,342	3.35
Amusements	796	0.61
Corporation	3,390	2.62
Hunting and fishing	8,572	6.62
Motor vehicle	78,875	60.93
Motor vehicle operators	10,252	7.92
Public utility	(X)	(X)
Occupation and business, NEC	41,147	31.79
Other	1,363	1.05
Other taxes	1,192,698	921.38
Individual income	1,072,810	828.77
Corporation net income	77,366	59.77
Death and gift	23,420	18.09
Documentary and stock transfer	19,102	14.76
Severance	(X)	(X)
Other	(X)	(X)

37ECONOMIC POLICY

The Finance Authority of Maine (FAME) encourages industrial and recreational projects by insuring mortgage loans, selling tax-exempt bonds to aid industrial development and natural-resource enterprises, authorizing municipalities to issue such revenue bonds, and guaranteeing loans to small businesses, veterans, and natural-resource enterprises. The Department of Economic and Community Development (DECD), created in 1987, provides technical, financial, training, and marketing assistance for existing Maine businesses and companies interested in establishing operations in the state. The DECD offers programs in the areas of business development, tourism, and community development. In 2002, more than $500,000 were awarded to Maine's eight tourist regions, over 1,400 Maine companies received on-going assistance from a network of development specialists; and about 70 communities received federal assistance under the Community Development Block Grant (CDBG) program.

38HEALTH

The overall death rate of 981.6 per 100,000 inhabitants in 2000 was significantly higher than the US rate of 873.1, reflecting the state's higher than average elderly population. The infant mortality rate was 4.9 per 1,000 live births in 2000, ranking 49th nationally. During 1999, 2,427 legal abortions were performed in Maine for an average rate of 9 per 1,000 women. Of the population age 18 and older, 23.8% were classified as smokers in 2000. A total of 1,004 AIDS cases were reported through 2001. Major causes of death in 2000 were heart disease, occurring at a rate of 270.1 per 100,000 population, and cerebrovascular disease, occurring at a rate of 66.2. In 2000, the rate of chronic lower respiratory disease, 61 per 100,000 population, was highest in the nation. The national rate was 44.3.

Maine's 37 community hospitals had 148,612 admissions and 3,844 beds in 2001. There were 5,076 full-time registered nurses and 362 full-time licensed practical nurses in 2001 and 277 physicians per 100,000 population in 2000. The average expense of a community hospital for care was $1,473 per inpatient day in 2001.

Federal government grants to cover the Medicare and Medicaid services in 2001 totaled $941 million; 219,310 enrollees received Medicare benefits that year. At least 10.3% of the population was uninsured in 2002.

39 SOCIAL WELFARE

In 2001, the average weekly unemployment benefit was $217.10. Average monthly participation in the food stamp program in FY2002 comprised 111,147 persons (56,376 households). The average monthly benefit was $73.06, and the sum total of benefits paid in FY2002 was $97,446,679.

With the enactment of the Personal Responsibility and Work Opportunity Reconciliation Act of 1996, the US government has changed the form and regulations for many of its social welfare programs. Most significantly, it replaces Aid to Families with Dependent Children (AFDC), an open-ended entitlement program, with Temporary Assistance for Needy Families (TANF), a limited system of assistance funded largely through federal block grants. The reform act also impacts the food stamp program, the Supplemental Security Income program, and the child nutrition program. The law took effect on 1 July 1997 and provided $16.38 billion in block grants for fiscal years 1997–2002. The grants are to be divided among the states based on an equation involving the numbers of former AFDC recipients in each state.

Reauthorization of the 1996 social welfare legislation, scheduled for 2002, was delayed, and the original law had been extended three times as of July 2003, with the most recent extension running through September 2003. Maine's TANF work program is called Additional Support for People in Retraining and Employment (ASPIRE). In June 2000 the state had 148,13 welfare recipients. State expenditures on the TANF program in FY2002 totaled $25,693,113.

Despite Maine's relatively low personal income and large proportion of residents below the poverty level, welfare payments per capita generally fall short of the national norms. In December 2001, Social Security benefits were paid to 253,810 Maine residents. This number included 154,910 retired workers, 25,860 widows and widowers, 36,200 disabled workers, 14,910 spouses, and 21,930 children. Social Security beneficiaries represented 19.7% of the total state population and 95.2% of the state's population age 65 and older. Retired workers (excluding persons with special benefits) received an average monthly payment of $805; widows and widowers, $780; disabled workers, $743; and spouses, $410. Payments for children of retired workers averaged $411 per month; children of deceased workers, $573; and children of disabled workers, $201.

Federal Supplemental Security Income payments in December 2001 went to 30,138 Maine residents, averaging $331 a month.

40 HOUSING

Housing for Maine families has improved substantially since 1960, when the federal census categorized 57,000 of Maine's 364,650 housing units as deteriorated or dilapidated. Between 1970 and 1980, over 115,000 new units were built. However, about 32% of the entire housing stock was built in 1939 or earlier.

There were an estimated 664,613 housing units in Maine in 2002. Approximately 536,194 of the total units were occupied, with 72% being owner-occupied. About 67.7% of all units are single-family, detached homes. Fuel oils and kerosene are the primary heating fuel for most units. It was estimated that 9,630 units lacked telephone service, 5,081 lacked complete plumbing facilities, and 4,058 lacked complete kitchen facilities. The average household size was 2.35 people.

In 2002, 7,207 privately owned units were authorized for construction. About one-seventh of all Maine homes are for seasonal rather than year-round use. The median home value is $121,036. The median monthly cost for mortgage owners was $971. Renters paid a median of $552 per month. During 2002, Maine received over $31 million in community planning and development aid from the US Department of Housing and Urban Development.

41 EDUCATION

In 2000, 85.4% of Maine residents age 25 and older were high school graduates; 22.9% had obtained a bachelor's degree or higher.

The total enrollment for fall 1999 in Maine's public schools stood at 209,253. Of these, 148,744 attended schools from kindergarten through grade eight, and 60,479 attended high school. Minority students made up approximately 3% of the total enrollment in public elementary and secondary schools in 2001. Total enrollment was estimated at 213,461 in fall 2000 and expected to drop to 198,000 by fall 2005. Enrollment in nonpublic schools in fall 2001 was 18,287. Expenditures for public education in 2000/01 were estimated at $1,634,197.

As of fall 2000, there were 67,216 students enrolled in institutions of higher education. In the same year Maine had 33 degree-granting institutions. In 1997, minority students comprised 4.5% of total postsecondary enrollment. Since 1968, the state's public colleges and universities have been incorporated into a single University of Maine System. The original land grant campus is at Orono; the other major campus in the system is the University of Southern Maine at Portland and Gorham. The state also operates the Maine Maritime Academy at Castine and the Maine Technical College System, comprised of six technical colleges. Of the state's 16 private colleges and professional schools, Bowdoin College in Brunswick, Colby College in Waterville, and Bates College in Lewiston are the best known.

42 ARTS

Maine has long held an attraction for painters and artists, Winslow Homer and Andrew Wyeth among them. The state abounds in summer theaters, the oldest and most famous of which is at Ogunquit. The Portland Symphony (est. 1923) is Maine's leading orchestra. Augusta and Bangor also host symphonies. The Maine State Ballet Company is based in Westbrook. The Portland Ballet is also well known in the state. The Bossov Ballet Theatre in Pittsfield is part of a boarding school for high school students looking for rigorous pre-professional training in dance. One of the newest additions to Maine's cultural life is the Maine Grand Opera Company (est. 2001), based at the Camden Opera House. There are many local theater groups.

Some well-known festivals include the Arcady Summer Music Festival (est. 1980), specializing in chamber music, and the annual Bowdoin Summer Music Festival (est. 1964), presented at Bowdoin College in Brunswick.

In 1979, Maine became the first state to allow inheritance taxes to be paid with qualified artworks. The Maine Arts Commission is an independent state agency funded in part by the Maine State Legislature and the National Endowment for the Arts. The state Department of Educational and Cultural Services has an Arts and Humanities Bureau that provides funds to artists in residence, Maine touring artists, and community arts councils. In 2003, the Maine Arts Commission and other Maine arts organizations received grants totaling $983,900 from the National Endowment for the Arts. Additional funds come from the state and other private sources. Arts education is offered by the state to about 11,600 schoolchildren.

The Maine Humanities Council (MHC), founded in 1975, has distributed over $4 million in grants since its inception. Several ongoing reading programs sponsored in part by MHC include Born to Read, for children and youth; New Books, New Readers, for adult learners; and Let's Talk About It, for adult readers. In 2000, the state received $1,059,661 from the National Endowment for the Humanities.

43 LIBRARIES AND MUSEUMS

In 2000, Maine public libraries had 5,683,000 volumes and a combined circulation of 8,124,000. Leading libraries and their book holdings in 1998 included the Maine State Library at Augusta (150,000 volumes), Bowdoin College at Brunswick (901,589), and the University of Maine School of Law (300,000). Total public library income in 2000 was $26,059,000 including $286,649 in state grants.

Maine has at least 121 museums and historic sites. The Maine State Museum in Augusta houses collections in history, natural history, anthropology, marine studies, mineralogy, science, and technology. The privately supported Maine Historical Society in Portland maintains a research library and the Wadsworth Longfellow House, the boyhood home of Henry Wadsworth Longfellow. The largest of several maritime museums is in Bath.

44 COMMUNICATIONS

In 2001, 97.7% of occupied housing units had telephones.

Maine had 33 major commercial radio stations (5 AM, 33 FM) in 2003, along with 12 major television stations. Educational television stations broadcast from Augusta, Biddeford, Calais, Orono, and Presque Isle.

By 2000, a total of 25,583 Internet domain names had been registered in Maine.

45 PRESS

Maine had seven daily newspapers in 2002 and four papers with Sunday editions. The most widely read newspapers with approximate 2002 circulation numbers are as follows:

AREA	NAME	DAILY	SUNDAY
Augusta	Kennebec Journal	14,566	13,699
Bangor	Daily News	64,799	76,103(wknd)
Portland	Press Herald/Sunday Telegram	76,603	123,386

Regional interest magazines include Maine Times and Down East.

46 ORGANIZATIONS

In 2003, there were about 841 regional, national, and international organizations within the state. Among the organizations with headquarters in Maine are the Maine Potato Council (Presque Isle), the Maine Lobstermen's Association (Stonington), the Wild Blueberry Association of North America (Bar Harbor), and the Potato Association of America (Orono).

State and local organizations for arts and education include the Bluegrass Music Association of Maine, Maine Arts Commission, the Maine Folklife Center, the Maine Historical Society, the Maine Humanities Council, Maine Preservation, and the National Poetry Foundation, based at the University of Maine. There are a number of smaller local arts organizations and municipal and regional historical societies as well.

47 TOURISM, TRAVEL, AND RECREATION

In 2001, the state of Maine hosted over 43 million travelers who spent about $5.6 billion dollars. About 34 million travelers were on day-trips throughout the state, with nearly 71% of tourist activity involved out-of-state travelers. Though Maine is a year-round resort destination, 59% of travelers arrive during the months of July, August, and September. Sightseeing and outdoor activities are the primary tourist attractions.

In the summer, the southern coast offers sandy beaches, icy surf, and several small harbors for sailing and saltwater fishing. Northeastward, the scenery becomes more rugged and spectacular, and sailing and hiking are the primary activities. Hundreds of lakes, ponds, rivers, and streams offer opportunities for freshwater bathing, boating, and fishing. Whitewater canoeing lures the adventurous along the Allagash Wilderness Waterway in northern Maine. Maine has always attracted hunters, especially during the fall deer season. Wintertime recreation facilities include nearly 60 ski areas and countless opportunities for cross-country skiing.

There are 12 state parks and beaches. Baxter State Park, in central Maine, includes Mount Katahdino. Acadia National Park is a popular attraction, along with other wildlife areas, refuges, and forests. The state fair is held at Bangor.

48 SPORTS

Maine has no major league professional sports team. The Portland Pirates (a minor league hockey team) of the American Hockey League play on their home ice at the Cumberland County Civic Center in Portland. Minor league baseball's Sea Dogs of the Double-A Eastern League play their games at Hadlock Field, which opened in 1994. Harness racing is held at Scarborough Downs and other tracks and fairgrounds throughout the state. Sailing is a popular participant sport with a Windsummer Festival held each July at Boothbay Harbor and a Retired Skippers Race at Castine in August. Joan Benoit-Samuelson, famous distance runner during the 1980s, was born in Cape Elizabeth.

49 FAMOUS MAINERS

The highest federal officeholders born in Maine were Hannibal Hamlin (1809–91), the nation's first Republican vice president, under Abraham Lincoln, and Nelson A. Rockefeller (1908–79), governor of New York State from 1959 to 1973 and US vice president under Gerald Ford. James G. Blaine (b.Pennsylvania, 1830–93), a lawyer and politician, served 13 years as a US representative from Maine and a term in the Senate; on his third try, he won the Republican presidential nomination in 1884 but lost to Grover Cleveland, later serving as secretary of state (1889–92) under Benjamin Harrison. Edmund S. Muskie (1914–96), leader of the Democratic revival in Maine in the 1950s, followed two successful terms as governor with 21 years in the Senate until appointed secretary of state by President Jimmy Carter in 1980.

Other conspicuous state and national officeholders have included Rufus King (1755–1827), a member of the Continental Congress and Constitutional Convention and US minister to Great Britain; William King (1768–1852), leader of the movement for Maine statehood and the state's first governor; Thomas Bracket Reed (1839–1902), longtime speaker of the US House of Representatives; and Margaret Chase Smith (1897–1995), who served longer in the US Senate—24 years—than any other woman.

Names prominent in Maine's colonial history include those of Sir Ferdinando Gorges (b.England, 1566–1647), the founder and proprietor of the colony; Sir William Phips (1651–95), who became the first American knight for his recovery of a Spanish treasure, later serving as royal governor of Massachusetts; and Sir William Pepperrell (1696–1759), who led the successful New England expedition against Louisburg in 1745, for which he became the first American-born baronet.

Maine claims a large number of well-known reformers and humanitarians: Dorothea Lynde Dix (1802–87), who led the movement for hospitals for the insane; Elijah Parish Lovejoy (1802–37), an abolitionist killed while defending his printing press from a proslavery mob in St. Louis, Missouri; Neal Dow (1804–97), who drafted and secured passage of the Maine prohibition laws of 1846 and 1851, later served as a Civil War general, and ran for president on the Prohibition Party ticket in 1880; and Harriet Beecher Stowe (b.Connecticut, 1811–96), whose *Uncle Tom's Cabin* (1852) was written in Maine.

Other important writers include poet Henry Wadsworth Longfellow (1807–82), born in Portland while Maine was still part of Massachusetts; humorist Artemus Ward (Charles Farrar Browne, 1834–67); Sarah Orne Jewett (1849–1909), novelist and short-story writer; Kate Douglas Wiggin (1856–1923), author of *Rebecca of Sunnybrook Farm;* Kenneth Roberts (1885–1957), historical novelist; and Robert Peter Tristram Coffin (1892–1955), poet, essayist, and novelist. Edwin Arlington Robinson (1869–1935) and Edna St. Vincent Millay (1892–1950) were both Pulitzer Prize-winning poets, and novelist Marguerite Yourcenar (b.Belgium, 1903–1987), a resident of Mt. Desert Island, became in 1980 the first woman ever elected to the Académie Française. Richard Russo (b.New York, 1949), whose *Empire Falls* won the Pulitzer Prize for fiction in 2002, lives in Camden. Stephen King (b.1947), perhaps Maine's best-known writer of popular fiction, lives in Bangor. Winslow Homer (b.Massachusetts, 1836–1910) had a summer home at Prouts Neck, where he painted many of his seascapes.

50BIBLIOGRAPHY

Alampi, Gary, ed. *Gale State Rankings Reporter.* Detroit: Gale Research, Inc., 1994.

Bearse, Ray, ed. *Maine: A Guide to the Vacation State.* 2nd ed., rev. Boston: Houghton Mifflin, 1969.

Beem, Edgar Allen. *Maine: the Spirit of America.* New York: Harry N. Abrams, 2000.

Churchill, Edwin A., Joel W. Eastman, and Richard W. Judd, eds. *Maine: The Pine Tree State from Prehistory to the Present.* Orono: University of Maine Press, 1995.

Clark, Charles E. *Maine: A Bicentennial History.* New York: Norton, 1977.

Council of State Governments. *The Book of the States, 1994–1995 Edition.* Vol. 30. Lexington, Kentucky: The Council of State Governments, 1994.

FDIC, Division of Research and Statistics. *Statistics on Banking: A Statistical Profile of the United States Banking Industry.* Washington, D.C.: Federal Deposit Insurance Corporation, 1993.

Gould, John. *Maine's Golden Road: A Memoir.* New York: Norton, 1995.

Isaacson, Dorris, ed. *Maine: A Guide "Down East."* 2nd ed. Rockland: Courier-Gazette, Inc., for the Maine League of Historical Societies and Museums, 1970 (orig. 1937).

McAuliffe, Emily. *Maine Facts and Symbols.* New York: Hilltop Books, 2000.

Maine, State of. State Development Office. *Maine: A Statistical Summary.* Augusta, 1984.

Morris, Gerald E., ed. *The Maine Bicentennial Atlas.* Portland: Maine Historical Society, 1976.

Osborn, William C. *The Paper Plantation.* New York: Grossman, 1974.

Palmer, Kenneth T. *Maine Politics & Government.* Lincoln: University of Nebraska Press, 1992.

Rich, Louise Dickinson. *State O' Maine.* New York: Harper & Row, 1964.

Rowe, William H. *The Maritime History of Maine.* New York: Norton, 1948.

Schmittroth, Linda, ed. *Cities of the United States.* 3rd ed. Detroit: Gale Research, Inc., 1997.

Smith, David C. *Studies in the Land: The Northeast Corner.* New York: Routledge, 2002.

U.S. Department of Education, National Center for Education Statistics. Office of Educational Research and Improvement. *Digest of Education Statistics, 1993.* Washington, D.C.: U.S. Government Printing Office, 1993.

U.S. Department of the Interior, U.S. Fish and Wildlife Service. *Endangered and Threatened Species Recovery Program.* Washington, D.C.: U.S. Government Printing Office, 1990.

MARYLAND

State of Maryland

ORIGIN OF STATE NAME: Named for Henrietta Maria, queen consort of King Charles I of England. **NICKNAME:** The Old Line State and the Free State. **CAPITAL:** Annapolis. **ENTERED UNION:** 28 April 1788 (7th). **SONG:** "Maryland, My Maryland." **MOTTO:** *Fatti maschii, parole femine* (Manly deeds, womanly words). **FLAG:** Bears the quartered arms of the Calvert and Crossland families (the paternal and maternal families of the founders of Maryland). **OFFICIAL SEAL:** REVERSE: A shield bearing the arms of the Calverts and Crosslands is surmounted by an earl's coronet and a helmet and supported by a farmer and fisherman. The state motto (originally that of the Calverts) appears on a scroll below. The circle is surrounded by the Latin legend *Scuto bon voluntatis tu coronasti nos,* meaning "With the shield of thy favor hast thou compassed us," and "1632," the date of Maryland's first charter. OBVERSE: Lord Baltimore is seen as a knight in armor on a charger. The surrounding inscription, in Latin, means "Cecilius, Absolute Lord of Maryland and Avalon New Foundland, Baron of Baltimore." **BIRD:** Baltimore oriole. **FISH:** Rockfish. **REPTILE:** Diamondback terrapin. **CRUSTACEAN:** Blue crab. **DOG:** Chesapeake Bay retriever. **INSECT:** Baltimore checkerspot butterfly. **FLOWER:** Black-eyed Susan. **TREE:** White oak. **BEVERAGE:** Milk. **SPORT:** Jousting. **BOAT:** The skipjack. **LEGAL HOLIDAYS:** New Year's Day, 1 January; Birthday of Martin Luther King, Jr., 3rd Monday in January; Lincoln's Birthday, 12 February; Washington's Birthday, 3rd Monday in February; Maryland Day, 25 March; Good Friday, March or April; Memorial Day, 30 May; Independence Day, 4 July; Labor Day, 1st Monday in September; Defenders' Day, 12 September; Columbus Day, 12 October; Election Day, 1st Tuesday after 1st Monday in November, even-numbered years; Veterans Day, 11 November; Thanksgiving Day, 4th Thursday in November; Christmas Day, 25 December. **TIME:** 7 AM EST = noon GMT.

¹LOCATION, SIZE, AND EXTENT

Located on the eastern seaboard of the US in the South Atlantic region, Maryland ranks 42nd in size among the 50 states.

Maryland's total area—10,460 sq mi (27,092 sq km)—comprises 9,837 sq mi (25,478 sq km) of land and 623 sq mi (1,614 sq km) of inland water. The state extends 199 mi (320 km) E-W and 126 mi (203 km) N-S.

Maryland is bordered on the N by Pennsylvania; on the E by Delaware and the Atlantic Ocean; on the S and SW by Virginia, the District of Columbia, and West Virginia (with the line passing through the Chesapeake Bay and Potomac River); and on the extreme W by West Virginia. Important islands in Chesapeake Bay, off Maryland's Eastern Shore (the Maryland sector of the Delmarva Peninsula), include Kent, Bloodsworth, South Marsh, and Smith.

The total boundary length of Maryland is 842 mi (1,355 km), including a general coastline of 31 mi (50 km); the total tidal shoreline extends 3,190 mi (5,134 km). The state's geographic center is in Prince George's County, 4.5 mi (7.2 km) NW of Davidsonville.

²TOPOGRAPHY

Three distinct regions characterize Maryland's topography. The first and major area, falling within the Atlantic Coastal Plain, is nearly bisected by the Chesapeake Bay, dividing Maryland into the Eastern Shore and the Western Shore. The Piedmont Plateau, west of the coastal lowlands, is broad, rolling upland with several deep gorges cut by rivers. Further west, from the Catoctin Mountains in Frederick County to the West Virginia border, is the Appalachian Mountain region, containing the state's highest hills. Backbone Mountain, in Garrett County in westernmost Maryland, is the state's highest point, at 3,360 ft (1,025 m).

A few small islands lie in the Chesapeake Bay, Maryland's dominant waterway. Extending 195 mi (314 km) inland from the Atlantic and varying in width from 3 to 20 mi (5–32 km), the bay comprises 3,237 sq mi (8,384 sq km), of which 1,726 sq km (4,470 sq km) are under Maryland's jurisdiction. Principal rivers include the Potomac, forming much of the southern and western border; the Patapsco, which runs through Baltimore; the Patuxent, draining the Western Shore; and the Susquehanna, crossing the Pennsylvania border and emptying into the Chesapeake Bay in northeastern Maryland. The state has 23 rivers and other bays, as well as many lakes and creeks, none of any great size.

³CLIMATE

Despite its small size, Maryland exhibits considerable climatic diversity. Temperatures vary from an annual average of 48°F (9°C) in the extreme western uplands to 59°F (15°C) in the southeast, where the climate is moderated by the Chesapeake Bay and the Atlantic Ocean. The daily mean temperature for Baltimore is 55°F (13°C), ranging from 33°F (1°C) in January to 77°F (25°C) in July. The record high temperature for the state is 109°F (43°C), set on 10 July 1936 in Cumberland and Frederick counties; the record low, –40°F (–40°C), occurred on 13 January 1912 at Oakland in Garrett County.

Precipitation averages about 49 in (124 cm) annually in the southeast, but only 36 in (91 cm) in the Cumberland area west of the Appalachians; Baltimore averaged 41.9 in (106 cm) annually 1971–2000. As much as 100 in (254 cm) of snow falls in western Garrett County, while 8–10 in (20–25 cm) is average for the Eastern Shore; and Baltimore receives about 22 in (56 cm).

⁴FLORA AND FAUNA

Maryland's three life zones—coastal plain, piedmont, and Appalachian—mingle wildlife characteristic of both North and South. Most of the state lies within a hardwood belt in which red and white oaks, yellow poplar, beech, blackgum, hickory, and white ash are represented; shortleaf and loblolly pines are the leading softwoods. Honeysuckle, Virginia creeper, wild grape, and wild raspberry are also common. Wooded hillsides are rich with such wild flowers as Carolina cranesbill, trailing arbutus, Mayapple, early blue violet, wild rose, and goldenrod. Seven plant species were listed as threatened or endangered in 2003, including Canby's dropwort, sandplain gerardia, northeastern bulrush, and harperella.

The white-tailed (Virginia) deer, eastern cottontail, raccoon, and red and gray foxes are indigenous to Maryland, although urbanization has sharply reduced their habitat. Common small mammals are the woodchuck, eastern chipmunk, and gray squirrel. The brown-headed nuthatch has been observed in the extreme south, the cardinal and tufted titmouse are common in the piedmont, and the chestnut-sided warbler and rose-breasted grosbeak are native to the Appalachians. Among saltwater species, shellfish—especially oysters, clams, and crabs—have the greatest economic importance. Nineteen Maryland animal species were listed as threatened or endangered in 2003, including the Indiana bat, Maryland darter, bald eagle, Delmarva Peninsula fox squirrel, three species of whale, and five species of turtle.

⁵ENVIRONMENTAL PROTECTION

The Maryland Department of the Environment (MDE) serves as the state's primary environmental protection agency. MDE protects and restores the quality of Maryland's land, air, and water by assessing, preventing and controlling sources of pollution for the benefit of public health, the environment and future generations. MDE regulations control the storage, transportation, and disposal of hazardous wastes and ensure long-term, environmentally sound solid waste recycling and disposal capabilities. In 2003, Maryland had 168 hazardous waste sites listed in the Environmental Protection Agency's database, 18 of which were on the National Priorities List.

MDE has broad regulatory, planning, and management responsibility for water quality, air quality, solid and hazardous waste management, stormwater management, sediment control, wetlands and waterways management, and water allocation. MDE also plays a pivotal role in Maryland's initiatives to protect and restore the Chesapeake Bay and has divided the state into ten major tributary watershed basins, each of which have specific nutrient reduction strategies designed to give the Bay added protection from the effects of stormwater run-off, airborne pollutants, and direct discharges. Additionally, Maryland's Department of Natural Resources manages water allocation, fish and wildlife, state parks and forests, land reclamation and open space.

MDE operates an innovative infrastructure financing program that leverages federal, state, and local funds to upgrade wastewater treatment plants, connect residents to public sewer systems, and improve water supply facilities. In addition, the Maryland Environmental Service, a quasi-public agency, contracts with local governments to design, construct, finance, and operate wastewater treatment plants, water supply systems, and recycling facilities.

The Maryland Department of Natural Resources (DNR) is responsible for the management, enhancement, and preservation of the state's living and natural resources. Utilizing an ecosystem approach to land, waterway, and species management, DNR programs and services support the health of the Chesapeake Bay and its tributaries, sustainable populations of fishery and wildlife species, and an integrated network of public lands and open space.

The Maryland Office of Planning's mission is to plan for the most effective development of the state and all of its resources. The Office assists state agencies and local governments to more effectively achieve environmental, agricultural, and natural resource objectives by integrating them with comprehensive planning and land use management. The state has recently embarked on a Neighborhood Conservation and Smart Growth initiative to encourage population and economic growth in priority funding areas, and to use a Rural Legacy Program to preserve agricultural, forest, and other rural lands from development. In 2001, Maryland received $91,169,000 in federal grants from the Environmental Protection Agency; EPA expenditures for procurement contracts in Maryland that year amounted to $61,152,000.

⁶POPULATION

Maryland ranked 18th in population in the US with an estimated total of 5,458,137 in 2002, an increase of 3.1% since 2000. Between 1990 and 2000, Maryland's population grew from 4,781,468 to 5,296,486, an increase of 10.8%. The population is projected to reach 5,467,000 by 2005 and 6.3 million by 2025.

In 2000 the median age was 36. Persons under 18 years old accounted for 25.6% of the population while 11.3% were age 65 or older.

The state's population doubled between 1940 and 1970 and increased 7.5% between 1970 and 1980. The enormous expansion of the federal government and exodus of people from Washington, D.C., to the surrounding suburbs contributed to the rapid growth that made Maryland the 17th most populous state in 1980, with 4,216,446 residents. There was an increase of 13.4% between 1980 and 1990, when Maryland held the 19th ranking, with 4,781,468 people. The population density in 2000 was 541.9 persons per sq mi, the 5th-highest among the 50 states.

Almost all the growth since World War II has occurred in the four suburban counties around Washington, D.C., and Baltimore. Metropolitan Baltimore, embracing Carroll, Howard, Hartford, Anne Arundel, and Baltimore counties, expanded from 2,244,700 to 2,491,254 between 1984 and 2000; the city of Baltimore, on the other hand, declined from 763,570 to 736,000 during the same period, and to an estimated 638,614 in 2002. Baltimore is the state's only major city; several west-central counties belong to the Washington metropolitan area, and Cecil County, in the northeast, is part of metropolitan Wilmington, Delaware.

⁷ETHNIC GROUPS

Blacks, numbering 1,477,411 in 2000, constitute the largest racial minority in Maryland. About one-third of Maryland's black population lives in the city of Baltimore.

Hispanics and Latinos, mostly from Puerto Rico and Central America, numbered 227,000 in 2000 (4.3% of the total population), up from 125,000. In 2000, the Asian population was relatively large: 39,155 Koreans, 49,400 Chinese (nearly double the 1990 total of 26,479), 26,608 Filipinos, 6,620 Japanese, and 16,744 Vietnamese (up from 7,809 in 1990); the total Asian population was estimated at 210,929 in 2000. Pacific Islanders numbered 2,303.

Foreign-born residents numbered 518,315, or 9.8% of the total population, in 2000, up from 313,494, or 6.5%, in 1990. Many immigrated to Maryland in the 1970s. A significant proportion of the state's German, Polish, and Russian immigrants were Jewish refugees arriving just before and after World War II. In 2000, the combined Native American population (including Eskimos and Aleuts) was estimated at 15,423.

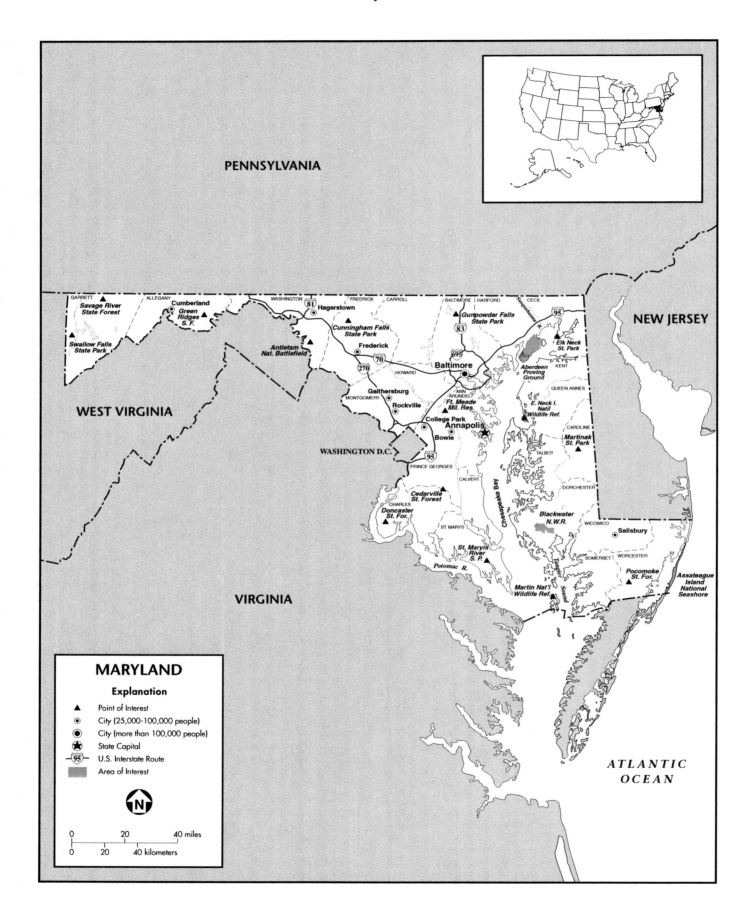

8LANGUAGES

Several Algonkian tribes originally inhabited what is now Maryland. There are some Indian place-names, such as Potomac, Susquehanna, and Allegheny.

The state's diverse topography has contributed to unusual diversity in its basic speech. Geographical isolation of the Delmarva Peninsula, proximity to the Virginia piedmont population, and access to southeastern and central Pennsylvania helped to yield a language mixture that now is dominantly Midland and yet reflects earlier ties to Southern English.

Regional features occur as well. In the northeast are found eastern Pennsylvania *pavement* (sidewalk) and *baby coach* (baby carriage). In the north and west are *poke* (bag), *quarter till, sick on the stomach, openseed peach* (freestone peach), and Pennsylvania German *ponhaws* (scrapple). In the southern portion are found *light bread* (white bread), *curtain* (shade), *carry* (escort), *crop* as /krap/, and *bulge* with the vowel of *put*. East of Chesapeake Bay are *mosquito hawk* (dragonfly), *paled fence* (picket fence), *poor* (rhyming with *mower*), and *Mary* with the vowel of *mate*. In central Maryland, an earthworm is a *baitworm*.

In 2000, 4, 322,329 residents, or 87.% of the population five years old or older (down from 91.1% in 1990), spoke only English at home.

The following table gives selected statistics from the 2000 census for language spoken at home by persons five years old and over. The category "African languages" includes Amharic, Ibo, Twi, Yoruba, Bantu, Swahili, and Somali. The category "Other Asian languages" includes Dravidian languages, Malayalam, Telugu, Tamil, and Turkish. The category "Other Indic languages" includes Bengali, Marathi, Punjabi, and Romany.

LANGUAGE	NUMBER	PERCENT
Population 5 years and over	4,945,043	100.0
Speak only English	4,322,329	87.4
Speak a language other than English	622,714	12.6
Speak a language other than English	622,714	12.6
Spanish or Spanish Creole	230,829	4.7
French (incl. Patois, Cajun)	42,838	0.9
Chinese	41,883	0.8
African languages	36,967	0.7
Korean	32,937	0.7
German	23,796	0.5
Tagalog	18,495	0.4
Russian	17,584	0.4
Vietnamese	14,891	0.3
Italian	13,798	0.3
Other Asian languages	12,405	0.3
Persian	11,951	0.2
Hindi	11,389	0.2
Other Indic languages	11,345	0.2
Greek	10,717	0.2
Arabic	10,458	0.2

9RELIGIONS

Maryland was founded as a haven for Roman Catholics, who still make up the largest single religious group in the states although their political supremacy ended in 1692, when Anglicanism (now the Episcopal Church) became the established religion. Laws against "popery" were enacted by 1704 and Roman Catholic priests were harassed; the state constitution of 1776, however, placed all Christian faiths on an equal footing. The state's first Lutheran church was built in 1729, the first Baptist church in 1742, and the earliest Methodist church in 1760. Jews settled in Baltimore in the early 1800s, with a much larger wave of Jewish immigration in the late 19th century.

As of 2000, there were 952,389 Roman Catholics in Maryland. Adherents of the major Protestant denominations included United Methodists, 297,729; Southern Baptists, 142,401; Evangelical Lutherans,103,644; and Episcopalians,

81,061. In 2000, there were an estimated 216,000 Jews and about 52,867 Muslims. Though membership numbers were unavailable, reports indicate there were about 32 Buddhist congregations and 26 Hindu congregations in 2000. Over 3 million people (about 56.7% of the population) were not counted as members of any religious organization.

10TRANSPORTATION

Some of the nation's earliest efforts toward the development of a reliable transportation system began in Maryland. In 1695, a public postal road was opened from the Potomac River through Annapolis and the Eastern Shore to Philadelphia. Construction on the National Road (now US 40) began at Cumberland in 1811; within seven years, the road was a conduit for settlers in Ohio. The first commercial steamboat service from Baltimore started in 1813, and steamboats were active all along the Chesapeake during the 1800s. The Delaware and Chesapeake Canal, linking Chesapeake Bay and the Delaware River, opened in 1829.

Maryland's first railroad, the Baltimore and Ohio (B&O), was started in 1828; in 1835, it provided the first passenger train service to Washington, DC, and Harpers Ferry, Virginia (now West Virginia). By 1857, the line was extended to St. Louis, and its freight capacity helped build Baltimore into a major center of commerce. In the 1850s, the Pennsylvania Railroad began to buy up small Maryland lines and provide direct service to northern cities.

Today Consolidated Rail, CSX Transportation, and Norfolk Southern are the Class I railroads operating in the state, along with one regional, one Canadian, four Local, and two switching and terminal railroads. As of 2000, total rail miles in Maryland amounted to 1,235 mi (1,987 km), including about 835 mi (1,343 km) of Class I track. The Maryland Transportation Department's Railroad Administration subsidizes four commuter lines, as well as freight lines in western Maryland and on the Eastern Shore. Amtrak operated six stations and about 70 daily trains on 94 mi (151 km) of track through the state in 1998.

The Maryland Mass Transit Administration inaugurated Baltimore's first subway line on 21 November 1983. The combined underground-elevated line ran for 8 mi (13 km) from downtown Baltimore to Reisterstown Plaza; later, the Baltimore Metro was extended for 6 mi (10 km) to Owings Mills, just outside the city limits. The Metro cost nearly $1 billion to build. In 1984, the Washington, DC, mass transit system was extended to the Maryland suburbs, including Bethesda and Rockville.

About half of Maryland's roads serve metropolitan Baltimore and Washington. As of 2000, there were 30,494 mi (49,075 km) of public roadway. The major toll road is the John F. Kennedy Memorial Highway (I-95), linking Baltimore with Wilmington, Delaware, and the New Jersey Turnpike. There were 3,382,451 licensed drivers and 3,847,538 motor vehicles registered in Maryland in 2000.

The Port of Baltimore handled 37.2 million tons of cargo in 2000, including 23 million tons of foreign cargo and 14.2 million tons of domestic cargo. There are 155 airports in Maryland. The Department of Transportation operates Baltimore-Washington International (BWI) Airport, the major air terminal in the state. Another 71 airfields (64 heliports, 1 stolport, and 6 seaplane bases) also served the state in 2002.

11HISTORY

The Indian tribes living in the region that was to become Maryland were Algonkian-speakers: the Accomac, Nanticoke, and Wicomico on the Eastern Shore, and the Susquehannock, Yacomico, and Piscataway on the Western Shore. The Susquehannock, the most powerful tribe at the time of English colonization, claimed all the land lying between the Susquehanna and Potomac rivers. Although the Algonkian Indians hunted for much of their food, many tribes (including the Susquehannock) also had permanent settlements where they cultivated corn (maize), vegetables, tobacco, and other crops. George Alsop, in his Character of the Province of Maryland (1666), noted that Susquehannock women "are the Butchers, Cooks, and Tillers of the ground but the men think it below the honour of a Masculine to stoop to any thing but that which their Gun, or Bow and Arrows can Command." European penetration of the Chesapeake region began early in the 16th century, with the expeditions of Giovanni da Verrazano, a Florentine navigator, and the Spaniard Lucas Vázquez de Ayllón. Captain John Smith, leader of the English settlement at Jamestown, Virginia, was the first English explorer of Chesapeake Bay (1608) and produced a map of the area that was used for years.

The founding of Maryland is intimately tied to the career of another Englishman, George Calvert. A favorite of King James I, Calvert left the Church of England in 1624 to become a Roman Catholic. He announced his conversion in 1625 and—because Catholics were not allowed to hold public office in England at that time—then resigned his post as secretary of state and, against the king's wishes, retired from the royal court. As a reward for Calvert's service, the king bestowed upon him large Irish estates and a peerage with the title of Baron of Baltimore. Two years later, Calvert sailed for the New World, landing in Newfoundland, to which he had received title in 1621. After a severe winter, however, Calvert decided to seek his fortunes where the weather was warmer—in Virginia. Not well-received there because of his religion, Calvert returned to England and asked King Charles I (James's successor) for land south of Virginia; instead he received a grant north of the Potomac. Virginia's agents in England contested Calvert's right to this land strenuously but unsuccessfully, and when he died in 1632, the title passed to his son Cecilius Calvert, 2nd Baron Baltimore (usually called Lord Baltimore), who named the region Maryland after the queen consort of Charles I, Henrietta Maria. At this time, the land grant embraced not only present-day Maryland but also the present State of Delaware, a large part of Pennsylvania, and the valley between the north and south branches of the Potomac River. Not until the 1760s was the final boundary between Pennsylvania and Maryland (as surveyed by Charles Mason and Jeremiah Dixon) established by royal decree, and nearly a century passed before Maryland conceded to Virginia the land between the north and south branches of the Potomac.

The government of provincial Maryland was absolute, embodying the most extensive grant of royal powers to a colonial settlement. Lord Baltimore's main source of income as lord proprietary was the quitrents settlers paid for their land; in return for his authority, Calvert had to give the king only two Indian arrows yearly. Lord Baltimore assigned to his half-brother, Leonard Calvert, the task of organizing the settlement of the colony. On 22 November 1633, Calvert and approximately 250 settlers, including many Roman Catholics and two Jesuit priests, set sail for America on two ships, the Ark and the Dove. They landed at St. Clements Island on 25 March 1634. Two days later, Calvert purchased a site from the Indians, named it St. Marys (the first capital of Maryland), and assumed the governorship of the colony.

The early days of settlement were tumultuous. The refusal by a Virginia colonist, William Claiborne of Kent Island, to acknowledge Lord Baltimore's charter led to a small war that ended in 1638 with a temporary victory for Governor Calvert. The conflict in England during the 1640s found an echo in the struggle between Puritans and Roman Catholics in Maryland, a conflict that saw the two-year exile of Governor Calvert to Virginia, the assumption of power by English representatives (including Claiborne and one of the Puritan leaders) in 1652, a subsequent civil war, and finally the recognition of Lord Baltimore's charter by Oliver Cromwell in 1657.

Cecilius Calvert died in 1675. His successor was Charles Calvert, 3rd Baron Baltimore and the next lord proprietary. His tenure, which lasted until 1715, saw a decisive change in the character of the province. In 1689, with Protestants ascendant in both England and Maryland, the British crown assumed direct control over the province, and in 1692, the Church of England became Maryland's established religion. When Charles Calvert died, his successor, Benedict Leonard Calvert, 4th Baron Baltimore, was granted full proprietary rights—but only because he had embraced the Protestant faith. Proprietary rule continued through his legitimate heirs until the eve of the American Revolution.

Throughout this period, the upper and lower houses of the colonial assembly—consisting, respectively, of the governor and his council and of delegates elected from the counties—quarreled over taxation and the extension of English statutes to free Marylanders. Having already secured most rights from the proprietor, the lower house was somewhat reluctant to vote for independence from the British crown, on whose authority the proprietary government now rested. After its initial hesitancy, however, Maryland cast its lot with the Revolution and sent approximately 20,000 soldiers to fight in the war. The Continental Congress met in Baltimore from December 1776 to March 1777 and in Annapolis from November 1783 to June 1784. These cities were thus among the eight that served as US capitals before the designation of a permanent seat of government in Washington, DC.

Maryland was one of the last states to sign the Articles of Confederation, not ratifying them until other states dropped their claims to what later became the Northwest Territory. On 28 April 1788, Maryland became the 7th state to ratify the federal Constitution. The state constitution, drawn up in 1776, was weighted heavily in favor of property holders and the rural counties, at the expense of the propertyless and the city of Baltimore; the legislature removed the property qualifications in 1810.

Maryland's prosperity during the colonial and early federal period waxed and waned according to the world price of tobacco, the staple crop of tidewater and southern Maryland. Planters increasingly employed slave labor on farms and plantations, and the black population grew rapidly in the 18th century. German immigrants began moving into western Maryland, where wheat became the primary crop. The cultivation of wheat also helped make Baltimore's fortune. Founded in 1729 and incorporated in 1796, the city of Baltimore was blessed with a harbor well suited to the export and import trade. As commerce developed, shipbuilding emerged as a major economic activity. By the early 19th century, Baltimore was already the state's major center of commerce and industry.

The city and harbor were the site of extensive naval and military operations during the War of 1812. It was during the bombardment of Ft. McHenry in 1814 that Francis Scott Key, detained on the British frigate, composed "The Star-Spangled Banner," which became the US national anthem in March 1931.

After the War of 1812, Maryland history was marked by the continued growth of Baltimore and increasing division over immigration, slavery, and secession. The chartering in 1827 of the Baltimore and Ohio (B&O) Railroad, which eventually linked Maryland with the markets of the Ohio Valley and the West, added to the city's economic vitality. But distrust of the thousands of newcomers—especially of Irish immigrants and their Roman Catholicism—and fear of the economic threat they supposedly represented spurred the rise of nativist political groups, such as the Know-Nothings, who persecuted the immigrants and dominated Maryland politics in the 1850s.

Although not many Marylanders were in favor of secession, they were hostile to the idea of using force against the secessionist states. On 19 April 1861, as the 6th Massachusetts Regiment passed through Baltimore, it was attacked by a mob of southern sympathizers in a riot that left four soldiers and 12 civilians dead. Ten days later, the Maryland house of delegates, following the lead of Governor Thomas Hicks, rejected a bill of secession. Throughout the Civil War, Maryland was largely occupied by Union troops because of its strategic location and the importance for the northern cause of the B&O Railroad. Marylanders fought on both sides during the war, and one major battle took place on Maryland soil—the Battle of Antietam (1862), during which a Union army thwarted a Confederate thrust toward the north, but at an enormous cost to both sides. Confederate armies invaded the state on two other occasions, when General Robert E. Lee brought his troops through the state on the way to Gettysburg in 1863 and when Lieutenant General Jubal Early ravaged the Hagerstown area and threatened Baltimore in 1864. The Maryland legislature, almost totally pro-Union by 1864, passed a new constitution, which among other things abolished slavery.

The state's economic activity increased during Reconstruction, as Maryland, and especially Baltimore, played a major role in rebuilding the South. Maryland's economic base gradually shifted from agriculture to industry, with shipbuilding, steelmaking, and the manufacture of clothing and shoes leading the way. The decades between the Civil War and World War I were also notable for the philanthropic activities of such wealthy businessmen as Johns Hopkins, George Peabody, and Enoch Pratt, who endowed some of the state's most prestigious cultural and educational institutions. The years after World War I saw the emergence of a political figure without equal in Maryland's more recent history: Albert C. Ritchie, a Democrat who won election to the governorship in 1919 and served in that office until 1935, just one year before his death. Stressing local issues, states' rights, and opposition to prohibition, Ritchie remained in power until Harry W. Nice, a Republican but an advocate of New Deal reforms, defeated him in 1934.

The decades after World War II were marked by significant population growth. From 1980 to 1990 alone, Maryland grew by 13.4%, well above the national rate of 9.8%. Baltimore, which, though still the hub of the state's economy, had fallen into decay and became the focus of a redevelopment project. Much of the downtown area and harbor facilities were revitalized by urban projects, begun in the late 1970s and continued into the 1990s. These featured the Charles Center development, the waterfront renovation of the Inner Harbor, Oriole Park at Camden Yards, and a new $150-million convention center at the Inner Harbor.

Although Maryland's economy declined less than those of other states during the recession of the late 1980s, the state suffered from the contraction of defense industry. Nevertheless, service industry employment, primarily in the Baltimore-Washington corridor, gave Maryland the 5th-highest state income in the country as of the mid-1990s—a ranking it maintained as of 1998. Federal government and high-tech employment accounted for many of these jobs.

Maryland's 370-year history of tobacco farming appeared to be drawing to a close in 2000. Nearly 90% of the state's tobacco farmers indicated they would accept a government buyout later that year. The crop that had settled the Chesapeake had become risky, with the tobacco industry under attack for the health hazards of its products. The state by 2003 had implemented a tobacco buyout program, whereby the state agrees to pay farmers $1 per pound of tobacco that they would sell for the following ten years based on the average amount of tobacco they sold between 1996 and 1998. Farmers agree to plant alternative crops instead of tobacco. As of January 2004, 785 growers were to participate in the buyout program, representing 80% of eligible growers and 7.3 million pounds of tobacco.

The environmental clean-up of Chesapeake Bay, begun in the mid-1980s, was slated to continue into the 21st century. In an effort to further protect the bay's ecosystem, in 1999 Maryland Governor Parris Glendening announced a plan to protect 60,000 forested acres on the Eastern Shore from development. Nevertheless, the bay faced more immediate threats such as the April 2000 oil spill into the Patuxent River, which flows into the Chesapeake. Federal officials faulted Maryland Power Company for its efforts to clean up the spill, the worst in the company's 104-year history. Governor Robert Ehrlich, elected in 2002, pledged to continue the clean-up of the Chesapeake Bay in 2003.

12STATE GOVERNMENT

Maryland's first state constitution was enacted in 1776. Subsequent constitutions were ratified in 1851, 1864, and 1867. By January 2003, it had 218 amendments.

Under the 1867 constitution, as amended, the general assembly, Maryland's legislative body, consists of two branches: a 47-member senate and a 141-member house of delegates. Legislative sessions begin the 2nd Wednesday of January of each year and are limited to 90 calendar days. Special sessions, which are limited to 30 calendar days, may be called by a petition of the majority in each house. All legislators serve four-year terms and must have been residents of the state for at least a year and of their district for at least six months prior to election. Senators must be at least 25 years old, delegates 21. The legislative salary was $31,591 in 2002.

Executives elected statewide are the governor and lieutenant governor (who run jointly), the comptroller of the treasury, and the attorney general; all serve four-year terms. The state treasurer is elected by joint ballot of the general assembly, while the secretary of state is appointed by the governor. The governor, who may serve no more than two four-year terms in succession, also appoints other members of the executive council (cabinet) and the heads of major boards and commissions. The chief executive must be a US citizen at least 30 years old, must have been a resident of Maryland for five years before election, and must have been a registered voter in the state for five years. In 2002 the governor's salary was $120,000, unchanged from 1999.

Bills passed by majority vote of both houses of the assembly become law when signed by the governor or if left unsigned for six days while the legislature is in session or 30 days if the legislature has adjourned. The only exception is the budget bill, which becomes effective immediately upon legislative passage. Gubernatorial vetoes may be overridden by three-fifths votes of the elected members in both houses. Proposed constitutional amendments also require approval by three-fifths of both houses of the legislature before submission to the voters at the next general election.

Eligible voters are US citizens who are at least 18 years old and are residents of the Maryland county in which they will vote. Restrictions apply to convicted felons and those declared mentally incompetent by the court.

13POLITICAL PARTIES

The Republican and Democratic parties are the dominant political groups in Maryland. Before the Civil War, the Democrats drew much of their strength from the slaveholding Eastern Shore, while their opponents, the Whigs, were popular in Baltimore and other centers of antislavery activity. The collapse of the Whigs on both the national and local levels corresponded with the rise in Maryland of the Native American ("Know-Nothing") Party, whose anti-immigrant and anti-Catholic attitudes appealed to Marylanders who saw their livelihood threatened by Roman Catholic immigrants. The Know-Nothings swept Baltimore in 1855 and won the governorship in 1857; Maryland was the only state to cast its electoral votes for the Know-Nothing presidential candidate, former President Millard Fillmore, in 1856. The Native American Party declined rapidly, however, and by 1860, Maryland was back in the Democratic column, voting for the secessionist John Breckinridge.

Revelations of influence peddling and corruption afflicted both major parties during the 1970s. In 1973, Republican Spiro T. Agnew, then vice president of the US, was accused of taking payments from people who had done business with the state government while he was Baltimore County executive and then governor of Maryland until 1969. Agnew pleaded nolo contendere to a federal charge of income tax evasion and resigned from the vice-presidency on 10 October 1973. His gubernatorial successor, Democrat Marvin Mandel, was convicted of mail fraud and racketeering in 1977 for having used the powers of his office to assist the owners of a now-defunct racetrack in exchange for $350,000 in gifts and favors; he served 20 months of a 36-month prison sentence before receiving a presidential pardon in 1981.

Maryland was one of the few states carried by President Jimmy Carter in the November 1980 presidential election, but four years later the state went for President Ronald Reagan in the national Republican landslide. In 2000, Maryland gave 57% of its vote to Democrat Al Gore, 40% to Republican George W. Bush, and 3% to Green Party candidate Ralph Nader.

In the 1994 governor's race, one of the closest in Maryland history, Democrat Parris N. Glendening won; he was reelected in 1998. Republican Governor Robert L Ehrlich, Jr. was elected in 2002. The two senators from Maryland, Barbara Mikulski and Paul S. Sarbanes, both Democrats, were reelected in 1998 and 2000, respectively. In 2002 there were 3,928,223 registered voters. In 1998, 58% of registered voters were Democratic, 20% Republican, and 12% unaffiliated or members of other parties.

Following the November 2002 elections, Maryland's US congressional delegation consisted of six Democrats and two Republicans. In mid-2003 there were 33 Democrats and 14 Republicans in the state senate, and 98 Democrats and 43 Republicans in the state house. The state had 10 electoral votes in the 2000 presidential election.

14LOCAL GOVERNMENT

As of 2002, there were 23 counties, 157 municipal governments, and 85 special districts in Maryland. Most counties have charter governments, in which voters elect a county executive and council members. The other counties, which tend to be rural, are governed by boards of county commissioners. County government is highly developed in Maryland, and there are numerous appointed county officials with responsibilities ranging from civil defense to liquor licensing.

The city of Baltimore is the only one in Maryland not contained within a county. It provides the same services as a county, and shares in state aid according to the same allocation formulas. The city (not to be confused with Baltimore County, which surrounds the city of Baltimore but has its county seat at Towson) is governed by an elected mayor and city council. Other cities and towns are each governed by a mayor, with or without a council, depending on the local charter. In 2002 Maryland had 39 public school systems.

15STATE SERVICES

To address the continuing threat of terrorism and to work with the federal Department of Homeland Security (created in 2002 following the terrorist attacks of 11 September 2001), homeland security in Maryland in 2003 operated under the authority of the governor; the governor's chief of staff was designated as the state homeland security advisor.

The State Ethics Commission, established in 1979, monitors compliance by state officeholders and employees with the Maryland public ethics law in order to avoid conflicts of interest; the Joint Committee on Legislative Ethics, created in 1972, has similar responsibilities with respect to general assembly members. The Fair Campaign Financing Commission provides for the public financing of elections and sets campaign spending limits.

The State Board of Education is an independent policymaking body whose nine members are appointed by the governor; its responsibilities include selection of a superintendent of schools to run the Education Department. The growth and development of postsecondary institutions are the responsibility of the State Board for Higher Education. The Department of Transportation oversees air, road, rail, bridge, and mass transit. The Department of Health and Mental Hygiene coordinates public health programs, regulates in-state medical care, and supervises the 24

Maryland Presidential Vote by Political Parties, 1948–2000

YEAR	ELECTORAL VOTE	MARYLAND WINNER	DEMOCRAT	REPUBLICAN	PROGRESSIVE	STATE'S RIGHTS DEMOCRAT	SOCIALIST
1948	8	Dewey (R)	286,521	294,814	9,983	2,467	2,941
1952	9	*Eisenhower (R)	395,337	499,424	7,313	—	—
1956	9	*Eisenhower (R)	372,613	559,738	—	—	—
1960	9	*Kennedy (D)	565,808	489,538	—	—	—
1964	10	*Johnson (D)	730,912	385,495	—	—	—
					AMERICAN IND.		
1968	10	Humphrey (D)	538,310	517,995	178,734	—	—
					AMERICAN		
1972	10	*Nixon (R)	505,781	829,305	18,726	—	—
1976	10	*Carter (D)	759,612	672,661	—		—
						LIBERTARIAN	
1980	10	Carter (D)	726,161	680,606	—	14,192	—
1984	10	*Reagan (R)	787,935	879,918	—	5,721	—
1988	10	*Bush (R)	826,304	876,167	5,115	6,748	—
							IND. (PEROT)
1992	10	*Clinton (D)	988,571	707,094	2,786	4,715	281,414
1996	10	*Clinton (D)	966,207	681,530	—	8,765	115,812
					GREEN		**REFORM**
2000	10	Gore (D)	1,145,782	813,797	53,768	5,310	4,248

* Won US presidential election.

local health departments. Social services and public assistance programs as well as employment security lie within the jurisdiction of the Department of Human Resources. The Department of Housing and Community Development assures the provision of low-cost housing. The Department of Business and Economic Development advances job opportunities and works to bring new businesses into the state. It also serves in a public relations capacity at home and abroad to stimulate international trade and tourism, and also invests in the arts and promotes sports events.

Maryland's Department of Public Safety and Correctional Services has statewide responsibility for the supervision and rehabilitation of adjudicated individuals, while the Department of Labor, Licensing, and Regulation supervises employment training, job match services, unemployment insurance, and many of the state's licensing and regulatory boards for businesses and trades. The Department of State Police enforces state motor vehicle and criminal laws, preserves public peace, maintains safe traffic on public streets and highways, enforces laws relating to narcotics, and incorporates the office of the State Fire Marshal. Other organizations include the departments of agriculture, assessments and taxation, natural resources, personnel, and rehabilitation services (for those with disabilities).

[16]JUDICIAL SYSTEM

The court of appeals, the state's highest court, comprises a chief judge and six associate judges. Each is appointed to the court by the governor but must be confirmed by the voters within two years of appointment. Most criminal appeals are decided by the court of special appeals, consisting of a chief judge and 12 associate judges, selected in the same manner as judges of the high court; each case must be heard by a panel of at least three judges of the high court. All state judges serve 10-year terms.

In 1971, 12 district courts took the place of all justices of the peace, county trial judges, magistrates, people's courts, and the municipal court of Baltimore. District courts handle all criminal, civil, and traffic cases, with appeals being taken to one of eight circuit courts. Circuit court judges are appointed by the governor and stand for election to 15-year terms; district court judges are appointed by the governor and confirmed by the senate to 10-year terms. The city of Baltimore and all counties except Montgomery and Hartford have orphans' courts composed of two judges and one chief judge, all of them elected to four-year terms.

According to the FBI Crime Index for 2001, Maryland had a crime rate of 4,866.8 per 100,000 population, including a total of 42,088 violent crimes and 219,512 crimes against property in that year. Maryland has the death penalty, and 15 prisoners were being held under the death sentence as of 2003. The state executed 71 people since 1930, only three of whom were put to death between 1977 and 2003. There were 23,970 prisoners in state and federal prisons in June 2001, an increase of 1.1% over the previous year. The state's incarceration rate stood at 432 per 100,000 inhabitants.

[17]ARMED FORCES

As of 2002, there were 30,928 active US military personnel in Maryland. Ft. Meade is located in Baltimore, and the Aberdeen Proving Ground is in Harford County. Perhaps Maryland's best-known defense installation is Andrews Air Force Base in Camp Springs, a military airlift center. Annapolis is the home of the US Naval Academy. Total military personnel at all naval facilities, including the National Naval Medical Center at Bethesda, was 15,853 in 2002. Federal defense contract awards to Maryland firms were approximately $4.9 billion in 2001.

There were 524,230 veterans of US military service in Maryland as of 2000, of whom 87,442 served in World War II;

55,875 in the Korean conflict; 150,518 during the Vietnam era; and 73,287 during 1990–2000 (including the Persian Gulf War). A total of $836 million in veterans' benefits were paid in 2002.

In 2000, the Maryland State Police employed 1,575 full-time sworn officers.

[18]MIGRATION

Maryland's earliest white settlers were English; many of them farmed lands on the Eastern Shore. As tobacco crops wore out the soil, these early immigrants moved on to the fertile Western Shore and piedmont. During the 19th century, Baltimore ranked 2nd only to New York as a port of entry for European immigrants. First to come were the Germans, followed by the Irish, Poles, East European Jews, and Italians; a significant number of Czechs settled in Cecil County during the 1860s. After the Civil War, many blacks migrated to Baltimore, both from rural Maryland and from southern states.

Since World War II, intrastate migration has followed the familiar urban/suburban pattern: both the Baltimore metropolitan area and the Maryland part of the metropolitan Washington, DC, area have experienced rapid growth while the inner cities have lost population. Overall, Maryland experienced a net loss from migration of about 36,000 between 1970 and 1980, much of it to Pennsylvania, Virginia, and Florida; the out-migration stopped during the 1980s, however, with a net gain of over 200,000 from 1980 to 1990. Between 1990 and 1998, Maryland had a net loss of 49,000 in domestic migration and a net gain of 118,000 in international migration. Maryland's foreign-born population totaled 412,000, or 8% of the total population, in 1996. In 1998, 15,561 foreign immigrants arrived in the state—the 10th-highest total of any state for that year. Between 1990 and 1998, the state's overall population increased 7.4%. In the period 1995–2000, 495,152 people moved into the state and 514,875 moved out, for a net loss of 19,723, many of whom moved to Virginia.

[19]INTERGOVERNMENTAL COOPERATION

Maryland is active in several regional organizations, including the Southern Regional Education Board, Atlantic States Marine Fisheries Commission, Mid-Atlantic Fishery Management Council, Interstate Mining Compact Commission, Appaalachian Regional Commission, Susquehanna River Basin Commission (with Pennsylvania and New York), and the Potomac River Fisheries Commission (with Virginia). Representatives of Maryland, Virginia, and the District of Columbia form the Washington Metropolitan Area Transit Authority, which coordinates regional mass transit. Other cooperation focuses on the Chesapeake Bay, and on the creation of the Woodrow Wilson Bridge and Tunnel. The Delmarva Advisory Council, representing Delaware, Maryland, and Virginia, works with local organizations on the Delmarva Peninsula to develop and implement economic improvement programs. In 2001, federal grants to Maryland totaled over $7.5 billion.

[20]ECONOMY

Throughout the colonial period, Maryland's economy was based on one crop—tobacco. Not only slaves but also indentured servants worked the fields, and when they earned their freedom, they too secured plots of land and grew tobacco for the European market. By 1820, however, industry was rivaling agriculture for economic preeminence. Shipbuilding, metalworking, and commerce transformed Baltimore into a major city; within 60 years, it was a leading manufacturer of men's clothing and had the largest steel making plant in the US.

Although manufacturing output continues to rise, the biggest growth areas in Maryland's economy are government, construction, trade, and services. Maryland employees are the best educated in the nation, with more than one-third of those over age 25 possessing a bachelor's degree in 2000. With the expansion of federal employment in the Washington metropolitan area by 40% from 1961 to 1980, many US government workers settled in suburban Maryland, primarily Prince George's and Montgomery counties; construction and services in those areas expanded accordingly. The growth of state government boosted employment in Anne Arundel and Baltimore counties. However, from 1992 to 2000, Maryland lost 17% of its federal employment in Washington DC. Also of importance to the economy are fishing and agriculture (primarily dairy and poultry farming) on the Eastern Shore and coal mining in Garrett and Allegheny counties. Manufacturing has shifted toward high technology, information, and health-related products. While manufacturing output has continued to grow (total of 6.5% from 1997 to 2001) its relative weight in the gross state product has fallen (from 8.5% in 1997 to 7.2% in 2001), as, over this same period, output from general services rose 33.7%, from financial services, 27.2%, from government services, 24.7%, and from the wholesale and retail trade sector, 21.4%. Annual growth rates averaged 6.2% 1998 to 2000, and only fell to 5.4% in the national recession and slowdown of 2001. Increased federal government spending, particularly in defense-related industries, is expected assure Maryland's economic recovery in 2002, and into 2003.

Maryland's gross state product was $195 billion in 2001, the 15th highest in the nation, to which general service contributed $48.4 billion; financial services, $42 billion; government, $34.3 billion, trade, $28.7 billion; transportation and utilities, $14.2 billion, manufacturing, $14 billion; and construction, $11.3 billion. The public sector constituted 17.6% of Maryland's gross state product in 2001, compared to a national state average of only 12%.

21 INCOME

According to the Bureau of Economic Analysis, in 2001, Maryland had a per capita personal income (PCPI) of $35,279 which ranked 6th in the United States (including the District of Columbia) and was 116% of the national average, $30,413. The 2001 PCPI reflected an increase of 3.6% from 2000 compared to the national change of 2.2%. In 2001, Maryland had a total personal income (TPI) of $190,014,792,000 which ranked 15th in the United States and accounted for 2.2% of the national total. The 2001 TPI reflected an increase of 5.0% from 2000 compared to the national change of 3.3%.

Earnings of persons employed in Maryland increased from $116,064,382,000 in 2000 to $122,248,013,000 in 2001, an increase of 5.3%. The largest industries in 2001 were services, 33.4% of earnings; state and local government, 11.3%; and federal civilian government, 9.7%. Of the industries that accounted for at least 5% of earnings in 2001, the slowest growing from 2000 to 2001 was wholesale trade (5.3% of earnings in 2001), which increased 0.8%; the fastest was construction (7.3% of earnings in 2001), which increased 8.0%.

According to data released by the US Census Bureau, in 2000, the median household income was $51,695 compared to the national average of $42,148. In 2001, the median income for a family of four was $82,879 compared to the national average of $63,278. For the period 1999 to 2001, the average poverty rate was 7.3% which placed it 3rd among the 50 states and the District of Columbia ranked lowest to highest.

22 LABOR

According to Bureau of Labor Statistics (BLS) provisional estimates, in July 2003 the seasonally adjusted civilian labor force in Maryland numbered 2,937,100, with approximately 135,300 workers unemployed, yielding an unemployment rate of 4.6%, compared to the national average of 6.2% for the same period. Since the beginning of the BLS data series in 1978, the highest unemployment rate recorded was 8.7% in January 1982. The historical low was 3.5% in January 2000. In 2001, an estimated 6.5% of the labor force was employed in construction; 6.8% in manufacturing; 5.6% in transportation, communications, and public utilities; 17.6% in trade; 5.8% in finance, insurance, and real estate; 28.8% in services; 21.9% in government; and 1.4% in agriculture.

Baltimore was a leading trade union center by the early 1830s although union activity subsided after the Panic of 1837. The Baltimore Federation of Labor was formed in 1889, and by 1900, the coal mines had been organized by the United Mine Workers. In 1902, Maryland passed the first workers' compensation law in the US; it was declared unconstitutional in 1904 but was subsequently revived. The US Department of Labor reported that in 2002, 346,000 of Maryland's 2,460,000 employed wage and salary workers were members of unions. This represented 14.1% of those so employed, up from 13.8% in 2001 but down from 16.1% in 1998. The national average is 13.2%. In all, 415,000 workers (16.9%) were represented by unions. In addition to union members, this category includes workers who report no union affiliation but whose jobs are covered by a union contract.

23 AGRICULTURE

Maryland ranked 36th among the 50 states in agricultural income in 2001, with estimated receipts of $1,596 million, about 41% of that in crops.

Until the Revolutionary War, tobacco was the state's only cash crop; in 2002, Maryland produced an estimated 2,380,000 lb of tobacco, down from 8,265,000 lb in 2000. Corn and cereal grains are grown mainly in southern Maryland. Production in 2002 included 32,300,000 bushels of corn for grain; 10,810,000 bushels of soybeans, $62,158,000; 11,880,000 bushels of wheat, $37,442,000, and 3,362,000 bushels of barley, $4,371,000. Commercial vegetables, cultivated primarily on the Eastern Shore, were valued at $54 million in 2002. Fruits are also cultivated.

Maryland had some 12,200 farms covering 2,100,000 acres (850,000 hectares) in 2002.

24 ANIMAL HUSBANDRY

The Eastern Shore is an important dairy and poultry region; cattle are raised in north-central and western Maryland, while the central region is notable for horse breeding. In 2001, poultry farmers produced an estimated 9.5 million lb (4.3 million kg) of chickens and 1.38 billion lb (0.63 billion kg) of broilers for around $552.6 million. Also in 2001, Maryland farmers produced an estimated 870 million eggs worth around $44 million.

An estimated 1.3 billion lb (0.6 billion kg) of milk was produced in 2001 from 82,000 dairy cows. Maryland farms and ranches had an estimated 240,000 cattle and calves worth around $235 million in 2003. In 2002, there were an estimated 45,000 hogs and pigs, worth $3.1 million.

25 FISHING

A leading source of oysters, clams, and crabs, Maryland had a total commercial catch in 1998 of 61,468,000 lb, valued at $67,190,000 (2.1% of US total). Ocean City is the state's leading fishing port. Shellfish landings in 1998 included blue crab, 30.5 million lb; surf clams, 3.8 million lb; and soft clams, 219,000 lb. Bigeye and yellowfin tuna together are the most important finfish, followed by menhaden, dogfish shark, swordfish, and sea bass. The state's 126 seafood-processing and wholesale plants employed 2,012 persons during 1997.

The Fisheries Administration of the Department of Natural Resources monitors fish populations and breeds and implants oysters; it also stocks inland waterways with finfish. Maryland had 374,548 licensed sport anglers in 1998.

[26]FORESTRY

Maryland's 2,566,000 acres (1,139,000 hectares) of forestland covers about 40% of the state's land area. More than 90% of that (2,372,000 acres/961,570 hectares) was classified as commercial forest, 90% of it privately owned. Hardwoods predominate, with red and white oaks and yellow poplar among the leading hardwood varieties. Lumber production in 2002 was 268 million board feet.

Forest management and improvement lie within the jurisdiction of the Maryland Department of Natural Resources Forest Service.

[27]MINING

The estimated value of nonfuel mineral production in Maryland in 2001 was $356 million, a marginal decrease from 2000. Maryland ranked 33rd among the states and accounted for almost 1% of the national nonfuel mineral production value. Crushed stone, cement (portland and masonry), and crushed sand and gravel together accounted for almost 99% of the state's total nonfuel mineral value.

According to preliminary figures, crushed stone (output 24 million metric tons, valued at $139 million) was the leading nonfuel mineral commodity, followed by portland cement (1.7 million metric tons, $123 million) and construction sand and gravel (12.7 million metric tons, $83.5 million). Maryland also produces significant quantities of dimension stone.

[28]ENERGY AND POWER

Maryland's installed electrical capacity (utility and nonutility) was 11.8 million kW in 1999; production of electricity exceeded 51.7 billion kWh in the same year. More than 99% of the generating capacity was privately owned, and about 57% of the state's electricity was produced by coal-fired plants. The Calvert Cliffs Nuclear Plant in Lusby, operated by Baltimore Gas and Electric, had a capacity of 1,685 MW in 2001; in 1999 it produced about 26% of the state's electricity. In 2000 Maryland's total per capita energy consumption was 287 million Btu (72.3 million kcal), ranking it 40th among the 50 states.

Coal, Maryland's lone fossil fuel resource, is mined in Allegheny and Garrett counties, along the Pennsylvania border. Recoverable reserves in 2000 were estimated at 72 million tons of bituminous coal; the 2000 output of 16 coal mines totaled 4.5 million tons. Marketed production of natural gas totaled 32 million cu ft (0.9 billion cu m) in 2001.

[29]INDUSTRY

During the early 1800s, Maryland's first industries centered around the Baltimore shipyards. Small ironworks cast parts for sailing vessels, and many laborers worked as shipbuilders. By the 1850s, Baltimore was also producing weather-measuring instruments and fertilizers, and by the 1930s, it was a major center of metal refining. The city remains an important manufacturer of automobiles and parts, steel, and instruments. Manufacturing is led by the printing and publishing industry, the food industry, the machinery industry, and the chemical industry.

Value of shipments by manufacturers in 1997 was $38 billion. About one-third of all manufacturing activity (by value) takes place in the city of Baltimore, followed by Baltimore County, Montgomery County, and Prince George's County. Maryland is

the headquarters for six Fortune 500 companies: Lockheed Martin, Marriott International, Black and Decker, Giant Food, USF&G, and BG&E. Other major employers as of the year 2000 included ARINC, Bethlehem Steel, Computer Sciences Corp., General Motors, McCormick and Co., Northrop Grumman, and Perdue Farms, Inc.

Earnings of persons employed in Maryland increased from $95.2 billion in 1997 to $101.4 billion in 1998, an increase of 6.5%. The largest industries in 1998 were services, 33.0% of earnings; state and local government, 10.9%; and retail trade, 9.5%. Of the industries that accounted for at least 5% of earnings in 1998, the slowest growing from 1997 to 1998 was state and local government, which increased 2.3%; the fastest was finance, insurance, and real estate (8.1% of earnings in 1998), which increased 9.7%.

[30]COMMERCE

In 1997, wholesale sales totaled $58 billion; from 7,433 wholesale establishments. Professional and commercial equipment (e.g., computers, software and related peripherals, ophthalmic goods, photographic equipment, etc.); motor vehicles, parts and supplies; and machinery, equipment lead in number of establishments. Groceries and related products, paper and paper goods, and petroleum and petroleum products lead in establishments among the non-durables.

Retail sales in 1997 totaled $48 billion. The state's 27,422 retail establishments in 1997 sold $48 billion in merchandise. Leading retail activity centers on food stores (11% of est.), automobiles and services stations (11%), and restaurants and taverns (28%). Food sales accounted for $8.6 billion in profits, and general merchandise sales took in $5.7 billion. More than 75% of Maryland's retail facilities are located in the Baltimore metropolitan area and Montgomery and Prince George's counties surrounding Washington, DC. These counties are home to about 90% of Maryland's five million residents. The Washington-Baltimore Consolidated Metropolitan Statistical Area is the nation's 4th-largest retail market.

Exports by Maryland companies totaled $4.7 billion in 1997. While export activities in established markets such as Europe and Canada are still predominant, strong inroads have been made in targeted trade areas of Asia and Latin America.

[31]CONSUMER PROTECTION

The state agency responsible for controlling unfair and deceptive trade practices is the Division of Consumer Protection within the Attorney General's Office. The consumer credit commissioner, within the Department of Licensing and Regulation, is responsible for enforcing a number of state acts. The Consumer Services Division of the Motor Vehicle Administration, under the Department of Transportation, licenses motor vehicle dealers and manufacturers and professional driving schools; the division is also responsible for school bus safety inspections.

[32]BANKING

Maryland's 134 insured banks in 2002 reported total assets of $60 billion. Sixty-one of those banks were state-chartered.

Fourteen savings institutions in Maryland were enrolled in the Resolution Trust Corporations (RTC) joint regulatory oversight program in 1999—these institutions had combined assets of over $8 billion and combined deposits exceeding $5.5 billion through nearly 842,000 accounts. In 1995, the RTC successfully resolved 14 institutions, at a cost of $1.5 billion.

All state-chartered savings and loan associations are regulated by the Commissioner of Financial Regulation, within the Department of Labor, Licensing and Regulation.

In 2002, a reduction in short-term interest rates helped lower banks' funding costs and offset the decline in asset yields reflecting declines in long-term interest rates. Funding costs were at near historic lows in 2002. Following the start of the 2001 US recession, the median past-due loan ratio for insured institutions headquartered in Maryland increased, but subsequently declined as of the end of 2002. At that time, the ratio was significantly below the national average. As of September 2002, over 40% of the state's insured institutions had a high level of traditionally higher-risk loans.

33INSURANCE

In 2001 there were 3.4 million ordinary life insurance policies in force with a total value of $218.9 billion; total value for all categories of life insurance (ordinary, group, industrial, and credit) was $346.7 billion. Death benefits paid that year totaled $883.9 million. As of 2000, there were 49 property and casualty and 13 life and health insurance companies incorporated or organized in the state. In 2001, property and casualty insurers wrote premiums totaling $6.1 billion. That year, there were 50,144 flood insurance policies in force in the state, with a total value of $5.8 million.

The Maryland Automobile Insurance Fund, a quasi-independent agency created in 1972, pays claims against uninsured motorists (i.e., hit-and-run drivers, out-of-state uninsured motorists, and state residents driving in violation of Maryland's compulsory automobile insurance law), and sells policies to Maryland drivers unable to obtain insurance from private companies.

The State Insurance Division of the Department of Licensing and Regulation licenses all state insurance companies, agents, and brokers, and must approve all policies for sale in the state.

34SECURITIES

There are no securities or commodities exchanges in Maryland. There are 772 broker-dealers organizations selling securities in Maryland with 8,967 employees. Some 306 investment advisory companies are registered to provide services. Securities dealers in Maryland are regulated by the Division of Securities within the Attorney General's Office. Maryland has the headquarters of 99 NASDAQ companies, five NASDAQ market makers, and 10 AMEX companies. Approximately 36 NYSE companies were incorporated in Maryland, the top five according to revenues being Lockheed Martin Corp., Marriott International, Black&Decker Corp., Sodexho, and Allegheny Energy.

35PUBLIC FINANCE

The state budget, prepared by the Department of Budget and Management, is submitted annually by the governor to the general assembly for amendment and approval. The fiscal year runs from 1 July to 30 June.

Since 1995, Maryland has implemented over 25 different tax cuts, the most dramatic of which was a 10% income tax cut. Despite the cuts in revenue; in 1999, fiscal revenues exceeded estimates by $320 million, and year 2000 revenues were expected to exceed estimates by $575 million. Total revenues for 2001 were forecast at $19.6 billion. In December 2000, a special commission concluded that that the state needed to increase education spending to avoid law suits about equitable funding. By 2001/02, however, the main concern was about budget shortfalls. Maryland had begun 2000/01 with a starting balance equal to 13.6% of expenditures. By 2000/01, the starting balance had dropped to 7.8% of expenditures, and continued to drop, to 5.3% of expenditures in 2002/03, and to 4.7% in 2003/04, as the government grappled with revenue shortfalls and rising costs. For 2002/03, Maryland's budget deficit was estimated at 5.5% of the

state budget, and for 2003/04, it was projected to increase to 11% of the state budget.

The following table from the US Census Bureau contains information on revenues, expenditures, indebtedness, and cash/securities for 2001.

	($000)	PERCENT	PER CAPITA
Population (thousands, 2001)	5,386	(X)	(X)
Total Revenue	20,938,683	100.00	3,887.61
General revenue	19,041,973	90.94	3,535.46
Utility revenue	95,274	0.46	17.69
Liquor store revenue	—	—	—
Insurance trust revenue	1,801,436	8.60	334.47
Exhibit: Salaries and wages	3,670,296	17.08	681.45
Total expenditure	21,484,098	100.00	3,988.88
General expenditure	19,243,614	89.57	3,572.90
Education	6,190,289	28.81	1,149.33
Public welfare	4,293,965	19.99	797.25
Hospitals	365,404	1.70	67.84
Health	1,199,211	5.58	222.65
Highways	1,486,752	6.92	276.04
Police protection	334,336	1.56	62.08
Correction	978,505	4.55	181.68
Natural resources	401,093	1.87	74.47
Parks and recreation	258,917	1.21	48.07
Government administration	838,729	3.90	155.72
Interest on general debt	851,788	3.96	158.15
Other and unallocable	2,044,625	9.52	379.62
Utility expenditure	418,584	1.95	77.72
Liquor store expenditure	—	—	—
Insurance trust expenditure	1,821,900	8.48	338.27
Debt at end of fiscal year	11,661,413	100.00	2,165.13
Cash and security holdings	42,038,440	100.00	7,805.13

36TAXATION

In 2002, Maryland reduced its top individual income tax rate from 4.85% to 4.75%. The lowest rate on the four-bracket schedule is 2%, applicable up t to $1000 of taxable income, and the highest rate applies to taxable income above $3,000. The current federal definition of adjusted gross income can be used as the tax base. The corporate income tax rate is 7%. The state general sales and use tax is 5% with exemptions for food and other basic items, and no local sales taxes permitted. The state also imposes a full array of excise taxes covering motor fuels, tobacco products, insurance premiums, public utilities, alcoholic beverages, amusements, pari-mutuels, and other selected items. Maryland has enacted its own estate tax (maximum rate 10%) so it is unaffected by the scheduled phase-out of the federal estate tax credit by 2007. Maryland's 10% inheritance tax-exempts close (Class A) relatives. Death and gift taxes accounted for 0.7% of state tax collected in 2002. Other state taxes include property taxes including a motor vehicle use tax, various license and franchise fees, and stamp taxes. All county and some local governments levy property taxes. The counties also tax personal income at rates ranging from 30% to 60% of those imposed by the state; the city of Baltimore taxes personal income at rates equal to 50% of the state levy. Local income tax rates have a cap of 3.1%. In 2002, localities collected 43.6% of total state and local taxes.

The state collected $10.821 billion in taxes in 2002, of which 43.5% came from individual income taxes, 24.9% from the general sales tax, 18.5% from selective sales taxes, 4% from license fees, and 3.3% from corporate income taxes. In 2003, Maryland ranked 27th among the states in terms of state and local tax burden, which amounted to about 9.5% of income.

The following table from the US Census Bureau provides a summary of taxes collected by the state in 2002.

	($000)	PER CAPITA
Total Taxes	10,821,276	1,982.60
Property taxes	272,806	49.98
Sales and gross receipts	4,699,086	860.93
General sales and gross receipts	2,690,434	492.92
Selective sales taxes	2,008,652	368.01
Alcoholic beverage	25,754	4.72
Amusements	4,794	0.88
Insurance Premiums	197,306	36.15

	($000)	PER CAPITA
Motor fuels	703,390	128.87
Pari-mutuels	3,122	0.57
Public utilities	140,895	25.81
Tobacco products	209,881	38.45
Other selective sales	723,510	132.56
Licenses	435,967	79.87
Alcoholic beverages	573	0.1
Amusements	22	0
Corporation	14,606	2.68
Hunting and fishing	11,099	2.03
Motor vehicle	199,651	36.58
Motor vehicle operators	20,139	3.69
Public utility	(X)	(X)
Occupation and business, NEC	187,728	34.39
Other	2,149	0.39
Other taxes	5,413,417	991.81
Individual income	4,704,368	861.9
Corporation net income	359,420	65.85
Death and gift	182,753	33.48
Documentary and stock transfer	124,160	22.75
Severance	(X)	(X)
Other	42,716	7.83

37 ECONOMIC POLICY

The Department of Business and Economic Development (DBED), created in 1995, encourages new firms to locate in Maryland and established firms to expand their in-state facilities, promotes the tourist industry, and disseminates information about the state's history and attractions. The department helps secure industrial mortgage loans for businesses that create new jobs, and also provides small-business loans, low-interest construction loads, assistance in plant location and expansion; and supports the Division of Business and Industrial Development to allow companies to maximize their use of state services. In addition, the department assists local governments in attracting federal funds for economic development and maintains programs to encourage minority businesses, the marketing of seafood, and the use of Ocean City Convention Hall. The DBED maintains a representative in Brussels to promote European investment in Maryland. The Department of State Planning oversees state and regional development programs and helps local governments develop planning goals.

During the 1930s, Maryland pioneered in urban design with the new town of Greenbelt, in Prince George's County. A wholly planned community, Columbia, was built in Howard County during the 1960s. More recently, redevelopment of Baltimore's decaying inner city has been aggressively promoted. Harborplace, a waterside pavilion featuring hundreds of shops and restaurants, formally opened in 1980, and an industrial park was developed in a high-unemployment section of northwest Baltimore during the early 1980s. Not far from Harborplace are the 33-story World Trade Center and the National Aquarium. Urban restoration has also been encouraged by urban homesteading: a Baltimorean willing to make a commitment to live in an old brick building and fix it up can submit a closed bid to buy it. An analogous "shopsteading" program to attract merchants has also been encouraged.

In 1982, Maryland initiated a program of state enterprise zones to encourage economic growth by focusing state and local resources on designated areas requiring economic stimulus. Five of these enterprise zones were located in western Maryland, four in the central part of the state, and one on the Eastern Shore. There were 34 state enterprise zones in 2000. In 2001, Maryland had the highest percent of professional and technology workers among the states, and Johns Hopkins was ranked first among hospitals. With Delaware, Virginia, and Washington DC, Maryland has been recognized as part of an international life sciences hub, dubbed the BioCapital hub. Maryland companies and agencies participate in bioscience "hotbed" campaigns, including ones in 2003, concerted efforts by groups made up of government development agencies, pharmaceutical and bioscience companies, research institutes, universities, and non-profits to attract capital, personnel and resources to develop a life sciences cluster. Over 500 foreign-based businesses have been established in Maryland, creating over 75,000 jobs. The Office of International Business (OIB) within the DBED, offers assistance to foreign companies for location, relocation, and expansion, in addition to providing assistance to Maryland exporters.

38 HEALTH

The infant mortality rate for 2000 was 7.6 per 1,000 live births, above the US average of 6.9. There were 11,164 legal abortions in 1999—a rate of 9 per 1,000 women.

In 2000, Maryland's overall death rate (838.4 per 100,000 population) was below the national norm of 873.1. The leading causes of death in 2000 were heart disease (236.6 per 100,000 population) and cerebrovascular diseases (56.6)—both rates below the US average for these categories. Death from diabetes mellitus and HIV were higher than the national rates in 2000. The rate of HIV-related deaths stood at 10.6 per 100,000 population, above the national average of 5.3 in 2000. There were 23,537 AIDS cases reported through 2001. Among persons ages 18 and older, 20.6% were current smokers in 2000. Death from lung disease occurred at a rate of 73.2 per 100,000 population in 2000. The Alcoholism Control Administration monitors rehabilitation programs for alcoholics while the Drug Abuse Administration oversees all drug treatment programs.

Maryland's 49 community hospitals had 608,165 admissions and 11,234 beds in 2001. There were 15,595 full-time registered nurses and 758 full-time licensed practical nurses in 2001 and 406 physicians per 100,000 population in 2000. The average expense of a community hospital for care was $1,180.50 per inpatient day in 2001.

Federal government grants to cover the Medicare and Medicaid services in 2001 totaled $1.9 billion; 654,607 enrollees received Medicare benefits that year. At least 12.3% of the population was uninsured in 2002.

Maryland's two medical schools are at Johns Hopkins University, which operates in connection with the Johns Hopkins Hospital and has superbly equipped research facilities, and at the University of Maryland—both located in Baltimore. Federal health centers located in Bethesda include the National Institutes of Health and the National Naval Medical Center.

39 SOCIAL WELFARE

In 2001, the average weekly unemployment benefit was $236.95. Average monthly participation in the food stamp program in FY2002 comprised 228,329 persons (104,795 households). The average monthly benefit was $78.54, and the sum total of benefits paid in FY2002 was $215,189,301.

With the enactment of the Personal Responsibility and Work Opportunity Reconciliation Act of 1996, the US government has changed the form and regulations for many of its social welfare programs. Most significantly, it replaces Aid to Families with

Dependent Children (AFDC), an open-ended entitlement program, with Temporary Assistance for Needy Families (TANF), a limited system of assistance funded largely through federal block grants. The reform act also impacts the food stamp program, the Supplemental Security Income program, and the child nutrition program. The law took effect on 1 July 1997 and provided $16.38 billion in block grants for fiscal years 1997–2002. The grants are to be divided among the states based on an equation involving the numbers of former AFDC recipients in each state.

Reauthorization of the 1996 social welfare legislation, scheduled for 2002, was delayed, and the original law had been extended three times as of July 2003, with the most recent extension running through September 2003. Maryland's TANF program is called the Family Investment Program (FIP). In June 2000 the state had 70,910 welfare recipients. State expenditures on the TANF program in FY2002 totaled $88,226,334.

In December 2001, Social Security benefits were paid to 733,940 Maryland residents. This number included 480,880 retired workers, 77,710 widows and widowers, 73,930 disabled workers, 38,610 spouses, and 62,810 children. Social Security beneficiaries represented 13.7% of the total state population and 88.6% of the state's population age 65 and older. Retired workers (excluding persons with special benefits) received an average monthly payment of $880; widows and widowers, $835; disabled workers, $851; and spouses, $453. Payments for children of retired workers averaged $447 per month; children of deceased workers, $580; and children of disabled workers, $263.

Federal Supplemental Security Income payments in December 2001 went to 89,180 Marylanders, averaging $379 a month.

40 HOUSING

Maryland has sought to preserve many of its historic houses. Block upon block of two-story brick row houses, often with white stoops, fill the older parts of Baltimore, and stone cottages built to withstand rough winters are still found in the western counties. Greenbelt and Columbia exemplify changing modern concepts of community planning.

There were an estimated 2,197,126 housing units in Maryland in 2002, of which 1,019,463 were occupied; 69.1% were owner-occupied. About 52.2% of all units are single-family, detached homes. Most units rely on utility gas and electricity for heating. It was estimated that 50,167 units lacked telephone service, 11,601 lacked complete plumbing facilities, and 7,833 lacked complete kitchen facilities. The average household size was 2.64 people.

In 2002, 29,293 privately owned units were authorized for construction. The median home value was $165,784. The median monthly cost for mortgage owners was $1,366. Renters paid a median of $738 per month. During 2002, Maryland received over $82.2 million in community planning and development aid from the US Department of Housing and Urban Development.

The Department of Housing and Community Development, formed in 1987, oversees all housing and cultural resource areas, providing neighborhood rehabilitation and revitalization, development financing, historical and cultural programs, and information technology. The Maryland Housing Fund of the Department insures qualified lending institutions against losses on home mortgage loans.

41 EDUCATION

Partly because of Maryland's large number of government and professional workers, educational attainments compare favorably with those of the other South Atlantic states. As of 2000, 83.8% of all Marylanders had completed high school, and 31.4% had at least four years of college (the US average was 24.4%). Maryland students must pass state competency exams in order to graduate from high school.

The total enrollment for fall 1999 in Maryland's public schools stood at 846,582. Of these, 607,125 attended schools from kindergarten through grade eight, and 239,457 attended high school. Minority students made up approximately 47% of the total enrollment in public elementary and secondary schools in 2001. Total enrollment was estimated at 853,406 in fall 2000 and is expected to reach 862,000 by fall 2005. Enrollment in nonpublic schools in fall 2001 was 144,131. Expenditures for public education in 2000/01 were estimated at $6,633,406.

As of fall 2000, there were 354,477 students enrolled in college or graduate school. In the same year Maryland had 57 degree-granting institutions. In 1997, minority students comprised 33.3% of total postsecondary enrollment. The institutions of higher education in Maryland are organized as follows: (1) the public four-year colleges and universities, (2) the community colleges, (3) the independent colleges and universities, and (4) the private career schools.

The state's public four-year institutions include the University of Maryland System, Morgan State University, and St. Mary's College of Maryland. The University of Maryland System is comprised of 13 separate degree-granting institutions located throughout the state. In addition, there are two research and public service institutions reporting to the System—the Center for Environmental and Estuarine Studies and the University of Maryland Biotechnology Institute. These institutions are governed by a single board of regents and a system administration. Morgan State University, the designated public urban teaching university, is governed by a single board of regents. Morgan is one of Maryland's four historically black institutions. St. Mary's College of Maryland, the state's public honors college, is the state's only "state-related" institution. As such, the college has more operational autonomy than the other public four-year institutions, particularly concerning procurement, budget, and personnel administration.

The 16 community colleges are two-year, open-admission institutions with courses and programs leading to certificates and associate degrees, as well as career-oriented and continuing education/community service programs. They receive their funding from three sources: 1) state funding through a funding formula; 2) local funding through a negotiated budget process; and 3) students' tuition and fees. Baltimore City Community College became a state institution in 1990/91 and receives the majority of its funding from the state. The state provides funding to 15 independent colleges and universities in Maryland under a statutory formula. Eligible independent institutions must meet certain standards concerning the date of establishment, type of degrees conferred, accreditation, and affirmative action programs.

St. John's College in Annapolis is known for its unique program that includes study of the ancient Greek and Latin classics in their original languages. Private career schools in Maryland provide job preparatory training for students in a wide variety of fields, including business, computers, travel, truck driving, mechanics, electronics, allied health, cosmetology, and barbering.

The Maryland Higher Education Commission serves as the state's agency that provides, as part of its primary mission, coordination, regulatory oversight, and program approval for Maryland's postsecondary education system. The State Scholarship Administration oversees 18 different state scholarship programs.

42 ARTS

Although close to the arts centers of Washington, D.C., Maryland has its own cultural attractions. Baltimore, a major theatrical center in the 1800s, still has many legitimate theaters. Center Stage in Baltimore is the designated state theater of Maryland,

and the Olney Theatre in Montgomery County is the official state summer theater. Arts organizations are aided by the 11-member Maryland Arts Council.

The state's leading orchestra is the Baltimore Symphony. Baltimore is also the home of the Baltimore Opera Company, and its jazz clubs were the launching pads for such musical notables as Eubie Blake, Ella Fitzgerald, and Cab Calloway. Annapolis hosts a symphony, an opera company, and the Ballet Theatre of Maryland. The National Ballet (est. 1948) is the oldest professional ballet company in the state. One of the newest additions to the arts community is the Maryland Symphony Orchestra in Hagerstown, established in 1982. The Peabody Institute of Johns Hopkins University in Baltimore is one of the nation's most distinguished music schools. Both the Maryland Ballet Company and Maryland Dance Theater are nationally known.

In 2003, the Maryland State Arts Council (est. 1967) and other arts organizations received grants totaling $2,404,700 from the National Endowment for the Arts (NEA). The Maryland Humanities Council (MHC) was founded in 1974. Ongoing programs of the MHC include Family Matters, a family-oriented reading and discussion group, and History Matters!, which promotes heritage tourism. In 2000, the state received 12 grants, totaling $2,855,540, from the National Endowment for the Humanities. The state makes arts education available to nearly 170,000 schoolchildren. There are about 1,000 state and 25 local arts associations in Maryland.

43LIBRARIES AND MUSEUMS

Maryland's 24 public library systems and 15 bookmobiles held 15,387,000 volumes in 2000 and had a combined circulation of 45,393,000. The center of the state library network is the Enoch Pratt Free Library in the city of Baltimore; founded in 1886, it had 28 branches, over 2.8 million volumes, and a circulation of over 1.5 million in 1999. Each county also has its own library system. The largest academic libraries are those of Johns Hopkins University (2,507,232 volumes in 1999) and the University of Maryland at College Park (2.2 million). The Maryland Historical Society Library specializes in genealogy, heraldry, and state history. The Maryland State Archives houses government records, private manuscripts, maps, and photographs. Maryland is also the site of several federal libraries, including the National Agricultural Library at Beltsville, with over two million volumes; the National Library of Medicine at Bethesda, 2,200,000; and the National Oceanic and Atmospheric Administration Library at Rockville, with about one million volumes in 1999. Total income for the public library system in 2000 was $174,458,000; including $2,267,954 in federal grants and $23,551,830 in state grants. Per capita spending was $32.55 in 1999.

Of the approximately 147 museums and historic sites in the state, the major institutions are the US Naval Academy Museum in Annapolis and Baltimore's Museum of Art, National Aquarium Seaport and Maritime Museum, Maryland Academy of Sciences, the Maryland Historical Society Museum, and Peale Museum, the oldest museum building in the US. Important historic sites include Ft. McHenry National Monument and Shrine in Baltimore (inspiration for "The Star-Spangled Banner") and Antietam National Battlefield Site near Sharpsburg.

44COMMUNICATIONS

In 2001, 95.5% of Maryland's occupied housing units had telephones.

The state had 12 major AM and 35 major FM radio stations in 2003. Maryland has 13 major television stations, including public broadcasting stations in Annapolis, Baltimore, Frederick, Hagerstown, Oakland, and Salisbury. Maryland also receives the signals of many Washington, DC. broadcast stations. The Baltimore area had almost one million television households, 68% of which received cable.

45PRESS

The *Maryland Gazette,* established at Annapolis in 1727, was the state's first newspaper. It wasn't until 1773 that Baltimore got its first paper, the *Maryland Journal and Baltimore Advertiser,* but by 1820 there were five highly partisan papers in the city. The *Baltimore Sun,* founded in 1837, reached its heyday after 1906, when H. L. Mencken became a staff writer. Mencken, who was also an important editor and critic, helped found the *American Mercury* magazine in 1924.

As of 2002, Maryland had 10 morning and 4 afternoon dailies, as well as 8 Sunday papers. The most influential newspaper published in Baltimore is the *Sun* (daily, 306,341; Sunday, 474,230). The *Washington Post* (759,864 daily; 1,059,646 Sundays) is also widely read in Maryland.

46ORGANIZATIONS

In 2003, there were about 2,894 regional, national, and international organizations within the state.

National medically oriented organizations with headquarters in Maryland include the National Federation of the Blind and the American Urological Association, both in Baltimore; the American Association of Colleges of Pharmacy, the American Institute of Nutrition, the American Occupational Therapy Association, and the National Foundation for Cancer Research, Bethesda; the American Speech-Language-Hearing Association and the Cystic Fibrosis Foundation, Rockville; and the National Association of the Deaf and the American Music Therapy Association, Silver Spring.

Leading commercial, professional, and trade groups include the Aircraft Owners and Pilots Association and the American Fisheries Society, Bethesda; the International Association of Chiefs of Police, Gaithersburg; and the Retail Bakers of America, Hyattsville.

Lacrosse, a major sport in the state, is represented by the Lacrosse Foundation in Baltimore and the US Intercollegiate Lacrosse Association in Chestertown. The National Rifle Association of America is based in Silver Spring. The National Amateur Baseball Federation and the National 4-H Council are also based in the state.

A number of military organizations are based in Maryland, including the Air Force Historical Foundation, the American Military Society, AMVETS (American Veterans of World War II, Korea, and Vietnam), the Black Military History Institute of America, the Vietnam Veterans of America, and the Blue Star Mothers of America. The National Flag Day Foundation is based in Baltimore.

Historical and cultural organizations include the Baltimore and Ohio Railroad Historical Society, the Edgar Allan Poe Society of Baltimore, and the Folk Alliance. There are also a number of county and regional historical societies. Education and research associations on the national level include the Jane Goodall Institute for Wildlife Research, Education, and Conservation, and the Wildlife Society.

Social action and civil rights organizations based in Maryland include the National Association for the Advancement of Colored People, Catholic Relief Services, and Goodwill Industries International.

47TOURISM, TRAVEL, AND RECREATION

In 2001, the state hosted over 19.4 million travelers. About 80% of all travelers were residents of one of the following states: Maryland, Pennsylvania, Virginia, New York, New Jersey, Florida, North Carolina, California, Ohio, Delaware, West Virginia. Total travel expenditures for 2001 were about $8.5

billion, which included support for about 105,400 travel-related jobs.

Attractions include parks, historical sites, and national seashore (Assateague Island). Annapolis, the state capital, is the site of the US Naval Academy. On Baltimore's waterfront are monuments to Francis Scott Key and Edgar Allan Poe, historic Ft. McHenry, and many restaurants serving the city's famed crab cakes and other seafood specialties. Ocean City is the state's major seaside resort, and there are many resort towns along Chesapeake Bay. The Office of Tourism promotes such historical attractions as the Civil War, War of 1812, and National Road. It also is expanding investment in multi-cultural tourism, sports marketing, and nature tourism. There are 19 state parks with camping facilities and 10 recreation areas.

48 SPORTS

Maryland has two major league professional sports teams: the Baltimore Orioles of Major League Baseball, and the Baltimore Ravens of the National Football League. The Ravens (formerly the Browns) moved from Cleveland after the 1995 season, and have begun playing in a new downtown stadium near Oriole Park at Camden Yards. The NFL's Washington Redskins have begun play in a new stadium, Jack Kent Cooke Stadium, in Landover, but will still be considered a team of the District of Columbia. The Orioles won the World Series in 1966, 1970, and 1983, and American League titles in 1969, 1971, and 1979.

There are several minor league baseball teams in the state, including teams in Bowie, Frederick, Delmarva, and Hagerstown.

Ever since 1750, when the first Arabian thoroughbred horse was imported by a Maryland breeder, horse racing has been a popular state pastime. The major tracks are Pimlico (Baltimore), Bowie, and Laurel; Pimlico is the site of the Preakness Stakes, the second leg of racing's Triple Crown. Harness racing is held at Ocean Downs in Ocean City; quarter-horse racing takes place at several tracks throughout the state; and several steeplechase events, including the prestigious Maryland Hunt Cup, are held annually.

In collegiate basketball, the University of Maryland won the NCAA Championship in 2002 and the National Invitation Tournament in 1972. Morgan State took the NCAA Division II title in 1974. Another major sport is lacrosse: Johns Hopkins, the Naval Academy, and the University of Maryland all have performed well in intercollegiate competition. In fact, Johns Hopkins has won the NCAA National Championship seven times, with the last title coming in 1987.

Every weekend from April to October, Marylanders compete in jousting tournaments held in four classes throughout the state. In modern jousting, designated as the official state sport, horseback riders attempt to pick up small rings with long, lancelike poles. The state championship is held in October.

Babe Ruth, perhaps the greatest baseball player to ever play the game, was one of many star athletes to be born in the state.

49 FAMOUS MARYLANDERS

Maryland's lone US vice president was Spiro Theodore Agnew (1918–96), who served as governor of Maryland before being elected as Richard Nixon's running mate in 1968. Reelected with Nixon in 1972, Agnew resigned the vice-presidency in October 1973 after a federal indictment had been filed against him. Roger Brooke Taney (1777–1864) served as attorney general and secretary of the treasury in Andrew Jackson's cabinet before being confirmed as US chief justice in 1836; his most historically significant case was the *Dred Scott* decision in 1856, in which the Supreme Court ruled that Congress could not exclude slavery from any territory.

Three associate justices of the US Supreme Court were also born in Maryland. Thomas Johnson (1732–1819), a signer of the

Declaration of Independence, served as the first governor of the State of Maryland before his appointment to the Court in 1791. Samuel Chase (1741–1811) was a Revolutionary leader, another signer of the Declaration of Independence, and a local judicial and political leader before being appointed to the high court in 1797; impeached in 1804 because of his alleged hostility to the Jeffersonians, he was acquitted by the Senate the following year. As counsel for the National Association for the Advancement of Colored People, Thurgood Marshall (1908–93), argued the landmark *Brown v. Board of Education* school desegregation case before the Supreme Court in 1954; President Lyndon Johnson appointed him to the Court 13 years later.

Other major federal officeholders born in Maryland include John Hanson (1721–83), a member of the Continental Congress and first president to serve under the Articles of confederation (1781–82); Charles Carroll of Carrollton (1737–1832), a signer of the Declaration of Independence and US senator from 1789 to 1792; John Pendleton Kennedy (1795–1870), secretary of the Navy under Millard Fillmore and a popular novelist known by the pseudonym Mark Littleton; Reverdy Johnson (1796–1876), attorney general under Zachary Taylor; Charles Joseph Bonaparte (1851–1921) secretary of the Navy and attorney general in Theodore Roosevelt's cabinet; and Benjamin Civiletti (b.New York, 1935), attorney general under Jimmy Carter. Among the many important state officeholders are William Paca (1740–99), a signer of the Declaration of Independence and later governor; Luther Martin (b.New Jersey, 1748–1826), Maryland's attorney general from 1778 to 1805 and from 1818 to 1822, as well as defense counsel in the impeachment trial of Chase and in the treason trial of Aaron Burr; John Eager Howard (1752–1827), Revolutionary soldier, governor, and US senator; and Albert C. Ritchie (1876–1936), governor from 1919 to 1935. William D. Schaefer (b.1921) was mayor of Baltimore from 1971–87; he was elected governor in 1987.

Lawyer and poet Francis Scott Key (1779–1843) wrote "The Star-Spangled Banner"—now the national anthem—in 1814. The prominent abolitionists Frederick Douglass (Frederick Augustus Washington Bailey, 1817?–95) and Harriet Tubman (1820?–1913) were born in Maryland, as was John Carroll (1735–1815), the first Roman Catholic bishop in the US and founder of Georgetown University. Elizabeth Ann Bayley Seton (b.New York, 1774–1821), canonized by the Roman Catholic Church in 1975, was the first native-born American saint. Stephen Decatur (1779–1820), a prominent naval officer, has been credited with the toast "Our country, right or wrong!"

Prominent Maryland business leaders include Alexander Brown (b.Ireland, 1764–1834), a Scotch-Irish immigrant who built the firm that is now the 2nd-oldest private investment banking house in the US; George Peabody (b.Massachusetts, 1795–1869), founder of the world-famous Peabody Conservatory of Music (now the Peabody Institute of Johns Hopkins University); and Enoch Pratt (b.Masachusetts, (1808–96) who endowed the Enoch Pratt Free Library in Baltimore. Benjamin Banneker (1731–1806), a free black, assisted in surveying the new District of Columbia and published almanacs from 1792 to 1797. Ottmar Mergenthaler (b.Germany, 1854–99), who made his home in Baltimore, invented the linotype machine.

Financier-philanthropist Johns Hopkins (1795–1873) was a Marylander, and educators Daniel Coit Gilman (b.Connecticut, 1831–1908) and William Osler (b.Canada, 1849–1919, also a famed physician), were prominent in the establishment of the university and medical school named in Hopkins' honor. Peyton Rous (1879–1970) won the 1966 Nobel Prize for physiology or medicine.

Maryland's best-known modern writer was H(enry) L(ouis) Mencken (1880–1956), a Baltimore newspaper reporter who was also a gifted social commentator, political wit, and student of the American language. Edgar Allan Poe (b.Massachusetts, 1809–49), known for his poems and eerie short stories, died in Baltimore, and novelist-reformer Upton Sinclair (1878–1968) was born there. Other writers associated with Maryland include James M. Cain (1892–1976), Leon Uris (b.1924), John Barth (b.1930), and Russell Baker (b.1925). Painters John Hesselius (b.Pennsylvania, 1728–78) and Charles Willson Peale (1741–1827) are also linked with the state.

Most notable among Maryland actors are Edwin Booth (1833–93) and his brother John Wilkes Booth (1838–65), notorious as the assassin of President Abraham Lincoln. Maryland was the birthplace of several jazz musicians, including James Hubert "Eubie" Blake (1883–1983), William Henry "Chick" Webb (1907–39), and Billie Holiday (1915–59).

Maryland was home to a number of well-known sports figures. Probably the greatest baseball player of all time, George Herman "Babe" Ruth (1895–1948) was born in Baltimore. Other prominent ballplayers include Robert Moses "Lefty" Grove (1900–75), James Emory "Jimmy" Foxx (1907–67), and Al Kaline (b.1934, and Cal Ripken, Jr. (b.1960), who played in 2,632 consecutive major league baseball games (ending 20 September 1998), setting a new record. Former lightweight boxing champion Joe Gans (1874–1910) was a Maryland native.

50 BIBLIOGRAPHY

Alampi, Gary, ed. *Gale State Rankings Reporter.* Detroit: Gale Research, Inc., 1994

Bode, Carl. *Maryland: A Bicentennial History.* New York: Norton, 1978.

Cohen, Richard M., and Jules Witcover. *A Heartbeat Away: The Investigation and Resignation of Vice President Spiro T. Agnew.* New York: Viking, 1974.

Council of State Governments. *The Book of the States, 1994–1995 Edition.* Vol. 30. Lexington, Ky.: The Council of State Governments, 1994.

Coursey, Denise Hawkins and Matthew Coursey. *Frommer's Maryland & Delaware.* Foster City, CA: IDG Books Worldwide, 2000.

Dozer, Donald. *Portrait of the Free State: A History of Maryland.* Cambridge, Md.: Tidewater, 1976.

FDIC, Division of Research and Statistics. *Statistics on Banking: A Statistical Profile of the United States Banking Industry.* Washington, D.C.: Federal Deposit Insurance Corporation, 1993.

Fields, Barbara J. *Slavery and Freedom on the Middle Ground: Maryland during the Nineteenth Century.* New Haven, Conn.: Yale University Press, 1985.

Fuke, Richard Paul. *Imperfect Equality: African Americans and the Confines of White Racial Attitudes in Post-Emancipation Maryland.* New York: Fordham University Press, 1999.

Gilland, Steve. *Early Families of Frederick County, Maryland, and South Central Pennsylvania.* Westminster, Md.: Willow Bend Books, 2000.

Maryland, State of. Department of Economic and Community Development. *Maryland Statistical Abstract 1993-94.* Annapolis: State of Maryland, 1995.

Maryland, State of. Department of General Services. Hall of Records Commission. Archives Division. *Maryland Manual 1985-1986.* Edited by Gregory A. Stiverson. Annapolis: State of Maryland, 1985.

McCormac, Eugene Irving. *White Servitude in Maryland, 1634-1820.* Westminster, Md. : Willow Bend Books, 2002.

Mencken, H. L. *A Choice of Days: Essays from "Happy Days," "Newspaper Days," and "Heathen Days."* Selected by Edward L. Galligan. New York: Knopf, 1980.

Papenfuse, Edward C. et al. *Maryland: A New Guide to the Old Line State.* Baltimore: Johns Hopkins University Press, 1976.

Schmittroth, Linda, and Mary Kay Rosteck, ed. *Cities of the United States.* 2nd ed. Detroit: Gale Research, Inc., 1994.

U.S. Department of Education, National Center for Education Statistics. Office of Educational Research and Improvement. *Digest of Education Statistics, 1993.* Washington, D.C.: U.S. Government Printing Office, 1993.

U.S. Department of the Interior, U.S. Fish and Wildlife Service. *Endangered and Threatened Species Recovery Program.* Washington, D.C.: U.S. Government Printing Office, 1990.

Walsh, Richard, and William Lloyd Fox, ed. *Maryland: A History.* Baltimore: Maryland Hall of Records, 1983.

Warner, William. *Beautiful Swimmers: Watermen, Crabs, and the Chesapeake Bay.* Boston: Little, Brown, 1976.

MASSACHUSETTS

Commonwealth of Massachusetts

ORIGIN OF STATE NAME: Derived from the name of the Massachuset Indian tribe that lived on Massachusetts Bay; the name is thought to mean "at or about the Great Hill." **NICKNAME:** The Bay State. **CAPITAL:** Boston. **ENTERED UNION:** 6 February 1788 (6th). **SONG:** "All Hail to Massachusetts." **FOLK SONG:** "Massachusetts." **POEM:** "Blue Hills of Massachusetts." **MOTTO:** *Ense petit placidam sub libertate quietem* (By the sword we seek peace, but peace only under liberty). **COAT OF ARMS:** On a blue shield, an Indian depicted in gold holds in his right hand a bow and in his left an arrow pointing downward. Above the bow is a five-pointed silver star. The crest shows a bent right arm holding a broadsword. Around the shield beneath the crest is a banner with the state motto in green. **FLAG:** The coat of arms on a white field. **OFFICIAL SEAL:** Same as the coat of arms, with the inscription *Sigillum Reipublicae Massachusettensis* (Seal of the Republic of Massachusetts). **HEROINE:** Deborah Sampson. **BIRD:** Chickadee. **HORSE:** Morgan horse. **DOG:** Boston terrier. **MARINE MAMMAL:** Right whale. **FISH:** Cod. **INSECT:** Ladybug. **FLOWER:** Mayflower (ground laurel). **TREE:** American elm. **GEM:** Rhodonite. **MINERAL:** Babingtonite. **ROCK:** Roxbury puddingstone. **HISTORICAL ROCK:** Plymouth Rock. **EXPLORER ROCK:** Dighton Rock. **BUILDING AND MONUMENT STONE:** Granite. **FOSSIL:** Theropod dinosaur tracks. **BEVERAGE:** Cranberry juice. **LEGAL HOLIDAYS:** New Year's Day, 1 January; Birthday of Martin Luther King, Jr., 3rd Monday in January; Washington's Birthday, 3rd Monday in February; Patriots' Day, 3rd Monday in April; Lafayette Day, 20 May; Memorial Day, last Monday in May; Independence Day, 4 July; Labor Day, 1st Monday in September; Columbus Day, 2nd Monday in October; Veterans Day, 11 November; Thanksgiving Day, appointed by the governor, customarily the 4th Thursday in November; Christmas Day, 25 December. **TIME:** 7 AM EST = noon GMT.

¹LOCATION, SIZE, AND EXTENT

Located in the northeastern US, Massachusetts is the 4th largest of the six New England states and ranks 45th in size among the 50 states.

The total area of Massachusetts is 8,284 sq mi (21,456 sq km), of which land comprises 7,824 sq mi (20,265 sq km) and inland water occupies 460 sq mi (1,191 sq km). Massachusetts extends about 190 mi (306 k) E-W; the maximum N-S extension is about 110 mi (177 km). Massachusetts is bordered on the N by Vermont and New Hampshire; on the E by the Atlantic Ocean; on the S by the Atlantic Ocean and by Rhode Island and Connecticut; and on the W by New York.

Two important islands lie south of the state's fishhook-shaped Cape Cod peninsula: Martha's Vineyard (108 sq mi or 280 sq km) and Nantucket (57 sq mi or 148 sq km). The Elizabeth Islands, SW of Cape Cod and NW of Martha's Vineyard, consist of 16 small islands separating Buzzards Bay from Vineyard Sound. The total boundary length of Massachusetts is 515 mi (829 km), including a general coastline of 192 mi (309 km); the tidal shoreline, encompassing numerous inlets and islands, is 1,519 mi (2,444 km). The state's geographic center is located in Worcester County, in the northern section of the city of Worcester.

²TOPOGRAPHY

Massachusetts is divided into four topographical regions: coastal lowlands, interior lowlands, dissected uplands, and residuals of ancient mountains. The coastal lowlands, located on the state's eastern edge, extend from the Atlantic Ocean 30–50 mi (48–80 km) inland and include Cape Cod and the offshore islands. The northern shoreline of the state is characterized by rugged high slopes, but at the southern end, along Cape Cod, the ground is flatter and covered with grassy heaths.

The Connecticut River Valley, characterized by red sandstone, curved ridges, meadows, and good soil, is the main feature of west-central Massachusetts. The Berkshire Valley to the west is filled with streams in its northern end, including the two streams that join below Pittsfield to form the Housatonic River.

East of the Connecticut River Valley are the eastern uplands, an extension of the White Mountains of New Hampshire. From elevations of 1,100 ft (335 m) in midstate, this ridge of heavily forested hills slopes down gradually toward the rocky northern coast.

In western Massachusetts, the Taconic Range and Berkshire Hills (which extend southward from the Green Mountains of Vermont) are characterized by numerous hills and valleys. Mt. Greylock, close to the New York border, is the highest point in the state, at 3,487 ft (1,064 m). Northeast of the Berkshires is the Hoosac Range, an area of plateau land. Its high point is Spruce Hill, at 1,974 ft (602 m).

There are more than 4,230 mi (6,808 km) of rivers in the state. The Connecticut River, the longest, runs southward through west-central Massachusetts; the Deerfield, Westfield, Chicopee, and Millers rivers flow into it. Other rivers of note include the Charles and the Mystic, which flow into Boston harbor; the Taunton, which empties into Mount Hope Bay at Fall River; the Blackstone, passing through Worcester on its way to Rhode Island; the Housatonic, winding through the Berkshires; and the Merrimack, flowing from New Hampshire to the Atlantic Ocean via the state's northeast corner. Over 1,100 lakes dot the state; the largest, the artificial Quabbin Reservoir in central Massachusetts, covers 24,704 acres (9,997 ha). The largest natural lake is Assawompset Pond in southern Massachusetts, occupying 2,656 acres (1,075 ha).

318

Hilly Martha's Vineyard is roughly triangular in shape, as is Nantucket Island to the east. The Elizabeth Islands are characterized by broad, grassy plains.

Millions of years ago, three mountainous masses of granite rock extended northeastward across the state. The creation of the Appalachian Mountains transformed limestone into marble, mud, and gravel into slate and schist, and sandstone into quartzite. The new surfaces were worn down several times. Then, during the last Ice Age, retreating glaciers left behind the shape of Cape Cod as well as a layer of soil, rock, and boulders.

³CLIMATE

Although Massachusetts is a relatively small state, there are significant climatic differences between its eastern and western sections. The entire state has cold winters and moderately warm summers, but the Berkshires in the west have both the coldest winters and the coolest summers. The normal January temperature in Pittsfield in the Berkshires is 22°F (–6°C), while the normal July temperature is 68°F (20°C). The interior lowlands are several degrees warmer in both winter and summer; the normal July temperature is 71°F (22°C). The coastal sections are the warmest areas of the state; the normal January temperature for Boston is 30°F (–1°C), and the normal July temperature is 74°F (23°C). The record high temperature in the state is 107°F (42°C), established at Chester and New Bedford on 2 August 1975; the record low is –35°F (–37°C), registered at Chester on 12 January 1981.

Precipitation ranges from 39 to 46 in (99 to 117 cm) annually, with an average for Boston (1971–2000) of 42.5 in (108 cm). The average snowfall for Boston is 42 in (107 cm), with the range in the Berkshires considerably higher. Boston's average wind speed is 13 mph (21 km/hr).

⁴FLORA AND FAUNA

Maple, birch, beech, oak, pine, hemlock, and larch cover the Massachusetts uplands. Common shrubs include rhodora, mountain laurel, and shadbush. Various ferns, maidenhair and osmund among them, grow throughout the state. Typical wildflowers include the Maryland meadow beauty and false loosestrife, as well as several varieties of orchid, lily, goldenrod, and aster. Listed as threatened or endangered plants in 2003 were northeastern bulrush, sandplain gerardia, and small whorled pogonia.

As many as 76 species of mammals, 74 of them native species, have been counted in Massachusetts. Common native mammals include the white-tailed deer, bobcat, river otter, striped skunk, mink, ermine, fisher, raccoon, black bear, gray fox, muskrat, porcupine, beaver, red and gray squirrels, snowshoe hare, little brown bat, and masked shrew. Among the Bay State's 336 resident bird species are the mallard, ruffed grouse, bobwhite quail, ring-necked pheasant, herring gull, great horned and screech owls, downy woodpecker, blue jay, mockingbird, cardinal, and song sparrow. Native inland fish include brook trout, chain pickerel, brown bullhead, and yellow perch; brown trout, carp, and smallmouth and largemouth bass have been introduced. Native amphibians include the Jefferson salamander, red-spotted newt, eastern American toad, gray tree frog, and bullfrog. Common reptiles are the snapping turtle, stinkpot, spotted turtle, northern water snake, and northern black racer. The venomous timber rattlesnake and northern copperhead are found mainly in Norfolk, Hampshire, and Hampden counties. The Cape Cod coasts are rich in a variety of shellfish, including clams, mussels, shrimps, and oysters. Twenty-one Massachusetts animal species were classified as threatened or endangered in 2003. Among them were the American burying beetle, the bald eagle, puma, shortnose sturgeon, five species of whale, and four species of turtle.

⁵ENVIRONMENTAL PROTECTION

All environmentally related programs are administered by the Executive Office of Environmental Affairs (EOEA) and its five agencies: the Department of Environmental Management (DEM); the Department of Environmental Protection (DEP); the Department of Fisheries, Wildlife and Environmental Law Enforcement (DFWELE); the Department of Food and Agriculture (DFA); and the Metropolitan District Commission (MDC).

EOEA agencies protect the state's more than 3,100 lakes and ponds covering about 150,000 acres (61,000 hectares); some 2,000 rivers and streams flowing 10,700 mi (17,200 km); 810,000 acres (about 328,000 hectares) of medium- and high-yield aquifers underlying about a sixth of the state; a half-million acres (about 200,000 hectares) of wetlands covering about a tenth of the state; and 1,500 mi (2,400 km) of coastal capes, coves, and estuaries.

With disposal of treated sewage sludge in Boston Harbor halted in 1991 and with improved sewage treatment, the harbor today is markedly cleaner than before. In 1988, 10% of the flounder caught in Boston Harbor had liver tumors caused by toxic chemicals; as of 1993, no flounder tested had tumors. In 1994, the state opened a new primary water treatment plant, and in 1996, a second new treatment facility also began operation.

Between 1978 and 1985, Massachusetts averaged 24 air pollution (i.e., ozone) violation days per year; between 1985 and 1993, the average dropped to 14. Since 1990, the state has averaged 7 violation days per year. With the adoption of Massachusetts acid rain legislation in 1985, sulfur dioxide output from Massachusetts sources has been cut by 17%. Additional decreases, particularly from out-of-state power plants, are expected to further cut sulfur dioxide emissions in half by 2000. In response to the Massachusetts Toxic Use Reduction Program and certain federal requirements, toxic air emissions were reduced by about a third between 1989 and 1996.

The state's solid waste recycling and composting rate stood at 28% in 1994; its goal for 2000 was 46%. In the mid-1990s, 341 of the state's 351 communities had some type of recycling program, and about 49% of solid waste was incinerated. In 2003, Massachusetts had 411 hazardous waste sites listed in the Environmental Protection Agency's database, 31 of which were on the National Priorities List.

Of the state's native vertebrate animals, 17% are endangered or threatened; among reptiles 55% are so listed. Wildlife management has restored populations of wild turkeys, white-tailed deer, bears, peregrine falcons, bald eagles, ospreys, Atlantic sturgeon, and Atlantic salmon.

Since about 1900, the Commonwealth has protected 528,400 acres (208,730 hectares) through acquisitions or restrictions, an area equal to 10% of the total land mass of the state. In 1993/94, the state added 8,930 acres (3,614 hectares) to its stock of protected land, expending $41 million in the effort. Federal, county, local, and private nonprofit agencies and organizations provide another 375,680 acres (152,038 hectares) of open space. In 2001, Massachusetts received a total of $131,856,000 in federal grants from the Environmental Protection Agency; EPA expenditures for procurement contracts in Massachusetts that year amounted to $76,126,000.

⁶POPULATION

As New England's most populous state, Massachusetts has seen its population grow steadily since colonial times. However, since the early 1800s, its growth rate has often lagged behind the rest of the nation's. Massachusetts's population, according to the 1990 federal census, was 6,016,425 (13th in the US), an increase of 4.9% over 1980, and much better than the 0.8% growth rate of the 1970s. Reasons behind the population lag include a

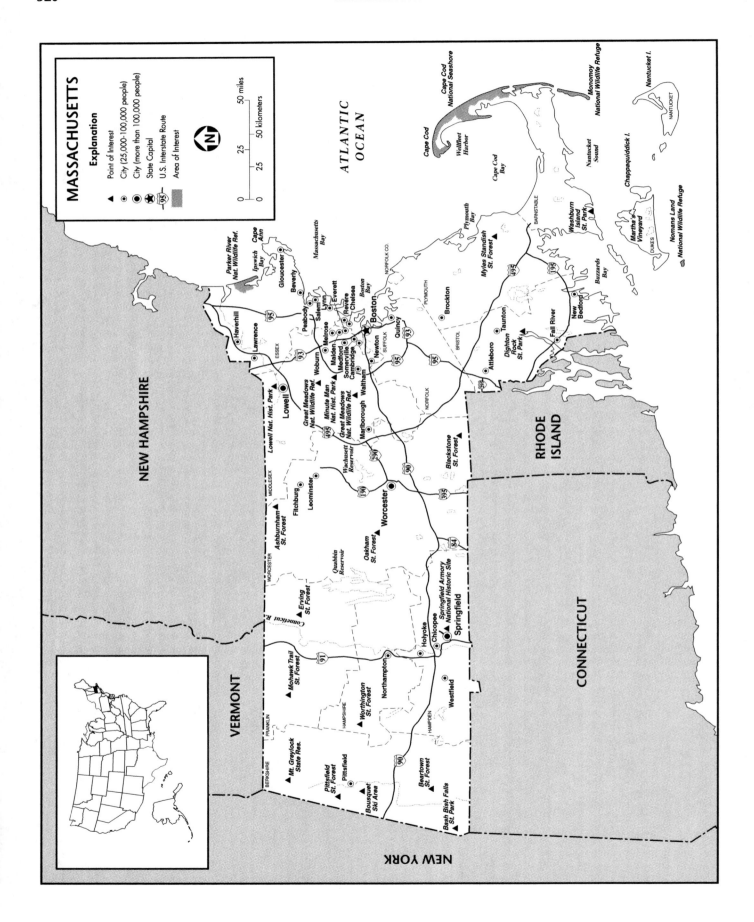

birthrate well below the US average, and a net out-migration of 301,000 people between 1970 and 1983, the largest drop of all New England states.

Massachusetts ranked 13th in population in the US with an estimated total of 6,427,137 in 2002, an increase of 1.2% since 2000. Between 1990 and 2000, Massachusetts's population grew from 6,016,425 to 6,349,097, an increase of 5.5%. The population is projected to reach 6.9 million by 2025. The population density in 2000 was 809.8 persons per sq mi, the 3rd highest in the nation.

In 2000 the median age was 36.5. Persons under 18 years old accounted for 23.6% of the population while 13.5% were age 65 or older.

The state's biggest city is Boston, which ranked 20th among the largest US cities with a population of 589,281 in 2002, up from an estimated 547,725 in 1994. Other large cities (with their 2002 estimated populations) are Worcester, 174,962, and Springfield, 151,915. More than two-thirds of all state residents live in the Greater Boston area, which in 1999 had an estimated metropolitan population of 5,667,225.

7ETHNIC GROUPS

Early industrialization helped make Massachusetts a mecca for many European migrants, particularly the Irish. As late as 1990 more than half of the population identified with at least one single ancestry group. As of 2000 the largest were the Irish (22.5% of the population), Italian (13.5%), English (11.4%), French (8%), Polish (5.1%), and Portuguese (4.4%). In that year, the foreign born numbered 772,983, or 12.2% of the state's population.

Massachusetts has always had a black population, and has contributed such distinguished figures as poet Phillis Wheatley and NAACP founder W.E.B. DuBois (the first black Ph.D. from Harvard) to US cultural and public life. A sizable class of black professionals has developed, and the 20th century has seen an influx of working-class blacks from southern states. In 2000 there were 343,454 black Americans in Massachusetts, 5.4% of the population. Blacks constituted more than 25% of Boston's population. The state also had 428,729 Hispanics and Latinos in 2000, predominantly Puerto Rican and Dominican.

Greater Boston has a small, well-organized Chinatown; in the suburbs reside many Chinese professionals and businesspeople, as well as those connected with the region's numerous educational institutions. Statewide, there were 84,392 Chinese in 2000 (up from 47,245 in 1990), 33,962 Vietnamese (up from 13,101 in 1990), 19,696 Cambodians, 17,369 Koreans, and 10,539 Japanese. In 2000, the total Asian population was estimated at 238,124, and the Native American population (including Eskimos and Aleuts) totaled an estimated 15,015. Pacific Islanders numbered 2,489. Cape Cod has settlements of Portuguese fishermen, as has New Bedford.

8LANGUAGES

Some general Algonkian loanwords and a few place-names—such as Massachusetts itself, Chicopee, Quebbin, and Naukeag—are the language echoes of the Massachuset, Pennacook, and Mahican Indians so historically important in the founding of Massachusetts Bay Colony and Old Colony, now Plymouth.

On the whole, Massachusetts English is classed as Northern, but early migration up the Connecticut River left that waterway a sometimes sharp, sometimes vague boundary, setting off special variations within the eastern half of the state. Two conspicuous but now receding features long held prestige because of the cultural eminence of Boston: the absence of /r/ after a vowel, as in *fear* and *port,* and the use of a vowel halfway between the /ah/ in *half* and *past* and as well as in *car* and *park* and the short /a/ of *cat.* Eastern Massachusetts speakers are likely to have /ah/ in *orange*

and to pronounce *on* and *fog* with the same vowel as in *form.* In the east, a sycamore is a *buttonwood,* a tied and filled quilt is a *comforter,* a *creek* is a saltwater inlet, and pancakes may be called *fritters.*

Around Boston are heard the intrusive /r/ as in "the lawr of the land," the /oo/ vowel in *butcher, tonic* for soft drink, *submarine* for a large sandwich, and *milkshake* for a concoction lacking ice cream. West of the Connecticut River are heard the /aw/ sound in *orange,* /ah/ in *on* and *fog,* and the short /a/ of *cat* in *half* and *bass; buttonball* is a sycamore, and *comfortable* is a tied quilt.

In 2000, 81.3% of the population five years of age or older (down from 84.8% in 1990) spoke only English at home.

The following table gives selected statistics from the 2000 census for language spoken at home by persons five years old and over.

LANGUAGE	NUMBER	PERCENT
Population 5 years and over	**5,954,249**	**100.0**
Speak only English	4,838,679	81.3
Speak a language other than English	1,115,570	18.7
Speak a language other than English	**1,115,570**	**18.7**
Spanish or Spanish Creole	370,011	6.2
Portuguese or Portuguese Creole	159,809	2.7
French (incl. Patois, Cajun)	84,484	1.4
Chinese	71,412	1.2
Italian	59,811	1.0
French Creole	43,519	0.7
Russian	32,580	0.5
Vietnamese	30,400	0.5
Greek	28,819	0.5
Polish	27,631	0.5
Mon-Khmer, Cambodian	21,549	0.4
German	20,029	0.3
Arabic	18,742	0.3

9RELIGIONS

While Protestant sects have contributed greatly to the state's history and development, more than half the state's population is Roman Catholic, a fact that has had a profound effect on Massachusetts politics and policies.

Both the Pilgrims, who landed on Plymouth Rock in 1620, and the Puritans, who formed the Massachusetts Bay Company in 1629, came to the land to escape harassment by the Church of England. These early communities were based on strict religious principles and forbade the practice of differing religions. Religious tolerance was included in the Charter of 1692, to protect the Baptists, Anglicans, and Catholics who had by then arrived in the colony.

The major influx of Roman Catholics came in the 1840s with the arrival of the Irish in Boston. By the 1850s, they had migrated to other towns and cities and formed the backbone of the state's industrial workforce. Later migration by Italian Catholics, German Catholics, and Eastern European Jews turned the state, by 1900, into a melting pot of religions and nationalities, although many of these minorities did not win substantial acceptance from the Protestant elite until the World War II era.

As of 2000, there were 3,092,296 Roman Catholics in Massachusetts, representing nearly half of the total population. The largest Protestant denominations were: the United Church of Christ, 121,826 adherents; the Episcopal Church, 98,963; the American Baptists (USA), 52,716,156; and the United Methodist Church, 64,028. The 2nd-largest religious affiliation is Judaism, with about 275,000 adherents in 2000. The Muslim population the same year was about 41,497 people. Though membership numbers were not available, reports noted that there were about 57 Buddhist congregations and 20 Hindu congregations throughout the state. About 35% of the population were not counted as members of any religious organization.

Although small, the Church of Christ, Scientist, is significant to Massachusetts's history. Its first house of worship was founded in 1879 in Boston by Mary Baker Eddy, who four years earlier had published the Christian Science textbook *Science and Health with Key to the Scriptures*. In Boston, the church continues to publish an influential newspaper, the *Christian Science Monitor*.

10 TRANSPORTATION

The first rail line in the US, a 3-mi (5-km) stretch from the Neponset River to the granite quarries in Quincy, was built in 1826. The first steam railroad in New England, connecting Boston and Lowell, was completed seven years later. By the late 1830s, tracks were laid from Boston to Worcester and to Providence, Rhode Island, and during the next two decades, additional railroad lines opened up new cities for industrial expansion.

As of 2000, 10 railroads transported freight through Massachusetts: CSX Transportation, the state's sole Class I railroad; Providence & Worcester and Guilford Rail, the state's regional railroads; and seven other local and switching and terminal railroads. At the end of 2000, the state had 1,233 rail mi (1,984 km) of railroad. Boston is the northern terminus of Amtrak's Northeast Corridor, linking New England with Washington, DC, via New York City and Philadelphia.

Commuter service is coordinated by the Massachusetts Bay Transportation Authority (MBTA), formed in 1964 to consolidate bus, commuter rail, high-speed trolley, and subway services to the 79 cities and towns in the Greater Boston area. The Boston subway, which began operation in 1897, is the oldest subway system in the US. Boston also is one of the few cities in the US with an operating trolley system. About 40% of all Bostonians commute to work by public transportation, the 2nd-highest percentage in the nation, following New York City.

In 2000, 35,311 mi (56,827 km) of public roadways crisscrossed the state. The major highways, which extend from and through Boston like the spokes of a wheel, include I-95, which runs north–south; the Massachusetts Turnpike (I-90), which runs west to the New York State border; I-93, which leads north to New Hampshire; State Highway 3 to Cape Cod; and State Highway 24 to Fall River. The other major road in the state is I-91, which runs north–south through the Connecticut River Valley. More than $3 billion was spent by all units of government for highways in 1997. In 2000, 5,372,117 motor vehicles were registered in the state, of which 3,673,638 were automobiles; 1,579,827 were trucks; and 11,934 were buses; there also were 106,718 motorcycles. The state issued 4,489,695 driver's licenses in 2000.

Because it is the major American city closest to Europe, Boston is an important shipping center for both domestic and foreign cargo. In 2000, 20.8 million tons of cargo passed through the Port of Boston. All port activity is under the jurisdiction of the Massachusetts Port Authority, which also operates Logan International Airport and Hanscom Field in Bedford. Other important ports and their 2000 cargo totals were Fall River, 3.4 million tons, and Salem, 1.2 million tons.

There were 76 airports and 129 heliports in Massachusetts in 2002. Logan International, near Boston, is the busiest airport in the state, with 13,613,507 passengers enplaned in 2000.

11 HISTORY

Some 15,000 years ago, when the last of the glaciers receded from the land we call Massachusetts, what remained was a rocky surface scoured of most of its topsoil. In time, however, forests grew to support a rich variety of wildlife. When the first Indians arrived from the south, game abounded and fish were plentiful in streams and along the coast. These first Indians were hunter-gatherers; their successors not only foraged for food but also cleared fields for planting corn (maize) and squash. Periodically they burned away the woodland underbrush, a technique of forest management that stimulated the vegetation that supported game. When English settlers arrived, they encountered five main Algonkian tribes: the Nauset, a fishing people on Cape Cod; the Wampanoag in the southeast; the Massachusetts in the northeast; the Nipmuc in the central hills; and the Pocumtuc in the west.

The earliest European explorers—including the Norsemen, who may have reached Cape Cod—made no apparent impact on these Algonkian groups, but in the wake of John and Sebastian Cabot's voyages (1497 and following), fishermen from England, France, Portugal, and Spain began fishing off the Massachusetts coast. By the mid-16th century, they were regularly going ashore to process and pack their catch. Within 50 years, fur trading with the Indians was established.

Permanent English settlement, which would ultimately destroy the Algonkian peoples, began in 1620 when a small band of Puritans left their haven at Leiden in the Netherlands to start a colony in the northern part of Virginia lands, near the Hudson River. Their ship, the Mayflower, was blown off course by an Atlantic storm, and they landed on Cape Cod before settling in an abandoned Wampanoag village they called Plymouth. Ten years later, a much larger Puritan group settled the Massachusetts Bay Colony, some miles to the north in Salem. Between 1630 and 1640, about 20,000 English people, chiefly Puritans, settled in Massachusetts with offshoots moving to Connecticut and Rhode Island.

The leaders of the Massachusetts settlement, most notably John Winthrop, a country gentleman with some legal training, intended to make their colony an exemplary Christian society. Though church and state were legally separate, they were mutually reinforcing agencies; thus, when Roger Williams and Anne Hutchinson were separately found guilty of heresy in the 1630s, they were banished by the state. All male church members had a voice in both church and state leadership, though both institutions were led by college-educated men. In order to provide for future leaders, Harvard College (now Harvard University) was founded in 1636.

After the beginning of the English revolution in 1640, migration to Massachusetts declined abruptly. Farming soon overtook fishing and fur trading in economic importance; after the trade in beaver skins was exhausted, the remaining Indian tribes were decimated in King Philip's War (1675–76). Shipbuilding and Atlantic commerce also brought prosperity to the Massachusetts Bay Colony, which was granted a new charter by King William and Queen Mary in 1692, merging Massachusetts and the colony of Plymouth. In that year, 19 people were executed for witchcraft on the gallows at Salem before Massachusetts authorities put a stop to the proceedings.

During the 18th century, settlement spread across the entire colony. Boston, the capital, had attained a population of 15,000 by 1730; it was an urbane community of brick as well as wooden buildings, with nearly a dozen church spires distinguishing its skyline by the 1750s. Religious revivals, also occurring elsewhere in America, swept Massachusetts in the 1730s and 1740s, rekindling piety and dividing the inhabitants into competing camps. Although the conflicts had ebbed by the 1750s, Massachusetts did not achieve unity again until the resistance to British imperial actions during the next two decades.

Up to this time, imperial government had rested lightly on Massachusetts, providing more advantages than drawbacks for commerce. The colony had actively supported British expeditions against French Canada, and supply contracts during the French and Indian War had enriched the economy. But the postwar recession after 1763 was accompanied by a new imperial policy that put pressure on Massachusetts as well as other colonies. None of the crown's three objectives—tight regulation of trade, the raising of revenue, and elimination of key areas of colonial political autonomy—were popular among the merchants, tradespeople, and farmers of Massachusetts. From 1765, when Bostonians violently protested the Stamp Act, Massachusetts was in the vanguard of the resistance.

At first, opposition was largely confined to Boston and surrounding towns, although the legislature, representing the entire colony, was active in opposing British measures. By December 1773, when East India Company tea was dumped into Boston harbor to prevent its taxation, most of the colony was committed to resistance. Newspaper polemics composed by Samuel Adams and his cousin John, among others, combined with the persuasive activities of the Boston Committee of Correspondence, helped convince a majority of Massachusetts residents that the slogan "no taxation without representation" stood for the preservation of their communities. When Parliament retaliated for the Tea Party by closing the port of Boston in 1774, rescinding the colony's 1692 charter, and remaking the government to put it under London's control, Massachusetts was ready to rebel. Military preparations began immediately on both sides. After almost a year of confrontation, battle began at Lexington and Concord on 19 April 1775. By this time, Massachusetts had the backing of the Continental Congress.

For Massachusetts, the battlefield experience of the Revolution was largely confined to 1775, the climaxes being the Battle of Bunker Hill and the British evacuation of Boston the following year. Thereafter, Massachusetts soldiers were active throughout the colonies, but the theater of action shifted southward. A new republican constitution, adopted in 1780, was the first state constitution to be submitted to the electorate for ratification.

Social and economic conditions in post-Revolutionary Massachusetts were much like those of the colonial era. Although the Shays Rebellion, an uprising of central and western farmers led by Daniel Shays in 1786–87, challenged the political hegemony of commercially oriented eastern leaders, the latter succeeded in maintaining their hold on the state. Massachusetts, which entered the Union on 6 February 1788, was the center of Federalism from 1790 until the mid-1820s. Although Jeffersonian Republicans and Jacksonian Democrats achieved substantial followings, Federalist policies, embodied in the Whigs in the 1830s and the Republicans from the late 1850s, were dominant. This political continuity was based on the importance of national commercial and industrial development to the state.

Even before 1800, it was clear that Massachusetts could not sustain growth in agriculture. Its soil had never been excellent, and the best lands were tired, having been worked for generations with little regard for conservation. Much of the state's population departed for New York, Ohio, and beyond during the first decades of the 19th century. Those who stayed maintained productive agriculture, concentrating more and more on fruits and dairying, but they also developed commerce and industry. At Waltham, Lowell, and Lawrence the first large-scale factories in the US were erected, and smaller textile mills throughout the state helped to make Massachusetts a leader in the cloth industry. At Springfield and Watertown, US armories led the way in metalworking, while shoes and leather goods brought prosperity to Lynn, and whale products and shipbuilding to New Bedford. By the 1850s, steam engines and clipper ships were both Bay State products.

The industrial development of Massachusetts was accompanied by a literary and intellectual flowering that was partly in reaction to the materialism and worldliness associated with urban and industrial growth. Concord, the home of Ralph Waldo Emerson, Henry David Thoreau, and a cluster of others, became the center of the transcendentalist movement in philosophy. Social reform also represented an assertion of moral values, whether in the field of education, health care, temperance, or penology. Abolitionism, the greatest of the moral reform efforts, found some of its chief leaders in Massachusetts, among them William Lloyd Garrison and Wendell Phillips, as well as a host of supporters.

In the years following the Civil War, Massachusetts emerged as an urban industrial state. Its population, fed by immigrants from England, Scotland, Germany, and especially Ireland, grew rapidly in the middle decades of the century. Later, between 1880 and 1920, another wave of immigrants came from French Canada, Italy, Russia, Poland, Scandinavia, Portugal, Greece, and Syria. Still later, between 1950 and 1970, black southerners and Puerto Ricans settled in the cities.

From the election of Lincoln in 1860 through the 1920s, Massachusetts was led by Protestant Yankee Republicans; most Democrats were Catholics. Class, ethnic, and religious tensions were endemic, occasionally erupting into open conflict. Three such episodes gained national attention. In 1912, immigrant textile workers in Lawrence were pitted against Yankee capitalists. A highly publicized strike of 1919 had the largely Irish-American police force rebelling against Yankees in city and state government, and brought Governor Calvin Coolidge—who suppressed the strike and refused to reinstate the striking policemen—to national prominence. In 1921, Nicola Sacco and Bartolomeo Vanzetti, Italian immigrant anarchists, were convicted for a payroll robbery and murder, though there was bitter controversy regarding the quality of the evidence against them. Before they were executed in 1927, their case and the issues it raised polarized political opinion throughout the US. Subsequently, electoral competition between Democrats and Republicans emerged as a less divisive outlet for class and ethnic tensions. Since 1959, the Democrats have enjoyed ascendance statewide, and Republicans have won only when their candidates stood close to the Democrats on the issues. Party loyalties as such have waned, however.

The Massachusetts economy, relatively stagnant between 1920 and 1950, revived in the second half of the 20th century through a combination of an educated and skilled workforce, capital resources, and political clout. As the old industries and the mill cities declined, new high-technology manufacturing developed in Boston's suburban perimeter, centering on start-up manufacturing firms along Route 128 outside Boston. Electronics, computers, and defense-oriented industries led the way, stimulating a general prosperity in which service activities such as banking, insurance, health care, and higher education were especially prominent. As a result, white-collar employment and middle-class suburbs flourished, though run-down mill towns and Yankee dairy farms and orchards still dotted the landscape.

In this respect, as in its politics, Massachusetts resembled many other areas of the Northeast. It was a multiracial state in which the general welfare was defined by shifting coalitions of ethnic groups and special interests. From a national perspective, Massachusetts voters appeared liberal; the Bay State was the only one to choose Democrat George McGovern over President Richard M. Nixon in 1972, and, since the 1970s, has been a perennially secure base for Senator Edward M. Kennedy. Yet Boston was also the site of some of the most extreme anti-integration tension during the same era; Massachusetts was simultaneously a center of efforts in favor of the Equal Rights Amendment and against abortion.

Massachusetts's defiance of political categories continued into the 1990s. In 1990, blaming the current governor, Democrat Michael Dukakis, for the economy's decline, Massachusetts voters elected a Republican, William Weld, as governor. Yet Weld in fact espoused a blend of liberal and conservative positions. A fiscal conservative who called for cutting taxes and reducing programs such as Medicaid and state employee pension plans, Weld took a liberal stance on social issues, supporting gay rights, abortion rights, and strict protection of the environment. In August 1997, Weld resigned as governor to pursue an appointment as ambassador to Mexico.

Beginning in 1989, the Massachusetts economy declined dramatically, losing 14% of its total jobs in three years. Like other parts of New England, Massachusetts was hit hard by the recession of the early 1990s, and the state's economic woes were aggravated by the collapse in the late 1980s of speculative real estate ventures. The saturation of the real estate market forced retrenchments not only of that industry but of construction as well. By 1992, a number of indications suggested that a recovery had begun to take hold, aided in part by the privatization of highway maintenance, prison health care, and some other state-run operations.

By the mid-1990s, the Massachusetts economy was in the midst of a vigorous upturn, credited largely to the strength of its leading local industries, including software and mutual funds, and the health of the US economy as a whole. In 1996 the state's unemployment level fell to 4%, the lowest it had been since 1989. By 1999 the unemployment rate had dropped further, to 3.2%. Its 1998 per capita income of $32,902 was the 3rd highest in the nation and had grown at the 2nd-fastest rate (2nd only to that of Wyoming).

The thriving economy came to an abrupt halt in 2001, as the US entered a recession marked by a large increase in job losses. As of mid-2003, Massachusetts had a $3 billion budget deficit. Issues facing the legislature in 2003 included Medicaid spending and a prescription drug program for senior citizens. The state Senate had approved a measure calling for a ban on smoking in the workplace, which was being considered by the House of Representatives. In addition, the state was considering the legality of same-sex marriages. Republican Governor Mitt Romney, a business executive and fiscal conservative elected in 2002, took a liberal stand on some social issues, such as supporting abortion choice and gay rights, but he also advocated reinstatement of the death penalty.

Balancing development with environmental conservation was among the issues the state grappled with at the dawn of the 21st century. In 2000 the legislature approved a statewide initiative to preserve open space through local land-acquisition funds. The funds were to come from a $20 surcharge on all transactions at the Registry of Deeds and Land Court; communities would also be given the option to allow voters to approve a property tax increase of up to 3% to support the measure.

The state was the setting of a national controversy in April 2000: in a report condemning lax oversight of the largest public works project in US history, a federal task force charged that managers of Boston's multibillion-dollar highway project intentionally concealed cost overruns. Known as "Big Dig," the massive project includes building a 10-lane expressway under Boston and extending the Massachusetts Turnpike beneath Boston Harbor to Logan International Airport. State officials had revealed in February that the project, which began in 1991, was $1.4 billion over its $10.8 billion budget, making it more expensive than the Boston Harbor clean-up. The project to restore the harbor, considered the nation's filthiest in 1990, was drawing to a successful close in 2000, in spite of cost overruns. Portions of the highway project, including the extention of I-90 through the Ted Williams Tunnel to Logan Airport were completed in January 2003. The entire project was expected to be completed by 2004.

Massachusetts was at the center of the sexual abuse scandals plaguing the Catholic Church in the early 2000s. Cardinal Bernard F. Law stepped down as Archbishop of Boston in December 2002 after widespread criticism of his handling of charges that priests sexually abused children, and of allegations of cover-ups. The Vatican replaced Law with Sean Patrick O'Malley as Archbishop of Boston in 2003.

12 STATE GOVERNMENT

The first state constitution, drawn up soon after the signing of the Declaration of Independence, was rejected by the electorate. A revised draft was not approved by the state voters until 15 June 1780, following two constitutional conventions. This constitution, as amended (120 times by January 2003), governs Massachusetts and is, according to the state, the oldest written constitution in the world still in effect.

The legislature of Massachusetts, known as the General Court, is composed of a 40-member senate and 160-member house of representatives, all of whom are elected every two years in even-numbered years. Annual legislative sessions begin the first Wednesday in January and must conclude by November 15 one year and by July 31 the following year. Additionally, legislators may petition to convene special sessions. Members of the senate must have resided in Maine for at least five years and must be residents of their districts; representatives must have lived in their districts for at least one year prior to election. The minimum age for all legislators is 18. The legislative salary was $50,123 in 2002.

The governor and lieutenant governor are elected jointly every four years. The governor appoints all state and local judges, as well as the heads of the 10 executive offices. Both the governor and lieutenant governor must have resided in the state for at least seven years; there is no minimum age specified for the offices. In 2002 the governor's salary was $135,000. Other elected officials include the attorney general, secretary of the commonwealth, treasurer and receiver-general, and auditor of the commonwealth. All serve four-year terms.

Any Massachusetts citizen may file a bill through a state legislator, or a bill may be filed directly by a legislator or by the governor. To win passage, a bill must gain a majority vote of both houses of the legislature. After a bill is passed, the governor has 10 days in which to sign it, return it for reconsideration (usually with amendments), veto it, or hold onto it until after the legislature adjourns ("pocket veto"). A veto may be overridden by a two-thirds vote of the members present in both houses.

Amendments to the constitution may be introduced by any house or senate member (legislative amendment) or by a petition signed by 3% of the total votes cast for governor in the last state election, which must be at least 25,000 qualified voters, and that is presented in a joint session of the General Court. If it is approved by two successive sessions of the legislature, the amendment is then submitted to the voters at the next general election.

To vote in a Massachusetts district, a person must be a US citizen, at least 18 years old, and a state resident. Those convicted of corrupt practices with respect to elections and those under guardianship with respect to voting may not vote.

13 POLITICAL PARTIES

The Federalist Party, represented nationally by John Adams, dominated Massachusetts in the late 18th and early 19th centuries. The state turned to the Whig Party in the second quarter of the 19th century. Predominantly Yankee in character, the Whigs supported business growth, promoted protective tariffs, and favored such enterprises as railroads and factories. The new Republican Party, to which most Massachusetts Whigs gravitated when their party split in the 1850s, was a prime mover of abolitionism and played an important role in the election of Abraham Lincoln as president in 1860. Republicans held most of the major state elective offices, as well as most US congressional seats, until the early 1900s.

The Democratic Party's rise starting in the 1870s was tied directly to massive Irish immigration. Other immigrant groups also gravitated toward the Democrats, and in 1876, the state's first Democratic congressman was elected. In 1928, the state voted for Democratic presidential candidate Alfred E. Smith, a Roman Catholic, the first time the Democrats won a majority in a Massachusetts presidential election. Democrats have subsequently, for the most part, dominated state politics. In 1960, John F. Kennedy, who had been a popular US senator from Massachusetts, became the first Roman Catholic president in US history. Since then the state has voted for all Democratic presidential candidates except Republican Ronald Reagan in 1980 and 1984; in 1972, it was the only state carried by Democrat George McGovern. Massachusetts chose its native son, Democratic Governor Michael Dukakis, for president in 1988 and voted again for a Democrat in the next three elections, giving Al Gore 60% of the vote, Republican George W. Bush 33%, and Green Party candidate Ralph Nader 6%. In 2002 there were 3,972,651 registered voters. In 1998, 37% of registered voters were Democratic, 13% Republican, and 50% unaffiliated or members of other parties. The state had 12 electoral votes in the 2000 presidential election.

From 1990 to 1997, the governorship was held by a Republican, William Weld. Weld resigned in 1997 to pursue an appointment as ambassador to Mexico, at which time he was succeeded by lieutenant governor and fellow Republican Argeo Paul Cellucci. Cellucci was elected in his own right in November 1998. In 2002, Republican Mitt Romney was elected governor. Following the 2002 election, the US Senate seats for Massachusetts were held by Democrats Edward Kennedy (last elected in 2000) and John Kerry (last elected in 2002). In 2003, Kerry had launched a campaign for the presidency. The 10-member US House delegation following the 2002 elections again consisted entirely of Democrats. In mid-2003 the Massachusetts state senate had 34 Democrats and six Republicans while the state house of representatives had 136 Democrats, 23 Republicans, and one Independent.

14LOCAL GOVERNMENT

As of 2002, Massachusetts had 5 counties, 45 cities, and 306 townships, 82 public school districts, and 403 special districts.

In most counties, which mostly serve judicial purposes, executive authority is vested in commissioners elected to four-year terms. Other county officials include the register of probate and family court, sheriff, clerk of courts, county treasurer, and register of deeds.

All Massachusetts cities are governed by mayors and city councils. Towns are governed by selectmen, who are usually elected to either one- or two-year terms. Town meetings—a carryover from the colonial period, when every taxpayer had an equal voice in town government—still take place. By state law, to be designated a city, a place must have at least 12,000 residents. Towns with more than 6,000 inhabitants may hold representative town meetings limited to elected officials.

15STATE SERVICES

To address the continuing threat of terrorism and to work with the federal Department of Homeland Security (created in 2002 following the terrorist attacks of 11 September 2001), homeland security in Massachusetts in 2003 operated under the authority of the governor; activities were overseen by the homeland security director.

State services are provided through the 12 executive offices and major departments that constitute the governor's cabinet. The heads of these departments are appointed by the governor. The Ethics in Massachusetts State Government organization distributes information on state government scandals.

Educational services are administered by the Executive Office of Education. Included under its jurisdiction are the State Board of Education and Board of Regents of Higher Education, the Massachusetts community college and state college systems, the University of Massachusetts, the Council of the Arts and Humanities, and the State Library.

The Executive Office of Transportation and Construction supervises the Department of Public Works and has responsibility for the planning and development of transportation systems within the state, including the Massachusetts Port Authority, the Massachusetts Highway Department, the Massachusetts Turnpike Authority, the Massachusetts Bay Transportation Authority, and the Massachusetts Aeronautics Commission.

All public health, mental health, youth, and veterans' programs are administered by the Executive Office of Health &

Massachusetts Presidential Vote by Political Party, 1948–2000

YEAR	ELECTORAL VOTE	MASSACHUSETTS WINNER	DEMOCRAT	REPUBLICAN	SOCIALIST LABOR	PROGRESSIVE
1948	16	*Truman (D)	1,151,788	909,370	5,535	38,157
1952	16	*Eisenhower (R)	1,083,525	1,292,325	1,957	4,636
1956	16	*Eisenhower (R)	948,190	1,393,197	5,573	—
1960	16	*Kennedy (D)	1,487,174	976,750	3,892	—
1964	14	*Johnson (D)	1,786,422	549,727	4,755	—
						AMERICAN IND.
1968	14	Humphrey (D)	1,469,218	766,844	6,180	87,088
					SOC. WORKERS	AMERICAN
1972	14	McGovern (D)	1,332,540	1,112,078	10,600	2,877
1976	14	*Carter (D)	1,429,475	1,030,276	8,138	7,555
					LIBERTARIAN	
1980	14	*Reagan (R)	1,048,562	1,054,213	21,311	—
1984	13	*Reagan	1,239,600	1,310,936	—	—
						NEW ALLIANCE
1988	13	Dukakis (D)	1,401,415	1,194,635	24,251	9,561
						IND. (PEROT)
1992	12	*Clinton (D)	1,318,639	805,039	9,021	630,731
1996	12	*Clinton (D)	1,571,763	718,107	20,426	227,217
						GREEN
2000	12	Gore (D)	1,616,487	878,502	16,366	173,564

*Won US presidential election.

Human Services. Also under its jurisdiction are the Department of Public Health and the Department of Correction. The Executive Office of Public Safety includes the Division of Civil Defense, Registry of Motor Vehicles, and Highway Safety Bureau.

The Executive Office of Consumer Affairs and Business Regulation regulates state standards and registers professional workers. The Department of Public Utilities and Alcoholic Beverages Control Commission are also part of this office, as are the divisions regulating banks and insurance. Housing services are provided through the Executive Office of Communities and Development. This office administers the Massachusetts Home Mortgage Finance Agency, the Housing Finance Agency, and the Bureaus of Housing Development and of Housing Management and Tenant Services.

The Executive Office of Environmental Affairs protects the state's marine and wildlife, and monitors the quality of its air, water, and food. Labor and industrial relations are monitored through the Executive Office of Labor, whose Department of Labor and Industries administers the minimum wage law, occupational safety laws, and child labor laws, among others. The Executive Office of Economic Affairs helps to improve the economic climate in the state and promotes exports and tourism. The Department of Elder Affairs plans and implements programs for the elderly, including nutrition, home care, and education programs.

16JUDICIAL SYSTEM

All statewide judicial offices are filled by the governor, with the advice and consent of the executive council.

The supreme judicial court, composed of a chief justice and six other justices, is the highest court in the state. It has appellate jurisdiction in matters of law and also advises the governor and legislature on legal questions. The superior courts, actually the highest level of trial court, have a chief justice and 79 other justices; these courts hear law, equity, civil, and criminal cases, and make the final determination in matters of fact. The appeals court, consisting of a chief justice and 13 other justices, hears appeals of decisions by district and municipal courts. There are also district and municipal courts and trial court judges. Other court systems in the state include the land court, probate and family court, housing court (with divisions in Boston and Hampden counties), and juvenile court (with divisions in Boston, Springfield, Worcester, and Bristol counties).

Massachusetts's total crime rate per 100,000 inhabitants was 3,098.6in 2001, including a total of 30,587 violent crimes and 167,079 crimes against property in that year. Massachusetts does not have a death penalty. Under Massachusetts gun control laws, all guns must be registered, and there is a mandatory one-year jail sentence for possession without a permit.

As of June 2001, there were 10,734 prisoners in state and federal correctional institutions, a decrease of 3.7% from the previous year. The state's incarceration rate stood at 247 per 100,000 inhabitants.

17ARMED FORCES

The military installations located in Massachusetts in 2002 had 2,427 active-duty military personnel. The largest installation in the state is the Laurence G. Hanscom Air Force Base in Bedford. Other installations include the Army reserve and development center at Natick, the Navy's South Weymouth Naval Air Station, and Westover Air Force Base. Defense contracts awarded in 2001 totaled $5.25 billion.

There were 558,933 military veterans living in the state in 2000. Veterans of World War II numbered 138,650,000; the Korean conflict, 78,706; the Vietnam era, 150,981; and during

1990–2000 (including the Persian Gulf War), 39,792. About $1.2 billion was paid in veterans' benefits in 2002.

In 2000, the Massachusetts State Police employed 2,221 full-time sworn officers.

18MIGRATION

Massachusetts was founded by the migration of English religious groups to its shores, and for over a century their descendants dominated all activity in the state. The first non-English to enter Massachusetts in significant numbers were the Irish, who migrated in vast numbers during the 1840s and 1850s. By 1860, one-third of Boston's population was Irish, while nearly one-fourth of Middlesex and Norfolk counties and one-fifth of the inhabitants of Berkshire, Bristol, Essex, and Hampden counties were Irish-born. Other ethnic groups—such as the Scottish, Welsh, Germans, and Poles—were also entering the state at this time, but their numbers were small by comparison. During the late 1880s and 1890s, another wave of immigrants—from Portugal, Spain, Italy, Russia, and Greece—arrived. Irish and Italians continued to enter the state during the 20th century.

A slow but steady migration from Massachusetts farm communities began during the mid–1700s and continued well into the 1800s. The first wave of farmers resettled in northern Connecticut, Vermont, New Hampshire, and Maine. Later farmers moved to New York's Mohawk Valley, Ohio, and points farther west. Out-migration has continued into recent times: from 1970 to 1990, Massachusetts lost nearly 400,000 residents in net migration to other states but experienced an overall net increase from migration of 59,000 due to migration from abroad. Between 1990 and 1998, the state had a net loss of 237,000 in domestic migration and a net gain of 135,000 in international migration. In 1996, Massachusetts's foreign-born population numbered 591,000, or nearly 10% of the state's total population. In 1998, 15,869 foreign immigrants arrived in Massachusetts, the 8th-highest total of any state for that year. Between 1990 and 1998, the state's overall population increased 2.2%. In the period 1995–2000, 446,849 people moved into the state and 501,557 moved out, for a net loss of 54,708, 14,434 of whom were age 65 or over and many of whom moved to Florida.

The only significant migration from other areas of the United States to Massachusetts has been the influx of southern blacks since World War II. According to census estimates, Massachusetts gained 84,000 blacks between 1940 and 1975; between 1990 and 1998, the black population grew from 300,000 to 395,000 persons, mostly in the Boston area.

19INTERGOVERNMENTAL COOPERATION

Massachusetts participates in numerous regional agreements, including the New England Interstate Corrections, Police, Board of Higher Education, Radiological Health Protection, and Interstate Water Pollution Control compacts. The state is also a party to the Atlantic States Marine Fisheries Commission, the Northeastern Forest Fire Protection Compact, the Connecticut River Valley Flood Control Compact, the Bay State-Ocean State Compact with Rhode Island, the Merrimack River Basin Flood Control Compact, the Thames River Flood Control Compact, and the Connecticut River Atlantic Salmon Compact.

Border agreements include the Connecticut-Massachusetts Boundary Compact (ratified by Massachusetts in 1908), the Massachusetts-New York Compact of 1853, and the Massachusetts-Rhode Island Compact of 1859. During 2001, the state received over $9.7 billion in federal grants.

20ECONOMY

From its beginnings as a farming and seafaring colony, Massachusetts became one of the most industrialized states in the country in the late 19th century and, more recently, a leader in the manufacture of high-technology products.

During the colonial and early national periods, the towns of Salem, Gloucester, Marblehead, and Boston, among others, gave the state strong fishing and shipbuilding industries. Boston was also an important commercial port and a leading center of foreign commerce. Agriculture was important, but productivity of the rocky soil was limited, and by the mid-1800s, farming could not sustain the expanding population. The opening of the Erie Canal, and subsequent competition with cheaper produce grown in the West, hastened agriculture's decline in the Bay State.

Massachusetts's rise as a center of manufacturing began in the early 1800s, when cottage industries developed in small farming communities. Large factories were then built in towns with water power. The country's first "company town," Lowell, was built in the early 1820s to accommodate the state's growing textile industry. Throughout the rest of the 19th century, the state supplied the nation with most of its shoes and woven goods.

Underbid by cheap labor in the south and in other countries, the shoe and textile industries died a slow and painful death. Manufacturing remained central to Massachusetts's economy, however. Fueled in part by a dramatic increase in the Pentagon's budget during the Reagan administration which focused on high-technology weaponry, as well as by significant advances in information technology, high-tech companies sprung up around the periphery of Boston in the 1970s and early 1980s. Wholesale and retail trade, transportation and public utilities also prospered. In the late 1980s, the boom ended. The minicomputer industry failed to innovate at the same pace as its competitors elsewhere at the same time that the market became increasingly crowded, and defense contractors suffered from cuts in military spending. Between 1988 and 1991, jobs in both high-tech and non–high tech manufacturing declined by 17%. The early 1980s also saw the rise of speculative real estate ventures which collapsed at the end of the decade when the market became saturated. Employment in construction dropped 44% between 1988 and 1991, and real estate jobs declined 23.8%. Wholesale and retail trade lost 100,000 jobs. Hurt by unsound loans, banks were forced to retrench. Unemployment rose to 9% in 1991.

The economy recovered in the 1990s, as evidenced by several banks' announcement of new lending programs as well as a reduction in the unemployment rate to 4% by 1997. Annual growth rates soared to 7.8% in 1998, 6.8% in 1999 and 9.8% in 2000 as Massachusetts benefited from information technology (IT) and stock market booms of the late 1990s. However, in the collapse of the dot.com bubble in the national recession of 2001, Massachusetts was the hardest hit among the New England economies, as growth abruptly plummeted to 1.7% in 2001. Continued weakness in national business investment and in equity markets continued to impede economic growth in Massachusetts in 2002.

Massachusetts's gross state product in 2001 was the 11th largest among the states at $287.8 billion, to which general services contributed $79.9 billion; financial services, $73.9 billion; trade, $42.2 billion; manufacturing, $34.4 billion; government, $26 billion, transportation and public utilities, $16.1 billion; and construction, $13.5 billion. Output from financial services increased 39% across the period 1997 to 2001, whereas output from general services increased 34%; from trade, 25%; and from both government services and the transportation and utilities sector, about 20%. Output from manufacturing increased 17% between 1997 and 2000, but then fell 9% in 2001. As a percent of total output, manufactures fell from 14.4% in 1997 to 12% in 2001. The public sector constituted 9% of gross state product in 2001, the 2nd-lowest percent among the states where the average was 12%.

21INCOME

According to the Bureau of Economic Analysis, in 2001, Massachusetts had a per capita personal income (PCPI) of $38,864 which ranked 3rd in the United States (including the District of Columbia) and was 128% of the national average, $30,413. The 2001 PCPI reflected an increase of 2.2% from 2000 compared to the national change of 2.2%. In 2001, Massachusetts had a total personal income (TPI) of $248,777,745,000 which ranked 10th in the United States and accounted for 2.9% of the national total. The 2001 TPI reflected an increase of 2.8% from 2000 compared to the national change of 3.3%.

Earnings of persons employed in Massachusetts increased from $184,521,088,000 in 2000 to $187,753,932,000 in 2001, an increase of 1.8%. The largest industries in 2001 were services, 36.4% of earnings; finance, insurance, and real estate, 12.4%; and durable goods manufacturing, 9.7%. Of the industries that accounted for at least 5% of earnings in 2001, the slowest growing from 2000 to 2001 was wholesale trade (6.1% of earnings in 2001), which decreased 8.9%; the fastest was construction (5.7% of earnings in 2001), which increased 9.9%.

According to data released by the US Census Bureau, in 2000, the median household income was $46,947 compared to the national average of $42,148. In 2001, the median income for a family of four was $80,247 compared to the national average of $63,278. For the period 1999 to 2001, the average poverty rate was 10.2% which placed it 23rd among the 50 states and the District of Columbia ranked lowest to highest.

22LABOR

According to Bureau of Labor Statistics (BLS) provisional estimates, in July 2003 the seasonally adjusted civilian labor force in Massachusetts numbered 3,450,000, with approximately 187,300 workers unemployed, yielding an unemployment rate of 5.4%, compared to the national average of 6.2% for the same period. Since the beginning of the BLS data series in 1978, the highest unemployment rate recorded was 9.6% in July 1991. The historical low was 2.5% in August 2000. In 2001, an estimated 4.9% of the labor force was employed in construction; 12.5% in manufacturing; 4.5% in transportation, communications, and public utilities; 17.8% in trade; 6.9% in finance, insurance, and real estate; 32.4% in services; 12.7% in government; and 1.0% in agriculture.

Some of the earliest unionization efforts took place in Massachusetts in the early 1880s, particularly in the shipbuilding and construction trades. However, the most important trade unions to evolve were those in the state's textile and shoe industries. The workers had numerous grievances: shoebinders' salaries of $1.60–$2.40 a week during the 1840s, workdays of 14 to 17 hours, wages paid in scrip that could be cashed only at company stores (which charged exorbitantly high prices), and children working at dangerous machinery. In 1867, a seven-week-long shoemakers' strike at Lynn, the center of the shoe business, was at that time the longest strike in US history.

After the turn of the century, the state suffered a severe decline in manufacturing, and employers sought to cut wages to make up for lost profits. This resulted in a number of strikes by both the United Textile Workers and the Boot and Shoe Workers Union. The largest strike of the era was at Lawrence in 1912, when textile workers (led by a radical labor group, the Industrial Workers of the World) closed the mills, and the mayor called in troops in an attempt to reopen them. Although the textile and shoe businesses are no longer major employers in the state, the United Shoe Workers of America, the Brotherhood of Shoe and Allied Craftsmen, the United Textile Workers, and the Leather Workers International Union of America have their headquarters in Massachusetts.

Massachusetts was one of the first states to enact child labor laws. In 1842, it established the 10-hour day for children under 12; in 1867, it forbade employment for children under 10. The nation's first Uniform Child Labor Law, establishing an 8-hour day for children ages 14 to 16, was enacted by Massachusetts in 1913. Massachusetts was also the first state to enact minimum wage guidelines (1912).

The US Department of Labor reported that in 2002, 428,000 of Massachusetts's 3,003,000 employed wage and salary workers were members of unions. This represented 14.2% of those so employed, down from 14.7% in 2001 and from 15.9% in 1998. The national average is 13.2%. In all, 469,000 workers (15.6%) were represented by unions. In addition to union members, this category includes workers who report no union affiliation but whose jobs are covered by a union contract.

23AGRICULTURE

As of 2002, there were 6,000 farms in Massachusetts, covering 560,000 acres (227,000 hectares). Farming was mostly limited to the western Massachusetts counties of Hampshire, Franklin, and Berkshire, and southern Bristol County. Total agricultural income for 2001 was estimated at $367 million (47th of the 50 states), of which crops provided 74%. Although the state is not a major farming area, it is a leading producer of cranberries in the US; production for 2002 was 141,600,000 lb about 26% of the US total. Output totals for other crops in 2002 were as follows: corn for silage, 315,000 tons; hay, 200,000 tons; and tobacco, 1,845,000 lb. While of local economic importance, these figures are tiny fractions of US totals.

24ANIMAL HUSBANDRY

Massachusetts is not a major producer of livestock. The state had 51,000 cattle and calves worth around $50 million in 2003, and an estimated 16,500 hogs and pigs worth $1.3 million in 2002. Also during 2001, poultry farmers sold 2.7 million lb (1.22 million kg) of chickens for $11 million, and the state produced an estimated 80 million eggs, worth around $4.4 million. An estimated 21,000 milk cows produced 358 million lb (162.4 million kg) of milk in 2001. During 2001, the state produced around 1.59 million lb (0.72 million kg) of turkeys worth $2.3 million.

25FISHING

Massachusetts's fish catch in 1998 was the 5th largest in the US, but the fishing industry is not as important to the state economy as it once was.

The early settlers earned much of their income from the sea. The first shipyard in Massachusetts opened at Salem Neck in 1637, and during the years before independence the towns of Salem, Newburyport, Plymouth, and Boston were among the colonies' leading ports. By 1807, Massachusetts's fishing fleet made up 88% of the US total; for much of the 19th century, Nantucket and, later, New Bedford were the leading US whaling centers. But with the decline of the whaling industry came a sharp drop in the importance of fishing to the livelihood of the state. By 1978, the fishing industry ranked 13th in importance of the 15 industries monitored by the state. However, the fishing ports of New Bedford and Gloucester were still among the busiest in the US in 1998, with the 2nd and 20th most valuable catches, respectively. In 1997, there were 376 fish processing and wholesale plants with an annual average of 5,120 employees in the state.

The value of the commercial catch in 1998—$204,408,000— was the highest among the New England states and the 4th highest in the US at 252,518,000 lb. In 1998, the lobster catch totaled 13.3 million lb, valued at $48.6 million, and quahog landings amounted to 19.2 million lb, valued at $8 million. About 5.8 million lb of sea scallops were landed in 1998.

The state's long shoreline and many rivers make sport fishing a popular pastime for both deepsea and freshwater fishermen. The fishing season runs from mid-April through late October, with the season extended through February for bass, pickerel, panfish, and trout. In 1998, there were 192,604 fishing license holders.

26FORESTRY

Forestry is a minor industry in the state. Forested lands cover about 3,126,000 acres (1,265,000 hectares), 76% of which are private lands. Wooded areas lost to urbanization in recent years have been offset by the conversion of inactive agricultural areas into forests. Red oak and white ash are found in the west; specialty products include maple syrup and Christmas trees. The wood and paper products industries require more pulp than the state currently produces.

Massachusetts has the 6th-largest state park system in the nation, with 38 state parks and 74 state forests totaling some 273,000 acres (110,000 hectares). There are no national forests in Massachusetts.

27MINING

The value of nonfuel mineral production in Massachusetts in 2001 was estimated at $209 million. This value represents a roughly 5% increase from 2000. Crushed stone and construction sand and gravel are the state's two leading mineral commodities. According to preliminary figures, in 2001 there were an estimated 14 million metric tons of crushed stone and 13.2 million metric tons of sand and gravel produced, worth $111 million and $81.3 million, respectively. Other mineral commodities produced include common clay, lime, and peat; industrial sand and gravel; and dimension stone. Nationally, the state ranked 6th in dimension stone. Industrial minerals processed or manufactured in the state include abrasives, graphite, gypsum, perlite, and vermiculite.

28ENERGY AND POWER

Massachusetts depends on oil for more than one-fourth of its electric generation and almost one-half of its home heating. Energy costs in the state are among the highest in the US. Nevertheless, this is an improvement from the early 1980s, when as much as 81% of the state's electric power output was generated from oil. In 2000 Massachusetts's total per capita energy consumption was 271 million Btu (68.3 million kcal), ranking it 42nd among the 50 states.

In 1999, about 41.5 billion kWh of electric power (utility and nonutility) was generated in state, and total installed capacity was over 11.8 million kW. Almost all generating capacity in the state is privately owned. As of 2001, Massachusetts had one operating nuclear plant, the single-unit Pilgrim plant in Plymouth, with a capacity of 667,000 kW. Boston Edison supplies electricity to the city of Boston; the rest of the state is served by 13 other companies, although a few municipalities do generate their own power. Power companies are regulated by the Department of Public Utilities, which establishes rates and monitors complaints from customers.

Massachusetts has no proven oil or coal reserves. After a lengthy court battle, oil exploration off the coast of Cape Cod began in 1979. Environmentalists and fishermen had sought to prevent development of an oil industry in the region, which is one of the richest fishing grounds in the country.

The state consumes but does not produce natural gas. In 2002 about 393 billion cu ft (11.1 billion cu m) of natural gas were delivered. Almost 35% of the gas sold was for residential use, 40% for industries and electricity generation, and 25% for commercial use.

There is one nuclear power plant in Plymouth, with an average operating capacity of 667 MW. Four pumped-storage hydroelectric plants have a combined capacity of 846 Mw. There were also 45 conventional hydroelectric generators, with a combined capacity of 151 MW in 1999.

The state encourages energy conservation and the development of alternative energy systems by granting tax credits to qualifying industries. Private researchers and the state have established demonstration projects for solar energy systems and other alternatives to fossil fuels.

29INDUSTRY

Massachusetts was the nation's first major industrial state, and during the later part of the 19th century, it was the US leader in shoemaking and textile production. By 1860, the state was a major producer of machinery and milled nearly one-fourth of the country's paper.

Massachusetts remains an important manufacturing center, ranking 17th among the 50 states in the value of manufacturers' shipments in 1997. Nearly all the major manufacturing sectors had plants in Massachusetts's eastern counties. Significant concentrations of industrial machinery employment are in Attleboro, Wilmington, Worcester, and the Springfield area. Much of the manufacturing industry is located along Route 128, a superhighway that circles Boston from Gloucester in the north to Quincy in the south and is unique in its concentration of high-technology enterprises. Although Massachusetts ranked 14th among the states in manufacturing employment in 1997 (at 441,770), nearly 3,200 manufacturing jobs had been lost from 1992 to 1997.

Massachusetts's future as a manufacturing center depends on its continued preeminence in the production of computers, optical equipment, and other sophisticated instruments. In 1997, the value of shipments by manufacturers was $83 billion. Important manufactures included: electronic and other electronic equipment, instruments and related products, industrial machinery and equipment, printing and publishing, chemicals and allied products, food and food products, and fabricated metals. As of 1997, the state was the headquarters for 16 Fortune 500 companies.

Earnings of persons employed in Massachusetts increased from $143.2 billion in 1997 to $154 billion in 1998, an increase of 7.5%. The largest industries in 1998 were services, 35.5% of earnings; durable goods manufacturing, 11.6%; and finance, insurance, and real estate, 10.3%. Of the industries that accounted for at least 5% of earnings in 1998, the slowest growing from 1997 to 1998 was state and local government (9.1% of earnings in 1998), which increased 4.1%; the fastest was services, which increased 8.7%.

30COMMERCE

Massachusetts's machinery and electrical goods industries are important components of the state's wholesale trade, along with motor vehicle and automotive equipment, and paper and paper products. In 1997, 11,423 wholesale establishments produced about $116 billion in sales. More than one-fourth of the wholesale establishments were located in Middlesex County. Retail sales brought in $63 billion in 1997, from 38,975 stores of all types. Food stores accounted for 11% of establishments; automotive dealers, 11%; and eating and drinking places, 32%. Food sales brought in $11 billion while general merchandise brought in $5.5 billion. In 1997, foreign exports totaled $16 billion, ranking 11th in the nation.

31CONSUMER PROTECTION

The cabinet-level Executive Office of Consumer Affairs and Business Regulation serves as an information and referral center for consumer complaints and oversees the activities of many regulatory agencies. The Office of the Attorney General also has a Consumer Protection and Antitrust Division that handles consumer complaints. The Massachusetts Consumer Council advises the governor and legislature; there are many local consumer councils.

32BANKING

By the mid-1800s, Boston had developed into a major banking center whose capital financed the state's burgeoning industries. Today banking remains an important sector of the state's economy, employing over 55,000 workers in 1999. As of 2002, Massachusetts had 217 insured banks, with assets of $193.5 billion.

More than 300 state chartered savings banks, trust companies, co-operative banks, credit unions, and over 4,000 other financial service providers, including mortgage lenders and brokers, debt collection agencies, foreign transmittal agencies, check cashers, and credit grantors, are examined by the state Division of Banks, within the Office of Consumer Affairs and Business Regulation. The division administers the state's banking laws and oversees bank and financial institution practices and policies.

In 2002, due to low mortgage rates, borrowers secured long-term fixed-rate loans at lower prices. During that year, median long-term assets to earning assets increased to 35%, the highest rate in a decade. Eighty-two percent of insured institutions headquartered in Massachusetts are savings institutions, and residential real estate loans make up 65% of the average loan portfolio. The Massachusetts economy continued to struggle in 2002, and there was an increase in residential and commercial real estate (CRE) delinquencies at some institutions.

33INSURANCE

Insurance is an important business in Massachusetts, and some of the largest life and property and casualty insurance companies in the nation have their headquarters in Boston. As of 2000, there were 56 property and casualty and 18 life and health insurance companies incorporated or organized in the state.

In 2001 there were 3.2 million ordinary life insurance policies in force with a total value of $277.2 billion; total value for all categories of life insurance (ordinary, group, industrial, and credit) was $475.7 billion. Death benefits paid that year totaled $1.2 billion. That year, property and casualty insurers wrote premiums totaling $7.3 billion. That year, there were 39,153 flood insurance policies in force in the state, with a total value of $5.6 million.

New England Mutual Life Insurance Co. of Boston was the first mutual company to be chartered in the US and remains one of the largest firms in the business. John Hancock Mutual Life, also of Boston, is one of the largest life insurance companies in the US.

In 1971, Massachusetts became the first state in the US to implement a no-fault automobile insurance law. All aspects of the insurance business in Massachusetts, including the licensing of agents and brokers and the examination of all insurance companies doing business in the state, are controlled by the Division of Insurance, under the Executive Office of Consumer Affairs and Business Regulation.

34SECURITIES

The Boston Stock Exchange, founded in 1834, is the only stock exchange in Massachusetts. The BSE has approximately 200 members, handles over 2,000 stocks, and is the fastest-growing stock exchange in the US (increasing trade volume tenfold during the 1990s). There are 1,623 securities brokers and dealers organizations in Massachusetts, with 54,795 employees; 593 investment advisory organizations operate in the state.

Massachusetts is the headquarters for 274 NASDAQ-listed companies, 11 NASDAQ market makers, 25 AMEX companies; and the state incorporated 101 companies on the NYSE. The top five companies on the NYSE are: Fleet Boston Financial Group, Raytheon, Gillette Co., TJX Companies, EMC Corp., and State St. Corp. Mutual funds originated in Boston during the 1920s.

The Securities Division of the Office of the Secretary of the Commonwealth is responsible for licensing and monitoring all brokerage firms in the state.

35PUBLIC FINANCE

The Massachusetts budget is prepared by the Executive Office of Administration and Finance and is presented by the governor to the legislature for revision and approval. The fiscal year runs from 1 July to 30 June.

From 1990 to 2000, tax reductions totaling an annual $3.6 billion had been enacted, and in the 2000 election, voters mandated a rollback in the income tax rate to 5% by 2003. Total fiscal year 2001 revenues were projected to be $21.3 billion. Actual general fund revenues overshot this, at $22.867 billion, which comfortably covered expenditures of $22.141 billion, but in 2002/03, revenues fell back to $22.68 billion while expenditures rose to $22.8 billion. In 2002/03, general fund revenues fell further, to $22.022 billion. Massachusetts's budget deficit for 2002/03 was estimated at a relatively mild 2.6% of the state budget, but projections for 2003/04 are for a budget deficit equal to 11% of the budget. In 2000/01, the state's starting balance was equal to 13.6% of expenditures; by 2002/03, the starting balance equaled only 1.4% of expenditures.

The following table from the US Census Bureau contains information on revenues, expenditures, indebtedness, and cash/securities for 2001.

	($000)	PERCENT	PER CAPITA
Population (thousands, 2001)	6,401	(X)	(X)
Total Revenue	29,303,913	100.00	4,578.02
General revenue	29,287,698	99.94	4,575.49
Utility revenue	105,833	0.36	16.53
Liquor store revenue	–	–	–
Insurance trust revenue	–89,618	–0.31	–14.00
Exhibit: Salaries and wages	4,158,099	12.82	649.60
Total expenditure	32,435,081	100.00	5,067.19
General expenditure	29,487,838	90.91	4,606.75
Education	6,564,905	20.24	1,025.61
Public welfare	7,263,888	22.40	1,134.81
Hospitals	510,744	1.57	79.79
Health	1,811,736	5.59	283.04
Highways	2,561,542	7.90	400.18
Police protection	327,536	1.01	51.17
Correction	1,033,143	3.19	161.40
Natural resources	296,254	0.91	46.28
Parks and recreation	267,457	0.82	41.78
Government administration	1,272,351	3.92	198.77
Interest on general debt	2,371,876	7.31	370.55
Other and unallocable	5,206,406	16.05	813.37
Utility expenditure	298,098	0.92	46.57
Liquor store expenditure	–	–	–
Insurance trust expenditure	2,649,145	8.17	413.86
Debt at end of fiscal year	42,149,219	100.00	6,584.79
Cash and security holdings	63,253,831	100.00	9,881.87

36TAXATION

The state levies a 12% tax on interest, dividends, and short-term capital gains, a 5% tax rate on capital gains from assets held between one and two years, a 2% rate on capital gains from assets held longer than that, and, in 2003, a flat 5.3% rate in on all other taxable personal income. The personal income tax rate has been reduced in steps from 5.95% in 1999. The corporate income tax rate is 9.5% with the franchise tax (at 0.26% per $1000 income) built into the tax rate. Commercial banks and other banking and trust companies pay a 10.5% tax on net income; savings and loans, 10.91%. There is a corporate minimum tax of $456 on public utilities, 6.5%.

The gross receipts tax on sales is 5%, but such necessities as food, clothing, and home heating fuel are exempt. Other levies include a room occupancy tax of 5.7%, with a local option of up to 4%, a cigarette tax, a gasoline tax, a deeds tax, and a motor vehicle excise tax. There is also a wide array of state and local selective (excise) taxes, including a room occupancy tax of 5.7%, with a local option of up to 4%, a motor vehicle excise tax, taxes covering motor fuels, tobacco products, insurance premiums, alcoholic beverages, amusements, pari-mutuels, and other selected items. In 2002 the gas tax was raised from 21 cents to 21.5 cents and the cigarette tax increased from 76 cents a pack to $1.51 a pack. In 1997, the estate tax changed from a separate system of estate taxation, in which estates were taxed from 5% to 16%, to a "sponge tax" system, whereby the amount of estate tax due was equal to the amount of the maximum federal credit for state death taxes. With the scheduled phase-out of the federal death tax credit by 2007, Massachusetts has reinstated its independent estate tax imposed only on estates worth $675,000 or more. Death and gift taxes accounted for 1.3% of state tax collected in 2002. Other state taxes include various license fees, a deeds tax, and a small property tax. Most property taxes are collected at the local level, although the tax system is relatively centralized, with the state collecting 67.9% of all state and local taxes in 2002.

The state collected $17.225 billion in taxes in 2002, of which 53.4% came from individual income taxes, 24.9% from the general sales tax, 10.2% from selective sales taxes, 5.2% from corporate income taxes (including built-in franchise fees) and 3.4% from license fees. In 2003, Massachusetts ranked 13th among the states in terms of state and local tax burden, which amounted to about 9.9% of income.

The following table from the US Census Bureau provides a summary of taxes collected by the state in 2002.

	($000)	PER CAPITA
Total Taxes	**14,819,794**	**2,305.58**
Property taxes	86	0.01
Sales and gross receipts	5,210,827	810.67
General sales and gross receipts	3,695,874	574.98
Selective sales taxes	1,514,953	235.69
Alcoholic beverage	65,927	10.26
Amusements	5,938	0.92
Insurance Premiums	360,676	56.11
Motor fuels	666,751	103.73
Pari-mutuels	6,856	1.07
Public utilities	(X)	(X)
Tobacco products	274,997	42.78
Other selective sales	133,808	20.82
Licenses	500,661	77.89
Alcoholic beverages	1,422	0.22
Amusements	468	0.07
Corporation	18,709	2.91
Hunting and fishing	6,194	0.96
Motor vehicle	270,336	42.06
Motor vehicle operators	57,800	8.99
Public utility	(X)	(X)
Occupation and business, NEC	87,002	13.54
Other	58,730	9.14
Other taxes	9,108,220	1,417.00
Individual income	7,912,934	1,231.05
Corporation net income	812,257	126.37
Death and gift	200,547	31.2
Documentary and stock transfer	182,482	28.39
Severance	(X)	(X)
Other	(X)	(X)

37 ECONOMIC POLICY

The Department of Economic Development (DED) is responsible for setting economic policy, promoting Massachusetts as a place to do business, increasing the job base, and generating economic activity in the Commonwealth.

The following agencies are within the Department of Economic Development: Massachusetts Office of Business Development, Massachusetts Office of International Trade and Investment, Massachusetts Office of Travel and Tourism, Office of Film and Video, and State Office of Minority and Women Business Assistance. The department also works closely with: the Massachusetts Development Finance Agency (Mass Development), the Corporation for Business, Work, and Learning, the Mass. Technology Collaborative, the Mass. Tech. Dev. Corp., the Department of Labor and Workforce Development, and the Department of Housing and Community Development.

Throughout most of the 1990s and up to 2002, the state economic development plan was guided by the 1993 report of the DED entitled "Choosing to Compete: A Statewide Strategy for Economic Growth and Job Creation." The Massachusetts Economic Development Incentive Program (EDIP), launched in 1993, was a series of initiatives geared to stimulate job creation, attract new businesses, and help firms expand. There were 34 Economic Target Areas (ETAs) throughout the state. Cities and towns, in partnership with the Commonwealth and private enterprises, also developed economic programs to attract new business. In October 2002, building on what was seen as the success of the Choosing to Compete campaign, the DEC issued a new framework entitled Toward a New Prosperity: Building Regional Competitiveness Across the Commonwealth. The approach divides the state economy into seven regional clusters, each with unique developmental needs and potentials. Six overall goals were stated: to improve the business climate for all business clusters; to support entrepreneurship and innovation; to prepare the workforce for the future; to build an information infrastructure for the 21st century; to ensure that economic growth is compatible with communities and the environment, and to improve the outcome from government actions.

38 HEALTH

Infant mortality was 4.6 per 1,000 live births in 2000. Well below the US rate of 6.9, Massachusetts ranked fiftieth in infant mortality. Also, in 1999, there were 26,852 abortions, for a rate of 19 per 1,000 women, above the US rate of 14 per 1,000 women,.

The overall death rate was 913.6 per 100,000 population in 2000, higher than the US rate of 873.1. In the same year, the major causes of death and their rates per 100,000 population were heart diseases, 246.8; cerebrovascular diseases, 56.6; accidents and adverse effects, 22.6; and suicide, 6.2. The rate of HIV-related deaths stood at 3.6 per 100,000 population, below the national rate of 5.3. A total of 17,008 AIDS cases had been reported through 2001.

Programs for treatment and rehabilitation of alcoholics are administered by the Division of Alcoholism of the Department of Health, under the Executive Office of Human Services. The Division of Communicable Disease Control operates venereal disease clinics throughout the state and provides educational material to schools and other groups. The Division of Drug Rehabilitation administers drug treatment from a statewide network of hospital agencies and self-help groups. The state also runs a lead-poisoning prevention program. Among persons ages 18 and older, 20.0% were current smokers in 2000.

In Massachusetts, all health-care facilities are registered by the Department of Public Health. The Division of Health Care Quality inspects and licenses hospitals, clinics, school infirmaries, and blood banks every two years. Licensing of nursing homes is also under its control. The state's 80 community hospitals had 766,708 admissions and 16,504 beds in 2001. There were 26,504 full-time registered nurses and 1,765 full-time licensed practical nurses in 2001 and 448 physicians per 100,000 population in 2000. The average expense of a community hospital for care was $1,889.80 per inpatient day in 2001.

Federal government grants to cover the Medicare and Medicaid services in 2001 totaled $3.6 billion; 961,409 enrollees received Medicare benefits that year. Only 8.2% of the population was uninsured in 2002.

Four prominent medical schools are located in the state: Harvard Medical School, Tufts University School of Medicine, Boston University School of Medicine, and the University of Massachusetts School of Medicine.

39 SOCIAL WELFARE

In 2001, the average weekly unemployment benefit was $334.26. Average monthly participation in the food stamp program in FY2002 comprised 242,542 persons (114,859 households). The average monthly benefit was $71.89, and the sum total of benefits paid in FY2002 was $209,235,751.

With the enactment of the Personal Responsibility and Work Opportunity Reconciliation Act of 1996, the US government has changed the form and regulations for many of its social welfare programs. Most significantly, it replaces Aid to Families with Dependent Children (AFDC), an open-ended entitlement program, with Temporary Assistance for Needy Families (TANF), a limited system of assistance funded largely through federal block grants. The reform act also impacts the food stamp program, the Supplemental Security Income program, and the child nutrition program. The law took effect on 1 July 1997 and provided $16.38 billion in block grants for fiscal years 1997–2002. The grants are to be divided among the states based on an equation involving the numbers of former AFDC recipients in each state.

Reauthorization of the 1996 social welfare legislation, scheduled for 2002, was delayed, and the original law had been extended three times as of July 2003, with the most recent extension running through September 2003. The Massachusetts TANF cash assistance program is called Transitional Aid to Families with Dependent Children (TAFDC), and the work program is called the Employment Services Program (ESP). In June 2000 the state had 93,890 welfare recipients. State expenditures on the TANF program in FY2002 totaled $354,317,143.

In December 2001, Social Security benefits were paid to 1,061,920 Massachusetts residents. This number included 696,240 retired workers, 102,450 widows and widowers, 128,510 disabled workers, 53,180 spouses, and 81,540 children. Social Security beneficiaries represented 16.6% of the total state population and 91.8% of the state's population age 65 and older. Retired workers (excluding persons with special benefits) received an average monthly payment of $879; widows and widowers, $853; disabled workers, $806; and spouses, $450. Payments for children of retired workers averaged $424 per month; children of deceased workers, $607; and children of disabled workers, $236.

Federal Supplemental Security Income payments in December 2001 went to 166,874 Massachusetts residents, averaging $410 a month.

40 HOUSING

Massachusetts's housing stock, much older than the US average, reflects the state's colonial heritage and its ties to English architectural traditions. Two major styles are common: colonial, typified by a wood frame, two stories, center hall entry, and center chimney; and Cape Cod, one-story houses built by fishermen, typified by shallow basements, shingled roofs, clapboard fronts, and unpainted shingled sides weathered gray by the salt air. Many new houses are also built in these styles.

As of 2002, there were an estimated 2,649,029 housing units in the state, of which 2,432,176 were occupied; 64% were owner-occupied. About 52.8% of all housing units were single-family, detached homes. About 35.6% of all units were built before or during 1939. Nearly 41% of all units rely on utility gas for heating and 35.8% use fuel oil or kerosene. It was estimated that 33,515 units lacked telephone service, 9,197 lacked complete plumbing facilities, and 11,111 lacked complete kitchen facilities. The average household size was 2.55 people.

In 2002, 17,465 new housing units were authorized for construction. The median home value was $249,161, the 3rd highest in the United States. The median monthly cost for mortgage owners was $1,486. Renters paid a median of $799 per month. During 2002, Massachusetts received over $175.9 million in community planning and development aid from the US Department of Housing and Urban Development.

The Executive Office of Communities and Development administers federal housing programs for the state. The Massachusetts Housing Finance Agency finances the construction and rehabilitation of housing by private and community groups.

41EDUCATION

Massachusetts has a long history of support for education. The Boston Latin School opened in 1635 as the first public school in the colonies. Harvard College—the first college in the US—was founded the following year. In 1647, for the first time, towns with more than 50 people were required by law to establish tax-supported school systems. More firsts followed: the country's first board of education, compulsory school attendance law, training school for teachers, state school for the retarded, and school for the blind. The drive for quality public education in the state was intensified through the efforts of educator Horace Mann, who during the 1830s and 1840s was also a leading force for the improvement of school systems throughout the US. Today the state boasts some of the most highly regarded private secondary schools and colleges in the country.

In 2000, 84.8% of state residents age 25 or older were high school graduates, and 33.2% had completed four or more years of college. Total public school enrollment for fall 1999 stood at 971,425. Of these, 706,251 attended schools from kindergarten through grade eight, and 265,174 attended high school. Minority students made up approximately 24% of the total enrollment in public elementary and secondary schools in 2001. Total enrollment was estimated at 985,000 in fall 2000 and is expected to reach 974,000 by fall 2005. State and local expenditures for public elementary and secondary pupils in 1999/2000 averaged $7,387 per pupil, well above the mean of $6,356. Expenditures for public education in 2000/01 were estimated at $9,050,308.

The early years of statehood saw the development of private academies, where the students could learn more than the basic reading and writing skills that were taught in the town schools at the time. Some of these private preparatory schools remain, including such prestigious institutions as Andover, Deerfield, and Groton. Enrollment in nonpublic schools in fall 2001 totaled 132,154.

As of fall 2000, there were 473,403 students enrolled in college or graduate school. In the same year Massachusetts had 117 degree-granting institutions. In 1997, minority students comprised 18.6% of total postsecondary enrollment. The major public university system is the University of Massachusetts, with campuses at Amherst, Boston, Dartmouth, and Lowell, and a medical school at Worcester. The Amherst campus was established in 1863, and the Boston campus in 1965. The state has a total of 15 public colleges and universities, while the

Massachusetts Board of Regional Community Colleges has 16 campuses.

Harvard University, which was established in Cambridge originally as a college for clergymen and magistrates, has grown to become one of the country's premier institutions. Also located in Cambridge are Radcliffe College (whose enrollment is included in Harvard's), founded in 1879, and the Massachusetts Institute of Technology, or MIT (1861). Mount Holyoke College, the first US college for women, was founded in 1837. Other prominent private schools and their dates of origin are Amherst College (1821); Boston College (1863); Boston University (1869); Brandeis University (1947); Clark University (1887); Hampshire College (1965); the New England Conservatory of Music (1867); Northeastern University (1898); Smith College (1871); Tufts University (1852); Wellesley College (1875); and Williams College (1793).

Among the tuition assistance programs available to state residents are the Massachusetts General Scholarships, awarded to thousands of college students annually, and Massachusetts Honor Scholarships, for outstanding performance on the Scholastic Aptitude Test. The State Board of Education establishes standards and policies for the public schools throughout the state; its programs are administered by the Department of Education. Higher education planning and programs are under the control of the Higher Education Coordinating Council.

The landmark Education Reform Act of 1993 established new systems of financial support for public elementary and secondary schools and instituted major reforms in governance, professional development, student educational goals, curricula, and assessments.

42ARTS

Boston is the center of artistic activity in Massachusetts, and Cape Cod and the Berkshires are areas of significant seasonal artistic activity. In 1979, Massachusetts became the first state to establish a lottery solely for funding the arts. Boston is the home of several small theaters, some of which offer previews of shows bound for Broadway. Well-known local theater companies include the American Repertory Theatre and the Huntington Theatre. Of the regional theaters scattered throughout the state, the Williamstown Theater in the Berkshires and the Provincetown Theater on Cape Cod are especially noteworthy.

The Boston Symphony, one of the major orchestras in the US, was founded in 1881, and its principal conductors have included Serge Koussevitzky, Charles Munch, Erich Leinsdorf, and Seiji Ozawa. Emmanuel Church in Boston's Back Bay is known for its early music concerts, and chamber music by first-rate local and internationally known performers is presented at the New England Conservatory's Jordan Hall and other venues throughout the city. During the summer, the Boston Symphony is the main attraction of the Berkshire Music Festival at Tanglewood in Lenox. An offshoot of the Boston Symphony, the Boston Pops Orchestra, gained fame under the conductorship of Arthur Fiedler. Its mixture of popular, jazz, and light symphonic music continued under the direction of Fiedler's successors, John Williams and Keith Lockhart. Boston is also the headquarters of the Boston Lyric Opera. Prominent in the world of dance are the Boston Ballet Company and the Jacob's Pillow Dance Festival in the Berkshires. *Ploughshares*, a literary journal published through Emerson College in Boston, has become well known nationally as a showplace for new writers.

The Massachusetts Cultural Council provides grants and services to support public programs in the arts, sciences, and the humanities. Grants are made to organizations, schools, communities and artists. In 2003, the Massachusetts Cultural Council and other arts organizations received grants totaling $3,315,100 from the National Endowment for the Arts (NEA).

The Massachusetts Foundation for the Humanities was founded in 1974. In 2000, the National Endowment for the Humanities contributed $5,880,267 to 72 state programs.

43 LIBRARIES AND MUSEUMS

The first public library in the US was established in Boston in 1653. Massachusetts has one of the most important university libraries in the country, and numerous museums and historical sites commemorate the state's rich colonial history. Six regional library systems served 351 towns and cities with a total number of volumes over 30 million in 2000. The major city libraries are in Boston, Worcester, and Springfield. State funding for public libraries was $17 million in 2000; total library income amounted to $205,569,000. Per capita spending came to $28.53.

The Boston Athenaeum, with 650,000 volumes, is the most noteworthy private library in the state. The American Antiquarian Society in Worcester has a 690,000-volume research library of original source material dating from colonial times to 1876.

Harvard University's library system is one of the largest in the world, with 14,311,152 volumes in 1999. Other major academic libraries are those of Boston University, the University of Massachusetts (Amherst), Smith College, and Boston College.

Boston houses a number of important museums, among them the Museum of Fine Arts with vast holdings of artwork including extensive Far East and French impressionists collections and American art and furniture, the Isabella Stewart Gardner Museum, the Museum of Science, the Massachusetts Historical Society, and the Children's Museum. Harvard University's museums include the Fogg Art Museum, the Peabody Museum of Archaeology and Ethnology, the Museum of Comparative Zoology, and the Botanical Museum. Other museums of note are the Whaling Museum in New Bedford, the Essex Institute in Salem, the Worcester Art Museum, the Clark Art Institute in Williamstown, the Bunker Hill Museum near Boston, and the National Basketball Hall of Fame in Springfield. In addition, many towns have their own historical societies and museums, including Historic Deerfield, Framingham Historical and Natural History Society, Ipswich Historical Society, Lexington Historical Society, and Marblehead Historical Society. Plymouth Plantation in Plymouth is a re-creation of life in the 17th century, and Old Sturbridge Village, a working historical farm, displays 18th- and 19th-century artifacts. The state had over 344 museums in 2000.

44 COMMUNICATIONS

The first American post office was established in Boston in 1639. Alexander Graham Bell first demonstrated the telephone in 1876 in Boston. As of 2001, 95.7% of the state's occupied housing units had telephones.

The state had 32 major AM stations and 63 major FM stations in 2003, when 10 major television stations were also in operation. In Boston, WGBH is a major producer of programming for the Public Broadcasting Service. In 2000, the Boston metropolitan area had 2,210,580 television-owning households, 80% of which received cable (the 2nd-highest penetration rate for any city).

In 2000, Massachusetts had 239,358 Internet domain name registrations, ranking 7th amongst all the states.

45 PRESS

Milestones in US publishing history that occurred in the state include the first book printed in the English colonies (Cambridge, 1640), the first regularly issued American newspaper, the *Boston News-Letter* (1704), and the first published American novel, William Hill Brown's *The Power of Sympathy* (Worcester, 1789). During the mid-1840s, two noted literary publications made their debut, the *North American Review* and the *Dial*, the latter under the editorial direction of Ralph Waldo Emerson and Margaret Fuller. The *Atlantic*, which began publishing in 1857, *Harvard Law Review, Harvard Business Review*, and *New England Journal of Medicine* are other influential publications.

As of 2002 there were 32 daily newspapers in the state (including 12 morning, 21 evening) and 16 papers with Sunday editions. The *Boston Globe*, the most widely read newspaper in the state, has won numerous awards for journalistic excellence on the local and national levels. The *Christian Science Monitor* is highly respected for its coverage of national and international news. Major daily newspapers and their average circulations in 2002 were:

AREA	NAME	DAILY	SUNDAY
Boston	*Christian Science Monitor* (m)	68,491	
	Globe (m,S)	471,199	704,852
	Herald (m,S)	259,228	160,172
Hyannis	*Cape Cod Times*	53,119	64,352
Worcester	*Telegram & Gazette*	103,565	124,722

Massachusetts is also a center of book publishing, with more than 100 publishing houses. Among them are Little, Brown and Co., Houghton Mifflin, Merriam-Webster, and Harvard University Press.

46 ORGANIZATIONS

In 2003, there were about 3,156 regional, national, and international organizations within the state.

Headquartered in Massachusetts are the National Association of Independent Schools, the National Commission for Cooperative Education, both in Boston, and the National Bureau of Economic Research in Cambridge. The Union of Concerned Scientists in Cambridge and the International Physicians for the Prevention of Nuclear War in Boston—recipient of the 1985 Nobel Peace Prize—are major public affairs associations based in the state.

Academic and scientific organizations headquartered in Boston include the American Meteorological Society, American Society of Law and Medicine, American Surgical Association, the Visiting Nurse Associations of America and Optometric Research Institute. The American Academy of Arts and Science is located in Cambridge, the National Association of Emergency Medical Technicians is in Newton Highlands, and the Protestant Guild for the Blind is in Belmont. Other education and research organizations with national scope and membership include the Albert Einstein Institution, the Albert Schweitzer Fellowship, the Bostonian Society, the Plymouth Rock Foundation, the Thoreau Society, and the Titanic Historical Society. There are numerous municipal and regional historical, preservations, and arts organizations.

Among the many professional, business, and consumer organizations based in Massachusetts are the American Institute of Management and the International Brotherhood of Police Officers in Quincy; the Wood Products Manufacturers Association in Gardner; and the National Consumer Law Center, Northern Textile Association, and Wool Manufacturers Council in Boston. The American Orchid Society and the Nieman Foundation are in Cambridge, the Shoe Suppliers Association of America is in East Bridgewater, and the United Textile Workers of America is in Lawrence.

The headquarters of the John Birch Society, an archconservative political association, is in Belmont. Oxfam-America, the US affiliate of the international humanitarian relief agency, is located in Boston. Students Against Destructive Decisions/Students Against Drunk Driving (SADD) is based in Marlborough. The Christian Science Publishing Society, which publishes the *Christian Science Monitor*, is located in Boston. The Unitarian Universalist Association of Congregations, a major body of the Unitarian Church, is also based in Boston.

Major sports associations in the state are the Eastern College Athletic Conference in Centerville and the American Hockey League in Springfield. The International Friendship League, which matches pen pals in 139 countries, has its headquarters in Boston.

⁴⁷TOURISM, TRAVEL, AND RECREATION

In 2001, there were over 26 million travelers to and within the state, with travel expenditures at about $11.7 billion. There were about 1.9 million international visitors to the state, with Canada and the United Kingdom being the largest markets. About 20% of all tourist activity involves residents traveling within the state. The travel industry supports over 147,600 jobs.

The greater Boston area was the most popular area for tourists in 2001, serving as the destination for about 43% of all trips. A trip to the city might include visits to such old landmarks as the Old North Church, the USS Constitution, and Paul Revere's House, and such newer attractions as the John Hancock Observatory, the skywalk above the Prudential Tower, Quincy Market, Faneuil Hall, and Copley Place. Boston Common, one of the oldest public parks in the country, is the most noteworthy municipal park.

About 19% of all trips are made to Cape Cod (Barnstable County). Among its many attractions are beaches, fishing, good dining spots, several artists' colonies with arts and crafts fairs, antique shops, and summer theaters. Beaches, fishing, and quaint villages are also the charms of Nantucket Island and Martha's Vineyard.

The Berkshires are the summer home of the Berkshire Music Festival at Tanglewood and the Jacob's Pillow Dance Festival in Lee, and during the winter also provide recreation for cross-country and downhill skiers. Essex County on the North Shore of Massachusetts Bay offers many seaside towns and the art colony of Rockport. Its main city, Salem, contains the Witch House and Museum as well as Nathaniel Hawthorne's House of Seven Gables. Middlesex County, to the west of Boston, holds the university city of Cambridge as well as the battlegrounds of Lexington and Concord. In Concord are the homes of Henry David Thoreau, Ralph Waldo Emerson, and Louisa May Alcott. Norfolk County, south of Boston, has the homes of three US presidents: John Adams and John Quincy Adams in Quincy and John F. Kennedy in Brookline. The seaport town and former whaling center of New Bedford and the industrial town of Fall River are in Bristol County. Plymouth County offers Plymouth Rock, Plymouth Plantation, and a steam-train ride through some cranberry bogs.

Massachusetts has about 79 operational state parks.

⁴⁸SPORTS

There are five major league professional sports teams in Massachusetts: the Boston Red Sox of Major League Baseball, the New England Patriots of the National Football League, the Boston Celtics of the National Basketball Association, the Boston Bruins of the National Hockey League, and the New England Revolution of Major League Soccer.

The Red Sox last won the World Series in 1918 but have appeared in it and lost five times since, most recently in 1986. The Patriots won the American Football Conference Championship in 1986 and 1997 but lost Super Bowls to the Chicago Bears and the Green Bay Packers, respectively. However, they reversed the trend by capturing the Super Bowl in 2002 with a dramatic win over the St. Louis Rams. The Celtics are the winningest team in NBA history; they have won the championship 16 times, including the seemingly unbeatable record of eight consecutive titles from 1959 to 1966. They last won an NBA championship in 1986. The Bruins won the Stanley Cup in 1929, 1939, 1941, 1970, and 1972. Additionally, there

are minor league hockey teams in Springfield, Worcester, and Lowell.

Suffolk Downs in East Boston features thoroughbred horse racing; harness racing takes place at the New England Harness Raceway in Foxboro. Dog racing can be seen at Raynham Park in Raynham, Taunton Dog Track in North Dighton, and Wonderland Park in Revere.

Probably the most famous amateur athletic event in the state is the Boston Marathon, a race of more than 26 mi (42 km) held every Patriots' Day (3rd Monday in April). It attracts many of the world's top long-distance runners. During the summer, a number of boat races are held. Rowing is also popular. Each October the traditional sport is celebrated in a regatta on the Charles River among college students in the Boston/Cambridge area.

In collegiate sports, the University of Massachusetts has become a nationally ranked basketball power; Boston College has appeared in 12 bowl games, highlighted by a victory in the Cotton Bowl in 1985; and the annual Harvard–Yale football game is one of the traditional rites of autumn.

⁴⁹FAMOUS BAY STATERS

Massachusetts has produced an extraordinary collection of public figures. Its four US presidents were John Adams (1735–1826), a signer of the Declaration of Independence; his son John Quincy Adams (1767–1848); John Fitzgerald Kennedy (1917–63); and George Herbert Walker Bush (b.Milton, 12 June 1924). All four served in Congress. John Adams was also the first US vice president; John Quincy Adams served as secretary of state under James Monroe, Calvin Coolidge (b.Vermont, 1872–1933) was governor of Massachusetts before his election to the vice-presidency in 1920 and his elevation to the presidency in 1923. George Bush was elected vice president on the Republican ticket in 1980 and reelected in 1984. Bush was elected president in 1988. Two others who held the office of vice president were another signer of the Declaration of Independence, Elbridge Gerry (1744–1814), for whom the political practice of gerrymandering is named, and Henry Wilson (b.New Hampshire, 1812–75), a US senator from Massachusetts before his election with Ulysses S. Grant.

Massachusetts's great jurists include US Supreme Court Justices Joseph Story (1779–1845), Oliver Wendell Holmes, Jr. (1841–1935), Louis D. Brandeis (b.Kentucky, 1856–1941), and Felix Frankfurter (b.Austria, 1882–1965). David Souter (b.1939), a Supreme Court justice appointed during the Bush administration, was born in Melrose. Stephen Breyer (b.California, 1939), another Supreme Court justice, was a Circuit Court of Appeals judge in Boston before his appointment. Important federal officeholders at the cabinet level were Henry Knox (1750–1806), the first secretary of war; Timothy Pickering (1745–1820), the first postmaster general and later secretary of war and secretary of state under George Washington and John Adams; Levi Lincoln (1749–1820), attorney general under Jefferson; William Eustis (1753–1825), secretary of war under Madison; Jacob Crowninshield (1770–1808), secretary of the navy under Jefferson, and his brother Benjamin (1772–1851), who held the same office under Madison; Daniel Webster (b.New Hampshire, 1782–1852), US senator from Massachusetts who served as secretary of state under William Henry Harrison, John Tyler, and Millard Fillmore; Edward Everett (1794–1865), a governor and ambassador who served as secretary of state under Fillmore; George Bancroft (1800–1891), a historian who became secretary of the Navy under James K. Polk; Caleb Cushing (1800–1879), attorney general under Franklin Pierce; Charles Devens (1820–91), attorney general under Rutherford B. Hayes; Christian Herter (1895–1966), secretary of state under Dwight Eisenhower; Elliot L. Richardson (1920–2000), secretary of health, education and welfare, secretary of defense, and attorney general under Richard Nixon; Henry Kissinger (b.Germany, 1923), secretary of state under Nixon and Gerald Ford and a Nobel Peace Prize winner in 1973; and Robert F. Kennedy (1925–68), attorney general under his brother John and later US senator from New York.

Other federal officeholders include some of the most important figures in American politics. Samuel Adams (1722–1803), the Boston Revolutionary leader, served extensively in the Continental Congress and was later governor of the Bay State. John Hancock (1737–93), a Boston merchant and Revolutionary, was the Continental Congress's first president and later became the first elected governor of the state. In the 19th century, Massachusetts sent abolitionist Charles Sumner (1811–74) to the Senate. As ambassador to England during the Civil War, John Quincy Adams's son Charles Francis Adams (1807–86) played a key role in preserving US-British amity. At the end of the century, Henry Cabot Lodge (1850–1924) emerged as a leading Republican in the US Senate, where he supported regulatory legislation, protectionist tariffs, and restrictive immigration laws, and opposed women's suffrage and the League of Nations; his grandson, also Henry Cabot Lodge (1902–85), was an internationalist who held numerous federal posts and was a US senator. Massachusetts has provided two US House speakers: John W. McCormack (1891–1980) and Thomas P. "Tip" O'Neill, Jr. (1912–94). Other well-known legislators include Edward W. Brooke (b.1919), the first black US senator since Reconstruction, and Edward M. Kennedy (b.1932), President Kennedy's youngest brother and a leading Senate liberal. Paul Tsongas (1941–97), a senator and presidential candidate during the 1992 election, was born in Lowell, Massachusetts. Michael S. Dukakis (b.1933), a former governor of the state and the 1988 Democratic nominee for president, was born in Brookline.

Among other historic colonial and state leaders were John Winthrop (b.England, 1588–1649), a founder of Massachusetts and longtime governor; William Bradford (b.England, 1590–1657), a founder of Plymouth, its governor, and author of its classic history; Thomas Hutchinson (1711–80), colonial lieutenant governor and governor during the 1760s and 1770s; and Paul Revere (1735–1818), the Patriot silversmith-courier, who was later an industrial pioneer.

Literary genius has flourished in Massachusetts. In the 17th century, the colony was the home of poets Anne Bradstreet (1612–72) and Edward Taylor (1645–1729) and of the prolific historian, scientist, theologian, and essayist Cotton Mather (1663–1728). Eighteenth-century notables include the theologian Jonathan Edwards (b.Connecticut, 1703–58), poet Phillis Wheatley (b.Senegal, 1753–84), and numerous political essayists and historians. During the 1800s, Massachusetts was the home of novelists Nathaniel Hawthorne (1804–64), Louisa May Alcott (b.Pennsylvania, 1832–88), Horatio Alger (1832–99), and Henry James (b.New York, 1843–1916); essayists Ralph Waldo Emerson (1803–82) and Henry David Thoreau (1817–62); and such poets as Henry Wadsworth Longfellow (b.Maine, 1807–82), John Greenleaf Whittier (1807–92), Oliver Wendell Holmes, Sr. (1809–94), James Russell Lowell (1819–91), and Emily Dickinson (1830–86). Classic historical writings include the works of George Bancroft (1800–91), William Hickling Prescott (1796–1859), John Lothrop Motley (1814–77), Francis Parkman (1823–93), and Henry B. Adams (1838–1918). Among 20th-century notables are novelists John P. Marquand (b.Delaware, 1893–1960) and John Cheever (1912–82); poets Elizabeth Bishop (1911–79), Robert Lowell (1917–77), Anne Sexton (1928–74), and Sylvia Plath (1932–63); and historian Samuel Eliot Morison (1887–1976). In philosophy, Charles Sanders Peirce (1839–1914) was one of the founders of pragmatism; Henry James's elder brother, William (b.New York, 1842–1910), was a pioneer in the field of psychology; and George Santayana (b.Spain, 1863–1952),

philosopher and author, grew up in Boston. Mary Baker Eddy (b.New Hampshire, 1821–1910) founded the Church of Christ, Scientist, during the 1870s.

Reformers have abounded in Massachusetts, especially in the 19th century. William Lloyd Garrison (1805–79), Wendell Phillips (1811–84), and Lydia Maria Child (1802–80) were outstanding abolitionists. Lucretia Coffin Mott (1793–1880), Lucy Stone (1818–93), Abigail Kelley Foster (1810–87), Margaret Fuller (1810–50), and Susan Brownell Anthony (1820–1906) were leading advocates of women's rights. Horace Mann (1796–1859), the state secretary of education, led the fight for public education; and Mary Lyon (1797–1849) founded Mount Holyoke, the first women's college.

Efforts to improve the care and treatment of the sick, wounded, and handicapped were led by Samuel Gridley Howe (1801–76), Dorothea Lynde Dix (1802–87), and Clara Barton (1821–1912), founder of the American Red Cross. The 20th-century reformer and NAACP leader William Edward Burghardt Du Bois (1868–1963) was born in Great Barrington.

Leonard Bernstein (1918–90) was a composer and conductor of worldwide fame. Arthur Fiedler (1894–79) was the celebrated conductor of the Boston Pops Orchestra. Composers include William Billings (1746–1800), Carl Ruggles (1876–1971), and Alan Hovhaness (1911–2000). Charles Bulfinch (1763–1844), Henry H. Richardson (b.Louisiana, 1838–86), and Louis Henri Sullivan (1856–1924) have been among the nation's important architects. Painters include John Singleton Copley (1738–1815), James Whistler (1834–1903), Winslow Homer (1836–1910), and Frank Stella (b.1936); Horatio Greenough (1805–52) was a prominent sculptor.

Among the notable scientists associated with Massachusetts are Nathaniel Bowditch (1773–1838), a mathematician and navigator; Samuel F. B. Morse (1791–1872), inventor of the telegraph; and Robert Hutchins Goddard (1882–1945), a physicist and rocketry pioneer.

Two professors at the Massachusetts Institute of Technology, in Cambridge, have won the Nobel Prize in economics—Paul A. Samuelson (b.Indiana, 1915), in 1970, and Franco Modigliani (b.Italy, 1918), in 1985. Other winners of the Nobel Prize include: Merton Miller (1923–2000), in economics; William Sharpe (b.1934), in economics; Douglass C. North (b.1920), 1993 co-recipient in economics; Elias James Corey (b.1928); Henry Kendall (1926–99), 1990 co-recipient in physics; and Joseph E. Murray (b.1919), the 1990 winner in medicine or physiology.

Massachusetts's most famous journalist has been Isaiah Thomas (1750–1831). Its great industrialists include textile entrepreneurs Francis Lowell (1775–1817) and Abbott Lawrence (1792–1855). Elias Howe (1819–67) invented the sewing machine.

Massachusetts was the birthplace of television journalists Mike Wallace (b.1918) and Barbara Walters (b.1931). Massachusetts-born show business luminaries include director Cecil B. DeMille (1881–1959); actors Walter Brennan (1894–1974), Jack Haley (1901–79), Ray Bolger (1904–84), Bette Davis (1908–84), and Jack Lemmon (1925–2001); and singers Donna Summer (b.1948) and James Taylor (b.1948). Outstanding among Massachusetts-born athletes was world heavyweight boxing champion Rocky Marciano (Rocco Francis Marchegiano, 1925–69), who retired undefeated in 1956.

50 BIBLIOGRAPHY

Bedford, Henry F., ed. *Their Lives and Numbers: The Condition of Working People in Massachusetts, 1870–1900.* Ithaca: Cornell University Press, 1995.

Brown, Richard D. *Massachusetts: A Concise History.* Amherst: University of Massachusetts Press, 2000.

Federal Writers' Project. *Massachusetts: A Guide to Its Places and People*. Reprint. New York: Somerset (orig. 1937).

Hunter, Phyllis Whitman. *Purchasing Identity in the Atlantic World: Massachusetts Merchants, 1670–1780*. Ithaca: Cornell University Press, 2001.

Mandell, Daniel R. *Behind the Frontier: Indians in Eighteenth-Century Eastern Massachusetts*. Lincoln: University of Nebraska Press, 1996.

Pletcher, Larry. *It Happened in Massachusetts*. Helena, Mont.: TwoDot, 1999.

Porter, Susan L., ed. *Women of the Commonwealth: Work, Family, and Social Change in Nineteenth-Century Massachusetts*. Amherst: University of Massachusetts Press, 1996.

Rothenberg, Winifred Barr. *From Market-Places to a Market Economy: The Transformation of Rural Massachusetts*. Chicago: University of Chicago Press, 1992.

Taymor, Betty. *Running Against the Wind: The Struggle of Women in Massachusetts Politics*. Boston: Northeastern University Press, 2000.

Tree, Christina. *Massachusetts, An Explorer's Guide: Beyond Boston and Cape Cod*. Woodstock, Vt.: Countryman Press, 1998.

Whitehall, Walter M., and Norman Kotker. *Massachusetts: A Pictorial History*. New York: Scribner, 1981.

MICHIGAN

State of Michigan

ORIGIN OF STATE NAME: Possibly derived from the Fox Indian word *mesikami*, meaning "large lake." **NICKNAME:** The Wolverine State. **CAPITAL:** Lansing. **ENTERED UNION:** 26 January 1837 (26th). **SONG:** "Michigan, My Michigan" (unofficial). **MOTTO:** *Si quaeris peninsulam amoenam circumspice* (If you seek a pleasant peninsula, look about you). **COAT OF ARMS:** In the center, a shield depicts a peninsula on which a man stands, at sunrise, holding a rifle. At the top of the shield is the word "Tuebor" (I will defend), beneath it is the state motto. Supporting the shield are an elk on the left and a moose on the right. Over the whole, on a crest, is an American eagle beneath the US motto, *E pluribus unum*. **FLAG:** The coat of arms centered on a dark blue field, fringed on three sides. **OFFICIAL SEAL:** The coat of arms surrounded by the words "The Great Seal of the State of Michigan" and the date "AD MDCCCXXXV" (1835, the year the first state constitution was adopted). **BIRD:** Robin. **FISH:** Trout. **REPTILE:** Painted turtle. **FLOWER:** Apple blossom. **TREE:** White pine. **GEM:** Chlorastrolite. **STONE:** Petoskey stone. **LEGAL HOLIDAYS:** New Year's Day, 1 January; Birthday of Martin Luther King, Jr., 3rd Monday in January; Lincoln's Birthday, 12 February; Washington's Birthday, 3rd Monday in February; Memorial Day, last Monday in May; Independence Day, 4 July; Labor Day, 1st Monday in September; Columbus Day, 2nd Monday in October; Veterans Day, 11 November; Thanksgiving Day, 4th Thursday in November; Christmas Day, 25 December. **TIME:** 7 AM EST = noon GMT; 6 AM CST = noon GMT.

¹LOCATION, SIZE, AND EXTENT

Located in the eastern north-central US, Michigan is the 3rd-largest state E of the Mississippi River and ranks 23rd in size among the 50 states.

The total area of Michigan (excluding Great Lakes waters) is 58,527 sq mi (151,585 sq km), of which land takes up 56,954 sq mi (147,511 sq km) and inland water 1,573 sq mi (4,074 sq km). The state consists of the upper peninsula adjoining three of the Great Lakes—Superior, Huron, and Michigan—and the lower peninsula, projecting northward between Lakes Michigan, Erie, and Huron. The upper peninsula extends 334 mi (538 km) E-W and 215 mi (346 km) N-S; the lower peninsula's maximum E-W extension is 220 mi (354 km), and its greatest N-S length is 286 mi (460 km).

Michigan's upper peninsula is bordered on the N and E by the Canadian province of Ontario (with the line passing through Lake Superior, the St. Marys River, and Lake Huron); on the S by Lake Huron, the Straits of Mackinac separating the two peninsulas, and Lake Michigan; and on the SW and W by Wisconsin (with the line passing through the Menominee, Brule, and Montreal rivers). The lower peninsula is bordered on the N by Lake Michigan, the Straits of Mackinac, and Lake Huron; on the E by Ontario (with the line passing through Lake Huron, the St. Clair River, Lake St. Clair, and the Detroit River); on the SE by Ontario and Ohio (with the line passing through Lake Erie); on the S by Ohio and Indiana; and on the W by Illinois and Wisconsin (with the line passing through Lake Michigan and Green Bay). The state's geographic center is in Wexford County, 5 mi (8 km) NNW of Cadillac.

Among the most important islands are Isle Royale in Lake Superior; Sugar, Neebish, and Drummond islands in the St. Marys River; Bois Blanc, Mackinac, and Les Cheneaux islands in Lake Huron; Beaver Island in Lake Michigan; and Belle Isle and Grosse Ile in the Detroit River.

The state's total boundary length is 1,673 mi (2,692 km). The total freshwater shoreline is 3,121 mi (5,023 km).

²TOPOGRAPHY

Michigan's two peninsulas are generally level land masses. Flat lowlands predominate in the eastern portion of both peninsulas and in scattered areas elsewhere. The state's lowest point, 572 ft (174 m), is found in southeastern Michigan along Lake Erie. Higher land is found in the western area of the lower peninsula, where elevations rise to as much as 1,600 ft (500 m); the hilly uplands of the upper peninsula attain elevations of 1,800 ft (550 m). The state's highest point, at 1,979 ft (603 m), is Mt. Arvon, in Baraga County.

Michigan's political boundaries extend into four of the five Great Lakes, giving Michigan jurisdiction over 16,231 sq mi (42,038 sq km) of Lake Superior, 13,037 sq mi (33,766 sq km) of Lake Michigan, 8,975 sq mi (23,245 sq km) of Lake Huron, and 216 sq mi (559 sq km) of Lake Erie, for a total of 38,459 sq mi (99,608 sq km). In addition, Michigan has about 35,000 inland lakes and ponds, the largest of which is Houghton Lake, on the lower peninsula, with an area of 31 sq mi (80 sq km).

The state's leading river is the Grand, about 260 mi (420 km) long, flowing through the lower peninsula into Lake Michigan. Other major rivers that flow into Lake Michigan include the St. Joseph, Kalamazoo, Muskegon, Pere Marquette, and Manistee. On the eastern side of the peninsula, the Saginaw River and its tributaries drain an area of some 6,000 sq mi (15,500 sq km), forming the state's largest watershed. Other important rivers that flow into Lake Huron include the Au Sable, Thunder Bay, and Cheboygan. In the southeast, the Huron and Raisin rivers flow into Lake Erie. Most major rivers in the upper peninsula (including the longest, the Menominee) flow southward into Lake Michigan and its various bays. Tahquamenon Falls, in the eastern part of the upper peninsula, is the largest of the state's more than 150 waterfalls.

Most of the many islands belonging to Michigan are located in northern Lake Michigan and in Lake Huron, although the largest, Isle Royale, about 44 mi (71 km) long by 8 mi (13 km) wide, is found in northern Lake Superior. In northern Lake

Michigan, Beaver Island is the largest, while Drummond Island, off the eastern tip of the upper peninsula, is the largest island in the northern Lake Huron area.

Michigan's geological development resulted from its location in what was once a basin south of the Laurentian Shield, a landmass covering most of eastern and central Canada and extending southward into the upper peninsula. Successive glaciers that swept down from the north dumped soil from the shield into the basin and eroded the basin's soft sandstone, limestone, and shale. With the retreat of the last glacier from the area about 6000 BC, the two peninsulas, the Great Lakes, and the islands in these lakes began to emerge, assuming their present shapes about 2,500 years ago.

3CLIMATE

Michigan has a temperate climate with well-defined seasons. The warmest temperatures and longest frost-free period are found most generally in the southern part of the lower peninsula; Detroit has a normal daily mean temperature of 49°F (9°C), ranging from 23°F (−5°C) in January to 72°F (22°C) in July. Colder temperatures and a shorter growing season prevail in the more northerly regions; Sault Ste. Marie has a normal daily mean of 40°F (4°C), ranging from 13°F (−11°C) in January to 64°F (18°C) in July. The coldest temperature ever recorded in the state is −51°F (−46°C), registered at Vanderbilt on 9 February 1934; the all-time high of 112°F (44°C) was recorded at Mio on 13 July 1936. Both sites are located in the interior of the lower peninsula, away from the moderating influence of the Great Lakes.

Detroit had an average annual precipitation (1971–2000) of 32.9 in (83.6 cm). The greatest snowfall is found in the extreme northern areas, where cloud cover created by cold air blowing over the warmer Lake Superior waters causes frequent heavy snow along the northern coast; Houghton and Calumet, on the Keweenaw Peninsula, average 183 in (465 cm) of snow a year, more than any other area in the state. Similarly, Lake Michigan's water temperatures create a snow belt along the west coast of the lower peninsula.

Cloudy days are more common in Michigan than in most states, in part because of the condensation of water vapor from the Great Lakes. Detroit has sunshine, on average, only 32% of the days in December and January, and only 49% year-round. The annual average relative humidity at Detroit is 81% at 7 AM, dropping to 60% at 1 PM; at Sault Ste. Marie, the comparable percentages are 85% and 67%, respectively. The southern half of the lower peninsula is an area of heavy thunderstorm activity. Late spring and early summer are the height of the tornado season.

4FLORA AND FAUNA

Maple, birch, hemlock, aspen, spruce, and fir predominate in the upper peninsula; maple, birch, aspen, pine, and beech in the lower. Once common in the state, elms have largely disappeared because of the ravages of disease, while the white pine (the state tree) and red pine, which dominated northern Michigan forests and were prime objects of logging operations, have been replaced in cutover lands by aspen and birch. The area south of a line from about Muskegon to Saginaw Bay formerly held the only significant patches of open prairie land (found chiefly in southwestern Michigan) and areas of widely scattered trees, called oak openings. Intensive agricultural development, followed by urban industrial growth, leveled much of this region's forests, although significant wooded acreage remains, especially in the less populated western regions.

Strawberries, raspberries, gooseberries, blueberries, and cranberries are among the fruit-bearing plants and shrubs that grow wild in many areas of the state, as do mushrooms and wild asparagus. The state flower, the apple blossom, calls to mind the importance of fruit-bearing trees and shrubs in Michigan, but wild flowers also abound, with as many as 400 varieties found in a single county. Eight Michigan plant species were listed as threatened or endangered as of 2003, including the American hart's-tongue fern, dwarf lake iris, Michigan Monkey-flower, and Eastern prairie fringed orchid.

Michigan's fauna, like its flora, has been greatly affected by settlement and, in a few cases, by intensive hunting and fishing. Moose are now confined to Isle Royale, as are nearly all the remaining wolves, which once roamed throughout the state. The caribou and passenger pigeon have been extirpated, but the elk and turkey have been successfully reintroduced in the 20th century. There is no evidence that the state's namesake, the wolverine, was ever found in Michigan, at least in historic times. Despite intensive hunting, the deer population remains high. Other game animals include the common cottontail, snowshoe hare, raccoon, and various squirrels. In addition to the raccoon, important native furbearers are the river otter and the beaver, once virtually exterminated but now making a strong comeback.

More than 300 types of birds have been observed. Aside from the robin (the state bird), the most notable bird is Kirtland's warbler, which nests only in a 60-sq-mi (155-sq-km) section of jack-pine forest in north-central Michigan. Ruffed grouse, bobwhite quail, American woodcock, and various ducks and geese are hunted extensively. Populations of ring-necked pheasant, introduced in 1895, have dropped at an alarming rate in recent decades. Reptiles include the massasauga, the state's only poisonous snake.

Whitefish, perch, and lake trout (the state fish) are native to the Great Lakes while perch, bass, and pike are indigenous to inland waters. In 1877, the carp was introduced, with such success that it has since become a nuisance. Rainbow and brown trout have also been planted, and in the late 1960s, the state enjoyed its most spectacular success with the introduction of several species of salmon.

The first Michigan list of threatened or endangered animals in 1976 included 64 species, 15 endangered and 49 threatened. In 2003, the US Fish and Wildlife Service listed 13 Michigan animals as threatened or endangered. These included the Indiana bat, two species of beetle, two species of butterfly, gray wolf, bald eagle, piping plover, and Kirland's warbler.

5ENVIRONMENTAL PROTECTION

The Michigan Department of Natural Resources (DNR) is the state's 4th-largest department employing approximately 3,700 persons. It is responsible for the administration of hundreds of programs affecting every aspect of the environment. These programs are based on state and federal laws calling for the protection and management of natural resources, including: air, water, fish, wildlife, recreational activities, wetlands, forests, minerals, oil, and gas. The regulatory programs operated by the DNR conserve and manage natural resources by controlling access or limiting their use and removal. Most of these programs rely on permit or license systems such as hunting or fishing licenses, forest use permits, and air/wastewater discharge permits.

Responding to citizens' concerns and new federal legislation, Michigan enacted programs to address water and air pollution as well as waste problems. At least 10 major environmental programs were established under Michigan law during the 1970s and 1980s, directing the DNR to assume new responsibilities and authorities. These included the Wetland Protection Act of 1980, Inland Lakes and Streams Act, the Resource Recovery Act, the Solid Waste Management Act, and the Hazardous Waste Management Act. In addition, changes in administrative rules and amendments to existing statutes greatly expanded the scope of some programs such as air and water pollution control (Air Pollution Control Act and Water Resources Commission Act).

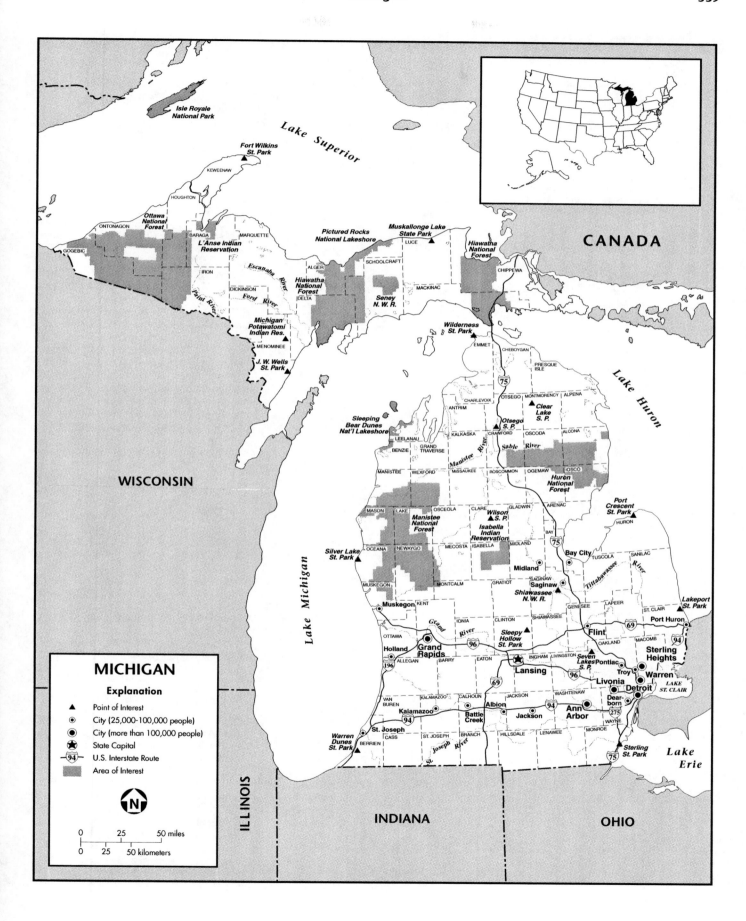

Isle Royale
National Park

Lake Superior

CANADA

Fort Wilkins
St. Park

KEWEENAW

HOUGHTON

Ottawa
National
Forest

ONTONAGON

GOGEBIC

BARAGA

MARQUETTE

L'Anse Indian
Reservation

Pictured Rocks
National Lakeshore

Muskallonge Lake
State Park

LUCE

Hiawatha
National
Forest

IRON

Escanaba River

DICKINSON

Ford River

ALGER

SCHOOLCRAFT

Hiawatha
National
Forest

DELTA

MACKINAC

CHIPPEWA

Seney
N. W. R.

Paint River

Michigan
Potawatomi
Indian Res.

MENOMINEE

J. W. Wells
St. Park

Wilderness
St. Park

EMMET

CHEBOYGAN

PRESQUE
ISLE

CANADA

Lake Huron

75

CHARLEVOIX

OTSEGO

MONTMORENCY

ALPENA

Sleeping
Bear Dunes
Nat'l Lakeshore

ANTRIM

Clear
Lake
S. P.

LEELANAU

BENZIE

GRAND
TRAVERSE

KALKASKA

Otsego
S. P.

CRAWFORD

OSCODA

ALCONA

Sable River

WISCONSIN

MANISTEE

WEXFORD

MISSAUKEE

ROSCOMMON

OGEMAW

IOSCO

Huron
National
Forest

MASON

LAKE

OSCEOLA

CLARE

GLADWIN

ARENAC

Port
Crescent
St. Park

Manistee
National
Forest

Wilson
S. P.

Isabella
Indian
Reservation

HURON

OCEANA

NEWAYGO

MECOSTA

ISABELLA

MIDLAND

BAY

75

Bay City

TUSCOLA

SANILAC

Tittabawassee River

Silver Lake
St. Park

MUSKEGON

MONTCALM

GRATIOT

SAGINAW

Midland

Saginaw

Shiawassee
N. W. R.

Lakeport
St. Park

ST. CLAIR

Lake Michigan

Muskegon

KENT

IONIA

CLINTON

SHIAWASSEE

GENESEE

LAPEER

69

Port Huron

Grand River

Sleepy
Hollow
St. Park

Flint

MACOMB

94

Holland

OTTAWA

Grand
Rapids

96

EATON

INGHAM

LIVINGSTON

Seven
Lakes
S. P.

Pontiac

OAKLAND

Sterling
Heights

ALLEGAN

BARRY

Lansing

69

96

Troy

Livonia

Warren

LAKE
ST. CLAIR

196

VAN
BUREN

KALAMAZOO

CALHOUN

JACKSON

WASHTENAW

Detroit

Dearborn

Kalamazoo

Albion

Jackson

94

Ann
Arbor

275

WAYNE

Battle
Creek

Warren
Dunes
St. Park

St. Joseph

BERRIEN

CASS

ST. JOSEPH

BRANCH

HILLSDALE

LENAWEE

MONROE

Sterling
St. Park

Lake
Erie

St. Joseph River

MICHIGAN

Explanation

▲ Point of Interest

⊙ City (25,000-100,000 people)

◉ City (more than 100,000 people)

★ State Capital

〔94〕 U.S. Interstate Route

▨ Area of Interest

N

| 0 | 25 | 50 miles |

| 0 | 25 | 50 kilometers |

ILLINOIS

INDIANA

OHIO

These legislated changes, coupled with reorganization measures enacted by executive order, greatly expanded the state's role in environmental protection matters and substantially increased the scope of DNR's mission.

Governor William Milliken decided Michigan would be better served if all environmental programs were under one roof. Executive Order 1973-2 transferred three programs from the Department of Public Health to the DNR, including sewage system maintenance and certification; solid waste disposal; and licensing of septic tank cleaners. Further transfers were accomplished under Executive Order 1973-2a, which changed the status of the Water Resources Commission (WRC), making it subordinate to the Natural Resources Commission (NRC). Additionally, Executive Order 1973-2a transferred the Air Pollution Control Commission to the DNR under the jurisdiction of the NRC. The Executive Order divided the DNR for the first time into two branches: the natural resources branch, and the environmental protection branch. The Executive Orders of 1973 clearly consolidated and defined the DNR's environmental protection responsibilities.

As the 1970s drew to a close, Michigan enacted two major pollution control laws: the Solid Waste Management Act and the Hazardous Waste Management Act. These acts provide the legal basis for the separate management of hazardous wastes under a detailed regulatory program. The two waste management laws substantially increased the DNR's enforcement and administrative responsibilities. In addition to these two acts, several other laws were enacted or amended by the legislature in the late 1970s and 1980s which had a major impact on the Department. For example, the Environmental Response Act provides for the identification of sites of environmental contamination throughout the state and an appropriation procedure to support the cleanup of contamination sites in the state. Other programs created by statute included the Clean Michigan Fund and the Leaking Underground Storage Tanks Act. Each of these statutes required the DNR to assume new program responsibilities and authorities in the 1980s.

As the policy body over the DNR, the NRC consists of seven members appointed by the governor, with the advice of the senate. The NRC sets the overall direction of the department and hires the director to carry out its policies. The department is organized both programmatically and geographically. The three program areas, each headed by a deputy director, include: resource management; environmental protection; and policy, budget, and administration. The three geographical regions split the state into the north, central, and south zones, each headed by a deputy director. The deputy directors report to the director of the DNR.

The mission of the department is to conserve and develop the state's natural resources and to protect and enhance the state's environmental quality in order to provide clean air, clean water, productive land, and healthy life. Additionally, the department seeks to provide quality recreational opportunities to the people of Michigan through the effective management of state recreational lands and parks, boating facilities, and population of fish and wildlife.

In 2003, Michigan had 343 hazardous waste sites listed in the Environmental Protection Agency's database, 66 of which were on the National Priorities List. In 2001, Michigan received $138,075,000 in federal grants from the Environmental Protection Agency; EPA expenditures for procurement contracts in Michigan that year amounted to $26,847,000.

6POPULATION

Michigan ranked 8th in population in the US with an estimated total of 10,050,446 in 2002, an increase of 1.1% since 2000. Between 1990 and 2000, Michigan's population grew from 9,295,297 to 9,938,444, an increase of 6.9%. The population is projected to reach 10.1 million by 2025. The population density in 2000 was 175 persons per sq mi.

Michigan was never inhabited by more than a few thousand Indians. As late as 1810, the non-Indian population of Michigan Territory was only 4,762. The late 1820s marked the start of steady, often spectacular, growth. The population increased from 31,639 people in 1830 to 212,267 in 1840 and 397,654 in 1850. Subsequently, the state's population grew by about 400,000 each decade until 1910, when its population of 2,810,173 ranked 8th among the 46 states. Industrial development sparked a sharp rise in population to 4,842,325 by 1930, pushing Michigan ahead of Massachusetts into 7th place.

In 2000, the national median age of Michigan's population was 35.5. In the same year, 26.1% of the population were under age 18 while 12.3% were age 65 or older. Approximately half of the state's population is concentrated in the Detroit metropolitan area.

Detroit has always been Michigan's largest city since its founding in 1701, but its growth, like the state's, was slow until well into the 19th century. The city's population grew from 21,019 in 1850 to 285,704 in 1900, when it ranked as the 13th-largest city in the country. Within the next 30 years, the booming automobile industry pushed the city up into 4th place, with a population of 1,568,662 in 1930. Since 1950, when the total reached 1,849,568, Detroit has lost population, dropping to 1,514,063 in 1970, 1,203,369 in 1980 and to 1,028,000 in 1990, when it held 7th place among US cities. The 2002 population was estimated at 925,051, putting Detroit in 10th place. As Detroit lost population, however, many of its suburban areas grew at an even greater rate. The Detroit metropolitan area totaled an estimated 5,469,312 in 1999, up from 4,320,203 in 1995 and 3,950,000 in 1960.

Other Michigan cities with estimated 2002 populations in excess of 100,000 include Grand Rapids with a population of 196,595; Warren, 137,672; Sterling Heights, 126,146; Flint, 121,007630; Lansing (the capital), 118,588; and Ann Arbor, 115,213.

7ETHNIC GROUPS

The 2000 census counted about 58,479 American Indians, including Eskimos and Aleuts. Most were scattered across the state, with a small number concentrated on the four federal reservations, comprising 16,635 acres (6,732 hectares). In the 1990s the Ottawa, Ojibwa, and Potawatomi were the principal groups with active tribal organizations.

In 2000, the black population of Michigan totaled an estimated 1,412,742. In 1980, nearly two-thirds lived in Detroit, where they made up 75.7% of the population, the highest percentage in any US city of one million or more. Detroit, which experienced severe race riots in 1943 and 1967, has had a black mayor since 1974.

The 2000 census found that 523,589 state residents (5.3%) were foreign born, up from 355,393 (3.8%) in 1990. There were 323,877 Hispanics and Latinos living in the state in 2000, of whom 220,769 were of Mexican descent. The state's Asian population has been increasing: as of 2000, the total number of Asians was 176,510. The census reported 54,631 Asian Indians (up from 18,100 in 1990), 17,377 Filipinos, 33,189 Chinese (up from 17,100 in 1990), 20,886 Koreans, 11,288 Japanese, and 13,673 Vietnamese (up from 5,229 in 1990). Pacific Islanders numbered 2,692.

Although state residents of first- or second-generation European descent are, almost without exception, decreasing in number and proportion, their influence remains great. Detroit continues to have numerous well-defined ethnic neighborhoods, and Hamtramck, a city surrounded by Detroit, is still dominated

Michigan Counties, County Seats, and County Areas and Populations

COUNTY	COUNTY SEAT	LAND AREA (SQ MI)	POPULATION (2002 EST.)	COUNTY	COUNTY SEAT	LAND AREA (SQ MI)	POPULATION (2002 EST.)
Alcona	Harrisville	679	11,455	Lapeer	Lapeer	658	90,776
Alger	Munising	912	9,796	Leelanau	Leland	341	21,722
Allegan	Allegan	832	109,336	Lenawee	Adrian	753	100,145
Alpena	Alpena	568	31,026	Livingston	Howell	575	168,862
Antrim	Bellaire	480	23,809	Luce	Newberry	905	7,027
Arenac	Standish	368	17,185	Mackinac	St. Ignace	1,025	11,505
Baraga	L'Anse	901	8,694	Macomb	Mt. Clemens	483	808,529
Barry	Hastings	560	57,943	Manistee	Manistee	543	25,082
Bay	Bay City	447	109,672	Marquette	Marquette	1,822	64,342
Benzie	Beulah	322	16,818	Mason	Ludington	495	28,879
Berrien	St. Joseph	576	162,285	Mecosta	Big Rapids	560	41,465
Branch	Coldwater	508	46,189	Menominee	Menominee	1,045	25,109
Calhoun	Marshall	712	138,375	Midland	Midland	525	84,119
Cass	Cassopolis	496	51,284	Missaukee	Lake City	565	14,950
Charlevoix	Charlevoix	421	26,386	Monroe	Monroe	557	149,253
Cheboygan	Cheboygan	720	27,072	Montcalm	Stanton	713	62,420
Chippewa	Sault Ste. Marie	1,590	38,898	Montmorency	Atlanta	550	10,560
Clare	Harrison	570	31,686	Muskegon	Muskegon	507	171,765
Clinton	St. Johns	573	66,668	Newaygo	White Cloud	847	49,013
Crawford	Grayling	559	14,734	Oakland	Pontiac	875	1,202,721
Delta	Escanaba	1,173	38,336	Oceana	Hart	541	27,650
Dickinson	Iron Mt.	770	27,325	Ogemaw	West Branch	569	21,758
Eaton	Charlotte	579	105,590	Ontonagon	Ontonagon	1,311	7,703
Emmet	Petoskey	468	32,329	Osceola	Reed City	569	23,500
Genesee	Flint	642	441,423	Oscoda	Mio	568	9,449
Gladwin	Gladwin	505	26,745	Otsego	Gaylord	516	24,155
Gogebic	Bessemer	1,105	17,407	Ottawa	Grand Haven	567	245,913
Grand Traverse	Traverse City	466	81,263	Presque Isle	Rogers City	656	14,320
Gratiot	Ithaca	570	42,365	Roscommon	Roscomon	528	25,818
Hillsdale	Hillsdale	603	46,980	Saginaw	Saginaw	815	210,087
Houghton	Houghton	1,014	35,883	St. Clair	Port Huron	734	167,712
Huron	Bad Axe	830	35,422	St. Joseph	Centreville	503	62,366
Ingham	Mason	560	281,362	Sanilac	Sandusky	964	44,535
Ionia	Ionia	577	62,941	Schoolcraft	Manistique	1,173	8,778
Iosco	Tawas City	546	26,979	Shiawassee	Corunna	541	72,122
Iron	Crystal Falls	1,163	12,736	Tuscola	Caro	812	58,249
Isabella	Mt. Pleasant	576	64,523	Van Buren	Paw Paw	612	77,235
Jackson	Mackson	705	160,972	Washtenaw	Ann Arbor	710	334,351
Kalamazoo	Kalamazoo	562	241,471	Wayne	Detroit	615	2,045,540
Kalkaska	Kalkaska	563	17,043	Wexford	Cadillac	566	30,777
Kent	Grand Rapids	862	587,951				
Keweenaw	Eagle River	544	2,204				
Lake	Balwin	568	11,623	TOTALS		56,954	10,050,446

by its Polish population. Elsewhere in Michigan, Frankenmuth is the site of an annual German festival, and the city of Holland has an annual tulip festival that attracts about 400,000 people each spring. In the upper peninsula, the Finnish culture dominates in rural areas; in the iron and copper mining regions, descendants of immigrants from Cornwall in England, the original mining work force, and persons of Scandinavian background predominate.

8 LANGUAGES

Before white settlement, Algonkian-language tribes occupied what is now Michigan, with the Menomini and Ojibwa in the upper peninsula and Ottawa on both sides of the Straits of Mackinac. Numerous place-names recall their presence: Michigan itself, Mackinaw City, Petoskey, Kalamazoo, Muskegon, Cheboygan, and Dowagiac.

Except for the huge industrial area in southeastern Michigan, English in the state is remarkably homogeneous in its retention of the major Northern dialect features of upper New York and western New England. Common are such Northern forms as *pail, wishbone, darning needle* (dragonfly), *mouth organ* (harmonica), *sick to the stomach, quarter to four* (3:45), and *dove* as past tense of *dive*. Common also are such pronunciations as the /ah/ vowel

in *fog, frog,* and *on;* the /aw/ vowel in *horrid, forest,* and *orange; creek* as /krik/; *root* and *roof* with the vowel of *put;* and *greasy* with an /s/ sound. *Swale* (a marsh emptying into a stream) and *clock shelf* (mantel) are dying Northern words not carried west of Michigan. *Pank* (to pack down, as of snow) is confined to the upper peninsula, and *pasty* (meat-filled pastry) is borrowed from Cornish miners and heard in the upper peninsula and a few other areas. A minister is a *dominie* in the Dutch area around Holland and Zeeland.

Southern blacks have introduced into the southeastern automotive manufacturing areas a regional variety of English that, because it has class connotations in the North, has become a controversial educational concern. Three of its features are perhaps more widely accepted than others: the coalescence of /e/ and /i/ before a nasal consonant, so that *pen* and *pin* sound alike; the loss of /r/ after a vowel, so that *cart* and *cot* also sound alike; and the lengthening of the first part of the diphthong /ai/, so that *time* and *Tom* sound alike, as do *ride* and *rod*.

In 2000, 91.6% of the state's population five years old or older spoke only English at home, down from 93.4% in 1990.

The following table gives selected statistics from the 2000 census for language spoken at home by persons five years old and over. The category "Other Indo-European languages" includes Albanian, Gaelic, Lithuanian, and Rumanian. The category "Other Slavic languages" includes Czech, Slovak, and Ukrainian. The category "Other Asian languages" includes Dravidian languages, Malayalam, Telugu, Tamil, and Turkish. The category "Other Indic languages" includes Bengali, Marathi, Punjabi, and Romany.

LANGUAGE	NUMBER	PERCENT
Population 5 years and over	9,268,782	100.0
Speak only English	8,487,401	91.6
Speak a language other than English	781,381	8.4
Speak a language other than English	781,381	8.4
Spanish or Spanish Creole	246,688	2.7
Arabic	75,412	0.8
German	52,366	0.6
Polish	40,372	0.4
French (incl. Patois, Cajun)	38,914	0.4
Other and unspecified languages	32,189	0.3
Italian	30,052	0.3
Other Indo-European languages	27,241	0.3
Chinese	26,955	0.3
Other Slavic languages	14,682	0.2
Other Asian languages	14,611	0.2
Other Indic languages	14,140	0.2
Korean	13,314	0.1
Serbo-Croatian	11,950	0.1
Tagalog	11,917	0.1
Vietnamese	11,776	0.1
Russian	11,701	0.1
Japanese	11,480	0.1
Greek	11,167	0.1

[9] RELIGIONS

The Roman Catholic Church was the only organized religion in Michigan until the 19th century. Detroit's St. Anne's parish, established in 1701, is the second-oldest Catholic parish in the country. In 1810, a Methodist society was organized near Detroit. After the War of 1812, as settlers poured in from the east, Presbyterian, Congregational, Baptist, Episcopal, and Quaker churches were founded. The original French Catholics, reduced to a small minority by the influx of American Protestants, were soon reinforced by the arrival of Catholic immigrants from Germany, Ireland, and, later, from eastern and southern Europe. The Lutheran religion was introduced by German and Scandinavian immigrants; Dutch settlers were affiliated with the Reformed Church in America. The first Jewish congregations were organized in Detroit by German Jews, with a much greater number of eastern European Jews arriving toward the end of the 1800s. The Orthodox Christian Church and the Islamic religion have been introduced by immigrants from the Near East during the 20th century.

Michigan had 2,019,926 Roman Catholics in 2000. Among Protestant denominations, the largest groups were the Missouri Synod Lutherans, with about 244,231 adherents, and the United Methodists, with about 222,269 adherents. Evangelical Lutherans numbered about 160,836 adherents. The Christian Reformed Church had about 112,711 members and the Presbyterian Church USA had 104,471. The Seventh Day Adventists, who had their world headquarters in Battle Creek from 1855 to 1903, numbered 37,712 in 2000. The Jewish community had about 110,000 members. Over 5.7 million people (about 58% of the population) were not counted as members of any religious organization.

[10] TRANSPORTATION

Because of Michigan's location, its inhabitants have always depended heavily on the Great Lakes for transportation. Not until the 1820s did land transportation systems begin to be developed. Although extensive networks of railroads and highways now reach into all parts of the state, the Great Lakes remain major avenues of commerce.

The first railroad company in the Midwest was chartered in Michigan in 1830, and six years later the Erie and Kalamazoo, operating between Toledo, Ohio, and Adrian, became the first railroad in service west of the Appalachians. Between 1837 and 1845, the state government sought to build three lines across southern Michigan, before abandoning the project and selling the two lines it had partially completed to private companies. The pace of railroad construction lagged behind that in other midwestern states until after the Civil War. Only then did the combination of federal and state aid and Michigan's booming economy lead to an enormous expansion in trackage, from fewer than 800 mi (1,300 km) in 1860 to a peak of 9,021 mi (14,518 km) in 1910. With the economic decline of northern Michigan and the resulting drop in railroad revenues, however, Class I trackage declined to 2,228 rail mi (3,585 km) by 2000. Most railroad passenger service is provided by Amtrak, which operates five trains through the state. Freight is carried by the state's 26 railroads. The Michigan state government, through the Department of Transportation, has helped to revive the railroad system through its Rail Program.

Railroads have been used only to a limited degree in the Detroit area as commuter carriers, although efforts have been made to improve this service. In the early 1900s, more than 1,000 mi (1,600 km) of inter-urban rail lines provided rapid transit service in southern Michigan, but automobiles and buses drove them out of business, and the last line shut down in 1934. Street railway service began in a number of cities in the 1860s, and Detroit took over its street railways in 1922. Use of these public transportation systems declined sharply after World War II. By the 1950s, streetcars had been replaced by buses, but by 1960 many small communities had abandoned city bus service altogether. During the 1970s, with massive government aid, bus service was restored to many cities and was improved in others, and the number of riders generally increased. In fiscal year 1995/96, local public transit systems handled 82.5 million passengers while inter-city bus systems carried an estimated 350,000 passengers.

As of 2000, the state had 91,927 mi (147,942 km) of rural roads and 30,007 mi (48,291 km) of urban roads. Major expressways included I-94 (Detroit to Chicago), I-96 (Detroit to Grand Rapids), and I-75 (from the Ohio border to Sault Ste. Marie). In 2000, there were 5,023,421 registered passenger cars, 3,386,473 trucks, 25,827 buses, and 183,592 motorcycles. Licensed drivers numbered 6,925,246 during the same year.

The completion in 1957 of the Mackinac Bridge, the 4th-longest suspension span in the world, eliminated the major barrier to easy movement between the state's two peninsulas. The International Bridge at Sault Ste. Marie, the Blue-Water Bridge at Port Huron, the Ambassador Bridge at Detroit, and the Detroit-Windsor Tunnel link Michigan with Canada.

The opening of the St. Lawrence Seaway in 1959 made it possible for a large number of oceangoing vessels to dock at Michigan ports. In 2000, the port of Detroit handled 17.3 million tons of cargo; Presque Isle, 10.7 million tons; Escanaba, 8.6 million tons;and the limestone-shipping port of Calcite, 8.5 million tons.

Michigan was a pioneer in developing air transportation service. The Ford Airport at Dearborn in the 1920s had one of the first air passenger facilities and was the base for some of the first regular airmail service. In 2002, the state had 380 airports, 85 heliports, 2 stolports, and 7 seaplane bases. The major airport is Detroit Metropolitan Wayne County Airport, with 17,326,775 enplaned passengers in 2000.

¹¹HISTORY

Indian hunters and fishermen inhabited the region now known as Michigan as early as 9000 BC; these peoples were making use of copper found in the upper peninsula—the first known use of a metal by peoples anywhere in the western hemisphere. Around 1000 BC, their descendants introduced agriculture into southwestern Michigan. In the latter part of the prehistoric era, the Indians appear to have declined in population.

In the early 17th century, when European penetration began, Michigan's lower peninsula was inhabited by tribes of Native Americans who may have moved west of Lake Michigan for temporary periods during periods of war. In the upper peninsula there were small bands of Ojibwa along the St. Marys River and the Lake Michigan shore; in the west, Menomini Indians lived along the present Michigan-Wisconsin border. Both tribes were of Algonkian linguistic stock, as were most Indians who later settled in the area, except for the Winnebago of the Siouan group in the Green Bay region of Lake Michigan, and the Huron of Iroquoian stock in the Georgian Bay area of Canada. In the 1640s, the Huron were nearly wiped out by other Iroquois tribes from New York, and the survivors fled westward with their neighbors to the north, the Ottawa Indians. Eventually, both tribes settled at the Straits of Mackinac before moving to the Detroit area early in the 18th century. During the same period, the Potawatomi and Miami Indians moved from Wisconsin into southern Michigan.

For two centuries after the first Europeans came to Michigan, the Indians remained a vital force in the area's development. They were the source of the furs that the whites traded for, and they also were highly respected as potential allies when war threatened between the rival colonial powers in North America. However, after the War of 1812, when the fur trade declined and the possibility of war receded, the value of the Indians to the white settlers diminished. Between 1795 and 1842, Indian lands in Michigan were ceded to the federal government, and the Huron, Miami, and many Potawatomi were removed from the area. Some Potawatomi were allowed to remain on lands reserved for them, along with most of the Ojibwa and Ottawa Indians in the north.

The first European explorer known to have reached Michigan was a Frenchman, Etienne Brulé, who explored the Sault Ste. Marie area around 1620. Fourteen years later, Jean Nicolet explored the Straits of Mackinac and the southern shore of the upper peninsula en route to Green Bay. Missionary and fur trading posts, to which were later added military forts, were established at Sault Ste. Marie by Father Jacques Marquette in 1668, and then at St. Ignace in 1671. By the 1680s, several temporary posts had been established in the lower peninsula. In 1701, Antoine Laumet de la Mothe Cadillac founded a permanent settlement at the site of present-day Detroit.

Detroit and Michigan grew little at first, however, because the rulers of the French colony of New France were obsessed with the fur trade, which did not attract large numbers of settlers. After France's defeat in the French and Indian War, fears that the British would turn the area over to English farmers from the coastal colonies, with the consequent destruction of the Indian way of life, led the Indians at Detroit to rebel in May 1763, under the leadership of the Ottawa chief Pontiac. Other uprisings resulting from similar grievances soon spread throughout the west but ended in failure for the Indians. Pontiac gave up his siege of Detroit after six months, and by 1764 the British were in firm control. Nevertheless, the British authorities did not attempt to settle the area. The need to protect the fur trade placed the people of Michigan solidly on the British side during the American Revolution, since a rebel triumph would likely mean the migration of American farmers into the west, converting the wilderness to cropland. The British occupied Michigan and other western areas for 13 years after the Treaty of Paris in 1783 had assigned these territories to the new United States. The US finally got possession of Michigan in the summer of 1796.

Michigan became a center of action in the War of 1812. The capture of Detroit by the British on 16 August 1812 was a crushing defeat for the Americans. Although Detroit was recaptured by the Americans in September 1813, continued British occupation of the fort on Mackinac Island, which they had captured in 1812, enabled them to control most of Michigan. The territory was finally returned to American authority under the terms of the Treaty of Ghent at the end of 1814. With the opening in 1825 of the Erie Canal, which provided a cheap, all-water link between Michigan and New York City, American pioneers turned their attention to these northern areas, and during the 1820s settlers for the first time pushed into the interior of southern Michigan.

Originally part of the Northwest Territory, Michigan had been set aside in 1805 as a separate territory, but with boundaries considerably different from those of the subsequent state. On the south, the territory's boundary was a line set due east from the southernmost point of Lake Michigan; on the north, only the eastern tip of the upper peninsula was included. In 1818 and 1834, areas as far west as Iowa and the Dakotas were added to the territory for administrative purposes. By 1833, Michigan had attained a population of 60,000, qualifying it for statehood. The territorial government's request in 1834 that Michigan be admitted to the Union was rejected by Congress, however, because of a dispute over Michigan's southern boundary. When Indiana became a state in 1816, it had been given a 10-mi (16-km) strip of land in southwestern Michigan, and Michigan now refused to accede to Ohio's claim that it should be awarded lands in southeastern Michigan, including the present site of Toledo. In 1835, Michigan militia defeated the efforts of Ohio authorities to take over the disputed area during the so-called Toledo War, in which no one was killed. Nevertheless, Ohio's superior political power in Congress ultimately forced Michigan to agree to relinquish the Toledo Strip. In return, Congress approved the state government that the people of Michigan had set up in 1835. As part of the compromise that finally brought Michigan into the Union on 26 January 1837, the new state was given land in the upper peninsula west of St. Ignace as compensation for the loss of Toledo.

Youthful Stevens T. Mason, who had led the drive for statehood, became Michigan's first elected governor, but he and the Democratic Party fell out of grace when the new state was plunged into financial difficulties during the depression of the late 1830s. The party soon returned to power and controlled the state until the mid-1850s. In Michigan, as elsewhere, it was the slavery issue that ended Democratic dominance. In July 1854, antislavery Democrats joined with members of the Whig and Free-Soil parties at a convention in Jackson to organize the Republican Party. In the elections of 1854, the Republicans swept into office in Michigan, controlling the state, with rare exceptions, until the 1930s.

Abraham Lincoln was not the first choice of Michigan Republicans for president in 1860, but when he was nominated, they gave him a solid margin of victory that fall and again in 1864. Approximately 90,000 Michigan men served in the Union army, taking part in all major actions of the Civil War. Michigan's Zachariah Chandler was one of the leaders of the Radical Republicans in the US Senate who fought for a harsh policy toward the South during Reconstruction.

Michigan grew rapidly in economic importance. Agriculture sparked the initial growth of the new state and was responsible for its rapid increase in population. By 1850, the southern half of the lower peninsula was filling up, with probably 85% of the state's population dependent in some way on agriculture for a living. Less than two decades later, exploitation of vast pine forests in northern Michigan had made the state the top lumber producer in the US. Settlers were also attracted to the same area by the discovery of rich mineral deposits, which made Michigan for a time the nation's leading source of iron ore, copper, and salt.

Toward the end of the 19th century, as timber resources were being exhausted and as farming and mining reached their peak stages of development, new opportunities in manufacturing opened up. Such well-known Michigan companies as Kellogg, Dow Chemical, and Upjohn had their origins during this period. The furniture industry in Grand Rapids, the paper industry in Kalamazoo, and numerous other industries were in themselves sufficient to ensure the state's increasing industrial importance. But the sudden popularity of Ransom E. Olds's Oldsmobile runabout, manufactured first in Lansing, inspired a host of Michiganians to produce similar practical, relatively inexpensive automobiles. By 1904, the most successful of the new models, Detroit's Cadillac and the first Fords, together with the Oldsmobile, had made Michigan the leading automobile producer in the country—and, later, in the world. The key developments in Michigan's auto industry were the creation of General Motors by William C. Durant in 1908; Henry Ford's development of the Model T in 1908, followed by his institution of the moving assembly line in 1913–14; and Walter P. Chrysler's 1925 formation of the automobile corporation named after him.

Industrialization brought with it urbanization; the census of 1920 for the first time showed a majority of Michiganians living in towns and cities. Nearly all industrial development was concentrated in the southern third of the state, particularly the southeastern area, around Detroit. The northern two-thirds of the state, where nothing took up the slack left by the decline in lumber and mining output, steadily lost population and became increasingly troubled economically. Meanwhile, the Republican Party, under such progressive governors as Fred Warner and Chase Osborn—and, in the 1920s, under a brilliant administrator, Alexander Groesbeck—showed itself far better able than the Democratic opposition to adjust to the complexities of a booming industrial economy.

The onset of the depression of the 1930s had devastating effects in Michigan. The market for automobiles collapsed; by 1932, half of Michigan's industrial workers were unemployed. The ineffectiveness of the Republican state and federal governments during the crisis led to a landslide victory for the Democrats. In traditionally Republican areas of rural Michigan, the defection to the Democratic Party in 1932 was only temporary, but in the urban industrial areas, the faith of the factory workers in the Republican Party was, for the great majority, permanently shaken. These workers, driven by the desire for greater job security, joined the recruiting campaign launched by the new Congress of Industrial Organizations (CIO). By 1941, with the capitulation of Ford Motor, the United Automobile Workers (UAW) had organized the entire auto industry, and Michigan had been converted to a strongly pro-union state.

Eventually, the liberal leadership of the UAW and of other CIO unions in the state allied itself with the Democratic Party to provide the funds and organization the party needed to mobilize worker support. The coalition elected G. Mennen Williams governor in 1948 and reelected him for five successive two-year terms. By the mid-1950s, the Democrats controlled virtually all statewide elective offices. Because legislative apportionment still reflected an earlier distribution of population, however, the Republicans maintained their control of the legislature and frustrated the efforts of the Williams administration to institute social reforms. In the 1960s, as a result of US Supreme Court

rulings, the legislature was reapportioned on a strictly equal-population basis. This shifted a majority of legislative seats into urban areas, enabling the Democrats generally to control the legislature at that time.

In the meantime, Republican moderates, led by George Romney, gained control of their party's organization. Romney was elected governor in 1962 and served until 1969, when he was succeeded by William G. Milliken, who held the governorship for 14 years. When Milliken chose not to run in the 1982 election, the statehouse was captured by the Democrats, ending 20 years of Republican rule. The new governor, James J. Blanchard, faced the immediate tasks of saving Michigan from bankruptcy and reducing the unemployment rate, which had averaged more than 15% in 1982 (60% above the US average).

The nationwide recession of the early 1980s hit Michigan harder than most other states because of its effect on the auto industry, which had already suffered heavy losses primarily as a result of its own inability to foresee the demise of the big luxury cars and because of the increasing share of the American auto market captured by foreign, mostly Japanese, manufacturers. In 1979, Chrysler had been forced to obtain $1.2 billion in federally guaranteed loans to stave off bankruptcy, and during the late 1970s and the first two years of the 1980s, US automakers were forced to lay off hundreds of thousands of workers, tens of thousands of whom left the state. Many smaller businesses, dependent on the auto industry, closed their doors, adding to the unemployment problem and to the state's fiscal problem; as the tax base shrank, state revenues plummeted, creating a budget deficit of nearly $1 billion. Two months after he took office in January 1983, Governor Blanchard was forced to institute budget cuts totaling $225 million and lay off thousands of government workers; at his urging, the state legislature increased Michigan's income tax by 38%.

As the recession eased in 1983, Michigan's economy showed some signs of improvement. The automakers became profitable, and Chrysler was even able to repay its $1.2 billion in loans seven years before it was due, rehire 100,000 workers, and make plans to build a $500-million technological center in the northern Detroit suburb of Auburn Hills. By May 1984, Michigan's unemployment rate had begun to drop, but the state faced the difficult task of restructuring its economy to lessen its dependence on the auto industry.

By the late 1980s, there were signs that Michigan had succeeded in diversifying its economy. Fewer than one in four wage earners worked in factories in 1988, a drop from 30% in 1978. Despite continued layoffs and plant closings by auto manufacturers between 1982 and 1988, Michigan added half a million more jobs than it lost. Many of the new jobs were in small engineering and applied technology companies, which found opportunities in the big manufacturers' efforts to automate. The state established a $100-million job retraining program to upgrade the skills of displaced factory workers, and contributed $5 million to a joint job training program created by General Motors and the United Automobile Workers. In the mid-1990s, the manufacture of transportation equipment was still Michigan's most important industry, with 28% of domestic automobiles produced in the state. Employment, wages, exports, and housing starts were all on the rise.

In the late 1990s prosperity across the nation had boosted Americans' appetite for new automobiles, including gas-guzzling sports utility vehicles. Combined with sales of other light trucks, SUVs bolstered the Big Three, now leaner and more competitive than in the pre-recession era. In 1998 Chrysler Corporation merged with German-based Daimler-Benz to form DaimlerChrysler, with headquarters in Michigan and Germany. Construction in the state was boosted by numerous road improvement projects during the late 1990s, a new Northwest Airlines terminal at Detroit Metropolitan Airport, voter-approved casinos in Detroit, and demand for new housing. In 1999, the robust economy had resulted in a low unemployment rate of 3.8%. In 2000 the state led the nation in home ownership, exceeding the national average by as much as 10%.

Republican Governor John Engler, first elected in 1990 and winning his third term in 1998, aggressively courted business during his administration. He was criticized by some for doing so at the expense of the state's environment. Engler had also, early on, garnered intense opposition to his plan to cut the state's welfare role. Nevertheless, he continued to be reelected. Among the state's challenges in 2000 were education reform (and the question of school vouchers), preserving farmlands in the face of development and urban sprawl, and, in conjunction with neighboring states and Canada, further clean-up and conservation of the Great Lakes system.

In 2002, Jennifer Granholm was elected Michigan's first female governor and the first Democrat to win the office since John Engler took office. In her 2003 State of the State Address, Granholm pledged to balance the state's budget (the state had a $1.8 billion deficit for fiscal year 2003/04), planned to create a corridor to attract technology companies to Michigan (particularly in the biotech and pharmaceutical sectors), to support education, and to purchase prescription drugs in bulk.

Michigan was one of the states affected by the 14 August 2003 massive power blackout in Canada, the Northeast and mid-western states. The largest electrical outage in US history affected 9,300 square miles and a population of over 50 million.

12 STATE GOVERNMENT

Michigan has had four constitutions. The first, adopted in 1835 when Michigan was applying for statehood, was followed by constitutions adopted in 1850, 1908, and 1963. By January 2003, there were 23 amendments.

The legislature consists of a senate of 38 members, elected for terms of four years, and a house of representatives of 110 members, elected for two-year terms. The legislature meets annually, beginning the 2nd Wednesday of January, for a session of indeterminate length. Special sessions may only be called by the governor. Legislation may be adopted by a majority of each house, but to override a governor's veto a two-thirds vote of the elected and serving members of each house is required. A legislator must be at least 21 years old, a US citizen, and a qualified voter of the district in which he or she resides. The legislative salary was $77,400 in 2002.

Elected executive officials include the governor and lieutenant governor (who run jointly), secretary of state, and attorney general, all serving four-year terms. Elections are held in even-numbered years between US presidential elections. The governor and lieutenant governor must be at least 30 years old and must have been registered voters in the state for at least four years prior to election. In 2002 the governor's salary was $177,000. The governor, who is limited to serving two consecutive terms, appoints the members of the governing boards and/or directors of executive departments, with the exception of the Department of Education, whose head is appointed by the elected State Board of Education. The trustees of Michigan State University, the University of Michigan, and Wayne State University are also elected by the state's voters. Trustees serve eight-year terms.

Legislative action is completed when a bill has been passed by both houses of the legislature and signed by the governor. A bill also becomes law if not signed by the governor after a 14-day period when the legislature is in session. The governor may stop passage of a bill by vetoing it or, if the legislature adjourns before the 14-day period expires, by refusing to sign it.

The constitution may be amended by a two-thirds vote of both houses of the legislature and a majority vote at the next general election. An amendment also may be proposed by registered voters through petition and submission to the general electorate; the petition must be signed by 10% of total voters for all candidates at the last gubernatorial election. Every 16 years, the question of calling a convention to revise the constitution must be submitted to the voters; the question was put on the ballot in 1978 and was rejected.

A voter in Michigan must be a US citizen, at least 18 years old, and must have been a resident of the state and city or township for 30 days prior to election day. Those confined to jail after conviction and sentencing are ineligible to vote.

13 POLITICAL PARTIES

From its birth in 1854 through 1932, the Republican Party dominated state politics, rarely losing statewide elections and developing strong support in all parts of the state, both rural and urban. The problems caused by the economic depression of the 1930s revitalized the Democratic Party and made Michigan a strong two-party state. Democratic strength was concentrated in metropolitan Detroit, while Republicans maintained their greatest strength in "outstate" areas, except for the mining regions of the upper peninsula, where the working class, hit hard by the depression, supported the Democrats.

Most labor organizations, led by the powerful United Automobile Workers union, have generally supported the Democratic Party since the 1930s. But in recent years, moderate Republicans have had considerable success in attracting support among previously Democratic voters.

Among minor parties, only Theodore Roosevelt's Progressive Party, which captured the state's electoral vote in 1912, has succeeded in winning a statewide contest. George Wallace captured 10% of the total vote cast for president in 1968; Ross Perot almost doubled that showing in 1992 with 19% of the vote.

Between 1948 and 1992, the Republican candidate for president carried Michigan in nine out of 13 elections, but Michiganians gave Democrat Bill Clinton 44% of the vote in 1992 and 52% in 1996. In 2000, Democrat Al Gore received 51% of the presidential vote to Republican George W. Bush's 47%. Green Party candidate Ralph Nader won 2%. The state had 18 electoral votes in the 2000 presidential election.

In the 1994 mid-term elections, Republican governor John Engler was reelected. Engler was voted in again in 1998, beginning a third term, which expired in January 2003. (Michigan limits its governors to serving two consecutive terms, but the law became effective after Engler's election, so he was grandfathered.) In November 2002, Democrat Jennifer Granholm became Michigan's first female governor. In 2002 there were 6,797,293 registered voters; there is no party registration in the state.

Four-term Democratic Senator Carl Levin was reelected in 2002. Republican Spencer Abraham was elected to the Senate in 1994, replacing retiring Democrat Donald Riegel. Abraham sought a second term in 2000, but failed to win reelection. He was named President George W. Bush's Secretary of Energy in 2001. After the 2002 elections, the state's 15-member US House delegation consisted of six Democrats and nine Republicans. On the state level, in mid-2003 there were 22 Democrats and 16 Republicans in the senate, and 47 Democrats and 63 Republicans in the house.

14 LOCAL GOVERNMENT

In 2002 there were 2,804 separate units of local government in Michigan, including 83 counties, 533 municipal governments, 1,242 townships, 580 public school districts, and 366 special districts. Each county is administered by a county board of commissioners whose members, ranging in number from 3 to 35 according to population, are elected for two-year terms. Executive authority is vested in officers (the sheriff, prosecuting attorney, treasurer, clerk, and register of deeds), who are generally elected for four-year terms. Some counties place overall administrative responsibility in the hands of a county manager or administrator.

Most cities are governed by home-rule legislation, adopted in 1909, enabling them to establish their own form of government under an adopted charter. Some charters provide for the election of a mayor, who usually functions as the chief executive officer of the city. Other cities have chosen the council-manager system. with a council appointing the manager to serve as chief executive and the office of mayor being largely ceremonial. Many villages are incorporated under home-rule legislation in order to provide services such as police and fire protection.

Township government, its powers strictly limited by state law, consists of a supervisor, clerk, treasurer, and up to four trustees, all elected for four-year terms and together forming the township board.

15STATE SERVICES

To address the continuing threat of terrorism and to work with the federal Department of Homeland Security (created in 2002 following the terrorist attacks of 11 September 2001), homeland security in Michigan in 2003 operated under the authority of the executive order; the state police director was designated as the state homeland security advisor.

Educational services are handled in part by the Department of Education, which distributes state school-aid funds, certifies teachers, and operates the School for the Deaf at Flint, the School for the Blind at Lansing, the State Technical Institute and Rehabilitation Center at Plainwell, and the state library system. The 13 state-supported colleges and universities are independent of the department's control, each being governed by an elected or appointed board. Although most of the funds administered by the Department of Transportation go for highway construction and maintenance, some allocations support improvements of railroad, bus, ferry, air, and port services.

Health and welfare services are provided by the Department of Community Health, the Department of Metal Health, the Family Independence Agency, and the Department of Civil Rights, as well as through programs administered by the Department of Labor, the Commission on Services to the Aging, the Department of Environmental Quality, the Michigan Women's Commission, the Indian Affairs Commission, the Spanish-Speaking Affairs Commission, and the Veterans Trust Fund. The state's Army and Air National Guard units are maintained by the Department of Military Affairs. Civil defense is part of the Department of State Police, and state prisons and other correctional facilities are maintained by the Department of Corrections.

Housing services are provided by the State Housing Development Authority. The Department of Labor establishes and enforces rules and standards relating to safety, wages, licenses, fees, and conditions of employment Security Commission administers unemployment benefits and assists job seekers.

16JUDICIAL SYSTEM

Michigan's highest court is the state supreme court, consisting of seven justices elected for eight-year terms; the chief justice is elected by the members of the court. The high court hears cases on appeal from lower state courts and also administers the state's entire court system. The 1963 constitution provided for an 18-member court of appeals to handle most of the cases that previously had clogged the high court's calendar. Unless the supreme court agrees to review a court of appeals ruling, the latter's decision is final. As of 1999, 28 appeals court justices are elected from each of four districts for six-year terms. The supreme court appoints a chief judge of the appeals court.

The major trial courts in the state as of 1999 were the circuit courts, encompassing 210 judicial seats, with the judges elected for six-year terms. The circuit courts have original jurisdiction in all felony criminal cases, civil cases involving sums of more than $10,000, and divorces. As of January 1998, the circuit courts have a "family" division to better serve families and individuals.

Michigan Presidential Vote by Political Parties, 1948–2000

YEAR	ELECTORAL VOTE	MICHIGAN WINNER	DEMOCRAT	REPUBLICAN	PROGRESSIVE	SOCIALIST	PROHIBITION
1948	19	Dewey (R)	1,003,448	1,038,595	46,515	6,063	13,052
						SOC. WORKERS	
1952	20	*Eisenhower (R)	1,230,657	1,551,529	3,922	655	10,331
1956	20	*Eisenhower (R)	1,359,898	1,713,647	—	—	6,923
					SOC. LABOR		
1960	20	*Kennedy (D)	1,687,269	1,620,428	1,718	4,347	2,029
1964	21	*Johnson (D)	2,136,615	1,060,152	1,704	3,817	
							AMERICAN IND.
1968	21	Humphrey (D)	1,593,082	1,370,665	1,762	4,099	331,968
							AMERICAN
1972	21	*Nixon (R)	1,459,435	1,961,721	2,437	1,603	63,321
					PEOPLE'S		LIBERTARIAN
1976	21	Ford (R)	1,696,714	1,893,742	3,504	1,804	5,406
					CITIZENS	COMMUNIST	
1980	21	*Reagan (R)	1,661,532	1,915,225	11,930	3,262	41,597
1984	20	*Reagan (R)	1,529,638	2,251,571	1,191	—	10,055
					NEW ALLIANCE	WORKERS LEAGUE	
1988	20	*Bush (R)	1,675,783	1,965,486	2,513	1,958	18,336
					IND. (PEROT)	TISCH IND. CITIZENS	
1992	18	*Clinton (D)	1,871,182	1,554,940	824,813	8,263	10,175
1996	18	*Clinton (D)	1,989,653	1,481,212	336,670	—	27,670
						GREEN	
2000	18	Gore (D)	2,170,418	1,953,139	—	84,165	16,711

*Won US presidential election

The circuit courts also hear appeals from lower courts and state administrative agencies. Probate courts have original jurisdiction in cases involving juveniles and dependents, and also handle wills and estates, adoptions, and commitments of the mentally ill. The 1963 constitution provided for the abolition of justice-of-the-peace courts and nearly all municipal courts, although the Detroit "Recorders Court" was not abolished until 1996 in a controversial move supported by the Republican governor and legislative majority but opposed by most Democratic leaders. To replace them, 101 district courts, some consisting of two or more divisions, have been established. These courts handle civil cases involving sums of less than $10,000, minor criminal violations, and preliminary examinations in all felony cases.

Prisoners in state or federal correctional facilities numbered 48,371 in June 2001, an increase of 2.2% over the previous year. The state's incarceration rate stood at 484 per 100,000 inhabitants. Detroit received adverse publicity during the 1970s as the "murder capital of the world," with more murders and other violent crimes than any other US city. Violent crimes (murder, non-negligent manslaughter, forcible rape, and aggravated assault) reached a peak of 2,226 offenses per 100,000 population in 1976. Michigan had an overall 2001 crime rate of 4,081.5 per 100,000 population, including a rate of 554.7 for violent crime and 3,526.8 for property crime.

In 1846, Michigan became the first state to abolish capital punishment, and recent efforts to restore capital punishment have failed.

[17]ARMED FORCES

In 2002, there were 1,173 active-duty military personnel and 8,038 civilian personnel in Michigan. The Detroit Arsenal at Warren is the state's largest center for civilians. In 2001 Michigan firms received over $2.28 billion in defense contracts.

As of 2002, there were 913,573 veterans of US military service living in Michigan. Of these, 186,516 served in World War II; 118,636 in the Korean conflict; 276,749 during the Vietnam era, and during 1990–2000 (including the Persian Gulf War), 82,180. Veterans' benefits exceeded $855 million in 2002.

In 2000, the Michigan State Police employed 2,102 full-time sworn officers.

[18]MIGRATION

The earliest European immigrants were the French and English. The successive opening of interior lands for farming, lumbering, mining, and manufacturing proved an irresistible attraction for hundreds of thousands of immigrants after the War of 1812, principally Germans, Canadians, English, Irish, and Dutch. During the second half of the 19th century, lumbering and mining opportunities in northern Michigan attracted large numbers of Cornishmen, Norwegians, Swedes, and Finns. The growth of manufacturing in southern Michigan at the end of the century brought many Poles, Italians, Russians, Belgians, and Greeks to the state. After World War II, many more Europeans immigrated to Michigan, plus smaller groups of Mexicans, other Spanish-speaking peoples from Latin America, and large numbers of Arabic-speaking peoples, particularly in Detroit, who by the late 1970s were more numerous there than in any other US city.

The first large domestic migration into Michigan came in the early 19th century after the War of 1812. Heavy immigration took place in the 1920s and 1930s, especially from northeastern states, particularly New York and Pennsylvania, and from Ohio. Beginning in 1916, the demand for labor in Michigan's factories started the second major domestic migration to Michigan, this time by southern blacks who settled mainly in Detroit, Flint, Pontiac, Grand Rapids, and Saginaw. During World War II, many southern whites migrated to the same industrial areas. Between 1940 and 1970, a net total of 518,000 migrants were drawn to

Michigan. The economic problems of the auto industry in the 1970s and 1980s caused a significant reversal of this trend, with the state suffering a net loss of 496,000 by out-migration in the 1970s and over 460,000 in the 1980s. Between 1990 and 1998, Michigan had a net loss of 190,000 in domestic migration and a net gain of 87,000 in international migration. In 1996, Michigan's foreign-born population totaled 491,000, or 5% of its total population. In 1998, 13,943 foreign immigrants entered the state, the 11th-highest total for any state that year. Michigan's overall population increased 5.6% between 1990 and 1998. In the period 1995–2000, 467,638 people moved into the state and 559,568 moved out, for a net loss of 91,930, 21,949 of whom were age 65 or over. A total of about 74,949 moved from Michigan to Florida.

Intrastate migration has been characterized since the late 19th century by a steady movement from rural to urban areas. Most parts of northern Michigan have suffered a loss of population since the early years of this century although a back-to-the-land movement, together with the growth of rural Michigan as a retirement area, appeared to reverse this trend beginning in the 1970s. Since 1950, the central cities have experienced a steady loss of population to the suburbs, in part caused by the migration of whites from areas that were becoming increasingly black. By 1998, Michigan's black population numbered 1,405,000, of whom over 1,100,000 lived in the Detroit–Ann Arbor–Flint metropolitan area.

[19]INTERGOVERNMENTAL COOPERATION

The Commission on Intergovernmental Cooperation of the Michigan legislature represents the state in dealings with the Council of State Governments and its allied organizations. Since 1935, the state has joined at least 21 interstate compacts, dealing mainly with such subjects as gas and oil problems, law enforcement, pest control, civil defense, tax reciprocity, and water resources. Compacts include the Boundary Compact Between Minnesota, Wisconsin, and Michigan; Interstate Compact for Juveniles, and the Great Lakes Commission. In 1985, Michigan, seven other Great Lakes states, and the Canadian provinces of Quebec and Ontario signed the Great Lakes Charter, designed to protect the lakes' water resources.

The International Bridge Authority, consisting of members from Michigan and Canada, operates a toll bridge connecting Sault Ste. Marie, Mich., and Sault Ste. Marie, Ontario. Federal grants to Michigan totaled close to $10.9 billion in 2001.

[20]ECONOMY

On the whole, Michigan benefited from its position as the center of the auto industry during the first half of the 20th century when Detroit and other south Michigan cities were the fastest-growing industrial areas in the US. But the state's dependence on automobile production has caused grave and persistent economic problems since the 1950s. Michigan's unemployment rates in times of recession have far exceeded the national average, since auto sales are among the hardest hit in such periods. Even in times of general prosperity, the auto industry's emphasis on labor-saving techniques and its shifting of operation from the state have reduced the number of jobs available to Michigan workers. Although the state was relatively prosperous during the record automotive production years of the 1960s and 1970s, the high cost of gasoline and the encroachment of imports on domestic car sales had disastrous effects by 1980, when it became apparent that the state's future economic health required greater diversification of industry. Agriculture, still dominant in the rural areas of southern Michigan, remains an important element in the state's economy, and in northern Michigan, forestry and mining continue but generally at levels far below earlier boom periods. Output from manufactures peaked in 1999 at close to $84 billion, about 27% of gross state product, but in 2001, after an 11.85% fall from 2000 levels, manufacturing output accounted for only 23.1% of gross state product. By contrast, services of various sorts accounted for over 70% of total output in 2001. In 2002, Michigan lagged the national economy, and was not expected to recover in the short-term, while it manufacturing sector goes through restructuring.

Michigan's gross state product in 2001 was the 9th largest among the states at $320.5 billion, to which manufacturing contributed $73.9 billion; general services, $66.4 billion; trade, $54 billion; financial services, $50.3 billion; government, $35.2 billion, transportation and public utilities, $20.8 billion; and construction, $16 billion. The public sector constituted 11% of gross state product in 2001.

21INCOME

According to the Bureau of Economic Analysis, in 2001, Michigan had a per capita personal income (PCPI) of $29,629 which ranked 19th in the United States (including the District of Columbia) and was 97% of the national average, $30,413. The 2001 PCPI reflected an increase of 0.8% from 2000 compared to the national change of 2.2%. In 2001, Michigan had a total personal income (TPI) of $296,480,397,000 which ranked 9th in the United States and accounted for 3.4% of the national total. The 2001 TPI reflected an increase of 1.3% from 2000 compared to the national change of 3.3%.

Earnings of persons employed in Michigan decreased from $213,701,415,000 in 2000 to $211,954,612,000 in 2001, a decrease of 0.8%. The largest industries in 2001 were services, 26.0% of earnings; durable goods manufacturing, 21.8%; and state and local government, 11.8%. Of the industries that accounted for at least 5% of earnings in 2001, the slowest growing from 2000 to 2001 was durable goods manufacturing, which decreased 8.4%; the fastest was finance, insurance, and real estate (5.9% of earnings in 2001), which increased 6.0%.

According to data released by the US Census Bureau, in 2000, the median household income was $46,181 compared to the national average of $42,148. In 2001, the median income for a family of four was $68,337 compared to the national average of $63,278. For the period 1999 to 2001, the average poverty rate was 9.7% which placed it 17th among the 50 states and the District of Columbia ranked lowest to highest.

22LABOR

According to Bureau of Labor Statistics (BLS) provisional estimates, in July 2003 the seasonally adjusted civilian labor force in Michigan numbered 5,130,300, with approximately 377,600 workers unemployed, yielding an unemployment rate of 7.4%, compared to the national average of 6.2% for the same period. Since the beginning of the BLS data series in 1978, the highest unemployment rate recorded was 16.3% in November 1982. The historical low was 3.1% in March 2000. In 2001, an estimated 5.1% of the labor force was employed in construction; 21.5% in manufacturing; 3.7% in transportation, communications, and public utilities; 19.6% in trade; 5.0% in finance, insurance, and real estate; 24.7% in services; 12.5% in government; and 1.9% in agriculture.

Michigan's most powerful and influential industrial union since the 1930s has been the United Automobile Workers (UAW); its national headquarters is in Detroit. Under its long-time president Walter Reuther and his successors, Leonard Woodcock, Douglas Fraser, Owen Bieber, and Stephen Yokich, the union has been a dominant force in the state Democratic Party. In recent years, as government employees and teachers have been organized, unions and associations representing these groups have become increasingly influential. Under the Michigan Public

Employment Relations Act of 1965, public employees have the right to organize and to engage in collective bargaining, but are prohibited from striking. However, strikes of teachers, college faculty members, and government employees have been common since the 1960s, and little or no effort was made to enforce the law.

Certain crafts and trades were organized in Michigan in the 19th century, with one national labor union, the Brotherhood of Locomotive Engineers, having been founded at meetings in Michigan in 1863, but efforts to organize workers in the lumber and mining industries were generally unsuccessful. Michigan acquired a reputation as an open-shop state, and factory workers showed little interest in unions at a time when wages were high. But the catastrophic impact of the depression of the 1930s completely changed these attitudes. With the support of sympathetic state and federal government officials, Michigan workers were in the forefront of the greatest labor-organizing drive in American history. The successful sit-down strike by the United Automobile Workers against General Motors in 1936–37 marked the first major victory of the new Congress of Industrial Organizations. Since then, a strong labor movement has provided manufacturing workers in Michigan with some of the most favorable working conditions in the country.

The US Department of Labor reported that in 2002, 914,000 of Michigan's 4,335,000 employed wage and salary workers were members of unions. This represented 21.1% of those so employed, down from 21.7% in 2001 and from 22.6% in 1998. The national average is 13.2%. Michigan is one of only four states with a union membership rate over 20%. In all, 953,000 workers (22.0%) were represented by unions. In addition to union members, this category includes workers who report no union affiliation but whose jobs are covered by a union contract.

23AGRICULTURE

In 2001, Michigan's agricultural income was estimated at nearly $3.5 billion, placing Michigan 24th among the 50 states. About 57% came from crops and the rest from livestock and livestock products; dairy products, nursery products, cattle, corn, and soybeans were the principal commodities. The state in 2002 ranked 2nd in output of tart cherries, 3rd in apples, and 4th in prunes and plums.

The growing of corn and other crops indigenous to North America was introduced in Michigan by the Indians around 100 BC, and early French settlers tried to develop European-style agriculture during the colonial era. But little progress was made until well into the 19th century, when farmers from New York and New England poured into the interior of southern Michigan. By mid-century, 34,000 farms had been established, and the number increased to a peak of about 207,000 in 1910. The major cash crop at first was wheat, until soil exhaustion, insect infestations, bad winters, and competition from huge wheat farms to the west forced a de-emphasis on wheat and a move toward agricultural diversity. Both the number of farms and the amount of farm acreage had declined by 2002 to 52,000 farms and 10,400,000 acres (4,200,000 hectares).

The southern half of the lower peninsula is the principal agricultural region, and the area along Lake Michigan is a leader in fruit growing. Potatoes are profitable in northern Michigan, while eastern Michigan (the "Thumb" area near Lake Huron) is a leading bean producer. The Saginaw Valley leads the state in sugar beets. The south-central and southeastern counties are major centers of soybean production. Leading field crops in 2002 included 232,300,000 bushels of corn for grain, valued at $534,290,000; 73,710,000 bushels of soybeans, worth $386,978,000; and 30,780,000 bushels of wheat, worth

$78,155,000. Output of commercial apples totaled 500,000,000 lb (227,000,000 kg).

24ANIMAL HUSBANDRY

The same areas of southern Michigan that lead in crop production also lead in livestock and livestock products, except that the northern counties are more favorable for dairying than for crop production.

In 2003, there were an estimated 990,000 cattle and calves, valued at $871.2 million. The state had an estimated 860,000 hogs and pigs in 2002, valued at $68.8 million.

In 2001, dairy farmers had an estimated 303,000 milk cows which produced around 5.6 million lb (2.5 million kg) of milk. Poultry farmers produced nearly 1.7 billion eggs, valued at around $61 million, in 2001.

25FISHING

Commercial fishing, once an important factor in the state's economy, is relatively minor today; the commercial catch in 1998 was 14,831,000 lb (6,727,00 kg) valued at $8,862,000. Principal species landed are silver salmon and alewives.

Sport fishing continues to flourish and is one of the state's major tourist attractions. A state salmon-planting program, begun in the mid-1960s, has made salmon the most popular game fish for Great Lakes sport fishermen. The state has also sought, through breeding and stocking programs, to bring back the trout, which was devastated by an invasion of lamprey. In 1998, the state issued 1,346,910 sport fishing licenses.

A bitter dispute raged during the 1970s between state officials and Ottawa and Ojibwa commercial fishermen, who claimed that Indian treaties with the federal government exempted them from state fishing regulations. The state contended that without such regulations, Indian commercial fishing would have a devastating impact on the northern Great Lakes' fish population. A federal court in 1979 upheld the Indians' contention; but in 1985, the state secured federal court approval of a compromise settlement intended to satisfy both Indian and non-Indian groups.

26FORESTRY

In 2002, Michigan's forestland totaled 19.3 million acres (7.8 million hectares), or more than half the state's total land area. Approximately 96% of it is classified as timberland, about two-thirds of it privately owned. The major forested regions are in the northern two-thirds of the state, where great pine forests enabled Michigan to become the leading lumber-producing state in the last four decades of the 19th century. These cutover lands regenerated naturally or were reforested in the 20th century. Lumber production was 744 million board feet in 2002.

State and national forests covered 6.9 million acres (2.8 million hectares), or about one-fifth of the state's land area.

27MINING

Nonfuel mineral production was valued at an estimated $1.62 billion in 2001 in Michigan, up 1% from 2000. The state ranked 6th nationally in value of nonfuel minerals produced during 2001, accounting for more than 4% of the national total. Michigan was first nationally in magnesium chloride produced and ranked 2nd in the production of peat, industrial sand and gravel, bromine, and iron ore (after Minnesota). It ranked 3rd in construction sand and gravel and potash; 4th in portland cement; and 7th in masonry cement. According to preliminary figures, in 2001, the production of 5.8 million metric tons of portland cement was worth $452 million. Over 77 million metric tons of construction sand and gravel were valued at $279 million. Crushed stone production, at 42.5 million metric tons, was worth $154 million.

Diamond, copper, and gold exploration have been conducted in the Upper Peninsula, and natural gas exploration in Crawford, Montmorency, Oscoda, and Otsego counties.

28ENERGY AND POWER

Michigan's energy supply is provided primarily by private utility companies. In 2000, energy consumption per capita totaled 314 million Btu (79.1 million kcal), which ranked Michigan 36th among the 50 states. Coal is the principal source of fuel used in generating electric power, while natural gas is the major fuel used for other energy needs.

The installed electric generating capacity of electric utilities and industrial plants in 1999 was 25.5 million kW; total electric energy production totaled 103.4 billion kWh. Hydroelectric plants, which had produced more than 10% of the state's electric energy in 1947, yielded less than 0.5% in 1999; coal-fired steam units produced 68%, nuclear-powered units 14%, gas-fired generators 13%, and other units less than 5%. As of 2001, Michigan had four operating nuclear reactors, two at the Donald C. Cook plant in Berrion County, one at the Enrico Fermi plant near Detroit, and one at the Palisades facility near South Haven.

The two major electric utilities are Detroit Edison, serving the Detroit area and portions of the eastern part of the lower peninsula, and Consumers Power, serving most of the remainder of the lower peninsula. Rates of the utility companies are set by the Public Service Commission.

Michigan is dependent on outside sources for most of its fuel needs. Petroleum production in 2000 totaled 20,000 barrels per day; natural gas marketed production in 2002 was 275.4 billion cu ft (7.8 billion cu m), less than one-fourth of the natural gas consumed in the state. Proved petroleum reserves were 46 million barrels at the end of 2001, natural gas reserves, 3 trillion cu ft (0.08 trillion cu m). Bituminous coal reserves (estimated at 127.7 million tons) remain in southern Michigan, but production is negligible.

29INDUSTRY

Manufacturing, a minor element in Michigan's economy in the mid-19th century, grew rapidly in importance until, by 1900, an estimated 25% of the state's jobholders were factory workers. The rise of the auto industry in the early 20th century completed the transformation of Michigan into one of the most important manufacturing areas in the world. In 1997, the value of shipments totaled $218 billion.

Motor vehicles and equipment dominate the state's economy, representing more than one-fourth of the state's manufacturing payroll; the value of shipments by automotive manufacturers was almost half of the total. Production of nonelectrical machinery, primary and fabricated metal products, and metal forgings and stampings was directly related to automobile production.

The Detroit metropolitan area is the major industrial region: this area includes not only the heavy concentration of auto-related plants in Wayne, Oakland, and Macomb counties, but also major steel, chemical, and pharmaceutical industries, among others. Flint, Grand Rapids, Saginaw, Ann Arbor, Lansing, and Kalamazoo are other major industrial centers.

Because the auto industry's "Big Three"—General Motors (GM), Ford, and Chrysler—have their headquarters in the Detroit area, Michigan has had for many years three of the nation's largest industrial corporations. In 2000, General Motors was the leader among all manufacturers in the world. In 1997, Michigan hosted the headquarters of 14 Fortune 500 companies, including General Motors, Ford, and Chrysler (ranked 1st, 2nd, and 9th, respectively).

The auto industry's preponderance in Michigan manufacturing has come to be viewed in recent years as more of a liability than an asset. When times are good, as they were in the 1960s and early 1970s, automobile sales soar to record levels and Michigan's economy prospers. But when the national economy slumps, these sales plummet, pushing the state into a far deeper recession than is felt by the nation as a whole. Michigan is the top vehicle manufacturing state in the nation, accounting for 23% of all US car and truck production in 1998. It made 31% of the automobiles produced for the US that year and 16.5% of the trucks.

Earnings of persons employed in Michigan increased from $181.9 billion in 1997 to $192 billion in 1998, an increase of 5.6%. The largest industries in 1998 were durable goods manufacturing, 24.8% of earnings; services, 24.2%; and state and local government, 11.3%. Of the industries that accounted for at least 5% of earnings in 1998, the slowest growing from 1997 to 1998 was nondurable goods manufacturing (6.4% of earnings in 1998), which increased 2.9%; the fastest was construction (5.3% of earnings in 1998), which increased 8.3%.

30COMMERCE

In 1997, Michigan had 16,060 wholesale establishments, with sales of $165 billion. Leading categories were motor vehicles and automobile parts and supplies (accounting for nearly one-fifth of all sales by value), groceries, metals and minerals, and machinery.

In 1997, Michigan's 55,276 retail establishments had sales of $97 billion, 7th among the states. The Detroit–Ann Arbor–Flint area had retail sales accounting for about half of the state's total. The importance of retail sales to the economy was greatest in northern Michigan. Of the total, food stores accounted for 12% of all establishments; automotive dealers and service stations, 13%; and restaurants and bars, 30%. Retail sales in food stores came to $13 billion in 1997 while general merchandise sales came to $16 billion.

With its ports open to oceangoing vessels through the St. Lawrence Seaway, Michigan is a major exporting and importing state for foreign as well as domestic markets. Exports of Michigan's manufactured goods totaled $29 billion in 1998, 5th in the US.

31CONSUMER PROTECTION

The Michigan Consumer's Council—composed of the attorney general, secretary of state, director of the Department of Commerce, and three members appointed by the governor and three by the legislature—was established in 1966 to protect consumers from harmful products, false advertising, and deceptive sales practices. The Council was dissolved in 1990 as a budget-cutting measure. Other state agencies, such as the Attorney General and the Public Service Commission, also are responsible for protecting consumers.

A number of local governments have instituted consumer affairs offices, with Detroit's being especially active.

32BANKING

Michigan's banks in the territorial and early statehood years were generally wildcat speculative ventures. More restrained banking activities date from the 1840s when the state's oldest bank, the Detroit Bank and Trust, was founded. A crisis that developed in the early 1930s forced Governor William Comstock to close all banks in February 1933 in order to prevent collapse of the entire banking system. Federal and state authorities supervised a reorganization and reform of the state's banks that has succeeded in preventing any major problems from arising since that time.

There were 180 insured banks in 2002, with assets of $166.9 billion. One hundred thirty-three of those banks were state-chartered. Banks with less than $1 billion in assets ("community banks") account for 82% of the state's insured institutions, but larger banks hold 80% of the state's assets. Community banks in

2002 had relatively high net interest margins (NIMs) (the difference between the lower rates offered to savers and the higher rates charged on loans), largely due to higher loan levels, especially commercial and industrial (C and I) and commercial real estate (CRE) loans.

33INSURANCE

In 2001 there were 4.7 million ordinary life insurance policies in force with a total value of $300.2 billion; total value for all categories of life insurance (ordinary, group, industrial, and credit) was $556.1 billion. Death benefits paid that year totaled $1.84 billion. As of 2000, there were 70 property and casualty and 19 life and health insurance companies incorporated or organized in the state. In 2001, property and casualty insurers wrote premiums totaling $13.2 billion. That year, there were 24,527 flood insurance policies in force in the state, with a total value of $2.7 million.

34SECURITIES

There are no securities or commodity exchanges in Michigan. There are 1,320 securities dealers in the state, with 9,454 employees; 295 investment advisory organizations operate in Michigan. The state is home to 88 NASDAQ-listed companies, 3 market makers, 14 AMEX-listed companies; and has incorporated 43 NYSE-listed companies. The top five according to revenues are GM, Ford, K-Mart, Dow Chemical Co., Lear Corp., and Whirlpool.

35PUBLIC FINANCE

The state constitution requires the governor to submit a budget proposal to the legislature each year. This executive budget, prepared by the Department of Management and Budget, is reviewed, revised, and passed by the legislature. During the fiscal year, which extends from 1 October to 30 September, if actual revenues drop below anticipated levels, the governor, in consultation with the legislative appropriations committees, must reduce expenditures to meet the constitutional requirement that the state budget be kept in balance.

In 1977, the legislature created a budget stabilization fund; a portion of tax revenues collected in good times is held in reserve to be used during periods of recession, when the funding of essential state services is threatened. In 1978, a tax limitation amendment put a lid on government spending by establishing a fixed ratio of state revenues to personal income in the state. Further efforts to limit taxes were rejected by the voters in 1980 and 1984.

Tax cuts have taken place every year during the 1990s. Michigan's 2001 fiscal budget recommendation included a personal income tax reduction from 4.4% to 4.2% in 2000. Total revenues were forecast at $37 billion, of which 25% was to come from federal aid, 21% from income tax, 21% from sales and use taxes, and the remainder from other sources. General fund revenues were forecast at $9.6 billion, but the actual amount was only $8.702 billion, a $637 million shortfall. To cover the budget gap, the legislature among other steps made withdrawals from the state's $1 billion rainy day fund. In 2001/02, general fund revenues fell further, to $8.702 billion, and in 2002/03, to $8.299 billion. In 2002/03, Michigan's state budget deficit was estimated at about 6.5% of the state budget, and was projected to reach 19.6% of the state budget in 2003/04. Allocations from the general fund are distributed, by function, to education (about 38%), community health (23%), family independence agency (9.6%), transportation (8%), and general government (7%).

The following table from the US Census Bureau contains information on revenues, expenditures, indebtedness, and cash/securities for 2001.

	($000)	PERCENT	PER CAPITA
Population (thousands, 2001)	10,006	(X)	(X)
Total Revenue	43,346,782	100.00	4,332.08
General revenue	40,619,411	93.71	4,059.51
Utility revenue	–	–	–
Liquor store revenue	592,084	1.37	59.17
Insurance trust revenue	2,135,287	4.93	213.40
Exhibit: Salaries and wages	6,416,564	13.75	641.27
Total expenditure	46,657,684	100.00	4,662.97
General expenditure	42,252,320	90.56	4,222.70
Education	18,745,402	40.18	1,873.42
Public welfare	9,103,944	19.51	909.85
Hospitals	1,247,150	2.67	124.64
Health	2,721,049	5.83	271.94
Highways	2,688,407	5.76	268.68
Police protection	312,540	0.67	31.24
Correction	1,675,379	3.59	167.44
Natural resources	480,943	1.03	48.07
Parks and recreation	135,422	0.29	13.53
Government administration	879,136	1.88	87.86
Interest on general debt	1,059,004	2.27	105.84
Other and unallocable	3,203,944	6.87	320.20
Utility expenditure	–	–	–
Liquor store expenditure	485,475	1.04	48.52
Insurance trust expenditure	3,919,889	8.40	391.75
Debt at end of fiscal year	20,114,054	100.00	2,010.20
Cash and security holdings	78,142,349	100.00	7,809.55

36 TAXATION

Until the 1930s, Michigan relied mainly on the property tax for revenues to support both local and state governments. A state sales tax, first imposed in 1933, and a state income tax, first levied in 1967, are now the main sources of state revenues. Property taxes are reserved entirely to local governments.

The state income tax was 4% on taxable income for 2003, down from 4.2% in 2000 and 4.1% in 2001, and scheduled to be further reduced to 3.9% in 2004. There is no corporate income tax in Michigan, but there is a gross receipts tax which has also been gradually reduced since 1998, from 2.3% to 1.9% in 2002 on income over $45,000. In 1998, the gross receipts tax was set on a course of elimination in 23 years, decreasing 0.1% a year. However, if the Budget Stabilization Fund drops below $250 million, as was the case in 2002, the next rate reduction is cancelled. Companies must file if gross receipts are over $250,000 after a deduction of $45, 000. Financial institutions are assessed .10% of income. The state sales and use tax is 6% on most retail purchases, except food, medicines and some other basic goods. Local sales taxes are not permitted. The state also imposes a full array of excise taxes covering motor fuels, tobacco products, insurance premiums, public utilities, alcoholic beverages (the state controls all sales), amusements, pari-mutuels, and other selected items. In 2002, Michigan was one of 20 states to increase the tax on a pack of cigarettes, raising its excise from 75¢ a pack to $1.25 a pack. An estate tax ranging from 2% to 17% is levied on estates of more than $100, with the first $65,000 to the spouse and the first $10,000 to other close relatives being exempt. The Michigan estate tax is independent of the federal tax credit for state death taxes, and so is unaffected by the scheduled phase-out of the federal estate tax credit by 2007. Death and gift taxes accounted for 0.6% of state collections in 2002. Other state taxes include oil and gas severance taxes, various license fees, stamp taxes and state property taxes. Most property taxes are collected at the local level, although the tax system is relatively centralized, with the state collecting 65.5% of all state and local taxes in 2002.

The state collected $21.864 billion in taxes in 2002, of which 35.6% came from the general sales tax, 28% from individual income taxes, 10.4% from selective sales taxes, 9.4% from corporate income taxes, 8.6% from state property taxes, and 5.9% from license fees. In 2003, Michigan ranked 29th among the states in terms of state and local tax burden, which amounted to about 9.4% of income.

The following table from the US Census Bureau provides a summary of taxes collected by the state in 2002.

	($000)	PER CAPITA
Total Taxes	21,864,052	2,175.43
Property taxes	1,890,783	188.13
Sales and gross receipts	10,069,290	1,001.87
General sales and gross receipts	7,784,308	774.52
Selective sales taxes	2,284,982	227.35
Alcoholic beverage	138,310	13.76
Amusements	91,915	9.15
Insurance Premiums	227,081	22.59
Motor fuels	1,089,813	108.43
Pari-mutuels	12,481	1.24
Public utilities	25,005	2.49
Tobacco products	670,022	66.67
Other selective sales	30,355	3.02
Licenses	1,297,312	129.08
Alcoholic beverages	12,208	1.21
Amusements	(X)	(X)
Corporation	12,172	1.21
Hunting and fishing	49,047	4.88
Motor vehicle	890,951	88.65
Motor vehicle operators	43,136	4.29
Public utility	17,403	1.73
Occupation and business, NEC	223,085	22.2
Other	49,310	4.91
Other taxes	8,606,667	856.35
Individual income	6,125,270	609.45
Corporation net income	2,065,241	205.49
Death and gift	131,029	13.04
Documentary and stock transfer	253,075	25.18
Severance	31,688	3.15
Other	364	0.04

37 ECONOMIC POLICY

The Michigan Economic Development Corporation (MEDC) has a long tradition of promoting economic development. Through the Michigan Careersite web page, economic development and job training programs are outlined. The mission of MEDC is to work with businesses, state government, and local communities to make Michigan more business-friendly. MEDC is a corporation, not a traditional government agency. As of 2003, Michigan had ranked first in the country for new plants and expansions for five years in a row, according to Site Selection magazine.

Michigan is part of the so-called Rust Belt, the region of the country dominated by steel-based industries from the 1940s to the 1980s. To focus economic development on new industries, Michigan has taken a number of steps, including cutting taxes for individuals and businesses. In the 1990s, Michigan taxpayers, both individuals and businesses, benefited from 21 tax cuts. The result has been the 13th-lowest tax burden in the country for 2000 and a robust economy with unemployment levels lower than the national average since 1995.

Michigan's Economic Growth Authority offers generous tax breaks to firms that locate a facility in Michigan, and offers substantial employment opportunities to Michigan workers. The state's Renaissance Zone program exempts companies and individuals within designated areas throughout the state from all state and local taxes as an incentive to rebuild and revitalize specific areas. Renaissance Zones include urban, rural, and former military installation sites. In 2003, Michigan also had eleven designated Smart Zones, which are collaborations between universities, industry, research organizations, government, and other community institutions to stimulate growth of technology-based businesses, particularly those focused on commercializing ideas and patents that result from R&D efforts.

38HEALTH

Infant mortality for the 12 months ending with December 2000 was 8.2 per 1,000 live births. In 1999, 26,207 legal abortions were performed (down from 64,200 in 1982), or about 12 per 1,000 women.

Major causes of death in 2000 (with their rates per 100,000 population) included heart disease, 275.5; cerebrovascular diseases, 59.1; accidents and adverse effects, 32.5; motor vehicle accidents, 15.2; and suicide, 9.8. In the same year, the overall death rate of 876.7 per 100,000 population was slightly above the national rate of 873.1. The HIV-related death rate for 2000 was only 2.5 per 100,000 population; the US rate was 5.3 per 100,000 that same year. A total of 11,863 AIDS cases were reported through 2001. Among persons ages 18 and older, 24.2% were current smokers in 2000.

Michigan's 145 community hospitals had 1,122,004 admissions and 25,630 beds in 2001. There were 34,053 full-time registered nurses and 3,982 full-time licensed practical nurses in 2001 and 250 physicians per 100,000 population in 2000. The average expense of a community hospital for care was $1,390.40 per inpatient day in 2001.

Federal government grants to cover the Medicare and Medicaid services in 2001 totaled $4.2 billion; 1,414,054 enrollees received Medicare benefits that year. At least 10.4% of the population was uninsured in 2002.

39SOCIAL WELFARE

Until the 1930s, Michigan's few limited welfare programs were handled by the counties, but the relief load during the Depression shifted the burden to the state and federal levels. In recent decades there have been enormous increases in social welfare programs. In 2001, the average weekly unemployment benefit was $261.03. Average monthly participation in the food stamp program in FY2002 comprised 750,037 persons (327,853 households). The average monthly benefit was $71.62, and the sum total of benefits paid in FY2002 was $644,577,181.

With the enactment of the Personal Responsibility and Work Opportunity Reconciliation Act of 1996, the US government has changed the form and regulations for many of its social welfare programs. Most significantly, it replaces Aid to Families with Dependent Children (AFDC), an open-ended entitlement program, with Temporary Assistance for Needy Families (TANF), a limited system of assistance funded largely through federal block grants. The reform act also impacts the food stamp program, the Supplemental Security Income program, and the child nutrition program. The law took effect on 1 July 1997 and provided $16.38 billion in block grants for fiscal years 1997–2002. The grants are to be divided among the states based on an equation involving the numbers of former AFDC recipients in each state.

Reauthorization of the 1996 social welfare legislation, scheduled for 2002, was delayed, and the original law had been extended three times as of July 2003, with the most recent extension running through September 2003. Michigan's TANF program is called the Family Independence Program (FIP). In June 2000 the state had 195,101 welfare recipients. State expenditures on the TANF program in FY2002 totaled $372,117,686.

In December 2001, Social Security benefits were paid to 1,658,480 Michigan residents. This number included 1,026,770 retired workers, 188,510 widows and widowers, 192,100 disabled workers, 106,640 spouses, and 144,460 children. Social Security beneficiaries represented 16.6% of the total state population and 96.1% of the state's population age 65 and older. Retired workers (excluding persons with special benefits) received an average monthly payment of $941; widows and widowers, $881; disabled workers, $879; and spouses, $474. Payments for children of retired workers averaged $458 per month; children of deceased workers, $614; and children of disabled workers, $258.

Federal Supplemental Security Income payments in December 2001 went to 210,492 Michigan residents, averaging $399 a month.

40HOUSING

In 2002, there were an estimated 4,331,986 housing units in Michigan, 3,844,635 of which were occupied. Michigan ranked 4th in the country for the number of units, 74%, which were owner-occupied in 2002. About 70.4% of all units were single-family, detached homes. Most homes rely on utility gas for heating. It was estimated that 172,371 units lacked telephone service, 15,456 lacked complete plumbing facilities, and 14,917 lacked complete kitchen facilities. The average household size was 2.55 people.

In 2002, 49,968 privately owned units were authorized for construction. The median home value was $133,270. The median monthly cost for mortgage owners was $1,085. Renters paid a median of $585 per month. During 2002, Michigan received over $244.6 million in community planning and development aid from the US Department of Housing and Urban Development. A limited amount of state aid for low-income housing is available through the State Housing Development Authority.

41EDUCATION

Historically, Michigan has strongly supported public education, which helps account for the fact that the percentage of students attending public schools is among the highest in the US. But the cost of maintaining this extensive public educational system has become a major problem in recent years because of the declining school-age population. In 2000, 83.4% of Michigan residents age 25 and older were high school graduates, and 21.8% had obtained a bachelor's degree or higher.

The total enrollment for fall 1999 in Michigan's public schools stood at 1,725,617. Of these, 1,244,586 attended schools from kindergarten through grade eight, and 481,031 attended high school. Minority students made up approximately 27% of the total enrollment in public elementary and secondary schools in 2001. Total enrollment was estimated at 1,705,800 in fall 2000 and is expected to drop to 1,665,000 by fall 2005. In 1999/2000, per pupil expenditures for public schools amounted to $7,483, well above the US mean of $6,356. Expenditures for public education in 2000/01 were estimated at $13,722,604.

Enrollment in nonpublic schools in fall 2001 was 179,579. The largest number of these students were enrolled in Catholic schools. Lutherans, Seventh-Day Adventists, and Reformed and Christian Reformed churches also have maintained schools for some time; in the 1970s, a number of new Christian schools, particularly those of fundamentalist Baptist groups, were established.

As of fall 2000, there were 635,836 students enrolled in college or graduate school. In the same year Michigan had 108 degree-granting institutions. In 1997, minority students comprised 17.9% of total postsecondary enrollment. The oldest state school is the University of Michigan, originally established in Detroit in 1817; its Ann Arbor campus was founded in 1835, and classes there began in 1841. Among the public universities are the University of Michigan, including the Dearborn and Flint campuses, Michigan State University, and Wayne State University. Among the state's private colleges and universities, the University of Detroit Mercy, a Jesuit school, is one of the largest. Kalamazoo College (founded in 1833), Albion College (1835), Hope College (1866) and Alma College (1886) are some of the oldest private liberal arts colleges in the state.

42ARTS

Michigan's major center of arts and cultural activities is the Detroit area. The city's refurbished Orchestra Hall is the home of the Detroit Symphony Orchestra as well as chamber music concerts and other musical events. The Music Hall and the Masonic Auditorium present a variety of musical productions; the Fisher Theater is the major home for Broadway productions; and the Detroit Cultural Center supports a number of cultural programs. The new Detroit Opera House is sponsored by the Michigan Opera Theatre. Nearby Meadow Brook, in Rochester, has a summer music program. At the University of Michigan, in Ann Arbor, the Power Center for the Performing Arts and Hill Auditorium host major musical, theatrical, and dance presentations.

Programs relating to the visual arts tend to be academically centered; the University of Michigan, Michigan State, Wayne State, and Eastern Michigan University have notable art schools. The Cranbrook Academy of Arts, which was created by the architect Eliel Saarinen, is a significant art center, and the Ox-bow School at Saugatuck is also outstanding. The Ann Arbor Art Fair, begun in 1959, is the largest and most prestigious summer outdoor art show in the state, and one of the best-known events of its type in the country. The Waterfront Film Festival in Saugatuck and the touring Ann Arbor Film Festival promote the art of independent filmmaking.

The Meadow Brook Theater at Rochester is perhaps the largest professional theater company; Detroit has a number of little theater groups. Successful summer theaters include the Cherry County Playhouse at Traverse City and the Star Theater in Flint.

The Detroit Symphony Orchestra, founded in 1914, is nationally known. Grand Rapids and Kalamazoo have regional orchestras that perform on a part-time, seasonal basis. The National Music Camp at Interlochen is a mecca for young musicians in the summer, and a prestigious private high school for the arts year round.

There are local ballet and opera groups in Detroit and in a few other communities. Michigan's best-known contribution to popular music was that of Berry Gordy, Jr., whose Motown recording company in the 1960s popularized the "Detroit sound" and featured such artists as Diana Ross and the Supremes, Smokey Robinson and the Miracles, Aretha Franklin, the Four Tops, the Temptations, and Stevie Wonder, among many others. In the 1970s however, Gordy moved his operations to California.

The state of Michigan generates federal and state funds for its arts programs. In 2003, the Michigan Council for the Arts and other Michigan arts organizations received grants totaling $1,601,500 from the National Endowment for the Arts. Private sources also provided funding for the activities of the Council. There are more than 1,000 state and over 100 local arts associations in Michigan. The Michigan Humanities Council was founded in 1974. One of its ongoing programs is the Great Outdoors Culture Tour, which includes performing artists and cultural interpreters/educators. In 2000, the National Endowment for the Humanities contributed $1,985,658 to state programs.

43LIBRARIES AND MUSEUMS

In 2000, public libraries in the state had a total of nearly 27 million volumes and a circulation exceeding 50 million. The Library of Michigan in Lansing functions as the coordinator of library facilities in the state. The largest public library is the Detroit Public Library, which in 1999 had over 2.5 million books and print materials in its main library and 26 branches. Outstanding among its special collections are the Burton Historical Collection, a major center for genealogical research, the National Automotive History Collection, and the E. Azalia Hackley Collection, a notable source for material pertaining to

African Americans in the performing arts, especially music. Grand Rapids, Kalamazoo, Lansing, Flint, and Ann Arbor are among the larger public libraries. Total public library income came to $288,142,000 in 2000, including $1,152,568 in state grants.

Among academic libraries, the University of Michigan at Ann Arbor, with 6,283,385 volumes and 56,663 periodical subscriptions in 1999, features the William L. Clements collection of books and manuscripts on the colonial period, the Labadie Collection relating to the history of American radicalism, and the Bentley Library's distinctive collection of books and manuscripts, particularly the one on Michigan, the largest such collection.

In 1980, the Gerald R. Ford Presidential Library was opened on U-M's Ann Arbor campus. The Michigan State University Library at East Lansing had 4,274,375 volumes and 27,314 periodical subscriptions in 1999. At Wayne State University in Detroit, the Walter P. Reuther Library houses the largest collection of labor history records in the US, as well as primary materials relating to social, economic, and political reform and urban affairs.

The Detroit Institute of Arts is the largest art museum in the state and has an outstanding collection of African art. It is located in the Detroit Cultural Center, along with the Public Library and the Detroit Historical Museum, one of the largest local history museums in the country. The Kalamazoo Institute of Art, the Flint Institute of Art, the Grand Rapids Art Museum, and the Hackley Art Gallery in Muskegon are important art museums. The University of Michigan and the Cranbrook Academy of Arts in Bloomfield Hills also maintain important collections.

The Detroit Historical Museum heads 229 museums in the state, including the State Historical Museum in Lansing and museums in Grand Rapids, Flint, Kalamazoo, and Dearborn. In the latter city, the privately run Henry Ford Museum and Greenfield Village are leading tourist attractions. In 1996 the world's largest museum of African American history was established in Detroit. A major Holocaust Memorial Center is located in the West Bloomfield Hills area of metropolitan Detroit.

The major historical sites open to the public include the late-18th-century fort on Mackinac Island and the reconstructed early-18th-century fort at Mackinaw City. The latter site has also been the scene of an archaeological program that has accumulated one of the largest collections of 18th-century artifacts in the country. Major investigations of prehistoric Indian sites have also been conducted in recent years.

44COMMUNICATIONS

Michigan's remote position in the interior of the continent hampered the development of adequate communications services, and the first regular postal service was not instituted until the early 19th century.

Telephone service began in Detroit in 1877. By 2001, 94.7% of the occupied housing units in the state had telephones.

Michigan had 63 major AM radio stations and 168 major FM stations in 2003. Radio station WWJ, originally owned by the Detroit News, began operating in 1920 as one of the country's first commercial broadcasting stations, and the News also started Michigan's first television station in 1947. As of 2003 there were 33 major television stations in the state. In the Detroit area, 68% of 1,855,500 television households had cable, and in the Grand Rapids-Kalamazoo-Battle Creek area, 62% of 671,320 television households had cable.

By 2000, a total of 145,596 Internet domain names had been registered in Michigan.

[45]PRESS

The first newspaper to appear in Michigan was Father Richard's *Michigan Essay or Impartial Observer*, published in August 1917. Continuous newspaper coverage in Michigan dates from the appearance of the weekly *Detroit Gazette*, also in 1817. The state's oldest paper still being published is the *Detroit Free Press*, founded in 1831 and the state's first daily paper since 1835.

In 2002 there were 49 daily newspapers in Michigan, with Sunday editions published in the state. Two of the state's largest newspapers—Knight Ridder's *Detroit Free Press* and Gannett's *Detroit News*—entered into a joint operating agreement (JOA) in 1989. The advertising, business, delivery, and production of each paper joined forces in a company called Detroit Newspapers; the editorial and news operations remain separate and report to their respective parent companies. During a labor dispute in the mid-1990s, the *Detroit Journal* was published weekly by locked-out newspaper workers. The *News* had the 6th-largest daily circulation of any paper in the US in 1994, and ranked 7th. In 2001, however, the *News* had dropped to number 42 nationwide and the *Free Press* was at number 18.

The following table shows leading daily newspapers in Michigan with average daily and Sunday circulation in 1998:

AREA	NAME	DAILY	SUNDAY
Detroit	*News* and *Free Press* (m,S)	614,116	749,113
Flint	*Journal* (e,S)	88,817	104,503
Grand Rapids	*Press* (e,S)	139,800	191,435
Kalamazoo	*Gazette* (e,S)	56,754	74,001
Lansing	*State Journal* (m,S)	70,845	89,505
Pontiac	*Oakland Press* (m,S)	70,767	84,361
Saginaw	*News* (e,S)	47,586	58,236

[46]ORGANIZATIONS

In 2003, there were about 4,411 regional, national, and international organizations within the state. The most important trade association headquartered in Michigan is the Motor Vehicle Manufacturers Association, with offices in Detroit. Its labor union counterpart—the United Automobile, Aerospace and Agricultural Implement Workers of America (UAW)—also has its international headquarters in that city.

Others with headquarters in the state include the American Concrete Institute, the Detroit; Society of Manufacturing Engineers, Dearborn; American Society of Agricultural Engineers, St. Joseph; the American Board of Emergency Medicine, East Lansing, and the National Association of Investment Corporations, Madison Heights.

Organizations for arts and education include the Association of College Honor Societies, the Children's Literature Association, Interlochen Center for the Arts, and the Institute for Social Research There are also a number of municipal and regional arts groups and historical societies. Several organizations focus on regional environmental issues, including the Great Lakes Maritime Institute and the Great Lakes Commission. The American Amateur Baseball Congress and the United Kennel Club are sports and hobby organizations with national memberships.

Charitable organizations include the Good Fellows, based in Detroit. Founded in 1914, the organization was called the Newsboys, since its first members were newspaper carriers. Though the group participates in a number of charitable causes, its primary program is A Christmas for Every Needy Child. There are chapters of Good Fellows nationwide. The W. K. Kellogg Foundation based in Battle Creek also supports a number of community, national, and international projects. The Islamic Assembly of North America, which serves as a coordinating body for US Islamic centers and organizations, is based in Ann Arbor.

[47]TOURISM, TRAVEL, AND RECREATION

Tourism has been an important source of economic activity in Michigan since the 19th century and now rivals agriculture as the second most important segment of the state's economy. In 2001, the state hosted over 67 million visitors, up from 58.8 million in 2000. About 54% of all travel is in the form of day-trips for state residents or visitors from neighboring states. The current slogan for tourism in Michigan is "Great Lakes, Great Times."

Michigan's tourist attractions are diverse and readily accessible to much of the country's population. The opportunities offered by Michigan's water resources are the number one attraction; no part of the state is more than 85 mi (137 km) from one of the Great Lakes, and most of the population lives only a few miles away from one of the thousands of inland lakes and streams. Southwestern Michigan's sandy beaches along Lake Michigan offer sunbathing and swimming on 5,000 km of Great Lakes coastline. Inland lakes numbering 11,000 in southern Michigan are favored by swimmers while the Metropolitan Beach on Lake St. Clair, northeast of Detroit, claims to be the largest artificial-lake beach in the world. Camping has enjoyed an enormous increase in popularity; in addition to the extensive public camping facilities, there are many private campgrounds.

Although the tourist and resort business has been primarily a summer activity, the rising popularity of ice fishing, skiing, and other winter sports, autumn scenic tours, hunting, and spring festivals has made tourism a year-round business in many parts of the state. Historic attractions have been heavily promoted in recent years, following the success of Dearborn's Henry Ford Museum and Greenfield Village; such as the Motown Historical Museum. Tours of Detroit automobile factories and other industrial sites, such as Battle Creek's breakfast-food plants, are also important tourist attractions. The Spirit of Ford, a 50,000 sq ft center in Dearborn, offers a "behind the scenes" look at how the automaker designs, engineers, tests, and produces cars and trucks.

Camping and recreational facilities are provided by the federal government at three national forests comprising 1.1 million hectares (2.8 million acres), three facilities operated by the National Park Service (Isle Royale National Park, the Pictured Rocks National Lakeshore, and Sleeping Bear Dunes National Lakeshore), and several wildlife sanctuaries. A wild African-style village covering 28.3 hectares (70 acres) at the Binder Park Zoo in Battle Creek features giraffes, zebras, and ostrich, plus a variety of endangered African species roaming freely on the grassy savannah.

State-operated facilities include 64 parks and recreational areas with 172,343 acres (69,747 hectares), and state forests and wildlife areas totaling 4,250,000 acres (1,720,000 hectares). Holland and Warren Dunes state parks, located on Lake Michigan, have the largest annual park attendances; Ludington State Park, also on Lake Michigan, attracts the largest number of campers.

[48]SPORTS

Michigan has five major league professional sports teams, all of them centered in Detroit: the Tigers of Major League Baseball, the Lions of the National Football League, the Pistons of the National Basketball Association, the Shock of the Women's National Basketball Association, and the Red Wings of the National Hockey League. The Tigers won the World Series in 1935, 1945, 1968, and 1984. The Pistons won the NBA Championship in 1989 and 1990. The Red Wings, arguably the most renowned hockey club ever, won the Stanley Cup in 1936, 1937, 1943, 1950, 1952, 1954, 1955, 1997, 1998, and 2002.

The state also has minor league hockey teams in Detroit, Flint, Grand Rapids, Muskegon, Kimball, and Saginaw; and baseball teams in Grand Rapids, Battle Creek, Comstock Park, and Lansing.

Horse racing, Michigan's oldest organized spectator sport, is controlled by the state racing commissioner, who regulates thoroughbred and harness-racing seasons at tracks in the Detroit area and at Jackson. Attendance and betting at these races is substantial, although the modest purses rarely attract the nation's leading horses. Auto racing is also popular in Michigan. The state hosts four major races: the Tenneco Automotive Grand Prix of Detroit, the Michigan 500 Indy car races on the CART circuit, and the Kmart 400 and Pepsi 400 NASCAR Winston Cup races.

Interest in college sports centers on the football and basketball teams of the University of Michigan and Michigan State University, which usually are among the top-ranked teams in the country. The University of Michigan football team was named National Champion in 1901 (with Harvard), 1902, 1903, 1904 (with Penn), 1918 (with Pittsburgh), 1923 (with Illinois), 1932, 1933, 1947, 1948, and 1997. The team won the Rose Bowl in 1948, 1951, 1965, 1981, 1989, 1993, and 1998, the Citrus Bowl in 1999, and the Orange Bowl in 2000. Michigan State won the Rose Bowl in 1954, 1956, and 1988, and was named National Champion in 1952 (with Georgia Tech), 1965 (with Alabama), and 1966 (with Notre Dame). The University of Michigan basketball team won the NCAA tournament in 1989, and Michigan State won it in 1979 and 2000. Michigan also advanced to the championship game in 1965, 1976, 1992, and 1993.

Other colleges also have achieved national rankings in basketball, hockey, baseball, and track. Elaborate facilities have been built for sporting competitions in Michigan; for example the University of Michigan's football stadium, seating 107,501, is one of the largest college-owned stadiums in the country.

Other annual sporting events include the Snowmobile Poker Runs in St. Ignace and, in July, the yacht races from Chicago and Port Huron to Mackinac Island.

⁴⁹FAMOUS MICHIGANIANS

Only one Michiganian has held the offices of US president and vice president. Gerald R. Ford (Leslie King, Jr., b.Nebraska, 1913), the 38th US president, was elected to the US House as a Republican in 1948 and served continuously until 1973, becoming minority leader in 1965. Upon the resignation of Vice President Spiro T. Agnew in 1973, President Richard M. Nixon appointed Ford to the vice-presidency. When Nixon resigned on 9 August 1974, Ford became president, the first to hold that post without having been elected to high national office. Ford succeeded in restoring much of the public's confidence in the presidency, but his pardoning of Nixon for all crimes he may have committed as president helped cost Ford victory in the presidential election of 1976. Ford subsequently moved his legal residence to California.

Lewis Cass (b.New Hampshire, 1782–1866), who served as governor of Michigan Territory, senator from Michigan, secretary of war and secretary of state, is the only other Michigan resident nominated by a major party for president; he lost the 1848 race as the Democratic candidate. Thomas E. Dewey (1902–72), a native of Owosso, was the Republican presidential nominee in 1944 and 1948, but from his adopted state of New York.

Two Michiganians have served as associate justices of the Supreme Court: Henry B. Brown (b.Massachusetts, 1836–1913), author of the 1896 segregationist decision in *Plessy v. Ferguson*; and Frank Murphy (1890–1949), who also served as US attorney general, mayor of Detroit, governor of Michigan, and was a notable defender of minority rights during his years on the court. Another justice, Potter Stewart (1915–85), was born in Jackson but appointed to the court from Ohio.

Other Michiganians who have held high federal office include Robert McClelland (b.Pennsylvania, 1807–80), secretary of the interior; Russell A. Alger (b.Ohio, 1836–1907), secretary of war; Edwin Denby (b.Indiana, 1870–1929), secretary of the Navy, who was forced to resign because of the Teapot Dome scandal; Roy D. Chapin (1880–1936), secretary of commerce; Charles E. Wilson (b.Ohio, 1890–1961), and Robert S. McNamara (b.California, 1916), secretaries of defense; George Romney (b.Mexico, 1907–96), secretary of housing and urban development; Donald M. Dickinson (b.New York, 1846–1917) and Arthur E. Summerfield (1899–1972), postmasters general; and W. Michael Blumenthal (b.Germany, 1926), secretary of the treasury.

Zachariah Chandler (b.New Hampshire, 1813–79) served as secretary of the interior but is best remembered as a leader of the Radical Republicans in the US Senate during the Civil War era. Other prominent US senators have included James M. Couzens (b.Canada, 1872–1936), a former Ford executive who became a maverick Republican liberal during the 1920s; Arthur W. Vandenberg (1884–1951), a leading supporter of a bipartisan internationalist foreign policy after World War II; and Philip A. Hart, Jr. (b.Pennsylvania, 1912–76), one of the most influential senators of the 1960s and 1970s. Recent well-known US representatives include John Conyers, Jr. (b.1929), and Martha W. Griffiths (b.Missouri, 1912), a representative for 20 years who served as the state's lieutenant governor from 1983–91.

In addition to Murphy and Romney, important governors have included Stevens T. Mason (b.Virginia, 1811–43), who guided Michigan to statehood; Austin Blair (b.New York, 1818–94), Civil War governor; Hazen S. Pingree (b.Maine, 1840–1901) and Chase S. Osborn (b.Indiana, 1860–1949), reform-minded governors; Alexander Groesbeck (1873–1953); G. Mennen Williams (1911–88); and William G. Milliken (b.1922), governor from 1969 to January 1983. From 1974 to 1994, Detroit's first black mayor, Coleman A. Young (b.Alabama, 1918–97), promoted programs to revive the city's tarnished image.

The most famous figure in the early development of Michigan is Jacques Marquette (b.France, 1637–75). Other famous historical figures include Charles de Langlade (1729–1801), a leader of the Ottawa people and a French-Indian soldier in the French and Indian War and the American Revolution; the Ottawa chieftain Pontiac (1720?–69), leader of an ambitious Indian uprising; and Gabriel Richard (b.France, 1769–1832), an important pioneer in education and the first Catholic priest to serve in Congress. Laura Haviland (b.Canada, 1808–98) was a noted leader in the fight against slavery and for black rights, while Lucinda Hinsdale Stone (b.Vermont, 1814–1900) and Anna Howard Shaw (b.England, 1847–1919) were important in the women's rights movement.

Nobel laureates from Michigan include diplomat Ralph J. Bunche (1904–71), winner of the Nobel Peace Prize in 1950; Glenn T. Seaborg (1912–99), Nobel Prize winner in chemistry in 1951; and Thomas H. Weller (b.1915) and Alfred D. Hershey (1908–97), Nobel Prize winners in physiology or medicine in 1954 and 1969, respectively. Among leading educators, James B. Angell (b.Rhode Island, 1829–1916), president of the University of Michigan, led that school to the forefront among American universities while John A. Hannah (1902–91), longtime president of Michigan State University, successfully strove to expand and diversify its programs. General Motors executive Charles S. Mott (b.New Jersey, 1875–1973) contributed to the growth of continuing education programs through huge grants of money.

In the business world, William C. Durant (b.Massachusetts, 1861–1947), Henry Ford (1863–1947) and Ransom E. Olds (b.Ohio, 1864–1950) are the three most important figures in making Michigan the center of the American auto industry. Ford's grandson, Henry Ford II (1917–87), was the dominant personality in the auto industry from 1945 through 1979. Two brothers, John Harvey Kellogg (1852–1943) and Will K. Kellogg (1860–1951), helped make Battle Creek the center of the breakfast-food industry. William E. Upjohn (1850–1932) and Herbert H. Dow (b.Canada, 1866–1930) founded major pharmaceutical and chemical companies that bear their names, James E. Scripps (b.England, 1835–1906), founder of the *Detroit News,* was a major innovator in the newspaper business. Pioneer aviator Charles A. Lindbergh (1902–74) was born in Detroit.

Among prominent labor leaders in Michigan were Walter Reuther (b.West Virginia, 1907–70), president of the United Automobile Workers, and his controversial contemporary, James Hoffa (b.Indiana, 1913–1975?), president of the Teamsters Union, whose disappearance and presumed murder remain a mystery.

The best-known literary figures who were either native or adopted Michiganians include Edgar Guest (b.England, 1881–1959), writer of enormously popular sentimental verses; Ring Lardner (1885–1933), master of the short story; Edna Ferber (1885–1968), best-selling novelist; Paul de Kruif (1890–1971), popular writer on scientific topics; Steward Edward White (1873–1946), writer of adventure tales; Howard Mumford Jones (1892–1980), critic and scholar; and Bruce Catton (1899–1978), Civil War historian.

Other prominent Michiganians past and present include Frederick Stuart Church (1842–1924), painter; Liberty Hyde Bailey (1858–1954), horticulturist and botanist; Albert Kahn (b.Germany, 1869–1942), noted architect and innovator in factory design; and (Gottlieb) Eliel Saarinen (b.Finland, 1873–1950), architect and creator of the Cranbrook School of Art, and his son Eero (1910–61), designer of the General Motors Technical Center in Warren and many distinctive structures throughout the US. Malcolm X (Malcolm Little, b.Nebraska, 1925–65) developed his black separatist beliefs while living in Lansing.

Popular entertainers born in Michigan include Danny Thomas (Amos Jacobs, 1914–91), David Wayne (1914-91), Betty Hutton (b.1921), Ed McMahon (b.1923), Julie Harris (b.1925), Ellen Burstyn (Edna Rae Gilhooley, b.1932), Della Reese (Dellareese Patricia Early, b.1932), William "Smokey" Robinson (b.1940), Diana Ross (b.1944), Bob Seger (b.1945), and Stevie Wonder (Stevland Morris, b.1950), along with film director Francis Ford Coppola (b.1939).

Among sports figures who had notable careers in the state were Fielding H. Yost (b.West Virginia, 1871–1946), University of Michigan football coach; Joe Louis (Joseph Louis Barrow, b.Alabama, 1914-81), heavyweight boxing champion from 1937 to 1949; "Sugar Ray" Robinson (1921-89), who held at various times the welterweight and middleweight boxing titles; and baseball Hall of Famers Al Kaline (b.Maryland, 1934) and Tyrus Raymond ("Ty") Cobb (b.Georgia, 1886–1961), who won 12 batting titles, were Detroit Tigers stars. Earvin "Magic" Johnson (b.1959), who broke Oscar Robertson's record for most assists, was born in Lansing, Michigan.

[50]BIBLIOGRAPHY

Barnett, LeRoy, ed. *Michigan's Early Military Forces: A Roster and History of Troops Activated Prior to the American Civil War.* Detroit: Wayne State University Press, 2003.

Browne, William Paul. *Michigan Politics and Government: Facing Change in a Complex State.* Lincoln: University of Nebraska Press, 1995.

Dunbar, Willis F., and George S. May. *Michigan: A History of the Wolverine State.* 3rd rev. ed. Grand Rapids: Eerdmans, 1995.

Federal Writers' Project. *Michigan: A Guide to the Wolverine State.* Reprint. New York: Somerset, 1981 (orig. 1941).

Fine, Sidney. *Civil Rights and the Michigan Constitution of 1963.* Ann Arbor: Bentley Historical Library, University of Michigan, 1996.

Folsom, Burton W. *Empire Builders: How Michigan Entrepreneurs Helped Make America Great.* Traverse City, MI: Rhodes & Easton, 1998.

Fuller, George N., ed. *Michigan: A Centennial History of the State.* 5 vols. Chicago: Lewis, 1939.

Hershock, Martin John. *Liberty and Power in the Old Northwest: Michigan, 1850–1867.* N.p., 1996.

The Legislative Process in Michigan: A Student's Guide. Lansing: Legislative Service Bureau, 1995.

Loepp, Daniel. *Sharing the Balance of Power: An Examination of Shared Power in the Michigan House of Representatives, 1993–94.* Ann Arbor: University of Michigan Press, 1999.

Moore, Elizabeth. *The State We're In: A Citizen's Guide to Michigan State Government.* Lansing: League of Women Voters of Michigan, 1995.

Rubenstein, Bruce A. *Michigan, A History of the Great Lakes State.* Wheeling, Ill.: Harlan Davidson, 1995.

MINNESOTA

State of Minnesota

ORIGIN OF STATE NAME: Derived from the Sioux Indian word *minisota*, meaning "sky-tinted waters." **NICKNAME:** The North Star State. **CAPITAL:** St. Paul. **ENTERED UNION:** 11 May 1858 (32nd). **SONG:** "Hail! Minnesota." **MOTTO:** *L'Etoile du Nord* (The North Star). **FLAG:** On a blue field bordered on three sides by a gold fringe, a version of the state seal is surrounded by a wreath with the statehood year (1858) the year of the establishment of Ft. Snelling (1819), and the year the flag was adopted (1893); five clusters of gold stars and the word "Minnesota" fill the outer circle. **OFFICIAL SEAL:** A farmer, with a powder horn and musket nearby, plows a field in the foreground, while in the background, before a rising sun, an Indian on horseback crosses the plains; pine trees and a waterfall represent the state's natural resources. The state motto is above and the whole is surrounded by the words "The Great Seal of the State of Minnesota 1858." Another version of the seal in common use shows a cowboy riding across the plains. **BIRD:** Common loon. **BUTTERFLY:** Monarch. **FISH:** Walleye. **FLOWER:** Pink and white (or showy) lady slipper. **TREE:** Red (Norway) pine. **GRAIN:** Wild rice. **MUSHROOM:** Morel or sponge mushroom. **DRINK:** Milk. **GEM:** Lake Superior agate. **LEGAL HOLIDAYS:** New Year's Day, 1 January; Birthday of Martin Luther King, Jr., 3rd Monday in January; Washington's and Lincoln's Birthdays, 3rd Monday in February; Memorial Day, last Monday in May; Independence Day, 4 July; Labor Day, 1st Monday in September; Columbus Day, 2nd Monday in October; Veterans Day, 11 November; Thanksgiving Day, 4th Thursday in November; Christmas Day, 25 December. By statute, schools hold special observances on Susan B. Anthony Day, 15 February; Arbor Day, last Friday in April; Minnesota Day, 11 May; Frances Willard Day, 28 September; Leif Erikson Day, 9 October. **TIME:** 6 AM CST = noon GMT.

¹LOCATION, SIZE, AND EXTENT

Situated in the western north-central US, Minnesota is the largest of the midwestern states and ranks 12th in size among the 50 states.

The total area of Minnesota is 84,402 sq mi (218,601 sq km), of which land accounts for 79,548 sq mi (206,029 sq km) and inland water 4,854 sq mi (12,572 sq km). Minnesota extends 406 mi (653 km) N-S; its extreme E-W extension is 358 mi (576 km).

Minnesota is bordered on the N by the Canadian provinces of Manitoba and Ontario (with the line passing through the Lake of the Woods, Rainy River, Rainy Lake, a succession of smaller lakes, the Pigeon River, and Lake Superior); on the E by Michigan and Wisconsin (with the line passing through Lake Superior and the St. Croix and Mississippi rivers); on the S by Iowa; and on the W by South Dakota and North Dakota (with the line passing through Big Stone Lake, Lake Traverse, the Bois de Sioux River, and the Red River of the North).

The length of Minnesota's boundaries totals 1,783 mi (2,870 km). The state's geographic center is in Crow Wing County, 10 mi (16 km) SW of Brainerd.

²TOPOGRAPHY

Minnesota, lying at the northern rim of the Central Plains region, consists mainly of flat prairie, nowhere flatter than in the Red River Valley of the west. There are rolling hills and deep river valleys in the southeast; the northeast, known as Arrowhead Country, is more rugged and includes the Vermilion Range and the Mesabi Range, with its rich iron deposits. Eagle Mountain, in the extreme northeast, rises to a height of 2,301 ft (702 m), the highest point in the state; the surface of nearby Lake Superior, 600 ft (183 m) above sea level, is the state's lowest elevation.

With more than 15,000 lakes and extensive wetlands, rivers, and streams, Minnesota has more inland water than any other state except Alaska. Some of the inland lakes are quite large: Lower and Upper Red Lake, 451 sq mi (1,168 sq km); Mille Lacs, 207 sq mi (536 sq km); and Leech Lake, 176 sq mi (456 sq km). The Lake of the Woods, 1,485 sq mi (3,846 sq km), is shared with Canada, as is Rainy Lake, 345 sq mi (894 sq km). A total of 2,212 sq mi (5,729 sq km) of Lake Superior lies within Minnesota's jurisdiction.

Lake Itasca, in the northwest, is the source of the Mississippi River, which drains about three-fifths of the state and, after meeting with the St. Croix below Minneapolis–St. Paul, forms part of the eastern boundary with Wisconsin. The Minnesota River, which flows across the southern part of the state, joins the Mississippi at the Twin Cities. The Red River of the North, which forms much of the boundary with North Dakota, is part of another large drainage system; it flows north, crosses the Canadian border above St. Vincent, and eventually empties into Lake Winnipeg in Canada.

Most of Minnesota, except for small areas in the southeast, was covered by ice during the glacial ages. When the ice melted, it left behind a body of water known as Lake Agassiz, which extended into what we now call the Dakotas and Canada and was larger than the combined Great Lakes are today; additional melting to the north caused the lake to drain away, leaving flat prairie in its wake. The glaciers also left behind large stretches of pulverized limestone, enriching Minnesota's soil, and the numerous shallow depressions that have developed into its modern-day lakes and streams.

³CLIMATE

Minnesota has a continental climate, with cold, often frigid winters and warm summers. The growing season is 160 days or more in the south-central and southeastern regions, but 100 days or less in the northern counties. Normal daily mean temperatures range from 7°F (−14°C) in January to 66°F (19°C) in July for Duluth, and from 12°F (−11°C) in January to 74°F (23°C) in July for Minneapolis-St. Paul, often called the Twin Cities. The lowest temperature recorded in Minnesota was −60°F (−51°C), at Tower on 2 February 1996; the highest, 114°F (46°C), at Moorhead on 6 July 1936.

Annual precipitation (1971–2000) averaged 31 in (79 cm) at Duluth and 29.4 in (75 cm) at Minneapolis-St. Paul. Precipitation is lightest in the northwest, where it averaged 19 in (48 cm) per year. Heavy snowfalls occur from November to April, averaging about 70 in (178 cm) annually in the northeast and 30 in (76 cm) in the southeast. Blizzards hit Minnesota twice each winter on the average. Tornadoes occur mostly in the south; on average there are 18 tornadoes in the state each year.

[4] FLORA AND FAUNA

Minnesota is divided into three main life zones: the wooded lake regions of the north and east, the prairie lands of the west and southwest, and a transition zone in between. Oak, maple, elm, birch, pine, ash, and poplar still thrive although much of the state's woodland has been cut down since the 1850s. Common shrubs include thimbleberry, sweetfern, and several varieties of honeysuckle. Familiar among some 1,500 native flowering plants are puccoon, prairie phlox, and blazing star; the pink and white (showy) lady slipper is the state flower. White and yellow water lilies cover the pond areas, with bulrushes and cattails on the shore. Three plant species were listed as threatened in 2003, including Leedy's roseroot, prairie bush-clover, and western prairie fringed orchid; the Minnesota dwarf trout lily was listed as endangered that year.

Among Minnesota's common mammals are the opossum, eastern and starnose moles, little brown bat, raccoon, mink, river otter, badger, striped and spotted skunks, red fox, bobcat, 13-lined ground squirrel (also known as the Minnesota gopher, symbol of the University of Minnesota), beaver, porcupine, eastern cottontail, moose, and white-tailed deer. The common loon (the state bird), western meadowlark, Brewer's blackbird, Carolina wren, and Louisiana water thrush are among some 240 resident bird species; introduced birds include the English sparrow and ring-necked pheasant. Teeming in Minnesota's many lakes are such game fishes as walleye, muskellunge, northern pike, and steelhead, rainbow, and brown trouts. The two poisonous snakes in the state are the timber rattler and the massasauga.

Classification of rare, threatened, and endangered species is delegated to the Minnesota Department of Natural Resources. Among rare species noted by the department are the white pelican, short-eared owl, rock vole, pine marten, American elk, woodland caribou, lake sturgeon, and paddlefish; threatened species include the bobwhite quail and piping plover. Eight species were listed as threatened or endangered in 2003 by the US Fish and Wildlife Service, including the gray wolf, bald eagle, piping plover, Topeka shiner, and Higgins' eye pearlymussel.

[5] ENVIRONMENTAL PROTECTION

The state's northern forests have been greatly depleted by fires, lumbering, and farming, but efforts to replenish them began as early as 1876, with the formation of the state's first forestry association. In 1911, the legislature authorized a state nursery, established forest reserves and parks, and created the post of chief fire warden to oversee forestry resources and promote reforestation projects. Minnesota divides its environmental programs among three agencies: the Minnesota Pollution Control Agency, the Department of Natural Resources, and the Office of Waste Management (newly reorganized as the Office of Environmental Assistance). The Conservation Department, created in 1931, evolved into the present Department of Natural

Resources, which is responsible for the management of forests, fish and game, public lands, minerals, and state parks and waters. The department's Soil and Water Conservation Board has jurisdiction over the state's 92 soil and water conservation districts. A separate Pollution Control Agency enforces air and water quality standards and oversees solid waste disposal and pollution-related land-use planning. The Environmental Quality Board coordinates conservation efforts among various state agencies.

Minnesotans dump 4,400 tons of waste a year (0.99 tons per capita) into 53 municipal landfills. In 1994, the state implemented the Minnesota Landfill Cleanup Program to ensure the proper care of 106 closed or closing municipal landfills. Beginning in 1996, the state began construction on 25 new municipal landfills and instituted a planning effort to manage all existing and closed sites. In 2003, Minnesota had 81 hazardous waste sites listed in the Environmental Protection Agency's database, 24 of which were on the National Priorities List. To control the state's solid waste stream, Minnesotans have established 488 curbside recycling programs. In 1997, the state had some 9.5 million acres (3.8 million hectares) of wetlands. The Wetlands Conservation Act of 1991 set the ambitious goal of no wetland loss in the future. The Reserve Mining Co. complied with a court order in 1980 by ending the dumping of taconite wastes, a possible carcinogen, into Lake Superior. Other pollution problems came to light during the 1970s with the discovery of asbestos in drinking water from Lake Superior, of contaminants from inadequately buried toxic wastes at St. Louis Park, and of the killing by agricultural pesticides of an estimated 100,000 fish in two southeastern Minnesota brooks. During the early 1980s, the state's Pollution Control Agency approved plans by FMC, a munitions maker, to clean up a hazardous waste site at Fridley (near Minneapolis), which the Environmental Protection Agency (EPA) claimed was the country's most dangerous hazardous waste area. The Minnesota Mining and Manufacturing Co. in 1983 began to remove chemical wastes from three dumps in Oakdale (a suburb of St. Paul), where the company had disposed of hazardous wastes since the late 1940s. Each cleanup project was to cost the respective companies at least $6 million. In 2001, Minnesota received $67,104,000 in federal grants from the EPA; EPA expenditures for procurement contracts in Minnesota that year amounted to $3,582,000.

[6] POPULATION

Minnesota ranked 21st in population in the US with an estimated total of 5,019,720 in 2002, an increase of 2% since 2000. Between 1990 and 2000, Minnesota's population grew from 4,375,099 to 4,919,479, an increase of 12.4%. The population is projected to reach 5.5 million by 2025. The population density in 2000 was 61.8 persons per sq mi.

Minnesota was still mostly wilderness until a land boom in 1848 attracted the first substantial wave of settlers, mainly lumbermen from New England, farmers from the Middle Atlantic states, and tradespeople from eastern cities. The 1850 census recorded a population of 6,077 in what was then Minnesota Territory. With the signing of major Indian treaties and widespread use of the steamboat, large areas were opened to settlement, and the population exceeded 150,000 by the end of 1857. Attracted by fertile farmland and enticed by ambitious recruitment programs overseas, large numbers of European immigrants came to settle in the new state from the 1860s onward. In 1880, the state population totaled 780,733; by 1920 (when overseas immigration virtually ceased), the state had 2,387,125 residents. Population growth leveled off during the 1920s and has fallen below the national average since the 1940s. As of 2000, Minnesotans had a median age of 35.4 years. Nearly

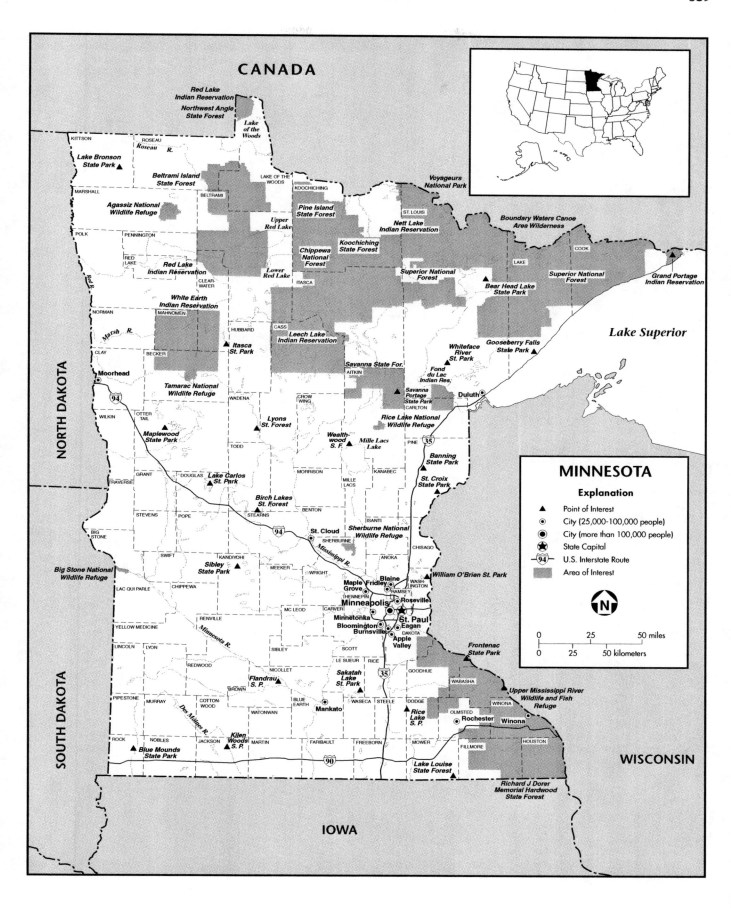

CANADA

Red Lake
Indian Reservation

Northwest Angle
State Forest

Lake
of the
Woods

KITTSON

ROSEAU
Roseau R.

Lake Bronson
State Park

Beltrami Island
State Forest

LAKE OF THE
WOODS

KOOCHICHING

Voyageurs
National Park

MARSHALL

BELTRAMI

ST. LOUIS

Agassiz National
Wildlife Refuge

Pine Island
State Forest

Boundary Waters Canoe
Area Wilderness

POLK

PENNINGTON

Upper Red Lake

Nett Lake
Indian Reservation

COOK

RED
LAKE

Chippewa
National
Forest

Koochiching
State Forest

LAKE

Superior
National
Forest

Red Lake
Indian Reservation

CLEAR-
WATER

Lower
Red Lake

Superior National
Forest

Grand Portage
Indian Reservation

ITASCA

Superior National
Forest

NORMAN

White Earth
Indian Reservation

Bear Head Lake
State Park

MAHNOMEN

HUBBARD

CASS

Lake Superior

CLAY

BECKER

Itasca
St. Park

Leech Lake
Indian Reservation

Whiteface
River
St. Park

Gooseberry Falls
State Park

Moorhead

Marsh R.

WADENA

Savanna State For.

Fond
du Lac
Indian Res.

Tamarac National
Wildlife Refuge

AITKIN

Savanna
Portage
State Park

Duluth

NORTH DAKOTA

WILKIN

OTTER
TAIL

CROW
WING

CARLTON

Maplewood
State Park

Lyons
St. Forest

Rice Lake National
Wildlife Refuge

94

TODD

Wealth-
wood
S. F.

Mille Lacs
Lake

PINE

35

Banning
State Park

GRANT

DOUGLAS

Lake Carlos
St. Park

MORRISON

MILLE
LACS

KANABEC

St. Croix
State Park

TRAVERSE

Birch Lakes
St. Forest

BENTON

STEVENS

POPE

STEARNS

ISANTI

BIG
STONE

94

St. Cloud

Sherburne National
Wildlife Refuge

CHISAGO

SWIFT

KANDIYOHI

SHERBURNE

Mississippi R.

ANOKA

Big Stone National
Wildlife Refuge

MEEKER

Sibley
State Park

WRIGHT

William O'Brien St. Park

LAC QUI PARLE

CHIPPEWA

Blaine

Maple Fridley
Grove

WASH-
INGTON

MC LEOD

HENNEPIN

RAMSEY

Roseville

CARVER

Minneapolis

YELLOW MEDICINE

RENVILLE

Minnetonka

St. Paul

Minnesota R.

Bloomington Eagan
Burnsville

DAKOTA

LINCOLN

LYON

REDWOOD

SIBLEY

Apple
Valley

SCOTT

LE SUEUR

RICE

35

Frontenac
State Park

Flandrau
S. P.

Sakatah
Lake
St. Park

GOODHUE

PIPESTONE

MURRAY

COTTON-
WOOD

BROWN

NICOLLET

WABASHA

Des Moines R.

BLUE
EARTH

WASECA

STEELE

DODGE

Upper Mississippi River
Wildlife and Fish
Refuge

Mankato

OLMSTED

WINONA

Rice
Lake
S. P.

Rochester

Winona

ROCK

NOBLES

JACKSON

Kilen
Woods
S. P.

MARTIN

FARIBAULT

FREEBORN

MOWER

FILLMORE

HOUSTON

Blue Mounds
State Park

90

Lake Louise
State Forest

WISCONSIN

Richard J Dorer
Memorial Hardwood
State Forest

SOUTH DAKOTA

IOWA

MINNESOTA

Explanation

▲ Point of Interest

⊙ City (25,000-100,000 people)

◉ City (more than 100,000 people)

✪ State Capital

94 U.S. Interstate Route

Area of Interest

N

| 0 | 25 | 50 miles |
| 0 | 25 | 50 kilometers |

26.2% of the population was under age 18, while 12.1% was age 65 or older.

The Minneapolis–St. Paul metropolitan area had an estimated population of 2,872,109 in 1999, up from an estimated 2,723,137 in 1995. The city of Minneapolis itself had an estimated 375,635 residents in 2002, down from 354,590 in 1994; St. Paul had an estimated 284,037. Other leading cities include Duluth and Rochester.

7ETHNIC GROUPS

Minnesota was settled during the second half of the 19th century, primarily by European immigrants, chiefly Germans, Swedes, Norwegians, Danes, English, and Poles, along with the Irish and some French Canadians. The Swedish newcomers were mainly farmers; Norwegians concentrated on lumbering while the Swiss worked for the most part in the dairy industry. In 1890, Finns and Slavs were recruited to work in the iron mines; the state's meat-packing plants brought in Balkan nationals, Mexicans, and Poles after the turn of the century. By 1930, 50% of the population was foreign-born. Among first- and second-generation Minnesotans of European origin, Germans and Scandinavians are still the largest groups. The state has more ethnic Norwegians than any other, and is 2nd in number of ethnic Swedes, behind California. The other ethnic groups are concentrated in Minneapolis–St. Paul or in the iron country of the Mesabi Range, where ethnic enclaves still persist. As of 2000, foreign-born residents of Minnesota numbered 260,463, or 5.3% of the state total, up from 113,039 (2.5%) in 1990.

As of 2000 there were 54,967 American Indians in Minnesota, with 35,282 living on 13 of the state's 14 Indian reservations (one was unpopulated). Besides those living on reservations and in villages, a cluster of Indian urban dwellers (chiefly Ojibwa) lived in St. Paul. The reservation with the largest 2000 population was Leech Lake, with 10,205 people. Other reservations included Fond du Lac (3,728) and Mille Lacs (4,704). Indian lands totaled 764,000 acres (309,000 hectares) in 1982, of which 93% were tribal lands.

There were only 39 black Americans in Minnesota in 1850; by 1990, blacks numbered 95,000, or 2.1% of the total population, and as of 2000, the black population had jumped to 171,731 (3.5%). In 2000 there were 141,968 Asian and Pacific residents, including 41,800 Hmong (2nd-largest total in the US), 18,824 Vietnamese, 16,887 Asian Indians, 16,060 Chinese, 12,584 Koreans, and 9,940 Laotians. In 2000, Pacific Islanders numbered 1,979. In 2000, there also were 143,382 Hispanics and Latinos, 2.9% of the state population.

8LANGUAGES

Many place-names echo the languages of the Yankton and Santee Sioux Indian tribes and of the incoming Algonkian-language Ojibwa, or Chippewa, from whom most of the Sioux fled to Dakota Territory. Such place-names as Minnesota itself, Minnetonka, and Mankato are Siouan in origin; Kabetogama and Winnibigoshish, both lakes, are Ojibwan.

English in the state is essentially Northern, with minor infiltration of Midland terms because of early movement up the Mississippi River into southern Minnesota and also up the Great Lakes into and beyond Duluth. Among older residents, traces of Scandinavian intonation persist, and on the Iron Range several pronunciation features reflect the mother tongues of mine workers from eastern Europe.

Although some minor variants now compete in frequency, on the whole Minnesota speech features such dominant Northern terms as *andirons*, *pail*, *mouth organ* (harmonica), *comforter* (tied and filled bedcover), *wishbone*, *clingstone peach*, *sweet corn*, *angleworm* (earthworm), *darning needle or mosquito hawk* (dragonfly), and *sick to the stomach*. Minnesotans call the grass strip between street and sidewalk the *boulevard* and a rubber band a *rubber binder*, and many *cook coffee* when they brew it. Three-fourths of a sample population spoke *root* with the vowel of *put*; one third, through school influence, pronounced /ah/ in *aunt* instead of the usual Northern short /a/, as in *pants*. Many younger speakers pronounce *caller* and *collar* alike.

In 2000, 4,201,503 Minnesotans—91.5%—five years old or older spoke only English at home.

The following table gives selected statistics from the 2000 census for language spoken at home by persons five years old and over. The category "African languages" includes Amharic, Ibo, Twi, Yoruba, Bantu, Swahili, and Somali. The category "Scandinavian languages" includes Danish, Norwegian, and Swedish.

LANGUAGE	NUMBER	PERCENT
Population 5 years and over	4,591,491	100.0
Speak only English	4,201,503	91.5
Speak a language other than English	389,988	8.5
Speak a language other than English	389,988	8.5
Spanish or Spanish Creole	132,066	2.9
Miao, Hmong	41,673	0.9
German	35,072	0.8
African languages	24,747	0.5
Vietnamese	16,503	0.4
French (incl. Patois, Cajun)	15,744	0.3
Scandinavian languages	12,722	0.3
Chinese	12,578	0.3
Russian	9,629	0.2
Laotian	7,987	0.2

9RELIGIONS

Minnesota's first Christian church was organized by Presbyterians in Ft. Snelling in 1835; the first Roman Catholic church, the Chapel of St. Paul, was dedicated in 1841 at a town then called Pig's Eye but now known by the same name as the chapel. Immigrants arriving in subsequent decades brought their religions with them, with Lutherans and Catholics predominating.

As of 2000, Protestant groups were predominant with the largest denominations being the Evangelical Lutheran Church in America, 853,448 adherents; the Lutheran Church—Missouri Synod, 203,863 adherents; and the United Methodist Church, 117,990 adherents. Other Lutheran, Presbyterian, and Baptist denominations were also somewhat prominent. The Episcopal Church had 30,547 adherents. The Church of Jesus Christ of Latter-Day Saints (Mormons) had about 20,000 members. There were about 42,000 adherents to Judaism and 12,300 adherents of Islam. Over 1.8 million people (about 38.3% of the population) were not counted as members of any religious organization.

Minnesota is the headquarters for three national Lutheran religious groups: the American Lutheran Church, the Church of the Lutheran Brethren, and the Association of Free Lutheran Congregations.

10TRANSPORTATION

The development of an extensive railroad network after the Civil War was a key factor in the growth of lumbering, iron mining, wheat growing, and other industries. By 2000, Minnesota had a total of 5,680 rail mi (9,141 km). In 2000, 35,362,987 tons of metallic ores originated from Minnesota, and accounted for 51% of the total rail tonnage originated within the state. Amtrak serves Minneapolis–St. Paul en route from Chicago to Seattle.

Planning and supervision of mass transportation in the Twin Cities metropolitan area are under the jurisdiction of the Metropolitan Transit Commission, a public corporation. The national Greyhound bus line was founded in Hibbing in 1914.

Minnesota had 132,250 mi (212,835 km) of public roads and streets in 2000, of which 116,232 mi (187,057 km) were rural and 16,018 mi (25,778 km) urban. I-35 links Minneapolis–St. Paul with Duluth, and I-94 connects the Twin Cities with Moorhead and Fargo, North Dakota. In 2000, there were 2,625,595 registered automobiles, 1,989,580 trucks, and 14,765 buses; there were 2,940,789 licensed drivers in that year.

The first settlements grew up around major river arteries, especially in the southeast; early traders and settlers arrived first by canoe or keelboat, later by steamer. The port of Duluth–Superior, at the western terminus of the Great Lakes–St. Lawrence Seaway (officially opened in 1959) handled 42.2 million tons of domestic and international cargo in 2000, including bulk grain, coal, metallic ores, and refrigerated commodities. The ports of Minneapolis and St. Paul handle a combined cargo tonnage greater than seven million each year, with agricultural products and scrap iron moving downstream and petroleum products, chemicals, and cement moving upstream.

As of 2002, the state had 380 airports, 74 seaplane bases, 52 heliports, and 1 stolport. Minneapolis–St. Paul International is the state's largest and busiest airport, with 16,959,014 passengers enplaned in 2000.

11HISTORY

People have lived on the land that is now Minnesota for at least 10,000 years. The earliest inhabitants—belonging to what archaeologists classify as the Paleo-Indian (or Big Game) culture—hunted large animals, primarily bison, from which they obtained food, clothing, and materials for shelter. A second identifiable cultural tradition, from around 5000 BC, was the Eastern Archaic (or Old Copper) culture. These people hunted small as well as large game animals and fashioned copper implements through a cold hammering process. The more recent Woodland Tradition (1000 BC–AD 1700) was marked by the introduction of pottery and of mound burials. From the 1870s to the early 1900s, more than 11,000 burial mounds were discovered in Minnesota—the most visible remains of prehistoric life in the area. Finally, overlapping the Woodland culture in time was the Mississippian Tradition, beginning around AD 1000, in which large villages with permanent dwellings were erected near fertile river bottoms; their residents, in addition to hunting and fishing, raising corn, beans, and squash. There are many sites from this culture throughout southern Minnesota.

At the time of European penetration in the 17th and early 18th centuries, the two principal Indian nations were the Dakota, or Minnesota Sioux, and, at least after 1700, the Ojibwa, or Chippewa, who were moving from the east into northern Minnesota and the Dakota homelands. Friendly relations between the two nations were shattered in 1736, when the Dakota slew a party of French missionaries and traders (allies of the Ojibwa) and their Cree Indian guides (distant relatives of the Ojibwa) at the Lake of the Woods, an act the Ojibwa viewed as a declaration of war. There followed more than 100 years of conflict between Dakota and Ojibwa, during which the Dakota were pressed toward the south and west, with the Ojibwa establishing themselves in the north.

Few scholars accept the authenticity of the Kensington Rune Stone, found in 1898, the basis of the claim that Minnesota was visited in 1362 by the Vikings. The first white men whose travels through the region have been documented were Pierre Esprit Radisson and his brother-in-law, Médart Chouart, Sieur de Groseilliers, who probably reached the interior of northern Minnesota in the 1650s. In 1679, Daniel Greysolon, Sieur Duluth, held council with the Dakota near Mille Lacs and formally claimed the region for King Louis XIV of France. The following year, Duluth negotiated the release of three captives of the Dakota Indians, among them a Belgian explorer and missionary, Father Louis Hennepin, who named the falls of the Mississippi (the site of present-day Minneapolis) after his patron saint, Anthony of Padua, and returned to Europe to write an exaggerated account of his travels in the region.

Duluth was in the vanguard of the French, English, and American explorers, fur traders, and missionaries who came to Minnesota during the two centuries before statehood. Among the best known was Nicolas Perrot, who built Ft. Antoine on the east side of Lake Pepin in 1686. In 1731, Pierre Gaultier de Varennes, Sieur de la Verendrye, journeyed to the Lake of the Woods, along whose shores he erected Ft. St. Charles; subsequently, he or his men ventured farther west than any other known French explorer, reaching the Dakotas and the Saskatchewan Valley. His eldest son was among those slain by Dakota Indians at the Lake of the Woods in 1736.

Competition for control of the upper Mississippi Valley ended with the British victory in the French and Indian War, which placed the portion of Minnesota east of the Mississippi under British control; the land west of the Mississippi was ceded by France to Spain in 1762. Although the Spanish paid little attention to their northern territory, the British immediately sent in fur traders and explorers. One of the best known was Jonathan Carver, who spent the winter of 1766–67 with the Dakota on the Minnesota River. His account of his travels—a mixture of personal observations and borrowings from others—quickly became a popular success.

There was little activity in the region during the Revolutionary War, and for a few decades afterward, the British continued to pursue their interests there. The North West Company built a major fur-trading post at Grand Portage, which quickly became the center of a prosperous inland trade, and other posts dotted the countryside. The company hired David Thompson away from the Hudson's Bay Company to map the area from Lake Superior west to the Red River; his detailed and accurate work, executed in the late 1790s, is still admired today. After the War of 1812, the US Congress passed an act curbing British participation in the fur trade, and the North West Company was eventually replaced by the American Fur Company, which John Jacob Astor had incorporated in 1808.

Under the Northwest Ordinance of 1787, Minnesota east of the Mississippi became part of the Northwest Territory; most of western Minnesota was acquired by the US as part of the Louisiana Purchase of 1803. The Red River Valley became a secure part of the US after an agreement with England on the northern boundary was reached in 1818.

In 1805, the US War Department sent Lieutenant Zebulon Pike and a detachment of troops to explore the Mississippi to its source. Pike failed to locate the source, but he concluded a treaty with a band of Dakota for two parcels of land along the river. Later, additional troops were sent in to establish US control, and in 1819, a military post was established in part of Pike's land, on a bluff overlooking the junction of the Mississippi and Minnesota rivers. First called Ft. St. Anthony, it was renamed in 1825 for Colonel Josiah Snelling, who supervised the construction of the permanent fort. For three decades, Ft. Snelling served as the principal center of civilization in Minnesota and the key frontier outpost in the northwest.

In 1834, Henry H. Sibley was appointed a manager of the American Fur Company on the upper Mississippi. He settled comfortably at Mendota, a trading post across the river from Ft. Snelling, and enjoyed immediate success. The company's fortunes took a downward turn in 1837, however—partly because of a financial panic but, even more important, because the first of a series of treaties with the Dakota and Ojibwa transferred large areas of Indian land to the US government and thus curtailed the profitable relationship between fur traders and Indians. The treaties opened the land for lumbering, farming, and settlement. Lumbering spawned many of the early permanent settlements, such as Marine and Stillwater, on the St. Croix River, and St. Anthony (later Minneapolis) at the falls of the Mississippi. Another important town, St. Paul (originally Pig's Eye), developed as a trading center at the head of navigation on the Mississippi.

In 1849, Minnesota Territory was established. It included all of present-day Minnesota, along with portions of North and South Dakota east of the Missouri River. Alexander Ramsey, a Pennsylvania Whig, was appointed as the first territorial governor, and in 1851, the legislature named St. Paul the capital. Stillwater was chosen for the state prison, while St. Anthony was selected as the site for the university. As of 1850, the new territory had slightly more than 6,000 inhabitants, but as lumbering grew and subsequent Indian treaties opened up more land, the population boomed, reaching a total of more than 150,000 by 1857, with the majority concentrated in the southeast corner, close to the rivers.

On 11 May 1858, Minnesota officially became the 32nd state, with its western boundaries pruned from the Missouri to the Red River. Henry Sibley, a Democrat, narrowly defeated Alexander Ramsey, running as a Republican, to become the state's first governor. But under Ramsey's leadership, the fast-growing Republican Party soon gained control of state politics and held it firmly through the early 20th century. In the first presidential election in which Minnesota participated, Abraham Lincoln, the Republican candidate, easily carried the state, and when the Civil War broke out, Minnesota was the first state to answer Lincoln's call for troops. In all, Minnesota supplied more than 20,000 men to defend the Union.

More challenging to the defense of Minnesota was the Dakota War of 1862. Grieved by the loss of their lands, dissatisfied with reservation life, and ultimately brought to a condition of near starvation, the Dakota appealed to US Indian agencies without success. The murder of five whites by four young Dakota Indians ignited a bloody uprising in which more than 300 whites and an unknown number of Indians were killed. In the aftermath, 38 Dakota captives were hanged for "voluntary participation in murders and massacres," and the Dakota remaining in Minnesota were removed to reservations in Nebraska. (Some later returned to Minnesota.) Meanwhile, the Ojibwa were relegated to reservations on remnants of their former lands.

Also during 1862, Minnesota's first railroad joined St. Anthony (Minneapolis) and St. Paul with 10 mi (16 km) of track. By 1867, the Twin Cities were connected with Chicago by rail; in the early 1870s, tracks crossed the prairie all the way to the Red River Valley. The railroads brought settlers from the eastern states (many of them Scandinavian and German in origin) to every corner of Minnesota; the settlers, in turn, grew produce for the trains to carry back to the cities of the east. The railroads soon ushered in an era of large-scale commercial farming. Wheat provided the biggest cash crop, as exports rose from 2 million bushels in 1860 to 95 million in 1890. Meanwhile, the falls of St. Anthony became the major US flour-milling center; by 1880, 27 Minneapolis mills were producing more than 2 million barrels of flour annually.

Despite these signs of prosperity, discontent grew among Minnesota farmers, who were plagued by high railroad rates, damaging droughts, and a deflationary economy. The first national farmers' movement, the National Grange of the Patrons of Husbandry, was founded in 1867 by a Minnesotan, Oliver H. Kelley, and spread more rapidly in Minnesota than in any other state. The Farmers' Alliance movement, joining forces with the Knights of Labor, exerted a major influence on state politics in the 1880s. In 1898, the Populist Party—in which a Minnesotan, Ignatius Donnelly, played a leading role nationwide—helped elect John Lind to the governorship on a fusion ticket.

Most immigrants during the 1860s and 1870s settled on the rich farmland of the north and west, but after 1880 the cities and industries grew more rapidly. When iron ore was discovered in the 1880s in the sparsely settled northeast, even that part of the state attracted settlers, many of them immigrants from eastern and southern Europe. Before 1900, Duluth had become a major lake port, and by the eve of World War I, Minnesota had become a national iron-mining center.

The economic picture changed after the war. As the forests were depleted, the big lumber companies turned to the Pacific Northwest. An agricultural depression hit the region, and flour mills moved to the Kansas City area and to Buffalo, New York. Minnesotans adapted to the new realities in various ways. Farmers planted corn, soybeans, and sugar beets along with wheat, and new food-processing industries developed. To these were added business machines, electronics, computers, and other high-technology industries. In 1948, for the first time, the dollar value of all manufactured products exceeded total cash farm receipts. In 1950 the state's urban population exceeded its rural population for the first time. Minnesota was becoming an urban commonwealth.

In addition to heightened demand for its agricultural products, Minnesota prospered as a result of new defense-related, high-technology, and other industries that grew up following World War II. Over $1 billion was invested in plants to process low-grade iron ore, called taconite, after the state's supply of high-grade ore declined. By the 1970s, environmentalists were targeting the ore producers for polluting Lake Superior with mineral wastes, and in 1978 the Minnesota Supreme Court ordered Reserve Mining Company to comply with pollution-control standards.

A successful merger of Minnesota's Farmer-Labor and Democratic parties, engineered in 1943–44 by both local and national politicians, revived the state's progressivist tradition after World War II. Hubert Humphrey (later US vice president) and his colleagues Orville Freeman, Eugene McCarthy, and Eugenie Anderson emerged as leaders of this new coalition. Their political heir, Walter Mondale, was vice president in 1977–81 but, as the Democratic presidential candidate in 1984, lost the election in a Republican landslide, carrying only his native state and the District of Columbia.

In the 1990s, Minnesota continued its economic diversification as service industries, including finance, insurance, and real estate, became increasingly important. As a result, it closed the decade with a low unemployment rate of 2.8% (when the national average was just over 4%). Though Minnesota, led by the Twin Cities, enjoyed an unprecedented decade of economic prosperity, it was generally acknowledged that agriculture across the Great Plains was in crisis by the end of the 1990s.

For many farmers, their problems had been exacerbated by weather conditions. In 1988, Minnesota's agricultural producers suffered from the worst drought since the 1930s. As a result of the severe flooding of the Mississippi River in 1993, almost half of Minnesota's counties were designated as disaster areas. Again in 1997, some of the most severe flooding in the century occurred in the Red River and Minnesota River valleys.

The state legislature closed its 1999 session having passed the largest permanent tax cut and one-time rebate in the state's history, amounting to $2.9 billion in tax relief. Though the accomplishment was hailed as a result of a multi-partisan effort, discord soon befell Minnesota government. By October, activists were attempting to recall Governor Jesse Ventura, elected the previous year as a Reform Party candidate, only to align himself with the Independence Party of Minnesota shortly after taking office. The following legislative session (in 2000) saw more veto overrides than in any other session of the last half century.

Republican Governor Tim Pawlenty, elected in 2002, sponsored an internet privacy bill early in his term, and stressed the need for higher education standards and attracting more high-tech jobs to the state. In 2003, Minnesota faced the largest budget deficit in its history, $4.2 billion. The legislature that year passed a $28.3 billion budget marked by spending cuts and no new taxes. Democrats, farmers, and labor leaders feared Pawlenty's commitment to no new taxes would amount to large spending cuts in education, health care, and other areas.

12 STATE GOVERNMENT

The constitutional convention that assembled at St. Paul on 13 July 1857 was marked by such bitter dissension that the Democrats and Republicans had to meet in separate chambers; the final draft was written by a committee of five Democrats and five Republicans and then adopted by a majority of each party, without amendment. Since Democrats and Republicans were also unwilling to sign the same piece of paper, two separate documents were prepared, one on blue-tinted paper, the other on white. The constitution was ratified by the electorate on 13 October and approved by the US Congress on 11 May 1858. An amendment restructuring the constitution for easy reference and simplifying its language was approved in 1974; for purposes of constitutional law, however, the original document (incorporating numerous other amendments) remains authoritative. Through January 2003 there were 118 amendments.

As reapportioned by court order after the 1970 census, the Minnesota legislature consists of a 67-member senate and a 134-member house of representatives. Legislative sessions begin in January and are limited to 120 legislative days or to the first Monday after the 3rd Saturday in May. Sessions are to be held in only odd-numbered years, but the legislature may divide and meet in even-numbered years as well. Only the governor may call for special sessions. Senators serve four years and representatives two, at annual salaries of $31,140 as of 2002, unchanged from

1999. Legislators must be at least 18 years old, qualified voters, and must have resided in the state for one year and in the legislative district for six months preceding election.

The governor and lieutenant governor are jointly elected for four-year terms; both must be US citizens at least 25 years old, and must have been residents of Minnesota for a year before election. Other constitutional officers are the secretary of state, auditor, treasurer (will be abolished, as of 2003), and attorney general, all serving for four years. Numerous other officials are appointed by the governor, among them the commissioners of government departments and many heads and members of independent agencies. In 2002 the governor's salary was $120,303, unchanged from 1999.

Once a bill is passed by a majority of both houses, the governor may sign it, veto it in whole or in part, or pocket-veto it by failing to act within 14 days of adjournment. (When the legislature is in session, however, a bill becomes law if the governor fails to act on it within three days.) A two-thirds vote of the members of both houses overrides a veto. Constitutional amendments require the approval of a majority of both houses of the legislature and are subject to ratification by the electorate. Those voting in state elections must be at least 18 years old, US citizens, and state residents for at least 20 days prior to election day. Restrictions apply to convicted felons and those declared mentally incompetent by the court.

13 POLITICAL PARTIES

The two major political parties are the Democratic-Farmer-Labor Party (DFL) and the Republican Party (until 1995 called the Independent-Republican Party). The Republican Party dominated Minnesota politics from the 1860s through the 1920s, except for a period around the turn of the century. The DFL, formed in 1944 by merger between the Democratic Party and the populist Farmer-Labor Party, rose to prominence in the 1950s under US Senator Hubert Humphrey.

Minnesota Presidential Vote by Political Parties, 1948–2000

YEAR	ELECTORAL VOTE	MINNESOTA WINNER	DEMOCRAT[1]	REPUBLICAN[2]	PROGRESSIVE	SOCIALIST	SOCIALIST LABOR[3]
1948	11	*Truman (D)	692,966	483,617	27,866	4,646	2,525
1952	11	*Eisenhower (R)	608,458	763,211	2,666	—	2,383
						SOC. WORKERS	
1956	11	*Eisenhower (R)	617,525	719,302	—	1,098	2,080
1960	11	*Kennedy (D)I	779,933	757,915	—	3,077	962
1964	10	*Johnson (D)	991,117	559,624	—	1,177	2,544
							AMERICAN IND.
1968	10	Humphrey (D)	857,738	658,643	—	—	68,931
					PEOPLE'S		AMERICAN
1972	10	*Nixon (R)	802,346	898,269	2,805	4,261	31,407
					LIBERTARIAN		
1976	10	*Carter (D)	1,070,440	819,395	3,529	4,149	13,592
						CITIZENS	
1980	10	Carter (D)	954,173	873,268	31,593	8,406	6,136
1984	10	Mondale (D)	1,036,364	1,032,603	2,996	1,219	—
					MINNESOTA PROGRESSIVE		SOCIALIST WORKERS
1988	10	Dukakis (D)	1,109,471	962,337	5,109	5,403	2,155
					IND. (Perot)		CONSTITUTION
1992	10	*Clinton (D)	1,020,997	747,841	3,373	562,506	3,363
							GREEN (Nader)
1996	10	*Clinton (D)	1,120,438	766,476	8,271	257,704	24,908
					REFORM		
2000	10	Gore (D)	1,168,266	1,109,659	5,282	22,166	126,696

*Won US presidential election.
1 Called Democratic-Farmer-Labor Party in Minnesota.
2 Independent-Republican party called Republican Party as of 1995.
3 Appeared as Industrial Government Party on the ballot.

The DFL is the heir to a long populist tradition bred during the panic of 1857 and the early days of statehood, a tradition perpetuated by a succession of strong, though transient, third-party movements. The Grange, a farmers' movement committed to the cause of railroad regulation, took root in Minnesota in 1868; it withered in the panic of 1873, but its successors, the Anti-Monopoly Party and the Greenback Party, attracted large followings for some time afterward. They were followed by a new pro-silver group, the Farmers' Alliance, which spread to Minnesota from Nebraska in 1881 and soon became associated with the Minnesota Knights of Labor. The Populist Party also won a foothold in Minnesota, in alliance with the Democratic Party in the late 1890s.

The Farmer-Labor Party, the most successful of Minnesota's third-party movements, grew out of a socialist and isolationist movement known at first as the Non-Partisan League. Founded in North Dakota with the initial aim of gaining control of the Republican Party in that state, the league moved its headquarters to St. Paul and competed in the 1918 elections under the name Farmer-Labor Party, hastily adopted to attract what party leaders hoped would be its two main constituencies. The party scored a major success in 1922 when its candidate, Henrik Shipstead, a Glenwood dentist, defeated a nationally known incumbent, Republican Senator Frank B. Kellogg; Farmer-Labor candidate Floyd B. Olson won the governorship in 1930. The decline of the party in the late 1930s was hastened by the rise of Republican Harold Stassen, an ardent internationalist, who won the governorship in 1938 and twice won reelection.

The first DFL candidate to become governor was Orville Freeman in 1954. The DFL held the governorship from 1963 to 1967 and from 1971 to 1978, when US Representative Al Quie (IR) defeated his DFL opponent, Rudy Perpich; however, Perpich regained the governorship for the DFL in 1982. Perpich served four terms. He lost to Independent-Republican Arne Carlson in 1990, and Carlson was reelected in 1994. The 1998 gubernatorial election in Minnesota made national headlines; it was won by Reform candidate and former World Wrestling Federation personality Jesse Ventura. After gaining office, Ventura switched allegiances to the Independence Party of Minnesota. Tim Pawlenty, a Republican, won the governorship in 2002.

Minnesota is famous as a breeding ground for presidential candidates. Governor Harold Stassen contended seriously for the Republican nomination in 1948 and again in 1952. Vice President Hubert Humphrey was the Democratic presidential nominee in 1968, losing by a narrow margin to Richard Nixon. During the same year, US Senator Eugene McCarthy unsuccessfully sought the Democratic presidential nomination on an antiwar platform; his surprising showings in the early primaries against the incumbent, Lyndon B. Johnson, helped persuade Johnson to withdraw his candidacy. Eight years later, McCarthy ran for the presidency as an independent, drawing 35,490 votes in Minnesota (1.8% of the total votes cast) and 756,631 votes (0.9%) nationwide. Walter Mondale, successor to Hubert Humphrey's seat when Humphrey became Johnson's vice president in 1964, was chosen in 1976 by Jimmy Carter as his vice-presidential running mate; he again ran with Carter in 1980, when the two lost their bid for reelection. In the 1984 election, Minnesota was the only state to favor the Mondale-Ferraro ticket. Minnesotans gave the Republican Party a majority in the state's house of representatives for the first time since 1970, but the Democrats retained control of the state senate.

In 2000, Democrat Al Gore won 48% of the presidential vote; Republican George W. Bush gained 46%; and Green Party candidate Ralph Nader received 5%. In 2002 there were 2,844,428 registered voters; there is no party registration in the state. The state had 10 electoral votes in the 2000 presidential election.

In 1994, US Senator David Durenberger retired, partly a result of having been "denounced" by the Senate in 1990, and Rod Grams, a 46-year-old Republican was elected to the seat. In 2000, Democrat Mark Dayton was elected to the Senate. In 1996 Democrat Paul Wellstone successfully defended his Senate seat against a challenge by Republican Rudy Boschwitz, from whom he had won the seat in 1990. Wellstone died in a plane crash in October 2002, along with his wife and daughter, three staff members, and two pilots. Republican Norm Coleman won Wellstone's Senate seat in 2002, defeating Walter Mondale, who stepped in to run after Wellstone's death. Following the 2002 elections, Minnesota's delegation to the US House was split between four Democrats and four Republicans. In mid-2003, there were 35 Democrats 31 Republicans, and one Independent serving in the Minnesota state senate. Party representation in the state house consisted of 52 Democrats, and 82 Republicans.

14LOCAL GOVERNMENT

Minnesota was divided into 87 counties as of 2002, with 1,793 townships (more than any other state), 854 municipal governments, 345 public school districts, and 403 special districts.

Each of Minnesota's counties is governed by a board of commissioners, ordinarily elected for four-year terms. Other elected officials include the auditor, treasurer, recorder, sheriff, attorney, and coroner; an assessor and engineer are customarily appointed. Besides administering welfare, highway maintenance, and other state programs, the county is responsible for planning and development and, except in large cities, for property assessment. During the 1970s, counties also assumed increased responsibility for solid waste disposal and shoreline management.

Each regional development commission, or RDC, consists of local officials (selected by counties, cities, townships, and boards of education in the region) and of representatives of public interest groups (selected by the elected officials). RDCs prepare and adopt regional development plans and review applications for loans and grants.

Cities either have home-rule charters or are statutory cities, which are restricted to the systems of government prescribed by state law. In either case, the mayor-council system is the most common. Besides providing such traditional functions as street maintenance and police and fire protection, some cities operate utilities, sell liquor, or run hospitals, among other services. Each township is governed by a board of supervisors and by other elected officials.

15STATE SERVICES

To address the continuing threat of terrorism and to work with the federal Department of Homeland Security (created in 2002 following the terrorist attacks of 11 September 2001), homeland security in Minnesota in 2003 operated under the authority of the governor; the public safety commissioner was designated as the state homeland security advisor.

Minnesota's ombudsman for corrections investigates complaints about corrections facilities or the conduct of prison officials. A six-member Ethical Practices Board supervises the registration of some 1,300 lobbyists, monitors the financing of political campaigns, and sees that some 1,000 elected and appointed state officials observe regulations governing conflict of interest and disclosure of personal finances. Minnesota law also provides that legislative meetings of any kind must be open to the public.

The state-aided public school system is under the jurisdiction of the Department of Children, Families, and Learning, which carries out the policies of a nine-member Board of Education appointed by the governor with the advice and consent of the senate. Responsible for higher education are the University of Minnesota Board of Regents, elected by the legislature; the boards of trustees of the Minnesota State Colleges and Universities (MNSCU), appointed by the governor; and other agencies. The Department of Transportation maintains roads and bridges, enforces public transportation rates, inspects airports, and has responsibility for railroad safety.

Minnesota's Department of Health investigates health problems, disseminates health information, regulates hospitals and nursing homes, and inspects restaurants and lodgings. Health regulations affecting farm produce are administered by the Department of Agriculture. State facilities for the mentally retarded are operated by the Department of Human Services, which administers state welfare programs and provides social services to the aged, the handicapped, and others in need.

The Department of Public Safety registers motor vehicles, licenses drivers, enforces traffic laws, and regulates the sale of liquor. The Department of Military Affairs has jurisdiction over the Minnesota National Guard, and the Department of Corrections operates prisons, reformatories, and parole programs. The Housing Finance Agency aids the construction and rehabilitation of low- and middle-income housing. Laws governing occupational safety, wages and hours, and child labor are enforced by the Department of Labor and Industry, while the Department of Economic Security supervises public employment programs and administers unemployment insurance. Other departments focus on agriculture, commerce, corrections, employee relations, finance, natural resources, public service, revenue, and trade and economic development.

16JUDICIAL SYSTEM

Minnesota's highest court is the supreme court, consisting of a chief justice and six associate justices; all are elected without party designation for six-year terms, with vacancies being filled by gubernatorial appointment. The district court, divided into 10 judicial districts with 254 judges in 1999, is the court of original jurisdiction. Each judicial district has at least three district judges, elected to six-year terms. The governor designates a chief judge for a three-year term.

County courts, operating in all counties of the state except two—Hennepin (Minneapolis) and Ramsey (St. Paul), which have municipal courts—assume functions formerly exercised by probate, family, and local courts. They exercise civil jurisdiction in cases where the amount in contention is $5,000 or less, and criminal jurisdiction in preliminary hearings and misdemeanors. They also hear cases involving family disputes, and have concurrent jurisdiction with the district court in divorces, adoptions, and certain other proceedings. The probate division of the county court system presides over guardianship and incompetency proceedings and all cases relating to the disposing of estates. All county judges are elected for six-year terms.

Minnesota's federal and state correctional institutions had a total population of 6,514 in June 2001, an increase of 4.7% over the previous year. The state's incarceration rate stood at 131 per 100,000 population.

Crime rates are generally below the national average. In 2001, Minnesota's total crime rate per 100,000 inhabitants was 3,583.7, including a total of 13,145 violent crimes and 165,046 crimes against property in that year. Minnesota has no death penalty statute. The Crime Victims Reparations Board offers compensation to innocent victims of crime or to their dependent survivors.

17ARMED FORCES

In 2002, there were 702 active-duty military personnel and 2,576 civilian personnel in Minnesota. In 2001 Minnesota firms received about $1.39 billion in defense contracts.

As of 2002, there were 464,968 veterans of US military service living in Minnesota. Of these, 90,206 served in World War II; 62,681 in the Korean conflict; 146,799 during the Vietnam era; and 38,395 during 1990–2000 (including the Persian Gulf War). Veterans' benefits exceeded $1.2 billion in 2002.

In 2000, the Minnesota Highway Patrol employed 548 full-time sworn officers

18MIGRATION

A succession of migratory waves began in the 17th and 18th centuries with the arrival of the Dakota and Ojibwa, among other Indian groups, followed during the 19th century by New England Yankees, Germans, Scandinavians, and finally southern and eastern Europeans. Especially since 1920, new arrivals from other states and countries have been relatively few, and the state experienced a net loss from migration of 80,000 between 1970 and 1980. The trend was almost halted in the 1980s when immigration nearly equaled emigration. Between 1990 and 1998, Minnesota had net gains of 71,000 in domestic migration and 47,000 in international migration. In 1998, 6,981 foreign immigrants entered the state. Minnesota's overall population increased 8% between 1990 and 1998.

Within the state, there has been a long-term movement to metropolitan areas, especially to the suburbs of major cities; from 1970 to 1983, the state's metropolitan population grew by nearly 1% annually. The urban population increased from 66.8% to 69.9% during the 1980s and, leveling off somewhat, ranged between 68.8% and 69.7% in the 1990s. From 1980 to 1990, the population of the Minneapolis-St. Paul metropolitan area grew 15.5%; it grew another 8.9% between 1990 and 1996. In the period 1995–2000, 355,250 people moved into the state and 326,081 moved out, for a net gain of 29,169, of whom were from Wisconsin.

19INTERGOVERNMENTAL COOPERATION

Relations with the Council of State Governments are conducted through the Minnesota Commission on Interstate Cooperation. consisting of five members from each house of the state legislature and five administrative officers or other state employees; in addition, the governor, the president of the senate, and the speaker of the house are nonvoting members. Minnesota also participates in the Great Lakes Charter, which it formed with seven other states in 1985 to preserve the lakes' water supply, and in other regional compacts. Minnesota is a party to the Boundary Compact Between Michigan, Wisconsin, and Minnesota; the Great Lakes Commission; the Midwest Interstate Low-Level Radioactive Waste Compact Commission; and the Midwestern Higher Education Compact. In 2001, Minnesota received over $5.2 billion in federal grants.

20ECONOMY

Furs, wheat, pine lumber, and high-grade iron ore were once the basis of Minnesota's economy. As these resources diminished, however, the state turned to wood pulp, dairy products, corn and soybeans, taconite, and manufacturing, often in such food-related industries as meat-packing, canning, and the processing of dairy products. The leading sources of income in Minnesota have shifted again in recent years. Manufacturing as a percent of total state output fell from 18.5% in 1997 to 15.8% in 2001, a relative decline accelerated by a –8.2% fall in manufacturing output in 2001. Net growth in manufacturing output 1997 to 2001 was 5.8% compared to an output growth of 32.5% from general services; 27.9% from the trade sector; 26.1% from financial services; and 25.8% from government services. Minnesota's economy grew robustly at the end of the 1990—7% in 1997; 5.2% in 1999, and 8.5% in 2000—, but the annual growth rate plummeted to 1% in the recession of 2001. In 2002, employment declined more rapidly than in the country as a whole because of the large share of Minnesota workers in sectors most affected by the national slowdown: manufacturing, information technology and airline industries. Office vacancy rates in metropolitan areas increased from 12.2% in 2001 to 19.6% in 2002, above the national average of 16.5%. On the other hand, having escaped the drought conditions that afflicted many other states, corn and soybean harvests were large in 2002, and Minnesota growers were in a position to benefit from drought-induced higher prices for both crops. The dairy sector, however, faced historically low prices, increasing the number of dairy producers leaving the industry.

Minnesota's gross state product in 2001 was $188.1 billion, the 17th largest among the states, to which general services contributed $40.6 billion; financial services, $36.3 billion; trade, $33.7 billion; manufacturing, $29.8 billion; government, 20.2 billion; transportation and public utilities, $!3.5 billion, and construction, $10 billion. In 2001, the public sector constituted 10.8% of the gross state product.

21INCOME

According to the Bureau of Economic Analysis, in 2001, Minnesota had a per capita personal income (PCPI) of $33,059 which ranked 9th in the United States (including the District of Columbia) and was 109% of the national average, $30,413. The 2001 PCPI reflected an increase of 2.6% from 2000 compared to the national change of 2.2%. In 2001, Minnesota had a total personal income (TPI) of $164,784,335,000 which ranked 17th in the United States and accounted for 1.9% of the national total. The 2001 TPI reflected an increase of 3.6% from 2000 compared to the national change of 3.3%.

Earnings of persons employed in Minnesota increased from $117,378,224,000 in 2000 to $120,934,233,000 in 2001, an increase of 3.0%. The largest industries in 2001 were services, 27.6% of earnings; state and local government, 11.3%; and durable goods manufacturing, 10.8%. Of the industries that accounted for at least 5% of earnings in 2001, the slowest growing from 2000 to 2001 was durable goods manufacturing, which decreased 4.1%; the fastest was finance, insurance, and real estate (9.8% of earnings in 2001), which increased 9.5%.

According to data released by the US Census Bureau, in 2000, the median household income was $50,865 compared to the national average of $42,148. In 2001, the median income for a family of four was $72,635 compared to the national average of $63,278. For the period 1999 to 2001, the average poverty rate was 6.8% which placed it 2nd among the 50 states and the District of Columbia ranked lowest to highest.

22LABOR

According to Bureau of Labor Statistics (BLS) provisional estimates, in July 2003 the seasonally adjusted civilian labor force in Minnesota numbered 2,937,500, with approximately 135,500 workers unemployed, yielding an unemployment rate of 4.6%, compared to the national average of 6.2% for the same period. Since the beginning of the BLS data series in 1978, the highest unemployment rate recorded was 9.2% in February 1983. The historical low was 2.4% in April 1999. In 2001, an estimated 5.0% of the labor force was employed in construction; 15.3% in manufacturing; 5.0% in transportation, communications, and public utilities; 18.5% in trade; 6.4% in finance, insurance, and real estate; 25.5% in services; 12.2% in government; and 4.3% in agriculture.

The history of unionization in the state includes several long and bitter labor disputes, notably the Iron Range strike of 1916, the Teamsters' strike of 1934, and the Hormel strike of 1985–86. The earliest known unions—two printers' locals, established in the late 1850s—died out during the Civil War, and several later unions faded in the panic of 1873. The Knights of Labor were the dominant force of the 1880s; the next decade saw the rise of the Minnesota State Federation of Labor, whose increasing political influence bore fruit in the landmark Workmen's Compensation Act of 1913 and the subsequent ascension of the Farmer-Labor Party. The legislature enacted a fair employment practices law in 1955 and passed a measure in 1973 prescribing collective-bargaining procedures for public employees and granting them a limited right to strike.

The US Department of Labor reported that in 2002, 439,000 of Minnesota's 2,503,000 employed wage and salary workers were members of unions. This represented 17.6% of those so employed, unchanged from 2001 but down from 18.8% in 1998. In all, 457,000 workers (18.3%) were represented by unions. In addition to union members, this category includes workers who report no union affiliation but whose jobs are covered by a union contract.

23AGRICULTURE

Cash receipts from farm marketings totaled over $8.1 billion in 2001, placing Minnesota 6th among the 50 states; crops made up about 47% of the total value. For 2002, Minnesota ranked 1st in the production of oats, sugar beets, sweet corn for processing, and green peas for processing; 2nd in flaxseed; 3rd in spring wheat, corn and soybeans; 4th in corn and sunflowers; 5th in hay and 6th in barley.

The early farmers settled in the wooded hills and valleys in the southeastern quarter of the state, where they had to cut down trees and dig up stumps to make room for crops. With the coming of the railroads, farmers began planting the prairies with wheat, which by the late 1870s took up 70% of all farm acreage. In succeeding decades, wheat prices fell and railroad rates soared, fanning agrarian discontent. Farmers began to diversify, with dairy farming, oats, and corn becoming increasingly important. Improved corn yields since the 1940s have spurred the production of hogs and beef cattle and the growth of meat-packing as a major industry.

As of 2002, the state had 79,000 farms, covering 28,400,000 acres (11,500,000 hectares), or 56% of the state's total land area; the average farm had 361 acres (146 hectares). The number of people living on farms steadily declined from 624,000 in 1960 to 482,000 in 1970, and then to only 207,956, or 4.75% of the total population, by 1991. The value of farmland rose between 1998 and 2002, from $1,040 per acre to $1,450. Minnesota's farmers faced acute financial troubles during the early 1980s as a result of heavy debts, high interest rates, and generally low crop prices.

The main farming areas are in southern Minnesota, where corn, soybeans, and oats are important, and in the Red River Valley along the western border, where wheat, barley, sugar beets, and potatoes are among the chief crops.

Agribusiness is Minnesota's largest basic industry, with about one-fourth of the state's labor force employed in agriculture or agriculture-related industries, most notably food processing.

24ANIMAL HUSBANDRY

Excluding the northeast, livestock-raising is dispersed throughout the state, with cattle concentrated particularly in west-central Minnesota and in the extreme southeast, and hogs along the southern border.

In 2003, the state had an estimated 2.5 million cattle and calves, valued at nearly $1.9 billion. The state had 5.9 million hogs and pigs, valued at $501.5 million in 2002. Minnesota produced more turkey in 2001 than any other state except North Carolina: 1.1 billion lb (0.5 billion kg), worth $385.7 million. Also during 2001, the state produced 16.8 million lb (7.1 million kg) of sheep and lambs, which brought in a total of nearly $11.6 million.

The state's total of 8.8 billion lb (4 billion kg) of milk outproduced all but four states in 2001. Production of broilers in 2001 was 219.5 million lb (99.6 million kg), worth around $85.6 million, and egg output in the same year was 3.1 billion, worth $112.8 million.

25 FISHING

Commercial fishermen in 1998 landed 427,000 lb (194,000 kg) of fish, valued at $224,000. The catch included herring and smelts from Lake Superior, whitefish and yellow pike from large inland lakes, and carp and catfish from the Mississippi and Minnesota rivers. Sport fishing attracts some 1.5 million anglers annually to the state's 2.6. million acres (1.1 million hectares) of fishing lakes and 7,000 mi (11,000 km) of fishing streams, which are stocked with trout, bass, pike, muskellunge, and other fish by the Division of Fish and Wildlife of the Department of Natural Resources. Fish farms distributed 177.1 million walleye and 2.1 million trout within the state in 1998.

26 FORESTRY

Forests, which originally occupied two-thirds of Minnesota's land area, have been depleted by lumbering, farming, and forest fires. As of 2002, forestland covered 16,680,000 acres (6,750,000 hectares), or about 36% of the state's total land area. Most of the forestland is in the north, especially in Arrowhead Country in the northeast. Of the 14,723,000 acres (5,958,000 hectares) of commercial timberland, less than half is privately owned and more than one-third is under state, county, or municipal jurisdiction. In 2002, lumber production totaled 272 million board feet, 49% hardwoods and 51% softwoods. Over half of the timber that is harvested is used in paper products, and about one-third for wood products. Mills that process raw logs account for half of all forest and forest-product employment in Minnesota.

The state's two national forests are Superior (2,092,097 acres—846,671 hectares) and Chippewa (666,325 acres—267,661 hectares). The Department of Natural Resources, Division of Forestry, promotes effective management of the forest environment and seeks to restrict forest fire occurrence to 1,100 fires annually, burning no more than 30,000 acres (12,000 hectares) in all.

More than 3 million acres (1.2 million hectares) are planted each year with trees by the wood fiber industry, other private interests, and federal, state, and county forest services—more than enough to replace those harvested or destroyed by fire, insects, or disease.

27 MINING

The value of nonfuel mineral production in Minnesota in 2001 was estimated to be about $1.44 billion, an increase of about 3.5% from 2000. Iron ore, Minnesota's leading mineral commodity, accounted for $1.16 billion of this total mineral value. Iron ore is found along a belt that runs through Itasca and St. Louis counties. The combined value of lime, industrial sand and gravel, dimension granite, and limestone was $43.3 million in 2001. The estimated value of crushed stone was $85 million. The state ranked 8th nationally in value of nonfuel minerals produced during the year. Minnesota ranked 1st nationally in iron ore and 3rd in peat. Iron ore mined in Minnesota accounted for 70% of all domestic shipments to US steel manufacturers in 2001. Minnesota's output of construction and industrial sand and gravel and dimension stone is also significant.

28 ENERGY AND POWER

Minnesota produced 48.6 billion kWh of electricity (utility and nonutility) in 1999, when total installed capacity reached 10.2 million kW. Conventional thermal plants accounted for about 75% of total installed capacity; most plants were coal-fired. There are three nuclear reactors (one at Monticello, two at the Prairie Island facility), all owned by the Northern States Power Co. In 2000 Minnesota's total per capita energy consumption was 343 million Btu (86.4 million kcal), ranking it 25th among the 50 states.

Minnesota's 7 million acres (2.8 million hectares) of peat lands, the state's only known fossil fuel resource, constitute nearly half of the US total (excluding Alaska). If burned directly, the accessible fuel-quality peat deposit could substantially supplement Minnesota's energy needs.

29 INDUSTRY

Minnesota's vast wealth of natural resources, especially the state's extensive timberlands and fertile prairie, was the basis for Minnesota's early industrial development. In the late 19th century, Minneapolis was the nation's flour milling center. By the early 20th century, canning and meat packing were among the state's largest industries.

While food and food products remain an important part of the state's economy, the state's economy has diversified significantly from these early beginnings. Today, the state looks primarily to high technology industries such as computer manufacturing, printing and publishing, scientific instrument manufacturing, and fabricated metal production, for revenues.

The total value of shipments by manufacturers in 1997 exceeded $78 billion. Industry is concentrated in the state's southeast region, especially in the Twin Cities area. Minnesota was the headquarters of 13 Fortune 500 companies as of 2000.

Earnings of persons employed in Minnesota increased from $93.8 billion in 1997 to $101.5 billion in 1998, an increase of 8.2%. The largest industries in 1998 were services, 26.3% of earnings; durable goods manufacturing, 12.6%; and state and local government, 10.8%. Of the industries that accounted for at least 5% of earnings in 1998, the slowest growing from 1997 to 1998 was state and local government, which increased as 2.9%; the fastest was transportation and public utilities (6.5% of earnings in 1998), which increased 9.5%.

30 COMMERCE

Access to the Great Lakes, the St. Lawrence Seaway, and the Atlantic Ocean, as well as to the Mississippi River and the Gulf of Mexico, helps make Minnesota a major marketing and distribution center for the upper Midwest. Sales by wholesale establishments totaled $103 billion in 1997, up by 43% during the previous five years, with the 11th highest growth rate in the country. As of 1997, the state's 10,915 wholesale trade establishments had payroll totals of $5.5 billion. Retail sales totaled $49 billion in 1997. The 28,378 retail establishments in 1997 had payroll totals slightly higher than $5.4 billion. Eating and drinking establishments accounted for 28% of the total number of establishments; auto dealers, 14%; and food stores, 9%. Much of this volume was concentrated in the Twin Cities metropolitan region.

Exports of manufactured goods to foreign countries amounted to $9.1 billion in 1998. Manufactured exports included computers and computer software, electronic equipment, scientific instruments, and transportation equipment. Dairy products, feed grains, soybeans, and wheat were the largest agricultural commodity exports; the total value estimated at $2.4

billion in 1998, making Minnesota the 7th largest agricultural exporter in the US. Exports went primarily to Canada, Japan, Germany, and the UK.

31 CONSUMER PROTECTION

The Minnesota Attorney General's Office enforces Minnesota's laws against false advertising, consumer fraud, and deceptive trade practices. The Consumer Protection Division answers consumer questions and mediates consumer complaints, attempting to resolve the complaints through a voluntary mediation program. The Attorney General's office also produces brochures and booklets on a wide variety of consumer topics, including landlords and tenants, new-car buying, home building, credit, and debt collection.

32 BANKING

As of 2002, Minnesota had 488 insured banks; the total assets of the state's insured banks in 2002 were over $108.8 billion. Three-hundred forty-five of those banks were state-chartered.

As of 2002, many insured banks headquartered in Minnesota relied upon commercial real estate (CRE) loans, and a soft real estate market negatively affected banks' credit quality. Community banks (those with less than $1 billion in assets) experienced declining net interest margins (NIMs) (the difference between the lower rates offered to savers and the higher rates charged on loans) in the 1990s and into the 2000s, due to increasing loan and funding competition. The lowering of interest rates by the Federal Reserve in 2001/02 caused fluctuations in NIMs, but did not signal an end to the long-term downward trend of NIMs.

33 INSURANCE

Minnesotans held 2.3 million life insurance policies valued at $200.8 billion as of 2001; total value for all categories of life insurance (ordinary, group, industrial, and credit) was $378.2 billion. Death benefits paid that year totaled $739.8 million. As of 2000 54, there were property and casualty and 18 life and health insurance companies incorporated or organized in the state. In 2001, property and casualty insurers wrote premiums totaling $6.5 billion. That year, there were 10,155 flood insurance policies in force in the state, with a total value of $1,187,884.

No-fault automobile insurance was enacted in 1974.

34 SECURITIES

The Minneapolis Grain Exchange, founded in 1881 as the Minneapolis Chamber of Commerce, is the state's major commodity exchange. The MGE is used primarily for the pricing of grains. Enforcement of statutes governing securities, franchises, and corporate takeovers (as well as charitable organizations, public cemeteries, collection agencies, and bingo) is the responsibility of the Securities Division of the Department of Commerce.

Approximately 1,104 securities dealers operate in Minnesota, with 18,901 employees; 238 investment advisory organizations do business in the state. Minnesota is headquarters to 197 NASDAQ companies, 15 NASDAQ market makers; and is the incorporator of 45 NYSE companies. The top five companies in terms of revenues are Target, Supervalue Inc., United Health Group Inc., Minnesota Mining and Manufacturing Co., and Best Buy Co., Inc.

35 PUBLIC FINANCE

Minnesota spends a relatively large amount on state government and local assistance, especially on a per capita basis. The state budget is prepared by the Department of Finance and submitted biennially by the governor to the legislature for amendment and approval. The fiscal year runs from 1 July to 30 June.

The fiscal year 2000–01 biennium budget for Minnesota included general fund revenues of $24.6 and spending of $23.4 billion. The tobacco lawsuit brought in revenues of almost one billion, which was set aside for tobacco use prevention, public health, and medical education. Personal income tax rates were cut from 6% to 5.5%, 8% to 7.25%, and 8.5% to 8%; as well as property taxes, sales taxes, and health care provider taxes. Investments were scheduled in the areas of education, health and human services, agriculture, criminal justice, economic development, government operations, and transportation.

The governor's 2000–01 budget reduced taxes by almost $1.4 billion, with the biggest cuts coming from income tax reductions. Tax revenues for 2000/01 were forecast at $12.6 billion, but the actual collection was only $12.15 billion, well short of expenditures of $12.703 billion. However, the gap was covered by previous surpluses: 2000/01 began with a starting balance of $2.125 billion and ended with a balance of $1.594 billion, all in the state's revenue stabilization fund. In 2001/02, however, revenues only reached $12.31 billion, while expenditures increased to $12.75 billion, and in 2002/03, the gap was more than $900 million: $13.046 billion in general fund revenues vs. $13.997 billion in general fund expenditures. Minnesota's budget deficit for 2002/03, was estimated at 10.7% of the state budget, and for 2003/04, was projected to increase to 18.7% of the state budget. Minnesota had gone from a starting balance equal to 12.4% of expenditures in 2000/01 to a starting balance in 2002/03 equal to only 1.3% of expenditures.

The following table from the US Census Bureau contains information on revenues, expenditures, indebtedness, and cash/securities for 2001.

	($000)	PERCENT	PER CAPITA
Population (thousands, 2001)	4,985	(X)	(X)
Total Revenue	26,135,477	100.00	5,242.82
General revenue	21,750,282	83.22	4,363.15
Utility revenue	–	–	–
Liquor store revenue	–	–	–
Insurance trust revenue	4,385,195	16.78	879.68
Exhibit: Salaries and wages	3,607,801	14.66	723.73
Total expenditure	24,612,196	100.00	4,937.25
General expenditure	21,958,545	89.22	4,404.92
Education	8,459,037	34.37	1,696.90
Public welfare	5,978,430	24.29	1,199.28
Hospitals	211,154	0.86	42.36
Health	473,095	1.92	94.90
Highways	1,505,330	6.12	301.97
Police protection	168,712	0.69	33.84
Correction	381,037	1.55	76.44
Natural resources	531,448	2.16	106.61
Parks and recreation	135,983	0.55	27.28
Government administration	693,478	2.82	139.11
Interest on general debt	337,027	1.37	67.61
Other and unallocable	3,083,814	12.53	618.62
Utility expenditure	–	–	–
Liquor store expenditure	–	–	–
Insurance trust expenditure	2,653,651	10.78	532.33
Debt at end of fiscal year	5,623,878	100.00	1,128.16
Cash and security holdings	53,464,608	100.00	10,725.10

36 TAXATION

Corporate profits are taxed at a flat rate of 9.8%. There is an alternative minimum tax (AMT) with a 5.8% rate. Effective 2001/02, personal income tax rates on Minnesota's three-bracket schedule were lowered, the lowest rate from 5.5% to 5.3% (on taxable income up to $18,710 for singles, and up to $27,350 for couples), and the highest from 8% to 7.85% (on taxable income above $61,461 for single, and $108,661 for couples). Personal exemptions and the standard deduction are the same as for federal income tax, and tax brackets are indexed for inflation. A refundable earned income credit is provided for low-income workers. The state of Minnesota also levies a 6.5% state sales tax, with local-option sales taxes permitted up to 1%. Food, medicines and other basics are exempted. The state also imposes a full array of excise taxes covering motor fuels, tobacco products, insurance premiums, public utilities, alcoholic beverages, amusements, pari-mutuels, and many other selected items. In 1980, Minnesota tied its estate tax to the federal exemption for state death taxes, but has reinstated its independent tax since the federal estate tax credit has been scheduled to be phased out by 2007. Death and gift taxes accounted for 0.6% of state taxes collected in 2002. Other state taxes include per ton severance taxes (for taconite, iron sulphides, agglomerate, and semi-taconite), various license fees, and stamp taxes.

Real property (commercial, industrial, and residential) is subject to the property tax, which accounts for 95% of total tax collections by local governing units. In Minnesota's classified property tax system, commercial, industrial, and rental properties are taxed at considerably higher rates than owned homes. Minnesota's "circuit breaker" system refunds property tax payments to homeowners and renters whose residential property taxes are high relative to their income. In 2002, about 37% of total state and local taxes were collected at the local level.

Total state tax collections in Minnesota in 2002 were $12.936 billion, of which 42.1% was generated by the state income tax, 28.9% by the state general sales and use tax, 15.7% by state excise taxes, 6.7% by state license fees, and 4.3% by the state corporate income tax. In 2003, Minnesota ranked 11th among the states in terms of state and local tax burden, which amounted to about 11% of income.

The following table from the US Census Bureau provides a summary of taxes collected by the state in 2002.

	($000)	PER CAPITA
Total Taxes	12,936,369	2,577.11
Property taxes	8,124	1.62
Sales and gross receipts	5,766,710	1,148.81
General sales and gross receipts	3,740,660	745.19
Selective sales taxes	2,026,050	403.62
Alcoholic beverage	57,495	11.45
Amusements	55,853	11.13
Insurance Premiums	163,110	32.49
Motor fuels	620,241	123.56
Pari-mutuels	1,340	0.27
Public utilities	52	0.01
Tobacco products	173,544	34.57
Other selective sales	954,415	190.13
Licenses	863,927	172.11
Alcoholic beverages	956	0.19
Amusements	403	0.08
Corporation	4,640	0.92
Hunting and fishing	51,204	10.2
Motor vehicle	493,482	98.31
Motor vehicle operators	31,082	6.19
Public utility	(X)	(X)
Occupation and business, NEC	248,439	49.49
Other	33,721	6.72
Other taxes	6,297,608	1,254.57
Individual income	5,444,715	1,084.67
Corporation net income	542,771	108.13
Death and gift	66,291	13.21
Documentary and stock transfer	230,354	45.89
Severance	13,477	2.68
Other	(X)	(X)

37ECONOMIC POLICY

Minnesota's Department of Trade and Economic Development (DTED) offers a variety of programs to encourage expansion of existing industries and to attract new industry to the state. The Department extends loans to small businesses for capital investments which create or retain jobs. It awards grants to new or expanding companies in rural areas and provides limited guarantees to private lenders for loans given to start-up companies. A Tourism Loan Program offers low-interest loans to tourism-related businesses to upgrade existing facilities or develop new ones. The Minnesota Export Finance Authority assists with the financing of small business exports. The state offers grants to depressed communities to help them retain or attract business or to rebuild their infrastructure. Minnesota's corporate income tax is structured to favor companies having relatively large payrolls and property (as opposed to sales) within the state. In 2003, a new initiative called Positively Minnesota was guiding economic development efforts. The primary goal was to capture a great share of business expansions. As a group, Positively Minnesota included economic developers, utilities and private firms as well as the DTED. In mid-2003, particular attention was being given to developing the state as part of a biosciences hub.

38HEALTH

Shortly after the founding of Minnesota Territory, promoters attracted new settlers partly by proclaiming the tonic benefits of Minnesota's soothing landscape and cool, bracing climate; the area was trumpeted as a haven for retirees and for those afflicted with malaria or tuberculosis.

In 2000, the infant mortality was relatively low, with a rate of 5.6 per 1,000 live births. There were 14,342 legal abortions in 1999, averaging 14 abortions per 1,000 women. In 2000, the overall death rate of 780.7 per 100,000 population was below the national rate of 873.1. Also in 2000, 19.8% of Minnesota residents were smokers. The rate of death from lung disease stood at 56.9 per 100,000 population in 2000. The death rates per 100,000 population for heart disease and cerebrovascular disease in 2000 were 184.0 and 68.4, respectively. HIV-related deaths occurred at a rate of 1.5 per 100,000 population in 2000; 3,919 AIDS cases had been reported through 2001.

Minnesota's 133 community hospitals had 586,016 admissions and 16,508 beds in 2001. There were 16,483 full-time registered nurses and 2,776 full-time licensed practical nurses in 2001 and 284 physicians per 100,000 population in 2000. The average expense of a community hospital for care was $1,421.30 per inpatient day in 2001.

Federal government grants to cover the Medicare and Medicaid services in 2001 totaled $2.1 billion; 660,399 enrollees received Medicare benefits that year. Only 8% of Minnesota residents were uninsured in 2002, the 2nd-lowest percentage in the US.

The Mayo Clinic, developed by Drs. Charles H. and William J. Mayo in the 1890s and early 1900s, was the first private clinic in the US and became a world-renowned center for surgery; today it is owned and operated by a self-perpetuating charitable foundation. The separate Mayo Foundation for Medical Education and Research, founded and endowed by the Mayo brothers in 1915, was subsequently affiliated with the University of Minnesota, which became the first US institution to offer graduate education in surgery and other branches of clinical medicine.

39SOCIAL WELFARE

In 2001, the average weekly unemployment benefit was $302.44. Average monthly participation in the food stamp program in FY2002 comprised 216,960 persons (101,820 households). The average monthly benefit was $77.07, and the sum total of benefits paid in FY2002 was $200,648,921.

With the enactment of the Personal Responsibility and Work Opportunity Reconciliation Act of 1996, the US government has changed the form and regulations for many of its social welfare programs. Most significantly, it replaces Aid to Families with Dependent Children (AFDC), an open-ended entitlement program, with Temporary Assistance for Needy Families (TANF), a limited system of assistance funded largely through federal block grants. The reform act also impacts the food stamp program, the Supplemental Security Income program, and the child nutrition program. The law took effect on 1 July 1997 and provided $16.38 billion in block grants for fiscal years 1997–2002. The grants are to be divided among the states based on an equation involving the numbers of former AFDC recipients in each state.

Reauthorization of the 1996 social welfare legislation, scheduled for 2002, was delayed, and the original law had been extended three times as of July 2003, with the most recent extension running through September 2003. Minnesota's TANF program is called Minnesota Family Investment Program (MFIP). In June 2000 the state had 116,589 welfare recipients. State expenditures on the TANF program in FY2002 totaled $372,117,686.

In December 2001, Social Security benefits were paid to 746,100 Minnesota residents. This number included 495,620 retired workers, 80,960 widows and widowers, 70,680 disabled workers, 49,250 spouses, and 49,590 children. Social Security beneficiaries represented 15% of the total state population and 94.5% of the state's population age 65 and older. Retired workers (excluding persons with special benefits) received an average monthly payment of $867; widows and widowers, $838; disabled workers, $797; and spouses, $443. Payments for children of retired workers averaged $449 per month; children of deceased workers, $618; and children of disabled workers, $244.

Federal Supplemental Security Income payments in December 2001 went to 65,538 Minnesota residents, averaging $366 a month.

40HOUSING

In 2002, Minnesota had 2,132,632 housing units, of which 1,992,524 were occupied. Minnesota had the highest rate of homeownership in the nation with 74.9% of all housing units being owner-occupied. About 69% of all units were single-family, detached homes. Most units rely on utility gas and electricity for heating. It was estimated that 35,226 units lacked telephone service, 8,823 lacked complete plumbing facilities, and 9,221 lacked complete kitchen facilities. The average household size was 2.45 people.

In 2002, 38,977 new units were authorized for construction. The median home value was $155,212. The median monthly cost for mortgage owners was $1,167. Renters paid a median of $651 per month. During 2002, Minnesota received over $97.2 million in community planning and development aid from the US Department of Housing and Urban Development.

41EDUCATION

Minnesota's first public school system was authorized in 1849, but significant growth in enrollment did not occur until after the Civil War. Today, Minnesota has one of the best-supported systems of public education in the US. In 2000, 87.9% of Minnesotans age 25 or older were high school graduates; 27.4% had obtained a bachelor's degree or higher.

The total enrollment for fall 1999 in Minnesota's public schools stood at 854,034. Of these, 580,363 attended schools from kindergarten through grade eight, and 273,671 attended high school. Minority students made up approximately 18% of the total enrollment in public elementary and secondary schools in 2001. Total enrollment was estimated at 847,000 in fall 2000 but is expected to drop to 840,000 by fall 2005. In 1999/2000, state expenditures per pupil totaled $7,326. Expenditures for public education in 2000/01 were estimated at $7,159,543. Enrollment in nonpublic schools in fall 2001 was 92,775.

As of fall 2000, there were 269,258 students enrolled in college or graduate school. In the same year Minnesota had 113 degree-granting institutions. The state's public postsecondary education system is overseen by Minnesota State Colleges and Universities (MNSCU) and includes three areas: the state university system—with campuses at Bemidji, Mankato, Marshall, Minneapolis-St. Paul, Moorhead, St. Cloud, and Winona; the community college system, consisting of 18 two-year colleges and 3 centers; and a statewide network of 33 area vocational-technical institutes. The University of Minnesota (founded as an academy in 1851) has campuses in the Twin Cities, Duluth, Morris, and Crookston. The state's oldest private college, Hamline University in St. Paul, was founded in 1854 and is affiliated with the United Methodist Church. There are more than 20 private colleges, many of them with ties to Lutheran or Roman Catholic religious authorities. Carleton College, at Northfield, is a notable independent institution. In 1997, minority students comprised 9.2% of total postsecondary enrollment.

Minnesota has an extensive program of student grants, work-study arrangements, and loan programs, in addition to reciprocal tuition arrangements with Wisconsin, North Dakota, and South Dakota.

42ARTS

The new Ordway Music Theater in St. Paul, which has two concert halls, opened in January 1985. The Ordway is the home of the Minnesota Orchestra, the Minnesota Opera Company, and the St. Paul Chamber Orchestra. The privately owned, nonprofit theater was built for about $45 million and was founded by Minnesota Mining and Manufacturing Corp. and other private sources. In 1999, the Ordway received funding from the National Endowment for the Arts to use interactive video-conferencing technology to develop an "electronic field trip" accessible to student audiences across the state.

The St. Olaf College Choir, at Northfield, has a national reputation. The Tyrone Guthrie Theater, founded in Minneapolis in 1963, is one of the nation's most prestigious repertory companies. The Minnesota Ballet is based in Duluth.

Literary arts are active in the state. The Loft, founded in 1974 in Minneapolis, is considered to be one of the nation's largest and most comprehensive literary centers. Milkweed Editions is a well-known, award-winning, nonprofit literary publisher of books on cultural diversity, environmental stewardship, poetry, and literature for adults and children in the middle grades.

The Walker Art Center in Minneapolis is an innovative museum with an outstanding contemporary collection, while the Minneapolis Institute of Arts exhibits more traditional works. The Weisman Art Museum of the University of Minnesota is in Minneapolis, and the Minnesota Museum of Art is in St. Paul.

State and regional arts groups as well as individual artists are supported by state and federal grants administered through the State Arts Board, an 11-member panel appointed by the governor. In 2003, the Minnesota State Arts Board and other Minnesota arts organizations received grants totaling $4,227,800 from the National Endowment for the Arts. The State Arts Board was also given funding from the state and from private sources. The state offers arts education to about 50,000 schoolchildren, with approximately 2,500 teachers participating in the programs. Local art associations as well as state art associations continue to contribute to the art education programs. The Minnesota Humanities Commission was founded in 1971. In 2000, the National Endowment for the Humanities contributed $1,812,839 to 19 state programs.

43LIBRARIES AND MUSEUMS

Minnesota has 12 county and seven multi-county public library systems. The total number of books and audiovisual items was 16,000,000 in 2000 when public library circulation reached 44,009,000. The largest single public library system is the Minneapolis Public Library and Information Center (founded in 1885), which had 2,515,545 volumes in 1999. The leading academic library, with 5,747,805 volumes, is that maintained by the University of Minnesota at Minneapolis. Special libraries include the James Jerome Hill Reference Library (devoted to commerce and transportation) and the library of the Minnesota Historical Society, both located in St. Paul. Nearly all public, academic, school, and special libraries participate in one of the seven library system networks that facilitate resource sharing. Total public library income for 2000 came to $146,199,000, including over $9 million in state grants. Per capita spending was $28.13.

There are more than 164 museums and historic sites. In addition to several noted museums of the visual arts, Minnesota is home to the Mayo Medical Museum at the Mayo Clinic in Rochester. The Minnesota Historical Society Museum offers rotating exhibits on varied aspects of the state's history. In May 1996, the Mille Lacs Indian Museum and Trading Post opened its doors. Historic sites include the Split Rock Lighthouse on the north shore of Lake Superior, Historic Fort Snelling in the Twin Cities, the boyhood home of Charles Lindbergh in Little Falls, and the Sauk Centre home of Sinclair Lewis.

44COMMUNICATIONS

As of 2001, 97.7% of Minnesota's occupied housing units had telephones. Commercial broadcasting began with the opening of the first radio station in 1922; as of 2003 there were 136 major radio stations—33 AM and 103 FM—and 20 major television stations. The Minneapolis-St. Paul metropolitan area had 1,481,050 television households, 54% of which received cable.

By the year 2000, a total of 116,792 Internet domain names had been registered in Minnesota.

45PRESS

The *Minnesota Pioneer,* whose first issue was printed on a small hand press and distributed by the publisher himself on April 28, 1849, in St. Paul, vies with the *Minnesota Register* (its first issue was dated earlier but may have appeared later) for the honor of being Minnesota's first newspaper. Over the next 10 years, in any case, nearly 100 newspapers appeared at locations throughout the territory, including direct ancestors of many present-day publications. In April 1982, Minneapolis's daily newspapers were merged into the *Minneapolis Star Tribune.* As of 2002, the state had 15 morning dailies, 10 evening dailies, and 14 Sunday papers. The following table lists the leading dailies, with their average circulations in 2002:

AREA	NAME	DAILY	SUNDAY
Duluth	*News Tribune* (m,S)	47,027	71,019
Minneapolis	*Star Tribune* (m,S)	340,445	671,359
St. Paul	*Pioneer Press* (m,S)	195,042	251,129

As of 1997, 337 weekly newspapers and 176 periodicals were being published in Minnesota. Among the most widely read magazines published in Minnesota were *Family Handyman,* appearing 10 times a year; *Catholic Digest,* a religious monthly; and *Snow Goer,* published five times a year for snowmobile enthusiasts.

46ORGANIZATIONS

In 2003, there were about 2,996 regional, national, and international organizations within the state.

The Minnesota Historical Society, founded in 1849, is the oldest educational organization in the state and the official custodian of its history. The society is partly supported by state funds, as are such other semistate organizations as the Academy of Science (which promotes interest in science among high school students), the Minnesota State Horticultural Society, and the Humane Society. The Sons of Norway and American Swedish Institute, both with headquarters in Minneapolis, seek to preserve the state's Scandinavian heritage.

Among the various professional, commercial, educational, and hobbyist associations with headquarters in Minnesota are the American Collectors Association and the National Scholastic Press Association, Minneapolis; the American Board of Radiology, the American Ophthalmological Society, and the American Board of Physical Medicine and Rehabilitation, Rochester; and World Pen Pals, St. Paul. The North American Fishing Club and North American Hunting Club are located in Minnetonka.

The National Marrow Donor Program is based in Minneapolis, as is the National Council of the United States, International Organization of Good Templars.

47TOURISM, TRAVEL, AND RECREATION

In 2001, the state hosted about 24 million travelers, with about 52% of all tourist activity involving Minnesota residents touring their own state. About 11.7 visitors were from out of state, primarily from one of the following states: Wisconsin, Iowa, North Dakota, Illinois, California, South Dakota, Michigan, Texas, Missouri, and Florida. Shopping was the most popular tourist activity for out-of-state visitors. Total travel expenditures for 2001 reached about $9.8 billion, which included support for over 135,400 jobs.

With its lakes and parks, ski trails and campsites, and historical and cultural attractions, Minnesota provides ample recreational opportunities for residents and visitors alike. Minnesota's attractions include the 220,000-acre (80,000-hectare) Voyageurs National Park, near the Canadian border; Grand Portage National Monument, in Arrowhead Country, a former fur-trading center with a restored trading post; and Pipestone National Monument, in southwestern Minnesota, containing the red pipestone quarry used by Indians to make peace pipes. Lumbertown USA, a restored 1870s lumber community, is in Brainerd, and the US Hockey Hall of Fame is in Eveleth.

The state maintains and operates 66 parks, 9240 mi (14,870 km) of trails, 10 scenic and natural areas, 5 recreation areas, and 18 canoe and boating routes. Minnesota also has 288 primary wildlife refuges. Many visitors hunt deer, muskrat, squirrel, beaver, duck, pheasant, and grouse. Others enjoy boating each year on Minnesota's scenic waterways. Winter sports have gained in popularity, and many parks are now used heavily all year round. Snowmobiling, though it has declined somewhat since the mid-1970s, still attracts enthusiasts annually, and cross-country skiing has rapidly accelerated in popularity.

48SPORTS

Five of the major league professional sports currently have teams in Minnesota: the Minnesota Twins of Major League Baseball, the Minnesota Vikings of the National Football League, the Minnesota Lynx of the Women's National Basketball Association, and the Minnesota Timberwolves of the National Basketball Association. The Twins won the World Series in 1987 and 1991. The Vikings have gone to the Super Bowl four times, losing each one. The Minnesota North Stars of the National Hockey League moved to Dallas in 1993, but a new NHL team, the Minnesota Wild, joined the league in 2000.

In collegiate sports, the University of Minnesota Golden Gophers compete in the Big Ten Conference. The football team won the Rose Bowl in 1962, while the basketball team won the

Big Ten title and advanced to the NCAA Final Four in 1997. The university is probably best known for its ice hockey team, which won the NCAA title three times during the 1970s and supplied the coach, Herb Brooks, and many of the players for the gold medal–winning US team in the 1980 Winter Olympics.

Other annual sporting events include the John Beargrease Sled Dog Race between Duluth and Grand Marais in January or early February, and auto racing at the Brainerd International Raceway in July and August. Alpine and cross-country skiing are popular.

Tracy Caulkins, Roger Maris, and Kevin McHale, past stars in swimming, baseball and basketball, respectively, were all born in Minnesota.

49FAMOUS MINNESOTANS

No Minnesotan has been elected to the US presidency, but several have sought the office, including two who served as vice president. Hubert Horatio Humphrey (b.South Dakota, 1911–78) was vice president under Lyndon Johnson and a serious contender for the presidency in 1960, 1968, and 1972. A onetime mayor of Minneapolis, the "Happy Warrior" entered the US Senate in 1949, winning recognition as a vigorous proponent of liberal causes; after he left the vice presidency, Humphrey won reelection to the Senate in 1970. Humphrey's protégé, Walter Frederick "Fritz" Mondale (b.1928), a former state attorney general, was appointed to fill Humphrey's Senate seat in 1964, was elected to it twice, and after an unsuccessful try for the presidency, became Jimmy Carter's running mate in 1976; four years later, Mondale and Carter ran unsuccessfully for reelection, losing to Ronald Reagan and George Bush. Mondale won the Democratic presidential nomination in 1984 and chose US Representative Geraldine A. Ferraro of New York as his running mate, making her the first woman to be nominated by a major party for national office; they were overwhelmingly defeated by Reagan and Bush, winning only 41% of the popular vote and carrying only Minnesota and the District of Columbia. Warren Earl Burger (1907–95) of St. Paul was named chief justice of the US Supreme Court in 1969. Three other Minnesotans have served on the court: Pierce Butler (1866–1939), William O. Douglas (1898–1980), and Harry A. Blackmun (b.Illinois, 1908–97).

Senator Frank B. Kellogg (b.New York, 1856–1937), who as secretary of state helped to negotiate the Kellogg-Briand Pact renouncing war as an instrument of national policy (for which he won the 1929 Nobel Peace Prize), also served on the Permanent Court of International Justice. Other political leaders who won national attention include Governors John A. Johnson (1861–1909), Floyd B. Olson (1891–1936), and Harold E. Stassen (1907–2001), a perennial presidential candidate since 1948 but a serious contender in his early races. Eugene J. McCarthy (b.1916), who served in the US Senate, was the central figure in a national protest movement against the Vietnam war and, in that role, unsuccessfully sought the 1968 Democratic presidential nomination won by Humphrey. McCarthy also ran for the presidency as an independent in 1976.

Several Minnesotans besides Kellogg have served in cabinet posts. Minnesota's first territorial governor, Alexander Ramsey (1815–1903), later served as a secretary of war, and Senator William Windom (1827–91) was also secretary of the treasury. Others serving in cabinet posts have included William DeWitt Mitchell (1874–1955), attorney general; Maurice H. Stans (b.1908), secretary of commerce; James D. Hodgson (b.1915), secretary of labor; and Orville Freeman (1918–2003) and Bob Bergland (b.1928), both secretaries of agriculture. The first woman ambassador in US history was Eugenie M. Anderson (Iowa, 1909–97), like Humphrey an architect of the Democratic-Farmer-Labor Party.

Notable members of Congress include Knute Nelson (b.Norway, 1843–1923), who served in the Senate from 1895 to

his death; Henrik Shipstead (1881–1960), who evolved into a leading Republican isolationist during 24 years in the Senate; Representative Andrew J. Volstead (1860–1947), who sponsored the 1919 prohibition act that bears his name; and Representative Walter Judd (b.1898–1994), a prominent leader of the so-called China Lobby.

The Mayo Clinic was founded in Minnesota by Dr. William W. Mayo (b.England, 1819–1911) and developed through the efforts of his sons, Drs. William H. (1861–1939) and Charles H. (1865–1939) Mayo. Oil magnate J. Paul Getty (1892–1976) was a Minnesota native, as was Richard W. Sears (1863–1914), founder of Sears, Roebuck.

Prominent literary figures, besides Sinclair Lewis, include Ignatius Donnelly (b.Pennsylvania, 1831–1901), a writer, editor, and Populist Party crusader; F. Scott Fitzgerald (1896–1940), well known for classic novels including *The Great Gatsby*; and Ole Edvart Rølvaag (b.Norway, 1876–1931), who conveyed the reality of the immigrant experience in his *Giants in the Earth*. The poet and critic Allen Tate (b.Kentucky, 1899–1979) taught for many years at the University of Minnesota.

Journalist Westbrook Pegler (1894–1969) and cartoonist Charles Schulz (1922–2000) were both born in Minnesota as was radio personality and author Garrison Keillor (b.1942), who gained nationwide fame playfully satirizing his home state through the fictitious town of Lake Wobegon. Architects LeRoy S. Buffington (1847–1937) and Cass Gilbert (b.Ohio, 1859–1934) and economist Thorstein Veblen (b.Wisconsin, 1857–1929) influenced their fields well beyond the state's borders, as did Minnesota artists Wanda Gag (1893–1946) and Adolph Dehn (1895–1968).

Minnesota born entertainers include Judy Garland (Frances Gumm, 1922–69) and Bob Dylan (Robert Zimmerman, b.1941). Football star William "Pudge" Heffelfinger (1867–1954) was a Minnesota native, and Bronislaw "Bronco" Nagurski (b.Canada, 1908–1990) played for the University of Minnesota.

Daniel Greysolon, Sieur Duluth (b.France, 1636–1710), Father Louis Hennepin (b.Flanders, 1640?–1701), and Jonathan Carver (b.Massachusetts, 1710–80) were among the early explorers and chroniclers of what is now the State of Minnesota. Fur trader Henry H. Sibley (b.Michigan, 1811–91) was a key political leader in the territorial period and became the state's first governor; he also put down the Sioux uprising of 1862. Railroad magnate James J. Hill (b.Canada, 1838–1916) built one of the greatest corporate empires of his time, and Oliver H. Kelley (b.Massachusetts, 1826–1913), a Minnesota farmer, organized the first National Grange. John Ireland (b.Ireland, 1838–1918) was the first Roman Catholic archbishop of St. Paul, while Henry B. Whipple (b.New York, 1822–1901), longtime Episcopal bishop of Minnesota, achieved particular recognition for his work among Indians in the region.

The first US citizen ever to be awarded the Nobel Prize for literature was Sinclair Lewis (1885–1951), whose novel *Main Street* (1920) was modeled on life in his hometown of Sauk Centre. Philip S. Hench (b.Pennsylvania, 1896–1965) and Edward C. Kendall (b.Connecticut, 1886–1972), both of the Mayo Clinic, shared the 1950 Nobel Prize for medicine, and St. Paul native Melvin Calvin (1911–97) won the 1961 Nobel Prize for chemistry.

50BIBLIOGRAPHY

Aby, Anne J., ed. *The North Star State: A Minnesota History Reader*. St. Paul, Minn.: Minnesota Historical Society Press, 2002.

Hauser, Tom. *Inside the Ropes with Jesse Ventura*. Minneapolis: University of Minnesota Press, 2002.

Lass, William E. *Minnesota: A History*. New York: W.W. Norton & Co., 1998.

Lewis, Anne Gillespie. *The Minnesota Guide*. Golden, Colo.: Fulcrum Pub., 1999.

Meyer, Roy. Rev. ed. *History of the Santee Sioux: United States Indian Policy on Trial*. Lincoln: University of Nebraska Press, 1993.

Radicalism in Minnesota, 1900–1960: A Survey of Selected Sources. St. Paul, Minn.: Minnesota Historical Society Press, 1994.

Rueter, Theodore. *The Minnesota House of Representatives and the Professionalization of Politics*. Lanham, Md.: University Press of America, 1994.

Schwartz, George M., and G. A. Thiel. *Minnesota's Rocks and Waters: A Geological Story*. Minneapolis: University of Minnesota Press, 1954.

Spadaccini, Victor M., ed. *Minnesota Pocket Data Book, 1985–86*. St. Paul, Minn.: Blue Sky, 1983.

Stuhler, Barbara. *Gentle Warriors: Clara Ueland and the Minnesota Struggle for Woman Suffrage*. St. Paul, Minn.: Minnesota Historical Society Press, 1994.

Upham, Warren. *Minnesota Geographic Names: Their Origin and Historic Significance*. St. Paul, Minn.: Minnesota Historical Society, 1969 (orig. 1920).

MISSISSIPPI

State of Mississippi

ORIGIN OF STATE NAME: Derived from the Ojibwa Indian words *misi sipi*, meaning "great river." **NICKNAME:** The Magnolia State. **CAPITAL:** Jackson. **ENTERED UNION:** 10 December 1817 (20th). **SONG:** "Go, Mississippi." **MOTTO:** *Virtute et armis* (By valor and arms). **COAT OF ARMS:** An American eagle clutches an olive branch and a quiver of arrows in its talons. **FLAG:** Crossed blue bars, on a red field, bordered with white and emblazoned with 13 white stars—the motif of the Confederate battle flag—cover the upper left corner. The field consists of three stripes of equal width, blue, white, and red. **OFFICIAL SEAL:** The seal consists of the coat of arms surrounded by the words "The Great Seal of the State of Mississippi." **MAMMAL:** White-tailed deer. **WATER MAMMAL:** Porpoise. **BIRD:** Mockingbird. **WATERFOWL:** Wood duck. **FISH:** Largemouth or black bass. **INSECT:** Honeybee. **FLOWER:** Magnolia. **TREE:** Magnolia. **STONE:** Petrified wood. **FOSSIL:** Prehistoric whale. **BEVERAGE:** Milk. **LEGAL HOLIDAYS:** New Year's Day, 1 January; Birthdays of Robert E. Lee and Martin Luther King, Jr., 3rd Monday in January; Washington's Birthday, 3rd Monday in February; Confederate Memorial Day, last Monday in April; Jefferson Davis's Birthday, 1st Monday in June; Independence Day, 4 July; Labor Day, 1st Monday in September; Veterans Day, 11 November; Thanksgiving Day, 4th Thursday in November; Christmas Day, 25 December. **TIME:** 6 AM CST = noon GMT.

1 LOCATION, SIZE, AND EXTENT

Located in the eastern south-central US, Mississippi ranks 32nd in size among the 50 states.

The total area of Mississippi is 47,689 sq mi (123,514 sq km), of which land takes up 47,233 sq mi (122,333 sq km) and inland water 456 sq mi (1,181 sq km). Mississippi's maximum E-W extension is 188 mi (303 km); its greatest N-S distance is 352 mi (566 km).

Mississippi is bordered on the N by Tennessee; on the E by Alabama; on the S by the Gulf of Mexico and Louisiana; and on the W by Louisiana (with the line partially formed by the Pearl and Mississippi rivers) and Arkansas (with the line formed by the Mississippi River). Several small islands lie off the coast.

The total boundary length of Mississippi is 1,015 mi (1,634 km). The state's geographic center is in Leake County, 9 mi (14 km) WNW of Carthage.

2 TOPOGRAPHY

Mississippi lies entirely within two lowland plains. Extending eastward from the Mississippi River, the Mississippi Alluvial Plain, popularly known as the Delta, is very narrow south of Vicksburg but stretches as much as a third of the way across the state farther north. The Gulf Coastal Plain, covering the rest of the state, includes several subregions, of which the Red Clay Hills of north-central Mississippi and the Piney Woods of the south and southeast are the most extensive. Mississippi's generally hilly landscape ascends from sea level at the Gulf of Mexico to reach its maximum elevation, 806 ft (246 m), at Woodall Mountain, in the extreme northeastern corner of the state.

The state's largest lakes—Grenada, Sardis, Enid, and Arkabutla—are all manmade. Numerous smaller lakes—called oxbow lakes because of their curved shape—extend along the western edge of the state; once part of the Mississippi River, they were formed when the river changed its course. Mississippi's longest inland river, the Pearl, flows about 490 mi (790 km) from the eastern center of the state to the Gulf of Mexico, its lower reaches forming part of the border with Louisiana. The Big Black River, some 330 mi (530 km) long, begins in the northeast and

cuts diagonally across the state, joining the Mississippi about 20 mi (32 km) below Vicksburg. Formed by the confluence of the Tallahatchie and Yalobusha rivers at Greenwood, the Yazoo flows 189 mi (304 km) southwest to the Mississippi just above Vicksburg.

3 CLIMATE

Mississippi has short winters and long, humid summers. Summer temperatures vary little from one part of the state to another. Biloxi, on the Gulf coast, averages 82°F (28°C) in July, while Oxford, in the north-central part of the state, averages 80°F (27°C). During the winter, however, because of the temperate influence of the Gulf of Mexico, the southern coast is much warmer than the north; in January, Biloxi averages 52°F (11°C) to Oxford's 41°F (5°C). The lowest temperature ever recorded in Mississippi was –19°F (–28°C) on 30 January 1966 in Corinth; the highest, 115°F (46°C), was set on 29 July 1930 at Holly Springs.

Precipitation in Mississippi increases from north to south. The north-central region averages 53 in (135 cm) of precipitation a year; the coastal region, 62 in (157 cm). Annual annual precipitation at Jackson (1971–2000) was 56 in (142 cm). Some snow falls in northern and central sections. Mississippi lies in the path of hurricanes moving northward from the Gulf of Mexico during the late summer and fall. On 17–18 August 1969, Hurricane Camille ripped into Biloxi and Gulfport and caused more than 100 deaths throughout the state. Two tornado alleys cross Mississippi from the southwest to northeast, from Vicksburg to Oxford and McComb to Tupelo.

4 FLORA AND FAUNA

Post and white oaks, hickory, maple, and magnolia grow in the forests of the uplands; various willows and gums (including the tupelo) in the Delta; and longleaf pine in the Piney Woods. Characteristic wild flowers include the green Virginia creeper, black-eyed Susan, and Cherokee rose. Listed as threatened in 2003 was Price's potato-bean; listed as endangered were the Louisiana quillwort, pondberry, and American chaffseed.

Common among the state's mammals are the opossum, eastern mole, armadillo, coyote, mink, white-tailed deer, striped skunk, and diverse bats and mice. Birds include varieties of wren, thrush, warbler, vireo, and hawk, along with numerous waterfowl and seabirds, Franklin's gull, the common loon, and the wood stork among them. Black bass, perch, and mullet are common freshwater fish. Rare species in Mississippi include the hoary bat, American oystercatcher, mole salamander, pigmy killifish, Yazoo darker, and five species of crayfish. Listed as threatened or endangered in 2003 were 34 species, including the American and Louisiana black bears, eastern indigo snake, Indiana bat, Mississippi sandhill crane, bald eagle, Mississippi gopher frog, brown pelican, red-cockaded woodpecker, five species of sea turtle, and the bayou darter.

5ENVIRONMENTAL PROTECTION

Except for the drinking water program, housed in the State Health Department, and regulation of noncommercial oil field waste disposal activities, assigned to the State Oil and Gas Board, the Mississippi Department of Environmental Quality (MDEQ) is responsible for environmental regulatory programs in the state. MDEQ regulates surface and groundwater withdrawals through its Office of Land and Water Resources and surface mining reclamation through its Office of Geology. All other environmental regulatory programs, including those federal regulatory programs delegated to Mississippi by the US Environmental Protection Agency (EPA), are administered through MDEQ's Office of Pollution Control. The state has primacy for almost all federally delegable programs; the one notable exception is the federal hazardous waste corrective action program (under the federal Hazardous and Solid Waste Amendments of 1984). MDEQ implements one of the premier Pollution Prevention programs in the nation.

In 2003, Mississippi had 83 hazardous waste sites listed in the Environmental Protection Agency's database, two of which were on the National Priorities List. In 1996, wetlands accounted for 13% of the state's lands. The Natural Heritage Program identifies and inventories priority wetlands. In 2001, Mississippi received $43,254,000 in federal grants from the EPA; EPA expenditures for procurement contracts in Mississippi that year amounted to $45,000.

6POPULATION

Mississippi ranked 31st in population in the US with an estimated total of 2,871,782 in 2002, an increase of 1% since 2000. Between 1990 and 2000, Mississippi's population grew from 2,573,216 to 2,844,658, an increase of 10.5%. The population is projected to reach 2,908,000 by 2005 and 3.1 million by 2025.

After remaining virtually level for 30 years, Mississippi's population during the 1970s grew 13.7%, but increased only 2.1% from 1980 to 1990. In 2000, the median age of Mississippians was 33.8. In the same year, 27.3% of the population were under the age of 18 while 12.1% were age 65 or older. The population density in 2000 was 61.8 persons per sq mi.

Mississippi remains one of the most rural states in the US, although the urban population has increased fivefold since 1920, when only 13% of state residents lived in cities. Mississippi's largest city, Jackson, had an estimated 2002 population of 180,881, down from 193,097 in 1994. Biloxi and Gulfport are other major cities with large populations. The Jackson metropolitan area had an estimated population of 432,647 in 1999.

7ETHNIC GROUPS

Since 1860, blacks have constituted a larger proportion of the population of Mississippi than of any other state. By the end of the 1830s, blacks outnumbered whites 52% to 48%, and from the 1860s through the early 20th century, they made up about three-fifths of the population. Because of out-migration, the proportion of black Mississippians had declined to about 36% in 2000 (still the highest in the country), when the state had 1,746,099 whites, 1,033,809 blacks, 18,626 Asians, 11,652 American Indians, and 667 Pacific Islanders. In 2000, there were 39,569 (1.4%) Hispanics and Latinos.

Until the 1940s, the Chinese, who numbered 3,099 in 2000, were an intermediate stratum between blacks and whites in the social hierarchy of the Delta Counties. There also were 5,387 Vietnamese and 2,608 Filipinos in 2000. Although the number of foreign-born almost tripled in the 1970s, Mississippi still had the nation's smallest percentage of foreign-born residents (1.4%, or 39,908) in 2000.

Mississippi has only a small Indian population remaining—0.4% of the state's population in 2000 (11,652). Many of them live on the Choctaw reservation in the east-central region.

8LANGUAGES

English in the state is largely Southern, with some South Midland speech in northern and eastern Mississippi because of population drift from Tennessee. Typical are the absence of final /r/ and the lengthening and weakening of the diphthongs /ai/ and /oi/ as in ride and oil. South Midland terms in northern Mississippi include tow sack (burlap bag), dog irons (andirons), plum peach (clingstone peach), snake doctor (dragonfly), and stone wall (rock fence). In the eastern section are found jew's harp (harmonica) and croker sack (burlap bag). Southern speech in the southern half features gallery for porch, mosquito hawk for dragonfly, and press peach for clingstone peach. Louisiana French has contributed armoire (wardrobe).

In 2000, 96.4% of Mississippi residents five years old and older spoke only English in the home, down from 97.2% in 1990.

The following table gives selected statistics from the 2000 census for language spoken at home by persons five years old and over. The category "Other Native North American languages" includes Apache, Cherokee, Choctaw, Dakota, Keres, Pima, and Yupik.

LANGUAGE	NUMBER	PERCENT
Population 5 years and over	**2,641,453**	**100.0**
Speak only English	2,545,931	96.4
Speak a language other than English	95,522	3.6
Speak a language other than English	**95,522**	**3.6**
Spanish or Spanish Creole	50,515	1.9
French (incl. Patois, Cajun)	10,826	0.4
Other Native North American languages	5,654	0.2
German	5,501	0.2
Vietnamese	4,916	0.2
Chinese	2,506	0.1
Tagalog	2,005	0.1
Korean	1,485	0.1
Italian	1,336	0.1
Arabic	1,081	0.0

9RELIGIONS

Protestants have dominated Mississippi since the late 18th century. The Baptists are the leading denomination and many adherents are fundamentalists. Partly because of the strong church influence, Mississippi was among the first states to enact prohibition and among the last to repeal it.

In 2000, membership in the two principal Protestant denominations was: the Southern Baptist Convention, 916,440 known adherents and the United Methodist Church, 240,576. There were about 115,760 Roman Catholics, an estimated 3,919 Muslims, and about 1,400 Jews. Over 1.2 million people (about 45.4% of the population) did not claim any religious affiliation.

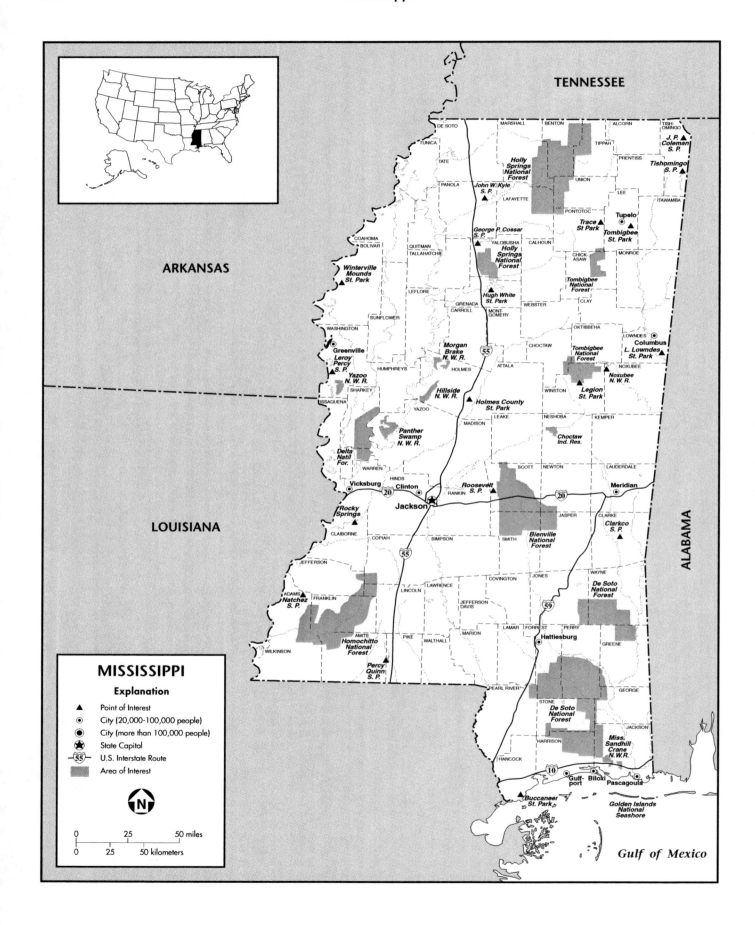

TENNESSEE

ARKANSAS

LOUISIANA

ALABAMA

Gulf of Mexico

MISSISSIPPI

Explanation

▲ Point of Interest
⊙ City (20,000-100,000 people)
◉ City (more than 100,000 people)
★ State Capital
—55— U.S. Interstate Route
▨ Area of Interest

[10]TRANSPORTATION

At the end of 2000, there were 2,707 rail mi (4,356 km) of mainline railroad track in the state, including 2,011 mi (3,236 km) operated by Class I railroads, which, in 2000, included the Burlington Northern, CSX, Illinois Central, Kansas City Southern, and Norfolk Southern lines. Rail passenger service providers include the City of New Orleans, which operates over Illinois Central's rails and serves the cities of Greenwood, Yazoo, Jackson, Hazlehurst, Brookhaven, and McComb in Mississippi on its route between Chicago and New Orleans; and the Crescent, which operates over the Norfolk Southern rail line and serves Meridian, Laurel, Hattiesburg, and Picayune in Mississippi on its route between Atlanta and New Orleans.

Mississippi had 73,498 mi (118,283 km) of public roads—65,443 mi (105,320 km) rural and 8,055 mi (12,963 km) urban—as of 2000. Interstate highways 55, running north–south, and 20, running east–west, intersect at Jackson. I-220 provides a loop from I-55 north of Jackson to I-20 west of Jackson. I-10 runs across the Mississippi Gulf Coast, and I-110 provides a connector from I-10 to US Highway 90 in Biloxi. I-59 runs diagonally through the southeastern corner of Mississippi from Meridian to New Orleans.

Mileage of four-lane highways is increasing daily under a "pay-as-you-go" public works program passed by the Mississippi legislature in 1987 to provide a four-lane highway within 30 minutes or 30 mi (48 km) of every citizen in the state. Originally, the $1.6 billion, three-phase agenda called for the creation of four lanes for 1,077 mi (1,733 km) of highway by the year 2001. During the 1994 regular legislative session, an additional 619 mi (996 km), known as Phase IV, were added to the program at an expected cost of $1.3 billion. As of 1996, 322 mi (518 km) of new four-lane highway were in place with an additional 332 mi (534 km) under contract. In 2000, there were 2,007,746 licensed drivers in Mississippi and 2,321,270 registered motor vehicles, including 1,318,648 automobiles and 960,389 trucks.

Mississippi's ports and waterways serve a surrounding 16-state market where nearly 40% of the nation's total population is located. Mississippi has two deepwater seaports, Gulfport and Pascagoula, both located on the Gulf of Mexico. In 2000, Gulfport handled 2.2 million tons of cargo, and Pascagoula handled 28.6 million tons. Much of Pascagoula's heavy volume consists of oil and gas imports. Other ports located on the Gulf include Port Bienville in Hancock County and Biloxi in Harrison County. Biloxi handled 2.5 million tons of cargo in 2000.

The Mississippi River flows along the western border of the state, linking the Gulf of Mexico to inland river states as far away as Minneapolis, Minnesota. The Mississippi is the largest commercial river in the country and the 3rd-largest river system in the world, and it carries the majority of the nation's inland waterway tonnage. Approximately 409 mi (658 km) of the Mississippi River flow through the state, with ports in Natchez, Vicksburg, Yazoo County, Greenville, and Rosedale. In 2000, the Port of Vicksburg handled 5 million tons of cargo; the Port of Greenville, 3.1 million tons.

To the east of Mississippi lies the Tennessee-Tombigbee (Tenn-Tom) Waterway, completed in 1984, which links the Tennessee and Ohio rivers with the Gulf of Mexico. Stretching 95 mi (153 km) through Mississippi from the northeast corner of the state down to a point just south of Columbus, the Tenn-Tom Waterway's overall length is 232 mi (373 km). Five local ports are located on the waterway: Yellow Creek, Itawamba, Amory, Aberdeen, and Columbus-Lowndes County. In 1999, about 10 million tons of commodities were shipped on the Tenn-Tom Waterway, compared with 8.9 million tons in 1996, 8.7 million tons in 1995, and 7.9 million tons in 1994.

In 2002, there were 76 public-use airports in Mississippi. They provide access to the nation's system of airports and are a major factor in the economic development of the state and of the communities where they are located. In addition, there are approximately 108 airports and 35 heliports in the state that are for private use.

[11]HISTORY

The earliest record of human habitation in the region that is now the state of Mississippi goes back perhaps 2,000 years. The names of Mississippi's pre-Columbian inhabitants are not known. Upon the appearance of the first Spanish explorers in the early 16th century, Mississippi Indians numbered some 30,000 and were divided into 15 tribes. Soon after the French settled in 1699, however, only three large tribes remained: the Choctaw, the Chickasaw, and the Natchez. The French destroyed the Natchez in 1729–30 in retaliation for the massacre of a French settlement on the Natchez bluffs.

Spanish explorers, of whom Hernando de Soto in 1540–41 was the most notable, explored the area that is now Mississippi in the first half of the 16th century. De Soto found little of the mineral wealth he was looking for, and the Spanish quickly lost interest in the region. The French explorer Robert Cavelier, Sieur de la Salle, penetrated the lower Mississippi Valley from New France (Canada) in 1682. La Salle discovered the mouth of the Mississippi and named the entire area Louisiana in honor of the French king, Louis XIV.

An expedition under French-Canadian Pierre Lemoyne, Sieur d'Iberville, established a settlement at Biloxi Bay in 1699. Soon the French opened settlements at Mobile (1702), Natchez (1716), and finally New Orleans (1718), which quickly eclipsed the others in size and importance. After losing the French and Indian War, France ceded Louisiana to its Spanish ally in 1762. The following year, Spain ceded the portion of the colony that lay east of the Mississippi to England, which governed the new lands as West Florida. During the American Revolution, the Spanish, who still held New Orleans and Louisiana, marched into Natchez, Mobile, and Pensacola (the capital) and took West Florida by conquest.

Although the US claimed the Natchez area after 1783, Spain continued to rule it. However, the Spanish were unable to change the Anglo-American character of the settlement. Spain agreed to relinquish its claim to the Natchez District by signing the Treaty of San Lorenzo on 27 October 1795, but did not evacuate its garrison there for another three years.

The US Congress organized the Mississippi Territory in 1798. Between 1798 and 1817, the territory grew enormously in population, attracting immigrants mainly from the older states of the South but also from the Middle Atlantic states and even from New England. During this period, the territory included all the land area that is today within the borders of Mississippi and Alabama. However, sectionalism and the territory's large size convinced Congress to organize the eastern half as the Alabama Territory in 1817. Congress then offered admission to the western half, which became the nation's 20th state-Mississippi on 10 December.

Until the Civil War, Mississippi exemplified the American frontier; it was bustling, violent, and aggressive. By and large, Mississippians viewed themselves as westerners, not southerners. Nor was Mississippi, except for a few plantations around Natchez, a land of large planters. Rather, Mississippi's antebellum society and government were dominated by a coalition of prosperous farmers and small landowners. At the time of statehood, the northern two-thirds of Mississippi, though nominally under US rule since 1783, remained in the hands of the Choctaw and Chickasaw and was closed to settlement. Under intense pressure from the state government and from Andrew Jackson's presidential administration, these tribes signed three treaties between 1820 and 1832, ceding their Mississippi lands and agreeing to move to what is now Oklahoma.

The opening of fertile Indian lands for sale and settlement produced a boom of speculation and growth unparalleled in Mississippi history. Cotton agriculture and slavery—introduced by the French and carried on by the British and Spanish, but hitherto limited mostly to the Natchez area—swept over the state. As the profitability and number of slaves increased, so did attempts by white Mississippians to justify slavery morally, socially, and economically. The expansion of slavery also produced a defensive attitude which focused the minds of white Mississippians on two dangers: that the slaves outnumbered the whites and would threaten white society unless kept down by slavery; and that any attack on slavery, whether from the abolitionists or from Free-Soilers like Abraham Lincoln, was a threat to white society. The danger, they believed, was so great that no price was too high to pay to maintain slavery, even secession and civil war.

After Lincoln's election to the US presidency, Mississippi became, on 9 January 1861, the second southern state to secede. When the war began, Mississippi occupied a central place in Union strategy. The state sat squarely astride the major Confederate east-west routes of communication in the lower South, and the Mississippi River twisted along the state's western border. Control of the river was essential to Union division of the Confederacy. The military campaign fell into three phases: the fight for northeastern Mississippi in 1862, the struggle for Vicksburg in 1862–63, and the battle for east Mississippi in 1864–65. The Union advance on Corinth began with the Battle of Shiloh (Tenn.) in April 1862. The first Union objective was the railroad that ran across the northeastern corner of Mississippi from Corinth to Iuka and linked Memphis, Tenn., to Atlanta, Ga. Losses in the ensuing battle of Shiloh, which eventually led to the occupation of Corinth by Union troops, exceeded 10,000 men on each side.

The campaign that dominated the war in Mississippi—and, indeed, along with Gettysburg provided the turning point of the Civil War—was Vicksburg. Perched atop high bluffs overlooking a bend in the Mississippi and surrounded by hills on all sides, Vicksburg provided a seemingly impregnable fortress. Union forces maneuvered before Vicksburg for more than a year before Grant besieged the city and forced its surrender on 4 July 1863. Along with Vicksburg went the western half of Mississippi. The rest of the military campaign in the state was devoted to the fight for the east, which Union forces still had not secured when the conflict ended in 1865. Of the 78,000 Mississippians who fought in the Civil War, nearly 30,000 died.

Ten years of political, social, and economic turmoil followed. Reconstruction was a tumultuous period during which the Republican Party encouraged blacks to vote and hold political office, while the native white Democrats resisted full freedom for their former slaves. The resulting confrontation lasted until 1875, when, using violence and intimidation, the Democrats recaptured control of the state from the Republicans and began a return to the racial status quo antebellum. However, Reconstruction left its legacy in the minds of Mississippians: to the whites it seemed proof that blacks were incapable of exercising political power; to the blacks it proved that political and social rights could not long be maintained without economic rights.

The era from the end of Reconstruction to World War II was a period of economic, political, and social stagnation for Mississippi. In many respects, white Mississippians pushed blacks back into slavery in all but name. Segregation laws and customs placed strict social controls on blacks, and a new state constitution in 1890 removed the last vestiges of their political rights. Mississippi's agricultural economy, dominated by cotton and tenant farming, provided the economic equivalent of slavery for black sharecroppers. As a continuing agricultural depression ground down the small white farmers, many of them also were driven into the sharecropper ranks; in 1890, 63% of all Mississippi farmers were tenants. Whether former planter-aristocrats like John Sharp Williams or small-farmer advocates like James K. Vardaman (1908–12) and Theodore Bilbo (1916–20 and 1928–32) held office as governor, political life was dominated by the overriding desire to keep the blacks subservient. From Reconstruction to the 1960s, white political solidarity was of paramount importance. Otherwise, the whites reasoned, another Reconstruction would follow. According to the Tuskegee Institute, 538 blacks were lynched in Mississippi between 1883 and 1959, more than in any other state.

The Great Depression of the 1930s pushed Mississippians, predominantly poor and rural, to the point of desperation, and the state's agricultural economy to the brink of disaster. In 1932, cotton sank to 5 cents a pound, and one-fourth of the state's farmland was forfeited for nonpayment of taxes. World War II unleashed the forces that would later revolutionize Mississippi's economic, social, and political order, bringing the state its first prosperity in a century. By introducing outsiders to Mississippi and Mississippians to the world, the armed forces and the war began to erode the state's insularity. It also stimulated industrial growth and agricultural mechanization and encouraged an exodus of blacks to better-paying jobs in other states. By the early 1980s, according to any standard, Mississippi had become an industrial state. In the agricultural sector, cotton had been dethroned and crop diversification accomplished. Politics in Mississippi also changed considerably after World War II. Within little more than a generation, from 1945 to 1975, legal segregation was destroyed, and black people exercised their political rights for the first time since Reconstruction. The "Mississippi Summer" (also called Freedom Summer) civil rights campaign—and the violent response to it, including the abduction and murder of three civil rights activists in June 1964—helped persuade white Mississippians to accept racial equality. Charles Evers, the brother of slain civil rights leader Medgar Evers, was elected mayor of Fayette in 1969, becoming Mississippi's first black mayor since Reconstruction.

Following the 1990 redistricting that boosted the number of blacks in the Mississippi house of representatives, the Mississippi legislature was nearly 23% black in a state in which blacks constituted 33% of the population. In 1998 African Americans accounted for 36% of the state's population.

In 1988 reformist governor Ray Mabus, elected in 1987, enacted the nation's largest teacher pay increase to date. Nevertheless, teacher salaries in 1992 were still, on average, the 2nd-lowest in the nation and public education remained a priority for the state in the early 2000s. Democratic Governor Ronnie Musgrove, elected in 2000, was able to win additional teacher pay increases from the legislature in 2001. Education was Musgrove's main focus in his 2003 State of the State Address, as he proposed a program that would place children in school two months before kindergarten, and one that would attempt to keep top faculty members at Mississippi's state colleges and universities.

Mississippi's economy was hard hit by the 1986 decline in oil and gas prices. Unemployment in the state rose to 13%. By 1992 it had fallen to about 8%. The 1990s saw increasing industrial diversification and rising personal incomes, although many agricultural workers in the Mississippi Delta area remained jobless due to the increasing mechanization of farm work. By 1999 the jobless rate had dropped to 5.1%, though still above the national average of 4.2%. Nevertheless, the state remained among the nation's poorest, with 17.6% of its population living below the poverty level as of 1998. Only three states had higher poverty rates. In 2003, Mississippi was facing a budget shortfall of at least $500 million.

¹²STATE GOVERNMENT

Mississippi has had four state constitutions. The first (1817) accompanied Mississippi's admission to the Union. A second constitution (1832) was superseded by that of 1868, redrafted under Republican rule to allow Mississippi's readmission to the Union after the Civil War. The state's present constitution, as amended, dates from 1890. By January 2003 it had 121 amendments.

Mississippi's bicameral legislature includes a 52-member senate and a 122-member house of representatives. Annual sessions begin in January and extend 90 calendar days, except in the first year of a gubernatorial administration, when they run 125 calendar days. Sessions may be extended, by a maximum of 30 days, by a two-thirds vote of the legislature. However, there is no limit to the number of extensions. All state legislators are elected to 4-year terms. State representatives must be at least 21 years old and senators 25. Representatives must be qualified voters and must have been Mississippi residents for four years and residents of their district for at least two years before election. Senators must have been qualified voters for at least four years and residents of their district for at least two years before election. The legislative salary was $10,000 in 2002, unchanged from 1999.

The governor and lieutenant governor (separately elected), secretary of state, attorney general, state treasurer, state auditor, commissioner of insurance, and the commissioner of agriculture and commerce all serve four-year terms. (Voters also elect three transportation commissioners and three public service commissioners, who also serve four-year terms.) The governor and lieutenant governor must be at least 30 years old, a US citizen for 20 years, and a Mississippi resident for five years before election. In 2002 the governor's salary was $101,800, unchanged from 1999. The governor is limited to a maximum of two consecutive terms.

A bill passed by both houses is sent to the governor, who has five days to veto or sign it before it becomes law. If the legislature adjourns, the governor has 15 days after the bill was presented to him to act on it before the measure becomes law. The governor's veto can be overridden by a two-thirds vote of the elected members of both houses. Constitutional amendments must first receive the approval of two-thirds of the members of each house of the legislature. The electorate may also initiate amendments, provided petitions are signed by 12% of total votes for all candidates for governor at the last election. A majority of voters must approve the amendment on a statewide ballot. The constitution also provides for the calling of a constitutional convention, by majority vote of each house.

Every US citizen over the age of 18 may vote in Mississippi upon producing evidence of 30 days of residence in the state and county (and city, in some cases). Restrictions apply to those convicted of certain crimes and to those judged by the court as mentally incompetent to vote.

¹³POLITICAL PARTIES

Mississippi's major political parties are the Democratic Party and the Republican Party, each an affiliate of the national party organization, but the Republicans are weak below the national level. Mississippi Democrats have often been at odds with each other and with the national Democratic Party. In the 1830s, party affiliation in the state began to divide along regional and economic lines: woodsmen and small farmers in eastern Mississippi became staunch Jacksonian Democrats, while the conservative planters in the western river counties tended to be Whigs. An early demonstration of the power of the state capital from Natchez in 1821 to a new city named after Andrew Jackson. During the pre-Civil War years, the secessionists were largely Democrats; the Unionists, western Whigs.

During Reconstruction, Mississippi had its first Republican governor. After the Democrats returned to power in 1875, they systematically deprived blacks of the right to vote, specifically by inserting into the constitution of 1890 a literacy clause that could be selectively interpreted to include illiterate whites but exclude blacks. A poll tax and convoluted residency requirements also

Mississippi Presidential Vote by Political Parties, 1948–2000

YEAR	ELECTORAL VOTE	MISSISSIPPI WINNER	DEMOCRAT	REPUBLICAN	STATES' RIGHTS DEMOCRAT	SOCIALIST WORKERS	LIBERTARIAN
1948	9	Thurmond (SRD)	19,384	4,995	167,538	—	—
1952	8	Stevenson (D)	172,553	112,966	—	—	—
					INDEPENDENT		
1956	8	Stevenson (D)	144,453	60,683	42,961	—	—
					UNPLEDGED		
1960	8	Byrd**	108,362	73,561	116,248	—	—
1964	7	Goldwater (R)	52,616	356,512	—	—	—
					AMERICAN IND.		
1968	7	Wallace (AI)	150,644	88,516	415,349		
					AMERICAN		
1972	7	*Nixon (R)	126,782	505,125	11,598	2,458	—
1976	7	*Carter (D)	381,309	366,846	6,678	2,805	2,788
					WORKERS' WORLD		
1980	7	*Reagan (R)	429,281	441,089	2,402	2,240	4,702
1984	7	*Reagan (R)	352,192	582,377		—	2,336
1988	7	*Bush (R)	363,921	557,890			3,329
					IND. (Perot)	**NEW ALLIANCE**	
1992	7	Bush (R)	400,258	487,793	85,626	2,625	2,154
1996	7	Dole (R)	394,022	439,838	52,222	—	2,809
					(Nader)	**REFORM**	
2000	7	*Bush, G. W. (R)	404,614	572,844	8,122	2,265	2,009

* Won US presidential election.
** Unpledged electors won plurality of votes and cast Mississippi's electoral votes for Senator Harry F. Byrd of Virginia.

restricted the electorate. Voter registration among blacks fell from 130,607 in 1880 to 16,234 by 1896.

In 1948, Mississippi Democrats seceded from the national party over the platform, which opposed racial discrimination. That November, Mississippi voters backed the States' Rights Democratic (Dixiecrat) presidential ticket. At the national Democratic convention in 1964, the black separatist Freedom Democratic Party asked to be allotted 40% of Mississippi's seats but was turned down. A further division in the party occurred during the 1960s between the (black) Loyalist Democrats and the (white) Regular Democrats, who were finally reunited in 1976. During the 1950s and early 1960s, the segregationist White Citizens' Councils were so widespread and influential in the state as to rival the major parties in political importance.

Since the passing of the federal Voting Rights Act of 1965, black Mississippians have registered and voted in substantial numbers. According to estimates by the Voter Education Project, only 5% of voting-age blacks were registered in 1960; by 1992, 23% were registered.

Mississippi was one of the most closely contested states in the South during the 1976 presidential election, and that again proved to be the case in 1980, when Ronald Reagan edged Jimmy Carter by a plurality of fewer than 12,000 votes. In 1984, however, Reagan won the state by a landslide, polling 62% of the vote. In the 2000 election, Republican George W. Bush won 57% of the vote; Democrat Al Gore received 42%; and Independent Ralph Nader garnered 1%. In 2002 there were 1,754,560 registered voters; there is no party registration in the state. The state had seven electoral votes in the 2000 presidential election.

Elected in 1991, Mississippi's governor Kirk Fordice was the first Republican governor since Reconstruction. But a Democrat soon regained the office: David Ronald Musgrove was elected governor in 1999. Following the 2002 elections, the state's two US senators were Republicans Trent Lott and Thad Cochran. Lott became majority leader of the Senate in 1996 following the departure of Bob Dole (R-Kansas); he stepped down from that post in December 2002 following controversy over remarks he made praising former South Carolina Senator Strom Thurmond's 1948 segregationist campaign for the presidency . All five of Mississippi's US representatives were Democrats until the 1994 midterm elections when Republican Roger Wicker won a House seat that had been in Democratic hands since Reconstruction. Following the 2002 elections, the House delegation comprised two Democrats and two Republicans. Before November 2003 elections, the state senate comprised 33 Democrats, 18 Republicans, and one vacancy; the state house had 86 Democrats, 35 Republicans, and three Independents.

14LOCAL GOVERNMENT

Each of Mississippi's 82 counties (2002) is divided into 5 districts, each of which elects a member to the county board of supervisors. As of 2002, Mississippi had 296 municipal governments (incorporated as cities, towns, or villages), typically administered by a mayor and council. Some smaller municipalities were run by a commission or by a city manager, appointed by council members. There were 164 public school districts and 458 special districts in 2002.

15STATE SERVICES

To address the continuing threat of terrorism and to work with the federal Department of Homeland Security (created in 2002 following the terrorist attacks of 11 September 2001), homeland security in Mississippi in 2003 operated under the authority of the governor; the emergency management director was designated as the state homeland security advisor.

The Mississippi Ethics Commission, established by the state legislature in 1979, is composed of eight members who administer a code of ethics requiring all state officials and elected local officials to file statements of sources of income.

The Mississippi Department of Education is primarily a planning and service organization whose role is to assist local schools from kindergarten through junior college and adult education. A separate Board of Trustees of Institutions of Higher Learning administers Mississippi's public college and university system. The Department of Health administers a statewide system of public health services, but other bodies, including the Department of Mental Health, also have important functions in this field. The Department of Public Welfare provides welfare services in the areas of assistance payments, child support, food stamp distribution, and such social services as foster home care.

Public protection is afforded by the Office of the Attorney General, Civil Defense Council, Military Department, Bureau of Narcotics, Department of Public Safety (including the Highway Safety Patrol), and Department of Corrections.

16JUDICIAL SYSTEM

The Mississippi supreme court consists of a chief justice, two presiding justices, and eight associate justices, all elected to eight-year terms. The constitution stipulates that the supreme court must hold two sessions a year in the state capital; one session is to commence on the 2nd Monday of September, the other on the 1st Monday of March. A new court of appeals was created in 1995. It consists of one chief judge, two presiding judges, and seven judges. Principal trial courts are the circuit courts, which try both civil and criminal cases; their 49 judges are elected to four-year terms. Municipal court judges are appointed. Small-claims courts are presided over by justices of the peace, who need not be lawyers.

There were 20,672 prisoners in state and federal prisons in Mississippi as of June 2001, an increase of 7.3% over the previous year. The state's incarceration rate stood at 689 per 100,000 inhabitants.

In 2001, Mississippi had a total FBI Crime Index rate of 4,185.2 per 100,000 population, including a total of 10,006 violent crimes and 109,609 crimes against property in that year. The death penalty was reinstated in 1977, and since then six persons have been executed. In 2003, 67 persons were under sentence of death.

17ARMED FORCES

In 2002, there were 14,005 active-duty military personnel and 9,289 civilian personnel stationed in Mississippi. There were two major US Air Force bases, Keesler (Biloxi) and Columbus. Among the four US naval installations were an oceanographic command at Bay St. Louis, an air station at Meridian, and a construction battalion center at Gulfport. In 2001, Mississippi received about $1.43 billion in federal defense contracts.

There were 249,431 veterans of US military service living in Mississippi as of 2000. Of those who served in wartime, 43,547 were veterans of World War II; 29,796 of the Korean conflict; 66,703 of the Vietnam era; and during 1990–2000 (including the Persion Gulf War), 36,848. Benefits totaling some $741 million were paid to Mississippi veterans during 2002.

In 2000, the Mississippi Highway State Patrol employed 532 full-time sworn officers.

18MIGRATION

In the late 18th century, most Mississippians were immigrants from the South and predominantly of Scotch-Irish descent. The opening of lands ceded by the Indians beginning in the 1820s brought tens of thousands of settlers into northern and central

Mississippi, and a resulting population increase between 1830 and 1840 of 175% (including an increase of 197% in the slave population).

After the Civil War, there was little migration into the state, but much out-migration, mainly of blacks. The exodus from Mississippi was especially heavy during the 1940s and 1950s, when at least 720,000 people, nearly three-quarters of them black, left the state. During the 1960s, between 267,000 and 279,000 blacks departed while net white out-migration came to an end. Black out-migration slowed considerably during the 1970s, and more whites settled in the state than left. Also during the 1970s there was considerable intrastate migration to Hinds County (Jackson) and the Gulf Coast. Between 1980 and 1990, Mississippi had a net loss from migration of 144,128 (38% whites). Only 12 of the state's 82 counties recorded a net gain from migration during the 1980s, mostly in Rankin, DeSoto, Madison, and Hancock counties. Between 1990 and 1998, Mississippi had net gains of 43,000 in domestic migration and 6,000 in international migration. In 1998, the state admitted 701 foreign immigrants. Between 1990 and 1998, Mississippi's overall population increased 6.9%. In the period 1995–2000, 226,788 people moved into the state and 199,858 moved out, for a net gain of 26,930, 2,433 of whom were age 65 or over.

19INTERGOVERNMENTAL COOPERATION

The Mississippi Commission on Interstate Cooperation oversees and encourages the state's participation in interstate bodies, especially the Council of State Governments and the National Conference of State Legislatures. Mississippi also participates in the Appalachian Regional Commission, Arkansas-Mississippi Great River Bridge Construction Compact, Highway 82 Four Lane Construction Compact, Mississippi-Alabama Railroad Authority Compact, Gulf States Marine Fisheries Commission, Southeastern Forest Fire Protection Compact, Southern Growth Policies Board, Southern States Energy Board, Southern Regional Education Board, and Tennessee-Tombigbee Waterway Development Authority. Mississippi received over $4.2 billion in federal aid in 2001.

20ECONOMY

Between the Civil War and World War II, Mississippi's economy remained poor, stagnant, and highly dependent on the market for cotton—a bitter legacy from which the state is only now beginning to recover. As in the pre–Civil War years, Mississippi exports mainly raw materials and imports mainly manufactures. In the 1930s, state leaders began to realize the necessity of diversifying the economy. By the mid-1960s, many more Mississippians recognized that political and economic inequality and racial conflict did not provide an environment attractive to the industries the state needed.

Once the turmoil of the 1950s and early 1960s had subsided, the impressive industrial growth of the immediate postwar years resumed. By the mid-1960s, manufacturing—attracted to the state, in part, because of low wage rates and a weak labor movement—surpassed farming as a source of jobs. During the following decade, the balance of industrial growth changed somewhat. The relatively low-paying garment, textile, and wood-products industries, based on cotton and timber, grew less rapidly in both value added and employment than a number of heavy industries, including transportation equipment and electric and electronic goods. The debut of casino gambling in the state in 1992 stimulated Mississippi's economy in the early and mid-1990s, and by 2002 accounted for 2.7% of total state employment (close to 31,000). In early 1995, however, the manufacturing sector began losing jobs, contributing to a deceleration in annual growth rates in the late 1990s, from 5% in

1998 to 4.1% in 1999 to 3% in 2000 to 1.5% in the national recession of 2001. Total employment began falling from the third quarter of 2000, and did not show any increase until the fourth quarter of 2002, with an uptick of 0.2%. Losses in the manufacturing sector created stress in other sectors, particularly in the retail trade and transportation and public utilities sectors. Areas of moderate growth in 2002 were business services and government. The number of personal bankruptcies in the state set a record in 2002, but the growth rate in filings moderated to 1.2%, down from 19.5% in 2001. The opening of a $1.4 billion Nissan plant near Jackson, scheduled for mid-2003 and projected to hire between 4,000 and 5,300 workers, should give the economy a boost. Southern Mississippi, where the Ship System division of Northrop Grumman, Keesler Air Force Base, and the Stennis Space Center are located, should also benefit from increased national defense spending. In 2001, the public sector accounted for 17.2% of the state gross product, the 6th-highest percent among the states.

Mississippi's gross state product in 2001 was $188.1 billion, the 35th largest among the states, to which general services and manufacturing each contributed about $12 billion; government, $11.5 billion; wholesale and retail trade, $11.2 billion; financial services, $8.2 billion; transportation and public utilities, $6.4 billion, and construction, $3.1 billion. From 1997 to 2001, the government sector grew 25.9% and general services 21%, while the level of manufacturing output fell –4.5%.

21INCOME

According to the Bureau of Economic Analysis, in 2001, Mississippi had a per capita personal income (PCPI) of $21,653 which ranked 51st in the United States (including the District of Columbia) and was 71% of the national average, $30,413. The 2001 PCPI reflected an increase of 3.5% from 2000 compared to the national change of 2.2%. In 2001, Mississippi had a total personal income (TPI) of $61,922,038,000 which ranked 33rd in the United States and accounted for 0.7% of the national total. The 2001 TPI reflected an increase of 3.9% from 2000 compared to the national change of 3.3%.

Earnings of persons employed in Mississippi increased from $39,429,472,000 in 2000 to $40,188,051,000 in 2001, an increase of 1.9%. The largest industries in 2001 were services, 24.0% of earnings; state and local government, 15.8%; and durable goods manufacturing, 11.3%. Of the industries that accounted for at least 5% of earnings in 2001, the slowest growing from 2000 to 2001 was durable goods manufacturing, which decreased 7.2%; the fastest was state and local government, which increased 5.6%.

According to data released by the US Census Bureau, in 2000, the median household income was $31,528 compared to the national average of $42,148. In 2001, the median income for a family of four was $46,810 compared to the national average of $63,278. For the period 1999 to 2001, the average poverty rate was 16.8% which placed it 49th among the 50 states and the District of Columbia ranked lowest to highest.

22LABOR

According to Bureau of Labor Statistics (BLS) provisional estimates, in July 2003 the seasonally adjusted civilian labor force in Mississippi numbered 1,335,900, with approximately 96,200 workers unemployed, yielding an unemployment rate of 7.2%, compared to the national average of 6.2% for the same period. Since the beginning of the BLS data series in 1978, the highest unemployment rate recorded was 13.8% in February 1983. The historical low was 4.7% in February 1999. In 2001, an estimated 5.0% of the labor force was employed in construction; 18.5% in manufacturing; 5.3% in transportation, communications, and public utilities; 18.7% in trade; 4.7% in finance, insurance, and real estate; 20.5% in services; 16.4% in government; and 2.0% in agriculture.

The US Department of Labor reported that in 2002, 69,000 of Mississippi's 1,052,000 employed wage and salary workers were members of unions. This represented 6.6% of those so employed, up from 5.5% in 2001 but down from 9.7% in 1998. The national average is 13.2%. In all, 84,000 workers (8.0%) were represented by unions. In addition to union members, this category includes workers who report no union affiliation but whose jobs are covered by a union contract. Mississippi is one of 22 states with a right-to-work law.

23 AGRICULTURE

In 2001, Mississippi ranked 26th among the states in income from agriculture, with marketings of over $3.1 billion; crops accounted for $900,000 and livestock and livestock products $2.2 billion.

The history of agriculture in the state is dominated by cotton, which from the 1830s through World War II was Mississippi's principal cash crop. During the postwar period, however, as mechanized farming replaced the sharecropper system, agriculture became more diversified. In 2002 Mississippi ranked 2nd in upland cotton and 4th in rice production. About 1,980,000 bales of cotton worth $380 million were harvested in 2002. Soybean output in 2002 totaled 44,000,000 bushels, worth $243 million, and rice production was 16,192,000 hundredweight in 2002, with a value of $62.3 million.

Federal estimates for 2002 showed some 43,000 farms with a total area of 11 million acres (4.5 million hectares. The richest soil is in the Delta, where most of the cotton is raised. Livestock has largely taken over the Black Belt, a fertile area in the northwest.

24 ANIMAL HUSBANDRY

Cattle are raised throughout the state, though principally in the Black Belt and Delta. The main chicken-raising area is in the eastern hills.

In 2003, there were around 1.07 million cattle and calves, valued at $609.9 million. In 2002, there were around 275,000 hogs and pigs, valued at $20.6 million. Mississippi is a leading producer of broilers, ranking 5th in 2001; some 3.8 billion lb (1.7 billion kg) of broilers, worth $1.49 billion, were produced in that year.

25 FISHING

In 1998, Mississippi ranked 8th among the 50 states in size of commercial fish landings, 210.8 million lb (95.6 million kg), with a value of $48,834,000. Of this total, 193.2 million lb (87.6 million kg) or 92% of the catch was landed at Pascagoula-Moss Point, the nation's 8th-largest port for commercial landings in 1998. Shrimp and blue crab made up the bulk of the commercial landings. The saltwater catch also includes mullet and red snapper; the freshwater catch is dominated by buffalo fish, carp, and catfish. Mississippi ranks 1st among the states in catfish farming, mostly from ponds in the Yazoo River basin. There are 396 catfish farms in operation, covering about 104,250 acres (47,288 hectares) of water surface, with a combined 2000 inventory of 805 million fingerlings and 561.5 million stocker-sized catfish. Sales of catfish in 1997 totaled $290 million. In 1998, the state issued 408,272 sport fishing licenses.

26 FORESTRY

Mississippi had approximately 18,580,000 acres (7,519,000 hectares) of forested land in 2002, about 60% of the total land area of the state. Six national forests extend over 1.1 million acres (445,000 hectares). The state's most heavily forested region is the Piney Woods in the southeast. Of the state's total commercial timberland, 90% is privately owned. Some of this land was also used for agricultural purposes (grazing). Lumber production in 2002 totaled 2.5 billion board feet (8th in the US).

27 MINING

Mississippi's nonfuel mineral production in 2001 was valued at an estimated $177 million, a decrease of 6.9% from 2000. Construction sand and gravel was the leading nonfuel mineral in 2001, accounting for 37% of the state's total nonfuel mineral production value. Mississippi ranked 2nd among the states in production of fuller's earth and 4th in bentonite and ball clay. Crushed stone was the 2nd most valuable nonfuel mineral commodity produced in 2001, followed by fuller's earth and industrial sand and gravel. According to preliminary figures, in 2001, 484,000 metric tons of common clay was produced for a value of $2.19 million; 12.4 million metric tons of construction sand and gravel produced were worth $65.6 million. A quantity of 3.3 million metric tons of crushed stone was worth $31.8 million.

28 ENERGY AND POWER

There were 21 electric generating plants in Mississippi in 1999, with a total installed capacity (utility and nonutility) of 8.9 million kW, almost all coal-fired or gas-fired. Total production in the same year was 34.9 billion kWh. The Grand Gulf Nuclear Station boiling-water reactor, built by Mississippi Power Company in Claiborne County, continues to provide power to consumers within Mississippi.

The Tennessee Valley Authority, the nation's largest producer of electricity, has negotiated and signed a contract with CRSS, Inc., to purchase electric power from a planned lignite power plant, known as the Red Hills Power Project, to be developed in Choctaw County.

Mississippi is a major petroleum producer, ranking 10th in the US in 2002. In that year, there were 1,474 producing wells located within the state. Production of petroleum in 1999 totaled 49,000 barrels per day, and there were proved reserves of 167 million barrels. Mississippi produced 112.8 billion cu ft (3.19 billion cu m) of natural gas during 2002, and proved reserves were estimated at 661 billion cu ft (18.7 billion cu m). Most production comes from the south-central part of the state. In 2000 Mississippi's total per capita energy consumption was 402 million Btu (101.3 million kcal), ranking it 14th among the 50 states.

29 INDUSTRY

In 1997, the value of shipments by Mississippi manufacturers totaled $41 billion. The state's biggest manufacturing concern is Litton Industries' Ingalls shipyard at Pascagoula. In addition to merchant vessels, this yard builds US Navy ships, including nuclear-powered submarines. In 1997, Mississippi was the headquarters for one Fortune 500 company, Worldcom.

Earnings of persons employed in Mississippi increased from $34.5 billion in 1997 to $36.7 billion in 1998, an increase of 6.5%. The largest industries in 1998 were services, 23.2% of earnings; state and local government, 13.7%; and durable goods manufacturing, 13.5%. Of the industries that accounted for at least 5% of earnings in 1998, the slowest growing from 1997 to 1998 was nondurable goods manufacturing (8.3% of earnings in 1998), which increased 1.8%; the fastest was services, which increased 7.9%.

30 COMMERCE

In 1997, a federal census counted 3,881 wholesale establishments in Mississippi, with $20 billion in sales. Retail sales totaled $21 billion in 1997, conducted by 15,786 establishments. Food stores accounted for 15% of all establishments; automotive dealers, 17%; and eating and drinking places, 20%. Food sales totaled $3.9 billion, and general merchandise sales totaled $3.4 billion. Exports from Mississippi totaled $2.3 billion in 1998.

31 CONSUMER PROTECTION
The Consumer Protection Division of the Office of the Attorney General, established in 1974, may investigate complaints of unfair or deceptive trade practices and, in specific cases, may issue injunctions to halt them. Under 1994 amendments, a violation of the Consumer Protection Act is now a criminal misdemeanor.

32 BANKING
Mississippi's 106 insured banks had assets of $38 billion by September 2002. Seventy-eight of those banks were state-chartered.

By the end of 2001, median past-due loan levels peaked at 3.78% of total loans, especially in the manufacturing sector; they subsequently declined by the third quarter 2002. Median net interest margins (NIMs) (the difference between the lower rates offered to savers and the higher rates charged on loans) reached their highest level by September 2002 since August 2000, largely due the wide spread between short- and long-term interest rates. This improvement occurred among banks of various types and sizes, as well as in varied geographic locations.

33 INSURANCE
At the end of 2000, 35 life and health and 17 property and casualty insurance companies were domiciled in Mississippi. In 2001 there were 1.8 million ordinary life insurance policies in force with a total value of $81.3 billion; total value for all categories of life insurance (ordinary, group, industrial, and credit) was $123.3 billion. Death benefits paid that year totaled $421.9 million. In 2001, property and casualty insurers wrote premiums totaling $2.9 billion. That year, there were 41,555 flood insurance policies in force in the state, with a total value of $3.7 million.

34 SECURITIES
There are no securities exchanges in Mississippi. There are 253 securities brokers and dealers in Mississippi, with over 1,000 employees. Approximately 40 securities investment advisory firms are registered. The state headquarters 18 NASDAQ companies, and incorporated eight NYSE-listed companies, including (in order of revenues size) Bancorp South Inc., Mississippi Chemical Corporation, Hancock Fabrics, Inc., ChemFirst Inc., and Delta & Pine Land Co.

35 PUBLIC FINANCE
Two state budgets are prepared annually—one by the State Department of Finance and Administration, for the executive branch; and one by the Joint Legislative Budget Committee, for the legislative branch—and submitted to the legislature for reconciliation and approval. The fiscal year runs from 1 July through 30 June.

During the 2000 Mississippi legislative session, lawmakers discussed their concern over the state's budget for fiscal year 2001 because revenue collections had fallen below projections. The legislature had adopted a budget of more than $10 billion overall, while general funds were set at $3.6 billion. Actual receipts were only $3.444 billion, however. The gap was met with withdrawals from the state rainy day fund, other fund transfers, and expenditure cuts of $106.9 million. In 2001/02, however, general fund revenues decreased further, to $3.371 billion, prompting more across the board budget cuts, withdrawals from the rainy day fund and other adjustments. In 2002/03, revenues

increased to $3.378 billion, though still behind expenditures, at $3.509 billion. Mississippi's budget deficit for 2002/03 was estimated at 2.8% of the state budget, but projections for 2003/04 had not been released by the state as of early 2003.

The following table from the US Census Bureau contains information on revenues, expenditures, indebtedness, and cash/securities for 2001.

	($000)	PERCENT	PER CAPITA
Population (thousands, 2001)	2,860	(X)	(X)
Total Revenue	11,692,949	100.00	4,088.44
General revenue	10,320,074	88.26	3,608.42
Utility revenue	—	—	—
Liquor store revenue	168,855	1.44	59.04
Insurance trust revenue	1,204,020	10.30	420.99
Exhibit: Salaries and wages	1,608,937	13.72	562.57
Total expenditure	11,727,422	100.00	4,100.50
General expenditure	10,610,118	90.47	3,709.83
Education	3,662,650	31.23	1,280.65
Public welfare	2,856,361	24.36	998.73
Hospitals	690,264	5.89	241.35
Health	281,956	2.40	98.59
Highways	862,068	7.35	301.42
Police protection	71,659	0.61	25.06
Correction	271,627	2.32	94.97
Natural resources	213,993	1.82	74.82
Parks and recreation	73,404	0.63	25.67
Government administration	203,444	1.73	71.13
Interest on general debt	188,821	1.61	66.02
Other and unallocable	1,233,871	10.52	431.42
Utility expenditure	—	—	—
Liquor store expenditure	136,641	1.17	47.78
Insurance trust expenditure	980,663	8.36	342.89
Debt at end of fiscal year	3,819,476	100.00	1,335.48
Cash and security holdings	23,109,542	100.00	8,080.26

36 TAXATION
The state income tax for both individuals and corporations ranges from 3% on the first $5,000 of net income to 5% on amounts over $10,000; the corporate income tax rate is one of the lowest in the nation. Mississippi also imposes severance taxes on oil, natural gas, timber and salt. The state also imposes a full array of excise taxes covering motor fuels, tobacco products, insurance premiums, public utilities, alcoholic beverages amusements, pari-mutuels, and other selected items. A 7% retail sales tax is levied, with local-option sales taxes permitted only up to 0.25%. The state also imposes a full array of excise taxes covering motor fuels, tobacco products, insurance premiums, public utilities, alcoholic beverages amusements, pari-mutuels, and many other selected items. Mississippi's estate tax is tied to the federal exemption for state death taxes, and is therefore set to be phased out in tandem with the phasing out of the federal estate tax exemption by 2007, unless the state takes positive action to establish an independent estate tax. Mississippi's revenue losses from the phasing out of its estate tax are estimated at -$13 million for 2002/03, -$20 million for 2003/04 and -$30 million for 2006/07. Death and gift taxes accounted for 0.6% of state collections in 2002. Other state taxes include various license fee and state property taxes, though most property taxes are collected at the local level. In 2002, local collections accounted for 38.7% of total state and local tax revenue.

The state collected $4.729 billion in taxes in 2002, of which 49.4% came from the general sales tax, 20.8% from individual income taxes, 17.8% from selective sales taxes, 6.37% from state license fees, and 4.1% from corporate income taxes. In 2003, Mississippi ranked 24th among the states in terms of combined state and local tax burden, which amounted to about 9.6% of income.

The following table from the US Census Bureau provides a summary of taxes collected by the state in 2002.

	($000)	PER CAPITA
Total Taxes	4,728,905	1,646.68
Property taxes	1,246	0.43
Sales and gross receipts	3,183,323	1,108.48
General sales and gross receipts	2,340,474	814.99
Selective sales taxes	842,849	293.49
Alcoholic beverage	39,690	13.82
Amusements	184,157	64.13
Insurance Premiums	130,241	45.35
Motor fuels	410,258	142.86
Pari-mutuels	(X)	(X)
Public utilities	16,031	5.58
Tobacco products	55,612	19.36
Other selective sales	6,860	2.39
Licenses	301,354	104.94
Alcoholic beverages	2,232	0.78
Amusements	1,356	0.47
Corporation	61,886	21.55
Hunting and fishing	13,369	4.66
Motor vehicle	111,683	38.89
Motor vehicle operators	23,620	8.22
Public utility	9,627	3.35
Occupation and business, NEC	76,898	26.78
Other	683	0.24
Other taxes	1,242,982	432.83
Individual income	985,117	343.03
Corporation net income	195,814	68.19
Death and gift	30,154	10.5
Documentary and stock transfer	(X)	(X)
Severance	31,897	11.11
Other	(X)	(X)

37ECONOMIC POLICY

In 1936, the state began implementing a program called Balance Agriculture with Industry (BAWI), designed to attract manufacturing to Mississippi. The BAWI laws offered industry substantial tax concessions and permitted local governments to issue bonds to build plants that would be leased to companies for a 20-year period, after which the company would own them. Mississippi continues to offer low tax rates and numerous tax incentives to industry.

The Department of Economic and Community Development is charged with encouraging economic growth in the specific fields of industrial development, marketing of state products, and development of tourism. A high-technology asset is the National Space and Technology Laboratory in Hancock County.

38HEALTH

In 2000, Mississippi's infant mortality rate was the highest in the US at 10.7 per 1,000 population, significantly higher than the national rate of 6.9. There were 3,878 legal abortions in the state in 1999, averaging 6 per 1,000 women. In 2000, Mississippi's overall rate of death was amongst the highest in the nation, 1,028.1 per 100,000 population. Also in that same year, Mississippi's death rates from heart diseases (332.1 per 100,000 population) and cerebrovascular diseases (71.7) exceeded national rates. The death rate for motor vehicle accidents was the highest in the nation, 33.5, more than double the national rate of 15.7. In the same year, the HIV-related death rate (5.7 per 100,000 population) also exceeded the national rate of 5.3; a total of 4,877 AIDS cases had been reported through 2001. Among persons ages 18 and older, 23.5% were smokers in 2000.

Mississippi's 96 community hospitals had 436,100 admissions and 13,670 beds in 2001. There were 11,279 full-time registered nurses and 2,344 full-time licensed practical nurses in 2001 and only 181 physicians per 100,000 population in 2000. The average expense of a community hospital for care was $1,264.70 per inpatient day in 2001.

Federal government grants to cover the Medicare and Medicaid services in 2001 totaled $2.0 billion; 423,436 enrollees received Medicare benefits that year. Approximately 16.4% of the state's adult population had no health insurance in 1998.

39SOCIAL WELFARE

In 2001, the average weekly unemployment benefit was $163.26. Average monthly participation in the food stamp program in FY2002 comprised 324,852 persons (126,389 households). The average monthly benefit was $76.43, and the sum total of benefits paid in FY2002 was $297,924,799.

With the enactment of the Personal Responsibility and Work Opportunity Reconciliation Act of 1996, the US government has changed the form and regulations for many of its social welfare programs. Most significantly, it replaces Aid to Families with Dependent Children (AFDC), an open-ended entitlement program, with Temporary Assistance for Needy Families (TANF), a limited system of assistance funded largely through federal block grants. The reform act also impacts the food stamp program, the Supplemental Security Income program, and the child nutrition program. The law took effect on 1 July 1997 and provided $16.38 billion in block grants for fiscal years 1997–2002. The grants are to be divided among the states based on an equation involving the numbers of former AFDC recipients in each state.

Reauthorization of the 1996 social welfare legislation, scheduled for 2002, was delayed, and the original law had been extended three times as of July 2003, with the most recent extension running through September 2003. In June 2000 the state had 33,781 welfare recipients. State expenditures on the TANF program in FY2002 totaled $21,724,308.

In December 2001, Social Security benefits were paid to 523,460 Mississippians. This number included 275,660 retired workers, 60,430 widows and widowers, 90,150 disabled workers, 26,830 spouses, and 70,390 children. Social Security beneficiaries represented 18.2% of the total state population and 91.9% of the state's population age 65 and older. Retired workers (excluding persons with special benefits) received an average monthly payment of $792; widows and widowers, $690; disabled workers, $759; and spouses, $381. Payments for children of retired workers averaged $370 per month; children of deceased workers, $508; and children of disabled workers, $215.

Federal Supplemental Security Income payments in December 2001 went to 128,449 Mississippi residents, averaging $336 a month.

40HOUSING

The 2002, Mississippi had 1,195,133 housing units, of which 1,047,324 were occupied; 71.4% were owner-occupied. About 69.9% of all units were single-family, detached homes; 14.7% were mobile homes. Utility gas and electricity were the most common energy sources to all units. It was estimated that 69,226 units lacked telephone service, 9,338 lacked complete plumbing facilities, and 5,723 lacked complete kitchen facilities. The average household size was 2.65 people.

In 2002, 11,276 privately owned units were authorized for construction. The median home value was $79,425, the 2nd lowest in the country. The median monthly cost for mortgage owners was $827. Renters paid a median of $511 per month. During 2002, Mississippi received over $67.6 million in community planning and development aid from the US Department of Housing and Urban Development.

41EDUCATION

Only 72.9% of Mississippians age 25 and older had completed high school in 2000, an improvement from 1980, when 55% of the adult population were graduates, but still below the national average of 80.4%. Only 19.5% had obtained a bachelor's degree or higher in 2000.

Mississippi's reaction to the US Supreme Court decision in 1954 mandating public school desegregation was to repeal the constitutional requirement for public schools and to foster the development of segregated private schools. In 1964, the state's schools did begin to integrate, and compulsory school attendance was restored 13 years later. As of 1980, 26% of minority (nonwhite) students were in schools in which minorities represented less than 50% of the student body, and 19% were in 99–100% minority schools—a considerable degree of de facto segregation, but less so than in some northern states. In 1982, the compulsory school age was raised to 14, and as of 2001, it was 17; also in 1982, a system of free public kindergartens was established for the first time.

The total enrollment for fall 1999 in Mississippi's public schools stood at 500,716. Of these, 365,357 attended schools from kindergarten through grade eight, and 135,359 attended high school. Minority students made up approximately 53% of the total enrollment in public elementary and secondary schools in 2001. Total enrollment was estimated at 499,362 in fall 2000 and is expected to reach 514,000 by fall 2005. Enrollment in nonpublic schools in fall 2001 was 51,369. Expenditures for public education in 2000/01 were estimated at $2,637,923.

As of fall 2000, there were 152,997 students enrolled in college or graduate school. In the same year Mississippi had 42 degree-granting institutions: 8 public universities, 17 community colleges, and 17 private colleges (including 4 Bible colleges and theological seminaries). In 1997, minority students comprised 33.3% of total postsecondary enrollment. Important institutions of higher learning in Mississippi include the University of Mississippi, established in 1844, Mississippi State University, and the University of Southern Mississippi. Predominantly black institutions include Tougaloo College, Alcorn State University, Jackson State University, and Mississippi Valley State University.

42ARTS

Jackson has two ballet companies, a symphony orchestra, and two opera companies. Opera South, an integrated but predominantly black company, presents free operas during its summer tours and mounts two major productions yearly. The Mississippi Opera instituted a summer festival during its 1980/81 season. There are local symphony orchestras in Meridian, Starkville, Tupelo, and Greenville.

The established professional theaters in the state are the Sheffield Ensemble in Biloxi and the New Stage in Jackson. The Greater Gulf Coast Arts Center has been very active in bringing arts programs into the coastal area.

A distinctive contribution to US culture is the music of black sharecroppers from the Delta, known as the blues. The Delta Blues Museum in Clarksdale has an extensive collection documenting blues history. The annual Mississippi Delta Blues and Heritage Festival is held in Greenville.

In 2003, the Mississippi Arts Commission and other Mississippi arts organizations received grants totaling $660,200 from the National Endowment for the Arts. The commission also receives significant sums from the state and private sources. In 2000, the National Endowment for the Humanities contributed $689,624 to 11 state programs.

43LIBRARIES AND MUSEUMS

There were 47 county or multi-county (regional) libraries, serving all counties in 2000. There were 5.6 million volumes in Mississippi libraries, and total circulation was over 8.4 million. The finest collection of Mississippiana is at the Mississippi State Department of Archives and History in Jackson. In the Vicksburg-Warren County Public Library are collections on the Civil War and state history and oral history collections. Tougaloo College has special collections of African materials, civil rights

papers, and oral history. The Gulf Coast Research Library of Ocean Springs has a marine biology collection. Total public library income amounted to $35,998,000 in 2000. In 1998; per capita spending was $11.66, one of the lowest of all states.

There are 65 museums, including the distinguished Mississippi State Historical Museum at Jackson. Pascagoula, Laurel, and Jackson all have notable art museums. The Mississippi Museum of Natural Science in Jackson has been designated the state's official natural science museum by the legislature. Also in Jackson is the Mississippi Agriculture and Forestry Museum. In Meridian is a museum devoted to country singer Jimmie Rodgers, and in Jackson one to pitcher Dizzy Dean.

Beauvoir, Jefferson Davis's home at Biloxi, is a state shrine and includes a museum. The Mississippi governor's mansion—completed in 1845, restored in 1975, and purportedly the 2nd-oldest executive residence in the US—is a National Historical Landmark.

44COMMUNICATIONS

In 2001, only 88.1% of the state's occupied housing units had telephones, the lowest rate in the US. In 2003, the state had 64 major operating radio stations (7 AM, 57 FM), and 14 major television stations. A total of 17,234 Internet domain names had been registered in Mississippi by the year 2000.

45PRESS

In 2002, Mississippi had 23 daily newspapers: 9 morning dailies and 14 evening dailies. There were 18 Sunday papers in the state. The state's leading newspaper is in Jackson, owned by the Gannett Co.: the *Clarion–Ledger*, a morning daily with a weekday circulation of 95,584 (114,223 Sunday). Other leading dailies with approximate 2002 circulation rates are:

AREA	NAME	DAILY	SUNDAY
Biloxi-Gulfport	*Sun Herald*	47,100	55,582
Tupelo	*Northeast Mississippi Daily Journal*	34,332	34,332

A monthly, *Mississippi Magazine*, is published in Edwards, and a bimonthly, *Mississippi: A View of the Magnolia State*, is published in Jackson.

46ORGANIZATIONS

In 2003, there were about 848 regional, national, and international organizations within the state.

The National Association for the Advancement of Colored People (NAACP), the Congress of Racial Equality, the Southern Christian Leadership Conference, and the Student Nonviolent Coordinating Committee (SNCC, later the Student National Coordinating Committee) were among the organizations that played key roles in the civil rights struggles in Mississippi during the 1950s and 1960s. Of the national civil rights organizations still active in Mississippi, the NAACP is the largest, with members in every county.

In contrast to the 1960s, most civil rights activities in the state are now organized around local social and economic programs, such as Head Start. The Freedom Information Service is a clearinghouse for information about civil rights activities in the state. The Citizens' Councils of America, headquartered in Jackson, is a states' rights group.

Other organizations with headquarters in Mississippi are the American Association of Public Health Physicians (Greenwood), the Sons of Confederate Veterans (Hattiesburg), the Sacred Heart League (Wallis), the National Band Association (Hattiesburg), and the Amateur Field Trial Clubs of America (Hernando).

47TOURISM, TRAVEL, AND RECREATION

In 2001, there were about 35 million overnight travelers in Mississippi, with about 83% of all visitors traveling from out of state. Estimated results from FY 2002 indicate total travel expenditures of $6.4 billion, which supported over 92,700 travel-related jobs. Gaming jobs represented about one-third of the total tourism and recreation jobs.

Among Mississippi's major tourist attractions are its floating riverboat casinos and its mansions and plantations, many of them in the Natchez area. In 2001, there were 30 licensed state casinos. About 75% of casino patrons are out-of-state visitors. McRaven plantation, in Vicksburg, was built in 1797. The Delta and Pine Land Co. plantation near Scott is one of the largest cotton plantations in the US. At Greenwood is the Florewood River Plantation, a museum re-creating 19th-century plantation life. The Mississippi State Fair is held annually in Jackson during the second week in October.

National parks include the Natchez Trace Parkway, Gulf Islands National Seashore, and Vicksburg National Military Park. There are also 6 national forests and 27 state parks.

48SPORTS

There are no major league professional teams in Mississippi. Jackson has a minor league baseball team, the Senators, of the Central League. There is also a minor league hockey team in Biloxi, as well as teams in Jackson and Tupelo. The University of Mississippi has long been prominent in college football. "Ole Miss" teams won the Sugar Bowl in 1958, 1960, 1961, 1963, and 1970, and the Cotton Bowl in 1956. The Rebels play in the Southeastern Conference, as do the Mississippi State Bulldogs. Southern Mississippi is a member of Conference USA.

Other annual sporting events of interest include the Dixie National Livestock Show and Rodeo, held in Jackson in February, and the Southern Farm Bureau Classic, held in Madison in October and November l.

Football greats Walter Payton and Jerry Rice, along with boxing legend Archie Moore, were born and raised in Mississippi.

49FAMOUS MISSISSIPPIANS

Mississippi's most famous political figure, Jefferson Davis (b.Kentucky, 1808–89), came to the state as a very young child, was educated at West Point, and served in the US Army from 1828 to 1835. He resigned a seat in Congress in 1846 to enter the Mexican War from which he returned home a hero after leading his famous regiment, the 1st Mississippi Rifles, at the Battle of Buena Vista, Mexico. From 1853 to 1857, he served as secretary of war in the cabinet of President Franklin Pierce. Davis was representing Mississippi in the US Senate in 1861 when the state withdrew from the Union. In February 1861, he was chosen president of the Confederacy, an office he held until the defeat of the South in 1865. Imprisoned for two years after the Civil War (though never tried), Davis lived the last years of his life at Beauvoir, an estate on the Mississippi Gulf Coast given to him by an admirer. There he wrote *The Rise and Fall of the Confederate Government*, completed eight years before his death in New Orleans.

Lucius Quintus Cincinnatus Lamar (b.Georgia, 1825–93) settled in Oxford in 1855 and only two years later was elected to the US House of Representatives. A supporter of secession, he served as Confederate minister to Russia in 1862. After the war, Lamar was the first Mississippi Democrat returned to the House; in 1877, he entered the US Senate. President Grover Cleveland made Lamar his secretary of the interior in 1885, later appointing him to the US Supreme Court. Lamar served as associate justice from 1888 until his death.

Some of the foremost authors of 20th-century America had their origins in Mississippi. Supreme among them is William Faulkner (1897–1962), whose literary career began in 1924 with the publication of *The Marble Faun*, a book of poems. His novels included such classics as *The Sound and the Fury* (1929), *Light in August* (1932), and *Absalom, Absalom!* (1936). Faulkner received two Pulitzer Prizes (one posthumously), and in 1949 was awarded the Nobel Prize for literature.

Richard Wright (1908–60), born near Natchez, spent his childhood years in Jackson. He moved to Memphis as a young man, and from there migrated to Chicago; he lived his last years in Paris. A powerful writer and a leading spokesman for the black Americans of his generation, Wright is best remembered for his novel *Native Son* (1940) and for *Black Boy* (1945), an autobiographical account of his Mississippi childhood.

Other native Mississippians of literary renown (and Pulitzer Prize winners) are Eudora Welty (1909–2001), Tennessee Williams (Thomas Lanier Williams, 1911–83), and playwright Beth Henley (b.1952). Welty's work, like Faulkner's, is set in Mississippi; her best-known novels include *Delta Wedding* (1946), *The Ponder Heart* (1954), and *Losing Battles* (1970). Although Tennessee Williams spent most of his life outside Mississippi, some of his most famous plays are set in the state. Other Mississippi authors are Hodding Carter (b.Louisiana, 1907–72), Shelby Foote (b.1916), Walker Percy (b.Alabama, 1916–1990), and Willie Morris (1934–99).

Among the state's numerous musicians are William Grant Still (1895–1978), a composer and conductor, and Leontyne Price (Mary Leontine Price, b.1927), a distinguished opera singer. Famous blues singers are Charlie Patton (1887–1934), William Lee Conley "Big Bill" Broonzy (1898–1958), Howlin' Wolf (Chester Arthur Burnett, 1910–1976), Muddy Waters (McKinley Morganfield, 1915–83), John Lee Hooker (1917–2001), and Riley "B. B." King (b.1925). Mississippi's contributions to country music include Jimmie Rodgers (1897–1933), Conway Twitty (1933–1994), and Charley Pride (b.1939). Elvis Presley (1935–77), born in Tupelo, was one of the most popular entertainers in US history.

50BIBLIOGRAPHY

Alampi, Gary, ed. *Gale State Rankings Reporter*. Detroit: Gale Research, Inc., 1994.

Ballard, Michael B. *Civil War Mississippi: A Guide*. Jackson: University Press of Mississippi, 2000.

Bettersworth, John K. *Your Mississippi*. Austin, Tex.: SteckVaughn, 1975.

Bond, Bradley G. *Political Culture in the Nineteenth-century South: Mississippi, 1830–1900*. Baton Rouge: Louisiana State University, 1995.

Brooks, Cleanth. *William Faulkner: The Yoknapatawpha Country*. New Haven, Conn.: Yale University Press, 1963.

Coleman, Mary DeLorse. *Legislators, Law, and Public Policy: Political Change in Mississippi and the South*. Westport, Conn.: Greenwood Press, 1993.

Council of State Governments. *The Book of the States, 1994–1995 Edition*. Vol. 30. Lexington, Ky.: The Council of State Governments, 1994.

Dittmer, John. *Local People: The Struggle for Civil Rights in Mississippi*. Urbana: University of Illinois Press, 1994.

FDIC, Division of Research and Statistics. *Statistics on Banking: A Statistical Profile of the United States Banking Industry*. Washington, D.C.: Federal Deposit Insurance Corporation, 1993.

Federal Writers' Project. *Mississippi: A Guide to the Magnolia State*. New York: Somerset, n.d. (orig. 1938).

Hendrickson, Paul. *Sons of Mississippi: A Story of Race and Its Legacy*. New York: Alfred A. Knopf, 2003.

McLemore, Richard A., ed. *A History of Mississippi*. 2 vols. Hattiesburg: University and College Press of Mississippi, 1973.

Nelson, Lawrence J. *King Cotton's Advocate: Oscar G. Johnston and the New Deal.* Knoxville: University of Tennessee Press, 1999.

Schmittroth, Linda, and Mary Kay Rosteck (eds.). *Cities of the United States.* 2nd ed. Detroit: Gale Research, Inc., 1994.

U.S. Department of Education, National Center for Education Statistics. Office of Educational Research and Improvement. *Digest of Education Statistics, 1993.* Washington, D.C.: U.S. Government Printing Office, 1993.

U.S. Department of the Interior, U.S. Fish and Wildlife Service. *Endangered and Threatened Species Recovery Program.* Washington, D.C.: U.S. Government Printing Office, 1990.

Welty, Eudora. *One Time, One Place: Mississippi in the Depression.* New York: Random House, 1971.

Wharton, Vernon L. *The Negro in Mississippi, 1865-90.* New York: Harper and Row, 1965 (orig. 1947).

Woodruff, Nan Elizabeth. *American Congo: The African American Freedom Struggle in the Delta.* Cambridge, Mass.: Harvard University Press, 2003.

MISSOURI

State of Missouri

ORIGIN OF STATE NAME: Probably from the Iliniwek Indian word *missouri,* meaning "owners of big canoes." **NICKNAME:** The Show Me State. **CAPITAL:** Jefferson City. **ENTERED UNION:** 10 August 1821 (24th). **SONG:** "Missouri Waltz." **MOTTO:** *Salus populi suprema lex esto* (The welfare of the people shall be the supreme law). **COAT OF ARMS:** Two grizzly bears standing on a scroll inscribed with the state motto support a shield portraying an American eagle and a constellation of stars, a grizzly bear on all fours, and a crescent moon, all encircled by the words "United We Stand, Divided We Fall." Above are a six-barred helmet and 24 stars; below, the roman numeral MDCCCXX (1820), when Missouri's first constitution was adopted. **FLAG:** Three horizontal stripes of red, white, and blue, with the coat of arms, encircled by 24 white stars on a blue band, in the center. **OFFICIAL SEAL:** The coat of arms surrounded by the words "The Great Seal of the State of Missouri." **BIRD:** Bluebird. **INSECT:** Honeybee. **FLOWER:** White Hawthorn blossom. **TREE:** Flowering dogwood. **ROCK:** Mozarkite (chert or flint rock). **MINERAL:** Galena. **LEGAL HOLIDAYS:** New Year's Day, 1 January; Birthday of Martin Luther King, Jr., 3rd Monday in January; Lincoln's Birthday, 12 February; Washington's Birthday, 3rd Monday in February; Harry S. Truman's Birthday, 8 May; Memorial Day, last Monday in May; Independence Day, 4 July; Primary Election Day; 1st Tuesday after 1st Monday in August (every four years); Labor Day, 1st Monday in September; Columbus Day, 2nd Monday in October; Election Day, 1st Tuesday after 1st Monday in November (every four years); Veterans Day, 11 November; Thanksgiving Day, 4th Thursday in November; Christmas Day, 25 December. Though not a legal holiday, Missouri Day, the 3rd Wednesday in October, is commemorated in schools each year. **TIME:** 6 AM CST = noon GMT.

¹LOCATION, SIZE, AND EXTENT

Located in the western north-central US, Missouri ranks 19th in size among the 50 states.

The total area of Missouri is 69,697 sq mi (180,516 sq km), of which land takes up 68,945 sq mi (178,568 sq km) and inland water 752 sq mi (1,948 sq km). Missouri extends 284 mi (457 km) E-W; its greatest N-S extension is 308 mi (496 km).

Missouri is bounded on the N by Iowa (with the line in the extreme NE defined by the Des Moines River); on the E by Illinois, Kentucky, and Tennessee (with the line passing through the Mississippi River); on the S by Arkansas (with a "boot heel" in the SE bounded by the Mississippi and St. Francis rivers); and on the W by Oklahoma, Kansas, and Nebraska (the line in the NW being formed by the Missouri River).

The total boundary length of Missouri is 1,438 mi (2,314 km). The state's geographic center is in Miller County, 20 mi (32 km) SW of Jefferson City.

²TOPOGRAPHY

Missouri is divided into four major land regions. The Dissected Till Plains, lying north of the Missouri River and forming part of the Central Plains region of the US, comprise rolling hills, open fertile flatlands, and well-watered prairie. The Osage Plains cover the western part of the state, their flat prairie monotony broken by low rounded hills. The Mississippi Alluvial Plain, in the southeastern corner, is made up of fertile black lowlands whose floodplain belts represent both the present and former courses of the Mississippi River. The Ozark Plateau, which comprises most of southern Missouri and extends into northern Arkansas and northeastern Oklahoma, constitutes the state's largest single region. The Ozarks contain Taum Sauk Mountain, at 1,772 ft (540 m) the highest elevation in the state. Along the St. Francis River, near Cardwell, is the state's lowest point, 230 ft (70 m).

Including a frontage of at least 500 mi (800 km) along the Mississippi River, Missouri has more than 1,000 mi (1,600 km) of navigable waterways. The Mississippi and Missouri rivers, the two largest in the US, respectively form the state's eastern border and part of its western border; Kansas City is located at the point where the Missouri bends eastward to cross the state, while St. Louis developed below the junction of the two great waterways. The White, Grand, Chariton, St. Francis, Current, and Osage are among the state's other major rivers. The largest lake is the artificial Lake of the Ozarks, covering a total of 93 sq mi (241 sq km).

Missouri's exceptional number of caves and caverns were formed during the last 50 million years through the erosion of limestone and dolomite by melting snows bearing vegetable acids. Coal, lead, and zinc deposits date from the Pennsylvanian era, beginning some 250 million years ago. The Mississippi Valley area is geologically active: massive earthquakes during 1811 and 1812 devastated the New Madrid area of the southeast.

³CLIMATE

Missouri has a continental climate, but with considerable local and regional variation. The average annual temperature is 50°F (10°C) in the northwest, but about 60°F (16°C) in the southeast. Kansas City has a normal daily mean temperature of 54°F (12°C), ranging from 26°F (–3°C) in January to 79°F (26°C) in July; St. Louis has an annual mean of 56°F (13°C) with 29°F (–2°C) in January and 80°F (27°C) in July.

The coldest temperature ever recorded in Missouri was –40°F (–40°C), set at Warsaw on 13 February 1905; the hottest, 118°F (48°C), at Warsaw and Union on 14 July 1954. A 1980 heat wave caused 311 heat-related deaths in Missouri, the highest toll in the country; most were elderly residents of St. Louis and Kansas City.

Fifty-one more heat-related deaths occurred in St. Louis during a 1983 heat wave.

The average annual precipitation for Kansas City (1971–2000) was 40 in (100 cm), with some rain or snow falling about 110 days a year. The heaviest precipitation is in the southeast, averaging 48 in (122 cm); the northwest usually receives 35 in (89 cm) yearly. Snowfall averages 20 in (51 cm) in the north, 10 in (25 cm) in the southeast. During the winter, northwest winds prevail; the air movement is largely from the south and southeast during the rest of the year. Springtime is the peak tornado season.

4 FLORA AND FAUNA

Representative trees of Missouri include the shortleaf pine, scarlet oak, smoke tree, pecan (Carya illinoensis), and peachleaf willow, along with species of tupelo, cottonwood, cypress, cedar, and dogwood (the state tree). American holly, which once flourished in the southeastern woodlands, is now considered rare; various types of wild grasses proliferate in the northern plains region. Missouri's state flower is the hawthorn blossom; other wild flowers include Queen Anne's lace, meadow rose, and white snakeroot. Showy and small white lady's slipper, green adder's-mouth, purslane, corn salad, dotted monardo, and prairie white-fringed orchid are rare in Missouri. Among the eight threatened or endangered plants listed in 2003 were the decurrent false aster, running buffalo clover, pondberry, Missouri bladderpod, and western prairie fringed orchid.

Indigenous mammals are the common cottontail, muskrat, white-tailed deer, and gray and red foxes. The state bird is the bluebird; other common birds are the cardinal, solitary vireo, and the prothonotary warbler. A characteristic amphibian is the plains leopard frog; native snakes include garter, ribbon, and copperhead. Bass, carp, perch, jack salmon (walleye), and crayfish abound in Missouri's waters. The chigger, a minute insect, is a notorious pest.

In 2003, 17 species were listed as threatened or endangered in Missouri, including three species of bat (Ozark big-eared, gray, and Indiana), bald eagle, pallid sturgeon, gray wolf, and three varieties of mussel.

5 ENVIRONMENTAL PROTECTION

Missouri's first conservation law, enacted in 1874, provided for a closed hunting season on deer and certain game birds. In 1936, the state established a Conservation Commission to protect the state's wildlife and forest resources. Today, Missouri's principal environmental protection agencies are the Department of Conservation, which manages the state forests and fish hatcheries and maintains wildlife refuges, the Department of Natural Resources, responsible for state parks, energy conservation, and environmental quality programs, including air pollution control, water purification, land reclamation, soil and water conservation, and solid and hazardous waste management. The State Environmental Improvement and Energy Resources Authority, within the Department of Natural Resources, is empowered to offer financial aid to any individual, business, institution, or governmental unit seeking to meet pollution control responsibilities.

An important environmental problem is soil erosion; the state loses 71 million tons of topsoil each year. Residents approved a 0.1% sales tax in 1984 and 1988 to create a fund to address this problem. As of 1982, 42 sites in Missouri were found to have unsafe concentrations of dioxin, a highly toxic by-product of hexachlorophene, manufactured in a Verona chemical plant; in that year, an evacuation was begun (completed in 1985) of the 2,000 residents of Times Beach, a community 30 mi (48 km) west of St. Louis that was declared a federal disaster area. St. Louis ranks high among US cities for the quantities of lead and

suspended particles found in the atmosphere, but conditions improved between the mid-1970s and early 1980s.

In 2003, Missouri had 503 hazardous waste sites listed in the Environmental Protection Agency's database, 23 of which were on the National Priorities List. In 1996, it had 643,000 acres (260,000 hectares) of wetlands, or about 1.4% of the state's lands. In 2001, Missouri received $101,560,000 in federal grants from the Environmental Protection Agency; EPA expenditures for procurement contracts in Missouri that year amounted to $2,137,000.

6 POPULATION

Missouri ranked 17th in population in the US (down from 15th in 1990) with an estimated total of 5,672,579 in 2002, an increase of 1.4% since 2000. Between 1990 and 2000, Missouri's population grew from 5,117,073 to 5,595,211, an increase of 9%. The population is projected to reach 5,718,000 by 2005 and 6.3 million by 2025. The population density in 2000 was 81.2 persons per sq mi.

In 1830, the first year in which Missouri was enumerated as a state, the population was 140,455. Missouri's population just about doubled each decade until 1860, when the growth rate subsided; the population surpassed the 2 million mark at the 1880 census, 3 million in 1900 (when it ranked 5th in the US), and 4 million during the early 1950s.

In 2000, the median age for Missourians was 36.1. In the same year, 25.5% of the population were under age 18 while 13.5% were age 65 or older.

More than half of all Missourians live in urban areas. The largest cities and their estimated 2002 populations are Kansas City, 443,471, and St. Louis, 338,353—both well below the 1980 figures. The St. Louis metropolitan area, embracing parts of Missouri and Illinois, comprised an estimated 2,569,029 people in 1999 while metropolitan Kansas City, in Missouri and Kansas, had a population of 1,755,899.

7 ETHNIC GROUPS

After the flatboat and French traders and settlers had made possible the earliest development of Missouri and its Mississippi shore, the river steamer, the Civil War, the Homestead Act (1862), and the railroad changed the character of the state ethnically as well as economically. Germans came in large numbers, developing small diversified industries, and they were followed by Czechs and Italians. The foreign-born numbered 151,196 in 2000, up from 83,633 in 1990.

Black Americans have represented a rising proportion of Missouri's population in recent decades: 9% in 1960, 10.3% in 1970, 10.5% in 1980, 10.7% in 1990, and 11.2% in 2000. Kansas City's black community supported a flourishing jazz and urban blues culture between the two world wars, while St. Louis was the home of Scott Joplin and W. C. Handy in the early years of the century. Of the 629,391 black residents of Missouri in 2000, 178,266 lived in St. Louis, which was 51.2% black. In 2000 Missouri also had 118,592 Hispanics and Latinos, nearly double the 1990 figure of 62,000, and including 77,887 of Mexican ancestry. The total Asian population as of 2000 was 61,595; in that year there were 13,667 Chinese, 7,735 Filipinos, 6,767 Koreans, 3,337 Japanese, and 12,169 Vietnamese (triple the 1990 figure of 4,030). Pacific Islanders numbered 3,178.

Only a few American Indians remained in Missouri after 1836. The 2000 census showed an Indian population of 25,076. The state has no Indian reservations.

Of those claiming descent from at least one specific ancestry group in 2000, 1,313,951 named German, 528,935 English, and 711,995 Irish.

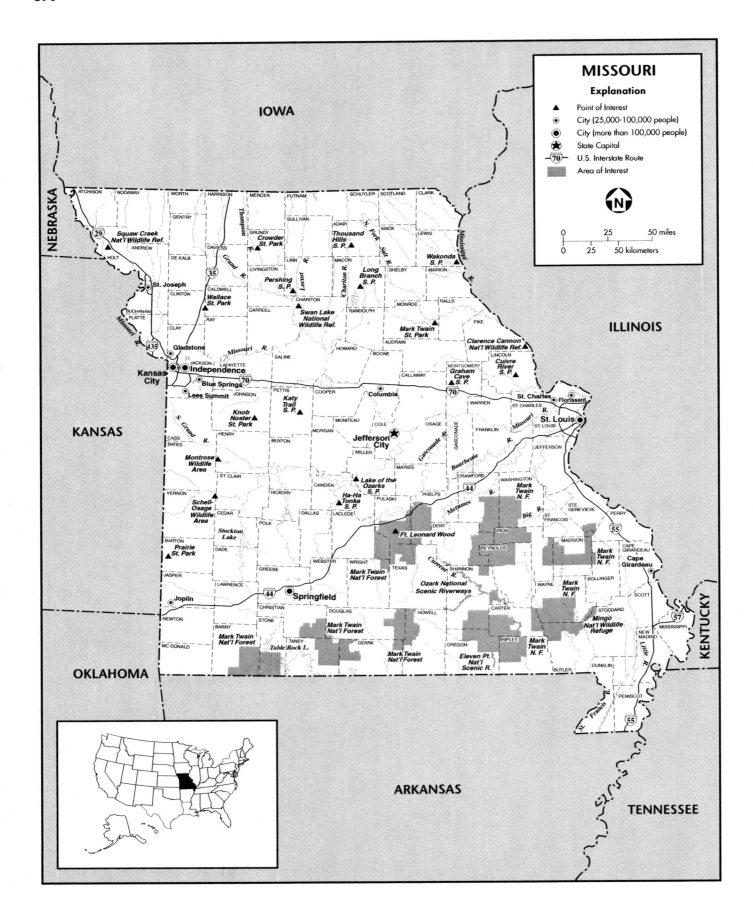

[8] LANGUAGES

White pioneers found Missouri Indians in the northern part of what is now Missouri Osage in the central portion, and Quapaw in the south. Long after these tribes' removal to Indian Territory, only a few place-names echo their heritage: Missouri itself, Kahoka, Wappapello.

Four westward-flowing language streams met and partly merged in Missouri. Northern and North Midland speakers settled north of the Missouri River and in the western border counties, bringing their Northern *pail* and *sick to the stomach* and their North Midland *fishworm* (earthworm), *gunnysack* (burlap bag), and *sick at the stomach*. But *sick in the stomach* occurs along the Missouri River from St. Louis to Kansas City and along the Mississippi south of St. Louis. South of the Missouri River, and notably in the Ozark Highlands, South Midland dominates, though with a few Southern forms, especially in the cotton-growing floodplain of the extreme southeast. *Wait on* (wait for), *light bread* (white bread), and *pullybone* (wishbone) are critical dialect markers for this area, as are *redworm* (earthworm), *towsack* (burlap bag), *snap beans* (string beans), *how* and *now* sounding like /haowl/ and /naowl/, and Missouri ending with the vowel of *me* rather than the final vowel of /uh/ heard north of the Missouri. In the extreme southeast are Southern *loaf bread*, *grass sack* (burlap bag), and *cold drink* as a term for a soft drink. In the eastern half of the state, a soft drink is generally *soda* or *sody*; in the western half, *pop*.

In 2000, 94.9% of state residents five years old or older spoke only English at home, down from 96% in 1990.

The following table gives selected statistics from the 2000 census for language spoken at home by persons five years old and over. The category "African languages" includes Amharic, Ibo, Twi, Yoruba, Bantu, Swahili, and Somali. The category "Other West Germanic languages" includes Dutch, Pennsylvania Dutch, and Afrikaans.

LANGUAGE	NUMBER	PERCENT
Population 5 years and over	5,226,022	100.0
Speak only English	4,961,741	94.9
Speak a language other than English	264,281	5.1
Speak a language other than English	264,281	5.1
Spanish or Spanish Creole	110,752	2.1
German	30,680	0.6
French (incl. Patois, Cajun)	19,547	0.4
Chinese	11,631	0.2
Vietnamese	9,420	0.2
Serbo-Croatian	8,350	0.2
Italian	6,710	0.1
Russian	5,469	0.1
Arabic	5,137	0.1
African languages	5,117	0.1
Other West Germanic languages	4,822	0.1
Korean	4,753	0.1
Tagalog	4,645	0.1

[9] RELIGIONS

Beginning in the late 17th century, French missionaries brought Roman Catholicism to what is now Missouri; the first permanent Roman Catholic church was built about 1755 at St. Genevieve. Immigration from Germany, Ireland, Italy, and Eastern Europe swelled the Catholic population during the 19th century and Roman Catholicism remains the largest single Christian denomination today, though the Evangelical Protestants collectively outnumber Catholics. Baptist preachers crossed the Mississippi River into Missouri in the late 1790s, and the state's first Methodist church was organized about 1806. Immigrants from Germany included not only Roman Catholics, but also many Lutherans, the most conservative of whom organized the Lutheran Church—Missouri Synod in 1847.

In 2000, Missouri had 856,964 Roman Catholics. The 2nd-largest single religious groups were the principal Protestant denominations of the Southern Baptist Convention, with 797,732 adherents; the United Methodist Church, 226,578; the Lutheran Church—Missouri Synod, 140,315; and the Christian Church (Disciples of Christ), 105,583. The same year, the estimated number of Jews was 62,315 and Muslims numbered about 19,359. About 2.7 million people (48.3% of the population) were not counted as members of any religious organization.

[10] TRANSPORTATION

Centrally located, Missouri is the leading US transportation center. Both St. Louis and Kansas City are hubs of rail, truck, and airline transportation.

In 1836, delegates from 11 counties met in St. Louis to recommend construction of two railroad lines and to petition Congress for a grant of 800,000 acres (324,000 hectares) of public land on which to build them. More than a dozen companies were incorporated by the legislature, but they all collapsed with the financial panic of 1837. Interest in railroad construction revived during the following decade, and in 1849 a national railroad convention was held in St. Louis at which nearly 1,000 delegates from 13 states recommended the construction of a transcontinental railroad. By 1851, three railroad lines had been chartered, and construction by the Pacific Railroad at St. Louis was under way; the Pacific line reached Kansas City in 1865, and a bridge built over the Missouri River four years later enabled Kansas City to link up with the Hannibal and St. Joseph Railroad, providing a freight route to Chicago that did not pass through St. Louis. In 2000, there were 4,541 rail mi (7,308 km) of track in the state, including 3,616 rail mi (5,819 km) of Class I track. In 1996, Amtrak provided eight passenger trains running directly from Chicago to St. Louis and to Kansas City, en route to San Antonio and Los Angeles, and two daily Kansas City–St. Louis round trips. Amtrak trains made eight other Missouri stops between St. Louis and Kansas City.

The first road developed in colonial Missouri was probably a trail between the lead mines and Ste. Genevieve in the early 1700s. A two-level cantilever bridge—the first in the world to have a steel superstructure—spanning the Mississippi at St. Louis was dedicated on 4 July 1874. By 1940, no place in Missouri was more than 10 mi (16 km) from a highway. In 2000, there were 123,039 mi (198,012 km) of public roads in Missouri. The main interstate highways were I-70, linking St. Louis with Kansas City; I-44, connecting St. Louis with Springfield and Joplin; I-55, linking St. Louis with Chicago, Illinois, to the north and paralleling the course of the Mississippi between St. Louis and Memphis, Tennessee; I-35, connecting Kansas City with Des Moines, Iowa; and I-29, paralleling the Missouri River north of Kansas City. Motor vehicle registration for the state in 2000 was 4,640,569, including 2,715,215 passenger cars, 1,851,429 trucks, and 12,985 buses; 3,856,271 driver's licenses were in force during the same year.

The Mississippi and Missouri rivers have long been important transportation routes. Pirogues, keelboats, and flatboats plied these waterways for more than a century before the first steamboat, the *New Orleans*, traveled down the Mississippi in 1811. The Mississippi still serves considerable barge traffic, making metropolitan St. Louis an active inland port area, with 33.3 million tons of cargo handled in 2000.

Pioneering aviators in Missouri organized the first international balloon races in 1907 and the first US-sponsored international aviation meet in 1910. Five St. Louis pilots made up the earliest US Army air corps, and a barnstorming pilot named Charles A. Lindbergh, having spent a few years in the St. Louis area, had the backing of businessmen from that city when he flew his *Spirit of St. Louis* across the Atlantic in 1927. Today, Kansas

City International Airport and Lambert-St. Louis Municipal Airport are among the busiest airports in the country.

11HISTORY

The region we now call Missouri has been inhabited for at least 4,000 years. The prehistoric Woodland peoples left low burial mounds, rudimentary pottery, arrowheads, and grooved axes; remains of the later Mississippian Culture include more sophisticated pottery and finely chipped arrowheads. When the first Europeans arrived in the late 17th century, most of the few thousand Indians living in Missouri were relatively recent immigrants, pushed westward across the Mississippi River because of pressures from eastern tribes and European settlers along the Atlantic coast. Indians then occupying Missouri belonged to two main linguistic groups: Algonkian-speakers, mainly the Sauk, Fox, and Iliniwek (Illinois) in the northeast; and a Siouan group, including the Osage, Missouri, Iowa, Kansas, and other tribes, to the south and west. Of greatest interest to the Europeans were the Osage, among whom were warriors and runners of extraordinary ability. The flood of white settlers into Missouri after 1803 forced the Indians to move into Kansas and into what became known as Indian Territory (present-day Oklahoma). During the 1820s, the US government negotiated treaties with the Osage, Sauk, Fox, and Iowa tribes whereby they surrendered, for the most part peaceable, all their lands in Missouri. By 1836, few Indians remained.

The first white men to pass through land eventually included within Missouri's boundaries apparently were Jacques Marquette and Louis Joliet, who in 1673 passed the mouth of the Missouri River on their journey down the Mississippi; so did Robert Cavelier, Sieur de la Salle, who claimed the entire Mississippi Valley for France in 1682. Probably the first Frenchman to explore the Missouri River was Louis Armand de Lom d'Arce, Baron de Lahontan, who in 1688 claimed to have reached the junction of the Missouri and Osage rivers. The French did little to develop the Missouri region during the first half of the 18th century, although a few fur traders and priests established posts and missions among the Indians. A false report that silver had been discovered set off a brief mining boom in which no silver but some lead—available in abundance—was extracted. Missouri passed into Spanish hands with the rest of the Louisiana Territory in 1762, but development was still guided by French settlers; in 1764, the French fur trader Pierre Laclède established a trading post on the present site of St. Louis.

Although Spain fortified St. Louis and a few other outposts during the American Revolution and beat back a British-Indian attack on St. Louis in 1780, the Spanish did not attempt to settle Missouri. However, they did allow Americans to migrate freely into the territory. Spanish authorities granted free land to the new settlers, relaxed their restrictions against Protestants, and welcomed slaveholding families from southern states—especially important after 1787, when slavery was banned in the Northwest Territory. Pioneers such as Daniel Boone arrived from Kentucky, and the Chouteau fur-trading family gained a lucrative monopoly among the Osage. Spanish rule ended abruptly in 1800 when Napoleon forced Spain to return Louisiana to France. Included in the Louisiana Purchase, Missouri then became part of the US in 1803. After the Lewis and Clark expedition (1804–6) had successfully explored the Missouri River, Missouri in general— and St. Louis in particular—became the gateway to the West.

Missouri was part of the Louisiana Territory (with headquarters at St. Louis) until 1 October 1812, when the Missouri Territory (including present-day Arkansas, organized separately in 1819) was established. A flood of settlers between 1810 and 1820 more than tripled Missouri's population from 19,783 to 66,586, leading Missourians to petition the US Congress for statehood as early as 1818. But Congress, divided over the slavery issue, withheld permission for three years, finally approving statehood for Maine and Missouri under the terms of the Missouri Compromise (1820), which sanctioned slavery in the new state but banned it in the rest of the former Louisiana Territory north of Arkansas. Congress further required that Missouri make no effort to enforce a state constitutional ban on the immigration of free Negroes and mulattos; once the legislature complied, Missouri became the 24th state on 10 August 1821, Alexander McNair became the state's first governor, and Thomas Hart Benton was one of the state's first two US senators; Benton remained an important political leader for more than three decades.

Aided by the advent of steamboat travel on the Mississippi and Missouri rivers, settlers continued to arrive in the new state, whose population surpassed 1 million by 1860. The site for a new capital, Jefferson City, was selected in 1821, and five years later the legislature met there for the first time. French fur traders settled the present site of Kansas City in 1821 and established a trading post at St. Joseph in 1827. Mormons came to Independence during the early 1830s but were expelled from the state and crossed the Mississippi back into Illinois. For much of the antebellum period, the state's economy flourished, with an emphasis on cotton, cattle, minerals (especially lead and zinc), and commerce—notably the outfitting of wagon trains for the Santa Fe and Oregon trails. On the eve of the Civil War, more than half the population consisted of Missouri natives; 15% of the white population was foreign-born, chiefly German and Irish. Black slaves represented only 9% of the total population—the lowest proportion of any slave state except Delaware—while only about 25,000 Missourians were slave holders. Nevertheless, there was a great deal of proslavery sentiment in the state, and thousands of Missourians crossed into neighboring Kansas in the mid-1850s to help elect a proslavery government in that territory. State residents were also active in the guerrilla warfare between proslavery forces and Free Staters that erupted along the border with "bleeding Kansas." The slavery controversy was exacerbated by the US Supreme Court's 1857 decision in the case of Dred Scott, a slave formerly owned by a Missourian who had temporarily brought him to what is now Minnesota, where slavery was prohibited; Scott's suit to obtain his freedom was denied by the Court on the grounds that it was unconstitutional to restrict the property rights of slave holders, in a decision that voided the Missouri Compromise reached 37 years earlier.

During the Civil War, Missouri remained loyal to the Union, though not without difficulty. When the conflict began, Governor Claiborne Fox Jackson called out the state militia "to repel the invasion" of federal forces, but pro-Union leaders such as Francis P. Blair deposed Jackson on 30 July 1861. Missouri supplied some 110,000 soldiers to the Union and 40,000 to the Confederacy. As devastating as the 1,162 battles or skirmishes fought on Missouri soil—more than in any other state except Virginia and Tennessee—was the general lawlessness that prevailed throughout the state; pro-Confederate guerrilla bands led by William Quantrill and Cole Younger, as well as Unionist freebooters, murdered and looted without hindrance. In October 1864, a Confederate army under Major General Sterling Price was defeated at the Battle of Westport, on the outskirts of Kansas City, ending the main military action. Some 27,000 Missourians were killed during the war. At a constitutional convention held in January 1865, Missouri became the first slave state to free all blacks.

During Reconstruction, the Radical Republicans sought to disfranchise all citizens who failed to swear that they had never aided or sympathized with the Confederacy. But the harshness of this and other measures caused a backlash, and Liberal Republicans such as Benjamin Gratz Brown and Carl Schurz, allied with the Democrats, succeeded in ousting the Radicals by

1872. The subsequent decline of the Liberal Republicans inaugurated a period during which Democrats occupied the governorship uninterruptedly for more than three decades.

The 1870s saw a period of renewed lawlessness, typified by the exploits of Jesse and Frank James, that earned Missouri the epithet of the "robber state." Of more lasting importance were the closing of the frontier in Missouri, the decline of the fur trade and steamboat traffic, and the rise of the railroads, shifting the market economy from St. Louis to Kansas City, whose population tripled during the 1880s, while St. Louis was eclipsed by Chicago as a center of finance, commerce, transportation, and population. Missouri farmers generally supported the movement for free silver coinage, along with other Populist policies such as railroad regulation. Reform Governor Joseph W. Folk (1905–09) and his immediate successors in the statehouse, Herbert S. Hadley (1909–13) and Elliott W. Major (1913–17), introduced progressive policies to Missouri. However, the ideal of honest government was soon subverted by Kansas City's corrupt political machine, under Thomas J. Pendergast, the most powerful Democrat in the state between the two world wars. Machine politics did not prevent capable politicians from rising to prominence—among them Harry S Truman, Missouri's first and thus far only native son to serve in the nation's highest office.

The state's economy increasingly shifted from agriculture to industry, and Missouri's rural population declined from about three-fourths of the total in 1880 to less than one-third by 1970. Although the overall importance of mining declined, Missouri remained the world's top lead producer, and the state has emerged as 2nd only to Michigan in US automobile manufacturing. Postwar prosperity was threatened beginning in the 1960s by the deterioration of several cities, notably St. Louis, which lost 47% of its population between 1950 and 1980; both St. Louis and Kansas City subsequently undertook urban renewal programs to cope with the serious problems of air pollution, traffic congestion, crime, and substandard housing. During the early 1980s, millions of dollars in federal, state, and private funds were used to rehabilitate abandoned and dilapidated apartment buildings and houses.

Missouri was affected by the farm crisis of the 1980s, and many farms in the state failed. With the weakening of trade restrictions, the state's industries also suffered during this period. However, Missouri's economy improved in the 1990s, initially at a rate that outpaced much of the country. By 1999 the state's jobless rate had fallen below the national average to 3.4%. Due largely to the weak US economy in the early 2000s, Missouri's unemployment rate rose to 5.8% by July 2003, albeit below the national average of 6.2%.

Times Beach and other parts of the state were found to be contaminated by high levels of dioxin in the early 1980s. The federal government purchased the homes and businesses that had to be abandoned by community residents and in 1991 began a several-year clean-up program.

In the spring and summer of 1993, Missouri was hit by devastating floods. The Illinois, Mississippi, and Missouri rivers reached record crests, rising in some areas to twice the height considered to be flood level. Over half the state was declared a disaster area, and 19,000 people were evacuated from their homes. Damage to the state was estimated at $3 billion.

In 2000, the state's popular governor, Mel Carnahan, died in a plane crash while running for the US Senate. He was replaced by Democrat Bob Holden, who became the first governor to appoint a state head of homeland security following the 11 September 2001 terrorist attacks on the US. In 2003, Missouri legislators adopted a measure requiring women seeking abortions to consult a doctor and comply with a 24-hour waiting period. Holden was expected to veto the measure as of May 2003. Twenty states as of that date had enacted 24-hour waiting periods for abortions.

12 STATE GOVERNMENT

Missouri's first constitutional convention met in St. Louis on 12 May 1820, and on 19 July a constitution was adopted. The constitution was rewritten in 1865 and again in 1875, the latter document remaining in effect until 1945, when another new constitution was enacted and the state government reorganized. A subsequent reorganization, effective 1 July 1974, replaced some 90 independent agencies with 13 cabinet departments and the Office of Administration. The 1945 constitution is still in effect today, with a total of 103 amendments through January 2003.

The legislative branch, or general assembly, consists of a 34-member senate and a 163-seat house of representatives. Annual sessions begin in early January and must conclude by May 30. Special sessions may be called by petition of three-quarters of the members of each house; such sessions are limited to 30 calendar days. Senators are elected to staggered four-year terms, representatives for two; the minimum age for a senator is 30, for a representative 24. Legislators must have been residents of their districts for one year prior to election; senators must have been qualified voters for a minimum of three years, representatives a minimum of two years. The legislative salary was $31,561 in 2002.

The state's elected executives are the governor and lieutenant governor (who run separately), secretary of state, auditor, treasurer, and attorney general; all serve four-year terms. The governor is limited to two terms in office, consecutive or not. The governor must be at least 30 years old and must have been a US citizen for 15 years and a Missouri resident for 10 years prior to election. In 2002, the governor's salary was $120,087.

A bill becomes law when signed or not vetoed by the governor within 15 days of legislative passage. A two-thirds vote by the elected members of both houses is required to override a gubernatorial veto. The governor has 45 days to act on a bill if the house adjourns. If he or she fails to do so, the bill becomes law. Except for appropriations or emergency measures, laws may not take effect until 90 days after the end of the legislative session at which they were enacted. Constitutional amendments require a majority vote of both houses or may be proposed by 8% of the legal voters for all candidates at the last election. Ratification by the voters is required.

To vote in Missouri, one must be a US citizen, at least 18 years old, and a state resident. Restrictions apply to convicted felons and those declared mentally incompetent by the court.

13 POLITICAL PARTIES

The major political groups in Missouri are the Democratic Party and the Republican Party, each affiliated with the national party organization. Before 1825, the state had no organized political parties, and candidates ran as independents; however, each of Missouri's first four governors called himself a Jeffersonian Republican, allying himself with the national group from which the modern Democratic Party traces its origins. Except for the Civil War and Reconstruction periods, the Democratic Party held the governorship from the late 1820s to the early 1900s. Ten Democrats and seven Republicans served in the statehouse from 1908 through 1985. The outstanding figures of 20th century Missouri politics were both Democrats: Thomas Pendergast, the Kansas City machine boss whose commitment to construction projects bore no small relation to his involvement with a concrete manufacturing firm, and Harry S. Truman, who began his political career as a Jackson County judge in the Kansas City area and in 1945 became 33rd president of the United States.

After voting consistently for Republican presidential candidates in the 1980s, Missouri was carried by Democrat Bill Clinton in 1996. In the 2000 presidential election, Missourians once again voted Republican, with George W. Bush receiving

51% of the vote to Democrat Al Gore's 47%. Green Party candidate Ralph Nader won 2% of the vote. In 2002 there were 3,681,844 registered voters; there is no party registration in the state. The state had 11 electoral votes in the 2000 presidential election.

Democrat Mel Carnahan was reelected to the governorship in 1996. In October 2000, Carnahan was running for the US Senate against Republican John Ashcroft when he died in a plane crash with his son and a political aide. Carnahan was elected posthumously to the Senate in November, and his wife Jean accepted an appointment to his seat. She served until 2002, when she was defeated by former US Representative and Republican Jim Talent in an extremely close race. As of 2003, Missouri's US senators were both Republicans—Talent, and Christopher Bond, reelected in 1998. In 2000, Democrat Bob Holden was elected governor. Following the 2002 elections, four of the state's US representatives were Democrats; five were Republicans. In the state senate in mid-2003, there were 14 Democrats and 20 Republicans; in the state house, there were 73 Democrats and 90 Republicans.

14LOCAL GOVERNMENT

As of 2002, Missouri had 114 counties, 946 municipalities, 312 townships, 536 public school districts, and 1,514 special districts. Elected county officials generally include commissioners, public administrator, prosecuting attorney, sheriff, collector of revenue, assessor, treasurer, and coroner. The city of St. Louis, which is administratively independent of any county, has an elected mayor, a comptroller, and a board of aldermen; the circuit attorney, city treasurer, sheriff, and collector of revenue, also elected, perform functions analogous to county officers. Most other cities are governed by an elected mayor and council. The state was the first in the union to grant home rule to cities.

15STATE SERVICES

To address the continuing threat of terrorism and to work with the federal Department of Homeland Security (created in 2002 following the terrorist attacks of 11 September 2001), homeland security in Missouri in 2003 operated under executive order; a special advisor was appointed to oversee the state's homeland security activities.

Under the 1974 reorganization plan, educational services are provided through the Department of Elementary and Secondary Education and the Department of Higher Education. Within the former's jurisdiction are the state schools for the deaf, the blind, and the severely handicapped; adult education programs; teacher certification; and the general supervision of instruction in the state. The department is headed by a board of education whose eight members are appointed by the governor to eight-year terms; the board, in turn, appoints the commissioner of education, the department's chief executive officer. The Department of Higher Education—governed by a nine-member appointive board that selects the commissioner of higher education—sets financial guidelines for state colleges and universities, authorizes the establishment of new senior colleges and residency centers, and establishes academic, admissions, residency, and transfer policies. Transportation services are under the direction of the Department of Transportation, which is responsible for aviation, railroads, mass transit, water transport, and the state highway system. The Department of Revenue licenses all road vehicles and motor vehicle operators and is responsible for the administration of all state taxes and local-option sales taxes.

Health and welfare services are provided primarily through the Department of Social Services, which oversees all state programs concerning public health (including operating a chest hospital and a cancer hospital), public assistance, youth corrections, probation and parole, veterans' affairs, and the aging. The Department of Mental Health operates 5 state mental hospitals, 3 community mental health centers, and 19 other facilities throughout the state, providing care for the emotionally disturbed, the mentally retarded, alcoholics, and drug abusers. Among the many responsibilities of the Attorney General within the Department of Consumer Affairs, Regulations, and Licensing were enforcement of antidiscrimination laws, development of low- and moderate-income housing, and provision of financial aid to private nonprofit hospitals and higher-education facilities. In 1984, however, a constitutional amendment created a new Department of Economic Development, which inherited most of the responsibilities of the former department.

Administered within the Department of Public Safety are the Missouri State Highway Patrol, National Guard, and civil defense, veterans' affairs, highway and water safety, and alcoholic

Missouri Presidential Vote by Political Parties, 1948–2000

YEAR	ELECTORAL VOTE	MISSOURI WINNER	DEMOCRAT	REPUBLICAN	PROGRESSIVE	SOCIALIST
1948	15	*Truman (D)	917,315	655,039	3,998	2,222
1952	13	*Eisenhower (R)	929,830	959,429	—	—
1956	13	Stevenson (D)	918,273	914,289	—	—
1960	13	*Kennedy (D)	972,201	962,218	—	—
1964	12	*Johnson (D)	1,164,344	653,535	—	—
					AMERICAN IND.	
1968	12	*Nixon (R)	791,444	811,932	206,126	—
1972	12	*Nixon (R)	698,531	1,154,058	—	—
1976	12	*Carter (D)	998,387	927,443	—	—
					LIBERTARIAN	SOC. WORKERS
1980	12	*Reagan (R)	931,182	1,074,181	14,422	1,515
1984	11	*Reagan (R)	848,583	1,274,188	—	—
						NEW ALLIANCE
1988	11	*Bush (R)	1,001,619	1,084,953	434	6,656
						IND. (Perot)
1992	11	*Clinton (D)	1,053,873	811,159	7,497	518,741
1996	11	*Clinton (D)	1,025,935	890,016	10,522	217,188
						GREEN
2000	11	*Bush, G. W. (R)	1,111,138	1,189,924	7,436	38,515

*Won US presidential election.

beverage control programs. The Department of Labor and Industrial Relations (DOLIR) administers unemployment insurance benefits, workers' compensation, and other programs. The Department of Corrections and Human Resources is responsible for corrections, probation, and parole of adult offenders. The Department of Agriculture enforces state laws regarding agribusiness products, and the Department of Conservation provides environmental aid. The lieutenant governor is designated as state ombudsman and volunteer coordinator.

16JUDICIAL SYSTEM

The supreme court, the state's highest court, consists of seven judges and three commissioners. Judges are selected by the governor from three nominees proposed by a nonpartisan judicial commission; after an interval of at least 12 months, the appointment must be ratified by the voters on a separate nonpartisan ballot. The justices, who serve 12-year terms, select one of their number to act as chief justice. The mandatory retirement age is 70 for all judges in state courts.

The court of appeals, consisting of 32 judges in three districts, assumed its present structure by constitutional amendment in 1970. All appellate judges are selected for 12-year terms in the same manner as the supreme court justices.

The circuit court is the only trial court and has original jurisdiction over all cases and matters, civil and municipal. Circuit court judges, numbering 135 in 1999, serve 6-year terms. Although many circuit court judges are still popularly elected, judges in St. Louis, Kansas City, and some other areas are selected on a nonpartisan basis. Many circuit courts have established municipal divisions, presided over by judges paid locally.

In 2001, Missouri had a total FBI Crime Index rate of 4,776.1 per 100,000 population, including a total of 30,472 violent crimes and 238,411 crimes against property in that year.

As of June 2001, there were 28,167 inmates in state and federal correctional institutions, an increase of 3.2% over the previous year. Two community release centers are located in St. Louis and Kansas City. There are also Missouri inmates housed in Texas jails through a cell leasing program, as well as inmates in an electronic monitoring program. The state's incarceration rate stood at 500 per 100,000 inhabitants in June 2001. Missouri has a death penalty and has executed 60 persons since 1977. In 2003, 70 prisoners were under sentence of death.

17ARMED FORCES

Missouri has played a key role in national defense since World War II, partly because of the influence of Missouri native Stuart Symington, first as secretary of the Air Force (1947–50) and later as an influential member of the Senate Armed Services Committee. In 2002, there were 16,119 active-duty military personnel and 9,330 civilian personnel stationed in the state. Installations include Ft. Leonard Wood, near Rolla, and Whiteman AFB, Knob Noster. The Defense Mapping Agency Aerospace Center is in St. Louis. Defense contract awards for 2001 totaled nearly $5.19 billion.

There were about 592,271 veterans living in the state as of 2000. Of these, 114,795 served in World War II; 77,455 in the Korean conflict; 173,656 during the Vietnam era; and 60,764 during 1990–2000 (including the Persian Gulf War). Veterans' benefits amounted to about $1.4 billion in 2002.

In 2000, the Missouri State Highway Patrol employed 1,080 full-time sworn officers.

18MIGRATION

Missouri's first European immigrants, French fur traders and missionaries, began settling in the state in the early 18th century. Under Spain, Missouri received few Spanish settlers but many immigrants from the eastern US. During the 19th century, newcomers continued to arrive from the South and the East–slave-owning southerners (with their black slaves) as well as New Englanders opposed to slavery. They were joined by a wave of European immigrants, notably Germans and, later, Italians. By 1850, one out of three St. Louis residents was German-born; of all foreign-born Missourians in the late 1800s, more than half came from Germany.

More recently, the state has been losing population through migration—322,000 people were lost to net migration between 1940 and 1970, followed by a net gain of 22,000 during the 1970s and a net loss of nearly 100,000 during the 1980s. Between 1990 and 1998, Missouri had net gains of 94,000 in domestic migration and 34,000 in international migration. In 1998, 3,588 foreign immigrants arrived in the state. The dominant intrastate migration pattern has been the concentration of blacks in the major cities, especially St. Louis and Kansas City, and the exodus of whites from those cities to the suburbs and, more recently, to small towns and rural areas. As of 1996, 82.4% of the population lived in metropolitan areas while 17.6% lived in non-metropolitan areas, up from 17.2% in 1990. Missouri's overall population increased 6.3% between 1990 and 1998. In the period 1995–2000, 473,369 people moved into the state and 427,316 moved out, for a net gain of 46,053.

19INTERGOVERNMENTAL COOPERATION

The Commission on Interstate Cooperation, established by the state legislature in 1941, represents Missouri before the Council of State Governments and its allied organizations. Regional agreements in which the state participates include boundary compacts with Arkansas, Iowa, Nebraska, and Kansas and various accords governing bridges across the Mississippi and Missouri rivers. The state is a signatory to the Bi-State Development Agency Compact with Illinois. Representatives from both Missouri and Kansas take part in the Kansas City Area Transportation Authority, which operates public transportation in the metropolitan region, the Metropolitan Culture District Compact, and the Kansas-Missouri Waterworks Compact. Missouri also belongs to the Southern States Energy Board, Southern Growth Policies Board, Midwest Interstate Low-Level Radioactive Waste Compact Commission, and many other multistate bodies. Federal grants to state and local governments in 2001 amounted to over $6.8 billion.

20ECONOMY

Missouri's central location and access to the Mississippi River contributed to its growth as a commercial center. By the mid–1700s, the state's first permanent settlement at Ste. Genevieve was shipping lead, furs, salt, pork, lard, bacon, bear, grease, feathers, flour and grain, and other products to distant markets. The introduction of steamboat traffic on the Mississippi, western migration along the Santa Fe and Oregon trails, and the rise of the railroads spurred the growth of commerce during the 19th century. Flour and grist mills, breweries and whiskey distilleries, and meat-packing establishments were among the state's early industrial enterprises. Lead mining has been profitable since the early 19th century. Grain growing was well established by the mid-18th century, and tobacco was a leading crop 100 years later.

Missouri's economy remains diversified, with manufacturing, farming, trade, tourism, services, government, and mining as prime sources of income. Today, automobile and aerospace manufacturing are the state's leading industries, while soybeans and meat and dairy products are the most important agricultural commodities. The state's historic past, varied topography, and modern urban attractions—notably the Gateway Arch in St. Louis—have made tourism a growth industry in recent decades. Mining, employing less than 1% of the state's nonagricultural workers, is no longer as important as it once was. Missouri posted moderate growth rates in the late 1990s, averaging 4.36% 1998 to 2000, and falling to 2.5% in the national recession and slowdown of 2001. Manufacturing output fell nearly 6% between 1997 and 2000, while output from financial services, including insurance and real estate, increased 29.2%; output from general services increased 25%; and from government services, 22.6%. Missouri began losing jobs in the first quarter 2001, four months ahead of the US as a whole. More than 12,000 jobs were lost in 2001, 62% in the manufacturing sector. Unemployment peaked at 5.4% in June 2002, but manufacturing unemployment continued above 6%. Office vacancy rates in St. Louis and Kansas City in 2002, at 17.7% and 18.6%, respectively, were above the national average of 16.5%. Missouri's farm sector was also afflicted by drought in 2002, which contributed to 22% decrease in corn production, and a 17% decrease in soybean production, compared to 2001. Cattle production was also disrupted by the drought-induced shortages of hay and pasture. Stress on the farming sector persisted into the winter of 2002–2003 as drought conditions continued.

Missouri's gross state product was $181.5 billion in 2001. General services contributed $38.6 billion, trade, $30.8 billion; manufacturing contributed $30.4 billion; financial services, $30 billion; government, $21.6 billion; transportation and public utilities, $17.8 billion, and construction, $9.6 billion. In 2001, the public sector accounted for 11.9% of gross state product.

21INCOME

According to the Bureau of Economic Analysis, in 2001, Missouri had a per capita personal income (PCPI) of $28,221, which ranked 31st in the United States (including the District of Columbia) and was 93% of the national average, $30,413. The 2001 PCPI reflected an increase of 2.6% from 2000 compared to the national change of 2.2%. In 2001, Missouri had a total personal income (TPI) of $159,093,214,000 which ranked 18th in the United States and accounted for 1.8% of the national total. The 2001 TPI reflected an increase of 3.2% from 2000 compared to the national change of 3.3%.

Earnings of persons employed in Missouri increased from $110,983,573,000 in 2000 to $113,595,014,000 in 2001, an increase of 2.4%. The largest industries in 2001 were services, 27.9% of earnings; state and local government, 11.3%; and retail trade, 9.2%. Of the industries that accounted for at least 5% of earnings in 2001, the slowest growing from 2000 to 2001 was durable goods manufacturing (9.1% of earnings in 2001), which decreased 3.0%; the fastest was state and local government, which increased 6.3%.

According to data released by the US Census Bureau, in 2000, the median household income was $47,462 compared to the national average of $42,148. In 2001, the median income for a family of four was $61,036 compared to the national average of $63,278. For the period 1999 to 2001, the average poverty rate was 10.2%, which placed it 24th among the 50 states and the District of Columbia ranked lowest to highest.

22LABOR

According to Bureau of Labor Statistics (BLS) provisional estimates, in July 2003 the seasonally adjusted civilian labor force in Missouri numbered 2,978,000, with approximately 165,700 workers unemployed, yielding an unemployment rate of 5.6%, compared to the national average of 6.2% for the same period. Since the beginning of the BLS data series in 1978, the highest unemployment rate recorded was 10.6% in April 1983. The historical low was 2.9% in January 2000. In 2001, an estimated 6.9% of the labor force was employed in construction; 13.8% in manufacturing; 6.8% in transportation, communications, and public utilities; 19.5% in trade; 6.1% in finance, insurance, and

real estate; 24.9% in services; 13.2% in government; and 2.6% in agriculture.

As early as the 1830s, journeyman laborers and mechanics in St. Louis, seeking higher wages and shorter hours, banded together to form trade unions and achieved some of their demands. Attempts to establish a workingman's party were unsuccessful, however, and immigration during subsequent decades ensured a plentiful supply of cheap labor. Union activity increased in the 1870s, partly because of the influence of German socialists. The Knights of Labor took a leading role in the labor movement from 1879 to 1887, the year that saw the birth of the St. Louis Trades and Labor Assembly; one year later, the American Federation of Labor came to St. Louis for its 3rd annual convention, with Samuel Gompers presiding. The Missouri State Federation of Labor was formed in 1891, at a convention in Kansas City. By 1916, the state had 915 unions. Union activity in Missouri declined in the 1990s and early 2000s. The US Department of Labor reported that in 2002, 332,000 of Missouri's 2,514,000 employed wage and salary workers were members of unions. This represented 13.2% of those so employed, down from 14.2% in 2001. The national average is 13.2%. In all, 366,000 workers (14.5%) were represented by unions. In addition to union members, this category includes workers who report no union affiliation but whose jobs are covered by a union contract.

23AGRICULTURE

Missouri had 107,000 farms (2nd in the US) covering 29.8 million acres (12.1 million hectares) in 2002. About 12,449,000 acres (5,038,000 hectares) were actually harvested in 1997. Missouri's agricultural income reached $4.8 billion in 2001, 15th among the 50 states.

In 2002, Missouri was 4th among the states in grain sorghum production and 6th in soybean and rice production. Soybean production is concentrated mainly in the northern counties and in the extreme southeast, with Mississippi County a leading producer. Stoddard County is a major source for corn and wheat production, as is New Madrid for grain sorghum.

The cash value of all crops totaled $2.1 billion in 2001, including $918 million from soybeans, $501 million from hay, $695 million from corn, $108 million from wheat, $38 million from grain sorghum, and $118.6 million from cotton. The value of rice production in 2002 was $39 million. Farmers harvested 170 million bushels of soybeans, 284 million bushels of corn, 34.2 million bushels of wheat, 15.7 million bushels of grain sorghum, 610,000 bales of cotton, and 7.8 million tons of hay in 2002. That year, 11.0 million hundredweight (494.9 million kg) of rice was harvested. Tobacco, oats, rye, apples, peaches, grapes, watermelons, and various seed crops are also grown in commercial quantities.

24ANIMAL HUSBANDRY

In Missouri, hog raising is concentrated north of the Missouri River, cattle raising in the western counties, and dairy farming in the southwest.

In 2003, Missouri farms and ranches had an estimated 4.5 million cattle and calves, valued at $3 billion. In 2002, there were around 3.1 million hogs and pigs, valued at $180 million. During 2001, Missouri farmers produced 560 million lb (254 million kg) of turkey (ranked 4th in the nation), valued at around $270 million. Also in 2001, poultry farmers produced 1.8 million eggs, valued at $75.6 million. The state's 145,000 milk cows yielded nearly 1.9 million lb (0.86 million kg) of milk in 2001.

25FISHING

Commercial fishing takes place mainly on the Mississippi, Missouri, and St. Francis rivers. Sport fishing is enjoyed throughout the state, but especially in the Ozarks, whose waters harbor walleye, rainbow trout, bluegill, and largemouth bass. In 1998, Missouri issued 926,357 sport fishing licenses. Fish farms distributed 2.4 million trout, 364,000 catfish, and 484,000 bass within Missouri in 1998 for restoration or conservation purposes.

26 FORESTRY

At one time, Missouri's forests covered 30 million acres (12 million hectares), more than two-thirds of the state. As of 2002, Missouri had 13,992,000 acres (5,663,000 hectares) of forestland (about 30% of the land area in the state), of which more than 95% was commercial forest, 85% of it privately owned. Most of Missouri's forestland is in the southeastern third of the state. Of the commercial forests, approximately three-fourths are of the oak/hickory type; shortleaf pine and oak/pine forests comprise about 5%, while the remainder consists of cedar and bottomland hardwoods.

According to the Forestry Division of the Department of Conservation, Missouri leads the US in the production of charcoal, red cedar novelties, gunstocks, and walnut bowls and nutmeats; railroad ties, hardwood veneer and lumber, wine and bourbon casks, and other forest-related items are also produced. Lumber production in 2002 totaled 616 million board feet, most of it hardwoods.

Conservation areas managed by the Forestry Division are used for timber production, wildlife and watershed protection, hunting, fishing, and other recreational purposes. A state-run nursery sells seedling trees and shrubs to Missouri landowners. Missouri's one national forest, Mark Twain in the southeast, encompassed 1,494,000 acres (604,621 hectares) of National Forest System lands as of 2001.

27 MINING

Nonfuel mineral production in Missouri was estimated at $1.34 billion in 2001, essentially unchanged from 2000. In the same year, crushed stone, portland cement, lead, and lime accounted for 88% of the total value. Crushed stone, by value, has been Missouri's leading nonfuel mineral commodity since 1997, when it surpassed portland cement and lead, the state's 2nd and 3rd top minerals in 2001. Except for several years in the mid-1980s and during 1993–95, lead had been the leading nonfuel mineral since 1969. Restrictions on the use of lead in paint and gasoline, along with prolonged labor strikes, caused lead production in Missouri to decline in the 1980s. Nevertheless in 2001 Missouri was still the nation's top lead producer, contributing well over half the lead produced in the US. The state also ranked 1st in lime and fire clay production, 2nd in iron oxide pigments, 3rd in zinc, and 5th in portland cement. Items of high value in 2001, according to preliminary figures, included crushed stone ($410 million, 75.3 million metric tons); portland cement ($381 million, 5 million metric tons); and construction sand and gravel ($45.4 million, 11.5 million metric tons). Missouri ranked 10th nationally in nonfuel mineral value.

28 ENERGY AND POWER

Missouri's electric power plants had an installed generating capacity (utility and nonutility) of 16.9 million kW in 1999. Electrical output totaled 73.8 billion kWh in the same year, and retail sales of electric power totaled 69 billion kWh. Coal-fired plants accounted for 83% of all power production, and nuclear plants for 12%.

Fossil fuel resources are limited. Reserves of bituminous coal totaled 6 billion tons in 1998, but only a small portion (3 million tons) was considered recoverable; 436,000 tons were mined in 2000, all from four surface mines. Small quantities of crude petroleum are also produced commercially; in 2002, production

was 260 barrels per day. In 2000 Missouri's total per capita energy consumption was 296 million Btu (74.6 million kcal), ranking it 38th among the 50 states.

29 INDUSTRY

In 1997, the value of shipments for manufactured goods in Missouri was $96 billion. St. Louis County, the city of St. Louis, and Jackson County (Kansas City) led the state in manufacturing employment. McDonnell Douglas has its headquarters in St. Louis; its aerospace products have included all the Mercury capsules and Gemini space capsules, the DC-9 and DC-10 commercial jet aircraft, and the Tomahawk cruise missile. As of 1997, the state was the headquarters for 14 Fortune 500 companies.

Earnings of persons employed in Missouri increased from $94.9 billion in 1997 to $99.2 billion in 1998, an increase of 4.6%. The largest industries in 1998 were services, 26.5% of earnings; durable goods manufacturing, 11.0%; and state and local government, 10.0%. Of the industries that accounted for at least 5% of earnings in 1998, the slowest growing from 1997 to 1998 was retail trade (9.3% of earnings in 1998), which increased 4.3%; the fastest was finance, insurance, and real estate (7.3% of earnings in 1998), which increased 7.7%.

30 COMMERCE

Missouri has been one of the nation's leading trade centers ever since merchants in Independence (now part of the Kansas City metropolitan area) began provisioning wagon trains for the Santa Fe Trail. In 1997, Missouri had 11,260 wholesale establishments, with sales of $96 billion. Retail sales totaled $52 billion in 1997 from 32,757 establishments. Automotive dealers accounted for 16% of establishments; food stores, 10%; and eating and drinking places, 29%. Food sales accounted for $8.8 billion in revenues, while general merchandise took in $8 billion. Foreign exports of Missouri products exceeded $5.7 billion in 1998.

31 CONSUMER PROTECTION

The Missouri Department of Insurance handles consumer complaints related to insurance matters. The office has a consumer services division that accepts complaints regarding violations of state insurance laws and regulations, unfair claim practices, advertising, and mandated benefits, policy language, and offers. The Attorney General's office has a Consumer Protection Division which investigates and prosecutes allegations of fraud in connection with the sale or offer for sale (advertising) of goods and services. The Office of the Public Counsel represents utility consumers in proceedings before and appeals from the Missouri Public Service Commission (PSC), which regulates the rates and services of utilities.

32 BANKING

The first banks in Missouri, the Bank of St. Louis (established in 1816) and the Bank of Missouri (1817), had both failed by the time Missouri became a state, and the paper notes they had distributed proved worthless. Not until 1837 did the Missouri state government again permit a bank within its borders, and then only after filling its charter with elaborate restrictions. The Bank of Missouri, chartered for 20 years, kept its reputation for sound banking by issuing notes bearing the portrait of US Senator Thomas Hart Benton, nicknamed "Old Bullion" because of his extreme fiscal conservatism. In 2002, 385 insured banks were operating in Missouri, 303 of which were state-chartered. The state's insured banks had assets totaling $77.5 billion.

As of 2002, commercial lenders in metropolitan areas of Missouri were negatively affected by softened commercial real estate markets. Past-due loan levels remained moderate among most community banks (those with assets of less than $1 billion).

Net interest margins (NIMs) (the difference between the lower rates offered to savers and the higher rates charged on loans) declined in the 1990s, due to strong loan and funding competition, in addition to depopulation trends in rural areas. The lowering of interest rates in 2001/02 by the Federal Reserve led to NIM fluctuations, but did not signal an end to overall NIM decline.

33INSURANCE

In 2001 there were 3.5 million ordinary life insurance policies in force with a total value of $198.7 billion; total value for all categories of life insurance (ordinary, group, industrial, and credit) was $364.9 billion. Death benefits paid that year totaled $1.0 billion. In 2000, 42 life and insurance companies were domiciled in Missouri, and 62 property and casualty insurance companies.

Direct premiums written by all property and casualty companies in Missouri totaled $6.58 billion in 2001. That year, there were 22,032 flood insurance policies in force in the state, with a total value of $2.3 million, $1.6 of which were written through the National Flood Insurance Program (NFIP).

34SECURITIES

The Missouri Uniform Securities Act, also known as the "Blue Sky Law" and administered by the Securities Division of the Office of Secretary of State, requires the registration of stocks, bonds, debentures, notes, investment contracts, and oil, gas, and mining interests intended for sale in the state. In cases of fraud, misrepresentation, or other failure to comply with the act, the Missouri investor has the right to sue to recover the investment, plus interest, costs, and attorney fees. Government securities, mutual funds, stocks listed on the principal national exchanges, and securities sold under specific transactional agreements are exempt from registration.

Missouri has 1,042 broker-dealers with 17,669 employees, and 185 investment advisory organizations. The state is the headquarters for 71 NASDAQ-listed companies, 12 NASDAQ market makers, and is the incorporator of 44 NYSE-listed companies. The top five in order of revenues are: Sprint, Utilicorp United Inc., Emerson Electric Co., May Dept. Stores, and Pharmacia Corp. Kansas City has a commodity exchange, the Board of Trade, which deals in grains, including futures and storage. The world's largest winter-wheat market is in Kansas City.

35PUBLIC FINANCE

The Missouri state budget is prepared by the Office of Administration's Division of Budget and Planning and submitted annually by the governor to the general assembly for amendment and approval. The fiscal year runs from 1 July to 30 June. Missouri's constitutional revenue and spending limit provides that over time, the growth in state revenues and spending cannot exceed the growth in Missouri personal income.

The fiscal year 2001 budget included total funds of $17 billion. The 1998 tobacco settlement was expected to bring in over $4 billion during the following 25 years, to be spent on health-related issues. General fund revenues were projected at $7.6 billion. Actual receipts in general fund revenue were $7.669 billion in 2000/01, sufficient to comfortably cover general fund expenditures of $7.643. In 2001/02, general fund revenues only increased marginally, to $7.699 billion and in 2002/03, they declined to $7.646 billion, creating widening gaps with expenditures. In 2002/03, Missouri's budget deficit was estimated at 10.7% of the state budget, and for 2003/04, was projected to increase to 13.1% of the state budget.

The following table from the US Census Bureau contains information on revenues, expenditures, indebtedness, and cash/securities for 2001.

	($000)	PERCENT	PER CAPITA
Population (thousands, 2001)	5,637	(X)	(X)
Total Revenue	20,133,937	100.00	3,571.75
General revenue	17,527,810	87.06	3,109.42
Utility revenue	–	–	–
Liquor store revenue	–	–	–
Insurance trust revenue	2,606,127	12.94	462.33
Exhibit: Salaries and wages	3,166,495	16.76	561.73
Total expenditure	18,888,113	100.00	3,350.74
General expenditure	17,123,078	90.66	3,037.62
Education	6,432,878	34.06	1,141.19
Public welfare	4,678,233	24.77	829.92
Hospitals	711,157	3.77	126.16
Health	612,744	3.24	108.70
Highways	1,545,353	8.18	274.14
Police protection	177,903	0.94	31.56
Correction	604,714	3.20	107.28
Natural resources	312,028	1.65	55.35
Parks and recreation	41,493	0.22	7.36
Government administration	520,170	2.75	92.28
Interest on general debt	583,219	3.09	103.46
Other and unallocable	903,186	4.78	160.22
Utility expenditure	–	–	–
Liquor store expenditure	–	–	–
Insurance trust expenditure	1,765,035	9.34	313.12
Debt at end of fiscal year	11,373,216	100.00	2,017.60
Cash and security holdings	44,991,145	100.00	7,981.40

36TAXATION

The Missouri's 10-bracket personal income tax schedule ranges from 1.5% on taxable income up to $1,000 to 6% on taxable income over $9,000. Individuals may deduct up to $5,000 of federal taxes paid from their state liability. The corporate tax rate is 6.25% of net income, with 50% of federal corporate taxes paid deductible. The rate for financial institutions is 7%. The basic state sales tax is 4.225%, but is lowered to 1.225% for food and beverages. Prescription drugs are exempt. Local-option sales taxes range from 0.5% to 4.125%. The state also imposes a full array of excise taxes covering motor fuels, tobacco products, insurance premiums, public utilities, alcoholic beverage, amusements, and other selected items. Missouri's estate tax is tied to the federal exemption for state death taxes, and is therefore set to expire in tandem with the phasing out of the federal estate tax credit absent positive action by the state to establish an independent estate tax. Missouri's' revenue losses from the phasing out of its estate tax are estimated at -$30 million for 2002/03, -$72 million for 2003/04, and -$187 million for 2006/07. Death and gift taxes accounted for 1.5% of state collections in 2002. Other state taxes include an assessment on surface mining, various license fees and franchise taxes, and state property taxes, although most property taxes are collected locally. Property and sales taxes are the leading sources of local revenue. In 2002, 44.6% of all state and local taxes were collected locally.

The state collected $8.677 billion in taxes in 2002, of which 41.6% came from individual income taxes, 32.9% came from the general sales tax, 14.8% from selective sales taxes, 5.36% from license fees, and 3.5% from corporate income taxes. In 2003, Missouri ranked 34th among the states in terms of combined state and local tax burden, which amounted to about 9.2% of income.

The following table from the US Census Bureau provides a summary of taxes collected by the state in 2002.

	($000)	PER CAPITA
Total Taxes	8,678,611	1,529.92
Property taxes	20,459	3.61
Sales and gross receipts	4,140,210	729.86
General sales and gross receipts	2,854,718	503.25
Selective sales taxes	1,285,492	226.62
Alcoholic beverage	25,907	4.57
Amusements	220,474	38.87
Insurance Premiums	217,173	38.28
Motor fuels	692,448	122.07
Pari-mutuels	(X)	(X)
Public utilities	304	0.05
Tobacco products	106,817	18.83
Other selective sales	22,369	3.94
Licenses	465,484	82.06
Alcoholic beverages	4,396	0.77
Amusements	877	0.15
Corporation	18,343	3.23
Hunting and fishing	28,716	5.06
Motor vehicle	237,166	41.81
Motor vehicle operators	21,060	3.71
Public utility	19,199	3.38
Occupation and business, NEC	125,910	22.2
Other	9,817	1.73
Other taxes	4,052,458	714.39
Individual income	3,615,417	637.35
Corporation net income	302,301	53.29
Death and gift	134,256	23.67
Documentary and stock transfer	(X)	(X)
Severance	33	0.01
Other	451	0.08

37 ECONOMIC POLICY

Primary responsibility for economic development is vested in the Department of Economic Development, and especially in its Office of International Marketing, which seeks outside investment in the state, promotes the national and international marketing of Missouri products, provides technical assistance to existing businesses, and maintained offices in Germany, Japan, Brazil, Chile, Korea, Mexico, Ghana, Taiwan, Thailand, and the UK as of 2000. Its Enterprise Zone Program provides a variety of tax credits, exemptions, and other incentives to businesses that locate in designated areas. The division also offers grants, information, technical aid, and other public resources to foster local and regional development. Special programs are provided for the Ozarks region and to rehabilitate urban neighborhoods. Loan and bond guarantees are provided to selected businesses by the Missouri Economic Development Commission and direct loans by the Missouri Industrial Development Authority. A nonprofit Missouri Business Modernization and Technology Corporation, provides support for research and development and for the development of new technologies.

38 HEALTH

The infant mortality rate in Missouri for the 12 months ending with December 2000 was 7.2 per 1,000 live births, above the national rate of 6.9. There were 8,113 legal abortions performed in 1999, a rate of 7 abortions per 1,000 women.

The overall death rate of 997.1 per 100,000 population in 2000 was one of the highest in the US—a phenomenon attributable in part to the relatively high proportion of elderly Missourians in the population as a whole. Deaths from heart disease, cerebrovascular disease, accidents and adverse effects, and motor vehicle accidents were all above the national rate. The suicide rate of 12.6 per 100,000 population was also higher than the national average.

In 2000, the rate of death from HIV-related infection stood at 3.0 per 100,000 population, below the US rate of 5.3; a total of 9,654 AIDS cases had been reported in Missouri through 2001.

In 2000, 27.2% of Missouri residents were smokers. The rate of death from lung disease stood at 81.9 per 100,000 inhabitants.

Missouri's 117 community hospitals had 800,648 admissions and 19,257 beds in 2001. There were 24,587 full-time registered nurses and 3,469 full-time licensed practical nurses in 2001 and 246 physicians per 100,000 population in 2000. The average expense of a community hospital for care was $1,619.80 per inpatient day in 2001.

Federal government grants to cover the Medicare and Medicaid services in 2001 totaled $3.1 billion; 866,815 enrollees received Medicare benefits that year. At least 10.2% of Missouri's adult population was uninsured in 2002.

39 SOCIAL WELFARE

In 2001, the average weekly unemployment benefit was $199.58. Average monthly participation in the food stamp program in FY2002 comprised 515,006 persons (220,639 households). The average monthly benefit was $77.17, and the sum total of benefits paid in FY2002 was $476,894,198.

With the enactment of the Personal Responsibility and Work Opportunity Reconciliation Act of 1996, the US government has changed the form and regulations for many of its social welfare programs. Most significantly, it replaces Aid to Families with Dependent Children (AFDC), an open-ended entitlement program, with Temporary Assistance for Needy Families (TANF), a limited system of assistance funded largely through federal block grants. The reform act also impacts the food stamp program, the Supplemental Security Income program, and the child nutrition program. The law took effect on 1 July 1997 and provided $16.38 billion in block grants for fiscal years 1997–2002. The grants are to be divided among the states based on an equation involving the numbers of former AFDC recipients in each state.

Reauthorization of the 1996 social welfare legislation, scheduled for 2002, was delayed, and the original law had been extended three times as of July 2003, with the most recent extension running through September 2003. Missouri's TANF program is called Beyond Welfare. In June 2000 the state had 122,930 welfare recipients. State expenditures on the TANF program in FY2002 totaled $123,426,440.

In December 2001, Social Security benefits were paid to 1,012,790 Missouri residents. This number included 624,910 retired workers, 109,710 widows and widowers, 130,3000 disabled workers, 59,340 spouses, and 88,530 children. Social Security beneficiaries represented 18% of the total state population and 94.4% of the state's population age 65 and older. Retired workers (excluding persons with special benefits) received an average monthly payment of $863; widows and widowers, $816; disabled workers, $797; and spouses, $429. Payments for children of retired workers averaged $435 per month; children of deceased workers, $568; and children of disabled workers, $227.

Federal Supplemental Security Income payments in December 2001 went to 113,258 Missouri residents, averaging $326 a month.

40 HOUSING

In 2002, Missouri had an estimated 2,503,187 housing units, of which 2,252,604 were occupied; 70% were owner-occupied. About 69.6% of all units were single-family, detached homes. Utility gas and electricity were the most common energy sources for heating. It was estimated that 74,604 units lacked telephone services, 8,942 lacked complete plumbing facilities, and 10,470 lacked complete kitchen facilities. The average household size was 2.44 people.

In 2002, 28,355 new privately owned units were authorized for construction. The median home value was $102,252. The median monthly cost for mortgage owners was $946. Renters paid a median of $538 per month. During 2002, Missouri received over $73 million in community planning and developments aid from the US Department of Housing and Urban Development.

The Missouri Housing Development Commission of the Department of Economic Development is empowered to make and insure loans to encourage the construction of residential housing for persons of low or moderate income; funds for mortgage financing are provided through the sale of tax-exempt notes and bonds issued by the commission. Construction of multi-unit public housing stagnated during the 1970s. In 1972, municipal authorities ordered the demolition of two apartment buildings in St. Louis's Pruitt-Igoe public housing complex, built 18 years earlier and regarded by many commentators as a classic case of the failure of such high-rise projects to offer a livable environment; the site remained vacant in the early 1980s. Only 5.5% of St. Louis's housing units in 1990 had been built during the 1980s; during the 1970s, many units were abandoned.

41EDUCATION

Although the constitution of 1820 provided for the establishment of public schools, it was not until 1839 that the state's public school system became a reality through legislation creating the office of state superintendent of common schools and establishing a permanent school fund. Missouri schools were officially segregated from 1875 to 1954, when the US Supreme Court issued its landmark ruling in Brown v. Board of Education; the state's school segregation law was not taken off the books until 1976. In that year, nearly 37% of all black students were in schools that were 99–100% black, a condition fostered by the high concentration of black Missourians in the state's two largest cities. In 1983, a desegregation plan was adopted for St. Louis-area public schools that called for 3,000 black students to be transferred from city to county schools.

In 2000, 81.3% of all Missourians 25 years of age or older were high school graduates, and 21.6% had obtained bachelor's degrees or higher. The total enrollment for fall 1999 in Missouri's public schools stood at 914,110. Of these, 648,758 attended schools from kindergarten through grade eight, and 265,352 attended high school. Minority students made up approximately 21% of the total enrollment in public elementary and secondary schools in 2001. Total enrollment was estimated at 897,081 in fall 2000 but expected to drop to 914,000 by fall 2005. Enrollment in nonpublic schools in fall 2001 was 122,387. Expenditures for public education in 2000/01 were estimated at $5,385,046.

As of fall 2000, there were 319,515 students enrolled in college or graduate school. In 1997, minority students comprised 14.1% of total postsecondary enrollment. Missouri has 30 public and 26 private institutions of higher education. The University of Missouri, established in 1839, was the first state-supported university west of the Mississippi River. It has four campuses: Columbia (site of the world's oldest and one of the best-known journalism schools), Kansas City, Rolla, and St. Louis. The Rolla campus, originally founded in 1870 as a mining and engineering school, is still one of the nation's leading universities specializing in technology. The majority of students attend the Columbia facility.

Lincoln University, a public university for blacks until segregation ended in 1954, is located in Jefferson City. There are five regional state universities, at Warrensburg, Maryville, Cape Girardeau, Springfield, and Kirksville, and three state colleges, at St. Louis, St. Joseph, and Joplin. Two leading independent universities, Washington and St. Louis, are located in St. Louis, as is the Concordia Seminary, an affiliate of the Lutheran Church-Missouri Synod and the center of much theological and political controversy during the 1970s. The Department of Higher Education offers grants and guaranteed loans to Missouri students.

42ARTS

Theatrical performances are offered throughout the state, mostly during the summer. In Kansas City, productions of Broadway musicals and light opera are staged at the Starlight Theater, which seats 7,860 in an open-air setting. The Missouri Repertory Theater, on the University of Missouri campus in Kansas City, also has a summer season. In St. Louis, the 12,000-seat Municipal Opera puts on outdoor musicals, while the Goldenrod, built in 1909 and said to be the largest showboat ever constructed (seating capacity 289), is used today for vaudeville, melodrama, and ragtime shows. Other notable playhouses are the 8,000-seat Riverfront Amphitheater in Hannibal, and the 344-seat Lyceum Theater in Arrow Rock (population 89).

Leading orchestras are the St. Louis Symphony and Kansas City Symphony; Independence, Liberty, Columbia, Kirksville, St. Joseph, and Springfield also have orchestras. The Opera Theatre of St. Louis and the Lyric Opera of Kansas City are distinguished musical organizations. Springfield has a regional opera company.

Between World Wars I and II, Kansas City was the home of a thriving jazz community that included Charlie Parker and Lester Young; leading bandleaders of that time were Benny Moten, Walter Page, and, later, Count Basie. Country music predominates in rural Missouri in places like the Ozark Opry at Osage Beach. There are over 40 performing venues in Branson, where over 5.8 million visitors take in performances annually.

In 2003, Missouri arts organizations received grants totaling $2,303,700 from the National Endowment for the Arts. There are about 350 arts associations and over 50 local associations in Missouri. The state provides arts education in all of the approximately 550 public school districts. In 1994, the Missouri General Assembly established the Missouri Cultural Trust, a state endowment for the arts, with the goal of building it into a $200 million operational endowment in 10 years. The Trust is one of only a few such trusts in the nation, and the only one that receives dedicated annual tax revenues.

The Missouri Humanities Council sponsors an annual weeklong summer history festival on various themes. The festival is generally in a different community each year. In 2000, the National Endowment for the Humanities contributed $1,020,678 for 24 state programs.

43LIBRARIES AND MUSEUMS

Missouri had 48 county and 14 regional library systems in 2000, when the combined book stock of all public libraries in the state was 22,697,000, and their combined circulation 38,458,000. The Missouri State Library, in Jefferson City, is the center of the state's interlibrary loan network. It also serves as the only public library for the population who live in areas without public libraries; it has 79,761 books. The largest public library systems, those of Kansas City and St. Louis County, had 1,204,992 and 2,777,056 volumes, respectively; the public library system of the city of St. Louis had 2,505,182 in 15 branches. The University of Missouri-Columbia has the leading academic library, with 2,850,747 volumes in 1998. The State Historical Society of Missouri Library in Columbia contains 453,000 volumes. The federally-administered Harry S. Truman Library and Museum is at Independence. The total income of public libraries in Missouri came to $146,528,000 in 2000; including $2,344,448 in federal grants and $3,223,616 in state grants.

Missouri has well over 162 museums and historic sites. The William Rockhill Nelson Gallery/Atkins Museum of Fine Arts in Kansas City and the St. Louis Art Museum each house distinguished general collections, while the Springfield Art Museum specializes in American sculpture, paintings, and relics of the westward movement. The Mark Twain Home and Museum in Hannibal has a collection of manuscripts and other memorabilia. Also notable are the Museum of Art and Archaeology, Columbia; the Kansas City Museum of History and Science; the Pony Express Stables Museum, St. Joseph; and the Jefferson National Expansion Memorial, Missouri Botanical Garden, St. Louis Center Museum of Science and Natural History and McDonnell Planetarium, National Museum of Transport, and a zoo, all in St. Louis. Kansas City, Springfield, and Eldon also have zoos.

44COMMUNICATIONS

In 1858, John Hockaday began weekly mail service by stagecoach between Independence and Salt Lake City, and John Butterfield, with a $600,000 annual appropriation from Congress, established semi-monthly mail transportation by coach and rail from St. Louis to San Francisco. On 3 April 1860, the Pony Express was launched, picking up mail arriving by train at St. Joseph and racing it westward on horseback; the system ceased in October 1861, when the Pacific Telegraph Co. began operations. The first experiment in airmail service took place at St. Louis in 1911; Charles Lindbergh was an airmail pilot on the St. Louis-Chicago route in 1926.

As of 2001, Missouri had approximately 96.6% of all state residences had telephone service.

Radio broadcasting in Missouri dates from 1921, when a station at St. Louis University began experimental programming. On Christmas Eve 1922, the first midnight Mass ever to be put on the air was broadcast from the Old Cathedral in St. Louis. The voice of a US president was heard over the air for the first time on 21 June 1923, when Warren G. Harding gave a speech in St. Louis. FM broadcasting began in Missouri during 1948. As of 2003 there were 36 major commercial AM stations and 96 major FM stations in service. Missouri's first television station, KSD-TV in St. Louis, began in 1947, with WDAF-TV in Kansas City following in 1949. As of 2003, Missouri had 25 major television stations. The St. Louis area had 1,114,370 television households, and only 56% of those received cable (one of the lowest penetration rates of all cities). Kansas City had a 65% penetration rate in 802,580 television households.

A total of 84,512 Internet domain names had been registered in Missouri by the year 2000.

45PRESS

The *Missouri Gazette*, published in St. Louis in 1808 by the politically independent and controversial Joseph Charless, was the state's first newspaper; issued to 174 subscribers, the paper was partly in French. In 1815, a group of Charless's enemies raised funds to establish a rival paper, the *Western Journal*, and brought in Joshua Norvell from Nashville to edit it. By 1820 there were five newspapers in Missouri.

Since that time, many Missouri newspapermen have achieved national recognition. The best known is Sam Clemens (later Mark Twain), who started out as a "printer's devil" in Hannibal at the age of 13. Hungarian-born Joseph Pulitzer began his journalistic career in 1868 as a reporter for a German-language daily in St. Louis. Pulitzer created the *St. Louis Post–Dispatch* from the merger of two defunct newspapers in 1878, endowed the Columbia University School of Journalism in New York City, and established by bequest the Pulitzer Prizes, which annually honor journalistic and artistic achievement.

As of 2002 there were 13 morning newspapers, 30 evening dailies, and 23 Sunday papers. The following table shows Missouri's leading dailies with their approximate 2002 circulations:

AREA	NAME	DAILY	SUNDAY
Kansas City	*Star* (e,S)	259,612	377,765
St. Louis	*Post–Dispatch* (m,S)	290,615	485,984

Periodicals include the St. Louis-based *Sporting News*, the bimonthly "bible" of baseball fans; *VFW Magazine*, put out monthly in Kansas City by the Veterans of Foreign Wars; and the *Missouri Historical View*, a quarterly with offices in Columbia.

46ORGANIZATIONS

In 2003, there were about 2,861 regional, national, and international organizations within the state. Among the national and international organizations with headquarters in Kansas City are the Veterans of Foreign Wars of the USA, the American Gulf War Veterans Association, Camp Fire Inc., People-to-People International, the American Academy of Family Physicians, the American Business Women's Association, the American Nurses Association, the Fellowship of Christian Athletes, the National Association of Intercollegiate Athletics, the American Humor Studies Association, and Professional Secretaries International.

Headquartered in St. Louis are the American Association of Orthodontists, the American Optometric Association, the Catholic Health Association of the US, the Danforth Foundation, the International Consumer Credit Association, National Garden Clubs, and the National Hairdressers and Cosmetologists Association. Children International and DeMolay International are based in Kansas City. Two major religious organizations based in the state are the Baptist Bible Fellowship International and the Gospel Missionary Union. The General Society, Sons of the Revolution is based in Independence. State culture is represented in part by the Kansas City Barbeque Society and the Scott Joplin International Ragtime Foundation, both of which have national memberships. The Negro Leagues Baseball Museum is located in Kansas City.

Other organizations include the Accrediting Council on Education in Journalism and Mass Communications (Columbia), the National Christmas Tree Association (St. Louis), and the American Cat Fanciers Association (Branson).

47TOURISM, TRAVEL, AND RECREATION

In 2002, the state hosted about 35.6 million domestic travelers, with 69% of all visitors coming from out-of-state. About 42% of all visitors came to visit family or friends. Of those traveling strictly for leisure activities, shopping was the major attraction. Total travel revenues were at about $5.5 billion dollars and the industry supported over 192,159 jobs. The most popular vacation areas are the St. Louis region (40% of all visits) and the Kansas City area (23%).

The principal attraction in St. Louis is the Gateway Arch, at 630 feet (192 meters) the tallest man-made national monument in the US. Designed by Eero Saarinen in 1948 but not constructed until 1964, three years after his death, the arch and the Museum of Westward Expansion form part of the Jefferson National Expansion Memorial on the western shore of the Mississippi River.

In the Kansas City area are the modern Crown Center hotels and shopping plaza, Country Club Plaza, the Truman Sports Complex, Ft. Osage near Sibley, Jesse James's birthplace near Excelsior Springs, and Harry Truman's hometown of Independence. Memorabilia of Mark Twain are housed in and around Hannibal, in the northeast, and the birthplace and childhood home of George Washington Carver, a national monument, is in Diamond.

The Lake of the Ozarks, with 1,375 mi (2,213 km) of shoreline, is one of the most popular vacation spots in mid-America. Other attractions are the Silver Dollar City handicrafts center near Branson; the Pony Express Stables and Museum at St. Joseph; Wilson's Creek National Battlefield at Republic, site of a

Confederate victory in the Civil War; and the "Big Springs Country" of the Ozarks, in the southeast. The state fair is held in Sedalia each August.

Missouri has 27 state parks. Operated by the Department of Natural Resources, they offer camping, picnicking, swimming, boating, fishing, and hiking facilities. Lake of the Ozarks State Park is the largest, covering 16,872 acres (6,828 hectares). There are also 27 historic sites; state parks and historic sites cover 105,000 acres (43,050 hectares). Hunting and fishing are popular recreational activities in state parks.

48 SPORTS

There are six major league professional sports teams in Missouri: the Kansas City Royals and St. Louis Cardinals of Major League Baseball; the Kansas City Chiefs and St. Louis Rams of the National Football League; the St. Louis Blues of the National Hockey League; and the Kansas City Wizards of Major League Soccer.

The Cardinals won the World Series in 1931, 1934, 1942, 1944, 1946, 1964, 1967, and 1982. The Royals have won the World Series once, in 1985, against their cross-state rivals, the St. Louis Cardinals. The Chiefs appeared in Super Bowl I in 1967, losing to the Green Bay Packers. They won the Super Bowl in their next appearance, in 1970. The Rams moved to St. Louis from Los Angeles after the 1994 season and now play in the 66,000-seat Trans World Dome, which opened in 1995. They won the Super Bowl in 2000 with a dramatic 23–16 victory over the Tennessee Titans.

Horse racing has a long history in Missouri. In 1812, St. Charles County sportsmen held two-day horse races; by the 1820s, racetracks were laid out in nearly every city and in crossroads villages.

In collegiate sports, the University of Missouri competes in the Big Twelve Conference.

49 FAMOUS MISSOURIANS

Harry S Truman (1884–1972) has been the only native-born Missourian to serve as US president or vice president. Elected US senator in 1932, Truman became Franklin D. Roosevelt's vice-presidential running mate in 1944 and succeeded to the presidency upon Roosevelt's death on 12 April 1945. The "man from Independence"—whose tenure in office spanned the end of World War II, the inauguration of the Marshall Plan to aid European economic recovery, and the beginning of the Korean conflict—was elected to the presidency in his own right in 1948, defeating Republican Thomas E. Dewey in one of the most surprising upsets in US political history. Charles Evans Whittaker (b.Kansas, 1901–73) was a federal district and appeals court judge in Missouri before his appointment as Supreme Court associate justice in 1957. Among the state's outstanding US military leaders are Generals John J. Pershing (1860–1948) and Omar Bradley (1893–1981).

Other notable federal officeholders from Missouri include Edward Bates (b.Virginia, 1793–1869), Abraham Lincoln's attorney general and the first cabinet official to be chosen from a state west of the Mississippi River; Montgomery Blair (b.Kentucky, 1813–83), postmaster general in Lincoln's cabinet; and Norman Jay Colman (b.New York, 1827–1911), the first secretary of agriculture. Missouri's best-known senator was Thomas Hart Benton (b.North Carolina, 1782–1858), who championed the interests of Missouri and the West for 30 years. Other well-known federal legislators include Francis P. Blair, Jr. (b.Kentucky, 1821–75), antislavery congressman, pro-Union leader during the Civil War, and Democratic vice-presidential nominee in 1868; Benjamin Gratz Brown (b.Kentucky, 1826–85), senator from 1863 to 1867 and later governor of the state and Republican vice-presidential nominee (1872); Carl Schurz

(b.Germany, 1829–1906), senator from 1869 to 1875 and subsequently US secretary of the interior, as well as a journalist and Union military leader; William H. Hatch (b.Kentucky, 1833–96), sponsor of much agricultural legislation as a US representative from 1879 to 1895; Richard P. Bland (b.Kentucky, 1835–99), leader of the free-silver bloc in the US House of Representatives; James Beauchamp "Champ" Clark (b.Kentucky, 1850–1921), speaker of the House from 1911 to 1919; W. Stuart Symington (b.Massachusetts, 1901–88), senator from 1953 to 1977 and earlier the nation's first secretary of the Air Force; and Thomas F. Eagleton (b.1929), senator since 1969 and, briefly, the Democratic vice-presidential nominee in 1972, until publicity about his having received electroshock treatment for depression forced him off the ticket. (Eagleton announced in 1984 that he would not seek reelection to the Senate in 1986.)

Outstanding figures in Missouri history include two pioneering fur traders: William Henry Ashley (b.Virginia, 1778–1838), who later became a US representative, and Manuel Lisa (b.Louisiana, 1772–1820), who helped establish trade relations with the Indians. Meriwether Lewis (b.Virginia, 1774–1809) and William Clark (b.Virginia, 1770–1838) explored Missouri and the West during 1804–6; Lewis later served as governor of Louisiana Territory, with headquarters at St. Louis, and Clark was governor of Missouri Territory from 1813 to 1821. Dred Scott (b.Virginia, 1795–1858), a slave owned by a Missourian, figured in a Supreme Court decision that set the stage for the Civil War. Missourians with unsavory reputations include such desperadoes as Jesse James (1847–82), his brother Frank (1843–1915), and Cole Younger (1844–1916), also a member of the James gang. Another well-known native was Kansas City's political boss, Thomas Joseph Pendergast (1872–1945), a power among Missouri Democrats until convicted of income tax evasion in 1939 and sent to Leavenworth prison.

Among notable Missouri educators were William Torrey Harris (b.Connecticut, 1835–1909), superintendent of St. Louis public schools, US commissioner of education, and an authority on Hegelian philosophy; James Milton Turney (1840–1915), who helped establish Lincoln University for blacks at Jefferson City; and Susan Elizabeth Blow (1843–1916), cofounder with Harris of the first US public kindergarten at St. Louis in 1873. Distinguished scientists include agricultural chemist George Washington Carver (1864–1943), astronomers Harlow Shapley (1885–1972) and Edwin P. Hubble (1889–1953), Nobel Prize-winning nuclear physicist Arthur Holly Compton (b.Ohio, 1892–1962), and mathematician-cyberneticist Norbert Wiener (1894–1964). Engineer and inventor James Buchanan Eads (b.Indiana, 1820–87) supervised construction during 1867–74 of the St. Louis bridge that bears his name. Charles A. Lindbergh (b.Michigan 1902–74) was a pilot and aviation instructor in the St. Louis area during the 1920s before wining worldwide acclaim for his solo New York-Paris flight.

Prominent Missouri businessmen include brewer Adolphus Busch (b.Germany, 1839–1913); William Rockhill Nelson (b.Indiana, 1847–1915), who founded the *Kansas City Star* (1880); Joseph Pulitzer (b.Hungary, 1847–1911), who merged two failed newspapers to establish the *St. Louis Post-Dispatch* (1878) and later endowed the journalism and literary prizes that bear his name; and James Cash Penney (1875–1971), founder of the J. C. Penney Co. Noteworthy journalists from Missouri include newspaper and magazine editor William M. Reedy (1862–1920), newspaper reporter Herbert Bayard Swope (1882–1958), and television newscaster Walter Cronkite (b.1916). Other distinguished Missourians include theologian Reinhold Niebuhr (1892–1971), civil rights leader Roy Wilkins (1901–81), and medical missionary Thomas Dooley (1927–61).

Missouri's most popular author is Mark Twain (Samuel Langhorne Clemens, 1835–1910), whose *Adventures of Tom*

Sawyer (1876) and *Adventures of Huckleberry Finn* (1884) evoke his boyhood in Hannibal. Novelist Harold Bell Wright (b.New York, 1872–1944) wrote about the people of the Ozarks; Robert Heinlein (1907–88) is a noted writer of science fiction, and William S. Burroughs (1914–97) an experimental novelist. Poet-critic T(homas) S(tearns) Eliot (1888–1965), awarded the Nobel Prize for literature in 1948, was born in St. Louis but became a British subject in 1927. Other Missouri-born poets include Sara Teasdale (1884–1933), Marianne Moore (1887–1972), and Langston Hughes (1902–67). Popular novelist and playwright Rupert Hughes (1872–1956) was a Missouri native, as was Zoe Akins (1886–1958), a Pulitzer Prize-winning playwright.

Distinguished painters who lived in Missouri include George Caleb Bingham (b.Virginia, 1811–79), who also served in several state offices; James Carroll Beckwith (1852–1917); and Thomas Hart Benton (1889–1975), the grandnephew and namesake of the state's famous political leader. Among the state's important musicians are ragtime pianist-composers Scott Joplin (b.Texas, 1868–1917) and John William "Blind" Boone (1864–1927); W(illiam) C(hristopher) Handy (b.Alabama, 1873–1958), composer of "St. Louis Blues," "Beale Street Blues," and other classics; composer-critic Virgil Thomson (1896–1989), known for his operatic collaborations with Gertrude Stein; jazzman Coleman Hawkins (1907–69); and popular songwriter Burt Bacharach (b.1929). Photographer Walker Evans (1903–75) was a St. Louis native.

Missouri-born entertainers include actors Wallace Beery, (1889–1949), Vincent Price (1911–93), and Edward Asner (b.1929); actresses Jean Harlow (Harlean Carpenter, 1911–37), Jane Wyman (b.1914), Betty Grable (1916–73), and Shelley Winters (b.1922); dancers Sally Rand (1904–79) and Josephine Baker (1906–75); actress-dancer Ginger Rogers (1911–95); film director John Huston (1906–84); and opera stars Helen Traubel (1903–72), Gladys Swarthout (1904–69), and Grace Bumbry (b.1937). In popular music, the state's most widely known singer-songwriter is Charles "Chuck" Berry (b.California, 1926), whose works had a powerful influence on the development of rock 'n' roll.

St. Louis Cardinals stars who became Hall of Famers include Jerome Herman "Dizzy" Dean (b.Arkansas, 1911–74), Stanley Frank "Stan the Man" Musial (b.Pennsylvania, 1920), Robert "Bob" Gibson (b.Nebraska, 1935), and Louis "Lou" Brock (b.Arkansas, 1939). Among the native Missourians who achieved stardom in the sports world are baseball manager Charles Dillon "Casey" Stengel (1890–1975), catcher Lawrence Peter "Yogi" Berra (b.1925), sportscaster Joe Garagiola (b.1926), and golfer Tom Watson (b.1949).

50 BIBLIOGRAPHY

Burnett, Robyn. *German Settlement in Missouri: New Land, Old Ways.* Columbia: University of Missouri Press, 1996.

Christensen, Lawrence O. et al., ed. *Dictionary of Missouri Biography.* Columbia: University of Missouri Press, 1999.

Greene, Lorenzo J., et al. *Missouri's Black Heritage.* Rev. ed. Columbia: University of Missouri Press, 1993.

Hall, Leonard. *Stars Upstream: Life Along an Ozark River.* Columbia: University of Missouri Press, 1991.

Harlan, James. *Atlas of Lewis and Clark in Missouri.* Columbia: University of Missouri Press, 2003.

Larsen, Lawrence Harold. *Federal Justice in Western Missouri: The Judges, the Cases, the Times.* Columbia: University of Missouri Press, 1994.

Truman, Harry S. *Memoirs.* 2 vols. Garden City, N.Y.: Doubleday, 1955–56.

MONTANA

State of Montana

ORIGIN OF STATE NAME: Derived from the Latin word meaning "mountainous." **NICKNAME:** The Treasure State. **CAPITAL:** Helena. **ENTERED UNION:** 8 November 1889 (41st). **SONG:** "Montana." **BALLAD:** "Montana Melody." **MOTTO:** *Oro y Plata* (Gold and silver). **FLAG:** A blue field, fringed in gold on the top and bottom borders, surround the state coat of arms, with "Montana" in gold letters above the coat of arms. **OFFICIAL SEAL:** In the lower center are a plow and a miner's pick and shovel; mountains appear above them on the left, the Great Falls of the Missouri River on the right, and a state motto on a banner below. The words "The Great Seal of the State of Montana" surround the whole. **ANIMAL:** Grizzly bear. **BIRD:** Western meadowlark. **FISH:** Black-spotted (cutthroat) trout. **FLOWER:** Bitterroot. **TREE:** Ponderosa pine. **GRASS:** Bluebunch wheatgrass. **GEMS:** Yogo sapphire; Montana agate. **FOSSIL:** Duck-billed dinosaur. **LEGAL HOLIDAYS:** New Year's Day, 1 January; Birthday of Martin Luther King, Jr., 3rd Monday in January; Lincoln's Birthday, 12 February; Washington's Birthday, 3rd Monday in February; Memorial Day, last Monday in May; Independence Day, 4 July; Labor Day, 1st Monday in September; Columbus Day, 2nd Monday in October; State Election Day, 1st Tuesday after the 1st Monday in November in even-numbered years; Veterans Day, 11 November; Thanksgiving Day, 4th Thursday in November; Christmas Day, 25 December. **TIME:** 5 AM MST = noon GMT.

1 LOCATION, SIZE, AND EXTENT

Located in the northwestern US, Montana is the largest of the 8 Rocky Mountain states and ranks 4th in size among the 50 states.

The total area of Montana is 147,046 sq mi (380,849 sq km), of which land takes up 145,388 sq mi (376,555 sq km) and inland water 1,658 sq mi (4,294 sq km). The state's maximum E-W extension is 570 mi (917 km); its extreme N-S distance is 315 mi (507 km).

Montana is bordered on the N by the Canadian provinces of British Columbia, Alberta, and Saskatchewan; on the E by North Dakota and South Dakota; on the S by Wyoming and Idaho; and on the W by Idaho. The total boundary length of Montana is 1,947 mi (3,133 km). The state's geographic center is in Fergus County, 12 mi (19 km) W of Lewistown. Nearly 30% of the state's land belongs to the federal government.

2 TOPOGRAPHY

Montana, as mountainous in parts as its name implies, has an approximate mean elevation of 3,400 ft (1,037 m). The Rocky Mountains cover the western two-fifths of the state, with the Bitterroot Range along the Idaho border; the high, gently rolling Great Plains occupy most of central and eastern Montana. The highest point in the state is Granite Peak, at an elevation of 12,799 ft (3,904 m), located in south-central Montana, near the Wyoming border. The lowest point, at 1,800 ft (549 m), is in the northwest, where the Kootenai River leaves the state at the Idaho border. The Continental Divide passes in a jagged pattern through the western part of the state, from the Lewis to the Bitterroot ranges.

Ft. Peck Reservoir is Montana's largest body of inland water, covering 375 sq mi (971 sq km); Flathead Lake is the largest natural lake. The state's most important rivers are the Missouri, rising in southwest Montana and flowing north and then east across the state, and the Yellowstone, which crosses southeastern Montana to join the Missouri in North Dakota near the Montana border. Located in Glacier National Park is the Triple Divide, from which Montana waters begin their journey to the Arctic and Pacific oceans and the Gulf of Mexico.

3 CLIMATE

The Continental Divide separates the state into two distinct climatic regions: the west generally has a milder climate than the east, where winters can be especially harsh. Montana's maximum daytime temperature averages 27°F (–2°C) in January and 85°F (29°C) in July. Great Falls has a normal daily mean temperature of 45°F (7°C), ranging from 21°F (–6°C) in January to 69°F (21°C) in July. The all-time low temperature in the state, –70°F (–57°C), registered at Rogers Pass on 20 January 1954, is the lowest ever recorded in the conterminous US; the all-time high, 117°F (47°C), was set at Medicine Lake on 5 July 1937. During the winter, Chinook winds from the eastern Rocky Mountains can bring rapid temperature increases of 40–50°F within a few minutes. Great Falls received an average annual precipitation (1971–2000) of 14.9 in (37.8 cm), but much of north-central Montana is arid. About 58.5 in (148.6 cm) of snow descends on Great Falls each year.

4 FLORA AND FAUNA

Montana has three major life zones: subalpine, montane, and plains. The subalpine region, in the northern Rocky Mountains, is rich in wild flowers during a short midsummer growing season. The montane flora consists largely of coniferous forests, principally alpine fir, and a variety of shrubs. The plains are characterized by an abundance of grasses, cacti, and sagebrush species. Three plant species were threatened as of 2003: Ute ladies'-tresses, Spalding's catchfly, and water howellia.

Game animals of the state include elk, moose, white-tailed and mule deers, pronghorn antelope, bighorn sheep, and mountain goat. Notable among the amphibians is the axolotl; rattlesnakes and other reptiles occur in most of the state. Thirteen species were listed as threatened or endangered in 2003, including the grizzly bear, black-footed ferret, Eskimo curlew, two species of sturgeon, gray wolf, and whooping crane.

5ENVIRONMENTAL PROTECTION

Montana's major environmental concerns are management of mineral and water resources and reclamation of strip-mined land. The 1973 Montana Resource Indemnity Trust Act, by 1975 amendment, imposes a coal severance tax of 30% on the contract sales price, with the proceeds placed in a permanent tax trust fund. This tax, in conjunction with the Montana Environmental Policy Act (1971) and the Major Facilities Siting Act (1973) reflects the determination of Montanans to protect the beauty of the Big Sky Country while maintaining economic momentum.

In 2003, Montana had 71 hazardous waste sites listed in the Environmental Protection Agency's database, 14 of which were on the National Priorities List. Only a tiny fraction of the state's lands are wetlands. The Water Quality Bureau of the Montana Department of Health and Environmental Sciences is responsible for managing wetlands. In 2001, Montana received $46,753,000 in federal grants from the Environmental Protection Agency; EPA expenditures for procurement contracts in Montana that year amounted to $140,000.

6POPULATION

Montana ranked 44th in population in the US with an estimated total of 909,453 in 2002, an increase of 0.8% since 2000. Between 1990 and 2000, Montana's population grew from 799,065 to 902,195, an increase of 12.9%. The population is projected to reach 1,006,000 by 2005 and 1.1 million by 2025. The population density in 2000 was 6.2 persons per sq mi, the 3rd-lowest in the country.

In 2000, the median age of all Montana residents was 37.5. In the same year, 25.5% of the populace were under the age of 18 while 13.4% were age 65 or older.

Montana had no cities with populations exceeding 100,000 in 2002. The largest cities and their estimated populations are Billings, 89,847, and Great Falls, 56,690.

7ETHNIC GROUPS

According to the 2000 census, there were approximately 56,068 American Indians in Montana, of whom the Blackfeet and Crow are the most numerous. The Blackfeet and Crow reservations had populations of, respectively, 10,100 and 6,894 in 2000.

The foreign born, numbering 16,396, made up 1.8% of Montana's 2000 census population, a decrease of 24% since 1980. Canada, Germany, the United Kingdom, and Mexico were the leading places of origin. As of 2000, the black and Asian populations were just 2,692 and 4,691, respectively. In 2000, 18,081 residents were Hispanic or Latino, representing 2% of the total population.

8LANGUAGES

English in Montana fuses Northern and Midland features, the Northern proportion declining from east to west. Topography has given new meaning to *basin, hollow, meadow,* and *park* as kinds of clear spaces in the mountains.

In 2000, the number of Montanans who spoke only English at was 803,031, representing about 95% of the resident population five years of age or older. There was no change in the overall percentage of English speakers from 1990 to 2000.

The following table gives selected statistics from the 2000 census for language spoken at home by persons five years old and over. The category "Other Native North American languages" includes Apache, Cherokee, Choctaw, Dakota, Keres, Pima, and Yupik. The category "Scandinavian languages" includes Danish, Norwegian, and Swedish. The category "Other Slavic languages" includes Czech, Slovak, and Ukrainian.

LANGUAGE	NUMBER	PERCENT
Population 5 years and over	847,362	100.0
Speak only English	803,031	94.8
Speak a language other than English	44,331	5.2
Speak a language other than English	**44,331**	**5.2**
Spanish or Spanish Creole	12,953	1.5
German	9,416	1.1
Other Native North American languages	9,234	1.1
French (incl. Patois, Cajun)	3,298	0.4
Scandinavian languages	1,335	0.2
Italian	759	0.1
Japanese	711	0.1
Russian	610	0.1
Other Slavic languages	570	0.1
Chinese	528	0.1

9RELIGIONS

In 2000, there was a nearly equal number of Protestants versus Catholics within the state. The Catholic Church was the largest single Christian denomination with about 169,250 adherents. Leading Protestant denominations were the Evangelical Lutheran Church in America, 50,287; the Church of Jesus Christ of the Latter-Day Saints (Mormons), 32,726; the United Methodist Church, 17,993; Assemblies of God, 16,385; the Lutheran Church—Missouri Synod, 15,441.and the Southern Baptist Convention, 15,318. There were about 850 Jews and 614 Muslims in the state.

Though relatively small in terms of membership, several religious groups within the state experienced significant growth throughout 1990–2000. Friends–USA (Quakers) reported a membership growth from 77 in 1990 to 160 in 2000. The Free Lutheran Congregations grew from 75 members to 427 members and the Salvation Army reported a total of 1,414 members in 2000, up from 551 in 1990. About 493,703 people (55% of the population) were not counted as members of any religious organization.

10TRANSPORTATION

Montana's first railroad, the Utah and Northern, entered the state in 1880. Today, Montana is served by two Class I railroads (Burlington Northern and Santa Fe, and Union Pacific), two regional railroads, and three local railroads, operating on 3,310 rail mi (5,326 km) of track. Amtrak operates one long-distance route (Chicago–Seattle/Portland) through the state, which serves 12 stations.

Because of its large size, small population, and difficult terrain, Montana was slow to develop a highway system. In 2000, the state had 69,567 mi (111,957 km) of public roads, streets, and highways. There were 1,052,737 registered motor vehicles in 2000, including 466,659 automobiles, 556,772 trucks, and 2,795 buses. There were 678,899 licensed drivers in the same year.

Montana had 222 airports, 28 heliports, 2 stolports, and 2 seaplane bases in 2002. The leading airport is at Billings, with 346,375 passengers enplaned in 2000.

11HISTORY

Much of Montana's prehistory has only recently been unearthed. The abundance of fossils of large and small dinosaurs, marine reptiles, miniature horses, and giant cave bears indicates that, from 100 million to 60 million years ago, the region had a tropical climate. Beginning some 2 million years ago, however, dramatic temperature changes profoundly altered what we now call Montana. At four different times, great sheets of glacial ice moved south through Canada to cover much of the north. The last glacial retreat, about 10,000 years ago, did much to carve the state's present topographic feature. Montana's first humans probably came from across the Bering Strait; their fragmentary remains indicate a presence dating between 10,000 and 4000 BC.

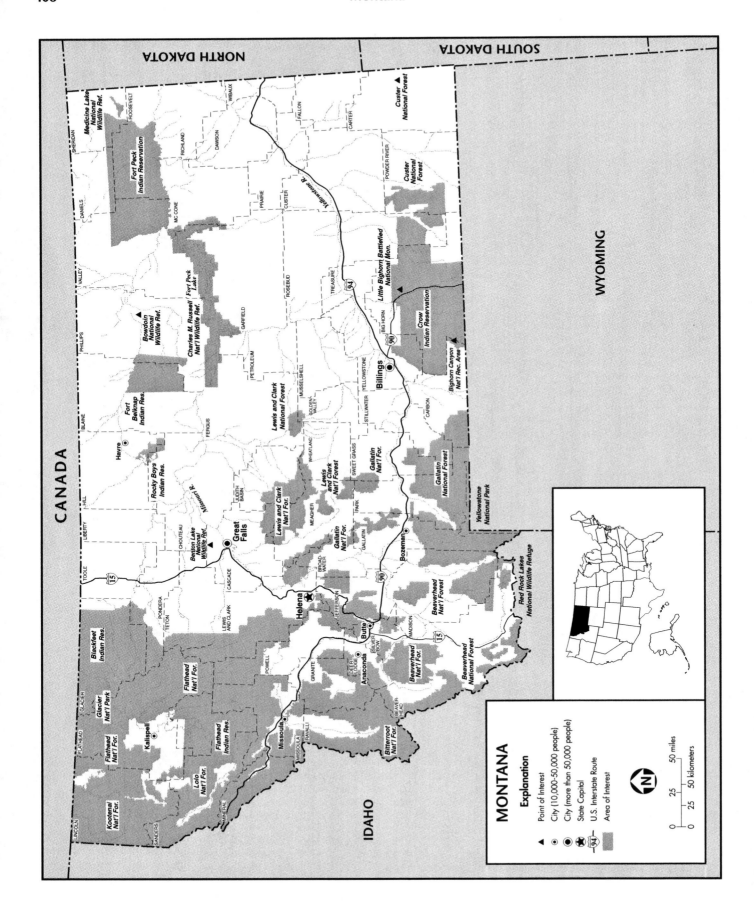

The Indians encountered by Montana's first white explorers—probably French traders and trappers from Canada—arrived from the east during the 17th and 18th centuries, pushed westward into Montana by the pressure of European colonization. In January 1743, two traders, Louis-Joseph and Francois Vérendrye, crossed the Dakota plains and saw before them what they called the "shining mountains," the eastern flank of the northern Rockies. However, it was not until 1803 that the written history of Montana begins. In that year, the Louisiana Purchase gave the United States most of Montana, and the Lewis and Clark expedition, dispatched by President Thomas Jefferson in 1804 to explore the upper reaches of the Missouri River, added the rest. On 25 April 1805, accompanied by a French trapper named Toussaint Charbonneau and his Shoshoni wife, Sacagawea, Meriwether Lewis and William Clark reached the mouth of the Yellowstone River near the present-day boundary with North Dakota. Shortly thereafter, the first American trappers, traders, and settlers entered Montana.

The fur trade dominated Montana's economy until 1858, when gold was discovered near the present community of Drummond. By mid-1862, a rush of miners from the gold fields of California, Nevada, Colorado, and Idaho had descended on the state. The temporary gold boom brought not only the state's first substantial white population but also an increased demand for government. In 1863, the eastern and western sectors of Montana were joined as part of Idaho Territory, which, in turn, was divided along the Bitterroot Mountains to form the present boundary between the two states. On 26 May 1864, President Abraham Lincoln signed the Organic Act, which created Montana Territory.

The territorial period was one of rapid and profound change. By the time Montana became a state on 8 November 1889, the remnants of Montana's Indian culture had been largely confined to federal reservations. A key event in this transformation was the Battle of the Little Big Horn River on 25 June 1876, when Lieutenant Colonel George Custer and his 7th US Cavalry regiment of fewer than 700 men were overwhelmed as they attacked an encampment of 15,000 Sioux and Northern Cheyenne led by Crazy Horse and Chief Gall. The following year, after a four-month running battle that traversed most of the state of Montana, Chief Joseph of the Nez Percé tribe surrendered to federal forces, signaling the end of organized Indian resistance.

As the Indian threat subsided, stockmen wasted little time in putting the seemingly limitless open range to use. By 1866, Nelson Story had driven the first longhorns up from Texas, and by the mid-1870s, sheep had also made a significant appearance on the open range. In 1886, at the peak of the open-range boom, approximately 664,000 head of cattle and nearly a million sheep grazed Montana's rangeland. Disaster struck during the "hard winter" of 1886/87, however, when perhaps as many as 362,000 head of cattle starved trying to find the scant forage covered by snow and ice. That winter marked the end of a cattle frontier based on the "free grass" of the open range and taught the stockmen the value of a secure winter feed supply.

Construction of Montana's railroad system between 1880 and 1909 breathed new life into mining as well as the livestock industry. Moreover, the railroads created a new network of market centers at Great Falls, Billings, Bozeman, Missoula, and Havre. By 1890, the Butte copper pits were producing more than 40% of the nation's copper requirements. The struggle to gain financial control of the enormous mineral wealth of Butte Hill led to the "War of the Copper Kings," in which the Amalgamated Copper Co., in conjunction with Standard Oil gave up its copper holdings. The new company, Anaconda Copper Mining, virtually controlled the press, politics, and governmental processes of Montana until changes in the structure of the international copper market and the diversification of Montana's economy in the 1940s and 1950s reduced the company's power. Anaconda Copper was absorbed by the Atlantic Richfield Co. in 1976, and the name was changed to Anaconda Minerals in 1982.

The railroads also brought an invasion of agricultural homesteaders. Montana's population surged from 243,329 in 1900 to 548,889 by 1920, while the number of farms and ranches increased form 13,000 to 57,000. Drought and a sharp drop in wheat prices after World War I brought an end to the homestead boom. By 1926, half of Montana's commercial banks had failed. Conditions worsened with the drought and depression of the early 1930s, until the New Deal—enormously popular in Montana—helped revive farming and silver mining and financed irrigation and other public works projects.

The decades after World War II saw moderate growth in Montana's population, economy, and social services. Although manufacturing developed slowly, the state's fossil fuels industry grew rapidly during the national energy crisis of the 1970s. However, production of coal, crude oil, and natural gas leveled off after the crisis and even declined in the early 1980s.

In 1983 the Anaconda Copper Mining Company shut down its mining operations in Butte. Farm income also suffered in the 1980s as a result of falling prices, drought, and insect damage. Growth in manufacturing and construction and recovery in the agricultural sector improved Montana's economy in the 1990s. However, even in the midst of a sustained economic boom, the state had the 8th-highest unemployment rate in the nation, 5.2% as of 1999. Other indicators also showed the state was not benefiting from the sustained national economic expansion of recent years. Montana faced a $230 million budget deficit in 2003, but lawmakers were able to balance the budget with a series of program reductions, new taxes, and budget transfers.

Tourism, air quality, and wildlife in parts of Montana were affected by the 1988 forest fires that burned for almost three months in Yellowstone National Park. Some Montana residents had to be evacuated from their homes. The state was among those afflicted by raging wildfires the summer of 2000, the worst fire season in more than a decade. In 2001, 2002 and 2003, wildfires broke out in the west once again. In the summer of 2002, wildfires burned over 7.1 million acres of public and private land in the US, most of it in the west. By August 2003, 36 wildfires had destroyed over 400,000 acres in Montana, equivalent to half the state of Rhode Island. Both Yellowstone and Glacier National Parks had to close sections of the parks due to fires.

In 1992 Montana's delegation to the US House of Representatives was reduced from two members to one, based on the results of the 1990 Census. The state remains one of the least populated in the nation, with an estimated 902,195 residents in 2000—or about six people per square mile.

12 STATE GOVERNMENT

Montana's original constitution, dating from 1889, was substantially revised by a 1972 constitutional convention, effective 1 July 1973. Under the present document, which had been amended 27 times by January 2003, the state legislature consists of 50 senators, elected to staggered four-year terms, and 100 representatives, who serve for two years. Legislators must be at least 18 years old and have lived in the state for a year and in their district for six months prior to election. In 2002 legislators received about $72 per diem during regular sessions. Sessions are held only in odd-numbered years, beginning the first Monday of January and lasting no more than 90 legislative days. An amendment passed by voters in 2002 requires the governor to give advance notice of special sessions, which have no time limit and may be called by petition of a majority in each house.

The only elected officers of the executive branch are the governor and lieutenant governor (who run jointly), secretary of state, attorney general, superintendent of public instruction, and auditor; each serves a four-year term. Without exception, the governor is limited to serving eight out of every 16 years. Candidates for governor must be at least 25 years old, a citizen of both the US and Montana, and must have resided in the state for at least two years. In 2002 the governor's salary was $88,190.

To become law, a bill must pass both houses by a simple majority and be signed by the governor, remain unsigned for 10 days (25 days if the legislature adjourns), or be passed over the governor's veto by a two-thirds vote of the members present in both houses. The state constitution may be amended by constitutional convention, by legislative referendum (a two-thirds vote of both houses), or by voter initiative (10% of qualified electors, as determined by number of votes cast for governor at the last election). To be adopted, each proposed amendment must be ratified at the next general election.

To vote in Montana, one must be a US citizen, at least 18 years old, and a state and county resident for 30 days prior to election day. Restrictions apply to convicted felons and those declared of unsound mind.

13POLITICAL PARTIES

Since statehood, Democrats generally dominated in contests for the US House and Senate, and Republicans in elections for state and local offices and in national presidential campaigns (except during the New Deal years). Although the erosion of Montana's rural population since the 1920s diluted the Republicans' agrarian base, the party has gained increasing financial and organizational backing from corporate interests, particularly from the mining and energy-related industries.

The strength of the Democratic Party, on the other hand, lies in the strong union movement centered in Butte and its surrounding counties, augmented by smaller family farms throughout the state. Urbanization also benefited the Democrats. Montanans voted overwhelmingly for Republican President Ronald Reagan in November 1984 and for Republican George Bush in 1988, but Democrat Bill Clinton carried the state in 1992. However, in 1996 Clinton lost the state to Republican Bob Dole. In 2000, Republican George W. Bush won an overwhelming victory over Democrat Al Gore, 58% to 34%. Green Party candidate Ralph Nader won 6% of the vote. In 2002 there were 624,548 registered voters; there is no party registration in the state. The state had three electoral votes in the 2000 presidential election.

Montana Governor Marc Racicot, Republican, was elected in 1992 and reelected in 1996. Republican Judy Martz was elected Montana's first female governor in 2000. Republican Conrad Burns was elected to the Senate in 1988 and reelected in 1994 and 2000, and Democrat Max Baucus won reelection in 2002. The state's sole seat in the US House was retained by a Republican in the 2002 election. Before November 2003 elections, there were 29 Republicans and 21 Democrats in the state senate. The Republicans continued to control the state house with 53 seats to the Democrats' 47.

14LOCAL GOVERNMENT

As of 2002, Montana had 54 counties, 129 municipalities, 592 special districts, and 352 public school districts. Typical elected county officials are three county commissioners (or a city manager), attorney, sheriff, clerk and recorder, school superintendent, treasurer, assessor, and coroner. Unified city-county governments include Anaconda-Deer Lodge and Butte-Silver Bow.

Montana Presidential Vote by Major Political Parties, 1948–2000

YEAR	ELECTORAL VOTE	MONTANA WINNER	DEMOCRAT	REPUBLICAN
1948	4	*Truman (D)	119,071	96,770
1952	4	*Eisenhower (R)	106,213	157,394
1956	4	*Eisenhower (R)	116,238	154,933
1960	4	Nixon (R)	134,891	141,841
1964	4	*Johnson (D)	164,246	113,032
1968	4	*Nixon (R)	114,117	138,835
1972	4	*Nixon (R)	120,197	183,976
1976	4	Ford (R)	149,259	173,703
1980	4	*Reagan (R)	118,032	206,814
1984	4	*Reagan (R)	146,742	232,450
1988	4	*Bush (R)	168,936	190,412
1992**	3	*Clinton (D)	154,507	144,207
1996**	3	Dole (R)	167,922	179,652
2000	3	*Bush, G. W. (R)	137,126	240,178

*Won US presidential election.
** Independent candidate Ross Perot received 107,225 votes in 1992 and 55,229 votes in 1996.

15STATE SERVICES

To address the continuing threat of terrorism and to work with the federal Department of Homeland Security (created in 2002 following the terrorist attacks of 11 September 2001), homeland security in Montana in 2003 operated under executive order; the emergency management director was designated as the state homeland security advisor.

The Citizens' Advocate Office, established in 1973, serves as a clearinghouse for problems, complaints, and questions concerning state government. The commissioner of higher education administers the state university system, while the superintendent of public instruction is responsible for the public schools. The Department of Transportation is the main transportation agency. Health and welfare programs are the province of the Department of Public Health and Human Services. Other departments deal with agriculture, commerce, justice, labor and industry, livestock, and natural resources and human services.

16JUDICIAL SYSTEM

Montana's highest court, the supreme court, consists of a chief justice and six associate justices. District courts are the courts of general jurisdiction. Justice of the peace courts are essentially county courts whose jurisdiction is limited to minor civil cases, misdemeanors, and traffic violations. Montana has seven supreme court justices elected on nonpartisan ballots for eight-year terms and 37 district court judges elected for six years.

Montana's total crime rate in 2001 stood at 3,688.7 per 100,000, including a total of 3,187 violent crimes and 30,175 crimes against property in that year. The state rarely enforces the death penalty; only eight convicted persons have been executed since 1930, and two since 1977. Six persons were under sentence of death in 2003.

In June 2001 there were 3,250 inmates in state and federal correctional facilities, an increase of 6.9% over the previous year. The state's incarceration rate stood at 359 per 100,000 inhabitants.

17ARMED FORCES

In 2002, there were 3,511 active-duty military personnel and 1,187 civilian personnel stationed in Montana. The principal military facility in Montana is Malmstrom Air Force Base (Great Falls), a Strategic Air Command facility. Total defense contracts in 2001 amounted to $127.4 million.

An estimated 108,476 veterans of US military service were living in Montana in 2000. Of these, 20,413 served in World War II; 12,885 in the Korean conflict; 34,199 during the Vietnam era; and 11,602 during 1990–2000 (including the Persian Gulf War). In 1999, expenditures on veterans totaled $216 million.

In 2000, the Montana Highway Patrol employed 205 full-time sworn officers.

18MIGRATION

Montana's first great migratory wave brought Indians from the east during the 17th and 18th centuries. The gold rush of the 1860s and a land boom between 1900 and 1920 resulted in surges of white settlement. The economically troubled 1920s and 1930s produced a severe wave of out-migration that continued through the 1960s. The trend reversed between 1970 and 1980, however, when Montana's net gain from migration was 16,000; from 1980 to 1989, the state had a net loss of 43,000 residents from migration. Between 1990 and 1998, Montana had net gains of 48,000 in domestic migration and 3,000 in international migration. In 1998, the state admitted 299 foreign immigrants. Between 1990 and 1998, the state's overall population increased 10.2%. In the period 1995–2000, 111,530 people moved into the state and 116,696 moved out, for a net loss of 5,166, 3,031 many of whom moved to Washington.

19INTERGOVERNMENTAL COOPERATION

Among the interstate agreements in which Montana participates are the Interstate Oil and Gas Compact, Western Interstate Corrections Compact, Western Interstate Energy Compact, Western Interstate Commission for Higher Education, Interstate Compact for Juveniles, Northwest Power and Conservation Council (with Idaho, Oregon, and Washington), and Yellowstone River Compact (with North Dakota and Wyoming). Federal grants to the state and local governments in 2001 totaled over $1.6 billion.

20ECONOMY

Resource industries (agriculture, mining, lumbering) traditionally dominated Montana's economy, although they have declined during the past decade. A lawsuit with the federal government over the federal lands which supplied much of the state's timber placed the timber industry's future in question, as did the selling by Champion International of its two mills and of its timber lands. While Stimson Lumber purchased the mills from Champion, it rehired only two-thirds of the employers. The mining industry in western Montana was hurt by low international price levels. The closure of Troy Mine, which produced silver, lead and zinc, resulted in the idling of 300 workers. Employment in the services industries has overtaken manufacturing and mining during the 1990s. Diversification into business, engineering, health, and tourism services has stimulated the economy. Annual growth rates averaged 4.67% 1998 to 2000, and the state economy was little affected by the national recession and slowdown in 2001, posting a growth rate of 4.3%. In November 2002, Montana's nonagricultural employment was up 1.1% above the year before, above the national rate. Employment increased in construction, financial and general services, and fell slightly in the manufacturing and transportation and utilities sectors. The announced closing of Stimson Lumber in Libby is expected to cost 300 mill jobs, and another 410 related jobs. Montana's farm sector, contributing directly less than 3% to gross state product, has been severely stressed by a four-year drought. Wheat crop yields in 2002 were the lowest since 1988. Government subsidy payments to Montana farmers, the 4th-highest in the country, amounted to 157% of their net income (that is, net income would have been negative without the subsidies).

Montana's gross state product in 2001 was $22.6 billion, the 4th lowest among the states, to which general services contributed $4.8 billion; government, $3.9; trade, $3.7 billion, financial services, $3.2 billion; transportation and public utilities, $2.5 billion, and construction, $1.3 billion. The public sector in 2001 constituted 17.1% of gross state product, the 7th highest percent among the states.

21INCOME

According to the Bureau of Economic Analysis, in 2001, Montana had a per capita personal income (PCPI) of $24,044 which ranked 46th in the United States (including the District of Columbia) and was 79% of the national average, $30,413. The 2001 PCPI reflected an increase of 4.7% from 2000 compared to the national change of 2.2%. In 2001, Montana had a total personal income (TPI) of $21,769,095,000 which ranked 46th in the United States and accounted for 0.3% of the national total. The 2001 TPI reflected an increase of 4.9% from 2000 compared to the national change of 3.3%.

Earnings of persons employed in Montana increased from $13,400,525,000 in 2000 to $14,069,660,000 in 2001, an increase of 5.0%. The largest industries in 2001 were services, 27.7% of earnings; state and local government, 14.9%; and retail trade, 11.3%. Of the industries that accounted for at least 5% of earnings in 2001, the slowest growing from 2000 to 2001 was federal civilian government (5.7% of earnings in 2001), which increased 0.6%; the fastest was state and local government, which increased 11.0%.

According to data released by the US Census Bureau, in 2000, the median household income was $32,045 compared to the national average of $42,148. In 2001, the median income for a family of four was $48,078 compared to the national average of $63,278. For the period 1999 to 2001, the average poverty rate was 14.4% which placed it 43rd among the 50 states and the District of Columbia ranked lowest to highest.

22LABOR

According to Bureau of Labor Statistics (BLS) provisional estimates, in July 2003 the seasonally adjusted civilian labor force in Montana numbered 478,000, with approximately 22,300 workers unemployed, yielding an unemployment rate of 4.7%, compared to the national average of 6.2% for the same period. Since the beginning of the BLS data series in 1978, the highest unemployment rate recorded was 9.2% in March 1983. The historical low was 4.0% in April 2003. In 2001, an estimated 4.9% of the labor force was employed in construction; 6.1% in manufacturing; 4.6% in transportation, communications, and public utilities; 21.6% in trade; 4.2% in finance, insurance, and real estate; 22.6% in services; 18.1% in government; and 6.6% in agriculture.

The US Department of Labor reported that in 2002, 51,000 of Montana's 362,000 employed wage and salary workers were members of unions. This represented 14.1% of those so employed, up from 13.2% in 2001 and 15.3% in 1998. The national average is 13.2%. In all, 56,000 workers (15.5%) were represented by unions. In addition to union members, this category includes workers who report no union affiliation but whose jobs are covered by a union contract.

23AGRICULTURE

Montana's farms numbered 28,000 in 2002, with average acreage of 2,090 (846 hectares). Farm income totaled nearly $1.8 billion in 2001. In 2002, Montana was the nation's 4th-leading wheat producer, with an output of 109.9 million bu, valued at $466.7 million. Other major crops were barley (3rd in the US) with 39.9 million bu, valued at $115.7 million; sugar beets (6th) with 1.1 million bu, valued at $44.6 million; and hay (12th) with 4.6 million tons, valued at $379.1 million.

24ANIMAL HUSBANDRY

In 2003, Montana's farms and ranches had around 2.4 million cattle and calves, valued at $2 million. There were an estimated 185,000 hogs and pigs, valued at $13.7 million in 2002. During 2001, Montana farmers produced around 31.7 million lb (14.4 million kg) of sheep and lambs that grossed $18.6 million in income.

25FISHING

Montana's designated fishing streams offer some 10,000 mi (16,000 km) of good to excellent freshwater fishing. Fish farms distributed over 4.4 million trout within Montana in 1998, when the state issued 367,478 sport fishing licenses.

26FORESTRY

As of 2002, 23,293,000 acres (9,427,000 hectares) in Montana were classified as forestland. There were 10 national forests, comprising 16,893,339 acres (6,836,734 hectares) in 1999. The lumbering industry produced 1.2 billion board feet in 2002.

27MINING

The estimated value of nonfuel mineral production for Montana in 2001 rose to $503 million, a decrease of about 15% from 2000. Metallic minerals—copper, gold, iron ore, lead, molybdenum, platinum group metals, silver, and zinc—accounted for 67% of the state's total nonfuel mineral production value. Most metal mining—especially for gold, silver, and copper—occurs in the southwest region, in the vicinity of Helena and Butte. In 2001, Montana ranked 29th nationally in the value of nonfuel minerals, compared with its ranking of 18th in 1992.

Palladium was Montana's leading mineral by value in 2001, followed by gold, platinum, portland cement, and construction sand and gravel. Montana is the only state to produce primary platinum and palladium, and is 1st in the production of talc; 2nd in bentonite; 3rd in garnet; 5th in zinc and lead; and 6th in gold and silver. According to preliminary figures, production and value in 2001 included construction sand and gravel, 11 million metric tons ($45.6 million); palladium, 12,000 kg ($177 million); platinum, 3,600 kg ($52.8 million); and zinc, 24,000 metric tons ($23.8 million). Production of gold in 2000 was 9,310 kg ($83.8 million).

28ENERGY AND POWER

In 1999, Montana generated 31.5 billion kWh of electricity (utility and nonutility), 44% from hydropower and 54% by coal burning; total installed capacity was 5.8 million kW.

In 2002, the state produced 46,000 barrels per day crude oil; proved reserves totaled 260 million barrels in 2001 (10th-largest among the states). Natural gas production in 2002 totaled 84.3 billion cu ft (2.39 billion cu m), with proved reserves in 2001 amounting to 898 billion cu ft (25.4 billion cu m). As of 2001, recoverable coal reserves were estimated at 1.2 billion tons. Production of coal in 2000 totaled 38.3 million tons. In 2000 Montana's total per capita energy consumption was 659 million Btu (166 million kcal), ranking it 4th among the 50 states.

29INDUSTRY

Montana's major manufacturing industries process raw materials from mines, forests, and farms. The total value of shipments by manufacturers in 1997 amounted to $5.2 billion.

Earnings of persons employed in Montana increased from $11.3 billion in 1997 to $12 billion in 1998, an increase of 5.8%. The largest industries in 1998 were services, 27.2% of earnings; state and local government, 13.4%; and retail trade, 12.6%. Of the industries that accounted for at least 5% of earnings in 1998, the slowest growing from 1997 to 1998 was state and local government, which increased 2.7%; the fastest was construction (7.7% of earnings in 1998), which increased 6.1%.

30COMMERCE

In 1997, 1,939 wholesale establishments had sales of $8.2 billion. That year, 7,387 retail stores had sales of $8 billion. In 1997, wholesale establishments employed 17,417 workers, and had a payroll of $439 million, while 75,840 retailers had a payroll of $919 million. Approximately 9% of stores sold primarily food, 13% sold cars and automobile services, and one-third were restaurants or bars. Montana's foreign exports in 1998 totaled $421 million, second to last, before Hawaii. Wheat is the leading export item.

31CONSUMER PROTECTION

Montana's consumer protection laws are administered by the Department of Administration's Consumer Protection Division. The office enforces Montana consumer protection laws and regulations relating to the Telemarketing Registration and Fraud Act, New Vehicle Warranty Act, Consumer Protection Act, Personal Solicitation Sales Act, and the Unfair Trade Practices Act.

32BANKING

In 2002, Montana had 84 insured banks, of which 64 were state-chartered. Assets of the insured banks totaled $13.9 billion.

Many of Montana's banks hold high concentrations of agricultural loans. Loan delinquency levels among farm lenders was at a relatively high level in 2002. Construction and development (C and D) lending increased in 2002, largely driven by housing construction. Lower interest rates during 2001 and 2002 caused Montana's banks to report lower earnings performance.

33INSURANCE

In 2001 there were 341,000 ordinary life insurance policies in force with a total value of $24.4 billion; total value for all categories of life insurance (ordinary, group, industrial, and credit) was $36.3 billion. Death benefits paid that year totaled $110.4 million. As of 2000, there were four property and casualty and three life and health insurance companies incorporated or organized in the state. Property and liability insurers wrote premiums of $1.1 billion in 2001. That year, there were 3,065 flood insurance policies in force in the state, with a total value of $314,676.

34SECURITIES

There are no securities exchanges in Montana. There are 192 broker-dealer companies in Montana, with 997 employees. About 24 firms are registered to market advisory services concerning investment in securities. The state headquarters nine NASDAQ-listed companies, one NASDAQ market maker, and incorporated one NYSE company: the Montana Power Company.

35PUBLIC FINANCE

The Montana state budget is prepared biennially by the Office of Budget and Program Planning and submitted by the governor to the legislature for amendment and approval. The fiscal year runs from 1 July to 30 June. Effective fiscal year 1995, certain public school revenues were to be deposited in general fund, increasing general fund revenues and public school appropriations.

Revenues for fiscal year 2003/04 in the general fund were forecast at $1.228 billion. General appropriations included $261.75 million for human services, $104.22 million for corrections, $442.35 million for public schools, $136.69 million for higher education, and $139.81 million for other agencies.

The following table from the US Census Bureau contains information on revenues, expenditures, indebtedness, and cash/securities for 2001.

	($000)	PERCENT	PER CAPITA
Population (thousands, 2001)	905	(X)	(X)
Total Revenue	4,224,359	100.00	4,667.80
General revenue	3,602,354	85.28	3,980.50
Utility revenue	–	–	–
Liquor store revenue	40,878	0.97	45.17
Insurance trust revenue	581,127	13.76	642.13
Exhibit: Salaries and wages	644,896	15.93	712.59
Total expenditure	4,048,049	100.00	4,472.98
General expenditure	3,619,417	89.41	3,999.36
Education	1,205,168	29.77	1,331.68
Public welfare	602,847	14.89	666.13
Hospitals	47,272	1.17	52.23
Health	233,868	5.78	258.42
Highways	427,498	10.56	472.37
Police protection	40,971	1.01	45.27
Correction	106,955	2.64	118.18
Natural resources	218,327	5.39	241.25
Parks and recreation	11,199	0.28	12.37
Government administration	220,802	5.45	243.98
Interest on general debt	146,389	3.62	161.76
Other and unallocable	358,121	8.85	395.71
Utility expenditure	–	–	–
Liquor store expenditure	35,196	0.87	38.89
Insurance trust expenditure	393,436	9.72	434.74
Debt at end of fiscal year	2,739,648	100.00	3,027.24
Cash and security holdings	9,756,638	100.00	10,780.82

36 TAXATION

Montana's 10-bracket personal income tax, which has been indexed to inflation since 1981, ranges from 2% to 11%. The corporate income tax is 6.75% on net income, with a minimum tax of $50; for small business corporations, $10. The rate for corporations filing on a water's-edge-basis (that is, only counting its operations within the boundaries of the US plus a number of tax havens and not its operations other foreign jurisdictions) is 7%. There is no state sales and use tax, but Montana imposes a full array of excise taxes covering motor fuels, tobacco products, insurance premiums, public utilities, alcoholic beverages (the state controls all sales), amusements, pari-mutuels, and other selected items. In 2002, the state tax on gas was raised from $0.27 a gallon to $0.2775¢ a gallon. Montana's estate tax, with a maximum rate of 32%, is tied to the federal exemption for state death taxes, and is therefore set to be phased out in tandem with the phasing out of the federal estate tax credit by 2007, unless the state takes positive action to establish an independent estate tax. Montana's revenue losses from the phasing out of its estate tax are estimated at -$900,000 for 2002/03, -$2.7 million for 2003/04 and -$3.9 million for 2006/07. Death and gift taxes accounted for 0.9% of state collections in 2002. Severance taxes in Montana include a coal severance tax, a metalliferous mines license tax, oil and gas producers' severance tax, a micaceous minerals license tax, a cement license tax and a mineral mining tax. Severance taxes constituted 6.2% of state taxes collected in 2002. Other state taxes include various license fees and a state property tax, although property taxes are also collected at the local level. In Montana's relatively centralized state tax system, 64.5% of all state and local taxes were collected at the state level.

The state collected $1.443 billion in taxes in 2002, of which 35.8% came from individual income taxes, 25.7% from selective sales taxes, 13.8% from license fees, 12.5% from state property taxes, and 3.5% from corporate income taxes. In 2003, Montana ranked 37th among the states in terms of combined state and local tax burden, which amounted to about 9.1% of income.

The following table from the US Census Bureau provides a summary of taxes collected by the state in 2002.

	($000)	PER CAPITA
Total Taxes	1,442,731	1,586.37
Property taxes	181,501	199.57
Sales and gross receipts	370,801	407.72
General sales and gross receipts	(X)	(X)
Selective sales taxes	370,801	407.72
Alcoholic beverage	18,388	20.22
Amusements	43,673	48.02
Insurance Premiums	51,084	56.17
Motor fuels	191,440	210.5
Pari-mutuels	115	0.13
Public utilities	31,251	34.36
Tobacco products	13,281	14.6
Other selective sales	21,569	23.72
Licenses	199,479	219.34
Alcoholic beverages	2,153	2.37
Amusements	3,977	4.37
Corporation	1,692	1.86
Hunting and fishing	33,013	36.3
Motor vehicle	127,164	139.82
Motor vehicle operators	4,343	4.78
Public utility	5	0.01
Occupation and business, NEC	25,991	28.58
Other	1,141	1.25
Other taxes	690,950	759.74
Individual income	517,568	569.1
Corporation net income	68,173	74.96
Death and gift	13,816	15.19
Documentary and stock transfer	(X)	(X)
Severance	88,882	97.73
Other	2,511	2.76

37 ECONOMIC POLICY

The Economic Development Division of the state's Department of Commerce offers a variety of programs aimed at improving and enhancing Montana's economic and business climate. Working closely with other state agencies and federal and private programs, the department's aim is to assist start-up and existing businesses with the technical and financial assistance necessary for their success. Relationships with local development groups, chambers of commerce, and similar organizations help Montana communities develop their full potential. Montana micro-business companies with fewer than 10 full-time equivalent employees and annual gross revenues under $500,000 can receive loans of up to $35,000. Other qualifying businesses can borrow under several other state and federal development loan programs. The Economic Development Division's trade program assists businesses in pursuing domestic and worldwide trade. The Small Business Development Center (SBDC) program and the State Data Center program both operate statewide networks of service centers. In 2003, the state was offering marketing simulations as part of its small business development program. The governor chose to use the discretionary component of federal Workforce Investment Act to continue a program to provide grants of workforce training. The governor also created a new agency, the Montana Economic Development Advisory Agency, to provide the Martz administration with advice concerning economic development matters. At the 2003 Montana Economic Development Summit in May 2003 the main focus was on the creation of quality jobs.

38 HEALTH

The infant mortality rate was 6.1 per 1,000 live births in 2000. In 1999, 2,499 abortions were performed; the abortion rate stood at 14 per 1,000 women. In 2000, the overall death rate was 911.8, well above the national rate of 873.1. Major causes of death (with their rates per 100,000 population) were heart disease,

204.8; cerebrovascular diseases, 65.7; accidents and adverse effects, 55.8 (highest in the nation); motor vehicle accidents, 26.4; and suicide, 17.8. The first rate was below the national norm; the rest were well above national norms. In 2000, 18.9% of the population were smokers. Death from lung disease occurred at a rate of 73 per 100,000 inhabitants in 1997.

Montana has one of the lowest AIDS rates per 100,000 population in the country. As of 2001, there had been only 341 AIDS cases reported.

Montana's 53 community hospitals had 103,346 admissions and 4,463 beds in 2001. There were 2,989 full-time registered nurses and 666 full-time licensed practical nurses in 2001 and 236 physicians per 100,000 population in 2000. The average expense of a community hospital for care was $1,345.10 per inpatient day in 2001.

Federal government grants to cover the Medicare and Medicaid services in 2001 totaled $414 million; 138,266 enrollees received Medicare benefits that year. At least 13.6% of Montana's residents were uninsured in 2002.

39SOCIAL WELFARE

Montana played an important role in the development of social welfare. It was one of the first states to experiment with workers' compensation, enacting a compulsory compensation law in 1915. Eight years later, Montana and Nevada became the first states to provide for old age pensions.

In 2001, the average weekly unemployment benefit was $166.44. Average monthly participation in the food stamp program in FY2002 comprised 63,347 persons (26,865 households). The average monthly benefit was $76.19, and the sum total of benefits paid in FY2002 was $57,920,257.

With the enactment of the Personal Responsibility and Work Opportunity Reconciliation Act of 1996, the US government has changed the form and regulations for many of its social welfare programs. Most significantly, it replaces Aid to Families with Dependent Children (AFDC), an open-ended entitlement program, with Temporary Assistance for Needy Families (TANF), a limited system of assistance funded largely through federal block grants. The reform act also impacts the food stamp program, the Supplemental Security Income program, and the child nutrition program. The law took effect on 1 July 1997 and provided $16.38 billion in block grants for fiscal years 1997–2002. The grants are to be divided among the states based on an equation involving the numbers of former AFDC recipients in each state.

Reauthorization of the 1996 social welfare legislation, scheduled for 2002, was delayed, and the original law had been extended three times as of July 2003, with the most recent extension running through September 2003. Montana's TANF program is called Families Achieving Independence in Montana (FAIM). In June 2000 the state had 14,001 welfare recipients. State expenditures on the TANF program in FY2002 totaled $14,700,643.

In December 2001, Social Security benefits were paid to 159,180 Montana residents. This number included 100,010 retired workers, 17,690 widows and widowers, 17,490 disabled workers, 11,460 spouses, and 12,530 children. Social Security beneficiaries represented 17.6% of the total state population and 94% of the state's population age 65 and older. Retired workers (excluding persons with special benefits) received an average monthly payment of $845; widows and widowers, $812; disabled workers, $800; and spouses, $424. Payments for children of retired workers averaged $386 per month; children of deceased workers, $556; and children of disabled workers, $229.

Federal Supplemental Security Income payments in December 2001 went to 14,206 Montana residents, averaging $350 a month.

40HOUSING

In 2002, Montana had an estimated 417,106 housing units, of which 357,296 were occupied; 70.2% were owner-occupied. About 68.9% of all units were single-family, detached homes; about 13% were mobile homes. Utility gas and electricity were the most common energy sources for heating. It was estimated that 11,057 units lacked telephone service, 2,653 lacked complete plumbing facilities, and 2,577 lacked complete kitchen facilities. The average household size was 2.48 people.

In 2002, 35,74 new privately owned units were authorized for construction. The median home value was $106,735. The median monthly cost for mortgage owners was $908. Renters paid a median of $478 per month. During 2002, Montana received over $16.7 million in community planning and development aid from the US Department of Housing and Urban Development.

41EDUCATION

In 2000, 87.2% of Montana residents age 25 and older were high school graduates; 24.4% (exactly the national average) had obtained a bachelor's degree or higher.

The total enrollment for fall 1999 in Montana's public schools stood at 157,556. Of these, 107,490 attended schools from kindergarten through grade eight, and 50,066 attended high school. Minority students made up approximately 14% of the total enrollment in public elementary and secondary schools in 2001. Total enrollment was estimated at 155,860 fall 2000 and expected to reach 164,000 by fall 2005. Enrollment in nonpublic schools in fall 2001 was 8,711. Expenditures for public education in 2000/01 were estimated at $995,900.

As of fall 2000, there were 51,255 students enrolled in college or graduate school. In the same year Montana had 24 degree-granting institutions. In 1997, minority students comprised 11.5% of total postsecondary enrollment. The University of Montana has campuses at Missoula, Montana Tech, and Western Montana College. Montana State University encompasses the Bozeman, Billings, and Northern campuses.

42ARTS

The C. M. Russell Museum in Great Falls honors the work of Charles Russell, whose mural *Lewis and Clark Meeting the Flathead Indians* adorns the capitol in Helena. Other fine art museums include the Museum of the Rockies in Bozeman, Yellowstone Art Center at Billings, and the Missoula Museum of the Arts. Orchestras are based in Billings and Bozeman. The Equinox Theater Company is also a popular attraction in Bozeman.

In 2003, the Montana Arts Council and other Montana arts organizations received grants totaling $782,600 from the National Endowment for the Arts (NEA). The Council has also received funding from state and private sources. Montana has an estimated 500 arts associations and 20 local arts groups. The Montana Arts Council assists the Missoula Museum of the Arts and the Judith Cultural Committee.

The Montana Committee for the Humanities (MCH) was founded in 1972. In 2000, the MCH sponsored its first annual Montana Festival of the Book in downtown Missoula, bringing together writers, readers, and entertainers from across the state. In 2000, the National Endowment for the Humanities contributed $558,952 to 12 state programs.

43LIBRARIES AND MUSEUMS

Montana has 79 public libraries, 28 public library branches, 6 institutional libraries, 52 special libraries, and 573 school libraries serving 56 counties. The combined book stock of all Montana public libraries is 2,638,000, and their combined circulation is 4,819,000. Distinguished collections include those of the University of Montana (Missoula), with over 850,000 volumes; Montana State University (Bozeman), 597,609; and the Montana State Library and Montana Historical Society Library, both in Helena. Total public library income for 2000 was $16,021,000, including $112,147 in federal grants and $336,441 in state grants.

Among the state's 74 museums are the Montana Historical Society Museum, Helena; World Museum of Mining, Butte; Western Heritage Center, Billings; and Museum of the Plains Indian, Browning. National historic sites include Big Hole and Little Big Horn battlefields and the Grant-Kohrs Ranch at Deer Lodge, west of Helena.

44COMMUNICATIONS

In 2001, 95.3% of the state's households had telephone service. There were 43 major commercial radio stations (14 AM, 29 FM) in 2003, and 16 major television stations. During the same year, Billings Tele-Communications, Inc. was the major provider of cable television service. A total of 15,300 Internet domain names were registered in Montana in 2000.

45PRESS

As of 2002, Montana had eight morning dailies, three evening dailies, and seven Sunday newspapers. The leading papers were the *Billings Gazette* (46,802 mornings, 53,166 Sundays), *Great Falls Tribune* (33,499 mornings, 38,541 Sundays), and the *Missoulian* (29,787 mornings, 36,728 Sundays).

46ORGANIZATIONS

In 2003, there were about 863 regional, national, and international organizations within the state. Among the organizations headquartered in Montana are the American Simmental Association (Bozeman) and Bikecentennial: The Bicycle Travel Association (Missoula).

Regional arts, history, and culture are represented in part through the Boone and Crockett Club, the Butte Jazz Society, the Custer Battlefield Historical and Museum Association, and the Lewis and Clark Trail Heritage Foundation. Conservation and outdoors recreation organizations include the Greater Yellowstone Coalition, Montana Outfitters and Guides Association, the National Forest Foundation, and the Yellowstone Park Foundation.

The Indian Law Resource Center, founded in 1978 and based in Helena, serves as a legal, environmental, and human rights organization promoting the welfare of Indian tribes and other indigenous peoples in North America.

47TOURISM, TRAVEL, AND RECREATION

Many tourists seek out the former gold rush camps, ghost towns, and dude ranches. Scenic wonders include all of Glacier National Park, covering 1,013,595 acres (410,202 hectares), which is the US portion of Waterton-Glacier International Peace Park; part of Yellowstone National Park, which also extends into Idaho and Wyoming; and Bighorn Canyon National Recreation Area.

In 2002, about 10 million nonresident travelers spent $1.8 billion dollars on visits to the state. The tourist industry sponsors over 33,500 jobs for the state. Tourism promotion and development are funded primarily through a 4% lodging tax, which generates about $11 million dollars per year.

48SPORTS

There are no major league professional sports teams in Montana, although there is minor league baseball in Billings, Butte, and Missoula. The University of Montana Grizzlies and Montana State University Bobcats both compete in the Big Sky Conference. Skiing is a very popular participation sport. The state has world-class ski resorts in Big Sky. Other annual sporting events include the Seeley-Lincoln 100/200 Dog Sled Race between Seely Lake and Lincoln in January and many rodeos statewide.

49FAMOUS MONTANANS

Prominent national officeholders from Montana include US Senator Thomas Walsh (b.Wisconsin, 1859–1933), who directed the investigation that uncovered the Teapot Dome scandal; Jeannette Rankin (1880–1973), the first woman member of Congress and the only US representative to vote against American participation in both world wars; Burton K. Wheeler (b.Mass., 1882–1975), US senator from 1923 to 1947 and one of the most powerful politicians in Montana history; and Michael Joseph "Mike" Mansfield (b.New York, 1903–2001), who held the office of majority leader of the US Senate longer than anyone else.

Chief Joseph (b.Oregon, 1840?–1904), a Nez Percé Indian, repeatedly outwitted the US Army during the late 1870s; Crazy Horse (1849?–77) led a Sioux-Cheyenne army in battle at Little Big Horn. The town of Bozeman is named for explorer and prospector John M. Bozeman (b.Georgia, 1835–67).

Creative artists from Montana include Alfred Bertram Guthrie, Jr. (b.Indiana, 1901–91), author of *The Big Sky* and the Pulitzer Prize-winning *The Way West*; Dorothy Johnson (b.Iowa, 1905–84), whose stories have been made into such notable Western movies as *The Hanging Tree*, *The Man Who Shot Liberty Valance*, and *A Man Called Horse*; and Charles Russell (b.Missouri, 1864–1926), Montana's foremost painter and sculptor. Hollywood stars Gary Cooper (Frank James Cooper, 1901–61) and Myrna Loy (1905–93) were born in Helena. Newscaster Chet Huntley (1911–74) was born in Cardwell.

50BIBLIOGRAPHY

Dougherty, Michael. *The Ultimate Montana Atlas and Travel Encyclopedia*. Bozeman, Mont.: Ultimate Press, 2001.

Farr, William, and K. Ross Toole. *Montana: Images of the Past*. Boulder, Colo.: Pruett, 1984.

Federal Writer's Project. *Montana: A State Guide Book*. Reprint. New York: Somerset, n.d. (orig. 1939).

Malone, Michael P., and Richard B. Roeder. *Montana: A History of Two Centuries*. Rev. ed. Seattle: University of Washington Press, 1991.

Rowles, Genevieve, ed. *Adventure Guide to Montana*. Edison, N.J.: Hunter, 2000.

Sateren, Shelley Swanson. *Montana Facts and Symbols*. Mankato, Minn.: Hilltop Books, 2000.

Schrems, Suzanne H. *Uncommon Women, Unmarked Trails: The Courageous Journey of Catholic Missionary Sisters in Frontier Montana*. Norman, Okla.: Horse Creek Publications, 2003.

Small, Lawrence F., ed. *Religion in Montana: Pathways to the Present*. Billings, Mont.: Rocky Mountain College, 1992.

Spence, Clark C. *Montana: A Bicentennial History*. New York: Norton, 1978.

Toole, Kenneth R. *Montana: An Uncommon Land*. Norman: University of Oklahoma Press, 1984.

———. *Twentieth-Century Montana: A State of Extremes*. Norman: University of Oklahoma Press, 1983.

Wright, John B. *Montana Ghost Dance: Essays on Land and Life*. Austin: University of Texas Press, 1998.

NEBRASKA

State of Nebraska

ORIGIN OF STATE NAME: From the Oto Indian word *nebrathka*, meaning "flat water" (for the Platte River). **NICKNAME:** The Cornhusker State. **CAPITAL:** Lincoln. **ENTERED UNION:** 1 March 1867 (37th). **SONG:** "Beautiful Nebraska." **MOTTO:** Equality Before the Law. **FLAG:** The great seal appears in the center in gold and silver on a field of blue. **OFFICIAL SEAL:** Agriculture is represented by a farmer's cabin, sheaves of wheat, and growing corn; the mechanic arts by a blacksmith. Above is the state motto; in the background, a steamboat plies the Missouri River and a train heads toward the Rockies. The scene is surrounded by the words "Great Seal of the State of Nebraska, March 1st 1867." **BIRD:** Western meadowlark. **INSECT:** Honeybee. **FLOWER:** Goldenrod. **TREE:** Western cottonwood. **GRASS:** Little bluestem. **GEM:** Blue agate. **ROCK:** Prairie agate. **FOSSIL:** Mammoth. **LEGAL HOLIDAYS:** New Year's Day, 1 January; Birthday of Martin Luther King, Jr., 3rd Monday in January; Presidents' Day, 3rd Monday in February; Arbor Day, 22 April; Memorial Day, last Monday in May; Independence Day, 4 July; Labor Day, 1st Monday in September; Columbus Day, 2nd Monday in October; Veterans Day, 11 November; Thanksgiving, 4th Thursday in November and following Friday; Christmas Day, 25 December. **TIME:** 6 AM CST = noon GMT; 5 AM MST = noon GMT.

¹LOCATION, SIZE, AND EXTENT

Located in the western north-central US, Nebraska ranks 15th in size among the 50 states. The total area of the state is 77,355 sq mi (200,349 sq km), of which land takes up 76,644 sq mi (198,508 sq km) and inland water 711 sq mi (1,841 sq km). Nebraska extends about 415 mi (668 km) E-W and 205 mi (330 km) N-S.

Nebraska is bordered on the N by South Dakota (with the line formed in part by the Missouri River); on the E by Iowa and Missouri (the line being defined by the Missouri River); on the S by Kansas and Colorado; and on the W by Colorado and Wyoming. The boundary length of Nebraska totals 1,332 mi (2,143 km). The state's geographic center is in Custer County, 10 mi (16 km) NW of Broken Bow.

²TOPOGRAPHY

Most of Nebraska is prairie; more than two-thirds of the state lies within the Great Plains proper. The elevation slopes upward gradually from east to west, from a low of 840 ft (256 m) in the southeast to 5,424 ft (1,654 m) in Kimball County. Rolling alluvial lowlands in the eastern portion of the state give way to the flat, treeless plain of central Nebraska, which in turn rises to a tableland in the west. The Sand Hills of the north-central plain is an unusual region of sand dunes anchored by grasses that cover about 18,000 sq mi (47,000 sq km).

The Sand Hills region is dotted with small natural lakes; in the rest of the state, the main lakes are artificial. The Missouri River—which, with its tributaries, drains the entire state—forms the eastern part of the northern boundary of Nebraska. Three rivers cross the state from west to east: the wide, shallow Platte River flows through the heart of the state for 310 mi (499 km); the Niobrara River traverses the state's northern region; and the Republican River flows through southern Nebraska.

³CLIMATE

Nebraska has a continental climate, with highly variable temperatures from season to season and year to year. The central region has an average annual normal temperature of 50°F (10°C), with a normal monthly maximum of 76°F (24°C) in July and a normal monthly minimum of 22°F (–6°C) in January. The record low for the state is –47°F (–44°C), registered in Morrill County on 12 February 1899; the record high of 118°F (48°C) was recorded at Minden on 24 July 1936.

Average yearly precipitation (1971–2000) in Omaha was 30 in (76 cm); in the semiarid panhandle in the west, 17 in (43 cm); and in the southeast, 30 in (76 cm). Snowfall in the state varies from about 21 in (53 cm) in the southeast to about 45 in (114 cm) in the northwest corner. Blizzards, droughts, and windstorms have plagued Nebraskans throughout their history.

⁴FLORA AND FAUNA

Nebraska's deciduous forests are generally oak and hickory; conifer forests are dominated by western yellow (ponderosa) pine. The tallgrass prairie may include various slough grasses and needlegrasses, along with big bluestem and prairie dropseed. Mixed prairie regions abound with western wheatgrass and buffalo grass. The prairie region of the Sand Hills supports a variety of bluestems, gramas, and other grasses. Common Nebraska wild flowers are wild rose, phlox, petunia, columbine, goldenrod, and sunflower. Rare species of Nebraska's flora include the Hayden penstemon, yellow ladyslipper, pawpaw, and snow trillium. Three species were threatened as of 2003, Ute ladies'-tresses, western prairie fringed orchid, and Colorado butterfly plant; blowout penstemon was listed as endangered that year.

Common mammals native to the state are the pronghorn sheep, white-tailed and mule deer, badger, kit fox, coyote, striped ground squirrel, prairie vole, and several skunk species. There are more than 400 kinds of birds, the mourning dove, barn swallow, and western meadowlark (the state bird) among them. Carp, catfish, trout, and perch are fished for sport. Rare animal species include the least shrew, least weasel, and bobcat. The US Fish and Wildlife Service listed nine animal species as threatened or endangered in 2003, including the American burying beetle, bald eagle, whooping crane, black-footed ferret, Topeka shiner, pallid sturgeon, and Eskimo curlew.

5ENVIRONMENTAL PROTECTION

The Department of Environmental Quality was established in 1971 to protect and improve the quality of the state's water, air, and land resources. The Agricultural Pollution Control Division of the Department regulates disposal of feedlot wastes and other sources of water pollution by agriculture. The Water and Waste Management Division is responsible for administering the Federal Clean Water Act, the Federal Resources Conservation and Recovery Act, portions of the Federal Safe Drinking Water Act, and the Nebraska Environmental Protection Act as it relates to water, solid waste, and hazardous materials. In 2003, Nebraska had 255 hazardous waste sites listed in the Environmental Protection Agency's database, 11 of which were on the National Priorities List.

A program to protect groundwater from such pollutants as nitrates, synthetic organic compounds, hydrocarbons, pesticides, and other sources, was outlined in 1985. In 1996, the state spent $3.2 million on its Soil and Water Conservation Program. In 1994, the state imposed a tax on commercial fertilizers to create the Natural Resources Enhancement Fund, which distributes funds to local natural resource districts for water quality improvement programs. The Engineering Division regulates wastewater treatment standards and assists municipalities in securing federal construction grants for wastewater facilities. The Air Quality Division is responsible for monitoring and securing compliance with national ambient air quality standards.

The state has three wetlands of international importance as migrational and breeding grounds for waterfowl and nongame birds. While these areas are protected, the state has lost about 1 million acres (405,000 hectares) of wetlands since pre-European settlement times. In 2001, Nebraska received $35,617,000 in federal grants from the Environmental Protection Agency; EPA expenditures for procurement contracts in Nebraska that year amounted to $55,000.

6POPULATION

Nebraska ranked 38th in population in the US with an estimated total of 1,729,180 in 2002, an increase of 1% since 2000. Between 1990 and 2000, Nebraska's population grew from 1,578,385 to 1,711,263, an increase of 8.4%. The population was projected to reach 1,761,000 by 2005 and 1.9 million by 2025. The population density in 2000 was 22.3 persons per sq mi.

In 2000, the median age of all Nebraskans was 35.3. In the same year, 26.3% of the populace were under age 18 while 13.6% were age 65 or older. The largest cities in 2002 were Omaha, which ranked 43rd among the nation's cities, with an estimated population of 399,357, and Lincoln, with 232,362.

7ETHNIC GROUPS

Among Nebraskans reporting at least one specific ancestry in the 2000 census, 661,133 identified their ancestry as German, 163,651 as English, 229,805 as Irish, 93,286 as Czech, and 84,294 as Swedish. The 2000 population also included 68,541 black Americans, 21,931 Asians, and 836 Pacific Islanders. There were 94,425 Hispanics and Latinos in 2000, representing 5.5% of the total population. Foreign-born residents numbered 74,638, or 4.4% of the total population, in 2000.

There were 14,896 American Indians in Nebraska as of 2000, down from around 16,000 in 1990. The three Indian reservations maintained for the Omaha, Winnebago, and Santee Sioux tribes had the following populations as of 2000: Omaha, 5,194, and Winnebago, 2,588, and Santee Sioux, 603.

8LANGUAGES

Many Plains Indians of the Macro-Siouan family once roamed widely over what is now Nebraska. Place-names derived from the Siouan language include Omaha, Ogallala, Niobrara, and Keya Paha. In 1990, about 1,300 Nebraskans claimed Indian tongues as their first languages.

Nebraska English, except for a slight South Midland influence in the southwest and some Northern influence from Wisconsin and New York settlers in the Platte River Valley, is almost pure North Midland. A few words, mostly food terms like *kolaches* (fruit-filled pastries), are derived from the language of the large Czech population. Usual pronunciation features are *on* and *hog* with the /o/ or *order, cow*, and *now* as /kaow/ and /naow/, because with the /ah/ vowel, *cot* and *caught* as sound-alikes, and a strong final /r/. *Fire* sounds almost like *far*, and *our* like *are*; *greasy* is pronounced /greezy/.

In 2000, 1, 469,046 Nebraskans—92.1% of the resident population five years old or older—spoke only English at home, down from 95.2% in 1990.

The following table gives selected statistics from the 2000 census for language spoken at home by persons five years old and over. The category "Other Slavic languages" includes Czech, Slovak, and Ukrainian. The category "African languages" includes Amharic, Ibo, Twi, Yoruba, Bantu, Swahili, and Somali.

LANGUAGE	NUMBER	PERCENT
Population 5 years and over	**1,594,700**	**100.0**
Speak only English	1,469,046	92.1
Speak a language other than English	125,654	7.9
Speak a language other than English	**125,654**	**7.9**
Spanish or Spanish Creole	77,655	4.9
German	8,865	0.6
Vietnamese	5,958	0.4
Other Slavic languages	4,236	0.3
French (incl. Patois, Cajun)	3,631	0.2
Chinese	2,409	0.2
Arabic	1,628	0.1
Russian	1,559	0.1
African languages	1,472	0.1
Polish	1,420	0.1
Italian	1,419	0.1
Tagalog	1,311	0.1
Japanese	1,274	0.1

9RELIGIONS

Nebraska's religious history derives from its patterns of immigration. German and Scandinavian settlers tended to be Lutheran; Irish, Polish, and Czech immigrants were mainly Roman Catholic. Methodism and other Protestant religions were spread by settlers from other Midwestern states.

Though Protestants collectively outnumber Catholics, the Roman Catholic Church is the largest single Christian denomination within the state with about 372,791 adherents. Lutherans constituted the largest Protestant group with 117,419 adherents of the Missouri Synod, 128,570 of the Evangelical Lutheran Church in America, and 5,829 of the Wisconsin Evangelical Lutheran Synod. A total of 117,277 people were United Methodists and 39,420 were Presbyterians–USA. The Jewish population was estimated at 7,100 in 2000 and Muslims numbered about 3,115. There were 704,403 people (about 41% of the population) who were not counted as members of any religious organization.

10TRANSPORTATION

Nebraska's development was profoundly influenced by two major railroads, the Union Pacific and the Burlington Northern, both of which were major landowners in the state in the late 1800s. As of 2000, these lines still operated in Nebraska, Burlington Northern combined with Santa Fe Railway. Altogether, there were 12 lines with 3,614 rail mi (5,816 km) of track in the state in 2000. Railroad freight traffic increased from 74,770,000 tons in 1970, to 168,463,000 tons in 1981, to

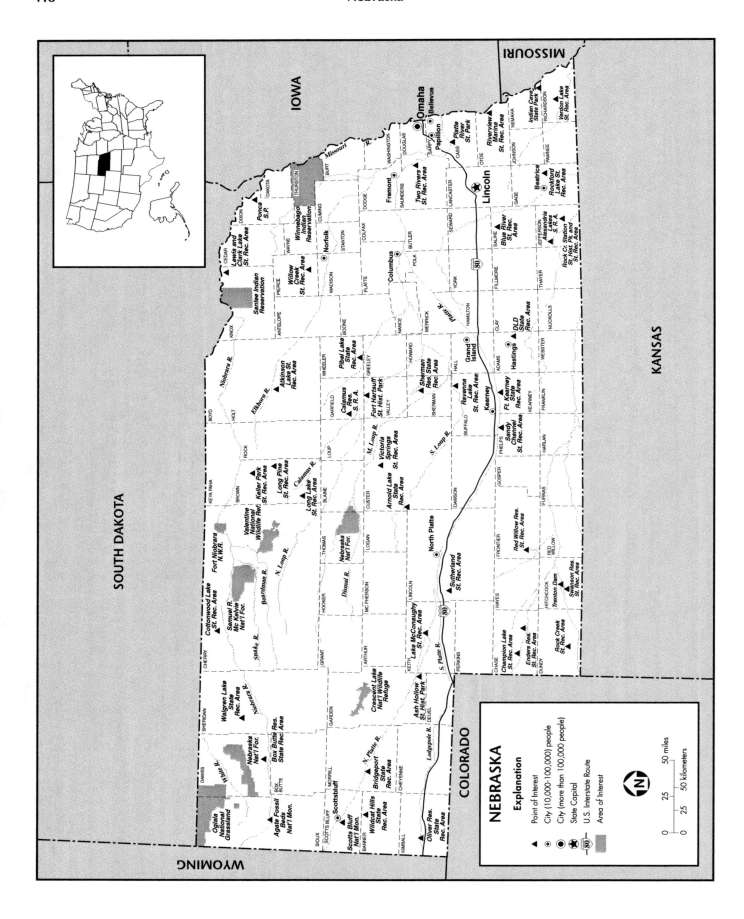

NEBRASKA

Explanation

▲ Point of Interest
⊙ City (10,000-100,000) people)
◉ City (more than 100,000 people)
✪ State Capital
80 U.S. Interstate Route
▨ Area of Interest

0   25   50 miles
0   25   50 kilometers

321,674,989 tons in 1995, to 388,733,750 tons in 1998. The state originated 16,085,629 rail tons of farm products in 2000, which accounted for 66% of all rail tonnage originating within Nebraska that year.

The state's road system, estimated at 92,791 mi (149,332 km) in 2000, is dominated by Interstate 80, the major east–west route and the largest public investment project in the state's history. A total of 2,464,571 motor vehicles were registered in 2000, of which 852,481 were automobiles and 760,420 trucks. About 1,195,219 people held driver's licenses in the same year.

There were 180 private and 87 public airports in the state in 2002. Eppley Airfield, Omaha's airport, is by far the busiest in the state, with 1,861,057 passengers enplaned in 2000.

11 HISTORY

Nebraska's first inhabitants, from about 10,000 BC, were nomadic Paleo-Indians. Successive groups were more sedentary, cultivating corn and beans. Archaeological excavations indicate that prolonged drought and dust storms before the 16th century caused these inhabitants to vacate the area. In the 16th and 17th centuries, other Indian tribes came from the East, some pushed by enemy tribes, others seeking new hunting grounds. By 1800, semisedentary Pawnee, Ponca, Omaha, and Oto, along with several nomadic groups, were in the region.

The Indians developed amiable relations with the first white explorers, French and Spanish fur trappers and traders who traveled through Nebraska in the 18th century, using the Missouri River as a route to the West. The area was claimed by both Spain and France and was French territory at the time of the Louisiana Purchase, when it came under US jurisdiction. It was explored during the first half of the 19th century by Lewis and Clark, Zebulon Pike, Stephen H. Long, and John C. Frémont.

The Indian Intercourse Act of 1834 forbade white settlement west of the Mississippi River, reserving the Great Plains as Indian Territory. Nothing prevented whites from traversing Nebraska, however, and from 1840 to 1866, some 350,000 persons crossed the area on the Oregon, California, and Mormon trails, following the Platte River Valley, a natural highway to the West. Military forts were established in the 1840s to protect travelers from Indian attack.

The Kansas-Nebraska Act of 1854 established Nebraska Territory, which stretched from Kansas to Canada and from the Missouri River to the Rockies. The territory assumed its present shape in 1861. Still sparsely populated, Nebraska escaped the violence over the slavery issue that afflicted Kansas. The creation of Nebraska Territory heightened conflict between Indians and white settlers, however, as Indians were forced to cede more and more of their land. From mid-1860 to the late 1870s, western Nebraska was a battleground for Indians and US soldiers. By 1890, the Indians were defeated and moved onto reservations in Nebraska, South Dakota, and Oklahoma.

Settlement of Nebraska Territory was rapid, accelerated by the Homestead Act of 1862, under which the US government provided 160 acres (65 hectares) to a settler for a nominal fee, and the construction of the Union Pacific, the first transcontinental railroad. The Burlington Railroad, which came to Nebraska in the late 1860s, used its vast land grants from Congress to promote immigration, selling the land to potential settlers from the East and from Europe. The end of the Civil War brought an influx of Union veterans, bolstering the Republican administration, which began pushing for statehood. On 1 March 1867, Nebraska became the 37th state to join the Union. Farming and ranching developed as the state's two main enterprises. Facing for the first time the harsh elements of the Great Plains, homesteaders in central and western Nebraska evolved what came to be known as the sod-house culture, using grassy soil to construct sturdy insulated homes. They harnessed the wind with windmills to pump water, constructed fences of barbed wire, and developed dry-land farming techniques.

Ranching existed in Nebraska as early as 1859, and by the 1870s, it was well established in the western part of the state. Some foreign investors controlled hundreds of thousands of acres of the free range. The cruel winter of 1886–87 killed thousands of cattle and bankrupted many of these large ranches.

By 1890, depressed farm prices, high railroad shipping charges, and rising interest rates were hurting the state's farmers, and a drought in the 1890s exacerbated their plight. These problems contributed to the rise of populism, a pro-agrian movement. Many Nebraska legislators embraced populism, helping to bring about the first initiative and referendum laws in the US, providing for the regulation of stockyards and telephone and telegraph companies and instituting compulsory education.

World War I created a rift among Nebraskans as excessive patriotic zeal was directed against residents of German descent. German-language newspapers were censored, ministers were ordered to preach only in English (often to congregations that understood only German), and three university professors of German origin were fired. A Nebraska law (1919) that prohibited the teaching of any foreign language until high school was later declared unconstitutional by the US Supreme Court.

Tilling of marginal land to take advantage of farm prices that had been inflated during World War I caused economic distress during the 1920s. Nebraska's farm economy was already in peril when the dust storms of the 1930s began, and conditions worsened as drought, heat, and grasshopper invasions plagued the state. Thousands of people, particularly from the southwest counties in which dust-bowl conditions were most severe, fled Nebraska for the west coast. Some farmers joined protest movements—dumping milk, for example, rather than selling at depressed prices—while others marched on the state capital to demand a moratorium on farm debts, which they received. In the end, federal aid saved the farmers.

The onset of World War II brought prosperity to other sectors. Military airfields and war industries were placed in the state because of its safe inland location, bringing industrial growth that extended into the postwar years. Much of the new industry that developed during the postwar era was agriculture-related, including the manufacture of mechanized implements and irrigation equipment.

Farm output and income increased dramatically into the 1970s through wider use of hybrid seed, pesticides, fungicides, chemical fertilizers, close-row planting, and irrigation, but contaminated runoff adversely affected water quality and greater water use drastically lowered water-table levels. Many farmers took on large debt burdens to finance expanded output, their credit buoyed by strong farm-product prices and exports. When prices began to fall in the early 1980s, many found themselves overextended. By spring 1985, an estimated 10% of all farmers were reportedly close to bankruptcy. In the early 1990s farm prices rose; the average farm income in Nebraska rose more than 10% between 1989 and the mid-1990s. Increasingly, the state had fewer, larger, and more-mechanized farms. The growth of small industries and tourism also bolstered Nebraska's economy in the 1990s. By 1999 the state enjoyed one of the lowest unemployment rates in the nation—2.9%. But farmers were struggling again; by June 2000, areas of the state had had no substantial rain in a year. The previous autumn and winter were the driest on record. Drought conditions prevailed. Even with mitigation efforts, much of the state's corn crop was lost.

A wildfire in the Sandhills of Nebraska's panhandle in 1999 scorched 74,840 acres and claimed 25,000 trees; it was the largest fire in the state's history.

Challenges facing the state include a loss of population in rural areas, urban decay, and tension among various ethnic groups. In

1998 there were more Hispanics, accounting for 4.4% of the population, in the state than there were African Americans; Nebraska also has a small Native American population. Water conservation to avoid depletion of the state's aquifers for irrigation purposes remains a major priority. In 2003, the state legislature was considering the legalization of up to eight gambling casinos, a raise in the minimum wage, tax incentives, and a concealed-weapon law. Governor Mike Johanns urged lawmakers not to raise income or sales taxes, and to cut state agencies by 10%. Nebraska was facing its worst recession since the 1980s in 2003, along with severe drought.

12 STATE GOVERNMENT

The first state constitution was adopted in 1866; a second, adopted in 1875, is still in effect. A 1919–20 constitutional convention proposed—and voters passed—41 amendments; by January 2003, the document had been revised an additional 219 times.

Nebraska's legislature is unique among the states; since 1934, it has been a unicameral body of 49 members elected on a nonpartisan basis. Members, who go by the title of senator, are chosen in even-numbered years for four-year terms. Legislative sessions begin in early January each year and are limited to 90 legislative days in odd-numbered years and to 60 legislative days in even-numbered years. Sessions may be extended by a four-fifths vote of members. Special sessions, not formally limited in duration, may be called by petition of two-thirds of the legislators. Legislators must be qualified voters, at least 21 years old, and should have lived in their district for a year prior to election. The legislative salary was $12,000 in 2002, unchanged from 1999.

Elected executives are the governor, lieutenant governor, secretary of state, auditor, treasurer, and attorney general, all of whom serve four-year terms. The governor and lieutenant governor are jointly elected; each must be a US citizen for at least five years, at least 30 years old, and have been a resident and citizen of Nebraska for at least five years. After serving two consecutive terms, the governor is ineligible for the office for four years. In 2002 the governor's salary was $65,000, unchanged from 1999.

A bill becomes law when passed by a majority of the legislature and signed by the governor. If the governor does not approve, the bill is returned with objections, and a three-fifths vote of the members of the legislature is required to override the veto. A bill automatically becomes law if the governor does not take action within five days of receiving it.

A three-fifths majority of the legislature is required to propose an amendment to the state constitution. The people may propose an amendment by presenting a petition signed by 10% of total votes for governor at last election. The amendments are then submitted for approval at the next regular election or at a special election that can be called by a four-fifths vote of the legislature.

Voters in Nebraska must be US citizens, at least 18 years old, and state residents. Restrictions apply to convicted felons and those officially found mentally incompetent.

13 POLITICAL PARTIES

In the 2000 presidential elections, Republican candidate George W. Bush secured 63% of the vote; Democrat Al Gore, 33%; and Green Party candidate Ralph Nader, 3%. In 2002 there were 1,083,544 registered voters. In 1998, 37% of registered voters were Democratic, 49% Republican, and 14% unaffiliated or members of other parties. The state had five electoral votes in the 2000 presidential election.

In the 2000 elections, Democrat Ben Nelson was elected to the Senate; Republican Chuck Hagel won election to the Senate in 1996 and was reelected in 2002. In 1998 Republican Mike

Johanns was elected to succeed Nelson as governor; Johanns was reelected in 2002. Republicans won all three of the state's seats in the US House of Representatives in 1994, 1996, 1998, 2000, and 2002. Nebraska's unicameral state legislature is nonpartisan.

Nebraska Presidential Vote by Major Political Parties, 1948–2000

YEAR	ELECTORAL VOTE	NEBRASKA WINNER	DEMOCRAT	REPUBLICAN
1948	6	Dewey (R)	224,165	264,774
1952	6	*Eisenhower (R)	188,057	421,603
1956	6	*Eisenhower (R)	199,029	378,108
1960	6	Nixon (R)	232,542	380,553
1964	5	*Johnson (D)	307,307	276,847
1968	5	*Nixon (R)	170,784	321,163
1972	5	*Nixon (R)	169,991	406,298
1976	5	Ford (R)	233,692	359,705
1980	5	*Reagan (R)	166,424	419,214
1984	5	*Reagan (R)	187,866	460,054
1988	5	*Bush (R)	259,235	397,956
1992**	5	Bush (R)	217,344	344,346
1996**	5	Dole (R)	236,761	363,467
2000	5	*Bush, G. W. (R)	231,780	433,862

* Won US presidential election.
** Independent candidate Ross Perot received 174,687 votes in 1992 and 71,278 votes in 1996.

14 LOCAL GOVERNMENT

In 2002, Nebraska had 93 counties, 446 townships, 531 municipalities, and 575 public school districts. Some 1,146 special districts covered such services as fire protection, housing, irrigation, and sewage treatment. Boards of supervisors or commissioners, elected by voters, administer at the county level. Municipalities are generally governed by mayor (or city manager) and council. Villages elect trustees to governing boards.

15 STATE SERVICES

To address the continuing threat of terrorism and to work with the federal Department of Homeland Security (created in 2002 following the terrorist attacks of 11 September 2001), homeland security in Nebraska in 2003 operated under the authority of the governor; the lieutenant governor was designated as the state homeland security advisor.

As of 1 June 1971, the Office of Public Counsel (Ombudsman) was empowered to investigate complaints from citizens in relation to the state government. The Accountability and Disclosure Commission, established in 1977, regulates the organization and financing of political campaigns and investigates reports of conflicts of interest involving state officials.

The eight-member state Board of Education, elected on a nonpartisan basis, oversees elementary and secondary public schools and vocational education. The Board of Regents, which also consists of eight elected members, governs the University of Nebraska system. Special examining boards license architects, engineers, psychologists, and land surveyors. The Coordinating Commission for Postsecondary Education works to develop a statewide plan for an educationally and economically sound, progressive, and coordinated system of postsecondary education.

The Department of Roads maintains and builds highways, and the Department of Aeronautics regulates aviation, licenses airports, and registers aviators. The Department of Motor Vehicles provides vehicle and driver services. Natural resources are protected by the Forest Service, Energy Office, Game and Parks Commission, and the Natural Resources Commission.

Public assistance, child welfare, medical care for the indigent, and a special program of services for children with disabilities are the responsibility of the Health and Human Service System, which also operates community health services, provides nutritional services, and is responsible for disease control.

The state's huge agricultural industry is aided and monitored by the Department of Agriculture, which is empowered to protect livestock, inspect food-processing areas, conduct research into crop development, and encourage product marketing. The Corn Development, Utilization and Marketing Board works to enhance the profitability of the corn producer.

16JUDICIAL SYSTEM

The state's highest court is the supreme court, consisting of a chief justice and six other justices, all of whom are initially appointed by the governor. They must be elected after serving three years, and every six years thereafter, running unopposed on their own record. Below the supreme court are the district courts; 53 judges serve 21 districts in the state. These are trial courts of general jurisdiction. County courts handle criminal misdemeanors and civil cases involving less than $5,000. In addition, there are a court of industrial relations, a worker's compensation court, two conciliation courts (family courts), two municipal courts (in Omaha and Lincoln), and juvenile courts in three counties.

In June 2001, prison inmates in state and federal prisons numbered 3,944, an increase of 7.7% over the previous year. The state's incarceration rate stood at 225 per 100,000 inhabitants. Seven persons were executed between 1930 and 1997, three of whom were put to death between 1977 and 2003; seven were under sentence of death in 2003. In 2001, Nebraska had a total crime rate of 4,329.6 per 100,000, including a total of 5,214 violent crimes and 68,963 crimes against property in that year.

17ARMED FORCES

The US military presence in the state is concentrated near Omaha, where Offutt Air Force Base serves as the headquarters of the US Strategic Air Command. In 2002, Nebraska firms were awarded $190.9 million in defense contracts. In the same year, there were 7,793 active-duty military personnel and 3,365 civilian personnel stationed in Nebraska.

A total of 173,189 veterans of US military service resided in Nebraska as of 2000. Of these, 33,450 served in World War II; 24,117 in the Korean conflict; 50,708 in the Vietnam era; and 21,751 during 1990–2000 (including the Persian Gulf War). In 2002, a total of more than $424 million was spent on veterans' benefits.

In 2000, the Nebraska State Patrol employed 462 full-time sworn officers.

18MIGRATION

The pioneers who settled Nebraska in the 1860s consisted mainly of Civil War veterans from the North and foreign-born immigrants. Some of the settlers migrated from the East and easterly parts of the Midwest, but many came directly from Europe to farm the land. The Union Pacific and Burlington Northern railroads, which sold land to the settlers, actively recruited immigrants in Europe. Germans were the largest group to settle in Nebraska (in 1900, 65,506 residents were German-born), then Czechs from Bohemia, and Scandinavians from Sweden, Denmark, and Norway. The Irish came to work on the railroads in the 1860s and stayed to help build the cities. Another wave of Irish immigrants in the 1880s went to work in the packinghouses of Omaha. The city's stockyards also attracted Polish workers. The 1900 census showed that over one-half of all Nebraskans were either foreign-born or the children of foreign-born parents. For much of the 20th century, Nebraska was in a period of out-migration. From 1930 to 1960, the state suffered a net loss of nearly 500,000 people through migration, with more than one third of the total leaving during the dust-bowl decade,

1930–40. This trend continued, with Nebraska experiencing a net out-migration of 27,400 for the period 1985–90. Between 1990 and 1998, the state had net gains of 2,000 in domestic migration and 14,000 in international migration. In 1998, 1,267 foreign immigrants arrived in Nebraska. The state's overall population increased 5.3% between 1990 and 1998. In the period 1995–2000, 154,025 people moved into the state and 169,378 moved out, for a net loss of 15,353, many of whom moved to Iowa.

19INTERGOVERNMENTAL COOPERATION

Nebraska's Commission on Intergovernmental Cooperation represents the state in the Council of State Governments. As an oil-producing state, Nebraska is a member of the Interstate Compact to Conserve Oil and Gas. In addition, the state belongs to several regional commissions. Of particular importance are the Republican River Compact with Colorado and Kansas, the Big Blue River Compact with Kansas, the South Platte River Compact with Colorado, the Ponca Creek Nebraska-South Dakota-Wyoming Water Compact, and the Upper Niobrara River Compact with Wyoming. The Nebraska Boundary Commission was authorized in 1982 to enter into negotiations to more precisely demarcate Nebraska's boundaries with Iowa, South Dakota, and Missouri. Nebraska is also a member of the Central Interstate Low-Level Radioactive Waste Compact, under which Nebraska, Kansas, Oklahoma, Louisiana, and Arkansas have located a suitable disposal site for such waste. Boundary pacts are in effect with Iowa, Missouri, and South Dakota. In 2001, the state received over $2 billion in federal grants.

20ECONOMY

Agriculture has historically been the backbone of Nebraska's economy, with cattle, corn, hogs, and soybeans leading the state's list of farm products. However, Nebraska is attempting to diversify its economy and has been successful in attracting new business, in large part because of its location near western coal and oil deposits. The largest portion of the state's labor force is employed in agriculture, either directly or indirectly—as farm workers, as factory workers in the food-processing and farm-equipment industries, or as providers of related services. The service sector, which includes not only the servicing of equipment but also the high growth areas of health and business services and telemarketing, expanded at an annual rate of 4.4 percent during the 1980s. The trend intensified in the late 1990s, as general services grew at an average annual rate of 7.7% 1998 to 2001, and financial services grew at an average rate of 5.7%. Nebraska was not deeply involved in the information technology (IT) boom of the 1990s, and therefore was not deeply affected by its bust in 2001. Coming into the 21st century, the state economy grew an a moderate average rate of about 4.1% (1998 to 2000), which fell to 2.4% in 2001. In 2001, declines in manufacturing employment were off-set by increases in the services and government sectors. The job losses became more severe in 2002, by the 8th quarter, the unemployment rate had eased to 3.3%, down from 3.9% in April 2002.

With technological advances in farming and transportation, and consolidation in the agricultural sector, Nebraska's rural counties have been losing population since the 1970s. In 2002, 66 of Nebraska's 93 counties had lower populations than in the 1970s, and in 21of these, population loss accelerated during the 1990s. Drought conditions in 2002 disrupted cattle production because of shortages of hay and pasture. Drought persisted into the winter of 2002–03, and the state is likely to face long-term water shortages.

Nebraska's gross state product in 2001 was $57 billion, the 36th highest among the states, to which general services contributed $11.5 billion; trade, $13 billion; financial services, $9 billion; government, $8.2 billion; manufacturing, $7 billion; transportation and public utilities, $6.3 billion, and construction, $2.7 billion. The public sector in 2001 constituted 14.4% of gross state product, above the average of 12% for all the states.

21 INCOME

According to the Bureau of Economic Analysis, in 2001, Nebraska had a per capita personal income (PCPI) of $28,861 which ranked 24th in the United States (including the District of Columbia) and was 95% of the national average, $30,413. The 2001 PCPI reflected an increase of 3.9% from 2000 compared to the national change of 2.2%. In 2001, Nebraska had a total personal income (TPI) of $49,642,391,000 which ranked 36th in the United States and accounted for 0.6% of the national total. The 2001 TPI reflected an increase of 4.3% from 2000 compared to the national change of 3.3%.

Earnings of persons employed in Nebraska increased from $34,101,943,000 in 2000 to $35,240,341,000 in 2001, an increase of 3.3%. The largest industries in 2001 were services, 27.1% of earnings; state and local government, 12.8%; and transportation and public utilities, 9.9%. Of the industries that accounted for at least 5% of earnings in 2001, the slowest growing from 2000 to 2001 was durable goods manufacturing (6.0% of earnings in 2001), which decreased 7.1%; the fastest was state and local government, which increased 7.5%.

According to data released by the US Census Bureau, in 2000, the median household income was $38,574 compared to the national average of $42,148. In 2001, the median income for a family of four was $60,626 compared to the national average of $63,278. For the period 1999 to 2001, the average poverty rate was 9.7% which placed it 18th among the 50 states and the District of Columbia ranked lowest to highest.

22 LABOR

According to Bureau of Labor Statistics (BLS) provisional estimates, in July 2003 the seasonally adjusted civilian labor force in Nebraska numbered 983,500, with approximately 38,000 workers unemployed, yielding an unemployment rate of 3.9%, compared to the national average of 6.2% for the same period. Since the beginning of the BLS data series in 1978, the highest unemployment rate recorded was 7.1% in January 1983. The historical low was 2.1% in June 1990. In 2001, an estimated 4.4% of the labor force was employed in construction; 11.1% in manufacturing; 5.2% in transportation, communications, and public utilities; 19.8% in trade; 7.2% in finance, insurance, and real estate; 24.0% in services; 14.3% in government; and 7.1% in agriculture.

The US Department of Labor reported that in 2002, 63,000 of Nebraska's 793,000 employed wage and salary workers were members of unions. This represented 7.9% of those so employed, up from 7.7% in 2001 and 10.3% in 1998. The national average is 13.2%. In all, 88,000 workers (11.1%) were represented by unions. In addition to union members, this category includes workers who report no union affiliation but whose jobs are covered by a union contract. Nebraska is one of 22 states with a right-to-work law.

23 AGRICULTURE

With total cash receipts from farm marketings at over $9.5 billion in 2001, Nebraska ranked 4th among the 50 states. About $6.1 billion of all farm marketings came from livestock production, and $3.4 billion from cash crops. In 2002, corn accounted for 24% of farm receipts.

Territorial Nebraska was settled by homesteaders. Farmers easily adapted to the land and the relatively rainy eastern region, and corn soon became their major crop. In the drier central and western prairie regions, settlers were forced to learn new farming

methods to conserve moisture in the ground. Droughts in the 1890s provided impetus for water conservation. Initially, oats and spring wheat were grown along with corn, but by the end of the 19th century, winter wheat became the main wheat crop. The drought and dust storms of the 1930s, which devastated the state's agricultural economy, once again drove home the need for water and soil conservation. In 1997, a total of 6.9 million acres (2.8 million hectares) were irrigated, a 22% increase from 1987. In 2002, there were 52,000 farms covering 46.4 million acres (18.8 million hectares).

Crop production in 2002 (in bushels) included: corn, 941 million; sorghum grain, 15 million; wheat, 48.6 million; soybeans, 176.3 million; oats, 2.4 million; and barley, 215,000. Hay production was 6.0 million tons; and potato production, 8.6 million hundredweight, (390.1 million kg). In 2002, Nebraska ranked 4th among the states in production of corn for grain and sorghum for grain; and 7th in winter wheat.

Farms in Nebraska are major businesses requiring large land holdings to justify investments. The value of the average farm in 2002 was $673,692. Nebraska farms still tend to be owned by single persons or families rather than by large corporations. The strength of state support for the family farm was reflected in the passage of a 1982 constitutional amendment, initiated by petition, prohibiting the purchase of Nebraska farm and ranch lands by other than a Nebraska family farm corporation.

24 ANIMAL HUSBANDRY

In 2003, Nebraska ranked 3rd behind Texas and Kansas in the total number of cattle on farms (6.2 million), including 72,000 milk cows. Nebraska farmers had around 2.9 million hogs and pigs, valued at $217.5 million in 2002. During 2001, the state produced an estimated 10.4 million lb (4.7 million kg) of sheep and lambs, which grossed $8.7 million in income for Nebraska farmers. Dairy products included 1.16 billion lb (0.5 billion kg) of milk produced.

25 FISHING

Commercial fishing is negligible in Nebraska. The US Fish and Wildlife Service maintains 87 public fishing areas. In 1998, the state had 211,248 fishing-license holders. The North Platte and Valentine State Fish Hatcheries provide fish for anglers.

26 FORESTRY

Arbor Day, now observed throughout the US, originated in Nebraska in 1872 as a way of encouraging tree planting in the sparsely forested state. Forestland occupies 947,000 acres (383,000 hectares), or 2% of all Nebraska. Ash, boxelder, hackberry, cottonwood, honey locust, red and bur oaks, walnut, elm, and willow trees are common to eastern and central Nebraska, while ponderosa pine, cottonwood, eastern red cedar, and Rocky Mountain juniper prevail in the west. The state's two national forests—Nebraska and Samuel R. McKelvie—are actually primarily grassland and are managed for livestock grazing. In 1999, the National Forest Service maintained 257,468 acres (104,197 hectares) of forestland.

27 MINING

The value of nonfuel mineral production in Nebraska in 2001 was estimated at $91.4 million, a decrease of about 9% from 2000.

All nonfuel minerals produced in Nebraska, with the exception of gemstones, were basic construction materials and production continued to reflect construction trends in the state. Most clay mining occurs in the southeast region, but sand and gravel mining takes place throughout the state. Industrial sand was used in the production of glass and had some applications outside of construction activities. According to preliminary figures, leading nonfuel minerals in 2001 were, in order of value, portland cement, crushed stone, and construction sand and gravel.

In 2001, 10.7 million metric tons of construction sand and gravel were mined, for a value of $36.3 million. That same year, 8.1 million metric tons of crushed stone and 133 metric tons of clay were mined, with values of $53.6 million and $340,000, respectively.

28 ENERGY AND POWER

In 2000 Nebraska's total per capita energy consumption was 341 million Btu (85.9 million kcal), ranking it 27th among the 50 states.

Nebraska is the only state with an electric power system owned by the public through regional, cooperative, and municipal systems. The state's installed capacity (utility and nonutility) was 5.8 million kW in 1999; total electricity generation totaled 30.1 billion kWh, a new all-time record. Electricity from coal accounted for 59% of the total (17.8 billion kWh). Nuclear power generation (one reactor at the Cooper plant in Brownsville and one at Fort Calhoun) accounted for 33% (10.1 billion kWh), hydropower generation accounted for 5.7% (1.7 million kWh), and less than 3% of the electricity was produced from natural gas or oil units.

About 58% of all electricity in 1998 was sold for commercial and industrial use, 37% for residential use, and the remaining 7% for other uses.

Crude oil production in 2002 in Nebraska was 8,000 barrels per day; in 2001 proved reserves totaled 15 million barrles. Oil is produced in 17 counties, primarily in the southwest and panhandle areas of the state. In 2002, natural gas production in Nebraska totaled 1.2 billion cu ft (0.03 billion cu m). Nebraska has no commercial coal industry.

29 INDUSTRY

Nebraska has a small but growing industrial sector. In 1997, there were 2,039 manufacturing establishments with 111,098 employees, and a payroll of $3.2 billion. The value of shipments for manufactured goods for Nebraska in 1997 was $28 billion.

More than one-third of all manufacturing establishments in Nebraska are in the Omaha metropolitan area, including ConAgra, the nation's largest flour miller and a producer of broiler chickens and crop-protection chemicals. Other manufacturing centers are Lincoln and the Sioux City, Iowa, metropolitan area in Nebraska. As of 1997, there were 6 Fortune 500 companies headquartered in Nebraska.

Earnings of persons employed in Nebraska increased from $29.7 billion in 1997 to $31.2 billion in 1998, an increase of 4.9%. The largest industries in 1998 were services, 24.8% of earnings; state and local government, 12.4%; and transportation and public utilities, 9.7%. Of the industries that accounted for at least 5% of earnings in 1998, the slowest growing from 1997 to 1998 was farm (5.4% of earnings in 1998), which decreased 35.2%; the fastest was transportation and public utilities, which increased 14.8%.

30 COMMERCE

In 1997, Nebraska had 3,894 wholesale trade establishments, with sales of $40 billion, and annual payrolls totaling $1.34 billion.

Retail sales totaled $16.4 billion in 1997, from 11,286 establishments. Automotive dealers numbered 16% that year; food stores, 10%; and restaurants and bars, 30%. In 1997, Nebraska's retail establishments had total annual payrolls of $1.8 billion. Food sales totaled $3.3 billion, while general merchandise sales totaled $2 billion.

Nebraska's exports of goods produced within the state totaled $2.3 billion in 1999. Major export items included: food ($1 billion), electronic equipment ($201 million), agricultural crops ($193 million), transport equipment ($166 million), and chemicals ($116 million). The majority of exports went to Japan, Canada, and Mexico.

31 CONSUMER PROTECTION

Nebraska has no separate state agency in charge of consumer protection. The Office of the Attorney General has a Consumers Protection Division. The Nebraska Public Service Commission regulates railroads, telephone companies, motor transport companies, and other common carriers operating in the state.

32 BANKING

In 2002, there were 284 insured banks in Nebraska, of which 195 were state-chartered. Insured banks held assets of $47.9 billion.

As of 2002, severe drought conditions in Nebraska, along with low crop prices, left many farm banks holding significant levels of debt as loan delinquency levels increased.

In the 1990s and into the 2000s, net interest margins (NIMs) (the difference between the lower rates offered to savers and the higher rates charged on loans) declined, due in large measure to loan and funding competition. As of 2002, the lowering of interest rates by the Federal Reserve caused fluctuations in NIMs, but did not signal an end to the longer-term downward trend of NIMs.

33 INSURANCE

The insurance industry is important in Nebraska's economy. The major company in the state is Mutual of Omaha. In 2001 there were 1.1 million ordinary life insurance policies in force with a total value of $73.2 billion; total value for all categories of life insurance (ordinary, group, industrial, and credit) was $111.7 billion. Death benefits paid that year totaled $319.4 million. Twenty-seven life and health and 43 property and casualty insurance companies were based in the state in 2000. Property and liability insurers wrote premiums of $2.32 billion in 2001. That year, there were 13,062 flood insurance policies in force in the state, with a total value of $1,175,242.

34 SECURITIES

The Bureau of Securities within the Department of Banking and Finance regulates the sale of securities. There are no stock exchanges in the state. Securities are sold in Nebraska by 336 broker-dealers through 2,141 employees; 56 investment advisory firms also are registered. The state houses 20 NASDAQ companies, one NASDAQ market maker, and incorporated nine NYSE-listed companies. The five with the most revenues are: ConAgra, Berkshire Hathaway, Union Pacific, Inacom, and the Commercial Federal Corp.

35 PUBLIC FINANCE

Nebraska's Constitution prohibits the state from incurring debt in excess of $100,000. However, there is a provision in the Constitution that permits the issuance of revenue bonds for highway and water conservation and management structure construction. There are $10 million of bonds payable by a separate legal entity that has been blended into the financial activity of the state. These bonds do not represent a general obligation of the state and are secured by revenues from the equipment that the debt was incurred to purchase.

The Constitution also authorizes the Board of Regents of the University of Nebraska, the Board of Trustees of the Nebraska State Colleges, and the State Board of Education to issue revenue bonds to construct, purchase, or remodel educational buildings and facilities. The payment of these bonds is generally made from revenue collected from use of the buildings and facilities. The Legislature has authorized the creation of two financing authorities that are not subject to state Constitutional restrictions on the incurrence of debt. These financing authorities were organized to assist in providing funds for the construction of capital improvement projects at the colleges and the University. Although the state has no legal responsibility for the debt of these financing authorities, they are considered part of the reporting entity.

The Nebraska state budget is prepared by the Budget Division of the Department of Administrative Services and is submitted annually by the governor to the legislature. The fiscal year runs from 1 July to 30 June.

The bulk of general fund monies in 2000/01 were put towards: local tax relief (38%), government (20%), aid to individuals (20%), and post-secondary education (17%). For 2000/01, the general fund was forecast with revenues of almost $2.4 billion, which actually totaled $2.457 billion. In 2001/02, however, general fund revenues fell to $2.363 billion while expenditures shot up to $2.599 billion. In 2002/03, Nebraska's state budget deficit was estimated at 5.9% of the state budget and for 2003/04, it was projected to reach between 21.25 and 28.2% of the state budget.

The following table from the US Census Bureau contains information on revenues, expenditures, indebtedness, and cash/securities for 2001.

	($000)	PERCENT	PER CAPITA
Population (thousands, 2001)	1,720	(X)	(X)
Total Revenue	5,943,922	100.00	3,455.77
General revenue	5,874,524	98.83	3,415.42
Utility revenue	–	–	–
Liquor store revenue	–	–	–
Insurance trust revenue	69,398	1.17	40.35
Exhibit: Salaries and wages	1,634,335	26.74	950.19
Total expenditure	6,111,217	100.00	3,553.03
General expenditure	5,842,608	95.60	3,396.87
Education	2,083,264	34.09	1,211.20
Public welfare	1,508,251	24.68	876.89
Hospitals	177,365	2.90	103.12
Health	323,252	5.29	187.94
Highways	477,265	7.81	277.48
Police protection	67,378	1.10	39.17
Correction	176,136	2.88	102.40
Natural resources	170,593	2.79	99.18
Parks and recreation	27,078	0.44	15.74
Government administration	189,669	3.10	110.27
Interest on general debt	116,122	1.90	67.51
Other and unallocable	526,235	8.61	305.95
Utility expenditure	–	–	–
Liquor store expenditure	–	–	–
Insurance trust expenditure	268,609	4.40	156.17
Debt at end of fiscal year	1,799,628	100.00	1,046.30
Cash and security holdings	9,285,224	100.00	5,398.39

36TAXATION

A constitutional amendment in 1967 prohibited the use of property tax revenues for state government. This forced the passage of both a sales and use tax and an income tax, which had long been resisted by fiscal conservatives in the state. The sales and use tax became effective in 1967, the income tax in 1968.

The state income tax is four-bracket schedule ranging between 2.56% (for a single individual, up to $2,400 of taxable income) and 6.84% (on taxable income above $26,500). Federal adjusted gross income as defined 19 April 2002 can be used as an individual's tax base. The corporate tax rate is 5.58% on the first $50,000 of net income and 7.81% on net income over $50,000. The state sales tax rate was raised temporarily from 5% to 5.5% in 2002, scheduled to fall back to 5% 1 October 2003. Nebraska exempts both foodstuffs and prescription drugs from its general sales tax. Local sales taxes range from none to 1.5%. The state imposes a full array of excise taxes covering motor fuels, tobacco

products, insurance premiums, alcoholic beverages, amusements, public utilities, pari-mutuels, and other selected items. In 2002, the cigarette tax was temporarily increased from 34 cents a pack to 64 cents a pack, scheduled to return to 34¢ 1 October 2004. Nebraska's gasoline tax is indexed for inflation, and revised quarterly. The state estate tax (maximum rate 18%) is independent of the federal estate tax, and therefore is unaffected by the latter's scheduled phase-out by 2007. There is also an inheritance tax, collected at the county level. State death and gift taxes constituted 0.5% of state taxes collected in 2002. Other state taxes include an oil and gas severance tax, an oil and gas conservation tax, a uranium severance tax (state severance tax receipts in 2002 totaled $1,221), various license and franchise fees, stamp taxes, and state property taxes. Most property taxes are collected locally. Local tax collections accounted for 43.4% of total state and local totals, in 2000.

The state collected $2.992 billion in taxes in 2002, of which 38.5% came from individual income taxes, 35.7% from the general sales tax, 14.6% from selective sales taxes, 6.5% from license fees, and 3.6% from corporate income taxes. In 2003, Nebraska ranked 16th among the states in terms of its combined state and local tax burden, which amounted to about 9.8% of income.

The following table from the US Census Bureau provides a summary of taxes collected by the state in 2002.

	($000)	PER CAPITA
Total Taxes	2,992,522	1,730.60
Property taxes	6,383	3.69
Sales and gross receipts	1,505,266	870.51
General sales and gross receipts	1,069,185	618.32
Selective sales taxes	436,081	252.19
Alcoholic beverage	17,534	10.14
Amusements	6,280	3.63
Insurance Premiums	38,107	22.04
Motor fuels	308,147	178.2
Pari-mutuels	945	0.55
Public utilities	2,878	1.66
Tobacco products	44,164	25.54
Other selective sales	18,026	10.42
Licenses	195,762	113.21
Alcoholic beverages	274	0.16
Amusements	(X)	(X)
Corporation	6,419	3.71
Hunting and fishing	13,606	7.87
Motor vehicle	85,268	49.31
Motor vehicle operators	8,157	4.72
Public utility	(X)	(X)
Occupation and business, NEC	61,414	35.52
Other	20,624	11.93
Other taxes	1,285,111	743.19
Individual income	1,153,444	667.05
Corporation net income	107,628	62.24
Death and gift	15,611	9.03
Documentary and stock transfer	7,207	4.17
Severance	1,221	0.71
Other	(X)	(X)

37ECONOMIC POLICY

The Department of Economic Development (DED)was created in 1967 to plan, promote, and develop the economy of the state. Nebraska offers loans for businesses which create or maintain employment for persons of low and moderate income. It provides tax credits to companies which increase investment and add jobs. The main operational divisions within the DED are provide assistance for businesses start-up, financing and planning, for business expansion, community and housing development, international trade, filming Nebraska, travel and tourism, and workforce development. From 1999 to 2001, ambitions to increase the state's exports were furthered in five trade missions, four to Asia (including one to Australia), and one to Latin

America. In September 2003, the DED issued a report it had commissioned from the Milken Institute the highlight of which showed that Nebraska, while rather low among the states in terms of R& D inputs, entrepreneurial infrastructure, human capital investment and other development-relevant categories, was 11th among the states in terms of technology and science workforce, suggesting a competitive advantage to be exploited.

38HEALTH

Nebraska's infant mortality in 2000 was 7.3 per 1,000 live births. In 1999, there were 5,807 abortions performed in the state, a ratio of 15 per 1,000 women. In 2000, the overall death rate stood at 897.5 per 1,000 population, above the national rate of 873.1.

Major causes of death in 2000 were heart disease (251.3 per 100,000 residents), cerebrovascular diseases (65.3), pneumonia (25.9), accidents and adverse effects (38.3), and suicide (11.6). The rate of HIV-related deaths in 2000 was 1.5 per 100,000, much lower than the US average of 5.3; a total of 1,167 AIDS cases had been reported through 2001. Also in 2000, 21.4% of adults 18 years and older were smokers. The rate of death from lung disease was 65.5 per 100,000 population in 2000.

University Hospital and University of Nebraska Medical Center are in Omaha. Nebraska's 84 community hospitals had 206,700 admissions and 8,324 beds in 2001. There were 7,304 full-time registered nurses and 1,369 full-time licensed practical nurses in 2001 and 245 physicians per 100,000 population in 2000. The average expense of a community hospital for care was $1,543.90 per inpatient day in 2001.

Federal government grants to cover the Medicare and Medicaid services in 2001 totaled $752 million; 254,680 enrollees received Medicare benefits that year. Only 9.5% of Nebraska's adult residents were uninsured in 2002, the lowest percentage of any state.

39SOCIAL WELFARE

In 2001, the average weekly unemployment benefit was $203.78. Average monthly participation in the food stamp program in FY2002 comprised 88,459 persons (37,570 households). The average monthly benefit was $70.07, and the sum total of benefits paid in FY2002 was $74,382,259.

With the enactment of the Personal Responsibility and Work Opportunity Reconciliation Act of 1996, the US government has changed the form and regulations for many of its social welfare programs. Most significantly, it replaces Aid to Families with Dependent Children (AFDC), an open-ended entitlement program, with Temporary Assistance for Needy Families (TANF), a limited system of assistance funded largely through federal block grants. The reform act also impacts the food stamp program, the Supplemental Security Income program, and the child nutrition program. The law took effect on 1 July 1997 and provided $16.38 billion in block grants for fiscal years 1997– 2002. The grants are to be divided among the states based on an equation involving the numbers of former AFDC recipients in each state.

Reauthorization of the 1996 social welfare legislation, scheduled for 2002, was delayed, and the original law had been extended three times as of July 2003, with the most recent extension running through September 2003. Nebraska's TANF program is called Employment First. In June 2000 the state had 26,841 welfare recipients. State expenditures on the TANF program in FY2002 totaled $22,944,891.

In December 2001, Social Security benefits were paid to 285,900 Nebraska residents. This number included 187,360 retired workers, 31,850 widows and widowers, 26,730 disabled workers, 20,450 spouses, and 19,510 children. Social Security beneficiaries represented 16.7% of the total state population and

94.6% of the state's population age 65 and older. Retired workers (excluding persons with special benefits) received an average monthly payment of $856; widows and widowers, $847; disabled workers, $772; and spouses, $442. Payments for children of retired workers averaged $454 per month; children of deceased workers, $596; and children of disabled workers, $228.

Federal Supplemental Security Income payments in December 2001 went to 21,471 Nebraska residents, averaging $339 a month.

40HOUSING

In 2002, there were 738,870 housing units in Nebraska, 677,159 of which were occupied; 67.7% were owner-occupied. About 72.7% of all units were single-family, detached homes. Utility gas and electricity were the most common heating energy sources. It was estimated that 24,565 units lacked telephone service, 1,811 lacked complete plumbing facilities, and 3,156 lacked complete kitchen facilities. The average household size was 2.48 people.

In 2002, 9,278 new privately owned units were authorized for construction. The median home value was $94,191. The median monthly cost for mortgage owners was $977. Renters paid a median of $536 per month. During 2002, Nebraska received over $33.7 million in community planning and development aid from the US Department of Housing and Urban Development.

41EDUCATION

In 2000, 86.6% of Nebraskans age 25 and older were high school graduates; 23.7% had obtained a bachelor's degree or higher.

The total enrollment for fall 1999 in Nebraska's public schools stood at 288,261. Of these, 197,014 attended schools from kindergarten through grade eight, and 91,247 attended high school. Minority students made up approximately 18% of the total enrollment in public elementary and secondary schools. Total enrollment was estimated at 286,176 in fall 2000 and expected to rise to 287,000 by fall 2005. Enrollment in nonpublic schools in fall 2001 was 42,141. Expenditures for public education in 2000/01 were estimated at $2,017,561.

As of fall 2000, there were 112,315 students enrolled in college or graduate school. In the same year Nebraska had 38 degree-granting institutions. In 1997, minority students comprised 8.7% of total postsecondary enrollment. In 2000 Nebraska had 7 public 4-year colleges, 15 independent colleges and universities, and 7 community colleges. The University of Nebraska is the state's largest postsecondary institution, with campuses in Kearney, Lincoln, and Omaha.

42ARTS

The 15-member Nebraska Arts Council (NAC), appointed by the governor, is empowered to receive federal and state funds and to plan and administer statewide and special programs in all the arts. Funds are available for arts education, organizational support, multicultural arts projects, special arts-related programs, touring, and fellowships. Affiliation with the Mid-America Arts Alliance allows the council to help sponsor national and regional events. In 2003, the NAC and other Nebraska arts organizations received grants totaling $863,000 from the National Endowment for the Arts.

The Nebraska Humanities Council, founded in 1972, sponsors two annual festivals: The Great Plains Chautauqua and the Nebraska Book Festival. In 2000, the National Endowment for the Humanities contributed $687,812 to seven programs in the state.

The Omaha Theater Company for Young People sponsors a number of theatrical performances as well as the Omaha Theater Ballet Company. The Omaha Symphony was founded in 1921, and Opera Omaha was founded in 1958. The Lied Center for

Performing Arts in Lincoln sponsors a wide variety of dance, theater, and musical programs.

The biennial Great Plains Film Festival serves as a showcase for film and video artists from the heartlands of both the U.S. and Canada. It is staged at the Mary Riepma Ross Media Arts Center of the University of Nebraska at Lincoln.

The state of Nebraska supports over 20 major art museums and art centers, 15 professional orchestras and ensembles, dance companies, opera, and theaters, and maintains over 100 local arts presenters, community theaters, and volunteer exhibition spaces.

43LIBRARIES AND MUSEUMS

The Nebraska Library Commission coordinates library services. In 2000, the state had 12 county and multi-county library systems. A total of 5,605,000 volumes were in the public library system in 2000; total circulation was 11,176,000. Total income for the public library system came to $34,635,000 in 2000; including $207,810 in federal grants and $450,255 in state grants. The Omaha public library system had 916,560 books and 2,471 periodical subscriptions in nine branches.

The Joslyn Art Museum in Omaha is the state's leading museum. Other important museums include the Nebraska State Museum of History, the University of Nebraska State Museum (natural history), and the Sheldon Memorial Art Gallery, all in Lincoln; the Western Heritage Museum in Omaha; the Stuhr Museum of the Prairie Pioneer in Grand Island; and the Hastings Museum in Hastings. In all, the state had 107 museums in 2000. The Agate Fossil Beds National Monument in northwestern Nebraska features mammal fossils from the Miocene era and a library of paleontological and geologic material.

44COMMUNICATIONS

Telephone service is regulated by the Public Service Commission. About 96.5% of the state's occupied housing units had telephones in 2001.

In 2003, 52 major FM stations and 19 major AM stations were operating. There were 8 major network TV stations. A total of 23,752 Internet domain names were registered in the state.

45PRESS

In 2002, Nebraska had 6 morning dailies, 12 evening dailies, and 6 Sunday newspapers. The leading newspaper is the *Omaha World–Herald*, with a daily circulation in 2001 of 196,326 and a Sunday circulation of 242,631. The *Lincoln Journal–Star* had a daily circulation of 75,292 and a Sunday circulation of 82,957.

46ORGANIZATIONS

In 2003, there were about 1,076 regional, national, and international organizations within the state. Among the organizations based in Nebraska are the Great Plains Council at the University of Nebraska (Lincoln), the American Shorthorn Society (Omaha), the Morse Telegraph Club (Lincoln), Girls and Boys Town (Boys Town), Wellness Councils of America (Omaha), the United States Amateur Confederation of Roller Skating (Lincoln), and the National Arbor Day Foundation (Nebraska City). The state's arts, culture, and history are represented in part by the Nebraska Humanities Council and the Nebraska State Historical Society.

47TOURISM, TRAVEL, AND RECREATION

Tourism is Nebraska's 3rd largest source of outside revenue (after agriculture and manufacturing). In 2002, the state hosted about 19.6 million travelers. Out-of-state visitors were primarily from Kansas, Iowa, Colorado, Missouri, South Dakota, Illinois, and Minnesota. Total travel expenditures were at about $2.8 billion. The industry supports nearly 46,000 jobs.

The 8 state parks, 9 state historical parks, 12 federal areas, and 55 recreational areas are main tourist attractions; fishing, swimming, picnicking, and sightseeing are the principal activities. The most attended Nebraska attractions in 2002 were: Omaha's Henry Doorly Zoo (1,420,556 visitors), Cabela's in Sidney (1,025,000), Eugene T. Mahoney State Park (1,100,000), Lake McConaughy State Recreation Area (859,624), Fort Robinson State Park (357,932), Joslyn Art Museum (186,646), Strategic Air and Space Museum (173,889), the Great Platte River Road Archway Monument (163,000), University of Nebraska State Museum (133,343), and Scotts Bluff National Monument (111,293).

48SPORTS

There are no major league professional sports teams in Nebraska. Minor league baseball's Omaha Golden Spikes play in the Triple-A Pacific Coast League. The most popular spectator sport is college football. Equestrian activities, including racing and rodeos, are popular. Major annual sporting events are the NCAA College Baseball World Series at Rosenblatt Stadium and the River City Roundup and Rodeo, both held in Omaha. Pari-mutuel racing is licensed by the state.

The University of Nebraska Cornhuskers compete in the Big Twelve Conference. The football team often places high in national rankings and was named National Champion in 1970 (with Texas), 1971, 1994, 1995, and 1997. The Cornhuskers won the Orange Bowl in 1964, 1971, 1972, 1973, 1983, 1995, 1997, and 1998; the Cotton Bowl in 1974 (January); the Sugar Bowl in 1974 (December), 1985, and 1987; the Bluebonnet Bowl in 1976; the Liberty Bowl in 1977; the Sun Bowl in 1980; the Alamo Bowl in 2001; and the Fiesta Bowl in 1996 and 2000.

The Nebraska basketball team won the National Invitational Tournament in 1996.

49FAMOUS NEBRASKANS

Nebraska was the birthplace of only one US president, Gerald R. Ford (Leslie King, Jr., b.1913). When Spiro Agnew resigned the vice-presidency in October 1973, President Richard M. Nixon appointed Ford, then a US representative from Michigan, to the post. Upon Nixon's resignation on 9 August 1974, Ford became the first nonelected president in US history.

Four native and adoptive Nebraskans have served in the cabinet. J. Sterling Morton (b.New York, 1832–1902), who originated Arbor Day, was secretary of agriculture under Grover Cleveland. William Jennings Bryan (b.Illinois, 1860–1925), a US representative from Nebraska, served as secretary of state and was three times the unsuccessful Democratic candidate for president. Frederick A. Seaton (b.Washington, 1909–74) was Dwight Eisenhower's secretary of the interior, and Melvin Laird (b.1922) was Richard Nixon's secretary of defense.

George W. Norris (b.Ohio, 1861–1944), the "fighting liberal," served 10 years in the US House of Representatives and 30 years in the Senate. Norris's greatest contributions were in rural electrification (his efforts led to the creation of the Tennessee Valley Authority), farm relief, and labor reform; he also promoted the unicameral form of government in Nebraska. Theodore C. Sorensen (b.1928) was an adviser to President John F. Kennedy.

Indian leaders important in Nebraska history include Oglala Sioux chiefs Red Cloud (1822–1909) and Crazy Horse (1849?–77). Moses Kinkaid (b.West Virginia, 1854–1920) served in the US House and was the author of the Kinkaid Act, which encouraged homesteading in Nebraska. Educator and legal scholar Roscoe Pound (1870–1964) was also a Nebraskan. In agricultural science, Samuel Aughey (b.Pennsylvania, 1831–1912) and Hardy W. Campbell (b.Vermont, 1850–1937) developed dry-land farming techniques. Botanist Charles E.

Bessey (b.Ohio, 1845–1915) encouraged forestation. Father Edward Joseph Flanagan (b.Ireland, 1886–1948) was the founder of Boys Town, a home for underprivileged youth. Two native Nebraskans became Nobel laureates in 1980: Lawrence R. Klein (b.1920) in economics and Val L. Fitch (b.1923) in physics.

Writers associated with Nebraska include Willa Cather (b.Virginia, 1873–1947), who used the Nebraska frontier setting of her childhood in many of her writings and won a Pulitzer Prize in 1922; author and poet John G. Neihardt (b.Illinois, 1881–1973), who incorporated Indian mythology and history in his work; Mari Sandoz (1901–66), who wrote of her native Great Plains; writer-photographer Wright Morris (1910–98); and author Tillie Olsen (b.1912). Rollin Kirby (1875–1952) won three Pulitzer Prizes for political cartooning. Composer-conductor Howard Hanson (1896–1982), born in Wahoo, won a Pulitzer Prize in 1944.

Nebraskans important in entertainment include actor-dancer Fred Astaire (Fred Austerlitz, 1899–1984); actors Harold Lloyd (1894–1971), Henry Fonda (1905–82), Robert Taylor (Spangler Arlington Brugh, (1911–69), Marlon Brando (b.1924), and Sandy Dennis (1937–93); television stars Johnny Carson (b.Iowa, 1925) and Dick Cavett (b.1936); and motion-picture producer Darryl F. Zanuck (1902–79).

50 BIBLIOGRAPHY

Calloway, Bertha W., and Alonzo N. Smith. *Visions of Freedom on the Great Plains: An Illustrated History of African Americans in Nebraska*. Virginia Beach, Va.: Donning Co., 1998.

Iowa Nebraska Travel-Smart. Santa Fe, N.Mex.: John Muir Publications, 2000.

Luebke, Frederick C. *Nebraska: An Illustrated History*. Lincoln: University of Nebraska Press, 1995.

Olson, James C., and Ronald C. Naugle. *History of Nebraska*. 3rd ed. Lincoln: University of Nebraska Press, 1997.

Spence, Polly. *Moving Out: A Nebraska Woman's Life*. Lincoln: University of Nebraska Press, 2002.

State of Nebraska. Department of Economic Development. *Nebraska Statistical Handbook, 1993–1994*. Lincoln, 1994.

Wishart, David J. *An Unspeakable Sadness: The Dispossession of the Nebraska Indians*. Lincoln: University of Nebraska Press, 1994.

NEVADA

State of Nevada

ORIGIN OF STATE NAME: Named for the Sierra Nevada, *nevada* meaning "snow-covered" in Spanish. **NICKNAME:** The Silver State; also, the Sagebrush State and the Battle Born State. **CAPITAL:** Carson City. **ENTERED UNION:** 31 October 1864 (36th). **SONG:** "Home Means Nevada." **MOTTO:** All for Our Country. **FLAG:** On a blue field, two sprays of sagebrush and a golden scroll in the upper lefthand corner frame a silver star encircled by the word "Nevada"; the scroll, reading "Battle Born," recalls that Nevada was admitted to the Union during the Civil War. **OFFICIAL SEAL:** An ore-crushing mill, ore cart, and mine tunnel symbolize Nevada's mining industry; a plow, sickle, and sheaf of wheat represent its agricultural resources. In the background are a railroad, a telegraph line, and a sun rising over the mountains. Encircling this scene are 36 stars and the state motto. The words "The Great Seal of the State of Nevada" surround the whole. **ANIMAL:** Desert bighorn sheep. **BIRD:** Mountain bluebird. **FISH:** Lahontan cutthroat trout. **FLOWER:** Sagebrush. **TREE:** Bristlecone pine and single-leaf pinon. **GRASS:** Indian ricegrass. **METAL:** Silver. **FOSSIL:** Ichthyosaur. **LEGAL HOLIDAYS:** New Year's Day, 1 January; Birthday of Martin Luther King, Jr., 3rd Monday in January; Washington's Birthday, 3rd Monday in February; Memorial Day, last Monday in May; Independence Day, 4 July; Labor Day, 1st Monday in September; Nevada Day, 31 October; Veterans Day, 11 November; Thanksgiving Day, 4th Thursday in November; Christmas Day, 25 December. **TIME:** 4 AM PST = noon GMT.

¹LOCATION, SIZE, AND EXTENT

Situated between the Rocky Mountains and the Sierra Nevada in the western US, Nevada ranks 7th in size among the 50 states.

The total area of Nevada is 110,561 sq mi (286,352 sq km), with land comprising 109,894 sq mi (284,624 sq km) and inland water covering 667 sq mi (1,728 sq km). Nevada extends 320 mi (515 km) E–W; the maximum N–S extension is 483 mi (777 km).

Nevada is bordered on the N by Oregon and Idaho; on the E by Utah and Arizona (with the line in the SE formed by the Colorado River); and on the S and W by California (with part of the line passing through Lake Tahoe). The total boundary length of Nevada is 1,480 mi (2,382 km). The state's geographic center is in Lander County, 26 mi (42 km) SE of Austin.

²TOPOGRAPHY

Almost all of Nevada belongs physiographically to the Great Basin, a plateau characterized by isolated mountain ranges separated by arid basins. These ranges generally trend north–south; most are short, up to 75 mi (121 km) long and 15 mi (24 km) wide, and rise to altitudes of 7,000–10,000 ft (2,100–3,000 m). Chief among them are the Schell Creek, Ruby, Toiyabe, and Carson (within the Sierra Nevada). Nevada's highest point is Boundary Peak, 13,140 ft (4,007 m), in the southwest.

Nevada has a number of large lakes and several large saline marshes known as sinks. The largest lake is Pyramid, with an area of 188 sq mi (487 sq km), in the west. Nevada shares Lake Tahoe with California, and Lake Mead, created by Hoover Dam on the Colorado River, with Arizona. The streams of the Great Basin frequently disappear during dry spells; many of them flow into local lakes or sinks without reaching the sea. The state's longest river, the Humboldt, flows for 290 mi (467 km) through the northern half of the state into the Humboldt Sink. The Walker, Truckee, and Carson rivers drain the western part of Nevada. The canyon carved by the mighty Colorado, the river that forms the extreme southeastern boundary of the state, is the site of Nevada's lowest elevation, 479 ft (146 m).

³CLIMATE

Nevada's climate is sunny and dry, with wide variation in daily temperatures. The normal daily temperature at Reno is 49°F (9°C), ranging from 32°F (0°C) in January to 69°F (21°C) in July. The all-time high, 125°F (52°C), was set at Laughlin on 29 June 1994; the record low, –50°F (–46°C), at San Jacinto on 8 January 1937.

Nevada is the driest state in the US, with overall average annual precipitation (1971–2000) of 7.5 in (19 cm) at Reno. Snowfall is abundant in the mountains, however, reaching 60 in (152 cm) a year on the highest peaks.

⁴FLORA AND FAUNA

Various species of pine—among them the single-leaf pinon, the state tree—dominate Nevada's woodlands. Creosote bush is common in southern Nevada, as are many kinds of sagebrush throughout the state. Wildflowers include shooting star and white and yellow violets. Eight plant species were listed as threatened or endangered in 2003. Endangered species that year were Amargosa niterwort and steamboat buckwheat.

Native mammals include the black bear, white-tailed and mule deer, pronghorn antelope, Rocky Mountain elk, cottontail rabbit, and river otter. Grouse, partridge, pheasant, and quail are the leading game birds, and a diversity of trout, char, salmon, and whitefish thrive in Nevada waters. Rare and protected reptiles are the Gila monster and desert tortoise. The US Fish and Wildlife Service listed 30 Nevada animal species as threatened or endangered in 2003, including the desert tortoise, six species of dace, three species of pupfish, woundfin, and three species of chub.

⁵ENVIRONMENTAL PROTECTION

Preservation of the state's clean air, scarce water resources, and no longer abundant wildlife are the major environmental challenges facing Nevada. The Department of Fish and Game sets quotas on the hunting of deer, antelope, bighorn sheep, and other game animals. The Department of Conservation and Natural

Resources has broad responsibility for environmental protection, state lands, forests, and water and mineral resources. The Division of Environmental Protection within the department has primary responsibility for the control of air pollution, water pollution, waste management, and groundwater protection. In 2003, Nevada had 33 hazardous waste sites listed in the Environmental Protection Agency's database, one of which was on the National Priorities List. Although wetlands cover only about 1% of the mainly barren state, they are some of the most valuable lands in the state. In 2001, Nevada received $32,498,000 in federal grants from the Environmental Protection Agency; EPA expenditures for procurement contracts in Nevada that year amounted to $846,000.

6POPULATION

Nevada ranked 35th in population in the US (up from 39th in 1990) with an estimated total of 2,173,491 in 2002, an increase of 8.8% since 2000 (the greatest increase in the country for this time period). Between 1990 and 2000, Nevada's population grew from 1,201,833 to 1,998,257, an increase of 66.3%, the decade's largest increase by far among the 50 states (followed by 40% for Arizona). It was also the fourth consecutive decade in which Nevada was the country's fastest-growing state and had a population growth rate over 50%. As of 1995 the population was projected to reach 2.3 million by 2025, but more recent increases suggest that the figure will be higher.

In 2000, the median age of Nevada residents was 35. In the same year, nearly 25.6% of the populace were under the age of 18 while 11% were age 65 or older.

With a population density of 18.2 persons per sq mi in 2000 (up from 15.9 in 1998), Nevada remains one of the most sparsely populated states. Approximately 90% of Nevada residents live in cities, the largest of which, Las Vegas, had an estimated 508,604 residents in 2002. Henderson had an estimated population of 206,153, and Reno had 190,248. The Greater Las Vegas metropolitan area had an estimated 1,381,086 residents in 1999; the Reno metropolitan area had an estimated 319,816.

7ETHNIC GROUPS

Some 135,477 black Americans made up about 6.8% of Nevada's population, up sharply from 79,000 in 1990, although the percentage has remained about the same. The American Indian population was 26,420 in 2000, down from 31,000 in 1990. In 1990, tribal landholdings totaled 1,138,462 acres (460,721 hectares). Major tribes are the Washo, Northern Paiute, Southern Paiute, and Shoshoni.

Both the number and percentage of foreign-born residents rose sharply in the 1990s, from 104,828 persons (8.7%) in 1990 to 316,593 state residents (15.8%) in 2000—the 6th-highest percentage of foreign born in the 50 states. In 2000, Hispanics and Latinos numbered 393,970 (19.7% of the state total), and 285,764 reported Mexican ancestry, up sharply from 72,281 in 1990.

8LANGUAGES

Midland and Northern English dialects are so intermixed in Nevada that no clear regional division appears; an example of this is the scattered use of both Midland *dived* (instead of dove) as the past tense of *dive* and the Northern /krik/ for *creek*. In 2000, 1,425,748 Nevadans—76.9% of the resident population five years old or older— spoke only English at home, down from 86.8% in 1990.

The following table gives selected statistics from the 2000 census for language spoken at home by persons five years old and over. The category "Other Pacific Island languages" includes Chamorro, Hawaiian, Ilocano, Indonesian, and Samoan.

LANGUAGE	NUMBER	PERCENT
Population 5 years and over	1,853,720	100.0
Speak only English	1,425,748	76.9
Speak a language other than English	427,972	23.1
Speak a language other than English	427,972	23.1
Spanish or Spanish Creole	299,947	16.2
Tagalog	29,476	1.6
Chinese	11,787	0.6
German	10,318	0.6
French (incl. Patois, Cajun)	7,912	0.4
Korean	6,634	0.4
Italian	6,169	0.3
Japanese	5,678	0.3
Other Pacific Island languages	4,552	0.2
Vietnamese	3,808	0.2
Thai	3,615	0.2

9RELIGIONS

In 2000, Nevada had 331,844 Roman Catholics, representing an increase in membership by 111% from 1990. The 2nd-largest single denomination was the Church of Jesus Christ of Latter-day Saints (Mormons) with 116,925 adherents. Other major Protestant groups include Southern Baptists, 40,233; Assemblies of God, 22,699 (an increase of 220% from 1990); Evangelical Lutherans, 10,663; and United Methodists, 10,452. The Salvation Army, though still relatively small, experienced membership growth of 145% from 1990 to report a total of 1,239 adherents in 2000. Also in 2000, there were an estimated 77,100 Jews living in Nevada, representing an increase of 277% from 1990. Muslims numbered about 2,291 and there were about 1,124 adherents to the Baha'i faith. About 1.3 million people (about 65.7% of the population) did not claim any religious affiliation.

10TRANSPORTATION

As of 2000, Nevada had 1,916 rail mi (3,083 km) of railroads. Amtrak provides passenger service across northern Nevada en route from Chicago to Oakland.

In 2000, there were 37,854 mi (60,920 km) of public roads and streets. Also in 2000, there were 1,244,637 registered vehicles, 655,592 of which were automobiles, 562,296 trucks, and 1,837 buses. Licensed drivers numbered 1,370,643. The major highways, I-80 and I-15, link Salt Lake City with Reno and Las Vegas, respectively. There were 95 airports in 2002 and 29 heliports. The leading commercial air terminals are McCarran International Airport in Las Vegas (17,425,214 passengers enplaned in 2000) and Reno-Tahoe International Airport (2,732,837 passengers enplaned in 2000).

11HISTORY

The first inhabitants of what is now Nevada arrived about 12,000 years ago. They were fishermen, as well as hunters and food gatherers, for the glacial lakes of the ancient Great Basin were then only beginning to recede. Numerous sites of early human habitation have been found, the most famous being Pueblo Grande de Nevada (also known as Lost City). In modern times, four principal Indian groups have inhabited Nevada: Southern Paiute, Northern Paiute, Shoshoni, and Washo.

Probably the first white explorer to enter the state was the Spanish priest Francisco Garces, who apparently penetrated extreme southern Nevada in 1776. The year 1826 saw Peter Skene Ogden of the British Hudson's Bay Company enter the northeast in a prelude to his later exploration of the Humboldt River; the rival American trapper Jedediah Smith traversed the state in 1826–27. During 1843–44, John C. Frémont led the first of his several expeditions into Nevada.

Nevada's first permanent white settlement, Mormon Station (later Genoa), was founded in 1850 in what is now western Nevada, a region that became part of Utah Territory the same

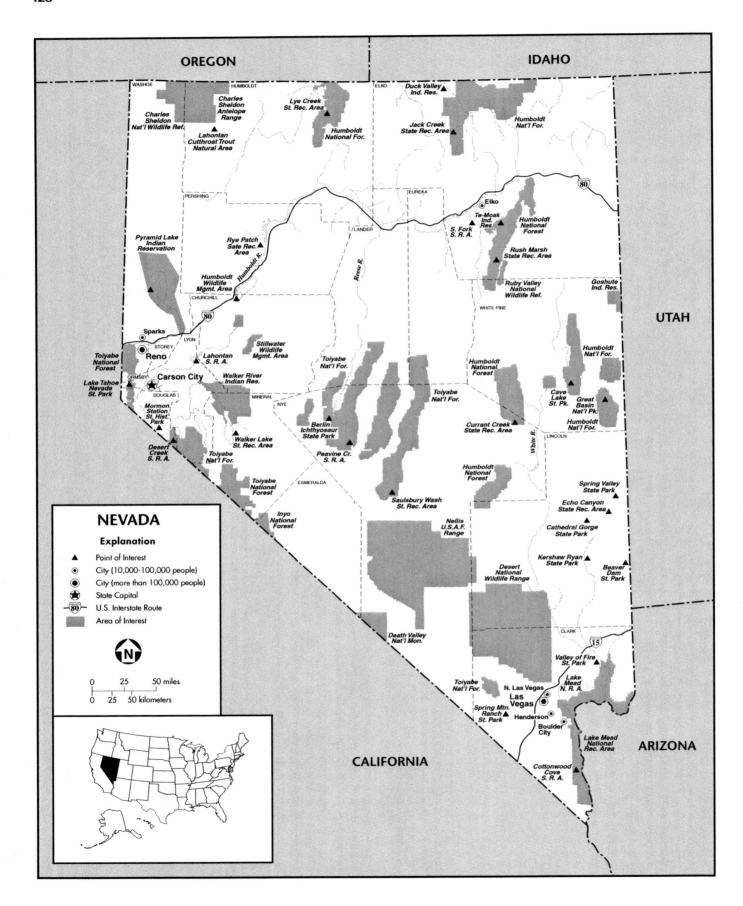

NEVADA

Explanation

▲ Point of Interest

◉ City (10,000-100,000 people)

◉ City (more than 100,000 people)

★ State Capital

🛡80 U.S. Interstate Route

▨ Area of Interest

year. (The southeastern tip of Nevada was assigned to the Territory of New Mexico.) Soon other Mormon settlements were started there and in Las Vegas Valley. The Las Vegas mission failed, but the farming communities to the northwest succeeded, even though friction between Mormons and placer miners in that area caused political unrest. Most of the Mormons in western Nevada departed in 1857, when Salt Lake City was threatened by an invasion of federal troops.

A separate Nevada Territory was established in 1861; only three years later, on 31 October 1864, Nevada achieved statehood, although the present boundaries were not established until 18 January 1867. Two factors accelerated the creation of Nevada: the secession of the southern states, whose congressmen had been blocking the creation of new free states, and the discovery, in 1859, of the Comstock Lode, an immense concentration of silver and gold which attracted thousands of fortune seekers and established the region as a thriving mining center.

Nevada's development during the rest of the century was determined by the economic fortunes of the Comstock, whose affairs were dominated, first, by the Bank of California (in alliance with the Central Pacific Railroad) and then by the "Bonanza Firm" of John W. Mackay and his partners. The lode's rich ores were exhausted in the late 1870s, and Nevada slipped into a 20-year depression. A number of efforts were made to revive the economy, one being an attempt to encourage mining by increasing the value of silver. To this end, Nevadans wholeheartedly supported the movement for free silver coinage during the 1890s, and the Silver Party reigned supreme in state politics for most of the decade.

Nevada's economy revived following new discoveries of silver at Tonopah and gold at Goldfield early in the 20th century. A second great mining boom ensued, bolstered and extended by major copper discoveries in eastern Nevada. Progressive political ferment in this pre-World War I period added recall, referendum, and initiative amendments to the state constitution and brought about the adoption of women's suffrage (1914).

The 1920s was a time of subdued economic activity; mining fell off, and not even the celebrated divorce trade, centered in Reno, was able to compensate for its decline. Politically, the decade was conservative and Republican, with millionaire George Wingfield dominating state politics through a so-called bipartisan machine. Nevada went Democratic during the 1930s, when the hard times of the Depression were alleviated by federal public-works projects, most notably the construction of the Hoover (Boulder) Dam, and by state laws aiding the divorce business and legalizing gambling.

Gaming grew rapidly after World War II, becoming by the mid-1950s not only the mainstay of Nevada tourism but also the state's leading industry. Revelations during the 1950s and 1960s that organized crime had infiltrated the casino industry and that casino income was being used to finance narcotics and other rackets in major East Coast cities led to a state and federal crackdown and the imposition of new state controls.

From 1960 to 1980, Nevada was the fastest-growing of the 50 states, increasing its population by 70% in the 1960s and 64% in the 1970s. In the mid-1980s the state's population growth continued to outpace that of the nation, reaching 14% in the first half of the 1980s in contrast to the national average of 4%. Much of this growth was associated with expansion of the gambling industry—centered in the casinos of Las Vegas and Reno—and of the military. In the 1980s, Nevada began to try to reduce its dependence on gambling by diversifying its economy. In an attempt to attract new businesses, particularly in the high-tech industry, the state promoted such features as its absence of state, corporate, or personal income taxes, inexpensive real estate, low wages, and its ready access by air or land to California.

In the first half of the 1990s, Nevada was once again the nation's fastest growing state, increasing its population by nearly 25%; by 2001 the state's population exceeded 2.1 million. Efforts to diversify the state's economy yielded results as its industrial base expanded. In the early 1990s, Nevada was the only state reporting an increase in manufacturing jobs. Meanwhile Las Vegas continued to prosper, expanding its offerings to attract new visitors. During the decade, several extravagant new hotel and casino complexes opened, many of them featuring amusement parks and other family-oriented entertainment. The booming Las Vegas economy helped push Nevada unemployment to an all-time low of 3.1% in December 1999, one-half a percentage point below the prior record of 3.6% set in 1962. Due in large measure to the 2001 US recession and its aftermath, however, Nevada faced a $704 million budget deficit in 2003, and the unemployment rate stood at 5.4% in July 2003, albeit below the national average of 6.2%.

Nevadans' opposition to the Yucca Mountain nuclear waste disposal site, first proposed by Congress in 1987, continued into 2003. In 2002, US Energy Secretary Spencer Abraham recommended the Yucca Mountain site to President George W. Bush as a nuclear waste repository, which Bush approved. Nevada Governor Kenny Guinn vetoed the project, but the US Congress overrode his veto. President Bush signed Congress's joint resolution into law, and Yucca Mountain became the nation's nuclear waste repository site. Nevada filed major lawsuits against the US Department of Energy, the Nuclear Regulatory Commission, President Bush, and Secretary Abraham. Nevada's lawsuits were set for oral argument before the District of Columbia's Court of Appeals in September 2003.

12STATE GOVERNMENT

Nevada's 1864 constitution, as amended (131 times by January 2003), continues to govern the state. In 2002 voters gave final approval to an amendment defining marriage as a union between a man and a woman. The state legislature consists of a senate with 21 members, each elected to a four-year term, and a house of representatives with 42 members, each serving two years. Legislative sessions are held in odd-numbered years only, beginning in early January and lasting no more than 60 calendar days. Only the governor may call special sessions, which are indirectly limited to 20 calendar days. Legislators must be qualified voters, at least 21 years old, and should have lived in the state and in their district for at least a year prior to election. The legislative salary was $130 per diem during regular sessions in 2002, unchanged from 1999.

Executive officials elected statewide include the governor and lieutenant governor (who run separately), secretary of state, attorney general, treasurer, and comptroller, all of whom serve for four years. The governor is limited to a maximum of two consecutive terms. Candidates for governor must be at least 25 years old and must have been a citizen and resident of the state for at least two years prior to election. In 2002 the governor's salary was $117,000, unchanged from 1999.

Bills approved by the legislature are sent to the governor, who has five days when the legislature is in session (or 10 days if adjourned) to sign or veto it. If the governor does not act within the required time period, the bill automatically becomes law. A two-thirds vote of the elected members of each house is required to override a gubernatorial veto.

Constitutional amendments may be submitted to the voters for ratification if the proposed amendments have received majority votes in each house in two successive sessions or under an initiative procedure calling for petitions signed by 10% of those who voted in the last general election. Legislative amendments need a majority vote; initiative amendments require majorities in two consecutive elections. Voters must be US citizens, at least 18 years old, continuous state residents, and county residents for at least 30 days and precinct residents for at least 10 days prior to election day. Restrictions apply to convicted felons and those declared mentally incompetent by the court.

13POLITICAL PARTIES

Since World War II neither the Democrats nor the Republicans have dominated state politics, which are basically conservative. As of 2002, there were 869,859 registered voters. In the 2000 presidential election, Republican George W. Bush received 49% of the vote to Democrat Al Gore's 46%. Republican Kenny Guinn, first elected governor in 1998, was reelected in 2002. Democrat Harry Reid was elected US Senator in 1986; he was reelected in 1992 and 1998. Republican Senator John Ensign was elected in 2000. Following the 2002 elections, Nevada sent one Democrat and two Republicans to the US House of Representatives. As of mid-2003, there were 13 Republicans and 8 Democrats in the state senate, and 23 Democrats and 19 Republicans in the state house.

Nevada Presidential Vote by Major Political Parties, 1948–2000

YEAR	ELECTORAL VOTE	NEVADA WINNER	DEMOCRAT	REPUBLICAN
1948	3	*Truman (D)	31,290	29,357
1952	3	*Eisenhower (R)	31,688	50,502
1956	3	*Eisenhower (R)	40,640	56,049
1960	3	*Kennedy (D)	54,880	52,387
1964	3	*Johnson (D)	79,339	56,094
1968	3	*Nixon (R)	60,598	73,188
1972	3	*Nixon (R)	66,016	115,750
1976	3	Ford (R)	92,479	101,273
1980	3	*Reagan (R)	66,666	155,017
1984	4	*Reagan (R)	91,655	188,770
1988	4	*Bush (R)	132,738	206,040
1992**	4	*Clinton (D)	189,148	175,828
1996**	4	*Clinton (D)	203,974	199,244
2000	4	*Bush, G. W. (R)	279,978	301,575

* Won US presidential election.
** Independent candidate Ross Perot received 132,580 votes in 1992 and 43,986 votes in 1996.

14LOCAL GOVERNMENT

As of 2002, Nevada was subdivided into 16 counties and 19 municipalities, most of them county seats. The state had 17 public school districts and 158 special districts that year. The county is the primary form of local government. Elected county officials include commissioners, public administrator, district attorney, and sheriff. Most municipalities use the mayor-council system of government.

15STATE SERVICES

To address the continuing threat of terrorism and to work with the federal Department of Homeland Security (created in 2002 following the terrorist attacks of 11 September 2001), homeland security in Nevada in 2003 operated under the authority of the governor; a special advisor was appointed to oversee the state's homeland security activities.

The Executive Ethics Commission was created in 1977 to oversee financial disclosure by state officials. The Department of Education and the University of Nevada System are the main state educational agencies. The Department of Human Resources has divisions covering public health, rehabilitation, mental hygiene and mental retardation, welfare, youth services, and programs for the elderly. Regulatory functions are exercised by the Commerce Department (insurance, banking, consumer affairs, real estate), the Public Service Commission, the Gaming

Control Board, and other state agencies. Other organizations include the Bureau of Mines and Geology, the Commission on Tourism, the Division of Wildlife, and the Nuclear Waste Project Office.

16JUDICIAL SYSTEM

Nevada's supreme court consists of a chief justice and six other justices. There are 51 district court judges organized into nine judicial districts. All judges are elected by nonpartisan ballot to six-year terms.

Nevada's overall crime rate in 2001 was 4,266.0 per 100,000 persons, including a total of 12,359 violent crimes and 77,486 for property crime. There were 10,291 inmates in state and federal correctional facilities in June 2001, an increase of 3.7% over the previous year. The state's incarceration rate stood at 485 per 100,000 inhabitants.

Nevada has a death penalty and has executed nine people between 1977 and 2003. In 2003, 86 persons were under sentence of death.

17ARMED FORCES

In 2002, there were 8,462 active-duty military personnel and 2,072 civilian personnel stationed in Nevada. The largest installation is the Nellis Air Force Base near Las Vegas. The state has been the site of both ballistic missile and atomic weapons testing. In 2001, Nevada firms received about $324 million in federal defense contracts.

As of 2000, 238,128 military veterans were living in the state, including 36,062 of World War II; 28,441 of the Korean conflict; 71,415 from the Vietnam era; and 29,080 of 1990–2000 (including the Persian Gulf War). Veterans' benefits in 2002 totaled more than $347 million.

In 2000, the Nevada Highway Patrol employed 414 full-time sworn officers.

18MIGRATION

In 1870, about half of Nevada's population consisted of foreign immigrants, among them Chinese, Italians, Swiss, British, Irish, Germans, and French Canadians. Though their origins were diverse, their numbers were few—no more than 21,000 in all. Not until the 1940s did migrants come in large volume. Between 1940 and 1980, Nevada gained a total of 507,000 residents through migration, equal to 63% of the 1980 population; there was an additional net gain from migration of 233,000 during the 1980s, accounting for 75% of the net population increase. Between 1990 and 1998, Nevada had net gains of 397,000 in domestic migration and 45,000 in international migration. In 1998, the state admitted 6,106 foreign immigrants, of whom 2,881 were from Mexico. Between 1990 and 1998, the state's overall population grew 45.4%, making it the fastest growing state in the nation. In the period 1995–2000, 466,123 people moved into the state and 232,189 moved out, for a net gain of 233,934, of whom 22,189 were age 65 or over.

19INTERGOVERNMENTAL COOPERATION

Nevada takes part in the Colorado River Compact, the Tahoe Regional Planning Authority, and the California-Nevada Interstate Compact, under which the two states administer water rights involving Lake Tahoe and the Carson, Truckee, and Walker rivers. Other river compacts influence use of the Upper Niobrara river, and the boundary between Arizona and Nevada on the Colorado River. The state also is a signatory to the Interstate Oil and Gas Compact, the Western Interstate Commission for Higher Education, and the Western Interstate Energy Compact. Federal grants in 2001 totaled over $1.4 billion.

²⁰ECONOMY

Nevada is disadvantaged by aridity and a shortage of arable land but blessed with a wealth of mineral resources—gold, silver, copper, and other metals. Mining remains important, though overshadowed since World War II by tourism and gambling, which generate more than 50% of the state's income. Legalized gaming alone produces nearly half of Nevada's tax revenues. Throughout the 1990s, employment growth averaged 5.2% annually. The state economy roared into the 21st century, posting annual growth rates of 7.7% in 1998, 9% in 1999, and 8.6% in 2000. The national recession and slowdown in 2001 caused the pace of job growth to fall to 2.4% and the overall the growth rate to fall to 4.9%, but these remain well above national averages. Job growth in Nevada has been centered on growth in services, the retail trade, government and the construction sector.

Nevada's gross state product in 2001 was $79.2 billion, the 32nd highest among the states, to which general services contributed $25.2 billion; financial services, $14.9 billion; trade, $12.1 billion; government, $8.3 billion; construction, $7.5 billion; transportation and public utilities, $5.8 billion, and manufacturing, $3 billion. The public sector in 2001 constituted 10.5% of gross state product, below the average of 12% for all the states.

²¹INCOME

According to the Bureau of Economic Analysis, in 2001, Nevada had a per capita personal income (PCPI) of $30,128 which ranked 18th in the United States (including the District of Columbia) and was 99% of the national average, $30,413. The 2001 PCPI reflected an increase of 1.1% from 2000 compared to the national change of 2.2%. In 2001, Nevada had a total personal income (TPI) of $63,200,370,000 which ranked 32nd in the United States and accounted for 0.7% of the national total. The 2001 TPI reflected an increase of 5.1% from 2000 compared to the national change of 3.3%.

Earnings of persons employed in Nevada increased from $44,299,834,000 in 2000 to $46,554,959,000 in 2001, an increase of 5.1%. The largest industries in 2001 were services, 39.2% of earnings; state and local government, 11.4%; and retail trade, 10.1%. Of the industries that accounted for at least 5% of earnings in 2001, the slowest growing from 2000 to 2001 was construction (10.1% of earnings in 2001), which increased 3.1%; the fastest was state and local government, which increased 8.3%.

According to data released by the US Census Bureau, in 2000, the median household income was $44,755 compared to the national average of $42,148. In 2001, the median income for a family of four was $59,283 compared to the national average of $63,278. For the period 1999 to 2001, the average poverty rate was 9.0% which placed it 14th among the 50 states and the District of Columbia ranked lowest to highest.

²²LABOR

According to Bureau of Labor Statistics (BLS) provisional estimates, in July 2003 the seasonally adjusted civilian labor force in Nevada numbered 1,112,200, with approximately 59,500 workers unemployed, yielding an unemployment rate of 5.4%, compared to the national average of 6.2% for the same period. Since the beginning of the BLS data series in 1978, the highest unemployment rate recorded was 11.6% in February 1983. The historical low was 3.7% in June 1978. In 2001, an estimated 8.3% of the labor force was employed in construction; 4.2% in manufacturing; 6.2% in transportation, communications, and public utilities; 18.5% in trade; 4.9% in finance, insurance, and real estate; 38.3% in services; 11.4% in government; and 1.4% in agriculture.

The US Department of Labor reported that in 2002, 147,000 of Nevada's 971,000 employed wage and salary workers were members of unions. This represented 15.2% of those so employed, down from 17.0% in 2001. The national average is 13.2%. In all, 162,000 workers (16.7%) were represented by unions. In addition to union members, this category includes workers who report no union affiliation but whose jobs are covered by a union contract. Nevada is one of 22 states with a right-to-work law.

²³AGRICULTURE

Agricultural income in 2001 totaled $425 million (45th in the US), of which $153 million was from crops and $271 million from livestock and animal products. Chief crops in 2002 included 405,000 bushels of wheat, 1.52 million tons of hay, and 340,000 hundredweight of potatoes. Nevada's barley crop in 2002 was 194,000 bushels, down from 2,700,000 in 1983. Virtually all of the state's cropland requires irrigation.

²⁴ANIMAL HUSBANDRY

In 2003, Nevada ranches and farms had 510,000 cattle and calves, valued at $382.5 million. In 2001, the state produced 3.13 million lb (1.4 million kg) of sheep and lambs which brought in around $2.8 million in gross income. In 2002, the shorn wool production was an estimated 590,000 lb (267,600 kg) of wool. Nevada's total milk yield in 2001 was 485 million lb (220 million kg) from 25,000 milk cows.

²⁵FISHING

There is no commercial fishing industry in Nevada. In 1998, fish farms distributed 3 million trout for conservation or restoration purposes. The Lahontan National Fish Hatchery also distributes cutthroat trout within the state. In 1998, Nevada issued 163,855 sport fishing licenses.

²⁶FORESTRY

Nevada in 2002 had 10,204,000 acres (4,130,000 hectares) of forestland. In 1999, six national forests had 5,832,769 acres (2,368,522 hectares) in the National Forest System. Less than 2% of all forested land in Nevada was classified as commercial timberland.

²⁷MINING

In 2001, the value of nonfuel mineral production in Nevada was estimated at $2.93 billion, a decrease of about 1.6% from that reported in 2000. Overall, Nevada accounted for 7.5% of the national nonfuel mineral production value. Gold production was 264,000 kg in 2001, and silver production was 612 metric tons. The state's mines provided 75% and 33% of the nation's gold and silver in 2001, respectively. Nevada remained the leading state in the production of gold, silver, mercury, barite, and lithium, and 2nd in the production of diatomite. It was the sole producer of mined magnesite, which is used in making refractories and magnesia. Nevada also ranked 5th in lead, 6th in perlite, and 7th in lime. Nevada ranked 2nd among the states in 2001 production value of nonfuel minerals.

Gold remained Nevada's most valuable mineral commodity, accounting for 81% of the state's total nonfuel value, or about $2.38 billion. Construction sand and gravel and silver were the state's next most valuable minerals ($157 and $98.3 million, respectively).

²⁸ENERGY AND POWER

Nevada had an installed electrical capacity (utility and nonutility) of 7 million kW in 1999; 32.8 billion kWh of power were produced in the same year. About half the electrical energy is sold in the state; the remainder is exported, principally to California.

Hoover Dam, anchored in the bedrock of Black Canyon east of Las Vegas, is the state's largest hydroelectric installation, with an installed capacity of 1,039,000 kW in 1999. The first six of the dam's eight turbines came onstream during 1936–38, while the other two were added in 1944 and 1961. In 2002, total oil production was 2,000 barrels per day. In 2000 Nevada's total per capita energy consumption was 317 million Btu (79.9 million kcal), ranking it 34th among the 50 states.

29INDUSTRY

Industry in Nevada is limited but diversified, producing communications equipment, pet food, chemicals, and sprinkler systems, among other products. The total value of shipments by manufacturers in 1997 was $6.7 billion, with the 3rd highest growth rate in the country between 1992 and 1997 (102%).

Earnings of persons employed in Nevada increased from $34.3 billion in 1997 to $37.2 billion in 1998, an increase of 8.5%. The largest industries in 1998 were services, 40.7% of earnings; construction, 11.6%; and state and local government, 10.0%. Of the industries that accounted for at least 5% of earnings in 1998, the slowest growing from 1997 to 1998 was finance, insurance, and real estate (7.0% of earnings in 1998), which increased 6.1%; the fastest was construction, which increased 9.9%.

30COMMERCE

Nevada had 2,672 wholesale establishments with sales of $14 billion in 1997, according to the Census of Wholesale Trade. Sales between 1992 and 1997 recorded a growth rate of 80%; the highest in the nation for wholesale trade. Retail trade amounted to $19 billion in 1997, conducted by 9,002 establishments, ranking 2nd only to South Dakota in terms of growth between 1992 and 1997. The ratio of food stores and automotive dealers was 10% each, followed by eating and drinking places with one-third of the total number of establishments. Food sales totaled $3.7 billion, and general merchandise sales totaled $2.4 billion. Foreign exports in 1998 totaled $688 million.

31CONSUMER PROTECTION

The Bureau of Consumer Protection at the Office of the Attorney General was created in 1997 by the Nevada Legislature to protect consumers from deceptive or fraudulent sales practices and represent consumers' interests in government.

32BANKING

In 2002, there were 36 insured banks in Nevada, with total assets of $39 billion. Twenty-seven of these banks were state-chartered.

During 2001 and 2002, close to 9 of every 1,000 people in Nevada filed for personal bankruptcy, a significantly higher percentage than the rest of the nation. Nevada's insured banks reported weak earnings through third quarter 2002, due in large measure to a high proportion (70%) of newly-chartered institutions (less than nine years old).

33INSURANCE

Nevadans held 572,000 ordinary life insurance policies in 2001 with a total value of $58.4 billion; total value for all categories of life insurance (ordinary, group, industrial, and credit) was $101.6 billion. Death benefits paid that year totaled $236.6 million. As of 2000, there were six property and casualty and three life and health insurance companies incorporated or organized in the state. Property and liability insurers wrote over $2.69 billion in premiums. That year, there were 12,988 flood insurance policies in force in the state, with a total value of $2.1 billion.

34SECURITIES

There are no securities exchanges in Nevada. Approximately 553 brokers and dealers organizations perform securities transactions

in Nevada, involving over 1,000 employees. Additionally, 47 organizations are registered to vend advice regarding investment in securities. The state headquarters 38 NASDAQ-listed companies, and has incorporated nine NYSE-listed companies; the top five in terms of revenues being: Harrah's Entertainment, Mandalay Resort Group, MGM Grand, Sierra Health Services, and Boyd Gaming Corp.

35PUBLIC FINANCE

The budget is prepared biennially by the Budget Division of the Department of Administration and submitted by the governor to the legislature, which has unlimited power to change it.

Nevada's two largest revenue sources, sales and gaming taxes, surged during the mid-1990s. Percentage fee collections, the State's largest source of gaming revenue, had gains of at least 6% every year between 1993 and 1996. Growth in the general fund occurred at comparable levels throughout the 1990s.

General fund appropriations for 2002/03 totaled $1.89 billion, including $990.4 million for education, $544 million for human services, and $207 million for public safety. For the 2003/04 appropriations totaled $2.35 billion, including $1.29 billion for education, $645 million for human services, and $224 million for public safety.

The following table from the US Census Bureau contains information on revenues, expenditures, indebtedness, and cash/securities for 2001.

	($000)	PERCENT	PER CAPITA
Population (thousands, 2001)	2,098	(X)	(X)
Total Revenue	6,643,897	100.00	3,166.78
General revenue	5,776,331	86.94	2,753.26
Utility revenue	151,041	2.27	71.99
Liquor store revenue	–	–	–
Insurance trust revenue	716,525	10.78	341.53
Exhibit: Salaries and wages	1,031,246	15.28	491.54
Total expenditure	6,747,035	100.00	3,215.94
General expenditure	5,871,195	87.02	2,798.47
Education	2,333,818	34.59	1,112.40
Public welfare	844,518	12.52	402.53
Hospitals	117,135	1.74	55.83
Health	146,394	2.17	69.78
Highways	620,179	9.19	295.60
Police protection	62,011	0.92	29.56
Correction	235,568	3.49	112.28
Natural resources	83,417	1.24	39.76
Parks and recreation	17,308	0.26	8.25
Government administration	194,688	2.89	92.80
Interest on general debt	254,402	3.77	121.26
Other and unallocable	961,757	14.25	458.42
Utility expenditure	168,879	2.50	80.50
Liquor store expenditure	–	–	–
Insurance trust expenditure	706,961	10.48	336.97
Debt at end of fiscal year	3,387,247	100.00	1,614.51
Cash and security holdings	18,527,483	100.00	8,831.02

36TAXATION

Nevada has neither an individual nor a corporate income tax. Almost 85% of state-level tax collections come from general and selective sales (excise) taxes. Nevada levies a 6.5% state sales and use tax, with localities levying additional amounts ranging from none to 3.125%. There is a full array of state excise taxes covering amusements (almost 60% of Nevada's excise tax receipts), motor fuels, tobacco products, insurance premiums, public utilities, and other selected items. In 2002, contrary to trends in other states, Nevada lowered its gasoline tax a penny, from 24 cents to 23 cents a gallon. Nevada's estate tax is tied to the federal exemption for state death taxes, and is therefore on track to be phased out in tandem with the phasing out of the federal estate tax credit by 2007, absent countervailing action by the state to preserve its tax. Nevada's revenue losses from the phasing out of its estate tax are estimated at -$14 million for 2002/03, -$23 million for 2003/04 and -$39 million for 2006/07. Death and gift taxes accounted for 0.76% of state collections in 2002. Other state taxes include various license and franchise fees, state property taxes (although most property taxes are collected locally), severance taxes (a minerals extraction tax and a oil and gas conservation tax accounting for 0.5% of state-level tax revenue in 2002), and stamp taxes. Almost half of total state and local taxes (47.2% in 2000) in Nevada are collected at the local level.

The state collected $3.945 billion in taxes in 2002, of which 52.5% came from the general sales tax, 32% from selective sales taxes, 11.1% from license fees, and 2.8% from state property taxes. In 2003, Nevada ranked 41st among the states in terms of combined state and local tax burden, which amounted to about 8.9% of income.

The following table from the US Census Bureau provides a summary of taxes collected by the state in 2002.

	($000)	PER CAPITA
Total Taxes	**3,945,329**	**1,815.20**
Property taxes	112,613	51.81
Sales and gross receipts	3,337,996	1,535.78
General sales and gross receipts	2,070,013	952.39
Selective sales taxes	1,267,983	583.39
Alcoholic beverage	16,717	7.69
Amusements	720,732	331.6
Insurance Premiums	156,412	71.96
Motor fuels	266,101	122.43
Pari-mutuels	(X)	(X)
Public utilities	11,159	5.13
Tobacco products	63,739	29.33
Other selective sales	33,123	15.24
Licenses	438,756	201.87
Alcoholic beverages	(X)	(X)
Amusements	92,233	42.44
Corporation	36,138	16.63
Hunting and fishing	6,557	3.02
Motor vehicle	129,657	59.65
Motor vehicle operators	13,064	6.01
Public utility	(X)	(X)
Occupation and business, NEC	157,124	72.29
Other	3,983	1.83
Other taxes	55,964	25.75
Individual income	(X)	(X)
Corporation net income	(X)	(X)
Death and gift	30,088	13.84
Documentary and stock transfer	4,383	2.02
Severance	21,493	9.89
Other	(X)	(X)

37ECONOMIC POLICY

Federal projects have played an especially large role in Nevada's development. During the depression of the 1930s, Hoover (Boulder) Dam was constructed to provide needed jobs, water, and hydroelectric power for the state. Other public works—Davis Dam (Lake Mohave) and the Southern Nevada Water Project—have served similar purposes. The fact that some 87% of Nevada land is owned by the US government further increases the federal impact on the economy. Gaming supplies a large proportion of state revenues.

The Nevada Commission on Economic Development (NCED) offers a number of incentives to encourage the growth of primary businesses in Nevada, and to promote economic diversification. There is no corporate or personal income tax and other state taxes are low. The Department of Commerce issues tax-exempt industrial development bonds which provide low-interest financing of new construction or improvement of manufacturing facilities and other projects. The Development Corporation, a private financial corporation certified by the US Small Business Administration, offers long-term loans for expanding or new businesses. Rural small businesses can obtain loans from the Rural Nevada Development Corporation and the Nevada Revolving Loan Fund Program. A report in 2003 indicated that Nevada was the only state in the country in which manufacturing jobs grew July 2002 to December 2002; Nevada's workforce grew 1,400. A Made in Nevada program was featured by the NCED in 2003, which also collaborated in publishing the Nevada Investment Guide for Japanese Companies. Almost 30% of foreign-based companies in Nevada are Japanese.

38HEALTH

Infant mortality during the 12 months ending with December 2000 was 6.5 per 1,000 live births. In 1999, 5,807 abortions were performed, a rate of 15 per 1,000 women. The overall death rate in 2000 was 811.6 per 1,000 population, with heart disease and cerebrovascular disease the leading causes of death. Deaths by accident (including motor vehicle accidents) were above the national rate. In 2000, Nevada had the 2nd-highest suicide rate among the states, at 21.3 per 100,000 population; Alaska's rate was the highest at 22.0.

Nevada also had the 2nd-highest smoking prevalence in the US in 2000, at 29.1% of the adult population ages 18 and older. The HIV-related death rate was slightly lower than the national average in 2000 (4.7 per 100,000 population); a total of 4,665 AIDS cases were reported through 2001.

Nevada's 24 community hospitals had 207,844 admissions and 4,099 beds in 2001. There were 4,746 full-time registered nurses and 481 full-time licensed practical nurses in 2001 and only 196 physicians per 100,000 population in 2000. The average expense of a community hospital for care was $991.30 per inpatient day in 2001.

Federal government grants to cover the Medicare and Medicaid services in 2001 totaled $371 million; 250,543 enrollees received Medicare benefits that year. At least 16.1% of adults in Nevada were uninsured in 2002, the 4th-highest percentage of uninsured residents among the states.

39SOCIAL WELFARE

In 2001, the average weekly unemployment benefit was $225.76. Average monthly participation in the food stamp program in FY2002 comprised 97,035 persons (43,556 households). The average monthly benefit was $82.02, and the sum total of benefits paid in FY2002 was $95,508,198.

With the enactment of the Personal Responsibility and Work Opportunity Reconciliation Act of 1996, the US government has changed the form and regulations for many of its social welfare programs. Most significantly, it replaces Aid to Families with Dependent Children (AFDC), an open-ended entitlement program, with Temporary Assistance for Needy Families (TANF), a limited system of assistance funded largely through federal block grants. The reform act also impacts the food stamp program, the Supplemental Security Income program, and the child nutrition program. The law took effect on 1 July 1997 and provided $16.38 billion in block grants for fiscal years 1997–2002. The grants are to be divided among the states based on an equation involving the numbers of former AFDC recipients in each state.

Reauthorization of the 1996 social welfare legislation, scheduled for 2002, was delayed, and the original law had been extended three times as of July 2003, with the most recent extension running through September 2003. In June 2000 the state had 16,478 welfare recipients. State expenditures on the TANF program in FY2002 totaled $25,488,834.

In December 2001, Social Security benefits were paid to 299,910 Nevada residents. This number included 204,130 retired workers, 25,360 widows and widowers, 34,000 disabled workers, 15,100 spouses, and 21,320 children. Social Security beneficiaries represented 14.2% of the total state population and 91.6% of the state's population age 65 and older. Retired workers (excluding persons with special benefits) received an average monthly payment of $882; widows and widowers, $857; disabled workers, $873; and spouses, $437. Payments for children of retired workers averaged $420 per month; children of deceased workers, $594; and children of disabled workers, $257.

Federal Supplemental Security Income payments in December 2001 went to 27,161 Nevada residents, averaging $365 a month.

40 HOUSING

In 2002, there were an estimated 901,597 housing units, of which 808,077 were occupied; 60.1% were owner-occupied. About 54.5% of all units were single-family, detached dwellings; 19.5% were in buildings containing 3–9 units. Over 1,700 units were listed in a category of boats, RVs, vans, etc. Utility gas and electricity were the most common heating energy sources. It was estimated that 37,588 units lacked telephone service, 874 lacked complete plumbing facilities, and 3,229 lacked complete kitchen facilities. The average household size was 2.65 people.

In 2002, 35,615 new privately owned units were authorized for construction. The median home value was $157,407. The median monthly cost for mortgage owners was $1,267. Renters paid a median of $762 per month. During 2002, Nevada received over $27.8 million in community planning and development aid from the US Department of Housing and Urban Development.

41 EDUCATION

In 2000, 80.7% of Nevada residents age 25 and older were high school graduates; 18.2% had obtained a bachelor's degree or higher.

The total enrollment for fall 1999 in Nevada's public schools stood at 325,610. Of these, 239,625 attended schools from kindergarten through grade eight, and 85,985 attended high school. Minority students made up approximately 45% of the total enrollment in public elementary and secondary schools in 2001. Total enrollment was estimated at 340,707 in fall 2000 and expected to reach 378,000 by fall 2005. Enrollment in nonpublic schools in fall 2001 was 13,926. Expenditures for public education in 2000/01 were estimated at $1,918,795.

As of fall 2000, there were 98,631 students enrolled in college or graduate school, nearly all of them in the University of Nevada system, which has campuses in Las Vegas and Reno. In the same year Nevada had 15 degree-granting institutions, including Sierra Nevada College. In 1997, minority students comprised 24.6% of total postsecondary enrollment.

42 ARTS

Major exhibits are mounted by the Las Vegas Arts League and the Sierra Arts Foundation in Reno. The Nevada Opera, Reno Chamber Orchestra, and the Nevada Festival Ballet are all based in Reno. The Las Vegas Philharmonic, founded in 1998, has quickly become one of the largest arts organizations in the state. The Western Folklife Center in Elko presents an annual Cowboy Poetry Gathering in the last week of January.

In 2003, the Nevada State Council on the Arts and other Nevada arts organizations received grants totaling $642,400 from the National Endowment for the Arts (NEA). The state also gave substantial funding to the Arts Council. There are approximately 200 arts associations in Nevada and 15 local arts associations. The Nevada Humanities council sponsors annual programs that include a Chautauqua in Reno, Boulder City and Lake Tahoe, and the Vegas Valley Book Festival. In 2000, the National Endowment for the Humanities contributed $687,097 to 17 state programs.

43 LIBRARIES AND MUSEUMS

Nevada's public library, consisting of 12 county, nine district, and two city systems in 2000, had a combined book stock of 4,136,000 volumes and a circulation of 8,992,000. The University of Nevada had 956,282 books in its Reno campus library system and 861,362 at Las Vegas. The Nevada State Library in Carson City had 76,445. Total public library income amounted to $63,119,000 in 2000; including $504,942 in federal grants and $883,666 in state grants. Spending per capita was $22.24.

There are some 29 museums and historic sites. Notable are the Nevada State Museum in Carson City and Las Vegas; the museum of the Nevada Historical Society and the Fleischmann Planetarium, University of Nevada, in Reno; and the Museum of Natural History, University of Nevada, at Las Vegas.

44 COMMUNICATIONS

In 2001, 95.2% of Nevada's occupied housing units had telephones. In 2003, broadcast facilities comprised 27 major radio stations (7 AM, 20 FM) and 8 network television stations. In 2000, at least two large cable television systems served the Las Vegas and Reno areas. A total of 72,183 Internet domain names were registered in the state.

45 PRESS

In 2002, the state had four morning newspapers, four evening papers, and four Sunday papers. The leading newspaper was the *Las Vegas Review–Journal*, with a daily circulation of 165,754 and a Sunday circulation of 217,419. The *Reno Gazette–Journal*, with a daily circulation of 66,919 and Sunday circulation of 84,981, is the most influential newspaper in the northern half of the state. The regional interest *Nevada* magazine is published six times a year.

46 ORGANIZATIONS

In 2003, there were about 732 regional, national, and international organizations within the state. Notable national organizations with headquarters in Nevada include the Western History Association, the American Chess Association, the American Gem Society, the Gaming Standards Association, and the North American Boxing Federation.

Local arts and history are represented in part by the Central Nevada Historical Society, the Lake Tahoe Arts Council, the National Association for Outlaw and Lawman History, and the Nevada Opera Association.

The Confederate National Congress, founded in 1865, is based in North Las Vegas. The group, which has reported a membership of 2 million, supports a movement for Southern independence and the reestablishment of the Confederate States of America.

47 TOURISM, TRAVEL, AND RECREATION

Tourism remains Nevada's most important industry, employing over 228,000 people. In 2002, approximately 47.9 million travelers visited the state. About 25 million people visited state and national parks. A majority of all tourists flock to "Vegas" for gambling and for the top-flight entertainers who perform there. The gaming industry had total revenues of about $9.4 billion in 2002. The Nevada Commission on Tourism has branch offices in Japan, the United Kingdom, and Seoul, Korea.

Nevada attractions include Pyramid Lake, Lake Tahoe, Lake Mead, and Lehman Caves National Monument. There are 21 state parks and recreation areas, and the Great Basin National Park. Lake Mead National Recreation Area attracts 43% of all park visitors (totaling over 24 million people in 1999). Grand Canyon National Park is the 2nd most popular parks destination, with 18% of all parks visitors.

48 SPORTS

There are no major league professional sports teams in Nevada. Las Vegas has a minor league baseball team, the 51s, in the Triple-A Pacific Coast League. Las Vegas and Reno have hosted many professional boxing title bouts. Golfing and rodeo are also popular.

The basketball team at the University of Nevada-Las Vegas emerged as a national power in the late 1980s and early 1990s. The Runnin' Rebels won the National Championship in 1990.

Other annual sporting events include the Greens.com Open at Reno-Tahoe in Reno in August, the Invensys Classic at Las Vegas in October, the Nationals Finals Rodeo staged in Las Vegas each December, and the Carsdirect.com 400 at Las Vegas in March.

Among those born in Nevada, Andre Agassi is the most well known. He is one of the top tennis stars in the world.

49 FAMOUS NEVADANS

Nevadans who have held important federal offices include Raymond T. Baker (1877–1935) and Eva B. Adams (1908–91), both directors of the US Mint, and Charles B. Henderson (b.California, 1873–1954), head of the Reconstruction Finance Corporation. Prominent US senators have been James W. Nye (b.New York, 1815–76), also the only governor of Nevada Territory; William M. Stewart (b.New York, 1827–1909), author of the final form of the 15th Amendment to the US Constitution, father of federal mining legislation, and a leader of the free-silver-coinage movement in the 1890s; and Francis G. Newlands (b.Mississippi, 1848–1917), author of the federal Reclamation Act of 1902.

Probably the most significant state historical figure is George Wingfield (b.Arkansas, 1876–1959), a mining millionaire who exerted great influence over Nevada's economic and political life in the early 20th century. Among the nationally recognized personalities associated with Nevada is Howard R. Hughes (b.Texas, 1905–76), an aviation entrepreneur who became a casino and hotel owner and wealthy recluse in his later years.

Leading creative and performing artists have included operatic singer Emma Nevada (Emma Wixon, 1862–1940); painter Robert Caples (1908–79); and, among writers, Dan DeQuille (William Wright, b.Ohio, 1829–98); Lucius Beebe (b.Massachusetts, 1902–66); and Walter Van Tilburg Clark (b.Maine, 1909–71). Professional tennis player, Andre Kirk Agassi (b.1960) has been a lifelong resident of Las Vegas.

50 BIBLIOGRAPHY

Bowers, Michael Wayne. *The Sagebrush State: Nevada's History, Government, and Politics.* Reno: University of Nevada Press, 2002.

Bushnell, Eleanore, and Don W. Driggs. *The Nevada Constitution: Origin and Growth.* 5th ed. Reno: University of Nevada Press, 1980.

Davies, Richard O., ed. *The Maverick Spirit: Building the New Nevada.* Reno: University of Nevada Press, 1999.

Driggs, Don W. *Nevada Politics and Government: Conservatism in an Open Society.* Lincoln: University of Nebraska Press, 1996.

Fox, William L. *Playa Works: The Myth of the Empty.* Reno: University of Nevada Press, 2002.

Laxalt, Robert. *Nevada: A Bicentennial History.* New York: Norton, 1977.

Peck, Donna. *Nevada: Off the Beaten Path.* Old Saybrook, Conn.: Globe Pequot Press, 1999.

Toll, David W. *The Complete Nevada Traveler.* Virginia City, Nev.: Gold Hill, 1981.

NEW HAMPSHIRE

State of New Hampshire

ORIGIN OF STATE NAME: Named for the English county of Hampshire. **NICKNAME:** The Granite State. **CAPITAL:** Concord. **ENTERED UNION:** 21 June 1788 (9th). **SONG:** "Old New Hampshire." **MOTTO:** Live Free or Die. **FLAG:** The state seal, surrounded by laurel leaves with nine stars interspersed, is centered on a blue field. **OFFICIAL SEAL:** In the center is a broadside view of the frigate *Raleigh*; in the left foreground is a granite boulder, in the background a rising sun. A laurel wreath and the words "Seal of the State of New Hampshire 1776" surround the whole. **STATE EMBLEM:** Within an elliptical panel appears a replica of the Old Man of the Mountains, with the state name above and motto below. **ANIMAL:** White-tailed deer. **BIRD:** Purple finch. **BUTTERFLY:** Karner blue. **INSECT:** Ladybug. **FLOWER:** Purple lilac. **TREE:** White birch. **GEM:** Smoky quartz. **SPORT:** Skiing. **LEGAL HOLIDAYS:** New Year's Day, 1 January; Civil Rights Day, 3rd Monday in January; Washington's Birthday, 3rd Monday in February; Memorial Day, 30 May; Independence Day, 4 July; Labor Day, 1st Monday in September; Columbus Day, 2nd Monday in October; Election Day, Tuesday following 1st Monday in November in even-numbered years; Veterans Day, 11 November; Thanksgiving Day, 4th Thursday in November; Christmas Day, 25 December. **TIME:** 7 AM EST = noon GMT.

¹LOCATION, SIZE, AND EXTENT

Situated in New England in the northeastern US, New Hampshire ranks 44th in size among the 50 states. The total area of New Hampshire is 9,279 sq mi (24,033 sq km), comprising 8,993 sq mi (23,292 sq km) of land and 286 sq mi (741 sq km) of inland water. The state has a maximum extension of 93 mi (150 km) E-W and 180 mi (290 km) N-S. New Hampshire is shaped roughly like a right triangle, with the line from the far N to the extreme SW forming the hypotenuse.

New Hampshire is bordered on the N by the Canadian province of Quebec; on the E by Maine (with part of the line formed by the Piscataqua and Salmon Falls rivers) and the Atlantic Ocean; on the S by Massachusetts; and on the W by Vermont (following the west bank of the Connecticut River) and Quebec (with the line formed by Halls Stream).

The three southernmost Isles of Shoals lying in the Atlantic belong to New Hampshire. The state's total boundary line is 555 mi (893 km). Its geographic center lies in Belknap County, 3 mi (5 km) E of Ashland.

²TOPOGRAPHY

The major regions of New Hampshire are the coastal lowland in the southeast; the New England Uplands, covering most of the south and west; and the White Mountains (part of the Appalachian chain) in the north, including Mt. Washington, at 6,288 ft (1,918 m), the highest peak in the northeastern US. With a mean elevation of about 1,000 ft (305 m), New Hampshire is generally hilly, rocky, and in many areas densely wooded.

There are some 1,300 lakes and ponds, of which the largest is Lake Winnipesaukee, covering 70 sq mi (181 sq km). The principal rivers are the Connecticut (forming the border with Vermont), Merrimack, Salmon Falls, Piscataqua, Saco, and Androscoggin. Near the coast are the nine rocky Isles of Shoals, three of which belong to New Hampshire.

³CLIMATE

New Hampshire has a changeable climate, with wide variations in daily and seasonal temperatures. Summers are short and cool, winters long and cold. Concord has a normal daily mean

temperature of 46°F (8°C), ranging from 21°F (–6°C) in January to 70°F (21°C) in July. The record low temperature, –46°F (–43°C), was set at Pittsburg on 28 January 1925; the all-time high, 106°F (41°C) at Nashua, 4 July 1911. Annual precipitation at Concord (1971–2000) averaged 37.6 in (95.5 cm); the average snowfall in Concord is 65 in (165 cm) a year, with more than 100 in (254 cm) yearly in the mountains. The strongest wind ever recorded, other than during a tornado—231 mph (372 kph)—occurred on Mt. Washington on 12 April 1934.

⁴FLORA AND FAUNA

Well forested, New Hampshire supports an abundance of elm, maple, beech, oak, pine, hemlock, and fir trees. Among wild flowers, several orchids are considered rare. Three New Hampshire plant species were listed as threatened or endangered in 2003; the small whorled pogonia was threatened and Jesup's milk-vetch and Northeastern bulrush were endangered.

Among native New Hampshire mammals are the white-tailed deer, muskrat, beaver, porcupine, and snowshoe hare. Nine animal species were listed as threatened or endangered in 2003, including the Karner blue butterfly, bald eagle, dwarf wedgemussel, finback whale, and leatherback sea turtle.

⁵ENVIRONMENTAL PROTECTION

State agencies concerned with environmental protection include the Fish and Game Department, the Department of Resources and Economic Development (DRED), and the Department of Environmental Services (DES). DRED oversees the state's forests, lands and parks and, in the late 1980s, DRED was the lead state agency in the acquisition and long-term protection of open space. DES was created in 1987, consolidating several preexisting commissions and boards into four divisions which protect the environmental quality of air, groundwater, the state's surface waters, and solid waste. In the 1990s, DES has focused on such issues as ground-level ozone, landfill closures, groundwater remediation and protection of lakes, rivers, and other wetlands in New Hampshire. In 2003, New Hampshire had 91 hazardous waste sites listed in the Environmental Protection Agency's database, 18 of which were on the National Priorities List. In

2001, the state received $41,926,000 in federal grants from the Environmental Protection Agency; EPA expenditures for procurement contracts in New Hampshire that year amounted to just $1,000.

6POPULATION

New Hampshire ranked 41st in population in the US with an estimated total of 1,275,056 in 2002, an increase of 11% since 2000. Between 1990 and 2000, New Hampshire's population grew from 1,109,252 to 1,235,786, an increase of 11.4%. The population is projected to reach 1,281,000 by 2005 and 1.4 million by 2025. The population density in 2000 was 137.8 persons per sq mi.

In 2000 the median age was 37.1. Persons under 18 years old accounted for 25% of the population while 12% were age 65 or older. Leading cities with their 2000 estimated populations are Manchester, 107,066; Nashua, 86,605; and Concord, the capital, 40,687. All three are located in the southeastern region, where more than two-thirds of all state residents live.

7ETHNIC GROUPS

In 2000, a total of 223,026 New Hampshirites claimed English ancestry. Those claiming French ancestry numbered 180,947, and Irish 240,804. There are also about 127,153 French Canadians. In 2000, there were 9,035 black Americans, 15,931 Asians, 371 Pacific Islanders, and 2,964 Native Americans living in New Hampshire. In the same year, there were 20,489 residents of Hispanic origin, or 1.7% of the total population. The foreign-born population numbered 54,154, or 4.4% of the total population, in 2000.

8LANGUAGES

Some place-names, such as Ossipee, Mascoma, and Chocorua, preserve the memory of the Pennacook and Abnaki Algonkian tribes living in the area before white settlement.

New Hampshire speech is essentially Northern, with the special features marking eastern New England, especially the loss of the final /r/, as in *park* and *father*, and /yu/ in *tube* and *new*. *Raspberries* sounds like /rawzberries/, a wishbone is a *luckybone*, gutters are *eavespouts*, and cows are summoned by "Loo!" Canadian French is heard in the northern region.

In 2000, 91.7% of all state residents aged five and above—a total of 935,825—spoke only English at home.

The following table gives selected statistics from the 2000 census for language spoken at home by persons five years old and over. The category "Other Indo-European languages" includes Albanian, Gaelic, Lithuanian, and Rumanian. The category "Other Asian languages" includes Dravidian languages, Malayalam, Telugu, Tamil, and Turkish.

LANGUAGE	NUMBER	PERCENT
Population 5 years and over	1,160,340	100.0
Speak only English	1,064,252	91.7
Speak a language other than English	96,088	8.3
Speak a language other than English	96,088	8.3
French (incl. Patois, Cajun)	39,551	3.4
Spanish or Spanish Creole	18,647	1.6
German	4,788	0.4
Greek	3,411	0.3
Chinese	3,268	0.3
Italian	2,649	0.2
Portuguese or Portuguese Creole	2,394	0.2
Polish	2,094	0.2
Other Indo-European languages	1,468	0.1
Arabic	1,462	0.1
Vietnamese	1,449	0.1
Other Asian languages	1,240	0.1
Korean	1,228	0.1
Serbo-Croatian	1,182	0.1
Russian	1,009	0.1

9RELIGIONS

The first settlers of New Hampshire were Separatists, precursors of the modern Congregationalists (United Church of Christ) and their first church was probably built around 1633. The first Episcopal church was built in 1638 and the first Quaker meetinghouse in 1701; Presbyterians, Baptists, and Methodists built churches later in the 18th century. The state remained almost entirely Protestant until the second half of the 19th century, when Roman Catholics (French Canadian, Irish, and Italian) began arriving in significant numbers, along with some Greek and Russian Orthodox Christians.

In 2000, Roman Catholics were the largest single Christian denomination with about 431,259 adherents. Leading Protestant denominations were the United Church of Christ, 34,299; the United Methodist Church, 18,927; the American Baptist Churches–USA, 16,359; and the Episcopal Church, 16,148. There were about 10,020 Jews and 3,782 Muslims throughout the state. A few small groups have reported considerable growth since 1990. These include the Salvation Army, which went from 763 members in 1990 to 2,651 members in 2000. The International Church of the Foursquare Gospel grew from 51 adherents in 1990 to 1,203 in 2000 and the Christian Churches and Churches of Christ reported a membership of 1,503 in 2000, up from 396 in 1990.

10TRANSPORTATION

New Hampshire's first railroad, between Nashua and Lowell, Massachusetts, was chartered in 1835 and opened in 1838. Two years later, Exeter and Boston were linked by rail. The state had more than 1,200 mi (1,900 km) of track in 1920, but by 2000, the total route mileage in New Hampshire was only 415 mi (667 km).

In 2000, the state had a total of 15,211 mi (24,479 km) of roads, of which 12,273 mi (19,751 km) were rural and 2,938 mi (4,728 km) urban; the main north–south highway is I-93. As of 2001, there were 670,394 automobiles, 379,624 trucks, 48,651 motorcycles, and 1,733 buses registered in the state, as well as 929,630 licensed drivers. New Hampshire had 53 airports, 53 heliports, and 6 seaplane bases. The main airport is Manchester Municipal Airport.

11HISTORY

The land called New Hampshire has supported a human population for at least 10,000 years. Prior to European settlement, Indian tribes of the Algonkian language group lived in the region. During the 17th century, most of New Hampshire's Indians, called Pennacook, were organized in a loose confederation centered along the Merrimack Valley.

The coast of New England was explored by Dutch, English, and French navigators throughout the 16th century. Samuel de Champlain prepared the first accurate map of the New England coast in 1604, and Captain John Smith explored the Isles of Shoals in 1614. By this time, numerous English fishermen were summering on New England's coastal banks, using the Isles of Shoals for temporary shelter and to dry their catch.

The first English settlement was established along the Piscataqua River in 1623. From 1643 to 1680, New Hampshire was a province of Massachusetts, and the boundary between them was not settled until 1740. During the 18th century, as settlers moved up the Merrimack and Connecticut river valleys, they came into conflict with the Indians. By 1760, however, the Pennacook had been expelled from the region.

Throughout the provincial period, people in New Hampshire made their living through fishing, farming, cutting and sawing timber, shipbuilding, and coastal and overseas trade. By the first quarter of the 18th century, Portsmouth, the provincial capital, had become a thriving commercial port. New Hampshire's terrain

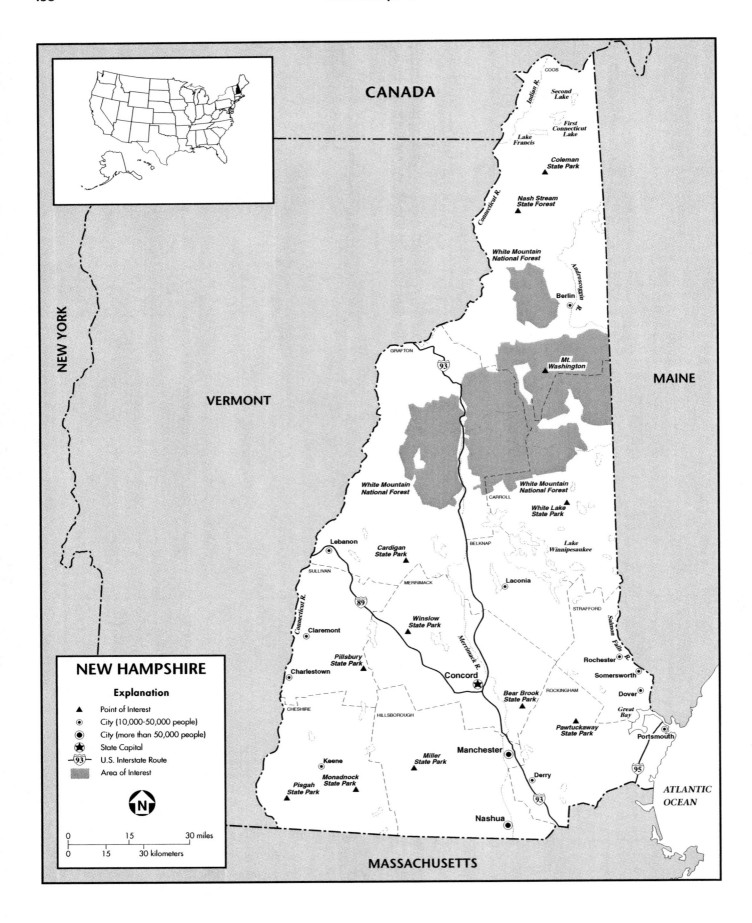

CANADA

NEW YORK

VERMONT

MAINE

COOS

Indian R.

Second Lake

First Connecticut Lake

Lake Francis

Coleman State Park

Connecticut R.

Nash Stream State Forest

White Mountain National Forest

Androscoggin R.

Berlin

GRAFTON

Mt. Washington

White Mountain National Forest

White Mountain National Forest

CARROLL

White Lake State Park

Lebanon

Cardigan State Park

BELKNAP

Lake Winnipesaukee

SULLIVAN

MERRIMACK

Laconia

Connecticut R.

Claremont

Winslow State Park

STRAFFORD

Pillsbury State Park

Merrimack R.

Rochester

Salmon Falls R.

Charlestown

Somersworth

Concord

Dover

CHESHIRE

HILLSBOROUGH

Bear Brook State Park

ROCKINGHAM

Great Bay

Pawtuckaway State Park

Portsmouth

Keene

Miller State Park

Manchester

Derry

Monadnock State Park

Pisgah State Park

ATLANTIC OCEAN

Nashua

MASSACHUSETTS

NEW HAMPSHIRE

Explanation

▲ Point of Interest
⊙ City (10,000-50,000 people)
◉ City (more than 50,000 people)
★ State Capital
〔93〕 U.S. Interstate Route
▓ Area of Interest

N

0   15   30 miles
0   15   30 kilometers

worked against Portsmouth's commercial interests, however, by dictating that roads (and later railroads) run in a north-south direction—making Boston, and not Portsmouth, New England's primary trading center. During the Revolutionary War, extensive preparations were made to protect the harbor from a British attack that never came. Although nearly 18,500 New Hampshire men enlisted in the war, no battle was fought within its boundaries. New Hampshire was the first of the original 13 colonies to establish an independent government—on 5 January 1776, six months before the Declaration of Independence.

During the 19th century, as overseas trade became less important to the New Hampshire economy, textile mills were built, principally along the Merrimack River. By midcentury, the Merrimack Valley had become the social, political, and economic center of the state. So great was the demand for workers in these mills that immigrant labor was imported during the 1850s; a decade later, French Canadian workers began pouring south from Quebec.

Although industry thrived, agriculture did not; New Hampshire hill farms could not compete against Midwestern farms. The population in farm towns dropped, leaving a maze of stone walls, cellar holes, and new forests on the hillsides. The people who remained began to cluster in small village centers.

World War I, however, marked a turning point for New Hampshire industry. As wartime demand fell off, the state's old textile mills were unable to compete with newer cotton mills in the South, and New Hampshire's mill towns became as depressed as its farm towns; only in the north, the center for logging and paper manufacturing, did state residents continue to enjoy moderate prosperity. Industrial towns in the southern counties responded to the decline in textile manufacture by making other items, particularly shoes, but the collapse of the state's railroad network spelled further trouble for the slumping economy. The growth of tourism aided the rural areas primarily, as old farms became spacious vacation homes for "summer people," who in some cases paid the bulk of local property taxes.

During the 1960s, New Hampshire's economic decline began to reverse, except in agriculture. In the 1970s and early 1980s, growth in the state's northern counties remained modest, but the combination of Boston's urban sprawl, interstate highway construction, and low state taxes encouraged people and industry—notably high-technology businesses—to move into southern New Hampshire. The state's population doubled between 1960 and 1988, from 606,921 to 1.1 million. Most of the arrivals were younger, more affluent, and better educated than the natives. The newcomers shared the fiscally conservative views of those born in New Hampshire but tended to be more liberal on social questions such as gun control and abortion. The rise in population strained government services, prompted an increase in local taxes, and provoked concern over the state's vanishing open spaces. The state's population has held fairly steady since 1988, with an estimated 1.25 million people in 2001.

Like other New England states, New Hampshire was hard hit by the recession of the early 1990s, with the unemployment rate rising to 10% by 1992. But by the mid-1990s a recovery was underway, and about 30,000 of the more than 60,000 jobs lost during the recession had been regained. By 1999 the state enjoyed the 2nd-lowest unemployment rate in the nation—just 2.7%. Population growth in the state threatened to do away with the annual town meeting. A study released in 2000 showed that more towns had replaced the celebrated tradition with the official ballot form of governance.

In 2000 New Hampshire Chief Justice David Brock faced an unprecedented trial on charges he influenced a lower-court judge about a powerful state senator's case, allowed a Supreme Court colleague to have a say in the handling of his own divorce, permitted disqualified justices to participate in cases, and lied to a house committee investigating the court. Brock was the first New Hampshire official impeached in 210 years and his trial was to be the first in the state's history. The last impeachment of a New Hampshire official was in 1790; Supreme Court Justice Woodbury Langdon resigned before he was tried. Brock was acquitted by the New Hampshire Senate in October 2000.

Like other New England states in the early 2000s, New Hampshire faced record-breaking budget deficits. Governor Craig Benson vetoed a June 2003 two-year budget passed by the state legislature, saying it would increase the deficit and raise taxes. Benson, elected in 2002, also signed two gun control bills in 2003 that he said would protect gun ownership.

12 STATE GOVERNMENT

New Hampshire's constitution, adopted in 1784 and extensively revised in 1792, is the second-oldest state-governing document still in effect. Every 10 years, the people vote on the question of calling a convention to revise it; proposed revisions must then be approved by two-thirds of the voters at a referendum. Amendments may also be placed on the ballot by a three-fifths vote of both houses of the state legislature. If placed on the ballot, an amendment must be approved by two-thirds of the voters on the amendment in order to be ratified. The constitution was amended 143 times by January 2003.

The state legislature, called the General Court, consists of a 24-member senate and a 400-seat house of representatives, larger than that of any other state. Legislative sessions begin each January and are limited to 45 legislative days. Special sessions, indirectly limited to 15 legislative days, may be called by a two-thirds vote of the members of each house. Senators must be at least 30 years old, representatives 18. The state residency requirement for senators is a minimum of seven years and for representatives a minimum of two. Legislators, who must reside in their districts, serve two-year terms, for which they were paid $200 ($100 per year) as of 2002, unchanged from 1999.

The only executive elected statewide is the governor, who serves a two-year term and is assisted by a five-member executive council, elected for two years by district. As of 2000, New Hampshire and Vermont were the only two states whose governors served two-year terms. The council must approve all administrative and judicial appointments. The secretary of state and state treasurer are elected by the legislature. The governor must be at least 30 years old and must have been a state resident for seven years before election. In 2002, the governor's salary was $100,690.

A bill becomes law if signed by the governor, if passed by the legislature and left unsigned by the governor for five days while the legislature is in session, or if passed over a gubernatorial veto by two-thirds of the elected legislators in each house. A voter must be at least 18 years old, a US citizen, and must have a permanent established domicile in the state of New Hampshire. Restrictions apply to convicted felons. As of 2003, New Hampshire was the only state that did not allow voters to register by mail.

13 POLITICAL PARTIES

New Hampshire has almost always gone with the Republican presidential nominee in recent decades, but the Democratic and Republican parties were much more evenly balanced in local and state elections. New Hampshire's quadrennial presidential preference primary, traditionally the first state primary of the campaign season, accords to New Hampshirites a degree of national political influence and a claim on media attention far out of proportion to their numbers. In the 1992 presidential election, New Hampshire voters defied their tradition and chose Democrat Bill Clinton over Republican incumbent George Bush by a scant 6,556 votes. Clinton won the state again in 1996. In the 2000 presidential election, Republican George W. Bush received 48% of the vote to Democrat Al Gore's 47%; Green Party candidate Ralph Nader garnered 4% of the vote. In 2002 there were 690,159 registered voters. In 1998, 27% of registered voters were Democratic, 36% Republican, and 36% unaffiliated or members of other parties. The state had four electoral votes in the 2000 presidential election.

As of 2003, both of New Hampshire's senators, John Sununu (elected in 2002) and Judd Gregg (reelected in 1998), were Republicans. Following the 2002 election, both House seats were held by Republicans. In 2002 Republican Craig Benson was elected governor. The New Hampshire state senate in mid-2003 had 18 Republicans and 6 Democrats, and the state house had 281 Republicans and 119 Democrats.

New Hampshire Presidential Vote by Major Political Parties, 1948–2000

YEAR	ELECTORAL VOTE	NEW HAMPSHIRE WINNER	DEMOCRAT	REPUBLICAN
1948	4	Dewey (R)	107,995	121,299
1952	4	*Eisenhower (R)	106,663	166,287
1956	4	*Eisenhower (R)	90,364	176,519
1960	4	Nixon (R)	137,772	157,989
1964	4	*Johnson (D)	182,065	104,029
1968	4	*Nixon (R)	130,589	154,903
1972	4	*Nixon (R)	116,435	213,724
1976	4	Ford (R)	147,635	185,935
1980	4	*Reagan (R)	108,864	221,705
1984	4	*Reagan (R)	120,347	267,050
1988	4	*Bush (R)	163,696	281,537
1992**	4	*Clinton (D)	209,040	202,484
1996**	4	*Clinton (D)	246,214	196,532
2000	4	*Bush, G. W. (R)	266,348	273,559

* Won US presidential election.
** Independent candidate Ross Perot received 121,337 votes in 1992, and 48,390 votes in 1996.

14LOCAL GOVERNMENT

New Hampshire has 10 counties (2002), each governed by three commissioners. Other elected county officials include the sheriff, attorney, treasurer, registrar of deeds, and registrar of probate.

As of 2002, New Hampshire also had 13 municipalities and 221 townships, 167 public school districts, and 148 special districts. Most municipalities have elected mayors and councils. Some municipal charters provide for the council-manager or commission system of government. The basic unit of town government is the traditional town meeting, held once a year, when selectmen and other local officials are chosen.

15STATE SERVICES

To address the continuing threat of terrorism and to work with the federal Department of Homeland Security (created in 2002 following the terrorist attacks of 11 September 2001), homeland security in New Hampshire in 2003 operated under the authority of the governor; the emergency management director was designated as the state homeland security advisor.

The Department of Education, governed by the State Board of Education (which appoints an education commissioner), has primary responsibility for public instruction. The Department of Transportation and the Port Authority share transport responsibilities, while the Department of Health and Human Services oversees public health and mental health and welfare. Executive branch departments include the departments of agriculture, cultural affairs, fish and game, justice, revenue, and parks and recreation. Authorities, boards, and commissions include the Liquor Commission and the Sweepstakes Commission.

16JUDICIAL SYSTEM

All judges in New Hampshire are appointed by the governor, subject to confirmation by the executive council; appointments are to age 70, with retirement compulsory at that time. The state's highest court, the supreme court, consists of a chief justice and four associate justices. The main trial court is the superior court for which there were 28 judges in 1999.

New Hampshire's total crime rate in 2001 was 2,321.6 per 100,000 inhabitants, including a total of 2,144 violent crimes and 27,089 property crimes in that year. In June 2001, there were 2,323 inmates in state and federal correctional facilities, an increase of 3.1% over the previous year. The state's incarceration rate stood at 184 per 100,000 inhabitants.

New Hampshire imposes the death penalty but has executed only one person since 1930. No prisoners were under sentence of death in 2003.

17ARMED FORCES

In 2002, there were 326 active-duty military personnel and 1,051 civilian personnel stationed in New Hampshire. The principal military installation is the Portsmouth Naval Shipyard. Firms in the state received nearly $489 million in defense contract awards in 2001. As of 2000, veterans living in New Hampshire numbered 139,038, of whom 24,594 were veterans of World War II; 16,880, the Korean conflict; 42,815, the Vietnam era; and 12,770 served during 1990–2000 (including the Persian Gulf War). Veterans' benefits totaled more than $227 million in 2002.

In 2000, the New Hampshire State Police employed 315 full-time sworn officers.

18MIGRATION

From the time of the first European settlement until the middle of the 19th century, the population of New Hampshire was primarily of British origin. Subsequently, immigrants from Quebec and from Ireland, Italy, and other countries began arriving in significant numbers. New Hampshire's population growth since 1960 has been fueled by migrants from other states. The net gain from migration was 74,000 from 1985 to 1990. Between 1990 and 1998, New Hampshire had net gains of 19,000 in domestic migration and 6,000 in international migration. In 1998, the state admitted 1,010 foreign immigrants. Between 1990 and 1998, the state's overall population increased 6.8%. In the period 1995–2000, 162,250 people moved into the state and 134,347 moved out, for a net gain of 27,903, of whom came from Massachusetts.

19INTERGOVERNMENTAL COOPERATION

New Hampshire participates in the American and Canadian French Cultural Exchange Commission, Atlantic States Marine Fisheries Commission, Connecticut River Valley Flood Control Compact, Maine-New Hampshire Interstate School Compact, Northeastern Forest Fire Protection Compact, and various New England regional compacts (including compacts on radiological health protection, higher education, corrections, police, trucking fees and permits, water pollution control, sewage and garbage disposal, fire protection, and the lotto). Federal grants to New Hampshire totaled almost $1.3 billion in 2001.

20ECONOMY

New Hampshire is one of the most industrialized states in the US, ranking well above the national median in proportion of labor force employed in manufacturing and in value added by manufacture. Between 1977 and 1982, manufacturing employment rose 13%, to 107,500, as many high-technology firms moved into the southern portion of the state. Since World War II, tourism has been one of the state's fastest-growing sources of income. Coming into the 21st century, the New Hampshire economy was booming, posting annual growth rates of 8.2% in 1998, 7% in 1999, and 9.3% in 2000. It was clearly headed for a correction, and in the national recession and slowdown of 2001 it was one of the few states that experienced a contraction for the year, albeit a small –0.4% contraction. Due to the large growth of information technology (IT) related jobs in southern New Hampshire in the 1990s, this was the region of New England that saw the greatest fall in personal income between mid-2000 and mid-2002.

New Hampshire's gross state product in 2001 was $47.2 billion, the 38th highest among the states, to which financial services contributed $11.8 billion; general services, $10.2 billion; trade, $8.3 billion; manufacturing, $7.6 billion; government, $3.8 billion; transportation and public utilities, $2.8 billion, and construction, $2.3 billion. The public sector in 2001 constituted 9.1% of gross state product, the 4th-lowest percent among the states.

[21]INCOME

According to the Bureau of Economic Analysis, in 2001, New Hampshire had a per capita personal income (PCPI) of $33,969 which ranked 7th in the United States (including the District of Columbia) and was 112% of the national average, $30,413. The 2001 PCPI reflected an increase of 2.1% from 2000 compared to the national change of 2.2%. In 2001, New Hampshire had a total personal income (TPI) of $42,778,997,000 which ranked 37th in the United States and accounted for 0.5% of the national total. The 2001 TPI reflected an increase of 3.7% from 2000 compared to the national change of 3.3%.

Earnings of persons employed in New Hampshire increased from $27,488,487,000 in 2000 to $28,315,411,000 in 2001, an increase of 3.0%. The largest industries in 2001 were services, 30.1% of earnings; durable goods manufacturing, 14.1%; and retail trade, 11.8%. Of the industries that accounted for at least 5% of earnings in 2001, the slowest growing from 2000 to 2001 was durable goods manufacturing, which decreased 5.6%; the fastest was construction (7.5% of earnings in 2001), which increased 11.8%.

According to data released by the US Census Bureau, in 2000, the median household income was $48,928 compared to the national average of $42,148. In 2001, the median income for a family of four was $72,606 compared to the national average of $63,278. For the period 1999 to 2001, the average poverty rate was 6.2% which placed it 1st among the 50 states and the District of Columbia ranked lowest to highest.

[22]LABOR

According to Bureau of Labor Statistics (BLS) provisional estimates, in July 2003 the seasonally adjusted civilian labor force in New Hampshire numbered 716,900, with approximately 30,900 workers unemployed, yielding an unemployment rate of 4.3%, compared to the national average of 6.2% for the same period. Since the beginning of the BLS data series in 1978, the highest unemployment rate recorded was 7.9% in July 1982. The historical low was 2.2% in March 1988. In 2001, an estimated 5.6% of the labor force was employed in construction; 17.8% in manufacturing; 4.3% in transportation, communications, and public utilities; 21.0% in trade; 5.2% in finance, insurance, and real estate; 25.2% in services; 11.6% in government; and 1.5% in agriculture.

The US Department of Labor reported that in 2002, 60,000 of New Hampshire's 613,000 employed wage and salary workers were members of unions. This represented 9.7% of those so employed, down from 10.0% in 2001 and from 12.6% in 1998. The national average is 13.2%. In all, 69,000 workers (11.2%) were represented by unions. In addition to union members, this category includes workers who report no union affiliation but whose jobs are covered by a union contract.

[23]AGRICULTURE

Only Rhode Island and Alaska generate less income from farming than New Hampshire. Farm income in 2001 was $155 million, 58% of which was crops.

In 2001 there were about 3,100 farms occupying about 410,000 acres (166,000 hectares). Leading crops and their output in 2002 were hay, 72,000 tons, and commercial apples, 24 million lb (10.8 million kg).

[24]ANIMAL HUSBANDRY

Dairy and poultry products are the mainstays of New Hampshire's agriculture. In 2001, the state had 18,000 milk cows, with a total milk yield of 323 million lb (147 million kg). Poultry items included 889,000 lb (403,000 kg) of chickens, sold for $35,000; 129,000 lb (58,500 kg) of turkey, valued at $190,000, and 42 million eggs, valued at $3.1 million.

[25]FISHING

New Hampshire's commercial catch in 1998 consisted of 10,143,000 lb (4,600,000 kg), much of it cod and lobster, worth $11,178,000. The state's 38 fish processors and wholesalers employed 495 persons in 1997. In 1998, the state issued 162,626 sport fishing licenses.

[26]FORESTRY

New Hampshire had 4,818,000 acres (1,950,000 hectares) of forestland in 2002, of which 4,503,000 acres (1,822,000 hectares) were considered suitable for commercial use. Of that total, 83% was privately owned. Forests cover about 86% of New Hampshire. Lumber production in 2002 was 287 million board feet.

[27]MINING

The value of nonfuel mineral production in New Hampshire in 2001 was estimated to be about $60 million, an incease of about 5.5% over 2000. The total dollar values reported in 2001 were artificially low because information was withheld to protect company confidentiality.

Construction sand and gravel remained the state's most important nonfuel mineral in 2001, accounting for about 75% of total value. According to preliminary figures, in that year 9.5 million metric tons of construction sand and gravel were mined, worth $46.1 million. There were 3.3 million metric tons of crushed stone mined, worth $14.2 million. Dimension stone, common clay, and gem stones collected by hobbyists accounted for the remainder of the state's mineral value. Sand and gravel are mined in every county, and dimension granite is quarried in Hillsborough, Merrimack, and Coos counties. Crude gypsum, imported into the state, was calcined at two plants to manufacture wallboard.

[28]ENERGY AND POWER

About 90% of all New Hampshire's electrical power was generated by water in the 1930s. By 1999, however, about 20% of the state's electricity came from coal-fired plants, another 10% from oil-fired plants, and 8% from hydroelectric facilities. Power production (utility and nonutility) totaled 16.2 billion kWh in 1999, when total installed capacity was 2.8 million kW. In 1990, the controversial nuclear power plant at Seabrook, being built by Public Service Co. of New Hampshire, began operating. Originally planned as a two-reactor, 2,300-Mw facility, Seabrook was scaled back to one 1,150 MW reactor whose cost was about five times the original $1 billion two-reactor estimate. As of 2001, the plant had a capacity of 1,161 MW and was the largest reactor in New England. Nuclear power supplied 54% of the state's electricity in 1999. In 2000 New Hampshire's total per capita energy consumption was 266 million Btu (67 million kcal), ranking it 44th among the 50 states.

29INDUSTRY

During the provincial era, shipbuilding was New Hampshire's major industry. By 1870, cotton and woolen mills, concentrated in the southeast, employed about one-third of the labor force and accounted for roughly half the value of all manufactures.

The value of shipments by manufacturers in 1997 was $20 billion, exhibiting a growth of 79% from 1992 (4th in the nation in terms of growth). As of 1997, there was one Fortune 500 company headquartered in New Hampshire, Tyco International.

Earnings of persons employed in New Hampshire increased from $21.4 billion in 1997 to $23.2 billion in 1998, an increase of 8.2%. The largest industries in 1998 were services, 27.6% of earnings; durable goods manufacturing, 16.6%; and retail trade, 11.6%. Of the industries that accounted for at least 5% of earnings in 1998, the slowest growing from 1997 to 1998 was state and local government (9.2% of earnings in 1998), which increased 4.4%; the fastest was wholesale trade (7.0% of earnings in 1998), which increased 13.4%.

30COMMERCE

New Hampshire wholesalers had $12 billion in sales in 1997. Retailers had sales of $16 billion, the leading sectors in terms of numbers of establishments being food stores and automotive dealers, 12% each; and restaurants and taverns, 26%. Foreign exports of goods originating in New Hampshire totaled $1.7 billion in 1998.

31CONSUMER PROTECTION

The Consumer Protection and Antitrust Bureau of the Attorney General's Office is responsible for enforcing New Hampshire's consumer protection laws.

32BANKING

New Hampshire had 32 insured banks in 2002, nine of which were state-chartered. Total assets for insured banks that year amounted to $29 billion.

Twenty percent of New Hampshire's banks have long-term asset concentrations greater than 30% of earnings assets. This is due in large measure to the large percentage of thrifts and residential lenders in the state, given the fact that mortgage rates in 2001/02 remained low, and borrowers secured long-term fixed-rate loans at lower rates for refinancing purposes. Over one-half of all insured banks in New Hampshire are savings institutions, and residential real estate loans make up 53% of the average loan portfolio in the state.

Personal bankruptcy filings increased in 2002, due to slow income growth rates. Over 45% of New Hampshire's banks report high-risk loan concentration.

33INSURANCE

In 2001 there were 631,000 ordinary life insurance policies in force in New Hampshire, with a total value of $48.1 billion; total value for all categories of life insurance (ordinary, group, industrial, and credit) was $78.6 billion. Death benefits paid that year totaled $195.1 million. As of 2000, there were 35 property and casualty and six life and health insurance companies incorporated or organized in the state. Property and liability insurers wrote over $1.5 billion in premiums. That year, there were 4.885 flood insurance policies in force in the state, with a total value of $576,143.

34SECURITIES

New Hampshire has no securities exchanges. There are over 237 broker-dealer firms doing business in the state, involving over 1,000 employees; 74 investment advisory organizations operate in New Hampshire. The state is home to 19 NASDAQ-listed companies, and has incorporated nine NYSE-listed companies; the top five in terms of revenue being: Fisher Scientific International, Cabletron Systems, Timberland, Standex International Corp., and General Chemical Group.

35PUBLIC FINANCE

The New Hampshire state budget is drawn up biennially by the Department of Administrative Services and then submitted by the governor to the legislature for amendment and approval. The fiscal year runs from 1 July to 30 June.

The biennial New Hampshire budget for 2000/01 ($2.8 billion) presaged the lowest capital budget since 1989, avoiding both an increase in taxes and the addition of executive branch employees, in preparation for a slowdown in economic growth. In 2000/01, New Hampshire had a comfortable starting balance the equaled 5.2% of expenditures, but since 2001/02 it has been running deficits due to revenue shortfalls and increasing costs. The starting balance in 2001/02 was a deficit equal to 3.2% of expenditures, and in 2002/03, the starting balance was a deficit equal to 4.8% of expenditures.

The following table from the US Census Bureau contains information on revenues, expenditures, indebtedness, and cash/securities for 2001.

	($000)	PERCENT	PER CAPITA
Population (thousands, 2001)	1,259	(X)	(X)
Total Revenue	4,574,828	100.00	3,633.70
General revenue	3,999,543	87.42	3,176.76
Utility revenue	99	–	0.08
Liquor store revenue	306,394	6.70	243.36
Insurance trust revenue	268,792	5.88	213.50
Exhibit: Salaries and wages	656,985	14.89	521.83
Total expenditure	4,411,243	100.00	3,503.77
General expenditure	3,890,457	88.19	3,090.12
Education	1,320,844	29.94	1,049.12
Public welfare	1,063,926	24.12	845.06
Hospitals	44,227	1.00	35.13
Health	141,764	3.21	112.60
Highways	361,214	8.19	286.91
Police protection	41,482	0.94	32.95
Correction	83,968	1.90	66.69
Natural resources	41,887	0.95	33.27
Parks and recreation	7,713	0.17	6.13
Government administration	187,107	4.24	148.62
Interest on general debt	252,294	5.72	200.39
Other and unallocable	344,031	7.80	273.26
Utility expenditure	141	–	0.11
Liquor store expenditure	262,590	5.95	208.57
Insurance trust expenditure	258,055	5.85	204.97
Debt at end of fiscal year	5,607,884	100.00	4,454.24
Cash and security holdings	9,255,107	100.00	7,351.16

36TAXATION

New Hampshire has neither state sales tax nor a state income tax, it does levy a flat 8.5% corporate income tax on net corporate income. The state also imposes a full array of excise taxes, on motor fuels, tobacco products, insurance premiums, public utilities, alcoholic beverages (the state controls all sales), amusements, pari-mutuels, and many other selected items. Interest and dividend income are taxed at 5%, and there is an 18% inheritance tax for non-linear inheritors. New Hampshire's estate tax is tied to the federal exemption for state death taxes, and is therefore set to be phased out in tandem with the phasing out of the federal estate tax credit by 2007 unless the state takes positive action to preserve an estate tax. New Hampshire's revenue losses from the phasing out of its inheritance tax are estimated at -$7 million for 2002/03, -$9.4 million for 2003/04 and -$31 million for 2006/07. Death and gift taxes accounted for 2.9% of state collections in 2002. Other taxes include various license and franchise fees, stamp taxes, and state property taxes. Most property taxes are collected locally. About 42% (42.1% in 2000) of total state and local taxes are collected locally.

The state collected $1.88 billion in taxes in 2002, of which 32% came from the selective sales taxes, 26.6% from state property taxes, 20% from corporate net income taxes, 9.1% from state license fees, and 5.3% from stamp taxes (documentary and stock transfers). In 2003, New Hampshire ranked 49th among the states in terms of state and local tax burden, which amounted to only 6.6% of income.

The following table from the US Census Bureau provides a summary of taxes collected by the state in 2002.

	($000)	PER CAPITA
Total Taxes	**1,883,924**	**1,477.52**
Property taxes	501,703	393.48
Sales and gross receipts	605,386	474.79
General sales and gross receipts	(X)	(X)
Selective sales taxes	605,386	474.79
Alcoholic beverage	11,882	9.32
Amusements	1,759	1.38
Insurance Premiums	69,331	54.37
Motor fuels	120,006	94.12
Pari-mutuels	4,376	3.43
Public utilities	63,605	49.88
Tobacco products	82,625	64.8
Other selective sales	251,802	197.48
Licenses	171,491	134.5
Alcoholic beverages	3,545	2.78
Amusements	363	0.28
Corporation	4,350	3.41
Hunting and fishing	8,016	6.29
Motor vehicle	76,625	60.1
Motor vehicle operators	13,763	10.79
Public utility	5,415	4.25
Occupation and business, NEC	57,080	44.77
Other	2,334	1.83
Other taxes	605,344	474.76
Individual income	71,433	56.02
Corporation net income	377,313	295.92
Death and gift	55,955	43.88
Documentary and stock transfer	100,643	78.93
Severance	(X)	(X)
Other	(X)	(X)

37 ECONOMIC POLICY

Business incentives in New Hampshire include a generally favorable tax climate (which includes the absence of sales, personal income, and capital gains taxes), specific tax incentives and exemptions, and relatively low wage rates. The state has offered loan programs through the New Hampshire Business Finance Authority since 1992, aimed at encouraging economic development and job creation and at assisting small businesses. The state also participates in a joint venture with Maine and Vermont which provides loans to export companies. Foreign Trade Zone No. 81 provides economic incentives to companies doing business in the international markets. New Hampshire's Division of Economic Development (DED), within the Department of Resources and Economic Development, has the main responsibility for state support of programs to increase jobs and revenues in the state. In 2003, the main operational units within the DED were focused on assistance for business relocations and expansions; New Economy Ventures (on which New Hampshire was rated by the Milken Institute as ninth among the states); community development; internet development; exports of states products, imports of state products and tourism. Under the program NH Works, employers were offered free assistance on all facets of hiring the right employees.

38 HEALTH

Infant mortality in New Hampshire for 2000 stood at 5.7 per 1,000 live births, among the lowest rates among the states. Abortions numbered 2,300 in 1996, or 8 per 1,000 women. The overall death rate in 2000 was 797.5 per 100,000 population, well below the national rate. Rates for death by heart disease, cerebrovascular diseases, accidents and adverse effects, motor vehicle accidents, homicide, and firearm injuries were lower than the US rates; rates for death by suicide and chronic obstructive and pulmonary diseases were higher in 2000. A total of 919 AIDS cases had been reported through 2001. Among persons ages 18 and older, 25.4% were smokers in 2000.

New Hampshire's 28 community hospitals had 116,071 admissions and 2,853 beds in 2001. There were 4,173 full-time registered nurses and 240 full-time licensed practical nurses in 2001 and 275 physicians per 100,000 population in 2000. The average expense of a community hospital for care was $1,285 per inpatient day in 2001.

Federal government grants to cover the Medicare and Medicaid services in 2001 totaled $483 million; 172,704 enrollees received Medicare benefits that year. At least 9.4% of New Hampshire's adult population were uninsured in 2002.

39 SOCIAL WELFARE

In 2001, the average weekly unemployment benefit was $240.83. Average monthly participation in the food stamp program in FY2002 comprised 41,053 persons (20,452 households). The average monthly benefit was $70.35, and the sum total of benefits paid in FY2002 was $34,656,997.

With the enactment of the Personal Responsibility and Work Opportunity Reconciliation Act of 1996, the US government has changed the form and regulations for many of its social welfare programs. Most significantly, it replaces Aid to Families with Dependent Children (AFDC), an open-ended entitlement program, with Temporary Assistance for Needy Families (TANF), a limited system of assistance funded largely through federal block grants. The reform act also impacts the food stamp program, the Supplemental Security Income program, and the child nutrition program. The law took effect on 1 July 1997 and provided $16.38 billion in block grants for fiscal years 1997–2002. The grants are to be divided among the states based on an equation involving the numbers of former AFDC recipients in each state.

Reauthorization of the 1996 social welfare legislation, scheduled for 2002, was delayed, and the original law had been extended three times as of July 2003, with the most recent extension running through September 2003. New Hampshire's TANF program for work-exempt families is called the Family Assistance Program (FAP), while aid to work-mandated families under TANF is called the New Hampshire Employment Program (NHEP). In June 2000 the state had 13,862 welfare recipients. State expenditures on the TANF program in FY2002 totaled $32,287,453.

In December 2001, Social Security benefits were paid to 204,140 New Hampshire residents. This number included 135,720 retired workers, 18,520 widows and widowers, 23,600 disabled workers, 9,750 spouses, and 16,550 children. Social Security beneficiaries represented 16.1% of the total state population and 97.5% of the state's population age 65 and older. Retired workers (excluding persons with special benefits) received an average monthly payment of $891; widows and widowers, $869; disabled workers, $815; and spouses, $460. Payments for children of retired workers averaged $454 per month; children of deceased workers, $632; and children of disabled workers, $254.

Federal Supplemental Security Income payments in December 2001 went to 11,942 New Hampshire residents, averaging $350 a month.

40 HOUSING

In 2002, there were 561,178 housing units in New Hampshire, 485,903 of which were occupied; 71.7% were owner-occupied. About 63.5% of all units were single-family, detached homes. Fuel oil and kerosene were the most common heating energy sources. It was estimated that 7,163 units lacked telephone service, 2,398 lacked complete plumbing facilities, and 1,648 lacked complete kitchen facilities. The average household size was 2.55 people.

In 2002, 8,708 new privately owned units were authorized for construction. The median home value was $173,699. The median monthly cost for mortgage owners was $1,377. Renters paid a median of $732. During 2002, New Hampshire received over $20.8 million in community planning and development aid from the US Department of Housing and Urban Development.

41 EDUCATION

New Hampshire residents have a long-standing commitment to education. In 2000, 87.4% of New Hampshire residents age 25 and older were high school graduates. Some 28.7% had obtained a bachelor's degree or higher.

The total enrollment for fall 1999 in New Hampshire's public schools stood at 206,783. Of these, 146,854 attended schools from kindergarten through grade eight, and 59,929 attended high school. Minority students made up approximately 5% of the total enrollment in public elementary and secondary schools in 2001. Total enrollment was estimated at 210,454 in fall 2000 but expected to drop to 202,000 by fall 2005. The 1999/2000 per pupil expenditure for public elementary and secondary schools was $6,306, slightly below the US mean of $6,356. Expenditures for public education in 2000/01 were estimated at $1,536,740. Enrollment in nonpublic schools in fall 2001 was 23,383.

As of fall 2000, there were 74,832 students enrolled in college or graduate school. In the same year New Hampshire had 25 degree-granting institutions. The best-known institution of higher education is Dartmouth College, which originated in Connecticut in 1754 as Moor's Indian Charity School and was established at Hanover in 1769. When the state of New Hampshire attempted to amend Dartmouth's charter to make the institution public in the early 19th century, the US Supreme Court handed down a precedent-setting ruling prohibiting state violation of contract rights. The University of New Hampshire, the leading public institution, was founded at Hanover in 1866 and relocated at Durham in 1891. The university also has a campus in Manchester. Other colleges include Franklin Pierce College, Keene State College, and Southern New Hampshire University. In 1997, minority students comprised 5.7% of total postsecondary enrollment.

42 ARTS

Hopkins Center at Dartmouth College features musical events throughout the year. Theater by the Sea at Portsmouth presents classical and modern plays, and there is a year-round student theater at Dartmouth. Ballet groups include Ballet New England in Portsmouth, City Center Ballet in Lebanon, Granite State Ballet Company in Nashua, and Petit Papillon in Concord. Opera groups include the Granite State Opera in Temple, Opera North in Hanover, and OPERAFEST! of NH, based at the Adams Memorial Opera House in Derry. Classical music groups include the Nashua Chamber Orchestra, the Nashua Symphony Orchestra, the Granite State Symphony in Concord, Lakes Region Symphony Orchestra in Meredith, the New England Wind Ensemble in Franklin, and the New Hampshire

Philharmonic Orchestra and New Hampshire Symphony Orchestra (both in Manchester).

The New Hampshire Music Festival in Center Harbor serves as a year-round educational institute and performing arts center and sponsors an annual summer festival featuring the New Hampshire Music Festival Orchestra. Monadnock Music in Peterborough is an organization sponsoring a variety of musical programs, including an annual summer festival featuring the Monadnock Chorus and Orchestra.

New Hampshire's poet laureate from 1999 to 2004 has been Marie Harris, author of Weasel in the Turkey Pen, Your Sun, Manny: A Prose Poem Memoir, and the children's book G is for GRANITE: A New Hampshire Alphabet. The artist laureate as of 2002 was Marguerite Mathews, who has worked in theater and has been an active participant in Council of the Arts education programs.

Principal galleries include the Currier Gallery of Art in Manchester, the Arts and Science Center in Nashua, the University Art Galleries at the University of New Hampshire in Durham, the Dartmouth College Museum and Galleries at Hanover, and the Lamont Gallery at Phillips Exeter Academy in Exeter.

In 2003, the New Hampshire State Council on the Arts and other New Hampshire arts organizations received grants totaling $745,700 from the National Endowment for the Arts. State and private sources also contributed substantial funding to the state's arts programs. New Hampshire has about 275 statewide arts associations and 8 local arts councils.

The New Hampshire Humanities Council sponsors a number of ongoing programs including What Is New Hampshire Reading This Month?, a statewide reading program; The Giving Frame Of Mind, a reading/discussion series; Connections, a literacy program for adult new readers; and an annual summer Chautauqua. In 2000, the National Endowment for the Humanities contributed $1,344,638 to 15 state programs.

43 LIBRARIES AND MUSEUMS

New Hampshire public libraries had a total book stock of 5,506,000 volumes and a combined circulation of 8,778,000 volumes in 2000. Leading academic and historical collections include Dartmouth College's Baker Memorial Library in Hanover (2,309,626 volumes); the New Hampshire State Library (519,319) and New Hampshire Historical Society Library (50,000), both in Concord; and the University of New Hampshire's Ezekiel W. Diamond Library (1,151,203) in Durham. Total income for the public library system in 2000 was $33,217,000; spending per capita was $28.27.

Among the more than 76 museums and historic sites are the Museum of New Hampshire History in Concord and the Franklin Pierce Homestead in Hillsboro.

44 COMMUNICATIONS

In 2001, 97.8% of New Hampshire's occupied housing units had telephones. In 2003, the state had 32 major radio stations (7 AM, 25 FM), and 8 television stations. State residents also receive broadcasts from neighboring Massachusetts, Vermont, and Maine. A total of 38,887 Internet domain names were registered in the state in 2000.

45 PRESS

In 2002, New Hampshire had seven morning newspapers, five evening newspapers, and eight Sunday papers. The best-known newspaper in the state is the Manchester Union Leader (63,517 daily and 84,855 Sunday), published by conservative William Loeb until his death in 1981. In the capital, the Concord Monitor circulates 20,592 papers daily and 23,290 on Sundays. The Dover Foster's Daily Democrat has a circulation of 23,376 for its weekday evening edition and 30,051 for the Sunday edition. The Nashua *Telegraph* has a circulation of 26,348 daily and 32,684 Sundays.

46 ORGANIZATIONS

In 2003, there were about 1,118 regional, national, and international organizations within the state. Organizations with headquarters in New Hampshire include the Student Conservation Association (Charlestown), the American Association of Commodity Traders (Concord), the American Society of Environmental Education (Hanover), Interhostel (Durham), the Academy of Applied Science (Concord), and the Natural Organic Farmers Association (Antrim). There are a number of municipal and county historical societies.

47 TOURISM, TRAVEL, AND RECREATION

Tourism is a major part of the economy of New Hampshire. It has been estimated that the industry brings in revenues of about $8.6 billion dollars per year and sponsors over 65,000 jobs.

Skiing, camping, hiking, and boating are the main outdoor attractions. Other attractions include Strawberry Banke, a restored village in Portsmouth, Daniel Webster's birthplace near Franklin, and the Mt. Washington Cog Railway. Merrimack Valley is the most visited area, generating about 36% of all tourism.

48 SPORTS

There are no major league professional sports teams in New Hampshire. Major national and international skiing events are frequently held in the state, as are such other winter competitions as snowmobile races and the Annual World Championship Sled Dog Derby in Laconia. Thoroughbred, harness, and greyhound racing are the warm-weather spectator sports. The annual Whaleback Yacht Race is held in early August.

Dartmouth College competes in the Ivy League, and the University of New Hampshire belongs to the America East Conference, both Division I-AA Conferences.

The New Hampshire International Speedway, which opened in Loudon in 1994, plays host to a NASCAR Winston Cup stock car race in July and September.

49 FAMOUS NEW HAMPSHIRITES

Born in Hillsboro, Franklin Pierce (1804–69), the nation's 14th president, serving from 1853 to 1857, was the only US chief executive to come from New Hampshire. Henry Wilson (Jeremiah Jones Colbath, 1812–75), US vice president from 1873 to 1875, was a native of Farmington.

US Supreme Court chief justices Salmon P. Chase (1808–73), Harlan Fiske Stone (1872–1946), and David Souter (b.1939) were New Hampshirites, and Levi Woodbury (1789–1851) was a distinguished associate justice. John Langdon (1741–1819) was the first president pro tempore of the US Senate; two other US senators from New Hampshire, George Higgins Moses (b.Maine, 1869–1944) and Henry Styles Bridges (b.Maine, 1898–1961), also held this position. US cabinet members from New Hampshire included Henry Dearborn (1751–1829), secretary of war; Daniel Webster (1782–1852), secretary of state; and William E. Chandler (1835–1917), secretary of the Navy. Other political leaders of note were Benning Wentworth (1696–1770), royal governor Meshech Weare (1713–86), the state's leader during the American Revolution; Josiah Bartlett (b.Massachusetts, 1729–95), a physician, governor, and signer of the Declaration of Independence; Isaac Hill (b.Massachusetts, 1789–1851), a

publisher, governor, and US senator; and John Parker Hale (1806–73), senator, antislavery agitator, minister to Spain, and presidential candidate of the Free Soil Party. John Sununu, a former governor of New Hampshire (b.Cuba, 1939) was chief of staff during the George H. W. Bush administration.

Military leaders associated with New Hampshire during the colonial and Revolutionary periods include John Stark (1728–1822), Robert Rogers (b.Massachusetts, 1731–95), and John Sullivan (1710–95). Among other figures of note are educator Eleazar Wheelock (b.Connecticut, 1711–79), the founder of Dartmouth College; physicians Lyman Spaulding (1775–1821), Reuben D. Mussey (1780–1866), and Amos Twitchell (1781–1850), as well as Samuel Thomson (1769–1843), a leading advocate of herbal medicine; religious leaders Hosea Ballou (1771–1852), his grandnephew of the same name (1796–1861), and Mary Baker Eddy (1821–1910), founder of Christian Science; George Whipple (1878–1976), winner of the 1934 Nobel Prize for physiology or medicine; and labor organizer and US Communist Party leader Elizabeth Gurley Flynn (1890–1964).

Sarah Josepha Hale (1788–1879), Horace Greeley (1811–72), Charles Dana (1819–97), Thomas Bailey Aldrich (1836–1907), Bradford Torrey (b.Massachusetts, 1843–1912), Alice Brown (1857–1948), and J(erome) D(avid) Salinger (b.New York, 1919) are among the writers and editors who have lived in New Hampshire, along with poets Edna Dean Proctor (1829–1923), Celia Laighton Thaxter (1826–94), Edward Arlington Robinson (b.Maine, 1869–1935), and Robert Frost (b.California, 1874–1963), one of whose poetry volumes is entitled *New Hampshire* (1923). Painter Benjamin Champney (1817–1907) and sculptor Daniel Chester French (1850–1931) were born in New Hampshire, while Augustus Saint-Gaudens (b.Ireland, 1848–1907) created much of his sculpture in the state.

Vaudevillian Will Cressey (1863–1930) was a New Hampshire man. More recent celebrities include newspaper publisher William Loeb (b.New York, 1905–81) and astronaut Alan B. Shepard, Jr. (1923–98).

50 BIBLIOGRAPHY

Belman, Felice, and Mike Pride, eds. *The New Hampshire Century.* Hanover, N.H.: University Press of New England, 2001.

Casanave, Suki. *Natural Wonders of New Hampshire: Exploring Wild and Scenic Places.* Lincolnwood, Ill.: Country Roads Press, 1998.

Clark, Charles E. *The Eastern Frontier: The Settlement of Northern New England, 1610–1763.* New York: Knopf, 1970.

Dubois, Muriel L. *New Hampshire Facts and Symbols.* Mankato, Minn.: Hilltop Books, 2000.

Harris, Patricia. *New Hampshire: The Spirit of America.* New York: H. N. Abrams, 2000.

Morison, Elizabeth Forbes, and Elting E. Morison. *New Hampshire: A Bicentennial History.* New York: Norton, 1976.

Smith, Clyde H. *New Hampshire: A Scenic Discovery.* Dublin, N.H.: Yankee Books, 1985.

Squires, J. Duane. *The Granite State of the United States: A History of New Hampshire from 1623 to the Present.* 4 vols. New York: American Historical Co., 1956.

Stacker, Ann P., and Nancy C. Hefferman. *Short History of New Hampshire.* Grantham, N.H.: Thompson and Rutter, 1985.

Taylor, William L., ed. *Readings in New Hampshire and New England History.* New York: Irvington, 1981.

NEW JERSEY

State of New Jersey

ORIGIN OF STATE NAME: Named for the British Channel Island of Jersey. **NICKNAME:** The Garden State. **CAPITAL:** Trenton. **ENTERED UNION:** 18 December 1787 (3rd). **MOTTO:** Liberty and Prosperity. **COLORS:** Buff and Jersey blue. **COAT OF ARMS:** In the center is a shield with three plows, symbolic of agriculture; a helmet above indicates sovereignty, and a horse's head atop the helmet signifies speed and prosperity. The state motto and the date "1776" are displayed on a banner below. **FLAG:** The coat of arms on a buff field. **OFFICIAL SEAL:** The coat of arms surrounded by the words "The Great Seal of the State of New Jersey." **ANIMAL:** Horse. **BIRD:** Eastern goldfinch. **INSECT:** Honeybee. **FLOWER:** Violet. **TREE:** Red oak. **MEMORIAL TREE:** Dogwood. **SHELL:** Knobbed whelk. **LEGAL HOLIDAYS:** New Year's Day, 1 January; Birthday of Martin Luther King, Jr. 3rd Monday in January; Lincoln's Birthday, 12 February; Washington's Birthday, 3rd Monday in February; Good Friday, March or April; Memorial Day, last Monday in May; Independence Day, 4 July; Labor Day, 1st Monday in September; Columbus Day, 2nd Monday in October; Election Day, 1st Tuesday after 1st Monday in November; Veterans Day, 11 November; Thanksgiving Day, 4th Thursday in November; Christmas Day, 25 December. **TIME:** 7 AM EST = noon GMT.

¹LOCATION, SIZE, AND EXTENT

Situated in the northeastern US, New Jersey is the smallest of the Middle Atlantic states and ranks 46th among the 50 states.

The total area of New Jersey is 7,787 sq mi (20,168 sq km), of which 7,468 sq mi (19,342 sq km) constitute land and 319 sq mi (826 sq km) are inland water. New Jersey extends 166 mi (267 km) N-S; the extreme width E-W is 57 mi (92 km).

New Jersey is bordered on the N and NE by New York State (with the boundary formed partly by the Hudson River, New York Bay, and Arthur Kill, and passing through Raritan Bay); on the E by the Atlantic Ocean; on the S and SW by Delaware (with the line passing through Delaware Bay); and on the W by Pennsylvania (separated by the Delaware River). Numerous barrier islands lie off the Atlantic coast.

New Jersey's total boundary length is 480 mi (773 km), including a general coastline of 130 mi (209 km); the tidal shoreline is 1,792 mi (2,884 km). The state's geographic center is in Mercer County, near Trenton.

²TOPOGRAPHY

Although small, New Jersey has considerable topographic variety. In the extreme northwest corner of the state are the Appalachian Valley and the Kittatinny Ridge and Valley. This area contains High Point, the state's peak elevation, at 1,803 ft (550 m) above sea level. To the east and south is the highlands region, an area of many natural lakes and steep ridges, including the Ramapo Mountains, part of the Appalachian chain. East of the highlands is a flat area broken by the high ridges of the Watchungs and Sourlands and—most spectacularly—by the Palisades, a column of traprock rising some 500 ft (150 m) above the Hudson River. The Atlantic Coastal Plain, a flat area with swamps and sandy beaches, claims the remaining two-thirds of the state. Its most notable feature is the Pine Barrens, 760 sq mi (1,968 sq km) of pitch pines and white oaks. Sandy Hook, a peninsula more than 5 mi (8 km) long, extending northward into the Atlantic from Monmouth County, is part of the Gateway National Recreation Area.

Major rivers include the Delaware, forming the border with Pennsylvania, and the Passaic, Hackensack, and Raritan. The largest natural lake is Lake Hopatcong, about 8 mi (13 km) long.

Some 550 to 600 million years ago, New Jersey's topography was the opposite of what it is now, with mountains to the east and a shallow sea to the west. Volcanic eruptions about 225 million years ago caused these eastern mountains to sink and new peaks to rise in the northwest; the lava flow formed the Watchung Mountains and the Palisades. The shoreline settled into its present shape at least 10,000 years ago.

³CLIMATE

Bounded by the Atlantic Ocean and the Delaware River, most of New Jersey has a moderate climate with cold winters and warm, humid summers. Winter temperatures are slightly colder and summer temperatures slightly milder in the northwestern hills than in the rest of the state.

In Atlantic City, the average mean temperature is 53°F (12°C), ranging from 31°F (−1°C) in January to 75°F (24°C) in July. Precipitation is plentiful, averaging 46 in (117 cm) annually; snowfall totals about 16 in (41 cm). At Atlantic City, annual precipitation (1971–2000) was 40.6 cm (103 cm). The annual average humidity is 81% at 7 AM, reaching a normal high of 87% in September.

Statewide, the record high temperature is 110°F (43°C), set in Runyon on 10 July 1936; the record low is −34°F (−37°C), set in River Vale on 5 January 1904. A 29.7-in. (75.4-cm) accumulation on Long Beach Island in 1947 was the greatest 24-hour snowfall in the state's recorded history. Occasional hurricanes and violent spring storms have damaged beachfront property over the years, and floods along northern New Jersey rivers especially in the Passaic River basin, are not uncommon. A serious drought occurs, on average, about once every 15 years.

⁴FLORA AND FAUNA

Although highly urbanized, New Jersey still provides a diversity of natural regions, including a shady coastal zone, the hilly and wooded Allegheny zone, and the Pine Barrens in the south. Birch, beech, hickory, and elm all grow in the state, along with black locust, red maple, and 20 varieties of oak; common shrubs include the spicebush, staggerbush, and mountain laurel. Vast stretches beneath pine trees are covered with pyxie, a small creeping evergreen shrub. Common wild flowers include meadow

446

rue, butterflyweed, black-eyed Susan, and the ubiquitous eastern (common) dandelion. Among rare plants are Candy's lobelia, floating heart, and pennywort. Six plant species were listed as threatened or endangered in 2003, including the American chaffseed and small whorled pogonia.

Among mammals indigenous to New Jersey are the white-tailed deer, black bear, gray and red foxes, raccoon, woodchuck, opossum, striped skunk, eastern gray squirrel, eastern chipmunk, and common cottontail. The herring gull, sandpiper, and little green and night herons are common shore birds, while the red-eyed vireo, hermit thrush, English sparrow, robin, cardinal, and Baltimore oriole are frequently sighted inland. Anglers prize the northern pike, chain pickerel, and various species of bass, trout, and perch. Declining or rare animals include the whippoorwill, hooded warbler, eastern hognose snake, northern red salamander, and northern kingfish. Seventeen animal species were listed as threatened or endangered in 2003, including four species of turtle, the Indiana bat, bald eagle, shortnose sturgeon, roseate tern, and three species of whale.

5ENVIRONMENTAL PROTECTION

Laws and policies regulating the management and protection of New Jersey's environment and natural resources are administered by the Department of Environmental Protection (DEP). The state devoted 1.4% of its total budget appropriations, or $225.1 million, to environmental protection in 1996/97.

The proximity of the populace to industrial plants and to the state's expansive highway system makes air pollution control a special concern in the state. New Jersey had one of the most comprehensive air pollution control programs in the US, maintaining a network of 105 air pollution monitoring stations, as well as 60 stations that monitor just for particulates and 10 that monitor for radiation.

The DEP reported that a 1984 review of water quality in the state showed that water quality degradation had been halted and that the quality of streams had been stabilized or improved. The greatest improvements had been made in certain bays and estuaries along the Atlantic coast, where the elimination of discharges from older municipal sewage treatment plants resulted in the reopening of shellfish-harvesting grounds for the first time in 20 years. However, some rivers in highly urbanized areas were still severely polluted.

Approximately 1,500 treatment facilities discharge waste water into New Jersey's surface and groundwaters. Nearly 80% of these facilities comply with the requirements of federal and state clean water laws. Solid waste disposal in New Jersey became critical as major landfills reached capacity. In 1977, the state had more than 300 operating landfills; in 1991 there were about 50 landfills. The state's solid waste stream is 1,100 tons per capita. Some counties and municipalities were implementing recycling programs in 1985, and the state legislature was considering a bill to make recycling mandatory. By the mid-1990s the state of New Jersey had about 30 curbside recycling programs.

New Jersey's toxic waste cleanup program is among the most serious in the US. In 2003, New Jersey had 551 hazardous waste sites listed in the Environmental Protection Agency's database, three of which were on the National Priorities List including the worst site in the nation (a landfill near Pitman). The state has received over $1 billion in Superfund money for site cleanup.

The New Jersey Spill Compensation Fund was established by the state legislature in 1977 and amended in 1980. A tax based on the transfer of hazardous substances and petroleum products is paid into the fund and used for the cleanup of spills.

New Jersey was the first state to begin a statewide search for sites contaminated by dioxin, a toxic by-product in the manufacture of herbicides.

New Jersey first acquired land for preservation purposes in 1907. Since 1961, the state has bought more than 240,000 acres (97,000 hectares) under a "Green Acres" program for conservation and recreation. In 1984, an $83-million Green Trust Fund was established to expand land acquisition. The Green Acres Program has assisted county and municipal governments in acquiring over 70,000 acres (28,000 hectares). Additionally, Green Acres is assisting nonprofit conservation groups in acquiring over 20,000 acres (8,000 hectares) in a 50% matching grant program established in 1989. The US Congress designated 1.1 million acres (445,000 hectares) in the southern part of the state as the Pinelands National Reserve in 1978. Since then, the state has purchased more than 60,000 acres (24,000 hectares) in the region, bringing the state open-space holding in the Pinelands to more than 270,000 acres (109,000 hectares). As of 1 July 1993, there were approximately 790,000 acres (319,000 hectares) of preserved public open space and recreation land in New Jersey. In 2001, New Jersey received $109,601,000 in federal grants from the Environmental Protection Agency; EPA expenditures for procurement contracts in New Jersey that year amounted to $31,736,000.

6POPULATION

New Jersey ranked 9th in population in the US with an estimated total of 8,590,300 in 2002, an increase of 2.1% since 2000. Between 1990 and 2000, New Jersey's population grew from 7,730,188 to 8,414,350, an increase of 8.9%. In 2000 New Jersey had the highest population density among the 50 states: 1,134.4 persons per sq mi. The population is projected to reach 9.6 million by 2025.

In 2000 the median age was 36.7. Persons under 18 years old accounted for 24.8% of the population while 13.2% were age 65 or older.

Sparsely populated at the time of the Revolutionary War, New Jersey did not pass the one million mark until the 1880 census. Most of the state's subsequent growth came through migration, especially from New York during the period after 1950 when the New Jersey population stood at 4,835,329. The most significant population growth came in older cities in northern New Jersey and in commuter towns near New York and Philadelphia. The average annual population growth declined from 2.3% in the

New Jersey Counties, County Seats, and County Areas and Populations

COUNTY	COUNTY SEAT	LAND AREA (SQ MI)	POPULATION (2002 EST.)
Atlantic	Mays Landing	568	259,423
Bergen	Hackensack	237	895,091
Burlington	Mt. Holly	808	437,871
Camden	Camden	223	511,957
Cape May	Cape May	263	102,013
Cumberland	Bridgeton	498	147,768
Essex	Newark	127	798,301
Gloucester	Woodbury	327	262,049
Hudson	Jersey City	46	611,439
Hunterdon	Flemington	427	125,795
Mercer	Trenton	227	359,463
Middlesex	New Brunswick	316	775,549
Monmouth	Freehold	472	629,836
Morris	Morristown	470	478,730
Ocean	Toms River	641	537,065
Passaic	Paterson	187	496,646
Salem	Salem	338	64,438
Somerset	Somerset	305	309,886
Sussex	Newton	525	148,680
Union	Elizabeth	103	530,763
Warren	Belvidere	359	107,537
TOTALS		7,468	8,590,300

1950s to 1.7% in the 1960s, and the state actually experienced a net loss from migration of 275,000 during the 1970s. Total growth rose to 5% during the 1980s.

New Jersey's major population centers, with estimated 2002 population figures, are Newark, 277,000; Jersey City, 240,100; Paterson, 150,750; and Elizabeth, 123,279.

7ETHNIC GROUPS

New Jersey is one of the most ethnically heterogeneous states. As of 2000, 1,476,327 New Jerseyites (17.5% of the state's population) were of foreign birth. The leading countries of origin were Italy, 7.3%; Cuba, 6.5%; India, 5.4%; and Germany, 4.4%. As of 2001, New Jersey had the 3rd-highest percentage of foreign-born residents among the 50 states, surpassed only by California and New York.

Blacks first came to New Jersey as slaves in the 1600s; the state abolished slavery in 1804, one of the last of the northern states to do so. Today black people constitute the state's largest (13.6%) ethnic minority, 1,141,821 as of 2000. Newark elected its first black mayor, Kenneth Gibson, in 1970, three years after the city was torn by racial disorders that killed 26 people and injured some 1,500 others.

The estimated Hispanic and Latino population in 2000 was 1,117,191 (up from 868,000 in 1996), or 13.3% of the total. The Puerto Rican population, which increased from 55,361 in 1960 to 366,788 in 2000, lived mostly in Newark, Jersey City, Elizabeth, Paterson, and Passaic. There were 77,337 Cubans in 2000, many of them in Union City and Elizabeth; their numbers were augmented by the migration of Cuban refugees in 1980. Smaller Spanish-speaking groups included Colombians and Dominicans.

The estimated number of Asians living in New Jersey in 2000 was 480,276, the 5th-largest total among the 50 states. Pacific Islanders numbered 273,000. The largest group of Asians reported was from India (169,180 in 2000, up from 54,039 in 1990); there were 85,245 Filipinos, 100,355 Chinese (more than double the 1990 figure of 47,068), 65,349 Koreans, and 14,672 Japanese.

The state's total Native American population, including Eskimos and Aleuts, numbered 19,492 in 2000. Among the state's Indians is a group claiming to be descended from Dutch settlers, black slaves, British and German soldiers, and Leni-Lenape and Tuscarora Indians; incorporated as the Ramapough Mountain Indians in 1978, they live in the Ramapo hills near Ringwood and Mahwah.

8LANGUAGES

European settlers found New Jersey inhabited largely by the Leni-Lenape Indians, whose legacy can still be found in such place-names as Passaic, Totowa, Hopatcong, Kittatinny, and Piscataway.

English in New Jersey is rather evenly divided north and south between Northern and Midland dialects. Special characteristics of some New York metropolitan area speech occur in the northeast portion, such as the absence of /r/ after a vowel, a consonant like /d/ or /t/ instead of the /th/ sounds in *this* or *thin*, and pronunciations as *coop* rhyming with *stoop*, *food* with *good*, and *goal* and *fool*; *faucet* has the vowel of *father*. Dominant in the southern half are *run* (small stream), *baby coach* (baby carriage) in the Philadelphia trading area, *winnering owl* (screech owl), and *eel worm* (earthworm). Heard also are *out* as /aot/, *muskmelon* as /muskmillon/, and *keg* rhyming with *bag*, *scarce* with *fierce*, *spook* with *book*, and *haunted* with *panted*.

In 2000, 5,854,578 New Jerseyites—74.5% of the resident population five years old or older—spoke only English at home, down from 80.5% in 1990.

The following table gives selected statistics from the 2000 census for language spoken at home by persons five years old and over. The category "Other Asian languages" includes Dravidian languages, Malayalam, Telugu, Tamil, and Turkish. The category "Other Indic languages" includes Bengali, Marathi, Punjabi, and Romany. The category "African languages" includes Amharic, Ibo, Twi, Yoruba, Bantu, Swahili, and Somali.

LANGUAGE	NUMBER	PERCENT
Population 5 years and over	7,856,268	100.0
Speak only English	5,854,578	74.5
Speak a language other than English	2,001,690	25.5
Speak a language other than English	2,001,690	25.5
Spanish or Spanish Creole	967,741	12.3
Italian	116,365	1.5
Chinese	84,345	1.1
Polish	74,663	1.0
Portuguese or Portuguese Creole	72,870	0.9
Tagalog	66,851	0.9
Korean	55,340	0.7
Gujarathi	47,324	0.6
French (incl. Patois, Cajun)	47,225	0.6
Arabic	47,052	0.6
German	41,025	0.5
Russian	38,566	0.5
Other Asian languages	36,573	0.5
Other Indic languages	35,718	0.5
Hindi	31,395	0.4
French Creole	28,783	0.4
Greek	26,566	0.3
African languages	21,514	0.3

9RELIGIONS

With a history of religious tolerance, New Jersey has welcomed many denominations to its shores. Dutch immigrants founded a Reformed Church in 1662, the first in the state. After the English took control, Puritans came from New England and Long Island, Congregationalists from Connecticut, and Baptists from Rhode Island. Quaker settlements in Shrewsbury and western New Jersey during the early 1670s predated the better-known Quaker colony in Pennsylvania. Episcopalians, Presbyterians, German Lutherans, and Methodists arrived during the 18th century. The state's first synagogue was established in 1848, in Newark.

About the only religion not tolerated by New Jerseyites was Catholicism; the first Catholic parish was not organized until 1814 and laws excluding Catholics from holding office were on the books until 1844. The Catholics' numbers swelled as a result of Irish immigration after 1845, and even more with the arrival of Italians after 1880. Today, Roman Catholics constitute the state's single largest religious group. Passaic is the headquarters of the Byzantine-Ruthenian Rite in the Byzantine Catholic Church.

In 2000, the number of Roman Catholics within the state was at about 3,403,020. The next largest group were Jewish, with about 468,000 members. The largest Protestant denomination was the United Methodist Church, with 140,133 adherents, followed by the Presbyterian Church USA, with 119,735; the Episcopal Church, 91,964; and the Evangelical Lutheran Church in America, 79,264. There were about 120,724 Muslims in the state. Nearly 3.5 million people (about 42.3% of the population) were not counted as members of any religious organization.

10TRANSPORTATION

Ever since the first traders sought the fastest way to get from New York to Philadelphia, transportation has been of central importance to New Jersey and has greatly shaped its growth. In the mid-1820s, Hoboken engineer John Stevens built the first steam locomotive operated in the US; over the protests of the dominant stagecoach operators, his son Robert obtained a charter in 1830 for the Camden and Amboy Railroad. The line opened in 1834, and six years later it held a monopoly on the

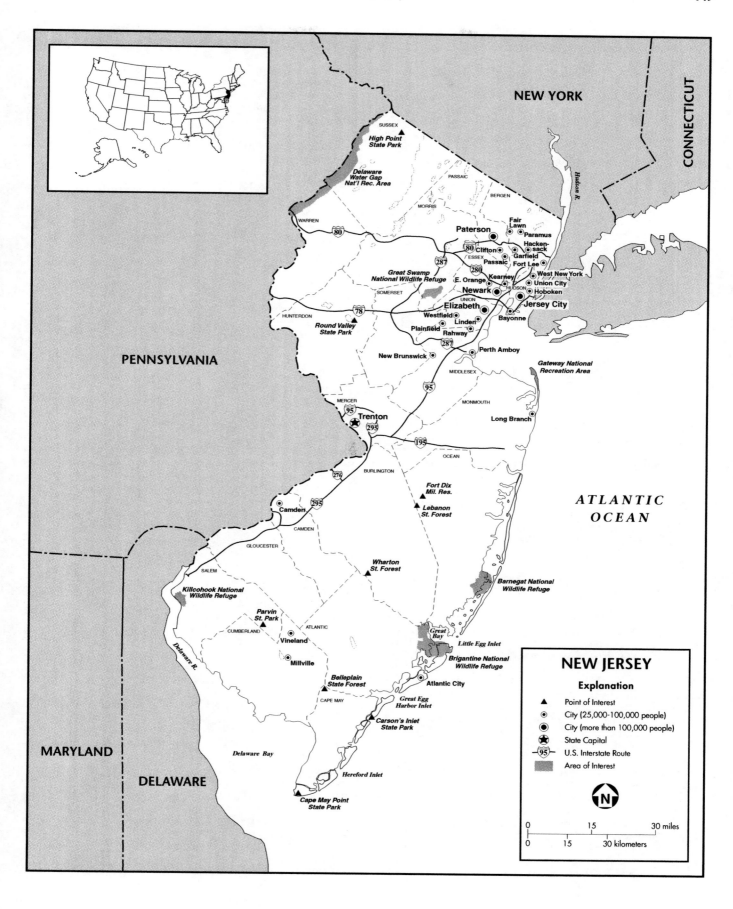

NEW YORK

CONNECTICUT

PENNSYLVANIA

SUSSEX
High Point
State Park

Delaware
Water Gap
Nat'l Rec. Area

PASSAIC

BERGEN

MORRIS

WARREN

80

Hudson R.

Fair
Lawn
Paterson
Paramus
80 Clifton
Hacken-
sack
287
Garfield
Passaic
Fort Lee
ESSEX
West New York
280
Kearney
Union City
Great Swamp
National Wildlife Refuge
E. Orange
Newark
Hoboken
SOMERSET
HUDSON
Jersey City
UNION
Elizabeth
78
Westfield
HUNTERDON
Linden
Bayonne
Plainfield
Round Valley
State Park
Rahway
287
New Brunswick
Perth Amboy
Gateway National
Recreation Area
MIDDLESEX

MONMOUTH
95
MERCER
95
Trenton
Long Branch
295
195

OCEAN

BURLINGTON
276
Fort Dix
Mil. Res.
295
Lebanon
St. Forest
Camden

ATLANTIC
OCEAN

CAMDEN
Wharton
St. Forest
GLOUCESTER

SALEM
Barnegat National
Wildlife Refuge
Killcohook National
Wildlife Refuge

Parvin
St. Park
ATLANTIC
CUMBERLAND
Vineland
Great
Bay
Little Egg Inlet
Millville
Brigantine National
Wildlife Refuge
Belleplain
State Forest
Atlantic City
CAPE MAY
Great Egg
Harbor Inlet
Delaware R.
Carson's Inlet
State Park
Delaware Bay
Hereford Inlet
Cape May Point
State Park

MARYLAND

DELAWARE

NEW JERSEY

Explanation

▲ Point of Interest
◉ City (25,000-100,000 people)
● City (more than 100,000 people)
✪ State Capital
95 U.S. Interstate Route
Area of Interest

N

0   15   30 miles
0   15   30 kilometers

lucrative New York–Philadelphia run. Other lines—such as the Elizabeth and Somerville, the Morris and Essex, the Paterson and Hudson, and the Jersey Central—were limited to shorter runs, largely because the Camden and Amboy's influence with the legislature gave it a huge competitive advantage. Camden and Amboy stock was leased to the Pennsylvania Railroad in 1871, and the ensuing controversy over whether New Jersey transit should be entrusted to an "alien" company led to the passage of a law opening up the state to rail competition. Industry grew around the rail lines, and the railroads became a vital link in the shipment of products from New York and northern New Jersey.

As of 2000, the major freight operations were run by Consolidated Rail (owned by CSX and Northfolk Southern), representing a consolidation of several bankrupt freight carriers, including the Penn Central, Central of New Jersey, Erie-Lackawanna, Reading, Lehigh Valley, and Lehigh and Hudson River railroads. In 2000, there were 2,353 route mi (3,786 km) of track in the state, more than 70% of which was Class I track. In addition, there were one regional, one Canadian, seven local, and six switching and terminal railroads operating in the state. About 90 daily Amtrak trains linked Newark, Trenton, and a few other New Jersey cities along the main eastern rail corridor. But the bulk of interstate passenger traffic consists of commuters to New York and Philadelphia on trains operated by the Port Authority of New York and New Jersey (PA) and the Port Authority Transit Corp. (PATCO), a subsidiary of the Delaware River Port Authority.

The New Jersey Transit Corporation, called NJ TRANSIT, is a public corporation created under the Public Transportation Act of 1979. The corporation is charged with coordinating and improving bus and rail services throughout the state. It is the nation's 3rd-largest pubic transit agency, providing 223 million passenger trips annually. It operates 711 daily trains on 11 rail lines, and 2,027 buses on 236 routes throughout the state. It also owns and operates the Newark City Subway, a 4.3-mile light rail system providing service through downtown Newark.

Although associated more with the West, the first stagecoach service began in New Jersey, as part of a New York–Philadelphia trek that took some five days in 1723. For a time, colonial law required towns along the way to provide taverns for the passengers, and it was not uncommon for coach operators who were also tavern owners to find some way to prolong the journey an extra night. They traveled on roads that were barely more passable than the Leni-Lenape trails from which they originated. Improvement was slow, but by 1828, the legislature had granted 54 turnpike charters.

Road building has continued ever since. In 2000, there were 36,022 mi (57,971 km) of public roads in the state: 11,838 km mi (19,051 km) of county roads and 24,184 mi (38,920 km) of municipal roads. The major highways are the New Jersey Turnpike, opened in 1952 and extending 133 mi (214 km) between Bergen and Salem counties, and the Garden State Parkway, completed in 1955 and stretching 173 mi (278 km) from the New York State line to Cape May. There were 6,501,884 registered vehicles in the state in 2000, including 4,450,719 automobiles, 1,917,774 trucks, and 21,538 buses. There were 5,654,973 licensed New Jersey drivers in the same year.

Many bridges and tunnels link New Jersey with New York State, Pennsylvania, and Delaware. Twenty-seven bridges cross the Delaware River, connecting New Jersey with Pennsylvania and Delaware.

At the gateway to New York Harbor, ports at Elizabeth and Newark have overtaken New York City ports in cargo volume, and contribute greatly to the local economy. Operated by the Port Authority of New York and New Jersey, Port Newark has almost 4 mi (6.4 km) of berthing space along Newark Bay, while nearby

Port Elizabeth, with better than 3 mi (4.8 km) of berths, is a major handler of containerized cargo. Private piers in Jersey City and Bayonne handle both containerized and bulk cargoes. The tonnage handled by northern New Jersey port facilities, taken as a whole, make it the largest port on the east coast, and 2nd-largest overall in the United States. The Ports of Philadelphia and Camden, Inc., headquartered in Philadelphia, operates facilities along the Delaware River including the Beckett Street and Broadway Terminals in Camden formerly operated by the South Jersey Port Corporation. The port facility at Paulsboro is the most active in the state, with 26.9 million tons of cargo (primarily petroleum) handled in 2000. The Camden ports handled some 5.2 million tons during the same period.

The state's early aviation centers were Lakehurst and Newark. Lakehurst, whose dirigible operations attracted crowds of spectators during the 1920s and 1930s, was the scene of the crash on 6 May 1937 of the Hindenburg, a disaster that killed 26 people and spelled the end of commercial airship flights in the US. The state's first airmail service began in 1924 from New Brunswick's Hadley Field. Newark Airport in the late 1920s billed itself as the busiest air terminal in the world. The PA took over its operation from the city of Newark in 1948. Rebuilt during the 1960s and 1970s, Newark International Airport has become the state's busiest by far in 2000, with 17,212,226 passengers enplaned that year. Statewide in 2002, there were 118 airports, 242 heliports, and 10 seaplane bases.

11 HISTORY

The first known inhabitants of what is now New Jersey were the Leni-Lenape (meaning "Original People"), who arrived in the land between the Hudson and Delaware rivers about 6,000 years ago. Members of the Algonkian language group, the Leni-Lenape were an agricultural people supplementing their diet with freshwater fish and shellfish. The peace-loving Leni-Lenape believed in monogamy, educated their children in the simple skills needed for wilderness survival, and clung rigidly to a tradition that a pot of food must always be warm on the fire to welcome all strangers.

The first European explorer to reach New Jersey was Giovanni da Verrazano, who sailed into what is now Newark Bay in 1524. Henry Hudson, an English captain sailing under a Dutch flag, piloted the Half Moon along the New Jersey shore and into Sandy Hook Bay in the late summer of 1609, a voyage that established a Dutch claim to the New World. Hollanders came to trade in what is now Hudson County as early as 1618, and in 1660, they founded New Jersey's first town, called Bergen (now part of Jersey City). Meanwhile, across the state, Swedish settlers began moving east of the Delaware River in 1639. Their colony of New Sweden had only one brief spurt of glory, from 1643 to 1653, under Governor Johan Printz.

The Leni-Lenape lost out to the newcomers, whether Dutch, Swedish, or English, despite a series of treaties that the Europeans thought fair. State and local records describe these agreements: huge tracts of land exchanged for trinkets, guns, and alcohol. The guns and alcohol, combined with smallpox (another European import), doomed the "Original People." In 1758, when a treaty established an Indian reservation at Brotherton (now the town of Indian Mills), only a few hundred Indians remained.

England assumed control in March 1664, when King Charles II granted a region from the Connecticut River to the Delaware River to his brother James, the Duke of York. The duke, in turn, deeded the land between the Hudson and Delaware rivers, which he named New Jersey, to his court friends John Berkeley, 1st Baron Berkeley of Stratton, and Sir George Carteret, on 23 June 1664. Lord Berkeley and Sir George became proprietors, owning the land and having the right to govern its people. Subsequently, the land passed into the hands of two boards of proprietors in two provinces called East Jersey and West Jersey, with their capitals in Perth Amboy and Burlington, respectively. East Jersey was settled mainly by Puritans from Long Island and New England, West Jersey by Quakers from England. The split cost the colony dearly in 1702, when Queen Anne united East and West Jersey but placed them under New York rule. The colony did not get its own "home rule" until 1738, when Lewis Morris was named the first royal governor.

By this time, New Jersey's divided character was already established. Eastern New Jersey looked toward New York, western New Jersey toward Philadelphia. The level plain connecting those two major colonial towns made it certain that New Jersey would serve as a pathway. Along the makeshift roads that soon crossed the region—more roads than in any other colony—travelers brought conflicting news and ideas. During the American Revolution, the colony was about equally divided between Revolutionists and Loyalists. William Franklin (illegitimate son of Benjamin Franklin), royal governor from 1763 until 1776, strove valiantly to keep New Jersey sympathetic to England, but failed and was arrested. Throughout the Revolutionary period, he remained a leading Loyalist; after the war, he left for England.

Franklin's influence caused New Jersey to dally at first over independence, but in June 1776, the colony sent five new delegates to the Continental Congress—Abraham Clark, John Hart, Frances Hopkinson, Richard Stockton, and the Reverend John Witherspoon—all of whom voted for the Declaration of Independence. Two days before the Declaration was proclaimed, New Jersey adopted its first state constitution. William Livingston, a fiery anti-British propagandist, was the first elected governor of the state.

New Jersey played a pivotal role in the Revolutionary War, for the side that controlled both New York and Philadelphia would almost certainly win. George Washington and his battered troops made their winter headquarters in the state three times during the first four years of the war, twice in Morristown and once in Somerville. Five major battles were fought in New Jersey, the most important being the Battle of Trenton on 26 December 1776 and the Battle of Monmouth on 28 June 1778. At war's end, Princeton became the temporary capital of the US from 26 June 1783 to 4 November 1783.

The state languished after the Revolution, with many of its pathway towns ravaged by the passing of competing armies, its trade dependent on New York City, and its ironworks (first established in 1676) shut down because of decreased demand. The state's leaders vigorously supported a federation of the 13 states, in which all states, regardless of size, would be represented equally in one national legislative body. This so-called New Jersey Plan led to the establishment of the US Senate.

Railroads and canals brought life to the state in the 1830s and set it on a course of urbanization and industrialization. The 90-mi (145-km) Morris Canal linked northern New Jersey with the coal fields of Pennsylvania. Considered one of the engineering marvels of the 19th century, the canal rose to 914 feet (279 meters) from sea level at Newark Bay to Lake Hopatcong, then fell 760 feet (232 meters) to a point on the Delaware River opposite Easton, Pa. Old iron mines beside the canal found markets, the dyeing and weaving mills of Paterson prospered, and Newark, most affected by the emerging industries, became the state's first incorporated city in 1836. Another canal, the Delaware and Raritan, crossed the relatively flat land from Bordentown, Trenton, and New Brunswick boomed. Princeton, whose leaders fought to keep the canal away from the town, settled into a long existence as a college community built around the College of New Jersey, founded in Elizabeth in 1746 and transferred to Princeton in 1756.

The canals were doomed by railroad competition almost from the start. The Morris Canal was insolvent long before World War I, and the Delaware Canal, although operative until 1934, went into a long, slow decline after the Civil War. The first railroad, from Bordentown to South Amboy, closely paralleled the Delaware and Raritan Canal and in 1871 became an important part of the Pennsylvania Railroad. The coal brought in on railroad cars freed industry from waterpower; factories sprang up wherever the rails went. The Hudson County waterfront, eastern terminus for most of the nation's railway systems, became the most important railroad area in the US. Rail lines also carried vacationers to the Jersey shore, building an important source of income for the state.

The Civil War split New Jersey bitterly. Leaders in the Democratic Party opposed the war as a "Black Republican" affair. Prosperous industrialists in Newark and Trenton feared that their vigorous trade with the South would be impaired, Cape May innkeepers fretted about the loss of tourists from Virginia, and even Princeton students were divided. As late as the summer of 1863, after the Battle of Gettysburg, many state "peace Democrats" were urging the North to make peace with the Confederacy. Draft calls were vigorously opposed in 1863, yet the state sent its full quota of troops into service throughout the conflict. Most important, New Jersey factories poured forth streams of munitions and other equipment for the Union army. At war's end, political leaders stubbornly opposed the 13th, 14th, and 15th Amendments to the US Constitution, and blacks were not permitted to vote in the state until 1870.

During the last decades of the 19th century, New Jersey developed a reputation for factories capable of making the components necessary for thousands of other manufacturing enterprises. Few factories were large, although in 1873, Isaac M. Singer opened a huge sewing machine plant at Elizabeth that employed 3,000 persons. Oil refineries on the Hudson County waterfront had ever-expanding payrolls, pottery firms in Trenton thrived, and Newark gained strength from many diversified manufacturers and also saw its insurance companies become nationally powerful.

Twentieth-century wars stimulated New Jersey's industries. During World War I, giant shipyards at Newark, Kearny, and Camden made New Jersey the nation's leading shipbuilding state. The Middlesex County area refined 75% of the nation's copper, and nearly 75% of US shells were loaded in the state. World War II revived the shipbuilding and munitions industries, while chemical and pharmaceutical manufacturing, spawned by the World War I cutoff of German chemicals, showed further growth during the second world conflict. Paterson, preeminent in locomotive building during the 19th century, became the nation's foremost airplane engine manufacturing center. Training and mobilization centers at Ft. Dix and Camp Kilmer moved millions of soldiers into the front lines.

The US Census Bureau termed New Jersey officially "urban" in 1880, when the state population rose above 1 million for the first time. Urbanization intensified throughout the 20th century and especially after World War II, as people left the old cities in New Jersey and other northeastern states to buy homes in developments on former farmlands. Places like Cherry Hill, Woodbridge, Clifton, and Middletown Township boomed after 1945, increasing their population as much as sixfold in the decades that followed. New Jersey has also experienced many of the problems of urbanization. Its cities have declined; traffic congestion is intense in the morning, when commuters stream into urban areas to work, and again in the evening, when they return home to what once was called "the country." That country now knows the problems of urban growth: increased needs for schools, sewers, police and fire protection, and road maintenance, along with rising taxes.

The state has not surrendered to its problems, however. In 1947, voters overwhelmingly approved a new state constitution, a terse, comprehensive document that streamlined state government, reformed the state's chaotic court system, and mandated equal rights for all. Governor Alfred E. Driscoll promptly integrated the New Jersey National Guard, despite strong federal objectives; integration of all US armed forces soon followed. After 1950 voters passed a wide variety of multi-million-dollar bond issues to establish or rebuild state colleges. Funds were allocated for the purchase and development of new park and forest lands. Large bond issues have financed the construction of highways, reservoirs, and rapid transit systems. In mid-2000 the state legislature approved the largest construction program in New Jersey history. Settling a long-running battle over how to rebuild the state's deteriorating and overcrowded schools, lawmakers agreed to spend $12 billion system-wide, with benefits to be seen in inner cities as well as in suburbs.

In the 1970s and early 1980s, New Jersey experienced a recession. The unemployment rate climbed to almost 10%. Over 270,000 people left the state. The state's cities were hit particularly hard, suffering both from the loss of manufacturing jobs and from a flight of retailing to suburban malls. The economy of New Jersey in these decades also underwent a dramatic restructuring. While the state lost over 200,000 manufacturing jobs it gained 670,000 jobs in service industries. The economy rebounded during the 1980s, but began to contract again at the end of the decade, declining further during the recession of early 1990s. In 1996 the state's unemployment rate fell below 6% for the first time in six years. By 1999 it had dropped to 4.6%. Observers credited the recovery of the 1990s in part to a skilled workforce that attracted pharmaceutical, biotechnology, electronics, and other high-tech firms to the state. Tax and economic incentives also helped bring business to the state. The state ranked 2nd in the nation in both per capita personal income ($33,953) and low poverty rate (8.6%) in 1998. However, the state faced a budget deficit nearing $5 billion in 2003.

In September 1999 New Jersey experienced one of the worst natural disasters in its history; Hurricane Floyd damaged more than 8,000 homes and destroyed several hundred more. A federal aid package approved in 2000 promised victims some relief.

During the second half of the 1900s New Jersey had no predictable political pattern. It gave huge presidential majorities to Republican Dwight D. Eisenhower and Democrat Lyndon B. Johnson, narrowly supported Democrat John F. Kennedy, favored Republican Gerald Ford over Democrat Jimmy Carter by a small margin, gave two big majorities to Republican Ronald Reagan, favored Democrat Bill Clinton in the 1990s, and favored Democrat Al Gore over George W. Bush in 2000. For more than 20 years, the state's two US senators, Clifford B. Case (R) and Harrison A. Williams (D), were recognized as like-minded liberals. Democrat Bill Bradley, former Princeton University and New York Knickerbockers basketball star, was elected to Case's seat in 1978. (In 1999 Bradley made a run for the presidency. Though gaining considerable support from the electorate, he dropped his bid for the Democratic nomination in the face of competition from Vice President Al Gore.)

Republican Governor Thomas Kean, who served from 1983–89, helped improve the public image of New Jersey, long perceived as dominated by smoke-belching factories and troubled cities. Kean was succeeded by Democrat Jim Florio who sought to redistribute wealth throughout the state by doubling the income tax of those in the top bracket, raising the sales tax, lowering property taxes for middle- and low-income homeowners and renters, and shifting state aid from public schools in affluent areas to schools in poor and moderate income communities. In 1992, Florio lost his bid for reelection to Republican Christine

Todd Whitman, who promised to lower income taxes by 30%. As soon as she took office, Whitman implemented a 5% cut and pushed through another 10% cut as part of her budget package in 1993. Whitman won a second term in the 1996 election. Whitman was named President George W. Bush's head of the Environmental Protection Agency; she took office in January 2001 and resigned in May 2003.

12 STATE GOVERNMENT

New Jersey's first state constitution took effect in 1776. A second constitution was written in 1844, and a third in 1947. This last document, as amended (54 times as of January 2003), continues to govern the state today.

The state legislature consists of a 40-member senate and an 80-member general assembly. Annual legislative sessions begin in early January and are not limited in length. Special sessions, also of unlimited duration, may be called by petition of a majority of the members in each house. Senators, elected to four-year terms, must be at least 30 years old and have been New Jersey residents for four years and district residents for a year. Assembly members, elected to two-year terms, must be at least 21 years old and have been New Jersey residents for two years and district residents for a year. All legislators must be qualified voters prior to election. Both houses of the legislature meet in unlimited annual sessions. The legislative salary was $49,000 in 2003.

New Jersey is one of only four states—the others are Maine, New Hampshire, and Tennessee—in which the governor is the only statewide elected administrative official. Given broad powers by the state constitution, the governor appoints the heads or commissioners of the major state departments with the advice and consent of the senate; not subject to senate approval are more than 500 patronage positions. The governor is also commander-in-chief of the state's armed forces, submits the budget to the legislature each January, presents an annual message on the condition of the state, and may grant pardons and, with the aid of the Parole Board, grant executive clemency. Elected to a four-year term in the odd-numbered year following the presidential election, the governor may run for a second term but not for a third until four years have passed. A candidate for governor must be at least 30 years old and must have been a US citizen for 20 years and a New Jersey citizen for seven years in order to qualify for the ballot. In 2003 the governor's salary was $157,000.

A bill may be introduced in either house of the legislature. Once passed, it goes to the governor, who may sign it, return it to the legislature with recommendations for change, or veto it in its entirety. A two-thirds vote by the members in each house is needed to override a veto. If the governor neither signs nor vetoes a bill, it becomes law after 45 days as long as the legislature is in session.

Amendments to the state constitution may originate in either house. If, after public hearings, both houses pass the proposal by a three-fifths vote, the amendment is placed on the ballot at the next general election. If approved by a majority, but by less than a three-fifths vote in both houses, the amendment is referred to the next session of the legislature, at which time, if again approved by a majority, it is placed on the ballot. The amendment goes into effect 30 days after ratification by the electorate.

To vote in New Jersey, one must be at least 18 years old, a US citizen, and a New Jersey and county resident for at least 30 days prior to election day. Restrictions apply to those convicted of crimes in New Jersey or another state.

13 POLITICAL PARTIES

From the 1830s through the early 1850s, Democrats and Whigs dominated the political life of New Jersey. Exercising considerable, though subtle, influence in the decade before the Civil War was the Native American (Know-Nothing) Party, an anti-immigrant, anti-Catholic group that won several assembly and senate seats. Wary of breaking ties with the South and ambivalent about the slavery issue, New Jerseyites, especially those in Essex and Bergen counties, did not lend much support to the abolitionist cause. Early Republicans thus found it advantageous to call themselves simply "Opposition;" the state's first Opposition governor was elected in 1856. Republicans controlled the state for most of the 1860s; but with heavy support from business leaders, the Democrats regained control in 1869 and held the governorship through 1896. They were succeeded by a series of Progressive Republican governors whose efforts were largely thwarted by a conservative legislature. Sweeping reforms-including a corrupt-practices act, a primary election law, and increased support for public education-were implemented during the two years that Woodrow Wilson, a Democrat, served as governor before being elected to the presidency. Between 1913 and 1985, Democrats held the statehouse almost two-thirds of the time.

New Jersey's unenviable reputation for corruption in government dates back at least to 1838, when ballot tampering resulted in the disputed election of five Whigs to the US House of Representatives. (After a House investigation, the Whigs were barred and their Democratic opponents given the seats.) Throughout the rest of the century, corruption was rampant in local elections: Philadelphians, for example, were regularly imported to vote in Atlantic City elections, and vote buying was a standard election-day procedure in Essex and Hudson counties. Wilson's 1911 reform bill eliminated some of these practices, but not the bossism that had come to dominate big-city politics. Frank Hague of Jersey City controlled patronage and political leaders on the local, state, and national level from 1919 to 1947; during the 1960s and 1970s, Hague's successor John V. Kenny, Jersey City mayor Thomas Whelan, and Newark mayor Hugh Addonizio, along with numerous other state and local officials, were convicted of corrupt political dealings. From 1969 to mid-

1975, federal prosecutors indicted 148 public officials, securing 72 convictions. Brendan Byrne, who had never before held elective office, won the governorship in 1973, mainly on the strength of a campaign that portrayed him as the "judge who couldn't be bought." On the national level, New Jersey Representative Peter Rodino gained a reputation for honesty and fairness when he chaired the House Judiciary Committee's impeachment hearings against Richard Nixon. However, the state's image suffered a further blow in 1980, when, as a result of the FBI's "ABSCAM" investigation, charges of influence peddling were brought against several state officials, including members of the Casino Control Commission, whose function was to prevent corruption and crime in Atlantic City's gambling establishments.

Later in the year, New Jersey Democrat Harrison Williams became the nation's first US senator to be indicted, on charges of bribery and conspiracy, as a result of the ABSCAM probe. He was convicted in 1981 and sentenced to prison. As a result of the same investigation, US Representative Frank Thompson, Jr., was convicted in 1980 on bribery and conspiracy charges. A New Jerseyite, Raymond Donovan, was named secretary of labor by President Ronald Reagan in 1981, but he resigned in 1985 after being indicted late in 1984 for allegedly seeking to defraud the New York City Transit Authority while serving as vice president of the Schiavone Construction Company in Secaucus.

In the 2000 presidential voting, Democrat Al Gore defeated Republican George W. Bush, picking up 56% of the vote to Dole's 41%. Independent Ralph Nader garnered 3%. In 2002 there were 4,654,897 registered voters. In 1998, 25% of registered voters were Democratic, 19% Republican, and 56% unaffiliated or members of other parties. The state had 15 electoral votes in the 2000 presidential election.

In 1993, New Jersey elected its first woman as governor, Republican Christine Todd Whitman; she was reelected in 1997. In late 2000 she was named President George W. Bush's head of the Environmental Protection Agency, a post she resigned in June

New Jersey Presidential Vote by Political Parties, 1948–2000

YEAR	ELECTORAL VOTES	NEW JERSEY WINNER	DEMOCRAT	REPUBLICAN	PROGRESSIVE	SOCIALIST	PROHIBITION	SOCIALIST LABOR	SOCIALIST WORKERS
1948	16	Dewey (R)	895,455	981,124	42,683	10,521	10,593	3,354	5,825
1952	16	*Eisenhower (R)	1,015,902	1,373,613	5,589	8,593	—	5,815	3,850
					CONSTITUTION				
1956	16	*Eisenhower (R)	850,337	1,606,942	5,317	—	9,147	6,736	4,004
					CONSERVATIVE				
1960	16	*Kennedy (D)	1,385,415	1,363,324	8,708	—	—	4,262	11,402
1964	17	*Johnson (D)	1,867,671	963,843	—	—	—	7,075	8,181
					AMERICAN IND.	PEACE & FREEDOM			
1968	17	*Nixon (R)	1,264,206	1,325,467	262,187	8,084	—	6,784	8,667
						PEOPLE'S	AMERICAN		
1972	17	*Nixon (R)	1,102,211	1,845,502	—	5,355	34,378	4,544	2,233
						US LABOR	LIBERTARIAN		COMMUNIST
1976	17	Ford (R)	1,444,653	1,509,688	7,716	1,650	9,449	3,686	1,662
1980	17	*Reagan (R)	1,147,364	1,546,557	8,203	—	20,652	2,198	2,555
						WORKERS WORLD			
1984	16	*Reagan (R)	1,261,323	1,933,630	—	8,404	6,416	—	1,564
					NEW ALLIANCE	PEACE & FREEDOM		CONSUMER	SOCIALIST
1988	16	* Bush (R)	1,320,352	1,743,192	5,139	9,953	8,421	3,454	2,587
						IND. (Perot)		IND. (Bradford)	TAXPAYERS
1992	15	* Clinton (D)	1,436,206	1,356,865	3,513	521,829	6,822	4,749	2,670
					GREEN (Nader)				
1996	15	*Clinton (D)	1,652,329	1,103,078	32,465	262,134	14,763	—	—
					IND. (Buchanan)				
2000	15	Gore (D)	1,788,850	1,284,173	94,554	6,989	6,312	—	—

* Won US presidential election.

2003. Democrat James McGreevey was elected New Jersey's governor in 2001. Democratic Senator Jon Corzine was elected in 2000. Democrat Frank Lautenberg, first elected to the Senate in 1982, and reelected in 1988 and 1994, returned to the Senate in 2002 after having retired in 2000. Following 2002 elections, the state's delegation to the US House consisted of seven Democrats and six Republicans. In mid-2003 the state senate was divided evenly between Democrats and Repubicans (20–20), while the General Assembly had 43 Democrats, 36 Republicans, and one independent.

14 LOCAL GOVERNMENT

As of 2002, New Jersey had 21 counties, 324 municipal governments, 242 townships, 549 public school districts, and 276 special districts. Counties are classed by population and whether or not they border the Atlantic Ocean.

Cities, boroughs, and towns may employ the mayor-council system, council-manager system, commission system, or other forms of their own devising. Most townships and villages are governed by committee or by a council and a mayor with limited powers. Cities, like counties, are classed by population and location: first-class cities are those over 150,000 in population; second-class, 12,000–150,000; third-class, all others except ocean resorts; and fourth-class, ocean resorts.

The budgets of all local units are supervised by the New Jersey Department of Community Affairs, which also offers municipal aid programs.

15 STATE SERVICES

To address the continuing threat of terrorism and to work with the federal Department of Homeland Security (created in 2002 following the terrorist attacks of 11 September 2001), homeland security in New Jersey in 2003 operated under executive order; a counterterrorism office director was named to oversee the state's homeland security activities.

The constitution of 1947 limited the number of state government departments to 20. New Jersey in 1974 became the first state to establish a Public Advocate Department, empowered to provide legal assistance for indigent criminal defendants, mental patients, and any citizen with a grievance against a government agency or regulated industry. A Code of Ethics, adopted by the legislature in 1976, seeks to prevent state employees from using their positions for personal gain. By executive order, more than 500 state executive officials must file financial disclosure statements.

The Education Department administers state and federal aid to all elementary and secondary schools, oversees pupil transportation, and has jurisdiction over the state library, museum, and historical commission. State-run colleges and universities and higher education policy are the province of the Department of Higher Education. All state-maintained highways and bus and rail transportation are the responsibility of the Department of Transportation, which also operates New Jersey Transit, whose function is to acquire and operate public transportation services.

The Human Services Department administers welfare, Medicaid, mental health, and mental retardation programs, as well as veterans' institutions and programs and other state-supported social services. Alcohol, drug abuse, and many other health-related programs are monitored by the Health Department, which also oversees hospitals and compiles statewide health statistics.

The Office of the Attorney General, officially titled the Department of Law and Public Safety, is the statewide law enforcement agency. Its functions include criminal justice, consumer affairs, civil rights, alcoholic beverage control, and gaming enforcement; also within this department are the State Police, State Racing Commission, Violent Crimes Compensation Board, and a number of regulatory boards. The Defense Department controls the Army and Air National Guard. Correctional institutions, training schools, treatment centers, and parole offices are administered by the Corrections Department.

The Department of Energy monitors the supply and use of fuel and administers the state master plan for energy use and conservation; its Board of Public Utilities has broad regulatory jurisdiction, ranging from garbage collection to public broadcasting. Other agencies are the departments of agriculture, banking, civil service, commerce and economic development, community affairs, environmental protection, insurance, labor and industry, state, and treasury.

16 JUDICIAL SYSTEM

All judges in New Jersey, except municipal court judges, are appointed by the governor with the consent of the senate. Initial terms for supreme and superior court judges are seven years; after reappointment, judges may serve indefinitely.

The supreme court, the state's highest, consists of six associate justices and a chief justice, who is also the administrative head of the state court system. As the court of highest authority, the supreme court hears appeals on constitutional questions and on certain cases from the superior court, which comprises three divisions: chancery, law, and appellate. The chancery division has original jurisdiction over general equity cases, most probate cases, and divorce actions. All other original cases are tried within the law division. The appellate division hears appeals from the chancery and law divisions, from lower courts, and from most state administrative agencies. A state tax court, empowered to review local property tax assessments, equalization tables, and state tax determinations, has been in operation since 1979; by statute, it may have from 6 to 12 judges. Municipal court judges, appointed by local governing bodies for three-year terms, hear minor criminal matters, motor vehicle cases, and violations of municipal ordinances.

The legislature approved a sweeping reform of the state's criminal law code in 1978. Strict sentencing standards were established, and one result was an overcrowding of the state's prison system. Governor Brendan Byrne signed a law in 1981 imposing a minimum three-year sentence on anyone committing a crime with a gun. In 1982, Governor Thomas Kean signed legislation establishing a death penalty by lethal injection; New Jersey became the ninth state to use that method, although the sentence has yet to be imposed. As of 2003, 15 persons were under sentence of death.

According to the FBI Crime Index, in 2001 New Jersey had a total crime rate of 3,225.3 per 100,000 persons, including a total of 33,094 violent crimes and 240,551 crimes against property in that year. Prisoners under jurisdiction of state and federal correctional authorities in New Jersey numbered 28,108 in June 2001, a decrease of 9.6% from the previous year. The state's incarceration rate stood at 331 per 100,000 inhabitants.

17 ARMED FORCES

In 2002, there were 6,306 active-duty military personnel and 13,943 civilian personnel stationed in New Jersey. The largest installation in the state is McGuire Air Force Base in Wrightstown. The US Coast Guard operates a training center in Cape May. New Jersey firms received over $2.8 billion in defense contracts awards in 2002.

Of the 672,217 veterans living in New Jersey according to the 2000 census, World War II veterans numbered 170,074; Korean conflict, 97,585; Vietnam era, 180,497; and those who served 1990–2000 (including the Persian Gulf War), 44,908. Veterans' benefits in 2002 totaled more than $862 million.

In 2000, the New Jersey State Police employed 2,569 full-time sworn officers.

[18]MIGRATION

New Jersey's first white settlers were inter-colonial migrants: Dutch from New Amsterdam, Swedes from west of the Delaware River, and Puritans from New England and Long Island. By 1776, New Jersey's population was about 138,000, of whom perhaps 7% were black slaves.

Population growth lagged during the early 19th century, as discouraged farmers left their worn-out plots for more fertile western soil; farmers in Salem County, for example, went off to found new Salems in Ohio, Indiana, Iowa, and Oregon. Not until the rapid industrial growth of the mid-1800s did New Jersey attract great waves of immigrants. Germans and Irish were the first to arrive, the latter comprising 37% of Jersey City's population by 1870. The late 1800s and early 1900s brought newcomers from Eastern Europe, including many Jews, and a much larger number of Italians to the cities. By 1900, 43% of all Hudson County residents were foreign-born. More recently, migration from Puerto Rico and Cuba has been substantial. In 1990, 143,974 New Jersey residents age five and older had lived in Puerto Rico in 1985. In 1996, 1,152,000 New Jersey residents, or 14%, were foreign born. In 1998, 35,091 foreign immigrants entered the state, the 5th-highest total for any state that year.

From World War I on, there has been a steady migration of blacks from southern states; Newark's black population grew by 130,000 between 1950 and 1970. Black as well as Hispanic newcomers settled in major cities just as whites were departing for the suburbs. New Jersey's suburbs were also attractive to residents of New York City, Philadelphia, and other adjacent areas, who began a massive move to the state just after World War II; nearly all of these suburbanites were white. From 1940 to 1970, New Jersey gained a net total of 1,360,000 residents. Between 1970 and 1990, however, the state lost about 250,000 residents through migration. Between 1990 and 1998, New Jersey had a net loss of 350,000 in domestic migration and a net gain of 360,000 in international migration. While the black, Hispanic, and Asian populations were still rising, whites were departing from New Jersey in increasing numbers. As of 1998, New Jersey's black population numbered 1,188,000; Hispanic, 866,000; and Asian, 453,000. Between 1990 and 1998, the state's overall population increased 4.7%. In the period 1995–2000, 534,578 people moved into the state and 717,407 moved out, for a net loss of 182,829. About 118,905 people moved to Florida.

[19]INTERGOVERNMENTAL COOPERATION

New Jersey participates in such regional bodies as the Interstate Sanitation Commission, Atlantic States Marine Fisheries Commission, and Mid-Atlantic Fishery Management Council. Of primary importance to the state are its relations with neighboring Pennsylvania and New York. With Pennsylvania, New Jersey takes part in the Delaware Valley Regional Planning Commission, Delaware River Joint Toll Bridge Commission, and Delaware River Port Authority; with New York, the Port Authority of New York and New Jersey, the Palisades Interstate Park Commission, and the Waterfront Commission, established to eliminate corruption and stabilize employment at the Hudson River ports. The Delaware River Basin Commission manages the water resources of the 12,750-sq mi (33,000-sq km) basin under the jurisdiction of Delaware, New Jersey, New York, and Pennsylvania. The Delaware River and Bay Authority operates a bridge and ferry between New Jersey and Delaware. In 2001, the state received almost $8.5 billion in federal grants.

[20]ECONOMY

New Jersey was predominantly agricultural until the mid-1800s, when the rise of the railroads stimulated manufacturing in northern New Jersey and opened the Jersey shore to resort development. The steady growth of population in the 1900s fostered the growth of service-related industries, construction, and trade, for which the state's proximity to New York and Philadelphia had long been advantageous.

During the 1970s, New Jersey's economy followed national trends, except that the mid-decade recession was especially severe. Conditions in most areas improved in the latter part of the decade, particularly in Atlantic City, with the construction of gambling casinos and other entertainment facilities. Manufacturing in the central cities declined, however, as industries moved to suburban locations.

Although petroleum refining, chemicals and pharmaceuticals, food processing, apparel, fabricated metals, electric and electronic equipment, and other machinery are all important, the state is more noteworthy for the diversity of its manufacturers in 2000, than for any dominant company or product. The service sector of the economy, led by wholesale and retail trade, continued to grow rapidly during the 1990s. The heaviest concentrations of jobs are in and near metropolitan New York and Philadelphia, but employment opportunities in the central and north-central counties have been increasing. Fresh market vegetables are the leading source of farm income. Overall growth in the state economy was robust coming into the 21st century, with annual growth rates averaging over 6% 1998 to 2000. The national recession and slowdown of 2001 slowed annual growth to 2.2%, but in 2002 the state economy was showing resiliency. Employment losses for the state as a whole started later and were milder than for the nation as a whole.

New Jersey's gross state product in 2001 was $365.4 billion, the 8th highest among the states, to which financial services contributed $90.1 billion; general services, $83.5 billion; trade, $62.8 billion; manufacturing, $42.1 billion; government, $35.9 billion; transportation and public utilities, $33 billion, and construction, $17.7 billion. The public sector in 2001 constituted 9.8% of gross state product, the 5th-lowest percent among the states.

[21]INCOME

According to the Bureau of Economic Analysis, in 2001, New Jersey had a per capita personal income (PCPI) of $38,625 which ranked 4th in the United States (including the District of Columbia) and was 127% of the national average, $30,413. The 2001 PCPI reflected an increase of 2.4% from 2000 compared to the national change of 2.2%. In 2001, New Jersey had a total personal income (TPI) of $328,742,929,000 which ranked 7th in the United States and accounted for 3.8% of the national total. The 2001 TPI reflected an increase of 3.3% from 2000 compared to the national change of 3.3%.

Earnings of persons employed in New Jersey increased from $218,793,481,000 in 2000 to $222,367,909,000 in 2001, an increase of 1.6%. The largest industries in 2001 were services, 31.0% of earnings; state and local government, 11.2%; and finance, insurance, and real estate, 10.5%. Of the industries that accounted for at least 5% of earnings in 2001, the slowest growing from 2000 to 2001 was nondurable goods manufacturing (9.0% of earnings in 2001), which decreased 12.3%; the fastest was construction (5.1% of earnings in 2001), which increased 10.0%.

According to data released by the US Census Bureau, in 2000, the median household income was $51,032 compared to the national average of $42,148. In 2001, the median income for a family of four was $80,577 compared to the national average of $63,278. For the period 1999 to 2001, the average poverty rate was 7.7% which placed it 6th among the 50 states and the District of Columbia ranked lowest to highest.

22LABOR

According to Bureau of Labor Statistics (BLS) provisional estimates, in July 2003 the seasonally adjusted civilian labor force in New Jersey numbered 4,442,200, with approximately 271,000 workers unemployed, yielding an unemployment rate of 6.1%, compared to the national average of 6.2% for the same period. Since the beginning of the BLS data series in 1978, the highest unemployment rate recorded was 9.4% in May 1992. The historical low was 3.4% in February 2001. In 2001, an estimated 4.8% of the labor force was employed in construction; 13.0% in manufacturing; 7.4% in transportation, communications, and public utilities; 18.2% in trade; 8.6% in finance, insurance, and real estate; 28.1% in services; 13.4% in government; and 0.8% in agriculture.

Although migrant workers are still employed at south Jersey tomato farms and fruit orchards, the number of farm workers coming into the state is declining with the increased use of mechanical harvesters.

The state's first child labor law was passed in 1851, and in 1886, workers were given the right to organize. Labor's gains were slow and painful, however. In Paterson, no fewer than 137 strikes were called between 1881 and 1900, every one of them a failure. A 1913 strike of Paterson silkworkers drew nationwide headlines but, again, few results. Other notable strikes were a walkout at a Carteret fertilizer factory in 1915, during which six picketers were killed by guards; a yearlong work stoppage by Passaic textile workers in 1926; and another Paterson silkworkers' strike in 1933, this one finally leading to union recognition and significant wage increases. That year, the state enacted a law setting minimum wages and maximum hours for women. This measure was repealed in 1971, in line with the trend toward nonpreferential labor standards.

The US Department of Labor reported that in 2002, 749,000 of New Jersey's 3,870,000 employed wage and salary workers were members of unions. This represented 19.4% of those so employed, down slightly from 19.5% in 2001. The national average is 13.2%. In all, 799,000 workers (20.6%) were represented by unions. In addition to union members, this category includes workers who report no union affiliation but whose jobs are covered by a union contract.

23AGRICULTURE

New Jersey is a leading producer of fresh fruits and vegetables. Its total farm income was $821 million in 2001. In 2000, New Jersey ranked 3rd in the US in the production of escarole/endive. In 2002,it ranked 3rd in cranberries, 6th in fresh market tomatoes, 7th in fresh market vegetables.

Some 820,000 acres (about 332,000 hectares) were in 9,600 farms in 2002. The major farm counties are: Warren for grain and milk production, Gloucester and Cumberland for fruits and vegetables, Atlantic for blueberries, Burlington for nursery production and berries, Salem for processing vegetables, and Monmouth for nursery and equine.

In 2002, New Jersey produced 290,700 tons of fresh market vegetables. Leading crops (in hundredweight units) were: bell peppers, 962,000; cabbage, 624,000; sweet corn, 791,000; tomatoes, 759,000; and head lettuce, 150,000. New Jersey farmers also produced 56,340 tons of vegetables for processing. Fruit crops in 2002 (in pound units) included apples, 35,000,000, and peaches, 62,000,000. In 2002, cranberry and strawberry production were 43 million and 1.8 million pounds respectively. The expansion of housing and industry has increased the value of farm acreage and buildings in New Jersey to over $8,000 per acre, the highest in the nation.

24ANIMAL HUSBANDRY

In 2003, New Jersey had an estimated 46,000 cattle and calves, valued at $46.5 million. During 2002, New Jersey farmers had an estimated 15,000 hogs and pigs valued at $1.3 million. In 2001, poultry farmers produced 893,000 million lb (405 million kg) of turkey, 2 million lb (0.9 million kg) of chickens, and 556 million eggs. The state's total milk yield was 233 million lb (105.7 million kg) in 2001.

25FISHING

New Jersey had a commercial fish catch of 195,918,000 lb (9th in the US) in 1998, worth $90.9 million. Cape May–Wildwood was the 14th-largest fishing port in the US by volume, bringing in 94 million lb of fish, worth $29.2 million. Clams, scallops, swordfish, tuna, squid, lobster, and flounder are the most valuable species. In 1998, landings of surf clams totaled 44.8 million lb; ocean quahog (a species of clam), 15.7 million lb; and Atlantic mackerel, 18.4 million lb.

The US Fish and Wildlife Service of the Department of the Interior maintains a total of 190,000 acres (76,900 hectares) on 12 different sites with boating access.

Recreational fishermen catch finfish and shellfish along the Atlantic coast and in the rivers and lakes of northern New Jersey. In 1998, the state issued 219,541 sport fishing licenses.

26FORESTRY

Over 42% of New Jersey's land area, or 2,132,000 acres (863,000 hectares), was forested in 2002. Of that total, 1,876,000 acres (759,200 hectares) were classified as commercial timberland, most of it privately owned. The forests of New Jersey are important for their function in conservation and recreation. Wood that is harvested contributes to specialty markets and quality veneer products. State forests cover 382,000 acres (155,000 hectares).

27MINING

The value of nonfuel mineral production in New Jersey in 2001 was estimated to be $348 million, up nearly 20% from 2000. According to preliminary figures, in 2001, 31 million metric tons of crushed stone were produced, for a total value of $218 million, up $174 million from the previous year. Other mineral resources mined or recovered included construction sand and gravel (17.9 million metric tons, worth $94.8 million), industrial sand and gravel (1.69 million metric tons, worth $35.5 million), common and fire clays, greensand, peat, titanium, and zircon concentrates. New Jersey continued to be the only state that produced greensand, also known as the mineral glauconite, which is processed and sold mainly as a water-softening filtration medium to remove soluble iron and manganese from well water. A secondary use is as an organic conditioner for soils.

28ENERGY AND POWER

Although it contains some of the largest oil refineries in the US, New Jersey produces little of its own energy, importing much of its electric power and virtually all of its fossil fuels.

In 1999, there were 31 electric generating plants in New Jersey; installed capacity (utility and nonutility) totaled 16.7 million kW. Power production amounted to 57 billion kWh. In 2000 New Jersey's total per capita energy consumption was 322 million Btu (81.1 million kcal), ranking it 33rd among the 50 states.

New Jersey had four nuclear reactors in operation in 2001. Two of them, at Salem, are operated by Public Service Electric and Gas (PSEandG), the state's largest utility. Another reactor, at Hope Creek, began operation in 1986, and the Oyster Creek reactor received its operating license in 1991. Nuclear generating stations accounted for 51% of the electric power generated in the state in 1999, up from only 16.5% in 1983.

29 INDUSTRY

New Jersey's earliest industries were glassmaking and iron working. In 1791, Alexander Hamilton proposed the development of a planned industrial town at the Passaic Falls. The Society for Establishing Useful Manufactures, an agency charged with developing the town, tried but failed to set up a cotton mill at the site, called Paterson, in 1797. By the early 1800s, however, Paterson had become the country's largest silk manufacturing center; by 1850, it was producing locomotives as well. On the eve of the Civil War, industry already had a strong foothold in the state. Newark had breweries, hat factories, and paper plants; Trenton, iron and paper; Jersey City, steel and soap; and Middlesex, clays and ceramics. The late 1800s saw the birth of the electrical industry, the growth of oil refineries on Bayonne's shores, and emerging chemical, drug, paint, and telephone manufacturing centers. All these products retain their places among the state's diverse manufactures.

In 1997, the value of shipments for manufactured goods totaled $101 billion. Nearly every major US corporation has facilities in the state. As of 1997, there were 23 Fortune 500 companies headquartered in New Jersey.

Earnings of persons employed in New Jersey increased from $179,371,115,000 in 1997 to $190,545,721,000 in 1998, an increase of 6.2%. The largest industries in 1998 were services, 30.7% of earnings; state and local government, 11.8%; and nondurable goods manufacturing, 10.0%. Of the industries that accounted for at least 5% of earnings in 1998, the slowest growing from 1997 to 1998 was durable goods manufacturing (5.6% of earnings in 1998), which increased 2.9%; the fastest was finance, insurance, and real estate (8.9% of earnings in 1998), which increased 7.3%.

30 COMMERCE

With one of the nation's busiest ports, one of the busiest airports (Newark), the largest length of highways and railroads per state area, and many regional distribution centers, New Jersey is an important commercial state.

In 1997, New Jersey had 19,595 wholesale establishments, with sales of $233 billion. Retail sales were conducted by 49,551 establishments and totaled $82 billion in 1997. The major categories of establishments were food stores, 13%; automotive dealers, 11%; and restaurants and bars, 30%. The state's wholesale trade is largely concentrated near manufacturing centers and along the New Jersey Turnpike.

Bergen, Union, and Essex counties accounted for more than one half of wholesale trade. Other large shopping centers are in Burlington, Eatontown, Lawrenceville, Livingston, Menlo Park, and Woodbridge. Three of the nation's largest supermarket chains have their headquarters in New Jersey: Great Atlantic and Pacific Tea Co. (A&P) in Montvale, Supermarkets General (Pathmark) in Woodbridge, and Grand Union in Elmwood Park. The toy store chain Toys R Us is headquartered in Rochelle Park.

Port Newark and the Elizabeth Marine Terminal, foreign-trade zones operated by the Port Authority of New York and New Jersey, have been modernized and enlarged in recent years, and together account for most of the cargo unloaded in New York Harbor. In 1998, New Jersey exported $15 billion to foreign countries. In 1999, the figure was $23 billion, ranking 9th in the nation. The leading exports were chemicals, electronics, and industrial machinery. Most exports went to Canada, Japan, the UK, and Mexico.

31 CONSUMER PROTECTION

Consumer fraud cases are handled by the Division of Consumer Affairs of the Department of Law and Public Safety (created in 1966 and integrated in 1971). The Offices of Consumer Protection and Weights and Measures, the Bureau of Securities, and a number of professional and occupational boards that license nearly 80 occupations and professions, work together to protect New Jerseyites from fraud and deceit.

32 BANKING

The colonies' first bank of issue opened in Gloucester in 1682. New Jersey's first chartered bank, the Newark Banking and Insurance Co., was the first of many banks to open in that city. By the mid-1800s, Newark was indisputably the financial center of the state. For the most part, commercial banking in New Jersey is overshadowed by the great financial centers of New York City and Philadelphia.

In 2002, there were 152 insured banks having their principal office in New Jersey. Deposits of these banks exceeded $132 billion. Fifty-nine of these banks were state-chartered.

Regulation of all state chartered banks, savings banks, savings and loan associations and limited purpose trust companies is the responsibility of the Department of Banking and Insurance. National banks are regulated by the Office of Comptroller of the Currency. The principal regulator of federally chartered savings and loan associations is the Office of Thrift Supervision.

During 2001/02, the Federal Reserve lowered interest rates considerably, causing fluctuations in net interest margins (NIMs) (the difference between the lower rates offered to savers and the higher rates charged on loans). Long-term interest rates neared historic lows by the end of 2002, and short-term interest rates stabilized, leading to a decline in banks' asset yields greater than the decline in funding costs. A large number of New Jersey's banks are residential lenders, and the widespread use of long-term mortgages in 2002 resulted in higher concentrations of long-term assets in New Jersey—twice that reported by other banks elsewhere in the nation.

As of September 2002, 40% of the state's insured banks held high concentrations of higher-risk loans. Almost 50% of these institutions were chartered during the 1990s expansion, and until the early 2000s, had not experienced an economic slowdown. Loan delinquency rates remained low in 2002.

33 INSURANCE

In 2001 there were 4.5 million ordinary life insurance policies in force in New Jersey, with a total value of $414.3 billion; total value for all categories of life insurance (ordinary, group, industrial, and credit) was $688.7 billion. Death benefits paid that year totaled $2.13 billion.

As of 2000, there were 76 property and casualty insurance companies headquartered in the state along with eight life and health domestic insurers. Property and liability insurers wrote over $12.7 billion in premiums. That year, there were 178,117 flood insurance policies in force in the state, with a total value of $25.8 million.

No-fault automobile insurance has been compulsory in New Jersey since 1973. All insurance agents, brokers, and companies in the state are licensed and regulated by the Department of Banking and Insurance.

34 SECURITIES

There are no stock or commodity exchanges in New Jersey. Regulation of securities trading in the state is under the control of the Bureau of Securities of the Division of Consumer Affairs, within the Department of Law and Public Safety.

About 1,803 broker-dealers organizations sell securities within New Jersey, involving 40,447 employees; registered investment advisory companies number 411. The state headquarters 231 NASDAQ companies, 38 NASDAQ market makers, 36 AMEX-listed companies; and has incorporated 112 NYSE-listed companies, including (the top five in revenues) Lucent Technologies, Merck & Co., Inc., Johnson & Johnson, Honeywell, Intl., and American Home Products Corp.

35 PUBLIC FINANCE

The annual budget, prepared by the Treasury Department's Division of Budget and Accounting, is submitted by the governor to the legislature for approval. The fiscal year runs from 1 July to 30 June.

Adjusted appropriations from New Jersey's general fund totaled $16.251 billion in 2002/03, including appropriations, by purpose, for direct state services ($5.284 billion), grants-in-aid ($6.139 billion), state aid ($3.923 billion), capital construction ($1.024 billion), and debt service ($434 million). New Jersey's budget deficit for 2002/03 was estimated at 25.6% of the state budget, and for 2003/04, was projected at 19% of the state budget.

The following table from the US Census Bureau contains information on revenues, expenditures, indebtedness, and cash/securities for 2001.

	($000)	PERCENT	PER CAPITA
Population (thousands, 2001)	8,511	(X)	(X)
Total Revenue	42,788,178	100.00	5,027.40
General revenue	34,372,985	80.33	4,038.65
Utility revenue	525,640	1.23	61.76
Liquor store revenue	–	–	–
Insurance trust revenue	7,889,553	18.44	926.98
Exhibit: Salaries and wages	5,330,587	14.15	626.32
Total expenditure	37,659,554	100.00	4,424.81
General expenditure	30,476,649	80.93	3,580.85
Education	10,397,395	27.61	1,221.64
Public welfare	5,813,422	15.44	683.05
Hospitals	1,257,365	3.34	147.73
Health	905,061	2.40	106.34
Highways	2,176,802	5.78	255.76
Police protection	404,771	1.07	47.56
Correction	1,206,768	3.20	141.79
Natural resources	352,582	0.94	41.43
Parks and recreation	430,370	1.14	50.57
Government administration	1,253,729	3.33	147.31
Interest on general debt	1,189,192	3.16	139.72
Other and unallocable	5,089,192	13.51	597.95
Utility expenditure	1,885,997	5.01	221.60
Liquor store expenditure	–	–	–
Insurance trust expenditure	5,296,908	14.07	622.36
Debt at end of fiscal year	29,727,858	100.00	3,492.87
Cash and security holdings	85,791,237	100.00	10,080.04

36 TAXATION

New Jersey's personal income tax is the largest single source of revenues, and the 6% retail sales tax is the 2nd largest. The personal income tax schedule has six brackets ranging from 1.4% (up to taxable income $20,000 for singles) to 6.37% (above $75,000; $150,000 for joint filers), with intermediate rates of 1.75%, 2.45%, 3.5%, and 5.25%. The net income of business corporations and banks is taxed at a rate of 7.5% for net income of less than $100,000, and 9% for higher net incomes. The state also imposes a full array of excise taxes covering motor fuels, tobacco products, insurance premiums, public utilities, alcoholic beverages (the state controls all sales), amusements, pari-mutuels, and other selected items. In 2002, the legislature raised both the gas tax (from 10.5 cents to 14.5 cents a gallon) and the cigarette tax (80 cents to $1.50 a pack). There are no local sales taxes. New Jersey has its own estate tax (maximum 18%), which is not affected by the scheduled phase-out of the federal exemption for state death taxes by 2007. The state graduated inheritance tax

applies mainly to property passing out of the direct family line. Death and gift taxes accounted for 2.8% of state taxes collected in 2002. Other state taxes include various license and franchise fees, stamp taxes and state property taxes. Most property taxes are collected locally. A large percent (43.8% in 2000) of total non-federal tax revenues are collected at local levels.

The 566 New Jersey municipalities are dependent on the local property tax, state grants, and state aid for their finances. Non-senior citizens with gross incomes under $40,000 are eligible for a Homestead Rebate of 490 (homeowner) or $30 (tenant). Citizens age 65 and over with incomes under $100,000 are eligible for rebates ranging from $100–500 (homeowners) and $35–500 (tenants). Over $323 million in property tax relief is provided through this program each year. In addition, about $60 million per year is directed towards offsetting local property tax bills for senior citizens, veterans, and surviving spouses.

The state collected $18.777 billion in taxes in 2002, of which 37.3% came from individual income taxes, 32.7% came from the general sales tax, 15.2% from selective sales taxes, 6% from corporate income taxes and 5.2% from license fees. In 2003, New Jersey ranked 19th among the states in terms of combined state and local tax burden, which amounted to about 9.8% of income.

The following table from the US Census Bureau provides a summary of taxes collected by the state in 2002.

	($000)	PER CAPITA
Total Taxes	18,328,814	2,133.66
Property taxes	3,303	0.38
Sales and gross receipts	8,777,442	1,021.79
General sales and gross receipts	5,996,839	698.09
Selective sales taxes	2,780,603	323.69
Alcoholic beverage	81,280	9.46
Amusements	350,977	40.86
Insurance Premiums	345,816	40.26
Motor fuels	523,819	60.98
Pari-mutuels	(X)	(X)
Public utilities	831,861	96.84
Tobacco products	406,856	47.36
Other selective sales	239,994	27.94
Licenses	957,176	111.43
Alcoholic beverages	6,364	0.74
Amusements	63,552	7.4
Corporation	122,367	14.24
Hunting and fishing	13,643	1.59
Motor vehicle	371,830	43.28
Motor vehicle operators	32,333	3.76
Public utility	(X)	(X)
Occupation and business, NEC	344,491	40.1
Other	2,596	0.3
Other taxes	8,590,893	1,000.07
Individual income	6,836,992	795.9
Corporation net income	1,101,296	128.2
Death and gift	510,367	59.41
Documentary and stock transfer	142,238	16.56
Severance	(X)	(X)
Other	(X)	(X)

37 ECONOMIC POLICY

New Jersey's controlled budget and relatively low business tax burden have helped encourage new businesses to enter the state. In addition, the state Department of Commerce and Economic Development administers a number of development programs designed to retain and attract business and jobs. The state's Economic Development Authority (EDA) is an independent authority established to provide financing programs, including loans, loan guarantees, and tax-free and taxable bond packages.

The Urban Enterprise Zone Program seeks to revitalize urban areas by granting tax incentives and relaxing some government regulations. The Office of Business Development identifies and assists firms that have expansion needs or are experiencing difficulties. The Economic Development Marketing Office fosters New Jersey's business-friendly environment through marketing and advertising initiatives, including targeted industry assistance programs. The Division of Development for Small Businesses, Women and Minority Businesses supports the start-up, growth and expansion of smaller firms and women and minority-owned enterprises. The Division of International Trade seeks to boost the state's exports and bring more foreign companies into the state. Other offices within the department promote tourism and motion picture production. In 2000, Governor Whitman announced a $165 million package called "New Jersey Jobs for a New Economy," to increase high technology in the state. In 2003, EDA was offering over 20 different programs for businesses. Besides financing, EDA offered a full range of real estate development services, training for entrepreneurs, and technical support. Specific categories targeted for assistance were small and mid-size businesses, high-tech businesses, non-profits, and brownfields. There were also separate divisions for advocating Smart Growth principles and for trade adjustment assistance.

38 HEALTH

During the 12 months ending with December 2000, the infant mortality rate in New Jersey was 6.3 per 1,000 live births, below the national average of 6.9. There were 35,126 abortions in 1999, averaging a rate of 20 per 1,000 women. In 2000, the overall death rate stood at 911.7 per 100,000 inhabitants, above the national average of 873.1.

The leading cause of death in the state is heart disease, for which New Jersey ranks above the national average. Mortality rates per 100,000 residents in 2000 were as follows: diseases of the heart, 289.2; cerebrovascular disease, 52.6; accidents and adverse effects, 27.8; motor vehicle accidents, 9.4; and suicide, 6.8. The HIV-related death rate was slightly lower than the national average in 2000 (9.3 per 100,000 population). A total of 43,824 AIDS cases had been reported through 2001. Among persons ages 18 and older, 21.0% were smokers in 2000.

New Jersey's 78 community hospitals had 1,083,798 admissions and 24,580 beds in 2001. There were 28,835 full-time registered nurses and 2,333 full-time licensed practical nurses in 2001 and 323 physicians per 100,000 population in 2000. The average expense of a community hospital for care was $1,381 per inpatient day in 2001.

Federal government grants to cover the Medicare and Medicaid services in 2001 totaled $3.6 billion; 1,207,663 enrollees received Medicare benefits that year. At least 13.1% of New Jersey's residents were uninsured in 2002.

The state's only medical school, the University of Medicine and Dentistry of New Jersey, is a public institution that combines three medical schools, one dental school, a school of allied professions, and a graduate school of biomedical sciences.

39 SOCIAL WELFARE

Through the Department of Human Services, New Jersey administers the major federal welfare programs, as well as several programs specifically designed to meet the needs of New Jersey minority groups. Among the latter in the 1990s was the Cuban-Haitian Entrant Program. Additional assistance went to refugees from such areas as Southeast Asia and Eastern Europe.

In 2001, the average weekly unemployment benefit was $302.95. Average monthly participation in the food stamp program in FY2002 comprised 319,799 persons (147,077 households). The average monthly benefit was $81.89, and the sum total of benefits paid in FY2002 was $314,258,247.

With the enactment of the Personal Responsibility and Work Opportunity Reconciliation Act of 1996, the US government has changed the form and regulations for many of its social welfare programs. Most significantly, it replaces Aid to Families with Dependent Children (AFDC), an open-ended entitlement program, with Temporary Assistance for Needy Families (TANF), a limited system of assistance funded largely through federal block grants. The reform act also impacts the food stamp program, the Supplemental Security Income program, and the child nutrition program. The law took effect on 1 July 1997 and provided $16.38 billion in block grants for fiscal years 1997–2002. The grants are to be divided among the states based on an equation involving the numbers of former AFDC recipients in each state.

Reauthorization of the 1996 social welfare legislation, scheduled for 2002, was delayed, and the original law had been extended three times as of July 2003, with the most recent extension running through September 2003. New Jersey's TANF program is called Work First New Jersey (WFNJ). In June 2000 the state had 125,258 welfare recipients. State expenditures on the TANF program in FY2002 totaled $410,326,128.

In December 2001, Social Security benefits were paid to 1,355,570 New Jersey residents. This number included 930,570 retired workers, 133,720 widows and widowers, 131,350 disabled workers, 60,770 spouses, and 99,160 children. Social Security beneficiaries represented 16% of the total state population and 92.5% of the state's population age 65 and older. Retired workers (excluding persons with special benefits) received an average monthly payment of $965; widows and widowers, $912; disabled workers, $878; and spouses, $474. Payments for children of retired workers averaged $462 per month; children of deceased workers, $627; and children of disabled workers, $274.

Federal Supplemental Security Income payments in December 2001 went to 147,747 New Jersey residents, averaging $388 a month.

40 HOUSING

Before 1967, New Jersey took a laissez-faire attitude toward housing. With each locality free to fashion its own zoning ordinances, large tracts of rural land succumbed to "suburban sprawl"—single-family housing developments spread out in two huge arcs from New York City and Philadelphia. Meanwhile, the tenement housing of New Jersey's central cities was left to deteriorate. Because poor housing was at least one of the causes of the Newark riot in 1967, the state established the Department of Community Affairs to coordinate existing housing aid programs and establish new ones. The state legislature also created the Mortgage Finance Agency and Housing Finance Agency to stimulate home buying and residential construction. In an effort to halt suburban sprawl, local and county planning boards were encouraged during the 1970s to adopt master plans for controlled growth. Court decisions in the late 1970s and early 1980s challenged the constitutionality of zoning laws that precluded the development of low-income housing in suburban areas.

In 2002, the state had an estimated 3,372,572 housing units, of which 3,081,928 were occupied; 65.9% were owner-occupied. About 54.2% of all units were single-family, detached homes. Nearly 46% of the entire housing stock was built before 1969. Utility gas is the most common heating energy source, followed by fuel oil and kerosene. It was estimated that 69,464 units lacked telephone service, 12,764 lacked complete plumbing facilities, and 14,958 lacked complete kitchen facilities. The average household size was 2.72 people.

In 2002, 30,441 new privately owned units were authorized for construction. The median home value was $210,483, the 5th-highest in the country. The median monthly cost for mortgage owners was $1,672. Renters paid a median of $808. During 2002, New Jersey received over $177.5 million in community planning and development aid from the US Department of Housing and Urban Development.

41EDUCATION

Public education in New Jersey dates from 1828, when the legislature first allocated funds to support education; by 1871, a public school system was established statewide. In 2000, the state was above the US norms in both the proportion of persons over age 25 who were high school graduates (82.1%) and the percentage of persons with four or more years of college (29.8%).

The total enrollment for fall 1999 in New Jersey's public schools stood at 1,890,256. Of these, 953,766 attended schools from kindergarten through grade eight, and 335,490 attended high school. Minority students made up approximately 40% of the total enrollment in public elementary and secondary schools in 2001. Total enrollment was estimated at 1,309,839 in fall 2000 and is expected to reach 1,279,000 by fall 2005. The state ranked first nationwide in expenditures per pupil ($9,775) in 1999/2000. Expenditures for public education in 2000/01 were estimated at $14,129,045. Enrollment in nonpublic schools in fall 2001 was 198,631.

As of fall 2000, there were 470,302 students enrolled in institutions of higher education. In the same year New Jersey had 58 degree-granting institutions. Rutgers, the state university, began operations as Queen's College in 1766 and was placed under state control in 1956, encompassing the separate colleges of Rutgers, Douglass, Livingston, and Cook, among others. As of 2000 the university had campuses at New Brunswick, Camden, and Newark. Altogether, New Jersey has 14 public four-year colleges, 19 two-year community colleges, and 21 private colleges. The major private university in the state and one of the nation's leading institutions is Princeton University, founded in 1746. Other major private universities are Seton Hall (1856); Stevens Institute of Technology (1870); and Fairleigh Dickinson (1942), with three main campuses. In 1997, minority students comprised 30.6% of total postsecondary enrollment.

The New Jersey Department of Higher Education offers tuition aid grants and scholarships to state residents who attend colleges and universities in the state. Guaranteed loans for any qualified resident are available through the New Jersey Higher Education Assistance Authority.

42ARTS

During the late 1800s and early 1900s, New Jersey towns, especially Atlantic City and Newark, were tryout centers for shows bound for Broadway. The New Jersey Theater Group, a service organization for nonprofit professional theaters, was established in 1978; 20 theaters—including the Tony Award–winning McCarter Theater at Princeton and Paper Mill Playhouse in Millburn—are members of the Theater Group.

Around the turn of the century, Ft. Lee was the motion picture capital of the world. Most of the best-known "silents"—including the first, *The Great Train Robbery,* and episodes of *The Perils of Pauline*—were shot there, and in its heyday the state film industry supported 21 companies and 7 studios. New Jersey's early preeminence in cinema, an era that ended with the rise of Hollywood, stemmed partly from the fact that the first motion picture system was developed by Thomas Edison at Menlo Park in the late 1880s. The state created the New Jersey Motion Picture and Television Commission in 1977; in the next six years, production companies spent $57 million in the state. Notable productions during this period included two Woody Allen pictures, *Broadway Danny Rose* and *The Purple Rose of Cairo.*

The state's long history of support for classical music dates at least to 1796, when William Dunlap of Perth Amboy wrote the libretto for *The Archers,* the first American opera to be commercially produced. There are over 60 professional and community orchestras throughout the state. The state's leading orchestra is the New Jersey Symphony, which makes its home in the new New Jersey Performing Arts Center in Newark; there are other symphony orchestras in Plainfield and Trenton. The New Jersey State Opera performs in Newark's Symphony Hall, while the Opera Festival of New Jersey makes its home in Lawrenceville. Noteworthy dance companies include the American Repertory Ballet, New Jersey Ballet, and the Nai N. Chen Dance Company.

The jazz clubs of northern New Jersey and the seaside rock clubs in Asbury Park have helped launch the careers of many local performers. Famous stars perform in the casinos and hotels of Atlantic City.

In 2003, the New Jersey State Council on the Arts and other New Jersey arts organizations received grants totaling $1,210,700 from the National Endowment for the Arts. State and private sources also contributed funding to New Jersey's arts programs; the state offered arts education programs to approximately 25,000 schoolchildren. The New Jersey Council for the Humanities was founded in 1973. In 2000, the National Endowment for the Humanities contributed $2,212,614 to 43 state programs.

43LIBRARIES AND MUSEUMS

Statewide, 13 public library systems in 2000 housed more than 28 million volumes. The Newark Public Library was the largest municipal system with 1,452,336 volumes and 10 branches. Distinguished by special collections on African-American studies, art and archaeology, economics, and international affairs, among many others, Princeton University's library is the largest in the state, with 4,973,619 volumes and 34,182 periodical subscriptions in 1998; Rutgers University ranked 2nd with 3,238,416. The New Jersey State Library in Trenton contained 470,000 volumes, mostly on the state's history and government. One of the largest business libraries, emphasizing scientific and technical data, is the AT&T Bell Laboratories' library system, based in Murray Hill. The public library system as a whole had an income of approximately $299,426,000; including $1,796,556 in federal grants and $10,180,484 in state grants.

New Jersey has more than 177 museums, historic sites, botanical gardens and arboretums. Among the most noteworthy museums are the New Jersey Historical Society in Newark and New Jersey State Museum in Trenton; the Newark Museum, containing both art and science exhibits; Princeton University's Art Museum and Museum of Natural History; and the Jersey City Museum. Also of interest are the early waterfront homes and vessels of Historic Gardner's Basin in Atlantic City, as well as Grover Cleveland's birthplace in Caldwell; the Campbell Museum in Camden (featuring the soup company's collection of bowls and utensils); Cape May County Historical Museum; Clinton Historical Museum Village; US Army Communications-Electronics Museum at Ft. Monmouth; Batsto Village, near Hammonton; Morristown National Historic Park (where George Washington headquartered during the Revolutionary War); Sandy Hook Museum; and one of the most popular attractions, the Edison National Historic Site, formerly the home and workshop of Thomas Edison, in West Orange. In 1984, the grounds at the Skylands section of Ringwood State Park were designated as the official state botanical garden.

44COMMUNICATIONS

Many communications breakthroughs—including Telstar, the first communications satellite—have been achieved by researchers at Bell Labs in Holmdel, Whippany, and Murray Hill. Three Bell Labs researchers shared the Nobel Prize in physics (1956) for developing the transistor, a device that has revolutionized communications and many other fields. In 1876, at Menlo Park, Thomas Edison invented the carbon telephone transmitter, a device that made the telephone commercially feasible.

The first mail carriers to come to New Jersey were, typically enough, on their way between New York and Philadelphia. Express mail between the two cities began in 1737, and by 1764, carriers could speed through the state in 24 hours. In colonial times, tavern keepers generally served as the local mailmen. The nation's largest bulk-mail facility is in Jersey City. In 2001, 95.9% of the state's occupied housing units had telephones.

Because the state lacks a major television broadcasting outlet, New Jerseyites receive more news about events in New York City and Philadelphia than in their own towns and cities. In 2003 there were 60 major radio stations (8 AM, 52 FM) and 15 television stations, none of which commanded anything like the audiences and influence of the stations across the Hudson and Delaware rivers. In 1978, in cooperation with public television's WNET (licensed in Newark but operated in New York), New Jersey's public stations began producing New Jersey's first nightly newscast.

A total of 251,401 Internet domain names were registered in New Jersey in the year 2000.

45 PRESS

New Jersey has not been known for having a very powerful press. In 1702, Queen Anne banned printers from the colony. The state's first periodical, founded in 1758, died two years later. New Jersey's first daily paper, the *Newark Daily Advertiser,* did not arrive until 1832.

Many present-day newspapers, most notably the *Newark Star–Ledger,* have amassed considerable circulation. However, no newspaper has been able to muster statewide influence or match the quality and prestige of the nearby *New York Times* or *Philadelphia Inquirer,* both of which are read widely in the state, along with other New York City and Philadelphia papers. In 2002, there were 17 morning dailies, 1 evening, and 15 Sunday papers. Most of the largest papers are owned by either Gannett Co., Inc (of Virginia) or Advance Publications (of New York).The following table shows leading New Jersey dailies with their approximate 2002 circulation:

AREA	NAME	DAILY	SUNDAY
Atlantic City	*Press*(m,S)	76,083	96,215
Burlington	*Courier-Post**(m,S)	80,550	96,513
Hackensack	*Record* (m,S)	178,029	226,091
Neptune	*Asbury Park Press**(m,S)	170,229	231,882
Newark	*Star–Ledger*+(m,S)	410,547	608,542
Trenton	*Times* +(m,S)	78,005	85,647

*owned by Gannett Co., Inc.
+owned by Advance Publications.

Numerous scholarly and historical works have been published by the university presses of Princeton and Rutgers. Prentice-Hall's offices are in Englewood Cliffs, and those of Silver Burdett, a textbook publisher, are in Morristown. Several New York City publishing houses maintain their production and warehousing facilities in the state. Periodicals published in New Jersey include *Home, Medical Economics, New Jersey Monthly, Personal Computing,* and *Tiger Beat.*

46 ORGANIZATIONS

In 2003, there were about 3,649 regional, national, and international organizations within the state.

Princeton is the headquarters of several education-related groups, including the Educational Testing Service, Graduate Record Examinations Board, Independent Educational Services, and Woodrow Wilson National Fellowship Foundation. Seeing Eye of Morristown was one of the first organizations to provide seeing-eye dogs for the blind. Other medical and health-related organizations are National Industries for the Blind (Wayne), the American Headache Society (Mount Royal), the Multiple Sclerosis Association of America (Cherry Hill), and the American

Association of Veterinary State Boards (Teaneck). Birthright USA, an anti-abortion counseling service, has its headquarters in Woodbury; the National Council on Crime and Delinquency is in Ft. Lee.

Among the many trade and professional organizations are the Hobby Industry Association of America in Elmwood Park, Science Fiction Writers of America in Wharton, the Institute of Electrical and Electronics Engineers in Piscataway, and American Littoral Society in Highlands.

Hobby and sports groups include the US Golf Association, the International Golf Federation, and the World Amateur Golf Council in Far Hills; US Equestrian Team in Gladstone; Babe Ruth Baseball/Softball in Trenton; the International Boxing Federation in East Orange; and National Intercollegiate Women's Fencing Association in Upper Montclair. The Miss America Organization, established in 1921, sponsors the annual Miss America competition in Atlantic City. The American Vegan Society is based in Malaga.

Several religious organizations have base offices in New Jersey, including the American Coptic Association, the Blue Army of Our Lady of Fatima, U.S.A., and the Xaverian Missionaries of the United States. The American Atheists organization is also based in the state.

There are numerous arts and cultural organizations. Some of national interest include the Music Critics Association of North America, the Musical Heritage Society, the National Music Council, the Royal Academy of Dance, and the World Congress of Teachers of Dancing. There are a number of local historical societies. The Heritage Institute of Ellis Island is located in Jersey City.

47 TOURISM, TRAVEL, AND RECREATION

Tourism is a leading industry in New Jersey, accounting for a sizeable part of the state's revenues. In 2002, there were about 60.8 million visitors to the state, 57% of which were day-trip travelers. About 34% of all trips are made by residents within the state. Nearly 25% of all visitors are from New York and about 19% are from Pennsylvania. The Jersey shore has been a popular attraction since 1801, when Cape May began advertising itself as a summer resort. Dining, entertainment, and gambling are also popular.

Of all the shore resorts, the largest has long been Atlantic City, which by the 1890s was the nation's most popular resort city and by 1905 was the first major city with an economy almost totally dependent on tourism. That proved to be its downfall, as improvements in road and air transportation made more modern resorts in other states easily accessible to easterners. By the early 1970s, the city's only claims to fame were the Miss America pageant and the game of Monopoly, whose standard version uses its street names. In an effort to restore Atlantic City to its former luster and revive its economy, New Jersey voters approved a constitutional amendment in 1976 to allow casinos in the resort. Some 33 million people visit Atlantic City annually. Casino taxes were earmarked to reduce property taxes of senior citizens.

State attractions include ten ski areas in northwestern New Jersey (on Hamburg Mountain alone, more than 50 slopes are available), canoeing and camping at the Delaware Water Gap National Recreation Area, three national wildlife refuges, 31 public golf courses, and 30 amusement parks, including Great Adventure in central Jersey. Dutch Neck Village, created in 1976, includes a living museum and the Old Hickory Arboretum. Jersey Greens, the largest outlet mall in New Jersey, opened in 1999, anticipating revenues of $5.6 million annually.

48 SPORTS

New Jersey did not have a major league professional team until 1976, when the New York Giants of the National Football League moved across the Hudson River into the newly completed

Giants Stadium in the Meadowlands Sports Complex at East Rutherford. The NFL's New York Jets began playing their home games at the Meadowlands in 1984. The Continental Airlines Arena, located at the same site, is the home of the New Jersey Nets of the National Basketball Association and the New Jersey Devils of the National Hockey League. As New York teams who no longer play in their home state, the Giants and the Jets are scorned by some New York sports purists. When the Giants won the Super Bowl in 1987, New York's then mayor, Ed Koch, refused them the ticker-tape parade traditionally given to local sports champions on the grounds that since they play in New Jersey they are not a New York team.

The state did celebrate a championship it could call its own, however, when the Devils won the Stanley Cup in 1995. The Devils repeated their success with two more Stanley Cup victories in 2000 and 2003.

The New Jersey Nets have made a surge in the recent past, becoming one of the most successful teams in the NBA. They captured births in consecutive NBA Finals in 2002–03, falling short on both occasions, however.

The Meadowlands is also the home of a dual thoroughbred–harness-racing track. Other racetracks are Garden State Park (Cherry Hill), Monmouth Park (Oceanport), and Atlantic City Race Course for thoroughbreds, and Freehold Raceway for harness racing. Auto racing is featured at speedways in Bridgeport, East Windsor, and New Egypt. Trenton has a minor league baseball team, the Thunder, in the Eastern League. New Jersey has several world-class golf courses, including Baltusrol, the site of seven US Opens, the latest in 1993. Numerous championship boxing matches have been held in Atlantic City.

New Jersey is historically significant in the births of two major national sports. Princeton and Rutgers played what is claimed to be the first intercollegiate football game on 6 November 1869 at New Brunswick. (Princeton was named national champion several times around the turn of the century, for the last time in 1911). The first game of what we know today as baseball was also played in New Jersey: at the Elysion Field in Hoboken between the Knickerbockers and the New York Nine on June 19, 1846. Several important college games are held at Giants Stadium each fall. In college basketball, Seton Hall placed high in the rankings repeatedly in the late 1980s and early 1990s. In 1989 they made it to the finals, losing to Michigan by one point in overtime. Rutgers had a formidable team in the 1970s, making it to the Final Four in 1976.

Other annual sporting events include the New Jersey Offshore Grand Prix Ocean Races held at Point Pleasant Beach in July and the National Marbles Tournament in Wildwood.

⁴⁹FAMOUS NEW JERSEYITES

While only one native New Jerseyite, (Stephen) Grover Cleveland (1837–1908), has been elected president of the US, the state can also properly claim (Thomas) Woodrow Wilson (b.Virginia, 1856–1924), who spent most of his adult life there. Cleveland left his birthplace in Caldwell as a little boy, winning his fame and two terms in the White House (1885–89, 1893–97) as a resident of New York State. After serving as president, he retired to Princeton, where he died and is buried. Wilson, a member of Princeton's class of 1879, returned to the university in 1908 as a professor and became its president in 1902. Elected governor of New Jersey in 1910, Wilson pushed through a series of sweeping reforms before entering the White House in 1913. Wilson's two presidential terms were marked by his controversial decision to declare war on Germany and his unsuccessful crusade for US membership in the League of Nations after World War I.

Two vice presidents hail from New Jersey: Aaron Burr (1756–1836) and Garret A. Hobart (1844–99). Burr, born in Newark and educated at what is now Princeton University, is best remembered for killing Alexander Hamilton in a duel at Weehawken in 1804. Hobart was born in Long Branch, graduated from Rutgers College, and served as a lawyer in Paterson until elected vice president in 1896; he died in office.

Four New Jerseyites have become associate justices of the US Supreme Court: William Paterson (b.Ireland, 1745–1806), Joseph P. Bradley (1813–92), Mahlon Pitney (1858–1924), and William J. Brennan, Jr. (1906-1997). Among the relatively few New Jerseyites to serve in the US cabinet was William E. Simon (1927), secretary of the treasury under Gerald Ford.

Few New Jerseyites won important political status in colonial years because the colony was so long under New York's political and social domination. Lewis Morris (b.New York, 1671–1746) was named the first royal governor of New Jersey when severance from New York came in 1738. Governors who made important contributions to the state included William Livingston (b.New York, 1723–90), first governor after New Jersey became a state in 1776; Marcus L. Ward (1812–84), a strong Union supporter; and Alfred E. Driscoll (1902–75), who persevered in getting New Jersey a new state constitution in 1947 despite intense opposition from the Democratic Party leadership. Other important historical figures are Molly Pitcher (Mary Ludwig Hays McCauley, 1754?–1832), a heroine of the American Revolution, and Zebulon Pike (1779–1813), the noted explorer.

Two New Jersey persons have won the Nobel Peace Prize: Woodrow Wilson in 1919, and Nicholas Murray Butler (1862–1947) in 1931. A three-man team at Bell Laboratories in Murray Hill won the 1956 physics award for their invention of the transistor: Walter Brattain (b.China, 1902–87), John Bardeen (b.Wisconsin, 1908–91), and William Shockley (b.England, 1910–89). Dr. Selman Waksman (b.Russia, 1888–1973), a Rutgers University professor, won the 1952 prize in medicine and physiology for the discovery of streptomycin. Dickinson Woodruff (1895–1973) won the medicine and physiology prize in 1956, and Joshua Lederberg (b.1925) was a co-winner in 1958. Theoretical physicist Albert Einstein (b.Germany, 1879–1955), winner of a Nobel Prize in 1921, spent his last decades in Princeton. One of the world's most prolific inventors, Thomas Alva Edison (b.Ohio, 1847–1931) patented over 1,000 devices from workshops at Menlo Park and West Orange. David Dinkins (b.1927), first African-American mayor of New York was born in Trenton, New Jersey. Norman Schwarzkopf (b.1934), commander of US forces in Desert Storm (Gulf War), was born August 22, 1934 in Trenton, New Jersey. Michael Chang (b.1972), 1989 French Open tennis champion, was born in Hoboken.

The state's traditions in the arts began in colonial times. Patience Lovell Wright (1725–86) of Bordentown was America's first recognized sculptor. Jonathan Odell (1737–1818) was an anti-Revolutionary satirist, while Francis Hopkinson (b.Pennsylvania, 1737–91), lawyer, artist, and musician, lampooned the British. Authors of note after the Revolution included William Dunlap (1766–1839), who compiled the first history of the stage in America; James Fenimore Cooper (1789–1851), one of the nation's first novelists; Mary Mapes Dodge (b.New York, 1838–1905), noted author of children's books; Stephen Crane (1871–1900), famed for *The Red Badge of Courage* (1895); and Albert Payson Terhune (1872–1942), beloved for his collie stories.

Quite a number of prominent 20th-century writers were born in or associated with New Jersey. They include poets William Carlos Williams (1883–1963) and Allen Ginsberg (1926-1997); satirist Dorothy Parker (1893–1967); journalist-critic Alexander Woollcott (1887–1943); Edmund Wilson (1895–1972), influential critic, editor, and literary historian; Norman Cousins (1912–90); Norman Mailer (b.1923); Thomas Fleming (b.1927); John McPhee (b.1931); Philip Roth (b.1933); Imamu Amiri

Baraka (LeRoi Jones, b.1934); and Peter Benchley (b.New York, 1940).

Notable 19th-century artists were Asher B. Durand (1796–1886) and George Inness (b.New York, 1825–94). The best-known 20th-century artist associated with New Jersey was Ben Shahn (1898–1969); cartoonist Charles Addams (1912–88) was born in Westfield. Noted photographers born in New Jersey include Alfred Stieglitz (1864–1946) and Dorothea Lange (1895–1965). Important New Jersey composers were Lowell Mason (b.Massachusetts, 1792–1872), called the "father of American church music," and Milton Babbitt (b.Pennsylvania, 1916), long active at Princeton. The state's many concert singers include Anna Case (1889–1984), Paul Robeson (1898–1976), and Richard Crooks (1900–72). Popular singers include Francis Albert "Frank" Sinatra (1915–98), Sarah Vaughan (1924–1990), Dionne Warwick (b.1941), Paul Simon (b.1942), and Bruce Springsteen (b.1949). Jazz musician William "Count" Basie (1904–84) was born in Red Bank.

Other celebrities native to New Jersey are actors Jack Nicholson (b.1937), Michael Douglas (b.1944), Meryl Streep (b.1948), and John Travolta (b.1954). Comedians Lou Costello (1906–59), Ernie Kovacs (1919–62), Jerry Lewis (b.1926), and Clerow "Flip" Wilson (1933–98) were also born in the state. New Jersey-born athletes include figure skater Richard "Dick" Button (b.1929), winner of two Olympic gold medals.

[50]BIBLIOGRAPHY

Amick, George. *The American Way of Graft.* Princeton, NJ: Center for Analysis of Public Issues, 1987.

Cohen, David. *The Folklore and Folklife of New Jersey.* New Brunswick, NJ.: Rutgers University Press, 1983.

Cunningham, John T. *This is New Jersey.* 4th ed. New Brunswick, N.J.: Rutgers University Press, 1994.

Federal Writers' Project. *New Jersey: A Guide to the Present and Past.* Reprint. New York: Somerset, n.d. (orig. 1939).

Fleming, Thomas. *The Forgotten Victory: The Battle for New Jersey.* New York: Reader's Digest, 1973.

———. *New Jersey: A Bicentennial History.* New York: Norton, 1977.

Gillette, William. *Jersey Blue: Civil War Politics in New Jersey, 1854–1865.* New Brunswick, N.J.: Rutgers University Press, 1995.

League of Women Voters of New Jersey. *New Jersey: Spotlight on New Jersey Government.* 6th ed. New Brunswick, N.J.: Rutgers University Press, 1992.

Lee, Francis Bazley, ed. *Genealogical and Memorial History of the State of New Jersey: A Record of the Achievements of Her People in the Making of a Commonwealth and the Founding of a Nation.* Baltimore, Md.: reprinted for Clearfield Company, Inc. by Genealogical Pub. Co., 2000.

Link, Arthur F. *The Road to the White House.* Princeton, N.J.: Princeton University Press, 1947.

McPhee, John. *The Pine Barrens.* New York: Farrar, Straus & Giroux, 1981.

A New Jersey Anthology. Newark: New Jersey Historical Society, 1994.

New Jersey, State of Economic Policy Council and Office of Economic Policy. *1985 Economic Outlook for New Jersey.* Trenton, 1984.

Roberts, Russell. *Discover the Hidden New Jersey.* New Brunswick, N.J.: Rutgers University Press, 1995.

Rosenthal, Alan, and John Blydenburgh (eds.). *Politics in New Jersey.* New Brunswick, N.J.: Rutgers University Press, 1975.

Santelli, Robert. *Guide to the Jersey Shore: from Sandy Hook to Cape May.* Guilford, Conn.: Globe Pequot Press, 2000.

Siegel, Alan A. *Beneath the Starry Flag: New Jersey's Civil War Experience.* New Brunswick, N.J.: Rutgers University Press, 2001.

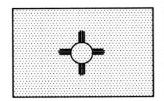

NEW MEXICO

State of New Mexico

ORIGIN OF STATE NAME: Spanish explorers in 1540 called the area "the new Mexico." **NICKNAME:** Land of Enchantment. **CAPITAL:** Santa Fe. **ENTERED UNION:** 6 January 1912 (47th). **SONGS:** "O Fair New Mexico" and "Así Es Nuevo México." **MOTTO:** *Crescit eundo* (It grows as it goes). **FLAG:** The sun symbol of the Indians of Zia Pueblo appears in red on a yellow field. **OFFICIAL SEAL:** An American bald eagle with extended wings grasps three arrows in its talons and shields a smaller eagle grasping a snake in its beak and a cactus in its talons (the emblem of Mexico; and thus symbolic of the change in sovereignty over the state). Below the scene is the state motto; the words "Great Seal of the State of New Mexico 1912" surround the whole. **ANIMAL:** Black bear. **BIRD:** Roadrunner (chaparral bird). **FISH:** Cutthroat trout. **FLOWER:** Yucca (Our Lord's Candles). **VEGETABLES:** Frijol; chile. **TREE:** Piñon pine. **FOSSIL:** *Coelophysis* dinosaur. **GEM:** Turquoise. **LEGAL HOLIDAYS:** New Year's Day, 1 January; Birthday of Martin Luther King, Jr., 3rd Monday in January; Lincoln's Birthday, 12 February; Washington's Birthday, 3rd Monday in February; Memorial Day, 30 May; Independence Day, 4 July; Labor Day, 1st Monday in September; Columbus Day, 2nd Monday in October; Veterans Day, 11 November; Thanksgiving Day, 4th Thursday in November; Christmas Day, 25 December. **TIME:** 5 AM MST = noon GMT.

¹LOCATION, SIZE, AND EXTENT

New Mexico is located in the southwestern US. Smaller only than Montana of the eight Rocky Mountain states, it ranks 5th in size among the 50 states. The area of New Mexico is 121,593 sq mi (314,926 sq km), of which land comprises 121,335 sq mi (314,258 sq km) and inland water 258 sq mi (668 sq km). Almost square in shape except for its jagged southern border, New Mexico extends about 352 mi (566 km) E-W and 391 mi (629 km) N-S.

New Mexico is bordered on the N by Colorado; on the E by Oklahoma and Texas; on the S by Texas and the Mexican state of Chihuahua (with a small portion of the south-central border formed by the Rio Grande); and on the W by Arizona. The total boundary length of New Mexico is 1,434 mi (2,308 km).

The geographic center of the state is in Torrance County, 12 mi (19 km) SSW of Willard.

²TOPOGRAPHY

The Continental Divide extends from north to south through central New Mexico. The north-central part of the state lies within the Southern Rocky Mountains, and the northwest forms part of the Colorado Plateau. The eastern two-fifths of the state fall on the western fringes of the Great Plains.

Major mountain ranges include the Southern Rockies, the Chuska Mountains in the northwest, and the Caballo, San Andres, San Mateo, Sacramento, and Guadalupe ranges in the south and southwest. The highest point in the state is Wheeler Peak, at 13,161 ft (4,014 m); the lowest point, 2,842 ft (867 m), is at Red Bluff Reservoir.

The Rio Grande traverses New Mexico from north to south and forms a small part of the state's southern border with Texas. Other major rivers include the Pecos, San Juan, Canadian, and Gila. The largest bodies of inland water are the Elephant Butte Reservoir and Conchas Reservoir, both created by dams.

The Carlsbad Caverns, the largest known subterranean labyrinth in the world, penetrate the foothills of the Guadalupes in the southeast. The caverns embrace more than 37 mi (60 km) of connecting chambers and corridors and are famed for their stalactite and stalagmite formations.

³CLIMATE

New Mexico's climate ranges from arid to semiarid, with a wide range of temperatures. Average January temperatures vary from about 35°F (2°C) in the north to about 55°F (13°C) in the southern and central regions. July temperatures range from about 78°F (26°C) at high elevations to around 92°F (33°C) at lower elevations. The record high temperature for the state is 122°F (50°C), set most recently on 27 July 1994 at Lakewood; the record low, −50°F (−46°C), was set on 1 February 1951 at Gavilan.

Average annual precipitation (1971–2000) was 9.5 in (24 cm) in Albuquerque in the desert; at high elevations, annual precipitation averaged over 20 in (50 cm). Nearly one-half the annual rainfall comes during July and August, and thunderstorms are common in the summer. Snow is much more frequent in the north than in the south; Albuquerque gets about 10 in (25 cm) of snow per year, and the northern mountains receive up to 100 in (254 cm).

⁴FLORA AND FAUNA

New Mexico is divided into the following six life zones: lower Sonoran, upper Sonoran, transition, Canadian, Hudsonian, and arctic-alpine.

Characteristic vegetation in each zone includes, respectively, desert shrubs and grasses; piñon/juniper woodland, sagebrush, and chaparral; ponderosa pine and oak woodlands; mixed conifer and aspen forests; spruce/fir forests and meadows; tundra wild flowers and riparian shrubs. The yucca has three varieties in New Mexico and is the state flower. Thirteen plant species were listed as threatened or endangered in 2003, including Sacramento prickly poppy, Moncos milk-vetch, and two species of cacti.

Indigenous animals include pronghorn antelope, javelina, and black-throated sparrow in the lower Sonoran zone; mule and white-tailed deer, ringtail, and brown towhee in the upper Sonoran zone; elk and wild turkey in the transition zone; black bear and hairy woodpecker in the Canadian zone; pine marten and blue grouse in the Hudsonian zone; and bighorn sheep, pika, ermine, and white-tailed ptarmigan in the arctic-alpine zone. Among notable desert insects are the tarantula, centipede, and vinegarroon. The coatimundi, Baird's sparrow, and brook stickleback are among rare animals. Twenty-nine New Mexican animal species were classified as threatened or endangered in 2003, including two species of bat, whooping crane, bald eagle, southwestern willow flycatcher, Mexican spotted owl, three species of shiner, and razorback sucker.

⁵ENVIRONMENTAL PROTECTION

Agencies concerned with the environment include the New Mexico Environment Department (NMED), the Environmental Improvement Board, the Water Quality Control Commission, and the Energy, Minerals and Natural Resources Department. As the state's leading environmental agency, the NMED's mission is to preserve, protect, and perpetuate New Mexico's environment for present and future generations. The Department is comprised of four divisions, 14 bureaus, four districts, and 17 field offices. Each entity is responsible for different areas and functions of environmental protection (or administrative support) concerning air, water, and land resources. Under the authority of state/federal laws and regulations, the NMED fulfills its mission through the judicious application of statewide regulatory, technical assistance, planning, enforcement, educational, and related functions in the service of its citizens. In 2003, New Mexico had 120 hazardous waste sites listed in the Environmental Protection Agency's database, 11 of which were on the National Priorities List. In 1996, it had 482,000 acres (0.6%) of wetlands. In 2001, New Mexico received $39,453,000 in federal grants from the Environmental Protection Agency; EPA expenditures for procurement contracts in New Mexico that year amounted to $1,486,000.

⁶POPULATION

New Mexico ranked 36th in population in the US with an estimated total of 1,855,059 in 2002, an increase of 2% since 2000. Between 1990 and 2000, New Mexico's population grew from 1,515,069 to 1,819,046, an increase of 20.1%. The population is projected to reach 2,016,000 by 2005 and 2.6 million by 2025. The population density in 2000 was 15 persons per sq mi.

In 2000 the median age was 34.6. Persons under 18 years old accounted for 28% of the population while 11.7% were age 65 or older.

In 2000, an estimated 463,874 people lived in Albuquerque; an estimated 678,820, more than one-third of New Mexico's total population, lived in the Albuquerque metropolitan area in 1999. Santa Fe, the 2nd-largest city and state capital, had 62,203 inhabitants in 2000.

⁷ETHNIC GROUPS

New Mexico has two large minorities: Indians and Hispanics. In 2000, the estimated American Indian population was 173,483 (9.5% of the total population—the 2nd-highest percentage of any state). Part of Arizona's great Navaho reservation extends across the border into New Mexico. New Mexico's Navaho population was recorded as 67,397 in 2000. There are 2 Apache reservations, 19 Pueblo villages (including one for the Zia in Sandoval County), and lands allotted to other tribes. Altogether, Indian lands cover 8,152,895 acres (3,299,477 hectares), 10.5% of New Mexico's area (2nd only to Arizona in proportion of Indian lands). In 2000 the Zuni lands had a population of 7,758, and the Acoma reservation had 2,802 residents.

The Hispanic population is an old one, descending from Spanish-speaking peoples who lived there before the territory was annexed by the US. In 2000, Hispanics and Latinos (including a small number of immigrants from modern Mexico) numbered 765,386 or 42.1% of the total state population.

As of 2000, an estimated 19,255 Asians, 1,503 Pacific Islanders, and 34,343 black Americans lived in the state.

⁸LANGUAGES

New Mexico has large Indian and Spanish-speaking populations. But just a few place-names, like Tucumcari and Mescalero, echo in English the presence of the Apache, Zuni, Navaho, and other tribes living there. Numerous Spanish borrowings include *vigas* (rafters) in the northern half, and *canales* (gutters) and *acequia* (irrigation ditch) in the Rio Grande Valley. New Mexico English is a mixture of dominant Midland, with some Northern features (such as *sick to the stomach*) in the northeast, and Southern and South Midland features such as *spoonbread* and *carry* (escort) in the eastern agricultural fringe.

In 2000, 1,072,947 New Mexicans—63.5% of the resident population five years of age and older—spoke only English at home, down slightly from 64.5% in 1990.

The following table gives selected statistics from the 2000 census for language spoken at home by persons five years old and over. The category "Other Native North American languages" includes Apache, Cherokee, Choctaw, Dakota, Keres, Pima, and Yupik.

LANGUAGE	NUMBER	PERCENT
Population 5 years and over	**1,689,911**	**100.0**
Speak only English	1,072,947	63.5
Speak a language other than English	616,964	36.5
Speak a language other than English	**616,964**	**36.5**
Spanish or Spanish Creole	485,681	28.7
Navajo	68,788	4.1
Other Native North American languages	26,880	1.6
German	7,871	0.5
French (incl. Patois, Cajun)	4,332	0.3
Chinese	2,983	0.2
Vietnamese	2,523	0.1
Italian	1,931	0.1
Tagalog	1,603	0.1
Japanese	1,263	0.1
Korean	1,197	0.1
Arabic	980	0.1

⁹RELIGIONS

The first religions in New Mexico were practiced by Pueblo and Navaho Indians. Franciscan missionaries arrived at the time of Coronado's conquest in 1540, and the first Roman Catholic church in the state was built in 1598. Roman Catholicism has long been the dominant religion, though from the mid-1800s there has also been a steady increase in the number of Protestants. The first Baptist missionaries arrived in 1849, the Methodists in 1850, and the Mormons in 1877.

The state's Roman Catholic churches had about 670,511 members in 2000. Protestants included 132,675 Southern Baptists, 41,597 United Methodists, 22,070 members of Assemblies of God, 18,985 members of Churches of Christ, and 13,224 Presbyterians (USA). The Church of Jesus Christ of Latter-Day Saints reported about 42,261 members. The Jewish population was estimated at 10,500 and the Muslim congregations had 2,604 adherents. About 761,218 people (about 41.8% of the population) were not counted as members of any religious organization.

¹⁰TRANSPORTATION

Important early roads included El Camino Real, extending from Mexico City, Mexico, up to Santa Fe and the Santa Fe Trail, leading westward from Independence, Missouri. By 2000, New Mexico had 59,927 mi (96,443 km) of public roads and streets.

In 2000, a total of 1,557,064 motor vehicles were registered in the state, of which 729,727 were automobiles, 795,343 trucks, 28,554 motorcycles, and 3,440 buses.

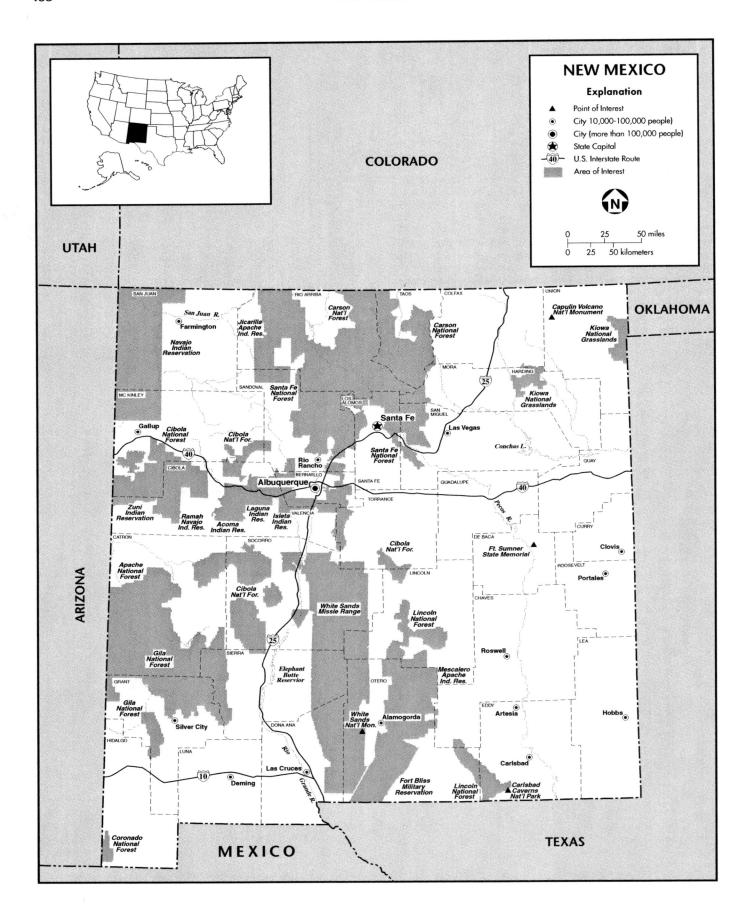

Rail service did not begin in New Mexico until 1879. New Mexico had 2,390 rail mi (3,846 km) of track in 2000, with Class I road making up close to 95% of that total. The main rail lines serving the state are the Union Pacific and Burlington Northern and Santa Fe. Amtrak provides passenger service en route from Chicago to Los Angeles and from New Orleans to Los Angeles.

In 2002, there were 145 airports, 25 heliports, and 1 seaplane base. Albuquerque International is the state's main airport, with 2,148,780 passengers enplaned in 2000.

11HISTORY

The earliest evidence of human occupation in what is now New Mexico, dating from about 20,000 years ago, has been found in Sandia Cave near Albuquerque. This so-called Sandia man was later joined by other nomadic hunters—the Clovis and Folsom people from the northern and eastern portions of the state, and the Cochise culture, which flourished in southwestern New Mexico from about 10,000 to 500 BC. The Mogollon people tilled small farms in the southwest from 300 BC to about 100 years before Columbus came to the New World. Also among the state's early inhabitants were the Basket Makers, a seminomadic people who eventually evolved into the Anasazi, or Cliff Dwellers. The Anasazi, who made their home in the Four Corners region (where present-day New Mexico meets Colorado, Arizona, and Utah), were the predecessors of the modern Pueblo Indians.

The Pueblo people lived along the upper Rio Grande, except for a desert group east of Albuquerque, who lived in the same kind of apartment-like villages as the river Pueblos. During the 13th century, the Navajo settled in the Four Corners area to become farmers, sheepherders, and occasional enemies of the Pueblos. The Apache, a more nomadic and warlike group who came at about the same time, later posed a threat to all the non-Indians who arrived in New Mexico during the Spanish, Mexican, and American periods.

Francisco Vásquez de Coronado led the earliest major expedition to New Mexico, beginning in 1540, 80 years before the Pilgrims landed at Plymouth Rock. In 1598, Don Juan de Onate led an expedition up the Rio Grande, where, one year later, he established the settlement of San Gabriel, near present-day Espanola; in 1610, the Spanish moved their center of activity to Santa Fe. For more than two centuries, the Spaniards, who concentrated their settlements, farms, and ranches in the upper Rio Grande Valley, dominated New Mexico, except for a period from 1680 to about 1693, when the Pueblo Indians temporarily regained control of the region.

In 1821, Mexico gained its independence from Spain, and New Mexico came under the Mexican flag for 25 years. The unpopularity of government officials sent from Mexico City and the inability of the new republic to control the Apache led to the revolt of 1837, which was put down by a force from Albuquerque led by General Manuel Armijo. In 1841, as governor of the Mexican territory, Armijo defeated an invading force from the Republic of Texas, but he later made a highly controversial decision not to defend Apache Pass east of Santa Fe during the Mexican-American War, instead retreating and allowing US forces under the command of General Stephen Watts Kearny to enter the capital city unopposed on 18 August 1846.

Kearny, without authorization from Congress, immediately attempted to make New Mexico a US territory. He appointed the respected Indian trader Charles Bent, a founder of Bent's Fort on the Santa Fe Trail, as civil governor, and then led his army on to California. After Kearny's departure, a Mexican and Indian revolt in Taos resulted in Bent's death; the suppression of the Taos uprising by another US Army contingent secured American control over New Mexico, although the area did not officially become a part of the US until the Treaty of Guadalupe-Hidalgo ended the Mexican-American War in 1848.

New Mexico became a US territory as part of the Compromise of 1850, which also brought California into the Union as a free state. Territorial status did not bring about rapid or dramatic changes in the lives of those who were already in New Mexico. However, an increasing number of people traveling on the Santa Fe Trail—which had been used since the early 1820s to carry goods between Independence, Mo., and Santa Fe—were Americans seeking a new home in the Southwest. One issue that divided many of these new settlers from the original Spanish-speaking inhabitants was land. Native New Mexicans resisted, sometimes violently, the efforts of new Anglo residents and outside capital to take over lands that had been allocated during the earlier Spanish and Mexican periods. Anglo lawyers such as Thomas Benton Catron acquired unprecedented amounts of land from native grantees as payment of legal fees in the prolonged litigation that often accompanied these disputes. Eventually, a court of private land claims, established by the federal government, legally processed 33 million acres (13 million hectares) of disputed land from 1891 to 1904.

Land disputes were not the only cause of violence during the territorial period. In 1862, Confederate General Henry Hopkins Sibley led an army of Texans up the Rio Grande and occupied Santa Fe; he was defeated at Glorieta Pass in northern New Mexico by a hastily assembled army that included volunteers from Colorado and New Mexico and Union regulars, in a battle that has been labeled the Gettysburg of the West. The so-called Lincoln County War of 1878–81, a range war pitting cattlemen against merchants and involving, among other partisans, William H. Bonney (Billy the Kid), helped give the territory the image of a lawless region unfit for statehood.

Despite the tumult, New Mexico began to make substantial economic progress. In 1879, the Atchison, Topeka & Santa Fe Railroad entered the territory. General Lew Wallace, who was appointed by President Rutherford B. Hayes to settle the Lincoln County War, was the last territorial governor to enter New Mexico by stagecoach and the first to leave it by train.

By the end of the 19th century, the Indian threat that had plagued the Anglos, like the Spanish-speaking New Mexicans before them, had finally been resolved. New Mexicans won the respect of Theodore Roosevelt by enlisting in his Rough Riders during the Spanish-American War, and when he became president, he returned the favor by working for statehood. New Mexico finally became a state on 6 January 1912, under President William H. Taft.

In March 1916, irregulars of the Mexican revolutionary Pancho Villa crossed the international boundary into New Mexico, killing, robbing, and burning homes in Columbus. US troops under the command of General John J. Pershing were sent into Mexico on a long and unsuccessful expedition to capture Villa, while National Guardsmen remained on the alert in the Columbus area for almost a year.

The decade of the 1920s was characterized by the discovery and development of new resources. Potash salts were found near Carlsbad, and important petroleum reserves in the southeast and northwest were discovered and exploited. Oil development made possible another important industry, tourism, which began to flourish as gasoline became increasingly available. This period of prosperity ended, however, with the onset of the Great Depression.

World War II revived the economy, but at a price. In 1942, hundreds of New Mexicans stationed in the Philippines were among the US troops forced to make the cruel "Bataan march" to Japanese prison camps. Scientists working at Los Alamos ushered in the Atomic Age with the explosion of the first atomic bomb at White Sands Proving Ground in June 1945.

The remarkable growth that characterized the Sunbelt during the postwar era has been noticeable in New Mexico. Newcomers from many parts of the country moved to the state, a demographic shift with profound social, cultural, and political consequences. Spanish-speaking New Mexicans, once an overwhelming majority, became a minority. As of the 2000 census, Hispanics accounted for 42% of the state's population, and Native Americans accounted for 9.5% of the population.

Defense-related industries have been a mainstay of New Mexico's economy in the postwar period. Income from this sector declined in the early 1990s due to reductions in military spending following the end of the Cold War. However, this decline was offset by New Mexico's diversification into nonmilitary production, including such high-tech projects as Intel's Rio Rancho plant, which, in the mid-1990s, was the world's largest computer-chip factory. Tourism also played a major role in New Mexico's economy through the 1990s, and the state remains a leading center of space and nuclear research.

Today New Mexico's leaders struggle with two persistent problems—poverty and crime. In 1998, with 20.4% of its residents living below the poverty level (the highest percentage in the nation), the state's children were found to be suffering. More than one in four children in New Mexico was poor, posing the immediate problems of hunger and malnutrition, lack of education, and a strain on the public health system as well as the long-term challenge to the juvenile justice system. Government figures in 1998 showed the state ranked as the most violent in the nation, with 961 crimes per 100,000 residents.

The state's public education system also posed a major issue in 2000, with the debate centering on proposed voucher legislation that would help parents pay for private schools. Opponents, including New Mexico's Democratic Party, argued in favor of legislation that would boost to public schools instead—increasing teacher pay, reducing class sizes, and improving early childhood education.

In recent years New Mexico has remained at the bottom of national rankings—ranking number one in crime, poverty, and dependence upon federal assistance, last in quality of education, 47th in livability, 44th in teachers' salaries, and 46th in health coverage.

Governor Bill Richardson, elected in 2002, came to the job with a long list of political credentials: former US Representative, UN ambassador, and Energy Secretary. In 2003 he focused on tax cuts, teachers' raises, school reform, job creation, water projects, changes in Medicaid, prescription drug coverage, and efforts to combat drunk driving.

12 STATE GOVERNMENT

The constitution of New Mexico was drafted in 1910, approved by the voters in 1911, and came into effect when statehood was achieved in 1912. A new constitution drawn up by a convention of elected delegates was rejected by the voters in 1969. By January 2003, the 1912 document had been amended 146 times.

The legislature consists of a 42-member senate and a 70-member house of representatives. Senators must be at least 25 years old and residents of their districts; they serve four-year terms. House members must be 21 years old and residents of their districts; they serve two-year terms. The legislature meets every year, for 60 calendar days in odd-numbered years and 30 calendar days in even-numbered years. The legislature may call special sessions, limited to 30 calendar days, by petition of three-fifths of the members of each house. Legislators do not receive a salary from the state.

The executive branch consists of the governor and lieutenant governor (elected jointly), secretary of state, auditor, treasurer, attorney general, and commissioner of public lands. They are elected for four-year terms; none may serve more than two successive terms. Candidates for governor must be 30 years old, US citizens, qualified voters, and residents of New Mexico for at least five years prior to election. In 2002 the governor's salary was $90,000, unchanged from 2000. Three elected members of the Corporation Commission, which has various regulatory and revenue-raising responsibilities, serve six-year terms.

A bill passed by the legislature becomes law if signed by the governor, if left unsigned by the governor for three days while the legislature is in session, or if passed over the governor's veto by two-thirds of the members present in each house. If the governor does not act on a bill after the legislature adjourns, the bill dies after 20 days.

In general, constitutional amendments must be approved by majority vote in each house and by a majority of the electorate. Amendments dealing with voting rights, school lands, and linguistic requirements for education can be proposed only by three-fourths of each house, and subsequently must be approved by three-fourths of the total electorate and two-thirds of the electorate in each county.

In order to vote in state elections, a person must be 18 years old, a US citizen, and a state resident. Restrictions apply to convicted felons and those declared mentally incompetent by the court.

13 POLITICAL PARTIES

Although Democrats hold a very substantial edge in voter registration—53% of registered voters to the Republicans' 33% as of 1998—New Mexico has been a "swing state" in US presidential elections since it entered the Union. Between 1948 and 1992, New Mexicans voted for Democratic presidential candidates four times and Republican presidential candidates eight times, choosing in every election except 1976 and 1992 the candidate who was also the presidential choice of voters nationwide. In the 2000 presidential election, Democrat Al Gore beat Republican candidate George W. Bush by a mere 366 votes, out of approximately 615,000 cast statewide. In 2002 there were 950,274 registered voters. The state had five electoral votes in the 2000 presidential election.

New Mexico's US senators in 1999 were Democrat Jeff Bingaman, elected in 2000 to his fourth term, and Republican Peter V. Domenici, who was elected to his sixth term in 2002. Following the 2002 elections, New Mexico's US House delegation consisted of two Republicans and one Democrat. As of mid-2003 there were 24 Democrats and 18 Republicans in the state senate and 43 Democrats and 27 Republicans in the state house. Governor Bill Richardson, Democrat, was first elected in 2002. He had previously served as a US Representative, UN ambassador, and Energy Secretary under President Bill Clinton.

14 LOCAL GOVERNMENT

There were 33 counties in New Mexico as of 2002. Each is governed by commissioners elected for two-year terms. Other county officers include the clerk, assessor, treasurer, surveyor, sheriff, and probate judge. Municipalities are incorporated as cities, towns, or villages. As of 2002, there were 101 municipalities, 96 public school districts, and 628 special districts.

The Indian Reorganization Act of 1934 reaffirmed the right of Indians to govern themselves, adopt constitutions, and form corporations to do business under federal law. Indians also retain the right to vote in state and federal elections. Pueblo Indians elect governors from each pueblo to form a coalition called the All-Indian Pueblo Council. The Apache elect a tribal council headed by a president and vice-president. The Navajo—one-third of whom live in New Mexico—elect a chairman, vice-chairman, and council members from their reservation in New Mexico and Arizona.

15STATE SERVICES

To address the continuing threat of terrorism and to work with the federal Department of Homeland Security (created in 2002 following the terrorist attacks of 11 September 2001), homeland security in New Mexico in 2003 operated under the authority of the governor; the public safety secretary was designated as the state homeland security advisor.

Agencies supervising the state transportation system include the Department of Aviation, the Civil Air Patrol, the State Highway Commission, the Department of Motor Transportation, the Department of Motor Vehicles, and the Traffic Safety Commission.

Welfare services are provided through the Human Services Department. Related service agencies include the Office of Indian Affairs and Human Rights Commission. Health services are provided by the Department of Health and Environment. The various public protection agencies include the Office of Civil and Defense Mobilization of the Attorney General's Office, the Department of Public Safety, the State Human Rights Commission, the Department of Corrections, and the New Mexico State Police. Education is regulated by the Department of Education.

The state's natural resources are protected by the Fish and Wildlife Service, the State Forest Conservation Commission, the Environment Department, the Energy Minerals and Natural Resources Department, the Bureau of Mines and Mineral Resources, the Water Quality Control Commission, and the State Park and Recreation Commission.

16JUDICIAL SYSTEM

The judicial branch consists of a supreme court, an appeals court, district courts, probate courts, magistrate courts, and other inferior courts as created by law.

The supreme court is composed of a chief justice and four associate justices; the appeals court, created to take over some of the supreme court's caseload, is composed of 10 judges. All are elected for eight-year terms.

The state's 33 counties are divided into 13 judicial districts, served by 72 district judges, each elected for a six-year term. District courts have unlimited general jurisdiction and are commonly referred to as trial courts. They also serve as courts of review for decisions of lower courts and administrative agencies.

Each county has a probate court, served by a probate judge who is elected from within the county for a two-year term.

In 2001, New Mexico had a total crime rate of 5,324.0 per 100,000 persons, including a total of 14,288 violent crimes and 83,095 crimes against property in that year. In June 2001, there were 5,288 inmates held in state and federal correctional facilities, an increase of 0.2% over the previous year. The state's incarceration rate stood at 281 per 100,000 inhabitants.

New Mexico imposes the death penalty but has only executed one person since 1976. In 2003, there were three prisoners under sentence of death.

17ARMED FORCES

In 2002, there were 11,254 active-duty military personnel and 6,704 civilian personnel stationed in New Mexico, 10,732 of whom were in the Air Force. The major installations are Kirtland Air Force Base in the Albuquerque area, Holloman Air Force Base at Alamogordo, and White Sands Missile Range north of Las Cruces. Defense contract awards totaled more than $ 763 million in 2002.

There were 190,718 veterans living in New Mexico according to the 2000 Census. Of these, 32,699 served in World War II; 21,942 in the Korean conflict; 57,340 during the Vietnam era; and 24,374 during 1990–2000 (including the Persian Gulf War). In 2002 total federal expenditures for veterans' programs amounted to nearly $545 million.

In 2000, the New Mexico State Police employed 525 full-time sworn officers.

18MIGRATION

Prior to statehood, the major influx of migrants came from Texas and Mexico; many of these immigrants spoke Spanish as their primary language.

Wartime prosperity during the 1940s brought a wave of Anglos into the state. New Mexico experienced a net gain through migration of 78,000 people during 1940–60, a net loss of 130,000 during the economic slump of the 1960s, and another net gain of 154,000 between 1970 and 1983. In the 1980s, New Mexico had a net gain from migration of 63,000 residents, accounting for 28% of the state's population increase during those years. Between 1990 and 1998, the state had net gains of 55,000 in domestic migration and 36,000 in international migration. In 1998, 2,199 foreign immigrants entered New

New Mexico Presidential Vote by Political Parties, 1948–2000

YEAR	ELECTORAL VOTE	NEW MEXICO WINNER	DEMOCRAT	REPUBLICAN	PROGRESSIVE
1948	4	*Truman (D)	105,240	80,303	1,037
1952	4	*Eisenhower (R)	105,435	132,170	225
					CONSTITUTION
1956	4	*Eisenhower (R)	106,098	146,788	364
1960	4	*Kennedy (D)	156,027	153,733	570
1964	4	*Johnson (D)	194,015	132,838	1,217
					AMERICAN IND.
1968	4	*Nixon (R)	130,081	169,692	25,737
					AMERICAN
1972	4	*Nixon (R)	141,084	235,606	8,767
					SOC. WORKERS
1976	4	Ford (R)	201,148	211,419	2,462
					LIBERTARIAN
1980	4	*Reagan (R)	167,826	250,779	4,365
1984	4	*Reagan (R)	201,769	307,101	4,459
1988	4	*Bush (R)	244,497	270,341	3,268
1992**	5	*Clinton (D)	261,617	212,824	1,615
1996**	5	*Clinton (D)	273,495	232,751	2,996
2000	5	Gore (D)	286,783	286,417	2,058

* Won US presidential election.

** Independent candidate Ross Perot received 91,895 votes in 1992 and 32,257 votes in 1996.

Mexico. The state's overall population increased 14.6% between 1990 and 1998. In the period 1995–2000, 205,267 people moved into the state and 235,212 moved out, for a net loss of 29,945, many of whom moved to Texas.

19INTERGOVERNMENTAL COOPERATION

New Mexico participates in the Interstate Oil and Gas Compact; Interstate Compact for Juveniles; Western Interstate Commission for Higher Education; Western Interstate Corrections Compact; Western Interstate Nuclear Compact; compacts governing use of the Rio Grande and the Canadian, Costilla, Colorado, La Plata, and Pecos rivers; and other interstate agreements including the Cumbres and Toltec Scenic Railroad Compact. It is an associate member of the Interstate Mining Compact. In 2001, New Mexico received almost $3.6 billion in government grants.

20ECONOMY

New Mexico was primarily an agricultural state until the 1940s, when military activities assumed major economic importance. Currently, major industries include manufacturing, petroleum, and food. Tourism also continues to flourish. Major employers range from Wal-Mart, Intel, Kirtland Air Force Base, to Los Alamos National Laboratory, and Honeywell, Inc. New Mexico's economy has an unusually large public sector, accounting for over 18% of total state product in 2001, compared to the state average of 12%. The state was relatively unaffected by both the boom of the late 1990s and the bust of 2001. In 1998 and 1999, the state posted anemic growth rates of 1.4% and 1.5%, and although this picked up to a strong 6.8% in 2000, growth continued at 5.4% in the recession year of 2001. The basis for the improvement—growth in general services, the government, transportation and utilities sector, and financial services offsetting steady losses in mining, manufacturing and construction—continued into 2002. As was true with the previous national recession in the early 1990s, New Mexico has not experienced net job losses.

New Mexico's gross state product in 2001 was $55.4 billion, the 37th highest among the states. General services contributed $25.4 billion; government, $10 billion; manufacturing, $7.5 billion; financial services, $7.4 billion; trade, $7.2 billion; transportation and public utilities, $4.1 billion, and construction, $2.4 billion. The public sector in 2001 constituted 18.1% of gross state product, the 3rd-largest among the states, after Hawaii and Alaska.

21INCOME

According to the Bureau of Economic Analysis, in 2001, New Mexico had a per capita personal income (PCPI) of $23,081 which ranked 48th in the United States (including the District of Columbia) and was 76% of the national average, $30,413. The 2001 PCPI reflected an increase of 5.9% from 2000 compared to the national change of 2.2%. In 2001, New Mexico had a total personal income (TPI) of $42,260,462,000 which ranked 38th in the United States and accounted for 0.5% of the national total. The 2001 TPI reflected an increase of 6.5% from 2000 compared to the national change of 3.3%.

Earnings of persons employed in New Mexico increased from $27,626,516,000 in 2000 to $29,404,755,000 in 2001, an increase of 6.4%. The largest industries in 2001 were services, 27.5% of earnings; state and local government, 19.2%; and retail trade, 10.1%. Of the industries that accounted for at least 5% of earnings in 2001, the slowest growing from 2000 to 2001 was retail trade, which increased 3.7%; the fastest was state and local government, which increased 13.0%.

According to data released by the US Census Bureau, in 2000, the median household income was $35,254 compared to the national average of $42,148. In 2001, the median income for a

family of four was $46,596 compared to the national average of $63,278. For the period 1999 to 2001, the average poverty rate was 18.8% which placed it 51st among the 50 states and the District of Columbia ranked lowest to highest.

22LABOR

According to Bureau of Labor Statistics (BLS) provisional estimates, in July 2003 the seasonally adjusted civilian labor force in New Mexico numbered 902,700, with approximately 55,400 workers unemployed, yielding an unemployment rate of 6.1%, compared to the national average of 6.2% for the same period. Since the beginning of the BLS data series in 1978, the highest unemployment rate recorded was 11.7% in February 1983. The historical low was 4.6% in March 2001. In 2001, an estimated 5.8% of the labor force was employed in construction; 6.4% in manufacturing; 4.9% in transportation, communications, and public utilities; 21.3% in trade; 3.7% in finance, insurance, and real estate; 23.2% in services; 21.2% in government; and 2.6% in agriculture.

The US Department of Labor reported that in 2002, 48,000 of New Mexico's 723,000 employed wage and salary workers were members of unions. This represented 6.6% of those so employed, down from 7.8% in 2001 and 9.4% in 1998. The national average is 13.2%. In all, 63,000 workers (8.7%) were represented by unions. In addition to union members, this category includes workers who report no union affiliation but whose jobs are covered by a union contract.

23AGRICULTURE

The first farmers of New Mexico were the Pueblo Indians, who raised corn, beans, and squash. Wheat and barley were introduced from Europe, and indigo and chiles came from Mexico.

In 2001, New Mexico's total farm marketings were $2.2 billion. About 25% came from crops and 75% from livestock products. Leading crops included hay and wheat. In 2002, hay production was 1,684,000 tons, valued at $233,200,000, and wheat production was 3,740,000 bushels, valued at $12,903,000. The state also produced 8,820,000 bushels of corn for grain, and 660,000 hundredweight of potatoes in 2002.

24ANIMAL HUSBANDRY

Meat animals, especially cattle, represent the bulk of New Mexico's agricultural income. In 2003, there were nearly 1.59 million cattle and calves, valued at $1.29 billion. In 2002, there were an estimated 3,000 hogs and pigs, valued at $228,000 on New Mexico farms. During 2001, New Mexico farms and ranches produced around 11 million lb (5 million kg) of sheep and lambs which brought in a gross income of some $8.6 million. The main stock-raising regions are in the east, northeast, and northwest.

25FISHING

There is no commercial fishing in New Mexico. In 1998, the state issued 249,236 sport fishing licenses. The native cutthroat trout is prized by sport fishermen, however, and numerous species have been introduced into state lakes and reservoirs. In 1998, seven aquacultural facilities distributed over 4.2 million trout within the state.

26FORESTRY

Lumber production was 111 million board feet in 2002. Although lumbering ranks low as a source of state income, the forests of New Mexico are of crucial importance because of the role they play in water conservation and recreation.

In 2002, 16,682 acres (675,120 hectares), or more than 20% of New Mexico's land area, was forestland. Of the state total,

9,522,000 acres (3,854,000 hectares) were federally owned or managed, and 825,000 acres (334,000 hectares) were owned by the state. Privately owned lands accounted for 6,331,000 acres (2,562,000 hectares).

27 MINING

In 2001, New Mexico ranked 24th nationally in total nonfuel mineral value, down from 18th place in 2000. In the same year, according to preliminary figures, nonfuel mineral production was valued at $614 million, down 22% from 2000. In 2001, New Mexico remained 3rd, behind Arizona and Utah, of 13 copper-producing states. Copper is the 3rd most widely used metal, after iron and aluminum, and one that is employed in electrical and telecommunications products, building construction, industrial machinery, transportation, consumer products, and in strategic military applications. Copper and potash again led other mineral commodities in New Mexico, and, along with construction sand and gravel and portland cement, accounted for about 88% of the state's total nonfuel mineral value.

The state continued to lead the country in perlite production with the largest output of six producing states, and the main markets for New Mexico's perlite were its uses in building construction, as filter aids, as a filler, and in agriculture. New Mexico also ranked 1st in production of potash and zeolites, 2nd in pumice and pumicite, 3rd in crude mica, and 5th in molybdenum and was an important producer of construction sand and gravel. According to the state, the vast majority of the potash finds its way as a soil amendment in agriculture; the remainder is used in industry for such things as manufacturing television tubes, chinaware, soaps, and synthetic rubber.

28 ENERGY AND POWER

New Mexico is a major producer of oil and natural gas, and has significant reserves of low-sulfur bituminous coal.

In 2000, the state consumed, per capita, 341 million Btu of energy (85.9 kcal), 26th among the 50 states. In 1999, total electrical capacity (utility and nonutility) was 5.5 million kW; total production was 32.6 billion kWh.

Most of New Mexico's natural gas and oil fields are located in the southeastern counties of Eddy, Lea, and Chaves, and in the northwestern counties of McKinley and San Juan. In 2002, 184,000 barrels per day of crude petroleum were produced; there were proven reserves of 715 million barrels in 2001. Natural gas marketed production in 2002 totaled 1.6 trillion cu ft (0.05 trillion cu m). Proved reserves in 2001 totaled 17.4 trillion cu ft (0.49 trillion cu m).

In 2000, 27.3 million tons of coal were mined.

29 INDUSTRY

The value of shipments by manufacturers in New Mexico exceeded $18 billion in 1997, with the highest growth rate of all states (114%) from 1992 to 1997. Major industries include electric equipment, petroleum and coal, food, printing and publishing, stone, glass, and clay products, and tourism.

More than 50% of the manufacturing jobs in the state are located in and around Albuquerque, in Bernalillo County. Other counties with substantial manufacturing activity include Santa Fe, San Juan, Otero, McKinley, and Dona Ana. Leading manufacturing employers include Honeywell and G.E. Aircraft, Intel Corp., Levi Strauss Co., Transportation Manufacturing Corp., Digital Equipment Corp., Philips Semiconductors, and General Mills.

Earnings of persons employed in New Mexico increased from $24.1 billion in 1997 to $25.3 billion in 1998, an increase of 5.2%. The largest industries in 1998 were services, 27.6% of earnings; state and local government, 16.9%; and retail trade, 11.3%. Of the industries that accounted for at least 5% of

earnings in 1998, the slowest growing from 1997 to 1998 was federal civilian government (5.8% of earnings in 1998), which increased 1.6%; the fastest was durable goods manufacturing (5.9% of earnings in 1998), which increased 11.7%.

30 COMMERCE

In 1997, New Mexico's 2,640 wholesale establishments had sales of nearly $8.4 billion. In 1997, wholesale establishments in the state registered total personal incomes of $726 million. Leading sectors of wholesale trade included petroleum and petroleum products; food and food products; machinery, equipment, and supplies; lumber and construction materials; and farm products. Retail sales totaled $16 billion in 1997 and the 10,176 retail establishments had total personal incomes of $1.8 billion. Leading types of retail trading establishments included food stores, 9%; eating and drinking establishments, 29%, and automotive dealers, 14%. Wal-Mart is the largest private sector employer in the state, with 9,270 employees, and a large distribution center in Los Lunas.

New Mexico's foreign exports totaled $1.9 million in 1998, 40th in the US. Intel is a major exporter of computer chips from New Mexico.

31 CONSUMER PROTECTION

Consumer protection in New Mexico is regulated by the Attorney General's Consumer Protection Division. This office may commence civil and criminal proceedings, represent the state before regulatory agencies, administer consumer protection programs, and handle consumer complaints.

32 BANKING

New Mexico's first bank, the First National Bank of Santa Fe, was organized in 1870. After the turn of the century, banking establishments expanded rapidly in the state, mainly because of growth in the livestock industry. In 2002, there were 61 insured banks headquartered in New Mexico, with total assets of $18 billion. Thirty-seven of these banks were state-chartered.

New Mexico's banks had low funding costs in 2002. Residential real estate was showing signs of stress that year, however, as home foreclosure rates were high. Despite the low nationwide commercial real estate (CRE) sector, insured banks in New Mexico had their highest level of CRE exposure on record in 2002. That year, New Mexico's per capita bankruptcy rates were at a 30-year high.

33 INSURANCE

As of 2000, there was one property and casualty, but no life and health insurance companies incorporated or organized in the state.

In 2001, 662,000 ordinary life insurance policies were in force in the state, and their total value was $45.4 billion; total value for all categories of life insurance (ordinary, group, industrial, and credit) was $76.9 billion. Death benefits paid that year totaled $214.1 million. Property and liability insurers wrote over $1.7 billion in premiums. That year, there were 11,640 flood insurance policies in force in the state, with a total value of $1,187,577.

The insurance industry is regulated by the State Insurance Board.

34 SECURITIES

There are no securities exchanges in New Mexico. Approximately 272 broker-dealer organizations conduct securities transactions in the state, involving 1,526 employees. There are also 36 registered securities investment advisory firms that provide services. New Mexico is the headquarters of 11 NASDAQ-listed companies, and has incorporated 6 NYSE-listed companies: Horizon/CMS Healthcare Corp., Nord Resources

Corp., Public Service Company of New Mexico, Security Capital Group, Inc., Sun Healthcare Group, Inc., and Thornbuy Mortgage Inc.

35PUBLIC FINANCE

The governor of New Mexico submits a budget annually to the legislature for approval. The fiscal year runs 1 July–30 June.

For the fiscal year 1999, total recurring general fund revenue equaled approximately $3.1 billion, exhibiting a growth rate of 3.7% from the previous year. The form of revenue that experienced the most growth was the income from personal income taxes, at a rate of almost 9%, even though total employment growth decelerated during the same period. Total general fund revenue was recorded at approximately $3.2 billion. General fund revenue was expected to grow at a rate of 6.0% during the whole of 2000, and 5.4% for the whole of 2001; revenue was expected to come primarily from sales taxes and personal income taxes.

For 2003/04, general fund appropriations totaled $4.018 billion, distributed, in terms of government agencies, to public schools ($1.858 billion), higher education and other education agencies ($628 million), health and human services ($845 million), public safety ($276 million), executive ($134 million), judicial branch ($133 million), agriculture and natural resources ($59 million), commerce and industry ($45 million), the legislature ($14.5 million), and transportation (0: funds derived from the states transportation fund.).

The following table from the US Census Bureau contains information on revenues, expenditures, indebtedness, and cash/securities for 2001.

	($000)	PERCENT	PER CAPITA
Population (thousands, 2001)	1,831	(X)	(X)
Total Revenue	9,099,224	100.00	4,969.54
General revenue	8,753,051	96.20	4,780.48
Utility revenue	–	–	–
Liquor store revenue	–	–	–
Insurance trust revenue	346,173	3.80	189.06
Exhibit: Salaries and wages	1,370,027	14.93	748.24
Total expenditure	9,173,756	100.00	5,010.24
General expenditure	8,399,238	91.56	4,587.24
Education	3,261,752	35.56	1,781.40
Public welfare	1,745,521	19.03	953.32
Hospitals	368,272	4.01	201.13
Health	323,794	3.53	176.84
Highways	849,800	9.26	464.12
Police protection	86,949	0.95	47.49
Correction	223,023	2.43	121.80
Natural resources	130,651	1.42	71.35
Parks and recreation	45,940	0.50	25.09
Government administration	335,880	3.66	183.44
Interest on general debt	190,205	2.07	103.88
Other and unallocable	837,451	9.13	457.37
Utility expenditure	–	–	–
Liquor store expenditure	–	–	–
Insurance trust expenditure	774,518	8.44	423.00
Debt at end of fiscal year	4,304,803	100.00	2,351.07
Cash and security holdings	33,072,291	100.00	18,062.42

36TAXATION

New Mexico's personal income tax schedule has seven brackets ranging from 1.7% (up to $5,500 of taxable income) to 8.2% (above $65,000). The corporate tax rate has three brackets, ranging from 4.8% on the first $500,000 of net income to 7.6% on net income above $1 million. The same rates apply to financial institutions. The state of New Mexico levies a gross receipts tax on goods and a broad range of services of 5%, with additional local rates ranging from 0.125% to 2.25%. The state also imposes a full array of excise taxes covering motor fuels, tobacco products, insurance premiums, public utilities, alcoholic beverages, amusements, pari-mutuels, and other selected items. New Mexico's estate tax is tied to the federal exemption for state death taxes, and is therefore set to be phased out in tandem with the phasing out of the federal estate tax credit by 2007 unless the state takes positive action to preserve an estate tax. New Mexico's revenue losses from the phasing out of its inheritance tax are estimated at -$7.5 million for 2002/03, -$12 million for 2003/04 and -$20 million for 2006/07. Death and gift taxes accounted for 0.5% of state collections in 2002. A larger source of state revenues is severance and conservation taxes imposed on oil and gas production, and at various rates on other substances. Other state taxes include license and franchise fees, and state property taxes. There are local property and sales taxes, but tax collection is highly centralized in New Mexico with three-quarters of total non-federal tax revenue collected at the state level.

The state collected $3.638 billion in taxes in 2002 (down from $4 billion in 2001), of which 36.9% came from the general sales tax, 27.1% from individual income taxes, 13.4% from selective sales taxes, 12.5% from severance taxes, 4.7% from license fees, 3.4% from corporate income taxes, and 1.4% from state property taxes. In 2003, New Mexico ranked 21st among the states in terms of combined state and local tax burden, which amounted to about 9.7% of income.

The following table from the US Census Bureau provides a summary of taxes collected by the state in 2002.

	($000)	PER CAPITA
Total Taxes	3,628,055	1,955.76
Property taxes	52,779	28.45
Sales and gross receipts	1,822,878	982.65
General sales and gross receipts	1,337,321	720.9
Selective sales taxes	485,557	261.75
Alcoholic beverage	35,471	19.12
Amusements	32,391	17.46
Insurance Premiums	51,705	27.87
Motor fuels	199,515	107.55
Pari-mutuels	1,154	0.62
Public utilities	12,945	6.98
Tobacco products	17,780	9.58
Other selective sales	134,596	72.56
Licenses	171,396	92.39
Alcoholic beverages	873	0.47
Amusements	263	0.14
Corporation	2,239	1.21
Hunting and fishing	17,245	9.3
Motor vehicle	117,459	63.32
Motor vehicle operators	5,935	3.2
Public utility	71	0.04
Occupation and business, NEC	27,244	14.69
Other	67	0.04
Other taxes	1,581,002	852.27
Individual income	982,891	529.84
Corporation net income	124,327	67.02
Death and gift	19,291	10.4
Documentary and stock transfer	(X)	(X)
Severance	453,397	244.41
Other	1,096	0.59

37ECONOMIC POLICY

The Economic Development Department promotes industrial and community development through such measures as tax-free bonds for manufacturing facilities; tax credits for investment and for job training, venture capital funds; and community development block grants. The state also seeks export markets for New Mexico's products and encourages use of the state by the film industry. Total incentives to employ 100 workers in a rural area, exporting most of the product, and investing at least $15 million amounted to almost $4 billion in 2000. The Economic Development Division, the biggest part of the Economic Development Department, focuses on business and community development. Separate divisions include International Trade, the Film Office, and the New Mexico Office for Space Commercialization (NMOSC).

38HEALTH

New Mexico's infant death rate was 6.6 per 1,000 live births for the 12 months ending with December 2000. In 1999, there were 5,098 legal abortions, or 14 per 1,000 women. In 2000, the overall death rate stood at 768.1 per 100,000 population, well below the national rate of 873.1.

New Mexico has the distinction of being the state with the 2nd-lowest death rate from heart diseases. The rate per 100,000 population in 1998 was 182.6, as compared with the national rate of 258.2. Among adults ages 18 and older, 23.6% were smokers in 2000. The death rate for lung disease among New Mexicans stood at 65.1 per 100,000 inhabitants in 1997. The rate of death from HIV-related infections (1.8 per 100,000 population) was also below the national rate in 2000. A total of 2,187 AIDS cases had been reported through 2001.

New Mexico's 35 community hospitals had 164,461 admissions and 3,584 beds in 2001. There were 4,703 full-time registered nurses and 705 full-time licensed practical nurses in 2001 and 238 physicians per 100,000 population in 2000. The average expense of a community hospital for care was $1,201.60 per inpatient day in 2001.

Federal government grants to cover the Medicare and Medicaid services in 2001 totaled $1.2 billion; 238,418 enrollees received Medicare benefits that year. At least 20.7% of New Mexico's residents were uninsured in 2002, the 2nd-highest percentage in the US.

39SOCIAL WELFARE

In 2001, the average weekly unemployment benefit was $198.92. Average monthly participation in the food stamp program in FY2002 comprised 170,457 persons (65,875 households). The average monthly benefit was $75.47, and the sum total of benefits paid in FY2002 was $154,364,768.

With the enactment of the Personal Responsibility and Work Opportunity Reconciliation Act of 1996, the US government has changed the form and regulations for many of its social welfare programs. Most significantly, it replaces Aid to Families with Dependent Children (AFDC), an open-ended entitlement program, with Temporary Assistance for Needy Families (TANF), a limited system of assistance funded largely through federal block grants. The reform act also impacts the food stamp program, the Supplemental Security Income program, and the child nutrition program. The law took effect on 1 July 1997 and provided $16.38 billion in block grants for fiscal years 1997–2002. The grants are to be divided among the states based on an equation involving the numbers of former AFDC recipients in each state.

Reauthorization of the 1996 social welfare legislation, scheduled for 2002, was delayed, and the original law had been extended three times as of July 2003, with the most recent extension running through September 2003. New Mexico's TANF program is called NM Works. In June 2000 the state had 67,950 welfare recipients. State expenditures on the TANF program in FY2002 totaled $32,748,302.

In December 2001, Social Security benefits were paid to 285,250 New Mexico residents. This number included 169,460 retired workers, 30,240 widows and widowers, 33,290 disabled workers, 22,750 spouses, and 29,510 children. Social Security beneficiaries represented 15.4% of the total state population and 89.4% of the state's population age 65 and older. Retired workers (excluding persons with special benefits) received an average monthly payment of $816; widows and widowers, $762; disabled workers, $783; and spouses, $390. Payments for children of retired workers averaged $361 per month; children of deceased workers, $476; and children of disabled workers, $226.

Federal Supplemental Security Income payments in December 2001 went to 47,579 New Mexico residents, averaging $350 a month.

The state maintains the Carrie Tingley Crippled Children's Hospital in Truth or Consequences, the Miners' Hospital of New Mexico in Raton, and the New Mexico School for the Visually Handicapped in Alamogordo.

40HOUSING

In 2002, New Mexico had an estimated 805,293 housing units, 681,931 of which were occupied; 69.3% were owner-occupied. About 38% of all housing units in New Mexico were built from 1970 to 1989. In 2002, about 61.5% of all units were single-family, detached homes; 18% were mobile homes. Utility gas and electricity were the most common heating energy sources. It was estimated that 63,185 units lacked telephone service, 12,152 lacked complete plumbing facilities, and 8,402 lacked complete kitchen facilities. The average household size was 2.67 people.

In 2002, 12,066 new privately owned units were authorized for construction. The median home value was $116,080. The median monthly cost for mortgage owners was $963. Renters paid a median of $528 per month. During 2002, New Mexico received more than $34.9 million in community planning and development aid from the US Department of Housing and Urban Development.

41EDUCATION

In 2000, 78.9% of New Mexicans age 25 and older were high school graduates. Some 23.5% had obtained a bachelor's degree or higher.

The total enrollment for fall 1999 in New Mexico's public schools stood at 324,495. Of these, 228,592 attended schools from kindergarten through grade eight, and 95,903 attended high school. Minority students made up approximately 65% of the total enrollment in public elementary and secondary schools in 2001. Total enrollment was estimated at 316,548 in fall 2000 and is expected to reach 371,000 by fall 2005. Direct expenditure per pupil for public elementary and secondary schools was $5,172 in the 1999/2000 school year. Expenditures for public education in 2000/01 were estimated at $2,045,977. Enrollment in nonpublic schools in fall 2001 was 23,055.

As of fall 2000, there were 120,265 students enrolled in institutions of higher education. In the same year New Mexico had 44 degree-granting institutions. New Mexico has 16 institutions of higher education. The leading public institutions are the University of New Mexico, with its main campus at Albuquerque, and New Mexico State University in Las Cruces. In 1997, minority students comprised 45.9% of total postsecondary enrollment.

42ARTS

New Mexico is a state rich in Indian, Spanish, Mexican, and contemporary art. Major exhibits can be seen at the University of New Mexico Art Museum in Albuquerque, and the Art Museum of the Harwood Foundation in Taos. Taos itself is an artists' colony of renown.

The Santa Fe Opera, one of the nation's most distinguished regional opera companies, has its season during July and August. The New Mexico Symphony Orchestra (also called the Albuquerque Symphony Orchestra, established in 1932) and the Orchestra Chorus present a variety of musical programs from classical to pops.

The Santa Fe Chamber Music Festival began in 1972 and has since become quite well known nationwide. Following the annual event, festival ensembles have traveled throughout the country.

There is also an annual Santa Fe Jazz and International Music Festival.

In 2003, New Mexico Arts and other New Mexico arts organizations received grants totaling $978,800 from the National Endowment for the Arts (NEA). State and private sources also contribute funding to the state's arts programs. The state offers arts education programs to approximately 26,600 schoolchildren. New Mexico has about 200 arts associations and 55 local arts councils. New Mexico Arts has contributed funding to promote multicultural arts programs that reflect the Spanish and American Indian cultural influences of the area. The Arts Division also sponsors the Dance on Tour Initiative to help traveling dance companies. The New Mexico Endowment for the Humanities was founded in 1972. In 2000, the National Endowment for the Humanities contributed $1,1225,076 for 13 state programs.

43 LIBRARIES AND MUSEUMS
Public libraries in New Mexico had a combined total of 4,029,595 volumes and a circulation of 7,807,000 volumes in 2000. The largest municipal library is the Albuquerque Public Library, with over 1,235,211 volumes. The largest university library is that of the University of New Mexico, with 1,882,136 volumes. There is a scientific library at Los Alamos and a law library at Santa Fe. Total public library income came to $29,416,000 in 2000.

New Mexico has 109 museums. Especially noteworthy are the Maxwell Museum of Anthropology at Albuquerque; the Museum of New Mexico, Museum of International Folk Art, and Institute of American Indian Arts Museum, all in Santa Fe; and several art galleries and museums in Taos. Historic sites include the Palace of the Governors (1610), the oldest US capitol and probably the nation's oldest public building, in Santa Fe; Aztec Ruins National Monument, near Aztec; and Gila Cliff Dwellings National Monument, 44 mi (71 km) north of Silver City. A state natural history museum, in Albuquerque, opened in 1985.

44 COMMUNICATIONS
The first regular monthly mail service between New Mexico and the other US states began in 1849. In 2001, 93.6% of the state's occupied housing units had telephones. In 2003 there were 5 major AM radio stations and 38 major FM stations. There were 10 major network television stations in 2003. The Albuquerque-Santa Fe area had 568,650 television households, 57% of which had cable. A total of 29,730 Internet domain names were registered in the state in 2000.

45 PRESS
The first newspaper published in New Mexico was *El Crep£sculo de la Libertad* (Dawn of Liberty), a Spanish-language paper established at Santa Fe in 1834. The *Santa Fe Republican*, established in 1847, was the first English-language newspaper.

In 2002, there were 8 morning, 10 evening, and 13 Sunday newspapers in the state. The leading dailies include the *Albuquerque Journal*, with a morning circulation of 108,668 (152,889 on Sundays); and the *Santa Fe New Mexican*, with a morning circulation of 25,268 (27,235 on Sundays).

La Herencia, (est. 1994) and *Tradición Revista* are magazines devoted to regional Hispanic history, art, and culture.

46 ORGANIZATIONS
In 2003, there were about 941 regional, national, and international organizations within the state. National organizations with headquarters in New Mexico include the National Association of Consumer Credit Administrators (Santa Fe), the American Indian Law Students Association, the American Holistic Medical Association, and Futures for Children, all located in Albuquerque.

The state is home to several organizations focusing on the rights and welfare of Native Americans. These include the National Indian Youth Council, the All Indian Pueblo Council, Gathering of Nations, the Inter-Tribal Indian Ceremonial Association, and the National Tribal Environmental Council.

Art and cultural organizations include the El Paso Symphony Orchestra Association, the Indian Arts and Crafts Association, the Institute of American Indian Arts, the New Mexico Art League, the New Mexico Ballet Company, and Spanish Colonial Arts.

47 TOURISM, TRAVEL, AND RECREATION
The development of New Mexico's natural recreational resources has made tourism a leading economic activity. In 2002, the state hosted about 11.5 million travelers. About 28.6% of all trips were instate travel by residents. About 53% of visitors came from the following states: Texas, Colorado, California, Arizona, and Oklahoma. The most popular vacation area was the Albuquerque-Sante Fe region (with 22.9% of all visitors), followed by El Paso (10.8%). Shopping, outdoor activities, and historical sites were the most popular attractions.

Hunting, fishing, camping, boating, and skiing are among the many outdoor attractions. The state has a national park—Carlsbad Caverns—and 13 national monuments: Aztec Ruins, Bandelier, Capulin Mountain, Chaco Canyon, El Morro (Inscription Rock), Fort Union, Gila Cliff Dwellings, Gran Quivira, Pecos, and White Sands. In 1984, the US House of Representatives designated 27,840 acres (11,266 hectares) of new wilderness preserves in New Mexico's San Juan basin, including a 2,720-acre (1,100-hectare) "fossil forest."

48 SPORTS
New Mexico has no major league professional sports teams, though Albuquerque does have a minor league baseball team in the Class-AAA Pacific Coast League. Thoroughbred and quarter-horse racing with pari-mutuel betting is an important spectator sport. Sunland Park, south of Las Cruces, has a winterlong schedule. From May to August there is racing and betting at Ruidoso Downs, Sun Ray Park, and the Downs at Albuquerque.

The Lobos of the University of New Mexico compete in the Mountain West Conference, while the Aggies of New Mexico State belong to the Big West Conference. New Mexico State finished third in the 1970 NCAA basketball tournament.

Other annual sporting events include the Great Overland Windsail Race in Lordsburg in June, the Silver City RPCA Wild, Wild West Rodeo Week in Gila in June, and the International Balloon Fiesta in Albuquerque in October.

49 FAMOUS NEW MEXICANS
Among the earliest Europeans to explore New Mexico were Francisco Vasquez de Coronado (b.Spain, 1510–54) and Juan de Oñate (b.Mexico, 1549?–1624?), the founder of New Mexico. Diego de Vargas (b.Spain, 1643–1704) reconquered New Mexico for the Spanish after the Pueblo Revolt of 1680, which was led by Popé (d.1685?), a San Juan Pueblo medicine man. Later Indian leaders include Mangas Coloradas (1795?–1863) and Victorio (1809?–80), both of the Mimbreño Apache. Two prominent native New Mexicans during the brief period of Mexican rule were Manuel Armijo (1792?–1853), governor at the time of the American conquest, and the Taos priest José Antonio Martinez (1793–1867).

Army scout and trapper Christopher Houston "Kit" Carson (b.Kentucky, 1809–68) made his home in Taos, as did Charles Bent (b.Virginia, 1799–1847), one of the builders of Bent's Fort, a famous landmark on the Santa Fe Trail. A pioneer of a different kind was Jean Baptiste Lamy (b.France, 1814–88), the first Roman Catholic bishop in the Southwest; his life inspired Willa Cather's novel *Death Comes for the Archbishop*. Among the more notorious of the frontier figures in New Mexico was Billy the Kid (William H. Bonney, b.New York, 1859–81); his killer was New Mexico lawman Patrick Floyd "Pat" Garrett (b.Alabama, 1850–1908).

Notable US senators from New Mexico were Thomas Benton Catron (b.Missouri, 1840–1921), a Republican who dominated New Mexico politics during the territorial period; Albert Bacon Fall (b.Kentucky, 1861–1944), who later, as secretary of the interior, gained notoriety for his role in the Teapot Dome scandal; Dennis Chavez (1888–1962), the most prominent and influential native New Mexican to serve in Washington; Carl A. Hatch (b.Kansas, 1889–1963), best known for the Hatch Act of 1939, which limited partisan political activities by federal employees; and Clinton P. Anderson (b.South Dakota, 1895–1975) who was also secretary of agriculture.

New Mexico has attracted many artists and writers. Painters Bert G. Phillips (b.New York, 1868–1956) and Ernest Leonard Blumenschein (b.Ohio 1874–1960) started the famous Taos art colony in 1898. Mabel Dodge Luhan (b.New York, 1879–1962) did much to lure the creative community to Taos through her writings; the most famous person to take up residence there was English novelist D. H. Lawrence (1885–1930). Peter Hurd (1940–84) was a muralist, portraitist, and book illustrator. New Mexico's best-known artist is Georgia O'Keeffe (b.Wisconsin, 1887–1986). Maria Povera Martinez (1887?–1980) was known for her black-on-black pottery.

Other prominent persons who have made New Mexico their home include rocketry pioneer Robert H. Goddard (b.Massachusetts, 1882–1945), Pulitzer Prize-winning editorial cartoonist Bill Mauldin (b.1921), novelist and popular historian Paul Horgan (b.New York, 1903–95), novelist N. Scott Momaday (b.Oklahoma, 1934), and golfer Nancy Lopez-Melton (b.California, 1957). Al Unser Sr. (b.1939), four-time winner of the Indianapolis 500, was born in Albuquerque.

50 BIBLIOGRAPHY

Beck, W. A. *New Mexico: A History of Four Centuries*. Reprint. Norman: University of Oklahoma Press, 1979.

Enchanted Lifeways: The History, Museums, Arts & Festivals of New Mexico. Compiled by the New Mexico Office of Cultural Affairs. Santa Fe, N. Mexico.: New Mexico Magazine, 1995.

Federal Writers' Project. *New Mexico: A Guide to the Colorful State*. Reprint. New York: Hastings House, 1962.

Kessell, John L. *Spain in the Southwest: A Narrative History of Colonial New Mexico, Arizona, Texas, and California*. Norman: University of Oklahoma Press, 2002.

Montgomery, Charles H. *The Spanish Redemption: Heritage, Power, and Loss on New Mexico's Upper Rio Grande*. Berkeley: University of California Press, 2002.

Preston, Christine, Douglas Preston, and José Antonio Esquibel. *The Royal Road: El Camino Real from Mexico City to Santa Fe*. Albuquerque: University of New Mexico Press, 1998.

Reeve, Frank, and Alice Cleaveland. *New Mexico: Land of Many Cultures*. Rev. ed. Boulder, Colo.: Pruett, 1979.

Religion in Modern New Mexico. Edited by Richard W. Etulain and Ferenc M. Szasz. Albuquerque: University of New Mexico Press, 1997.

Samora, Julian, and Patricia Vandel Simon. *A History of the Mexican-American People*. Rev. ed. Notre Dame, Ind.: University of Notre Dame Press, 1993.

Simmons, Marc. *New Mexico: A Bicentennial History*. New York: Norton, 1977.

Staats, Todd. *New Mexico: Off the Beaten Path*. Guilford, Conn.: Globe Pequot Press, 1999.

NEW YORK

State of New York

ORIGIN OF STATE NAME: Named for the Duke of York (later King James II) in 1664. **NICKNAME:** The Empire State. **CAPITAL:** Albany. **ENTERED UNION:** 26 July 1788 (11th). **SONG:** "I Love New York" (unofficial). **MOTTO:** *Excelsior* (Ever upward). **COAT OF ARMS:** Liberty and Justice stand on either side of a shield showing a mountain sunrise; surmounted on the shield is an eagle on a globe. In the foreground are a three-masted ship and a Hudson River sloop, both representing commerce. Liberty's left foot has kicked aside a royal crown. Beneath the shield is the state motto. **FLAG:** Dark blue with the coat of arms in the center. **OFFICIAL SEAL:** The coat of arms surrounded by the words "The Great Seal of the State of New York." **ANIMAL:** Beaver. **BIRD:** Bluebird. **FISH:** Brook or speckled trout. **FLOWER:** Rose. **TREE:** Sugar maple. **FRUIT:** Apple. **BEVERAGE:** Milk. **GEM:** Garnet. **FOSSIL:** Sea scorpion (Eurypterus remipes). **LEGAL HOLIDAYS:** New Year's Day, 1 January; Birthday of Martin Luther King, Jr., 3rd Monday in January; Lincoln's Birthday, 12 February; Washington's Birthday, 3rd Monday in February; Memorial Day, last Monday in May; Flag Day, 2nd Sunday in June; Independence Day, 4 July; Labor Day, 1st Monday in September; Columbus Day, 2nd Monday in October; General Election Day, 1st Tuesday after the 1st Monday in November; Veterans Day, 11 November; Thanksgiving Day, 4th Thursday in November; Christmas Day, 25 December. **TIME:** 7 AM EST = noon GMT.

¹LOCATION, SIZE, AND EXTENT

Located in the northeastern US, New York State is the largest of the three Middle Atlantic states and ranks 30th in size among the 50 states.

The total area of New York is 49,108 sq mi (127,190 sq km), of which land takes up 47,377 sq mi (122,707 sq km) and the remaining 1,731 sq mi (4,483 sq km) consist of inland water. New York's width is about 320 mi (515 km) E-W, not including Long Island, which extends an additional 118 mi (190 km) SW-NE; the state's maximum N-S extension is about 310 mi (499 km). New York State is shaped roughly like a right triangle: the line from the extreme NE to the extreme SW forms the hypotenuse, with New York City as the right angle.

Mainland New York is bordered on the NW and N by the Canadian provinces of Ontario (with the boundary line passing through Lake Ontario and the St. Lawrence River) and Quebec; on the E by Vermont (with part of the line passing through Lake Champlain and the Poultney River), Massachusetts, and Connecticut; on the S by the Atlantic Ocean, New Jersey (part of the line passes through the Hudson River), and Pennsylvania (partly through the Delaware River); and on the W by Pennsylvania (with the line extending into Lake Erie) and Ontario (through Lake Erie and the Niagara River).

Two large islands lie off the state's SE corner. Long Island is bounded by Connecticut (through Long Island Sound) to the N, Rhode Island (through the Atlantic Ocean) to the NE, the Atlantic to the S, and the East River and the Narrows to the W. Staten Island (a borough of New York City) is separated from New Jersey by Newark Bay in the N, Raritan Bay in the S, and Arthur Kill channel in the W, and from Long Island by the Narrows to the E. Including these two islands, the total boundary length of New York State is 1,430 mi (2,301 km). Long Island, with an area of 1,396 sq mi (3,616 sq km), is the largest island belonging to one of the 48 coterminous states.

The state's geographic center is in Madison County, 12 mi (19 km) S of Oneida.

²TOPOGRAPHY

Two upland regions—the Adirondack Mountains and the Appalachian Highlands—dominate the topography of New York State.

The Adirondacks cover most of the northeast and occupy about one-fourth of the state's total area. The Appalachian Highlands, including the Catskill Mountains and Kittatinny Mountain Ridge (or Shawangunk Mountains), extend across the southern half of the state, from the Hudson River Valley to the basin of Lake Erie. Between these two upland regions, and also along the state's northern and eastern borders, lies a network of lowlands, including the Great Lakes Plain; the Hudson, Mohawk, Lake Champlain, and St. Lawrence valleys; and the coastal areas of New York City and Long Island.

The state's highest peaks are found in the Adirondacks: Mt. March, 5,344 feet (1,629 meters), and Algonquin Peak, 5,114 feet (1,559 meters). Nestled among the Adirondacks are many scenic lakes, including Lake Placid, Saranac Lake, and Lake George. The region is also the source of the Hudson and Ausable rivers. The Adirondack Forest Preserve covers much of this terrain, and both public and private lakes are mainly for recreational use.

The highest peak in the Catskills is Slide Mountain, at 4,204 feet (1,281 meters). Lesser upland regions of New York include the Hudson Highlands, projecting into the Hudson Valley; the Taconic Range, along the state's eastern border; and Tug Hill Plateau, set amid the lowlands just west of the Adirondacks.

Three lakes—Erie, Ontario, and Champlain—form part of the state's borders. The state has jurisdiction over 594 sq mi (1,538 sq km) of Lake Erie and 3,033 sq mi (7,855 sq km) of Lake Ontario. New York contains some 8,000 lakes; the largest lake wholly within the state is Oneida, about 22 mi (35 km) long, with a maximum width of 6 mi (10 km) and an area of 80 sq mi (207 sq km). Many smaller lakes are found in the Adirondacks and in the Finger Lakes region in west-central New York, renowned for its vineyards and great natural beauty. The 11 Finger Lakes themselves (including Owasco, Cayuga, Seneca, Keuka,

Canadaigua, and Skaneateles) are long and narrow, fanning southward from a line that runs roughly from Syracuse westward to Geneseo.

New York's longest river is the Hudson, extending from the Adirondacks to New York Bay for a distance of 306 mi (492 km). The Mohawk River flows into the Hudson north of Albany. The major rivers of central and western New York State—the Black, Genesee, and Oswego—all flow into Lake Ontario. Rivers defining the state's borders are the St. Lawrence in the north, the Poultney in the east, the Delaware in the southeast, and the Niagara in the west. Along the Niagara River, Niagara Falls forms New York's most spectacular natural feature. The falls, with an estimated mean flow rate of more than 1,585,000 gallons (60,000 hectoliters) per second, are both a leading tourist attraction and a major source of hydroelectric power.

About 2 billion years ago, New York State was entirely covered by a body of water that periodically rose and fell. The Adirondacks and Hudson River Palisades were produced by undersea volcanic action during this Grenville period. At about the same time, the schist and other crystalline rock that lie beneath Manhattan were formed. The Catskills were worn down by erosion from what was once a high, level plain. Glaciers from the last Ice Age carved out the inland lakes and valleys and determined the surface features of Staten Island and Long Island.

3CLIMATE

Although New York lies entirely within the humid continental zone, there is much variation from region to region. The three main climatic regions are the southeastern lowlands, which have the warmest temperatures and the longest season between frosts; the uplands of the Catskills and Adirondacks, where winters are cold and summers cool; and the snow belt along the Great Lakes Plain, one of the snowiest areas of the US. The growing (frost-free) season ranges from 100 to 120 days in the Adirondacks, Catskills, and higher elevations of the hills of southwestern New York to 180–200 days on Long Island.

Among the major population centers, New York City has an annual mean temperature of 55°F (13°C), with a normal maximum of 62°F (17°C) and a normal minimum of 47°F (8°C). Albany has an annual mean of 47°F (8°C), with a normal maximum of 58°F (14°C) and a normal minimum of 37°F (3°C). The mean in Buffalo is 48°F (9°C), the normal maximum 56°F (13°C), and the normal minimum 39°F (4°C). The record low temperature for the state is –52°F (–47°C), recorded at Stillwater Reservoir in the Adirondacks on 9 February 1934 and at Old Forge on 18 February 1979; the record high is 108°F (42°C), registered at Troy on 22 July 1926.

Annual precipitation ranges from over 50 in (127 cm) in the higher elevations to about 30 in (76 cm) in the areas near Lake Ontario and Lake Champlain, and in the lower half of the Genesee River Valley. New York City had an average annual precipitation (1971–2000) of 49.7 in (126 cm), with a mean annual snowfall of 29 in (74 cm); Albany received an average annual precipitation of 38.6 in (98 cm); and Buffalo, 40.5 in (102.9 cm). In the snow belt, Buffalo receives 92 in (234 cm) of snow. Rochester averages 86 in (218 cm), and Syracuse 110 in (279 cm). New York City has fewer days of precipitation than other major populated areas (120 days annually, compared with 168 for Buffalo). Buffalo is the windiest city in the state, with a mean hourly wind speed of about 12 mph (19 km/hr). Tornadoes are rare, but hurricanes and tropical storms sometimes cause heavy damage to Long Island.

4FLORA AND FAUNA

New York has some 150 species of trees. Post and willow oak, laurel magnolia, sweet gum, and hop trees dominate the Atlantic shore areas, while oak, hickory, and chestnut thrive in the Hudson and Mohawk valleys and the Great Lakes Plain. Birch, beech, basswood, white oak, and commercially valuable maple are found on the Appalachian Plateau and in the foothills of the Adirondack Mountains. The bulk of the Adirondacks and Catskills is covered with red and black spruce, balsam fir, and mountain ash, as well as white pine and maple. Spruce, balsam fir, paper birch, and mountain ash rise to the timberline while only the hardiest plant species grow above it. Larch, mulberry, locust, and several kinds of willow are among the many varieties that have been introduced throughout the state. Apple trees and other fruit-bearing species are important in western New York and the Hudson Valley.

Common meadow flowers include several types of rose (the state flower), along with dandelion, Queen Anne's lace, goldenrod, and black-eyed Susan. Wild sarsaparilla, Solomon's seal, Indian pipe, bunchberry, and goldthread flourish amid the forests. Cattails grow in profusion along the Hudson, and rushes cover the Finger Lakes shallows. Among protected plants are all species of fern, bayberry, lotus, all native orchids, five species of rhododendron (including azalea), and trillium. Six plant species were listed as threatened or endangered in 2003, including the sandplain gerardia, American hart's-tongue fern, and Leedy's roseroot.

Some 600 species of mammals, birds, amphibians, and reptiles are found in New York, of which more than 450 species are common. Mammals in abundance include many mouse species, the snowshoe hare, common and New England cottontails, woodchuck, squirrel, muskrat, and raccoon. The deer population has been estimated at as many as 500,000, making them a pest causing millions of dollars annually in crop damage. The wolverine, elk, and moose were all wiped out during the 19th century, and the otter, mink, marten, and fisher populations were drastically reduced; but the beaver, nearly eliminated by fur trappers, had come back strongly by 1940.

More than 260 bird species have been observed. The most common year-round residents are the crow, hawk, and several types of woodpecker. Summer visitors are many, and include the bluebird (the state bird). The wild turkey, which disappeared during the 19th century, was successfully reestablished in the 1970s. The house (or English) sparrow has been in New York since its introduction in the 1800s.

The common toad, newt, and several species of frog and salamander inhabit New York waters. Garter snakes, water snakes, grass snakes, and milk snakes are common; rattlesnakes formerly thrived in the Adirondacks. There are 210 known species of fish; 130 species are found in the Hudson, 120 in the Lake Ontario watershed. Freshwater fish include species of perch, bass, pike, and trout (the state fish). Oysters, clams, and several saltwater fish species are found in Long Island Sound. Of insect varieties, the praying mantis is looked upon as a friend (since it eats insects that prey on crops and trees) while the gypsy moth has been singled out as an enemy in periodic state-run pest-control programs.

In 2003, twenty animal species were classified as threatened or endangered, including the Indiana bat, Karner blue butterfly, piping plover, bald eagle, shortnose sturgeon, three species of whale, and five species of turtle.

5ENVIRONMENTAL PROTECTION

New York was one of the first states to mount a major conservation effort. In the 1970s, well over $1 billion was spent to reclaim the state from the ravages of pollution. State conservation efforts date back at least to 1885, when a forest preserve was legally established in the Adirondacks and Catskills. Adirondack Park was created in 1892, Catskill Park in 1904. Then, as now, the issue was how much if any state forestland would be put to commercial use. Timber cutting in the forest

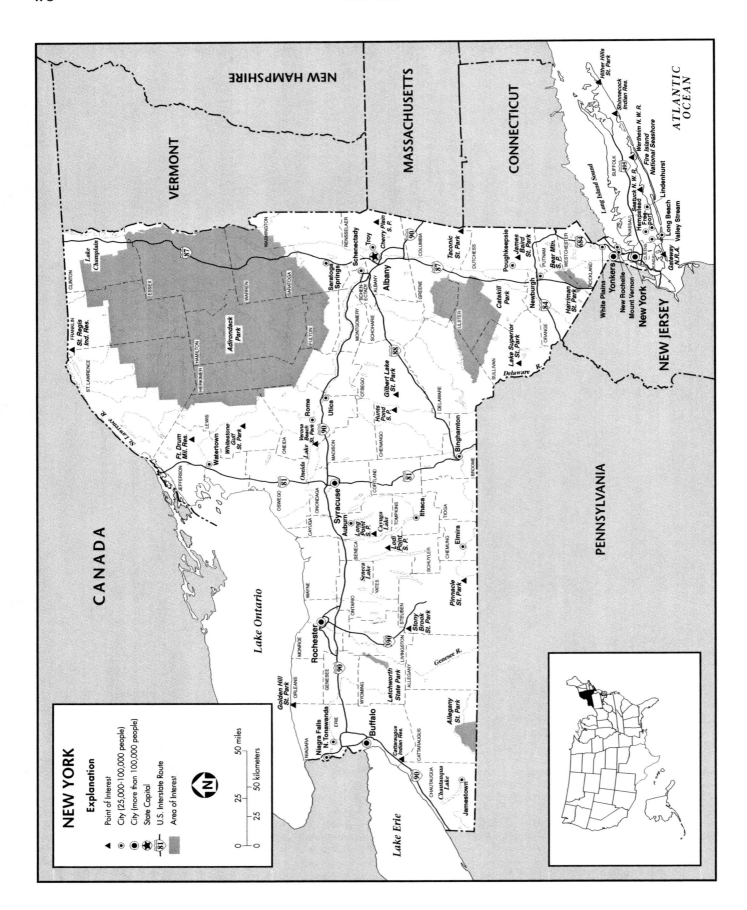

New York Counties, County Seats, and County Areas and Populations

COUNTY	COUNTY SEAT	LAND AREA (SQ MI)	POPULATION (2002 EST.)	COUNTY	COUNTY SEAT	LAND AREA (SQ MI)	POPULATION (2002 EST.)
Albany	Albany	584	296,173	Niagara	Lockport	526	218,099
Allegany	Belmont	1,032	50,181	Oneida	Utica	1,819	234,966
Bronx	Bronx	42	1,354,068	Onondaga	Syracuse	785	460,776
Broome	Binghamton	712	200,324	Ontario	Canandaigua	644	101,567
Cattaraugus	Little Valley	1,306	83,269	Orange	Goshen	826	356,773
Cayuga	Auburn	695	81,562	Orleans	Albion	391	43,891
Chautauqua	Mayville	1,064	138,332	Oswego	Oswego	954	122,932
Chemung	Elmira	411	90,614	Otsego	Cooperstown	1,004	62,070
Chenango	Norwich	897	51,324	Putnam	Carmel	231	98,257
Clinton	Plattsburgh	1,043	81,069	Queens	Queens	109	2,237,815
Columbia	Hudson	628	63,532	Rensselaer	Troy	655	153,299
Cortland	Cortland	500	48,814	Richmond	Staten Island	59	457,383
Delaware	Delhi	1,440	47,302	Rockland	New City	175	291,835
Dutchess	Poughkeepsie	804	287,752	St. Lawrence	Canton	2,728	111,173
Erie	Buffalo	1,046	945,049	Saratoga	Ballston Spa	810	207,135
Essex	Elizabethtown	1,806	38,935	Schenectady	Schenectady	206	147,120
Franklin	Malone	1,648	50,964	Schoharie	Schoharie	624	31,855
Fulton	Johnstown	497	55,049	Schuyler	Watkins Glen	329	19,375
Genesee	Batavia	495	59,799	Seneca	Waterloo	327	34,976
Greene	Catskill	648	48,538	Steuben	Bath	1,396	99,313
Hamilton	Lake Pleasant	1,721	5,295	Suffolk	Riverhead	911	1,458,655
Herkimer	Herkimer	1,416	63,741	Sullivan	Monticello	976	74,273
Jefferson	Watertown	1,273	108,160	Tioga	Owego	519	51,772
Kings	Brooklyn	70	2,488,194	Tompkins	Ithaca	477	99,207
Lewis	Lowville	1,283	26,673	Ulster	Kingston	1,131	179,986
Livingston	Geneseo	633	64,824	Warren	Town of Queensbury*	882	63,906
Madison	Wampsville	656	69,789	Washington	Hudson Falls**	836	61,195
Monroe	Rochester	663	738,422	Wayne	Lyons	605	94,078
Montgomery	Fonda	404	49,387	Westchester	White Plains	438	937,279
Nassau	Mineola	287	1,344,892	Wyoming	Warsaw	595	43,165
New York	New York	22	1,546,856	Yates	Penn Yan	339	24,523
				TOTALS		47,377	19,157,532

* Mail Lake George.   ** Mail Fort Edward.

preserve was legalized in 1893, but the constitution of 1895 forbade the practice. By the late 1930s, the state had spent more than $16 million on land purchases and controlled 2,159,795 acres (874,041 hectares) in the Adirondacks and some 230,000 acres (more than 93,000 hectares) in the Catskills. The constitutional revision of 1894 expressly outlawed the sale, removal, or destruction of timber on forestlands. That requirement was modified by constitutional amendment in 1957 and 1973, however, and the state is now permitted to sell forest products from the preserves in limited amounts.

All state environmental programs are run by the Department of Environmental Conservation (DEC), established in 1970. The department oversees pollution control programs, monitors environmental quality, manages the forest preserves, and administers fish and wildlife laws (including the issuance of hunting and fishing licenses). The state's national parks totaled 35,914 acres (14,534 hectares). State parks and recreational areas totaled 258,000 acres (104,000 hectares). Wetlands covered 2.5 million acres of the state as of 2000. About one-half of the 160 species identified as endangered or threatened by the Department of Environmental Conservation are wetlands-dependent.

The chief air-quality problem areas are Buffalo, where levels of particles (especially from the use of coke in steelmaking) are high, and New York City, where little progress has been made in cutting carbon monoxide emissions from motor vehicles.

Despite air-quality efforts, acid rain has been blamed for killing fish and trees in the Adirondacks, Catskills, and other areas. In 1984, the legislature passed the first measure in the nation designed to reduce acid rain, calling for a cut of 12% in sulfur dioxide emissions by 1988 and further reductions after that. In 2000, the state legislature passed the Air Pollution Mitigation

Law, which penalized New York utilities for selling sulfur dioxide allowances to other states; the law was overturned in April 2002, when a federal district court ruled that the law both restricted interstate commerce and was preempted by the federal Clean Air Act.

Before the 1960s, the condition of New York's waters was a national scandal. Raw sewage, arsenic, cyanide, and heavy metals were regularly dumped into the state's lakes and rivers, and fish were rapidly dying off. Two Pure Waters Bond Acts during the 1960s, the Environmental Quality Bond Act of 1972, and a state fishery program have helped reverse the damage. The state has also taken action against corporate polluters, including a $7-million settlement with General Electric over that company's discharge of toxic polychlorinated biphenyls (PCBs) into the Hudson. In addition, the state and federal government spent perhaps $45 million between 1978 and 1982 on the cleanup of the Love Canal area of Niagara Falls, which was contaminated by the improper disposal of toxic wastes, and on the relocation of some 400 families that had lived there. Remaining problems include continued dumping of sewage and industrial wastes into New York Bay and Long Island Sound, sewage overflows into the Lower Hudson, industrial dumping in the Hudson Valley, nuclear wastes in West Valley in Cattaraugus County, and contamination of fish in Lake Erie. Toxic pollutants, such as organic chemicals and heavy metals, appear in surface and groundwater to an extent not yet fully assessed.

In 2003, New York had 485 hazardous waste sites listed in the Environmental Protection Agency's database, 90 of which were on the National Priorities List. A 1982 law requires a deposit on beer and soft-drink containers sold in the state, to encourage return and recycling of bottles and cans. In 2001, New York received $253,408,000 in federal grants from the Environmental Protection Agency; EPA expenditures for procurement contracts in New York that year amounted to $34,453,000.

⁶POPULATION

New York is no longer the most populous state, having lost that position to California in the 1970 census. However, New York City remains the most populous US city, as it has been since at least 1790. New York state ranked 3rd in population in the US with an estimated total of 19,157,532 in 2002, an increase of 1% since 2000. Between 1990 and 2000, New York's population grew from 17,990,455 to 18,976,457, an increase of 5.5%. The population is projected to reach 19.8 million by 2025. New York's population density in 2000 was 401.9 persons per sq mi, the 6th-highest in the nation. In 2000, the median age for New Yorkers was 35.9, with nearly 24.7% of the populace under age 18 and 12.9% over 65.

First in the state as well as the nation in population was New York City, with 8,084,316 residents in 2002 (up from 7,323,000 in 1990). Other leading cities, with their estimated 2002 populations were Buffalo, 287,698; Rochester, 217,158; Yonkers, 197,234; and Syracuse, 145,164. All these cities have lost population since the 1970s.

With 20,196,649 people, the tri-state New York City metropolitan area remained the nation's largest in 1999; other major metropolitan areas included those of Buffalo, with an estimated 1,175,000 people, and Rochester, with 1,079,073. Albany, the state capital, had an estimated metropolitan population of 869,474 in 1999.

The growth of New York City has been remarkable. In 1790, when the first national census was taken, the city had 49,401 residents. By 1850, its population had boomed to 696,115; by 1900, to 3,437,202, double that of Chicago, the city's closest rival. Manhattan alone housed more people in 1900 than any city outside New York. In 1990, if Brooklyn, Queens, Manhattan, and the Bronx had each been a separate city, they would still have ranked 3rd, 4th, 6th, and 7th in the nation, respectively.

⁷ETHNIC GROUPS

During the 19th and 20th centuries, New York was the principal gateway for European immigrants. In the great northern migration that began after World War I, large numbers of blacks also settled there; more recently there has been an influx of Hispanics and Latinos and, to a lesser extent, of Asians. As of 2000, New York had the largest black and 2nd-largest Asian population among the 50 states, and the 2nd-highest percentage of foreign-born residents.

According to the US Bureau of the Census, New York had 82,461 Indians in 2000. In 1996, there were an estimated 16,014 Indians living on or adjacent to the reservations of the following seven tribes: the Cayuga, Oneida, Onondaga, Seneca, and Tuscarora nations, the St. Regis Mohawk Tribe, and the Tonawanda Band of Senecas.

Blacks have been in New York since 1624. All black slaves were freed by a state law in 1827. Rochester was a major center of the antislavery movement; Frederick Douglass, a former slave, settled and published his newspaper North Star there, while helping to run the Underground Railroad. After World War I, blacks moving into New York City displaced the Jews, Italians, Germans, and Irish then living in Harlem, which went on to become the cultural capital of black America. The black population of New York State was 3,014,385 as of 2000—15.9% of the state's population. The black population of New York City alone was 2,129,762, larger than the black populations of all but four of the 50 states, and representing 26.6% of all city residents.

The population of Hispanics and Latinos as of 2000 was 2,867,583, or 15% of the state population. Of this total, New York City accounted for roughly 75%. Puerto Ricans in New York state numbered 1,050,293. Cubans, Dominicans, Colombians, Central Americans, and Mexicans are also present in growing numbers, including a large but undetermined number of illegal immigrants.

New York's Asian population is surpassed only by that of California. In 2000 it was estimated at 1,044,976, up from 694,000 in 1990. Pacific Islanders numbered 8,818. In 2000, state residents included 424,774 Chinese, 251,724 Asian Indians (up from 80,430 a decade earlier), 119,846 Koreans, 81,681 Filipinos, 37,279 Japanese, and 23,818 Vietnamese (up from 12,116 in 1990). New York City has the 2nd-largest Chinatown in the US.

In 2000 there were 3,868,133 foreign-born New Yorkers (20.4% of the total state population), a million more than there had been in 1990 (2,851,861, or 15.8%) and more than any other state except California. Among persons who reported at least one specific ancestry group, 2,122,620 named German; 2,737,146 Italian; 2,454,469 Irish; 1,140,036 English; 986,141 Polish; and 460,261 Russian. These figures do not distinguish the large numbers of European Jewish immigrants who would identify themselves as Jews rather than by their country of origin.

The ethnic diversity of the state is reflected in such Manhattan neighborhoods as Harlem, Chinatown, Little Italy, and "Spanish," or East, Harlem, with its large Puerto Rican concentration. Many of the more successful ethnics have moved to the suburbs; on the other hand, new immigrants still tend to form ethnic communities, often in the outer boroughs, such as Asians and South Americans in certain parts of Queens and Russian Jews in south Brooklyn. Outside New York City there are also important ethnic enclaves in the Buffalo metropolitan area, with its large populations of Polish and Italian origin.

⁸LANGUAGES

Just as New York for three centuries has channeled immigrant speakers of other languages into the English-speaking population, so it has helped to channel some of their words into English, with much more rapid dissemination because of the concentration of publishing and communications industries in New York City.

Little word-borrowing followed contacts by European settlers with the unfriendly Iroquois, who between the 14th and 17th centuries had dispersed the several Algonkian tribes of Montauk, Delaware, and Mahican Indians. In New York State, the effect on English has been almost entirely the adoption of such place-names as Manhattan, Adirondack, Chautauqua, and Skaneateles.

Although the speech of metropolitan New York has its own characteristics, in the state as a whole the Northern dialect predominates. New York State residents generally say /hahg/ and /fahg/ for hog and fog, /krik/ for creek, greasy with an /s/ sound, and half and path with the vowel of cat. They keep the /r/ after a vowel, as in far and cord; sharply differentiate horse and hoarse by pronouncing the former with the vowel of haw and the latter with the vowel of hoe; and call a clump of hard maples a sugarbush.

There are many regional variations. In the Hudson Valley, horse and hoarse tend to be pronounced alike, and a sugarbush is called a sap bush. In the eastern sector, New England piazza for porch and buttonball for sycamore are found, as is the Hudson Valley term nightwalker for a large earthworm. In the Niagara peninsula, Midland eavespout (gutter) and bawl (how a calf sounds) have successfully moved north from Pennsylvania to invade Northern speech. In the North Country, some Canadian influence survives in stook (shock), boodan (liver sausage), and shivaree (wedding celebration). In the New York City area, many speakers pronounce bird almost as if it were /boyd/, do not sound the /h/ in *whip* or the /r/ after a vowel—although the trend now is toward the /r/ pronunciation—may pronounce initial /th/ almost like /t/ or /d/, *stand on line* (instead of in a line) while waiting to buy a huge sandwich they call a *hero* and may even pronounce *Long Island* with an inserted /g/ as / long giland/. From the high proportion of New York Yiddish speakers (nearly 40% of all those in the US in 1990) have come such terms as *schlock*, *schmaltz*, and *chutzpah*.

Serious communication problems have arisen in New York City, especially in the schools, because of the major influx since World War II of Spanish speakers from the Caribbean region, speakers of so-called black English from the South, and, more recently, Asians, in addition to the ever-present large numbers of speakers of other languages. As a result, schools in some areas have emphasized teaching English as a second language.

According to the 2000 census, 72% of all New Yorkers five years of age or older spoke only English at home, down from 76.7% in 1990.

The following table gives selected statistics from the 2000 census for language spoken at home by persons five years old and over. The category "Other Indic languages" includes Bengali, Marathi, Punjabi, and Romany. The category "Other Indo-European languages" includes Albanian, Gaelic, Lithuanian, and Rumanian. The category "African languages" includes Amharic, Ibo, Twi, Yoruba, Bantu, Swahili, and Somali. The category "Other Asian languages" includes Dravidian languages, Malayalam, Telugu, Tamil, and Turkish. The category "Other Slavic languages" includes Czech, Slovak, and Ukrainian. The category "Other West Germanic languages" includes Dutch, Pennsylvania Dutch, and Afrikaans. The category "Scandinavian languages" includes Danish, Norwegian, and Swedish.

LANGUAGE	NUMBER	PERCENT
Population 5 years and over	**17,749,110**	**100.0**
Speak only English	12,786,189	72.0
Speak a language other than English	4,962,921	28.0
Speak a language other than English	**4,962,921**	**28.0**
Spanish or Spanish Creole	2,416,126	13.6
Chinese	374,627	2.1
Italian	294,271	1.7
Russian	218,765	1.2
French (incl. Patois, Cajun)	180,809	1.0
French Creole	114,747	0.6
Yiddish	113,514	0.6
Polish	111,730	0.6
Korean	102,105	0.6
Other Indic languages	97,212	0.5
German	92,709	0.5
Greek	86,659	0.5
Arabic	69,959	0.4
Hebrew	67,675	0.4
Tagalog	65,506	0.4
Other Indo-European languages	61,128	0.3
African languages	54,271	0.3
Other Asian languages	53,400	0.3
Urdu	52,448	0.3
Portuguese or Portuguese Creole	41,378	0.2
Hindi	41,151	0.2
Other Slavic languages	39,619	0.2
Japanese	34,569	0.2
Serbo-Croatian	31,553	0.2
Persian	25,975	0.1
Vietnamese	20,249	0.1
Hungarian	18,421	0.1
Gujarathi	16,908	0.1
Other West Germanic languages	13,415	0.1
Scandinavian languages	11,974	0.1

⁹RELIGIONS

Before the 1800s, Protestant sects dominated the religious life of New York, although religion did not play as large a role in the public life of New Netherland as it did in New England, with its Puritan population. The first Jews were permitted by the Dutch to settle in New Amsterdam in 1654, but their numbers remained small for the next 200 years. Both the Dutch and later the English forbade the practice of Roman Catholicism. Full religious freedom was not permitted until the constitution of 1777, and there was no Roman Catholic church in upstate New York until 1797. During the early 19th century, Presbyterian, Methodist, Universalist, Baptist, and Quaker pioneers carried their faith westward across the state. Many Protestant churches took part enthusiastically in the abolitionist movement, and the blacks who fled northward out of slavery formed their own Protestant churches and church organizations.

For Roman Catholics and Jews, the history of the 19th century is the story of successive waves of immigration: Roman Catholics first from Ireland and Germany, later from Italy and Poland, Jews first from Germany, Austria, and England, later (in vast numbers) from Russia and other Eastern European nations. The Jews who settled in New York City tended to remain there, the Roman Catholic immigrants were more dispersed throughout the state, with a large German and Eastern European group settling in Buffalo. Irish Catholics were the first group to win great political influence, but since World War II, Jews and Italian Catholics have played a leading role, especially in New York City.

As of 2000, New York had 7,550,491 Roman Catholics, representing about 39.8% of the total population. The same year, there were 1,653,870 adherents of Jewish congregations. Membership of leading Protestant denominations in included United Methodists, 403,362; Episcopalians, 201,797; Presbyterians (USA), 162,227; and Evangelical Lutherans, 169,329. About 39.6% of the population were not counted as members of any religious organization.

Because of diversified immigration, New York City has small percentages but significant numbers of Buddhists, Muslims, Hindus, and Orthodox Christians. There were about 223,968 members of Muslim congregations. Though exact membership numbers were not available, there were about 121 Buddhist congregations and 83 Hindu congregations statewide. There is also a wide variety of religious-nationalist sects and cults, including the World Community of Islam in the West, also called the Nation of Islam (Black Muslims), the Hare Krishna group, and the Unification Church of the Reverend Sun Myung Moon.

¹⁰TRANSPORTATION

New York City is a major transit point for both domestic and international passenger and freight traffic. The Port of New York and New Jersey is among the nation's busiest harbors; New York City hosts two major airports, Kennedy International and La Guardia, both in Queens. New York City is connected with the rest of the state by an extensive network of good roads, although road and rail transport within the metropolitan region is sagging with age.

The first railroad in New York State was the Mohawk and Hudson, which made its initial trip from Albany to Schenectady on 9 August 1831. A series of short inter-city rail lines, built during the 1830s and 1840s, were united into the New York Central in 1853. Cornelius Vanderbilt gained control of the New York Central in 1867 and by 1873 had connected New York with Chicago. Under Vanderbilt and his son William, rail links were also forged between New York and Boston, Buffalo, Montreal, and western Pennsylvania.

The height of the railroads' power and commercial importance came during the last decades of the 19th century. After World War I, road vehicles gradually replaced the railroads as freight carriers. In 2000, New York had 4,796 mi (7,718 km) of track. In the same year, there were 2 Class I lines, 2 Canadian lines, 4 regional, 19 local, and 8 switching and terminal railroads.

The decline in freight business, and the railroads' inability to make up the loss of passenger traffic, led to a series of reorganizations and failures: the best known is the merger of the New York Central with the Pennsylvania Railroad, and the subsequent bankruptcy of the Penn Central. Today, much of New York's rail network is operated by Conrail, a federally assisted private corporation that among its operations provides commuter service up the Hudson and to New Jersey and Connecticut. Conrail is now owned by CSX Transportation and Norfolk & Southern Railroad. The National Railroad Passenger Corporation (Amtrak) owns and operates lines along the eastern corridor from Boston through New York City to Washington, DC. In 1996, it regularly operated 110 daily trains through New York State, stopping at 25 stations. New York City's Penn Station is the busiest station in the entire Amtrak system. The Long Island Railroad, an important commuter carrier, is run by the Metropolitan Transportation Authority (MTA), which also operates the New York City subways. Construction of the New York City subway system began in 1900; service started on 27 October 1904. The route network is about 230 mi (370 km) long, of which 137 mi (220 km) are underground.

The only other mass-transit rail line in the state is Buffalo's 6.4 mi (10.3 km) light rail system, of which 5.2 mi (8.4 km) is underground. In 1984, regular trolley service resumed in Buffalo for the first time since 1950 on the other 1.2 mi (1.9 km) of track, running through the downtown shipping district. Among cities served by municipal, county, or metropolitan-area bus systems are Albany, Binghamton, Buffalo, Elmira, and Syracuse.

In 2000, 10,342,017 motor vehicles were registered in New York State, including 7,501,343 automobiles, 54,083 buses, and 2,679,105 trucks. In addition 107,486 motorcycles were registered. As of 2000, the state had 112,783 mi (181,506 km) of public roads and highways; nearly two-thirds of the mileage was rural. The major toll road, and the nation's longest toll superhighway, is the Thomas E. Dewey Thruway, operated by the New York State Thruway Authority, which extends 559 mi (900 km) from just outside New York City to Buffalo and the Pennsylvania border in southwestern New York. Toll-free expressways include the Adirondack Northway (I-87), from Albany to the Canadian border, and the North–South Expressway (I-81), from the Canadian to the Pennsylvania border.

A number of famous bridges and tunnels connect the five boroughs of New York City with each other and with New Jersey. The Verrazano–Narrows Bridge, opened to traffic in 1964, spans New York Harbor between Brooklyn and Staten Island. Equally famous, and especially renowned for their beauty, are the Brooklyn Bridge (1883), the city's first suspension bridge, and the George Washington Bridge (1931). The Holland (1927) and Lincoln (1937–57) tunnels under the Hudson River link Manhattan with New Jersey. Important links among the five boroughs include the Triborough Bridge, Manhattan Bridge, Williamsburg Bridge, Queensboro Bridge, Bronx-Whitestone Bridge, Throgs Neck Bridge, Brooklyn-Battery Tunnel, and Queens-Midtown Tunnel. The Staten Island Ferry conveys passengers and autos between the borough and lower Manhattan.

Until the early 1800s, almost all the state's trade moved on the Atlantic Ocean, Hudson River, and New York Bay. This waterway transportation system was expanded starting in the 1820s. Off the Hudson, one of the country's major arteries, branched the main elements of the New York Barge Canal System: the Erie Canal, linking the Atlantic with Lake Erie, and New York City with Buffalo; the Oswego Canal, connecting the Erie Canal with Lake Ontario; the Cayuga and Seneca Canal, connecting the Erie Canal with Cayuga and Seneca lakes; and the Champlain Canal, extending the state's navigable waterways from the Hudson to Lake Champlain, and so to Vermont and Quebec Province. By 1872, New York's canal system was carrying over 6 million tons of cargo per year; however, an absolute decline in freight tonnage began after 1890 (the relative decline had begun 40 years earlier, with the rise of the railroads). By the mid-1980s, the canals carried less than 10% of the tonnage for 1880.

Buffalo, on Lake Erie, is the most important inland port. In 2000, it handled 2.2 million tons of cargo. Albany, the major port on the Hudson, handled 6.1 million tons of cargo, and Port Jefferson, on Long Island Sound, handled 2.8 million tons in 2000.

It would be difficult to exaggerate the historic and economic importance of New York Harbor—haven for explorers, point of entry for millions of refugees and immigrants, and the nation's greatest seaport until recent years, when it was surpassed by Greater New Orleans and Houston in terms of cargo tonnage. Harbor facilities, including those of Bayonne, Jersey City, and Newark, New Jersey, add up to 755 mi (1,215 km) of frontage, with some 700 piers and wharves. The entire port is under the jurisdiction of the Port Authority of New York and New Jersey. In 2000, it handled 138.7 million tons of cargo. In the mid-1990s, the port was served by 1,000 trucking companies, 80 steamship lines, and 12 intermodal rail terminals.

In 2002, New York State had 555 airfields, including 381 airports, 154 heliports, and 20 seaplane bases. By far the busiest airports in the state are John F. Kennedy International (16,155,437 passengers enplaned in 2000) and La Guardia (12,697,208 passengers enplaned), both in New York City. The Greater Buffalo International Airport, with 2,140,002 enplaned passengers in 2000, is the largest in the state outside New York City.

[11]HISTORY

The region now known as New York State has been inhabited for about 10,000 years. The first Indians probably came across the Bering Strait and most likely reached New York via the Niagara Peninsula. Remains have been found in southwestern New York of the Indians called Mound Builders (for their practice of burying their dead in large mounds), who cultivated food crops and tobacco. The Mound Builders were still living in the state well after AD 1000, although by that time most of New York was controlled by later migrants of the Algonkian linguistic group. These Algonkian tribes included the Mahican in the northeast, the Wappinger in the Hudson Valley and on Long Island, and the Leni-Lenape (or Delaware) of the Delaware Valley.

Indians of the Iroquoian language group invaded the state from the north and west during the early 14th century. In 1570, after European explorers had discovered New York but before the establishment of any permanent European settlements, the main Iroquois tribes—the Onondaga, Oneida, Seneca, Cayuga, and Mohawk—established the League of the Five Nations. For the next 200 years, members of the League generally kept peace among themselves but made war on other tribes, using not only traditional weapons but also the guns they were able to get from the French, Dutch, and English. In 1715, a sixth nation joined the League—the Tuscarora, who had fled the British in North Carolina. For much of the 18th century, the Iroquois played a skillful role in balancing competing French and British interests.

The first European known to have entered New York Harbor was the Florentine navigator Giovanni da Verrazano, on 17 April 1524. The Frenchman Samuel de Champlain began exploring the St. Lawrence River in 1603. While Champlain was aiding the Huron Indians in their fight against the League in 1609, the English mariner Henry Hudson, in the service of the Dutch East India Company, entered New York Bay and sailed up the river that would later bear his name, reaching about as far as Albany.

To the Dutch the area did not look especially promising, and there was no permanent Dutch settlement until 1624, three years after the Dutch West India Company had been founded. The area near Albany was first to be settled. The Dutch were mainly interested in fur trading, and agriculture in the colony—named New Netherland—was slow to develop. New Amsterdam was founded in 1626, when Director-General Peter Minuit bought Manhattan (from the Indian word manahatin, "hill island") from the Indians for goods worth—as tradition has it—about $24.

New Amsterdam grew slowly, and by 1650 had no more than 1,000 people. When the British took over New Netherland in 1664, only 8,000 residents lived in the colony. Already, however, the population was remarkably diverse: there were the Dutch and English, of course, but also French, Germans, Finns, Swedes, and Jews, as well as black slaves from Angola. The Swedes lived in what had been New Sweden, a territory along the Delaware River ceded to the Netherlands during the administration of Peter Stuyvesant. Equally famed for his wooden leg and his hot temper, Stuyvesant had become director general of the New Netherland colony in 1647. Three years later, after skirmishes with the English settlers of New England, the colony gave up all claims to the Connecticut Valley in the Treaty of Hartford.

Though small and weak, New Netherland was an annoyance to the English. The presence of Dutch traders in New York Bay made it difficult for England to enforce its monopolies under the Navigation Acts. Moreover, the Dutch colony was a political barrier between New England and two other English colonies, Maryland and Virginia. So, in 1664, King Charles II awarded "all the land from the west side of the Connecticutte River to the East Side of De La Ware Bay" to his brother, the Duke of York and Albany, the future King James II. The British fleet arrived in New York Bay on 18 August 1664. Stuyvesant wanted to fight, but his subjects refused, and the governor had no choice but to surrender. The English agreed to preserve the Dutch rights of property and inheritance, and to guarantee complete liberty of conscience. Thus New Netherland became New York. It remained an English colony for the next 112 years, except for a period in 1673 when Dutch rule was briefly restored.

The first decades under the English were stormy. After repeated demands from the colonists, a general assembly was called in 1683. The assembly adopted a Charter of Liberties and Privileges, but the document, approved by James before his coronation, was revoked after he became king in 1685. The assembly itself was dissolved in 1686, and James II acted to place New York under the dominion of New England. The plan was aborted by the Glorious Revolution of 1688, when James was forced to abdicate. Power in New York fell to Jacob Leisler, a German merchant with local backing. Leisler ruled until 1691, when a new royal governor arrived and had Leisler hanged for treason.

The succeeding decades were marked by conflict between the English and French and by the rising power of the provincial assembly in relations with the British crown. As early as 1690, a band of 150 Frenchmen and 100 Indians attacked and burned Schenectady. New York contributed men and money to campaign against the French in Canada in 1709 and 1711 (during Queen Anne's War) and in 1746 (during King George's War). In 1756, the English determined to drive the French out of the region once and for all. After some early reverses, the English defeated the French in 1760. The Treaty of Paris (1763), ending the French and Indian War, ceded all territory east of the Mississippi to England, except for New Orleans and two islands in the mouth of the St. Lawrence River. The Iroquois, their power weakened during the course of the war, signed treaties giving large areas of their land to the New York colony.

The signing of the Treaty of Paris was followed by English attempts to tighten control over the colonies, in New York as elsewhere. New York merchants vehemently protested the Sugar Act and Stamp Act, and the radical Sons of Liberty made their first appearance in the colony in October 1765. Later, in 1774, after Paul Revere brought news of the Boston Tea Party to New York City, British tea was also dumped into that city's harbor. Nevertheless, New York hesitated before committing itself to independence. The colony's delegates to the Continental Congress in Philadelphia were not permitted by the Third Provincial Congress in New York to vote either for or against the Declaration of Independence on 4 July 1776. The Fourth Provincial Congress, meeting at White Plains, did ratify the Declaration five days later. On 6 February 1778, New York became the second state to ratify the Articles of Confederation.

Nearly one-third of all battles during the Revolutionary War took place on New York soil. The action there began when troops under Ethan Allen captured Fort Ticonderoga in May 1775, and Seth Warner and his New England forces took Crown Point. Reverses came in 1776, however, when George Washington's forces were driven from Long Island and Manhattan by the British; New York City was to remain in British hands for the rest of the war. Troops commanded by British General John Burgoyne recaptured Ticonderoga in July 1777, but were defeated in October at Saratoga, in a battle that is often considered the turning point of the war. In 1778, General Washington made his headquarters at West Point, which General Benedict Arnold tried unsuccessfully to betray to the British in 1780. Washington moved his forces to Newburgh in 1782, and marched into New York City on 25 November 1785, the day the British evacuated their forces. On 4 December, he said farewell to his officers at Fraunces Tavern in lower Manhattan, a landmark that still stands.

Even as war raged, New York State adopted its first constitution on 20 April 1777. The constitution provided for an elected governor and house of assembly, but the franchise was limited to property holders. The first state capital was Kingston, but the capital was moved to Albany in January 1797. After much debate, in which the Federalist Alexander Hamilton played a leading role, the state ratified the US Constitution (with amendments) on 26 July 1788. New York City served as the seat of the US government from 11 January 1785 to 12 August 1790, and the first US president, George Washington, was inaugurated in the city on 30 April 1789.

George Clinton was the state's first elected governor, serving from 1777 to 1795 and again from 1801 to 1804. The achievements under his governorship were considerable. Commerce and agriculture expanded, partly because of Clinton's protectionist policies and partly because of the state's extremely favorable geographical situation.

The end of the War of 1812 signaled the opening of an era of unprecedented economic expansion for the state. By this time, the Iroquois were no longer a threat (most had sided with the British during the Revolutionary War, and many later fled to Canada). Migrants from New England were flocking to the state, which the census of 1810 showed was the most populous in the country. Small wonder that New York was the site of the early 19th century's most ambitious engineering project: construction of the Erie Canal. Ground was broken for the canal in 1817, during the first term of Governor De Witt Clinton, the nephew of George Clinton; the first vessels passed through the completed canal in 1825.

Actually, New York had emerged as the nation's leading commercial center before the canal was even started. The textile industry had established itself by the mid-1820s, and the dairy industry was thriving. The effects of the canal were felt most strongly in foreign trade—by 1831, 50% of US imports and 27% of US exports passed through the state—and in the canal towns of Utica, Syracuse, Rochester, and Buffalo, where business boomed.

Commercial progress during this period was matched by social and cultural advancement. New York City became a center of literary activity during the 1820s, and by the 1840s was already the nation's theatrical capital. A new state constitution drafted in 1821 established universal white male suffrage, but retained the property qualifications for blacks. Slavery was abolished as of 4 July 1827 (few slaves actually remained in the state by this time), and New Yorkers soon took the lead in the growing antislavery movement. The first women's rights convention in the US was held in Seneca Falls in 1848—though women would have to wait until 1917 before winning the right to vote in state elections. Also during the 1840s, the state saw the first of several great waves of European immigration. The Irish and Germans were the earliest major arrivals during the 19th century, but before World War I they would be joined—not always amicably—by Italians and European Jews.

New Yorkers voted for Abraham Lincoln in the presidential election of 1860 and were among the readiest recruits to the Union side. Enthusiasm for the conflict diminished during the next two years, however. When the military draft reached New York City on 11 July 1863, the result was three days of rioting in which blacks were lynched and the homes of prominent abolitionists were burned. But New York was not a wartime battleground, and overall the war and Reconstruction were very good for business.

The decades after the Civil War ushered in an era of extraordinary commercial growth and political corruption. This was the Gilded Age, during which entrepreneurs became multimillionaires and New York was transformed from an agricultural state to an industrial giant. In 1860, the leading manufactures in the state were flour and meal, men's clothing, refined sugar, leather goods, liquor, and lumber; 90 years later, apparel, printing and publishing, food, machinery, chemicals, fabricated metal products, electrical machinery, textiles, instruments, and transportation equipment had became the dominant industries.

The key to this transformation was the development of the railroads. The boom period for railroad construction started in the 1850s and reached its high point after 1867, when "Commodore" Cornelius Vanderbilt, who had been a steamboat captain in 1818, took over the New York Central. During the 1860s, native New Yorkers like Jay Gould and Russell Sage made their fortunes through investment and speculation. Especially during the century's last two decades, corporate names that today are household words began to emerge: Westinghouse Electric in 1886, General Electric (as Edison Electric) in 1889, Eastman Kodak in 1892. In 1882, another native New Yorker, John D. Rockefeller, formed the Standard Oil Trust; although the trust would eventually be broken up, the Rockefeller family would help shape New York politics for many decades to come.

The period immediately following the Civil War also marked a new high in political influence for the Tammany Society (or "Tammany Hall"), founded in 1789 as an anti-Federalist organization. From 1857 until his exposure by the press in 1871, Democrat William March "Boss" Tweed ruled Tammany and effectively dominated New York City by dispersing patronage, buying votes, and bribing legislators and judges. Tammany went into temporary eclipse after the Tweed Ring was broken up, and Republicans swept the state in 1872. The first result was a series of constitutional changes, including one abolishing the requirement that blacks hold property in order to vote. A new constitution approved in 1894, and effective in 1895, remains the basic law of New York State today.

During the Union's first 100 years, New York's political life had projected into national prominence such men as Alexander Hamilton, John Jay, George and De Witt Clinton, Martin Van Buren, and Millard Fillmore. The state's vast population—New York held more electoral votes than any other state between 1812 and 1972—coupled with its growing industrial and financial power, enhanced the prestige of state leaders during the nation's second century. Grover Cleveland, though born in New Jersey, became mayor of Buffalo, then governor of New York, and finally the 22nd US president in 1885. Theodore Roosevelt was governor of New York, then became vice president and finally president of the US in 1901. In 1910, Charles Evans Hughes resigned the governorship to become an associate justice of the US Supreme Court; he also served as secretary of state, and in 1930 was appointed chief justice of the US. By the 1920s, Tammany had rebounded from the Tweed Ring breakup and from another scandal during the 1890s to reach its peak of prestige: Alfred E. Smith, a longtime member of Tammany, as well as an able and popular official, was four times elected governor and in 1928 became the first Roman Catholic candidate to be nominated by a major party for the presidency of the US. That year saw the election of Franklin D. Roosevelt as governor of New York.

The 1930s, a period of depression, ushered in a new wave of progressive government. From 1933 until 1945, FDR was in the White House. Roosevelt's successor in the statehouse was Herbert H. Lehman, whose Little New Deal established the basic pattern of present state social welfare policies that had begun on a much more modest scale during Smith's administration. The Fusion mayor of New York City at this time—propelled into office by yet another wave of exposure of Tammany corruption— was the colorful and popular Fiorello H. La Guardia.

The decades following World War II saw extraordinary expansion of New York social services, including construction of the state university system, but also an erosion of the state's industrial base. Fiscal crises were not new to the state—reformers in the 1920s railed against New York City's "spendthrift" policies—but the greatly increased scale of government in the 1970s made the fiscal crisis of 1975 unprecedented in its scope and implications. The city's short-term debt grew from virtually zero to about $6 billion between 1970 and 1975, although its government reported consistently balanced budgets. Eventually a package totaling $4.5 billion in aid was needed to avoid bankruptcy. The decreasing pace of population and industrial growth during the 1950s and 1960s, and the decline during the 1970s, also led to a dimming of New York's political fortunes. The single dominant political figure in New York after World War II, Nelson A. Rockefeller (governor, 1958–73), tried and failed three times to win the Republican presidential nomination before his appointment to the vice-presidency in 1974. Unable to overcome the hostility of his party's conservative wing, he was not renominated for the vice-presidency in 1976. In 1984, however, US Representative Geraldine Ferraro of Queens was the Democratic Party's vice-presidential standard-bearer, and Governor Mario M. Cuomo emerged as an influential Democratic spokesman. After serving for 12 years, Cuomo was replaced in 1995 by State Senator George Pataki, the first Republican elected New York governor since 1970.

From the late 1970s through the late 1980s, New York enjoyed an economic boom, particularly in finance, insurance, real estate and construction. The state budget increased in constant dollars by 20%. While much of that increase compensated for cuts in federal aid to states and was directed at education, municipalities, schools and prisons, some went to meet new needs such as homelessness and AIDS victims. Prosperity did not reach all sectors of the economy or the population, however. In 1984, 25% of the residents of New York City lived below the poverty line. The collapse of the stock market in October of 1987, in which the market plunged 36% in two months, not only forced a retrenchment on Wall Street but also signaled the end of the boom and the beginning of a recession that was quite severe in New York, exacerbated by the curtailment of federal funding by the Reagan and Bush administrations. Unemployment peaked in 1992, and by 1994 a recovery was under way.

The boom economy of the late 1990s boosted Wall Street, with the bulls dominating the stock market despite some historic losses, particularly in the technology sector, which analysts later categorized as "market corrections." In 1998 New York had the 4th-highest per capita income in the nation ($31,679) but it also had more people living below the poverty level than 45 other states, again indicating prosperity had not reached into all sectors.

The 1990s witnessed the settlement of the lawsuits surrounding Love Canal in Buffalo, where leaking chemical wastes in the 1970s and early 1980s had prompted the state and federal governments to pay to move families from the area. In the largest legal settlement in New York's history, in 1994 Occidental Petroleum Corp. agreed to pay $98 million in damages for the dumping of hazardous wastes at Love Canal, ending 16 years of litigation.

The state, which dropped from the nation's 2nd to 3rd most populous in 1994, retained the ranking in 2003. According to Census Bureau estimates, the state had over 19 million people in 2001—surpassed only by California and Texas. New York's Hispanic population was estimated to be roughly the same in number as its African American population (African Americans 15.9%; Hispanics 15.1%).

In mid-1999, in the midst of a budget impasse in the state legislature, the government determined it would sell state facilities. A resulting deal, reached in 2000, saw the state selling two nuclear plants for a total asking price of $967 million. It was the largest privatization of state assets in New York history.

Transportation in and around New York City was the focus of the statehouse and legislature in 2000. Governor George Pataki and New Jersey Governor Christine Todd Whitman, a fellow Republican, had squared off over issues surrounding the Port Authority, which the states jointly control. The governors resolved their differences in June 2000. They cleared the way for the construction of a $200-million cargo hub for the world's largest ocean carrier (Maersk Sealand) and reopened the possibility that the World Trade Center, which the Port Authority still controlled, could be turned over to a private developer. Meanwhile, lawmakers heard arguments for and against a proposed $17-billion project to be undertaken by the Metropolitan Transit Authority (MTA). Advocates argued the public works plan, which would result in the largest sale of municipal bonds in US history, was necessary to build a new generation of subways, buses, and trains to serve the greater New York area. Opponents believed the project would pose disaster for the MTA, burying the agency under a mountain of debt and rendering it unable to maintain the existing transportation systems.

New York City was one site of the nation's worst terrorist attacks on 11 September 2001, when hijackers from the al-Qaeda terrorist organization flew two passenger airliners into the North and South Towers of the World Trade Center, destroying them. Another aircraft hit the Pentagon building in Washington, D.C., and a fourth crashed into a field in Stony Creek Township, Pennsylvania. Officials estimated that as of 2002, 3,066 people had died, were missing, or presumed dead as a result of the attacks. The city and the nation went into a long period of mourning.

Berlin-based architect Daniel Libeskind's design for rebuilding "Ground Zero" (the site of the demolished World Trade Center) was accepted in 2003; New Yorkers had expressed dissatisfaction with the original designs, which were thought to be uninspiring.

Construction at the site was not to begin until 2005 at the earliest. Libeskind's design features a complex of angular towers and a spire that would be among the world's tallest structures.

New York was one of the states affected by the 14 August 2003 massive power blackout in Canada, the Northeast and midwestern states. The largest electrical outage in US history affected 9,300 square miles and a population of over 50 million.

Following the decline of the stock market on Wall Street and the US recession in the early 2000s, New York in 2003 was plagued with economic woes. The state faced a budget deficit of $10 billion in 2003.

12 STATE GOVERNMENT

New York has had four constitutions, adopted in 1777, 1822, 1846, and 1895. The 1895 constitution was extensively revised in 1938, and the basic structure of state government has not changed since then, although the document had been amended 215 times by January 2003. In 1993 the Temporary State Commission on Constitutional Revision was created in anticipation of a referendum on a constitutional convention in 1997.

The legislature consists of a 61-member senate and 150-member assembly. Senators and assembly members serve two-year terms and are elected in even-numbered years. Each house holds regular annual sessions, which begin in January and are not formally limited in length; special sessions may be called by the governor or initiated by petition of two-thirds of the membership of each body. All legislators must be at least 18 years old, US citizens, and must have been residents of the state for at least five years and residents of their districts for at least one year prior to election. The legislative salary was $79,500 in 2002, unchanged from 1999.

Either senators or assembly members may introduce or amend a bill; the governor may introduce a budget bill. To pass, a bill requires a majority vote in both houses; a two-thirds majority (of the elected members in each house) is required to override the governor's veto. If the governor neither signs nor vetoes a bill, it becomes law after 10 days, as long as the legislature is in session.

The state's only elected executives are the governor, lieutenant governor, comptroller, and attorney general. Each serves a four-year term. The governor and lieutenant governor are jointly elected; there is no limit to the number of terms they may serve. The governor must be at least 30 years old, a US citizen, and a resident of the state for five years prior to the date of election. The lieutenant governor is next in line for the governorship (should the governor be unable to complete his or her term in office) and presides over the senate. In 2002 the governor's salary was $179,000, unchanged from 1999.

The governor appoints the heads of most of the major executive departments, with some of the appointments requiring the advice and consent of the senate. The exceptions are the comptroller and attorney general, who are elected by the voters; the commissioner of education, who is named by the Regents of the University of the State of New York; the commissioner of social services, elected by the Board of Social Services; and the chief of the Executive Department, which the governor heads ex officio.

A bill becomes law when passed by both houses of the legislature and signed by the governor. While the legislature is in session, a bill may also become law if the governor fails to act on it within 10 days of its receipt. The governor may veto a bill or, if the legislature has adjourned, may kill a bill simply by taking no action on it for 30 days.

A proposed amendment to the state constitution must receive majority votes in both houses of the legislature during two successive sessions. Amendments so approved are put on the ballot in November and adopted or rejected by majority vote.

The constitution also provides that the voters must be permitted every 20 years to decide whether a convention should be called to amend the present constitution. Voters in New York must be US citizens, at least 18 years old, residents of the county (or New York City) for 30 days prior to election day, and unable to claim the right to vote elsewhere. Restrictions apply to convicted felons and those declared mentally incompetent by the court.

13 POLITICAL PARTIES

In addition to the Democratic and Republican parties, the major political groups, there has always been a profusion of minor parties in New York, some of which have significantly influenced the outcomes of national and state elections.

Party politics in the state crystallized into their present form around 1855. Up to that time, a welter of parties and factions—including such short-lived groups as the Anti-Masons, Bucktails, Clintonians, Hunkers, and Barnburners (split into Hardshell and Softshell Democrats), Know-Nothings (Native American Party), Wooly Heads and Silver-Grays (factions of the Whigs), and the Liberty Party—jockeyed for power in New York State.

Roughly speaking, the Democratic Party evolved out of the Democratic Republican factions of the old Republican Party and had become a unified party by the 1850s. The Democratic power base was—and has remained—the big cities, especially New York City. The most important big-city political machine from the 1860s through the 1950s, except for a few brief periods, was the Tammany Society ("Tammany Hall"). Tammany controlled the Democratic Party in New York City and, through that party, the city itself.

The Republican Party in New York State emerged in 1855 as the heir of the Whigs, the Liberty Party, and the Softshell Democratic faction. The Republican Party's power base includes the state's rural counties, the smaller cities and towns, and

(though not so much in the 1970s and early 1980s as in earlier decades) the New York City suburbs. Although New York Republicans stand to the right of the Democrats on social issues, they have usually been well to the left of the national Republican Party. The liberal "internationalist" strain of Republicanism was personified during the 1960s by Governor Nelson Rockefeller, US Senator Jacob Javits, and New York City Mayor John V. Lindsay (who later became a Democrat).

The disaffection of more conservative Republicans and Democrats within the state led to the formation of the Conservative Party in 1963. At first intended as a device to exert pressure on the state Republican establishment, the Conservative Party soon became a power in its own right, electing a US senator, James Buckley, in 1970. Its power decreased in the late 1970s as the Republican Party embraced some of its positions. The Conservative Party has its left-wing counterpart in the Liberal Party, which was formed in 1944 by dissidents in the American Labor Party who claimed the ALP was Communist-influenced. Tied strongly to labor interests, the Liberals have normally supported the national Democratic ticket. Their power, however, has waned considerably in recent years.

Minor parties have sometimes meant the difference between victory and defeat for major party candidates in state and national elections. The Liberal Party line provided the victory margin in the state, and therefore the nation, for Democratic presidential candidate John F. Kennedy in 1960. Other significant, though not victorious, minor-party presidential candidates have included the American Labor Party with Henry Wallace in 1948 (8% of the vote), the Courage Party with George Wallace in 1968 (5%), and the Liberal Party with John Anderson in 1980 (7%). Among radical parties, the Socialists qualified for the presidential ballot continuously between 1900 and 1952, reaching a peak of 203,201 votes (7% of the total) in 1920.

New York Presidential Vote by Political Parties, 1948–2000

YEAR	ELECTORAL VOTE	NEW YORK WINNER	DEMOCRAT	LIBERAL[1]	REPUBLICAN	PROGRESSIVE[2]	SOCIALIST	SOCIALIST WORKERS	PEACE AND FREEDOM
1948	47	Dewey (R)	2,557,642	222,562	2,841,163	509,559	40,879	2,675	—
1952	45	*Eisenhower (R)	2,687,890	416,711	3,952,815	64,211	2,664	2,212	—
1956	45	*Eisenhower (R)	2,458,212	292,557	4,340,340	—	—	—	—
1960	45	*Kennedy (D)	3,423,909	406,176	3,446,419	—	—	14,319	—
							SOC. LABOR		
1964	43	*Johnson (D)	4,570,670	342,432	2,243,559		6,118	3,228	—
						AMERICAN IND.[3]			
1968	43	Humphrey (D)	3,066,848	311,622	3,007,932	358,864	8,432	11,851	24,517
						CONSERVATIVE[4]			COMMUNIST
1972	41	*Nixon (R)	2,767,956	183,128	3,824,642	368,136	4,530	7,797	5,641
							LIBERTARIAN		
1976	41	*Carter (D)	3,244,165	145,393	2,825,913	2,724,878	12,197	6,996	10,270
								RIGHT TO LIFE	CITIZENS
1980	41	*Reagan (R)	2,728,372	467,801	2,637,700	256,131	52,648	24,159	23,186
									COMMUNIST
1984	36	*Reagan (R)	3,001,285	118,324	3,376,519	288,244	11,949	—	4,226
								NEW ALLIANCE	
1988	36	Dukakis (D)	3,255,487	92,395	2,838,414	243,457	12,109	15,845	20,497
1992[5]	22	*Clinton (D)	3,346,894	97,556	2,041,690	177,000	13,451	15,472	11,318
								FREEDOM[4]	GREEN (NADER)
1996[5]	33	*Clinton (D)	3,649,630	106,547	1,738,707	183,392	12,220	11,393	75,956
2000	33	Gore (D)	3,942,215	77,087	2,258,877	144,797	7,649	—	244,030

* Won US presidential election.

[1] Supported Democratic candidate except in 1980, when John Anderson ran on the Liberal line.

[2] Ran in the state as the American Labor Party.

[3] Appeared on the state ballot as the Courage Party.

[4] Supported Republican candidate.

[5] Independent candidate Ross Perot received 1,090,721 votes in 1992 and 503,458 votes in 1996.

Democrat Mario M. Cuomo was defeated in his run for a fourth term as governor in November 1994 by Republican George Pataki; Pataki was elected to a third term in 2002. In 2003 New York's US senators were Democrat Charles Schumer, elected to his first term in 1998 to succeed three-term Republican Alphonse D'Amato, and Democrat Hillary Rodham Clinton, first elected in 2000. Following the 2002 elections, New York's US representatives included 19 Democrats and 10 Republicans. Republicans held 37 seats in the state senate while Democrats held 25. In the state assembly there were 103 Democrats and 47 Republicans.

In the November 1980 presidential elections, Republican nominee Ronald Reagan (with Conservative Party backing) won the state's then-41 electoral votes, apparently because John Anderson, running in New York State on the Liberal Party line, siphoned enough votes from the Democratic incumbent, Jimmy Carter, to give Reagan a plurality. Reagan carried the state again in 1984, despite the presence on the Democratic ticket of US Representative Geraldine Ferraro of Queens as the running mate of Walter Mondale; Ferraro was the first woman candidate for president or vice president on a major party ticket. New Yorkers chose Democratic nominees Michael Dukakis and Bill Clinton in 1988 and 1992, respectively, and Clinton again won the state in 1996. In the 2000 presidential election, Democrat Al Gore won 60% of the vote to Republican George W. Bush's 35%; Green Party candidate Ralph Nader garnered 4% of the vote. In 2002 there were 11,246,362 registered voters. In 1998, 47% of registered voters were Democratic, 29% Republican, and 24% unaffiliated or members of other parties. The state had 33 electoral votes in the 2000 presidential election.

In November 1993, New York City mayor David Dinkins, a Democrat and New York's first black mayor, who had served since 1990, was defeated by Republican Rudolph Giuliani. Giuliani was legally barred from seeking a third term, and billionaire media tycoon Michael Bloomberg won the mayoral contest in 2001.

14 LOCAL GOVERNMENT

The state constitution, endorsing the principle of home rule, recognizes many different levels of local government. In 2002, New York had 57 counties, 616 municipal governments, 929 townships, and 683 public school districts.

Cities are contained within counties, with one outstanding exception: New York City is made up of five counties, one for each of its five boroughs. Traditionally, counties are run by an elected board of supervisors or county legislature; however, a growing number of counties have vested increased powers in a single elected county executive. With the exception of some counties within New York City, each county has a county attorney and district attorney, sheriff, fiscal officer (treasurer), county clerk, and commissioner of social services.

Towns are run by a town board; the town supervisor is the board's presiding officer and acts as town treasurer. A group of people within a town or towns may also incorporate themselves into a village, with their own elected mayor and elected board of trustees. Some villages have administrators or managers. Members of the village remain members of the town, and must pay taxes to both jurisdictions. The constitution grants the state legislature the power to decide which taxes the local governments may levy and how much debt they may incur.

New York City is governed by a mayor and city council, but much practical power resides in the Board of Estimate. On this board sit the city's three top elected officials—the mayor, comptroller, and city council president. The board also includes the five borough presidents, elected officials who represent (and, to a limited extent, govern) each of the five boroughs. New York City government is further complicated by the fact that certain essential services are provided not by the city itself but by independent "authorities." The special district of the Port Authority of New York and New Jersey, for example, operates New York Harbor, sets interstate bridge and tunnel tolls, and supervises the city's bus and air terminals; it is responsible not to the mayor but to the governors of New York and New Jersey. Similarly, the Metropolitan Transportation Authority, which controls the city's subways and some of its commuter rail lines, is an independent agency responsible to the state rather than the city. There were 1,135 other special districts in 2002, of which nearly 900 were for fire prevention.

15 STATE SERVICES

To address the continuing threat of terrorism and to work with the federal Department of Homeland Security (created in 2002 following the terrorist attacks of 11 September 2001), homeland security in New York in 2003 operated under executive order; the public security director was designated as the state homeland security advisor.

Educational services are provided through the Education Department. Under this department's jurisdiction are the State Library, the State Museum, the State Archives, the New York State School for the Blind at Batavia, and the New York State School for the Deaf at Rome. The Education Department also issues licenses for 20 professions, including architecture, engineering and land surveying, massage, pharmacy, public accountancy, social work, and various medical specialties. The state university system is administered by a separate agency headed by a chancellor.

Transportation services are under the direction of the Department of Transportation, which has responsibility for highways, aviation, mass transit, railroads, water transport, transportation safety, and intrastate rate regulation. The Department of Motor Vehicles licenses all road vehicles, motor vehicle dealers, motor vehicle operators, and driving schools.

Human services are provided through several state departments. Among the programs and facilities operated by the Department of Health are three research and treatment facilities; the New York State Veterans' Home at Oxford, Roswell Park Memorial Institute at Buffalo, and Helen Hayes Hospital at West Haverstraw. The state provides care for the mentally ill, retarded, and alcoholics and other substance-dependent persons through the Department of Mental Hygiene. It maintains 30 psychiatric centers, and 18 developmental centers for retardation and developmental disabilities. The Department of Social Services supervises and sets standards for locally administered public and private welfare and health programs, including Medicaid and Aid to Families with Dependent Children; it has special responsibilities for the blind and visually handicapped and over Indian affairs. Other human services are provided through the Division of Veterans' Affairs, the Division of Human Rights, the Division for Youth, and the Office for the Aging, all within the Executive Department.

Public protection services include state armed forces, corrections, and consumer protection. Included within the Division of Military and Naval Affairs, in the Executive Department, are the Army National Guard, Air National Guard, Naval Militia, State Civil Defense Commission, and Disaster Preparedness Commission. The Division of State Police operates within the Executive Department, while prisons are administered by the separate Department of Correctional Services, which in 1985 operated 46 correctional facilities. The State Consumer Protection Board (Executive Department) coordinates the consumer protection activities of the various agencies and departments. The major legal role in consumer protection is played by the attorney general.

Housing services are provided through the Division of Housing and Community Renewal of the Executive Department, and through the quasi-independent New York State Housing Finance Agency, State of New York Mortgage Agency, and New York State Urban Development Corporation. The Division of Economic Opportunity (Department of State) acts as the state representative of the economically disadvantaged in dealing with local, state, and federal agencies. The Department of Commerce has an Office of Minority and Women's Business.

Natural resources protection services are centralized in the Department of Environmental Conservation. The administration of the state park and recreation system is carried out by the Office of Parks, Recreation and Historic Preservation, in the Executive Department. The Department of Agriculture and Markets serves the interests of farmers and also administers the state's Pure Food Law. Energy is the province of the Department of Public Service. The quasi-independent Power Authority of the State of New York finances, builds, and operates electricity-generating and transmission facilities.

The Department of Labor provides most labor services for the state. Its responsibilities include occupational health and safety, human resource development and allocation, administration of unemployment insurance and other benefit programs, and maintenance of labor standards, including enforcement of minimum wage and other labor laws. The Employment Relations Board tries to settle labor disputes and prevent work stoppages.

16JUDICIAL SYSTEM

New York's highest court is the court of appeals, in Albany, with appellate jurisdiction only. The court of appeals consists of a chief judge and six associate judges, appointed by the governor and approved by the senate for 14-year terms. Below the court of appeals is the supreme court, with nearly 570 justices in 12 judicial districts. The supreme court of New York State does not sit as one body; instead, most supreme court justices are assigned original jurisdiction in civil and criminal matters, while 56 justices are assigned to the appellate division of supreme court and 15 to appellate terms of supreme court. Supreme court justices are elected by district and serve 14-year terms.

The New York court of claims sits in Albany, with judges appointed by the governor to nine-year terms, along with judges sitting as acting Supreme Court justices in felony trials. This special trial court hears civil cases involving claims by or against the state.

Outside New York City, each county has its own county court to handle criminal cases, although some are delegated to be handled by lower courts. County court judges are elected to 10-year terms. Many counties have a surrogate's court to handle such matters as wills and estates; surrogates are elected to 10-year terms except in New York City counties, where they are elected to 14-year terms. Each county has its own family court. In New York City, judges are appointed by the mayor for 10-year terms; elsewhere they are elected for 10 years. A county's district attorney has authority in criminal matters. Most cities (including New York City) have their own court systems; in New York City, the mayor appoints judges of city criminal and family courts. Village police justices and town justices of the peace handle minor violations and other routine matters.

The Department of Correctional Services maintains correctional facilities throughout the state, as well as regional parole offices. In June 2001, 69,158 inmates were in state and federal facilities, a decrease of 3.5% from the previous year. The state's incarceration rate stood at 364 per 100,000 inhabitants.

New York had an FBI Crime Index total of 2,925.1 per 100,000 inhabitants in 2001, including a total of 98,103 violent crimes and 458,003 crimes against property in that year.

New York abolished the death penalty in 1965 and reinstated it in 1995. No one has been executed under the new law; the last execution in the state occurred under the old law in 1963. No prisoners were under sentence of death as of 2003.

17ARMED FORCES

The US Military Academy at West Point was founded in 1802. In 2002, there were 20,882 active-duty military personnel and 11,220 civilian personnel stationed in New York, more than half of whom were at Fort Drum. In 2002, New York firms received more than $3.4 billion in defense contracts.

According to the 2000 Census, there were 1,361,164 veterans of US military service in the state. Allowing for overlapping (some veterans served in more than one war), the statistics for living veterans of wartime service were as follows: World War II, 332,779; Korea, 196,018; Vietnam era, 364,061; 1990–2000 (including the Persian Gulf War), 104,128. Veterans' benefits totaling nearly $2.7 billion were paid to New Yorkers during 2002.

In 2000, the New York State Police employed 4,112 sworn officers.

18MIGRATION

Since the early 1800s, New York has been the primary port of entry for Europeans coming to the US. The Statue of Liberty—dedicated in 1886 and beckoning "your tired, your poor, /Your huddled masses yearning to breathe free" to the shores of America—was often the immigrants' first glimpse of America. The first stop for some 20 million immigrants in the late 19th and early 20th centuries was Ellis Island, where they were processed, often given Americanized names, and sent onward to an uncertain future.

The first great wave of European immigrants arrived in the 1840s, impelled by the potato famine in Ireland. By 1850, New York City had 133,730 Irish-born inhabitants, and by 1890, 409,224. Although smaller in number, German immigration during this period was more widespread; during the 1850s, German-speaking people were the largest foreign-born group in Rochester and Buffalo, and by 1855 about 30,000 of Buffalo's 74,000 residents were German.

The next two great waves of European immigration—Eastern European Jews and Italians—overlapped. Vast numbers of Jews began arriving from Eastern Europe during the 1880s, by which time some 80,000 German-speaking Jews were already living in New York City. By 1910, the Jewish population of the city was about 1,250,000, growing to nearly 2,000,000 by the mid-1920s. The flood of Italians began during the 1800s, when the Italian population of New York City increased from 75,000 to more than 200,000; in 1950, nearly 500,000 Italian-born immigrants were living in the state. Migration from the 1840s onward followed a cyclical pattern: as one group dispersed from New York City throughout the state and the nation, it was replaced by a new wave of immigrants.

Yankees from New England made up the first great wave of domestic migration. Most of the migrants who came to New York between 1790 and 1840 were Yankees; it has been estimated that by 1850, 52,000 natives of Vermont (20% of that state's population) had become residents of New York. There was a slow, steady migration of African Americans from slave states to New York before the Civil War, but massive black migration to New York, and especially to New York City, began during World War I and continued well into the 1960s. The third great wave of domestic migration came after World War II, from Puerto Rico. Nearly 40,000 Puerto Ricans settled in New York City in 1946, and 58,500 in 1952–53. By 1960, the census showed well over 600,000 New Yorkers of Puerto Rican birth or parentage. As of 1990, Puerto Rican-born New Yorkers numbered 143,974.

Nearly 41,800 state residents in 1990 had lived in Puerto Rico in 1985. Many other Caribbean natives—especially Dominicans, Jamaicans, and Haitians—followed. In 1996, there were a reported 3,232,000 state residents who were foreign-born (about 17% of the state's population). In 1998, 96,559 foreign immigrants entered New York, the 2nd-highest total of any state (surpassed only by California) and over 15% of the total immigration for that year.

The fourth and most recent domestic migratory trend is unique in New York history—the net outward migration from New York to other states. During the 1960s, New York suffered a net loss of more than 100,000 residents through migration; between 1970 and 1980, the estimated net loss was probably in excess of 1,500,000, far greater than that in any other state: probably 80% of the migration was from New York City. From 1980 to 1990, net loss from migration exceeded 340,000. Between 1990 and 1998, New York had a net loss of 1,722,000 in domestic migration. These general estimates hide a racial movement of historic proportions: during the 1960s, while an estimated net total of 638,000 whites were moving out of the state, 396,000 blacks were moving in; during 1970–75, according to Census Bureau estimates, 701,000 whites left New York, while 60,000 blacks were arriving. According to a private study, a net total of 700,000 whites and 50,000 blacks left the state during 1975–80. It appears that many of the white emigrants went to suburban areas of New Jersey and Connecticut, but many also went to two Sunbelt states, Florida and California. Overwhelmingly, the black arrivals came from the South. During the 1980s, the black population of the New York City area increased by 16.4%. By 1997, blacks comprised 19.4% of the New York City area's total population.

Intrastate migration has followed the familiar pattern of rural to urban, urban to suburban. In 1790, the state was 88% rural; the rural population grew in absolute terms (though not as a percentage of the total state population) until the 1880s when the long period of decline began. New York's farm population decreased by 21% during the 1940s, 33% during the 1950s, 38% during the 1960s, and 49% during the 1970s. By 1990, 84% of all New Yorkers lived in urban areas; by 1996, 91.8%. Meanwhile, the suburban population has grown steadily. In 1950, 3,538,620 New Yorkers (24% of the state total) lived in suburbs; by 1980, this figure had grown to 7,461,161 (42% of all state residents). It should be remembered, of course, that this more than doubling of the suburban population reflects natural increase and direct migration from other states and regions, as well as the intrastate migratory movement from central cities to suburbs. Between 1990 and 1998, New York's overall population only increased by 1%.

In the period 1995–2000, 726,477 people moved into the state and 1,600,725 moved out, for a net loss of 874,248. Of those who left the state, about 308,230 went to Florida, 206,979 went to New Jersey, 112,214 went to Pennsylvania, 100,727 went to North Carolina, and 95,952 went to California. The largest immigration came from New Jersey, with 97,584 people moving to New York.

19INTERGOVERNMENTAL COOPERATION

New York State is a member of the Council of State Governments and its allied organizations. The state participates in many interstate regional commissions (and in commissions with the Canadian provinces of Ontario and Quebec). Among the more active interstate commissions are the Appalachian Regional Commission, Atlantic States Marine Fisheries Commission, Delaware River Basin Commission, Great Lakes Commission, Interstate Oil and Gas Compact Commission, Mid-Atlantic Fishery Management Council, New England Interstate Water Pollution Control Commission, Northeastern Forest Fire

Protection Commission, and the Ohio River Valley Water Sanitation Commission. In 1985, New York joined seven other Great Lakes states and two Canadian provinces in the Great Lakes Charter, for the purpose of protecting the lakes' water reserves.

The three most important interstate bodies for the New York metropolitan area are the Palisades Interstate Park Commission, Interstate Sanitation Commission, and Port Authority of New York and New Jersey. The Palisades Interstate Park Commission was founded in 1900 (with New Jersey) in order to preserve the natural beauty of the Palisades region. The Interstate Sanitation Commission (with New Jersey and Connecticut; established in 1961) monitors and seeks to control pollution within the tri-state Interstate Sanitation District. The Port Authority of New York and New Jersey, created in 1921 and the most powerful of the three, is a public corporation with the power to issue its own bonds. Its vast holdings include 4 bridges, 2 tunnels, 5 airports and heliports, 2 motor vehicle terminals, 6 marine terminals, the trans-Hudson rapid transit system, an industrial park in the Bronx, and the 110-story twin-towered World Trade Center in lower Manhattan, until it was destroyed in 2001. Bridge compacts include those on the Buffalo and Fort Erie bridge, the Ogdensburg bridge and port, and the Canada and New York International bridge. Other compacts include the New York-Connecticut Railroad Service, and the Susquehanna River Basin Compact (with Maryland and Pennsylvania). Federal grants to New York state and local governments totaled almost $32.9 billion in 2001, higher than for any other state, except California.

20ECONOMY

From the Civil War through the 1950s, New York State led the nation in just about every category by which an economy can be measured. In the colonial and early national periods, New York was a leading wheat-growing state. When the wheat crop declined, dairying and lumbering became the state's mainstays. New York then emerged as the national leader in wholesaling, retailing, and manufacturing—and remained so well into the 1960s.

By 1973, however, the state was running neck and neck with California by most output measures, or had already been surpassed. The total labor force, the number of workers in manufacturing, and the number of factories all declined during the 1960s and 1970s. New York City's manufacturing base and its skilled laborers have been emigrating to the suburbs and to other states since World War II. Between 1969 and 1976, the city lost 600,000 jobs. With the departure of much of the middle class, the city's tax base shrank, a factor that contributed to the fiscal crisis of 1975, when a package of short-term aid from Congress, the state government, and the labor union pension funds saved the city from default.

The 1980s saw the state's fortunes on the rise. A shift in dependence from manufacturing to services, and particularly to finance, helped the state and New York City weather the 1981–82 recession. In 1983, the state's three largest industrial and commercial employers (excluding public utilities) were all banks based in New York City. From 1980 to 1990, the state's economy acquired approximately one million jobs, in contrast to 50,000 the previous decade. Financial services led the city's economic expansion, adding 100,000 jobs from 1980 to 1987. Long Island also experienced growth in the first half of the decade, benefiting from the defense build-up by the federal government in the early and mid-eighties.

New York's economy not only grew during the eighties but also underwent a restructuring. Manufacturing witnessed a decline in its share of total employment from 20% in 1980 to 14% in 1990. Apparel, industrial machinery and equipment, and primary metals accounted for 40% of the total loss of jobs.

Industrial output, however, increased 10.1% between 1980 and 1987. Productivity gains produced both the rise in output and the decline in employment. Construction boomed from 1982–89, increasing its share of employment from 2.9% to 3.8%. The service sector, particularly business-related, health care, education and social services grew 52% in the decade, increasing services' share of employment from 24% in 1980 to 29% in 1990. Finance, insurance, and the real estate industry expanded 64%. The surge in financial services employment ended with the crash of the stock market in October of 1987, in which stock prices dropped 36% in two months. The crash prompted the layoff of 9,000 employees on Wall Street and a downsizing of the banking and securities industries. More than $1 trillion in financial transactions took place per day on the NYSE in 2000.

About 1 in 11 New York City residents received some form of public assistance (including Medicaid and Supplemental Security Income benefits) in 1994. The high number of people on welfare prompted the New York State government to turn the welfare program into a "workfare" program that put the able-bodied to work. By 1998, the welfare role call had been reduced by over 600,000 from 1995 numbers, a 35% decrease. Job growth rose steadily through the 1990s. Coming into the 21st century, the state economy was growing briskly, with annual growth rates of 8.3% in 1998, 3.5% in 1999, and 7.3%. Even in the national recession of 2001, and with the events of 9/11, the state economy posted 3.5% annual growth. Employment growth in the state lagged the nation as a whole during 2001 and 2002, but was close to the national average by the end of 2002. New York City's rate of job losses, however, continued to exceed the state and the nation. However, office vacancy rates in New York City in the fourth quarter 2002, at 8% for midtown, and 12% for downtown (where twin towers had been located), were well below the national average of 16.5%. The state's manufacturing sector, which had been contracting for decades, fell from 10.8% of gross state product in 1997 to 9.4% of the total in 2001. In 2002, the highest percentages of manufacturing job losses were in the cities of Buffalo, Rochester and Syracuse.

New York's gross state product in 2001 was $826.5 billion, 2nd only to California, to which financial services contributed $282.9 billion; general services, $190.2 billion; trade, $103.5 billion; government, $81.2 billion; manufacturing, $77.7 billion; transportation and public utilities, $59.3 billion, and construction, $17.4 billion. The public sector in 2001 constituted 9.8% of gross state product, tied with New Jersey for the 5th-lowest percent among the states where the average was 12%.

21 INCOME

According to the Bureau of Economic Analysis, in 2001, New York had a per capita personal income (PCPI) of $35,878 which ranked 5th in the United States (including the District of Columbia) and was 118% of the national average, $30,413. The 2001 PCPI reflected an increase of 2.4% from 2000 compared to the national change of 2.2%. In 2001, New York had a total personal income (TPI) of $684,703,928,000 which ranked 2nd in the United States and accounted for 7.9% of the national total. The 2001 TPI reflected an increase of 2.8% from 2000 compared to the national change of 3.3%.

Earnings of persons employed in New York increased from $501,698,617,000 in 2000 to $514,032,731,000 in 2001, an increase of 2.5%. The largest industries in 2001 were services, 31.1% of earnings; finance, insurance, and real estate, 23.2%; and state and local government, 11.6%. Of the industries that accounted for at least 5% of earnings in 2001, the slowest growing from 2000 to 2001 was wholesale trade (5.2% of earnings in 2001), which decreased 2.5%; the fastest was services, which increased 3.3%.

According to data released by the US Census Bureau, in 2000, the median household income was $41,605 compared to the national average of $42,148. In 2001, the median income for a family of four was $66,498 compared to the national average of $63,278. For the period 1999 to 2001, the average poverty rate was 14.1% which placed it 41st among the 50 states and the District of Columbia ranked lowest to highest.

22 LABOR

According to Bureau of Labor Statistics (BLS) provisional estimates, in July 2003 the seasonally adjusted civilian labor force in New York numbered 9,365,400, with approximately 571,600 workers unemployed, yielding an unemployment rate of 6.1%, compared to the national average of 6.2% for the same period. Since the beginning of the BLS data series in 1978, the highest unemployment rate recorded was 9.2% in April 1983. The historical low was 3.9% in April 1988. In 2001, an estimated 4.7% of the labor force was employed in construction; 10.9% in manufacturing; 5.6% in transportation, communications, and public utilities; 17.3% in trade; 7.5% in finance, insurance, and real estate; 29.5% in services; 16.4% in government; and 1.1% in agriculture.

The labor force participation rate of women increased from 42.0% in 1974 to 55.8% in 1998. Over the same period, participation rates for men declined from 75.9% to 71.4%. Among minority groups, the unemployment rate in 1998 was 11.4% for blacks and 8.9% for Hispanics.

At the turn of the 20th century, working conditions in New York were among the worst in the country. The flood of immigrants into the labor market and the absence of labor laws to protect them led to the development in New York City of cramped, ill-lit, poorly ventilated, and unhealthy factories—the sweatshops for which the garment industry became notorious. Since that time working conditions in the garment factories have improved, primarily through the efforts of the International Ladies' Garment Workers Union and, later, its sister organization, the Amalgamated Clothing and Textiles Workers Union.

According to the US Census Bureau, 1,899,800 workers belonged to unions in 1998. That figure represented nearly 25.4% of the work force; 19.5% of workers in the private manufacturing sector belonged to unions in 1998. Under the Taylor Law, public employees do not have the right to strike. Penalties for striking may be exacted against both the unions and their leaders.

The US Department of Labor reported that in 2002, 1,987,000 of New York's 7,844,000 employed wage and salary workers were members of unions. This represented 25.3% of those so employed, down from 26.4% in 2001. The national average is 13.2%. New York, one of only four states with union membership over 20%, ranked first in the nation in union membership. New York ranked 2nd to California in the largest number of union members. In all, 2,088,000 workers (26.6%) were represented by unions. In addition to union members, this category includes workers who report no union affiliation but whose jobs are covered by a union contract.

23 AGRICULTURE

New York ranked 25th in farm income in 2001, with cash receipts from farming at over $3.4 billion. About 65% came from livestock products, mostly dairy goods. In 2002, the state ranked 2nd in apples, 3rd in the production of corn for silage, 3rd in cauliflower, 3rd in tart cherries, 3rd in snap beans, 7th in onions, and 10th in oats.

Corn was the leading crop for the Indians and for the European settlers of the early colonial period. During the early 1800s, however, wheat was the major crop grown in eastern New York. With the opening of the Erie Canal, western New York (especially the Genesee Valley) became a major wheat-growing center as well. By the late 1850s, when the state's wheat crop began to decline, New York still led the nation in barley, flax, hops, and potato production and was a significant grower of corn and oats. The opening of the railroads took away the state's competitive advantage, but as grain production shifted to the Midwest, the state emerged as a leading supplier of meat and dairy products.

New York remains an important dairy state, but urbanization has reduced its overall agricultural potential. In 1997, 15.6% of the state's land area was devoted to crop growing; in 2002, there were only 37,000 farms, with 7.6 million acres (3.1 million hectares).

The west-central part of the state is the most intensively farmed. Chautauqua County, in the extreme southwest, leads the state in grape production, while Wayne County, along Lake Ontario, leads in apples and cherries. The dairy industry is concentrated in the St. Lawrence Valley; grain growing dominates the plains between Syracuse and Buffalo. Potatoes are grown mostly in Suffolk County, on eastern Long Island.

Leading filed crops in 2002 included Hay, of which 3.7 million tons were produced, worth $374 million; corn, 43.7 million bushels worth $124 million; oats, 3.6 million bushels worth $5.9 million; and wheat, 7.4 million bushels, worth $24.1 million.

Farms in 2002 also produced 138,200 tons of vegetables. Leading vegetable crops were cabbage, onions, sweet corn, and snap beans. State vineyards produced 156,000 tons of grapes for wine and juice in 2002, while the apple crop totaled 650 million lb.

24ANIMAL HUSBANDRY

The St. Lawrence Valley is the state's leading cattle-raising region, followed by the Mohawk Valley and Wyoming County, in western New York. The poultry industry is more widely dispersed. In 2003, an estimated 1.46 million cattle and calves were worth around $1.39 billion. There were an estimated 86,000 hogs and pigs, worth $6 million in 2002. During 2001, around 11 million lb (5 million kg) of chickens were produced, worth $11 million, and 11.1 million lb (5 million kg) of turkey, worth $4.5 million.

New York is a leading dairy state. In 2001, New York was 3rd in the US in milk production with 11.8 million lb (5.3 million kg) of milk from 672,000 milk cows.

Also during 2001, New York farmers produced around 3.8 million lb (1.7 million kg) of sheep and lambs, which brought in around $3.7 million in gross income. The state produced around 1.14 billion eggs, valued at $54 million in 2001. Duck raising is an industry of local importance on Long Island.

25FISHING

Fishing, though an attraction for tourists and sportsmen, plays only a marginal role in the economic life of the state. In 1998, the commercial catch by New York fishers was 57,532,000 lb, less than 1% of the US total and far below the 1880 peak of 335,000,000 lb. The catch was valued at $84,323,000. Important species for commercial use are menhaden and, among shellfish, clams and oysters. Virtually all of New York's commercial fishing takes place in the Atlantic waters off Long Island. Montauk, on the eastern end of Long Island, is the state's leading fishing port.

Pollution and poor wildlife management have seriously endangered the state's commercial and sport fishing in the ocean, rivers, and lakes. Commercial fishing for striped bass in the Hudson River was banned in 1976 because of contamination by polychlorinated biphenyls (PCBs). Commercial fishing in the river for five other species—black crappie, brown bullhead, carp, goldfish, and pumpkinseed—was banned in 1985. Also banned in 1985 was commercial fishing for striped bass in New York Harbor and along both shores of western Long Island.

In recent decades, however, the Department of Environmental Conservation has taken an active role in restocking New York's inland waters. The US Fish and Wildlife Service distributes large numbers of lake trout and Atlantic salmon fingerlings and rainbow and brook trout fry throughout the state.

26FORESTRY

About 61% of New York's surface area is forestland. The most densely forested counties are Hamilton, Essex, and Warren in the Adirondacks, and Delaware, Greene, and Ulster in the Catskills. The total forested area was about 18,432,000 acres (7,459,000 hectares) in 2002, of which 15,389,000 acres (6,228,000 hectares) were classified as commercial forest, meaning they were available for the harvest of wood products such as sawlogs, veneer, and pulpwood or firewood. In 2002, lumber production totaled 464 million board feet.

Finger Lakes National Forest, the only national forest within the state, covered 16,175 acres (6,546 hectares) in 2001. The state Department of Environmental Conservation manages about 3,000,000 acres (1,200,000 hectares) in the Catskills and Adirondacks as Forest Preserves, and an additional 800,000 acres in State Forests and Wildlife Management Areas (where timber harvesting is allowed as part of their management plans).

27MINING

The value of nonfuel mineral production in New York in 2001 was estimated to be $1.05 billion, an increase of 4% from that of 2000. In 2001, crushed stone was New York's leading nonfuel mineral, based on value. About 93% of the total value came from industrial minerals and mineral products, primarily crushed stone, salt, construction sand and gravel, portland cement, and wollastonite. According to preliminary figures, the value of crushed stone in 2001 was $322 million; salt, $224 million; construction sand and gravel, $162 million; and common clays, $7.8 million.

Other commodities produced included masonry cement, garnet, gypsum, peat, industrial sand, dimension stone, talc, and byproduct lead and silver. The combined value of cement, abrasive garnet, crude gypsum, lead, peat, industrial sand and gravel, silver, talc and pyrophyllite, wollastonite, and zinc in 2001 was $94.3 million.

Nationally, the state ranked 14th overall in the value of nonfuel minerals produced. New York was the only state in the nation that produced wollastonite and one of only two states where garnet was mined. Major uses of wollastonite (a type of calcium silicate) are as a filler in ceramic tile, marine wallboard, paint, plastics, and refractory liners in steel mills.

28ENERGY AND POWER

Although New York State's fossil fuel resources are limited, the state ranked 6th in the US in electric power production in 1999. About 16% of the state's annual electric power output came from hydroelectric plants built and operated by the Power Authority of the State of New York. Almost 10% came from oil-fired units, 15% from coal-fired units, 32% from gas-fired units, 26% from nuclear power plants, and about 2% from other sources. Installed capacity (utility and nonutility) in 1999 was 33.7 million kW. Electrical output totaled nearly 144.6 billion kWh. Electric bills for New York City are the highest in the nation, and customers in Buffalo and Rochester also pay above the national median. Sales of public and private electric power totaled 131.8 billion kWh in 1998, of which 40% went to commercial users, 19% to industrial purchasers, 31% to residential users, and 10% for other purposes.

The largest nonfederal hydroelectric plant in the US is the Niagara Power Project, which had a capacity of 2,160,000 kW at the beginning of 1999. The New York side of the St. Lawrence River Power Project had a capacity of 912,000 kW in the same year. Both plants were built and are operated by the Power Authority of the State of New York, which also built and operates a pumped-storage plant in Schoharie County (1,000,000 kW) and a nuclear power plant on Lake Ontario near Oswego (883,000 kW). Other nuclear plants in the state include two reactors at Indian Point (one operated by Consolidated Edison, and one by the State Power Authority), and units operated by the Niagara Mohawk Power Co. and the Rochester Gas and Electric Co. The State Energy Research and Development Authority manages the only commercial nuclear fuel reprocessing plant in the US, at West Valley in Cattaraugus County.

Estimated reserves of petroleum in New York State are much less than 1% of the US total. Oil output in 2002 was 452 barrels per day—also a tiny fraction of the national total. Because New York has a large number of motor vehicles and because more than half of all occupied housing units in the state are heated by oil, the state is a very large net importer of petroleum products.

The state's estimated natural gas reserves as of 2001 were 318 billion cu ft (9 billion cu m); marketed production in the same year totaled 27.8 billion cu ft (0.79 billion cu m). Although the state's natural gas output has risen steadily since 1966, both production and reserves represent only a tiny fraction of US totals.

29INDUSTRY

Until the 1970s, New York was the nation's foremost industrial state, ranking 1st in virtually every general category. However, US Commerce Department data show that by 1975 the state had slipped in manufacturing to 2nd in number of employees, payroll, and value added, 4th in value of shipments of manufactured goods, and 6th in new capital spending. Manufacturing shipments in 1998 totaled $168 billion, or 7th in the nation. Important sectors are instruments and related products, industrial machinery and equipment, electronic and electric equipment, printing and publishing, and textiles.

The Buffalo region, with its excellent transport facilities and abundant power supply, is the main center for heavy industry in the state. Plants in the region manufacture iron and steel, aircraft, automobile parts and accessories, and machinery, as well as flour, animal feed, and various chemicals. The Buffalo area's biggest private industrial employer, Bethlehem Steel, closed its Lackawanna plant in 1983. Republic Steel also closed its plant, and General Motors cut employment at its Tonawanda facility by two-thirds. Light industry is dispersed throughout the state. Rochester is especially well known for its photographic (Kodak) and optical equipment (Bausch & Lomb) and office machines (Xerox); the city is the world headquarters of the Eastman Kodak Co., a world leader in photography with sales of $15.968 billion in 1997. The state's leadership in electronic equipment is in large part attributable to the International Business Machines Corp. (IBM), which was founded in 1911 at Endicott, near Binghamton. In 1997, IBM ranked as the 6th-leading US industrial corporation, with sales of $75.9 billion. Its world headquarters is at Armonk, in Westchester County, and it has important facilities at Endicott, Kingston, and Poughkeepsie. The presence of two large General Electric plants has long made Schenectady a leader in the manufacture of electric machinery.

New York City excels not only in the apparel and publishing trades but also in food processing, meat packing, chemicals, leather goods, metal products, and many other manufactures. In addition, the city serves as headquarters for many large industrial corporations whose manufacturing activities often take place entirely outside New York. In all, 61 Fortune 500 firms had their headquarters in New York State in 1997.

Earnings of persons employed in New York increased from $407.4 billion in 1997 to $432.6 billion in 1998, an increase of 6.2%. The largest industries in 1998 were services, 31.4% of earnings; finance, insurance, and real estate, 20.0%; and state and local government, 12.2%. Of the industries that accounted for at least 5% of earnings in 1998, the slowest growing from 1997 to 1998 was state and local government, which increased 2.3%; the fastest was finance, insurance, and real estate, which increased 9.0%.

30COMMERCE

New York was 2nd in sales from wholesale trade in 1997; the sales from wholesale trade in the New York City metropolitan area (including portions of nearby New Jersey, Connecticut, and Pennsylvania) alone exceeded that of any state. The state ranked 3rd in retail trade, behind California and Texas.

In 1997, state wholesale sales totaled $329 billion, or 10% of the US total. The most valuable categories of goods traded were petroleum and petroleum products, apparel, piece goods and notions, groceries and related products, jewelry, watches, diamonds and other precious stones, woven goods, grain, machinery, equipment and supplies, minerals and metals, and electrical goods. Except for apparel, woven goods, jewelry, and perhaps electrical goods, this list appears to reflect the importance of New York City as a port and transportation center rather than the makeup of state or city industries.

According to the Census of Retail Sales of 1997, 109,098 retail establishments in New York had sales of $149 billion, or 5.9% of the US total. Food stores accounted for 15% of establishments; automotive dealers, 9%; and eating and drinking places, 31%. Food sales added up to $25 billion, and general merchandise sales, $13 billion.

The state's long border with Canada, its important ports on Lakes Erie and Ontario, and its vast harbor on New York Bay ensure it a major role in US foreign trade. About one-quarter of US waterborne imports and exports pass through the New York Customs District (including New York City, Albany, and Newark and Perth Amboy, N.J.). Exports of goods from New York totaled $37 billion in 1998, 4th among the states.

31CONSUMER PROTECTION

The State Consumer Protection Board in the Executive Department was created in 1970, and is headed by an executive director appointed by the governor with the advice and consent of the senate. The CPB is divided into three organizations—the Consumer Assistance Unit, "Do Not Call" Telemarketing Law Investigation and Enforcement Unit, and the Office of Strategic Programs (which in turn is composed of an Outreach and Education Unit, and a Utility Intervention Unit). The board coordinates the activities of all state agencies performing consumer protection functions, represents consumer interests before federal, state, and local bodies (including the Public Service Commission), and encourages consumer education and research, but it has no enforcement powers. These are vested in the Bureau of Consumer Frauds and Protection within the Department of Law, under the direction of the attorney general. The Department of Public Service has regulatory authority over several areas of key interest to consumers, including gas, electric, and telephone rates.

State law outlaws unfair or deceptive trade practices and provides for small-claims courts, where consumers can take action at little cost to themselves. New York licenses and regulates automobile repair services, permits advertising of prescription drug prices, and requires unit pricing. A "cooling-off" period for home purchase contracts is mandated, and standards have been established for mobile-home construction. New York has no-fault automobile insurance. In 1974, the legislature outlawed sex discrimination in banking, credit, and insurance policy transactions; the state's fair-trade law, which allowed price fixing on certain items, was repealed in 1975. The Fair Credit Reporting Act passed in 1977, allows consumers access to their credit bureau files. A 1984 "lemon law" entitles purchasers of defective new cars to repairs, a refund, or a replacement under specified circumstances. A similar law for used cars requires a written warranty for most essential mechanical components.

Extremely influential both within the state and throughout the US is the Consumers Union (CU), established as a nonprofit corporation at Mt. Vernon in 1936. CU derives its income solely from sales of its magazine, Consumer Reports, and other publications. The magazine embraces many consumer interests, but the bulk of each issue consists of product reports on items as varied as stereos and canned chili. Product tests are conducted by CU's own research staff. Ratings of products may not be cited in advertising or used by product manufacturers or distributors for any commercial purpose.

32 BANKING

New York City is the major US banking center. Banking is one of the state's leading industries, ranking first in the US. As of 2002, New York's 212 insured banks held total assets of about $1.58 trillion, and New York led the nation in both assets and deposits.

In 2002, New York's large insured banks (those with assets over $10 billion) reported increases in past-due loan ratios. A deterioration in the corporate lending sector occurred, largely due to exposure to the telecommunications and airline industries. Although smaller community banks (those with assets less than $1 billion) also reported weak credit quality, the average loan delinquency rate was lower than that for large banks.

The Federal Reserve in 2001/02 lowered long-term interest rates to near historic lows, leading to a decline in asset yields. Although short-term interest rates also declined, banks' funding costs were already near historic lows and did not have room to decline further. Therefore, the net interest margin (NIM) (the difference between the lower rates offered to savers and the higher rates charged on loans) was projected to be limited in 2003.

New York has a higher percentage of residential mortgage lenders than the rest of the nation, and its median ratio of long-term assets-to-average earning assets remains above that of the nation.

33 INSURANCE

Like banking, insurance is big business in New York. Three of the ten top US life insurance companies—Metropolitan Life, New York Life, and Equitable Life Assurance—have their headquarters in New York. As of 2000, there were 222 property and casualty and 103 life and health insurance companies incorporated or organized in the state.

Property and liability insurers wrote over $25.2 billion in premiums in 2001. That year, there were 93,859 flood insurance policies in force in the state, with a total value of $14.1 million.

Automobile insurance is compulsory for all owners of motor vehicles in the state. A no-fault system is in effect.

In 2001, New Yorkers held 9.2 million ordinary life insurance policies with a value of $783.4 billion; total value for all categories of life insurance (ordinary, group, industrial, and credit) was $1,296 billion. Death benefits paid that year totaled $3.73 billion.

34 SECURITIES

New York City is the capital of the US securities market. Nearly 6,330 broker-dealers organizations conduct business in the state, with 187,624 employees; 1,172 investment advisory organizations operate in New York. The state is the headquarters for 411 NASDAQ-listed companies, 216 NASDAQ market makers, 92 AMEX-listed companies (over 14% of the nation's total); and is the incorporator of 309 NYSE-listed companies. The top five companies in terms of revenues are: Citigroup, Phillip Morris Companies, AT&T, American International Group, and Texaco.

The New York Stock Exchange (NYSE) is by far the largest organized securities market in the nation and the world; over 50 million individual investors and 10,000 institutional investors buy and sell securities issued by nearly 3,085 companies, including 382 foreign companies. There are about 414 firms with 1,366 seats on the NYSE. The exchange began as an agreement among 24 brokers, known as the Buttonwood Agreement, in 1792; the exchange adopted its first constitution in 1817 and took on its present name in 1863. A clear sign of the growth of the NYSE is the development of its communications system. Stock tickers were first introduced in 1867; a faster ticker, installed in 1930, was capable of printing 500 characters a minute. By 1964, this was no longer fast enough, and a 900-character-a-minute ticker was introduced. Annual registered share volume increased from 1.8 billion in 1965 to 7.6 billion in 1978 following the introduction in 1976 of a new data line capable of handling 36,000 characters a minute. In August 2000, the NYSE switched to a decimal system. The New York Futures Exchange was incorporated in 1979 as a wholly owned subsidiary of the NYSE and began trading in 1980. It also deals in options on futures.

The American Stock Exchange (AMEX) is the 2nd leading US securities floor-based market, but the AMEX ranks far below the NYSE in both volume and value of securities. The AMEX traces its origins to the outdoor trading in unlisted securities that began on Wall and Hanover streets in the 1840s, the exchange was organized as the New York Curb Agency in 1908; the exchange moved indoors, but continued to use the hand signals developed by outdoor traders. The AMEX adopted its current name in 1953. Constitutional changes in 1976 for the first time permitted qualified issues to be traded on both the AMEX and the NYSE as well as on other exchanges. This Intermarket Trading System (ITS) began in 1978. In 1996, the hand signals used in trading on the AMEX for over 100 years were replaced by a computerized communication system. AMEX has 661 regular trading members, and 203 options members.

The National Association of Securities Dealers Automated Quotations (NASDAQ), created in 1971, is a highly active exchange for over-the-counter securities. New York City is also a major center for trading in commodity futures. Leading commodity exchanges are the New York Coffee and Sugar Exchange; the New York Cocoa Exchange; the New York Cotton Exchange; the Commodity Exchange, Inc. (COMEX), specializing in gold, silver, and copper futures; and the New York Mercantile Exchange, which trades in futures for potatoes, platinum, palladium, silver coins, beef, and gold, among other items. Bonds may be issued in New York by cities, counties, towns, villages, school districts, and fire districts, as well as by quasi-independent authorities.

35 PUBLIC FINANCE

New York State has the 2nd-largest budget (behind California) of all states in the US. The New York State budget is prepared by the Division of the Budget and submitted annually by the governor to the legislature for amendment and approval. The fiscal year runs from 1 April to 31 March.

The 2000/01 state budget announced tax cuts of $6.8 billion over a period of five years (adding to a cumulative total, including previously enacted tax cuts, to more than $100 billion over the same time period), while attacking the state debt and increasing reserves. The 2000/01 budget included more than 30 tax cuts totaling nearly $1.4 billion in new tax relief, including the elimination of taxes on energy for industry and business, a college tuition deduction, and the elimination of the sales tax on the transmission and distribution of gas and electricity for commercial customers. In 2002/03, however, much of this had to be reversed. Fiscal 2002, a turbulent year financially for most states, presented New York with particularly serious challenges as it was impacted by the collapse of the stock market boom, the national recession, the trauma of 9/11, and on-going problems in the financial services sector. To help close the budget gap that emerged in 2001/02 from lower-than-expected revenues and increased costs, $578 million in cuts were made in the budget after it was enacted. New York also raised its sales tax rate (from 4% to 4.5%), raised taxes on cigarettes and gasoline, increased a number of fees (projected to produce additional revenue of $435.4 million in 2002/03, and $471.6 million in 2003/04), made spending cuts, instituted a hiring freeze and early retirement programs to cut the number of state personnel, and made a number of administrative adjustments to save money, including restructuring the state's debt to take advantage of lowered interest rates, and made other administrative adjustments to save money. The government also secured the future proceeds from the New York's share of the tobacco settlement, estimated to raise $3.8 billion in revenues for 2003/04. In 2002/03, the state budget deficit was estimated at $2.5 billion (about 6.3% of total expenditures), and for 2003/04, the budget deficit was projected at $7 to $10 billion (17% to 24.3% of total expenditures) In the enacted state budget for 2003-04, General Fund disbursements totaled $40.84 billion, up$1.32 billion or 3.4% from 2001/02-03. Decreases in expenditures for state operations and higher education were more than offset by increases for Medicaid, welfare, public health, pensions and insurance. The largest appropriations were for school aid (30.1%); state operations (17.6%); Medicaid (15.4%); general state charges (7.8%); higher education (3.6%); handicapped/other education (3.2%); welfare (2.8%); and public health (1.4%). The General Fund constitutes approximately 41% of all state disbursements, and receives almost all state taxes and other resources not specifically dedicated to other purposes. For 2003-04, 68% of the enacted General Fund budget was for local assistance, 18% for state operations, 8% for general state charges, 4% for debt service, and 2% for capital projects and other expenditures.

The following table from the US Census Bureau contains information on revenues, expenditures, indebtedness, and cash/securities for 2001.

	($000)	PERCENT	PER CAPITA
Population (thousands, 2001)	19,084	(X)	(X)
Total Revenue	112,438,570	100.00	5,891.77
General revenue	91,801,777	81.65	4,810.41
Utility revenue	2,985,298	2.66	156.43
Liquor store revenue	–	–	–
Insurance trust revenue	17,651,495	15.70	924.94
Exhibit: Salaries and wages	12,005,091	11.26	629.07
Total expenditure	106,598,603	100.00	5,585.76
General expenditure	89,236,585	83.71	4,675.99
Education	23,568,538	22.11	1,234.99
Public welfare	32,220,931	30.23	1,688.37
Hospitals	3,281,523	3.08	171.95
Health	4,249,606	3.99	222.68
Highways	3,437,042	3.22	180.10
Police protection	496,925	0.47	26.04
Correction	2,566,911	2.41	134.51
Natural resources	427,800	0.40	22.42
Parks and recreation	535,208	0.50	28.04

	($000)	PERCENT	PER CAPITA
General expenditure (continued)			
Government administration	3,928,341	3.69	205.84
Interest on general debt	3,684,100	3.46	193.05
Other and unallocable	10,839,660	10.17	568.00
Utility expenditure	6,142,983	5.76	321.89
Liquor store expenditure	–	–	–
Insurance trust expenditure	11,219,035	10.52	587.88
Debt at end of fiscal year	80,384,892	100.00	4,212.16
Cash and security holdings	221,202,888	100.00	11,591.01

36 TAXATION

In terms of combined state and local taxes as a percent of income, New York, at 12.2% in 2003, is 2nd only to Maine in the US. Personal income tax is the state's largest source of revenue. The five-bracket personal income tax schedule ranges from 4% to 6.85%. The basic corporate tax is 9% on net income, but only 6.85% for businesses with net income under $200,000. Effective 1 June 2003, New York's general sales tax rate was raised to 4.5% from 4%. Local governments impose additional sales taxes ranging from none to 4.25%. The state also imposes a full array of excise taxes covering motor fuels, tobacco products, insurance premiums, public utilities, alcoholic beverages, amusements, pari-mutuels, and other selected items. In 2002 New York increased both its gas tax (from 8 cents a gallon to 32.35 cents a gallon) and its cigarette tax (from $1.11 to $1.50 a pack). There is no inheritance tax and New York's estate tax is tied to the federal tax exemption for state death taxes. In 2002, death and gift taxes accounted for 1.8% of total state taxes collected. Other state taxes include license fees and stamp taxes. There are no state property taxes, which are all collected locally. The state collects less than half (45.6% in 2000) of total non-federal taxes paid in New York.

The state collected $19.158 billion in taxes in 2002, of which 59.1% came from individual income taxes, 19.9% came from the general sales tax, 10.4% from selective sales taxes, 5.2% from corporate income taxes, and 2.4% from license fees.

The following table from the US Census Bureau provides a summary of taxes collected by the state in 2002.

	($000)	PER CAPITA
Total Taxes	43,262,137	2,258.23
Property taxes	(X)	(X)
Sales and gross receipts	13,120,783	684.89
General sales and gross receipts	8,607,718	449.31
Selective sales taxes	4,513,065	235.58
Alcoholic beverage	177,991	9.29
Amusements	673	0.04
Insurance Premiums	585,444	30.56
Motor fuels	492,185	25.69
Pari-mutuels	38,034	1.99
Public utilities	1,154,612	60.27
Tobacco products	1,010,949	52.77
Other selective sales	1,053,177	54.97
Licenses	1,040,091	54.29
Alcoholic beverages	31,985	1.67
Amusements	201	0.01
Corporation	66,287	3.46
Hunting and fishing	33,627	1.76
Motor vehicle	661,059	34.51
Motor vehicle operators	106,169	5.54
Public utility	22,044	1.15
Occupation and business, NEC	112,761	5.89
Other	5,958	0.31
Other taxes	29,101,263	1,519.05
Individual income	25,573,667	1,334.91
Corporation net income	2,257,935	117.86
Death and gift	767,689	40.07
Documentary and stock transfer	501,972	26.2
Severance	(X)	(X)
Other	(X)	(X)

[37]ECONOMIC POLICY

New York has created a number of incentives for business to foster new jobs and encourage economic prosperity. Among these are government-owned industrial park sites, state aid in the creation of county and city master plans, state recruitment and screening of industrial employees, programs for the promotion of research and development, and state help in bidding on federal procurement contracts. Through Empire State Development (ESD), New York State provides a full range of technical assistance. Representatives of the Division of International Commerce call on firms in Canada, Asia, and Europe; the division maintains offices in London, Tokyo, Montreal, Toronto, and Frankfurt, Germany. The Strategic Business Division, through its ten regional offices, encourages the retention and expansion of existing facilities and the attraction of new job-creating investments. Other divisions aid small business and minority and women's business.

The state administers a number of financial programs to attract or retain businesses. Among these are low interest loans and grants for small businesses or for firms that create substantial numbers of jobs; grants and low cost loans for the development of industrial parks; and working capital loans to help companies at risk of downsizing. The state awards both grants and loans to manufacturing companies to encourage productivity improvements and modernization. It also seeks to encourage economic development in distressed rural communities with low interest loans for small businesses located in such areas. To promote technological innovation, the state provides debt and equity financing for technology based start-up companies.

In June 2002, the ESD announced that to assist businesses affected by the World Trade Center (WTC) tragedy, it was implementing a Community Development Block Grant (CDBG) program with funds provided by the federal government. The funds were to be made available in the form of loans and grants to affected businesses that committed to job retention, job creation and investment in New York City, with priority on Lower Manhattan. Other WTC assistance programs of the ESD included a Disaster Assistance Program for Individuals, Disaster Recovery Resources for Small Businesses, Liberty Zone Tax Benefits, a New York Liberty Bond Program, and the World Trade Center Relief Fund. The Lower Manhattan Development Corporation (LMDC), created after 9/11, was charged with planning and coordinating the rebuilding and revitalization of lower Manhattan.

[38]HEALTH

Health presents a mixed picture in New York State. The state has some of the finest hospital and medical education facilities in the US, but it also has large numbers of the needy with serious health problems.

The infant death rate stood at 6.4 per 1,000 live births in 2000, below the national rate of 6.9. New York State was one of the first states to liberalize its abortion laws, in 1970. A total of 137,234 legal abortions were performed in the state in 1999, most of which were in New York City. The 1997 state ratio of 34 legal abortions per 1,000 women was higher than that of any other state except California.

The overall death rate of 865.5 per 100,000 residents in 2000 was slightly below the national average of 873.1. The state ranks above the national average rates in deaths due to heart disease and malignant neoplasms (cancer), but below the national average in deaths due to cerebrovascular diseases, suicide, and accidents. Major causes of death in 2000 (with their rates per 100,000 population) included heart disease, 314.4; cancer, 203.5; cerebrovascular diseases, 43.8; accidents and adverse effects, 23.2; and suicide, 6.2. In 2000, New York had the lowest suicide rate compared to the national rate of 10.7. The HIV-related death rate was 12.2 per 100,000 residents in 2000, significantly higher than the national rate of 5.3; a total of 149,341 AIDS cases had been reported through 2001, more than in any other state. Among adults ages 18 and older, 21.6% were smokers in 2000.

Major public health issues in the 1990s included emerging infections, such as multidrug-resistant TB; chronic diseases, such as those related to smoking; HIV/AIDS; violent and abusive behavior; and the care of vulnerable populations.

New York's 212 community hospitals had 2,410,906 admissions and 67,296 beds in 2001. There were 73,234 full-time registered nurses and 8,580 full-time licensed practical nurses in 2001 and 409 physicians per 100,000 population in 2000. The average expense of a community hospital for care was $1,807 per inpatient day in 2001.

Federal government grants to cover the Medicare and Medicaid services in 2001 totaled $16.7 billion; 2,728,967 enrollees received Medicare benefits that year. At least 15.5% of New York's residents were uninsured in 2002.

[39]SOCIAL WELFARE

A 1938 New York constitutional provision mandated that the care and support of the needy shall be a state concern. Social welfare is a major public enterprise in the state; the growth of poverty relief programs has been enormous. In 2001, the average weekly unemployment benefit was $271.18. Average monthly participation in the food stamp program in FY2002 comprised 1,346,644 persons (685,572 households). The average monthly benefit was $91.50, and the sum total of benefits paid in FY2002 was $1,478,662,757.

With the enactment of the Personal Responsibility and Work Opportunity Reconciliation Act of 1996, the US government has changed the form and regulations for many of its social welfare programs. Most significantly, it replaces Aid to Families with Dependent Children (AFDC), an open-ended entitlement program, with Temporary Assistance for Needy Families (TANF), a limited system of assistance funded largely through federal block grants. The reform act also impacts the food stamp program, the Supplemental Security Income program, and the child nutrition program. The law took effect on 1 July 1997 and provided $16.38 billion in block grants for fiscal years 1997–2002. The grants are to be divided among the states based on an equation involving the numbers of former AFDC recipients in each state.

Reauthorization of the 1996 social welfare legislation, scheduled for 2002, was delayed, and the original law had been extended three times as of July 2003, with the most recent extension running through September 2003. New York's TANF program is called the Family Assistance Program (FA). In June 2000 the state had 693,012 welfare recipients. State expenditures on the TANF program in FY2002 totaled $1,174,803,344.

In December 2001, Social Security benefits were paid to 3,014,910 New York residents. This number included 1,965,790 retired workers, 295,210 widows and widowers, 345,880 disabled workers, 158,460 spouses, and 249,570 children. Social Security beneficiaries represented 15.9% of the total state population and 89.5% of the state's population age 65 and older. Retired workers (excluding persons with special benefits) received an average monthly payment of $928; widows and widowers, $868; disabled workers, $862; and spouses, $447. Payments for children of retired workers averaged $434 per month; children of deceased workers, $599; and children of disabled workers, $247.

Federal Supplemental Security Income payments in December 2001 went to 622,764 New York residents, averaging $435 a month.

⁴⁰HOUSING

In 2002, the state had an estimated 7,754,508 housing units, of which 7,060,516 were occupied. An estimated 3,223,004 units, or 41.5%, are located in New York City (NYC). The housing stock in New York is relatively old. About 33% of all units in the state were built before or during 1939; 51% were built between 1940 and 1979. In NYC, 70% of all housing units were built before 1960; in Buffalo, 75% of all units were built before 1939.

Statewide in 2002, 41.9% of all units were single-family, detached homes. In NYC, however, only 10% were single, detached units; 47.7% of the city's housing units are located in buildings of 20 units or more. Housing differences in New York City offer far greater contrasts than units per structure: the posh apartment houses of Manhattan and the hovels of the South Bronx both count as multi-unit dwellings. New York State had the 2nd-lowest percentage of owner-occupied housing in the country, at 53.8% in 2002 (only the District of Columbia was lower). Characteristic of housing in New York is a system of rent controls that began in 1943. It was estimated that 137,919 units in NYC lacked telephone service, 17,901 lacked complete plumbing facilities, and 22,711 lacked complete kitchen facilities. These figures represent roughly half of the statewide total.

The tight housing market—which may have contributed to the exodus of New Yorkers from the state—was not helped by the slump in housing construction from the mid-1970s to the mid-1980s. In New York City, more units were demolished than built every year from 1974 to 1981. The drop in construction of multi-unit dwellings was even more noticeable: from 64,959 units in 1972 to 11,740 units in 1982. In 1993, only 7,723 multi-unit dwellings were authorized. The overall decline in construction was coupled with a drastic drop in new public housing. In 1972, permits were issued for 111,282 units valued at $2.1 billion. By 1975, however, only 32,623 units worth $756 million were authorized; in 1982 there were only 25,280 units worth $1.1 billion, and in 1996, 34,895 units valued at $3.1 billion were authorized. In 1998, numbers were on the rebound with 38,400 new privately owned housing units.

In 2002, 49,149 new privately owned housing units were authorized for construction. The median home value for the state was $176,438, 9th in the country. The median home value in NYC was $277,237. The median monthly cost for mortgage owners statewide was $1,411; renters paid a median of $727 per month. In NYC, the median monthly cost for mortgage owners was $1,695; renters paid a median of $771 per month.

Direct state aid for housing is limited. Governmental and quasi-independent agencies dealing with housing include the following: the Division of Housing and Community Renewal of the Executive Department, which makes loans and grants to municipalities for slum clearance and construction of low-income housing, supervises the operation of more than 400 housing developments, and administers rent-control and rent-stabilization laws; the New York State Housing Finance Agency, which is empowered to issue notes and bonds for various construction projects, not limited to housing; the State of New York Mortgage Agency, which may purchase existing mortgage loans from banks in order to make funds available for the banks to make new mortgage loans, and which also offers mortgage insurance; and the New York State Urban Development Corporation (UDC), a multibillion dollar agency designed to raise capital for all types of construction, including low-income housing. During 2002, New York received more than $657.8 million in community planning and development aid from the US Department of Housing and Urban Development.

⁴¹EDUCATION

The Board of Regents and the State Education Department govern education from pre-kindergarten to graduate school. They are constitutionally responsible for setting educational policy, standards, and rules and legally required to ensure that the entities they oversee carry them out. The board and department also provide vocational and educational services to people with disabilities.

In 2000, 79.1% of New Yorkers age 25 and older were high school graduates. Some 27.4% had obtained a bachelor's degree or higher.

The total enrollment for fall 1999 in New York's public schools stood at 2,887,776. Of these, 2,33,748 attended schools from kindergarten through grade eight, and 854,028 attended high school. Minority students made up approximately 45% of the total enrollment in public elementary and secondary schools in 2001. Total enrollment was estimated at 2,940,000 in fall 2000 and is expected to reach 2,961,000 by fall 2005. Expenditures for public education in 2000/01 were estimated at $29,209,562. Enrollment in nonpublic schools in fall 2001 was 475,942.

As of fall 2000, there were 1,301,375 students enrolled in institutions of higher education. In the same year New York had 325 degree-granting institutions. In 2000 New York had 44 public two-year institutions. In 1997, minority students comprised 32.1% of total postsecondary enrollment.

There are two massive public university systems: the State University of New York (SUNY) and the City University of New York (CUNY). Established in 1948, SUNY is one of the largest university systems in the country and encompasses university colleges of arts and sciences, specialized colleges, agricultural and technical colleges, statutory colleges (allied with private universities), health sciences centers, and locally sponsored community colleges. University centers include Buffalo, Albany, and Binghamton. The City University of New York was created in 1961, although many of its component institutions (including 12 four-year institutions) were founded much earlier. Under an open-enrollment policy adopted in 1970, every New York City resident with a high school diploma is guaranteed the chance to earn a college degree within the CUNY system (which CUNY campus the student attends is determined by grade point average).

The oldest private university in the state is Columbia University, founded in New York City as Kings College in 1754. Also part of Columbia are Barnard College (all women) and Columbia University Teachers College. Other major private institutions are Cornell University in Ithaca (1865); Fordham University in Manhattan and the Bronx (1841); New York University in Manhattan (1831); Rensselaer Polytechnic Institute in Troy (1824); St. John's University in Queens (1870); Syracuse University (1870); and the University of Rochester (1850). Among the state's many smaller but highly distinguished institutions are Hamilton College, the Juilliard School, the New School for Social Research, Rockefeller University, Sarah Lawrence College, Vassar College, and Yeshiva University.

Unique features of education in New York are the "Regents exams," uniform subject examinations administered to all high school students, and the Regents Scholarships Tuition Assistance Program (TAP), a higher-education aid program. The state passed a "truth in testing" law in 1979, giving students the right to see their graded college and graduate school entrance examinations, as well as information on how the test results were validated.

⁴²ARTS

New York City is the cultural capital of the state, and leads the nation in both the creative and the performing arts. The state's foremost arts center is Lincoln Center for the Performing Arts, in Manhattan. Facilities at Lincoln Center include Avery Fisher Hall (which opened as Philharmonic Hall in 1962), the home of the New York Philharmonic; the Metropolitan Opera House (1966), where the Metropolitan Opera Company performs; and the New York State Theater, which presents both the New York City Opera and the New York City Ballet. Also at Lincoln Center are the Julliard School and the Library and Museum of the Performing Arts. The best-known arts center outside New York City is the Saratoga Performing Arts Center at Saratoga Springs. During the summer, the Saratoga Center presents performances by the New York City Ballet and the Philadelphia Orchestra. Artpark, a state park at Lewiston, has a 2,324-seat theater for operas and musicals, and offers art exhibits during the summer. Classical music, opera, and plays are performed at the Chautauqua Festival, which has been held every summer since 1874.

In 2003, the New York State Council on the Arts and other New York arts organizations received grants totaling over $15 million from the National Endowment for the Arts. The Council on the Arts also receives funding from the state as well as contributions from private sources. Audiences for the state's arts programs total well over 200 million, and there are more than 1.5 million contributing artists. The state offers arts education programs to about one million schoolchildren. The state of New York has approximately 2,000 arts associations and 90 local art groups. The New York State Council on the Arts contributed to the Arts Connection of New York City and to the National Book Foundation.

The New York Council for the Humanities was established in 1975. In 2000, the National Endowment for the Humanities contributed over $12 million to 140 state programs.

In addition to its many museums, New York City has more than 350 galleries devoted to the visual and plastic arts. The city's most famous artists' district is Greenwich Village, which still holds an annual outdoor art show, although after the 1950s many artists moved to SoHo (Manhattan on the West Side between Canal and Houston Streets), NoHo (immediately north of Houston Street), the East Village, and Tribeca (between Canal Street and the World Trade Center). By the early 1980s, artists seeking space at reasonable prices were moving to Long Island City in Queens, to areas of Brooklyn, or out of the city entirely, to places such as Hoboken and Paterson in New Jersey. During the late 1940s and early 1950s, abstract painters—including Jackson Pollock, Mark Rothko, and Willem de Kooning—helped make the city a center of the avant garde.

At the same time, poets such as Frank O'Hara and John Ashbery sought verbal analogues to developments in the visual arts, and an urbane, improvisatory literature was created. New York has enjoyed a vigorous poetic tradition throughout its history, most notably with the works of Walt Whitman (who served as editor of the Brooklyn Eagle from 1846 to 1848) and through Hart Crane's mythic vision of the city in his long poem The Bridge. The emergence of New York as the center of the US publishing and communications industries fostered the growth of a literary marketplace, attracting writers from across the country and the world. Early New York novelists included Washington Irving, Edgar Allan Poe, and Herman Melville; among the many who made their home in the city in the 20th century were Thomas Wolfe and Norman Mailer. The simultaneous growth of the Broadway stage made New York City a vital forum for playwriting, songwriting, and theatrical production.

There are more than 35 Broadway theaters—large theaters in midtown Manhattan presenting full-scale, sometimes lavish productions with top-rank performers. "Off Broadway" productions are often of high professional quality, though typically in smaller theaters, outside the midtown district, often with smaller casts and less costly settings. "Off-Off Broadway" productions range from small experimental theaters on the fringes of the city to performances in nightclubs and cabarets. The New York metropolitan area has hundreds of motion picture theaters—more than 65 in Manhattan alone, not counting special series at the Museum of Modern Art and other cultural institutions. In the 1970s, New York City made a determined and successful effort to attract motion picture production companies.

New York's leading symphony orchestra is the New York Philharmonic, whose history dates back to the founding of the Philharmonic Society of New York in 1842. Among the principal conductors of the orchestra have been Gustav Mahler, Josef Willem Mengelberg, Wilhelm Furtwangler, Arturo Toscanini, Leonard Bernstein, Pierre Boulez, Zubin Mehta, and Kurt Masur. Leading US and foreign orchestras and soloists appear at both Avery Fisher Hall and Carnegie Hall, built in 1892 and famed for its acoustics. In 2003 the New York Philharmonic announced that it would leave Lincoln Center and move back to Carnegie Hall sometime during or after 2005. Important orchestras outside New York City include the Buffalo Philharmonic, which performs at Kleinhans Music Hall, the Rochester Philharmonic, and the Eastman Philharmonia, the orchestra of the Eastman School of Music (University of Rochester).

New York City is one of the world centers of ballet. Of special renown is the New York City Ballet, whose principal choreographer until his death in 1983 was George Balanchine. Many other ballet companies, including the American Ballet Theatre and the Alvin Ailey American Dance Theatre, make regular appearances in New York. Rochester, Syracuse, Cooperstown, Chautauqua, and Binghamton have opera companies, and Lake George has an opera festival. Jazz and popular artists perform at more than 60 nightspots in New York City. The Westbury Music Fair (Long Island) presents a wide-ranging annual program of musical entertainment, and resorts in the Catskills offer both music and comedy to their patrons. New York City is a major link in the US songwriting, music publishing, and recording industries.

43 LIBRARIES AND MUSEUMS

New York State has three of the world's largest libraries, and New York City has several of the world's most famous museums. The New York State Library in Albany coordinates 23 public library systems covering every county in the state in 2000, with book holdings of 71,776,093 volumes and a combined circulation of 122,147,000 volumes. The public libraries received $834,402,000 during that year (the most of any state), of which $6,675,216 came from the federal government, $50,064,120 from the state government, and the rest from local sources. Per capita spending was $42.54, the 2nd-highest rate in the country.

The leading public library systems and their operating statistics as of 1999 were the New York Public Library, 17,762,034 volumes in 127 branches; Brooklyn Public Library, 6,800,000 volumes and 10,077,559 circulation; Queens Borough Public Library, 8,668,948 volumes and 14,829,837 circulation; and Buffalo and Erie County system, 5,240,965 volumes and 8,734,854 circulation.

Chartered in 1895, the New York Public Library (NYPL) is the most complete municipal library system in the world. The library's main branch, at 5th Avenue and 42nd Street, is one of the city's best-known landmarks; serving the needs of Manhattan, the Bronx, and Staten Island. The NYPL is a repository for every book published in the US. The NYPL also operates the Library and Museum of the Performing Arts at Lincoln Center; the Schomburg Center for Research in Black Culture; and the Science, Industry, and Business Library that opened in May 1996.

Two private university libraries—at Columbia University (7,018,408 volumes in 1999) and Cornell University (6,617,242)—rank among the world's major libraries. Other major university libraries in the state, with their 1999 book holdings, are Syracuse University, 2,650,995; New York University, 2,987,062; the State University of New York at Buffalo, 2,534,500; and the University of Rochester, 2,446,729.

There are about 671 museums in New York State; about 150 are major museums, of which perhaps 80% are in New York City. In addition, some 579 sites of historic importance are maintained by local historical societies. Major art museums in New York City include the Metropolitan Museum of Art, with more than one million art objects and paintings from virtually every period and culture; the Cloisters, a branch of the Metropolitan Museum devoted entirely to medieval art and architecture; the Frick collection; the Whitney Museum of American Art; the Brooklyn Museum; and two large modern collections, the Museum of Modern Art and the Solomon R. Guggenheim Museum (the latter designed by Frank Lloyd Wright in a distinctive spiral pattern). The Jewish Museum, the Museum of the American Indian, and the museum and reference library of the Hispanic Society of America specialize in cultural history.

The sciences are represented by the American Museum of Natural History, famed for its dioramas of humans and animals in natural settings and for its massive dinosaur skeletons; the Hayden Planetarium; the New York Botanical Garden and New York Zoological Society Park (Bronx Zoo), both in the Bronx. Also of interest are the Museum of the City of New York, the Museum of the New-York Historical Society, the South Street Seaport Museum, and the New York Aquarium.

The New York State Museum in Albany contains natural history collections and historical artifacts. Buffalo has several museums of note, including the Albright-Knox Art Gallery (for contemporary art), the Buffalo Museum of Science, and the Buffalo and Erie County Historical Society museum.

Among the state's many other fine museums, the Everson Museum of Art (Syracuse), the Rochester Museum and Science Center, the National Baseball Hall of Fame and Museum (Cooperstown), and the Corning Museum of Glass deserve special mention. Buffalo, New Rochelle, Rochester, Syracuse, and Utica have zoos.

44COMMUNICATIONS

New York City is the hub of the entire US communications network. Postal service was established in New York State in 1692; at the same time, the first General Letter Office was begun in New York City. By the mid-19th century, postal receipts in the state accounted for more than 20% of the US total. "Fast mail" service by train started in the 1870s, with the main routes leading from New York City to either Chicago or St. Louis via Indianapolis and Cincinnati. Mail was carried by air experimentally from Garden City to Mineola, Long Island, in 1911; the first regular airmail service in the US started in 1917, between New York City and Washington, D.C., via Philadelphia.

Telephone service in New York is provided primarily by the New York Telephone Co., but also by more than 40 smaller companies throughout the state. As of 2001, 94.9% of New York's occupied housing units had telephones.

Until 31 December 1983, New York Telephone was part of the Bell System, whose parent organization was the American Telephone and Telegraph Co. (AT&T). Effective 1 January 1984, as the result of a US Justice Department antitrust suit, AT&T divested itself of 22 Bell operating companies, which regrouped into seven independent regional telephone companies to provide local telephone service in the US. One of these companies, NYNEX, is the parent company of New York Telephone. AT&T, which continued to supply long-distance telephone services to New Yorkers (along with competitive carriers such as MCI, ITT, and GTE), is headquartered in New York City.

Domestic telegraph service is provided by the Western Union Telegraph Co., ITT World Communications, RCA Global Communications, and Western Union International. All four companies have their headquarters in New York City. New York State had 57 major AM stations and 180 major FM stations operating in 2003. New York City operates its own radio stations, WNYC-AM and FM, devoted largely to classical music and educational programming. There were 46 major television stations in the state in 2003. The city is the headquarters for most of the major US television networks, including the American Broadcasting Co. (now part of Walt Disney Corp.), Columbia Broadcasting System (owned by the Westinghouse Corp.), National Broadcasting Co. (owned by General Electric), Westinghouse Broadcasting (Group W), Metromedia, and the Public Broadcasting Service (PBS). The metropolitan area's PBS affiliate, WNET (licensed in Newark, N.J.), is a leading producer of programs for the PBS network. As of 2000, the New York metropolitan area had 6,874,990 television households, 74% of which received cable. The Buffalo region had 621,460 television homes, with a 77% cable penetration rate.

A total of 589,963 Internet domain names were registered in the state in the year 2000; the 2nd-highest number of all states.

45PRESS

A pioneer in the establishment of freedom of the press, New York is the leader of the US newspaper, magazine, and book-publishing industries. The first major test of press freedom in the colonies came in 1734, when a German-American printer, John Peter Zenger, was arrested on charges of sedition and libel. In his newspaper, the *New-York Weekly Journal*, Zenger had published articles criticizing the colonial governor of New York. Zenger's lawyer, Andrew Hamilton, argued that because the charges in the article were true, they could not be libelous. The jury's acceptance of this argument freed Zenger and established the right of the press to criticize those in power. Two late decisions involving a New York newspaper also struck blows for press freedom. In *New York Times v. Sullivan* (1964), the US Supreme Court ruled that a public official could not win a libel suit against a newspaper unless he could show that its statements about him were not only false but also malicious or in reckless disregard of the truth. In 1971, the *New York Times* was again involved in a landmark case when the federal government tried—and failed—to prevent the newspaper from publishing the Pentagon Papers, a collection of secret documents concerning the war in Vietnam.

All of New York City's major newspapers have claims to fame. The *Times* is the nation's "newspaper of record," excelling in the publication of speeches, press conferences, and government reports. It is widely circulated to US libraries and is often cited in research. In 2001, the *Times* Sunday edition was the number one Sunday newspaper in the nation, based on circulation figures. The *New York Post*, founded in 1801, is the oldest US newspaper published continuously without change of name. The *Wall Street Journal*, published Monday through Friday, is a truly national paper, presenting mostly business news in four regional editions. In 2001, the *Wall Street Journal*, the *Times*, the New York *Daily News*, the Long Island *Newsday*, and the *Post* were among the top ten largest daily newspapers in the nation. Many historic New York papers first merged and then—bearing compound names like the *Herald-Tribune*, *Journal-American*, and *World-Telegram & Sun*—died in the 1950s and 1960s. In 2001, the Syracuse *Herald-American* and *Herald-Journal* merged to form the *Post-Standard*

In 2002, New York had 35 morning newspapers, 24 evening papers, and 37 Sunday editions. The following table shows leading papers in New York, with their average daily and Sunday circulations in 2002:

AREA	NAME	DAILY	SUNDAY
Albany	*Times–Union* (m,S)	98,543	145,299
Buffalo	*News* (all day,S)	218,781	304,434
Long Island	*Newsday*(m,S)	577,354	675,619
New York City	*Daily News* (m,S)	734,473	802,215
	Post (m,S)	533,860	401,365
	Times (m,S)	1,109,371	1,668,650
	Wall Street Journal	1,780,605	
Rochester	*Democrat and Chronicle*(m,S)	176,040	238,888
Syracuse	*Post-Standard* (m,S)	126,761	180,624

There are two Spanish dailies published in New York City: *El Diario La Prensa,* with a circulation of 56,938 daily and 36,758 Sundays; and *Hoy,* with a circulation of 65,768 daily and 21,567 Sundays. The leading newspaper chain is the Gannett Co., Inc. (headquarters in Virginia). Other groups include Ogden Newspapers, Inc. (West Virginia), Hearst Newspapers (New York), and Johnson Newspaper Corp. (New York). All the major news agencies have offices in New York City, and the Associated Press has its headquarters there.

Many leading US magazines are published in New York City, including the newsmagazines *Time* and *Newsweek,* business journals like *Fortune, Forbes,* and *Business Week,* and hundreds of consumer and trade publications. *Reader's Digest* is published in Pleasantville. Two weeklies closely identified with New York are of more than local interest. While the *New Yorker* carries up-to-date listings of cultural events and exhibitions in New York City, the excellence of its journalism, criticism, fiction, and cartoons has long made it a literary standard-bearer for the entire nation. *New York* magazine influenced the writing style and graphic design of the 1960s and set the pattern for a new wave of state and local magazines that avoided boosterism in favor of independent reporting and commentary. Another weekly, the *Village Voice* (actually a tabloid newspaper), became the prototype for a host of alternative or "underground" journals during the 1960s.

New York City is also the center of the nation's book-publishing industry. New York publishers include McGraw–Hill, Macmillan, Simon & Schuster, and Random House; many book publishers are subsidiaries of other companies.

46 ORGANIZATIONS

In 2003, there were over 8,076 regional, national, and international organizations within the state.

The United Nations is the best-known organization to have its headquarters in New York. The UN Secretariat, completed in 1951, remains one of the most familiar landmarks of New York City. Hundreds of US nonprofit organizations also have their national headquarters in New York City. General and service organizations operating out of New York City include the American Field Service, Boys Clubs of America, Girls Clubs of America, Girl Scouts of the USA, Young Women's Christian Associations of the USA (YWCA), and Associated YM-YWHAs of Greater New York (the Jewish equivalent of the YMCA and YWCA).

Among the cultural and educational groups of national interest are the American Academy of Arts and Letters, Authors League of America, Children's Book Council, Modern Language Association of America, and PEN American Center. State organizations include the Folk Music Society of New York, the New York Center for Books and Reading, the New York Academy of Sciences, the New York Drama Critics Circle, and the New York State Historical. The Statue of Liberty–Ellis Island Foundation sponsors educational programs as well as maintaining the monument and museum. There are numerous

local musical and theater groups. There are also several regional historical societies.

Among the national environmental and animal welfare organizations with headquarters in the city are the American Society for the Prevention of Cruelty to Animals (ASPCA), Friends of Animals, Fund for Animals, National Audubon Society, Bide-A-Wee Home Association, Environmental Defense Fund, and American Kennel Club. State groups include the New York City Community Garden Coalition, the New York Conservation Foundation, and the New York State Conservation Council.

Many medical, health, and charitable organizations have their national offices in New York City, including Alcoholics Anonymous, American Foundation for the Blind, National Society to Prevent Blindness, CARE, American Cancer Society, United Cerebral Palsy Associations, Child Welfare League of America, American Diabetes Association, National Multiple Sclerosis Society, Muscular Dystrophy Association, and Planned Parenthood Federation of America.

Leading ethnic and religious organizations based in the city include the American Bible Society, National Conference of Christians and Jews, Hadassah, United Jewish Appeal, American Jewish Committee, American Jewish Congress, National Association for the Advancement of Colored People (NAACP), United Negro College Fund, Congress of Racial Equality, and National Urban League.

There are many commercial, trade, and professional organizations headquartered in New York City. Among the better known are the Actors' Equity Association, American Arbitration Association, American Booksellers Association, American Federation of Musicians, American Institute of Chemical Engineers, American Society of Civil Engineers, American Society of Composers, Authors, and Publishers (ASCAP), American Society of Journalists and Authors, American Insurance Association, Magazine Publishers Association, American Management Associations, American Society of Mechanical Engineers, and American Institute of Physics.

Sports organizations centered in New York City include the National Football League, the American and the National Leagues of Professional Baseball Clubs, National Basketball Association, and the US Tennis Association.

Influential political and international affairs groups include the American Civil Liberties Union, Council on Foreign Relations, Trilateral Commission, United Nations Association of the USA, and US Committee for UNICEF.

Major organizations with their headquarters outside New York City include the Consumers Union of the United States (Mt. Vernon), US Chess Federation (New Windsor), and the Thoroughbred Racing Association (Lake Success). Virtually every other major US organization has one or more chapters within the state.

47 TOURISM, TRAVEL, AND RECREATION

New York City is the primary travel destination in the state. In 2001, there were 35.2 million visitors to New York City, including 5.7 million international visitors. A typical visit to New York City might include a boat ride to the Statue of Liberty—a three-hour boat ride around Manhattan; visits to the World Trade Center, the Empire State Building, the UN, Rockefeller Center, and the New York Stock Exchange; walking tours of the Bronx Zoo, Chinatown, and the theater district; and a sampling of the city's many museums, restaurants, shops, and shows.

Second to New York City as a magnet for tourists comes Long Island, with its beaches, racetracks, and other recreational facilities. Attractions of the Hudson Valley include the US Military Academy (West Point), the Franklin D. Roosevelt home at Hyde Park, Bear Mountain State Park, and several wineries.

North of Hudson Valley is Albany, with its massive government center, Governor Nelson A. Rockefeller Plaza, often called the Albany Mall; Saratoga Springs, home of an arts center, racetrack, and spa; and the Adirondack region, with its forest preserve, summer and winter resorts, and abundant hunting and fishing. Northwest of the Adirondacks, in the St. Lawrence River, are the Thousand Islands—actually some 1,800 small islands extending over about 50 mi (80 km), and popular among freshwater fishermen and summer vacationers.

Scenic sites in central New York include the resorts of the Catskills and the scenic marvels of the Finger Lakes region, including Taughannock Falls in Trumansburg, the highest waterfall east of the Rockies. Further west lie Buffalo and Niagara Falls. South of the Niagara Frontier is the Southwest Gateway, among whose dominant features are Chautauqua Lake and Allegany State Park, the state's largest. The Office of Parks, Recreation and Historic Preservation operates state parks, historic sites, and boat-launching sites.

48 SPORTS

New York has eleven major league professional sports teams: the New York Yankees and the New York Mets of Major League Baseball; the New York Giants, the New York Jets (although the Giants' and Jets' stadiums are located in New Jersey), and the Buffalo Bills of the National Football League; the New York Knickerbockers (usually called the Knicks) of the National Basketball Association; the New York Islanders, the New York Rangers, and the Buffalo Sabres of the National Hockey League; the New York Liberty of the Women's National Basketball Association, and the New York–New Jersey Metro Stars of Major League Soccer.

The Yankees have a record of excellence spanning most of the twentieth century. They won the American League Pennant 36 times and the World Series 25 times, most recently in 2000, when they defeated the New York Mets in five games. The series was coined the "Subway Series" because both teams were from New York City. Other championship streaks include the American League Pennant in 1927 and 1928; 1936–39; 1941–43; 1949–53; 1955–58; and 1960–64. In the 28 years between 1936 and 1964, the Yankees competed in 23 World Series, winning 16. The Mets have played in four World Series, winning in 1969 and 1986. The Giants won Super Bowls in 1987 and 1991, and the Jets did so in 1969 in a memorable upset victory over the Baltimore Colts. The Buffalo Bills won the American Football Conference Championship in 1991, 1992, 1993, and 1994, losing the Super Bowl each time. The Knicks won the NBA championship in 1973, and lost in the NBA finals in 1951, 1952, 1953, 1972, 1994, and 1999. The Islanders won the Stanley Cup in 1980, 1981, 1982, and 1983. The Rangers won it in 1928, 1933, 1940, and 1994.

Three New York teams, the Nets, Giants, and Jets, moved to New Jersey during the 1970s and 1980s. The Giants and Jets remained, in name, New York teams (unlike the Nets, who are now the New Jersey Nets), although the move remains controversial. In 1987, when the Giants won the Super Bowl, then mayor of New York Ed Koch refused them the ticker-tape parade through the city traditionally given in honor of championship teams on the grounds that, their name notwithstanding, they are a New Jersey team.

The state also has 14 minor league baseball teams and five minor league hockey teams.

Horse racing is important to New York State, both as a sports attraction and because of the tax revenues that betting generates. The main thoroughbred racetracks are Aqueduct in Queens, Belmont in Nassau County, and the Saratoga Race Course in Saratoga Springs. Belmont is the home of the Belmont Stakes, one of the three jewels in the Triple Crown of US racing. Saratoga Springs also has a longer harness-racing season at its Saratoga Equine Sports Center facility. Thoroughbred racing is also offered at the Finger Lakes track in Canandaigua. The top track for harness racing is Monticello Raceway (in the Catskills).

The New York City Off-Track Betting Corporation (OTB), which began operations in April 1971, takes bets on races at the state's major tracks, as well as on some out-of-state races. Off-track betting services operate on a smaller scale on Long Island and in upstate New York.

New York City hosts several major professional tennis tournaments every year, including the US Open in Flushing Meadows; the Last Minute Travel.com Masters (men) in Central Park, and the Chase Championships of the WTA Tour (women) at Madison Square Garden.

Among other professional sports facilities, the Watkins Glen automobile racetrack was, until recently, the site of a Grand Prix race every October. It now hosts a NASCAR Winston Cup race in August. Lake Placid, an important winter-sports region, hosted the 1932 and 1980 Winter Olympics, and continues to host amateur winter sports competitions, such as bobsled racing and ski jumping. New York City's Madison Square Garden is a leading venue for professional boxing and hosts many other sporting events.

In collegiate sports, basketball is perhaps most popular. Historically, the City College of New York produced many nationally ranked teams including the NCAA champions of 1950; that year they also won the NIT (National Invitational Basketball Tournament). St. John's and Syracuse have produced more contemporary nationally prominent teams, including the 1989 St. John's team that won the NIT. The 2003 National Championship was won in a dramatic victory by the Syracuse Orangemen.

The US Military Academy at West Point (Army) won college football national championships in 1944 and 1945, and, as of 1997, ranked 12th all-time among Division I-A teams with more than 600 victories.

Hockey and lacrosse are popular sports at the collegiate level and have been well represented by New York colleges and univesities. Both the Syracuse Orangemen and Cornell Big Red have captured multiple national championships on the Division-I level. Cornell has been equally successful on the ice, advancing to the Frozen Four on a number of occasions (most recently 2003). The Big Red captured the national championship in both 1967 and 1970.

In 1978, New York became the first state to sponsor a statewide amateur athletic event, the Empire State Games. More than 50,000 athletes now compete for a place in the finals, held each summer; the Winter Games, held each February in Lake Placid, host more than 1,000.

The New York City marathon, which is held in late October or early November, has become one of the largest, most prestigious marathons in the world.

Other annual sporting events include the Adirondack Hot Air Balloon Festival in Glens Falls in September and the Westminster Kennel Club Dog Show in New York City in February. The Baseball Hall of Fame is located in Cooperstown.

49 FAMOUS NEW YORKERS

New York State has been the home of five US presidents, eight US vice presidents (three of whom also became president), many statesmen of national and international repute, and a large corps of writers and entertainers.

Martin Van Buren (1782–1862), the 8th US president, became governor of New York in 1828. He was elected to the vice presidency as a Democrat under Andrew Jackson in 1832, and succeeded Jackson in the election of 1836. An unpopular president, Van Buren ran for reelection in 1840 but was defeated, losing even his home state. The 13th US president, Millard Fillmore (1800–74), was elected vice president under Zachary Taylor in 1848. He became president in 1850 when Taylor died. Fillmore's party, the Whigs, did not renominate him in 1852; four years later, he unsuccessfully ran for president as the candidate of the Native American (or Know-Nothing) Party.

Chester Alan Arthur (1829–86), a transplanted New Yorker born in Vermont, became the 21st US president when James Garfield was assassinated. New York's other US presidents had more distinguished careers. Although he was born in New Jersey, Grover Cleveland (1837–1908) served as mayor of Buffalo and as governor of New York before his election to his first presidential term in 1884; he was again elected president in 1892. Theodore Roosevelt (1858–1919), a Republican, was elected governor in 1898. He won election as vice president under William McKinley in 1900, and became the nation's 26th president after McKinley was murdered in 1901. Roosevelt pursued an aggressive foreign policy, but also won renown as a conservationist and trustbuster. Reelected in 1904, he was awarded the Nobel Peace Prize in 1906 for helping to settle a war between Russia and Japan. Roosevelt declined to run again in 1908. However, he sought the Republican nomination in 1912 and, when defeated, became the candidate of the Progressive (or Bull Moose) Party, losing the general election to Woodrow Wilson.

Franklin Delano Roosevelt (1882–1945), a fifth cousin of Theodore Roosevelt, first ran for national office in 1920, when he was the Democratic vice-presidential choice. A year after losing that election, FDR was crippled by poliomyelitis. He then made an amazing political comeback: he was elected governor of New York in 1928 and served until 1932, when US voters chose him as their 32nd president. Reelected in 1936, 1940, and 1944, FDR is the only president ever to have served more than two full terms in office. Roosevelt guided the US through the Great Depression and World War II, and his New Deal programs greatly enlarged the federal role in promoting social welfare.

In addition to Van Buren, Fillmore, and Theodore Roosevelt, five US vice presidents were born in New York: George Clinton (1739–1812), who was also New York State's first elected governor; Daniel D. Tompkins (1774–1825); William A. Wheeler (1819–87); Schuyler Colfax (1823–85); and James S. Sherman 1855–1912). Two other US vice presidents, though not born in New York, were New Yorkers by the time they became vice president. The first was Aaron Burr (1756–1836), perhaps best known for killing Alexander Hamilton in a duel in 1804; Hamilton (b.Nevis, West Indies, 1757–1804) was a leading Federalist, George Washington's treasury secretary, and the only New York delegate to sign the US Constitution in 1787. The second transplanted New Yorker to become vice president was Nelson Aldrich Rockefeller (1908–79). Born in Maine, Rockefeller served as governor of New York State from 1959 to 1973, was for two decades a major force in national Republican politics, and was appointed vice president by Gerald Ford in 1974, serving in that office through January 1977. Alan Greenspan (b.1926), a chairman of the Federal Reserve, was born in New York City.

Two native New Yorkers have become chief justices of the US: John Jay (1745–1829) and Charles Evans Hughes (1862–1948). A third chief justice, Harlan Fiske Stone (1872–1946), born in New Hampshire, spent most of his legal career in New York City and served as dean of Columbia University's School of Law. Among New Yorkers who became associate justices of the US Supreme Court, Benjamin Nathan Cardozo (1870–1938) is noteworthy. Ruth Bader Ginsberg (b.1933) was President Bill Clinton's first appointment to the Supreme Court.

Other federal officeholders born in New York include US secretaries of state William Henry Seward (1801–72), Hamilton Fish (1808–93), Elihu Root (1845–1937), Frank B. Kellogg

(1856–1937), and Henry L. Stimson (1867–1950). Prominent US senators have included Robert F. Wagner (1877–1953), who sponsored many New Deal laws; Robert F. Kennedy (1925–68), who though born in Massachusetts was elected to represent New York in 1964; Jacob K. Javits (1904–86), who served continuously in the Senate from 1957 through 1980; and Daniel Patrick Moynihan (1927–2003), a scholar, author, and former federal bureaucrat who represented New York 1977–2001. Colin Powell (b.1937), first African American to lead the Armed Forces and to serve as Secretary of State, attended the City University of New York.

The most important—and most colorful—figure in colonial New York was Peter Stuyvesant (b.Netherlands, 1592–1672); as director general of New Netherland, he won the hearty dislike of the Dutch settlers. Signers of the Declaration of Independence in 1776 from New York were Francis Lewis (1713–1803); Philip Livingston (1716–78); Lewis Morris (1726–98), the half-brother of the colonial patriot Gouverneur Morris (1752–1816); and William Floyd (1734–1821).

Other governors who made important contributions to the history of the state include DeWitt Clinton (1769–1828); Alfred E. Smith (1873–1944); Herbert H. Lehman (1878–1963); W. Averell Harriman (1891–1986), who has also held many US diplomatic posts; and Thomas E. Dewey (1902–71). Mario M. Cuomo (b.1932) served three terms as governor from 1982–94. Robert Moses (b.Connecticut, 1888–1981) led in the development of New York's parks and highway transportation system. One of the best-known and best-loved mayors in New York City history was Fiorello H. La Guardia (1882–1947), a reformer who held the office from 1934 to 1945. Edward I. Koch (b.1924) was first elected to the mayoralty in 1977.

Native New Yorkers have won Nobel prizes in every category. Winners of the Nobel Peace Prize besides Theodore Roosevelt were Elihu Root in 1912 and Frank B. Kellogg in 1929. The lone winner of the Nobel Prize for literature was Eugene O'Neill (1888–1953) in 1936. The chemistry prize was awarded to Irving Langmuir (1881–1957) in 1932, John H. Northrop (1891–1987) in 1946, and William Howard Stein (1911–80) in 1972. Winners in physics include Carl D. Anderson (1905–91) in 1936, Robert Hofstadter (1915–90) in 1961, Richard Phillips Feynman (1918–88) and Julian Seymour Schwinger (1918–94) in 1965, Murray Gell-Mann (b.1929) in 1969, Leon N. Cooper (b.1930) in 1972, Burton Richter (b.1931) in 1976, and Steven Weinberg (b.1933) and Sheldon L. Glashow (b.1932) in 1979.

The following New Yorkers have been awarded the Nobel Prize for physiology or medicine: Hermann Joseph Muller (1890–1967) in 1946, Arthur Kornberg (b.1918) in 1959, George Wald (1906–97) in 1967, Marshall Warren Nirenberg (b.1927) in 1968, Julius Axelrod (b.1912) in 1970, Gerald Maurice Edelman (b.1929) in 1972, David Baltimore (b.1938) in 1975, Baruch Samuel Blumberg (b.1925) and Daniel Carlton Gajdusek (b.1923) in 1976, Rosalyn Sussman Yalow (b.1921) in 1977, and Hamilton O. Smith (b.1931) in 1978.

The Nobel Prize for economic science was won by Kenneth J. Arrow (b.1921) in 1972, Milton Friedman (b.1912) in 1976, Richard Stone (1928–91) in 1984, and Robert Fogel (b.1926) in 1993. New York is also the birthplace of national labor leader George Meany (1894–1980) and economist Walter Heller (1915–87). Other distinguished state residents were physicist Joseph Henry (1797–1878), Mormon leader Brigham Young (b.Vermont, 1801–77), botanist Asa Gray (1810–88), inventor-businessman George Westinghouse (1846–1914), and Jonas E. Salk (1914–95), developer of a poliomyelitis vaccine. Melvin Schwartz (b.New York City, 1932) was a co-recipient of the 1988 Nobel prize in physics. Gertrude Belle Elion (1918–99), Nobel Prize winner in medicine 1988, was born in New York City. Leon

Max Lederman (b.1922) was a co-recipient of the 1988 Nobel Prize in physics.

Writers born in New York include the storyteller and satirist Washington Irving (1783–1859); poets Walt Whitman (1819–92) and Ogden Nash (1902–71); and playwrights Eugene O'Neill (1888–1953), Arthur Miller (b.1915), Paddy Chayefsky (1923–81), and Neil Simon (b.1927). Two of America's greatest novelists were New Yorkers: Herman Melville (1819–91), who was also an important poet, and Henry James (1843–1916), whose short stories are equally well known. Other novelists include James Fenimore Cooper (b.New Jersey, 1789–1851), Henry Miller (1891–1980), James Michener (1907–97), J(erome) D(avid) Salinger (b.1919), Joseph Heller (1923–99), James Baldwin (1924–87), and Gore Vidal (b.1925). Lionel Trilling (1905–75) was a well-known literary critic; Barbara Tuchman (1912–89), a historian, has won both scholarly praise and popular favor. New York City has produced two famous journalist-commentators, Walter Lippmann (1889–1974) and William F. Buckley, Jr. (b.1925), and a famous journalist-broadcaster Walter Winchell (1897–1972).

Broadway is the showcase of American drama and the birthplace of the American musical theater. New Yorkers linked with the growth of the musical include Jerome Kern (1885–1945), Lorenz Hart (1895–1943), Oscar Hammerstein 2nd (1895–1960), Richard Rodgers (1902–79), Alan Jay Lerner (1918–86), and Stephen Sondheim (b.1930). George Gershwin (1898–1937), whose *Porgy and Bess* raised the musical to its highest artistic form, also composed piano and orchestral works. Other important US composers from New York include Irving Berlin (b.Russia, 1888–1989), Aaron Copland (1900–90), Elliott Carter (b.1908), and William Schuman (1910–92). New York was the adopted home of ballet director and choreographer George Balanchine (b.Russia, 1904–83); his associate Jerome Robbins (1918–99) was born in New York City, as was choreographer Agnes De Mille (1905–93). Leaders in the visual arts include Frederic Remington (1861–1909), the popular illustrator Norman Rockwell (1894–1978), Willem de Kooning (b.Netherlands, 1904–97), and the photographer Margaret Bourke-White (1906–71).

Many of America's best-loved entertainers come from the state. A small sampling would include comedians Groucho Marx (Julius Marx, 1890–1977), Mae West (1892–1980), Eddie Cantor (Edward Israel Iskowitz, 1892–1964), James "Jimmy" Durante (1893–1980), Bert Lahr (Irving Lahrheim, 1895–1967), George Burns (1896–1996), Milton Berle (Berlinger, 1908–2002), Lucille Ball (1911–1989), Danny Kaye (David Daniel Kominsky, 1913–87), and Sid Caesar (b.1922); comedian-film directors Mel Brooks (Melvin Kaminsky, b.1926) and Woody Allen (Allen Konigsberg, b.1935); stage and screen stars Humphrey Bogart (1899–1957), James Cagney (1904–86), Zero Mostel (Samuel Joel Mostel, 1915–77), and Lauren Bacall (Betty Joan Perske, b.1924); pop, jazz, and folk singers Cab Calloway (1907–90), Lena Horne (b.1917), Pete Seeger (b.1919), Sammy Davis, Jr. (1925–90), Harry Belafonte (b.1927), Joan Baez (b.1941), Barbra Streisand (b.1942), Carly Simon (b.1945), Arlo Guthrie (b.1947), Billy Joel (b.1951), and Mariah Carey, Grammy Award-winning pop singer (b.1969); and opera stars Robert Merrill (b.1919), Maria Callas (Kalogeropoulos, 1923–77), and Beverly Sills (Belle Silverman, b.1929). Also noteworthy are producers Irving Thalberg (1899–1936), David Susskind (1920–87), Joseph Papp (1921–91), and Harold Prince (b.1928) and directors George Cukor (1899–1983), Stanley Kubrick (1928–99), John Frankenheimer (b.1930), Peter Bogdanovich (b.1939), and actor Tom Cruise (b.1962) was born in Syracuse.

Among many prominent sports figures born in New York are first-baseman Lou Gehrig (1903–41), football coach Vince Lombardi (1913–70), pitcher Sanford "Sandy" Koufax (b.1935),

and basketball stars Kareem Abdul-Jabbar (Lew Alcindor, b.1947) and Julius Erving (b.1950). Orel Leonard Hershiser IV (b.1958), who set the record for most consecutive scoreless innings pitched, was born in Buffalo, New York.

⁵⁰BIBLIOGRAPHY

Auletta, Ken. *The Streets Were Paved with Gold*. New York: Random House, 1980.

Barlow, Elizabeth, *Frederick Law Olmsted's New York*. New York: Praeger, 1972.

Bellush, Jewel, and Stephen M. David. *Race and Politics in New York City*. New York: Praeger, 1971.

Berle, Beatrice Bishop. *80 Puerto Rican Families in New York City*. New York: Arno Press, 1975.

Berrol, Selma Cantor. *The Empire City: New York and Its People, 1624-1996*. Westport, Conn.: Praeger, 1997.

Bliven, Bruce. *New York*. New York: Norton, 1981.

Brown, Claude. *Manchild in the Promised Land*. New York: Macmillan, 1965.

Caro, Robert A. *The Power Broker: Robert Moses and the Fall of New York*. New York: Vintage, 1975.

Colby, Peter W. (ed.). *New York State Today: Politics, Government, Public Policy*. 2nd ed. Albany: State University of New York Press, 1989.

Cuomo, Mario M. *Diaries of Mario M. Cuomo: The Campaign for Governor*. New York: Random House, 1984.

Edmiston, Susan, and Linda D. Cirino. *Literary New York: A History and Guide*. Boston, Houghton Mifflin, 1976.

Ellis, David M. *New York: State and City*. Ithaca: Cornell University Press, 1979.

Ellis, David M., James A. Frost, Harold C. Syrett, and Harry J. Carman. *A History of New York State*. Rev. ed. Ithaca: Cornell University Press, 1967.

Ellis, David M., James A. Frost, and William B. Fink. *New York: The Empire State*. 4th ed. Englewood Cliffs, N.J.: Prentice-Hall, 1975.

Fabend, Firth Haring. *Zion on the Hudson: Dutch New York and New Jersey in the Age of Revivals*. New Brunswick, N.J.: Rutgers University Press, 2000.

Federal Writers' Project. *New York City Guide*. New York: Somerset, n.d. (orig. 1939).

Flick, Alexander C. (ed.). *History of the State of New York*. Port Washington, N.Y.: Ira J. Friedman, 1969 (orig. 1860).

Furer, Howard B. *New York: A Chronological and Documentary History: 1524–1970*. Dobbs Ferry, N.Y.: Oceana Publications, 1974.

Galie, Peter J. *The New York State Constitution: A Reference Guide*. New York, Greenwood Press, 1991.

———. *Ordered Liberty: A Constitutional History of New York*. New York: Fordham University Press, 1996.

Hacker, Andrew, *The New Yorkers: A Profile of an American People*. New York: Mason/Charter, 1975.

Hansen, Joyce and Gary McGowan. *Breaking Ground, Breaking Silence: The Story of New York's African Burial Ground*. New York: Henry Holt, 1998.

Heckscher, August, with Phyllis Robinson. *When La Guardia Was Mayor: New York's Legendary Years*. New York: Norton, 1978.

Henderson, Mary C. *The City and the Theatre: New York Playhouses from Bowling Green to Times Square*. Clifton, N.J.: J. T. White, 1975.

Hevesi, Alan G. *Legislative Politics in New York State*. New York: Praeger, 1975.

Homberger, Eric. *The Historical Atlas of New York City: A Visual Celebration of Nearly 400 Years of New York City's History*. New York: H. Holt and Co., 1996.

Howe, Irving. *World of Our Fathers.* New York: Harcourt Brace Jovanovich, 1976.

Irving, Washington. *A History of New York.* Edited by Michael L. Black and Nancy B. Black. Boston: Twayne Publishers, 1984.

Kammen, Michael. *Colonial New York: A History.* Millwood, N.Y.: Kraud, 1975.

Kennedy, William. *O Albany!* New York: Viking, 1983.

Kenney, Alice P. *Stubborn for Liberty: The Dutch in New York.* Syracuse: Syracuse University Press, 1975.

Klein, Milton M., ed. *The Empire State: A History of New York.* Ithaca, N.Y.: Cornell University Press, 2001.

Koch, Edward I., and William Rauch. *Mayor: An Autobiography.* New York: Simon & Schuster, 1984.

Kouwenhoven, John A. *The Columbia Historical Portrait of New York: An Essay in Graphic History.* New York: Harper & Row, 1972 (orig. 1952).

League of Women Voters of New York State. *A Guide to New York State Government.* Edited by Mary Jo Fairbanks. Croton-on Hudson, N.Y.: Policy Studies Associates, 1995.

Lopez, Manual D. *New York: A Guide to Information and Reference Sources.* Metuchen, N.J.: Scarecrow, 1980.

Myers, Gustavus. *The History of Tammany Hall.* New York: Burt Franklin, 1967 (orig. 1901).

Nelson A. Rockefeller Institute of Government, in cooperation with the New York State Division of the Budget. *New York State Statistical Yearbook, 1984–1985.* Albany: Rockefeller Institute, 1985.

Newfield, Jack, and Paul DuBrul. *Abuse of Power: The Permanent Government and the Fall of New York.* New York: Viking, 1977.

Peirce, Neal R. *The Megastates of America: People, Politics, and Power in the Ten Great States.* New York: Norton, 1972.

Ravitch, Diane. *The Great School Wars: New York City 1805–1973.* New York: Basic Books, 1974.

Schneider, David Moses, and Albert Deutsch. *The History of Public Welfare in New York State.* Montclair, N.J.: Patterson, Smith, 1969.

Talese, Gay. *The Kingdom and the Power.* New York: World, 1969.

Torres, Andrés. *Between Melting Pot and Mosaic: African Americans and Puerto Ricans in the New York Political Economy.* Philadelphia: Temple University Press, 1995.

Zimmerman, Joseph F. *The Government and Politics of New York State.* New York: New York University Press, 1981.

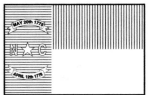

NORTH CAROLINA

State of North Carolina

ORIGIN OF STATE NAME: Named in honor of King Charles I of England. **NICKNAME:** The Tar Heel State and Old North State. **CAPITAL:** Raleigh. **ENTERED UNION:** 21 November 1789 (12th). **SONG:** "The Old North State." **MOTTO:** *Esse quam videri* (To be rather than to seem). **FLAG:** Adjacent to the fly of two equally sized bars, red above and white below, is a blue union containing a white star in the center, flanked by the letters N and C in gold. Above and below the star are two gold scrolls, the upper one reading "May 20th 1775," the lower one "April 12th 1776." **OFFICIAL SEAL:** Liberty, clasping a constitution and holding aloft on a pole a liberty cap, stands on the left, while Plenty sits beside a cornucopia on the right; behind them, mountains run to the sea, on which a three-masted ship appears. "May 20, 1775" appears above the figures; the words "The Great Seal of the State of North Carolina" and the state motto surround the whole. **MAMMAL:** Gray squirrel. **BIRD:** Cardinal. **FISH:** Channel bass. **DOG:** Plott hound. **REPTILE:** Eastern box turtle. **INSECT:** Honeybee. **FLOWER:** Dogwood. **TREE:** Long leaf pine. **VEGETABLE:** Sweet potato. **BEVERAGE:** Milk. **SHELL:** Scotch bonnet. **PRECIOUS STONE:** Emerald. **ROCK:** Granite. **LEGAL HOLIDAYS:** New Year's Day, 1 January; Birthday of Martin Luther King, Jr., 3rd Monday in January; Easter Monday, March or April; Memorial Day, last Monday in May; Independence Day, 4 July; Labor Day, 1st Monday in September; Veterans Day, 11 November; Thanksgiving Day, 4th Thursday in November, and the day following; Christmas Eve, 24 December; Christmas Day, 25 December. **TIME:** 7 AM EST = noon GMT.

¹LOCATION, SIZE, AND EXTENT

Located in the southeastern US, North Carolina ranks 28th in size among the 50 states.

The total area of North Carolina is 52,669 sq mi (136,413 sq km), of which land accounts for 48,843 sq mi (126,504 sq km) and inland water 3,826 sq mi (9,909 sq km). North Carolina extends 503 mi (810 km) E-W; the state's maximum N-S extension is 187 mi (301 km).

North Carolina is bordered on the N by Virginia; on the E by the Atlantic Ocean; on the S by South Carolina and Georgia; and on the W by Tennessee. A long chain of islands or sand banks, called the Outer Banks, lies off the state's Atlantic coast. The total boundary line of North Carolina is 1,270 mi (2,044 km), including a general coastline of 301 mi (484 km); the tidal shoreline extends 3,375 mi (5,432 km). The state's geographic center is in Chatham County, 10 mi (16 km) NW of Sanford.

²TOPOGRAPHY

North Carolina's three major topographic regions belong to the Atlantic Coastal Plain, the Piedmont Plateau, and the Appalachian Mountains.

The Outer Banks, narrow islands of shifting sandbars, screen most of the coastal plain from the ocean. Treacherous navigation conditions and numerous shipwrecks have earned the name of "Graveyard of the Atlantic" for the shoal waters off Cape Hatteras, which, like Cape Lookout and Cape Fear, juts out from the banks into the Atlantic. Cape Hatteras Lighthouse is the tallest in the US, rising 208 ft (63 m). The shallow Pamlico and Albemarle sounds and broad salt marshes lying behind the Outer Banks serve not only as valuable habitats for marine life but as further hindrances to water transportation.

On the mainland, the coastal plain extends westward from the sounds for 100 to 140 mi (160–225 km) and upward from sea level to nearly 500 ft (150 m). Near the ocean, the outer coastal plain is very flat and often swampy; this region contains all the

natural lakes in North Carolina, the largest being Lake Mattamuskeet (67 sq mi/174 sq km), followed by lakes Phelps and Waccamaw. The inner coastal plain is more elevated and better drained. Infertile sand hills mark its southwestern section, but the rest of the region constitutes the state's principal farming country.

The Piedmont is a rolling plateau of red clay soil roughly 150 mi (240 km) wide, rising from 30 to 600 ft (90–180 m) in the east to 1,500 ft (460 m) in the west. The fall line, a sudden change in elevation, separates the piedmont from the coastal plain and produces numerous rapids in the rivers that flow between the regions.

The Blue Ridge, a steep escarpment that parallels the Tennessee border, divides the piedmont from North Carolina's westernmost region, containing the highest and most rugged portion of the Appalachian chain. The two major ranges are the Blue Ridge itself, which averages 3,000–4,000 ft high (900–1,200 m), and the Great Smoky Mountains, which have 43 peaks higher than 6,000 ft (1,800 m). Several smaller chains intersect these two ranges; one of them, the Black Mountains, contains Mt. Mitchell, at 6,684 ft (2,039 m) the tallest peak east of the Mississippi River.

No single river basin dominates North Carolina. The Hiwassee, Little Tennessee, French Broad, Watauga, and New rivers flow from the mountains westward to the Mississippi River system. East of the Blue Ridge, the Chowan, Roanoke, Tar, Neuse, Cape Fear, Yadkin, and Catawba drain the piedmont and coastal plain. The largest artificial lakes are Lake Norman on the Catawba, Lake Gaston on the Roanoke, and High Rock Lake on the Yadkin.

³CLIMATE

North Carolina has a humid, subtropical climate. Winters are short and mild, while summers are usually very sultry; spring and fall are distinct and refreshing periods of transition. In most of North Carolina, temperatures rarely go above 100°F (38°C) or fall below 10°F (–12°C), but differences in altitude and proximity to the ocean create significant local variations. Average January temperatures range from 36°F (21°C) to 48°F (9°C), with an average daily maximum January temperature of 51°F (11°C) and minimum of 29°F (–2°C). Average July temperatures range from 68°F (20°C) to 80°F (27°C), with an average daily high of 87°F (31°C) and a low of 66°F (19°C). The coldest temperature ever recorded in North Carolina was –34°F (–37°C), registered on 21 January 1985 on Mt. Mitchell; the hottest, 110°F (43°C), occurred on 21 August 1983 at Fayetteville.

In the southwestern section of the Blue Ridge, moist southerly winds rising over the mountains drop more than 80 in (203 cm) of precipitation per year, making this region the wettest in the eastern states; the other side of the mountains receives less than half that amount. Average annual precipitation at Charlotte (1971–2000) was 43.5 in (110.5 cm). The piedmont gets between 44 and 48 in (112 to 122 cm) of precipitation per year, while 44 to 56 in (112 to 142 cm) annually fall on the coastal plain. Average winter snowfalls vary from 50 in (127 cm) on Mt. Mitchell to only a trace amount at Cape Hatteras. In the summer, North Carolina weather responds to the Bermuda High, a pressure system centered in the mid-Atlantic. Winds from the southwest bring masses of hot humid air over the state; anticyclones connected with this system frequently lead to upper-level thermal inversions, producing a stagnant air mass that cannot disperse pollutants until cooler, drier air from Canada moves in. During late summer and early autumn, the eastern region is vulnerable to high winds and flooding from hurricanes. Hurricane Diana struck the Carolina coast in September 1984, causing $36 million in damage. A series of tornadoes in March of that year killed 61 people, injured over 1,000, and caused damage exceeding $120 million. Hurricanes Hugo (1989) and Fran (1996) caused major damage.

4FLORA AND FAUNA

North Carolina has approximately 300 species and subspecies of trees and almost 3,000 varieties of flowering plants. Coastal plant life begins with sea oats predominating on the dunes and saltmeadow and cordgrass in the marshes, then gives way to wax myrtle, yaupon, red cedar, and live oak further inland. Blackwater swamps support dense stands of cypress and gum trees. Pond pine favors the peat soils of the Carolina bays, while longleaf pine and turkey oak cover the sand hills and other well-drained areas. Weeds take root when a field is abandoned in the piedmont, followed soon by loblolly, shortleaf, and Virginia pine; sweet gum and tulip poplars spring up beneath the pines, later giving way to an oak-hickory climax forest. Dogwood decorates the understory, but kudzu—a rank, weedy vine introduced from Japan as an antierosion measure in the 1930s—is a less attractive feature of the landscape. The profusion of plants reaches extraordinary proportions in the mountains. The deciduous forests on the lower slopes contain Carolina hemlock, silver bell, yellow buckeye, white basswood, sugar maple, yellow birch, tulip poplar, and beech, in addition to the common trees of the piedmont. Spruce and fir dominate the high mountain peaks. There is no true treeline in the North Carolina mountains, but unexplained treeless areas called "balds" appear on certain summits. Twenty-seven plant species were listed as threatened or endangered in 2003, including Blue Ridge goldenrod, bunched arrowhead, Heller's blazingstar, Virginia spiraea, seabeach amaranth, and rough-leaved loosestrife.

The white-tailed deer is the principal big-game animal of North Carolina, and the black bear is a tourist attraction in the Great Smoky Mountains National Park. The wild boar was introduced to the mountains during the 19th century; beavers have been reintroduced and are now the state's principal furbearers. The largest native carnivore is the bobcat.

North Carolina game birds include the bobwhite quail, mourning dove, wild turkey, and many varieties of duck and goose. Trout and smallmouth bass flourish in North Carolina's clear mountain streams, while catfish, pickerel, perch, crappie, and largemouth bass thrive in fresh water elsewhere. The sounds and surf of the coast yield channel bass, striped bass, flounder, and bluefish to anglers. Among insect pests, the pine bark beetle is a threat to the state's forests and forest industries.

The gray wolf, elk, eastern cougar, and bison are extinct in North Carolina; the American alligator, protected by the state, has returned in large numbers to eastern swamps and lakeshores. Thirty-six animal species were listed as threatened or endangered in 2003, including Indiana and Virginia big-eared bats, bald eagle, red-cockaded woodpecker, four species of whale, and five species of sea turtle.

5ENVIRONMENTAL PROTECTION

State actions to safeguard the environment began in 1915 with the purchase of the summit of Mt. Mitchell as North Carolina's first state park. North Carolina's citizens and officials worked actively (along with those in Tennessee) to establish the Great Smoky Mountains National Park during the 1920s, the same decade that saw the establishment of the first state agency for wildlife conservation. In 1937, a state and local program of soil and water conservation districts began to halt erosion and waste of natural resources.

Interest in environmental protection intensified during the 1970s. In 1971, the state required its own agencies to submit environmental impact statements in connection with all major project proposals; it also empowered local governments to require such statements from major private developers. Voters approved a $150 million bond issue in 1972 to assist in the construction of wastewater treatment facilities by local governments. The Coastal Management Act of 1974 mandated comprehensive land-use planning for estuaries, wetlands, beaches, and adjacent areas of environmental concern. The most controversial environmental action occurred mid-decade, when a coalition of state officials, local residents, and national environmental groups fought the proposed construction of a dam that would have flooded the New River Valley in northwestern North Carolina. Congress quashed the project when it designated the stream as a national scenic river in 1976.

Air quality in most of North Carolina's eight air-quality-control regions is good, although the industrialized areas of the piedmont and mountains experience pollution from vehicle exhausts and coal-fired electric generating plants. Water quality ranges from extraordinary purity in numerous mountain trout streams to serious pollution in major rivers and coastal waters. Soil erosion and municipal and industrial waste discharges have drastically increased the level of dissolved solids in some piedmont streams, while runoffs from livestock pastures and nitrates leached from fertilized farmland have overstimulated the growth of algae in slow-moving eastern rivers. Pollution also has made certain areas of the coast unsafe for commercial shellfishing. About 5.7 million acres (2.3 million hectares) of the state are wetlands; since 1997 the North Carolina Wetlands Partnership has overseen wetlands conservation. About 70% of North Carolina's rare and endangered plants and animals are considered wetland-dependent.

The Department of Environment, Health and Natural Resources, the state's main environmental agency, issues licenses to industries and municipalities and seeks to enforce clean air and water regulations. In 2003, North Carolina had 311 hazardous waste sites listed in the Environmental Protection Agency's database, 28 of which were on the National Priorities List. In 2001, North Carolina received $99,797,000 in federal grants from the Environmental Protection Agency; EPA expenditures for

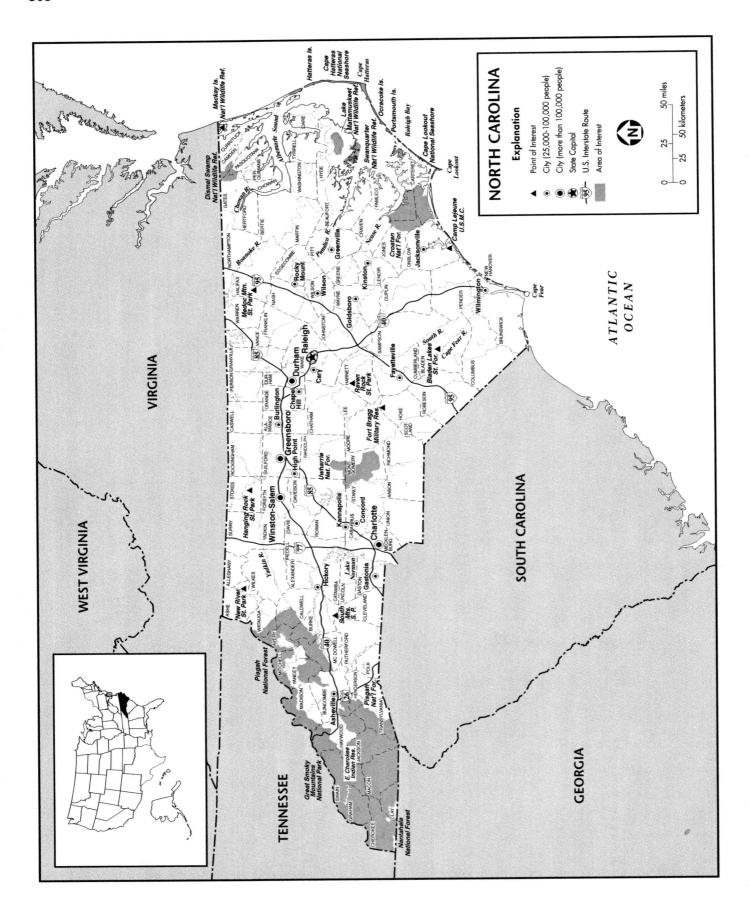

North Carolina Counties, County Seats, and County Areas and Populations

COUNTY	COUNTY SEAT	LAND AREA (SQ MI)	POPULATION (2002 EST.)	COUNTY	COUNTY SEAT	LAND AREA (SQ MI)	POPULATION (2002 EST.)
Alamance	Graham	433	135,893	Jones	Trenton	470	10,259
Alexander	Taylorsville	259	34,400	Lee	Sanford	259	49,521
Alleghany	Sparta	234	10,837	Lenoir	Kinston	402	59,073
Anson	Wadesboro	533	25,351	Lincoln	Lincolnton	298	66,598
Ashe	Jefferson	426	24,796	Macon	Franklin	517	30,752
Avery	Newland	247	17,610	Madison	Marshall	451	20,004
Beaufort	Washington	826	45,571	Martin	Williamston	461	25,062
Bertie	Windsor	701	19,697	McDowell	Marion	437	42,880
Bladen	Elizabethtown	879	32,509	Mecklenburg	Charlotte	528	737,950
Brunswick	Bolivia	861	78,567	Mitchell	Bakersville	222	15,844
Buncombe	Asheville	659	211,201	Montgomery	Troy	490	27,288
Burke	Morganton	505	29,638	Moore	Carthage	701	78,191
Cabarrus	Concord	364	140,182	Nash	Nashville	540	89,286
Caldwell	Lenoir	471	78,513	New Hanover	Wilmington	185	165,712
Camden	Camden	241	7,456	Northampton	Jackson	538	21,803
Carteret	Beaufort	525	60,232	Onslow	Jacksonville	763	149,003
Caswell	Yanceyville	427	23,555	Orange	Hillsborough	400	120,458
Catawba	Newton	396	146,690	Pamlico	Bayboro	341	12,882
Chatham	Pittsboro	708	53,893	Pasquotank	Elizabeth City	228	35,445
Cherokee	Murphy	452	24,869	Pender	Burgaw	875	42,734
Chowan	Edenton	181	14,525	Perquimans	Hertford	246	11,486
Clay	Hayesville	214	9,186	Person	Roxboro	398	36,610
Cleveland	Shelby	468	97,960	Pitt	Greenville	656	137,240
Columbus	Whiteville	939	54,930	Polk	Columbus	238	18,845
Craven	New Bern	702	91,926	Randolph	Asheboro	789	134,217
Cumberland	Fayetteville	657	303,328	Richmond	Rockingham	477	46,841
Currituck	Currituck	256	19,623	Robeson	Lumberton	949	125,351
Dare	Manteo	391	32,106	Rockingham	Wentworth	569	92,778
Davidson	Lexington	548	151,238	Rowan	Salisbury	519	133,359
DAvie	Mocksville	267	36,734	Rutherford	Rutherfordton	568	63,287
Duplin	Kenansville	819	50,800	Sampson	Clinton	947	61,256
Durham	Durham	298	234,199	Scotland	Laurinburg	319	36,109
Edgecombe	Tarboro	506	55,007	Stanly	Albemarle	396	58,553
Forsyth	Winston-Salem	412	314,933	Stokes	Danbury	452	44,984
Franklin	Louisburg	494	50,449	Surry	Dobson	539	72,211
Gaston	Gastonia	357	193,443	Swain	Bryson City	526	13,137
Gates	Gatesville	338	10,635	Transylvania	Brevard	378	29,499
Graham	Robbinsville	289	8,045	Tyrrell	Columbia	407	4,193
Granville	Oxford	534	50,946	Union	Monroe	639	139,611
Greene	Snow Hill	266	19,416	Vance	Henderson	249	44,348
Guilford	Greensboro	651	430,937	Wake	Raleigh	854	675,518
Halifax	Halifax	724	56,606	Warren	Warrenton	427	19,914
Harnett	Lillington	601	97,045	Washington	Plymouth	332	13,526
Haywood	Waynesville	555	54,831	Watauga	Boone	314	42,857
Henderson	Hendersonville	375	92,526	Wayne	Goldsboro	554	112,954
Hertford	Winton	356	22,037	Wilkes	Wilkesboro	752	66,773
Hoke	Racford	391	36,032	Wilson	Wilson	374	74,942
Hyde	Swanquarter	624	5,702	Yadkin	Yadkinville	336	37,329
Iredell	Statesville	574	130,178	Yancey	Burnsville	314	17,959
Jackson	Sylva	490	33,763				
Johnston	Smithfield	795	133,159	TOTALS		48,843	8,320,146

procurement contracts in North Carolina that year amounted to $100,928,000.

⁶POPULATION

North Carolina ranked 11th in population in the US with an estimated total of 8,320,146 in 2002, an increase of 3.4 % since 2000. Between 1990 and 2000, North Carolina's population grew from 6,628,637 to 8,049,313, an increase of 21.4%, making North Carolina the 6th-fastest-growing state of the decade. The population is projected to reach 9.3 million by 2025. The population density in 2000 was 165.2 persons per sq mi.

At the time of the first census in 1790, North Carolina ranked 3rd among the 13 states, with a population of 393,751, but it slipped to 10th by 1850. In the decades that followed, North Carolina grew slowly by natural increase and suffered from net out-migration, while the rest of the nation expanded rapidly. Out-migration abated after 1890, however, and North Carolina's overall growth rate in the 20th century was slightly greater than that of the nation as a whole.

As of 2000, the state's population had a median age of 35.3. In the same year, 24.4% of the populace were under the age of 18 while 12% were age 65 or older. Most North Carolinians live in and around a relatively large number of small and medium-sized cities and towns, many of which are concentrated in the Piedmont Crescent, between Charlotte, Greensboro, and Raleigh. Leading cities in 2002 were Charlotte, 580,597; Raleigh, 306,944; Greensboro, 228,217; Durham, 195,914; Winston-Salem, 188,934. The Charlotte metropolitan area had an estimated 1,417,217 people in 1999.

7ETHNIC GROUPS

North Carolina's white population is descended mostly from English settlers who arrived in the east in the 17th and early 18th centuries and from Scottish, Scots-Irish, and German immigrants who poured into the piedmont in the middle of the 18th century. Originally very distinct, these groups assimilated with one another in the first half of the 19th century to form a relatively homogeneous body of native-born white Protestants. By 1860, North Carolina had the lowest proportion of foreign-born whites of any state; more than a century later, in 1990, only 1.7% (115,077) of North Carolina residents were foreign born, mostly from Germany, the United Kingdom, and Mexico. Within the following decade, however, the foreign-born population increased dramatically, to 430,000 (5.3%) in 2000. In the same year, the estimated Hispanic and Latino population was 378,963 (4.7% of the state total), up from 161,000 (2.1%) in 1990.

According to the 2000 federal census there were some 99,551 Native Americans (including Eskimos and Aleuts) living in North Carolina, the 6th-largest number in any state, and the largest number in any state east of the Mississippi. The Lumbee of Robeson County and the surrounding area are the major Indian group. The total population of their lands in 2000, including non-Indians, was 474,100. Their origins are mysterious, but they are probably descended from many small tribes, decimated by war and disease, that banded together in the Lumber River swamps in the 18th century. The Lumbee have no language other than English, have no traditional tribal culture, and are not recognized by the Bureau of Indian Affairs.

The Haliwa, Waccamaw Siouan, Coharie, and Person County Indians are smaller groups in eastern North Carolina who share the Lumbee's predicament. The only North Carolina Indians with a reservation, a tribal language and culture, and federal recognition are the Cherokee, whose ancestors hid in the Smokies when the majority of their tribe was removed to Indian Territory (now Oklahoma) in 1838. The North Carolina Cherokee have remained in the mountains ever since, living in a community that now centers on the Qualla Boundary Reservation near Great Smoky Mountains National Park.

The 1,737,545 blacks in North Carolina made up 21.6% of its total population in 2000. Black slaves came to North Carolina from the 17th century through the early 19th; like most white immigrants, they usually arrived in North Carolina after previous residence in other colonies. Although black slaves performed a wide variety of tasks and lived in every county of the state, they were most often field laborers on the large farms in the eastern region. The distribution of black population today still reflects the patterns of plantation agriculture: the coastal plain contains a much higher than average concentration of black inhabitants. The overall proportion of blacks in North Carolina rose throughout the 19th century but fell steadily in the 20th, until about 1970, as hundreds of thousands migrated to northern and western states. Some of the earliest demonstrations of the civil rights movement, most notably a 1960 lunch counter sit-in at Greensboro, took place in the state.

In 2000 North Carolina's Asian population numbered 113,689, including 26,197 Asian Indians, 18,984 Chinese, 15,596 Vietnamese, 12,600 Koreans, 9,592 Filipinos, and 7,093 Hmong. Pacific Islanders numbered 3,983.

8LANGUAGES

Although most of the original Cherokee Indians were removed to Indian Territory around 1838, descendants of those who resisted and remained have formed a strong Indian community in the Appalachian foothills. Among Indian place-names are Pamlico, Nantahala, and Cullasaja.

Many regional language features are widespread, but others sharply distinguish two subregions: the western half, including the piedmont and the Appalachian Highlands, and the eastern coastal plain. Terms common to South Midland and Southern speech occur throughout the state: both *dog irons* and *firedogs* (andirons), *bucket* (pail), *spicket* (spigot), *seesaw*, *comfort* (tied and filled bedcover), *pullybone* (wishbone), *ground squirrel* (chipmunk), *branch* (small stream), *light bread* (white bread), *polecat* (skunk), and *carry* (escort). Also common are *greasy* with the /z/ sound, *new* as /nyoo/ and *due* as /dyoo/, *swallow it* as /swaller it/, *can't* rhyming with *paint*, *poor* with the vowel sound /aw/, and *horse* and *hoarse* with different vowels.

Distinct to the western region are *snake feeder* (dragonfly), *blinds* (roller shades), *poke* (paper bag), *redworm* (earthworm), a *little piece* (a short distance), *plum peach* (clingstone peach), *sick on the stomach* (also found in the Pee Dee River Valley), *boiled* as /bawrld/, *fog* as /fawg/, *Mary* sounding like *merry* and *bulge* with the vowel of *good*. Setting off eastern North Carolina are *lightwood* (kindling), *mosquito hawk* (dragonfly), *earthworm*, *press peach* (instead of plum peach), *you-all* as second-person plural, and *sick in the stomach*. Distinctive eastern pronunciations include the loss of /r/ after a vowel, *fog* as /fagh/, *scarce* and *Mary* with the vowel of *gate*, *bulge* with the vowel sound /ah/. Along the coast, peanuts are *goobers* and a screech owl is a *shivering owl*.

In 2000, 6,909,648 North Carolinians—92% of the population five years of age and older—spoke only English at home, down from 96.1% in 1990.

The following table gives selected statistics from the 2000 census for language spoken at home by persons five years old and over. The category "African languages" includes Amharic, Ibo, Twi, Yoruba, Bantu, Swahili, and Somali.

LANGUAGE	NUMBER	PERCENT
Population 5 years and over	7,513,165	100.0
Speak only English	6,909,648	92.0
Speak a language other than English	603,517	8.0
Speak a language other than English	603,517	8.0
Spanish or Spanish Creole	378,942	5.0
French (incl. Patois, Cajun)	33,201	0.4
German	28,520	0.4
Chinese	15,698	0.2
Vietnamese	13,594	0.2
Korean	11,386	0.2
Arabic	10,834	0.1
African languages	9,181	0.1
Miao, Hmong	7,493	0.1
Tagalog	6,521	0.1
Greek	6,404	0.1
Japanese	6,317	0.1
Italian	6,233	0.1

9RELIGIONS

The Church of England was the established church of colonial North Carolina but was never a dominant force among the early immigrants. Scottish Presbyterians settled in the upper Cape Fear Valley, and Scots-Irish Presbyterians occupied the piedmont after 1757. Lutheran Evangelical Reformed Germans later moved into the Yadkin and Catawba valleys of the same region. The Moravians, a German sect, founded the town of Salem (later merging with Winston to become Winston-Salem) in 1766 as the center of their utopian community at Wachovia. Methodist circuit riders and Separate Baptists missionaries won thousands of converts among blacks and whites, strengthening their appeal in the Great Revival of 1801. In the subsequent generation, a powerful evangelical consensus dominated popular culture. After the Civil War, blacks left the white congregations to found their own churches, but the overall strength of Protestantism persisted. When many North Carolinians left their farms at the end of the 19th century, they moved to mill villages that were well supplied with churches, often at the mill owners' expense.

The majority of North Carolinians are Protestant. The churches of the Southern Baptist Convention reported 1,512,058 adherents in 2000; the United Methodist Church claimed 638,785; and the Presbyterian Church USA, 203,647. The next largest Protestant denominations were the Evangelical Lutheran Church in America, 88,830 adherents; the Church of God (Cleveland, Tennessee), 81,037; the Episcopal Church, 80,068; the United Church of Christ, 50,088; the International Pentecostal Holiness Church, 50,265; the Original Free Will Baptists, 46,020; Independent Charismatic Churches, 42,559; and the Church of Jesus Christ of Latter-Day Saints (Mormons) 40,936. In 2000, the state had 315,606 Roman Catholics, an estimated 25,545 Jews, and about 20,137 Muslims. There are still about 18,180 Moravians in the state. Over 4.3 million people (about 54.6% of the population) were not counted as members of any religious organization.

10 TRANSPORTATION

The history of North Carolina's growth and prosperity has been inextricably linked to the history of transportation in the state, especially the history of highway development. North Carolina has the largest state-maintained highway system in the nation. To provide and maintain this system, North Carolina relies strictly on user-related sources of funds, such as motor fuel taxes and state license and registration fees.

The early settlers widened and improved the Indian trails into bridle trails and then dirt roads. In colonial times, waterways were the avenues of commerce. Almost all products moved on rivers and streams within the state, and most manufactured goods arrived by sea. When it became necessary to transport goods farther inland, local laws were passed which directed that a road be built to the nearest landing. By this piecemeal process, the state slowly acquired a system of dirt roads.

As the population of the state grew, so did the demand for roads. From 1830 onward, a new element was introduced into the picture—railroads, representing the newest and most efficient means of travel. In the 1850s, transportation took yet another turn when the state invested in plank roads, which did not prove financially practical.

With the coming of the Civil War, transportation improvements in North Carolina ground to a halt. During the war, the existing railroads were used heavily for military purposes. Renovations and improvements were delayed during the early years of the Reconstruction period because of poor economic conditions in the state. By 1870, the state gave up on assistance to railroads and left their further development to private companies. In 1895, the Southern Railway acquired a 99-year lease on the piedmont section of the North Carolina Railroad while eastern routes fell to the Atlantic Coast Line and the Seaboard Air Line Railway.

In the early years of the 20th century, the principal emphasis was on the further development of the investor-owned railroads. In 1911, there were railroads covering 4,608 mi (7,414 km); by 1937 this figure had increased, if only slightly, to a total of 4,763 (7,663 km). By 2000, railroad track in North Carolina had decreased to 3,360 route mi (5,407 km). Two Class I railroads operate in the state, along with 14 local and eight switching and terminal lines. In 1998, these railroads shipped more than 122 million tons of rail freight through the state. The Carolinian and Piedmont, both state-owned trains, provide daily, round-trip passenger-rail service between Charlotte and Raleigh. The Carolinian also offers continuing service to the Northeast. Amtrak provides passenger service to most large North Carolina cities. Each year more than 325,000 rail passengers begin or end their trips at one of North Carolina's 16 Amtrak stations.

By the second decade of the century, the building of roads received new emphasis. It was during this period that North Carolina earned the label "the Good Roads State." In 1915, the Highway Commission was created, and in 1921 the General Assembly approved a $40 million state highway bond to construct a system of hard-surface roads connecting each of the 100 county seats with all of the others. The new hard-surface roads soon proved ideal for automobiles and trucks. More highway bonds were approved to pay for a statewide system of paved highways, giving the state more roads by the end of the decade than any other southern state except Texas. The state government took over the county roads in 1931.

In 2000, North Carolina had 99,813 mi (160,633 km) of public roads. There were 6,305,150 motor vehicles registered in the same year, including 3,743,066 automobiles, 2,448,806 trucks, and 30,631 buses. Licensed drivers numbered 5,690,494. The major interstate highways are I-95, which stretches north–south across the coastal plain, and I-85, which parallels it across the piedmont. I-40 leads from the mountains to the coast at Wilmington, and I-26 and I-77 handle north–south traffic in the western section. I-73 and I-74 add 325 mi (523 km) of interstate highway and will handle north–south traffic in the eastern section of the state.

Transportation 2001, a plan to speed up highway construction and complete key corridors, eliminate the road maintenance backlog, and develop a master plan for public transportation, was unveiled in 1994. A $950 million highway bond was approved by North Carolina voters in 1996 to accelerate construction of urban loops and intrastates and to pave secondary roads. Transit 2001, the master plan to improve public transportation was unveiled in February 1997. A major incentive has been placed on high-speed rail service from Raleigh to Charlotte, reducing travel time to two hours by 2000.

There are nine types of public transportation currently operating in North Carolina: human service transportation, rural general public transportation, urban transit, regional transit, vanpool and carpool programs, inter-city buses, inter-city rail passenger service, pupil transportation, and passenger ferry service. There are 17 publicly owned urban transit systems operating in North Carolina. More than three million North Carolinians have access to rural public transportation services operating in approximately 45 counties and towns.

The Atlantic Intracoastal Waterway follows sounds, rivers, and canals down the entire length of eastern North Carolina. The North Carolina ferry system, the 2nd-largest in the nation, transports more than 23 million passengers and 820,000 vehicles each year. Twenty-four ferry vessels move passengers and vehicles between the state's coastal communities. Seventeen of the vessels feature the colors and seals of North Carolina's public and private colleges and universities to promote the ferry system. There are major ports at Morehead City and Wilmington. Morehead City handled 4.4 million tons of cargo in 2000; Wilmington, 6.7 million tons.

North Carolina has 76 publicly owned and 225 privately owned airports. Fifteen airports have regularly scheduled airline service; four are international. There are more than 6,000 private aircraft based in the state, flown by more than 15,000 certified pilots. More than 36 million passengers fly to and from North Carolina each year, and more than 650 million pounds of air freight originate annually in the state. There are three major airline hubs in North Carolina. North Carolina has larger airports at Asheville, Charlotte, Fayetteville, Greensboro, Kinston, Raleigh/Durham, Wilmington, and Winston-Salem.

11 HISTORY

Paleo-Indian peoples came to North Carolina about 10,000 years ago. These early inhabitants hunted game with spears and gathered nuts, roots, berries, and freshwater mollusks. Around 500 BC, with the invention of pottery and the development of agriculture, the Woodland Culture began to emerge. The Woodland way of life—growing corn, beans, and squash, and hunting game with bows and arrows—prevailed on the North Carolina coast until the Europeans arrived.

Living in North Carolina by this time were Indians of the Algonkian-, Siouan-, and Iroquoian-language families. The Roanoke, Chowanoc, Hatteras, Meherrin, and other Algonkian-speaking tribes of the coast had probably lived in the area the longest; some of them belonged to the Powhatan Confederacy of Virginia. The Siouan groups were related to larger tribes of the Great Plains. Of the Iroquoian-speakers, the Cherokee probably had lived in the mountains since before the beginning of the Christian era, while the Tuscarora had entered the upper coastal plain somewhat later. After their defeat by the colonists in the Tuscarora War of 1711–13, the tribe fled to what is now upper New York State to become the sixth member of the Iroquois Confederacy.

Contact with whites brought war, disease, and enslavement of the Algonkian and Siouan tribes. Banding together, the survivors probably gave rise to the present-day Lumbee and to the other Indian groups of eastern North Carolina. The Cherokee tried to avoid the fate of the coastal tribes by selectively adopting aspects of white culture. In 1838, however, the federal government responded to the demands of land-hungry whites by expelling most of the Cherokee to Indian Territory along the so-called Trail of Tears.

European penetration began when Giovanni da Verrazano, a Florentine navigator in French service, discovered the North Carolina coast in 1524. Don Lucas Vásquez de Ayllón led an unsuccessful Spanish attempt to settle near the mouth of the Cape Fear River two years later. Hernando de Soto tramped over the North Carolina mountains in 1540 in an unsuccessful search for gold, but the Spanish made no permanent contribution to the colonization of North Carolina.

Sixty years after Verrazano's voyage, North Carolina became the scene of England's first experiment in American empire. Sir Walter Raleigh, a courtier of Queen Elizabeth I, gained the queen's permission to send out explorers to the New World. They landed on the Outer Banks in 1584 and returned with reports so enthusiastic that Raleigh decided to sponsor a colony on Roanoke Island between Albemarle and Pamlico sounds. After a second expedition returned without founding a permanent settlement, Raleigh sent out a third group in 1587 under John White as governor. The passengers included White's daughter Eleanor and her husband, Ananias Dare. Shortly after landfall, Eleanor gave birth to Virginia Dare, the first child born of English parents in the New World. Several weeks later, White returned to England for supplies, but the threat of the Spanish Armada prevented his prompt return. By the time White got back to Roanoke in 1590, he found no trace of the settlers—only the word "Croatoan" carved on a tree. The fate of this "Lost Colony" has never been satisfactorily explained.

The next English venture focused on the more accessible Jamestown colony in the Chesapeake Bay area of Virginia. England tended to ignore the southern region until 1629, when Charles I laid out the territory between 30° and 36°N, named it Carolana for himself, and granted it to his attorney general, Sir Robert Heath. Heath made no attempt to people his domain, however, and Carolana remained empty of whites until stragglers drifted in from the mid-17th century onward. Events in England transformed Virginia's outpost into a separate colony. After the execution of Charles I in 1649, England had no ruling monarch until a party of noblemen invited Charles II back to England in 1660. Charles thanked eight of his benefactors three years later by making them lord proprietors of the province, now called Carolina. The vast new region eventually stretched from northern

Florida to the modern boundary between North Carolina and Virginia, and from the Atlantic to the Pacific Ocean.

The proprietors divided Carolina into three counties and appointed a governor for each one. Albemarle County embraced the existing settlements in northeastern North Carolina near the waters of Albemarle Sound; it was the only one that developed a government within the present state boundaries. From the beginning, relations between the older pioneers and their newly imposed government were stormy. The English philosopher John Locke drew up the Fundamental Constitutions of Carolina, but his political blueprints proved unworkable. The proprietors' arbitrary efforts to collect royal customs touched off factional violence, culminating in Culpepper's Rebellion of 1677, one of the first American uprisings against a corrupt regime.

For a few years afterward, local residents had a more representative government, until the proprietors attempted to strengthen the establishment of the Anglican Church in the colony. In 1711, Cary's Rebellion was touched off by laws passed against the colony's Quakers. During the confusion, Tuscarora Indians launched a war against the white intruders on their lands. The whites won the Tuscarora War in 1713 with assistance from South Carolina, but political weakness in the north persisted. Proprietary officials openly consorted with pirates—including the notorious Edward Teach, alias Blackbeard—and royal inspectors questioned the fitness of proprietary government. South Carolina officially split off in 1719 and received a royal governor in 1721. Ten years later, all but one of the proprietors relinquished their rights for £2,500 each, and North Carolina became a royal colony. The remaining proprietor, Lord Granville, gave up his governing rights but retained ownership of one-eighth of the original grant; the Granville District thus included more than half of the unsettled territory in the North Carolina colony.

In the decades that followed, thousands of new settlers poured into North Carolina; by 1775 the population had swollen to 345,000, making North Carolina the 4th most populous colony. Germans and Scots-Irish trekked down the Great Wagon Road from Pennsylvania to the Piedmont. Scottish Highlanders spread over the upper Cape Fear Valley as more Englishmen filled up the coastal plain. Backcountry settlers practiced self-sufficient farming, but eastern North Carolinians used slave labor to carve out rice and tobacco plantations. The westerners were often exploited by an eastern-dominated colonial assembly that sent corrupt and overbearing officials to govern them. Organizing in 1768 and calling themselves Regulators, unhappy westerners first petitioned for redress and then took up arms. Royal Governor William Tryon used eastern militia to crush the Regulators in a two-hour pitched battle at Alamance Creek in 1771.

The eastern leaders who dominated the assembly opposed all challenges to their authority, whether from the Regulators or from the British ministry. When England tightened its colonial administration, North Carolinians joined their fellow colonists in protests against the Stamp Act and similar impositions by Parliament. Meeting at Halifax in April 1776, the North Carolina provincial congress resolved in favor of American independence, the first colonial representative body to do so. Years later, citizens of Mecklenburg County recalled a gathering in 1775 during which their region declared independence, but subsequent historians have not verified their claim. The two dates on the North Carolina state flag nevertheless commemorate the Halifax Resolves and the "Mecklenburg Declaration of Independence."

Support for Britain appeared among recent Scottish immigrants, who answered the call to aid the royal governor but were ambushed by patriot militia at Moore's Creek Bridge on 27 February 1776. The incident effectively prevented a planned British invasion of the South. There was little further military action in North Carolina until late in the War for Independence, when Gen. Charles Cornwallis invaded the state from South

Carolina in the fall of 1780. Guerrilla bands harassed his troops, and North Carolina militia wiped out a Loyalist detachment at King's Mountain. Pursuing the elusive American army under Gen. Nathanael Greene, Cornwallis won a costly victory at Guilford Courthouse in March 1781 but could neither eliminate his rival nor pacify the countryside. For the rest of 1781, Cornwallis wearied his men in marches and countermarches across North Carolina and Virginia before he finally succumbed to a trap set at Yorktown, Va., by an American army and a French fleet.

Numerous problems beset the new state. The government had a dire need of money, but when the victors sought to pay debts by selling land confiscated from the Loyalists, conservative lawyers objected strenuously, and a bitter political controversy ensued. Suspicious of outside control, North Carolina leaders hesitated before joining the Union. The state waited until November 1789 to ratify the US Constitution—a delay that helped stimulate the movement for adoption of a Bill of Rights. In 1789, North Carolina relinquished its lands beyond the Great Smokies in 1789 (after an unsuccessful attempt by settlers to create a new state called Franklin), and thousands of North Carolinians migrated to the new western territories. The state did not share in the general prosperity of the early federal period. Poor transportation facilities hampered all efforts to expand commercial agriculture, and illiteracy remained widespread. North Carolina society came to appear so backward that some observers nicknamed it the "Rip Van Winkle state."

In 1815, state senator Archibald D. Murphey of Orange County began to press for public schools and for improved transportation to open up the Piedmont. Most eastern planters resisted Murphey's suggestions, partly because they refused to be taxed for the benefit of the westerners and partly because they feared the destabilizing social effects of reform. As long as the east controlled the general assembly, the ideas of Murphey and his sympathizers had little practical impact, but in 1835, as a result of reforms in the state constitution, the west obtained reapportionment and the political climate changed. North Carolina initiated a program of state aid to railroads and other public works, and established the first state—supported system of common schools in the South.

Like other southern whites, North Carolina's white majority feared for the security of slavery under a national Republican administration, but North Carolinians reacted to the election of Abraham Lincoln with caution. When South Carolina and six other states seceded and formed the Confederate States of America in 1861, North Carolina refused to join, instead making a futile attempt to work for a peaceful settlement of the issue. However, after the outbreak of hostilities at Ft. Sumter, S.C., and Lincoln's call for troops in April 1861, neutrality disappeared and public opinion swung to the Confederate side. North Carolina became the last state to withdraw from the Union, joining the Confederacy on 20 May 1861.

North Carolina provided more troops to the Confederacy than any other state, and its losses added up to more than one-fourth of the total for the entire South, but support for the war was mixed. State leaders resisted the centralizing tendencies of the Richmond government, and even Governor Zebulon B. Vance opposed the Confederacy's conscription policies. North Carolina became a haven for deserters from the front lines in Virginia. William W. Holden, a popular Raleigh editor, organized a peace movement when defeat appeared inevitable, and Unionist sentiment flourished in the mountain counties; nevertheless, most white North Carolinians stood by Vance and the dying Confederate cause. At the war's end, Gen. Joseph E. Johnston surrendered the last major Confederate army to Gen. William T. Sherman at Bennett House near Hillsborough on 26 April 1865.

Reconstruction was marked by a bitter political and social struggle in North Carolina. United in the Conservative Party, most of the prewar slaveholding elite fought to preserve as much as possible of the former system, but a Republican coalition of blacks and nonslaveholding white Unionists defended freedmen's rights and instituted democratic reforms for the benefit of both races. After writing a new constitution in 1868, Republicans elected Holden as governor, but native whites fought back with violence and intimidation under the robes of the Ku Klux Klan. Holden's efforts to restore order were ineffectual, and when the Conservatives recaptured the general assembly in 1870, they impeached him and removed him from office. Election of a Conservative governor in 1876 signaled the end of the Reconstruction era.

Once in power, the Conservatives—or Democrats, as they renamed themselves—slashed public services and enacted legislation to guarantee the power of landlords over tenants and sharecroppers. They cooperated with the consolidation of railroads under northern ownership, and they supported a massive drive to build cotton mills on the swiftly flowing streams of the Piedmont. By 1880, industry had surpassed its prewar level. But it was not until 1900 that blacks and their white allies were entirely eliminated as contenders for political power.

As the Industrial Revolution gained ground in North Carolina, small farmers protested their steadily worsening condition. The Populist Party expressed their demands for reform, and for a brief period in the 1890s shared power with the Republican Party in the Fusion movement. Under the leadership of Charles Brantley Aycock, conservative Democrats fought back with virulent denunciations of "Negro rule" and a call for white supremacy. In 1900, voters elected Aycock governor and approved a constitutional amendment that barred all illiterates from voting, except for those whose ancestors had voted before 1867. This literacy test and "grandfather clause" effectively disenfranchised blacks, while providing a temporary loophole for uneducated whites. To safeguard white rights after 1908 (the constitutional limit for registration under the grandfather clause), Aycock promised substantial improvements in the school system to put an end to white illiteracy.

In the decades after Aycock's election, an alliance of business interests and moderate-to-conservative Democrats dominated North Carolina politics. The industrial triumvirate of textile, tobacco, and furniture manufacturers, joined by banks and insurance companies, controlled the state's economy. The Republican Party shrank to a small remnant among mountain whites as blacks were forced out of the electorate.

In the years after World War II, North Carolina took its place in the booming Sunbelt economy. The development of Research Triangle Park—equidistant from the educational facilities of Duke University, North Carolina State University, and the University of North Carolina at Chapel Hill—provided a home for dozens of scientific and technology laboratories for government and business. New industries, some of them financed by foreign capital, appeared in formerly rural areas, and a prolonged population drain was effectively reversed.

The process of development has not been smooth or uniform, however. The late 1980s and early 1990s saw a shift in employment patterns as financial and high-technology industries boomed while jobs in the state's traditional industries, notably textiles and tobacco, declined. North Carolina possessed both the largest percentage of manufacturing jobs in the country and the lowest manufacturing wages. In 1990, 30% of all jobs paid annual wages below the poverty line for a family of four, resulting in 13% of North Carolinians living below the nationally established poverty line. Despite widespread prosperity in the 1990s, North Carolina was one of only 15 states where poverty—and child poverty—were on the rise. The rate had climbed to 14% by 1998.

The excellence of many of North Carolina's universities contrasted with the inferior education provided by its primary and secondary public schools. North Carolina students' SAT scores placed them last nationally in 1989. In the ongoing effort to improve the public school system, in 2000 Democratic Governor Jim Hunt's top two priorities were raising teacher pay by 6.5% and funding the Smart Start (early childhood education) program. But Hunt's stance was not popular with the state's workers, who were lobbying the governor and the General Assembly for pay raises.

Racial tensions have created divisions within the state, which has one of the highest levels of Ku Klux Klan activity in the country. While Charlotte integrated its schools peacefully in 1971 through court-ordered busing, the militancy of black activists in the late 1960s and early 1970s provoked a white backlash. That backlash, along with the identification of the Democratic party in the early 1970s with liberal causes and with opposition to the Vietnam War, helped the conservative wing of the Republican party gain popularity in a state whose six military bases had given it a hawkish tradition. In 1972, North Carolina elected its first Republican US senator (Jesse A. Helms) and governor (James E. Holshouser, Jr.) since Fusion days, and Republican strength continued to build into the mid-1990s. But after 1998 elections, the state was leaning toward a more bipartisan representation: Democratic candidate John Edwards took the state's second Senate seat while conservative Republican Helms retained the other; and voters sent seven Republicans and five Democrats to represent them in the US House.

Rising crime rates were among the leading public policy issues in the 1990s. The state legislature enacted laws imposing tough penalties on adults who supply guns to minors, and mandating life imprisonment without parole for three-time violent offenders.

Mother Nature has posed serious problems for North Carolinians in recent times. In September 1999, successive hurricanes moved onshore, water logging the low-lying eastern part of the state. The worst flooding in North Carolina history was intensified by more rainfall in the weeks that followed. The death toll climbed to 40 while property damages and agricultural losses rose. Preliminary damage estimates reached $1.3 billion and were expected to rise. Clean-up of the state's waterways, which were polluted by waste from pigs and other livestock as well as from flooded sewage plants, remained a major health concern. In January 2000 the same region was blanketed in record snowfalls, adding further hardships to those who were struggling to recover. A month earlier, in an emergency legislative session, the General Assembly approved Governor Jim Hunt's plan to send $836 million to flood victims. By July 2000 the federal government had approved more than $1 billion in aid to the state. But it was estimated that the conditions had put thousands of farmers permanently out of business. North Carolina experienced a harsh winter in 2002–03, with some of the heaviest snowfalls since 1989.

The state's agricultural producers were also facing the declining demand for tobacco. The documented health hazards of smoking, state and federal excise taxes, ongoing lawsuits, and declining exports combined to cut cigarette production (also hurting the state's manufacturing sector in the process). With Kentucky, North Carolina farmers produced more than 65% of the total US crop. The state's historical dependency on the cash crop caused lawmakers to allocate half the funds from the national tobacco settlement to tobacco communities—to support educational and job training programs, provide employment assistance for farmers and displaced laborers, fund rural health care and social service programs, and invest in local public works and economic development projects to attract new businesses to areas that had been dependent on tobacco. The other half of the settlement was evenly divided between statewide health care and a trust fund for (former) tobacco growers and farm laborers.

Governor Mike Easley set his 2003 executive agenda on education, proposing a state lottery to fund education. The state was considering a moratorium on the death penalty in 2003, due to concerns over racial bias.

12 STATE GOVERNMENT

North Carolina has operated under three constitutions, adopted in 1776, 1868, and 1971, respectively. The first was drafted hurriedly under wartime pressures and contained several inconsistencies and undemocratic features. The second, a product of Reconstruction, was written by native white Republicans and a sprinkling of blacks and northern-born Republicans. When conservative whites regained power, they left the basic framework of this constitution intact, though they added the literacy test, poll tax, and grandfather clause to it.

A century after the Civil War, the document had become unwieldy and partially obsolete. A constitutional study commission submitted to the general assembly in 1969 a rewritten constitution, which the electorate ratified, as amended, in 1971. As of January 2003, the document had been amended a total of 31 times. One amendment permits the governor and lieutenant governor to serve a maximum of two successive four-year terms.

Under the 1971 constitution, the general assembly consists of a 50-member senate and a 120-member house of representatives. Regular sessions are held in odd-numbered years, with the provision that the legislature may (and in practice, does) divide to meet in even-numbered years. Sessions begin in January and are not formally limited in length. Special sessions may be called by three-fifths petition of each house. Senators must be at least 25 years old, must be qualified voters of the state, and must have been residents of the state for at least two years and residents of their districts for at least one year prior to election. Representatives must be qualified voters of the state and must have lived in their district for at least a year; the constitution establishes 21 as the minimum age for elective office. All members of the general assembly serve two-year terms. The legislative salary was $13,951 in 2002, unchanged from 1999.

The governor and lieutenant governor (who run separately) must be 30 years old; each must have been a US citizen for five years and a state resident for two. In 2002 the governor's salary was $118,430. North Carolina's chief executive has powers of appointment, supervision, veto, and budgetary recommendation. The voters also elect a secretary of state, treasurer, auditor, superintendent of public instruction, attorney general, and commissioners of agriculture, insurance, labor, and public lands; all serve four-year terms. These officials preside over their respective departments and sit with the governor and lieutenant governor as the council of state. The governor appoints the heads of the other executive departments.

Bills become law when they have passed three readings in each house of the general assembly, and take effect 30 days after adjournment. Bills that are not signed or vetoed by the governor become law after 10 days when the legislature is in session and after 30 days if the legislature adjourns. A three-fifths vote of the elected members in each house is required to override a gubernatorial veto. Constitutional amendments may be proposed by a convention called by a two-thirds vote of both houses and a majority of the voters, or may be submitted directly to the voters by a three-fifths consent of each house. In either case, the proposed amendments must be ratified by a popular majority before becoming part of the constitution.

To vote in North Carolina a person must be a US citizen, at least 18 years old, a resident of the state and county for at least

30 days prior to election day, and not registered to vote in another state. Restrictions apply to convicted felons.

13 POLITICAL PARTIES

Prior to the Civil War, Whigs and Democrats were the two major political groups in North Carolina. The Republican Party emerged during Reconstruction as a coalition of newly enfranchised blacks, northern immigrants, and disaffected native whites, especially from non-slaveholding areas in the mountains. The opposing Conservative Party, representing a coalition of antebellum Democrats and former Whigs, became the Democratic Party after winning the governorship in 1876; from that time and for most of the 20th century, North Carolina was practically a one-party state.

Beginning in the 1930s, however, as blacks reentered the electorate as supporters of the New Deal and the liberal measures associated with Democratic presidents, the Republican Party attracted new white members who objected to national Democratic policies. Republican presidential candidates picked up strength in the 1950s and 1960s, and Richard Nixon carried North Carolina in 1968 and 1972, when Republicans also succeeded in electing Governor James E. Holshouser, Jr., and US Senator Jesse A. Helms. The Watergate scandal cut short this movement toward a revitalized two-party system, and in 1976, Jimmy Carter became the first Democratic presidential candidate to carry the state since 1964.

Republican presidential candidate Ronald Reagan narrowly carried North Carolina in 1980, and a second Republican senator, John P. East, was elected that year. In 1984, the Republican Party had its best election year in North Carolina. Reagan won the state by a landslide, Helms won a third term—defeating two-term Governor James B. Hunt in the most expensive race to date in Senate history (more than $26 million was spent)—and Republican James G. Martin, a US representative, was elected governor, succeeding Hunt. In 1990, Helms was reelected to the Senate, defeating black mayor Harvey Gantt in a bitterly contested race. In 1996 Gantt challenged Helms again, and once again Helms was the victor. Helms subsequently announced he would not run for reelection in 2002, and Republican Elizabeth H. Dole won his seat. In 2000,

Republican George W. Bush won 56% of the presidential vote, to Democrat Al Gore's 43%.

But by the mid-1990s the states' Democrats were influential again. In 1993 Democrat James B. Hunt returned to the governor's office after a hiatus of eight years. He was elected to his third term (having served the first two between 1977 and 1985) in the 1992 election, and went on to a fourth term following the 1996 elections. Having served the limit, Hunt was leaving the gubernatorial race open for 2000, and Democrat Mike Easley won the governorship in 2000. In 1998 elections the second US Senate seat, which had been won by Republican Lauch Faircloth in 1992, was won by Democrat John Edwards. In 2003 Edwards was running for president and had announced he would not seek reelection in 2004.

In 2002 there were 5,058,021 registered voters. In 1998, 53% of registered voters were Democratic, 34% Republican, and 14% unaffiliated or members of other parties. The state had 14 electoral votes in the 2000 presidential election.

Following the 2002 elections, seven of North Carolina's 13 US Representatives were Republicans, and six were Democrats. In mid-2003 the state assembly was divided evenly between Democrats and Republicans (60–60), and there were 22 Republicans and 28 Democrats in the state senate.

Minor parties have had a marked influence on the state. George Wallace's American Independent Party won 496,188 votes in 1968, placing second with more than 31% of the total vote. In 1992, Independent Ross Perot captured 14% of the vote.

14 LOCAL GOVERNMENT

As of 2002, North Carolina had 100 counties, 541 municipalities, and 175 special districts. That year the state has 319 public school systems.

Counties have been the basis of local government in North Carolina for more than 300 years, and are still the primary governmental units for most citizens. All counties are led by boards of commissioners; commissioners serve either two- or four-year terms, and most are elected at large rather than by district. Most boards elect their own chairman from among their members, but voters in some counties choose a chairman separately. More than half the counties employ a county manager to supervise day-to-day operations of county government. Other

North Carolina Presidential Vote by Political Parties, 1948–2000

YEAR	ELECTORAL VOTE	NORTH CAROLINA WINNER	DEMOCRAT	REPUBLICAN	STATES' RIGHTS DEMOCRAT	PROGRESSIVE
1948	14	*Truman (D)	459,070	258,572	69,652	3,915
1952	14	Stevenson (D)	652,803	558,107	—	
1956	14	Stevenson (D)	590,530	575,069	—	—
1960	14	*Kennedy (D)	713,136	655,420	—	—
1964	13	*Johnson (D)	800,139	624,841	—	—
						AMERICAN IND.
1968	13	*Nixon (R)	464,113	627,192	—	496,188
						American
1972	13	*Nixon (R)	438,705	1,054,889	—	25,018
					LIBERTARIAN	
1976	13	Carter (D)	927,365	741,960	2,219	5,607
1980	13	*Reagan (R)	875,635	915,018	9,677	
1984	13	*Reagan (R)	824,287	1,346,481	3,794	—
						NEW ALLIANCE
1988	13	*Bush (R)	890,167	1,237,258	1,263	5,682
						IND. (Perot)
1992	14	Bush (R)	1,114,042	1,134,661	5,171	357,864
1996	14	Dole (R)	1,107,849	1,225,938	8,740	168,059
						REFORM
2000	14	*Bush, G. W. (R)	1,257,692	1,631,163	12,307	8,874

*Won US presidential election.

elected officials are the sheriff, register of deeds, and the school board. Counties are subdivided into townships, but these are for administrative convenience only; they do not exercise any independent government functions.

County and municipal governments share many functions, but the precise allocation of authority varies in each case. Although the city of Charlotte and Mecklenburg County share a common school system, most often schools, streets, sewers, garbage collection, police and fire protection, and other services are handled separately. Most cities use the council-manager form of government, with council members elected from the city at large. Proliferation of suburban governments was hampered by a 1972 constitutional amendment that forbids the incorporation of a new town or city within 1 mi (1.6 km) of a city of 5,000–9,999 people, within 3 mi (4.8 km) of a city of 10,000–24,999, within 4 mi (6.4 km) of a city of 25,000–49,999, and within 5 mi (8 km) of a city of 50,000 or more unless the general assembly acts to do so by a three-fifths vote of all members of each house.

15STATE SERVICES

To address the continuing threat of terrorism and to work with the federal Department of Homeland Security (created in 2002 following the terrorist attacks of 11 September 2001), homeland security in North Carolina in 2003 operated under the authority of the governor; the crime control/public safety secretary was designated as the state homeland security advisor.

The Department of Public Instruction administers state aid to local public school systems, a board of governors directs the 16 state-supported institutions of higher education, and the Department of Community Colleges administers the 58 community colleges. The Department of Cultural Resources offers a variety of educational and enrichment services to the public, maintaining historical sites, operating two major state museums, funding the North Carolina Symphony, and providing for the State Library. The Department of Transportation plans, builds, and maintains state highways; registers motor vehicles; develops airport facilities; administers public transportation activities; and operates 15 ferries.

Within the Department of Health and Human Resources, the Division of Mental Health, Mental Retardation, and Substance Abuse Services operates 4 regional psychiatric hospitals, 5 regional mental retardation centers, and 3 alcoholic rehabilitation centers; it also coordinates 41 area mental health programs that include community mental health centers, group homes for the mentally retarded and emotionally disturbed, shelter workshops, halfway houses, a special-care facility, and 2 reeducation programs for emotionally disturbed children and adolescents. The Division of Social Services administers public assistance programs, and other divisions license medical facilities, promote public health, administer programs for juvenile delinquents and the vocationally handicapped, and operate a school for the blind and visually impaired and three schools for the deaf. The Department of Agriculture and Consumer Services protects the consumer.

The Department of Crime Control and Public Safety includes the Highway Patrol and the National Guard, while the Department of Correction manages the prison system. Local law enforcement agencies receive assistance from the Department of Justice's State Bureau of Investigation and the Police Information Network. The Community Assistance Division of the Department of Environment and Natural Resources offers a variety of planning services to local government in the areas of housing, neighborhood renewal, and fiscal resources. The Department of Labor administers the state Occupational Safety and Health Act; inspects boilers, elevators, amusement rides, mines, and quarries; offers conciliation, mediation, and arbitration services to settle labor disputes; and enforces state laws governing child labor, minimum wages, maximum working hours, and uniform wage payment.

16JUDICIAL SYSTEM

North Carolina's general court of justice is a unified judicial system that includes appellate courts (court of appeals) and trial courts (superior court). District court judges are elected to four-year terms; judges above that level are elected for eight years.

The state's highest court, the supreme court, consists of a chief justice and six associate justices. It hears cases from the court of appeals as well as certain cases from lower courts. The court of appeals comprises 12 judges who hear cases in 3-judge panels. Superior courts, in 44 districts, have original jurisdiction in most major civil and criminal cases. There are 99 superior court judges appointed by the governor to eight-year terms. All superior court justices rotate between the districts within their divisions. District courts try misdemeanors, civil cases involving less than $5,000, and all domestic cases. They have no juries in criminal cases, but these cases may be appealed to superior court and be given a jury trial de novo; in civil cases, jury trial is provided on demand.

North Carolina had 31,142 prisoners in state and federal correctional institutions in June 2001, an increase of 0.2% from the previous year. The state's incarceration rate stood at 329 per 100,000 population. In 2001 North Carolina's overall crime rate per 100,000 persons was 4,938.0, including a total of 40,465 violent crimes and 363,777 crimes against property in that year.

North Carolina punishes crime severely. From 1930 to 1997, the state executed 271 persons, and executed 25 people between 1977 and 2003. The US Supreme Court invalidated North Carolina's death penalty statute in 1976, and the sentences of all inmates then on death row reverted to life imprisonment. The state passed a new capital punishment statute in 1977 that apparently assuaged the Court's objections. Two persons were executed in 1984—the state's first executions since 1961. One of the prisoners executed that year, Velma Barfield, was the first woman executed in the US since 1962 and the first in North Carolina since 1944. In 2003, there were 217 persons under sentence of death.

17ARMED FORCES

North Carolina holds the headquarters of the 3rd Army at Ft. Bragg in Fayetteville and a major training facility for the Marine Corps at Camp Lejeune in Jacksonville. The Marine Corps air stations at Cherry Point and New River and Seymour Johnson Air Force Base in Goldsboro are the state's other important military installations. North Carolina firms received nearly $1.48 billion in defense contract awards in 2002. In 2002, there were 94,296 active duty military personnel and 16,444 civilian personnel stationed in North Carolina, most of whom were at Ft. Bragg.

There were 792,646 veterans living in North Carolina according to the 2000 Census. Of these, 129,478 saw service in World War II; 89,290 in the Korean conflict; 226,806 during the Vietnam era; and 118,357 during 1990–2000 (including the Persian Gulf War). Veterans' benefits totaled more than $1.6 billion in 2002.

In 2000, the North Carolina State Highway Patrol employed 1,416 full-time sworn officers.

18MIGRATION

For most of the state's history, more people have moved away every decade than have moved into the state, and population growth has come only from net natural increase. In 1850, one-third of all free, native-born North Carolinians lived outside the state, chiefly in Tennessee, Georgia, Indiana, and Alabama. The state suffered a net loss of population from migration in every decade from 1870 to 1970.

Before 1890, the emigration rate was higher among whites than among blacks; since then, the reverse has been true, but the number of whites moving into North Carolina did not exceed the number of white emigrants until the 1960s. Between 1940 and 1970, 539,000 more blacks left North Carolina than moved into the state; most of these emigrants sought homes in the North and West. After 1970, however, black out-migration abruptly slackened as economic conditions in eastern North Carolina improved. Net migration to North Carolina was estimated at 278,000 (6th among the states) from 1970 to 1980, at 83,000 (9th among the states) from 1980 to 1983; and 347,000 (5th among the states) from 1985 to 1990. Between 1990 and 1998, the state had net gains of 501,000 in domestic migration and 49,000 in international migration. In 1998, 6,415 foreign immigrants arrived in North Carolina. The state's overall population increased 13.8% between 1990 and 1998. In the period 1995–2000, 919,336 people moved into the state and 581,453 moved out, for a net gain of 337,883, 20,922 of whom were age 65 or over.

[19]INTERGOVERNMENTAL COOPERATION

North Carolina adheres to at least 23 interstate compacts, including four that promote regional planning and development. The oldest of the four, establishing the Board of Control for Southern Regional Education, pools the resources of southern states for the support of graduate and professional schools. The Southeastern Forest Fire Protection Compact promotes regional forest conservation, while the Southern States Energy Board fosters cooperation in nuclear power development. The Southern Growth Policies Board, formed in 1971 at the suggestion of former North Carolina Governor Terry Sanford, collects and publishes data for planning purposes from its headquarters in Research Triangle Park. The Tennessee Valley Authority operates four dams in western North Carolina to aid in flood control, generate hydroelectric power, and assist navigation downstream on the Tennessee River; most of the electricity generated is exported to Tennessee. North Caroline also belongs to the Mid-Atlantic Fishery Management Council, the Atlantic States Marine Fisheries Commission, the Ohio River Basin Commission, and the Appalachian Regional Commission. Total federal grants in 2001 were over $9.1 billion.

[20]ECONOMY

North Carolina's economy was dominated by agriculture until the closing decades of the 19th century, with tobacco the major cash crop; today, tobacco is still the central factor in the economy of the coastal plain. In the piedmont, industrialization accelerated after 1880 when falling crop prices made farming less attractive. During the "cotton mill crusade" of the late 19th and early 20th centuries, local capitalists put spinning or weaving mills on swift streams throughout the region, until nearly every hamlet had its own factory. Under the leadership of James B. Duke, the American Tobacco Co. (now American Brands, with headquarters in New York City) expanded from its Durham headquarters during this same period to control, for a time, virtually the entire US market for smoking products. After native businessmen had established a successful textile boom, New England firms moved south in an effort to cut costs, and the piedmont became a center of southern industrial development.

As more and more Tar Heels left agriculture for the factory, their per capita income rose from 47% of the national average in 1930 to slightly less than 100% of the national average in 2000. The biggest employers are the textile and furniture industries. State government has made a vigorous effort to recruit outside investment and to improve the state's industrial mix. Major new firms now produce electrical equipment, processed foods, technical instruments, fabricated metals, plastics, and chemicals. The greatest industrial growth, however, has come not from wholly new industries but from fields related to industries that were firmly established. Apparel manufacture spread across eastern North Carolina during as an obvious extension of the textile industry, and other new firms produce chemicals and machinery for the textile and furniture business. Manufacturing remains the dominant sector in the state's economy, peaking at an output of nearly $62 billion (23.8% of total output) in 1999, as the overall state economy grew at a rate of 8.8% in 1998 and 8% in 1999. A decline in manufacturing output of 4.9% by 2001 was accompanied by declining overall growth rates, of 4.7% in 2000, and 0.98% in the national recession of 2001. While the nation's unemployment rose 1.4 percentage points between the third quarter 1999 and third quarter 2002, the rise in North Carolina over this period was 6.4%, reflecting mainly layoffs in its manufacturing sector.

North Carolina's gross state product in 2001 was $275.6 billion, twelfth among the states, to which manufacturing contributed $53.9 billion; financial services, $52.3 billion; general services, $48 billion; trade, $41.9 billion; government, $35.9 billion; transportation and public utilities, $18.8 billion, and construction, $14.1 billion. The public sector in 2001 constituted 13% of gross state product.

[21]INCOME

According to the Bureau of Economic Analysis, in 2001, North Carolina had a per capita personal income (PCPI) of $27,308 which ranked 33rd in the United States (including the District of Columbia) and was 90% of the national average, $30,413. The 2001 PCPI reflected an increase of 1.4% from 2000 compared to the national change of 2.2%. In 2001, North Carolina had a total personal income (TPI) of $224,093,955,000 which ranked 13th in the United States and accounted for 2.6% of the national total. The 2001 TPI reflected an increase of 2.9% from 2000 compared to the national change of 3.3%.

Earnings of persons employed in North Carolina increased from $158,315,629,000 in 2000 to $161,595,258,000 in 2001, an increase of 2.1%. The largest industries in 2001 were services, 24.7% of earnings; state and local government, 12.6%; and durable goods manufacturing, 10.3%. Of the industries that accounted for at least 5% of earnings in 2001, the slowest growing from 2000 to 2001 was durable goods manufacturing, which decreased 6.3%; the fastest was state and local government, which increased 6.2%.

According to data released by the US Census Bureau, in 2000, the median household income was $38,829 compared to the national average of $42,148. In 2001, the median income for a family of four was $56,500 compared to the national average of $63,278. For the period 1999 to 2001, the average poverty rate was 12.9% which placed it 38th among the 50 states and the District of Columbia ranked lowest to highest.

[22]LABOR

According to Bureau of Labor Statistics (BLS) provisional estimates, in July 2003 the seasonally adjusted civilian labor force in North Carolina numbered 4,185,400, with approximately 277,900 workers unemployed, yielding an unemployment rate of 6.6%, compared to the national average of 6.2% for the same period. Since the beginning of the BLS data series in 1978, the highest unemployment rate recorded was 10.0% in February 1983. The historical low was 3.0% in June 1999. It is estimated that in 2001, 6.6% of the labor force was employed in construction; 18.6% in manufacturing; 4.7% in transportation, communications, and public utilities; 19.3% in trade; 5.1% in finance, insurance, and real estate; 22.4% in services; 13.7% in government; and 2.5% in agriculture.

North Carolina working conditions have brought the state considerable notoriety over the years. North Carolina is one of 22 states with a right-to-work law, and public officials are legally barred from negotiating a collective bargaining agreement. The US Department of Labor reported that in 2002, 111,000 of North Carolina's 3,427,000 employed wage and salary workers were members of unions. This represented 3.2% of those so employed, down from 3.7% in 2001. The national average is 13.2%. North Carolina has the lowest union membership rate of all the states, a position it has held since the state data series became available. The national average is 13.2%. In all, 138,000 workers (4.0%) were represented by unions. In addition to union members, this category includes workers who report no union affiliation but whose jobs are covered by a union contract.

[23]AGRICULTURE

Farm marketings in North Carolina totaled over $7.7 billion in 2001, 7th among the 50 states, with 40% from crop marketings. North Carolina led the nation in the production of tobacco and sweet potatoes, ranked 4th in peanuts, and was also a leading producer of corn, grapes, pecans, apples, tomatoes, and soybeans. Farm life plays an important role in the culture of the state.

The number of farms fell from 301,000 in 1950 to 56,000 in 2002, while the number of acres in farms declined from 17,800,000 to 9,100,000 (7,203,000 to 3,682,000 hectares). At 163 acres (66 hectares), the average North Carolina farm was only 37% the size of the average US farm—a statistic that in part reflects the smaller acreage requirements of tobacco, the state's principal crop. The relatively large number of family farm owner-operators who depend on a modest tobacco allotment to make their small acreages profitable is the basis for North Carolina's opposition to the US government's antismoking campaign and its fight to preserve tobacco price supports.

Although farm employment continues to decline, a significant share of North Carolina jobs—perhaps more than one-third—are still linked to agriculture either directly or indirectly. North Carolina's most heavily agricultural counties are massed in the coastal plain, the center of tobacco, corn, and soybean production, along with a bank of northern piedmont counties on the Virginia border. Virtually all peanut production is in the eastern part of the state, while tobacco, corn, and soybean production spills over into the piedmont. Cotton is grown in scattered counties along the South Carolina border and in a band leading northward across the coastal plain. Beans, tomatoes, cucumbers, strawberries, and blueberries are commercial crops in selected mountain and coastal plain locations. Apples are important to the economy of the mountains, and the sand hills are a center of peach cultivation.

In 2002, tobacco production was 357,350,000 lb, 40% of US production. Production and value data for North Carolina's other principal crops were as follows: corn, 58,100,000 bushels, $168,490,000; soybeans, 30,080,000 bushels, $165,440,000; peanuts, 210,000,000 lb, $43,680,000; and sweet potatoes, 4,810,000 hundredweight, $62,530,000.

[24]ANIMAL HUSBANDRY

North Carolina farms and ranches had an estimated 920,000 cattle and calves in 2003, valued at $552 million. In 2002, the state had around 9.6 million hogs and pigs, valued at $556.8 million. During 2001, North Carolina led the nation in turkey production with 1.13 billion lb (0.5 billion kg) of turkey, worth $452 million; the state was 4th in broiler production with 4.2 billion lb (1.9 billion kg), worth $1.68 billion; egg production

totaled 2.54 billion eggs, worth $232.4 million. Milk cows numbered 67,000 in 2001 and they produced 1.16 million lb (0.53 million kg) of milk.

[25]FISHING

North Carolina's fishing industry ranks 2nd only to Virginia's among the South Atlantic states, but its overall economic importance has declined. The record landing for the state was in 1981, a total of 432 million lb; the 1998 catch was only 182.2 million lb, valued at $104.8 million. North Carolina had 835 commercial fishing boats and vessels in 1997. Flounder, menhaden, and sea trout are the most valuable finfish; shrimp, crabs, and clams are the most sought-after shellfish. The state's 152 fish processors and wholesalers employed 2,344 persons in 1997.

[26]FORESTRY

As of 2002, forests covered 19,302,000 acres (7,812,000 hectares) in North Carolina, or about 62% of the state's land area. North Carolina's forests constitute 2.5% of all US forestland, and 97% of the state's wooded areas have commercial value. The largest tracts are found along the coast and in the Western Mountains, where most counties are more than 70% tree-covered. Hardwoods make up 53% of the state's forests. Mixed stands of oak and pine account for an additional 14%. The remaining 33% is pine and other conifers. More than 90% of the acreage harvested for timber is reforested.

National forests cover 6% of North Carolina's timberlands, and state and local governments own another 2%. The remainder is privately owned. In the days of wooden sailing vessels, North Carolina pine trees supplied large quantities of "naval stores"— tar, pitch, and turpentine for waterproofing and other nautical purposes. Today, the state produces mainly saw logs, pulpwood, veneer logs, and Christmas trees.

In 2002, lumber production totaled 2.55 billion board feet, 7th in the US.

[27]MINING

The estimated 2001 value of minerals produced in North Carolina was essentially unchanged from that of 2000, remaining at $744 million. The state's leading mineral commodities remained crushed stone and phosphate rock. According to preliminary figures, crushed stone was valued at $485 million (about $7 million more than in 2000). Production was estimated at 68.4 million metric tons. Phosphate rock, in Beaufort County, and lithium minerals, mined in the Kings Mountain area of Gaston and Cleveland counties, were the next most valuable mineral commodities mined. North Carolina ranked 1st in the production of common clay, feldspar, crude mica, and pyrophyllite; 2nd in olivine lithium; 3rd in phosphate rock; 5th in kaolin; and 8th in industrial sand and gravel and crushed stone. Clay production amounted to 2.43 million metric tons, valued at $18.6 million. Two categories of clay, common clay, and shale and kaolin, were produced, the kaolin as a byproduct of feldspar and mica operations in Avery and Cleveland counties. Dimension stone production was 40,000 metric tons (valued at $16 million).

[28]ENERGY AND POWER

Except for a modest volume of hydroelectric power, the energy consumed in North Carolina comes from outside sources. In 1998 residential users consumed about 23% of North Carolina's energy in that year, commercial users 17%, industrial users 34%, and transportation 26%.

Installed electrical capacity (utility and nonutility) totaled 22.9 million kW in 1999, and production reached 117.6 billion kWh. The two Brunswick stations in Southport and the Harris plant in Wake County, operated by Carolina Power and Light, and the two Duke Power McGuire stations at Cowens Ford Dam were the only nuclear power units in operation in 2001. In 2000 North Carolina's total per capita energy consumption was 311 million Btu (78.4 million kcal), ranking it 37th among the 50 states.

No petroleum or natural gas has been found in North Carolina, but major companies have expressed interest in offshore drilling. There is no coal mining, and proved coal reserves are minor, at only 10.7 million tons.

[29] INDUSTRY

North Carolina had a predominantly industrial economy for most of the 20th century. Today, the state remains the nation's largest manufacturer of textiles, cigarettes, and furniture. The textile industry is the largest manufacturing sector, followed by tobacco manufacturers, chemicals and allied products, industrial machinery, food products, electronics/electrical equipment, furniture and fixtures, and rubber and plastics products. The total value of shipments by manufacturers exceeded $163 billion in 1997.

The industrial regions of North Carolina spread out from the piedmont cities; roughly speaking, each movement outward represents a step down in the predominant level of skills and wages and a step closer to the primary processing of raw materials. Burlington Industries (the world's largest textile company), Blue Bell Inc., Cannon Mills, and Cone Mills are major US textile corporations based in Greensboro; Fieldcrest Mills has its headquarters in Eden. The furniture industry is centered in the High Point-Thomasville and Hickory-Statesville areas. Charlotte's factories produce electrical appliances, textiles, and chemicals and machinery for the textile industry. Broad rural areas of the piedmont also have many industrial installations: Gaston County near Charlotte contains the largest concentration of textile factories in the US.

In 1997, North Carolina was the headquarters for seven Fortune 500 companies: Nationsbank Corp., First Union Corp., Lowe's, Duke Power, Wachovia Corp., Nucor, and Carolina Power and Light.

Earnings of persons employed in North Carolina increased from $130.5 billion in 1997 to $138.5 billion in 1998, an increase of 6.2%. The largest industries in 1998 were services, 22.2% of earnings; nondurable goods manufacturing, 12.2%; and durable goods manufacturing, 11.6%. Of the industries that accounted for at least 5% of earnings in 1998, the slowest growing from 1997 to 1998 was nondurable goods manufacturing, which increased 2.9%; the fastest was construction (6.7% of earnings in 1998), which increased 11.1%.

[30] COMMERCE

North Carolina had 14,502 wholesale establishments in 1997 with sales of over $103 billion. Wholesaling is concentrated in the Piedmont Crescent. Retail sales by 46,815 establishments in 1997 totaled $75 billion (ranked 5th in the state in terms of sales growth from 1992 to 1997, at 50%). The leading type of retail sales establishments in 1997 were automotive dealers, 15%; food stores, 11%; and eating and drinking places, 26%. Food sales came to $14 billion, while general merchandise sales amounted to $8.9 billion.

The state ports at Wilmington and Morehead City handle a growing volume of international trade. In 1998, North Carolina exported over $15.7 billion worth of its goods to foreign markets (10th in the US).

[31] CONSUMER PROTECTION

The Consumer Protection Office of the Attorney General has as its function the protection of North Carolina consumers from unfair and deceptive trade practices and dishonest and unethical business competition. Although it assists in the resolution of disputes, investigates cases of consumer fraud, and initiates action to halt proscribed trade practices, it does not represent individual consumers in court. It also represents the public before the North Carolina Utilities Commission.

[32] BANKING

North Carolina had 62 insured banks in 2002 with assets of $17.8 billion. Fifty-seven of those banks were state-chartered.

Net interest margins (NIMs) (the difference between the lower rates offered to savers and the higher rates charged on loans) improved for 38 insured banks in North Carolina in 2002, compared with 15 in 2001. Overall performance for community banks (those with less than $1 billion in assets) improved during 2002. Aggressive interest rate cuts by the Federal Reserve in 2001/02 lowered banks' funding costs, but compressed NIMs. Even though the economy was weak in 2002, loan growth increased rapidly, especially in commercial real estate (CRE) loans.

[33] INSURANCE

As of 2000, there were 52 property and casualty and eight life and health insurance companies incorporated or organized in the state.

In 2001, there were 6.6 million ordinary life insurance policies in force, with a total value of $314.3 billion; total value for all categories of life insurance (ordinary, group, industrial, and credit) was $517.3 billion. Death benefits paid that year totaled $1.43 billion. Property and liability insurers wrote over $8.6 billion in premiums. That year, there were 102,876 flood insurance policies in force in the state, with a total value of $14.9 million. There were also 48,896 beach and windstorm insurance policies against hurricane and other windstorm damage in force, with a total value of $11.3 billion.

[34] SECURITIES

There are no securities exchanges in North Carolina. The Securities Division of the Office of Secretary of State is authorized to protect the public against fraudulent issues and sellers of securities. The state has 985 broker-dealers organizations with 7,254 employees, and 176 investment advisory organizations. North Carolina is home to 82 NASDAQ-listed companies, two NASDAQ market makers, 11 AMEX-listed companies; and has incorporated 37 NYSE-listed companies. The top five companies by revenues are: First Union Corp., Duke Energy Corp., Lowe's Companies, Inc., Delhaize America, Inc., and Reynolds (R.J.) Tobacco Holdings.

[35] PUBLIC FINANCE

The North Carolina budget is prepared biennially by the governor and reviewed annually by the Office of State Budget and Management, in consultation with the Advisory Budget Commission, an independent agency composed of five gubernatorial appointees, five members from the senate, and five from the house of representatives. It is then submitted to the general assembly for amendment and approval. The fiscal year runs from 1 July to 30 June.

The state budget for the 1999 to 2001 biennium totaled $24.3 billion for 1999/00, and $23.9 billion for 2000/01. For the biennium, almost 60% of funds were to come from the general fund, 25% from the federal government, and 8% each from highway taxes and other government receipts.

The largest appropriations went to education, or $26 billion for the two fiscal years and 54% of the budget. Approximately $5.8 billion was allocated to health programs, $1.8 billion to the Department of Corrections.

Adjustments for the improved economic outlook in 2000 (GDP growth for 2000/01 was revised to 4.9%, from a forecast of only 2.4%) increased the prospects of meeting the requirements of the estimated budget.

The following table from the US Census Bureau contains information on revenues, expenditures, indebtedness, and cash/securities for 2001.

	($000)	PERCENT	PER CAPITA
Population (thousands, 2001)	8,206	(X)	(X)
Total Revenue	32,202,748	100.00	3,924.29
General revenue	29,391,844	91.27	3,581.75
Utility revenue	–	–	–
Liquor store revenue	–	–	–
Insurance trust revenue	2,810,904	8.73	342.54
Exhibit: Salaries and wages	5,013,082	15.85	610.90
Total expenditure	31,626,851	100.00	3,854.11
General expenditure	28,860,264	91.25	3,516.97
Education	11,960,237	37.82	1,457.50
Public welfare	6,202,780	19.61	755.88
Hospitals	1,266,440	4.00	154.33
Health	922,880	2.92	112.46
Highways	2,513,413	7.95	306.29
Police protection	338,731	1.07	41.28
Correction	937,572	2.96	114.25
Natural resources	623,002	1.97	75.92
Parks and recreation	158,100	0.50	19.27
Government administration	853,751	2.70	104.04
Interest on general debt	558,404	1.77	68.05
Other and unallocable	2,524,954	7.98	307.70
Utility expenditure	–	–	–
Liquor store expenditure	–	–	–
Insurance trust expenditure	2,766,587	8.75	337.14
Debt at end of fiscal year	9,998,034	100.00	1,218.38
Cash and security holdings	73,324,695	100.00	8,935.50

36 TAXATION

In 1921, North Carolina was one of the first states to adopt a graduated income tax. In 1923, it was one of the first to institute a statewide sales tax. The state and local tax system remains relative centralized, with about 60% of total non-federal taxes collected at the state level. All property taxes, however, are collected locally. In 2001, North Carolina temporarily added an 8.25% bracket for income above $120,000 to its three-bracket personal income tax schedule with rates 6% (up to $12,750 taxable income), 7% and 7.75% ($60,000 to $120,000). The rates are scheduled to decline after 2003. The corporate income tax is a flat rate of 6.9% of net income. Financial institutions are taxed on the basis of their assets ($30 for each $1 million in assets). In 2001, North Carolina increased its state sales and use tax from 4% to 4.5%. Local governments also impose sales taxes, ranging from 2 to 3%. Food, prescription drugs, and certain other articles are exempt from the state sales tax or have lowered rates, but food may be subject to local sales taxes. The state also imposes a wide array of excise taxes covering motor fuels, tobacco products, insurance premiums, public utilities, alcoholic beverages (the state controls all sales), amusements, and other selected items. The cigarette tax, at 5 cents a pack, is the 3rd-lowest in the country (after Virginia and Kentucky). The gasoline tax is indexed to inflation, and contrary to trend elsewhere, was reduced from 24.3 cents a gallon to 22.1 cents a gallon in 2002. The state estate tax, with a maximum rate of 17%, has been de-linked from the exemption for state death taxes in the federal estate tax, which is scheduled to be phased out by 2007. Death and gift taxes accounted for 0.76% of state taxes collected in 2002. Other state taxes include an oil and gas production tax, a forest product assessment tax, various license fees, and stamp taxes.

The state collected $15.535 billion in taxes in 2002 (down from $15.6 billion in 2001), of which 46.7% came from individual income taxes, 21.5% from selective sales taxes 20.6% came from the general sales tax, 5.7% from license fees, and

4.3% from corporate income taxes. In 2003, North Carolina ranked mid-way (25th) among the states in terms of combined state and local tax burden, which amounted to about 9.5% of income.

The following table from the US Census Bureau provides a summary of taxes collected by the state in 2002.

	($000)	PER CAPITA
Total Taxes	15,535,277	1,867.19
Property taxes	(X)	(X)
Sales and gross receipts	6,562,496	788.75
General sales and gross receipts	3,212,098	386.06
Selective sales taxes	3,350,398	402.69
Alcoholic beverage	213,986	25.72
Amusements	11,130	1.34
Insurance Premiums	348,113	41.84
Motor fuels	1,209,386	145.36
Pari-mutuels	(X)	(X)
Public utilities	888,675	106.81
Tobacco products	41,531	4.99
Other selective sales	637,577	76.63
Licenses	884,085	106.26
Alcoholic beverages	6,817	0.82
Amusements	(X)	(X)
Corporation	273,669	32.89
Hunting and fishing	15,114	1.82
Motor vehicle	410,708	49.36
Motor vehicle operators	69,477	8.35
Public utility	(X)	(X)
Occupation and business, NEC	104,795	12.6
Other	3,505	0.42
Other taxes	8,088,696	972.18
Individual income	7,265,242	873.21
Corporation net income	668,124	80.3
Death and gift	118,141	14.2
Documentary and stock transfer	35,300	4.24
Severance	1,889	0.23
Other	(X)	(X)

37 ECONOMIC POLICY

North Carolina's government has actively stimulated economic growth ever since the beginning of the 19th century. During the administration of Governor Luther H. Hodges (1954–61), the state began to recruit outside investment directly, developing such forward-looking facilities as Research Triangle Park. Since the 1970s, other policies and legislation have been aimed at the fostering of development in rural areas, where per capita income is lower and unemployment is higher than elsewhere in the state. In 1996, under the administration of Governor James B. Hunt, the General Assembly adopted the William S. Lee Quality Jobs and Business Expansion Act. The act groups North Carolina's 100 counties into Enterprise Tiers, and provides for graduated tax credit amounts, depending upon Enterprise Tier location, for specific company activities including job creation, machinery and equipment investment, worker training, and research and development. The North Carolina Economic Development Board's goal in 1999 was to help the transformation of the economy from manufacturing to more high-technology enterprises.

The state also actively participates in programs involving industrial revenue bonds, state and federally assisted loan and grant programs, business energy loans, and assistance to local communities with shell buildings that can be customized to meet the needs of a company in a shorter period of time. In 2003, North Carolina's life-sciences industry was showcased at the industry's annual conference in Washington DC. More than 50 participants were included in the state's public-private collaboration. In February 2003, the Business and Industry ServiCenter, a one-stop information and resource center for businesses, began pilot operations. Later in the year, it was announced that it would expand to seven new locations.

38HEALTH

Health conditions and health care facilities in North Carolina vary widely from region to region. In the larger cities-and especially in proximity to the excellent medical schools at Duke University and the University of North Carolina at Chapel Hill—quality health care is as readily available as anywhere in the US.

Around 15% of North Carolinians were uninsured in 2002. The one million Medicare and 985,000 Medicaid recipients in North Carolina received respectively $3.7 and $2.7 billion dollars in health care in 1994.

In 2000 the infant mortality rate stood at 8.6 per 1,000 live births. In 1999, there were 32,081 legal abortions, or 19 per 1,000 women. The death rate for HIV-related infections was 6.0 per 100,000 population, higher than the US average of 5.3 in 2000. A total of 11,356 AIDS cases had been reported through 2001. The leading causes of death in North Carolina are similar to those in the rest of the US although, as of 2000, North Carolinians died less frequently from heart disease than other Americans, but more frequently from cerebrovascular disease, accidents, and suicide. The 2000 overall death rate of 928.5 per 100,000 inhabitants was above the national average of 873.1. Among North Carolina residents age 18 and older, 26.1% were smokers in 2000. Death resulting from lung disease occurred at a rate of 80.3 per 100,000 population in 2000.

A particularly serious public health problem in North Carolina is byssinosis, or brown lung disease. Caused by prolonged inhalation of cotton dust, byssinosis cripples the lungs of longtime textile workers, producing grave disability and even death. According to a study in 1980, the Brown Lung Association estimated that some 25,000 present or former North Carolina textile workers showed symptoms of byssinosis, and that between 10,000 and 15,000 North Carolinians were disabled by it; textile industry estimates ran to less than one-tenth of those figures.

North Carolina's 111 community hospitals had 973,451 admissions and 23,755 beds in 2001. There were 31,324 full-time registered nurses and 2,738 full-time licensed practical nurses in 2001 and 255 physicians per 100,000 population in 2000. The average expense of a community hospital for care was $1,297.90 per inpatient day in 2001.

Federal government grants to cover the Medicare and Medicaid services in 2001 totaled $4.1 billion; 1,154,864 enrollees received Medicare benefits that year. At least 14.4% of North Carolina's residents were uninsured in 2002.

The state acted to increase the supply of doctors in eastern North Carolina in the 1970s by the establishment of a new medical school at East Carolina University in Greenville. Medical schools and superior medical research facilities are also located at Duke University Medical Center in Durham, UNC Hospitals at the University of North Carolina in Chapel Hill, and the Bowman Gray School of Medicine at Wake Forest University in Winston-Salem.

39SOCIAL WELFARE

In 2001, the average weekly unemployment benefit was $250.15. Average monthly participation in the food stamp program in FY2002 comprised 574,369 persons (244,907 households). The average monthly benefit was $77.83, and the sum total of benefits paid in FY2002 was $536,423,418.

With the enactment of the Personal Responsibility and Work Opportunity Reconciliation Act of 1996, the US government has changed the form and regulations for many of its social welfare programs. Most significantly, it replaces Aid to Families with Dependent Children (AFDC), an open-ended entitlement program, with Temporary Assistance for Needy Families (TANF), a limited system of assistance funded largely through federal block grants. The reform act also impacts the food stamp program, the Supplemental Security Income program, and the child nutrition program. The law took effect on 1 July 1997 and provided $16.38 billion in block grants for fiscal years 1997–2002. The grants are to be divided among the states based on an equation involving the numbers of former AFDC recipients in each state.

Reauthorization of the 1996 social welfare legislation, scheduled for 2002, was delayed, and the original law had been extended three times as of July 2003, with the most recent extension running through September 2003. North Carolina's TANF program is called Work First. In June 2000 the state had 97,171 welfare recipients. State expenditures on the TANF program in FY2002 totaled $191,587,210.

In December 2001, Social Security benefits were paid to 1,373,880 North Carolina residents. This number included 853,740 retired workers, 134,940 widows and widowers, 200,240 disabled workers, 26,290 spouses, and 122,670 children. Social Security beneficiaries represented 16.8% of the total state population and 94.5% of the state's population age 65 and older. Retired workers (excluding persons with special benefits) received an average monthly payment of $846; widows and widowers, $748; disabled workers, $789; and spouses, $425. Payments for children of retired workers averaged $428 per month; children of deceased workers, $551; and children of disabled workers, $242.

Federal Supplemental Security Income payments in December 2001 went to 191,630 North Carolinians, averaging $326 a month.

40HOUSING

In 2002, there were an estimated 3,707,129 units of housing in North Carolina, of which 3,207,447 were occupied; 68.6% were owner-occupied. About 64.2% of all housing units were single-family, detached homes; 17% were mobile homes. Nearly 36% of the entire housing stock was built between 1970 and 1989. The most common energy source for heating was electricity. It was estimated that 141,700 units lacked telephone service, 16,346 lacked complete plumbing facilities, and 16,752 lacked complete kitchen facilities. The average household size was 2.51 people.

Also in 2002, 79,824 new privately owned units were authorized for construction. The median home value was $121,181. The median monthly cost for mortgage owners was $1,071. renters paid a median of $590 per month. During 2002, North Carolina received over $112.6 million in community planning and development aid from the US Department of Housing and Urban Development.

41EDUCATION

North Carolina's commitment to education has been strengthened in recent years with legislative and financial support for improving student achievement through high standards; teacher accountability; an emphasis on teaching the basics of reading, writing and mathematics; and moving state control of schools to the local, community level. Legislation passed in 1996 allowed for the state's first public charter schools, up to 100 of them, and the first ones approved began operating in 1997. In 2000, 78.1% of North Carolinians age 25 and older were high school graduates; 22.5% had obtained a bachelor's degree or higher.

North Carolina has a rich educational history, having started the first state university in the United States, in 1795, and the first free system of common schools in the South in 1839. North Carolina led the nation in the construction of rural schools in the 1920s. In 1957, Charlotte, Greensboro, and Winston-Salem were the first cities in the South to admit black students voluntarily to formerly all-white schools. But, as was the case throughout the South, widespread desegregation took much longer. In 1971, the US Supreme Court, in the landmark decision *Swann v. Charlotte-*

Mecklenburg Board of Education, upheld the use of busing to desegregate that school system. The remainder of the state soon followed suit.

North Carolina established a statewide testing program in 1977 and increased high school graduation requirements in 1983, becoming the first state to require that students pass Algebra I in order to earn a diploma. North Carolina has been active in providing special programs for gifted students. Governor's School, a summer residential program for the gifted, was founded in 1963. Other talented students are served by the highly regarded North Carolina School of the Arts in Winston-Salem, which began operating in 1965, and the North Carolina School of Science and Mathematics, located in Durham, which opened in 1980.

The total enrollment for fall 1999 in North Carolina's public schools stood at 1,275,925. Of these, 934,725 attended schools from kindergarten through grade eight, and 341,200 attended high school. Minority students made up approximately 40% of the total enrollment in public elementary and secondary schoolsin 2001. Total enrollment was estimated at 1,265,810 in fall 2000 and is expected to reach 1,390,000 by fall 2005. Expenditures for public education in 2000/01 were estimated at $7,630,436. Enrollment in nonpublic schools in fall 2001 was 96,262.

As of fall 2000, there were 462,275 students enrolled in college or graduate school. In the same year North Carolina had 120 degree-granting institutions. The University of North Carolina (UNC) was chartered in 1789 and opened at Chapel Hill in 1795. The state university system now embraces 16 campuses under a common board of governors. The three oldest and largest campuses, all of which offer research and graduate as well as undergraduate programs, are UNC-Chapel Hill, North Carolina State University in Raleigh (the first land-grant college for the study of agriculture and engineering), and UNC-Greensboro. North Carolina had 59 community colleges as of 2000.

Duke University in Durham is North Carolina's premier private institution and takes its place with the Chapel Hill and Raleigh public campuses as the third key facility in the Research Triangle. In addition to the public institutions and community colleges, there are also 42 private, four-year schools, of which Wake Forest University in Winston-Salem and Davidson College in Davidson are most noteworthy. Additionally, the state has two private junior colleges, plus seven theological seminaries. In 1997, minority students comprised 25.7% of total postsecondary enrollment.

42ARTS

North Carolina has been a pioneer in exploring new channels for state support of the arts. It was the first state to fund its own symphony, to endow its own art museum, to found a state school of the arts, to create a statewide arts council, and to establish a cabinet-level Department of Cultural Resources. Its state arts council, created in 1964, reaches the pubic through a network of over 100 community arts councils and over 600 arts organizations each year.

The North Carolina Symphony, based in Raleigh, gives free concerts to more than 150,000 public schoolchildren and performs 175 concerts annually. The North Carolina Museum of Art, which is visited by about 230,000 people each year, features one of the finest collections of early European master paintings in the country. The museum's collection spans 5,000 years and includes work by Dutch masters, Renaissance masterpieces, Egyptian artifacts, classical statues, and tribal and contemporary art.

At least 200 arts-related festivals are held in North Carolina each year. Summer dance and music festivals, as well as professional theaters and historical outdoor dramas, galleries and museums, and the crafts community all serve as anchors for the

state's tourism industry. North Carolina's Pulitzer Prize–winning playwright Paul Green created the genre of historical drama with the 1937 production of *The Lost Colony.* North Carolina's stages nine outdoor historical dramas (double the number of any other state).

Based for 20 years in Durham, the American Dance Festival has commissioned new dance works, preserved dance history, trained dancers, and presented the best in contemporary dance. The African American Dance Ensemble, based in North Carolina, performs for over 350,000 people across the United States each year. Flat Rock Playhouse, the state theater of North Carolina, performs for over 60,000 people.

Folk and traditional arts thrive across North Carolina in all disciplines. The North Carolina Folk Heritage Awards are given to recognize the state's leading folk artists. Penland School of Crafts, the John C. Campbell Folk School, the Southern Highland Guild, Qualla Arts and Crafts Mutual, Inc., the Core Sound Waterfowl Museum, and the North Carolina Pottery Center are but a few of the organizations in North Carolina that help to keep the craft traditions alive.

In 2003, North Carolina arts organizations received grants totaling $1,328,100 from the National Endowment for the Arts. North Carolina has over 2,000 arts organizations. About 34,000 artists work in all disciplines, and over 18,000,000 citizens and visitors participate in the arts programs. The North Carolina Humanities Council is active in a number of programs. In 2000, the National Endowment for the Humanities contributed $2,674,639 to 40 state programs.

For 30 years, the North Carolina Arts Council has supported artists in the schools to teach, perform, and encourage creative expression. The council was instrumental in funding two of the first arts-based curriculum experiments in the state; there are now 27 elementary schools teaching core curriculum through the arts and interdisciplinary instruction. The Arts Council's Grassroots Arts Program, established in 1977, was the nation's first per capita funding program for the local arts initiatives in which decision making remained at the local level. The program has invested over $21 million in community-based programming over the past 25 years.

43LIBRARIES AND MUSEUMS

Public libraries, open in nearly every North Carolina community, are linked together through the State Library, ensuring that users in all parts of the state can have access to printed, filmed, and recorded materials. Total volumes in the 75 public libraries numbered 14,812,562 in 2000, when circulation reached 42,539,000. Major university research libraries are located at the Chapel Hill, Raleigh, and Greensboro campuses of the University of North Carolina and at Duke University in Durham. The North Carolina Collection and Southern Historical Collection at the Chapel Hill campus are especially noteworthy. Total public library income in 2000 was $145,107,000; including $1,596,177 in federal grants and $17,267,773 in state grants.

North Carolina had 188 museums and historical sites in 2000. Established in 1956, the North Carolina Museum of Art, in Raleigh, is one of only two state-supported art museums in the US (the other is in Virginia); the museum had an attendance of 233,893 in 1999. The North Carolina Museum of History is in Raleigh, with an annual attendance of 239,642. The Department of Cultural Resources administers 20 state historical sites and Tryon Place Restoration in New Bern. The Museum of Natural History in Raleigh is maintained by the state Department of Agriculture; smaller science museums exist in Charlotte, Greensboro, and Durham.

44COMMUNICATIONS

Government postal service in North Carolina began in 1755 but did not become regular until 1771, with the establishment of a central post office for the southern colonies. Mails were slow and erratic, and many North Carolinians continued to entrust their letters to private travelers until well into the 19th century. Rural free delivery in the state began on 23 October 1896 in Rowan County.

Telephone service began in Wilmington and Raleigh in October 1879, and long distance connections between Wilmington and Petersburg, Va., began later that same year. In 2001, 93.9% of the state's occupied housing units had telephones.

There were 49 major AM radio stations in North Carolina in 2003, and 106 major FM stations. Major television stations numbered 33. The Greenville-Spartanburg-Asheville-Anderson area had 732,490 television households, 61% of which received cable. The Raleigh-Durham area had 858,490 television-viewing households, 62% of which had cable. Finally, the Greensboro-High Point-Winstom Salem viewing area boasted 64% of all television households with cable.

A total of 120,858 Internet domain names were registered in the state in the year 2000.

45PRESS

As of 2002, North Carolina had 30 morning newspapers, 17 evening dailies, and 39 Sunday papers. The following table shows the circulation of the largest dailies as of 2002:

AREA	NAME	DAILY	SUNDAY
Charlotte	*Observer* (m,S)	235,375	291,080
Greensboro	*News & Record* (m,S)	88,781	111,060
Raleigh	*News & Observer* (m,S)	162,869	208,407
Winston–Salem	*Journal* (m,S)	84,780	96,038

The *Charlotte Observer* won a 1981 Pulitzer Prize for its series on brown lung disease. The (Raleigh) *News & Observer* won a 1996 Pulitzer Prize for its series on the hog industry in North Carolina.

North Carolina has been the home of several nationally recognized "little reviews" of literature, poetry, and criticism, including *The Rebel, Crucible, Southern Poetry Review, The Carolina Quarterly, St. Andrews Review, The Sun, Pembroke Magazine*, and *Miscellany*. The *North Carolina Historical Review* is a quarterly scholarly publication of the Division of Archives and History.

46ORGANIZATIONS

In 2003, there were about 2,683 regional, national, and international organizations within the state.

The North Carolina Citizens Association serves as the voice of the state's business community. A teachers' organization, the North Carolina Association of Educators, is widely acknowledged as one of the most effective political pressure groups in the state, as is the North Carolina State Employees Association. Every major branch of industry has its own trade association; most are highly effective lobbying bodies. Carolina Action, the North Carolina Public Interest Research Group, the Kudzu Alliance, and the Brown Lung Association represent related consumer, environmental, antinuclear power, and public health concerns.

National organizations headquartered in the state include the American Board of Pediatrics, Association of Professors of Medicine, the American Senior Citizens Association, the Institute for Southern Studies, the Tobacco Association of the US, the US Power Squadrons, the Improved Benevolent Protective Order of Elks of the World, the Independent Order of Odd Fellows, the World Methodist Council, and the Center for Creative Leadership.

Cultural and educational organizations at the local and national levels include the American Dance Festival, the Appalachian Consortium, Art in the Public Interest, the Center for Urban and Regional Studies, the National Humanities Center, the National Institute of Statistical Sciences, the North Carolina Humanities Council, and Preservation North Carolina

47TOURISM, TRAVEL, AND RECREATION

In 2002, there were about 44.4 million visitors to North Carolina, with total travel expenditures reaching about $11.9 billion dollars. About 30% of all trips are made by residents traveling within the state. About 53% of visitors travel from the following states: Virginia, South Carolina, Georgia, Florida, Pennsylvania, Tennessee, New York, Maryland, and Ohio.

Tourists are attracted by North Carolina's coastal beaches, by golf and tennis opportunities (including the world-famous golf courses at Pinehurst), and parks and scenery in the North Carolina mountains. Sites of special interest are the Revolutionary War battlegrounds at Guilford Courthouse and Moore's Creek Bridge; Bennett Place, near Hillsborough, where the last major Confederate army surrendered; Ft. Raleigh, the site of the Lost Colony's misadventures; and the Wright Brothers National Memorial at Kitty Hawk. With more than 500 golf courses across the state, North Carolina is often nicknamed the "Golf Capital of the World."

Cape Hatteras and Cape Lookout national seashores, which protect the beauty of the Outer Banks, together cover 58,563 acres (23,700 hectares). The Blue Ridge Parkway, a scenic motor route operated by the National Park Service that winds over the crest of the Blue Ridge in Virginia, North Carolina, and Georgia, attracts millions of visitors to North Carolina yearly. Another popular attraction, Great Smoky Mountains National Park, straddles the North Carolina-Tennessee border. There are more than 1.2 million acres of national forest land located in North Carolina, 1,500 lakes of ten acres or more, and 37,000 miles of freshwater streams.

48SPORTS

There are three major league professional sports teams in North Carolina: the Charlotte Sting of the Women's National Basketball Association, the Carolina Panthers of the National Football League, and the Carolina Hurricanes of the National Hockey League, who relocated to Raleigh from Hartford, Connecticut, in 1997. The Charlotte Hornets, now located in New Orleans, left North Carolina in 2002. Minor league baseball's Carolina League is based in North Carolina, and 14 minor league teams call the state home. Additionally, there is minor league hockey in Charlotte, Fayetteville, Asheville, and Greensboro. Two other professional sports that figure prominently in the state are golf and stock-car racing. The Greater Greensboro Chrysler Classic in April is a major tournament on the Professional Golfers' Association tour. The North Carolina Motor Speedway in Rockingham hosts the Dura-Lube/KMart 400 and the Pop Secret Microwave Popcorn 400 annually on the NASCAR Winston Cup circuit, while the Lowe's Motor Speedway in Charlotte is the home of The Winston, the Coca-Cola 600, and the UAW-GM Quality 500 on the NASCAR Winston Cup circuit.

College basketball is the ruling passion of amateur sports fans in North Carolina. Organized in the Atlantic Coast Conference, the University of North Carolina at Chapel Hill, North Carolina State University, Wake Forest University, and Duke University consistently field nationally ranked basketball teams. North Carolina won the NCAA Championship in 1957, 1982, and 1993, North Carolina State captured the title in 1974 and 1983, and Duke won back-to-back championships in 1991 and 1992.

Other annual sporting events include the Stoneybrook Steeplechase in Southern Pines in April and the National Hollerin' Contest in Spivey's Corner, which tests farmers' ability to call livestock.

⁴⁹FAMOUS NORTH CAROLINIANS

Three US presidents had North Carolina roots, but all three reached the White House from Tennessee. Andrew Jackson (1767–1845), the 7th president, was born in an unsurveyed border region, probably in South Carolina, but studied law and was admitted to the bar in North Carolina before moving to frontier Tennessee in 1788. James K. Polk (1795–1849), the 11th president, was born in Mecklenburg County but grew up in Tennessee. Another native North Carolinian, Andrew Johnson (1808–75), was a tailor's apprentice in Raleigh before moving to Tennessee at the age of 18. Johnson served as Abraham Lincoln's vice president for six weeks in 1865 before becoming the nation's 17th president when Lincoln was assassinated. William Rufus King (1786–1853), the other US vice president from North Carolina, also served for only six weeks, dying before he could exercise his duties.

Three native North Carolinians have served as speaker of the US House of Representatives. The first, Nathaniel Macon (1758–1837), occupied the speaker's chair from 1801 to 1807 and served as president pro tem of the US Senate in 1826–27. The other two were James K. Polk and Joseph G. "Uncle Joe" Cannon (1836–1926), who served as speaker of the House from 1903 to 1911, but as a representative from Illinois.

Sir Walter Raleigh (or Ralegh, b.England, 1552?–1618) never came to North Carolina, but his efforts to found a colony there led state lawmakers to give his name to the new state capital in 1792. Raleigh's "Lost Colony" on Roanoke Island was the home of Virginia Dare (1587–?), the first child of English parents to be born in America. More than a century later, the infamous Edward Teach (or Thatch, b.England, ?–1716) made his headquarters at Bath and terrorized coastal waters as the pirate known as Blackbeard.

Principal leaders of the early national period included Richard Caswell (b.Maryland, 1729–89), Revolutionary War governor; William Richardson Davie (b.England, 1756–1820), governor of the state and founder of the University of North Carolina; and Archibald De Bow Murphey (1777–1832), reform advocate, legislator, and judge. Prominent black Americans of the 19th century who were born or who lived in North Carolina were John Chavis (1763–1838), teacher and minister; David Walker (1785–1830), abolitionist; and Hiram Revels (1827–1901), first black member of the US Senate.

North Carolinians prominent in the era of the Civil War and Reconstruction included antislavery author Hinton Rowan Helper (1829–1909), Civil War governor Zebulon B. Vance (1830–94), Reconstruction governor William W. Holden (1818–92), and "carpetbagger" judge Albion Winegar Tourgee (b.Ohio, 1838–1905). Among major politicians of the 20th century are Furnifold McLendell Simmons (1854–1940), US senator from 1901 to 1931; Charles Brantley Aycock (1859–1912), governor from 1901 to 1905; Frank Porter Graham (1886–1972), University of North Carolina president, New Deal adviser, and US senator, 1949–50; Luther H. Hodges (b.Virginia, 1898–1974), governor from 1954 to 1960, US secretary of commerce from 1961 to 1965, and founder of Research Triangle Park; Samuel J. Ervin, Jr. (1896–1985), US senator from 1954 to 1974 and chairman of the Senate Watergate investigation; Terry Sanford (1917–98), governor from 1961 to 1965, US presidential aspirant, and president of Duke University; and Jesse Helms (b.1921), senator since 1973. Civil rights leader Jesse Jackson (b.1941) began his career as a student activist in Greensboro. The most famous North Carolinian living today is probably evangelist Billy Graham (b.1918).

James Buchanan Duke (1856–1925) founded the American Tobacco Co. and provided the endowment that transformed Trinity College into Duke University. The most outstanding North Carolina-born inventor was Richard J. Gatling (1818–1903), creator of the "Gatling gun," the first machine gun. The Wright brothers, Wilbur (b.Indiana, 1867–1912) and Orville (b.Ohio, 1871–1948), achieved the first successful powered airplane flight at Kitty Hawk, on the Outer Banks, on 17 December 1903. Psychologist Joseph Banks Rhine (b.Pennsylvania, 1895–1980) was known for his research on extrasensory perception. Kary Mullis (b.1944), 1993 winner of the Nobel Prize for chemistry, was born in Lenoir, North Carolina.

A number of North Carolinians have won fame as literary figures. They include Walter Hines Page (1855–1918), editor and diplomat; William Sydney Porter (1862–1910), a short-story writer who used the pseudonym O. Henry; playwright Paul Green (1894–1984); and novelists Thomas Wolfe (1900–38) and Reynolds Price (b.1933). Major scholars associated with the state have included sociologist Howard W. Odum (b.Georgia, 1884–1954) and historians W. J. Cash (1901–41) and John Hope Franklin (b.Oklahoma, 1915). Journalists Edward R. Murrow (1908–65), Tom Wicker (b.1926), and Charles Kuralt (1934–97) were all North Carolina natives. Harry Golden (Harry L. Goldhurst, b.New York, 1903–81), a Jewish humorist, founded the *Carolina Israelite*.

Jazz artists Thelonious Monk (1918–82), John Coltrane (1926–67), and Nina Simone (b.1933) were born in the state, as were pop singer Roberta Flack (b.1939), folksinger Arthel "Doc" Watson (b.1923), bluegrass banjo artist Earl Scruggs (b.1924), and actor Andy Griffith (b.1926). North Carolina athletes include former heavyweight champion Floyd Patterson (b.1935), NASCAR driver Richard Petty (1937–2000), football quarterbacks Sonny Jurgenson (b.1934) and Roman Gabriel (b.1940), baseball pitchers Gaylord Perry (b.1938) and Jim "Catfish" Hunter (1946–99), and basketball player Meadowlark Lemon (b.1932), long a star with the Harlem Globetrotters. Michael Jordan (b.Brooklyn, N.Y., 1963) played college basketball at the University of North Carolina, and went on to fame as a National Basketball Association star.

⁵⁰BIBLIOGRAPHY

Ausband, Stephen C. *Byrd's Line: A Natural History.* Charlottesville: University of Virginia Press, 2002.

Byrd, William L. *In Full Force and Virtue: North Carolina Emancipation Records, 1713–1860.* Bowie, Md.: Heritage Books, 1999.

Chafe, William H. *Civilities and Civil Rights: Greensboro, North Carolina and the Black Struggle for Freedom.* New York: Oxford University Press, 1980.

Clay, James W., Douglas M. Orr, Jr., and Alfred W. Stuart (eds.). *North Carolina Atlas: Portrait of a Changing Southern State.* Chapel Hill: University of North Carolina Press, 1975.

Crow, Jeffrey J., Paul D. Escott, and Flora J. Hatley. *A History of African Americans in North Carolina.* Raleigh: North Carolina Department of Cultural Resources, Office of Archives and History, 2002.

Davis, Anita Price, compiler. *North Carolina During the Great Depression: A Documentary Portrait of a Decade.* Jefferson, N.C.: McFarland, 2003.

Fleer, Jack D. *North Carolina Government & Politics.* Lincoln, Nebr.: University of Nebraska, 1994.

Jones, H.G. *North Carolina History: An Annotated Bibliography.* Westport, Conn.: Greenwood Press, 1995.

Lefler, Hugh T., and Albert Ray Newsome. *North Carolina: The History of a Southern State.* 3rd ed., rev. Chapel Hill: University of North Carolina Press, 1973.

Morley, Margaret Warner. The Carolina Mountains. Alexander, N.C.: Land of the Sky Books, 2002.

Nathans, Sydney. *The Quest for Progress: The Way We Lived in North Carolina, 1870–1920.* Chapel Hill: University of North Carolina Press, 1983.

North Carolina Handbook. Chico, Calif.: Moon Publications, 1999.

Powell, William S. *North Carolina: A Bicentennial History.* New York: Norton, 1977.

State of North Carolina. Office of State Budget and Management. *North Carolina State Government Statistical Abstract, 1984.* 5th ed. Raleigh, 1984.

NORTH DAKOTA

State of North Dakota

ORIGIN OF STATE NAME: The state was formerly the northern section of Dakota Territory; *dakota* is a Siouan word meaning "allies." **NICKNAME:** Peace Garden State. **CAPITAL:** Bismarck. **ENTERED UNION:** 2 November 1889 (39th). **SONG:** "North Dakota Hymn." **MARCH:** "Flickertail March." **MOTTO:** Liberty and Union, Now and Forever, One and Inseparable. **FLAG:** The flag consists of a blue field with yellow fringes; on each side is depicted an eagle with outstretched wings, holding in one talon a sheaf of arrows, in the other an olive branch, and in his beak a banner inscribed with the words "*E Pluribus Unum.*" Below the eagle are the words "North Dakota"; above it are 13 stars surmounted by a sunburst. **OFFICIAL SEAL:** In the center is an elm tree; beneath it are a sheaf of wheat, a plow, an anvil, and a bow and three arrows, and in the background an Indian chases a buffalo toward a setting sun. The depiction is surrounded by the state motto and the words "Great Seal State of North Dakota October 1st 1889" encircle the whole. **BIRD:** Western meadowlark. **FISH:** Northern pike. **FLOWER:** Wild prairie rose. **TREE:** American elm. **GRASS:** Western wheatgrass. **BEVERAGE:** Milk. **FOSSIL:** Teredo petrified wood. **LEGAL HOLIDAYS:** New Year's Day, 1 January; Birthday of Martin Luther King, Jr., 3rd Monday in January; George Washington's Birthday, 3rd Monday in February; Good Friday, March or April; Memorial Day, last Monday in May; Independence Day, 4 July; Labor Day, 1st Monday in September; Veterans Day, 11 November; Thanksgiving Day, 4th Thursday in November; Christmas Day, 25 December. **TIME** 6 AM CST = noon GMT; 5 AM MST = noon GMT.

¹LOCATION, SIZE, AND EXTENT

Located in the western north-central US, North Dakota ranks 17th in size among the 50 states.

The total area of North Dakota is 70,703 sq mi (183,121 sq km), comprising 69,300 sq mi (179,487 sq km) of land and 1,403 sq mi (3,634 sq km) of inland water. Shaped roughly like a rectangle, North Dakota has three straight sides and one irregular border on the E. Its maximum length E-W is about 360 mi (580 km), its extreme width N-S about 210 mi (340 km).

North Dakota is bordered on the N by the Canadian provinces of Saskatchewan and Manitoba; on the E by Minnesota (with the line formed by the Red River of the North); on the S by South Dakota; and on the W by Montana. The total boundary length is 1,312 mi (2,111 km). The state's geographic center is in Sheridan County, 5 mi (8 km) SW of McClusky.

²TOPOGRAPHY

North Dakota straddles two major US physiographic regions: the Central Plains in the east and the Great Plains in the west. Along the eastern border is the generally flat Red River Valley, with the state's lowest point, 750 ft (229 m); this valley was once covered by the waters of a glacial lake. Most of the eastern half of North Dakota consists of the Drift Prairie, at 1,300–1,600 ft (400–500 m) above sea level. The Missouri Plateau occupies the western half of the state and has the highest point in North Dakota—White Butte, 3,506 ft (1,069 m)—in Slope County in the southwest. Separating the Missouri Plateau from the Drift Prairie is the Missouri Escarpment, which rises 400 ft (122 m) above the prairie and extends diagonally from northwest to southeast.

North Dakota has two major rivers: the Red River of the North, flowing northward into Canada; and the Missouri River, which enters in the northwest and then flows east and, joined by the Yellowstone River, southeast into South Dakota.

³CLIMATE

North Dakota lies in the northwestern continental interior of the US. Characteristically, summers are hot, winters very cold, and rainfall sparse to moderate, with periods of drought. The average annual temperature is 40°F (4°C), ranging from 7°F (-14°C) in January to 69°F (21°C) in July. The record low temperature, -60°F (-51°C), was set at Parshall on 15 February 1936; the record high, 121°F (49°C), at Steele on 6 July 1936.

The average yearly precipitation (1971–2000) was about 16.8 in (42.7 cm) at Bismarck. The total annual snowfall averages 44 in (112 cm) at Bismarck.

⁴FLORA AND FAUNA

North Dakota is predominantly a region of prairie and plains, although the American elm, green ash, box elder, and cottonwood grow there. Cranberries, juneberries, and wild grapes are also common. Indian, blue, grama, and buffalo grasses grow on the plains; the wild prairie rose is the state flower. The western prairie fringed orchid was the only plant species classified as threatened in 2003; no plant species were listed as endangered that year by the US Fish and Wildlife Service.

Once on the verge of extinction, the white-tailed and mule deers and pronghorn antelope have been restored. The elk and grizzly bear, both common until about 1880, had disappeared by 1900; bighorn sheep, reintroduced in 1956, are beginning to flourish. North Dakota claims more wild ducks than any other state except Alaska, and it has the largest sharptailed grouse population in the United States. Seven animal species were listed as threatened or endangered in North Dakota in 2003, including the bald eagle, Eskimo curlew, pallid sturgeon, least tern, and whooping crane.

⁵ENVIRONMENTAL PROTECTION

North Dakota has little urban or industrial pollution. An environmental issue confronting the state in the mid-1980s and early 1990s was how to use its coal resources without damaging the land through strip mining or polluting the air with coal-fired industrial plants. Major environmental issues confronting the state are importation of non-hazardous and hazardous solid wastes for treatment or disposal, non-point surface water pollution from agricultural and native land, groundwater contamination by fuel storage tanks and by irrigation, and air pollution by energy conversion plants.

The Environmental Health Section of the North Dakota Department of Health oversees programs to ensure water and air quality. North Dakota has little urban air pollution with one exception: motor vehicle traffic is causing excess ambient carbon monoxide in an area within the city of Fargo. The major industrial sources of air contaminants within the state are seven coal-fired electrical generating plants, a coal gasification plant, a refinery, and agricultural commodity processing facilities. The ambient air quality has been in compliance with federal standards, although an epidemiological study has associated certain air contaminants with a higher incidence of respiratory illness among persons living in the vicinity of coal-burning plants.

To conserve water and provide irrigation, nearly 700 dams have been built, including Garrison Dam, completed in 1960. The Garrison Diversion Project, authorized by the US Congress in 1965, was intended to draw water from Lake Sakakawea, the impoundment behind Garrison Dam.

Diversion of household waste to recycling grew to about nearly 15% of the waste stream. Yard wastes, household appliances, and scrap tires are also diverted for compost, recycling, or fuel, respectively. In 2003, North Dakota had 17 hazardous waste sites listed in the Environmental Protection Agency's database, but none was on the National Priorities List. In 2001, North Dakota received $24,606,000 in federal grants from the Environmental Protection Agency; EPA expenditures for procurement contracts in North Dakota that year amounted to $70,000.

6 POPULATION

North Dakota ranked 48th in population in the US with an estimated total of 634,110 in 2002, a decrease of 1.3% from 2000. Between 1990 and 2000, North Dakota's population grew from 638,800 to 642,200, an increase of 0.5%. The population is projected to reach 677,000 by 2005 and 729,000 by 2025. The population density in 2000 was 9.3 persons per sq mi, the 4th-lowest in the nation.

In 2000, the median age in North Dakota was 36.2; 25% of the populace were under age 18 while 14.7% were age 65 or older.

North Dakota is one of the most rural states in the US, with over half of its population living outside metropolitan areas. Leading cities are Fargo, with a 2000 population of 90,599; Bismarck, the capital, 55,532; and Grand Forks, 49,321.

7 ETHNIC GROUPS

As of 2000, about 92.4% of the state's population was white. The American Indian population was 31,329, or about 4.9% of the total, and there were some 3,916 blacks, representing 0.6% of the population. Among Americans of European origin, the leading groups were Germans, who made up 44% of the total population, and Norwegians, who made up 30%. Only about 1.9% of the state's population (12,114) was foreign born as of 2000, predominantly from neighboring Canada. In the same year, the Asian population totaled 3,606, with 230 Pacific Islanders. In 2000, 7,786 North Dakotans were Hispanic or Latino, representing 1.2% of the state's total population.

8 LANGUAGES

Although a few Indian words are used in the English spoken near the reservations where Ojibwa and Sioux live in North Dakota, the only general impact of Indian speech on English is in such place-names as Pembina, Mandan, Wabek, and Anamoose.

A few Norwegian food terms like *lefse* and *lutefisk* have entered the Northern dialect that is characteristic of North Dakota, and some Midland terms have intruded from the south.

In 2000, 93.7% of the population five years old or older spoke only English at home, down slightly from 92.1% in 1990.

The following table gives selected statistics from the 2000 census for language spoken at home by persons five years old and over. The category "Scandinavian languages" includes Danish, Norwegian, and Swedish. The category "Other Native North American languages" includes Apache, Cherokee, Choctaw, Dakota, Keres, Pima, and Yupik. The category "African languages" includes Amharic, Ibo, Twi, Yoruba, Bantu, Swahili, and Somali.

LANGUAGE	NUMBER	PERCENT
Population 5 years and over	603,106	100.0
Speak only English	565,130	93.7
Speak a language other than English	37,976	6.3
Speak a language other than English	37,976	6.3
German	14,931	2.5
Spanish or Spanish Creole	8,263	1.4
Scandinavian languages	3,193	0.5
Other Native North American languages	2,536	0.4
French (incl. Patois, Cajun)	1,597	0.3
Other Slavic languages	1,350	0.2
Serbo-Croatian	825	0.1
African languages	459	0.1
Polish	452	0.1
Chinese	437	0.1
Russian	331	0.1
Tagalog	330	0.1

9 RELIGIONS

Most of the state population is Mainline Protestant, with the leading denominations being the Evangelical Lutheran Church in America with 174,554 adherents (in 2000) and the Untied Methodist Church with 20,159 adherents. The Lutheran Church—Missouri Synod had about 23,720 members. The Catholic Church had about 179,349 members. There were an estimate 920 Muslims and 730 Jews in the state in 2000. About 26.8% of the population were not counted as members of any religious organization.

10 TRANSPORTATION

In 2000, there were 3,956 mi (6,366 km) of rail trackage in North Dakota. The largest railroad lines are the Burlington Northern and Santa Fe (BNSF) and the Soo Line. Farm products and coal accounted for most of the tonnage originated and carried within the state. Amtrak passenger service was provided by the Chicago–Seattle/Portland route.

There were 86,609 mi (139,383 km) of public roads, streets, and highways in North Dakota in 2000. There were also 710,895 registered motor vehicles and 458,944 licensed drivers in the state.

In 2002, there were 322 private airports, 94 public airports, and 16 heliports in North Dakota. More than 237,234 passengers were enplaned from Hector International Airport at Fargo in 2000.

11 HISTORY

Human occupation of what is now North Dakota began about 13,000 BC in the southwestern corner of the state, which at that time was covered with lush vegetation. Drought drove away the aboriginal hunter-gatherers, and it was not until about 2,000 years ago that Indians from the more humid regions to the east moved into the easternmost third of the Dakotas. About AD 1300 the Mandan Indians brought an advanced agricultural economy

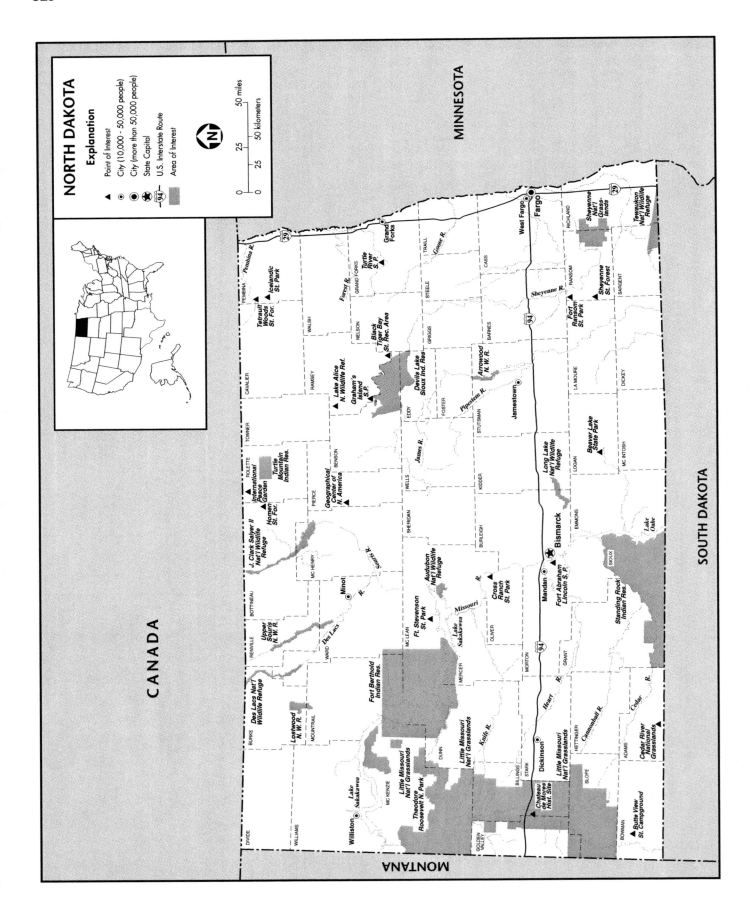

up the Missouri River. They were joined by the Hidatsa and Arikara about three or four centuries later. Moving from the Minnesota forests during the 17th century, the Yanktonai Sioux occupied the southeastern quarter of the state. Their cousins west of the Missouri River, the Teton Sioux, led a nomadic life as hunters and mounted warriors. The Ojibwa, who had driven the Sioux out of Minnesota, settled in the northeast.

European penetration of the Dakotas began in 1738, when Pierre Gaultier de Varennes, Sieur de la Vérendrye, of Trois Riviéres in New France, traded for furs in the Red River region. Later the fur trade spread farther into the Red and Missouri river valleys, especially around Pembina, where the North West Company and the Hudson's Bay Company had their posts. After the Lewis and Clark expedition (1804–06) explored the Missouri, the American Fur Company traded there, with buffalo hides the leading commodity.

In 1812, Scottish settlers from Canada moved up the Red River to Pembina. This first white farming settlement in North Dakota also attracted numerous métis, half-breeds of mixed Indian and European ancestry. An extensive trade in furs and buffalo hides, which were transported first by heavy carts and later by steamboats, sprang up between Pembina, Ft. Garry (Winnipeg, Canada), and St. Paul, Minn.

Army movements against the Sioux during and after the Civil War brought white men into central North Dakota, which in 1861 was organized as part of the Dakota Territory, including the present-day Dakotas, Montana, and Wyoming. The signing of treaties confining the agricultural Indians to reservations, the arrival of the Northern Pacific Railroad at Fargo in 1872, and its extension to the Missouri the following year led to the rise of homesteading on giant "bonanza farms." Settlers poured in, especially from Canada. This short-lived "Great Dakota boom" ended in the mid-1880s with drought and depressed farm prices. As many of the original American and Canadian settlers left in disgust, they were replaced by Norwegians, Germans, and other Europeans. By 1910, North Dakota, which had entered the Union in 1889, was among the leading states in percentage of foreign-born residents.

From the time of statehood onward, Republicans dominated politics in North Dakota. Their leader was Alexander McKenzie, a Canadian immigrant who built a reputation as an agent of the railroads, protecting them from regulation. Between 1898 and 1915, the "Second Boom" brought an upsurge in population and railroad construction. In politics, Republican Progressives enacted reforms, but left unsolved the basic problem of how North Dakota farmers could stand up to the powerful grain traders of Minneapolis-St. Paul. Agrarian revolt flared in 1915, when Arthur C. Townley organized the Farmers' Nonpartisan Political League. Operating through Republican Party machinery, Townley succeeded in having his gubernatorial candidate, Lynn J. Frazier, elected in 1916. State-owned enterprises were established, including the Bank of North Dakota, the Home Building Association, the Hail Insurance Department, and a mill and grain elevator. However, the league was hurt by charges of "socialism" and, after 1917, by allegations of pro-German sympathies in World War I, as well as of mismanagement. In 1921, Frazier and Attorney General William Lemke were removed from office in the nation's first recall election.

The 1920s, a period of bank failures, low farm prices, drought, and political disunity, saw the beginnings of an exodus from the state. Matters grew worse during the Great Depression. Elected governor by hard-pressed farmers in 1932, William Langer took spectacular steps to save farms from foreclosure and to raise grain prices, until a conflict with the Roosevelt administration led to his removal from office on charges that he had illegally solicited political contributions.

World War II brought a quiet prosperity to North Dakota that lasted into the following decades. The Arab oil embargo of 1973 and the rise of oil prices throughout the decade spurred drilling for oil, encouraged the mining of lignite for electrical generation, and led to the construction of the nation's first coal gasification plant, at a cost of $2 billion, in a lignite mining area near Beulah. In the 1980s, however, North Dakota's economy suffered a setback when oil prices dropped. In addition, a drought that began in 1987 damaged over 5.3 million acres of land by 1988 and persisted into the 1990s and early 2000s. Agricultural production was strong in early 1990s. However, severe storms and flooding in 1994 damaged about $600 million in crops. The state continued to experience extreme weather conditions. Drought was followed by flooding rains in early summer 2000, destroying crops.

The state's economy was boosted by the 1991 repeal of the "blue laws" enforcing the closing of all retail businesses on Sundays. Republican Governor Ed Schafer, elected in 1992 and reelected in 1996, set an aggressive plan for the state's economic development, resulting in an estimated 10% increase in the number of jobs and record-low unemployment. By 2000 Fargo boasted one of the lowest unemployment rates in the nation. Nevertheless, poverty was on the rise in the 1990s. With 15.1% of its residents living below the nationally established poverty line, North Dakota ranked as the 9th-poorest in the US in 1998. The state had begun the decade ranked nineteenth, with a 13.7% rate. It was also one of just 15 states where child poverty was on the rise—one in five children lived in poverty in 1998.

Census Bureau figures in 2000 showed the state (population 642,200) continued to be one of the least populated in the nation—only Alaska, Vermont, and Wyoming had fewer residents. Stemming the tide of North Dakotans moving out of state was a top priority. The state enjoyed the rank of safest in the nation in 1999, with only 89 crimes per 100,000 people.

As of 2003, it was illegal for unmarried couples to cohabitate; however, the legislature was considering the repeal of that law. Lawmakers were debating tobacco-related issues in 2003, including banning smoking in public and nonpublic workplaces, and outlawing the sale of flavored cigarettes. Republican Governor John Hoeven in 2003 was calling for budget proposals to combine economic growth and education.

12 STATE GOVERNMENT

North Dakota is governed by the constitution of 1889, as amended (144 times by January 2003). The constitution may be amended by a majority vote in the legislature; a majority vote of the state electorate is required for ratification. Amendments may also be proposed by initiative (by petition of 4% of the state's population).

State elected officials are the governor and lieutenant governor (elected jointly), secretary of state, auditor, treasurer, attorney general, superintendent of public instruction, three public service commissioners, and the commissioners of labor, insurance, taxation, and agriculture. With the exception of the public service commissioners, who serve six-year terms, all terms are four years. Candidates for governor must be 30 years old, US citizens, qualified voters, and state residents for at least five years prior to election. In 2002 the governor's salary was $83,013.

The legislature, which convenes every two years (in odd-numbered years) beginning in early January, is bicameral, with a 49-member senate and a 98-member house of representatives. Regular sessions are limited to 80 legislative days. Only the governor may call for a special session. All legislators must be at least 18 years old, state residents for at least one year, and qualified voters in their districts prior to election; they serve four-year terms. In 2002 legislators received a per diem salary during regular sessions of $125 per calendar day. A two-thirds vote of the elected members of each house is required to override a gubernatorial veto. Bills that are not vetoed or signed by the governor become law after three days (or after 15 days if the legislature adjourns).

Voters in North Dakota must be US citizens, at least 18 years old, and must have been residents of the state at least 30 days prior to the election. The state does not require voters to register.

13POLITICAL PARTIES

Between 1889 and 1960, Republicans held the governorship for 58 years. North Dakota politics were not monolithic, however, for aside from the Populist and Democratic opposition, the Republican Party was itself torn by factionalism, with Progressive and Nonpartisan League challenges to the conservative, probusiness party establishment. Between 1960 and 1980, the statehouse was in Democratic hands. In the early and mid-nineties, the Republican party increased its influence at the state level, gaining dominance in both houses of the state legislature, having wrestled control of the senate away from the Democrats in the November 1994 election. The state had 481,351 registered voters in 2002, 49% of whom turned out to vote. Following the 2002 election, the state senate had 31 Republicans and 16 Democrats. The state house was dominated by the Republicans, who held 66 seats, while the Democrats had 28.

In the 2000 presidential election, Republican George W. Bush won 61% of the vote to Democrat Al Gore's 33%. Independent candidate Ralph Nader and Reform Party candidate Pat Buchanan each received 3% of the vote. North Dakota had three electoral votes in the 2000 presidential election.

Republican John Hoeven was elected governor in 2000. North Dakota's US senators in 2003 were Kent Conrad, a Democrat elected in 1992 to fill a seat vacated by the death of Quentin D. Burdick and reelected to full terms in 1994 and 2000, and Democrat Byron Dorgan, who was also reelected for a second term in 1998. Following the 2002 elections, North Dakota's sole representative to the US House was a Democrat.

North Dakota Presidential Vote by Major Political Parties, 1948–2000

YEAR	ELECTORAL VOTE	N. DAKOTA WINNER	DEMOCRAT	REPUBLICAN
1948	4	Dewey (R)	95,812	115,139
1952	4	*Eisenhower (R)	76,694	191,712
1956	4	*Eisenhower (R)	96,742	156,766
1960	4	Nixon (R)	123,963	154,310
1964	4	*Johnson (D)	149,784	108,207
1968	4	*Nixon (R)	94,769	138,669
1972	3	*Nixon (R)	100,384	174,109
1976	3	Ford (R)	136,078	153,470
1980	3	*Reagan (R)	79,189	193,695
1984	3	*Reagan (R)	104,429	200,336
1988	3	*Bush (R)	127,739	166,559
1992**	3	Bush (R)	99,168	136,244
1996**	3	Dole (R)	106,905	125,050
2000	3	*Bush, G. W. (R)	95,284	174.852

*Won US presidential election.

** Independent candidate Ross Perot received 71,084 votes in 1992 and 32,515 votes in 1996.

14LOCAL GOVERNMENT

North Dakota in 2002 had 2,735 units of local government, including 53 counties, 360 municipalities (all designated as cities regardless of size), 1,332 townships, 226 public school districts, and 764 special districts. Typical elected county officials are commissioners, sheriff, court clerk, county judge, county justice, and state's attorney. Counties are divided into townships, each with its own elected administrative officers. Most municipalities operate by the mayor-council system of government.

15STATE SERVICES

To address the continuing threat of terrorism and to work with the federal Department of Homeland Security (created in 2002 following the terrorist attacks of 11 September 2001), homeland security in North Dakota in 2003 operated under the authority of the governor; the emergency management director was designated as the state homeland security advisor.

Educational services are under the jurisdiction of the Department of Public Instruction and the Board of Higher Education; there are state schools for the deaf, blind, handicapped, and mentally retarded. Health and welfare agencies include the State Health Department, Department of Agriculture, Department of Economic Development and Finance, Council on the Arts, Veterans Affairs Department, Social Service Board, and Indian Affairs Commission. Agricultural services include an extensive program of experiment and extension stations. The state bank, mill, and grain elevator established under Nonpartisan League influence remain to this day.

16JUDICIAL SYSTEM

North Dakota has a supreme court of five justices, seven district courts with 43 justices, and a system of local (county) courts. Supreme court justices are elected for 10-year terms, district court judges for 6-year terms.

According to the FBI Crime Index, in 2001 North Dakota had a total crime rate of 2,417.7 crimes per 100,000 population, including a total of 505 violent crimes and 14,834 crimes against property in that year.). As of June 2001, there were 1,080 inmates held in state and federal correctional facilities, an increase of 7.6% over the previous year. The state's incarceration rate stood at 158 per 100,000 population.

North Dakota does not have a death penalty. It was abolished in 1973, and the last execution in that state took place in 1930. North Dakota does provide for life without parole.

17ARMED FORCES

In 2002, there were 7,465 active-duty military personnel and 1,621 civilian personnel stationed in North Dakota, the majority of whom were stationed at the Strategic Air Command bases at Minot and Grand Forks. North Dakota firms received more than $159 million in defense contract awards in 2002.

According to the 2000 Census, 61,365 veterans were living in North Dakota, including 11,604 from World War II; 8,174 from the Korean conflict; 18,780 from the Vietnam era; and 7,805 during 1990–2000 (including the Persian Gulf War). A total of more than $152 million was spent on major veterans' benefit programs in the state in 2002.

In 2000, the North Dakota Highway Patrol employed 126 full-time sworn officers.

18MIGRATION

During the late 19th century, North Dakota was largely settled by immigrants of German and Scandinavian stock. The state reached a peak population in 1930, but then suffered steady losses until well into the 1970s because of out-migration. This trend has shown some signs of abating, however. From 1980 to 1983, the state's population grew 4.3%, in part because of a net gain in migration of about 5,000 people. Also during the 1980s, the urban population grew to outnumber the rural population, rising from 48.8% to 53.3% of the total populace. From 1985 to 1990, North Dakota had a net loss of 44,142 from migration. Between 1990 and 1998, the state had a net loss of 30,000 in domestic migration but a net gain of 4,000 in international migration. In 1998, the state admitted 472 foreign immigrants. North Dakota's overall population decreased by 0.1% between 1990 and 1998. In the period 1995–2000, 60,252 people moved into the state and

85,459 moved out, for a net loss of 25,207, many of whom moved to Minnesota.

[19] INTERGOVERNMENTAL COOPERATION

North Dakota participates in such interstate agreements as the Yellowstone River Compact, Western Interstate Commission for Higher Education, Interstate Compact for Juveniles, and Interstate Oil and Gas Compact. A Minnesota–North Dakota Boundary Compact was ratified in 1961. Federal grants in 2001 totaled almost $1.3 billion.

[20] ECONOMY

North Dakota has been and still is an important agricultural state, especially as a producer of wheat, much of which finds its way onto the world market. Many segments of the economy are affected by agriculture; for example, a substantial wholesale trade is involved in moving grain and livestock to market. Like other Midwestern farmers, North Dakotans suffered from high interest rates and a federal embargo on grain shipments to the Soviet Union in the early 1980s. Farm numbers have continued to decline, posing a threat to the vitality of the state's rural lifestyle. From 1970, 43 of North Dakota's 53 counties have lost population, and for 23 of these the population decline accelerated in the 1990s. The exodus has been aggravated by prolonged drought conditions, which in 2002 helped reduce wheat production (representing a quarter of the states total agricultural revenues) by 24% and disrupted cattle production. Not being deeply involved in the dot.com frenzy of the 1990s, North Dakota was only slightly affected by the national recession and slowdown of 2001 and 2002. By December 2002, state unemployment which had risen to 3.6% in October, had fallen back to 3%.

Growth industries for the state include petroleum and the mining of coal, chiefly lignite; North Dakota has more coal resources than any other state. Manufacturing is concentrated to a great extent on farm products and machinery.

North Dakota's gross state product in 2001 was $19 billion, smallest among the 50 states, to which general services contributed $3.7 billion; trade, $3.5 billion; government, $3 billion; financial services, $2.8 billion; transportation and public utilities, $1.9 billion, and construction, $896 million. The public sector in 2001 constituted 15.7% of gross state product, the 9th-highest among the states.

[21] INCOME

According to the Bureau of Economic Analysis, in 2001, North Dakota had a per capita personal income (PCPI) of $25,798 which ranked 39th in the United States (including the District of Columbia) and was 85% of the national average, $30,413. The 2001 PCPI reflected an increase of 3.2% from 2000 compared to the national change of 2.2%. In 2001, North Dakota had a total personal income (TPI) of $16,421,689,000 which ranked 50th in the United States and accounted for 0.2% of the national total. The 2001 TPI reflected an increase of 2.5% from 2000 compared to the national change of 3.3%.

Earnings of persons employed in North Dakota increased from $11,227,477,000 in 2000 to $11,426,137,000 in 2001, an increase of 1.8%. The largest industries in 2001 were services, 26.1% of earnings; state and local government, 13.8%; and retail trade, 9.6%. Of the industries that accounted for at least 5% of earnings in 2001, the slowest growing from 2000 to 2001 was construction (6.5% of earnings in 2001), which increased 0.2%; the fastest was state and local government, which increased 15.7%.

According to data released by the US Census Bureau, in 2000, the median household income was $35,349 compared to the national average of $42,148. In 2001, the median income for a family of four was $55,138 compared to the national average of $63,278. For the period 1999 to 2001, the average poverty rate was 12.4% which placed it 33rd among the 50 states and the District of Columbia ranked lowest to highest.

[22] LABOR

According to Bureau of Labor Statistics (BLS) provisional estimates, in July 2003 the seasonally adjusted civilian labor force in North Dakota numbered 350,500, with approximately 12,600 workers unemployed, yielding an unemployment rate of 3.6%, compared to the national average of 6.2% for the same period. Since the beginning of the BLS data series in 1978, the highest unemployment rate recorded was 6.7% in May 1986. The historical low was 2.3% in October 1997. In 2001, an estimated 4.7% of the labor force was employed in construction; 7.3% in manufacturing; 5.2% in transportation, communications, and public utilities; 20.3% in trade; 4.7% in finance, insurance, and real estate; 23.6% in services; 17.9% in government; and 8.5% in agriculture.

The US Department of Labor reported that in 2002, 24,000 of North Dakota's 291,000 employed wage and salary workers were members of unions. This represented 8.1% of those so employed, up from 7.5% in 2001 but down from 9.1% in 1998. The national average is 13.2%. In all, 28,000 workers (9.8%) were represented by unions. In addition to union members, this category includes workers who report no union affiliation but whose jobs are covered by a union contract. North Dakota is one of 22 states with a right-to-work law.

[23] AGRICULTURE

North Dakota's farm marketings totaled $2.98 billion in 2001. Typically, North Dakota is the number one producer of hard spring wheat, durum wheat, sunflowers, barley, oats, flax, all dry edible beans, and pinto beans. In 2002, North Dakota led the nation in spring wheat, drum wheat, barley, dry edible beans, sunflowers, and was 2nd in the nation in overall wheat production. production.

The total number of farms has declined over the years as the average size of farming operations has increased. In 2002, the state had approximately 30,000 farms and ranches occupying 39.4 million acres (16 million hectares) and producing 216.6 million bushels of wheat, 57.0 million bushels of barley, 1.71 billion lb of sunflowers, 12.7 million bushels of oats, 10.6 hundredweight of dry edible beans, 114.4 million bushels of corn, 4.8 million tons of sugar beets, and 23.5 million hundredweight of potatoes. The average farm is 1,313 acres (531 hectares).

[24] ANIMAL HUSBANDRY

North Dakota farms and ranches had an estimated 1.9 million cattle and calves, valued at $1.58 billion in 2003. During 2002, there were around 154,000 hogs and pigs, worth $11.4 million. North Dakota farmers produced nearly 9.1 million lb (4.1 million kg) of sheep and lambs, which brought in $5.8 million in gross income in 2001, and nearly 42 million lb (19.1 million kg) of turkey were produced in that same year.

[25] FISHING

There is little commercial fishing in North Dakota. In 1998, the state issued 139,162 sport fishing licenses.

[26] FORESTRY

The dispersed forests on the rolling prairie are not a dominant feature of the landscape; North Dakota's climate is more favorable to grassland ecosystems. At the time of settlement, native forests covered about 700,000 acres (283,000 hectares). In 2002, there were 672,000 acres (272,000 hectares) of forestland, with 441,000 acres (178,000 hectares) classified as viable timberland. Agricultural clearing, inundation by reservoirs, and other land use changes have resulted in a 9% reduction in total forestland since 1954.

27MINING

The value of nonfuel minerals produced in North Dakota in 2001 was estimated at about $39 million, up about 12% from 2000. Construction sand and gravel accounted for more than 70% of the value ($27.6 million) of North Dakota's nonfuel mineral output, from a production of 10.6 million metric tons. Recovered elemental sulfur is the 2nd most important mineral produced in North Dakota, in terms of value. Sulfur and other byproducts such as krypton, xenon, anhydrous ammonia, and liquid nitrogen are recovered during natural gas processing at five plants in the western part of the state. Lapidary and collectible materials such as petrified wood, agates, jasper, and flint are also found in North Dakota.

28ENERGY AND POWER

Power stations in North Dakota (utility and nonutility) generated 31.4 billion kWh of electricity in 1999 and had 4.7 million kW of installed electric generating capacity. Energy consumption per capita in 2000 amounted to 569 million Btu (143.3 million kcal) (5th among the states).

Recoverable coal reserves totaled 1,151 million tons in 2001, when North Dakota produced 31,270,000 tons of coal. Proved petroleum reserves in 2001 totaled 328 million barrels; production was 85,000 barrels per day in 2002. In 2001, natural gas reserves totaled 443 billion cu ft (12.5 billion cu m); marketed production was 56.9 billion cu ft (1.6 billion cu m) in 2002.

29INDUSTRY

By number of employees, the leading manufacturing industries in North Dakota in 1997 were food and food products; industrial machinery and equipment; printing and publishing; electronic and other electric equipment; transportation equipment; and fabricated metal products. Value of shipments of manufactures in 1997 were estimated at over $5.2 billion, exhibiting the 9th fastest growth in shipments between 1992 and 1997.

Earnings of persons employed in North Dakota increased from $9.1 billion in 1997 to $10.2 in 1998, an increase of 11.5%. The largest industries in 1998 were services, 26.2% of earnings; state and local government, 12.4%; and retail trade, 10.5%. Of the industries that accounted for at least 5% of earnings in 1998, the slowest growing from 1997 to 1998 was construction (6.9% of earnings in 1998), which increased 1.9%; the fastest was durable goods manufacturing (5.1% of earnings in 1998), which increased 11.9%.

30COMMERCE

In 1997, North Dakota had 1,963 wholesale establishments, with sales of $9.5 billion. The leading wholesale lines by sales volume were farm-product raw materials, machinery, equipment, and supplies (especially farm machinery), groceries and related products, and petroleum and petroleum products. The state's 4,810 retail establishments recorded $6.4 billion in sales during 1997. Exports of North Dakota origin totaled $750 million in 1998, ranked 45th of all states.

31CONSUMER PROTECTION

Allegations of consumer fraud and other illegal business practices are handled by the Consumer Protection and Antitrust Division of the State Attorney General's Office.

32BANKING

As of 2002, North Dakota's 107 insured banks had assets of $19.5 billion. Eighty-nine of those banks were state-chartered.

Despite the economic downturn that started in 2001, community banks (those with assets of less than $1 billion) headquartered in North Dakota reported sound assets, as past-due loan levels moderated as of late 2002. Although many farm banks had high loan delinquency levels due to low crop prices from 1998–2002, government support helped curb loan defaults.

During 2001/02, the Federal Reserve cut interest rates considerably, leading to fluctuations in net interest margins (NIMs) (the difference between the lower rates offered to savers and the higher rates charged on loans), but they did not signal an end to a long-term decline in NIMs since the 1990s.

33INSURANCE

In 2001, North Dakota had 317,000 life insurance policies in force, worth $25.3 billion; total value for all categories of life insurance (ordinary, group, industrial, and credit) was $40.9 billion. Death benefits paid that year totaled $89.3 million. As of 2000, there were 17 property and casualty and four life and health insurance companies incorporated or organized in the state. Property and casualty insurers wrote over $875 million in premiums. That year, there were 6,586 flood insurance policies in force in the state, with a total value of $815,604.

34SECURITIES

North Dakota has no securities exchanges. There are 117 broker-dealers industries with over 500 employees, and nine investment advisory organizations in North Dakota. Six NASDAQ-listed companies are headquartered and one NYSE-listed company—RDO Equipment Co.—is incorporated in the state.

35PUBLIC FINANCE

Total expenditures for 1995–97 (including federal and special funds) totaled approximately $3.6 billion, including $500 million for transportation, a total of $1.1 billion for health and human services, and a total of $1.3 billion for education. North Dakota has the only state-owned bank and state-owned mill, contributing $50 million and $3 million, respectively, to the general fund during the 1999–2001 biennium.

For the biennial 2003–2005 budget, legislative appropriations for the $1.804 billion general fund budget included, by function, 34.9% for elementary and secondary education, 23.9% for health and human services, 20% for higher education, 8.4% for general government and grants, 6.1% for public safety, 4.1% for agriculture and economic development, 1.4% for natural resources, and 1.2% for regulatory agencies. The following table from the US Census Bureau contains information on revenues, expenditures, indebtedness, and cash/securities for 2001.

	($000)	PERCENT	PER CAPITA
Population (thousands, 2001)	637	(X)	(X)
Total Revenue	3,373,244	100.00	5,295.52
General revenue	2,840,380	84.20	4,459.00
Insurance trust revenue	532,864	15.80	836.52
Exhibit: Salaries and wages	4,939,301	170.44	7,754.00
Total expenditure	2,897,950	100.00	4,549.37
General expenditure	2,673,193	92.24	4,196.54
Education	902,302	31.14	1,416.49
Public welfare	600,415	20.72	942.57
Hospitals	44,212	1.53	69.41
Health	50,017	1.73	78.52
Highways	322,484	11.13	506.25
Police protection	9,815	0.34	15.41
Correction	37,605	1.30	59.03
Natural resources	101,487	3.50	159.32
Parks and recreation	10,805	0.37	16.96
Government administration	96,974	3.35	152.24
Interest on general debt	85,986	2.97	134.99
Other and unallocable	411,091	14.19	645.35
Insurance trust expenditure	224,757	7.76	352.84
Debt at end of fiscal year	1,549,350	100.00	2,432.26
Cash and security holdings	6,777,927	100.00	10,640.39

36TAXATION

For filers using North Dakota's regular long form, the five-bracket personal income schedule ranges from 2.67% to 12.0%, with federal taxes paid deductible. The rates for the state's short form (Form 375) are lower: 2.1% (up to taxable income of $27,050) to 5.54% (above $297,350), but without deductions for federal taxes paid. Effective in 2002, the lower rates on the short form replaced a tax of 14% of adjusted federal income tax liability. The corporate income tax schedule has six brackets ranging from 3% (up to $3,000 net income) to 10.5% (above $50,000 net income).Banks have a minimum tax of $50. The state sales and use tax rate is 5%, with exemptions for food and prescription drugs, and lower rates on certain items. Local sales taxes range from none to 2.5%. The state also imposes a full array of excise taxes covering motor fuels, tobacco products, insurance premiums, public utilities, alcoholic beverages, amusements, pari-mutuels, and other selected items. Severance taxes—the oil and gas gross production tax, the coal severance tax, and the oil extraction tax—generate a substantial portion of state revenue. North Dakota's inheritance tax was repealed in 1927 and replaced with an estate tax tied to the exemption for state death taxes in the federal estate tax (enacted in 1926).The federal exemption is scheduled to be phased out by 2007, and with it, North Dakota's estate tax unless countervailing action is taken by the state legislature. North Dakota's revenue losses from the phasing out of its estate tax are estimated at -$1.5 million for 2002/03, -$4 million for 2003/04 and -$5.5 million for 2006/07. Death and gift taxes accounted for 0.5% of state collections in 2002. Other state taxes include various license fees and state property taxes. Most state and local revenues are collected at the state level (64.4% in 2000).

Total state tax collections in North Dakota in 2002 were $1.117 billion (down $57 million from 2001, which, in turn, had been over $850 million below projections), of which 30% was generated by the state general sales and use tax, 25.4% by state excise taxes, 17.8% by personal income taxes, 12.3% by severance taxes, 9.2% license fees, and 4.4% by the corporate income tax. In 2003, combined state and local taxes amounted to 9.8% of income, and North Dakota ranked 17th in the country.

The following table from the US Census Bureau provides a summary of taxes collected by the state in 2002.

	($000)	PER CAPITA
Total Taxes	1,117,299	1,762.00
Property taxes	1,375	2.17
Sales and gross receipts	619,974	977.71
General sales and gross receipts	335,613	529.27
Selective sales taxes	284,361	448.44
Alcoholic beverage	5,494	8.66
Amusements	14,054	22.16
Insurance Premiums	25,999	41
Motor fuels	110,848	174.81
Pari-mutuels	2,531	3.99
Public utilities	32,808	51.74
Tobacco products	21,573	34.02
Other selective sales	71,054	112.05
Licenses	102,792	162.1
Alcoholic beverages	252	0.4
Amusements	242	0.38
Hunting and fishing	10,384	16.38
Motor vehicle	52,234	82.37
Motor vehicle operators	3,639	5.74
Public utility	5	0.01
Occupation and business, NEC	36,036	56.83
Other	(X)	(X)
Other taxes	393,158	620.02
Individual income	199,590	314.76
Corporation net income	49,990	78.83
Death and gift	5,334	8.41
Severance	138,244	218.01

37ECONOMIC POLICY

The North Dakota Economic Development and Finance Division of the Department of Commerce seeks to attract new industry, retain and expand existing industry, promote start-up businesses, and develop markets for state products. The state uses a local approach to provide business incentives, including job training, financing, and tax-abatement programs. In 2003, the main operating units within the division included the Rural Development Council, Research, Marketing, and Business Development. Other divisions within the Department of Commerce focused on Community Services, Tourism and Workforce Development.

38HEALTH

In 2000, the infant mortality rate was 8.1 per 1,000 population. The Centers for Disease Control estimate that in 1999 there were 1,345 abortions performed, or 10 per 1,000 women. The mortality rate for all major causes (930.6 per 100,000 population) in North Dakota in 2000 was significantly higher than the national average of 873.1. For 100,000 population, 266.8 residents died of heart disease in that same year.

In 1998, the rate of death from HIV-related infection stood at 3.0 per 100,000 population, below the US rate of 5.3. A total of 110 AIDS cases had been reported in North Dakota through 2000, less than in any other state. In 2000, 23.3% of North Dakota residents were smokers. The rate of death from lung disease stood at 81.9 per 100,000 inhabitants.

North Dakota's 40 community hospitals had 91,530 admissions and 3,717 beds in 2001. There were 2,937 full-time registered nurses and 785 full-time licensed practical nurses in 2001 and 242 physicians per 100,000 population in 2000. The average expense of a community hospital for care was $1,924 per inpatient day in 2001.

Federal government grants to cover the Medicare and Medicaid services in 2001 totaled $308 million; 103,126 enrollees received Medicare benefits that year. Only 9.6% of North Dakota's residents were uninsured in 2002.

39SOCIAL WELFARE

In 2001, the average weekly unemployment benefit was $196.34. Average monthly participation in the food stamp program in FY2002 comprised 36,781 persons (15,899 households). The average monthly benefit was $71.08, and the sum total of benefits paid in FY2002 was $31,374,657.

With the enactment of the Personal Responsibility and Work Opportunity Reconciliation Act of 1996, the US government has changed the form and regulations for many of its social welfare programs. Most significantly, it replaces Aid to Families with Dependent Children (AFDC), an open-ended entitlement program, with Temporary Assistance for Needy Families (TANF), a limited system of assistance funded largely through federal block grants. The reform act also impacts the food stamp program, the Supplemental Security Income program, and the child nutrition program. The law took effect on 1 July 1997 and provided $16.38 billion in block grants for fiscal years 1997–2002. The grants are to be divided among the states based on an equation involving the numbers of former AFDC recipients in each state.

Reauthorization of the 1996 social welfare legislation, scheduled for 2002, was delayed, and the original law had been extended three times as of July 2003, with the most recent extension running through September 2003. North Dakota's TANF program is called Training, Employment, Education Management (TEEM). In June 2000 the state had 7,734 welfare recipients. State expenditures on the TANF program in FY2002 totaled $9,069,360.

In December 2001, Social Security benefits were paid to 114,380 North Dakota residents. This number included 70,470 retired workers, 16,640 widows and widowers, 9,560 disabled workers, 10,590 spouses, and 7,120 children. Social Security beneficiaries represented 18% of the total state population and 95% of the state's population age 65 and older. Retired workers (excluding persons with special benefits) received an average monthly payment of $817; widows and widowers, $798; disabled workers, $765; and spouses, $408. Payments for children of retired workers averaged $398 per month; children of deceased workers, $514; and children of disabled workers, $233.

Federal Supplemental Security Income payments in December 2001 went to 8,129 North Dakota residents, averaging $310 a month.

40HOUSING

In 2002, North Dakota had 294,165 housing units, 254,689 of which were occupied; 65.9% were owner-occupied. About 61.5 % of all housing units were single-family, detached homes. Utility gas and electricity were the most common energy sources for heating. It was estimated that 6,850 units lacked telephone services, 1,880 lacked complete plumbing facilities, and 1,279 lacked complete kitchen facilities. The average household size was 2.4 people.

In 2002, 3,265 new privately owned units were authorized for construction. The median home value was $80,317, one of the lowest in the nation. The median monthly cost for mortgage owners was $852. Renters paid a median of $433 per month. During 2002, North Dakota received over $12.6 million in community planning and development aid from the US Department of Housing and Urban Development.

41EDUCATION

In 2000, 83.9% of North Dakota residents age 25 and older were high school graduates; 22% had obtained a bachelor's degree or higher.

The total enrollment for fall 1999 in North Dakota's public schools stood at 112,751. Of these, 74,968 attended schools from kindergarten through grade eight, and 37,782 attended high school. Minority students made up approximately 11% of the total enrollment in public elementary and secondary schools in 1997. Total enrollment was estimated at 106,635 in fall 2000. Enrollment in nonpublic schools in fall 2001 was 7,148. Expenditures for public education in 2000/01 were estimated at $809,204

As of fall 2000, there were 38,937 students enrolled in college or graduate school. In the same year North Dakota had 21 degree-granting institutions. The chief universities are the University of North Dakota in Grand Forks and North Dakota State University in Fargo. The North Dakota Student Financial Assistance Program offers scholarships for North Dakota college students, and the state Indian Scholarship Board provides aid to Native Americans attending college in the state. In 1997, minority students comprised 8% of total postsecondary enrollment.

42ARTS

The North Dakota Council on the Arts, a branch of the North Dakota state government, provides grants to local artists and groups such as the Trollwood Performing Arts School and the Annual United Tribes Indian Art Expo; encourages visits by out-of-state artists and exhibitions; and provides information and other services to the general public.

The historic Fargo Theater present live theatrical performances as well as films and sponsors the annual Fargo Film Festival. Fargo is also the center for the Fargo-Moorhead Opera and the Fargo-Moorhead Symphony. The Northern Plains Ballet is based

in Bismarck but tours to Sioux Falls, Fargo, Billings, and Grand Forks.

Two popular musical events are the Old Time Fiddlers Contest (at Dunseith in June) and the Medora Musical (Medora, June through Labor Day); the latter features Western songs and dance.

In 2003, the North Dakota Council of the Arts and other North Dakota arts organizations received grants totaling $609,100 from the National Endowment for the Arts. The state also provided the council with funding. The North Dakota Humanities Council was established in 1973. In 2000, the National Endowment for the Humanities contributed $596,714 to 12 state programs. The state offers arts education to approximately 14,000 schoolchildren.

43LIBRARIES AND MUSEUMS

During 2000, North Dakota public libraries had 2,126,285 volumes and a total circulation of 3,902,000. The leading academic library was that of the University of North Dakota (Grand Forks), with 1,221,953 items. Total public library income for 2000 was $8,134,000; including $544,978 in state grants. State libraries spent 59.8% of income on staff, and 18.9% on collections.

Among the most notable of the state's 50 museums are the Art Galleries and Zoology Museum of the University of North Dakota and the North Dakota Heritage Center at Bismarck, which has an outstanding collection of Indian artifacts. Theodore Roosevelt National Park contains relics from the Elkhorn ranch where Roosevelt lived in the 1880s.

44COMMUNICATIONS

In 2001, 97.3% of North Dakota's occupied housing units had telephones. There were 28 major radio stations (10 AM, 18 FM) in 2003. As of 2003, nine major network television stations were in operation. A total of 15,091 Internet domain names were registered in North Dakota in 2000.

45PRESS

As of 2002, there were six morning dailies and four evening dailies. There were also seven Sunday papers in the state. The leading dailies were the *Fargo Forum,* with a daily circulation of 51,244, Sunday, 63,522; the *Grand Forks Herald,* 32,790 morning, 33,998 Sunday; the *Minot Daily News,* 22,620 morning, 23,555 Sunday; and the *Bismarck Tribune,* 26,865 morning, 30,153 Sunday. In addition, there were about 15 periodicals. The leading historical journal is *North Dakota Horizons,* a quarterly founded in 1971.

46ORGANIZATIONS

In 2003, there were about 769 regional, national, and international organizations within the state. Two of the state's largest organizations are the Friends (Service Club) and the Northwest Farm Managers Association, both headquartered in Fargo.

State organizations focusing on arts, culture, history, and the environment include Arts on the Prairie, ArtWise, the Bluegrass and Old Time Music Association of North Dakota, the Crazy Horse Memorial Foundation, Fargo Garden Society, the North Dakota Council on Arts, and the North Dakota Wildlife Federation. The North Dakota Academy of Science is located in Grand Forks.

Other notable organizations include the National Sunflower Association in Bismarck and the Cracker Jack Collectors Association in Grand Forks.

47TOURISM, TRAVEL, AND RECREATION

North Dakota's 17 state parks and other state recreational areas received 1,069,762 visitors in 1999, including a record 267,000 visitors at Lake Sakakawea State Park near Pick City. Nearly 43% of all park users come from other states and countries.

Among the leading tourist attractions is the International Peace Garden, covering 2,200 acres (890 hectares) in North Dakota and Manitoba and commemorating friendly relations between the US and Canada. Ft. Abraham Lincoln State Park, south of Mandan, has been restored to evoke the 1870s, when General Custer left the area for his "last stand" against the Sioux. The most spectacular scenery in North Dakota is found in the Theodore Roosevelt National Park. The so-called "badlands," an integral part of the park, consist of strangely colored and intricately eroded buttes and other rock formations. Hunting and fishing are major recreational activities in North Dakota. The Maah Daah Hey Trail is a 100-mile non-motorized trail that runs through Theodore Roosevelt Park and the Little Missouri National Grasslands.

48SPORTS

There are no major professional sports teams in North Dakota. In collegiate football, the University of North Dakota Fighting Sioux and the North Dakota State University Bison compete in the North Central Conference. The University of North Dakota also competes in collegiate ice hockey, winning NCAA championships in 1959, 1963, 1980, 1982, 1987, 1997, and 2000.

Other annual sporting events include the PWT Championship (a walleye fishing tournament) in Bismarck in September, and several rodeos throughout the state. Former New York Yankee slugger Roger Maris grew up in Fargo, North Dakota.

49FAMOUS NORTH DAKOTANS

Preeminent among North Dakota politicians known to the nation was Gerald P. Nye (b.Wisconsin, 1892–1971), a US senator and a leading isolationist opponent of President Franklin D. Roosevelt's foreign policy, as was Senator William Langer (1886–1959). Another prominent senator, Porter J. McCumber (1858–1933), supported President Woodrow Wilson in the League of Nations battle. US Representative William Lemke (1878–1950) sponsored farm-relief legislation and in 1936 ran for US president on the Union Party ticket. Usher L. Burdick (1879–1960), a maverick isolationist and champion of the American Indian, served 18 years in the US House of Representatives.

Vilhjalmur Stefansson (b.Canada, 1879–1962) recorded in numerous books his explorations and experiments in the high Arctic. Orin G. Libby (1864–1952) made a significant contribution to the study of American history. Other North Dakota–nurtured writers and commentators include Maxwell Anderson (b.Pennsylvania, 1888–1959), a Pulitzer Prize–winning

playwright; Edward K. Thompson (Minnesota, 1907–96), editor of *Life* magazine and founder-editor of *Smithsonian;* radio and television commentator Eric Severeid (1912–1992); and novelist Larry Woiwode (b.1941).

To the entertainment world North Dakota has contributed band leaders Harold Bachman (1892–1972), Lawrence Welk (1903–92), and Tommy Tucker (Gerald Duppler, 1908–89); jazz vocalist Peggy Lee (Norma Delores Egstrom, 1920–2002) and country singer Lynn Anderson (b.1947); and actresses Dorothy Stickney (1900–98) and Angie Dickinson (Angeline Brown, b.1931).

Sports personalities associated with the state include outfielder Roger Maris (1934–85), who in 1961 broke Babe Ruth's record for home runs in one season.

50BIBLIOGRAPHY

Crawford, Lewis F. *History of North Dakota.* 3 vols. Chicago: American Historical Society, 1931.

DeLorme Mapping Company. *North Dakota Atlas & Gazetteer: Topo Maps of the Entire State: Back Roads, Outdoor Recreation.* Yarmouth, Me.: DeLorme, 1999.

Federal Writers' Project. *North Dakota: A Guide to the Northern Prairie State.* Reprint. New York: Somerset, 1980 (orig. 1938).

Goodman, L. R., and R. J. Eidem. *The Atlas of North Dakota.* Fargo: North Dakota Studies, Inc., 1976.

Hintz, Martin. *North Dakota.* New York: Children's Press, 2000.

Hoover, Herbert T. *The Sioux and Other Native American Cultures of the Dakotas: An Annotated Bibliography.* Westport, Conn.: Greenwood Press, 1993.

McMacken, Robin. *The Dakotas: Off the Beaten Path.* Old Saybrook, Conn.: Globe Pequot Press, 1998.

North Dakota Economic Development Commission. *North Dakota Growth Indicators.* Bismarck, 1984.

Raaen, Aagot. *Grass of the Earth: Immigrant Life in Dakota Country.* St. Paul, Minn.: Minnesota Historical Society Press, 1994.

Robinson, Elwyn B. *History of North Dakota.* Lincoln: University of Nebraska Press, 1966.

Tweton, D. Jerome, and Theodore Jelliff. *North Dakota—The Heritage of a People.* Fargo: North Dakota Institute for Regional Studies, 1976.

———. and Daniel F. Rylance. *The Years of Despair: North Dakota in the Depression.* Grand Forks: Oxcart Press, 1973.

University of North Dakota. Bureau of Business and Economic Research. *Statistical Abstract of North Dakota 1983.* Grand Forks: University of North Dakota Press, 1983.

Wilkins, Robert P., and Wynona H. *North Dakota: A Bicentennial History.* New York: Norton, 1977.

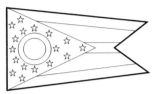

OHIO

State of Ohio

ORIGIN OF STATE NAME: From the Iroquois Indian word *oheo*, meaning "beautiful." **NICKNAME:** The Buckeye State. **CAPITAL:** Columbus. **ENTERED UNION:** 1 March 1803 (17th). **SONG:** "Beautiful Ohio." **MOTTO:** With God All Things Are Possible. **FLAG:** The flag is a burgee, with three red and two white lateral stripes; at the staff is a blue triangular field covered with 17 stars (signifying Ohio's order of entry into the Union) grouped around a red disk superimposed on a white circular "O." **OFFICIAL SEAL:** In the foreground are a sheaf of wheat and a sheaf of 17 arrows; behind, a sun rises over a mountain range, indicating that Ohio is the 1st state west of the Alleghenies. Surrounding the scene are the words "The Great Seal of the State of Ohio." **ANIMAL:** White-tailed deer. **BIRD:** Cardinal. **INSECT:** Ladybug. **REPTILE:** Black racer snake. **FLOWER:** Scarlet carnation. **TREE:** Buckeye. **BEVERAGE:** Tomato juice. **STONE:** Ohio flint. **LEGAL HOLIDAYS:** New Year's Day, 1 January; Birthday of Martin Luther King, Jr., 3rd Monday in January; Presidents' Day, 3rd Monday in February; Memorial Day, last Monday in May; Independence Day, 4 July; Labor Day, 1st Monday in September; Columbus Day, 2nd Monday in October; Veterans Day, 11 November; Thanksgiving Day, 4th Thursday in November; Christmas Day, 25 December. **TIME:** 7 AM EST = noon GMT.

¹LOCATION, SIZE, AND EXTENT

Located in the eastern north-central US, Ohio is the 11th largest of the 12 midwestern states and ranks 35th in size among the 50 states.

The state's total area is 41,330 sq mi (107,044 sq km), of which land comprises 41,004 sq mi (106,201 sq km) and inland water 326 sq mi (823 sq km). Ohio extends about 210 mi (338 km) E-W; its maximum N-S extension is 230 mi (370 km).

Ohio is bordered on the N by Michigan and the Canadian province of Ontario (with the line passing through Lake Erie); on the E by Pennsylvania and West Virginia (with the Ohio River forming part of the boundary); on the S by West Virginia and Kentucky (with the entire line defined by the Ohio River); and on the W by Indiana.

Five important islands lie off the state's northern shore, in Lake Erie: the three Bass Islands, Kelleys Island, and Catawba Island. Ohio's total boundary length is 997 mi (1,605 km).

The state's geographic center is in Delaware County, 25 mi (40 km) NNE of Columbus.

²TOPOGRAPHY

Ohio has three distinct topographical regions: the foothills of the Allegheny Mountains in the eastern half of the state; the Erie lakeshore, extending for nearly three-fourths of the northern boundary; and the central plains in the western half of the state.

The Allegheny Plateau in eastern Ohio consists of rugged hills and steep valleys that recede gradually as the terrain sweeps westward toward the central plains. The highest point in the state is Campbell Hill (1,549 ft/472 m), located in Logan County about 50 mi (80 km) northwest of Columbus.

The Erie lakeshore, a band of level lowland that runs across the state to the northwestern corner on the Michigan boundary, is distinguished by sandy beaches. The central plains extend to the western boundary with Indiana. In the south, undulating hills decline in altitude as they reach the serpentine Ohio River, which forms the state's southern boundary with Kentucky and West Virginia. The state's lowest point is on the bands of the Ohio River in the southwest, where the altitude drops to 455 ft (139 m) above sea level.

Most of Ohio's 2,500 lakes are situated in the east, and nearly all are reservoirs backed up by river dams. The largest, Pymatuning Reservoir, on the Pennsylvania border, has an area of 14,650 acres (5,929 ha). Grand Lake (St. Mary's), located near the western border, covering 12,500 acres (5,059 ha), is the largest lake wholly within Ohio.

Ohio has two drainage basins separated by a low ridge extending from the northeast corner to about the middle of the western border with Indiana. North of the ridge, more than one-third of Ohio's area is drained by the Maumee, Portage, Sandusky, Cuyahoga, and Grand rivers into Lake Erie. South of the ridge, the remaining two-thirds of the state is drained mainly by the Muskingum, Hocking, Raccoon, Scioto, Little Miami, and Miami rivers into the Ohio River, which winds for about 450 mi (725 km) along the eastern and southern borders.

Ohio's bedrock of sandstone, shale, and limestone was formed during the Paleozoic era some 300–600 million years ago. The oldest limestone rocks are found in the Cincinnati anticline, a ridge of sedimentary rock layers about 3,000 ft (900 m) thick that extends from north to south in west-central Ohio. Inland seas filled and receded periodically to form salt and gypsum, also creating peat bogs that later were pressurized into the coal beds of southeastern Ohio. At the end of the Paleozoic era, the land in the eastern region uplifted to form a plateau that was later eroded by wind and water into hills and gorges.

About two million years ago, glaciers covering two-thirds of the state leveled the western region into plains and deposited fertile limestone topsoil. As the glaciers retreated, the melting ice formed a vast lake, which overflowed southward into the channels that became the Ohio River. Perhaps 15,000 years ago, during the last Ice Age, the glacial waters ran off and reduced Lake Erie to its present size. Limestone rocks in Glacier Grooves State Park on Kelley's Island bear the marks of the glaciers' movements.

³CLIMATE

Lying in the humid continental zone, Ohio has a generally temperate climate. Winters are cold and summers mild in the eastern highlands. The southern region has the warmest temperatures and longest growing season—198 days on the average, compared with 150 to 178 days in the remainder of the state. More than half of the annual rainfall occurs during the growing season, from May to October.

Among the major cities, Columbus, in the central region, has an annual mean temperature of 51°F (11°C), with a normal maximum of 61°F (16°C) and a normal minimum of 42°F (6°C). Cleveland, in the north, has an annual mean of 50°F (10°C), with a normal maximum of 59°F (15°C) and minimum of 41°F (5°C). The mean temperature in Cincinnati, in the south, is 53°F (12°C), the normal maximum 63°F (17°C), and the normal minimum 43°F (6°C). Cleveland has an average of 127 days per year in which the temperature drops to 32° (0°C) or lower, Columbus 124 days, and Cincinnati 99 days. The record low temperature for the state is −39°F (−39°C), set at Milligan on 10 February 1899. The record high is 113°F (45°C), registered near Gallipolis on 21 July 1934.

Cleveland has an average annual snowfall of 56.3 in (143 cm), while Columbus receives 28 in (71 cm), and Cincinnati 24 in (61 cm). Cincinnati had the most average annual precipitation (1971–2000), with 42.6 in (108 cm), compared with 38.5 in (97.8 cm) for Columbus and 38.7 in (98.3 cm) for Cleveland. Because of its proximity to Lake Erie, Cleveland is the windiest city, with winds that average 11 mph (18 km/hr).

⁴FLORA AND FAUNA

More than 2,500 plant species have been found in Ohio. The southeastern hill and valley region supports pitch pine, bigleaf magnolia, and sourwood, with undergrowths of sassafras, witch-hazel, pawpaw, hornbeam, and various dogwoods. At least 14 species of oak, 10 of maple, 9 of poplar, 9 of pine, 7 of ash, 7 of elm, 6 of hickory, 5 of birch, and 2 of beech grow in the state, along with butternut, eastern black walnut, wild black cherry, black locust, and sycamore. A relative of the horse chestnut (introduced to Ohio from Asia), the distinctive buckeye—first called the Ohio buckeye and now the official state tree—is characterized by its clusters of cream-colored flowers that bloom in spring and later form large, brown, thick-hulled nuts. Five Ohio plant species were listed as threatened in 2003, including eastern prairie fringed orchid, northern wild monkshood, and lakeside daisy; the running buffalo clover was listed as endangered that year by the US Fish and Wildlife Service.

The Buckeye State is rich in mammals. White-tailed deer, badger, mink, raccoon, red and gray foxes, coyote, beaver, eastern cottontail, woodchuck, least shrew, and opossum are found throughout the state's five wildlife districts; the bobcat, woodland jumping mouse, and red-backed mole are among many species with more restricted habitats. Common birds include the eastern great blue heron, green-winged teal, mourning dove, eastern belted kingfisher, eastern horned lark, blue-gray gnatcatcher, eastern cowbird, and a great variety of ducks, woodpeckers, and warblers; the cardinal is the state bird, and the ruffed grouse, mostly confined to the Allegheny Plateau, is a favorite game species. Bass, pickerel, perch, carp, pike, trout, catfish, sucker, and darter thrive in Ohio's lakes and streams. The snapping, midland painted, and spiny soft-shelled turtles, five-lined skink, northern water snake, midland brown snake, eastern hognose, and eastern milk snake appear throughout Ohio. The northern copperhead, eastern massasauga (swamp rattler), and timber rattlesnake are Ohio's only poisonous reptiles. Fowler's toad, bullfrog, green pickerel frog, and marbled and red-backed salamanders are common native amphibians.

Acting on the premise that the largest problem facing wildlife is the destruction of their habitat, the Division of Wildlife of the Department of Natural Resources has instituted an ambitious endangered species program. The US Fish and Wildlife Service listed 20 Ohio animal species as threatened or endangered in 2003, including the bald eagle, Indiana bat, Scioto madtom, and piping plover.

⁵ENVIRONMENTAL PROTECTION

Early conservation efforts in Ohio were aimed at controlling the ravages of spring floods and preventing soil erosion. After the Miami River floods of March 1913, which took 361 lives and resulted in property losses of more than $100 million in Dayton alone, the Miami Conservancy District was formed; five earth dams and 60 mi (97 km) of river levees were completed by 1922, at a cost of $40 million, to hold back cresting water. In the Muskingum Conservancy District in eastern Ohio, construction of flood-control dams has prevented spring flooding and the washing away of valuable topsoil into the Ohio River.

In recent years, the state's major environmental concerns have been to reverse the pollution of Lake Erie, control the air pollution attributable to industries and automobiles, clean up dumps for solid and hazardous wastes, improve water quality, and prevent pollution. Of recent concern is the problem with so-called "brownfields"—polluted industrial sites whose cleanup costs present barriers to development. In November 2000, voters approved the Clean Ohio Fund; it will provide $200 million to help revitalize abandoned commercial and industrial sites, promoting reuse of existing infrastructure, and helping to reduce sprawl. The Clean Ohio Revitalization Fund awarded nearly $40 million to 17 projects in its first round of funding.

The state's regulatory agency for environmental matters is the Ohio Environmental Protection Agency (EPA), established in 1972. The agency has long-range programs to deal with pollution of air, water, and land resources. Ohio EPA also coordinates state, local, and federal funding of environmental programs. In 2001, Ohio received $73,963,000 in federal grants from the EPA; EPA expenditures for procurement contracts in Ohio that year amounted to $59,880,000.

Since 1972, antipollution efforts in Lake Erie have focused on reducing the discharge of phosphorus into the lake from sewage and agricultural wastes; sewage treatment facilities have been upgraded with the aid of more than $750 million in federal grants, and efforts have been made to promote reduced-tillage farming to control runoff. By the early 1980s, numerous beaches had been reopened, and sport fishing was once again on the increase. Since 1972, Ohio industries spent billions of dollars on efforts to control air pollution. Peak ozone levels have dropped by 25% overall and by up to 50% in some urban areas. Lead levels in the outdoor air have dropped 98% since 1978 and particulate levels have dropped 80%. From 1967 to 1983, through the efforts of local health departments and with the eventual help of the EPA, over 1,300 open garbage dumps were closed down and more than 200 sanitary landfills constructed to replace them.

In 1980, Ohio passed its first legislation aimed at controlling hazardous wastes, and by the mid-1980s, with the aid of more than $11 million in federal Superfund grants, cleanup had been completed or begun at 16 major sites. In 2003, Ohio had 318 hazardous waste sites listed in the Environmental Protection Agency's database, 28 of which were on the National Priorities List.

Another agency, the Ohio Department of Natural Resources, is responsible for the development and use of the state's natural resources. The state's parks and recreational areas totaled 208,000 acres (84,000 hectares). The department also assists in soil conservation, issues permits for dams, promotes conservation of oil and gas, and allocates strip-mining licenses.

⁶POPULATION

Ohio ranked 7th in population in the US with an estimated total of 11,421,267 in 2002, an increase of 0.6% since 2000. Between

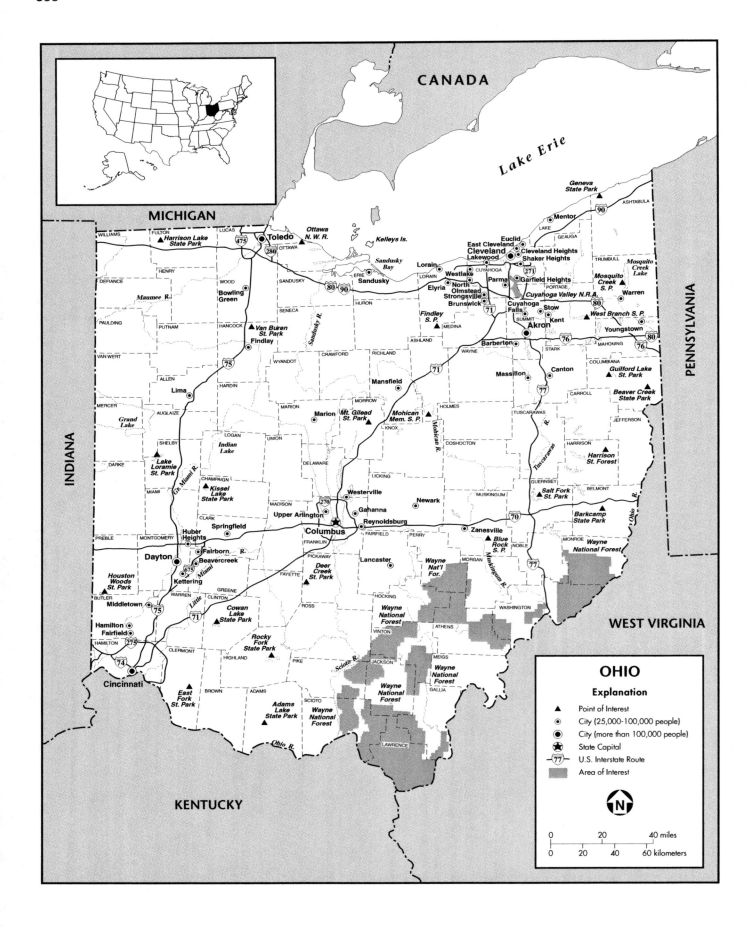

Ohio Counties, County Seats, and County Areas and Populations

COUNTY	COUNTY SEAT	LAND AREA (SQ MI)	POPULATION (2002 EST.)	COUNTY	COUNTY SEAT	LAND AREA (SQ MI)	POPULATION (2002 EST.)
Adams	West Union	586	27,804	Logan	Bellefontaine	458	46,262
Allen	Lima	405	108,120	Lorain	Elyria	495	288,360
Ashland	Ashland	424	52,900	Lucas	Toledo	341	453,506
Ashtabula	Jefferson	703	102,515	Madison	London	467	40,365
Athens	Athens	508	63,256	Mahoning	Youngstown	417	253,308
Auglaize	Wapakoneta	398	46,464	Marion	Marion	403	66,028
Belmont	St. Clairsville	537	69,448	Medina	Medina	422	158,439
Brown	Georgetown	493	43,464	Meigs	Pomeroy	432	23,111
Butler	Hamilton	469	340,543	Mercer	Celina	457	40,815
Carroll	Carrollton	393	29,166	Miami	Troy	410	99,596
Champaign	Urbana	429	39,121	Monroe	Woodsfield	458	14,973
Clark	Springfield	398	143,416	Montgomery	Dayton	458	554,470
Clermont	Batavia	456	183,352	Morgan	McConnelsville	420	14,749
Clinton	Wilmington	410	41,090	Morrow	Mt. Gilead	406	32,976
Columbiana	Lisbon	534	111,806	Muskingum	Zanesville	654	85,349
Coshocton	Coshocton	566	36,836	Noble	Caldwell	399	14,088
Crawford	Bucyrus	403	46,420	Ottawa	Port Clinton	253	41,049
Cuyahoga	Cleveland	459	1,379,049	Paulding	Paulding	419	19,841
Darke	Greenville	600	52,966	Perry	New Lexington	412	34,408
Defiance	Defiance	414	39,334	Pickaway	Circleville	503	53,437
Delaware	Delaware	443	125,399	Pike	Waverly	443	27,921
Erie	Sandusky	264	79,207	Portage	Ravenna	493	153,886
Fairfield	Lancaster	506	129,161	Preble	Eaton	426	42,680
Fayette	Washington Ct. House	405	28,176	Putnam	Ottawa	484	34,736
Franklin	Columbus	542	1,086,814	Richland	Mansfield	497	128,004
Fulton	Wauseon	407	42,573	Ross	Chillicothe	692	74,469
Gallia	Gallipolis	471	31,301	Sandusky	Fremont	409	61,698
Geauga	Chardon	408	92,980	Scioto	Portsmouth	614	78,041
Greene	Xenia	415	149,964	Seneca	Tiffin	553	58,077
Guernsey	Cambridge	522	40,987	Shelby	Sidney	409	48,516
Hamilton	Cincinnati	412	833,721	Stark	Canton	574	377,940
Hancock	Findlay	532	72,286	Summit	Akron	412	546,381
Hardin	Kenton	471	31,731	Trumbull	Warren	612	223,518
Harrison	Cadiz	400	15,890	Tuscarawas	New Philadelphia	569	91,490
Henry	Napoleon	415	29,478	Union	Marysville	437	43,010
Highland	Hillsboro	553	41,851	Van Wert	Van Wert	410	29,399
Hocking	Logan	423	28,481	Vinton	McArthur	414	13,128
Holmes	Millersburg	424	40,375	Warren	Lebanon	403	175,133
Huron	Norwalk	495	60,020	Washington	Marietta	640	62,561
Jackson	Jackson	420	32,854	Wayne	Wooster	557	112,704
Jefferson	Steubenville	410	72,402	Williams	Bryan	422	39,020
Knox	Mt. Vernon	529	56,037	Wood	Bowling Green	619	122,387
Lake	Painesville	231	229,004	Wyandot	Upper Sandusky	406	22,773
Lawrence	Ironton	457	62,172				
Licking	Newark	686	148,731	TOTALS		41,004	11,421,267

1990 and 2000, Ohio's population grew from 10,847,115 to 11,353,140, an increase of 4.7%. The population is projected to reach 11.7 million by 2025. The population density in 2000 was 277.3 persons per sq mi, the 9th-highest among the 50 states.

Ohio's population grew slowly during the colonial period and totaled 45,365 persons in 1800. Once the territory became a state in 1803, settlers flocked to Ohio and the population quintupled to 230,760 by 1810. The state's population doubled again by 1820, approached 2,000,000 in 1850, and totaled 3,198,062 by 1880. Ohio's annual rate of population increase slowed considerably after 1900, when its population was 4,157,545; nevertheless, in the period between 1900 and 1960, the total population more than doubled to 9,706,397. A slow rate of population increase during the 1970s, and a population decline during 1980–85, resulted from a net migration loss and a declining birthrate.

In 2000, the median age in Ohio was 36.2. In the same year, more than 25.4% of the populace were under age 18 while 13.3% were age 65 or older.

As of the 1990 census, Columbus became Ohio's largest city, with a population of 632,910, trading 2nd place with Cleveland, which had 505,616 residents. Whereas Columbus increased its population by 12% during the 1980s, Cleveland's population decreased by 11.9%. The 2002 estimated populations of the two cities were Columbus, 725,228, and Cleveland, 467,851. Cincinnati and other large cities also lost population during this period, largely because of the shift of the middle class from the inner cities to the suburbs or to other states. In 2002, Cincinnati's estimated population was 323,885, followed by Toledo, 309,106; Akron, 214,349; and Dayton, 162,669.

Ohio's three most populated cities and their suburbs ranked among the 30 largest metropolitan areas in the US in 1996. In 1999, metropolitan Cleveland (including Akron and Lorain) had an estimated population of 2,910,616; metropolitan Cincinnati (including some portions of Kentucky and Indiana), 1,960,995; and the metropolitan area of Columbus, 1,489,487.

7ETHNIC GROUPS

Ohio was first settled by migrants from the eastern states and from the British Isles and northern Europe, especially Germany. Cincinnati had such a large German population that its public schools were bilingual until World War I. With the coming of the railroads and the development of industry, Slavic and other south Europeans were recruited in large numbers.

By 2000, however, only about 3% of Ohioans were foreign born, the major places of origin being Germany, Italy, and the United Kingdom. Ethnic clusters persist in the large cities, and some small communities retain a specific ethnic flavor, such as Fairport Harbor on Lake Erie, with its large Finnish population.

As of 2000 there were 1,301,307 blacks, representing 11.5% of the population. Most lived in the larger cities, especially Cleveland, which in 2000 had a black population of 243,939, or 51.0% of the city total. Historically, Ohio was very active in the antislavery movement. Oberlin College, established in 1833 by dissident theological students, admitted blacks from its founding and maintained a "station" on the Underground Railroad. Cleveland elected its first black mayor, Carl B. Stokes, in 1967.

Some 217,123 people in Ohio (1.9% of the total population) were Hispanic or Latino in 2000, up from 140,000 in 1990. The largest number (90,663) were of Mexican descent, but there were also many Puerto Ricans. In 2000, American Indians numbered about 24,486. In 2000, Asians were estimated to number 132,633, including 30,425 Chinese (up from 16,829 in 1990), 12,393 Filipinos, 10,732 Japanese, and 13,376 Koreans. Pacific Islanders numbered 2,749.

Except for small Iroquoian groups like the Erie and Seneca, most of the Indian population before white settlement comprised four Algonkian tribes: Delaware, Miami, Wyandot, and Shawnee. Indian place-names include Ohio, Coshocton, Cuyahoga, and Wapakoneta.

8LANGUAGES

Ohio English reflects three post-Revolutionary migration paths. Into the Western Reserve south of Lake Erie came Northern speech from New York and Connecticut. Still common there are the Northern pronunciation of the *ow* diphthong, as in *cow*, with a beginning like the /ah/ vowel in *father*, and the use of the /ah/ in *fog* and *college*; /krik/ is more common than /kreek/ for *creek*. A dragonfly is a *devil's darning needle*; doughnuts may be *fried cakes*; a boy throws himself face down on a sled in a *bellyflop (per)*; and a tied and filled bedcover is a *comforter*.

Most of nonurban Ohio has North Midland speech from Pennsylvania. Generally, except in the northern strip, *cot* and *caught* are sound-alikes, and *now* is /naow/, south of Columbus, because of the influence of South Midland patterns from Kentucky and extreme southern Pennsylvania, corn bread may be *corn pone*, lima beans are *butter beans*, and a tied quilt is a *comforter*. *Spouting*, yielding to *gutters*, barely reaches across to Indiana; and *sick at the stomach*, *dived*, and *wait on me* are competing with expanding Northern *to the stomach*, *dove*, and *wait for me*. A new Midland term, *bellybuster*, originated around Wheeling and has spread north to compete with *bellyflop*. Northern and Midland merge in the mixed dialect west of Toledo.

From Kentucky, South Midland speakers took *you-all* into Ohio River towns, and in the southwestern tip of the state can be heard their *evening* for *afternoon*, *terrapin* for *tortoise*, and *frogstool* for *toadstool*. Recent northward migration has introduced South Midland speech and black English, a southern dialect, into such industrial centers as Cleveland, Toledo, and Akron.

Localisms have developed. For the grass strip between sidewalk and street, Akron has *devil-strip* and Cleveland has *treelawn*. Foreign-language influence appears in such Pennsylvania Germanisms as *clook* (hatching hen), *snits* (dried apples), *smearcase* (cottage cheese), and *got awake*.

Of Ohioans aged five years or older 93.9% spoke only English at home in 2000, down from 94.6% in 1990.

The following table gives selected statistics from the 2000 census for language spoken at home by persons five years old and over. The category "Other West Germanic languages" includes Dutch, Pennsylvania Dutch, and Afrikaans. The category "Other Slavic languages" includes Czech, Slovak, and Ukrainian. The category "African languages" includes Amharic, Ibo, Twi, Yoruba, Bantu, Swahili, and Somali. The category "Other Indo-European languages" includes Albanian, Gaelic, Lithuanian, and Rumanian.

LANGUAGE	NUMBER	PERCENT
Population 5 years and over	10,599,968	100.0
Speak only English	9,951,475	93.9
Speak a language other than English	648,493	6.1
Speak a language other than English	648,493	6.1
Spanish or Spanish Creole	213,147	2.0
German	72,647	0.7
French (incl. Patois, Cajun)	44,594	0.4
Italian	27,697	0.3
Other West Germanic languages	26,372	0.2
Chinese	25,704	0.2
Arabic	22,647	0.2
Other Slavic languages	21,230	0.2
Polish	16,462	0.2
Russian	16,030	0.2
Greek	13,656	0.1
African languages	13,261	0.1
Serbo-Croatian	12,577	0.1
Hungarian	11,859	0.1
Other Indo-European languages	11,070	0.1
Korean	11,028	0.1

9RELIGIONS

The first religious settlement in Ohio territory was founded among Huron Indians in 1751 by a Roman Catholic priest near what is now Sandusky. Shortly afterward, Moravian missionaries converted some Delaware Indians to Christianity; the first Protestant church was founded by Congregationalist ministers at Marietta in 1788. Dissident religious sects such as the Shakers, Amish, and Quakers moved into Ohio from the early 18th century onward, but the majority of settlers in the early 19th century were Presbyterians, Methodists, Baptists, Disciples of Christ, and Episcopalians.

The first Roman Catholic priest to be stationed permanently in Ohio was Father Edward Fenwick, who settled in Cincinnati in 1817. When the Protestant settlers there did not allow him to build a Catholic church in the town, he founded Christ Church (now St. Francis Church) just outside Cincinnati. In 1821, Father Fenwick became the first Catholic bishop in Ohio. The large influx of Irish and German immigrants after 1830 greatly increased the Catholic constituency in Cleveland, Cincinnati, Columbus, and Toledo. Among the German immigrants were many Lutherans and large number of Jews, who made Cincinnati a center of Reform Judaism. In the mid-19th century, Cincinnati had the nation's 3rd-largest Jewish community; the Union of American Hebrew Congregations, the most important Reform body, was founded there in 1873, and Hebrew Union College, a rabbinical training school and center of Jewish learning, was founded two years later. The Church of Jesus Christ of Latter-Day Saints (Mormons), founded in 1930 by Joseph Smith, Jr. of New York, built its first permanent place of worship in Kirtland, Ohio, in 1933. The Kirtland Temple, as it has been called, is still open today.

In 2000, Ohio had a Roman Catholic population of about 2,231,832. During the same year, the state's Jewish population was estimated at 142,255. Leading Jewish communities were in

Cleveland, Cincinnati, and Columbus. The Muslim population was at about 41,281 people. Ohio communities of Amish and Mennonites are among the largest in the nation with over 24,000 Amish and over 20,000 Mennonites in the state (primarily central Ohio).

The largest Protestant denominations and their adherents in 2000 were the United Methodist Church, 566,084; the Evangelical Lutheran Church in America, 301,749; the Southern Baptist Convention, 187,227; the Presbyterian Church USA, 160,800; the United Church of Christ, 157,180; Christian Churches and Churches of Christ, 142,571; and the American Baptist Churches USA, 117,757. About 6.2 million people (55.1% of the population) were not counted as members of any religious organization.

[10] TRANSPORTATION

Sandwiched between two of the country's largest inland water systems, Lake Erie and the Ohio River, Ohio has long been a leader in water transport. With its numerous terminals on the Ohio River and deepwater ports on Lake Erie, Ohio ranks as one of the major US states for shipping.

The building of railroads in the mid-19th century greatly improved transportation within the state by connecting inland counties with Lake Erie and the Ohio River. The Mad River and Lake Erie Railroad, between Dayton and Sandusky, was completed in 1844, and two years later, it was joined with the Little Miami Railroad, to provide through service to Cincinnati. Also in 1846, Cleveland was connected by rail with Columbus and Pittsburgh. Railroad building in the state reached a peak in the 1850s; at the outbreak of the Civil War, Ohio had more miles of track than any other state. By 1900, railroads were by far the most important system of transport.

In 2000, Class I railroads operated 4,526 rail mi (7,283 km) of track in the state; 6,494 mi (10,451 km) of track was in service, utilized by 33 railroads, including 3 Class I railroads. Freight service on branch lines to counties has been maintained through a state subsidy program.

Mass transit in Ohio's cities began in 1859 with horse-drawn carriages carrying paying passengers in Cleveland and Cincinnati, which added a cable car on rails about 1880. The electric trolley car, introduced to Cleveland in 1884, soon became the most popular mass transit system for the large cities. Inter-urban electric railways carried passengers to and from rural towns that had been bypassed by the railroads; there were 2,809 mi (4,521 km) of interurban track in the state by 1907. The use of electric railways declined with the development of the motor car in the 1920s, and by 1939, for example, the seven interurban lines serving Columbus had been abandoned. Today, suburbanites commute to their workplaces in Columbus and other cities by automobile and bus lines. In the mid-1990s, Amtrak operated four regularly scheduled trains through Ohio on 631 mi (1,016 km) of track.

Rough roads were used by settlers in the early 19th century. The National Road was built from Wheeling, West Virginia, to Zanesville in 1826, and was extended to Columbus by 1833. The increasing use of the automobile in the 1930s led to massive state and federal road-building programs in Ohio as elsewhere. The major interstate highways across Ohio connect Cleveland and the Toledo area in the north (I-80, I-90); link Columbus with Dayton, Zanesville, and Wheeling (I-70) and with Cincinnati and Cleveland (I-71); and extend north–south from Cleveland and Akron to Marietta in the east (I-77), and from Toledo to Dayton and Cincinnati in the west (I-75).

In 2000, Ohio had 116,964 mi (188,235 km) of roads: 83,419 mi (134,249 km) rural and 33,545 mi (53,985 km) urban. Also in 2000, 6,709,706 automobiles, 3,720,187 trucks, 254,666 motorcycles, and 37,583 buses were registered in the state; there were 8,205,524 licensed drivers.

Inland waterways have long been important for transport and commerce in Ohio. The first settlers traveled into Ohio by flatboat down the Ohio River to establish such towns as Marietta and Cincinnati. Lake Erie schooners brought the founders of Cleveland and Sandusky. Steamboat service began on the Ohio River in 1811, and at Lake Erie ports in 1818. The public demand for water transportation in the interior of the state, where few rivers were navigable, led to construction of the Ohio and Erie Canal from Cincinnati to Dayton; both were opened to traffic in 1827 but not completed for another 14 years. The canals gave Ohio's farmers better access to eastern and southern markets. Water transportation is still a principal means of shipping Ohio's products through the St. Lawrence Seaway to foreign countries, and the method by which millions of tons of cargo, particularly coal, are moved via the Ohio River to domestic markets.

Ohio's ports rank among the busiest of the 50 states in volume. In 2000, the state's most active ports were Cleveland, with 14.4 million tons of cargo handled; Cincinnati, 14.3 million tons; Lorain, 14.2 million tons; and Toledo, 13.3 million tons.

Ohioans consider Dayton to be the birthplace of aviation because it was there that Wilbur and Orville Wright built the first motor-powered airplane in 1903. In 2002, there were 526 airports in the state. The major air terminals are the Greater Cincinnati airport (actually located across the Ohio River in Kentucky) and Hopkins International in Cleveland.

[11] HISTORY

The first people in Ohio, some 11,000 years ago, were hunters. Their stone tools have been found with skeletal remains of long-extinct mammoths and mastodons. Centuries later, Ohio was inhabited by the Adena people, the earliest mound builders. Their descendants, the Hopewell Indians, built burial mounds, fortifications, and ceremonial earthworks, some of which are now preserved in state parks.

The first European travelers in Ohio, during the 17th century, found four Indian tribes: Wyandot and Delaware in northern Ohio, Miami and Shawnee in the south. All were hunters who followed game trails that threaded the dense Ohio forest. All together, these four tribes numbered about 15,000 people. European exploration was begun by a French nobleman, Robert Cavelier, Sieur de la Salle, who, with Indian guides and paddlers, voyaged from the St. Lawrence River to the Ohio, which he explored in 1669–70. In the early 1700s, French and English traders brought knives, hatchets, guns, blankets, tobacco, rum, and brandy to exchange for the Indians' deer and beaver skins.

Both the French and the English claimed possession of Ohio, the French claim resting on La Salle's exploration, while the British claimed all territory extending westward from their coastal colonies. To reinforce the French claim, Celeron de Bienville led an expedition from Canada to Ohio in 1749 to warn off English traders, win over the Indians, and assert French possession of the land. Traveling by canoe, with marches overland, he found the Indians better disposed at that time to the English than to the French. The following year, a company of Virginia merchants sent Christopher Gist to map Ohio trade routes and to make friendship and trade agreements with the tribes. The clash of ambitions brought on the French and Indian War—during which the Indians fought on both sides—ending in 1763 with French defeat and the ceding of the vast western territory to the British. During the Revolutionary War, the American militiaman George Rogers Clark, with a small company of woodsmen-soldiers, seized British posts and trading stations in Ohio, and, in the Battle of Piqua, defeated Indian warriors allied with the British. It was largely Clark's campaigns that won the Northwest Territory for the US.

The new nation had a huge public domain, extending from the Allegheny Mountains to the Mississippi River. To provide future government and development of the territory northwest of the Ohio River, the US Congress enacted the Land Ordinance of 1785 and the Northwest Ordinance of 1787. The Land Ordinance created a survey system of rectangular sections and townships, a system begun in Ohio and extended to all new areas in the expanding nation. The farsighted Northwest Ordinance provided a system of government under which territories could achieve statehood on a basis equal with that of the original colonies. When a specified area had a population of 60,000 free adult males, it could seek admission to the Union as a state.

The first permanent settlement in Ohio was made in 1788 by an organization of Revolutionary War veterans who had received land warrants as a reward for their military service. They trekked by ox-drawn wagons over the mountains and by flatboat down the Ohio River to the mouth of the Muskingum, where they built the historic town of Marietta. John Cleves Symes, a New Jersey official, brought pioneer settlers to his Miami Purchase in southwestern Ohio; their first settlement, in 1789, eventually became the city of Cincinnati. Access to the fertile Ohio Valley was provided by the westward-flowing Ohio River, which carried pioneer settlers and frontier commerce. Flatboats made a one-way journey, as families floated toward what they hoped would be new settlements. Keelboats traveled both downstream and upstream—an easy journey followed by a hard one. The keelboat trade, carrying military supplies and frontier produce, created an enduring river lore. Its legendary hero is burly, blustering Mike Fink, "half horse and half alligator," always ready for a fight or a frolic, for riot or rampage.

Increasing settlement of the Ohio Valley aroused Indian resistance. War parties raided outlying villages, burned houses, and drove families away. Two military expeditions against the Indians were shattered by Chief Little Turtle and his Miami warriors. Then, in 1793, Maj. Gen. "Mad Anthony" Wayne took command in the west. He built roads and forts in the Miami Valley, and trained a force of riflemen. On a summer morning in 1794, Wayne routed allied tribesmen, mostly Miami and Shawnee, in the decisive Battle of Fallen Timbers. In the ensuing Treaty of Greenville, Indian leaders surrendered claim to the southern half of Ohio, opening that large domain to uncontested American occupation.

When, in 1800, Connecticut ceded to the US a strip of land along Lake Erie claimed by its colonial charter and called the Western Reserve, that region became a part of the Northwest Territory. Now the future seemed unclouded, and from the older colonies came a great migration to the promised land. By 1802, Ohio had enough population to seek statehood, and in November, a constitutional convention assembled at Chillicothe. In 25 days and at a total cost of $5,000, the 35 delegates framed a constitution that vested most authority in the state legislature and gave the vote to all white male taxpayers. On 1 March 1803, Ohio joined the Union as the 17th state.

Beyond Ohio's western border, Indians still roamed free. In 1811, the powerful Shawnee chief Tecumseh led a tribal resistance movement (supported by the British) seeking to halt the white man's advance into the new territory and to regain lands already lost to the Americans. Ohio militia regiments led by Gen. William Henry Harrison repulsed an Indian invasion near Toledo in the battle of Tippecanoe on 7 November 1811. Control of Lake Erie and of Great Lakes commerce was at stake when Commodore Oliver Hazard Perry won a decisive naval victory over a British fleet in western Lake Erie during the War of 1812. Tecumseh was slain in the Battle of Thames in Canada on 5 October 1813.

With peace restored in 1815, "Ohio fever" spread through New England. In a great migration, people streamed over the mountains and the lakes to a land of rich soil, mild climate, and beckoning opportunities. Across the Atlantic, especially in England, Ireland, and Germany, thousands of immigrants boarded ship for America. At newly opened land offices, public land was sold at $1.25 an acre. Forest became fields, fields became villages and towns, towns became cities. By 1850, Ohio was the 3rd most populous state in the Union.

Having cleared millions of acres of forest, Ohioans turned to economic development. Producing more than its people consumed, the state needed transportation routes to eastern markets. The National Road extended across the central counties in the 1830s, carrying stagecoach passengers and wagon commerce from Pennsylvania and Maryland. The Ohio canal system, created between 1825 and 1841, linked the Ohio River and Lake Erie, providing a waterway to the Atlantic via New York's Erie Canal. In 1826, state lands were valued at $16 million; 15 years later, their value exceeded $100 million. The chief products were wheat, corn, pork, beef, salt, wool, and leather. By 1850, when farm and factory production outstripped the capacity of mule teams and canal barges, railroad building had begun. In the next decade, railroads crisscrossed the state.

In 1861, Ohio, like the rest of the nation, was divided. The northern counties, teeming with former New Englanders, were imbued with abolitionist zeal. But Ohio's southern counties had close ties with Virginia and Kentucky across the river. From southeastern Ohio came Clement L. Vallandigham, leader of the Peace Democrats—called Copperheads by their opponents—who defended states' rights, opposed all of President Lincoln's policies, and urged compromise with the Confederacy. While Ohio surpassed its quota by providing a total of 320,000 Union Army volunteers, the Copperhead movement grew strong enough to nominate Vallandigham for state governor in 1863. Responding to the news of Vallandigham's defeat by the rugged Unionist John Brough, Lincoln telegraphed: "Ohio has saved the nation." Ohio became directly involved in the war for two weeks in 1863, when Confederate Gen. John Hunt Morgan led a Kentucky cavalry force on a daring but ineffectual raid through the southern counties.

Ohio gave the Union its greatest generals—Ulysses S. Grant, William Tecumseh Sherman, and Philip H. Sheridan—each of whom won decisive victories at crucial times. Also essential to the Union cause was the service of Ohio men in Lincoln's cabinet, including Treasury Secretary Salmon P. Chase and War Secretary Edwin M. Stanton.

Mid-19th-century Ohio was primarily an agricultural state, but war demands stimulated Ohio manufacturing, and in the decade following the war, the state's industrial products surpassed the value of its rich farm production. The greatest commercial development came in northern Ohio, where heavy industry grew dramatically. To Toledo, Cleveland, and Youngstown via Lake Superior came iron ore that was converted into iron and steel with coal from the Ohio Valley. In the 1870s, John D. Rockefeller of Cleveland organized the Standard Oil Co., which soon controlled oil refining and distribution throughout the nation. At the same time, B. F. Goodrich of Akron began making fire hose, the first rubber product in an industry whose prodigious growth would make Akron the "rubber capital of the world." In the middle of the state, the capital city, Columbus, became a center of the brewing, railroad equipment, and farm implement industries. Cincinnati factories made steamboat boilers, machine tools, meat products, railroad cars, and soap. Dayton became known for its paper products, refrigerators, and cash registers. With industrial growth came political power. In the next half century, Ohio virtually took possession of the White House. Presidents Grant, Rutherford B. Hayes, James A.

Garfield, Benjamin Harrison, William McKinley, William Howard Taft, and Warren G. Harding were all Ohioans.

The four great business pursuits—agriculture, commerce, mining, and manufacturing—were remarkably balanced in Ohio. Its ethnic strains were various. Following the earlier English, Irish, and German influx came Italian, Czech, Dutch, Finnish, Greek, Hungarian, Polish, Russian, Serbian, and Ukrainian immigrants, along with a growing number of blacks from the rural South. Thus Ohio provided an advantageous background for a president; to any segment of the nation, an Ohio candidate did not seem alien. In the 1920 campaign, both the Republican and Democratic nominees—Harding and James M. Cox—were Ohio men. Norman Thomas, a perennial Socialist candidate, was likewise an Ohioan.

During World War I, Ohio's heavy industry expanded and its cities grew. Progressivism developed in Toledo and Cleveland, under their respective mayors, Samuel M. "Golden Rule" Jones and Tom L. Johnson, whose reforms resulted in the city-manager form of government that spread to other Ohio cities. In the postwar 1920s, Ohio's oil, rubber, and glass industries kept pace with accelerating automobile production. Yet none of these industries was immune to the prolonged depression of the 1930s. Widespread unemployment and a stagnant economy were not relieved until the outbreak of World War II. The war swept 641,000 Ohioans into military service and gave Ohio industry military contracts totaling $18 billion.

The state's economy prospered after World War II, with highway building, truck and tractor production, aircraft manufacture, and airport construction leading the field. The completion of the St. Lawrence Seaway in 1959 made active international ports of Toledo and Cleveland. Major problems during this period involved pollution created by the dumping of industrial wastes (especially in Lake Erie) and urban decay resulting from the departure of middle-class families to the suburbs, an exodus that left the central cities to growing numbers of the poor and underprivileged. Related to these problems were troubles in the Ohio school system. Deteriorating neighborhoods produced inadequate revenues for schools and public services, and attempts at racial integration brought controversy and disturbance. When political offices were won by minority leaders—in 1967, for example, Carl Stokes of Cleveland became the first black mayor of any major US city—friction and tension continued. A further shock to Ohioans was the May 1970 shooting of 13 Kent State University students, four of whom died, by national guardsmen who had been sent to the campus to preserve order during a series of demonstrations against US involvement in Indochina (Vietnam).

During the early 1980s, Ohio was still beset by serious social and economic problems. While the state's population remained static, the unemployment rate in 1982 and 1983 reached 14%. A decline in manufacturing jobs was only partly offset by the employment brought by a growing service sector. In 1983, the state established the Thomas Edison Program to provide start-up companies with venture capital funds. The legislation helped jumpstart the state's economy. But by the end of the 1980s, economic progress slowed again. Unemployment rose in the recession of the early 1990s, reaching 6.9% in 1992. Within two years, as part of a national recovery, it had rebounded to 4.9%. In March 1995, Ohio was the site of the largest work stoppage in the auto industry in a quarter century, when almost 178,000 employees were laid off in response to a 17-day strike by auto workers at two General Motors plants in Dayton. In 1999 the economy was holding steady with an unemployment rate of 4.3%, in line with the national average. In July 2003, the unemployment rate stood at 6.2%, again on par with the national average. Ohio, like the rest of the nation, was experiencing heavy job losses due to a weak economy just beginning to recover from the 2001 recession.

Hunger and homelessness were on the rise in the late 1990s and early 2000s. A 1999 report by the Ohio Hunger Task Force found that nearly one million children in low-income family faced hunger, while the Coalition on Homelessness and Housing reported that need for emergency shelters for families had grown, stretching resources in the state's 10 largest counties.

In January 1999, newly elected Governor Robert Taft, the great grandson of President William Howard Taft, took office. His administration moved quickly to address the problem highlighted in a 1996 federal study that revealed the state had the worst school facilities in the nation. His plan to spend $23 billion on school repairs over 12 years was boosted in November 1999 by voters who approved Issue 1, a ballot initiative allowing Ohio to borrow money less expensively for school construction. The governor was also pushing for tougher gun control.

Conservancy programs at the state level encompassed the watersheds of the Muskingum and Miami rivers, which became models for such undertakings in other states in the 1980s. Pollution in Lake Erie, where poor water conditions had made national headlines, was successfully reversed through a coalition of government efforts. By the end of the 1990s, the state was viewed as a national leader in improving waterways. But, as the Environmental Protection Agency lined up partners to clean up the Cuyahoga River, Ohio still faced serious environmental threats. A study released in 2000 indicated air pollution in the Ohio River Valley was worse than that on the nation's East Coast. It was reported earlier that rain contaminated with mercury from coal-fired electric plants was polluting Midwest lakes and rivers. In 2000 the EPA released a study citing the state for failing to meet tighter federal ozone limits. Illegal dumping also posed a persistent problem, with an estimated 30 to 40 million tires having been unlawfully deposited at nearly 100 sites around the state.

In 2000 the state remained among the most populous in the nation, with its more than 11.3 million people giving it a rank of 7th among the states.

Ohio was one of the states affected by the 14 August 2003 massive power blackout in Canada, the Northeast, and Midwestern states. The largest electrical outage in US history affected 9,300 square miles and a population of over 50 million. An initial power failure in Ohio was later found to be the trigger for the outage. Many areas of Cleveland were without safe drinking water for a number of days.

12 STATE GOVERNMENT

The Ohio constitution of 1803 was replaced by a second constitution in 1851. Amendments proposed by a constitutional convention in 1912 and subsequently approved by the voters so heavily revised the 1851 constitution as to make it virtually a new document. This modified constitution, with subsequent amendments (a total of 160 by January 2003), provides for county and municipal home rule, direct primary elections, recall of elected officials, and constitutional amendments by initiative and referendum.

Ohio's general assembly consists of a 99-member house of representatives, elected for two years, and a senate of 33 members serving four-year terms (half the members are chosen every two years). Regular sessions of the legislature convene the first Monday in January of each year and are not formally limited in length. The presiding officers of both houses may issue a joint call to convene a special session. Legislators must be at least 18 years old and have lived in their districts for at least one year. The legislative salary was $51,674 in 2002. Each house may introduce legislation, and both houses must approve a bill before it can be signed into law by the governor. The governor's veto of a bill can be overridden by three-fifths majority votes of the elected members of each houses. Bills not signed or vetoed by the governor become law after 10 days.

Officials elected statewide are the governor and lieutenant governor (elected jointly), secretary of state, attorney general, auditor, and treasurer, all of whom serve four-year terms. (The 19 members of the state Board of Education, who serve six-year terms, are also elected by voters.) Effective in 1959, a constitutional amendment changed the governor's term from two to four years and forbade a governor from serving more than two successive terms. The governor appoints the heads of executive departments, as well as the adjutant general and members of most statutory boards. Candidates for governor must be 18 years old, US citizens, qualified voters, and state residents. In 2002, the governor's salary was $126,485.

The constitution may be amended legislatively by a three-fifths vote of each house; the proposed amendment must then receive majority approval by the voters at the next general election. Amendments may also be proposed by petition of 10% of the electors who voted for governor in the last general election; a majority vote in a subsequent referendum is required for passage.

The constitution provides that every 20 years (from 1932 onward), the voters must be given the chance to choose whether a constitutional convention should be held. Voters rejected this option in 1932, 1952, 1972, and again in 1992.

To vote in Ohio, one must be a US citizen, at least 18 years old, and have been a state resident for at least 30 days prior to election day. Restrictions apply to convicted felons and those declared mentally incompetent by the court.

¹³POLITICAL PARTIES

Ohio has sent seven native sons and one other state resident to the White House—equaling Virginia as the "mother of presidents." The state's two major political parties, Democratic and Republican, have dominated the political scene since 1856.

Ohioans scattered their votes among various political factions until 1836, when they rallied behind state resident William Henry Harrison and the Whig Party; they again supported Harrison in 1840, helping him win his second bid for the presidency. Whigs and Democrats divided the votes in 1844, 1848, and 1852; in 1856, however, Ohio supported the newly formed Republican Party, and after the Civil War, seven of the country's next 12 presidents were Ohio-born Republicans, beginning with Grant and ending with Harding. From 1856 to 1984, Ohioans voted for the Republican candidate in all presidential elections except those in which the following six Democrats were elected: Woodrow Wilson (twice), Franklin D. Roosevelt (three times), Harry S. Truman, Lyndon B. Johnson, Jimmy Carter, and Bill Clinton (twice). In 1920, when the presidential candidates of both major parties were Ohioans, the Republican, Warren G. Harding, carried Ohio as well as the nation.

Political bossism flourished in Ohio during the last quarter of the 19th century, when the state government was controlled by Republicans Mark Hanna in Cleveland and George B. Cox in Cincinnati. Hanna played an influential role in Republican national politics; in 1896, his handpicked candidate, William McKinley, was elected to the presidency. But the despotism of the bosses and the widespread corruption in city governments led to public demands for reform. In Toledo, a reform mayor, Samuel "Golden Rule" Jones, began to clean house in 1897. Four years later, another group of reformers, led by Mayor Tom L. Johnson, ousted the Hanna machine and instituted honest government in Cleveland. At the time, journalist Lincoln Steffens called Cleveland "the best-governed city in the US" and Cincinnati "the worst." The era of bossism ended for Cincinnati in 1905, when the voters overthrew the Cox machine, elected a reform mayor on a fusion ticket, and instituted reforms that in 1925 made Cincinnati the first major US city with a nonpartisan city-manager form of government.

With the decline of big-city political machines, ticket splitting has become a regular practice among Ohio voters in state and local contests. Governor Frank J. Lausche, a Democrat, was elected to an unprecedented five two-year terms (1945–47, 1949–57), and Republican James A. Rhodes served four four-year terms (1963–71, 1975–83). In 1982, Ohioans elected a Democratic governor, Richard F. Celeste, and Democrats swept all state offices and won control of both houses of the state legislature. Republican George Voinovich won the governorship in 1990 and again in 1994. In 1998 elections, Republican candidate Bob Taft won the governor's office; he was reelected in 2002. In 2003 the Republicans also dominated the state senate (22 seats as opposed to the Democrats' 11), and they retained control over the House—there were 62 Republicans and 37 Democrats in the state house.

Ohio Presidential Vote by Political Parties, 1948–2000

YEAR	ELECTORAL VOTE	OHIO WINNER	DEMOCRAT	REPUBLICAN	PROGRESSIVE	SOC. LABOR	COMMUNIST	LIBERTARIAN
1948	25	*Truman (D)	1,452,791	1,445,684	37,487	—	—	—
1952	25	*Eisenhower (R)	1,600,367	2,100,391	—	—	—	—
1956	25	*Eisenhower (R)	1,439,655	2,262,610	—	—	—	—
1960	25	Nixon (R)	1,944,248	2,217,611	—	—	—	—
1964	26f	*Johnson (D)	2,498,331	1,470,865	—	—	—	—
					AMERICAN IND.			
1968	26	*Nixon (R)	1,700,586	1,791,014	467,495	—	—	—
					AMERICAN			
1972	25	*Nixon (R)	1,558,889	2,441,827	80,067	7,107	6,437	—
						SOC. WORKERS		
1976	25	*Carter (D)	2,011,621	2,000,505	15,529	4,717	7,817	8,961
					CITIZENS			
1980	25	*Reagan (R)	1,745,103	2,203,139	8,979	4,436	5,030	49,604
1984	25	*Reagan (R)	1,825,440	2,678,560	—	—	—	5,886
						WORKER'S LEAGUE	NEW ALLIANCE	
1988	25	*Bush (R)	1,939,629	2,416,549	—	5,432	12,017	11,989
					IND. (Perot)	POPULIST/AMERICA FIRST		
1992	21	*Clinton (D)	1,984,942	1,894,310	1,036,426	4,698	6,411	7,252
1996	21	*Clinton (D)	2,148,222	1,859,883	483,207	—	—	12,851
					IND. (Nader)	IND. (Buchanan)		
2000	21	*Bush, G. W. (R)	2,186,190	2,351,209	117,857	26,724	—	13,475

* Won US presidential election.

Following November 2002 elections, there were six Democrats and 12 Republicans serving as US Representatives. In 1992 both Ohio senators—John Glenn, elected to a fourth term in 1992, and Howard Metzenbaum, elected to a third term in 1988—were Democrats. However, in 1994 Metzenbaum retired and a Republican, Mike DeWine, took the seat (he was reelected in 2000). In 1998, the seat held by retiring Senator John Glenn was won by former Ohio governor, Republican George Voinovich.

In general, third parties have fared poorly in Ohio since 1856. Exceptions were the 1968 presidential election, in which American Independent Party candidate George Wallace garnered nearly 12% of Ohio's popular vote, and the 1992 presidential election, when Independent Ross Perot captured 21% of the vote. A more typical voting pattern was displayed in the 1976 presidential election when the two major parties together received 97.7% of the total votes cast, and only 2.3% of the votes were split among minor parties and independents. In 2000, independent candidate Ralph Nader took 3% of the vote, and independent candidate Pat Buchanan won 1%.

The result was not nearly so close in 1980, when Ronald Reagan, the Republican presidential nominee, won 51% of the popular vote to 41% for Jimmy Carter (with 6% going to John Anderson and 2% to minor party candidates), or in 1984, when Reagan won 59% of the popular vote to defeat Walter Mondale in the state. Republican George Bush won 55% of the vote in 1988. In 1992, however, Bush lost the state to Democratic nominee Bill Clinton, who captured 40% of the vote to Bush's 38%. In 1996, Clinton won 47% of the vote, Republican Bob Dole won 41%, and Independent Ross Perot received 11%. In 2000, Republican George W. Bush won 50% of the vote to Democrat Al Gore's 46%. In 2002 there were 7,104,549 registered voters. In 1998, 17% of registered voters were Democratic, 18% Republican, and 65% unaffiliated or members of other parties. The state had 21 electoral votes in the 2000 presidential election.

14LOCAL GOVERNMENT

Local government in Ohio is exercised by 88 counties, 942 cities and villages, and 1,308 townships (2002). In 2002 there were 667 public school districts and 631 special districts.

Each county is administered by a board of commissioners, elected to four-year terms, whose authority is limited by state law. The county government is run by officials elected to four-year terms: auditor or financial officer, clerk of courts, coroner, engineer, prosecuting attorney, recorder, sheriff, and treasurer.

Within each county are incorporated areas with limited authority to govern their own affairs. Thirty voters in an area may request incorporation of the community as a village. A village reaching the population of 5,000 automatically becomes a city, which by law must establish executive and legislative bodies. There are three types of city government: the mayor-council plan, which is the form adopted by a majority of the state's cities; the city-manager form, under which the city council appoints a professional manager to conduct nonpartisan government operations; and the commission type, in which a board of elected commissioners administers the city government. In practice, most large cities have adopted a home-rule charter that permits them to select the form of government best suited to their requirements.

Cleveland experimented with the city-manager form of government from 1924 to 1932, at which time public disclosures of municipal corruption led the city's voters to return to the mayor-council plan. In 1967, Cleveland became the first major US city to elect a black mayor; Carl Stokes served two two-year terms but retired from politics in 1971. Cleveland again attracted national attention in 1978 when its 31-year-old mayor, Dennis J. Kucinich, publicly disputed the city's financial policies with

members of the city council, and the city defaulted on $15 million in bank loans. Mayor Kucinich narrowly survived a recall election; in 1979, he was defeated for reelection.

Cincinnati has retained the city-manager form of government since 1925. The mayor, elected by the city council from among its members, has no administrative duties. Instead, the council appoints a city manager to a term as chief executive. Columbus, the state capital since 1816, has a mayor-council form of government.

Townships are governed by three trustees and a clerk, all elected to staggered four-year terms. These elected officials oversee zoning ordinances, parks, road maintenance, fire protection, and other matters within their jurisdiction.

15STATE SERVICES

To address the continuing threat of terrorism and to work with the federal Department of Homeland Security (created in 2002 following the terrorist attacks of 11 September 2001), homeland security in Ohio in 2003 operated under the authority of the governor; the lieutenant governor was designated as the state homeland security advisor.

The State Department of Education administers every phase of public school operations, including counseling and testing services, the federal school lunch program, and teacher education and certification. The department also oversees special schools for the blind and deaf. The department's chief administrator is the superintendent of public instruction.

Health and welfare services are provided by several departments. The Department of Health issues and enforces health and sanitary regulations. Violations of health rules are reviewed by a Public Health Council of seven members, including three physicians and a pharmacist. The Department of Mental Health administers mental health institutions; develops diagnostic, prevention, and rehabilitation programs; and trains mental health professionals. The Department of Human Services helps the poor through aid to families with dependent children, public assistance payments, food stamps, and Medicaid. The Bureau of Employment Services and the Bureau of Workers' Compensation administer labor benefit programs.

Public protection services include those of the State Highway Patrol and the Bureau of Motor Vehicles, both within the Department of Highway Safety; the Department of Rehabilitation and Correction, which operates penal institutions; the Department of Youth Services, which administers juvenile correction centers; and the Environmental Protection Agency.

16JUDICIAL SYSTEM

The supreme court of Ohio, the highest court in the state, reviews proceedings of the lower courts and of state agencies. The high court has a chief justice and six associate justices elected to six-year terms. Below the supreme court are 12 courts of appeals, which exercise jurisdiction over their respective judicial districts. Each court has at least three judges elected to six-year terms; the district including Cleveland has nine appeals court judges, and the Cincinnati district has six.

Trial courts include 88 courts of common pleas, one in each county; judges are elected to six-year terms. Probate courts, domestic relations courts, and juvenile courts often function as divisions of the common pleas courts. In 1957, a system of county courts was established by the legislature to replace justices of the peace and mayor's courts at the local level. Large cities have their own municipal, juvenile, and police courts.

In June 2001, state and federal prisons in Ohio had 45,684 inmates, a decrease of 2.5% from the previous year. The state's incarceration rate stood at 402 per 100,000 inhabitants. According to FBI data for 2001, Ohio's crime index total stood at

4,177.6 per 100,000 population, including a total of 40,023 violent crimes and 435,115 crimes against property in that year.

Ohio executed 172 persons between 1930 and 1977, and another 14 people between 1977 and 2003. In 2003, 208 persons were under sentence of death.

[17]ARMED FORCES

In 2002, there were 6,899 active-duty military personnel and 22,080 civilian personnel stationed in Ohio, the vast majority of whom were at Wright-Patterson Air Force Base near Dayton. In 2002, the Defense Department awarded over $3.3 billion in defense contracts to Ohio companies.

According to the 2000 Census, Ohio had 1,144,007 living veterans, of whom 237,430 had served in World War II; 144,768 during the Korean conflict; 335,572 during the Vietnam era; and 109,397 during 1990–2000 (including the Persian Gulf War). In 2002, the Veterans Administration expended more than $2 billion in pensions, medical assistance, and other major veterans' benefits.

In 2000, the Ohio State Highway Patrol employed 1,382 full-time sworn officers.

[18]MIGRATION

After the Ohio country became a US territory in 1785, Virginians, Connecticut Yankees, and New Jerseyites began arriving in significant numbers; tens of thousands of settlers from New England, Pennsylvania, and some southern states thronged into Ohio in subsequent decades. The great migration from the eastern states continued throughout most of the 19th century, and was bolstered by new arrivals from Europe. The Irish came in the 1830s, and many Germans began arriving in the 1840s. Another wave of European immigration brought about 500,000 people a year to Ohio during the 1880s, many of them from southern and eastern Europe. Former slaves left the South for Ohio following the Civil War, and a larger migratory wave brought blacks to Ohio after World War II to work in the industrial cities. In the 1910s, many emigrants from Greece, Albania, and Latvia settled in Akron to work in the rubber industry.

The industrialization of Ohio in the late 19th and the 20th centuries encouraged the migration of Ohioans from the farms to the cities. The large number of Ohioans who lived in rural areas and worked on farms declined steadily after 1900, with the farm population decreasing to under 1,000,000 during World War II and then to fewer than 400,000 by 1979. A more recent development has been the exodus of urbanites from Ohio's largest cities. From 1970 to 1990, Cleveland lost 245,000 residents, Cincinnati 90,000, Dayton 61,000, Akron 52,000, and Toledo 50,000. Columbus was the only major city to gain residents—93,000—during this period. Ohio lost more than one million people through migration during the period 1970–83. Net migration loss for the state from 1985 to 1990 came to 72,000. Between 1990 and 1998, Ohio had a net loss of 144,000 in domestic migration and a net gain of 48,000 in international migration. In 1998, 7,697 foreign immigrants arrived in Ohio; of these, the greatest number, 900, came from India. The state's overall population increased 3.3% between 1990 and 1998. In the period 1995–2000, 588,650 people moved into the state and 705,590 moved out, for a net loss of 116,940, many of whom (90,833) moved to Florida.

[19]INTERGOVERNMENTAL COOPERATION

The Ohio Commission on Interstate Cooperation represents the state in dealings with the Council of State Governments and its allied organizations. Ohio is a signatory to interstate compacts covering the Ohio River Valley, Pymatuning Reservoir, and the Great Lakes Basin, including the Great Lakes Charter signed in

February 1985. The state also participates in the Interstate Mining Compact Commission, the Appalachian Regional Commission, the Midwest Interstate Low-Level Radioactive Waste Compact Commission, the Interstate Oil and Gas Compact, and other compacts. Federal grants to Ohio exceeded $11.7 billion in the 2001 fiscal year.

[20]ECONOMY

Ohio's economy has shown remarkable balance over the years. In the mid-19th century, Ohio became a leader in agriculture, ranking 1st among the states in wheat production in 1840, and 1st in corn and wool by 1850. With industrialization, Ohio ranked 4th in value added by manufacturing in 1900.

Coal mining in the southeastern part of the state and easy access to Minnesota's iron ore via the Great Lakes contributed to the growth of the iron and steel industry in the Cleveland-Youngstown area; Ohio led the nation in the manufacture of machine tools and placed 2nd among the states in steel production in the early 1900s. Automobile manufacturing and other new industries developed after World War I. Hit hard by the depression of the 1930s, the state diversified its industrial foundation and enjoyed prosperity during and after World War II, as its population increased and its income grew.

In the 1970s, however, growth began to lag. By 1980, per capita income in Ohio had fallen well behind the national average. While the gross national product in constant dollars grew 99% from 1960 to 1980, the gross state product expanded only 66%. Manufacturing, which traditionally accounted for more than one-third of the gross state product, was shrinking, as demand for durable goods declined. Manufacturing employment peaked at 1.4 million in 1969; by 1982, the total was down to 1.1 million, and it was believed that many of these jobs would be permanently lost because of a reorientation of Ohio's economy from manufacturing toward services. With unemployment reaching peak levels, the state was forced to borrow from the federal government to fund the soaring cost of unemployment benefits.

Steel was produced primarily in Youngstown, automotive and aircraft parts in Cleveland, automobile tires and other rubber products in Akron, and office equipment in Dayton. Recessionary trends in 1980 led to the closing of a US Steel plant in Youngstown and of two Firestone tire and rubber factories in the Akron area, and to widespread layoffs in the auto parts industry. This bad economic news was partially offset when in 1983 the Honda Motor Co. opened Japan's first US automobile assembly plant at Marysville near Columbus, where Honda had already been manufacturing motorcycles. Honda suppliers also began establishing plants in the state.

Despite its shrinking size, manufacturing remains dominant in Ohio's economy. The sector centers on durable goods. Among manufacturers, transportation equipment and industrial machinery are the largest employers. Both durable and nondurable goods (instruments, chemicals, printing and lumber) enjoyed the greatest gains in employment between 1987 and 1993. However, durable goods' share of the gross state product, particularly primary metals, motor vehicles, and industrial machinery, fell 4.5% between 1977 and 1990 while nondurable goods industries' share of the gross state product remained constant and services, particularly business services, increased their share by 2.5%. In 2002, durable made up two-thirds of Ohio's manufacturing output. Output from Ohio's manufacturing sector peaked in 1998 at approximately $90.4 billion (about 26.1% of gross state product), and had fallen 11.9% by 2001, including a 7.1% dip in the national recession of 2001. Output from manufacturing in 2001 constituted only 21.3% of gross state product. The fall in manufacturing output helped bring down the state's annual growth rates down from

6.5% in 1998 to an average of 3.3% 1999-2000, and then to 0.83% in 2001. In 2002, Ohio lagged the rest of the nation in employment performance because of significant losses in manufacturing, employing 18% of the state's labor force. Employment losses were sharpest among manufacturers of durable goods (which make up two-thirds of Ohio's manufactures), falling 8.4% between the fourth quarter of 2000 and the fourth quarter of 2002. Ohio's recovery hinges on recovery in its durable manufacturing sector.

In 2001, Ohio's gross state product gross state product was $373.7 billion, the 7th-largest among the states, to which manufacturing contributed $79.6 billion; general services, $73.3 billion; financial services, $17.8 billion; trade, $63.8 billion; government, $42.8 billion; transportation and public utilities, $26.2 billion, and construction, $16.5 billion. The public sector in 2001 constituted 11.4% of gross state product, close to the 12% average for the states.

21INCOME

According to the Bureau of Economic Analysis, in 2001, Ohio had a per capita personal income (PCPI) of $28,699 which ranked 26th in the United States (including the District of Columbia) and was 94% of the national average, $30,413. The 2001 PCPI reflected an increase of 2.0% from 2000 compared to the national change of 2.2%. In 2001, Ohio had a total personal income (TPI) of $326,876,143,000 which ranked 8th in the United States and accounted for 3.8% of the national total. The 2001 TPI reflected an increase of 2.3% from 2000 compared to the national change of 3.3%.

Earnings of persons employed in Ohio increased from $227,799,531,000 in 2000 to $230,606,619,000 in 2001, an increase of 1.2%. The largest industries in 2001 were services, 26.6% of earnings; durable goods manufacturing, 15.2%; and state and local government, 12.2%. Of the industries that accounted for at least 5% of earnings in 2001, the slowest growing from 2000 to 2001 was durable goods manufacturing, which decreased 6.8%; the fastest was finance, insurance, and real estate (7.3% of earnings in 2001), which increased 6.2%.

According to data released by the US Census Bureau, in 2000, the median household income was $43,894 compared to the national average of $42,148. In 2001, the median income for a family of four was $64,282 compared to the national average of $63,278. For the period 1999 to 2001, the average poverty rate was 10.8% which placed it 29th among the 50 states and the District of Columbia ranked lowest to highest.

22LABOR

According to Bureau of Labor Statistics (BLS) provisional estimates, in July 2003 the seasonally adjusted civilian labor force in Ohio numbered 5,895,900, with approximately 367,300 workers unemployed, yielding an unemployment rate of 6.2%, compared to the national average of 6.2% for the same period. Since the beginning of the BLS data series in 1978, the highest unemployment rate recorded was 13.8% in January 1983. The historical low was 3.6% in March 2001. In 2001, an estimated 4.7% of the labor force was employed in construction; 17.1% in manufacturing; 5.0% in transportation, communications, and public utilities; 20.5% in trade; 5.3% in finance, insurance, and real estate; 26.8% in services; 12.7% in government; and 1.6% in agriculture.

The first workers' organization in Ohio was formed by Dayton mechanics in 1811. The Ohio Federation of Labor was founded in 1884; the American Federation of Labor (AFL) was founded in Columbus in 1886, and Ohio native William Green became president of the AFL in 1924. But it was not until the 1930s that labor unions in Ohio were formed on a large scale. In 1934, the United Rubber Workers began to organize workers in Akron; through a successful series of sit-down strikes at the city's rubber plants, the union grew to about 70,000 members by 1937. In that year, the United Steelworkers struck seven steel plants in the Youngstown area and won the right to bargain collectively for 50,000 steelworkers. The number of union members increased from about 25% of the state's non-farm employees in 1939 to 32% in 1980 when about 1.4 million workers belonged to labor organizations.

Progressive labor legislation in the state began in 1852 with laws regulating working hours for women and children and limiting men to a 10-hour workday. In 1890, Ohio became the first state to establish a public employment service. Subsequent labor legislation included a workers' compensation act in 1911 and child labor and minimum wage measures in the 1930s. In 1983, a law was passed giving public employees, other than police officers and fire fighters, a limited right to strike.

The US Department of Labor reported that in 2002, 858,000 of Ohio's 5,123,000 employed wage and salary workers were members of unions. This represented 16.7% of those so employed, down from 17.7% in 2001. The national average is 13.2%. In all, 918,000 workers (17.9%) were represented by unions. In addition to union members, this category includes workers who report no union affiliation but whose jobs are covered by a union contract.

23AGRICULTURE

Despite increasing urbanization and industrialization, agriculture retains its economic importance. Ohio ranked 17th in net farm income among the 50 states in 2001. In that year, the state's production of crops, dairy products, and livestock was valued at nearly $4.7 billion.

The number of farms in 2002 was 78,000, down from 234,000 in 1940. The average size of farms increased from 94 acres (38 hectares) in 1940 to 188 acres (76 hectares) in 2002

Grain is grown and cattle and hogs are raised on large farms in the north-central and western parts of the state, while smaller farms predominate in the hilly southeastern region. Truck farming has continued to expand near the large cities.

Ohio was the 3rd-leading producer of tomatoes for processing in 2002 with 158,710 tons. Field crops in 2002 (in bushels) included corn for grain, 252,560,000; soybeans, 141,300,000; wheat, 50,220,000; and oats, 3,720,000. The most valuable crops included soybeans, with sales of $770,085,000, and corn, $631,400,000. These two crops accounted for over 30% of Ohio's farm receipts in 2002. Ohio farmers also produced 3,750,000 tons of hay and 36,000 tons of sugar beets in 2002.

24ANIMAL HUSBANDRY

Cattle and hogs are raised in the central and western regions. In 2003, Ohio had 1.25 million cattle and calves, worth $988.2 million. In 2002, Ohio farmers had 1.5 million hogs and pigs, valued at $109.4 million. During 2001, Ohio farmers produced nearly 12.7 million lb (5.8 million kg) of sheep and lambs.

Dairying is common in most regions of the state, but especially in the east and southeast. In 2001, Ohio's 260,000 milk cows produced 4.32 billion lb (1.96 billion kg) of milk. The poultry industry is dispersed throughout the state. Ohio ranked 2nd among the states in production of eggs with 7.9 billion eggs in 2001. Poultry farmers in Ohio also produced 181.8 million lb (82.5 million kg) of turkey and sold 57.9 million lb (26.3 million kg) of chickens in 2001.

25FISHING

Commercial fishing, which once flourished in Lake Erie, has declined during the 20th century. Only 4,733,000 lb of fish, worth $2,618,000, were landed in 1998, up from 3,980,000 lb and $917,000 in 1984, but far from the record catch of 31,083,000 lb in 1936.

A statewide fish hatchery system annually produces and stocks up to 30 million fry and yearling size fish—mostly walleye, saugeye, trout, catfish, bass, sunfish, muskellunge, and pike. In 1998 the state issued 1,144,261 sport fishing licenses.

26FORESTRY

In 2002, Ohio had 7,855,000 acres (3,179,000 hectares) of forestland, representing 30% of the state's total land area, but only 1% of all US forests. Although scattered throughout the state, hardwood forests are concentrated in the hilly region of the southeast. Commercial timberlands in 2002 totaled 7,568,000 acres (3,063,000 hectares), of which over 90% was privately owned.

The state's lumber and wood products industry supplies building materials, household furniture, and paper products. In 2002, total lumber production was 381 million board feet. In 2002 there were about 690,000 acres (279,000 hectares) of federal, state, county, and municipal forestland in Ohio.

27MINING

The value of nonfuel mineral production in Ohio in 2001 was an estimated $1.07 billion, up about 7% from 2000. Crushed stone and construction sand and gravel were the leading mineral commodities produced in Ohio. According to preliminary figures, the combined production of these two commodities (about 135 million metric tons) accounted for about 60%, or about $646 million, of the state's nonfuel value. Crushed stone, the state's leading mineral commodity, showed a production total of about 80 million metric tons. In 2001, Ohio ranked 2nd in fire clays, 4th in salt, 5th in common clays (1.37 million metric tons, valued at $7.38 million) and construction sand and gravel (55 million metric tons, $280 million), 7th in crushed stone, and 9th in industrial sand and gravel. Lime production was 1.72 million metric tons, worth $103 million. The combined value of fire clays, gypsum, peat, and salt was $171 million. Overall, Ohio ranked 12th in the US in the value of nonfuel mineral production, accounting for slightly more than 2.5% of the US total.

28ENERGY AND POWER

Ohio has abundant energy resources. The state government estimates that Ohio's coal reserves are sufficient to meet demand for 500 years and that oil and natural gas reserves are also ample.

In 1999, Ohio ranked 7th among all states in electric power production. In that year, installed electric power capacity (utility and nonutility) was 27.4 million kW, and electrical output totaled 142.4 billion kWh.

With energy consumption of 353 million Btu per capita (89 million kcal), Ohio ranked 23rd among the 50 states in 2000. In 1998 industries consumed 40%, residential users 22%, commercial establishments 16%, and transportation 22%.

In the 1880s, petroleum was discovered near Lima and natural gas near Toledo, both in the northwest; these fossil fuels have since been found and exploited in the central and eastern regions. In 2002, the state produced 16,000 barrels per day of crude petroleum; proved reserves were estimated at approximately 46 million barrels in 2001. About 100.1 billion cu ft (2.8 billion cu m) of natural gas were extracted in 2001, with reserves estimated at 970 billion cu ft (27.5 billion cu m). At the end of 2001 there were 33,917 producing gas wells.

Coalfields lie beneath southeastern Ohio, particularly in Hocking, Athens, and Perry counties. In 2000, Ohio's coal production was 22.3 million tons. Reserves were estimated at 450 million tons as of 2001. In 1998, 75 surface mines produced 48% of the state's coal; eight underground mines supplied the remainder. A potential energy source is the rich bed of shale rock, underlying more than half of Ohio, which was estimated to contain more than 200 trillion cu ft (5.7 trillion cu m) of natural gas; but much research is needed before the gas could be extracted economically.

As of September 2003, only one of Ohio's two nuclear facilities, Perry in Lake County, was in operation. The Davis-Besse plant in Ottawa County was shut down in February 2002 after it was discovered that boric acid had eaten a hole through the steel cap covering the reactor vessel. The plant had been scheduled to return to service in the spring of 2003, but the reopening was delayed repeatedly due to other problems.

In January 1985, three Ohio utilities halted construction of the Zimmerman nuclear power plant, after spending $1.7 billion on the project; plans were announced to convert the plant to coal use, at an estimated cost of another $1.7 billion. In June 1985, a nuclear reactor at Oak Park was closed down after an accident involving the failure of 14 pieces of equipment; no radiation release or major damage was reported.

29INDUSTRY

Ohio has been a leading manufacturing state since the mid-1800s. During the last two decades of the 20th century, Ohio became the nation's leader in machine-tool manufacturing, the 2nd leading steel producer, and a pioneer in oil refining and in the production of automobiles and automotive parts, such as rubber tires.

In recent decades, Ohio has become important as a manufacturer of glassware, soap, matches, paint, business machines, refrigerators—and even comic books and Chinese food products. In 1997, the value of manufacturing shipments was estimated at $246 billion, ranked 3rd in the nation. In 1997, Ohio was the headquarters to 29 Fortune 500 companies.

Earnings of persons employed in Ohio increased from $197.6 billion in 1997 to $208.4 billion in 1998, an increase of 5.3%. The largest industries in 1998 were services, 24.9% of earnings; durable goods manufacturing, 18.5%; and state and local government, 10.5%. Of the industries that accounted for at least 5% of earnings in 1998, the slowest growing from 1997 to 1998 was durable goods manufacturing, which increased 3.6%; the fastest was finance, insurance, and real estate (6.4% of earnings in 1998), which increased 9.4%.

30COMMERCE

Ohio is a major commercial state. In 1997, 20,099 wholesale establishments had sales of over $127 billion. The chief categories of wholesale goods traded are groceries and related products, machinery, equipment. and supplies, motor vehicles and automotive parts, metals and minerals (except petroleum), petroleum and oil products. chemicals, electrical goods, grains and other agricultural raw materials, hardware, plumbing, and heating equipment, and lumber and construction materials. Retail sales amounted to $107 billion in 1997 (7th in the country). The principal retail store groups were automotive, 13%; food stores, 11%; and eating and drinking places, 31%.

In 1998, Ohio ranked 7th in the US as an exporter of goods, with exports worth $25 billion, or 4% of the US total. Transportation equipment, nonelectric machinery, chemicals, electric and electronic equipment, primary metals, fabricated metal products, stone, clay, and glass products, and rubber and plastic products account for most of the export value.

31CONSUMER PROTECTION

Agencies involved in consumer protection include the Agriculture Department's Division of Food Safety, which operates inspection programs to protect consumers, and the Commerce Department's Office of Consumer Affairs (created in 2002), which protects consumers from abusive lending practices through education, fielding complaints, referring borrowers to organizations that can assist them, and initiating enforcement action if lending laws are violated. The Ohio Consumers' Counsel acts to protect the interests of residential consumers of public utilities and works to educate consumers about utility issues and resolve consumer complaints. The Attorney General's Office resolves consumer complaints and enforces consumer protection laws.

[32]BANKING

Ohio's first banks, in Marietta and Chillicothe, were incorporated in 1808, and a state bank was authorized in 1845. There were318 insured banks in Ohio in 2002, with total assets of $582 billion. One hundred fourteen of these banks were state-chartered. There were 62 savings and loans in Ohio in 2002. At the end of 1995, the Resolution Trust Corporation had resolved 18 institutions at a cost of $664 million. Ohio ranks 4th in the nation for percentage of total assets held and 9th in the number of banks.

Many of Ohio's banks have large concentrations of commercial real estate (CRE) or non-residential real estate loans. Ohio's large banks saw significantly higher delinquencies in one-to-four family loans than community banks (those with assets of less than $1 billion). Although large bank delinquencies in nonresidential real estate loans also increased as of 2002, the increase was not as dramatic.

[33]INSURANCE

In 2001, there were 7.0 million ordinary life insurance policies in force, with a total value of $417.3 billion; total value for all categories of life insurance (ordinary, group, industrial, and credit) was $702.2 billion. Death benefits paid that year totaled $2.1 billion. In 2000, 46 life and health insurance companies had headquarters in Ohio.

At the end of 2000, 131 property and casualty insurance companies were domiciled in Ohio. In 2001, property and casualty insurers wrote over $13.6 billion in premiums. That year, there were 33,830 flood insurance policies in force in the state, with a total value of $3.1 million.

[34]SECURITIES

Ohio has 1,498 broker-dealers organizations with 3,634 employees; 488 investment advisory organizations do business in the state. Ohio provides headquarters for 160 NASDAQ-listed companies, 9 NASDAQ market makers, 19 AMEX-listed companies, and has incorporated 68 NYSE-listed companies. The most important revenue makers are: Kroger, Proctor & Gamble, Cardinal Health, TRW, Inc., and Goodyear Tire and Rubber Corp.

The Cincinnati Stock Exchange (CSE) was organized on 11 March 1885 by 12 stockbrokers who agreed to meet regularly to buy and sell securities. In the mid-1990s, the Cincinnati Stock Exchange moved to Chicago and ceased operations in Ohio.

The Ohio securities marketplace is overseen by the Ohio Division of Securities of the Ohio Department of Commerce. The division provides investor protection, enhances capital formation, and protects the integrity of the securities marketplace by administering and enforcing the Ohio Securities Act, which was enacted in 1913. It requires that all securities sold in Ohio be registered with the division or properly exempted from registration and requires that each person transacting business in securities in Ohio be licensed by the division. It also imposes anti-fraud standards in connection with the sale of securities.

[35]PUBLIC FINANCE

The state budget is prepared on a biennial basis by the Office of Budget and Management. It is submitted by the governor to the state legislature, which must act on it by the close of the current fiscal year (30 June).

The general assembly has nearly total discretion in allocating general revenues, which are used primarily to support education, welfare, mental health facilities, law enforcement, property tax relief, and government operations. The assembly also allocates money from special revenue funds by means of specific legislative acts. More than one-half of all state expenditures come from the general fund.

Ohio's total biennium appropriations for 2004/05 of its general revenue fund total $48.787 billion, distributed in terms of function to Medicaid (37.2%), other health and human services (8.5%), primary and secondary education (26.9%), higher and other education (10.3%), public safety and protection (7.2%), general government and tax relief (6.8%), environment, development and transportation (1.9%), executive, legislative and judicial (1.3%). In 2002/03, Ohio's budget deficit was estimated at just under $2 billion (8.4% of the state budget), and for 2003/04 the deficit is projects at just over $2 billion (about 9.2% of the state budget).

The following table from the US Census Bureau contains information on revenues, expenditures, indebtedness, and cash/securities for 2001.

	($000)	PERCENT	PER CAPITA
Population (thousands, 2001)	11,390	(X)	(X)
Total Revenue	52,802,649	100.00	4,635.88
General revenue	38,195,700	72.34	3,353.44
Utility revenue	–	–	–
Liquor store revenue	506,767	0.96	44.49
Insurance trust revenue	14,100,182	26.70	1,237.94
Exhibit: Salaries and wages	2,771,496	5.79	243.33
Total expenditure	47,880,092	100.00	4,203.70
General expenditure	39,034,887	81.53	3,427.12
Education	14,556,698	30.40	1,278.02
Public welfare	10,424,962	21.77	915.27
Hospitals	1,198,907	2.50	105.26
Health	1,757,178	3.67	154.27
Highways	3,042,469	6.35	267.12
Police protection	239,383	0.50	21.02
Correction	1,581,349	3.30	138.84
Natural resources	363,358	0.76	31.90
Parks and recreation	102,535	0.21	9.00
Government administration	1,208,262	2.52	106.08
Interest on general debt	1,038,977	2.17	91.22
Other and unallocable	3,520,809	7.35	309.11
Utility expenditure	–	–	–
Liquor store expenditure	321,664	0.67	28.24
Insurance trust expenditure	8,523,541	17.80	748.34
Debt at end of fiscal year	18,748,257	100.00	1,646.03
Cash and security holdings	156,985,724	100.00	13,782.77

[36]TAXATION

The state income tax was enacted in 1972. The nine-bracket schedule is adjusted yearly for inflation. For 2002, the personal income tax rates ranged from 0.743% (up to $5,000 of taxable income) to 7.5% (above $200,000). Rates for each tax year are determined in July. The corporate income tax rate is 5.1%, and 8.5% on funds over $50,000.The state sales and use tax, 5% on retail sales (excepting groceries and prescription drugs), rental of personal property, and selected services, was raised temporarily to 6%, effective 1 July 2003. A number of personal services (like dry-cleaning and hair cutting), previously untaxed, were added to the sales tax base as of 1 August 2003. Telecommunications services are scheduled to be taxed from 1 January 2004. Ohio's cities, counties, villages and school districts can impose sales taxes, and local taxes add 0.25% to 2% to the state rate. The state also collects excise taxes on motor fuels, tobacco products, insurance premiums, public utilities, alcoholic beverages, and pari-mutuels. In 2002, Ohio was one of 20 states to raise its cigarette tax, and one of seven to more that double it, going from 24 cents a pack to 55 cents a pack. The public utility excise tax, on intrastate business receipts of public utilities, is 4.75% for most utilities. The state also imposes taxes on estates (of 3% to 7% of assets over $45,000), which is independent of the federal tax exemption for state death taxes, and so not affected by the scheduled phase out of this exemption by 2007. Each estate receives a tax credit, which was $13,900 for deaths in 2002. Death and gift taxes accounted for 0.6% of state taxes collected in 2002. Other state taxes include a resources severance tax, and various license fees. The state collects just over half (54.3% in 2000) of total state and local revenues.

The state collected $19.616 billion in taxes in 2002 (down about $1.4 million from 2001), of which 42.5% came from individual income taxes, 32.6% came from the general sales tax, 12.35% from selective sales taxes, 8% from license fees, and 3.8% from corporate income taxes. In 2003, Ohio ranked 10th among the states in terms of combined state and local tax burden, which amounted to about 10.3% of income.

The following table from the US Census Bureau provides a summary of taxes collected by the state in 2002.

	($000)	PER CAPITA
Total Taxes	19,616,569	1,717.55
Property taxes	18,498	1.62
Sales and gross receipts	8,814,121	771.73
General sales and gross receipts	6,391,475	559.61
Selective sales taxes	2,422,646	212.12
Alcoholic beverage	85,837	7.52
Amusements	(X)	(X)
Insurance Premiums	365,734	32.02
Motor fuels	1,372,423	120.16
Pari-mutuels	17,411	1.52
Public utilities	299,950	26.26
Tobacco products	281,291	24.63
Other selective sales	(X)	(X)
Licenses	1,562,432	136.8
Alcoholic beverages	24,489	2.14
Amusements	(X)	(X)
Corporation	264,484	23.16
Hunting and fishing	27,870	2.44
Motor vehicle	618,327	54.14
Motor vehicle operators	42,442	3.72
Public utility	2,425	0.21
Occupation and business, NEC	575,593	50.4
Other	6,802	0.6
Other taxes	9,221,518	807.4
Individual income	8,335,554	729.83
Corporation net income	761,050	66.63
Death and gift	116,259	10.18
Documentary and stock transfer	(X)	(X)
Severance	8,655	0.76
Other	(X)	(X)

37 ECONOMIC POLICY

Although Ohio seeks to attract new industries, a substantial portion of the state's annual economic growth stems from the expansion of existing businesses.

Ohio offers numerous business incentives to spur industrial development. The state encourages capital investment by offering private developers property tax abatements for commercial redevelopment. A 1976 state law permits municipal corporations to exempt certain property improvements from real property taxes for periods of up to 30 years. The state's guaranteed-loan program for industrial developers provides repayment guarantees on 90% of loans up to $1 million. The state also offers revenue bonds to finance a developer's land, buildings, and equipment at interest rates below the going mortgage interest rates.

The Ohio Department of Development (ODOD) consists of several divisions, including the: Economic Development Division, Office of Business Development, Office of Tax Incentives, Office of Financial Incentives, Office of Industrial Training, and Office of Small and Developing Business. These organizations administer plans for economic growth in cooperation with city and county governments. They inform companies about opportunities and advantages in the state and promote the sale of Ohio's exports abroad. In the 1990s, the departments instituted research and development programs at state universities in such fields as biotechnology, clean coat technologies, welding and joining technologies, robotics, polymers, and artificial intelligence. In 2002, special attention was paid to the development of Ohio's growing life science industry under the BioOhio 2002 rubric. In 2003, the Governor announced the Third Frontier Internship Program, designed to keep Ohio's college graduates in the state by connecting them with Ohio businesses through student internships.

38 HEALTH

The infant death rate for 2000 was 7.6 per 1,000 live births, higher than the national rate of 6.9. In 1999, 37,041 legal abortions were performed in Ohio, a rate of 15 per 1,000 women. In 2000, the overall death rate stood at 959.4, well above the national rate of 873.1.

Ohio ranks above the national rate in deaths due to heart disease, cerebrovascular diseases, and cancer, but below the US average for deaths caused by accidents and suicide. The major causes of death in 1998 (with rates per 100,000 population) included heart disease, 290.3; malignant neoplasms, 213.9; cerebrovascular diseases, 60.9; accidents and adverse effects, 31.0; motor vehicle accidents, 12.9; and suicide, 9.7. The HIV mortality rate was 2.2 per 100,000, less than half the national average. A total of 11,958 AIDS cases had been reported in Ohio through 2001 Among adults ages 18 and older, 26.3% were smokers in 2000, well above the median US rate of 23.3% .

Ohio's 166 community hospitals had 1,439,252 admissions and 33,310 beds in 2001. There were 46,026 full-time registered nurses and 5,018 full-time licensed practical nurses in 2001 and 262 physicians per 100,000 population in 2000. The average expense of a community hospital for care was $1,570.80 per inpatient day in 2001.

Federal government grants to cover the Medicare and Medicaid services in 2001 totaled $5.2 billion; 1,705,333 enrollees received Medicare benefits that year. Only 11.2% of Ohio's residents were uninsured in 2002.

39 SOCIAL WELFARE

The growth of welfare programs in the state was remarkably rapid during the 1970s and early 1980s. From 1970 to 1978, for example, Aid to Families with Dependent Children (AFDC) nearly tripled, to $446 million; by 1996, there were 552,000 AFDC recipients; the average payment per family was $421. In 2001, the average weekly unemployment benefit was $245.56. Average monthly participation in the food stamp program in FY2002 comprised 734,679 persons (330,844 households). The average monthly benefit was $82.38, and the sum total of benefits paid in FY2002 was $726,310,158.

With the enactment of the Personal Responsibility and Work Opportunity Reconciliation Act of 1996, the US government has changed the form and regulations for many of its social welfare programs. Most significantly, it replaces Aid to Families with Dependent Children (AFDC), an open-ended entitlement program, with Temporary Assistance for Needy Families (TANF), a limited system of assistance funded largely through federal block grants. The reform act also impacts the food stamp program, the Supplemental Security Income program, and the child nutrition program. The law took effect on 1 July 1997 and provided $16.38 billion in block grants for fiscal years 1997–2002. The grants are to be divided among the states based on an equation involving the numbers of former AFDC recipients in each state.

Reauthorization of the 1996 social welfare legislation, scheduled for 2002, was delayed, and the original law had been extended three times as of July 2003, with the most recent extension running through September 2003. Ohio's TANF program is called Ohio Works First (OWF). In June 2000 the state had 238,351 welfare recipients. State expenditures on the TANF program in FY2002 totaled $406,829,976.

In December 2001, Social Security benefits were paid to 1,921,920 Ohio residents. This number included 1,178,840 retired workers, 250,020 widows and widowers, 201,160 disabled workers, 145,800 spouses, and 146,100 children. Social Security beneficiaries represented 16.8% of the total state population and 93.5% of the state's population age 65 and older. Retired workers (excluding persons with special benefits) received an average monthly payment of $891; widows and widowers, $858; disabled workers, $811; and spouses, $452. Payments for children of retired workers averaged $442 per month; children of deceased workers, $591; and children of disabled workers, $234.

Federal Supplemental Security Income payments in December 2001 went to 241,763 Ohio residents, averaging $392 a month.

40 HOUSING

In 2002, Ohio had an estimated 4,875,496 housing units, 4,447,307 of which were occupied; 69.3% were owner-occupied. About 67.2% of all units were single-family, detached homes. About 24% of the housing units were built in 1939 or earlier; 44.6% were built between 1950 and 1979. In 2002, it was estimated that 145,923 units lacked telephone service, 18,220 lacked complete plumbing facilities, and 21,856 lacked complete kitchen facilities. Utility gas was the most common energy source for heating. About 585 units were equipped for solar energy. The average household size was 2.5 people.

In 2002, 51,246 new privately owned units were authorized for construction. The median home value was $113,072. The median monthly cost for mortgage owners was $1,028. Renters paid a median of $557 per month. During 2002, Ohio received over $257.2 million in community planning and development aid from the US Department of Housing and Urban Development.

41 EDUCATION

In 2000, 83% of Ohio residents age 25 and older were high school graduates; 21.1% had obtained a bachelor's degree or higher.

Ohio claims a number of "firsts" in US education: the first kindergarten, established by German settlers in Columbus in 1838; the first junior high school, also at Columbus, in 1909; the first municipal university, the University of Cincinnati, founded in 1870; and the first college to grant degrees to women, Oberlin, in 1837. The state's earliest school system was organized in Akron in 1847.

The total enrollment in Ohio's public schools for fall 1999 stood at 1,836,554. Of these, 1,296,450 attended schools from kindergarten through grade eight, and 540,104 attended high school. Minority students made up approximately 20% of the total enrollment in public elementary and secondary schools in 2001. Total enrollment was estimated at 1,821,200 in fall 2000 and is expected to drop to 1,802,000 by fall 2005. Expenditures for public education in 2000/01 were estimated at $12,400,000. Enrollment in nonpublic schools in fall 2001 was 254,494.

As of fall 2000, there were 652,393 students enrolled in college or graduate school. In the same year Ohio had 175 degree-granting institutions. There are 12 state universities, including Ohio State University (Columbus), Ohio University (Athens), Miami University (Oxford), and other state universities at Akron, Bowling Green, Cincinnati, Cleveland, Dayton, Kent, Toledo, Wilberforce, and Youngstown. The largest, Ohio State, was chartered in 1870 and also has campuses at Lima, Mansfield, Marion, Newark, and Wooster. Ohio has 37 public two-year colleges. Well-known private colleges and universities include Antioch (Yellow Springs), Case Western Reserve (Cleveland), Kenyon (Gambier), Muskingum (New Concord), Oberlin, Wittenberg (Springfield), and Wooster. The conservatories at both Oberlin and the Cleveland Institute of Music have national reputations. In 1997, minority students comprised 14.1% of total postsecondary enrollment.

Ohio residents enrolled as full-time students at an eligible institution within the state may apply for instructional grants from the Student Assistance Office of the Ohio Board of Regents. Guaranteed loans are provided through the Ohio Student Loan Commission.

42 ARTS

The earliest center of artistic activities in Ohio was Cincinnati, where a group of young painters did landscapes and portraits as early as 1840. The state's first art gallery was established there in 1854; the Cincinnati Art Academy was founded in 1869, and the Art Museum in 1886. Famous American artists who worked in Cincinnati during part of their careers include Thomas Cole, a founder of the "Hudson River School" of landscape painting, and Columbus-born George Bellows, whose realistic Stag at Sharkey's is displayed at the Cleveland Museum of Art (founded in 1913). Other notable centers for the visual arts include the Akron Art Institute, Columbus Museum of Art, Dayton Art Institute, Toledo Museum of Art, and museums or galleries in Marion, Oberlin, Springfield, Youngstown, and Zanesville.

Cincinnati also was an early center for the theater; the Eagle Theater opened there in 1839, and shortly afterward, the first showboat on the Ohio River began making regular stops at the city. The first US minstrel show appeared in Ohio in 1842. Ohio has three professional theatrical companies: the Cincinnati Playhouse, the Cleveland Play House (the nation's oldest permanent repertory theater), and the Great Lakes Theatre Festival. The Ohio Community Theater Association included groups in Akron, Canton, Columbus, Mansfield, Toledo, and Youngstown.

The Cincinnati Symphony was founded in 1895 and reorganized in 1909 with Leopold Stokowski as conductor. The Cincinnati Pops Orchestra acquired a new summer home in 1984 at the newly opened Riverbend Music Center. The Cincinnati Opera Association, founded in 1920, is the 2nd-oldest opera company in the United States. Cincinnati is also the host of the annual Cincinnati May Festival, a classical music event that is considered to be the oldest continuous choral festival in the Western Hemisphere.

The Cleveland Orchestra, founded in 1918, has risen to world-class stature since 1946, when George Szell began his 24-year tenure as conductor and music director. Blossom Music Center, the Cleveland Orchestra's summer home located between Cleveland and Akron, has been a center for both classical and popular music in Northeast Ohio since opening in 1968. In 2002/2003 Blossom underwent major improvements to its structures and landscaping. A $36.7 million renovation and expansion of the orchestra's main home, Severance Hall, had been completed three years earlier.

Smaller professional musical groups in Cleveland include Apollo's Fire (the Cleveland Baroque Orchestra), the Cleveland Chamber Orchestra, and the Cleveland Pops Orchestra. The Cleveland Opera finds its home at the State Theatre and the Lyric Opera Cleveland is a resident of Playhouse Square, the nation's largest performing arts center outside of New York.

There are civic symphony orchestras in Columbus, Dayton, Toledo, and Youngstown. Ballet companies are based in Cincinnati, Dayton, and Toledo. E. J. Thomas Hall in Akron is the home of the Ohio Ballet and the Akron Symphony. Operas are performed by resident companies in Cleveland, Columbus, Cincinnati, Toledo, and Dayton. There are numerous local arts festivals and craft shows.

The nation's first college music department was established at Oberlin College in 1865; the Cincinnati Conservatory of Music was established in 1867, the Baldwin-Wallace College Conservatory in 1899, and the Cleveland Institute of Music in 1920. The Baldwin-Wallace Bach Festival, begun in 1932, is the oldest collegiate Bach festival in the country. Bach's four major choral works are performed at the festival in four-year cycles (one per year). Baldwin-Wallace is also home to the Riemenschneider Bach Institute.

The Cleveland International Piano Competition, held biennially at the Cleveland Institute of Music since 1975, has become one of the foremost events of its type, drawing contestants from 19 countries throughout the world in 2003.

In 2003, the Ohio Arts Council and other Ohio arts organizations received grants totaling $1,617,800 from the National Endowment for the Arts. State and private sources contributed funds to arts programming as well. The Ohio Humanities Council presents a number of historical and literary programs, including Booked for the Day: Literary Retreats for Working Professionals. In 2000, the National Endowment for the Humanities contributed $2,821,510 to 50 state programs. The state has over 2,000 arts associations and about 100 local arts groups.

[43]LIBRARIES AND MUSEUMS

Ever since early settlers traded coonskins for books and established, in 1804, the Coonskin Library (now on display at the Ohio Historical Center in Columbus), Ohioans have stressed the importance of the public library system. In 2000, the state public library system of seven regions had 44,766,042 volumes, and a circulation of 144,911,000.

Major public library systems include those of Cincinnati, with 4,721,766 volumes in 1998; Cleveland, 3,782,419; Cuyahoga County, 3,085,123; Dayton, 1,782,419; and Columbus, 2,433,636. Leading academic libraries include those of Ohio State University, over seven million books; Case Western Reserve University, 1,304,852 books; and the University of Cincinnati, over three million books. The State Library of Ohio in Columbus, founded in 1817, provides research and information services for Ohio's state government and agencies with more than two million books and periodicals. Total public libraries income for 2000 came to $680,401,000 (3rd in the nation), including $1,360,802 in federal grants and $49,465,000 in state grants. Per capita spending was the highest in the nation, at $50.05.

Among the state's more than 284 museums are the Museum of Art, Natural History Museum, and Western Reserve Historical Society Museum in Cleveland; the Museum of Natural History, Art Museum, and Taft Museum in Cincinnati; the Dayton Art Institute; and the Center of Science and Industry and Ohio Historical Center in Columbus. The Zanesville Art Center has collections of ceramics and glass made in the Zanesville area. Also noteworthy are the US Air Force Museum near Dayton, the Neil Armstrong Air and Space Museum at Wapakoneta, and the Ohio River Museum in Marietta. Cincinnati has a conservatory of rare plants, while Cleveland has botanical gardens and an aquarium; both cities have zoos. The National First Ladies' Library in Canton features the artwork and artifacts of First Lady Caroline Harrison.

Historical sites in Ohio include the Schoenbrunn Village State Memorial, a reconstruction of the state's first settlement by Moravian missionaries, near New Philadelphia; the early-19th-century Piqua Historical Area, with exhibits of Indian culture; and the Fort Meigs reconstruction at Perrysburg. Archaeological sites include the "great circle" mounds, built by the Hopewell

Indians at present-day Newark, and Inscription Rock, marked by prehistoric Indians, on Kelley's Island.

[44]COMMUNICATIONS

In 2001, 96.7% of Ohio's occupied housing units had telephones.

Many of the state's radio stations were established in the early 1920s, when the growth of radio broadcasting was fostered by the availability of low-priced sets manufactured by Crosley Radio of Cincinnati. In 2003 there were 44 major AM stations, 158 major FM stations, and 42 commercial and 12 noncommercial television stations. The Cleveland area had 1,479,020 television households, 72% of which received cable. The Cincinnati area had 820,000 television households, 64% receiving cable. Finally, of the Columbus area's 757,860 television-viewing families, 66% watched cable. A total of 168,083 Internet domain names were registered in Ohio in 2000.

[45]PRESS

The first newspaper published in the region north and west of the Ohio River was the *Centinel of the North–Western Territory,* which was written, typeset, and printed in Cincinnati by William Maxwell in 1793. The oldest newspaper in the state still published under its original name is the *Scioto Gazette,* which appeared in 1800. The oldest extant weekly, the *Lebanon Western Star,* began publication in 1807, and the first daily, the *Cincinnati Commercial Register,* appeared in 1826. By 1840 there were 145 newspapers in Ohio.

Two of the state's most influential newspapers, the *Cleveland Plain Dealer* and the *Cincinnati Enquirer,* were founded in 1841. In 2001, the *Cleveland Plain Dealer* was the twentieth-largest daily newspaper in the country. In 1878, Edward W. Scripps established the Cleveland *Penny Press* (later called the *Press*), the first newspaper in what would become the extensive Scripps-Howard chain (though the *Press* folded in 1982). He later added to his newspaper empire the *Cincinnati Post* (1881) and the *Columbus Citizen* (1899), as well as papers in Akron, Toledo, and Youngstown.

In 2002, the state had 26 mornings dailies, 59 evening editions, and 42 Sunday editions. With a total of 84 daily newspapers, Ohio has the 3rd-largest number of daily papers in the country (following California and Texas). The following table lists leading Ohio newspapers with their approximate daily circulation in 2002:

AREA	NAME	DAILY	SUNDAY
Akron	*Beacon Journal* (m,S)	141,073	190,444
Cincinnati	*Enquirer* (m,S)	188,173	204,890
	Post (e)	49,779	68,910 (Sat.)
Cleveland	*Plain Dealer* (m,S)	359,978	477,515
Columbus	*Dispatch* (m,S)	244,204	367,546
Dayton	*Daily News* (m,S)	135,818	152,613
Toledo	*Blade* (m,S)	140,406	191,593
Youngstown	*Vindicator* (e,S)	70,152	100,502

Sun Newspapers, a weekly newspaper which produces 25 regional editions to serve 81 communities in the greater Cleveland and Akron areas, had a weekly circulation of 239,773. *Crain's Cleveland Business* has reported a readership of about 87,000 per week. Regional interest periodicals include *Cleveland Magazine, Cincinnati Magazine, Ohio Magazine,* and *Northern Ohio Live.*

[46]ORGANIZATIONS

In 2003, there were about 5,627 regional, national, and international organizations within the state. Service organizations with headquarters in Ohio include the Army and Navy Union, USA, at Kent, and the National Exchange Club, in Toledo.

Commercial and professional organizations include the American Ceramic Society and Order of United Commercial

Travelers of America, both in Columbus; American Society for Metals International in Materials Park; the United States Police Canine Association in Springboro; and Association for Systems Management and Brotherhood of Locomotive Engineers, both in Cleveland.

Sports associations operating out of Ohio are the Lighter-Than-Air Society and Professional Bowlers Association, Akron; American Motorcyclist Association, Westerville; the Amateur Trapshooting Association, Vandalia; the International Soap Box Derby, Akron; US Boomerang Association, Delaware; US Flag and Touch Football League, Mentor; US Speedskating, Westlake; and Indoor Sports Club, Napoleon. The American Coaster Enthusiasts are based in Russell Township.

Arts, culture, and history are promoted in the state through such organizations as the American Indian Lore Association, the Botanical Society of America, the American Classical League, the Guild of Carilloneurs in North America, Music Teachers National Association, the Ohio and Erie Canal Association, the Ohio Art League, the Ohio Arts Council, and the Ohio Valley Art League. There are also numerous local arts groups and historical societies.

47TOURISM, TRAVEL, AND RECREATION

Ohio visitors spend more than $27.1 billion annually on travel and tourism and the industry supports nearly 700,000 travel-related positions. Visitors spend more than one billion annually in Ashtabula County alone. It is known as the Covered Bridge Capital (16) and the Wine Capital (11) of Ohio, and offers more campsites than any other county in Ohio (18).

Cleveland, Columbus, and Cincinnati all offer major attractions of museums, restaurants, shopping, parks, and concerts. The Rock and Roll Hall of Fame and Museum and the Great Lakes Science Center, both in Cleveland, are major attractions. The NFL Hall of Fame is located in Canton. Popular amusement parks include Cedar Point in Sandusky, King's Island in Cincinnati, and Six Flags Worlds of Adventure in Aurora.

Beaches and parks in the Lake Erie region are especially popular with tourists during the summer, including the Mentor Headlands State Park. The Cuyahoga Valley National Recreation Area is also a popular attraction, linking the urban center of Cleveland and Akron. The Cleveland Metroparks system creates an "Emerald Necklace" around the greater Cleveland area.

Ohio state parks comprise 204,274 acres (84,000 hectares). Among the most visited state parks are Alum Creek, East Harbor and Kelleys Island (both on Lake Erie), Grand Lake, St. Mary's, Hocking Hills, Hueston Woods, Mohican, Pymatuning (on the Pennsylvania border), Rocky Fork, Salt Fork, Scioto Trail, and West Branch.

The most popular sport fish are bass, catfish, bullhead, carp, perch, and rainbow trout. The deer-shooting season is held in late November; hunters are limited to one deer per season. However, because of the growing deer population in Ohio, hunters have been able to take two deer per season recently. Also the season times vary for shotgun, primitive arms, and bows. The bow season lasts several months.

The eastern Allegheny region has several ski resorts for winter sports enthusiasts. Popular tourist attractions here include the Amish settlement around Millersburg, the National Road-Zane Grey Museum near Zanesville, and the restored Roscoe Village on the Ohio-Erie Canal. The southern region offers scenic hill country and the showboat Majestic, the last of the original floating theaters, in Cincinnati.

In the western region, tourist sites include the Wright brothers' early flying machines in Dayton's Carillon Park, the Ohio Caverns at West Liberty, and the Zane Caverns near Bellefontaine. The central region is "Johnny Appleseed" country; the folk hero (a frontiersman whose real name was John Chapman) is commemorated in Mansfield by the blockhouse to which he directed settlers in order to save them from an Indian raid. At Columbus are the reconstructed Ohio Village and the Exposition Center, site of the annual Ohio State Fair, held for 13 days in mid-August.

Other leading tourist attractions include Ohio's presidential memorials and homes: the William Henry Harrison Memorial at North Bend, Ulysses S. Grant's birthplace at Point Pleasant, the James A. Garfield home at Mentor, the Rutherford B. Hayes home at Fremont, the William McKinley Memorial at Canton, the Taft National Historic Site in Cincinnati, and the Warren G. Harding home in Marion. Also of interest are the Thomas A. Edison birthplace at Milan, and Malabar Farm, in Richland County, home of author and conservationist Louis Bromfield.

48SPORTS

There are eight major league professional sports teams in Ohio: the Cleveland Indians and the Cincinnati Reds of Major League Baseball, the Columbus Crew of Major League Soccer, the Cincinnati Bengals and the Cleveland Browns of the National Football League, the Cleveland Rockers of the Women's National Basketball Association, and the Cleveland Cavaliers of the National Basketball Association. In fall 2000, the Columbus Blue Jackets began playing in the National Hockey League.

The state is also home to Triple-A minor league baseball teams in Columbus and Toledo, and a Double-A team in Akron. A new team, the Lake County Captains, began play in 2003 and are a Single-A affiliate of the Indians. The state also fields a team in the Midwest League and the New York Penn League. A professional indoor soccer team, the Force, makes its home in Cleveland. The club was formerly known as the Crunch. In addition, there is minor league hockey in Cleveland, Columbus, Dayton, and Toledo.

The Cincinnati Reds (traditionally short for Redstockings) were the first professionally organized baseball team, playing their first season in 1869. Their record was 64–0. The Reds won the World Series in 1919, 1940, 1975, 1976, and in 1990. The Indians won the World Series in 1920 and 1948. In 1995, the Indians won their first American League pennant since 1954, but lost to the Atlanta Braves in the World Series. They returned to the Series in 1997, this time losing to the Florida Marlins. The original Cleveland Browns, who moved to Baltimore in 1995, won four NFL titles, football's championship prior to the Super Bowl, the last in 1964. An expansion or relocation NFL team began play as the Browns in a new stadium in Cleveland beginning in 1999. The Bengals won the American Football Conference Championship in both 1981 and 1988, but lost each year's Super Bowl.

Akron has been headquarters for the Professional Bowlers Association (PBA) since its founding in 1958. The PBA's top tournament is played there each year, and the PBA Hall of Fame is also located in Akron. The NEC Invitational is played annually in Akron, and the Memorial Golf Tournament in Dublin.

Major horse-racing tracks include Cleveland's Thistledown, Cincinnati's River Downs, Columbus's Scioto Downs, and other tracks at Toledo, Lebanon, Grove City, and Northfield. The Cleveland Gold Cup race is held annually at Thistledown, as is the Ohio Derby. The Little Brown Jug classic for three-year-old pacers takes place every year at the Delaware Fairgrounds, and the Ohio State race for two-year-old trotters is held during the state fair at Columbus.

Several new facilities have been constructed, including the new Cleveland Browns Stadium in 1999, Jacobs Field in 1994 (home of the Indians), Columbus Crew Stadium, and most recently, the Great American Ballpark in Cincinnati (2003). The Cincinnati Reds make it their home park.

In collegiate sports, Ohio State University has long been a football power, winning over 25 Big Ten titles. Ohio State won the Rose Bowl in 1950, 1955, 1958, 1969, 1974, and 1997. The Buckeyes were named national champions in 1942, 1954 (with UCLA), 1957 (with Auburn), 1968, and in 2003 after upsetting Miami (Fl) in the Fiesta Bowl. Ohio State also has won NCAA championships in baseball, basketball, fencing, golf, gymnastics, and swimming, while Cincinnati and Dayton universities have had highly successful basketball teams. The Pro Football Hall of Fame is located in Canton, where the sport was first organized professionally in 1920.

Other annual sporting events include the grand tournament of the American Trapshooting Association in Vandalia, the Grand Prix or Cleveland Indy car race, and the All-American Soap Box Derby in Akron, a nationally covered event in which 9- to 15-year-olds compete.

49 FAMOUS OHIOANS

Ohio has been the native state of seven US presidents and the residence of another. Inventions by Ohioans include the incandescent light, the arc light, and the airplane.

William Henry Harrison (b.Virginia, 1773–1841), the 9th US president, came to Ohio as a US Army ensign in territorial times. After serving in the Indian wars under Gen. Anthony Wayne, he became secretary of the Northwest Territory. As the territorial delegate to Congress, he fostered the Harrison Land Act, which stimulated settlement of the public domain. Named territorial governor in 1800, Harrison conducted both warfare and peace negotiations with the Indians. After the defeat of British and Indian forces in 1813, he became known as the "Washington of the West." After settling at North Bend on the Ohio River, he began a political career that carried him to the White House in 1841. Harrison caught a chill from a cold March wind and died of pneumonia exactly one month after his inauguration.

From 1869 to 1881, the White House was occupied by three Ohioans. All were Republicans who had served with distinction as Union Army generals. The first, Ulysses Simpson Grant (Hiram Ulysses Grant, 1822–85), the 18th US president, was an Ohio farm boy educated at West Point. After service in the Mexican War, he left the US Army, having been charged with intemperance. He emerged from obscurity in 1861, when he was assigned to an Illinois regiment. Grant rose quickly in command; after victories at Shiloh and Vicksburg, he was commissioned major general. In 1864, he directed the Virginia campaign that ended with Confederate surrender, and this rumpled, slouching, laconic man became the nation's hero. In 1868, he was elected president, and he was reelected in 1872. His second term was rocked with financial scandals, though none were directly connected to Grant. After leaving the presidency in 1877, he went bankrupt, and to discharge his debts, he wrote his memoirs. That extraordinary book was completed four days before his death from throat cancer in 1885. Grant is buried in a monumental tomb in New York City.

Rutherford B. Hayes (1822–93), the 19th US president, was born in Delaware, Ohio, and educated at Kenyon College and Harvard Law School. Following Army service, he was elected to Congress, and in 1876 became the Republican presidential nominee. In a close and disputed election, he defeated New York's Governor Samuel J. Tilden. Hayes chose not to run for re-election, returning instead to Ohio to work on behalf of humanitarian causes. In 1893, Hayes died in Fremont, where the Hayes Memorial was created—the first presidential museum and library in the nation.

James A. Garfield (1831–81), 20th US president, was born in a log cabin in northern Ohio. Between school terms, he worked as a farmhand and a mule driver on the Ohio Canal. After holding several Civil War commands, he served in Congress for 18 years. Elected president in 1880, he held office but a few months; he was shot by a disappointed office seeker in the Washington, D.C. railroad station on 2 July and died 11 weeks later.

Benjamin Harrison (1833–1901), 23rd US president and grandson of William Henry Harrison, was born in North Bend. After graduation from Miami University, he studied law and began to practice in Indianapolis. Military command in the Civil War was followed by service in the US Senate and the Republican presidential nomination in 1888. As president, Harrison gave impetus to westward expansion, moved toward annexation of Hawaii, and enlarged the civil-service system.

US presidents in the 20th century include three more native Ohioans. William McKinley (1843–1901) was born in Niles. Elected in 1896 as the 25th president, he established the gold standard and maintained tariff protection for US manufactures. Early in his second term, while greeting a throng of people, he was shot to death by a young anarchist. William Howard Taft (1857–1930), of Cincinnati, was the 27th US president. He gained a national reputation in 1904 as President Theodore Roosevelt's secretary of war; five years later, he succeeded Roosevelt in the White House. Defeated in 1912, Taft then left Washington for a law professorship at Yale. In 1921, under President Warren G. Harding (1865–1923), he became US chief justice, serving in that office until a month before his death. Harding, the last Ohioan to win the White House, was born in Blooming Grove. He went into politics from journalism, after serving as editor of the *Marion Star*. After eight years in the US Senate, he was a dark-horse candidate for the Republican presidential nomination in 1920. He won the election from James M. Cox (1870–1957), another Ohio journalist-politician, and became the 29th US president. Harding, who died in office, was surrounded by graft and corruption in his own cabinet.

Three US vice presidents were natives of Ohio. Thomas A. Hendricks (1819–85) was elected on the Democratic ticket with Grover Cleveland in 1884. Charles W. Fairbanks (1852–1918) served from 1905 to 1909 under Theodore Roosevelt. Charles Gates Dawes (1865–1951) became vice president under Calvin Coolidge in 1925, the same year the Dawes Plan for reorganizing German finances brought him the Nobel Peace Prize; from 1929 to 1932, he served as US ambassador to Great Britain.

Three Ohioans served as chief justice on the Supreme Court: Salmon P. Chase (b.New Hampshire, 1808–73), Morrison R. Waite (b.Connecticut, 1816–88), and Taft. Most notable among nearly 40 cabinet officers from Ohio were Secretary of State Lewis Cass (b.New Hampshire, 1783–1866), Treasury Secretaries Chase and John Sherman (1823–1900), and Secretary of War Edwin M. Stanton (1814–69). William Tecumseh Sherman (1820–91) was a Union general in the Civil War whose Georgia campaign in 1864 helped effect the surrender of the Confederacy. Although disappointed in his quest for the presidency, US Senator Robert A. Taft (1889–1953) was an enduring figure, best remembered for his authorship of the Taft-Hartley Labor Management Relations Act of 1947.

Nobel Prize winners from Ohio include Dawes and physicists Arthur Compton (1892–1962) and Donald Glaser (b.1926). Notable Pulitzer Prize winners include novelist Louis Bromfield (1896–1956), dramatist Russell Crouse (1893–1966), historian Paul Herman Buck (1899–1979), and historian and biographer Arthur Schlesinger, Jr. (b.1917). Ohio writers of enduring fame are novelists William Dean Howells (1837–1920), Zane Grey (1875–1939), and Sherwood Anderson (1876–1941), whose short story collection *Winesburg, Ohio* was set in his hometown of Clyde; poets Paul Laurence Dunbar (1872–1906) and Hart Crane (1899–1932); and humorist James Thurber (1894–1961). Toni Morrison (b.1931), winner of the 1988 Pulitzer Prize for literature and the 1993 Nobel Prize for literature, was born in Lorain, Ohio. Among Ohio's eminent journalists are Whitelaw

Reid (1837–1912), satirists David R. Locke (1833–88) and Ambrose Bierce (1842–1914), columnist O. O. McIntyre (1884–1938), newsletter publisher W. M. Kiplinger (1891–1967), and James Reston (b.Scotland, 1909–95), an editor and columnist for the *New York Times* along with author-commentator Lowell Thomas (1892–1981). Important in the art world were painters Thomas Cole (b.England, 1801–48), Frank Duveneck (b.Kentucky, 1848–1919), and George Bellows (1882–1925), as well as architects Cass Gilbert (1859–1934) and Philip Johnson (b.1906). Defense lawyer Clarence Darrow (1857–1938) was also an Ohioan.

Ohio educators whose books taught reading, writing, and arithmetic to the nation's schoolchildren were William Holmes McGuffey (b.Pennsylvania, 1800–73), Platt R. Spencer (1800–64), and Joseph Ray (1807–65). In higher education, Horace Mann (b.Massachusetts, 1796–1859) was the first president of innovative Antioch College, and William Rainey Harper (1856–1906) founded the University of Chicago.

Several Ohio-born inventor-scientists have furthered the nation's industrial progress. Thomas A. Edison (1847–1931) produced the incandescent lamp, the phonograph, and the movie camera. Charles Brush (1849–1929) invented the arc light. John H. Patterson (1844–1922) helped develop the cash register. The Wright brothers, Orville (1871–1948) and Wilbur (b.Indiana, 1867–1912), made the first flight in a powered aircraft. Charles F. Kettering (1876–1958) invented the automobile self-starter. Ohio's leading industrialist was John D. Rockefeller (b.New York, 1839–1937), founder of Standard Oil of Ohio. Harvey S. Firestone (1868–1938) started the tire company that bears his name. Edward "Eddie" Rickenbacker (1890–1973), an ace pilot in World War I, was president of Eastern Airlines.

The most notable Ohioans in the entertainment field are markswoman Annie Oakley (Phoebe Anne Oakley Mozee, 1860–1926); movie actors Clark Gable (1901–60) and Roy Rogers (Leonard Slye, 1912–98); movie director Stephen Spielberg (b.1947); comedian Bob Hope (Leslie Townes Hope, b.England, 1903–2003); actors Paul Newman (b.1925), Hal Holbrook (b.1925), and Joel Grey (b.1932); jazz pianist Art Tatum (1910–56); and composer Henry Mancini (1924–94).

Leading sports figures from Ohio are boxing champion Jim Jeffries (1875–1953), racing driver Barney Oldfield (1878–1946), baseball pitcher Cy Young (1867–1955), baseball executive Branch Rickey (1881–1965), baseball star Peter "Pete" Rose (b.1941) who broke Ty Cobb's record for the most hits, track star Jesse Owens (b.Alabama, 1912–80), jockey George Edward "Eddie" Arcaro (1916–97), and golfer Jack Nicklaus (b.1940).

Astronauts from Ohio include John Glenn (b.1921), the first American to orbit the earth, who was elected US senator from Ohio in 1974; and Neil Armstrong (b.1930), the first man to walk on the moon.

50 BIBLIOGRAPHY

Bromfield, Louis. *The Farm*. New York: Harper, 1933.

Condon, George E. *Cleveland: The Best Kept Secret*. Garden City, N.Y.: Doubleday, 1967.

Curtin, Michael F. *The Ohio Politics Almanac*. Kent: Kent State University Press, 1996.

Downes, Randolph C. *Frontier Ohio: 1788–1803*. Columbus: Ohio State Archaeological and Historical Society, 1935.

Ellis, William D. *The Cuyahoga*. New York: Holt, 1966.

Feagler, Dick. *Feagler's Cleveland*. Cleveland: Gray & Co., 1996.

Federal Writers' Project. *The Ohio Guide*. Reprint. New York: Somerset, n.d. (orig. 1940).

Galbreath, Charles B. *History of Ohio*. 5 vols. Chicago and New York: American Historical Society, 1925.

A Geography of Ohio. Edited by Leonard Peacefull. Kent: Kent State University Press, 1996.

Havighurst, Walter. *Ohio: A Bicentennial History*. New York: Norton, 1976.

Hopkins, Charles E. *Ohio the Beautiful and Historic*. Boston: Page, 1931.

Howe, Henry, *Historical Collections of Ohio*. 2 vols. Columbus: Henry Howe & Son, 1889.

Howells, William Dean. *A Boy's Town*. New York: Harper, 1890.

Hulbert, Archer B. *The Ohio River: A Course of Empire*. New York and London: Putnam, 1906.

Jones, Robert L. *The History of Agriculture in Ohio to Eighteen Eighty*. Kent: Kent State University Press, 1983.

Leech, Margaret. *In the Days of McKinley*. New York: Harper & Row, 1959.

Longworth de Chambrun, Clara. *Cincinnati: The Story of the Queen City*. New York: Scribner, 1939.

McCormick, Richard P. *The Second American Party System: Party Formation in the Jacksonian Era*. Chapel Hill: University of North Carolina Press, 1966.

Morgan, H. Wayne. *From Hayes to McKinley*. Syracuse, N.Y.: Syracuse University Press, 1969.

The National Road. Edited by Karl Raitz. Baltimore, Md.: Johns Hopkins University Press, 1996.

Notestein, Lucy. *Wooster of the Middle West*. New Haven, Conn.: Yale University Press, 1937.

Ohio Politics. Edited by Alexander P. Lamis. Kent: Kent State University Press, 1994.

Ohio State. Department of State. *Constitution of the State of Ohio*. Columbus: Anderson, 1979.

Ohio State. Secretary of State. *Official Roster, 1983–1984*. Columbus, 1984.

Owen, Lorrie K., ed. *Dictionary of Ohio Historic Places*. St. Clair Shores, Mich.: Somerset Publishers, 1999.

Patterson, James T. *Mr. Republican: A Biography of Robert A. Taft*. Boston: Houghton Mifflin, 1972.

Reid, Whitelaw. *Ohio in the War: Her Statesmen, Generals, and Soldiers*. 2 vols. Cincinnati: Moore, Wilstach & Baldwin, 1868.

Roseboom, Eugene Holloway, and Francis P. Weisenburger. *A History of Ohio*. New York: Prentice-Hall, 1934.

Shriver, Phillip R., and Clarence E. Wunderlin, Jr., ed. *The Documentary Heritage of Ohio*. Athens: Ohio University Press, 2000.

Thurber, James. *My Life and Hard Times*. New York: Harper, 1933.

Warner, Hoyt Landon. *Progressivism in Ohio 1897–1917*. Columbus: Ohio State University Press, 1964.

Wittke, Carl, ed. *History of the State of Ohio*. 6 vols. Columbus: Ohio State Archaeological and Historical Society, 1941–44.

OKLAHOMA

State of Oklahoma

ORIGIN OF STATE NAME: Derived from the Choctaw Indian words *okla humma*, meaning "land of the red people." **NICKNAME:** The Sooner State. **CAPITAL:** Oklahoma City. **ENTERED UNION:** 16 November 1907 (46th). **SONG:** "Oklahoma!" **POEM:** "Howdy Folks." **MOTTO:** *Labor omnia vincit* (Labor conquers all things). **FLAG:** On a blue field, a peace pipe, and an olive branch cross an Osage warrior's shield, which is decorated with small crosses and from which seven eagle feathers descend; the word "Oklahoma" appears below. **OFFICIAL SEAL:** Each point of a five-pointed star incorporates the emblem of an Indian nation: (clockwise from top) Chickasaw, Choctaw, Seminole, Creek, and Cherokee. In the center, a frontiersman and Indian shake hands before the goddess of justice; behind them are symbols of progress, including a farm, train, and mill. Surrounding the large star are 45 small ones and the words "Great Seal of the State of Oklahoma 1907." **ANIMAL:** American buffalo (bison). **BIRD:** Scissor-tailed flycatcher. **FISH:** White bass (sand bass). **REPTILE:** Collared lizard (mountain boomer). **FLORAL EMBLEM:** Mistletoe. **TREE:** Redbud. **GRASS:** Indian grass. **STONE:** Barite rose (rose rock). **LEGAL HOLIDAYS:** New Year's Day, 1 January; Birthday of Martin Luther King, Jr., 3rd Monday in January; Washington's Birthday, 3rd Monday in February; Memorial Day, last Monday in May; Independence Day, 4 July; Labor Day, 1st Monday in September; Columbus Day, 2nd Monday in October; Veterans Day, 11 November; Thanksgiving Day, 4th Thursday in November; Christmas Day, 25 December. **TIME:** 6 AM CST = noon GMT.

¹LOCATION, SIZE, AND EXTENT

Situated in the western south-central US, Oklahoma ranks 18th in size among the 50 states.

The total area of Oklahoma is 69,956 sq mi (181,186 sq km), of which land takes up 68,655 sq mi (177,817 sq km) and inland water 1,301 sq mi (3,369 sq km). Oklahoma extends 464 mi (747 km) E-W including the panhandle in the NW, which is about 165 mi (266 km) long. The maximum N-S extension is 230 mi (370 km).

Oklahoma is bordered on the N by Colorado and Kansas; on the E by Missouri and Arkansas; on the S and SW by Texas (with part of the line formed by the Red River); and on the extreme W by New Mexico. The total estimated boundary length of Oklahoma is 1,581 mi (2,544 km). The state's geographic center is in Oklahoma County, 8 mi (13 km) N of Oklahoma City.

²TOPOGRAPHY

The land of Oklahoma rises gently to the west from an altitude of 289 ft (88 m) at Little River in the southeastern corner to a height of 4,973 ft (1,517 m) at Black Mesa, on the tip of the panhandle. Four mountain ranges cross this Great Plains state: the Boston Mountains (part of the Ozark Plateau) in the northeast, the Quachitas in the southeast, the Arbuckles in the south-central region, and the Wichitas in the southwest. Much of the northwest belongs to the High Plains, while northeastern Oklahoma is mainly a region of buttes and valleys.

Not quite two-thirds of the state is drained by the Arkansas River, and the remainder by the Red River. Within Oklahoma, the Arkansas is joined by the Verdigris, Grand (Neosho), and Illinois rivers from the north and northeast, and by the Cimarron and Canadian rivers from the northwest and west. The Red River, which marks most of the state's southern boundary, is joined by the Washita, Salt Fork, Blue, Kiamichi, and many smaller rivers. There are few natural lakes but many artificial ones, of which the largest is Lake Eufaula, covering 102,500 acres (41,500 ha).

³CLIMATE

Oklahoma has a continental climate with cold winters and hot summers. Normal daily mean temperatures in Oklahoma City range from 37°F (3°C) in January to 82°F (28°C) in July. The record low temperature of –27°F (–33°C) was set at Watts on 18 January 1930; the record high, 120°F (49°C), occurred at Tipton on 27 June 1994.

Dry, sunny weather generally prevails throughout the state. Precipitation varies from an average of 15 in (38 cm) annually in the panhandle to over 50 in (127 cm) in the southeast. Average annual precipitation in Oklahoma City (1971–2000) was 35.9 in (91.2 cm). Snowfall averages 9 in (23 cm) a year in Oklahoma City, which is also one of the windiest cities in the US, with an average annual wind speed of 12.3 mph (19.8 km/hr).

Oklahoma is tornado-prone. One of the most destructive windstorms was the tornado that tore through Ellis, Woods, and Woodward counties on 9 April 1947, killing 101 people and injuring 782 others.

⁴FLORA AND FAUNA

Grasses grow in abundance in Oklahoma. Bluestem, buffalo, sand lovegrass, and grama grasses are native, with the bluestem found mostly in the eastern and central regions, and buffalo grass most common in the western counties, known as the "short grass country." Deciduous hardwoods stand in eastern Oklahoma, and red and yellow cactus blossoms brighten the Black Mesa area in the northwest. The western prairie fringed orchid was listed as threatened in 2003; there were no plant species listed as endangered that year in Oklahoma.

The white-tailed deer is found in all counties, and Rio Grande wild turkeys are hunted across much of the state. Pronghorn antelope inhabit the panhandle area, and elk survive in the Wichita Mountains Wildlife Refuge, where a few herds of American buffalo (bison) are also preserved. The bobwhite quail, ring-necked pheasant, and prairie chicken are common game birds. Native sport fish include largemouth, smallmouth, white, and spotted bass; catfish; crappie; and sunfish.

Among the state's 19 endangered or threatened species of wildlife in 2003 were three species of bat (Ozark big-eared, Indiana, and gray), bald eagle, whooping crane, black-capped vireo, red-cockaded woodpecker, Eskimo curlew, and Neosho madtom.

5ENVIRONMENTAL PROTECTION

The Oklahoma Department of Environment Quality has overall responsibility for coordinating all pollution control activities by other state agencies and for developing a comprehensive water quality management program for Oklahoma. The Oklahoma Conservation Commission is responsible for conservation of renewable natural resources through landuse planning, small watershed upstream flood control, reclamation of abandoned mine land, water quality monitoring and soil and water conservation, as well as environmental education and wetlands conservation. The Department of Wildlife Conservation manages wildlife resources and habitat specifically for hunters, anglers, and others who appreciate wildlife.

The Department of Health is responsible for the monitoring of air quality standards; the enforcement of regulations covering control of industrial and solid waste; the enforcement of regulations covering radioactive materials at the Kerr-McGee processing facility at Gore and elsewhere; and the maintenance of standards at all public waterworks and sewer systems. The Water Resources Board has broad statutory authority to protect the state's waters.

Toxic industrial wastes remain an environmental concern, and old mines in the Tar Creek area of northeastern Oklahoma still exude groundwater contaminated by zinc, iron, and cadmium. In 2003, Oklahoma had 165 hazardous waste sites listed in the Environmental Protection Agency's database, 10 of which were on the National Priorities List; among these were Compass Industries, Sand Springs Petro Chemical Complex, and Criner.

Lands devastated by erosion during the droughts of the 1930s were purchased by the federal government and turned over to the Soil Conservation Service for restoration. When grasses were firmly established in the mid-1950s, the land was turned over to the US Forest Service and is now leased for grazing. In 2003, the state had about 890,000 acres of wetlands—about 2% of the land. In 2001, Oklahoma received $65,159,000 in federal grants from the EPA; EPA expenditures for procurement contracts in Oklahoma that year amounted to $3,307,000.

6POPULATION

Oklahoma ranked 28th in population in the US with an estimated total of 3,493,714 in 2002, an increase of 1.2% since 2000. Between 1990 and 2000, Oklahoma's population grew from 3,145,585 to 3,450,654, an increase of 9.7%. The population is projected to reach 4.1 million by 2025. The population density in 2000 was 50.3 persons per sq mi.

In 2000 the median age in Oklahoma was 35.5; 25.9% of the population were under age 18 while 13.2% were age 65 or older.

The largest city is Oklahoma City, which in 2002 had an estimated 519,034 inhabitants in the inner city (up from 463,201 in 1994) and a 1999 estimated population of 1,046,283 in the metropolitan statistical area. Tulsa, the 2nd-largest city, had a 2002 estimated population of 391,908 in the inner city and a 1999 estimated population of 786,117 in the metropolitan area. Lawton ranked 3rd with a population of 92,757 in 2000.

7ETHNIC GROUPS

According to the 1990 Census, Oklahoma had more American Indians—252,420—than any other state, but by 1998 its estimated American Indian population of 281,000 had been surpassed by California's (292,000), and it remained in 2nd place in 2000, with an Indian population of 273,230, or 7.9% of the

state's total population—the 4th-highest percentage ranking in the US. Oklahoma was also home to some of the nation's largest Indian reservations, including those of the Creek, Cherokee, Chickasaw, and Choctaw Indians.

Black slaves came to Oklahoma (then known as Indian Territory) with their Indian masters after Congress forced the resettlement of Indians from the southeast to lands west of the Mississippi River in 1830. By the time of the Civil War, there were 7,000 free Negroes in Oklahoma. After the depression of the 1930s, blacks left the farms and small towns and concentrated in Oklahoma City and Tulsa. In 2000, the black population of 260,968 was smaller than the American Indian population.

Mexicans came to Oklahoma during the 19th century as laborers on railroads and ranches, and in coal mines. Later they worked in the cotton fields until the depression of the 1930s and subsequent mechanization reduced the need for seasonal labor. Today, most first- and second-generation Mexicans live in Oklahoma City, Tulsa, and Lawton. In 2000, Oklahomans who were classified as Hispanics or Latinos numbered 179,304 and represented 5.2% of the state's total population. Of this total, 132,813 were Mexican.

Italians, Czechs, Germans, Poles, Britons, Irish, and others of European stock also came to Oklahoma during the 19th century. Foreign immigration has been small since that time, however, and in 2000, less than 4% of the population consisted of the foreign born (who numbered 131,747). Persons claiming at least one specific ancestry group in 2000 included English, 291,553; German, 435,245; and Irish, 354,802. In 2000, the Asian population numbered 46,767 and there were 2,372 Pacific Islanders.

8LANGUAGES

Once the open hunting ground of the Osage, Commanche, and Apache Indians, what is now Oklahoma later welcomed the deported Cherokee and other transferred eastern tribes. The diversity of tribal and linguistic backgrounds is reflected in numerous place-names such as Oklahoma itself, Kiamichi, and Muskogee. Almost equally diverse is Oklahoma English, with its uneven blending of features of North Midland, South Midland, and Southern dialects.

In 2000, 2,977,187 Oklahomans—92.6% of the resident population five years or older—spoke only English at home, down from 95% in 1990. The following table gives selected statistics from the 2000 census for language spoken at home by persons five years old and over. The category "Other Native North American languages" includes Apache, Cherokee, Choctaw, Dakota, Keres, Pima, and Yupik. The category "Other Asian languages" includes Dravidian languages, Malayalam, Telugu, Tamil, and Turkish. The category "African languages" includes Amharic, Ibo, Twi, Yoruba, Bantu, Swahili, and Somali.

LANGUAGE	NUMBER	PERCENT
Population 5 years and over	3,215,719	100.0
Speak only English	2,977,187	92.6
Speak a language other than English	238,532	7.4
Speak a language other than English	238,532	7.4
Spanish or Spanish Creole	141,060	4.4
Other Native North American languages	18,871	0.6
German	13,445	0.4
Vietnamese	11,330	0.4
French (incl. Patois, Cajun)	8,258	0.3
Chinese	6,413	0.2
Korean	3,948	0.1
Arabic	3,265	0.1
Other Asian languages	3,134	0.1
Tagalog	2,888	0.1
Japanese	2,546	0.1
African languages	2,546	0.1

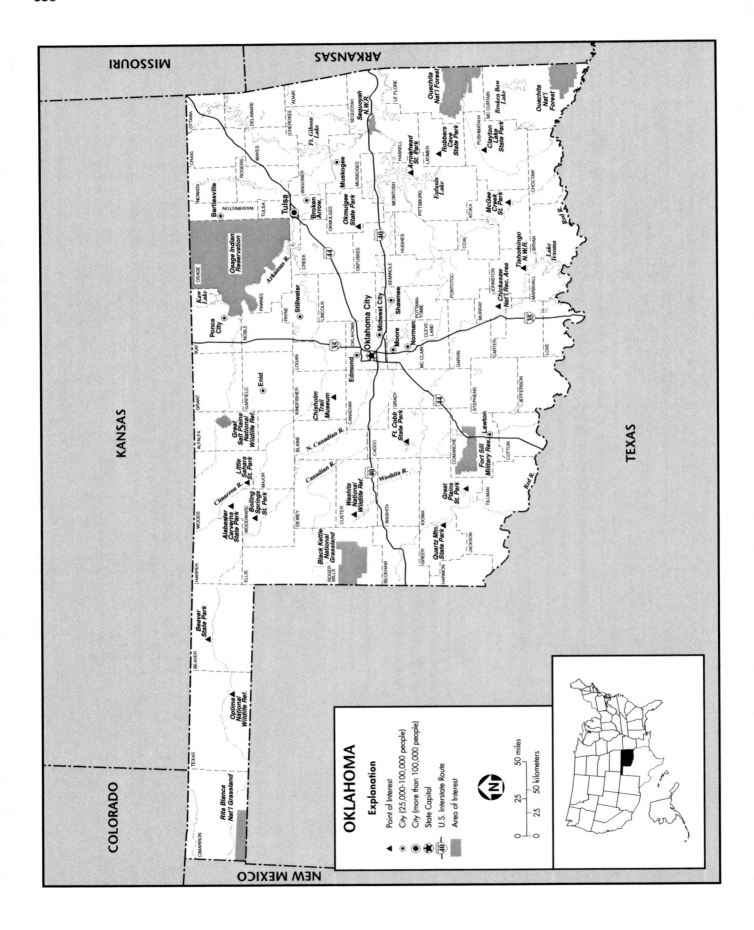

9RELIGIONS

Evangelical Protestant groups predominate in Oklahoma with adherents representing about 41.4% of the total population in 2000. This group was influential in keeping the state "dry"—that is, banning the sale of all alcoholic beverages—until 1959 and resisting legalization of public drinking until 29 counties voted to permit the sale of liquor by the drink in 1985.

The leading Protestant group in 2000 was the Southern Baptist Convention with 967,223 adherents. Other leading Evangelical Protestant denominations include the Assemblies of God, 88,301 adherents; the Churches of Christ, 83,047; the Christian Church (Disciples of Christ), 53,729; and the Christian Churches, 42,708. Free Will Baptists, Nazarenes, Missouri Synod Lutherans, and those of various other Pentecostal traditions are also fairly well represented. The largest Mainline Protestant denominations are the United Methodist Church, with 322,794 adherents, and the Presbyterian Church USA, with 35,211 adherents. In 2000, there were 168,625 Roman Catholics, 6,145 Muslims, and about 5,050 Jews throughout the state. About 39.2% of the population did not claim any religious affiliation.

Oral Roberts, a popular minister, has established a college and faith-healing hospital in Tulsa, and his "Tower of Faith" broadcasts by radio and television have made him a well-known preacher throughout the United States.

10TRANSPORTATION

In 1930, the high point for railroad transportation in Oklahoma, there were 6,678 mi (10,747 km) of railroad track in the state. In 2000, there were 3,903 rail mi (6,281 km) of track; Burlington Northern and Santa Fe had the most track, followed by Union Pacific. Kansas City Southern was the other Class I railroad operating in the state in 2000. In 1979, Amtrak terminated the state's last passenger train. Inter-urban transit needs, formerly served by streetcars (one of the most popular routes operated between Oklahoma City and Norman), are now supplied by buses.

The Department of Transportation is responsible for construction and maintenance of the state road system, which in 2000 included state roads and highways, and interstate highways. The main east-west highways are I-44, connecting Tulsa and Oklahoma City, and I-40; the major north-south route is I-35, which links Oklahoma City with Topeka, Kansas and Dallas–Ft. Worth, Texas. Overall in 2000, Oklahoma had 112,634 mi (181,266 km) of roadway. A total of 3,072,137 motor vehicles were registered in 2000, including 1,587,115 automobiles and 1,410,783 trucks. There were 2,295,036 licensed drivers.

The opening of the McClellan–Kerr Arkansas River Navigation System in 1971 linked Oklahoma with the Mississippi River and thus to Gulf coast ports. Tulsa, Port of Catoosa, is the chief port on the system, handling 1.9 million tons of cargo in 2000.

Oklahoma had 339 airports, 92 heliports, 1 stolport, and 1 seaplane base in 2002. Will Rogers World Airport in Oklahoma City and Tulsa International Airport are the state's largest airports.

11HISTORY

There is evidence—chiefly from the Spiro Mound in eastern Oklahoma, excavated in 1930—that an advanced Indian civilization inhabited the region around AD 900–1100. By the time the Spanish conquistadores, led by Hernando de Soto and Francisco Vasquez de Coronado, arrived there in the 16th century, however, only a few scattered tribes remained. Two centuries later, French trappers moved up the rivers of Oklahoma.

Except for the panhandle, which remained a no-man's-land until 1890, all of present-day Oklahoma became part of US territory with the Louisiana Purchase in 1803. Under the Indian Removal Act of 1830, Indian tribes from the southeastern US were resettled in what was then known as Indian Country. Although 4,000 Indians died along the "Trail of Tears" (from Georgia to Oklahoma) between the time of removal and the Civil War, the Five Civilized Tribes— Cherokees, Chickasaw, Choctaw, Creek, and Seminole—prospered in the new land. The eastern region that they settled, comprising not quite half of modern Oklahoma and known as Indian Territory since the early 19th century (although not formally organized under that name until 1890), offered rich soil and luxurious vegetation. White settlers also came to farm the land, but their methods depleted the soil, preparing the way for the dust bowl of the 1930s. Meanwhile, the increasing movement of people and goods between Santa Fe and New Orleans spurred further growth in the region. Military posts such as Ft. Gibson, Ft. Supply, and Ft. Towson were established between 1824 and the 1880s, with settlements growing up around them.

During the early Civil War period, the Five Civilized Tribes— some of whose members were slaveholders—allied with the Confederacy. After Union troops captured Ft. Gibson in 1863, the Union Army controlled one-half of Indian Territory. From the end of the Civil War to the 1880s, the federal government removed the eastern tribes from certain lands that were especially attractive to the railroads and to interested white settlers. Skirmishes between the Indians and the federal troops occurred, culminating in a massacre of Cheyenne Indians on 27 November 1868 by Colonel George Custer and his 7th Cavalry at the Battle of the Washita.

Amid a clamor for Indian lands, Congress opened western Oklahoma—formerly reserved for the Cherokee, Cheyenne, Fox, and other tribes—to homesteaders in 1889. Present-day Oklahoma City, Norman, Guthrie, Edmond, and Stillwater represent the eastern boundary for the 1889 "run" on Oklahoma lands; eight more runs were to follow. The greatest was in 1893, when about 100,000 people stormed onto the newly opened Cherokee outlet. The drive to get a land claim was fierce, and thousands of "Sooners" staked their claims before the land was officially opened. The western region became Oklahoma Territory, governed by a territorial legislature and a federally appointed governor in 1890; Guthrie was named the capital. Most of eastern Oklahoma continued to be governed by the Five Civilized Tribes.

Although an Oklahoma statehood bill was introduced in Congress as early as 1892, the Five Civilized Tribes resisted all efforts to unite Indian Territory until their attempt to form their own state was defeated in 1905. Congress passed an enabling act in June 1906, and Oklahoma became the 46th state on 16 November 1907 after a vote of the residents of both territories. Oklahoma City was named the state capital in 1910.

When President Theodore Roosevelt signed the statehood proclamation, Oklahoma's population was about 1,500,000— 75% rural, 25% urban—most of them drawn by the state's agricultural and mineral resources. The McAlester coal mines had opened in 1871, and lead and zinc were being mined in Ottawa County. But it was oil that made the state prosperous. Prospecting began in 1882, and the first commercial well was drilled at Bartlesville in 1897. The famous Glenn Pool gusher, near Tulsa, was struck in 1905. Oil wells were producing more than 40 million barrels annually when Oklahoma entered the Union, and the state led all others in oil production until 1928.

Generally, the decade of the 1920s was a tumultuous period for Oklahoma. A race riot in Tulsa in 1921 was put down by the National Guard. (In February 2000, a state commission recommended that the surviving victims be compensated for what has been called the nation's most violent instance of racial oppression. The recommendation launched an intense debate over whether today's taxpayers should have to pay restitution for yesterday's crimes.) Also in 1921, the Ku Klux Klan claimed close to 100,000 Oklahomans. The Klan was outlawed when Governor John C. Walton declared martial law in 1923, during a period of turmoil and violence that culminated in Walton's impeachment and conviction on charges of incompetence, corruption, and abuse of power. The 1930s brought a destructive drought, dust storms, and an exodus of "Okies," many of them to California. Colorful Governor William "Alfalfa Bill" Murray led the call for federal relief for the distressed dust bowl region—though he insisted on his right to administer the funds. When Oklahoma oil fields were glutting the market at 15 cents a barrel, Murray placed 3,106 producing wells under martial law from August 1931 to April 1933. Kansas, New Mexico, and Texas also agreed to control their oil production and under the leadership of Governor E. W. Marland, the Interstate Oil Compact was created in 1936 to conserve petroleum and stabilize prices.

Oklahoma's first native-born governor, Robert Kerr (later a senator for 14 years) held the statehouse during World War II and brought the state national recognition by promoting Oklahoma as a site for military, industrial, and conservation projects. Under early postwar governors Roy Turner, Johnston Murray, and Raymond Gary, tax reductions attracted industry, major highways were built, a loyalty oath for state employees was declared unconstitutional, and Oklahoma's higher educational facilities were integrated. The term of Governor Howard Edmondson saw the repeal of prohibition in 1959, the establishment of merit and central purchasing systems, and the introduction of a state income tax withholding plan.

Oil and gas again brought increased wealth to the state in the 1960s, 1970s, and early 1980s, as state revenues from oil and gas increased from $72 million in 1972 to $745 million in 1982. Nearly $1 billion was spent for new highways, schools, and state offices; new police were hired; and teacher salaries were raised to nationally competitive levels. Unemployment fell to 3.6% in 1981 while an influx of job seekers from other states made Oklahoma one of the fastest-growing states in the nation in the early 1980s.

In 1983, as oil prices fell in the face of a growing worldwide oil glut, the oil boom suddenly ended. Between 1982 and 1986, jobs in the extraction of oil and gas dropped by 50%. The failure of 24 banks, home mortgage foreclosures, and mounting distress among the state's farmers added to Oklahoma's financial woes. Falling state revenues and a balanced budget requirement in the state constitution compelled Governor George Nigh in 1983 to cut appropriations and to preside over a series of tax increases that lost for Oklahoma its claim to one of the lowest tax burdens in the nation.

The oil bust did not entirely devastate the Oklahoma economy. Those industries with a national rather than a regional base, such as distribution, transportation, food processing, and light manufacturing, continued to prosper, and the state's leaders made a concerted effort to diversify Oklahoma's industries even further by attracting both private enterprise and defense contracts. By the end of the decade, the economy had begun to recover, and recovery continued into the 1990s. By 1999 the unemployment rate had dropped to 3.4%, below the national average. Poverty was on the decline in the state: 15.6% of Oklahomans lived below the federal poverty level in 1990; in 1998 the rate dipped to 14.1%. But with the 10th-lowest median income in the nation, the state's income levels lagged behind, causing some analysts to predict that Oklahoma might have problems competing in a strong economy.

On 19 April 1995, the Alfred P. Murrah Federal Building in Oklahoma City was destroyed in a bomb blast that claimed 168 lives and constituted the most serious act of terrorism in the history of the United States. Governor Frank Keating was commended for his strong leadership during the crisis. A memorial to the victims was unveiled in April 2000, the five-year anniversary of the tragedy.

In 2003 Oklahoma faced its largest budget deficit in state history ($600 million). Democratic Governor Brad Henry pledged to eliminate taxes on retirement income for senior citizens, provide access to affordable prescription drugs, retain jobs in the state, improve Oklahoma schools, and increase teachers' salaries. Henry proposed a state lottery to fund education.

[12]STATE GOVERNMENT

Oklahoma's first and only constitution became effective on 16 November 1907. By January 2003, that document had been amended 165 times (including five amendments that were subsequently nullified by the courts).

The Oklahoma legislature consists of two chambers, a 48-member senate and a 101-member house of representatives. To serve in the legislature one must be a qualified voter; also, senators must be at least 25 years old and representatives at least 21. Senators hold office for four years, representatives for two. The legislature meets annually, beginning in early February, for a session limited to 160 calendar days. Special sessions may be called by a vote of two-thirds of the members of each house. The legislative salary in 2002 was $38,400, unchanged from 1999.

State elected officials are the governor, lieutenant governor, attorney general, auditor, state treasurer, superintendent of public instruction, commissioner of labor, and commissioner of insurance, all of whom serve four-year terms, and three corporation commissioners, who serve staggered six-year terms. The governor is limited to serving two consecutive terms. A candidate for governor must be a US citizen at least 31 years old and must have been a qualified voter in Oklahoma for at least 10 years preceding election. In 2002 the governor's salary was $101,040, unchanged from 1999.

Any member of either house may introduce legislation. A bill passed by the legislature becomes law if signed by the governor, if left unsigned by the governor for five days while the legislature is in session, or if passed over the governor's veto by two-thirds of the elected members of each house (three-fourths in the case of emergency bills). A bill dies after 15 days if the governor takes no action and the legislature has adjourned. Constitutional amendments may be placed on the ballot by majority vote in both houses, by initiative petition of 15% of the electorate, or by constitutional convention. To be ratified, proposed amendments must receive a majority vote of the electorate.

To vote in Oklahoma, one must be a US citizen, at least 18 years old, and a state resident. Restrictions apply to convicted felons and those declared mentally incapacitated by the court.

[13]POLITICAL PARTIES

The history of the two major political groups in Oklahoma, the Democratic and Republican parties, dates back to 1890, when Indian Territory and Oklahoma Territory were separately organized. Indian Territory was dominated by Democrats, reflecting the influence of southern immigrants, while Oklahoma Territory was primarily Republican because of immigration from the northern states. When the two territories joined for admission to the Union in 1907, Democrats outnumbered Republicans, as they have ever since. Democrats have continued to dominate the lesser state offices, but the Republicans won the governorship three times between 1962 and 1990, and the Republican presidential nominee out-polled his Democratic counterpart in ten of twelve presidential elections between 1948 and 1992. The best showing by a minor party in a recent presidential race was 25% garnered by Independent Ross Perot in 1992.

Oklahomans cast 60% of their popular vote for Republican George W. Bush in the 2000 presidential election, and 38% for Al

Gore. In 2002 there were 2,008,036 registered voters. In 1998, 57% of registered voters were Democratic, 35% Republican, and 8% unaffiliated or members of other parties. The state had eight electoral votes in the 2000 presidential election.

Democrat Brad Henry was elected governor in 2002. Republican Senator James Inhofe, first elected in a special election in 1994, was reelected to full terms in 1996 and 2002. Republican Senator Don Nickles, first elected in 1980, was reelected in 1998 to a fourth term. In 2002, Oklahoma sent four Republicans and one Democrat to the US House of Representatives. Democrats controlled the state house and senate in 2003—there were 28 Democrats and 20 Republicans in the house, and 53 Democrats and 48 Republicans in the senate.

Oklahoma Presidential Vote by Political Parties, 1948–2000

YEAR	ELECTORALOKLAHOMA VOTE WINNER	DEMOCRAT	REPUBLICAN
1948	10*Truman (D)	452,782	2687,817
1952	8*Eisenhower (R)	430,939	518,045
1956	8*Eisenhower (R)	385,581	473,769
1960	8Nixon (R)	370,111	533,039
1964	8*Johnson (D)	519,834	412,665
1968	8*Nixon (R)	301,658	449,697
1972	8*Nixon (R)	247,147	759,025
1976	8Ford (R)	532,442	545,708
1980	8*Reagan (R(	402,026	695,570
1984	8*Reagan (R)	385,080	861,530
1988	8*Bush (R)	483,423	678,367
1992**	8Bush (R)	473,066	592,929
1996**	8Dole (R)	488,105	582,315
2000***	8*Bush, G. W. (R)	474,276	744,337

* Won US presidential election.
** Independent candidate Ross Perot received 319,878 votes in 1992 and 130,788 votes in 1996.

14LOCAL GOVERNMENT

As of 2002, local governmental units in Oklahoma included 77 counties, 590 incorporated cities and towns, and several hundred unincorporated areas. There were 571 public school districts and 560 special districts that year.

County government consists of three commissioners elected by districts, a county clerk, assessor, treasurer, sheriff, surveyor, and (in most counties) superintendent of schools. Towns of 1,000 population or more may incorporate as cities. Any city of 2,000 or more people may vote to become a home-rule city, determining its own form of government, by adopting a home-rule charter. Cities electing not to adopt a home-rule charter operate under aldermanic, mayor-council, or council-manager systems. A large majority of home-rule cities have council-manager systems.

15STATE SERVICES

To address the continuing threat of terrorism and to work with the federal Department of Homeland Security (created in 2002 following the terrorist attacks of 11 September 2001), homeland security in Oklahoma in 2003 operated under state statute; the safety/security secretary was designated as the state homeland security advisor.

The Oklahoma Department of Education, functioning under a six-member appointed Board of Education and an elected superintendent of public instruction, has responsibility for all phases of education through the first 12 grades. Postsecondary study is under the general authority of the Oklahoma State Regents for Higher Education and 16 separate boards of regents associated with one or more institutions. Vocational and technical education, a federal-state cooperative program, is administered in Oklahoma under the Department of Vocational and Technical Education. The Department of Transportation has authority over the planning, construction, and maintenance of the state highway system. The Oklahoma Corporation Commission regulates transportation and transmission companies, public utilities, motor carriers, and the oil and gas industry, while the Oklahoma Aeronautics Commission participates in financing airports.

The Department of Health has as a major function the control and prevention of communicable diseases; it administers community health program funds and licenses most health-related facilities. The Department of Human Services oversees the care of neglected children, delinquent youths, and the mentally retarded and operates various facilities and programs for the handicapped, the elderly, and the infirm.

Protective services are supplied through the Oklahoma Military Department, which administers the Army and Air National Guard; the Department of Corrections, overseeing the state penitentiary and reformatory, nine adult correctional centers, and eight community treatment centers; and the Department of Public Safety, with general safety and law enforcement responsibilities, among which are licensing drivers and patrolling the highways. Natural resource protection services are centered principally in the Oklahoma Conservation Commission. The Department of Wildlife Conservation and the Wildlife Conservation Commission administer the game and fish laws.

16JUDICIAL SYSTEM

In 1967, following some of the worst judicial scandals in the history of the state, in which one supreme court justice was imprisoned for income tax evasion and another impeached on charges of bribery and corruption, Oklahoma approved a constitutional amendment to reform the state's judicial system. Under the new provisions, the supreme court, the state's highest court, consists of nine justices initially elected to six-year terms, but with additional terms pursuant to nonpartisan, noncompetitive elections; if a justice is rejected by the voters, the vacancy is filled by gubernatorial appointment, subject to confirmation by the electorate. The court's appellate jurisdiction includes all civil cases (except those which it assigns to the courts of appeals), while its original jurisdiction extends to general supervisory control over all inferior courts and agencies created by law.

The highest appellate court for criminal cases is the court of criminal appeals, a five-member body filled in the same manner as the supreme court. Courts of civil appeals, created by the legislature in 1968, are located in Tulsa and Oklahoma City; each has six elective judges with powers to hear civil cases assigned to them by the supreme court. When final, their decisions are not appealable to any other state court, a system unique to Oklahoma.

District courts have original jurisdiction over all judicial matters and some review powers over administrative actions. There are 26 districts with 131 district judges who are elected to four-year terms. Municipal courts hear cases arising from local ordinances. As of June 2001, over 23,139 prisoners were under the jurisdiction of state and federal authorities, an increase of 0.6% over the previous year. The state's incarceration rate stood at 669 per 100,000 inhabitants.

In 2001 the FBI reported a crime index total of 4,607.0 crimes per 100,000 population, including a total of 17,726 violent crimes and 141,679 crimes against property in that year. Oklahoma law permits capital punishment by lethal injection for several felony crimes. A total of 65 persons were executed between 1977 and 2003. In 2003, 114 prisoners were under sentence of death.

[17]ARMED FORCES

In 2002, there were 23,664 active-duty military personnel and 21,972 civilian personnel stationed in Oklahoma, the majority of whom were at Ft. Sill, near Lawton, the training facility for the Artillery Branch. A total of nearly $1.6 billion in prime military contracts was received by local businesses in 2002.

According to the 2000 Census, 376,062 veterans were living in Oklahoma, of whom 66,698 saw service in World War II; 42,946 in the Korean conflict; 116,672 during the Vietnam era; and 48,681 during 1990–2000 (including the Persian Gulf War). Veterans' benefits for 2002 were more than $1 billion.

In 2000, the Oklahoma Highway Patrol employed 782 full-time sworn officers.

[18]MIGRATION

Early immigrants to what is now Oklahoma included explorers, adventurers, and traders who made the country conscious of the new territory, and Indian tribes forcibly removed from the East and Midwest. The interior plains of Oklahoma remained basically unchanged until white settlers came in the late 1880s.

Coal mining brought miners from Italy to the McAlester and Krebs area in the 1870s, and Poles migrated to Bartlesville to work in the lead and zinc smelters. British and Irish coal miners came to Indian Territory because they could earn higher wages there than in their native countries, and Czechs and Slovaks arrived from Nebraska, Kansas, Iowa, and Texas when railroad construction began. Mexicans also worked as railroad laborers, ranch hands, and coal miners before statehood. The oil boom of the early 20th century brought an influx of workers from the eastern and Midwestern industrial regions. In 1907, the population of Oklahoma was 75% rural and 25% urban; by 1990, however, 67.7% of all inhabitants resided in urban areas. Oklahoma lost population during the 1930s because of dust bowl and drought conditions, and the trend toward out-migration continued after World War II; from 1940 through 1960, the net loss from migration was 653,000. Migration patterns were reversed, however, after 1960. From 1960 to 1970 nearly 21,000 more people moved into the state than out of it. In the period 1970–80, a total of 293,500 more people came than left, the migration accounting for nearly two-thirds of Oklahoma's total increase of 466,000 persons in that decade. From 1980 to 1983, Oklahoma ranked 4th among the states with a total net gain from migration of 186,000 people. From 1985 to 1990, a net migration loss of about 95,500 was reported. Between 1990 and 1998, the state had net gains of 48,000 in domestic migration and 26,000 in international migration. In 1998, 2,273 foreign immigrants arrived in Oklahoma. The state's overall population increased 6.4% between 1990 and 1998. In the period 1995–2000, 322,500 people moved into the state and 305,613 moved out, for a net gain of 16,887, many whom were from Texas.

[19]INTERGOVERNMENTAL COOPERATION

Oklahoma participates in a number of regional intergovernmental agreements, among them the Arkansas River Compact, Arkansas River Basin Compact, Canadian River Compact, Interstate Oil and Gas Compact, Red River Compact, South Central Interstate Forest Fire Protection Compact, Southern Growth Policies Board, Southern States Energy Board, Southern Regional Education Board, Interstate Mining Compact Commission, and the Central Interstate Low-Level Radioactive Waste Compact. Federal grants in 2001 totaled over $4.1 billion.

[20]ECONOMY

Primarily an agricultural state through the first half of the 20th century, Oklahoma has assumed a broader economic structure since the 1950s. Manufacturing heads the list of growth sectors, followed by wholesale and retail trade, services, finance, insurance, and real estate. Oil and gas extraction continues to play a major role. The oil industry boomed from the mid-1970s through the mid-1980s. In 1985, however, the boom ended. Prices dropped from $27 a barrel to $13 a barrel within a month in 1985. In 1998, gas and oil production was valued at only $3.4 billion; one-third of what it was worth in the mid-1980s. Oklahoma's unemployment rate, which averaged about 3% in the early 1980s, jumped to 9% in 1983, and then fell to 7% in 1985, and rose again, to 8%, in 1986. Since then, the economy has undergone a slow but steady recovery. Unemployment was at 3.4% in 1999. Gains in manufacturing made up for the losses in mining. Manufacturing output, however, peaked in 1999, and by 2001 had fallen 9.2%. The state's overall growth rate, which accelerated from 3.5% in 1998 to 3.9% in 1999 to 6.5% in 2000, fell back to 3.2% in the national recession and slowdown of 2001. The main growth sectors in terms of output coming into the 21st century (1997 to 2001) were general services (up 26.8%), government (up 24.2%), financial services (up 2.5%) and trade (up 21.3%). The impact of the national slowdown is expected to be mitigated by Oklahoma's military installations (Fort Sill and Tinder Air Force Base are two of the state's top five employers) in a time of rising defense spending, and by its oil and gas industry as prices reach new highs in 2003.

In 2001, Oklahoma's gross state product gross state product was $93.9 billion, the 29th largest among the states, to which general services contributed $17.6 billion; government, $15.8 billion; trade, $15.4 billion; manufacturing, $13 billion; financial services, $11.9 billion; transportation and public utilities, $8.8 billion; and construction, $3.9 billion. The public sector in 2001 constituted 16.8% of gross state product, well above the 12% average for the states.

[21]INCOME

According to the Bureau of Economic Analysis, in 2001, Oklahoma had a per capita personal income (PCPI) of $24,945 which ranked 40th in the United States (including the District of Columbia) and was 82% of the national average, $30,413. The 2001 PCPI reflected an increase of 3.9% from 2000 compared to the national change of 2.2%. In 2001, Oklahoma had a total personal income (TPI) of $86,549,589,000 which ranked 29th in the United States and accounted for 1% of the national total. The 2001 TPI reflected an increase of 4.4% from 2000 compared to the national change of 3.3%.

Earnings of persons employed in Oklahoma increased from $57,597,895,000 in 2000 to $59,936,900,000 in 2001, an increase of 4.1%. The largest industries in 2001 were services, 24.3% of earnings; state and local government, 13.7%; and retail trade, 9.4%. Of the industries that accounted for at least 5% of earnings in 2001, the slowest growing from 2000 to 2001 was durable goods manufacturing (8.1% of earnings in 2001), which decreased 7.6%; the fastest was state and local government, which increased 11.5%.

According to data released by the US Census Bureau, in 2000, the median household income was $32,445 compared to the national average of $42,148. In 2001, the median income for a family of four was $53,949 compared to the national average of $63,278. For the period 1999 to 2001, the average poverty rate was 14.3% which placed it 42nd among the 50 states and the District of Columbia ranked lowest to highest.

[22]LABOR

According to Bureau of Labor Statistics (BLS) provisional estimates, in July 2003 the seasonally adjusted civilian labor force in Oklahoma numbered 1,703,400, with approximately 93,600 workers unemployed, yielding an unemployment rate of 5.5%, compared to the national average of 6.2% for the same period. Since the beginning of the BLS data series in 1978, the highest unemployment rate recorded was 9.7% in May 1983. The historical low was 2.9% in February 2000. In 2001, an estimated 5.2% of the labor force was employed in construction; 13.2% in manufacturing; 5.7% in transportation, communications, and public utilities; 18.2% in trade; 4.4% in finance, insurance, and real estate; 23.6% in services; 16.4% in government; and 3.4% in agriculture.

The US Department of Labor reported that in 2002, 127,000 of Oklahoma's 1,421,000 employed wage and salary workers were members of unions. This represented 8.9% of those so employed, up from 8.4% in 2001. The national average is 13.2%. In all, 150,000 workers (10.6%) were represented by unions. In addition to union members, this category includes workers who report no union affiliation but whose jobs are covered by a union contract. Oklahoma became the 22nd state with a right-to-work law when its legislature adopted both a constitutional amendment and passed a law in 2001 .

23AGRICULTURE

Agriculture remains an important economic activity in Oklahoma, even though its relative share of personal income and employment has declined since 1950. Total farm income, estimated at $4.03 billion, ranked 20th in the US in 2001. Crop marketings contributed $874 million, livestock $3.13 billion.

As of 2002, Oklahoma had 87,000 farms and ranches covering 34,000,000 acres (13,760,000 hectares). The state ranked 5th in the US for wheat production in 2002, with 98,000,000 bushels worth $343 million. Peanut production ranked 6th in 2002, with 159,600,000 lb, valued at $27,132,000. Other 2002 crop figures include sorghum for grain, 14,850,000 bushels, $34,927,000; soybeans, 7,000,000 bushels, $37,800,000; corn for grain, 24,700,000 bushels, $60,515,000; and oats, 1,110,000 bushels, $2,220,000.

Virtually all of Oklahoma's wheat production is located in the western half of the state; cotton (200,000 bales in 2002) is grown in the southwest corner. Sorghum-producing regions include the panhandle, central to southwestern Oklahoma, and the northeast corner of the state.

24ANIMAL HUSBANDRY

In 2003, there were 5.4 million cattle and calves, worth $3.5 billion. During 2002, Oklahoma farmers had 2.49 million hogs and pigs, valued at $146.9 million. In 2001, the state produced around 3.2 million lb (1.5 million kg) of sheep and lambs which brought in nearly $2.2 million in gross income. Also during 2001, poultry farmers produced 1.11 billion lb (0.5 billion kg) of broilers, and 926 million eggs valued at $65 million. Oklahoma's 89,000 dairy cows produced an estimated 1.29 billion lb (0.59 billion kg) of milk in 2001.

25FISHING

Commercial fishing is of minor importance in Oklahoma. The prolific white bass (sand bass), Oklahoma's state fish, is abundant in most large reservoirs. Smallmouth and spotted bass, bluegill, and channel catfish have won favor with fishermen. Rainbow trout are stocked year round in the Illinois River, and walleye and sauger are stocked in most reservoirs. In 1998, the state issued 637,557 sport fishing licenses.

26FORESTRY

While Oklahoma is not generally known as a forested state, a significant amount of forest is found there. Oklahoma's forests cover approximately 7,665,000 acres (3,102,000 hectares) or nearly 17% of the state's land area. Approximately 65% of this is commercially productive forestland. These forests are about 95% privately owned. They are intensively utilized for lumber, plywood, paper, fuelwood, and other products. They also provide

high quality drinking water for the state's two largest cities, excellent wildlife habitat, substantial protection against soil erosion, and numerous recreational opportunities.

Oklahoma's forests play a vital role in the economy in the eastern half of the state. Much of the timber harvested in Oklahoma is shipped to processing plants in western Arkansas. Nearly two million acres of the loblolly-shortleaf pine and shortleaf pine-oak forests support several major wood processing plants in the southeastern corner of the state. Hardwood processing is scattered over the entire forested area in smaller sawmills. In the late 1980s and early 1990s, Oklahoma's eastern red cedar forests and woodlands supported a surge in processing plants.

In 1999 roundwood output from Oklahoma's forests totaled 120 million cu ft (3.4 million cu m). Mill byproducts generated from primary manufacturers totaled 51 million cu ft (1.44 million cu m). In the same year, Oklahoma had 67 primary processing plants.

27MINING

Large deposits of limestone are found throughout northeastern Oklahoma, while gypsum is extracted in the northwest, the west-central region, and the four southwesternmost counties. Oklahoma was a leading producer of lead and zinc until the 1970s.

The value of nonfuel mineral production in Oklahoma in 2001 was estimated at $530 million, a 7.3% increase over 2000. Crushed stone continued as the state's leading mineral commodity, accounting for about 40% of the total nonfuel mineral value in 2001. Together with construction sand and gravel and gypsum it accounted for more than 50% of the total. Oklahoma remained the only state producing crude iodine, with a value of $20.9 million for the production of 1,340 metric tons. The state remained first of 20 states producing crude gypsum, with 2.65 million metric tons worth $23.3 million in 2001. It was 2nd of four states producing tripoli, 3rd in crude helium, and 5th in feldspar. The combined value of cement, feldspar, helium, lime, salt, and tripoli was $187 million. In 2001, Oklahoma ranked 31st in the US in nonfuel mineral value.

28ENERGY AND POWER

Electric power production in Oklahoma in 1999 (utility and nonutility) was 55 billion kWh, based on an installed capacity of 13.5 million kW. Coal-fired steam units accounted for 61%, natural gas-fired units 33%, and hydroelectricity 6%. There were no nuclear power plants as of 1 January 1999. In 2000 Oklahoma's total per capita energy consumption was 406 million Btu (102.3 million kcal), ranking it 12th among the 50 states.

Oklahoma is rich in fossil fuel resources, producing oil, natural gas, and coal. Crude oil production declined from 223.6 million barrels in 1968, to 150.5 million barrels in 1978, to 70.6 million barrels in 1999. Production was 183,000 barrels per day in 2002. Proved reserves of crude oil were estimated at 556 million barrels at the close of 2001. In 2002, Oklahoma's natural gas output was 1.62 trillion cu ft (0.05 trillion cu m), leaving reserves of 13.56 trillion cu ft (0.038 trillion cu m).

Production of bituminous coal fell from a record high of 6.1 million tons in 1978 to 1.6 million tons in 2000. Of eight coal mines in the state, all but one were surface mines. Recoverable reserves totaled 19 million tons in 2001.

29INDUSTRY

Oklahoma's earliest manufactures were based on agricultural and petroleum production. As late as 1939, the food-processing and petroleum-refining industries together accounted for one-third of the total value added by manufacture. Although resource-related industries continue to predominate, manufacturing was much more diversified in 1997. The total value of shipments of manufactured goods was more than $38 billion, with only 10% from fuel extraction and refining, and 10% from food. In 1997, four Fortune 500 companies were headquartered in Oklahoma: Fleming, Phillips Petroleum, Williams, and Mapco.

Earnings of persons employed in Oklahoma increased from $48.3 billion in 1997 to $51.1 billion in 1998, an increase of 5.9%. The largest industries in 1998 were services, 24.6% of earnings; state and local government, 12.4%; and durable goods manufacturing, 10.4%. Of the industries that accounted for at least 5% of earnings in 1998, the slowest growing from 1997 to 1998 was state and local government, which increased 2.8%; the fastest was services, which increased 6.8%.

30COMMERCE

In 1997, Oklahoma had 6,037 wholesale establishments, with sales of over $30 billion. Retail sales totaled $28 billion in 1997. Retail establishments had personal incomes totaling $3 billion in 1997. Automotive dealers accounted for 15% of the total number of establishments in 1997, followed by food stores, 13%; and eating and drinking places, 28%. Food sales totaled $4.3 billion, while general merchandise sales totaled $4.2 billion. The value of foreign exports produced within Oklahoma in 1998 was $2.9 billion. Major exports included industrial machinery (33%) to Europe, and transportation equipment (20%) to Canada.

31CONSUMER PROTECTION

A Uniform Consumer Credit Code, passed in 1969, prohibits discrimination because of sex or marital status. It is administered by the Commission on Consumer Credit, which also maintains a program of consumer education and has the power to require lawful and businesslike procedures by lending agencies. The attorney general is responsible for enforcing the state's Consumer Protection Act through the Consumer Protection Division.

32BANKING

In 2002, Oklahoma had 280 insured banks, of which 181 were state-chartered. That same year, the state's insured banks had assets totaling $54.7 billion. The failure of the Penn Square Bank in 1982 led to a series of mergers between strong institutions and distressed smaller ones and a 1983 revision of the state's banking laws which allowed for the restructuring of the industry. Concurrently, Oklahoma's banks were adversely affected by proposals to ease restrictions on reciprocal interstate banking in Missouri and Texas.

The State Banking Department has the responsibility for supervising all state-chartered banks, savings and loan associations, credit unions, and trust companies.

Although the residential and commercial real estate sectors in Oklahoma were weak in 2002, insured banks in the state performed well. Banks reported their highest nine-month average return on assets (ROA) ratio (the measure of earnings in relation to all resources) in a decade as of September 2002.

Oklahoma is the only state in the Southwest region in which the per capita bankruptcy rate was higher than the national average. As of 2002, consumer debt and bankruptcy filings trended upward, which was projected to weaken banks' credit quality. Due to significant levels of government support, agricultural banks reported strong conditions in 2002.

33INSURANCE

As of 2000, there were 55 property and casualty and 29 life and health insurance companies incorporated or organized in the state. In 2001, property and casualty insurers wrote over $3.8 billion in premiums. That year, there were 14,537 flood insurance policies in force in the state, with a total value of $1.4 million.

In 2001, there were 1.6 million ordinary life insurance policies in force, with a total value of $91.0 billion; total value for all categories of life insurance (ordinary, group, industrial, and credit) was $149.7 billion. Death benefits paid that year totaled $513.1 million.

34SECURITIES

There are no stock or commodity exchanges in Oklahoma. The state has 713 broker-dealers companies with 3,634 employees; 71 investment advisory organizations do business in Oklahoma. The state is home to 32 NASDAQ companies, two NASDAQ market makers, 11 AMEX companies; and Oklahoma has incorporated nine NYSE-listed companies. The top five are: Auto Nation, Inc., Waste Management, Intl., OGE Energy Corp., SLI, Inc., and Parker Drilling.

35PUBLIC FINANCE

The Oklahoma budget is prepared by the director of state finance and submitted by the governor to the legislature each February. Article 10, section 23 of the Oklahoma Constitution requires a balanced budget. The constitution establishes a "Rainy Day" Fund into which general revenue fund revenues in excess of the certified estimate are deposited for emergency appropriation at a later date. All funds are "appropriated" pursuant to the constitution. In addition, state law authorizes a cash-flow reserve fund that can be up to 10% of the approved budget. The fiscal year is 1 July–30 June.

Taxes in Oklahoma provide over half of total treasury funds. In 2000/01, general fund revenues, at $5.055 billion, were comfortably above expenditures, which were $4.819 billion. In 2002/03, however, revenues dropped to $4.791 billion, and Oklahoma has since been faced with serious budget problems, particularly as costs have continued to rise. Across-the-board cuts have been mandated, as are required by the constitution. In 2001/02, the legislature made cuts totaling $173.7 million in the budget after it was enacted; in 2002/03, post-enactment cuts reached $427.2 million. Oklahoma's budget deficit was estimated at 20.6% of its state budget for 2002/03, and was projected at 15.9% of the state budget for 2003/04. In 2000/01, Oklahoma had a starting balance equal to 13.1% of expenditures. By 2002/03, the starting balance had dropped to 1% of expenditures.

The following table from the US Census Bureau contains information on revenues, expenditures, indebtedness, and cash/securities for 2001.

	($000)	PERCENT	PER CAPITA
Population (thousands, 2001)	3,470	(X)	(X)
Total Revenue	12,745,926	100.00	3,673.18
General revenue	12,193,457	95.67	3,513.96
Utility revenue	331,088	2.60	95.41
Insurance trust revenue	221,381	1.74	63.80
Exhibit: Salaries and wages	2,055,605	18.01	592.39
Total expenditure	11,416,492	100.00	3,290.06
General expenditure	9,797,462	85.82	2,823.48
Education	4,979,111	43.61	1,434.90
Public welfare	708,873	6.21	204.29
Hospitals	166,664	1.46	48.03
Health	379,888	3.33	109.48
Highways	1,294,774	11.34	373.13
Police protection	81,281	0.71	23.42
Correction	486,255	4.26	140.13
Natural resources	253,499	2.22	73.05
Parks and recreation	77,846	0.68	22.43
Government administration	436,448	3.82	125.78
Interest on general debt	251,903	2.21	72.59
Other and unallocable	680,920	5.96	196.23
Utility expenditure	299,172	2.62	86.22
Insurance trust expenditure	1,319,858	11.56	380.36
Debt at end of fiscal year	5,985,516	100.00	1,724.93
Cash and security holdings	24,581,619	100.00	7,084.04

³⁶TAXATION

The state income tax on Oklahoma's 8-bracket schedule ranges from 0.5% to 7%. The corporate tax on net income is 6.0%, and the franchise tax equals $1.25 per $1,000 invested in Oklahoma. The state levies a sales and use tax of 4.5%, and many municipalities levy their own sales taxes, ranging from none to 6%. The typical city in Oklahoma has an 8% or 9% sales tax, but collections are reduced by competition from Indian reservations where there is little or no sales tax. The state also imposes a full array of excise taxes covering motor fuels, tobacco products, insurance premiums, public utilities, alcoholic beverages, amusements, pari-mutuels, and other selected items. It is estimated, however, that about a third of all cigarettes are bought in Indian territories where the state excises do not apply. The severance tax on oil and gas is 7% of gross value; on uranium, 5%; and on asphalt and minerals, up to 1%. The gas conservation excise tax is 7 cents per million cu ft. There is no inheritance tax, but the state estate tax is tied to the federal tax exemption for state death taxes, and is thus scheduled to be phased out in tandem with the federal exemption by 2007 unless the legislature takes countervailing action. Oklahoma's revenue losses from the phasing out of its estate tax are estimated at -$4.6 million for 2002/03, -$10.3 million for 2003/04 and -$11.5 million for 2006/07. Death and gift taxes accounted for 1.4% of state collections in 2002. Other state taxes include various license fees and stamp taxes. Property taxes, although the third lowest per capita in the US (next to New Mexico and Alabama), are collected only at the local level and remain the principal source of revenue for local governments. In 2000, the local level governments collected 38.2% of total state and local revenues.

Total state tax collections in Oklahoma in 2002 were $6.053 billion (down almost $300 million from 2001). In 2003, combined state and local taxes amounted to 9.1% of income, and Oklahoma was ranked 35th highest rate in the country in terms of state and local tax burden.

The following table from the US Census Bureau provides a summary of taxes collected by the state in 2002.

	($000)	PER CAPITA
Total Taxes	6,052,680	1,732.45
Property taxes	(X)	(X)
Sales and gross receipts	2,272,729	650.52
General sales and gross receipts	1,529,465	437.78
Selective sales taxes	743,264	212.74
Alcoholic beverage	64,729	18.53
Amusements	7,002	2
Insurance Premiums	149,018	42.65
Motor fuels	410,353	117.45
Pari-mutuels	3,078	0.88
Public utilities	19,771	5.66
Tobacco products	71,501	20.47
Other selective sales	17,812	5.1
Licenses	823,394	235.68
Alcoholic beverages	5,502	1.57
Amusements	5,907	1.69
Corporation	43,528	12.46
Hunting and fishing	16,079	4.6
Motor vehicle	568,820	162.81
Motor vehicle operators	12,272	3.51
Public utility	5	0
Occupation and business, NEC	170,916	48.92
Other	365	0.1
Other taxes	2,956,557	846.25
Individual income	2,286,110	654.35
Corporation net income	173,701	49.72
Death and gift	85,976	24.61
Documentary and stock transfer	9,511	2.72
Severance	364,459	104.32
Other	36,800	10.53

³⁷ECONOMIC POLICY

Pro-business measures in Oklahoma include comparatively low property tax rates, limits on annual increases in property tax rates, and requirements that tax increases be submitted to a vote of the people or pass the legislature with a 75% vote.

Business incentives include wage rebates of up to 5% for 10 years for qualifying basic firms that add at least $2.5 million of new payroll in the state over a three-year period. This incentive, known as the Oklahoma Quality Jobs Program, was adopted in July 1993. Since that time, more than 130 firms have received in excess of $35 million in incentive payments while adding more than 26,000 jobs to the Oklahoma economy. More than 55,000 jobs were planned to be added by the year 2005.

Other incentives include a job tax credit of $1,000 per year for five years for new manufacturing jobs in state enterprise zones; a 30% investment tax credit for investment in qualifying agricultural processing ventures or cooperatives; and free customized training for qualifying firms from the Oklahoma Department of Vocational and Technical Education through its Training in Industry Program (TIP). In 2002, the state put emphasis on the Oklahoma Main Street Program, a statewide downtown revitalization program providing training, resources, and technical assistance to 36 targeted Main Street communities. The Oklahoma Main Street Program was first created in late 1985. From 1986 to 2002, 44 communities received technical assistance and training through the program.

³⁸HEALTH

In 2000, the infant mortality rate was 8.5 per 1,000 live births, higher than the national rate of 6.9. In 1998, there were 6,769 legal abortions performed in Oklahoma, a ratio of 10 per 1,000 women. The overall death rate for 2000was one of the highest in the US at 1,037.8 per 100,000 inhabitants, well above the national rate of 873.1. The leading causes of death in Oklahoma in 2000 (with their death rates per 100,000 population) were heart disease, 334.2; cancer, 219.0; accidents, 46.3; and cerebrovascular disease, 73.8. The HIV mortality rate was 3.3 per 100,000. A total of 4,030 AIDS cases had been reported in Oklahoma through 2001. Among adults ages 18 and older, 23.3% were smokers in 2000, equal with the median US rate of 23.3% .

Oklahoma's 108 community hospitals had 434,831 admissions and 11,207 beds in 2001. There were 10,264 full-time registered nurses and 2,807 full-time licensed practical nurses in 2001 and only 184 physicians per 100,000 population in 2000. The average expense of a community hospital for care was $1,075.80 per inpatient day in 2001.

Federal government grants to cover the Medicare and Medicaid services in 2001 totaled $1.6 billion; 510,582 enrollees received Medicare benefits that year. At least 18.3% of Oklahoma's residents were uninsured in 2002.

³⁹SOCIAL WELFARE

In 2001, the average weekly unemployment benefit was $229.29. Average monthly participation in the food stamp program in FY2002 comprised 316,684 persons (129,934 households). The average monthly benefit was $75.90, and the sum total of benefits paid in FY2002 was $288,441,518.

With the enactment of the Personal Responsibility and Work Opportunity Reconciliation Act of 1996, the US government has changed the form and regulations for many of its social welfare programs. Most significantly, it replaces Aid to Families with Dependent Children (AFDC), an open-ended entitlement program, with Temporary Assistance for Needy Families (TANF), a limited system of assistance funded largely through federal block grants. The reform act also impacts the food stamp program, the Supplemental Security Income program, and the child nutrition program. The law took effect on 1 July 1997 and provided $16.38 billion in block grants for fiscal years 1997–2002. The grants are to be divided among the states based on an equation involving the numbers of former AFDC recipients in each state.

Reauthorization of the 1996 social welfare legislation, scheduled for 2002, was delayed, and the original law had been extended three times as of July 2003, with the most recent extension running through September 2003. In June 2000 the state had 13,606 welfare recipients. State expenditures on the TANF program in FY2002 totaled $61,076,784.

In December 2001, Social Security benefits were paid to 597,270 Oklahoma residents. This number included 367,050 retired workers, 72,010 widows and widowers, 68,900 disabled workers, 39,230 spouses, and 50,080 children. Social Security beneficiaries represented 17.3% of the total state population and 93% of the state's population age 65 and older. Retired workers (excluding persons with special benefits) received an average monthly payment of $835; widows and widowers, $790; disabled workers, $802; and spouses, $414. Payments for children of retired workers averaged $420 per month; children of deceased workers, $552; and children of disabled workers, $237.

Federal Supplemental Security Income payments in December 2001 went to 72,756 Oklahoma residents, averaging $349 a month.

40 HOUSING

Indian tepees and settlers' sod houses dotted the Oklahoma plains when the "eighty-niners" swarmed into the territory; old neighborhoods in cities and towns of Oklahoma still retain some of the modest frame houses they built. Oklahomans continue to prefer single-family dwellings, despite a recent trend toward condominiums. Modern underground homes and solar-heated dwellings can be seen in the university towns of Norman and Stillwater.

In 2002, there were an estimated 1,541,518 housing units, of which 1,338,651 were occupied; 68.7% were owner-occupied. About 72.2% of all units were single-family, detached homes. Utility gas and electricity were the most common energy sources for heating. It was estimated that 81,042 units lacked telephone service, 8,856 lacked complete plumbing facilities, and 7,351 lacked complete kitchen facilities. The average household size was 2.52 people.

In 2002, 12,979 new privately owned units were authorized for construction. The median home value was $79,839. The median monthly cost for mortgage owners was $832. Renters paid a median of $503 per month. During 2002, Oklahoma received over $59.3 million in community planning and development aid from the US Department of Housing and Urban Development.

41 EDUCATION

In 2000, 80.6% of all Oklahomans 25 years of age or older were high school graduates; during the same year, 20.3% of adult state residents had obtained a bachelor's degree or higher.

The total enrollment for fall 1999 in Oklahoma's public schools stood at 627,032. Of these, 446,719 attended schools from kindergarten through grade eight, and 180,313 attended high school. Minority students made up approximately 34% of the total enrollment in public elementary and secondary schools. Total enrollment was estimated at 625,577 in fall 2000 and is expected to drop to 596,000 by fall 2005. Education is the largest expenditure item in the state budget. Expenditures for public education in 2000/01 were estimated at $625,577. Enrollment in nonpublic schools in fall 2001 was 31,276.

As of fall 2000, there were 203,262 students enrolled in college or graduate school. In the same year Oklahoma had 50 degree-granting institutions. Public higher education institutions include 2 comprehensive institutions, 6 regional campuses, 18 senior and junior colleges, and a professional college. The comprehensive institutions, the University of Oklahoma (Norman) and Oklahoma State University (Stillwater), also offer major graduate-level programs. There are 21 private colleges and universities. Well-known institutions include Oral Roberts University and the University of Tulsa. In 1997, minority students comprised 21.9% of total postsecondary enrollment.

42 ARTS

Major arts centers are located in Tulsa and Oklahoma City, but there are many arts and crafts museums throughout the state. Oklahoma City's leading cultural institution is the Oklahoma City Philharmonic. The Tulsa Philharmonic, Tulsa Ballet Theater, and Tulsa Opera all appear at the Tulsa Performing Arts Center, a municipally owned and operated facility. This six-level center consists of a 2,500-seat concert hall, 450-seat theater, and two multilevel experimental theaters.

There are five other ballet companies located in Oklahoma City, Bartlesville, Clinton, Lawton, and Norman. The intermingling of Native American, American West, and Euro-American art traditions infuses all aspects of Oklahoma culture. Native American contributions to the arts include achievements in art and sculpture, as well as the international acclaim accorded to ballerinas Maria and Marjorie Tallchief, Rosella Hightower, and Moscelyne Larkin.

Bartlesville is home to a symphony orchestra, a show choir, a civic ballet, and a theater guild. It is also the host of the annual OK Mozart International Festival, established in 1985, which features the Solisti New York Orchestra and attracts world-class guest artists.

In 2003, the State Arts Council of Oklahoma and other Oklahoma arts organizations received grants totaling $715,000 from the National Endowment for the Arts. The State Arts Council of Oklahoma also received funding from the state and private sources. Among the organizations that typically benefit from federal funding are the Metropolitan Library Commission of Oklahoma Country, the Red Earth Native American Cultural Festival, and the Theater of North Tulsa. The Oklahoma Humanities Council was founded in 1971. In 2000, the National Endowment for the Humanities contributed $686,699 for 10 state programs. There are about 400 arts associations and 70 local arts councils in Oklahoma.

43 LIBRARIES AND MUSEUMS

Six multi-county, two city-county, and six county libraries serve 42 counties, while five bookmobiles aid in serving counties without libraries of their own. In 2000 a total of 6,383,236 volumes occupied public library shelves; total circulation was 16,214,000. The Five Civilized Tribes Museum Library in Muskogee has a large collection of Indian documents and art, while the Cherokee archives are held at the Cherokee National Historical Society in Tahlequah. The Morris Swett Library at Ft. Sill has a special collection on military history, particularly field artillery. The Oklahoma Department of Libraries in Oklahoma City has holdings covering law, library science, Oklahoma history, and other fields. Large academic libraries include those of the University of Oklahoma (Norman), with 3,642,653 volumes and 10,496 periodical subscriptions in 1998, and Oklahoma State University Library (Stillwater), with 2,025,168. Total public library income in 2000 was $61,141,000, including $550,269 in federal grants and $1,834,230 in state grants. Per capita spending was $14.87.

Oklahoma has 113 museums and historic sites. The Philbrook Art Center in Tulsa houses important collections of Indian, Renaissance, and Oriental art. Also in Tulsa are the Thomas

Gilcrease Institute of American History and Art. Major museums in Norman are the University of Oklahoma's Museum of Art and the Stovall Museum of Science and Industry. The Oklahoma Art Center, National Cowboy Hall of Fame and Western Heritage Center, Oklahoma Heritage Association, Oklahoma Historical Society Museum, Oklahoma Museum of Art, State Museum of Oklahoma, and the Omniplex Science Museum are major attractions in Oklahoma City. Other museums of special interest include the Museum of the Great Plains in Lawton, the Will Rogers Memorial in Claremore, Cherokee National Museum in Tahlequah, and the Woolaroc Museum in Bartlesville.

44 COMMUNICATIONS

The Butterfield Stage and Overland Mail delivered the mail to Millerton on 18 September 1858 as part of the first US transcontinental postal route. After the Civil War, the early railroads delivered mail and parcels to the Oklahoma and Indian territories.

In 2001, 93.0% of Oklahoma's occupied housing units had telephones. In 2003, Oklahoma had 24 major AM and 55 major FM radio stations, and 19 major television channels. Oklahoma City had 600,240 television households, 63% of which received cable. A total of 44,743 Internet domain names were registered in the state in 2000.

45 PRESS

In 2002, Oklahoma had 12 morning dailies, 31 evening dailies, and 36 Sunday newspapers. Leading dailies and their approximate circulation in 2002 were as follows:

AREA	NAME	DAILY	SUNDAY
Oklahoma City	*Oklahoman* (m,S)	195,454	283,519
Tulsa	*Tulsa World* (m,S)	139,383	201,130

As of 1997 there were 153 newspapers that appeared weekly or up to three times a week; most had circulations of less than 10,000 copies.

Tulsa and Oklahoma City each have monthly city-interest publications and the University of Oklahoma has a highly active university press.

46 ORGANIZATIONS

In 2003, there were about 1,461 regional, national, and international organizations within the state. Among the organizations headquartered in Oklahoma are the Football Writers Association of America, Edmond; the International Professional Rodeo Association, Pauls Valley; the National Judges Association, Maud; the National Pigeon Association, Newalla; the Amateur Softball Association of America and the International Softball Federation, both in Oklahoma City; and the American Association of Petroleum Geologists, the Gas Processors Association, and the US Jaycees, all located in Tulsa.

Organizations focusing on the arts include the American Choral Directors Association and Sweet Adelines International. Historical and cultural organizations include the Cherokee National Historical Society, the Institute of the Great Plains, and the National Cowboy and Western Heritage Museum. Organizations dedicated to the rights and welfare of Native Americans include the American Indian Institute, American Indian Research and Development, and the Institute for the Development of Indian Law.

47 TOURISM, TRAVEL, AND RECREATION

Tourism has become a growing sector of Oklahoma's economy. Domestic travelers spent $3.8 billion on overnight and day trips in 2000, a 5.2% increase over 1999. The travel industry employed over 71,700 people in the same year.

Oklahoma's 45 state parks and recreational areas draw some 16 million visitors annually. The national park service maintains one facility in Oklahoma—Chickasaw National Recreation Area, centering on artificial Lake Arbuckle.

The state also maintains and operates the American Indian Hall of Fame, in Anadarko; Black Kettle Museum, in Cheyenne; the T. B. Ferguson Home in Watonga; the Murrell Home, south of Tahlequah; the Pawnee Bill Museum, in Pawnee; the Pioneer Woman Statue and Museum, in Ponca City; the Chisholm Trail Museum, in Kingfisher; and the Western Trails Museum, in Clinton.

National wildlife refuges include Optima, Salt Plains, Sequoyah, Tishomingo, Washita, and Wichita Mountains; they have a combined area of 140,696 acres (56,938 hectares).

48 SPORTS

Oklahoma has no major league professional sports teams. The class-AAA baseball Red Hawks play in Oklahoma City, and the Tulsa Drillers play in the AA Texas League. Collegiate sports, however, is the primary source of pride for Oklahomans. As of 2003, the University of Oklahoma Sooners had won seven national football titles. They won the Orange Bowl in 1954, 1956, 1958, 1959, 1968, 1976, 1979, 1980, 1981, 1986, and 1987. They have also produced championships in wrestling, baseball, and gymnastics. Recently, the Sooners have had a resurgence in basketball as well. The Oklahoma State University Cowboys have captured NCAA and Big Eight titles in basketball, baseball, and golf, and are a perennial national contender in wrestling.

Oklahoma City hosts the rodeo at the Oklahoma state fair every September and October. In golf, Tulsa has been the site of several US Open tournaments. The Softball Hall of Fame is in Oklahoma City.

Jim Thorpe, possibly the greatest athlete of all time, was born in Oklahoma, as were baseball greats Mickey Mantle and Johnny Bench.

49 FAMOUS OKLAHOMANS

Carl Albert (1908–2000), a McAlester native, has held the highest public position of any Oklahoman. Elected to the US House of Representatives in 1947, he became majority leader in 1962 and served as speaker of the House from 1971 until his retirement in 1976. Patrick Jay Hurley (1883–1963), the first Oklahoman appointed to a cabinet post, was secretary of war under Herbert Hoover and later ambassador to China.

William "Alfalfa Bill" Murray (b.Texas, 1869–1956) was president of the state constitutional convention and served as governor from 1931 to 1935. Robert S. Kerr (1896–1963), founder of Kerr-McGee Oil, was the state's first native-born governor, serving from 1943 to 1947; elected to the US Senate in 1948, he became an influential Democratic leader. A(lmer) S(tillwell) Mike Monroney (1902–80) served as US representative from 1939 to 1951 and senator from 1951 to 1969.

Oklahomans have been prominent in literature and the arts. Journalist and historian Marquis James (b.Missouri, 1891–1955) won a Pulitzer Prize in 1930 for his biography of Sam Houston and another in 1938 for Andrew Jackson; John Berryman (1914–72) won the 1965 Pulitzer Prize in poetry for *77 Dream Songs, 1964*; and Ralph Ellison (1914–94) won the 1953 National Book Award for his novel *Invisible Man*. The popular musical *Oklahoma!* by Richard Rodgers and Oscar Hammerstein 2nd is based on *Green Grow the Lilacs* by Oklahoman Lynn Riggs (1899–1954). N(avarre) Scott Momaday (b.1934), born in Lawton, received a Pulitzer Prize in 1969 for *House Made of Dawn*. Woodrow Crumbo (1912–89) and Allen Houser (1914–94) wereprominent Indian artists born in the state.

Just about the best-known Oklahoman was William Penn Adair "Will" Rogers (1879–1935), the beloved humorist and writer who spread cheer in the dreary days of the Depression.

Part Cherokee, Rogers was a horse rider, trick roper, and stage and movie star until he was killed in a plane crash in Alaska. Among his gifts to the American language are the oft-quoted expressions "I never met a man I didn't like" and "All I know is what I read in the newspapers." Other prominent performing artists include singer-songwriter Woody Guthrie (1912–67), composer of "This Land Is Your Land," among other classics; ballerina Maria Tallchief (b.1925); popular singer Patti Page (b.1927); and operatic soprano Roberta Knie (b.1938). Famous Oklahoma actors include (Francis) Van Heflin (1910–71), Ben Johnson (1918–96), Jennifer Jones (b.1919), Tony Randall (b.1920), James Garner (James Baumgardner, b.1928), and Cleavon Little (1939–92). Paul Harvey (b.1918) is a widely syndicated radio commentator. James Francis "Jim" Thorpe (1888–1953) became known as the "world's greatest athlete" after his pentathlon and decathlon performances at the 1912 Olympic Games; of Indian ancestry, Thorpe also starred in baseball, football, and other sports. Bud Wilkinson (b.Minnesota, 1916–94) coached the University of Oklahoma football team to a record 47-game unbeaten streak in the 1950s. Baseball stars Paul Warner (1903–65) and his brother Lloyd (1906–82), Mickey Mantle (1931–95), Wilver Dornel "Willie" Stargell (1941–2001), and Johnny Bench (b.1947) are native Oklahomans.

50BIBLIOGRAPHY

Bicha, Karel D. *The Czechs in Oklahoma*. Norman: University of Oklahoma Press, 1980.

Blessing, Patrick. *The British and Irish in Oklahoma*. Norman: University of Oklahoma Press, 1980.

Brown, Kenny L. *Italians in Oklahoma*. Norman: University of Oklahoma Press, 1978.

Fischer, John. *From the High Plains*. New York: Harper & Row, 1978.

Franklin, Jimmie Lewis. *Blacks in Oklahoma*. Norman: University of Oklahoma Press, 1980.

Gibson, Arrell M. *The Oklahoma Story*. Norman: University of Oklahoma Press, 1978.

Goble, Danney. *Progressive Oklahoma: The Making of A New Kind of State*. Norman: University of Oklahoma Press, 1980.

Harris, LaDonna. *LaDonna Harris: A Comanche Life*. Lincoln: University of Nebraska Press, 2000.

Morgan, Anne, H. Wayne, and Anne Hodges. *Oklahoma: A Bicentennial History*. New York: Norton, 1977.

Morgan, Anne and H. Wayne. *Oklahoma: New Views of the Forty-sixth State*. Norman: University of Oklahoma Press, 1982.

Rohrs, Richard. *Germans in Oklahoma*. Norman: University of Oklahoma Press, 1980.

Smith, Michael. *Mexicans in Oklahoma*. Norman: University of Oklahoma Press, 1980.

Stein, Howard F., and Robert F. Hill, eds. *The Culture of Oklahoma*. Norman: University of Oklahoma Press, 1993.

Strain, Jack M. *An Outline of Oklahoma Government*. Edmond, Okla.: Central State University, 1978.

Strickland, Rennard. *Indians in Oklahoma*. Norman: University of Oklahoma Press, 1980.

Sullivan, Lynn M. *Adventure Guide to Oklahoma*. Edison, N.J.: Hunter Publishing, 1999.

Tobias, Henry J. *Jews in Oklahoma*. Norman: University of Oklahoma Press, 1980.

OREGON

State of Oregon

ORIGIN OF STATE NAME: Unknown; name first applied to the river now known as the Columbia. **NICKNAME:** The Beaver State. **CAPITAL:** Salem. **ENTERED UNION:** 14 February 1859 (33rd). **SONG:** "Oregon, My Oregon." **DANCE:** Square dance. **MOTTO:** She Flies With Her Own Wings. **COLORS:** Navy-blue and gold. **FLAG:** The flag consists of a navy-blue field with gold lettering and illustrations. Obverse: the shield from the state seal, supported by 33 stars, with the words "State of Oregon" above and the year of admission below. Reverse: a beaver. **OFFICIAL SEAL:** A shield, supported by 33 stars and crested by an American eagle, depicts mountains and forests, an elk, a covered wagon and ox team, wheat, a plow, a pickax, and the state motto; in the background, as the sun sets over the Pacific, an American merchant ship arrives as a British man-o'-war departs. The words "State of Oregon 1859" surround the whole. **ANIMAL:** American beaver. **BIRD:** Western meadowlark. **FISH:** Chinook salmon. **INSECT:** Oregon swallowtail butterfly. **FLOWER:** Oregon grape. **BEVERAGE:** Milk. **TREE:** Douglas fir. **ROCK:** Thunderegg (geode). **GEM:** Sunstone. **LEGAL HOLIDAYS:** New Year's Day, 1 January; Birthday of Martin Luther King, Jr., 3rd Monday in January; Lincoln's Birthday, 1st Monday in February; Washington's Birthday, 3rd Monday in February; Memorial Day, last Monday in May; Independence Day, 4 July; Labor Day, 1st Monday in September; Veterans Day, 11 November; Thanksgiving Day, 4th Thursday in November; Christmas Day, 25 December. Designated as commemoration days are Oregon's Admission into the Union, 14 February, and Columbus Day, 12 October. **TIME:** 5 AM MST = noon GMT; 4 AM PST = noon GMT.

¹LOCATION, SIZE, AND EXTENT

Located on the Pacific coast of the northwestern US. Oregon ranks 10th in size among the 50 states.

The total area of Oregon is 97,073 sq mi (251,419 sq km), with land comprising 96,184 sq mi (249,117 sq km) and inland water 889 sq mi (2,302 sq km). Oregon extends 395 mi (636 km) E-W; the state's maximum N-S extension is 295 mi (475 km).

Oregon is bordered on the N by Washington (with most of the line formed by the Columbia River); on the E by Idaho (with part of the line defined by the Snake River); on the S by Nevada and California; and on the W by the Pacific Ocean. The total boundary length of Oregon is 1,444 mi (2,324 km), including a general coastline of 296 mi (476 km); the tidal shoreline extends 1,410 mi (2,269 km). The state's geographic center is in Crook County, 25 mi (40 km) SSE of Prineville.

²TOPOGRAPHY

The Cascade Range, extending north-south, divides Oregon into distinct eastern and western regions, each of which contains a great variety of landforms.

At the state's western edge, the Coast Range, a relatively low mountain system, rises from the beaches, bays, and rugged headlands of the Pacific coast. Between the Coast and Cascade ranges lie fertile valleys, the largest being the Willamette Valley, Oregon's heartland. The two-thirds of the state lying east of the Cascade Range consists generally of arid plateaus cut by river canyons, with rolling hills in the north-central portion giving way to the Blue Mountains in the northeast. The Great Basin in the southeast is characterized by fault-block ridges, weathered buttes, and remnants of large prehistoric lakes.

The Cascades, Oregon's highest mountains, contain nine snow-capped volcanic peaks more than 9,000 ft (2,700 m) high, of which the highest is Mt. Hood, at 11,239 ft (3,428 m). A dormant volcano, Mt. Hood last erupted in 1865. (Mt. St. Helen's, which erupted in 1980, is only 60 mi/97 km to the northwest, in Washington.) The Blue Mountains include several rugged subranges interspersed with plateaus, alluvial basins, and deep river canyons. The Klamath Mountains in the southwest form a jumble of ridges where the Coast and Cascade ranges join.

Oregon is drained by many rivers, but the Columbia, demarcating most of the northern border with Washington, is by far the biggest and most important. Originating in Canada, it flows more than 1,200 mi (1,900 km) to the Pacific Ocean. With a mean flow rate of 250,134 cu ft per second, the Columbia is the 3rd-largest river in the US. It drains some 58% of Oregon's surface by way of a series of northward-flowing rivers, including the Deschutes, John Day, and Umatilla. The largest of the Columbia's tributaries in Oregon, and longest river entirely within the state, is the Willamette, which drains a fertile valley more than 100 mi (160 km) long. Better than half of Oregon's eastern boundary with Idaho is formed by the Snake River, which flows through Hell's Canyon, one of the deepest canyons in North America.

Oregon has 19 natural lakes with a surface area of more than 3,000 acres (1,200 ha), and many smaller ones. The largest is Upper Klamath Lake, which covers 58,922 acres (23,845 ha) and is quite shallow. The most famous, however, is Crater Lake, which formed in the crater created by the violent eruption of Mt. Mazama several thousand years ago and is now a national park. Its depth of 1,932 ft (589 m)—greater than any other lake in the US—and its nearly circular expanse of bright-blue water, edged by the crater's rim, make it a natural wonder.

³CLIMATE

Oregon has a generally temperate climate, but there are marked regional variations. The Cascade Range separates the state into two broad climatic zones: the western third, with relatively heavy precipitation and moderate temperatures, and the eastern two-thirds, with relatively little precipitation and more extreme temperatures. Within these general regions, climate depends largely on elevation and land configuration.

In January, normal daily mean temperatures range from more than 45°F (7°C) in the coastal sections to between 25°F (−4°C) and 28°F (−2°C) in the southeast. In July, the normal daily means range between 65°F (18°C) and 70°F (21°C) in the plateau regions and central valleys and between 70°F (21°C) and 78°F (26°C) along the eastern border. Oregon's record low temperature, −54°F (−48°C), was registered at Seneca on 10 February 1933; the all-time high, 119°F (48°C), at Pendleton on 10 August 1898.

The Cascades serve as a barrier to the warm, moist winds blowing in from the Pacific, confining most precipitation to western Oregon. The average annual rainfall (1971–2000) in Portland was 37 in (94 cm); rainfall elsewhere varied from less than 8 in (20 cm) in the drier plateau regions to as much as 200 in (508 cm) at locations on the upper west slopes of the Coast Range. In the Blue Mountains and the Columbia River Basin, totals are about 15 in (38 cm) to 20 in (51 cm). In Portland, fog is common, and the sun shines, on average, during only 39% of the daylight hours—one of the lowest such percentages for any major US city. From 300 in (760 cm) to 550 in (1,400 cm) of snow falls each year in the highest reaches of the Cascades.

4FLORA AND FAUNA

With its variety of climatic conditions and surface features, Oregon has a diverse assortment of vegetation and wildlife, including 78 native tree species. The coastal region is covered by a rain forest of spruce, hemlock, and cedar rising above dense underbrush. A short distance inland, the stands of Douglas fir—Oregon's state tree and dominant timber resource—begin, extending across the western slopes to the summit of the Cascade Range. Where the Douglas fir has been destroyed by fire or logging, alder and various types of berries grow. In the high elevations of the Cascades, Douglas fir gives way to pines and true firs. Ponderosa pine predominates on the eastern slopes, while in areas too dry for pine the forests give way to open range, which, in its natural state, is characterized by sagebrush, occasional juniper trees, and sparse grasses. The state's many species of smaller indigenous plants include Oregon grape—the state flower—as well as salmonberry, huckleberry, blackberry, and many other berries. Eighteen Oregon plant species were listed as threatened or endangered in 2003 (up from eight in 1997), including the Willamette daisy, Western lily, Malheur wire-lettuce, rough popcornflower, and MacFarlane's four-o'clock.

More than 130 species of mammal are native to Oregon, of which 28 are found throughout the state. Many species, such as the cougar and bear, are protected, either entirely or through hunting restrictions. The bighorn sheep, once extirpated—deliberately exterminated—in Oregon, has been reintroduced in limited numbers; the Columbian white-tailed deer, with an extremely limited habitat along the Columbia River, is still classified as endangered. Deer and elk are popular game mammals, with herds managed by the state: mule deer predominate in eastern Oregon, black-tailed deer in the west. Among introduced mammals, the nutria and opossum are now present in large numbers. At least 60 species of fish are found in Oregon, including five different salmon species, of which the Chinook is the largest and the coho most common. Salmon form the basis of Oregon's sport and commercial fishing, although dams and development have blocked many spawning areas, causing a decline in numbers and heavy reliance on hatcheries to continue the runs. Hundreds of species of birds inhabit Oregon, either year-round or during particular seasons. The state lies in the path of the Pacific Flyway, a major route for migratory waterfowl, and large numbers of geese and ducks may be found in western Oregon and marshy areas east of the Cascades. Extensive bird refuges have been established in various parts of the state. Thirty-six Oregon animal species were classified as threatened or endangered in 2003 (up from 21 in 1997),

including the short-tailed albatross, bald eagle, Fender's blue butterfly, three species of chub, brown pelican, northern spotted owl, and three species of sea turtle.

5ENVIRONMENTAL PROTECTION

Oregon has been among the most active states in environmental protection. In 1938, the polluted condition of the Willamette River led to the enactment, by initiative, of one of the nation's first comprehensive water pollution control laws, which helped restore the river's quality for swimming and fishing. An air pollution control law was enacted in 1951, and air and water quality programs were placed under the Department of Environmental Quality (DEQ), established in 1969. This department is Oregon's major environmental protection agency, enforcing standards for air and water quality and solid and hazardous waste disposal. A vehicle inspection program has been instituted to reduce exhaust emissions in the Portland area and in Rogue Valley. The DEQ also operates an asbestos program to protect the public from asbestos in buildings that are being demolished or remodeled. The DEQ monitors 18 river basins for water quality and issues permits to businesses, industries, and government bodies that discharge waste water into public waters. In 2003, Oregon had 112 hazardous waste sites listed in the Environmental Protection Agency's database, 10 of which were on the National Priorities List.

In 1973, the legislature enacted what has become known as the Oregon Bottle Bill, the first state law prohibiting the sale of nonreturnable beer or soft-drink containers. The DEQ estimates that more than 95% of beverage containers are returned for recycling. The success of the Bottle Bill was partly responsible for the passage in 1983 of the Recycling Opportunity Act, which reduces the amount of solid waste generated. Furthermore, all cities with 5,000 or more residents are required to provide curbside recycling services. In 2001, Oregon received $51,925,000 in federal grants from the Environmental Protection Agency; EPA expenditures for procurement contracts in Oregon that year amounted to $3,288,000.

6POPULATION

Oregon ranked 27th in population in the US with an estimated total of 3,521,515 in 2002, an increase of 2.9% since 2000. Between 1990 and 2000, Oregon's population grew from 2,842,321 to 3,421,399, an increase of 20.4%, making it one of the fastest-growing states in the nation. The population is projected to reach 3,613,000 by 2005 and 4.3 million by 2025.

In 2000 the median age was 36.3. Persons under 18 years old accounted for 24.7% of the population while 12.8% were age 65 or older.

Like other western states, Oregon experienced more rapid population growth than that of the US as a whole in the 1970s, when population expanded 26%. The 1990 census figure represented a 7.9% increase over the 1980 census population. The population density in 2000 was 35.6 persons per sq mi.

As of 2000, more than half of all Oregonians lived in the Portland region, while much of the remainder also lived in the Willamette Valley, particularly in and around Salem and Eugene. The city of Portland had an estimated 539,438 residents in 2002; the Portland Consolidated Metropolitan Statistical Area (which includes Vancouver, Washington) had an estimated 1999 population of 2,180,996. The estimated population of Salem was 140,977 and Eugene's was 140,395.

7ETHNIC GROUPS

In 2000, the estimated number of American Indians was 45,211, with most of the population living in urban areas. The state's four reservations (with estimated 1995 population) are the Umatilla (2,154), Siletz (1,778), Spokane (1,416), and Kalispel (170).

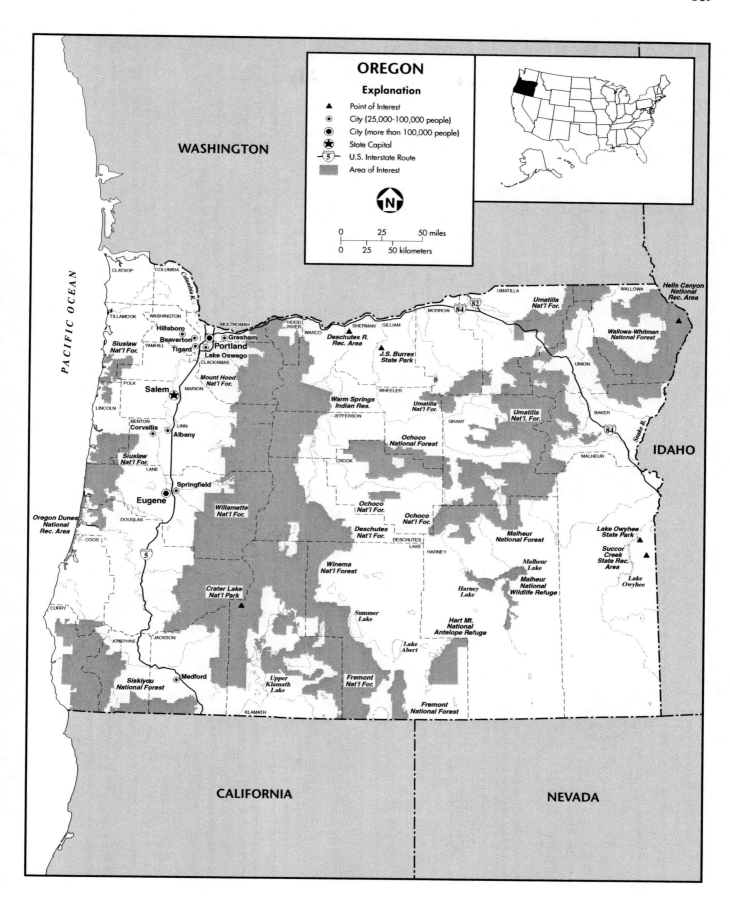

OREGON

Explanation

▲ Point of Interest

⊙ City (25,000-100,000 people)

◉ City (more than 100,000 people)

★ State Capital

⑤ U.S. Interstate Route

▨ Area of Interest

Ⓝ

0   25   50 miles

0   25   50 kilometers

WASHINGTON

PACIFIC OCEAN

CLATSOP

COLUMBIA

Columbia R.

TILLAMOOK

WASHINGTON

MULTNOMAH

Hillsboro

Beaverton

Siuslaw Nat'l For.

YAMHILL

Tigard

Lake Oswego

Gresham

Portland

CLACKAMAS

HOOD RIVER

WASCO

SHERMAN

GILLIAM

Deschutes R. Rec. Area

J.S. Burres State Park

UMATILLA

MORROW

84

82

Umatilla Nat'l For.

WALLOWA

Hells Canyon National Rec. Area

Wallowa-Whitman National Forest

POLK

Salem

MARION

Mount Hood Nat'l For.

Warm Springs Indian Res.

WHEELER

Umatilla Nat'l For.

UNION

UMATILLA

BAKER

84

LINCOLN

BENTON

Corvallis

LINN

Albany

JEFFERSON

Umatilla Nat'l For.

Ochoco National Forest

GRANT

Snake R.

IDAHO

Siuslaw Nat'l For.

LANE

Springfield

Eugene

Willamette Nat'l For.

CROOK

Ochoco Nat'l For.

Ochoco Nat'l For.

Malheur National Forest

MALHEUR

Lake Owyhee State Park

Oregon Dunes National Rec. Area

DOUGLAS

5

Deschutes Nat'l For.

DESCHUTES

LAKE

HARNEY

Malheur Lake

Succor Creek State Rec. Area

Lake Owyhee

COOS

Winema Nat'l Forest

Malheur National Wildlife Refuge

Crater Lake Nat'l Park

Summer Lake

Harney Lake

CURRY

Hart Mt. National Antelope Refuge

JOSEPHINE

JACKSON

Upper Klamath Lake

Lake Abert

Fremont Nat'l For.

Siskiyou National Forest

Medford

Fremont National Forest

KLAMATH

CALIFORNIA

NEVADA

Important salmon fishing rights in the north are reserved under treaty.

About 55,662 blacks were estimated to live in Oregon in 2000, up from 46,000 in 1990; most blacks reside in the Portland area. In 2000, Hispanics and Latinos numbered about 275,314, or 8% of the state total population, up from 113,000 in 1990. In the same year Asians numbered 101,350. There were 20,930 Chinese, 12,131 Japanese, 12,387 Koreans, 10,627 Filipinos, 18,890 Vietnamese (up from 8,130 in 1990), 9,575 Asian Indians (more than triple the 1990 population of 2,726), and 4,392 Laotians. Pacific Islanders numbered 7,976.

French Canadians have lived in Oregon since the opening of the territory, and they have continued to come in a small but steady migration. As of 2000, 31,354 Oregonians reported French Canadian ancestry. In all, the 2000 census counted some 289,702 Oregonians of foreign birth, accounting for 8.5% of the population (up from 139,307, or 4.9%, in 1990).

8LANGUAGES

Place-names such as Umatilla, Coos Bay, Klamath Falls, and Tillamook reflect the variety of Indian tribes that white settlers found in Oregon territory.

The midland dialect dominates Oregon English, except for an apparent Northern dialect influence in the Willamette Valley. Throughout the state, *foreign* and *orange* have the /aw/ vowel, and *tomorrow* has the /ah/ of *father*.

In 2000, 2,810,654 Oregonians—87.9 of the population five years old or older—spoke only English at home, down from 92.7% in 1990.

The following table gives selected statistics from the 2000 census for language spoken at home by persons five years old and over. The category "Other Indo-European languages" includes Albanian, Gaelic, Lithuanian, and Rumanian. The category "Other Slavic languages" includes Czech, Slovak, and Ukrainian. Samoan. The category "Other Asian languages" includes Dravidian languages, Malayalam, Telugu, Tamil, and Turkish. The category "Scandinavian languages" includes Danish, Norwegian, and Swedish.

LANGUAGE	NUMBER	PERCENT
Population 5 years and over	3,199,323	100.0
Speak only English	2,810,654	87.9
Speak a language other than English	388,669	12.1
Speak a language other than English	388,669	12.1
Spanish or Spanish Creole	217,614	6.8
German	18,400	0.6
Vietnamese	17,805	0.6
Russian	16,344	0.5
Chinese	15,504	0.5
French (incl. Patois, Cajun)	11,837	0.4
Japanese	9,377	0.3
Korean	9,185	0.3
Tagalog	6,181	0.2
Other Indo-European languages	5,945	0.2
Other Slavic languages	5,630	0.2
Other Pacific Island languages	4,331	0.1
Other Asian languages	4,109	0.1
Arabic	3,723	0.1
Scandinavian languages	3,276	0.1
Italian	3,104	0.1

9RELIGIONS

Just over one-third of Oregon's population is affiliated with an organized religion. About 2.3 million people, 68% of the population, were not counted as members of any religious organization in a 2000 survey. In 2000, the leading Christian denominations were the Roman Catholic church, with 348,239 members, and the Church of Jesus Christ of Latter-day Saints (Mormon), with 104,312 adherents. Other major Protestant groups, were the Assemblies of God, 49,357; the Evangelical Lutheran Church in America, 46,807; Christian Churches and Churches of Christ, 39,011; United Methodists, 34,101; Presbyterians (USA), 33,909; and Southern Baptists, 32,433. The International Church of the Foursquare Gospel (established in California in 1923) had 44,826 members in Oregon in 2000. Jewish Oregonians were estimated to number 31,625, a figure which represents a 195% increase from 1990. There were about 5,225 Muslims throughout the state.

10TRANSPORTATION

With the state's major deepwater port and international airport, Portland is the transportation hub of Oregon. The state has 2,638 rail mi (4,245 km) of track and is served by two major rail systems: Union Pacific and Burlington Northern/Santa Fe. Lumber and wood products are the major commodities originating in Oregon. Farm products and chemicals are the major commodities terminating in Oregon, primarily at the Port of Portland. Amtrak provides passenger service north–south through Portland, Salem, and Eugene.

Starting with pioneer trails and toll roads, Oregon's roads and highways had become a network extending 66,902 mi (107,668 km) by 2000. The main interstate highways are I-5, running the length of the state north-south connecting the major cities, and I-84, running northwest from Ontario in eastern Oregon and then along the northern border. In 2000, there were 3,091,042 registered vehicles, including 1,541,253 passenger cars registered in Oregon, with 2,495,059 licensed drivers.

The Columbia River forms the major inland waterway for the Pacific Northwest, with barge navigation possible for 464 mi (747 km) upstream to Lewiston, Idaho, via the Snake River. Wheat from eastern Oregon and Washington is shipped downstream to Portland for reloading onto oceangoing vessels. The Port of Portland owns five major cargo terminals and handled more than 34.3 million tons of cargo in 2000. Oregon also has several important coastal harbors, including Astoria, Newport, and Coos Bay.

In 2000, Oregon had 435 airfields (103 public, 332 private). The state's largest and busiest airport is Portland International, with 6,754,514 passengers enplaned in 2000.

11HISTORY

The land now known as Oregon has been inhabited for at least 10,000 years, the age assigned to woven brush sandals found in caves along what was once the shore of a large inland lake. Later, a variety of Indian cultures evolved. Along the coast and lower Columbia River lived peoples of the Northern Coast Culture, who ate salmon and other marine life, built large dugout canoes and cedar plank houses, and possessed a complex social structure, including slavery, that emphasized status and wealth. East of the Cascade Range were hunter-gatherers who migrated from place to place as the food supply dictated.

The first European to see Oregon was probably Sir Francis Drake. In 1578, while on a raiding expedition against the Spanish, Drake reported sighting what is believed to be the Oregon coast before being forced to return southward by "vile, thick and stinking fogges." For most of the next 200 years, European contact was limited to occasional sightings by mariners, who considered the coast too dangerous for landing. In 1778, however, British Captain James Cook, on his third voyage of discovery, visited the Northwest and named several Oregon capes. Soon afterward, American ships arrived in search of sea otter and other furs. A Yankee merchant captain, Robert Gray, discovered the Columbia River (which he named for his ship) in 1792, contributing to the US claim to the Northwest.

The first overland trek to Oregon was the Lewis and Clark Expedition, which traveled from St. Louis to the mouth of the Columbia, where it spent the winter of 1805–06. In 1811, a party of fur traders employed by New York merchant John Jacob Astor arrived by ship at the mouth of the Columbia and built a trading post named Astoria. The venture was not a success and was sold three years later to British interests, but some of the Astor party stayed, becoming Oregon's first permanent white residents. For the next 20 years, European and US interest in Oregon focused on the quest for beaver pelts. Agents of the British North West Company (which merged in 1821 with the Hudson's Bay Company) and some rival American parties explored the region, mapped trails, and established trading posts. Although Britain and the US had agreed to a treaty of joint occupation in 1818, the de facto governor from 1824 to the early 1840s was Dr. John McLoughlin, the Hudson's Bay Company chief factor at Ft. Vancouver in Washington.

Another major influence on the region was Protestant missionary activity, which began with the arrival of Jason Lee, a Methodist missionary, in 1834. Lee started his mission in the Willamette Valley, near present-day Salem. After a lecture tour of the East, he returned to Oregon in 1840 with 50 settlers and assistants. While Lee's mission was of little help to the local Indians, most of whom had been killed off by white men's diseases, it served as a base for subsequent American settlement and as a counterbalance to the Hudson's Bay Company.

The first major wagon trains arrived by way of the Oregon Trail in the early 1840s. On 2 May 1843, as a "great migration" of 875 men, women, and children was crossing the plains, about 100 settlers met at the Willamette Valley community of Champoeg and voted to form a provisional government. That government remained in power until 1849, when Oregon became a territory, three years after the Oregon Treaty between Great Britain and the US established the present US-Canadian boundary. As originally constituted, Oregon Territory included present-day Washington and much of Montana, Idaho, and Wyoming. A constitution prepared by an elected convention was approved in November 1857, and after a delay caused by North-South rivalries, on 14 February 1859, Congress voted to make Oregon, reduced to its present borders, the 33rd state.

Oregon remained relatively isolated until the completion of the first transcontinental railroad link in 1883. State politics, which had followed a pattern of venality and influence buying, underwent an upheaval in the early 1900s. Reformers led by William S. U'Ren instituted what became known as the "Oregon System" of initiative, referendum, and recall, by which voters could legislate directly and removed corrupt elected officials.

Oregon's population grew steadily in the 20th century as migration into the state continued. (By 1999, its population topped 3.3 million.) Improved transportation helped make the state the nation's leading lumber producer and a major exporter of agricultural products. Development was also aided by hydroelectric projects, many undertaken by the federal government. The principal economic changes after World War II were the growth of the aluminum industry, a rapid expansion of the tourist trade, and the creation of a growing electronics industry. The dominant industries in the Oregon economy, however, remained those centered on its abundant natural resources—agriculture, timber, and coal. These industries suffered in the late 1970s and 1980s when interest rates skyrocketed, reducing demand for houses and therefore for wood. Employment in the lumber and wood industry dropped from 81,000 jobs in 1979 to 64,000 in 1985. High interest rates, by boosting the value of the dollar, also lowered foreign demand for lumber and produce.

It was hoped that the construction of high-technology plants in the mid-1980s would help immunize Oregon from the fluctuating fortunes of the extractive (mining and timber) and agricultural industries. However, a slump in the computer industry delayed the building of planned facilities in the state. By the early 1990s,

Oregon did boast a burgeoning electronics industry, but the greatest job growth had occurred in the service sector. Agricultural industries also helped boost the state's economy. By 1994, unemployment stood at a 25-year low of 5%. Nevertheless, by 1999 it had increased to 5.7%, well above the national average (it was the 3rd-highest jobless rate in the nation). Other statistics pointed out problems in Oregon. Poverty was on the rise during the decade—climbing from 9.2% in 1990 to 15% in 1998. The dramatic increase came as levels in most other states were on the decline, so that Oregon began the decade as the 43rd poorest (one of the best-off states) in the nation and was set to close the decade as the 10th-poorest state. Children were a large part of these statistics: Oregon's child poverty rate shot up 25% between 1993 and 1998 alone, so that in 1998 one in five children in the state was living in poverty.

By 1990, the struggle between environmentalists and the timber industry over logging in Oregon's forests had become a major public policy debate. Federal legislation passed in 1993 set limits on commercial exploitation of older forests that were home to the spotted owl. With the shift in focus from timber production to protecting habitat, timber harvests in national forests declined 70% during the 1990s. The decline of logging resulted in severe economic downturns in rural areas and a loss of school funding, which the National Education Association called a "crisis for many forest county education systems" in western states, including Oregon. To assist communities affected by the downturn, Congress was considering disparate proposals—from requiring the US Forest Service to generate more income (a portion of which, by a 1908 law, funds schools) from logging on public lands to issuing US Treasury payments to afflicted counties as they transition from logging-based economies. Conservationists were being backed by analysts who forecasted the state's greatest job growth would come from the environmentally friendly high-tech sector and the environmentally dependent tourism industry.

In 2003, Oregon faced a $2.5 billion budget deficit. Upon being elected in 2002, Democratic Governor Ted Kulongoski supported a temporary income tax increase, which voters rejected in a January 2003 referendum. The state then had to face cuts of over $300 million in education, health care, and other programs in order to balance the $11.6 billion budget for 2003–05.

12 STATE GOVERNMENT

The Oregon constitution—drafted and approved in 1857, effective in 1859, and amended 234 times by January 2003—governs the state today. The first decade of the 20th century saw the passage of numerous progressive amendments, including provisions for the direct election of senators, the rights of initiative, referendum, recall, and a direct primary system.

The constitution establishes a 60-member house of representatives, elected for two years, and a senate of 30 members, serving four-year terms. Legislative sessions, which are not formally limited in length, begin in January of odd-numbered years. Special sessions may be called by the majority petition of each house. Legislators must be US citizens, at least 21 years old, and must have lived in their districts for at least one year. In 2002 the legislative salary was $15,396.

State elected officials are the governor, secretary of state, attorney general, state treasurer, superintendent of public instruction, and a commissioner of labor and industries, all elected for four-year terms. The governor, who may serve no more than eight years in any 12-year period, must be a US citizen, must be at least 30 years old, and must have been a resident of the state for three years before assuming office. In 2002 the governor's salary was $93,600. Much policy in Oregon is set by boards and commissions whose members are appointed by the governor, subject to confirmation by the senate.

Bills become law when approved by a majority of the house and senate and either signed by the governor or left unsigned for five days when the legislature is in session or for 30 days after it has adjourned. Measures presented to the voters by the legislature or by petition become law when approved by a majority of the electorate. The governor may veto a legislative bill, but the legislature may override a veto by a two-thirds vote of those present in each house. Proposed constitutional amendments require voter approval to take effect, and they may be placed on the ballot either by the legislature or by initiative petition (8% of total votes for all candidates for governor at last election).

To vote in Oregon a person must be a US citizen, age 18 or older, and a state resident.

13POLITICAL PARTIES

Oregon has two major political parties, Democratic and Republican. Partly because of the role the direct primary system plays in choosing nominees, party organization is relatively weak. There is a strong tradition of political independence, evidenced in 1976 when Oregon gave independent presidential candidate Eugene McCarthy 3.9% of the vote—his highest percentage in any state—a total that probably cost Jimmy Carter Oregon's then six electoral votes. Another independent, John Anderson, won 112,389 votes (9.5%) in the 1980 presidential election.

Democrat Barbara Roberts was elected governor in 1990. She did not run for reelection in 1994, and Dr. John Kitzhaber, a Democrat who designed Oregon's health care rationing system, defeated Republican congressman Denny Smith to become governor. Kitzhaber won a second term in 1998. In 2002, Democrat Ted Kulongoski won the governorship.

Oregonians elected two US senators in 1996. In a special election in January, Democrat Ron Wyden was chosen to serve the remainder of Robert Packwood's term after Packwood resigned from the Senate due to allegations of sexual misconduct; Wyden was elected to his first full term in 1998. In the November 1996 election, Republican Gordon Smith won the seat vacated by five-term senator Mark Hatfield; he was reelected in 2002. Following 2002 elections, all but one of the state's five US representatives were Democrats.

In mid-2003 there were an equal number of Democrats and Republicans in the state senate (15 each) and 35 Republicans and 25 Democrats in the state house. In 2000, Oregon voters gave Democratic presidential candidate Al Gore a very slight victory over Republican George W. Bush. (Gore won by a margin of 6,765 votes out of over 1.5 million cast statewide.) In 2002 there were 1,872,615 registered voters. In 1998, 40% of registered voters were Democratic, 36% Republican, and 24% unaffiliated or members of other parties. The state had seven electoral votes in the 2000 presidential election.

14LOCAL GOVERNMENT

As of 2002, Oregon had 36 counties, 240 municipal governments, 236 public school districts, and 927 special districts. Towns and cities enjoy home rule, the right to choose their own form of government and enact legislation on matters of local concern. In 1958, home rule was extended to counties. Most of Oregon's larger cities have council-manager forms of government while smaller communities are governed by a city council and mayor. At the county level, typical elected officials are commissioners, judge, assessor, district attorney, sheriff, and treasurer.

The state constitution gives voters strong control over local government revenue by requiring voter approval of property tax levies.

15STATE SERVICES

To address the continuing threat of terrorism and to work with the federal Department of Homeland Security (created in 2002 following the terrorist attacks of 11 September 2001), homeland security in Oregon in 2003 operated under the authority of the governor; the state police superintendent was designated as the state homeland security advisor.

Special offices within the governor's office include the Office of the Citizens' Representative, the state Affirmative Action Office, and the Long-Term Care Ombudsman. The Oregon Government Ethics commission is a citizens' panel, established in 1974, to investigate conflicts of interest involving public officials and to levy civil penalties for infractions. Responsibility for educational matters is divided among the Board of Education, which oversees

Oregon's Presidential Vote by Political Parties, 1948–2000

YEAR	ELECTORAL VOTE	OREGON WINNER	DEMOCRAT	REPUBLICAN	PROGRESSIVE	SOCIALIST	LIBERTARIAN
1948	6	Dewey (R	243,147	260,904	14,978	5,051	—
1952	6	*Eisenhower (R)	270,579	420,815	3,665	—	—
1956	6	Eisenhower (R)	329,204	406,393	—	—	—
1960	6	Nixon (R	367,402	408,065	—	—	—
1964	6	*Johnson (D)	501,017	282,779	—	—	—
						AMERICAN IND.	
1968	6	*Nixon (R)	358,866	408,433	—	49,683	—
						AMERICAN	
1972	6	*Nixon (R)	392,760	486,686	—	46,211	—
1976	6	Ford (R	490,407	492,120	—	—	—
						CITIZENS	
1980	6	*Reagan (R)	456,890	571,044	—	13,642	25,838
1984	7	*Reagan (R)	536,479	685,700	—	—	—
					NEW ALLIANCE		
1988	7	Dukakis (D)	678,367	483,423	2,985	—	6,261
						IND. (Perot)	
1992	7	*Clinton (D)	621,314	475,757	3,030	354,091	4,277
					GREEN		
1996	7	*Clinton (D)	649,641	538,152	49,415	121,221	8,903
						IND. (Buchanan)	
2000	7	Gore (D)	720,342	713,577	77,357	7,063	7,447

* Won US presidential election.

primary and secondary schools and community colleges; the Board of Higher Education, which controls the state college and university system; and the Educational Coordinating Commission, which monitors programs and advises the governor and legislature on policy. The economy is guided by the departments of agriculture, consumer and business services, revenue, and economic development.

State highways, airfields, and public transit systems are under the jurisdiction of the Department of Transportation, which is headed by an appointed commission. The largest state agency is the Department of Human Resources; nearly one-fourth of the state's budget and work force is committed to this department's 250 programs, which include corrections, children's services, adult and family services, health, mental health, and vocational rehabilitation. State agencies involved in environmental matters include the Department of Environmental Quality, the Department of Land Conservation and Development, and the departments of Energy, Forestry, Fish and Wildlife, and Water Resources. State-owned lands are administered through the Land Board.

16 JUDICIAL SYSTEM

Oregon's highest court is the supreme court, consisting of seven justices who elect one of their number to serve as chief justice. It accepts cases on review from the 10-judge court of appeals, which has exclusive jurisdiction over all criminal and civil appeals from lower courts and over certain actions of state agencies. Circuit courts and tax courts are the trial courts of original jurisdiction for civil and criminal matters. The 30 more-populous counties also have district courts, which hear minor civil, criminal, and traffic matters. In 1998, the circuit courts and district courts were merged; the circuit courts are thus the only state-level trial courts. Thirty localities retain justices of the peace, also with jurisdiction over minor cases. State judges and local justices of the peace are elected by nonpartisan ballot for six-year terms.

Oregon's penal system is operated by the Oregon Department of Corrections. There were 11,077 inmates in state correctional facilities as of June 2001, an increase of 7.4% over the previous year. The state's incarceration rate stood at 319 per 100,000 population. As measured by the FBI Crime Index, Oregon's total crime rate in 2001, stood at 5,044.1 per 100,000 inhabitants, including a total of 10,650 violent crimes and 164,524 crimes against property in that year. Oregon imposes the death penalty, and there were 29 persons under sentence of death in 2003. There have been two executions in Oregon since 1977.

17 ARMED FORCES

In 2002, there were 705 active duty military personnel and 3,121 civilian personnel stationed in Oregon. The US Coast Guard does maintain search-and-rescue facilities, and the Army Corps of Engineers operates a number of hydroelectric projects in the state. Military contract awards in 2002 totaled nearly $393 million.

According to the 2000 Census, 388,990 military veterans were living in Oregon, of whom 76,939 served in World War II; 43,849 during the Korean conflict; 123,113 during the Vietnam era; and 36,587 during 1990–2000 (including the Persian Gulf War). Federal veterans' benefits totaled more than $805 million in 2002.

In 2000, the Oregon State Police employed 826 full-time sworn officers.

18 MIGRATION

The Oregon Trail was the route along which thousands of settlers traveled to Oregon by covered wagon in the 1840s and 1850s. This early immigration was predominantly from Midwestern states. After the completion of the transcontinental railroad, northeastern states supplied an increasing proportion of the newcomers.

Foreign immigration began in the 1860s with the importation of Chinese contract laborers, and reached its peak about 1900. Germans and Scandinavians (particularly after 1900) were the most numerous foreign immigrants; Japanese, who began arriving in the 1890s, met a hostile reception in some areas. Canadians have also come to Oregon in significant numbers. Nevertheless, immigration from other states has predominated. Between 1970 and 1980, the state's net gain from migration was about 341,000; from 1980 to 1983, however, the state suffered a net loss of about 37,000, and from 1985 to 1990, the net migration gain was 123,500. Between 1990 and 1998, Oregon had net gains of 260,000 in domestic migration and 58,000 in international migration. In 1998, 5,909 foreign immigrants arrived in Oregon; of these, the greatest number, 1,879, came from Mexico. The state's overall population increased 15.5% between 1990 and 1998, making it one of the fastest growing states in the nation. In the period 1995–2000, 399,328 people moved into the state and 324,663 moved out, for a net gain of 74,665, many of whom came from California.

19 INTERGOVERNMENTAL COOPERATION

Oregon participates in such regional accords as the Columbia River Compact (between Oregon and Washington on fishing), Columbia River Gorge Compact, Columbia River Boundary Compact, Klamath River Compact (with California), Pacific States Marine Fisheries Commission, Pacific Ocean Resources Compact, Northwest Power and Conservation Council (with Idaho, Montana, and Washington), and several western groups concerned with corrections, education, and energy matters.

While Oregon receives federal assistance for a variety of programs, federal involvement is particularly heavy in the areas of energy and natural resources, through federal development, operation, and marketing of hydroelectric power and federal ownership of forest and grazing lands. Approximately 49% of Oregon's land area is owned by the federal government. Federal grants to Oregon totaled more than $4.3 billion in 2001.

20 ECONOMY

Since early settlement, Oregon's natural resources have formed the basis of its economy. Vast forests have made lumber and wood products the leading industry in the state. Since World War II, however, the state has striven to diversify its job base. The aluminum industry has been attracted to Oregon, along with computer and electronics firms, which now constitute the fastest-growing manufacturing sector. Development, principally in the "Silicon Forest" west of Portland, was expected to bring as many as 3,000 jobs a year during the mid- and late 1980s. Meanwhile, the trend in employment has been toward white-collar and service jobs, with agriculture and manufacturing holding a declining share of the civilian labor force. Tourism and research-related businesses growing out of partnerships between government and higher education are on the rise.

A large portion of manufacturing jobs outside the Portland area are in the lumber and wood products field, making them dependent on the health of the US construction industry. Jobs are plentiful when US housing starts rise, but unemployment increases when nationwide construction drops off. The cyclical changes in demand for forest products are a chronic problem, with rural areas and small towns particularly hard hit by the periodic closing of local lumber and plywood mills. State efforts at diversification in the 1990s were very effective, however, resulting in an astounding 79.8% growth in output from the electronics field of manufactures 1997 to 2000, the main component in an overall increase in output from manufactures of 43% across this period. Oregon was almost unique among the states in that growth in manufacturing, instead of services, led overall growth coming into the 21st century, with the state economy's annual growth rate accelerating from 5.6% in 1998, to 7.2% in 1999 to 10% in 2000. Oregon's economy was clearly headed for a correction, which came abruptly in the national recession of 2001, in which year manufacturing output fell 7.7% and the state economy contracted overall -1.1% (one of the few states to register negative growth for the year). As of the third quarter 2002, the personal bankruptcy rate in Oregon was the 12th highest in the country, and foreclosures were running at rates not seen since the mid-1980s. By the end of 2002, employment in the electronic products and industrial machinery manufacturing sectors (which produce semiconductors and computers) had fallen 3%, and Oregon was posting the 2nd-highest unemployment rate in the country (7%).

In 2001, Oregon's gross state product gross state product was $120.4 billion, the 27th largest among the states, to which manufacturing contributed $30.6 billion (down 9.2% from the peak in 2000); general services, $21.8 billion; trade, $18.5 billion; financial services, $17.6 billion; government, $14.65 billion; transportation and public utilities, $7.75 billion, and construction, $5.9 billion. The public sector in 2001 constituted 12.2% of gross state product, close to the 12% average for the states.

21INCOME

According to the Bureau of Economic Analysis, in 2001, Oregon had a per capita personal income (PCPI) of $28,222 which ranked 30th in the United States (including the District of Columbia) and was 93% of the national average, $30,413. The 2001 PCPI reflected an increase of 1.4% from 2000 compared to the national change of 2.2%. In 2001, Oregon had a total personal income (TPI) of $98,026,048,000 which ranked 28th in the United States and accounted for 1.1% of the national total. The 2001 TPI reflected an increase of 2.6% from 2000 compared to the national change of 3.3%.

Earnings of persons employed in Oregon increased from $68,401,157,000 in 2000 to $69,035,322,000 in 2001, an increase of 0.9%. The largest industries in 2001 were services, 26.6% of earnings; durable goods manufacturing, 13.8%; and state and local government, 13.5%. Of the industries that accounted for at least 5% of earnings in 2001, the slowest growing from 2000 to 2001 was durable goods manufacturing, which decreased 8.1%; the fastest was state and local government, which increased 8.2%.

According to data released by the US Census Bureau, in 2000, the median household income was $42,440 compared to the national average of $42,148. In 2001, the median income for a family of four was $58,737 compared to the national average of $63,278. For the period 1999 to 2001, the average poverty rate was 11.8% which placed it 30th among the 50 states and the District of Columbia ranked lowest to highest.

22LABOR

According to Bureau of Labor Statistics (BLS) provisional estimates, in July 2003 the seasonally adjusted civilian labor force in Oregon numbered 1,848,200, with approximately 150,300 workers unemployed, yielding an unemployment rate of 8.1%, compared to the national average of 6.2% for the same period. Since the beginning of the BLS data series in 1978, the highest unemployment rate recorded was 12.4% in January 1983. The historical low was 4.4% in March 1995. In 2001, an estimated 5.2% of the labor force was employed in construction; 14.4% in manufacturing; 5.3% in transportation, communications, and public utilities; 19.0% in trade; 4.7% in finance, insurance, and real estate; 24.4% in services; 13.8% in government; and 4.2% in agriculture.

The US Department of Labor reported that in 2002, 227,000 of Oregon's 1,460,000 employed wage and salary workers were members of unions. This represented 15.5% of those so employed, down slightly from 15.6% in 2001 (and from 16.1% in 1998). The national average is 13.2%. In all, 242,000 workers (16.6%) were represented by unions. In addition to union members, this category includes workers who report no union affiliation but whose jobs are covered by a union contract.

23AGRICULTURE

Oregon ranked 27th in the US in agricultural output in 2001, with cash receipts of $3.1 billion. Crops accounted for 74% of the total. While wheat has been Oregon's leading crop since the state was first settled, in recent years nursery and greenhouse products, valued at more than $842 million, have taken over the number-one spot, followed by hay and ryegrass production which bring in $231 million and $138 million respectively. Additionally, more than 170 farm and ranch commodities are commercially produced in the state. Oregon leads the nation in the production of hazelnuts, peppermint oil, blackberries, black raspberries, boysenberries, loganberries, several grass and seed crops, and Christmas trees.

Farmland covers about 17.2 million acres (7 million hectares), or 28% of Oregon's total area. Oregon's average farm is 420 acres (170 hectares), around the same size as the national average. In 2002, the state had some 41,000 farms. Quantity and value of selected crops in 2002 were as follows: hay, 5.03 million tons (valued at $358 million); wheat, 34.1 million bushels (valued at $135.5 million); potatoes, 501,000 hundred weight (valued at $24.9 million); pears, 198,000 tons (valued at $67.9 million).

Oregon produces the nation's entire supply of ryegrass seed, with the seed selling for $58 per hundredweight in 2002. In recent years, the growth of Oregon's wine industry has become noteworthy.

24ANIMAL HUSBANDRY

Most beef cattle are raised on the rangeland of eastern Oregon, while dairy operations are concentrated in the western portion of the state. Sheep and poultry are also raised largely in the west.

Cattle and calf production is Oregon's leading agricultural activity in terms of value, although income varies greatly with market conditions. Ranchers lease large tracts of federally owned grazing land under a permit system.

In 2003, Oregon ranches and farms had around 1.36 million cattle and calves, worth an estimated $1.03 billion. During 2001, the state produced nearly 13 million lb (5.9 million kg) of sheep and lambs, which brought in $8.1 million in gross income; in 2002 shorn wool production was an estimated 1.3 million lb (0.6 million kg) of wool. The 2001 milk output was estimated at 1.71 billion lb (0.8 billion kg). Oregon's poultry farmers produced nearly 4.4 million lb (2 million kg) of chickens in 2001, and 818 million eggs.

25FISHING

Oregon's fish resources have long been of great importance to its inhabitants. For centuries, salmon provided much of the food for Indians, who gathered at traditional fishing grounds when the salmon were returning upstream from the ocean to spawn.

In 1998, Oregon ranked 7th among the states in the total amount of its commercial catch, at 230,125,000 lb (104,385,000 kg), valued at $50,341,000. The catch included salmon, especially chinook and silver; groundfish such as flounder, rockfish, and lingcod; shellfish such as shrimp and oysters; and albacore tuna. Salmon landings totaled 1.8 million lb (0.8 million kg), valued at $2.5 million; sablefish, 3.9 million lb (1.8 million kg), $4.6 million; dungeness crab, 7.4 million lb (3.3 million kg); and shrimp, 6.2 million lb (2.8 million kg). Newport, Astoria, and Coos Bay–Charleston were the leading commercial fishing ports in 1998, with landings of 117.6 million, 87.7 million, and 14.6 million lb (53.3 million, 39.8 million, and 6.6 million kg), respectively. Oregon's commercial fishing fleet consisted of 1,060 boats and vessels in 1997, and supplied the state's 63 fish processing and wholesale plants.

Sport fishing, primarily for salmon and trout, is a major recreational attraction. In 1998, the state issued 653,292 sport fishing licenses. An estimated 168,000 coastal residents, along with 13,000 inland Oregonians and 51,000 residents of other states, participated in 649,000 recreational marine fishing trips in 1998, catching some 1,712,000 fish (mainly rockfish).

Hatchery production of salmon and steelhead has taken on increased importance, as development has destroyed natural fishspawning areas.

26FORESTRY

About 48% (29.7 million acres/12 million hectares) of Oregon is forested. Oregon's forests are divided into two major geographic regions. Douglas-fir is a primary conifer species in western Oregon, with western hemlock and sitka spruce found along the coast. In eastern Oregon, ponderosa pine is the main species. Several species of true fir, larch, and lodgepole pine also grow east of the Cascades. Noncommercial forests are found along the crest of the Cascade Range and in the high-desert country of eastern Oregon. These species include alpine fir, mountain hemlock and western juniper.

Over 60% of Oregon's forests are publicly owned. National Forest Service lands cover 17.5 million acres (7.1 million hectares). Most of these are federal lands. Federal timber harvest levels have steadily declined over the last several years as timber sales have been appealed and forest set-asides for habitat protection have increased. Reduced revenues have affected local services and infrastructure—where a percentage of harvest tax dollars are reinvested—and the overall structure and funding of federal agencies. The Oregon Department of Forestry manages about 786,000 acres (318,000 hectares) of forestland. About 654,000 acres (265,000 hectares) are managed by the department for the counties, and a further 132,000 acres (53,000 hectares) are Common School Fund forestlands, managed for the State Land Board. State forestlands are not managed with the same "multiple-use" strategy as lands managed by the US Forest Service. According to statute, state lands are managed to produce sustainable revenue for counties, schools, and local taxing districts. About 80% of the state's forestland, or 23.8 million acres (9.6 million hectares), is land capable of producing timber for commercial harvest. However, less than 60% of this commercial land is available for full-yield timber production. The remaining forestland base contains commercial forest, but at reduced levels, and provides vital environmental and recreational functions.

Forestland available for commercial timber management has decreased since the 1970s. Estimates show that Oregon's commercial land base has decreased by more than 24% since 1945. Private forestland has been lost due to urban expansion and other non-timber uses. Private forestlands, however, have assumed a much more important role as Oregon's timber supplier due to harvest limitations placed on federal forestland. Timber harvest levels on non-industrial forestlands—parcels typically smaller than 5,000 acres (2,000 hectares) and owned by individuals, not corporations—have more than doubled since 1981, and harvest levels on industry-owned forestlands have also increased during the same period. The relative percentage of overall harvest, however, emphasizes the importance of Oregon's private forestlands.

In 2002, Oregon led the nation in total lumber production, with 6.4 billion board feet, and contributed about 13% to the national total. Nearly all of the timber harvested from private forestlands is second-growth—trees originating from 1920 to

1940. Private forestlands are being reforested and play a major role in sustaining Oregon's long-term timber supply. Oregon law has required reforestation following timber harvesting since 1941. Oregon was the first state to pass a Forest Practices Act, in 1971. About 100 million seedlings are planted in Oregon each year.

27MINING

The estimated value of Oregon's nonfuel mineral production in 2001 was $326 million, up 9% from 2000. Industrial minerals account for all of the nonfuel mineral production value in 2001. Construction sand and gravel and crushed stone were, respectively, Oregon's leading nonfuel mineral commodities, accounting for almost 65% of the state's total nonfuel mineral value in 2001. According to preliminary figures, in 2001, Oregon produced 19.8 million metric tons of crushed stone, worth $96.9 million. Construction sand and gravel production was 19 million metric tons ($114 million). Oregon was the nation's sole producer of nickel until 1998, when the Nickel Mountain Mine near Riddle closed. It ranked 1st nationally in the quantity of pumice produced, 2nd in perlite, 3rd in the quantity of diatomite and zeolites, and 5th in talc. Zeolites are processed and sold for ammonia absorbent in aquarium systems, animal feed supplement, anticaking agents, fungicide carriers, odor control, and wastewater treatment. In 2001 Oregon ranked 36th in the US in overall nonfuel mineral production.

28ENERGY AND POWER

Oregon ranks 3rd in the US in hydroelectric power development, and hydropower supplies nearly half of the state's energy needs. Multipurpose federal projects, including four dams on the Columbia River and eight in the Willamette Basin, and projects owned by private or public utilities give Oregon a hydroelectric capacity of over 8,100,000 kW. In recent decades, low-cost power from dams has proved inadequate to meet the state's energy needs, and nuclear and coal-fired steam plants have been built to supply additional electric power. As of 2001, however, there were no nuclear power plants in operation.

Hydropower provided 82% of electricity in 1999; coal and gas-fired thermal plants produced nearly 16%. Oregon's total electric power production (utility and nonutility) in 1999 was 56.7 billion kWh; total installed capacity was 11.2 million kW. The Bonneville Power Administration, the federal power-marketing agency, operates a power distribution grid interconnecting Oregon, Washington, and parts of Idaho and Montana.

Energy consumption per capita was 316 million Btu (79.6 million kcal) in 2000 (35th in the US).

29INDUSTRY

Manufacturing in Oregon is dominated by the lumber and wood products industry (one-fifth of total shipments). In 1997, the total value of shipments of manufactured goods was $50 billion, exhibiting a 56% growth from 1992 to 1997, 8th fastest in the nation. More than half of Oregon's industrial workers are employed in the Portland area. The Willamette Valley is the site of one of the nation's largest canning and freezing industries.

In 1997, Oregon was the headquarters of 6 Fortune 500 companies: Nike, Thrifty Payless Holdings, Pacificorp, Fred Meyer, Willamette Industries, and US Bancorp.

Earnings of persons employed in Oregon increased from $57.1 billion in 1997 to $60.1 billion in 1998, an increase of 5.2%. The largest industries in 1998 were services, 25.4% of earnings; durable goods manufacturing, 15.1%; and state and local government, 11.5%. Of the industries that accounted for at least 5% of earnings in 1998, the slowest growing from 1997 to 1998 was state and local government, which increased 4.5%; the fastest was finance, insurance, and real estate (6.7% of earnings in 1998), which increased 11.3%.

30 COMMERCE

Wholesalers numbered 6,929 in 1997, with sales of over $45 billion. Retail establishments numbering 20,920 in 1997 had combined sales of $34 billion. Automotive dealers accounted for 11% of establishments; food stores, 11%; and restaurants and taverns, 32%. Exports moving through Oregon were valued at almost $9 billion in 1998. Exports went primarily to Canada, Japan, Korea, and the Philippines.

31 CONSUMER PROTECTION

The Department of Consumer and Business Services (DCBS) is the state's largest regulatory and consumer protection agency. The department administers laws and rules regarding workmen's compensation, occupational safety and health, building codes, financial institutions and insurance companies, and securities offerings. The Financial Fraud/Consumer Protection Section of the Department of Justice coordinates consumer services carried on by other government agencies, conducts studies and research in consumer services, and advises executive and legislative branches in matters affecting consumer interests. Also responsible for consumer protection are the Department of Agriculture (measurement standards division); and the public utility commission.

32 BANKING

Consolidations and acquisitions transformed Oregon's banking system from one characterized by a large number of local banks into one dominated by two large chains—the US National Bank of Oregon and Wells Fargo.

In all, the state had 39 insured banks in 2002, with total assets of $22.9 billion. Thirty-one of these banks were state-chartered. By 1996, the Resolution Trust Corporation had resolved three institutions at a cost of $393 million.

As of 2002, a disproportionate share of Oregon's insured banks held high concentrations of commercial real estate (CRE) loans, especially in the high-risk construction and development (C and D) sectors. At that time, the demand for commercial real estate had declined, challenging the credit quality of many banks.

Although steep interest rate cuts by the Federal Reserve in 2001/02 initially hampered net interest margins (NIMs) (the difference between the lower rates offered to savers and the higher rates charged on loans), banks' funding costs declined dramatically during 2002, which contributed to improved NIMs.

33 INSURANCE

In 2001, there were 1.1 million ordinary life insurance policies in force, with a total value of $103.6 billion; total value for all categories of life insurance (ordinary, group, industrial, and credit) was $166.6 billion. Death benefits paid that year totaled $451.6 million. As of the end of 2000, there were 16 property and casualty and three life and health insurance companies incorporated or organized in the state. In 2001, property and casualty insurers wrote over $4.1 billion in premiums. That year, there were 25,909 flood insurance policies in force in the state, with a total value of $3.8 million.

34 SECURITIES

There are no securities or commodities exchanges in Oregon. The state has 610 broker-dealer firms, with 4,585 employees; 118 investment advisory organizations operate in Oregon. The state headquarters 74 NASDAQ companies, five NASDAQ market makers, and has incorporated six NYSE-listed companies: Cascade Corp., Nike, Precision Cast Parts Corp., Stancorp Financial Group, Inc., Tektronix, Inc., and Willamette Industries, Inc.

35 PUBLIC FINANCE

Oregon's biennial budget, covering a period from 1 July of each odd-numbered year to 30 June of the next odd-numbered year, is prepared by the Executive Department and submitted by the governor to the legislature for amendment and approval. Unlike some state budgets, Oregon's is not contained in a single omnibus appropriations bill; instead, each agency appropriation is considered as a separate measure. When the legislature is not in session, an emergency board of 17 legislators considers fiscal problems; this board may adjust budgets, allocate money from a special emergency fund, and establish new expenditure limitations, but it cannot enact new general fund appropriations. The Oregon constitution prohibits a state budget deficit and requires that all general obligation bond issues be submitted to the voters.

The Oregon state budget for 1999–2001 receives its revenues primarily from the general fund (34%) and the federal government (19%). Other funds are received and directly allocated to certain purposes, such as the highways, employment, and forests. Total expenditures for 1999–2001 were forecast at almost $30 billion. General fund resources available for allocation were estimated at a total of $10 billion for 1999–2001. In 2000/01, general fund revenues totaled $5.238, in line with the estimates for the biennium budget, and expenditures, at $5.249 billion, were readily covered even thought Medicaid Upper Payment Limit (MUPL) funds had been removed from the calculation. However, in 2001/02, the shortfall was dramatic as general fund revenue only reached $4.326 billion. A total of $801.4 million was cut from the biennial budget after it was enacted, as the legislature met in five special sessions to explore how to deal with the budget shortfalls facing the state. In 2002/03, general fund revenues only reached $5.03 billion, and the legislature made cuts totaling $465 million in the enacted budget, with no program held exempt. Oregon's budget deficit in 2002/03 was estimated at 4.6% of the state budget, and for 2003/04, was projected to reach between 20.4% and 27.2% of the state budget. Allocations from the general fund include, by function, education (about 30%), human resources (27%), economic development (9%), and public safety and transportation (about 7% each). The following table from the US Census Bureau contains information on revenues, expenditures, indebtedness, and cash/securities for 2001.

	($000)	PERCENT	PER CAPITA
Population (thousands, 2001)	3,473	(X)	(X)
Total Revenue	18,218,617	100.00	5,245.79
General revenue	14,196,386	77.92	4,087.64
Liquor store revenue	241,355	1.32	69.49
Insurance trust revenue	3,780,876	20.75	1,088.65
Exhibit: Salaries and wages	2,650,269	16.24	763.11
Total expenditure	16,321,295	100.00	4,699.48
General expenditure	13,546,387	83.00	3,900.49
Education	4,670,857	28.62	1,344.91
Public welfare	3,330,343	20.40	958.92
Hospitals	982,096	6.02	282.78
Health	528,364	3.24	152.13
Highways	824,037	5.05	237.27
Police protection	184,537	1.13	53.13
Correction	575,836	3.53	165.80
Natural resources	337,582	2.07	97.20
Parks and recreation	53,268	0.33	15.34
Government administration	833,747	5.11	240.07
Interest on general debt	408,611	2.50	117.65
Other and unallocable	817,109	5.01	235.27
Utility expenditure	4,458	0.03	1.28
Liquor store expenditure	121,332	0.74	34.94
Insurance trust expenditure	2,649,118	16.23	762.78
Debt at end of fiscal year	6,417,534	100.00	1,847.84
Cash and security holdings	35,096,584	100.00	10,105.55

36 TAXATION

Oregon's chief source of general revenue is the personal income tax, adopted in 1929; the tax has three brackets, ranging from 5% on taxable income up to $2,500 to 9% on taxable income above $6,250. A corporate income tax of 6.6% is also levied, with a $10 minimum tax. Oregon is one of five states without a general sales tax, but it does levy excise taxes on motor fuels, tobacco products, insurance premiums, public utilities, alcoholic beverages, pari-mutuels, and amusements. Oregon has a state inheritance tax and an estate tax tied to the federal exemption for state death taxes (which is scheduled to be phased out by 2007, which would cost Oregon an $46 million in revenues if the legislature does not act to preserve Oregon's estate tax). Death and gift taxes accounted for 1.3% of state collections in 2002. Severance taxes in Oregon include a forest products harvest tax, an oil and gas production tax, and privilege taxes on Eastern and Western Oregon timber. Other state taxes include various license fees and stamp taxes. There are no state property taxes. Instead they are collected exclusively by local governments. About 40% of total state and local revenue is collected at the local level.

The state constitution gives voters the right to vote on any substantial tax increase, either by the state or by local governments. State tax measures may be placed on the ballot by the legislature or by petition; local levies must be voted on yearly unless voter approval has been secured for a tax base that may increase by 6% a year without an additional vote.

The state collected $5.892 billion in taxes in 2002, of which 71.5% came from individual income taxes, 12.7% from selective sales taxes, 9.7% from license fees, 3.8% from corporate income taxes, and 0.6% from severance taxes. In 2003, Oregon ranked 39th among the states in terms of combined state and local tax burden, which amounted to about 9% of income.

The following table from the US Census Bureau provides a summary of taxes collected by the state in 2002.

	($000)	PER CAPITA
Total Taxes	5,139,322	1,459.41
Property taxes	(X)	(X)
Sales and gross receipts	650,297	184.66
General sales and gross receipts	(X)	(X)
Selective sales taxes	650,297	184.66
Alcoholic beverage	12,684	3.6
Amusements	3	0
Insurance Premiums	53,737	15.26
Motor fuels	398,309	113.11
Pari-mutuels	1,915	0.54
Public utilities	8,615	2.45
Tobacco products	175,034	49.7
Other selective sales	(X)	(X)
Licenses	496,378	140.96
Alcoholic beverages	2,800	0.8
Amusements	1,912	0.54
Corporation	367	0.1
Hunting and fishing	33,200	9.43
Motor vehicle	266,138	75.57
Motor vehicle operators	27,357	7.77
Public utility	13,047	3.7
Occupation and business, NEC	148,596	42.2
Other	2,961	0.84
Other taxes	3,992,647	1,133.79
Individual income	3,674,962	1,043.57
Corporation net income	196,257	55.73
Death and gift	65,200	18.51
Documentary and stock transfer	26,616	7.56
Severance	29,612	8.41
Other	(X)	(X)

37 ECONOMIC POLICY

Oregon actively seeks balanced economic growth in order to diversify its industrial base, reduce its dependence on the wood products industry, and provide jobs for a steadily growing labor force. The Economic Development Department offers a variety of financial assistance and incentives to companies which create jobs, particularly for low-income residents. It extends loans and issues industrial development bonds for manufacturing, processing and tourism-related facilities in Oregon. The bonds are exempt from federal taxes. The Department enables banks to make loans to projects that carry higher than conventional risk by creating reserve accounts which function as insurance for the banks. To promote new technologies, the Oregon Resource and Technology Development Corporation invests in applied research. Enterprise zones offer incentives for new businesses. The state offers tax credits to encourage businesses to use pollution control facilities, to invest in energy conservation and to employ renewable energy resources. In 2003, the Department developed a Guidebook and Readiness Assessment Tool to help communities assess their economic development potentials.

38 HEALTH

In 2000, the infant mortality rate was 5.6 infant deaths per 1,000 live births, well below the national rate of 6.9. In 1999, 14,145 legal abortions were performed in Oregon, a rate of 20 abortions per 1,000 women. The HIV mortality rate per 100,000 population was 1.8, well below the national average of 5.3 in 2000. A total of 5,056 AIDS cases had been reported in Oregon through 2001. Major causes of death in 2000 (with rates per 100,000 population) were heart disease, 212.3; cancer, 208.0; cerebrovascular diseases, 71.9; accidents and adverse effects, 38.2; motor vehicle accidents, 14.3 and suicide, 14.8. The overall death rate of 884.5 per 100,000 population is higher than the national rate of 873.1. At least 20.8% of Oregon residents 18 and older smoked in 2000.

Oregon's 60 community hospitals had 334,862 admissions and 6,660 beds in 2001. There were 11,266 full-time registered nurses and 575 full-time licensed practical nurses in 2001 and 265 physicians per 100,000 population in 2000. The average expense of a community hospital for care was $1,137.80 per inpatient day in 2001.

Federal government grants to cover the Medicare and Medicaid services in 2001 totaled $1.8 billion; 495,704 enrollees received Medicare benefits that year. At least 12.8% of Oregon's residents were uninsured in 2002.

The only medical and dental schools in the state are at the University of Oregon Health Sciences University in Portland.

39 SOCIAL WELFARE

The Department of Human Resources was created in 1971 to coordinate social service activities. In 2001, the average weekly unemployment benefit was $261.89. Average monthly participation in the food stamp program in FY2002 comprised 359,705 persons (177,291 households). The average monthly benefit was $74.13, and the sum total of benefits paid in FY2002 was $319,462,072.

With the enactment of the Personal Responsibility and Work Opportunity Reconciliation Act of 1996, the US government has changed the form and regulations for many of its social welfare programs. Most significantly, it replaces Aid to Families with Dependent Children (AFDC), an open-ended entitlement program, with Temporary Assistance for Needy Families (TANF), a limited system of assistance funded largely through federal block grants. The reform act also impacts the food stamp program, the Supplemental Security Income program, and the child nutrition program. The law took effect on 1 July 1997 and provided $16.38 billion in block grants for fiscal years 1997–2002. The grants are to be divided among the states based on an equation involving the numbers of former AFDC recipients in each state.

Reauthorization of the 1996 social welfare legislation, scheduled for 2002, was delayed, and the original law had been extended three times as of July 2003, with the most recent extension running through September 2003. Oregon's TANF program is called JOBS (Job Opportunities and Basic Skills). In June 2000 the state had 42,374 welfare recipients. State expenditures on the TANF program in FY2002 totaled $83,107,655.

In December 2001, Social Security benefits were paid to 577,570 Oregon residents. This number included 383,590 retired workers, 57,860 widows and widowers, 61,470 disabled workers, 36,860 spouses, and 37,790 children. Social Security beneficiaries represented 16.4% of the total state population and 95.6% of the state's population age 65 and older. Retired workers (excluding persons with special benefits) received an average monthly payment of $884; widows and widowers, $865; disabled workers, $812; and spouses, $448. Payments for children of retired workers averaged $444 per month; children of deceased workers, $595; and children of disabled workers, $252.

Federal Supplemental Security Income payments in December 2001 went to 54,099 Oregon residents, averaging $370 a month.

40 HOUSING

During the 1970s and early 1980s, a growing percentage of new construction went for rental units. Between 1970 and 1980, the proportion of the housing stock in single-family units fell from 77% to 68%. In 2002, there were an estimated 1,495,582 housing units in Oregon, of which 1,409,433 were occupied; 63.7% owner-occupied. About 62.6% of all units were single-family, detached homes. Electricity and utility gas were the most common energy sources for heat; about 1,058 units were equipped for solar power. It was estimated that 40,452 units lacked telephone service, 6,950 lacked complete plumbing facilities, and 12,734 lacked complete kitchen facilities. The average household size was 2.44 people.

In 2002, 22,186 new privately owned units were authorized for construction. The median home value was $160,185. The median monthly cost for mortgage owners was $1,217. Renters paid a median of $663 per month. During 2002, Oregon received over $62.3 million in community planning and development aid from the US Department of Housing and Urban Development. The Housing Division of the Department of Commerce offers housing purchase assistance (through interest rates below the prevailing market) and construction subsidies to build units for disabled and for low- and moderate-income renters.

41 EDUCATION

Passed by Oregon's legislature in 1991, the Educational Act for the 21st Century set into motion an extensive restructuring of the state's kindergarten through 12th grade public school system. Key components of the Act include raising academic standards for all students, increasing student skills and abilities needed in the workplace, involving parents in decision-making, assessing student performance, requiring accountability for results, emphasizing early childhood education, providing learning opportunities in partnership with communities, and giving local schools more freedom and autonomy.

In 2000, 85.1% of Oregon residents age 25 and older were high school graduates. Some 25.1% had obtained a bachelor's degree or higher. The total enrollment for fall 1999 in Oregon's public schools stood at 545,033. Of these, 378,474 attended schools from kindergarten through grade eight, and 166,559 attended high school. Minority students made up approximately 21% of the total enrollment in public elementary and secondary schools in 2001. Total enrollment was estimated at 547,200 in fall 2000 and is expected to reach 564,000 by fall 2005. Expenditures for public education in 2000/01 were estimated at $4,026,000. Enrollment in nonpublic schools in fall 2001 was 45,352.

As of fall 2000, there were 204,811 students enrolled in college or graduate school. In the same year Oregon had 56 degree-granting institutions. Higher education in Oregon comprises 21 community colleges, 19 independent institutions, and a state higher education system of 8 institutions. The University of Oregon in Eugene has the highest regular enrollment, followed by Portland State University in Portland, and Oregon State University in Corvallis. The Oregon State Scholarship Commission administers an extensive financial aid program for state college students. In 1997, minority students comprised 13.2% of total postsecondary enrollment.

Major private higher education institutions include Willamette University, Salem; George Fox College, Newberg; Linfield College, McMinnville; and University of Portland, Reed College, Lewis and Clark College, and Oregon Graduate Institute of Science and Technology, all in Portland.

42 ARTS

The Portland Art Museum, with an associated art school, is the city's center for the visual arts. The University of Oregon in Eugene has an art museum specializing in Oriental art.

The state's most noted theatrical enterprise is the annual Oregon Shakespeare Festival in Ashland, with a complex of theaters drawing actors and audiences from around the nation. The Portland Center for the Performing Arts is home to the Oregon Symphony Orchestra, the Portland Opera, Oregon Ballet Theatre, Oregon Children's Theatre, Portland Center Stage, Portland Youth Philharmonic, Tears of Joy Puppet Theatre, and Broadway in Portland. Salem and Eugene have small symphony orchestras of their own.

The Oregon Arts Commission was established in 1967 and became a division of the Oregon Economic and Community Development Department in 1993. The Commission operates a program of direct-mail marketing of fine art prints created by artists from the Northwest. The Commission and the Department of Education jointly administer a program of Young Writers Fellowships.

In 2003, the Oregon Arts Commission and other Oregon arts organizations received grants totaling $1,124,200 from the National Endowment for the Arts. The state and private sources contribute funding for the arts as well. The Oregon Council for the Humanities has a number of annual historical and literary programs. In 2000, the National Endowment for the Humanities contributed $1,016,207 for 13 state programs. The state has approximately 300 arts associations and 60 local arts groups.

43 LIBRARIES AND MUSEUMS

In 2000, Oregon had 17 library systems; the total book stock of all public libraries was 8,895,249, and their combined circulation was 34,814,000. Most cities and counties in Oregon have public library systems, the largest being the Multnomah County library system in Portland, with 14 branches and 1,288,634 volumes in 1999. The State Library in Salem serves as a reference agency for state government. Total public library income in 2000 was $109 million, including $759,878 in federal grants and $651,324 in state grants. Per capita spending was $30.00.

Oregon has 105 museums, historic sites, botanical gardens and arboretums. Historical museums emphasizing Oregon's pioneer heritage appear throughout the state, with Ft. Clatsop National Memorial—featuring a replica of Lewis and Clark's winter headquarters—among the notable attractions. The Oregon Historical Society operates a major historical museum in Portland, publishes books of historical interest, and issues the Oregon Historical Quarterly. In Portland's Washington Park area are the Oregon Museum of Science and Industry, Washington Park Zoo, Western Forestry Center, and an arboretum and other gardens.

44COMMUNICATIONS

As of 2001, 96.2% of Oregon's households had telephones. Oregon had 37 major AM and 86 major FM commercial radio stations in 2003; and 24 major television stations. A state-owned broadcasting system provides educational radio and television programming. The Portland area had over one million television households, 62% of which ordered cable. A total of 97,453 Internet domain names were registered in the state by the year 2000.

45PRESS

Oregon's first newspaper was the weekly *Oregon Spectator,* which began publication in 1846. Early newspapers engaged in what became known as the "Oregon style" of journalism, characterized by intemperate, vituperative, and fiercely partisan comments. As of 2002, 6 morning, 14 evening, and 11 Sunday newspapers were published in Oregon. The state's largest newspaper, the *Oregonian,* published in Portland, is owned by Advance Publications. The following table lists leading Oregon newspapers with their approximate 2002 circulations:

AREA	NAME	DAILY	SUNDAY
Eugene	*Register–Guard* (m,S)	73,091	77,597
Portland	*Oregonian* (all day,S)	351,303	430,551
Salem	*Statesman–Journal* (m,S)	57,827	66,587

46ORGANIZATIONS

In 2003, there were about 2,166 regional, national, and international organizations within the state. Among the many forestry-related organizations in Oregon are the International Woodworkers of America (AFL-CIO), Association of Western Pulp and Paper Workers, Pacific Lumber Exporters Association, Western Forest Industries Association, and Western Wood Products Association, all with their headquarters in Portland. The American Lumberjack Association is based in West Linn. State and national conservation issues are represented in part by the Native Fish Society, the Native Forest Council, and the Natural Areas Association.

Other national organizations based in the state are the Hop Growers of America and the North American Bungee Association. Local history is represented in part through the Big Butte Historical Society and the Oregon Trail Travelers, as well as several other regional historical societies.

47TOURISM, TRAVEL, AND RECREATION

Oregon's abundance and variety of natural features and recreational opportunities make the state a major tourist attraction. Travel and tourism is the state's 3rd-largest employer, generating over 94,500 jobs. In 2002, travel revenues reached about $6.2 billion dollars. The Oregon Tourism Commission maintains an active tourist advertising program, and Portland hotels busily seek major conventions.

Among the leading attractions are the rugged Oregon coast, with its offshore salmon fishing; Crater Lake National Park; the Rogue River, for river running and fishing; the Columbia Gorge, east of Portland; the Cascades wilderness; and Portland's annual Rose Festival. Oregon has one national park, Crater Lake, and three other areas—John Day Fossil Beds National Monument, Oregon Caves National Monument and Ft. Clatsop National Memorial—managed by the National Park Service. The US Forest Service administers the Oregon Dunes National Recreation Area, on the Oregon coast; the Lava Lands Visitor Complex near Bend; and the Hells Canyon National Recreation Area, east of Enterprise. Oregon has one of the nation's most extensive state park systems: 225 parks and recreation areas cover 90,000 acres (36,400 hectares).

48SPORTS

Oregon has one major league team, based in Portland. The Portland Trail Blazers, winners of the National Basketball Association championship in 1977, play in the NBA. The city did have a WNBA franchise, the Fire, but it folded following the 2002 season. The state fields three teams that compete in baseball's class-A Northwest League, in Eugene, Portland, and Keizer.

Horse racing takes place at Portland Meadows in Portland and, in late August and early September, at the Oregon State Fair in Salem; there is greyhound racing at the Multnomah Greyhound Park near Portland. Pari-mutuel betting is permitted at the tracks, but off-track betting is prohibited.

The University of Oregon and Oregon State University belong to the Pacific 10 Conference. The Oregon State Ducks won the Rose Bowl in 1942 and appeared in it but lost in 1965. Oregon was a surprise winner at the Pac-10 in 1994, and made its first Rose Bowl appearance in 37 years. The Ducks lost to Penn State in the 1995 Rose Bowl. Since 1996, the Ducks have won several bowl contests, highlighted by a victory over the Colorado Buffaloes in the 2002 Fiesta Bowl. Oregon finished the season as the 2nd-ranked team in the nation.

Other annual sporting events include sled dog races in Bend and Union Creek, the All-Indian Rodeo in Tygh Valley in May (one of many rodeos), and the Cycle Oregon Bike Ride.

49FAMOUS OREGONIANS

Prominent federal officeholders from Oregon include Senator Charles McNary (1874–1944), a leading advocate of federal reclamation and development projects and the Republican vice-presidential nominee in 1940; Senator Wayne Morse (b.Wisconsin, 1900–74), who was an early opponent of US involvement in Vietnam; Representative Edith Green (1910–84), a leader in federal education assistance; and Representative Al Ullman (b.Montana, 1914–86), chairman of the House Ways and Means Committee until his defeat in 1980. Recent cabinet members from Oregon have been Douglas McKay (1893–1959), secretary of the interior; and Neil Goldschmidt (b.1940) secretary of transportation.

A major figure in early Oregon history was sea captain Robert Gray (b.Rhode Island. 1755–1806), discoverer of the Columbia River. Although never holding a government position, fur trader Dr. John McLoughlin (b.Canada, 1784–1857) in effect ruled Oregon from 1824 to 1845; he was officially designated the "father of Oregon" by the 1957 state legislature. Also of importance in the early settlement was Methodist missionary Jason Lee (b.Canada, 1803–45). Oregon's most famous Indian was Chief Joseph (1840?–1904), leader of the Nez Percé in northeastern Oregon; when tension between the Nez Percé and white settlers erupted into open hostilities in 1877, Chief Joseph led his band of about 650 men, women, and children from the Oregon-Idaho border across the Bitterroot Range evading three army detachments before being captured in northern Montana.

Other important figures in the early days of statehood were Harvey W. Scott (b.Illinois 1838–1910), longtime editor of the Portland *Oregonian,* and his sister, Abigail Scott Duniway (b.Illinois, 1823–1915), the Northwest's foremost advocate of women's suffrage, a cause her brother strongly opposed. William Simon U'Ren (b.Wisconsin, 1859–1949) was a lawyer and reformer whose influence on Oregon politics and government endures to this day. Journalist and Communist John Reed (1887–1920), author of *Ten Days That Shook the World,* an eyewitness account of the Bolshevik Revolution, was born in Portland, and award-winning science-fiction writer Ursula K. LeGuin (b.California, 1929) is a Portland resident. Linus Pauling (1901–94), two-time winner of the Nobel Prize (for chemistry in 1954, for peace in 1962), was another Portland native. Other scientists prominent in the state's history include botanist David Douglas (b.Scotland, 1798–1834), who made two trips to Oregon and after whom the Douglas fir is named; and geologist and paleontologist Thomas Condon (b.Ireland, 1822–1907), discoverer of major fossil beds in eastern Oregon.

⁵⁰BIBLIOGRAPHY

Blair, Karen J. *Northwest Women: An Annotated Bibliography of Sources on the History of Oregon and Washington Women, 1787–1970.* Pullman, Wash.: Washington State University Press, 1997.

Cogswell, Philip. *Capitol Names: Individuals Woven into Oregon's History.* Portland: Oregon Historical Society, 1977.

Corning, Howard. *Dictionary of Oregon History.* Portland: Binfords & Mort, 1956.

Dodds, Gordon B. *Oregon: A Bicentennial History.* New York: Norton, 1977.

Federal Writers' Project. *Oregon: End of the Trail.* 1941. Reprint, New York: Somerset, n.d.

Johansen, Dorothy, and Charles Gates. *Empire of the Columbia: A History of the Pacific Northwest.* 2nd ed. New York: Harper & Row, 1967.

Loy, William. *Atlas of Oregon.* Eugene: University of Oregon Books, 1976.

McCartney, Laton. *Across the Great Divide: Robert Stuart and the Discovery of the Oregon Trail.* New York: Free Press, 2003.

Parkman, Francis, Jr. *The Oregon Trail.* New York: Penguin, 1982.

Throckmorton, Arthur L. *Oregon Argonauts: Merchant Adventurers on the Western Frontier.* Portland: Oregon Historical Society, 1961.

Vaughan, Thomas, and Terrence O'Donnell. *Portland: A Historical Sketch and Guide.* Portland: Oregon Historical Society, 1976.

Webber, Bert, and Margie Webber. *Awesome Caverns of Marble in the Oregon Caves National Monuement.* Medford, Ore.: Webb Research Group Publishers, 1998.

Yuskavitch, Jim, and Leslie D. Cole. *The Insider's Guide to Bend & Central Oregon.* Helena, Mont.: Falcon Pub., Inc., 1999.

PENNSYLVANIA

Commonwealth of Pennsylvania

ORIGIN OF STATE NAME: Named for Admiral William Penn, father of the founder of Pennsylvania. **NICKNAME:** The Keystone State. **CAPITAL:** Harrisburg. **ENTERED UNION:** 12 December 1787 (2nd). **SONG:** "Pennsylvania." **MOTTO:** Virtue, Liberty and Independence. **COAT OF ARMS:** A shield supported by two horses displays a sailing ship, a plow, and three sheaves of wheat; an eagle forms the crest. Beneath the shield an olive branch and a cornstalk are crossed and below them is the state motto. **FLAG:** The coat of arms appears in the center of a blue field. **OFFICIAL SEAL:** OBVERSE: A shield displays a sailing ship, a plow, and three sheaves of wheat with a cornstalk to the left, an olive branch to the right, and an eagle above, surrounded by the inscription "Seal of the State of Pennsylvania." REVERSE: A woman representing Liberty holds a wand topped by a liberty cap in her left hand and a drawn sword in her right as she tramples a lion representing Tyranny; the legend "Both Can't Survive" encircles the design. **ANIMAL:** White-tailed deer. **BIRD:** Ruffed grouse. **DOG:** Great Dane. **FISH:** Brook trout. **INSECT:** Firefly. **FLOWER:** Mountain laurel. **TREE:** Hemlock. **BEAUTIFICATION AND CONSERVATION PLANT:** Penngift crownvetch. **BEVERAGE:** Milk. **FOSSIL:** Phacops rana. **LEGAL HOLIDAYS:** New Year's Day, 1 January; Birthday of Martin Luther King, Jr., 3rd Monday in January; Presidents' Day, 3rd Monday in February; Memorial Day, last Monday in May; Flag Day, 14 June; Independence Day, 4 July; Labor Day, 1st Monday in September; Columbus Day, 2nd Monday in October; Veterans Day, 11 November; Thanksgiving Day, 4th Thursday in November; Christmas Day, 25 December. **TIME:** 7 AM EST = noon GMT.

¹LOCATION, SIZE, AND EXTENT

Located in the northeastern US, the Commonwealth of Pennsylvania is the 2nd largest of the three Middle Atlantic states and ranks 33rd in size among the 50 states.

The total area of Pennsylvania is 45,308 sq mi (117,348 sq km), of which land occupies 44,888 sq mi (116,260 sq km) and inland water 420 sq mi (1,088 sq km). The state extends 307 mi (494 km) E-W and 169 mi (272 km) N-S. Pennsylvania is rectangular in shape, except for an irregular side on the E and a break in the even boundary in the NW where the line extends N-E for about 50 mi (80 km) along the shore of Lake Erie.

Pennsylvania is bordered on the N by New York; on the E by New York and New Jersey (with the Delaware River forming the entire boundary); on the SE by Delaware; on the S by Maryland and West Virginia (demarcated by the Mason-Dixon line); on the W by West Virginia and Ohio; and on the NW by Lake Erie. The total boundary length of Pennsylvania is 880 mi (1,416 km). The state's geographical center lies in Centre County, 2.5 mi (4 km) SW of Bellefonte.

²TOPOGRAPHY

Pennsylvania may be divided into more than a dozen distinct physiographic regions, most of which extend in curved bands from east to south. Beginning in the southeast, the first region (including Philadelphia) is a narrow belt of coastal plain along the lower Delaware River; this area, at sea level, is the state's lowest region. The next belt, dominating the southeastern corner, is the Piedmont Plateau, a wide area of rolling hills and lowlands. The Great Valley, approximately 10–15 mi (16–24 km) in width, runs from the middle of the state's eastern border to the middle of its southern border. The eastern, central, and western parts of the Great Valley are known as the Lehigh, Lebanon, and Cumberland valleys, respectively. West and north of the Great Valley, the Pocono Plateau rises to about 2,200 ft (700 m). Next, in a band 50–60 mi (80–100 km) wide, most of the way from the north-

central part of the eastern border to the west-central part of the southern border are the Appalachian Mountains, a distinctive region of parallel ridges and valleys.

The Allegheny High Plateau, part of the Appalachian Plateaus, makes up the western and northern parts of the state. The Allegheny Front, the escarpment along the eastern edge of the plateau, is the most striking topographical feature in Pennsylvania, dissected by many winding streams to form narrow, steep-sided valleys; the southwestern extension of the Allegheny High Plateau contains the state's highest peak, Mt. Davis, at 3,213 ft (980 m). A narrow lowland region, the Erie Plain, borders Lake Erie in the extreme northwestern part of the state.

According to federal sources, Pennsylvania has jurisdiction over 735 sq mi (1,904 sq km) of Lake Erie; the state government gives a figure of 891 sq mi (2,308 sq km). Pennsylvania contains about 250 natural lakes larger than 20 acres (8 ha), most of them in the glaciated regions of the northeast and northwest. The largest natural lake within the state's borders is Conneaut Lake, about 30 mi (48 km) south of the city of Erie, with an area of less than 1.5 sq mi (39 sq km); the largest manmade lake is Lake Wallenpaupack, in the Poconos, occupying about 9 sq mi (23 sq km). Pennsylvania claims more than 21 sq mi (54 sq km) of the Pymatuning Reservoir on the Ohio border.

The Susquehanna River and its tributaries drain more than 46% of the area of Pennsylvania, much of it in the Appalachian Mountains. The Delaware River forms Pennsylvania's eastern border and, like the Susquehanna, flows southeastward to the Atlantic Ocean. Most of the western part of the state is drained by the Allegheny and Monongahela rivers, which join at Pittsburgh to form the Ohio. The Beaver, Clarion, and Youghiogheny rivers are also important parts of this system.

During early geological history, the topography of Pennsylvania had the reverse of its present configurations, with mountains in the southeast and a large inland sea covering the rest of the state. This sea, which alternately expanded and contracted, interwove layers of vegetation (which later became coal) with layers of sandstone and shale.

³CLIMATE

Although Pennsylvania lies entirely within the humid continental zone, its climate varies according to region and elevation. The regions with the warmest temperatures and the longest growing seasons are the low-lying southwest Ohio valley and the Monongahela valley in the southeast. The region bordering Lake Erie also has a long growing season, as the moderating effect of the lake prevents early spring and late autumn frosts. The first two areas have hot summers, while the Erie area is more moderate. The rest of the state, at higher elevations, has cold winters and cool summers.

Among the major population centers, Philadelphia has an annual mean temperature of 54°F (12°C), with a normal minimum of 45°F (7°C) and a normal maximum of 64°F (18°C). Pittsburgh has an annual mean of 50°F (10°C), with a minimum of 41°F (5°C) and a maximum of 60°F (16°C). In the cooler northern areas, Scranton has a normal annual mean ranging from 41°F (5°C) to 59°F (15°C); Erie, from 42°F (6°C) to 58°F (14°C). The record low temperature for the state is –42°F (–41°C), set at Smethport on 5 January 1904; the record high, 111°F (44°C), was reached at Phoenixville on 10 July 1936.

Philadelphia had about 42 in (107 cm) of precipitation annually (1971–2000), and Pittsburgh had 37.8 in (96 cm). Pittsburgh, however, has much more snow—44 in (112 cm), compared with 21 in (53 cm) for Philadelphia. The snowfall in Erie, in the snow belt, exceeds 54 in (137 cm) per year, with heavy snows sometimes experienced late in April. In Philadelphia, the sun shines an average of 56% of the time; in Pittsburgh, 44%.

The state has experienced several destructive floods. On 31 May 1889, the South Fork Dam near Johnstown broke after a heavy rainfall, and its rampaging waters killed 2,200 people and devastated the entire city in less than 10 minutes. On 19–20 July 1977, Johnstown experienced another flood, resulting in 68 deaths. Three tornadoes raked the southwestern part of the commonwealth on 23 June 1944, killing 45 persons and injuring another 362. Rains from Hurricane Agnes in June 1972 resulted in floods that caused 48 deaths and more than $1.2 billion worth of property damage in the Susquehanna Valley.

⁴FLORA AND FAUNA

Maple, walnut, poplar, oak, pine, ash, beech, and linden trees fill Pennsylvania's extensive forests, along with sassafras, sycamore, weeping willow, and balsam fir (Abies fraseri). Red pine and paper birch are found in the north while the sweet gum is dominant in the extreme southwest. Mountain laurel (the state flower), June-berry, dotted hawthorn, New Jersey tea, and various dogwoods are among the shrubs and small trees found in most parts of the state, and dewberry, wintergreen, wild columbine, and wild ginger are also common. In 2003, the small whorled pogonia and Virginia spirea were classified as threatened, with the northeastern bulrush as endangered.

Numerous mammals persist in Pennsylvania, among them the white-tailed deer (the state animal), black bear, red and gray foxes, opossum, raccoon, muskrat, mink, snowshoe hare, common cottontail, and red, gray, fox, and flying squirrels. Native amphibians include the hellbender, Fowler's toad, and the tree, cricket, and true frogs; among reptilian species are the five-lined and black skinks and five varieties of lizard. The ruffed grouse, a common game species, is the official state bird; other game birds are the wood dove, ring-necked pheasant, bobwhite quail, and mallard and black ducks. The robin, cardinal, English sparrow, red-eyed vireo, cedar waxwing, tufted titmouse, yellow-shafted flicker, barn swallow, blue jay, and killdeer are common

non-game birds. More than 170 types of fish have been identified in Pennsylvania, with brown and brook trout, grass pickerel, bigeye chub, pirate perch, and white bass among the common native varieties.

In 1978, the Pennsylvania Game Commission and the US Fish and Wildlife Service signed a cooperative agreement under which the federal government provides two dollars for each dollar spent by the state to determine the status of and improve conditions for threatened or endangered species. On the threatened or endangered list in 2003 were 14 species, including the Indiana bat, bald eagle, orangefoot pimpleback pearly mussel, dwarf wedgemussel, and pink mucket pearlymussel.

⁵ENVIRONMENTAL PROTECTION

Pennsylvania's environment was ravaged by uncontrolled timber cutting in the 19th century, and by extensive coal mining and industrial development until recent times. Pittsburgh's most famous landmarks were its smokestacks, and it was said that silverware on ships entering the port of Philadelphia would tarnish immediately from the fumes of the Delaware River. The anthracite-mining regions were filled with huge, hideous culm piles, and the bituminous and anthracite fields were torn up by strip-mining. In 1979, a different kind of threat to Pennsylvania's environment received worldwide attention when the nuclear power plant at Three Mile Island seriously malfunctioned.

In 1895, Pennsylvania appointed its first commissioner of forestry, in an attempt to repair some of the earlier damage. Gifford Pinchot, who twice served as governor of Pennsylvania, was the first professionally trained forester in the US (he studied at the École National Forestiere in Paris), developed the US Forest Service, and served as Pennsylvania forest commissioner from 1920 to 1922. In 1955, the state forests were put under scientific management.

In 1972, Pennsylvania voters ratified a state constitutional amendment adopted 18 May 1971, acknowledging the people's "right to clean air, pure water, and to the preservation of the natural, scenic, historic, and esthetic values of the environment" and naming the state as trustee of these resources. Passage of the amendment came only two years after establishment of the Pennsylvania Department of Environmental Resources, which in the 1990s was reorganized into two separate entities. The Department of Conservation and Natural Resources (DCNR) was established on 1 July 1995 to maintain and preserve the state's 116 state parks, manage the 2.1 million acres of state forest land, and provide information on the state's ecological and geologic resources. The DCNR also oversees environmental education and provides assistance and grants for preserving rivers, community trails, parks, and recreation. The Pennsylvania Department of Environmental Protection (DEP) was established to protect the state's air, land, and water from pollution and to provide a cleaner environment for the health and safety of Pennsylvania's citizens. After miners were trapped (and subsequently successfully rescued) in an accident at Quecreek Mine in July 2002, the DEP launched a program to build a database of abandoned mine locations to minimize the risk of another such accident occurring.

As of the early 1990s, sewage and industrial wastes were the major pollutants in areas with high industrial and population concentrations. In western and parts of central Pennsylvania, drainage from abandoned bituminous coal mines created serious water quality problems; active mines in this region were also potentially polluting. A similar situation prevailed in the anthracite areas of northeastern Pennsylvania. Oil and gas well operations, located primarily in the northwestern portion of the commonwealth, were additional pollution sources. In 2003, Pennsylvania had 572 hazardous waste sites listed in the Environmental Protection Agency's database, 94 of which were

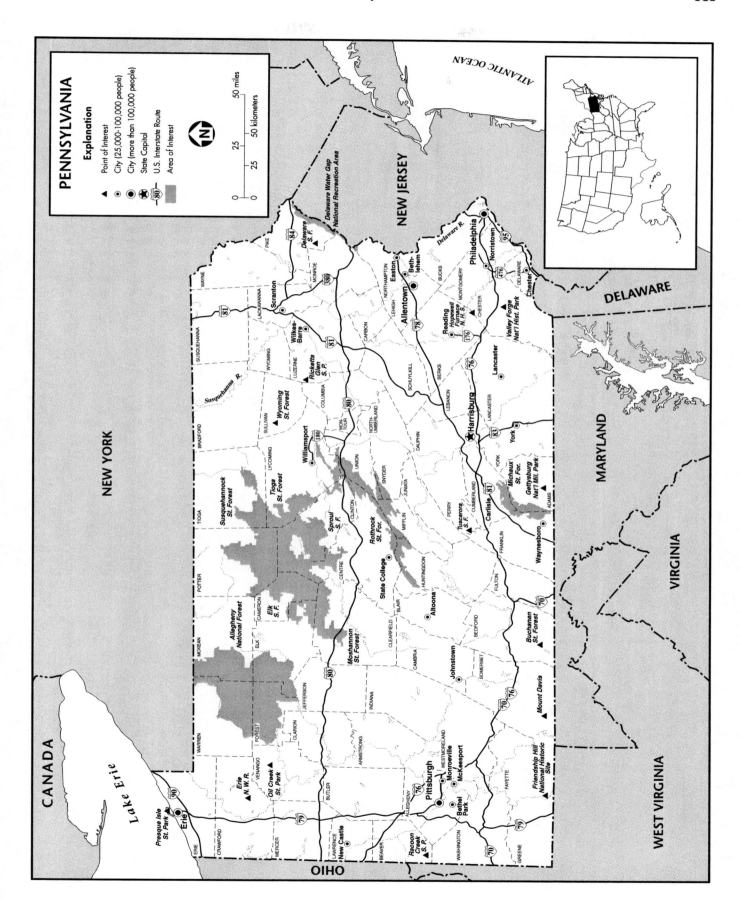

on the National Priorities List. In 1996, there were 404,000 acres of wetlands in the state.

In March 1979, Pennsylvania suffered the worst nuclear-power accident in US history when a nuclear reactor on Three Mile Island malfunctioned and radioactive gases escaped. A second reactor was shut down immediately even though it was not damaged. The cleanup of radioactive waste cost about $1 billion, and it was not until late 1985 that the undamaged unit was placed back in operation.

An oil spill at Marcus Hook, near the Delaware Border, released 435,000 gallons of crude oil into the Delaware River in September 1985; damage to birds and wetlands was more extensive in Delaware than in Pennsylvania.

In 2001, Pennsylvania received $197,186,000 in federal grants from the Environmental Protection Agency; EPA expenditures for procurement contracts in Pennsylvania that year amounted to $63,078,000.

6 POPULATION

Pennsylvania ranked 6th in population in the US with an estimated total of 12,335,091 in 2002, an increase of 0.4% since 2000. Between 1990 and 2000, Pennsylvania's population grew from 11,881,643 to 12,281,054, an increase of 3.4%. The population is projected to reach 12.7 million by 2025.

As recently as 1940, Pennsylvania was the 2nd most populous state in the US. By the 1980 census, however, the state had slipped to 4th place, with a population of 11,863,895; it dropped to 5th place in 1990 with a population of 11,881,643.

In 2000, the median age for Pennsylvanians was 38. In the same year, 23.8% of the populace was under age 18 while 15.6% were age 65 or older. The population density in 2000 was 274 persons per sq mi.

The largest city in the state, Philadelphia, was the 5th-largest US city as of 2002, with a population of 1,492,231. Philadelphia's population has declined since 1970, when 1,949,996 people lived there. The population of its metropolitan area also declined during the 1970s, but then increased from 4,716,559 in 1980 to 4,922,257 in 1990 and stood at an estimated 4,949,867 in 1999. Further, the larger Philadelphia–Wilmington (Del.)–Trenton (N. J.) consolidated metropolitan area increased from 5,680,509 in 1980 to an estimated 5,999,034 in 1999. Pittsburgh's population declined from 616,806 in 1950 to an estimated 327,898 in 2002 in the city proper, and the Pittsburgh metropolitan area population decreased from 2,348,000 in 1970 to 2,331,336 in 1999.

The 2002 estimated populations of Pennsylvania's other major cities were Allentown, 106,105, and Erie, 102,122. Other cities with large populations include Reading, Scranton, Bethlehem, Lancaster, Harrisburg, Altoona, and Wilkes-Barre.

7 ETHNIC GROUPS

During the colonial period, under the religious tolerance of a Quaker government, Pennsylvania was a haven for dissident sectarians from continental Europe and the British Isles. Some German sectarians, including the Amish, have kept up their traditions to this day. An initially friendly policy toward the Indians waned in the late 18th century under the pressures of population growth and the anxieties of the French and Indian War. The famous Carlisle Indian School (1879–1918) educated many leaders from various tribes throughout the US. In

Pennsylvania Counties, County Seats, and County Areas and Populations

COUNTY	COUNTY SEAT	LAND AREA (SQ MI)	POPULATION (2002 EST.)	COUNTY	COUNTY SEAT	LAND AREA (SQ MI)	POPULATION (2002 EST.)
Adams	Gettysburg	521	94,437	Lancaster	Lancaster	952	478,561
Allegheny	Pittsburgh	727	1,269,904	Lawrence	New Castle	363	94,104
Armstrong	Kittanning	646	71,673	Lebanon	Lebanon	363	121,199
Beaver	Beaver	436	179,351	Lehigh	Allentown	348	317,533
Bedford	Bedford	1,017	49,944	Luzerne	Wilkes-Barre	891	314,643
Berks	Reading	861	382,108	Lycoming	Williamsport	1,237	119,000
Blair	Hollidaysburg	527	127,840	McKean	Smethport	1,237	44,884
Bradford	Towanda	1,152	62,810	Mercer	Mercer	672	119,514
Bucks	Doylestown	610	610,440	Mifflin	Lewistown	413	46,435
Butler	Butler	789	178,078	Monroe	Stroudsburg	609	148,839
Cambria	Ebensburg	691	150,452	Montgomery	Norristown	486	766,517
Cameron	Emporium	398	5,843	Montour	Danville	131	18,214
Carbon	Jim Thorpe	384	59,688	Northhampton	Easton	376	273,324
Centre	Bellefonte	1,106	138,524	Northumberland	Sunbury	461	93,371
Chester	West Chester	758	450,160	Perry	New Bloomfield	557	43,876
Clarion	Clarion	607	41,316	Philadelphia	Philadelphia	136	1,492,231
Clearfield	Clearfield	1,149	83,203	Pike	Milford	550	50,095
Clinton	Lock Haven	891	37,680	Potter	Coudersport	1,081	18,217
Columbia	Bloomsburg	486	64,134	Schuylkill	Pottsville	782	148,505
Crawford	Meadville	1,011	89,856	Snyder	Middleburg	329	37,828
Cumberland	Carlisle	547	217,743	Somerset	Somerset	1,073	79,456
Dauphin	Harrisburg	528	252,933	Sullivan	Laporte	451	6,482
Delaware	Media	184	553,425	Susquehanna	Montrose	826	42,082
Elk	Ridgeway	830	34,454	Tioga	Wellsboro	1,131	41,461
Erie	Erie	804	280,370	Union	Lewisburg	317	42,006
Fayette	Uniontown	794	146,654	Venango	Franklin	679	56,810
Forest	Tionesta	428	4,888	Warren	Warren	885	43,290
Franklin	Chambersburg	774	131,598	Washington	Washington	858	204,110
Fulton	McConnellsburg	438	14,365	Wayne	Honesdale	731	48,889
Greene	Waynesburg	577	42,520	Westmoreland	Greensburg	1,033	368,428
Huntingdon	Huntingdon	877	45,707	Wyoming	Tunkhannock	399	27,801
Indiana	Indiana	829	88,780	York	York	906	389,209
Jefferson	Brookville	657	45,818				
Juniata	Mifflintown	392	22,760	TOTALS		45,150	12,335,091
Lackawanna	Scranton	461	210,711				

Pennsylvania itself, however, there were only 18,348 American Indians in 2000, up from 15,000 in 1990.

Modest numbers of black slaves were utilized as domestics, field workers, and iron miners in colonial Pennsylvania. Antislavery sentiment was stirred in the 18th century through the efforts of a Quaker, John Woolman, and other Pennsylvanians. The Gradual Abolition of Slavery Act was passed in 1780, and the important antislavery newspaper *The Liberator* appeared in Philadelphia in 1831. As of 2000, black Americans numbered 1,224,612 (10% of the total state population), and were concentrated in the large cities. Philadelphia was 43.2% black in 2000, with 655,824 African American residents.

The late 19th and early 20th centuries brought waves of immigrants from Ireland, Wales, various Slavic nations, and the eastern Mediterranean and the Balkans. Many of the new immigrants settled in the east-central anthracite coal-mining region. In 2000, 508,291 Pennsylvania residents, or 4.1% of the total population, were foreign born, up from 3.1% in 1990. Italy, Germany, the United Kingdom, India, the former Soviet Union, Korea, and Poland were the leading countries of origin. In the valleys surrounding Pittsburgh there are still self-contained ethnic enclaves, and there has been increased interest in preserving distinctive ethnic traditions.

Hispanics and Latinos in Pennsylvania numbered 394,088 in 2000 (3.2%), up from 232,000 in 1990. Most were Puerto Ricans, with smaller numbers of Cubans and Central Americans. In 2000, Asians numbered 219,813; the Asian population included 50,650 Chinese (almost double the 1990 total of 25,908), 31,612 Koreans, 57,241 Asian Indians (almost triple the 1990 figure of 19,769), 14,506 Filipinos, and 30,037 Vietnamese, up sharply from 14,126 in 1990. Pacific Islanders numbered 3,417.

[8]LANGUAGES

Once home to several Algonkian tribes, Pennsylvania still has such Algonkian place-names as Punxsutawney, Aliquippa, Pocono, Towanda, Susquehanna, and Shamokin. An Iroquoian tribe gave its name to the Conestoga region. The word came to identify first the pioneers' covered wagons manufactured in the area and then, in shortened form, a cheap cigar called a *stogie*.

Although not quite homogeneous, Pennsylvania's North Midland dialect is significant as the source of much midwestern and western speech. The only non-Midland sector is the northern tier of counties, settled from southern New York State, where features of the northern dialect predominate.

On the whole, Pennsylvania North Midland is distinguished by the presence of *want off* a tram or bus, *snake feeder* (dragonfly), *run* (small stream), *waterspouts* and *spouts* (gutters), and *creek* as /krik/. With these features are found others that commonly occur in Southern Pennsylvania, such as *corn pone, roasting ears*, and *spiket* (spigot). Western Pennsylvania, however, contrasts with the eastern half by the dominance of /nawthing/ for *nothing*, /greezy/ for *greasy*, /kao/ for *cow*, sugar tree (sugar maple), *hap* (quilt), and *clothes press* (closet), as well as by the influential merging of the /ah/ vowel and the /aw/ vowel so that *cot* and *caught* sound alike. Southern Pennsylvania has *flannel cakes* for pancakes and *ground hackie* for chipmunk. Within this region, Philadelphia and its suburbs have distinctive *baby coach* for baby carriage, *pavement* for sidewalk, *hoagie* for a large sandwich, the vowel of *put* in *broom* and *Cooper*, and the vowel of *father* in *on* and *fog*. In the east and northeast, a doughnut is a *cruller*, one is *sick in the stomach*, and *syrup* has the vowel of *sit*.

In much of central Pennsylvania, descendants of the colonial Palatinate German population retain their speech as Deutsch, often misnamed Pennsylvania Dutch, which has influenced English in the state through such loanwords as *toot* (bag),

rainworm (earthworm), *snits* (dried apples), and *smearcase* (cottage cheese).

In 2000, 10,583,054 Pennsylvanians—91.6% of the population five years old or older—spoke only English at home, down slightly from 92.7% in 1990.

The following table gives selected statistics from the 2000 census for language spoken at home by persons five years old and over. The category "Other West Germanic languages" includes Dutch, Pennsylvania Dutch, and Afrikaans. The category "Other Slavic languages" includes Czech, Slovak, and Ukrainian. The category "Other Asian languages" includes Dravidian languages, Malayalam, Telugu, Tamil, and Turkish. The category "Other Indic languages" includes Bengali, Marathi, Punjabi, and Romany. The category "Other Indo-European languages" includes Albanian, Gaelic, Lithuanian, and Rumanian.

LANGUAGE	NUMBER	PERCENT
Population 5 years and over	11,555,538	100.0
Speak only English	10,583,054	91.6
Speak a language other than English	972,484	8.4
Speak a language other than English	972,484	8.4
Spanish or Spanish Creole	356,754	3.1
Italian	70,434	0.6
German	68,672	0.6
Other West Germanic languages	51,073	0.4
French (incl. Patois, Cajun)	47,735	0.4
Chinese	42,790	0.4
Russian	32,189	0.3
Polish	31,717	0.3
Korean	25,978	0.2
Vietnamese	25,880	0.2
Other Slavic languages	24,423	0.2
Arabic	19,557	0.2
Greek	17,348	0.2
Other Asian languages	16,196	0.1
Other Indic languages	12,297	0.1
Other Indo-European languages	11,656	0.1
Hindi	10,045	0.1

[9]RELIGIONS

With a long history of toleration, Pennsylvania has been a haven for numerous religious groups. The first European settlers were Swedish Lutherans; German Lutherans began arriving 1703. William Penn brought the Quakers to Pennsylvania during the 1680s and the climate of religious liberty soon attracted other dissident groups, including German Mennonites, Dunkars, Moravians, and Schwenkfelders; French Huguenots; Scots-Irish Presbyterians; and English Baptists. Descendants of the 16th-century Anabaptists, the Mennonites for the most part settled as farmers; they and the Quakers were the first religious groups openly to advocate abolition of slavery and to help runaway slaves to freedom via the Underground Railroad. The Amish-Mennonite followers of Jacob Amman continue to dress in black clothing, shun the use of mechanized tools, automobiles and electrical appliance, and observe Sundays by singing 16th-century hymns.

The Presbyterians, who built their first church in the state in 1704, played a major role both in the establishment of schools in the colony and in the later development of Pittsburgh and other cities in the western part of the state. Methodists held their first services in Philadelphia in 1768; for many years thereafter, Methodist circuit riders proselytized throughout the state.

Immigration during the 19th century brought a major change in patterns of worship. The Quakers gradually diminished in number and influence, while Roman Catholic and Greek Orthodox churches and Jewish synagogues opened in many of the mining and manufacturing centers. The bulk of the Jewish migration came, after 1848, from Germany and, after 1882, from East Europe and Russia. The Gilded Age saw the founding of a new group in Pittsburgh by clergyman Charles Taze Russell; first called the Russellites, members of this group (established in 1872) are known today as Jehovah's Witnesses.

As of 2000, Roman Catholics constituted the largest religious group in the state, with a total membership of about of 3,802,524. The largest Protestant denomination in 2000 was the United Methodists, with 659,350 adherents. Other major Protestant groups were the Evangelical Lutheran Church in America, 611,913; the Presbyterian Church USA, 324,714; the United Church of Christ, 241,844; the American Baptist Church USA, 132,858; and the Episcopal Church, 116,511. The historically important Mennonites, of various traditions, had over 68,000 adherents in 2000. Amish communities had over 25,000 members and Moravians numbered over 10,000. Friends USA (Quakers) reported a membership of about 11,844. Jewish congregations included an estimated 283,000 members and the Muslim congregations had about 71,190 adherents. About 5.1 million people (42.1% of the population) were not counted as members of any religious organization.

¹⁰TRANSPORTATION

Like so many of its industrial assets, Pennsylvania's well-developed road and rail networks are showing signs of old age. Nevertheless, the state remains an important center of transportation, and its ports are among the busiest in the US.

The early years of railroad building left Pennsylvania with more miles of track than any other state. The first railroad charter, issued in 1819, provided for a horse-drawn railroad from the Delaware Valley to the headwaters of the Lehigh River. The state authorized construction of a line between Columbia and Philadelphia in 1828, and partial service began four years later as part of the State Works. The roadbed was state-owned, and private rail car companies paid a toll to use the rails. During this time, Pennsylvanians John Jervis and Joseph Harrison were developing steam-powered locomotives. Taking advantage of the new technology were separate rail lines connecting Philadelphia with Germantown (1834), Trenton, New Jersey (1838), and Reading (1839), with the Lehigh Valley (1846), and with New York City (1855). In December 1852, the Pennsylvania Central completed lines connecting Philadelphia and Pittsburgh. Five years later, the Pennsylvania Railroad purchased the State Works, eliminating state competition and tolls. By 1880, the company (which had added many smaller coal hauling lines to its holdings) was the world's largest corporation, with more than 30,000 employees and $400 million in capital. Although railroad revenues declined with the rise of the automobile, the Pennsylvania Railroad remained profitable until the 1960s, when the line merged with the New York Central to form the Penn Central. In 1970, the Penn Central separated its real estate holdings from its transportation operation, on which it declared bankruptcy.

As of 2000, the major (Class I) lines using the state's 6,795 rail mi (10,935 km) of track were the Consolidated Rail Corp., or Conrail (which took over much of Penn Central's business), owned by CSX Transportation and Norfolk Southern, which each operated independently as well. In 2000, Pennsylvania had 60 railroads in operation, more than any other state. Coal accounted for most of the 120,978,349 tons carried by rail that year—in both tonnage originated and terminated within the state. Amtrak operates around 100 daily trains through Pennsylvania, offering passenger service to Philadelphia, Pittsburgh, and other cities along the east–west route, and from Philadelphia to New York and Washington, DC, along the northeast corridor.

Mass transit systems exist in metropolitan Philadelphia and Pittsburgh, in Bucks, Chester, Delaware, Montgomery, and Philadelphia counties, and in Altoona, Allentown, Erie, Harrisburg. Johnstown, Lancaster, Reading, Scranton, State College, and Wilkes-Barre. The Philadelphia Rapid Transit System, the state's first subway, was established in 1902 and is operated by the Southeastern Pennsylvania Transportation Authority, (SEPTA), which also runs buses, trolleys, trackless trolleys, and commuter trains in Bucks, Chester, Delaware, Montgomery, and Philadelphia counties. In 1985, a 1.1-mile (1.8-km) subway was opened in Pittsburgh as part of a 10.5-mile (16.9-km) light-rail (trolley) transit system linking downtown Pittsburgh with the South Hills section of the city.

Throughout its history, Pennsylvania has been a pioneer in road transportation. One of the earliest roads in the colonies was a "king's highway," connecting Philadelphia to Delaware in 1677; a "queen's road" from Philadelphia to Chester opened in 1706. A flurry of road building connected Philadelphia with other eastern Pennsylvania communities between 1705 and 1735. The first interior artery, the Great Conestoga Road, was opened in 1741 and linked Philadelphia with Lancaster. Indian trails in western Pennsylvania were developed into roadways, and a thoroughfare to Pittsburgh was completed in 1758. During the mid-1700s, a Lancaster County artisan developed an improved wagon for transporting goods across the Alleghenies; called a Conestoga wagon after the region from which it came, this vehicle later became the prime means of transport for westward pioneers. Another major improvement in land transportation came with the opening in 1792 of the Philadelphia and Lancaster Turnpike, one of the first stone-surfaced roads in the US. The steel-cable suspension bridge built by John Roebling over the Monongahela River at Pittsburgh in 1846 revolutionized bridge building, leading to the construction of spans longer and wider than had previously been thought possible. During the 1920s, Pennsylvania farmers were aided by the building of inexpensive rural roads connecting them with their markets.

A major development in automotive transport, the limited-access highway came to fruition with the Pennsylvania Turnpike, which opened in 1940 and was the first high-speed, multilane highway in the US. In 1995, this 470-mi (756-km) toll highway received $297.6 million from motorists, or 74% of the total receipts for state-administered toll road and crossing facilities in Pennsylvania. In 2000, Pennsylvania had 119,642 mi (192,545 km) of public roads, including 85,392 mi (137,425 km) of rural roads and 34,250 mi (55,120 km) of urban streets. In 1997, total road and highway expenditures from all units of government came to almost $4.1 billion, with nearly $1.7 billion of that amount for maintenance. Besides the Turnpike, the major highways are I-80 (Keystone Shortway), crossing the state from East Stroudsburg to the Ohio Turnpike; I-81, from the New York to the Maryland border via Scranton, Wilkes–Barre, and Harrisburg; and I-79, from Erie to the West Virginia border via Pittsburgh. As of 2000, there were 9,475,704 motor vehicles registered, including 6,032,058 automobiles, 3,192,210 trucks, and 35,699 buses. The total of 8,229,490 licensed drivers as of 2000 was the 5th highest in the US.

Blessed with access to the Atlantic Ocean and the Great Lakes and with such navigable waterways as the Delaware, Monongahela, Allegheny, and Ohio rivers, Pennsylvania was an early leader in water transportation, and Philadelphia, Pittsburgh, and Erie all developed as major ports. The peak period of canal building came during the 1820s and 1830s, which saw the completion of the Main Line of Public Works, used to transport goods between Philadelphia and Pittsburgh from 1834 to 1854. This system used waterways and a spectacular portage railroad that climbed over and cut through, via a tunnel, the Allegheny Mountains. Monumental as it was, the undertaking was largely a failure. Built too late to challenge the Erie Canal's domination of east–west trade, the Main Line was soon made obsolete by the railroads, as was the rest of the state's 800-mi (1,300-km) canal system.

Philadelphia, Pittsburgh, and Erie are the state's major shipping ports. The Philadelphia Harbor (including ports in the Philadelphia metropolitan area) handled 43.9 million tons of cargo in 2000. Although no longer the dominant gateway to the Mississippi, Pittsburgh is still a major inland port, and handled 53.9 million tons of cargo that year. Erie is the state's port on the Great Lakes, with 1.5 million tons of cargo handled in 2000.

In 2002, Pennsylvania had 781 airfields, including 461 airports, 307 heliports, 10 seaplane bases, and 3 stolports. The busiest air terminal in the state is the Philadelphia International Airport, followed by the Greater Pittsburgh Airport.

11 HISTORY

Soon after the glacier receded from what is now Pennsylvania, about 20,000 years ago, nomadic hunters from the west moved up the Ohio River, penetrated the passes through the Allegheny Mountains, and moved down the Susquehanna and Delaware rivers. By about AD 500, the earliest Indians, already accustomed to fishing and gathering nuts, seeds, fruit, and roots, were beginning to cultivate the soil, make pottery, and build burial mounds. Over the next thousand years, the Indians became semisedentary, or only seasonal, nomads.

Woodland Indians living in Pennsylvania, mostly of the Algonkian language family, were less inclined toward agriculture than other Indian tribes. The first Europeans to sail up the Delaware River found the Leni-Lenape ("original people"), who, as their name signified, had long occupied that valley, and whom the English later called the Delaware. Other Algonkian tribes related to the Leni-Lenape were the Nanticoke, who ranged along the Susquehanna River, and the Shawnee, who were scattered throughout central Pennsylvania. The other major Indian language group in Pennsylvania was Iroquoian. This group included the Susquehanna (Conestoga), living east of the Susquehanna River and south to the shores of Chesapeake Bay; the Wyandot, along the Allegheny River; and the Erie, south of Lake Erie. Proving that tribes related by language could be deadly enemies, the Iroquoian Confederacy of the Five Nations, located in what is now New York, destroyed the Iroquoian-speaking Erie in the 1640s and the Susquehanna by 1680. The confederacy conquered the Leni-Lenape by 1720 but failed to destroy them.

The first European to reach Pennsylvania was probably Cornelis Jacobssen, who in 1614 entered Delaware Bay for Dutch merchants interested in the fur trade. In 1638, the Swedes began planting farms along the Delaware River; they lived in peace with the Leni-Lenape and Susquehanna, with whom they traded for furs. Under Governor Johan Printz, the Swedes expanded into present-day Pennsylvania with a post at Tinicum Island (1643) and several forts along the Schuylkill River. The Dutch conquered New Sweden in 1655, but surrendered the land in 1664 to the English, led by James, Duke of York, the brother of King Charles II and the future King James II.

The English conquest was financed partly by Admiral William Penn, whose son, also named William, subsequently joined the Society of Friends (Quakers), a radical Protestant sect persecuted for espousing equality and pacifism. Dreaming of an ideal commonwealth that would be a refuge for all persecuted peoples, Penn asked Charles II, who had not paid the debt owed to Penn's father, to grant him land west of the Delaware. The Duke of York willingly gave up his claim to that land, and Charles II granted it in 1681 as a proprietary colony to the younger Penn and named it Pennsylvania in honor of Penn's father.

As proprietor of Pennsylvania, Penn was given enormous power to make laws and wars (subject to approval by the king and the freemen of Pennsylvania), levy taxes, coin money, regulate commerce, sell land, appoint officials, administer justice, and construct a government. From the beginning, Penn virtually gave up his lawmaking power and granted suffrage to property

holders of 50 acres or £50. Even before coming to Pennsylvania, he forged his first Frame of Government, a document that went into effect 25 April 1682 but lasted less than a year. Under it, a 72-member council, presided over by a governor, monopolized executive, legislative, and judicial power, although a 200-member assembly could veto or amend the council's legislation. Arriving in the colony in October 1682, Penn approved the location and layout of Philadelphia, met with the Leni-Lenape to acquire land and exchange vows of peace, called for elections to select an assembly, and proposed a Great Law that ranged from prescribing weights and measures to guaranteeing fundamental liberties.

When the First Frame proved unwieldy, Penn on 2 April 1683 approved a Second Frame, which created an 18-member council and a 36-member assembly. A conspicuous friend of the deposed James II, Penn lost control of Pennsylvania from 1692 to 1694, and it was during this period that the legislature began to assert its rights. Penn returned to the colony in 1699, and on 28 October 1701 approved yet another constitution, called the Charter of Privileges. This document lodged legislative power in an annually elected unicameral assembly, executive power in a governor and council, which he now appointed, and judicial power in appointed provincial judges and an elected county judiciary. The Charter of Privileges remained in force until 1776.

As Pennsylvania's government evolved, its population grew steadily. Most of the first immigrants were from the British Isles and Germany. From 1681 to 1710, numerous English and Welsh Quaker migrants populated a 25-mi (40-km) zone surrounding Philadelphia. By 1750, most German immigrants were settled in a semicircular zone some 25–75 mi (40–120 km) from Philadelphia. A third and outermost ring, extending roughly 75 mi (120 km) west and north of the Germans, was populated beginning in 1717 by the Scots-Irish, who were indifferent farmers, but known as aggressive pioneers. By 1776, each of the major groups—which remained quite distinct—constituted roughly a third of the 300,000 Pennsylvanians. Minorities included about 10,000 Scots, 10,000 Irish Catholics, 8,000 French Huguenots, 8,000 black slaves (despite Quaker hostility to slavery), and 1,000 Jews.

A key issue during the pre-Revolutionary period was the size and extent of the colony. Conflicting colonial charters, reflecting vague English ideas of American geography, brought all of Pennsylvania's boundaries except the Delaware River into dispute. After a protracted struggle, Pennsylvania and Maryland agreed upon a basis for Charles Mason and Jeremiah Dixon to run the famous line (1763–67) that divided North and South. Although Virginia and Pennsylvania both claimed the area around Pittsburgh, a joint commission agreed in 1779 to extend the Mason-Dixon line west the full five degrees prescribed in Penn's original charter. Five years earlier, the Penn family had abandoned to New York land north of the 42nd parallel. This was confirmed as Pennsylvania's northern border in 1782, when the US Congress rejected Connecticut's claim to the Wyoming Valley area, where skirmishes (called the Yankee-Pennamite wars) had been going on since the 1760s.

Pennsylvania moved rapidly toward independence after the British victory in the French and Indian War. The Proclamation of 1763, preventing settlement west of the Alleghenies, outraged western Pennsylvania, while the Stamp Act (1765), Townshend Acts (1767), and Tea Act (1773) incensed Philadelphians. Although the Continental Congress began meeting in Philadelphia in September 1774, Pennsylvania revolted reluctantly. In July 1776, only three Pennsylvania delegates to the Second Continental Congress voted for independence, while two were opposed and two absented themselves from the vote. Nevertheless, the Declaration of Independence was proclaimed from Independence Hall, Pennsylvania's State House, on 4 July 1776. As the headquarters of the Congress, Philadelphia was an important British target. The American defeat at the Battle of Brandywine Creek on 11 September 1777 led to the British occupation of the city. The provisional capital was moved first to Lancaster and then to York, where the Articles of Confederation were drafted. Following battles at Germantown and Whitemarsh, General George Washington set up winter headquarters at Valley Forge, remaining there from December 1777 to June 1778. Faced with the threat of French naval power intervening on behalf of the Americans, the British evacuated Philadelphia during the spring of 1778, and Congress reconvened there on 2 July. Philadelphia would serve as the US capital until 1783, and again from 1790 to 1800.

With independence, Pennsylvania adopted the state constitution of 1776, which established a powerful unicameral assembly elected annually by all freemen supporting the Revolution, a weak administrative supreme executive council (with a figurehead president), an appointed judiciary, and a council of censors meeting every seven years in order to take a census, reapportion the assembly, and review the constitutionality of state actions. In 1780, Pennsylvania passed the first state law abolishing slavery. Seven years later, Pennsylvania became the second state to ratify the US Constitution and join the Union. In 1790, Pennsylvania adopted a new constitution, modeled on the federal one, allowing all taxpaying males to vote. This document provided for a powerful governor, elected for a three-year term and eligible to succeed himself twice, a bicameral legislature (with senators elected every four years and a house elected annually), and an appointed judiciary.

Opposition to national taxes was evidenced by two disturbances in the 1790s. In 1794, western Pennsylvania settlers, opposed to a federal excise tax on distilled spirits, waged the Whiskey Rebellion. The insurrection was soon quashed by state troops under federal command. The levying of a federal property tax inspired the unsuccessful Fries Rebellion (1799) among Pennsylvania Germans.

By 1800, the first stages of industrialization were at hand. Pittsburgh's first iron furnace was built in 1792, and the increasing use of coal as fuel made its mining commercially feasible. The completion of the Main Line of Public Works, a canal and rail system connecting Philadelphia with Pittsburgh, was a major development of the early 19th century, which was otherwise a period of political turmoil and shifting party alliances.

By 1838, Pennsylvania adopted a new constitution curtailing the governor's power (he could serve only two three-year terms in a nine-year period), making many judgeships elective for specific terms, restricting the charter of banks, and disenfranchising black people. The 1840s saw not only an influx of Irish immigrants but also the rise of the Native American (Know-Nothing) Party, an anti-Catholic movement. The antislavery crusade, which gave birth to the Republican Party, influenced state politics during the following decade.

Although a Pennsylvania Democrat, James Buchanan, carried the state and won the presidency in 1856, the Republicans captured Pennsylvania for Abraham Lincoln in 1860, partly by their strong support for a protective tariff. Protectionism attracted Pennsylvania because, in addition to its enormously productive farms, it was heavily industrialized, leading the nation in the production of iron, lumber, textiles, and leather.

Pennsylvania rallied to the Union cause, supplying some 338,000 men, a figure exceeded only by New York. The state was the scene of the Battle of Gettysburg (1–3 July 1863), a turning point in the war for the Union cause. Under General George Gordon Meade, the Union troops (one-third of whom were Pennsylvanians) defeated Confederate forces under General Robert E. Lee, who was then forced to lead a retreat to Virginia.

The Civil War left the Republican Party dominant in Pennsylvania, but, in the postwar years, the Republicans were themselves dominated by industry, particularly the Pennsylvania Railroad. Between 1890 and 1900, the state was the nation's chief producer of coal, iron, and steel, and for much of that period the main source of petroleum and lumber. Farmers' sons and daughters joined immigrants from abroad in flocking to the anthracite and bituminous coal regions and to Philadelphia, Pittsburgh, and other urban centers to work in mines, mills, and factories. As the state's industrial wealth increased, education, journalism, literature, art, and architecture flourished in Philadelphia and Pittsburgh. The 1876 Centennial Exhibition at Philadelphia illustrated America's advancement in the arts and industry.

Pennsylvania adopted a reform constitution in 1873, increasing the size of the senate and house to reduce the threat of bribery, prescribing rules to prevent treachery in legislation and fraud at the polls, equalizing taxation, limiting state indebtedness, restricting the governor to one four-year term in eight years, and creating the office of lieutenant governor. None of this, however, seriously hampered the Republican political machine, led by Simon Cameron, Matthew Quay, and Boies Penrose, which dominated the state from the 1860s to the 1920s. Though Progressive reforms were enacted in subsequent years, the Penrose machine grew ever more efficient, while industrial leaders—supported both by the Pennsylvania state government and by society at large—smashed labor's efforts to unite, particularly in the great steel strike of 1919.

During the nationwide boom years of the 1920s, Pennsylvania did little more than hold its own economically, and its industrial growth rate was low. The state's share of the nation's iron and steel output no longer exceeded that of the rest of the country combined. Coal, textiles, and agriculture—all basic to the state's economy—were depressed. When Penrose died in 1921, at least five factions sought to control the powerful Pennsylvania Republican Party. In this confusion, Gifford Pinchot, a Progressive disciple of Theodore Roosevelt, won the governorship for 1923–27 and reorganized the state's administration, but failed in his attempt to enforce prohibition and to regulate power utilities.

The disastrous depression of the 1930s brought major changes to Pennsylvania. Serving again as governor (1931–35), Pinchot fought for state and federal relief for the unemployed. The Republican organization's lack of enthusiasm for Pinchot and Progressivism helped revive the state Democratic Party long enough to secure the election in 1934—for the first time since 1890—of its gubernatorial nominee, George H. Earle. As governor, Earle successfully introduced a Little New Deal, supporting labor, regulating utilities, aiding farmers, and building public works. With government support, coal miners, steelworkers, and other organized labor groups emerged from the Depression strong enough to challenge industry. Full employment and prosperity returned to Pennsylvania with the unprecedented demands on it for steel, ships, munitions, and uniforms during World War II.

Despite their professed opposition to government control, the Republican administrations (1939–55) that succeeded the Earle regime espoused and even enlarged Earle's program. They regulated industry, improved education, and augmented social services, at the same time increasing state bureaucracy, budgets, and taxes. Markets, transportation, banks, factories, machinery, and skilled labor remained abundant. Two Democratic governors were able to attract new industries to the state during the 1950s and early 1960s. However, the economy was still not healthy in 1963, when Republican William W. Scranton entered the statehouse (1963–67). Scranton continued both to enlarge state responsibilities (through increased taxes) and to secure federal aid for economic and social programs. He was rewarded with four years of steady economic growth. Pennsylvania's unemployment level, 2nd highest in the nation from 1950 to 1962, had dropped below the national average by 1966. The 1873 constitution was extensively revised at a constitutional convention held in 1967–68, during the administration of Raymond P. Shafer (1967–71), Scranton's Republican successor.

Pennsylvania faced an unresolved financial crisis in 1971 when Democrat Milton J. Shapp became governor. During his first term (1971–75), Shapp weathered the storm by securing passage of a state income tax. He virtually eliminated state patronage by signing union contracts covering state employees. Not only did he continue to attract business to Pennsylvania, but he also championed the consumer with no-fault auto insurance, adopted in 1974. Shapp's second term, however, was wrecked by his pursuit of the 1976 presidential nomination and by rampant corruption among Pennsylvania Democrats. Shapp's successor, Republican Richard L. Thornburgh, had scarcely been seated in the governor's chair before the release of radioactive gases resulting from the malfunction of one of the two nuclear reactors at Three Mile Island in March 1979 confronted him—and others—with vexing questions concerning the safety and wisdom of atomic power. Nevertheless, in September 1985, during Thornburgh's second term, and following six years of cleanup of radioactive waste, the undamaged reactor at Three Mile Island was restarted.

In the mid-1980s, Pennsylvania found itself confronted with the problem of completing the transition from a manufacturing to a service economy. While some parts of the state, namely southeastern Pennsylvania and Philadelphia, had successfully negotiated the transition, the economies of Pittsburgh, Lehigh Valley, Scranton, and Wilkes-Barre remained centered on the depressed steel and coal industries. Under Governor Robert Casey, who took office in 1987, Pennsylvania created an organization called the Governor's Response Team to assist ailing industries in the state. The team helped companies obtain low-interest loans and subsidized companies that sought to retrain their workers. In the first year of its existence, the team reached out to assist 214 companies, saved 10,000 existing jobs, and created 10,000 new ones.

In the mid-1990s, steel was no longer the mainstay of industry in Pennsylvania, although the state still led the nation in production of specialty steel. Important manufacturing sectors included food processing and chemicals, especially pharmaceuticals. Philadelphia had become a center for high-technology industries, while Pittsburgh was a mecca for corporate headquarters. By 2000 the state's economy was described as "relentlessly strong" by one newspaper, and legislators considered $643.5 million in tax cuts to residents and businesses along with increased spending in education and health care. As in many other regions of the nation, one of the by-products of Pennsylvania's robust economy was urban sprawl. A landmark in the anti-sprawl movement, in June 2000 Republican Governor Tom Ridge signed into law a plan that encouraged local governments to work together, allowed them to determine growth areas, and required state agencies to comply with community development guidelines.

In 1996 Governor Ridge approved the deregulation of the state's electrical utilities. Four years later, a report indicated the move had helped the economy (by lower consumer bills) but would result in lower tax revenues (due to restructuring and lower prices). While computer models forecasted that by 2004 reductions in electric rates under deregulation would lead to $1.9 billion in additional economic output, a $1.4-billion increase in personal income, and 36,000 new jobs, legislators had not yet addressed the projected shortfall in tax revenues, which would affect public transportation and municipalities.

The state remained one of the nation's most populous, ranking 5th both in the 1990 census and 1995 estimates, before slipping to 6th (with over 12.2 million people) in 2000.

Following the 11 September 2001 terrorist attacks on the United States, President George Bush proposed the creation of a cabinet-level Department of Homeland Security. Former Governor Tom Ridge was named first secretary of the department.

Democratic Governor Ed Rendell, elected in 2002, was the first former Philadelphia mayor to become Pennsylvania governor in 90 years. Rendell pledged to lower property taxes by one-third during his first year in office, raise income taxes, and to provide prescription drug coverage for senior citizens. He favored the introduction of slot machines at the state's racetracks and increasing school spending. In 2003, Pennsylvania faced a $2.4 billion budget deficit for fiscal year 2003/04.

12 STATE GOVERNMENT

The 1873 constitution, substantially reshaped by a constitutional convention in 1967–68, is the foundation of state government in Pennsylvania. Between 1968 and January 2003, 28 amendments had been adopted.

The general assembly consists of a 50-member senate, elected to staggered four-year terms, and a 203-member house of representatives, elected every two years. Each house meets annually, beginning in January, and there are no limits to the length of each session. Special sessions may be called by the majority petition of each house. To qualify for the general assembly, a person must have been a district resident for at least one year; senators must be at least 25 years old, representatives at least 21. The legislative salary was $61,889 in 2002.

As head of the executive branch and chief executive officer of the state, the governor of Pennsylvania has the power to appoint heads of administrative departments, boards, and commissions, to approve or veto legislation, to grant pardons, and to command the state's military forces. The governor, who may serve no more than two four-year terms in succession, must be a US citizen, be at least 30 years old, and have been a Pennsylvania resident for at least seven years before election. Elected with the governor is the lieutenant governor, who serves as president of the senate and chairman of the board of pardons, and assumes the powers of the governor if the governor becomes unable to continue in that office. In 2002, the governor's salary was $144,410.

Other state elected officials are the auditor general, who oversees all state financial transactions; the state treasurer, who receives and keeps records of all state funds; and the attorney general, who heads the Department of Justice. All other department heads, or secretaries, are appointed by the governor and confirmed by a majority of the senate.

A bill may be introduced in either house of the general assembly. After the measure is passed by majority vote in each house, the governor has 10 days including Sundays (or 30 days, including Sundays, if the legislature has adjourned) in which to sign it, refuse to sign it (in which case it automatically becomes law), or veto it. Vetoes may be overridden by a two-thirds vote of the elected members of each house. A bill becomes effective 60 days after enactment.

A proposed constitutional amendment must be approved by a majority of both house and senate members in two successive legislatures before it can be placed on the ballot. If approved by a majority of the voters in a general election, the amendment then becomes part of the constitution.

To vote in state elections a person must be a US citizen for at least one month before the next election, at least 18 years old, and a resident of Pennsylvania and of the district for at least 30 days preceding the election. Restrictions apply to convicted felons.

13 POLITICAL PARTIES

The Republican Party totally dominated Pennsylvania politics from 1860, when the first Republican governor was elected, to the early 1930s. During this period, there were 16 Republican and only two Democratic administrations. Most of the Republicans were staunchly probusiness, though one Republican Progressive, Gifford Pinchot, was elected governor in 1922 and again in 1930. A Democrat, George Earle, won the governorship in 1934, in the depths of the Depression, but from 1939 through 1955, Republicans again held the office without interruption. Only since the mid-1950s has Pennsylvania emerged as a two-party state, with Democrats electing governors in 1954, 1958, 1970, 1974, 1986 and 1990, and Republicans winning the governorships in 1962, 1966, 1978, 1982, and 1994. In 1998, Tom Ridge, the Republican first elected to the office in 1994, won a second term as governor. He was named the first secretary of the newly-created Department of Homeland Security in November 2002, after having served as the first administrator of the Office of Homeland Security from September 2001. In 2002, Democrat Ed Rendell was elected governor.

Both US Senate seats were held by Republicans from 1968 to 1991. In November of 1991, a little-known Democrat and former college president named Harris Wofford defeated former governor Richard Thornburgh for the seat of Senator John Heinz, who died in 1991. In 1994, Republican Rick Santorum, a congressman from the Pittsburgh area, defeated Wofford; Santorum was reelected in 2000. Pennsylvania's other senator, Republican Arlen Specter, was elected to his fourth term in 1998. In 2003, Pennsylvania's 19 US House seats were held by seven Democrats and 12 Republicans. In mid-2003, there were 29 Republicans and 21 Democrats in the state senate, and 109 Republicans and 94 Democrats in the state house.

Democratic voters were heavily concentrated in metropolitan Philadelphia and Pittsburgh. Pennsylvania, a pivotal state for Jimmy Carter in 1976, was swept by the Republican tide in the 1980 presidential election; Ronald Reagan, the Republican nominee, won nearly 50% of the popular vote. In 1984, President Reagan received 53% of the popular vote, while Democrat

Walter Mondale received 46%. In 1988, Republican and former vice president George Bush won 51% of the popular vote. Democratic nominee Bill Clinton garnered 45% of the vote in 1992, and in 1996, Clinton won 49% of the vote. In 2000, Democrat Al Gore won 51% of the vote to Republican George W. Bush's 47%; Green Party candidate Ralph Nader won 2% of the vote. In 2002 there were 7,835,775 registered voters. In 1998, 48% of registered voters were Democratic, 42% Republican, and 9% unaffiliated or members of other parties. The state had 23 electoral votes in the 2000 presidential election.

14 LOCAL GOVERNMENT

As of 2002, Pennsylvania had 66 counties, 1,018 municipal governments, 1,546 townships, 516 public school districts, and 1,885 authorities (special districts). Under home-rule laws, municipalities may choose to draft and amend their own charter.

Pennsylvania counties are responsible for state law enforcement, judicial administration, and the conduct of state elections: counties also are involved in public health, regional planning, and solid waste disposal. Counties can also maintain hospitals, homes for the aged, community colleges, libraries, and other community facilities. The chief governing body in each county is a three-member board of commissioners, each elected to a four-year term. Other elected officials generally include the sheriff, district attorney, notary, clerk of courts, register of wills, recorder of deeds, jury commissioners, auditor or controller, and treasurer. Among the appointed officials is a public defender. Counties are divided by law into nine classes, depending on population. Philadelphia's county offices were merged with the city government in 1952, pursuant to the home-rule charter of 1951.

There are four classes of cities. The only first-class city, Philadelphia, is governed by a mayor and city council. Other elected officials are the controller, district attorney, sheriff, register of wills, and three city commissioners. Major appointed officials include managing director, director of finance, city representative, and city solicitor. Both Pittsburgh and Scranton

Pennsylvania Presidential Vote by Political Parties, 1948–2000

YEAR	ELECTORAL VOTE	PENNSYLVANIA WINNER	DEMOCRAT	REPUBLICAN	PROGRESSIVE	SOCIALIST	PROHIBITION	SOC. LABOR
1948	35	Dewey (R)	1,752,426	1,902,197	55,161	11,325	10,538	1,461
						SOC. WORKERS		
1952	32	*Eisenhower (R)	2,146,269	2,415,789	4,222	1,508	8,951	1,377
1956	32	*Eisenhower (R)	1,981,769	2,585,252	—	2,035	—	7,447
1960	32	*Kennedy (D)	2,556,282	2,439,956	—	2,678	—	7,158
1964	29	*Johnson (D)	3,130,954	1,673,657	—	10,456	—	5,092
						PEACE & FREEDOM	AMERICAN IND.	
1968	29	Humphrey (D)	2,259,403	2,090,017	7,821	4,862	378,582	4,977
								AMERICAN
1972	27	*Nixon (R)	1,796,951	2,714,521	—	4,639	—	70,593
					COMMUNIST			US LABOR
1976	27	*Carter (D)	2,328,677	2,205,604	1,891	3,009	25,344	2,744
						LIBERTARIAN	SOC. WORKERS	
1980	27	*Reagan (R)	1,937,540	2,261,872	5,184	33,263	20,291	—
1984	25	*Reagan (R)	2,228,131	2,584,323	21,628	6,982	—	—
					CONSUMER		NEW ALLIANCE	POPULIST
1988	25	*Bush (R)	2,194,944	2,300,087	19,158	12,051	4,379	3,444
								IND. (Perot)
1992	23	*Clinton (D)	2,239,164	1,791,164		21,477	4,661	902,667
1996	23	*Clinton (D)	2,215,819	1,801,169	—	28,000	—	430,984
					GREEN		REFORM	
2000	23	Gore (D)	2,485,967	2,281,127	103,392	11,248	16,023	

*Won US presidential election.

(classified as second-class cities) are governed under mayor-council systems that give the mayors strong discretionary powers.

Boroughs are governed under mayor-council systems giving the council strong powers. Other elected officials are the tax assessor, tax collector, and auditor or controller. The state's first-class townships, located mostly in metropolitan areas, are governed by elected commissioners who serve four-year overlapping terms. Second-class townships, most of them located in rural areas, have three supervisors who are elected at large to six-year terms.

15 STATE SERVICES

To address the continuing threat of terrorism and to work with the federal Department of Homeland Security (created in 2002 following the terrorist attacks of 11 September 2001), homeland security in Pennsylvania in 2003 operated under executive order; a homeland security director was appointed to oversee the state's homeland security activities.

Executive agencies under the governor's jurisdiction are the Pennsylvania Council on Aging, Human Relations Commission, Governor's Council on the Hispanic Community, Commission for Women, and State Ethics Commission. The Liquor Control Board operates state liquor stores and claims to be the world's largest single purchaser of liquors and wines.

The Department of Education administers the school laws of Pennsylvania, oversees community colleges, licenses and regulates private schools, and administers the state public library program. Educational policy is the province of the State Board of Education, a panel with 17 members appointed by the governor to six-year terms. Also within the department are various boards that make policies for and review developments within the state's higher educational system.

The Department of Transportation maintains state-operated highways, mass transit, rail service, and aviation facilities. The State Highway and Bridge Authority and the Pennsylvania Turnpike Commission also have responsibilities related to transportation. Agencies and departments providing health and welfare services include the Department of Aging, Department of Community and Economic Development, and Department of Health. All public assistance, social service, mental health, and mental retardation programs are administered by the Department of Public Welfare.

The Office of Attorney General has divisions on criminal law, legal services, and public protection. The National Guard, Bureau for Veterans' Affairs, and state veterans' homes are under the Department of Military Affairs; the Pennsylvania State Police is a separate state agency. The Pennsylvania Commission on Crime and Delinquency, created in 1978, allocates federal funds for crime control, juvenile justice, and delinquency prevention. The Pennsylvania Emergency Management Agency (formerly the State Council of Civil Defense) provides assistance in emergency situations resulting from natural or manmade disasters.

All state park and forest preservation programs, ecological and geological resource information programs, and community conservation partnerships are under the supervision of the Department of Conservation and Natural Resources and the Department of Environmental Protection. Land and water environmental protection programs are under the supervision of the Department of Environmental Protection. The Governor's Energy Council seeks to augment the state's energy security through the planned development and conservation of energy resources. The Department of Labor and Industry administers safety, employment, and industrial standards; operates vocational rehabilitation and workers' compensation programs; and mediates labor disputes.

16 JUDICIAL SYSTEM

Since 1968, all Pennsylvania courts have been organized under the Unified Judicial System. The highest court in the state is the supreme court, which, having been established in 1722, is the oldest appellate court in the US. The supreme court consists of seven justices, elected to ten-year terms; the justice with the longest continuous service on the court automatically becomes chief justice. In general, the supreme court hears appeals from the commonwealth court. A separate appellate court, called the superior court, hears appeals from the courts of common pleas. There are 15 superior court judges, also elected to 10-year terms, as are the commonwealth and common pleas, which have original jurisdiction over all civil and criminal cases not otherwise specified.

In counties other than Philadelphia, misdemeanors and other minor offenses are tried by district justices, formerly known as justices of the peace. The Philadelphia municipal court consists of 22 judges, all of whom must be lawyers; the six judges who constitute the Philadelphia traffic court need not be lawyers. Pittsburgh's magistrates' court, appointed by the mayor, comprises five to eight judges who need not be lawyers. All of Pennsylvania's judges, except traffic court judges and Pittsburgh's magistrates, are initially elected on a partisan ballot and thereafter on a nonpartisan retention ballot.

Pennsylvania's overall crime rate in 2001 was 2,961.1 per 100,000 people, including a total of 50,432 violent crimes and 313,408 crimes against property in that year. In June 2001, there were 37,105 inmates held in state and federal correctional facilities, an increase of 1.3% over the previous year. The state's incarceration rate stood at 302 per 100,000 population.

Pennsylvania imposes the death penalty and executed three persons between 1977 and 2003. In 2003, there were 244 persons under sentence of death.

17 ARMED FORCES

In 2002, there were 3,098 active-duty military personnel and 24,920 civilian personnel stationed in Pennsylvania. The US Army War College is in Carlisle, and there are army depots in Chambersburg, Harrisburg, and Scranton. Defense contracts worth more than $4.2 billion were awarded to Pennsylvania firms in 1997.

According to the 2000 Census, there were 1,280,788 veterans living in the state, of whom 316,088 served in World War II; 177,394 in the Korean conflict; 350,055 during the Vietnam era; and 95,741 during 1990–2000 (including the Persian Gulf War). Veterans' benefits totaled more than $2 billion in 2002.

In 2000, the Pennsylvania State Police employed 4,152 full-time sworn officers.

18 MIGRATION

When William Penn's followers arrived in Pennsylvania, they joined small groups of Dutch, Swedish, and Finnish immigrants who were already settled along the Delaware River. By 1685, 50% of Pennsylvania's European population was British. In 1683, the Frankfort Land Co. founded the Mennonite community of Germantown on 6,000 acres (2,400 hectares) east of the Schuylkill River. One hundred years later there were 120,000 Germans, about one-fourth of the state's census population; the Moravians, from Saxony, settled primarily in Bethlehem and Nazareth, and the Amish in Lancaster and Reading.

During the 19th century, more immigrants settled in Pennsylvania than in any other state except New York. Between 1840 and 1890, the anthracite mines in east-central Pennsylvania attracted the Irish, Welsh, and Slavs; Scots-Irish, Italian, Austrian, Hungarian, and Polish (and, after 1880, Russian) immigrants worked the western coal fields. The cities attracted Italian,

French, and Slavic workers. East European and Russian Jews settled in Philadelphia and Pittsburgh between 1882 and 1900. By the turn of the century, the urban population surpassed the rural population.

During the 20th century, these patterns have been reversed. The trend among whites, particularly since World War II, has been to move out—from the cities to the suburbs, and from Pennsylvania to other states. Blacks, who began entering the state first as slaves and then as freemen, continued to migrate to the larger cities until the early 1970s, when a small out-migration began. Overall, between 1940 and 1980, Pennsylvania lost a net total of 1,759,000 residents through migration; it lost an additional 98,000 residents between 1980 and 1983. From 1985 to 1990, Pennsylvania had a net migration gain of nearly 21,000. Between 1990 and 1998, the state had a net loss of 219,000 in domestic migration but a net gain of 104,000 in international migration. In 1996, about 3% of Pennsylvania's population (421,000) was foreign-born. In 1998, 11,942 foreign immigrants arrived in the state; of these, the greatest number, 1,127, came from India. Pennsylvania's overall population increased only 1% between 1990 and 1998. In the period 1995–2000, 668,753 people moved into the state and 800,049 moved out, for a net loss of 131,296, 92,385 of whom moved to Florida.

[19]INTERGOVERNMENTAL COOPERATION

Pennsylvania participates in such regional bodies as the Atlantic States Marine Fisheries Commission, Susquehanna River Basin Commission, Ohio River Valley Water Sanitation Commission, Wheeling Creek Watershed Protection and Flood Prevention Commission, and Great Lakes Commission. In 1985, Pennsylvania, seven other Great Lakes states, and the Canadian provinces of Quebec and Ontario signed the Great Lakes Compact to protect the lakes' water reserves. Other agreements include the Mid-Atlantic Fishery Management Council, Interstate Mining Compact Commission, Ohio River Basin Coimmission, Appalachian Regional Commission, Brandywine River Valley Compact, New Jersey-Pennsylvania Turnpike Bridge Compact, Potomac Valley Conservancy District, Pymatuning Lake Compact, and the Tri-State Agreement on the Chesapeake Bay.

Some of the most important interstate agreements concern commerce and development along the Delaware River. The Delaware River Basin Commission involves the governors of Delaware, New Jersey, New York, and Pennsylvania in the utilization and conservation of the Delaware and its surrounding areas. Through the Delaware River Port Authority, New Jersey and Pennsylvania control an interstate mass transit system. The two states also are signatories to the Delaware River Joint Toll Bridge Compact and Delaware Valley Regional Planning Commission. During 2001, Pennsylvania received over $14.8 billion in federal grants (4th among the 50 states).

[20]ECONOMY

Dominated by coal and steel, Pennsylvania is an important contributor to the national economy, but its role diminished considerably during the 20th century. The state reached the height of its economic development by 1920, when its western oil wells and coal fields made it the nation's leading energy producer. By that time, however, Pennsylvania's oil production was already on the decline, and demand for coal had slackened. No longer did the state dominate US steel production: Pennsylvania produced 60% of the US total in 1900, but only 30% in 1940 and 24% in 1960. Philadelphia, a diversified manufacturing center, began to lose many of its textile and apparel factories. The Depression hastened the decline. Industrial production in 1932 was less than half the 1929 level, and mineral production, already in a slump throughout the 1920, dropped more than 50% in value between 1929 and 1933. By 1933, 37% of the workforce was unemployed.

Massive federal aid programs and the production of munitions stimulated employment during the 1940s, but some sections of the state have never fully recovered from the damage of the Depression years. Declines in coal and steel production and the loss of other industries to the Sunbelt have not yet been entirely counterbalanced by gains in other sectors, despite a steady expansion of machinery production, increased tourism, and the growth of service-related industries and trade. Manufacturing, the 2nd-largest employer in Pennsylvania—providing one million jobs in the 1990s—lost about 350,000 jobs during the 1980s. The outlook for the steel industry remained uncertain in the 1990s, as Pennsylvania's aging factories faced severe competition from foreign producers. Services, in contrast, recorded about as much growth as manufacturing lost. The fastest growing service industries were concentrated in the medical and health fields. Coming into the 21st century, the annual growth rate for Pennsylvania's economy averaged 4.75% (1998 to 2000), which was then more than halved to 2.2% in the national recession of 2001. Manufacturing output, which grew 5.2% from 1997 to 2000 (although decreasing as a share of total output from 20.1% to 18.4%), fell -7.2% in 2001 (decreasing its share to 16.7%). The strongest growth in output was in various service sectors, with output from general services up 28% from 1997 to 2001; from financial services, up 22.1%, and from trade, up 19.5%.

In 2001, Pennsylvania's gross state product gross state product was $408.4 billion, the 6th largest among the states, to which general services contributed $98.6 billion; financial services, $79.3 billion; manufacturing, $68.3 billion; trade, $62.3 billion; government, $41.4 billion; transportation and public utilities, $35 billion, and construction, $18.5 billion. The public sector in 2001 constituted 10% of gross state product, below the 12% average for the states.

[21]INCOME

According to the Bureau of Economic Analysis, in 2001, Pennsylvania had a per capita personal income (PCPI) of $30,752 which ranked 16th in the United States (including the District of Columbia) and was 101% of the national average, $30,413. The 2001 PCPI reflected an increase of 3.3% from 2000 compared to the national change of 2.2%. In 2001, Pennsylvania had a total personal income (TPI) of $378,350,395,000 which ranked 6th in the United States and accounted for 4.4% of the national total. The 2001 TPI reflected an increase of 3.5% from 2000 compared to the national change of 3.3%.

Earnings of persons employed in Pennsylvania increased from $251,749,824,000 in 2000 to $258,915,007,000 in 2001, an increase of 2.8%. The largest industries in 2001 were services, 31.4% of earnings; durable goods manufacturing, 10.0%; and state and local government, 9.7%. Of the industries that accounted for at least 5% of earnings in 2001, the slowest growing from 2000 to 2001 was durable goods manufacturing, which decreased 4.4%; the fastest was construction (6.0% of earnings in 2001), which increased 5.5%.

According to data released by the US Census Bureau, in 2000, the median household income was $43,742 compared to the national average of $42,148. In 2001, the median income for a family of four was $66,130 compared to the national average of $63,278. For the period 1999 to 2001, the average poverty rate was 9.2% which placed it 16th among the 50 states and the District of Columbia ranked lowest to highest.

[22]LABOR

According to Bureau of Labor Statistics (BLS) provisional estimates, in July 2003 the seasonally adjusted civilian labor force in Pennsylvania numbered 6,195,200, with approximately 347,800 workers unemployed, yielding an unemployment rate of 5.6%, compared to the national average of 6.2% for the same period. Since the beginning of the BLS data series in 1978, the highest unemployment rate recorded was 13.1% in February 1983. The historical low was 4.0% in April 2000. It is estimated that in 2001, 4.5% of the labor force was employed in construction; 16.2% in manufacturing; 5.6% in transportation, communications, and public utilities; 19.0% in trade; 5.9% in finance, insurance, and real estate; 28.7% in services; 11.4% in government; and 1.7% in agriculture.

The history of unionism in Pennsylvania dates back to 1724 when Philadelphia workers organized the Carpenters' Company, the first crafts association in the colonies. Its Carpenters' Hall gained fame as the site of the First Continental Congress in 1774; the carpenters were also responsible for the first strike in the United States in 1791. The nation's first labor union was organized by Philadelphia shoemakers in 1794. By 1827, the Mechanics' Union of Trade Associations, the country's first central labor body, was striking for a 10-hour workday and was the impetus behind the formation of the Organized Workingman's Party. Nine years later there were no fewer than 58 labor organizations in Philadelphia and 13 in Pittsburgh, but the Panic of 1837 resulted in a sharp decline of union strength and membership for many years. Union ranks were further depleted by the Civil War, despite the efforts of Pennsylvania labor leader William Sylvis, who later became an important figure in the national labor reform movement. After the Civil War ended, the Noble Order of the Knights of Labor was established in Philadelphia in 1869.

The coal fields were sites of violent organizing struggles. In 1835, low wages and long hours sparked the first general mine strikes, which, like a walkout by anthracite miners in 1849, proved unsuccessful. During the 1850s and 1870s, a secret society known as the Molly Maguires led uprisings in the anthracite fields, but its influence ended after the conviction of its leaders for terrorist activities. The demise of the Molly Maguires did not stop the violence, however. Eleven persons were killed during a mine strike at Connellsville in 1891, and a strike by Luzerne County miners in 1897 resulted in 20 deaths. Finally, a five-month walkout by anthracite miners in 1902 led to increased pay, reduced hours, and an agreement to employ arbitration to settle disputes.

Steelworkers, burdened for many years by 12-hour workdays and 7-day workweeks, called several major strikes during this period. An 1892 lockout at Andrew Carnegie's Homestead steel mill led to a clash between workers and Pinkerton guards hired by the company; after several months, the strikers went back to work, their resources exhausted. A major strike in 1919, involving half of the nation's steelworkers, shut down the industry for more than three months, but it too produced no immediate gains. The Steel Workers Organizing Committee, later the United Steelworkers, finally won a contract and improved benefits from US Steel in 1937, although other steel companies held out until the early 1940s, when the Supreme Court forced recognition of the union.

The US Department of Labor reported that in 2002, 847,000 of Pennsylvania's 5,452,000 employed wage and salary workers were members of unions. This represented 15.5% of those so employed, down from 17.0% in 2001. The national average is 13.2%. In all, 907,000 workers (16.6%) were represented by unions. In addition to union members, this category includes workers who report no union affiliation but whose jobs are covered by a union contract. The most important union in the state is the United Steelworkers of America, headquartered in Pittsburgh.

23AGRICULTURE

Pennsylvania ranked 18th among the 50 states in agricultural income in 2001, with receipts of $4.46 billion.

During the colonial period, German immigrants farmed the fertile land in southeastern Pennsylvania, making the state a leader in agricultural production. Unlike farmers in other states, who worked the soil until it was depleted and then moved on, these farmers carefully cultivated the same plots year after year, using crop rotation techniques that kept the land productive. As late as 1840, the state led the nation in wheat production, thanks in part to planting techniques developed and largely confined to southeastern Pennsylvania. However, westward expansion and the subsequent fall in agricultural prices hurt farming in the state, and many left the land for industrial jobs in the cities. Today, most farms in the state produce crops and dairy items for Philadelphia and other major eastern markets.

As of 2002 there were about 59,000 farms averaging 131 acres (53 hectares) in size. The leading farm areas were all in southeastern Pennsylvania. Lancaster County is by far the most productive, followed by the counties of Chester, Berks, Franklin, and Lebanon.

Field crops in 2002 included: hay, 3,560,000 tons (valued at $473 million); corn for grain, 59 million bushels (valued at $174.5 million); soybeans, 9.1 million bushels (valued at $51.9 million); wheat, 20 million bushels (valued at $33.5 million); oats, 7 million bushels (valued at $13.3 million); and barley, 4.4 million (valued at $7.1 million).

Pennsylvania is a major producer of mushrooms and greenhouse and nursery crops. Other crops are fresh vegetables, potatoes, strawberries, apples, pears, peaches, grapes, and cherries (sweet and tart). The value of fresh market vegetables exceeded $30.4 million in 2002; the value of vegetables for processing, $10.5 million.

24ANIMAL HUSBANDRY

Most of Pennsylvania's farm income stems from livestock production, primarily in Lancaster County.

In 2003, there were an estimated 1.63 million cattle and calves, valued at $1.5 billion. During 2002, there were around 1.1 million hogs and pigs, worth $72.4 million. In 2001 the state produced 5.8 million lb (2.6 million kg) of sheep and lambs, which brought in $4 million in gross income.

Pennsylvania is a leading producer of chickens in the US, selling 53.9 million lb (24.4 million kg) in 2001. An estimated 10.8 billion lb (4.9 billion kg) of milk (4th among the 50 states) was produced from 599,000 milk cows in the same year.

25FISHING

Although there is little commercial fishing in Pennsylvania—the 1998 catch of 338,000 lb was worth only $53,000—the state's many lakes and streams make it a popular area for sport fishing. All recreational fishing in the state is supervised by the Fish Commission, established in 1866 and one of the oldest conservation agencies in the US. Walleye, trout, and salmon were the leading species. In 1998, Pennsylvania issued 1,089,693 sport fishing licenses.

26FORESTRY

Pennsylvania's richly diverse forests dominate the landscape, covering 59% (16,905,000 acres/6,841,000 hectares) of the total land area. For the northeastern United States, public ownership is high at 26% (4,403,000 acres/1,782,000 hectares), mostly owned by the commonwealth. The 1989 Forest Inventory identified 90 different tree species; most of the 2,076 species of native vascular plants are forest related. Eagles and ospreys are making a comeback, there is a resident elk herd (the largest east of the

Mississippi), coyotes have moved in, and river otters and fishers have been reintroduced. Some species of forest birds which are experiencing declines regionally have increasing populations in Pennsylvania's forests.

The forest products industry and forest-based recreation are very important to Pennsylvania's economy. Ten commercial tree species dominate the average annual net growth, producing 74% of the wood grown each year. In 2002, the total lumber production was 1,109 million board feet, or 2.3% of the US total.

Camping, fishing, hiking, and hunting are traditional Pennsylvania pastimes and the clean streams, vistas, and flora and fauna of the forest provide a focal point for these activities.

27MINING

The value of nonfuel mineral production in Pennsylvania in 2001 was estimated at about $1.27 billion, up about 2% from 2000. According to preliminary figures, the most valuable nonfuel mineral was crushed stone, which amounted to 101 million metric tons, worth $553 million (2nd in the US). Other important minerals were portland cement (3rd in US), 6.66 million metric tons ($477 million); lime (6th in US), 1.22 million metric tons ($74.6 million); and construction sand and gravel, 20.1 million metric tons ($125 million). Together, crushed stone, cement, and lime accounted for almost 90% of the total nonfuel mineral production value.

Pennsylvania ranked 11th among the states in value of nonfuel minerals, accounting for more than 3% of total US value. Although no metals were mined in Pennsylvania, the state retained its position as the nation's 4th-leading producer of raw steel, processing about 5.22 million metric tons in 2001.

28ENERGY AND POWER

Installed capacity at Pennsylvania's electric power plants (utility and nonutility) in 1999 was 36.6 million kW, all of it privately owned. In the same year, total electricity generation was 195.6 billion kWh. In 2000, energy consumption was 390 million Btu (98.3 million kcal) per capita, ranking Pennsylvania 16th among the 50 states. Electric energy sales in the state in 1998 exceeded 127.5 billion kHz, of which 38% was industrial, 33% residential, and 29% commercial.

Pennsylvania's nuclear power production dropped abruptly on 28 March 1979, when a malfunction at the 906,000-kW Unit 2 plant operated by Metropolitan Edison (a subsidiary of General Public Utilities) at Three Mile Island near Harrisburg caused the reactor's containment building to fill up with radioactive water. Some radioactive steam was vented into the atmosphere, and thousands of residents of nearby areas were temporarily evacuated. A 12-member panel appointed by President Jimmy Carter to investigate the accident found serious flaws in the design of the plant's safety systems and in federal regulation of the nuclear power industry. Metropolitan Edison's 819,000-kW Unit I plant was also shut down after the accident but was reopened in fall 1985.

Operating nuclear plants in Pennsylvania as of 2001 were the Peach Bottom Units 2 and 3 (combined capacity 2,090,000 kW), 85% of which is owned jointly by Philadelphia Electric and Public Service Electric and Gas; Beaver Valley Units 1 and 2 (combined capacity 1,640,000 kW), at Shippingport, 69% owned by Duquesne Light and Ohio Edison; Susquehanna Units 1 and 2 (2,100,000 kW), 90% owned by Pennsylvania Power and Light; Limerick Units 1 and 2 (with capacities of 1,134,000 each) near Philadelphia; and Unit 1 of the Three Mile Island plant, with a capacity of 816,000 kW.

The nation's first oil well was struck in Titusville in 1859, and for the next five decades Pennsylvania led the nation in oil production. Reserves totaled 10 million barrels in 2001, and output dropped to 6,000 barrels per day in 2001. Marketed natural gas production in 2001 was 157 billion cu ft (4.44 million cu m); estimated reserves as of 2001 were 1,775 billion cu ft (50.3 billion cu m). Virtually all the state's commercial oil and gas reserves lie beneath the Allegheny High Plateau, in western Pennsylvania.

Coal is the state's most valuable mineral commodity, accounting for more than two-thirds of all mine income; the state's output in 1998 represented 7.2% of US production. In 2000, Pennsylvania's mining companies produced 74,619,000 tons of coal. Pennsylvania is the only major US producer of anthracite coal, with an output of 4,572,000 tons in 2000; bituminous coal production totaled 70,046,000 tons. Bituminous coal is mined in Washington, Clearfield, Greene, Cambria, Armstrong, Somerset, Clarion, Allegheny, and 19 other counties in the western part of the state; anthracite mining is concentrated in Schuylkill, Luzerne, Lackawanna, Northumberland, Carbon, Columbia, Sullivan, and Dauphin counties in the east. In 1998, there were 375 active coal mines, 97 underground and 278 surface. Recoverable reserves as of 2001 were 541 million tons of bituminous and 16 million tons of anthracite.

29INDUSTRY

At different times throughout its history, Pennsylvania has been the nation's principal producer of ships, iron, chemicals, lumber, oil, textiles, glass, coal, and steel. Although it is still a major manufacturing center, Pennsylvania's industrial leadership has diminished steadily during this century.

The first major industry in colonial Pennsylvania was shipbuilding, centered in Philadelphia. Iron works, brick kilns, candle factories, and other small crafts industries also grew up around the city. By 1850, Philadelphia alone accounted for nearly half of Pennsylvania's manufacturing output, with an array of products including flour, preserved meats, sugar, textiles, shoes, furniture, iron, locomotives, pharmaceuticals, and books. The exploitation of the state's coal and oil resources and the discovery of new steel-making processes helped build Pittsburgh into a major industrial center.

From 1977 to 1991, the value of shipments of manufactured goods grew from $79.8 billion to $134 billion. In 1997, the value of shipments for manufactured goods was $177 billion. In 1997, Pennsylvania was headquarters for 32 Fortune 500 companies.

Earnings of persons employed in Pennsylvania increased from $214.2 billion in 1997 to $226.7 billion in 1998, an increase of 5.9%. The largest industries in 1998 were services, 30.0% of earnings; durable goods manufacturing, 12.2%; and state and local government, 9.7%. Of the industries that accounted for at least 5% of earnings in 1998, the slowest growing from 1997 to 1998 was state and local government, which increased 2.8%; the fastest was services, which increased 7.0%.

30COMMERCE

A major component in Philadelphia's early economy, trade remains important to the state.

According to federal data, sales from wholesale trade in 1997 totaled $167 billion, 8th highest in the US. The main items sold were groceries and related products; machinery, equipment, and supplies; motor vehicles and automotive parts and supplies; metals and minerals (excluding petroleum); electrical goods; and petroleum and petroleum products.

Pennsylvania ranked 5th in the US in sales from retail trade in 1997, with almost $113 billion. The top categories in terms of numbers of businesses were automotive dealers, 12%; food stores, 11%; and restaurants or taverns, 30%. Philadelphian John Wanamaker opened the world's first department store in 1876; by 1997, Pennsylvania had over 1,600 shopping centers, about one-third of them in the Philadelphia and Pittsburgh metropolitan areas.

During the colonial era, Philadelphia was one of the busiest Atlantic ports and the leading port for the lucrative Caribbean trade. Philadelphia remains one of the country's leading foreign trade centers; the main import suppliers are the United Kingdom, Indonesia, Saudi Arabia, Venezuela, and Algeria. In 1998, total exports of Pennsylvania goods had a value of $16 billion (10th in the US).

³¹CONSUMER PROTECTION

The Bureau of Consumer Protection is part of the Public Protection Division of the Office of Attorney General. The Bureau investigates and mediates complaints. Also within the Office of Attorney General is the Charitable Trusts and Organizations section. Pennsylvanians are encouraged to report instances of fraud, waste, or mismanagement of state funds through a toll-free telephone service run by the Auditor General. Additionally, the Department of Insurance and the Department of Banking protect state residents against insurance fraud and banking fraud, respectively.

³²BANKING

Philadelphia is the nation's oldest banking center, and Third Street between Chestnut and Walnut has been called the cradle of American finance. The first chartered commercial bank in the US was the Bank of North America, granted its charter in Philadelphia by the federal government in December 1781 and by Pennsylvania in April 1782.

The First Bank of the US was headquartered in Philadelphia from its inception in 1791 to 1811, when its charter was allowed to expire. Its building was bought by Stephen Girard, a private banker whose new institution quickly became one of the nation's largest banks. Girard's bank was closed after he died in 1831, but a new Girard Bank was opened in 1832; it merged with Philadelphia National Bank in 1926.

By the early 1800s, Philadelphia had reached its zenith as the nation's financial center. It was the home of the Bank of Pennsylvania, founded in 1793; the Bank of Philadelphia (1804); the Farmers and Mechanics Bank (1809); the Philadelphia Savings Fund Society (1816), the first mutual savings bank; and, most powerful of all, the Second Bank of the US (1816). After 1823, under the directorship of Nicholas Biddle, this bank became an international leader and the only rival to New York City's growing banking industry. When President Jackson vetoed the bank's recharter in 1831, Philadelphia lost its preeminence as a banking center.

Pittsburgh also rose to prominence during the Gilded Age, in great part because of the efforts of its most successful financier, Andrew Mellon. In March 1982, the state legalized multibank holding companies; subsequently, the Mellon Bank acquired Centre County Bank of State College, Girard Bank, and Northwest Bank. Other major institutions are Pittsburgh National Bank, part of PNC Financial, and Philadelphia National Bank. First Pennsylvania, in financial difficulty for several years, was saved from possible failure early in 1980 through a loan package engineered by the Federal Deposit Insurance Corporation.

In 2002, Pennsylvania had 285 insured banks with $283 billion in assets. Ninety-four of these banks were state-chartered.

The Federal Reserve made steep cuts in interest rates in 2001/02, and net interest margins (NIMs) (the difference between the lower rates offered to savers and the higher rates charged on loans) in Pennsylvania declined by the end of 2002. Banks' funding costs were already at historic lows when short-term interest rates stabilized, limiting further significant improvement in NIMs. The lower long-term interest rates resulted in consumers increased refinancing with long-term fixed-rate mortgage loans. If interest rates were to rise in 2004, those insured banks with high concentrations of long-term assets might experience NIM compression.

Pennsylvania's banks had lower past-due loan ratios than the rest of the nation in 2002, except for commercial real estate (CRE) loans. CRE markets were soft in 2002, and CRE loan delinquency levels were projected to increase.

³³INSURANCE

In 2001, there were 8.9 million ordinary life insurance policies in force, with a total value of $450.3 billion; total value for all categories of life insurance (ordinary, group, industrial, and credit) was $768.9 billion. Death benefits paid that year totaled $2.3 billion.

There were 37 life and health and 210 property and casualty insurance companies headquartered in Pennsylvania in 2000. In 2001, property and casualty insurers wrote over $14.7 billion in premiums. That year, there were 61,267 flood insurance policies in force in the state, with a total value of $6.8 million.

³⁴SECURITIES

Formally established in 1790, the Philadelphia Stock Exchange (PHLX) is the oldest stock exchange in the US. It was also the nation's most important exchange until the 1820s, when the New York Stock Exchange eclipsed it. Since World War II, the Philadelphia exchange has merged with stock exchanges in Baltimore (1949), Washington, DC (1953), and Pittsburgh (1969). As the primary odd-lot market for Government National Mortgage Association securities and as a leading market for odd-lot government securities and stock options, PHLX ranks after only the New York and American exchanges in trading volume. PHLX was the first exchange in the US to trade foreign currency options (1982) and the National Over-the-Counter Index (1985). Over 2,600 stocks are traded on the exchange, and over 800 options.

Pennsylvania has 1,870 brokers and dealers organizations doing business in the state through 27,113 employees; investment advisory services are provided by 505 firms. The state provides headquarters for 215 NASDAQ-listed companies, 12 NASDAQ market makers, 28 AMEX-listed companies; and has incorporated 49 NYSE companies, the largest being: Rite Aid, Sunoco, Heinz, PPG Industries, and Mellon Financial Corp.

Sales of securities are regulated by the Pennsylvania Securities Commission, which also licenses all securities dealers, agents, and investment advisors in the state.

³⁵PUBLIC FINANCE

Pennsylvania's budget is prepared annually by the Office of Budget and submitted by the governor to the general assembly for amendment and approval. By law, annual operating expenditures may not exceed available revenues and surpluses from prior years. The fiscal year runs from 1 July to 30 June.

For 2003/04, allocations from Pennsylvania's general fund were for education (42.8%), health and human services (35.7%), protection (11.8%), regulation and direction (4.1%), other programs, including general government (2.9%) and economic development (2.7%). In 2002/03, Pennsylvania's budget deficit was estimated at 2.4% of the state budget, and for 2003/04, the deficit was projected at 2.4% to 9.6% of the state budget.

The following table from the US Census Bureau contains information on revenues, expenditures, indebtedness, and cash/securities for 2001.

	($000)	PERCENT	PER CAPITA
Population (thousands, 2001)	12,303	(X)	(X)
Total Revenue	45,887,490	100.00	3,729.78
General revenue	44,180,616	96.28	3,591.04
Utility revenue	–	–	–
Liquor store revenue	911,128	1.99	74.06
Insurance trust revenue	795,746	1.73	64.68
Exhibit: Salaries and wages	5,447,349	10.58	442.77
Total expenditure	51,488,402	100.00	4,185.03
General expenditure	45,517,170	88.40	3,699.68
Education	13,691,837	26.59	1,112.89
Public welfare	15,067,500	29.26	1,224.70
Hospitals	1,676,160	3.26	136.24
Health	1,655,602	3.22	134.57
Highways	3,759,193	7.30	305.55
Police protection	828,177	1.61	67.32
Correction	1,558,157	3.03	126.65
Natural resources	694,626	1.35	56.46
Parks and recreation	151,727	0.29	12.33
Government administration	1,431,360	2.78	116.34
Interest on general debt	1,107,325	2.15	90.00
Other and unallocable	3,895,506	7.57	316.63
Utility expenditure	–	–	–
Liquor store expenditure	840,206	1.63	68.29
Insurance trust expenditure	5,131,026	9.97	417.05
Debt at end of fiscal year	19,249,044	100.00	1,564.58
Cash and security holdings	104,570,955	100.00	8,499.63

36TAXATION

Pennsylvania's personal income tax, adopted in 1971, is levied at a rate of 2.8% (the flat rate is dictated by the "uniformity clause" in the 1923 state constitution). Business taxes include a corporate net income tax of 9.99%, capital stock and franchise taxes, and taxes on public utilities, insurance premiums, and financial institutions. Pennsylvania's 6% sales and use tax exempts essential items like clothing, groceries, and medicines. Local sales taxes are limited to 1%. Programs such as the Target Jobs Tax Credit and the Employment Incentive Payment program provide tax credits for hiring welfare recipients or persons from specified groups that have special employment needs or high unemployment rates. The state has an inheritance tax and has taken action to disconnect its estate tax from the federal tax exemption, which is scheduled to expire in 2007. Gift and death taxes account for a comparatively substantial part of state tax collections: 6.2% in 2001 and 3.44% in 2002. Other state taxes include various license fees and stamp taxes. Most property taxes are collected by local government, which collects about 40% of all state and local revenues in Pennsylvania.

The state collected $22.135 billion in taxes in 2002 (down $436 million from 2001), of which 33.1% came from the general sales tax, 30.4% came from individual income taxes, 16.3% from selective sales taxes, 9.4% from license fees, and 5.4% from corporate income taxes. In 2003, Pennsylvania ranked 36th among the states in terms of combined state and local tax burden, which amounted to about 9.1% of income.

The following table from the US Census Bureau provides a summary of taxes collected by the state in 2002.

	($000)	PER CAPITA
Total Taxes	22,135,537	1,794.52
Property taxes	50,949	4.13
Sales and gross receipts	10,948,136	887.56
General sales and gross receipts	7,330,422	594.27
Selective sales taxes	3,617,714	293.29
Alcoholic beverage	197,426	16.01
Amusements	685	0.06
Insurance Premiums	503,155	40.79
Motor fuels	1,753,338	142.14
Pari-mutuels	29,049	2.35
Public utilities	732,262	59.36
Tobacco products	317,442	25.73
Other selective sales	84,357	6.84

	($000)	PER CAPITA
Licenses	2,078,209	168.48
Alcoholic beverages	14,400	1.17
Amusements	163	0.01
Corporation	697,815	56.57
Hunting and fishing	60,175	4.88
Motor vehicle	771,420	62.54
Motor vehicle operators	53,865	4.37
Public utility	48,048	3.9
Occupation and business, NEC	418,899	33.96
Other	13,424	1.09
Other taxes	9,058,243	734.35
Individual income	6,734,729	545.98
Corporation net income	1,198,438	97.16
Death and gift	761,812	61.76
Documentary and stock transfer	342,710	27.78
Severance	(X)	(X)
Other	20,554	1.67

37ECONOMIC POLICY

The Bureau of Economic Assistance directs and controls the Commerce Department's economic assistance activities, including the administration and management of the Revenue Bond and Mortgage Program, the Pennsylvania Industrial Development Authority, the Job Training Partnership Act, and the Pennsylvania Capital Loan Fund. Among the activities of the Bureau of Domestic and International Commerce are supervising projects encouraging industrial development, attracting both domestic and foreign investment to the state, and providing export assistance to Pennsylvania companies. Pennsylvania had about 27,000 acres of "Opportunity Zones;" virtually tax-free areas for new businesses, in 2000.

The Pennsylvania Industrial Development Authority Board and the Pennsylvania Minority Business Development Authority provide loans to businesses that want to build new facilities or renovate and expand older ones. The Office of Minority Business Enterprise seeks to strengthen minority businesses by helping them obtain contracts with the state. The Small Business Action Center aids small businesses by providing a network of informational sources. The Bureau of Technological Development directs all phases of the Department of Commerce's scientific and technological activities and monitors advanced technology initiatives and growth throughout the state. Additional services are provided by the Bureau of Statistics, Research and Planning, the Bureau of Appalachian Development, the Bureau of Travel Development, the Bureau of Motion Picture and Television Development, the Bureau of Management and Administration, the Financial Analysis Office, and the Nursing Home Loan Agency.

38HEALTH

Pennsylvania's infant mortality rate in 2000 was 7.1 per 1,000 live births. In 1999, there were 34,494 legal abortions performed, a rate of 14 per 1,000 women. In 2000, mortality rates for the leading causes of death—heart disease, cancer, and stroke—were well above the US averages. Death rates per 100,000 population were as follows: heart disease, 339.7; cancer, 210.4; cerebrovascular disease, 74.7; accidents, 38.2; and suicide, 11.3. The overall death rate in 2000 was 1,091.5 per 100,000 population, one of the highest among the states. Among Pennsylvania residents 18 and older, 24.3% were smokers in 2000; the rate of death from lung disease stood at 68.4 per 100,000 population in 2000. The HIV mortality rate per 100,000 population was 1.8, well below the national average of 5.3 in 2000. A total of 26,369 AIDS cases had been reported in Pennsylvania through 2001.

Pennsylvania's 205 community hospitals had 1,808,531 admissions and 42,131 beds in 2001. There were 51,312 full-time registered nurses and 6,215 full-time licensed practical nurses in

2001 and 318 physicians per 100,000 population in 2000. The average expense of a community hospital for care was $1,600.70 per inpatient day in 2001.

Federal government grants to cover the Medicare and Medicaid services in 2001 totaled $6.2 billion; 2,095,453 enrollees received Medicare benefits that year. Only 9.2% of Pennsylvania's residents were uninsured in 2002.

The University of Pennsylvania School of Medicine, which originated as the medical school of the College of Philadelphia in 1765, is the nation's oldest medical school. One of the nation's newest is the Hershey Medical Center of Pennsylvania State University. Other medical schools in Pennsylvania are the University of Pittsburgh School of Medicine, Temple University's School of Medicine, the Medical College of Pennsylvania, and Allegheny University, the last three in Philadelphia. The state also aids colleges of osteopathic medicine, podiatric medicine, and optometry—all in Philadelphia. Among the many medical certification boards located in Philadelphia are the boards of allergy and immunology, internal medicine, ophthalmology, and surgery.

39SOCIAL WELFARE

In 2001, the average weekly unemployment benefit was $276.64. Average monthly participation in the food stamp program in FY2002 comprised 766,615 persons (350,838 households). The average monthly benefit was $76.13, and the sum total of benefits paid in FY2002 was $700,337,384.

With the enactment of the Personal Responsibility and Work Opportunity Reconciliation Act of 1996, the US government has changed the form and regulations for many of its social welfare programs. Most significantly, it replaces Aid to Families with Dependent Children (AFDC), an open-ended entitlement program, with Temporary Assistance for Needy Families (TANF), a limited system of assistance funded largely through federal block grants. The reform act also impacts the food stamp program, the Supplemental Security Income program, and the child nutrition program. The law took effect on 1 July 1997 and provided $16.38 billion in block grants for fiscal years 1997–2002. The grants are to be divided among the states based on an equation involving the numbers of former AFDC recipients in each state.

Reauthorization of the 1996 social welfare legislation, scheduled for 2002, was delayed, and the original law had been extended three times as of July 2003, with the most recent extension running through September 2003. In June 2000 the state had 232,976 welfare recipients. State expenditures on the TANF program in FY2002 totaled $407,125,600.

In December 2001, Social Security benefits were paid to 2,658,850 Pennsylvania residents. This number included 1,452,510 retired workers, 283,180 widows and widowers, 229,190 disabled workers, 146,220 spouses, and 161,750 children. Social Security beneficiaries represented 19.2% of the total state population and 93.6% of the state's population age 65 and older. Retired workers (excluding persons with special benefits) received an average monthly payment of $899; widows and widowers, $867; disabled workers, $831; and spouses, $459. Payments for children of retired workers averaged $453 per month; children of deceased workers, $599; and children of disabled workers, $235.

Federal Supplemental Security Income payments in December 2001 went to 294,467 Pennsylvania residents, averaging $408 a month.

40HOUSING

In 2002, there were 5,328,251 housing units in Pennsylvania, 4,821,279 of which were occupied; 71.7% were owner-occupied. About 56.9% of all units were single-family, detached homes.

About 31.7% of all units were built in 1939 or earlier. Faced with a decaying housing stock, Philadelphia during the 1970s and 1980s encouraged renovation of existing units along with the construction of new ones, effectively revitalizing several neighborhoods. About 22% of all units were built statewide in the period from 1970 to 1989. In 2002, utility gas and fuel oil were the most common sources of energy for heating. It was estimated that 95,671 units lacked telephone services, 20,146 lacked complete plumbing facilities, and 28,034 lacked complete kitchen facilities.

In 2002, 45,114 new privately owned housing units were authorized for construction. The median home value was $102,871. The median monthly cost for mortgage owners was $1,062. Renters paid a median of $577 per month. During fiscal year 2002, Pennsylvania received over $277.7 million in community planning and development aid from the US Department of Housing and Urban Development.

41EDUCATION

Pennsylvania lagged behind many of its neighbors in establishing a free public school system. From colonial times until the 1830s, almost all instruction in reading and writing took place in private schools. Called "dame schools" in the cities and "neighborhood schools" in rural areas, they offered primary courses, usually taught by women in their own homes. In addition, the Quakers, Moravians, and Scots-Irish Presbyterians all formed their own private schools, emphasizing religious study. Many communities also set up secondary schools, called academies, on land granted by the state; by 1850, there were 524 academies, some of which later developed into colleges. A public school law passed in 1834 was not mandatory in the school districts but was still unpopular. Thaddeus Stevens, then a state legislator, is credited with saving the law from repeal in 1835. Two years later, more than 40% of the state's children were in public schools.

As of 2000, 81.9% of the population 25 years old and older had completed four years of high school, and 22.4% had finished four or more years of college.

The total enrollment for fall 1999 in Pennsylvania's public schools stood at 1,816,716. Of these, 1,262,181 attended schools from kindergarten through grade eight, and 554,535 attended high school. Minority students made up approximately 22% of the total enrollment in public elementary and secondary schools in 2001. Total enrollment was estimated at 1,811,030 in fall 2000. Expenditures for public education in 2000/01 were estimated at $15,070,000. Enrollment in nonpublic schools in fall 2001 was 339,484.

As of fall 2000, there were 703,163 students enrolled in college or graduate school. In the same year Pennsylvania had 263 degree-granting institutions. Indiana University of Pennsylvania, established in 1872, accounted for about 15% of this enrollment. Four universities have nonprofit corporate charters but are classified as state-related: Pennsylvania State University, Temple University, the University of Pittsburgh, and Lincoln University. Of these, Penn State is by far the largest. Founded in 1855 as the Farmers' High School of Pennsylvania, Penn State now has its main campus at University Park and 23 smaller campus locations statewide. In 2000 there were 21 community colleges and one technical institute.

There are eight state-aided private institutions receiving designated grants from the legislature. The largest of these schools is the University of Pennsylvania, founded in 1740 by Benjamin Franklin as the Philadelphia Academy and Charitable School; among its noteworthy professional schools is the Wharton School of Business. Other private colleges and universities, also eligible to receive state aid through a per-pupil funding formula, include Bryn Mawr College (founded in 1880), Bucknell University (1846) in Lewisburg, Carnegie-Mellon

University (1900) in Pittsburgh, Dickinson College (1733) in Carlisle, Duquesne University (1878) in Pittsburgh, Haverford College (1833), Lafayette College (1826), Lehigh University (1865), Swarthmore College (1864), and Villanova University (1842). In 1997, minority students comprised 14.7% of total postsecondary enrollment. The Pennsylvania Higher Education Assistance Agency offers higher education grants, guarantees private loans, and administers work-study programs for Pennsylvania students.

42ARTS

Philadelphia was the cultural capital of the colonies and rivaled New York as a theatrical center during the 1800s. In 1984, Philadelphia had five fully developed resident theaters, ranking 3rd in the nation after New York and California. A number of regional and summer stock theaters are scattered throughout the state, the most noteworthy being in Bucks County, Lancaster, and Pittsburgh.

Pennsylvania's most significant contribution to the performing arts has come through music. One of America's first important songwriters, Stephen Foster, grew up in Pittsburgh. The Pittsburgh Symphony, which began performing in 1896, first achieved prominence under Victor Herbert. Temporarily disbanded in 1910, the symphony was revived under Fritz Reiner in 1927; subsequent music directors have included William Steinberg and Andre Previn. Even more illustrious has been the career of the Philadelphia Orchestra, founded in 1900. Among this orchestra's best-known permanent conductors have been Leopold Stokowski and Eugene Ormandy, both of whom recorded extensively.

An important dance company, the Pennsylvania Ballet, is based in Philadelphia, which also has the Curtis Institute of Music, founded in 1924. Pittsburgh also hosts a ballet company. The National Choreographic Center was established in the mid-1980s in Carlisle in conjunction with the Central Pennsylvania Youth Ballet School. Opera companies include the Pennsylvania Opera Theater, Pittsburgh Opera, and Opera Company of Philadelphia.

Expressions '80, a minorities arts festival in Philadelphia that attracted artists from a six-state area, was the first regional festival of its kind in the Northeast. The Pennsylvania Writers Collective, an initiative program of the Pennsylvania Council on the Arts, supports the work of the state's creative writers. The American Poetry Review, published out of Philadelphia, has become one of the nation's premier poetry journals. Favorite tourist sites featuring the arts include the Andy Warhol Museum in Pittsburgh and Fallingwater, a home created by Frank Lloyd Wright in Bear Run.

In 2003, the Pennsylvania Council on the Arts and other Pennsylvania arts organizations received grants totaling $2,753,400 from the National Endowment for the Arts. The Pennsylvania Humanities Council was established in 1973. In 2000, the National Endowment for the Humanities contributed $3,692,993 for 45 state programs. The state and various private sources also provided funding for arts programs. Pennsylvania has an estimated 3,000 arts associations and 75 local arts groups, with over 400,000 contributing artists.

43LIBRARIES AND MUSEUMS

Pennsylvania's public libraries stocked 28,000,000 volumes during 2000, with a total circulation of 54,560,000. The largest public library in the state, and one of the oldest in the US, is the Free Library of Philadelphia, with 6,700,000 volumes in 73 branches. The Carnegie Library in Pittsburgh has 3,439,666 volumes and 18 branches. Harrisburg offers the State Library of Pennsylvania, which had 1,000,494 volumes in 1998. The Alverthorpe Gallery Library in Jenkintown contains the Rosenwald collection of illustrated books dating from the 15th century. Total public library income came to $235,416,000 in 2000, including $2.6 million in federal grants and about $44 million in state grants. Per capita spending was $17.95.

Philadelphia is the site of the state's largest academic collection, the University of Pennsylvania Libraries, with 4,791,342 volumes. Other major academic libraries are at the University of Pittsburgh, 3,968,106 volumes; Penn State, over 2.5 million; Temple, 2,445,164; Carnegie-Mellon, 906,069; and Bryn Mawr, 1,062,594.

Pennsylvania has 362 museums and public gardens, with many of the museums located in Philadelphia. The Franklin Institute, established in 1824 as an exhibition hall and training center for inventors and mechanics, is a leading showcase for science and technology. Other important museums are the Philadelphia Museum of Art, Academy of Natural Sciences, Pennsylvania Academy of the Fine Arts, Afro-American Historical and Cultural Museum, American Catholic Historical Society, American Swedish Historical Foundation Museum, and Museum of American Jewish History.

The Carnegie Institute in Pittsburgh is home to several major museums, including the Carnegie Museum of Natural History and the Museum of Art. Also in Pittsburgh are the Buhl Planetarium and Institute of Popular Science and the Frick Art Museum. Other institutions scattered throughout the state include the Moravian Museum, Bethlehem; US Army Military History Institute, Carlisle; Erie Art Center, Museum, and Old Custom House; Pennsylvania Lumber Museum, Galeton; Pennsylvania Historical and Museum Commission and William Penn Memorial Museum, Harrisburg; Pennsylvania Dutch Folk Culture Society, Lenhartsville; Schwenkfelder Museum, Pennsburg; and Railroad Museum of Pennsylvania, Strasburg. A new exhibit at the Pittsburgh Zoo and Aquarium opened in June of 2000, featuring a $16.8 million aquarium that was twice as big as the old Aqua Zoo, and included 500 species of sea creatures.

Several old forts commemorate the French and Indian War, and George Washington's Revolutionary headquarters at Valley Forge is now a national historical park. Brandywine Battlefield (Chadds Ford) is another Revolutionary War site. Gettysburg National Military Park commemorates the Civil War. Other historic sites are Independence National Historical Park, Philadelphia; the Daniel Boone Homestead, Birdsboro; John Brown's House, Chambersburg; James Buchanan's home, Lancaster; and Ft. Augusta, Sunbury, a frontier outpost.

44COMMUNICATIONS

Philadelphia already had mail links to surrounding towns and to Maryland and Virginia by 1737, when Benjamin Franklin was named deputy postmaster of the city, but service was slow and not always reliable. During the remainder of the century, significant improvements in delivery were made, but some townspeople devised ingenious ways of transmitting information even faster than the mails. Philadelphia stock exchange brokers, for instance, communicated with agents in New York by flashing coded signals with mirrors and lights from a series of high points across New Jersey, thereby receiving stock prices on the same day they were transacted. By 1846, the first telegraph service in the state linked Harrisburg and Lancaster.

In 2001, 97.0% of Pennsylvania's households had telephones.

Pittsburgh's KDKA became the world's first commercial radio station in 1920. By 2003, it was one of 52 major AM and 144 major FM radio stations. In addition, there were 34 major television stations. WQED in Pittsburgh pioneered community-sponsored educational television when it began broadcasting in 1954. In 2000, the Philadelphia area had 2,670,710 households, 79% with cable; the Pittsburgh area had a 79% penetration rate in 1,135,290 households; and the Harrisburg-Lancaster-Lebanon-York area had 599,930 households, 78% with cable.

A total of 217,724 Internet domain names were registered in the state by the year 2000.

[45] PRESS

Benjamin Franklin may have been colonial Pennsylvania's most renowned publisher, but its first was Andrew Bradford, whose *American Weekly Mercury*, established in 1719, was the third newspaper to appear in the colonies. Founded nine years later, the *Pennsylvania Gazette* was purchased by Franklin in 1730 and served as the springboard for *Poor Richard's Almanack*.

During the 1800s, newspapers sprang up in all the major cities and many small communities. By 1880, Pittsburgh had 10 daily newspapers—more than any other city its size. After a series of mergers and closings, however, it is left with only one paper today—the *Post-Gazette*. Philadelphia has two newspapers, the *Inquirer* and the *Daily News*. The *Inquirer*, founded in 1829, has won numerous awards for its investigative reporting.

In 2002, Pennsylvania had 47 morning newspapers, 36 evening newspapers, and 41 Sunday papers. The following table shows the approximate circulation of some of the leading dailies in 2002:

AREA	NAME	DAILY	SUNDAY
Allentown	*Morning Call* (m)	128,204	171,651
Erie	*Times-News* (m,S)	60,764	88,722
Harrisburg	*Patriot-News* (m,S)	99,871	151,603
Philadelphia	*Inquirer* (m,S)	365,154	732,412
	Daily News (m)	152,435	77,104 (Sat.)
Pittsburgh	*Post-Gazette* (m,S)	242,141	409,352
Wilkes-Barre	*Citizens' Voice* (m,S)	33,017	29,733
	Times Leader (m,S)	43,684	64,110

Farm Journal and *Current History*, both monthlies, are published in Philadelphia, and there are monthlies named for both Philadelphia and Pittsburgh. Of more specialized interest are the gardening, nutrition, and health magazines and books from Rodale Press in Emmaus, and automotive guides from the Chilton Co. in Radnor.

[46] ORGANIZATIONS

In 2003, there were about 5,513 regional, national, and international organizations within the state.

Philadelphia is the home for two major service organizations: Big Brothers/Big Sisters of America and the Grand United Order of Odd Fellows. Cultural and educational organizations in that city include the American Academy of Political and Social Science, the Academy of Natural Sciences, the American Philosophical Society, and Middle States Association of Colleges and Schools. The Association for Children with Learning Disabilities is located in Pittsburgh, the College Placement Council in Bethlehem, and the American Philatelic Society in State College. Also in State College is the Environmental Coalition on Nuclear Power. The Society for Animal Rights, a humane organization, is in Clarks Summit.

State arts organizations include Dance Theatre of Pennsylvania, the Pittsburgh Center for the Arts, the Folk Heritage Institute. State environmental organizations include Preservation Pennsylvania and the Rodale Institute.

Commercial and trade groups in the state include the American Mushroom Institute, Kennett Square; Insurance Institute of America, Malvern; the American College of Physicians–American Society of Internal Medicine, Philadelphia; and the Society of Automotive Engineers, Warrendale. The Gray Panthers, a senior citizens' activist group, and Women's Strike for Peace are in Philadelphia. Valley Forge is the home of the Patriotic Order of the Sons of America.

Among the many sports organizations headquartered in Pennsylvania are the US Squash Racquets Association, in Bala-Cynwyd; National Trotting and Pacing Association, Hanover; Pop Warner Football and US Rowing Association, Philadelphia; and Little League Baseball, Williamsport. The Major League Umpires Association is also based in the state.

The Jewish Publication Society is based in Philadelphia. The Mennonite Central Committee, a major international relief and service organization, is based in Akron.

[47] TOURISM, TRAVEL, AND RECREATION

Tourism is the 2nd-largest industry in the state of Pennsylvania, which hosted about 117.5 million travelers in 2002. Of these, about 1.3 million were international visitors with the majority from Canada, the United Kingdom, and Germany. Most out-of-state visitors are from New York, New Jersey, Ohio, Maryland, and Virginia. The total economic impact from travel expenditures was $34.1 billion in 2002. The industry supported over 563,440 jobs.

Philadelphia—whose Independence National Historical Park has been called the most historic square mile in America—offers the Liberty Bell, Independence Hall, Carpenter's Hall, and many other sites. North of Philadelphia, in Bucks County, is the town of New Hope, with its numerous crafts and antique shops.

The Lancaster area is "Pennsylvania Dutch" country, featuring tours and exhibits of Amish farm life. Gettysburg contains not only the famous Civil War battlefield but also the home of Dwight D. Eisenhower, opened to the public in 1980. Among the most popular sites are Chocolate World and Hershey Park in the town of Hershey and Valley Forge National Historic Park. Annual parades and festivals include the Mummers Parade on 1 January in Philadelphia and the Kutztown Folk Festival, commemorating Pennsylvania Dutch life, held the first week of July.

No less an attraction are the state's outdoor recreation areas. By far the most popular for both skiing and camping are the Delaware Water Gap and the Poconos, also a favorite resort region. The state park system includes 116 state parks, 20 state forests, one national forest, and 3 environmental education centers.

[48] SPORTS

Pennsylvania has seven major league professional sports teams: the Philadelphia Phillies and the Pittsburgh Pirates of Major League Baseball, the Philadelphia Eagles and the Pittsburgh Steelers of the National Football League, the Philadelphia 76ers of the National Basketball Association, and the Pittsburgh Penguins and Philadelphia Flyers of the National Hockey League.

The Phillies won the World Series in 1980; they won the National League Championship in 1993, but lost the World Series to the Toronto Blue Jays. The Pirates won the World Series in 1909, 1925, 1960, 1971, and 1979. The Steelers established a legendary football dynasty in the 1970s, winning Super Bowls in 1975, 1976, 1979, and 1980. They also played in the 1996 Super Bowl, losing to the Dallas Cowboys. The Eagles won the National Football Conference championship in 1981, but lost to Oakland in that year's Super Bowl. The 76ers won the NBA championship in 1947, 1956, 1967, and 1983, and lost the championship series in 1977, 1980, and 1982. The Flyers won the Stanley Cup in 1974 and 1975 and lost in the finals in 1976, 1980, 1985, 1987, and 1997. The Penguins won the Stanley Cup in 1991 and 1992.

There are also minor league baseball teams in Harrisburg, Scranton, Altoona, Reading, Williamsport, Allentown, and Erie, and minor league hockey teams in Hershey, Johnstown, Wilkes-Barre, and Philadelphia.

Horse racing is conducted at Keystone Race Track in Bucks County, Penn National Race Course in Dauphin County, and Commodore Downs in Erie County. Harness-racing tracks include Liberty Bell Park in northeast Philadelphia, the Meadows in Washington County, and Pocono Downs in Luzerne County. Each June, Pennsylvania hosts a major auto race, the Pocono 500. Each July, the state hosts a second NASCAR Winston Cup event, the Pennsylvania 500. The Penn Relays, an important amateur track meet, are held in Philadelphia every April.

In collegiate sports, football is most prominent. The University of Pittsburgh Panthers were named national champions in 1918, 1937, and 1976. Penn State was named champion in 1982 and 1986 and joined the Big Ten in 1990. The Nittany Lions won the Rose Bowl in 1995, the Sugar Bowl in 1983, the Orange Bowl in 1969, the Florida Citrus Bowl in 1994, the Fiesta Bowl in 1997, the Outback Bowl in 1996 and 1999, and the Cotton Bowl in 1972, to name just a few of their bowl victories. The University of Pennsylvania, members of the Ivy League, field traditionally strong teams in football and basketball. Villanova, located in Philadelphia, won the NCAA basketball championship in 1985.

Each summer, Williamsport hosts baseball's Little League World Series.

⁴⁹FAMOUS PENNSYLVANIANS

Johan Printz (b.Sweden, 1592–1663), the 400-lb, hard-drinking, hard-swearing, and hard-ruling governor of New Sweden, was Pennsylvania's first European resident of note. The founder of Pennsylvania was William Penn (b.England, 1644–1718), a Quaker of sober habits and deep religious beliefs. Most extraordinary of all Pennsylvanians, Benjamin Franklin (b.Massachusetts, 1706–90), a printer, author, inventor, scientist, legislator, diplomat, and statesman, served the Philadelphia, Pennsylvania, and US governments in a variety of posts.

Only one native Pennsylvanian, James Buchanan (1791–1868), has ever become US president. Buchanan was a state assemblyman, five-term US representative, two-term US senator, secretary of state, and minister to Russia and then to Great Britain before entering the White House as a 65-year-old bachelor in 1857. As president, he tried to maintain the Union by avoiding extremes and preaching compromise, but his toleration of slavery was abhorrent to abolitionists and his desire to preserve the Union was obnoxious to secessionists. Dwight D. Eisenhower (b.Texas, 1890–1969) retired to a farm in Gettysburg after his presidency was over. George M. Dallas (1792–1864), Pennsylvania's only US vice president, was James K. Polk's running mate.

The six Pennsylvanians who have served on the US Supreme Court have all been associate justices: James Wilson (1742–98), Henry Baldwin (1780–1844), Robert C. Grier (1794–1870), William Strong (1808–95), George Shiras, Jr. (1832–1924), and Owen J. Roberts (1875–1955). Supreme Court nominee Robert Heron Bork (b.1927) served as a federal judge for many years, but his Supreme Court nomination was not confirmed.

Many other Pennsylvanians have held prominent federal positions. Albert Gallatin (b.Switzerland, 1761–1849), brilliant secretary of the treasury under Thomas Jefferson and James Madison, later served as minister to France and then to Great Britain. Richard Rush (1780–1859) was Madison's attorney general and John Quincy Adams's secretary of the treasury. A distinguished jurist, Jeremiah Sullivan Black (1810–83) was Buchanan's attorney general and later his secretary of state. John Wanamaker (1838–1922), an innovative department store merchandiser, served as postmaster general under Benjamin Harrison. Philander C. Knox (1853–1921) was Theodore Roosevelt's attorney general and William Howard Taft's secretary of state. Financier Andrew C. Mellon (1855–1937) was secretary of the treasury under Warren G. Harding, Calvin Coolidge, and Herbert Hoover. Recent Pennsylvanians in high office include Richard Helms (1913–2002), director of the US Central Intelligence Agency from 1966 to 1973, and Alexander Haig (b.1924), former commander of NATO forces in Europe, chief of staff under Richard Nixon, and Ronald Reagan's first choice for secretary of state.

Three US senators, Simon Cameron (1799–1889), Matthew Quay (1833–1904), and Boies Penrose (1860–1921), are best known as leaders of the powerful Pennsylvania Republican machine. Senator Joseph F. Guffey (1870–1959) sponsored legislation to stabilize the bituminous coal industry. After serving as reform mayor of Philadelphia, Joseph S. Clark (1901–1990) also distinguished himself in the Senate, and Hugh Scott (1900–94) was Republican minority leader from 1969 to 1977. Outstanding representatives from Pennsylvania include Thaddeus Stevens (1792–1868), leader of radical Republicans during the Civil War era; David Wilmot (1814–68), author of the proviso attempting to prohibit slavery in territory acquired from Mexico; and Samuel J. Randall (1828–90), speaker of the House of Representatives from 1876 to 1881.

Other notable historical figures were Joseph Galloway (b.Maryland, 1729?–1803), a loyalist; Robert Morris (England, 1734–1806), a Revolutionary financier; and Betsy Ross (Elizabeth Griscom, 1752–1836), the seamstress who allegedly stitched the first American flag. Pamphleteer Thomas Paine (England, 1737–1809), pioneer Daniel Boone (1734–1820), and General Anthony Wayne (1745–96) also distinguished themselves during this period. In the Civil War, General George B. McClellan (1826–85) led the Union army on the Peninsula and at the Battle of Antietam, while at the Battle of Gettysburg, Generals George Gordon Meade (b.Spain, 1815–72) and Winfield Scott Hancock (1824–86) both showed their military prowess.

Important state governors include John W. Geary (1819–73), Samuel W. Pennypacker (1843–1916), Robert E. Pattison (b.Maryland, 1850–1904), Gifford Pinchot (b.Connecticut 1865–1946), James H. Duff (1883–1969), George H. Earle (1890–1974), Milton J. Shapp (Ohio, 1912–88), William W. Scranton (b.Connecticut, 1917), George M. Leader (b.1918), and Richard L. Thornburgh (b.1932).

Pennsylvanians have won Nobel Prizes in every category except literature. General George C. Marshall (1880–1959), chief of staff of the US Army in World War II and secretary of state when the European Recovery Program (Marshall Plan) was adopted, won the 1953 Nobel Peace Prize. Simon Kuznets (b.Russia, 1901–85) received the 1971 Nobel Prize in economic science for work on economic growth, and Herbert A. Simon (b.Wisconsin, 1916–2001) received the 1978 award for work on decision making in economic organizations; in 1980, Lawrence R. Klein (b.Nebraska, 1920) was honored for his design and application of econometric models. In physics, Otto Stern (b.Germany, 1888–1969) won the 1943 prize for work on the magnetic momentum of protons. In chemistry, Theodore W. Richards (1868–1928) won the 1914 Nobel Prize for determining the atomic weight of many elements, and Christian Boehmer Anfinsen (1916–95) won the 1972 award for pioneering studies in enzymes. In physiology or medicine, Philip S. Hench (1896–1965) won in 1950 for his discoveries about hormones of the adrenal cortex, Haldane K. Hartline (1903–83) won in 1967 for work on the human eye, and Howard M. Temin (1934–94) was honored in 1975 for the study of tumor viruses.

Many other Pennsylvanians were distinguished scientists. Ebenezer Kinnersly (1711–78) studied electricity, and Benjamin Franklin's grandson Alexander Dallas Bache (1806–67) was an expert on magnetism. Caspar Wistar (b.Germany, 1761–1818) and Thomas Woodhouse (1770–1809) pioneered the study of chemistry, while William Maclure (b.Scotland, 1763–1840) and James Mease (1771–1846) were early geologists. David Rittenhouse (1732–96) was a distinguished astronomer. John Bartram (1699–1777) and his son William (1739–1823) won international repute as botanists. Benjamin Rush (1745–1813) was Pennsylvania's most distinguished physician. Philip Syng

Physick (1768–1837) was a leading surgeon, and Nathaniel Chapman (b.Virginia, 1780–1853) was the first president of the American Medical Association. Rachel Carson (1907–64), a marine biologist and writer, became widely known for her crusade against the use of chemical pesticides. Noted inventors born in Pennsylvania include steamboat builder Robert Fulton (1765–1815) and David Thomas (1794–1882), the father of the American anthracite iron industry.

Pennsylvania played a large role in the economic development of the US. In addition to Mellon, outstanding bankers include Stephen Girard (b.France, 1750–1831), Nicholas Biddle (1786–1844), Anthony J. Drexel (1826–93), and John J. McCloy (1895–1985). Andrew Carnegie (b.Scotland, 1835–1919) and his lieutenants, including Henry Clay Frick (1849–1919) and Charles M. Schwab (1862–1939), created the most efficient steel-manufacturing company in the 19th century. Wanamaker, Frank W. Woolworth (b.New York, 1852–1919), and Sebastian S. Kresge (1867–1966) were pioneer merchandisers.

Other prominent businessmen born in Pennsylvania are automobile pioneer Clement Studebaker (1831–1901), chocolate manufacturer Milton S. Hershey (1857–1945), and retired Chrysler chairman Lee A. Iacocca (b.1924).

Pennsylvania labor leaders include Uriah S. Stephens (1821–82) and Terence V. Powderly (1849–1924), leaders of the Knights of Labor; Philip Murray (b.Scotland, 1886–1952), president of the CIO; and David J. MacDonald (1902–79), leader of the steelworkers. Among economic theorists, Henry George (1839–97) was the unorthodox advocate of the single tax. Florence Kelley (1859–1932) was an important social reformer, as is Bayard Rustin (1910–1987).

Important early religious leaders, all born in Germany, include Henry Melchior Muhlenberg (1711–87), organizer of Pennsylvania's Lutherans; Count Nikolaus Ludwig von Zinzendorf (1700–1760), a Moravian leader; and Johann Conrad Beissel (1690–1768), founder of the Ephrata Cloister. Charles Taze Russell (1852–1916), born a Congregationalist, founded the group that later became Jehovah's Witnesses. Among the state's outstanding scholars are historians Henry C. Lee (1825–1909), John Bach McMaster (1852–1932), Ellis Paxson Oberholtzer (1868–1936), and Henry Steele Commager (1902–98); anthropologist Margaret Mead (1901–78); behavioral psychologist B(urrhus) F(rederic) Skinner (1904–1990); urbanologist Jane Jacobs (b.1916); and language theorist Noam Chomsky (b.1928). Thomas Gallaudet (b.1787–1851) was a pioneer in education of the deaf.

Pennsylvania has produced a large number of distinguished journalists and writers. In addition to Franklin, newspapermen include John Dunlap (b.Ireland, 1747–1812), Benjamin Franklin Bache (1769–98), William L. McLean (1852–1931), and Moses L. Annenberg (1878–1942). Magazine editors were Sarah Josepha Buell Hale (b.New Hampshire, 1788–1879), Cyrus H. K. Curtis (b.Maine, 1850–1933), Edward W. Bok (b.Netherlands, 1863–1930), and I(sidor) F(einstein) Stone (1907–89). Ida M. Tarbell (1857–1944) was perhaps Pennsylvania's most famous muckraker. Among the many noteworthy Pennsylvania-born writers are Charles Brockden Brown (1771–1810), Bayard Taylor (1825–78), novelist and physician Silas Weir Mitchell (1829–1914), Charles Godfrey Leland (1824–1903), Owen Wister (1860–1938), Richard Harding Davis (1864–1916), Gertrude Stein (1874–1946), Mary Roberts Rinehart (1876–1958), Hervey Allen (1889–1949), Christopher Morley (1890–1957), Conrad Richter (1890–1968), John O'Hara (1905–70), Donald Barthelme (1931–89), and John Updike (b.1932). James Michener (b.New York, 1907–97) was raised in the state. Pennsylvania playwrights include James Nelson Barker (1784–1858), Maxwell Anderson (1888–1959), George S. Kaufman (1889–1961), Marc Connelly (1890–1980), Clifford Odets

(1906–63), and Ed Bullins (b.1935). Among Pennsylvania poets are Francis Hopkinson (1737–91), Philip Freneau (b.New York, 1753–1832), Thomas Dunn English (1819–1902), Thomas Buchanan Read (1822–72), and Wallace Stevens (1879–1955).

Composers include Stephen Collins Foster (1826–64), Ethelbert Woodbridge Nevin (1862–1901), Charles Wakefield Cadman (1881–1946), and Samuel Barber (1910–81). Among Pennsylvania painters prominent in the history of American art are Benjamin West (1738–1820), renowned as the father of American painting; Charles Willson Peale (1741–1827), who was also a naturalist; Thomas Sully (b.England, 1783–1872); George Catlin (1796–1872); Thomas Eakins (1844–1916); Mary Cassatt (1845–1926); Man Ray (1890–1976); Andrew Wyeth (b.1917); and Andy Warhol (1927–87). Outstanding sculptors include William Rush (1756–1833), George Grey Barnard (1863–1938), and Alexander Calder (1898–1976).

Pennsylvania produced and patronized a host of actors, including Edwin Forrest (1806–72) Lionel (1878–1954), Ethel (1879–1959), and John (1882–1942) Barrymore; W. C. Fields (William Claude Dukenfield, 1880–1946); Ed Wynn (Isaiah Edwin Leopold, 1886–1966); William Powell (1892–1987); Ethel Waters (1896–1977); Janet Gaynor (1906–84); James Stewart (1908–97); Broderick Crawford (1911–86); Gene Kelly (1912–96); Charles Bronson (Charles Buchinsky, b.1922); Mario Lanza (1925–59); Shirley Jones (b.1934); and comedian Bill Cosby (b.1937). Film directors Joseph L. Mankiewicz (1909–93), Arthur Penn (b.1922), and Sidney Lumet (b.1924) and film producer David O. Selznick (1902–65) also came from Pennsylvania.

Pennsylvania has produced outstanding musicians. Four important Pennsylvania-born vocalists are Marian Anderson (b.1897–1993), Blanche Thebom (b.1919), Marilyn Horne (b.1934), and Anna Moffo (b.1934). Pianists include the versatile Oscar Levant (1906–72) and jazz interpreters Earl "Fatha" Hines (1905–83) and Erroll Garner (1921–77). Popular band leaders include Fred Waring (1900–84), Jimmy Dorsey (1904–57) and his brother Tommy (1905–56), and Les Brown (b.1912). Perry Como (1913–2001), Daryl Hall (b.1949), and John Oates (b.New York, 1948) have achieved renown as popular singers. Dancers and choreographers from Pennsylvania include Martha Graham (1893–1991), Paul Taylor (b.1930), and Gelsey Kirkland (b.1952).

Of the many outstanding athletes associated with Pennsylvania, Jim Thorpe (b.Oklahoma, 1888–1953) was most versatile, having starred in Olympic pentathlon and decathlon events and football. Baseball Hall of Famers include Honus Wagner (1874–1955), Stan Musial (b.1920), and Roy Campanella (1921–1993). Outstanding Pennsylvania football players include Harold "Red" Grange (1903–91), George Blanda (b.1927), John Unitas (1933–2002), Joe Namath (b.1943), and Tony Dorsett (b.1954). Other stars include basketball's Wilt Chamberlain (1936–99); golf's Arnold Palmer (b.1929), tennis's Bill Tilden (1893–1953); horse racing's Bill Hartack (b.1932); billiards' Willie Mosconi (1913–93); swimming's Johnny Weissmuller (1904–84); and track and field's Bill Toomey (b.1939).

Pennsylvania has also been the birthplace of a duchess—Bessie Wallis Warfield, the Duchess of Windsor (1896–1986)—and of a princess—Grace Kelly, Princess Grace of Monaco (1929–82).

⁵⁰BIBLIOGRAPHY

Billinger, Robert D. *Pennsylvania's Coal Industry.* Gettysburg: Pennsylvania Historical Association, 1954.

Binder, Frederick Moor. *Coal Age Empire: Pennsylvania Coal and its Utilization to 1860.* Harrisburg: Pennsylvania Historical and Museum Commission. 1974

Blockson, Charles L. *African Americans in Pennsylvania: A History and Guide*. Baltimore: Black Classic, 1994.

Bremer, Francis J., and Dennis B. Downey (ed.). *A Guide to the History of Pennsylvania*. Westport, Conn.: Greenwood, 1994.

Bridenbaugh, Carl. *Cities in Revolt: Urban Life in America, 1743–76*. New York: Knopf, 1955.

Cochran, Thomas C. *Pennsylvania: A Bicentennial History*. New York: Norton, 1978.

Commonwealth of Pennsylvania. Bureau of Statistics. Research, and Planning. *1984 Pennsylvania Statistical Abstract*. 26th ed. Harrisburg, 1984.

Federal Writers' Project. *Pennsylvania: A Guide to the Keystone State*. Reprint. New York: Somerset, 1980 (orig. 1940).

Klein, Philip S., and Ari Hoogenboom. *A History of Pennsylvania*. Rev. ed. University Park: Pennsylvania State University Press, 1980.

Miller, Arthur P., Jr., and Marjorie L. Miller. *Pennsylvania Battlefields and Military Landmarks*. Mechanicsburg, Pa.: Stackpole Books, 2000.

Miller, E. Willard, ed. *A Geography of Pennsylvania*. University Park: Pennsylvania State University Press, 1995.

Murphy, Raymond E., and Marion Murphy. *Pennsylvania: A Regional Geography*. Harrisburg: Pennsylvania Book Service, 1937.

Pennsylvania, Commonwealth of. Department of General Services. *The Pennsylvania Manual, 1995*. Vol 112. Harrisburg, 1995.

Pennsylvania Chamber of Commerce. *Pennsylvania Government Today*. State College, Pa: Pennsylvania Valley Publishers, 1973.

Root, Douglas. *Pennsylvania*. Oakland, Calif.: Compass American Guides, 2000.

Soderland, Jean R., and Richard S. Dunn (eds.). *William Penn and the Founding of Pennsylvania, 1680–1684: A Documentary History*. Philadelphia: University of Pennsylvania Press, 1983.

Wallace, Paul A. W. *Pennsylvania: Seed of a Nation*. New York: Harper & Row, 1962.

RHODE ISLAND

State of Rhode Island and Providence Plantations

ORIGIN OF STATE NAME: Named for Rhode Island in Narragansett Bay, which was likened to the isle of Rhodes in the Mediterranean Sea. **NICKNAME:** The Ocean State; also, Little Rhody. **CAPITAL:** Providence. **ENTERED UNION:** 29 May 1790 (13th). **SONG:** "Rhode Island." **MOTTO:** Hope. **COAT OF ARMS:** A golden anchor on a blue field. **FLAG:** In the center of a white field is a golden anchor and beneath it is a blue ribbon with the state motto in gold letters, all surrounded by a circle of 13 gold stars. **OFFICIAL SEAL:** The anchor of the arms is surrounded by four scrolls, the topmost bearing the state motto: the words "Seal of the State of Rhode Island and Providence Plantations 1636" encircle the whole. **ANIMAL:** Quahaug. **BIRD:** Rhode Island Red. **FLOWER:** Violet. **TREE:** Red maple. **MINERAL:** Bowenite. **ROCK:** Cumberlandite. **LEGAL HOLIDAYS:** New Year's Day, 1 January; Birthday of Martin Luther King, Jr., 3rd Monday in January; Washington's Birthday, 3rd Monday in February; Memorial Day, last Monday in May; Independence Day, 4 July; Victory Day, 2nd Monday in August; Labor Day, 1st Monday in September; Columbus Day, 2nd Monday in October; Election Day, 1st Tuesday after 1st Monday in November, in even-numbered years; Veterans Day, 11 November; Thanksgiving Day, 4th Thursday in November; Christmas Day, 25 December. **TIME:** 7 AM EST = noon GMT.

¹LOCATION, SIZE, AND EXTENT

One of the six New England states in the northeastern US, Rhode Island is the smallest of all the 50 states. Rhode Island occupies only 0.03% of the total US area, and could fit inside Alaska, the largest state, nearly 486 times.

The total area of Rhode Island is 1,212 sq mi (3,139 sq km), of which land comprises 1,055 sq mi (2,732 sq km), and inland water 157 sq mi (407 sq km). The state extends 37 mi (60 km) E-W and 48 mi (77 km) N-S.

Rhode Island is bordered on the N and E by Massachusetts; on the S by the Atlantic Ocean (enclosing the ocean inlet, Narragansett Bay); and on the W by Connecticut (with part of the line formed by the Pawcatuck River). Three large islands—Prudence, Aquidneck (officially known as Rhode Island), and Conanicut—are situated within Narragansett Bay. Block Island, with an area of about 11 sq mi (28 sq km), lies some 9 mi (14 km) SW of Pt. Judith, on the mainland. There are 38 islands in all.

The total boundary length of Rhode Island is 160 mi (257 km). The state's geographic center is in Kent County, 1 mi (1.6 km) SSW of Cranston.

²TOPOGRAPHY

Rhode Island comprises two main regions. The New England Upland Region, which is rough and hilly and marked by forests and lakes, occupies the western two-thirds of the state, while the Seaboard Lowland, with its sandy beaches and salt marshes, occupies the eastern third. The highest point in the state is Jerimoth Hill, at 812 ft (248 m), in the northwest.

Rhode Island's principal river, the Blackstone, flows from Woonsocket past Pawtucket and thence into the Providence River, which, like the Sakonnet, is an estuary of Narragansett Bay; the Pawcatuck River flows into Block Island Sound. The state has 38 islands, the largest being Aquidneck (Rhode Island), with an area of about 45 sq mi (117 sq km).

³CLIMATE

Rhode Island has a humid climate, with cold winters and short summers. The average annual temperature is 50°F (10°C). At Providence the temperature ranges from an average of 28°F (–2°C) in January to 73°F (23°C) in July. The record high temperature, 104°F (40°C), was registered in Providence on 2 August 1975; the record low, –23°F (–31°C), at Kingston on 11 January 1942. In Providence, the average annual precipitation (1971–2000) was 46.5 in (118 cm); snowfall averages 37 in (94 cm) a year. Rhode Island's weather is highly changeable, with storms and hurricanes an occasional threat. On 21 September 1938, a hurricane and tidal wave took a toll of 262 lives; Hurricane Carol, on 31 August 1954, left 19 dead, and property damage was estimated at $90 million. A blizzard on 6–7 February 1978 dropped a record 28.6 in (73 cm) of snow on the state, as measured at Warwick, and caused 21 storm-attributed deaths.

⁴FLORA AND FAUNA

Though small, Rhode Island has three distinct life zones: sand-plain lowlands, rising hills, and highlands. Common trees are the tuliptree, pin and post oaks, and red cedar. Cattails are abundant in marsh areas, and 40 types of fern and 30 species of orchid are indigenous to the state. In 2003, the small whorled pogonia was threatened, the sandplain gerardia endangered.

Urbanization and industrialization have taken their toll of native mammals. Swordfish, bluefish, lobsters, and clams populate coastal waters; brook trout and pickerel are among the common freshwater fish. Fifteen Rhode Island animal species were listed as threatened or endangered in 2003, including the American burying beetle, bald eagle, finback and humpback whale, and four species of sea turtle.

⁵ENVIRONMENTAL PROTECTION

The Department of Environmental Management (DEM) coordinates all of the state's environmental protection and management programs. The Air, Solid Waste, and Hazardous Materials Section enforces controls on solid waste disposal, hazardous waste management facilities, industrial air pollution, and site remediation; the Water Quality Management Section regulates waste-treatment facilities, the discharge of industrial and oil wastes into state waters and public sewer facilities, groundwater protection, freshwater wetlands, dam maintenance, and home sewage disposal systems; the Natural Resources Management Section oversees fish, wildlife and estuarine resources, forest management, parks and recreation, and the enforcement of conservation laws; Planning and Administrative Services assists industry in pollution prevention, administers recycling programs, administers land preservation programs, and coordinates land acquisitions. The department also oversees water supply management. In 2003, the DEM, working the Department of Health, operated a Mosquito Abatement Coordination Office to help citizens minimize the risk of contracting West Nile virus from the mosquito population.

In 2003, Rhode Island had 187 hazardous waste sites listed in the Environmental Protection Agency's database, 12 of which were on the National Priorities List. In 1996, 10% of the state's area was wetland. In 2001, Rhode Island received $28,618,000 in federal grants from the Environmental Protection Agency; EPA expenditures for procurement contracts in Rhode Island that year amounted to $2,128,000.

6POPULATION

Rhode Island ranked 43rd in population in the US with an estimated total of 1,069,725 in 2002, an increase of 2% since 2000. Between 1990 and 2000, Rhode Island's population grew from 1,003,464 to 1,048,319, an increase of 4.5%. The population is projected to reach 1.1 million by 2025. The population density in 2000 was 1,003.2 persons per sq mi, making Rhode Island the nation's 2nd most densely populated state, after New Jersey.

In 2000 the median age was 36.7. Persons under 18 years old accounted for 23.6% of the population while14.5 % were age 65 or older.

Providence, the capital, is the leading city, with an estimated population in 2002 of 175,901 (compared to the 1940 peak of 253,504). In 1999, the Providence-Fall River-Warwick metropolitan area had an estimated population of 1,125,639. Other cities with large populations include Pawtucket and Woonsocket.

7ETHNIC GROUPS

Rhode Island's black population numbered 46,908 in 2000, up from 39,000 in 1990 (and 4.5% of the state total). In 2000 there were 90,820 Hispanics and Latinos (8.7% of the total population), nearly twice the 1990 census count of 46,000. In 2000, there were 5,121 American Indians, up from 4,000 in 1990. The Asian population was 23,665; the 2000 census reported 4,974 Chinese, 4,522 Cambodians, 2,942 Asian Indians, and 2,062 Filipinos. Pacific Islanders numbered 567. The foreign born made up 11.4% of the population, or 119,277 persons, up from 9.5% of the population in 1990.

8LANGUAGES

Many place-names in Rhode Island attest to the early presence of Mahican Indians: for instance, Sakonnet Point, Pawtucket, Matunuck, Narragansett.

English in Rhode Island is of the Northern dialect, with the distinctive features of eastern New England: absence of final /r/, and a vowel in *part* and *bath* intermediate between that in *father* and that in *bat*.

Rhode Island's immigrant tradition is reflected in the fact that in 2000, 20% of the state's residents reported speaking a language other than English in the home, up from 18% in 1990.

The following table gives selected statistics from the 2000 census for language spoken at home by persons five years old and over. The category "African languages" includes Amharic, Ibo, Twi, Yoruba, Bantu, Swahili, and Somali.

LANGUAGE	NUMBER	PERCENT
Population 5 years and over	985,184	100.0
Speak only English	788,560	80.0
Speak a language other than English	196,624	20.0
Speak a language other than English	196,624	20.0
Spanish or Spanish Creole	79,443	8.1
Portuguese or Portuguese Creole	37,437	3.8
French (incl. Patois, Cajun)	19,385	2.0
Italian	13,759	1.4
Mon-Khmer, Cambodian	5,586	0.6
French Creole	4,337	0.4
Chinese	3,882	0.4
Laotian	3,195	0.3
Polish	2,966	0.3
German	2,841	0.3
African languages	2,581	0.3
Arabic	2,086	0.2

9RELIGIONS

The first European settlement in Rhode Island was founded by an English clergyman, Roger Williams, who left Massachusetts to find freedom of worship. The Rhode Island Charter of 1663 proclaimed that a "flourishing civil state may stand and best be maintained with full liberty in religious concernments." Rhode Island has maintained this viewpoint throughout its history, and has long been a model of religious pluralism. The first Baptist congregation in the United States was established in 1638 in Providence. In Newport stands the oldest synagogue (1763) and the oldest Quaker meetinghouse (1699) in the United States.

A majority of the population of Rhode Island is Catholic, reflecting heavy immigration from Italy, Ireland, Portugal, and French Canada. In 2000, there were 542,244 Roman Catholics, accounting for 51.7% of the total state population. The largest Protestant denominations were Episcopalians, with 26,756 adherents, and American Baptists USA, with 20,997. An estimated 16,10 Jews resided in the state the same in 2000, as did about 1,827 Muslims. Friends–USA (Quakers) had only 599 members. About 36.5% of the population were not counted as members of any religious organization.

10TRANSPORTATION

As of 2000, Providence & Worcester was the only freight-hauling railroad in operation, utilizing 102 rail mi (164 km) of track. In the same year, chemicals accounted for most of the 598,410 tons of freight brought into or hauled from the state. In 1996, Amtrak operated 16 daily trains through Rhode Island.

In 2000, there were 6,052 mi (9,739 km) of public highways and roads; 779,054 motor vehicles were registered in 2000, and 654,035 drivers' licenses were in force. The major route through New England, I-95, crosses Rhode Island. The Rhode Island Public Transit Authority provides commuter bus service connecting urbanized areas.

Some of the best deepwater ocean ports on the east coast are in Narragansett Bay. The port at Providence handled 8.9 million tons of cargo in 2000.

There were 26 airfields in 2002, including 10 airports, 15 heliports, and 1 seaplane base. Theodore Francis Green Airport is the major air terminal, with 2,684,204 passengers enplaned in 2000.

11HISTORY

Before the arrival of the first white settlers, the Narragansett Indians inhabited the area from what is now Providence south along Narragansett Bay. Their principal rivals, the Wampanoag, dominated the eastern shore region.

In 1524, Florentine navigator Giovanni da Verrazano, sailing in the employ of France, became the first European to explore Rhode Island. The earliest permanent settlement was established at Providence in 1636 by English clergyman Roger Williams and

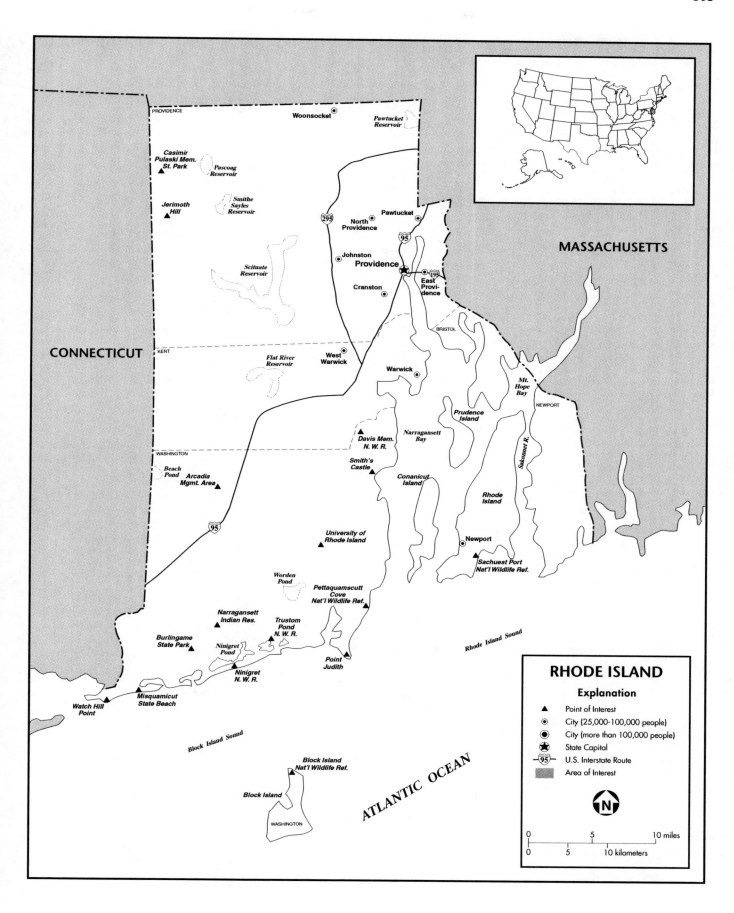

MASSACHUSETTS

CONNECTICUT

PROVIDENCE

Woonsocket

Pawtucket
Reservoir

Casimir
Pulaski Mem.
St. Park

Pascoag
Reservoir

Smithe
Sayles
Reservoir

Jerimoth
Hill

I-295

North
Providence

Pawtucket

95

Johnston

Providence

Scituate
Reservoir

195

East
Provi-
dence

Cranston

BRISTOL

KENT

Flat River
Reservoir

West
Warwick

Warwick

Mt.
Hope
Bay

NEWPORT

Prudence
Island

Narragansett
Bay

Davis Mem.
N. W. R.

WASHINGTON

Smith's
Castle

Conanicut
Island

Rhode
Island

Beach
Pond

Arcadia
Mgmt. Area

Sakonnet R.

95

University of
Rhode Island

Newport

Sachuest Port
Nat'l Wildlife Ref.

Worden
Pond

Pettaquamscutt
Cove
Nat'l Wildlife Ref.

Narragansett
Indian Res.

Trustom
Pond
N. W. R.

Burlingame
State Park

Ninigret
Pond

Point
Judith

Rhode Island Sound

Ninigret
N. W. R.

Misquamicut
State Beach

Watch Hill
Point

Block Island Sound

Block Island
Nat'l Wildlife Ref.

ATLANTIC OCEAN

Block Island

WASHINGTON

RHODE ISLAND

Explanation

▲ Point of Interest

⊙ City (25,000–100,000 people)

◉ City (more than 100,000 people)

★ State Capital

95 U.S. Interstate Route

▨ Area of Interest

N

| 0 | 5 | 10 miles |

| 0 | 5 | 10 kilometers |

a small band of followers who left the repressive atmosphere of the Massachusetts Bay Colony to seek freedom of worship. Other nonconformists followed, settling Portsmouth (1638), Newport (1639), and Warwick (1642). In 1644, Williams journeyed to England, where he secured a parliamentary patent uniting the four original towns into a single colony, the Providence Plantations. This legislative grant remained in effect until the Stuart Restoration made it prudent to seek a royal charter. The charter, secured for Rhode Island and the Providence Plantations from Charles II in 1663, guaranteed religious liberty, permitting significant local autonomy, and strengthened the colony's territorial claims. Encroachments by white settlers on Indian lands led to the Indian uprising known as King Philip's War (1675–76), during which the Indians were soundly defeated.

The early 18th century was marked by significant growth in agriculture and commerce, including the rise of the slave trade. Having the greatest degree of self-rule, Rhode Island had the most to lose from British efforts after 1763 to increase the mother country's supervision and control over the colonies. On 4 May 1776, Rhode Island became the first colony formally to renounce all allegiance to King George III. Favoring the weak central government established by the Articles of Confederation, the state quickly ratified them in 1778, but subsequently resisted the centralizing tendencies of the federal constitution. Rhode Island withheld ratification until 29 May 1790, making it the last of the original 13 states to join the Union.

The principal trends in 19th-century Rhode Island were industrialization, immigration, and urbanization. The state's royal charter (then still in effect) contained no procedure for its amendment, gave disproportionate influence to the declining rural towns, and conferred almost unlimited power on the legislature. In addition, suffrage was restricted by the general assembly to owners of real estate and their eldest sons. Because earlier, moderate efforts at change had been virtually ignored by the assembly, political reformers decided to bypass the legislature and convene a People's Convention. Thomas Wilson Dorr, who led this movement, became the principal draftsman of a progressive "People's Constitution," ratified in a popular referendum in December 1841. A coalition of Whigs and rural Democrats used force to suppress the movement now known as Dorr's Rebellion, but they bowed to popular pressure and made limited changes via a new constitution, effective May 1843.

The latter half of the 19th century was marked by continued industrialization and urbanization. Immigration increased and became more diverse. Politically the state was dominated by the Republican Party until the 1930s. The Democrats, having seized the opportunity during the New Deal, consolidated their power during the 1940s, and from that time onward have captured most state and congressional elections. Present-day Rhode Island, though predominantly Catholic and Democratic, retains an ethnic and cultural diversity surprising in view of its size but consistent with its pluralist traditions. Rhode Island's residents have been moving from the cities to the suburbs, and in 1980 the state lost its ranking as the most urban state in the country to New Jersey. In the mid-1990s Rhode Island was still the nation's 2nd most densely populated state, with more than three-quarters of its residents living within 15 mi (25 km) of the capital city of Providence.

From the 1950s to the 1980s, 30% of the workforce were in manufacturing jobs; in the 1990s many of these were still low-paid jobs in the jewelry and textile industries. Rhode Island experienced a real estate boom in the 1980s thanks to federal savings and loan deregulation and the state's proximity to the thriving Boston metropolitan area. However, real estate values declined at the end of the decade, and Rhode Island entered the 1990s with a banking crisis that forced its government to spend taxpayer dollars propping up uninsured financial institutions.

The state was also hard hit by the recession of the early 1990s. By 1994 a slow recovery was under way, with unemployment fluctuating between 6% and 8%. Though the state's economy grew less quickly than that of its New England neighbors, it experienced a full recovery by the end of the 1990s and successfully made the transition from a manufacturing-based system to one reliant on the service sector. Further, it had done so without widening the gap between rich and poor, an achievement that had eluded other states. As of 1999, Rhode Island's unemployment was 4.1%, in line with the national average. Between January 1999 and January 2000 alone, the state added 10,300 jobs. By 2001, however, the nation was in the grip of recession, and Rhode Island's unemployment rate by July 2003 was 5.6%, albeit below the national average of 6.2%. The state faced a $200 million budget deficit that year.

Rhode Island was the setting for a landmark lawsuit settlement in 1999. Three years earlier, the worst oil spill in the state's history contaminated waters and destroyed lobsters in Block Island Sound. Under the federal Oil Spill Act of 1990, those responsible for the spill settled separately with local lobstermen and the state, which was to direct $18 million in ongoing clean-up and recovery efforts. The cases were expected to set the standard for future negotiations in the wake of oil spills.

Republican Governor Donald Carciere, elected in 2002, allowed a minimum wage increase of 60 cents to become law without his signature in 2003. Rhode Island's minimum wage law effective January 2004 was to be $6.75 per hour. In 2003, Carciere pledged to revamp state government, create jobs, and balance the budget without raising taxes.

12 STATE GOVERNMENT

Rhode Island has had two constitutions: the first based on the colonial charter (1842) and a revision (1986). In 1986, 8 amendments and a revision of the constitution were approved; subsequently, the constitution has been known as the 1986 Constitution. From 1986 through January 2003 there have been 7 amendments; total amendments since 1842 number 59.

Legislative authority is vested in the general assembly, a bicameral body composed of 50 senators and 100 representatives. All legislators are elected for two-year terms from districts that are apportioned equally according to population after every federal decennial census. Annual sessions begin in January and are limited to 60 legislative days. The legislature may not call for a special session. Legislators must be qualified voters. Among the more important checks enjoyed by the assembly is the power to override the governor's veto by a three-fifths vote of its members and the power to establish all courts below the supreme court. The legislative salary in 2002 was $11,235.

State elected officials are the governor and lieutenant governor (elected separately), attorney general, secretary of state, and general treasurer. All are elected, in the odd-numbered year following presidential elections, for four-year terms. The governor is limited to serving two consecutive terms. The governor and lieutenant governor must be qualified voters in Rhode Island; no minimum age is specified for the offices. In 2002 the governor's salary was $95,000, unchanged from 1999.

A bill passed by the legislature becomes law if signed by the governor, if left unsigned by the governor for six days while the legislature is in session (10 days if the legislature adjourns), or if passed over the governor's veto by three-fifths of the members present in each house. Legislation becomes effective upon enactment. Constitutional amendments are made by majority vote of the whole membership of each house of the legislature, and by a simple majority at the next general election.

Voters must be US citizens, 18 years old or over, and must have been residents of the state at least 30 days prior to an election.

Restrictions apply to convicted felons and those declared mentally incompetent by the court.

[13]POLITICAL PARTIES

For nearly five decades, Rhode Island has been one of the nation's most solidly Democratic states. It has voted for the Republican presidential candidate only four times since 1928, elected only one Republican (former Governor John H. Chafee) to the US Senate since 1934, and sent no Republicans to the US House from 1940 until 1980, when one Republican and one Democrat were elected. (They were reelected in 1982 and 1984.) Also in 1980, Rhode Island was one of only six states to favor Jimmy Carter. However, in 1984, Republican Edward DiPrete was elected governor, and Ronald Reagan narrowly carried the state in the presidential election. In the 2000 presidential election, Democrat Al Gore won 61% of the vote to Republican George W. Bush's 32%; independent candidate Ralph Nader took 6% of the popular vote.

In 1994, Republican John H. Chafee won a fourth term in the US Senate. Republican Lincoln D. Chafee was named Senator in November 1999 upon the death of his father; he was elected to his first full term in 2000. In 1996, Democrat Jack Reed won the Senate seat vacated by Claiborne Pell after 36 years in office; Reed was reelected in 2002. Both US representatives were Democrats in 2003. Among state officeholders, in mid-2003 there were 32 Democrats and six Republicans in the state senate, and 63 Democrats, 11 Republicans and one Independent in the state house. The governor's office is held by Republican Donald L. Carcieri, elected in 2002.

Rhode Island Presidential Vote, 1948–2000

YEAR	ELECTORAL VOTE	RHODE ISLAND WINNER	DEMOCRAT	REPUBLICAN
1948	4	*Truman (D)	188,736	135,787
1952	4	*Eisenhower (R)	203,293	210,935
1956	4	*Eisenhower (R)	161,790	225,819
1960	4	*Kennedy (D)	258,032	147,502
1964	4	*Johnson (D)	315,463	74,615
1968	4	Humphrey (D)	246,518	122,359
1972	4	*Nixon (R)	194,645	220,383
1976	4	*Carter (D)	227,636	181,249
1980	4	Carter (D)	198,342	154,793
1984	4	*Reagan (R)	197,106	212,080
1988	4	Dukakis (D)	225,123	177,761
1992**	4	*Clinton (D)	213,299	131,601
1996**	4	*Clinton (D)	233,050	104,683
2000	4	Gore (D)	249,508	130,555

*Won US presidential election.
** Independent candidate Ross Perot received 105,045 votes in 1992 and 43,723 votes in 1996.

[14]LOCAL GOVERNMENT

As of 2002, Rhode Island was subdivided into eight municipalities and 31 townships, the main units of local government. As of 2003, there were four public school districts and 75 special districts.

Many smaller communities retain the New England town meeting form of government, under which the town's eligible voters assemble to enact the local budget, set the tax levy, and approve other local measures. Larger cities and towns are governed by a mayor and/or city manager and a council.

[15]STATE SERVICES

To address the continuing threat of terrorism and to work with the federal Department of Homeland Security (created in 2002 following the terrorist attacks of 11 September 2001), homeland security in Rhode Island in 2003 operated under the authority of the governor; the adjutant general was designated as the state homeland security advisor.

The Department of Education, with the Board of Regents for Elementary and Secondary Education and the Board of Governors for Higher Education oversee all state educational services. Railroads, motor vehicle administration, and highway and bridge management come under the jurisdiction of the Department of Transportation. Health and welfare services are provided through the Department of Corrections; Department of the Attorney General; Department of Children, Youth, and Families; Department of Elderly Affairs; Department of Health; Department of Mental Health, Retardation, and Hospitals; and the Department of Human Services.

[16]JUDICIAL SYSTEM

The five-member supreme court is the state's highest appellate tribunal; it may also issue, upon request, advisory opinions on the constitutionality of a questioned act to the governor or either house of the legislature. Supreme court justices are chosen by the legislature and, like other state judges, hold office for life ("during good behavior"), but in actuality they can be removed by a mere resolution of the general assembly. In 1935, all five justices were ousted in this manner when a Democratic legislature replaced a court previously appointed by Republicans. In 1994, Chief Justice Thomas Fay resigned under impeachment pressure.

The general trial court is the superior court, with 1,012 justices in 1999. The state's trial court hears all jury trials in criminal cases and in civil matters involving more than $5,000, but can also hear non-jury cases. Superior court and district court judges are appointed by the governor with the consent of the senate.

District courts do not hold jury trials. Civil matters that involve $5,000 or less, small claims procedures, and non-jury criminal cases, including felony arraignments and misdemeanors, are handled at the district level. All cities and towns appoint judges to operate probate courts for wills and estates. Providence and a few other communities each have a municipal or police court.

According to the FBI Crime Index for 2001, the total crime rate stood at 3,684.9 per 100,000 persons, including a total of 3,278 violent crimes and 35,742 crimes against property in that year. There were 3,147 prisoners in state and federal prisons in June 2001, a decrease of 1.2% from the previous year. The state's incarceration rate stood at 179 per 100,000 inhabitants. Rhode Island does not have a death penalty.

[17]ARMED FORCES

In 2002, there were 2,974 active duty military personnel and 4,346 civilian personnel stationed in Rhode Island, most of whom were at the US Naval Education and Training Center and Naval War College in Newport. Rhode Island firms received more than $283 million in defense contracts during 2002.

According to the 2000 Census, there were 102,494 US veterans living in the state, of whom 25,187 saw military service during World War II; 13,548 in the Korean conflict; 27,967 during the Vietnam era; and 8,001 during 1990–2000 (including the Persian Gulf War). Veterans' benefits totaled approximately $226 million in 2002.

In 2000, the Rhode Island State Police employed 221 full-time sworn officers.

[18]MIGRATION

During the 19th and early 20th centuries, the major immigrant groups who came to work in the state's growing industries were Irish, Italian, and French-Canadian. Significant numbers of British, Portuguese, Swedish, Polish, and German immigrants also moved to Rhode Island. Between 1940 and 1970, however, 2,000 more people left the state than moved to it, and between

1970 and 1983 there was a net loss of about 42,000. From 1985 to 1990, there was a net gain from migration of nearly 34,000. Between 1990 and 1998, Rhode Island had a net loss of 64,000 in domestic migration and a net gain of 16,000 in international migration. In 1998, 1,976 foreign immigrants arrived in the state. Rhode Island's overall population decreased 1.5% between 1990 and 1998.

During the 1980s, the urban proportion of the population remained virtually unchanged, dropping from 87% to 86%. By 1996, the metropolitan population had reached 93.8%. In the period 1995–2000, 96,980 people moved into the state and 93,744 moved out, for a net gain of 3,236, many of whom were from Massachusetts.

19INTERGOVERNMENTAL COOPERATION

Rhode Island participates in many interstate regional bodies, including the Atlantic States Marine Fisheries Commission, Interstate Compact for Juveniles, New England Interstate Water Pollution Control Commission, and Northeastern Forest Fire Protection Commission. New England regional agreements include those on tuberculosis control, radiological health protection, higher education, police, and dairy products. Federal grants to Rhode Island state and local governments exceeded $1.6 billion in 2001.

20ECONOMY

Rhode Island's economy was historically based overwhelmingly on industry; agriculture, mining, forestry, and fishing making only small contributions. The state's leading manufactured products were jewelry, silverware, machinery, primary metals, textiles, and rubber products. In the late 1990s, manufacturing declined steadily as a contributor to state economic output, falling from 14.7% in 1997 to 11.1% in 2001. The recession of 2001only accelerated the contraction in the Rhode Island's manufacturing output to 3.3% from its previous rates of about 2% a year. The strongest growth sectors in terms of output coming into the 21st century (1997 to 2001) were financial services (up 44.3%); trade (up 28.5%); general services (up 25.6%); and government (up 20.6%). Unemployment rates in Rhode Island exceeded those of the US throughout the 1970s, and the state's economic growth lagged behind that of the nation as a whole. Unemployment fell dramatically in 1983 and 1984, rose again to 8.7% in 1992, and but had fallen to around 5% by 1996. Manufacturing employment declined 23% between 1983 and 1992 while service jobs increased 36%. In all, only about 1,000 jobs were lost between 1988 and 1998, mostly in the manufacturing sector, while service-related jobs rose, accounting for about half of all personal income in 1998. The impact of the 2001 national recession and slowdown on Rhode Island's employment and income was the mildest among the New England states. By mid-2002, job growth had surpassed the peak reached in 2000.

In 2001, Rhode Island's gross state product gross state product was $36.9 billion, 8th smallest among the states, to which financial services contributed $10.9 billion; general services, $7.9 billion; trade, $5.1 billion; government, $4.4 billion; manufacturing, $4.1 billion; transportation and public utilities, $2.3 billion, and construction, $1.9 billion. The public sector in 2001 constituted 11.8% of gross state product, close to the 12% average for the states.

21INCOME

According to the Bureau of Economic Analysis, in 2001, Rhode Island had a per capita personal income (PCPI) of $30,256 which ranked 17th in the United States (including the District of Columbia) and was 99% of the national average, $30,413. The 2001 PCPI reflected an increase of 3.4% from 2000 compared to the national change of 2.2%. In 2001, Rhode Island had a total personal income (TPI) of $32,060,552,000 which ranked 43rd in the United States and accounted for 0.4% of the national total. The 2001 TPI reflected an increase of 4.3% from 2000 compared to the national change of 3.3%.

Earnings of persons employed in Rhode Island increased from $19,899,129,000 in 2000 to $20,566,915,000 in 2001, an increase of 3.4%. The largest industries in 2001 were services, 32.2% of earnings; state and local government, 12.7%; and durable goods manufacturing, 10.0%. Of the industries that accounted for at least 5% of earnings in 2001, the slowest growing from 2000 to 2001 was durable goods manufacturing, which decreased 2.9%; the fastest was finance, insurance, and real estate (8.7% of earnings in 2001), which increased 9.0%.

According to data released by the US Census Bureau, in 2000, the median household income was $42,973 compared to the national average of $42,148. In 2001, the median income for a family of four was $70,446 compared to the national average of $63,278. For the period 1999 to 2001, the average poverty rate was 10.0% which placed it 20th among the 50 states and the District of Columbia ranked lowest to highest.

22LABOR

According to Bureau of Labor Statistics (BLS) provisional estimates, in July 2003 the seasonally adjusted civilian labor force in Rhode Island numbered 573,600, with approximately 32,200 workers unemployed, yielding an unemployment rate of 5.6%, compared to the national average of 6.2% for the same period. Since the beginning of the BLS data series in 1978, the highest unemployment rate recorded was 10.9% in October 1982. The historical low was 2.7% in May 1988. In 2001, an estimated 4.1% of the labor force was employed in construction; 15.5% in manufacturing; 4.9% in transportation, communications, and public utilities; 20.1% in trade; 6.3% in finance, insurance, and real estate; 29.8% in services; 12.8% in government; and 1.0% in agriculture.

The US Department of Labor reported that in 2002, 81,000 of Rhode Island's 471,000 employed wage and salary workers were members of unions. This represented 17.2% of those so employed, down from 17.8% in 2001 and from 19% in 1998. The national average is 13.2%. In all, 84,000 workers (17.9%) were represented by unions. In addition to union members, this category includes workers who report no union affiliation but whose jobs are covered by a union contract.

23AGRICULTURE

The state's total receipts from farm marketings were $47 million in 2001, 50th in the US. Rhode Island had only about 700 farms in 1998 with an average size of just 86 acres (35 hectares), with the smallest area devoted to crops (21,000 acres, or 8,500 hectares) of any state. Nursery and greenhouse products were the main agricultural commodity. Total crop marketings amounted to $40 million in 2001.

24ANIMAL HUSBANDRY

In 2003, Rhode Island had around 5,500 cattle and calves, valued at $4.95 million. During 2002, there were some 2,900 hogs and pigs, valued at $215,000. In 2001, the state produced 23.2 million lb (10.5 million kg) of milk, from 1,400 milk cows.

25FISHING

The commercial catch in 1998 was 131.4 million lb, valued at $71.1 million. Point Judith is the main fishing port, with landings of 75.1 million lb in 1998, ranking 18th in the US for size of catch that year. The commercial fishing fleet consisted of 2,777 boats and vessels in 1997, supplying the state's 77 processing and wholesale plants. The most valuable edible fish and shellfish caught are whiting, fluke and yellowtail flounders, cod, scup lobster, squid, and clams. Landings of Atlantic mackerel in 1998 totaled 5.8 million lb, 88% of the national total.

In 1998, Rhode Island issued 34,487 sport fishing licenses. Three hatcheries distributed nearly 326,000 lb of trout within the state that year.

26FORESTRY

In 2002, forests covered 385,000 acres (159,000 hectares), about 60% of the state's land area. Some 340,000 acres (138,000 hectares) were usable as commercial timberland.

27MINING

The value of nonfuel mineral production in Rhode Island in 2001 was estimated to be $28.3 million, an 8.1% decrease from 2000. According to preliminary figures, crushed stone (3.3 million metric tons, worth $19.3 million) and construction sand and gravel (1.12 million metric tons, worth $9 million) accounted for, respectively, about 68% and 31% of the state's production. Small amounts of industrial sand and gemstones were also mined.

28ENERGY AND POWER

Rhode Island is part of the New England regional power grid and imports most of its electric power. The state's installed capacity (utility and nonutility) was 981,000 kW in 1999, and power production totaled 6.4 billion kWh; both figures were the lowest in the US. Electric utility sales in Rhode Island in 1998 were 6.6 billion kWh, of which 2.4 billion kWh went for residential users, 2.6 billion kWh for commercial purchasers, and nearly all the rest for industry. In 2000 Rhode Island's total per capita energy consumption was 239 million Btu (60.2 million kcal), ranking it 49th among the 50 states.

29INDUSTRY

The Industrial Revolution began early in Rhode Island. The first spinning jenny in the US was built at Providence in 1787; three years later, in Pawtucket, Samuel Slater opened a cotton mill, one of the first modern factories in America. By the end of the 18th century, textile, jewelry, and metal products were being manufactured in the state.

Over 1,000 manufacturers in the state produce finished jewelry and jewelry parts. Prominent manufacturing firms in the state include AT Cross and Shaeffer (pens), Fort (novelty gift and collector items), and Swarovski (rhinestones and crystal boutique items). Hasbro, one of the world's largest toy manufacturers, is headquartered in Pawtucket.

Electronic and related products manufactured in the state include online lottery machines, circuit boards, and meteorological, navigational, and medical equipment. Chemicals and allied products made in the state include pigments and dyes, drugs and biomedical products, and liquid and aerosol consumer products. The total value of shipments of manufactured products in 1997 was $11 billion.

Earnings of persons employed in Rhode Island increased from $16.9 billion in 1997 to $17.9 billion in 1998, an increase of 5.9%. The largest industries in 1998 were services, 32.1% of earnings; durable goods manufacturing, 12.1%; and state and local government, 11.6%. Of the industries that accounted for at least 5% of earnings in 1998, the slowest growing from 1997 to 1998 was nondurable goods manufacturing (7.0% of earnings in 1998), which increased 3.3%; the fastest was finance, insurance, and real estate (7.4% of earnings in 1998), which increased 11.2%.

30COMMERCE

Approximately 1,802 wholesalers in 1997 had sales of $8 billion. In that year, retail establishments had sales of $8.2 billion. Of

total establishments, 12% were food stores, 12% were automotive dealers, and 34% were eating and drinking places. Foreign exports of manufactured goods were $1.1 billion in 1998.

31CONSUMER PROTECTION

The Consumer Protection Unit of the Department of the Attorney General and the Consumer's Council bear primary responsibility for enforcing consumer laws and regulations. In 2003, legislation to create an Office of Ratepayer Advocate was being considered. The office would represent consumers before the Public Utilities Commission on issues regarding the rates and services of utilities.

32BANKING

In 2002, Rhode Island had 14 insured banks with combined assets of $196.7 billion. Three of these banks were state-chartered.

As of 2002, the 30-year mortgage rate was below 7%, and refinancing activity was strong among consumers securing long-term fixed-rate loans at low rates. In Rhode Island, median long-term assets to earning assets rose to a 10-year high. Close to 50% of the state's banks have long-term asset concentrations of greater than 40%. Savings banks represent 50% of insured banks in Rhode Island and residential real estate loans made up 56% of the average loan portfolio in 2002.

Residential and commercial real estate (CRE) loan delinquencies increased in late 2002. One-fourth of Rhode Island's insured banks have high-risk (commercial, construction, commercial real estate, and multifamily loans) loan concentrations of at least 300% of capital.

33INSURANCE

In 2001, 518,000 ordinary life insurance policies worth $41.0 billion were in force in Rhode Island; total value for all categories of life insurance (ordinary, group, industrial, and credit) was $73.3 billion. Death benefits paid that year totaled $174.6 million. As of 2000, there were 20 property and casualty and five life and health insurance companies incorporated or organized in the state. In 2001, property and casualty insurers wrote over $1.4 billion in premiums. That year, there were 11,261 flood insurance policies in force in the state, with a total value of $1.6 million.

34SECURITIES

Rhode Island has no securities exchanges. There are 177 broker-dealers, involving over 1,000 employees, and 36 investment advisory companies. Rhode Island is home to 14 NASDAQ companies, two NASDAQ market makers, and three NYSE-listed companies: Fleet Boston Financial Corp., Nortek, and Providence Energy.

35PUBLIC FINANCE

The annual budget is prepared by the State Budget Office in conjunction with the governor, and submitted to the legislature for approval. The fiscal year runs from 1 July to 30 June.

The 2000/01 Rhode Island budget increased by 1.9% from 2000, to $4.7 billion. Resources totaled $2.3 billion; a budgetary shortfall was forecast for the year, increasing the already high recurring state debt. A Capital Improvement Plan for 2000/01–2005 focuses on reducing the debt from $1.8 billion to $1.65 billion. Nevertheless, increases in funding for education, public safety, and the environment were scheduled for 2001. In 2000/01, general fund revenues reached $2.533 billion, sufficient to cover expenditures of $2.483 billion. The starting balance for 2001/02, at $92 million in 2000/01, had increased to $131 million. General fund revenues in 2002/03, however, were almost $50 million less than expenditures. The government made cuts in the budget after it was enacted totaling $1.4 million to cover the gap and also secured its tobacco settlement proceeds to obtain immediate cash. In 2002/03, Rhode Island's budget deficit was estimated at $300 million or about 11.2% for the state budget, but projections for 2003/04 were for a deficit to fall to a more manageable 3.8% to 4.9% of the state budget.

The following table from the US Census Bureau contains information on revenues, expenditures, indebtedness, and cash/securities for 2001.

	($000)	PERCENT	PER CAPITA
Population (thousands, 2001)	1,060	(X)	(X)
Total Revenue	5,483,128	100.00	5,172.76
General revenue	4,764,967	86.90	4,495.25
Utility revenue	12,100	0.22	11.42
Liquor store revenue	–	–	–
Insurance trust revenue	706,061	12.88	666.10
Exhibit: Salaries and wages	858,053	16.04	809.48
Total expenditure	5,350,551	100.00	5,047.69
General expenditure	4,652,841	86.96	4,389.47
Education	1,346,644	25.17	1,270.42
Public welfare	1,393,687	26.05	1,314.80
Hospitals	135,791	2.54	128.10
Health	137,275	2.57	129.50
Highways	249,291	4.66	235.18
Police protection	46,948	0.88	44.29
Correction	151,172	2.83	142.62
Natural resources	42,338	0.79	39.94
Parks and recreation	39,170	0.73	36.95
Government administration	274,822	5.14	259.27
Interest on general debt	355,701	6.65	335.57
Other and unallocable	480,002	8.97	452.83
Utility expenditure	77,421	1.45	73.04
Liquor store expenditure	–	–	–
Insurance trust expenditure	620,289	11.59	585.18
Debt at end of fiscal year	5,832,702	100.00	5,502.55
Cash and security holdings	12,021,798	100.00	11,341.32

[36]TAXATION

In 2003, Rhode Island's state income tax was set equal to 25% (down from 26% in 2001) of the taxpayer's federal income tax liability as it stood prior to the enactment of the federal Economic Growth and Tax Relief Reconciliation Act (EGTRRA) of 2001. The basic corporate tax rate is 9%. The state sales and use tax is 7% with local add-ons prohibited. The state imposes a full array of excise taxes covering motor fuels, tobacco products, insurance premiums, public utilities, alcoholic beverages, pari-mutuels and other specified items. Before New York and Wisconsin raised their gasoline tax in 2002, Rhode Island had the highest in the country, at 28 cents a gallon. In 2002, Rhode Island raised its cigarette tax from 71 cents a pack to $1.32. Rhode Island's estate tax is independent of the federal estate tax exemption for state death taxes, and thus is not scheduled to expire with this exemption in 2007. Death and gift taxes accounted for 0.9% of state collections in 2002. Other state taxes include various license fees, stamp taxes, and state property taxes. Most property taxes, which are among the highest in the country, are collected at the local level. About 35% of Rhode Island's total state and local taxes are collected by local governments.

The state collected $$2,128 billion in taxes in 2002 (down $119 million from 2001), of which 38.7% came from individual income taxes, 34.4% came from the general sales tax, 20% from selective sales taxes, 4.4% from license fees, and 1.3% from corporate income taxes. In 2003, Rhode Island ranked 4th among the states in terms of combined state and local tax burden, which amounted to about 11% of income.

The following table from the US Census Bureau provides a summary of taxes collected by the state in 2002.

	($000)	PER CAPITA
Total Taxes	2,127,609	1,988.93
Property taxes	1,139	1.06
Sales and gross receipts	1,160,626	1,084.98
General sales and gross receipts	731,597	683.91
Selective sales taxes	429,029	401.06
Alcoholic beverage	10,271	9.6
Amusements	(X)	(X)
Insurance Premiums	32,062	29.97
Motor fuels	130,134	121.65
Pari-mutuels	5,435	5.08
Public utilities	79,844	74.64
Tobacco products	83,099	77.68
Other selective sales	88,184	82.44
Licenses	92,463	86.44
Alcoholic beverages	78	0.07
Amusements	315	0.29
Corporation	11,884	11.11
Hunting and fishing	1,364	1.28
Motor vehicle	53,197	49.73
Motor vehicle operators	580	0.54
Public utility	(X)	(X)
Occupation and business, NEC	24,288	22.7
Other	757	0.71
Other taxes	873,381	816.45
Individual income	823,521	769.84
Corporation net income	28,273	26.43
Death and gift	18,848	17.62
Documentary and stock transfer	2,651	2.48
Severance	(X)	(X)
Other	88	0.08

[37]ECONOMIC POLICY

The Rhode Island Economic Development Corporation (RIEDC) exists to preserve and expand Rhode Island businesses, and to attract new businesses to the state. Some of the services available to businesses through RIEDC are: job training assistance; financial assistance; government contracting assistance; site selection; and exporting assistance. In 2003, the RIEDC emphasized job training grant programs, including a Job Creation Grant Fund, an Excellence Through Training Grant Program, an Employee Investment Grant Program, and an Export Management Training Grant Program.

[38]HEALTH

As of 2000, Rhode Island's infant mortality rate was 6.3 per 1,000 live births. Despite the state's heavy Catholic population, 5,004 abortions were performed in 1999, a ratio of 23 per 1,000 women, the nation's 7th-highest rate. Death rates from heart disease (312.7 per 100,000 population) and cancer (244.3)—the leading causes of death in 2000—were well above the national averages. In the same year, the overall death rate of 1006.6 per 100,000 ranked well above the national rate of 873.1.

The rate of death from HIV-related infections stood at 3.8 per 100,000 population, below the US average of 5.3 in 2000. A total of 2,153 AIDS cases had been reported in Rhode Island through 2001. Among Rhode Island adults ages 18 and older, 23.5% were smokers. The death rate due to lung disease stood at 71.5 per 100,000 population in 2000.

Rhode Island's 11 community hospitals had 120,901 admissions and 2,449 beds in 2001. There were 3,066 full-time registered nurses and 294 full-time licensed practical nurses in 2001 and 357 physicians per 100,000 population in 2000. The average expense of a community hospital for care was $1,503.70 per inpatient day in 2001.

Federal government grants to cover the Medicare and Medicaid services in 2001 totaled $711 million; 171,822 enrollees received Medicare benefits that year. Only 7.7% of Rhode Island residents were uninsured in 2002.

39 SOCIAL WELFARE

In 2001, the average weekly unemployment benefit was $297.33. Average monthly participation in the food stamp program in FY2002 comprised 71,933 persons (33,370 households). The average monthly benefit was $74.44, and the sum total of benefits paid in FY2002 was $64,256,422.

With the enactment of the Personal Responsibility and Work Opportunity Reconciliation Act of 1996, the US government has changed the form and regulations for many of its social welfare programs. Most significantly, it replaces Aid to Families with Dependent Children (AFDC), an open-ended entitlement program, with Temporary Assistance for Needy Families (TANF), a limited system of assistance funded largely through federal block grants. The reform act also impacts the food stamp program, the Supplemental Security Income program, and the child nutrition program. The law took effect on 1 July 1997 and provided $16.38 billion in block grants for fiscal years 1997–2002. The grants are to be divided among the states based on an equation involving the numbers of former AFDC recipients in each state.

Reauthorization of the 1996 social welfare legislation, scheduled for 2002, was delayed, and the original law had been extended three times as of July 2003, with the most recent extension running through September 2003. Rhode Island's TANF program is called the Family Independence Program (FIP). In June 2000 the state had 44,826 welfare recipients. State expenditures on the TANF program in FY2002 totaled $63,230,033.

In December 2001, Social Security benefits were paid to 191,520 Rhode Island residents. This number included 129,650 retired workers, 16,030 widows and widowers, 23,990 disabled workers, 7,250 spouses, and 14,600 children. Social Security beneficiaries represented 18.2% of the total state population and 93.6% of the state's population age 65 and older. Retired workers (excluding persons with special benefits) received an average monthly payment of $874; widows and widowers, $857; disabled workers, $797; and spouses, $437. Payments for children of retired workers averaged $409 per month; children of deceased workers, $586; and children of disabled workers, $222.

Federal Supplemental Security Income payments in December 2001 went to 28,623 Rhode Island residents, averaging $402 a month.

40 HOUSING

In 2002, there were an estimated 443,761 housing units, 408,272 of which were occupied; 61.4% were owner-occupied. About 55% of all units were single-family, detached homes; 37.4% of all units were built in 1939 or earlier. In 2002, utility gas and fuel oil were the most common energy sources for heating. It was estimated that 8,859 units lacked telephone service, 1,225 lacked complete plumbing facilities, and 1,465 lacked complete kitchen facilities. The average household size was 2.52 people.

In 2002, 2,848 new privately owned housing units were authorized for construction. Much of the new residential construction has taken place in the suburbs south and west of Providence. The median home value was $165,458. The median monthly cost for mortgage owners was $1,305. Renters paid a median of $622. During 2002, Rhode Island received over $18.8 million in community planning and development aid from the US Department of Housing and Urban Development.

41 EDUCATION

In 2000, 78% of Rhode Islanders age 25 and older were high school graduates. Approximately 25.6% had obtained a bachelor's degree or higher.

The total enrollment for fall 1999 in Rhode Island's public schools stood at 156,454. Of these, 111,520 attended schools from kindergarten through grade eight, and 42,934 attended high school. Minority students made up approximately 26% of the total enrollment in public elementary and secondary schools. Total enrollment was estimated at 158,141 in fall 2000 and is expected to drop to 149,000 by fall 2005. Expenditures for public education in 2000/01 were estimated at $1,504,648. Enrollment in nonpublic schools in fall 2001 was 24,738.

As of fall 2000, there were 84,009 students enrolled in college or graduate school. In the same year Rhode Island had 13 degree-granting institutions. Leading institutions include Brown University (1764) in Providence; the University of Rhode Island (1892) in Kingston; and Providence College (1917). The Rhode Island School of Design (1877) is located in Providence. In 1997, minority students comprised 13.6% of total postsecondary enrollment.

42 ARTS

Newport and Providence have notable art galleries and museums, including the museum at the Rhode Island School of Design in Providence. Theatrical groups include the Trinity Repertory Company in Providence. The Rhode Island Philharmonic performs throughout the state. Newport is the site of the internationally famous Newport Jazz Festival and the Newport Music Festival. The Festival Ballet Providence and the State Ballet of Rhode Island are prominent dance groups. The Providence Performing Arts Center, restored to its original 1920s splendor in the late 1990s (and now listed on the National Register of Historic Places), hosts touring Broadway shows as well as concerts by a variety of performers.

The WaterFire public art installation on the riverfront in downtown Providence has played a key role in the revitalization of the city. The lighting of bonfires in 97 braziers placed in three rivers that flow through Providence has drawn thousands to the downtown area to enjoy music and other entertainment.

The success of the installation, begun as a one-time commemorative event in 1994, inspired a grassroots movement to make WaterFire an ongoing event, with regularly scheduled lightings sponsored by local business and civic groups throughout the summer.

In 2003, the Rhode Island State Council on the Arts and other Rhode Island arts organizations received grants totaling $885,400 from the National Endowment for the Arts (NEA). The Rhode Island Council for the Humanities (est. 1973) has awarded over $2.5 million to community and academic organizations since its inception. In 2000, the National Endowment for the Humanities contributed $1,096,719 for nine state programs. The state, the New England Foundation for the Arts, and various private sources also provide funding for arts activities. Rhode Island has about 1,000 arts associations and six local arts councils.

43 LIBRARIES AND MUSEUMS

In 2000, Rhode Island had one consolidated library system. In 2000, public libraries had a book stock of 4,100,000, and a combined circulation of 6,521,000. The Providence Public Library maintains several special historical collections. The Brown University Libraries, containing more than 2.6 million books and periodicals, include the Annmary Brown Memorial Library, with its collection of rare manuscripts, and the John Carter Brown Library, with an excellent collection of early Americana.

Among the state's more than 53 museums and historic sites are the Haffenreffer Museum of Anthropology in Bristol, the Museum of Art of the Rhode Island School of Design in Providence, the Roger Williams Park Museum, also in Providence, the Nathanael Greene Homestead in Coventry, and the Slater Mill Historic Site in Pawtucket. Providence has the Roger Williams Park Zoo.

44COMMUNICATIONS

The first automated post office in the US postal system was opened in Providence in 1960. As of 2001, 95.7% of the state's occupied housing units had telephones. In 2003, the state had 6 major AM and 9 major FM radio stations. Rhode Island had seven television stations, including one public broadcasting affiliate operated by the state's Public Telecommunications Authority. The Providence-New Bedford area had 565,230 television-viewing homes, 79% with cable. A total of 23,508 Internet domain names were registered in Rhode Island by the year 2000.

45PRESS

The *Rhode Island Gazette*, the state's first newspaper, appeared in 1732. In 1850, Paulina Wright Davis established *Una*, one of the first women's rights newspapers in the country.

In 2002, Rhode Island had six daily newspapers with three Sunday editions. The following table shows the approximate circulation for the state's leading dailies in 2002:

AREA	NAME	DAILY	SUNDAY
Newport	*Daily News* (e)	12,853	12,853 (Sat.)
Pawtucket	*Times* (m)	13,605	13,605 (Sat.)
Providence	*Journal* (m,S)	165,880	233,751
Woonsocket	*The Call* (m,S)	14,504	19,729

Regional interest periodicals include *Providence Monthly* and *Rhode Island Monthly*.

46ORGANIZATIONS

In 2003, there were about 517 regional, national, and international organizations within the state. Among the organizations with headquarters in Rhode Island are the US Surfing Federation, Barrington; the Rooster Class Yacht Racing Association, Wakefield; the Foundation for Gifted and Creative Children and the Foster Parents Plan USA, both in Warwick; the American Mathematical Society and the Manufacturing Jewelers and Silversmiths of America, both in Providence; and the US International Sailing Association and US Yacht Racing Union, both in Newport. The International Tennis Hall of Fame is in Newport. State art organizations include the Alliance of Artists' Communities, the Art League of Rhode Island, and the Summer Arts and Festival Organization .

47TOURISM, TRAVEL, AND RECREATION

Tourism is the 2nd-largest and fastest-growing industry in Rhode Island. In 2000, the state hosted 15.7 million visitors, generating total revenues of about $3.26 billion (a figure that represents an increase of 16.4% from 1999. The industry supports over 38,000 jobs.

Historic sites—especially the mansions of Newport and Providence—and water sports (particularly the America's Cup yacht races) are the main tourist attractions. Block Island is a popular resort. The Providence Place Mall, a 13-acre mega shopping complex with 150 specialty shops, restaurants, and cinemas opened in 1999. An architectural marvel, the shopping complex spans a highway, a river, and a train track bed. Rhode Island's state parks and recreational areas total 8,063 acres (3,263 hectares).

48SPORTS

Rhode Island has no major league professional sports teams. Pawtucket has a AAA minor league baseball team and Providence has a minor league team in the American Hockey League. Providence College has competed successfully in collegiate basketball, winning National Invitational Tournament titles in 1961 and 1963, and advancing to the NCAA Final Four in 1973 and 1987.

Historically, Rhode Island has played an important part in the development of both yachting and tennis. The Newport Yacht Club hosted the America's Cup, international sailing's most prestigious event, from 1930 until 1983, when an Australian yacht won the race. It was the first time since 1851 that the cup had been won by a non-American. The cup was returned to America in 1987, but by a yacht from San Diego. Lawn tennis was first played in America at the Newport Casino, which was also the site of the United States Tennis championship from 1881 until 1915. Today it is home to the International Tennis Hall of Fame. The Museum of Yachting is located in Newport as well. Dog racing at Lincoln and jai alai at Newport are popular spectator sports with pari-mutuel betting.

Other annual sporting events include the Tennis Hall of Fame Championships in Newport in July, the Annual Tuna Tournament near Galilee and Narragansett in September, the Rhode Island Marathon in Newport in November, and summer college baseball league play on Martha's Vineyard.

49FAMOUS RHODE ISLANDERS

Important federal officeholders from Rhode Island have included US Senators Nelson W. Aldrich (1841–1915), Henry Bowen Anthony (1815–84), Theodore Francis Green (1867–1966), and John O. Pastore (b.1907), and US Representative John E. Fogarty (1913–67). J. Howard McGrath (1903–66) held the posts of US senator, solicitor general, and attorney general.

Foremost among Rhode Island's historical figures is Roger Williams (b.England, 1603?–83), apostle of religious liberty and founder of Providence. Other significant pioneers, also born in England, include Anne Hutchinson (1591–1643), religious leader and cofounder of Portsmouth, and William Coddington (1601–78), founder of Newport. Other 17th-century Rhode Islanders of note were Dr. John Clarke (b.England, 1609–76), who secured the colony's royal charter, and Indian leader King Philip, known also as Metacomet (1639?–76). Important participants in the War for Independence were Commodore Esek Hopkins (1718–1802) and General Nathanael Greene (1742–86). The 19th century brought to prominence Thomas Wilson Dorr (1805–54), courageous leader of Dorr's Rebellion; social reformer Elizabeth Buffum Chace (1806–99); and naval officers Oliver Hazard Perry (1785–1819), who secured important US victories in the War of 1812, and his brother, Matthew C. Perry (1794–1858), who led the expedition that opened Japan to foreign trade in 1854. Among the state's many prominent industrialists and inventors are Samuel Slater (b.England, 1768–1835), pioneer in textile manufacturing, and silversmith Jabez Gorham (1792–1869). Other significant public figures include Unitarian theologian William Ellery Channing (1780–1842); political boss Charles R. Brayton (1840–1910); Roman Catholic bishop and social reformer Matthew Harkins (b.Massachusetts, 1845–1921); and Dr. Charles V. Chapin (1856–1941), pioneer in public health.

Rhode Island's best-known creative writers are Gothic novelists H. P. Lovecraft (1890–1937) and Oliver La Farge (1901–63), and its most famous artist is portrait painter Gilbert Stuart (1755–1828). Popular performing artists include George M. Cohan (1878–1942), Nelson Eddy (1901–67), Bobby Hackett (1915–76), Van Johnson (b.1916), and Spalding Gray (b.1941).

Important sports personalities include Baseball Hall of Famers Hugh Duffy (1866–1954), Napoleon Lajoie (1875–1959), and Charles "Gabby" Hartnett (1900–1972).

50BIBLIOGRAPHY

Carroll, Charles. *Rhode Island: Three Centuries of Democracy.* 4 vols. New York: Lewis, 1932.

Conley, Patrick T. *Democracy in Decline: Rhode Island's Constitutional Development, 1775–1841*. Providence: Rhode Island Historical Society, 1977.

———. *Rhode Island Profile*. Providence: Rhode Island Publications Society, 1983.

Conley, Patrick T., and Matthew J. Smith. *Catholicism in Rhode Island*. Providence: Diocese of Providence, 1976.

Federal Writers' Project. *Rhode Island: A Guide to the Smallest State*. Reprint. New York: Somerset, n.d. (orig. 1937).

James, Sydney V. *Colonial Rhode Island: A History*. White Plains, N.Y.: Kraus International, 1975.

McLoughlin, William G. *Rhode Island: A Bicentennial History*. New York: Norton, 1978.

Méras, Phyllis, and Tom Gannon. *Rhode Island, An Explorer's Guide*. Woodstock, Vt.: Countryman Press; New York: Distributed by W.W. Norton, 2000.

Providence Journal-Bulletin. *1985. Journal-Bulletin Rhode Island Almanac*. 99th ed. Providence, n.d.

Rhode Island, Department of Economic Development, Economic Research Division. *Rhode Island: Basic Economic Statistics 1982–1983*. Providence, 1983.

Rhode Island, Secretary of State. *Rhode Island Manual 1983–84*. Edited by Edward F. Walsh. Providence, 1983.

Sherman, Steve. *Country Roads of Connecticut and Rhode Island: Day Trips and Weekend Excursions*. Lincolnwood, Ill.: Country Roads Press, 1999.

Steinberg, Sheila, and Cathleen McGuigan. *Rhode Island: An Historical Guide,* Providence: Rhode Island Bicentennial Commission, 1976.

SOUTH CAROLINA

State of South Carolina

ORIGIN OF STATE NAME: Named in honor of King Charles I of England. **NICKNAME:** The Palmetto State. **CAPITAL:** Columbia. **ENTERED UNION:** 23 May 1788 (8th). **SONG:** "Carolina" and "South Carolina on My Mind." **OPERA:** "Porgy and Bess." **MOTTO:** *Animis opibusque parati* (Prepared in mind and resources) and *Dum spiro spero* (While I breathe, I hope). **COAT OF ARMS:** A palmetto stands erect, with a ravaged oak (representing the British fleet) at its base; 12 spears, symbolizing the first 12 states, are bound crosswise to the palmetto's trunk by a hand bearing the inscription "Quis separabit" (Who shall separate?). Two shields bearing the inscriptions "March 26" (the date in 1776 when South Carolina established its first independent government) and "July 4," respectively, hang from the tree; under the oak are the words "Meliorem lapsa locavit" (Having fallen, it has set up a better one) and the year "1776." The words "South Carolina" and the motto *Animis opibusque parati* surround the whole. **FLAG:** Blue field with a white palmetto in the center and a white crescent at the union. **OFFICIAL SEAL:** The official seal consists of two ovals showing the original designs for the obverse and the reverse of South Carolina's great seal of 1777. LEFT (OBVERSE): same as the coat of arms. RIGHT (REVERSE): as the sun rises over the seashore, Hope, holding a laurel branch, walks over swords and daggers; the motto *Dum spiro spero* is above her, the word "Spes" (hope) below. **ANIMAL:** White-tailed deer. **BIRD:** Carolina wren. **WILD GAME BIRD:** Wild turkey. **FISH:** Striped bass. **FLOWER:** Yellow jessamine. **FRUIT:** Peach. **BEVERAGE:** Milk. **HOSPITALITY BEVERAGE:** Tea. **TREE:** Palmetto. **GEM:** Amethyst. **STONE:** Blue granite. **LEGAL HOLIDAYS:** New Year's Day, 1 January; Birthday of Martin Luther King, Jr., 3rd Monday in January; Lee's Birthday, 19 January; Washington's Birthday, 3rd Monday in February; Jefferson Davis's Birthday, 3 June; Independence Day, 4 July; Labor Day, 1st Monday in September; Election Day, 1st Tuesday after 1st Monday in November (even-numbered years); Veterans Day, 11 November; Thanksgiving Day, 4th Thursday in November; Christmas Eve, 24 December, when declared by the governor; Christmas Day, 25 December; day after Christmas. **TIME:** 7 AM EST = noon GMT.

¹LOCATION, SIZE, AND EXTENT

Situated in the southeastern US, South Carolina ranks 40th in size among the 50 states.

The state's total area is 31,113 sq mi (80,583 sq km), of which land takes up 30,203 sq mi (78,226 sq km) and inland water 910 sq mi (2,357 sq km). South Carolina extends 273 mi (439 km) E-W; its maximum N-S extension is 210 mi (338 km).

South Carolina is bounded on the N and NE by North Carolina; on the SE by the Atlantic Ocean; and on the SW and W by Georgia (with the line passing through the Savannah and Chattooga rivers).

Among the 13 major Sea Islands in the Atlantic off South Carolina are Bull, Sullivans, Kiawah, Edisto, Hunting, and Hilton Head, the largest island (42 sq mi—109 sq km) on the Atlantic seaboard between New Jersey and Florida. The total boundary length of South Carolina is 824 mi (1,326 km), including a general coastline of 187 mi (301 km); the tidal shoreline extends 2,876 mi (4,628 km). The state's geographic center is located in Richland County, 13 mi (21 km) SE of Columbia.

²TOPOGRAPHY

South Carolina is divided into two major regions by the fall line that runs through the center of the state from Augusta, Georgia, to Columbia and thence to Cheraw, near the North Carolina border. The area northwest of the line, known as the upcountry, lies within the Piedmont Plateau; the region to the southeast, called the low country, forms part of the Atlantic Coastal Plain. The rise of the land from ocean to the fall line is very gradual: Columbia, 120 mi (193 km) inland, is only 135 ft (41 m) above sea level. In the extreme northwest, the Blue Ridge Mountains

cover about 500 sq mi (1,300 sq km); the highest elevation, at 3,560 ft (1,086 m), is Sassafras Mountain.

Among the many artificial lakes, mostly associated with electric power plants, is Lake Marion, the state's largest, covering 173 sq mi (48 sq km). Three river systems—the Pee Dee, Santee, and Savannah—drain most of the state. No rivers are navigable above the fall line.

³CLIMATE

South Carolina has a humid, subtropical climate. Average temperatures range from 68°F (20°C) on the coast to 58°F (14°C) in the northwest, with colder temperatures in the mountains. Summers are hot: in the central part of the state, temperatures often exceed 90°F (32°C), with a record of 111°F (44°C) set at Camden on 28 June 1954. In the northwest, temperatures of 32°F (0°C) or less occur from 50 to 70 days a year; the record low for the state is –20°F (– 29°C), set at Caesars Head Mountain on 18 January 1977. The daily mean temperature at Columbia is 44°F (7°C) in January and 81°F (27°C) in July.

Rainfall is ample throughout the state, averaging 48.3 in (122.7 cm) annually at Columbia (1971–2000) and ranging from 38 in (97 cm) in the central region to 52 in (132 cm) in the upper piedmont. Snow and sleet (averaging 2 in/5 cm a year at Columbia) occur about three times annually, but more frequently and heavily in the mountains.

⁴FLORA AND FAUNA

Principal trees of South Carolina include palmetto (the state tree), balsam fir, beech, yellow birch, pitch pine, cypress, and several types of maple, ash, hickory, and oak; longleaf pine grows mainly south of the fall line. Rocky areas of the piedmont contain a wide mixture of moss and lichens. The coastal plain has a diversity of land formations—swamp, prairie, savannah, marsh, dunes—and, accordingly, a great number of different grasses, shrubs, and vines. Azaleas and camellias, not native to the state, have been planted profusely in private and pubic gardens. Twenty plant species were listed as threatened or endangered in 2003, including smooth coneflower, Schweinitz's sunflower, black spored quillwort, pondberry, and persistent trillium.

South Carolina mammals include white-tailed deer (the state animal), black bear, opossum, gray and red foxes, cottontail and marsh rabbits, mink, and woodchuck. Three varieties of raccoon are indigenous, one of them unique to Hilton Head Island. The state is also home to Bachman's shrew, originally identified in South Carolina by John Bachman, one of John J. Audubon's collaborators. Common birds include the mockingbird and Carolina wren (the state bird). Twenty-two animal species were listed as threatened or endangered in South Carolina in 2003, including the Indiana bat, Carolina heelsplitter, bald eagle, five species of sea turtle, wood stork, and shortnose sturgeon.

5ENVIRONMENTAL PROTECTION

The Department of Health and Environmental Control, established in 1973, is South Carolina's primary environmental protection agency. The agency's responsibilities were broadened in 1993 by government restructuring, which brought all natural resources permitting under the DHEC umbrella. The former Land Resources Commission and Water Resources Commission were dissolved by restructuring. The DHEC's areas of responsibility include all programs dealing with surface and groundwater protection; air quality; solid, hazardous, infectious and nuclear waste; mining; dam safety; public drinking water protection; shellfish; public swimming pool inspection; and environmental laboratory certification, among other things. In 2002, more than 99% of the state's 1,520 federally defined public water systems had complied with drinking water regulatory requirements.

South Carolina has an aggressive environmental compliance program in all media. Recent convictions for criminal violations have moved the state to the national forefront in this area.

The state has implemented an innovative river basin planning program for the modeling, permitting and protection of its surface water resources. South Carolina's five major river basins are to be studied, modeled, and subsequent permits renewed on a five-year rotating basis. The state's goal is to use the environmental permitting process to assess and control the overall health of the basin systems. In 2002 DHEC implemented programs to help citizens minimize risk of contracting West Nile virus, transmitted by mosquitoes.

South Carolina, as the rest of the nation, is preparing to implement an aggressive air quality permitting program. The state has in place an industrial fee system to support the air program which will include both stationary and mobile source activities.

In 1992, South Carolina passed the Solid Waste Management and Policy Act requiring county and regional solid waste planning to be in conformance with the State Solid Waste Management Plan. The state has in place innovative programs for source reduction, waste minimization, and recycling. Regulations have been approved for municipal and industrial waste land disposal systems, incineration, construction, and land clearing debris and other solid waste activities.

South Carolina has implemented aggressive regulatory reform. Coupled with "streamlined permitting," customer-friendly programs promote economic development without sacrificing environmental protection. In 2003, South Carolina had 194 hazardous waste sites listed in the Environmental Protection Agency's database, 25 of which were on the National Priorities List. In 2001, South Carolina received $57,098,000 in federal grants from the Environmental Protection Agency; EPA expenditures for procurement contracts in South Carolina that year amounted to $14,000.

6POPULATION

South Carolina ranked 25th in population in the US with an estimated total of 4,107,183 in 2002, an increase of 2.4% since 2000. Between 1990 and 2000, South Carolina's population grew from 3,486,703 to 4,012,012, an increase of 15.1%. The population is projected to reach 4.6 million by 2025.

In 2000, the median age for South Carolinians was 35.4.In the same year, 25.2% of the populace was under age 18 while 12.1% was age 65 or older. The population density in 2000 was 133.2 persons per sq mi.

In 2002, Columbia was the largest city proper, with 117,394 residents. Other cities with large population concentrations include Charleston, Greenville, and Spartanburg. In 1999, the Columbia metropolitan area had an estimated 516,251 residents, and the Charleston metropolitan area had 552,803.

7ETHNIC GROUPS

The white population of South Carolina is mainly of Northern European stock; the great migratory wave from Southern and Eastern Europe during the late 19th century left South Carolina virtually untouched. As of 2000, 115,978, or 2.9%, of South Carolinians were foreign born (up from 1.4% in 1990).

In 2000, the black population was 1,185,216, or 29.5% of the state's population (the 3rd-highest percentage in the nation). In the coastal regions and offshore islands there still can be found some vestiges of African heritage, notably the Gullah dialect. South Carolina has always had an urban black elite, much of it of mixed racial heritage. After 1954, racial integration proceeded relatively peacefully, with careful planning by both black and white leaders.

The 2000 census counted 13,718 American Indians, up from 8,000 in 1990. In 1983, a federal appeals court upheld the Indians' claim that 144,000 acres (58,275 hectares) of disputed land still belonged to the Catawba tribe, who numbered an estimated 1,597 in 1995. In 2000, there were 95,076 Hispanics and Latinos (2.4% of the total population), nearly double the 1990 figure of 50,000 (1.3%). In 2000, the census reported 52,871 Mexicans and 12.211 Puerto Ricans (up from 4,282 in 1990) in South Carolina. In the same year, South Carolina had 36,014 Asians, including 6,423 Filipinos, 2,448 Japanese, and 3,665 Koreans. Pacific Islanders numbered 1,628.

8LANGUAGES

English settlers in the 17th century encountered first the Yamasee Indians and then the Catawba, both having languages of the Hokan-Siouan family. Few Indians remain today, and a bare handful of their place-names persist: Cherokee Falls, Santee, Saluda.

South Carolina English is marked by a division between the South Midland of the upcountry and the plantation Southern of the coastal plain, where dominant Charleston speech has extensive cultural influence even in rural areas. Many upcountry speakers of Scotch-Irish background retain /r/ after a vowel, as in *hard*, a feature now gaining acceptance among younger speakers in Charleston. At the same time, a longtime distinctive Charleston feature, a centering glide after a long vowel, so that *date* and *eight* sound like /day-uht/ and /ay-uht/, is losing ground among younger speakers. Along the coast and on the Sea Islands, some blacks still use the Gullah dialect, based on a Creole mixture of pre-Revolutionary English and African speech. The dialect is rapidly dying in South Carolina, though its influence on local pronunciations persists.

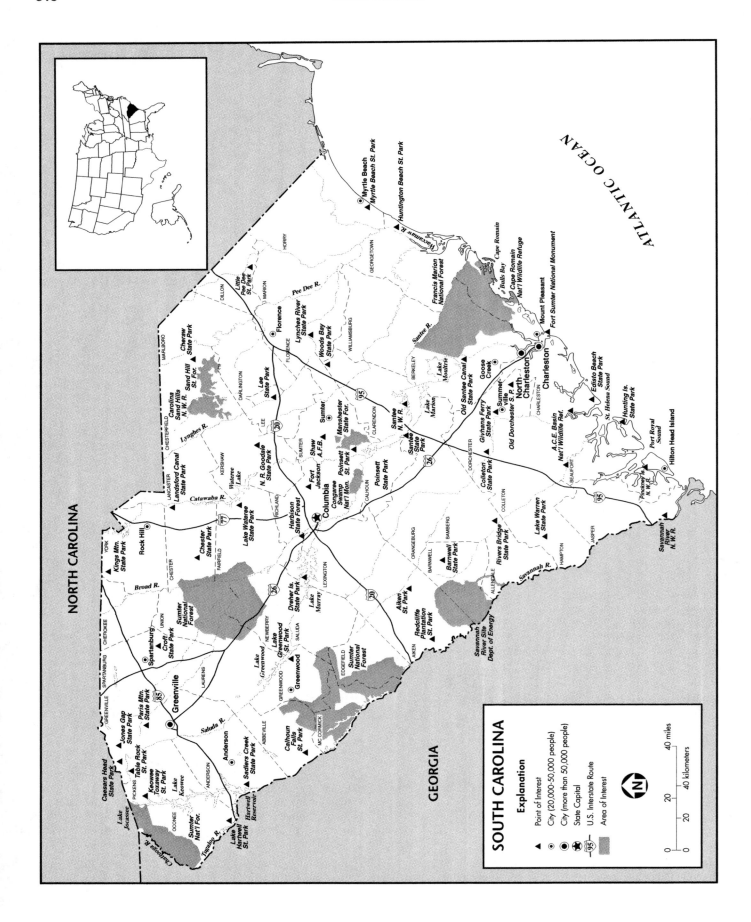

ATLANTIC OCEAN

NORTH CAROLINA

GEORGIA

SOUTH CAROLINA

Explanation

▲ Point of Interest
◉ City (20,000–50,000 people)
◎ City (more than 50,000 people)
✪ State Capital
─95─ U.S. Interstate Route
▨ Area of Interest

N

0   20   40 miles
0   20   40 kilometers

In 2000, 94.8% of all state residents five years of age and older reported speaking English at home, up from 96.5% in 1990.

The following table gives selected statistics from the 2000 census for language spoken at home by persons five years old and over.

LANGUAGE	NUMBER	PERCENT
Population 5 years and over	3,748,669	100.0
Speak only English	3,552,240	94.8
Speak a language other than English	196,429	5.2
Speak a language other than English	196,429	5.2
Spanish or Spanish Creole	110,030	2.9
French (incl. Patois, Cajun)	19,110	0.5
German	15,195	0.4
Chinese	5,648	0.2
Tagalog	4,496	0.1
Vietnamese	3,772	0.1
Korean	3,294	0.1
Italian	3,091	0.1
Japanese	2,807	0.1
Greek	2,566	0.1
Arabic	2,440	0.1
Gujarathi	2,101	0.1
Russian	1,618	0.0

9 RELIGIONS

Evangelical Protestants account for a majority of the religiously active residents in the state. The largest single Christian denomination in 2000 was the Southern Baptist Convention with 928,341 adherents. The next largest of the Evangelical denominations were the Church of God (Cleveland, Tennessee) with 56,612 adherents and the Pentecostal Holiness Church with 33,820 adherents. The largest Mainline Protestant denominations were the United Methodist Church, 302,528; the Presbyterian Church USA, 103,883; and the Evangelical Lutheran Church in America, 61,380. The Episcopal Church had great influence during colonial times, but in 2000 it had only 52,486 members. There were 136,719 Roman Catholics, an estimated 11,000 Jews, 17,586 adherents to the Baha'i faith, and 5,761 Muslims. About 2.1 million people (52.4% of the population) were not counted as members of any religious organization.

10 TRANSPORTATION

Since the Revolutionary War, South Carolina has been concerned with expanding the transport of goods between the upcountry and the port of Charleston and the midwestern US. Several canals were constructed north of the fall line, and the 136-mi (219-km) railroad completed from Charleston to Hamburg (across the Savannah River from Augusta, Georgia) in 1833 was the longest in the world at that time. Three years earlier, the *Best Friend of Charleston* had become the first American steam locomotive built for public railway passenger service; by the time the Charleston–Hamburg railway was completed, however, the *Best Friend* had blown up, and a new engine, the *Phoenix*, had replaced it. Many other efforts were made to connect Charleston to the interior by railway, but tunnels through the mountains were never completed. Today, most freight service is furnished by Norfolk Southern and CSX Transportation. In 2000, there were 2,507 rail mi (4,034 km) of track, utilized by 2 Class I, 10 local, and 2 switching and terminal railroads. About 19% (2,907,544 tons) of the rail tonnage in 2000 originating within the state was lumber and wood products, and also that year, coal represented 42% (13,951,600 tons) of the rail tonnage terminated in South Carolina. Amtrak passenger trains pass north–south through the state, providing limited service to Charleston, Columbia, and other cities.

The public road network in 2000 was made up of 54,300 mi (87,387 km) of rural roads and 10,621 mi (17,092 km) of urban roads. Highway I-26, running northwest–southeast from the upcountry to the Atlantic, intersects I-85 at Spartanburg, I-20 at Columbia, and I-95 on its way toward Charleston. There were 1,924,398 passenger vehicles, 1,154,113 trucks, and 16,218 buses registered in 2000 when the number of licensed drivers totaled 2,842,553. City bus service is most heavily used in the Charleston and Columbia systems.

The state has three deepwater seaports. Charleston is one of the major ports on the Atlantic, handling 19.9 million tons of cargo in 2000, and the harbors of Georgetown and Port Royal also handle significant waterborne trade. The Atlantic Intracoastal Waterway, crossing the state slightly inward form the Atlantic Ocean, is a major thoroughfare.

South Carolina had 149 airports in 2002. Charleston, Myrtle Beach, Columbia, and Greenville–Spartanburg are the major airports within the state; however, many travelers also enter South Carolina via the air terminals at Savannah, Augusta, and Atlanta, Georgia, and at Charlotte, North Carolina.

11 HISTORY

Prior to European settlement, the region now called South Carolina was populated by several Indian groups. Indians of Iroquoian stock, including the Cherokee, inhabited the northwestern section, while those of the Siouan stock—of whom the Catawba were the most numerous—occupied the northern and eastern regions. Indians of Muskogean stock lived in the south.

In the early 1500s, long before the English claimed the Carolinas, Spanish sea captains explored the coast. The Spaniards made an unsuccessful attempt to establish a settlement in 1526 at Winyah Bay, near the present city of Georgetown. Thirty-six years later, a group of French Huguenots under Jean Ribault landed at a site near Parris Island, but the colony failed after Ribault returned to France. The English established the first permanent settlement in 1670 under the supervision of the eight lords proprietors who had been granted "Carolana" by King Charles II. At first the colonists settled at Albemarle Point on the Ashley River: 10 years later, they moved across the river to the present site of Charleston.

Rice cultivation began in the coastal swamps, and black slaves were imported as field hands. The colony flourished, and by the mid-1700s, new areas were developing inland. Germans, Scots-Irish, and Welsh, who differed markedly from the original aristocratic settlers of the Charleston area, migrated to the southern part of the new province. Although the upcountry was developing and was taxed, it was not until 1770 that the settlers there were represented in the government. For the most part, the colonists had friendly relations with the Indians. In 1715, however, the Yamasee were incited by Spanish colonists at St. Augustine, Fla., to attack the South Carolina settlements. The settlers successfully resisted, with no help from the proprietors.

The original royal grant had made South Carolina a very large colony, but eventually the separate provinces of North Carolina and Georgia were established, two moves that destined South Carolina to be a small state. The colonists were successful in having the proprietors overthrown in 1719 and the government transferred to royal rule by 1721.

Skirmishes with the French, Spanish, Indians, and pirates, as well as a slave uprising in 1739, marked the pre-Revolutionary period. South Carolina opposed the Stamp Act of 1765 and took an active part in the American Revolution. The first British property seized by American Revolutionary forces was Ft. Charlotte in McCormick County in 1775. Among the many battles fought in South Carolina were major Patriot victories at Ft. Moultrie in Charleston (1776), Kings Mountain (1780), and Cowpens (1781), the last two among the war's most important engagements. Delegates from South Carolina, notably Charles Cotesworth Pinckney, were leaders at the federal constitutional convention of 1787. On 23 May 1788, South Carolina became the 8th state to ratify the Constitution.

Between the Revolutionary War and the Civil War, two issues dominated South Carolinians' political thinking: tariffs and slavery. Senator John C. Calhoun took an active part in developing the nullification theory by which a state claimed the right to abrogate unpopular federal laws. Open conflict over tariffs during the early 1830s was narrowly averted by a compromise on the rates, but in 1860, on the issue of slavery, no compromise was possible. At the time of secession, on 20 December 1860, more than half the state's population consisted of black slaves. The first battle of the Civil War took place at Ft. Sumter in Charleston Harbor on 12 April 1861. Federal forces soon captured the Sea Islands, but Charleston withstood a long siege until February 1865. In the closing months of the war, Union troops under General William Tecumseh Sherman burned Columbia and caused widespread destruction elsewhere. South Carolina contributed about 63,000 soldiers to the Confederacy out of a white population of some 291,000. Casualties were high: nearly 14,00 men were killed in battle or died after capture.

Federal troops occupied South Carolina after the war. During Reconstruction, as white South Carolinians saw it, illiterates, carpetbaggers, and scalawags raided the treasury, plunging the state into debt. The constitution was revised in 1868 by a convention in which blacks outnumbered whites by 76 to 48; given the franchise, blacks attained the offices of lieutenant governor and US representative. In 1876, bands of white militants called Red Shirts, supporting the gubernatorial candidacy of former Confederate General Wade Hampton, rode through the countryside urging whites to vote and intimidating potential black voters. Hampton, a Democrat, won the election, but was not permitted by the Republican incumbent to take office until President Rutherford B. Hayes declared an end to Reconstruction and withdrew federal troops from the state in April 1877.

For the next 100 years, South Carolina suffered through political turmoil, crop failures, and recessions. A major political change came in the 1880s with a large population increase upcountry and the migration of poor whites to cities. These trends gave farmers and industrial workers a majority of votes, and they found their leader in Benjamin Ryan "Pitchfork Ben" Tillman, a populist who stirred up class and racial hatreds by attacking the "Charleston ring." Tillman was influential in wresting control of the state Democratic Party from the coastal aristocrats; he served as governor from 1890 to 1894 and then as US senator until his death in 1918. However, his success inaugurated a period of political and racial demagoguery that saw the gradual (though not total) disfranchisement of black voters.

The main economic transformation after 1890 was the replacement of rice and cotton growing by tobacco and soybean cultivation and truck farming, along with the movement of tenant farmers, or sharecroppers, from the land to the cities. There they found jobs in textile mills, and textiles became the state's leading industry after 1900. With the devastation of the cotton crop by the boll weevil in the 1920s, farmers were compelled to diversify their crops, and some turned to raising cattle. Labor shortages in the North during and after World War II drew many thousands of African Americans from South Carolina to Philadelphia, Washington, D.C., New York, and other cities.

In the postwar period, industry took over the dominant role formerly held by agriculture in South Carolina's economy, and the focus of textile production shifted from cotton to synthetic fabrics. In the 1990s the major industries were textiles and chemicals, and foreign investment played a major role in the state's economy. BMW, the German automobile company, established their North American plant in Greenville. Tourism also played a role, with the coastal areas drawing visitors from around the nation. In the early 2000s, South Carolina, along with other tobacco-producing states, was in the midst of a transition away from tobacco production.

Public school desegregation after the Brown vs. Board of Education ruling of 1954 proceeded peacefully, but very slowly, and blacks were gradually accepted alongside whites in the textile mills and other industries. In 1983, for the first time in 95 years, a black state senator was elected; the following year, four blacks were elected to the reapportioned senate. Despite these changes, most white South Carolinians remained staunchly conservative in political and social matters, as witnessed by the 1999–2000 firestorm over the display of the Confederate flag on the dome of the State House. The controversy prompted the NAACP (National Association for the Advancement of Colored People) to call for a tourism boycott of the state. A January 2000 protest drew nearly 50,000 demonstrators, black and white, against the flag. Legislators brokered a compromise that moved the flag, viewed as a symbol of oppression by African Americans, to a spot in front of the capitol, where it flies from a 30-ft pole. The "solution," though favored by most South Carolinians who were polled, did not satisfy most of the black community. Tourism officials called for the NAACP to lift its boycott, but the organization refused to do so, maintaining the flag's only place is in a museum of history.

In the postwar period, the Democrats' traditional control of the state weakened, and, beginning with Barry Goldwater, Republican presidential candidates have carried the state in every election except that of 1976, in which Southerner Jimmy Carter prevailed. Well-known conservative Republican Strom Thurmond represented South Carolina in the US Senate from 1954 to 2003, when he died at age 100. But his Democratic counterpart, Ernest Hollings (also a former governor) has been in the Senate since 1966.

In 1989, Hurricane Hugo, the 10th-strongest hurricane to hit the United States coast in the 20th century, struck South Carolina, packing 135-mph (217-kph) winds. Ripping roofs off buildings and sweeping boats onto city streets, the storm killed 37 people and produced over $700 million worth of property damage. Seven South Carolina counties were declared disaster areas. In 1993, flooding, followed by a record-breaking drought, caused an estimated $226 million in crop damage.

In response to a Supreme Court ruling, The Citadel (in Charleston), one of only two state-supported military schools in the country, admitted its first female cadet, Shannon Faulkner, in 1995. Faulkner left the institution after only six days. In 1997 two of four women attending the institution quit, alleging hazing and sexual harassment by their male peers. In May 1999 the institution graduated its first female cadet. By the following August, there were 75 female cadets enrolled at the Citadel—the first in its 156-year history, as the school fought a sexual harassment lawsuit of a former cadet.

In 1999 a settlement was reached in the worst oil spill in the state's history. A record $7-million fine was to be paid by a national pipeline company that admitted its negligence caused nearly one million gallons of diesel fuel to pollute the Upstate River.

South Carolina finished fiscal year 2003 with a $68.8 million budget deficit, down from the $248.8 million deficit at the end of fiscal year 2002. In 2003, Republican Governor Mark Sanford, elected in 2002, urged state legislators to reform the way the government conducts its business, from allowing state officials to hire and fire employees more easily, to funding schools with block grants rather than line items.

12STATE GOVERNMENT

South Carolina has had seven constitutions, dating from 1776, 1778, 1790, 1861, 1865, 1868, and 1895, respectively. Beginning in 1970, most articles of the 1895 constitution were rewritten. The present document had been amended 484 times as of January 2003.

The general assembly consists of a senate of 46 members, elected for four-year terms, and a house of representatives of 124 members, elected for two-year terms. Senators must be 25 years old, representatives 21; all legislators must be qualified voters in the districts they represent. The legislative salary was $10,400 in 2002, unchanged from 1999.

Officials elected statewide are the governor and lieutenant governor (elected separately), attorney general, secretary of state, comptroller general, treasurer, adjutant general, secretary of agriculture, and superintendent of education, all elected to four-year terms in odd-numbered years following presidential elections. The governor is limited to serving two consecutive terms. Eligibility requirements for the governor include a minimum age of 30, US citizenship for at least five years, and a five-year state residency as well as a qualified voter. In 2002 the governor's salary was $106,078, unchanged from 1999.

Legislative sessions are held annually, beginning in January and ending no later than June. Bills may be introduced in either house, except for revenue measures, which are reserved to the house of representatives. The governor has a regular veto and an item veto on appropriation matters, either of which may be overridden by a two-thirds vote of those present in each house of the legislature. Bills automatically become law after five days if the governor takes no action. The constitution may be amended by a two-thirds vote of each house of the general assembly and by a majority of those casting ballots at the next general election. To take effect, however, the amendment must then be ratified by a majority vote of the next general assembly.

US citizens 18 years old and older who are residents of the state are eligible to vote. Restrictions apply to convicted felons and those declared mentally incompetent by the court.

13POLITICAL PARTIES

South Carolina's major political organizations are the Democratic and Republican parties. From the end of Reconstruction, the Democratic Party dominated state politics. Dissatisfaction with the national party's position on civil rights in 1948 led to the formation of the States' Rights Democrat faction, whose candidate, South Carolina Governor J. Strom Thurmond, carried the state in 1948. Thurmond's subsequent switch to the Republicans while in the US Senate was a big boost for the state's Republican Party, which since 1964 has captured South Carolina's eight electoral votes in eight of the nine presidential elections. In 2000, Republican George W. Bush received 57% of the vote to Democrat Al Gore's 41%. Independent candidate Ralph Nader garnered 2% of the popular vote.

South Carolina's US senators are Democrat Ernest F. Hollings, who was last reelected in 1998, and Republican Lindsey Graham, elected in 2002. Senator Hollings announced in August 2003 that he would retire at the end of his term. Republican Strom Thurmond, who was reelected in 1996 at the age of 93—was the oldest senator in the country's history. Thurmond died in June 2003 at the age of 100. As of 2003, there were two Democrats and four Republicans serving as US representatives. The state senate had 21 Democrats and 25 Republicans; while in the state house there were 73 Republicans and 51 Democrats as of mid-2003. In 2002 voters elected a Republican, Mark Sanford, to the governor's office.

Voters do not register according to political party in South Carolina. Instead, at primary elections, they simply take an oath that they have not participated in another primary. In 2002 there were 2,047,368 registered voters and the state held eight electoral votes for the 2000 presidential election.

14LOCAL GOVERNMENT

As of 2002, South Carolina had 46 counties, 269 incorporated municipalities, 85 public school districts, and 301 special districts of various types. Ten regional councils provide a broad range of technical and advisory services to county and municipal governments.

Under legislation enacted in 1975, all counties and municipalities have the same powers, regardless of size. Most municipalities operate under the mayor-council or city manager system; more than half the counties have a county administrator or manager. Customarily, each county has a council or commission, attorney, auditor, clerk of court, coroner, tax collector, treasurer, and sheriff. Many of these county officials are

South Carolina Presidential Vote by Political Parties, 1948–2000

YEAR	ELECTORAL VOTE	SOUTH CAROLINA WINNER	DEMOCRAT	REPUBLICAN	STATES' RIGHTS DEMOCRAT	LIBERTARIAN
1948	8	Thurmond (SRD)	34,423	5,386	102,607	—
1952	8	Stevenson (D)	172,957	168,043	—	—
					UNPLEDGED	
1956	8	Stevenson (D)	136,278	75,634	88,509	—
1960	8	*Kennedy (D)	198,121	188,558	—	—
1964	8	Goldwater (R)	215,723	309,048	—	—
					AMERICAN IND.	
1968	8	*Nixon (R)	197,486	254,062	215,430	—
					AMERICAN	
1972	8	*Nixon (R)	1,868,824	477,044	10,075	—
1976	8	*Carter (D)	450,807	346,149	2,996	—
						LIBERTARIAN
1980	8	*Reagan (R)	430,385	441,841	—	4,975
1984	8	*Reagan (R)	344,459	615,539	—	4,359
1988	8	*Bush (R)	370,554	606,443	—	4,935
					IND. (Perot)	
1992	8	Bush (R)	479.514	577,507	138,872	2,719
1996	8	Dole (R)	506,283	573,458	64,386	4,271
					UNITED CITIZENS	
2000	8	*Bush, G., W. (R)	565,561	785,937	20,200	4,876

* Won US presidential election.

elected, but the only municipal officers elected are the mayor and the members of the council.

While the state shares revenues from many different sources with the counties and, municipalities, these local units derive virtually all their direct revenue from the property tax. The state's school districts have rapidly increased their own property tax levies, squeezing the counties' and municipalities' revenue base.

15 STATE SERVICES

To address the continuing threat of terrorism and to work with the federal Department of Homeland Security (created in 2002 following the terrorist attacks of 11 September 2001), homeland security in South Carolina in 2003 operated under state statute; a homeland security director was appointed to oversee the state's homeland security activities.

The State Ethics Commission establishes rules covering possible conflicts of interest, oversees election campaign practices, and provides for officeholders' financial disclosure.

The Department of Education administers state and federal aid to the public schools, while the State Commission on Higher Education oversees the public colleges and universities, and the State Board for Technical and Comprehensive Education is responsible for postsecondary technical training schools. The state also runs special schools for the deaf and blind. Complementing both public and higher education is a state educational television network, under the jurisdiction of the South Carolina Educational Television Commission. Transportation services are provided by the Department of Transportation, which maintains most major roads, issues drivers' licenses, and has jurisdiction over the Highway Patrol. The Department of Public Safety regulates traffic, motor vehicles, and commercial vehicles. The Department of Commerce Division of Aeronautics oversees airport development.

Through a variety of agencies, South Carolina offers a broad array of human services in the fields of mental health, mental retardation, vocational rehabilitation, veterans' affairs, care of the blind, and adoptions. An ombudsman for the aging handles complaints about nursing homes, which are licensed by the state. The South Carolina Law Enforcement Division provides technical aid to county sheriffs and municipal police departments. Emergency situations are handled by the Emergency Preparedness Division, Office of Disaster Assistance, and the National Guard.

The State Housing Authority is authorized to subsidize interest rates on mortgages for middle- and low-income families. The Employment Security Commission oversees unemployment compensation and job placement, while the Department of Labor offers arbitration and mediation services and enforces health and safety standards. The Human Affairs Commission looks into unfair labor practices based on sex, race, or age.

16 JUDICIAL SYSTEM

South Carolina's unified judicial system is headed by the chief justice of the supreme court, who, along with four associate justices, is elected by the general assembly to a 10-year term. The supreme court is the final court of appeal. A five-member intermediate court of appeals for criminal cases was established in 1979, but legal questions (specifically, about the election of general assembly members to four of the five seats) prevented the court from convening until 1981; the court became a permanent constitutional court in 1984.

Sixteen circuit courts hear major criminal and civil cases. As of 1999 there were 154 circuit court judges, all of them elected by the general assembly to six-year terms. The state also has a system of family courts for domestic and juvenile cases. In addition, there are magistrates' courts (justices of the peace) in all counties, municipal courts, and county probate judges.

The state penal system is rapidly becoming centralized under the state Department of Corrections; there is a separate state system for juvenile offenders. In June 2001, there were 22,267 inmates in state and federal correctional institutions, an increase of 0.5% over the previous year. The state's incarceration rate stood at 526 per 100,000 population. South Carolina's total crime rate for 2001 was 4,752.7 crimes per 100,000 inhabitants, including a total of 29,265 violent crimes and 163,838 crimes against property in that year. South Carolina has a death penalty statute. In 2003 there were 77 inmates on death row. Between 1912 and 1962 there were 241 executions, and there were 28 between 1977 and 2003.

17 ARMED FORCES

In 2002, there were 37,943 active duty military personnel and 9,370 civilian personnel stationed in South Carolina. Ft. Jackson, in Columbia, is the Army's largest major training center. Air Force bases at Charleston and Sumter are major installations. Parris Island has long been one of the country's chief Marine Corps training bases. South Carolina firms received about $1.03 billion in defense contract awards during 2002.

Veterans in South Carolina according to the 2000 Census totaled 420,971, including 63,607 from World War II; 44,816 from the Korean conflict; 122,615 who served during the Vietnam era; and 63,972 who served during 1990–2000 (including the Persian Gulf War). Veterans' benefits during 2002 amounted to nearly $908 million.

In 2000, the South Carolina Highway Patrol employed 977 full-time sworn officers.

18 MIGRATION

The original European migration into South Carolina consisted mostly of German, Welsh, and Scotch-Irish settlers. During the 19th century, many of the original settlers emigrated westward to Alabama, Mississippi, and Texas. In the 20th century, many blacks left the state for cities in the North. Between 1940 and 1970, South Carolina's net loss from migration was 601,000. During 1970–80, however, the state enjoyed a net gain of 210,000; in the 1980s, the net gain from migration was nearly 200,000. Between 1990 and 1998, the state had net gains of 119,000 in domestic migration and 16,000 in international migration. In 1998, 2,125 foreign immigrants arrived in South Carolina. The state's overall population increased 10% between 1990 and 1998. In the period 1995–2000, 442,449 people moved into the state and 310,244 moved out, for a net gain of 132,205, of whom 15,760 were age 65 or over.

19 INTERGOVERNMENTAL COOPERATION

The South Carolina Interstate Cooperation Commission represents the state before the Council of State Governments. South Carolina also participates in the Atlantic States Marine Fisheries Commission, Southeastern Forest Fire Protection Compact, Southern Growth Policies Board, Southern States Energy Board, Appalachian Regional Commission, Interstate Mining Compact Commission, and Southern Regional Education Board. In 2001, the state received over $4.7 billion in federal grants.

20 ECONOMY

During its early days, South Carolina was one of the country's richest areas. Its economy depended on foreign commerce and agriculture, especially indigo, rice, and later cotton. After the Civil War, the state suffered severe economic depression. Not until the 1880s did the textile industry—today the state's major employer— begin to develop.

Textiles and farming completely dominated the economy until after World War II, when efforts toward economic diversification attracted paper, chemical, and other industries to the state. During the postwar period, the state spent sizable amounts to improve its three ports, especially the harbor facilities of Charleston.

By 1999, manufacturing had become the most important sector in the South Carolina economy. Almost 25% of the labor force worked in manufacturing, well above the national average of 17%. The top ten manufacturers in the state employed over 40,000 workers. The Westinghouse Savannah River Site military base accounts for a significant portion of the state's manufacturing base. Employment at those facilities grew significantly during the 1980s when the Reagan administration increased military expenditures. In the 1990s, however, the federal government began cutting staff at the bases and considered phasing them out. Rising foreign and domestic investment, coupled with an abundance of first-class tourist facilities along the coast, contributed to the continuing growth of South Carolina's economy in the 1980s and were only temporarily hurt by the national recession of the early nineties. The state economy's annual growth rate, averaging 5.5% 1998 to 2000, dropped to 2.6% in the national recession of 2001. Manufacturing output, nearly flat from 1997 to 2001, dropped as a share of total state output from 24.5% to 20%. The strongest output growth was in the transportation and public utilities sector (up 41.9% 1997 to 2001); in general services, including health, business, tourist, personal and educational services (up 30.3%); financial services, including insurance and real estate (up 28%); and government services (up 25.7%). Employment peaked in June 2000, and as of October 2002, was still nearly 2% below this level.

In 2001, South Carolina's gross state product gross state product was $115.2 billion, the 28th largest among the states, to which manufacturing contributed $23.1 billion; general services, $19.6 billion; trade, $19.3 billion; government, $17.9 billion; financial services, $16.6 billion; transportation and public utilities, $10.3 billion, and construction, $6.8 billion. The public sector in 2001 constituted 15.5% of gross state product, above the 12% average for the states.

²¹INCOME

According to the Bureau of Economic Analysis, in 2001, South Carolina had a per capita personal income (PCPI) of $24,840 which ranked 42nd in the United States (including the District of Columbia) and was 82% of the national average, $30,413. The 2001 PCPI reflected an increase of 2.6% from 2000 compared to the national change of 2.2%. In 2001, South Carolina had a total personal income (TPI) of $100,901,536,000 which ranked 27th in the United States and accounted for 1.2% of the national total. The 2001 TPI reflected an increase of 3.6% from 2000 compared to the national change of 3.3%.

Earnings of persons employed in South Carolina increased from $67,736,812,000 in 2000 to $69,306,154,000 in 2001, an increase of 2.3%. The largest industries in 2001 were services, 23.2% of earnings; state and local government, 14.8%; and retail trade, 10.4%. Of the industries that accounted for at least 5% of earnings in 2001, the slowest growing from 2000 to 2001 was nondurable goods manufacturing (10.3% of earnings in 2001), which decreased 3.7%; the fastest was services, which increased 6.0%.

According to data released by the US Census Bureau, in 2000, the median household income was $37,119 compared to the national average of $42,148. In 2001, the median income for a family of four was $59,212 compared to the national average of $63,278. For the period 1999 to 2001, the average poverty rate was 12.7% which placed it 36th among the 50 states and the District of Columbia ranked lowest to highest.

²²LABOR

According to Bureau of Labor Statistics (BLS) provisional estimates, in July 2003 the seasonally adjusted civilian labor force in South Carolina numbered 2,036,800, with approximately 143,300 workers unemployed, yielding an unemployment rate of 7.0%, compared to the national average of 6.2% for the same period. Since the beginning of the BLS data series in 1978, the highest unemployment rate recorded was 11.7% in February 1983. The historical low was 3.3% in March 1998. It is estimated that in 2001, 5.9% of the labor force was employed in construction; 17.2% in manufacturing; 5.5% in transportation, communications, and public utilities; 20.0% in trade; 4.5% in finance, insurance, and real estate; 21.9% in services; 17.1% in government; and 1.3% in agriculture.

South Carolina has one of the lowest work stoppage rates in the nation and only a small percentage of the total labor force is organized. Textile, clothing, and ladies' garment workers' unions make up the bulk of the membership, followed by transportation and electrical workers. Several large textile companies have made major efforts to prevent their workers from organizing unions; conflicts between management and workers have continued for years, but without serious violence.

The US Department of Labor reported that in 2002, 81,000 of South Carolina's 1,643,000 employed wage and salary workers were members of unions. This represented 4.9% of those so employed, up from 4.5% in 2001. Despite the increase, South Carolina is 2nd only to North Carolina in having the lowest union membership rate in the nation. The national average is 13.2%. In all, 101,000 workers (6.1%) were represented by unions. In addition to union members, this category includes workers who report no union affiliation but whose jobs are covered by a union contract. South Carolina is one of 22 states with a right-to-work law.

²³AGRICULTURE

Agriculture is an integral part of the state's economy. The total cash receipts for agriculture were about $1.6 billion in 2002, but that figure represents only a fraction of the impact of agriculture and agribusiness in the state. Agriculture (food and fiber) along with forestry and forestry products contribute about 25% to the gross state product (GSP). Some 18% of all jobs in South Carolina are from agriculture and agribusiness. As of 2002 there were about 24,500 farms in the state, occupying 4.8 million acres (1.9 million hectares) with an average size of 196 acres (79 hectares). Agriculture in South Carolina supplies not only food for consumption, but also cotton for clothing and soybean oil for newsprint ink.

The main farming area is a 50-mi (80-km) band across the upper coastal plain. The Pee Dee region in the east is the center for tobacco production. Cotton is grown mostly south of the fall line, and feed crops thrive in the coastal and sand hill counties. Tobacco is the leading crop by value; in 2002, farmers in the state produced 59.48 million lb (26.98 million kg) of tobacco on 30,500 acres (12,300 hectares). Soybean and cotton production in that year were 7.1 million bushels and 130,000 bales, respectively. Peach production in 2002 was 160 million lb (72.5 million kg). Greenhouse and nursery products contributed 16.3% to total farm receipts in 2002.

South Carolina farmers and agribusinesses also produce apples, barley, beans, berries, canola, corn, cucumbers, hay, kiwifruit, mushrooms, oats, peanuts, pecans, popcorn, rye, sorghum, sweet potatoes, tea, turf grasses, tomatoes, ornamental trees, and wheat. As more people relocate and retire to the state, demand for agricultural products is increasing in order to supply restaurant, hotel, and landscaping businesses. The South Carolina Department of Agriculture operates three state farmers' markets in Columbia, Florence, and Greenville.

24ANIMAL HUSBANDRY

In 2003, there were an estimated 435,000 cattle and calves, worth $257 million. During 2002, there were around 300,000 hogs and pigs, valued at $17.4 million. Dairy farmers produced around 367 million lb (166.5 million kg) of milk from 21,000 milk cows in 2001. Poultry farmers produced 1.4 billion eggs, worth some $79.5 million in the same year, and 16.5 million lb (7.5 million kg) of chicken, 1.05 billion lb (475.8 million kg) of broilers, and 325.7 million lb (147.7 million kg) of turkey.

25FISHING

The state's oceanfront saltwater inlets and freshwater rivers and lakes provide ample fishing opportunities. Major commercial fishing is restricted to saltwater species of fish and shellfish, mainly shrimp, crabs, clams, and oysters. In 1998, the commercial catch totaled 17.3 million lb (7.8 million kg), valued at $28,292,000. The state issued 511,811 sport fishing licenses at that time.

26FORESTRY

South Carolina had 12,495,000 acres (5,057,000 hectares) of forestland in 2002—about two-thirds of the state's area and 1.7% of all US forests. The state's two national forests, Francis Marion and Sumter, comprised 5% of the forested area. Nearly all of South Carolina's forests are classified as commercial timberland, about 90% of it privately owned. Several varieties of pine, loblolly, longleaf, and shortleaf, are the major source of timber and of pulp for the paper industry. Total lumber production in 2002 was 1.4 billion board feet.

27MINING

The estimated 2001 value of nonfuel mineral commodities produced in South Carolina decreased by about 4% from 2000 to $531 million, 27th in the nation.

Portland and masonry cement were the leading mineral commodities produced in South Carolina in 2001 by value. According to preliminary figures, some 33.1 million metric tons were produced, valued at $255 million. Two companies in Orangeburg County and one in Dorchester County produced portland cement. Crushed stone, the 2nd leading mineral, consisted primarily of granite and limestone with minor amounts of dolomite, marl, and shell. Its estimated value in 2001 was $180 million, with 27.2 million metric tons produced. Production of gold, a major component of South Carolina's nonfuel mineral sector, ceased when Kennecott Minerals's Ridgeway Mine closed down operations in 1999. Construction sand and gravel was the 3rd most valuable nonfuel mineral produced in 2001, with 10.1 million metric tons, valued at $40.5 million. Kaolin was the 4th most valuable mineral commodity produced (422,000 metric tons, $20.6 million). Common clay and shale and fuller's earth were other varieties of clay mined. South Carolina remained the 2nd-leading state in vermiculite production, 3rd in the production of kaolin, fire clays, and mica, 4th in masonry cement, 8th in portland cement, and 11th in industrial sand and gravel (755,000 metric tons, valued at $18.6 million).

28ENERGY AND POWER

Although it lacks fossil fuel resources, South Carolina produces more electricity than it consumes. Installed electric capacity (utility and nonutility) totaled 18.2 million kW in 1999, when power production reached 90.3 billion kWh. About 56% of electric output came from nuclear reactors, 40% from coal-fired plants, 1% from hydropower, and 3% from other sources. Major power suppliers are six private companies and the state-owned Public Service Authority, known as Santee-Cooper. Gas utilities sold 183.5 million cu ft (5.2 million cu m) of natural gas—all of it imported—in 2001. In 2000, South Carolina's total per capita energy consumption was 368 million Btu (92.7 million kcal), ranking it 21st among the 50 states.

South Carolina is heavily engaged in nuclear energy. It is the nation's 3rd-largest generator of nuclear power. As of 2001, the state had seven nuclear reactors in operation, two at the Catawba plant (the state's largest), three at the Oconee facility near Greenville, one at the H. B. Robinson plant near Hartsville, and one at the Virgil C. Summer plant near Jenkinsville. The vast Savannah River plant in Aiken County produces most of the plutonium for the nation's nuclear weapons; Chem-Nuclear Systems in Barnwell County stores about half of the country's low-level nuclear wastes; and a Westinghouse plant in Richland County makes fuel assemblies for nuclear reactors.

29INDUSTRY

South Carolina's principal industry beginning in the 1880s was textiles, but many textile mills were closed during the 1970s and early 1980s because of the importation of cheaper textiles from abroad. The economic slack was made up, however, by the establishment of new industries, especially paper and chemical manufactures, and by increasing foreign investment in the state. Overseas investments totaled $17 billion in South Carolina in 1997, or more than half of total industrial investment in the state. Principal overseas investment came from Switzerland, Germany, the United Kingdom, and Japan. South Carolina's major manufacturing centers are concentrated north of the fall line and in the piedmont. The total value of shipments for manufactured goods in 1997 was $72 billion. In 1997, Sonoco Products was the only Fortune 500 company headquartered in South Carolina.

Earnings of persons employed in South Carolina increased from $56.7 billion in 1997 to $60.4 billion in 1998, an increase of 6.5%. The largest industries in 1998 were services, 21.9% of earnings; nondurable goods manufacturing, 14.4%; and state and local government, 13.6%. Of the industries that accounted for at least 5% of earnings in 1998, the slowest growing from 1997 to 1998 was nondurable goods manufacturing, which increased 3.3%; the fastest was wholesale trade (5.0% of earnings in 1998), which increased 10.0%.

30COMMERCE

South Carolina had 5,965 wholesale establishments in 1997, with sales of $37 billion, exhibiting the 3rd-fastest growth rate for sales in the country (68%) between 1992 and 1997. Tobacco wholesale markets and warehouses are centered in the Pee Dee region, while soybean sales and storage facilities cluster around the port of Charleston; truck crops, fruits, and melons are sold in large quantities at the state farmers' market in Columbia. Sales from 24,572 retail establishments in 1997 totaled $35 billion, of which food stores accounted for 11% of establishments, automotive dealers, 15%; and eating and drinking places, 26%. In 1998, foreign exports were valued at $7.7 billion. Exports, mostly machinery, transportation equipment, and electronics; went primarily to Canada, Mexico, and Germany.

31CONSUMER PROTECTION

The Department of Consumer Affairs, established in 1974, has the authority to take, process, and investigate consumer complaints for probable basis and merit, represent the public at regulatory proceedings, and enforce consumer credit laws and consumer-related licensing laws.

32BANKING

In 2002, the state's 69 insured banks had total assets of $10 billion. Forty-five of these banks were state-chartered.

South Carolina's community banks (those with assets under $1 billion) saw weakened performance in 2002. The return on assets (ROA) (the measure of earnings in relation to all resources) ratio declined by September 2002 to its lowest point in 12 quarters. The Federal Reserve's steep cuts in interest rates in 2001/02 lowered banks' funding costs, but they also compressed net interest margins (NIMs) (the difference between the lower rates offered to savers and the higher rates charged on loans) as long-term rates declined and short-term rates stabilized. Although the economy was weak in 2002, loan growth stood at 16%, and there was a shift toward higher-yielding commercial real estate (CRE) loans.

33INSURANCE

The South Carolina Department of Insurance licenses and supervises the insurance companies doing business in the state. Most of these represent national insurance organizations. In 2001, 3.6 million ordinary life insurance policies worth $134.8 billion were in force in South Carolina; total value for all categories of life insurance (ordinary, group, industrial, and credit) was $223.6 billion. Death benefits paid that year totaled $711.8 million. As of 2000, there were 26 property and casualty and 14 life and health insurance companies incorporated or organized in the state. In 2001, property and casualty insurers wrote over $5.2 billion in premiums. That year, there were 133,039 flood insurance policies in force in the state, with a total value of $22.6 million. There were also 16,322 beach and windstorm insurance policies against hurricane and other windstorm damage in force, with a total value of $4.0 million.

A tort system of automobile insurance is in effect.

34SECURITIES

There are no securities exchanges in South Carolina, but there are 445 broker-dealers there, involving some 2,487 employees; registered investment advisors number 60. South Carolina houses 37 NASDAQ companies, and has incorporated five NYSE-listed companies: Liberty Corp., Policy Management Systems Corp., SCANA Corp., Sonoco Products Corp., and Springs Industries Inc. Enforcement of the state Securities Act is vested in the securities commissioner within the Office of the Attorney General.

35PUBLIC FINANCE

South Carolina's governor submits the annual budget to the General Assembly in January as the basis for enactment of an appropriation bill, effective for the fiscal year beginning July 1.

The state constitution requires that budget appropriations not exceed expected revenues. A General Reserve Fund (equaling three percent of General Fund revenues) is maintained to cover operating deficits. In addition, approximately 25% of projected revenue growth is set-aside and may be used as a surplus at the end of the fiscal year. Many tax revenues are earmarked for specific purposes and are deposited in accounts other than the general fund: all gasoline taxes and related charges are designated for highways, and a portion of the sales tax goes directly to public education. In addition, public education accounts for more than half of all general fund expenditures. The state shares tax collections with its subdivisions (counties and municipalities), which determine how their share of the money will be spent.

For 1999/00, the total state budget for South Carolina was $13 billion, of which $4.9 billion came from general funds and $3.5 billion came from federal funds. General fund revenues for 2000/01 actually came to over $5 billion, but expenditures reached $5.5 billion, a gap that was largely covered by a starting balance of $573 million from the previous year. In 2001/02, however, general fund revenues fell to $4.93 billion. The government met the shortfall with across-the-board cuts and drawings on its rainy day fund. A total of $326.4 million was cut from the budget after it was enacted. In 2002/03, general fund revenues reached only $5.01 billion. Cuts in the budget totaled $416.6 million with only

the debt service and capital reserve funds exempted. More drawings were made on the South Carolina's rainy day fund. The budget deficit for 2002/03 was estimated at 6.1% of the state budget, and was projected at 13.6% of the budget for 2003/04. Its starting balance in 2000/01 had been 3% of expenditures. In 2002/03 the starting balance was only 0.8% of expenditures. Total appropriations of the state budget include approximately 35% to health and social projects, 20% to primary and secondary education, 19% to higher education, 7% to transportation, and 6% to correctional institutions and public safety.

The following table from the US Census Bureau contains information on revenues, expenditures, indebtedness, and cash/securities for 2001.

	($000)	PERCENT	PER CAPITA
Population (thousands, 2001)	4,062	(X)	(X)
Total Revenue	16,865,229	100.00	4,151.95
General revenue	13,872,539	82.26	3,415.20
Utility revenue	862,415	5.11	212.31
Liquor store revenue	–	–	–
Insurance trust revenue	2,130,275	12.63	524.44
Exhibit: Salaries and wages	3,059,775	16.92	753.27
Total expenditure	18,078,717	100.00	4,450.69
General expenditure	15,674,885	86.70	3,858.91
Education	5,448,935	30.14	1,341.44
Public welfare	3,866,330	21.39	951.83
Hospitals	847,267	4.69	208.58
Health	680,276	3.76	167.47
Highways	1,222,064	6.76	300.85
Police protection	219,115	1.21	53.94
Correction	480,952	2.66	118.40
Natural resources	276,422	1.53	68.05
Parks and recreation	69,479	0.38	17.10
Government administration	566,984	3.14	139.58
Interest on general debt	290,863	1.61	71.61
Other and unallocable	1,706,198	9.44	420.04
Utility expenditure	899,903	4.98	221.54
Liquor store expenditure	–	–	–
Insurance trust expenditure	1,503,929	8.32	370.24
Debt at end of fiscal year	9,560,312	100.00	2,353.60
Cash and security holdings	26,854,349	100.00	6,611.11

36TAXATION

In the prosperity of the late 1990's, South Carolinian legislators cut taxes at a rate to removed an estimated $714 million a year from the income and sales tax base, and another $450 million a year from the property tax base. The six-bracket personal income tax schedule ranges from 2% (on taxable income up to $2,400) to 7% (above $12,000). The corporate income tax rate is 5% (4.5% for banks, 6% for savings and loan associations). The state sales and use tax rate 5% sales tax; with allowable local add-ons up to 2%. Prescription drugs are exempted, and the list of other special exemptions runs about 10 pages in the tax code (but does not include food). The state imposes a full array of selective sales (excise) taxes, covering motor fuels, tobacco products, insurance premiums, public utilities, alcoholic beverages, amusements, and other specified items. South Carolina has no inheritance tax, and its estate tax is tied to the federal exemption for state death taxes, and is therefore set to be phased out in tandem with the phasing out of the federal estate tax credit by 2007 unless the state takes positive action to preserve an estate tax. South Carolina's revenue losses from the phasing out of its estate tax are estimated at -$12 million for 2002/03, -$24 million for 2003/04 and.-$48 million for 2006/07. Death and gift taxes accounted for 1.1% of state collections in 2002. Other state taxes include various license fees, stamp taxes and state property taxes. Most property taxes are collected by local governments, however. In addition to the property tax, municipalities and counties may impose business license fees, plus charges for such services as garbage collection and water supply. Particularly in the tourist-attraction coastal areas, there are some local option sales and accommodations taxes. Over 40% (41.8% in 2000) of total state and local revenues are collected by local governments.

The state collected $5.749 billion in taxes in 2002 (down over $666 million from 2001), of which 40.6% came from the general sales tax, 34% came from individual income taxes, 14.3% from selective sales taxes, 5.4% from license fees, and 3.8% from corporate income taxes. In 2003, South Carolina ranked 38th among the states in terms of combined state and local tax burden, which amounted to about 9% of income.

The following table from the US Census Bureau provides a summary of taxes collected by the state in 2002.

	($000)	PER CAPITA
Total Taxes	5,748,585	1,399.64
Property taxes	12,746	3.1
Sales and gross receipts	3,157,804	768.85
General sales and gross receipts	2,335,170	568.56
Selective sales taxes	822,634	200.29
Alcoholic beverage	124,110	30.22
Amusements	28,996	7.06
Insurance Premiums	113,139	27.55
Motor fuels	411,074	100.09
Pari-mutuels	(X)	(X)
Public utilities	42,680	10.39
Tobacco products	26,627	6.48
Other selective sales	76,008	18.51
Licenses	310,759	75.66
Alcoholic beverages	6,894	1.68
Amusements	1,639	0.4
Corporation	59,183	14.41
Hunting and fishing	14,623	3.56
Motor vehicle	91,089	22.18
Motor vehicle operators	20,888	5.09
Public utility	(X)	(X)
Occupation and business, NEC	100,087	24.37
Other	16,356	3.98
Other taxes	2,267,276	552.03
Individual income	1,952,498	475.39
Corporation net income	217,327	52.91
Death and gift	63,647	15.5
Documentary and stock transfer	33,804	8.23
Severance	(X)	(X)
Other	(X)	(X)

37ECONOMIC POLICY

The Department of Commerce seeks to encourage economic growth and to attract new industries; it has been successful in attracting foreign companies, especially to the Piedmont. The state's Small Business Development Center, Economic Developers' Association, and Governor's Office of Minority Business help companies to get started.

The state exempts all new industrial construction from local property taxes (except the school tax) for five years. Moreover, industrial properties are assessed very leniently for tax purposes. State and local governments have cooperated in building necessary roads to industrial sites, providing water and sewer services, and helping industries to meet environmental standards. Counties are authorized to issue industrial bonds at low interest rates. Generally conservative state fiscal policies, relatively low swage rates, and an anti-union climate also serve as magnets for industry. In 2003, the Department of Commerce scheduled a series of six regional meetings in an Open Door Tour to connect with local economic developers, county councils, and business leaders.

38HEALTH

South Carolina's infant mortality rate has improved significantly in recent years but was still higher than the nation's average rate in 2000: 8.7 per 1,000 live births, as compared to the national rate of 6.9. In 1999, 7,687 abortions were performed, or 9 per 1,000 women. Impeding efforts to further improve health standards are a shortage of doctors (especially in rural areas and small towns), inadequate public education, poor housing, and improper sanitation.

As of 2000, the leading causes of death (with their mortality rates per 100,000 population were heart disease, 252.1; cancer, 210.2; and accidents and adverse effects, 50.3. The state has mounted major programs to detect heart disease and high blood pressure, reduce infant mortality, and expand medical education. In 2000, the state's overall death rate of 941.5 per 100,000 inhabitants was well above the national average.

The death rate due to HIV-related infections stood at 6.7 per 100,000 population, higher than the US average of 5.3 in 2000. A total of 10,237 AIDS cases had been reported in South Carolina through 2001.

South Carolina's 62 community hospitals had 505,294 admissions and 11,282 beds in 2001. There were 14,354 full-time registered nurses and 1,999 full-time licensed practical nurses in 2001 and 234 physicians per 100,000 population in 2000. The average expense of a community hospital for care was $1,282.70 per inpatient day in 2001.

Federal government grants to cover the Medicare and Medicaid services in 2001 totaled $2.2 billion; 579,597 enrollees received Medicare benefits that year. At least 12.3% of South Carolina's residents were uninsured in 2002.

39SOCIAL WELFARE

In 2001, the average weekly unemployment benefit was $207.76. Average monthly participation in the food stamp program in FY2002 comprised 379,310 persons (154,584 households). The average monthly benefit was $77.26, and the sum total of benefits paid in FY2002 was $351,661,564.

With the enactment of the Personal Responsibility and Work Opportunity Reconciliation Act of 1996, the US government has changed the form and regulations for many of its social welfare programs. Most significantly, it replaces Aid to Families with Dependent Children (AFDC), an open-ended entitlement program, with Temporary Assistance for Needy Families (TANF), a limited system of assistance funded largely through federal block grants. The reform act also impacts the food stamp program, the Supplemental Security Income program, and the child nutrition program. The law took effect on 1 July 1997 and provided $16.38 billion in block grants for fiscal years 1997–2002. The grants are to be divided among the states based on an equation involving the numbers of former AFDC recipients in each state.

Reauthorization of the 1996 social welfare legislation, scheduled for 2002, was delayed, and the original law had been extended three times as of July 2003, with the most recent extension running through September 2003. South Carolina's TANF program is called Family Independence. In June 2000 the state had 35,721 welfare recipients. State expenditures on the TANF program in FY2002 totaled $35,926,740.

In December 2001, Social Security benefits were paid to 703,930 South Carolina residents. This number included 421,330 retired workers, 70,860 widows and widowers, 107,120 disabled workers, 32,540 spouses, and 72,080 children. Social Security beneficiaries represented 17.3% of the total state population and 92.8% of the state's population age 65 and older. Retired workers (excluding persons with special benefits) received an average monthly payment of $844; widows and widowers, $740; disabled workers, $803; and spouses, $428. Payments for children of retired workers averaged $424 per month; children of deceased workers, $540; and children of disabled workers, $240.

Federal Supplemental Security Income payments in December 2001 went to 106,881 Pennsylvania residents, averaging $339 a month.

40 HOUSING

In 2002, there were an estimated 1,825,531 housing units, 1,563,144 of which were occupied; 70.2% were owner-occupied. About 61.4% of all housing units were single-family, detached homes; nearly 19.6% were mobile homes. Electricity and utility gas were the most common energy sources for heating. It was estimated 82,402 units lacked telephone service, 4,327 lacked complete plumbing facilities, and 5,233, lacked complete kitchen facilities. The average household size was 2.54 people.

In 2002, 34,104 new privately owned housing units were authorized for construction. The median home value was $116,614. The median monthly cost for mortgage owners was $995. Renters paid a median of $565 per month. During 2002, South Carolina received over $70.1 million in community planning and development aid from the US Department of Housing and Urban Development.

South Carolina has made a determined effort to upgrade housing. The State Housing Authority, created in 1971, is empowered to issue bonds to provide mortgage subsidies for low- and middle-income families.

41 EDUCATION

For decades, South Carolina ranked below the national averages in most phases of education, including expenditures per pupil, median years of school completed, teachers' salaries, and literacy levels. During the 1970s, however, significant improvements were made through the adoption of five-year achievement goals, enactment of a statewide educational funding plan, provision of special programs for exceptional children and of kindergartens for all children, measurement of students' achievements at various stages, and expansion of adult education programs. As a result, South Carolina high school graduates now score only slightly lower than the national averages on standardized examinations. South Carolina's educational funding is higher in relation to per capita income than that of most other states. As of 2000, 76.3% of all residents 25 years or older had completed high school, and 20.4% had attended four or more years of college.

The total enrollment for fall 1999 in South Carolina's public schools stood at 666,780. Of these, 483,725 attended schools from kindergarten through grade eight, and 136,055 attended high school. Minority students made up approximately 45% of the total enrollment in public elementary and secondary schools. Total enrollment was estimated at 647,000 in fall 2000 and is expected to drop to 635,000 by fall 2005. Expenditures for public education in 2000/01 were estimated at $4,263,599. Enrollment in nonpublic schools in fall 2001 was 55,612.

As of fall 2000, there were 178,529 students enrolled in college or graduate school. In the same year South Carolina had 62 degree-granting institutions. The state has three major universities: the University of South Carolina, with its main campus in Columbia; Clemson University, at Clemson; and the Medical University of South Carolina in Charleston. In addition, there are four-year state colleges, as well as four-year and two-year branches of the University of South Carolina. The state also has 23 four-year private colleges and universities; most are church-affiliated. The Lutheran Theological Southern Seminary in Columbia is the only major private graduate institution. There are 6 private junior colleges. South Carolina has an extensive technical education system, supported by both state and local funds. In 1997, minority students comprised 26.9% of total postsecondary enrollment. Tuition grants are offered for needy South Carolina students enrolled in private colleges in the state.

42 ARTS

South Carolina's three major centers for the visual arts are the Gibbes Art Gallery in Charleston, the Columbia Museum of Art and Science, and the Greenville County Museum of Art. Local theater groups in the larger municipalities produce five or six plays a year; Columbia's Town Theater claims to be the nation's oldest continuous community playhouse.

Augusta is home to the Augusta Opera, the Augusta Symphony, and the Augusta Jazz Project. Charleston and Charlotte also have orchestras. Perhaps South Carolina's best-known musical event is the Spoleto Festival—held annually in Charleston during May and June and modeled on the Spoleto Festival in Italy—at which artists of international repute perform in original productions of operas and dramas.

The South Carolina Arts Commission, created in 1967, has developed apprenticeship programs in which students learn from master artists. In 2003, the South Carolina Arts Commission and other South Carolina arts organizations received grants totaling $1,184,800 from the National Endowment for the Arts (NEA). In 2000, the National Endowment for the Humanities contributed $1,025,487 for 14 state programs. The state and various private sources also provided funding for the council's activities. The state of South Carolina has approximately 200 arts associations and 50 local arts groups.

43 LIBRARIES AND MUSEUMS

Public library systems numbering 40 in South Carolina had a combined book stock of 7,731,724 volumes and a total circulation of 17,476,000 in 2000. The State Library in Columbia works to improve library services throughout the state and also provides reference and research services for the state government. The University of South Carolina and Clemson University libraries, with more than 3,067,457 and 1,024,289 volumes, respectively, have the most outstanding academic collections. Special libraries are maintained by the South Carolina Historical Society in Charleston and the Department of Archives and History in Columbia; the South Caroliniana Society at the University of South Carolina is a friends' group devoted to the USC library. Total public library income amounted to $71,918,000 in 2000; including $647,262 in federal grants and $6,616,456 in state grants

There are 131 museums and historic sites, notably the State Museum in Columbia, with collections reflecting all areas of the state; Charleston Museum (specializing in history, natural history, and anthropology); and the University of South Carolina McKissick Museums (with silver, lapidary, and military collections) also in Columbia. Charleston is also famous for its many old homes, streets, churches, and public facilities; at the entrance to Charleston Harbor stands Ft. Sumter, where the Civil War began. Throughout the state, numerous battle sites of the American Revolution have been preserved; many antebellum plantation homes have been restored, especially in the low country. Restoration projects have proceeded in Columbia and Charleston, where the restored Exchange Building, dating to the Revolutionary War, was opened to the public in 1981.

Among the state's best-known botanical gardens are the Cypress, Magnolia, and Middleton gardens in the Charleston area. Edisto Garden in Orangeburg is renowned for its azaleas and roses, and Brookgreen Gardens near Georgetown displays a wide variety of plants, animals, and sculpture.

44 COMMUNICATIONS

In 2001, 94.9% of South Carolina's occupied housing units had telephones. The state had 62 major radio stations (26 AM, 36 FM) and 20 major television stations in 2003. South Carolina has one of the most highly regarded educational television systems in the nation, with ten stations serving the public schools, higher education institutions, state agencies, and the general public through a multichannel closed-circuit network and seven open channels. The Charlotte area alone had 880,570 television households, 67% receiving cable. Some 45,839 Internet domain names were registered in the state by the year 2000.

45 PRESS

Charleston *Courier*, founded in 1803, and the *Post*. founded in 1894 merged to form the Charleston *Post and Courier* in 1991. The Spartanburg *Herald-Journal* was founded in 1844 and the Greenville *News* began publication in 1874. Overall, as of 2002, South Carolina had 13 morning newspapers, 2 evening dailies, and 14 Sunday newspapers. Leading dailies and their approximate 2002 circulation rates are as follows:

AREA	NAME	DAILY	SUNDAY
Charleston	*Post and Courier*	103,162	113,567
Columbia	*The State*	117,423	152,873
Greenville	*News*	92,731	127,218
Spartanburg	*Herald-Journal*	51,797	60,659

46 ORGANIZATIONS

In 2003, there were about 1,695 regional, national, and international organizations within the state. National organizations with headquarters in the state include the Association of Social and Behavioral Scientists, in Orangeburg, and the International Studies Association and the US Collegiate Sports Council, in Columbia. State educational organizations include the South Carolina Historical Society and the South Carolina Humanities Council. There are several local arts councils.

47 TOURISM, TRAVEL, AND RECREATION

In 2001, the tourism and travel industry ranked first in the state as the largest employer and the largest "export." That year, the state hosted about 29 million visitors with total visitor spending at about $7.1 billion. Approximately 132,400 South Carolinians are directly employed by the tourism industry. About 75% of travelers are from out-of-state. Nearly one-third of all trips are day-trips. About 75% of out-of-state tourist revenue is spent by vacationers in Charleston and at the Myrtle Beach and Hilton Head Island resorts.

The Cowpens National Battlefield and the Ft. Sumter and Kings Mountain national military sites are popular tourist attractions. Golf is a major attraction, generating more income than any other single entertainment or recreational activity. In 2001, visiting golfers generated a total annual economic impact of about $1.5 billion.

There are 46 state parks and nine welcome centers in the state.

48 SPORTS

There are no major league professional sports teams in South Carolina. Minor league baseball teams are located in Fort Mill, Myrtle Beach, Greenville, Columbia, and Charleston. There is also minor league hockey in North Charleston, Greenville, and Florence. Several steeplechase horse races are held annually in Camden, and important professional golf and tennis tournaments are held at Hilton Head Island.

In collegiate football, the Clemson Tigers of the Atlantic Coast Conference won the AP and UPI National Championship in 1981; the University of South Carolina of the Southeastern Conference and South Carolina State of the Mid-Eastern Athletic Conference also have football programs. Under the tutelage of former Notre Dame coach Lou Holtz, the South Carolina Gamecocks saw a turnaround in their football program, highlighted by consecutive Outback Bowl victories over Ohio State in 2001 and 2002.

Fishing, water-skiing, and sailing are popular participant sports. There are two major stock car races held at Darlington each year: the Mall.com 400 in March and the Southern 500 on Labor Day weekend.

Other annual sporting events include Polo Games held from February through Easter in Aiken, and the Governor's Annual Frog Jumping Contest held in Springfield on the Saturday, before Easter.

49 FAMOUS SOUTH CAROLINIANS

Many distinguished South Carolinians made their reputations outside the state. Andrew Jackson (1767–1845), the 7th US president, was born in a border settlement probably inside present-day South Carolina, but studied law in North Carolina before establishing a legal practice in Tennessee. Identified more closely with South Carolina is John C. Calhoun (1782–1850), vice president from 1825 to 1832; Calhoun also served as US senator and was a leader of the South before the Civil War.

John Rutledge (1739–1800), the first governor of the state and a leader during the America Revolution, served a term as US chief justice but was never confirmed by the Senate. Another Revolutionary leader, Charles Cotesworth Pinckney (1746–1825), was also a delegate to the US constitutional convention. A strong Unionist, Joel R. Poinsett (1779–1851) served as secretary of war and as the first US ambassador to Mexico; he developed the poinsettia, named after him, from a Mexican plant. Benjamin R. Tillman (1847–1918) was governor, US senator, and leader of the populist movement in South Carolina. Bernard M. Baruch (1870–1965), an outstanding financier, statesman, and adviser to presidents, was born in South Carolina. Another presidential adviser, James F. Byrnes (1879–1972), also served as US senator, associate justice of the Supreme Court, and secretary of state. The state's best-known recent political leader is J(ames) Strom Thurmond (1902–2003), who ran for the presidency as a States' Rights Democrat ("Dixiecrat") in 1948, winning 1,169,134 popular votes and 39 electoral votes, and has served in the Senate since 1955.

Famous military leaders native to the state are the Revolutionary War General Francis Marion (1732?–95), known as the Swamp Fox, and James Longstreet (1821–1904), a Confederate lieutenant general during the Civil War, Mark W. Clark (b.New York, 1896–1984), US Army general and former president of the Citadel, lived in South Carolina after 1954. General William C. Westmoreland (b.1914) was commander of US forces in Vietnam.

Notable in the academic world are Francis Lieber (b.Germany, 1800–1872), a political scientist who taught at the University of South Carolina and, later, Columbia University in New York City, and wrote for the US the world's first comprehensive code of military laws and procedures; Mary McLeod Bethune (1875–1955), founder of Bethune-Cookman College in Florida and of the National Council of Negro Women; John B. Watson (1878–1958), a pioneer in behavioral psychology; and Charles H. Townes (b.1915), awarded the Nobel Prize in physics in 1964. South Carolinians prominent in business and the professions include architect Robert Mills (1781–1855), who designed the Washington Monument and many other buildings; William Gregg (b.Virginia, 1800–1867), a leader in establishing the textile industry in the South; David R. Coker (1870–1938), who developed many varieties of pedigreed seed; and industrial builder Charles E. Daniel (1895–1964), who helped bring many new industries to the state.

South Carolinians who made significant contributions to literature include William Gilmore Simms (1806–70), author of nearly 100 books; Julia Peterkin (1880–1961), who won the Pulitzer Prize for *Scarlet Sister Mary*; DuBose Heyward (1885–1940), whose novel *Porgy* was the basis of the folk opera *Porgy and Bess;* and James M. Dabbs (1896–1970), a writer who was also a leader in the racial integration movement.

Entertainers born in the state include singer Eartha Kitt (b.1928) and jazz trumpeter John Birks "Dizzy" Gillespie (1917–1993). Tennis champion Althea Gibson (b.1927) is another South Carolina native.

50 BIBLIOGRAPHY

Alampi, Gary, ed. *Gale State Rankings Reporter.* Detroit: Gale Research, Inc., 1994.

Barefoot, Daniel W. *Touring South Carolina's Revolutionary War Sites.* Winston-Salem, N.C.: John F. Blair, 1999.

Barry, John M. *Natural Vegetation of South Carolina.* Columbia: University of South Carolina Press, 1979.

Cauthen, Charles E. *South Carolina Goes to War, 1860–65.* Chapel Hill: University of North Carolina Press, 1950.

Council of State Governments. *The Book of the States, 1994–1995 Edition.* Vol. 30. Lexington, Ky.: The Council of State Governments, 1994.

FDIC, Division of Research and Statistics. *Statistics on Banking: A Statistical Profile of the United States Banking Industry.* Washington, D.C.: Federal Deposit Insurance Corporation, 1993.

Graham, Cole Brease. *South Carolina Politics & Government.* Lincoln, Nebr.: University of Nebraska Press, 1994.

Jones, Lewis P. *South Carolina: A Synoptic History for Laymen.* Orangeburg, S.C.: Sandlapper Publishing, 1979.

Lander, Ernest M. *A History of South Carolina, 1856–1960.* 2nd ed. Columbia: University of South Carolina Press, 1970.

McAuliffe, Bill. *South Carolina Facts and Symbols.* New York: Hilltop Books, 1999.

McCaslin, Richard B. *Photographic History of South Carolina in the Civil War.* Fayetteville, Ark.: University of Arkansas Press, 1994.

Rhyne, Nancy, ed. *Voices of Carolina Slave Children.* Orangeburg, S.C.: Sandlapper Pub. Co., 1999.

Rogers, George C. *A South Carolina Chronology, 1497–1992.* Columbia, S.C.: University of South Carolina Press, 1994.

Schmittroth, Linda, and Mary Kay Rosteck, ed. *Cities of the United States.* 2nd ed. Detroit: Gale Research, Inc., 1994.

Sirmans, M. Eugene. *Colonial South Carolina: A Political History, 1663–1763.* Chapel Hill: University of North Carolina Press, 1966.

South Carolina, State of. Division of Research and Statistical Services. *South Carolina Statistical Abstract, 1984.* Columbia, 1984.

Taylor, Rosser H. *Ante-Bellum South Carolina: A Social and Cultural History.* New York: Da Capo Press, 1970.

US Department of Education, National Center for Education Statistics. Office of Educational Research and Improvement. *Digest of Education Statistics, 1993.* Washington, D.C.: US Government Printing Office, 1993.

US Department of the Interior, US Fish and Wildlife Service. *Endangered and Threatened Species Recovery Program.* Washington, D.C.: US Government Printing Office, 1990.

Wallace, David Duncan. *History of South Carolina.* 4 vols. New York: American Historical Society, 1934.

Wood, Peter H. *Black Majority: Negroes in Colonial South Carolina from 1670 through the Stono Rebellion.* New York: Knopf, 1974.

Wright, Louis B. *South Carolina: A Bicentennial History.* New York: Norton, 1976.

Zuczek, Richard. *State of Rebellion: Reconstruction in South Carolina.* Columbia, S.C.: University of South Carolina Press, 1996.

SOUTH DAKOTA

State of South Dakota

ORIGIN OF STATE NAME: The state was formerly the southern part of Dakota Territory; *dakota* is a Sioux word meaning "friend." **NICKNAME:** Mt. Rushmore State or the Coyote State. **CAPITAL:** Pierre. **ENTERED UNION:** 2 November 1889 (40th). **SONG:** "Hail, South Dakota." **MOTTO:** Under God the People Rule. **COAT OF ARMS:** Beneath the state motto, the Missouri River winds between hills and plains; symbols representing mining (a smelting furnace and hills), commerce (a steamboat), and agriculture (a man plowing, cattle, and a field of corn) complete the scene. **FLAG:** The state seal, centered on a white or light-blue field and encircled by a serrated sun, is surrounded by the words "South Dakota" above and "The Mount Rushmore State" below. **OFFICIAL SEAL:** The words "State of South Dakota Great Seal 1889" encircle the arms. **ANIMAL:** Coyote. **BIRD:** Chinese ring-necked pheasant. **INSECT:** Honeybee. **FISH:** Walleye. **FLOWER:** American pasque (also called the May Day flower). **TREE:** Black Hills spruce. **GRASS:** Western wheatgrass. **GEM:** Fairburn agate. **MINERAL:** Rose quartz. **LEGAL HOLIDAYS:** New Year's Day, 1 January; Birthday of Martin Luther King, Jr., 3rd Monday in January; Washington's Birthday, 3rd Monday in February; Memorial Day, last Monday in May; Independence Day, 4 July; Labor Day, 1st Monday in September; Columbus Day, 2nd Monday in October; Veterans Day, 11 November; Thanksgiving Day, 4th Thursday in November; Christmas Day, 25 December. **TIME** 6 AM CST = noon GM; 5 AM MST = noon GMT.

¹LOCATION, SIZE, AND EXTENT

Situated in the western north-central US, South Dakota ranks 16th in size among the 50 states.

The state has a total area of 77,121 sq mi (199,730 sq km), comprising 75,896 sq mi (196,715 sq km) of land and 1,164 sq mi (3,015 sq km) of inland water. Shaped roughly like a rectangle with irregular borders on the E and SE, South Dakota extends about 380 mi (610 km) E-W and has a maximum N-S extension of 245 mi (394 km).

South Dakota is bordered on the N by North Dakota; on the E by Minnesota and Iowa (with the line in the NE passing through the Bois de Sioux River, Lake Traverse, and Big Stone Lake, and in the SE through the Big Sioux River); on the S by Nebraska (with part of the line formed by the Missouri River and Lewis and Clark Lake); and on the W by Wyoming and Montana.

The total boundary length of South Dakota is 1,316 mi (2,118 km). The state's geographic center is in Hughes County, 8 mi (13 km) NE of Pierre. The geographic center of the US, including Alaska and Hawaii, is at 44°58' N, 103°46' W, in Butte County, 17 mi (27 km) W of Castle Rock.

²TOPOGRAPHY

The eastern two-fifths of South Dakota is prairie, belonging to the Central Lowlands. The western three-fifths falls within the Missouri Plateau, part of the Great Plains region; the High Plains extend into the southern fringes of the state. The Black Hills, an extension of the Rocky Mountains, occupy the southern half of the state's western border; the mountains, which tower about 4,000 ft (1,200 m) over the neighboring plains, include Harney Peak, at 7,242 ft (2,209 m) the highest point in the state. East of the southern Black Hills are the Badlands, a barren, eroded region with extensive fossil deposits. South Dakota's lowest elevation, 966 ft (295 m), is at Big Stone Lake, in the northeastern corner. Flowing south and southeast, the Missouri River cuts a huge swath through the heart of South Dakota before forming part of the southeastern boundary. Tributaries of the Missouri include the Grand, Cheyenne, Bad, Moreau, and White rivers in the west and the James, Vermillion, and Big Sioux

in the east. The Missouri River itself is controlled by four massive dams—Gavins Point, Ft. Randall, Big Bend, and Oahe—which provide water for irrigation, flood control, and hydroelectric power. Major lakes in the state include Traverse, Big Stone, Lewis and Clark, Francis Case, and Oahe.

³CLIMATE

South Dakota has an interior continental climate, with hot summers, extremely cold winters, high winds, and periodic droughts. The normal January temperature is 12°F (−11°C); the normal July temperature, 74°F (23°C). The record low temperature is −58°F (−50°C), set at McIntosh on 17 February 1936; the record high, 120°F (49°C), at Gannvalley on 5 July 1936.

Normal annual precipitation (1971–2000) averaged 24.7 in (62.7 cm) in Sioux Falls in the southeast, decreasing to less than 13 in (33 cm) in the northwest. Sioux Falls receives an average of 41 in (104 cm) of snow per year.

⁴FLORA AND FAUNA

Oak, maple, beech, birch, hickory, and willow are all represented in South Dakota's forests while thickets of chokecherry, wild plum, gooseberry, and currant are found in the eastern part of the state. Pasqueflower (Anemone ludoviciana) is the state flower; other wild flowers are beardtongue, bluebell, and monkshood. No South Dakota plant species were listed as threatened or endangered in 2003.

Familiar native mammals are the coyote (the state animal), porcupine, raccoon, bobcat, buffalo, white-tailed and mule deer, white-tailed jackrabbit, and black-tailed prairie dog. Nearly 300 species of birds have been identified; the sage grouse, bobwhite quail, and ring-necked pheasant are leading game birds. Trout, catfish, pike, bass, and perch are fished for sport. In 2003, twelve South Dakota animal species were listed as threatened or endangered, including the American burying beetle, whooping crave, Eskimo curlew, black-footed ferret, Topeka shiner, pallid sturgeon, least tern, and bald eagle.

[5] ENVIRONMENTAL PROTECTION

The mission of the Department of the Environment and Natural Resources (DENR), the primary environmental agency in South Dakota, is to provide environmental services in a customer-oriented manner that promotes economic development; conserves natural resources; helps municipalities, industry, and citizens comply with regulations; and protects public health and the environment. In 2003, South Dakota had 39 hazardous waste sites listed in the Environmental Protection Agency's database, two of which were on the National Priorities List. In 2001, South Dakota received $33,633,000 in federal grants from the Environmental Protection Agency; EPA expenditures for procurement contracts in South Dakota that year amounted to $14,000.

[6] POPULATION

South Dakota ranked 46th in population in the US with an estimated total of 761,063 in 2002, an increase of 0.8% since 2000. Between 1990 and 2000, South Dakota's population grew from 696,004 to 754,844, an increase of 8.5%. The population is projected to reach 810,000 by 2005 and 866,000 by 2025.

In 2000, the median age for South Dakotans was 35.6. In the same year, more than 26.8% of the populace was under the age of 18 while 14.3% were age 65 or older. The population density in 2000 was 9.9 persons per sq mi, making it the 5th most sparsely populated state in the nation.

The leading cities were Sioux Falls, with an estimated 2002 population of 130,491; and Rapid City, with 59,607 residents as of 2000.

[7] ETHNIC GROUPS

According to the 2000 census, South Dakota's population included some 62,283 American Indians, or 8.3% of the total state population—the 3rd-highest percentage among the 50 states. Many lived on the 5,099,000 acres (2,063,500 hectares) of Indian lands in 1982, but Rapid City also had a large Indian population. Among the state's largest reservations, with their populations as of 2000, are the Pine Ridge (15,521), Rosebud (10,469), and Cheyenne River (8,470) reservations.

As of 2000, the black population was 4,685, up from 3,000 recorded in the 1990 census. The estimated number of Asian residents was 4,378. Pacific Islanders numbered 261. Of the South Dakotans who reported at least one specific ancestry in the 2000 census, 307,309 listed German, 115,292 Norwegian, 78,481 Irish, 53,2141 English, and 35,655 Dutch. In the same year, 13,495 South Dakotans—1.8% of the population—were foreign born, up from 7,731 in 1990. In 2000, the number of Hispanics and Latinos was 10,903, or 1.4% of the population.

[8] LANGUAGES

Despite hints given by such place-names as Dakota, Oahe, and Akaska, English has borrowed little from the language of the Sioux still living in South Dakota. *Tepee* is such a loanword, and *tado* (jerky) is heard near Pine Ridge. South Dakota English is transitional between the Northern and Midland dialects. Diffusion throughout the state is apparent, but many terms contrast along a curving line from the southeast to the northwest corner.

In 2000, 658,245 South Dakotans—93.5% of the resident population five years of age or older—spoke only English at home. The following table gives selected statistics from the 2000 census for language spoken at home by persons five years old and over. The category "Other Native North American languages" includes Apache, Cherokee, Choctaw, Dakota, Keres, Pima, and Yupik. The category "Other Slavic languages" includes Czech, Slovak, and Ukrainian. The category "African languages" includes Amharic, Ibo, Twi, Yoruba, Bantu, Swahili, and Somali.

The category "Scandinavian languages" includes Danish, Norwegian, and Swedish.

LANGUAGE	NUMBER	PERCENT
Population 5 years and over	703,820	100.0
Speak only English	658,245	93.5
Speak a language other than English	45,575	6.5
Speak a language other than English	45,575	6.5
German	13,422	1.9
Other Native North American languages	11,246	1.6
Spanish or Spanish Creole	10,052	1.4
French (incl. Patois, Cajun)	1,256	0.2
Other Slavic languages	1,055	0.1
African languages	1,042	0.1
Scandinavian languages	1,024	0.1
Serbo-Croatian	573	0.1
Chinese	569	0.1
Vietnamese	553	0.1
Tagalog	457	0.1
Russian	411	0.1
Arabic	384	0.1

[9] RELIGIONS

In 2000, the largest single denomination in the state was the Roman Catholic Church, with 181,434 adherents, or about 24% of the population. Leading Protestant denominations were the Evangelical Lutheran Church in America, with 121,871 adherents; the United Methodist Church, 37,280; and the Lutheran Church—Missouri Synod, 31,524. The Jewish population was estimated at 350 adherents. A few religious groups, though still relatively small in numbers, reported significant growth in membership since 1990. The Salvation Army grew from 732 members in 1990 to 2,804 in 2000, a difference of 283%. Likewise, the International Church of the Foursquare Gospel grew from 466 adherents in 1990 to 1,518 in 2000, a difference of 225%. The Church of Jesus Christ of Latter-Day Saints reported a membership of about 5,998 adherents. About 242,950 people (32.3% of the population) were not counted as members of any religious organization.

[10] TRANSPORTATION

In 2000, 1,908 mi (3,070 km) of railroad track were operated in South Dakota by nine railroads. The Burlington Northern/Santa Fe (BNSF) and Soo Line were Class I railroads in operation in 2000 when 11.7 million tons of freight were hauled in the state. The freight was primarily agricultural products (originating) and coal (terminating). Class I trackage amounted to 986 mi (1,586 km). The remaining track was operated by eight other regional, local, and switching and terminal railroads.

Public highways, streets, and roads covered 83,471 mi (134,333 km) in 2000 when the state had 821,714 registered motor vehicles and 543,817 licensed drivers. There are 180 airfields, of which Joe Foss Field at Sioux Falls is the most active.

[11] HISTORY

People have lived in what is now South Dakota for at least 25,000 years. The original inhabitants, who hunted in the northern Great Plains until about 5000 BC, were the first of a succession of nomadic groups, followed by a society of semisedentary mound builders. After them came the prehistoric forebears of the modern riverine groups-Mandan, Hidatsa, and Arikara-who were found gathering, hunting, farming, and fishing along the upper Missouri River by the first European immigrants. These groups faced no challenge until the Sioux, driven from the Minnesota woodlands, began to move westward during the second quarter of the 18th century, expelling all other Native American groups form South Dakota by the mid-1830s.

Significant European penetration of South Dakota followed the Lewis and Clark expedition of 1804–06. White men came to

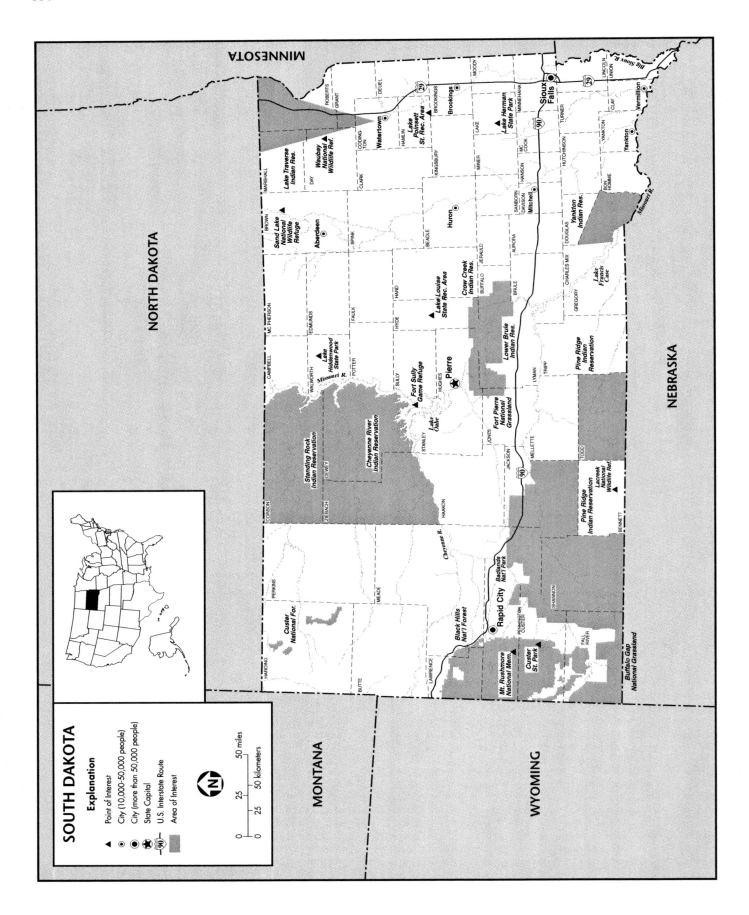

SOUTH DAKOTA

Explanation

▲　Point of Interest

⊙　City (10,000-50,000 people)

◉　City (more than 50,000 people)

✪　State Capital

⑨　U.S. Interstate Route

▨　Area of Interest

50 miles

50 kilometers

N

assert US sovereignty, to negotiate Indian treaties, to "save Indian souls," and to traffic in hides and furs. Among the most important early merchants were Manuel Lisa, who pressed up the Missouri from St. Louis, and Pierre Chouteau, Jr., whose offices in St. Louis dominated trade on both the upper Mississippi and upper Missouri rivers from 1825 until his death in 1865, by which time all major sources of hides and furs were exhausted, negotiations for Indian land titles were in progress, and surveyors were preparing ceded territories for non-Indian settlers.

The Dakota Territory, which included much of present-day Wyoming and Montana as well as North and south Dakota, was established in 1861, with headquarters first at Yankton (1861–83) and later at Bismarck (1883–89). The territory was reduced to just the Dakotas in 1868; six years later, a gold rush brought thousands of prospectors and settlers to the Black Hills. South Dakota emerged as a state in 1889, with the capital in Pierre. Included within the state were nine Indian reservations, established, after protracted negotiations and three wars with the Sioux, by Indian Office personnel. Five reservations were established west of the Missouri for the Teton and Yanktonai Sioux, and four reserves east of the Missouri for the Yankton and several Isanti Sioux tribes. Sovereignty was thus divided among Indian agents, state officials, and tribal leaders, a division that did not always make for efficient government. Through the late 19th and early 20th centuries, South Dakotans had limited economic opportunities, for they depended mainly on agriculture. Some 30,000 Sioux barely survived on farming and livestock production, supplemented by irregular government jobs and off-reservation employment. The 500,000 non-Indians lived mainly off cattle-feeding enterprises and small grain sales east of the Missouri, mineral production (especially gold) in the Black Hills, and various service industries at urban centers throughout South Dakota.

The period after World War I saw extensive road building, the establishment of a tourist industry, and efforts to subdue and harness the waters of the Missouri. Like other Americans, South Dakotans were helped through the drought and depression of the 1930s by federal aid. Non-Indians were assisted by food relief, various work-relief programs, and crop-marketing plans, while Indians enjoyed an array of federal programs often called the "Indian New Deal." The economic revival brought about by World War II persisted into the postwar era. Rural whites benefited from the mechanization of agriculture, dam construction along the Missouri, rural electrification, and arid-land reclamation. Federal programs were organized for reservation Indians, relocating them in urban centers where industrial jobs were available, establishing light industries in areas already heavily populated by Indians, and improving education and occupational opportunities on reservations.

Meanwhile, the Sioux continued to bring their historic grievances to public attention. For 70 days in 1973, some 200 armed Indians occupied Wounded Knee, on the Pine Ridge Reservation, where hundreds of Sioux had been killed by US cavalry 83 years earlier. In 1980, reviewing one of several land claims brought by the Sioux, the US Supreme Court upheld compensation of $105 million for land in the Black Hills taken from the Indians by the federal government in 1877. But members of the American Indian Movement (AIM) opposed this settlement and demanded the return of the Black Hills to the Sioux. The economic plight of South Dakota's Indians worsened during the 1980s after the federal government reduced job training programs, and conditions on reservations remained bad in the 1990s, with unemployment in some cases as high as 70%.

In sharp contrast, the state economy as a whole showed strength under the direction of Republican Governor William Janklow, elected in 1978 and reelected in 1982 and, after an eight-year hiatus, in 1994. Janklow, noted for his strong

opposition to Indian claims, developed the state's water resources, revived railroad transportation, and attracted new industry to South Dakota, including Citicorp, the largest bank-holding company in the US, which set up a credit-card operation in Sioux Falls and bought controlling interest in the American State Bank of Rapid City. In the 1990s, farm income had risen; record corn and soybean yields were reported in 1994, in spite of major flooding the year before that resulted in parts of the state being declared disaster areas. Manufacturing also prospered, expanding by up to 10% each year in the early 1990s. Legalized casino gambling has become an important source of government revenue since it was authorized in 1989.

Although the state had budget problems in 2003, they were not as severe as other states. Republican Governor Mike Rounds, elected in 2002, asked legislators in 2003 to increase state aid to schools by $15 million and to create a prescription drug program. He planned a full-scale review of the state department of education.

In 2003 South Dakota was experiencing severe drought conditions once again, after a damaging drought in 2002 ruined crops, kept grass from growing, and led ranchers to sell off their cattle.

12 STATE GOVERNMENT

South Dakota is governed by the constitution of 1889, which had been amended 112 times by January 2003. The legislature consists of a 35-seat senate and 70-seat house of representatives; all members serve two-year terms. Convening every January, regular sessions are limited to 40 legislative days in odd-numbered years and 35 legislative days in even-numbered years. To run for the legislature, a person must be at least 21 years old, a US citizen, a qualified voter in their district, and must have resided in the state for at least two years prior to election. As of 2002 the legislative salary was $12,000 for two years.

Executives elected statewide are the governor and lieutenant governor (elected jointly), secretary of state, attorney general, treasurer, auditor, and commissioner of school and public lands, all of them elected for four-year terms. (Voters also elect three public utility commissioners and the 15 members of the Board of Education, who all serve six-year terms.) A candidate for governor must be at least 18 years old and have been a resident of the state for at least two years and a US citizen for at least two years prior to election. The governor is limited to serving two consecutive terms. In 2002 the governor's salary was $95,389.

A bill passed by the legislature becomes law if signed by the governor, if left unsigned by the governor for five days (including Sundays) while the legislature is in session (15 days, including Sundays, if has adjourned), or if passed over the governor's veto by two-thirds of the elected members of each house. Constitutional amendments may be proposed by the legislature with a majority vote in both houses. If the amendment is approved by a majority of voters during general elections, it becomes part of the constitution. Amendments may also be proposed by initiative (by petition of 10% of total votes for governor at last election).

Voters must be US citizens, at least 18 years old, and state residents. Restrictions apply to convicted felons and those declared mentally incompetent by the court.

13 POLITICAL PARTIES

For the most part, South Dakota has voted Republican in presidential elections, even when native-son George McGovern was the Democratic candidate in 1972. Conservatism runs strong at the local level, although between the two world wars, populist groups gained a broad agrarian following. South Dakotans chose George Bush in 1988 and again in 1992, and in 1996 they gave Republican Bob Dole 46% of the vote. In 2000, Republican

George W. Bush received 60% of the vote to Democrat Al Gore's 38%. In 2002 there were 475,984 registered voters. In 1998, 40% were Democratic, 48% Republican, and 12% unaffiliated or members of other parties. The state had three electoral votes in the 2000 presidential election.

In 1994 voters elected Republican William Janklow to the governor's office; Janklow had earlier served in that capacity for two terms, 1979–83 and 1983–87. He was again elected to the job in 1998. Republican Mike Rounds was elected governor in 2002 (Janklow had reached his term limit). Janklow was elected South Dakota's US Representative in 2002, and in August 2003, he was charged with second-degree manslaughter in a fatal automobile collision with a motorcyclist. He also faced charges of failure to stop, speeding, and reckless driving. Janklow had a history of speeding.

Democrat Thomas Daschle won a third term in the Senate in 1998. In 1996, South Dakota's US representative, Democrat Tim Johnson, won the US Senate seat of Larry Pressler, who was seeking a fourth term. There were 25 Republicans, 9 Democrats, and one vacancy in the state senate, and 49 Republicans and 21 Democrats in the state house in mid-2003.

South Dakota Presidential Vote by Major Political Parties, 1948–2000

YEAR	ELECTORAL VOTE	SOUTH DAKOTA WINNER	DEMOCRAT	REPUBLICAN
1948	4	Dewey (R)	117,653	129,651
1952	4	*Eisenhower (R)	90,426	203,857
1956	4	*Eisenhower (R)	122,288	171,569
1960	4	Nixon (R)	128,070	178,417
1964	4	*Johnson (D)	163,010	130,108
1968	4	*Nixon (R)	118,023	149,841
1972	4	*Nixon (R)	139,945	166,476
1976	4	Ford (R)	147,068	151,505
1980	4	*Reagan (R)	103,855	198,343
1984	3	*Reagan (R)	116,113	200,267
1988	3	*Bush (R)	145,560	165,415
1992**	3	Bush (R)	124,888	136,718
1996**	3	Dole (R)	139,333	150,543
2000	3	*Bush, G. W. (R)	118,804	190,700

* Won US presidential election.
** Independent candidate Ross Perot received 73,295 votes in 1992 and 31,250 votes in 1996.

14LOCAL GOVERNMENT
As of 2002, South Dakota had 1,866 units of local government, including 66 counties, 308 municipalities, 940 townships, 176 public school districts, and 376 special districts, most of them concerned with agricultural issues such as soil conservation. Typical county officials include a treasurer, auditor, state's attorney, sheriff, register of deeds, and clerk of courts.

15STATE SERVICES
To address the continuing threat of terrorism and to work with the federal Department of Homeland Security (created in 2002 following the terrorist attacks of 11 September 2001), homeland security in South Dakota in 2003 operated under the authority of the governor; a homeland security coordinator was appointed to oversee the state's homeland security activities.

The Department of Education and Cultural Affairs oversees all elementary, secondary, higher, vocational, and cultural education programs.

The Department of Human Services administers a variety of welfare programs, the Department of Labor aids the unemployed and underemployed, and the Department of Vocational Rehabilitation serves disabled South Dakotans. Special agencies within the executive branch include the Office of Indian Affairs, the Office of Economic Development, and the Office of Energy Policy.

16JUDICIAL SYSTEM
South Dakota has a supreme court with five justices, and eight circuit courts with 167 judges; all are elected on a nonpartisan ballot to staggered eight-year terms.

In 2001, South Dakota's crime index total was 2,332.0 crimes per 100,000 inhabitants, including a total of 1,171 violent crimes and 16,473 crimes against property in that year. In June 2001, there were 2,673 inmates in state and federal correctional facilities, an increase of 4.0% over the previous year. The state's incarceration rate stood at 353 per 100,000 inhabitants. South Dakota imposes the death penalty but has only executed one person since 1930. In 2003, there were four persons under sentence of death.

17ARMED FORCES
In 2002, there were 3,350 active duty military personnel and 1,219 civilian personnel stationed in South Dakota, almost all of whom were at Ellsworth Air Force Base, near Rapid City, the state's only defense installation. South Dakota firms received more than $118 million in federal defense contracts in 2002.

According to the 2000 Census, 79,370 veterans were living in the state, including 14,709 from World War II; 11,738 from the Korean conflict; 22,660 from the Vietnam era; and 9,821 from 1990–2000 (including the Persian Gulf War). Veterans' benefits totaled nearly $283 million during 2002.

In 2000, the South Dakota Highway Patrol employed 153 full-time sworn officers.

18MIGRATION
Since the 1930s, more people have left South Dakota than have settled in the state. Between 1940 and 1990, the net loss from migration amounted to almost 340,000. In 1980, the urban population stood at 46.4%, but had grown to equal the rural population (at 50%) by 1990. Between 1990 and 1998, South Dakota had net gains of 6,000 in domestic migration and 4,000 in international migration. In 1998, the state admitted 356 foreign immigrants. Between 1990 and 1998, the state's overall population increased 6.1%. In the period 1995–2000, 72,548 people moved into the state and 85,016 moved out, for a net loss of 12,468, many of whom moved to Minnesota.

19INTERGOVERNMENTAL COOPERATION
South Dakota participates in the Belle Fourche River Compact (with Wyoming), the Interstate Oil and Gas Compact, and the Western Interstate Commission for Higher Education, among other organizations; there are, in addition, boundary compacts with Minnesota and Nebraska. In 2001, South Dakota received over $1.2 billion in federal grants.

20ECONOMY
Agriculture has traditionally dominated South Dakota's economy. Grains and livestock have been the main farm products, and processed foods and farm equipment the leading manufactured items. However, since 1970, 44 of South Dakota's 67 counties have lost population, and for five these counties, the rate of depopulation accelerated during the 1990s. The prolonged drought affecting many western states and which helped to reduce the state's corn production 10% and soybean production 6% in 2002 and disrupted cattle production, worsened in the winter of 2002–03, threatening another below-average season. The historically important mining sector was contributing less than 1% of total state product in 2001. South Dakota's tax free environment was designed in part to attract high-technology,

financial, and manufacturing investments during the 1990s. Manufacturing output grew at a substantial 16.9% 1997 to 2000, but then plummeted 10% in the recession year of 2001, reducing the manufacturing share in gross state product from about 13% to 11.3%. The strongest growth in output has been in various services sectors. Coming into the 21st century (1997 to 2001), output from financial services increased 42.6%; from government services, 29.4%; from general services, 28.7% and from wholesale and retail trade, 21.4%.

In 2001, South Dakota's gross state product gross state product was $24.3 billion, the 5th smallest among the states, to which financial services contributed $5.4 billion; general services, $4.2 billion; trade, $4.16 billion; government, $3.3 billion; manufacturing, $2.7 billion; transportation and public utilities, $1.8 billion, and construction, $963 million. The public sector in 2001 constituted 13.5% of gross state product, compared to the 12% average for the states.

21INCOME

According to the Bureau of Economic Analysis, in 2001, South Dakota had a per capita personal income (PCPI) of $26,566 which ranked 37th in the United States (including the District of Columbia) and was 87% of the national average, $30,413. The 2001 PCPI reflected an increase of 2.9% from 2000 compared to the national change of 2.2%. In 2001, South Dakota had a total personal income (TPI) of $20,145,602,000 which ranked 47th in the United States and accounted for 0.2% of the national total. The 2001 TPI reflected an increase of 3.3% from 2000 compared to the national change of 3.3%.

Earnings of persons employed in South Dakota increased from $13,486,211,000 in 2000 to $13,749,822,000 in 2001, an increase of 2.0%. The largest industries in 2001 were services, 24.9% of earnings; state and local government, 12.5%; and retail trade, 10.1%. Of the industries that accounted for at least 5% of earnings in 2001, the slowest growing from 2000 to 2001 was farm (6.1% of earnings in 2001), which decreased 18.8%; the fastest was state and local government, which increased 19.6%.

According to data released by the US Census Bureau, in 2000, the median household income was $36,172 compared to the national average of $42,148. In 2001, the median income for a family of four was $59,718 compared to the national average of $63,278. For the period 1999 to 2001, the average poverty rate was 9.0% which placed it 15th among the 50 states and the District of Columbia ranked lowest to highest.

22LABOR

According to Bureau of Labor Statistics (BLS) provisional estimates, in July 2003 the seasonally adjusted civilian labor force in South Dakota numbered 422,900, with approximately 14,100 workers unemployed, yielding an unemployment rate of 3.3%, compared to the national average of 6.2% for the same period. Since the beginning of the BLS data series in 1978, the highest unemployment rate recorded was 6.3% in February 1983. The historical low was 1.9% in March 2000. In 2001, an estimated 4.4% of the labor force was employed in construction; 10.4% in manufacturing; 4.3% in transportation, communications, and public utilities; 19.1% in trade; 6.3% in finance, insurance, and real estate; 22.5% in services; 15.8% in government; and 9.1% in agriculture.

The US Department of Labor reported that in 2002, 19,000 of South Dakota's 350,000 employed wage and salary workers were members of unions. This represented 5.6% of those so employed, down from 6.0% in 2001. The national average is 13.2%. In all, 24,000 workers (6.9%) were represented by unions. In addition to union members, this category includes workers who report no union affiliation but whose jobs are covered by a union contract. South Dakota is one of 22 states with a right-to-work law.

23AGRICULTURE

South Dakota ranked 19th among the 50 states in 2001 in agricultural income, with receipts of $4.1 billion. In 2002 there were an estimated 32,500 farms and ranches in the state, covering about 44.0 million acres (17.8 million hectares).

Leading crops and their values during 2002 were hay, 4.8 million tons, $353.0 million; wheat, 42.2 million bushels, $170.2 million; corn for grain, 304.0 million bushels, $668.8 million; soybeans, 133.4 million bushels, $653.6 million; oats, 4.5 million bushels, $8.5 million; and barley, 1.9 million bushels, $3.4 million.

24ANIMAL HUSBANDRY

The livestock industry is of great importance in South Dakota, particularly in the High Plains. In 2003 the state had an estimated 3.7 million cattle and calves, valued at around $2.9 billion. During 2002, there were 1.3 million hogs and pigs, valued at $99.3 million. In 2001 the state produced 27.6 million lb (12.5 million kg) of sheep and lambs, 166 million lb (75.3 million kg) of turkeys, 575 million eggs, and 2.3 million lb (1 million kg) of chickens. Dairy farmers produced nearly 1.58 billion lb (0.7 billion kg) of milk from around 99,000 milk cows in the same year.

25FISHING

Virtually all fishing is recreational. Sport fishing is popular; the state manages the maintenance of 5 million angler days of recreation per year. In 1998, South Dakota issued 229,360 sport fishing licenses.

26FORESTRY

In terms of geography and forests, east meets west in South Dakota in a rather dramatic way. The Prairie Plains in the east gradually give way to the grasslands of the Great Plains in the west as elevation increases by some 1,500 ft (450 m) between the Minnesota border and Rapid City.

The forests in the Plains regions are primarily associated with water-reservoirs, lakes, and the dominating Missouri River and its major tributaries such as the Cheyenne, Big White, Moreau, Grand, and Bad rivers. Collectively these forests make up only 10% of the total forestland in the state and consist primarily of tree species associated with the eastern hardwood forests—elm, ash, basswood, and so forth. In the far western portion of the state and spilling over into northeastern Wyoming are the Black Hills. The forests in the Black Hills and at higher elevations west of the 103rd meridian to the southeast and north of the "Hills" are typically "western," consisting principally of ponderosa pine. About 90% of the forestland in South Dakota occurs west of the 103rd meridian, and most of it is in the Black Hills. Three counties, Pennington, Lawrence, and Custer, account for most of the State's forest area, which totals roughly 1,619,000 acres (655,209 million hectares).

The public sector owns 66% of South Dakota's forestland. The Black Hills and Custer National Forests administer about 90% of the public forestland. The rest is under the jurisdiction of the State and the US Department of the Interior, Bureau of Land Management (BLM). Most of the state-owned land is in the Custer State Park. East of Rapid City the 226,300 acres (91,500 hectares) of forestland is primarily privately owned.

Nonreserved timberland is the primary component of the state's forestland and occupies 1,511,000 acres (612,000 hectares). Woodland covers an additional 23,000 acres (9,300 hectares). Of the forestland, 1% contained primarily in national parks is reserved from harvesting wood products. Ponderosa pine is the state's predominant species. The 2nd most predominant species is the bottomland hardwood group (elm/ash).

Sawtimber stands occupy 964,700 acres (390,400 hectares), which is more than half the total forested area; 675,000 acres (273,000 hectares) of this area is found in national forests. Poletimber stands account for a fifth of the timberland base, and sapling and seedling stands account for an additional 118,700 acres (48,000 hectares) of timberland.

South Dakota's timberland is not very productive when compared to other western states. Less than one-fifth of the state's timberland has the potential to produce greater than 50 cu ft (1.42 cu m) per acre per year. However, this is not to say that the state's timberland, and in particular the Black Hills area, has not been a good timber producer. The Black Hills have, for nearly a century, been successfully producing and supplying sawlogs, fuelwood, pulpwood, posts, and poles.

27MINING

The estimated value of nonfuel mineral production for South Dakota in 2001 was $255 million, a decrease of about 9% from the amount reported in 2000, and down 24% from the record $337 million of 1993. Most of the decrease was due to a significant decline in gold prices. Metals, including iron ore and silver, accounted for over one-third of the total nonfuel mineral value. Gold remained the leading commodity by value, followed by cement (portland and masonry), construction sand and gravel, crushed stone, and granite dimension stone.

The 125-year-old Homestake Mining Company mined its last gold ore in South Dakota at the end of 2001, closing what was at one time the Western Hemisphere's largest gold mine. Homestake was planning a merger with Barrick Gold Corporation, which would create the world's 3rd-largest gold mining company. In 2000 the major gold-mining operations in South Dakota processed 8,230 kg (worth $74.2 million) of gold. In the same year, 1 metric ton (worth $227,000) of silver was recovered.

According to preliminary figures, in 2001, South Dakota quarries produced 11.5 million metric tons of construction sand and gravel, and 5.4 million metric tons of crushed stone, with respective values of $42.5 million and $26 million. South Dakota ranked 2nd nationally in production of granite dimension stone, 5th in gold and crude mica, and 7th in feldspar. Milbank Granite, a dark- to medium-red granite found in the northeastern part of the state, has been quarried continuously since 1907 and is the major source of dimension stone in the state.

28ENERGY AND POWER

In 1999, South Dakota had an installed electrical capacity (utility and nonutility) of 2.89 million kW and produced 10.6 billion kWh of electricity, more than half of it sold to customers in other states. Over 63% of the power output came from hydroelectric sources and almost all the remainder from coal-fired plants. South Dakota marketed 1.1 billion cu ft (0.03 billion cu m) of natural gas in 2001. In 2000 South Dakota's total per capita energy consumption was 325 million Btu (81.9 million kcal), ranking it 31st among the 50 states.

South Dakota has very modest fossil-fuel resources. Lignite reserves were 366,100,000 tons; production of lignite and petroleum was negligible in 1998, however.

29INDUSTRY

The total value of shipments of manufactured goods in 1997 was $12 billion (with the 2nd highest growth rate in the country between 1992 and 1997). In 1997, South Dakota was headquarters to one Fortune 500 company, Gateway 2000. Both Citibank and 3M have large operations in South Dakota.

Earnings of persons employed in South Dakota increased from $11.1 billion in 1997 to $11.9 billion in 1998, an increase of 6.9%. The largest industries in 1998 were services, 24.6% of earnings; retail trade, 10.8%; and state and local government,

10.2%. Of the industries that accounted for at least 5% of earnings in 1998, the slowest growing from 1997 to 1998 was farm (8.0% of earnings in 1998), which decreased 25.1%; the fastest was durable goods manufacturing (9.6% of earnings in 1998), which increased 9.9%.

30COMMERCE

Wholesalers in South Dakota numbered 1,796 in 1997 and had sales totaling $10 billion (showing the 5th highest growth in sales between 1992 and 1997 in the country). The state had $9.9 billion in sales from retail trade that year; automotive dealers accounted for 16% of establishments; food stores, 10%; and eating and drinking places, 29%. Growth in retail sales between 1992 and 1997 was the largest in the country (at 93%). The state's exports were valued at $446 million in 1998, ranked as the 3rd-smallest export market in the country.

31CONSUMER PROTECTION

The Division of Consumer Protection of the Office of the Attorney General enforces South Dakota's Deceptive Trade Practices Act, prosecutes cases of fraud and other illegal activities, and registers Charitable Solicitation organizations and Buying Clubs. Disputes are mediated between consumers and businesses.

32BANKING

South Dakota in 2002 had 97 insured banks with total assets of $72 billion. Seventy-four of these institutions were state-chartered.

As of 2003, much of South Dakota was experiencing severe drought conditions, following years of very low crop prices that left many agricultural banks holding substantial levels of debt. It was projected that South Dakota's farm banks would see higher loan delinquency levels in the drought-affected areas.

33INSURANCE

In 2001 there were 403,000 ordinary life insurance policies worth $29.7 billion were in force in South Dakota; total value for all categories of life insurance (ordinary, group, industrial, and credit) was $40.7 billion. Death benefits paid that year totaled $103.8 million. As of 2000, there were 16 property and casualty and two life and health insurance companies incorporated or organized in the state. In 2001, property and casualty insurers wrote over $1.0 billion in premiums. That year, there were 3,225 flood insurance policies in force in the state, with a total value of $323.6 million.

34SECURITIES

There are 153 investment advisory firms in the state, with over 500 employees. Over ten investment advisory organizations operate in South Dakota. The state headquarters six NASDAQ companies, and has incorporated two NYSE-listed companies: AMCOL Intl. Corp., and Black Hills Corp.

35PUBLIC FINANCE

The governor must submit the annual budget to the state legislature by 1 December; the fiscal year begins the following 1 July. The legislature may amend the budget at will, but the governor has an item veto.

The governor's 2000/01 South Dakota State budget totaled $2.26 billion, with $769 million in general funds and $880 million in federal funds. Approximately $536 million was set aside for personal services, and $1.7 billion for operating expenses. In 2000/01 general fund revenues came in over target, at $814 million, to cover expenditures of $803 million. In 2001/02, general fund revenues increased to $843 million, but expenditures climbed faster, to $850 million. The state transferred $13.3 million from the Budget Reserve Fund (South

Dakota's rainy day fund) and made other fund transfers to close the budget gap. In 2002/03, however, the gap widened, as general fund revenues of $865 million were matched with general fund expenditures of $886 million. Again, the South Dakota's budget deficit for 2003 was estimated at 4.1% of the state budget, and for 2003/04 was projected at 6.4% of the state budget. In 2000/01, South Dakota had a starting balance equal to 18.8% of expenditures. For 2003/04, the starting balance is at 10.3% of projected expenditures.

The following table from the US Census Bureau contains information on revenues, expenditures, indebtedness, and cash/securities for 2001.

	($000)	PERCENT	PER CAPITA
Population (thousands, 2001)	758	(X)	(X)
Total Revenue	3,170,959	100.00	4,183.32
General revenue	2,584,159	81.49	3,409.18
Utility revenue	–	–	–
Liquor store revenue	–	–	–
Insurance trust revenue	586,800	18.51	774.14
Exhibit: Salaries and wages	428,462	15.93	565.25
Total expenditure	2,690,165	100.00	3,549.03
General expenditure	2,491,580	92.62	3,287.04
Education	734,750	27.31	969.33
Public welfare	553,651	20.58	730.41
Hospitals	43,589	1.62	57.51
Health	67,183	2.50	88.63
Highways	459,212	17.07	605.82
Police protection	18,999	0.71	25.06
Correction	66,745	2.48	88.05
Natural resources	96,869	3.60	127.80
Parks and recreation	24,075	0.89	31.76
Government administration	100,810	3.75	132.99
Interest on general debt	124,145	4.61	163.78
Other and unallocable	201,552	7.49	265.90
Utility expenditure	–	–	–
Liquor store expenditure	–	–	–
Insurance trust expenditure	198,585	7.38	261.99
Debt at end of fiscal year	2,215,512	100.00	2,922.84
Cash and security holdings	7,712,237	100.00	10,174.46

³⁶TAXATION

South Dakota has no personal or corporate income tax, with the exception of a 6% tax levied on financial institutions. Personal property taxes have been reduced since 1978, continuing into 2000 with a 30% property tax reduction. A state sales and use tax of 4% supplies more than two-thirds of South Dakota's general-fund receipts. Taxes are also levied on gasoline sales, alcoholic beverages, tobacco products, mineral severance, inheritances, insurance premiums, and other items. A large proportion of total state and local revenues are collected by local government (43.2% in 2000).

The state collected $977 million in taxes in 2002, of which 52.7% came from the general sales tax, 24.8% from selective sales taxes, 14.3% from license fees, 4.4% from corporate income taxes, 3.6% from severance taxes, and 0.2% from death and gift taxes. In 2003, South Dakota ranked 42nd among the states in terms of combined state and local tax burden, which amounted to about 7.7% of income.

The following table from the US Census Bureau provides a summary of taxes collected by the state in 2002.

	($000)	PER CAPITA
Total Taxes	976,596	1,283.20
Property taxes	(X)	(X)
Sales and gross receipts	777,174	1,021.17
General sales and gross receipts	523,001	687.2
Selective sales taxes	254,173	333.97
Alcoholic beverage	11,143	14.64
Amusements	21	0.03
Insurance Premiums	45,012	59.14

	($000)	PER CAPITA
Motor fuels	123,427	162.18
Pari-mutuels	1,345	1.77
Public utilities	2,700	3.55
Tobacco products	18,724	24.6
Other selective sales	51,801	68.06
Licenses	133,058	174.83
Alcoholic beverages	279	0.37
Amusements	142	0.19
Corporation	2,271	2.98
Hunting and fishing	21,760	28.59
Motor vehicle	41,185	54.12
Motor vehicle operators	2,327	3.06
Public utility	834	1.1
Occupation and business, NEC	55,693	73.18
Other	8,567	11.26
Other taxes	66,364	87.2
Individual income	(X)	(X)
Corporation net income	40,547	53.28
Death and gift	23,482	30.85
Documentary and stock transfer	144	0.19
Severance	2,191	2.88
Other	(X)	(X)

³⁷ECONOMIC POLICY

Efforts to attract industry to South Dakota and to broaden the state's economic base are under the jurisdiction of the Governor's Office of Economic Development. Among the advantages noted by the agency are the absence of corporate or personal income taxes, the low level of property taxes, the availability of community development corporations to finance construction of new facilities, various property tax relief measures, inventory tax exemptions, personal property tax exemptions, and a favorable labor climate in which work stoppages are few and union activity is limited by a right-to-work law. South Dakota is one of the few states to have enacted a statute of limitations on product liability—in this case, six years—a measure cited as further proof of the state's attempt to create an atmosphere conducive to manufacturing.

³⁸HEALTH

Infant mortality in 2000 averaged 5.5 per 1,000 live births. In 1999, only 740 legal abortions were performed, for a rate of 5 per 1,000 women, the 2nd lowest in the US. In 2000, the overall death rate was 952.3 per 100,000 inhabitants, well above the US rate of 873.1. In the same year, 22.0% of persons 18 years of age and older were smokers; the rate of death from lung disease was 60.6 per 100,000 population in 2000. Death caused by heart disease occurred at a rate of 285.5 per 100,000 population in 2000; the mortality rate for cerebrovascular disease was 76.0. A total of 191 AIDS cases had been reported in South Dakota through 2001

South Dakota's 50 community hospitals had 103,907 admissions and 4,465 beds in 2001. There were 3,472 full-time registered nurses and 338 full-time licensed practical nurses in 2001 and only 214 physicians per 100,000 population in 2000. The average expense of a community hospital for care was $1,462.20 per inpatient day in 2001.

Federal government grants to cover the Medicare and Medicaid services in 2001 totaled $341 million; 120,019 enrollees received Medicare benefits that year. Only 9.3% of South Dakota's residents were uninsured in 2002.

³⁹SOCIAL WELFARE

In 2001, the average weekly unemployment benefit was $184.73. Average monthly participation in the food stamp program in FY2002 comprised 47,663 persons (18,474 households). The average monthly benefit was $79.24, and the sum total of benefits paid in FY2002 was $45,323,818.

With the enactment of the Personal Responsibility and Work Opportunity Reconciliation Act of 1996, the US government has changed the form and regulations for many of its social welfare programs. Most significantly, it replaces Aid to Families with Dependent Children (AFDC), an open-ended entitlement program, with Temporary Assistance for Needy Families (TANF), a limited system of assistance funded largely through federal block grants. The reform act also impacts the food stamp program, the Supplemental Security Income program, and the child nutrition program. The law took effect on 1 July 1997 and provided $16.38 billion in block grants for fiscal years 1997–2002. The grants are to be divided among the states based on an equation involving the numbers of former AFDC recipients in each state.

Reauthorization of the 1996 social welfare legislation, scheduled for 2002, was delayed, and the original law had been extended three times as of July 2003, with the most recent extension running through September 2003. In June 2000 the state had 6,702 welfare recipients. State expenditures on the TANF program in FY2002 totaled $8,575,000.

In December 2001, Social Security benefits were paid to 136,560 South Dakota residents. This number included 86,210 retired workers, 16,450 widows and widowers, 12,260 disabled workers, 10,550 spouses, and 11,090 children. Social Security beneficiaries represented 18.1% of the total state population and 96.7% of the state's population age 65 and older. Retired workers (excluding persons with special benefits) received an average monthly payment of $802; widows and widowers, $784; disabled workers, $742; and spouses, $409. Payments for children of retired workers averaged $372 per month; children of deceased workers, $530; and children of disabled workers, $221.

Federal Supplemental Security Income payments in December 2001 went to 12,698 South Dakota residents, averaging $327 a month.

40 HOUSING

In 2002, there were an estimated 322,360 housing units, of which 291,851 were occupied; 69.4% were owner-occupied. About 66.8% of all units were single-family, detached homes. Utility gas was the most common energy source for heating. It was estimated that 9,442 units lacked telephone service, 1,348 lacked complete plumbing facilities, and 2,936 lacked complete kitchen facilities. The average household size was 2.51 people.

In 2002, 4,816 new privately owned housing units were authorized for construction. The median home value was $90,022. The median monthly cost for mortgage owners was $895. Renters paid a median of $481 per month. During 2002, South Dakota received more than $14.7 million in community planning and development aid from the US Department of Housing and Urban Development.

41 EDUCATION

As of 2000, 84.6% of South Dakotans 25 years of age or older were high school graduates, and 21.5% had four or more years of college.

The total enrollment for fall 1999 in South Dakota's public schools stood at 131,037. Of these, 89,590 attended schools from kindergarten through grade eight, and 41,447 attended high school. Minority students made up approximately 14% of the total enrollment in public elementary and secondary schools. Total enrollment was estimated at 128,133 in fall 2000 but expected to drop to 141,000 by fall 2005. Expenditures for public education in 2000/01 were estimated at $783,489. Enrollment in nonpublic schools in fall 1997 was 9,794.

As of fall 2000, there were 42,894 students enrolled in college or graduate school. In the same year South Dakota had 25 degree-granting institutions. There are eight state-supported colleges and universities, of which the largest are the University of South Dakota and South Dakota State University. In addition, the state has 11 private institutions of higher education. In 1997, minority students comprised 9.2% of total postsecondary enrollment.

42 ARTS

Artworks and handicrafts are displayed at the Dacotah Prairie Museum (Aberdeen), South Dakota Art Center (Brookings), Sioux Indian Museum and Crafts Center (Rapid City), Civic Fine Arts Association (Sioux Falls), Cultural Heritage Center (Pierre), and W. H. Over Museum (Vermillion). Several tribal councils present annual cultural and arts events or pow-wows.

Symphony orchestras include the South Dakota Symphony in Sioux Falls and the Rapid City Symphony Orchestra. The Sioux Falls Jazz and Blues Society sponsors an annual festival. There are at least 10 municipal band organizations across the state. Sioux Falls, Rapid City, and Pierre all have theater groups. The annual Laura Ingalls Wilder Pageant in DeSmit includes outdoor performances as well as activities to re-create pioneer history.

The South Dakota Arts Council, located at Pierre, and the South Dakota Humanities Council, at Brookings, aid and coordinate arts and humanities activities throughout the state. In 2003, the South Dakota Arts Council and other South Dakota arts organizations received grants totaling $640,900 from the National Endowment for the Arts (NEA). In 2000, the National Endowment for the Humanities contributed $632,964 for two state projects. The state and various private sources also provided funding for the council's activities. South Dakota provides about 50,000 of its schoolchildren with arts education programs. The state has approximately 350 arts associations and 40 local arts groups.

43 LIBRARIES AND MUSEUMS

In 2000, South Dakota had 20 public library systems with a combined total of 2,600,000 volumes and 4,596,000 circulation. Leading collections, each with more than 100,000 volumes, were those of South Dakota State University (Brookings), Northern State College and Alexander Mitchell Library (Aberdeen), Augustana College (Sioux Falls), the University of South Dakota (Vermillion), the South Dakota State Library (Pierre), and the Sioux Falls and Rapid City public libraries. Total public library income for 2000 was $13,618,000; per capita spending equaled $23.89.

South Dakota has 81 museums and historic sites, including the Cultural Heritage Museum (Pierre), Siouxland Heritage Museums and Delbridge Museum of Natural History (Sioux Falls), and the Shrine to Music Museum (Vermillion). Badlands National Park and Wind Cave National Park also display interesting exhibits.

44 COMMUNICATIONS

In 2001, 94.6% of South Dakota's occupied housing units had telephones. There were 64 major radio stations (21 AM, 43 FM) and 16 major television stations in 2003. Cable television service was mainly provided by Midcontinent Cable Company in the Sioux Falls area. Some 8,919 Internet domain names were registered in the state by the year 2000.

45 PRESS

In 2002, South Dakota had six morning newspapers, five evening papers, and four Sunday papers. Leading newspapers included the *Rapid City Journal*, mornings 29,726, Sundays 33,730; and the Sioux Falls *Argus Leader*, mornings 53,558, Sundays 75,696.

46 ORGANIZATIONS

In 2003, there were about 662 regional, national, and international organizations within the state. Among the organizations headquartered in South Dakota are the National Buffalo Association, Custer; Federal Court Clerks Association and Evangelical Lutheran Good Samaritan Society, Sioux Falls); and the National Trail Council, Brookings.

There are several organizations focusing on the local and national interests of Native Americans. These include the Association of Community Tribal Schools, the Association on American Indian Affairs, and the Lakota Student Alliance. The South Dakota State Historical Society is located in Pierre. There are a number of municipal and county historical societies as well. There are also several local arts councils. Environmental groups include the Keep South Dakota Green Association and the South Dakota Wildlife Federation.

47 TOURISM, TRAVEL, AND RECREATION

Tourism is the state's largest industry. Travelers spent an estimated $663 million in South Dakota in 2002. The travel industry accounts for 31,022 jobs across the state.

Most of the state's tourist attractions lie west of the Missouri River, especially in the Black Hills region. Mt. Rushmore National Memorial consists of the heads of four US presidents—George Washington, Thomas Jefferson, Abraham Lincoln, and Theodore Roosevelt—carved in granite in the mountainside. Wind Cave National Park and Jewel Cave National Monument are also in the Black Hills region. Just to the east is Badlands National Monument, consisting of fossil beds and eroded cliffs almost bare of vegetation.

48 SPORTS

There are no major league professional sports teams in South Dakota. However, the Sioux Falls Canaries are a minor league baseball club playing in the independent Northern League. Sioux Falls also hosts a minor league hockey team. The University of South Dakota Coyotes and the Jackrabbits of South Dakota State both compete in the North Central Conference. Skiing and hiking are popular in the Black Hills. Other annual sporting events include the Black Hills Motorcycle Classic in Sturgis and many rodeos, including the Days of '76 in Deadwood. Former Olympic gold medalist Billy Mills and Football Hall of Famer Norm van Brocklin are among those athletes born in South Dakota.

49 FAMOUS SOUTH DAKOTANS

The only South Dakotan to win high elective office was Hubert H. Humphrey (1911–78), a native of Wallace who, after rising to power in Minnesota Democratic politics, served as US senator for 16 years before becoming vice president under Lyndon Johnson (1965–69).

Other outstanding federal officeholders from South Dakota were Newton Edmunds (1819–1908), second governor of the Dakota Territory; Charles Henry Burke (b.New York, 1861–1944), who as commissioner of Indian affairs improved education and health care for Native Americans; and Vermillion-born Peter Norbeck (1870–1936), a Progressive Republican leader, first while governor (1917–21) and then as US senator until his death. The son of a German-American father and a Brulé Indian mother, Benjamin Reifel (1906-1990) was the first American Indian elected to Congress from South Dakota; he later served as the last US commissioner of Indian affairs. George McGovern (b.1922) served in the US Senate from 1963 through 1980; an early opponent of the war in Vietnam, he ran unsuccessfully as the Democratic presidential nominee in 1972.

Associated with South Dakota are several distinguished Indian leaders. Among them were Red Cloud (b.Nebraska 1822–1909), an Oglala warrior; Spotted Tail (b.Wyoming, 1833?–1881), the Brulé chief who was a commanding figure on the Rosebud Reservation; Sitting Bull (1834–90), a Hunkpapa Sioux most famous as the main leader of the Indian army that crushed George Custer's Seventh US Cavalry at the Battle of the Little Big Horn (1876) in Montana; and Crazy Horse (1849?–1877), an Oglala chief who also fought at Little Big Horn.

Ernest Orlando Lawrence (1901–58), the state's only Nobel Prize winner, received the physics award in 1939 for the invention of the cyclotron. The business leader with the greatest personal influence on South Dakota's history was Pierre Chouteau, Jr. (b.Missouri, 1789–1865), a fur trader after whom the state capital is named.

South Dakota artists include George Catlin (b.Pennsylvania, 1796–1872), Karl Bodmer (1809–93), Harvey Dunn (1884–1952), and Oscar Howe (1915–83). Gutzon Borglum (b.Idaho, 1871–1941) carved the faces on Mt. Rushmore. The state's two leading writers are Ole Edvart Rölvaag (b.Norway, 1876–1931), author of *Giants in the Earth* and other novels, and Frederick Manfred (b.Iowa, 1912–94), a Minnesota resident who served as writer-in-residence at the University of South Dakota and has used the state as a setting for many of his novels.

50 BIBLIOGRAPHY

Amerson, Robert. *From the Hidewood: Memories of a Dakota Neighborhood.* St. Paul: Minnesota Historical Society Press, 1996.

Daum, Ann. *The Prairie in Her Eyes.* Minneapolis, Minn.: Milkweed, 2001.

Federal Writers' Project. *South Dakota: A Guide to the State.* 1938. Reprint, New York: Somerset, 1952.

Hasselstrom, Linda M. *Feels Like Far: A Rancher's Life on the Great Plains.* New York: Lyons Press, 1999.

Kingsbury, George W. *History of Dakota Territory.* 2 vols. Chicago: Clarke, 1915.

Milton, John R., ed. *The Literature of South Dakota.* Vermillion: Dakota Press, 1976

———. *South Dakota: A Bicentennial History.* New York: Norton, 1977.

Nelson, Paula. *The Prairie Winnows Out Its Own: The West River Country of South Dakota in the Years of Depression and Dust.* Iowa City: University of Iowa Press, 1996.

Parker, Watson. *Gold in the Black Hills.* Norman: University of Oklahoma Press, 1966.

Schell, Herbert. *History of South Dakota.* 3rd ed. Lincoln: University of Nebraska Press, 1975.

Shaff, Howard and Audrey. *Six Wars at a Time.* Sioux Falls, S.D.: Center for Western Studies at Augustana College, 1985.

Welsbacher, Anne. *South Dakota.* Minneapolis, Minn.: Abdo & Daughters, 1998.

TENNESSEE

State of Tennessee

ORIGIN OF STATE NAME: Probably from Indian name *Tenase,* which was the principal village of the Cherokee. **NICKNAME:** The Volunteer State. **CAPITAL:** Nashville. **ENTERED UNION:** 1 June 1796 (16th). **SONGS:** "When It's Iris Time in Tennessee," "The Tennessee Waltz," "My Homeland, Tennessee," "Rocky Top," and "My Tennessee." **POEM:** "Oh Tennessee, My Tennessee." **FOLK DANCE:** Square dance. **MOTTO:** Agriculture and Commerce. **FLAG:** On a crimson field separated by a white border from a blue bar at the fly, three white stars on a blue circle edged in white represent the state's three main general divisions— East, Middle, and West Tennessee. **OFFICIAL SEAL:** The upper half consists of the word "Agriculture," a plow, a sheaf of wheat, a cotton plant, and the roman numeral XVI, signifying the order of entry into the Union; the lower half comprises the word "Commerce" and a boat. The words "The Great Seal of the State of Tennessee 1796" surround the whole. The date commemorates the passage of the state constitution. **WILD ANIMAL:** Raccoon. **BIRD:** Mockingbird. **AMPHIBIAN:** Tennessee cave salamander. **REPTILE:** Box turtle. **INSECTS:** Ladybug, firefly, and honeybee. **CULTIVATED FLOWER:** Iris. **WILD FLOWER:** Passion flower. **TREE:** Tulip poplar. **GEM:** Freshwater pearl. **ROCKS:** Limestone, agate. **LEGAL HOLIDAYS:** New Year's Day, 1 January; Birthday of Martin Luther King, Jr., 3rd Monday in January; Washington's Birthday, 3rd Monday in February; Good Friday, March or April; Decoration Day, last Monday in May; Independence Day, 4 July; primary and county elections, 1st Thursday in August in even-numbered years; Labor Day, 1st Monday in September; Columbus Day, 2nd Monday in October; General Election Day, 1st Tuesday after 1st Monday in November in even-numbered years; Veterans Day, 11 November; Thanksgiving Day, 4th Thursday in November; Christmas Day, 25 December. **TIME:** 7 AM EST = noon GMT; 6 AM CST = noon GMT.

¹LOCATION, SIZE, AND EXTENT

Situated in the eastern south-central US, Tennessee ranks 34th in size among the 50 states.

The total area of the state is 42,144 sq mi (109,152 sq km), of which land occupies 41,155 sq mi (106,591 sq km) and inland water 989 sq mi (2,561 sq km). Tennessee extends about 430 mi (690 km) E-W and 110 mi (180 km) N-S.

Tennessee is bordered on the N by Kentucky and Virginia; on the E by North Carolina; on the S by Georgia, Alabama, and Mississippi; and on the W by Arkansas and Missouri (with the line formed by the Mississippi River). The boundary length of Tennessee totals 1,306 mi (2,102 km). The state's geographic center lies in Rutherford County, 5 mi (8 km) NE of Murfreesboro.

²TOPOGRAPHY

Long, narrow, and rhomboidal, Tennessee is divided topographically into six major physical regions: the Unaka Mountains, the Great Valley of East Tennessee, the Cumberland Plateau, the Highland Rim, the Central Basin, and the Gulf Coastal Plain. In addition, there are two minor physical regions: the Western Valley of the Tennessee River and the Mississippi Flood Plains.

The easternmost region is the Unaka Mountains, part of the Appalachian chain. The Unakas actually include several ranges, the most notable of which is the Great Smoky Mountains. The region constitutes the highest and most rugged surface in the state and covers an area of about 2,600 sq mi (6,700 sq km). Several peaks reach a height of 6,000 ft (1,800 m) or more: the tallest is Clingmans Dome in the Great Smokies, which rises to 6,643 ft (2,026 m) and is the highest point in the state.

Lying due west of the Unakas is the Great Valley of East Tennessee. Extending from southwestern Virginia into northern

Georgia, the Great Valley is a segment of the Ridge and Valley province of the Appalachian Highlands, which reach from New York into Alabama. This region, consisting of long, narrow ridges with broad valleys between them, covers more than 9,000 sq mi (23,000 sq km) of Tennessee. Since the coming of the Tennessee Valley Authority (TVA) in 1933, the area has been dotted with artificial lakes and dams, which supply electric power and aid in flood control.

The Cumberland Plateau, which extends in its entirety from southern Kentucky into central Alabama, has an area of about 5,400 sq mi (14,000 sq km) in Middle Tennessee. The plateau is a region of contrasts, including both the Cumberland Mountains, which rise to a height of 3,500 ft (1,100 m), and the Sequatchie Valley, the floor of which lies about 1,000 ft (300 m) below the surface of the adjoining plateau.

The Highland Rim, also in Middle Tennessee, is the state's largest natural region, consisting of more than 12,500 sq mi (32,400 sq km) and encircling the Central Basin. The eastern section is a gently rolling plain some 1,000 ft (300 m) lower than the Cumberland Plateau. The western part has an even lower elevation and sinks gently toward the Tennessee River.

The Central Basin, an oval depression with a gently rolling surface, has been compared to the bottom of an oval dish, of which the Highland Rim forms the broad, flat brim. With its rich soil, the region has attracted people from the earliest days of European settlement and is more densely populated than any other area in the state.

The westernmost of the major regions is the Gulf Coastal Plain. It embraces practically all of West Tennessee and covers an area of 9,000 sq mi (23,000 sq km). It is a broad plain, sloping gradually westward until it ends abruptly at the bluffs overlooking the Mississippi Flood Plains. In the northwest corner is Reelfoot Lake, the only natural lake of significance in the state, formed by a series of earthquakes in 1811 and 1812. The state's lowest point, 178 ft (54 m) above sea level, is on the banks of the Mississippi in the southwest.

Most of the state is drained by the Mississippi River system. Waters from the two longest rivers—the Tennessee, with a total length of 652 mi (1,049 km), and the Cumberland, which is 687 mi (1,106 km) long—flow into the Ohio River in Kentucky and join the Mississippi at Cairo, Illinois. Formed a few miles north of Knoxville by the confluence of the Holston and French Broad rivers, the Tennessee flows southwestward through the Great Valley into northern Alabama, then curves back into the state and flows northward into Kentucky. Other tributaries of the Tennessee are the Clinch, Duck, Elk, Hiwassee, and Sequatchie rivers. The Cumberland River rises in southeastern Kentucky, flows across central Tennessee, and then turns northward back into Kentucky; its principal tributaries are the Harpeth, Red, Obey, Caney Fork, and Stones rivers and Yellow Creek. In the western part of the state, the Forked Deer and Wolf rivers are among those flowing into the Mississippi, which forms the western border with Missouri and Arkansas.

³CLIMATE

Generally, Tennessee has a temperate climate, with warm summers and mild winters. However, the state's varied topography leads to a wide range of climatic conditions.

The warmest parts of the state, with the longest growing season, are the Gulf Coastal Plain, the Central Basin, and the Sequatchie Valley. In the Memphis area in the southwest, the average date of the last killing frost is 20 March, and the growing season is about 235 days. Memphis has an annual mean temperature of 62°F (17°C), 40°F (4°C) in January, and 83°F (28°C) in July. In the Nashville area, the growing season lasts about 225 days. Nashville has an annual mean of 59°F (15°C), ranging from 36°F (2°C) in January to 79°F (26°C) in July. The Knoxville area has a growing season of 220 days. The city's annual mean temperature is 60°F (16°C), with averages of 41°F (5°C) in January and 78°F (26°C) in July. In some parts of the mountainous east, where the temperatures are considerably lower, the growing season is as short as 130 days. The record high temperature for the state is 113°F (45°C), set at Perryville on 9 August 1930; the record low, −32°F (−36°C), was registered at Mountain City on 30 December 1917.

Severe storms occur infrequently. The greatest rainfall occurs in the winter and early spring, especially March; the early fall months, particularly September and October, are the driest. Average annual precipitation (1971–2000) was 54.7 in (138.9 cm) in Memphis and 48 in (122 cm) in Nashville. Snowfall varies and is more prevalent in East Tennessee than in the western section; Nashville gets about 10 in (25.4 cm) a year, Memphis only 5 in (12.7 cm).

⁴FLORA AND FAUNA

With its varied terrain and soils, Tennessee has an abundance of flora, including at least 150 kinds of native trees. Tulip poplar (the state tree), shortleaf pine, and chestnut, black, and red oaks are commonly found in the eastern part of the state while the Highland Rim abounds in several varieties of oak, hickory, ash, and pine. Gum maple, black walnut, sycamore, and cottonwood grow in the west, and cypress is plentiful in the Reelfoot Lake area. In East Tennessee, rhododendron, mountain laurel, and wild azalea blossoms create a blaze of color in the mountains. More than 300 native Tennessee plants, including digitalis and ginseng have been utilized for medicinal purposes. In 2003, 20 plant species were listed as threatened or endangered in Tennessee, including the Blue Ridge goldenrod, Cumberland rosemary and sandwort, Roan Mountain bluet, and Tennessee purple coneflower.

Tennessee mammals include the raccoon (the state animal), white-tailed deer, black bear bobcat, muskrat, woodchuck, opossum, and red and gray foxes; the European wild boar was introduced by sportsmen in 1912. More than 250 bird species reside in Tennessee. Bobwhite quail, ruffed grouse, mourning dove, and mallard duck are the most common game birds. The state's 56 amphibian species include numerous frogs, salamanders, newts, and lizards; 58 reptile species include three types of rattlesnake. Of the 186 fish species in Tennessee's lakes and streams, catfish, bream, bass, crappie, pike, and trout are the leading game fish.

Tennessee's Wildlife Resources Agency conducts an endangered and threatened species protection program. Seventy-six animal species were listed as endangered or threatened as of 2003, including the seven species of darter, gray and Indiana bats, pallid sturgeon, bald eagle, Carolina northern flying squirrel, least tern, and white wartyback pearlymussel. The snail darter, cited by opponents of the Tellico Dam following the passage of the Endangered Species Act in 1973, is probably Tennessee's most famous threatened species.

⁵ENVIRONMENTAL PROTECTION

Tennessee is historically an agricultural state but is geologically varied with mountains in the east, rolling hills in the central part of the state, and the wide floodplain of the Mississippi in the west.

The Great Smoky Mountains in east Tennessee are sensitive to changes in air quality. In 1997 the state forged an agreement with the US National Park Service and the US Forest Service to ensure that the process for issuing permits for new industries in the area take into account both business and environmental concerns.

The first conservationists were agricultural reformers who, even before the Civil War, recommended terracing to conserve the soil and curtail erosion. Such conservation techniques as crop rotation and contour plowing were discussed at county fairs and other places where farmers gathered. In 1854, the legislature established the State Agricultural Bureau, which sought primarily to protect farmlands from floods. The streams of west Tennessee were extensively channelized for flood control beginning in the late 1800s, with a negative impact on both habitat and cropland. As of 2003, the state was working with local citizens and the US Army Corps of Engineers to reverse this process by restoring the natural meandering flow to the tributaries of the Mississippi.

The Department of Environment and Conservation is responsible for air, land, and water protection in Tennessee. The department also manages the state park system and state natural areas. In 1996, Tennessee had approximately one million acres of wetlands. The Tennessee Wetland Act of 1986 authorized the acquisition of wetlands through the use of real estate taxes. In 1997, the state created four new natural areas.

When many of the first environmental laws were written in the 1970s, pollution of the air and water was widespread and severe. The early laws focused on tough enforcement tools and strict compliance measures to address this problem. In 1993, the Division of Pollution Prevention Assistance was established to provide information and support to industries attempting to reduce their pollution and waste. In 2003, Tennessee had 245 hazardous waste sites listed in the Environmental Protection Agency's database, 12 of which were on the National Priorities List. In 2001, Tennessee received $31,235,000 in federal grants from the Environmental Protection Agency; EPA expenditures for procurement contracts in Tennessee that year amounted to $2,491,000.

⁶POPULATION

Tennessee ranked 16th in population in the US with an estimated total of 5,797,290 in 2002, an increase of 1.9% since 2000.

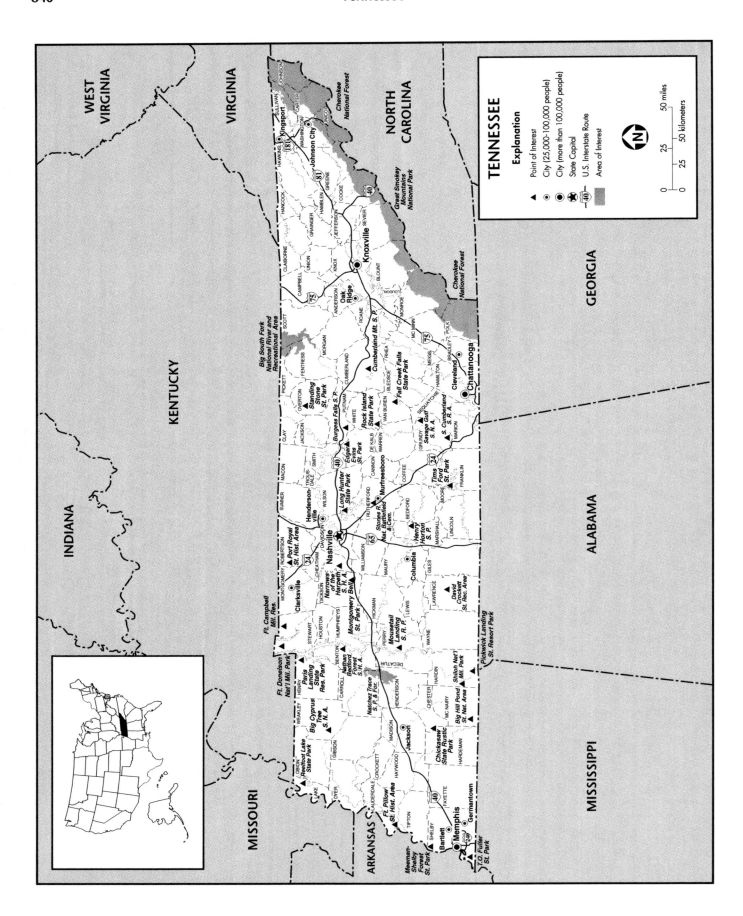

TENNESSEE

Explanation

Point of Interest
City (25,000-100,000 people)
City (more than 100,000 people)
State Capital
U.S. Interstate Route
Area of Interest

50 miles
50 kilometers

WEST VIRGINIA

VIRGINIA

KENTUCKY

INDIANA

MISSOURI

ARKANSAS

MISSISSIPPI

ALABAMA

GEORGIA

NORTH CAROLINA

JOHNSON

CARTER

Cherokee National Forest

SULLIVAN

Kingsport

WASHINGTON

Johnson City

HAWKINS

UNICOI

HANCOCK

GREENE

Great Smokey Mountains National Park

GRAINGER

HAMBLEN

COCKE

CLAIBORNE

UNION

JEFFERSON

SEVIER

Knoxville

CAMPBELL

KNOX

BLOUNT

Oak Ridge

ANDERSON

ROANE

MONROE

Cherokee National Forest

SCOTT

MORGAN

CUMBERLAND

RHEA

MC MINN

POLK

Big South Fork National River and Recreational Area

FENTRESS

Cumberland Mt. S.P.

MEIGS

BRADLEY

Cleveland

Chattanooga

HAMILTON

PICKETT

Standing Stone St. Park

PUTNAM

WHITE

Fall Creek Falls State Park

BLEDSOE

SEQUATCHIE

OVERTON

Burgess Falls S.P.

Rock Island State Park

VAN BUREN

S. Cumberland S.R.A.

Savage Gulf S.N.A.

MARION

CLAY

JACKSON

DE KALB

WARREN

GRUNDY

Edgar Evins St. Park

CANNON

COFFEE

MACON

SMITH

Long Hunter State Park

MOORE

Tims Ford St. Park

FRANKLIN

SUMNER

TROUSDALE

WILSON

Hendersonville

RUTHERFORD

Murfreesboro

BEDFORD

LINCOLN

Henry Horton S.P.

MARSHALL

Stones R. Nat. Battlefield & Cem.

ROBERTSON

Port Royal St. Hist. Area

Nashville

DAVIDSON

Columbia

GILES

MONTGOMERY

CHEATHAM

WILLIAMSON

MAURY

LAWRENCE

David Crockett St. Rec. Area

Clarksville

DICKSON

Narrows of the Harpeth S.H.A.

HICKMAN

LEWIS

Ft. Campbell Mil. Res.

STEWART

HOUSTON

Montgomery Bell St. Park

HUMPHREYS

PERRY

WAYNE

Mousetail Landing S.R.P.

Pickwick Landing St. Resort Park

Ft. Donelson Nat'l Mil. Park

HENRY

Paris Landing State Res. Park

BENTON

Nathan Bedford Forrest S.H.A.

DECATUR

HARDIN

Shiloh Nat'l Mil. Park

WEAKLEY

CARROLL

HENDERSON

CHESTER

MC NARY

Big Hill Pond St. Nat. Area

OBION

Reelfoot Lake State Park

GIBSON

MADISON

Jackson

Chickasaw State Rustic St. Park

HARDEMAN

Big Cypress Tree S.N.A.

LAKE

DYER

CROCKETT

HAYWOOD

Natchez Trace S.P. & For.

LAUDERDALE

Ft. Pillow St. Hist. Area

TIPTON

FAYETTE

SHELBY

Memphis

Germantown

Bartlett

Meeman-Shelby Forest St. Park

T.O. Fuller St. Park

Between 1990 and 2000, Tennessee's population grew from 4,877,185 to 5,689,283, an increase of 16.7%. The population is projected to reach 7,249,000 by 2005 and 6.7 million by 2025. The population density in 1998 was 138 persons per sq mi.

In 2000 the median age was 35.9. Persons under 18 years old accounted for 24.6% of the population while 12.4% were age 65 or older.

The first permanent white settlements in the state were established in the 1760s, when people from North Carolina and Virginia crossed the Unaka Mountains and settled in the fertile valleys. Between 1790 and 1800, the population increased threefold, from 35,690 to 105,600, and it doubled during each of the next two decades. After the Civil War, the population continued to increase, though at a slower rate, tripling between 1870 and 1970.

A pronounced urban trend became apparent after World War II. In 1960, for the first time in the state's history, census figures showed slightly more people living in urban than in rural areas. In the 1990s, approximately 70% of all Tennesseans lived in metropolitan areas. Memphis is the state's largest city; in 2002, it had an estimated population of 648,882. Nashville (Davidson County) had 545,915, followed by Knoxville, 173,661, and Chattanooga, 155,404. The Memphis metropolitan area, including parts of Arkansas and Mississippi, had an estimated 1,105,058 residents in 1999, while metropolitan Nashville had 1,171,755.

7ETHNIC GROUPS

For nearly a century after the earliest white settlements, Tennessee was inhabited by three ethnoracial populations: whites of English and Scotch-Irish descent, Cherokee Indians, and black Americans. Settlers crossing the Appalachians met Indian resistance as early as the late 1700s. Eventually, however, nearly all the Cherokee were forced to leave; in 2000 there were an estimated 15,152 American Indians in Tennessee, up from 10,000, the number recorded by the 1990 census.

Blacks, originally brought into the state as slaves to work in the cotton fields of West Tennessee, made up about 10% of the population in 1790. White Tennesseans were divided on the issue of slavery. The small farmers of the eastern region were against it, and in the late 1820s and 1830s there were more antislavery societies in Tennessee than in any other southern state except North Carolina. The planters and merchants of southwest Tennessee, however, linked their sentiments and interests with those of the proslavery planters of the Mississippi Valley. The introduction of the cotton gin gave impetus to the acquisition of more slaves; by 1840, blacks accounted for 26% of the population, and Memphis had become a major market for the shipment of black slaves to large plantations farther south.

Immediately after the Civil War, many blacks, now free, migrated from Virginia and North Carolina to East Tennessee to become farmers, artisans, and owners of small businesses. After 1880, however, the black proportion of the population declined steadily. In 2000, the estimated black population was 932,809 (16% of the state total), up from 778,000 in 1990. In 2000, there were an estimated 56,662 Asians residing in the state; 12,835 Asian Indians constituted the largest group. Pacific Islanders numbered 2,205.

Descendants of European immigrants make up about half the population of Tennessee, the largest groups being of English and German descent. In 2000, 159,004 residents—2.8% of the population—were foreign-born, more than twice the 1990 total of 59,114 (1.2%). In 2000, there were 123,838 Hispanics and Latinos, representing 2.2% of the total population, up from 62,000 (1.1%) in 1990.

8LANGUAGES

White settlers found Tennessee inhabited by Cherokee Indians in the eastern mountains, Shawnee in most of the eastern and central region, and Chickasaw in the west—all of them speakers of Hokan-Siouan languages. Subsequently removed to Indian Territory, they left behind such place-names as Chickamauga, Chattanooga, and Chilhowee, as well as Tennessee itself.

Tennessee English represents a mixture of North Midland and South Midland features brought into the northeastern and northcentral areas, of South Midland and Southern features introduced by settlers from Virginia and the Carolinas, and of a few additional Southern terms in the extreme western fringe, to which they were carried from Mississippi and Louisiana. Certain pronunciations exhibit a declining frequency from the Appalachians to the Mississippi River, such as /r/ after a vowel in the same syllable, as in *form* and *short,* and a rounded /aw/ before /r/ in *arm* and *barbed.* Others occur statewide, such as the /ah/ vowel in *forest* and *foreign, coop* and *Cooper* with the vowel of *book,* and simplification of the long / i/ vowel, so that *lice* sounds like *lass.* Common are such non-Northern terms as *wait on* (wait for), *pullybone* (along with Northern wishbone), *nicker* (neigh), *light bread* (white bread), and *snake feeder* (dragonfly), as well as *Jew's harp, juice harp,* and *French harp* (all for harmonica). In eastern Tennessee are found *goobers* (peanuts), *tote* (carry), *plum peach* (clingstone peach), *ash cake* (a kind of cornbread), *fireboard* (mantel), *redworm* (earthworm), *branch* (stream), and *peckerwood* (woodpecker). Appearing in western Tennessee are *loaf bread, cold drink* (soft drink), and *burlap bag.* In Memphis, a large, long sandwich is a *poorboy.*

In 2000, 5,059,404 Tennesseans five years old and over—95.2% of the population in that age group—spoke only English at home, down from 97% in 1990.

The following table gives selected statistics from the 2000 census for language spoken at home by persons five years old and over. The category "African languages" includes Amharic, Ibo, Twi, Yoruba, Bantu, Swahili, and Somali. The category "Other Indo-European languages" includes Albanian, Gaelic, Lithuanian, and Rumanian.

LANGUAGE	NUMBER	PERCENT
Population 5 years and over	5,315,920	100.0
Speak only English	5,059,404	95.2
Speak a language other than English	256,516	4.8
Speak a language other than English	256,516	4.8
Spanish or Spanish Creole	133,931	2.5
German	20,267	0.4
French (incl. Patois, Cajun)	17,557	0.3
Chinese	7,492	0.1
Vietnamese	6,625	0.1
Korean	6,550	0.1
Arabic	6,482	0.1
Laotian	4,496	0.1
African languages	4,480	0.1
Japanese	4,423	0.1
Other Indo-European languages	4,250	0.1
Tagalog	3,386	0.1
Italian	3,134	0.1

9RELIGIONS

Baptist and Presbyterian churches were organized on the frontier soon after permanent settlements were made. Many divisions have occurred in both groups. The Cumberland Presbyterian Church, which spread into other states, was organized near Nashville in 1810 because of differences within the parent church. Both the Baptists and the Presbyterians divided over slavery. Methodist circuit riders arrived with the early settlers, and they quickly succeeded in attracting many followers. Controversies over slavery and other sectional issues also developed within the Methodist Church and, as with the Baptists and Presbyterians, divisions emerged during the 1840s. The Methodists, however, were able to resolve their differences and regroup. The United Presbyterian Church and the Presbyterian Church in the US finally ended their 122-year separation in 1983, reuniting to form the Presbyterian Church (USA).

Two other Protestant groups with large followings in the state had their origin on the Tennessee frontier in the first half of the 19th century: the Disciples of Christ and the Church of Christ. Both groups began with the followers of Thomas and Alexander Campbell and Barton W. Stone, among others, who deplored formal creeds and denominations and sought to return to the purity of early Christianity. As their numbers grew, these followers divided into Progressives, who supported missionary societies and instrumental music in church, and Conservatives, who did not. In 1906, a federal census of religions listed the Conservatives for the first time as the Church of Christ and the Progressives as the Disciples of Christ. The latter, now the Christian Church (Disciples of Christ) had 28,108 known adherents in 2000. The Church of God (Cleveland, Tennessee) was established in the state in 1886 as a result of the greater Pentecostal movement.

Tennessee has long been considered part of the Bible Belt because of the influence of fundamentalist Protestant groups that believe in the literal accuracy of the Bible. Evangelical Protestants still account for a majority of the religiously active population. In 2000, the largest single religious group in the state was the Southern Baptist Convention with 1,414,199 adherents. Other Evangelical groups were the Churches of Christ, 216,648; the Church of God (Cleveland, Tennessee), 66,136; Independent, Non-Charismatic Churches, 50,003; and Assemblies of God, 40,430. The major Mainline Protestant denominations were the United Methodist Church, 393,994; the Presbyterian Church USA, 67,800; and the Episcopal Church, 35,037. There were 183,161 Roman Catholics, 18,464 Muslims, and an estimated 18,250 Jews in the state. About 2.7 million people (48,9% of the population) were not counted as members of any religious organization.

10 TRANSPORTATION

Memphis, Nashville, Knoxville, and Chattanooga are the focal points for rail, highway, water, and air transportation. All are located on important rivers and interstate highways, and all have airports served by the major airlines.

Railroad building began in Tennessee as early as the 1820s. During the 1850s, the basis for 20th-century rail transportation was laid: the Louisville and Nashville Railroad linked Tennessee to the northern states, and the Memphis and Charleston line established ties with the East Coast. In 2000, Tennessee had 2,929 rail mi (4,713 km) of track, of which 2,331 mi (3,751 km) were Class I track. No east-west passenger trains operate in the state today (Amtrak serves Memphis on the Chicago–New Orleans route), but considerable freight is hauled.

The first roads—such as the Natchez Trace, which connected Nashville with the southwestern part of the state—often followed Indian trails. Many roads in the early 1800s were constructed by private individuals or chartered turnpike companies. The introduction of the automobile shortly after the beginning of the 20th century brought the development of modern roads and highways. After 1916, the federal government began to share the high cost of highway construction, and the 1920s were a decade of extensive road building.

In 2000, Tennessee had 69,679 mi (112,137 km) of rural roads and 17,740 mi (28,549 km) of urban roads. The major interstate highway is I-40, crossing east-west from Knoxville to Nashville and Memphis. In 2000, 4,890,883 motor vehicles were registered in the state, and 4,251,228 Tennesseans held drivers' licenses.

The principal means of transportation during Tennessee's early history was water, and all the early settlements were built on or near streams. The introduction of steamboats on the Cumberland River in the early 19th century helped make Nashville the state's largest city and its foremost trading center. By mid-century, however, Memphis, on the Mississippi River, had surpassed Nashville in population and trade, largely because of cotton. Tennessee has about 1,000 mi (1,600 km) of navigable waterways. The completion in 1985 of the 234-mi (377-km) Tennessee-Tombigbee Waterway gave Tennessee shippers a direct north-south route for all vessels between the Tennessee River and the Gulf of Mexico via the Black Warrior River in Alabama. Although none of the waterway runs through Tennessee, the northern terminus is on the Tennessee River near the common borders of Tennessee, Alabama, and Mississippi. In 2000, the ports of Memphis and Nashville handled 18.3 million and 4.5 million tons of freight, respectively.

In 2002, there were 185 public and private airports, 87 heliports, 8 stolports, and 2 seaplane bases in the state. As of 2000, Memphis International Airport was among the world's busiest cargo-handling facilities; it was also the state's major air terminal in terms of enplanement. Nashville International retains the lead in terms of aircraft operations.

11 HISTORY

The lower Tennessee Valley was heavily populated with hunter-gatherers some 10,000 years ago. Their descendants, called Paleo-Indians, were succeeded by other native cultures, including the Archaic Indians, Woodland Indians, and Early Mississippians. When the first Spanish arrived in the early 16th century, Creek Indians were living in what is now East Tennessee, along with the Yuchi. About 200 years later, the powerful Cherokee—the largest single tribe south of the Ohio River, occupying parts of North Carolina, South Carolina, Georgia, and East Tennessee—drove the Creek and Yuchi out of the area and established themselves as the dominant tribe. Their settlements, varying in size from a dozen families to more than 200, were known as the Upper or Overhill Towns. The Cherokee retained their tribal dominance until they were forced out by the federal government in the 1830s. In West Tennessee, the Chickasaw were the major group. They lived principally in northern Mississippi but used Tennessee lands as a hunting ground. Shawnee occupied the Cumberland Valley in Middle Tennessee until driven north of the Ohio River by the Cherokee and Chickasaw.

Explorers and traders from continental Europe and the British Isles were in Tennessee for well over 200 years before permanent settlements were established in the 1760s. Hernando de Soto, a Spaniard, came from Florida to explore the area as early as 1540. He was followed during the 17th century by the French explorers Jacques Marquette, Louis Jolliet, and Robert Cavelier, Sieur de la Salle. Englishmen were not far behind: by the mid-1700s, hundreds—perhaps thousands—had crossed the Appalachian barrier and explored the transmontane country beyond, which was claimed first by the colony of Virginia and later assigned to North Carolina. They came in search of pelts, furs, and whatever else of value they might find. A fiercely independent breed, they were accustomed to hardship and unwilling to settle in a civilized community. Perhaps the best known was Daniel Boone, who by 1760 had found his way into present-day Washington County.

With the conclusion of the French and Indian War in 1763, many people from North Carolina and Virginia began to cross the Alleghenies. Elisha Walden was among those who first led groups of "long hunters" into the wilderness. By 1770, small pockets of white settlement were developing in the valley between the Unaka and Cumberland mountains. In the two decades that followed, more than 35,000 people settled on soil soon to become the State of Tennessee.

Two major areas of settlement developed. The larger one-in the northeast along the Holston, Nolichucky, and Watauga rivers-was organized as the Watauga Association in 1791. The second major area was in the Cumberland Basin, where James Robertson, under the sponsorship of the Transylvania Company (formed by eastern land speculators), established a settlement he called Nashborough (now Nashville) in 1779. There more than 250 adult males signed the Cumberland Compact, which established a government. They pledged to abide by the will of the majority and expressed their allegiance to North Carolina.

The Revolutionary War did not reach as far west as Tennessee, but many of the frontiersmen fought in the Carolinas and Virginia. The most famous battle involving these early Tennesseans was that of Kings Mountain, in South Carolina, where Colonel John Sevier and others defeated a superior force of British soldiers and captured more than 1,000 prisoners. Hardly was the Revolution over when Tennesseans began to think about statehood for themselves. As early as 1784, leaders in three mountain counties—Greene, Sullivan, and Washington—established the Free State of Franklin. John Sevier was chosen as governor, and an assembly was formed. Only after border warfare developed and factionalism weakened their cause did Franklin's leaders abandon their plans and return their allegiance to North Carolina. But the spirit of independence—indeed, defiance—persisted.

In 1790, less than two years after Franklin collapsed, North Carolina ceded its western lands to the US. Tennessee became known as the Southwest Territory, with William Blount, a prominent North Carolina speculator and politician, as its governor. During his six-year tenure, a government was organized and a capital established at Knoxville. The population doubled to more than 70,000 in 1795, and steps were taken to convert the territory into a state. When the territorial legislature presented Congress with a petition for statehood, a lively debate ensued in the US Senate between Jeffersonian Democratic-Republicans, who urged immediate admission, and Federalists, who opposed it. The Jeffersonians triumphed, and on 1 June 1796, President George Washington signed a bill admitting Tennessee as the 16th state. Sevier became governor of the new state, Blount was elected to the US Senate, and Andrew Jackson became the state's first US representative.

Sevier dominated state politics for the first two decades of statehood, and he had little difficulty in thwarting the ambitions of Andrew Jackson and others who sought to challenge his leadership. Tennessee's population, about 85,000 when Sevier became governor, was more than 250,000 when he left the statehouse in 1809. Under Sevier's governorship, Nashville, Knoxville, and other early settlements became thriving frontier towns. Churches and schools were established, industry and agriculture developed, and Tennessee became a leading iron producer.

Andrew Jackson's rise to prominence came as a result of the Battle of New Orleans, fought at the conclusion of the War of 1812. Jackson, who had little difficulty raising troops in a state where volunteers for military service have always been abundant, lost only about a half dozen of his men, while British casualties exceeded 2,000. He returned to Nashville a hero, built a fine house that he named The Hermitage, received thousands of congratulatory messages, and conferred with friends about his political and military future. In 1823, Jackson was elected to the US Senate. Defeated the following year in a four-man race for the presidency, he ran again, this time successfully, in 1828, serving in that office for eight years.

Jackson alienated himself from many people in the state after 1835, when he announced his support of Martin Van Buren for president instead of Knoxvillian Hugh Lawson White, an avowed candidate. A majority of Tennesseans joined the new Whig Party,

which arose in opposition to Jackson's Democratic Party, and voted in the 1836 presidential election for White instead of for Van Buren. The Whigs won every presidential election in Tennessee from 1836 to 1852, including the election of 1844, which sent Tennessean James Knox Polk, a Democrat, to the White House. Polk's term (1845–49) brought another war, this one with Mexico. Although Tennessee's quota was only 2,800, more than 25,000 men volunteered for service. Among the heroes of that war were William Trousdale and William B. Campbell, both of whom later were elected governor.

Social reform and cultural growth characterized the first half of the 19th century. A penitentiary was built, and the penal code made somewhat more humane. Temperance newspapers were published, temperance societies formed, and laws passed to curtail the consumption of alcoholic beverages. In 1834, a few women, embracing the feminist cause, were influential in giving the courts, rather than the legislature, the right to grant divorces. Many important schools were established, including the Nashville Female Academy, the University of Nashville, and more than two dozen colleges.

More than most other southern states, antebellum Tennessee was divided over the issue of slavery. Slaves had accompanied their owners into Tennessee in the 18th century, and by 1850, they constituted about one-fourth of the state's population. Although slaveholders lived in all sections of the state, they predominated in the west, where cotton was grown profitably, as well as in Middle Tennessee. In East Tennessee, where blacks made up less than 10% of the population, antislavery sentiment thrived. Most of those who supported emancipation urged that it be accomplished peacefully, gradually, and with compensation to the slave owners. Frances Wright, the Scottish reformer, founded the colony of Nashoba near Memphis in the 1820s as a place where freed blacks could learn self-reliance. After a few years the colony failed, however, and Wright took her colonists to Haiti. At the constitutional convention of 1834, hundreds of petitions were presented asking that the legislature be empowered to free the slaves. But while the convention endorsed several measures to democratize the constitution of 1796—abolishing property qualifications as a condition for holding office, for example—it decided against emancipation.

Considerable economic growth took place during this period. West Tennessee became a major cotton-growing area immediately after it was purchased form the Chickasaw in 1818, and Memphis, established in 1821, became the principal cotton-marketing center. The Volunteer State's annual cotton crop grew from less than 3,000 bales in 1810 to nearly 200,000 bales by midcentury. The counties of the Highland Rim produced tobacco in such abundance that, by 1840, Tennessee ranked just behind Kentucky and Virginia in total production. East Tennessee farmers practiced greater crop diversification, growing a variety of fruits and vegetables for market. Silk cultivation flourished briefly in the 1830s and 1840s.

Tennessee became a major battleground during the Civil War, as armies from both North and South crossed the state several times. Most Tennesseans favored secession. But the eastern counties remained staunchly Unionist, and many East Tennesseans crossed over into Kentucky to enlist in the Union Army. General Albert Sidney Johnston, the Confederate commander of the western theater, set up lines of defense across the northern border of the state and built forts on both the Cumberland and Tennessee rivers. In February 1862, Ft. Donelson and Ft. Henry were taken by General Ulysses S. Grant and naval Captain Andrew H. Foote, thereby opening the state to Union armies. Within two weeks Nashville was in the hands of the enemy. Northern troops pushed farther south and west, taking key positions on the Mississippi River. Less than two months later, on 6 April, Union forces near the Mississippi state line engaged Johnston's army in the Battle of Shiloh. Both sides suffered tremendous losses, including Johnston himself, who bled to death after sustaining a thigh wound. In the meantime President Abraham Lincoln had established a military government for the conquered state and appointed Andrew Johnson to head it. Johnson, who had served two terms as governor a decade earlier, had been elected to the US Senate in 1858; he remained there in 1861, the only southern senator to do so, refusing to follow his state into the Confederacy. In 1864, he was elected vice president under Lincoln.

Johnson's governorship did not mean the end of Confederate activities in Tennessee. Late in December 1862, Confederate forces made the first of two vigorous attempts to rid the state of the invader. General Braxton Bragg, who replaced Johnston as Confederate commander, established himself at Murfreesboro, 30 mi (48 km) southwest of Nashville, and threatened to retake the capital city. But at the Battle of Stones River, Union troops under General William S. Rosecrans forced Bragg to retreat to the southeast. Fighting did not resume until 19–20 September 1863, when the Confederates drove Union troops back to Chattanooga in the Battle of Chickamauga, one of the bloodiest engagements of the war. The second major Confederate drive occurred in November and December 1864, when General John B. Hood, commanding the Confederate Army of Tennessee, came out of Georgia and attacked the Union forces at Franklin and Nashville. Hood's army was destroyed, and these battles were the last major engagements in the state.

Returning to the Union in 1866, Tennessee was the only former Confederate state not to have a military government during Reconstruction. Economic readjustment was not as difficult as elsewhere in the South, and within a few years agricultural production exceeded antebellum levels. Extensive coal and iron deposits in East Tennessee attracted northern capital, and by the early 1880s, flour, woolen, and paper mills were established in all the urban areas. By the late 1890s, Memphis was a leading cotton market and the nation's foremost producer of cottonseed oil. Politically, the Democratic Party became firmly entrenched, and would remain so until the 1950s.

As the 20th century dawned, the major issue in Tennessee was the crusade against alcohol, a movement with deep roots in the 19th century. Though the major cities still were "wet," earlier legislation had dried up the rural areas and small towns, and the Tennessee Anti-Saloon League and Women's Christian Temperance Union (WCTU) kept the matter in the public eye. In 1908, with "wet" forces controlling the state government, Edward Ward Carmack—a rabid prohibitionist, powerful politician, newspaper editor, and former US senator—was shot and killed in the street of Nashville. His assailants were convicted but pardoned immediately by the governor. In the following year, with Carmack as a martyr to their cause, "dry" forces enacted legislation that, in effect, imposed prohibition on the entire state. The dominant Democratic Party was divided and demoralized to such an extent that a Republican governor was elected-only the second since Reconstruction. The prohibition movement helped promote the cause of women's suffrage. A proposed state constitutional amendment giving women the right to vote failed in 1915, but in 1919, they were granted the franchise in municipal elections. One year later, Tennessee became the 36th state to ratify the 19th Amendment to the US Constitution, thereby granting women the right to vote nationwide.

The 1920s brought a resurgence of religious fundamentalism. When, in 1925, the legislature enacted a measure that prohibited the teaching of the theory of evolution in the public schools, a high school teacher named John T. Scopes decided to challenge the law. Three-time presidential candidate and fundamentalist spokesman William Jennings Bryan arrived in the tiny town of Dayton to aid in Scopes's prosecution, while the great civil

liberties lawyer Clarence Darrow came from Chicago to lead the defense. The Scopes trial gave the Volunteer State unwanted notoriety throughout the civilized world. Scopes was convicted, and it was not until 1967 that the law was repealed.

The 1930s brought depression, but they also brought the Tennessee Valley Authority. Before TVA, residents of the Tennessee River Valley could boast of the beauty of the landscape, but of little else. The soil was so thin that little other than subsistence agriculture was possible, and many people lived on cash incomes of less than $100 a year. There were some senators, such as George Norris of Nebraska and Tennessee's own Kenneth D. McKellar, who saw great possibilities in valley development. Harnessing the Tennessee River with dams could not only generate electricity inexpensively but also greatly improve navigation; aid flood control, soil conservation, and reforestation; and produce nitrate fertilizer. Efforts to establish such a program failed, however, until Franklin D. Roosevelt included it in his New Deal. The law establishing the TVA was passed a few weeks after Roosevelt's inauguration in 1933, and dam construction began almost immediately. Before TVA, people in the valley consumed only 1.5 billion kWh of electricity annually; but consumption increased to 11.5 billion kWh by 1945 and to 57.5 billion kWh by 1960. Fewer than 2% of rural families in Tennessee had electricity in 1933; but by the late 1930s, power lines were being strung into remote areas, bringing to practically everyone the advantages that hitherto only urban residents had enjoyed. Inexpensive power became a magnet for industry, and industrial employment in the region nearly doubled in two decades. The building of a plant for the production of atomic weapons at Oak Ridge in 1942 was due in large measure to the availability of TVA power.

The TVA notwithstanding, the depression caused many manufacturers to close or curtail operations, and farm prices declined drastically. Cotton, which had earlier brought farmers more than 30 cents a pound, declined to 5.7 cents, and the prices of corn, tobacco, and other crops fell proportionately. The state still was in the grip of financial depression when World War II began. Thousands of men volunteered for service before conscription was introduced; when the US entered the war in 1941, several training posts were established in Tennessee. Tennessee firms manufacturing war materiel received contracts amounting to $1.25 billion and employed more than 200,000 people during the war. Industrial growth continued during the postwar period, while agriculture recovered and diversified. The chemical industry, spurred by high demand during and after World War II, became a leading sector, along with textiles, apparel, and food processing. Cotton and tobacco continued to be major crops, but by the early 1970s, soybeans had taken the lead, accounting for 22% of estimated farm income in 1980. Beef and dairy production also flourished.

Democratic boss Edward H. Crump, who ran an efficient political machine in Memphis, dominated state politics for most of the period between 1910 and the early 1950s, an era that saw the elevation of many Tennessee Democrats to national prominence. Considerable progress was made toward ending racial discrimination during the postwar years, although the desegregation of public schools was accomplished only after outbursts of violence at Clinton, Nashville, and Memphis. The killing of civil rights leader Martin Luther King, Jr., in Memphis in 1968 resulted in rioting by blacks in that city. The most notable political development during the 1970s was the resurgence of the Republican Party, making Tennessee one of the few true two-party states in the South.

The early 1980s saw the exposure of corruption in high places: former governor Ray Blanton and several aides were convicted for conspiracy to sell liquor licenses, and banker and former gubernatorial candidate Jacob F. "Jake" Butcher was convicted for fraud in the aftermath of the collapse of his banking empire. On the brighter side, there was a successful World's Fair in 1982, the Knoxville International Energy Exposition, and a fairly resilient state economy, bolstered by the much-heralded openings of the Nissan truck-assembly plant in Smyrna in 1983 and the General Motors Saturn plant in Spring Hill in 1990.

Manufacturing in Tennessee continued to grow throughout the 1980s, aided by the completion of the Tennessee-Tombigbee Waterway in 1985. The state gained nearly 45,000 manufacturing jobs between 1982 and 1992, many of them in the automotive and other transport-related industries. Tennessee's unemployment rate fell to a 16-year low of 4.7% in 1994.

The state legislature passed school reform laws in 1992 and, in 1993, a healthcare package mandating the creation of TennCare, an insurance program designed to replace Medicaid coverage for 1.5 million uninsured residents of the state.

Democratic Governor Phil Bredesen, elected in 2002, served two terms as Nashville mayor and hoped in 2003, despite the state's budget problems, to repeat statewide the significant economic growth he spearheaded in Nashville. The state was a leader in the nation in attempting to collect internet and mail-order sales taxes. Tennessee officials estimated the state could lose up to $300 million in uncollected internet and mail-order sales taxes in 2003.

12 STATE GOVERNMENT

Tennessee's first constitution was adopted in 1796, just before the state was admitted to the Union. It vested executive authority in a governor, elected for two years, who had to be at least 25 years old and own at least 500 acres (202 hectares) of land. The governor could approve or veto bills adopted by the legislature, as commander-in-chief of the militia, and could grant pardons and reprieves, among other powers. Legislative power was placed in a general assembly, consisting of a house and senate, whose members served terms of two years. Candidates for the legislature were required to fulfill residence and age requirements and to own at least 200 acres (81 hectares). Property qualifications were not required for voting, and all freemen—including free blacks—could vote.

The basic governmental structure established in 1796 remains the fundamental law today. The constitution has been amended 36 times as of January 2003, however. The spirit of Jacksonian democracy prompted delegates at the constitutional convention of 1834 to remove property qualifications as a requirement for public office, reapportion representation, transfer the right to select county officials from justices of the peace to the voters, and reorganize the court system. At the same time, though, free blacks were disfranchised. In 1870, another constitutional convention confirmed the abolition of slavery and the enfranchisement of black men but imposed a poll tax as a requirement for voting. Membership of the house was fixed at 99 and the senate at 33-numbers, these numbers are retained today. Assembling each January, regular sessions are limited to 90 legislative days. Special sessions, limited to 30 legislative days, may be called by petition of two-thirds of each house. All legislators must be US citizens, qualified voters in their districts, citizens of the state, and must have lived in the state for at least three years. Senators are required to be at least 30 years old and representatives 21. The legislative salary in 2002 was $16,500, unchanged from 1999.

In the constitutional convention held in 1953, delegates increased the gubernatorial term from two to four years, gave the governor item-veto, eliminated the poll tax, authorized home rule for cities, and provided for the consolidation of county and city functions. Later conventions extended the term of state senators from two to four years, sought to improve and streamline county government, and placed a constitutional limit on state spending. A limited convention in 1965 required the apportionment of the legislature according to population. This change greatly increased the weight of urban, and particularly black, votes.

The governor, the only executive elected statewide, appoints a cabinet of 21 members. The speaker of the state senate automatically becomes lieutenant governor; the secretary of state, treasurer, and comptroller of the treasury are chosen by the legislature. The governor is limited to serving two consecutive terms. A candidate for governor must be at least 30 years old, a US citizen, and must have been a state citizen for at least seven years prior to election. In 2002 the governor's salary was $85,000, unchanged from 1999.

Legislation is enacted after bills are read and approved three times in each house and signed by the governor. If the governor vetoes a measure, the legislature may override the veto by majority vote of the elected members of each house. If the governor does not act on a bill, it becomes law after 10 days. Not more often than once every six years the legislature may submit to the voters the question of calling a convention to amend the constitution. If the vote is favorable, delegates are chosen. Changes proposed by the convention must be approved by a majority vote in a subsequent election. To amend the constitution, a majority of the members elected to both houses must first approve the proposed change. A second (two-thirds) vote by the legislature is required before the measure is put before the state's voters for majority approval.

Voters must be US citizens, at least 18 years old, and state residents. Restrictions apply to convicted felons and those declared mentally incompetent by the court.

13 POLITICAL PARTIES

The major political groups are the Democratic and Republican parties. Minor parties have seldom affected the outcome of an election in Tennessee.

When Tennessee entered the Union in 1796, it was strongly loyal to the Democratic-Republican Party. The Jacksonian era brought a change in political affiliations, and for more than 20 years, Tennessee had a vibrant two-party system. Jackson's followers formed the Democratic Party, which prevailed for a decade over the National Republican Party led by John Quincy Adams and Henry Clay. But by 1835, Tennesseans had become disillusioned with Jackson, and they joined the new Whig Party in large numbers. A Whig governor was elected in that year, and Whig presidential nominees consistently garnered Tennessee's electoral votes until the party foundered over the slavery issue in the 1850s.

After the Civil War and Reconstruction, Tennessee was part of the solid Democratic South for nearly a century. Only three Republican governors were elected during that period, and only then because bitter factionalism had divided the dominant party. East Tennessee remained a Republican stronghold. However, the 2nd Congressional district, which includes Knoxville, was the only district in the country to elect a Republican continuously from 1860 on. Republicans Warren G. Harding and Herbert Hoover carried the state in the presidential elections of 1920 and 1928. But whereas the 1920s saw a tendency away from one-party domination, Franklin D. Roosevelt and the New Deal brought the Volunteer State decisively back into the Democratic fold. Tennesseans voted overwhelmingly Democratic in the four elections that Roosevelt won (1932–44).

After World War II, the one-party system in Tennessee was shaken anew. Dwight D. Eisenhower narrowly won the state in 1952 and 1956, although Tennessee Senator Estes Kefauver was the Democratic vice-presidential nominee in the latter year. Tennesseans chose Richard Nixon all three times he ran for president. In fact, between 1948 and 1976, the only Democratic nominees to carry the state came from the South (Lyndon

Johnson and Jimmy Carter) or from a border state (Harry Truman).

In state elections, the Republicans made deep inroads into Democratic power during the 1960s and 1970s. In 1966, Howard Baker became the first popularly elected Republican US senator in the state history. In 1970, voters elected Winfield Dunn as the first Republican governor in more than 50 years, and in the same year, they sent Republican Bill Brock to join Baker in the Senate. The Democrats regained the governorship in 1974 and Brock's seat in 1976, but Republicans again won the governorship in 1978 when Lamar Alexander defeated Jacob F. "Jake" Butcher. In 1982, Alexander became the first Tennessee governor to be elected to two successive four-year terms. Ned McWherter, a Democrat, was elected governor in 1990. Republican Don Sundquist became governor in 1994 and was reelected in 1998. Democrat Phil Bredesen was elected governor in 2002.

In 1994, Bill Frist, a heart surgeon, was elected to the US Senate on the Republican ticket, defeating Democrat James Sasser. He was reelected in 2000, and elected Senate Majority Leader in December 2002 after former Majority Leader Trent Lott aroused controversy by praising the 1948 presidential candidacy of segregationist Strom Thurmond. Democrat Harlan Matthews was appointed to fill the seat vacated by Al Gore in 1992 when Gore became vice president. In 1994, Republican Fred Thompson defeated Jim Cooper for the remaining two years of Gore's term. Thompson was elected to his first full term in 1996, but retired in 2002. That November, former Governor Lamar Alexander was elected US Senator from Tennessee. US representatives included four Republicans and five Democrats after the November 2002 elections. There were 18 Democrats and 15 Republicans in the state senate and 54 Democrats and 45 Republicans in the state house in mid-2003.

Tennessee voters, who gave Republican George Bush 57.4% of the vote in 1988, chose Bill Clinton in 1992 and 1996. In 2000, Republican George W. Bush received 51% of the vote to Democrat Al Gore's 48%. In 2002 there were 3,134,104 registered voters; there is no party registration in the state. The state had 11 electoral votes in the 2000 presidential election.

[14]LOCAL GOVERNMENT

In 2002, local government in Tennessee was exercised by 92 counties and 349 municipalities. The county, a direct descendant of the Anglo-Saxon shire, has remained remarkably unaltered in Tennessee since it was brought from Virginia and North Carolina in frontier days. The constitution specifies that county officials must include at least a register, trustee (the custodian of county funds), sheriff, and county clerk, all of whom hold office for four years. Other officials have been added by legislative enactment: county commissioners, county executives (known for many years as county judges or county chairmen), tax assessors, county court clerks, and superintendents of public schools.

City government is of more recent origin than county government. There are three forms of municipal government: mayor-council (or mayor-alderman), council-manager, and commission. The mayor-council system is the oldest and by far the most widely employed. There were 14 public school districts and 475 special districts in 2002.

[15]STATE SERVICES

To address the continuing threat of terrorism and to work with the federal Department of Homeland Security (created in 2002 following the terrorist attacks of 11 September 2001), homeland security in Tennessee in 2003 operated under executive order; the deputy to the governor was designated as the state homeland security advisor.

The commissioner of education oversees the public schools as well as special, higher, and vocational-technical education. Highways, aeronautics, mass transit, and waterways are the responsibility of the Department of Transportation. The Department of Safety, including the State Highway Patrol, is charged with enforcing the safety laws on all state roads and interstate highways. Railroad regulation and the setting of railroad rates are the duties of the Public Service Commission. Public protection services are provided by the Military Department, which includes the Army and Air National Guard. The Department of Correction maintains prisons for adult offenders, a work-release program, and correctional and rehabilitation centers for juveniles. The Department of

Tennessee Presidential Vote by Political Parties, 1948–2000

YEAR	ELECTORAL VOTE	TENNESSEE WINNER	DEMOCRAT	REPUBLICAN	STATES' RIGHTS DEMOCRAT	SOCIALIST	PROGRESSIVE	PROHIBITION
1948	11	*Truman (D)	270,402	202,914	73,815	1,288	1,864	—
					CONSTITUTION	—		
1952	11	*Eisenhower (R)	443,710	446,147	379	—	887	1,432
1956	11	*Eisenhower (R)	456,507	462,288	19,820		—	789
					NATL. STATES' RIGHTS			
1960	11	Nixon (R)	481,453	556,577	11,298	—	—	2,450
1964	11	*Johnson (D)	635,047	508,965	—	—	—	—
					AMERICAN IND.			
1968	11	*Nixon (R)	351,233	472,592	424,792	—	—	—
							AMERICAN	—
1972	10	*Nixon (R)	357,293	813,147	—		30,373	—
								LIBERTARIAN
1976	10	*Carter (D)	825,897	633,969	2,303	—	5,769	1,375
					NATL. STATESMAN		CITIZENS	
1980	10	*Reagan (R)	783,051	787,761	5,0211	—	1,112	7,116
1984	11	*Reagan (R)	711,714	990,212	—	—	978	3,072
1988	11	*Bush (R)	679,794	947,233	—	—	1,334	2,041
					IND. (Perot)			
1992	11	*Clinton (D)	933,521	841,300	199,968	1,356	727	1,847
1996	11	*Clinton (D)	909,146	863,530	105,918	—	—	5,020
					IND. (Nader)		IND. (Buchanan)	
2000	11	*Bush, G. W. (R)	981,720	1,061,949	19,781		4,250	4,284

*Won US presidential election.

Environment and Conservation concerns itself with the environment.

The Department of Health licenses medical facilities, provides medical care for the indigent, operates tuberculosis treatment centers, and administers pollution control programs. The Department of Mental Health and Mental Retardation supervises mental hospitals, mental health clinics, and homes for retarded children. The Department of Human Services administers aid to the blind, aged, disabled, and families with dependent children, and determines eligibility for families receiving food stamps. The Department of Employment Security administers unemployment insurance and provides job training and placement services. State laws governing workers' compensation, occupational and mine safety, child labor, and wage standards are enforced by the Department of Labor.

16JUDICIAL SYSTEM

The supreme court is the highest court in the state. It consists of five justices, not more than two of whom may reside in any one grand division of the state—East, Middle, or West Tennessee. The justices are elected by popular vote for terms of eight years and must be at least 35 years of age. The court has appellate jurisdiction only, holding sessions in Nashville, Knoxville, and Jackson. The position of chief justice rotates every 19 months.

Immediately below the supreme court are two appellate courts (each sitting in three divisions), established by the legislature to relieve the crowded high court docket. The court of appeals has appellate jurisdiction in most civil cases. The court of criminal appeals hears cases from the lower courts involving criminal matters. Judges on both appellate courts are elected for eight-year terms.

Circuit courts have original jurisdiction in both civil and criminal cases. Tennessee still has chancery courts, vestiges of the English courts designed to hear cases where there was no adequate remedy at law. They administer cases involving receiverships of corporations, settle disputes regarding property ownership, hear divorce cases, and adjudicate on a variety of other matters. In some districts, judges of the circuit and chancery courts, all of whom are elected for eight-year terms, have concurrent jurisdiction.

At the bottom of the judicial structure are general sessions courts. A comprehensive juvenile court system was set up in 1911. Other courts created for specific services include domestic relations courts and probate courts.

As of June 2001, federal and state prisons in Tennessee had 23,168 inmates, an increase of 2.7% over the previous year. The state's incarceration rate stood at 404 per 100,000 inhabitants.

According to the FBI Crime Index, Tennessee's total crime rate stood at 5,152.8 per 100,000 population, including a total of 42,778 violent crimes and 252,992 crimes against property in that year. Tennessee does implement the death penalty; there were 105 persons under sentence of death in 2003. There has only been one execution in the state since 1977.

17ARMED FORCES

Tennessee supplied so many soldiers for the War of 1812 and the Mexican War that it became known as the Volunteer State. During the Civil War, more than 100,000 Tennesseans fought for the Confederacy and about half that number for the Union. In World War I, some 91,000 men served in the armed forces, and in World War II, 316,000 Tennesseans saw active duty.

In 2002, there were 2,554 active-duty military personnel and 5,496 civilian personnel stationed in Tennessee, most of whom were at Millington Naval Air Station near Memphis. Tennessee firms were awarded defense contracts totaling almost $1.03 billion in 2002.

According to the 2000 Census, 560,141 veterans were living in Tennessee, of whom 91,043 served in World War II; 64,585 in the Korean conflict; 171,540 during the Vietnam era; and 70,025 during 1990–2000 (including the Persian Gulf War). Veterans' benefits totaled nearly $1.4 billion in fiscal year 2002.

In 2000, the Tennessee Department of Public Safety employed 899 full-time sworn officers.

18MIGRATION

The first white settlers in Tennessee, who came across the mountains from North Carolina and Virginia, were almost entirely of English extraction. They were followed by an influx of Scotch-Irish, mainly from Pennsylvania. About 3,800 German and Irish migrants arrived during the 1830s and 1840s. In the next century, Tennessee's population remained relatively stable, except for an influx of blacks immediately following the Civil War. There was a steady out-migration of blacks to industrial centers in the North during the 20th century. The state suffered a net loss through migration of 462,000 between 1940 and 1970 but gained over 465,000 between 1970 and 1990. Between 1990 and 1998, Tennessee had net gains of 338,000 in domestic migration and 27,000 in international migration. In 1998, 2,806 foreign immigrants arrived in the state, the greatest concentrations coming from Mexico (300) and India (291). Tennessee's overall population increased 11.3% between 1990 and 1998.

The major in-state migration has been away from rural areas and into towns and cities. Blacks, especially, have tended to cluster in large urban centers. The population of metropolitan Memphis, for example, was more than 42% black in 1997. In the period 1995–2000, 567,966 people moved into the state and 421,652 moved out, for a net gain of 146,314, with about 52,918 moving into the state from Florida.

19INTERGOVERNMENTAL COOPERATION

Tennessee participates in such interstate agreements as the Appalachian Regioanl Commission, Interstate Mining Compact Commission, Southeastern Forest Fire Protection Compact, Southern Regional Education Board, Southern Growth Policies Board, and the Southern States Energy Board. There are boundary accords with Arkansas, Kentucky, and Virginia, and an agreement with Alabama, Kentucky, and Mississippi governing development of the Tennessee-Tombigbee waterway.

Federal grants to Tennessee amounted to $7 billion in 2001.

20ECONOMY

Tennessee's economy is based primarily on industry. Since the 1930s, the number of people employed in industry has grown at a rapid rate, while the number of farmers has declined proportionately. The principal manufacturing areas are Memphis, Nashville, Chattanooga, Knoxville, and Kingsport-Bristol. With the construction in the 1980s of a Nissan automobile and truck plant and a General Motors automobile facility, both in the area southeast of Nashville, Tennessee has become an important producer of transportation equipment. Since 1995, however, employment in Tennessee's manufacturing sector has fallen, and since 1999, total output from the sector has fallen (-3.2% between 1999 and 2001). The pace of job loss in manufactures accelerated in the 2001 national recession and slowdown, with 36,000 jobs lost during the year, 42% higher than any previous year. Manufacturing as a share of the state gross product fell from 21.5% in 1997 to 18.7% in 2001. The influx of new residents, from which Tennessee's economy benefited throughout the 1990s, fell to an eleven-year low with the fall in job growth in 2001. As of the fourth quarter 2002, the manufacturing jobs made up 17% of total employment in Tennessee, still above the national average of 13%. Income from agricultural products currently comes more from dairy and beef cattle and soybeans than from traditional crops, tobacco, cotton, and corn. Coming into the 21st century (1997 to 2001) the strongest growth in terms of contributions to state gross product has been in the various services sectors: output from general services increased 27.4%; from financial services, 29.5%; from the transportation and utilities sector, 27.4%; from government, 22.8%; and from trade, 17.8%.

In 2001, Tennessee's gross state product gross state product was $182.5 billion, the 18th largest among the states, to which general services contributed $39.7 billion; manufacturing, $34.2 billion; trade, $33.5 billion; financial services, $27.5 billion; government, $21.6 billion; transportation and public utilities, $15.4 billion, and construction, $8.2 billion. The public sector in 2001 constituted 12% of gross state product, the same as the average for all the states.

[21] INCOME

According to the Bureau of Economic Analysis, in 2001, Tennessee had a per capita personal income (PCPI) of $26,808 which ranked 36th in the United States (including the District of Columbia) and was 88% of the national average, $30,413. The 2001 PCPI reflected an increase of 2.0% from 2000 compared to the national change of 2.2%. In 2001, Tennessee had a total personal income (TPI) of $154,129,629,000 which ranked 20th in the United States and accounted for 1.8% of the national total. The 2001 TPI reflected an increase of 2.8% from 2000 compared to the national change of 3.3%.

Earnings of persons employed in Tennessee increased from $110,654,536,000 in 2000 to $112,771,356,000 in 2001, an increase of 1.9%. The largest industries in 2001 were services, 29.2% of earnings; durable goods manufacturing, 10.7%; and retail trade, 10.4%. Of the industries that accounted for at least 5% of earnings in 2001, the slowest growing from 2000 to 2001 was durable goods manufacturing, which decreased 6.9%; the fastest was state and local government (10.3% of earnings in 2001), which increased 5.9%.

According to data released by the US Census Bureau, in 2000, the median household income was $33,885 compared to the national average of $42,148. In 2001, the median income for a family of four was $56,052 compared to the national average of $63,278. For the period 1999 to 2001, the average poverty rate was 13.2% which placed it 40th among the 50 states and the District of Columbia ranked lowest to highest.

[22] LABOR

According to Bureau of Labor Statistics (BLS) provisional estimates, in July 2003 the seasonally adjusted civilian labor force in Tennessee numbered 2,901,500, with approximately 146,000 workers unemployed, yielding an unemployment rate of 5.0%, compared to the national average of 6.2% for the same period. Since the beginning of the BLS data series in 1978, the highest unemployment rate recorded was 12.8% in December 1982. The historical low was 3.7% in March 2000. In 2001, an estimated 5.9% of the labor force was employed in construction; 16.5% in manufacturing; 6.8% in transportation, communications, and public utilities; 20.1% in trade; 4.9% in finance, insurance, and real estate; 22.8% in services; 13.5% in government; and 1.6% in agriculture.

The US Department of Labor reported that in 2002, 222,000 of Tennessee's 2,466,000 employed wage and salary workers were members of unions. This represented 9.0% of those so employed, up from 7.6% in 2001. The national average is 13.2%. In all, 258,000 workers (10.5%) were represented by unions. In addition to union members, this category includes workers who report no union affiliation but whose jobs are covered by a union contract. Tennessee is one of 22 states with a right-to-work law.

[23] AGRICULTURE

Tennessee ranked 32nd among the 50 states in 2001 with farm receipts of over $2.1 billion. There were 90,000 farms in 2002.

From the antebellum period to the 1950s, cotton was the leading crop, followed by corn and tobacco. But during the early 1960s, soybeans surpassed cotton as the principal source of income. In 2002, 34.7 million bushels of soybeans, valued at $197.9 million, were harvested. Tobacco production in 2002 was 72.5 million lb. The main types of tobacco are burley, a fine leaf used primarily for cigarettes, and eastern and western dark-fired, which are used primarily for cigars, pipe tobacco, and snuff. The corn harvest in 2002 was about 66.3 million bushels, valued at $169 million. In 2002, cotton production was 813,000 bales, valued at $159.9 million.

[24] ANIMAL HUSBANDRY

Cattle are raised throughout the state, but principally in middle and east Tennessee. In 1930, fewer than a million cattle and calves were raised on Tennessee farms; by 2003, there were an estimated 2.27 million cattle and calves, valued at $1.34 billion. During 2002, hogs and pigs numbered around 220,000 and were valued at $13.4 million. In 2001, Tennessee poultry farmers produced 932 million lb (422.7 million kg) of broilers, worth $363.5 million, and 294 million eggs, valued at $31.9 million. Tennessee dairy farmers produced 1.34 billion lb (0.6 billion kg) of milk from some 92,000 milk cows.

[25] FISHING

Fishing is a major attraction for sport but plays a relatively small role in the economic life of Tennessee. There are seventeen TVA lakes and seven other lakes, all maintained by the Army Corps of Engineers; 10 of these lakes span an area of 10,000 acres (4,000 hectares) or more, and there are thousands of miles of creeks and mountain streams, all of which attract anglers. Tennessee has no closed season, except on trout.

In the 1970s, pollution from industrial waste dumping killed millions of fish and seriously endangered sport fishing. By the 1980s, however, industrial establishments in the state were complying more fully with the 1974 Water Pollution Act. Aquacultural facilities distributed 2.4 million trout, 254,000 catfish, and 694,000 walleye for restoration or conservation purposes in 1998, when the state issued 968,807 sport fishing licenses.

[26] FORESTRY

Forests covered 14,396,000 acres (5,826,000 hectares) in 2002, or more than 50% of the state's total land area. Commercial timberlands in 2002 totaled 13,956,000 acres (5,648,000 hectares). In 2002, 86% of the forested area was privately owned, 10% federally owned, 3% state-owned, and 1% municipally owned. The counties of the Cumberland Plateau and Highland Rim are the major sources of timber products, and in Lewis, Perry, Polk, Scott, Sequatchie, Unicoi, and Wayne counties, more than 75% of the total area is commercial forest.

About 95% of Tennessee's timber is in hardwoods, and nearly one-half of that is in white and red oak. Of the softwoods, pine—shortleaf, loblolly, Virginia, pitch, and white—accounts for 80%. Red cedar accounts for about 5% of the softwood supply. Total lumber production in 2002 was 899 million board feet.

Wood products manufacturing is among the state's largest basic industries. The wood products industry in Tennessee falls into three main categories: paper and similar products, lumber and similar products, and furniture. Manufacturing uses only about a third of the wood grown by forests in Tennessee each year. The remaining two-thirds continues to accumulate on aging trees or is lost through decomposition of diseased and dead trees. The most common method of cutting timber in Tennessee has long been "high-grading," that is, cutting only the most valuable trees and leaving those of inferior quality and value. Clearcutting, patch cutting, and group selection are silviculturally preferable, but, with the exception of clearcutting on industry lands, are rarely practiced.

27MINING

The 2001 value of nonfuel mineral production in Tennessee decreased by 5% from 2000 to $708 million. Crushed stone remained, by value, the leading commodity, accounting for about half the total nonfuel mineral value. Nationally, Tennessee ranked 21st in the total value of nonfuel minerals produced in 2001. Crushed stone has been the leading nonfuel mineral commodity produced in Tennessee for over 20 years, except for 1981. According to preliminary figures, in 2001, production was 60.5 million metric tons, valued at $372 million. Major rock types quarried to produce crushed stone were limestone, dolomite, and sandstone. Zinc, the state's leading nonfuel mineral commodity until 1981, remained the 2nd-leading mineral produced. Zinc was mined in Knox and Jefferson counties. Estimated ball clay production increased to 715,000 metric tons, with an estimated value of $30 million. The production of construction sand and gravel decreased from 8.76 million metric tons valued at $47 million in 2000 to 7.91 million metric tons valued at $43.1 million in 2001. In 2001, Tennessee led the nation in the value of natural gemstones produced. Tennessee was also 1st in ball clay, 2nd in zinc, 3rd in barite, 8th in fuller's earth, and 10th in industrial sand and gravel. Gemstone production consisted almost entirely of cultured freshwater pearls and mother-of-pearl derived from freshwater mussel shells.

28ENERGY AND POWER

The Tennessee Valley Authority (TVA) is the principal supplier of power in the state, providing electricity to more than 100 cities and 50 rural cooperatives. In 1999, Tennessee's installed electrical generating capacity (utility and nonutility) was 18.4 million kW, virtually all of it publicly owned; electrical output totaled 94.4 billion kWh (99% public). There were two nuclear power facilities in operation as of 2001, the two-unit Sequoyah plant near Chattanooga and the single-unit Watts Bar facility between Chattanooga and Knoxville. In 2000 Tennessee's total per capita energy consumption was 352 million Btu (88.7 million kcal), ranking it 24th among the 50 states.

Between 1978 and 2000, declining demand for coal, conservationist opposition to surface mining, and other factors led to a drop in coal production from 10 million tons to 2.7 million tons. Reserves in 2001 totaled 24 million tons of recoverable coal. Surface mining, which had marred thousands of acres of land and which accounted for 59% of coal production in 1978, accounted for 61% in 1998. Surface mine operators are now required to reclaim mined land. Most of the coal mined in the state is used for producing electricity, although some is used for home heating.

Tennessee produced 1,000 barrels of crude oil per day in 2002; natural gas reserves were negligible.

29INDUSTRY

On the eve of the Civil War, only 1% of Tennessee's population was employed in manufacturing, mostly in the iron, cotton, lumber, and flour-milling industries. Rapid industrial growth took place during the 20th century, however, and by 1981, Tennessee ranked 3rd among the southeastern states and 15th in the US in value of shipments. Tennessee's four major metropolitan areas, Memphis, Nashville, Knoxville, and Chattanooga, employ about half of all the state's industrial workers.

From 1987 to 1992, 54 industrial and commercial machinery manufacturers announced new plant locations in Tennessee while 366 existing companies in the industry expanded plant facilities. The state ranks 4th nationally in auto production. Automotive jobs went from 3,000 in the early 1980s to more than 22,000 jobs in 1996. The state is the leading noncoastal state for foreign investment; $14.5 billion in foreign investment entered the state in 1998. The total value of shipments for manufactured goods was $100 billion in 1997. In 1997, Tennessee was headquarters to four Fortune 500 companies: Columbia/HCA Health care, Federal Express, Eastman chemical, and Service Merchandise.

Earnings of persons employed in Tennessee increased from $93.3 billion in 1997 to $98.6 billion in 1998, an increase of 5.7%. The largest industries in 1998 were services, 27.1% of earnings; durable goods manufacturing, 12.4%; and retail trade, 10.6%. Of the industries that accounted for at least 5% of earnings in 1998, the slowest growing from 1997 to 1998 was nondurable goods manufacturing (9.3% of earnings in 1998), which increased 2.0%; the fastest was finance, insurance, and real estate (6.2% of earnings in 1998), which increased 9.6%.

30COMMERCE

Tennessee has been an important inland commercial center for some 60 years. In 1997, the state's sales from wholesale trade amounted to $86 billion. In 1997, Tennessee's retail sales totaled $53 billion. The principal retail groups were: automotive dealers, 15%; food stores, 12%; and eating and drinking places, 25%. Tennessee's foreign exports of goods totaled nearly $9.6 billion in 1998. Major exports, in order of importance, included transportation equipment, chemicals, and non-electric machinery.

31CONSUMER PROTECTION

The Tennessee Division of Consumer Affairs is a division of the State Department of Commerce and Insurance. Its mission is to serve and protect consumers from deceptive business practices. The division's activities include consumer complaint mediation, litigation for violations of the Tennessee Consumer Protection Act, consumer education, investigation, registration of health clubs, and influence on legislation.

32BANKING

The first bank in Tennessee was the Bank of Nashville, chartered in 1807. Four years later, the Bank of the State of Tennessee was chartered at Knoxville; branches were established at Nashville, Jonesboro, Clarksville, and Columbia. In 1817, nearly a dozen more banks were chartered in various frontier towns. The Civil War curtailed banking operations, but the industry began again immediately after cessation of hostilities.

In 2002, Tennessee had 212 insured banks with total assets of over $112 billion. One hundred sixty-three of these institutions were state-chartered.

Tennessee ranked 4th nationwide in per capita bankruptcy filings as of September 2002. Past-due loan levels remained high in the consumer and agricultural loan categories while there was an improvement in the commercial loan categories. There was an improvement in net interest margins (NIMs) (the difference between the lower rates offered to savers and the higher rates charged on loans) for insured banks as the spread between short- and long-term interest rates was fairly wide.

33INSURANCE

In 2000, 34 property and casualty and 20 life insurance companies had home offices in Tennessee. Some 4.4 million ordinary life insurance policies worth $198.6 billion were in force in 1998; total value for all categories of life insurance (ordinary, group, industrial, and credit) was $343.2 billion. Death benefits paid that year totaled $1.0 billion. As of 2000, there were 34 property and casualty and 20 life and health insurance companies incorporated or organized in the state. In 2001, property and casualty insurers wrote over $6.2 billion in premiums. That year, there were 15,339 flood insurance policies in force in the state, with a total value of $1.8 million.

³⁴SECURITIES

There are no securities exchanges in Tennessee, but approximately 703 broker-dealers with 6,867 employees, and 99 investment advisory firms do business there. The state is the headquarters of 56 NASDAQ companies, three NASDAQ market makers; and has incorporated 16 NYSE-listed companies. The top five are: Saks, Union Planters Corp., First Tennessee National Corp., Clayton Homes, Inc., and Central Parking Corp.

³⁵PUBLIC FINANCE

The state budget is prepared annually by the Budget Division of the Tennessee Department of Finance and Administration and submitted by the governor to the legislature every January. The fiscal year lasts from 1 July to 30 June.

The total Tennessee State budget forecast for 2000/01 was $16.7 billion, of which $14 billion came from the general fund, and $1.3 billion came from the Department of Transportation. For 2000/01 general fund revenues totaled $7.159 billion, sufficient for the biennial budget, but in 2001/02 general fund revenues fell to $7.002 billion, while expenditures rose to $7.516 billion. Already at the end of 2001, the governor had closed some public parks for lack of funds, and in 2002 the legislature drew on the state's Reserve for Revenue Fluctuations (RRF, the rainy day fund) and made major transfers from other fund. The stage was set for a battle over whether Tennessee was going to finally going to get a personal income tax (a 3.75% flat tax), which ended in defeat for the income tax advocates and a hike in the state sales tax from 6% to 7%. In 2002/03 general fund revenue jumped to $7.895 billion thanks mainly to the increase sales rate, but expenditures jumped even more, to $8.2 billion. The state's budget deficit was estimated at 8.2% of the state budget for 2002/03. For 2004, the deficit is projected to reach 37.8% of the state's budget (about $896 million). The starting balance in 2000/01 equaled 3% of expenditures. This fell to 2.5% of expenditure in 2002/03, for both 2002/03 and 2003/04, the starting balance was at 0. Appropriations were scheduled for health and social services (approximately 23%), health care providers (18.4%), higher education (16%), general government (14.2%), primary and secondary education (14%), public safety (3.5%), economic development (3%), resources and regulations (3%), mental health services (2% million), children's services (1.2%), commission on aging (0.7%); and human services, health services, and mental retardation 0.3% each).

The following table from the US Census Bureau contains information on revenues, expenditures, indebtedness, and cash/securities for 2001.

	($000)	PERCENT	PER CAPITA
Population (thousands, 2001)	5,749	(X)	(X)
Total Revenue	17,344,232	100.00	3,016.91
General revenue	17,041,478	98.25	2,964.25
Utility revenue	–	–	–
Liquor store revenue	–	–	–
Insurance trust revenue	302,754	1.75	52.66
Exhibit: Salaries and wages	2,649,613	14.41	460.88
Total expenditure	18,385,079	100.00	3,197.96
General expenditure	17,135,629	93.20	2,980.63
Education	5,807,290	31.59	1,010.14
Public welfare	6,122,866	33.30	1,065.03
Hospitals	365,594	1.99	63.59
Health	706,657	3.84	122.92

	($000)	PERCENT	PER CAPITA
Highways	1,487,367	8.09	258.72
Police protection	126,207	0.69	21.95
Correction	491,727	2.67	85.53
Natural resources	226,895	1.23	39.47
Parks and recreation	115,219	0.63	20.04
Government administration	454,478	2.47	79.05
Interest on general debt	194,170	1.06	33.77
Other and unallocable	1,037,159	5.64	180.41
Utility expenditure	4,611	0.03	0.80
Liquor store expenditure	–	–	–
Insurance trust expenditure	1,244,839	6.77	216.53
Debt at end of fiscal year	3,387,622	100.00	589.25
Cash and security holdings	29,044,562	100.00	5,052.11

³⁶TAXATION

Tennessee is known for die-hard resistance to a state income tax. The major source of general state revenue is a sales and use tax (close to 60% of total state tax revenue), first levied in 1947. In 2002, the general rate was raised to 7%, with local add-ons allowed up to 2.5%. Food is taxed at lower rates. Other state taxes include a 6% levy on dividend and interest income, a 6% corporate income tax, and levies on inheritances (1.3% of state revenues in 2002), alcoholic beverages, tobacco, gross receipts, motor vehicle registration, and other items. There is no state property tax. Instead property taxes are collected by counties and municipalities, and are their major source of income. Almost half (47% in 2000) of total state and local revenues are collected by local governments and taxing units.

The state collected $7.798 billion in taxes in 2002 (down almost $250 million from 2001), of which 59.9% came from the general sales tax, 17.6% from selective sales taxes, 10.7% from license fees, and 6.4% from corporate income taxes. In 2003, Tennessee ranked 47th among the states in terms of combined state and local tax burden, which amounted to about 7.7% of income.

The following table from the US Census Bureau provides a summary of taxes collected by the state in 2002.

	($000)	PER CAPITA
Total Taxes	7,797,681	1,345.06
Property taxes	(X)	(X)
Sales and gross receipts	6,045,888	1,042.88
General sales and gross receipts	4,674,896	806.39
Selective sales taxes	1,370,992	236.49
Alcoholic beverage	80,107	13.82
Amusements	(X)	(X)
Insurance Premiums	282,623	48.75
Motor fuels	814,468	140.49
Pari-mutuels	(X)	(X)
Public utilities	5,183	0.89
Tobacco products	83,573	14.42
Other selective sales	105,038	18.12
Licenses	836,013	144.21
Alcoholic beverages	2,591	0.45
Amusements	31	0.01
Corporation	420,768	72.58
Hunting and fishing	24,819	4.28
Motor vehicle	236,559	40.81
Motor vehicle operators	40,057	6.91
Public utility	7,078	1.22
Occupation and business, NEC	99,945	17.24
Other	4,165	0.72
Other taxes	915,780	157.97
Individual income	146,293	25.23
Corporation net income	502,977	86.76
Death and gift	100,045	17.26
Documentary and stock transfer	134,932	23.28
Severance	1,120	0.19
Other	30,413	5.25

37 ECONOMIC POLICY

Since World War II, Tennessee has aggressively sought new business and industry. The Department of Economic and Community Development (ECD) helps prospective firms locate industrial sites in communities throughout the state, and its representatives work with firms in Canada, Europe, and the Far East, as well as with domestic businesses. The department also administers special Appalachian regional programs in 50 counties and directs the state Office of Minority Business Enterprise.

Tennessee's right-to-work law and relatively weak labor movement constitute important industrial incentives, as well as a low state tax burden. The counties and municipalities, moreover, offer tax exemptions on land, capital improvements, equipment, and machinery. In 2003, under the slogan "Prepare for Battle," the Tennessee ECD announced the 2003 Governor's Conference on Economic and Community Development, scheduled for September.

38 HEALTH

Tennessee's infant mortality rate in 2000 was 9.1 per 1,000 live births. In the same year, 16,924 legal abortions were performed, a rate of 14 per 1,000 women. The death rate due to HIV-related infections stood at 5.2 per 100,000 population, higher than the US average of 5.3 in 2000. A total of 9,166 AIDS cases had been reported through 2001. In 2000, the overall death rate stood at 998.4, significantly higher than the national average rate of 873.1.

The major causes of death in Tennessee in 2000 (with rates per 100,000 population) were heart disease, 292.3; cancer, 223.0; cerebrovascular diseases, 77.1; accidents, 49.6; and suicide, 13.2. Of all Tennessee residents 18 years of age or older, 25.7% were regular smokers in 2000. Lung disease occurred at a rate of 89.8 per 100,000 population in 2000.

Tennessee's 123 community hospitals had 751,495 admissions and 20,600 beds in 2001. There were 20,150 full-time registered nurses and 4,335 full-time licensed practical nurses in 2001 and 263 physicians per 100,000 population in 2000. The average expense of a community hospital for care was $1,418.70 per inpatient day in 2001.

Federal government grants to cover the Medicare and Medicaid services in 2001 totaled $3.7 billion; 842,264 enrollees received Medicare benefits that year. At least 11.3% of Tennessee's residents were uninsured in 2002.

Tennessee has four medical schools: two in Nashville (Vanderbilt University and Meharry Medical School), one at Johnson City (East Tennessee State University), and one at Memphis (University of Tennessee).

39 SOCIAL WELFARE

In 2001, the average weekly unemployment benefit was $196.22. Average monthly participation in the food stamp program in FY2002 comprised 598,012 persons (255,900 households). The average monthly benefit was $76.85, and the sum total of benefits paid in FY2002 was $551,508,090.

With the enactment of the Personal Responsibility and Work Opportunity Reconciliation Act of 1996, the US government has changed the form and regulations for many of its social welfare programs. Most significantly, it replaces Aid to Families with Dependent Children (AFDC), an open-ended entitlement program, with Temporary Assistance for Needy Families (TANF), a limited system of assistance funded largely through federal block grants. The reform act also impacts the food stamp program, the Supplemental Security Income program, and the child nutrition program. The law took effect on 1 July 1997 and provided $16.38 billion in block grants for fiscal years 1997–2002. The grants are to be divided among the states based on an equation involving the numbers of former AFDC recipients in each state.

Reauthorization of the 1996 social welfare legislation, scheduled for 2002, was delayed, and the original law had been extended three times as of July 2003, with the most recent extension running through September 2003. Tennessee's TANF program is called Families First. In June 2000 the state had 143,823 welfare recipients. State expenditures on the TANF program in FY2002 totaled $82,529,784.

In December 2001, Social Security benefits were paid to 1,010,900 Tennessee residents. This number included 588,420 retired workers, 117,210 widows and widowers, 148,610 disabled workers, 59,800 spouses, and 96,860 children. Social Security beneficiaries represented 17.5% of the total state population and 93.9% of the state's population age 65 and older. Retired workers (excluding persons with special benefits) received an average monthly payment of $842; widows and widowers, $760; disabled workers, $783; and spouses, $420. Payments for children of retired workers averaged $410 per month; children of deceased workers, $540; and children of disabled workers, $235.

Federal Supplemental Security Income payments in December 2001 went to 162,920 Tennessee residents, averaging $347 a month.

40 HOUSING

In 2002, there were an estimated 2,519,825 housing units in the state, 2,257,080 of which were occupied; 69.2% were owner-occupied. About 68.5% of all units were single-family, detached homes. Electricity and utility gas were the most common energy sources for heating. It was estimated that 82,457 units lacked telephone service, 11,715 lacked complete plumbing facilities, and 11,301 lacked complete kitchen facilities. The average household size was 2.5 people.

In 2002, 34,273 new privately owned housing units were authorized for construction. The median home value was $106,070. The median monthly cost for mortgage owners was $962. Renters paid a median of $537 per month. During 2002, Tennessee received more than $97 million in community planning and development aid from the US Department of Housing and Urban Development.

41 EDUCATION

The state assumed responsibility for education in 1873, when the legislature established a permanent school fund and made schools free to all persons between the ages of 6 and 21. In 1917, an eight-year elementary and four-year secondary school system was set up. Thirty years later, enactment of the state sales and use tax enabled state authorities to increase teachers' salaries by about 100% and to provide capital funds for a variety of expanded educational programs. In the early 1980s, Tennessee further improved its educational system by offering incentive pay to its teachers. more than half of the state's consolidated state budget is spent on education.

The 21st Century Schools Program adopted by the Tennessee General Assembly in 1992 provided K-12 public schools with nearly $1 billion in new state dollars—an increase of 90%. The program repealed 3,700 state rules and regulations, gave communities wide discretion over education decision-making, made local school systems more accountable for results, and funded 5,450 high-tech classrooms in Tennessee's public schools. In 1996/97, Tennessee pioneered a statewide network connecting every public school to museums, libraries, and databases available on the World Wide Web. Tennessee's Literacy 2000 initiative (begun in 1987) improved the adult literacy rate by 24% in its first four years.

In 2000, 75.9% of Tennessee residents age 25 and older were high school graduates; 19.6% had obtained a bachelor's degree or higher. The total enrollment for fall 1999 in Tennessee's public schools stood at 916,202. Of these, 664,393 attended schools from kindergarten through grade eight, and 251,809 attended high school. Minority students made up approximately 29% of the total enrollment in public elementary and secondary schools in 2001. Total enrollment is expected to reach 954,000 in fall 2000 and 987,000 by fall 2005. Public school expenditures per pupil were $5,255 in 1999/2000. Expenditures for public education in 2000/01 were estimated at $5,189,243. Enrollment in nonpublic schools in fall 2001 was 93,680.

As of fall 2000, there were 287,550 students enrolled in college or graduate school. In the same year Tennessee had 87 degree-granting institutions. The University of Tennessee system has principal campuses at Knoxville, Memphis, Martin, and Chattanooga. Components of the State University and Community College System of Tennessee include Memphis State University (the largest), Tennessee Technological University at Cookeville, East Tennessee State University at Johnson City, Austin Peay State University at Clarksville, Tennessee State University at Nashville, and Middle Tennessee State University at Murfreesboro, along with 14 two-year community colleges located throughout the state. Well-known private colleges are Vanderbilt University at Nashville, the University of the South at Sewanee, and Rhodes College at Memphis. Vanderbilt has schools of medicine, law, divinity, nursing, business, and education, as well as an undergraduate program. In 1997, minority students comprised 18.7% of total postsecondary enrollment. Loan and grant programs are administered by the Tennessee Student Assistance Corporation.

42ARTS

Each of Tennessee's major cities has a symphony orchestra. The best known are the Memphis Symphony and the Nashville Symphony, the latter of which makes its home in the Tennessee Performing Arts Center. Included in this complex are three performing arts theaters and the State Museum. The major operatic troupes are Opera Memphis, Nashville Opera, and Knoxville Opera.

Nashville is known as "Music City, USA"; the Grand Ole Opry, Country Music Hall of Fame, Ryman Auditorium, and numerous recording studios are located there. Among the leading art galleries are the Dixon Gallery and the Brooks Museum of Art in Memphis, the Cheekwood Museum of Art in Nashville, the Knoxville Museum of Art, and the Hunter Museum of Art in Chattanooga. Professional dance and theater groups are located in both urban and rural areas.

There are several state and local festivals reflecting the music and arts of the state. Elvis Week, in August, is celebrated each year in Memphis. Graceland is the site of the annual Elvis Presley Birthday Celebration (January) and Christmas at Graceland. The Dollywood theme park in Pigeon Force, created by singer Dolly Parton, presents several festivals and musical events each year. The Tennessee Association of Craft Artists presents three annual fairs. The Memphis in May International Festival includes the following programs: the Beale Street Music Festival, International Week, the World Championship Barbecue Cooking Contest, the Great Southern Food Festival, and Sunset Symphony (featuring the Memphis Symphony).

The state's arts programs attract a total audience of more than 5 million each year. The Tennessee Arts Commission, in partnership with the Tennessee Department of Education and the Tennessee Performing Arts Center, offers arts education programs to one-third of the state's 900,000 public school students. Tennessee has more than 300 arts groups. The Memphis Arts Council is active in promoting the cultural and economic growth of the city. Members help to encourage new businesses to relocate in Memphis based on the city's cultural advantages. Similar groups work in Tennessee's other urban centers, as well as dozens of suburban and rural areas. In 2003, the Tennessee Arts Commission and other Tennessee arts organizations received grants totaling $850,800 from the National Endowment for the Arts.

Humanities Tennessee sponsors a number of annual programs including the Southern Festival of Books, the Tennessee Young Writers' Workshop, Motheread Fatheread Tennessee, and the Tennessee Community Heritage Program. In 2000, the National Endowment for the Humanities contributed $1,121,433 for 11 state programs.

43LIBRARIES AND MUSEUMS

Libraries and library associations were formed soon after Tennessee became a state. The Dickson Library at Charlotte was founded in 1811, and the Nashville Library Company in 1813. Not until 1854, however, was the first state-maintained library established. Andrew Johnson, the governor, requested a library appropriation of $5,000, telling legislators that he wanted other Tennesseans to have the opportunities that had been denied him.

Today, the institution he founded, the State Library at Nashville, with more than 637,371 volumes, has a renowned collection of state materials and is the repository for state records. In all, there are 16 public library systems in Tennessee. Their combined book stock exceeds 9.6 million volumes, and their total circulation is over 21 million. The largest libraries are the Vanderbilt University Library at Nashville (2,512,072 volumes), Memphis-Shelby County Library (1,938,685), Memphis State University Libraries (1,067,624), University of Tennessee at Knoxville Library (2,013,273), Knoxville-Knox County Library (865,088), and Chattanooga-Hamilton County Library (806,285). Public library income in 2000 was $73,891,000; including $1,034,000 in federal funds and $1,477,000 in state funds. Per capita spending was one of the lowest of all states in the country.

Tennessee has more than 127 museums and historic sites. The Tennessee State Museum in Nashville displays exhibits on pioneer life, military traditions, evangelical religion, and presidential lore. The Museum of Appalachia, near Norris, attempts an authentic replica of early Appalachian life, with more than 20,000 pioneer relics on display in several log cabins. Displays of solar, nuclear, and other energy technologies are featured at the American Museum of Science and Energy, at Oak Ridge. There are floral collections at the Goldsmith Civic Garden Center in Memphis and the Tennessee Botanical Gardens and Fine Arts Center in Nashville.

44COMMUNICATIONS

The first postal service across the state, by stagecoach, began operations in the early 1790s. As of 2001, 94.5% of Tennessee's occupied housing units had telephones. Tennessee had 30 major AM stations and 79 major FM stations in 2003. There were 42 television stations in operation in 2003. The Nashville area had 826,090 television households, 63% of which received cable. The Memphis area had 623,110 television homes, 64% of which ordered cable. About 81,858 Internet domain names were registered in the state by the year 2000.

45PRESS

In 2002, there were 14 morning newspapers, 11 evening dailies, and 17 Sunday papers. The following table lists leading Tennessee newspapers with their approximate daily circulation in 2002:

AREA	NAME	DAILY	SUNDAY
Chattanooga	*Times Free Press* (m,S)	74,637	101,257
Knoxville	*News-Sentinel* (m,S)	114,989	156,208
Memphis	*Commercial Appeal* (m,S)	155,196	231,755
Nashville	*Tennessean* (m,S)	183,406	256,437

Several dozen trade publications, such as *Southern Lumberman*, appear in Nashville, the state's major publishing center, where there is also a thriving religious publishing industry.

46 ORGANIZATIONS

In 2003, there were about 2,121 regional, national, and international organizations within the state.

Nashville is a center for Tennessee cultural and educational organizations. Among them are the American Association for State and Local History, the International Bluegrass Music Association, the Western Music Association, the Country Music Association, the Tennessee Historical Commission, and the Gospel Music Association. The Center for Southern Folklore is based in Memphis. The Tennessee Folklore Society is in Murfreesboro.

Several national and regional trade and professional associations are based in Tennessee, including the Walking Horse Breeders' and Exhibitors' Association, Lewisburg. and the Walking Horse Trainers' Association, Shelbyville. Knoxville is the headquarters of the Burley Tobacco Stabilization Corporation, and Springfield is the home of the Eastern Dark-Fired Tobacco Growers Association. The offices of the Southern Cotton Association, National Cotton Council of America, and Southern Hardwood Lumber Manufacturing Association are in Memphis, as is the headquarters of the American Contract Bridge League. The American Board of Veterinary Practitioners and the Fraternal Order of Police Grand Lodge are located in Nashville.

Several Christian denominations and organizations have their headquarters or major departmental offices in Tennessee. These include AMG International, Church of God World Missions, Gideons International, the National Association of Free Will Baptists, the National Baptist Convention–U.S.A., the Presbyterian Evangelistic Fellowship, the United Methodist Youth Organization, and the World Convention of Churches of Christ.

47 TOURISM, TRAVEL, AND RECREATION

The natural beauty of Tennessee, combined with the activities of the Department of Tourist Development, has made tourism a major industry in the state. Tennessee was the first state to create a government department devoted solely to the promotion of tourism. In 1999, the state spent $11 million to attract tourists through advertising. In 1997, domestic visitors spent $9 billion on day trips and overnight stays in the state.

Leading tourist attractions include Fort Loudoun, built by the British in 1757; the American Museum of Science and Energy at Oak Ridge; the William Blount Mansion at Knoxville; the Beale Street Historic District in Memphis, home of W. C. Handy, the "father of the blues"; Graceland, the Memphis estate of Elvis Presley; and Opryland USA and the Grand Ole Opry at Nashville. There are three presidential homes—Andrew Johnson's at Greeneville, Andrew Jackson's Hermitage near Nashville, and James K. Polk's at Columbia. Pinson Mounds, near Jackson, offers outstanding archaeological treasures and the remains of an Indian city. Reservoirs and lakes attract thousands of anglers and water sports enthusiasts. The top attractions in 1998 included (with annual attendance records): Dollywood (2,200,000), Tennessee Aquarium (1,150,148), Bristol Motor Sports (1,050,000), Ober Gatlinburg (1,004,659), and Casey Jones Village (840,000).

There are 33 state parks, almost all of which have camping facilities. Altogether, they cover 88,160 acres (35,678 hectares). Among the most visited state parks are the Meeman-Shelby Forest in Shelby County, Montgomery Bell in Dickson County, Cedars of Lebanon in Wilson County, and Natchez Trace in Henderson and Carroll counties. Cherokee National Park is the most visited national park in Tennessee (10,500,000). Extending into North Carolina, the Great Smoky Mountains National Park covers 241,207 acres (97,613 hectares) in Tennessee and drew nearly ten million visitors in 1998. Other popular national parks include the TVA's Land Between the Lakes National Historic Park (2,081,053), Cumberland Gap National Historic Park (1,500,000), and Chickamauga-Chattanooga National Military Park (1,022,500).

48 SPORTS

Tennessee has two major league professional sports teams, the National Football League's Titans, who relocated to Nashville from Houston before the 1997 season, and the NHL's Nashville Predators, who began play in 1999. Minor league baseball teams play throughout the state including Chattanooga, Memphis, Elizabethton, Johnson City, Kingsport, Lynchburg, and Nashville.

Tennessee's colleges and universities provide the major fall and winter sports. The University of Tennessee Volunteers and Vanderbilt University Commodores, in the Southeastern Conference, compete nationally in football, basketball, and baseball. Austin Peay and Tennessee Technological universities belong to the Ohio Valley Conference. The University of Tennessee won the Sugar Bowl in 1943, 1971, 1986, and 1991, the Fiesta Bowl in 1999, and the Florida Citrus Bowl in 1996 and 1997. The Volunteers were named national champions in 1951 and then again in 1999. The University of Tennessee's women's basketball team, the Lady Vols, won NCAA titles in 1987, 1989, 1991, 1996, 1997, and 1998. They have won more games than any other NCAA basketball team in the country. Other annual sporting events include the Iroquois steeplechase in Nashville in May and two NASCAR races at the Bristol Motor Speedway, one in March and one in August. Basketball Hall of Fame member Oscar Robertson and track and field legend Wilma Rudolph were both born and raised in Tennessee.

49 FAMOUS TENNESSEANS

Andrew Jackson (b.South Carolina, 1767–1845), the 7th president, moved to Tennessee as a young man. He won renown in the War of 1812 and became the first Democratic president in 1828. Jackson's close friend and associate, James Knox Polk (b.North Carolina, 1795–1849), came to Tennessee at the age of 10. He was elected the nation's 11th president in 1844 and served one term. Andrew Johnson (b.North Carolina, 1808–75) also a Democrat, remained loyal to the Union during the Civil War and was elected vice president with Abraham Lincoln in 1864. He became president upon Lincoln's assassination in 1865 and served out his predecessor's second term. Impeached because of a dispute over Reconstruction policies and presidential power, Johnson escaped conviction by one vote in 1868. Albert Gore, Jr. (b.Washington, D.C., 1948), was elected vice president in 1992 and 1996 on the Democratic ticket with Bill Clinton; Gore, whose father was a prominent US senator from Tennessee, had previously served in the Senate as well.

Supreme Court justices from Tennessee include John Catron (b.Pennsylvania, 1786–1865), Howell Jackson (1832–95), James C. McReynolds (b.Kentucky, 1862–1946), and Edward T. Sanford (1865–1930). Tennesseans who became cabinet officials include Secretary of State Cordell Hull (1871–1955), secretaries of war John Eaton (1790–1856) and John Bell (1797–1869), Secretary of the Treasury George Campbell (b.Scotland, 1769–1848), and attorneys general Felix Grundy (b.Virginia, 1777–1840) and James C. McReynolds (1862–1946).

Other nationally prominent political figures from Tennessee are Cary Estes Kefauver (1903–63), two-term US senator who ran unsuccessfully for vice president in 1956 on the Democratic ticket; Albert Gore (1907–98), three-term member of the US Senate; and Howard Baker (b.1925), who in 1966 became the first popularly elected Republican senator in Tennessee history. Three Tennesseans have been speaker of the US House of

Representatives: James K. Polk, John Bell, and Joseph W. Byrns (1869–1936). Nancy Ward (1738–1822) was an outstanding Cherokee leader, and Sue Shelton White (1887–1943) played a major role in the campaign for women's suffrage.

Tennessee history features several military leaders and combat heroes. John Sevier (b.Virginia, 1745–1815), the first governor of the state, defeated British troops at Kings Mountain in the Revolution. David "Davy" Crockett (1786–1836) was a frontiersman who fought the British with Jackson in the War of 1812. Sam Houston (b.Virginia, 1793–1863) also fought in the War of 1812 and was governor of Tennessee before migrating to Texas. Nathan Bedford Forrest (1821–77) and Sam Davis (1842–63) were heroes of the Civil War. Sergeant Alvin C. York (1887–1964) won the Medal of Honor for his bravery in World War I.

Cordell Hull was awarded the Nobel Peace Prize in 1945 for his work on behalf of the United Nations. In 1971, Earl W. Sutherland, Jr. (b.Kansas 1915–75), a biomedical scientist at Vanderbilt University, won a Nobel Prize for his discoveries concerning the mechanisms of hormones. Outstanding educators include Philip Lindsey (1786–1855), a Presbyterian minister and first president of the University of Nashville, and Alexander Heard (b.Georgia, 1917), nationally known political scientist and chancellor of Vanderbilt University.

Famous Tennessee writers are Mary Noailles Murfree (1850–1922), who used the pseudonym Charles Egbert Craddock; influential poet and critic John Crowe Ransom (1888–1974); author and critic James Agee (1909–55), posthumously awarded a Pulitzer Prize for his novel *A Death in the Family*; poet Randall Jarrell (1914–65), winner of two National Book Awards; and Wilma Dykeman (b.1920), novelist and historian. Peter Taylor (Trenton, Tenn., 1917–94) won a Pulitzer in 1987 for *A Summons to Memphis*. Sportswriter Grantland Rice (1880–1954) was born in Murfreesboro.

Tennessee has long been a center of popular music. Musician and songwriter William C. Handy (1873–1958) wrote "St Louis Blues" and "Memphis Blues," among other classics. Bessie Smith (1898?–1937) was a leading blues singer. Elvis Presley (b.Mississippi, 1935–77) fused rhythm-and-blues with country-and-western styles to become one of the most popular entertainers in US history. Other Tennessee-born singers are Dinah Shore (1917–1994), Aretha Franklin (b.1942), and Dolly Parton (b.1946). Morgan Freeman, star of movies including *Driving Miss Daisy*, was born in Memphis in 1937.

50 BIBLIOGRAPHY

Abernethy, Thomas P. *From Frontier to Plantation in Tennessee*. Reprint. Westport, CT: Greenwood Press, 1979 (orig. 1932).

Atkins, Jonathan M. *Parties, Politics, and the Sectional Conflict in Tennessee, 1832–1861*. Knoxville: University of Tennessee Press, 1997.

Connelly, T. L. *Civil War Tennessee: Battles and Leaders*. Knoxville: University of Tennessee Press, 1979.

Corlew, Robert E. *Statehood for Tennessee*. Nashville: Tennessee Bicentennial Commission, 1976.

———. *Tennessee: A Short History*. 2nd ed. Knoxville: University of Tennessee Press, 1981.

Dykeman, Wilma. *Tennessee: A Bicentennial History*. New York: Norton, 1975.

Federal Writers' Project: *Tennessee: A Guide to the State*. New York: Somerset, n.d. (orig. 1939).

Feeney, Kathy. *Tennessee Facts and Symbols*. Mankato, Minn.: Bridgestone Books, 2000.

Finger, John R. *Tennessee Frontiers: Three Regions in Transition*. Bloomington: Indiana University Press, 2001.

Folmsbee, Stanley J., Robert E. Crolew, and Enoch Mitchell. *History of Tennessee*. 4 vols. New York: Lewis, 1960.

Goehring, Eleanor E. *Tennessee Folk Culture: An Annotated Bibliography*. Knoxville: University of Tennessee Press, 1982.

Greene, Lee S., et al. *Government in Tennessee*. 4th ed. Knoxville: University of Tennessee Press, 1982.

Hsiung, David C. *Two Worlds in the Tennessee Mountains: Exploring the Origins of Appalachian Stereotypes*. Lexington: University Press of Kentucky, 1997

Hubbard, Preston. *Origins of the TVA*. New York: Norton, 1968.

Lewis, Thomas M. N., and Madeline Kneberg. *Tribes That Slumber: Indians of the Tennessee Region*. Knoxville: University of Tennessee Press, 1958.

Mooney, Chase. *Slavery in Tennessee*. Bloomington: Indiana University Press, 1957.

Olmstead, Marty. *Hidden Tennessee*. Berkeley, Calif.: Ulysses Press, 1999.

Patterson, Christine P. *Haunting Memories: Echoes and Images of Tennessee's Past*. Knoxville: University of Tennessee Press, 1996.

Smith, Samuel B., ed. *Tennessee History: A Bibliography*. Knoxville: University of Tennessee Press, 1974.

Tennessee, State of. Secretary of State. *Tennessee Blue Book 1983/84*. Nashville, 1983.

Tennessee, University of. College of Business Administration. Center for Business and Economic Research. *Tennessee Statistical Abstract 1984/85*. Knoxville, 1984.

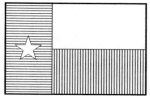

TEXAS

State of Texas

ORIGIN OF STATE NAME: Derived from the Caddo word *tavshas*, meaning "allies" or "friends." **NICKNAME:** The Lone Star State. **CAPITAL:** Austin. **ENTERED UNION:** 29 December 1845 (28th). **SONG:** "Texas, Our Texas." **MOTTO:** Friendship. **FLAG:** At the hoist is a vertical bar of blue with a single white five-pointed star; two horizontal bars of white and red cover the remainder of the flag. **OFFICIAL SEAL:** A five-pointed star encircled by olive and live oak branches, with the words "The State of Texas" surrounding. **BIRD:** Mockingbird. **FISH:** Guadalupe bass. **FLOWER:** Bluebonnet. **TREE:** Pecan. **PLANT:** Prickly pear cactus. **GRASS:** Sideoats grama. **DISH:** Chili. **GEM:** Topaz. **STONE:** Petrified palmwood. **SEASHELL:** Lightning whelk. **SPORT:** Rodeo. **LEGAL HOLIDAYS:** New Year's Day, 1 January; Confederate Heroes Day, 19 January; Birthday of Martin Luther King, Jr., 3rd Monday in January; Washington's Birthday, 3rd Monday in February; Texas Independence Day, 2 March: San Jacinto Day, 21 April; Memorial Day, last Monday in May; Emancipation Day, 19 June; Independence Day, 4 July; Lyndon B. Johnson's Birthday, 27 August; Labor Day, 1st Monday in September; Columbus Day, 2nd Monday in October; General Election Day, 1st Tuesday after 1st Monday in November; Veterans Day, 11 November; Thanksgiving Day, 4th Thursday in November; Christmas Day, 25 December. **TIME:** 6 AM CST = noon GMT.

¹LOCATION, SIZE, AND EXTENT

Located in the west south-central US, Texas is the largest of the 48 conterminous states. Texas's US rank slipped to 2nd when Alaska entered the Union in 1959.

The total area of Texas is 266,807 sq mi (691,030 sq km), of which land comprises 262,017 sq mi (678,624 sq km) and inland water 4,790 sq mi (12,406 sq km). The state's land area represents 8.8% of the US mainland and 7.4% of the nation as a whole. The state's maximum E-W extension is 801 mi (1,289 km); its extreme N-S distance is 773 mi (1,244 km).

Texas is bordered on the N by Oklahoma and Arkansas (with part of the line formed by the Red River); on the E by Arkansas and Louisiana (with part of the Louisiana line defined by the Sabine River); on the SE by the Gulf of Mexico; on the SW by the Mexican states of Tamaulipas, Nuevo León, Coahuila, and Chihuahua (with the line formed by the Rio Grande); and on the W by New Mexico. The state's geographic center is in McCulloch County, 15 mi (24 km) NE of Brady.

Large islands in the Gulf of Mexico belonging to Texas are Galveston, Matagorda, and Padre. The boundary length of the state totals 3,029 mi (4,875 km), including a general Gulf of Mexico coastline of 367 mi (591 km); the tidal shoreline is 3,359 mi (5,406 km).

²TOPOGRAPHY

Texas's major physiographic divisions are the Gulf Coastal Plain in the east and southeast; the North Central Plains, covering most of central Texas; the Great Plains, extending from west-central Texas up into the panhandle; and the mountainous trans-Pecos area in the extreme west.

Within the Gulf Coastal Plain are the Piney Woods, an extension of western Louisiana that introduces into East Texas for about 125 mi (200 km), and the Post Oak Belt, a flat region of mixed soil that gives way to the rolling prairie of the Blackland Belt, the state's most densely populated region. The Balcones Escarpment (so-called by the Spanish because its sharp profile suggests a balcony), a geological fault line running from the Rio Grande near Del Rio across central Texas, separates the Gulf Coastal Plain and Rio Grande Plain from the North Central

Plains and south-central Hill Country, and in so doing, divides East Texas from West Texas, watered Texas from dry Texas, and (culturally speaking) the Old South from the burgeoning West.

The North Central Plains extend from the Blackland Belt to the Cap Rock Escarpment, a natural boundary carved by erosion to heights of nearly 1,000 ft (300 m) in some places. Much of this plains region is rolling prairie, but the dude ranches of the Hill Country and the mineral-rich Burnet-Llano Basin are also found here. West of the Cap Rock Escarpment are the Great Plains, stretching north–south from the Panhandle Plains to the Edwards Plateau, just north of the Balcones Escarpment. Along the western edge of the panhandle and extending into New Mexico is the Llano Estacado (Staked Plains), an extension of the High Plains lying east of the base of the Rocky Mountains.

The trans-Pecos region, between the Pecos River and the Rio Grande, contains the highest point in the state: Guadalupe Peak, with an altitude of 8,749 ft (2,668 m), part of the Guadalupe Range extending southward from New Mexico into western Texas for about 20 mi (32 km). Also in the trans-Pecos region is the Diablo Plateau, which has no runoff to the sea and holds its scant water in lakes that often evaporate entirely. Farther south are the Davis Mountains, with a number of peaks rising above 7,000 ft (2,100 m), and Big Bend country (surrounded on three sides by the Rio Grande), whose canyons sometimes reach depths of nearly 2,000 ft (600 m). The Chisos Mountains, also exceeding 7,000 ft (2,100 m) at some points stand just north and west of the Rio Grande.

For its vast expanse, Texas boasts few natural lakes. Caddo Lake, which lies in Texas and Louisiana, is the state's largest natural lake, though its present length of 20 mi (32 km) includes waters added by dam construction in Louisiana. Two artificial reservoirs—Amistad (shared with Mexico), near Del Rio, and Toledo Bend (shared with Louisiana) on the Sabine River—have respective storage capacities exceeding 3 million and 4 million acre-ft, and the Sam Rayburn Reservoir (covering 179 sq mi/464 sq km) has a capacity of 2.9 million acre-ft. All together, the state contains close to 200 major reservoirs, eight of which can store more than 1 million acre-ft of water. From the air, Texas looks as well watered as Minnesota, but the lakes are artificial, and much of the soil is dry.

One reason Texas has so many reservoirs is that it is blessed with a number of major river systems, although none is navigable for more than 50 mi (80 km) inland. Starting from the west, the Rio Grande, a majestic stream in some places but a trickling trough in others, imparts life to the Texas desert and serves as the international boundary with Mexico. Its total length of 1,896 mi (3,051 km), including segments in Colorado and New Mexico, makes the Rio Grande the nation's 2nd-longest river, exceeded only by the Missouri-Mississippi river system. The Colorado River is the longest river wholly within the state, extending about 600 mi (970 km) on its journey across central and southeastern Texas to the Gulf of Mexico. Other important rivers include the Nueces, in whose brushy valley the range cattle industry began; the San Antonio, which stems from springs within the present city limits and flows, like most Texas rivers, to the Gulf of Mexico; the Brazos, which rises in New Mexico and stretches diagonally for about 840 mi (1,350 km) across Texas; the Trinity, which serves Fort Worth and Dallas; the San Jacinto, a short river but one of the most heavily trafficked in North America, overlapping the Houston Ship Channel, which connects the Port of Houston with the Gulf; the Neches, which makes an ocean port out of Beaumont; the Sabine, which has the largest water discharge (6,800,000 acre-ft) at its mouth of any Texas river; the Red, forming part of the northern boundary; and the Canadian, which crosses the Texas panhandle from New Mexico to Oklahoma, bringing moisture to the cattle raisers and wheat growers of that region. In all, Texas has about 3,700 identifiable streams, many of which dry up in the summer and flood during periods of rainfall.

Because of its extensive outcroppings of limestone, extending westward from the Balcones Escarpment, Texas contains a maze of caverns. Among the better-known caves are Longhorn Cavern in Burnet County; Wonder Cave, near San Marcos; the Caverns of Sonora, at Sonora; and Jack Pit Cave, in Menard County, which, with 19,000 ft (5,800 m) of passages, is the most extensive cave yet mapped in the state.

About 1 billion years ago, shallow seas covered much of Texas. After the seas receded, the land dropped gradually over millions of years, leaving a thick sediment that was then compressed into a long mountain range called the Ouachita Fold Belt. The sea was eventually restricted to a zone in West Texas called the Permian Basin, a giant evaporation pan holding gypsum and salt deposits hundreds of feet deep. As the mountain chain across central Texas eroded and the land continued to subside, the Rocky Mountains were uplifted, leaving deep cuts in Big Bend country and creating the Llano Estacado. The Gulf of Mexico subsided rapidly, depositing sediment accumulations several thousand feet deep, while salt domes formed over vast petroleum and sulfur deposits. All this geologic activity also deposited quicksilver in the Terlingua section of the Big Bend, built up the Horseshoe Atoll (a buried reef in west-central Texas that is the largest limestone reservoir in the nation), created uranium deposits in southern Texas, and preserved the oil-bearing Jurassic rocks of the northeast.

3CLIMATE

Texas's great size and topographic variety make climatic description difficult. Brownsville, at the mouth of the Rio Grande, has had no measurable snowfall during all the years that records have been kept, but Vega, in the panhandle, averages 23 in (58 cm) of snowfall per year. Near the Louisiana border, rainfall exceeds 56 in (142 cm) annually, while in parts of extreme West Texas, rainfall averages less than 8 in (20 cm). Average annual precipitation in Dallas (1971–2000) was 34.7 in

(88 cm); in El Paso, 9.4 in (23.9 cm); and in Houston, 47.8 in (121.4 cm).

Generally, a maritime climate prevails along the Gulf coast, with continental conditions inland; the Balcones Escarpment is the main dividing line between the two zones, but they are not completely isolated from each other's influence. Texas has two basic seasons—a hot summer that may last from April through October, and a winter that starts in November and usually lasts until March. When summer ends, the state is too dry for autumn foliage, except in East Texas. Temperatures in El Paso, in the southwest, range from a mean January minimum of 29°F (–2°C) to a mean July maximum of 96°F (36°C); at Amarillo, in the panhandle, from 23°F (–5°C) in January to 91°F (33°C) in July; and at Galveston, on the Gulf, from 48°F (9°C) in January to 88°F (31°C) in August. Perhaps the most startling contrast is in relative humidity, averaging 34% at noon in El Paso, 44% in Amarillo, and 72% in Galveston. In the Texas panhandle, the average date of the first freeze is 1 November; in the lower Rio Grande Valley, 16 December. The last freeze arrives in the panhandle on 15 April, and in the lower Rio Grande Valley on 30 January. The valley thus falls only six weeks short of having a 12-month growing season while the panhandle approximates the growing season of the upper Midwest.

Record temperatures range from –23°F (–31v) at Seminole, on 8 February 1933, to 120°F (49v) at Seymour in north-central Texas on 12 August 1936. The greatest annual rainfall was 109 in (277 cm), measured in 1873 at Clarksville, just below the Red River in northeast Texas; the least annual rainfall, 1.786 in (4.47 cm), was recorded at Wink, near the New Mexico line, in 1956. Thrall, in central Texas, received 38.2 in (97 cm) of rain in 24 hours on 9–10 September 1921. Alvin, in Brazoria County on the Gulf Coast, had 43 in (109 cm) of rain on 25–26 July 1979, a national record for the most rainfall during a 24-hour period. Romero, on the New Mexico border, received a record 65 in (165 cm) of snow in the winter of 1923–24, and Hale Center, near Lubbock, measured 33 in (84 cm) during one storm in February 1956. The highest sustained wind velocity in Texas history, 145 mph (233 km/hr), occurred when Hurricane Carla hit Matagorda and Port Lavaca along the Gulf coast on 11 September 1961.

Hurricanes strike the Gulf coast about once every decade, usually in September or October. A hurricane on 19–20 August 1886 leveled the port of Indianola; the town (near present-day Port Lavaca) was never rebuilt. Galveston was the site of the most destructive storm in US history: on 8–9 September 1900, a hurricane blew across the island of 38,000 residents, leaving at least 6,000 dead (the exact total has never been ascertained) and leveling most of the city. A storm of equal intensity hit Galveston in mid-August 1915, but this time, the city was prepared; its new seawall held the toll to 275 deaths and $50 million worth of property damage. Because of well-planned damage-prevention and evacuation procedures, Hurricane Carla—at least as powerful as any previous hurricane—claimed no more than 34 lives. More recent hurricanes have frequently passed over the coastal area with no loss of life at all. Texas also lies in the path of "Tornado Alley," stretching across the Great Plains to Canada. The worst tornado in recent decades struck downtown Waco on 11 May 1953, killing 114 persons, injuring another 597, and destroying or damaging some 1,050 homes and 685 buildings. At least 115 tornadoes—the greatest concentration on record— occurred with Hurricane Beulah during 19–23 September 1967; the 67 tornadoes on 20 September set a record for the largest number of tornadoes on one day in the state.

Floods and droughts have also taken their toll in Texas. The worst flood occurred on 26–28 June 1954, when Hurricane Alice moved inland up the Rio Grande for several hundred miles, dropping 27 in (69 cm) of rain on Pandale above Del Rio. The Rio Grande rose 50 to 60 ft (15–18 m) within 48 hours, as a wall

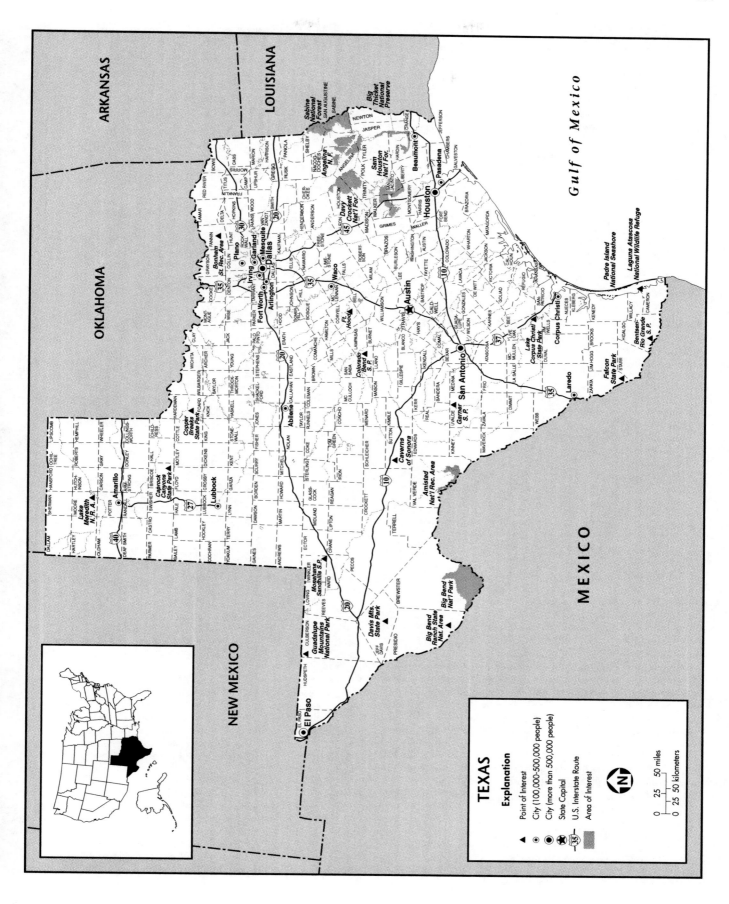

ARKANSAS

LOUISIANA

OKLAHOMA

NEW MEXICO

Gulf of Mexico

MEXICO

TEXAS

Explanation

Point of Interest

City (100,000–500,000 people)

City (more than 500,000 people)

State Capital

U.S. Interstate Route

Area of Interest

0   25   50 miles
0   25   50 kilometers

of water 86 ft (26 m) high in the Pecos River canyon fed it from the north. A Pecos River bridge built with a 50-ft (15-m) clearance was washed out, as was the international bridge linking Laredo with Mexico. Periodic droughts afflicted Texas in the 1930s and 1950s.

⁴FLORA AND FAUNA

More than 500 species of grasses covered Texas when the Spanish and Anglo-Americans arrived. Although plowing and lack of soil conservation destroyed a considerable portion of this rich heritage, grassy pastureland still covers about two-thirds of the state. Bermuda grass is a favorite ground cover, especially an improved type called Coastal Bermuda, introduced after World War II. The prickly pear cactus is a mixed blessing: like the cedar and mesquite, it saps moisture and inhibits grass growth, but it does retain moisture in periods of drought and will survive the worst dry spells, so (with the spines burned off) it can be of great value to ranchers as cattle feed in difficult times. The bean of the mesquite also provides food for horses and cattle when they have little else to eat, and its wood is a favorite in barbecues and fireplaces.

Texas has more than 20 native trees, of which the catclaw, flowering mimosa, huisache, black persimmon, huajillo, and weeping juniper (unique to the Big Bend) are common only in Texas. Cottonwood grows along streams in almost every part of the state, while cypress inhabits the swamps. The flowering dogwood in East Texas draws tourists to that region every spring, and the largest bois d'arc trees in the US are grown in the Red River Valley. Probably the most popular shade tree is the American (white) elm, which, like the gum tree, has considerable commercial importance. The magnolia is treasured for its grace and beauty; no home of substance in southeastern Texas would have a lawn without one. Of the principal hardwoods, the white oak is the most commercially valuable, the post oak the most common, and the live oak the most desirable for shade; the pecan is the state tree. Pines grow in two areas about 600 mi (970 km) apart—deep East Texas and the trans-Pecos region. In southeast Texas stands the Big Thicket, a unique area originally covering more than 3 million acres (1.2 million ha) but now reduced to about one-tenth of that by lumbering. Gonzales County, in south-central Texas, is the home of palmettos, orchids, and other semitropical plants not found anywhere else in the state. Texas wild rice and several cactus species are classified as endangered throughout the state.

In 2003, 28 Texas plant species were listed as threatened or endangered, including ashy dogweed, black lace cactus, large-fruited sand-verbena, South Texas ambrosia, Terlingua creek cats-eye, Texas snowbells, Texas trailing phlox, and Texas wild-rice.

Possibly the rarest mammal in Texas is the red wolf, which inhabits the marshland between Houston and Beaumont, one of the most thickly settled areas of the state; owing to human encroachment and possible hybridization with coyotes, the red wolf is steadily disappearing despite efforts by naturalists throughout the United States to save it. On the other hand, Texans claim to have the largest number of white-tailed deer of any state in the Union, an estimated 3 million. Although the Hill Country is the white-tailed deer's natural habitat, the species has been transplanted successfully throughout the state.

Perhaps the most unusual mammal in Texas is the nine-banded armadillo. Originally confined to the Rio Grande border, the armadillo has gradually spread northward and eastward, crossing the Red River into Oklahoma and the Mississippi River into the Deep South. It accomplished these feats of transport by sucking in air until it becomes buoyant and then swimming across the water. The armadillo is likewise notable for always having its young in litters of identical quadruplets. The chief mammalian predators are the coyote, bobcat, and mountain lion.

Texas attracts more than 825 different kinds of birds, with bird life most abundant in the lower Rio Grande Valley and coastal plains. Argument continues as to whether Texas is the last home of the ivory-billed woodpecker, which lives in inaccessible swamps, preferably in cutover timber. Somewhat less rare is the pileated woodpecker, which also inhabits the forested lowlands. Other characteristic birds include the yellow-trimmed hooded warbler, which frequents the canebrakes and produces one of the most melodious songs of any Texas bird; the scissor-tailed flycatcher, known popularly as the scissor-tail; Attwater's greater prairie chicken, now declining because of inadequate protection from hunters and urbanization; the mockingbird, the state bird; and the roadrunner, also known as paisano and chaparral. Rare birds include the Mexican jacana, with a flesh comb and bright yellow-green wings; the white-throated swift, one of the world's fastest flyers; the Texas canyon wren, with a musical range of more than an octave; and the Colima warbler, which breeds only in the Chisos Mountains. In the Aransas National Wildlife Refuge, along the central Gulf coast, lives the whooping crane, which has long been on the endangered list. Controversy surrounds the golden eagle, protected by federal law but despised by ranchers for allegedly preying on lambs and other young livestock.

Texas has its fair share of reptiles, including more than 100 species of snake, 16 of them poisonous, notably the deadly Texas coral snake. There are 10 kinds of rattlesnake, and some parts of West Texas hold annual rattlesnake roundups. Disappearing with the onset of urbanization are the horned toad, a small iguana-like lizard; the vinegarroon, a stinging scorpion; and the tarantula, a large, black, hairy spider that is scary to behold but basically harmless.

In addition to providing protection for the animals on federal lists of threatened and endangered species, the state has its own wildlife protection programs. Among the animals classified as non-game (not hunted) and therefore given special consideration are the lesser yellow bat, spotted dolphin, reddish egret, white-tailed hawk, wood stork, Big Bend gecko, rock rattlesnake, Louisiana pine snake, white-lipped frog, giant toad, toothless blindcat, and blue sucker. In 2003, 63 animal species were listed as threatened or endangered in Texas (up from 43 in 1997), including the Mexican long-nosed bat, Louisiana black bear, bald eagle, ocelot, Mexican spotted owl, Texas blind salamander, Houston toad, black-capped vireo, two species of whale, and five species of turtle.

Texas has 15 National Wildlife Refuges, with a total of 302,731 acres (122,511 ha). The Texas Parks and Wildlife Department administers an additional 19 wildlife management areas.

⁵ENVIRONMENTAL PROTECTION

Conservation in Texas officially began with the creation of a State Department of Forestry in 1915; 11 years later, this body was reorganized as the Texas Forest Service, the name it retains today. The state's Soil Conservation Service was created in 1935.

The scarcity of water is the one environmental crisis every Texan must live with. Much of the state has absorbent soils, a high evaporation rate, vast areas without trees to hold moisture, and a rolling terrain susceptible to rapid runoff. The Texas Water Commission and Water Development Board direct the state's water supply and conservation programs. Various county and regional water authorities have been constituted, as have several water commissions for river systems. Probably the most complete system is that of the three Colorado River authorities—lower, central, and upper. The oldest of these is the Lower Colorado River Authority, created in 1934 by the Texas legislature to "control, store, preserve, and distribute" the waters of the Colorado River and its feeder streams. The authority exercises control over a 10-county area stretching from above Austin to the Gulf coast, overseeing flood control, municipal and industrial water supplies, irrigation, hydroelectric power generation, soil conservation, and recreation.

The most powerful conservation agency in Texas is the Railroad Commission. Originally established to regulate railroads, the commission extended its power to regulate oil and natural gas by virtue of its jurisdiction over the transportation of those products by rail and pipeline. In 1917, the state legislature empowered the commission to prevent the waste of oil and gas. The key step in conservation arrived with the discovery of oil in East Texas in 1930. With a national depression in full swing and the price of oil dropping to $1 a barrel, the commission agreed to halt ruinous overproduction, issuing the first proration order in April 1931. In a field composed of hundreds of small owners, however, control was difficult to establish; oil was bootlegged, the commission's authority broke down, Governor Ross S. Sterling declared martial law, and the state's conservation edicts were not heeded until the federal government stepped in to enforce them. As os 2003, the Railroad Commission is comprised of four divisions that oversee the state's oil and gas industry, gas utilities, pipeline and rail safety, safety in the liquefied petroleum gas industry, and coal and uranium mining.

As in other states, hazardous wastes have become an environmental concern in Texas. In 1984, for example, a suit was brought against eight oil and chemical companies, including both Exxon and Shell Oil, alleging that they had dumped hazardous wastes at four sites in Harris County. The agency that oversees compliance with hazardous-waste statutes is the Hazardous and Solid Waste Division of the Texas Water Commission. In 2003, Texas had 298 hazardous waste sites listed in the Environmental Protection Agency's database, 41 of which were on the National Priorities List. The state has lost about one-half of its original wetlands, which reportedly covered about 5% of the state's total land area in 2003. The three agencies that define wetlands disagree on the total wetlands are in the state, with estimates ranging from about 6 million acres (2.4 million hectares) to 8 million acres (3.2 million hectares). In 2001, Texas received $348,780,000 in federal grants from the Environmental Protection Agency; EPA expenditures for procurement contracts in Texas that year amounted to $24,198,000.

6POPULATION

In 1998 Texas overtook New York as the nation's 2nd most populous state. Between 1990 and 2000 Texas's population grew from 16,986,510 to 20,851,820, a gain of 22.8%, and the 2nd-largest increase for the decade among the 50 states. The state had placed 4th in the 1970 census, with a population of 11,196,730, but had surpassed Pennsylvania in 1974. The estimated population as of 2002 was 21,779,893, an increase of 4.5% since 2000. The population is projected to reach 27.2 million by 2025. The population density in 2000 was 79.6 persons per sq mi.

At the first decennial census of 1850, less than five years after Texas had become a state, the population totaled 212,592. It reached 1,600,000 by the early 1880s (when the state ranked eleventh), passed 4,000,000 during World War I, and jumped to 7,700,000 by 1950. The slowest period of growth occurred during the Depression decade (1930–40) when the population rose only 10%, and the state was surpassed by California. The growth rate ranged between 17% and 27% for each decade from the 1940s through the 1970s; it was 19.4% between 1980 and 1990.

The Texas population has grown steadily older, a phenomenon linked to declining birthrates and increased life expectancies. In 1870, only one out of 68 Texans was 65 years of age or older; by 1990, the proportion was one out of 10. In 2000, the median age for Texans was 32.3. In the same year, 28.2% of the populace were under age 18 while 9.9% were age 65 or older.

The largest metropolitan area in 1999 was Dallas-Fort Worth (which traded places with Houston-Galveston-Brazoria in the national rank of the most populated metropolitan areas from 1980 to 1990), with an estimated 4,909,523 people. Close behind was the Houston-Galveston-Brazoria area, with 4,493,741 residents. San Antonio had an estimated 1,564,949. Houston, the largest city proper in Texas and 4th-largest in the US, had an estimated 2002 population of 2,009,834. Next was Dallas, with 1,211,467; followed by San Antonio, 1,194,222; Austin, 671,873; El Paso, 577,415; Fort Worth, 567,516; Arlington, 349,944; and Corpus Christi, 278,520. With the exception of El Paso, in the far western corner of the trans-Peco region, most of the larger cities are situated along the Gulf coast or on or near an axis that extends north-south from Wichita Falls to Corpus Christi, in the heart of the Blackland Belt.

7ETHNIC GROUPS

As white settlers pushed toward Texas during the 19th century, many Indian groups moved west and south into the region. The most notable tribes were the Comanche, Wichita, Kiowa, Apache, Choctaw, and Cherokee. Also entering in significant numbers were the Kickapoo and Potawatomi from Illinois, the Delaware and Shawnee from Missouri, the Quapaw from Arkansas, and the Creek from Alabama and Georgia. One of the few Texas tribes that has survived to the present time as an identifiable group is the Alabama-Coushatta, who inhabit a 4,351-acre (1,761-hectare) reservation in Polk County, 90 mi (145 km) northeast of Houston. The Tigua, living in Texas since the 1680s, were recognized by a federal law in 1968 that transferred all responsibility for them to the state of Texas. The two Indian reservations number about 500 persons each. Overall, at the 2000 census, there were 118,362 American Indians living in Texas.

Blacks have been integral to the history of Texas ever since a black Moor named Estevanico was shipwrecked near present-day Galveston in 1528. By 1860, Texas had 182,921 blacks, or 30% of the total population, of whom only 355 were free. Once emancipated, blacks made effective use of the franchise, electing two of their number to the state senate and nine to the house in 1868. After the return of the Democratic Party to political dominance, however, the power of blacks steadily diminished. Since then, their numbers have grown, but their proportion of the total population has dwindled, although Houston and Dallas were, respectively, about 25% and 26% black at the 2000 census. In 2000, 2,404,566 blacks lived in the state, which ranked 2nd behind New York in the size of its black population.

Hispanics and Latinos, the largest minority in Texas, numbered 6,669,666 in 2000, representing 32% of the population, an increase over 1990, when Texans of Hispanic origin represented 25.5% of the total. Mostly of Mexican ancestry, they are nevertheless a heterogeneous group, divided by history, geography, and economic circumstances. Hispanics have been elected to the state legislature and to the US Congress. In 1980, the Houston independent school district, the state's largest, reported more Hispanic students than Anglos for the first time in its history.

Altogether, Texas has nearly 30 identifiable ethnic groups. Certain areas of central Texas are heavily Germanic and Czech. The first permanent Polish colony in the US was established at Panna Maria, near San Antonio, in 1854. Texas has one of the largest colonies of Wends in the world, principally at Serbin in central Texas. Significant numbers of Danes, Swedes, and Norwegians have also settled in Texas.

Texas Counties, County Seats, and County Areas and Populations

COUNTY	COUNTY SEAT	LAND AREA (SQ MI)	POPULATION (2002 EST.)	COUNTY	COUNTY SEAT	LAND AREA (SQ MI)	POPULATION (2002 EST.)
Anderson	Palestine	1,077	54,585	Duval	San Diego	1,795	12,811
Andrews	Andrews	1,501	12,951	Eastland	Eastland	924	18,210
Angelina	Lufkin	807	80,582	Ector	Odessa	903	122,312
Aransas	Rockport	280	22,928	Edwards	Rocksprings	2,120	2,081
Archer	Archer City	907	8,996	Ellis	Waxahachie	939	120,052
Armstrong	Claude	910	2,145	El Paso	El Paso	1,014	697,562
Atascosa	Jourdanton	1,218	40,948	Erath	Stephenville	1,080	33,077
Austin	Bellville	656	24,596	Falls	Marlin	770	18,091
Bailey	Muleshoe	827	6,480	Fannin	Bonham	895	31,672
Bandera	Bandera	793	19,153	Fayette	La Grange	950	22,304
Bastrop	Bastrop	895	63,934	Fisher	Roby	897	4,246
Baylor	Seymour	862	3,929	Floyd	Floydada	992	7,455
Bee	Beeville	880	32,277	Foard	Crowell	703	1,545
Bell	Belton	1,055	244,668	Ft. Bend	Richmond	876	399,537
Bexar	San Antonio	1,248	1,446,333	Franklin	Mt. Vernon	294	9,699
Blanco	Johnson City	714	8,866	Freestone	Fairfield	888	18,595
Borden	Gail	900	701	Frio	Pearsall	1,133	16,249
Bosque	Meridian	989	17,535	Gaines	Seminole	1,504	14,312
Bowie	Boston	891	89,894	Galveston	Galveston	399	261,219
Brazoria	Angleton	1,407	257,256	Garza	Post	895	4,976
Brazos	Bryan	588	156,099	Gillespie	Fredericksburg	1,061	21,607
Brewster	Alpine	6,169	9,009	Glasscock	Garden City	900	1,369
Briscoe	Silverton	887	1,716	Goliad	Goliad	859	7,075
Brooks	Falfurrias	942	7,766	Gonzales	Gonzales	1,068	18,884
Brown	Brownwood	936	37,957	Gray	Pampa	921	22,088
Burleson	Caldwell	668	16,874	Grayson	Sherman	934	113,860
Burnet	Burnet	994	36,889	Gregg	Longview	273	113,255
Caldwell	Lockhart	546	35,050	Grimes	Anderson	799	24,740
Calhoun	Port Lavaca	540	20,595	Guadalupe	Seguin	713	94,215
Callahan	Baird	899	12,762	Hale	Plainview	1,005	35,900
Cameron	Brownsville	905	353,561	Hall	Memphis	876	3,662
Camp	Pittsburg	203	11,643	Hamilton	Hamilton	836	8,079
Carson	Panhandle	924	6,582	Hansford	Spearman	921	5,288
Cass	Linden	937	30,133	Hardeman	Quanah	688	4,490
Castro	Dimmitt	899	8,075	Hardin	Kountze	898	48,988
Chambers	Anahuac	616	27,244	Harris	Houston	1,734	3,557,055
Cherokee	Rusk	1,052	47,450	Harrison	Marshall	908	62,534
Childress	Childress	707	7,571	Hartley	Channing	1,462	5,464
Clay	Henrietta	1,085	11,396	Haskell	Haskell	901	5,909
Cochran	Morton	775	3,482	Hays	San Marcos	678	109,570
Coke	Robert Lee	908	3,844	Hemphill	Canadian	903	3,332
Coleman	Coleman	1,277	8,906	Henderson	Athens	888	75,797
Collin	McKenney	851	566,798	Hidalgo	Edinburg	1,569	614,474
Collingsworth	Wellington	909	3,103	Hill	Hillsboro	968	33,701
Colorado	Columbus	964	20,384	Hockley	Levelland	908	22,838
Comal	New Braunfels	555	85,109	Hood	Granbury	425	44,149
Comanche	Comanche	930	13,565	Hopkins	Sulphur Springs	789	32,299
Concho	Paint Rock	992	3,854	Houston	Crockett	1,234	23,225
Cooke	Gainesville	893	37,634	Howard	Big Spring	901	33,215
Coryell	Gatesville	1,057	74,495	Hudspeth	Sierra Blanca	4,566	3,341
Cottle	Paducah	895	1,797	Hunt	Greenville	840	79,361
Crane	Crane	782	3,874	Hutchinson	Stinnett	871	23,061
Crockett	Ozona	2,806	3,807	Irion	Mertzon	1,052	1,757
Crosby	Crosbyton	898	6,865	Jack	Jacksboro	920	8,965
Culberson	Van Horn	3,815	2,839	Jackson	Edna	844	14,364
Dallam	Dalhart	1,505	6,184	Jasper	Jasper	921	35,776
Dallas	Dallas	880	2,283,953	Jeff Davis	Ft. Davis	2,258	2,211
Dawson	Lamesa	903	14,712	Jefferson	Beaumont	937	248,890
Deaf Smith	Hereford	1,497	18,396	Jim Hogg	Hebbronville	1,136	5,173
Delta	Cooper	278	5,362	Jim Wells	Alice	867	39,945
Denton	Denton	911	488,481	Johnson	Cleburne	731	136,332
DeWitt	Cuero	910	20,067	Jones	Anson	931	20,284
Dickens	Dickens	907	2,702	Karnes	Karnes City	753	15,411
Dimmet	Carrizo Springs	1,307	10,200	Kaufman	Kaufman	788	77,954
Donley	Clarendon	929	3,887	Kendall	Boerne	663	25,390

Texas Counties, County Seats, and County Areas and Populations

COUNTY	COUNTY SEAT	LAND AREA (SQ MI)	POPULATION (2002 EST.)	COUNTY	COUNTY SEAT	LAND AREA (SQ MI)	POPULATION (2002 EST.)
Kenedy	Sarita	1,389	419	Refugio	Refugio	771	7,724
Kent	Jayton	878	807	Roberts	Miami	915	857
Kerr	Kerrville	1,107	44,857	Robertson	Franklin	864	16,044
Kimble	Junction	1,250	4,502	Rockwall	Rockwall	128	50,858
King	Guthrie	914	333	Runnels	Ballinger	1,056	11,123
Kinney	Brackettville	1,359	3,447	Rusk	Henderson	932	47,541
Kleberg	Kingsville	853	31,145	Sabine	Hemphill	486	10,370
Knox	Benjamin	845	4,061	San Augustine	San Augustine	524	8,922
Lamar	Paris	919	49,079	San Jacinto	Coldspring	572	23,247
Lamb	Littlefield	1,013	14,662	San Patricio	Sinton	693	67,492
Lampasas	Lampasas	714	18,846	San Saba	San Saba	1,136	6,148
La Salle	Cotulla	1,517	5,876	Schleicher	Eldorado	1,309	2,944
Lavaca	Hallettsville	971	18,935	Scurry	Snyder	900	15,877
Lee	Giddings	631	16,329	Shackelford	Albany	915	3,338
Leon	Centerville	1,078	15,885	Shelby	Center	791	25,439
Liberty	Liberty	1,174	73,739	Sherman	Stratford	923	3,285
Limestone	Groesbeck	931	22,263	Smith	Tyler	932	181,437
Lipscomb	Lipscomb	933	3,103	Somervell	Glen Rose	188	7,224
Live Oak	George West	1,057	12,014	Starr	Rio Grande City	1,226	56,686
Llano	Llano	939	17,758	Stephens	Breckenridge	894	9,453
Loving	Mentone	671	64	Sterling	Sterling City	923	1,346
Lubbock	Lubbock	900	247,574	Stonewall	Aspermont	925	1,493
Lynn	Tahoka	888	6,325	Sutton	Sonora	1,455	4,117
McCulloch	Brady	1,071	7,885	Swisher	Tulia	902	8,082
McLennan	Waco	1,031	217,713	Tarrant	Ft. Worth	868	1,527,366
McMullen	Tilden	1,163	856	Taylor	Abilene	917	125,647
Madison	Madisonville	473	13,105	Terrell	Sanderson	2,357	988
Marion	Jefferson	385	11,081	Terry	Brownfield	886	12,723
Martin	Stanton	914	4,673	Throckmorton	Throckmorton	912	1,711
Mason	Mason	934	3,771	Titus	Mt. Pleasant	412	28,405
Matagorda	Bay City	1,127	37,954	Tom Green	San Angelo	1,515	103,018
Maverick	Eagle Pass	1,287	48,651	Travis	Austin	989	850,813
Medina	Hondo	1,331	40,924	Trinity	Groveton	692	14,088
Menard	Menard	902	2,329	Tyler	Woodville	922	20,743
Midland	Midland	902	117,669	Upshur	Gilmer	587	36,499
Milam	Cameron	1,019	24,880	Upton	Rankin	1,243	3,287
Mills	Goldthwaite	748	5,133	Uvalde	Uvalde	1,564	26,508
Mitchell	ColoradoCity	912	9,348	Val Verde	Del Rio	3,150	45,903
Montague	Montague	928	19,237	Van Zandt	Canton	855	50,124
Montgomery	Conroe	1,047	328,449	Victoria	Victoria	887	84,932
Moore	Dumas	905	20,350	Walker	Huntsville	786	62,388
Morris	Daingerfield	256	13,240	Waller	Hempstead	514	34,057
Motley	Matador	959	1,336	Ward	Monahans	836	10,507
Nacogdoches	Nacogdoches	939	59,514	Washington	Brenham	610	30,626
Navarro	Corsicana	1,068	46,792	Webb	Laredo	3,363	207,611
Newton	Newton	935	14,946	Wharton	Wharton	1,086	41,329
Nolan	Sweetwater	915	15,172	Wheeler	Wheeler	905	5,022
Nueces	Corpus Christi	847	314,696	Wichita	Wichita Falls	606	129,964
Ochiltree	Perryton	919	9,048	Wilbarger	Vernon	947	14,027
Oldham	Vega	1,485	2,156	Willacy	Raymondville	589	19,990
Orange	Orange	362	84,364	Williamson	Georgetown	1,137	289,924
Palo Pinto	Palo Pinto	949	27,306	Wilson	Floresville	807	34,548
Panola	Carthage	812	22,734	Winkler	Kermit	840	6,892
Parker	Weatherford	902	94,618	Wise	Decatur	902	52,926
Parmer	Farwell	885	9,877	Wood	Quitman	689	38,053
Pecos	Ft. Stockton	4,776	16,421	Yoakum	Plains	800	7,305
Polk	Livingston	1,061	44,449	Young	Graham	919	17,725
Potter	Amarillo	902	116,093	Zapata	Zapata	999	12,788
Presidio	Marfa	3,857	7,681	Zavala	Crystal City	1,298	11,556
Rains	Emory	243	10,236				
Randall	Canyon	917	106,822	TOTALS		262,017	21,779,893
Reagan	Big Lake	1,173	3,182				
Real	Leakey	697	2,999				
Red River	Clarksville	1,054	13,941				
Reeves	Pecos	2,626	12,478				

As of 2000, foreign-born Texans numbered 2,899,642 (13.9% of the total population). In the same year, Asians numbered 562,319 (the 3rd-largest Asian population among the 50 states). The 2000 census counted 105,829 Chinese (nearly double the 1990 total of 55,023), 58,340 Filipinos, 129,365 Asian Indians (more than triple the 1990 figure of 40,506), 45,571 Koreans, 17,120 Japanese, and 10,114 Laotians. Of the 134,961 Vietnamese (up from 60,649 in 1990), many were refugees who resettled in Texas beginning in 1975. Pacific Islanders numbered 14,434 in 2000.

The term "Anglos" denotes all whites except Spanish-surnamed or Spanish-speaking individuals.

8LANGUAGES

The Indians of Texas are mostly descendants of the Alabama-Coushatta who came to Texas in the 19th century. The few Indian place-names include Texas itself, Pecos, Waco, and Toyah.

Most of the regional features in Texas English derive from the influx of South Midland and Southern speakers, with a noticeable Spanish flavor from older as well as more recent loans. Settlers from the Gulf Coast states brought such terms as *snap beans* (green beans), the widespread *pail* (here probably of Southern rather the Northern origin), and *carry* (escort), with a 47% frequency in north Texas and 22% in the south. Louisiana *praline* (pecan patty) is now widespread, but *banquette* (sidewalk) appears only in the extreme southeast corner.

Southern and South Midland terms were largely introduced by settlers from Arkansas, Missouri, and Tennessee; their use ranges from northeast to west, but with declining frequency in the trans-Pecos area. Examples are *clabber cheese* (cottage cheese), *mosquito hawk* (dragonfly), *croker sack* (burlap bag), *mouth harp* (harmonica), *branch* (stream), and *dog irons* (andirons). A dialect survey showed *pallet* (bed on the floor) with a 90% overall frequency; *light bread* (white bread) and *pullybone* (wishbone), each 78%; and *you-all*, more than 80%. General Midland terms also widespread in the state are *sook!* (call to calves), *blinds* (roller shades), *piece* (a certain distance), and *quarter till five* (4:45).

Some terms exhibit uneven distribution. Examples include *mott* (clump of trees) in the south and southwest, *sugan* (a wool-filled comforter for a cowboy's bedroll) in the west, Midland *draw* (dry streambed) in the west and southwest, South Midland *peckerwood* (woodpecker) in most of the state except west of the Pecos, *poke* (paper bag) in the central and northern areas, and *surly* (euphemism for bull) in the west. A curious result of dialect mixture is the appearance of a number of hybrids combining two different dialects, such as *freeseed peach* from *freestone* and *clearseed*, *fire mantel* and *mantel board* from *fireboard* and *mantel*, *flapcakes* from *flapjacks* and *pancakes*, and *horse doctor* from *horsefly* and *snake doctor*. The large sandwich is known as a *torpedo* in San Antonio and a *poorboy* in Houston.

Texas pronunciation is largely South Midland, with such characteristic forms as /caow/, and /naow/ for *cow* and *now* and /dyoo/ for *due*, although /doo/ is now more common in urban areas. In the German settlement around New Braunfels are heard a few loanwords such as *smearcase* (cottage cheese), *krebbel* (doughnut), *clook* (setting hen), and *oma* and *opa* for grandmother and grandfather.

Spanish has been the major foreign-language influence. In areas like Laredo and Brownsville, along the Rio Grande, as many as 90% of the people may be bilingual; in northeast Texas, however, Spanish is as foreign as French. In the days of the early Spanish ranchers, standard English adopted *hacienda*, *ranch*, *burro*, *canyon*, and *lariat*; in the southwestern cattle country are heard *la reata* (lasso), *remuda* (group of horses), and *resaca* (pond), along with the *acequia* (irrigation ditch), *pilon* (something extra, as a trip), and *olla* (water jar). The presence of

the large Spanish-speaking population was a major factor in the passage of the state's bilingual education law, as a result of which numerous school programs in both English and Spanish are now offered; in a ruling issued in January 1981, US District Judge William Wayne Justice ruled that by 1987, the state must expand such programs to cover all Spanish-speaking students. Legislation enacted in 1995 established a requirement for schools with a certain number of students with limited English proficiency to be required to have bilingual and/or English as a second language programs. About one-sixth of all Texas counties—and a great many cities—are named for Mexicans or Spaniards or after place-names in Spain or Mexico.

In 2000, 13,230,765 Texans—68.8% of the population five years old or older—spoke only English at home, down from 74.6% in 1990.

The following table gives selected statistics from the 2000 census for language spoken at home by persons five years old and over. The category "African languages" includes Amharic, Ibo, Twi, Yoruba, Bantu, Swahili, and Somali. The category "Other Asian languages" includes Dravidian languages, Malayalam, Telugu, Tamil, and Turkish. The category "Other Indic languages" includes Bengali, Marathi, Punjabi, and Romany. The category "Other Slavic languages" includes Czech, Slovak, and Ukrainian.

LANGUAGE	NUMBER	PERCENT
Population 5 years and over	**19,241,518**	**100.0**
Speak only English	13,230,765	68.8
Speak a language other than English	6,010,753	31.2
Speak a language other than English	**6,010,753**	**31.2**
Spanish or Spanish Creole	5,195,182	27.0
Vietnamese	122,517	0.6
Chinese	91,500	0.5
German	82,117	0.4
French (incl. Patois, Cajun)	62,274	0.3
Tagalog	39,988	0.2
Korean	38,451	0.2
African languages	36,087	0.2
Urdu	32,978	0.2
Arabic	32,909	0.2
Other Asian languages	32,780	0.2
Other Indic languages	24,454	0.1
Hindi	20,919	0.1
Gujarathi	19,140	0.1
Persian	17,558	0.1
Other Slavic languages	15,448	0.1
Japanese	14,701	0.1
Russian	11,574	0.1
Italian	11,158	0.1
Laotian	10,378	0.1

9RELIGIONS

Because of its Spanish heritage, Texas originally was entirely Roman Catholic except for unconverted Indians. Consequently, the early history of Texas is almost identical with that of the Roman Catholic Church in the area. Under the Mexican Republic, the Catholic Church continued as the sole recognized religious body. In order to receive the generous land grants given by the Mexicans, Anglo-American immigrants had to sign a paper saying that they followed the Catholic religion. With an average grant of 4,605 acres (1,864 hectares) as bait, many early Protestants and atheists must have felt little hesitancy about becoming instant Catholics.

The Mexican government was careless about enforcing adherence to the Catholic faith in Texas, however, and many Baptists, Methodists, and Presbyterians drifted in from the east. The Methodist practice of having itinerant ministers range over frontier areas was particularly well suited to the Texas scene and, in 1837, the church hierarchy sent three preachers to the new republic. The first presbytery had been formed by that date and

Baptists had organized in Houston by 1840. Swedish and German immigrants brought their Lutheranism with them; the first German Lutheran synod was organized in Houston in 1851.

Geographically, Texas tends to be heavily Protestant in the north and east and Catholic in the south and southwest. Leading Protestant denominations and their known adherents in 2000 were the Southern Baptist Convention, 3,519,459; the United Methodist Church, 1,022,342; Churches of Christ, 377,264; Assemblies of God, 228,098; the Presbyterian Church USA, 180,315; the Episcopal Church, 177,910; Independent Charismatic Churches, 159,449; the Church of Jesus Christ of Latter-Day Saints, 155,451; the Evangelical Lutheran Church in America, 155,019; Independent Non-Charismatic Churches, 145,249; and the Lutheran Church—Missouri Synod, 140,106. Roman Catholics numbered 4,368,969 in 2000. There were an estimated 128,000 Jews, 114,999 Muslims, and about 10,777 adherents to the Baha'i faith. There were about 9.2 million people (44.5% of the population) who were not counted as members of any religious organization.

10 TRANSPORTATION

Texas ranks first among the 50 states in total railroad mileage, highway mileage, and number of airports, and 2nd only to California in motor vehicle registrations and in number of general aviation aircraft.

Transportation has been a severe problem for Texas because of the state's extraordinary size and sometimes difficult terrain; one of the more unusual experiments in US transport history was the use of camels in southwestern Texas during the mid-1800s. The Republic of Texas authorized railroad construction as early as 1836, but the financial panic of 1837 helped kill that attempt. Not until 1853 did the state's first railroad—from Harrisburg (now incorporated into Houston) to Stafford's Point, 20 mi (32 km) to the west—come into service. At the outbreak of the Civil War, 10 railroads were operating, all but two connected with seaports. Although the state legislature in 1852 had offered railroad companies eight sections (5,120 acres/2,072 hectares) of land per mile of road construction and doubled that offer two years later, Texas lacked sufficient capital to satisfy its railroad-building needs until the war was over. The state generally held to the 10,240-acre (4,144-hectare) figure until all grants ceased in 1882. In all, Texas granted more than 50,000 sq mi (130,000 sq km) to railroad companies.

In 1870, Texas had fewer than 600 mi (970 km) of track; 10 years later, it had 3,026 mi (4,870 km); in 1890, 6,045 mi (9,729 km); and by 1920, 16,049 mi (25,828 km). A peak was reached in 1932, when there were 17,078 mi (27,484 km) of track; by the end of 2000, trackage had dwindled to 14,006 rail mi (22,540 km), with 11,377 mi (18,309 km) of the total being Class I railroad. Total rail mileage in Texas still ranks higher than any other state. Three carriers—Burlington Northern/Santa Fe, Kansas City Southern, and Union Pacific—control almost 85% of the mileage. The only rail passenger service in Texas is provided by Amtrak, which runs two routes—the Sunset Limited (New Orleans–Los Angeles) from Beaumont through Houston and San Antonio to El Paso, and the Texas Eagle (Chicago–San Antonio).

In mid-1983, Dallas-area voters approved the creation of the Dallas Area Rapid Transit system (DART) to serve the city and 13 suburbs. Surface rail routes, running 160 mi (257 km), were to be constructed and bus service doubled at an expense of some $8.9 billion over a 26-year period. Ft. Worth has the state's only true subway—a 1-mi (1.6-km) line from a parking lot to a downtown shipping and office center—although Dallas-Ft. Worth Regional Airport has its own rail shuttle system.

Texas has by far the most mileage of any state. In 2000, Texas had 301,035 mi (484,468 km) of public roadway, 218,641 mi (351,868 km) of it rural. In 1997, expenditures on roads and highways by federal, state, and local governments came to more than $7.5 billion, 2nd only to California. The leading interstate highways are I-10 and I-20, respectively linking Houston and the Dallas–Ft.Worth Areas with El Paso in the west, and I-35 and I-45, connecting Dallas–Ft. Worth with, respectively, San Antonio (via Austin) and Galveston (via Houston). There were 13,462,023 licensed drivers in 2000 (2nd highest). Registered motor vehicles in 2000 included 7,616,183 automobiles, 6,368,516 trucks, 187,174 motorcycles, and 85,397 buses.

River transport did not become commercially successful until the end of the 19th century, when the Houston Ship Channel was dredged along the San Jacinto River and Buffalo Bayou for more than 50 mi (80 km), and another channel was dredged down the Neches River to make a seaport out of Beaumont. With 13 major seaports and many shallow-water ports, Texas has been a major factor in waterborne commerce since the early 1950s. The Port of Houston is the nation's 2nd most active harbor, with over 158.8 million tons of cargo handled in 2000. The Gulf Intracoastal Waterway begins in Brownsville, at the mouth of the Rio Grande, and extends across Texas for 423 mi (681 km) on its way to Florida and its connections with a similar waterway on the Atlantic.

After American entry into World War I, Texas began to build airfields for training grounds; when the war ended, many US fliers returned to Texas and became civilian commercial pilots, carrying air mail (from 1926), dusting crops, and mapping potential oil fields. In 2002, the state had 1,805 landing facilities. In 2000, the Dallas–Ft. Worth Regional Airport, the nation's largest air terminal, serviced nearly half of the aircraft departures in Texas, with another sixth handled by George Bush Intercontinental Airport. In May 1999, the city of Austin formally opened the $585 million Austin-Bergstrom Airport.

11 HISTORY

Although a site near Lewisville, in Denton County, contains artifacts that might be more than 37,000 years old, the generally accepted date for the earliest human presence in the region now known as Texas is the Llano civilization, dating from 12,000 years ago. Prehistoric Indians in Texas failed to develop as complex technologies as their neighbors to the west and east. When the first Europeans arrived in the 16th century, the Indians had developed little in the way of pottery or basketry, and had shown little interest in agriculture except in the extreme east and northeast, and possibly west of the Pecos. They were still largely hunter-gatherers on whom the more technologically complex cultures of Mexico and the southeastern US had little effect.

Along the Gulf coast and overlapping into northeastern Mexico were the Coahuiltecan and Karankawa peoples. They lived in a hostile environment, consuming berries in season, animal dung, spiders, and an occasional deer, bison, or jabalina. In central Texas lived the Tonkawa, who hunted buffalo, slept in teepees, used dogs for hauling, and had a communal structure akin to that of the Plains Indians. Unlike the Karankawa, who were tall, the Tonkawa were of average height, tattooed, and dressed in breech-clouts-long for men, short for women. They proved extremely susceptible to European diseases and evidently died out, whereas the Karankawa migrated to northern Mexico.

About two dozen tribes of Caddo in eastern and northeastern Texas were at the time of European penetration the most technologically complex Indians living within the state's present borders. Having developed agriculture, the Caddo were relatively sedentary and village oriented. Those belonging to the Hasinai Confederation called each other tayshas, a term that translates as "allies" or "friends." When the Hasinai told Spanish explorers that they were tayshas, the Spaniards wrote the word as Tejas, which in time became Texas. The Caddo lived in the gentle portion of Texas, where woods, wild fruits, and berries abound, and where game was plentiful until the advent of European civilization. Life was so good, in fact, that several members of an expedition under Robert Cavelier, Sieur de la Salle, reaching Matagorda Bay on 15 February 1685, chose to desert to the Caddo rather than remain with their fellow Frenchmen. Henri de Tonti, who entered the region somewhat later, reported that one Caddo tribe had a woman as chief. The Caddo were also unusual in their belief that three women had created the world.

In trans-Pecos Texas, to the west, lived a fourth Indian group, the Jumano, probably descendants of the Pueblo cultures. Some of the Jumano were nomadic hunters in the Davis and Chisos mountains. Others became farmers along the Rio Grande and the lower Rio Conchos, making and using some pottery and raising good crops of corn, beans, squash, and possibly cotton. Probably the successive droughts so common to the region began to thin out their ranks, and the coming of the Spanish removed them from the historical picture altogether.

The first European to enter Texas was Spanish explorer Alonso Alvarez de Pineda, who sailed into the mouth of the Rio Grande in 1519. Basically, the Spanish left the Texas Indians alone for more than 150 years. Sometimes an accident placed Spaniards in Texas, or sometimes they entered by design, but generally, the Spanish looked on Texas as too remote from Florida and the Mexico highlands-where most of their colonizing occurred-for successful settlement. A remarkable episode of this period involves the survivors of the Pánfilo de Narváez expedition, which had been commissioned to occupy the Gulf of Mexico coast from Mexico to Florida. Four shipwrecked men, led by Álvar Nunez Cabeza de Vaca, were washed ashore on a Texas sandbar on 6 November 1528: three were Spaniards, and one was the Moor Estevanico. For eight years, they wandered virtually naked among the Texas Indians, sometimes as slaves and sometimes as free men, alternately blistered by the summer sun and freezing under winter ice storms. Using a deer bone as a needle, Cabeza removed an arrowhead from deep in an Indian's chest—a bit of surgical magic that earned him treatment as a demigod, for a time. Finally, the four Europeans reached the west coast of Mexico, from where Cabeza de Vaca returned home a hero. The other two Spaniards remained in Mexico, but Estevanico joined the Fray Marcos de Niza expedition as a guide, dying at the hands of Pueblo Indians in New Mexico in 1539. The trail he helped blaze through the High Plains of West Texas served as the route for the expedition a year later by Francisco Vásquez de Coronado. The first Texas towns and missions were begun by Spaniards in West Texas, outside present-day El Paso. Ysleta del Sur was founded in 1682, almost a decade before the earliest East Texas missions. But Ysleta was 500 mi (800 km) from anything else resembling a settlement in Texas, and the Spanish considered it a part of New Mexico.

What changed the Spaniards' attitude toward the colonization of Texas was the establishment of Ft. St. Louis by La Salle on the Gulf coast in 1685. Four years later, Capt. Alonso de León, governor of Coahuila, sent out an expedition to expel the French. Father Damien Massanet, a Coahuilan priest, accompanied the León expedition and was charged with establishing a mission near wherever the captain built a fort. During the next several decades these two men and their successors established a string of mission-forts across Texas. After fear of the French presence eased, Spain tended to neglect these establishments. But when the French entered Louisiana in force during the early 18th century, Spanish fears of French expansion were re-ignited. In 1718, the Spanish began to build a mission, San Antonio de Valero, and a fort, San Antonio de Bexar, at the site of the present city of San Antonio. As a halfway post between Mexico and the Louisiana border, San Antonio grew to be Texas's most important city during the Spanish period.

Until the 19th century, the US showed little interest in Texas. But the purchase of Louisiana Territory from the French by the US government in 1803 made Texas a next-door neighbor, and "filibusters" (military adventurers) began to filter across the border into Spanish territory. The best known is Philip Nolan, an Irish-born intriguer who started spending time in Texas as early as 1790. Ostensibly, he was trading horses with the Indians, but the Spanish associated him with Aaron Burr's schemes to excise the Spanish southwest from its owners. In the summer of 1800, the Spanish governor of Texas, Juan Bautista Elguezábal, ordered that Nolan should be arrested if he returned. In December of that year, Nolan returned with a small force of 20 men and built a fort near Nacogdoches; he was killed fighting the Spanish on 4 March 1801. Nolan is remembered for having drafted the first Anglo-American map of Texas.

In 1810–11, the Mexicans launched their revolution against Spain, and though only an outpost, Texas as a Spanish-Mexican colony was naturally involved. In 1813, Texas formally declared its independence of Spain and its intention of becoming a Mexican state, with its capital at San Antonio. Various Anglo-Americans entered the new state to serve on behalf of Mexico. Pirates also aided the Mexican cause: on Galveston Island, Luis Aury preyed on Spanish shipping, and after 1816, his place was taken by Jean Laffite, who privateered against both Spanish and US shipping until the US Navy drove him out.

The Spanish finally gave up on Mexico in 1821, leaving Texas as a Mexican province with a non-Indian population of about 7,000. The only towns of significant size were Goliad, San Antonio (commonly called Bexar), and Nacogdoches. A year earlier, Moses Austin of Missouri had received permission from Spanish authorities to introduce Anglo-American colonists into Texas, presumably as a barrier against aggression by the US. When Spanish rule ended, his son, Stephen F. Austin, succeeded his late father as head of the colonization movement, securing permission from the new Mexican government to settle 300 families in the area between the lower Colorado and Brazos rivers. After Austin had settled his "Old Three Hundred" in 1821, he received permission to settle more, and within a decade, his colonists numbered more than 5,000. The Mexicans invested Austin with the responsibilities and privileges of an empresario: authority to run commerce, maintain militia, administer justice, and hand out land titles. Other empresarios made similar arrangements. Green DeWitt, also of Missouri, settled several hundred families farther west and founded the town of Gonzales in 1825. Hayden Edwards received a grant to settle 800 families near Nacogdoches. Mexicans were also permitted to organize colonies. Texas thus began a pattern of growth from the outside that has continued to the present day.

Between 1821 and 1835, the population of non-Indian Texas expanded to between 35,000 and 50,000. Most new settlers were Anglo-Americans who often brought their prejudices against Mexico with them, whether they were from the North or the South. They disliked Mexican culture, Mexican folkways, Mexican justice—and the Protestants among them resented the omnipresence of the Roman Catholic Church. All of these Anglo-American settlers had ties to the US, and many undoubtedly longed for the time when they would live under the American flag again. The ineptitude of the Mexican government made the situation even worse. In 1826, Hayden Edwards organized the Republic of Fredonia and tried to drive the Mexicans from East Texas, but in the end, he had to flee the province himself. Troubled by the rising spirit of rebellion, the Mexican Congress enacted the Law of 1830, which forbade most immigration and imposed duties on all imports. Anglo-Americans in Texas responded with the same anger that New Englanders had once shown when Britain imposed tax restrictions on the original American colonies.

At first, the Anglo-Texans insisted they were opposing Mexican political excesses, not the Mexican nation. Their hope lay with Gen. Antonio López de Santa Anna, who was leading a liberal revolution against President Anastasio Bustamante. Skirmishes between the Anglo-Texans and Mexican officials remained sporadic and localized until 1833 when Santa Anna became president of Mexico and almost immediately dropped his liberal stance. Texans sent Austin to Mexico City to petition Santa Anna to rescind the Law of 1830, to allow the use of English in public business, and to make Texas (then an appendage of Coahuila) a separate state. After several months in Mexico City, Austin was arrested on his way back to Texas and was imprisoned for a year. When Santa Anna tried to enforce customs collections, colonists at Anahuac, led by William Barret Travis, drove the Mexican officials out of town. Santa Anna's answer was to place Texas under military jurisdiction. When the Mexican military commander, Col. Domingo de Ugartechea, sent his soldiers to Gonzales to take a cannon from the colonists, the Anglo-Texan civilians drove them off on 2 October 1835, in a battle that is generally considered to mark the start of the Texas Revolution.

On 3 November, a provisional government was formed. It called not for independence but for a return to the liberal Mexican constitution of 1824. Three commissioners, one of them Austin, were sent to Washington, D.C., to request aid from the US. Sam Houston, who only six years earlier had resigned the governorship of Tennessee (when his wife left him) and had come to Texas after stays in Oklahoma and Arkansas, was named commander in chief of the upstart Texas army. Hostilities remained at a standstill until February 1836, when Santa Anna led an army across the Rio Grande. The Mexicans concentrated outside San Antonio at a mission-fort called the Alamo, where 187 or so Texans, commanded by Colonel William Barret Travis, had holed up in defense. The Mexicans besieged the Alamo until 6 March, when Santa Anna's forces, now numbering more than 4,000, stormed the fortress. When the battle ended, all the Alamo's defenders, including several native Mexicans, were dead. Among those killed were Travis and two Americans who became legends—James Bowie and Davy Crockett.

Four days before the battle of the Alamo, other Texans gathered at Washington-on-the-Brazos and issued a declaration of independence. As so often happens, a fight that had started on principle-in this case, a constitutional issue-grew into a fight for independence. The men who died at the Alamo believed they were fighting for restoration of the constitution of 1824. But three weeks after the Alamo fell, on 27 March 1836, the Mexicans killed 342 Texans who had surrendered at Goliad, thinking they would be treated as prisoners of war. Coming on the heels of the Alamo tragedy, the "Goliad massacre" persuaded Texans that only total victory or total defeat would solve their problems with Santa Anna. The Texas army under Sam Houston retreated before Santa Anna's oncoming forces, which held a numerical advantage over Houston's of about 1,600 to 800. On 21 April 1836, however, the Texans surprised the Mexicans during their siesta period at San Jacinto (east of present-day Houston). Mexican losses were 630 killed, 280 wounded, and 730 taken prisoner, while the Texans had only 9 killed and 30 wounded. This decisive battle-fought to the cry of "Remember the Alamo, remember Goliad!" freed Texas from Mexico once and for all.

For 10 years, Texas existed as an independent republic, recognized by the US, Belgium, France, the United Kingdom, the Netherlands, and several German states. Sam Houston, the victorious commander at San Jacinto, became the republic's first nationally elected president. Although Texans are proud of their once-independent status, the fact is that the republic limped along like any new nation, strife-torn and short of cash. It was unable to reach agreement with Mexico on a treaty to clarify the border. Moreover, its original $1-million public debt increased eightfold in a decade, and its paper money depreciated alarmingly. Consequently, when Texas joined the Union on 29 December 1845, the date of the US congressional resolution recognizing the new state (the Lone Star flag, the republic's official banner, was not actually lowered and a governor inaugurated until 19 February 1846), its citizens looked on the action as a rescue. The annexation in great measure provoked the Mexican War, which in turn led to the conclusion of the Treaty of Guadalupe Hidalgo on 2 February 1848. Under the treaty, Mexico dropped its claim to the territory between the Rio Grande and the Nueces River. Later, in accordance with the Compromise of 1850, Texas relinquished, for $10 million, its claim on lands stretching into New Mexico, Colorado, Wyoming, Oklahoma, and Kansas.

With the coming of the Civil War, Texas followed its proslavery southern neighbors out of the Union into the Confederacy; Governor Houston, who opposed secession, was ousted from office. The state saw little fighting, and Texas thus suffered from the war far less than most of the South. The last battle of the war was fought on Texas soil at Palmito Ranch, near Brownsville, on 13 May 1865—more than a month after General Robert E. Lee's surrender at Appomattox Court House in Virginia.

During Reconstruction, Texas was governed briefly by a military occupation force and then by a Republican regime; the so-called carpetbag constitution of 1869, passed during this period, gave the franchise to blacks, a right that the Ku Klux Klan actively sought to deny them. Texas was allowed to rejoin the Union on 30 March 1870. Three years later, Republican Governor Edmund J. Davis was defeated at the polls by Richard Coke, and a Democratic legislature wrote a new constitution, which was approved by the voters in 1876.

While most southern states were economically prostrate, the Texas economy flourished because of the rapid development of the cattle industry. Millions of Texas cattle walked the trails to northern markets, where they were sold for hard cash, providing a bonanza for the state. The widespread use of barbed wire to fence cattle ranches in the 1880s ended the open range and encouraged scientific cattle breeding. By 1900, Texas began to transform its predominantly agricultural economy into an industrial one. This process was accelerated by the discovery of the Spindletop oil field—the state's first gusher—near Beaumont in 1901, and by the subsequent development of the petroleum and petrochemical industries. World War I saw the emergence of Texas as a military training center. The rapid growth of the aircraft industry and other high-technology fields contributed to the continuing industrialization of Texas during and after World War II.

Texas politics remained solidly Democratic during most of the modern era, and the significant political conflict in the state was between the liberal and conservative wings of the Democratic Party. Populist-style reforms were enacted slowly during the governorships of James E. Ferguson—impeached and removed from office during his second term in 1917—and of his wife, Miriam A. "Ma" Ferguson (1925–27, 1933–35), and more rapidly during the two administrations of James V. Allred (1935–39). During the 1960s and 1970s, the Republican Party gathered strength in the state, electing John G. Tower as US senator in 1961 and William P. Clements, Jr., as governor in 1978—the first Republicans to hold those offices since Reconstruction. In general, the state's recent political leaders, Democrats was well as Republicans, have represented property interests and taken a conservative line.

On the national level, Texans have been influential since the 1930s, notably through such congressional leaders as US House Speaker Sam Rayburn and Senate Majority Leader Lyndon B.

Johnson. Johnson, elected vice president under John F. Kennedy, was riding in the motorcade with the president when Kennedy was assassinated in Dallas on 22 November 1963. The city attained further national notoriety when Kennedy's alleged killer, Lee Harvey Oswald, was shot to death by Jack Ruby, a Dallas nightclub operator, two days later. Johnson served out the remainder of Kennedy's term, was elected to the presidency by a landslide in 1964, and presided over one of the stormiest periods in US history before retiring to his LBJ ranch in 1969. Memorials to him include the Lyndon B. Johnson Library at Austin and the renamed Lyndon B. Johnson Space Center, headquarters for the US manned spaceflight program, near Houston.

The most prominent Texans on the national scene since Johnson have been Republican George H.W. Bush and his son, George W. Bush. After failing in his bid for the Republican presidential nomination in 1980, George Bush Sr. became Ronald Reagan's running mate; Reagan and Bush won in 1980 and were reelected in 1984. Bush ran for and won the presidency in 1988, but was defeated in his 1992 bid for re-election by Bill Clinton. Bush's son, George W. Bush, was elected governor of Texas in 1994, succeeding Democrat Ann Richards, the second woman governor in Texas history. In 2000, George W. Bush was elected president in a contested election against then-Vice President Al Gore.

Texas benefited from a booming oil industry in the 1970s. The economy grew at an average of 6% a year, more than twice the national average. The boom collapsed in the early 1980s as overproduction caused world oil prices to plummet. The state's annual rate of population growth, 60% of which came from migration, dropped from 4% in 1982 to 1.3% in 1985. By 1986, the state had become a net exporter of population. Scrambling to make up the $100 million in revenues that the government estimated it lost for every $1 dollar decline in the price of a barrel of oil, the government in 1985 imposed or raised fees on everything from vanity license plates to day-care centers. The state also took steps to encourage economic diversification by wooing service, electronics, and high-technology companies to Texas. In 1985, the government and the University of Texas at Austin persuaded Microchips and Computer Corporation, which translates basic scientific research into computer innovations, to settle in Austin. In the late 1980s, a number of Texas's financial institutions collapsed, brought down by the slump in the oil industry and by unsound real estate loans.

Since 1986, oil prices have increased and stabilized, and the state has reaped the benefits of diversification efforts spurred by the oil price collapse earlier in the decade. Although the petroleum industry was still the state's leading economic sector in the mid-1990s, high-technology and service sector jobs had played a major role in rebuilding the Texas economy and reversing the population decline of the previous decade. High-tech companies were concentrated in the "Silicon Hills" area surrounding Austin.

In the early 2000s, Texas had the 2nd-largest population of any state, behind California. The high rate of migration into Texas which accompanied the oil boom had a profound effect on the state's population distribution and political profile. Newcomers to the state have tended to share the fiscally conservative values of native Texans but take more liberal positions on issues such as abortion, civil rights, and homosexuality. According to the 2000 census, 32% of the Texas population was of Hispanic or Latino origin.

On 19 April 1993, the 51-day confrontation between the FBI and the Branch Davidian cult near Waco ended tragically when the group's compound burned to the ground, killing at least 72 persons.

In early 2003, 51 Democratic state representatives fled Texas for Oklahoma to prevent the Republican-dominated state House of Representatives from passing a controversial redistricting plan that would favor Republicans. The tactic worked when the House failed to reach quorum and the redistricting bill died. State Democratic senators later also fled the state (for New Mexico) in July 2003 to break quorum and thus block a redistricting bill. Republican Governor Rick Perry had called special legislative sessions to take up the redistricting measures, but as of September 2003, they had failed.

12 STATE GOVERNMENT

Texas has been governed directly under eight constitutions: the Mexican national constitution of 1824, the Coahuila-Texas state constitution of 1827, the independent Republic of Texas constitution of 1836, and the five US state constitutions of 1845, 1861, 1866, 1869, and 1876. This last document, with 410 amendments (through 2002), is the foundation of the state government today. An attempt to replace it with eight propositions that in effect would have given Texas a new constitution was defeated at the polls in November 1975.

The state legislature consists of a senate of 31 members elected to four-year terms, and a house of representatives of 150 members elected to two-year terms. The legislature meets on the 2nd Tuesday in January of odd-numbered years for sessions of as many as 140 calendar days; the governor may also call special sessions, each limited to 30 calendar days. Senators and representatives receive the same pay, pursuant to a constitutional amendment of 1975: $7,200 per year (as of 2002, unchanged from 1999) and $124 per diem living expenses (as of 2002) while the legislature is in session. All legislators must be US citizens, qualified voters, and residents of their districts for at least one year. Further, senators are required to be at least 26 years old and to have lived in the state for a minimum of five years. Representatives must be at least 21 and must have lived in the state for at least two years before election.

The state's chief executives are the governor and lieutenant governor, separately elected to four-year terms. Other elected executives, also serving four-year terms, include the attorney general, comptroller, treasurer, commissioner of agriculture, and commissioner of the general land office. The remaining cabinet members are appointed by the governor, who also appoints members of the many executive boards and commissions. The governor, whose salary was $115,345 as of 2002 (unchanged from 1999), must be a US citizen, at least 30 years old, and must have resided in the state for at least five years prior to election. A uniquely important executive agency is the Texas Railroad Commission (TRC). Established in 1891 and consisting of three members elected for six-year terms, the commission regulates the state's railroads, oil and gas production, coal and uranium mining, and trucking industry. The TRC thus wields extraordinary economic power, and the alleged influence by the regulated industries over the commission has been a major source of political controversy in the state.

To become law, a bill must be approved by a majority of members present and voting in each house, with a quorum of two-thirds of the membership present, and either signed by the governor or left unsigned for 10 days while the legislature is in session or 20 days after it has adjourned. A gubernatorial veto may be overridden by a two-thirds vote of members present in the house of origin, followed by either a vote of two-thirds of members present in the lower house or two-thirds of the entire membership of the senate (the difference is the result of differing interpretations of an ambiguity in the state constitution). Overrides have been rare: the vote in April 1979 by state legislators to override the new Republican governor's veto of a minor wildlife regulation measure affecting only one county was the first successful attempt in 38 years. A constitutional amendment requires a two-thirds vote of the membership of each house and ratification by the voters at the next election.

In order to vote in Texas one must be a US citizen, at least 18 years old, and a resident in the county of registration. Restrictions apply to convicted felons and those declared mentally incompetent by the court.

13 POLITICAL PARTIES

Until recent years, the Democratic Party had dominated politics in Texas. William P. Clements, Jr., elected governor in 1978, was the first Republican since Reconstruction to hold that office. No Republican carried Texas in a presidential election until 1928, when Herbert Hoover defeated Democrat Al Smith, a Roman Catholic at a severe disadvantage in a Protestant fundamentalist state. Another Roman Catholic, Democratic presidential candidate John Kennedy, carried the state in 1960 largely because he had a Texan, Lyndon Johnson, on his ticket.

Prior to the Civil War, many candidates for statewide office ran as independents. After a period of Republican rule during Reconstruction, Democrats won control of the statehouse and state legislature in 1873. The major challenge to Democratic rule during the late 19th century came not from Republicans but from the People's Party, whose candidates placed 2nd in the gubernatorial races of 1894, 1896, and 1898, aided by the collapse of the cotton market; imposition of a poll tax in 1902 helped disfranchise the poor white farmers and laborers who were the base of Populist support. The Populists and the Farmers' Alliance probably exercised their greatest influence through a Democratic reformer, Governor James S. Hogg (1891–95), who fought the railroad magnates, secured lower freight rates for farmers and shippers, and curbed the power of large landholding companies. Another Democratic governor, James E. "Farmer Jim" Ferguson, was elected on an agrarian reform platform in 1914 and reelected in 1916, but was impeached and convicted the following year for irregular financial dealings. Barred from holding state office, he promoted the candidacy of his wife, Miriam "Ma" Ferguson, whose first term as governor (1925–27) marked her as a formidable opponent of the Ku Klux Klan. During her second term (1933–35), the state's first New Deal reforms were enacted, and prohibition was repealed. The

Fergusons came to represent the more liberal wing of the Democratic Party in a state where liberals have long been in the minority. After the progressive administration of Governor James V. Allred, during which the state's first old-age assistance program was enacted, conservative Democrats, sometimes called "Texas Tories," controlled the state until the late 1970s.

In the November 1994 elections, George W. Bush (son of former President George H. W. Bush), upset Ann Richards to become governor. Bush was reelected in 1998, shortly before announcing his run for the US presidency. Republican Kay Bailey Hutchison was elected in 1993 to fill the Senate seat vacated by Democrat Lloyd Bentsen, who resigned to become secretary of the treasury in the Clinton administration. In 1994, Hutchinson won reelection to a full term, and she was reelected once again in 2000. Republican John Cornyn was elected to the Senate in 2002. Following the 2002 elections, Texas Democrats held 17 seats in the US House of Representatives and the Republicans 15. As of mid-2003, the Republicans continued to control the state house by a margin of 88 to 62, and that had a majority of 19–12 over the Democrats in the state senate.

Republican and native son George H. W. Bush captured 56% of the vote in the 1988 presidential election and 41% in the 1992 election. In 2000, his son, George W. Bush, took 59% of the presidential popular vote to Democrat Al Gore's 38%, and Bush went on to become president. As of 2002 there were 12,563,459 registered voters in the state; there is no voter registration by party in Texas. The state had 32 electoral votes in the 2000 presidential election.

Aside from the Populists, third parties have played a minor role in Texas politics. The Native American (Know-Nothing) Party helped elect Sam Houston governor in 1859. In 1968, George Wallace of the American Independent Party won 19% of the Texas popular vote and in 1992 native son Ross Perot picked up 22% of the vote.

Following passage of the federal Voting Rights Act of 1965, registration of black voters increased to about 11.5% of the total population of voters. Between 1895 and 1967, no black person served as a state legislator. By 1993, however, there were 472 blacks holding elective office. At about the same time. Hispanic elected officials numbered 2,215. Democrat Henry Cisneros,

Texas Presidential Vote by Political Parties, 1948–2000

YEAR	ELECTORAL VOTE	TEXAS WINNER	DEMOCRAT	REPUBLICAN	STATES' RIGHTS DEMOCRAT	PROGRESSIVE	PROHIBITION
1948	23	*Truman (D)	750,700	282,240	106,909	3,764	2,758
					CONSTITUTION		
1952	24	*Eisenhower (R)	969,227	1,102,818	1,563	—	1,983
1956	24	*Eisenhower (R)	859,958	1,080,619	14,591	—	—
1960	24	*Kennedy (D)	1,167,935	1,121,693	18,170	—	3,868
1964	25	*Johnson (D)	1,663,185	958,566	5,060	—	—
					AMERICAN IND.		
1968	25	Humphrey (D)	1,266,804	1,227,844	584,269	—	—
					AMERICAN	SOC. WORKERS	
1972	26	*Nixon (R)	1,154,289	2,298,896	6,039	8,664	—
1976	26	*Carter (D)	2,082,319	1,953,300	11,442	1,723	—
					LIBERTARIAN		
1980	26	*Reagan (R)	1,881,147	2,510,705	37,643	—	—
1984	29	*Reagan (R)	1,949,276	3,433,428	—	—	—
						NEW ALLIANCE	
1988	29	*Bush (R)	2,352,748	3,036,829	30,355	7,208	—
						POPULIST/AMERICA FIRST	IND. (Perot)
1992	32	Bush (R)	2,281,815	2,496,071	19,699	505	1,354,781
1996	32	Dole (R)	2,549,683	2,736,167	20,256	—	378,537
						GREEN	IND. (Buchanan)
2000	32	*Bush, G. W. (R)	2,433,746	3,799,639	23,160	137,994	12,394

* Won US presidential election.

former mayor of San Antonio, served as Secretary of Housing and Urban Development in the Clinton Administration.

14 LOCAL GOVERNMENT

The Texas constitution grants considerable autonomy to local governments. As of 2002, Texas had 254 counties, a number that has remained constant since 1931. In 2002 there were 1,196 municipal governments, 1,089 public school districts (down from 8,600 in 1910), and 2,245 special districts.

Each county is governed by a commissioners' court, consisting of commissioners elected by precinct and a county judge or administrator elected at large. Other elected officials generally include a county clerk, attorney, treasurer, assessor-collector, and sheriff.

At the municipal level, cities with populations greater than 5,000 can adopt home rule.

15 STATE SERVICES

To address the continuing threat of terrorism and to work with the federal Department of Homeland Security (created in 2002 following the terrorist attacks of 11 September 2001), homeland security in Texas in 2003 operated under executive order; the lieutenant governor was designated as the state homeland security advisor.

The state of Texas provides environmental protection through its Natural Resource Conservation Commission. The Department of Housing and Human Affairs helps to provide shelter for all citizens. The Ethics Commission promotes individual participation and confidence in governmental processes by enforcing and administering applicable laws and by providing public official conduct information.

Educational services in the public schools are administered by the Texas Education Agency, which is run by a commissioner of education appointed by an elected State Board of Education; the State Textbook Committee, appointed by the board, oversees textbook purchases statewide. The Coordinating Board for the State College and University System, consisting of appointed members, oversees public higher education. Transportation facilities are regulated by the State Highway and Public Transportation Commission, the Texas Railroad Commission, and the Texas Aeronautics Commission.

Health and welfare services are offered by the Department of Health and the Department of Human Services, while public protection is the responsibility of the National Guard, Texas Department of Corrections, and Texas Youth Council, which maintains institutions for juvenile offenders. Labor services are provided by the Texas Employment Commission and the Department of Labor and Standards. Other departments deal with mental health and mental retardation, public safety, aging, banking, and agriculture.

16 JUDICIAL SYSTEM

The Texas judiciary comprises the supreme court, the state court of criminal appeals, 14 courts of appeals, and more than 380 district courts.

The highest court is the supreme court, consisting of a chief justice and eight justices, who are popularly elected to staggered six-year terms. The court of criminal appeals, which has final jurisdiction in most criminal cases, consists of a presiding judge and eight judges, also elected to staggered six-year terms.

Justices of the courts of appeals, numbering 80 in 1999, are elected to six-year terms and sit in 14 judicial districts; each court has a chief justice and at least two associate justices. There were 27 district court judges in 1999, each elected to a four-year term. County, justice of the peace, and municipal courts handle local matters.

As of June 2001, there were 164,465 offenders incarcerated within the Texas Department of Criminal Justice facilities, an decrease of 2.2% from the previous year. The state's incarceration rate stood at 731 per 100,000 inhabitants. According to the FBI Crime Index, Texas had a 2001 total crime rate of 5,152.7 per 100,000 population, including a total of 122,155 violent crimes and 976,654 crimes against property in that year. Texas criminal law provides for capital punishment by lethal intravenous injection for certain violent crimes. Between 1977 and 2003, 306 persons were executed in Texas, by far the highest number in the nation. As of 2003, there were 454 inmates under sentence of death.

17 ARMED FORCES

In few states do US military forces and defense-related industries play such a large role as in Texas, which as of 2002 had 115,000 active-duty military personnel and 37,238 civilian personnel employed at major US military bases. Also in 2002, Texas received prime defense contract awards worth more than $9.5 billion.

Ft. Sam Houston, at San Antonio, is headquarters of the US 5th Army, while Ft. Bliss, at El Paso, is the home of the US Army Air Defense Center. Ft. Hood, near Killeen, is headquarters of the 3rd Army Corps and other military units. It is the state's single largest defense installation. Ft. Sam Houston is also the headquarters of the US Army Health Services Command and the site of the Academy of Health Sciences, the largest US military medical school, enrolling more than 25,000 officers and enlisted personnel and providing correspondence courses for another 30,000 students. Brooke Army Medical Center, the 2nd-largest US Army hospital, is located at the same installation. William Beaumont Army Medical Center, at El Paso, is one of the nation's largest US Army hospitals and one of its most modern medical treatment centers.

Four principal Air Force bases are located near San Antonio: Brooks, Kelly, Lackland, and Randolph. Other major air bases are Dyess (Abilene); Ellington (southwest of Houston); Goodfellow (San Angelo); Laughlin (Del Rio); Reese (Lubbock); and Sheppard (Wichita Falls). All US-manned space flights are controlled from the Lyndon B. Johnson Space Center, operated by the National Aeronautics and Space Administration. Naval air training stations are located at Corpus Christi, Beeville, Dallas, and Kingsville. The Inactive Ships Maintenance Facility, at Orange, is home port for some of the US Navy's "mothball fleet."

Texas was a major military training center during World War II, when about one out of every 10 soldiers was trained there. Some 750,000 Texans served in the US armed forces during that war; the state's war dead numbered 23,022. Military veterans living in the state according to the 2000 Census totaled 1,754,809, including 284,485 who served in World War II; 179,512 during the Korean conflict; 533,801 during the Vietnam era; and 263,192 during 1990–2000 (including the Persian Gulf War). Expenditures on Texas veterans totaled nearly $3.7 billion in 2002.

The Texas Army National Guard has dual status as a federal and state military force. The Texas State Guard is an all-volunteer force available either to back up National Guard units or to respond to local emergencies.

The famous Texas Rangers, a state police force first employed in 1823 (though not formally organized until 1835) to protect the early settlers, served as scouts for the US Army during the Mexican War. Many individual rangers fought with the Confederacy in the Civil War; during Reconstruction, however, the rangers were used to enforce unpopular carpetbagger laws. Later, the rangers put down banditry on the Rio Grande. The force was reorganized in 1935 as a unit of the Department of Public Safety and is now called on in major criminal cases, helps control mob violence in emergencies, and sometimes assists local police officers. The Texas Rangers have been romanticized in fiction and films, but one of their less glamorous tasks has been to intervene in labor disputes on the side of management. In 2000, the Texas Department of Public Safety employed 3,119 full-time sworn officers.

[18]MIGRATION

Estimates of the number of Indians living in Texas when the first Europeans arrived range from 30,000 to 130,000. Eventually, they all were killed, fled southward or westward, or were removed to reservations. The first great wave of white settlers, beginning in 1821, came from nearby southern states, particularly Tennessee, Alabama, Arkansas, and Mississippi; some of these newcomers brought their black slaves to work in the cotton fields. During the 1840s, a second wave of immigrants arrived directly from Germany, France, and eastern Europe.

Interstate migration during the second half of the 19th century was accelerated by the Homestead Act of 1862 and the westward march of the railroads. Particularly notable since 1900 has been the intrastate movement from rural areas to the cities; this trend was especially pronounced from the end of World War II, when about half the state's population was rural, to the late 1970s, when nearly four out of every five Texans made their homes in metropolitan areas.

Texas's net gain from migration between 1940 and 1980 was 1,821,000, 81% of that during the 1970–80 period. A significant proportion of postwar immigrants were seasonal laborers from Mexico, remaining in the US either legally or illegally. By 1990, Texas had a foreign-born population of 1,524,436, representing 9% of the total. During 1980–83, Texas had the highest net migration gain—922,000—in the nation. From 1985 to 1990, the net gain from migration was 36,700. Between 1990 and 1998, the state had net gains of 541,000 in domestic migration and 656,000 in international migration. In 1996, the state's foreign-born population was 2,081,000, or 11% of the total population. In 1998, 44,428 foreign immigrants arrived in Texas, the 4th-highest total among the states. Of that total, the greatest number of immigrants (22,956) came from Mexico. Between 1990 and 1998, Texas's overall population increased 16.3%. In the period 1995–2000, 1,362,849 people moved into the state and 1,214,609 moved out, for a net gain of 148,240, 17,957 of whom were age 65 or over.

[19]INTERGOVERNMENTAL COOPERATION

The Texas Commission on Interstate Cooperation represents Texas before the Council of State Governments. Texas is a member of the Interstate Mining Compact Commission and Interstate Oil and Gas Compact Commission. The state also belongs to the Gulf States Marine Fisheries Commission, South Central Interstate Forest Fire Protection Compact, Southern Southern States Energy Board, and Southern Regional Education Board, and to accords apportioning the waters of the Canadian, Pecos, Red River, Pecos, and Sabine rivers and the Rio Grande.

During 2001, Texas received over $21.6 billion in federal grants (3rd largest after California and New York).

[20]ECONOMY

Traditionally, the Texas economy has been dependent on the production of cotton, cattle, timber, and petroleum. In recent years, cotton has declined in importance, cattle ranchers have suffered financial difficulties because of increased production costs, and lumber production has remained relatively stable. But in the 1970s, as a result of rising world petroleum prices, oil and natural gas emerged as by far the state's most important resource. The decades since World War II have also witnessed a boom in the electronics, computer, transport equipment, aerospace, and

communications industries, which has placed Texas 2nd only to California in manufacturing among all the states of the Sunbelt region. Between 1972 and 1982, the Texas economy grew 6 percent a year, twice the national average, led by a booming oil industry. Other factors that contributed to the Lone Star State's robust economy in the early 1980s were a plentiful labor market, high worker productivity, diversification of new industries, and less restrictive regulation of business activities than in most other states. The result was a steady increase in industrial production, construction values, retail sales, and personal income, coupled with a relatively low rate of unemployment. In 1982, however, Texas began to be affected by the worldwide recession. Lower energy demand, worldwide overproduction of oil, and the resulting fall in prices, caused a steep decline in the state's petroleum industry. Unemployment in Texas jumped from 6.9% in 1982 to 8% in 1983, a period during which the national rate fell 0.1%. Much of this unemployment was among persons who came to Texas seeking jobs, particularly from northern industrial states. The rise and fall in the oil industry's fortunes affected other industries as well. Thousands of banks had speculated in real estate in the early eighties. By the late eighties, many of their investments had become worthless, and numerous banks were declared insolvent.

In the wake of the oil-centered recession, Texas began attempts to diversify. The state government has successfully wooed high-tech industries to locate in Texas. The percentage of economic activity contributed by the oil and gas extraction industry dropped from about 20% to 6% between 1980 and 2000. Electronics, telecommunications, food processing, services and retail trade, on the other hand, saw substantial growth in the 1990s. While output from oil and gas extraction increased 7.4% between 1997 and 2001, output from general services rose 35.4%; from financial services, 32.5%; from retail and wholesale trade, 30.7%; from the transportation and public utilities sector, 26.4%; and from government, 24%. In the recession and slowdown of 2001 and 2002, employment growth in Texas followed the national trends, remaining negative through the fourth quarter of 2002. Shortfalls in state revenues following, particularly, the collapse of capital gains income, faced the state government with a serious budget deficit. Higher oil prices in 2003, following a Venezuelan oil strike and the US-led invasion of Iraq, should benefit the Texan economy.

In 2001, Texas's gross state product gross state product was $763.9 billion, the 3rd largest among the states, to which general services contributed $156.4 billion; trade, $131.7 billion; financial services, $118.2 billion; manufacturing, $93.8 billion; government, $85.4 billion; transportation and public utilities, $83 billion; mining (of which 97.9% was oil and gas extraction), $46.9 billion; and construction, $37.8 billion. The public sector in 2001 constituted 11.2% of gross state product, compared to the 12% average for the states.

[21]INCOME

According to the Bureau of Economic Analysis, in 2001, Texas had a per capita personal income (PCPI) of $28,472 which ranked 28th in the United States (including the District of Columbia) and was 94% of the national average, $30,413. The 2001 PCPI reflected an increase of 1.7% from 2000 compared to the national change of 2.2%. In 2001, Texas had a total personal income (TPI) of $608,465,986,000 which ranked 3rd in the United States and accounted for 7% of the national total. The 2001 TPI reflected an increase of 3.7% from 2000 compared to the national change of 3.3%.

Earnings of persons employed in Texas increased from $458,488,441,000 in 2000 to $474,958,148,000 in 2001, an increase of 3.6%. The largest industries in 2001 were services, 27.3% of earnings; state and local government, 10.5%; and transportation and public utilities, 9.4%. Of the industries that accounted for at least 5% of earnings in 2001, the slowest growing from 2000 to 2001 was wholesale trade (6.8% of earnings in 2001), which decreased 2.5%; the fastest was state and local government, which increased 6.0%.

According to data released by the US Census Bureau, in 2000, the median household income was $39,842 compared to the national average of $42,148. In 2001, the median income for a family of four was $56,606 compared to the national average of $63,278. For the period 1999 to 2001, the average poverty rate was 15.2% which placed it 45th among the 50 states and the District of Columbia ranked lowest to highest.

22LABOR

According to Bureau of Labor Statistics (BLS) provisional estimates, in July 2003 the seasonally adjusted civilian labor force in Texas numbered 11,008,800, with approximately 721,800 workers unemployed, yielding an unemployment rate of 6.6%, compared to the national average of 6.2% for the same period. Since the beginning of the BLS data series in 1978, the highest unemployment rate recorded was 9.4% in October 1986. The historical low was 3.8% in December 2000. In 2001, an estimated 6.5% of the labor force was employed in construction; 11.8% in manufacturing; 6.7% in transportation, communications, and public utilities; 20.3% in trade; 5.4% in finance, insurance, and real estate; 22.9% in services; 14.4% in government; and 2.9% in agriculture.

Organized labor has never been able to establish a strong base in Texas, and a state right-to-work law continues to make unionization difficult. The earliest national union, the Knights of Labor, declined in Texas after failing to win a strike against the railroads in 1886 when the Texas Rangers served as strike breakers. That same year, the American Federation of Labor (AFL) began to organize workers along craft lines. One of the more protracted and violent disputes in Texas labor history occurred in 1935 when longshoremen struck Gulf coast ports for 62 days. The Congress of Industrial Organizations (CIO) succeeded in organizing oil-field and maritime workers during the 1930s.

The US Department of Labor reported that in 2002, 451,000 of Texas's 8,818,000 employed wage and salary workers were members of unions. This represented 5.1% of those so employed, down from 5.5% in 2001 and 5.9% in 1998. The national average is 13.2%. Texas (the 2nd most populous state) had less than one-fourth as many union members as New York (the 3rd largest), despite having nearly one million more wage and salary employees. In all, 571,000 workers (6.5%) were represented by unions. In addition to union members, this category includes workers who report no union affiliation but whose jobs are covered by a union contract. Texas is one of 22 states with a right-to-work law.

23AGRICULTURE

Texas ranked 2nd among the 50 states in agricultural production in 2001, with farm marketings totaling over $13.8 billion; crops accounted for 32% of the total. Texas leads the nation in output of cotton, grain sorghum, hay, watermelons, cabbages, and spinach.

Since 1880, Texas has been the leading producer of cotton (producing both Upland and American-Pima), which accounted for 29% of total US production and 7.3% of the state's farm marketings in 2002. After 1900, Texas farmers developed bumper crops of wheat, corn, and other grains by irrigating dry land and transformed the "great Sahara" of West Texas into one of the nation's foremost grain-growing regions. Texans also grow practically every vegetable suited to a temperate or semitropical climate. Since World War II, farms have become fewer and larger,

more specialized in raising certain crops and meat animals, more expensive to operate, and far more productive.

About 131 million acres (53 million hectares) are devoted to farms and ranches, representing more than three-fourths of the state's total area. The number of farms declined from 420,000 in 1940 to fewer than 185,000 in 1978, but rose to 230,000 in 2002. The average farm was valued at $720 per acre in 2002.

Productive farmland is located throughout the state. Grains are grown mainly in the temperate north and west, and vegetables and citrus fruits in the subtropical south. Cotton has been grown in all sections, but in recent years, it has been extensively cultivated in the High Plains of the west and the upper Rio Grande Valley. Grain sorghum, wheat, corn, hay, and other forage crops are raised in the north-central and western plains regions. Rice is cultivated along the Gulf coast, and soybeans are raised mainly in the High Plains and Red River Valley.

Major crops in 2002 included: upland cotton, 4.4 million acres produced 5 million bales (valued at $919.2 million); wheat, 2.7 million acres produced 78.3 million bushels (valued at $234.9 million); hay, 5.6 million acres produced 13.9 million (valued at $930.4 million); sorghum, grain, 2.6 million acres produced 130.1 million bushels (valued at $305.9 million); corn, 1.8 million acres produced 205.7 million bushels (valued at $534.7 million); rice, 206,000 acres produced 14,616 hundred weight (valued at $61.4 million); vegetables, fresh, 91,800 acres produced 1.2 million tons (valued at $428.8 million); soybeans, 215,000 acres produced 6 million bushels (valued at $31.3 million).

The major vegetables and fruits, in terms of value, are onions, cabbages, watermelons, carrots, potatoes, cantaloupes, green peppers, honeydew melons, spinach, cucumbers, and lettuce. Cottonseed, barley, oats, peanuts, pecans, sugar beets, sugarcane, and sunflowers are also produced in commercial quantities.

The total value of farmland and buildings alone was estimated at $94.3 billion in 2002, higher than any other state.

Irrigated farmland in 1997 totaled 5.4 million acres (2.2 million hectares), of which about 65% was in the High Plains; other areas dependent on irrigation included the lower Rio Grande Valley and the trans-Pecos region. Approximately 80% of the irrigated land is supplied with water pumped from wells. Because more than half of the state's irrigation pumps are fueled by natural gas, the cost of irrigation increased significantly as gas prices rose during the 1970s.

24ANIMAL HUSBANDRY

About two-thirds of cattle fattened for market are kept in feedlots located in the Texas panhandle and northwestern plains. In 2003, Texas ranked first in number of cattle and calves with an estimated 14 million, valued at $8.4 billion. During 2002, Texas farms had around 930,000 hogs and pigs, valued at $57.7 million. In 2001, Texas's production of sheep and lambs was first in the US at 48 million lb (21.8 million kg), valued at $40.4 million; shorn wool production was an estimated 5.5 million lb (2.5 million kg) in 2002.

About 90% of the dairy industry is located in eastern Texas. In 2001, milk production was around 5.1 billion lb (2.3 billion kg) from 325,000 milk cows. Poultry production included 2.71 billion lb (1.2 billion kg) of broilers, valued at around $1.06 billion, and 4.7 billion eggs were produced, valued at $267 million.

Breeding of Palominos, Arabians, Appaloosas, Thoroughbreds, and quarter horses is a major industry in Texas. The animals are most abundant in the most heavily populated areas, and it is not unusual for residential subdivisions of metropolitan areas to include facilities for keeping and riding horses.

25FISHING

Texas in 1998 recorded a commercial catch of 89,217,000 lb, valued at $183,257,000 (5th). The leading commercial fishing ports are Brownsville-Port Isabel, Galveston, Aransas Pass-Rockport, and Freeport.

Shrimp accounted for about 81% of the total volume of the catch in 1995; other commercial shellfish include blue crabs and oysters. Species of saltwater fish with the greatest commercial value are yellowfin tuna, red snapper, swordfish, and flounder. Texas had 147 fish processing and wholesale plants employing 2,598 persons in 1997. Early in 1980, the US government banned shrimp fishing for 45 days, effective in the summer of 1981, in order to conserve shrimp supplies. Texas has since continued to close the Gulf to shrimping from about 1 June to 15 July.

The state manages fish stocks and habitats to maintain 40.4 million freshwater and 14.5 million marine angler days per year. In 1998, Texas issued 1,451,414 sport fishing licenses. Among the most sought-after native freshwater fish are large-mouth and white bass, crappie, sunfish, and catfish.

26FORESTRY

Texas forestland in 2002 covered 17,149,000 acres (6,940,000 hectares), representing 2.3% of the US total and over 10% of the state's land area. Commercial timberland comprised 11,774,000 acres (4,765,000 hectares), of which about 90% was privately owned. Timberlands managed by the federal government covered 794,000 acres (321,000 hectares). Most forested land, including practically all commercial timberland, is located in the Piney Woods region of east Texas.

In 2002, Texas timberlands yielded 1.6 billion board feet of lumber, tenth in the US. Primary forest products manufactured include plywood, waferboard, and pulpwood. Texas wood-treating plants process utility poles, crossties, lumber, and fence posts.

The Texas Forest Service, a member of the Texas A&M University System, provides direct, professional forestry assistance to private landowners, manages several state and federal reforestation and forest stewardship incentives programs, coordinates pest control activities, and assists in protecting against wildfires statewide. In addition, the state agency has an urban and community forestry program, forest products laboratory, two tree nurseries, and a genetics laboratory.

As of 2003 there were four national forests in Texas—Angelina, Davy Crockett, Sabine, and Sam Houston—with a total area of 637,434 acres (257,970 hectares). Texas also has five state forests: the E. O. Siecke, W. Goodrich Jones, I. D. Fairchild, John Henry Kirby, and Paul N. Masterson Memorial State Forests.

27MINING

According to preliminary estimates, 2001 nonfuel mineral production in Texas was valued at $2.21 billion, about 13% higher than the 2000 total. In the same year Texas rose from 4th to 3rd place in overall nonfuel mineral value. The major construction aggregates (crushed stone and sand and gravel) and portland cement grew in value, accounting for most of the overall increase. The leading commodities, in order of value, were crushed stone (145 million metric tons, valued at $612 million), construction sand and gravel (89 million metric tons, valued at $456 million), portland cement (10.7 million metric tons, valued at $788 million), industrial sand and gravel (1.75 million metric tons, valued at $45.2 million), and salt (10.8 million metric tons, valued at $104 million). These top minerals together accounted for about 94% of the state's total nonfuel mineral value.

In 2001, Texas ranked 1st nationally in crushed stone and portland cement; 2nd in construction sand and gravel, salt, crude helium (10 million cu m, valued at $11.1 million), common clay

(2.21 million metric tons, $9.46 million), ball clay, talc, zeolites, and brucite; 5th in lime (1.55 million metric tons, valued at $94.3 million) and dimension stone (84,700 metric tons, valued at $11.5 million); and 8th in masonry cement (250,000 metric tons, valued at $27.2 million).

28ENERGY AND POWER

Texas is an energy-rich state. Its vast deposits of petroleum and natural gas liquids account for nearly 30% of US proved liquid hydrocarbon reserves. Texas is also the largest producer and exporter of oil and natural gas to other states, and it leads the US in electric power production.

As of 1999, Texas power plants had a combined installed capacity (utility and nonutility) of 76.3 million kW; their power output was 359.4 billion kWh. Gas-fired steam plants accounted for 49% of the production; coal, 39%; and others 12%. In 1998, domestic sales of electricity totaled 301.3 million kWh, of which industrial plants used 33%, homes 36%, businesses 26%, and other consumers 5%. As of 2001, the state had four nuclear reactors in operation, two at the Comanche Peak plant and two at the South Texas plant (the largest commercial reactors in the US).

The state's first oil well was drilled in 1866 at Melrose in East Texas, and the first major oil discovery was made in 1894 at Corsicana, northwest of Melrose, in Navarro County. The famous Spindletop gusher, near Beaumont, was tapped on 10 January 1901. Another great oil deposit was discovered in the panhandle in 1921, and the largest of all, the East Texas field, in Rusk County, was opened in 1930. Subsequent major oil discoveries were made in West Texas, starting in Scurry County in 1948. Thirty years later, the state's crude-oil production exceeded 1 billion barrels. In 1983, production was 908.2 million barrels, averaging 2.5 million barrels per day. Production in 1999 was 449.2 million barrels (including over 1 million barrels from offshore wells), averaging 1.23 million barrels per day. Production in 2002 was down to 1.13 barrels per day. Proved petroleum reserves at the end of 2001 were estimated at more than 4.9 billion barrels, representing about one-fifth of total US reserves.

In 2002, Texas produced more than 5.3 trillion cu ft (0.15 trillion cu m)of natural gas. At the beginning of 2001, proved natural gas reserves were estimated at 43.5 trillion cu ft (1.23 trillion cu m).

Coal production totaled 49.5 million tons in 2000, all from 14 surface mines. Almost 99% of the coal was lignite, nearly all of it used as fuel for electric generating plants close to the mines. Recoverable coal reserves were estimated at 724 million tons in 2001. As of 1999, four nuclear reactors—South Texas Project 1 and 2, in Matagorda County, and Comanche Peak 1 and 2, in Somervell County—were in operation.

In 2000, energy consumption per capita in Texas was 555 million Btu (139.9 million kcal), 6th highest in the nation.

29INDUSTRY

Before 1900, Texas had an agricultural economy based, in the common phrase, on "cotton, cows, and corn." When the first US Census of Manufactures was taken in Texas in 1849, there were only 309 industrial establishments, with 1,066 wage earners; payrolls totaled $322,368, and the value added by manufacture was a mere $773,896. The number of establishments increased tenfold by 1899, when the state had 38,604 wage earners and a total value added of $38,506,130. During World War II, the value added passed the $1-billion mark, and by 1982, the total was $53.4 billion.

In 1997, the value of all shipments by manufacturers was $302 billion, 2nd only to California. Three of the state's leading industrial products—refined petroleum, industrial organic chemicals, and oil-field machinery—all stem directly from the petrochemical sector. Major oil refineries are located at Houston and other Gulf ports. Aircraft plants include those of North American Aviation and Chance-Vought at Grand Prairie, General Dynamics near Ft. Worth, and Bell Aircraft's helicopter division at Hurst. In 1997, Texas was the headquarters to 36 Fortune 500 companies, including Exxon, which ranked as the 3rd-largest industrial corporation.

Earnings of persons employed in Texas increased from $355.7 billion in 1997 to $388.3 billion in 1998, an increase of 9.2%. The largest industries in 1998 were services, 26.3% of earnings; state and local government, 10.3%; and transportation and public utilities, 9.1%. Of the industries that accounted for at least 5% of earnings in 1998, the slowest growing from 1997 to 1998 was state and local government, which increased 5.1%; the fastest was wholesale trade (6.7% of earnings in 1998), which increased 11.3%.

³⁰COMMERCE

Texas ranked 3rd among the 50 states in wholesale trade, with total sales of over $270 billion in 1997. The leading wholesaling centers are the Houston, Dallas-Ft. Worth, San Antonio, El Paso, Lubbock, Midland, Amarillo, Austin, and Corpus Christi metropolitan areas.

Texas ranked 2nd behind California in retail sales, which amounted to $183 billion in 1997. Of the retail stores total of 102,185; automotive dealers accounted for 14%; food stores, 13%; and restaurants and taverns, 28%.

Foreign exports through Texas during 1998 totaled $79 billion. The leading items shipped through Texas ports to foreign countries were grains, chemicals, fertilizers, and petroleum refinery products; principal imports included crude petroleum, minerals and metals (especially aluminum ores), liquefied gases, motor vehicles, bananas, sugar, and molasses. Texas ranked 2nd among the 50 states in 1998 as an exporter of goods produced in the state.

³¹CONSUMER PROTECTION

The Attorney General's Consumer Protection Division protects consumers and the legitimate business community by filing civil lawsuits under the Deceptive Trade Practices Act (DTPA) and other related statutes. The division is best known for its work in traditional areas of consumer protection litigation: false and deceptive advertising, defective merchandise, and home or appliance repair scams, for example.

The attorney general's litigation activities are supplemented by a highly effective mediation program that is available to Texas consumers who have complaints amenable to informal resolution. The Consumer Protection Division also disseminates a wide range of public information materials to educate consumers about their rights, alert them to trends in deceptive or unfair business practices, and prevent losses due to fraud before they occur. Over the years, the division has succeeded in winning funds for consumer education as part of the settlement of consumer protection litigation.

³²BANKING

Texas has the 2nd highest number of banks in the nation, behind Illinois. In 2002, Texas had 718 insured banks; bank assets totaled $211.8 billion.

Banking was illegal in the Texas Republic and under the first state constitution, reflecting the widespread fear of financial speculation like that which had caused the panic of 1837. Because both the independent republic and the new state government found it difficult to raise funds or obtain credit without a banking system, they were forced to borrow money from merchants, thus permitting banking functions and privileges

despite the constitutional ban. A formal banking system was legalized during the latter part of the 19th century.

Between 1986 and 1989, the number of bank closings in Texas rose from 26 per year to 134, or 64.7% of all US bank closings. By 1993, the number of failed banks fell to 10. In 1994 and 1995, no banks failed, but in 1996, there were 2 banks closed. In 1997, 98% of the 445 banks in the state banking system were in good condition. The statistics for the national banks in Texas paralleled state banking system numbers.

In 2002, the state's insured banks were performing well, in part due to lower funding costs. Texas banks reported the highest-level of commercial real estate (CRE) loans as of September 2002. However, Texas's metropolitan areas had high office vacancy rates, exposing banks to high risk. Residential foreclosures as of September 2002 were at a 30-month high, and the per capita bankruptcy rate was at an all-time high as well.

Although the Texas agricultural economy had been weak for several years, farm banks performed well in 2002 due to significant government support.

³³INSURANCE

The industry's most recent state-by-state comparison (year-end 2000) showed Texas ranked 2nd (behind Arizona) in number of domestic life and health insurance companies with 181, and 2nd (behind Vermont) in the number of domestic property and casualty companies with 245. In 2001, property and casualty insurers wrote over $24.9 billion in premiums. That year, there were 431,388 flood insurance policies in force in the state, with a total value of $63.4 million. Many residents of Texas also took out beach and windstorm insurance policies against hurricane and other windstorm damage in force. In 1998 the total value of this insurance was $11.6 billion.

In 2001, there were 10.2 million ordinary life insurance policies in force in Texas with a total value of $656.4 billion; total value for all categories of life insurance (ordinary, group, industrial, and credit) was $1,251.3 billion. Death benefits paid that year totaled $3.2 billion.

The insurance industry is regulated by the Texas Department of Insurance. TDI is headed by the commissioner of insurance, who is appointed by the governor and confirmed by the state senate for two-year terms beginning 1 February of odd-numbered years.

³⁴SECURITIES

Although there are no securities exchanges in Texas, 4,252 broker-dealers organizations conduct securities transactions, with the number of employees at 30,977. Securities investment advice is professionally marketed by 581 registered firms. Texas is the headquarters of 341 NASDAQ companies, 24 NASDAQ market makers, 71 AMEX companies (almost 11% of the national total); and the state has incorporated 53 NYSE-listed corporations. The top five in terms of revenues are: Electronic Data Systems Corp., TXU Corp., Reliant Energy Corp., Southwest Airlines Corp., and Allied Waste Industries, Inc. The State Securities Board, established in 1957, oversees the issuance and sale of stocks and bonds in Texas.

³⁵PUBLIC FINANCE

The Texas budget operates on a "pay as you go" basis in that expenditures cannot exceed revenue during the budget cycle. The state's budget period runs on a biennial basis from September 1 of each odd-numbered year to August 31 of the following odd-numbered year.

The state legislature meets from approximately January to May every odd-numbered year and writes a budget for the next two years. The appropriations committee in the house, and the finance committee in the senate are responsible for budget development. The primary legislative entity responsible for oversight of the budget when the legislature is not in session is the 10-member legislative budget board. Chaired by the lieutenant governor, the board prepares the initial budget that will be considered by the legislature.

The governor's office of budget and planning also prepares a budget for the Legislature's consideration. The governor has line-item veto authority over the budget and must sign the appropriations bill before it becomes law. The comptroller of public accounts must also sign the bill certifying that sufficient revenue will be available to fund the budget.

After running large budget surpluses in the early 1980s, the state experienced several years of budget shortfalls in the wake of falling oil prices. As the state's economy has diversified, the budget has shown greater ability to withstand minor economic fluctuations.

The governor's proposed state budget for the 2000–2001 biennium consisted of $96 billion, or a 9% increase from the previous biennium. In 2000/01 the state's starting balance was a comfortable $3.766 billion, equal to 14.4% of expenditures. General fund revenues totaled $29.36 billion, but in 2001/02, revenues fell nearly $1 billion to $28.4 billion while expenses were increasing. Texas has the highest percent of low-income uninsured children, so Medicaid and the Child's Health Insurance Program (CHIPS) have particularly large caseloads. No budget cuts were made in the face of the revenue short-fall in 2001/02, but in 2002/03, general fund revenues fell further, to $27.86 billion, and cuts made after the budget was enacted totaled $1.1 billion, 2nd in size only to the budget cuts being made by California. The governor called for 7% cuts across-the-board reductions while other options were being studied. The ending balance for 2002/03 (and the beginning balance for 2003/04) was –$1.796 billion. Projections in early 2003 estimated that the Texas deficit in 2003/04 would range from $2.5 billion to $8 billion, or 8.2% to 26.2% of the state budget. General funds are appropriated for education (48%), health and human services (30%), economic development (12%), public safety and criminal justice (8%), and general government (2%).

The following table from the US Census Bureau contains information on revenues, expenditures, indebtedness, and cash/securities for 2001.

	($000)	PERCENT	PER CAPITA
Population (thousands, 2001)	21,371	(X)	(X)
Total Revenue	65,525,245	100.00	3,066.08
General revenue	60,596,395	92.48	2,835.45
Utility revenue	–	–	–
Liquor store revenue	–	–	–
Insurance trust revenue	4,928,850	7.52	230.63
Exhibit: Salaries and wages	7,602,410	11.75	355.73
Total expenditure	64,685,858	100.00	3,026.81
General expenditure	58,183,264	89.95	2,722.53
Education	24,804,955	38.35	1,160.68
Public welfare	13,254,594	20.49	620.21
Hospitals	3,032,440	4.69	141.90
Health	1,725,889	2.67	80.76
Highways	4,875,993	7.54	228.16
Police protection	337,456	0.52	15.79
Correction	3,074,359	4.75	143.86
Natural resources	690,462	1.07	32.31
Parks and recreation	106,724	0.16	4.99
Government administration	1,494,589	2.31	69.94
Interest on general debt	1,014,301	1.57	47.46
Other and unallocable	3,771,502	5.83	176.48
Utility expenditure	–	–	–
Liquor store expenditure	–	–	–
Insurance trust expenditure	6,502,594	10.05	304.27
Debt at end of fiscal year	16,815,848	100.00	786.85
Cash and security holdings	176,316,695	100.00	8,250.28

36 TAXATION

The principal source of state tax revenue is the 6.25% sales and use tax. Both basic foodstuffs and drugs are exempted. Local sale taxes range from none to 2.5% add-ons. The state also imposes a full array of selective sales (excise) taxes, including ones on motor fuels, tobacco products, insurance premiums, public utilities, alcoholic beverages, amusements, pari-mutuels, and other selected items. There is no state inheritance tax, and the state estate tax is tied to the federal exemption for state death taxes, and is therefore scheduled to expire in tandem with the exemption in 2007, unless the state takes positive action to preserve the tax. Texas' revenue losses from the phasing out of its estate tax are estimated at -$81 million for 2002/03, -$159 million for 2003/04 and -$253 million for 2006/07. Death and gift taxes accounted for 1.1% of state collections in 2002. Other state levies include oil and gas severance taxes and various license fees. Property taxes are collected at the local level. Local property tax rates per $100 of assessed valuation vary widely throughout the state. The city sales tax is a major source of revenue for the municipalities. Almost half of total state and local revenues (47% in 2000) are collected at the local level.

The state collected $28.662 billion in taxes in 2002, of which 50.8% came from the general sales tax, 31.4% from selective sales taxes, 13.2% from license fees, and 3.4% from severance taxes. In 2003, Texas ranked 46th among the states in terms of combined state and local tax burden, which amounted to about 8.3% of income.

The following table from the US Census Bureau provides a summary of taxes collected by the state in 2002.

	($000)	PER CAPITA
Total Taxes	28,662,395	1,316.00
Property taxes	(X)	(X)
Sales and gross receipts	23,577,124	1,082.52
General sales and gross receipts	14,559,504	668.48
Selective sales taxes	9,017,620	414.03
Alcoholic beverage	560,197	25.72
Amusements	21,218	0.97
Insurance Premiums	972,325	44.64
Motor fuels	2,835,232	130.18
Pari-mutuels	12,739	0.58
Public utilities	722,187	33.16
Tobacco products	540,034	24.8
Other selective sales	3,353,688	153.98
Licenses	3,777,969	173.46
Alcoholic beverages	32,268	1.48
Amusements	7,119	0.33
Corporation	1,991,450	91.44
Hunting and fishing	64,273	2.95
Motor vehicle	985,568	45.25
Motor vehicle operators	114,978	5.28
Public utility	17,350	0.8
Occupation and business, NEC	535,787	24.6
Other	29,176	1.34
Other taxes	1,307,302	60.02
Individual income	(X)	(X)
Corporation net income	(X)	(X)
Death and gift	332,575	15.27
Documentary and stock transfer	(X)	(X)
Severance	974,727	44.75
Other	(X)	(X)

37 ECONOMIC POLICY

Texas state government has historically been pro business: regulation is less restrictive than in many states, and there is no corporate income tax. The state government actively encourages outside capital investment in Texas industries, and the state's industrial productivity has produced a generally high return on investment.

Texas Economic (TXED) (formerly the Texas Industrial Commission) helps businesses locate or expand their operations in the state. Its stated mission in 2003 was to market the Texas and assist communities to maximize their economic development opportunities. The main division within TXED are Business Development, Tourism, Economic Research, and Financial Incentives. A private organization, the Texas Industrial Development Council, in Bryan, also assists new and developing industries.

38HEALTH

Medical care ranges from adequate to excellent in the state's largest cities, but many small communities are without doctors and hospitals. Texas suffers from a general shortage of health care personnel: although the number of students enrolled in medical education programs more than doubled during the 1970s, many hospitals were functioning without adequate numbers of registered nurses, laboratory technicians, and therapists in the 1980s.

The infant mortality rate as of 2000 was 5.7 per 1,000 live births. In the same year, there were 80,739 legal abortions, or 18 per 1,000 women, 3rd-highest in the US.

The overall death rate in 2000 was 735.4 per 100,000 population. Texas ranked below the national average in deaths due to heart disease, cancer, cerebrovascular diseases, and suicide but above average in deaths from accidents. The leading causes of death in 2000, with their rates per 100,000 population, were heart disease, 211.0; cancer, 163.3; cerebrovascular disease, 52.4; and accidents, 36.3.

The HIV mortality rate was 5.3 per 100,000 population in 2000, equal to the US national rate. A total of 56,730 AIDS cases had been reported through 2001. According to the CDC, 22.0% of Texans 18 years of age and older were regular smokers in 2000.

Texas's 411 community hospitals had 2,461,016 admissions and 56,354 beds in 2001. There were 64,359 full-time registered nurses and 13,650 full-time licensed practical nurses in 2001 and 217 physicians per 100,000 population in 2000. The average expense of a community hospital for care was $1,214.80 per inpatient day in 2001.

Federal government grants to cover the Medicare and Medicaid services in 2001 totaled $7.7 billion; 2,299,599 enrollees received Medicare benefits that year. At least 23.5% of Texas's adult residents were uninsured in 2002, the highest percentage in the US.

There are 8 medical schools, 2 dental colleges, and 64 schools of nursing in the state. The University of Texas has medical colleges at Dallas, Houston, Galveston, San Antonio, and Tyler. The University of Texas Cancer Center at Houston is one of the nation's major facilities for cancer research. Houston is also noted as a center for cardiovascular surgery. On 3 May 1968, Houston surgeon Denton Cooley performed the first human heart transplant in the US.

39SOCIAL WELFARE

In 2001, the average weekly unemployment benefit was $239.77. Average monthly participation in the food stamp program in FY2002 comprised 1,554,428 persons (570,337 households). The average monthly benefit was $81.61, and the sum total of benefits paid in FY2002 was $1,522,292,908.

With the enactment of the Personal Responsibility and Work Opportunity Reconciliation Act of 1996, the US government has changed the form and regulations for many of its social welfare programs. Most significantly, it replaces Aid to Families with Dependent Children (AFDC), an open-ended entitlement program, with Temporary Assistance for Needy Families (TANF), a limited system of assistance funded largely through federal block grants. The reform act also impacts the food stamp program, the Supplemental Security Income program, and the

child nutrition program. The law took effect on 1 July 1997 and provided $16.38 billion in block grants for fiscal years 1997–2002. The grants are to be divided among the states based on an equation involving the numbers of former AFDC recipients in each state.

Reauthorization of the 1996 social welfare legislation, scheduled for 2002, was delayed, and the original law had been extended three times as of July 2003, with the most recent extension running through September 2003. Texas's TANF cash assistance program, run by the Department of Human Services, is called Texas Works; the work program, run by the Texas Workforce Commission, is called Choices. In June 2000 the state had 343,464 welfare recipients. State expenditures on the TANF program in FY2002 totaled $223,454,150.

In December 2001, Social Security benefits were paid to 2,672,950 Texans. This number included 1,605,330 retired workers, 339,910 widows and widowers, 268,460 disabled workers, 209,150 spouses, and 250,100 children. Social Security beneficiaries represented 12.5% of the total state population and 89.7% of the state's population age 65 and older. Retired workers (excluding persons with special benefits) received an average monthly payment of $851; widows and widowers, $793; disabled workers, $807; and spouses, $418. Payments for children of retired workers averaged $374 per month; children of deceased workers, $555; and children of disabled workers, $234.

Federal Supplemental Security Income payments in December 2001 went to 418,235 Texas residents, averaging $327 a month.

40HOUSING

The variety of Texas architectural styles reflects the diversity of the state's topography and climate. In the early settlement period, Spanish-style adobe houses were built in southern Texas. During the 1840s, Anglo-American settlers in the east erected primitive log cabins. These were later replaced by "dog-run" houses, consisting of two rooms linked by an open passageway covered by a gabled roof, so-called because pet dogs slept in the open, roofed shelter, as did occasional overnight guests. During the late 19th century, southern-style mansions were built in East Texas, and the familiar ranch house, constructed of stone and usually stuccoed or whitewashed, with a shingle roof and a long porch, proliferated throughout the state; the modern ranch house in southwestern Texas shows a distinct Mexican-Spanish influence. Climate affects such modern amenities as air conditioning: a new house in the humid eastern region is likely to have a refrigeration-style cooler, while in the dry west and south, an evaporating "swamp cooler" is the more common means of making hot weather bearable.

In 2002, Texas had an estimated 8,502,060 housing units, of which 7,521,712 were occupied; 64.2% were owner-occupied. About 64.7% of all units were single-family, detached homes. About 65% of all units were built between 1950 and 1989. Electricity and utility gas were the most common energy sources for heating. It was estimated that 344,430 units lacked telephone service, 42,127 lacked complete plumbing facilities, and 45,614 lacked complete kitchen facilities. The average household size was 2.82 people.

In 2002, 165,027 new privately owned housing units were authorized for construction. The median home value was $94,559. The median monthly cost for mortgage owners was $1,096. Renters paid a median of $629 per month. During 2002, Texas received over $439 million in community planning and development aid from the US Department of Housing and Urban Development.

41EDUCATION

Although public instruction began in Texas as early as 1746, education was slow to develop during the period of Spanish and

Mexican rule. The legislative foundation for a public school system was laid by the government of the Republic of Texas during the late 1830s, but funding was slow in coming. After annexation, in 1846, Galveston began to support free public schools, and San Antonio had at least four free schools by the time a statewide system of public education was established in 1854. Free segregated schooling was provided for black children beginning in the 1870s, but their schools were ill-maintained and underfinanced. School desegregation was accomplished during the 1960s, nonviolently for the most part.

In 2000, 75.7% of the population 25 years old and over had completed four years of high school, and 23.2% had four or more years of college. The total enrollment for fall 1999 in Texas public schools stood at 3,991,783. Of these, 2,895,853 attended schools from kindergarten through grade eight, and 1,095,930 attended high school. Minority students made up approximately 59% of the total enrollment in public elementary and secondary schools in 2001. Total enrollment was estimated at 4,033,697 in fall 2000 and is expected to reach 4,248,000 by fall 2005. Expenditures for public education in 2000/01 were estimated at $25,753,029. Enrollment in nonpublic schools in fall 2001 was 227,645.

As of fall 2000, there were 1,202,890 students enrolled in college or graduate school. In the same year Texas had 201 degree-granting institutions. Institutions of higher education include 42 public four-year colleges and universities, 67 public community college campuses, and more than 38 private institutions. The leading public universities are Texas A&M (College Station), which opened in 1876, and the University of Texas (Austin), founded in 1883. Each institution is now the center of its own university system, including campuses in several other cities. Oil was discovered on lands owned by the University of Texas in 1923, and beginning in 1924, the university and Texas A&M shared more than $1 billion in oil-related rentals and royalties. Other state-supported institutions include the University of Houston and Texas Tech University (Lubbock).

The first private college in Texas was Rutersville, established by a Methodist minister in Fayette County in 1840. The oldest private institution still active in the state is Baylor University (1845), at Waco. Other major private universities include Hardin-Simmons (Abilene), Rice (Houston), Southern Methodist or SMU (Dallas), and Texas Christian, or TCU (Ft. Worth). Well-known black-oriented institutions of higher learning include Texas Southern University in Houston and Prairie View A&M University. In 1997, minority students comprised 38.2% of total postsecondary enrollment.

Tuition charges to Texas colleges are among the lowest in the nation. The Texas Student Assistance Corp. administers a guaranteed-loan program and tuition equalization grants for needy students.

42ARTS

Although Texas has never been regarded as a leading cultural center, the arts have a long history in the state. The cities of Houston and Matagorda each had a theater before they had a church, and the state's first theater was active in Houston as early as 1838. Stark Young founded the Curtain Club acting group at the University of Texas in Austin in 1909 and the little-theater movement began in that city in 1921. The performing arts now flourish at Houston's Theater Center, Jones Hall of Performing Arts, and Alley Theater, as well as at Dallas's Theater Center, National Children's Theater, and Theater Three. The Margo Jones repertory company in Dallas has a national reputation, and there are major repertory groups in Houston and San Antonio. During the late 1970s, Texas also emerged as a center for motion picture production. The city pf Austin has since become the host for the Austin Film Festival and the South by Southwest (SXSW) Film festival.

Texas has 5 major symphony orchestras—the Dallas Symphony (performing in the Myerson Symphone Center since 1989), Houston Symphony, San Antonio Symphony, Austin Symphony, and Ft. Worth Symphony—and 25 orchestras in other cities. The Houston Grand Opera performs at Jones Hall, and in 1999 received a National Endowment for the Arts Access grant to provide free outdoor performances and artist residencies. Other opera companies perform regularly in Beaumont, Dallas, El Paso, Ft. Worth, and San Antonio.

Several cities have resident dance companies, including Abilene, Amarillo, Denton, Galveston, Garland, Longview, Lubbock, Midland-Odessa, and Pampa. The ballet groups in Fort Worth, Houston, Austin, and Corpus Christi are notable.

Popular music in Texas stems from early Spanish and Mexican folk songs, Negro spirituals, cowboy ballads, and German-language songfests. Texans pioneered a kind of country and western music that is more outspoken and direct than Nashville's commercial product, and a colony of country-rock songwriters and musicians were active in the Austin area during the 1970s. Texans of Mexican ancestry have also fashioned a Latin-flavored music ("Tejano") that is as distinctly "Tex-Mex" as the state's famous chili.

There are a number of groups for writers and storytellers, including the Writers' League of Texas and the Tejas Storytelling Association. In 2000, the National Center for Children's Illustrated Literature (chartered in 1997) opened in Abilene. Besides sponsoring its own museum of illustrated works, the Center provides educational programs and exhibits for teachers and other display venues.

In 2003, the Texas Commission on the Arts and other Texas arts organizations received grants totaling $1,655,600 from the National Endowment for the Arts (NEA). The Texas Council for the Humanities was established in 1965. In 2000, the National Endowment for the Humanities contributed $3,173,869 for 58 state programs. The state and private sources also provide funding to the Commission and other arts organizations. The state of Texas has over 2,000 arts associations.

43LIBRARIES AND MUSEUMS

In 2000, the Texas public library system had 49,746,793 volumes, with a total circulation of 78,370,000. Funding for public libraries in Texas comes from local cities, counties, school districts, and state and federal sources, with additional funding from donations, gifts, and corporate and foundation grants. Total public library income for 2000 was $294,967,000; including $1,474,000 in federal grants, and $1,179,000 in state grants.

The largest municipal libraries in Texas include the Houston Public Library with 4,573,356 volumes, and the Dallas Public Library with 2,568,852 volumes. The University of Texas at Austin, noted for outstanding collections in the humanities and in Latin American studies, had over seven million volumes in 1998. The Lyndon B. Johnson Presidential Library is also located in Austin, as is the Lorenzo de Zavala State Archives and Library Building. Other notable academic libraries include those of Texas A&M University, with over two million volumes, and the University of Houston, Rice University, Southern Methodist University, and Texas Tech University, all with collections of over one million volumes.

Among the state's 389 museums are Austin's Texas Memorial Museum; the Dallas Museum of Fine Arts and the Dallas Museum of Art; and the Amon Carter Museum of Western Art, the Ft. Worth Art Museums, and Kimbell Art Museum, all in Ft. Worth. Houston has the Museum of Fine Arts, Contemporary Arts Museum, and at least 30 galleries. Both Dallas-Ft. Worth and Houston have become major centers of art sales.

National historic sites in Texas are Ft. Davis (Jeff Davis County), President Johnson's boyhood home and Texas White House (Blanco and Gillespie counties), and the San Jose Mission (San Antonio). Other historic places include the Alamo, Dwight D. Eisenhower's birthplace at Denison, the Sam Rayburn home in Bonham, and the John F. Kennedy memorials in Dallas. A noteworthy prehistoric Indian site is the Alibates Flint Quarries National Monument, located in Potter County and accessible by guided tour.

44COMMUNICATIONS

In 2001, 94.3% of the occupied housing units in Texas had telephones. Dallas was one of Western Union's first US communications satellite stations, and it leads the state as a center for data communications.

The state has not always been in the communications vanguard, however. Texas passed up a chance to make a handsome profit from the invention of the telegraph when, in 1838, inventor Samuel F. B. Morse offered his newfangled device to the republic as a gift. When the Texas government neglected to respond, Morse withdrew the offer.

Texas had 309 major radio stations (72 AM, 237 FM) in 2003 and 87 major
television stations. The state's first radio station, WRR, was established by the city of Dallas in 1920. The first television station, WBAP, began broadcasting in Ft. Worth in 1948. The Dallas-Fort Worth area has 2,018,120 television households, only 51% receiving cable; the Houston area has 1,712,060 television households, 58% with cable; and the San Antonio area has 684,730 television homes, 66% with cable.

Approximately 439,135 Internet domain names were registered with the state in the year 2000; the 3rd most of any state.

45PRESS

The first newspaper in Texas was a revolutionary Spanish-language sheet published in May 1813 at Nacagdoches. Six years later, the *Texas Republican* was published by Dr. James Long in the same city. In 1835, the *Telegraph and Texas Register* became the official newspaper of the Texas Republic and it continued to publish until 1877. The first modern newspaper was the *Galveston News* (1842), a forerunner of the *Dallas Morning News* (1885).

In 2002, Texas had 45 morning dailies, 42 evening dailies, and 83 Sunday papers. Texas had the 2nd-largest number of daily newspapers in the country in 2002 (2nd to California). In 2001, the Houston *Chronicle* and the Dallas *Morning News* were ranked as the 9th- and 12th-largest daily newspapers nationwide. The newspapers with the largest daily circulations (2002 est.) were as follows:

AREA	NAME	DAILY	SUNDAY
Austin	*American-Statesman* (m,S)	183,873	238,624
Dallas	*Morning News* (m,S)	494,890	540,180
Fort Worth	*Star-Telegram* (m,S)	213,781	321,354
Houston	*Chronicle* (m,S)	551,854	744,009
San Antonio	*Express-News* (m,S)	208,951	349,280

In 1997, there were 437 weekly newspapers. The *Texas Almanac*, a comprehensive guide to the state, has been issued at regular intervals since 1857 by the A.H. Belo Corp., publishers of the *Dallas Morning News*. Leading magazines include the *Texas Monthly* and *Texas Observer*, both published in Austin.

46ORGANIZATIONS

In 2003, there were about 7,954 regional, national, and international organizations within the state.

Irving is the home of one of the nation's largest organizations, the Boy Scouts of America. The national headquarters of Little
People of America is in Lubbock. The National Temperance and Prohibition Council is in Richardson.

Important medical groups are the American Heart Association, in Dallas, and the National Association for Retarded Citizens, Arlington. Other national medical organizations based in Texas include the American Academy of Nurse Practitioners, the American Pediatric Society, the American Board of Obstetrics and Gynecology, and the American Board of Otolaryngology.

Professional societies include the American Association of Petroleum Landmen, Ft. Worth. The Noncommissioned Officers Association has its home office in San Antonio; the Airline Passengers Association is in Dallas. The Association of Space Explorers–U.S.A., based in Texas, is an international professional organization for astronauts who have made at least one orbit around the Earth.

Among the many organizations devoted to horse breeding are the American Quarter Horse Association, Amarillo; Palomino Horse Breeders of America, Mineral Wells; and the National Cutting Horse Association and American Paint Association, both in Ft. Worth. Ft. Worth is also the home of the Texas Longhorn Breeders Association of America.

The scholarly organization American Mensa is based in Arlington. National and state arts and cultural organizations include the American Cowboy Culture Association, the American Indian Arts Council, the Texas Folklore Society, the Texas International Theatrical Arts Society, the Texas Historical Foundation, and the Writers' League of Texas. National sports organizations based in Texas include the United States Professional Tennis Association and the United States Youth Soccer Association.

47TOURISM, TRAVEL, AND RECREATION

In 2001, the state hosted over 180 million visitors with direct travel spending at about $39.8 billion. The Industry supported about 468,000 jobs. Marketing for tourism and travel to Texas is the responsibility of Texas Economic Development Market Texas Tourism.

Each of the state's seven major tourist regions offers outstanding attractions. East Texas has one of the state's oldest cities, Nacogdoches, with the nation's oldest public thoroughfare and a reconstruction of the Old Stone Fort, a Spanish trading post dating from 1779. Jefferson, an important 19th-century inland port, has many old homes, including Excelsior House. Tyler, which bills itself as the "rose capital of the world," features a 28-acre (11-hectare) municipal rose garden and puts on a Rose Festival each October. The Gulf Coast region of southeastern Texas offers the Lyndon B. Johnson Space Center, the Astrodome sports stadium and adjacent Astroworld amusement park, and a profusion of museums, galleries, and shops, all in metropolitan Houston; Spindletop Park, in Beaumont, commemorating the state's first great oil gusher; Galveston's sandy beaches, deep-sea fishing, and Sea-Arama Marineworld; and the Padre Island National Seashore.

To the north, the Dallas-Ft. Worth metropolitan area (including Arlington) has numerous cultural and entertainment attractions, including the Six Flags Over Texas amusement park and the state fair held in Dallas each October. Old Abilene Town amusement park, with its strong western flavor, is also popular with visitors. The Hill Country of south-central Texas encompasses many tourist sites, including the state capitol in Austin, Waco's Texas Ranger Museum (Ft. Fisher), the Lyndon B. Johnson National Historic Site, and frontier relics in Bastrop and Bandera.

South Texas has the state's most famous historic site—the Alamo, in San Antonio, which also contains HemisFair Plaza and Brackenndge Park. The Rio Grande Valley Museum, at Harlingen, is popular with visitors, as is the King Ranch headquarters in Kleberg County. The Great Plains region of the Texas panhandle offers Palo Duro Canyon—Texas's largest state park, covering 16,402 acres (6,638 hectares) in Armstrong and Randall counties—the Prairie Dog Town at Lubbock, Old West exhibits at Matador, and the cultural and entertainment resources of Amarillo. In the extreme northwestern corner of the panhandle is the XIT Museum, recalling the famous XIT Ranch, at one time the world's largest fenced ranch, which formerly covered more than 3 million acres (1.2 million hectares). Outstanding tourist sites in the far west are the Big Bend and Guadalupe Mountains national parks, the Jersey Lilly Saloon and Judge Roy Bean visitor center in Langtry, and metropolitan El Paso.

Texas's park system includes Palo Duro Canyon, Big Creek (Ft. Bend County), Brazos Island (Cameron County), Caddo Lake (Harrison County), Dinosaur Valley (Somervell County), Eisenhower (Grayson County), Galveston Island, and Longhorn Cavern (Burnet County). State historical parks include San Jacinto Battleground (east Harris County), Texas State Railroad (Anderson and Cherokee counties), and Washington-on-the-Brazos (Washington County). Hunting and fishing are extremely popular in Texas. White-tailed deer are hunted as a way of cutting the wildlife population; thousands of jabalina and wild turkeys are shot annually.

48SPORTS

Texas has eleven major league professional sports teams: the Texas Rangers and Houston Astros of Major League Baseball; the Dallas Cowboys and Houston Texans of the National Football League; the Dallas Stars of the National Hockey League; the Houston Rockets, San Antonio Spurs, and Dallas Mavericks of the National Basketball Association; the Houston Comets and San Antonio Silver Stars of the Women's National Basketball Association, and the Dallas Burn of Major League Soccer. The Cowboys are, by far, the most consistently successful of Texas's teams. They have won the Super Bowl five times—in 1972, 1978, 1993, 1994, and 1996. They have appeared in it and lost an additional three times. The Houston Rockets won consecutive NBA Championships in 1994 and 1995. Houston lost the Oilers of the NFL, who moved to Tennessee after the 1996 season. However, an expansion team, the Texans, replaced them and began NFL play in 2002.

Pari-mutuel betting on horse races was legalized in Texas in the early 1990s, and thoroughbred tracks are open near Houston and Dallas. Quarter-horse racing is also popular and rodeo is a leading spectator sport. Participant sports popular with Texans include hunting, fishing, horseback riding, boating, swimming, tennis, and golf. State professional and amateur golf tournaments are held annually, as are numerous rodeos. The Texas Sports Hall of Fame was organized in 1951; new members are selected each year by a special committee of the Texas Sports Writers Association.

There are a plethora of colleges and universities in Texas, with many elite teams in football, basketball, and baseball. The University of Texas Longhorns are traditionally strong in football, having captured three national championships (1963, 1969, 1970) and made over 40 bowl game appearances. They also have a very solid baseball program. Texas A&M University in College Station also has an elite football program. Their team earned a national championship in 1939 and won 18 conference titles in the now-defunct Southwestern Conference. In 1998 the Aggies won the Big Twelve Conference title. Texas Tech's women's basketball team has been consistently ranked as a top team in the national polls. Baylor and Rice Universities, of the Big Twelve Conference and Western Athletic Conference, respectively, both field outstanding baseball teams. The teams are traditonally ranked high in the national polls. The Rice Owls won the 2003 College World Series.

49FAMOUS TEXANS

Two native sons of Texas have served as president of the US. Dwight D. Eisenhower (1890–1969), the 34th president, was born in Denison, but his family moved to Kansas when he was two years old. Lyndon Baines Johnson (1908–73), the 36th president, was the only lifelong resident of the state to serve in that office. Born near Stonewall, he occupied center stage in state and national politics for a third of a century as US representative, Democratic majority leader of the US Senate, and vice president under John F. Kennedy, before succeeding to the presidency after Kennedy's assassination. Reelected by a landslide, Johnson accomplished much of his Great Society program of social reform but saw his power and popularity wane because of the war in Viet Nam. His wife, Claudia Alta Taylor "Lady Bird" Johnson (b.1912), was influential in environmental causes as First Lady.

Texas's other native vice president was John Nance Garner (1868–1967), former speaker of the US House of Representatives. George Bush (b.Massachusetts, 1924), who founded his own oil development company and has served in numerous federal posts, was elected vice president in 1980 on the Republican ticket and reelected in 1984, then elected to the presidency in 1988. Tom C. Clark (1899–1977) served as an associate justice on the US Supreme Court from 1949 to 1967; he stepped down when his son Ramsey (b.1927) was appointed US attorney general, a post the elder Clark had also held.

Another prominent federal officeholder from Texas was Jesse H. Jones (1874–1956), who served as chairman of the Reconstruction Finance Corporation and secretary of commerce under Franklin D. Roosevelt. Oveta Culp Hobby (1905–95), publisher of the *Houston Post*, became the first director of the Women's Army Corps (WAC) during World War II and the first secretary of the Department of Health, Education, and Welfare under President Eisenhower. John Connally (1917–1993), a protégé of Lyndon Johnson's, served as secretary of the US Navy under Kennedy and, as governor of Texas, was wounded in the same attack that killed the president; subsequently, he switched political allegiance, was secretary of the treasury under Richard Nixon, and had been active in Republican Party politics. Other federal officials from Texas include "Colonel" Edward M. House (1858–1938), principal advisor to President Wilson, and Leon Jaworski (1905–82), the Watergate special prosecutor whose investigations led to President Nixon's resignation. Lloyd Bentsen, a senator and a secretary of the treasury, was born 11 February 1921 in Mission, Texas.

The state's most famous legislative leader was Sam Rayburn (1882–1961), who served the longest tenure in the nation's history as speaker of the US House of Representatives—17 years in three periods between 1940 and 1961. James Wright (b.1922) was Democratic majority leader of the House in the 1970s and early 1980s, and Barbara C. Jordan (1936–96) won national attention as a forceful member of the House Judiciary Committee during its impeachment deliberations in 1974.

Famous figures in early Texas history include Moses Austin (b.Connecticut, 1761–1821) and his son, Stephen F. Austin (b.Virginia, 1793–1836), often called the "father of Texas." Samuel "Sam" Houston (b.Virginia, 1793–1863), adopted as a youth by the Cherokee, won enduring fame as commander in chief of the Texas revolutionary army, as president of the Texas Republic, and as the new state's first US senator; earlier in his career, he had been governor of Tennessee. Mirabeau Bonaparte Lamar (b.Georgia, 1798–1859), the second president of the republic, founded the present state capital (now called Austin) in 1839. Anson Jones (b.Massachusetts, 1798–1858) was the last president of the republic.

Noteworthy state leaders include John H. Reagan (b.Tennessee, 1818–1905), postmaster general for the Confederacy; he dominated Texas politics from the Civil War to the 1890s, helping to write the state constitutions of 1866 and 1875, and eventually becoming chairman of the newly created Texas Railroad Commission. The most able Texas governor was probably James Stephen Hogg (1851–1906), the first native-born Texan to hold that office. Another administration with a progressive record was that of Governor James V. Allred (1899–1959), who served during the 1930s. In 1924 Miriam A. "Ma" Ferguson (1875–1961) became the first woman to be elected governor of a state, and she was elected again in 1932. With her husband, Governor James E. Ferguson (1871–1944), she was active in Texas politics for nearly 30 years. Texas military heroes include Audie Murphy (1924–71), the most decorated soldier of World War II (and later a film actor), and Admiral of the Fleet Chester W. Nimitz (1885–1966).

Figures of history and legend include James Bowie (b.Kentucky, 1796?–1836), who had a reputation as a brawling fighter and wheeler-dealer until he died at the Alamo: he is popularly credited with the invention of the bowie knife. David "Davy" Crockett (b.Tennessee, 1786–1836) served three terms as a US representative from Tennessee before departing for Texas; he, too, lost his life at the Alamo. Among the more notorious Texans was Roy Bean (b.Kentucky, 1825–1903), a judge who proclaimed himself "the law west of the Pecos." Gambler, gunman, and desperado John Wesley Hardin (1853–95) boasted that he "never killed a man who didn't deserve it." Bonnie Parker (1910–34) and Clyde Barrow (1909–34), second-rate bank robbers and murderers who were shot to death by Texas lawmen, achieved posthumous notoriety through the movie *Bonnie and Clyde* (1967).

Many Texas businessmen have profoundly influenced the state's politics and lifestyle. Clint Murchison (1895–1969) and Sid Richardson (1891–1959) made great fortunes as independent oil operators and spread their wealth into other enterprises: Murchison became owner-operator of the successful Dallas Cowboys professional football franchise, and Richardson, through the Sid Richardson Foundation, aided educational institutions throughout the Southwest. Oilman H(aroldson) L(afayette) Hunt (b.Illinois, 1889–1974), reputedly the wealthiest man in the US, was an avid supporter of right-wing causes. Howard Hughes (1905–79), an industrialist, aviation pioneer, film producer, and casino owner, became a fabulously wealthy eccentric recluse in his later years. Stanley Marcus (b.1905), head of the famous specialty store Neiman-Marcus, became an arbiter of taste for the world's wealthy and fashionable men and women. Rancher Richard King (b.New York, 1825–85) put together the famed King Ranch, the largest in the US at his death. Charles Goodnight (b.Illinois, 1836–1929) was an outstanding cattleman. H. Ross Perot, billionaire computer software developer and independent presidential candidate in 1992 and 1996, was born 27 June 1930 in Dallas.

Influential Texas historians include folklorist John A. Lomax (b.Mississippi, 1867–1948); Walter Prescott Webb (1888–1963), whose books *The Great Plains* and *The Great Frontier* helped shape American thought; and J. Frank Dobie (1888–1964), well-known University of Texas educator and compiler of Texas folklore. Dan Rather (b.1931) has earned a nationwide reputation as a television reporter and anchorman. Frank Buck (1884–1950), a successful film producer, narrated and appeared in documentaries showing his exploits among animals.

William Sydney Porter (b.North Carolina, 1862–1910) apparently embezzled funds from an Austin bank, escaped to Honduras, but returned to serve a three-year jail term—during which time he began writing short stories, later published under the pen name O. Henry. Katherine Anne Porter (1890–1980) also won fame as a short-story writer. Fred Gipson (1908–73) wrote *Hound Dog Man* and *Old Yeller*, praised by critics as a remarkable evocation of a frontier boy's viewpoint. Two novels

by Larry McMurtry (b.1936), *Horsemen, Pass By* (film title, *Hud*) and *The Last Picture Show*, became significant motion pictures. Robert Rauschenberg (b.1925) is a leading contemporary painter. Elisabet Ney (b.Germany, 1833–1907), a sculptor, came to Texas with a European reputation and became the state's first determined feminist; she wore pants in public, and seldom passed up an opportunity to transgress Texans' Victorian mores. E. Donnall Thomas, 1990 co-recipient of the Nobel Prize in medicine, was born 15 March 1920 in Mart, Texas.

Prominent Texans in the entertainment field include Mary Martin (1913–1990), who reigned over the New York musical comedy world for two decades; her son, Larry Hagman (b.1931), star of the *Dallas* television series; actress Debbie Reynolds (b.1931); movie director King Vidor (1894–1982); and Joshua Logan (1903–1988), director of Broadway plays and Hollywood movies. Texans who achieved national reputations with local repertory companies were Margo Jones (1912–55) and Nina Vance (1914–80), who founded and directed theater groups in Dallas and Houston, respectively; and Preston Jones (1936–79), author of *A Texas Trilogy* and other plays.

Among Texas-born musicians, Tina Turner (b.1941) is a leading rock singer, as was Janis Joplin (1943–70). Willie Nelson (b.1933) wedded progressive rock with country music to start a new school of progressive "outlaw" music. Bob Wills (b.Oklahoma, 1905–75) was the acknowledged king of western swing. Musicians Trini Lopez (b.1937), Freddy Fender (Baldemar Huerta, b.1937), and Johnny Rodriguez (b.1951) have earned popular followings based on their Mexican-American music. Charlie Pride (b.Mississippi, 1938) became the first black country-western star. Other country-western stars born in Texas are Waylon Jennings (b.1937) and Kenny Rogers (b.1938). In the jazz field, pianist Teddy Wilson (1912–86) was a member of the famed Benny Goodman trio in the 1930s. Trombonist Jack Teagarden (1905–64) and trumpeter Harry James (1916–83) have also been influential.

The imposing list of Texas athletes is headed by Mildred "Babe" Didrikson Zaharias (1913–56), who gained fame as an All-American basketball player in 1930, won two gold medals in track and field in the 1932 Olympics, and was the leading woman golfer during the 1940s and early 1950s. Another Texan, John Arthur "Jack" Johnson (1878–1946), was boxing's first black heavyweight champion. Texans who won fame in football include quarterbacks Sammy Baugh (b.1914), Don Meredith (b.1938), and Roger Staubach (b.Ohio, 1942); running back Earl Campbell (b.1955); and coaches Dana X. Bible (1892–1980). Darrell Royal (b.Oklahoma, 1924), and Thomas Wade "Tom" Landry (b.1924). Tim Brown (b.Dallas, Texas 1966), a wide receiver in the NFL, won the Heisman Trophy in 1987 as a member of the Fighting Irish of Notre Dame. Among other Texas sports greats are baseball Hall of Famers Tris Speaker (1888–1958) and Rogers Hornsby (1896–1963); golfers Ben Hogan (1912–97), Byron Nelson (b.1912), and Lee Trevino (b.1939); auto racing driver A(nthony) J(oseph) Foyt (b.1935); and jockey William Lee "Willie" Shoemaker (b.1931). Nolan Ryan, pitching giant, was born 31 January 1947 in Refugio, Texas.

50BIBLIOGRAPHY

Arbingast, Stanley A., et al. *Atlas of Texas.* Austin: University of Texas Press, 1979.

Bainbridge, John. *The Super-Americans.* New York: Doubleday. 1961.

Binkley, William C. *The Texas Revolution.* Austin: Texas State Historical Association, 1979.

Buenger, Walter L. (ed.) *Texas History.* Boston: American Press, 1983.

Caro, Robert A. *The Years of Lyndon Johnson: The Path to Power.* New York: Knopf, 1982.

Cartwright, Gary. *Turn Out the Lights: Chronicles of Texas in the 80s and 90s.* Austin: University of Texas Press, 2000.

Chipman, Donald E. *Spanish Texas, 1519–1821.* Austin: University of Texas Press, 1992.

Conaway, James. *The Texans.* New York: Knopf, 1976.

Connor, Seymour V. (ed.). *The Saga of Texas.* 6 vols. Austin: Steck-Vaughn, 1965.

Dobie, J. Frank. *Coronado's Children.* New York: Grosset & Dunlap, 1963.

———. *The Longhorns.* Boston: Little, Brown, 1941.

Duke, Cordia Sloan, and Joe B. Frantz. *6000 Miles of Fence: Life on the XIT Ranch of Texas.* Austin: University of Texas Press, 1981.

Federal Writers' Project. *Texas: A Guide to the Lone Star State.* Reprint. New York: Somerset, n.d. (orig. 1940).

Fehrenbach, T. R. *Lone Star: A History of Texas and the Texans.* New York: Crown, 1983.

Frantz, Joe B. *Texas: A Bicentennial History.* New York: Norton, 1976.

Frantz, Joe B., and Julian E. Choate, Jr. *The American Cowboy.* Norman: University of Oklahoma Press, 1955.

Friend, Llerena. *Sam Houston: The Great Designer.* Austin: University of Texas Press, 1954.

Gambrell, Herbert. *Anson Jones: The Last President of Texas.* Austin: University of Texas Press, 1964.

Handbook of Texas. 3 vols. Edited by Walter Prescott Webb and H. Bailey Carroll, with supplement edited by Eldon Stephen Brandon. Austin: Texas State Historical Association. 1952–76.

Horgan, Paul. *Great River: The Rio Grande in North American History.* New York: Holt, Rinehart & Winston, 1954.

James, Gary. *The Texas Guide.* Golden, Colo.: Fulcrum Pub., 2000.

Jones, Nancy Baker. *Capitol Women: Texas Female Legislators, 1923–1999.* Austin: University of Texas Press, 2000.

Jordan, Terry G. *Immigration to Texas.* Boston: American Press, 1981.

Kessell, John L. *Spain in the Southwest: A Narrative History of Colonial New Mexico, Arizona, Texas, and California.* Norman: University of Oklahoma Press, 2002.

Lack, Paul D. *The Texas Revolutionary Experience: A Political and Social History, 1835–1836.* College Station: Texas A&M University Press, 1992.

Sibley, Marilyn McAdams. *The Port of Houston: A History.* Austin: University of Texas Press, 1968.

Spratt, John S. *The Road to Spindletop: Economic Change in Texas, 1875–1901.* Austin: University of Texas Press, 1983.

Texas Almanac and State Industrial Guide, 1984–85. 50th ed. Dallas: A. H. Belo Corp., 1983.

Texas Fact Book, 1984. Edited by Joseph E. Pluta. Rita J. Wright and Midred C. Anderson. Austin: University of Texas, 1983.

Texas Government Today. Pacific Grove, Calif.: Brooks/Cole Pub. Co., 1992.

Tinkle, Lon. *Thirteen Days to Glory.* New York: McGraw-Hill, 1958.

Watson, Charles S. *Horton Foote: A Literary Biography.* Austin: University of Texas Press, 2003.

Webb, Walter Prescott. *The Texas Rangers: A Century of Frontier Defense.* Austin: University of Texas Press, 1965.

Wright, Rita J. *Texas Sources: A Bibliography.* Austin: University of Texas, 1976.

UTAH

State of Utah

ORIGIN OF STATE NAME: Named for the Ute Indians. **NICKNAME:** The Beehive State. **CAPITAL:** Salt Lake City. **ENTERED UNION:** 4 January 1896 (45th). **SONG:** "Utah, We Love Thee" and "Utah, This is the Place." **MOTTO:** Industry. **COAT OF ARMS:** In the center, a shield, flanked by American flags, shows a beehive with the state motto and six arrows above, sego lilies on either side, and the numerals "1847" (the year the Mormons settled in Utah) below. Perched atop the shield is an American eagle. **FLAG:** Inside a thin gold circle, the coat of arms and the year of statehood are centered on a blue field, fringed with gold. **OFFICIAL SEAL:** The coat of arms with the words "The Great Seal of the State of Utah 1896" surrounding. **ANIMAL:** Rocky Mountain elk. **BIRD:** California sea gull. **FISH:** Bonneville cutthroat trout. **INSECT:** Honeybee. **FLOWER:** Sego lily. **TREE:** Blue spruce. **GEM:** Topaz. **EMBLEM:** Beehive. **LEGAL HOLIDAYS:** New Year's Day, 1 January; Birthday of Martin Luther King, Jr., 3rd Monday in January; Lincoln's Birthday, 12 February; Washington's Birthday, 3rd Monday in February; Memorial Day, last Monday in May; Independence Day, 4 July; Pioneer Day, 24 July; Labor Day, 1st Monday in September; Columbus Day, 2nd Monday in October; Veterans Day, 11 November; Thanksgiving Day, 4th Thursday in November; Christmas Day, 25 December. **TIME:** 5 AM MST = noon GMT.

¹LOCATION, SIZE, AND EXTENT

Located in the Rocky Mountain region of the western US, Utah ranks 11th in size among the 50 states.

The area of Utah totals 84,899 sq mi (219,899 sq km), of which land comprises 82,073 sq mi (212,569 sq km) and inland water 2,826 sq mi (7,320 sq km). Utah extends 275 mi (443 km) E-W and 345 mi (555 km) N-S.

Utah is bordered on the N by Idaho; on the NE by Wyoming; on the E by Colorado; and on the S by Arizona (with the two borders joined at Four Corners); and on the W by Nevada. The total boundary length of Utah is 1,226 mi (1,973 km). The state's geographic center is in Sanpete County, 3 mi (5 km) N of Manti.

²TOPOGRAPHY

The eastern and southern two-thirds of Utah belong to the Colorado Plateau, a region characterized by deep river canyons; erosion has carved much of the plateau into buttes and mesas. The Rocky Mountains are represented by the Bear River, Wasatch, and Uinta ranges in the north and northeast. These ranges, rising well above 10,000 ft (3,000 m), hold the highest point in Utah—Kings Peak in the Uintas—at an altitude of 13,528 ft (4,126 m).

The arid, sparsely populated Great Basin dominates the western third of the state. Drainage in this region does not reach the sea, and streams often disappear in the dry season. To the north are the Great Salt Lake, a body of hypersaline water, and the Great Salt Lake Desert (containing the Bonneville Salt Flats), both remnants of a vast prehistoric lake that covered the region during the last Ice Age. The lowest point in Utah—2,000 ft (610 m) above sea level—occurs at Beaverdam Creek in Washington County, in the southwest corner of the state.

The western edge of the Wasatch Range, or Wasatch Front, holds most of Utah's major cities. It also attracts the greatest rainfall and snowfall, particularly in the north. Two regions rich in fossil fuels are the Kaiparowits Plateau, in southern Utah, and the Overthrust Belt, a geologic structural zone underlying the north-central part of the state.

The largest lake is the Great Salt Lake, which at the end of 1984 covered 2,250 sq mi (5,827 sq km) and was 34% larger than in 1976. In 1984, as a result of increased precipitation, the lake rose to 4,209.25 ft (1,283 m) above sea level, its highest level since 1877; the lake has been rising steadily since 1963, causing severe flooding, and its waters, diluted by runoff, have lost some salinity. Other major bodies of water are Utah Lake, Bear Lake (shared with Idaho), and Lake Powell, formed by the Glen Canyon Dam on the Colorado River. Other important rivers include the Green, flowing into the Colorado; the Sevier, which drains central and southern Utah; and the Bear, which flows into the Great Salt Lake.

³CLIMATE

The climate of Utah is generally semiarid to arid. Temperatures are favorable along the Wasatch Front, where there are relatively mild winters. At Salt Lake City, the normal daily mean temperature is 52°F (11°C), ranging from 28°F (–2°C) in January to 78°F (26°C) in July. The record high temperature, 117°F (47°C), was set at St. George on 5 July 1985; the record low temperature, –69°F (–56°C), in Peter's Sink, on 1 February 1985. The average annual precipitation varies from less than 5 in (12.7 cm) in the west to over 40 in (102 cm) in the mountains, with Salt Lake City receiving 16.5 in (42 cm) per year during the period (1971–2000). The annual snowfall is about 59 in (150 cm) and remains on the higher mountains until late summer.

⁴FLORA AND FAUNA

Botanists have recognized more than 4,000 floral species in Utah's six major life zones. Common trees and shrubs include four species of pine and three of juniper; aspen, cottonwood, maple, hawthorn, and chokecherry also flourish, along with the Utah oak, Joshua tree, and blue spruce (the state tree). Among Utah's wildflowers are sweet William and Indian paintbrush; the sego lily is the state flower. In 2003, 24 plant species were classified as threatened or endangered in Utah, including five species (San Rafael, Siler pincushion, Wright fishhook, Uinta Basin hookless, and Winkler) of cactus, dwarf bear-poppy, five species (Shivwitz, Deseret, Holmgren, heliotrope, and Welsh's) of milk-vetch, and autumn buttercup.

Mule deer are the most common of Utah's large mammals; other mammals include pronghorn antelope, Rocky Mountain bighorn sheep, lynx, grizzly and black bears, and white- and black-tailed jackrabbits. Among native bird species are the great horned owl, plain titmouse, and water ouzel; the golden eagle and great white pelican are rare species; and the sea gull (the state bird) is a spring and summer visitor from the California coast. The pygmy rattler is found in southwest Utah, and the Mormon cricket is unique to the state.

In 2003, 23 animal species were listed as threatened or endangered in Utah. Among them were the bald eagle, Utah prairie dog, three species (bonytail, humpback, and Virgin River) chub, whooping crane, two species of sucker, southwestern willow flycatcher, and woundfin. Many birds and fish have been killed or imperiled by the inundation of freshwater marshes with salt water from the flooding Great Salt Lake.

⁵ENVIRONMENTAL PROTECTION

Divisions of the Department of Natural Resources oversee water and mineral resources, parks and recreation, state lands and forests, and wildlife. The Department of Agriculture is concerned with soil conservation and pesticide control. The Department of Environmental Quality has separate divisions dealing with air quality, drinking water systems, water quality, and regulation of water pollution, radioactive, hazardous, and solid wastes.

Air pollution is a serious problem along the Wasatch Front where 70% of the state's population reside. Automobiles are a major contributor to the high levels of ozone and carbon monoxide impacting the communities in the Salt Lake, Weber, and Utah counties. Also of considerable concern is the quality of drinking water.

Other environmental issues of concern in the state are transportation safety of hazardous materials, chemical warfare agent storage and disposal, a proposed nuclear fuel storage site in the western part of the state (which, as of March 2003 had been approved despite widespread protests against it, but had not yet built), and interstate transportation of hazardous waste for disposal. Another environmental problem is the pollution of Great Salt Lake by industrial waste. In 1996, the lake and its surrounding wetlands were designated a Hemispheric Reserve in the Western Hemisphere Shorebird Reserve Network. The move was taken in recognition of the area's importance to migratory waterfowl and shorebirds. In 2003, Utah had 197 hazardous waste sites listed in the Environmental Protection Agency's database, 15 of which were on the National Priorities List. As of 2003, Utah' Carbon County was home to the 2nd-largest landfill in the United States. In 2001, Utah received $26,413,000 in federal grants from the Environmental Protection Agency; EPA expenditures for procurement contracts in Utah that year amounted to $210,000.

⁶POPULATION

Utah ranked 34th in population in the US with an estimated total of 2,316,256 in 2002, an increase of 3.7% since 2000. Between 1990 and 2000, Utah's population grew from 1,722,850 to 2,233,169, an increase of 29.6%, the 4th-highest percentage gain in the decade among the 50 states. The population is projected to reach 2,411,000 by 2005 and 2.9 million by 2025. The population density in 2000 was 27.2 persons per sq mi.

Because of the state's consistently high birthrate, Utahns tend to be much younger than the US population as a whole. In 2000, the median age was 27.1 (compared with the US average of 35.3). In the same year, more than 9.4% of state residents were under 5 years of age, and more than 32.2% were younger than 18 years of age (compared with the national average of 25.7%); only 8.5% of the populace were age 65 or older.

Nearly 90% of all Utahns live in cities and towns, mostly along the Wasatch Front. Salt Lake City is Utah's most populous urban center, with an estimated 2002 population of 181,266 in the city proper and a 1999 estimate of 1,275,076 in its metropolitan region. Other major cities with large populations include Provo, Ogden, and Orem.

⁷ETHNIC GROUPS

Hispanics and Latinos constitute the largest ethnic minority in Utah, with an estimated 2000 population of 201,559 or 9% of the total, up from 6.8% in 1990.

American Indians are the 3rd-largest minority group in Utah, numbering an estimated 29,684 in 2000, up from 24,000 in 1990. Indian lands covered 2,331,000 acres (943,000 hectares) in 1982, all but 35 acres (14 hectares) of which were tribal landholdings. The Uintah and Ouray Indian reservation, in the northeast (2000 population 19,182), and the Navaho Indian reservation, in the southeast, are the largest. Far smaller are the Skull Valley and Goshute reservations, in the west.

About 37,108 Asians resided in the state as of 2000, including 8,045 Chinese, 6,186 Japanese, and 5,968 Vietnamese. Pacific Islanders numbered 15,145. Utah also had an estimated black population of 17,657 as of 2000, up from 12,000 in 1990. Until 1978, blacks were denied full church membership as Mormons.

Utah had 158,664 residents who were foreign born, or 7.1% of the population, up from 58,600 in 1990. Among persons reporting at least one specific ancestry in 2000, 647,987 persons claimed English descent, 258,496 German, 163,048 Danish, 144,713 Irish, and 94,911 Swedish.

⁸LANGUAGES

Forebears of the Ute, Goshute, and Paiute contributed to English only a few place-names, such as Utah itself, Uinata (and Uintah), Wasatch, and Tavaputs.

Utah English is primarily that merger of Northern and Midland carried west by the Mormons, whose original New York dialect later incorporated features from southern Ohio and central Illinois. Conspicuous in Mormon speech in the central valley, although less frequent now in Salt Lake City, is a reversal of vowels, so that *farm* and *barn* sound like *form* and *born* and, conversely, *form* and *born* sound like *farm* and *barn*.

In 2000, 87.5% of all state residents five years of age or older spoke only English at home; this was a decrease from 92.2% in 1990.

The following table gives selected statistics from the 2000 census for language spoken at home by persons five years old and over. The category "Other Pacific Island languages" includes Chamorro, Hawaiian, Ilocano, Indonesian, and Samoan.

LANGUAGE	NUMBER	PERCENT
Population 5 years and over	2,023,875	100.0
Speak only English	1,770,626	87.5
Speak a language other than English	253,249	12.5
Speak a language other than English	253,249	12.5
Spanish or Spanish Creole	150,244	7.4
German	12,095	0.6
Navajo	9,373	0.5
Other Pacific Island languages	8,998	0.4
French (incl. Patois, Cajun)	7,905	0.4
Chinese	7,093	0.4
Portuguese or Portuguese Creole	5,715	0.3
Vietnamese	5,202	0.3
Japanese	5,032	0.2

⁹RELIGIONS

The dominant religious group in Utah, accounting for 66% of the entire state population in 2000, was the Church of Jesus Christ of Latter-Day Saints, popularly known as the Mormons. The church was founded by Joseph Smith, Jr., in 1830, the same year he published the Book of Mormon, the group's sacred text. The Mormons' arrival in Utah climaxed a long pilgrimage that began in New York State and led westward to Missouri, then back to Illinois (where Smith was lynched), and finally across Iowa,

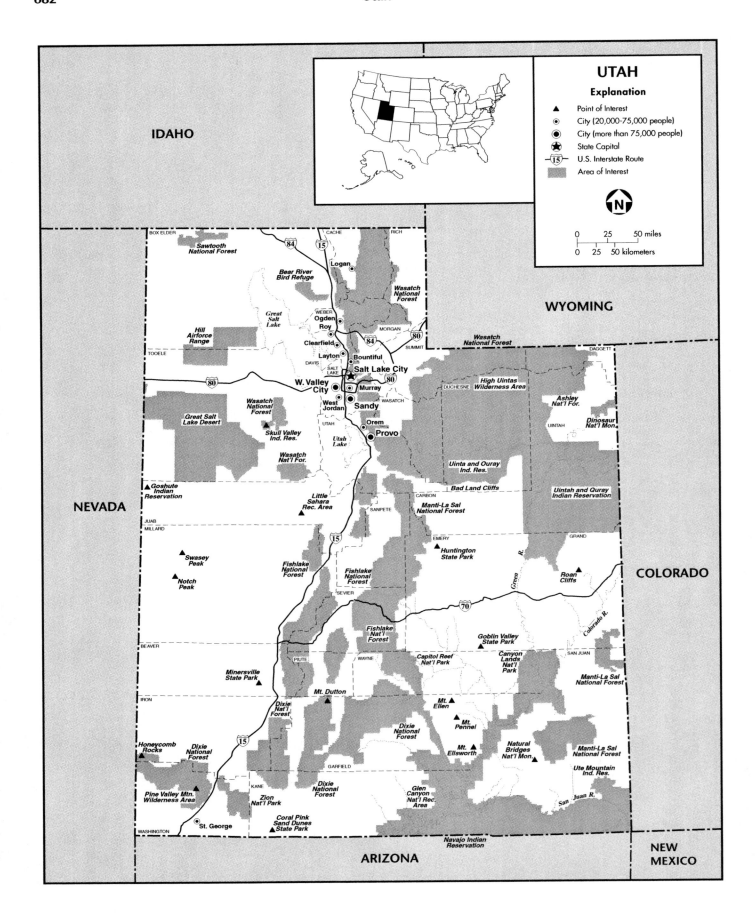

UTAH
Explanation
▲ Point of Interest
⊙ City (20,000-75,000 people)
◉ City (more than 75,000 people)
★ State Capital
15 U.S. Interstate Route
Area of Interest

IDAHO
NEVADA
WYOMING
COLORADO
ARIZONA
NEW MEXICO

BOX ELDER
Sawtooth National Forest
Bear River Bird Refuge
CACHE
RICH
Logan
Wasatch National Forest
Great Salt Lake
WEBER
Ogden
Roy
MORGAN
Clearfield
Layton
DAVIS
Bountiful
Salt Lake City
SALT LAKE
W. Valley City
Murray
West Jordan
Sandy
WASATCH
Orem
UTAH
Provo
Utah Lake
Hill Airforce Range
TOOELE
Wasatch National Forest
Great Salt Lake Desert
Skull Valley Ind. Res.
Wasatch Nat'l For.
SUMMIT
DUCHESNE
High Uintas Wilderness Area
Wasatch National Forest
DAGGETT
Ashley Nat'l For.
UINTAH
Dinosaur Nat'l Mon.
Uinta and Ouray Ind. Res.
Bad Land Cliffs
Uintah and Quray Indian Reservation
▲ Goshute Indian Reservation
JUAB
Little Sahara Rec. Area
CARBON
SANPETE
Manti-La Sal National Forest
MILLARD
▲ Swasey Peak
▲ Notch Peak
Fishlake National Forest
Fishlake National Forest
EMERY
▲ Huntington State Park
GRAND
Green R.
▲ Roan Cliffs
Colorado R.
SEVIER
Fishlake Nat'l Forest
70
BEAVER
PIUTE
WAYNE
Capitol Reef Nat'l Park
Goblin Valley State Park ▲
Canyon Lands Nat'l Park
SAN JUAN
Minersville State Park ▲
Mt. Dutton ▲
Mt. Ellen ▲
Mt. Pennel ▲
Manti-La Sal National Forest
IRON
Dixie Nat'l Forest
Dixie National Forest
▲ Honeycomb Rocks
Dixie National Forest
Mt. Ellsworth ▲
Natural Bridges Nat'l Mon. ▲
Manti-La Sal National Forest
Ute Mountain Ind. Res.
Pine Valley Mtn. Wilderness Area ▲
GARFIELD
KANE
Dixie National Forest
Glen Canyon Nat'l Rec. Area
San Juan R.
Zion Nat'l Park
St. George
Coral Pink Sand Dunes State Park ▲
WASHINGTON
Navajo Indian Reservation

84
15
80
0   25   50 miles
0   25   50 kilometers

Nebraska, and Wyoming to Salt Lake City in 1847. The Mormon Church and its leadership continue to play a central role in the state's political, economic, and cultural institutions. Among other assets in the state, the church owns Zion Cooperative Mercantile Institute (the largest department store in Salt Lake City), one of the leading newspapers, one television station, and holdings in banks, insurance companies, and real estate.

The Latter-Day Saints had 1,483,858 members in Utah in 2000. The next largest Christian groups were Roman Catholics, 97,085 and Southern Baptists, 13,258. In 2000, there were an estimated 4,500 Jews and 3,645 Muslims in the state. About 25.3% of the population were not counted as members of any religious organization.

[10]TRANSPORTATION

Utah, where the golden spike was driven in 1869 to mark the completion of the first transcontinental railroad, had 2,255 rail mi (3,629 km) of track in 2000. Major railroads are the Burlinton Northern/Santa Fe and the Union Pacific. Amtrak provides passenger service to Salt Lake City, Ogden, Milford, Provo, Helper, and Thompson.

The Utah Transit Authority, created in 1970, provides bus service for Salt Lake City, Provo, and Ogden. In 2000, Utah had 41,852 mi (67,354 km) of public roads and streets; there were 1,655,897 registered motor vehicles and 1,463,366 licensed drivers. The main east–west and north–south routes—I-80 and I-15, respectively—intersect at Salt Lake City. Utah had 95 airports in 2002. By far the busiest was Salt Lake City International Airport, with 9,522,344 passengers enplaned in 2000.

[11]HISTORY

Utah's historic Indian groups are primarily Shoshonean: the Ute in the eastern two-thirds of the state, the Goshute of the western desert, and the Southern Paiute of southwestern Utah. The Athapaskan-speaking Navaho of southeastern Utah migrated from western Canada, arriving not long before the Spaniards. The differing lifestyles of each group remained essentially unchanged until the introduction of the horse by the Spanish sometime after 1600. White settlement from 1847 led to two wars between whites and Indians-the Walker War of 1853–54 and the even more costly Black Hawk War of 1865–68-resulting finally in the removal of many Indians to reservations.

Mexicans and Spaniards are the first non-Indians known to have entered Utah, with Juan María Antonio Rivera reportedly arriving near present-day Moab as early as 1765. In July 1776, a party led by two Franciscan priests, Francisco Atanasio Domínguez and Silvestre Vélez de Escalanta, entered Utah from the east, traversed the Uinta basin, crossed the Wasatch Mountains, and visited the Ute encampment at Utah Lake. Trade between Santa Fe, the capital of the Spanish province of New Mexico, and the Indians of Utah was fairly well established by the early 1800s.

Until 1848, the 1,200-mi (1,900-km) Spanish Trail, the longest segment of which lies in Utah, was the main route through the Southwest. Following this trail, mountain men competing for fur explored vast areas of the American West, including most of Utah's rivers and valleys. In the 1840s, Utah was traversed by California-bound settlers and explorers, the most notable being John C. Frémont.

When Joseph Smith, Jr., founder of the Church of Jesus Christ of Latter-day Saints (Mormons), was lynched at Carthage, Ill., in June 1844, Brigham Young and other Mormon leaders decided to move west. By April 1847, the pioneer company of Mormons, including three blacks, was on its way to Utah, the reports of Frémont having influenced their choice of the Great Basin as a refuge. Advance scouts entered the Salt Lake Valley on 22 July, and the rest of the company two days later. Planting and irrigation were begun immediately. Natural resources were regarded as community property, and the church organization served as the first government.

After the Treaty of Guadalupe-Hidalgo (1848) gave the US title to much of the Southwest, the Mormons established the provisional state of Deseret. Congress refused to admit Deseret to the Union, choosing instead to create Utah Territory "with or without slavery." The territory encompassed, in addition to present-day Utah, most of Nevada and parts of Wyoming and Colorado; land cessions during the 1860s left Utah with its present boundaries.

The territorial period lasted for 46 years, marked by immigration, growth, and conflict. Reports that Utahns were in rebellion against federal authority led President James Buchanan to send an expeditionary force under Albert Sidney Johnston to Utah in 1857. On 11 September, Mormon militiamen and their Indian allies, caught up in an atmosphere of war hysteria, massacred some 120 California-bound migrants at Mountain Meadows—the darkest event in Utah history and the only major disaster of the so—called Utah War. Peace was attained in June 1858, and Alfred Cumming assumed civil authority, replacing Brigham Young as territorial governor. Cumming's appointment signaled the beginning of prolonged hostility between Mormon leaders and federal authorities.

Almost 98% of Utah's total population was Mormon until after 1870, and the Mormon way of life dominated politics, economics, and social and cultural activities. As church president, Brigham Young remained the principal figure in the territory until his death in 1877. He contracted in 1868 with the Union Pacific to lay part of the track for the transcontinental railroad in Utah, and on 10 May 1869, the Central (now Southern) Pacific and Union Pacific were joined at Promontory. During the 1870s, new rail lines connected many settlements with the capital, Salt Lake City, spurring commerce and mining. Young had discouraged mining until agriculture and manufacturing were firmly established. Not until 1863, with the rediscovery of silver-bearing ore in Bingham Canyon, did the boom in precious metals begin. Those connected with mining, mostly non-Mormons, began to exert influence in the territory's business, politics, and social life.

Several factors made the non-Mormon minority fearful of Mormon domination: communitarian economic practices, lack of free public schools, encouragement of immigration of Mormon converts, church authoritarianism, and the mingling of church and state. But the most sensational reason was the Mormon practice of polygamy. Congress passed the Anti-Bigamy Act in 1862, but it was generally not enforced. After the Edmunds Act of 1882 was upheld by the US Supreme Court, arrests for polygamy greatly increased. Finally, in 1887, the Edmunds-Tucker Act dissolved the Mormon Church as a corporate entity, thereby threatening the survival of all Mormon institutions.

In fall 1890, Mormon president Wilford Woodruff issued a manifesto renouncing the practice of polygamy. The following year, the Republican and Democratic parties were organized in Utah, effectively ending political division along religious lines. A constitutional convention was held in 1895, and statehood became a reality on 4 January 1896. The new state constitution provided for an elected governor and a bicameral legislature, and restored the franchise to women, a privilege they had enjoyed from 1870 until 1887, when the Edmunds-Tucker Act had disfranchised Utah women and polygamous men.

The early 20th century saw further growth of the mineral industry. Many of those who came to mine copper and coal were foreign immigrants. Militant union activity had begun slowly during the 1890s, until an explosion that killed 200 miners at Scofield on 1 May 1900 dramatized the plight of the miners and galvanized radical organizers in the state. It was in Utah in 1915 that a Swedish miner and songwriter named Joe Hill, associated with the Industrial Workers of the World ("Wobblies"), was executed for the murder of a Salt Lake City grocer and his son, a case that continues to generate controversy because of the circumstantial quality of the evidence against him.

Gradually, modern cities emerged, along with power plants, interurban railroads, and highways. By 1920, nearly half the population lived along the Wasatch Front. The influx of various ethnic groups diversified the state's social and cultural life, and the proportion of Mormons in the total population declined to about 68% in 1920.

Utah businesses enjoyed the postwar prosperity of the 1920s. On the other hand, mining and agriculture were depressed throughout the 1920s and 1930s, decades marked by increased union activity, particularly in the coal and copper industries. The depression of the 1930s hit Utah especially hard. Severe droughts hurt farmers in 1931 and 1934, and high freight rates limited the expansion of manufacturing. With the coming of World War II, increased demand for food revived Utah's agriculture, and important military installations and war-related industries brought new jobs to the state.

In the years since World War II, the state's population has more than doubled, while per capita income has declined relative to the national average-both trends indicative of a very high birthrate. Politics generally reflect prevailing Mormon attitudes and tend to be conservative. The state successfully opposed plans for storing nerve gas bombs in Utah and for the location in the western desert of an MX missile racetrack system. In 1967 work began on the Central Utah Project, a dam and irrigation program still under way in the early 2000s and intended to assure an adequate water supply for the state through the year 2020.

Utah had one of the nation's fastest growing economies in the 1990s and one of its lowest rates of unemployment. The state's leading industry was the manufacture of transport equipment, including aircraft parts and parts for missiles and rockets. At the beginning of the 21st century, Utahns were divided over the issue of protecting the state's natural areas from residential and commercial development.

Salt Lake City was the site of the 2002 Winter Olympic Games. The selection of Salt Lake City as the site for the games was controversial and mired in a scandal that broke in 1998, as bid leaders for Salt Lake City's selection were charged with bribing International Olympic Committee officials in exchange for their support of Salt Lake City's bid. Ten International Olympic Committee members either resigned or were expelled as a result of the scandal. The 2002 Winter Olympics generated $56 million in profits.

Governor Michael O. Leavitt became the second Utah governor to be elected to a third term in 2000, but as of mid-2003, he had not yet announced if he would run for an unprecedented fourth term. He was responsible for cutting income and property taxes, and in 2003, pledged to balance Utah's budget without raising taxes. In 2003, Leavitt maintained economic prosperity would be achieved through reforming Utah's education system, including adopting a competency standard for high school graduation. Wildfires and serious drought conditions plagued Utah in the early 2000s.

12 STATE GOVERNMENT

The state legislature, as established in the constitution of 1896, consists of a 29-member senate and a 75-seat house of representatives; senators serve for four years, representatives for two. Annual sessions begin in January and are limited to 45 calendar days. Legislators must be at least 25 years old, US citizens, state residents for at least three years, district residents for at least six months, and qualified voters in their districts. In 2002 legislators received a per diem salary of $120 during regular sessions.

The chief executive officers, all elected for four-year terms, include the governor, lieutenant governor (who also serves as secretary of state), attorney general, treasurer, and auditor. The governor must be at least 30 years old, a qualified voter, and must have been a state resident and citizen for at least five years. The governor and lieutenant governor are jointly elected and limited to serving three consecutive terms. In 2002 the governor's salary was $100,600.

A bill passed by the legislature becomes law if signed by the governor, if left unsigned by the governor for 10 days while the legislature is in session (20 if it has adjourned), or if passed over the governor's veto by two-thirds of the members of each house.

Amending the constitution requires a two-thirds vote of the legislature and ratification by majority vote at the next general election. The Utah Constitutional Revision Commission has been a permanent commission since 1977, recommending and drafting proposed constitutional changes. In 2002 voters approved the Commission's recommended constitution changes regarding taxation and state revenue. In 1994 Utah's voters approved constitutional amendment dealings with the rights of crime victims. The state's constitution had been amended 103 times by January 2003. Voters must be US citizens, at least 18 years old, and have been residents of the state 30 days prior to election day. Restrictions apply to those convicted of certain crimes and to those judged by the court as mentally incompetent to vote.

13 POLITICAL PARTIES

The Republican and Democratic parties are the state's leading political groups. Though there is no party registration in the state, Utah's voting record shows its voters to be heavily Republican. In the midterm elections of 2000, Orrin Hatch was reelected to a fifth term in the US Senate. Utah's other US senator, Republican Robert F. Bennett, was last elected in 1998. In the 2002 elections, voters sent two Republicans and one Democrat to Washington as their delegation in the US House. At the state level, Republicans continued to dominate the assembly, with 56 members to the Democrats' 19; while the state senate had 22 Republicans and 7 Democrats. Republican governor Michael O. Leavitt was first elected in 1992 and secured a third term in the 2000 election. In November 2000, true to form, Utahns cast 67% of their presidential votes for Republican George W. Bush; 26% for Democrat Al Gore; and 5% for Green Party candidate Ralph Nader. In 2002 there were 1,254,994 registered voters; there is no party registration in the state. The state had five electoral votes in the 2000 presidential election.

Utah Presidential Vote by Major Political Parties, 1948–2000

YEAR	ELECTORAL VOTE	UTAH WINNER	DEMOCRAT	REPUBLICAN
1948	4	*Truman (D)	149,151	124,402
1952	4	*Eisenhower (R)	135,364	194,190
1956	4	*Eisenhower (R)	118,364	215,631
1960	4	Nixon (R)	169,248	205,361
1964	4	*Johnson (D)	219,628	181,785
1968	4	*Nixon (R)	156,665	238,728
1972	4	*Nixon (R)	126,284	323,643
1976	4	Ford (R)	182,110	337,908
1980	4	*Reagan (R)	124,266	439,687
1984	5	*Reagan (R)	155,369	469,105
1988	5	*Bush (R)	207,343	428,442
1992**	5	Bush (R)	183,429	322,632
1996**	5	Dole (R)	221,633	361,911
2000	5	*Bush, G. W. (R)	203,053	515,096

* Won US presidential election.
** Independent candidate Ross Perot received 203,400 votes in 1992 and 66,461 votes in 1996.

[14]LOCAL GOVERNMENT

Utah has 29 counties (2002), governed by elected commissioners. Other elected county officials include clerk-auditor, sheriff, assessor, recorder, treasurer, county attorney, and surveyor. Counties are the most powerful form of local government, having administrative, judicial, and financial authority. They also are responsible for law enforcement, education, and welfare.

There were 236 municipal governments in 2002. Larger cities were run by an elected mayor and two commissioners while smaller communities were governed by mayor and city council. Nevertheless, the state's largest municipality, Salt Lake City, adopted the mayor-council system. Additionally, the state had 40 public school districts and 340 special districts in 2002.

[15]STATE SERVICES

To address the continuing threat of terrorism and to work with the federal Department of Homeland Security (created in 2002 following the terrorist attacks of 11 September 2001), homeland security in Utah in 2003 operated under state statute; the emergency management director was designated as the state homeland security advisor.

The Department of Public Education is responsible for public instruction, and the Utah State Board of Regents oversees the state college and university system. Highways and airports are the responsibility of the Department of Transportation.

The Department of Community and Economic Development supports economic and technological development programs in the state. Agencies dealing with the elderly, disabled, family services, mental health, assistance payments, and youth corrections are under the Department of Human Services. The Department of Health oversees public health and health care for the indigent. Other state departments deal with natural resources, business, labor, agriculture, corrections, and public safety.

[16]JUDICIAL SYSTEM

Utah's highest court is the supreme court, consisting of a chief justice and 4 other justices, each serving a 10-year term. As of 1999 there were 37 district court judges, each one serving a 6-year term. Supreme court justices and district court judges are appointed by the governor with the consent of the state senate. Appointments must be ratified by the voters at the next general election. In 1984, to ease the supreme court's caseload, residents approved a constitutional amendment allowing the legislature to create an intermediate court.

In 2001, the FBI reported a crime-index rate of 4,243.0 crimes per 100,000 inhabitants, including a total of 5,314 violent crimes and 90,993 crimes against property in that year. Utah has a death penalty statute providing for execution by lethal injection or firing squad. In 1977 it executed (by firing squad) a prisoner, Gary Gilmore, thus becoming the first state in a decade to carry out a sentence of capital punishment. Between 1977 and 2003, the state executed six persons in total. As of 2003, 11 persons were under sentence of death. Prisoners under jurisdiction of state and federal correctional facilities numbered 5,440 in June 2001, a decrease of 0.2% from the previous year. The state's incarceration rate stood at 235 per 100,000 inhabitants.

[17]ARMED FORCES

In 2002, there were 5,447 active-duty military personnel and 14,725 civilian personnel stationed in Utah, the majority of whom were at Hill Air Force Base near Ogden and, in the Great Salt Lake Desert, Tooele Army Depot. Dugway Proving Ground—where nerve gas tests have been conducted—and the USAF Utah Test and Training Range are near the Nevada line. State firms were awarded more than $1.25 billion in federal contracts during the same year.

According to the 2000 Census, there were 62,809 veterans living in Utah, of whom 32,309 were veterans of World War II; 19,993 of the Korean conflict; 46,045 of the Vietnam era; and 21,348 during 1990–2000 (including the Persian Gulf War). Veterans' benefits in 2002 totaled nearly $324 million.

In 2000, the Utah Highway Patrol employed 397 full-time sworn officers.

[18]MIGRATION

After the initial exodus of Latter-day Saints from the eastern United States to Utah, Mormon missionaries attracted other immigrants to the state, and some 90,000 foreign converts arrived between 1850 and 1905. Many non-Mormons were recruited from overseas to work in the mines, especially during the early 20th century. Utah had a net gain from migration of 176,000 between 1940 and 1985. From 1985 to 1990, there was a net loss from migration of 10,500. Between 1990 and 1998, the state had net gains of 86,000 in domestic migration and 27,000 in international migration. In 1998, 3,360 foreign immigrants arrived in Utah; of these, 1,035 came from Mexico. The state's population increased 21.9% between 1990 and 1998, making it the 4th-fastest growing state in the nation. In the period 1995–2000, 242,189 people moved into the state and 216,893 moved out, for a net gain of 25,296, of whom 2,096 were age 65 or over. Most new residents are from California.

[19]INTERGOVERNMENTAL COOPERATION

Utah participates in several regional agreements, including the Bear River Compact (with Idaho and Wyoming), Colorado River Compact, and the Upper Colorado River Basin Compact. The state is also a signatory to the Interstate Oil and Gas Compact, Western Interstate Corrections Compact, Western Interstate Commission for Higher Education, and Western Interstate Energy Compact. Federal grants in 2001 amounted to over $2.2 billion.

[20]ECONOMY

Trade replaced government as the leading employer in Utah in 1980. Nearly 14% of personal income in the state was derived from government sources in 1995, a proportion increased to 14.7% by 1997. With more than 70% of Utah lands under US control and some 37,750 civilian workers on federal payrolls—and others employed by defense industries or the military—the federal presence in Utah is both a major economic force and a controversial political issue. On the one hand, elected officials have sought federal funds for mammoth reclamation and power projects. On the other hand, they resent many federal programs concerned with social welfare, land use, or environmental protection. Employment in the 1990s shifted away from agriculture, mining, transportation, and communications toward government, trade, and service occupations, and to a much lesser extent, manufacturing. Utah suffered disproportionately from cuts in the federal military budget in the early nineties, but from 1997 to 2001, output from the government sector increased 27%, including a 30.7% increase from federal operations, civilian and military. Even stronger growth was shown in other service sectors, with financial services up 55%, and general services up 33.8%. Output from Utah's manufacturing sector increased 18% between 1997 and 2000, increasing its share in the gross state product from 14.1% to 15.6%, but then plummeted 11.7% in the national recession and slowdown of 2001, reducing its share in total state output to 11.5%. In 2002, Utah ranked seventh in the nation in job losses. Construction jobs were down 7% in part because of the end of work for the 2002 Winter Olympics held in Utah. Manufacturing jobs in December 2002 were down 3.2% year-on-year, and the loss of high-paying jobs in high-tech and venture capital fields was seriously impacting personal income in the state. As of September 2002, personal bankruptcy filings had increased 15% over the year before, as Utah continued to have among the highest foreclosure start and bankruptcy rates in the country.

In 2001, Utah's gross state product gross state product was $70.4 billion, the 33rd largest among the states, to which general services contributed $14.5 billion; general services, $14.1 billion; trade, $11.2 billion; government, $10.3 billion; manufacturing, $8.1 billion; transportation and public utilities, $85.6 billion, and construction, $4.4 billion. The public sector in 2001 constituted 14.7% of gross state product, compared to the 12% average for the states.

21INCOME

According to the Bureau of Economic Analysis, in 2001, Utah had a per capita personal income (PCPI) of $24,033 which ranked 47th in the United States (including the District of Columbia) and was 79% of the national average, $30,413. The 2001 PCPI reflected an increase of 2.7% from 2000 compared to the national change of 2.2%. In 2001, Utah had a total personal income (TPI) of $54,763,859,000 which ranked 35th in the United States and accounted for 0.6% of the national total. The 2001 TPI reflected an increase of 4.3% from 2000 compared to the national change of 3.3%.

Earnings of persons employed in Utah increased from $40,700,989,000 in 2000 to $42,234,478,000 in 2001, an increase of 3.8%. The largest industries in 2001 were services, 28.4% of earnings; state and local government, 12.8%; and retail trade, 9.7%. Of the industries that accounted for at least 5% of earnings in 2001, the slowest growing from 2000 to 2001 was durable goods manufacturing (8.6% of earnings in 2001), which decreased 1.8%; the fastest was state and local government, which increased 6.9%.

According to data released by the US Census Bureau, in 2000, the median household income was $45,230 compared to the national average of $42,148. In 2001, the median income for a family of four was $59,035 compared to the national average of $63,278. For the period 1999 to 2001, the average poverty rate was 8.0% which placed it 9th among the 50 states and the District of Columbia ranked lowest to highest.

22LABOR

According to Bureau of Labor Statistics (BLS) provisional estimates, in July 2003 the seasonally adjusted civilian labor force in Utah numbered 1,205,800, with approximately 63,100 workers unemployed, yielding an unemployment rate of 5.2%, compared to the national average of 6.2% for the same period. Since the beginning of the BLS data series in 1978, the highest unemployment rate recorded was 10.5% in April 1983. The historical low was 2.9% in March 1997. In 2001, an estimated 7.6% of the labor force was employed in construction; 12.5% in manufacturing; 5.3% in transportation, communications, and public utilities; 19.8% in trade; 5.0% in finance, insurance, and real estate; 24.1% in services; 15.4% in government; and 2.4% in agriculture.

Utah's union movement weakened in the 1980s as mining and heavy manufacturing industries mechanized, which resulted in the elimination of thousands of jobs. The US Department of Labor reported that in 2002, 60,000 of Utah's 973,000 employed wage and salary workers were members of unions. This represented 6.2% of those so employed, down from 6.8% in 2001. The national average is 13.2%. In all, 73,000 workers (7.5%) were represented by unions. In addition to union members, this category includes workers who report no union affiliation but whose jobs are covered by a union contract. Utah is one of 22 states with a right-to-work law.

23AGRICULTURE

Despite a dry climate and unpromising terrain, Utah ranked 37th in the US in value of farm marketings in 2001, with $1.1 billion. Crops accounted for $263 million; livestock and livestock products for $853 million. The first pioneers in Utah settled in fertile valleys near streams, which were diverted for irrigation. Today, Utah farmers and ranchers practice comprehensive soil and water conservation projects to help maximize crop yields and protect the natural resources. A farmland preservation movement is under way to protect valuable food-producing land from urban sprawl. In 2002 there were some 15,000 farms and ranches, covering 11,600,000 acres (4,700,000 hectares). The chief crops in 2002 were hay, 2.3 million tons; wheat, 4.9 million bushels; and tart cherries, 3 tons.

24ANIMAL HUSBANDRY

Livestock and livestock products account for over three-fourths of Utah's agricultural income. In 2003, there were an estimated 880,000 cattle and calves, valued at nearly $668.9 million on Utah farms and ranches. During 2002, hogs and pigs numbered 670,000 and were valued at around $50.9 million. Utah farms produced 25.3 million lb of sheep and lambs in 2001, and an estimated 2.65 million lb (1.2 million kg) of shorn wool in 2002. Dairy farms had around 93,000 milk cows, which produced 1.64 billion lb (0.74 billion kg) of milk.

25FISHING

Fishing in Utah is for recreation only. The state maintains egg-taking facilities at Bear Lake, Swan Creek, St. Charles, and Big Spring Creek to support 5.2 million angler days annually. Fish farms distributed 10.7 million trout for restoration or conservation purposes in 1998. In the same period, Utah issued 468,546 sport fishing licenses.

26FORESTRY

In 2002, Utah had 15,676,000 acres (6,344,000 hectares) of forestland. In 2001, 8,189,000 acres (3,314,000 hectares) were in the state's six national forests—Ashley, Dixie, Fishlake, Manti-La Sal, Uinta, and Wasatch-Cache. Only 4,683,000 acres (1,895,000 hectares) were classed as commercial timberland in 2002. In the same year, lumber production was 53 million board feet.

27MINING

The total value of nonfuel mineral production in Utah was approximately $1.53 billion in 2001, a decrease of about 5.6% from the previous year, accounted for partly by significant declines in the value of copper and magnesium compounds. The state was ranked in 9th place nationally in the output of nonfuel minerals. Approximately 60% of the value of production in the state was attributed to the metals sector, which included copper, gold, iron, magnesium, molybdenum, and silver. In addition, Utah mines produced significant quantities of beryllium, cement, magnesium compounds, sand and gravel, and salt. In 2001, Utah was 2nd in the nation in the output of magnesium metal and compounds, and potash; 3rd in molybdenum concentrates; 4th in crude perlite and phosphate rock; 5th in silver, gemstones, and bentonite; and 6th in salt. It was also the only US source of mined beryllium during the year. The largest operating beryllium mine in the world is in Juab County, located at Spor Mountain. Utah was also a significant producer of portland cement, construction sand and gravel (27.8 million metric tons, valued at $99.5 million), and lime.

28ENERGY AND POWER

In 1999, electric utilities in the state had an installed capacity (utility and nonutility) of 5.2 million kW; electricity production totaled 36.8 billion kWh. In 2000 Utah's total per capita energy consumption was 322 million Btu (81.1 million kcal), ranking it 32nd among the 50 states.

Proved oil reserves totaled 271 million barrels in 2001, and production was 42,000 barrels per day in 2002. Reserves of natural gas in 2001 amounted to 4,579 billion cu ft (129.6 billion cu m); marketed production, 282.1 billion cu ft (7.9 billion cu m). Early in 1980 there were large new natural gas finds in northeastern Utah. The state's recoverable reserves of bituminous coal were estimated at nearly 364 million tons in 2001, production reached 26.7 million tons in 2000. Utah is the only coal-producing state whose entire production comes from underground mines.

29 INDUSTRY

Utah's diversified manufacturing is concentrated geographically in Salt Lake City, Weber, Utah, and Cache counties. The total value of shipments by manufacturers in 1997 was $24 billion. In 1997, Utah was the headquarters for two Fortune 500 companies, American Stores and Smith's Food & Drug Centers. Utah has one truck-assembly plant, in Ogden.

Earnings of persons employed in Utah increased from $33.3 billion in 1997 to $35.5 billion in 1998, an increase of 6.7%. The largest industries in 1998 were services, 26.9% of earnings; state and local government, 11.6%; and retail trade, 10.9%. Of the industries that accounted for at least 5% of earnings in 1998, the slowest growing from 1997 to 1998 was durable goods manufacturing (10.5% of earnings in 1998), which increased 5.3%; the fastest was retail trade, which increased 9.7%.

30 COMMERCE

In 1997, Utah had 3,318 wholesale establishments, with sales of $23 billion. Utah's wholesale business had personal income exceeding $1.6 billion in 1997, when personal income from retail sales totaled $2.2 billion. Retail sales in 1997 totaled over $20 billion, with the 3rd-highest growth rate in the country for sales between 1992 and 1997. Retail and wholesale trading establishments are heavily concentrated in the Salt Lake City-Ogden metropolitan area. The leading wholesale trade categories were machinery, electrical goods, hardware, professional equipment, and construction materials. Foreign exports of Utah's manufactured goods totaled $3 billion in 1998.

31 CONSUMER PROTECTION

The Consumer Assistance Division in the Department of the Attorney General is charged with protecting Utah's consumers (particularly in the areas of enforcing federal and state antitrust laws, handling cybercrime, enforcing laws to protect consumers from fraud, identity fraud, and ensuring against Medicaid fraud), along with the Department of Commerce's Division of Consumer Protection. The protection division investigates and mediates complaints and allegations of unfair, deceptive, or fraudulent business practices. It also conducts ongoing consumer education programs to teach consumers how to recognize consumer fraud and how to avoid becoming a victim. The right's division supplies attorneys for subsequent legal action.

32 BANKING

Utah in 2002 had 60 insured banks with total assets of $134.8 billion. Forty-nine of these banks were state-chartered.

Utah had one of the nation's highest bankruptcy and foreclosure rates as of September 2002. The number of personal bankruptcy filings for 2002 was 15% higher than 2001. The office vacancy rate in the Salt Lake City area was close to 20% in late 2002, due in large measure to weaknesses in the high technology sector. Commercial real estate (CRE) market decline adversely affected Utah's banks, as most of them hold high CRE loan concentrations.

33 INSURANCE

Utahans held some 745,000 ordinary life insurance policies in 2001 with a total value of $78.5 billion; total value for all categories of life insurance (ordinary, group, industrial, and credit) was $108.2 billion. Death benefits paid that year totaled $258.7 million. As of 1997, there were 15 property and casualty and 17 life and health insurance companies incorporated or organized in the state. In 2001, property and casualty insurers wrote over $2.3 billion in premiums. That year, there were 2,351 flood insurance policies in force in the state, with a total value of $327,543.

34 SECURITIES

Utah has 318 brokerage firms doing business in the state via over 1,000 employees. Securities investment advisory services are provided by 64 firms. The state is the headquarters of 47 NASDAQ companies, four NASDAQ market makers; and Utah has incorporated six NYSE companies: CHS Electronics, Conoco Inc., Franklin Covey Co., Questar Corp., Union Pacific Corp., and Utah Medical Products, Inc.

35 PUBLIC FINANCE

The annual budget is prepared by the State Budget Office and submitted by the governor to the legislature for amendment and approval. The fiscal year runs from 1 July through 30 June.

The governor's 2000/01 State of Utah budget recommendations utilized total revenues of $6.7 billion, including $3.5 billion from the state's general fund. Actual general fund revenues in 2001 were $3.624 billion, above projections, but in 2001/02 the state began experiencing shortfalls, General fund revenues fell to $3.4 billion. Transfers from other funds, including $44.4 million from the tobacco settlement fund, were used to close the budget gap. In 2002/03, general fund revenues increased slightly to $3.45 billion, but expenditures were also increasing, and the state budget deficit was reported as $173 million or about 4.7% of the state budget. $25 million was cut from the state budget after its enactment with across-the-board cuts, furloughs, and partial freezes on travel, hiring and equipment purchases. The governor initiated a broader effort to cut $1.1 billion from the general budget, permanently reducing the size of the state government. The governor, however, pledged not to reduce education funds in 2003/04. Utah had the biggest family size and largest proportion of school-age children in the United States. In 2000/01, the state had a starting balance equal to 3.5% of expenditures. In 2001/02 and 2002/03 the start balance had equaled only 0.6% of expenditures.

The following table from the US Census Bureau contains information on revenues, expenditures, indebtedness, and cash/securities for 2001.

	($000)	PERCENT	PER CAPITA
Population (thousands, 2001)	2,279	(X)	(X)
Total Revenue	9,131,656	100.00	4,006.87
General revenue	8,171,229	89.48	3,585.44
Liquor store revenue	122,927	1.35	53.94
Insurance trust revenue	837,500	9.17	367.49
Exhibit: Salaries and wages	1,469,230	15.88	644.68
Total expenditure	9,253,469	100.00	4,060.32
General expenditure	8,488,561	91.73	3,724.69
Education	3,967,659	42.88	1,740.96
Public welfare	1,434,414	15.50	629.41
Hospitals	420,128	4.54	184.35
Health	277,794	3.00	121.89
Highways	883,759	9.55	387.78
Police protection	77,926	0.84	34.19
Correction	265,689	2.87	116.58
Natural resources	153,137	1.65	67.19
Parks and recreation	25,159	0.27	11.04
Government administration	428,668	4.63	188.09
Interest on general debt	195,527	2.11	85.80
Other and unallocable	358,701	3.88	157.39
Liquor store expenditure	91,427	0.99	40.12
Insurance trust expenditure	673,481	7.28	295.52
Debt at end of fiscal year	4,022,974	100.00	1,765.24
Cash and security holdings	18,105,334	100.00	7,944.42

36TAXATION

Utah's personal income tax is a six-bracket schedule ranging from 2.3% to 7% (the highest rate applicable to all taxable above $4,313). The corporate income tax rate is a flat 5%. The state's general sales and use tax rate is 4.75%, with local sales taxes adding on 1% to 3.5%. The state also levies a full array of excise taxes covering motor fuels, tobacco products, insurance premiums, public utilities, alcoholic beverages, pari-mutuels, and other selected items. The state's estate tax is related to the federal exemption for state death taxes, and is therefore scheduled to expire with the exemption in 2007, absent countervailing action by Utah. Utah's revenue losses from the phasing out of its estate tax are estimated at -$3 million for 2002/03, -$8 million for 2003/04 and -$16 million for 2006/07. Death and gift taxes accounted for 0.2% of state collections in 2002. Other state taxes include various state license fees and severance taxes. All property taxes are collected the local level. Property taxes are the main source of local revenue, with localities collecting about 35% of total state and local revenue in Utah. 53% of property taxes go to schools as does most of the state's budget. The government subsidizes water rates at the cost of about $20 million a year, and though Utah is the 2nd driest state, its water rates are among the lowest in the country.

The state collected $3.925 billion in taxes in 2002, of which 40.9% came from individual income taxes, 38.2% from the general sales tax, 13.3% from selective sales taxes, 3.76% from state license fees, 2.8% from corporate income taxes, and 0.7% from severance taxes. In 2003, Utah ranked 9th among the states in terms of combined state and local tax burden, which amounted to about 10.6% of income.

The following table from the US Census Bureau provides a summary of taxes collected by the state in 2002.

	($000)	PER CAPITA
Total Taxes	3,925,382	1,694.71
Property taxes	(X)	(X)
Sales and gross receipts	2,023,047	873.41
General sales and gross receipts	1,500,278	647.72
Selective sales taxes	522,769	225.7
Alcoholic beverage	26,080	11.26
Amusements	(X)	(X)
Insurance Premiums	87,838	37.92
Motor fuels	336,411	145.24
Pari-mutuels	(X)	(X)
Public utilities	1,797	0.78
Tobacco products	50,994	22.02
Other selective sales	19,649	8.48
Licenses	147,640	63.74
Alcoholic beverages	922	0.4
Amusements	(X)	(X)
Corporation	2,439	1.05
Hunting and fishing	21,714	9.37
Motor vehicle	85,734	37.01
Motor vehicle operators	9,132	3.94
Public utility	(X)	(X)
Occupation and business, NEC	24,690	10.66
Other	3,009	1.3
Other taxes	1,754,695	757.56
Individual income	1,605,310	693.06
Corporation net income	110,989	47.92
Death and gift	9,424	4.07
Documentary and stock transfer	(X)	(X)
Severance	28,972	12.51
Other	(X)	(X)

37ECONOMIC POLICY

The economic development of Utah has been dominated by two major forces: the relatively closed system of the original Mormon settlers and the more wide-open, speculative ventures of the state's later immigrants. The Mormons developed agriculture, industry, and a cooperative exchange system that excluded non-Mormons. The church actively opposed mining, and it was mostly with non-Mormon capital, by non-Mormon foreign immigrants, that the state's mineral industry was developed.

In the 1990s, these conflicts were supplanted by a widespread fiscal conservatism that supports business activities and opposes expansion of government social programs at all levels. One Utah politician, J. Bracken Lee, who served as governor from 1949 to 1957, and as mayor of Salt Lake City from 1960 to 72, became nationally famous for his call to repeal the federal income tax.

The Department of Community and Economic Development is the state agency responsible for the expansion of tourism and industry. The department's economic development programs include the Technology Finance Corporation, which uses private venture capital to provide loans for new technological investments. In 2003, the Utah Travel Council launched a new tourism database. Besides business and tourism, other division within the Department focus on Arts, Culture and Learning; Ethnic Affairs; and Community Resources.

38HEALTH

Health conditions in Utah are exceptionally good. In 2000, death rates per 100,000 population for heart disease (137.2), cancer (112.9), cerebrovascular disease (37.9), and accidents (34.0) were lower than the average national rates while the suicide rate (16.0) was above the national norm. The infant mortality rate—6.0 per 1,000 live births in 1996—was among the lowest in the US, and the overall death rate (563.1 per 100,000 persons in 1998) was well below the national average of 873.1. In 2000, Utah had the lowest proportion of adult smokers of any state, only 12.9% of residents 18 years of age and older. A total of 3,381 legal abortions were performed in 1999, or 7 per 1,000 women. The HIV mortality rate was 1.0 per 100,000 population in 2000, near the US national average of 5.3. A total of 2,097 AIDS cases had been reported through 2001.

Utah's 42 community hospitals had 203,037 admissions and 4,437 beds in 2001. There were 5,816 full-time registered nurses and 759 full-time licensed practical nurses in 2001 and 221 physicians per 100,000 population in 2000. The average expense of a community hospital for care was $988 per inpatient day in 2001.

Federal government grants to cover the Medicare and Medicaid services in 2001 totaled $688 million; 210,400 enrollees received Medicare benefits that year. At least 14.8% of Utah's residents were uninsured in 2002.

39SOCIAL WELFARE

In 2001, the average weekly unemployment benefit was $260.40. Average monthly participation in the food stamp program in FY2002 comprised 89,899 persons (36,005 households). The average monthly benefit was $73.89, and the sum total of benefits paid in FY2002 was $79,708,928.

With the enactment of the Personal Responsibility and Work Opportunity Reconciliation Act of 1996, the US government has changed the form and regulations for many of its social welfare programs. Most significantly, it replaces Aid to Families with Dependent Children (AFDC), an open-ended entitlement program, with Temporary Assistance for Needy Families (TANF), a limited system of assistance funded largely through federal block grants. The reform act also impacts the food stamp program, the Supplemental Security Income program, and the child nutrition program. The law took effect on 1 July 1997 and provided $16.38 billion in block grants for fiscal years 1997–2002. The grants are to be divided among the states based on an equation involving the numbers of former AFDC recipients in each state.

Reauthorization of the 1996 social welfare legislation, scheduled for 2002, was delayed, and the original law had been extended three times as of July 2003, with the most recent extension running through September 2003. Utah's TANF program is called the Family Employment Program (FEP). In June 2000 the state had 24,101 welfare recipients. State expenditures on the TANF program in FY2002 totaled $24,349,753.

In December 2001, Social Security benefits were paid to 246,330 Utah residents. This number included 159,570 retired workers, 21,840 widows and widowers, 22,810 disabled workers, 18,500 spouses, and 23,610 children. Social Security beneficiaries represented 10.8% of the total state population and 91.2% of the state's population age 65 and older. Retired workers (excluding persons with special benefits) received an average monthly payment of $878; widows and widowers, $867; disabled workers, $804; and spouses, $458. Payments for children of retired workers averaged $461 per month; children of deceased workers, $574; and children of disabled workers, $234.

Federal Supplemental Security Income payments in December 2001 went to 20,545 Utah residents, averaging $367 a month.

40 HOUSING

In 2002, there were an estimated 808,593 housing units in Utah, of which 744,627 were occupied; 71.7% were owner-occupied. Nearly 58.6% of all housing units were in the Salt Lake City–Ogden Area. About 67.5% of all units were single-family, detached homes. Utility gas was the most common energy source for heating; about 673 units were equipped for solar power. It was estimated that 17,291 units lacked telephone services, 734 lacked complete plumbing facilities, and 3,259 lacked complete kitchen facilities. The average household size was 3.06 people.

In 2002, 19,327 new privately owned housing units were authorized for construction. The median home value was $151,775. The median monthly cost for mortgage owners was $1,155. Renters paid a median of $667 per month. During 2002, Utah received more than $34.1 million in community planning and development aid from the US Department of Housing and Urban Development.

41 EDUCATION

Utah is among the nation's leaders in educational attainment. In 2000, 87.7% of Utah residents had graduated from high school; 26.1% had four or more years of college.

The total enrollment for fall 1999 in Utah's public schools stood at 480,255. Of these, 329,185 attended schools from kindergarten through grade eight, and 151,070 attended high school. Minority students made up approximately 15% of the total enrollment in public elementary and secondary schools. Total enrollment was estimated at 475,269 in fall 2000 and is expected to reach 512,000 by fall 2005. Expenditures for public education in 2000/01 were estimated at $2,077,668. Enrollment in nonpublic schools in fall 2001 was 12,614.

As of fall 2000, there were 186,743 students enrolled in college or graduate school. In the same year Utah had 24 degree-granting institutions. Major public institutions include the University of Utah; Utah State University; and Weber State College. Brigham Young University (Provo), founded in 1875 and affiliated with the Latter-day Saints, is the main private institution. In 1997, minority students comprised 6.9% of total postsecondary enrollment.

42 ARTS

Music has a central role in Utah's cultural life. The Mormon Tabernacle Choir has won world renown, and Ballet West is ranked among the nation's leading dance companies. The Utah Symphony (Salt Lake City) has also gained a national reputation. Opera buffs enjoy the Utah Opera Company, founded in 1976.

The Utah Arts Council sponsors exhibitions, artists in the schools, rural arts and folk arts programs, and statewide arts competitions in cooperation with arts organizations throughout the state. In addition, the partially state-funded Utah Arts Festival

is held each year in Salt Lake City. In 2003, Kenneth Brewer was named Utah's poet laureate. His books include The Place In Between (1998), Lake's Edge (1997), and Hoping for All, Dreading Nothing (1994).

Utah has about 25 art museums and galleries, including Utah State University's Nora Eccles Harrison Museum in Logan and the LDS Church Museum of Art and History in Salt Lake City. Other major facilities are the Brigham Young University Art Museum Collection, Provo; the Museum of Fine Arts of the University of Utah, Salt Lake City; and the Springville Art Museum.

Living Traditions: A Celebration of Salt Lake's Folk and Ethnic Arts is an annual festival that takes place on the weekend before Memorial Day. The three-day event attracts over 35,000 people and offers continuous music and dance on two stages, as well as crafts demonstrations and sales. The Sundance Institute, founded by Robert Redford in 1981, presents the annual Sundance Film Festival, which is widely regarded as one of the nation's most influential gatherings for independent filmmakers.

In 2003, the Utah Arts Council and other Utah arts organizations received grants totaling $1,020,500 from the National Endowment for the Arts. The Utah Humanities Council was established in 1975 and promotes several literacy and history-related programs and exhibits. In 2000, the National Endowment for the Humanities contributed $867,310 for 10 state programs. In addition, the state and private sources provide substantial contributions to the arts. Utah has over 450 arts associations and 60 local arts groups.

43 LIBRARIES AND MUSEUMS

In 2000, Utah had 13 public library systems with 5,942,200 volumes, and a circulation of 22,314,000. The Salt Lake County library system had 1,765,295 volumes (not including Salt Lake City, whose system has 704,123 volumes); the Weber County system (including Ogden) has 382,024. The leading academic libraries are the University of Utah (Salt Lake City), 2,350,297; and Brigham Young University (Provo), 2,500,849. Other collections are the Latter-Day Saints' Library-Archives and the Utah State Historical Society Library, both in Salt Lake City. During 2000, Utah had at least 60 museums, notably the Utah Museum of Natural History and Utah Museum of Fine Arts, Salt Lake City; Hill Aerospace Museum near Ogden; College of Eastern Utah Prehistoric Museum, Price; and Museum of Peoples and Cultures, Provo. Some are maintained as museums, including Beehive House and Wheeler Historic Farm, Salt Lake City, and Brigham Young's Winter Home, St. George. Total public library income for 2000 was $54,114,000; including $324,684 in federal funds, and $919,938 in state funds.

44 COMMUNICATIONS

In 2001, 96.5% of Utah's occupied houses had telephones. A total of 45 major radio stations broadcast in Utah in 2003; 14 were AM stations, 31 FM. There were 8 major television stations in 2003. The Salt Lake City area had 720,860 television households, 53% ordering cable. In the year 2000, Utah had registered 64,217 Internet domain names.

45 PRESS

In 2002, Utah had six daily newspapers and six Sunday papers. The following table shows leading daily newspapers as of 2002:

AREA	NAME	DAILY	SUNDAY
Ogden	Standard-Examiner (m,S)	61,324	65,585
Provo	Daily Herald (m,S)	30,547	31,270
Salt Lake City	Deseret News *(e,S)	66,804	69,831
	Tribune *(m,S)	134,712	160,124

*operated by Newspaper Agency Corp.

46ORGANIZATIONS

In 2003, there were about 913 regional, national, and international organizations within the state. Salt Lake City is the world headquarters of the Church of Jesus Christ of Latter-Day Saints (Mormon). The city is also home to the Mental Retardation Association of America, the National Energy Foundation, and Executive Women International.

The Utah Arts Council and the Utah State Historical Society are primary organizations for promoting arts and culture in the state.

47TOURISM, TRAVEL, AND RECREATION

In 2002, the state hosted about 17.5 million visitors spending a total of around $4.15 billion dollars. About 83% of all trips were made by residents within the state and by those traveling from California, Idaho, Nevada, Colorado, Texas, Wyoming, and Washington. International visitors account for about 3.1% of all travel to the state. The top international markets are Canada, Germany, the United Kingdom, and France. Also in 2002, nearly 5.8 million visitors came to state parks and 5.2 million came to national parks. Skier visits totaled 3 million. The industry supports over 130,000 jobs.

The top five tourist attractions in 2002 (by attendance) were Temple Square (5–7 million), Zion National Park (2.6 million), Glen Canyon National Recreation Center (2.1 million), Wasatch Mountain State Park (1.2 million), and Lagoon Amusement Park (1.1 million). Pioneer Trail State Park and Hogle Zoological Gardens are leading attractions of Salt Lake City, about 11 mi (18 km) east of the Great Salt Lake. At the Bonneville Salt Flats, experimental automobiles have set world land-speed records.

Utah has 41 state parks, 5 national parks, and 8 national monuments. Mountain and rock climbing, skiing, fishing, and hunting are major forms of recreation.

48SPORTS

Utah has one major league professional sports team, located in Salt Lake City: the Utah Jazz of the National Basketball Association, which moved from New Orleans at the close of the 1979 season. The Jazz, led by future hall of famers John Stockton and Karl Malone, advanced to the NBA Finals for the first time in 1997, but lost to the Chicago Bulls. The Jazz again advanced to the Finals in 1998, but were again defeated by the Chicago Bulls in Michael Jordan's last game. Utah did host a WNBA team, the Starzz, but the team was relocated to San Antonio prior to the 2003 season. Basketball is also popular at the college level. The University of Utah's Running Utes have had great success in the recent past and won the NCAA championship back in 1944 and the National Invitation Tournament in 1947, while the Cougars of Brigham Young won NIT titles in 1951 and 1966, and were named college football's national champions in 1984. Salt Lake City is also home to minor league baseball and hockey teams.

Other annual sporting events include the Easter Jeep Sandhill Climb in Moab, the Ute Stampede (a rodeo) in Nephi in July, and various skiing events at Utah's world-class resort in Park City. Salt Lake city hosted the Winter Olympics in 2002.

49FAMOUS UTAHNS

George Sutherland (b.England, 1862–1942) capped a long career in Utah Republican politics by serving as an associate justice of the US Supreme Court (1922–38). Other important federal officeholders from Utah include George Dern (b.Nebraska, 1872–1936), President Franklin D. Roosevelt's secretary of war from 1933 to 1936; Ezra Taft Benson (Idaho, 1899–1994), a high official of the Mormon Church and President Dwight Eisenhower's secretary of agriculture; and Ivy Baker Priest (1905–75), US treasurer during 1953–61. Prominent in the US Senate for 30 years was Republican tariff expert Reed Smoot (1862–1941),

also a Mormon Church official. The most colorful politician in state history. J(oseph) Bracken Lee (1899–1996), was mayor of Price for 12 years before serving as governor during 1949–57 and mayor of Salt Lake City during 1960–72. Jacob "Jake" Garn (b.1932), first elected to the US Senate in 1974, was launched into space aboard the space shuttle in 1985.

The dominant figure in Utah history is undoubtedly Brigham Young (b.Vermont, 1801–77), the great western colonizer. As leader of the Mormons for more than 30 years, he initiated white settlement of Utah in 1847 and, until his death, exerted almost complete control over life in the territory. Other major historical figures include Eliza R. Snow (b.Massachusetts, 1804–87), Mormon women's leader; Wakara, anglicized Walker (c.1808–55), the foremost Ute leader of the early settlement period; Colonel Patrick Edward Conner (b.Ireland, 1820–91), founder of Camp Douglas and father of Utah mining; George Q. Cannon (b.England, 1827–1901), editor, businessman, political leader, and a power in the Mormon Church for more than 40 years; and Lawrence Scanlan (b.Ireland, 1843–1915), first Roman Catholic bishop of Salt Lake City, founder of schools and a hospital.

Utah's most important scientist is John A. Widtsoe (b.Norway, 1872–1952), whose pioneering research in dryland farming revolutionized agricultural practices. Noted inventors are gunsmith John M. Browning (1855–1926) and television innovator Philo T. Farnsworth (1906–71). Of note in business are mining entrepreneurs David Keith (b.Canada, 1847–1918), Samuel Newhouse (b.New York, 1853–1930), Susanna Emery-Holmes (b.Missouri, 1859–1942), Thomas Kearns (b.Canada, 1862–1918), and Daniel C. Jackling (b.Missouri, 1869–1956). Labor leaders include William Dudley "Big Bill" Haywood (1869–1928), radical Industrial Workers of the World organizer, and Frank Bonacci (b.Italy, 1884–1954), United Mine Workers of America organizer.

Utah's artists and writers include sculptors Cyrus E. Dallin (1861–1944) and Mahonri M. Young (1877–1957), painter Henry L. A. Culmer (b.England, 1854–1914), author-critic Bernard A. DeVoto (1897–1955), poet-critic Brewster Ghiselin (b.Missouri, 1903), folklorist Austin E. Fife (b.Idaho, 1909–86), and novelists Maurine Whipple (b.1904), Virginia Sorensen (1912–91), and Edward Abbey (1927–1989).

Actors from Utah are Maude Adams (1872–1953), Robert Walker (1918–1951, Loretta Young (1913–2000), Laraine Day (b.1920). Donald "Donny" Osmond (b.1957) and his sister Marie (b.1959) are Utah's best-known popular singers. Emma Lucy Gates Bowen (1880–1951), an opera singer, founded her own traveling opera company, and William F. Christensen (1902–2001) founded Ballet West. Maurice Abravanel (b.Greece, 1903–1993) conducted the Utah Symphony for many years. Other musicians of note include jazz trumpeter Ernest Loring "Red" Nichols (1905–65).

Sports figures include former world middleweight boxing champion Gene Fullmer (b.1931), former Los Angeles Rams tackle Merlin Olsen (b.1940), and NFL quarterback Steve Young (b.1961) of the San Francisco 49ers.

50BIBLIOGRAPHY

Alexander, Thomas. *Mormons and Gentiles: A History of Salt Lake City.* Boulder, Colo.: Pruett Publishing, 1984.

Alter, J. Cecil. *Utah, the Storied Domain: A Documentary History.* 3 vols. Chicago: American Historical Society, 1932.

Arrington, Leonard J., and Davis Bitton. *The Mormon Experience: A History of the Latter-day Saints.* 2nd ed. Urbana: University of Illinois Press, 1992.

Bagley, Will. *Blood of the Prophets: Brigham Young and the Massacre at Mountain Meadows.* Norman: University of Oklahoma Press, 2002.

Cuch, Forrest S., ed. *A History of Utah's American Indians.* Salt Lake City, Utah: Utah State University Press, 2000.

Smart, William B., and Donna T. Smart, eds. *Over the Rim: the Parley P. Pratt Exploring Expedition to Southern Utah, 1849–50.* Logan: Utah State University Press, 1999.

Till, Tom. *Utah, Then & Now.* Englewood, Colo.: Westcliffe, 2000.

Utah History Encyclopedia. Salt Lake City: University of Utah Press, 1994.

Verdoia, Ken. *Utah: The Struggle for Statehood.* Salt Lake City: University of Utah Press, 1996.

Watkins, Tom H. *The Redrock Chronicles: Saving Wild Utah.* Baltimore, Md.: Johns Hopkins University Press, 2000.

VERMONT

State of Vermont

ORIGIN OF STATE NAME: Derived from the French words *vert* (green) and *mont* (mountain). **NICKNAME:** The Green Mountain State. **CAPITAL:** Montpelier. **ENTERED UNION:** 4 March 1791 (14th). **SONG:** "These Green Mountains." **MOTTO:** Freedom and Unity. **COAT OF ARMS:** Rural Vermont is represented by a pine tree in the center, three sheaves of grain on the left, and a cow on the right, with a background of fields and mountains; a deer crests the shield. Below are crossed pine branches and the state name and motto. **FLAG:** The coat of arms on a field of dark blue. **OFFICIAL SEAL:** Bisecting Vermont's golden seal is a row of wooded hills above the state name; the upper half has a spearhead, pine tree, cow, and two sheaves of wheat, while two more sheaves and the state motto fill the lower half. **ANIMAL:** Morgan horse. **BIRD:** Hermit thrush. **INSECT:** Honeybee. **FISH:** Brook trout (cold water); walleye pike (warm water). **FLOWER:** Red clover. **TREE:** Sugar maple. **BEVERAGE:** Milk. **LEGAL HOLIDAYS:** New Year's Day, 1 January; Birthday of Martin Luther King, Jr., 3rd Monday in January; Lincoln's Birthday, 12 February; Washington's Birthday, 3rd Monday in February; Town Meeting Day, 1st Tuesday in March; Memorial Day, 30 May; Independence Day, 4 July; Bennington Battle Day, 16 August; Labor Day, 1st Monday in September; Columbus Day, 2nd Monday in October; Veterans Day, 11 November; Thanksgiving Day, 4th Thursday in November; Christmas Day, 25 December. **TIME:** 7 AM EST = noon GMT.

¹LOCATION, SIZE, AND EXTENT

Situated in the northeastern US, Vermont is the 2nd largest of the six New England states, and ranks 43rd in size among the 50 states.

Vermont's total area of 9,614 sq mi (24,900 sq km) consists of 9,249 sq mi (23,955 sq km) of land and 365 sq mi (945 sq km) of inland water. Vermont's maximum E-W extension is 90 mi (145 km); its maximum N-S extension is 158 mi (254 km). The state resembles a wedge, wide and flat at the top and narrower at the bottom.

Vermont is bordered on the N by the Canadian province of Quebec; on the E by New Hampshire (separated by the Connecticut River); on the S by Massachusetts; and on the W by New York (with part of the line passing through Lake Champlain and the Poultney River).

The state's territory includes several islands and the lower part of a peninsula jutting south into Lake Champlain from the Canadian border, collectively called Grand Isle County. Vermont's total boundary length is 561 mi (903 km). Its geographic center is in Washington County, 3 mi (5 km) E of Roxbury.

²TOPOGRAPHY

The Green Mountains are the most prominent topographic region in Vermont. Extending north–south from the Canadian border to the Massachusetts state line, the Green Mountains contain the state's highest peaks, including Mansfield, 4,393 ft (1,340 m), the highest point in Vermont; Killington, 4,235 ft (1,293 m); and Elbow Mountain (Warren), 4,135 ft (1,260 m). A much lower range, the Taconic Mountains, straddles the New York-Vermont border for about 80 mi (129 km). To their north is the narrow Valley of Vermont; farther north is the Champlain Valley, a lowland about 20 mi (32 km) wide between Lake Champlain—site of the state's lowest point, 95 ft (29 m) above sea level—and the Green Mountains. The Vermont piedmont is a narrow corridor of hills and valleys stretching about 100 mi (161

km) to the east of the Green Mountains. The Northeast Highlands consist of an isolated series of peaks near the New Hampshire border.

Vermont's major inland rivers are the Missisquoi, Lamoille, and Winooski. The state includes about 66% of Lake Champlain on its western border and about 25% of Lake Memphremagog on the northern border.

³CLIMATE

Burlington's normal daily mean temperature is 45°F (7°C), ranging from 16°F (–9°C) in January to 71°F (22°C) in July. Winters are generally colder and summer nights cooler in the higher elevations of the Green Mountains. The record high temperature for the state is 105°F (41°C), registered at Vernon on 4 July 1911; the record low, –50°F (–46°C), at Bloomfield, 30 December 1933. Burlington's average annual precipitation (1971–2000) of 36 in (91 cm) was less than the statewide average of 40 in (102 cm). Annual snowfall in Burlington is 79 in (200 cm); elsewhere in the state snowfall ranges from 55 to 65 in (140–165 cm) in the lower regions, and from 100 to 125 in (254–318 cm) in the mountain areas.

⁴FLORA AND FAUNA

Common trees of Vermont are the commercially important sugar maple (the state tree), the butternut, white pine, and yellow birch. Other recognized flora include 15 types of conifer, 130 grasses, and 192 sedges. Two plant species, Jesup's milk-vetch and Northeastern bulrush, were endangered in 2003.

Native mammalian species include white-tailed deer, coyote, red fox, and snowshoe hare. Several species of trout are prolific. Characteristic birds include the raven (Corvus corax), gray or Canada jay, and saw-whet owl. In 2003, six animal species were listed as threatened or endangered in Vermont, including the Indiana bat, dwarf wedgemussel, and bald eagle.

5 ENVIRONMENTAL PROTECTION

All natural resource regulation, planning, and operation are coordinated by the Department of Environmental Conservation. The state is divided into 14 soil and water conservation districts operated by local landowners with the assistance of the state Natural Resources Conservation Council. Several dams on the Winooski and Connecticut rivers' drainage basins help control flooding. Legislation enacted in 1972 bans the use of throwaway beverage containers in Vermont, in an effort to reduce roadside litter. Billboards were banned in 1968. In the 1980s and early 1990s, the effects of acid rain became a source of concern in Vermont, as in the rest of the Northeast. In 2003, Vermont had 56 hazardous waste sites listed in the Environmental Protection Agency's database, nine of which were on the National Priorities List. By some estimates as much as 35% of Vermont's wetlands have been lost since colonization. As of 2002, about 4% of the state was designated as wetlands, and the government has established the Vermont Wetlands Conservation Strategy. In 2001, Vermont received $24,854,000 in federal grants from the Environmental Protection Agency; EPA expenditures for procurement contracts in Vermont that year amounted to $87,000.

6 POPULATION

Vermont ranked 49th in population in the US with an estimated total of 616,592 in 2002, an increase of 1.3% since 2000. Between 1990 and 2000, Vermont's population grew from 562,758 to 608,827, an increase of 8.2%. The population is projected to reach 638,000 by 2005 and 678,000 by 2025. The population density in 2000 was 65.8 persons per sq mi.

In 2000, the median age for Vermont residents was 37.7. In the same year, 24.2% of the populace were under age 18 while 12.7% were age 65 or older. The rural population increased 12% between 1970 and 1980; in the 1990s, Vermont had the highest percentage of rural dwellers in all states.

Vermont cities with the largest populations, all under 100,000, include Burlington, Rutland, and Montpelier.

7 ETHNIC GROUPS

There were 53,835 residents reporting French Canadian ancestry in 2000. These Vermonters are congregated chiefly in the northern counties and in such urban centers as Burlington, St. Albans, and Montpelier. Italians make up 6.4% of the population reporting at least one specific ancestry group. The foreign born numbered 23,245—3.8% of the population—in 2000. In 2000, Hispanics and Latinos numbered 5,504, just under 1% of the total.

The 1990 census counted few non-Caucasians. There were 5,217 Asians, 3,063 blacks, and 2,420 American Indians.

8 LANGUAGES

A few place-names and very few Indian-language speakers remain as evidence of the early Vermont presence of the Algonkian Mohawk tribe and of some Iroquois in the north. Vermont English, although typical of the Northern dialect, differs from that of New Hampshire in several respects, including retention of the final /r/ and use of *eavestrough* in place of eavespout.

In 2000, 540,767 Vermonters—94.1% of the population age five and over—spoke only English at home. The percent of the population who spoke only English at home remained constant from 1990 to 2000.

The following table gives selected statistics from the 2000 census for language spoken at home by persons five years old and over. The category "Scandinavian languages" includes Danish, Norwegian, and Swedish.

LANGUAGE	NUMBER	PERCENT
Population 5 years and over	574,842	100.0
Speak only English	540,767	94.1
Speak a language other than English	34,075	5.9
Speak a language other than English	34,075	5.9
French (incl. Patois, Cajun)	14,624	2.5
Spanish or Spanish Creole	5,791	1.0
German	2,612	0.5
Serbo-Croatian	1,600	0.3
Italian	1,198	0.2
Polish	977	0.2
Vietnamese	812	0.1
Chinese	782	0.1
Russian	554	0.1
Scandinavian languages	415	0.1

9 RELIGIONS

From the early days of settlement to the present, Congregationalists (now called the United Church of Christ) have played a dominant role in the state. They were the largest Protestant denomination in the state in 2000, with 21,597 known adherents in 2000. Other major Protestant groups include the United Methodists, 19,000; Episcopalians, 9,163; and American Baptists, 8,352. The largest single religious organization in Vermont is the Roman Catholic Church, with 147,918 members in 2000. There is a small Jewish population (estimated at 5,810 in 2000), most of whom live in Burlington.

Vermont was the birthplace of both Joseph Smith and Brigham Young, founders of the Church of Jesus Christ of Latter-Day Saints. The state had 3,046 Mormons in 2000. Over 370,000 people (about 60.9% of the population) were not counted as members of any religious organization.

10 TRANSPORTATION

Vermont's first railroad, completed in 1849, served more as a link to Boston than as an intrastate line; it soon went into receivership, as did many other early state lines. From a high of nearly 1,100 mi (1,770 km) of track in 1910, trackage shrank to 669 rail mi (1,076 km) in 2000, none of it Class I line. Ten railroads were operating within the state in 2000. Glass and stone made up 55% of the rail tonnage originating within the state, and lumber and wood products accounted for 29% of the rail tonnage terminated within Vermont that year. In 1996, Amtrak provided passenger service to eight stations.

Of the 14,273 mi (22,970 km) of public streets, roads, and highways in 2000, 12,894 mi (20,750 km) were rural and only 1,379 mi (2,219 km) urban. A total of 514,883 motor vehicles were registered in 2000, when there were 506,085 licensed drivers.

In 2002, Vermont had 12 public use airports. Burlington International Airport is the state's major air terminal.

11 HISTORY

Vermont has been inhabited continuously since about 10,000 BC. Archaeological finds suggest the presence of a pre-Algonkian group along the Otter River. Algonkian-speaking Abnaki settled along Lake Champlain and in the Connecticut Valley, and Mahican settled in the southern counties between AD 1200 and 1790. In 1609, Samuel de Champlain crossed the lake that now bears his name, becoming the first European explorer of Vermont. From the 1650s to the 1760s, French, Iroquois Indians from New York, Dutch, and English passed through the state over trails connecting Montreal with Massachusetts and New York. However, few settled there. In 1666 the French built and briefly occupied Ft. Ste. Anne on Isle La Motte, and in 1690 there was a short-lived settlement at Chimney Point. Ft. Dummer, built in 1724 near present-day Brattleboro, was the first permanent settlement.

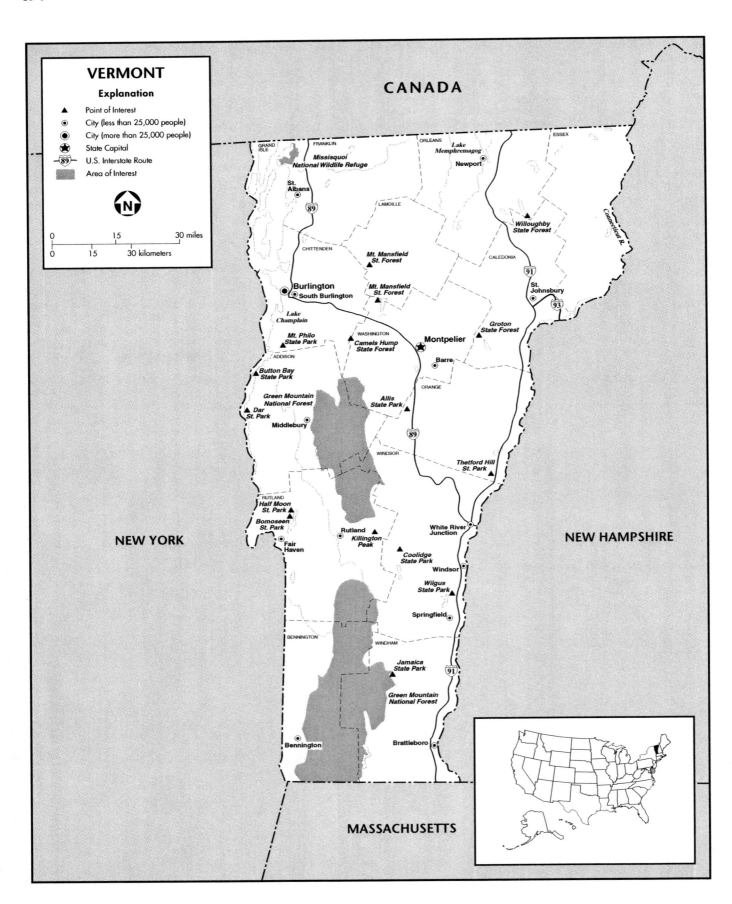

VERMONT

Explanation

▲ Point of Interest
⊙ City (less than 25,000 people)
◉ City (more than 25,000 people)
★ State Capital
—89— U.S. Interstate Route
▨ Area of Interest

N

0   15   30 miles
0   15   30 kilometers

CANADA

GRAND ISLE

FRANKLIN

ORLEANS

Lake Memphremagog

Newport

ESSEX

Missisquoi National Wildlife Refuge

St. Albans

LAMOILLE

Willoughby State Forest

Mt. Mansfield St. Forest

CHITTENDEN

CALEDONIA

91

Burlington
South Burlington

Mt. Mansfield St. Forest

St. Johnsbury

93

Lake Champlain

WASHINGTON

Groton State Forest

Mt. Philo State Park

Camels Hump State Forest

Montpelier

ADDISON

Barre

Button Bay State Park

Allis State Park

ORANGE

Green Mountain National Forest

Dar St. Park

Middlebury

89

WINDSOR

Thetford Hill St. Park

RUTLAND

Half Moon St. Park

Bomoseen St. Park

Rutland

White River Junction

NEW YORK

Fair Haven

Killington Peak

Coolidge State Park

NEW HAMPSHIRE

Windsor

Wilgus State Park

Springfield

BENNINGTON

WINDHAM

Jamaica State Park

91

Green Mountain National Forest

Bennington

Brattleboro

Connecticut R.

MASSACHUSETTS

Governor Benning Wentworth of New Hampshire, claiming that his colony extended as far west as did Massachusetts and Connecticut, had granted 131 town charters in the territory by 1764. In that year, the crown declared that New York's northeastern boundary was the Connecticut River. Owners of New Hampshire titles, fearful of losing their land, prevented New York from enforcing its jurisdiction. The Green Mountain Boys, organized by Ethan Allen in 1770–71, scared off the defenseless settlers under New York title and flouted New York courts.

Shortly after the outbreak of the Revolutionary War, Ethan Allen's men helped capture Ft. Ticonderoga, and for two years frontiersmen fought in the northern theater. On 16 August 1777, after a skirmish at Hubbardton, a Vermont contingent routed German detachments sent by British General Burgoyne toward Bennington—a battle that contributed to the general's surrender at Saratoga, New York. There were several British raids on Vermont towns during the war.

Vermont declared itself an independent republic with the name "New Connecticut" in 1777, promulgated a constitution abolishing slavery and providing universal manhood suffrage, adopted the laws of Connecticut, and confiscated Tory lands. Most Vermonters preferred to join the US, but the dominant Allen faction, with large holdings in the northwest, needed free trade with Canada, even at the price of returning to the British Empire. Political defeat of the Allen faction in 1789 led to negotiations that settled New York's claims and secured Vermont's admission to the Union on 4 March 1791.

With 30,000 people in 1781 and nearly 220,000 in 1810, Vermont was a state of newcomers spread evenly over the hills in self-sufficient homesteads. Second-generation Vermonters developed towns and villages with water-powered mills, charcoal-fired furnaces, general stores, newspapers, craft shops, churches, and schools. Those who ran these local institutions tended to be Congregationalist in religion and successively Federalist, Whig, and Republican in party politics. Dissidents in the early 1800s included minority Protestants suffering legal and social discrimination, hardscrabble farmers, and Jacksonian Democrats.

Northwestern Vermonters smuggled to avoid the US foreign trade embargo of 1808, and widespread trade continued with Canada during the War of 1812. In September 1814, however, Vermont soldiers fought in the Battle of Plattsburgh, New York, won by Thomas Macdonough's fleet built at Vergennes the previous winter. The Mexican War (1846–48) was unpopular in the state, but Vermont, which had strongly opposed slavery, was an enthusiastic supporter of the Union during the Civil War.

The opening of the Champlain-Hudson Canal in 1823, and the building of the early railroad lines in 1846–53, made Vermont more vulnerable to western competition, caused the demise of many small farms and businesses, and stimulated emigration. The remaining farmers' purchasing power steadily increased as they held temporary advantages in wool, then in butter and cheesemaking, and finally in milk production. The immigration of the Irish and French Canadians stabilized the population, and the expansion of light industry bolstered the economy.

During the 20th century, and especially after World War II, autos, buses, trucks, and planes took over most passengers and much freight from the railroads. Manufacturing, especially light industry, prospered in valley villages. Vermont's picturesque landscape began to attract city buyers of second homes. Still rural in population distribution, Vermont became increasingly suburban in outlook, as new highways made the cities and hills mutually accessible, and the state absorbed an influx of young professionals from New York and Massachusetts. Tourism thrived, especially in the Green Mountains and other ski resort areas. Longtime Vermonters, accustomed to their state's pristine beauty, were confronted in the 1980s with the question of how much development was necessary for the state's economic health.

The newcomers changed the political landscape as well. Whereas Vermont had long been dominated by the Republican Party, by the mid-1980s fully a third of the electorate voted Democratic. The Democratic presidential candidate carried Vermont in the 1988, 1992, 1996, and 2000 elections. In 1990, Vermont elected as its sole congressional representative a democratic socialist, Bernie Sanders, who called for reduced limits on campaign spending, a sharply progressive income tax, national health care, and 50% cuts in military spending over five years. Sanders's victory reflected, in part, voters' frustration with a downturn in the New England economy in the late 1980s. He was reelected in 2002.

In the early 1990s Vermont had the nation's highest percentage of women in its state legislature. With two-thirds of its population living in towns of 2,500 or fewer, it was the nation's most rural state. In 1993 Vermont passed legislation barring smoking in all public buildings, including most restaurants and hotels.

In 2003, Governor James H. Douglas, a Republican elected in 2002, pledged to create jobs and provide economic security to the state. He also emphasized higher education, and transportation spending. Douglas announced a substance abuse and interdiction program for Vermont's correctional facilities that would include random drug testing, including for those inmates out on furlough.

12 STATE GOVERNMENT

A constitution establishing Vermont as an independent republic was adopted in 1777. The constitution that governs the state today became effective on 9 July 1793. By January 2003, that document had been amended 53 times.

The general assembly consists of a 150-member house of representatives and a 30-member senate. All legislators are elected to two-year terms. Regular sessions are held in odd-numbered years, with the provision that the legislature may (and in practice, does) divide to meet in even-numbered years. Sessions begin in January and are not formally limited in length. Legislators must be at least 18 years old and residents of the state for at least two years and of their districts for at least one year. In 2003 the legislative salary was $536 per week, unchanged from 1999.

State elected officials are the governor and lieutenant governor (elected separately), treasurer, secretary of state, auditor of accounts, and attorney general, all of whom serve two-year terms. A governor must have been a state resident for at least four years prior to election; no minimum age is specified for the office. In 2002 the governor's salary was $88,026, unchanged from 1999.

All bills require a majority vote in each house for passage. Bills can be vetoed by the governor, and vetoes can be overridden by a two-thirds vote of those present in each legislative house. If the governor neither vetoes nor signs a bill within five days of receiving it, it becomes law. If the legislature has adjourned, an unsigned bill dies after three days. A constitutional amendment must first be passed by a two-thirds vote in the senate, followed by a majority in the house during the same legislative session. It must then receive majority votes in both houses before it can be submitted to the voters for approval. Amendments may only be submitted every four years.

Voters must be US citizens, at least 18 years old, and state residents.

13 POLITICAL PARTIES

The Republican Party, which originally drew strength from powerful abolitionist sentiment, gained control of Vermont state offices in 1856 and for more than 100 years dominated state politics. No Democrat was elected governor from 1853 until 1962.

In 1984, Democrat Madeleine M. Kunin was elected as Vermont's first woman governor and only the third Democratic governor in the state's history. Kunin served as governor for three terms, followed in 1990 by Republican Richard Snelling. When Snelling died in office in August 1991, Lieutenant Governor Howard Dean, a Democrat, became governor. Dean was elected to full two-year terms in November 1992, 1994, 1996, 1998, and 2000. (The state has no term limit for the office of governor.) Dean announced in 2001 that he would not seek reelection in 2002, and in May 2002, became the first candidate to enter the race for the Democratic nomination for president in 2004. Republican James Douglas was elected governor of Vermont in 2002.

Vermont's delegation to the US House of Representatives consists of one Independent. In mid-2003, Democrats controlled the state senate, with 19 seats out of 30. In the state house of representatives, the Democrats held 69 seats; the Republicans had 74; and Independents had 7. Following the 2002 election, Vermont had one Independent US senator, James Jeffords, elected in 1988 as a Republican and reelected in 2000 (he switched party affiliation from the Republican Party to independent status in 2001), and one Democratic senator, Patrick Leahy, who was elected to his fifth term in 1998. The state's sole representative in the US House, Bernard Sanders, is an Independent (elected 2002).

Vermont has often shown its independence in national political elections. In 1832, it was the only state to cast a plurality vote for the Anti-Masonic presidential candidate, William Wirt; in 1912, the only state besides Utah to vote for William Howard Taft; and in 1936, the only state besides Maine to prefer Alf Landon to Franklin D. Roosevelt. In 2000, Vermonters gave 51% of their presidential vote to Democratic candidate Al Gore; 41% to Republican George W. Bush; and 7% to Green Party candidate Ralph Nader. In 2002 there were 418,718 registered voters; there is no party registration in the state. The state had three electoral votes in the 2000 presidential election.

Vermont Presidential Vote by Major Political Parties, 1948–2000

YEAR	ELECTORAL VOTE	VERMONT WINNER	DEMOCRAT	REPUBLICAN
1948	3	Dewey (R)	45,557	75,926
1952	3	*Eisenhower (R)	43,355	109,717
1956	3	*Eisenhower (R)	42,549	110,390
1960	3	Nixon (R)	69,186	98,131
1964	3	*Johnson (D)	108,127	54,942
1968	3	*Nixon (R)	70,255	85,142
1972	3	*Nixon (R)	68,174	117,149
1976	3	Ford (R)	77,798	100,387
1980	3	*Reagan (R)	81,891	94,598
1984	3	*Reagan (R)	95,730	135,865
1988	3	*Bush (R)	115,775	124,331
1992**	3	*Clinton (D)	133,592	88,122
1996**	3	*Clinton (D)	137,894	80,352
2000	3	Gore (D)	149,022	119,775

* Won US presidential election.
** Independent candidate Ross Perot received 65,991 votes in 1992 and 31,024 votes in 1996.

¹⁴LOCAL GOVERNMENT

As of 2002, there were 14 counties, 47 municipal governments, and 237 townships in Vermont, as well as 283 public school districts and 152 special districts. County officers, operating out of shire towns (county seats), include the probate courts judge, assistant judges of the county court, county clerk, state's attorney, high bailiff, treasurer, and sheriff. All cities have mayor-council systems. Towns are governed by selectmen, who serve staggered terms. Larger towns also have town managers. The town meeting remains an important part of government in the state: citizens gather on the first Tuesday in March each year to discuss municipal issues and elect local officials.

¹⁵STATE SERVICES

To address the continuing threat of terrorism and to work with the federal Department of Homeland Security (created in 2002 following the terrorist attacks of 11 September 2001), homeland security in Vermont in 2003 operated under executive order; the civil/military affairs secretary was designated as the state homeland security advisor.

Vermont's Department of Education oversees public elementary, secondary, higher education, and adult education programs. The Agency of Transportation includes the Department of Motor Vehicles, Transportation Board, and Hazardous Materials Committee. The Agency of Human Services coordinates programs for nursing homes, veterans' affairs, social welfare, employment and training, health, corrections, and parole. The Agency of Housing and Community Affairs and the Agency of Commerce and Community Development administer federal housing programs and offers aid to localities. Other departments specialize in the areas of: personnel, natural resources, aging, agriculture, labor and industry, libraries, and liquor control.

¹⁶JUDICIAL SYSTEM

Vermont's highest court is the supreme court, which consists of a chief justice and four associate justices. Other courts include the superior, district, family, and environmental courts, with a total of 497 judges. All judges are appointed by the governor to six-year terms, subject to senate confirmation, from a list of qualified candidates prepared by the Judicial Nominating Board, which includes representatives of the governor, the legislature, and the Vermont bar. There are also 318 associate judges and 50 permissive associate judges.

In June 2001 there were 1,782 inmates in stage and federal correctional facilities, an increase of 7.7% over the previous year. The state's incarceration rate stood at 221 per 100,000 inhabitants.

According to the FBI Crime Index, Vermont had a 2001 total crime rate of 2,769.3 per 100,000 population, including a total of 644 violent crimes and 16,334 crimes against property in that year. There is no death penalty; the last execution in Vermont took place in 1954.

¹⁷ARMED FORCES

In 2002, there were 61 active-duty military personnel and 567 civilian personnel stationed in Vermont. Also in 2002, the government awarded almost $308 million in defense contracts to Vermont firms.

According to the 2000 Census, there were 62,809 veterans living in Vermont, of which 11,640 served in World War II; 8,090 in the Korean conflict; 19,060 during the Vietnam era; and 5,146 during 1990–2000 (including the Persian Gulf War). Veterans' benefits in 2002 totaled more than $166 million.

In 2000, the Vermont State Police employed 304 full-time sworn officers.

¹⁸MIGRATION

The earliest Vermont settlers were farmers from southern New England and New York; most were of English descent although some Dutch settlers moved to Vermont from New York. French Canadians came beginning in the 1830s; by 1850, several thousand had moved into Vermont. As milling, quarrying, and mining grew during the 19th century, other Europeans arrived—small groups of Italians and Scots in Barre, and Poles, Swedes, Czechs, Russians, and Austrians in the Rutland quarry areas. Irish immigrants built the railroads in the mid-19th century.

Steady out-migrations during the 19th and early 20th centuries kept population increases down, and in the decades 1910–20 and 1930–40, the population dropped. During the 1960s, the population of blacks more than doubled, though they still accounted for only 0.34% of the population in 1990. Between 1970 and 1983, 45,000 migrants settled in Vermont. From 1985 to 1990, Vermont had a net gain from migration of nearly 21,400. Falling from 33.8% in 1980, Vermont's urban population in 1990 was the lowest among the states at 32.2% and fell further to 27.7% in 1996. Between 1990 and 1998, the state had net gains of 5,000 in domestic migration and 4,000 in international migration. In 1998, Vermont admitted 513 foreign immigrants. Between 1990 and 1998, Vermont's overall population increased 5%. In the period 1995–2000, 69,748 people moved into the state and 67,494 moved out, for a net gain of 2,254. Most new residents were from New York.

[19] INTERGOVERNMENTAL COOPERATION

Vermont participates in New England compacts on corrections, higher education, water pollution control, police, and radiological health protection. The state also takes part in the Connecticut River Valley Flood Control Compact, Connecticut River Atlantic Salmon Compact, Interstatee Pest Control Compact, and Northeastern Forest Fire Protection Compact. The state has several agreements with New Hampshire regarding schools, and sewage and waste disposal.

Federal grants to Vermont amounted to just over one billion in 2001, 2nd lowest of all states (Delaware receives the fewest).

[20] ECONOMY

During its early years of statehood, Vermont was overwhelmingly agricultural, with beef cattle, sheep, and dairying contributing greatly to the state's income. After World War II, agriculture was replaced by manufacturing and tourism as the backbone of the economy. Durable goods manufacturing (primarily electronics and machine parts), construction, wholesale and retail trade, and other service industries have shown the largest growth in employment during the 1990s. Vermont's economy was little impacted by the national recession in 2001, as the growth rate of its gross state product, which had accelerated from 5.1% in 1998 to 5.3% in 1999, to 5.6% in 2000, actually improved to 5.7% in 2001. The main negative effect was an unexpected shortfall in tax revenues that followed the abrupt collapse in capital gains income, presenting Vermont, as with most states, with a state budget crisis. Payroll employment did decline, but the trough was reached by April 2002, and despite layoffs by IBM in late 2002, the state economy registered net job gains in fall 2002. Per capita income grew in the first half of 2002, and Vermont's bankruptcy rate was the lowest in New England.

In 2001, Vermont's gross state product gross state product was $19.1 billion, the 2nd smallest (after North Dakota) among the states, to which general services contributed $4.4 billion; financial services, $3.5 billion; trade, $3.02 billion; manufacturing, $2.99 billion; government, $2.5 billion; transportation and public utilities, $1.4 billion, and construction, $868 million. The public sector in 2001 constituted 13.3% of gross state product, compared to the 12% average for the states.

[21] INCOME

According to the Bureau of Economic Analysis, in 2001, Vermont had a per capita personal income (PCPI) of $28,756 which ranked 25th in the United States (including the District of Columbia) and was 95% of the national average, $30,413. The 2001 PCPI reflected an increase of 4.7% from 2000 compared to the national change of 2.2%. In 2001, Vermont had a total personal income (TPI) of $17,626,599,000 which ranked 49th in the United States and accounted for 0.2% of the national total.

The 2001 TPI reflected an increase of 5.2% from 2000 compared to the national change of 3.3%.

Earnings of persons employed in Vermont increased from $11,467,531,000 in 2000 to $12,018,771,000 in 2001, an increase of 4.8%. The largest industries in 2001 were services, 29.7% of earnings; durable goods manufacturing, 14.4%; and state and local government, 12.6%. Of the industries that accounted for at least 5% of earnings in 2001, the slowest growing from 2000 to 2001 was durable goods manufacturing, which increased 3.5%; the fastest was state and local government, which increased 8.6%.

According to data released by the US Census Bureau, in 2000, the median household income was $38,150 compared to the national average of $42,148. In 2001, the median income for a family of four was $62,938 compared to the national average of $63,278. For the period 1999 to 2001, the average poverty rate was 9.8% which placed it 19th among the 50 states and the District of Columbia ranked lowest to highest.

[22] LABOR

According to Bureau of Labor Statistics (BLS) provisional estimates, in July 2003 the seasonally adjusted civilian labor force in Vermont numbered 354,600, with approximately 14,600 workers unemployed, yielding an unemployment rate of 4.1%, compared to the national average of 6.2% for the same period. Since the beginning of the BLS data series in 1978, the highest unemployment rate recorded was 7.5% in May 1983. The historical low was 2.4% in July 1988. In 2001, 5.1% of the labor force was employed in construction; 15.6% in manufacturing; 4.0% in transportation, communications, and public utilities; 18.0% in trade; 4.1% in finance, insurance, and real estate; 27.0% in services; 12.8% in government; and 3.3% in agriculture.

The US Department of Labor reported that in 2002, 27,000 of Vermont's 289,000 employed wage and salary workers were members of unions. This represented 9.5% of those so employed, down from 10.8% in 2001. The national average is 13.2%. In all, 32,000 workers (11.0%) were represented by unions. In addition to union members, this category includes workers who report no union affiliation but whose jobs are covered by a union contract.

[23] AGRICULTURE

Although Vermont is one of the nation's most rural states, its agricultural income was only $557 million in 2001, 41st among the 50 states. More than 88% of that came from livestock and livestock products, especially dairy products. The leading crops in 2002 were corn for silage, 2,030,000 tons; hay, 2,286,000 tons; and apples, 8 million lb.

[24] ANIMAL HUSBANDRY

The merino sheep and the Morgan horse (a breed developed in Vermont) were common sights on pastures more than a century ago, but today they have been for the most part replaced by dairy cattle. In 2001, Vermont dairy farms had around 153,000 milk cows that produced 2.67 billion lb (1.2 billion kg) of milk. In 2003, the state had an estimated 280,000 cattle and calves, valued at $299.6 million.

[25] FISHING

Sport fishermen can find ample species of trout, perch, walleye pike, bass, and pickerel in Vermont's waters, many of which are stocked by the Department of Fish and Game. Fish farms distributed 1,046,000 trout for restoration in 1998. That year, the state issued 96,260 sport fishing licenses. There is little commercial fishing.

[26] FORESTRY

The Green Mountain State is covered by 4,618,000 acres (1,869,000 hectares) of forestland—77% of the state's total land area—much of it owned or leased by lumber companies. In 2002, lumber production totaled 206 million board feet.

The largest forest reserve in Vermont is the Green Mountain National Forest, with 374,092 acres (151,395 hectares) in 1999, managed by the US Forest Service.

[27] MINING

The value of nonfuel mineral production in Vermont in 2001 was estimated to be $68.9 million, a 3% increase over that of 2000. According to preliminary figures, the leading mineral commodity, in terms of value, was dimension stone ($26 million for 103,000 metric tons), which accounted for nearly 38% of the state's total nonfuel mineral value. However, construction sand and gravel ($21.3 million for 4.6 metric tons) accounted for the greatest part of the state's increase in nonfuel mineral value since 2000. Crushed stone ($21.6 million for 5.1 million metric tons) was the other leading commodity produced. Nationally, the state ranked 2nd in dimension stone and 3rd in talc. Granite is quarried near Barre, and slate is found in the Southwest. The West Rutland-Proctor area has the world's largest marble reserve, the Danby quarry.

[28] ENERGY AND POWER

Because of the state's lack of fossil fuel resources, utility bills are higher in Vermont than in most states. During 1999, 59 plants (utility and nonutility) with a capacity of 992,000 kW generated 5.7 billion kWh of power, more than 71% of which was produced by the state's single-unit nuclear plant at Vernon, operated by Vermont Yankee Nuclear Power Corp. In 2000 Vermont's total per capita energy consumption was 270 million Btu (68 million kcal), ranking it 43rd among the 50 states.

[29] INDUSTRY

The estimated value of shipments of manufactured goods was $8 billion in 1997. Scales, machine tools, and electronic components are important manufactured items.

Earnings of persons employed in Vermont increased from $9.4 billion in 1997 to $9.99 billion in 1998, an increase of 6.4%. The largest industries in 1998 were services, 28.3% of earnings; durable goods manufacturing, 14.9%; and state and local government, 12.2%. Of the industries that accounted for at least 5% of earnings in 1998, the slowest growing from 1997 to 1998 was nondurable goods manufacturing (5.6% of earnings in 1998), which increased 3.1%; the fastest was services, which increased 5.6%.

[30] COMMERCE

Wholesale trade in 1997 was over $4.5 billion. Retail trade totaled $6 billion (48th in the nation), of which the leading sectors in terms of number of establishments were food stores, 15%; automotive dealers, 13%; and eating and drinking places, 25%. Foreign exports of Vermont manufacturers were estimated at $3.7 billion for 1998.

[31] CONSUMER PROTECTION

The Consumer Protection Division of the Attorney General's Office handles most consumer complaints. The Vermont Public Service Department's Consumer Affairs Division monitors utility rates, and the Agency of Human Services' Department of Aging and Disabilities protects the rights of the state's senior citizens and adults with physical disabilities.

[32] BANKING

In 2002, there were 20 insured banks in Vermont, seven of them state-chartered. As of September 2002, Vermont's insured banks had assets of $7.2 billion. There was one savings institution at the end of 2002, and one savings and loan bank.

Due to the fact that 30-year mortgage rates were below 7% during 2001/02, refinancing activity was strong during that period, and consumers were able to secure long-term, fixed-rate loans at low rates. Close to one-fifth of Vermont's banks had high concentrations of long-term assets.

At the end of 2002, residential, consumer, and commercial delinquencies increased at many Vermont banks, and the median past-due ratio remained the highest among the New England states. Vermont during 2002 also had high concentrations of residential real estate.

[33] INSURANCE

Two life insurance and 377 property and casualty insurance companies have their home offices in Vermont. Vermont ranks first among the states in number of property and casualty insurance companies. In 2001, there were 324,000 ordinary life insurance policies in force in Vermont with a total value of $21.2 billion; total value for all categories of life insurance (ordinary, group, industrial, and credit) was $31.9 billion. Death benefits paid that year totaled $74.7 million. In 2001, property and casualty insurers wrote over $786.7 million in premiums. That year, there were 2,937 flood insurance policies in force in the state, with a total value of $311,448.

[34] SECURITIES

There are no stock or commodity exchanges in Vermont. Securities are sold by 103 brokers and dealers firms with over 500 employees; investment advisory organizations number 44. The state is home to 14 NASDAQ companies, and has incorporated four NYSE-listed companies: Bluegreen Corp., Central Vermont Public Services Corp., Chittenden Corp., and Green Mountain Power Company.

[35] PUBLIC FINANCE

The budgets for two fiscal years are submitted by the governor to the general assembly for approval during its biennial session. The fiscal year runs from 1 July to 30 June.

In 2002/03 Vermont began experiencing revenue shortfalls. $26.7 million in cuts were made in the budget after enacted in across-the-board cuts, and drawings were made on the state's rainy day fund. In 2002/03 more cuts were made on the enacted budget, totaling $13.1 million, in across-the-board cuts. In 2000/01, the state had a beginning balance that equaled 5.1% of expenditures. General fund revenues, at $896 million in 2000/01, fell to $835 million in 2002 and to $854 million in 2002/03. They are projected below the 2000/01 level for 2003/04, at $882 million. In 2001/02, the beginning balance was only 1.5% of expenditures; in 2002/03, 1.7% and in 2003/04, 1.8% of projected expenditures. Fiscal year 2003 base appropriations, combining funds from the general fund, the transportation fund, the education fund and special state funds including the tobacco settlement fund, were for K-12 education (49%), higher education (3%), human services (18%), corrections (4%), protection (6%), general government (7%), transportation (7%), debt service (3%), commerce (1%), and natural resources (2%).

The following table from the US Census Bureau contains information on revenues, expenditures, indebtedness, and cash/securities for 2001.

	($000)	PERCENT	PER CAPITA
Population (thousands, 2001)	613	(X)	(X)
Total Revenue	3,143,100	100.00	5,127.41
General revenue	3,106,668	98.84	5,067.97
Utility revenue	–	–	–
Liquor store revenue	32,864	1.05	53.61
Insurance trust revenue	3,568	0.11	5.82
Exhibit: Salaries and wages	535,854	15.90	874.15
Total expenditure	3,370,929	100.00	5,499.07
General expenditure	3,200,408	94.94	5,220.89
Education	1,315,939	39.04	2,146.72
Public welfare	763,765	22.66	1,245.95
Hospitals	9,205	0.27	15.02
Health	77,440	2.30	126.33
Highways	256,299	7.60	418.11
Police protection	43,112	1.28	70.33
Correction	71,988	2.14	117.44
Natural resources	82,291	2.44	134.24
Parks and recreation	13,572	0.40	22.14
Government administration	203,496	6.04	331.97
Interest on general debt	124,945	3.71	203.83
Other and unallocable	238,356	7.07	388.84
Utility expenditure	4,384	0.13	7.15
Liquor store expenditure	31,220	0.93	50.93
Insurance trust expenditure	134,917	4.00	220.09
Debt at end of fiscal year	2,325,609	100.00	3,793.82
Cash and security holdings	4,679,114	100.00	7,633.14

36 TAXATION

State and local taxes in Vermont are not only relatively heavy (in 2003, they amounted to 10.1% of income, and Vermont was ranked 12th highest in the country), but also variable (rates have been raised and lowered eight times since 1980) and highly centralized (over 78% of total state and local revenues are collected at the state level). In 2003, the Vermont's personal income tax also had the highest thresholds in the country: the five-bracket schedule ranged from 2.3% (on taxable income up to $27,950) to 9.5% (on taxable income above $307,050). Corporate income is taxed according to a four-bracket schedule ranging from 7% (on net income up to $10,000) to 9% (above $250,000), with a minimum corporate tax of $250. The state sales and use tax rate is 5%, with basics, including food and medicines, exempted, and local sales taxes limited to 1%. The state also imposes a full array of excise taxes covering motor fuels, tobacco products, insurance premiums, public utilities, alcoholic beverages, pari-mutuels, and other selected items. State property taxes are means-tested, and there is a broad property tax rebate program. There is no inheritance tax, but the Vermont legislature has taken action to preserve the state's estate tax independent of the scheduled phase-out of the federal tax exemption for state death taxes. Death and gift taxes accounted for 0.8% of state collections in 2002. Other state taxes include various license fees and stamp taxes.

The state collected $1.533 billion in taxes in 2002, of which 31.6% came from state property taxes, 24.4% from individual income taxes, 20.5% from selective sales taxes, 14% from the general sales tax, 4.5% from state license fees, and 2.4% from corporate income taxes.

The following table from the US Census Bureau provides a summary of taxes collected by the state in 2002.

	($000)	PER CAPITA
Total Taxes	**1,533,982**	**2,487.84**
Property taxes	484,306	785.46
Sales and gross receipts	529,638	858.98
General sales and gross receipts	214,841	348.43
Selective sales taxes	314,797	510.54
Alcoholic beverage	15,578	25.26
Amusements	(X)	(X)
Insurance Premiums	36,181	58.68
Motor fuels	86,440	140.19
Pari-mutuels	(X)	(X)

	($000)	PER CAPITA
Public utilities	10,893	17.67
Tobacco products	26,599	43.14
Other selective sales	139,106	225.6
Licenses	69,300	112.39
Alcoholic beverages	436	0.71
Amusements	144	0.23
Corporation	1,680	2.72
Hunting and fishing	6,393	10.37
Motor vehicle	40,974	66.45
Motor vehicle operators	2,711	4.4
Public utility	(X)	(X)
Occupation and business, NEC	15,524	25.18
Other	1,438	2.33
Other taxes	450,738	731.01
Individual income	374,445	607.28
Corporation net income	37,306	60.5
Death and gift	13,886	22.52
Documentary and stock transfer	21,691	35.18
Severance	(X)	(X)
Other	3,410	5.53

37 ECONOMIC POLICY

Incentives for industrial expansion include state and municipally financed industrial sites; state employment development and training funds; revenue bond financing; tax credits for investment in research and development and in capital equipment; loans and loan guarantees for construction and equipment; and financial incentives for locating plants in areas of high unemployment. There are also exemptions from inventory taxes and sales tax on new equipment and raw materials. Major economic development initiatives by the state in 2003 included streamlining the environmental permit process, funding for workforce development, an aggressive business recruitment campaign, infrastructural improvements, increased financial incentives for business, and a phase out of the corporate income tax.

38 HEALTH

In 2000, the infant mortality rate was 6.0 per 1,000 live births. In 1999, there were 1,748 legal abortions in Vermont, or 13 per 1,000 women.

Heart disease was the leading cause of death in 2000 though the rate of 240.5 per 100,000 population was below the US average. Also in 2000, the death rate from motor vehicle accidents was 12.7 per 100,000 population. Vermont's suicide rate of 12.9 per 100,000 population exceeded the national rate of 10.7 in 2000 and was the 2nd highest among the New England states in the same year. In 2000, 21.5% of residents 18 years of age of Vermont smoked. The state's HIV-related mortality rate was one of the lowest in the country in 2000; only 428 AIDS cases had been reported in the state through 2001.

Vermont's 14 community hospitals had 54,701 admissions and 1,694 beds in 2001. There were 1,538 full-time registered nurses and 308 full-time licensed practical nurses in 2001 and 375 physicians per 100,000 population in 2000. The average expense of a community hospital for care was $1,257.90 per inpatient day in 2001.

Federal government grants to cover the Medicare and Medicaid services in 2001 totaled $413 million; 90,049 enrollees received Medicare benefits that year. Most Vermont residents have health insurance; only 9.6% were uninsured in 2002.

39 SOCIAL WELFARE

In 2001, the average weekly unemployment benefit was $226.28. Average monthly participation in the food stamp program in FY2002 comprised 39,914 persons (19,809 households). The average monthly benefit was $71.51, and the sum total of benefits paid in FY2002 was $34,252,771.

With the enactment of the Personal Responsibility and Work Opportunity Reconciliation Act of 1996, the US government has changed the form and regulations for many of its social welfare programs. Most significantly, it replaces Aid to Families with Dependent Children (AFDC), an open-ended entitlement program, with Temporary Assistance for Needy Families (TANF), a limited system of assistance funded largely through federal block grants. The reform act also impacts the food stamp program, the Supplemental Security Income program, and the child nutrition program. The law took effect on 1 July 1997 and provided $16.38 billion in block grants for fiscal years 1997–2002. The grants are to be divided among the states based on an equation involving the numbers of former AFDC recipients in each state.

Reauthorization of the 1996 social welfare legislation, scheduled for 2002, was delayed, and the original law had been extended three times as of July 2003, with the most recent extension running through September 2003. Vermont's TANF cash assistance program is called Aid to Needy Families with Children (ANFC); the work program is called Reach Up. In June 2000 the state had 15,528 welfare recipients. State expenditures on the TANF program in FY2002 totaled $25,653,406.

In December 2001, Social Security benefits were paid to 105,330 Vermont residents. This number included 66,570 retired workers, 10,200 widows and widowers, 13,400 disabled workers, 6,080 spouses, and 9,080 children. Social Security beneficiaries represented 17.2% of the total state population and 95.6% of the state's population age 65 and older. Retired workers (excluding persons with special benefits) received an average monthly payment of $862; widows and widowers, $818; disabled workers, $787; and spouses, $421. Payments for children of retired workers averaged $421 per month; children of deceased workers, $584; and children of disabled workers, $225.

Federal Supplemental Security Income payments in December 2001 went to 12,554 Vermont residents, averaging $355 a month.

40HOUSING

As rustic farmhouses gradually disappear, modern units (many of them vacation homes for Vermonters and out-of-staters) are being built to replace them. In 2002, there were an estimated 299,570 housing units in Vermont (one of the lowest housing stocks in the country), 242,201 of which were occupied; 71% were owner-occupied. About 64.4% of all units were single-family, detached homes. Nearly 31% of all housing was built in 1939 or earlier. Fuel oil was the most common energy source for heating. It was estimated that 4,709 units lacked telephone service, 1,464 lacked complete plumbing facilities, and 778 lacked complete kitchen facilities. The average household size was 2.46 people.

In 2002, 3,072 new privately owned housing units were authorized for construction. The median home value was $130,492. The median monthly cost for mortgage owners was $1,082. Renters paid a median of $601 per month. During 2002, Vermont received over $14.2 million in community planning and development aid from the US Department of Housing and Urban Development.

41EDUCATION

In 2000, 86.4% of Vermont residents age 25 and older were high school graduates; 29.4% had obtained a bachelor's degree or higher.

The total enrollment for fall 1999 in Vermont's public schools stood at 104,559. Of these, 72,276 attended schools from kindergarten through grade eight, and 32,283 attended high school. Minority students made up approximately 4% of the total enrollment in public elementary and secondary schools in 2001. Total enrollment was estimated at 104,000 in fall 2000 but was expected to drop to 102,000 by fall 2005. Expenditures for public education in 2000/01 were estimated at $886,771. Enrollment in nonpublic schools in fall 2001 was 12,170.

As of fall 2000, there were 40,318 students enrolled in college or graduate school. In the same year Vermont had 25 degree-granting institutions. The state college system includes colleges at Castleton, Johnson, and Lyndonville, a technical college at Randolph Center, and the Community College of Vermont system with 12 branch campuses. The University of Vermont (Burlington) is a state-supported institution combining features of both a private and a state facility. Founded in 1791, it is the oldest higher educational institution in the state.

Notable private institutions include Bennington College, Champlain College (Burlington), Landmark College (Putney) serving students with ADHD and learning disabilities, Marlboro College (Marlboro), and Norwich University (Northfield), the oldest private military college in the US. The School for International Training (Brattleboro) is the academic branch of the Experiment in International Living, a student exchange program. Other notable institutions include St. Michael's College (Winooski) and Trinity College (Burlington). In 1997, minority students comprised 5% of total postsecondary enrollment.

The Vermont Student Assistance Corp. offers scholarships, incentive grants, and guaranteed loans for eligible Vermont students.

42ARTS

The Vermont State Crafts Centers at Frog Hollow (Middlebury) and Windsor display the works of Vermont artisans. The Vermont Symphony Orchestra, in Burlington, makes extensive statewide tours. Marlboro College is the home of the summer Marlboro Music Festival, co-founded by famed pianist Rudolf Serkin, who directed the festival from 1952 to 1992. Among the summer theaters in the state are those at Dorset and Weston and the University of Vermont Shakespeare Festival. The Middlebury College Bread Loaf Writers' Conference, founded in 1926, meets each August in Ripton.

The Flynn Center for the Performing Arts in Burlington serves as a major performance center for the area. The Center presents year-round FlynnArts classes in music, theater, and dance for children, teens, and adults. It is also home to the Lyric Stage, the Vermont Symphony Orchestra, the Vermont Stage Company, and the Burlington Discover Jazz Festival. Other musical performance and education venues include the Vermont Jazz Center in Brattleboro and the Vergennes Opera House, which presents concerts, films, dance and theater presentations, and various literary readings, as well as operas.

In 2003, the Vermont Council on the Arts and other Vermont arts organizations received grants totaling $1 million from the National Endowment for the Arts. The Vermont Humanities Council supports a number of literacy and history-related programs, as well as sponsoring annual Humanities Camps at schools throughout the state. In 2000, the National Endowment for the Humanities contributed $1,302,176 for nine state programs. The state provides over 18,000 schoolchildren with arts education programs. The state has approximately 100 arts associations and five local arts groups.

43LIBRARIES AND MUSEUMS

During 2000, the state's public libraries held 2,542,757 volumes and had a combined circulation of 3,899,000. The largest academic library was at the University of Vermont, with a book stock of 1,112,121, and 4,808 periodical subscriptions. Total library income in 2000 was $12,640,000, with 63.3% of this spent on staff, and 15.9% on collections.

Vermont has 89 museums and more than 65 historic sites. Among them are the Bennington Museum, with its collection of Early American glass, pottery, furniture, and Grandma Moses paintings, and the Art Gallery–St. Johnsbury Athenaeum, featuring 19th-century American artists. The Shelburne Museum, housed in restored Early American buildings, contains collections of American primitives and Indian artifacts. The Vermont Museum, in Montpelier, features historical exhibits concerning Indians, the Revolutionary War, rural life, and railroads and industry. Old Constitution House in Windsor offers exhibits on Vermont history.

44 COMMUNICATIONS

In 2001, about 97.2% of all occupied homes had telephones. There were 5 major AM and 19 major FM radio stations and eight television stations in operation in 2003. In the same year, Adelphia Cable was the state's major cable provider.

45 PRESS

In 2002, there were eight daily papers and three Sunday papers. A leading daily in 2002 was the *Burlington Free Press* (50,420 mornings, 60,659 Sundays). *Vermont Life* magazine is published quarterly under the aegis of the Agency of Development and Community Affairs.

46 ORGANIZATIONS

In 2003, there were about 537 regional, national, and international organizations within the state.

Associations headquartered in Vermont largely reflect the state's agricultural interests. Among these are Gardens for All (the National Association for Gardening), the American Chestnut Foundation, the Ayrshire Breeders' Association of America, the Holstein Association USA, and the International Maple Syrup Institute. The Vermont Arts Council is located in Montpelier. There are several local arts organizations and historical societies as well. The Bread Loaf Writers Conference, based at Middlebury College, sponsors educational programs that attract writers from across the country.

47 TOURISM, TRAVEL, AND RECREATION

With the building of the first ski slopes in the 1930s (Woodstock claims the first ski area in the United States) and the development of modern highways, tourism became a major industry in Vermont. In 2001, direct spending from about 13.9 million visitors totaled $2.84 billion, or 13% of the entire Vermont economy. Over 30% of all trips were day-trips. The tourism and travel industry supports 63,279 jobs (about 21% of all jobs in the state.

Summer and fall are the most popular seasons for visitors. Fall foliage trips account for about 28% of all travel. In the winter, the state's ski areas offer some of the finest skiing in the East. About 11,000 Vermonters work at a Vermont ski area. There are 52 state parks and over 100 campgrounds in the state. Historical sites, including several Revolutionary War battlefields, are popular attractions and shopping, particularly for Vermont made products such as maple syrup, is a major activity for all visitors.

48 SPORTS

Vermont has no major league professional sports teams. Skiing is, perhaps, the most popular participation sport, and Vermont ski areas have hosted national and international ski competitions in both Alpine and Nordic events. World Cup races have been run at Stratton Mountain, and the national cross-country championships have been held near Putney. Famous skiers Billy Kidd and Andrea Mead Lawrence, both Olympic medalists, grew up in Vermont and trained in the state.

49 FAMOUS VERMONTERS

Two US presidents, both of whom assumed office upon the death of their predecessors, were born in Vermont. Chester Alan Arthur (1829–86) became the 21st president after James A. Garfield's assassination in 1881 and finished his term. A machine politician, Arthur became a civil-service reformer in the White House. Calvin Coolidge (1872–1933), 28th president, was born in Plymouth Notch but pursued a political career in Massachusetts. Elected vice president in 1920, he became president on the death of Warren G. Harding in 1923 and was elected to a full term in 1924.

Other federal officeholders have included Matthew Lyon (1750–1822), a US representative imprisoned under the Sedition Act and reelected from a Vergennes jail; Jacob Collamer (1791–1865), who, after serving three terms in the US House, was US postmaster general and then a US senator; Justin Smith Morrill (1810–98), US representative and senator who sponsored the Morrill tariff in 1861 and the Land Grant College Act in 1862; Levi Parsons Morton (1824–1920), Benjamin Harrison's vice president from 1889 to 1893; George Franklin Edmunds (1828–1919), a US senator who helped draft the Sherman Antitrust Act; Redfield Proctor (1831–1908), secretary of war, US senator, state governor, and the founder of a marble company; John Garibaldi Sargent (1860–1939), Coolidge's attorney general; Warren Robinson Austin (1877–1963), US senator and head of the US delegation to the UN; and George David Aiken (1892–1984), US senator from 1941 to 1977.

Important state leaders were Thomas Chittenden (1730–97), leader of the Vermont republic and the state's first governor; Ethan Allen (1738–89), a frontier folk hero, leader of the Green Mountain Boys, and presenter of Vermont's claim to independence to the US Congress in 1778; Ira Allen (1751–1814), the brother of Ethan, who led the fight for statehood; Cornelius Peter Van Ness (b.New York, 1782–1852), who served first as Vermont chief justice and then as governor; and Erastus Fairbanks (1792–1864), a governor and railroad promoter.

Vermont's many businessmen and inventors include Thaddeus Fairbanks (1796–1886), inventor of the platform scale; Thomas Davenport (1802–51), inventor of the electric motor; plow and tractor manufacturer John Deere (1804–86); Elisha G. Otis (1811–61), inventor of a steam elevator and elevator safety devices; and Horace Wells (1815–48), inventor of laughing gas. Educator John Dewey (1859–1952) was born in Burlington. Donald James Cram (1919–2001), a professor of chemistry at the University of California at Los Angeles, was awarded a Nobel Prize in chemistry in 1987.

Robert Frost (b.California, 1874–1963) maintained a summer home near Ripton, where he helped found Middlebury College's Bread Loaf Writers' Conference. He was named poet laureate of Vermont in 1961. In 1992, Louise Gluck (b.1943) became the first Vermont woman to win a Pulitzer Prize for poetry. A famous Vermont performer is crooner and orchestra leader Rudy Vallee (Hubert Prior Rudy Vallee, 1901–1986).

50 BIBLIOGRAPHY

Albers, Jan. *Hands on the Land: A History of the Vermont Landscape.* Cambridge, Mass.: MIT Press, 2000.

Bassett, T. D. S. *Vermont.* Hanover, N.H.: University Press of New England, 1983.

Bearse, Ray, ed. *Vermont: A Guide to the Green Mountain State.* Boston: Houghton Mifflin, 1968.

Crockett, Walter H. *History of Vermont.* 5 vols. New York: Century, 1921.

Davis, Allen Freeman. *Postcards from Vermont: A Social History, 1905–1945.* Hanover, N.H.: University Press of New England, 2002.

Husher, Helen. *Off the Leash: Subversive Journeys Around Vermont*. Woodstock, Vt.: Countryman Press, 1999.

Klyza, Christopher McGrory, and Stephen C. Trombulak. *The Story of Vermont: A Natural and Cultural History*. Hanover, N.H.: University Press of New England, 1999.

Morrissey, Charles T. *Vermont: A Bicentennial History*. New York: Norton, 1981.

Sherman, Micheal, and Jennie Versteeg (eds.). *We Vermonters: Perspectives on the Past*. Montpelier: Vermont Historical Society, 1992.

VIRGINIA

Commonwealth of Virginia

ORIGIN OF STATE NAME: Named for Queen Elizabeth I of England, the "Virgin Queen." **NICKNAME:** The Old Dominion. **CAPITAL:** Richmond. **ENTERED UNION:** 25 June 1788 (10th). **SONG:** "Carry Me Back to Old Virginia" was formally retired from use in 1997 but has not yet been replaced. **MOTTO:** *Sic semper tyrannis* (Thus ever to tyrants). **FLAG:** On a blue field with a white border at the fly, the state seal is centered on a white circle. **OFFICIAL SEAL:** OBVERSE: the Roman goddess Virtus, dressed as an Amazon and holding a sheathed sword in one hand and a spear in the other, stands over the body of Tyranny, who is pictured with a broken chain in his hand and a fallen crown nearby. The state motto appears below, the word "Virginia" above, and a border of Virginia creeper encircles the whole. REVERSE: the Roman goddesses of Liberty, Eternity, and Fruitfulness, with the word "Perseverando" (By persevering) above. **ANIMAL:** Foxhound. **BIRD:** Cardinal. **FLOWER:** Dogwood. **TREE:** Dogwood. **SHELL:** Oyster. **BEVERAGE:** Milk. **LEGAL HOLIDAYS:** New Year's Day, 1 January; Lee-Jackson Day and Birthday of Martin Luther King, Jr., 3rd Monday in January; Washington's Birthday, 3rd Monday in February; Memorial Day, last Monday in May; Independence Day, 4 July; Labor Day, 1st Monday in September; Columbus Day and Yorktown Victory Day, 2nd Monday in October; Election Day, 1st Tuesday after 1st Monday in November; Veterans Day, 11 November; Thanksgiving Day, 4th Thursday in November; Christmas Day, 25 December. **TIME:** 7 AM EST = noon GMT.

¹LOCATION, SIZE, AND EXTENT

Situated on the eastern seaboard of the US, Virginia is the 4th largest of the South Atlantic states and ranks 36th in size among the 50 states.

The total area of Virginia is 40,767 sq mi (105,586 sq km), of which land occupies 39,704 sq mi (102,833 sq km) and inland water 1,063 sq mi (2,753 sq km). Virginia extends approximately 440 mi (710 km) E-W, but the maximum point-to-point distance from the state's noncontiguous Eastern Shore to the western extremity is 470 mi (756 km). The maximum N-S extension is about 200 mi (320 km).

Virginia is bordered on the NW by West Virginia; on the NE by Maryland and the District of Columbia (with the line passing through the Potomac River and Chesapeake Bay); on the E by the Atlantic Ocean; on the S by North Carolina and Tennessee; and on the W by Kentucky. The state's geographic center is in Buckingham County, 5 mi (8 km) SW of the town of Buckingham.

Virginia's offshore islands in the Atlantic include Chincoteague, Wallops, Cedar, Parramore, Hog, Cobb, and Smith. The boundaries of Virginia, including the Eastern Shore at the tip of the Delmarva Peninsula, total 1,356 mi (2,182 km), of which 112 mi (180 km) is general coastline; the tidal shoreline extends 3,315 mi (5,335 km).

²TOPOGRAPHY

Virginia consists of three principal physiographic areas: the Atlantic Coastal Plain, or Tidewater; the Piedmont Plateau, in the central section; and the Blue Ridge and Allegheny Mountains of the Appalachian chain, in the west and northwest.

The long, narrow Blue Ridge rises sharply from the piedmont, reaching a maximum elevation of 5,729 ft (1,747 m) at Mt. Rogers, the state's highest point. Between the Blue Ridge and the Allegheny Mountains of the Appalachian chain in the northwest lies the Valley of Virginia, consisting of transverse ridges and six

separate valleys. The floors of these valleys ascend in altitude from about 300 ft (90 m) in the northern Shenandoah Valley to 2,400 ft (730 m) in the Powell Valley. The Alleghenies average 3,000 ft (900 m) in height.

The Piedmont, shaped roughly like a triangle, varies in width from 40 mi (64 km) in the far north to 180 mi (290 km) in the extreme south. Altitudes in this region range from about 300 ft (90 m) at the fall line in the east to a maximum of about 1,000 ft (300 m) at the base of the Blue Ridge in the southwest. The Tidewater, which declines gently from the fall line to sea level, is divided by four long peninsulas cut by the state's four principal rivers—the Potomac, Rappahannock, York, and James—and the Chesapeake Bay. On the opposite side of the bay is Virginia's low-lying Eastern Shore, the southern tip of the Delmarva Peninsula. The Tidewater has many excellent harbors, notably the deep Hampton Roads estuary. Also in the southeast lies the Dismal Swamp, a drainage basin that includes Lake Drummond, about 7 mi (11 km) long and 5 mi (8 km) wide near the North Carolina border. Other major lakes in Virginia are Smith Mountain—at 31 sq mi (80 sq km) the largest lake wholly within the state—Claytor, and South Holston. The John H. Kerr Reservoir, covering 76 sq mi (197 sq km), straddles the Virginia–North Carolina line.

³CLIMATE

A mild, humid coastal climate is characteristic of Virginia. Temperatures, most equable in the Tidewater, become increasingly cooler with the rising altitudes as one moves westward. The normal daily mean temperature at Richmond is about 58°F (14°C), ranging from 36°F (2°C) in January to 78°F (26°C) in July. The record high, 110°F (43°C), was registered at Balcony Falls (near Glasgow) on 15 July 1954; the record low, –30°F (–34°C), was set at Mountain Lake on 22 January 1985. The frost-free growing season ranges from about 140 days in the mountains of the extreme west to over 250 in the Norfolk area.

Annual precipitation at Richmond (1971–2000) averaged 43.9 in (111.5 cm); at Norfolk, annual precipitation averaged 45.7 in (116 cm) during the same period. The average annual snowfall amounts to nearly 15 in (38 cm) at Richmond but only 8 in (20 cm) at Norfolk.

⁴FLORA AND FAUNA

Native to Virginia are 12 varieties of oak, 5 of pine, and 2 each of walnut, locust, gum, and popular. Pines predominate in the coastal areas, with numerous hardwoods on slopes and ridges inland; isolated stands of persimmon, ash, cedar, and basswood can also be found. Characteristic wild flowers include trailing arbutus, mountain laurel, and diverse azaleas and rhododendrons. In 2003, 15 plant species were listed as threatened or endangered in Virginia, including the Virginia round-leaf birch, harperella, Northeastern bulrush, and small whorled pogonia.

Among indigenous mammalian species are white-tailed (Virginia) deer, elk, black bear, bobcat, woodchuck, raccoon, opossum, nutria, red and gray foxes, and spotted and striped skunks, along with several species each of moles, shrews, bats, squirrels, deermice, rats, and rabbits; the beaver, mink, and river otter, once thought to be endangered, have returned in recent decades. Principal game birds include the ruffed grouse (commonly called pheasant in Virginia), wild turkey, bobwhite quail, mourning dove, woodcock, and Wilson's snipe. Tidal waters abound with croaker, hogfish, gray and spotted trout, and flounder; bass, bream, bluegill, sunfish, perch, carp, catfish, and crappie live in freshwater ponds and streams. Native reptiles include such poisonous snakes as the northern copperhead, eastern cottonmouth, and timber rattler.

In 2003, 56 animal species were listed as threatened or endangered in Virginia, including the Delmarva Peninsula fox and Virginia northern flying squirrels; Indiana, gray, and Virginia big-eared bats; bald eagle; red-cockaded woodpecker; Virginia fringed mountain snail; Lee County cave isopod; eight species of pearlymussel; three species of pigtoe; tan riffleshell; and three species of whale. At last one-fourth of the rare or endangered species in the state are found in the Dismal Swamp.

⁵ENVIRONMENTAL PROTECTION

The Virginia Department of Environmental Quality (DEQ), established in 1993, is under the jurisdiction of the Secretary of Natural Resources. The mission of the DEQ is to protect the environment of Virginia in order to promote the health and well-being of the citizens of the Commonwealth. The DEQ administers state and federal environmental programs; issues environmental permits and ensures compliance with regulations; and coordinates planning among Virginia's environmental programs. The DEQ provides staff support to assist the State Water Control Board in administering the federal Clean Water Act and enforcing state laws to improve the quality of surface water and groundwater for aquatic life and human health; the State Air Pollution Control Board in administering the federal Clean Air Act and enforcing state laws and regulations to improve air quality; and the Waste Management Board in administering waste management programs created by legislation such as the Resource Conservation and Recovery Act and the Virginia Waste Management Act. In 2002, Virginia waste treatment facilities received about 12% less total solid waste (municipal solid waste, construction and demolition debris, sludge and other types of waste), or about 824,000 tons less that they received in 2001. The Commission of Game and Inland Fisheries manages land wildlife and freshwater fish resources, while the Marine Resources Commission manages the wetlands,

commercial fishery resources, and the use of the marine environment in the Tidewater area. Virginia has implemented programs to improve air quality in the Northern Virginia, Richmond, and Hampton Roads regions; to enhance water quality monitoring for streams and lakes statewide; to continue restoration efforts for the Chesapeake Bay; and to promote voluntary cleanups of contaminated industrial sites. In 2003, Virginia had 250 hazardous waste sites listed in the Environmental Protection Agency's database, 30 of which were on the National Priorities List. About one million acres of the state is wetlands. These areas are regulated by the Virginia Water Protection Permit. In 2001, Virginia received $88,993,000 in federal grants from the Environmental Protection Agency; EPA expenditures for procurement contracts in Virginia that year amounted to $199,446,000.

⁶POPULATION

Virginia ranked 12th in population in the US with an estimated total of 7,293,542 in 2002, an increase of 3% since 2000. Between 1990 and 2000, Virginia's population grew from 6,187,358 to 7,078,515, an increase of 14.4%. The population is projected to reach 7,324,000 by 2005 and 8.5 million by 2025. The population density in 2000 was 178.8 persons per sq mi.

In 2000 the median age was 35.7. Persons under 18 years old accounted for 24.6% of the population while 11.2% were age 65 or older.

From the outset, Virginia was the most populous of the English colonies, with a population that doubled every 25 years and totaled more than 100,000 by 1727. By 1790, the time of the first US census, Virginia's population of 821,287 was about 21% of the US total and almost twice that of 2nd-ranked Pennsylvania. Although surpassed by New York State at the 1820 census, Virginia continued to enjoy slow but steady growth until the Civil War. During the 1860s, the loss of its western counties (which became the new state of West Virginia) and wartime devastation caused a decline of 23%. The population passed the 2 million mark in 1910, and the number of Virginians doubled between 1920 and 1970. The population growth rates for the five decades following 1940 were 23.9%, 19.5%, 17.2%, 15%, and 15.7%, in each case above the US average.

In the 1990s, approximately three-fourths of all Virginians lived in metropolitan areas, the largest of which in 1999 was the Norfolk–Virginia Beach–Newport News area, with an estimated 1,562,635 people; the Richmond–Petersburg metropolitan area had 961,416 people. Virginia's most populous cities proper with their estimated 2002 populations are Virginia Beach, 433,934; Norfolk, 239,036; Chesapeake, 206,665; Richmond, 197,456; Arlington, 189,927; Newport News, 180,272; Hampton, 145,921; and Alexandria, 130,804.

⁷ETHNIC GROUPS

When the first federal census was taken in 1790, more than 306,000 blacks—of whom only 12,000 were free—made up more than one-third of Virginia's total population. After emancipation, blacks continued to be heavily represented, accounting in 1870 for 512,841 (42%) of the 1,225,163 Virginians. Blacks numbered 1,390,293 in 2000, and their proportion of the total estimated population was 19.6%.

In 2000, Virginia had 329,540 Hispanic and Latino residents, chiefly Mexicans and Salvadorans. The 2000 census counted some 261,025 Asians, including 47,609 Filipinos, 45,279 Koreans, 36,966 Chinese, 37,309 Vietnamese, 48,815 Asian Indians, and 9,080 Japanese. In 2000, Pacific Islanders numbered 3,946. An estimated 570,279 Virginians—8.1% of all state residents—were of foreign birth in 2000, compared with 177,000 in 1980. The Native American population, including Eskimos and Aleuts, numbered 21,172 in 2000.

Virginia Counties, County Seats, and County Areas and Populations

COUNTY	COUNTY SEAT	LAND AREA (SQ MI)	POPULATION (2002 EST.)	COUNTY	COUNTY SEAT	LAND AREA (SQ MI)	POPULATION (2002 EST.)
Accomack	Accomac	476	39,007	King William	King William	278	13,822
Albemarle	Charlottesville	725	81,888	Lancaster	Lancaster	133	11,463
Allegheny	Covington	446	16,960	Lee	Jonesville	437	23,396
Amelia	Amelia	357	11,714	Loudoun	Leesburg	521	204,054
Amherst	Amherst	478	31,976	Louisa	Louisa	497	27,007
Appomattox	Appomattox	336	13,696	Lunenburg	Lunenburg	432	13,318
Arlington	Arlington	26	189,927	Madison	Madison	322	12,947
Augusta	Staunton	989	67,046	Mathews	Mathews	87	9,258
Bath	Warm Springs	537	5,063	Mecklenburg	Boydton	616	32,274
Bedford	Bedford	747	61,875	Middlesex	Saluda	134	10,178
Bland	Bland	359	6,916	Montgomery	Christiansburg	390	85,368
Botetourt	Fincastle	545	31,272	Nelson	Lovingston	475	14,727
Brunswick	Lawrenceville	563	18,250	New Kent	New Kent	213	14,157
Buchanan	Grundy	504	25,994	Northampton	Eastville	226	12,929
Buckingham	Buckingham	583	15,767	Northumberland	Heathsville	185	12,431
Campbell	Rustburg	505	51,471	Nottoway	Nottoway	317	15,861
Caroline	Bowling Green	536	22,622	Orange	Orange	342	27,298
Carroll	Hillsville	478	29,109	Page	Luray	313	23,310
Charles City	Charles City	181	7,239	Patrick	Stuart	481	19,455
Charlotte	Charlotte	476	12,209	Pittsylvania	Chatham	995	61,745
Chesterfield	Chesterfield	434	271,142	Powhatan	Powhatan	261	23,997
Clarke	Berryville	178	13,290	Prince Edward	Farmville	354	19,985
Craig	New Castle	330	5,118	Prince George	Prince George	266	34,135
Culpeper	Culpeper	382	36,893	Prince William	Manassas	3392	311,892
Cumberland	Cumberland	300	8,899	Pulaski	Pulaski	318	35,028
Dickenson	Clintwood	331	16,216	Rappahannock	Washington	267	7,206
Dinwiddie	Dinwiddie	507	24,747	Richmond	Warsaw	193	8,837
Essex	Tappahannock	263	9,993	Roanoke	Salem	251	85,937
Fairfax	Fairfax	393	997,580	Rockbridge	Lexington	603	20,777
Fauquier	Warrenton	651	59,245	Rockingham	Harrisonburg	865	68,648
Floyd	Floyd	381	14,248	Russell	Lebanon	479	28,974
Fluvanna	Palmyra	290	22,207	Scott	Gate City	536	23,136
Franklin	Rock Mount	683	48,462	Shenandoah	Woodstock	512	36,315
Frederick	Winchester	415	62,971	Smyth	Marion	452	32,827
Giles	Pearisburg	362	17,083	Southampton	Courtland	603	17,448
Gloucester	Gloucester	225	35,755	Spotsylvania	Spotsylvania	404	102,570
Goochland	Goochland	281	17,523	Stafford	Stafford	271	104,823
Grayson	Independence	446	16,612	Surry	Surry	281	7,107
Greene	Standardsville	157	16,269	Sussex	Sussex	496	12,221
Greensville	Emporia	300	11,572	Tazewell	Tazewell	522	44,011
Halifax	Halifax	816	36,973	Warren	Front Royal	219	32,910
Hanover	Hanover	468	92,050	Washington	Abingdon	578	51,331
Henrico	Richmond	238	268,270	Westmoreland	Montross	250	16,676
Henry	Martinsville	283	57,395	Wise	Wise	405	41,710
Highland	Monterey	416	2,415	Wythe	Wytheville	460	27.790
Isle of Wight	Isle of Wight	319	31,085	York	Yorktown	122	59,720
James City	Williamsburg	153	51,418	Independent Cities		1,605	
King and Queen	King and Queen	317	6,558				
King George	King George	180	17,657	TOTALS		39,704	7,293,542

[8] LANGUAGES

English settlers encountered members of the Powhatan Indian confederacy, speakers of an Algonkian language, whose legacy includes such place-names as Roanoke and Rappahannock.

Although the expanding suburban area south of the District of Columbia has become dialectically heterogeneous, the rest of the state has retained its essentially Southern speech features. Many dialect markers occur statewide, but subregional contrasts distinguish the South Midland of the Appalachians from the Southern of the piedmont and Tidewater. General are *batter bread* (a soft corn cake), *batter cake* (pancake), *comfort* (tied and filled bed cover), and *polecat* (skunk). Widespread pronunciation features include *greasy* with a /z/ sound; *yeast* and *east* as sound-alikes, *creek* rhyming with *peek*, and *can't* with *paint*; *coop* and *bulge* with the vowel of *book*; and *forest* with an /ah/ sound.

The Tidewater is set off by *creek* meaning a saltwater inlet, *fishing worm* for earthworm, and fog as /fahg/. Appalachian South Midland has *redworm* for earthworm, *fog* as /fawg/, *wash* as /wawsh/, *Mary* and *merry* as sound-alikes, and *poor* with the vowel of *book*. The Richmond area is noted also for having two variants of the long /i/ and /ow/ diphthongs as they occur before voiceless and voiced consonants, so that the vowel in the noun *house* is quite different from the vowel in the verb *house*, and the vowel in *advice* differs from that in *advise*. The Tidewater exhibits similar features.

In 2000, Virginia residents five years of age and over who spoke only English at home numbered 5,884,075, or 88.9% of the total population, down from 92.7% in 1990.

The following table gives selected statistics from the 2000 census for language spoken at home by persons five years old and over. The category "African languages" includes Amharic, Ibo, Twi, Yoruba, Bantu, Swahili, and Somali. The category "Other Indic languages" includes Bengali, Marathi, Punjabi, and

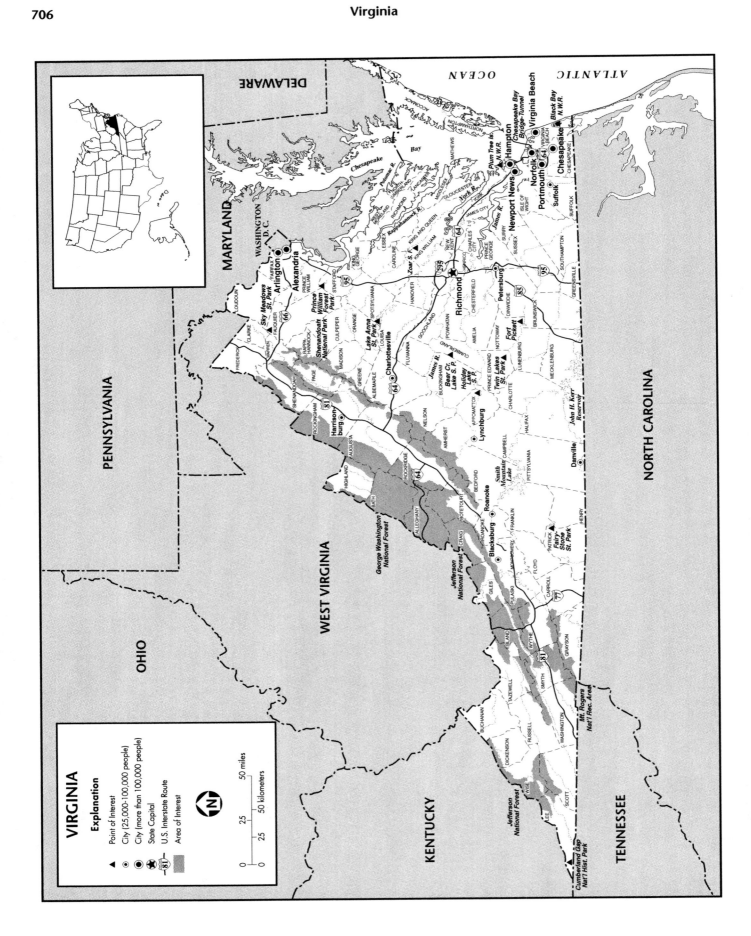

Romany. The category "Other Asian languages" includes Dravidian languages, Malayalam, Telugu, Tamil, and Turkish.

LANGUAGE	NUMBER	PERCENT
Population 5 years and over	6,619,266	100.0
Speak only English	5,884,075	88.9
Speak a language other than English	735,191	11.1
Speak a language other than English	735,191	11.1
Spanish or Spanish Creole	316,274	4.8
French (incl. Patois, Cajun)	40,117	0.6
Korean	39,636	0.6
Tagalog	33,598	0.5
German	32,736	0.5
Vietnamese	31,918	0.5
Chinese	29,837	0.5
Arabic	25,984	0.4
African languages	21,164	0.3
Persian	19,199	0.3
Urdu	15,250	0.2
Other Indic languages	13,767	0.2
Other Asian languages	12,115	0.2
Hindi	11,947	0.2
Italian	10,099	0.2

9RELIGIONS

The Anglican Church (later the Episcopal Church), whose members founded and populated Virginia Colony in the early days, was the established church during the colonial period. The first dissenters to arrive were Scotch-Irish Presbyterians in the late 17th century; they were followed by large numbers of German Lutherans, Welsh Baptists, and English Quakers, who settled in the Valley of Virginia in the early 18th century. The general assembly's adoption in 1785 of the Virginia Statute for Religious Freedom, drafted by Thomas Jefferson, disestablished the Episcopal Church and made religious toleration the norm in Virginia. Although the Episcopal and Presbyterian churches retained the allegiance of the landed gentry during the 19th century, the Methodists and Baptists became the largest church groups in the state.

Protestant denominations combined had the greatest number of known adherents in 2000, when the leading groups were the Southern Baptist Convention, with 774,673 adherents; the United Methodist Church, 470,381; the Presbyterian Church USA, 135,435; and the Episcopal Church, 126,874. As of 2000, there were 606,059 Roman Catholics in Virginia, representing a membership growth of 57% from 1990. The Jewish population was estimated at 76,140 and there were an estimated 51,021 Muslims. Over 4.1 million people (about 58.4% of the population) were not counted as members of any religious organization.

10TRANSPORTATION

Virginia has one of the nation's most extensive highway systems, one of the leading ports—Hampton Roads—and two of the nation's busiest air terminals.

Virginia was a leader in early railroad development. Rail lines were completed between Richmond and Fredericksburg in 1836, from Portsmouth to Roanoke in 1837, and from Richmond to Washington, DC, in 1872. Virginia's 1,290 mi (2,076 km) of track formed a strategic supply link for both the Confederate and Union armies during the Civil War. Railroads remained the primary system of transportation until the rise of the automobile in the 1920s. As of 2000, there were 10 rail companies operating in the state, two of them Class I railways with combined trackage of 3,033 rail mi (4,853 km). Principal (Class I) railroads were CSX Transportation and Norfolk Southern. These two, combined with one Canadian, five local, and two switching and terminal railroads, carried 37 million tons of freight originating in Virginia in 2000. In 2000, 50 million rail-tons of coal terminated in Virginia. Amtrak passenger trains served 21 communities.

Virginia's road network, at first built mainly for hauling tobacco to market, had expanded across the Blue Ridge by 1782, to the Cumberland Gap by 1795, and into the Shenandoah Valley by means of the Valley Turnpike in 1840. As of 2000, Virginia had 70,393 mi (112,629 km) of public roads, 6,019,194 registered vehicles, and 4,836,993 licensed drivers. Major interstate highways are I-95 extending north–south from Washington, DC, via Richmond to the North Carolina border (and, eventually, to Florida); I-81, connecting northern Virginia with the southwest; and I-64, linking the Hampton Roads area with West Virginia via Clifton Forge and Covington in the west. The 18-mi (29-km) Chesapeake Bay Bridge-Tunnel, completed in 1964, connects the Eastern Shore with the southeastern mainland. Popular scenic highways include the Blue Ridge Parkway, Colonial National Historical Parkway, and George Washington Memorial Parkway.

Virginia's District of Columbia suburbs are linked to the nation's capital by the Washington Metropolitan Area Transit Authority's bus and rail systems. Norfolk, Newport News-Hampton, and Richmond have extensive bus systems.

Virginia's Hampton Roads has one of the largest and strongest commercial port complexes in the world. Three state-owned general cargo marine terminals—Newport News Marine Terminal, Norfolk International Terminals, and Portsmouth Marine Terminal—share the harbor with more than 20 privately owned bulk terminals. Foreign and domestic waterborne coal shipments originating in Virginia totaled 22 short tons in 2000, accounting for 45% of all such shipments that year. Located on a naturally deep, ice-free harbor, 18 mi (29 km) from the open sea, Virginia's ports have the largest landside intermodal facilities on the US east coast. Each general cargo terminal in the port has on-site rail connections that offer single and double-stack train service from the docks. Virginia's mid-Atlantic location and transportation infrastructure offer users of the port access to two-thirds of the US population within 24 hours. In addition to the marine terminals, the Virginia Inland Port (VIP) terminal, just west of Washington, DC, in Front Royal, Virginia, offers daily rail service to the marine terminals in Hampton Roads and allows direct access to the international trade routes of the 75 international shipping lines calling at the ports. In addition to the movement of international export and import cargo, the VIP is a full-service domestic rail ramp for Norfolk Southern's domestic service.

Virginia's 275 public and private airports in 2000 included 55 licensed public-use airports and 220 private airports; there were 115 heliports and 5 seaplane bases. Each year, some 9.6 million passengers enplane at Dulles International Airport; over 7.5 million enplane at Ronald Reagan Washington National Airport (at Arlington), a major center for domestic flights.

11HISTORY

Distinctively fluted stone points found at Flint Run in Front Royal and at the Williamson Site in Dinwiddie County testify to the presence in what is now the Commonwealth of Virginia of nomadic Paleo-Indians after 8000 BC. Climatic changes and the arrival of other Indian groups about 3500 BC produced the Archaic Culture, which lasted until about AD 500. These Indians apparently were great eaters of oysters, and shell accumulations along riverbanks mark their settlement sites. The Woodland Period (AD 500–1600) marked the Indians' development of the bow and arrow and sophisticated pottery. At the time of English contact, early in the 17th century, Tidewater Virginia was occupied principally by Algonkian-speakers, planters as well as hunters and fishers, who lived in pole-framed dwellings forming small, palisaded towns. The piedmont area was the home of the Manahoac, Monacan, and Tutelo, all of Siouan stock. Cherokee lived in Virginia's far southwestern triangle.

The first permanent English settlement in America was established at Jamestown on 13 May 1607 in the new land named Virginia in honor of Elizabeth I, the "Virgin Queen." The successful settlement was sponsored by the London Company (also known as the Virginia Company), a joint-stock venture chartered by King James I in 1606. The charter defined Virginia as all of the North American coast between 30° and 45°N and extending inland for 50 mi (80 km). A new royal charter in 1609 placed Virginia's northern and southern boundaries at points 200 mi (320 km) north and south of Point Comfort, at the mouth of the James River, and extended its territory westward to the Pacific; a third charter issued in 1612 pushed Virginia eastward to embrace the Bermuda Islands. Thus, Virginia at one time stretched from southern Maine to California and encompassed all or part of 42 of the present 50 states, as well as Bermuda and part of the Canadian province of Ontario.

Upon landing at Jamestown, the 100 or more male colonists elected from among 12 royally approved councillors a governor and captain general, Edward Maria Wingfield. Much internal strife, conflict with the Indians, and a "starving time" that reduced the settlers to eating their horses caused them to vote to leave the colony in 1610, but just as they were leaving, three supply ships arrived; with them came Thomas West, Baron De La Warr (Lord Delaware), who stayed to govern the Virginia Colony until 1611. Finally, however, it was the energy, resourcefulness, and military skill of Captain John Smith that saved the colony from both starvation and destruction by the Indians. He also charted the coast and wrote the first American book, *A True Relation*, which effectively publicized English colonization of the New World.

Smith's chief Algonkian adversary was Powhatan, emperor of a confederacy in eastern Virginia that bore his name. Although Smith was taken prisoner by Powhatan, he was able to work out a tenuous peace later cemented by the marriage in 1614 of the emperor's favorite daughter, Pocahontas, to John Rolfe, a Jamestown settler who founded the colonial tobacco industry.

Three events marked 1619 as a red-letter year in Virginia history. First, women were sent to the colony in large numbers. Any man marrying one of a shipment of 90 "young maids" had to pay 120 lb of tobacco for the cost of her transportation. The women were carefully screened for respectability, and none had to marry if she did not find a man to her liking. The second key event was the arrival in Jamestown of the first blacks, probably as indentured servants, a condition from which slavery in the colony evolved (the first legally recognized slaveholder, in the 1630s, was Anthony Johnson, himself black). The third and most celebrated event of 1619 was the convening in Jamestown of the first representative assembly in the New World, consisting of a council chosen by the London Company and a house of burgesses elected by the colonists. Thus, self-government through locally elected representatives became a reality in America and an important precedent for the English colonies.

King James I, for whom the colonial capital was named, was at first content with colonization under the London Company's direction. But in 1624, he charged the company with mismanagement and revoked its charter. Virginia remained a royal colony until 1776, although royal governors such as Sir Francis Wyatt and Sir George Yeardley continued to convoke the general assembly without the Crown's assent. A serious challenge to self-government came in 1629–35 with Governor John Harvey's "executive offenses"—including the knocking out of a councillor's teeth and the detaining of a petition of protest to the king—which sparked a rebellion led by Dr. John Pott. Harvey was bloodlessly deposed by the council, which turned, significantly, to the house of burgesses for confirmation of the action the council had taken.

Despite serious setbacks because of Indian massacres in 1622 and 1644, the colony's population expanded rapidly along the James, York, Rappahannock, and Potomac rivers, and along the Eastern Shore. In 1653, the general assembly attempted to collect taxes from the Eastern Shore although that area had no legislative representation. At a mass meeting, Colonel Thomas Johnson urged resistance to taxation without representation. The resulting Northampton Declaration embodied this principle, which would provide the rallying cry for the American Revolution; the immediate result was the granting of representation to the Eastern Shore.

Virginia earned the designation Old Dominion through its loyalty to the Stuarts during England's Civil War, but the superior military and naval forces of Oliver Cromwell compelled submission to parliamentary commissioners in 1652. In the eight years that followed, the house of burgesses played an increasingly prominent role. Colonial governors, while at least nominally Puritan, usually conducted affairs with an easy tolerance that did not mar Virginia's general hospitality to refugee Cavaliers from the mother country.

With the restoration of the royal family in 1660, Sir William Berkeley, an ardent royalist who had served as governor before the colony's surrender to the Commonwealth, was returned to that office. In his first administration, his benign policies and appealing personality had earned him great popularity, but during his second term, his dictatorial and vindictive support of royal prerogatives made him the most hated man in the colony. When he seemed unable to defend the people against Indian incursions in 1676, they sought a general of their own. They found him in young Nathaniel Bacon, a charismatic planter of great daring and eloquence, whose leadership attracted many small planters impatient by this time with the privileged oligarchy directing the colony. Bacon's war against the Indians became a populist-style revolt against the governor, who fled to the Eastern Shore, and reform legislation was pushed by the burgesses. Berkeley regained control of the capital briefly, only to be defeated by Bacon's forces; but Jamestown was burned by the retreating Bacon, who died of fever shortly afterward. Berkeley's subsequent return to power was marked by so many hangings of offenders that the governor was summoned to the court of Charles II to answer for his actions. Bacon's Rebellion was cited as a precedent when the colonies waged war against George III a century later.

The 17th century closed on a note of material and cultural progress with the gubernatorial administration of Francis Nicholson. The College of William and Mary, the second institution of higher learning in America, was chartered in 1693, and Middle Plantation (renamed Williamsburg in 1722), the site of the college, became the seat of government when the capital was moved from Jamestown in 1699. The new capital remained small, although it was crowded when the legislature was in session. A new era of cultural and economic progress dawned with the administration of Alexander Spotswood (1710–22), sometimes considered the greatest of Virginia's colonial governors. He discouraged the colony's excessively heavy dependence on a single crop, tobacco; promoted industry, especially ironwork; took a humane interest in blacks and Indians' strengthened fortification; ended the depredations of the notorious pirate Edward Teach, better known as Blackbeard; and, by leading his "Knights of the Golden Horseshoe" across the Blue Ridge, dramatized the opening of the transmontane region.

In the decades that followed, eastern Virginians moving into the Valley of Virginia were joined by Scotch-Irish and Germans moving southward from Maryland and Pennsylvania. Virginians caught up in western settlement lost much of their awe of the mother country during the French and Indian War (1756–63). A young Virginia militiaman, Colonel George Washington, gave wise but unheeded advice to Britain's Major General Edward Braddock before the Battle of Monongahela, and afterward emerged as the hero of that action.

Virginia, acting independently and with other colonies, repeatedly challenged agents of the Crown. In 1765, the House of Burgesses, swept by the eloquence of Patrick Henry, adopted five resolutions opposing the Stamp Act, through which the English Parliament had sought to tax the colonists for their own defense. In 1768, Virginia joined Massachusetts in issuing an appeal to all the colonies for concerted action. The following year, Virginia initiated a boycott of British goods in answer to the taxation provisions of the hated Townshend Acts. In 1773, the Old Dominion became the first colony to establish an intercolonial Committee of Correspondence. And it joined the other colonies at the First Continental Congress, which met in Philadelphia in 1774 and elected Virginia's Peyton Randolph president.

Virginia was the first colony to instruct its delegates to move for independence at the Continental Congress of 1776. The congressional resolution was introduced by one native son, Richard Henry Lee, and the Declaration of Independence was written by another, Thomas Jefferson. In the same year, Virginians proclaimed their government a commonwealth and adopted a constitution and declaration of rights, prepared by George Mason. The declaration became the basis for the Bill of Rights in the US Constitution. Virginians were equally active in the Revolutionary War. George Washington was commander in chief of the Continental Army, and other outstanding Virginia officers were George Rogers Clark, Hugh Mercer, Henry "Light Horse Harry" Lee, William Campbell, Isaac Shelby, and an adopted son, Daniel Morgan. In addition, the greatest American naval hero was a Scottish-born Virginian, John Paul Jones. Virginia itself was a major battlefield, and it was on Virginia soil, at Yorktown on 19 October 1781, that British General Charles Cornwallis surrendered to Washington, effectively ending the war.

During the early federal period, Virginia's leadership was as notable as it had been during the American Revolution. James Madison is honored as the "father of the Constitution," and Washington, who was president of the constitutional convention, became the first US president in 1789. Indeed, Virginians occupied the presidency for all but four of the nation's first 28 years. Far more influential than most presidents was another Virginian, John Marshall, who served as US chief justice for 34 years, beginning in 1801.

During the first half of the 19th century, Virginians became increasingly concerned with the problem of slavery. From the early 1700s, the general assembly had repeatedly prohibited the importation of slaves, only to be overruled by the Crown, protecting the interests of British slave traders. In 1778, no longer subject to royal veto, the legislature provided that any slave brought into the state would automatically be freed upon arrival. (There was no immediate legal termination of the bondage of those already enslaved, or of their offspring.) The number of free blacks grew tenfold by 1810, and though some became self-supporting farmers and artisans, many could find no employment. Fearing that unhappy free blacks might incite those who were still slaves to rebellion, the general assembly in 1806 decreed that each slave emancipated in due course must then leave Virginia within a year or after reaching the age of 21. Nat Turner's slave revolt—which took the lives of at least 55 white men, women, and children in Southampton County in 1831—increased white fears of black emancipation. Nevertheless, legislation to end slavery in Virginia failed adoption by only seven votes the following year.

The slavery controversy did not consume all Virginians' energies in the first half of the 19th century, an era that saw the state become a leading center of scientific, artistic, and educational advancement. But this era ended with the coming of the Civil War, a conflict about which many Virginians had grave misgivings. Governor John Letcher was a Union man, and most of the state's top political leaders hoped to retain the federal tie. Even after the formation at Montgomery, Alabama, of the Confederate States of America, Virginia initiated a national peace convention in Washington, DC, headed by a native son and former US president, John Tyler. A statewide convention, assembled in Richmond in April 1861, adopted an ordinance of secession only after President Abraham Lincoln sought to send troops across Virginia to punish the states that had already seceded and called upon the commonwealth to furnish soldiers for that task. Virginia adopted secession with some regret and apprehension but with no agonizing over constitutional principles, for in ratifying the Constitution the state had reserved the right to secede. Shortly afterward, Richmond, the capital of Virginia since 1780, became the capital of the Confederacy. It was also the home of the Tredegar Ironworks, the South's most important manufacturer of heavy weaponry.

Robert E. Lee, offered field command of the Union armies, instead resigned his US commission in order to serve his native state as commander of the Army of Northern Virginia and eventually as chief of the Confederate armies. Other outstanding Virginian generals included Thomas Jonathan "Stonewall" Jackson, J. E. B. "Jeb" Stuart, Joseph E. Johnston, and A. P. Hill. Besides furnishing a greater number of outstanding Confederate generals than any other state, the Old Dominion supplied some of the Union's military leaders, George H. Thomas, the "Rock of Chickamauga," among them. More than 30 Virginians held the rank of brigadier general or major general in the federal forces.

Virginia became the principal battlefield of the Civil War, the scene of brilliant victories won by General Lee's army at Bull Run (about 30 mi/48 km southwest of Washington, DC), Fredericksburg, and Chancellorsville (Spotsylvania County). But the overwhelming numbers and industrial and naval might of the Union compelled Lee's surrender at Appomattox on 9 April 1865. Virginia waters were the scene of one of the most celebrated naval engagements in world history, the first battle of the ironclads, when the USS Monitor and CSS Virginia (Merrimac), rebuilt in the Portsmouth Shipyard, met at Hampton Roads. The war cost Virginia one-third of its territory when West Virginia was admitted to the Union as a separate state on 20 June 1863. Richmond was left in ruins, and agriculture and industry throughout the commonwealth were destroyed. Union General Philip H. Sheridan's systematic campaign of demolition in the Shenandoah Valley almost made good his boast that a crow flying over the valley would have to carry its own rations.

In 1867, Virginia was placed under US military rule. A constitutional convention held in Richmond under the leadership of carpetbaggers and scalawags drafted a constitution that disqualified the overwhelming majority of white Virginians from holding office and deprived about 95% of them of the right to vote. In this crisis, a compromise was negotiated under which white Virginians would accept Negro suffrage if they themselves were permitted to vote and hold office. The amended constitution, providing for universal manhood suffrage, was adopted in 1869, and Virginia was readmitted to the Union on 26 January 1870.

Although the bankrupt state was saddled with a debt of more than $45 million, the Conservative Democrats undertook repayment of the entire debt, including approximately one-third estimated to be West Virginia's share. Other Democrats, who came to be known as Readjusters, argued that the commonwealth could not provide education and other essential services to its citizens unless it disclaimed one-third of the debt and reached a compromise with creditors concerning the remainder. William Mahone, a railroad president and former Confederate major general, engineered victory for the Readjusters in 1880 with the aid of the Republicans. His election to the US Senate that year represented another success for the Readjuster-Republican coalition, which was attentive to the needs of both blacks and underprivileged whites.

Throughout the 1880s and 1890s, life in public places in Virginia continued in an unsegregated fashion that sometimes amazed visitors from northern cities. As the 19th century neared an end, however, Virginia moved toward legal separation of the races. In 1900, the general assembly by a one-vote majority enacted segregation on railroad cars. The rule became applicable the following year to streetcars and steamboats. In 1902, the Virginia constitutional convention enacted a literacy test and poll tax that effectively reduced the black vote to negligible size.

Two decades later, just when the Old Dominion seemed permanently set in the grooves of conservatism, two liberals, each with impeccable old-line backgrounds, found themselves battling for the governorship in a Democratic primary campaign that changed the course of Virginia's political history. Harry F. Byrd defeated G. Walter Mapp in the election of 1925 and immediately after taking office launched the state on an era of reform. In a whirlwind 60 days, the general assembly revised the tax system, revised balloting procedures, and adopted measures to lure industry to Virginia. The Anti-Lynch Act of 1927 made anyone present at the scene of a lynching who did not intervene guilty of murder; there has not been a lynching in Virginia since its passage. Byrd also reorganized the state government, consolidating nearly 100 agencies into 14 departments. Later, as US senator, Byrd became so renowned as a conservative that many people forgot his earlier career as a fighting liberal.

Following the depression of the 1930s, Virginia became one of the most prosperous states of the Southeast. It profited partly from national defense contracts and military and naval expansion, but also from increased manufacturing and from what became one of the nation's leading tourist industries. Few states made so great a contribution as Virginia to the US effort in World War II. More than 300,000 Virginians served in the armed forces; 9,000 lost their lives, and 10 were awarded the Medal of Honor. Virginians were proud of the fact that General George C. Marshall was a Virginia resident and a graduate of Virginia Military Institute, and even delighted in the knowledge that both General Dwight D. Eisenhower, commander in the European theater, and General Douglas MacArthur, commander in the Pacific, were sons of Virginia mothers.

The postwar period brought many changes in the commonwealth's public life. During the first administration of Governor Mills E. Godwin, Jr. (1966–70), the state abandoned its strict pay-as-you-go fiscal policy, secured an $81-million bond issue, and enacted a sales tax. Much of the increased revenue benefited the public school system; funding for the four-year colleges was greatly expanded, and a system of low-tuition community colleges was instituted.

In 1970, A. Linwood Holton, Jr., became the first Republican governor of Virginia since 1874. Pledging to "make today's Virginia a model in race relations," Holton increased black representation on state boards and in the higher echelons of government. He reversed the policies of his immediate predecessors, who had generally met the US Supreme Court's desegregation ruling in 1954 with a program of massive resistance, eschewing violence but adopting every legal expedient to frustrate integration. By the mid-1970s, public school integration in Virginia had been achieved to a degree not yet accomplished in many northern states.

The northeast and Virginia Beach/Norfolk area of Virginia boomed in the early 1980s, spurred by an expansion of federal jobs and a national military build-up. The population in Virginia Beach grew by 50% between 1980 and 1990. Non-agricultural employment rose by 29% between 1980 and 1988. The economies of rural parts of the state to the west and south, however, remained stagnant.

In the late 1980s, Virginia was hit by a recession. Douglas Wilder, the nation's first black governor and a moderate Democrat, responded to a significant shortfall in state revenues by refusing to raise taxes and by insisting on maintaining a $200 million reserve fund. Instead, Wilder reduced the budgets and staff of state services and of the state's college and university system. Wilder's cuts created particular hardship for the less affluent counties that relied heavily on state aid for their funding of schools, libraries, and road maintenance. Wilder, limited by law to one term in office, was succeeded in 1993 by conservative Republican Richard Allen. In 1994, nationwide attention was focused on the US Senate race in which the Democratic incumbent, Charles S. Robb, defeated Republican challenger Oliver North, known for his role in the Iran-contra affair of the 1980s.

In the mid-1990s Virginia's economy was strong, thanks to its diversified base of agriculture, manufacturing, and service industries (the latter dominated by federal government employment). Pollution from industry and agricultural chemicals remained a significant concern, and the state was investing in cleanup efforts in the Chesapeake Bay.

In 1994, the Walt Disney Company abandoned its much-publicized plan to build a history theme park, "Disney's America," in Virginia, following strong opposition from residents, environmentalists, and historians.

Virginia was in the midst of its worst state revenue performance in 40 years in 2003, but the state managed to arrive at a balanced budget. To help it overcome massive budget deficits in 2003, the state cut funding for higher education by more than 25% over the previous two years. Nearly all state universities raised tuition in response. Despite this fact, the State Council of Higher Education said Virginia needed to come up with an additional $350 million per year to maintain the quality of its public higher education system.

12STATE GOVERNMENT

Since 1776, Virginia has had six constitutions, all of which have expanded the power of the executive branch. The last constitution, framed in 1970 and effective 1 July 1971, governs the state today. As of January 2003, this document had been amended 38 times.

The general assembly consists of a 40-member senate, elected to four-year terms, and a 100-member house of delegates, serving for two-year terms. Senators and delegates must be at least 21 years old, residents of their districts, and qualified voters. The assembly convenes annually on the 2nd Wednesday in January for 60-day sessions in even-numbered years and 30-day sessions in odd-numbered years, with an option to extend the annual session for a maximum of 30 days or declare a special session by two-thirds vote of each house. In 2002 legislative salaries were $18,000 for state senators and $17,640 for delegates, unchanged from 1999.

The governor and lieutenant governor (elected separately), and attorney general, all serving four-year terms, are the only officials elected statewide. Elections for these offices are held in odd-numbered years, following presidential elections. The governor, who must be at least 30 years old, a US citizen, and a state resident and qualified voter for five years, may not serve two successive terms. In 2002, the governor's salary was $124,855, but the governor returns 10% of his or her salary to the state treasury. Most state officials—including the secretaries of administration and finance, commerce and resources, education, human resources, public safety, and transportation—are appointed by the governor but must be confirmed by both houses of the legislature.

Bills become law when signed by the governor or left unsigned for seven days (including Sundays) while the legislature is in session; a bill dies if left unsigned for 30 days after the legislature has adjourned. A two-thirds majority of those present in each house is needed to override a gubernatorial veto. The constitution may be amended by constitutional convention or by a majority vote of two sessions of the general assembly; ratification by the electorate is required.

Voters must be US citizens, at least 18 years old, and residents of their voting precinct. Restrictions apply to convicted felons and those declared mentally incompetent by the court.

[13]POLITICAL PARTIES

Virginia has exercised a unique role in US politics as the birthplace not only of representative government but also of one of America's two major parties. The modern Democratic Party traces its origins to the original Republican Party (usually referred to as the Democratic-Republican Party, or the Jeffersonian Democrats), led by two native sons of Virginia, Thomas Jefferson and James Madison. Virginians have also been remarkably influential in the political life of other states: a survey published in 1949 showed that 319 Virginia natives had represented 31 other states in the US Senate and House of Representatives.

From the end of Reconstruction through the 1960s, conservative Democrats dominated state politics, with few exceptions. Harry F. Byrd was the state's Democratic political leader for 40 years, first as a reform governor (1926–30) and then as a conservative senator (1933–95). During the 1970s, Virginians, still staunchly conservative, turned increasingly to the Republican Party, whose presidential nominees carried the state in every election from 1952 through 1984, except for 1964. Linwood Holton, the first Republican governor since Reconstruction, was elected in 1969. His Republican successor, Mills E. Godwin, Jr., the first governor since the Civil War to serve more than one term, had earlier won election as a Democrat. The election in 1977 of another Republican, John N.

Dalton, finally proved that Virginia had become a two-party state. In 1981, however, the governorship was won by Democrat Charles S. Robb, who appointed a record number of blacks and women to state offices. Robb, prohibited by law from seeking a consecutive second term, was succeeded by Democrat Gerald L. Baliles in 1985 when Virginians also elected L. Douglas Wilder as lieutenant governor and Mary Sue Terry as attorney general. Wilder became the highest-ranking black state official in the US, and Terry was the first woman to win a statewide office in Virginia. Wilder was elected governor in 1989, followed by Republican George Allen in 1993. Another Republican, James S. Gilmore III, was elected to the office in the 1997 election. Democrat Mark Warner was elected governor in 2001.

Former governor Robb won election to the US Senate in 1988 and reelection in 1994 when he was opposed by Republican Oliver North, a former Marine and Reagan White House aide who gained fame for his role in the Iran-contra affair. Republican George F. Allen won the seat in 2000. Senior Senator John Warner, a Republican, was elected to a fifth term in 2002.

After the 2002 elections, Virginia's delegation to the US House of Representatives consisted of three Democrats and eight Republicans. As of mid-2003, control of the state senate and house was in the hands of the Republicans. Republicans controlled the state house, 65–33, with 2 independents; the state senate was split 23–17, Republicans to Democrats.

In 2000, Republican George W. Bush won 52% of the presidential vote; Democrat Al Gore received 45%; and Green Party candidate garnered 2%. In 2002 there were 4,217,810 registered voters; there is no party registration in the state. The state had 13 electoral votes in the 2000 presidential election.

[14]LOCAL GOVERNMENT

As of 2002, Virginia had 95 counties and 229 municipal governments, as well as 196 special districts.

During the colonial period, most Virginians lived on plantations and were reluctant to form towns. In 1705, the general assembly approved the formation of 16 "free boroughs." Although only Jamestown, Williamsburg, and Norfolk chose at

Virginia Presidential Vote by Political Parties, 1948–2000

YEAR	ELECTORAL VOTE	VIRGINIA WINNER	DEMOCRAT	REPUBLICAN	STATES' RIGHTS DEMOCRAT	PROGRESSIVE	SOCIALIST	SOCIALIST LABOR
1948	11	*Truman (D)	200,786	172,070	43,393	2,047	726	234
1952	12	*Eisenhower (R)	268,677	349,037	—	—	504	1,160
1956	12	*Eisenhower (R)	267,760	386,459	CONSTITUTION 42,964	—	444	351
1960	12	Nixon (R)	362,327	404,521	VA. CONSERVATIVE 4,204	—	—	397
1964	12	*Johnson (D)	558,038	481,334`	—	—	—	2,895
1968	12	*Nixon (R)	442,387	590,319	AMERICAN IND. 320,272	—	PEACE & FREEDOM 1,680	4,671
1972	12	*Nixon (R)	438,887	988,493	AMERICAN 19,721	—	—	9,918
1976	12	Ford (R)	813,896	836,554	16,686	LIBERTARIAN 4,648	US LABOR 7,508	SOC. WORKERS 17,802
1980	12	*Reagan (R)	752,174	989,609	—	12,821	Citizens **14,024	1,9861
1984	12	*Reagan (R)	796,250	1,337,078	—	—	—	—
1988	12	*Bush (R)	859,799	1,309,162	NEW ALLIANCE 14,312	8,336	—	—
1992	13	Bush (R)	1,038,650	1,150,517	3,192	5,730	IND. (PEROT) 348,639	IND. (LAROUCHE) 11,937
1996	13	Dole (R)	1,091,060	1,138,350	—	9,174	159,861	—
2000	13	*Bush, G. W. (R)	1,217,290	1,437,490	GREEN 59,398	15,198		

* Won US presidential election.
**Candidates of the nationwide Citizens and Socialist Workers parties were listed as independents on the Virginia ballot; another independent, John Anderson, won 95,418 votes.

that time to avail themselves of the option and become independent municipalities, their decision laid the foundation for the independence of Virginia's present-day cities from county government. In 1842, Richmond became the commonwealth's first charter city. Cities elect their own officials (typically including council members and city managers), levy their own taxes, and are unencumbered by county obligations. Incorporated towns, on the other hand, remain part of the counties.

In general, counties are governed by elected boards of supervisors, with a county administrator or executive handling day-to-day affairs; other typical county officials are the clerk of the circuit court (chief administrator of the court), county treasurer, commissioner of the revenue, commonwealth's attorney, and sheriff. Incorporated towns have elected mayors and councils.

15STATE SERVICES

To address the continuing threat of terrorism and to work with the federal Department of Homeland Security (created in 2002 following the terrorist attacks of 11 September 2001), homeland security in Virginia in 2003 operated under executive order; a special assistant to the governor was designated as the state homeland security advisor.

Under the jurisdiction of the secretary of education are the Department of Education, which administers the public school system, and the State Council of Higher Education, which coordinates the programs of the state-controlled colleges and universities. The secretary of transportation oversees the Department of Transportation, Department of Transportation Safety, Department of Aviation, Virginia Port Authority, Department of Military Affairs (National Guard), Department of Motor Vehicles, and State Office of Emergency Services.

Within the purview of the secretary of human resources are the Department of Health, Department of Mental Health and Mental Retardation, Department of Health Regulatory Boards, Department of Social Services, and Department of Rehabilitative Services, as well as special offices dealing with problems that affect women, children, the elderly, and the disabled. The departments of State Police, Corrections, Criminal Justice Services, Fire Programs, and Alcoholic Beverage Control are under the aegis of the secretary of public safety.

The secretary of commerce and resources oversees the departments of Housing and Community Development, Labor and Industry, Commerce, Agriculture and Consumer Services, and Conservation and Recreation, as well as a profusion of boards, councils, offices, divisions, and commissions. The secretary of administration and finance exercises jurisdiction over budgeting, telecommunications, accounting, computer services, taxation, the state treasury, records, and personnel, as well as over the State Board of Elections. Regulatory functions are concentrated in the quasi-independent State Corporation Commission, consisting of three commissioners elected by the legislature to staggered six-year terms. The commission regulates all public utilities; licenses banks, savings and loan associations, credit unions, and small loan companies; enforces motor carrier and certain aviation laws and sets railroad rates; supervises the activities of insurance companies; and enforces laws governing securities and retail franchising. Natural resources are protected by the Department of Environmental Quality, the Department of Forestry, and the Department of Game and Inland Fisheries.

16JUDICIAL SYSTEM

The highest judicial body in the commonwealth is the supreme court, consisting of a chief justice and six other justices elected to 12-year terms by the General Assembly. The court of appeals has ten judges serving 8-year terms. The state is divided into 31 judicial circuits/districts. Each city and county has a circuit court, a general district court, and a juvenile and domestic relations district court. Circuit court judges are elected by the legislature for eight-year terms. General district courts hear all misdemeanors, including civil cases involving $1,000 or less, and have concurrent jurisdiction with the circuit courts in claims involving $1,000 to $15,000. General district courts also hold preliminary hearings concerning felony cases. Each of the 31 judicial districts has a juvenile and a domestic relations court, with judges elected by the general assembly to six-year terms. Each city or county has at least one local magistrate.

Virginia's state and federal prisons had 30,473 inmates in June 2001, an increase of 2.0% over the previous year. The state's incarceration rate stood at 415 per 100,000 population. According to the FBI Crime Index, the state's crime rate was 3,178.3 per 100,000, including a total of 20,939 violent crimes and 207,506 crimes against property in that year. A capital punishment statute providing for death by electrocution or lethal injection is in effect. Between 1930 and 1997, the state executed 138 persons, 88 of whom were put to death between 1977 and 2003. There were 26 prisoners under sentence of death in 2003.

17ARMED FORCES

In 2002, there were 90,851 active-duty military personnel and 77,119 civilian personnel stationed in Virginia. The Hampton Roads area, one of the nation's major concentrations of military facilities, includes Langley Air Force Base in Hampton, the Norfolk naval air station and shipyard, the naval air station at Virginia Beach, the Marine Corps air facility and command and staff college at Quantico, and Forts Eustis, Belvoir, and Lee. Norfolk is the home base of the Atlantic Fleet, and several major army and air commands are in Virginia. Virginia's major defense establishments also include an army base at Arlington. In 2002, Virginia firms received more than $18.4 billion in defense contracts.

According to the 2000 Census, there were 786,359 veterans of US military service living in Virginia. Of these, 103, 986 saw service in World War II; 71,521 during the Korean conflict; 226,908 during the Vietnam era; and 159,915 during 1990–2000 (including the Persian Gulf War). Veterans' benefits allocated to Virginia totaled about $1.3 billion in 2002.

In 2000, the Virginia State Police employed 1,883 full-time sworn officers.

18MIGRATION

Virginia's earliest European immigrants were English—only a few hundred at first, but 4,000 between 1619 and 1624, of whom fewer than 1,200 survived epidemics and Indian attacks. Despite such setbacks, Virginia's population increased, mostly by means of immigration, from about 5,000 in 1634 to more than 15,000 in 1642, including 300 blacks. Within 30 years, the population had risen to more than 40,000, including 2,000 blacks. In the late 17th and early 18th centuries, immigrants came not only from England but also from Scotland, Wales, Ireland, Germany, France, the Netherlands, and Poland. In 1701, about 500 French Huguenots fled Catholic France to settle near the present site of Richmond, and beginning in 1714, many Germans and Scotch-Irish moved from Pennsylvania into the Valley of Virginia.

By the early 19th century, Virginians were moving westward into Kentucky, Ohio, and other states; the 1850 census showed that 388,000 former Virginians (not including the many thousands of slaves sold to other states) were living elsewhere. Some of those who left—Henry Clay, Sam Houston, Stephen Austin—were among the most able men of their time. The Civil War era saw the movement of thousands of blacks to northern states, a trend that accelerated after Reconstruction and again after World War I. Since 1900, the dominant migratory trend has been intra-state, from farm to city. Urbanization has been most noticeable since World War II in the Richmond and Hampton Roads areas. At the same time, the movement of middle-income Virginians to the suburbs and increasing concentrations of blacks in the central cities have been evident in Virginia as in other states. During the 1980s, the urban population grew from 66% to 69.4% of the total population; during the 1990s it reached 77.9%.

Between 1940 and 1970, Virginia enjoyed a net gain from migration of 325,000. In the 1970s, the net gain was 239,000, and during 1985–90, 377,000 (4th highest among the states for that period). Between 1990 and 1998, Virginia had net gains of 68,000 in domestic migration and 131,000 in international migration. In 1996, 372,000, or about 6%, of the state's population was foreign-born. In 1998, 15,686 foreign immigrants arrived in Virginia, the 9th-highest total of any state. Of that total, 1,509 came from El Salvador, 921 from the Philippines, and 910 from India. Between 1990 and 1998, Virginia's overall population increased 9.7%. In the period 1995–2000, 821,738 people moved into the state and 746,008 moved out, for a net gain of 75,730. Most new residents were from Maryland.

19INTERGOVERNMENTAL COOPERATION

Regional bodies in which Virginia participates include the Atlantic States Marine Fisheries Commission, Ohio River Valley Water Sanitation Commission, Southern Growth Policies Board, Southern States Energy Board, Southeastern Forest Fire Protection Compact, Ohio River Basin Commission, Mid-Atlantic Fishery Management Council, Southern Regional Education Board, Appalachian Regional Commission, Potomac River Fisheries Commission (with Maryland) and Washington Metropolitan Area Transit Authority. The Delmarva Advisory Council, representing Delaware, Maryland, and Virginia, works with local organizations on the Delmarva Peninsula to develop and implement economic improvement programs. The state also has a number of border compacts, including ones with Maryland, West Virginia, District of Columbia, Kentucky, Maryland, North Carolina, and Tennessee. In 2001, Virginia received federal grants exceeding $5.9 billion.

20ECONOMY

Early settlements in Virginia depended on subsistence farming of native crops such as corn and potatoes. Tobacco, the leading export crop during the colonial era, was joined by cotton during the early statehood period. Although cotton was never "king" in Virginia, as it was in many other southern states, the sale of slaves to Deep South plantations was an important source of income for Virginians, especially during the 1830s, when some 118,000 slaves were exported for profit. Eventually, a diversified agriculture developed in the piedmont and the Shenandoah Valley. Manufacturing became significant during the 19th century, with a proliferation of cotton mills, tobacco-processing plants, ironworks, paper mills, and shipyards.

Services, trade, and government are important economic sectors today. Because of Virginia's extensive military installations and the large number of Virginia residents working for the federal government in the Washington, DC, metropolitan area, the federal government plays a larger role in the Virginia economy than in any other state except Hawaii. The industries that experienced the most growth in the 1990s were printing, transportation equipment, and electronic and other electrical equipment. Between 1992 and 2000, job growth in Virginia averaged 2.7% a year, and in northern Virginia, the rate was 4% a year. The state economy as a whole grew briskly, averaging 7.13% a year 1998 to 2000. However, the high concentration of high-technology industry in Virginia, with the two largest high-tech fields being computer and data processing services and electronic equipment, meant that the collapse of the dot.com bubble in the national recession of 2001 would have negative impacts even despite counter-cyclical increases in government spending. The growth rate moderated to 4.7%in 2001, employment contracted., and for 2000/01 tax revenue growth fell by more than half. By November 2002 employment was still 1.5% below the peak reached in March 2001. Tax revenues in 2001/02 declined 4%, facing the state with a billion dollar deficit after successive years of budget surpluses.

In 2001, Virginia's gross state product gross state product was $273.1 billion, the 13th largest among the states, to which general services contributed $64.5 billion; financial services, $51.8 billion; government, $48.3 billion; trade, $37.3 billion; manufacturing, $31.6 billion; transportation and public utilities, $22.6 billion, and construction, $13.3 billion. The public sector in 2001 constituted 17.7% of gross state product, the 4th highest among the states, which averaged 12%.

21INCOME

According to the Bureau of Economic Analysis, in 2001, Virginia had a per capita personal income (PCPI) of $32,338 which ranked 12th in the United States (including the District of Columbia) and was 106% of the national average, $30,413. The 2001 PCPI reflected an increase of 3.6% from 2000 compared to the national change of 2.2%. In 2001, Virginia had a total personal income (TPI) of $232,730,432,000 which ranked 12th in the United States and accounted for 2.7% of the national total. The 2001 TPI reflected an increase of 4.9% from 2000 compared to the national change of 3.3%.

Earnings of persons employed in Virginia increased from $161,906,976,000 in 2000 to $169,233,172,000 in 2001, an increase of 4.5%. The largest industries in 2001 were services, 32.2% of earnings; state and local government, 10.8%; and retail trade, 8.0%. Of the industries that accounted for at least 5% of earnings in 2001, the slowest growing from 2000 to 2001 was transportation and public utilities (6.6% of earnings in 2001), which decreased 1.0%; the fastest was finance, insurance, and real estate (7.5% of earnings in 2001), which increased 9.9%.

According to data released by the US Census Bureau, in 2000, the median household income was $50,069 compared to the national average of $42,148. In 2001, the median income for a family of four was $69,616 compared to the national average of $63,278. For the period 1999 to 2001, the average poverty rate was 8.0% which placed it 10th among the 50 states and the District of Columbia ranked lowest to highest.

22LABOR

According to Bureau of Labor Statistics (BLS) provisional estimates, in July 2003 the seasonally adjusted civilian labor force in Virginia numbered 3,806,200, with approximately 151,600 workers unemployed, yielding an unemployment rate of 4.0%, compared to the national average of 6.2% for the same period. Since the beginning of the BLS data series in 1978, the highest unemployment rate recorded was 8.0% in March 1982. The historical low was 2.1% in July 2000. In 2001, an estimated 6.5% of the labor force was employed in construction; 11.3% in manufacturing; 5.4% in transportation, communications, and public utilities; 17.8% in trade; 6.7% in finance, insurance, and real estate; 27.2% in services; 18.6% in government; and 1.8% in agriculture.

Although the state has no equal-employment statute, an equal-pay law does prohibit employers from wage discrimination on the basis of sex, and the Virginia Employment Contracting Act established as state policy the elimination of racial, religious, ethnic, and sexual bias in the employment practices of government agencies and contractors. The labor movement has grown slowly, partly because of past practices of racial segregation that prevented workers from acting in concert.

The US Department of Labor reported that in 2002, 189,000 of Virginia's 3,208,000 employed wage and salary workers were members of unions. This represented 5.9% of those so employed, up from 5.0% in 2001, but down from 6.8% in 1998. The national average is 13.2%. In all, 249,000 workers (7.8%) were represented by unions. In addition to union members, this category includes workers who report no union affiliation but whose jobs are covered by a union contract. Virginia is one of 22 states with a right-to-work law.

23AGRICULTURE

Virginia ranked 30th among the 50 states in 2002 with farm marketings of more than $2.4 billion. The commonwealth is an important producer of tobacco, soybeans, peanuts, cotton, tomatoes, potatoes, and peaches. There were an estimated 49,000 farms in 2002, covering 8.7 million acres (3.5 million hectares).

The Tidewater is an important farming region, as it has been since the early 17th century. Crops grown include corn, wheat, tobacco, cotton, peanuts and truck crops. Truck crops and soybeans are cultivated on the Eastern Shore. The piedmont is known for its apples and other fruits, while the Shenandoah Valley is one of the nation's main apple growing regions. In 2002, Virginia ranked 4th among states in tobacco, 7th in peanuts, and 6th in apples. The following table shows data for leading crops in 2002:

	ACRES (1,000s)	PRODUCTION	VALUE ($)
Tobacco	29,570	66,180,000 lb	—
Hay	1,370,000	2,050,000,000 tons	197,300,000
Soybeans	440,000	10,120,000 bushels	55,154,000
Corn for grain	305,000	20,130,000 bushels	55,358,000
Peanuts	57,000	119,700,000 lb	23,701,000[/
Wheat	230,000	10,710,000 bushels	29,988,000
Apples	—	250,000,000 lb	30,250,000
Tomatoes	3,800	1,520,000 hundredweight	41,040,000
Barley	65,000	3,080,000 bushels	4,312,000
Potatoes	6,300	220,000 hundredweight	304,920,000
Peaches	—	7,000,000 lb	2,800,000
Sweet potatoes	500	105,000 hundredweight	1,680,000
Cotton	98,000	99,000 (480lb bales)	19,388,000

24ANIMAL HUSBANDRY

In 2003, Virginia farms and ranches had 1.6 million cattle and calves, valued at $1.01 billion. During 2002, the state had around 400,000 hogs and pigs, valued at $23.6 million. The state produced 4.2 million lb (1.9 million kg) of sheep and lambs in 2001, and an estimated 255,000 lb of shorn wool in 2002.

Dairy farmers produced 1.88 billion lb (0.85 billion kg) of milk from 118,000 milk cows in 2001. That same year, poultry farmers produced 766 million eggs, worth around $61.3 million; 530 million lb (240 million kg) of turkey, worth almost $206.9 million; over 1.3 billion lb (603 million kg) of broilers, valued at $518.8 million; and 20 million lb (9 million kg) of chicken sold for over $1.5 million.

25FISHING

The relative importance of Chesapeake Bay and Atlantic fisheries to Virginia's economy has lessened considerably in recent decades, although the state continues to place high in national rankings. In 1998, Virginia's commercial fish landings totaled 591.9 million lb (3rd in the US), worth $112.7 million (7th). Landings at the Reedville port in 1998 totaled 509 million lb, valued at $42.6 million. The bulk of the catch consists of shellfish such as crabs, scallops, and clams, and finfish such as flounder and menhaden. The blue crab catch totaled 33 million tons in 1998, or 15% of the US total. Both saltwater and freshwater fish are avidly sought by sport fishermen. A threat to Virginia fisheries has been the chemical and oil pollution of the Chesapeake Bay and its tributaries. In 1998, the state issued 632,179 fishing licenses.

26FORESTRY

As of 2002, Virginia had 16,074,000 acres (6,505,000 hectares) of forestland, representing more than 63% of the state's land area and 2.1% of all US forests. Virtually every county has some commercial forestland and supports a wood products industry. In 2002, 1,502 million board feet of lumber were produced. Reforestation programs initiated by the Division of Forestry in 1971 have paid landowners to plant pine seedlings, and state-funded tree nurseries produce 60–70 million seedlings annually. The Division of Forestry's tree seed orchards have developed improved strains of loblolly, shortleaf, white, and Virginia pine for planting in cutover timberland. For recreational purposes, there were 2.59 million acres (1.05 million hectares) of forested public lands in 2002, including Shenandoah National Park, Washington and Jefferson National Forests, 24 state parks, and eight state forests.

27MINING

Virginia is one of the nation's most diverse producers of industrial minerals. In 2001, the state ranked 21st nationally in total nonfuel mineral production value. The value of nonfuel mineral production in Virginia in 2001 was about $751 million, a 9.2% increase from 2000. According to preliminary figures, in 2001, the combined output of crushed stone, construction sand and gravel, and lime accounted for 88% of the total value, and crushed stone alone (the state's leading mineral commodity) accounted for more than 60%. Virginia ranked 2nd in the nation in production of crude vermiculite, feldspar, titanium and zirconium; 9th in crushed stone; and 10th in lime. Virginia was also one of the top six states producing fuller's earth.

28ENERGY AND POWER

Virginia's installed electric utility net generating capacity (utility and nonutility) was approximately 18.8 million kW in 1999; total production of electricity totaled 74.1 billion kWh, almost all of it provided by private utilities. Electric power is supplied to the eastern, northeastern, and central parts of the state chiefly by Virginia Power; to the central and southwestern regions by American Electric Power; to the far southwest by Old Dominion Power; to the northwest by Potomac Edison; and to the Eastern Shore by Delmarva Power and Light. Sales of electric power in 1998 amounted to 89.9 billion kWh: 38% residential, 22% industrial, 29% commercial, and 11% other. In 2001 Virginia had four nuclear reactors in operation, two at the North Anna plant in Louisa County and two at the Surry plant, in the county of the same name.

Virginia has one major oil refinery at Yorktown that uses imported petroleum. The state is supplied with natural gas by three major interstate pipeline companies. Liquefied natural gas plants operate in Chesapeake, Roanoke, and Lynchburg, and a synthetic gas plant is in service at Chesapeake. There is one underground natural gas storage facility in Scott and Washington Counties, and a second was under development during 1997 in Saltville.

Coal-fired steam units accounted for 48% of electric power production in 1999. Oil-fired plants produced less than 5%, nuclear 38%, gas 6%, and other sources about 3%. The state has two nuclear power reactors, both owned by Virginia Power. Virginia's 173 coal mines (127 underground), all in the Appalachian Mountains area, produced 32.8 million tons in 2000. All the coal was bituminous.

Virginia's 3,521 gas wells produced 71.5 billion cu ft (2.02 billion cu m) of natural gas in 2001. The state produced 60 barrels per day of oil in 2002 (last among the 50 states).

29INDUSTRY

Beginning with the establishment of a glass factory at Jamestown in 1608, manufacturing grew slowly during the colonial era to include flour mills and, by 1715, an iron foundry. During the 19th century, the shipbuilding industry flourished, and many cotton mills, tanneries, and ironworks were built; light industries producing a wide variety of consumer goods developed later. The strength of the Commonwealth's diversified manufacturing sector is shown in its 10.2% employment increase between 1970 and 1993. During this time period, national manufacturing employment declined by 8.3%.

Richmond is a principal industrial area for tobacco processing, paper and printing, clothing, and food products; nearby Hopewell is a locus of the chemical industry. Newport News, Hampton, and Norfolk are centers for shipbuilding and the manufacture of other transportation equipment. In the western part of the state, Lynchburg is a center for electrical machinery, metals, clothing, and printing, and Roanoke for food, clothing, and textiles. In the south, Martinsville has a concentration of furniture and textile-manufacturing plants, and textiles are also dominant in Danville.

The total value of manufacturing shipments in 1997 totaled $87 billion, or 15th in the nation. In 1997, Virginia was the headquarters for 16 Fortune 500 companies.

Earnings of persons employed in Virginia increased from $129 billion in 1997 to $138.3 billion in 1998, an increase of 7.2%. The largest industries in 1998 were services, 29.6% of earnings; state and local government, 10.5%; and retail trade, 8.7%. Of the industries that accounted for at least 5% of earnings in 1998, the slowest growing from 1997 to 1998 was federal civilian government (7.0% of earnings in 1998), which increased 0.4%; the fastest was finance, insurance, and real estate (7.0% of earnings in 1998), which increased 9.9%.

30COMMERCE

Virginia's wholesale trade in 1997 totaled $65 billion, conducted by 9,697 establishments. Retail sales in 1997 amounted to $65 billion. The leading retail sales categories among establishments were food stores, 13%; automotive dealers 13%; and eating and drinking places, 26%. Virginia, a major container shipping center, handled import and export cargo worth nearly $23 billion combined in 1995, almost all through the Hampton Roads estuary. Coal is the leading exported commodity and residual fuel oil the principal import. Exports of goods originating within Virginia totaled $12.5 billion in 1998.

31CONSUMER PROTECTION

The Department of Agriculture and Consumer Services, Division of Consumer Protection, regulates food processors and handlers, product labeling, the use of pesticides, and product safety, and is also responsible for enforcement of consumer protection laws. The Office of the Attorney General is responsible for representing citizens in a variety of consumer protection issues.

32BANKING

In 2002, Virginia's 116 insured banks reported combined assets of $29 billion. Eighty-five of those institutions were state-chartered. As of the end of 1995, the Resolution Trust Corporation had resolved 18 institutions with combined assets of $11.5 billion at a resolution cost of $2.3 billion.

Net income for Virginia's banks rose 32% from 2001 to 2002, compared with 11% growth from 2000 to 2001. A series of deep cuts in interest rates on the part of the Federal Reserve during 2001–03 served to compress net interest margins (NIMs) (the difference between the lower rates offered to savers and the higher rates charged on loans). Loan growth was brisk at Virginia's smaller community banks (those with assets under $1 billion), especially in high-risk areas, such as commercial real estate (CRE) loans.

33INSURANCE

Virginians held 4.5 million ordinary life insurance policies worth $268.9 billion in 2001; total value for all categories of life insurance (ordinary, group, industrial, and credit) was $487.63 billion. Death benefits paid that year totaled $1.3 billion. As of 2000, there were 18 property and casualty and 15 life and health insurance companies incorporated or organized in the state. In 2001, property and casualty insurers wrote $7.5 billion in premiums. That year, there were 77,371 flood insurance policies in force in the state, with a total value of $10.9 million.

34SECURITIES

There are no securities exchanges in Virginia. Approximately 999 broker-dealer organizations conduct securities transactions in the Commonwealth through 8,995 employees. Investment advice on securities is provided by 275 registered advisors. The state headquarters 123 NASDAQ companies, nine NASDAQ market makers, 13 AMEX companies; and has incorporated 32 NYSE companies, including Phillip Morris Co., Circuit City, and CSX.

35PUBLIC FINANCE

Virginia's resources are divided equally into two portions: the general fund (which comes from general state taxes), and the non-general fund (which is used for set purposes). Total general funds for 2002 were forecast at over $12 billion, 64% from individual income taxes, 20% from sales taxes, and 4% from corporate taxes. Growth in receipts from each area was expected to average 10% annually between 1999 and 2002, except for corporate taxes, which were expected to decline. Non-general fund revenue was expected to total $11 billion in 2002, primarily from federal grants and contracts (40%), and institutional revenue (23%). The governor's 2000–02 budget emphasized a property tax phase-out, including others; it encouraged tourism attraction and economic development, technological expansion, educational funding, health care improvements, and transportation and environment stewardship. The following table from the US Census Bureau contains information on revenues, expenditures, indebtedness, and cash/securities for 2001.

	($000)	PERCENT	PER CAPITA
Population (thousands, 2001)	7,197	(X)	(X)
Total Revenue	22,760,130	100.00	3,162.45
General revenue	24,193,607	106.30	3,361.62
Liquor store revenue	319,363	1.40	44.37
Insurance trust revenue	−1,752,840	−7.70	−243.55
Exhibit: Salaries and wages	4,508,433	16.83	626.43
Total expenditure	26,786,593	100.00	3,721.91
General expenditure	24,869,440	92.84	3,455.53
Education	9,385,965	35.04	1,304.15
Public welfare	4,401,313	16.43	611.55
Hospitals	1,667,367	6.22	231.68
Health	706,790	2.64	98.21
Highways	2,616,685	9.77	363.58
Police protection	544,706	2.03	75.69
Correction	1,247,296	4.66	173.31
Natural resources	216,844	0.81	30.13
Parks and recreation	120,544	0.45	16.75
Government administration	1,061,261	3.96	147.46
Interest on general debt	848,467	3.17	117.89
Other and unallocable	2,052,202	7.66	285.15
Utility expenditure	25,743	0.10	3.58
Liquor store expenditure	288,119	1.08	40.03
Insurance trust expenditure	1,603,291	5.99	222.77
Debt at end of fiscal year	12,963,092	100.00	1,801.18
Cash and security holdings	55,169,437	100.00	7,665.62

36 TAXATION

The personal income tax schedule has four brackets ranging from 2% to 5.75% (on amounts over $17,000). The corporate income tax rate is a flat 6%. The state sales and use tax rate is 3.5%, but there is also a statewide local sales tax of 1%. Food is taxed at 3.5% as of 1 April 2003. There are many pages of exemptions from the general tax, and most services are not covered. The state imposes excise taxes covering motor fuels, tobacco products, insurance premiums, public utilities, alcoholic beverages, amusements, and other selected items. Virginia's two and a half cent tax on cigarettes is the lowest in the country. Virginia's estate tax accounted for 1% of state collections in 2002. Other state taxes include various license fees, stamp taxes, state property taxes, and severance taxes (total collection of $1,644 in 2002). Most property taxes are collected locally. In all, local governments and taxing units collect 40% of Virginia's total state and local revenue.

The state collected $12.781 billion in taxes in 2002, of which 52.5% came from individual income taxes, 21.9% from the general sales tax, 15.5% from selective sales taxes, 4.2% from state license fees, and 2.4% from corporate income taxes. In 2003, Virginia ranked 40th among the states in terms of combined state and local tax burden, which amounted to about 8.9% of income

The following table from the US Census Bureau provides a summary of taxes collected by the state in 2002.

	($000)	PER CAPITA
Total Taxes	12,781,149	1,752.39
Property taxes	20,557	2.82
Sales and gross receipts	4,782,295	655.69
General sales and gross receipts	2,799,526	383.84
Selective sales taxes	1,982,769	271.85
Alcoholic beverage	132,878	18.22
Amusements	54	0.01
Insurance Premiums	292,702	40.13
Motor fuels	848,528	116.34
Pari-mutuels	(X)	(X)
Public utilities	86,518	11.86
Tobacco products	15,125	2.07
Other selective sales	606,964	83.22
Licenses	542,724	74.41
Alcoholic beverages	7,288	1
Amusements	58	0.01
Corporation	30,293	4.15
Hunting and fishing	19,802	2.72
Motor vehicle	313,416	42.97
Motor vehicle operators	29,738	4.08
Public utility	(X)	(X)
Occupation and business, NEC	137,252	18.82
Other	4,877	0.67
Other taxes	7,435,573	1,019.47
Individual income	6,710,771	920.1
Corporation net income	308,554	42.31
Death and gift	133,660	18.33
Documentary and stock transfer	213,177	29.23
Severance	1,644	0.23
Other	67,767	9.29

37 ECONOMIC POLICY

The state government actively promotes a pro-business climate. Conservative traditions, low tax rates, low wage rates, a weak labor movement, and excellent access to eastern and overseas markets are the general incentives for companies to relocate into Virginia. Five duty-free foreign trade zones have been established in Virginia.

The Virginia Economic Development Corp. (VEDCORP), a privately financed and privately capitalized lending facility operating under special charter from the general assembly, extends low-interest loans to creditworthy companies to purchase land, buildings, and machinery if conventional financing is not available. The state also issues revenue bonds to finance industrial projects—a popular method of financing because the return to investors is tax-free. The bonds are issued for small as well as large companies and may be used to finance the installation of pollution control equipment. Localities allow total or partial tax exemptions for such equipment and for certified solar energy devices. The Virginia Small Business Financing Authority's loan guarantee program helps small companies obtain working capital by guaranteeing up to $150,000 of a bank loan.

Counties, cities, and incorporated towns may form local industrial development authorities to finance industrial projects and various other facilities, and may issue their own revenue bonds to cover the cost of land, buildings, machinery, and equipment. The authority's lease of the property normally includes an option to buy at a nominal price on the expiration of the lease. In addition, some 110 local development corporations have been organized. The Virginia Department of Housing and Community Development offers grants for projects which will generate employment in economically depressed areas, and the Virginia Coalfield Economic Development Authority extends loans to new or growing companies in southwestern Virginia. For minority-owned entrepreneurships, Virginia maintains the Office of Minority Business Enterprises to give advice on special problems. In 2003, the Governor announced new jobs and investments for Halifax County, and launched a Virginia Motorsports initiative. With Delaware, Maryland and Washington DC, Virginia has been recognized as part of an international life sciences hub, dubbed the BioCapital hub. In 2003, Virginia companies and agencies participated in bioscience "hotbed" campaigns, concerted efforts by groups made up of government development agencies, pharmaceutical and bioscience companies, research institutes, universities, and non-profits to attract capital, personnel and resources to develop a life sciences cluster.

38 HEALTH

Virginia's infant mortality rate in 2000 was 6.9 deaths per 1,000 live births, equal to the national rate. A total of 27,354 legal abortions were performed in 1999, or 17 per 1,000 women. In 2000, Virginia's death rate of 807.4 per 100,000 population was below the US average of 873.1. Mortality rates for the leading causes of death in 2000—heart disease, cancer, and stroke—were likewise below the national norms. Those rates (per 100,000 population in 2000) were as follows: diseases of the heart, 219.0; cancer, 194.1 and stroke, 58.9. The rate of HIV-related deaths stood at 4.1 per 100,000 inhabitants, lower than the national average of 5.3 in 2000. In the same year, 21.5% of persons 18 years of age and older were smokers. In Virginia 14,018 AIDS cases had been reported in the state through 2001.

Virginia's 87 community hospitals had 743,992 admissions and 16,775 beds in 2001. There were 21,524 full-time registered nurses and 3,120 full-time licensed practical nurses in 2001 and 272 physicians per 100,000 population in 2000. The average expense of a community hospital for care was $1,107.60 per inpatient day in 2001.

Federal government grants to cover the Medicare and Medicaid services in 2001 totaled $1.8 billion; 909,536 enrollees received Medicare benefits that year. At least 10.9% of Virginia's residents were uninsured in 2002.

39 SOCIAL WELFARE

In 2001, the average weekly unemployment benefit was $226.55. Average monthly participation in the food stamp program in FY2002 comprised 352,172 persons (157,703 households). The average monthly benefit was $71.86, and the sum total of benefits paid in FY2002 was $303,674,409.

With the enactment of the Personal Responsibility and Work Opportunity Reconciliation Act of 1996, the US government has changed the form and regulations for many of its social welfare programs. Most significantly, it replaces Aid to Families with Dependent Children (AFDC), an open-ended entitlement program, with Temporary Assistance for Needy Families (TANF), a limited system of assistance funded largely through federal block grants. The reform act also impacts the food stamp program, the Supplemental Security Income program, and the child nutrition program. The law took effect on 1 July 1997 and provided $16.38 billion in block grants for fiscal years 1997–2002. The grants are to be divided among the states based on an equation involving the numbers of former AFDC recipients in each state.

Reauthorization of the 1996 social welfare legislation, scheduled for 2002, was delayed, and the original law had been extended three times as of July 2003, with the most recent extension running through September 2003. Virginia's TANF program is called VIEW (Virginia Initiative for Employment, Not Welfare). In June 2000 the state had 67,388 welfare recipients. State expenditures on the TANF program in FY2002 totaled $124,058,733.

In December 2001, Social Security benefits were paid to 1,053,340 Virginians. This number included 651,010 retired workers, 115,420 widows and widowers, 133,540 disabled workers, 62,120 spouses, and 91,250 children. Social Security beneficiaries represented 14.7% of the total state population and 91.2% of the state's population age 65 and older. Retired workers (excluding persons with special benefits) received an average monthly payment of $852; widows and widowers, $782; disabled workers, $816; and spouses, $340. Payments for children of retired workers averaged $435 per month; children of deceased workers, $591; and children of disabled workers, $244.

Federal Supplemental Security Income payments in December 2001 went to 132,808 Virginia residents, averaging $344 a month.

40HOUSING

In 2002, Virginia had an estimated 3,006,877 housing units, 2,773,044 of them occupied; 67.8% were owner-occupied. About 60.7% of all units were single-family, detached homes. Electricity and utility gas were the most common energy sources for heating. It was estimated that 82,296 units lacked telephone service, 19,276 lacked complete plumbing facilities, and 11,128 lacked complete kitchen facilities. The average household size was 2.55 people.

In 2002, 59,445 new privately owned housing units were authorized for construction. The median home value was $145,437. The median monthly cost for mortgage owners was $1,228. Renters paid a median of $707 per month. During 2002, Virginia received more than $181 million in community planning and development aid from the US Department of Housing and Urban Development.

41EDUCATION

Although Virginia was the first English colony to found a free school (1634), the state's public school system developed very slowly. Thomas Jefferson proposed a system of free public schools as early as 1779, but it was not until 1851 that such a system was established—for whites only. Free schools for blacks were founded after the Civil War, but they were poorly funded. Opposition by white Virginians to the US Supreme Court's desegregation order in 1954 was marked in certain communities by public school closings and the establishment of all-white private schools. In Prince Edward County, the most extreme case, the school board abandoned public education and left black children without schools from 1959 to 1963. By the 1970s, however, school integration was an accomplished fact throughout the commonwealth.

Under a Literacy Passport program adopted in 1990, students must pass writing tests in reading, writing, and math in order to enter high school. In 2000, 81.5% of all state residents 25 years of age or older were high school graduates, and 29.5% had four or more years of college.

The total enrollment for fall 1999 in Virginia's public schools stood at 1,133,994. Of these, 817,143 attended schools from kindergarten through grade eight, and 316,851 attended high school. Minority students made up approximately 37% of the total enrollment in public elementary and secondary schools in 2001. Total enrollment was estimated at 1,144,054 in fall 2000 and is expected to reach 1,162,000 by fall 2005. Expenditures for public education in 2000/01 were estimated at $7,721,950. Enrollment in nonpublic schools in fall 2001 was 100,171.

As of fall 2000, there were 450,800 students enrolled in college or graduate school. In the same year Virginia had 96 degree-granting institutions. Virginia has had a distinguished record in higher education since the College of William and Mary was founded at Williamsburg (then called Middle Plantation) in 1693, especially after Thomas Jefferson established the University of Virginia at Charlottesville in 1819. There are 74 colleges and universities in the state, almost three-fifths of them full-time, and 24 community colleges. In addition to the University of Virginia and the College of William and Mary, public state-supported institutions include Virginia Polytechnic Institute and State University, Blacksburg; Virginia Commonwealth University, Richmond; Virginia Military Institute, Lexington; Old Dominion University, Norfolk; and George Mason University, Fairfax. Well-known private institutions include the Hampton Institute, Hampton; Randolph-Macon College, Ashland; University of Richmond; Sweet Briar College, Sweet Briar; and Washington and Lee University, Lexington. In 1997, minority students comprised 25.6% of total postsecondary enrollment. Tuition assistance grants and scholarships are provided through the State Council of Higher Education, while the Virginia Student Assistance Authority provides guaranteed student loans.

42ARTS

Richmond, Norfolk, and the northern Virginia metropolitan area are the principal centers for the creative and the performing arts in Virginia, although the arts flourish throughout the state. Richmond's Landmark Theatre (formerly known as The Mosque) has been the scene of concerts by internationally famous orchestras and soloists for generations. Theatre Virginia, located at the Virginia Museum of Fine Arts, presents new plays and classics with professional casts. The Barksdale Theatre and its repertory company present serious plays and occasionally give premiere performances of new works.

In Norfolk, the performing arts are strikingly housed in Scope, a large auditorium designed by Pier Luigi Nervi; Chrysler Hall, an elegant structure with gleaming crystal; and the Wells Theatre, an ornate building that has hosted such diverse performers as John Philip Sousa, Will Rogers, and Fred Astaire. The internationally recognized Virginia Opera Association is housed in the recently constructed Harrison Opera House.

Wolf Trap Foundation for the Performing Arts, in northern Virginia, provides theatrical, operatic, and musical performances featuring internationally celebrated performers. The John F. Kennedy Center for the Performing Arts in nearby Washington, D.C., is heavily patronized by Virginians. The College of William and Mary's Phi Beta Kappa Hall in Williamsburg is the site of the Virginia Shakespeare Festival, an annual summer event inaugurated in 1979. Abingdon is the home of the Barter Theatre, the first state-supported theatre in the United States, whose alumni include Ernest Borgnine and Gregory Peck. This repertory company has performed widely in the US and at selected sites abroad.

There are orchestras in Alexandria, Arlington, Fairfax, Lynchberg, Petersburg, and Roanoke. Richmond is home to the Richmond Ballet, Richmond Choral Society, Richmond Jazz Society, Richmond Philharmonic, and the Richmond Symphony. The Virginia Symphony, founded in 1920, has been recognized as one of the nation's leading regional symphony orchestras.

The annual Virginia Arts Festival has drawn national attention since its inception in 1997. In 2002, the festival presented 93 performances of music, theater, and dance in 25 days and had an attendance of over 76,000. The annual Shenandoah Valley Music Festival in Orkney Springs features arts and crafts presentations as well as musical performances.

In 2002, George Garrett (poet, novelist, essayist, humorist, critic, and editor) was named Virginia's poet laureate. His works include the nonfiction book Going to See the Elephant: Pieces of a Writing Life, the novel The King of Babylon Shall Not Come Against You, and a trilogy of historical novels, Death of the Fox (1971), The Succession: A Novel of Elizabeth and James (1983), and Entered from the Sun (1990).

In 2003, the Virginia Commission on the Arts and other Virginia arts organizations received grants totaling $1,321,300 from the National Endowment for the Arts. The Virginia Foundation for the Humanities was established in 1974 and has since sponsored over 40,000 humanities programs. In 2000, the National Endowment for the Humanities contributed $2,990,783 for 41 state programs. Arts education programs are offered to over 130,000 of the state's schoolchildren. Virginia has over 500 arts organizations.

43LIBRARIES AND MUSEUMS

A total of 108 county, city, town, and regional library systems served the population of Virginia in 2000; their combined book stock reached 17,006,421 volumes, and their combined circulation was 53,251,000. The Virginia State Library in Richmond and the libraries of the University of Virginia (Charlottesville) and the College of William and Mary (Williamsburg) have the personal papers of such notables as Washington, Jefferson, Madison, Robert E. Lee, William H. McGuffey, and William Faulkner. The University of Virginia also has an impressive collection of medieval illuminated manuscripts, and the library of colonial Williamsburg has extensive microfilms of British records. Total public library income in 2000 was $178,385,000, including $1.1 million in federal grants and nearly $17 million in state grants.

There were 260 museums in 1996–97. In Richmond, the Virginia Museum of Fine Arts, the first state museum of art in the US, has a collection that ranges from ancient Egyptian artifacts to mobile jewelry by Salvador Dali. The Science Museum of Virginia has a 280-seat planetarium that features a simulated excursion to outer space. Other museums in Richmond are Wilton, the Randolphs' handsome 18th-century mansion, and the Maymont and Wickham-Valentine houses, elaborate 19th-century residences; Agecroft Hall and Virginia House, Tudor manor houses that were moved from England, are also open to the public. Norfolk has the Chrysler Museum, with its famous glassware collection; Myers House, an early Federal period home with handsome art and furnishings; and the Hermitage Foundation Museum, noted for its Oriental art. The Mariners Museum in Newport News has a superb maritime collection, and the much smaller but quite select exhibits of the Portsmouth Naval Shipyard Museum are also notable. Perhaps the most extensive "museum" in the US is Williamsburg's mile-long Duke of Gloucester Street, with such remarkable restorations as the Christopher Wren Building of the College of William and Mary, Bruton Parish Church, the Governor's Palace, and the colonial capital.

More historic sites are maintained as museums in Virginia than in any other state. These include Washington's home at Mt. Vernon (Fairfax County), Jefferson's residence at Monticello (Charlottesville), and James River plantation houses such as Berkeley, Shirley, Westover, Sherwood Forest, and Carter's Grove. The National Park Service operates a visitors' center at Jamestown.

44COMMUNICATIONS

The state's communications network has expanded steadily since the first postal routes were established in 1738. Airmail service from Richmond to New York and Atlanta began in 1928.

In 2001, 95.8% of Virginia's occupied housing units had telephones. In 2003, broadcasters operated 24 major AM radio stations and 81 major FM stations. In the same year, Virginia had 26 major television stations. The Norfolk-Portsmouth-Newport News area had 629,100 television households, 76% of which ordered cable.

Approximately 187,445 Internet domain names were registered with the state in the year 2000.

45PRESS

Although the Crown forbade the establishment of a printing press in Virginia Colony, William Parks was publishing the Virginia Gazette at Williamsburg in 1736. Three newspapers were published regularly during the Revolutionary period, and in 1780 the general assembly declared that the press was "indispensable for the right information of the people and for the public service." The oldest continuously published Virginia daily, tracing its origins to 1784, is the Alexandria Gazette. The first Negro newspaper, The True Southerner, was started by a white man in 1865; several weeklies published and edited by blacks began soon after. By 1900 there were 180 newspapers in the state, but the number has declined drastically since then because of fierce competition, mergers, and rising costs.

USA Today, the nation's largest daily newspaper in 2001, is based in Arlington, Virginia. In 2002, the Arlington Journal and the Fairfax Journal merged to form the Northern Virginia Journal. In 2002, Virginia had 22 morning dailies, 4 evening, and 17 Sunday papers. Leading dailies and their approximate circulation rates were:

AREA	NAME	DAILY	SUNDAY
Arlington	USA Today(m)	2,149,933	
Alexandria	Northern Virginia Journal(m,S)	62,910	386,000
Newport News	Daily Press (m,S)	93,693	115,273
Norfolk	Virginian-Pilot (m,S)	195,583	232,721
Richmond	Times–Dispatch (m,S)*	190,509	230,313
Roanoke	Times (m,S)	98,916	113,101

*Absorbed Richmond's News Leader in 1992.

The newspaper group, Gannett Co, Inc, is based in Virginia. This group owns about 96 daily newspapers nationwide, including USA Today, as well as over 300 non-daily papers and shoppers bulletins. Gannett's UK subsidiary, Newsquest PLC, publishes 15 daily newspapers.

46ORGANIZATIONS

In 2003, there were about 2,235 regional, national, and international organizations within the state.

Service and educational groups headquartered in the state include the United Way of America, American Astronautical Society, American Society for Horticultural Science, American Geological Institute, and American Physical Therapy Association, all located in Alexandria; and the National Honor Society, Music Educators National Conference, and National Art Education Association, located in Reston.

Veterans' organizations include the Veterans of World War I of the USA and the Retired Officers Association, Alexandria, and the Military Order of the Purple Heart, Springfield. The United Daughters of the Confederacy has national offices in Richmond. Among the business and professional groups based in Virginia are the American Gas Association, Arlington, and the National Automobile Dealers Association, McLean.

Sports societies headquartered in the state include the American Canoe Association, Lorton; Boat Owners Association of the US, Alexandria; and National Rowing Foundation and the Walking Association, both in Arlington.

Other groups operating out of Virginia include the Future Farmers of America and the National Sojourners, Alexandria; American Automobile Association, Falls Church; Federation of Homemakers and National Alliance of Senior Citizens, Arlington; Association of Former Intelligence Officers, McLean; and the Moral Majority, Lynchburg.

47 TOURISM, TRAVEL, AND RECREATION

In 2001, travelers spent over $12.9 billion in Virginia on daytrips and overnight stays. The tourism and travel industry is the state's 3rd-largest employer, supporting over 211,000 jobs. Attractions in the coastal region alone include the Jamestown and Yorktown historic sites, the Williamsburg restoration, and the homes of George Washington and Robert E. Lee. Also featured are the National Aeronautics and Space Administration's Langley Research Center, Assateague Island National Seashore, and the resort pleasures of Virginia Beach.

The interior offers numerous Civil War Sites, including Appomattox; Thomas Jefferson's Monticello; Booker T. Washington's birthplace near Smith Mountain Lake; and the historic cities of Richmond, Petersburg, and Fredericksburg. In the west, the Blue Ridge Parkway and Shenandoah National Park, traversed by the breathtaking Skyline Drive, are favorite tourist destinations, as are Cumberland Gap and, in the Lexington area, the Natural Bridge, the home of Confederate General Thomas "Stonewall" Jackson, the George C. Marshall Library and Museum, and the Virginia Military Institute. A number of historic sites in Arlington and Alexandria attract many visitors to the Washington, D.C., area.

The state's many recreation areas include state parks, national forests, a major national park, scenic parkways, and thousands of miles of hiking trails and shoreline. Some of the most-visited sites are Mt. Rogers National Recreational Area, Prince William Forest Park, Chincoteague National Wildlife Refuge, and the Kerr Reservoir. Part of the famous Appalachian Trail winds through Virginia's Blue Ridge and Appalachian mountains. The commonwealth has more than 1,500 mi (2,400 km) of well-stocked trout streams.

48 SPORTS

Although Virginia has no major league professional sports teams, it does support two class-AAA baseball teams: the Richmond Braves and Norfolk Tides. Other minor league baseball teams play in Bristol, Danville, Pulaski, Salem, Martinsville, and Woodbridge. There is also minor league hockey in Richmond, Roanoke, and Hampton Roads.

In collegiate sports, the University of Virginia belongs to the Atlantic Coast Conference, and the Virginia Military Institute competes in the Southern Conference. Virginia won college basketball's NIT Tournament in 1980 and 1992; Virginia Tech won the NIT in 1973 and has appeared in ten postseason college football bowl games since 1993.

Stock car racing is also popular in the state. The Richmond International Raceway and Martinsville Speedway host four NASCAR Winston Cup races each year.

Participant sports popular with Virginians include tennis, golf, swimming, skiing, boating, and water skiing. The state has at least 180 public and private golf courses.

Among the many notable persons that call Virginia their home, several are legendary athletes. Arthur Ashe, Fran Tarkenton, and Sam Snead all were born and raised in the state.

49 FAMOUS VIRGINIANS

Virginia is the birthplace of eight US presidents and many famous statesmen, noted scientists, influential educators, distinguished writers, and popular entertainers.

The first president of the US, George Washington (1732–99), also led his country's armies in the Revolutionary War and presided over the convention that framed its Constitution. Washington—who was unanimously elected president in 1789 and served two four-year terms, declining a third—was not, as has sometimes been assumed, a newcomer to politics: his political career began at the age of 27 with his election to the house of burgesses.

Thomas Jefferson (1743–1826), the nation's 3rd president, offered this as his epitaph: "author of the Declaration of Independence and the Virginia Statute for Religious Freedom, and father of the University of Virginia." After serving as secretary of state under Washington and vice president under John Adams, he was elected president of the US in 1800 and reelected in 1804. Honored now as a statesman and political thinker, Jefferson was also a musician and one of the foremost architects of his time, and he has been called the first American archaeologist.

Jefferson's successor, James Madison (1751–1836), actually made his most important contributions before becoming chief executive. As a skillful and persistent negotiator throughout the Constitutional Convention of 1787, he earned the designation "father of the Constitution"; then, as coauthor of the Federalist papers, he helped produce a classic of American political philosophy. He was more responsible than any other statesman for Virginia's crucial ratification vote. Secretary of State during Jefferson's two terms, Madison occupied the presidency from 1809 to 1817.

Madison was succeeded as president in 1817 by James Monroe (1758–1831), who was reelected to a second term starting in 1821. Monroe—who had served as governor, US senator, minister to France, and secretary of state—is best known for the Monroe Doctrine, which has been US policy since his administration. William Henry Harrison (1773–1841) became the 9th president in 1841 but died of pneumonia one month after his inauguration; he had been a governor of Indiana Territory, a major general in the War of 1812, and a US representative and senator from Indiana. Harrison was succeeded by Vice President John Tyler (1790–1862), a native and resident of Virginia, who established the precedent that, upon the death of the president, the vice president inherits the title as well as the duties of the office.

Another native of Virginia, Zachary Taylor (1784–1850), renowned chiefly as a military leader, became the 12th US president in 1849 but died midway through his term. The eighth Virginia-born president, (Thomas) Woodrow Wilson (1856–1924), became the 28th president of the US in 1913 after serving as governor of New Jersey.

John Marshall (1755–1835) was the third confirmed chief justice of the US and is generally regarded by historians as the first great American jurist, partly because of his establishment of the principle of judicial review. Five other Virginians—John Blair (1732–1800), Bushrod Washington (1762–1829), Philip P. Barbour (1783–1841), Peter V. Daniel (1784–1860), and Lewis F. Powell, Jr. (1907–98)—have served as associate justices.

George Washington's cabinet included two Virginians, Secretary of State Jefferson and Attorney General Edmund Randolph (1753–1813), who, as governor of Virginia, had introduced the Virginia Plan—drafted by Madison and calling for a House of Representatives elected by the people and a Senate elected by the House—at the Constitutional Convention of 1787. Among other distinguished Virginians who have served in the cabinet are James Barbour (1775–1842), secretary of war; John Y. Mason (1799–1859), secretary of the Navy and attorney general; Carter Glass (1858–1946), secretary of the treasury, author of the Federal Reserve System, and US senator for 26 years; and Claude Augustus Swanson (1862–1939), secretary of the Navy and earlier, state governor and US senator.

Other prominent US senators from Virginia include Richard Henry Lee (1732–94), former president of the Continental Congress; James M. Mason (b.District of Columbia, 1798–1871), who later was commissioner of the Confederacy to the United Kingdom and France; John W. Daniel (1842–1910), a legal scholar and powerful Democratic Party leader; Thomas S. Martin (1847–1919), US Senate majority leader; Harry F. Byrd (1887–1966), governor of Virginia from 1926 to 1930 and US senator from 1933 to 1965; and Harry F. Byrd, Jr. (b.1914), senator from 1965 to 1982. In 1985, Virginia was represented in the senate by Republican John W. Warner (b.District of Columbia, 1927), former secretary of the Navy, and Republican Paul S. Trible, Jr. (b.Maryland, 1946), a US representative from 1976 to 1982.

Some native-born Virginians have become famous as leaders in other nations. Joseph Jenkins Roberts (1809–76) was the first president of the Republic of Liberia, and Nancy Langhorne Astor (1879–1964) was the first woman to serve in the British House of Commons.

Virginia's important colonial governors included Captain John Smith (b.England, 1580?–1631), Sir George Yeardley (b.England, 1587?–1627), Sir William Berkeley (b.England, 1606–77), Alexander Spotswood (b.Tangier, 1676–1740), Sir William Gooch (b.England, 1681–1751), and Robert Dinwiddie (b.Scotland, 1693–1770).

Virginia signers of the Declaration of Independence, besides Jefferson and Richard Henry Lee, were Carter Braxton (1736–97); Benjamin Harrison (1726?–1791), father of President William Henry Harrison; Francis Lightfoot Lee (1734–97); Thomas Nelson, Jr. (1738–89); and George Wythe (1726–1806). Wythe is also famous as the first US law professor and the teacher, in their student days, of Presidents Jefferson, Monroe, and Tyler, and Chief Justice Marshall. Virginia furnished both the first president of the Continental Congress, Peyton Randolph (1721–75), and the last, Cyrus Griffin (1748–1810).

Other notable Virginia governors include Patrick Henry (1736–99), the first governor of the commonwealth, though best remembered as a Revolutionary orator; Westmoreland Davis (1859–1942); Andrew Jackson Montague (1862–1937); and Mills E. Goodwin, Jr. (b.1914). A major historical figure who defies classification is Robert "King" Carter (1663–1732), greatest of the Virginia land barons, who also served as acting governor of Virginia and rector of the College of William and Mary.

Chief among Virginia's great military and naval leaders besides Washington and Taylor are John Paul Jones (b.Scotland, 1747–92); George Rogers Clark (1752–1818); Winfield Scott (1786–1866); Robert E. Lee (1807–70), the Confederate commander who earlier served in the Mexican War and as superintendent of West Point; Joseph E. Johnston (1807–91); George H. Thomas (1816–70); Thomas Jonathan "Stonewall" Jackson (1824–63); James Ewell Brown "Jeb" Stuart (1833–64); and George C. Marshall (b.Pennsylvania, 1880–1959). Virginians' names are also written high in the history of exploration. Daniel Boone (b.Pennsylvania, 1734–1820), who pioneered in Kentucky and Missouri, was once a member of the Virginia general assembly. Meriwether Lewis (1774–1809) and William Clark (1770–1838), both native Virginians, led the most famous expedition in US history, from St. Louis to the Pacific coast (1804–6). Richard E.

Byrd (1888–1957) was both an explorer of Antarctica and a pioneer aviator.

Woodrow Wilson and George C. Marshall both received the Nobel Peace Prize, in 1919 and 1953, respectively. Distinguished Virginia-born scientists and inventors include Matthew Fontaine Maury (1806–73), founder of the science of oceanography; Cyrus H. McCormick (1809–84), who perfected the mechanical reaper; and Dr. Walter Reed (1851–1902) who proved that yellow fever was transmitted by a mosquito. Among educators associated with the state are William H. McGuffey (b.Pennsylvania, 1800–1873), a University of Virginia professor who designed and edited the most famous series of school readers in American history; and Booker T. Washington (1856–1915), the nation's foremost black educator.

William Byrd II (1674–1744) is widely acknowledged to have been the most graceful writer in English America in his day, and Jefferson was a leading prose stylist of the Revolutionary period. Edgar Allen Poe (b.Massachusetts, 1809–49), who was taken to Richmond at the age of three and later educated at the University of Virginia, was the father of the detective story and one of America's great poets and short-story writers. Virginia is the setting of historical romances by three natives: John Esten Cooke (1830–86), Thomas Nelson Page (1853–1922), and Mary Johnston (1870–1936). Notable 20th-century novelists born in Virginia include Willa Cather (1873–1947), Ellen Glasgow (1874–1945), and James Branch Cabell (1879–1958). Willard Huntington Wright (1888–1939), better known as S. S. Van Dine, wrote many detective thrillers. Twice winner of the Pulitzer Prize for biography and often regarded as the greatest American master of that genre was Douglas Southall Freeman (1886–1953). Other important historians were Lyon Gardiner Tyler (1853–1935), son of President Tyler and also an eminent educator; Philip A. Bruce (1856–1933); William Cabell Bruce (1860–1946); Virginius Dabney (1901–95); and Alf J. Mapp, Jr. (b.1925). Some contemporary Virginia authors are television writer-producer Earl Hamner (b.1923); novelist William Styron (b.1925); and journalists Virginia Moore (1903–1993) and Tom Wolfe (Thomas Kennerly Wolfe, Jr., b. 1931).

Celebrated Virginia artists include sculptors Edward V. Valentine (1838–1930) and Moses Ezekiel (1844–1917), and painters George Caleb Bingham (1811–79) and Jerome Myers (1867–1940). A protégé of Jefferson's, Robert Mills (b.South Carolina, 1781–1855), designed the Washington Monument.

The roster of Virginians prominent in the entertainment world includes Bill "Bojangles" Robinson (1878–1949), Francis X. Bushman (1883–1966), Freeman Gosden (1899–1982), Randolph Scott (1903–1987), Joseph Cotten (1905–94), Margaret Sullavan (1911–60), John Payne (1912–1989), George C. Scott (1927–99), Shirley MacLaine (b.1934), and Warren Beatty (b.1938).

Outstanding musical performers include John Powell (1882–1963), whose fame as a pianist once equaled his prominence as a composer. Virginia's most eminent contemporary composer is Thea Musgrave (b.Scotland, 1928). Popular musical stars include Kathryn Elizabeth "Kate" Smith (1907–1986), Pearl Bailey (1918–1990), Ella Fitzgerald (1918–96), June Carter (1929–2003), Roy Clark (b.1933), and Wayne Newton (b.1942).

The Old Dominion's sports champions include golfers Bobby Cruickshank (1896–1975), Sam Snead (1912–2002), and Chandler Harper (b.1914); tennis star Arthur Ashe (1943–1993); football players Clarence "Ace" Parker (b.1912), Bill Dudley (b.1921), and Francis "Fran" Tarkenton (b.1940); and baseball pitcher Eppa Rixey (1891–1963). At age 15, Olympic swimming champion Melissa Belote (b.1957) won three gold medals. Helen Chenery "Penny" Tweedy (b.1922) is a famous breeder and racer of horses from whose stables have come Secretariat and other champions. Equestrienne Jean McLean Davis (b.1929) won 65 world championships.

50 BIBLIOGRAPHY

Adams, Stephen. *The Best and Worst Country in the World: Perspectives on the Early Virginia Landscape.* Charlottesville: University Press of Virginia, 2001.

Ashe, Dora J. (comp.). *Four Hundred Years of Virginia, 1584–1984: An Anthology.* Lanham, Md.: University Press of America, 1985.

Bruce, Philip Alexander. *Economic History of Virginia in the Seventeenth Century.* 2 vols. New York: Johnson Reprints. n.d. (orig. 1896).

———. *Social Life of Virginia in the Seventeenth Century.* Lynchburg, Va.: J. P. Bell, 1927.

Buni, Andrew. *The Negro in Virginia Politics, 1902–65.* Charlottesville: University Press of Virginia. 1967.

Dabney, Virginius. *Richmond: The Story of a City.* Rev. and enl. Charlottesville: University Press of Virginia, 1990.

———. *Virginia: The New Dominion.* Charlottesville: University Press of Virginia, 1983 (orig. 1971).

Davis, Richard Beale. *Intellectual Life in Jefferson's Virginia, 1790–1830.* Knoxville: University of Tennessee Press, 1972.

Diversity and Accommodation: Essays on the Cultural Composition of the Virginia Frontier. Knoxville: University of Tennessee Press, 1997.(orig. 1964).

Federal Writers' Project. *Virginia: A Guide to the Old Dominion.* New York: Somerset, 1980 (orig. 1940).

Friddell, Guy. *What Is It About Virginia?* Richmond: Dietz, 1983 (orig. 1966).

Goodwin, Bill. *Virginia.* London: Frommers/Transworld, 2000.

Malone, Dumas. *Jefferson and His Time.* Vols. 1 and 2. Boston: Little, Brown, 1948, 1951.

Mapp, Alf J., Jr. *Frock Coats and Epaulets: The Men Who Led the Confederacy.* Lanham, Md.: Madison Books, 1996.

———. *The Virginia Experiment: The Old Dominion's Role in the Making of America, 1607–1781.* 3rd ed. Lanham, Md.: Hamilton Press, 1987.

Moger, Allen W. *Virginia: Bourbonism to Byrd, 1870–1925.* Charlottesville: University Press of Virginia, 1968.

Morgan, Edmund S. *American Slavery, American Freedom: The Ordeal of Colonial Virginia.* New York: Norton, 1975.

Morton, Richard L. *Colonial Virginia.* 2 vols. Chapel Hill: University of North Carolina Press, 1960.

Pratt, Robert A. *The Color of Their Skin: Education and Race in Richmond, Virginia, 1954-89.* Charlottesville: University Press of Virginia, 1992.

Ragsdale, Bruce A. *A Planters' Republic: The Search for Economic Independence in Revolutionary Virginia.* Madison, Wis.: Madison House, 1996.

Rubin, Louis D., Jr. *Virginia: A Bicentennial History.* New York: Norton, 1977.

Saffell, William Thomas Roberts. *Records of the Revolutionary War: Containing the Military and Financial Correspondence of Distinguished Officers.* Bowie, Md.: Heritage Books, 1999.

Shade, William G. *Democratizing the Old Dominion: Virginia and the Second Party System, 1824-1861.* Charlottesville: University Press.

Smith, J. Douglas. *Managing White Supremacy: Race, Politics, and Citizenship in Jim Crow Virginia.* Chapel Hill: University of North Carolina Press, 2002.

Stanard, Mary Newton. *The Story of Virginia's First Century.* Philadelphia: Lippincott, 1938.

WASHINGTON

State of Washington

ORIGIN OF STATE NAME: Named for George Washington. **NICKNAME:** The Evergreen State. **CAPITAL:** Olympia. **ENTERED UNION:** 11 November 1889 (42nd). **SONG:** "Washington, My Home." **DANCE:** Square dance. **MOTTO:** Alki (Chinook for *By and by*). **FLAG:** The state seal centered on a dark green field. **OFFICIAL SEAL:** Portrait of George Washington surrounded by the words "The Seal of the State of Washington 1889." **BIRD:** Willow goldfinch. **FISH:** Steelhead trout. **FLOWER:** Coast rhododendron. **TREE:** Western hemlock. **GEM:** Petrified wood. **FRUIT:** Apple. **LEGAL HOLIDAYS:** New Year's Day, 1 January; Birthday of Martin Luther King, Jr., 3rd Monday in January; Presidents' Day, 2nd Monday in February; Memorial Day, last Monday in May; Independence Day, 4 July; Labor Day, 1st Monday in September; Veterans Day and State Admission Day, 11 November; Thanksgiving Day, 4th Thursday in November; Christmas Day, 25 December. **TIME:** 4 AM PST = noon GMT.

¹LOCATION, SIZE, AND EXTENT

Located on the Pacific coast of the northwestern US, Washington ranks 20th in size among the 50 states.

The total area of Washington is 66,582 sq mi (176,477 sq km), of which land takes up 66,511 sq mi (172,263 sq km) and inland water 1,627 sq mi (4,214 sq km). The state extends about 360 mi (580 km) E-W and 240 mi (390 km) N-S.

Washington is bounded on the N by the Canadian province of British Columbia (with the northwestern line passing through the Juan de Fuca Strait and the Haro and Georgia straits); on the E by Idaho (with the line in the southwest passing through the Snake River); on the S by Oregon (with most of the line defined by the Columbia River); and on the W by the Pacific Ocean.

Islands of the San Juan group, lying between the Haro and Rosario straits, include Orcas, San Juan, and Lopez; Whidbey is a large island in the upper Puget Sound. The state's boundary length totals 1,099 mi (1,769 km), including 157 mi (253 km) of general coastline; the tidal shoreline extends 3,026 mi (4,870 km). Washington's geographic center is in Chelan County, 10 mi (16 km) WSW of Wenatchee.

²TOPOGRAPHY

Much of Washington is mountainous. Along the Pacific coast are the Coast Ranges extending northward from Oregon and California. This chain forms two groups: the Olympic Mountains in the northwest, mainly on the Olympic Peninsula between the Pacific Ocean and Puget Sound, and the Willapa Hills in the southwest. The highest of the Olympic group is Mt. Olympus, at 7,965 ft (2,428 m). About 100 mi (160 km) inward from the Pacific coast is the Cascade Range, extending northward from the Sierra Nevada in California. This chain, 50–100 mi (80–100 km) wide, has peaks generally ranging up to 10,000 ft (3,000 m), except for such volcanic cones as Mt. Adams, Mt. Baker, Glacier Peak, Mt. St. Helen's, and Mt. Rainier, which at 14,410 ft (4,395 m) is the highest peak in the state.

Between the Coast and Cascade ranges lies a long, troughlike depression—the Western Corridor—where most of Washington's major cities are concentrated. The northern section of this lowland is carved by Puget Sound, a complex, narrow arm of the Pacific wending southward for about 80 mi (130 km) and covering an area of 561 sq mi (1,453 sq km). Of all the state's other major regions, only south-central Washington, forming part of the Columbia Plateau, is generally flat.

The Cascade volcanoes were dormant, for the most part, during the second half of the 19th century and most of the 20th. Early in 1980, however, Mt. St. Helen's began to show ominous signs of activity. On 18 May, the volcano exploded, blasting more than 1,300 ft (400 m) off a mountain crest that had been 9,677 ft (2,950 m) high. Tremendous plumes of steam and ash were thrust into the stratosphere, where prevailing winds carried volcanic dust thousands of miles eastward. The areas immediately surrounding Mt. St. Helen's were deluged with ash and mudflows, choking local streams and lakes, particularly Spirit Lake. About 150 sq mi (388 sq km) of trees and brush were destroyed; the ash fall also damaged crops in neighboring agricultural areas and made highway travel extremely hazardous. The eruption left 57 people dead or missing. Eruptions of lesser severity followed the main outburst; the mountain continued to pose a serious danger to life in the area as the estimated cost of the damage to property, crops, and livestock approached $3 billion. Another minor eruption, on 14 May 1984, shot ash 4 mi (6 km) high and caused a small mudflow down the mountain's flanks, but no injuries or other damage occurred. East of the Cascade Range, much of Washington is a plateau underlain by ancient basalt lava flows. In the northeast are the Okanogan Highlands; in the southeast, the Blue Mountains and the Palouse Hills. All these uplands form extensions of the Rocky Mountain system.

Among Washington's numerous rivers, the longest and most powerful is the Columbia, entering Washington from Canada in the northeast corner and flowing for more than 1,200 mi (1,900 km) across the heart of the state and then along the Oregon border to the Pacific. In average discharge, the Columbia ranks 2nd only to the Mississippi, with 262,000 cu ft (7,400 cu m) per second. Washington's other major river, the Snake, enters the state from Idaho in the southeast and flows generally westward, meeting the Columbia River near Pasco.

Washington has numerous lakes, of which the largest is the artificial Franklin D. Roosevelt Lake, covering 123 sq mi (319 sq km). Washington has some 90 dams, providing water storage, flood control, and hydroelectric power. One of the largest and most famous dams in the US is Grand Coulee on the upper Columbia River, measuring 550 ft (168 m) high and 4,173 ft

(1,272 m) long, with a storage capacity of more than 9.7 million acre-ft (11,960 cu m).

³CLIMATE

The Cascade Mountains divide Washington not only topographically but also climatically. Despite its northerly location, western Washington is as mild as the middle and southeastern Atlantic coast; it is also one of the rainiest regions in the world. Eastern Washington, on the other hand, has a much more continental climate, characterized by cold winters, hot summers, and sparse rainfall. Since the prevailing winds are from the west, the windward (western) slopes of the state's major mountains intercept most of the atmospheric moisture and precipitate it as rain or snow. Certain coastal areas, receiving more than 200 in (500 cm) of rain a year, support dense stands of timber in a temperate rain forest. But in the dry southeastern quadrant, there are sagebrush deserts.

Average January temperatures in western Washington range from a minimum of 20°F (–7°C) on the western slope of the Cascades to a maximum of 48°F (9°C) along the Pacific coast; July temperatures range from a minimum of 44°F (7°C) on the western slope of the Cascades to a maximum of 80°F (27°C) in the foothills. In the east the temperature ranges are much more extreme: in January, from 8°F (–13°C) in the northeastern Cascades to 40°F (4°C) on the southeastern plateau; in July, from 48°F (9°C) on the eastern slope of the Cascades to 92°F (33°C) in the south-central portion of the state. The normal daily mean temperature in Seattle is 52°F (11°C), ranging from 40°F (4°C) in January to 65°F (18°C) in July; Spokane averages 47°F (8°C), ranging from 27°F (–3°C) in January to 69°F (21°C) in July. The lowest temperature ever recorded in the state is –48°F (–44°C), set at Mazama and Winthrop on 30 December 1968; the highest, at Ice Harbor Dam on 5 August 1961, was 118°F (48°C).

In Seattle average annual precipitation (1971–2000) was 37 in (94 cm), falling most heavily from October through March; in the same period, Spokane received an average of only 16.7 in (42.4 cm) annually, more than half of that from November through February. Snowfall in Seattle averages 11.4 in (29 cm) annually; in Spokane, 49.4 in (125.5 cm). Paradise Ranger Station holds the North American record for the most snowfall in one season, when 1,122 in (2,850 cm) of snow fell during the winter of 1971–72. High mountain peaks, such as Mt. Adams, Mt. Baker, and Mt. Rainier, have permanent snowcaps or snowfields of up to 100 ft (30 m) deep.

⁴FLORA AND FAUNA

More than 1,300 plant species have been identified in Washington. Sand strawberries and beach peas are found among the dunes while fennel and spurry grow in salt marshes; greasewood and sagebrush predominate in the desert regions of the Columbia Plateau. Conifers include Sitka spruce, Douglas fir, western hemlock, and Alaska cedar; big-leaf maple, red alder, black cottonwood, and western yew are among the characteristic deciduous trees. Wild flowers include the deerhead orchid and wake-robin; the western rhododendron is the state flower. In 2003, six plant species were threatened, including golden paintbrush, Nelson's checker-mallow, Kincaid's lupine, Spalding's catchfly, Ute ladies'-tresses, and water howelia. That year, four species were endangered, including Bradshaw's desert-parsley, showy stickseed, Wenatchee Mountains checkermallow, and marsh sandwort.

Forest and mountain regions support Columbia black-tailed and mule deer, elk, and black bear; the Roosevelt elk, named after President Theodore Roosevelt, is indigenous to the Olympic Mountains. Other native mammals are the Canadian lynx, red fox, and red western bobcat. Smaller native mammals—western fisher, raccoon, muskrat, porcupine, marten, and mink—are

plentiful. The whistler (hoary) marmot is the largest rodent. Game birds include the ruffed grouse, bobwhite quail, and ring-necked pheasant. Sixteen varieties of owl have been identified; other birds of prey include the prairie falcon, sparrow hawk, and golden eagle. The bald eagle is more numerous in Washington than in any other state except Alaska. Washington is also a haven for marsh, shore, and water birds. Various salmon species thrive in coastal waters and along the Columbia River, and the octopus, hair seal, and sea lion inhabit Puget Sound.

Animals driven away from the slopes of Mt. St. Helen's by the volcanic eruption in 1980 have largely returned; more than 25 species of mammals and over 100 species of birds have been observed inhabiting the mountain again. The number of elk and deer in the vicinity was roughly the same as prior to the eruption although the mountain goat population reportedly had been killed off. Earlier, on 17 August 1982, the Mt. St. Helen's National Volcanic Monument was created by an act of Congress; it includes about 110,000 acres (44,500 ha) of the area that had been devastated by the original eruption.

In 2003, 30 animal species were listed as threatened or endangered in Washington, including the Columbian white-tailed deer, woodland caribou, short-tailed albatross, brown pelican, pygmy rabbit, humpback whale, nine species of salmon, and two species (green and leatherback) of sea turtle.

⁵ENVIRONMENTAL PROTECTION

The mission of the Department of Ecology (established in 1970) is to protect, preserve, and enhance Washington's environment and promote the wise management of its air, land, and water for the benefit of current and future generations. To fulfill this mission, the Department of Ecology: administers permit and authorization programs which ensure that pollutant discharges, waste management and clean-up, and resource uses are properly controlled; provides technical assistance on pollution control or resource development issues; and provides financial assistance through grant and loan programs to local governments for waste water and solid waste facilities. The Department of Ecology also reviews federal and state actions and plans for consistency with state laws and regulations for natural resource protection, maintains an ongoing program to monitor the quality of air and water resources, hazardous waste management, and toxic and nuclear clean-up actions; and reviews local government-permitting actions relating to the state's shorelands and to solid waste facilities. Furthermore, the Department of Ecology directly administers an automobile inspection program for the Seattle, Vancouver (Washington), and Spokane areas, an Estuarine Sanctuary program at Padilla Bay, the Conservation Corps employment program, and the Youth Corps litter control program.

Among other state agencies with environmental responsibilities are the State Conservation Commission, Environmental Hearings Office, State Parks and Recreation Commission, Department of Health, Department of Fish and Wildlife, and Department of Natural Resources.

Principal air pollutants in the state are particulate emissions, carbon monoxide, hydrocarbons, lead, and dioxides of nitrogen. Fuel combustion and industrial processes are responsible for most of the first two pollutants, transportation (especially the automobile) for most of the last four. Significant progress has been made since 1988 in reducing the amount of pollutants released to the air. In 1988, the total number of days air quality did not meet health standards was 25. In 1994, the total number of days was 15, and by 1999, the total had been reduced to seven days. In 1990, more than two million people were exposed to air that violated federal standards, but by 1999, the number had been reduced to 112,000.

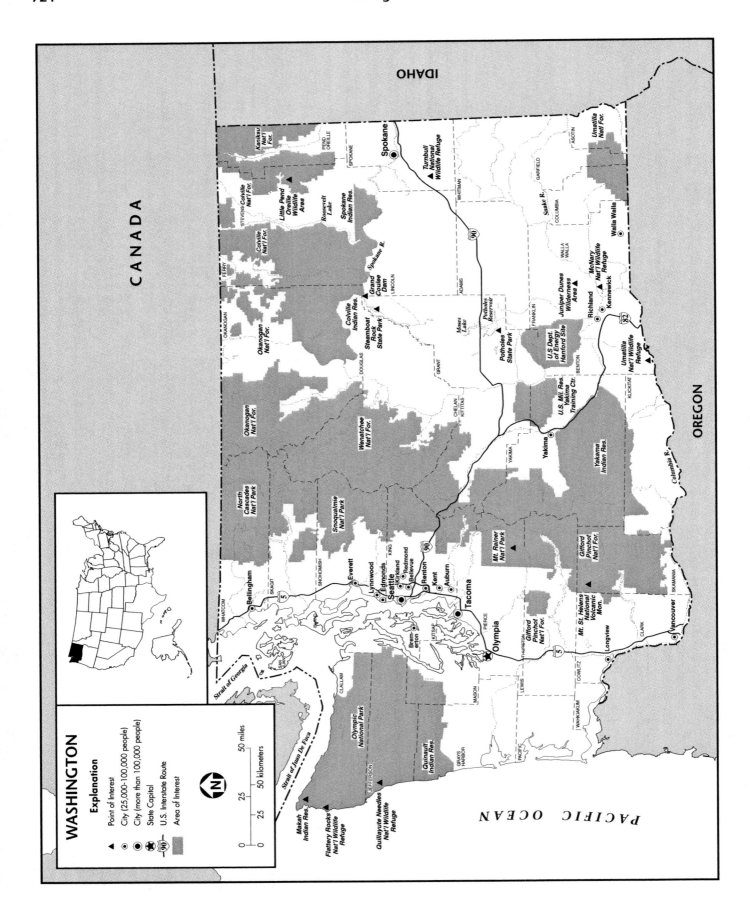

CANADA

IDAHO

OREGON

PACIFIC OCEAN

WASHINGTON

Explanation

▲ Point of Interest

⊙ City (25,000-100,000 people)

◉ City (more than 100,000 people)

✪ State Capital

⑨⓪ U.S. Interstate Route

▨ Area of Interest

50 miles

50 kilometers

25

25

0

0

Spokane

Kaniksu Nat'l For.

Colville Nat'l For.

Colville Nat'l For.

Little Pend Oreille Wildlife Area

Roosevelt Lake

Spokane Indian Res.

Tumbull National Wildlife Refuge

Umatilla Nat'l For.

Walla Walla

Okanogan Nat'l For.

Grand Coulee Dam

Colville Indian Res.

Steamboat Rock State Park

Spokane R.

Moses Lake

Potholes Reservoir

Potholes State Park

Juniper Dunes Wilderness Area

McNary Nat'l Wildlife Refuge

Richland

Kennewick

U.S. Dept. of Energy Hanford Site

Umatilla Nat'l Wildlife Refuge

Okanogan Nat'l For.

Wenatchee Nat'l For.

U.S. Mil. Res. Yakima Training Ctr.

Yakima

Yakama Indian Res.

North Cascades Nat'l Park

Snoqualmie Nat'l Park

Mt. Rainier Nat'l Park

Gifford Pinchot Nat'l For.

Bellingham

Everett

Lynnwood

Edmonds

Seattle

Kirkland

Redmond

Bellevue

Renton

Kent

Auburn

Tacoma

Brem-erton

Olympia

Mt. St. Helens National Volcanic Mon.

Gifford Pinchot Nat'l For.

Longview

Vancouver

Olympic National Park

Quinault Indian Res.

Makah Indian Res.

Flattery Rocks Nat'l Wildlife Refuge

Quillayute Needles Nat'l Wildlife Refuge

Strait of Juan De Fuca

Strait of Georgia

WHATCOM

SKAGIT

SNOHOMISH

SAN JUAN

CLALLAM

JEFFERSON

KING

KITSAP

MASON

GRAYS HARBOR

PACIFIC

THURSTON

PIERCE

LEWIS

COWLITZ

WAHKIAKUM

CLARK

SKAMANIA

KLICKITAT

YAKIMA

BENTON

FRANKLIN

WALLA WALLA

COLUMBIA

GARFIELD

ASOTIN

WHITMAN

SPOKANE

LINCOLN

ADAMS

GRANT

DOUGLAS

CHELAN

KITTITAS

OKANOGAN

FERRY

STEVENS

PEND OREILLE

Snake R.

Columbia R.

N

More than 6,500 sites in Washington are suspected or confirmed to be contaminated with toxic chemicals. At the Hanford Nuclear Site alone, contamination includes 1,500 places where radioactive and chemical wastes were disposed to the soil. From 1990–2002, clean-up was completed (nearly completed) at a majority of the high-priority sites.

Washington state has one of the highest overall recycling rates in the United States. In the mid-1980s, Bellingham began the state's first curbside recycling collection program. Seattle soon started its own program after being forced to close a municipal landfill and facing fierce opposition to construction of a garbage incinerator. In 1989, the state legislature passed the Waste-Not Washington Act, which defined a clear solid-waste management strategy and set a recycling goal of 50%; while this had not been achieved as of 2003, the rate of 40% was reported in in 1995, with 37% reported for 2001. (The national average is 30%.) In 2003, Washington had 236 hazardous waste sites listed in the Environmental Protection Agency's database, 47 of which were on the National Priorities List. In 2001, Washington received $71,549,000 in federal grants from the Environmental Protection Agency; EPA expenditures for procurement contracts in Washington that year amounted to $6,721,000.

6 POPULATION

Washington ranked 15th in population in the US (up from 18th in 1990) with an estimated total of 6,068,996 in 2002, an increase of 3% since 2000. Between 1990 and 2000, Washington's population grew from 4,866,692 to 5,894,121, an increase of 21.1%, making it one of the nation's 10 fastest-growing states. The population is projected to reach 6,258,000 by 2005 and 7.8 million by 2025. The population density in 2000 was 88.6 persons per sq mi.

In 2000 the median age was 35.3. Persons under 18 years old accounted for 25.7% of the population while 11.2% were age 65 or older.

Most Washingtonians live in the Western Corridor, a broad strip in western Washington running north–south between the Coast and Cascade ranges. The leading city in the Western Corridor is Seattle, with an estimated 2002 population of 570,426. Other leading cities with their 2002 population estimates are Tacoma, 197,553; Spokane, 196,305; Vancouver, 149,811; and Bellevue, 112,894. The Seattle-Tacoma-Bremerton metropolitan area had an estimated 1999 population of 3,465,760.

7 ETHNIC GROUPS

Washington is ethnically and racially heterogeneous. As of 2000, foreign-born Washingtonians made up 10.4% of the state's population (614,457), up from 6.6% in 1990. The largest minority group consists of Hispanics and Latinos, numbering 441,509, or 7.5% of the state population, according to the 2000 census, more than double the 1990 figure of 215,000. Most of the state's Spanish-speaking residents have arrived since World War II. Black Americans numbered 190,267 in 2000. Black immigration dates largely from World War II and postwar recruitment for defense-related industries.

Japanese-Americans have been farmers and small merchants in Washington throughout the 20th century. During World War II, the Nisei (Japanese Americans) of Washington were deported to internment camps. Chinese-Americans, imported as laborers in the mid-1800s, endured a wave of mob violence during the 1880s. As of 2000, the Asian population was estimated at 322,335, up from 281,000 in 1996. According to the 1990 census, there were 65,373 Filipinos, 35,985 Japanese, 59,914 Chinese, 46,880 Koreans, and 46,149 Vietnamese, up from 17,004 in 1990. Pacific Islanders numbered 23,953 in 2000, including 8,049 Samoans and 4,883 native Hawaiians.

Immigration from Southeast Asia was an importan demographic factor during the late 1970s and early 1980s.

There were 93,301 American Indians, Eskimos, and Aleuts living in Washington in 2000, the eighth-highest total in the nation. Indian lands in the state cover some 2.5 million acres (1 million hectares). The Yakama reservation had a population of 31,799 in 2000. A dispute developed in the 1970s over Indian fishing rights in the Puget Sound area; a decision in 1974 by US District Judge George Boldt that two 120-year-old treaties guaranteed the Indians 50% of the salmon catch in certain rivers was essentially upheld by the US Supreme Court in 1979.

8 LANGUAGES

Early settlers took from Chinook jargon some words like *potlatch* (gift-dispensing feast), *skookum* (strong), and *tillicum* (friend). Other language influences came from the many Indian tribes inhabiting Washington, especially such place-names as Chehalis, Walla Walla, Puyallup, Humptulips, and Spokane. Northern and Midland dialects dominate, with Midland strongest in eastern Washington and the Bellingham area, Northern elsewhere. In the urban areas, minor eastern variants have been lost; in rural sections, however, older people have preserved such terms as *johnnycake* (corn bread) and *mouth organ* (harmonica). One survey showed Northern *quarter* to dominant in the state with 81%, with Midland *quarter till* having only a 5% response; Northern *angleworm* (earthworm) had 63%, but Midland *fishworm* and *fishing worm* only 17%. The north coast of the Olympic Peninsula, settled by New Englanders who sailed around Cape Horn, retains New England /ah/ in *glass* and *aunt*. In Seattle, *fog* and *frog* are Midland /fawg/ and /frawg/, but *on* is Northern /ahn/; *cot* and *caught* sound alike, as in Midland; but the final /y/, as in *city* and *pretty*, has the Northern /ee/ sound rather than the Midland short /i/ as in pit.

In 2000, English was the language spoken at home by 86% of Washington residents five years old and older, down from 91% in 1990.

The following table gives selected statistics from the 2000 census for language spoken at home by persons five years old and over. The category "Other Pacific Island languages" includes Chamorro, Hawaiian, Ilocano, Indonesian, and Samoan. The category "Other Slavic languages" includes Czech, Slovak, and Ukrainian. The category "African languages" includes Amharic, Ibo, Twi, Yoruba, Bantu, Swahili, and Somali. The category "Scandinavian languages" includes Danish, Norwegian, and Swedish.

LANGUAGE	NUMBER	PERCENT
Population 5 years and over	5,501,398	100.0
Speak only English	4,730,512	86.0
Speak a language other than English	770,886	14.0
Speak a language other than English	**770,886**	**14.0**
Spanish or Spanish Creole	321,490	5.8
Chinese	48,459	0.9
Tagalog	41,674	0.8
Vietnamese	39,829	0.7
German	39,702	0.7
Korean	39,522	0.7
Russian	31,339	0.6
Japanese	24,055	0.4
French (incl. Patois, Cajun)	22,385	0.4
Other Pacific Island languages	16,199	0.3
Other Slavic languages	15,596	0.3
Mon-Khmer, Cambodian	14,559	0.3
African languages	12,420	0.2
Scandinavian languages	10,695	0.2

9 RELIGIONS

First settled by Protestant missionaries, Protestant denominations were only slightly predominant among the religiously active population in 2000. The leading denominations were the Church of Jesus Christ of Latter-Day Saints (Mormon), 178,000; Assemblies of God, 105,692; the Evangelical Lutheran Church in America, 127,854; the United Methodist Church, 76,648; and the Presbyterian Church USA, 74,338. There were 716,133 Roman Catholics, an estimated 43,500 Jews, and about 15,550 Muslims. Over 3.9 million people (about 67% of the population) were not counted as members of any religious organization.

[10] TRANSPORTATION

As of 2000, Washington had 2,330 rail mi (2,738 km) of freight railroad lines. In the same year, farm products totaling 14.6 million tons, accounted for 37% of rail tonnage terminated in the state. Amtrak provides service from Seattle down the coast to Los Angeles, and eastward via Spokane to St. Paul, Minnesota, and Chicago. More than half of all Amtrak passengers in the state board trains in Seattle.

Washington had 80,209 mi (128,334 km) of public roads in 2000, of which 62,012 mi (99,219 km) were rural. Principal interstate highways include I-90, connecting Spokane and Seattle, and I-5, proceeding north-south from Vancouver in British Columbia through Seattle and Tacoma to Vancouver, Washington, and Portland, Oregon. In 2000, the state had 4,154,501 licensed drivers and 5,166,904 registered motor vehicles, including 2,871,919 automobiles, 2,032,865, and 117,857 motorcycles.

Washington's principal ports include Seattle, Tacoma, and Anacortes, all part of the Puget Sound area and belonging to the Seattle Customs District; and Longview, Kalama, and Vancouver, along the Columbia River and considered part of the Portland (Oregon) Customs District. In 2000, Seattle handled 25.4 million tons of cargo; Tacoma, 21.1 million tons; Anacortes, 16.2 million tons; and Vancouver, 7.8 million tons.

Washington had 470 public and private airports, heliports, and seaplane bases in 2000; over 15 million passengers enplaned at Washington airports that year. Seattle-Tacoma (SEATAC) International Airport was by far the busiest in the state, with more than 13 million passengers enplaning there in 2000.

[11] HISTORY

The region now known as the State of Washington has been inhabited for at least 9,000 years, the first Americans having crossed the Bering Strait from Asia and entered North America via the Pacific Northwest. Their earliest known remains in Washington—burned bison bones and a human skeleton—date from approximately 7000 BC. Clovis points, a type of arrowhead, have been unearthed and determined to be approximately 30,000 years old.

The Cascades impeded communications between coastal Indians and those of the eastern plateau, and their material cultures evolved somewhat differently. Coastal Indians—belonging mainly to the Nootkin and Salishan language families—lived in a land of plenty, with ample fish, shellfish, roots, and berries. Timber was abundant for the construction of dugout canoes, villages with wooden dwellings, and some stationary wooden furniture. Warfare between villages was fairly common, with the acquisition of slaves the primary objective. The coastal Indians also emphasized rank based on wealth, through such institutions as the potlatch, a gigantic feast with extravagant exchanges of gifts. The plateau (or "horse") Indians, on the other hand, paid little attention to class distinctions. Social organization was simpler and intertribal warfare less frequent than on the coast. After the horse reached Washington around 1730, the plateau tribes (mainly of the Shahaptian language group) became largely nomadic, traveling long distances in search of food. Housing was portable, often taking the form of skin or mat teepees. In winter, circular pit houses were dug for protection from the wind and snow.

The first Europeans known to have sailed along the Washington coast were 18th-century Spaniards; stories of earlier voyages to the area by Sir Francis Drake in 1579 and Juan de Fuca in 1592 are largely undocumented. In 1774, Juan Pérez explored the northwestern coastline to the southern tip of Alaska; an expedition led by Bruno Heceta and his assistant, Juan Francisco de la Bodega y Quadra, arrived a year later. Men from this expedition made the first known landing on Washington soil, at the mouth of the Hoh River, but the venture ended in tragedy when the Indians seized the landing boat and killed the Spaniards.

English captain James Cook, on his third voyage of exploration, arrived in the Pacific Northwest in 1778 while searching for a northwest passage across America. He was the first of numerous British explorers and traders to be attracted by the luxuriant fur of the sea otter. Cook was followed in 1792 by another Englishman, George Vancouver, who mapped the Pacific coast and the Puget Sound area. In the same year, an American fur trader and explorer, Captain Robert Gray, discovered the mouth of the Columbia River. As the maritime fur trade began to prosper, overland traders moved toward the Northwest, the most active organizations being the British Hudson's Bay Company and the Canadian North West Company.

American interest in the area also increased. Several US maritime explorers had already visited the Northwest when President Thomas Jefferson commissioned an overland expedition to inspect the territory acquired from France through the Louisiana Purchase (1803). That expedition, led by Meriwether Lewis and William Clark, first sighted the Pacific Ocean in early November 1805 from the north bank of the Columbia River in what is now Pacific County. In time, as reports of the trip became known, a host of British and American fur traders followed portions of their route to the Pacific coast, and the interest of missionaries was excited. In 1831, a delegation visited Clark in St. Louis, Missouri, where he was then superintendent of Indian affairs, to persuade him to send teachers who could instruct the Indians in the Christian religion. When news of the visit became known, there was an immediate response from the churches.

The first missionaries to settle in Washington were Marcus and Narcissa Whitman, representing the Protestant American Board of Missions; their settlement, at Waiilatpu in southeastern Washington (near present-day Walla Walla), was established in 1836. Although the early Protestant missions had scant success in converting the Indians, the publicity surrounding their activities encouraged other Americans to journey to the Pacific Northwest, and the first immigrant wagons arrived at Waiilatpu in 1840. The Indian population became increasingly hostile to the missionaries, however, and on 29 November 1847, Marcus and Narcissa Whitman and 12 other Americans were massacred.

As early as 1843, an American provisional government had been established, embracing the entire Oregon country and extending far into the area that is now British Columbia, Canada. Three years later, after considerable military and diplomatic maneuvering, a US-Canada boundary along the 49th parallel was established by agreement with the British. Oregon Territory, including the present state of Washington, was organized in 1848. In the early 1850s, residents north of the Columbia River petitioned Congress to create a separate "Columbia Territory." The new territorial status was granted in 1853, but at the last minute the name of the territory (which embraced part of present-day Idaho) was changed to Washington.

President Franklin Pierce appointed Isaac I. Stevens as the first territorial governor. Stevens, who served at the same time as a US superintendent of Indian affairs, negotiated a series of treaties with the Northwest Indian tribes, establishing a system of reservations. Although the Indian situation had long been tense, it worsened after the treaties were concluded, and bloody uprisings by the Yakima, Nisqualli, and Cayuse were not suppressed until the late 1850s. Court battles over fishing rights spelled out in those treaties were not substantially resolved until 1980.

On the economic front, discoveries of gold in the Walla Walla area, in British Columbia, and in Idaho brought prosperity to the entire region. The completion in 1883 of the Northern Pacific Railroad line from the eastern US to Puget Sound encouraged immigration, and Washington's population, only 23,955 in 1870, swelled to 357,232 by 1890. In the political sphere, Washington was an early champion of women's suffrage. The territorial legislature granted women the vote in 1883; however, the suffrage acts were pronounced unconstitutional in 1887.

Cattle and sheep raising, farming, and lumbering were all established by the time Washington became the 42nd state in 1889. The Populist movement of the 1890s found fertile soil in Washington, and the financial panic of 1893 further stimulated radical labor and Granger activity. In 1896, the Fusionists—a coalition of Populists, Democrats, and Silver Republicans—swept the state. The discovery of gold in the Klondike, for which Seattle was the primary departure point, helped dim the Fusionists' prospects, and for the next three decades the Republican Party dominated state politics.

In 1909 Seattle staged the Alaska-Yukon-Pacific Exposition, celebrating the Alaska gold rush and Seattle's new position as a major seaport. World War I brought the state several major new military installations, and the Puget Sound area thrived as a shipbuilding center. The war years also saw the emergence of radical labor activities, especially in the shipbuilding and logging industries. Seattle was the national headquarters of the Industrial Workers of the World (IWW) and became, in 1919, the scene of the first general strike in the US, involving about 60,000 workers. The towns of Centralia and Everett were the sites of violent conflict between the IWW and conservative groups.

Washington's economy was in dire straits during the depression of the 1930s, when the market for forest products and field crops tumbled. The New Deal era brought numerous federally funded public works projects, notably the Bonneville and Grand Coulee dams on the Columbia River, providing hydroelectric power for industry and water for the irrigation of desert lands. Eventually, more than one million acres (400,000 hectares) were reclaimed for agricultural production. During World War II, Boeing led the way in establishing the aerospace industry as Washington's primary employer. Also during the war, the federal government built the Hanford Reservation nuclear research center; the Hanford plant was one of the major contractors in the construction of the first atomic bomb and later became a pioneer producer of atomic-powered electricity.

In 1962, "Century 21," the Seattle World's Fair, again promoted the area as the Alaska-Yukon-Pacific Exposition had a half-century earlier. The exhibition left Seattle a number of buildings—including the Space Needle and Coliseum—that have since been converted into a civic and performing arts center. The 1960s and 1970s, a period of rapid population growth (with Seattle and the Puget Sound area leading the way), also witnessed an effort by government and industry to reconcile the needs of an expanding economy with an increasing public concern for protection of the state's unique natural heritage. An unforeseen environmental hazard emerged in May 1980 with the eruption of Mt. St. Helens and the resultant widespread destruction.

Washington experienced a deep recession in 1979. The industries of logging and lumber, which lost market share to mills in the Southeast and in Canada, were particularly hard hit. Employment in wood products dropped 30% between 1978 and 1982. Nuclear waste also became an issue with the publication of a study in 1985 claiming that plutonium produced at the Hanford bomb fuel facility had leaked into the nearby Columbia

River. This claim was confirmed in 1990 by the federal government, which, together with the state, started a clean-up program expected to continue past the year 2000. The state's economy, strengthened by the expansion of Microsoft Corporation, Boeing, and Weyerhauser Paper in the 1980s, was still hampered by falling agricultural prices and weakness in the timber industry.

Speaker of the House Tom Foley, a Democrat and 30-year congressional veteran, lost his House seat in the 1994 mid-term elections in which Republicans prevailed in seven of the state's nine congressional districts.

In 2003, the state had a $2.6 billion budget deficit. Governor Gary Locke, a Democrat, was the nation's first governor of Chinese heritage; he won reelection in 2000. Under his administration, the state raised education spending by $1 billion.

12 STATE GOVERNMENT

Washington's constitution of 1889, as amended (95 times as of January 2003), continues to govern the state today. The legislative branch consists of a senate of 49 members elected to four-year terms, and a house of representatives with 98 members serving two-year terms. Legislators assemble annually in January, meeting for a maximum of 105 calendar days in odd-numbered years and 60 calendar days in even-numbered years. Special sessions, which are limited to 30 calendar days, may be called by a two-thirds vote of the members in each house. Legislators must be US citizens at least 18 years old and qualified voters in their districts. The legislative salary in 2002 was $32,064.

Executives elected statewide are the governor and lieutenant governor (who run separately), secretary of state, treasurer, attorney general, auditor, superintendent of public education, and officers of insurance and public land. The governor and lieutenant governor are elected separately and serve four-year terms. Candidates for these offices must be qualified voters in the state. The governor is limited to serving eight out of 14 years. In 2002 the governor's salary was $139,087.

A bill becomes law if passed by a majority of the elected members of each house and then signed by the governor or left unsigned for five days while the legislature is in session or 20 days after it has adjourned. A two-thirds vote of members present in each house is sufficient to override a gubernatorial veto. Constitutional amendments require a two-thirds vote of the legislature and ratification by the voters at the next general election.

Voters in Washington must be US citizens, at least 18 years old, and residents of the state, their county, and their precinct for at least 30 days prior to election day. Restrictions apply to those convicted of certain crimes and to those judged by the court as mentally incompetent to vote.

13 POLITICAL PARTIES

Washington never went for a full-fledged Democrat in a presidential election until 1932, when Franklin D. Roosevelt won the first of four successive victories in the state. Until then, Washington had generally voted Republican, the lone exceptions being 1896, when the state's Populist voters carried Washington for William Jennings Bryan, and 1912, when a plurality of the voters chose Theodore Roosevelt on the Progressive ticket.

The rise of the Democratic Party after World War II was linked to the careers of two US senators—Henry Jackson, who held his seat from 1953 until his death in 1983, and Warren Magnuson, defeated in 1980 after serving since 1945.

During the 1970s and 1980s the state tended to favor Republicans in presidential elections, but Democrats more than held their own in other contests. Washingtonians elected a Democratic governor, Dixy Lee Ray, in 1976, but in 1980 they chose a Republican, John Spellman; in 1984, they returned to the

Democratic column, electing Booth Gardner. Mike Lowry, also a Democrat, was elected governor in 1992. He was succeeded, in 1997, by fellow Democrat Gary Locke. Locke was reelected in 2000, but in 2003, announced he would not seek reelection in 2004.

In November 2000, Democrat Maria Cantwell was elected to the US Senate. Washington's other senator, Democrat Patty Murray, was elected to a second term in 1998. A stunning Republican victory in the 1994 mid-term elections saw, for the first time since 1860, a sitting Speaker of the US House of Representatives, Thomas S. Foley, lose his seat in the House. The winner was a little-known Republican, George Nethercutt, who called for change and received support from conservative national talk show hosts and former presidential candidate Ross Perot. Nethercutt was reelected in 1996, 1998, 2000, and 2002. Following the 2002 elections, three of Washington's nine US Representatives were Republicans; the other six were Democrats. There were 25 Republicans and 24 Democrats serving in the state senate, and 52 Democrats and 46 Republicans in the state house in mid-2003.

Democratic candidate Al Gore received 50% of Washington's popular vote in the 2000 presidential election; Republican George W. Bush received 45%, and Green Party candidate Ralph Nader garnered 4%. In 2002 there were 3,209,648 registered voters; there is no party registration in the state. The state had 11 electoral votes in the 2000 presidential election.

14 LOCAL GOVERNMENT

As of 2002, Washington had 39 counties, 279 municipal governments, 296 public school districts, and 1,173 special districts, including public utility, library, port, water, hospital, cemetery, and sewer districts.

Counties may establish their own institutions of government by charter; otherwise, the chief governing body is an elected board of commissioners. Other elected officials generally include the sheriff, prosecuting attorney, coroner, auditor, treasurer, and clerk. Cities and towns are governed under the mayor-council or council-manager systems. Larger cities, Seattle among them, generally have their own charters and elected mayors.

15 STATE SERVICES

To address the continuing threat of terrorism and to work with the federal Department of Homeland Security (created in 2002 following the terrorist attacks of 11 September 2001), homeland security in Washington in 2003 operated under the authority of the governor; the adjutant general was designated as the state homeland security advisor.

The Public Disclosure Commission, consisting of five members appointed by the governor and confirmed by the senate, provides disclosure of financial data in connection with political campaigns, lobbyists' activities, and the holdings of elected officials and candidates for public office. Each house of the legislature has its own board of ethics.

Public education in Washington is governed by a Board of Education and superintendent of public instruction; the Council for Postsecondary Education coordinates the state's higher educational institutions. The Department of Transportation oversees the construction and maintenance of highways, bridges, and ferries and assists locally owned airports.

The Department of Social and Health Services, the main human resources agency, oversees programs for adult corrections, juvenile rehabilitation, public and mental health, Medicaid, nursing homes, income maintenance, and vocational rehabilitation. Also involved in human resources activities are the Human Rights Commission, Department of Labor and Industries, Employment Security Department, Department of Veterans Affairs, and Council on Child Abuse and Neglect. Public protection services are provided by the Washington State Patrol, the Department of Emergency Services (civil defense), and the Military Department (Army and Air National Guard).

16 JUDICIAL SYSTEM

The state's highest court, the supreme court, consists of nine justices serving six-year terms; three justices are elected by nonpartisan ballot in each even-numbered year. The chief justice is elected to a four-year term by members of the court. The courts' senior judge holds the title of associate chief justice. Appeals of superior court decisions are usually heard in the court of appeals, whose 21 judges are elected to staggered six-year terms. The superior courts are the state's felony trial courts. There

Washington Presidential Vote by Political Parties, 1948–2000

YEAR	ELECTORAL VOTE	WASHINGTON WINNER	DEMOCRAT	REPUBLICAN	PROGRESSIVE	SOCIALIST	PROHIBITION	SOCIALIST LABOR	CONSTITUTION
1948	8	*Truman (D)	476,165	386,315	31,692	3,534	6,117	1,113	—
1952	9	*Eisenhower (R)	492,845	599,107	2,460	—	—	633	7,290
1956	9	*Eisenhower (R)	523,002	620,430	—	—	—	7,457	—
1960	9	Nixon (R)	599,298	629,273	—	—	—	10,895	1,401
1964	9	*Johnson (D)	779,699	470,366	—	—	—	7,772	—
					PEACE & FREEDOM		AMERICAN IND.		
1968	9	Humphrey (D)	616,037	588,510	1,669	—	96,900	491	—
					PEOPLE'S	LIBERTARIAN			AMERICAN
1972	9	*Nixon (R)	568,334	837,135	2,644	1,537	_	1,102	58,906
1976	9	Ford (R)	717,323	777,732	1,124	5,042	8,585	—	5,046
					CITIZENS			SOC. WORKERS	
1980	9	*Reagan (R)	650,193	865,244	9,403	29,213	—	1,137	—
1984	9	*Reagan (R)	807,352	1,051,670	1,891	8,844	—	—	—
					NEW ALLIANCE		WORKER'S WORLD		
1988	9	Dukakis (D)	933,516	903,835	3,520	17,240	1,440	1,290	—
					IND. (Perot)		TAXPAYERS	NATURAL LAW	POPULIST
1992	11	*Clinton (D)	993,037	731,234	541,780	7,533	2,354	2,456	4,854
					IND. (Nader)				
1996	11	*Clinton (D)	1,123,323	840,712	201,003	12,522	60,322	—	—
					FREEDOM (Buchanan)		GREEN (Nader)		
2000	11	Gore (D)	1,247,652	1,108,864	7,171	13,135	103,002	2,927	—

* Won US presidential election.

are 176 district and municipal courts; they hear traffic and misdemeanor matters.

Prisoners in state or federal correctional facilities numbered 15,242 in June 2001, an increase of 3.7% over the previous year. The state's incarceration rate stood at 251 per 100,000 population. In 2001, Washington's crime index rate was 5,151.9 per 100,000 inhabitants, including a total of 21,258 violent crimes and 287,234 crimes against property in that year. Washington imposes the death penalty and as of 2003 had 12 persons under sentence of death. There were four executions in the state between 1977 and 2003.

17ARMED FORCES

In 2002, there were 38,521 active-duty military personnel and 23,259 civilian personnel stationed in Washington, nearly half of whom were at Fort Lewis near Tacoma. Other chief facilities in Washington include a Trident nuclear submarine base at Bangor, Whidbey Island Naval Air Station, McChord Air Force Base (Tacoma), and Fairchild Air Force Base (Airway Heights). In 2002, federal defense contract awards totaled about $2.45 billion.

According to the 2000 Census, there were 670,628 veterans living in Washington, of whom 104,590 served during World War II; 64,921 in the Korean conflict; 212,968 during the Vietnam era; and 94,170 during 1990–2000 (including the Persian Gulf War). During 2002, veterans' benefits totaled more than $1.2 billion.

In 2000, the Washington State Patrol employed 987 full-time sworn officers.

18MIGRATION

The first overseas immigrants to reach Washington were Chinese laborers, imported during the 1860s; Chinese continued to arrive into the 1880s, when mob attacks on Chinese homes forced the territorial government to put Seattle under martial law and call in federal troops to restore order. The 1870s and 1880s brought an influx of immigrants from western Europe—especially Germany, Scandinavia, and the Netherlands—and from Russia and Japan.

In recent decades, Washington has benefited from a second migratory wave even more massive than the first. From 1970 to 1980, the state ranked seventh among the states in net migration with a gain of 719,000. From 1985 to 1990, the net migration gain was 317,832 (sixth among the states). Many of those new residents were drawn from other states by Washington's defense- and trade-related industries. In addition, many immigrants from Southeast Asia arrived during the late 1970s. Between 1990 and 1998, Washington had net gains of 374,000 in domestic migration and 121,000 in international migration. In 1996, the foreign-born population totaled 386,000, or 7% of the state's total population. In 1998, 16,920 immigrants from foreign countries entered Washington, the seventh-highest total of any state for that year. Of that total, 4,129 came from Mexico, 1,159 from the Philippines, and 940 from Vietnam. In the period 1995–2000, 618,395 people moved into the state and 543,065 moved out, for a net gain of 75,330. Most new residents were from California.

19INTERGOVERNMENTAL COOPERATION

Washington participates in the Columbia River Gorge Compact (with Oregon), Pacific States Marine Fisheries Commission, Western Interstate Corrections Compact, Western Interstate Energy Compact, Western Interstate Commission for Higher Education, Northwest Power and Conservation Council (with Idaho, Montana, and Oregon), Interstate Compact for the Supervision of Parolees and Probationers, Agreement on Qualification of Educational Personnel, Interstate Compact on Placement of Children, Multistate Tax Compact, and Driver License Compact, among other interstate bodies. The state has one boundary compact with Oregon. Federal grants in 2001 totaled over $6.7 billion.

20ECONOMY

The mainstays of Washington's economy are services, financial institutions, manufacturing (especially aerospace equipment, shipbuilding, food processing, and wood products), agriculture, lumbering, and tourism. Between 1971 and 1984, employment increased in such sectors as lumber and wood products, metals and machinery, food processing, trade, services, and government, while decreasing in aerospace—which remains, nevertheless, the state's single leading industry. The eruption of Mt. St. Helens in 1980 had an immediate negative impact on the forestry industry—already clouded by a slowdown in housing construction—crop growing, and the tourist trade. Foreign trade, especially with Canada and Japan, was an important growth sector during the 1990s. Leading manufacturers are the Boeing Aerospace Co. and Microsoft, Inc. In the 1990s, state economic growth was robust, with annual rates soaring to 9.6% in 1998 and 8.6% in 1999, before moderating to 4.6% in 2000. The driving forces in Washington's economy, the high-tech computer and aerospace sectors, became the main sources of its troubles after the collapse of the dot.com bubble on the stock market in 2001 and after the events of 11 September. Growth fell to 2.2% in 2001, and by the end of 2002, all sectors except government and financial services (including insurance and real estate) had lost jobs. In December 2002, Washington's unemployment rate of 6.8% was higher than all states except its neighbor, Oregon, and Alaska. Already having problems before 9/11, Boeing cut its workforce 18% in 2002, announcing plans to cut more jobs and/or relocate its operations out of Washington. Spokane continued to suffer the adverse effects of the bankruptcy of Kaiser Aluminum. Job losses in the high-paid dot.com, high-tech, and aerospace sectors had disproportionate impacts on personal income in Washington. In 2001, Washington's gross state product gross state product was $223 billion, the 14th largest among the states, to which general services contributed $52.1 billion; financial services, $41 billion; trade, $37.3 billion; government, $30.8 billion; manufacturing, $27.4 billion; transportation and public utilities, $18.1 billion, and construction, $11 billion. The public sector in 2001 constituted 13.8% of gross state product, above the 12% average for the states.

21INCOME

According to the Bureau of Economic Analysis, in 2001, Washington had a per capita personal income (PCPI) of $31,976 which ranked 14th in the United States (including the District of Columbia) and was 105% of the national average, $30,413. The 2001 PCPI reflected an increase of 1.2% from 2000 compared to the national change of 2.2%. In 2001, Washington had a total personal income (TPI) of $191,644,569,000 which ranked 14th in the United States and accounted for 2.2% of the national total. The 2001 TPI reflected an increase of 2.6% from 2000 compared to the national change of 3.3%.

Earnings of persons employed in Washington increased from $135,901,389,000 in 2000 to $137,199,518,000 in 2001, an increase of 1.0%. The largest industries in 2001 were services, 30.8% of earnings; state and local government, 12.6%; and durable goods manufacturing, 10.2%. Of the industries that accounted for at least 5% of earnings in 2001, the slowest growing from 2000 to 2001 was wholesale trade (5.7% of earnings in 2001), which decreased 2.1%; the fastest was state and local government, which increased 9.8%.

According to data released by the US Census Bureau, in 2000, the median household income was $42,024 compared to the national average of $42,148. In 2001, the median income for a family of four was $65,997 compared to the national average of $63,278. For the period 1999 to 2001, the average poverty rate was 10.4% which placed it 28th among the 50 states and the District of Columbia ranked lowest to highest.

22LABOR

According to Bureau of Labor Statistics (BLS) provisional estimates, in July 2003 the seasonally adjusted civilian labor force in Washington numbered 3,115,200, with approximately 234,000 workers unemployed, yielding an unemployment rate of 7.5%, compared to the national average of 6.2% for the same period. Since the beginning of the BLS data series in 1978, the highest unemployment rate recorded was 12.5% in November 1982. The historical low was 4.4% in November 1997. It is estimated that in 2001, 5.4% of the labor force was employed in construction; 11.4% in manufacturing; 5.8% in transportation, communications, and public utilities; 21.4% in trade; 5.6% in finance, insurance, and real estate; 24.8% in services; 14.8% in government; and 2.8% in agriculture.

Although state and federal authorities suppressed radical labor activities in the mines around the turn of the century, in the logging camps during World War I, and in Seattle in 1919, the impulse to unionize remained strong in Washington. The state's labor force is still one of the most organized in the United States although (in line with national trends) the unions' share of the non-farm work force declined from 45% in 1970 to 34% in 1980.

The US Department of Labor reported that in 2002, 471,000 of Washington's 2,553,000 employed wage and salary workers were members of unions. This represented 18.4% of those so employed; the national average is 13.2%. In all, 512,000 workers (20.0%) were represented by unions. In addition to union members, this category includes workers who report no union affiliation but whose jobs are covered by a union contract.

23AGRICULTURE

Orchard and field crops dominate Washington's agricultural economy, which yielded $5.2 billion in farm marketings in 2001, 12th among the 50 states. Fruits and vegetables are raised in the humid and irrigated areas of the state while wheat and other grains grow in the drier central and eastern regions.

Washington is the nation's leading producer of apples. The estimated 2002 crop, representing 54% of the US total, totaled 5.1 million tons. Among leading varieties, delicious apples ranked 1st, followed by golden delicious and winesap. The state also ranked 1st in production of hops, red raspberries, pears, and cherries; and 2nd in grapes and apricots. Other preliminary crop figures for 2002 included wheat, 129.7 million bushels, valued at $537.0 million; potatoes, 560,000 hundredweight, $533 million; barley, 18.4 million bushels, $47.7 million; and corn for grain, 13.3 million bushels, $38.5 million. Sugar beets, peaches, and various seed crops are also grown in Washington.

24ANIMAL HUSBANDRY

In 2003, Washington's farms and ranches had 1.13 million cattle and calves, valued at $957 million. During 2002, the state had approximately 24,000 hogs and pigs, valued at $2 million. The state produced 4.95 million lb (2.2 million kg) of sheep and lambs in 1997, which brought in $3.1 million in gross income.

Washington dairy farmers had 247,000 milk cows that produced 5.51 billion lb (2.5 billion kg) of milk in 2001. Poultry farmers sold 9.2 million lb (4.2 million kg) of chicken, and produced 1.34 billion eggs, valued at $62.4 million.

25FISHING

In 1998, Washington's production of food fish reached 419 million lb (190 million kg), valued at $123.2 million. The record catch was 527.8 million lb (239.4 million kg) in 1994. Oyster landings in 1998 amounted to over 6.5 million lb (2.9 million kg), 83% of the Pacific region's total. The shellfish catch in 1998 also included 21.3 million lb (9.7 million kg) of crab and 3.1 million lb (1.4 million kg) of shrimp. Most production of farm-raised oysters occurs in Washington although there are some smaller operations in the other Pacific coastal states. Salmon landings were 13.9 million lb (6.3 million kg), valued at $9.1 million, of which pink salmon accounted for 2%; chum, 51%; silver, 10%; sockeye, 23%; and chinook, 14%. Washington had 1,656 commercial fishing vessels in 1997. The leading fishing ports, by value of landings in 1998, were Seattle, $22.3 million; Bellingham, $16.7 million; and Westport, $12.8 million. In 1997, on average, some 3,927 workers were employed in the state's 96 fish processing plants, and 1,711 were engaged in 198 wholesale plants.

In 1998, 65 fish farms distributed nearly 837 million salmon and 239 million trout in Washington's streams and lakes. In 1998, Washington issued 681,656 fishing licenses.

26FORESTRY

Washington's forests, covering 21,790,000 acres (8,818,000 hectares), are an important commercial and recreational resource. Some 17,347,000 acres (7,020,000 hectares) are classified as commercial forestland. The largest federal forests are Wenatchee, Mt. Baker–Snoqualmie, and Okanogan.

Forest production is one of Washington's major manufacturing industries. In 2002, lumber production totaled 4.92 billion board feet (2nd in the US).

Restrictions on federal timberlands to protect the Northern spotted owl, which became effective in late 1990, reflect diverse public demands on forest values. The regulations impact Washington's forest industry and forest-based employment due to the sharp decline of federal timber supply. However, this scarcity of timber created by forest preservation practices will enhance the value of the state's timber resource. This will spur the trend toward more efficient wood use and higher value-added products.

Public ownership accounts for about 55% of Washington's forest, with the remaining 45% owned by the forest industry and other private owners. Lumber and plywood, logs for export, various chip products, pulp logs, and shakes and shingles are leading forest commodities. The largest forest industry company is Weyerhauser, with headquarters in Tacoma.

Since 1975, more acres have been planted or seeded than have been cut down. Washington's forest-fire control program covers some 12.5 million acres (5.1 million hectares). Leading causes of forest fires in lands under the jurisdiction of the Department of Natural Resources are (in order of frequency) burning debris, lightning, recreation, children, smokers, incendiary logging, and railroad operations.

27MINING

The estimated value of nonfuel mineral production for Washington in 2001 was $545 million, a roughly 10% decrease from that of 2000. Washington ranked 25th nationally in nonfuel mineral production value in 2001. In that year, the four leading nonfuel mineral commodities—construction sand and gravel, crushed stone, portland cement, and magnesium metal—together accounted for almost 90% of the total nonfuel mineral value. According to preliminary figures, crushed stone production was 18.1 million metric tons, valued at $120 million. That same year, construction sand and gravel quarried amounted to 41.1 million metric tons, valued at $221 million, and 116,000 metric tons of clays produced were worth $425,000. In 2001 Washington ranked 1st in magnesium metal, 2nd in olivine, 4th in diatomite, 7th in construction sand and gravel, and 8th in gold. In 2001, increasing energy costs led the state to close most of its seven aluminum smelters, dropping from 1st to 11th place in production of primary aluminum. In 1998 it had produced 31% of the national total.

28ENERGY AND POWER

In 2000 Washington's total per capita energy consumption was 369 million Btu (93 million kcal), ranking it 20th among the 50 states. Transportation's share of the energy consumed has increased steadily, owing to large increases in the number of people, cars, and miles driven per vehicle; declines in the real cost of fuel; and major increases in airplane travel. Transportation consumption is derived almost exclusively from petroleum, which is the major energy source in the state.

Washington has no indigenous sources of petroleum or natural gas, but it does have the largest hydroelectric generation base of any state in the nation, with a net generation capability (utility and nonutility) of 26.1 million kW in 1999. Electric plants in Washington generated 117.1 million kWh in 1999, 83% of that from hydroelectric facilities, which are largely publicly owned and operated. As of 2001, Washington had one nuclear plant, the single-unit Columbia Generating Station in Benton County. Almost all of the 4.3 million tons of coal mined in the state in 2000 were burned to generate electricity. Washington has five petroleum refineries with combined production of 608,000 barrels per day. The state has also been a pioneer in pursuing efficiency as a source of new energy. Significant savings have been captured since 1983.

Washington is one of the beneficiaries of the hydropower system owned by various federal entities and marketed by Bonneville Power Administration. While this results in both low power costs and the lowest power-related air emissions per capita of any state, there are associated responsibilities to ensure protection and preservation of fish.

29INDUSTRY

The 1990s were Washington's busiest years in terms of technology company start-ups. Software and computer-related businesses accounted for most of the activity but more traditional manufacturing companies were also emerging. Even today, computers, software, and related activities make up the largest single portion in Washington technology companies. Manufacturing of all types is another strong element.

Washington technology companies cross borders and many are world leaders. Boeing's airplane sales make that company one of the nation's leading exporters. Microsoft has offices around the world and its products are in use on every continent. However, even small firms benefit from foreign trade and over half of Washington's technology companies are in overseas markets. Aerospace/transportation equipment is the largest industry in Washington state, run primarily by Boeing.

The state's biotechnology firms are growing at a phenomenal rate, but many are still in the research and development stage. More than two-thirds are developing products for human health care. Most of the firms not focused on medical treatment are developing products and processes for the state's natural resource sectors: agriculture, food processing, forestry, veterinary medicine, marine industries, and environmental waste clean-up and management.

Washington state is one of the top 15 film-production states in the US. Film and video have grown to represent at least a $100-million-a-year industry. Washington state has approximately 1,500 film and video businesses which provide jobs for about 5,000 state residents. Washington film companies make feature films, television movies, TV series or episodes, TV commercials, documentaries, industrial films, and music videos. Out-of-state producers shoot over 100 film and video projects in Washington annually, contributing more than $40 million to the state's economy every year; $45 million is generated by in-state film and video companies.

The total value of shipments for manufactured goods in 1997 was $82 billion. In 1997, Washington was the headquarters for eight Fortune 500 companies: Boeing, Costco, Weyerhaeuser, Microsoft, Paccar, Nordstrom, Safeco, and Washington Mutual.

Earnings of persons employed in Washington increased from $108.1 billion in 1997 to $118.1 billion in 1998, an increase of 9.3%. The largest industries in 1998 were services, 28.4% of earnings; durable goods manufacturing, 13.0%; and state and local government, 11.8%. Of the industries that accounted for at least 5% of earnings in 1998, the slowest growing from 1997 to 1998 was state and local government, which increased 4.2%; the fastest was durable goods manufacturing, which increased 14.3%.

30COMMERCE

Wholesalers in 1997 had sales of $79 billion. Total retail sales in 1997 reached over $40 billion. Food stores accounted for 11% of establishments; automotive dealers, 12%; and eating and drinking establishments, 33%. The Seattle-Tacoma-Bremerton area had retail sales over half of the state's total.

In 1998, exports of goods originating from the state had a value of $38 billion, 3rd in the United States. The leading exports were aircraft and aircraft parts (accounting for more than one-half of the total), machinery, lumber and logs, fish and fish products, grains, motor vehicles and parts, fruits and vegetables, wood pulp, and paper products. Principal imports included crude petroleum, lumber, natural gas, passenger cars, truck chassis and bodies, newsprint, aluminum oxide, motorcycles, radios, and television sets.

31CONSUMER PROTECTION

The Office of the Attorney General, which enforces the state's 1961 Consumer Protection Act through the Consumer Protection Division, investigates consumer complaints and, when necessary, seeks court action in connection with retail sales abuses, unfair automobile sales techniques, false advertising, and other fraudulent or deceptive practices. Responsibilities of the Department of Agriculture include food inspection and labeling, sanitary food handling and storage, and accurate weights and measures.

32BANKING

As of September 2002, Washington had 102 insured banks, with assets of $71.7 billion. Sixty-five of those banks were state-chartered.

The state in 2001/02 was experiencing its worst recession since 1980/81. The weak economy caused demand for commercial property to weaken: office and industrial vacancy rates rose sharply from 2000 to 2003, particularly in the Seattle area. However, low interest rates caused a rise in housing prices. But loan delinquency ratios for commercial real estate (CRE) increased in 2002.

The median return on assets (ROA) (the measure of earnings in relation to all resources) among insured banks headquartered in Washington improved from 2001 to 2002. Net interest margins (NIMs) (the difference between the lower rates offered to savers and the higher rates charged on loans) widened during that period, contributing to the improvement in ROA ratios. However, median past-due loan levels increased from 1999 to 2002, particularly among Washington's community banks (those with assets under $1 billion). Agricultural banks experienced the most pressure with regard to past-due loan levels.

33INSURANCE

Washingtonians held 1.8 million ordinary life insurance policies with a total face value of $181.0 billion in 2001. Total value for all categories of life insurance (ordinary, group, industrial, and credit) was $323.5 billion. Death benefits paid that year totaled $729.2 million. As of 2000, there were 26 property and casualty and 14 life and health insurance companies incorporated or organized in the state. In 2001, property and casualty insurers wrote over $6.5 billion in premiums. That year, there were 27,083 flood insurance policies in force in the state, with a total value of $3.7 million.

The Office of the Insurance Commissioner and State Fire Marshal regulates insurance company operations, reviews insurance policies and rates, and examines and licenses agents and brokers. It also conducts fire safety inspections in hospitals, nursing homes, and other facilities, investigates fires of suspicious origin, and regulates the manufacture, sale, and public display of fireworks.

34SECURITIES

The Spokane Stock Exchange (founded 1897), specializing in mining stocks, is no longer operating. Approximately 1,187 broker-dealers and 9,299 employees conduct business in the state. Professional securities investment advice is available from 218 registered firms. The state houses 96 NASDAQ companies, six NASDAQ market makers, and has incorporated nine NYSE companies.

35PUBLIC FINANCE

Washington's biennial budget is prepared by the Office of Financial Management and submitted by the governor to the legislature for amendment and approval. The fiscal year runs from 1 July through 30 June.

The 1999–2001 State budget plan had resources totaling $20.7 billion and proposed expenditures of $20.6 billion. The majority of general funds were put towards education, $435 million towards health services, and $200 million to salmon recovery, amongst other initiatives. Total resources for 2001–03 were expected to reach $23 billion, with an expenditure limit of $22 billion. In 2002/03, the Washington's budget deficit was reported to be about $1.12 billion or about 5% of the state budget. Projections in early 2003 for 2003/04 were for a budget deficit ranging from $1.3 billion to $2.87 billion (11.5% to 25.3% of the state budget). Total resources for the 2003-05 biennium were projected at $22.979 billion appropriated to K-12 education (44.1%), higher education (11.6%), social and health services (28.2%), corrections (4.9%), bond retirement (5.5%), government operations (1.7%), natural resources (1.3%) and other, including the legislature and judiciary (2.7%)

The following table from the US Census Bureau contains information on revenues, expenditures, indebtedness, and cash/securities for 2001.

	($000)	PERCENT	PER CAPITA
Population (thousands, 2001)	5,993	(X)	(X)
Total Revenue	23,646,114	100.00	3,945.62
General revenue	22,418,306	94.81	3,740.75
Utility revenue	–	–	–
Liquor store revenue	342,556	1.45	57.16
Insurance trust revenue	885,252	3.74	147.71
Exhibit: Salaries and wages	4,610,966	16.57	769.39
Total expenditure	27,824,006	100.00	4,642.75
General expenditure	23,597,439	84.81	3,937.50
Education	9,720,289	34.93	1,621.94
Public welfare	5,509,101	19.80	919.26
Hospitals	926,711	3.33	154.63
Health	1,313,199	4.72	219.12
Highways	1,628,846	5.85	271.79
Police protection	224,377	0.81	37.44

	($000)	PERCENT	PER CAPITA
General expenditure (continued)			
Correction	730,116	2.62	121.83
Natural resources	637,305	2.29	106.34
Parks and recreation	105,346	0.38	17.58
Government administration	486,328	1.75	81.15
Interest on general debt	657,705	2.36	109.75
Other and unallocable	1,658,116	5.96	276.68
Utility expenditure	16,229	0.06	2.71
Liquor store expenditure	310,336	1.12	51.78
Insurance trust expenditure	3,900,002	14.02	650.76
Debt at end of fiscal year	12,607,489	100.00	2,103.70
Cash and security holdings	63,720,710	100.00	10,632.52

36TAXATION

Washington is one of seven states without income taxes, individual or corporate. The biggest source of state revenue is the general sales and use tax, set at 6.5% with local sales taxes adding on 0.5% to 2.4%. Food and prescription drugs are exempted. The state also imposes a full array of excise taxes covering motor fuels, tobacco products, insurance premiums, public utilities, alcoholic beverages, amusements, pari-mutuels, and other selected items. In 1982 Washington replaced its inheritance tax with an estate tax tied to the federal exemption for state death taxes, and since 2001, has taken action prevent its phase-out in tandem with the phase-out of the federal tax credit by 2007. In 2002, gift and death taxes accounted for 0.9% of total state collections. Other state taxes include various license fees, document and stock transfer fees, state property taxes, and severance taxes (0.3% of state collections in 2002). Most property taxes are collected locally. In all, about 42% of total state and local revenues are collected by local government and taxing units.

The state collected $12.629 billion in taxes in 2002, of which 62.5% came from the general sales tax, 16.2% from selective sales taxes, 11.5% from state property taxes, 5.% from state license fees, and 3.4% from document and stock transfer taxes. In 2003, Washington ranked 18th among the states in terms of combined state and local tax burden, which amounted to about 9.8% of income. The following table from the US Census Bureau provides a summary of taxes collected by the state in 2002.

	($000)	PER CAPITA
Total Taxes	12,628,567	2,080.83
Property taxes	1,457,432	240.14
Sales and gross receipts	9,949,859	1,639.46
General sales and gross receipts	7,904,003	1,302.36
Selective sales taxes	2,045,856	337.1
Alcoholic beverage	174,170	28.7
Amusements	85	0.01
Insurance Premiums	291,250	47.99
Motor fuels	742,699	122.38
Pari-mutuels	2,002	0.33
Public utilities	332,438	54.78
Tobacco products	330,730	54.5
Other selective sales	172,482	28.42
Licenses	630,801	103.94
Alcoholic beverages	9,139	1.51
Amusements	106	0.02
Corporation	15,540	2.56
Hunting and fishing	31,061	5.12
Motor vehicle	308,482	50.83
Motor vehicle operators	41,060	6.77
Public utility	15,366	2.53
Occupation and business, NEC	175,353	28.89
Other	34,694	5.72
Other taxes	590,475	97.29
Death and gift	114,173	18.81
Documentary and stock transfer	432,884	71.33
Severance	43,418	7.15
Other	(X)	(X)

[37] ECONOMIC POLICY

The Department of Trade and Economic Development seeks to promote a healthy state economy and to expand markets for Washington's products. The state has no corporate or personal income tax and no tax on interest, dividends, or capital gains. The department offers a tax credit program for companies that expand or locate in high unemployment areas and issues industrial development bonds with federal tax-exempt status for new capital construction. It extends loans to projects in distressed and timber-dependent areas and offers low interest loans to small and medium-sized Washington State forest products companies. The state helps communities finance infrastructure improvements to retain existing businesses or to attract new companies and provides special services for small and minority-owned enterprises. By 2003, in an effort to encourage international trade, Washington had created nine foreign trade zones. Other initiatives including workshops sponsored by the Small Business Development Center on starting and expanding small businesses in the state.

[38] HEALTH

Washington's infant mortality rate in 2000 was 5.2 per 1,000 live births, well below the national norm of 6.9. In 1999 there were 25,523 abortions performed, or 20 per 1,000 women. In 2000, the overall death rate, 756.2 per 100,000 population, was well below the national rate of 873.1; the rates for heart disease and cancer were lower than the national rates as well. The HIV mortality rate of 2.2 per 100,000 population was below the national rate in 2000; a total 10,005 AIDS cases had been reported through 2001. In the 2000, 20.7% of persons 18 years of age and older were smokers

Leading causes of death in 2000 were heart disease (195.7 deaths per 100,000 population), cancer (183.6 deaths per 100,000), accidents and adverse effects (35.3 deaths per 100,000), and suicide (12.5 deaths per 100,000).

Washington's 84 community hospitals had 522,624 admissions and 11,382 beds in 2001. There were 15,773 full-time registered nurses and 1,395 full-time licensed practical nurses in 2001 and 274 physicians per 100,000 population in 2000. The average expense of a community hospital for care was $1,164.30 per inpatient day in 2001.

Federal government grants to cover the Medicare and Medicaid services in 2001 totaled $2.5 billion; 745,859 enrollees received Medicare benefits that year. At least 13.1% of Washington's residents were uninsured in 2002.

[39] SOCIAL WELFARE

In 2001, the average weekly unemployment benefit was $319.61. Average monthly participation in the food stamp program in FY2002 comprised 350,373 persons (163,313 households). The average monthly benefit was $75.55, and the sum total of benefits paid in FY2002 was $317,651,773.

With the enactment of the Personal Responsibility and Work Opportunity Reconciliation Act of 1996, the US government has changed the form and regulations for many of its social welfare programs. Most significantly, it replaces Aid to Families with Dependent Children (AFDC), an open-ended entitlement program, with Temporary Assistance for Needy Families (TANF), a limited system of assistance funded largely through federal block grants. The reform act also impacts the food stamp program, the Supplemental Security Income program, and the child nutrition program. The law took effect on 1 July 1997 and provided $16.38 billion in block grants for fiscal years 1997–2002. The grants are to be divided among the states based on an equation involving the numbers of former AFDC recipients in each state.

Reauthorization of the 1996 social welfare legislation, scheduled for 2002, was delayed, and the original law had been extended three times as of July 2003, with the most recent extension running through September 2003. Washington's TANF program is called WorkFirst. In June 2000 the state had 146,375 welfare recipients. State expenditures on the TANF program in FY2002 totaled $260,893,184.

In December 2001, Social Security benefits were paid to 858,510 Washington residents. This number included 563,710 retired workers, 82,950 widows and widowers, 94,700 disabled workers, 56,670 spouses, and 60,480 children. Social Security beneficiaries represented 14.3% of the total state population and 93.4% of the state's population age 65 and older. Retired workers (excluding persons with special benefits) received an average monthly payment of $911; widows and widowers, $880; disabled workers, $823; and spouses, $465. Payments for children of retired workers averaged $452 per month; children of deceased workers, $616; and children of disabled workers, $264.

Federal Supplemental Security Income payments in December 2001 went to 104,700 Washington residents, averaging $414 a month.

[40] HOUSING

In 2002, there were an estimated 2,530,215 housing units in Washington, 2,358,892 of which were occupied; 64.3% were owner-occupied. About 61.2% of all units were single-family, detached homes. Electricity was the most common energy source for heating. It was estimated that 50,854 units lacked telephone service, 8,654 lacked complete plumbing, and 14,433 lacked complete kitchen facilities. The average household size was 2.51 people.

In 2002, 40,200 new privately owned housing units were authorized for construction. The median home value was $189,148. The median monthly cost for mortgage owners was $1,405. Renters paid a median of $710 per month. During 2002, Washington received more than $102 million in community planning and development aid from the US Department of Housing and Urban Development.

[41] EDUCATION

Washingtonians rank exceptionally high by most educational standards. As of 2000, 87.1% of all Washingtonians 25 years of age or older were high school graduates, and 27.7% had four or more years of college.

The total enrollment for fall 1999 in Washington's public schools stood at 1,003,714. Of these, 694,750 attended schools from kindergarten through grade eight, and 308,964 attended high school. Minority students made up approximately 26% of the total enrollment in public elementary and secondary schools in 2001. Total enrollment was estimated at 1,014,000 in fall 2000 and is expected to reach 1,036,000 by fall 2005. Expenditures for public schools in 1999/2000 were $6,126 per pupil. Expenditures for public education in 2000/01 were estimated at $6,557,294. Enrollment in nonpublic schools in fall 2001 was 76,885.

As of fall 2000, there were 358,414 students enrolled in college or graduate school. In the same year Washington had 79 degree-granting institutions. Washington has 35 colleges and universities (11 public, 24 private) and 34 community colleges. The largest institutions are the University of Washington (Seattle), founded in 1861, and Washington State University (Pullman). Other public institutions include the following: Eastern Washington University (Cheney); Central Washington University (Ellensburg); Western Washington University (Bellingham); and Evergreen State College (Olympia). Private institutions include Gonzaga University (Spokane); Pacific Lutheran University (Tacoma); Seattle University; Seattle Pacific College; University of Puget Sound

(Tacoma); Walla Walla College; and Whitworth College (Spokane). In 1997, minority students comprised 19.2% of total postsecondary enrollment.

42ARTS

The focus of professional performance activities in Washington is Seattle Center, home of the Seattle Symphony, Pacific Northwest Ballet Company, and Seattle Repertory Theater. The Seattle Opera Association (founded 1964), which also performs there throughout the year, is one of the nation's leading opera companies, offering five operas each season and presenting Richard Wagner's "Ring" cycle at the Pacific Northwest Festival in July. Tacoma and Spokane have notable local orchestras.

The Seattle Cherry Blossom and Japanese Cultural Festival has been a popular community event since its inception in 1975. The annual Diwali Festival, also in Seattle, is sponsored in part by the regional Cultural Society of India and the Washington State Arts Commission. It includes performances of traditional dance, music, and drama, as does the Hmong New Year Celebration, another popular cultural event in Seattle.

Among Washington's many museums, universities, and other organizations exhibiting works of art on a permanent or periodic basis are the Seattle Art Museum, with its Modern Art Pavilion, and the Henry Art Gallery of the University of Washington at Seattle. Others include the Washington State University Museum of Art at Pullman; the Whatcom Museum of History and Art (Bellingham); the Tacoma Art Museum; the State Capitol Museum (Olympia); and the Cheney Cowles Memorial Museum of the Eastern Washington State Historical Society (Spokane).

In 2003, the Washington State Arts Commission and other Washington arts organizations received grants totaling $1,947,900 from the National Endowment for the Arts. The state of Washington has approximately 230 arts associations and 75 local arts groups. In 2002, Humanities Washington (est. 1973) sponsored 1,349 programs in 32 of 39 counties in Washington state. In 2000, the National Endowment for the Humanities contributed $1,456,062 for 21 state programs. Contributions to the arts also come from state and private sources.

43LIBRARIES AND MUSEUMS

In 2000, Washington's system of public libraries held more than 19,355,962 volumes and had a combined circulation of nearly 53,307,000. Of Washington's 39 counties, 27 were served by the state's 21 county and multi-county libraries. Total library income in 2000 came to $218,086,000, most of that total derived from local funds.

The leading public library system is the Seattle Public Library, with 25 branches and 1,892,067 volumes in 1998. The principal academic libraries are at the University of Washington (Seattle) and Washington State University (Pullman), with 5,820,230 and 1,966,516 volumes, respectively. Olympia is the home of the Washington State Library, with a collection of 339,194 books and more than one million documents.

Washington has 160 museums and historic sites. The Washington State Historical Society Museum (Tacoma) features Native American and other pioneer artifacts; the State Capitol Museum (Olympia) and Cheney Cowles Memorial Museum (Spokane) also have important historical exhibits, as do the Thomas Burke Memorial Washington State Museum (Seattle) and the Pacific Northwest Indian Center (Spokane). Mt. Rainier National Park displays zoological, botanical, geological, and historical collections. The Pacific Science Center (Seattle) concentrates on aerospace technology; the Seattle Aquarium is a leading attraction of Waterfront Park. Also in Seattle is Woodland Park Zoological Gardens, while Tacoma has the Point Defiance Zoo and Aquarium.

44COMMUNICATIONS

As of 2001, 96.9% of Washington's households had telephones. During 2003, Washington had 146 major radio stations—50 AM, 96 FM—and 19 major television stations. The Seattle-Tacoma area had 1,591,100 television households, 74% of which ordered cable. About 206,961 Internet domain names were registered in the state by the year 2000.

45PRESS

In 2002, Washington had 16 morning newspapers, 8 evening dailies, and 18 Sunday papers. The following table shows the leading newspapers with their approximate 2002 circulations:

AREA	NAME	DAILY	SUNDAY
Seattle	*Post-Intelligencer* (m,S)	169,105	478,612*
	Times (e,S)	219,941	478,612*
Spokane	*Spokesman–Review* (m,S)	105,911	137,500
Tacoma	*News Tribune* (m,S)	127,786	144,125

*Sunday edition is a combination of *Post-Intelligencer* and *Times*.

46ORGANIZATIONS

In 2003, there were about 3,787 regional, national, and international organizations within the state.

Among the associations with headquarters in Washington are the American Plywood Association and the American Academy on Mental Retardation, Tacoma; the Center for the Defense of Free Enterprise and the Citizens Committee for the Right to Keep and Bear Arms, Bellevue; the Pacific International Trapshooting Association, Puyallup; the Northwest Mining Association, Spokane; and the Northwest Fisheries Association, the International Association for the Study of Pain, the International Conference of Symphony and Opera Musicians, and the Mountaineers, all located in Seattle. The national offices of the Freedom Socialist Party are based in Seattle.

47TOURISM, TRAVEL, AND RECREATION

Seattle Center—featuring the 605-foot (184-meter) Space Needle tower, Opera House, and Pacific Science Center—helps make Washington's largest city one of the most exciting on the West Coast. Nevertheless, scenic beauty and opportunities for outdoor recreation are Washington's principal attractions for tourists from out of the state.

Mt. Rainier National Park, covering 235,404 acres (95,265 hectares), encompasses not only the state's highest peak but also the most extensive glacial system in the conterminous US. Glaciers, lakes, and mountain peaks are also featured at North Cascades National Park (504,780 acres/204,278 hectares), while Olympic National Park (908,720 acres/367,747 hectares) is famous as the site of Mt. Olympus and for its dense rain forest and rare elk herds. Deception Pass is another popular park. Washington also offers two national historic parks (San Juan Island and part of Klondike Gold Rush), two national historic sites (Fort Vancouver and the Whitman Mission), and three national recreation areas (Coulee Dam, Lake Chelan, and Ross Lake).

Tourism is the fourth-largest industry in Washington state, after aerospace/transportation equipment, agriculture, and timber. Travelers pumped more than $10 billion into the economy in each year on overnight and day trips in Washington. The industry supplies over 126,800 jobs in the state annually. Washington has been consistently ranked among the nation's top 10 tourist destination states and attracts a significant proportion of the nation's international visitors.

Part of the state's strategy currently under development focuses on regional appeal and off-season activities. Areas such as the Yakima Valley, the Columbia River Gorge, the Olympic Peninsula and the Methow Valley were rural, undervisited tourist markets that have been able to draw travelers by promoting the region as opposed to a city within the region. High seasonality is one of the biggest problems facing Washington State. Spring, fall, and winter traditionally do not draw as many tourists as the summer.

48 SPORTS

Washington is home to four major league professional sports teams, all of which play in Seattle. The Mariners, of Major League Baseball; the Seahawks, of the National Football League; the Storm, of the Women's National Basketball Association; and the Supersonics, of the National Basketball Association. The Supersonics won the NBA Championship in 1979. The Mariners reached the American League Championship Series in 1995. In collegiate sports, the Huskies of the University of Washington won the Rose Bowl in 1960, 1961, 1978, 1982, and 1992. Skiing, boating, and hiking are popular participant sports.

Other annual sporting events include outboard hydroplane races in Electric City in June and the Ellensburg Rodeo in September.

49 FAMOUS WASHINGTONIANS

Washington's most distinguished public figure was US Supreme Court Justice William O. Douglas (b.Minnesota, 1898–1980), who grew up in Yakima and attended Whitman College in Walla Walla. In addition to his 37-year tenure on the Court, an all-time high, Douglas was the author of numerous legal casebooks as well as 27 other volumes on various subjects. Other federal officeholders from Washington include Lewis B. Schwellenbach (b.Wisconsin, 1894–1948), secretary of labor under Harry Truman, and Brockman Adams (b.Georgia, 1927), secretary of transportation under Jimmy Carter. Serving in the US Senate from 1945 to 1981), Warren G. Magnuson (Minnesota, 1905–89) held the chairmanship of the powerful Appropriations Committee. A fellow Democrat, Henry M. "Scoop" Jackson (1912–83) was first elected to the House in 1940 and to the Senate in 1952. Influential on the Armed Services Committee, Jackson ran unsuccessfully for his party's presidential nomination in 1976. William E. Boeing (b.Michigan, 1881–1956) pioneered Washington's largest single industry, aerospace technology.

Notable governors include Isaac I. Stevens (b.Massachusetts, 1818–62), Washington's first territorial governor; after serving as Washington's territorial representative to Congress, he died in the Civil War. Elisha P. Ferry (b.Michigan, 1825–95), territorial governor from 1872 to 1880, was elected as Washington's first state governor in 1889. John R. Rogers (b.Maine, 1838–1901), Washington's only Populist governor, was also the first to be elected for a second term. Clarence D. Martin (1886–1955) was governor during the critical New Deal period. Daniel J. Evans (b.1925) is the youngest man ever elected governor of Washington and also is the only one to have served three consecutive terms (1965–77).

Dixy Lee Ray (1914–93), governor from 1977 to 1981 and the only woman governor in the state's history, was a former head of the federal Atomic Energy Commission and a staunch advocate of nuclear power. Other notable women were Emma Smith DeVoe (b.New Jersey, 1848–1927), a leading proponent of equal suffrage, and Bertha Knight Landes (b.Massachusetts, 1868–1943), elected mayor of Seattle in 1926; Landes, the first woman to be elected mayor of a large US city, was also an outspoken advocate of moral reform in municipal government.

Thomas Stephen Foley, former Speaker of the House, was born on 6 March 1929 in Spokane.

Several Washington Indians attained national prominence. Seattle (1786–1866) was the first signer of the Treaty of Point Elliott, which established two Indian reservations; the city of Seattle is named for him. Kamiakin (b.Idaho, c.1800–80) was the leader of the Yakima tribe during the Indian Wars of 1855, and Leschi (d.1858) was chief of the Nisqualli Indians and commanded the forces west of the Cascades during the 1855 uprising; Leschi was executed by the territorial government after the uprising was suppressed.

Washington authors have made substantial contributions to American literature. Mary McCarthy (1912–1989) was born in Seattle, and one of her books, *Memories of a Catholic Girlhood* (1957), describes her early life there. University of Washington professor Vernon Louis Parrington (b.Illinois, 1871–1929) was the first Washingtonian to win a Pulitzer Prize (1928), for his monumental *Main Currents in American Thought.* Another University of Washington faculty member, Theodore Roethke (b.Michigan, 1908–63), won the Pulitzer Prize for poetry in 1953. Seattle-born Audrey May Wurdemann (1911–60) was awarded a Pulitzer Prize for poetry in 1934 for *Bright Ambush.* Max Brand (Frederick Schiller Faust, 1892–1944) wrote hundreds of Western novels. Norman Ramsey (b.Washington, 1915) 1989 Nobel Prize recipient for physics. Hans Georg Dehmelt (b.Germany, 1922) was a recipient of the 1989 Nobel Prize for physics as a member at the University of Washington. George Herbert Hitchings, Nobel Prize winner in medicine 1988, was born April 18, 1905 in Hoquiam, Washington.

Singer-actor Harry Lillis "Bing" Crosby (1904–77), born in Tacoma, remained a loyal alumnus of Spokane's Gonzaga University. Modern dance choreographers Merce Cunningham (b.1919) and Robert Joffrey (1930–88) are both Washington natives. Photographer Edward S. Curtis (b.Wisconsin, 1868–1952) did most of the work on the North American Indian series while residing in Seattle. Modern artists Mark Tobey (b.Wisconsin, 1890–1976) spent much of his productive life in Seattle, and Robert Motherwell (1915–91) was born in Aberdeen. Washington's major contribution to popular music is rock guitarist Jimi Hendrix (1943–70).

50 BIBLIOGRAPHY

Asher, Brad. *Beyond the Reservation: Indians, Settlers, and the Law in Washington Territory, 1853–1889.* Norman: University of Oklahoma Press, 1999.

Bancroft, H. H. *History of Washington, Idaho, and Montana.* San Francisco: History Co., 1890.

Blair, Karen J. *Northwest Women: An Annotated Bibliography of Sources on the History of Oregon and Washington Women, 1787–1970.* Pullman, Wash.: Washington State University Press, 1997.

Clark, Norman H. *Washington: A Bicentennial History.* New York: Norton, 1976.

Douglas, William O. *Of Men and Mountains.* New York: Harper & Row, 1950.

Drury, Clifford M. *Marcus and Narcissa Whitman and the Opening of Old Oregon.* 2 vols. Glendale, Calif.: Clark, 1973.

Ficken, Robert E. *Lumber and Politics: The Career of Mark E. Reed.* Seattle: University of Washington Press, 1980.

Johansen, Dorothy O., and Charles M. Gates. *Empire of the Columbia: A History of the Pacific Northwest.* 2nd ed. New York: Harper & Row, 1967.

Kirk, Ruth. *Washington State: National Parks, Historic Sites, Recreation Areas, and Natural Landmarks.* Seattle: University of Washington Press, 1974.

Lee, W. Storrs, ed. *Washington State: A Literary Chronicle.* New York: Funk & Wagnalls, 1969.

Mapes, Lynda. *Washington: the Spirit of the Land.* Stillwater, Minn.: Voyageur Press, 1999.

Meany, Edmond S. *History of the State of Washington.* New York: Macmillan, 1909.

Meinig, D. W. *The Great Columbia Plain: A Historical Geography, 1805–1910*. Seattle: University of Washington Press, 1968.

Seeberger, Edward D. *Sine Die: A Guide to the Washington State Legislative Process*. Seattle, Wash.: Washington State University Press, 1997.

Snowden, Clinton A. *History of Washington*. 6 vols. New York: Century History, 1911.

Stewart, Edgar I. *Washington, Northwest Frontier*. 4 vols. New York: Lewis, 1957.

The Washington Almanac. Portland, Or.: WestWinds Press, 1999.

WEST VIRGINIA

State of West Virginia

ORIGIN OF STATE NAME: The state was originally the western part of Virginia. **NICKNAME:** The Mountain State. **CAPITAL:** Charleston. **ENTERED UNION:** 20 June 1863 (35th). **SONGS:** "The West Virginia Hills," "West Virginia, My Home Sweet Home," and "This Is My West Virginia." **MOTTO:** *Montani semper liberi* (Mountaineers are always free). **COAT OF ARMS:** A farmer stands to the right and a miner to the left of a large ivy-draped rock bearing the date of the state's admission to the Union. In front of the rock are two hunters' rifles upon which rests a cap of liberty. The state motto is beneath and the words "State of West Virginia" above. **FLAG:** The flag has a white field bordered by a strip of blue, with the coat of arms in the center, wreathed by rhododendron leaves; across the top of the coat of arms are the words "State of West Virginia." **OFFICIAL SEAL:** The same as the coat of arms. **ANIMAL:** Black bear. **BIRD:** Cardinal. **FISH:** Brook trout. **FLOWER:** Rhododendron. **TREE:** Sugar maple. **FRUIT:** Apple. **COLORS:** Old gold and blue. **LEGAL HOLIDAYS:** New Year's Day, 1 January; Birthday of Martin Luther King, Jr., 3rd Monday in January; Lincoln's Birthday, 12 February; Washington's Birthday, 3rd Monday in February; Memorial Day, last Monday in May; West Virginia Day, 20 June; Independence Day, 4 July; Labor Day, 1st Monday in September; Columbus Day, 2nd Monday in October; Veterans Day, 11 November; Thanksgiving Day, 4th Thursday in November; Christmas Day, 25 December. **TIME:** 7 AM EST = noon GMT.

¹LOCATION, SIZE, AND EXTENT

Located in the eastern US, in the South Atlantic region, West Virginia ranks 41st in size among the 50 states.

The area of West Virginia totals 24,231 sq mi (62,758 sq km), including 24,119 sq mi (62,468 sq km) of land and 112 sq mi (290 sq km) of inland water. The state extends 265 mi (426 km) E-W; its maximum N-S extension is 237 mi (381 km). West Virginia is one of the most irregularly shaped states in the US, with two panhandles of land—the northern, narrower one separating parts of Ohio and Pennsylvania, and the eastern panhandle separating parts of Maryland and Virginia.

West Virginia is bordered on the N by Ohio (with the line formed by the Ohio River), Pennsylvania, and Maryland (with most of the line defined by the Potomac River); on the E and S by Virginia; and on the W by Kentucky and Ohio (with the line following the Ohio, Big Sandy, and Tug Fork rivers).

The total boundary length of West Virginia is 1,180 mi (1,899 km). The geographical center of the state is in the Elk River Public Hunting Area in Braxton County, 4 mi (6 km) E of Sutton.

²TOPOGRAPHY

West Virginia lies within two divisions of the Appalachian Highlands. Most of the eastern panhandle, which is crossed by the Allegheny Mountains, is in the Ridge and Valley region. The remainder, or more than two-thirds of the state, is part of the Allegheny Plateau, to the west of a bold escarpment known as the Allegheny Front, and tilts toward the Ohio River.

The mean elevation of West Virginia is 1,500 ft (458 m), higher than any other state east of the Mississippi River. Its highest point, Spruce Knob, towers 4,861 ft (1,483 m) above sea level. Major lowlands lie along the rivers, especially the Potomac, Ohio, and Kanawha. A point on the Potomac River near Harpers Ferry has the lowest elevation, only 240 ft (73 m) above sea level. West Virginia has no natural lakes.

Most of the eastern panhandle drains into the Potomac River. The Ohio and its tributaries—the Monongahela, Little Kanawha, Kanawha, Guyandotte, and Big Sandy—drain most of the Allegheny Plateau section. Subterranean streams have carved out numerous caverns—including Seneca Caverns, Smoke Hole Caverns, and Organ Cave—from limestone beds.

During the Paleozoic era, when West Virginia was under water, a 30,000-ft (9,000-m) layer of rock streaked with rich coal deposits was laid down over much of the state. Alternately worn down and uplifted during succeeding eras, most of West Virginia is thus a plateau where rivers have carved deep valleys and gorges and given the land a rugged character.

³CLIMATE

West Virginia has a humid continental climate, with hot summers and cool to cold winters. The climate of the eastern panhandle is influenced by its proximity to the Atlantic slope and is similar to that of nearby coastal areas. Mean annual temperatures vary from 56°F (13°C) in the southwest to 48°F (9°C) at higher elevations. The yearly average is 53°F (12°C). The highest recorded temperature, 112°F (44°C), was at Martinsburg on 10 July 1936; the lowest, –37°F (–38°C), at Lewisburg on 30 December 1917.

Prevailing winds are from the south and west, and seldom reach hurricane or tornado force. In Charleston, average annual precipitation (1971–2000) was 44 in (111.8 cm) annually and is slightly heavier on the western slopes of the Alleghenies. Accumulations of snow may vary from about 20 in (51cm) in the western sections to more than 50 in (127 cm) in the higher mountains.

⁴FLORA AND FAUNA

With its varied topography and climate, West Virginia provides a natural habitat for more than 3,200 species of plants in three life zones: Canadian, Alleghenian, and Carolinian. Oak, maple, poplar, walnut, hickory, birch, and such softwoods as hemlock, pine, and spruce are the common forest trees. Rhododendron, laurel, dogwood, redbud, and pussy willow are among the more than 200 flowering trees and shrubs. Rare plant species include the box huckleberry, Guyandotte beauty, and Kate's mountain clover. The Cranberry Glades, an ancient lake bed similar to a glacial bog, contains the bog rosemary and other plant species common in more northern climates. In 2003, four plant species were listed as endangered, including shale barren rock-cress, harperella, northeastern bulrush, and running buffalo clover. The Virginia spirea and small whorled pogonia were the two species listed as threatened that year.

West Virginia fauna includes at least 56 species and subspecies of mammals and more than 300 types of birds. The gray wolf, puma, elk, and bison of early times have disappeared. The white-tailed (Virginia) deer and the black bear (both protected by the state) as well as the wildcat are still found in the deep timber of the Allegheny ridges; raccoons, skunks, woodchucks, opossums, gray and red foxes, squirrels, and cottontail rabbits remain numerous. Common birds include the cardinal, tufted titmouse, brown thrasher, scarlet tanager, catbird, and a diversity of sparrows, woodpeckers, swallows, and warblers. Major game birds are the wild turkey, bobwhite quail, and ruffed grouse; hawks and owls are the most common birds of prey. Notable among more than 100 species of fish are smallmouth bass, rainbow trout, and brook trout (the state fish). The copperhead and rattlesnake are both numerous and poisonous. In 2003, 15 animal species were listed as threatened or endangered in West Virginia, including the bald eagle, three species (gray, Indiana, and Virginia big-eared) of bat, fanshell, flat-spired three-toothed snail, and several species of pearlymussel.

5ENVIRONMENTAL PROTECTION

Major responsibility for environmental protection in West Virginia rests with the Division of Environmental Protection (DEP). The DEP was established in October 1991 and became West Virginia's leading environmental agency in July 1992, with the consolidation of the state's major environmental regulatory programs. Today, the DEP is responsible for the oversight of the state's Abandoned Mine Lands, Air Quality, Mining and Reclamation, Oil and Gas, Waste Management, and Water Resources programs. A new DEP program is the Office of Environmental Advocate. The office was created to improve public access and input into DEP functioning.

Environmental issues confronting the state of West Virginia include the restoration of about 2,000 mi (3,218 km) of streams that are being impacted by acid mine damage. To combat the problem, the state has created a Stream Restoration program, which is using a variety of treatment methods, including limestone drum technology, to improve water quality. The first treatment station is under construction in the Blackwater River watershed, with plans to construct a second station in the Middlefork River watershed. The state is in the midst of an initiative that focuses on better planning and management of West Virginia's five major watersheds. In 1996, less than 1% of West Virginia's land was designated wetlands.

The proper disposal of solid waste had been addressed through requirements for landfills to meet environmental safety standards by the end of 1994 or face closure. West Virginia also mandates that cities with populations of 10,000 or more develop recycling programs. In 2003, West Virginia had 154 hazardous waste sites listed in the Environmental Protection Agency's database, nine of which were on the National Priorities List. In 2001, West Virginia received $67,280,000 in federal grants from the EPA; EPA expenditures for procurement contracts in West Virginia that year amounted to just $1,000.

6POPULATION

West Virginia ranked 37th in population in the US with an estimated total of 1,801,873 in 2002, an increase of 0.4% since 2000. Between 1990 and 2000, West Virginia's population grew from 1,793,477 to 1,808,344, an increase of 0.8%. The

population is projected to reach 1,849,000 by 2005 and 1.8 million by 2025. The population density in 2000 was 75.1 persons per sq mi.

West Virginia is a relatively old state. In 2000 the median age was 38.9, compared to the US average of 35.3. Persons under 18 years old accounted for 22.3% of the population (the national average was 25.7%) while 15.3% were age 65 or older (national average 12.4%).

The state's population grew rapidly in the 1880s and 1890s, as coal mining, lumbering, and railroads expanded to meet the needs of nearby industrial centers, but the pace of expansion slowed in the early 20th century. The population peaked at 2,005,552 in 1950; then mass unemployment, particularly in the coal industry, caused thousands of families to migrate to midwestern cities. An upswing began in the 1970s.

West Virginia's major cities, all with populations of less than 100,000, are Charleston (the largest city), Huntington, Wheeling, and Parkersburg. The Huntington-Ashland metropolitan region, which includes parts of eastern Kentucky and southern Ohio, had an estimated population of 312,447 in 1999; the Charleston region had 251,199.

7ETHNIC GROUPS

Nearly all Indian inhabitants had left the state before the arrival of European settlers. In the 2000 census, about 3,606 Indians were counted.

The 57,232 blacks in the state in 2000 constituted about 3.2% of the population. The majority lived in industrial centers and coal-mining areas. Only 19,390 West Virginians, or 1.1% of the population, were foreign born in 2000. In 2000, there were 12,279 Hispanics and Latinos, representing 0.7% of the total population. In the same year, there were 9,434 persons of Asian origin. Persons reporting at least one specific ancestry group in 2000 included 176,297 English, 253,388 Germans, 198,473 Irish, and 37,837 Dutch.

8LANGUAGES

With little foreign immigration and with no effect from the original Iroquois and Cherokee Indians, West Virginia maintains Midland speech. There is a secondary contrast between the northern half and the southern half, with the former influenced by Pennsylvania and the latter by western Virginia.

The basic Midland speech sounds the /r/ after a vowel as in *far* and *short*, and has /kag/ for *keg*, /greezy/ for *greasy, sofy* instead of sofa, and *nicker* in place of neigh. The northern part has /yelk/ for *yolk*, /loom/ for *loam*, an /ai/ diphthong so stretched that sat and *sight* sound very much alike, *run* for creek, and *teeter(totter)* for seesaw. The southern half pronounces *here* and *hear* as /hyeer/, *aunt* and *can't* as /aint/ and /kaint/, and uses *branch* for creek, and *tinter* for teeter.

In 2000, 1,661,036 West Virginians—97.3% of the population five years of age or over (virtually unchanged since 1990)—spoke only English at home.

The following table gives selected statistics from the 2000 census for language spoken at home by persons five years old and over. The category "Other Indic languages" includes Bengali, Marathi, Punjabi, and Romany. The category "Other Asian languages" includes Dravidian languages, Malayalam, Telugu, Tamil, and Turkish.

LANGUAGE	NUMBER	PERCENT
Population 5 years and over	1,706,931	100.0
Speak only English	1,661,036	97.3
Speak a language other than English	45,895	2.7
Speak a language other than English	45,895	2.7
Spanish or Spanish Creole	17,652	1.0
French (incl. Patois, Cajun)	5,693	0.3
German	5,040	0.3

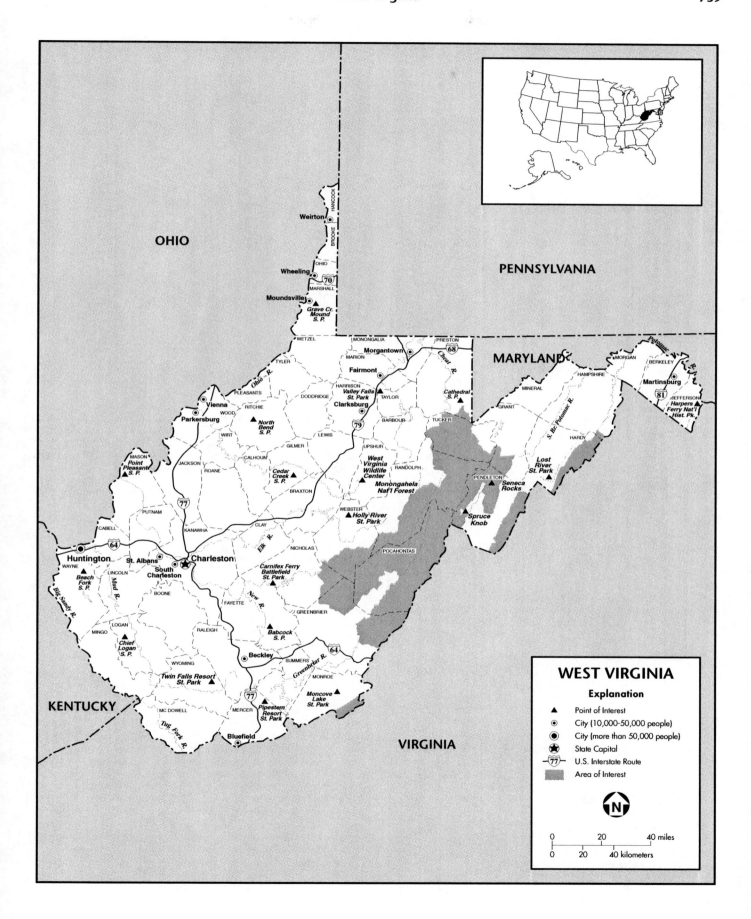

WEST VIRGINIA

Explanation

▲   Point of Interest

◉   City (10,000-50,000 people)

◉   City (more than 50,000 people)

★   State Capital

77   U.S. Interstate Route

     Area of Interest

0   20   40 miles

0   20   40 kilometers

LANGUAGE	NUMBER	PERCENT
Speak a language other than English (continued)		
Italian	2,815	0.2
Chinese	1,634	0.1
Arabic	1,563	0.1
Japanese	1,135	0.1
Tagalog	970	0.1
Greek	912	0.1
Other Indic languages	806	0.0
Other Asian languages	784	0.0
Polish	763	0.0
Korean	581	0.0

[9] RELIGIONS

Throughout its history, the religiously active population in West Virginia has been overwhelmingly Protestant. Most settlers before the American Revolution were Anglicans, Presbyterians, Quakers, or members of German sects, such as Lutherans, German Reformed, Dunkers, and Mennonites. The Great Awakening had a profound effect on these settlers and they avidly embraced its evangelism, emotionalism, and emphasis on personal religious experience. Catholics were mostly immigrants from Ireland and southern and eastern Europe.

In 2000, the major Protestant denominations and the number of their adherents were the United Methodist Church, 150,985; the American Baptist Churches USA, 108,087; the Southern Baptist Convention, 43,606; and the Presbyterian Church USA, 28,467. Other fundamentalist denominations included the Churches of Christ, 24,143; the Church of God (Cleveland, Tennessee), 21,657; and the Church of the Nazarene, 21,389. The Catholic population was 105,363 in 2000; there were an estimated at 2,400 Jews and 1,528 Muslims. Over 1.1 million people (about 64% of the population) were not counted as members of any religious organization.

[10] TRANSPORTATION

West Virginia has long been plagued by inadequate transportation. The first major pre–Civil War railroad line was the Baltimore and Ohio (B&O), completed to Wheeling in 1852. Later railroads, mostly built between 1880 and 1917 to tap rich coal and timber resources, also helped open up interior regions to settlement. Today, the railroads still play an important part in coal transportation. In 2000, CSX and Norfolk Southern were the state's Class I operators. In the same year, total rail mileage was 2,142 mi (3,427 km). Originated rail-tons of coal totaled 114.1 million tons, which accounted for 95% of all rail tonnage originating within the state that year; coal shipments terminating in West Virginia in 2000 totaled 23.7 million tons and accounted for 67% of the total that year. Amtrak provides passenger service for parts of the state.

In 2000, there were 27,276 mi (43,641 km) of public roads under the state system, 34,026 mi (54,441 km) of which were rural roads. The West Virginia Turnpike was completed from Charleston to Princeton in 1955. There were 1,418,862 registered motor vehicles in the state in 2000, 779,616 or which were automobiles, 612,638 were trucks, and 25,705 were motorcycles. In 2000, the state had 1,347,207 licensed drivers. The four major urban transit systems in 2000 were Kanawha Valley Transportation, Tri-State Authority (service between Huntington-Ashland and Kentucky and Ohio), Ohio Valley Regional Transportation Authority (serving Wheeling and Ohio), and Mid-Ohio Valley Transit Authority (serving Parkersburg and Ohio).

Major navigable inland rivers are the Ohio, Kanawha, and Monongahela; each has locks and dams. In 2000, West Virginia had 67 airports, 29 heliports, 10 seaplane bases, 1,992 active pilots, and 274 active flight instructors. Yeager Airport in Charleston is the state's main air terminal.

[11] HISTORY

Paleo-Indian cultures in what is now West Virginia existed some 15,000 years ago, when hunters pursued buffalo and other large game. About 7000 BC, they were supplanted by Archaic cultures, marked by pursuit of smaller game. Woodland (Adena) cultures, characterized by mound-building and agriculture, prevailed after about 1000 BC.

By the 1640s, the principal Indian claimants, the Iroquois and Cherokee, had driven out older inhabitants and made the region a vast buffer land. When European settlers arrived only a few Shawnee, Tuscarora, and Delaware Indian villages remained, but the area was still actively used as hunting and warring grounds, and European possession was hotly contested.

The fur trade stimulated early exploration. In 1671, Thomas Batts and Robert Fallam explored New River and gave England a claim to the Ohio Valley, to which most of West Virginia belongs. France also claimed the Ohio Valley by virtue of an alleged visit by Robert Cavelier, Sieur de la Salle, in 1669. England eventually prevailed as a result of the French and Indian War.

Unsubstantiated tradition credits Morgan Morgan, who moved to Bunker Hill in 1731, with the first settlement in the state. By 1750, several thousand settlers were living in the eastern panhandle. In 1769, following treaties with the Iroquois and Cherokee, settlers began to occupy the Greenbrier, Monongahela, and upper Ohio valleys, and movement into other interior sections continued into the Revolutionary War, although wars with Indians occurred sporadically until the 1790s. The area that is now West Virginia was part of Virginia at the time of that state's entry into the Union, 25 June 1788.

Serious differences between eastern and western Virginia developed after the War of 1812. Eastern Virginia was dominated by a slaveholding aristocracy, while small diversified farms and infant industries predominated in western Virginia. Westerners bristled under property qualifications for voting, inadequate representation in the Virginia legislature, and undemocratic county governments, as well as poor transportation, inadequate schools, inequitable taxes, and economic retardation. A constitutional convention in 1829–30 failed to effect changes, leaving the westerners embittered. In 1850–51 another convention met the west's political demands but exacerbated economic differences.

When Virginia seceded from the Union in 1861, western counties remaining loyal to the Union set up the Reorganized Government and consented to the separation of present-day West Virginia from Virginia. After approval by Congress and President Lincoln, West Virginia entered the Union on 20 June 1863 as the 35th state. West Virginia won control over Jefferson and Berkeley counties in the eastern panhandle in 1871, giving it a greater share of the Baltimore and Ohio Railroad lines in the state.

Both Bourbon Democratic and Republican governors after the Civil War sought to improve transportation, foster immigration, and provide tax structures attractive to business. Industrialists such as Democrats Henry Gassaway Davis and Johnson N. Camden, who amassed fortunes in coal, oil, railroads, and timber, sat in the US Senate and dominated party affairs in West Virginia. Similarly, industrialists Nathan Goff, Jr., and Stephen B. Elkins—Davis's son-in-law—wielded preponderant influence in the Republican Party from the 1870s until 1911. Native industrialists often collaborated with eastern interests to give the state a colonial economy dominated by absentee owners. Although Republican governors of the early 20th century were dominated by Elkins, they were attuned to Progressive ideas and were instrumental in the adoption of the direct primary, safety legislation for the coal mines, revision of corporate tax laws, and improvements in highways and education.

The Great Depression of the 1930s, from which West Virginia suffered acutely, ushered in a Democratic era. West Virginians embraced the New Deal and Fair Deal philosophies of presidents Franklin D. Roosevelt and Harry S. Truman.

World Wars I and II produced significant changes in West Virginia, particularly through stimulation of chemical, steel, and textile industries in the Kanawha and Ohio valleys and the eastern panhandle. These industries lessened the state's dependence on extractive industries, historically the backbone of its economy, and gave cities and towns a more cosmopolitan character.

Overshadowing the economic diversification was the plight of the coal-mining areas, where, after World War II, mechanization and strip-mining displaced thousands of miners and resulted in a large exodus to other states. By 1960, West Virginia was considered one of the most economically depressed areas of the country, primarily because of conditions in the mining regions. The antipoverty programs of the Kennedy and Johnson administrations provided some relief, but much of it was temporary, as was a brief upsurge in coal mining during the late 1970s.

Over the last several decades, West Virginia's manufacturing and mining sectors have shrunk dramatically. Automation, foreign competition, and the recession of the early 1980s caused employment in steel, glass, and chemical manufacturing and in coal mining to drop by a third between 1979 and 1985, when the state had the highest rate of unemployment in the nation.

West Virginia's economy improved in the 1990s. Coal and timber production expanded, and trade and tourism were boosted by the completion of Interstate Highway 64 in 1988. The state won a number of federal projects (including the FBI's fingerprint identification division), aided by the tenure of Democrat Robert C. Byrd as chairman of the US Senate Appropriations Committee from 1988 to 1995. As of 2003, he was ranking member on the committee.

In early 2003, Democratic Governor Bob Wise called for a special session of the legislature to prevent the state Workers' Compensation Fund from going bankrupt. The system provides medical care and cash benefits for workers injured on the job.

12 STATE GOVERNMENT

Since becoming a state, West Virginia has had two constitutions. The first, adopted in 1863, served until 1872, when the present constitution was adopted. As of January 2003, 70 amendments to this constitution had become law.

The legislature consists of a senate with 34 members and a house of delegates with 100 members. Senators and delegates must be at least 25 and 18 years old, respectively. All legislators must be qualified voters, state citizens, and residents of the state for at least five years and of their districts for at least one year before taking their seats. Senators are elected to staggered four-year terms, and delegates serve for two years. The legislature meets annually in 60-day sessions, beginning in January or February. Special sessions may be called by a petition signed by three-fifths of the members of each house. The legislative salary in 2002 was $15,000, unchanged from 1999.

Elected officials of the executive branch of government are the governor, secretary of state, auditor, attorney general, commissioner of agriculture, and treasurer, all elected for four-year terms. The governor, who may serve no more than two terms in succession, must be at least 30 years old, a registered voter, a citizen of the state for at least five years, and a resident for at least one. His successor is the president of the senate (there is no lieutenant governor). In 2002, the governor's salary was $90,000.

Bills passed by the legislature become law when signed by the governor or left unsigned for five days when the legislature is in session (or 15 days after it has adjourned). Bills vetoed by the governor become law if passed again by a majority of the elected members of each house. To override a gubernatorial veto of a revenue or appropriations bill, two-thirds of the elected members of each house must approve it. Either house may propose an amendment to the state constitution. If both houses approve it by a two-thirds majority, it is submitted to the voters at the next regular election or at a special election for adoption by majority vote.

Voters in West Virginia must live in the state, be US citizens, and at least 18 years old. Restrictions apply to those convicted of certain crimes and to those judged by the court as mentally incompetent to vote.

13 POLITICAL PARTIES

The Republican Party presided over the birth of West Virginia, but the Democrats have generally been in power for the past five decades. In 1940, a strong New Deal faction, headed by Matthew M. Neely and supported by organized labor, formed the "state-house machine," which became a dominant factor in state politics. Only two Republicans, Cecil H. Underwood (1957–61, 1997–2001) and Arch Moore, Jr. (1969–77, 1985–89), have been governor since 1933. Underwood was elected in 1996, having vacated the office 35 years earlier. Democrat Bob Wise unseated Underwood in 2001.

Democratic Senator Robert C. Byrd, first elected in 1958, was reelected to his eighth term in 2000. Democratic Senator John D. "Jay" Rockefeller IV, first elected in 1984, was reelected to his fourth term in 2002. Following the 2002 elections, West Virginia sent two Democrats and one Republican to the US House of Representatives. As of mid-2003, Democrats controlled both the state house and state senate. There were 24 Democrats and 10 Republicans in the state senate, and 68 Democrats and 32 Republicans in the state house.

Since the New Deal, Republican presidential candidates have carried West Virginia only in 1956, 1972, 1984, and 2000. In 2000, Republican George W. Bush received 52% of the popular vote to Democrat Al Gore's 46%; Green Party candidate Ralph Nader garnered 2% of the vote. In 2002 there were 1,060,892 registered voters. In 1998, 63% of registered voters were Democratic, 29% Republican, and 8% unaffiliated or members of other parties. The state had five electoral votes in the 2000 presidential election.

West Virginia Presidential Vote by Major Political Parties, 1948–2000

YEAR	ELECTORAL VOTE	WEST VIRGINIA WINNER	DEMOCRAT	REPUBLICAN
1948	8	*Truman (D)	429,188	316,251
1952	8	Stevenson (D)	453,578	419,970
1956	8	*Eisenhower (R)	381,534	449,297
1960	8	*Kennedy (D)	441,786	395,995
1964	7	*Johnson (D)	538,087	253,953
1968	7	Humphrey (D)	374,091	307,555
1972	6	*Nixon (R)	277,435	484,964
1976	6	*Carter (D)	435,914	314,760
1980	6	Carter (D)	367,462	334,206
1984	6	*Reagan (R)	328,125`	405,483
1988	6	Dukakis (D)	341,016	310,065
1992**	5	*Clinton (D)	331,001	241,974
1996**	5	*Clinton (D)	327,812	233,946
2000	5	*Bush, G. W. (R)	295,497	336,475

* Won US presidential election.
** Independent candidate Ross Perot received 108,829 votes in 1992, and 71,639 in 1996.

14 LOCAL GOVERNMENT

West Virginia has 55 counties (2002). The chief county officials are the three commissioners, elected for six-year terms, who serve on the county court; the sheriff, assessor, county clerk, and prosecuting attorney, elected for four-year terms; and the five-member board of education, elected for six-year terms. The sheriff is the principal peace officer but also collects taxes and disburses funds of the county court and board of education. The 234 cities, towns, and villages as of 2002 are divided into classes according to population. They are run by mayor and council or by council and city manager. There were 55 public school districts and 397 special districts in 2002.

15 STATE SERVICES

To address the continuing threat of terrorism and to work with the federal Department of Homeland Security (created in 2002 following the terrorist attacks of 11 September 2001), homeland security in West Virginia in 2003 operated under the authority of the governor; the public safety secretary was designated as the state homeland security advisor.

The Department of Education determines policy for public elementary and secondary schools, and the Board of Regents governs the state's colleges and universities. The Department of Transportation is responsible for construction and operation of state roads. Services of the Department of Health center around treatment of alcoholism and drug abuse, mental health, environmental health services, maternal and child care, family planning, and control of communicable diseases. The Department of Human Services administers a variety of economic, medical, and social services.

In the area of public protection, the Department of Public Safety enforces criminal and traffic laws, the Office of Emergency Services oversees civil defense and other emergency activities, and the Department of Corrections oversees prisons and other such facilities. The Public Service Commission regulates utilities. The Housing Development Fund concentrates on housing for low- and middle-income families and the elderly. The Division of Environmental Protection has the major responsibility for protection of forests, wildlife, water, and other resources, for reclamation projects, and for operation of state parks and recreational facilities.

Responsibility in labor matters is shared by the Department of Labor, Department of Employment Security, Department of Mines, Workers' Compensation Fund, and Labor-Management Relations Board.

16 JUDICIAL SYSTEM

The highest court in West Virginia, the supreme court of appeals, has five justices, including the chief justice, elected for 12-year terms. The court has broad discretionary appellate jurisdiction in both civil and criminal cases, and original jurisdiction in certain other cases.

West Virginia's general trial court is the circuit court, with 156 judges in 1999. Each circuit serves from one to four counties and has jurisdiction over civil cases in amounts that exceed $300 and criminal cases. Circuit courts also have jurisdiction over juveniles, domestic relations, and certain administrative appeals. Family law specialists conduct most domestic relations hearings.

Local courts include the county magistrate and municipal courts. Magistrate courts have original jurisdiction in criminal matters but may not convict or sentence in felony cases. All judges down to the magistrate level are popularly elected by partisan ballot. Municipal, police, or mayor's courts have authority to enforce municipal ordinances; unlike other courts, these are not part of the unified court system. Appeals from municipal and magistrate courts are to circuit courts, and from circuit courts are to the supreme court.

As of June 2001, there were 4,130 prisoners in state or federal correctional facilities, an increase of 8.7% over the previous year.

The state's incarceration rate stood at 225 per 100,000 inhabitants.

In 2001, West Virginia's crime rate was 2,559.5 per 100,000 persons, including a total of 5,035 violent crimes and 41,085 crimes against property in that year. The state abolished the death penalty in 1965.

17 ARMED FORCES

In 2002, there were 558 active duty military personnel and 1,783 civilian personnel stationed in West Virginia. The state has no military bases, academies, or training facilities. The Naval Telecommunications Station (Sugar Grove) is the main receiving facility for the Navy's global high-frequency radio communications and for point-to-point circuits destined for Washington, DC. In 2002, defense contracts awarded West Virginia totaled about $107 million.

According to the 2000 Census, there were 201,701 veteran living in West Virginia, of whom 41,041 served in World War II; 27,410 in the Korean conflict; 61,260 in the Vietnam era; and 18,723 in 1990–2000 (including the Persian Gulf War). In 2002, veterans received nearly $620 million in benefits.

In 2000, the West Virginia State Police employed 681 full-time sworn officers.

18 MIGRATION

West Virginia has considerable national and ethnic diversity. Settlers before the Civil War consisted principally of English, German, Scotch-Irish, and Welsh immigrants, many of whom came by way of Pennsylvania. A second wave of immigration from the 1880s to the 1920s brought thousands of Italians, Poles, Austrians, and Hungarians to the coal mines and industrial towns, which also attracted many blacks from the South. In 1980, 79% of the residents of the state were born in West Virginia (4th highest among states).

Between 1950 and 1970, West Virginia suffered a 13% loss in population, chiefly from the coal-mining areas; but between 1970 and 1980, population rose by almost 12%. According to federal estimates, the state had a net migration gain of 71,000 in the 1970s and a net migration loss of about 81,000 in the 1980s. Between 1990 and 1998, West Virginia had net gains of 8,000 in domestic migration and 3,000 in international migration. In 1998, the state admitted 375 foreign immigrants. Between 1990 and 1998, the state's overall population increased by 1%. In the period 1995–2000, 138,487 people moved into the state and 149,241 moved out, for a net loss of 10,754, many of whom moved to Ohio.

19 INTERGOVERNMENTAL COOPERATION

The West Virginia Commission on Interstate Cooperation participates in the Council of State Governments. West Virginia is a member of some 30 regional compacts, including the Ohio River Valley Water Sanitation and Potomac River Basin compacts, Interstate Mining Compact Commission, Wheeling Creek Watershed Protection and Flood Prevention Commission, Ohio River Basin Commission, Appalachian Regional Commission, Jennings Randolph Lake Project Compact, Southern Regional Education Board, Southern States Energy Board, and Southern Governors' Association. In 2001, federal grants to West Virginia totaled over $2.9 billion.

20 ECONOMY

Agriculture was the backbone of West Virginia's economy until the 1890s, when extractive industries (including coal, oil, natural gas, and timber) began to play a major role. World War I stimulated important secondary industries, such as chemicals, steel, glass, and textiles. The beauty of West Virginia's mountains and forests attracted an increasing number of tourists in the 1990s, but the state's rugged topography and relative isolation from major markets continued to hamper its economic development. West Virginia did not participate substantially in the high-tech boom of the 1990s, as the long-term decline of its critical coal mining sector continued. From 1997 to 2000, output from the general services and retail trade sectors grew 19% and 13.6%, respectively, while coal mining declined 17.6%, trends that meant the loss of coal mining jobs paying more than $53,000 a year and the increase in service jobs paying $14,000 to $24,000. Output from the manufacturing sector fell at the same rate as mining output (17.6%) 1997 to 2000, although from an high base($6.5 billion in 1997 vs. $2.4 billion from coal mining). Overall growth was sluggish in the late 1990s, reaching 3.8% in 1999 (up from 1.9% in 1998) but falling to 0.1% in 2000. In 2001, growth actually improved to 3.5%, including a 13.8% jump in output from coal mining. However, by 2002, the national economic slowdown had begun to impact West Virginia employment, and by October 2002, there had been year-on-year losses in jobs in every state economic sector except services and government (a sector that grew 24.5% 1997 to 2001). The overall decline in employment was 0.7%, ahead of the national average of 0.4%.

In 2001, West Virginia's gross state product gross state product was $42.4 billion, the 40th largest among the states, to which general services contributed $8.3 billion; government, $7.1 billion; trade, $14.9 billion; manufacturing, $5.2 billion; financial services, $5 billion; transportation and public utilities, $4.6 billion, and construction, $2.1 billion. The public sector in 2001 constituted 16.8% of gross state product, well above the 12% average for the states.

21 INCOME

According to the Bureau of Economic Analysis, in 2001, West Virginia had a per capita personal income (PCPI) of $22,862 which ranked 49th in the United States (including the District of Columbia) and was 75% of the national average, $30,413. The 2001 PCPI reflected an increase of 4.8% from 2000 compared to the national change of 2.2%. In 2001, West Virginia had a total personal income (TPI) of $41,173,821,000 which ranked 39th in the United States and accounted for 0.5% of the national total. The 2001 TPI reflected an increase of 4.4% from 2000 compared to the national change of 3.3%.

Earnings of persons employed in West Virginia increased from $24,648,169,000 in 2000 to $25,618,719,000 in 2001, an increase of 3.9%. The largest industries in 2001 were services, 26.6% of earnings; state and local government, 15.8%; and retail trade, 9.3%. Of the industries that accounted for at least 5% of earnings in 2001, the slowest growing from 2000 to 2001 was durable goods manufacturing (7.4% of earnings in 2001), which decreased 3.8%; the fastest was mining (6.0% of earnings in 2001), which increased 12.0%.

According to data released by the US Census Bureau, in 2000, the median household income was $29,052 compared to the national average of $42,148. In 2001, the median income for a family of four was $49,470 compared to the national average of $63,278. For the period 1999 to 2001, the average poverty rate was 15.6% which placed it 46th among the 50 states and the District of Columbia ranked lowest to highest.

22 LABOR

According to Bureau of Labor Statistics (BLS) provisional estimates, in July 2003 the seasonally adjusted civilian labor force in West Virginia numbered 808,500, with approximately 54,600 workers unemployed, yielding an unemployment rate of 6.8%, compared to the national average of 6.2% for the same period.

Since the beginning of the BLS data series in 1978, the highest unemployment rate recorded was 19.5% in February 1983. The historical low was 4.7% in October 2001. In 2001, an estimated 5.3% of the labor force was employed in construction; 11.8% in manufacturing; 6.2% in transportation, communications, and public utilities; 19.9% in trade; 3.7% in finance, insurance, and real estate; 26.6% in services; 15.9% in government; and 1.3% in agriculture.

Important milestones in the growth of unionism were the organization of the state as District 17 of the United Mine Workers of America (UMWA) in 1890 and the formation of the State Federation of Labor in 1903. The coal miners fought to gain union recognition by coal companies, and instances of violence were not uncommon in the early 1900s. Wages, working conditions, and benefits for miners improved rapidly after World War II. Membership in unions in 1980 was 222,000, or 34% of the work force, compared to 47% in 1970, an indication of the UMWA's waning strength.

The US Department of Labor reported that in 2002, 92,000 of West Virginia's 693,000 employed wage and salary workers were members of unions. This represented 13.3% of those so employed, down from 14.6% in 2001. The national average is 13.2%. In all, 97,000 workers (14.0%) were represented by unions. In addition to union members, this category includes workers who report no union affiliation but whose jobs are covered by a union contract.

23 AGRICULTURE

With estimated farm marketings of $408 million ($348 million from livestock and poultry), West Virginia ranked 46th among the 50 states in 2002. Poultry, meat animals, and dairy dominate the farm economy in the Mountain State.

Until about 1890 small, diversified farms were dominant, but, as in other states, farms have grown larger and the farm population has dropped. In 2002, the state had 3,600,000 acres (1,457,000 hectares), or 23% of its land, devoted to farming. Its 20,500 farms averaged 176 acres (71 hectares) in size. Major farm sections are the eastern panhandle, a tier of counties along the Virginia border, the upper Monongahela Valley, and the Ohio Valley. Leading crops produced in 2002 were hay, 1,061,000 tons; corn for grain, 3,150,000 bushels; corn for silage, 314,000 tons; commercial apples, 105,000,000 lb; and tobacco, 1,950,000 lb.

24 ANIMAL HUSBANDRY

In 2003, there were an estimated 405,000 cattle and calves, valued at $243 million. During 2002, the state had 11,000 hogs and pigs, valued at around $814,000. During 2001, poultry farmers produced 368.2 million lb (167 million kg) of broilers valued at $143.6 million, and 90.6 million lb of turkey, valued at $35 million. The dairy industry yielded 249 million lb (112.9 million kg) of milk and 235 million eggs.

25 FISHING

West Virginia fishing has little commercial importance. In 1998, aquacultural facilities distributed over 2.2 million trout within the state. Fishing licenses issues in that year numbered 282,750.

26 FORESTRY

In 2002, West Virginia had four-fifths, or 12.1 million acres (4.9 million hectares), of its land area in forestland and, of this, 11.9 million acres (4.8 million hectares) are classified as timberland.

In 1997, West Virginia's timber resource was the largest and of the highest quality of any time in the past 75 or more years, with 64% of its timberland being sawtimber size. Sawtimber volumes average 6,500 board feet per acre. About 92% of West Virginia forest species are hardwoods, with approximately 77% of the timberland being of the oak-hickory forest type. In all, West Virginia's forests contain more than 100 species of trees.

During the early 1900s, West Virginia became a lumbering giant. From 1908 to 1911, some 1,500 mills produced up to 1.5 billion board ft of lumber annually to feed the nation's needs. By 1920, the state was first in the production of cherry and chestnut lumber and 13th in total production. After the extensive logging and resulting debris came forest fires which devastated the remaining forest resource and caused extensive soil erosion. In the early 1930s, a cooperative fire prevention program was initiated in the state and later in the early 1950s, an educational and forestry technical assistance program was created to help forest landowners manage and protect their forests. The maturing forests of West Virginia languished in their contribution to the state's economy until the 1980s when annual production, which had averaged around 350 to 450 million board ft per year, began to increase significantly.

Production increased to 600 million board ft in 1988, and 724 million board ft by 2002. Employment in the forest industry is 2nd only to the chemical and primary metal manufacturing industries. However, it is estimated that growth still exceeded removals by a ratio of 1.34 to 1. Even more important, the net volume of all growing stock on timberland increased from 9.1 to 20.3 million cu ft between 1953 and 1997.

The state is encouraging the professional management of its forests so they will continue to produce a sustained array of benefits, such as wood products, jobs, clean water, oxygen, scenery, and diverse recreational opportunities like hunting, hiking, and tourism.

27MINING

The value of nonfuel mineral production in West Virginia in 2001 was about $185 million (up 7.5% from 2000). According to preliminary figures, in 2001 crushed stone accounted for about 35% ($65.4 million for 14.5 million metric tons) of the state's total value of nonfuel minerals. In the same year, construction sand and gravel production was 1.78 million short tons, worth $8.93 million.

28ENERGY AND POWER

West Virginia has long been an important supplier of energy in the form of electric power and fossil fuels. In 1999, installed capacity (utility and nonutility) was almost 15.1 million kW; net generation of electric energy was 94.8 billion kWh, of which nearly 99% was produced by coal-fired steam units. Out of 26.5 billion kWh of electricity sold in the state in 1998, 35% went to residential customers, 23% to commercial, and 42% to industrial consumers. The state's power facilities are all privately owned. The John Amos Plant, on the Kanawha River, is one of the world's largest investor-owned generating plants. In 2000 West Virginia's total per capita energy consumption was 411 million Btu (103.6 million kcal), ranking it 11th among the 50 states.

Major coal-mining regions lie within a north–south belt some 60 mi (97 km) wide through the central part of the state and include the Fairmount, New River-Kanawha, Pocahontas, and Logan-Mingo fields. In 1998, West Virginia was 2nd to Wyoming in coal production, with 346 mines producing 171.1 million tons (15% of the national total), all of it bituminous and 68% of it mined underground. In 2000, 37.6 million tons were produced in northern West Virginia, and 120.7 million tons in the southern part of the state. West Virginia produced 4,000 barrels per day of oil in 2002, and 250.9 billion cu ft (7.1 billion cu m) of natural gas in 2001. Proved crude oil reserves in 2001 totaled 8 million barrels; natural gas, 2.7 trillion cu ft (0.08 billion cu m).

29INDUSTRY

Known for its rich natural resources and strong industrial presence, the value of West Virginian shipments by manufacturers in 1997 was $19 billion.

Major industrial areas are the Kanawha, Ohio, and Monongahela valleys and the eastern panhandle. The largest industrial corporations with headquarters in West Virginia are Weirton Steel and Wheeling-Pittsburgh. Other major industrial companies with operations in West Virginia include E. I. du Pont de Nemours, Union Carbide, Ravenswood Aluminum, and Rhone Poulenc.

Earnings of persons employed in West Virginia increased from $21.9 billion in 1997 to $22.7 billion in 1998, an increase of 3.5%. The largest industries in 1998 were services, 25.0% of earnings; state and local government, 14.2%; and retail trade, 9.8%. Of the industries that accounted for at least 5% of earnings in 1998, the slowest growing from 1997 to 1998 was mining (7.0% of earnings in 1998), which decreased 2.3%; the fastest was services, which increased 5.5%.

30COMMERCE

In 1997, West Virginia's 9,697 wholesale trade establishments had sales of $65 billion. Retail sales of $65 billion in 1997 were executed by 38,588 businesses. Food stores made up 14% of the total number of enterprises; automotive dealers, 17%; and eating and drinking places, 26%. In 1998, West Virginia exported $2.1 billion worth of products, ranking it 37th in the nation.

31CONSUMER PROTECTION

The state attorney general's office, Division of Consumer Protection and Antitrust, is empowered to investigate, arbitrate, and litigate complaints by consumers alleging unfair and deceptive trade practices, and violations of the West Virginia Consumer Credit and Protection Act, the West Virginia Antitrust Act, and the Pre-need Funeral Contracts Act. There are five assistant attorneys general assigned to defend these laws.

The Public Service Commission, consisting of three members, regulates rates, charges, and services of utilities and common carriers. Since 1977, it has included one member who is supposed to represent the "average" wage earner.

32BANKING

West Virginia had 59 insured banks at the end of 2002, with assets worth $7 billion. Forty-three of those banks were state-chartered.

The state's insured banks reported increased return on assets (ROA) ratios (the measure of earnings in relation to all resources) in 2002, due to the relatively mild effect of the 2001 recession on the West Virginia economy. Net interest margins (NIMs) (the difference between the lower rates offered to savers and the higher rates charged on loans) were also higher during 2002.

There was a 3% growth rate in loans between 2001 and 2002, especially in the commercial real estate (CRE) sector.

33INSURANCE

In 1991, one life insurance company, three property and casualty insurance companies, and 11 farmers mutual fire insurance companies were domiciled in West Virginia. As of 2000, there were four property and casualty and two life and health insurance companies incorporated or organized in the state. In 2001, property and casualty insurers wrote over $1.8 billion in premiums. That year, there were 19,091 flood insurance policies in force in the state, at a total value of $1.4 million.

In 2001, there were 1.1 million ordinary life insurance policies in force with a total value of $39.5 billion; total value for all categories of life insurance (ordinary, group, industrial, and credit) was $69.4 billion. Death benefits paid that year totaled $264.5 million.

34SECURITIES

There are no securities exchanges in West Virginia. West Virginia has 154 broker-dealers organizations doing business in the state, with over 500 employees. There are 14 investment advisor firms registered in West Virginia. The state is headquarters to 14 NASDAQ companies.

35PUBLIC FINANCE

The state constitution requires the governor to submit to the legislature within 10 days after the opening of a regular legislative session a budget for the ensuing fiscal year (1 July–30 June).

Total revenue for 2000/01 was estimated at $8 billion, 35% from the general fund, 30% from federal funds, 23% from special revenue funds, and 12% from state road funds. Expenditures were expected to equal revenue, including: health and human resources (29%), education (22%), transportation (17%), higher education and the arts (14%), and public safety (3.4%).

The overall budget for 2003/04 was $8.1 billion. General fund expenditures were budgeted at $3.034 billion (equal to expected revenues), of which $1.56 billion (51.4%) were targeted for public education.

The following table from the US Census Bureau contains information on revenues, expenditures, indebtedness, and cash/securities for 2001.

	($000)	PERCENT	PER CAPITA
Population (thousands, 2001)	1,801	(X)	(X)
Total Revenue	8,296,556	100.00	4,606.64
General revenue	6,958,550	83.87	3,863.71
Utility revenue	374	–	0.21
Liquor store revenue	50,784	0.61	28.20
Insurance trust revenue	1,286,848	15.51	714.52
Exhibit: Salaries and wages	1,182,154	16.19	656.39
Total expenditure	7,300,483	100.00	4,053.57
General expenditure	6,165,244	84.45	3,423.23
Education	1,930,625	26.45	1,071.97
Public welfare	1,564,560	21.43	868.72
Hospitals	74,653	1.02	41.45
Health	145,136	1.99	80.59
Highways	1,187,038	16.26	659.10
Police protection	37,874	0.52	21.03
Correction	122,009	1.67	67.75
Natural resources	148,350	2.03	82.37
Parks and recreation	58,026	0.79	32.22
Government administration	316,539	4.34	175.76
Interest on general debt	216,642	2.97	120.29
Other and unallocable	363,792	4.98	201.99
Utility expenditure	4,025	0.06	2.23
Liquor store expenditure	44,112	0.60	24.49
Insurance trust expenditure	1,087,102	14.89	603.61
Debt at end of fiscal year	4,091,919	100.00	2,272.03
Cash and security holdings	10,313,189	100.00	5,726.37

36TAXATION

Personal income taxes range from 3.0% to 6.5%. The corporate income tax is 9%; and consumer sales taxes are 6% on goods and services including food. West Virginia has a business and occupations tax on gross income; the West Virginia Business and Occupation Tax is imposed on public utilities and generators of electric power. Counties and localities mainly tax real and personal property. Most state and local revenues—over 70%—is collected at the state level.

The state collected $3.552 billion in taxes in 2002, of which 29% came from individual income taxes, 27.1% from the general sales tax, 26.9% from selective sales taxes, 4.9% from state license fees, and 6.2% from corporate income taxes. In 2003,

West Virginia ranked 23rd among the states in terms of combined state and local tax burden, which amounted to about 9.7% of income

The following table from the US Census Bureau provides a summary of taxes collected by the state in 2002.

	($000)	PER CAPITA
Total Taxes	**3,551,756**	**1,971.15**
Property taxes	3,819	2.12
Sales and gross receipts	1,920,724	1,065.96
General sales and gross receipts	962,756	534.31
Selective sales taxes	957,968	531.65
Alcoholic beverage	8,621	4.78
Amusements	(X)	(X)
Insurance Premiums	88,586	49.16
Motor fuels	300,049	166.52
Pari-mutuels	11,973	6.64
Public utilities	186,902	103.73
Tobacco products	32,219	17.88
Other selective sales	329,618	182.93
Licenses	174,660	96.93
Alcoholic beverages	8,717	4.84
Amusements	14	0.01
Corporation	7,235	4.02
Hunting and fishing	16,434	9.12
Motor vehicle	87,320	48.46
Motor vehicle operators	3,940	2.19
Public utility	20,367	11.3
Occupation and business, NEC	30,387	16.86
Other	246	0.14
Other taxes	1,452,553	806.14
Individual income	1,034,665	574.22
Corporation net income	220,158	122.18
Death and gift	13,322	7.39
Documentary and stock transfer	7,315	4.06
Severance	177,093	98.28
Other	(X)	(X)

37ECONOMIC POLICY

The West Virginia Development Office supports business and industry in the state and assists new companies with site location and employee training programs as well as with the construction of plants and access roads and the provision of essential services. The West Virginia Economic Development Authority may make loans of up to 50% of the costs of land, buildings, and equipment at low interest rates for a normal term of 15 years. Tax incentives include a credit of 10% on industrial expansion and revitalization, applicable to the business and occupations tax over a 10-year period. The Development Office helps small business by investing in venture capital companies and by offering loans for venture capital purposes. In 2003, West Virginia has trade offices in Munich, Germany and Nagoya, Japan. The main emphasis of the Governor's program was work force development.

38HEALTH

West Virginia's infant mortality rate was 7.6 per 1,000 live births in 2000, above the national average rate of 6.9. In 1999, 2,498 abortions were performed, or 7 per 1,000 women. The overall death rate in West Virginia, 1,171.5 per 100,000 population in 2000, was the highest in the nation. Only 1,178 AIDS cases had been reported in West Virginia through 2001. In 2000, West Virginia had the highest death rate from cardiovascular disease of any state, at 357.0 per 100,000 inhabitants, and of cancer at 263.7. Other leading causes of death were stroke, accidents, chronic obstructive pulmonary diseases, pneumonia and flu, and diabetes. Pneumoconiosis (black lung) is an occupational hazard among coal miners. In the 2000, 26.1% of persons 18 years of age and older in West Virginia were smokers.

West Virginia's 57 community hospitals had 297,079 admissions and 7,906 beds in 2001. There were 8,512 full-time registered nurses and 1,877 full-time licensed practical nurses in 2001 and 238 physicians per 100,000 population in 2000. The average expense of a community hospital for care was $1,591.30 per inpatient day in 2001.

Federal government grants to cover the Medicare and Medicaid services in 2001 totaled $1.2 billion; 339,853 enrollees received Medicare benefits that year. At least 13.2% of West Virginia's residents were uninsured in 2002.

Medical education is provided by medical schools at West Virginia University and Marshall University and at the West Virginia School of Osteopathic Medicine.

39 SOCIAL WELFARE

Although rich in natural resources, West Virginia is a generally poor state. In 2001, the average weekly unemployment benefit was $201.46. Average monthly participation in the food stamp program in FY2002 comprised 2353,736 persons (100,359 households). The average monthly benefit was $70.00, and the sum total of benefits paid in FY2002 was $198,011,265.

With the enactment of the Personal Responsibility and Work Opportunity Reconciliation Act of 1996, the US government has changed the form and regulations for many of its social welfare programs. Most significantly, it replaces Aid to Families with Dependent Children (AFDC), an open-ended entitlement program, with Temporary Assistance for Needy Families (TANF), a limited system of assistance funded largely through federal block grants. The reform act also impacts the food stamp program, the Supplemental Security Income program, and the child nutrition program. The law took effect on 1 July 1997 and provided $16.38 billion in block grants for the next five fiscal years (1997–2002). The grants are to be divided among the states based on an equation involving the numbers of former AFDC recipients in each state.

Reauthorization of the 1996 social welfare legislation, scheduled for 2002, was delayed, and the original law had been extended three times as of July 2003, with the most recent extension running through September 2003. West Virginia's TANF program is called West Virginia Works. In June 2000 the state had 31,500 welfare recipients. State expenditures on the TANF program in FY2002 totaled $34,446,442.

In December 2001, Social Security benefits were paid to 394,510 West Virginians. This number included 201,500 retired workers, 58,860 widows and widowers, 64,210 disabled workers, 33,140 spouses, and 36,800 children. Social Security beneficiaries represented 22% of the total state population and 93.2% of the state's population age 65 and older. Retired workers (excluding persons with special benefits) received an average monthly payment of $862; widows and widowers, $786; disabled workers, $859; and spouses, $411. Payments for children of retired workers averaged $412 per month; children of deceased workers, $568; and children of disabled workers, $253.

Federal Supplemental Security Income payments in December 2001 went to 72,953 West Virginia residents, averaging $373 a month.

40 HOUSING

In 2002, West Virginia had an estimated 852,165 housing units, 719,655 of which were occupied; 74.1% were owner-occupied. About 70% of all units were single-family, detached homes; 16.9% were mobile homes. Utility gas and electricity were the most common energy sources for heating. It was estimated that 29,823 units lacked telephone service, 4,310 lacked complete plumbing facilities, and 3,175 lacked complete kitchen facilities. The average household size was 2.44 people.

In 2002, 4,890 new privately owned housing units were authorized for construction. The median home value was $81,695, one of the lowest in the country. The median monthly cost for mortgage owners was $762. Renters paid a median of $448 per month. During 2002, West Virginia received over $45 million in community planning and development aid from the US Department of Housing and Urban Development.

41 EDUCATION

West Virginia has generally ranked below national standards in education. In 2000, 75.2% of adult West Virginians were high school graduates, well below the national average of 80.4%. Only 14.8% had completed four or more years of college, also well below the national average of 24.4%.

The total enrollment for fall 1999 in West Virginia's public schools stood at 291,811. Of these, 203,475 attended schools from kindergarten through grade eight, and 88,336 attended high school. Minority students made up approximately 5% of the total enrollment in public elementary and secondary schools in 2001. Total enrollment was estimated at 285,169 in fall 2000 and is expected to drop to 290,000 by fall 2005. Expenditure per pupil in elementary and secondary public schools was $6,878 in the 1999/2000 school year. Expenditures for public education in 2000/01 were estimated at $2,157,163. Enrollment in nonpublic schools in fall 2001 was 15,895.

As of fall 2000, there were 92,329 students enrolled in college or graduate school. In the same year West Virginia had 36 degree-granting institutions. The state supports West Virginia University, Marshall University, and the West Virginia College of Graduate Studies (all offering graduate work), as well as 3 medical schools, 8 four-year colleges, and 3 public two-year institutions. There are also 10 private colleges. In 1997, minority students comprised 6.8% of total post-secondary enrollment.

42 ARTS

West Virginia is known for the quilts, pottery, and woodwork of its mountain artisans. Huntington Galleries, the Sunrise Foundation at Charleston, and Oglebay Park in Wheeling are major art centers. The Clay Center for the Arts and Sciences at Charleston includes a performing arts center that hosts the annual Stretched Strings Festival. Other musical attractions include the West Virginia Symphony Orchestra in Charleston, the Charleston Ballet, Charleston Light Opera Guild, the Wheeling Symphony, and a country music program at Wheeling. The Charleston Stage Company and the Children's Theater of Charleston are also popular. The Mountain State Art and Craft Fair is held each summer at Ripley.

In 2003, the West Virginia Department of Education's Division of Culture and History and other West Virginia arts organizations received grants totaling $644,100 from the National Endowment for the Arts. The West Virginia Humanities Council sponsors an active speaker's bureau and History Alive! program. In 2000, the National Endowment for the Humanities contributed $533,716 for seven state programs. Contributions to the arts also come from state and private sources. There are nearly 40,000 contributing artists, and approximately 25,000 schoolchildren receive arts education through the Department of Education's Arts and Humanities Section. The state has about 150 arts associations and 30 local arts groups.

43 LIBRARIES AND MUSEUMS

In 2000, West Virginia's public libraries had 4,850,472 volumes in 14 systems, with a combined circulation of 8,254,000. The largest was the Kanawha County Public Library system at Charleston, with 628,308 volumes. Of college and university libraries, the largest collection was at West Virginia University. Total public library income was $21,940,015 in 1999.

There were 51 museums in 2000, including the State Museum and the Sunrise Museum in Charleston, and Oglebay Institute-Mansion Museum in Wheeling. Point Pleasant marks the site of a battle between colonists and Indians, and Harpers Ferry is the site of John Brown's raid. Wheeling is the location of the Oglebay's Good Children's Zoo.

44COMMUNICATIONS

In 2001, 94.5% of West Virginian homes had telephones. In 2003, broadcasting facilities included 8 major AM and 46 major FM radio stations, and 13 major television stations. Approximately 13,062 Internet domain names were registered in the state by the year 2000.

45PRESS

In 2002, West Virginia had 22 daily newspapers and 12 Sunday newspapers. The following table shows leading West Virginia newspapers with their approximate 2002 circulations:

AREA	NAME	DAILY	SUNDAY
Charleston	*Gazette* (m,S)	50,194	91,834*
	Daily Mail (m,S)	35,802	91,834*
Huntington	*Herald–Dispatch* (m,S)	35,143	41,125
Wheeling	*Intelligencer/News Register*(m,e,S)	21,571	43,903

*The Sunday edition is a combination of the *Gazette* and the *Daily Mail*.

46ORGANIZATIONS

In 2003, there were about 979 regional, national, and international organizations within the state.

The Black Lung Association, based in Beckley, promotes safe working conditions in coalmines and benefits for disabled miners. The headquarters of the Appalachian Trail Conference is in Harpers Ferry, and the American Association of Zoological Parks and Aquariums is in Oglebay. There are city and county historical societies throughout the state. Some counties also sponsor arts councils.

47TOURISM, TRAVEL, AND RECREATION

In 2002, almost 23.9 million travelers visited West Virginia, representing an increase of 8.5% from 2000, with about 14.19 million visitors making day trips. Direct travel spending in 2002 was about $3.53 billion. About 250,000 whitewater rafting enthusiasts raft West Virginia waters each year, and more than 750,000 skiers venture down the slopes of the Appalachian Mountains. Major attractions are Harpers Ferry National Historical Park, New River Gorge National River, the Naval Telecommunications Station at Sugar Grove, and White Sulphur Springs, a popular mountain golfing resort. Nearly 80% of the state is covered by forest. Among the 37 state parks and state forests are Cass Scenic Railroad, which includes a restoration of an old logging line, and Prickett's Fort, with re-creations of pioneer life.

48SPORTS

No major league professional teams are based in West Virginia, but there are minor league baseball teams in Charleston, Bluefield, and Princeton, and there is minor league hockey in Wheeling. West Virginia University's basketball team won a National Invitation Tournament championship in 1942 and was NCAA Division 1 runner-up in 1959. In football, West Virginia produced a string of national contenders in the late 1980s and early 1990s. West Virginia won the Peach Bowl in 1981 and played for the national championship in the 1989 Fiesta Bowl, which they lost to Notre Dame. Marshall University has also risen to the elite among college football teams, having secured a string of several Mid-American Conference champions and having won five straight bowl game appearances from 1998 to 2002.

Horse-racing tracks operate in Chester and Charles Town. Greyhound races are run in Wheeling and Charleston. Other popular sports are skiing and white-water rafting.

Professional athletes who were born in West Virginia include George Brett, Mary Lou Retton, and Jerry West.

49FAMOUS WEST VIRGINIANS

Among West Virginians who have served in presidential cabinets are Nathan Goff, Jr. (1843–1920), navy secretary; William L. Wilson (1843–1900), postmaster general; John Barton Payne (1855–1935), interior secretary; and Newton D. Baker (1871–1937), secretary of war during World War I. Lewis L. Strauss (1896–1974) was commerce secretary and chairman of the Atomic Energy Commission, and Cyrus R. Vance (1917–2002) served as secretary of state. John W. Davis (1873–1955), an ambassador to Great Britain, ran as the Democratic presidential nominee in 1924. Prominent members of the US Senate have included Matthew M. Neely (1874–1958), who was also governor, Harley M. Kilgore (1893–1956), and Robert C. Byrd (b.1917).

Thomas J. "Stonewall" Jackson (1824–63) was a leading Confederate general during the Civil War. Brigadier General Charles E. "Chuck" Yeager (b.1923), a World War II ace, became the first person to fly faster than the speed of sound.

Major state political leaders, all governors (though some have held federal offices), have been E. Willis Wilson (1844–1905), Henry D. Hatfield (1875–1962), Arch A. Moore, Jr. (b.1923), and John D. "Jay" Rockefeller IV (b.New York, 1937).

The state's only Nobel Prize winner has been Pearl S. Buck (Pearl Sydenstricker, 1893–1973), who won the Nobel Prize for literature for her novels concerning China. Alexander Campbell (b.Ireland, 1788–1866), with his father, founded the Disciples of Christ Church and was president of Bethany College in West Virginia. Major labor leaders have included Walter Reuther (1907–70), president of the United Automobile Workers, and Arnold Miller (1923–85), president of the United Mine Workers.

Musicians include George Crumb (b.1929), a Pulitzer Prize-winning composer, and opera singers Eleanor Steber (1916–1990) and Phyllis Curtin (b.1922). Melville Davisson Post (1871–1930) was a leading writer of mystery stories. Important writers of the modern period include Mary Lee Settle (b.1918) and John Knowles (1926–2001). Jerry West (b.1938) was a collegiate and professional basketball star, and a pro coach after his playing days ended; Rod Hundley (b.1934) and Hal Greer (b.1936) also starred in the National Basketball Association. Mary Lou Retton (b.1968) won a gold medal in gymnastics at the 1984 Olympics. Another West Virginian of note is Anna Jarvis (1864–1948), founder of Mother's Day.

50BIBLIOGRAPHY

Duda, Mark Damian. *West Virginia Wildlife Viewing Guide.* Helena, Mont.: Falcon, 1999.

Forbes, Harold M. *West Virginia History: Bibliography and Guide to Studies.* Morgantown: West Virginia University Press, 1981.

Johnson, Clint. *In the Footsteps of Stonewall Jackson.* Winston-Salem, N.C.: John F. Blair, 2002.

Lilly, John, ed. *Mountains of Music: West Virginia Traditional Music from Goldenseal.* Urbana: University of Illinois Press, 1999.

———. *West Virginia: A History.* 2nd ed. Lexington, Ky.: University of Kentucky Press, 1993.

Shaffer, John W. *Clash of Loyalties: A Border County in the Civil War.* Morgantown: West Virginia University Press, 2003.

Thomas, Jerry Bruce. *An Appalachian New Deal: West Virginia in the Great Depression.* Lexington, Ky.: The University Press of Kentucky, 1998.

West Virginia Politics and Government. Edited by Richard A. Brisbin, Jr., et al. Lincoln, Nebr.: University of Nebraska Press, 1996.

WISCONSIN

State of Wisconsin

ORIGIN OF STATE NAME: Probably from the Ojibwa word *wishkonsing*, meaning "place of the beaver." **NICKNAME:** The Badger State. **CAPITAL:** Madison. **ENTERED UNION:** 29 May 1848 (30th). **SONG:** "On, Wisconsin!" **MOTTO:** Forward. **COAT OF ARMS:** Surrounding the US shield is the shield of Wisconsin, which is divided into four parts symbolizing agriculture, mining, navigation, and manufacturing. Flanking the shield are a sailor, representing labor on water, and a yeoman or miner, representing labor on land. Above is a badger and the state motto; below, a horn of plenty and a pyramid of pig lead. **FLAG:** A dark-blue field, fringed in yellow on three sides, surrounds the state coat of arms on each side, with "Wisconsin" in white letters above the coat of arms and "1848" below. **OFFICIAL SEAL:** Arms surrounded by the words "Great Seal of the State of Wisconsin" and 13 stars below. **ANIMAL:** Badger. **WILDLIFE ANIMAL:** White-tailed deer. **DOMESTIC ANIMAL:** Dairy cow. **BIRD:** Robin. **SYMBOL OF PEACE:** Mourning dove. **FISH:** Muskellunge. **INSECT:** Honeybee. **FLOWER:** Wood violet. **TREE:** Sugar maple. **ROCK:** Red granite. **MINERAL:** Galena. **SOIL:** Antigo silt loam. **BEVERAGE:** Milk. **GRAIN:** Corn. **DANCE:** Polka. **LEGAL HOLIDAYS:** New Year's Day, 1 January; Birthday of Martin Luther King, Jr., 3rd Monday in January; Lincoln and Washington Day, 3rd Monday in February; Good Friday, March or April; Memorial Day, last Monday in May; Independence Day, 4 July; Labor Day, 1st Monday in September; Primary Day, 2nd Tuesday in September in even-numbered years; Columbus Day, 2nd Monday in October; Election Day, 1st Tuesday after 1st Monday in November in even-numbered years; Veterans Day, 11 November; Thanksgiving Day, 4th Thursday in November; Christmas Day, 25 December. **TIME:** 6 AM CST = noon GMT.

¹LOCATION, SIZE, AND EXTENT

Located in the eastern north-central US, Wisconsin ranks 26th in size among the 50 states.

The total area of Wisconsin is 56,153 sq mi (145,436 sq km), of which 54,426 sq mi (140,963 sq km) is land and 1,727 sq mi is (4,473 sq km) inland water. The state extends 295 mi (475 km) E-W and 320 mi (515 km) N-S.

Wisconsin is bordered on the N by Lake Superior and the state of Michigan (with the northeastern boundary formed by the Menominee River); on the E by Lake Michigan; on the S by Illinois; and on the W by Iowa and Minnesota (with the line defined mainly by the Mississippi and St. Croix rivers).

Important islands belonging to Wisconsin are the Apostle Islands in Lake Superior, and Washington Island in Lake Michigan. The state's boundaries have a total length of 1,379 mi (2,219 km). Wisconsin's geographic center is in Wood County, 9 mi (14 km) SE of Marshfield.

²TOPOGRAPHY

Wisconsin can be divided into four main geographical regions, each covering roughly one-quarter of the state's land area. The most highly elevated of these is the Superior Upland, below Lake Superior and the border with Michigan. It has heavily forested rolling hills but no high mountains. Elevations range from about 700 ft (200 m) to slightly under 2,000 ft (600 m). A second upland region, called the Driftless Area, has a more rugged terrain, having been largely untouched by the glacial drifts that smoothed out topographical features in other parts of the state. Elevations here reach more than 1,200 ft (400 m). The third region is a large, crescent-shaped plain in central Wisconsin; its unglaciated portion is a sandstone plain, broken by rock formations that from a distance appear similar to the buttes and mesas of Colorado. Finally, in the east and southeast along Lake Michigan lies a large, glaciated lowland plain, fairly smooth in

the Green Bay-Winnebago area but more irregular on the Door Peninsula and in the south.

Wisconsin's mean altitude is 1,050 ft (320 m), with elevations generally higher in the north. The Gogebic Range, extending westward from Michigan's Upper Peninsula into northern Wisconsin, was an important center of iron mining in the early days of statehood. Timms Hill, in north-central Wisconsin, is the state's highest point, at 1,952 ft (595 m). The lowest elevation is 579 ft (177 m), along the Lake Michigan shoreline.

There are well over 8,000 lakes in Wisconsin. Lakes Michigan and Superior form part of the northern and eastern borders; the Wisconsin mainland has at least 575 mi (925 km) of lakeshore and holds jurisdiction over 10,062 sq mi (26,061 sq km) of lake waters. By far, the largest inland lake is Lake Winnebago, in eastern Wisconsin, covering an area of 215 sq mi (557 sq km).

The Mississippi River, which forms part of the border with Minnesota and the entire border with Iowa, is the main navigable river. The major river flowing through the state is the Wisconsin, which follows a south-southwest course for 430 mi (692 km) before meeting the Mississippi at the Iowa border. Other tributaries of the Mississippi are the St. Croix River, also part of the Minnesota border, and the Chippewa and Black rivers. Located on the Black River are Big Manitou Falls, at 165 ft (50 m) the highest of the state's many waterfalls. Waters from the Fox River and its major tributary, the Wolf, flow into Green Bay and then into Lake Michigan, as does the Menominee, which is part of the Michigan state line.

Except in the Driftless Area, glaciation smoothed out many surface features, gouged out new ones, and left deposits of rock and soil creating distinctively shaped hills and ridges. Oval mounds, called drumlins, are still scattered over the southeast; and moraines, formed by deposits left at the edges of glaciers, are a prominent feature of eastern, central, and northwestern Wisconsin. In one section, called the Dells, the Wisconsin River has cut a gorge through 8 mi (13 km) of sandstone, creating caves and interesting rock formations.

3CLIMATE

Wisconsin has a continental climate. Summers are warm and winters very cold, especially in the upper northeast and north-central lowlands, where the freeze-free (growing) season is around 80 days. The average annual temperature ranges from 39°F (4°C) in the north to about 50°F (10°C) in the south. At Danbury, in the northwest, the average January daily temperature over a 34-year period was 8°F (–13°C), and the average July daily temperature 68°F (20°C); at Racine, in the southeast, these figures were 21°F (–6°C) and 72°F (22°C), respectively. Over a 30-year period ending in 1990, Milwaukee had average daily temperatures ranging from 12°F (–11°C) to 26°F (–3°C) in January and from 62°F (17°C) to 80°F (27°C) in July. Among major US metropolitan areas, only Minneapolis-St. Paul is colder than Milwaukee. The lowest temperature ever recorded in Wisconsin was –55°F (–48.3°C), at Couderay on 4 February 1996; the highest, 114°F (46°C), at Wisconsin Dells on 13 July 1936.

Annual precipitation in the state ranges from about 34 in (86 cm) for parts of the northwest to about 28 in (71 cm) in the south-central region and the areas bordering Lake Superior and Lake Michigan. In Milwaukee average annual precipitation (1971–2000) was is 34.8 in (88.4 cm); April, June, and July are the rainiest months in Milwaukee. Milwaukee's annual snowfall averages 47 in (119 cm); the average wind speed is 12 mph (19 km/hr).

4FLORA AND FAUNA

Common trees of Wisconsin include four oaks—bur, black, white, and red—along with black cherry and hickory. Jack, red, and white pine, yellow birch, eastern hemlock, mountain maple, moosewood, and leatherwood grow in the north, with black spruce, black ash, balsam fir, and tamarack concentrated in the northern lowlands. Characteristic of southern Wisconsin's climax forests are sugar maple (the state tree), white elm, basswood, and ironwood, with silver maple, black willow, silver birch, and cottonwood on low, moist land. Prairies are thick with grasses; bogs and marshes are home to white and jack pines and jack oak. Forty-five varieties of orchid have been identified, as well as 20 types of violet, including the wood violet (the state flower). In 2003, six plant species were threatened, including the eastern prairie fringed orchid, prairie bush-clover, dwarf lake iris, Pitcher's thistle, Fassett's locoweed, and northern wild monkshood.

White-tailed deer, black bear, woodchuck, snowshoe hare, chipmunk, and porcupine are mammals typical of forestlands. The striped skunk, red and gray foxes, and various mice are characteristic of upland fields while wetlands harbor such mammals as the muskrat, mink, river otter, and water shrew. The badger, dwelling in grasslands and semi-open areas, is rarely seen today. Game birds include the ring-necked pheasant, bobwhite quail, Hungarian partridge, and ruffed grouse; among 336 bird species native to Wisconsin are 42 kinds of waterfowl and 6 types of shorebird that are also hunted. Reptiles include 23 varieties of snake, 13 types of turtle, and 4 kinds of lizard. Muskellunge (the state fish), northern pike, walleye, and brook trout are native to Wisconsin waterways.

In 2003, nine animal species were listed as threatened or endangered in Wisconsin, including the bald eagle, Kirtland's warbler, Karner blue butterfly, Hine's emerald dragonfly, Higgins' eye pearlymussel, piping plover, and gray wolf. The Bureau of Endangered Resources in the Department of Natural Resources develops programs designed to aid the recovery of threatened or endangered flora and fauna.

5ENVIRONMENTAL PROTECTION

Conservation has been a concern in Wisconsin for more than a century. In 1867, a legislative commission reported that depletion of the northern forests by wasteful timber industry practices and frequent forest fires had become an urgent problem, partly because it increased the hazards of flooding. In 1897, a forestry warden was appointed and a system of fire detection and control was set up. A reforestation program was instituted in 1911; at about the same time, the state university began planting rows of trees in plains areas to protect soil from wind erosion, a method that was widely copied in other states. Fish and game wardens were appointed in the 1880s. In 1927, the state began a program to clean its waters of industrial wastes, caused especially by pulp and paper mills and canneries. The legislature enacted a comprehensive antipollution program in 1966.

The present Department of Natural Resources (DNR), organized in 1967, brings together conservation and environmental protection responsibilities. The department supervises air, water, and solid-waste pollution control programs and deals with the protection of forest, fish, and wildlife resources.

Southeastern Wisconsin has experienced serious air quality problems since the 1970s. Reductions in industrial emissions have been offset by increases in emissions from transportation sources and consumer products. In 2002, the US Environmental Protection Agency implemented new requirements for reporting air quality, and the DNR developed procedures to help corporations comply.

Since water pollution became a serious problem in the 1920s, pulp and paper mills, cheese factories, and canneries have taken major steps to control and prevent harmful water pollution. Communities built new or upgraded existing sewage treatment plants to reduce the flow of sewage into rivers and streams. Pulp and paper mills spent millions of dollars to reduce suspended solids and other pollutants in their industrial effluent. Water quality and fisheries visibly improved, but problems caused by persistent toxic chemicals, such as PCBs (polychlorinated biphenyls) and mercury, arose that had to be addressed next. In the 1980s, the state identified five Areas of Concern on Lakes Michigan and Superior where toxic pollutants harmed fish or wildlife or impaired human use of the waterways. Efforts are underway to identify sources of contamination and clean-up options at these sites and inland areas suffering similar problems. Regulations controlling the discharge of toxic substances from both water and air were passed in the late 1980s, and water quality improved significantly by 2000.

Contaminated stormwater and run-off from agriculture, development, and other sources remain the most serious threats to Wisconsin's lakes, rivers, and streams. The state adopted rules to limit stormwater contamination in large municipalities, construction sites over five acres, and 10,000 industrial facilities. The DNR also formed a citizen advisory committee in 1994 to overhaul the state's animal waste regulations; new rules to control polluted runoff from agricultural, non-agricultural, and transportation sources went into effect 1 October 2002. Wetland protection regulations were upgraded in the late 1980s, and in 1991 the state became the first in the nation to legislate wetlands protection. Wisconsin has a Wetlands Restoration program administered by the US Department of Agriculture Natural Resources Conservation Service (NRCS) and the US Fish and Wildlife Service (FWS) with assistance from DNR. Between 1992 and 1998, approximately 11,312 acres of wetlands were restored.

Wisconsin passed a comprehensive groundwater protection law in 1984 to safeguard underground water supplies that serve two-thirds of the state's population. The law requires identification and clean-up of groundwater-damaging contamination sources, such as abandoned, leaking landfills;

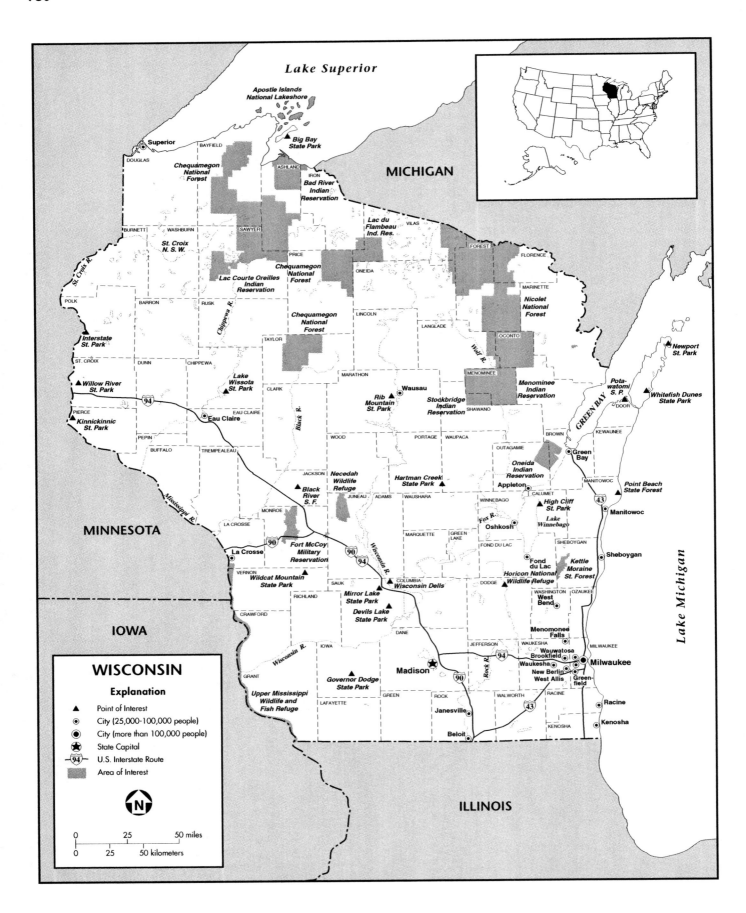

Lake Superior

Apostle Islands
National Lakeshore

Superior

Big Bay
State Park

BAYFIELD

DOUGLAS

ASHLAND

MICHIGAN

IRON

Chequamegon
National
Forest

Bad River
Indian
Reservation

BURNETT   WASHBURN

Lac du
Flambeau
Ind. Res.

VILAS

St. Croix
N. S. W.

SAWYER

PRICE

FOREST

FLORENCE

Chequamegon
National
Forest

ONEIDA

MARINETTE

Lac Courte Oreilles
Indian
Reservation

POLK

BARRON   RUSK

Chequamegon
National
Forest

LINCOLN

LANGLADE

Nicolet
National
Forest

Interstate
St. Park

TAYLOR

OCONTO

ST. CROIX

DUNN   CHIPPEWA

Lake
Wissota
St. Park

CLARK

MARATHON

MENOMINEE

Menominee
Indian
Reservation

Willow River
St. Park

Rib
Mountain
St. Park

Wausau

PIERCE

EAU CLAIRE

Eau Claire

Stockbridge
Indian
Reservation

SHAWANO

Kinnickinnic
St. Park

PEPIN

Black R.

WOOD

PORTAGE   WAUPACA

BROWN

GREEN BAY

KEWAUNEE

BUFFALO   TREMPEALEAU

OUTAGAMIE

Green
Bay

Newport
St. Park

Pota-
watomi
S. P.

DOOR

Whitefish Dunes
State Park

JACKSON

Necedah
Wildlife
Refuge

Hartman Creek
State Park

Oneida
Indian
Reservation

Appleton

MANITOWOC

Black
River
S. F.

JUNEAU   ADAMS   WAUSHARA

WINNEBAGO

CALUMET

Point Beach
State Forest

MONROE

Fox R.

High Cliff
St. Park

Manitowoc

MINNESOTA

LA CROSSE

MARQUETTE

GREEN
LAKE

Oshkosh

Lake
Winnebago

FOND DU LAC

SHEBOYGAN

Fort McCoy
Military
Reservation

La Crosse

Wisconsin R.

Sheboygan

Fond
du Lac

Kettle
Moraine
St. Forest

VERNON

Wildcat Mountain
State Park

SAUK

COLUMBIA

Wisconsin Dells

Horicon National
Wildlife Refuge

DODGE

WASHINGTON

OZAUKEE

West
Bend

IOWA

RICHLAND

Mirror Lake
State Park

CRAWFORD

Devils Lake
State Park

DANE

Menomonee
Falls

JEFFERSON

WAUKESHA

MILWAUKEE

Wauwatosa
Brookfield

Milwaukee

Wisconsin R.

IOWA

Madison

Waukesha

New Berlin

West Allis

Green-
field

Governor Dodge
State Park

GRANT

GREEN

ROCK

WALWORTH

RACINE

Racine

Upper Mississippi
Wildlife and
Fish Refuge

LAFAYETTE

Janesville

Kenosha

Beloit

KENOSHA

ILLINOIS

Lake Michigan

WISCONSIN

Explanation

▲ Point of Interest

⊙ City (25,000-100,000 people)

◉ City (more than 100,000 people)

★ State Capital

94 U.S. Interstate Route

Area of Interest

N

0   25   50 miles

0   25   50 kilometers

underground gasoline storage tanks; and illegal, hazardous waste dumps. The law also requires the state to establish groundwater protection and enforcement standards for various substances. Wisconsin has identified over 16,000 contamination sites that must be cleaned up to prevent environmental contamination and safety hazards. Over one-third of these sites have been cleaned up and no further action is deemed necessary.

In 1996, Wisconsin began administering a new program whereby owners of contaminated property could petition the state for clean-up waivers if they were able to demonstrate that contamination was being cleaned up by natural processes. Property owners would then be able to redevelop within strict guidelines and monitoring. By mid-1997, 51 properties had applied for such liability releases, 30 of which were approved.

Bacterial contamination of Wisconsin drinking water supplies did not pose much of a problem in the state until 1993 when 400,000 Milwaukee residents became ill from inadequately treated water drawn from Lake Michigan. The water was found to contain the protozoan Cryptosporidium. Water treatment procedures were changed immediately at 21 community drinking water treatment plants that drew water from the Great Lakes. The state also began a two-year Cryptosporidium monitoring effort to determine the presence and distribution of this protozoan in state waterways.

In the 1980s, more than 800 landfills in the state closed because they could not meet new federal environmental protection requirements. To ease the burden on the state's remaining landfills, Wisconsin passed a comprehensive waste reduction and recycling law, 1989 Wisconsin Act 335. The law required local units of government to set up effective programs to recycle more than 11 different items by 1995. State grants collected from a tax on businesses were awarded to local governments to aid in setting up local recycling programs. The legislature is expected to decide a permanent funding mechanism in a future legislative session.

In 2003, Wisconsin had 163 hazardous waste sites listed in the Environmental Protection Agency's database, 39 of which were on the National Priorities List. In 2001, Wisconsin received $87,268,000 in federal grants from the Environmental Protection Agency; EPA expenditures for procurement contracts in Wisconsin that year amounted to $7,229,000.

6POPULATION

Wisconsin ranked 20th in population in the US (down from 16th in 1990) with an estimated total of 5,441,196 in 2002, an increase of 1.4% since 2000. Between 1990 and 2000, Wisconsin's population grew from 4,891,769 to 5,363,675, an increase of 9.6%. The population is projected to reach 5.9 million by 2025. The population density in 2000 was 98.8 persons per sq mi.

During the 18th and early 19th centuries, the area that is now Wisconsin was very sparsely settled by perhaps 20,000 Indians and a few hundred white settlers, most of them engaged in the fur trade. With the development of lead mining, the population began to expand, reaching a total of 30,945 (excluding Indians) by 1840. During the next two decades, the population increased rapidly to 775,881, as large numbers of settlers from the East and German, British, and Scandinavian immigrants arrived. Subsequent growth has been steady, if slower. In the late 19th century, industry expanded and, by 1930, the population became predominantly urban.

In 2000, the median age for Wisconsinites was 36. In the same year, 25.5% of the populace were under age 18 while 13.1% were age 65 or older.

The majority of Wisconsinites live in urban areas, most of them in the heavily urbanized southeastern region. Milwaukee, the largest city in Wisconsin and the 19th largest in the US, had a

population of 590,895 in 2002. Other large cities, with their 2002 population estimates, were Madison, 215,211, and Green Bay, 101,515. Racine had 81,855 residents in 2000, and Kenosha had 90,352. The state's largest metropolitan area, Milwaukee-Racine, had an estimated 1,648,199 residents as of 1999.

7ETHNIC GROUPS

As early as 1839, Wisconsin attracted immigrants from Norway, Sweden, Denmark, and Finland, soon to be followed by large numbers of Germans and Irish. In 1850, the greatest number of foreign-born persons were English-speaking, but within a decade, the Germans had eclipsed them. Industrial development brought Belgians, Greeks, Hungarians, Lithuanians, Italians, and especially Poles, who continued to come steadily until the restriction of immigration in the early 1920s; in the 1930 census, Poles were the largest foreign-born group. In 2000, foreign-born residents numbered 193,751 (3.6% of the total).

Black Americans were in the region as early as 1822. Before World War I, however, there were no more than 3,000 blacks. Migration during and after that war brought the number to 10,739 by 1930; by 1990, blacks were the largest racial minority in the state, numbering 245,000 (5% of Wisconsin's population). As of 2000, the black population was 304,460, or 5.7% of the state total. Most black Wisconsinites live in Milwaukee, which was 37% black in 2000.

The Asian population in 2000 was 88,763. In that year Wisconsin had 33,791 Hmong (the nation's 3rd-largest Hmong community), 11,184 Chinese, 6,800 Koreans, 5,158 Filipinos, and 4,469 Laotians. Pacific Islanders numbered 1,630. As of 2000, there were 192,921 Hispanics and Latinos (3.6% of the total population), of whom 126,719 were of Mexican ancestry and 30,267 of Puerto Rican descent.

Wisconsin had an estimated 47,228 American Indians in 2000, up from 39,000 American Indians in 1990. The principal tribes are Oneida, Menominee, Ojibwa (Chippewa), and Winnebago. There were 11 reservations, the largest being that of the Menominee, which comprised Menominee County (345 sq mi, 896 sq km) and had a population of 3,225 in 2000. Indian reservations covered 634 sq mi (1,642 sq km).

8LANGUAGES

Early French and English fur traders found in what is now Wisconsin several Indian tribes of the Algonkian family: Ojibwa along Lake Superior, Sauk in the northeast, Winnebago and Fox south of them, and Kickapoo in the southwest. Numerous Indian place-names include Antigo, Kaukauna, Kewaunee, Menomonie, Oshkosh, Wausau, and Winnebago.

Wisconsin English is almost entirely Northern, like that of the areas that provided Wisconsin's first settlers—Michigan, northern Ohio, New York State, and western New England. Common are the Northern *pail, comforter* (tied and filled bed cover), *sick to the stomach, angleworm* (earthworm), *skip school* (play truant), and *dove* as the past of *dive*. Pronunciation features are *fog, frog,* and *on* with the vowel sound /ah/; and *orange, forest,* and *foreign* with the /aw/ vowel sound. Northern *fried cakes* is now yielding to *doughnuts,* and *johnnycake* is giving way to *corn bread.* Milwaukee has *sick in the stomach* and is known for the localism *bubbler* (drinking fountain). A small exception to Northern homogeneity is the cluster of South Midland terms brought by Kentucky miners to the southwestern lead-mining district, such as *dressing* (sweet sauce for a pudding), *eaves spout* as a blend of *eavestrough* and Midland *spouting, branch* for stream, and *fishworm* for earthworm.

In 2000, 92.7% (down from 94.2% in 1990) of the state population five years old and older spoke only English in the home.

The following table gives selected statistics from the 2000 census for language spoken at home by persons five years old and over. The category "Other West Germanic languages" includes Dutch, Pennsylvania Dutch, and Afrikaans. The category "Scandinavian languages" includes Danish, Norwegian, and Swedish. The category "Other Native North American languages" includes Apache, Cherokee, Choctaw, Dakota, Keres, Pima, and Yupik.

LANGUAGE	NUMBER	PERCENT
Population 5 years and over	5,022,073	100.0
Speak only English	4,653,361	92.7
Speak a language other than English	368,712	7.3
Speak a language other than English	368,712	7.3
Spanish or Spanish Creole	168,778	3.4
German	48,409	1.0
Miao, Hmong	30,569	0.6
French (incl. Patois, Cajun)	14,970	0.3
Polish	12,097	0.2
Chinese	7,951	0.2
Italian	6,774	0.1
Other West Germanic languages	5,870	0.1
Scandinavian languages	5,651	0.1
Russian	5,362	0.1

[9]RELIGIONS

The first Catholics to arrive were Jesuit missionaries seeking to convert the Huron Indians in the 17th century. Protestant settlers and missionaries of different sects, including large numbers of German Lutherans, came during the 19th century, along with Protestants from the east. Jews settled primarily in the cities. These groups often had conflicting aims. Evangelical sects favored strict blue laws and temperance legislation, which was enacted in many communities. The use of Protestant prayers and the King James Bible in public schools was another source of public discord until these practices were declared unconstitutional by the state supreme court in 1890. A constitutional amendment allowing parochial school students to ride in public school buses was defeated in 1946, amid great controversy; 19 years later, however, it was enacted with little opposition. By that time, religious conflicts appeared to be on the decline.

In 2000, there were 1,695,680 Roman Catholics in Wisconsin. Lutherans make up the largest Protestant group, though they are divided in denominations: the Evangelical Lutheran Church in American, 463,432; the Lutheran Church—Missouri Synod, 241,306; and the Wisconsin Evangelical Lutheran Synod, 241,306. Other leading Protestant groups include the United Methodists, 129,216, and the United Church of Christ, 83,768. There were an estimated 28,230 Jews in 2000, primarily in the Milwaukee area. The Muslim population had about 7,796 members. Though still relatively small in total membership, the Salvation Army reported growth from 2,574 members in 1990 to 12,951 members in 2000, a difference of 403%. Over 2.1 million people (about 39% of the population) were not counted as members of any religious organization.

[10]TRANSPORTATION

Wisconsin's first rail line was built across the state, from Milwaukee to Prairie du Chien, in the 1850s. Communities soon began vying with one another to be included on proposed railroad routes. Several thousand farmers mortgaged property to buy railroad stock; the state had to rescue them from ruin when companies went bankrupt. By the late 1860s, two railroads—the Chicago and North Western, and the Chicago, Milwaukee, and St. Paul—had become dominant in the state. However, Chicago emerged as the major rail center of the Midwest because of its proximity to eastern markets. In 1920, there were 35 railroads operating on 11,615 mi (18,700 km) of track; by 1998, there were just 12 railroads operating on 4,347 rail mi (6,955 km) of

track, with only 1,817 mi (2,907 km) for Class I lines. Nonmetallic minerals accounted for 23% of rail tonnage originating within the state in 2000; coal accounted for the largest percentage (51%) of rail tonnage terminating in the state. Amtrak provides passenger rail service to Milwaukee, La Crosse, Tomah, and several other cities throughout Wisconsin. As of 2003, the Hiawatha service between Chicago and Milwaukee fourteen trains daily.

As of 2000, Wisconsin had 112,362 mi (179.779 km) of public roadway, 95,709 mi (153,134 km) of which were rural. The private passenger vehicle continues to be the dominant mode of travel. In 2000, Wisconsin had 3,770,453 licensed drivers and 4,545,101 registered vehicles (2,526,849 automobiles and 1,825,056 trucks). Public transit includes large bus systems in Milwaukee and Madison. In 2000, Milwaukee County Transit System provided 71 million passenger trips annually, with an average of 237,000 passengers trips each weekday. Madison Metroprovided 10 million passenger trips annually, with an average of 35,000 passengers trips each weekday.

The opening of the St. Lawrence Seaway in 1959 allowed oceangoing vessels access to Wisconsin via the Great Lakes but failed to stimulate traffic to the extent anticipated. Overall, the state has 15 cargo-handling ports. The port of Superior (shared with Duluth, Minnesota) on Lake Superior is the busiest of all US Great Lakes ports. Its chief commodities are iron ore. Other important Wisconsin ports, all on Lake Michigan, are Milwaukee, Green Bay, Port Washington, Oak Creek, Manitowoc, and Sturgeon Bay; coal is the chief commodity. Overall, iron ore made up 25% of shipments originating in Wisconsin in 2000 and coal, 55%. On the Mississippi River, Prairie du Chien and La Crosse are the main ports. Ferry service across Lake Michigan is offered from Manitowoc to Ludington, Michigan.

As of 2000, Wisconsin had 443 public and private airports. Milwaukee's General Mitchell International Airport is the state's main air terminal; in 2000, there were 9 airports in the state providing commercial air service to 2,500 or more passengers annually; in addition, there were 11,275 active pilots in the state and 1,455 flight instructors.

[11]HISTORY

The region that is now Wisconsin has probably been inhabited since the end of the glacial period, 10,000 years ago. Some of the earliest inhabitants were ancestors of the Menominee; these early immigrants from the north built burial mounds, conical ones at first, then large effigy mounds shaped like different animals. Other peoples arrived from the south and east, including ancestors of the Winnebago Indians (about AD 1400) and a tribe that built flat-top earthen pyramids. During the 17th century, the Ojibwa, Sauk, Fox, Potawatomi, Kickapoo, and other tribes came to Wisconsin. These tribes engaged in agriculture, hunting, and fishing, but with the arrival of Europeans, they became increasingly dependent on the fur trade—a dependence that had serious economic consequences when the fur trade declined in the early 19th century.

The first European believed to have reached Wisconsin was Jean Nicolet, who in 1634 landed on the shores of Green Bay while in the service of Samuel de Champlain. Two decades later, Médard Chouart des Groseilliers and Pierre Esprit Radisson, both fur traders, explored northern Wisconsin; in 1673, the Jesuit priest Jacques Marquette and the explorer Louis Jolliet crossed the whole area that is now Wisconsin, via the Fox and Wisconsin rivers, on their way to the Mississippi. Other Jesuits established missions, and French fur traders opened up posts. The French were succeeded by the British after the French and Indian War (the British ruled Wisconsin as part of Quebec Province from 1774 to 1783). Although ceded to the US in 1783, it remained

British in all but name until 1816, when the US built forts at Prairie du Chien and Green Bay.

Under the Ordinance of 1787, Wisconsin became part of the Northwest Territory; it was subsequently included in the Indiana Territory, the Territory of Illinois, and then the Michigan Territory. In the early 1820s, lead mining brought an influx of white settlers called "Badgers." Indian resistance to white expansion collapsed after the 1832 Black Hawk War, in which Sauk and Fox Indians fleeing from Illinois were defeated and massacred by white militia near the site of present-day La Crosse, at the Battle of Bad Axe. Subsequently, the Winnebago and other tribes were removed to reservations outside the state, while the Ojibwa, Menominee, and some eastern tribes were among those resettled in reservations inside Wisconsin.

The Wisconsin Territory was formed in 1836. Initially it included all of Iowa and Minnesota, along with a portion of the Dakotas, but in 1838, these areas became part of a newly organized Iowa Territory. The 1830s also saw the beginning of a land boom, fueled by migration of Yankees from New England and southerners who moved to the lead-mining region of southwestern Wisconsin. The population and economy began to expand rapidly. Wisconsin voters endorsed statehood in 1846, and Congress passed enabling legislation that year. After a first constitution was rejected by the voters, a revised document was adopted on 13 March 1848, and on 29 May, President James K. Polk signed the bill that made Wisconsin the 30th state.

Transportation and industry did not develop as rapidly as proponents of statehood had expected. A canal was opened at the portage between the Fox and Wisconsin rivers in 1851, but the waterway was not heavily used. Railroads encountered difficulties in gaining financing, then suffered setbacks in the panic of 1857.

Wisconsinites took a generally abolitionist stand, and it was in Wisconsin—at Ripon, on 28 February 1854—that the Republican Party was formally established in the state. The new party developed an efficient political machine and later used much of its influence to benefit the railroads and lumber industry, both of which grew in importance in the decade following the Civil War. In that war, 96,000 Wisconsin men fought on the Union side, and 12,216 died. During the late 19th century, Wisconsin was generally prosperous; dairying, food processing, and lumbering emerged as major industries, and Milwaukee grew into an important industrial center.

Wisconsin took a new political turn in the early 20th century with the inauguration of Republican Robert "Fighting Bob" La Follette as governor and the dawning of the Progressive Era. An ardent reformer, La Follette fought against conservatives within his own party. In 1903, the legislature, under his prodding, passed a law providing for the nation's first direct statewide primary; other measures that he championed during his tenure as governor (1901–06) provided for increased taxation of railroads, regulation of lobbyists, creation of a civil service, and establishment of a railroad commission to regulate intrastate rates.

La Follette was also a conspicuous exponent of what came to be called the "Wisconsin idea": governmental reform guided by academic experts and supported by an enlightened electorate. Around the time he was governor, the philosophy of reform was energetically promoted at the University of Wisconsin (which had opened at Madison, the state capital, in 1849), and many professors were drafted to serve on government commissions and boards. In 1901, Wisconsin became the first state to establish a legislative reference bureau, intended to help lawmakers shape effective, forward-looking measures.

After La Follette left the governor's office to become a US senator, his progressivism was carried on by Republican governors James O. Davidson (1906–11) and especially by

Francis E. McGovern (1911–15). During one session in 1911, legislators enacted the first state income tax in the US and one of the first workers' compensation programs. Other legislation passed during the same year sought to regulate the insurance business and the use of water power, create forest reserves, encourage farmer cooperatives, limit and require disclosure of political campaign expenditures, and establish a board of public affairs to recommend efficiency measures for state and local governments. This outburst of activity attracted national attention, and many states followed in Wisconsin's footsteps.

While serving as US senator (1906–25), La Follette opposed involvement in World War I and was one of only six senators to vote against US entry into the war; as a result, he was censured by the state legislature and the faculty of the University of Wisconsin, and there was a move to expel him from the Senate. His renomination and reelection in 1922 served to vindicate him, however, and he carried Wisconsin when he ran in 1924 for president on the national League for Progressive Political Action ticket.

After his death in 1925, the reform tradition continued in Wisconsin. A pioneering old-age pension act was passed in 1925; seven years later, Wisconsin enacted the nation's first unemployment compensation act, with the encouragement of La Follette's son Philip, then serving his first term as governor. When Wisconsin went Democratic in November 1932, turning Philip out of office, he and his brother, Robert, Jr., a US senator, temporarily left the state Republican organization and in 1934 formed a separate Progressive Party; that party, with the support of President Franklin Roosevelt and the Socialists, swept the 1934 elections and returned both brothers to office. During his second and third terms as governor, Philip La Follette successfully pressed for the creation of state agencies to develop electric power, arbitrate labor disputes, and set rules for fair business competition; his so-called Little New Deal corresponded to the New Deal policies of the Roosevelt administration.

After World War II, the state continued a trend toward increased urbanization, and its industries prospered. The major figure on the national scene in the postwar era was Senator Joseph R. McCarthy, who served 10 years in the Senate, launching unsubstantiated attacks in the early 1950s on alleged communists and other subversives in the federal government. After McCarthy's censure by the US Senate in 1954 and death in 1957, the Progressive tradition began to recover strength, and the liberal Democratic Party grew increasingly influential in state politics. There was student unrest at the University of Wisconsin during the 1960s and early 1970s, and growing discontent among Milwaukee's black population. A major controversy in the 1970s concerned a court-ordered busing plan, implemented in 1979, aimed at decreasing racial imbalances in Milwaukee's public schools. In 1984, the Milwaukee school board filed suit in federal court, charging that the policies of the state and suburban schools had resulted in an unconstitutionally segregated school system that restricted blacks to city schools. Two years later, the city school board and nine suburban districts agreed on a plan by which minority students from the city would transfer voluntarily to the nine suburbs, and suburban students would attend Milwaukee schools.

Wisconsin's economy, with its strong manufacturing and agricultural sectors, remained sound throughout the 1980s and into the 1990s. The dairy industry, traditionally a mainstay of the economy, was linked to two different environmental issues. The first was the 1993 contamination of Milwaukee's drinking water with harmful bacteria that made thousands of people sick and killed some of them. Some claimed that the organisms had come from agricultural runoff containing animal wastes. The second issue was the use of bovine growth hormone to bolster milk production.

Flooding of the Mississippi River in 1993 caused massive damage in Wisconsin. Forty-seven counties were declared federal disaster areas; four people were killed; and financial losses totaled $900 million.

In 2003, Wisconsin faced a $3.2 billion two-year budget deficit. Governor Jim Doyle, elected in 2002, became the first Democratic governor to be elected in Wisconsin in 16 years. Doyle, who advocated abortion rights, gun control, and environmental protection, was at odds with the Republican-controlled state legislature over issues of state spending on health care and public education, and on raising taxes. Doyle promised to counteract the budget shortfall with deep spending cuts, which might threaten local services.

12 STATE GOVERNMENT

Wisconsin's first constitutional convention, meeting in Madison in October 1846, was marked by controversy between conservative Whigs and allied Democrats on the one hand, and progressive Democrats with a constituency made up of miners, farmers, and immigrants on the other. The latter, who favored the popular election of judges and exemption of homesteads from seizure for debt, among other provisions, carried the day, but this version of the constitution failed to win ratification. A second constitutional convention, convened in December 1847, agreed on a new draft which made few major changes. This document, ratified by the electorate in 1848 and amended 133 times (two of which were subsequently nullified by the courts) as of January 2003, remains in effect today.

The Wisconsin legislature consists of a senate with 33 members elected for four-year terms, and an assembly of 99 representatives elected for two-year terms. Legislators must be state residents for one year prior to election, and residents of their districts at least 10 days before the election. Voters elect an assembly and half the senate membership in even-numbered years. Legislators must be at least 18 years old, qualified voters in their districts, and residents of the state for at least one year. Regular legislative sessions begin in January; session schedules are determined biennially (in odd-numbered years) by joint resolution. Each house elects its own presiding officer and other officers from among its members. The legislative salary in 2002 was $44,333.

There are six elected state officers: governor and lieutenant governor (elected jointly), secretary of state, state treasurer, attorney general, and superintendent of public instruction. Since 1970, all have been elected for four-year terms. The governor and lieutenant governor must be qualified voters; there are no additional residency requirements. In 2002 the governor's salary was $122,406. As the chief executive officer, the governor exercises authority by the power of appointment, by presenting a budget bill and major addresses to the legislature, and by the power to veto bills and call special legislative sessions. Of 15 administrative departments in the executive branch, two—the Department of Justice and the Department of Public Instruction—are headed by the attorney general and the superintendent of public instruction, respectively. Eight departments are headed by secretaries appointed by the governor with the advice and consent of the senate, while the Department of Military Affairs is headed by the adjutant general, who is appointed by the governor alone; part-time boards appoint the heads of the four remaining departments. There were also 18 independent agencies in 1983, of which five were headed by individual commissioners and 13 by commissions or boards.

A bill may be introduced in either house of the legislature, but must be passed by both houses to become law. The governor has six days (Sundays excluded) to sign or veto a measure. If the governor fails to act and the legislature is still in session, the bill automatically becomes law. (If the legislature has adjourned, a bill automatically dies after six days unless the governor acts on

it.) Gubernatorial vetoes can be overridden by a two-thirds majority of those present in each house. Constitutional amendments may be introduced in either house. They must be approved by a simple majority of both houses in two legislatures and then ratified by a majority of the electorate at a subsequent election.

Voters must be US citizens, at least 18 years old, and must have resided in the state for at least 10 days before the election. Registration is not required. (The residency requirement is waived in voting for US president and vice-president.) Restrictions apply to those convicted of certain crimes and to those judged by the court as mentally incompetent to vote.

13 POLITICAL PARTIES

The Democratic Party dominated politics until the late 1850s; then the newly founded Republican Party held sway for almost 100 years. More recently, the parties remain relatively even in power at both the national and state levels.

Jacksonian democracy was strong in Wisconsin in the early days, and until 1856 all territorial and state governors were Democrats, except for one Whig. In 1854, however, a coalition of Whigs, antislavery Democrats, and Free Soilers formed a Republican Party in the state—a key event in the establishment of the national Republican Party. Republicans quickly gained control of most elective offices; from 1856 to 1959 there were only three Democratic governors. The Republican Party was dominated in the late 19th century by conservatives, who were sympathetic to the railroads and the lumbering industry but whose stands on pensions and jobs for Union veterans and ability to win federal funds for the state attracted support from farmers and small business. Then, in the 1890s, Progressives within the party, led by Robert La Follette, began a successful battle for control that culminated in La Follette's election as governor in 1900.

The La Follette brand of progressivism remained strong in the state, although not always under the umbrella of Republicanism. In 1924, La Follette ran for president on the Progressive ticket; 10 years later, his sons, Robert and Philip, also broke away from the GOP, to head a Progressive Party slate. However, their newly organized national third party faded and folded when Philip La Follette failed to be reelected governor, and World War II made isolationism unpopular. The Progressives rejoined the GOP in 1946.

Socialist parties have won some success in Wisconsin's political history. Socialists worked with progressive Republicans at the state level to pass important legislation in the early 20th century. In 1910, the Socialists scored two major political victories in Wisconsin: Emil Seidel was elected mayor of Milwaukee, becoming the first Socialist mayor of a major US city, and Victor Berger became the first Socialist ever elected to Congress. The state does not require voters to register. There were 3,045,730 voters registered in the state in 2002, however.

Wisconsin's senators, both Democrats, are Herb Kohl, reelected in 2000 and Russell Feingold, reelected in 1998. Wisconsin's US House delegation consists of four Republicans and four Democrats following 2002 elections. In mid-2003, there were 18 Republicans and 15 Democrats in the state senate, and 41 Democrats and 58 Republicans in the state assembly. Wisconsin's former Republican governor, Tommy Thompson, who was reelected to an unprecedented fourth four-year term in 1998, was named President George W. Bush's Secretary of Health and Human Services in 2001.

In the 2000 presidential election, Democrat Al Gore beat Republican George W. Bush by a mere 5,396 votes in Wisconsin; Green Party candidate Ralph Nader received 4% of the vote. The state had 11 electoral votes in the 2000 presidential election.

¹⁴LOCAL GOVERNMENT

Wisconsin had 72 counties, 585 municipal governments, 1,265 townships, and 442 public school districts as of 2002. There were also 684 special districts, each providing a certain local service, such as sewerage or fire fighting, usually across municipal lines.

Each county is governed by a board of supervisors (which in the most populous counties has more than 40 members), generally elected for two-year terms. Some counties have elected county executives, serving four-year terms; several others have an appointed administrator or similar official. County officials can include district attorneys, sheriffs, clerks, treasurers, coroners, registers of deeds, and surveyors.

Towns are civil subdivisions of counties equivalent to townships in other states. Each town is a unit of 6 sq mi (16 sq km) marked off for governmental purposes. Wisconsin towns are generally small units with populations under 2,500. Each town is governed by a board of supervisors elected every two years; a town supervisor carries out policies set at an annual town meeting. Cities and villages have home-rule powers limited by legislative review. Most cities are governed by a mayor-council system; a small percentage of cities have a council-manager system, which was first authorized in Wisconsin in 1923. Executive power in a village is vested in an elected president who presides over an elected board but has no veto power.

¹⁵STATE SERVICES

To address the continuing threat of terrorism and to work with the federal Department of Homeland Security (created in 2002 following the terrorist attacks of 11 September 2001), homeland security in Wisconsin in 2003 operated under the authority of the governor; the emergency management director was designated as the state homeland security advisor.

A six-member Ethics Board, appointed by the governor, administers an ethics code for public officials and employees and investigates complaints against them. The board may refer cases for criminal prosecution.

The Department of Public Instruction administers public elementary and secondary education in the state, and the Board of Regents of the University of Wisconsin System has jurisdiction over all public higher education. A Board of Vocational, Technical, and Adult Education supervises programs in these areas.

The Transportation Department plans, constructs, and maintains highways and licenses motor vehicles and drivers. Physical and mental health, corrections, public and medical assistance, service to the aged, children's services, and vocational rehabilitation fall within the purview of the Department of Health and Social Services. The Department of Employee Relations enforces antidiscrimination laws in employment as well as minimum standards for wages and working conditions, provides training for the unemployed and disadvantaged, and sets safety standards for buildings.

Public protection in general is provided by the Department of Justice, which is responsible for investigating crimes of statewide magnitude and offering technical assistance to local law enforcement agencies. Regulations to protect consumers are administered and enforced by the Trade and Consumer Protection Division of the Department of Agriculture, Trade, and Consumer Protection, in cooperation with the Justice Department. The Army and Air National Guard are under the Department of Military Affairs.

The Department of Commerce has responsibilities in the areas of community, economic, and housing development, promotion of trade and tourism, and small and minority business assistance.

¹⁶JUDICIAL SYSTEM

The judicial branch is headed by a supreme court, consisting of seven justices, elected statewide on a nonpartisan basis for terms of 10 years. Vacancies are filled by gubernatorial appointment until an open election day becomes available. The justice with the greatest seniority serves as chief justice. The supreme court, which is the final authority on state constitutional questions, hears appeals at its own discretion and has original jurisdiction in limited areas.

The state's next-highest court is the court of appeals, established by constitutional amendment in 1977. Its 16 judges

Wisconsin Presidential Vote by Political Party, 1948–2000

YEAR	ELEC. VOTE	WISCONSIN WINNER	DEMOCRAT	REPUBLICAN	PROGRESSIVE	SOCIALIST	SOC. WORKERS	SOCIALIST LABOR
1948	12	*Truman (D)	647,310	590,959	25,282	12,547	—	399
1952	12	*Eisenhower (R)	622,175	979,744	2,174	1,157	1,350	770
					CONSTITUTION			
1956	12	*Eisenhower (R)	586,768	954,844	6,918	754	564	710
1960	12	Nixon (R)	830,805	895,175	—	—	1,792	1,310
1964	12	*Johnson (D)	1,050,424	638,495	—	—	1,692	1,204
1968	12	*Nixon (R)	748,804	809,997	—	—	1,222	1,338
					AMERICAN IND.	AMERICAN		
1972	11	*Nixon (R)	810,174	989,430	127,835	47,525	—	998
						SOCIALIST		LIBERTARIAN
1976	11	*Carter (D)	1,040,232	1,004,967	8,552	4,298	1,691	3,814
							Citizens	
1980	11	*Reagan (R)	981,584	1,088,845	**1,519	—	7,767	29,135
1984	11	*Reagan (R)	995,740	1,198,584	—	—	—	4,883
					POPULIST	SOC. WORKERS	NEW ALLIANCE	
1988	11	Dukakis (D)	1,126,794	1,047,499	3,056	2,574	1,953	5,157
						IND. (Perot)	TAXPAYERS	
1992	11	*Clinton (D)	1,041,066	930,855	2,311	544,479	1,772	2,877
							IND. (Nader)	
1996	11	*Clinton (D)	1,071,971	845,029	—	227,339	28,723	7,929
					CONSTITUTION	IND. (Buchanan)	GREEN (Nader)	
2000	11	Gore (D)	1,242,987	1,237,279	2,042	11,471	94,070	6,640

*Won US presidential election.
**Listed as Constitution Party on Wisconsin ballot.

are elected by district on a nonpartisan basis and serve staggered six-year terms. Vacancies are filled by the governor until a successor is elected. Judges sit in panels of three for most cases, although some cases can be heard by a single judge. Decisions by the court of appeals may be reviewed by the supreme court.

The circuit court, the trial court of general jurisdiction, also hears appeals from municipal courts. Circuit court boundaries coincide with county boundaries, except that three judicial circuits comprise two counties each; thus, there are 69 judicial circuits. Trial judges are elected by district on a nonpartisan basis for six-year terms. All justices at the circuit court level or higher must have at least five years' experience as practicing attorneys and be less than 70 years old in order to qualify for office. Vacancies are filled by the governor until a successor is elected.

Wisconsin's 200 municipal courts have jurisdiction over local matters. Municipal judges are elected for terms of two or four years, generally serve on a part-time basis, and need not be attorneys.

Wisconsin's crime rate in 2001 was 3,321.2 per 100,000 population, including a total of 12,486 violent crimes and 166,924 crimes against property in that year. Inmates in federal and state prisons totaled 20,931 in June 2001, an increase of 0.7% over the previous year. The state's incarceration rate stood at 373 per 100,000 inhabitants. Wisconsin does not have a death penalty.

[17]ARMED FORCES

In 2002, there were 532 active-duty military personnel and 3,074 civilian personnel stationed in Wisconsin. Prime military contracts amounted to more than $911 million in the same fiscal year.

A total of 3,932 Wisconsinites were killed in World War I; 7,980 in World War II; 800 in Korea; and 1,142 in Vietnam. According to the 2000 Census, there were 514,213 veterans were living in Wisconsin. Of these, 104,290 saw service in World War II; 69,651 in the Korean conflict; 150,679 in the Vietnam era; and 46,415 in 1990–2000 (including the Persian Gulf War). Wisconsin veterans received benefits of nearly $875 million in 2002.

In 2000, the Wisconsin State Patrol employed 508 full-time sworn officers.

[18]MIGRATION

Until the early 19th century, Wisconsin was inhabited mainly by Indians; the French and British brought few permanent settlers. In the 1820s, southerners began to arrive from the lower Mississippi, and in the 1830s easterners poured in from New York, Ohio, Pennsylvania, and New England.

Foreign immigrants began arriving in the 1820s, either directly from Europe or after temporary settlement in eastern states. Most of the early immigrants were from Ireland and England. Germans also came in large numbers, especially after the Revolution of 1848, and by 1860 they were predominant in the immigrant population, which was proportionally larger than in any other state except California. The state soon became a patchwork of ethnic communities—Germans in the counties near Lake Michigan, Norwegians in southern and western Wisconsin, Dutch in the lower Fox Valley and near Sheboygan, and other groups in other regions.

After the Civil War, and especially in the 1880s, immigration reached new heights, with Wisconsin receiving a large share of Germans and Scandinavians. The proportion of Germans declined, however, as new immigrants arrived from Finland, Russia and from southern and eastern Europe, especially Poland, before World War I. Despite this overseas immigration, Wisconsin suffered a net population loss from migration beginning in 1900 as Wisconsinites moved to other states.

Between 1970 and 1983 alone, this loss totaled 154,000. From 1985 to 1990, the net loss from migration amounted to 3,150. Between 1990 and 1998, Wisconsin had net gains of 84,000 in domestic migration and 21,000 in international migration. In 1998, 3,724 foreign immigrants arrived in Wisconsin; of these, the greatest number (680) came from Mexico. The state's overall population increased 6.8% between 1990 and 1998.

A significant trend since 1970 has been the decline in population in Milwaukee and other large cities; at the same time, suburbs have continued to grow, as have many other areas, especially in parts of northern Wisconsin. In the period 1995–2000, 338,108 people moved into the state and 330,826 moved out, for a net gain of 7,282.

[19]INTERGOVERNMENTAL COOPERATION

The Commission on Interstate Cooperation represents the state in its dealings with the Council of State Governments. Wisconsin also participates in the Education Commission of the States, Great Lakes Commission, Midwest Interstate Low-Level Radioactive Waste Compact Commission, and Mississippi River Parkway Commission. In 1985, Wisconsin, seven other Great Lakes states, and the Canadian provinces of Quebec and Ontario signed the Great Lakes Compact to protect the lakes' water reserves. In 2001, Wisconsin received over $5.8 billion in federal grants.

[20]ECONOMY

With the coming of the first Europeans, fur trading became a major economic activity; as more settlers arrived, agriculture prospered. Although farming—preeminently dairying—remains important, manufacturing is the mainstay of today's economy. Wisconsin's industries are diversified, with nonelectrical machinery and food products the leading items. Other important industries are paper and pulp products, transportation equipment, electrical and electronic equipment, and fabricated metals. Economic growth has been concentrated in the southeast. There, soils and climate are favorable for agriculture; a skilled labor force is available to industry; and capital, transportation, and markets are most readily accessible.

As happened to the country at large, Wisconsin in 1981–82 experienced the worst economic slump since the Great Depression, with the unemployment rate rising to 11.7% in late 1982. Manufacturing was hard hit, and the loss of jobs in this sector was considered permanent. Nevertheless, manufacturing has remained Wisconsin's dominant sector, accounting for 27% of total state output in 1997, and growing close to 2.7% a year 1997 to 2000 (although falling to 25% of total output), before falling 2.9% in the national recession of 2001 (and falling to 21% of total output). The strongest growth in the period, as in most of the rest of the country, was in various categories of services, with output from general services up 29.1%; from financial services, up 25.2%, from government, trade and the transportation and utilities sectors, all up more than 20% 1997 to 2001. The diversity of Wisconsin's economy could be expected moderate the impact of the national recession and slowdown in 2001 and 2002, and by the end of 2002, the rebound of employment in the state was outpacing that of the nation overall.

In 2001, Wisconsin's gross state product gross state product was $177.4 billion, the 20th largest among the states, to which manufacturing contributed $42 billion; general services, $32.9 billion; financial services, $29.2 billion; trade, $28 billion; government, $20.4 billion; transportation and public utilities, $12.5 billion, and construction, $8.6 billion. The public sector in 2001 constituted 11.5% of gross state product, close to the 12% average for the states.

21 INCOME

According to the Bureau of Economic Analysis, in 2001, Wisconsin had a per capita personal income (PCPI) of $29,196 which ranked 21st in the United States (including the District of Columbia) and was 96% of the national average, $30,413. The 2001 PCPI reflected an increase of 2.8% from 2000 compared to the national change of 2.2%. In 2001, Wisconsin had a total personal income (TPI) of $157,831,749,000 which ranked 19th in the United States and accounted for 1.8% of the national total. The 2001 TPI reflected an increase of 3.4% from 2000 compared to the national change of 3.3%.

Earnings of persons employed in Wisconsin increased from $106,673,167,000 in 2000 to $109,311,907,000 in 2001, an increase of 2.5%. The largest industries in 2001 were services, 24.9% of earnings; durable goods manufacturing, 14.8%; and state and local government, 12.9%. Of the industries that accounted for at least 5% of earnings in 2001, the slowest growing from 2000 to 2001 was durable goods manufacturing, which decreased 5.9%; the fastest was state and local government, which increased 7.9%.

According to data released by the US Census Bureau, in 2000, the median household income was $45,349 compared to the national average of $42,148. In 2001, the median income for a family of four was $65,441 compared to the national average of $63,278. For the period 1999 to 2001, the average poverty rate was 8.6% which placed it 12th among the 50 states and the District of Columbia ranked lowest to highest.

22 LABOR

According to Bureau of Labor Statistics (BLS) provisional estimates, in July 2003 the seasonally adjusted civilian labor force in Wisconsin numbered 3,099,200, with approximately 174,300 workers unemployed, yielding an unemployment rate of 5.6%, compared to the national average of 6.2% for the same period. Since the beginning of the BLS data series in 1978, the highest unemployment rate recorded was 12.7% in January 1983. The historical low was 2.8% in June 1999. In 2001, an estimated 5.7% of the labor force was employed in construction; 21.0% in manufacturing; 4.5% in transportation, communications, and public utilities; 19.3% in trade; 5.5% in finance, insurance, and real estate; 23.3% in services; 11.1% in government; and 3.3% in agriculture.

Labor began to organize in the state after the Civil War. The Knights of St. Crispin, a shoemakers' union, grew into what was at that time the nation's largest union, before it collapsed during the Panic of 1873. In 1887, unions of printers, cigarmakers, and iron molders organized the Milwaukee Federated Trades Council, and in 1893 the Wisconsin State Federation of Labor was formed. A statewide union for public employees was established in 1932. In 1977, the state's legislature granted public employees (except public safety personnel) the right to strike, subject to certain limitations.

The US Department of Labor reported that in 2002, 398,000 of Wisconsin's 2,554,000 employed wage and salary workers were members of unions. This represented 15.6% of those so employed, down from 16.2% in 2001 and 18.7% in 1998. The national average is 13.2%. In all, 420,000 workers (16.4%) were represented by unions. In addition to union members, this category includes workers who report no union affiliation but whose jobs are covered by a union contract.

23 AGRICULTURE

Farm marketings in 2001 amounted to $5.9 billion, 10th among the 50 states; over $4.5 billion in farm marketings came from dairy products and livestock. Wisconsin led the US in 2002 in the production of snap beans for processing, cranberries, processing beets, corn for silage, and cabbage for kraut. It also ranked 2nd for oat production, 3rd in sweet corn, peas, tart cherries, and carrots for processing, 4th in oats and fall potatoes, 10th in hay, and 6th in corn for grain.

In the early years, Wisconsin developed an agricultural economy based on wheat, some of which was exported to eastern states and overseas via the port of Milwaukee. Farmers also grew barley and hops, finding a market for these products among early Milwaukee brewers. After the Civil War, soil exhaustion and the depredations of the chinch bug forced farmers to turn to other crops, including corn, oats, and hay, which could be used to feed hogs, sheep, cows, and other livestock.

Although agricultural income has continued to rise in recent years and the average size of farms has increased, farm acreage and the number of farms have declined. In 2002 there were 15.9 million acres (6.4 million hectares) of land in farms, nearly 50% of the total land area, distributed among 77,000 farms, a decline of 4,100 from 1986. Farmland is concentrated in the southern two-thirds of the state, especially in the southeast. Potatoes are grown mainly in central Wisconsin, cranberries in the Wisconsin River Valley, and cherries in the Door Peninsula.

Leading field crops (in bushels) in 2002 were corn for grain, 391,500,000; oats 15,000,000; wheat, 10,771,000; and barley, 1,800,000. About 5,340,000 tons of dry hay and 11,680,000 tons of corn for silage were harvested that year. Potato production was 375,000 hundredweight. In 2002, Wisconsin farmers produced for processing 473,000 tons of sweet corn, 317,070 tons of snap beans, 67,230 tons of green peas, 3,190,000 barrels of cranberries, and 4 tons of tart cherries, and 433,000 lb (196,000 kg) of spearmint and peppermint for oil. Some 31,750 tons of cucumber pickles were produced in 2002; 55,670 tons of beets for canning and 81,470 tons of cabbage for kraut were also grown in 2001.

24 ANIMAL HUSBANDRY

Aided by the skills of immigrant cheesemakers and by the encouragement of dairy farmers who emigrated from New York—especially by the promotional effort of the agriculturist and publisher William D. Hoard—Wisconsin turned to dairying in the late 19th century. In 1997, Wisconsin ranked 2nd (after California) in the number of milk cows with 1.29 million milk cows which produced nearly 22.2 billion lb (10 billion kg) of milk. Dairy farms are prominent in nearly all regions, but especially in the Central Plains and Western Uplands. Wisconsin ranchers also raise livestock for meat production.

In 2003, the state had 3.3 million cattle and calves, valued at $3.27 billion. During 2002, Wisconsin farms had about 520,000 hogs and pigs, valued at $35.4 million. Poultry farmers sold 7.9 million lb (3.6 million kg) of chicken in 2001. Also during 2001, there were 1.24 billion eggs produced, valued at $51.5 million.

25 FISHING

In 1998, Wisconsin ranked 2nd among the Great Lakes states in the value of its commercial fishing; 6,991,000 lb (3,171,000 kg) of fish were landed (not including Mississippi River landings), at a total value of $4,418,000. In 1998, fish farms distributed over 35.4 million walleye and 7 million trout into Wisconsin's waters. The muskellunge is the premier game fish of Wisconsin's inland waters; Coho and chinook salmon, introduced to Lake Michigan, now thrive there. The largest concentration of lake sturgeon in the US is in Lake Winnebago. In 1998, the state issued 1,468,061 fishing licenses.

26 FORESTRY

Wisconsin was once about 85% forested. Although much of the forest was depleted by forest fires and wasteful lumber industry practices, vast areas reseeded themselves naturally, and more than 820,000 acres (332,000 hectares) have been replanted. In 2002,

Wisconsin had 15,963,000 acres (6,460,000 hectares) of forest, covering 46% of the state's land area; 70% of all forestlands are privately owned. Hardwoods make up about 80% of the sawtimber. The most heavily forested region is in the north. The timber industry reached its peak in the late 19th century. In 2002, lumber production totaled 583 million board feet.

Wisconsin's woods have recreational as well as commercial value. Two national forests—Chequamegon and Nicolet, both located in northern Wisconsin—cover 1,522,485 acres (616,150 hectares). The 10 state forests cover 471,329 acres (190,741 hectares).

Forest management and fire control programs are directed by the Department of Natural Resources. The US Forest Service operates a Forest Products Laboratory at Madison, in cooperation with the University of Wisconsin.

[27]MINING

In 2001 the estimated value of nonfuel mineral commodities produced in Wisconsin decreased marginally from the previous year to $368 million. According to preliminary figures, construction sand and gravel (37.3 million metric tons, valued at $143 million) was the leading mineral commodity produced in Wisconsin, followed by crushed stone (34 million metric tons, also valued at $143 million). Each accounted for almost 39% of the state's total nonfuel mineral value, followed by lime (610,000 metric tons, $37.1 million), which accounted for about 10%. In 2001 Wisconsin was 3rd nationally in dimension stone, 4th in industrial sand and gravel, and 8th in construction sand and gravel.

[28]ENERGY AND POWER

The state's first hydroelectric plant was built at Appleton in 1882; many others were built later, especially along the Wisconsin River. Because Wisconsin itself has no coal, oil, or natural gas resources, the state has been active in developing alternative energy resources to increase its energy independence. Biomass energy is being developed for the production of ethanol; and waste wood is being used for utility generation and as fuel in industrial processes. Hydropower is a significant source of electricity generation in the paper industry and for electric utility generation.

In 1999, electric generation (utility and nonutility) totaled 58.5 billion kWh, and total installed generating capacity was 13.1 million kW. Of Wisconsin's power generation in 1999, 70% came from coal, more than 19% from nuclear energy, and the remainder from oil, gas, hydroelectric, and other sources. The state has three nuclear power reactors: Point Beach Units 1 and 2, operated by Wisconsin Electric Power Company; and the Kewaunee plant, operated by the Wisconsin Public Service Co. In 2000 Wisconsin's total per capita energy consumption was 333 million Btu (83.9 million kcal), ranking it 29th among the 50 states.

[29]INDUSTRY

Industrial activity is concentrated in the southeast, especially the Milwaukee metropolitan area. Milwaukee has lost some of its luster as a brewery center; Miller and Pabst still have breweries there, but Schlitz beer is no longer made in Wisconsin, and Blatz and Old Style are brewed by G. Heileman in La Crosse.

Of the state's three biggest paper and lumber products firms, Consolidated Paper is located in Wisconsin Rapids, and Fort Howard Paper in Green Bay. Johnson & Son (wax products) and J. I. Case (agricultural equipment), the latter a subsidiary of Tenneco, are in Racine. Oscar Mayer (meat-packing and food products), located in Madison, is now a subsidiary of General Foods. Parker Pen Co. is in Janesville.

In 1997, the total value of shipments for manufactured goods in Wisconsin was $119 billion. Wisconsin is headquarters for eight Fortune 500 companies: Northwestern Mutual Life, Johnson Controls, Manpower, Case, American Family Insurance Group, Aid Association for Lutherans, Harnischfeger Industrial, and Roundy's.

Earnings of persons employed in Wisconsin increased from $90.3 billion in 1997 to $96 billion in 1998, an increase of 6.4%. The largest industries in 1998 were services, 23.1% of earnings; durable goods manufacturing, 17.7%; and state and local government, 11.6%. Of the industries that accounted for at least 5% of earnings in 1998, the slowest growing from 1997 to 1998 was state and local government, which increased 4.0%; the fastest was wholesale trade (6.2% of earnings in 1998), which increased 8.0%.

[30]COMMERCE

Wholesale trade in 1997 totaled $61 billion. Retail sales for 1997 amounted to $51 billion. Statewide, automotive dealers accounted for 14% of establishments; food stores, 8%; and eating and drinking places, 35%.

The state engages in foreign as well as domestic trade through the Great Lakes ports of Superior-Duluth, Milwaukee, Green Bay, and Kenosha. Iron ore and grain are shipped primarily from Superior-Duluth, while Milwaukee handles the heaviest volume of general merchandise. Wisconsin exported about $10 billion in goods (18th in the US) in 1998. Greater Milwaukee is a foreign-trade zone where goods can enter duty-free under certain conditions.

[31]CONSUMER PROTECTION

The Department of Agriculture, Trade, and Consumer Protection monitors food production, inspects meat, and administers grading programs; its Trade and Consumer Protection Division administers laws governing product safety and trade practices, in cooperation with the state Department of Justice. The Office of the Commissioner of Banking administers laws governing consumer credit, and the Department of Transportation's Motor Vehicles Division investigates complaints from buyers of new and used automobiles. The Department of Justice's Office of Consumer Protection Division provides protection against deceptive and fraudulent business practices through its consumer protection unit.

[32]BANKING

As of 2002 there were 316 insured banks in the state, with assets of $102 billion. Two hundred twenty-nine of those banks were state-chartered. The Office of the Commissioner of Banking licenses and charters banks, loan and collection companies, and currency exchanges. The Office of the Commissioner of Savings and Loan supervises state-chartered savings and loan associations. The Office of the Commissioner of Credit Unions enforces laws relating to credit unions.

The 2001 recession in the United States only moderately affected Wisconsin, and banking performance in the state was strong in 2002. Wisconsin ranks 10th in the nation with regard to the total number of insured banks. Loan delinquencies remained a risk for Wisconsin banks in 2002, especially among agricultural banks. As well, community banks (those with less than $1 billion in assets) saw a shift in loan portfolios to higher-yielding, riskier lending, which required banks to implement effective risk management strategies.

[33]INSURANCE

In 2001, there were 2.8 million ordinary life insurance policies in force with a total value of $184.8 billion; total value for all categories of life insurance (ordinary, group, industrial, and credit) was $311.4 billion. Death benefits paid that year totaled $911.8 million. As of 2000, there were 175 property and casualty and 28 life and health insurance companies incorporated or organized in the state. In 2001, property and casualty insurers wrote over $6.2 billion in premiums. That year, there were 12,714 flood insurance policies in force in the state, with a total value of $1.3 million.

The Office of the Commissioner of Insurance licenses insurance agents, enforces state and federal regulations, responds to consumer complaints, and develops consumer education programs and literature. The office also operates the State Life Insurance Fund, which sells basic life insurance (maximum $10,000) to state residents; and the Local Government Property Insurance Fund, which insures properties of local government units on an optional basis.

34SECURITIES

Wisconsin has no securities exchanges. Approximately 857 brokers and dealers firms conduct business in the state by means of 8,358 employees. Professional securities investment advice is available through 171 firms. Wisconsin acts as the headquarters for 56 NASDAQ-listed companies, 3 NASDAQ market makers; and has incorporated 20 NYSE-listed companies. The sale of securities is regulated by the Department of Financial Institutions, Division of Securities.

35PUBLIC FINANCE

Budget estimates are prepared by departments and sent to the governor or governor-elect in the fall of each even-numbered year; the following January, the governor presents a biennial budget to the legislature, which passes a budget bill, often after many amendments. Most appropriations are made separately for each year of the biennium. The fiscal year begins 1 July. Expenditures by state and local governments alike have risen dramatically since 1960. At one time, the state was constitutionally prohibited from borrowing money; this provision was at first circumvented by the use of private corporations and then, in 1969, eliminated by constitutional amendment. As of 1995, state indebtedness exceeded $8.2 billion. As of 2000, the state was required to maintain a budget balance equal to 1% of gross appropriations and the compensation reserve each year. The governor proposed raising the percentage to 1.1% for 2000/01, and 2% over the following five years.

The Wisconsin budget for 2000/01 was set at approximately $22 billion. General purpose revenue made up about 53% of total revenues, federal revenue 24%, program revenue 13%, and segregated revenue 10%. General purpose revenue went to primary and secondary education (39%), tax relief (10%), medical assistance (9%), the UW system (8%), correctional services (7%), and tax credits (6%). About 60% of general purpose revenue went to local assistant programs, 16% to individuals, 15% to state agencies, and 9% to the University of Wisconsin.

In 2001/02, revenue shortfalls and increased expenses let to total cuts in Wisconsin's biennial budget of $324.4 million. Across-the-board cuts were mandated, state employees were laid off and the state raised funds through by securing future tobacco settlement proceeds. Revenue shortfalls in 2002/03 led to $89.6 million in cuts in the budget after it was enacted, including further layoffs and across-the-board cuts. As a percent of expenditures, the state's starting balance dropped from 1.9% of expenditures in 2000/01, to 0.5% in 2001/02, to –2.6% in 2002/03. The state's starting balance for 2003/04 was 0.4% of projected expenditures. Allocations by purpose in 2003/04 were 58% for local assistance, 20% for aid to individuals, 8% for state universities, 6% for corrections, and 8% for other state operations.

The following table from the US Census Bureau contains information on revenues, expenditures, indebtedness, and cash/securities for 2001.

	($000)	PERCENT	PER CAPITA
Population (thousands, 2001)	5,406	(X)	(X)
Total Revenue	18,826,011	100.00	3,482.43
General revenue	21,883,865	116.24	4,048.07
Utility revenue	–	–	–
Liquor store revenue	–	–	–
Insurance trust revenue	–3,057,854	–16.24	–565.64
Exhibit: Salaries and wages	3,013,983	12.13	557.53
Total expenditure	24,857,238	100.00	4,598.08
General expenditure	21,693,978	87.27	4,012.94
Education	8,169,640	32.87	1,511.22
Public welfare	4,630,773	18.63	856.60
Hospitals	593,927	2.39	109.86
Health	549,415	2.21	101.63
Highways	1,634,446	6.58	302.34
Police protection	126,512	0.51	23.40
Correction	932,819	3.75	172.55
Natural resources	369,284	1.49	68.31
Parks and recreation	64,561	0.26	11.94
Government administration	608,860	2.45	112.63
Interest on general debt	706,143	2.84	130.62
Other and unallocable	3,307,598	13.31	611.84
Utility expenditure	–	–	–
Liquor store expenditure	–	–	–
Insurance trust expenditure	3,163,260	12.73	585.14
Debt at end of fiscal year	12,172,209	100.00	2,251.61
Cash and security holdings	71,507,450	100.00	13,227.42

36TAXATION

The largest single source of state revenue is the income tax on individuals. Most local tax revenue comes from property taxes, and most of that goes for education. Personal income tax rates on net taxable income ranges from 4.77% to 6.77%. The corporate tax rate is 7.9% of net income. The general sales tax is 5%. Other state taxes are those on gasoline, cigarettes, liquor, wine, beer, motor vehicles, insurance companies, estates (limited to the amount of credit allowed under the federal estate tax), real estate transfers, and public utilities.

The state collected $11.814 billion in taxes in 2002, of which 42.1% came from individual income taxes, 31.3% came from the general sales tax, 14.7% from selective sales taxes, 5.5% from license fees, and 4.4% from corporate income taxes. In 2003, Michigan ranked 7th among the states in terms of state and local tax burden, which amounted to about 10.7% of income.

The following table from the US Census Bureau provides a summary of taxes collected by the state in 2002.

	($000)	PER CAPITA
Total Taxes	11,813,832	2,171.18
Property taxes	91,703	16.85
Sales and gross receipts	5,427,664	997.51
General sales and gross receipts	3,695,796	679.22
Selective sales taxes	1,731,868	318.29
Alcoholic beverage	45,581	8.38
Amusements	385	0.07
Insurance Premiums	107,352	19.73
Motor fuels	955,404	175.59
Pari-mutuels	2,104	0.39
Public utilities	314,769	57.85
Tobacco products	302,701	55.63
Other selective sales	3,572	0.66
Licenses	650,971	119.64
Alcoholic beverages	490	0.09
Amusements	566	0.1
Corporation	12,247	2.25
Hunting and fishing	58,683	10.78
Motor vehicle	312,993	57.52
Motor vehicle operators	33,388	6.14
Public utility	(X)	(X)

	($000)	PER CAPITA
Licenses (continued)		
Occupation and business, NEC	230,470	42.36
Other	2,134	0.39
Other taxes	5,643,494	1,037.18
Individual income	4,973,615	914.07
Corporation net income	521,584	95.86
Death and gift	82,635	15.19
Documentary and stock transfer	51,176	9.41
Severance	3,460	0.64
Other	11,024	2.03

37 ECONOMIC POLICY

The state seeks to promote the relocation of new industries to Wisconsin, as well as the expansion of existing ones, by providing advice and assistance through the Division of Economic Development and some 280 local development corporations. It supports businesses that promise to substantially improve the economy of a community or the state; extends loans to small businesses; helps with the training or retraining of employees; and offers financial assistance for applied research that results in a new product or production process. To revitalize economically depressed areas, the state provides tax benefits to businesses locating or expanding operations in such areas and helps finance local economic development projects. Communities are authorized to issue tax-exempt bonds to enable industries to finance new equipment. In addition, all machinery and equipment used in goods production is tax-exempt under state law. In 2003, the Division was contained of three main operating bureaus: the Bureau of Business Development, the Bureau of Business Finance, and Bureau of Minority Business Development.

38 HEALTH

Wisconsin's infant mortality rate was 6.6 per 1,000 live births in 2000, slightly below the national rate of 6.9. In 1999, there were 11,013 legal abortions performed in the state, a ratio of 10 abortions for every 1,000 women. State law prohibits the use of public funds for abortions, except in cases of incest or rape or for grave health reasons. The state does provide funds for family-planning counseling.

The overall death rate in 2000 was 877.4 per 100,000 population. In the same year, Wisconsin ranked above the nation as a whole in death rates for cerebrovascular disease, accidents, and suicide but below the national averages for heart disease. Leading causes of death in 2000 were heart disease (256.8 deaths per 100,000 population), cancer (200.9), and cerebrovascular disease (67.9). Among Wisconsin adult 18 years of age and older, 23.4% were regular smokers in 1998. The HIV mortality rate of 1.4 per 100,000 population was below the national rate in 2000; a total 3,768 AIDS cases had been reported through 2001.

Wisconsin's 121 community hospitals had 579,089 admissions and 15,597 beds in 2001. There were 16,762 full-time registered nurses and 1,316 full-time licensed practical nurses in 2001 and 257 physicians per 100,000 population in 2000. The average expense of a community hospital for care was $1,329.70 per inpatient day in 2001.

Federal government grants to cover the Medicare and Medicaid services in 2001 totaled $2.4 billion; 787,442 enrollees received Medicare benefits that year. Only 7.7% of Wisconsin's residents were uninsured in 2002.

Medical degrees are granted by the University of Wisconsin at Madison and by the Medical College of Wisconsin (formerly part of Marquette University). The Division of Health, a branch of the State Department of Health and Social Services, has responsibility for planning and supervising health services and facilities, enforcing state and federal regulations, administering medical assistance programs, and providing information to the public. State laws provide for generic drug substitution and require continuing physician education.

39 SOCIAL WELFARE

In 2001, the average weekly unemployment benefit was $235.58. Average monthly participation in the food stamp program in FY2002 comprised 262,310 persons (105,747 households). The average monthly benefit was $62.69, and the sum total of benefits paid in FY2002 was $197,330,085.

With the enactment of the Personal Responsibility and Work Opportunity Reconciliation Act of 1996, the US government has changed the form and regulations for many of its social welfare programs. Most significantly, it replaces Aid to Families with Dependent Children (AFDC), an open-ended entitlement program, with Temporary Assistance for Needy Families (TANF), a limited system of assistance funded largely through federal block grants. The reform act also impacts the food stamp program, the Supplemental Security Income program, and the child nutrition program. The law took effect on 1 July 1997 and provided $16.38 billion in block grants for fiscal years 1997–2002. The grants are to be divided among the states based on an equation involving the numbers of former AFDC recipients in each state.

Reauthorization of the 1996 social welfare legislation, scheduled for 2002, was delayed, and the original law had been extended three times as of July 2003, with the most recent extension running through September 2003. Wisconsin's TANF program is called Wisconsin Works (W-2). In June 2000 the state had 37,381 welfare recipients. State expenditures on the TANF program in FY2002 totaled $159,075,067.

In December 2001, Social Security benefits were paid to 905,890 Wisconsin residents. This number included 608,890 retired workers, 94,480 widows and widowers, 85,830 disabled workers, 53,680 spouses, and 62,570 children. Social Security beneficiaries represented 16.8% of the total state population and 96.8% of the state's population age 65 and older. Retired workers (excluding persons with special benefits) received an average monthly payment of $896; widows and widowers, $870; disabled workers, $807; and spouses, $456. Payments for children of retired workers averaged $480 per month; children of deceased workers, $607; and children of disabled workers, $244.

Federal Supplemental Security Income payments in December 2001 went to 85,333 Wisconsin residents, averaging $359 a month.

40 HOUSING

In 2002, there were an estimated 2,386,848 housing units, 2,142,645 of which were occupied; 68.7% were owner-occupied. About 64.8% of all units were single-family, detached homes. Rural areas had a higher proportion of deficient housing than urban areas, and substandard conditions were three times as common in units built before 1939, which account for about 24% of the existing housing stock. In 2002, utility gas was the most common energy source for heating; about 804 units were equipped for solar power. It was estimated that 53,261 units lacked telephone service, 10,703 lacked complete plumbing facilities, and 11,711 lacked complete kitchen facilities. The average household size was 2.47 people.

In 2002, 38,208 new privately owned housing units were authorized for construction. The median home value was $122,259. The median monthly cost for mortgage owners was $1,088. Renters paid a median of $580 per month. During 2002, Wisconsin received more than $235.3 million in community planning and development aid from the US Department of Housing and Urban Development.

The Department of Veterans Affairs makes home loans to veterans. The Housing Finance Authority, created by the legislature in 1971, raises money through the sale of tax-exempt bonds and makes loans directly or indirectly to low- and moderate-income home buyers. Wisconsin's state building code, developed in 1913 to cover construction of all dwellings with three or more units, was revised in the late 1970s to cover new one- and two-family dwellings. Local housing codes prescribing standards for structural upkeep and maintenance in existing buildings are in force in all large cities and in many smaller cities and villages.

41EDUCATION

Wisconsin has a tradition of leadership in education. The state's constitution, adopted in 1848, provided for free public education; however, there was no state tax for schools until 1885. A compulsory education law was passed in 1879 and strengthened in 1903 and 1907. The first kindergarten in the United States was established in Watertown, Wisconsin, in 1856.

General public elementary and secondary education is administered under the overall supervision of the Department of Public Instruction, which is headed by a state superintendent elected on a nonpartisan basis. As of 2000, 85.1% of all Wisconsinites 25 years or older had completed high school, well above the US average of 80.4%. More than 22% had obtained a bachelor's degree or higher.

The total enrollment for fall 1999 in Wisconsin's public schools stood at 877,753. Of these, 596,439 attended schools from kindergarten through grade eight, and 281,314 attended high school. Minority students made up approximately 20% of the total enrollment in public elementary and secondary schools in 2001. Total enrollment is expected to reach 883,000 in fall 2000 but drop to 869,000 by fall 2005. Expenditures for public education in 2000/01 were estimated at $7,327,962. Enrollment in nonpublic schools in fall 2001 was 139,455.

As of fall 2000, there were 328,537 students enrolled in college or graduate school. In the same year Wisconsin had 68 degree-granting institutions. The University of Wisconsin (UW) system is comprised of 13 degree-granting campuses, 13 two-year centers, and the University of Wisconsin-Extension, which has outreach and continuing education activities on all 26 UW campuses and in all 72 Wisconsin counties. All 13 universities award bachelor's and master's degrees. University of Wisconsin-Madison and University of Wisconsin-Milwaukee also confer doctoral degrees. UW-Madison, one of the world's largest and most respected institutions of higher learning, was chartered by the state's first legislature in 1848. UW-Milwaukee was the system's 2nd-largest campus. The 11 other universities are Eau Claire, Green Bay, La Crosse, Oshkosh, Parkside (at Kenosha-Racine), Platteville, River Falls, Stevens Point, Stout (at Menomonie), Superior, and Whitewater.

Wisconsin's private institutions of higher education encompass a broad range of schools. There were 34 private 4-year institutions in 2000, including such leading institutions as Marquette University, Lawrence University, Ripon College, and Beloit College. In addition, there are 4 technical and professional schools, and 5 theological seminaries. Wisconsin also has a system of technical colleges, the Wisconsin Technical College System. In 1911, the legislature enacted the first system of state support for vocational, technical, and adult education in the nation. One in eight Wisconsin citizens attends a technical college. The system includes 16 technical colleges, each governed by a local board. At the same time, each college is part of a statewide system governed by an independent board. In 1997, minority students comprised 9.9% of total postsecondary enrollment.

42ARTS

Wisconsin offers numerous facilities for drama, music, and other performing arts, including the four-theater Performing Arts Center in Milwaukee and the Dane County Exposition Center in Madison. Milwaukee has a repertory theater, and there are many other theater groups around the state. Summer plays are performed at an unusual garden theater at Fish Creek in the Door Peninsula. There is also an annual music festival at that site.

The Pro Arte String Quartet in Madison and the Fine Arts Quartet in Milwaukee have been sponsored by the University of Wisconsin, which has also supported many other musical activities. Milwaukee is the home of the Great Lakes Opera Company, the Milwaukee Ballet Company, the Milwaukee Chamber Orchestra, and the Milwaukee Symphony. Madison is home to the Madison Symphony, the Madison Opera, and the Wisconsin Chamber Orchestra.

The Wisconsin Arts Board, consisting of 15 members appointed by the governor for three-year terms, aids artists and performing groups and assists communities in developing arts programs. In 2003, the Wisconsin Arts Board and other Wisconsin arts organizations received grants totaling $1,033,800 from the National Endowment for the Arts. The Wisconsin Humanities Council was founded in 1972. In 2000, the National Endowment for the Humanities contributed $1,979,499 for 29 state programs. State and private sources contribute funding to supplement federal assistance. The state has over 1,000 arts associations and over 150 local groups.

43LIBRARIES AND MUSEUMS

In 2000, the state library system had a total of 18 million volumes and circulation of 46 million. The Milwaukee Public Library, founded in 1878, maintained 12 branches and had 2,504,461 bound volumes as of 1998; the Madison Public Library had seven branches and over 815,686 volumes. The largest academic library is that of the University of Wisconsin at Madison, with six million bound volumes. The best-known special library is that of the State Historical Society of Wisconsin at Madison, with 3.6 million books and over 60,000 cu ft (1,700 cu m) of government publications and documents. Total public library income in 2000 was $156,649,000, including $5.3 million in state grants.

Wisconsin had 208 museums and historical sites in 2000. The State Historical Society maintains a historical museum in Madison and other historical sites and museums around the state. The Milwaukee Public Museum contains collections on history, natural history, and art. The Milwaukee Art Center, founded in 1888, a major museum of the visual arts, emphasizes European works of the 17th to 19th centuries. The Madison Art Center, founded in 1901, has European, Japanese, Mexican, and American paintings and sculpture, as well as 17th-century Flemish tapestries. The Charles Allis Art Library in Milwaukee, founded in 1947, houses collections of Chinese porcelains, French antiques, and 19th-century American landscape paintings. Other leading art museums include the Elvehjem Museum of Art in Madison and the Theodore Lyman Wright Art Center at Beloit College.

The Circus World Museum at Baraboo occupies the site of the original Ringling Brothers Circus. Other museums of special interest include the Dard Hunter Paper Museum (Appleton), the National Railroad Museum (Green Bay), and the Green Bay Packer Hall of Fame. More than 500 species of animals are on exhibit at the Milwaukee County Zoological Park; Madison and Racine also have zoos. Historical sites in Wisconsin include Villa Louis, a fur trader's mansion at Prairie du Chien; the Old Wade House in Greenbush; Old World Wisconsin, an outdoor ethnic museum near Eagle; Pendarvis, focusing on lead mining at

Mineral Point; and the Taliesin estate of architect Frank Lloyd Wright, in Spring Green.

44COMMUNICATIONS

About 95.6% of the state's households had telephones in 2001. In 2003 there were 34 major AM and 98 major FM radio stations. The state also had 28 major television stations. The Milwaukee area had 815,640 television households, 63% of which subscribed to cable. A total of 77,862 Internet domain names were registered with the state in the year 2000.

45PRESS

The state's first newspaper was the *Green Bay Intelligencer,* founded in 1833. Some early papers were put out by rival land speculators who used them to promote their interests. Among these was the *Milwaukee Sentinel,* launched in 1837 and a major daily newspaper today. As immigrants poured in from Europe in succeeding decades, German, Norwegian, Polish, Yiddish, and Finnish papers sprang up. Wisconsin journalism has a tradition of political involvement. The *Milwaukee Leader,* founded as a Socialist daily by Victor Berger in 1911, was denied the use of the US mails because it printed antiwar articles; the *Madison Capital Times,* still important today, also started as an antiwar paper. Founded in 1882 by Lucius Nieman, the *Milwaukee Journal* won a Pulitzer Prize in 1919 for distinguished public service and remains the state's largest-selling and most influential newspaper.

In 2002, Wisconsin had 11 morning papers, 24 evening papers, and 18 Sunday papers. The following table shows leading dailies with their approximate 2002 circulations:

AREA	NAME	DAILY	SUNDAY
Green Bay	*Press–Gazette* (m,S)	54,244	80,810
Madison	*Wisconsin State Journal* (m,S)	100,300	100,300
Milwaukee	*Journal Sentinel* (m,S)	255,098	455,862

As of 1997 there were also 27 semiweekly newspapers and weeklies, as well as 318 periodicals directed to a wide variety of special interests. Among the largest are *Hoard's Dairyman,* founded by William D. Hoard in 1885, with a paid semimonthly circulation of 139,600; *Model Railroader,* monthly 224,732; *Bowling Magazine,* monthly 150,000; *Coin Prices,* bimonthly 83,011; *Coin,* monthly 15,044; and *Old Cars Weekly,* 85,000. Other notable periodicals are the *Wisconsin Magazine of History,* published quarterly in Madison by the state historical society; and *Wisconsin Trails,* another quarterly, also published in Madison.

46ORGANIZATIONS

In 2003, there were about 3,195 regional, national, and international organizations within the state.

The State Historical Society of Wisconsin, founded in 1846, is one of the largest organizations of its kind. It has a museum, a library, and research collections in Madison and is a prominent publisher of historical articles and books. There are several city and county historical societies throughout the state as well. The Forest Products Research Society, in Madison, has an international membership of about 5,000.

Other national organizations based in Wisconsin include the American Bowling Congress, American Society of Agronomy, Conservation Education Association, Crop Science Society of America, Experimental Aircraft Association, Inter-Varsity Christian Fellowship/USA, the John Birch Society, Master Brewers Association of the Americas, the National Association of Congregational Christian Churches, Model Railroad Industry Association, the Seventh Day Baptist General Conference, the National Funeral Directors Association, the United States Curling Association, Wilderness Watch, and World Council of Credit Unions.

47TOURISM, TRAVEL, AND RECREATION

Wisconsin had estimated tourism revenues of $11.6 billion in 2002, reflecting a 2% increase over the previous year. The tourism industry directly and indirectly supports 323,759 jobs in the state.

The state has ample scenic attractions and outdoor recreational opportunities. In addition to the famous Wisconsin Dells gorge, visitors are attracted to the Cave of the Mounds at Blue Mounds, the sandstone cliffs along the Mississippi River, the rocky Lake Michigan shoreline of the Door Peninsula, the lakes and forests of the Rhinelander and Minocqua areas in the north, and Lake Geneva, a resort, in the south. Several areas in southern and northwestern Wisconsin, preserved by the state as the Ice Age National Scientific Reserve, still exhibit drumlins, moraines, and unusual geological formations.

There are three national parks in Wisconsin: Apostle Islands National Lakeshore, on Lake Superior, and the St. Croix and Lower St. Croix scenic riverways. There are 48 state parks, covering 65,483 acres (26,193 hectares).

48SPORTS

Wisconsin has three major league teams: the Milwaukee Brewers of Major League Baseball, the Green Bay Packers of the National Football League, and the Milwaukee Bucks of the National Basketball Association. The Brewers won the American League Pennant in 1982 but lost the World Series to St. Louis. The Brewers have since been realigned and now play in the National League. The Packers won five league championships prior to the establishment of the Super Bowl and then won Super Bowls I, II, and XXXI in 1967, 1968, and 1997, respectively. The Bucks won the NBA Championship in 1971. Milwaukee is the site of the Greater Milwaukee Open in professional golf. There are also numerous minor league baseball, basketball, and hockey teams in the state.

The University of Wisconsin Badgers compete in the Big Ten Conference. Badger ice hockey teams won the NCAA championship in 1973, 1977, 1981, 1983, and 1990. In football, they won the Rose Bowl in 1994, 1999, and 2000 after losing their first three appearances, in 1953, 1960, and 1963. Overall, they have eight bowl game victories. The basketball team from Marquette University in Milwaukee won the NCAA Division I title in 1977 and the National Invitation Tournament championship in 1970. They advanced to the NCAA Final Four in 2003.

Other annual sporting events include ski jumping tournaments in Iola, Middleton, and Wetsby; the World Championship Snowmobile Derby in Eagle River in January; the American Birkebeiner Cross-Country Race at Cable and Hayward in February; and the Great Wisconsin Dells Balloon Race in the Dells. Famous athletes native to Wisconsin include Eric Heiden, Elroy (Crazy Legs) Hirsch, and Chris Witty.

49FAMOUS WISCONSINITES

Wisconsinites who have won prominence as federal judicial or executive officers include Jeremiah Rusk (b.Ohio, 1830–93), a Wisconsin governor selected as the first head of the Agriculture Department in 1889; William F. Vilas (b.Vermont, 1840–1908), who served as postmaster general under Grover Cleveland; Melvin Laird (b.Nebraska, 1922–92), a congressman who served as secretary of defense from 1969–73; and William Rehnquist (b.1924), named to the Supreme Court in 1971.

The state's best-known political figures achieved nationwide reputations as members of the US Senate. John C. Spooner (b.Indiana, 1843–1919) won distinction as one of the inner circle of Senate conservatives before he retired in 1907 amid an upsurge of Progressivism within his party. Robert La Follette (1855–1925) embodied the new wave of Republican Progressivism—and, later, isolationism—as governor and in the Senate. His sons, Robert, Jr. (1895–1953), and Philip (1897–1965), carried on the Progressive tradition as US senator and governor, respectively. Joseph R. McCarthy (1908–57) won attention in the Senate and throughout the nation for his anti-communist crusade. William Proxmire (b.Illinois, 1915), a Democrat, succeeded McCarthy in the Senate and eventually became chairman of the powerful Senate Banking Committee. Representative Henry S. Reuss (1912–2002), also a Democrat, served in the House for 28 years and was chairman of the Banking Committee. Democrat Clement Zablocki (1912–83), elected to the House in 1948, was chairman of the Foreign Affairs Committee. Victor L. Berger (b.Transylvania, 1860–1929), a founder of the Social-Democratic Party, was first elected to the House in 1910; during World War I, he was denied his seat and prosecuted because of his antiwar views.

Besides the La Follettes, other governors who made notable contributions to the state include James D. Doty (b.New York, 1799–1865), who fought to make Wisconsin a separate territory and became the territory's second governor; William D. Hoard (b.New York, 1836–1918), a tireless promoter of dairy farming, as both private citizen and chief executive; James O. Davidson (b.Norway, 1854–1922), who attempted to improve relations between conservatives and progressives; Francis E. McGovern (1866–1946), who pushed through the legislature significant social and economic reform legislation; and Walter J. Kohler (1875–1940), an industrialist who, as governor, greatly expanded the power of the office.

Prominent figures in the state's early history include the Jesuit Jacques Marquette (b.France, 1637–75) and the explorer Louis Jolliet (b.Canada, 1645–1700); and the Sauk Indian leader Black Hawk (b.Illinois, 1767–1838), who was defeated in the Battle of Bad Axe. John Bascom (b.New York, 1827–1911) was an early president of the University of Wisconsin. Charles Van Hise (1857–1918), a later president, promoted the use of academic experts as government advisers; John R. Commons (b.Ohio, 1862–1945), an economist at the university, drafted major state legislation. Philetus Sawyer (b.Vermont, 1816–1900), a prosperous lumberman and US senator, led the state Republican Party for 15 years, before Progressives won control. Carl Schurz (b.Germany, 1829–1906) was a prominent Republican Party figure in the years immediately before the Civil War. Lucius W. Nieman (1857–1935) founded the *Milwaukee Journal*, and Edward P. Allis (b.New York, 1824–89) was an important iron industrialist.

Wisconsin was the birthplace of several Nobel Prize winners, including Herbert S. Gasser (1888–1963), who shared a 1944 Nobel Prize for research into nerve impulses; William P. Murphy (1892–1987), who shared a 1934 prize for research relating to anemia; John Bardeen (1908–91), who shared the physics award in 1956 for his contribution to the development of the transistor; and Herbert A. Simon (1916–2001), who won the 1978 prize in economics. Stephen Babcock (b.New York, 1843–1931) was an agricultural chemist who did research important to the dairy industry. In addition, Wisconsin was the birthplace of the child psychologist Arnold Gesell (1880–1961), and of naturalist and explorer Chapman Andrews (1884–1960). John Muir (b.Scotland, 1838–1914), another noted naturalist and explorer, lived in Wisconsin in his youth. Conservationist Aldo Leopold (1887–1948) taught at the University of Wisconsin and wrote *A Sand County Almanac*.

Frederick Jackson Turner (1861–1932), historian of the American frontier, was born in Wisconsin, as were the economist and social theorist Thorstein Veblen (1857–1929) and the diplomat and historian George F. Kennan (b.1904). Famous journalists include news commentator H. V. Kaltenborn (1878–1965), award-winning sports columnist Red Smith (Walter Wellesley Smith, 1905–82), and television newsman Tom Snyder (b.1936).

Thornton Wilder (1897–1975), a novelist and playwright best known for *The Bridge of San Luis Rey* (1927), *Our Town* (1938), and *The Skin of Our Teeth* (1942), each of which won a Pulitzer Prize, heads the list of literary figures born in the state. Hamlin Garland (1860–1940), a novelist and essayist, was also a native, as were the poet Ella Wheeler Wilcox (1850–1919) and the novelist and playwright Zona Gale (1874–1938). The novelist Edna Ferber (b.Michigan, 1887–1968) spent her early life in the state.

Wisconsin is the birthplace of architect Frank Lloyd Wright (1869–1959) and the site of his famous Taliesin estate (Spring Green), Johnson Wax Co. headquarters (Racine), and first Unitarian Church (Madison). The artist Georgia O'Keefe (1887–1986) was born in Sun Prairie. Wisconsin natives who have distinguished themselves in the performing arts include Alfred Lunt (1893–1977), Frederic March (Frederick Bickel, 1897–1975), Spencer Tracy (1900–1967), Agnes Moorehead (1906–74), and Orson Welles (1915–85). Magician and escape artist Harry Houdini (Ehrich Weiss, b.Hungary, 1874–1926) was raised in the state, and piano stylist Liberace (Wlad Ziu Valentino Liberace, 1919–1987) was born there. Speed skater Eric Heiden (b.1958), a five-time Olympic gold medalist in 1980, is another Wisconsin native.

50 BIBLIOGRAPHY

Abrams, Lawrence and Kathleen. *Exploring Wisconsin*. Skokie, Ill.: Rand McNally, 1983.

Current, Richard N. *The History of Wisconsin*. Vol. 2: *The Civil War Era, 1848–73*. Madison: State Historical Society of Wisconsin, 1976.

Current, Richard N. *Wisconsin: A History*. Urbana: University of Illinois Press, 2001.

Davenport, Don. *Natural Wonders of Wisconsin: Exploring Wild and Scenic Places*. Lincolnwood, Ill.: Country Roads Press, 1999.

Dictionary of Wisconsin Biography. Madison: State Historical Society of Wisconsin, 1960.

Federal Writers' Project. *Wisconsin: A Guide to the Badger State*. Reprint, New York: Somerset, n.d.

Gara, Larry. *A Short History of Wisconsin*. Madison: State Historical Society of Wisconsin, 1962.

Klement, Frank L. *Wisconsin in the Civil War: The Home Front and the Battle Front, 1861–1865*. Madison: State Historical Society of Wisconsin, 1997.

Nesbit, Robert C. *Wisconsin: A History*. Madison: University of Wisconsin Press, 1973.

Pederson, Jane Marie. *Between Memory and Reality: Family and Community in Rural Wisconsin, 1870–1970*. Madison: University of Wisconsin Press, 1992.

Risjord, Norman K. *Wisconsin: The Story of the Badger State*. Madison: Wisconsin Trails, 1995.

Ritzenthaler, Robert E. *Prehistoric Indians of Wisconsin*. Milwaukee: Milwaukee Public Museum, 1953.

Smith, Alice E. *The History of Wisconsin. From Exploration to Statehood*. Vol. 1. Madison: State Historical Society of Wisconsin, 1973.

State of Wisconsin, Legislative Reference Bureau. *Blue Book*. Madison, n.d.

Still, Bayrd. *Milwaukee: The History of a City*. Madison: State Historical Society of Wisconsin, 1948.

Thelen, David P. *Robert M. La Follette and the Insurgent Spirit*. Boston: Little, Brown, 1976.

Yatzeck, Richard. *Hunting the Edges*. Madison: University of Wisconsin Press, 1999.

WYOMING

State of Wyoming

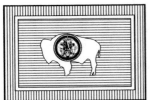

ORIGIN OF STATE NAME: Derived from the Delaware Indian words *maugh-wau-wa-ma,* meaning "large plains." **NICKNAMES:** The Equality State and The Cowboy State. **CAPITAL:** Cheyenne. **ENTERED UNION:** 10 July 1890 (44th). **SONG:** "Wyoming." **MOTTO:** Equal Rights. **FLAG:** A blue field with a white inner border and a red outer border (symbolizing, respectively, the sky, purity, and the Indians) surrounds a bison with the state seal branded on its side. **OFFICIAL SEAL:** A female figure holding the banner "Equal Rights" stands on a pedestal between pillars topped by lamps symbolizing the light of knowledge; two male figures flank the pillars, on which are draped banners that proclaim "Livestock," "Grain," "Mines," and "Oil." At the bottom is a shield with an eagle, star, and Roman numerals XLIV, flanked by the dates 1869 and 1890. The whole is surrounded by the words "Great Seal of the State of Wyoming." **ANIMAL:** Bison. **BIRD:** Western meadowlark. **FLOWER:** Indian paintbrush. **TREE:** Cottonwood. **GEM:** Jade. **LEGAL HOLIDAYS:** New Year's Day, 1 January; Birthday of Martin Luther King, Jr., 3rd Monday in January; Presidents' Day, 3rd Monday in February; Memorial Day, last Monday in May; Independence Day, 4 July; Labor Day, 1st Monday in September; Columbus Day, 2nd Monday in October; Election Day, 1st Tuesday after 1st Monday in November in even-numbered years; Veterans Day, 11 November; Thanksgiving Day, 4th Thursday in November; Christmas Day, 25 December. **TIME:** 5 AM MST = noon GMT.

¹LOCATION, SIZE, AND EXTENT

Located in the Rocky Mountain region of the northwestern US, Wyoming ranks 9th in size among the 50 states.

The total area of Wyoming is 97,809 sq mi (253,325 sq km), of which land comprises 96,989 sq mi (251,201 sq km) and inland water 820 sq mi (2,124 sq km). Shaped like a rectangle, Wyoming has a maximum E-W extension of 365 mi (587 km); its extreme distance N-S is 265 mi (426 km).

Wyoming is bordered on the N by Montana; on the E by South Dakota and Nebraska; on the S by Colorado and Utah; and on the W by Utah, Idaho, and Montana. The boundary length of Wyoming totals 1,269 mi (2,042 km). The state's geographic center lies in Fremont County, 58 mi (93 km) ENE of Lander.

²TOPOGRAPHY

The eastern third of Wyoming forms part of the Great Plains; the remainder belongs to the Rocky Mountains. Much of western Wyoming constitutes a special geomorphic province known as the Wyoming Basin. It represents a westward extension of the Great Plains into the Rocky Mountains, separating the Middle and Southern Rockies. Extending diagonally across the state from northwest to south is the Continental Divide, which separates the generally eastward-flowing drainage system of North America from the westward-flowing drainage of the Pacific states.

Wyoming's mean elevation is 6,700 ft (2,044 m), 2nd only to Colorado's among the 50 states. Gannett Peak, in western Wyoming, at 13,804 ft (4,210 m), is the highest point in the state. With the notable exception of the Black Hills in the northeast, the eastern portion of Wyoming is generally much lower. The lowest point in the state—3,099 ft (945 m)—occurs in the northeast, on the Belle Fourche River.

Wyoming's largest lake—Yellowstone—lies in the heart of Yellowstone National Park. In Grand Teton National Park to the south are two smaller lakes, Jackson and Jenny. All but one of Wyoming's major rivers originate within its boundaries and flow into neighboring states. The Green River flows into Utah; the Yellowstone, Big Horn, and Powder rivers flow into Montana; the Snake River, into Idaho; the Belle Fourche and Cheyenne rivers, into South Dakota; and the Niobrara and Bear rivers, into Nebraska. The lone exception, the North Platte River, enters Wyoming from Colorado and eventually exits into Nebraska.

³CLIMATE

Wyoming is generally semiarid, with local desert conditions. Normal daily temperatures in Cheyenne range from 15°F (–9°C) to 38°F (3°C) in January, and 55°F (13°C) to 82°F (28°C) in July. The record low temperature, –66°F (–54°C), was set 9 February 1933 at Riverside; the record high, 114°F (46°C), 12 July 1900 at Basin. In Cheyenne, average annual precipitation (1971–2000) was 15.5 in (39.4 cm) a year, most of that falling between March and September; the snowfall in Cheyenne averages 56 in (142 cm) annually.

⁴FLORA AND FAUNA

Wyoming has more than 2,000 species of ferns, conifers, and flowering plants. Prairie grasses dominate the eastern third of the state; desert shrubs, primarily sagebrush, cover the Great Basin in the west. Rocky Mountain forests consist largely of pine, spruce, and fir. In 2003, only one plant species was endangered, blowout penstemon. Three species were listed as threatened by the US Fish and Wildlife Service, including Colorado butterfly plant, Ute ladies'-tresses, and desert yellowhead.

The mule deer is the most abundant game mammal; others include the white-tailed deer, pronghorn antelope, elk, and moose. The jackrabbit, antelope, and raccoon are plentiful. Wild turkey, bobwhite quail, and several grouse species are leading game birds; more than 50 species of non-game birds also inhabit Wyoming all year long. There are 78 species of fish, of which rainbow trout is the favorite game fish. In 2003, 13 Wyoming animal species were listed as threatened or endangered, including the black-footed ferret, grizzly bear, whooping crane, razorback sucker, Kendall Warm Springs dace, and Wyoming toad.

⁵ENVIRONMENTAL PROTECTION

The state's principal environmental concerns are conservation of scarce water resources and preservation of air quality. The

Environmental Quality Council, a seven-member board appointed by the governor, hears and decides all cases arising under the regulations of the Department of Environmental Quality, which was established in 1973 and reorganized in 1992. The department enforces measures to prevent pollution of Wyoming's surface water and groundwater, and it administers 21 air-monitoring sites to maintain air quality. Wyoming typically spends the most money per capita on the environment and natural resources relative to all the states in the union. Programs to dispose of hazardous waste and assure safe drinking water are administered by the federal Environmental Protection Agency (EPA); in 2002–2005, the federal program to fund infrastructure for safe drinking water allocated 1% of its budget to Wyoming. In 2003, Wyoming had 42 hazardous waste sites listed in the Environmental Protection Agency's database, two of which were on the National Priorities List. Wetlands cover about 1.25 million acres of Wyoming and are administered and protected by the Wyoming Wetlands Act. In 2001, Wyoming received $28,059,000 in federal grants from the Environmental Protection Agency; however, there were no EPA expenditures for procurement contracts in Wyoming that year.

[6] POPULATION

Wyoming ranked 50th in population in the US with an estimated total of 498,703 in 2002, an increase of 1% since 2000. Between 1990 and 2000, Wyoming's population grew from 453,588 to 493,782, an increase of 8.9%. The population is projected to reach 702,000 by 2005.

In 2000 the median age was 36.2. Persons under 18 years old accounted for 26.1% of the population while 11.7% were age 65 or older.

Wyoming ranks 49th in population density (5.1 persons per sq mi in 2000); only Alaska is more sparsely populated. However, during the 1970s Wyoming was the 3rd-fastest growing state; its population grew by 41%, from 332,416 at the 1970 census to 469,557 according to the 1980 census, largely from in-migration. The growth rate reversed during the 1980s, shrinking the population to 453,588 in 1990 (–3.4%).

Leading cities, all with populations of less than 100,000, are Cheyenne, Casper, and Laramie.

[7] ETHNIC GROUPS

There were some 11,133 American Indians residing in Wyoming in 2000, up from 9,000 at the 1990 census. The largest tribe is the Arapaho. Wind River (2000 population 23,250) is the state's only reservation; tribal lands covered 1,793,000 acres (726,000 hectares) in 1982.

The black population was 3,722 in 2000. Also in 2000, the Asian population was 2,771; the largest group was the Chinese, who numbered 609. In 2000, 92.1% of the population was white and mostly of European descent, the largest groups being German, English, and Irish.

[8] LANGUAGES

Some place-names—Oshoto, Shoshoni, Cheyenne, Uinta—reflect early contacts with regional Indians.

Some terms common in Wyoming, like *comforter* (tied quilt) and *angleworm* (earthworm), evidence the Northern dialect of early settlers from New York State and New England, but generally Wyoming English is North Midland with some South Midland mixture, especially along the Nebraska border. Geography has changed the meaning of *hole, basin, meadow,* and *park* to signify mountain openings.

In 2000, over 433,000 Wyomingites—93.6% of the residents five years old or older (down slightly from 94.3% in 1990)—spoke only English at home.

The following table gives selected statistics from the 2000 census for language spoken at home by persons five years old and over. The category "Other Native North American languages" includes Apache, Cherokee, Choctaw, Dakota, Keres, Pima, and Yupik.

LANGUAGE	NUMBER	PERCENT
Population 5 years and over	462,809	100.0
Speak only English	433,324	93.6
Speak a language other than English	29,485	6.4
Speak a language other than English	29,485	6.4
Spanish or Spanish Creole	18,606	4.0
German	2,382	0.5
Other Native North American languages	1,795	0.4
French (incl. Patois, Cajun)	1,618	0.3
Japanese	518	0.1
Chinese	512	0.1

[9] RELIGIONS

The religiously active population in Wyoming is somewhat closely split between Protestants and Catholics. In 2000, the Catholic Church had about 80,421 members. The next largest single denomination was the Church of Jesus Christ of Latter-Day Saints (Mormons), with 47,129 members. Other leading denominations included the Southern Baptist Convention, 17,101; the United Methodist Church. 11,431; the Lutheran Church—Missouri Synod, 11,113; and the Evangelical Lutheran Church in America, 10,038. Wyoming also had an estimated 430 Jews and 263 Muslims. There were 263,057 people (about 53% of the population) who were not counted as members of any religious organization.

[10] TRANSPORTATION

Wyoming is served chiefly by the Burlington Northern/Santa Fe and Union Pacific railroads. The total trackage of these two Class I railroads in 2000 was 1,919 rail mi (3,070 km). In 2000, coal was the top commodity in both rail tonnage originated (310.7 million tons, or 95%) and terminated (13.3 million tons, or 92%) within the state. Amtrak passenger rail service in and through the state was discontinued on 10 May 1997. Public highways and rural and urban roads, totaling 27,327 mi (43,722 km) crossed the state as of 2000. That year, there were 573,500 registered motor vehicles and 370,740 licensed drivers.

As of 2000, Wyoming had 115 airports (10 of which offered commercial passenger service to at least 2,500 passengers per year) and heliports; that year there were 1,812 active pilots and 195 flight instructors in Wyoming.

[11] HISTORY

The first human inhabitants of what is now Wyoming probably arrived about 11,500 BC. The forebears of these early Americans had most likely come by way of the Bering Strait and then worked their way south. Sites of mammoth kills south of Rawlins and near Powell suggest that the area was well populated. Artifacts from the period beginning in 500 BC include, high in the Big Horn Mountains of northern Wyoming, the Medicine Wheel monument, a circle of stones some 75 ft (23 m) in diameter with 28 "spokes" that were apparently used to mark the seasons.

The first Europeans to visit Wyoming were French Canadian traders. The Vérendrye brothers, Francois and Louis-Joseph, probably reached the Big Horn Mountains in 1743; nothing came of their travels, however. The first effective discovery of Wyoming was made by an American fur trader, John Colter, earlier a member of the Lewis and Clark expedition. In 1806–07, Colter traversed much of the northwestern part of the state, probably crossing what is now Yellowstone Park, and came back to report on the natural wonders of the area. After Colter, trappers and fur traders crisscrossed Wyoming. By 1840, the major rivers and

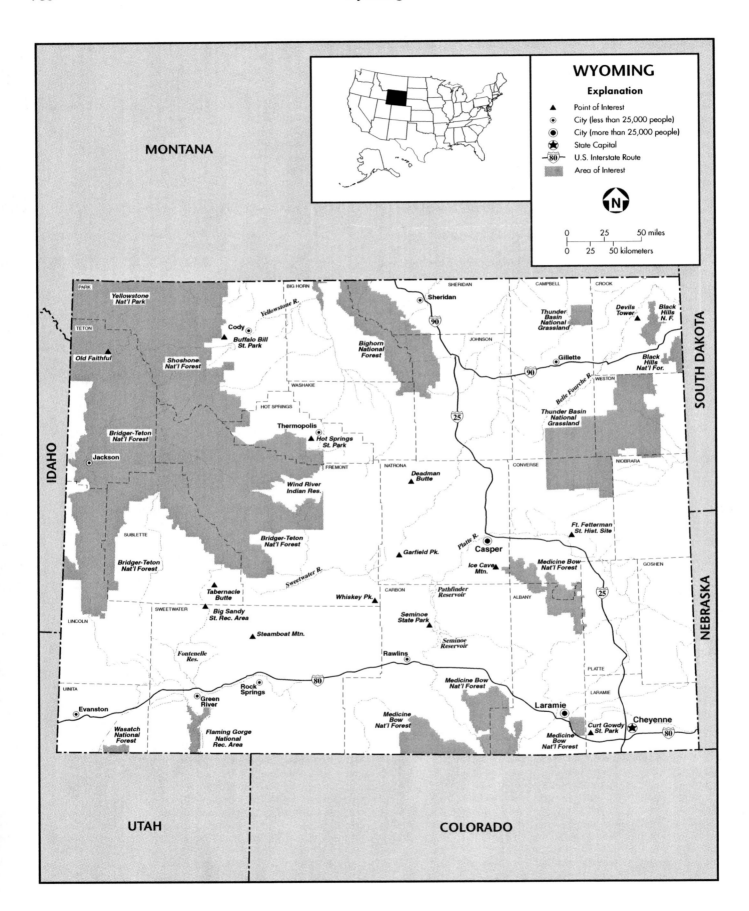

mountains were named, and the general topography of the region was well documented.

Between 1840 and 1867, thousands of Americans crossed Wyoming on the Oregon Trail, bound for Oregon or California. Migration began as a trickle, but with the discovery of gold in California in 1848, the trickle became a flood. In 1849 alone it is estimated that more than 22,000 "forty-niners" passed through the state via the Oregon Trail. Fort Laramie in the east and Fort Bridger in the west were the best-known supply points; between the two forts, immigrants encountered Independence Rock, Devil's Gate, Split Rock, and South Pass, all landmarks on the Oregon Trail. Although thousands of Americans crossed Wyoming during this period, very few stayed in this harsh region.

The event that brought population as well as territorial status to Wyoming was the coming of the Union Pacific Railroad. Railroad towns such as Cheyenne, Laramie, Rawlins, Rock Springs, and Evanston sprang up as the transcontinental railroad leapfrogged across the region in 1867 and 1868; in the latter year, Wyoming was organized as a territory. The first territorial legislature distinguished itself in 1869 by passing a women's suffrage act, the first state or territory to do so. Wyoming quickly acquired the nickname the Equality State.

After hostile Indians had been subdued by the late 1870s, Wyoming became a center for cattlemen and foreign investors who hoped to make a fortune from free grass and the high price of cattle. Thousands of Texas longhorn cattle were driven to the southeastern quarter of the territory. In time, blooded cattle, particularly Hereford, were introduced. As cattle "barons" dominated both the rangeland and state politics, the small rancher and cowboy found it difficult to go into the ranching business. However, overgrazing, low cattle prices, and the dry summer of 1886 and harsh winter of 1886/87 all proved disastrous to the speculators. The struggle between the large landowners and small ranchers culminated in the so-called Johnson County War of 1891–92, in which the large landowners were arrested by federal troops after attempting to take the law into their own hands.

Wyoming became a state in 1890, but growth remained slow. Attempts at farming proved unsuccessful in this high, arid region, and Wyoming to this day remains a sparsely settled ranching state. What growth has occurred has been primarily through the minerals industry, especially the development of coal, oil, and natural gas resources during the 1970s because of the national energy crisis. However, the world's oil glut in the early 1980s slowed the growth of the state's energy industries; in 1984, the growth of the state's nonfuel mineral industry slowed as well.

Wyoming's population, which had risen 41% during the minerals boom of the 1970s, declined, leaving the state ranking 50th in population in the 1990 census, having ceded 49th place to Alaska in the decade since 1980. In the 1990s, Wyoming's economy has been spurred by a rise in oil prices and expanding coal production, as well as increased tourism.

In the summer of 1988, wild fires raged through Yellowstone National Park, damaging nearly one-third of the park's total area. Gray wolves, eradicated from the mountains of Wyoming and Idaho in the 1930s, were reintroduced to Yellowstone National Park and central Idaho in 1995 and 1996 as part of the US Fish and Wildlife Service's wolf reintroduction program. The program was initiated to fulfill a goal of the Endangered Species Act, passed in 1973. It was subjected to legal challenge in 1997, but the wolf reintroduction program was ruled legal in 2000. In 2003, the US Fish and Wildlife Service reclassified the gray wolves in the northern Rockies from an "endangered" to a "threatened" species, due to the growing wolf populations in those areas.

In 2003, Wyoming had a $169 million budget surplus, largely due to an increase in mineral revenues. Rising health care costs and the need to pay for new state buildings and schools caused Democratic Governor Dave Freudenthal, elected in 2002, to call for increases in property taxes.

12 STATE GOVERNMENT

Wyoming's state constitution was approved by the voters in November 1889 and accepted by Congress in 1890. By January 2003 it had been amended 91 times. Constitutional amendments require a two-thirds vote of the legislature and ratification by the voters at the next general election.

The legislature consists of a 30-member senate and a 60-member house of representatives. Senators are elected to staggered four-year terms. The entire house of representatives is elected every two years for a two-year term. Legislators must be US citizens, citizens and residents of Wyoming, and residents of their districts for at least one year prior to election. The minimum age for senators is 25 and for representatives 21. Regular sessions begin in January or February and are limited to 40 legislative days in odd-numbered years and 20 legislative days in even-numbered years. The legislature may not call special sessions. In 2003 the legislative salary was $125 per diem during regular sessions, unchanged from 1999.

Heading the executive branch are five elected officials: the governor, secretary of state, auditor, treasurer, and superintendent of public instruction. Each serves a four-year term and, under Wyoming's cabinet form of government, is also a member of seven state boards and commissions. The governor is limited to serving two consecutive terms. His successor is the secretary of the senate, as there is no lieutenant governor. A governor must be at least 30 years old, a US citizen, a qualified voter, and at least a five-resident of the state. In 2002 the governor's salary was $130,000.

A bill passed by the legislature becomes law if signed by the governor, if left unsigned by the governor for three days while the legislature is in session (or 15 days after it has adjourned), or if passed over the governor's veto by two-thirds of the elected members of each house.

Voters must be US citizens, at least 18 years old, and bona fide residents of Wyoming. Convicted felons and those adjudicated as mentally incompetent may not vote.

13 POLITICAL PARTIES

The Republicans currently dominate Wyoming politics at the federal and state level, although the state elected a Democratic governor in 2002. There were 241,200 registered voters in 2002. Governor Dave Freudenthal's victory in 2002 was seen as a Democratic victory in a solidly Republican state . Both of Wyoming's senators, Craig Thomas (reelected in 2000) and Mike Enzi (elected in 1996 to succeed Alan Simpson and reelected in 2002), are Republicans, as is Wyoming's US Representative, Barbara Cubin, reelected in 2002.

As of mid-2003, there were 20 Republicans and 10 Democrats in the state senate; 45 Republicans and 15 Democrats in the state house. Republican George W. Bush received 69% of the vote in the 2000 presidential election, while Democratic candidate Al Gore won 28%. In 1998, 30% of registered voters were Democratic, 59% Republican, and 11% unaffiliated or members of other parties. The state had three electoral votes in the 2000 presidential election.

14 LOCAL GOVERNMENT

In 2003 Wyoming was subdivided into 23 counties, 98 municipalities, 55 public school districts, and 546 special districts and authorities.

Counties, which can be geographically vast and include a relatively small population, are run by commissioners. Each county has a clerk, treasurer, assessor, sheriff, attorney, coroner,

Wyoming Presidential Vote by Major Political Parties 1948–2000

YEAR	ELECTORAL VOTE	WYOMING WINNER	DEMOCRAT	REPUBLICAN
1948	3	*Truman (D)	52,354	47,947
1952	3	*Eisenhower (R)	47,934	81,049
1956	3	*Eisenhower (R)	49,554	74,573
1960	3	Nixon (R)	63,331	77,451
1964	3	*Johnson (D)	80,718	61,998
1968	3	*Nixon (R)	45,173	70,927
1972	3	*Nixon (R)	44,358	100,464
1976	3	Ford (R)	62,239	92,717
1980	3	*Reagan (R)	49,427	110,700
1984	3	*Reagan (R)	53,370	133,241
1988	3	*Bush (R)	67,113	106,867
1992**	3	Bush (R)	68,160	79,347
1996**	3	Dole (R)	77,934	105,388
2000	3	*Bush, G. W. (R)	60,481	147,947

* Won US presidential election.
** Independent candidate Ross Perot received 51,263 votes in 1992 and 25,928 votes in 1996.

district court clerk, and from one to five county judges or justices of the peace. Municipalities may decide their own form of government, including mayor-council and council-manager.

15 STATE SERVICES

To address the continuing threat of terrorism and to work with the federal Department of Homeland Security (created in 2002 following the terrorist attacks of 11 September 2001), homeland security in Wyoming in 2003 operated under executive order; the adjutant general was designated as the state homeland security advisor.

The Board of Education has primary responsibility for educational services in Wyoming. Transportation services are provided by the Wyoming Department of Transportation; health and welfare matters fall under the jurisdiction of the Departments of Health and Family Services. Among the many state agencies concerned with natural resources are the Department of Environmental Quality, Board of Land Commissioners, Oil and Gas Conservation Commission, and Water Development Commission. The Department of Employment is responsible for labor services.

16 JUDICIAL SYSTEM

Wyoming's judicial branch consists of a supreme court with a chief justice and 4 other justices, district courts with a total of 222 judges, and county judges and justices of the peace. Supreme court justices are appointed by the governor but must stand for retention at the next general election; once elected, they serve eight-year terms.

Wyoming's prison population totaled 1,679 in June 2001, a decrease of 2.5% from the previous year. The state's incarceration rate stood at 340 per 100,000 population. Wyoming's total crime rate in 2001 was 3,517.6 per 100,000 persons, including a total of 1,272 violent crimes and 16,120 crimes against property in that year. Wyoming has a death penalty, and as of 2003 there were two persons under sentence of death. Wyoming executed one inmate between 1977 and 2003.

17 ARMED FORCES

In 2002, there were 3,292 active-duty military personnel and 1,004 civilian personnel stationed in Wyoming, nearly all of whom were at Wyoming's only US military installation—the Francis E. Warren Air Force Base at Cheyenne. Total defense contracts awarded that year totaled more than $92 million.

According to the 2000 Census, there were 57,860 military veterans living in Wyoming. Of these, 9,377 were veterans of World War II; 6,454 of the Korean conflict; 19,083 of the Vietnam era; and 8,327 of 1990–2000 (including the Persian Gulf War). Veterans' benefits totaled nearly $145 million in 2002.

In 2000, the Wyoming Highway Patrol employed 148 full-time sworn officers.

18 MIGRATION

Many people have passed through Wyoming, but relatively few have come to stay. Not until the 1970s, a time of rapid economic development, did the picture change. Between 1970 and 1983, Wyoming gained a net total of 45,500 residents through migration. In the 1980s, the state's total population grew only by 1.1%, primarily offset by the net loss from migration of 52,000 persons. The urban population increased from 62.8% of the state's total in 1980 to 65% in 1990. Between 1990 and 1998, Wyoming had a net loss of less than 500 in domestic migration but a net gain of 2,000 in international migration. In 1998, the state admitted 159 foreign immigrants. Between 1990 and 1998, the state's overall population increased 6%. In the period 1995–2000, 72,834 people moved into the state and 85,361 moved out, for a net loss of 12,527, many of whom moved to Colorado.

19 INTERGOVERNMENTAL COOPERATION

Emblematic of Wyoming's concern for water resources is the fact that it belongs to seven compacts with neighboring states concerning the Bear, Belle Fourche, Colorado, Upper Colorado, Snake, Upper Niobrara, and Yellowstone rivers.

Wyoming has also joined the Interstate Oil and Gas Compact, the Western Interstate Energy Compact, the Western States Water Council, the Western Interstate Commission for Higher Education, and numerous other multistate bodies, including the Council of State Governments. Federal grants in 2001 totaled over $1.2 billion.

20 ECONOMY

The economic life of Wyoming is largely sustained by agriculture—chiefly feed grains and livestock—and mining, including petroleum and gas production. Mining and petroleum production mushroomed during the 1970s, leading to a powerful upsurge in population. In the early 1980s, unemployment remained low, per capita income was high, and the inflation rate declined. The absence of personal and corporate income taxes helped foster a favorable business climate during the 1990s. The state economy's annual growth rate accelerated coming into the 21st century, from 1.1% in 1998 to 3.6% in 1999 to 12.3% in 2000. Not heavily involved in the information technology (IT) boom of the 1990s, Wyoming was relatively unaffected by its bust in 2001, registering annual growth of 6.8% for the year. The main growth sectors have been various categories of services, with output from general services up 37.9% 1997 to 2001; from trade, up 29.1%; from the government sector, up 24.3%, and from financial services, up 23.6%.

In 2001, Wyoming's gross state product gross state product was $20.4 billion, the 3rd-smallest among the states, to which government contributed $2.8 billion; transportation and public utilities, $2.6 billion; general services, $2.4 billion; financial services, $2.35 billion; trade, $2.3 billion; manufacturing, $1.5 billion; and construction, $1.1 billion. The public sector in 2001 constituted 13.7% of gross state product, above the 12% average for the states.

21 INCOME

According to the Bureau of Economic Analysis, in 2001, Wyoming had a per capita personal income (PCPI) of $29,587 which ranked 20th in the United States (including the District of

Columbia) and was 97% of the national average, $30,413. The 2001 PCPI reflected an increase of 5.9% from 2000 compared to the national change of 2.2%. In 2001, Wyoming had a total personal income (TPI) of $14,608,814,000 which ranked 51st in the United States and accounted for 0.2% of the national total. The 2001 TPI reflected an increase of 5.8% from 2000 compared to the national change of 3.3%.

Earnings of persons employed in Wyoming increased from $9,006,059,000 in 2000 to $9,625,372,000 in 2001, an increase of 6.9%. The largest industries in 2001 were services, 20.3% of earnings; state and local government, 16.8%; and mining, 14.9%. Of the industries that accounted for at least 5% of earnings in 2001, the slowest growing from 2000 to 2001 was transportation and public utilities (7.9% of earnings in 2001), which increased 0.9%; the fastest was state and local government, which increased 9.7%.

According to data released by the US Census Bureau, in 2000, the median household income was $39,026 compared to the national average of $42,148. In 2001, the median income for a family of four was $58,541 compared to the national average of $63,278. For the period 1999 to 2001, the average poverty rate was 10.3% which placed it 26th among the 50 states and the District of Columbia ranked lowest to highest.

22 LABOR

According to Bureau of Labor Statistics (BLS) provisional estimates, in July 2003 the seasonally adjusted civilian labor force in Wyoming numbered 276,000, with approximately 11,300 workers unemployed, yielding an unemployment rate of 4.1%, compared to the national average of 6.2% for the same period. Since the beginning of the BLS data series in 1978, the highest unemployment rate recorded was 10.7% in February 1987. The historical low was 2.2% in April 1979. In 2001, an estimated 6.0% of the labor force was employed in construction; 4.5% in manufacturing; 6.3% in transportation, communications, and public utilities; 19.0% in trade; 3.7% in finance, insurance, and real estate; 17.5% in services; 20.7% in government; and 5.8% in agriculture.

The US Department of Labor reported that in 2002, 17,000 of Wyoming's 219,000 employed wage and salary workers were members of unions. This represented 7.8% of those so employed, down from 8.9% in 2001 and 9.6% in 1998. The national average is 13.2%. In all, 22,000 workers (9.8%) were represented by unions. In addition to union members, this category includes workers who report no union affiliation but whose jobs are covered by a union contract. Wyoming is one of 22 states with a right-to-work law.

23 AGRICULTURE

Agriculture—especially livestock and grain—is one of Wyoming's most important industries. In 2002, Wyoming had about 9,200 farms and ranches covering almost 34.6 million acres (14 million hectares). The state's average of 3,761 acres (1,522 hectares) per farm ranked 2nd in the US after Arizona. The value of the lands and buildings of Wyoming's farms and ranches in 2002 was over $9.9 billion. Total farm marketings in 2002 amounted to $983 million, ranking 38th among the 50 states. Of this, livestock and animal products accounted for $837 million; crops, $145 million.

Field crops in 2002 included barley, 4,900,000 bu; wheat, 2,376,000 bu; oats, 810,000 bu; potatoes, 375,000 hundred weight (cwt); sugar beets, 659,000 tons; dry beans, 624,000 cwt; and hay, 1,600,000 tons.

24 ANIMAL HUSBANDRY

For most of Wyoming's territorial and state history, cattle ranchers have dominated the economy, even though the livestock industry is not large by national standards. In 2003, Wyoming

had an estimated 1.29 million cattle and calves, valued at $980.4 million. During 2002, there were 115,000 hogs and pigs, valued at $9.66 million. Wyoming farms and ranches produced 33.8 million lb (15.3 million kg) of sheep and lambs in 2001, and an estimated 3.75 million lb (1.7 million kg) of shorn wool in 2002. In 2001, Wyoming farmers sold 41,000 lb (18,600 kg) of chicken and produced 63 million lb (28.6 million kg) of milk.

25 FISHING

There is no important commercial fishing in Wyoming. Fishing is largely recreational, and fish hatcheries and fish-planting programs keep the streams well stocked. Wyoming's streams annually provide 1.3 million angler days and 3.4 million fish; lakes generate 1.6 million angler days and a harvest of 4.1 million fish. In 1998, the state issued 280,634 fishing licenses. That year, fish farms distributed nearly 3.3 million trout and 9.9 million trout eggs within the state.

26 FORESTRY

Wyoming has 10,995,000 acres (4,450,000 hectares) of forested land, equal to 17.8% of the state's land area. Of this, 5,739,000 acres (2,323,000 hectares) are usable as commercial timberland. As of 2001, the state's four national forests—Bighorn, Bridger-Teton, Medicine Bow, and Shoshone—covered a total of 9,238,000 acres (3,739,000 hectares). In 2002, lumber production totaled 230 million board feet. Ponderosa pine accounts for about 50% of the annual cut, and lodgepole pine most of the rest. The remainder consists of Douglas fir, larch, Engelmann spruce, and other species.

27 MINING

The estimated value of nonfuel mineral production for Wyoming in 2001 was nearly $986 million, an increase of about 1% over 2000. According to preliminary figures, in 2001 Wyoming produced 3.16 million metric tons of bentonite, worth $131 million, as well as 5 million metric tons of crushed stone, valued at $21.5 million. No metal production has been reported since 1984. Wyoming ranked 15th nationally in the value of nonfuel mineral production. Wyoming continued to rank 1st in the nation in bentonite production. In 2001, major uses of Wyoming bentonite were as pet waste absorbent, drilling mud, pelletizing iron ore, in foundry sand, and as a waterproof sealant. Wyoming also continued to lead the nation in soda ash production from the world's largest known resource of trona, a natural sodium carbonate-bicarbonate. Trona mined in Wyoming was used to produce soda ash, caustic soda, sodium sulfite, sodium bicarbonate, sodium cyanide, and calcined trona. Grade-A helium production increased slightly; of the four states that produced grade-A helium, Wyoming ranked 2nd. The combined value of portland cement, common clays, crude gypsum, grade-A helium, lime, and soda ash in 2001 was $809 million.

28 ENERGY AND POWER

Wyoming is comparatively energy-rich, ranking 1st among the states in coal production and 7th in output of crude oil. The state's production of petroleum declined in the early 1990s as the result of declining reserves. Production in 2002 was 150,000 barrels per day; proved reserves totaled 489 million barrels. In 2001, reserves of natural gas were estimated at 18.4 trillion cu ft (0.52 trillion cu m); natural gas production totaled 1.44 trillion cu ft (0.04 trillion cu m) in 2002.

Wyoming has the three largest producing coal mines in the US and total recoverable coal reserves estimated at 6,100 million tons. In 1970, Wyoming's coal production accounted for only 1% of the US total. By 1998 the state's production had risen to 28% of national production. The Black Thunder mine in the Powder River Basin is the largest coal producer in the nation, with an output of 36.1 million tons in 1995. In 2000, the state's active mines produced 338.9 million tons of coal.

Electric power production (utility and nonutility) in 1999 totaled 43.6 billion kWh; total installed capacity was 6.1 million kW. In 1998, sales of electricity totaled 12.1 billion kWh. In 2000 Wyoming's total per capita energy consumption was 844 million Btu (212.7 million kcal), ranking it 3rd among the 50 states, behind Alaska and Louisiana. However, exported energy is counted as intrastate consumption, thus inflating per capita energy usage.

29 INDUSTRY

Although manufacturing increased markedly in Wyoming from 1977 to 1991—value of shipments by manufacturers more than doubled from $1,287 million to $2,733 million—it remains insignificant by national standards. Total value added by manufacture in 1997 was $3 billion.

Earnings of persons employed in Wyoming increased from $7.6 billion in 1997 to $7.8 billion in 1998, an increase of 3.1%. The largest industries in 1998 were services, 18.9% of earnings; state and local government, 16.5%; and mining, 15.7%. Of the industries that accounted for at least 5% of earnings in 1998, the slowest growing from 1997 to 1998 was state and local government, which increased 2.3%; the fastest was mining, which increased 9.8%.

30 COMMERCE

In 1997, sales from wholesale trade were over $2.5 billion, and retailers had sales of over $3.6 billion. Of the 1997 total, automotive dealers accounted for 17% of establishments; food stores, 7%; and restaurants or taverns, 29%. Wyoming's exports of products to other countries were valued at $500 million in 1998, ranking 47th amongst all states.

31 CONSUMER PROTECTION

The Attorney General's Consumer Protection Unit enforces the Wyoming Consumer Protection Act, which includes provisions regulating the promotional advertising of prizes and telephone solicitation, and creates a telemarketer "no-call" list. The Unit also enforces statutes prohibiting price discrimination and regarding pyramid schemes.

32 BANKING

In 2002, Wyoming had 50 insured banks with total assets of $7.5 billion. Twenty-six of those institutions were state-chartered. Wyoming had two insured savings banks in 2002.

The median net interest margin (NIM) (the difference between the lower rates offered to savers and the higher rates charged on loans) increased from 2001 to 2002, although high overhead expenses and lower non-interest income offset that margin. The past-due loan ratio remained below the national average in 2002, but was showing some signs of weakness.

Close to one-fourth of all insured Wyoming banks had high concentrations of commercial real estate (CRE) loans in 2002. Construction and development (C and D) loans contributed significantly to this trend.

33 INSURANCE

In 2001, there were 221,000 ordinary life insurance policies in force in Wyoming with a total value of $15.5 billion; total value for all categories of life insurance (ordinary, group, industrial, and credit) was $23.0 billion. Death benefits paid that year totaled $79.1 million. As of 2000, there were two property and casualty and no life and health insurance companies incorporated or organized in the state. In 2001, property and casualty insurers wrote over $559 million in premiums. That year, there were 1,887 flood insurance policies in force in the state, with a total value of $244,671.

34 SECURITIES

Securities transactions are conducted by about 117 firms and over 500 employees; 17 investment advisory organizations provide services in Wyoming. The state headquarters seven NASDAQ companies, and has incorporated one NYSE company: the Frontier Oil Corp.

35 PUBLIC FINANCE

Wyoming's biennial budget is prepared by the governor and submitted to the legislature at the beginning of each even-numbered calendar year. The fiscal year is 1 July–30 June.

For the 2003/04 biennium, executive recommendations were for a total general fund budget of $1.315 billion, with $430.3 million for education, $392.6 million for health services, $211.9 million for public safety, $158.8 million for human services, $86.7 million for general government, $51.1 million for economic development, and $38.5 for natural resources. For 2003/04, general fund revenues were projected to be $614 million and expenditures $779 million, with adjustments to be made in the course of the biennium.

The following table from the US Census Bureau contains information on revenues, expenditures, indebtedness, and cash/securities for 2001.

	($000)	PERCENT	PER CAPITA
Population (thousands, 2001)	494	(X)	(X)
Total Revenue	2,880,176	100.00	5,830.32
General revenue	2,726,669	94.67	5,519.57
Utility revenue	–	–	–
Liquor store revenue	47,292	1.64	95.73
Insurance trust revenue	106,215	3.69	215.01
Exhibit: Salaries and wages	390,453	14.76	790.39
Total expenditure	2,645,226	100.00	5,354.71
General expenditure	2,330,920	88.12	4,718.46
Education	772,461	29.20	1,563.69
Public welfare	329,318	12.45	666.64
Hospitals	30,118	1.14	60.97
Health	98,184	3.71	198.75
Highways	329,077	12.44	666.15
Police protection	21,593	0.82	43.71
Correction	80,018	3.02	161.98
Natural resources	132,902	5.02	269.03
Parks and recreation	18,893	0.71	38.24
Government administration	89,269	3.37	180.71
Interest on general debt	72,782	2.75	147.33
Other and unallocable	356,305	13.47	721.27
Utility expenditure	6,565	0.25	13.29
Liquor store expenditure	41,028	1.55	83.05
Insurance trust expenditure	266,713	10.08	539.90
Debt at end of fiscal year	1,346,322	100.00	2,725.35
Cash and security holdings	9,515,826	100.00	19,262.81

36 TAXATION

Sales tax is 4%, while use taxes vary from 4% to 6%. Other taxes include cigarette taxes, estate taxes, lodging taxes, severance taxes, railroad car tax, ad valorem taxes, and public utility assessments. Wyoming has no personal or corporate income tax.

The state collected $1.094 billion in taxes in 2002, of which 40.7% came from the general sales tax, 27.5% from severance taxes, 13.2% from property taxes, 9% from selective sales taxes, and 8.7% from corporate income taxes. In 2003, Michigan ranked 43rd among the states in terms of state and local tax burden, which amounted to about 8.5% of income.

The following table from the US Census Bureau provides a summary of taxes collected by the state in 2002.

	($000)	PER CAPITA
Total Taxes	**1,094,402**	**2,194.50**
Property taxes	143,975	288.7
Sales and gross receipts	543,844	1,090.52
General sales and gross receipts	445,479	893.28
Selective sales taxes	98,365	197.24
Alcoholic beverage	1,149	2.3
Amusements	(X)	(X)
Insurance Premiums	14,604	29.28
Motor fuels	75,053	150.5
Pari-mutuels	208	0.42
Public utilities	2,284	4.58
Tobacco products	5,067	10.16
Other selective sales	(X)	(X)
Licenses	95,088	190.67
Alcoholic beverages	6	0.01
Amusements	(X)	(X)
Corporation	7,704	15.45
Hunting and fishing	26,050	52.24
Motor vehicle	51,616	103.5
Motor vehicle operators	2,570	5.15
Public utility	(X)	(X)
Occupation and business, NEC	6,131	12.29
Other	1,011	2.03
Other taxes	311,495	624.61
Individual income	(X)	(X)
Corporation net income	(X)	(X)
Death and gift	9,901	19.85
Documentary and stock transfer	(X)	(X)
Severance	301,594	604.76
Other	(X)	(X)

37 ECONOMIC POLICY

State policy in Wyoming has traditionally favored fiscal, social, and political conservatism. A pro-business and pro-family climate has generally prevailed. For example, Wyoming does not have a state personal income tax, a state business income tax, nor a business inventory tax. Not until 1969 was the minerals industry compelled to pay a severance tax on the wealth it was extracting from Wyoming soils. The state's leading industry is tourism, (the federal government owns over 50% of Wyoming's land), and Wyoming is first among US states in coal and iron production. The Wyoming Department of Commerce, Division of Economic and Community Development encourages entrepreneurship, emphasizes community development, and supports retention and expansion of existing Wyoming businesses. Grant and loan programs also assist Wyoming communities and businesses. In 2003, the Wyoming Business Council maintained six regional offices around the state to provide personalized and localized technical assistance. These were part of a statewide network of partners, offering one-on-one business assistance.

38 HEALTH

The infant mortality rate in 2000 was 6.7 deaths per 1,000 live births, below the national rate of 6.9. Wyoming has the lowest number, ratio, and rate of abortions of all the states—110 in 1999, or 1 per 1,000 women. In 2000, the state's overall death rate—815.1 per 100,000 population—was well below the national rate of 873.1. The death rates for heart disease, cerebrovascular diseases and cancer were well below the national norm in 2000, but the rates for motor vehicle accidents, suicide and accidental deaths were above it.

Among residents 18 years of age and older, 23.8% were reported to be regular smokers in 2000 The rate of death due to lung disease was 74.0 per 100,000 population in 2000. The rate of HIV-related deaths in Wyoming was one of the lowest in the nation in 2000 a total of just 192 AIDS cases had been reported through 2001.

Wyoming's 24 community hospitals had 47,587 admissions and 1,920 beds in 2001. There were 1,608 full-time registered nurses and 295 full-time licensed practical nurses in 2001 and 197 physicians per 100,000 population in 2000. The average expense of a community hospital for care was $1,129.80 per inpatient day in 1998.

Federal government grants to cover the Medicare and Medicaid services in 2001 totaled $186 million; 66,439 enrollees received Medicare benefits that year. At least 15.9% of Wyoming's residents were uninsured in 2002.

39 SOCIAL WELFARE

In 2001, the average weekly unemployment benefit was $213.65. Average monthly participation in the food stamp program in FY2002 comprised 23,530 persons (9,545 households). The average monthly benefit was $76.28, and the sum total of benefits paid in FY2002 was $21,538,153.

With the enactment of the Personal Responsibility and Work Opportunity Reconciliation Act of 1996, the US government has changed the form and regulations for many of its social welfare programs. Most significantly, it replaces Aid to Families with Dependent Children (AFDC), an open-ended entitlement program, with Temporary Assistance for Needy Families (TANF), a limited system of assistance funded largely through federal block grants. The reform act also impacts the food stamp program, the Supplemental Security Income program, and the child nutrition program. The law took effect on 1 July 1997 and provided $16.38 billion in block grants for fiscal years 1997–2002. The grants are to be divided among the states based on an equation involving the numbers of former AFDC recipients in each state.

Reauthorization of the 1996 social welfare legislation, scheduled for 2002, was delayed, and the original law had been extended three times as of July 2003, with the most recent extension running through September 2003. Wyoming's TANF program is called POWER (Personal Opportunities With Employment Responsibility). In June 2000 the state had 1,103 welfare recipients. State expenditures on the TANF program in FY2002 totaled $7,425,022.

In December 2001, Social Security benefits were paid to 78,420 Wyoming residents. This number included 51,440 retired workers, 7,200 widows and widowers, 8,520 disabled workers, 5,150 spouses, and 6,110 children. Social Security beneficiaries represented 15.6% of the total state population and 95.3% of the state's population age 65 and older. Retired workers (excluding persons with special benefits) received an average monthly payment of $871; widows and widowers, $851; disabled workers, $822; and spouses, $442. Payments for children of retired workers averaged $462 per month; children of deceased workers, $604; and children of disabled workers, $227.

Federal Supplemental Security Income payments in December 2001 went to 5,790 Wyoming residents, averaging $343 a month.

40 HOUSING

In 2002, there were an estimated 227,941 housing units in Wyoming, ranking the state as having the lowest housing stock in the country. About 199,848 units were occupied; 69.3% were owner-occupied. About 62.7% of all units were single-family, detached homes; 16% were mobile homes. It was estimated that 10,207 units lacked telephone service, 1,057 lacked complete plumbing facilities, and 1,281 lacked complete kitchen facilities. Utility gas was the most common energy source for heating. The average household size was 2.43 people.

In 2002, 2,045 new privately owned housing units were authorized for construction. The median home value was $110,586. The median monthly cost for mortgage owners was $913. Renters paid a median of $481 per month. In 2002, Wyoming received over $8.4 million in community planning and development aid from the US Department of Housing and Urban Development.

41 EDUCATION

In 2000, 87.9% of Wyoming residents age 25 and older were high school graduates; 21.9% had obtained a bachelor's degree or higher.

The total enrollment for fall 1999 in Wyoming's public schools stood at 92,105. Of these, 61,654 attended schools from kindergarten through grade eight, and 30,451 attended high school. Minority students made up approximately 13% of the total enrollment in public elementary and secondary schools in 2001. Total enrollment was estimated at 95,000 by fall 2000 and is expected to remain at that level as of fall 2005. Expenditures for public education in 2000/01 were estimated at $710,000. Enrollment in nonpublic schools in fall 2001 was 2,221.

As of fall 2000, there were 29,697 students enrolled in college or graduate school. In the same year Wyoming had 9 degree-granting institutions. Wyoming has seven community colleges. The state controls and funds the University of Wyoming in Laramie, as well as the seven community colleges. There are no private colleges or universities, although the National Outdoor Leadership School, based in Lander, offers courses in mountaineering and ecology. In 1997, minority students comprised 7.9% of total postsecondary enrollment.

42 ARTS

The Grand Teton Music Festival (formerly the Jackson Hole Fine Arts Festival) was established in 1962 and has continued to present an annual program of symphonic and chamber music performed by some of the nation's top artists. The Cheyenne Civic Center serves as a venue for a variety of musical and theatrical groups, including the Cheyenne Symphony Orchestra. Theater Wyoming offers summer performances in Cheyenne, Cody, and Jackson.

The Wyoming Council on the Arts, consisting of 10 members appointed by the governor to three-year terms, funds local activities and organizations in the visual and performing arts, including painting, music, theater, and dance. In 2003, the Wyoming Arts Council and other Wyoming arts organizations received grants totaling $612,100 from the National Endowment for the Arts (NEA). The Wyoming Council for the Humanities has an active speaker's bureau and ongoing history programs, as well as sponsoring a Native American Language Preservation program. In 2000, the National Endowment for the Humanities contributed $478,127 for nine state programs. Contributions to the arts also came from state and private sources. The state of Wyoming offers arts education programs to approximately 33,000 schoolchildren.

43 LIBRARIES AND MUSEUMS

Wyoming was served by 23 county public library systems, with 2,359,732 volumes, in 2000. Public library circulation was 3,711,000 during the same period. The University of Wyoming, in Laramie, had 1,227,000 volumes and 12,960 periodical subscriptions in 2000. Total public library income in 2000 was $14,539,000; including $72,695 in federal funds. Libraries spent 70.5% of this income on staff, and 11.5% on collections.

There are at least 53 museums and historic sites, including the Wyoming State Museum in Cheyenne; the Buffalo Bill Historical Center (Cody), which exhibits paintings by Frederic Remington; and the anthropological, geological, and art museums of the University of Wyoming at Laramie.

44 COMMUNICATIONS

In 2001, 95% of all Wyoming households had telephones. In 2003, Wyoming had 28 major radio stations, 7 AM and 21 FM, plus 17 television stations. A total of 7,279 Internet domain names were registered in the state by 2000.

45 PRESS

There were nine daily newspapers and five Sunday newspapers in Wyoming in 2002. The major daily and its 2001 circulation was the *Casper Star–Tribune*, 31,074 (33,959 on Sunday).

46 ORGANIZATIONS

In 2003, there were about 467 regional, national, and international organizations within the state. National organizations with headquarters within the state include the Dude Ranchers' Association, the National Park Academy of the Arts, and the Yellowstone Association. Local arts, history, and the environment are represented in part through the Arts Council (in Cheyenne), the Wyoming Blues and Jazz Society, and the Wyoming Wildlife Initiative.

47 TOURISM, TRAVEL, AND RECREATION

In 2001, the state hosted 7 million overnight visitors and 17.9 million day-trip travelers. Direct spending on travel within the state totaled about $1.82 billion and accounted for 12.7% of total sales tax revenue. The tourism and travel industry supports over 32,300 jobs.

There are two national parks in Wyoming—Yellowstone and Grand Teton—and nine national forests. Devils Tower and Fossil Butte are national monuments, and Fort Laramie is a national historic site. Yellowstone National Park, covering 2,219,791 acres (898,349 hectares), mostly in the northwestern corner of the state, is the oldest (1 March 1872) and largest national park in the US. The park features some 3,000 geysers and hot springs, including the celebrated Old Faithful. Just to the south of Yellowstone is Grand Teton National Park, 309,993 acres (125,454 hectares).

Adjacent to Grand Teton is the National Elk Refuge, the feeding range of the continent's largest known herd of elk. Devils Tower, a rock formation in the northeast, looming 5,117 feet (1,560 meters) high, is the country's oldest national monument (24 September 1906).

48 SPORTS

There are no major league professional sports teams in Wyoming. Participation sports in Wyoming are typically Western. Skills developed by ranch hands in herding cattle are featured at rodeos held throughout the state. Cheyenne Frontier Days is the largest of these rodeos. Skiing is also a major sport, with Jackson Hole being the largest, best-known resort.

In collegiate sports, the University of Wyoming competes in the Mountain West Conference. They won the Sun Bowl in 1956 and 1958, and they appeared in, but lost, the Holiday Bowl in 1987 and 1988.

49 FAMOUS WYOMINGITES

The most important federal officeholder from Wyoming was Willis Van Devanter (b.Indiana, 1859–1941), who served on the US Supreme Court from 1910 to 1937. Many of Wyoming's better-known individuals are associated with the frontier: John Colter (b.Virginia, 1775?–1813), a fur trader, was the first white man to explore northwestern Wyoming; and Jim Bridger (b.Virginia, 1804–81), perhaps the most famous fur trapper in the West, centered his activities in Wyoming. Late in life, William F. "Buffalo Bill" Cody (b.Iowa, 1846–1917) settled in the Big Horn Basin and established the town of Cody. A number of outlaws made their headquarters in Wyoming. The most famous were "Butch Cassidy" (George Leroy Parker, b.Utah, 1866–1908) and the "Sundance Kid" (Harry Longabaugh, birthplace in dispute, 1863?–1908), who, as members of the Wild Bunch, could often be found there.

Two Wyoming women, Esther Morris (b.New York, 1814–1902) and Nellie Taylor Ross (b.Missouri, 1880–1979), are recognized as the first woman judge and the first woman governor, respectively, in the US; Ross also was the first woman to serve as director of the US Mint. Few Wyoming politicians have received national recognition, but Francis E. Warren (b.Massachusetts, 1844–1929), the state's first governor, served 37 years in the US Senate and came to wield considerable influence and power.

Without question, Wyoming's most famous businessman was James Cash Penney (b.Missouri, 1875–1971). Penney established his first "Golden Rule" store in Kemmerer and eventually built a chain of department stores nationwide. The water-reclamation accomplishments of Elwood Mead (b.Indiana, 1858–1936) and the botanical work in the Rocky Mountains of Aven Nelson (b.Iowa, 1859–1952) were highly significant. Jackson Pollock (1912–56), born in Cody, was a leading painter in the abstract expressionist movement.

50 BIBLIOGRAPHY

Athearn, Robert G. *Union Pacific Country*. New York: Rand McNally, 1971.

Bishop, Tom. *The Real West: Wyoming at Century, a Personal View*. Bloomington, Ind.: 1st Books Library, 2002.

Burt, Nathaniel. *Wyoming*. New York: Compass American Guides, 2002.

Dubois, Muriel L. *Wyoming Facts and Symbols*. Mankato, Minn.: Hilltop Books, 2000.

Gottberg, John. *Hidden Wyoming*. Berkeley, Calif.: Ulysses Press, 1999.

Larson, T. A. *History of Wyoming*. 2nd ed., rev. Lincoln: University of Nebraska Press, 1978.

———. *Wyoming: A History*. New York: Norton, 1984.

Lavender, David. *Westward Vision: The Story of the Oregon Trail*. New York: McGraw-Hill, 1963.

Mead, Jean. *Wyoming in Profile*. Boulder, Colo.: Pruett, 1982.

Woods, L. Milton. *The Wyoming Country Before Statehood*. Worland, Wyo.: Worland Press, 1971.

Wyoming, Department of Administration and Fiscal Control, Division of Research and Statistics. *Wyoming Data Handbook 1983*. 6th ed. Cheyenne, 1983.

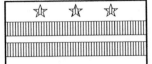

DISTRICT OF COLUMBIA

District of Columbia

ORIGIN OF NAME: From "Columbia," a name commonly applied to the United States in the late 18th century, ultimately deriving from Christopher Columbus. **BECAME US CAPITAL:** 1 December 1800. **MOTTO:** *Justitia omnibus* (Justice for all). **FLAG:** The flag, based on George Washington's coat of arms, consists of three red stars above two horizontal red stripes on a white field. **OFFICIAL SEAL:** In the background, the Potomac River separates the District of Columbia from the Virginia shore, over which the sun is rising. In the foreground, Justice, holding a wreath and a tablet with the word "Constitution," stands beside a statue of George Washington. To her left is the Capitol; to her right, an eagle and various agricultural products. Below is the District motto and the date 1871; above are the words "District of Columbia." **BIRD:** Wood thrush. **FLOWER:** American beauty rose. **TREE:** Scarlet oak. **LEGAL HOLIDAYS:** New Year's Day, 1 January; Birthday of Martin Luther King, Jr., 3rd Monday in January; Washington's Birthday, 3rd Monday in February; Memorial Day, last Monday in May; Independence Day, 4 July; Labor Day, 1st Monday in September; Columbus Day, 2nd Monday in October; Veterans Day, 11 November; Thanksgiving Day, 4th Thursday in November; Christmas Day, 25 December. **TIME:** 7 AM EST = noon GMT.

¹LOCATION, SIZE, AND EXTENT

Located in the South Atlantic region of the US, the District of Columbia has a total area of 69 sq mi (179 sq km), of which land takes up 63 sq mi (163 sq km) and inland water 6 sq mi (16 sq km). The District is bounded on the N, E, and S by Maryland, and on the W by the Virginia shore of the Potomac River. The total boundary length is 37 mi (60 km).

For statistical purposes, the District of Columbia (coextensive since 1890 with the city of Washington, D.C.) is considered part of the Washington, D.C., metropolitan area, which since 1985 has embraced Calvert, Charles, Frederick, Montgomery, and Prince George's counties in Maryland, and Arlington, Fairfax, Loudoun, Prince William, and Stafford counties in Virginia, along with a number of other Virginia jurisdictions, most notably the city of Alexandria.

²TOPOGRAPHY

The District of Columbia, an enclave of western Maryland, lies wholly within the Atlantic Coastal Plain. The major topographical features are the Potomac River and its adjacent marshlands; the Anacostia River, edged by reclaimed flatlands to the south and east; Rock Creek, wending its way from the northwestern plateau to the Potomac; and the gentle hills of the north. The District's average elevation is about 150 ft (46 m). The highest point—410 ft (125 m)—is in the northwest, at Tenleytown; the low point is the Potomac, only 1 ft (30 cm) above sea level.

³CLIMATE

The climate of the nation's capital is characterized by chilly, damp winters and hot, humid summers. The normal daily mean temperature is 58°F (14°C), ranging from 35°F (2°C) in January to 80°F (27°C) in July. The record low, –15°F (–26°C), was set on 11 February 1899; the all-time high, 106°F (41°C), on 20 July 1930. Precipitation averaged 39.4 in (100 cm) yearly during 1971–2000; snowfall, 17 in (43 cm). The average annual relative humidity is 75% at 7 AM and 53% at 1 PM.

⁴FLORA AND FAUNA

Although most of its original flora has been obliterated by urbanization, the District has long been known for its beautiful parks, where about 1,800 varieties of flowering plants and 250 shrubs grow. Boulevards are shaded by stately sycamores, pin and red oaks, American lindens, and black walnut trees. Famous among the introduced species are the Japanese cherry trees around the Tidal Basin. Magnolia, dogwood, and gingko are also characteristic. The District's fauna is less exotic, with squirrels, cottontails, English sparrows, and starlings predominating. Two species (Hay's Spring amphipod and the puma) were listed as endangered and one (the bald eagle) as threatened by the US Fish and Wildlife Service as of August 2003.

⁵ENVIRONMENTAL PROTECTION

The Environmental Regulation Administration (ERA) administers district and federal laws, regulations and mayoral initiatives governing the environment and natural resources of the District of Columbia and the surrounding metropolitan area. The main duty is the protection of human health and the environment as they relate to pesticides, hazardous waste, underground storage tanks, water, air, soils, and fisheries programs. The ERA is responsible for administrating over 30 statutes and regulations. In 1996, the District had about 250 acres of wetlands, all palustrine (marsh) or riverine. In 2003, the Environmental Protection Agency's database listed 29 hazardous waste sites, one of which was on the National Priorities List, in the District. In 2001, the District of Columbia received $116,325,000 in federal grants from the Environmental Protection Agency; EPA expenditures for procurement contracts in the District that year amounted to $82,213,000.

⁶POPULATION

In 2002 the District of Columbia had a larger population than the last-ranked state of Wyoming, with an estimated 570,898, an decrease of 0.2% since 2000. Between 1990 and 2000, the District's population declined from 606,900 to 572,059, an decrease of 5.7%. The population is projected to reach 655,000 by 2025.

In 2000 the median age was 34.6. Persons under 18 years old accounted for 20.1% of the population while 12.2% were age 65 or older.

In 1990 the District of Columbia outranked three states in population, with a census total of 606,900, a decline of almost 5% from 1980. Considered as a city, the District ranked 23rd in the US in 2002. The population density in 2000 was 9,316.4 persons per sq mi, the 7th-highest of any city in the US (behind Philadelphia and ahead of Baltimore).

Even as the capital's population has declined, the number of Washington, D.C., metropolitan area residents has been increasing, from 3,040,000 in 1970 to 3,251,000 in 1980, to 3,924,000 in 1990, and to an estimated 4,739,999 in 1999. The District's population is 100% urban and extremely mobile.

7 ETHNIC GROUPS

Black Americans have long been the largest ethnic or racial group in the District of Columbia, accounting for 60% of the population in 2000 (when they numbered 343,312), among the highest percentages of any major US city.

Between 1970 and 1980, the population of groups other than white and black almost quadrupled within the Washington metropolitan area, reaching 134,209 in 1980. Southeast Asians made up a significant proportion of the immigrants, as did Mexicans and Central and South Americans. The District's racial and ethnic minorities in 2000 included 44,953 Hispanics and Latinos (up from 33,000 in 1990) and 15,189 Asians (including 3,734 Chinese and 2,845 Asian Indians). There also were 1,713 American Indians living in the District.

There were 73,561 foreign-born residents, accounting for 12.9% of the District's total population, in 2000. In addition, the many foreign-born residents attached to foreign embassies and missions contribute to Washington's ethnic diversity.

8 LANGUAGES

Dialectically, the Washington, D.C., area is extremely heterogeneous. In 2000, 83.2% of all District of Columbia residents five years of age or older spoke only English at home, down from 87% in 1990.

The following table gives selected statistics from the 2000 census for language spoken at home by persons five years old and over. The category "African languages" includes Amharic, Ibo, Twi, Yoruba, Bantu, Swahili, and Somali.

LANGUAGE	NUMBER	PERCENT
Population 5 years and over	539,658	100.0
Speak only English	449,241	83.2
Speak a language other than English	90,417	16.8
Speak a language other than English	90,417	16.8
Spanish or Spanish Creole	49,461	9.2
French (incl. Patois, Cajun)	9,085	1.7
African languages	5,181	1.0
Chinese	2,913	0.5
German	2,695	0.5
Arabic	2,097	0.4
Italian	1,723	0.3
Vietnamese	1,610	0.3
Tagalog	1,356	0.3
Russian	1,110	0.2
Portuguese or Portuguese Creole	1,013	0.2

9 RELIGIONS

As of 2000, the largest number of religious adherents in Washington, D.C., were Roman Catholic, with about 160,048 adherents in 42 congregations. Mainline Protestants were next in numbers with the American Baptist Churches in the USA claiming 51,836 adherents in 62 congregations and the Episcopal Church claiming 19,698 adherents in 34 congregations. The Southern Baptist Convention had 38,852 adherents in about 49 congregations. The Jewish population was estimated at 25,500. About 26.8% of the population were not counted as members of any religious organization.

The Washington National Cathedral was established by Congress through an 1893 charter with the Protestant Episcopal Cathedral Foundation. The charter was signed by President Benjamin Harrison. The building was completed in 1912.

10 TRANSPORTATION

Union Station, located north of the Capitol, is the District's one rail terminal, from which Amtrak provides passenger service to the northeast corridor and southern points. In the mid-1990s, Amtrak operated about 75 trains per day into Union Station. In all, four railroads operate 45 rail mi (72 km) of track. The Washington Metropolitan Area Transit Authority, or Metro, operates bus and subway transportation within the city and its Maryland and Virginia suburbs. About 40% of working District residents commute by public transportation. In 1994–95, the federal Transit Authority awarded grants of $199 million for the Metro.

Within the District, as of 2000, were 1,425 mi (2,293 km) of public streets and roads; 243,557 motor vehicles were registered, and 348,216 driver's licenses were in force. Three major airports handle the District's commercial air traffic: Ronald Reagan Washington National Airport, just south of the city in Virginia; Dulles International Airport in Virginia; and Baltimore-Washington International Airport in Maryland. Washington National Airport was officially renamed Ronald Reagan Washington National Airport in February 1998 by the US Congress and President Clinton.

11 HISTORY

Algonkian-speakers were living in what is now the District of Columbia when Englishmen founded the Jamestown, Va., settlement in 1607. The first white person known to have set foot in the Washington area was the English fur trader Henry Fleete, who in 1622 was captured by the Indians and held there for several years. Originally part of Maryland Colony, the region had been carved up into plantations by the latter half of the 17th century.

After the US Constitution (1787) provided that a tract of land be reserved for the seat of the federal government, both Maryland and Virginia offered parcels for that purpose; on 16 July 1790, Congress authorized George Washington to choose a site not more than 10 mi (16 km) square along the Potomac River. President Washington made his selection in January 1791 and then appointed Andrew Ellicott to survey the area and employed Pierre Charles L'Enfant, a French military engineer who had served in the Continental Army, to draw up plans for the federal city. L'Enfant's masterful design called for a wide roadway (now called Pennsylvania Avenue) to connect the Capitol with the President's House (Executive Mansion, now commonly called the White House) a mile away, and for other widely separated public buildings with spacious vistas. However, L'Enfant was late in completing the engraved plan of his design, and he also had difficulty in working with the three commissioners who had been appointed to direct a territorial survey; for these and other reasons, L'Enfant was dismissed and Ellicott carried out the plans. Construction was delayed by lack of adequate financing. Only one wing of the Capitol was completed, and the President's House was still under construction when President John Adams and some 125 government officials moved into the District in 1800. Congress met there for the first time on 17 November, and the District officially became the nation's capital on 1 December. On 3 May 1802, the city of Washington was incorporated (the District also included other local entities), with an elected council and a mayor appointed by the president.

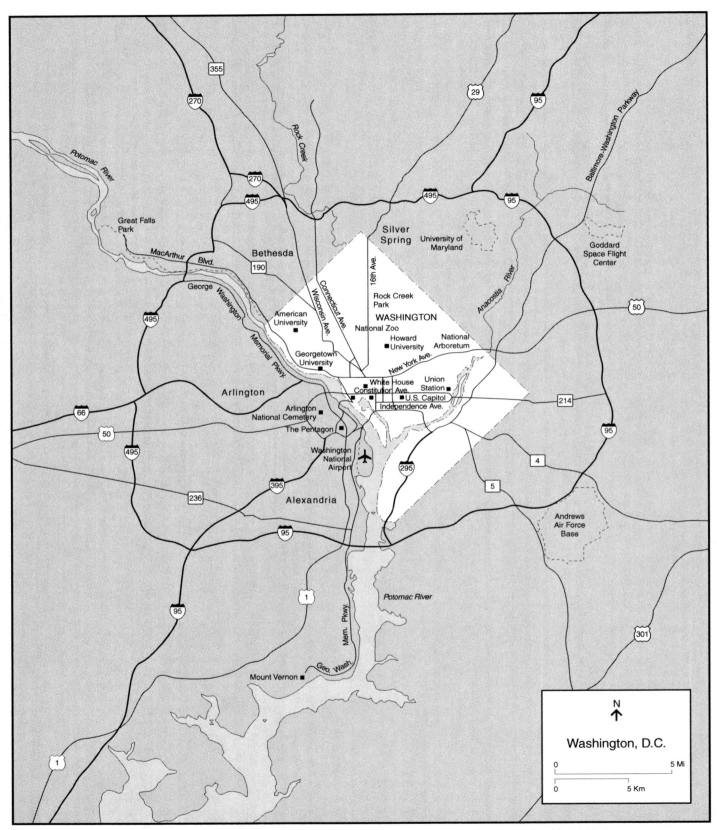

Washington, D.C.

N

0   5 Mi

0   5 Km

LOCATION: 38° 47′ to 39° N; 76° 55′ to 77° 07′ W. **BOUNDARIES:** Maryland line, 25 mi (40 km); Virginia line, 12 mi (19 km).

Construction proceeded slowly, while the city's population grew to about 24,000 by 1810. In August 1814, during the War of 1812, British forces invaded and burned the Capitol, the President's House, and other public buildings. These were rebuilt within five years, but for a long time, Washington remained a rude, rough city. In 1842, English author Charles Dickens described it as a "monument raised to a deceased project," consisting of "spacious avenues that begin in nothing and lead nowhere." At the request of its residents, the Virginia portion was retroceded in 1846, thus confining the federal district to the eastern shore of the Potomac. The Civil War brought a large influx of Union soldiers, workers, and escaped slaves, and the District's population rose sharply from 75,080 in 1860 to 131,700 by the end of the decade, spurring the development of modern Washington.

In 1871, Congress created a territorial form of government; this territorial government was abolished three years later because of alleged local extravagances, and in 1878, a new form of government was established, headed by three commissioners appointed by the president. During the same decade, Congress barred District residents from voting in national elections or even for their own local officials. In the 1890s, Rock Creek Park and Potomac Park were established, and during the early 1900s, city planners began to rebuild the monumental core of Washington in harmony with L'Enfant's original design. The New Deal period brought a rise in public employment, substantial growth of federal facilities, and the beginnings of large-scale public housing construction and slum clearance. After World War II, redevelopment efforts concentrated on demolishing slums in the city's southwest section. The White House was completely renovated in the late 1940s, and a huge building program coincided with the expansion of the federal bureaucracy during the 1960s.

Because it is the residence of the president, Washington, D.C., has always been noted for its public events, in particular the Presidential Inauguration and Inaugural Ball. The District has also been the site of many historic demonstrations: the appearance in 1894 of Coxey's Army—some 300 unemployed workers; the demonstrations in 1932 of the Bonus Marchers—17,000 Army veterans demanding that the government cash their bonus certificates; the massive March on Washington by civil rights demonstrators in 1963; the march on the Pentagon in 1967 by antiwar activists and later Vietnam-era protests; and, in 1995, the Million Man March organized by the controversial Nation of Islam leader Louis Farrakhan.

In recent years, the District's form of government has undergone significant changes. The 23rd Amendment to the US Constitution, ratified on 3 April 1961, permits residents to vote in presidential elections, and beginning in 1971, the District was allowed to send a nonvoting delegate to the US House of Representatives. Local self-rule began in 1975, when an elected mayor and council took office. The District both prospered and suffered in the 1980s and 1990s. In spite of an expanding economy, the city has been wracked by poverty, drug-bred crime, and even gang warfare. In 1989, the federal government mandated $80 million for a program to combat drug abuse in the nation's capital. Crime in Washington has included corruption in high places. In the mid-1980s, the federal government launched an investigation into allegations of bribery, fraud, and racketeering in the award of millions of dollars in municipal and federal contracts. The investigation produced the conviction of 11 city officials. In 1990, the District's mayor of twelve years, Marion Barry, was videotaped smoking crack and was convicted of possessing cocaine. Barry was succeeded that year by Sharon Pratt Dixon, a black lawyer and former power company executive, but reelected in 1994. In 1998 he announced he would not run for reelection, completing four terms of office.

Since the 1970s, many of Washington's residents have supported statehood for the District of Columbia. A proposal for statehood won the majority of votes in a 1980 election, and the name "New Columbia" was approved by voters two years later. In 1992, the US House of Representatives passed a measure approving statehood for the capital, but the Senate refused to consider it.

Mayor Anthony A. Williams was reelected to a second term in November 2002. He pledged to target education, expand opportunities for all district residents, and to keep neighborhoods safe.

¹²STATE GOVERNMENT

The District of Columbia is the seat of the federal government and is home to the principal organs of the legislative, executive, and judicial branches. Both the US Senate and House have subcommittees (of the Appropriations Committees) to oversee federal spending within the District. The District's residents have only limited representation in the House, where an elected delegate may participate in discussions and votes on bills within the District of Columbia subcommittees but may not vote on measures on the floor of the House. The District has no representation in the Senate. In 1978 Congress approved an amendment to the US Constitution granting the District two US senators and at least one representative; however, the amendment failed to become law when it was not ratified by the necessary 38 state legislatures by August 1985 (by that time only 16 states had approved the amendment).

In 1982 elected delegates to a District of Columbia statehood convention drafted a constitution for the proposed State of New Columbia. The petition for statehood was approved by voters within the District and sent to Congress. But in 1993 Congress voted on and rejected District statehood by 63 votes (277 against, 153 for, and four not voting). The bill, which polls have shown has wide public support within the District, can be reintroduced.

The Council of the District of Columbia, the unicameral legislative body for the district, is comprised of 13 representatives who serve four-year terms. Council members must be district residents and qualified voters. Prior to 1973, the mayor and council members were appointed by the US president; since 1973, they have been elected by the District's voters. The body was given full legislative powers in 1974. The council meets every year, beginning in January. In 2002 the legislative salary was $92,500 per year.

Voters must be US citizens, at least 18 years old, residents of Washington, D.C. for at least 30 days prior to election day, and not able to claim the right to vote elsewhere. Restrictions apply to convicted felons and those declared mentally incompetent by the court.

¹³POLITICAL PARTIES

Washington, D.C., is the headquarters of the Democratic and Republican parties, the nation's major political organizations. The District itself is overwhelmingly Democratic: in 1992 and again in 1996, Democratic presidential candidate Bill Clinton garnered an impressive 85% of the District's voters. Democrat Al Gore repeated this performance in 2000, capturing 85% of the vote to Republican candidate George W. Bush's 9% and Green Party candidate Ralph Nader's 5%. In fact, since 1964, when they were first permitted to vote for president, D.C. voters have unfailingly cast their ballots for the Democratic nominee. In 2002 there were 363,211 registered voters. As of 2003, the district had three electoral votes.

The first mayor, Walter Washington, was defeated for reelection in 1978 by Marion S. Barry, Jr., who was reelected in 1982 and again in 1986. Sharon Pratt Dixon was elected mayor in 1990. In 1994, Marion S. Barry Jr., returning to political life after serving a six-month jail term for a 1990 drug conviction, defeated Republican Carol Schwartz in the mayoral contest. Schwartz previously lost to Barry in the mayoral election of 1986. Anthony Williams was elected mayor in 1998 and reelected in 2002.

Eleanor Holmes Norton serves as the District's delegate to the House of Representatives.

D.C. Presidential Vote by Major Parties, 1964–2000

YEAR	ELECTORAL VOTE	D.C. WINNER	DEMOCRAT	REPUBLICAN
1964	3	*Johnson (D)	169,796	28,801
1968	3	Humphrey (D)	139,566	31,012
1972	3	McGovern (D)	127,627	35,226
1976	3	*Carter (D)	137,818	27,873
1980	3	Carter (D)	124,376	21,765
1984	3	Mondale (D)	180,408	29,009
1988	3	Dukakis (D)	159,407	27,590
1992	3	*Clinton (D)	192,619	20,698
1996	3	*Clinton (D)	158,220	17,339
2000	3	Gore (D)	171,923	18,073

* Won US presidential election.

14 LOCAL GOVERNMENT

Local government in the District of Columbia operates under authority delegated by Congress. In 1973, for the first time in more than a century, Congress provided the District with a home-rule charter, allowing Washington, D.C., residents to elect their own mayor and city council. Residents of the District approved the charter on 7 May 1974, and a new elected government took office on 1 January 1975.

The mayor has traditionally been the District's chief executive, and the council is the legislative branch; however, under constitutional authority, Congress can enact laws on any subject affecting the District, and all legislation enacted by the District is subject to congressional veto. In response to both a managerial and budgetary crisis, Congress passed the District of Columbia Financial Responsibility and Management Assistance Act of 1995. This law established a Control Board that has broad powers to review all actions of the D.C. government and must approve the financial plans and budget for the city before submission to Congress. Home rule was further eroded when in 1997 Congress took responsibility for most major agencies away from the mayor and gave them to the Control Board.

The council consists of 13 members: the council chairman and 4 members elected at large, and 8 elected by wards. The 12-member Board of Education consists of eight officials elected by ward and four elected at-large, including one at-large member elected by students. They serve for four years. As of 2002, there were two public school systems in the District. The charter also provides for 36 neighborhood advisory commissions, whose seats are filled through nonpartisan elections.

15 STATE SERVICES

To address the continuing threat of terrorism and to work with the federal Department of Homeland Security (created in 2002 following the terrorist attacks of 11 September 2001), homeland security in the District of Columbia in 2003 operated under the executive order; the deputy mayor for public safety was designated as the state homeland security advisor for the District.

Public education in the District is the responsibility of a chief executive officer and board of trustees appointed by the Control Board and the University of the District of Columbia Board of Trustees. The elected Board of Education is left with very little authority. Transportation services are provided through the Department of Transportation and the Washington Metropolitan Area Transit Authority, while health and welfare services fall within the jurisdiction of the Department of Human Resources.

The Office of Consumer and Regulatory Affairs, Department of Corrections, District of Columbia National Guard, and Metropolitan Police Department provide public protection services, and the Department of Housing and Community Development is the main housing agency. Employment and job training programs are offered through the Department of Employment Services.

16 JUDICIAL SYSTEM

All judges in Washington, DC, are nominated by the president of the US from a list of persons recommended by the District of Columbia Nomination Commission, and appointed upon the advice and consent of the Senate. The US Court of Appeals for the District of Columbia functions in a manner similar to that of a state supreme court; it also has original jurisdiction over federal crimes. The court consists of a chief judge and 8 associate judges, all serving 15-year terms. The Superior Court of the District of Columbia, the trial court, consisted in 1999 of five divisions and 16 judges, also serving for 15 years. Washington, DC, is the site of the US Supreme Court and the US Department of Justice. The District of Columbia is the only US jurisdiction where the US Attorney's Office, an arm of the Justice Department, and not the local government, prosecutes criminal offenders for nonfederal crimes.

According to the FBI Crime Index, the total crime rate in the District of Columbia in 2001 was 7,709.6 per 100,000 population, including a total of 9,931 violent crimes and 34,154 property crimes in that year. DC prisoners numbered 5,388 in June 2001, a decrease of 37.2% from the previous year. The incarceration rate stood at 592 per 100,000 inhabitants. The last execution took place in 1957. DC residents voted 2-1 against the death penalty in 1992. There is a provision for life without parole.

17 ARMED FORCES

In 2002, there were 12,767 active-duty military personnel stationed in the District of Columbia, the vast majority of whom were at the Pentagon, the headquarters of the US Department of Defense, which covers 34 acres (14 hectares) of Arlington, Virginia, across the Potomac. An Air Force installation (Bolling AFB), the Army's Fort McNair, and Walter Reed Medical Center were also within the District. Firms in the District received $1.4 billion in federal defense contract awards in 2001.

There were 44,484 veterans of US military service in the District as of 2000, of whom 9,269 served in World War II; 5,430 in the Korean conflict; 11,816 during the Vietnam era; and 4,942 during 1990–2000 (including the Persian Gulf War). Veterans' benefits totaled $1.7 billion during 2002.

Because Washington is often the scene of political demonstrations and because high federal officials and the District's foreign embassy personnel pose special police-protection problems, the ratio of police personnel to residents is higher than in any state. In 2000, 3,963 police employees were employed in the District.

18 MIGRATION

The principal migratory movements have been an influx of southern blacks after the Civil War and, more recently, the rapid growth of the Washington, D.C., metropolitan area, coupled with shrinkage in the population of the District itself. Between 1950 and 1970, the District suffered a net loss from migration of as much as 260,000, much of it to Maryland and Virginia; there was, however, an estimated net inflow of 87,000 blacks in this period. Net emigration totaled between 150,000 and 190,000 during the 1970s, and roughly 23,000 more during 1981–83.

From 1985 to 1990, the District had a net loss from migration of over 30,000. Between 1990 and 1998, there was a net loss of

139,000 in domestic migration and a net gain of 28,000 in international migration. In 1998, 2,377 foreign immigrants arrived in Washington, D.C. The District's overall population decreased 13.8% between 1990 and 1998. In the period 1995–2000, 113,029 people moved into the state and 158,360 moved out, for a net loss of 45,331.

[19]INTERGOVERNMENTAL COOPERATION

The District of Columbia, a member of the Council of State Governments and its allied organizations, also participates in such interstate regional bodies as the Washington Metropolitan Area Transit Authority Commission, and Potomac Valley Commission. Counties and incorporated cities in the Washington area are represented on the Metropolitan Washington Council of Governments, established in 1957. The District relies heavily on federal grants, which came to over $4 billion in fiscal year 2001.

[20]ECONOMY

During the 1990s, the number of jobs in the service sector grew by about 50%. Other sectors, however, declined in that decade. The small manufacturing sector went from 2.3% of the gross state product in 1997 to 1.2% in 2001. Not surprisingly, the public sector has a greater weight in DC's economy than is found in any of the 50 states, where the average contribution from the public sector in 2001 was 12% compared to 35.2% in DC. Also distinct from most of the states, the District's economy was not adversely affected by the national recession of 2001, as the strong annual growth rates at the end of the 20th century—6.2% in 1999 and 8.2% in 2000—continued into the 21st, averaging 7.5% for 2001. In 2002, the military build-up for the war in Iraq was one of the major growth points in an otherwise slowed national economy reeling from a precipitous drops in both domestic and foreign private investment. The recession and slowed economy also meant more work for government agencies.

[21]INCOME

According to the Bureau of Economic Analysis, in 2001, District of Columbia had a per capita personal income (PCPI) of $40,539 which ranked 2nd in the United States (including the District of Columbia) and was 133% of the national average, $30,413. The 2001 PCPI reflected an increase of 1.4% from 2000 compared to the national change of 2.2%. In 2001, District of Columbia had a total personal income (TPI) of $23,262,315,000 which ranked 45th in the United States and accounted for 0.3% of the national total. The 2001 TPI reflected an increase of 1.8% from 2000 compared to the national change of 3.3%.

Earnings of persons employed in District of Columbia increased from $46,950,429,000 in 2000 to $49,161,209,000 in 2001, an increase of 4.7%. The largest industries in 2001 were services, 42.6% of earnings; federal civilian government, 33.4%; and finance, insurance, and real estate, 6.0%. Of the industries that accounted for at least 5% of earnings in 2001, the slowest growing from 2000 to 2001 was federal civilian government, which increased 3.3%; the fastest was services, which increased 7.5%.

According to data released by the US Census Bureau, in 2000, the median household income was $38,752 compared to the national average of $42,148. In 2001, the median income for a family of four was $61,799 compared to the national average of $63,278. For the period 1999 to 2001, the average poverty rate was 16.1% which placed it 47th among the 50 states and the District of Columbia ranked lowest to highest.

[22]LABOR

According to Bureau of Labor Statistics (BLS) provisional estimates, in July 2003 the seasonally adjusted civilian labor force in the District of Columbia numbered 309,700, with approximately 20,000 workers unemployed, yielding an unemployment rate of 6.5%, compared to the national average of 6.2% for the same period. Since the beginning of the BLS data series in 1978, the highest unemployment rate recorded was 11.9% in July 1983. The historical low was 4.4% in November 1988. It is estimated that in 2001, 3.9% of the labor force was employed in construction; 2.7% in manufacturing; 5.9% in transportation, communications, and public utilities; 9.6% in trade; 5.5% in finance, insurance, and real estate; 39.9% in services; 26.1% in government; and 0.6% in agriculture.

The District of Columbia serves as the headquarters of many labor organizations. The US Department of Labor reported that in 2002, 36,000 of the District of Columbia's 260,000 employed wage and salary workers were members of unions. This represented 13.8% of those so employed, down from 16.2% in 2001. The national average is 13.2%. In all, 46,000 workers (17.8%) were represented by unions. In addition to union members, this category includes workers who report no union affiliation but whose jobs are covered by a union contract.

[23]AGRICULTURE

There is no commercial farming in the District of Columbia.

[24]ANIMAL HUSBANDRY

The District of Columbia has no livestock industry.

[25]FISHING

There is no commercial fishing in the District of Columbia. Recreational fishing is accessible via a boat-launching facility on the Anacostia River. The Mammoth Spring National Fish Hatchery in Arkansas distributed 1,200 channel catfish within the district in 1995/96.

[26]FORESTRY

There is no forestland or forest products industry in the District of Columbia.

[27]MINING

There is no mining in the District of Columbia, although a few mining firms have offices there.

[28]ENERGY AND POWER

The District of Columbia had an installed electric-energy capacity (utility and nonutility) of 806,000 kW in 1999 from four oil-fired plants, all privately owned. Electrical output totaled 230 million kWh. In 2000 the District's total per capita energy consumption was 291 million Btu (73.3 million kcal).

[29]INDUSTRY

Value of shipments by manufacturers in 1997 reached $2.4 billion. Within the District is the Government Printing Office (established by Congress in 1860), which operates one of the largest printing plants in the US. Also in the District is the Washington Post Co., publisher of the newspaper of that name and of Newsweek magazine; the company also owns television stations.

Earnings of persons employed in District of Columbia increased from $38.9 billion in 1997 to $40.6 billion in 1998, an increase of 4.3%. The largest industries in 1998 were services, 41.6% of earnings; federal civilian government, 33.1%; and finance, insurance, and real estate, 5.7%. Of the industries that accounted for at least 5% of earnings in 1998, the slowest growing from 1997 to 1998 was state and local government (5.3% of earnings in 1998), which decreased 3.7%; the fastest was finance, insurance, and real estate, which increased 6.6%.

30COMMERCE

Sales from wholesaling totaled over $3.3 billion in 1997. Retail sales totaled over $3.6 billion that same year. Among retail establishments, eating and drinking establishments accounted for 43%; food stores, 11%; and automotive dealers and service stations, 5.4%. Washington, D.C. exported $350 million in merchandise in 1998.

31CONSUMER PROTECTION

The Department of Consumer and Regulatory Affairs has primary responsibility for consumer protection in the District. The Department regulates businesses; land and building use; occupational and professional standards; rental housing and condominiums; health and social service care facilities; and the natural environment.

32BANKING

Banking in the District of Columbia began with the chartering of the Bank of Alexandria in 1792 and the Bank of Columbia in 1793; both banks terminated in the early 19th century. The oldest surviving bank in the District is the National Bank of Washington, founded as the Bank of Washington in 1809.

Overall, there were 22 federally insured financial institutions in 2002, regulated by the D.C. Department of Banking and Financial Institutions.

33INSURANCE

In 2001, District of Columbia policyholders held 385,000 ordinary life insurance policies worth $19.7 billion; total value for all categories of life insurance (ordinary, group, industrial, and credit) was $80.3 billion. Death benefits paid that year totaled $114.2 million. As of 2003, there were eight property and casualty and four life and health insurance companies incorporated or organized in the District of Columbia. In 2001, property and casualty insurers wrote over $1 billion in premiums. That year, there were 441 flood insurance policies in force in the District of Columbia, with a total value of $55,791.

34SECURITIES

There are no securities exchanges in the District of Columbia. Securities transactions are conducted by about 1,418 firms by over 10,000 employees; 48 investment advisory organizations operate in the district. D.C. headquarters 16 NASDAQ companies, and three NASDAQ market makers.

35PUBLIC FINANCE

The budget for the District of Columbia is prepared in conjunction with the mayor's office and reviewed by the city council, but is subject to review and approval by Congress. The fiscal year runs from 1 October through 30 September.

The local tax base is limited by a shortage of taxable real estate, much of the District being occupied by government buildings and federal reservations. Moreover, Congress has not allowed the District to tax the incomes of people who work in Washington but live in the suburbs, an objective the District government has urgently sought.

The District of Columbia Financial Responsibility and Management Assistance Authority was created in 1995 in order to deal with the district's massive debt, and is in charge of the district's budget and financial planning. The 2001 budget had revenues of $4.87 billion, and expenditures of $4.86 billion, with an accumulated surplus of over $250 million.

36TAXATION

The District of Columbia is in the process of making yearly reductions in the rates on its three-bracket personal income tax schedule. The top rate was reduced from 9.5% to 9.3% in 2001,

to 9% in 2002, to 8.7% in 2003, with further reductions scheduled for 2004. For 2003, the lowest rate was lowered from 5% to 4.5% and is scheduled to fall to 4% in 2004. The corporate income tax, set to be reduced to 9% in 2003 and to 8.5% in 2004., had not been reduced according to schedule, and was at 9.975% (which includes a surtax) in 2003. There is a minimum corporate tax of $100. The District levies a 5.75% general sales and use tax, various excise taxes, plus real and personal property taxes. Until 2001, the District's estate tax was equal to the federal exemption for state estate taxes, but after the federal estate (or death) tax was set to be phased out, the District enacted its own stand-alone estate tax law.

37ECONOMIC POLICY

The District's Office of Business and Economic Development (OBED) administers a revolving loan fund that helps small businesses in need of investment capital. The Local Development Corporation administers the federal Small Business Administration's loan guarantee program for plant and equipment. OBED also assists business in applying for federal urban development action grant funds. Federal community development block grant funds are available as well. By District law, 35% of all construction and procurement contracts by District government agencies must go to minority-owned business enterprises.

38HEALTH

Health conditions in the nation's capital are no source of national pride. The infant mortality rate was 12.0 per 1,000 live births in 2000. Legal abortions numbered 7,373 within the District in 1999. In 2000, the District had an overall death rate of 1,157.7 per 100,000 population, higher than any state except West Virginia. In addition, the death rate from cardiovascular diseases was among highest in the nation, at 338.8 per 100,000 in 2000. The death rates for cerebrovascular diseases, motor vehicle accidents, and suicide, however, were below the overall US rates. Firearm-related deaths in the District, 28.7 per 100,000, far exceeded the national rate of 10.4 in 2000. The homicide rate of 35.5 per 100,000 also remains the highest in the country. Of the residents 18 years of age and older 20.9% were smokers in 2000. In 2000, the HIV-related death rate (45.6 per 100,000 population) was the highest in the US. AIDS cases numbering 13,969 had been reported through 2001.

The District of Columbia's 10 community hospitals had 131,906 admissions and 3,372 beds in 2001. There were 4,577 full-time registered nurses and 292 full-time licensed practical nurses in 2001 and 718 physicians per 100,000 population in 2000. The average expense of a community hospital for care was $3,772.50 per inpatient day.

Federal government grants to cover the Medicare and Medicaid services in 2001 totaled $701 million; 74,701 enrollees received Medicare benefits that year.

39SOCIAL WELFARE

In 2001, the average weekly unemployment benefit was $253.21. Average monthly participation in the food stamp program in FY2002 comprised 74,271 persons (34,554 households). The average monthly benefit was $84.90, and the sum total of benefits paid in FY2002 was $75,667,818.

With the enactment of the Personal Responsibility and Work Opportunity Reconciliation Act of 1996, the US government has changed the form and regulations for many of its social welfare programs. Most significantly, it replaces Aid to Families with Dependent Children (AFDC), an open-ended entitlement program, with Temporary Assistance for Needy Families (TANF), a limited system of assistance funded largely through federal block grants. The reform act also impacts the food stamp

program, the Supplemental Security Income program, and the child nutrition program. The law took effect on 1 July 1997 and provided $16.38 billion in block grants for fiscal years 1997–2002. The grants are to be divided among the states based on an equation involving the numbers of former AFDC recipients in each state.

Reauthorization of the 1996 social welfare legislation, scheduled for 2002, was delayed, and the original law had been extended three times as of July 2003, with the most recent extension running through September 2003. State expenditures on the TANF program in FY2002 totaled $74,877,637.

In December 2001, Social Security benefits were paid to 73,390 District of Columbia residents. This number included 48,090 retired workers, 7,440 widows and widowers, 8,560 disabled workers, 4,820 spouses, and 6,480 children. Social Security beneficiaries represented 12.8% of the District's total population and 78.6% of the District's population age 65 and older. Retired workers (excluding persons with special benefits) received an average monthly payment of $741; widows and widowers, $685; disabled workers, $760; and spouses, $384. Payments for children of retired workers averaged $351 per month; children of deceased workers, $445; and children of disabled workers, $230.

Federal Supplemental Security Income payments in December 2001 went to 19,973 District of Columbia residents, averaging $395 a month.

40 HOUSING

In 2002, the District of Columbia had an estimated 272,636 housing units, of which 242,095 were occupied. Only 39.9% were owner-occupied, ranking the District as having the least number of homeowners in the nation. About 38% of all units dated from 1939 or earlier. Only 13% of all units were single-family, detached homes. About 30% were in buildings of 20 units or more. It was estimated that about 6,046 units were without telephone service, 985 lacked complete plumbing facilities, and 543 lacked complete kitchen facilities. Most households relief on gas and electricity for heating.

In 2002, 1,591 new privately owned housing units were authorized for construction. The median home value was $212,428, placing the District as 4th in the nation for highest home values. The median monthly cost for mortgage owners was $1,549 while renters paid a median of $693 per month. During 2002, Washington, D.C., received more than $42 million in community planning and development aid from the US Department of Housing and Urban Development.

41 EDUCATION

The District of Columbia's first public schools were opened in 1805. Until 1954, public schools for whites and blacks were operated separately. Although legally integrated, the public school system remains virtually segregated. Most white and many black students attend private schools. In 2000, 77.8% of all residents 25 years of age or older were high school graduates, and 36.1% were college graduates.

The total enrollment for fall 1999 in the District of Columbia's public schools stood at 77,194. Of these, 59,917 attended schools from kindergarten through grade eight, and 17,277 attended high school. Minority students made up approximately 96% of the total enrollment in public elementary and secondary schools in 1997. Total enrollment was estimated at 78,751 in fall 2000 and but expected to drop to 72,000 by fall 2005. Enrollment in nonpublic schools in fall 2001 was 16,690. Expenditures for public education in 2000/01 were estimated at $807,381.

As of fall 2000, there were 59,498 students enrolled in college or graduate school. In the same year the District of Columbia had 17 degree-granting institutions, 16 private and 1 public. In

1997, minority students comprised 44.5% of total postsecondary enrollment. Some of the best-known private universities are American, Georgetown, George Washington, and Howard. The University of the District of Columbia, created in 1976 from the merger of three institutions, has an open admissions policy for District freshman undergraduate students. It has five academic colleges. The US Department of Agriculture Graduate School also operates within the District.

42 ARTS

The District of Columbia Commission on the Arts and Humanities was founded in 1968 and is a partner with the Mid-Atlantic Arts Foundation. In 2003, District arts organizations received $3,454,260 in grants from the National Endowment for the Arts. The Humanities Council of Washington, D.C., was established in 1980 and awards about $125,000 each year to support local programs. In 2000, the National Endowment for the Humanities contributed $3,499,044 for 30 programs within the District.

Recent by the National Endowment for the Humanities include $400,000 to the Historical Society of Washington, D.C., for community educational programs and exhibits, humanities fellowships of $149,565 to the American Councils for International Education in 2002, and $378,000 to the Folger Shakespeare Library in 2003. The Humanities Council of Washington, D.C., presents Humanities Salons throughout the year that feature distinguished guest speakers, films, and discussions related to the humanities.

The John F. Kennedy Center for the Performing Arts, officially opened on 8 September 1971, is the District's principal performing arts center. Its five main halls—the Opera House, Concert Hall, Eisenhower Theater, Terrace Theatre, and American Film Institute Theater—display gifts from at least 30 foreign governments, ranging from stage curtains and tapestries to sculptures and crystal chandeliers. Major theatrical productions are also presented at the Arena Stage-Kreeger Theater, National Theatre, Folger Theatre, and Ford's Theatre. Rep, Inc. is one of the few professional black theatres in the US; the New Playwrights' Theatre of Washington is a nonprofit group presenting new plays by American dramatists.

The District's leading symphony is the National Symphony Orchestra, which performs from October through April at the Concert Hall of the Kennedy Center. On a smaller scale, the Phillips Collection, National Gallery of Art, and Library of Congress offer concerts and recitals. The Washington Opera performs at the Kennedy Center's Opera House.

During the summer months, the Carter Barron Amphitheater presents popular music and jazz. Concerts featuring the US Army, US Navy, and US Marine Corps bands, and the Air Force Symphony Orchestra are held throughout the District.

43 LIBRARIES AND MUSEUMS

Washington, D.C., is the site of the world's largest library, the Library of Congress, with a 1998 collection of more than 80 million items, including 26 million books and pamphlets. The Library, which is also the cataloging and bibliographic center for libraries throughout the US, has on permanent display a 1455 Gutenberg Bible, Thomas Jefferson's first draft of the Declaration of Independence, and Abraham Lincoln's first two drafts of the Gettysburg Address. Also in its permanent collection are the oldest known existing film (Thomas Edison's *The Sneeze*, lasting three seconds), maps believed to date from the Lewis and Clark expedition, original musical scores by Charles Ives, and huge libraries of Russian and Chinese texts. The Folger Shakespeare Library contains not only rare Renaissance manuscripts but also a full-size re-creation of an Elizabethan theater. The District's own public library system has a main library and 26 branches—

including the Martin Luther King Memorial Library—with 2,863,296 volumes in 1998.

The District of Columbia was home to at least 93 museums in 2000. The Smithsonian Institution—endowed in 1826 by an Englishman, James Smithson, who had never visited the US—operates a vast museum and research complex that includes the National Air and Space Museum, National Museum of Natural History, National Museum of History and Technology, many of the District's art museums, and the National Zoological Park. Among the art museums operated by the Smithsonian are the National Gallery of Art, housing one of the world's outstanding collections of Western art from the 13th century to the present; the Freer Gallery of Art, housing a renowned collection of Near and Far Eastern treasures, along with one of the largest collections of the works of James McNeill Whistler, whose Peacock Room is one of the museum's highlights; the National Collection of Fine Arts; the National Portrait Gallery; and the Hirshhorn Museum and Sculpture Garden. Among the capital's other distinguished art collections are the Phillips Collection, the oldest museum of modern art in the US; the Museum of African Art, located in the Frederick Douglass Memorial Home; and the Corcoran Gallery of Art, devoted primarily to American paintings, sculpture, and drawings of the last 300 years. Washington is also the site of such historic house-museums as Octagon House, Decatur House, Dumbarton Oaks, and the Woodrow Wilson House. Many national associations maintain exhibitions relevant to their areas of interest. The US National Arboretum, US Botanic Garden, and National Aquarium are in the city. In 1999, lawmakers debated plans to build a memorial for Reverend Dr. Martin Luther King Jr. between the Jefferson and Lincoln memorials in D.C.

44COMMUNICATIONS

Washington, D.C., is the headquarters of the US Postal Service. As of 2001, about 93.8% of households had telephones. In 2000, the District had 7 AM and 13 FM radio stations and 13 television stations. The District had 1,999,870 television households, 70% of which ordered cable. A total of 47,433 Internet were registered in the District in 2000.

45PRESS

Because the District of Columbia is the center of US government activity, hundreds of US and foreign newspapers maintain permanent news bureaus there. The District has one major newspaper, the *Washington Post*. In 2002, the *Post*, a morning paper, had an average daily circulation of 759,864 and a Sunday circulation of 1,059,646. In 2001, the *Post* had the 5th-largest daily circulation and the third-largest Sunday circulation in the country. The *Washington Times*, also published on weekday mornings, had a circulation of 103,505 (48,534 on Sunday).

Press clubs active within the District include the National Press Club, Gridiron Club, American Newspaper Women's Club, Washington Press Club, and White House Correspondents Association.

There are more than 30 major Washington-based periodicals. Among the best known are the *National Geographic, U.S. News & World Report, Smithsonian,* and *New Republic.* Important periodicals covering the workings of the federal government are the *Congressional Quarterly* and its companion, *CQ Weekly Report.*

46ORGANIZATIONS

In 2003, there were over 3,000 regional, national, and international organizations represented within the District. Service and patriotic organizations with headquarters in the District include the Air Force Association, Daughters of the American Revolution, and the 4-H Program. Among the cultural,

scientific, and educational groups are the American Film Institute, American Theatre Association, Federation of American Scientists, American Association for the Advancement of Science, National Academy of Sciences, National Geographic Society, Association of American Colleges, American Council on Education, National Education Association, American Association of University Professors, American Association of University Women, and US Student Association.

District cultural and educational organizations include the Cultural Alliance of Greater Washington and the Historical Society of Washington, D.C.

Among the environmental and animal protection organizations in the District are the Animal Welfare Institute, Humane Society of the US, and National Wildlife Federation. Medical, health, and charitable organizations include the American Red Cross. Groups dealing with the elderly include the National Association of Retired Federal Employees and the American Association of Retired Persons. Among ethnic and religious bodies with headquarters in the District are the National Association of Arab Americans, B'nai B'rith International, and the US Catholic Conference.

Trade, professional, and commercial organizations include the American Advertising Federation, American Federation of Police, American Youth Hostels, National Aeronautic Association, Air Line Pilots Association, American Bankers Association, National Cable Television Association, Chamber of Commerce of the US, American Chemical Society, International Association of Firefighters, Health Insurance Association of America, American Council of Life Insurance, National Association of Manufacturers, American Petroleum Institute, and National Press Club.

Virtually every major public interest group maintains an office in Washington, D.C. Notable examples are the Consumer Federation of America, National Consumers League, National Abortion Rights Action League, National League of Cities, Common Cause, US Conference of Mayors, National Organization for Women, and National Rifle Association of America.

Among the important world organizations with headquarters in the District are the Organization of American States, International Monetary Fund, and International Bank for Reconstruction and Development.

47TOURISM, TRAVEL, AND RECREATION

As the nation's capital, the District of Columbia is one of the world's leading tourist centers. Tourism in Washington, D.C. generates over $10 billion in direct spending each year and sustains about 260,000 jobs. In 2002, there were over 17.6 million visitors.

The most popular sites are The National Air and Space Museum, the National Museum of Natural History, National Gallery of Art, Museum of American History, the National Zoo, the US Holocaust Memorial Museum, Smithsonian Castle, the Vietnam Veterans Memorial, Lincoln Memorial, Library of Congress, White House, and US Capitol tours.

Across the Potomac, in Virginia, are Arlington National Cemetery, site of the Tomb of the Unknown Soldier and the grave of John F. Kennedy, and George Washington's home at Mt. Vernon.

48SPORTS

There are five major league professional sports teams in Washington, D.C.: the Redskins of the National Football League, the Wizards (formerly the Bullets), of the National Basketball Association, the Mystics of the Women's National Basketball Association, the Capitals of the National Hockey League, and DC United of Major League Soccer. Hockey and basketball are played in downtown Washington at the MCI Arena, which was opened for the 1997–98 season. The Redskins began the 1997 season in the new Jack Kent Cooke Stadium in Landover, Maryland. The Redskins have reached football's Super Bowl five times, winning in 1983, 1988, and 1992. The Bullets won the NBA championship in 1978.

In collegiate sports the Georgetown Hoyas were a dominant force in basketball during the 1980s, reaching the NCAA championship game in 1982, 1984, and 1985, and winning the title in 1984.

49FAMOUS WASHINGTONIANS

Although no US president has been born in the District of Columbia, all but George Washington (b.Virginia, 1732–99) lived there while serving as chief executive. Seven presidents died in Washington, D.C., including three during their term of office: William Henry Harrison (b.Virginia, 1773–1841), Zachary Taylor (b.Virginia, 1784–1850), and Abraham Lincoln (b.Kentucky, 1809–65). In addition, John Quincy Adams (b.Massachusetts, 1767–1848), who served as a congressman for 17 years after he left the White House, died at his desk in the House of Representatives; and William Howard Taft (b.Ohio, 1857–1930) passed away while serving as US chief justice. Retired presidents Woodrow Wilson (b.Virginia, 1856–1924) and Dwight D. Eisenhower (b.Texas, 1890–1969) also died in the capital. Federal officials born in Washington, D.C., include John Foster Dulles (1888–1959), secretary of state; J(ohn) Edgar Hoover (1895–1972), director of the FBI; and Robert C. Weaver (1907–97), who as secretary of housing and urban development during the administration of President Lyndon B. Johnson was the first black American to hold cabinet rank. Walter E. Fauntroy (b.1933) was the District's first delegate to Congress in the 20th century, appointed when that office was reestablished in 1971.

Among the outstanding scientists and other professionals associated with the District were Cleveland Abbe (b.New York, 1838–1916), a meteorologist who helped develop the US Weather Service; inventor Alexander Graham Bell (b.Scotland, 1842–1922), president of the National Geographic Society (NGS) in his later years; Henry Gannett (b.Maryland, 1846–1914), chief geographer with the US Geological Survey, president of the NGS and a pioneer in American cartography; Charles D. Walcott (b.New York, 1850–1927), director of the Geological Survey and secretary of the Smithsonian Institution; Emile Berliner (b.Germany, 1851–1929), a pioneer in the development of the phonograph; Gilbert H. Grosvenor (b.Turkey, 1875–1966), editor in chief of *National Geographic* magazine; and Charles R. Drew (1904–50), developer of the blood bank concept. Leading business executives who have lived or worked in the District include William W. Corcoran (1798–1888), banker and philanthropist, and Katharine Graham (b.New York, 1917–2001), publisher of the *Washington Post* and chairman of its parent company; the two *Post* reporters who received much of the credit for uncovering the Watergate scandal are Carl Bernstein (b.1944), a native Washingtonian, and Robert "Bob" Woodward (b.Illinois, 1943). Mary Elizabeth "Tipper" Gore (b.1948), wife of Vice President Al Gore, was born in Washington, D.C. Washingtonians who achieved military fame include Benjamin O. Davis (1877–1970), the first black to become an Army general, and his son, Benjamin O. Davis, Jr. (1912–2002), who was the first black to become a general in the Air Force. John Shalikashvili (b.Poland, 1936) was the first foreign born commander in chief of the joint chiefs of staff.

The designer of the nation's capital was Pierre Charles L'Enfant (b.France, 1754–1825), whose grave is in Arlington National Cemetery; also involved in laying out the capital were surveyor Andrew Ellicott (b.Pennsylvania, 1754–1820) and mathematician-astronomer Benjamin Banneker (b.Maryland, 1731–1806), a black who was an early champion of equal rights. Among Washingtonians to achieve distinction in the creative arts were John Philip Sousa (1854–1932), bandmaster and composer; Herblock (Herbert L. Block, b. Illinois, 1909–2001), political cartoonist; and playwright Edward Albee (b.1928), winner of the Pulitzer Prize for drama in 1967 and 1975. Famous performers born in the District of Columbia include composer-pianist-bandleader Edward Kennedy "Duke" Ellington (1899–1974) and actress Helen Hayes (Helen Hayes Brown, 1900–92). Alice Roosevelt Longworth (b.New York, 1884–1980) dominated the Washington social scene for much of this century.

50BIBLIOGRAPHY

Allen, Thomas B. *The Washington Monument: It Stands for All.* New York: Discovery Books, 2000.

Caroli, Betty Boyd. *Inside the White House: America's Most Famous Home.* Pleasantville, N.Y.: Reader's Digest Association, Inc., 1999.

Cary, Francine Curro, ed. *Urban Odyssey: A Multicultural History of Washington, D.C.* Washington, D.C.: Smithsonian Institution, 1996.

Federal Writer's Project. *Washington, D.C.: A City and Capital.* Reprint. New York: Somerset, n.d. (orig. 1942).

Goode, James M. *Capital Losses: A Cultural History of Washington's Destroyed Buildings.* Washington, D.C.: Smithsonian Books, 2003.

Greene, Constance M. *Washington: A History of the Capital.* Princeton, N.J.: Princeton University Press, 1976.

Gurney, Gene, and Harold Wise. *The Official Washington, D.C., Directory.* New York: Crown, 1977.

Gutheim, Frederick. *Worthy of the Nation: The Planning and Development of the National Capital City.* Washington, D.C.: Smithsonian, 1977.

Katharine Graham's Washington. New York: Alfred A. Knopf, 2002.

Lewis, David L. *District of Columbia: A Bicentennial History.* New York: Norton, 1976.

Moore, John L. *Speaking of Washington: Facts, Firsts, and Folklore.* Washington, D.C.: Congressional Quarterly, 1993.

Shidler, Atlee E. *Trends and Issues in the Greater Washington Region: A Preliminary Report.* Washington, D.C.: Center for Municipal and Metropolitan Research, 1979.

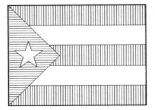

PUERTO RICO

Commonwealth of Puerto Rico
Estado Libre Asociado de Puerto Rico

ORIGIN OF NAME: Spanish for "rich port." **NICKNAME:** Island of Enchantment. **CAPITAL:** San Juan. **BECAME A COMMONWEALTH:** 25 July 1952. **SONG:** *La Borinquena.* **MOTTO:** *Joannes est nomen ejus.* (John is his name.) **FLAG:** From the hoist extends a blue triangle, with one white star; five horizontal stripes—three red, two white—make up the balance. **OFFICIAL SEAL:** In the center of a green circular shield, a lamb holding a white banner reclines on the book of the Apocalypse. Above are a yoke, a cluster of arrows, and the letters "F" and "I," signifying King Ferdinand and Queen Isabella, rulers of Spain at the time of discovery; below is the commonwealth motto. Surrounding the shield, on a white border, are the towers of Castile and lions symbolizing Spain, crosses representing the conquest of Jerusalem, and Spanish banners. **ANIMAL:** Coqui. **BIRD:** Reinita. **FLOWER:** Maga. **TREE:** Ceiba. **LEGAL HOLIDAYS:** New Year's Day, 1 January; Three Kings Day (Epiphany), 6 January; Birthday of Eugenio Maria de Hostos, 11 January; Birthday of Martin Luther King, Jr., 3rd Monday in January; Washington's Birthday, 3rd Monday in February; Abolition Day, 22 March; Good Friday, March or April; Birthday of José de Diego, 16 April; Memorial Day, last Monday in May; Independence Day, 4 July; Birthday of Luis Muñoz Rivera, 17 July; Constitution Day, 25 July; Birthday of José Celso Barbosa, 27 July; Labor Day, 1st Monday in September; Anniversary of the "Grito de Lares," 23 September; Discovery of America, 12 October; Veterans Day, 11 November; Discovery of Puerto Rico Day, 19 November; Thanksgiving Day, 4th Thursday in November, Christmas Day, 25 December. **TIME:** 8 AM Atlantic Standard Time = noon GMT.

¹LOCATION, SIZE, AND EXTENT

Situated on the NE periphery of the Caribbean Sea, about 1,000 mi (1,600 km) SE of Miami, Puerto Rico is the easternmost and smallest island of the Greater Antilles group. Its total area is 3,515 sq mi (9,104 sq km), including 3,459 sq mi (8,959 sq km) of land and 56 sq mi (145 sq km) of inland water.

Shaped roughly like a rectangle, the main island measures 111 mi (179 km) E-W and 36 (58 km) N-S. Offshore and to the E are two major islands, Vieques and Culebra.

Puerto Rico is bounded by the Atlantic Ocean to the N, the Virgin Passage and Vieques Sound to the E, the Caribbean Sea to the S, and the Mona Passage to the W. Puerto Rico's total boundary length is 378 mi (608 km).

²TOPOGRAPHY

About 75% of Puerto Rico's land area consists of hills or mountains too steep for intensive commercial cultivation. The Cordillera Central range, separating the northern coast from the semiarid south, has the island's highest peak, Cerro de Punta (4,389 feet–1,338 meters). Puerto Rico's best-known peak, El Yunque (3,496 feet–1,066 meters), stands to the east, in the Luquillo Mountains (Sierra de Luquillo). The north coast consists of a level strip about 100 mi (160 km) long and 5 mi (8 km) wide. Principal valleys are located along the east coast, from Fajardo to Cape Mala Pascua, and around Caguas, in the east-central region. Off the eastern shore are two small islands: Vieques, with an area of 51 sq mi (132 sq km), and Culebra, covering 24 sq mi (62 sq km). Uninhabited Mona Island (19 sq mi–49 sq km), off the southwest coast, is a breeding ground for wildlife.

Puerto Rico has 50 waterways large enough to be classified as rivers, but none is navigable by large vessels. The longest river is the Rio de la Plata, extending 46 mi (74 km) from Cayey to Dorado, where it empties into the Atlantic. There are few natural lakes but numerous artificial ones, of which Dos Bocas, south of Arecibo, is one of the most beautiful. Phosphorescent Bay, whose luminescent organisms glow in the night, is a tourist attraction on the south coast.

Like many other Caribbean islands, Puerto Rico is the crest of an extinct submarine volcano. About 45 mi (72 km) north of the island lies the Puerto Rico Trench, at over 28,000 feet (8,500 meters) one of the world's deepest chasms.

³CLIMATE

Tradewinds from the northeast keep Puerto Rico's climate equable, although tropical. San Juan has a normal daily mean temperature of 80°F (27°C), ranging from 77°F (25°C) in January to 82°F (28°C) in July; the normal daily minimum is 73°F (23°C), the maximum 86°F (30°C). The lowest temperature ever recorded on the island is 39°F (4°C), at Aibonito, the highest 103°F (39°C), at San Lorenzo. The recorded temperature in San Juan has never been lower than 60°F (16°C) or higher than 98°F (37°C).

Rainfall varies by region. Ponce, on the south coast, averages only 32 in (81 cm) a year, while the highlands average 108 in (274 cm); the rain forest on El Yunque receives an annual average of 183 in (465 cm). San Juan's average annual rainfall is 54 in (137 cm), the rainiest months being May through November.

The word "hurricane" derives from *hurakán,* a term the Spanish learned from Puerto Rico's Taino Indians. Nine hurricanes have struck Puerto Rico in this century, the most recent being the devasting Hurricane Georges in 1998. On 7 October 1985, torrential rains created a mud slide that devastated the hillside barrio of Mameyes, killing hundreds of people; not only was this Puerto Rico's worst disaster of the century, but it was the single most destructive landslide in US history.

⁴FLORA AND FAUNA

During the 19th century, forests covered about three-fourths of Puerto Rico. Today, however, only one-fourth of the island is forested. Flowering trees still abound, and the butterfly tree, African tulip, and flamboyán (royal poinciana) add bright reds and pinks to Puerto Rico's lush green landscape. Among hardwoods, now rare, are nutmeg, satinwood, Spanish elm, and Spanish cedar. Pre-Columbian peoples cultivated yucca, yams, peanuts, hot peppers, tobacco, and cotton. Pineapple guava, tamarind, and cashews are indigenous, and such fruits as mamey, jobo guanábana, and quenepa are new to most visitors. Coconuts, coffee, sugarcane, plantains, mangoes, and most citrus fruits were introduced by the Spanish.

The only mammal found on the island by the conquistadores was a kind of barkless dog, now extinct. Virtually all present-day mammals have been introduced, including horses, cattle, cats, and dogs. The only troublesome mammal is the mongoose, brought in from India to control reptiles in the cane fields and now wild in remote rural areas. Mosquitoes and sand flies are common pests, but the only dangerous insect is the giant centipede, whose sting is painful but rarely fatal. Perhaps the island's best-known inhabitant is the golden coqui, a tiny tree frog whose call of "ko-kee, ko-kee" is heard all through the night; it is a threatened species. Marine life is extraordinarily abundant, including many tropical fish, crabs, and corals. Puerto Rico has some 200 bird species, many of which live in the rain forest. Thrushes, orioles, grosbeaks, and hummingbirds are common, and the reinita and pitirre are distinctive to the island. Several parrot species are rare, and the Puerto Rican parrot is endangered. Also on the endangered list are the yellow-shouldered blackbird and the Puerto Rican plain pigeon, Puerto Rican whippoorwill, Culebra giant anole, Puerto Rican boa, and Monita gecko. The Mona boa and Mona ground iguana are threatened. There are three national wildlife refuges, covering a total of 2,425 acres (981 hectares).

5ENVIRONMENTAL PROTECTION

US environmental laws and regulations are applicable in Puerto Rico. Land-use planning, overseen by the Puerto Rico Planning Board, is an especially difficult problem, since residential, industrial, and recreational developers are all competing for about 30% of the total land area on an island that is already more densely populated than any state of the US except New Jersey. Pollution from highland latrines and septic systems and from agricultural and industrial wastes is a potential hazard; the rum industry, for example, has traditionally dumped its wastes into the ocean. Moreover, the US requirement that sewage receive secondary treatment before being discharged into deep seas may be unrealistic in view of the commonwealth government's claim, in the late 1970s, that it could not afford to build secondary sewage treatment facilities when 45% of its population lacks primary sewage treatment systems. As of 2003, sewage discharges into the ocean remained a problem: in August 2000, the US Environmental Protection Agency (EPA) granted the Puerto Rico Aqueduct and Sewage Authority's Aguadilla treatment plant a 20-year waiver for discharging primary treated sewage into the ocean, threatening coral reefs.

About 300,000 tons of hazardous waste are generated annually, and 16,000 tons of chemical substances are released into the air, water, and soil each year. In January 1994, 750,000 gallons of oil were spilled off the coast of Puerto Rico, resulting in a fine of over $75 million levied against the three companies responsible. Wetlands on the island have been devastated by development, but in recent years, efforts have been mounted to save and expand these resources.

6POPULATION

Puerto Rico's population was estimated at 3,885,877 in mid-2003, up from 3,528,000 in 1990. With a population density of 1,025 per sq mi (465 per sq km), Puerto Rico is one of the most densely populated areas of the world.

In 2003, there were 93 Puerto Rican males for every 100 females. That year, about 22.9% of the population was under 15

years of age, 65.2% were 15–64 years of age, and 11.9% were 65 years or over. The birthrate declined steadily from 38.9 live births per 1,000 population in 1950 to 18.2 in 1991 to 15 by 2003. The death rate, on the other hand, was 7.4 per 1,000 population in 1990 and 7.68 per 1,000 population in 2003.

The population was estimated to be 75.2% urban and 24.8% rural in 2000. San Juan is Puerto Rico's capital and largest city, with an estimated 2002 population of 433,412, followed by Bayamon, 224,670; Carolina, 187,468; Ponce, 186,112; and Caguas, 141,693.

7ETHNIC GROUPS

Three main ethnic strands reflect the heritage of Puerto Rico: the Taino Indians, most of whom fled or perished after the Spanish conquest; black Africans, imported as slaves under Spanish rule; and the Spanish themselves. With an admixture of Dutch, English, Corsicans, and other Europeans, Puerto Ricans today enjoy a distinct Hispanic-Afro-Antillean heritage.

Less than two-thirds of all ethnic Puerto Ricans live on the island. Virtually all the remainder reside on the US mainland; in 2000 there were 3,407,000 people who identified themselves as Puerto Rican in the 50 states. The state of New York had the largest US ethnic Puerto Rican population (some 1.1 million) and ethnic Puerto Ricans made up 5.5% of that state's total population. Florida's total ethnic population in 2000 stood 2nd to New York's, at approximately one-half million.

8LANGUAGES

Spanish is the official language of Puerto Rico; English is required in schools as a second language. From 1898 through the 1920s, US authorities unsuccessfully sought to make English the island's primary language.

Taino Indian terms that survive in Puerto Rican Spanish include such place-names as Arecibo, Guayama, and Mayagüez, as well as *hamaca* (hammock) and *canoa* (canoe). Among many African borrowings are food terms like *quimbombó* (okra), *guince* (banana), and *mondongo* (a spicy stew).

9RELIGIONS

During the first three centuries of Spanish rule, Roman Catholicism was the only religion permitted in Puerto Rico. More than 85% of the population was still Roman Catholic in mid-2003, and the Church maintains numerous hospitals and schools on the island. Most of the remaining Puerto Ricans belong to other Christian denominations, which have been allowed on the island since the 1850s. Pentecostal churches have attracted a significant following, particularly among the urban poor of the barrios.

10TRANSPORTATION

Puerto Rico's inland transportation network consists primarily of roads and motor vehicles. A system of public buses operated by the Metropolitan Bus Authority (MBA) provides intercity passenger transport in the capital of San Juan and nearby cities. As of 2000, the bus service carried 135,000 daily passengers, up from 60,000 daily passengers in 1995, a 125% increase. The *públicos,* a privately owned jitney service of small buses and cars, offers transportation between fixed destinations in cities and towns.

In 2000, Puerto Rico had 14,695 mi (23,649 km) of state highways and municipal roads. In 2000, the territory had approximately two million registered automobiles.

The rail transit system under development by Puerto Rico Highway and Transportation Authority (PRHTA), known as the *Tren Urbano* (Urban Train), was scheduled to begin operations in September 2003. *Tren Urbano* was expected to operate 74 vehicles, to serve about 115,000 passengers per day at 16 stations along a 10.7-mi (17-km), 30-minute route. The cost of the *Tren*

Urbano project had risen from $1.25 billion in 1996 to $2.3 billion by 2003; these escalating costs and logistical problems delayed the completion of the project as of August 2003.

In 1996/97, the PRHTA invested nearly $750 million to complete the strategic highway network system around the island, as well as other roads that connect small towns with the nearby cities. By 2000, the majority of the projects to improve the highway system had been completed, including improvements to Highways 2, 3, 22, 26, 30, and 52. The PR-10 Expressway crosses from the north to the central moutainous region. The PR-53 toll road provides a new route for the towns of the northeast. The Baldorioty de Castro Expressway allows rapid travel between the main airport and the capital. In 2000, a $200 million master plan for a new north-south expressway was being developed, which would involve the Martinez Nadal Expressway (Highway 20), improvements to Highway 1 to Caguas, an intersection in Caparra, and the Kennedy Expressway. The project was to be completed by 2008.

San Juan, the island's principal port and a leading containerized cargo-handling facility, handled 9.6 million tons of cargo in 2001. Ponce and Mayagüez handle considerable tons of cargo as well. Ferries link the main island with the islands of Vieques and Culebra.

As of 2003, plans were underway to develop the "Port of the Americas," a world-class transshipment port and adjoining free industrial zone extending from Ponce to Guayanilla. Extensive tracts of land and the natural deep-water bay were to create an advantageous site for the port. The port was designed to handle all of Puerto Rico's foreign trade, and a good deal of its international container traffic crossing the Caribbean. The government was expecting to select a port development firm by the end of 2003. It was expected that 20,000 jobs would be created with the establishment of the port.

Puerto Rico receives flights from 38 US mainland cities, and from the Virgin Islands, the British West Indies, Jamaica, the Dominican Republic, Great Britain, France, Spain, and the Netherlands. Luis Muñoz Marin International Airport in San Juan enplaned 10.4 million passengers in 2002. Puerto Rico shipped 495.8 million tons of air cargo in 2002. San Juan had 1.29 million passenger airline seats in January 2003. Other leading air terminals are located at Ponce, Mayagüez, and Aguadilla. There were 31 airports in Puerto Rico in mid-2002, 19 of which had paved runways. As of 2003, 52 airlines serviced Puerto Rico.

11 HISTORY

Archaeological finds indicate that at least three Indian cultures flourished on the island now known as Puerto Rico long before its discovery by Christopher Columbus on 19 November 1493. The first group, belonging to the Archaic Culture, is believed to have come from Florida. Having no knowledge of agriculture or pottery, it relied on the products of the sea; the remains of its members have been found mostly in caves. The second group, the Igneri, came from northern South America. Descended from Arawak stock, the Igneri brought agriculture and pottery to the island; their remains are found mostly in the coastal areas. The third culture, the Taino, also of Arawak origin, combined fishing with agriculture. A peaceful, sedentary tribe, the Taino were adept at stonework and lived in many parts of the island; Taino relics have been discovered not only along the coastal perimeter but also high in the mountains, where the Taino performed ritual games in ball parks that have been restored in recent times. To the Indians, the island was known as Boriquén.

Columbus, accompanied by a young nobleman named Juan Ponce de León, landed at the western end of the island—which he called San Juan Bautista (St. John the Baptist)—and claimed it for Spain. Not until colonization was well under way would the

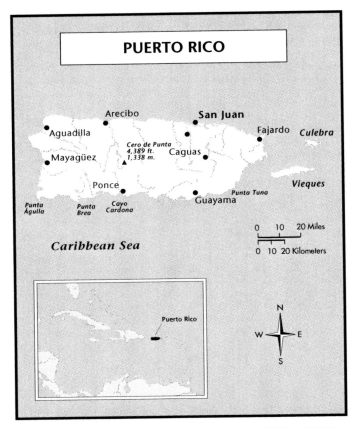

LOCATION: (main island only): 18°04′15′′ to 18°31N; 65°35′30′′ to 67°15′9w.
BOUNDARIES: Total coastline, 378 mi (608 km).

island acquire the name Puerto Rico (literally, "rich port"), with the name San Juan Bautista applied to the capital city. The first settlers arrived on 12 August 1508, under the able leadership of Ponce de León, who sought to transplant and adapt Spanish civilization to Puerto Rico's tropical habitat. The small contingent of Spaniards compelled the Taino, numbering perhaps 30,000, to mine for gold; the rigors of forced labor and the losses from rebellion reduced the Taino population to about 4,000 by 1514, by which time the mines were nearly depleted. With the introduction of slaves from Africa, sugarcane growing became the leading economic activity. Since neither mining nor sugarcane was able to provide sufficient revenue to support the struggling colony, the treasury of New Spain began a subsidy, known as the *situado*, which until the early 19th century defrayed the cost of the island's government and defense.

From the early 16th century onward, an intense power struggle for control of the Caribbean marked Puerto Rico as a strategic base of the first magnitude. After a French attack in 1528, construction of La Fortaleza (still in use today as the governor's palace) was begun in 1533, and work on El Morro fortress in San Juan commenced six years later. The new fortifications helped repel a British attack led by Sir Francis Drake in 1595; a second force, arriving in 1598 under George Clifford, Earl of Cumberland, succeeded in capturing San Juan, but the British were forced to withdraw by tropical heat and disease. In 1625, a Dutch attack under the command of Boudewijn Hendrikszoon was repulsed, although much of San Juan was sacked and burned by the attackers. By the 18th century, Puerto Rico had become a haven for pirates, and smuggling was the major economic activity. A Spanish envoy who came to the island in 1765 was appalled, and his report to the crown inaugurated a period of economic, administrative, and military reform. The creation of a native militia helped Puerto Rico withstand a fierce British assault on San Juan in 1797, by which time the island had more than 100,000 inhabitants.

Long after most of the Spanish colonies in the New World had obtained independence, Puerto Rico and Cuba remained under Spanish tutelage. Despite several insurrection attempts, most of them inspired by the liberator, Simón Bolívar, Spain's military might concentrated on these islands precluded any revolution.

Puerto Rico became a shelter for refugees from Santo Domingo, Haiti, and Venezuela who were faithful to Spain, fearful of disturbances in their own countries, or both. As in Cuba, the sugar industry developed in Puerto Rico during this period under policies that favored foreign settlers. As a result, a new landowner class emerged—the *hacendados*—who were instrumental in strengthening the institution of slavery on the island. By 1830, the population was 300,000. Sugar, tobacco, and coffee were the leading export crops, although subsistence farming still covered much of the interior. Sugar found a ready market in the US, and trade steadily developed, particularly with the northeast.

The 19th century also gave birth, however, to a new Puerto Rican civil and political consciousness. Puerto Rican participation in the short-lived constitutional experiments in Spain (1812–14 and 1820–23) fostered the rise of a spirit of liberalism, expressed most notably by Ramón Power y Giralt, at one time vice president of the Spanish Cortes (parliament). During these early decades, Spain's hold on the island was never seriously threatened. Although the Spanish constitution of 1812 declared that the people of Puerto Rico were no longer colonial subjects but were full-fledged citizens of Spain, the crown maintained an alert, centralized, absolutist government with all basic powers concentrated in the captain general.

Toward the middle of the 19th century, a *criollo* generation with strong liberal roots began a new era in Puerto Rican history. This group, which called for the abolition of slavery and the introduction of far-reaching economic and political reforms, at the same time developed and strengthened Puerto Rican literary tradition. The more radical reformers espoused the cause of separation from Spain and joined in a propaganda campaign in New York on behalf of Cuban independence. An aborted revolution, beginning in the town of Lares in September 1868 (and coinciding with an insurrection in Spain that deposed Queen Isabella II), though soon quelled, awakened among Puerto Ricans a dormant sense of national identity. "El Grito de Lares" (the Cry of Lares) helped inspire a strong anti-Spanish separatist current that was unable to challenge Spanish power effectively but produced such influential leaders as Ramón Emeterio Betances and Eugenio Maria de Hostos.

The major reform efforts after 1868 revolved around abolitionism and *autonomia*, or self-government. Slavery was abolished in 1873 by the First Spanish Republic, which also granted new political rights to the islanders. The restoration of the Spanish monarchy two years later, however, was a check to Puerto Rican aspirations. During the last quarter of the century, leaders such as Luis Muñoz Rivera sought unsuccessfully to secure vast new powers of self-government. By this time, Puerto Rico was an island with a distinct Antillean profile, strong Hispanic roots, and a mixed population that, borrowing from its Indian-Spanish-African background and an influx of Dutch, English, Corsicans, and other Europeans, had developed its own folkways and mores.

The imminence of war with the US over Cuba, coupled with autonomist agitation within Puerto Rico, led Spain in November 1897 to grant to the island a charter with broad powers of self-rule. Led by Luis Muñoz Rivera, Puerto Ricans began to establish new organs of self-government; but no sooner had an elected government begun to function in July 1898 than US forces, overcoming Spanish resistance, took over the island. A cease-fire was proclaimed on 13 August, and sovereignty was formally transferred to the US with the signing in December of the Treaty of Paris, ending the Spanish-American War. The US government swept aside the self-governing charter granted by Spain and established military rule from 1898 to 1900. Civilian government was restored in 1900 under a colonial law, the Foraker Act, that gave the federal government full control of the executive and legislative branches, leaving some local representation in the lower chamber, or house of delegates. Under the Jones Act, signed into law by President Woodrow Wilson on 2 March 1917, Congress extended US citizenship to the islanders and granted them an elective senate, but still reserved vast powers over Puerto Rico to the federal bureaucracy.

The early period of US rule saw an effort to Americanize all insular institutions, even to the point of superseding the Spanish language as the vernacular. In the meantime, American corporate capital took over the sugar industry, developing a plantation economy so pervasive that, by 1920, 75% of the population relied on the cane crop for its livelihood. Glaring irregularities of wealth resulted, sharpening social and political divisions. This period also saw the development of three main trends in Puerto Rican political thinking. One group favored the incorporation of Puerto Rico into the US as a state; a second group, fearful of cultural assimilation, favored self-government; while a third group spoke for independence.

The Depression hit Puerto Rico especially hard. With a population approaching 2 million by the late 1930s and with few occupational opportunities outside the sugar industry, the island's economy deteriorated, and mass unemployment and near-starvation were the results. Controlling the Puerto Rican legislature from 1932 to 1940 was a coalition of the Socialist Party, led by Santiago Iglesias, a Spanish labor leader who became a protégé of the American Federation of Labor, and the Republican Party, which had traditionally espoused statehood and had been founded in Puerto Rico by José Celso Barbosa, a black physician who had studied in the US. The coalition was unable to produce any significant improvement, although under the New Deal a US government effort was made to supply emergency relief for the "stricken island."

Agitation for full political and economic reform or independence gained ground during this period. A violent challenge to US authority in Puerto Rico was posed by the small Nationalist Party, led by Harvard-educated Pedro Albizu Campos. A broader attack on the island's political and economic ills was led by Luis Muñoz Marin and the Popular Democratic Party (PDP), founded in 1938; within two years, the PDP won control of the senate. Under Muñoz Marin, a new era began in Puerto Rico. Great pressure was put on Washington for a change in the island's political status, while social and economic reform was carried to the fullest extent possible within the limitations of the Jones Act. Intensive efforts were made to centralize economic planning, attract new industries through local tax exemptions (Puerto Rico was already exempt from federal taxation), reduce inequality of income, and improve housing, schools, and health conditions. Meanwhile, a land distribution program helped the destitute peasants who were the backbone of the new party. All these measures—widely publicized as Operation Bootstrap—coupled with the general US economic expansion after World War II, so transformed Puerto Rico's economy that income from manufacturing surpassed that from agriculture by 1955 and was five times as great by 1970. Annual income per capita rose steadily from $296 in 1950 to $1,384 in 1970.

The PDP, the dominant force in Puerto Rican politics from 1940 to 1968, favored a new self-governing relationship with the US, distinct from statehood or independence. The party succeeded not only in bringing about significant social and economic change but also in obtaining from Congress in 1950 a law allowing Puerto Ricans to draft their own constitution with full local self-government. This new constitution, approved in a general referendum on 3 March 1952, led to the establishment on 25 July of the Commonwealth of Puerto Rico (Estado Libre Asociado de Puerto Rico), which, according to a resolution approved in 1953 by the United Nations Committee on Information from Non-Self-Governing Territories, was constituted as an autonomous political entity in voluntary association with the United States.

An island-wide plebiscite in 1967 showed that 60% of those voting favored continuation and improvement of the commonwealth relationship, 39% preferred statehood, and less than 1% supported independence; the turnout among eligible voters was 65%. The result of the plebiscite, held to support a movement for additional home-rule powers, met with indifference from the US executive branch and outright opposition from the pro-statehood minority in Puerto Rico. Consequently, efforts to obtain passage by Congress of a "Compact of Permanent Union between Puerto Rico and the United States," although approved at the subcommittee level by the House of Representatives, failed to produce any change in the commonwealth arrangement.

The result was renewed agitation for either statehood or independence, with growing internal political polarization. The island's Republican Party rearranged itself after the plebiscite as the New Progressive Party (NPP), and came to power in 1968 as a result of a split in PDP ranks that led to the creation of the splinter People's Party. The two major blocs have been evenly balanced since that time, with the PDP returning to power in 1972 but losing to the NPP in 1976 and again, by a very narrow margin, in 1980, before regaining the governorship in 1984. The independence movement, in turn, divided into two wings: the moderates favored social democracy, while the radicals pursued close ties with the Fidel Castro regime in Cuba. Capitalizing on the increased power of Third World countries in the United Nations, and with Soviet support, the radicals challenged US policies and demanded a full transfer of sovereign rights to the people of Puerto Rico. Their position won the support of the UN Special Committee on the Situation with Regard to the Implementation of the Declaration on the Granting of Independence to Colonial Countries and Peoples (more generally known as the Committee of 24), which on 15 August 1979 reaffirmed "the inalienable right of the people of Puerto Rico to self-determination and independence...." The US government replied that the people of Puerto Rico had already exercised their right of self-determination in the 1967 plebiscite, and noted that Congress in 1979 had restated its "commitment to respect and support the right of the people of Puerto Rico to determine their own political future through peaceful, open and democratic processes."

More advanced than most Caribbean countries in education, health, and social development, Puerto Rico suffered from growing political tensions in the early 1980s, with occasional terrorist attacks on US military installations and personnel. These tensions may have been exacerbated by the national recession of 1980–81, which had a particularly severe impact on Puerto Rico. The commonwealth's gross national product declined by 6% in 1982 and 1983, and federal budget cuts ended a jobs program and reduced access to food stamps. At the same time, the island's economy experienced a structural shift. Whereas 50% of jobs in Puerto Rico had been in agriculture in 1940, by 1989 that figure had dropped to 20%. Manufacturing jobs, in contrast, rose from 5 to 15% of total employment between 1940 and 1989. Although Puerto Rico's economy began to expand in the mid-

1980s, growing at an annual rate of 3.6%, the island continued to depend heavily on the federal government, which in 1989 employed 25% of Puerto Rican workers. The economy grew at an estimated rate of 2.2% in 2001. (Due to adverse conditions in the global economy, however, the GDP growth rate stood at 0.5% in 2002).

Puerto Rico's political status remains a source of controversy. Statehood would give Puerto Rico representation in the US Congress and would make the island eligible for billions of dollars more a year in food stamps, medical insurance, and income support payments, which are currently set at levels far below those of states. However, statehood would also incur the loss of tax benefits. Under current federal tax law for the commonwealth, individuals pay no federal income tax. More importantly, corporations pay no federal tax on profits, which has persuaded many companies, particularly manufacturers of pharmaceuticals, chemicals, and electronics, to build plants in Puerto Rico. In 1993 and 1998 plebiscites, a slight majority of Puerto Rican voters chose to maintain the island's status as an American commonwealth rather than opt for statehood or independence.

In 1989, Hurricane Hugo caused 12 deaths and $1 billion in damage in Puerto Rico. In 1994, the island suffered its worst drought in almost 30 years, and narrowly avoided serious damage to its beaches and wildlife when over half a million gallons (2.3 million liters) of heavy oil were spilled by a barge that ran aground on a coral reef. In October 1998, Hurricane Georges ravaged the island, causing damage estimated in the billions of dollars.

Pedro Rosselló was reelected governor in 1994; he announced in 1999 that he would not seek a third term in elections of fall 2000. In the 2000 election, Sila M. Calderón was elected the island's first woman governor. In May 2003, however, she announced she would not run for reelection in 2004.

In 1999 one Puerto Rican civilian was killed and four others were seriously wounded in an accident during a US military training exercise on the island of Vieques. Widespread protests following the accident led US president Bill Clinton to temporarily suspend military training on the island pending an investigation, and subsequent exercises used inert weapons only. The residents of Vieques, however, maintained that the military exercises were responsible for health and environmental problems. Governor Calderón, who opposed the US Navy manoeuvres, pressured President George W. Bush to halt the activity. On 1 May 2003, the US Navy withdrew from Vieques, and approximately 15,000 acres of land previously used by the military were turned over to the US Department of the Interior's Fish and Wildlife Service, to be dedicated to a wildlife refuge closed to the public.

Although Puerto Rico banned capital punishment in 1929, in 2003, two men who were charged with first degree murder and extortion were being considered for execution under the 1994 Federal Death Penalty Act, which broadened the range of crimes punishable by death. Many Puerto Ricans claimed the imposition of the death penalty would infringe upon the commonwealth's right to self-government.

12 STATE GOVERNMENT

Since 1952, Puerto Rico has been a commonwealth of the US, governed under the Puerto Rican Federal Relations Act and under a constitution based on the US model. The Puerto Rican constitution specifically prohibits discrimination "on account of race, color, sex, birth, social origin or condition, or political ideas." The consitution has been amended a number of times, and in 2002, plans to hold a constitutional assembly to amend the constitution were proposed, providing for the elimination of the

house of representatives and the senate and the creation of a unicameral legislature.

The commonwealth legislature comprises a senate *(Senado)* of 27 or more members, 2 from each of 8 senatorial districts, and 11 elected at large; and a house of representatives *(Cámara de Representantes)* of 51 or more members, 1 from each of 40 districts and 11 at large. Each senate district consists of five house districts. The Law of Minorities holds that if a single party wins two-thirds or more of the seats in either house, but does not win two-thirds of the vote in the gubernatorial election, the opposition parties are eligible for additional seats, in order to give the opposition (collectively) one-third of the seats in either house. The number of seats therefore, can be expanded (up to a limit of 9 in the senate and 17 in the house), if opposition parties receive at least 3% of the gubernatorial vote. In the 2000 election, one seat was added to the senate according to this law, but no seats were added to the house of representatives. Senators must be at least 30 years of age, representatives must be 25. Legislators must have been commonwealth residents for two years and district or municipal residents for one year. All legislators serve four-year terms.

The governor, who may serve an unlimited number of four-year terms, is the only elected executive. Candidates for the governorship must be US citizens for at least five years, must be at least 35 years of age, and must have resided in Puerto Rico for at least five years.

A bill becomes law if approved by both houses and either signed by the governor or left unsigned for 10 days while the legislature is in session. A two-thirds vote of the elected members of each house is sufficient to override a gubernatorial veto. The governor can employ the item veto or reduce amounts in appropriations bills. The governor also has the power to declare martial law in cases of rebellion, invasion, or immediate danger of rebellion or invasion. The constitution may be amended by a two-thirds vote of the legislature and ratification by popular majority vote.

Residents of Puerto Rico may not vote in US presidential elections. A Puerto Rican who settles in one of the 50 states automatically becomes eligible to vote for president; conversely, a state resident who migrates to Puerto Rico forfeits such eligibility. Puerto Rico has no vote in the US Senate or House of Representatives, but a nonvoting resident delegate, elected every four years,

may speak on the floor of the House, introduce legislation, and vote in House committees.

Qualified voters must be US citizens, be at least 18 years of age, and have registered 50 days before a general election; absentee registration is not allowed.

13 POLITICAL PARTIES

Taking part in Puerto Rican elections during recent years were two major and three smaller political parties. The Popular Democratic (PPD), founded in 1938, favors the strengthening and development of commonwealth status. The New Progressive Party (PNP), created in 1968 as the successor to the Puerto Rican Republican Party, is pro-statehood. The National Republican Party of Puerto Rico is led by Luis Ferré. Two smaller parties, each favoring independence for the island, were the Puerto Rican Independence Party (PIP), founded in the mid-1940s and committed to democratic socialism, and the more radical Puerto Rican Socialist Party, which had close ties with Cuba until it became defunct. A breakaway group, the Renewal Party, led by the mayor of San Juan, Hernán Padilla, left the PNP and took part in the 1984 elections.

In 1980, Governor Carlos Romero Barceló of the PNP, who had pledged to actively seek Puerto Rico's admission to the Union if elected by a large margin, retained the governorship by a plurality of fewer than 3,500 votes, in the closest election in the island's history, while the PPD won control of the legislature and 52 out of 78 mayoralty contests. Former governor Rafael Hernández Colón defeated Romero Barceló's bid for reelection in 1984 by more than 54,000 votes. Colón was reelected in 1988 and was succeeded in 1992 by Pedro Rosselló, a New Progressive and a supporter of statehood, who was reelected in 1996. In 2000, Sila M. Calderón was elected Puero Rico's first female governor, with 48.6% of the vote.

The question of Puerto Rico's status remains controversial. Governor Rosselló called a plebiscite in November of 1993 to enable voters to choose between independence, commonwealth or statehood. A narrow majority of Puerto Rican voters decided to maintain the island's status as an American commonwealth. However, they conditioned their vote on a demand that the terms of the island's commonwealth status be modified. Such modifications would include eliminating the federal limits on food stamps and expanding Supplemental Security Income to encompass

Puerto Rico Gubernatorial Vote by Political Parties, 1948–2000

YEAR	WINNER	POPULAR DEMOCRAT (PPD)	NEW PROGRESSIVE (PNP)	PUERTO RICAN REPUBLICAN	INDEPENDENCE (PIP)	SOCIALIST	LIBERAL REFORMIST
1948	Luis Muñoz Marin (PPD)	392,033	—	88,819	66,141	64,121	28,203
1952	Luis Muñoz Marin (PPD)	429,064	—	85,172	125,734	21,655	—
1956	Luis Muñoz Marin (PPD)	433,010	—	172,838	86,386	—	—
1960	Luis Muñoz Marin (PPD)	457,880	—	252,364	24,103	—	—
						CHRISTIAN ACTION	
1964	Roberto Sanchez Vitella (PPD)	487,280	—	284,627	22,201	26,867	—
						PEOPLE'S	
1968	Luis A Ferré (PNP)	367,903	390,623	4,057	24,713	87,844	—
							PR UNION
1972	Rafael Hernández Colón (PPD)	609,670	524,039	—	52,070	2,910	1,608
1976	Carlos Romero Barceló (PNP)	634,941	682,607	—	58,556	9,761	—
1980	Carlos Romero Barceló (PNP)	756,434	759,868	—	87,275	5,225	—
							RENEWAL
1984	Rafael Hernández Colón (PPD)	822,040	767,710	—	61,101	—	68,536
1988	Rafael Hernández Colón (PPD)	865,309	813,448	—	96,230	—	—
1992	Pedro Rosselló (PNP)	845,372	919,029	—	76,357	—	—
1996	Pedro Rosselló (PNP)	1,006,331	875,852	—	75,304	—	—
2000	Sila María Calderón (PPD)	978,860	919,194	—	104,705	—	—

* Residents of Puerto Rico are barred from voting in US presidential elections.

elderly and handicapped Puerto Ricans. Puerto Rican voters also requested that recent changes in Federal Tax Law 936, which had lowered by 60% the exemptions corporations could claim from taxes on profits, be removed and that the law be restored to its original form. Although Puerto Ricans have no vote in US presidential elections, the island does send voting delegates to the national conventions of the Democratic and Republican parties. In 1980, for the first time, those delegates were chosen by presidential preference primary.

Puerto Rico's political parties have generally committed themselves to peaceful change through democratic methods. One exception was the pro-independence Nationalist Party, whose followers were involved in an attempt to assassinate US president Harry S. Truman in 1950 and in an outbreak of shooting in the House of Representatives that wounded five congressman in 1954. A US-based terrorist group, the Armed Forces of Puerto Rican National Liberation (FALN), claimed credit during the late 1970s for bombings in New York and other major cities. FALN members briefly took over the Statue of Liberty in New York Harbor on 25 October 1977. Another group, the Macheteros, apparently based on the island, claimed responsibility for an attack on a US Navy bus in 1980 and for blowing up eight US Air Force planes at a Puerto Rico Air National Guard installation early in 1981.

[14]LOCAL GOVERNMENT

The Commonweath of Puerto Rico had 78 municipalities in 2003, each governed by a mayor and municipal assembly elected every four years. In fact, these governments resemble US county governments in that they perform services for both urban and rural areas. Many of the functions normally performed by municipal governments in the US—for instance, fire protection, education, water supply, and law enforcement—are performed by the commonwealth government directly.

[15]STATE SERVICES

The executive branch of Puerto Rico's highly centralized government is organized into departments, agencies, and public corporations. The departments are as follows: agriculture, consumer affairs, correction and rehabilitation, economic development and commerce, education, family services, health, housing, justice, labor and human resources, natural resources and the environment, recreation and sports, state, transportation and public works, and treasury. Lodged within the Office of the Governor are the Office of Management and Budget, Planning Board, Commission on Women's Affairs, and Environmental Quality Board, as well as offices of economic opportunity, energy, youth affairs, cultural affairs, labor affairs, child development, and development of the disabled, and commissions for the protection and strengthening of the family and of agricultural planning and action.

Puerto Rico is more heavily socialized than any US state. Almost one-fourth of all those employed work for the commonwealth government, which operates hotels, marine transports, the telephone company, and all sugar mills, among other enterprises.

[16]JUDICIAL SYSTEM

Puerto Rico's highest court, the Supreme Court, consists of a chief justice and six associate justices, appointed, like all other judges, by the governor with the consent of the senate and serving until compulsory retirement at age 70. The court may sit in separate panels for some purposes, but not in cases dealing with the constitutionality of commonwealth law, for which the entire body convenes. Decisions of the Supreme Court of Puerto Rico regarding US constitutional questions may be appealed to the US Supreme Court.

The Circuit Court of Appeals consists of 33 justices named by the governor with the consent of the senate. Decisions of the court may revise those of the trial courts of first instance. The Circuit Court of Appeals was created in 1994 as an intermediary tribunal between the courts of first instance and the Supreme Court. The tribunal sits in San Juan.

The nine superior courts are the main trial courts; superior court judges are appointed to 12-year terms. In 2003, superior courts were divided into 13 districts. These courts have original jurisdiction in civil cases not exceeding $10,000 and in minor criminal cases. District courts also hear preliminary motions in more serious criminal cases. Municipal judges, serving for five years, and justices of the peace, in rural areas, decide cases involving local ordinances.

San Juan is the seat of the US District Court for Puerto Rico, which has the same jurisdiction as federal district courts on the US mainland.

The death penalty is constitutionally forbidden; however, in 2003, the 1994 Federal Death Penalty Act was being invoked in a case involving two men accused of murder and extortion. The last execution in Puerto Rico took place in 1927.

[17]ARMED FORCES

Military expenditures in 1998–99 totaled $940 million or 9.6% of gross domestic product. In 2002, there were 2,796 active-duty military personnel stationed in Puerto Rico. Principal of the four US military installations in Puerto Rico are the Roosevelt Roads Naval Reservation, near Ceiba, and the Naval Security Station at Sabana Seca. Ft. Buchanan, an army base, is in Guaynabo. Use of Vieques for training maneuvers, including shelling and bombing, forced many of that island's residents to move; the US Navy withdrew its forces in May 2003. Aerial and naval target practice on Culebra by the US Navy was halted by protests and legal action. Defense spending decreased dramatically in 2002: US defense agencies spent $133.8 million on procurement contracts greater than $25,000 during the first nine months of 2002. During all of 2001, the same agencies spent $297.5 million on such contracts.

As of 1996, 129,000 veterans of US military service were living on the island. Puerto Ricans suffered 731 combat deaths in Korea and 270 in Vietnam.

Reserve and national guard personnel in Puerto Rico totaled 18,123 in 1996, with the army accounting for the vast majority (16,306).

[18]MIGRATION

Although migration from Puerto Rico to the US mainland is not an entirely new phenomenon—several Puerto Rican merchants were living in New York City as early as 1830—there were no more than 70,000 islanders in the US in 1940. Mass migration, spurred by the booming postwar job market in the US, began in 1947. The out-migration was particularly large from 1951 through 1959, when the net outflow of migrants from the island averaged more than 47,000 a year. According to the 2000 census, 3,406,178 ethnic Puerto Ricans were living in the 50 states; at least 32 cities had Puerto Rican communities of 5,000 or more. Puerto Ricans are found in significant numbers not only in New York State but also in New Jersey, Illinois, Pennsylvania, California, Florida. Connecticut, and Massachusetts. Indeed, 58% of ethnic Puerto Ricans living in the 50 states were concentrated in the Northeast in 2002.

During the 1970s, in part because of the economic decline of many US urban centers, the migration trend slowed; official estimates show that the net flow of migrants from the island totaled only 65,900. But with the Puerto Rican economy worsening in the early 1980s, the net migration from early 1980 to mid-1983 was about 90,000. From 1990 to 1992, there was a net loss from migration of about 40,000.

One striking aspect of the US-Puerto Rico migration pattern is its fluidity. As US citizens, Puerto Ricans can move freely between the island and the mainland. Even in 1953, when the heaviest net outflow was recorded—74,603—fully 230,307 persons emigrated from the US mainland to Puerto Rico, as 304,910 Puerto Ricans were migrating the other way. In 2000, 242,973 people living on the US mainland said that they had lived in Puerto Rico in 1995, while 112,788 people living in the commonwealth in 2000 said that they had lived on the mainland in 1995. This extreme mobility, though sensitive to the job market, would not be possible were it not for the increased income available to Puerto Ricans on both the island and the US mainland, and the fact that Puerto Ricans who come to the continental US generally preserve their ties of family and friendship with those in the commonwealth, thus finding it easy to return, whether for a short stay at Christmastime or for a new job on the island.

[19] INTERGOVERNMENTAL COOPERATION

A member of the US Council of State Governments, Puerto Rico subscribes to the Compact for Education, the Interstate Compact for the Supervision of Parolees and Probationers, the Southern States Energy Board, and the Southern Growth Policies Compact. In its relations with the US government, the commonwealth is in most respects like a state, except in the key areas of taxation and representation. US laws are in effect, federal agencies regulate aviation and broadcasting, and Puerto Ricans participate in such federally funded programs as Social Security and food stamps. US grants to Puerto Rico totaled almost $3.9 billion in fiscal year 2001.

[20] ECONOMY

In 1940, annual income per capita was $118, and agricultural workers made as little as 6 cents an hour. By 1978, income per capita was $2,600, and the average hourly farm wage at least $1.65—in each case, far below the US average, but also in each case a vast improvement over former times.

The island's most important industrial products are pharmaceuticals, electronics, apparel, and food products. The sugar industry has gradually lost ground to dairy production and other livestock products in the agricultural sector. Tourism is the backbone of a large service industry, and the government sector has also grown. Tourist revenues and remittances from workers on the US mainland largely counterbalance Puerto Rico's chronic trade deficit. Federal funds to the government and directly to the people have been important to the Puerto Rican economy.

Puerto Rico's major problem is lack of jobs for an expanding population, a problem exacerbated when rising unemployment in the US persuades Puerto Ricans to return to the island. From its former dependence on subsistence agriculture, Puerto Rico became a center for low-wage textile manufacturing, then a home for refining cheap crude oil from abroad—mainly Venezuela. The sharp rise of overseas oil prices that began in 1973 devastated this economic sector. Since then, high-technology industries have become a major presence on the island. For instance, along with the development of the Port of the Americas on the southwestern coast of the island, a "techno-economic" corridor is being envisioned on the western coast, which will take advantage of the excellent highway system linking the port and the leading engineering university to the airport in Aguadilla, with the longest runway in the Caribbean.

Section 936 of the US internal revenue code, passed in 1976 and discontinued in 1996, established a substantial tax credit for income of US corporations doing business in Puerto Rico and possessions of the US. Some corporations were also allowed to import their products into the US duty-free. Section 936 was

replaced with Section 30A, which allowed companies to claim 60% of wages and capital investment as non-taxable income. Pharmaceutical companies and high-tech industries based in Puerto Rico were to have an advantage over NAFTA member Mexico, whose low wages in low-skill labor-intensive jobs competed with Puerto Rican jobs. Due to the elimination of Section 936, however, many companies in Puerto Rico closed.

The downturn in the US economy that began in 2001 negatively impacted the Puerto Rican economy more severely than the mainland economy. The 11 September 2001 terrorist attacks on the US also had an adverse effect on the Puerto Rican tourist industry. However, by 2003, the economy was showing signs of stabilizing: unemployment stood at 11.9% in the first quarter of 2003, down from over 13% in 2002. The GDP growth rate, at 0.5% in 2002, was forecast for 2003 at 2.7%.

[21] INCOME

Per capita personal income in Puerto Rico was $11,500 in 2002, far lower than in any of the 50 states during that year, but far exceeding that of its Caribbean neighbors. Total net income increased from $1.3 billion in 1960 to $5 billion in 1972, $9 billion in 1980, and $24.5 billion in 1996. The gross domestic product was estimated at $45.7 billion in 2002, with an estimated growth rate that year of 0.5%.

[22] LABOR

Puerto Rico's civilian labor force in July 2002 numbered 1,273,000. The unemployment rate averaged 13% in 2002, although it had decreased to 11.9% in the first quarter of 2003.

In March 1997, agriculture, forestry, and fishing accounted for about 3.1% of employment; mining, 0.1%; construction, 5.5%; manufacturing, 15.3%; wholesale and retail trade, 19.5%; finance, insurance, and real estate, 3.0%; transportation, communication, and public utilities, 5.5%; services, 25.5%; and government, 22.5%. In fiscal year 2002, approximately 276,600 people were employed in government, 215,000 in services, 212,800 in trade, 141,2000 in manufacturing, 70,400 in construction, and 46,900 in finance, insurance, and real estate.

Approximately 7% of the labor force belonged to trade unions in 1997. There are four main Puerto Rican unions represented on the island, the largest of which is the General Confederation of Puerto Rican Workers. Wages tend to adhere closely to the US statutory minimum, which applies to Puerto Rico.

[23] AGRICULTURE

In 1940, agriculture employed 43% of the work force; by 2000, about 3% of the Puerto Rican labor force had agricultural jobs. Nowhere is this decline more evident than in the sugar industry. Production peaked at 1,300,000 tons in 1952, when 150,000 cane cutters were employed; by 1978, however, production was 300,000 tons, fewer than 20,000 cutters were in the fields, and the industry was heavily subsidized. By 2000, only 2,500 people were employed in the sugar industry, mostly in the fields, and Puerto Rico was importing most of its sugar from the US mainland and the Dominican Republic. The hilly terrain makes mechanization difficult, and manual cutting contributes to production costs that are much higher than those of Hawaii and Louisiana. Despite incentives and subsidies, tobacco production has practically ceased, and coffee production—well adapted to the highlands—falls far short of domestic consumption, although about 10% of the best quality crops are exported to Asia, Europe, and the US. Plantains are an important crop, and ornamental plants, exotic fruits, mangoes, vegetables, and bananas are also grown on plots and on former sugar cane fields.

[24]ANIMAL HUSBANDRY

By the close of 1995 there were 429,000 cattle and 196,000 hogs and pigs on Puerto Rico farms and ranches. Production of meat animals in 1995 included 39.69 million lb (18,000 metric tons) of beef, and 33.075 million lb (15,000 metric tons) of pork. Sales of cattle and calves amounted to $51.6 million in 1992; hogs and pigs, $11.6 million.

Leading dairy and poultry products in 1995 were 822.465 million lb (373,000 metric tons) of milk, 39,690 lb (18 metric tons) of eggs, and 136.71 million lb (62,000 metric tons) of broilers. In 1995, there were about 14 million chickens on Puerto Rican poultry farms. Dairy and poultry sales in 1992 totaled $197.7 million and $98.9 million, respectively.

Approximately 23,473,000 lb of livestock products were produced in 2002, for a total value of $29,534,000. Although increases in dairy, beef, egg, pork, and poultry production have been realized in the early 2000s, those increases have not kept up with domestic demand, so these products are also imported.

[25]FISHING

Although sport fishing, especially for blue marlin, is an important tourist attraction, the waters surrounding Puerto Rico are too deep to lend themselves to commercial fishery. Tuna brought in from African and South American waters and processed on the western shore provides much of the canned tuna sold in eastern US markets. Landings in 1995 amounted to 3,892,000 lb, valued at $7.05 million. Leading species by quantity (and value) included: snappers, 1,119,000 lb ($2.3 million); tuna, 135,100 lb (179,300); dolphinfish (or mahi-mahi), 223,600 lb ($325,600); spiny lobster, 288,600 lb ($1.22 million); mackerel, 204,000 lb ($337,700); and conch (snail) meats, 221,900 lb ($499,800). In 1994, 86% of the total catch came from marine fishing.

Five aquacultural projects covering some 550 acres (220 hectares) were operating in 1992, including the largest freshwater prawn farm in the Americas. Other species produced by Puerto Rican aquaculture include saltwater shrimp, red tilapia fish, and ornamental species.

Approximately 4,497,000 lb of fish were produced in 2002, for a total value of $10,278,000.

[26]FORESTRY

Puerto Rico lost its self-sufficiency in timber production by the mid-19th century, as population expansion, increasing demand for food, and extraction of native and endemic woods for export led to massive deforestation. Today, Puerto Rico must import nearly all of its wood and paper products. The public forest system covers 86,095 acres (34,842 hectares), of which 58,249 acres (23,573 hectares) are part of the Puerto Rico State Forest system and 27,846 acres (11,269 hectares) are part of the Caribbean National Forest.

[27]MINING

The estimated value of nonfuel mineral commodities produced in Puerto Rico was $84.8 million in 1995, excluding the value of crushed stone, which accounts for approximately 30% of the commonwealth's mineral value and is the island's 2nd leading mineral commodity. In 1995, 10.9 million metric tons of crushed stone were produced, for a value of $80.8 million. Even with crushed stone being excluded, Puerto Rico's mineral value was greater than that of seven mainland states. Cement is the most valuable mineral commodity produced. Lime ($3,650,000) and clay ($370,000) production in 1995 posted changes of 23% and 9.4%, respectively, from the values reported in 1994.

A multiyear study of the island's known and undiscovered mineral resources indicated that at least 11 different types of metallic mineral deposits, including copper, iron, gold, manganese, silver, molybdenum, zinc, lead, and other minerals, occur on the island in additon to the industrial minerals (cement, stone, clay, and sand and gravel) currently being produced.

Approximately 1,500 people were employed in mining in 2002. Mining is currently limited to quarry operations.

[28]ENERGY AND POWER

Puerto Rico is almost totally dependent on imported crude oil for its energy needs, particularly electricity generation. Oil accounted for 93% of total primary energy consumption in 2001. The island has not yet developed any fossil fuel resources of its own, and its one experimental nuclear reactor, built on the south coast at Rincon in 1964, was shut down after a few years. Solar-powered hot-water heaters have been installed in a few private homes and at La Fortaleza. Inefficiency in the public transport system has encouraged commonwealth residents to rely on private vehicles, thereby increasing the demands for imported petroleum. In 2002, Puerto Rico imported and consumed 193,000 barrels per day of oil; the vast majority of its imports came from American and Caribbean suppliers.

As of 2003, the commonwealth's refining capacity was 93,000 barrels per day, from two operating refining facilities, the Caribbean Petroleum Refining facility on Bayamon, and the Shell Chemical's facility in Yabucoa. A third refinery at Guayama is used for storage. Puerto Rico also has petroleum storage at its Proterm facility.

Puerto Rico began importing liquefied natural gas in 2000 to feed its 540-MW EcoEléctrica gas-fired plant in Peñuelas.

As of 2001, Puerto Rico consumed 180,000 short tons of coal each year, all of it imported. Since becoming operational in 2002, a new 454-MW coal-fired plant in Guayama increased the use of coal. The plant was recognized as one of the cleanest coal-fired plants in the world.

The commonwealth generated approximately 19.4 billion kilowatt hours of electricity in 2001, mostly from five oil-fired generators, but a fraction came from small hydroelectric dams. The Puerto Rico Electric Power Authority (PREPA) is Puerto Rico's only distributor of electric power.

The first non-incineration waste-to-energy power plant in the United States was being developed as of 2003 in Caguas. The proposed plant is to use a gasification process that will break down approximately 3,300 tons of waste per day into basic elements and electricity.

[29]INDUSTRY

Value added by manufacture surpassed $8.6 billion in 1982, more than double the total for 1977. In 1949, about 55,200 Puerto Rican workers were employed in industrial jobs, 26% of them in sugar refining. By 1992, despite the loss of many jobs in the sugar industry, the number was 158,181 with a total payroll of $2.7 billion. The leading employment categories in 1992 were apparel and textiles, 30,700; chemicals and allied products, 25,400; food and kindred products, 21,000; electric and electronic equipment, 18,400; and instruments, 15,900. The growth areas were electric and electronic equipment, up 47% from 1977, and instruments and related products, up 60%.

According to the 1992 Census of Manufactures, the value of shipments amounted to $31 million, of which chemicals and allied products accounted for $13.3 billion; food and kindred products, $5.2 billion; and electronic and electric equipment, $2.8 billion.

There were more than 90 pharmaceutical plants representing 20 of the world's leading drug and health companies. The largest included Johnson & Johnson (Rio Piedras), Abbott Chemicals (Barceloneta), Bristol-Myers Squibb (Humacao), Warner-Lambert (Vega Baja), and Schering-Plough (Manati). In 1991, Baxter International (medical devices) was one of the commonwealth's largest non–locally based manufacturers, with 10 plants;

Westinghouse Electric (electric components) had 15; Sara Lee (men's underwear), 6; and Motorola (radio equipment), 4.

In addition to the production of pharmaceuticals, electrical and electronic products, and textiles, other industries include: bottling, chemicals, clay and glass, distilling, leather, metal (including precision instruments), printing, publishing, and software manufacturing.

Industries tend to be labor intensive. The construction industry has been a growth area in recent years; in 1997, construction growth was estimated at around 15%. By 2003, however, the construction sector saw a downward trend. Manufacturing in 2003 accounted for 40% of GDP, more than double the percentage share of the US mainland. In 2002, employment in manufacturing declined by 8.5%, compared with a decline of 6.9% on the mainland.

Puerto Rico has two foreign free-trade zones, in Mayagüez and San Juan. In January 1987, the Puerto Rico Industrial Incentives Act was passed to make more manufacturing and export service industries eligible for tax exemptions.

30COMMERCE

Wholesale trade in Puerto Rico in 1992 involved 2,651 establishments and major distributors, with sales of $10,187.7 million. Merchant wholesalers accounted for 90.8% of establishments and 83.4% of wholesale trade. Durable goods accounted for only 34.1% of sales. Wholesale trade in 2002 involved 2,674 businesses, 2,180 of which were firms employing fewer than 20 employees. There were 41,454 employees engaged in wholesale trade, which was a reduction of 3.8% compared with 2001.

Retail trade during 1992 involved 13,534 establishments, the major sectors being food and apparel stores. Total retail sales in 1992 amounted to $11,707 million. Two large shopping centers, Plaza las Americas and Plaza Carolina, are in the San Juan area. The San Juan area alone had retail sales of nearly $3.3 billion in 1992, or over 28.1% of the total. In 2002, 14,529 businesses were engaged in retail trade, 12,474 of which employed fewer than 20 persons. There were 172,619 employees involved in retail trade, which was a reduction of 0.5% compared with 2001.

Retail sales stood at approximately $15 billion in 2001, and several new retail chains established or expanded operations in 2002. Radio Shack announced at the end of 2002 that its best selling store in the world was the one at Plaza las Americas, with $6 million in revenue for fiscal year 2002.

Foreign trade is a significant factor in Puerto Rico's economy. Trade between the US and Puerto Rico is unrestricted. Puerto Rico is the US's 8th-largest trading partner and the world's 4th-largest purchaser of US goods per capita. In 2001, the island's imports were $29.1 billion and exports $46.9 billion. (In 2000, exports of pharmaceutical products reached $20.8 billion.) During 2001, the US received $41.4 billion of Puerto Rico's exports and supplied about $15.6 billion of its imports. The principal reason for the relative decline in imports from the continental US has been the heavy volume and cost of oil imports, especially from Venezuela, and auto imports and other goods from Japan. In 2002, Puerto Rico imported $6.3 billion in goods and services from Ireland, 2nd behind the US. Puerto Rico's 2nd largest export market behind the US was the United Kingdom ($731 million). More than 100 of US Fortune 500 multinational companies have industrial plants located in Puerto Rico.

31CONSUMER PROTECTION

Consumer protection is the responsibility of Puerto Rico's cabinet-level Department of Consumer Affairs.

32BANKING

Puerto Rico's first bank began operations in 1850. As of 2003, there were 14 commercial banks in Puerto Rico (most are local corporations, with the rest being US branches and foreign interests). The government owns and operates two banks, the Government Development Bank and the Economic Development Bank. Banco Popular de Puerto Rico continues to be the largest domestic bank in Puerto Rico, with $18 billion in assets and 200 branches (2003), followed by Banco Santander Puerto Rico, with $7.5 billion in assets in 2002 and 66 branches. Both are subsidiaries of bank holding companies, the former incorporated in Puerto Rico, the latter in Spain.

Since 1992, a new type of institution has flourished in Puerto Rico, promoted by the government: the international banking entity. International banking entities are completely tax-exempt but can only receive deposits from non-residents. As the end of 2002, there were 34 international banking entities in Puerto Rico with total combined assets of $50 billion. Citibank controls 40% of these assets.

The credit union industry is also thriving in Puerto Rico. There were 144 credit unions throughout the island in 2002.

US corporations no longer operate tax-free in Puerto Rico. Amendments made to the US Internal Revenue Code tax laws require the payment of federal taxes on a portion of their income.

In addition to the Government Development Bank, founded in 1948, the Economic Development Bank for Puerto Rico, created in 1985, fosters the development of local businesses engaged in agriculture, manufacturing, commerce, and other services, thus decreasing the need to import goods and services. The Economic Development Bank's loan portfolio was $128.7 million in 2003, and loan disbursements amounted to $82.7 million. The average of loan principal by sector in 2003 was: agriculture, 30%; services, 27%; business, 23%; manufacturing, 14%; and tourism, 6%. The Government Development Bank's liquidity increased 69.4% in fiscal year 2002, with $2.2 billion in reported capital.

Banks in Puerto Rico are insured by the Federal Deposit Insurance Corporation (FDIC). Automatic teller machines are located all across the island.

33INSURANCE

More than 200 Puerto Rican insurance companies collected revenues of $82.4 million (life insurance companies, $18.1 million; property and casualty, $64.3 million) in 1990/91, enforcing policies exceeding $1.5 billion. Due to Hurricane Hugo, the insurance industry suffered underwriting losses of $19.5 million in 1989. The largest life insurance company in 1990 was Seguro de Service de Salud de Puerto Rico, Inc., with written premiums exceeding $275 million. Hurricane Georges in 1998 caused $1 billion in insured property losses in Puerto Rico and the Virgin Islands.

34SECURITIES

There are no securities exchanges in Puerto Rico. Bonds issued by the Government Development Bank, exempt from federal income taxes and from the income taxes of all US states and cities, are offered for sale on the world securities market. The Puerto Rico Stock Index (PRSI) is a market-value-weighted index, composed of 10 businesses with their main headquarters or main places of business in Puerto Rico. The companies included in the index are traded on national stock markets, such as the NYSE and AMEX, and in the over-the-counter market (NASDAQ). There are several hundred broker-dealer firms registered to do business in Puerto Rico. Approximately 100 organizations providing security investment advice are registered in Puerto Rico.

35PUBLIC FINANCE

Puerto Rico's annual budget is prepared by the Bureau of Budget and Management and submitted by the governor to the legislature, which has unlimited power to amend it. The fiscal year extends from 1 July to 30 June.

In 1959/60, transfers from the US government amounted to $44 million, or less than 13% of all revenues. By 1972/73, receipts from the US government represented 23% of all revenues; by 1977/78, more than 29%. In 1995/96 intergovernmental transfers from the US government amounted to $2.9 billion, or 30.0% of the commonwealth government's receipts.

Puerto Rico's revenues were $6.7 billion, with expenditures of $9.6 billion during 1999/2000.

Of expenditures, 3.3% were assigned to economic development and 26.2% to public housing and welfare; education accounted for 25.4% of the central government's expenditures.

36 TAXATION

The Puerto Rican Federal Relations Act stipulates that the commonwealth is exempt from US internal revenue laws. The federal income tax is not levied on permanent residents of Puerto Rico, but federal Social Security and unemployment taxes are deducted from payrolls, and the commonwealth government collects an income tax. Corporations in Puerto Rico are also taxed, though some companies fell under Section 936 financing until it was repealed in 1996.

Section 936 of the Internal Revenue Code exempted certain corporations from paying taxes for periods ranging from 10 to 25 years, allowing subsidiaries of US corporations virtual exemption from US corporate income taxes. The exemption was passed in 1976 to encourage economic development on the island. At the time of repatriation of profits to the US stockholder, the Puerto Rican government imposed a "tollgate" of 5–10%. Section 936 was replaced with Section 30A in 1996, which reduced the amount of income companies could claim as non-taxable to 60% of wages and capital investment.

The government in 2001 also enacted a series of 27 laws to further economic development and foreign investment, primary among them Laws 145, 169, and 225. These provide incentives or tax credits that could in effect reduce corporate income tax to as low as 2%; a 10% income tax credit for companies that purchase locally produced goods for export, or to be used in local manufacturing for local consumption; and lower tax rates directed to businesses that establish hemispheric, global, or Latin American headquarters in Puerto Rico.

Property, excise, and franchise taxes are also levied by the government. Excise taxes on new and used cars are an important source of revenue for the government.

37 ECONOMIC POLICY

Inaugurated during the 1940s, Operation Bootstrap had succeeded by 1982 in attracting investments from more than 500 US corporations. The principal Puerto Rican agencies responsible for this transformation are the Administración de Fomento Económico, known as Fomento (Development), and its subsidiary, the Puerto Rico Industrial Development Co. (PRIDCO), which help select plant sites, build factories, hire and train workers, and arrange financing. Fomento reorganized certain industries, taking a direct role, for example, in promoting export sales of Puerto Rican rum. At first, Fomento brought in apparel and textile manufacturers, who needed relatively unskilled workers. More recently, with the improvement in Puerto Rico's educational system, Fomento has emphasized such technologically advanced industries as pharmaceuticals and electronics. Industrialization has also required heavy investment in roads, power, water facilities, and communications systems.

The primary incentives to investment in Puerto Rico have been lower wage scales than in the continental US and the exemption of up to 90% of corporate profits from island corporate and property taxes for five years, with a descending rate of exemption that could last as long as 235 years in some regions. The commonwealth government created a 218-acre (88-hectare) free-trade zone in the San Juan area that allows companies to assemble imports duty-free in government-built warehouses for export from the island.

The government's Economic Development Council reported in 2002 that by the end of fiscal year 2003, $3 billion would have been invested in manufacturing projects and $500 million in tourism. In 2002, $2 billion was invested in public works, and $2 billion was budgeted for 2003. Between 2001 and 2003, $4.3 billion was targeted for six economic development regions, including the Mayaguez-Ponce Expressway and the Santiago Channel.

PRIDCO reported that 253 new businesses were established in 2002 with 11,296 new jobs created with $1.1 billion in investment. Approximately 5,200 jobs were retained with a $170 million investment, and 110 projects were being promoted, with a possible 15,724 new jobs being created with $408 million in investment.

The government's plans for urban center rehabilitation in 2003 included $165.5 million for 80 revitalization projects in 18 municipalities. Economic development was being geared toward five sectors: pharmaceuticals, biotechnology, medical instruments, communication and information technology, and health services. The government launched "Puerto Rico 2025," a long-term economic and social development plan directed to ensuring the commonwealth's competitiveness in the global economy.

38 HEALTH

Health conditions in Puerto Rico have improved remarkably since 1940, when the average life expectancy was only 46 years. A resident of Puerto Rico born in 2003 could expect to live 77.26 years. Infant mortality declined from 113 per l,000 live births in 1940 to 9.38 in 1999. The leading causes of death in 1940 were diseases brought on by malnutrition or infection: diarrhea, enteritis, tuberculosis, and pneumonia. By 2002, the most common causes of death, in order of prevalence, were heart disease (139 per 100,000 population); cancer (115 per 100,000); and diabetes mellitus (56 per 100,000). In 1999, 93 people died as a result of work-related accidents. In 2000, there were 153,598 people with visual disabilities, and 191,997 with developmental problems.

There were 25,525 confirmed adult and adolescent cases of HIV/AIDS in 2001, and 395 confirmed child cases of AIDS. As of 2002, the annual number of registered cases of AIDS was 1,024.

In 2002, Puerto Rico had 45 private hospitals and 13 public hopitals. There were 12,178 hospital beds available in 2002There were 17.5 physicians per 10,000 people. Annual national health expenditure as a percentage of GDP was 6.03%. The budget for health in 1999/00 was $993.3 million; of that amount, $570.3 came from federal contributions.

As a result of health reform, the government now finances a medical insurance program contracted to the private sector. As of late 2000, all 78 municipalities had been incorporated into the health insurance plan, with 99% insured and 1.8 million participants in the plan.

39 SOCIAL WELFARE

Since the mid-1960s, residents of Puerto Rico have been eligible for most of the programs that apply throughout the 50 states. About one-fourth of the commonwealth's budget is appropriated for public housing and welfare. Federal grants, transfers, and expenditures in Puerto Rico amounted to nearly one-quarter of the GNP in 1990. The school lunch program received $117.7 million in 1996.

With the enactment of the Personal Responsibility and Work Opportunity Reconciliation Act of 1996, the US government has changed the form and regulations for many of its social welfare programs; most significantly, it replaces Aid to Families with

Dependent Children (AFDC), an open-ended entitlement program, with Temporary Assistance for Needy Families (TANF), a limited system of assistance funded largely through federal block grants. The reform act also impacts the food stamp program, the Supplemental Security Income program, and the child nutrition program. The law took effect on 1 July 1997 and provided $16.38 billion in block grants for fiscal years 1997–2002.

Because unemployment is high and wages are low, Social Security benefits are below the US average. In 2001, benefits averaging $577 per month were paid to 677,130 residents. Island residents are not eligible for Supplemental Security Income. Weekly unemployment benefits averaged $102.82 in 1999, lower than any of the 50 states.

40HOUSING

In 1990, there were a total of 1,184,382 housing units with 2.97 persons per unit, up from 867,697 units in 1980, when there were 3.66 persons per occupied unit. The total value of housing construction in 1992 was an estimated $632 million, down from $754 million in 1991. In 1993, 9,785 new units valued at $381.7 million were authorized. During 1995/96, Puerto Rico received $386.7 million in aid from the US Department of Housing and Urban Development, including $132.3 million in community development block grants.

Between 2001 and 2003, about $1.35 million was spent to renovate 139 public housing projects. Investment in elderly housing was $105 million for 994 units in 22 public housing projects. There were 15,985 housing units constructed during this period.

41EDUCATION

Puerto Rico has made enormous strides in public education. In 1900, only 14% of the island's school-age children were actually in school; the proportion had increased to 50% by 1940 and 85% by the late 1970s. The government encouraged school attendance among the poor in the 1940s and 1950s by providing inexpensive shoes, free lunches, school uniforms, and small scholarships. Today, education is compulsory for children between 6 and 16 years of age, and nearly two out of ten commonwealth budget dollars goes to education. About 93.8% of the population is literate (2001).

In the 2002/03 academic year there were 596,350 students attending public school, and 210,665 students attending private schools. Instruction is carried out in Spanish, but English is taught at all levels. In 2002/03, there were 1,532 public schools, and 545 private schools in Puerto Rico.

The main state-supported institution of higher learning is the University of Puerto Rico, with its main campus at Rico Piedras. The system also included doctorate-level campuses at Mayagüez and San Juan (for medical sciences), and four year colleges at Aguadilla, Arecibo, Bayamon, Carolina, Cayey, Humacao, Ponce, and Utuado. The 39 private institutions in 2002/03 included Inter-American University, with campuses at Hato Rey, San German, and other locations, and the Catholic University of Puerto Rico, at Ponce. In 2002/03, 191,552 students were enrolled at higher education institutions in Puerto Rico.

42ARTS

The Tapia Theater in Old San Juan is the island's major showcase for local and visiting performers, including the Taller de Histriones group and *zarzuela* (comic opera) troupes from Spain. The Institute of Puerto Rican Culture produces an annual theatrcal festival. The Fine Arts Center features entertainment ranging from ballet, opera, and symphonies to drama, jazz, and popular music.

Puerto Rico has its own symphony orchestra and conservatory of music. Both were formerly directed by Pablo Casals, and the annual Music Festival Casals, which he founded, still attracts world-renowned musicians to the island each May. The Opera de Camara tours several houses. Puerto Rico supports both a classical ballet company (the Ballets de San Juan), and the Areyto Folkloric Group, which performs traditional folk dances. Salsa, a popular style pioneered by Puerto Rican musicians like Tito Puente, influenced the development of pop music on the US mainland during the 1970s. Puerto Rico generated $805,000 in federal funds to support its arts programs in 1996. The NEA contributed $523,500 to the Institute of Puerto Rican Culture in 2002. The NEA has also contributed to the arts education programs developed by the Institute of Puerto Rican Culture, and supported the Opera de Camara in Old San Juan and the Ballet Concierto de Puerto Rico. The Puerto Rican Community Foundation, Inc., has received funding through the NEA's challenge grant program. In 2002, the Puerto Rican government devoted $25 million to a Public Arts Project, developing 97 works of art in 18 municipalities as part of an urban revitalization program.

43LIBRARIES AND MUSEUMS

In 1996/97, Puerto Rico's public libraries contained about 609,391 volumes and had a combined circulation of 479,133. The University of Puerto Rico Library at Rio Piedras held 1,804,010 books in 2003; the library of the Puerto Rico Conservatory of Music, in San Juan, has a collection of music written by Puerto Rican and Latin American composers. La Casa del Libro, also in San Juan, is a library-museum of typographic and graphic arts. There were some 50 museums in Puerto Rico in 2003, among them the Museo de Arte de Ponce (Luis A. Ferre Foundation) has paintings, sculptures, and archaeological artifacts, as well as a library. The Marine Station Museum in Mayagüez exhibits Caribbean marine specimens and sponsors research and field trips.

44COMMUNICATIONS

Puerto Rico is one of the most advanced and fastest growing telecommunications markets in the Caribbean region. The Puerto Rico Telephone Co. was founded in 1914 by two German sugar brokers, Sosthenes and Hernand Behn, best known today as the creators of International Telephone and Telegraph (ITT). In 1974 the Puerto Rican government bought the phone company from ITT. In 2002, there were an estimated 1.329 million telephone lines on the island. In 2002, there were an estimated 1.211 million cellular phone subscribers, which represented 47.7% of the total number of telephone subscribers.

On 12 September 1996, Law 213 (known as Puerto Rico's Telecommunications Act of 1996) was enacted. The Act created the Puerto Rico Telecommunications Regulatory Board with jurisdiction over all telecommunications companies providing services on the island. As of 2003, as a result of the 1996 law, 233 telecommunications companies had begun operations on the island. The Puerto Rico Telephone Co. has a 93% market share of the local telecommunications market, and Centennial of Puerto Rico holds the remaining 7%. However, the Puerto Rico Telecommunications Regulatory Board, as of 2003, was attempting to further competition within the telecommunications industry.

WKAQ, the island's first radio station, came on the air in 1923, and the first television station, WKAQ-TV, began broadcasting in 1954. As of 2003, there were 73 AM and 50 FM radio stations. In 2003, there were 4 commercial television channels/networks with 6 affiliates, 1 public broadcast television channel/network, 3 cable television service companies (with 360,579 subscribers), and 4 satellite television providers.

There were 76 internet service providers in 2000, and approximately 600,000 internet users in 2002.

45PRESS

Puerto Rico has five major dailies: *El Nuevo Dia, El Vocero, Primera Hora, El San Juan Star,* and the *San Juan Star.* There are 22 weekly newspapers, including *El Estrella de Puerto Rico,* and *Caribbean Business,* Puerto Rico's leading business publication. There are also eight monthly newspapers. The 2003 circulation for *El Nuevo Dia* (Puerto Rico's daily with the largest circulation), was 203,058 mornings, 242,318 Sundays. The English-language *San Juan Star* won a Pulitzer Prize in 1961.

46ORGANIZATIONS

Important organizations on the island include the Puerto Rico Medical Association, Puerto Rico Manufacturers' Association, and Puerto Rico Bar Association. Also maintaining headquarters in Puerto Rico are the Association of Island Marine Laboratories of the Caribbean, Puerto Rico Rum Producers Association, Caribbean Hotel Association, and Caribbean Studies Association.

US-based agencies such as the National Puerto Rican Forum and the Puerto Rican Community Development Project assist Puerto Ricans living on the mainland. "Hometown clubs" consisting of "absent sons" (*hilos ausentes*) of various Puerto Rican towns are a typical feature of the barrios in New York and other cities in the continental US.

47TOURISM, TRAVEL, AND RECREATION

Only government and manufacturing exceed tourism in importance to the Puerto Rican economy. The industry has grown rapidly, from 65,000 tourists in 1950 to 1,088,000 in 1970, to 5 million per year in the early 2000s. Tourism employs approximately 60,000 workers.

Many hotels are located in San Juan, though the eastern part of the island also features hotels and resorts. Most tourists come for sunning, swimming, deep-sea fishing, and the fashionable shops, night clubs, and casinos of San Juan's Condado Strip. Attractions of old San Juan include two fortresses, El Morro and San Cristobal, San Jose Church (one of the oldest in the New World), and La Fortaleza, the governor's palace. The government has been encouraging tourists to journey outside of San Juan to such destinations such as the Arecibo Observatory (with its radio telescope use for research astronomy, ionospheric studies, and radar mapping), the rain forest of El Yunque, Phosphorescent Bay, colonial-style San German, and the bird sanctuary and mangrove forest on the shores of Torrecilla Lagoon. The 53-acre (21-hectare) San Juan harbor fortifications are a national historic site.

As of 2002, there were 1,826,052 registrations in hotels and *paradores,* 1,032,629 of which came from the United States. The room occupancy rate was 61.8%. During 2000/01, visitors spent $2.7 billion in Puerto Rico, a 14.2% increase over 1999/00. The 11 September 2001 terrorist attacks on the US had a negative impact on the Puerto Rican tourist industry, however, as did the 2003 USS-led war in Iraq. The World Travel and Tourism Council estimated that the war in Iraq cost Puerto Rico $262 million in lost tourism revenue and 3,800 jobs.

48SPORTS

Baseball is very popular in Puerto Rico. There is a 6-team professional winter league, in which many ball players from American and National league teams participate. There were 50 games played in the league's six ballparks in 2002. Horse racing, cockfighting, boxing, and basketball are also popular. Puerto Rico, which has its own Olympic Committee, sent a delegation to the 1980 Olympics in Moscow despite the US boycott. Other annual sporting events include the Copa Velasco Regatta, the first

leg of the Caribbean Ocean Racing Triangle, and the International Billfish Tournament in San Juan.

49FAMOUS PUERTO RICANS

Elected to represent Puerto Rico before the Spanish Cortes in 1812, Ramón Power y Giralt (1775–1813), a liberal reformer, was the leading Puerto Rican political figure of the early 19th century. Power, appointed vice president of the Cortes, participated in the drafting of the new Spanish constitution of 1812. Ramón Emeterio Betances (1827–98) became well known not only for his efforts to alleviate a cholera epidemic in 1855 but also for his crusade to abolish slavery in Puerto Rico and as a leader of a separatist movement that culminated in 1868 in the "Grito de Lares." Eugenio Maria de Hostos (1839–1903), a writer, abolitionist, and educator, spent much of his adult life in Latin America, seeking to establish a free federation of the West Indies to replace colonial rule in the Caribbean. Luis Muñoz Rivera (1859–1916), a liberal journalist, led the movement that obtained for Puerto Rico the Autonomic Charter of 1897, and he headed the cabinet that took office in 1898. With the island under US rule, Muñoz Rivera served between 1911 and 1916 as Puerto Rico's resident commissioner to the US Congress. Other important Puerto Rican historical figures include Juan Alejo Arizmendi (1760?–1814), the first Puerto Rican–born bishop, appointed to the See of San Juan; José de Diego (1866–1918), a noted poet and gifted orator who, under the Foraker Act, became the first speaker of the island house of delegates and was a champion of independence for Puerto Rico.

The dominant political figure in 20th-century Puerto Rico was Luis Muñoz Marin (1898–1980), founder of the Popular Democratic Party in 1938 and president of the Puerto Rico senate from 1940 to 1948. Muñoz, the first native-born elected governor of the island (1948–64), devised the commonwealth relationship that has governed the island since 1952. Another prominent 20th-century figure, Antonio R. Barceló (1869–1939), led the Unionista Party after Muñoz Rivera's death, was the first president of the senate under the Jones Act, and was later the leader of the Liberal Party. In 1946, Jesús T. Pinero (1897–1952) became the first Puerto Rican appointed governor of the island by a US president; he had been elected as resident commissioner of Puerto Rico to the US Congress two years before. Pedro Albizu Campos (1891–1965), a Harvard Law School graduate, presided over the militant Nationalist Party and was until his death the leader of forces that advocated independence for Puerto Rico by revolution. In 1945, Gilberto Concepción de Gracia (1909–68), also a lawyer, helped found the more moderate Puerto Rican Independence Party. Herman Badillo (b.1929) was the first person of Puerto Rican birth to be a voting member of the US House of Representatives, as congressman from New York, and Maurice Ferré (b.1935), elected mayor of Miami in 1973, was the first native-born Puerto Rican to run a large US mainland city. Hernán Padilla (b.1938), mayor of San Juan, became the first Hispanic American elected to head the US Conference of Mayors (1984).

Women have participated actively in Puerto Rican politics. Ana Roqué de Duprey (1853–1933) led the Asociación Puertorriquena de Mujeres Sufragistas, organized in late 1926, while Milagros Benet de Mewton (1868–1945) presided over the Liga Social Sufragista, founded in 1917. Both groups actively lobbied for the extension of the right to vote to Puerto Rican women, not only in Puerto Rico but in the US and other countries as well. Felisa Rincón de Gautier (1897–1994), mayor of San Juan from 1946 to 1968, was named Woman of the Americas in 1954, the year she presided over the Inter-American Organization for Municipalities. Carmen Delgado Votaw (b.1935) was the first person of Puerto Rican birth to be elected president of the Inter-American Commission of Women, the oldest international organization in the field of women's rights. Sila María Calderón, elected in 2000, became the commonwealth's first female governor.

Manuel A. Alonso (1822–89) blazed the trail for a distinctly Puerto Rican literature with the publication, in 1849, of *El Gibaro*, the first major effort to depict the traditions and mores of the island's rural society. Following him in the development of a rich Puerto Rican literary tradition were, among many others, that most prolific of 19th-century Puerto Rican writers, Alejandro Tapia y Rivera (1826–82), adept in history, drama, poetry, and other forms of literary expression; essayist and critic Manuel Elzaburu (1852–92); novelist Manuel Zeno Gandia (1855–1930); and poets Lola Rodriguez de Tió (1843–1924) and José Gautier Benitez (1848–80). The former's patriotic lyrics, popularly acclaimed, were adapted to become Puerto Rico's national anthem. Among 20th-century Puerto Rican literary figures are poets Luis Lloréns Torres (1878–1944), Luis Palés Matos (1898–1959), and Julia de Burgos (1916–1953) and essayists and critics Antonio S. Pedreira (1898–1939), Tomás Blanco (b.1900), José A. Balseiro (b.1900), Margot Arce (b.1904), Concha Meléndez (b.1904), Nilita Vientós Gastón (b.1908), and Maria T. Babin (1910–89). In the field of fiction, René Marqués (1919–79), Abelardo Diaz Alfaro (1919–99), José Luis González (b.1926), and Pedro Juan Soto (b.1928) are among the best known outside Puerto Rico.

In the world of entertainment, Academy Award winners José Ferrer (1912–92) and Rita Moreno (b.1931) are among the most famous. Notable in classical music are cellist-conductor Pablo Casals (b.Spain, 1876–1973), a longtime resident of Puerto Rico; pianist Jesús Maria Sanromá (1902–84); and opera star Justino Diaz (b.1940). Well-known popular musicians include Tito Puente (b.New York, 1923—2000) and José Feliciano (b.1945).

Roberto Clemente (1934–72), one of baseball's most admired performers and a member of the Hall of Fame, played on 12 National League All-Star teams and was named Most Valuable Player in 1966.

50 BIBLIOGRAPHY

Babin, Maria Teresa. *The Puerto Ricans' Spirit: Their History, Life and Culture.* New York: Collier, 1971.

Carr, Raymond. *Puerto Rico: A Colonial Experiment.* New York: Vintage, 1984.

Colonial Dilemma: Critical Perspectives on Contemporary Puerto Rico. Boston: South End Press, 1993.

Fernandez, Ronald. *The Disenchanted Island: Puerto Rico and the United States in the Twentieth Century.* Westport, Conn.: Praeger, 1996.

———. *Puerto Rico Past and Present: An Encyclopedia.* Westport, Conn.: Greenwood Press, 1998.

Hostos, Adolfo de. *Diccionario Historico Bibliografico Comentado de Puerto Rico.* San Juan: Academia Puertorriquena de la Historia, 1976.

Morales Carrion, Arturo. *Puerto Rico and the Non-Hispanic Caribbean.* Rio Piedras: University of Puerto Rico, 1971.

———. *Puerto Rico: A Political and Cultural History.* New York: Norton, 1984.

Morris, Nancy. *Puerto Rico: Culture, Politics, and Identity.* Westport, Conn.: Praeger, 1995.

Puerto Rico Federal Affairs Administration. *Puerto Rico, U.S.A.* Washington, DC., 1979.

US Commission on Civil Rights. *Puerto Ricans in the Continental United States: An Uncertain Future.* Washington, D.C., 1976.

US Department of Commerce. *Economic Study of Puerto Rico.* 2 vols. Washingtion, D.C., 1979.

Vivo, Paquita. *The Puerto Ricans: An Annotated Bibliography.* New York: Bowker, 1973.

Votaw, Carmen Delgado. *Puerto Rican Women: Some Biographical Profiles.* Washington, D.C.: National Conference of Puerto Rican Woman, 1978.

Wagenheim, Kal. *Puerto Rico: A Profile.* 2nd ed. New York: Praeger, 1975.

———, and Olga Jimenez de Wagenheim (eds.). *The Puerto Ricans: A Documentary History.* Maplewood, N.J.: Waterfrom Press, 1988.

Wells, Henry. *The Modernization of Puerto Rico.* Cambridge, Mass.: Harvard University Press, 1969.

UNITED STATES
CARIBBEAN DEPENDENCIES

NAVASSA

Navassa, a 5-sq-km (2-sq-mi) island between Jamaica and Haiti, was claimed by the United States under the Guano Act of 1856. The island, located at 18°2′N and 75°1′W, is uninhabited except for a lighthouse station under the administration of the coast guard.

VIRGIN ISLANDS OF THE UNITED STATES

The Virgin Islands of the United States lie about 64 km (40 mi) n of Puerto Rico and 1,600 km (1,000 mi) SSE of Miami, between 17°40′ and 18°25′ N and 64°34′ and 65°3′ N. The island group extends 82 km (51 mi) N–S and 80 km (50 mi) E–W with a total area of at least 353 sq km (136 sq mi). Only 3 of the more than 50 islands and cays are of significant size: St. Croix, 218 sq km (84 sq mi) in area; St. Thomas, 83 sq km (32 sq mi); and St. John, 52 sq km (20 sq mi). The territorial capital, Charlotte Amalie, on St. Thomas, has one of the finest harbors in the Caribbean.

St. Croix is relatively flat, with a terrain suitable for sugarcane cultivation. St. Thomas is mountainous and little cultivated, but it has many snug harbors. St. John, also mountainous, has fine beaches and lush vegetation; about two-thirds of St. John's area has been declared a national park. The subtropical climate, with temperatures ranging from 21° to 32°C (70–90 °F) and an average temperature of 25°C (77°F), is moderated by northeast trade winds. Rainfall, the main source of fresh water, varies widely, and severe droughts are frequent. The average yearly rainfall is 114 cm (45 in), mostly during the summer months.

The population of the US Virgin Islands was estimated at 123,498 in 2002, up from 96,569 at the time of the 1980 census. St. Croix has two principal towns: Christiansted and Frederiksted. Economic development has brought an influx of new residents, mainly from Puerto Rico, other Caribbean islands, and the US mainland. Most of the permanent inhabitants are descendants of slaves who were brought from Africa in the early days of Danish rule, and about 80% of the population is black. English is the official and most widely spoken language.

Some of the oldest religious congregations in the Western Hemisphere are located in the Virgin Islands. St. Thomas Synagogue, founded in 1796, is the 2nd-oldest in the New World, and the Lutheran Congregation of St. Thomas, founded in 1666, is one of the three oldest congregations in the United States. As of 1999, Baptists made up an estimated 42% of the population, Roman Catholics 34%, and Episcopalians 17%.

In 2000, there were 856 km (531.6 mi) of roads in the US Virgin Islands; the road of the US Virgin Islands are the only US roads where driving is done of the left side of the road. Cargo-shipping services operate from Baltimore, Jacksonville, and Miami via Puerto Rico. In addition, weekly shipping service is available from Miami. Both St. Croix and St. Thomas have airports, with St. Croix's facility handling the larger number of jet flights from the continental United States and Europe.

Excavations at St. Croix in the 1970s uncovered evidence of a civilization perhaps as ancient as AD 100. Christopher Columbus, who reached the islands in 1493, named them for the martyred virgin St. Ursula. At this time, St. Croix was inhabited by Carib Indians, who were eventually driven from the island by Spanish

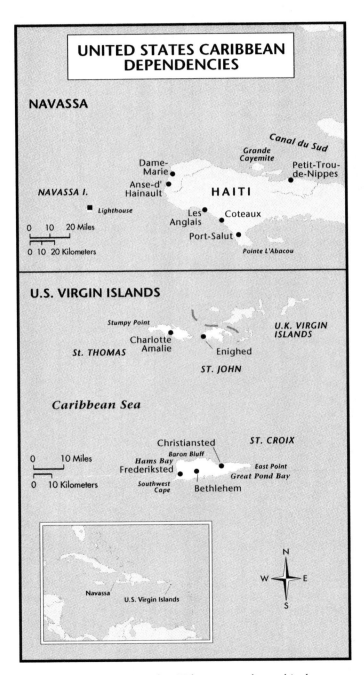

soldiers in 1555. During the 17th century, the archipelago was divided into two territorial units, one controlled by the British, the other (now the US Virgin Islands) controlled by Denmark. The separate history of the latter unit began with the settlement of St. Thomas by the Danish West India Company in 1672. St.

John was claimed by the company in 1683, and St. Croix was purchased from France in 1733. The holdings of the company were taken over as a Danish crown colony in 1754. Sugarcane, cultivated by slave labor, was the backbone of the islands' prosperity in the 18th and early 19th centuries. After brutally suppressing several slave revolts. Denmark abolished slavery in the colony in 1848. A long period of economic decline followed, until Denmark sold the islands to the United States in 1917 for $25 million. Congress granted US citizenship to the Virgin Islanders in 1927. In 1931, administration of the islands was transferred from the Department of the Navy to the Department of the Interior, and the first civilian governor was appointed. In the late 1970s, the Virgin Islands government began to consider ways to expand self-rule. A UN delegation in 1977 found little interest in independence, however, and a locally drafted constitution was voted down by the electorate in 1979.

The chief executive of the Virgin Islands is the territorial governor, elected by direct popular vote (prior to 1970, territorial governors were appointed by the US president). Constitutionally, the US Congress has plenary authority to legislate for the territory. Enactment of the Revised Organic Act of the Virgin Islands on 22 July 1954 vested local legislative power—subject to veto by the governor—in a unicameral legislature. Since 1972, the islands have sent one nonvoting representative to the US House of Representatives. Courts are under the US federal judiciary; the two federal district court judges are appointed by the US president. Territorial court judges, who preside over misdemeanor and traffic cases, are appointed by the governor and confirmed by the legislature. The district court has appellate jurisdiction over the territorial court.

Tourism, which accounts for approximately 70% of both GDP and employment is the islands' principal economic activity. The number of tourists rose dramatically throughout the late 1960s and early 1970s, from 448,165 in 1964 to over 2 million per year in the 1990s. Rum remains an important manufacture, with petroleum refining (on St. Croix) a major addition in the late 1960s. Economic development is promoted by the US-government-owned Virgin Islands Corp. In 2000 the gross domestic product per capita was $15,000. The unemployment rate was 4.9% in 1999, down from 6.2% in 1994. Exports for 1992 totaled $1.8 billion while imports totaled $2.2 billion. The island's primary export is refined petroleum products. Raw crude oil constitutes the Virgin Island's principal import. In 1990, median family income was $24,036. The total operating budget of the Virgin Islands government in 1994 was $364.4 million.

The territorial Department of Health provides hospital and medical services, public health services, and veterinary medicine. Education is compulsory. The College of the Virgin Islands is the territory's first institution of higher learning. There are about 62,000 main line telephones and 2,000 mobile cellular phones, 66,000 televisions, and 105,000 radios in use on the islands. The Virgin Islands had 16 radio stations (5 AM, 11 FM) and 2 television stations in 2002.

UNITED STATES PACIFIC DEPENDENCIES

AMERICAN SAMOA

American Samoa, an unincorporated and unorganized insular US territory in the South Pacific Ocean, comprises that portion of the Samoan archipelago lying E of longitude 171° w. (The rest of the Samoan islands comprise the independent state of Western Samoa.) While the Samoan group as a whole has an area of 3,121 sq km (1,205 sq mi), American Samoa consists of only seven small islands (between 14° and 15° s and 168° and 171° w) with a total area (land and water) of 197 sq km (76 sq mi). Five of the islands are volcanic, with rugged peaks rising sharply, and two are coral atolls.

The climate is hot and rainy; normal temperatures range from 24° C (75° F) in August to 32° C (90° F) during December–February; mean annual rainfall is 330 cm (130 in), the rainy season lasting from December through March. Hurricanes are common. The native flora includes flourishing tree ferns, coconut, hardwoods, and rubber trees. There are few wild animals.

As of mid-2002, the estimated population was 68,688, an increase over the 1986 population estimate of 37,500. However, the total population has remained relatively constant for many years because of the substantial number of Samoans who migrate to the United States. The inhabitants, who are concentrated on the island of Tutuila, are almost pure Polynesian. English is the official language, but Samoan is also widely spoken. Most Samoans are Christians.

The capital of the territory, Pago Pago, on Tutuila, has one of the finest natural harbors in the South Pacific and is a duty-free port. Passenger liners call there on South Pacific tours, and passenger and cargo ships arrive regularly from Japan, New Zealand, Australia, and the US west coast. There are regular air and sea services between American Samoa and Western Samoa, and scheduled flights between Pago Pago and Honolulu.

American Samoa was settled by Melanesian migrants in the 1st millennium BC. The Samoan islands were visited in 1768 by the French explorer Louis-Antoine de Bougainville, who named them the Îles des Navigateurs as a tribute to the skill of their native boatmen. In 1889, the United States, the United Kingdom, and Germany agreed to share control of the islands. The United Kingdom later withdrew its claim, and under the 1899 Treaty of Berlin, the United States was internationally acknowledged to have rights extending over all the islands of the Samoan group lying east of 171° w, while Germany was acknowledged to have similar rights to the islands west of that meridian. The islands of American Samoa were officially ceded to the United States by the various ruling chiefs in 1900 and 1904, and on 20 February 1929 the US Congress formally accepted sovereignty over the entire group. From 1900 to 1951, the territory was administered by the US Department of the Navy, and thereafter by the Department of the Interior. The basic law is the Constitution of 1966.

The executive branch of the government is headed by a governor who, along with the lieutenant governor, is elected by popular vote; before 1977, the two posts were appointed by the US government. Village, county, and district councils have full authority to regulate local affairs.

The legislature (Fono) is composed of the House of Representatives and the Senate. The 15 counties elect 18 *matais* (chiefs) to four-year terms in the senate, while the 20 house members are elected for two-year terms by popular vote within the counties. (There is one appointed member from Swains Island.) The secretary for Samoan affairs, who heads the Department of Local Government, is appointed by the governor. Under his administration are three district governors, the county chiefs, village mayors, and police officials. The judiciary, an independent branch of the government, functions through the high court and five district courts. Samoans living in the islands as of 17 April 1900 or born there since that date are nationals of the United States. The territory sends one delegate to the US House of Representatives.

The economy is primarily agricultural. Small plantations occupy about one-third of the land area; 90% of the land is communally owned. The principal crops are bananas, breadfruit, taro, papayas, pineapples, sweet potatoes, tapioca, coffee, cocoa, and yams. Hogs and poultry are the principal livestock raised; dairy cattle are few. The principal cash crop is copra (dried coconut meat). A third of the total labor force is employed by the federal and territorial government. The largest employers in the private sector, with more than 15% of the labor force, are two modern tuna canneries supplied with fish caught by Japanese, US, and Taiwanese fishing fleets. Between 80% and 90% of foreign trade is conducted with the United States.

Samoans are entitled to free medical treatment, including hospital care. Besides district dispensaries, the government maintains a central hospital, a tuberculosis unit, and a leprosarium. US-trained staff physicians work with Samoan medical practitioners and nurses. The LBJ Tropical Medical Center opened in 1986.

Education is a joint undertaking between the territorial government and the villages. School attendance is compulsory for all children from 6 through 18. The villages furnish the elementary-school buildings and living quarters for the teachers; the territorial government pays teachers' salaries and provides buildings and supplies for all but primary schools. Since 1964, educational television has served as a basic teaching tool in the school system. About 97% of the population is literate. In 1997, total enrollment in American Samoa's 29 public elementary and secondary schools was over 19,000. American Samoa Community College enrolled 1,178 in the fall of 2001.

Radiotelegraph circuits connect the territory with Hawaii, Fiji, and Western Samoa. Every village in American Samoa has telephone service.

GUAM

The largest and most populous of the Mariana Islands in the Western Pacific, Guam (13° 28′ N and 144° 44′ E) has an area, including land and water, of 540 sq km (208 sq mi) and is about 48 km (30 mi) long and from 6 to 12 km (4–7 mi) wide. The island is of volcanic origin; in the south, the terrain is mountainous, while the northern part is a plateau with shallow fertile soil. The central part of the island (where the capital, Agana, is located) is undulating country.

Guam lies in the typhoon belt of the Western Pacific and is occasionally subject to widespread storm damage. In May 1976, a typhoon with winds of 306 km/hr (190 mph) struck Guam, causing an estimated $300 million in damage and leaving 80% of the island's buildings in ruins. Guam has a tropical climate with little seasonal variation. Average temperature is 26°C (79°F); rainfall is substantial, reaching an annual average of more than 200 cm (80 in). Endangered species include the giant Micronesian kingfisher and Marianas crow.

The mid-2002 population, excluding transient US military and civilian personnel and their families, was estimated at 160,796, an increase over the 1986 estimate of 117,500. The increase was attributed largely to the higher birthrate and low mortality rate. The present-day Chamorro, who comprise about 37% of the permanent resident population, descend from the intermingling of the few surviving original Chamorro with the Spanish, Filipino, and Mexican settlers, plus later arrivals from the United States, United Kingdom, Korea, China, and Japan. Filipinos (26%) are the largest ethnic minority. English is the official language, although Chamorro is taught in the primary schools. The predominant religion is Roman Catholicism.

The earliest known settlers on Guam were the original Chamorro, who migrated from the Malay Peninsula to the Pacific around 1500 BC. When Ferdinand Magellan landed on Guam in 1521, it is believed that as many as 100,000 Chamorro lived on the island; by 1741, their numbers had been reduced to 5,000— most of the population either had fled the island or been killed through disease or war with the Spanish. A Spanish fort was established in 1565, and from 1696 until 1898, Guam was under Spanish rule.

Under the Treaty of Paris that ended the Spanish-American War in 1898, the island was ceded to the United States and placed under the jurisdiction of the Department of the Navy. During World War II, Guam was occupied by Japanese forces; the United States recaptured the island in 1944 after 54 days of fighting. In 1950, the island's administration was transferred from the Navy to the US Department of the Interior. Under the 1950 Organic Act of Guam, passed by the US Congress, the island was established as an unincorporated territory of the United States; Guamanians were granted US citizenship, and internal self-government was introduced.

The governor and lieutenant governor have been elected directly since 1970. A 15-member unicameral legislature elected for two years by adult suffrage is empowered to legislate on all local matters, including taxation and appropriations. The US Congress reserves the right to annul any law passed by the Guam legislature, but must do so within a year of the date it receives the text of any such law.

Judicial authority is vested in the district court of Guam, and appeals may be taken to the regular US courts of appeal and ultimately to the US Supreme Court. An island superior court and other specialized courts have jurisdiction over certain cases arising under the laws of Guam. The judge of the district court is appointed by the US president; the judges of the other courts are appointed by the governor. Guam's laws were codified in 1953.

Guam is one of the most important US military bases in the Pacific, and the island's economy has been profoundly affected by the large sums of money spent by the US defense establishment. During the late 1960s and early 1970s, when the United States took the role of a major combatant in the Vietnam conflict, Guam served as a base for long-range US bombers on sorties over Indochina. In 2001, there were 3,398 active-duty US military personnel stationed on the island.

Prior to World War II, agriculture and animal husbandry were the primary activities. By 1947, most adults were wage earners employed by the US armed forces, although many continued to cultivate small plots to supplement their earnings. Since World War II, agriculture has generally contributed less than 1% of the GNP, partly because a considerable amount of arable land is taken up by military installations. Fruits and vegetables are grown and pigs and poultry are raised for local consumption, but most food is imported. Current fish catches are insufficient to meet local demand.

Tourism has become a major industry and sparked a boom in the construction industry in the mid-1980s. The number of visitors grew rapidly from 6,600 in 1967 to around one million per year in the early 2000s, 90% of whom come from Japan. The stagnation in the Japanese economy since the early 1990s slowed the growth of Guam's tourism sector.

The Guam Rehabilitation Act of 1963 has funded the territory's capital improvement program. Further allocations in 1969 and 1977 provided over $120 million for additional capital improvements and development of the island's power installations. More than $200 million of federal funds were authorized for typhoon relief in 1977–78. Total expenditures by the government of Guam were $431 million in 2000; revenues were $420 million.

Guam's foreign trade usually shows large deficits. The bulk of Guam's trade is with the United States, Micronesia, and Japan.

US income tax laws are applicable in Guam; all internal revenue taxes derived by the United States from Guam are paid into the territory's treasury. US customs duties, however, are not levied. Guam is a duty-free port. In its trade with the US mainland, Guam is required to use US shipping.

Typical tropical diseases are practically unknown today in Guam. Tuberculosis, long the principal killer, was brought under control by the mid-1950s. The Guam Memorial Hospital has a capacity of 192 beds. Village dispensaries serve both as public health units and first-aid stations. In addition, there are a number of physicians in private practice. Specialists from the US Naval Hospital in Guam, assisting on a part-time basis, have made possible a complete program of curative medicine.

School attendance is compulsory from the age of 6 through 16. In 1998/99, 31,860 pupils were enrolled in public elementary and secondary schools. The University of Guam enrolled 3,748 students in 1998/99, and Guam Community College enrolled 4,404 students in the fall of 1998.

HOWLAND, BAKER, AND JARVIS ISLANDS

Howland Island (0°48′ N and 176°38′ W), Baker Island (0°14′ N and 176°28′ W), and Jarvis Island (0°23′ S and 160°1′ W) are three small coral islands, each about 2.6 sq km (1 sq mi) in area, belonging to the Line Islands group of the Central Pacific Ocean. All are administered directly from Washington as US unincorporated territories. Public entry is by special permit and generally restricted to scientists and educators. Howland was discovered in 1842 by US sailors, claimed by the United States in 1857, and formally proclaimed a US territory in 1935–36. It was worked for guano by US and British companies until about 1890.

Baker, 64 km (40 mi) S of Howland, and Jarvis, 1,770 km (1,100 mi) E of Howland, also were claimed by the United States in 1857, and their guano deposits were similarly worked by US and British enterprises. The United Kingdom annexed Jarvis in 1889. In 1935, the United States sent colonists from Hawaii to all three islands, which were placed under the US Department of the Interior in 1936 and are administered as part of the National Wildlife Refuge system. Baker was captured by the Japanese in 1942 and recaptured by the United States in 1944. The three islands lack fresh water and have no permanent inhabitants. They are visited annually by the US Coast Guard. A lighthouse on Howland Island is named in honor of the US aviatrix Amelia Earhart, who vanished en route to the island on a round-the-world flight in 1937.

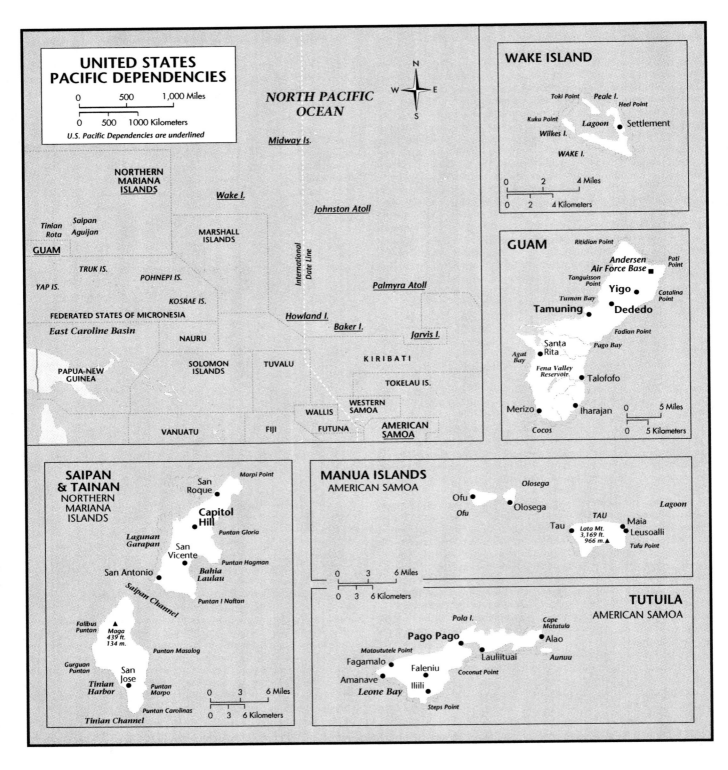

JOHNSTON ATOLL

Johnston Atoll, located in the North Pacific 1,151 km (715 mi) sw of Honolulu, consists of two islands, Johnston (16° 44′ N and 169° 31′ w) and Sand (16° 45′ N and 169° 30′ w), with a total land and water area of about 2.6 sq km (1 sq mi). The islands are enclosed by a semicircular reef. It was discovered by English sailors in 1807 and claimed by the United States in 1858. For many years, it was worked for guano and was a bird reservation.

Commissioned as a naval station in 1941, it remains an unincorporated US territory under the control of the US Department of the Air Force. In recent years, it has been used primarily for the testing of nuclear weapons.

As of January 2003, there were about 800 people living on the atoll; the population, usually standing at 1,100 government personnel and contractors, decreased significantly after the September 2001 departure of the US Army Chemical Activity

Pacific (USACAP). The atoll is equipped with an excellent satellite and radio telecommunications system.

MIDWAY

The Midway Islands (28° 12′ –17′ N and 177° 19′ –26′ w) consist of an atoll and two small islets, Eastern Island (177° 20′ w) and Sand Island (177° 22′ –24′ w), 2,100 km (1,300 mi) WNW of Honolulu. Total land and water area is 5 sq km (2 sq mi). As of 2002, 40 people made up the staff of the US Fish and Wildlife service on the atoll.

Discovered and claimed by the United States in 1859 and formally annexed in 1867, Midway became a submarine cable station early in the 20th century and an airlines station in 1935. Made a US naval base in 1941, Midway was attacked by the Japanese in December 1941 and January 1942. In one of the great battles of World War II, a Japanese naval attack on 3–6 June 1942 was repelled by US warplanes. Midway is a US unincorporated territory; there is a closed naval station, and the islands are important nesting places for seabirds. In 1993, administrative control of Midway was transferred from the US Department of the Navy to the US Department of the Interior's Fish and Wildlife Service.

NORTHERN MARIANAS

The Northern Marianas, a US commonwealth in the Western Pacific Ocean, is comprised of the Mariana Islands excluding Guam (a separate political entity). Located between 12° and 21° N and 144° and 146° E, it consists of 16 volcanic islands with a total land area of about 475 sq km (183.5 sq mi). Only six of the islands are inhabited, and most of the people live on the three largest islands—Rota, 85 sq km (33 sq mi); Saipan, 122 sq km (47 sq mi); and Tinian, 101 sq km (39 sq mi).

The climate is tropical, with relatively little seasonal change; temperatures average 21–29° C (70–85° F), and relative humidity is generally high. Rainfall averages 216 cm (85 in) per year. The southern islands, which include Rota, Saipan, and Tinian, are generally lower and covered with moderately heavy tropical vegetation. The northern islands are more rugged, reaching a high point of 959 m (3,146 ft) on Agrihan, and are generally barren due to erosion and insufficient rainfall. Pagan and Agrihan have active volcanos, and typhoons are common from August to November. Insects are numerous and ocean birds and fauna are abundant. The Marianas mallard is a local endangered species.

The Northern Marianas had an estimated population of 77,311 in mid-2002. Three-fourths of the population is descended from the original Micronesian inhabitants, known as Chamorros. There are also many descendants of migrants from the Caroline Islands and smaller numbers of Filipino and Korean laborers and settlers from the US mainland. English is the official language and Chamorro and Carolinian are taught in school. However, only 14% of the population speaks English in the home. About 90% of the people are Roman Catholic.

It is believed that the Marianas were settled by migrants from the Philippines and Indonesia. Excavations on Saipan have yielded evidence of settlement around 1500 BC. The first European to reach the Marianas, in 1521, was Ferdinand Magellan. The islands were ruled by Spain until the Spanish defeat by the United States in the Spanish-American War (1898). Guam was then ceded to the United States and the rest of the Marianas were sold to Germany. When World War I broke out, Japan took over the Northern Marianas and other German-held islands in the Western Pacific. These islands (the Northern Marianas, Carolines, and Marshalls) were placed under Japanese administration as a League of Nations mandate on 17 December 1920. Upon its withdrawal from the League in 1935, Japan began to fortify the islands, and in World War II they served as important military bases. Several of the islands were the scene of heavy fighting during the war. In the battle for control of Saipan

in June 1944, some 23,000 Japanese and 3,500 US troops lost their lives in one day's fighting. As each island was occupied by US troops, it became subject to US authority in accordance with the international law of belligerent occupation. The US planes that dropped atomic bombs on Hiroshima and Nagasaki, bringing an end to the war, took off from Tinian.

On 18 July 1947, the Northern Mariana, Caroline, and Marshall islands formally became a UN trust territory under US administration. This Trust Territory of the Pacific Islands was administered by the US Department of the Navy until 1 July 1951, when administration was transferred to the Department of the Interior. From 1953 to 1962, the Northern Marianas, with the exception of Rota, were administered by the Department of the Navy.

The people of the Northern Marianas voted to become a US commonwealth by a majority of 78.8% in a plebescite held on 17 June 1975. A covenant approved by the US Congress in March 1976 provided for the separation of the Northern Marianas from the Caroline and Marshall island groups, and for the Marianas' transition to a commonwealth status similar to that of Puerto Rico. The islands became internally self-governing in January 1978. On 3 November 1986, US president Ronald Reagan proclaimed the Northern Marianas a self-governing commonwealth; its people became US citizens. The termination of the trusteeship was approved by the UN Trusteeship Council in May 1986 and received the required approval from the UN Security Council. On 3 November 1986, the Constitution of the Commonwealth of the Northern Marianas Islands came into force.

A governor and a lieutenant governor are popularly elected for four-year terms. The legislature consists of 9 senators elected for four-year terms and 18 representatives elected for two-year terms. A district court handles matters involving federal law and a commonwealth court has jurisdiction over local matters.

The traditional economic activities were subsistence agriculture, livestock raising, and fishing, but much agricultural land was destroyed or damaged during World War II and agriculture has never resumed its prewar importance. Today, government employment and tourism are the mainstays of the economy. Tourism employs about 50% of the work force. The construction industry is also expanding, and there is some small-scale industry, chiefly handicrafts and food processing.

The Northern Marianas is heavily dependent on federal funds. The United States also pays to lease property on Saipan, Tinian, and Farallon de Medinilla islands for defense purposes. The principal exports are garments, milk, and meat; imports include foods, petroleum, construction materials, and vehicles. US currency is the official medium of exchange.

Health care is primarily the responsibility of the commonwealth government and has improved substantially since 1978. Tuberculosis, once the major health problem, has been controlled. There is a hospital on Saipan and health centers on Tinian and Rota. The largest hospital in the commonwealth is a 74 bed, 110,000 square foot facility.

Education is free and compulsory for children between the ages of 8 and 14, and literacy is high. Northern Marianas College had an enrollment of 982 in fall 2001. There are 2 AM, 1 FM, and 1 television stations.

PALMYRA ATOLL

Palmyra, an atoll in the Central Pacific Ocean, containing some 50 islets with a total area of some 10 sq km (4 sq mi), is situated about 1,600 km (1,000 mi) SSW of Honolulu at 5° 52′ N and 162° 5′ w. It was discovered in 1802 by the USS *Palmyra* and formally annexed by the United States in 1912, and was under the jurisdiction of the city of Honolulu until 1959, when Hawaii became the 50th state of the United States. It is now the responsibility of the US Department of the Interior. The atoll is privately owned by the Fullard-Leo family of Hawaii.

Kingman Reef, NW of Palmyra Atoll at 6° 25′ N and 162° 23′ N, was discovered by the United States in 1874, annexed by the United States in 1922, and became a naval reservation in 1934. Now abandoned, it is under the control of the US Department of the Navy. The reef only has an elevation of 1 m (3 ft) and is awash most of the time, making it hazardous for ships.

WAKE ISLAND

Wake Island, actually a coral atoll and three islets (Wake, Peale, and Wilkes) about 8 km (5 mi) long by 3.6 km (2.25 mi) wide, lies in the North Pacific 3,380 km (2,100 mi) W of Honolulu at 19° 17′ N and 166° 35′ E. The total land and water area is about 8 sq km (3 sq mi). Discovered by the British in 1796, Wake was long uninhabited.

In 1898, a US expeditionary force en route to Manila landed on the island. The United States formally claimed Wake in 1899. It was made a US naval reservation in 1934, and became a civil aviation station in 1935. Captured by the Japanese on 23 December 1941, Wake was subsequently the target of several US air raids. It was surrendered by the Japanese in September 1945 and has thereafter remained a US unincorporated territory under the jurisdiction, since 1972, of the Department of the Air Force.

As of October 2001, only around 200 contractor personnel inhabited Wake Island. The island was no longer being used for missile launches by the US Army's Space and Strategic Defense Command. It is a stopover and fueling station for civilian and military aircraft flying between Honolulu, Guam, and Japan.

UNITED STATES

United States of America

CAPITAL: Washington, D.C. (District of Columbia). **FLAG:** The flag consists of 13 alternate stripes, 7 red and 6 white; these represent the 13 original colonies. Fifty 5-pointed white stars, representing the present number of states in the Union, are placed in 9 horizontal rows alternately of 6 and 5 against a blue field in the upper left corner of the flag. **OFFICIAL SEAL:** OBVERSE: An American eagle with outstretched wings bears a shield consisting of 13 alternating white and red stripes with a broad blue band across the top. The right talon clutches an olive branch, representing peace; in the left are 13 arrows, symbolizing military strength. The eagle's beak holds a banner with the motto *"E pluribus unum"* (From many, one); overhead is a constellation of 13 five-pointed stars in a glory. REVERSE: Above a truncated pyramid is an all-seeing eye within a triangle; at the bottom of this triangle appear the roman numerals MDCCLXXVI (1776). The pyramid stands on a grassy ground, against a backdrop of mountains. The words *"Annuit Coeptis"* (He has favored our undertakings) and, on a banner, *"Novus Ordo Seclorum"* (A new order of the ages) surround the whole. **ANTHEM:** *The Star-Spangled Banner.* **MOTTO:** In God We Trust. **MONETARY UNIT:** The dollar ($) of 100 cents is a paper currency with a floating rate. There are coins of 1, 5, 10, 25, and 50 cents and 1 dollar, and notes of 1, 2, 5, 10, 20, 50, and 100 dollars. Although issuance of higher notes ceased in 1969, a limited number of notes of 500, 1,000, 5,000, and 10,000 dollars remain in circulation. A gold-colored 1 dollar coin featuring Sacagawea was introduced in 2000. **WEIGHTS AND MEASURES:** The imperial system is in common use; however, the use of metrics in industry is increasing, and the metric system is taught in public schools throughout the United States. Common avoirdupois units in use are the avoirdupois pound of 16 oz or 453.5924277 gm; the long ton of 2,240 lb or 35,840 oz; and the short ton, more commonly used, of 2,000 lb or 32,000 oz. (Unless otherwise indicated, all measures given in tons are in short tons.) Liquid measures: 1 gallon = 231 cu in = 4 quarts = 8 pints. Dry measures: 1 bushel = 4 pecks = 32 dry quarts = 64 dry pints. Linear measures: 1 ft = 12 in; 1 statute mi = 1,760 yd = 5,280 ft. Metric equivalent: 1 m = 39.37 in. **FEDERAL HOLIDAYS:** New Year's Day, 1 January; Birthday of Martin Luther King, Jr., 3rd Monday in January; Lincoln's Birthday, 12 February (only in the northern and western states); Washington's Birthday, 3rd Monday in February; Memorial or Decoration Day, last Monday in May; Independence Day, 4 July; Labor Day, 1st Monday in September; Columbus Day, 2nd Monday in October; Election Day, 1st Tuesday after the 1st Monday in November; Veterans or Armistice Day, 11 November; Thanksgiving Day, 4th Thursday in November; Christmas, 25 December. **TIME:** Eastern, 7 AM = noon GMT; Central, 6 AM = noon GMT; Mountain, 5 AM = noon GMT; Pacific (includes the Alaska panhandle), 4 AM = noon GMT; Yukon, 3 AM = noon GMT; Alaska and Hawaii, 2 AM = noon GMT; western Alaska, 1 AM = noon GMT.

¹LOCATION, SIZE, AND EXTENT

Located in the Western Hemisphere on the continent of North America, the United States is the fourth-largest country in the world. Its total area, including Alaska and Hawaii, is 9,629,091 sq km (3,717,813 sq mi). The conterminous United States extends 4,662 km (2,897 mi) ENE—WSW and 4,583 km (2,848 mi) SSE–NNW. It is bordered on the N by Canada, on the E by the Atlantic Ocean, on the S by the Gulf of Mexico and Mexico, and on the W by the Pacific Ocean, with a total boundary length of 17,563 km (10,913 mi). Alaska, the 49th state, extends 3,639 km (2,261 mi) E–W and 2,185 km (1,358 mi) N–S. It is bounded on the N by the Arctic Ocean and Beaufort Sea, on the E by Canada, on the S by the Gulf of Alaska, Pacific Ocean and Bering Sea, and on the W by the Bering Sea, Bering Strait, Chukchi Sea, and Arctic Ocean, with a total land boundary of 12,034 km (7,593 mi) and a coastline of 19,924 km (12,380 mi). The 50th state, Hawaii, consists of islands in the Pacific Ocean extending 2,536 km (1,576 mi) N–S and 2,293 km (1,425 mi) E–W, with a general coastline of 1,207 km (750 mi).

The nation's capital, Washington, D.C., is located on the mid-Atlantic coast.

²TOPOGRAPHY

Although the northern New England coast is rocky, along the rest of the eastern seaboard the Atlantic Coastal Plain rises gradually from the shoreline. Narrow in the north, the plain widens to about 320 km (200 mi) in the south and in Georgia merges with the Gulf Coastal Plain that borders the Gulf of Mexico and extends through Mexico as far as the Yucatán. West of the Atlantic Coastal Plain is the Piedmont Plateau, bounded by the Appalachian Mountains. The Appalachians—which extend from southwest Maine into central Alabama—with special names in some areas—are old mountains, largely eroded away, with rounded contours and forested, as a rule, to the top. Few of their summits rise much above 1,100 m (3,500 ft), although the highest, Mt. Mitchell in North Carolina, reaches 2,037 m (6,684 ft).

Between the Appalachians and the Rocky Mountains, more than 1,600 km (1,000 mi) to the west, lies the vast interior plain of the United States. Running south through the center of this plain and draining almost two-thirds of the area of the continental United States is the Mississippi River. Waters starting from the source of the Missouri, the longest of its tributaries, travel almost 6,450 km (4,000 mi) to the Gulf of Mexico. The eastern reaches of the great interior plain are bounded on the north by the Great Lakes, which are thought to contain about half the world's total supply of fresh water. Under US jurisdiction are 57,441 sq km (22,178 sq mi) of Lake Michigan, 54,696 sq km (21,118 sq mi) of Lake Superior, 23,245 sq km (8,975 sq mi) of Lake Huron, 12,955 sq km (5,002 sq mi) of Lake Erie, and 7,855 sq km (3,033 sq mi) of Lake Ontario. The five lakes are now accessible to oceangoing vessels from the Atlantic via the St. Lawrence Seaway. The basins of the Great Lakes were formed by the glacial ice cap that moved down over large parts of North America some 25,000 years ago. The glaciers also determined the direction of flow of the Missouri River and, it is believed, were responsible for carrying soil from what is now Canada down into the central agricultural basin of the United States. The great interior plain consists of two major subregions: the fertile Central Plains, extending from the Appalachian highlands to a line drawn approximately 480 km (300 mi) west of the Mississippi, broken by the Ozark Plateau; and the more arid Great Plains, extending from that line to the foothills of the Rocky Mountains. Although they appear flat, the Great Plains rise gradually from about 460 m (1,500 ft) to more than 1,500 m (5,000 ft) at their western extremity.

The Continental Divide, the Atlantic-Pacific watershed, runs along the crest of the Rocky Mountains. The Rockies and the ranges to the west are parts of the great system of young, rugged mountains, shaped like a gigantic spinal column, that runs along western North, Central, and South America from Alaska to Tierra del Fuego, Chile. In the continental United States, the series of western ranges, most of them paralleling the Pacific coast, are the Sierra Nevada, the Coast Ranges, the Cascade Range, and the Tehachapi and San Bernardino mountains. Between the Rockies and the Sierra Nevada—Cascade mountain barrier to the west lies the Great Basin, a group of vast arid plateaus containing most of the desert areas of the United States, in the south eroded by deep canyons. The coastal plains along the Pacific are narrow, and in many places the mountains plunge directly into the sea. The most extensive lowland near the west coast is the Great Valley of California, lying between the Sierra Nevada and the Coast Ranges. There are 71 peaks in these western ranges of the continental United States that rise to an altitude of 4,267 m (14,000 ft) or more, Mt. Whitney in California at 4,418 m (14,494 ft) being the highest. The greatest rivers of the Far West are the Colorado in the south, flowing into the Gulf of California, and the Columbia in the northwest, flowing to the Pacific. Each is more than 1,900 km (1,200 mi) long; both have been intensively developed to generate electric power, and both are important sources of irrigation.

Separated from the continental United States by Canadian territory, the state of Alaska occupies the extreme northwest portion of the North American continent. A series of precipitous mountain ranges separates the heavily indented Pacific coast on the south from Alaska's broad central basin, through which the Yukon River flows from Canada in the east to the Bering Sea in the west. The central basin is bounded on the north by the Brooks Range, which slopes down gradually to the Arctic Ocean. The Alaskan Peninsula and the Aleutian Islands, sweeping west far out to sea, consist of a chain of volcanoes, many still active. The state of Hawaii consists of a group of Pacific islands formed by volcanoes rising sharply from the ocean floor. The highest of these volcanoes, Mauna Loa, at 4,168 m (13,675 ft), is located on the largest of the islands, Hawaii, and is still active.

The lowest point in the United States is Death Valley in California, 86 m (282 ft) below sea level. At 6,194 m (20,320 ft), Mt. McKinley in Alaska is the highest peak in North America. These topographic extremes suggest the geological instability of the Pacific Coast region. Major earthquakes destroyed San Francisco in 1906 and Anchorage, Alaska, in 1964, and the San Andreas Fault in California still causes frequent earth tremors. Washington State's Mt. St. Helens erupted in 1980, spewing volcanic ash over much of the Northwest.

[3]CLIMATE

The eastern continental region is well watered, with annual rainfall generally in excess of 100 cm (40 in). It includes all of the Atlantic seaboard and southeastern states and extends west to cover Indiana, southern Illinois, most of Missouri, Arkansas, Louisiana, and easternmost Texas. The eastern seaboard is affected primarily by the masses of air moving from west to east across the continent rather than by air moving in from the Atlantic. Hence its climate is basically continental rather than maritime. The midwestern and Atlantic seaboard states experience hot summers and cold winters; spring and autumn are clearly defined periods of climatic transition. Only Florida, with the Gulf of Mexico lying to its west, experiences moderate differences between summer and winter temperatures. Mean annual temperatures vary considerably between north and south: Boston, 11°C (51°F); New York City, 13°C (55°F); Charlotte, N.C., 16°C (61°F); Miami, Fla., 24°C (76°F). The Gulf and South Atlantic states are often hit by severe tropical storms originating in the Caribbean in late summer and early autumn.

The prairie lands lying to the west constitute a subhumid region. Precipitation usually exceeds evaporation by only a small amount; hence the region experiences drought more often than

Outlying Areas of the United States[1]

NAME	AREA SQ MI	SQ KM	CAPITAL	YEAR OF ACQUISITION	POPULATION 1980	POPULATION 1999
Puerto Rico	3,515	9,104	San Juan	1898	3,196,520	3,887,652
Virgin Islands of the United States	136	352	Charlotte Amalie	1917	96,569	119,827
Trust Territory of the Pacific Islands, of which:	713	1,847	Saipan	1947	132,929	87,865
Northern Marianas[2]	182	471	Saipan[3]	–	16,780	69,398
Republic of Palau[2]	191	495	Koror[3]	–	12,116	18,467
Other Pacific territories:						
American Samoa	77	199	Pago Pago	1899	32,297	63,786
Guam	209	541	Agaña	1898	105,979	151,716
Midway Islands	2	5	–	1867	468	n.a.
Wake Island	3	8	–	1899	302	n.a.

[1]Excludes minor and uninhabited islands.

[2]Although governed under separate constitutional arrangements by the mid–1980s, these territories formally remained part of the Trust Territory of the Pacific Islands pending action by the US Congress, the US president, and the UN Security Council.

[3]Centers of constitutional government. The entire Trust Territory of the Pacific Islands is administered from Saipan.

excessive rainfall. Dryness generally increases from east to west. The average midwinter temperature in the extreme north—Minnesota and North Dakota—is about –13°C (9°F) or less, while the average July temperature is 18°C (65°F). In the Texas prairie region to the south, January temperatures average 10–13°C (50–55°F) and July temperatures 27–29°C (80–85°F). Rainfall along the western border of the prairie region is as low as 46 cm (18 in) per year in the north and 64 cm (25 in) in the south. Precipitation is greatest in the early summer—a matter of great importance to agriculture, particularly in the growing of grain crops. In dry years, the prevailing winds may carry the topsoil eastward (particularly from the southern region) for hundreds of miles in clouds that obscure the sun.

The Great Plains constitute a semiarid climatic region. Rainfall in the southern plains averages about 50 cm (20 in) per year and in the northern plains about 25 cm (10 in), but extreme year-to-year variations are common. The tropical air masses that move northward across the plains originate on the fairly high plateaus of Mexico and contain little water vapor. Periods as long as 120 days without rain have been experienced in this region. The rains that do occur are often violent, and a third of the total annual rainfall may be recorded in a single day at certain weather stations. The contrast between summer and winter temperatures is extreme throughout the Great Plains. Maximum summer temperatures of over 43°C (110°F) have been recorded in the northern as well as in the southern plains. From the Texas panhandle north, blizzards are common in the winter, and tornadoes at other seasons. The average minimum temperature for January in Duluth, Minn., is –19°C (–3°F).

The higher reaches of the Rockies and the mountains paralleling the Pacific coast to the west are characterized by a typical alpine climate. Precipitation as a rule is heavier on the western slopes of the ranges. The great intermontane arid region of the West shows considerable climatic variation between its northern and southern portions. In New Mexico, Arizona, and southeastern California, the greatest precipitation occurs in July, August, and September, mean annual rainfall ranging from 8 cm (3 in) in Yuma, Ariz., to 76 cm (30 in) in the mountains of northern Arizona and New Mexico. Phoenix has a mean annual temperature of 22°C (71°F), rising to 33°C (92°F) in July and falling to 11°C (52°F) in January. North of the Utah-Arizona line, the summer months usually are very dry; maximum precipitation occurs in the winter and early spring. In the desert valleys west of Great Salt Lake, mean annual precipitation adds up to only 10 cm (4 in). Although the northern plateaus are generally arid, some of the mountainous areas of central Washington and Idaho receive at least 152 cm (60 in) of rain per year. Throughout the intermontane region, the uneven availability of water is the principal factor shaping the habitat.

The Pacific coast, separated by tall mountain barriers from the severe continental climate to the east, is a region of mild winters and moderately warm, dry summers. Its climate is basically maritime, the westerly winds from the Pacific Ocean moderating the extremes of both winter and summer temperatures. Los Angeles in the south has an average temperature of 13°C (56 °F) in January and 21°C (69°F) in July; Seattle in the north has an average temperature of 4°C (39°F) in January and 18°C (65°F) in July. Precipitation in general increases along the coast from south to north, extremes ranging from an annual average of 4.52 cm (1.78 in) at Death Valley in California (the lowest in the United States) to more than 356 cm (140 in) in Washington's Olympic Mountains.

Climatic conditions vary considerably in the vastness of Alaska. In the fogbound Aleutians and in the coastal panhandle strip that extends southeastward along the Gulf of Alaska and includes the capital, Juneau, a relatively moderate maritime climate prevails. The interior is characterized by short, hot summers and long, bitterly cold winters, and in the region

bordering the Arctic Ocean a polar climate prevails, the soil hundreds of feet below the surface remaining frozen the year round. Although snowy in winter, continental Alaska is relatively dry.

Hawaii has a remarkably mild and stable climate with only slight seasonal variations in temperature, as a result of northeast ocean winds. The mean January temperature in Honolulu is 23°C (73°F); the mean July temperature 27°C (80°F). Rainfall is moderate—about 71 cm (28 in) per year—but much greater in the mountains; Mt. Waialeale on Kauai has a mean annual rainfall of 1,168 cm (460 in), highest in the world.

The lowest temperature recorded in the United States was -62°C (-79.8°F) at Prospect Creek Camp, Alaska, on 23 January 1971; the highest, 57°C (134°F) at Greenland Ranch, in Death Valley, Calif., on 10 July 1913. The record annual rainfall is 1,878 cm (739 in) recorded at Kukui, Maui in 1982; the previous record for a one-year period was 1,468 cm (578 in) recorded at Fuu Kukui, Maui, in 1950; in 1 hour, 30 cm (12 in), at Holt, Mo., on 22 June 1947, and on Kauai, Hawaii, on 24–25 January 1956.

[4]FLORA AND FAUNA

At least 7,000 species and subspecies of indigenous US flora have been categorized. The eastern forests contain a mixture of softwoods and hardwoods that includes pine, oak, maple, spruce, beech, birch, hemlock, walnut, gum, and hickory. The central hardwood forest, which originally stretched unbroken from Cape Cod to Texas and northwest to Minnesota—still an important timber source—supports oak, hickory, ash, maple, and walnut. Pine, hickory, tupelo, pecan, gum, birch, and sycamore are found in the southern forest that stretches along the Gulf coast into the eastern half of Texas. The Pacific forest is the most spectacular of all because of its enormous redwoods and Douglas firs. In the southwest are saguaro (giant cactus), yucca, candlewood, and the Joshua tree.

The central grasslands lie in the interior of the continent, where the moisture is not sufficient to support the growth of large forests. The tall grassland or prairie (now almost entirely under cultivation) lies to the east of the 100th meridian. To the west of this line, where rainfall is frequently less than 50 cm (20 in) per year, is the short grassland. Mesquite grass covers parts of west Texas, southern New Mexico, and Arizona. Short grass may be found in the highlands of the latter two states, while tall grass covers large portions of the coastal regions of Texas and Louisiana and occurs in some parts of Mississippi, Alabama, and Florida. The Pacific grassland includes northern Idaho, the higher plateaus of eastern Washington and Oregon, and the mountain valleys of California.

The intermontane region of the Western Cordillera is for the most part covered with desert shrubs. Sagebrush predominates in the northern part of this area, creosote in the southern, with saltbrush near the Great Salt Lake and in Death Valley.

The lower slopes of the mountains running up to the coastline of Alaska are covered with coniferous forests as far north as the Seward Peninsula. The central part of the Yukon Basin is also a region of softwood forests. The rest of Alaska is heath or tundra. Hawaii has extensive forests of bamboo and ferns. Sugarcane and pineapple, although not native to the islands, now cover a large portion of the cultivated land.

Small trees and shrubs common to most of the United States include hackberry, hawthorn, serviceberry, blackberry, wild cherry, dogwood, and snowberry. Wildflowers bloom in all areas, from the seldom-seen blossoms of rare desert cacti to the hardiest alpine species. Wildflowers include forget-me-not, fringed and closed gentians, jack-in-the-pulpit, black-eyed Susan, columbine, and common dandelion, along with numerous varieties of aster, orchid, lady's slipper, and wild rose.

An estimated 432 species of mammals characterize the animal life of the continental United States. Among the larger game

LOCATION: Conterminous United States: 66°57′ to 124°44′ W; 24°33′ to 49°23′ N. Alaska: 130°W to 172°28′ E; 51° to 71°23′ N. Hawaii: 154°48′ to 178°22′ W 18°55′ to 28°25′ N. BOUNDARY LENGTHS: Conterminous United States: Canada, 6,416 kilometers (3,987 miles); Atlantic Ocean, 3,330 kilometers (2,069 miles); Gulf of Mexico coastline, 2,625 kilometers (1,631 miles); Mexico, 3,111 kilometers (1,933 miles); Pacific coastline, 2,081 kilometers (1,293 miles). Alaska: Arctic Ocean coastline, 1,706 kilometers (1,060 miles); Canada, 2,475 kilometers (1,538 miles); Pacific coastline, including the Bering Sea and Strait and Chukchi coastlines, 8,980 kilometers (5,580 miles). Hawaii: coastline, 1,207 kilometers (750 miles).

animals are the white-tailed deer, moose, pronghorn antelope, bighorn sheep, mountain goat, black bear, and grizzly bear. The Alaskan brown bear often reaches a weight of 1,200–1,400 lbs. Some 25 important furbearers are common, including the muskrat, red and gray foxes, mink, raccoon, beaver, opossum, striped skunk, woodchuck, common cottontail, snowshoe hare, and various squirrels. Human encroachment has transformed the mammalian habitat over the last two centuries. The American buffalo (bison), millions of which once roamed the plains, is now found only on select reserves. Other mammals, such as the elk and gray wolf, have been restricted to much smaller ranges.

Year-round and migratory birds abound. Loons, wild ducks, and wild geese are found in lake country; terns, gulls, sandpipers, herons, and other seabirds live along the coasts. Wrens, thrushes, owls, hummingbirds, sparrows, woodpeckers, swallows, chickadees, vireos, warblers, and finches appear in profusion, along with the robin, common crow, cardinal, Baltimore oriole, eastern and western meadowlarks, and various blackbirds. Wild turkey, ruffed grouse, and ring-necked pheasant (introduced from Europe) are popular game birds.

Lakes, rivers, and streams teem with trout, bass, perch, muskellunge, carp, catfish, and pike; sea bass, cod, snapper, and flounder are abundant along the coasts, along with such shellfish as lobster, shrimp, clams, oysters, and mussels. Garter, pine, and milk snakes are found in most regions. Four poisonous snakes survive, of which the rattlesnake is the most common. Alligators appear in southern waterways and the Gila monster makes its home in the Southwest.

Laws and lists designed to protect threatened and endangered flora and fauna have been adopted throughout the United States. Generally, each species listed as protected by the federal government is also protected by the states, but some states may list species not included on federal lists or on the lists of neighboring states. (Conversely, a species threatened throughout most of the United States may be abundant in one or two states.) As of August 2003, the US Fish and Wildlife Service listed 987 endangered US species (up from 751 listed in 1996), including 65 mammals (64 in 1996), 78 birds (77 in 1996), 71 fish (69 in 1996), and 599 plants (432 in 1996); and 276 threatened species (209 in 1996), including 147 plants (94 in 1996). The agency listed another 517 endangered and 41 threatened foreign species by international agreement.

Threatened species, likely to become endangered if recent trends continue, include such plants as Lee pincushion cactus. Among the endangered floral species (in imminent danger of extinction in the wild) are the Virginia round-leaf birch, San Clemente Island broom, Texas wild-rice, Furbish lousewort, Truckee barberry, Sneed pincushion cactus, spineless hedgehog cactus, Knowlton cactus, persistent trillium, dwarf bear-poppy, and small whorled pogonia.

Endangered mammals included the red wolf, black-footed ferret, jaguar, key deer, northern swift fox, San Joaquin kit fox, jaguar, jaguarundi, Florida manatee, ocelot, Florida panther, Utah prairie dog, Sonoran pronghorn, and numerous whale species. Endangered species of rodents included the Delmarva Peninsula fox squirrel; beach mouse; salt-marsh harvest mouse; 7 species of bat (Virginia and Ozark big-eared Sanborn's and Mexican long-nosed, Hawaiian hoary, Indiana, and gray); the Morro Ba, Fresno, Stephens', and Tipton Kangaroo rats; and rice rat.

Endangered species of birds included the California condor, bald eagle, three species of falcon (American peregrine, tundra peregrine, and northern aplomado), Eskimo curlew, two species of crane (whooping and Mississippi sandhill), three species of warbler (Kirtland's, Bachman's, and golden-cheeked), dusky seaside sparrow, light-footed clapper rail, least tern, San Clemente loggerhead shrike, bald eagle (endangered in most states, but only threatened in the Northwest and the Great Lakes region), Hawaii creeper, Everglade kite, California clapper rail, and red-cockaded woodpecker. Endangered amphibians included four species of salamander (Santa Cruz long-toed, Shenandoah, desert slender, and Texas blind), Houston and Wyoming toad, and six species of turtle (green sea, hawksbill, Kemp's ridley, Plymouth and Alabama red-bellied, and leatherback). Endangered reptiles included the American crocodile, (blunt nosed leopard and island night), and San Francisco garter snake.

Aquatic species included the shortnose sturgeon, Gila trout, eight species of chub (humpback, Pahranagat, Yaqui, Mohave tui, Owens tui, bonytail, Virgin River, and Borax lake), Colorado River squawfish, five species of dace (Kendall Warm Springs, and Clover Valley, Independence Valley, Moapa and Ash Meadows speckled), Modoc sucker, cui-ui, Smoky and Scioto madtom, seven species of pupfish (Leon Springs, Gila Desert, Ash Meadows Amargosa, Warm Springs, Owens, Devil's Hole, and Comanche Springs), Pahrump killifish, four species of gambusia (San Marcos, Pecos, Amistad, Big Bend, and Clear Creek), six species of darter (fountain, watercress, Okaloosa, boulder, Maryland, and amber), totoaba, and 32 species of mussel and pearly mussel. Also classified as endangered were two species of earthworm (Washington giant and Oregon giant), the Socorro isopod, San Francisco forktail damselfly, Ohio emerald dragonfly, three species of beetle (Kretschmarr Cave, Tooth Cave, and giant carrion), Belkin's dune tabanid fly, and 10 species of butterfly (Schaus' swallowtail, lotis, mission, El Segundo, and Palos Verde blue, Mitchell's satyr, Uncompahgre fritillary, Lange's metalmark, San Bruno elfin, and Smith's blue).

Several species on the federal list of endangered and threatened wildlife and plants are found only in Hawaii. Endangered bird species in Hawaii included the Hawaiian dark-rumped petrel, Hawaiian gallinule, Hawaiian crow, three species of thrush (Kauai, Molokai, and puaiohi), Kauai 'o'o, Kauai nukupu'u, Kauai 'alialoa, 'akiapola'au, Maui'akepa, Molokai creeper, Oahu creeper, palila, and 'o'u.

Endangered plants in the United States include: aster, cactus, pea, mustard, mint, mallow, bellflower and pink family, snapdragon, and buckwheat.

Threatened fauna include the grizzly bear, southern sea otter, Newell's shearwater, eastern indigo snake, bayou darter, and several southwestern trout species. Species formerly listed as threatened or endangered that have been removed from the list include (with delisting year and reason) American alligator (1987, recovered); coastal cutthroat trout (2000, taxonomic revision); Bahama swallowtail butterfly (1984, amendment); gray whale (1994, recovered); brown pelican (1984, recovered); Rydberg milk-vetch (1987, new information); Lloyd's hedgehog cactus (1999, taxonomic revision), and Columbian white-tailed Douglas County Deer (2003, recovered).

⁵ENVIRONMENTAL PROTECTION

The Council on Environmental Quality, an advisory body contained within the Executive Office of the President, was established by the National Environmental Policy Act of 1969, which mandated an assessment of environmental impact for every federally funded project. The Environmental Protection Agency (EPA), created in 1970, is an independent body with primary regulatory responsibility in the fields of air and noise pollution, water and waste management, and control of toxic substances. Other federal agencies with environmental responsibilities are the Forest Service and Soil Conservation Service within the Department of Agriculture, the Fish and Wildlife Service and the National Park Service within the Department of the Interior, the Department of Energy, and the Nuclear Regulatory Commission. In addition to the 1969 legislation, landmark federal laws protecting the environment include the Clean Air Act Amendments of 1970 and 1990, controlling automobile and electric utility emissions; the Water Pollution Act of 1972, setting clean-water criteria for fishing and swimming; and the Endangered Species Act of 1973, protecting wildlife near extinction. A measure enacted in December 1980 established a $1.6-billion "Superfund," financed largely by excise taxes on chemical companies, to clean up toxic waste dumps such as the one in the Love Canal district of Niagara Falls, N.Y. In 2003, there were 1,232 hazardous waste sites on the Superfund's national priority list.

In 2003, the 2004 expenditure estimate for the Environmental Protection Agency was $7.6 billion. The EPA employed 17,850 workers.

The most influential environmental lobbies include the Sierra Club (founded in 1892; 700,000 members in 2003) and its legal arm, the Sierra Club Legal Defense Fund. Large conservation groups include the National Wildlife Federation (1936; over 4,000,000), the National Audubon Society (1905; 600,000), and the Nature Conservancy (1917; 1,000,000). Greenpeace USA (founded in 1979) has gained international attention by seeking to disrupt hunts for whales and seals.

Among the environmental movement's most notable successes have been the inauguration (and mandating in some states) of recycling programs; the banning in the United States of the insecticide dichlorodiphenyltrichloroethane (DDT); the successful fight against construction of a supersonic transport (SST); and the protection of more than 40 million hectares (100 million acres) of Alaska lands (after a fruitless fight to halt construction of the trans-Alaska pipeline); and the gradual elimination of chlorofluorocarbon (CFC) production by 2000. In March 2003, the US Senate narrowly voted to reject a Bush administration plan to begin oil exploration in the 19 million acre (7.7 million hectare) Arctic National Wildlife Refuge (ANWR).

Outstanding problems include acid rain (precipitation contaminated by fossil fuel wastes); inadequate facilities for solid waste disposal; air pollution from industrial emissions (the United States leads the world in carbon dioxide emissions from the burning of fossil fuels); the contamination of homes by radon, a radioactive gas that is produced by the decay of underground deposits of radium and can cause cancer; runoffs of agricultural pesticides, pollutants deadly to fishing streams and very difficult to regulate; continued dumping of raw or partially treated sewage from major cities into US waterways; falling water tables in many western states; the decrease in arable land because of depletion, erosion, and urbanization; the need for reclamation of strip-mined lands and for regulation of present and future strip mining; and the expansion of the US nuclear industry in the absence of a fully satisfactory technique for the handling and permanent disposal of radioactive wastes.

6POPULATION

At the time of the first federal census, in 1790, the population of the United States was 3,929,214. Between 1800 and 1850, the population almost quadrupled; between 1850 and 1900, it tripled; and between 1900 and 1950, it almost doubled. During the 1960s and 1970s, however, the growth rate slowed steadily, declining from 2.9% annually in 1960 to 2% in 1969 and to less than 1% in the 1980s. The population was estimated at 263,064,000 in mid-1995. The median age of the population increased from 16.7 years in 1820 to 22.9 years in 1900 and to 34.3 years in 1995.

The population of United States in 2003 was estimated by the United Nations at 294,043,000, which placed it as number 3 in population among the 193 nations of the world. In that year approximately 13% of the population was over 65 years of age, with another 21% of the population under 15 years of age. There were 97 males for every 100 females in the country in 2003. According to the UN, the annual population growth rate for 2000–2005 is 1.03%, with the projected population for the year 2015 at 329,669,000. The population density in 2002 was 30 per sq km (77 per sq mi). The major population concentrations are along the northeast Atlantic coast and the southwest Pacific coast. The population is most dense between New York City and Washington, D.C.

It was estimated by the Population Reference Bureau that 77% of the population lived in urban areas in 2001. Suburbs have absorbed most of the shift in population distribution since 1950. The capital city, Washington, D.C., had a population of 3,888,000 in that year. Other major metropolitan areas include the following: New York, 16,626,000; Los Angeles, 13,129,000; Chicago, 6,945,000; Dallas, 3,912,000; Houston, 3,365,000; Philadelphia, 2,607,000; San Diego, 2,983,000; and Phoenix, 2,607,000. Major cities can be found throughout the United States. According to the United Nations, the urban population growth rate for 2000–2005 was 1.0%.

7ETHNIC GROUPS

The majority of the population of the United States is of European origin, with the largest groups having primary ancestry traceable to the United Kingdom, Germany, and Ireland; many Americans report multiple ancestries. Major racial and national minority groups include blacks (either of US, African, or Caribbean parentage), Chinese, Filipinos, Japanese, Mexicans, and other Spanish-speaking peoples of the Americas. According to the 2000 Census, it was estimated that whites comprised 75.1% of the US population; Hispanics, 12.5%; blacks or African Americans, 12.3%; Asians and Pacific Islanders, 3.7%; and Native Americans (Amerindians—more commonly known as Indians, Eskimos, and Aleuts), 0.9%. Inequality in social and economic opportunities for ethnic minorities became a key public issue in the post–World War II period.

Some Native American societies survived warfare with land-hungry white settlers and retained their tribal cultures. Their survival, however, has been on the fringes of North American society, especially as a result of the implementation of a national policy of resettling Native American tribes on reservations. In 1890, according to the official census count, there were 248,253 Native Americans; in 1940, 333,909; and in 2000, 2,475,956 (including also Eskimos and Aleuts). Groups of Native Americans are found most numerously in the southwestern states of Oklahoma, Arizona, New Mexico, and California. The 1960s and 1970s saw successful court fights by Native Americans in Alaska, Maine, South Dakota, and other states to regain tribal lands or to receive cash settlements for lands taken from them in violation of treaties during the 1800s.

The black population in 2000 was estimated at 34,658,190, with the majority still residing in the South, the region that absorbed most of the slaves brought from Africa in the 18th and 19th centuries. Two important regional migrations of blacks have taken place: (1) a "Great Migration" to the North, commencing in 1915, and (2) a small but then unprecedented westward movement beginning about 1940. Both migrations were fostered by wartime demands for labor and by postwar job opportunities in northern and western urban centers. More than three out of four black Americans live in metropolitan areas, notably in Washington, D.C., Atlanta, Chicago, Detroit, New Orleans, Newark, Baltimore, and New York City, which had the largest number of black residents. Large-scale federal programs to ensure equality for African Americans in voting rights, public education, employment, and housing were initiated after the historic 1954 Supreme Court ruling that barred racial segregation in public schools. By 1966, however, in the midst of growing and increasingly violent expressions of dissatisfaction by black residents of northern cities and southern rural areas, the federal Civil Rights Commission reported that integration programs were lagging. Throughout the 1960s, 1970s, and 1980s, the unemployment rate among nonwhites in the United States was at least double that for whites, and school integration proceeded slowly, especially outside the South.

Also included in the US population are a substantial number of persons whose lineage can be traced to Asian and Pacific nationalities, chiefly Chinese, Filipino, Japanese, Indian, Korean, and Vietnamese. The Chinese population is highly urbanized and concentrated particularly in cities of over 100,000 population, mostly on the West Coast and in New York City. The Japanese population has risen steadily from a level of 72,157 in 1910.

State Areas, Entry Dates, and Populations

	TOTAL AREA				ORDER OF			POPULATION	
	SQ MI	SQ KM	RANK	CAPITAL	ENTRY	DATE OF ENTRY	AT ENTRY†	CENSUS 1990	CENSUS 2000
Alabama	51,705	133,916	19	Montgomery	22	14 December 1819	127,901	4,040,587	4,447,100
Alaska	591,004	1,530,699	1	Juneau	49	3 January 1959	226,167	550,043	626,932
Arizona	114,000	295,260	6	Phoenix	48	14 February 1912	204,354	3,665,228	5,130,632
Arkansas	53,187	137,754	27	Little Rock	25	15 June 1836	57,574	2,350,725	2,673,400
California	158,706	411,048	3	Sacramento	31	9 September 1850	92,597	29,760,021	33,871,648
Colorado	104,091	269,595	8	Denver	38	1 August 1876	39,864	3,294,394	4,301,261
Connecticut*	5,018	12,997	48	Hartford	5	9 January 1788	237,946	3,287,116	3,405,565
Delaware*	2,044	5,294	49	Dover	1	7 December 1787	59,096	666,168	783,600
Florida	58,664	151,940	22	Tallahassee	27	3 March 1845	87,445	12,937,926	15,982,378
Georgia*	58,910	152,577	21	Atlanta	4	2 January 1788	82,548	6,478,316	8,186,453
Hawaii	6,471	16,760	47	Honolulu	50	21 August 1959	632,772	1,108,229	1,211,537
Idaho	83,564	216,431	13	Boise	43	3 July 1890	88,548	1,006,749	1,293,953
Illinois	56,345	145,933	24	Springfield	21	3 December 1818	55,211	11,430,602	12,419,293
Indiana	36,185	93,719	38	Indianapolis	19	11 December 1816	147,178	5,544,159	6,080,485
Iowa	56,275	145,752	25	Des Moines	29	28 December 1846	192,214	2,776,755	2,926,324
Kansas	82,277	213,097	14	Topeka	34	29 January 1861	107,206	2,477,574	2,688,418
Kentucky	40,409	104,659	37	Frankfort	15	1 June 1792	73,677	3,685,296	4,041,769
Louisiana	47,752	123,678	31	Baton Rouge	18	30 April 1812	76,556	4,219,973	4,468,976
Maine	33,265	86,156	39	Augusta	23	15 March 1820	298,335	1,227,928	1,274,923
Maryland*	10,460	27,091	42	Annapolis	7	28 April 1788	319,728	4,781,468	5,296,486
Massachusetts*	8,284	21,456	45	Boston	6	6 February 1788	378,787	6,016,425	6,349,097
Michigan	58,527	151,585	23	Lansing	26	26 January 1837	212,267	9,295,297	9,938,444
Minnesota	84,402	218,601	12	St. Paul	32	11 May 1858	172,023	4,375,099	4,919,497
Mississippi	47,689	123,514	32	Jackson	20	10 December 1817	75,448	2,573,216	2,844,658
Missouri	69,697	180,515	19	Jefferson City	24	10 August 1821	66,586	5,117,073	5,595,211
Montana	147,046	380,849	4	Helena	41	8 November 1889	142,924	799,065	902,195
Nebraska	77,355	200,349	15	Lincoln	37	1 March 1867	122,993	1,578,385	1,711,263
Nevada	110,561	286,353	7	Carson City	36	31 October 1864	42,491	1,201,833	1,998,257
New Hampshire*	9,279	24,033	44	Concord	9	21 June 1788	141,885	1,109,252	1,235,786
New Jersey*	7,787	20,168	46	Trenton	3	18 December 1787	184,139	7,730,188	8,414,350
New Mexico	121,593	314,926	5	Santa Fe	47	6 January 1912	327,301	1,515,069	1,819,046
New York*	49,108	127,190	30	Albany	11	26 July 1788	340,120	17,990,455	18,976,457
North Carolina*	52,669	136,413	28	Raleigh	12	21 November 1789	393,751	6,628,637	8,049,313
North Dakota	70,702	183,118	17	Bismarck	39	2 November 1889	190,983	638,800	642,200
Ohio	41,330	107,045	35	Columbus	17	1 March 1803††	43,365	10,847,115	11,353,140
Oklahoma	69,956	181,186	18	Oklahoma City	46	16 November 1907	657,155	3,145,585	3,450,654
Oregon	97,073	251,419	10	Salem	33	14 February 1859	52,465	2,842,321	3,421,399
Pennsylvania*	45,308	117,348	33	Harrisburg	2	12 December 1787	434,373	11,003,464	12,281,054
Rhode Island*	1,212	3,139	50	Providence	13	29 May 1790	68,825	1,003,464	1,048,319
South Carolina*	31,113	80,583	40	Columbia	8	23 May 1788	393,751	3,486,703	4,012,012
South Dakota	77,116	199,730	16	Pierre	40	2 November 1889	348,600	696,004	754,844
Tennessee	42,144	109,153	34	Nashville	16	1 June 1796	35,691	4,877,185	5,689,283
Texas	266,807	691,030	2	Austin	28	29 December 1845	212,592	16,986,510	20,851,820
Utah	84,899	219,888	11	Salt Lake City	45	4 January 1896	276,749	1,722,850	2,233,169
Vermont	9,614	24,900	43	Montpelier	14	4 March 1791	85,425	562,758	608,827
Virginia*	40,767	105,586	36	Richmond	10	25 June 1788	747,610	6,187,358	7,078,515
Washington	68,139	176,480	20	Olympia	42	11 November 1889	357,232	4,866,692	5,894,121
West Virginia	24,231	62,758	41	Charleston	35	20 June 1863	442,014	1,793,477	1,808,344
Wisconsin	56,153	145,436	26	Madison	30	29 May 1848	305,391	4,891,769	5,363,675
Wyoming	97,809	253,325	9	Cheyenne	44	10 July 1890	62,555	453,588	493,782

†Census closest to entry date.
††Date fixed in 1953 by congressional resolution.
*One of original 13 colonies.

Hawaii has been the most popular magnet of Japanese emigration. Most Japanese in California were farmers until the outbreak of World War II, when they were interned and deprived of their landholdings; after the war, most entered the professions and other urban occupations.

Hispanics in 2003 made up the largest minority group in the United States. Although Mexicans in the 21st century were still concentrated in the Southwest, they have settled throughout the United States; Mexico was the largest source country for immigration in 2002. Spanish-speaking Puerto Ricans, who often represent an amalgam of racial strains, have largely settled in the New York metropolitan area, where they partake in considerable measure of the hardships and problems experienced by other immigrant groups in the process of settling in the United States.

Since 1959, many Cubans have settled in Florida and other eastern states.

8LANGUAGES

The primary language of the United States is English, enriched by words borrowed from the languages of Indians and immigrants, predominantly European. Spanish is also spoken by a sizable minority.

When European settlement began, Indians living north of Mexico spoke about 300 different languages now held to belong to 58 different language families. Only 2 such families have contributed noticeably to the American vocabulary: Algonkian in the Northeast and Aztec-Tanoan in the Southwest. From Algonkian languages, directly or sometimes through Canadian French, English has taken such words as *moose, skunk, caribou, opossum, woodchuck,* and *raccoon* for New World animals; *hickory, squash,* and *tamarack* for New World flora; and *succotash, hominy, mackinaw, moccasin, tomahawk, toboggan,* and *totem* for various cultural items. From Nahuatl, the language of the Aztecs, terms such as *tomato, mesquite, coyote, chili, tamale, chocolate,* and *ocelot* have entered English, largely by way of Spanish. A bare handful of words come from other Indian language groups, such as *tepee* from Dakota Siouan, *catalpa* from Creek, *sequoia* from Cherokee, *hogan* from Navaho, and *sockeye* from Salish, as well as *cayuse* from Chinook.

Professional dialect research, initiated in Germany in 1878 and in France in 1902, did not begin in the United States until 1931, in connection with the *Linguistic Atlas of New England* (1939–43). This kind of research, requiring trained field-workers to interview representative informants in their homes, subsequently was extended to the entire Atlantic Coast, the north-central states, the upper Midwest, the Pacific Coast, the Gulf states, and Oklahoma. The New England atlas, the *Linguistic Atlas of the Upper Midwest* (1973–76), and the first two fascicles of the *Linguistic Atlas of the Middle and South Atlantic States* (1980) have been published, along with three volumes based on Atlantic Coast field materials. Also published or nearing publication are atlases of the north-central states, the Gulf states, and Oklahoma. In other areas, individual dialect researchers have produced more specialized studies. The definitive work on dialect speech, the American Dialect Society's monumental *Dictionary of American Regional English,* began publication in 1985.

Dialect studies confirm that standard English is not uniform throughout the country. Major regional variations reflect patterns of colonial settlement, dialect features from England having dominated particular areas along the Atlantic Coast and then spread westward along the three main migration routes through the Appalachian system. Dialectologists recognize three main dialects—Northern, Midland, and Southern—each with subdivisions related to the effect of mountain ranges and rivers and railroads on population movement.

The Northern dialect is that of New England and its derivative settlements in New York; the northern parts of Ohio, Indiana, Illinois, and Iowa; and Michigan, Wisconsin, northeastern South Dakota, and North Dakota. A major subdivision is that of New England east of the Connecticut River, an area noted typically by the loss of /r/ after a vowel, and by the pronunciation of *can't, dance, half,* and *bath* with a vowel more like that in *father* than that in *fat.* Generally, however, Northern speech has a strong /r/ after a vowel, the same vowel in *can't* and *cat,* a conspicuous contrast between *cot* and *caught,* the /s/ sound in *greasy, creek* rhyming with *pick,* and *with* ending with the same consonant sound as at the end of *breath.*

Midland speech extends in a wide band across the United States: there are two main subdivisions, North Midland and South Midland. North Midland speech extends westward from New Jersey, Delaware, and Pennsylvania into Ohio, Illinois, southern Iowa, and northern Missouri. Its speakers generally end

with with the consonant sound that begins the word *thin,* pronounce *cot* and *caught* alike, and say *cow* and *down* as /caow/ and /daown/. South Midland speech was carried by the Scotch–Irish from Pennsylvania down the Shenandoah Valley into the southern Appalachians, where it acquired many Southern speech features before it spread westward into Kentucky, Tennessee, southern Missouri, Arkansas, and northeast Texas. Its speakers are likely to say *plum peach* rather than *clingstone peach* and *snake doctor* rather than *dragonfly.*

Southern speech typically, though not always, lacks the consonant /r/ after a vowel, lengthens the first part of the diphthong in *write* so that to Northern ears it sounds almost like *rat,* and diphthongizes the vowels in *bed* and *hit* so that they sound like /beuhd/ and /hiuht/. *Horse* and *hoarse* do not sound alike, and *creek* rhymes with *meek. Corn bread* is *corn pone,* and *you-all* is standard for the plural.

In the western part of the United States, migration routes so crossed and intermingled that no neat dialect boundaries can be drawn, although there are a few rather clear population pockets.

The majority of Spanish speakers live in the Southwest, Florida, and eastern urban centers. Refugee immigration since the 1950s has greatly increased the number of foreign-language speakers from Latin America and Asia.

Very early English borrowed from neighboring French speakers such words as *shivaree, butte, levee,* and *prairie;* from German, *sauerkraut, smearcase,* and *cranberry;* from Dutch, *stoop, spook,* and *cookie;* and from Spanish, *tornado, corral, ranch,* and *canyon.* From various West African languages, blacks have given English *jazz, voodoo,* and *okra.*

Educational problems raised by the presence of large blocs of non-English speakers led to the passage in 1976 of the Bilingual Educational Act, enabling children to study basic courses in their first language while they learn English. A related school problem is that of black English, a Southern dialect variant that is the vernacular of many black students now in northern schools.

9RELIGIONS

US religious traditions are predominantly Judeo-Christian, and most Americans identify themselves as Protestants (of various denominations), Roman Catholics, or Jews. As of 1995, 163 million Americans, about 63% of the total population, reported affiliation with a religious group. The largest Christian denomination is the Roman Catholic Church, with 1995 membership estimated at 59.9 million in 19,787 local congregations with some 50,000 clergy. Immigration from Ireland, Italy, Eastern Europe, French Canada, and the Caribbean accounts for the predominance of Roman Catholicism in the Northeast, Northwest, and some parts of the Great Lakes region, while Hispanic traditions and more recent immigration from Mexico and other Latin American countries account for the historical importance of Roman Catholicism in California and throughout most of the sunbelt. More than any other US religious body, the Roman Catholic Church maintains an extensive network of parochial schools.

Jewish immigrants settled first in the Northeast, where the largest Jewish population remains; at last estimates, nearly 6 million Jews (or 3.7% of those reporting religious affiliation in the United States) were affiliated with over 3,400 local congregation served by 6,500 clergy.

According to reported statistics, 94,612,579 persons in the United States reported affiliation with a Protestant denomination. Baptists predominate below the Mason-Dixon line and west to Texas. By far the nation's largest Protestant group, the Southern Baptist Convention had 15,892,000 adherents by 1997 estimates; the American Baptist Churches in the USA claimed 1,503,000 adherents in 1996. A concentration of Methodist groups extends westward in a band from Delaware to eastern Colorado; the largest of these groups, the United Methodist

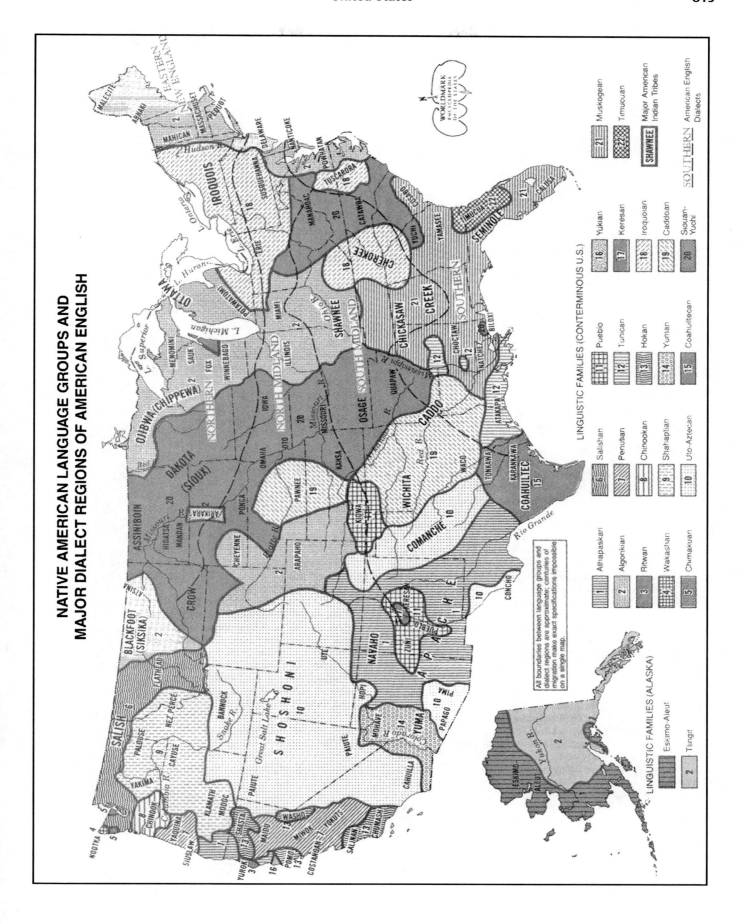

NATIVE AMERICAN LANGUAGE GROUPS AND
MAJOR DIALECT REGIONS OF AMERICAN ENGLISH

All boundaries between language groups and dialect regions are approximate; centuries of migration make exact specifications impossible on a simple map.

LINGUISTIC FAMILIES (CONTERMINOUS U.S.)

1	Athapaskan
2	Algonkian
3	Ritwan
4	Wakashan
5	Chimakuan

6	Salishan
7	Penutian
8	Chinookan
9	Shahaptian
10	Uto-Aztecan

11	Pueblo
12	Tunican
13	Hokan
14	Yuman
15	Coahuiltecan

16	Yukian
17	Keresan
18	Iroquoian
19	Caddoan
20	Siouan-Yuchi

| 21 | Muskogean |
| 22 | Timucuan |

SHAWNEE — Major American Indian Tribes

SOUTHERN — American English Dialects

LINGUISTIC FAMILIES (ALASKA)

| | Eskimo-Aleut |
| 2 | Tlingit |

Church had 8,646,595 adherents. Lutheran denominations, reflecting in part the patterns of German and Scandinavian settlement, are most highly concentrated in the north-central states, especially Minnesota and the Dakotas. Two Lutheran synods, the Lutheran Church in America and the American Lutheran Church, merged in 1987 to form the Evangelical Lutheran Church in America, with more than 5,185,000 adherents in 1997. In June 1983, the two major Presbyterian churches, the northern-based United Presbyterian Church in the USA and the southern-based Presbyterian Church in the United States, formally merged as the Presbyterian Church (USA), ending a division that began with the Civil War. This group claimed 3,611,000 adherents in 1997. Other Protestant denominations and their estimated adherents (by year) include the Episcopal Church 2,365,000 (1996); Churches of Christ 1,800,000 (1997); and the United Church of Christ 1,438,000 (1997). One Christian group, the Church of Jesus Christ of Latter-Day Saints (Mormon), with 4,923,000 members (1997), was organized in New York in 1830 and, since migrating westward has played a leading role in Utah's political, economic, and religious life. Notable during the 1970s and early 1980s was a rise in the fundamentalist, evangelical, and Pentecostal movements. In the first half of the 1990s, Pentecostal churches reported 10,281,559 adherents, representing over 6% of the population reporting religious affiliation.

Several million Muslims followers of various Asian religious, a multiplicity of small Protestant groups, and a sizable number of cults also participate in US religious life.

10TRANSPORTATION

Railroads have lost not only the largest share of intercity freight traffic, their chief source of revenue, but passenger traffic as well. Despite an attempt to revive passenger transport through the development of a national network (Amtrak) in the 1970s, the rail sector has continued to experience heavy losses and declining revenues. In 1998 there were 9 Class I rail companies in the United States, down from 13 in 1994, with a total of 178,222 employees and operating revenues of $32.2 billion. In 2002 there were 212,433 km (132,005 mi) of mainline routes, all standard gauge. In 2000, Amtrak carried 84.1 million passengers.

The most conspicuous form of transportation is the automobile, and the extent and quality of the United States road-transport system are without parallel in the world. Over 213 million vehicles—a record number—were registered in 2000, including more than 127.7 million passenger cars. In 2000, there were some 4,346,068 motorcycles registered as well.

The United States has a vast network of public roads, whose total length as of 1998 was 6.37 million km (3.9 million mi). Of that total, about 5,733,028 km (3,562,503 mi) were paved, including 74,091 km (46,040 mi) of expressways. In 1999, federal and state funds for highway construction were $95.5 billion. In 2000, federal funds for highway construction were $27.7 billion. The United States also has 41,009 km (25,483 mi) of navigable inland channels, exclusive of the Great Lakes.

Major ocean ports or port areas are New York, the Delaware River areas (Philadelphia), the Chesapeake Bay area (Baltimore, Norfolk, Newport News), New Orleans, Houston, and the San Francisco Bay area. The inland port of Duluth on Lake Superior handles more freight than all but the top-ranking ocean ports. The importance of this port, along with those of Chicago and Detroit, was enhanced with the opening in 1959 of the St. Lawrence Seaway. Waterborne freight consists primarily of bulk commodities such as petroleum and its products, coal and coke, iron ore and steel, sand, gravel and stone, grains, and lumber. The US merchant marine industry has been decreasing gradually since the 1950s. In 2002, the United States had a merchant shipping fleet of 258 vessels of more than 1,000 gross registered tons with a combined GRT of 8,259,914.

In 2001, the United States had an estimated 14,695 airports, of which 5,1631 had paved runways. Principal airports include Hartsfield at Atlanta; Logan International at Boston; O'Hare International at Chicago; Dallas-Fort Worth at Dallas; Detroit Metropolitan; Honolulu International; Houston Intercontinental; Los Angeles International; John F. Kennedy, La Guardia, and Newark International at or near New York; Philadelphia International; Orlando International; Miami International; San Francisco International; L. Munoz Marin at San Juan, Seattle-Tacoma at Seattle, and Dulles International at Washington. Revenue passengers carried by the airlines in 1940 totaled 2.7 million; by 2001, the figure exceeded 619 million for US domestic and international carriers, along with 28,042 million freight ton-km (17,425 million freight ton-mi).

11HISTORY

The first Americans—distant ancestors of the Native Americans—probably crossed the Bering Strait from Asia at least 12,000 years ago. By the time Christopher Columbus came to the New World in 1492 there were probably no more than 2 million Native Americans living in the land that was to become the United States.

Following exploration of the American coasts by English, Portuguese, Spanish, Dutch, and French sea captains from the late 15th century onward, European settlements sprang up in the latter part of the 16th century. The Spanish established the first permanent settlement at St. Augustine in the future state of Florida in 1565, and another in New Mexico in 1599. During the early 17th century, the English founded Jamestown in Virginia Colony (1607) and Plymouth Colony in present-day Massachusetts (1620). The Dutch established settlements at Ft. Orange (now Albany, N.Y.) in 1624, New Amsterdam (now New York City) in 1626, and at Bergen (now part of Jersey City, N.J.) in 1660; they conquered New Sweden—the Swedish colony in Delaware and New Jersey—in 1655. Nine years later, however, the English seized this New Netherland Colony and subsequently monopolized settlement of the East Coast except for Florida, where Spanish rule prevailed until 1821. In the Southwest, California, Arizona, New Mexico, and Texas also were part of the Spanish empire until the 19th century. Meanwhile, in the Great Lakes area south of present-day Canada, France set up a few trading posts and settlements but never established effective control; New Orleans was one of the few areas of the United States where France pursued an active colonial policy.

From the founding of Jamestown to the outbreak of the American Revolution more than 150 years later, the British government administered its American colonies within the context of mercantilism: the colonies existed primarily for the economic benefit of the empire. Great Britain valued its American colonies especially for their tobacco, lumber, indigo, rice, furs, fish, grain, and naval stores, relying particularly in the southern colonies on black slave labor.

The colonies had a large measure of internal self-government until the end of the French and Indian War (1745–63), which resulted in the loss of French Canada to the British. To prevent further troubles with the Indians, the British government in 1763 prohibited the American colonists from settling beyond the Appalachian Mountains. Heavy debts forced London to decree that the colonists should assume the costs of their own defense, and the British government enacted a series of revenue measures to provide funds for that purpose. But soon, the colonists began to insist that they could be taxed only with their consent and the struggle grew to become one of local versus imperial authority.

Widening cultural and intellectual differences also served to divide the colonies and the mother country. Life on the edge of the civilized world had brought about changes in the colonists' attitudes and outlook, emphasizing their remoteness from English life. In view of the long tradition of virtual self-government in the colonies, strict enforcement of imperial regulations and British efforts to curtail the power of colonial legislatures presaged inevitable conflict between the colonies and the mother country. When citizens of Massachusetts, protesting the tax on tea, dumped a shipload of tea belonging to the East India Company into Boston harbor in 1773, the British felt compelled to act in defense of their authority as well as in defense of private property. Punitive measures—referred to as the Intolerable Acts by the colonists—struck at the foundations of self-government.

In response, the First Continental Congress, composed of delegates from 12 of the 13 colonies—Georgia was not represented—met in Philadelphia in September 1774, and proposed a general boycott of English goods, together with the organizing of a militia. British troops marched to Concord, Mass., on 19 April 1775 and destroyed the supplies that the colonists had assembled there. American "minutemen" assembled on the nearby Lexington green and fired "the shot heard round the world," although no one knows who actually fired the first shot that morning. The British soldiers withdrew and fought their way back to Boston.

Voices in favor of conciliation were raised in the Second Continental Congress that assembled in Philadelphia on 10 May 1775, this time including Georgia; but with news of the Restraining Act (30 March 1775), which denied the colonies the right to trade with countries outside the British Empire, all hopes for peace vanished. George Washington was appointed commander in chief of the new American army, and on 4 July 1776, the 13 American colonies adopted the Declaration of Independence, justifying the right of revolution by the theory of natural rights.

British and American forces met in their first organized encounter near Boston on 17 June 1775. Numerous battles up and down the coast followed. The British seized and held the principal cities but were unable to inflict a decisive defeat on Washington's troops. The entry of France into the war on the American side eventually tipped the balance. On 19 October 1781, the British commander, Cornwallis, cut off from reinforcements by the French fleet on one side and besieged by French and American forces on the other, surrendered his army at Yorktown, Va. American independence was acknowledged by the British in a treaty of peace signed in Paris on 3 September 1783.

The first Constitution uniting the 13 original states—the Articles of Confederation—reflected all the suspicions that Americans entertained about a strong central government. Congress was denied power to raise taxes or regulate commerce, and many of the powers it was authorized to exercise required the approval of a minimum of nine states. Dissatisfaction with the Articles of Confederation was aggravated by the hardships of a postwar depression, and in 1787—the same year that Congress passed the Northwest Ordinance, providing for the organization of new territories and states on the frontier—a convention assembled in Philadelphia to revise the articles. The convention adopted an altogether new constitution, the present Constitution of the United States, which greatly increased the powers of the central government at the expense of the states. This document was ratified by the states with the understanding that it would be amended to include a bill of rights guaranteeing certain fundamental freedoms. These freedoms—including the rights of free speech, press, and assembly, freedom from unreasonable search and seizure, and the right to a speedy and public trial by an impartial jury—are assured by the first 10 amendments to the Constitution, adopted on 5 December 1791; the Constitution did however recognize slavery, and did not provide for universal suffrage. On 30 April 1789 George Washington was inaugurated as the first president of the United States.

During Washington's administration, the credit of the new nation was bolstered by acts providing for a revenue tariff and an excise tax; opposition to the excise on whiskey sparked the Whiskey Rebellion, suppressed on Washington's orders in 1794. Alexander Hamilton's proposals for funding the domestic and foreign debt and permitting the national government to assume the debts of the states were also implemented. Hamilton, the secretary of the treasury, also created the first national bank, and was the founder of the Federalist Party. Opposition to the bank as well as to the rest of the Hamiltonian program, which tended to favor northeastern commercial and business interests, led to the formation of an anti-Federalist party, the Democratic-Republicans, led by Thomas Jefferson.

The Federalist Party, to which Washington belonged, regarded the French Revolution as a threat to security and property; the Democratic-Republicans, while condemning the violence of the revolutionists, hailed the overthrow of the French monarchy as a blow to tyranny. The split of the nation's leadership into rival camps was the first manifestation of the two-party system, which has since been the dominant characteristic of the US political scene. (Jefferson's party should not be confused with the modern Republican Party, formed in 1854.)

The 1800 election brought the defeat of Federalist president John Adams, Washington's successor, by Jefferson; a key factor in Adam's loss was the unpopularity of the Alien and Sedition Acts (1798), Federalist-sponsored measures that had abridged certain freedoms guaranteed in the Bill of Rights. In 1803, Jefferson achieved the purchase from France of the Louisiana Territory, including all the present territory of the United States west of the Mississippi drained by that river and its tributaries; exploration and mapping of the new territory, notably through the expeditions of Meriwether Lewis and William Clark, began almost immediately. Under Chief Justice John Marshall, the US Supreme Court, in the landmark case of *Marbury v. Madison*, established the principle of federal supremacy in conflicts with the states and enunciated the doctrine of judicial review.

During Jefferson's second term in office, the United States became involved in a protracted struggle between Britain and Napoleonic France. Seizures of US ships and the impressment of US seamen by the British navy led the administration to pass the Embargo Act of 1807, under which no US ships were to put out to sea. After the act was repealed in 1809, ship seizures and impressment of seamen by the British continued, and were the ostensible reasons for the declaration of war on Britain in 1812 during the administration of James Madison. An underlying cause of the War of 1812, however, was land-hungry Westerners' coveting of southern Canada as potential US territory.

The war was largely a standoff. A few surprising US naval victories countered British successes on land. The Treaty of Ghent (24 December 1814), which ended the war, made no mention of impressment and provided for no territorial changes. The occasion for further maritime conflict with Britain, however, disappeared with the defeat of Napoleon in 1815.

Now the nation became occupied primarily with domestic problems and westward expansion. Because the United States had been cut off from its normal sources of manufactured goods in Great Britain during the war, textiles and other industries developed and prospered in New England. To protect these infant industries, Congress adopted a high-tariff policy in 1816.

Three events of the late 1810s and the 1820s were of considerable importance for the future of the country. The federal government in 1817 began a policy of forcibly resettling the Indians, already decimated by war and disease, in what later became known as Indian Territory (now Oklahoma); those Indians not forced to move were restricted to reservations. The Missouri Compromise (1820) was an attempt to find a nationally acceptable solution to the volatile dispute over the extension of black slavery to new territories. It provided for admission of Missouri into the Union as a slave state but banned slavery in territories to the west that lay north of 36°30′. As a result of the establishment of independent Latin American republics and

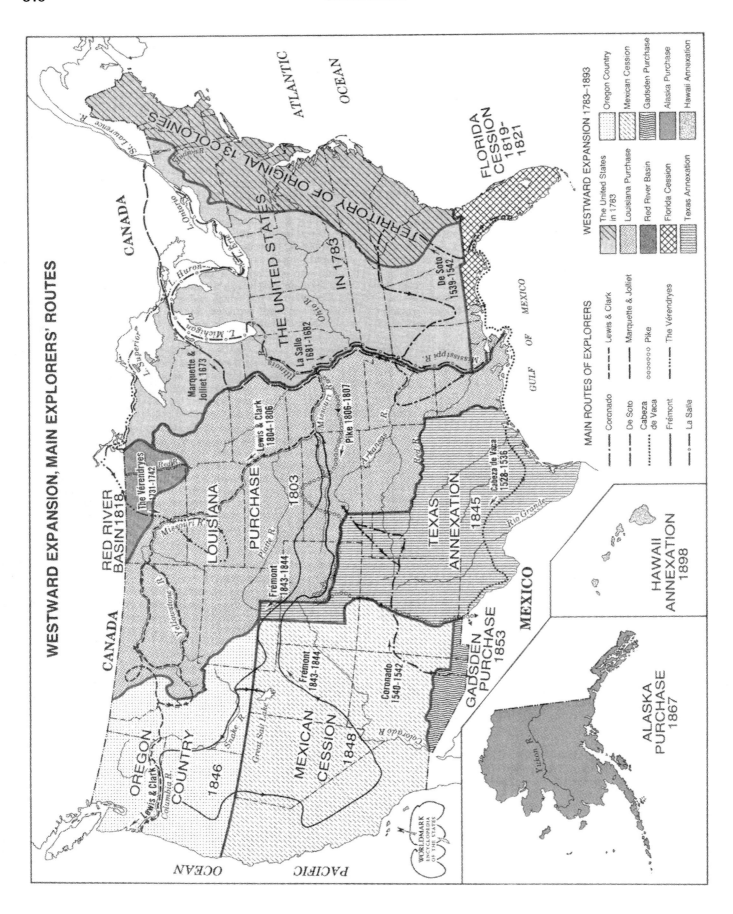

WESTWARD EXPANSION, MAIN EXPLORERS' ROUTES

TERRITORY OF ORIGINAL 13 COLONIES

THE UNITED STATES IN 1783

FLORIDA CESSION 1819–1821

De Soto 1539–1542

La Salle 1681–1682

Marquette & Joliet 1673

Lewis & Clark 1804–1806

Pike 1806–1807

LOUISIANA PURCHASE 1803

RED RIVER BASIN 1818

The Vérendryes 1731–1742

TEXAS ANNEXATION 1845

Cabeza de Vaca 1528–1536

Fremont 1843–1844

GADSDEN PURCHASE 1853

MEXICO

Fremont 1843–1844

Coronado 1540–1542

MEXICAN CESSION 1848

OREGON COUNTRY 1846

Lewis & Clark

CANADA

ATLANTIC OCEAN

GULF OF MEXICO

PACIFIC OCEAN

WESTWARD EXPANSION 1783–1893

	Oregon Country
	Mexican Cession
	Gadsden Purchase
	Alaska Purchase
	Hawaii Annexation

	The United States in 1783
	Louisiana Purchase
	Red River Basin
	Florida Cession
	Texas Annexation

MAIN ROUTES OF EXPLORERS

Coronado	Lewis & Clark
De Soto	Marquette & Joliet
Cabeza de Vaca	Pike
Frémont	The Vérendryes
La Salle	

HAWAII ANNEXATION 1898

ALASKA PURCHASE 1867

Yukon R.

WORLDMARK ENCYCLOPEDIA OF THE STATES

threats by France and Spain to reestablish colonial rule, President James Monroe in 1823 asserted that the Western Hemisphere was closed to further colonization by European powers. The Monroe Doctrine declared that any effort by such powers to recover territories whose independence the United States had recognized would be regarded as an unfriendly act.

From the 1820s to the outbreak of the Civil War, the growth of manufacturing continued, mainly in the North, and was accelerated by inventions and technological advances. Farming expanded with westward migration. The South discovered that its future lay in the cultivation of cotton. The cotton gin, invented by Eli Whitney in 1793, greatly simplified the problems of production; the growth of the textile industry in New England and Great Britain assured a firm market for cotton. Hence, during the first half of the 19th century, the South remained a fundamentally agrarian society based increasingly on a one-crop economy. Large numbers of field hands were required for cotton cultivation, and black slavery became solidly entrenched in the southern economy.

The construction of roads and canals paralleled the country's growth and economic expansion. The successful completion of the Erie Canal (1825), linking the Great Lakes with the Atlantic, ushered in a canal-building boom. Railroad building began in earnest in the 1830s, and by 1840, about 3,300 mi (5,300 km) of track had been laid. The development of the telegraph a few years later gave the nation the beginnings of a modern telecommunications network. As a result of the establishment of the factory system, a laboring class appeared in the North by the 1830s, bringing with it the earliest unionization efforts.

Western states admitted into the Union following the War of 1812 provided for free white male suffrage without property qualifications and helped spark a democratic revolution. As eastern states began to broaden the franchise, mass appeal became an important requisite for political candidates. The election to the presidency in 1829 of Andrew Jackson, a military hero and Indian fighter from Tennessee, was no doubt a result of this widening of the democratic process. By this time, the United States consisted of 24 states and had a population of nearly 13 million.

The relentless westward thrust of the United States population ultimately involved the United States in foreign conflict. In 1836, US settlers in Texas revolted against Mexican rule and established an independent republic. Texas was admitted to the Union as a state in 1845, and relations between Mexico and the United States steadily worsened. A dispute arose over the southern boundary of Texas, and a Mexican attack on a US patrol in May 1846 gave President James K. Polk a pretext to declare war. After a rapid advance, US forces captured Mexico City, and on 2 February 1848, Mexico formally gave up the unequal fight by signing the Treaty of Guadalupe Hidalgo, providing for the cession of California and the territory of New Mexico to the United States. With the Gadsden Purchase of 1853, the United States acquired from Mexico for $10 million large strips of land forming the balance of southern Arizona and New Mexico. A dispute with Britain over the Oregon Territory was settled in 1846 by a treaty that established the 49th parallel as the boundary with Canada. Thenceforth the United States was to be a Pacific as well as an Atlantic power.

Westward expansion exacerbated the issue of slavery in the territories. By 1840, abolition of slavery constituted a fundamental aspect of a movement for moral reform, which also encompassed women's rights, universal education, alleviation of working class hardships, and temperance. In 1849, a year after the discovery of gold had precipitated a rush of new settlers to California, that territory (whose constitution prohibited slavery) demanded admission to the Union. A compromise engineered in Congress by Senator Henry Clay in 1850 provided for California's admission as a free state in return for various concessions to the South. But enmities dividing North and South could not be silenced. The issue of slavery in the territories came to a head with the Kansas- Nebraska Act of 1854, which repealed the Missouri Compromise and left the question of slavery in those territories to be decided by the settlers themselves. The ensuing conflicts in Kansas between northern and southern settlers earned the territory the name "bleeding Kansas."

In 1860, the Democratic Party, split along northern and southern lines, offered two presidential candidates. The new Republican Party, organized in 1854 and opposed to the expansion of slavery, nominated Abraham Lincoln. Owing to the defection in Democratic ranks, Lincoln was able to carry the election in the electoral college, although he did not obtain a majority of the popular vote. To ardent supporters of slavery, Lincoln's election provided a reason for immediate secession. Between December 1860 and February 1861, the seven states of the Deep South—South Carolina, Mississippi, Florida, Alabama, Georgia, Louisiana, and Texas—withdrew from the Union and formed a separate government, known as the Confederate States of America, under the presidency of Jefferson Davis. The secessionists soon began to confiscate federal property in the South. On 12 April 1861, the Confederates opened fire on Ft. Sumter in the harbor of Charleston, S.C., and thus precipitated the US Civil War. Following the outbreak of hostilities, Arkansas, North Carolina, Virginia, and Tennessee joined the Confederacy.

For the next four years, war raged between the Confederate and Union forces, largely in southern territories. An estimated 360,000 men in the Union forces died of various causes, including 110,000 killed in battle. Confederate dead were estimated at 250,000, including 94,000 killed in battle. The North, with great superiority in manpower and resources, finally prevailed. A Confederate invasion of the North was repulsed at the battle of Gettysburg, Pennsylvania, in July 1863; a Union army took Atlanta in September 1864; and Confederate forces evacuated Richmond, the Confederate capital, in early April 1865. With much of the South in Union hands, Confederate General Robert E. Lee surrendered to General Ulysses S. Grant at Appomattox Courthouse in Virginia on 9 April.

The outcome of the war brought great changes in US life. Lincoln's Emancipation Proclamation of 1863 was the initial step in freeing some 4 million black slaves; their liberation was completed soon after the war's end by amendments to the Constitution. Lincoln's plan for the reconstruction of the rebellious states was compassionate, but only five days after Lee's surrender, Lincoln was assassinated by John Wilkes Booth as part of a conspiracy in which US Secretary of State William H. Seward was seriously wounded.

During the Reconstruction era (1865–77), the defeated South was governed by Union Army commanders, and the resultant bitterness of southerners toward northern Republican rule, which enfranchised blacks, persisted for years afterward. Vice President Andrew Johnson, who succeeded Lincoln as president, tried to carry out Lincoln's conciliatory policies but was opposed by radical Republican leaders in Congress, who demanded harsher treatment of the South. On the pretext that he had failed to carry out an act of Congress, the House of Representatives voted to impeach Johnson in 1868, but the Senate failed by one vote to convict him and remove him from office. It was during Johnson's presidency that Secretary of State Seward negotiated the purchase of Alaska (which attained statehood in 1959) from Russia for $7.2 million.

The efforts of southern whites to regain political control of their states led to the formation of organizations like the Ku Klux Klan, which employed violence to prevent blacks from voting. By the end of the Reconstruction era, whites had reestablished their political domination over blacks in the southern states and had begun to enforce patterns of segregation in education and social organization that were to last for nearly a century.

In many southern states, the decades following the Civil War were ones of economic devastation, in which rural whites as well as blacks were reduced to sharecropper status. Outside the South, however, a great period of economic expansion began. Transcontinental railroads were constructed, corporate enterprise spurted ahead, and the remaining western frontier lands were rapidly occupied and settled. The age of big business tycoons dawned. As heavy manufacturing developed, Pittsburgh, Chicago, and New York emerged as the nation's great industrial centers. The Knights of Labor, founded in 1869, engaged in numerous strikes, and violent conflicts between strikers and strikebreakers were common. The American Federation of Labor, founded in 1886, established a nationwide system of craft unionism that remained dominant for many decades. During this period, too, the woman's rights movement organized actively to secure the vote (although woman's suffrage was not enacted nationally until 1920), and groups outraged by the depletion of forests and wildlife in the West pressed for the conservation of natural resources.

During the latter half of the 19th century, the acceleration of westward expansion made room for millions of immigrants from Europe. The country's population grew to more than 76 million by 1900. As homesteaders, prospectors, and other settlers tamed the frontier, the federal government forced Native Americans west of the Mississippi to cede vast tracts of land to the whites, precipitating a series of wars with various tribes. By 1890, only 250,000 Native Americans remained in the United States, virtually all of them residing on reservations.

The 1890s marked the closing of the United States frontier for settlement and the beginning of US overseas expansion. By 1892, Hawaiian sugar planters of US origin had become strong enough to bring about the downfall of the native queen and to establish a republic, which in 1898, at its own request, was annexed as a territory by the United States. The sympathies of the United States with the Cuban nationalists who were battling for independence from Spain were aroused by a lurid press and by expansionist elements. A series of events climaxed by the sinking of the USS *Maine* in Havana harbor finally forced a reluctant President William McKinley to declare war on Spain on 25 April 1898. US forces overwhelmed those of Spain in Cuba, and as a result of the Spanish-American War, the United States added to its territories the Philippines, Guam, and Puerto Rico. A newly independent Cuba was drawn into the United States orbit as a virtual protectorate through the 1950s. Many eminent citizens saw these new departures into imperialism as a betrayal of the time-honored US doctrine of government by the consent of the governed.

With the marked expansion of big business came increasing protests against the oppressive policies of large corporations and their dominant role in the public life of the nation. A demand emerged for strict control of monopolistic business practice through the enforcement of antitrust laws. Two US presidents, Theodore Roosevelt (1901–09), a Republican and Woodrow Wilson (1913–21), a Democrat, approved of the general movement for reform, which came to be called progressivism. Roosevelt developed a considerable reputation as a trustbuster, while Wilson's program, known as the New Freedom, called for reform of tariffs, business procedures, and banking. During Roosevelt's first term, the United States leased the Panama Canal Zone and started construction of a 42-mi (68-km) canal, completed in 1914.

US involvement in World War I marked the country's active emergence as one of the great powers of the world. When war broke out in 1914 between Germany, Austria-Hungary, and Turkey on one side and Britain, France, and Russia on the other, sentiment in the United States was strongly opposed to participation in the conflict, although a large segment of the American people sympathized with the British and the French.

While both sides violated US maritime rights on the high seas, the Germans, enmeshed in a British blockade, resorted to unrestricted submarine warfare. On 6 April 1917, Congress declared war on Germany. Through a national draft of all able-bodied men between the ages of 18 and 45, some 4 million US soldiers were trained, of whom more than 2 million were sent overseas to France. By late 1917, when US troops began to take part in the fighting on the western front, the European armies were approaching exhaustion, and US intervention may well have been decisive in ensuring the eventual victory of the Allies. In a series of great battles in which US soldiers took an increasingly major part, the German forces were rolled back in the west, and in the autumn of 1918 were compelled to sue for peace. Fighting ended with the armistice of 11 November 1918. President Wilson played an active role in drawing up the 1919 Versailles Peace Treaty, which embodied his dream of establishing a League of Nations to preserve the peace, but the isolationist bloc in the Senate was able to prevent US ratification of the treaty.

In the 1920s, the United States had little enthusiasm left for crusades, either for democracy abroad or for reform at home; a rare instance of idealism in action was the Kellogg-Briand Pact (1928), an antiwar accord negotiated on behalf of the United States by Secretary of State Frank B. Kellogg. In general, however, the philosophy of the Republican administrations from 1921 to 1933 was expressed in the aphorism "The business of America is business," and the 1920s saw a great business boom. The years 1923–24 also witnessed the unraveling of the Teapot Dome scandal: the revelation that President Warren G. Harding's secretary of the interior, Albert B. Fall, had secretly leased federal oil reserves in California and Wyoming to private oil companies in return for gifts and loans.

The great stock market crash of October 1929 ushered in the most serious and most prolonged economic depression the country had ever known. By 1933, an estimated 12 million men and women were out of work; personal savings were wiped out on a vast scale through a disastrous series of corporate bankruptcies and bank failures. Relief for the unemployed was left to private charities and local governments, which were incapable of handling the enormous task.

The inauguration of the successful Democratic presidential candidate, Franklin D. Roosevelt, in March 1933 ushered in a new era of US history, in which the federal government was to assume a much more prominent role in the nation's economic affairs. Proposing to give the country a "New Deal," Roosevelt accepted national responsibility for alleviating the hardships of unemployment; relief measures were instituted, work projects were established, the deficit spending was accepted in preference to ignoring public distress. The federal Social Security program was inaugurated, as were various measures designed to stimulate and develop the economy through federal intervention. Unions were strengthened through the National Labor Relations Act, which established the right of employees' organizations to bargain collectively with employers. Union membership increased rapidly, and the dominance of the American Federation of Labor was challenged by the newly formed Congress of Industrial Organizations, which organized workers along industrial lines.

The depression of the 1930s was worldwide, and certain nations attempted to counter economic stagnation by building large military establishments and embarking on foreign adventures. Following German, Italian, and Japanese aggression, World War II broke out in Europe during September 1939. In 1940, Roosevelt, disregarding a tradition dating back to Washington that no president should serve more than two terms, ran again for reelection. He easily defeated his Republican opponent, Wendell Willkie, who, along with Roosevelt, advocated increased rearmament and all possible aid to victims of aggression. The United States was brought actively into the war by the Japanese attack on the Pearl Harbor naval base in Hawaii on 7 December 1941. The forces of Germany, Italy, and Japan were now arrayed over a vast theater of war against those of the United States and the British Commonwealth; in Europe, Germany was locked in a bloody struggle with the Soviet Union. US forces waged war across the vast expanses of the Pacific, in Africa, in Asia, and in Europe. Italy surrendered in 1943; Germany was successfully invaded in 1944 and conquered in May 1945; and after the United States dropped the world's first atomic bombs on Hiroshima and Nagasaki, the Japanese capitulated in August. The Philippines became an independent republic soon after the war, but the United States retained most of its other Pacific possessions, with Hawaii becoming the 50th state in 1959.

Roosevelt, who had been elected to a fourth term in 1944, died in April 1945 and was succeeded by Harry S Truman, his vice president. Under the Truman administration, the United States became an active member of the new world organization, the United Nations. The Truman administration embarked on large-scale programs of military aid and economic support to check the expansion of communism. Aid to Greece and Turkey in 1948 and the Marshall Plan, a program designed to accelerate the economic recovery of Western Europe, were outstanding features of US postwar foreign policy. The North Atlantic Treaty (1949) established a defensive alliance among a number of West European nations and the United States. Truman's Point Four program gave technical and scientific aid to developing nations. When, following the North Korean attack on South Korea on 25 June 1950, the UN Security Council resolved that members of the UN should proceed to the aid of South Korea. US naval, air, and ground forces were immediately dispatched by President Truman. An undeclared war ensued, which eventually was brought to a halt by an armistice signed on 27 June 1953.

In 1952, Dwight D. Eisenhower, supreme commander of Allied forces in Europe during World War II, was elected president on the Republican ticket, thereby bringing to an end 20 years of Democratic presidential leadership. In foreign affairs, the Eisenhower administration continued the Truman policy of containing the USSR and threatened "massive retaliation" in the event of Soviet aggression, thus heightening the Cold War between the world's two great nuclear powers. Although Republican domestic policies were more conservative than those of the Democrats, the Eisenhower administration extended certain major social and economic programs of the Roosevelt and Truman administrations, notably Social Security and public housing. The early years of the Eisenhower administration were marked by agitation (arising in 1950) over charges of Communist and other allegedly subversive activities in the United States—a phenomenon known as McCarthyism, after Republican Senator Joseph R. McCarthy of Wisconsin, who aroused much controversy with unsubstantiated allegations that Communists had penetrated the US government, especially the Army and the Department of State. Even those who personally opposed McCarthy lent their support to the imposition of loyalty oaths and the blacklisting of persons with left-wing backgrounds.

A major event of the Eisenhower years was the US Supreme Court's decision in *Brown v. Board of Education* of Topeka (1954) outlawing segregation of whites and blacks in public schools. In the aftermath of this ruling, desegregation proceeded slowly and painfully. In the early 1960s, sit-ins, "freedom rides," and similar expressions of nonviolent resistance by blacks and their sympathizers led to a lessening of segregation practices in public facilities. Under Chief Justice Earl Warren, the high court in 1962 mandated the reapportionment of state and federal legislative districts according to a "one person, one vote" formula. It also broadly extended the rights of defendants in criminal trials to include the provision of a defense lawyer at public expense for an accused person unable to afford one, and

established the duty of police to advise an accused person of his or her legal rights immediately upon arrest.

In the early 1960s, during the administration of Eisenhower's Democratic successor, John F. Kennedy, the Cold War heated up as Cuba, under the regime of Fidel Castro, aligned itself with the Soviet Union. Attempts by anti-Communist Cuban exiles to invade their homeland in the spring of 1961 failed despite US aid. In October 1962, President Kennedy successfully forced a showdown with the Soviet Union over Cuba in demanding the withdrawal of Soviet-supplied "offensive weapons"—missiles—from the nearby island. On 22 November 1963, President Kennedy was assassinated while riding in a motorcade through Dallas, Texas; hours later, Vice President Lyndon B. Johnson was inaugurated president. In the November 1964 elections, Johnson overwhelmingly defeated his Republican opponent, Barry M. Goldwater, and embarked on a vigorous program of social legislation unprecedented since Roosevelt's New Deal. His "Great Society" program sought to ensure black Americans' rights in voting and public housing, to give the underprivileged job training, and to provide persons 65 years of age and over with hospitalization and other medical benefits (Medicare). Measures ensuring equal opportunity for minority groups may have contributed to the growth of the woman's rights movement in the late 1960s. This same period also saw the growth of a powerful environmental protection movement.

US military and economic aid to anti-Communist forces in Vietnam, which had its beginnings during the Truman administration (while Vietnam was still part of French Indochina) and was increased gradually by presidents Eisenhower and Kennedy, escalated in 1965. In that year, President Johnson sent US combat troops to South Vietnam and ordered US bombing raids on North Vietnam, after Congress (in the Gulf of Tonkin Resolution of 1964) had given him practically carte blanche authority to wage war in that region. By the end of 1968, American forces in Vietnam numbered 536,100 men, but US military might was unable to defeat the Vietnamese guerrillas, and the American people were badly split over continuing the undeclared (and, some thought, ill-advised or even immoral) war, with its high price in casualties and materiel. Reacting to widespread dissatisfaction with his Vietnam policies, Johnson withdrew in March 1968 from the upcoming presidential race, and in November, Republican Richard M. Nixon, who had been the vice president under Eisenhower, was elected president. Thus, the Johnson years—which had begun with the new hopes of a Great Society but had soured with a rising tide of racial violence in US cities and the assassinations of civil rights leader Martin Luther King, Jr., and US senator Robert F. Kennedy, among others—drew to a close.

President Nixon gradually withdrew US ground troops from Vietnam but expanded aerial bombardment throughout Indochina, and the increasingly unpopular and costly war continued for four more years before a cease-fire—negotiated by Nixon's national security adviser, Henry Kissinger—was finally signed on 27 January 1973 and the last US soldiers were withdrawn. The most protracted conflict in American history had resulted in 46,163 US combat deaths and 303,654 wounded soldiers, and had cost the US government $112 billion in military allocations. Two years later, the South Vietnamese army collapsed, and the North Vietnamese Communist regime united the country.

In 1972, during the last year of his first administration, Nixon initiated the normalization of relations—ruptured in 1949—with the People's Republic of China and signed a strategic arms limitation agreement with the Soviet Union as part of a Nixon-Kissinger policy of pursuing détente with both major Communist powers. (Earlier, in July 1969, American technology had achieved a national triumph by landing the first astronaut on the moon.) The Nixon administration sought to muster a "silent majority" in support of its Indochina policies and its conservative social outlook in domestic affairs. The most momentous domestic development, however, was the Watergate scandal, which began on 17 June 1972 with the arrest of five men associated with Nixon's reelection campaign, during a break-in at Democratic Party headquarters in the Watergate office building in Washington, D.C. Although Nixon was reelected in 1972, subsequent disclosures by the press and by a Senate investigating committee revealed a complex pattern of political "dirty tricks" and illegal domestic surveillance throughout his first term. The president's apparent attempts to obstruct justice by helping his aides cover up the scandal were confirmed by tape recordings (made by Nixon himself) of his private conversations, which the Supreme Court ordered him to release for use as evidence in criminal proceedings. The House voted to begin impeachment proceedings, and in late July 1974, its Judiciary Committee approved three articles of impeachment. On 9 August, Nixon became the first president to resign the office. The following year, Nixon's top aides and former attorney general, John N. Mitchell, were convicted of obstruction and were subsequently sentenced to prison.

Nixon's successor was Gerald R. Ford, who in October 1973 had been appointed to succeed Vice President Spiro T. Agnew when Agnew resigned following his plea of *nolo contendere* to charges that he had evaded paying income tax on moneys he had received from contractors while governor of Maryland. Less than a month after taking office, President Ford granted a full pardon to Nixon for any crimes he may have committed as president. In August 1974, Ford nominated Nelson A. Rockefeller as vice president (he was not confirmed until December), thus giving the country the first instance of a nonelected president and an appointed vice president serving simultaneously. Ford's pardon of Nixon, as well as continued inflation and unemployment, probably contributed to his narrow defeat by a Georgia Democrat, Jimmy Carter, in 1976.

President Carter's forthright championing of human rights—though consistent with the Helsinki accords, the "final act" of the Conference on Security and Cooperation in Europe, signed by the United States and 34 other nations in July 1974—contributed to strained relations with the USSR and with some US allies. During 1978–79, the president concluded and secured Senate passage of treaties ending US sovereignty over the Panama Canal Zone. His major accomplishment in foreign affairs, however, was his role in mediating a peace agreement between Israel and Egypt, signed at the camp David, Md., retreat in September 1978. Domestically, the Carter administration initiated a national energy program to reduce US dependence on foreign oil by cutting gasoline and oil consumption and by encouraging the development of alternative energy resources. But the continuing decline of the economy because of double-digit inflation and high unemployment caused his popularity to wane, and confusing shifts in economic policy (coupled with a lack of clear goals in foreign affairs) characterized his administration during 1979 and 1980; a prolonged quarrel with Iran over more than 50 US hostages seized in Tehran on 4 November 1979 contributed to public doubts about his presidency. Exactly a year after the hostages were taken, former California Governor Ronald Reagan defeated Carter in an election that saw the Republican Party score major gains throughout the United States. The hostages were released on 20 January 1981, the day of Reagan's inauguration.

Reagan, who survived a chest wound from an assassination attempt in Washington, D.C., in 1981, used his popularity to push through significant policy changes. He succeeded in enacting income tax cuts of 25%, reducing the maximum tax rate on unearned income from 70% to 50%, and accelerating depreciation allowances for businesses. At the same time, he more than doubled the military budget, in constant 1985 dollars, between 1980 and 1989. Vowing to reduce domestic spending,

Reagan cut benefits for the working poor, reduced allocations for food stamps and Aid to Families With Dependent Children by 13%, and decreased grants for the education of disadvantaged children. He slashed the budget of the Environmental Protection Agency and instituted a flat rate reimbursement system for the treatment of Medicare patients with particular illnesses, replacing a more flexible arrangement in which hospitals had been reimbursed for "reasonable charges."

Reagan's appointment of Sandra Day O'Connor as the first woman justice of the Supreme Court was widely praised and won unanimous confirmation from the Senate. However, some of his other high-level choices were extremely controversial—none more so than that of his secretary of the interior, James G. Watt, who finally resigned on October 1983. To direct foreign affairs, Reagan named Alexander M. Haig, Jr., former NATO supreme commander for Europe, to the post of secretary of state; Haig, who clashed frequently with other administration officials, resigned in June 1982 and was replace by George P. Shultz. In framing his foreign and defense policy, Reagan insisted on a military buildup as a precondition for arms-control talks with the USSR. His administration sent money and advisers to help the government of El Salvador in its war against leftist rebels, and US advisers were also sent to Honduras, reportedly to aid groups of Nicaraguans trying to overthrow the Sandinista government in their country. Troops were also dispatched to Lebanon in September 1982, as part of a multinational peacekeeping force in Beirut, and to Grenada in October 1983 to oust a leftist government there.

Reelected in 1984, President Reagan embarked on his second term with a legislative agenda that included reduction of federal budget deficits (which had mounted rapidly during his first term in office), further cuts in domestic spending, and reform of the federal tax code. In military affairs, Reagan persuaded Congress to fund on a modest scale his Strategic Defense Initiative, commonly known as Star Wars, a highly complex and extremely costly space-based antimissile system. In 1987, the downing of an aircraft carrying arms to Nicaragua led to the disclosure that a group of National Security Council members had secretly diverted $48 million that the federal government had received in payment from Iran for American arms to rebel forces in Nicaragua. The disclosure prompted the resignation of two of the leaders of the group, Vice Admiral John Poindexter and Lieutenant Colonel Oliver North, as well as investigations by House and Senate committees and a special prosecutor, Lawrence Walsh. The congressional investigations found no conclusive evidence that Reagan had authorized or known of the diversion. Yet they noted that because Reagan had approved of the sale of arms to Iran and had encouraged his staff to assist Nicaraguan rebels despite the prohibition of such assistance by Congress, "the President created or at least tolerated an environment where those who did know of the diversion believed with certainty that they were carrying out the President's policies."

Reagan was succeeded in 1988 by his vice president, George Bush. Benefiting from a prolonged economic expansion, Bush handily defeated Michael Dukakis, governor of Massachusetts and a liberal Democrat. On domestic issues, Bush sought to maintain policies introduced by the Reagan administration. His few legislative initiatives included the passage of legislation establishing strict regulations of air pollution, providing subsidies for child care, and protecting the rights of the disabled. Abroad, Bush showed more confidence and energy. While he responded cautiously to revolutions in Eastern Europe and the Soviet Union, he used his personal relationships with foreign leaders to bring about comprehensive peace talks between Israel and its Arab neighbors, to encourage a peaceful unification of Germany, and to negotiate broad and substantial arms cuts with the Russians. Bush reacted to Iraq's invasion of Kuwait in 1990 by sending 400,000 soldiers to form the basis of a multinational coalition, which he assembled and which destroyed Iraq's main force within seven months. This conflict became known as the Gulf War.

One of the biggest crises that the Bush administration encountered was the collapse of the savings and loan industry in the late eighties. Thrift institutions were required by law to pay low interest rates for deposits and long-term loans. The creation of money market funds for the small investor in the eighties which paid higher rates of return than savings accounts prompted depositors to withdraw their money from banks and invest it in the higher yielding mutual funds. To finance the withdrawals, banks began selling assets at a loss. The deregulation of the savings and loan industry, combined with the increase in federal deposit insurance from $40,000 to $100,000 per account, encouraged many desperate savings institutions to invest in high-risk real-estate ventures, for which no state supervision or regulation existed. When the majority of such ventures predictably failed, the federal government found itself compelled by law to rescue the thrifts. It is estimated that this will cost to taxpayers $345 billion, in settlements that will continue through 2029.

In his bid for reelection in 1992, Bush faced not only Democratic nominee Bill Clinton, Governor of Arkansas, but also third-party candidate Ross Perot, a Dallas billionaire who had made his fortune in the computer industry. In contrast to Bush's first run for the presidency, when the nation had enjoyed an unusually long period of economic expansion, the economy in 1992 was just beginning to recover from a recession. Although data released the following year indicated that a healthy rebound had already begun in 1992, the public perceived the economy during election year as weak. Clinton took advantage of this perception in his campaign, focusing on the financial concerns of what he called "the forgotten middle class." He also took a more centrist position on many issues than more traditional Democrats, promising fiscal responsibility and economic growth. Clinton defeated Bush, winning 43% of the vote to Bush's 38%. Perot garnered 18% of the vote.

At its outset, Clinton's presidency was plagued by numerous setbacks, most notably the failure of his controversial health care reform plan, drawn up under the leadership of first lady Hillary Rodham Clinton. Major accomplishments included the passage, by a narrow margin, of a deficit-reduction bill calling for tax increases and spending cuts and Congressional approval of the North American Free Trade Agreement, which removed or reduced tariffs on most goods moving across the borders of the United States, Canada, and Mexico. Although supporters and critics agreed that the treaty would create or eliminate relatively few jobs—two hundred thousand—the accord prompted heated debate. Labor strenuously opposed the agreement, seeing it as accelerating the flight of factory jobs to countries with low labor costs such as Mexico, the 3rd-largest trading partner of the United States. Business, on the other hand, lobbied heavily for the treaty, arguing that it would create new markets for American goods and insisting that competition from Mexico would benefit the American economy.

By the fall of 1994, many American workers, still confronting stagnating wages, benefits, and living standards, had yet to feel the effects of the nation's recovery from the recession of 1990–91. The resulting disillusionment with the actions of the Clinton administration and the Democrat-controlled Congress, combined with the widespread climate of social conservatism resulting from a perceived erosion of traditional moral values led to an overwhelming upset by the Republican party in the 1994 midterm elections. The GOP gained control of both houses of Congress for the first time in over 40 years, also winning 11 gubernatorial races, for control of a total of 30 governorships nationwide. The Republican agenda—increased defense spending and cuts in taxes, social programs, and farm subsidies—had been popularized under the label "Contract with America," the title of a manifesto circulated during the campaign.

The ensuing confrontation between the nation's Democratic president and Republican-controlled Congress came to a head at the end of 1995, when Congress responded to presidential vetoes of appropriations and budget bills by refusing to pass stop gap spending measures, resulting in major shutdowns of the federal government in November and December. The following summer, however, the president and Congress joined forces to reform the welfare system through a bill replacing Aid to Families with Dependent Children with block grants through which welfare funding would largely become the province of the states.

The nation's economic recovery gained strength as the decade advanced, with healthy growth, falling unemployment, and moderate interest and inflation levels. Public confidence in the economy was reflected in a bull market on the stock exchange, which gained 60% between 1995 and 1997. Bolstered by a favorable economy at home and peace abroad, Clinton's faltering popularity rebounded and in 1996 he became the first Democratic president elected to a second term since Franklin D. Roosevelt in 1936, defeating the Republican candidate, former Senate majority leader Robert Dole, and Independent Ross Perot, whose electoral support was greatly reduced from its 1992 level. The Republicans retained control of both houses of Congress. In 1997, President Clinton signed into law a bipartisan budget plan designed to balance the federal budget by 2002 for the first time since 1969, through a combination of tax and spending cuts. In 1998–99, the federal government experienced two straight years of budget surpluses.

In 1998, special prosecutor Kenneth Starr submitted a report to Congress that resulted in the House of Representatives passing four articles of impeachment against President Clinton on charges that he obstructed justice and lied in a court proceeding to cover up an extramarital affair with a White House intern. In the subsequent trial in the Senate, the articles were defeated.

Regulation of the three large financial industries underwent significant change in late 1999. The Gramm-Leach-Bliley Act, (also known as the Financial Modernization Act) passed by Congress in November 1999. It cleared the way for banks, insurance companies, and securities companies to sell each other's services and to engage in merger and acquisition activity. Prior to the Act's passage, activities of the banking, insurance and securities industries were strictly limited by the Glass Steagall Act of 1933, which Gramm-Leach-Bliley repealed.

Health care issues received significant attention in 2000. On 23 November 1998, 46 states and the District of Columbia together reached a settlement with the large US tobacco companies over compensation for smoking-related health-care costs incurred by the states. Payments to the states, totaling $206 billion, were scheduled to be made over 25 years beginning in 1999. As of 2000, 44 states and the District of Columbia had passed Patients' Rights legislation; 39 passed legislation allowing Medicaid to pay for assisted-living care in qualifying cases; and all 50 states and the District of Columbia passed Children's Health Insurance Programs (CHIP) legislation to provide health care to children in low-income families.

The ongoing strong economy continued through the late 1990s and into 2000. Economic expansion set a record for longevity, and—except for higher gasoline prices during summer 2000, stemming from higher crude oil prices—inflation continued to be relatively low. By 2000, there was additional evidence that productivity growth had improved substantially since the mid-1990s, boosting living standards while helping to hold down increases in costs and prices despite very tight labor markets.

In 2000, Hispanics replaced African Americans as the largest minority group in the United States. (Hispanics numbered 35.3 million in 2000, or 12.5% of the population, compared with 34.7 million blacks, or 12.3% of the population.)

The 2000 presidential election was one of the closest in US history, pitting Democratic Vice President Al Gore against Republican Party candidate George W. Bush, son of former President George H. W. Bush. The vote count in Florida became the determining factor in the 7 November election, as each candidate needed to obtain the state's 25 electoral college votes in order to capture the 270 needed to win the presidency. When in the early hours of 8 November Bush appeared to have won the state's 25 votes, Gore called Bush to concede the election. He soon retracted the concession, however, after the extremely thin margin of victory triggered an automatic recount of the vote in Florida. The Democrats subsequently mounted a series of legal challenges to the vote count in Florida, which favored Bush. Eventually, the US Supreme Court, in *Bush v. Gore*, was summoned to rule on the election. On 12 December 2000, the US Supreme Court, divided 5–4, reversed the Florida state supreme court decision that had ordered new recounts called for by Al Gore. George W. Bush was declared president. Gore had won the popular vote, however, capturing 48.4% of votes cast to Bush's 47.9%.

Once inaugurated, Bush called education his top priority, stating that "no child should be left behind" in America. He affirmed support for Medicare and Social Security, and called for pay and benefit increases for the military. He called upon charities and faith-based and community groups to aid the disadvantaged. Bush announced a $1.6 trillion tax cut plan (subsequently reduced to $1.35 trillion) in his first State of the Union Address as an economic stimulus package designed to respond to an economy that had begun to falter. He called for research and development of a missile-defense program, and warned of the threat of international terrorism.

The threat of international terrorism was made all too real on 11 September 2001, when 19 hijackers crashed 4 passenger aircraft into the North and South towers of the World Trade Center, the Pentagon, and a field in Stony Creek Township in Pennsylvania. The World Trade Center towers were destroyed. As of 7 September 2002, 3,044 people were presumed dead as a result of all four 11 September 2001 attacks. The terrorist organization al-Qaeda, led by Saudi citizen Osama bin Laden, was believed to be responsible for the attacks, and a manhunt for bin Laden began.

On 7 October 2001, the United States and Britain launched air strikes against known terrorist training camps and military installations within Afghanistan, ruled by the Taliban regime that supported the al-Qaeda organization. The air strikes were supported by leaders of the European Union and Russia, as well as other nations. By December 2001, the Taliban were defeated, and Afghan leader Hamid Karzai was chosen to lead an interim administration for the country. Remnants of al-Qaeda still remained in Afghanistan and the surrounding region, and a year after the 2001 offensive more than 10,000 US soldiers remained in Afghanistan to suppress efforts by either the Taliban or al-Qaeda to regroup. As of mid-2003, Allied soldiers continued to come under periodic attack in Afghanistan.

As a response to the 11 September 2001 terrorist attacks, the US Congress that October approved the USA Patriot Act, proposed by the Bush administration. The act gave the government greater powers to detain suspected terrorists (or also immigrants), to counter money-laundering, and increase surveillance by domestic law enforcement and international intelligence agencies. Critics claimed the law did not provide for the system of checks and balances that safeguard civil liberties in the United States.

Beginning in late 2001, corporate America suffered a crisis of confidence. In December 2001, the energy giant Enron Corporation declared bankruptcy after massive false accounting practices came to light. Eclipsing the Enron scandal, telecommunications giant WorldCom in June 2002 disclosed that it had hid $3.8 billion in expenses over 15 months. The fraud led to WorldCom's bankruptcy, the largest in US history (the company had $107 billion in assets).

In his January 2002 State of the Union Address, President Bush announced that Iran, Iraq, and North Korea constituted an "axis of evil," sponsoring terrorism and threatening the United States and its allies with weapons of mass destruction. Throughout 2002, the United States pressed its case against Iraq, stating that the Iraqi regime had to disarm itself of weapons of mass destruction. In November 2002, the UN Security Council passed Resolution 1441, calling upon Iraq to disarm itself of any chemical, biological, or nuclear weapons or weapons capabilities it might possess, to comply with all previous UN Security Council resolutions regarding the country since the end of the Gulf War in 1991, and to allow for the immediate return of UN and International Atomic Energy Agency (IAEA) weapons inspectors (they had been expelled in 1998). UN and IAEA weapons inspectors returned to the country, but the United States and the United Kingdom expressed disatisfaction with their progress, and indicated military force might be necessary to remove the Iraqi regime, led by Saddam Hussein. France and Russia, permanent members of the UN Security Council, and Germany, a nonpermanent member, in particular, opposed the use of military force. The disagreement caused a diplomatic rift in the West that was slow to repair.

After diplomatic efforts at conflict resolution failed by March 2003, the United States, on 20 March, launched air strikes against targets in Baghdad, and war began. British forces moved into southern Iraq, around the city of Basra, and US ground forces began a march to Baghdad. On 9 April, Baghdad fell to US forces, and work began on restoring basic services to the Iraqi population, including providing safe drinking water, electricity, and sanitation. On 1 May, President Bush declared major combat operations had been completed. On 13 July 2003, a 25-member Iraqi interim Governing Council was formed. On 22 July, Saddam Hussein's two sons, Uday and Qusay, were killed by US forces in Mosul. US forces increasingly became the targets of attacks in Iraq, and by 1 August 2003, 52 US soldiers had been killed since combat was declared over on 1 May. By mid-August 2003, neither Saddam Hussein nor any weapons of mass destruction had been found in Iraq.

12 FEDERAL GOVERNMENT

The Constitution of the United States, signed in 1787, is the nation's governing document. In the first 10 amendments to the Constitution, ratified in 1791 and known as the Bill of Rights, the federal government is denied the power to infringe on rights generally regarded as fundamental to the civil liberties of the people. These amendments prohibit the establishment of a state religion and the abridgment of freedom of speech, press, and the right to assemble. They protect all persons against unreasonable searches and seizures, guarantee trial by jury, and prohibit excessive bail and cruel and unusual punishments. No person may be required to testify against himself, nor may he be deprived of life, liberty, or property without due process of law. The 13th Amendment (1865) banned slavery; the 15th (1870) protected the freed slaves' right to vote; and the 19th (1920) guaranteed the franchise to women. In all, there have been 27 amendments, the last of which, proposed in 1789 but ratified in 1992, denied the variation of the compensation of Senators and Representatives until an election intervened. The Equal Rights Amendment (ERA), approved by Congress in 1972, would have mandated equality between the sexes; only 35 of the required 38 states had ratified the ERA by the time the ratification deadline expired on 30 June 1982.

The United States has a federal form of government, with the distribution of powers between the federal government and the states constitutionally defined. The legislative powers of the federal government are vested in Congress, which consists of the House of Representatives and the Senate. There are 435 members of the House of Representatives. Each state is allotted a number of representatives in proportion to its population as determined by the decennial census. Representatives are elected for two-year terms in every even-numbered year. A representative must be at least 25 years old, must be a resident of the state represented, and must have been a citizen of the United States for at least seven years. The Senate consists of two senators from each state, elected for six-year terms. Senators must be at least 30 years old, must be residents of the states from which they are elected, and must have been citizens of the United States for at least nine years. One-third of the Senate is elected in every even-numbered year.

Congress legislates on matters of taxation, borrowing, regulation of international and interstate commerce, formulation of rules of naturalization, bankruptcy, coinage, weights and measures, post offices and post roads, courts inferior to the Supreme Court, provision for the armed forces, among many other matters. A broad interpretation of the "necessary and proper" clause of the Constitution has widened considerably the scope of congressional legislation based on the enumerated powers.

A bill that is passed by both houses of Congress in the same form is submitted to the president, who may sign it or veto it. If the president chooses to veto the bill, it is returned to the house in which it originated with the reasons for the veto. The bill may become law despite the president's veto if it is passed again by a two-thirds vote in both houses. A bill becomes law without the president's signature if retained for 10 days while Congress is in session. After Congress adjourns, if the president does not sign a bill within 10 days, an automatic veto ensues.

The president must be "a natural born citizen" at least 35 years old, and must have been a resident of the United States for 14 years. Under the 22nd Amendment to the Constitution, adopted in 1951, a president may not be elected more than twice. Each state is allotted a number of electors based on its combined total of US senators and representatives, and, technically, it is these electors who, constituted as the electoral college, cast their vote for president, with all of the state's electoral votes customarily going to the candidate who won the largest share of the popular vote of the state (the District of Columbia also has three electors, making a total of 538 votes). Thus, the candidate who wins the greatest share of the popular vote throughout the United States may, in rare cases, fail to win a majority of the electoral vote. If no candidate gains a majority in the electoral college, the choice passes to the House of Representatives.

The vice president, elected at the same time and on the same ballot as the president, serves as ex officio president of the Senate. The vice president assumes the power and duties of the presidency on the president's removal from office or as a result of the president's death, resignation, or inability to perform his duties. In the case of a vacancy in the vice presidency, the president nominates a successor, who must be approved by a majority in both houses of Congress. The Congress has the power to determine the line of presidential succession in case of the death or disability of both the president and vice president.

Under the Constitution, the president is enjoined to "take care that the laws be faithfully executed." In reality, the president has a considerable amount of leeway in determining to what extent a law is or is not enforced. Congress's only recourse is impeachment, to which it has resorted only three times, in proceedings against presidents Andrew Johnson, Richard Nixon, and Bill Clinton. Both the president and the vice president are removable from office after impeachment by the House and conviction at a Senate trial for "treason, bribery, or other high crimes and misdemeanors." The president has the power to grant reprieves and pardons for offenses against the United States except in cases of impeachment.

The president nominates and "by and with the advice and consent of the Senate" appoints ambassadors, public ministers, consuls, and all federal judges, including the justices of the Supreme Court. As commander in chief, the president is ultimately responsible for the disposition of the land, naval, and air forces, but the power to declare war belongs to Congress. The president conducts foreign relations and makes treaties with the advice and consent of the Senate. No treaty is binding unless it wins the approval of two-thirds of the Senate. The president's independence is also limited by the House of Representatives, where all money bills originate.

The president also appoints as his cabinet, subject to Senate confirmation, the secretaries who head the departments of the executive branch. As of 2003, the executive branch included the following cabinet departments: Agriculture (created in 1862), Commerce (1913), Defense (1947), Education (1980), Energy (1977), Health and Human Services (1980), Housing and Urban Development (1965), Interior (1849), Justice (1870), Labor (1913), State (1789), Transportation (1966), Treasury (1789), Veterans' Affairs (1989), and Homeland Security (2002). The Department of Defense—headquartered in the Pentagon, the world's largest office building—also administers the various branches of the military: Air Force, Army, Navy, defense agencies, and joint- service schools. The Department of Justice administers the Federal Bureau of Investigation, which originated in 1908; the Central Intelligence Agency (1947) is under the aegis of the Executive office. Among the several hundred quasi-independent agencies are the Federal Reserve System (1913), serving as the nation's central bank, and the major regulatory bodies, notably the Environmental Protection Agency (1970), Federal Communications Commission (1934), Federal Power Commission (1920), Federal Trade Commission (1914), and Interstate Commerce Commission (1887).

Regulations for voting are determined by the individual states for federal as well as for local offices, and requirements vary from state to state. In the past, various southern states used literacy tests, poll taxes, "grandfather" clauses, and other methods to disfranchise black voters, but Supreme Court decisions and congressional measures, including the Voting Rights Act of 1965, more than doubled the number of black registrants in Deep South states between 1964 and 1992. In 1960, only 29.1% of the black voting-age population was registered to vote; by the mid-1990s, that percentage had risen to over 65%. By 2003, there were over 12 million registered African American voters. The number of registered Hispanic voters increased from 2.5 million in 1972 to 7.6 million in 2000.

13 POLITICAL PARTIES

Two major parties, Democratic and Republican, have dominated national, state, and local politics since 1860. These parties are made up of clusters of small autonomous local groups primarily concerned with local politics and the election of local candidates to office. Within each party, such groups frequently differ drastically in policies and beliefs on many issues, but once every four years, they successfully bury their differences and rally around a candidate for the presidency. Minority parties have been formed at various periods in US political history, but most have generally allied with one of the two major parties, and none has achieved sustained national prominence. The most successful minority party in recent decades—that of Texas billionaire Ross Perot in 1992—was little more than a protest vote. Various extreme groups on the right and left, including a small US Communist Party, have had little political significance on a national scale; in 1980, the Libertarian Party became the first minor party since 1916 to appear on the ballot in all 50 states. The Green Party increased its showing in the 2000 election, with presidential candidate Ralph Nader winning 2.7% of the vote.

Independent candidates have won state and local office, but no candidate has won the presidency without major party backing.

Traditionally, the Republican Party is more solicitous of business interests and gets greater support from business than does the Democratic Party. A majority of blue-collar workers, by contrast, have generally supported the Democratic Party, which favors more lenient labor laws, particularly as they affect labor unions; the Republican Party often (though not always) supports legislation that restricts the power of labor unions. Republicans favor the enhancement of the private sector of the economy, while Democrats generally urge the cause of greater government participation and regulatory authority, especially at the federal level

Within both parties there are sharp differences on a great many issues; for example, northeastern Democrats in the past almost uniformly favored strong federal civil rights legislation, which was anathema to the Deep South; eastern Republicans in foreign policy are internationalist-minded, while midwesterners of the same party constituted from 1910 through 1940 the hard core of isolationist sentiment in the country. More recently, "conservative" headings have been adopted by members of both

parties who emphasize decentralized government power, strengthened private enterprise, and a strong US military posture overseas, while the designation "liberal" has been applied to those favoring an increased federal government role in economic and social affairs, disengagement from foreign military commitments, and the intensive pursuit of nuclear-arms reduction.

President Nixon's resignation and the accompanying scandal surrounding the Republican Party hierarchy had a telling, if predictable, effect on party morale, as indicated by Republican losses in the 1974 and 1976 elections. The latent consequences of the Vietnam and Watergate years appeared to take their toll on both parties, however, in growing apathy toward politics and mistrust of politicians among the electorate. As of 1992, Democrats enjoyed a large advantage over Republicans in voter registration, held both houses of congress, had a majority of state governorships, and controlled most state legislative bodies. Ronald Reagan's successful 1980 presidential bid cut into traditional Democratic strongholds throughout the United States, as Republicans won control of the US Senate and eroded state and local Democratic majorities. On the strength of an economic

US Popular Vote for President by National Political Parties, 1948–2000

YEAR	WINNER	TOTAL VOTES CAST	% OF ELIGIBLE VOTERS	DEMOCRAT	REPUBLICAN	PROHI-BITION	SOC. LABOR	SOC. WORKERS	SOCIALIST	PROGRES-SIVE	STATES' RIGHTS DEMOCRAT	CONSTI-TUTION	OTHER[1]
1948	Truman (D)	48,692,442	51	24,105,587	21,970,017	103,489	29,038	13,614	138,973	1,157,057	1,169,134	—	5,533
1952	Eisenhower (R)	61,551,118	62	27,314,649	33,936,137	73,413	30,250	10,312	20,065	140,416	—	17,200	8,676
1956	Eisenhower (R)	62,025,372	59	26,030,172	35,585,245	41,937	44,300	7,797	2,044	—	2,657	108,055	203,165
											NATL. STATES' RIGHTS		
1960	Kennedy (D)	68,828,960	63	34,221,344	34,106,761	44,087	47,522	40,166	—	—	209,314	—	159,856
											UNPLEDGED DEM.		
1964	Johnson (D)	70,641,104	62	43,126,584	27,177,838	23,266	45,187	32,701	—	—	6,953	210,732	17,843
								COMMUNIST	PEACE & FREEDOM	AMERICAN IND.		
1968	Nixon (R)	73,203,370	61	31,274,503	31,785,148	14,915	52,591	41,390	1,076	83,720[2]	9,901,151	—	48,876
									LIBERTARIAN		AMERICAN	
1972	Nixon (R)	77,727,590	55	29,171,791	47,170,179	12,818	53,811	94,415[2]	25,343	3,671	—	1,090,673	104,889
						US LABOR						
1976	Carter (D)	81,552,331	54	40,829,046	39,146,006	15,958	40,041	91,310	58,992	173,019	170,531	160,773	866,655[3]
						CITIZENS	RESPECT FOR LIFE					
1980	Reagan (R)	86,495,678	54	35,481,435	43,899,248	230,377	32,319	40,105	43,871	920,859	41,172	6,539	5,799,753[4]
							POPULIST			IND. ALLIANCE		
1984	Reagan (R)	92,652,793	53	37,577,137	54,455,074	72,200	66,336	24,706	36,386	228,314	46,852	13,161	132,627[5]
1988	Bush (R)	91,594,809	50	41,809,074	48,886,097	30,905	47,047	15,604	—	432,179	217,219	3,475	153,209
						US TAX-PAYER						
1992	Clinton (D)	104,426,659	55	44,909,889	39,104,545	43,398	107,002	23,091	39,163	291,628	73,708	3,875	19,830,360[6]
						US TAX-PAYER	GREEN			LIBERTARIAN	NATURAL LAW	
1996	Clinton (D)	96,277,223	49	47,402,357	39,198,755	184,658	684,902	8,476	4,765	485,798	113,668	1,847	8,196,762[7]
						REFORM						
2000	Bush, GW (R)	105,405,100	48	50,999,897	50,456,002	448,895	2,882,955	7,378	—	384,431	87,714	98,020	39,808

[1]Includes votes for state parties, independent candidates and unpledged electors.
[2]Total includes votes for several candidates in different states under the same party label.
[3]Includes 756,631 votes for Eugene McCarthy, an independent.
[4]Includes 5,719,437 votes for John Anderson, an independent.
[5]Includes 78,807 votes for Lyndon H. LaRouche, an independent.
[6]Includes 19,742,267 votes for Ross Perot, an independent.
[7]Includes 8,085,402 votes for Ross Perot, a Reform candidate.

recovery, President Reagan won reelection in November 1984, carrying 49 of 50 states (with a combined total of 525 electoral votes) and 58.8% of the popular vote; the Republicans retained control of the Senate, but the Democrats held on to the House. Benefiting from a six-year expansion of the economy, Republican George Bush won 54% of the vote in 1988. As Reagan had, Bush successfully penetrated traditionally Democratic regions. He carried every state in the South as well as the industrial states of the North.

Bush's approval rating reached a high of 91% in March of 1991 in the wake of the Persian Gulf War. By July of 1992, however, that rating had plummeted to 25%, in part because Bush appeared to be disengaged from domestic issues, particularly the 1991 recession. Bill Clinton, governor of Arkansas and twenty years younger than Bush, presented himself to the electorate as a "New Democrat." He took more moderate positions than traditional New Deal Democrats, including calling for a middle-class tax cut, welfare reform, national service, and such traditionally Republican goals as getting tough on crime. The presidential race took on an unpredictable dimension with the entrance of Independent Ross Perot, a Texas billionaire. Perot, who attacked the budget deficit and called for shared sacrifice, withdrew from the race in July and then re-entered it in October. Clinton won the election with 43% of the vote, Bush received 38%, and Perot captured 18%, more than any third-party presidential candidate since Theodore Roosevelt in 1912. In 1996 Bill Clinton became the first Democratic president since Franklin Roosevelt to be elected to a second term, with 49% of the popular vote to 41% for Republican Bob Dole, and 8% for Ross Perot, who once again ran as an Independent. Republicans retained control of the House and Senate.

Aided by a growing climate of conservatism on moral issues and popular discontent with the pace of economic recovery from the recent recession, the Republicans accomplished an historic upset in the 1994 midterm elections, gaining control of both houses of Congress for the first time since 1952. They gained 52 seats in the House, for a majority of 230–204, and 8 seats in the Senate, for a majority that came to 53–47 once Democrat Richard Shelby of Alabama changed parties shortly after the election. The Republicans also increased their power at the state level, winning 11 governorships, for a national total of 30. The number of state legislatures under Republican control increased from 8 to 19, with 18 controlled by the Democrats and 12 under split control. After the 1998 election, the Republican majority had eroded slightly in the House, with the 106th Congress including 223 Republicans, 210 Democrats, and 2 Independents; the Senate included 55 Republicans and 45 Democrats.

The 1984 election marked a turning point for women in national politics. Geraldine A. Ferraro, a Democrat, became the first female vice presidential nominee of a major US political party; no woman has ever captured a major-party presidential nomination. As of 2000, 9 women served in the US Senate, and 58 women held seats in the US House of Representatives.

The 1984 presidential candidacy of Jesse L. Jackson, election, the first black ever to win a plurality in a statewide presidential preference primary, likewise marked the emergence of African Americans as a political force, especially within the Democratic Party. In 1992 an African American woman, Democrat Carol Moseley Braun of Illinois, won election to the Senate, becoming the first black senator; Moseley Braun lost her reelection bid in 1998. There were 39 blacks and 17 Hispanics in the House as of 2000.

The candidates in the 2000 presidential were Republican George W. Bush, son of former president George Herbert Walker Bush; his vice presidential running mate was Dick Cheney. The Democratic candidate was Vice President Al Gore, Jr. (Clinton administration 1992–2000). Gore chose Joseph Lieberman, senator from Connecticut, as his running mate. Lieberman, an Orthodox Jew, became the first Jew to run for national office. Following the contested presidential election of 2000, George W. Bush emerged as president following a ruling by the US Supreme Court. Gore won the popular vote, with 48.4%, to 47.9% for Bush, but Bush won the electoral college vote, 271–266, with one blank vote in the electoral college cast.

Sectional and demographic shifts in party strength were evident in the 2000 election, with the Northeast, parts of the Midwest, and and the Pacific states voting Democratic, and the South, West, and rural communities voting Republican.

Following the November 2002 mid-term elections, Republicans held 229 of 435 seats in the House of Representatives, and there were 205 Democrats and 1 independent in the House. The Republicans held an extremely thin margin in the Senate, of 51 seats, to the Democrats' 48. There was one independent in the Senate, former Republican Jim Jeffords. Following the election, Nancy Pelosi became the Democratic Majority Leader in the House of Representatives, the first woman to head either party in Congress. As a result of the 2002 election, there were 60 women, 37 African Americans, and 22 Hispanics in the House of Representatives, and 14 women in the Senate. There were no African American or Hispanic senators following the 2002 election.

14 LOCAL GOVERNMENT

Governmental units within each state comprise counties, municipalities, and such special districts as those for water, sanitation, highways, and parks and recreation. There are more than 3,000 counties in the United States; more than 19,000 municipalities, including cities, villages, towns, and boroughs; nearly 15,000 school districts; and at least 31,000 special districts. Additional townships, authorities, commissions, and boards make up the rest of the nearly 85,000 local governmental units.

The 50 states are autonomous within their own spheres of government, and their autonomy is defined in broad terms by the 10th Amendment to the US Constitution, which reserves to the states such powers as are not granted to the federal government and not denied to the states. The states may not, among other restrictions, issue paper money, conduct foreign relations, impair the obligations of contracts, or establish a government that is not republican in form. Subsequent amendments to the Constitution and many Supreme Court decisions added to the restrictions placed on the states. The 13th Amendment prohibited the states from legalizing the ownership of one person by another (slavery); the 14th Amendment deprived the states of their power to determine qualifications for citizenship; the 15th Amendment prohibited the states from denying the right to vote because of race, color, or previous condition of servitude; and the 19th, from denying the vote to women.

Since the Civil War, the functions of the state have expanded. Local business—that is, business not involved in foreign or interstate commerce—is regulated by the state. The states create subordinate governmental bodies such as counties, cities, towns, villages, and boroughs, whose charters they either issue or, where home rule is permitted, approve. States regulate employment of children and women in industry, and enact safety laws to prevent industrial accidents. Unemployment insurance is a state function, as are education, public health, highway construction and safety, operation of a state highway patrol, and various kinds of personal relief. The state and local governments still are primarily responsible for providing public assistance, despite the large part the federal government plays in financing welfare.

Each state is headed by an elected governor. State legislatures are bicameral except Nebraska's, which has been unicameral since 1934. Generally, the upper house is called the senate, and the lower house the house of representatives or the assembly. Bills must be passed by both houses, and the governor has a suspensive veto, which usually may be overridden by a two-thirds vote.

The number, population, and geographic extent of the more than 3,000 counties in the United States—including the analogous units called boroughs in Alaska and parishes in Louisiana—show no uniformity from state to state. The county is the most conspicuous unit of rural local government and has a variety of powers, including location and repair of highways, county poor relief, determination of voting precincts and of polling places, and organization of school and road districts. City governments, usually headed by a mayor or city manager, have the power to levy taxes; to borrow; to pass, amend, and repeal local ordinances; and to grant franchises for public service corporations. Township government through an annual town meeting is an important New England tradition.

From the 1960s into the 21st century, a number of large cities began to suffer severe fiscal crises brought on by a combination of factors. Loss of tax revenues stemmed from the migration of middle-class residents to the suburbs and the flight of many small and large firms seeking to avoid the usually higher costs of doing business in urban areas. Low-income groups, many of them unskilled blacks and Hispanic migrants, came to constitute large segments of city populations, placing added burdens on locally funded welfare, medical, housing, and other services without providing the commensurate tax base for additional revenues.

15 STATE SERVICES

All state governments provide services in the fields of education, transportation, health and social welfare, public protection (including state police and prison personnel), housing, and labor. The 1970s saw an expansion of state services in four key areas: energy, environment, consumer protection, and governmental ethics. Each state provides some form of consumer advocacy, either through a separate department or agency or through the office of the attorney general. State government in the 1970s and early 1980s also showed the effects of the so-called post-Watergate morality. Laws mandating financial disclosure by public officials, once rare, had become common by 1983. Also notable were "sunshine laws," opening legislative committee meetings and administrative hearings to the public, and the use of an ombudsman either with general jurisdiction or with special powers relating, for example, to the problems of businesses, prisoners, the elderly, or racial minorities. Other trends in state administration, reflected on the federal level, include the separation of education from other services and the consolidation of social welfare programs in departments of human resources.

The distribution of federal funds to state, local, and territorial governments was estimated at more than $1.5 trillion in 1998. The largest outlays of aid were for retirement and disability funds, $507 billion; Medicare, $210 billion; Medicaid, $96 billion; supplemental security income, $28 billion; highways, $20 billion; housing assistance payments, $10 billion; compensatory education for the disadvantaged, $7.2 billion; urban mass transit, $4.6 billion; and unemployment insurance, $2 billion.

California received more funds than any other state, $87 billion, followed by New York state and Florida, at $58 billion each. Texas ($51), Pennsylvania ($45), Ohio ($33), and Illinois ($35), each received over $30 billion in federal funds.

16 JUDICIAL SYSTEM

The Supreme Court, established by the US Constitution, is the nation's highest judicial body, consisting of the chief justice of the United States and eight associate justices. All justices are appointed by the president with the advice and consent of the Senate. Appointments are for life "during good behavior," otherwise terminating only by resignation or impeachment and conviction.

The original jurisdiction of the Supreme Court is relatively narrow; as an appellate court, it is open to appeal from decisions of federal district courts, circuit courts of appeals, and the highest courts in the states, although it may dismiss an appeal if it sees fit to do so. The Supreme Court, by means of a writ of certiorari, may call up a case from a district court for review. Regardless of how cases reach it, the Court enforces a kind of unity on the decisions of the lower courts. It also exercises the power of judicial review, determining the constitutionality of state laws, state constitutions, congressional statutes, and federal regulations, but only when these are specifically challenged.

The Constitution empowers Congress to establish all federal courts inferior to the Supreme Court. On the lowest level and handling the greatest proportion of federal cases are the district courts—including one each in Puerto Rico, Guam, the Virgin Islands, the Northern Mariana Islands, and the District of Columbia—where all offenses against the laws of the United States are tried. Civil actions that involve cases arising under treaties and laws of the United States and under the Constitution, where the amount in dispute is greater than $5,000, also fall within the jurisdiction of the district courts. District courts have no appellate jurisdiction; their decisions may be carried to the courts of appeals, organized into 13 circuits. These courts also hear appeals from decisions made by administrative commissions. For most cases, this is usually the last stage of appeal, except where the court rules that a statute of a state conflicts with the Constitution of the United States, with federal law, or with a treaty. Special federal courts include the Court of Claims, Court of Customs and Patent Appeals, and Tax Court.

State courts operate independently of the federal judiciary. Most states adhere to a court system that begins on the lowest level with a justice of the peace and includes courts of general trial jurisdiction, appellate courts, and, at the apex of the system, a state supreme court. The court of trial jurisdiction, sometimes called the county or superior court, has both original and appellate jurisdiction; all criminal cases (except those petty in nature) and some civil cases are tried in this court. The state's highest court, like the Supreme Court of the United States, interprets the constitution and the laws of the state.

The grand jury is a body of from 13 to 24 persons that brings indictments against individuals suspected of having violated the law. Initially, evidence is presented to it by either a justice of the peace or a prosecuting county or district attorney. The trial or petit jury of 12 persons is used in trials of common law, both criminal and civil, except where the right to a jury trial is waived by consent of all parties at law. It judges the facts of the case, while the court is concerned exclusively with questions of law. The US accepts the compulsory jurisdiction of the International Court of Justice with reservations.

17 ARMED FORCES

The armed forces of the United States of America in 2002 numbered 1.41 million on active duty and 1.24 million in the Ready Reserve, a category of participation that allows regular training with pay and extended active duty periods for training. The Standby and Retired Reserve includes about 23,400 experienced officers and NCOs who can be recalled in a national emergency. Membership in all of these forces is voluntary and has been since 1973 when conscription expired as the Vietnam war was winding down. The active duty force includes 196,100 women, who serve in all grades and all occupational specialties except direct ground combat units and some aviation billets.

In the 1990s, the armed forces reduced their personnel numbers and force structure because of the diminished threat of a nuclear war with the former Soviet Union or a major conflict in central Europe. Despite the interlude of the Gulf War, 1990–91, the force reductions continued throughout the decade, forcing some restructuring of the active duty forces, with emphasis on rapid deployment to deter or fight major regional conflicts much like the Gulf War, in Korea, elsewhere in the Middle East, or Latin America (e.g. Cuba). The conventional force debate centered on whether the United States could or should maintain forces to fight two regional conflicts simultaneously. In the spring of 1999, the United States took part in the NATO air campaign in response to the crisis in Kosovo, and the ensuing US participation in peacekeeping operations in the region brought with it the prospect of another long-term overseas deployment.

For the purposes of administration, personnel management, logistics, and training, the traditional four military services in the Department of Defense remain central to strategic planning. The US Army numbers 485,500 (71,400 women) soldiers on active duty, divided roughly between 6 heavy (armored or mechanized) divisions, 4 light (infantry airborne, airmobile) divisions, and three independent infantry battalions as well as three armored cavalry regiments, five aviation brigades, and 11 air defense battalions. Army special operations missions go to Special Forces groups, an airborne ranger regiment, an aviation group, and a psychological warfare group with civil affairs and communications support units. The Army has 7,620 main battle tanks, 6,710 infantry fighting vehicles, 15,910 other tracked vehicles, almost 6,000 towed or self-propelled artillery, some 249 aircraft, and about 4,813 armed and transport helicopters. The Army National Guard (355,900) emphasizes the preparation of combat units up to division size for major regional conflicts while the Army Reserve (358,100) prepares individuals to fill active units or provide combat support or service support/technical/medical units upon mobilization. In addition, the National Guard retains a residual state role in suppressing civil disturbances and providing disaster relief.

The US Navy (385,400; 57,800 women) has shifted from its role in nuclear strategic deterrence and control of sea routes to Europe and Asia to the projection of naval power from the sea. Naval task forces normally combine three combat elements: air, surface, and subsurface. The Navy mans 24 nuclear-powered attack submarines with one configured for special operations; most of these boats can launch cruise missiles at land targets.

Naval aviation is centered on 12 carriers (9 nuclear-powered) and 11 carrier aircraft wings. Including its armed ASW helicopters and armed long-range ASW patrol aircraft—as well as a large fleet of communications and support aircraft—the Navy controls 1,510 aircraft and 506 armed helicopters. Naval aviation reserves provide additional wings for carrier deployment. The surface force includes 27 cruisers (22 with advanced anti-air suites), 54 destroyers, 37 frigates, 42 amphibious ships, 27 mine warfare ships, and 21 patrol and coastal combatants. More ships are kept in ready reserve or are manned by surface line reserve units. The fleet support force also includes specialized ships for global logistics that are not base-dependent.

The Marine Corps, a separate naval service, is organized into three active divisions and three aircraft wings of the Fleet Marine Force, which also include 3 Force Service Support groups. The Marine Corps (173,400; 10,500 women) emphasizes amphibious landings but trains for a wide-range of contingency employments. The marines have 403 main battle tanks, 1,321 amphibious armored vehicles, and about 1,000 towed artillery pieces.

The US Air Force (369,700; 56,400 women) has focused on becoming rapidly deployable rather than US-based. Almost all its aircraft are now dedicated to nonstrategic roles in support of forward deployed ground and naval forces. The Air Force stresses the missions of air superiority and interdiction with complementary operations in electronic warfare and reconnaissance, but it also includes 28 transport squadrons. Air Force personnel manage the US radar and satellite early-warning and intelligence effort. The Air Force Reserve and Air National Guard (roughly 183,100 active reserves) provides a wide range of flying and support units, and its flying squadrons have demonstrated exceptional readiness and combat skills on contingency missions. Air Force reserves, for example, provide the backbone of the air refueling and transport fleets.

The armed forces are deployed in functional unified or specified commands for actual missions. The Strategic Command controls the strategic nuclear deterrence forces: 550 ICMBs, 18 Navy fleet ballistic missile submarines, and 178 operational long-range bombers. These forces have undergone reduction to conform with the START arms limitation treaty of 1991, as amended in 1992, so that by the year 2003 the United States will have only 500 ICMBs, 1,728 SLBMs, and 95 nuclear-armed bombers. Strategic Command is complemented by Space Command/North American Air Defense Command. In 2002, the Treaty of Moscow was signed between the United States and Russia to reduce deployed nuclear weapons by two-thirds by the year 2012. As of 2002, the United States had more than 10,000 operational nuclear warheads.

The conventional forces are assigned to a mix of geographic and functional commands: Atlantic Command, European Command, Central Command, Southern Command, and Pacific Command, as well as Transportation Command and Special Operations Command. The Army also maintains a Forces Command for ground forces in strategic reserve in the United States. Major operational units are deployed to Germany, Korea, and Japan as part of collective security alliances. About one-third of active duty personnel are assigned to overseas billets (1–3 years) or serve in air, naval, and ground units that serve short tours on a rotational basis. Peacekeeping forces are stationed in Bosnia, East Timor, Ethiopia/Eritrea, Georgia, Hungary, Iraq/Kuwait, the Middle East, Tajikstan, Turkey, Uzbekistan, and Yugoslavia. Approximately 7,200 US troops are stationed in Afghanistan with Operation enduring Freedom.

Patterns of defense spending reflect the movement away from Cold War assumptions and confrontation with the former Soviet Union and the People's Republic of China. During the 1980s when defense spending hovered around $300 billion a year and increased roughly 30% over the decade, defense spending absorbed roughly 6% of the gross domestic spending, 25% of federal spending, and 16% of net public spending. In the early 1990s, when the defense budget slipped back to the $250–$260 billion level, the respective percentages were 4.5, 18, and 11, the lowest levels of support for defense since the Korean War (1950). In 1999, the defense budget was $276.7 million or 3.2% of GDP. US military assistance abroad shows similar trends. From 1981 to 1991 the United States sold $118 billion in arms abroad and provided some outright grants, military training, and other support services, most in dollar value to its NATOs allies, Sau'di Arabia, Israel, South Korea, and Japan. This spending also declined in the 1990s.

[18]MIGRATION

Between 1840 and 1930, some 37 million immigrants, the overwhelming majority of them Europeans, arrived in the United States. Immigration reached its peak in the first decade of the 20th century, when nearly 9 million came. Following the end of World War I, the tradition of almost unlimited immigration was abandoned, and through the National Origins Act of 1924, a quota system was established as the basis of a carefully restricted policy of immigration. Under the McCarran Act of 1952, one-sixth of 1% of the number of inhabitants from each European nation residing in the continental United States as of 1920 could be admitted annually. In practice, this system favored nations of northern and western Europe, with the UK, Germany, and Ireland being the chief beneficiaries. The quota system was radically reformed in 1965, under a new law that established an annual ceiling of 170,000 for Eastern Hemisphere immigrants and 120,000 for entrants from the Western Hemisphere; in

October 1978, these limits were replaced by a worldwide limit of 290,000, which was lowered to 270,000 by 1981. A major 1990 overhaul set a total annual ceiling of 700,000 (675,000 beginning in fiscal 1995), of which 480,000 would be family sponsored and 140,000 employment based.

In 2002, 1,063,732 immigrants entered the United States, of whom 416,860 were subject to the numerical limits. Some 342,099 immigrants in 2002 were from Asia; 404,437 were from North America; 74,506 were from South America; 174,209 from Europe; 60,269 from Africa, and 5,557 from Oceania. A direct result of the immigration law revisions has been a sharp rise in the influx of Asians (primarily Chinese, Filipinos, Indians, Japanese, and Koreans), of whom 2,738,157 entered the country during 1981–90, as compared with 153,249 during the entire decade of the 1950s. Most immigrants in 2002 came from Mexico (219,380).

Since 1961, the federal government supported and financed the Cuban Refugee Program; in 1995, new accords were agreed to by the two countries. More than 500,000 Cubans were living in southern Florida by 1980, when another 125,000 Cuban refugees arrived; by 1990, 4% of Florida's population was of Cuban descent. Some 169,322 Cubans arrived from 1991–2000, and 27,520 arrived in 2002. Between 1975 and 1978, following the defeat of the US-backed Saigon (Vietnam) government, several hundred thousand Vietnamese refugees came to the United States. Under the Refugee Act of 1980, a ceiling for the number of admissible refugees is set annually; in fiscal 2002, the ceiling for refugees was 70,000. Since Puerto Ricans are American citizens, no special authorization is required for their admission to the continental United States. The population of refugees, asylees, resettled refugees, and asylum-seekers with pending claims was estimated at 5,250,954 in June 2003, a 34% increase over June 2002. During the same year, the newly-formed Bureau of Citizenship and Immigration Services (BCIS—formerly the Immigration and Naturalization Service or INS) received 66,577 applications for asylum, a decline of 36% from 2002. UNHCR reports the United States as the leading destination of refugees, accounting for half of all resettlement worldwide.

Large numbers of aliens—mainly from Latin America, especially Mexico—have illegally established residence in the United States after entering the country as tourists, students, or temporary visitors engaged in work or business. In November 1986, Congress passed a bill allowing illegal aliens who had lived and worked in the United States since 1982 the opportunity to become permanent residents. By the end of fiscal year 1992, 2,650,000 of a potential 2,760,000 eligible for permanent residence under this bill had attained that status. In 1996 the number of illegal alien residents was estimated at 5 million, of which 2 million were believed to be in California. As of 2002, an estimated 33.1 million immigrants (legal and illegal) lived in the United States. Of this total, the Census Bureau estimated in 2000 that 8–9 million of them were illegal alien residents.

The major migratory trends within the United States have been a general westward movement during the 19th century; a long-term movement from farms and other rural settlements to metropolitan areas, which showed signs of reversing in some states during the 1970s; an exodus of southern blacks to the cities of the North and Midwest, especially after World War I; a shift of whites from central cities to surrounding suburbs since World War II; and, also during the post–World War II period, a massive shift from the North and East to the Sunbelt region of the South and Southwest.

19INTERNATIONAL COOPERATION

The United States, whose failure to join the League of Nations was a major cause of the failure of that body, is a charter member of the UN, having joined on 24 October 1945. The United States participates in ECE, ECLAC, ESCAP, and all the nonregional specialized agencies (it withdrew from UNESCO in 1984, charging the agency with mismanagement and with bias against Western nation, but rejoined in 2002). There are also policy differences between the United States and several other UN agencies. The US share of the total funds required for the upkeep of the UN is about 25% of the total, far more than any other nation; however, the United States withheld its payments during the 1990s. The US participates in more than 70 intergovernmental organizations, including the Asian Development Bank, OECD, the IMF and IBRD (World Bank), and international councils and commissions on various industries. The US also participates actively in the Permanent Court of Arbitration. Hemispheric agencies include the Inter-American Committee on the Alliance for Progress, IADB, and OAS.

NATO is the principal military alliance to which the United States belongs. The ANZUS alliance was a mutual defense pact between Australia, New Zealand, and the United States; in 1986, following New Zealand's decision to ban US nuclear-armed or nuclear-powered ships from its ports, the United States renounced its ANZUS treaty security commitments to New Zealand. The nation is a member of the WTO but refused to sign the Law of the Sea because of unwillingness to relinquish rights over seabed mining; in keeping with international practice, however, the United States does maintain a 200-mi coastal economic zone. In 1992, the United States, Canada, and Mexico signed the North American Free Trade Agreement (NAFTA), creating a free-trade zone among the three countries. It was ratified by all three governments in 1993 and took effect the following year. In 1986, the United States approved the 1948 UN convention against genocide.

20ECONOMY

In variety and quantity, the natural resources of the United States probably exceed those of any other nation, with the possible exception of the former Soviet Union. The United States is among the world's leading exporters of coal, wheat, corn, and soybeans. Because of its vast economic growth, however, the United States depends increasingly on foreign sources for a long list of raw materials including oil.

By the middle of the 20th century, the United States was a leading consumer of nearly every important industrial raw material. The industry of the United States produced about 40% of the world's total output of goods, despite the fact that the country's population comprised about 6% of the world total and its land area about 7% of the earth's surface. In recent decades, US production has continued to expand, though at a slower rate than that of most other industrialized nations.

In absolute terms the United States far exceeds every other nation in the size of its gross national product (GNP), which more than tripled between 1970 and 1983 to $3.3 trillion. In 1998 the nation's gross domestic product (GDP) reached a record $8.5 trillion in current dollars, with per capita GDP reaching $31,500. Per capita GDP stood at $37,600 in 2002, and the nation's GDP was $10.4 trillion.

Inflation has not been as significant a factor in the US economy in the 1990s as it was in the 1970s and 1980s. The US inflation rate tends to be lower than that of the majority of industrialized nations. For the period 1970–78, for example, consumer prices increased by an annual average of 6.7%, less than in every other Western country except Austria, Luxembourg, Switzerland, and West Germany, and well below the price increase in Japan. The double-digit inflation of 1979–81 came as a rude shock to most Americans, with economists and politicians variously blaming international oil price rises, federal monetary policies, and US government spending.

The United States entered the post–World War II era with the world's largest, and strongest, economy. Public confidence in both business and government was strong, the nation enjoyed the largest peacetime trade surplus in its history, and the gross national product grew to a record $482.7 billion by the end of the 1950s. In the sixties the country enjoyed the most sustained period of economic expansion it had known, accompanied by rising productivity and low unemployment. Real income rose 50% during the decade, and US investment in foreign countries reached $49 billion in 1965, up from $11.8 billion in 1950. Big business and big government were both powerful forces in the economy during this period, when large industrial corporations accounted for vast portions of the national income, and the federal government expanded its role in such areas as social welfare, scientific research, space technology, and development of the nation's highway system.

After two decades of prosperity, Americans experienced an economic downturn in the 1970s, a period known for the unprecedented combination of lagging economic growth and inflation that gave birth to the term *stagflation*. Foreign competitors in Japan and Europe challenged the global dominance of American manufacturers, and oil crises in 1973–74 and 1979 shook public confidence in the institutions of both government and business. The forced bailouts of Chrysler and Lockheed were symbolic of the difficult transition to a new economic era, marked by the growing importance of the service sector and the ascendancy of small businesses.

People in the 1980s also witnessed a crisis in the banking industry, caused by a combination of factors, including high inflation and interest rates, problem loans to developing countries, and speculative real estate ventures that caused thousands of banks to fail when the real estate boom of the early eighties collapsed.

During Ronald Reagan's first presidential term, from 1980 to 1984, the nation endured two years of severe recession followed by two years of robust recovery. The inflation rate was brought down, and millions of new jobs were created. The economic boom of the early and mid-eighties, however, coincided with a number of alarming developments. Federal budget deficits, caused by dramatic increases in the military budget and by rising costs of entitlement programs such as Medicaid and Medicare, averaged more than $150 billion annually. By 1992, the total deficit reached $290 billion, or $1,150 for every American. In addition, corporate debt rose dramatically, and household borrowing grew twice as fast as personal income.

The disparity between the affluent and the poor widened in at the end of the 20th century. The share of the nation's income received by the richest 5% of American families rose from 18.6% in 1977 to 24.5% in 1990, while the share of the poorest 20% fell from 5.7% to 4.3%. Externally, the nation's trade position deteriorated, as a high level of foreign investment combined with an uncompetitive US dollar to create a ballooning trade deficit. In 1990, the American economy plunged into a recession. Factors contributing to the slump included rising oil prices following Iraq's invasion of Kuwait, a sharp increase in interest rates, and declining availability of credit. Output fell 1.6% and 1.7 million jobs were cut. Unemployment rose from 5.2% in 1989 to 7.5% in 1991, but had fallen to 4.5% by 1998.

The recovery that began in March 1991 inaugurated a sustained period of expansion that, as of mid-2000, was the 3rd-longest since World War II, characterized by moderation in the key areas of growth, inflation, unemployment, and interest rates. Real GDP growth, which fluctuated between 2% and 3.5% throughout the period, was 3.9% for 1998. After peaking at 7.5%, unemployment declined steadily throughout the early and mid-1990s, falling to 5.6% in 1995, 5.3% at the end of 1996, and in 1998, remaining below 5%. After 1993/94, inflation mostly remained under 3%. One exception to the generally moderate character of the economy was the stock market, which rose 60% between 1995 and 1997, buoyed by the combination of

low unemployment and low inflation, as well as strong corporate earnings. By 1999/2000, stock market growth had slowed somewhat. Further cause for optimism was the bipartisan balanced-budget legislation enacted and signed into law in 1997. The plan, combining tax and spending cuts over a five-year period, was aimed at balancing the federal budget by 2002 for the first time since 1969. In early 2001, the government projected a budget surplus of $275 billion for the fiscal year ending that September. That projection would soon be reversed.

At the beginning of the 21st century, significant economic concerns—aside from the inevitable worry over how long the boom could last without an eventual downturn—included the nation's sizable trade deficit, the increasing medical costs of an aging population, and the failure of the strong economy to improve conditions for the poor. Since 1975, gains in household income were experienced almost exclusively by the top 20% of households. However, in the late 1990s and early 2000, productivity was continuing to grow, inflation was relatively low, and the labor market was tight.

Economic growth came to a standstill in the middle of 2001, largely due to the end of the long investment boom, especially in the information technology sector. The economy was in recession in the second half of 2001, and the service sector was affected as well as manufacturing. The 11 September 2001 terrorist attacks on the United States exacerbated the poor economic situation. Average real GDP growth rose by only 0.3% in 2001. The US economy, which had driven global economic growth during the 1990s, became the cause of a worldwide economic downturn, including in the rest of North America, Europe, Japan, and the developing economies of Latin America and Southeast Asia strongly influenced by trends in the US economy.

The economy began to recover, slowly, in 2002, with GDP growth estimated at 2.45%. Analysts attributed the modest recovery to the ability of business decision-makers to respond to economic imbalances based on real-time information, on deregulation, and on innovation in financial and product markets. Nevertheless, domestic confidence in the economy remained low, and coupled with major corporate failures (including Enron and WorldCom) and additional stock market declines, the recovery remained sluggish and uneven. Growth slowed at the end of 2002 and into 2003, and the unemployment rate rose to 6.3% in July 2003. The CPI inflation rate fell to under 1.5% at the beginning of 2003, which raised concerns over the risk of deflation. As well, there was a substantial rise in military spending as a result of the 2003 war in Iraq.

Following the war in Iraq, consumer spending rebounded, as did stock prices; the housing market remained strong; inflation was low; the dollar depreciated on world markets; additional tax cuts were passed; there was an easing of oil prices; and productivity growth was strong. As a result of these factors, many analysts predicted a more favorable economic climate for 2004. Nevertheless, in 2003, the federal budget deficit was projected to reach $455 billion, the largest shortfall on record.

21 INCOME

The US Central Intelligence Agency (CIA) reports that in 2001 the United States' gross domestic product (GDP) was estimated at $10.082 trillion. The per capita GDP was estimated at $36,300. The annual growth rate of GDP was estimated at 0.3%. The average inflation rate in 2001 was 2.8%. The CIA defines GDP as the value of all final goods and services produced within a nation in a given year and computed on the basis of purchasing power parity (PPP) rather than value as measured on the basis of the rate of exchange. It was estimated that agriculture accounted for 2% of GDP, industry 18%, and services 80%.

The World Bank reports that in 2000 per capita household consumption (in constant 1995 US dollars) was $21,707. Household consumption includes expenditures of individuals, households, and nongovernmental organizations on goods and services, excluding purchases of dwellings. It was estimated that for the same period private consumption grew at an annual rate of 4%. Approximately 13% of household consumption was spent on food, 9% on fuel, 4% on health care, and 6% on education. The richest 10% of the population accounted for approximately 30.5% of household consumption and the poorest 10% approximately 1.8%. It was estimated that in 2001 about 13% of the population had incomes below the poverty line.

22LABOR

About 144,863,000 persons constituted the country's civilian labor force in 2002. In July 2003, the unemployment rate was 6.2%. As of July 2003, agriculture engaged 1,126,000 Americans. Earnings of workers vary considerably with type of work and section of country. In the first quarter of 2003, the national average wage was $15.27 per hour for nonagricultural workers, with an average workweek of 33.8 hours. Workers in manufacturing had a national average wage of $15.64, (including overtime), with the longest average workweek of all categories of workers at 40.4 hours in the first quarter of 2003.

In 2002, 13.2% of wage and salary workers were union members—16.1 million US citizens belonged to a union that year. In 1983, union membership was 20.1%. In 2002, there were 34 national labor unions with over 100,000 members, the largest being the National Educational Association with 2.7 million members as of 2003. The most important federation of organized workers in the United States is the American Federation of Labor–Congress of Industrial Organizations (AFL–CIO), whose affiliated unions had 13 million members as of 2003, down from 14.1 million members in 1992. The major independent industrial and labor unions and their estimated 2002 memberships are the International Brotherhood of Teamsters, 1,398,412, and the United Automobile Workers, some 710,000 (the majority of whom work for General Motors, Ford, and Daimler-Chrylser). Most of the other unaffiliated unions are confined to a single establishment or locality. US labor unions exercise economic and political influence not only through the power of strikes and slowdowns but also through the human and financial resources they allocate to political campaigns (usually on behalf of Democratic candidates) and through the selective investment of multibillion-dollar pension funds.

The National Labor Relations Act of 1935 (the Wagner Act), the basic labor law of the United States, was considerably modified by the Labor-Management Relations Act of 1947 (the Taft-Hartley Act) and the Labor-Management Reporting and Disclosure Act of 1959 (the Landrum-Griffin Act). Closed-shop agreements, which require employers to hire only union members, are banned. The union shop agreement, however, is permitted; it allows the hiring of nonunion members on the condition that they join the union within a given period of time.

As of 2003, 23 states had right-to-work laws, forbidding the imposition of union membership as a condition of employment. Under the Taft-Hartley Act, the president of the United States may postpone a strike for 90 days in the national interest. The act of 1959 requires all labor organizations to file constitutions, bylaws, and detailed financial reports with the secretary of labor, and stipulates methods of union elections. The National Labor Relations Board seeks to remedy or prevent unfair labor practices and supervises union elections, while the Equal Employment Opportunity Commission seeks to prevent discrimination in hiring, firing, and apprenticeship programs.

The number of work stoppages and of workers involved reached a peak in the late 1960s and early 1970s, declining steadily thereafter. In 2002, there were 19 major stoppages involving 46,000 workers resulting in 660,000 workdays idle, compared with 1995, when there were 31 major stoppages involving 191,500 workers resulting in 5,771,000 days idle; a major stoppage was defined as one involving 1,000 workers or more for a minimum of one day or shift.

23AGRICULTURE

In 1999, the United States produced a substantial share of the world's agricultural commodities. Agricultural exports reached $56.7 billion in 2001. The United States had an agricultural trade surplus of $11.7 billion in 2001, 3rd after Australia and Brazil.

Between 1930 and 1998, the number of farms in the United States declined from 6,546,000 to an estimated 2,190,000. The total amount of farmland increased from 399 million hectares (986 million acres) in 1930 to 479 million hectares (1.18 billion acres) in 1959 but declined to 386 million hectares (954 million acres) in 1998. From 1930 to 1998, the size of the average farm tripled from 61 to 136 hectares (from 151 to 435 acres), a result of the consolidation effected by large-scale mechanized production. The farm population, which comprised 35% of the total US population in 1910, declined to 25% during the Great Depression of the 1930s, and dwindled to less than 2% by 1998.

A remarkable increase in the application of machinery to farms took place during and after World War II (1939–45). Tractors, trucks, milking machines, grain combines, corn pickers, and pickup bailers became virtual necessities in farming. In 1920 there was less than one tractor in use for every 400 hectares (1,000 acres) of cropland harvested; by 1997 there were five tractors per 400 hectares. Two other elements essential to US farm productivity are chemical fertilizers and irrigation. Fertilizers and lime represent more than 6% of farm operating expenses. Arable land under irrigation amounted to 12% of the total in 1998.

Substantial quantities of corn, the most valuable crop produced in the United States, are grown in almost every state; its yield and price are important factors in the economies of the regions where it is grown. Production of selected US crops in 1999 (in 1,000 metric tons), and their percent of world production were wheat, 62,662 (10.7%); corn, 239,719 (39.9%); rice, 9,546 (1.6%); soybeans, 71,928 (46.6%); cotton, 3,691 (20.2%); and tobacco, 576 (8.1%).

24ANIMAL HUSBANDRY

The livestock population in 2001 included an estimated 97.2 million head of cattle, 59.1 million hogs, and seven million sheep and lambs. That year, there were 1.9 billion chickens, and 88 million turkeys. Milk production totaled 75 million metric tons in that year, with Wisconsin, California, and New York together accounting for much of the total. Wisconsin, Minnesota, and California account for more than half of all US butter production, which totaled 558,700 metric tons in 2001; in that year, the United States was the world's largest producer of cheese, with more than four million metric tons (24% of the world's total). The United States produced an estimated 16% of the world's meat supply in 2001. In 2001, meat animals accounted for $6.7 billion in exports; dairy and eggs, $773 million.

25FISHING

The 2000 commercial catch was 4.74 million tons. Food fish make up 78% of the catch, and nonfood fish, processed for fertilizer and oil, 22%.

Alaska pollock, with landings of 1,182,438 tons, was the most important species in quantity among the commercial fishery landings in the United States in 2000. Other leading species by volume included Gulf menhaden, 591,434 tons; Atlantic menhaden, 207,122 tons; Pacific cod, 240,635 tons; North Pacific hake, 205,351 tons; and American cupped oyster, 197,072 tons. In 2000, exports of fish products totaled $3,055 million (3rd after Norway and China).

Aquacultural production consists mostly of catfish, oysters, trout, and crayfish. In 1998, there were 1,810 aquacultural farms in the United States.

Pollution is a problem of increasing concern to the US fishing industry; dumping of raw sewage, industrial wastes, spillage from oil tankers, and blowouts of offshore wells are the main threats to the fishing grounds. Overfishing is also a threat to the viability of the industry in some areas, especially Alaska.

26FORESTRY

US forestland covered about 226 million hectares (558.4 million acres) in 2000, or 24.7% of the land area. Major forest regions include the eastern, central hardwood, southern, Rocky Mountain, and Pacific coast areas. The National Forest Service lands account for approximately 19% of the nation's forestland. Extensive tracts of land (4 million acres or more) are under ownership of private lumber companies in Alabama, Arkansas, Florida, Georgia, Maine, Oregon, and Washington. During 1990–2000, forested area increased by an annual average of 38,000 hectares (93,900 acres) per year.

Domestic production of roundwood during 2000 amounted to 500.4 million cu m (17.7 billion cu ft), of which softwoods accounted for roughly 60%. Other forest products in 2000 included 58.5 million metric tons of wood pulp, 86.5 million metric tons of paper and paperboard (excluding newsprint), and 45.5 million cu m (1.6 billion cu ft) of wood-based panels. Rising petroleum prices in the late 1970s sparked a revival in the use of wood as home heating fuel, especially in the Northeast. Fuelwood and charcoal production amounted to 71.9 million cu m (2.5 billion cu ft) in 2000.

Throughout the 19th century, the federal government distributed forestlands lavishly as a means of subsidizing railroads and education. By the turn of the century, the realization that the forests were not inexhaustible led to the growth of a vigorous conservation movement, which was given increased impetus during the 1930s and again in the late 1960s. Federal timberlands are no longer open for private acquisition, although the lands can be leased for timber cutting and for grazing. In recent decades, the states also have moved in the direction of retaining forestlands and adding to their holdings when possible.

27MINING

Rich in a variety of mineral resources, the United States was a world leader in the production of many important mineral commodities, such as aluminum, cement, copper, pig iron, lead, molybdenum, phosphates, potash, salt, sulfur, uranium, and zinc. The leading mineral-producing states were Arizona (copper, sand and gravel, portland cement, molybdenum); California (portland cement, sand and gravel, gold, boron); Michigan (iron ore, portland cement, sand and gravel, magnesium compounds); Georgia (clays, crushed and broken stone, portland and masonry cement, sand and gravel); Florida (phosphate rock, crushed and broken stone, portland cement, sand and gravel); Utah (copper, gold, magnesium metal, sand and gravel); Texas (portland cement, crushed and broken stone, magnesium metal, sand and gravel); and Minnesota (iron ore, construction and industrial sand and gravel, crushed and broken stone). Oklahoma and New Mexico were important for petroleum and natural gas, and Kentucky, West Virginia, and Pennsylvania, for coal. Iron ore supported the nation's most basic nonagricultural industry, iron and steel manufacture; the major domestic sources were in the Lake Superior area, with Minnesota and Michigan leading all other states in iron ore yields.

28ENERGY AND POWER

The United States is the world's leading energy producer and consumer. With about 4.6% of the world's population, the United States consumed 24.3% of the world's energy in 1995. In 2002, US coal production was an estimated 1.98 billion short tons. Natural gas production was 552 billion cu m (19.5 trillion cu ft); oil production was 8.1 million barrels per day in the first nine months of 2002. Conventional thermal sources provided the greatest share of energy consumed in 2001: coal supplied 23%, natural gas 23%, and petroleum 39%. The rest was supplied by nuclear power, hydroelectric power, and renewable energy sources including geothermal, wind, photovoltaic, and wood and waste. Increased use of natural gas was the most spectacular development in the commercial marketing of fuel after World War II (1939–45); between 1950 and the peak in 1975, its share of total US energy production doubled from 20% to 40%; since then, production has stabilized at just under 30%.

Mineral fuel production in the United States dates to the early 1800s; by 1810–19 US coal production was about 230,000 tons, and fuelwood production equivalent to 26 million tons of coal. In 1854, a refinery opened in Brooklyn, New York, to process shale and coal to kerosene. In 1859, the United States recorded its first oil production, and in 1870, John D. Rockefeller established the Standard Oil Company in Cleveland, Ohio; the company controlled 90% of the Western oil market from 1880 to 1910, and was split into 33 independent companies in 1911 under the Sherman Antitrust Act.

Proved reserves of crude oil totaled an estimated 22.4 billion barrels at the start of 2002. Reserves of natural gas were about 5 trillion cu m (177 trillion cu ft) at the beginning of 2002, equivalent to more than 3% of the world's proved reserves. Recoverable coal reserves amounted to 275.1 billion tons at the end of 1998 (46% anthracite and bituminous), more than 20% of the world's total. The 1973 Arab oil embargo and subsequent fuel shortages prompted a host of governmental measures aimed at increasing development of oil and gas resources, including an easing of restrictions on oil drilling on the continental shelf. Since the mid-1980s, net petroleum imports have risen from 4.29 million barrels per day in 1985 to 10.3 million barrels daily in 2002, exceeding the record level of 8.56 million barrels per day set in 1977.

In 2000, public utilities and private industrial plants generated 3,802 billion kWh of electricity, of which 70.8% was from fossil fuels, 7.2% from hydropower, 19.8% from nuclear power, and 2.2% from other sources. Conventional steam and internal combustion plants produced most of the electricity. Coal accounted for 60% of generation by public utilities, nuclear power 20%, natural gas 10%, hydroelectricity 7%, oil 3%, and other sources less than 1%. Consumption of electricity in 2000 was 3.6 trillion kWh. Installed generating capacity at electric utilities totaled 812.7 million kW in 2001.

In 1957 the nuclear portion of domestic electricity generation accounted for less than 0.05% of the nation's total. By the mid-1990s it represented about 20% and, after a decline in the late 1990s, reached a similar level again in 2001, when nuclear power generation hit a record 769 billion kWh. The number of operable nuclear power units peaked at 112 units in 1990 but had declined to 104 by 2002. In 2000 the Nuclear Regulatory Commission granted its first-ever renewal of a nuclear facility's operating license, sending a positive message to the nuclear power industry, whose future had been in doubt since the 1980s due to cost and safety problems. In July 2002 the US Congress approved the creation of a permanent nuclear waste disposal site at Yucca Mountain, Nevada.

During the 1980s, increasing attention was focused on the development of solar power, synthetic fuels, geothermal resources, and other energy technologies. Such energy conservation measures as mandatory automobile fuel-efficiency standards and tax incentives for home insulation were promoted by the federal government, which also decontrolled oil and gas prices in the expectation that a rise in domestic costs to world-

MAJOR LAND-USE REGIONS AND MINERAL RESOURCES

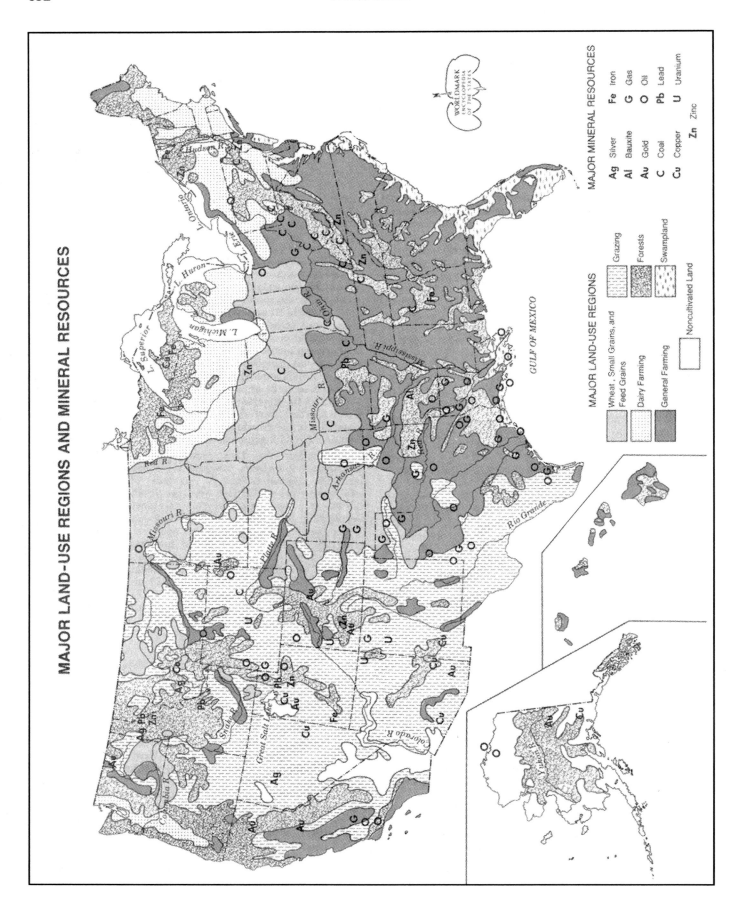

MAJOR LAND-USE REGIONS

Wheat, Small Grains, and Feed Grains

Dairy Farming

General Farming

Grazing

Forests

Swampland

Noncultivated Land

MAJOR MINERAL RESOURCES

Ag	Silver	Fe	Iron
Al	Bauxite	G	Gas
Au	Gold	O	Oil
C	Coal	Pb	Lead
Cu	Copper	U	Uranium
	Zn	Zinc	

market levels would provide a powerful economic incentive for consumers to conserve fuel. In 2001, the United States had 1,694 MW of installed wind power.

29INDUSTRY

Although the United States remains one of the world's preeminent industrial powers, manufacturing no longer plays as dominant a role in the economy as it once did.

Between 1979 and 1998, manufacturing employment fell from 20.9 million to 18.7 million, or from 21.8% to 14.8% of national employment. Throughout the 1960s, manufacturing accounted for about 29% of total national income; by 1987, the proportion was down to about 19%. In 2002, manufacturing was experiencing a decline due to the recession that began in March 2001, according to the Institute for Supply Management's (ISM) gauge of manufacturing activity.

Industrial activity within the United States has been expanding southward and westward for much of the 20th century, most rapidly since World War II. Louisiana, Oklahoma, and especially Texas are centers of industrial expansion based on petroleum refining; aerospace and other high technology industries are the basis of the new wealth of Texas and California, the nation's leading manufacturing state. The industrial heartland of the United States is the east–north–central region, comprising Ohio, Indiana, Illinois, Michigan, and Wisconsin, with steelmaking and automobile manufacturing among the leading industries. The Middle Atlantic states (New Jersey, New York, and Pennsylvania) and the Northeast are also highly industrialized; but of the major industrial states in these two regions, Massachusetts has taken the lead in reorienting itself toward such high-technology industries as electronics and information processing.

Large corporations are dominant especially in sectors such as steel, automobiles, pharmaceuticals, aircraft, petroleum refining, computers, soaps and detergents, tires, and communications equipment. The growth of multinational activities of US corporations has been rapid in recent decades.

The history of US industry has been marked by the introduction of increasingly sophisticated technology in the manufacturing process. Advances in chemistry and electronics have revolutionized many industries through new products and methods: examples include the impact of plastics on petrochemicals, the use of lasers and electronic sensors as measuring and controlling devices, and the application of microprocessors to computing machines, home entertainment products, and a variety of other industries. Science has vastly expanded the number of metals available for industrial purposes, notably such light metals as aluminum, magnesium, and titanium. Integrated machines now perform a complex number of successive operations that formerly were done on the assembly line at separate stations. Those industries have prospered that have been best able to make use of the new technology, and the economies of some states—in particular California and Massachusetts—have been largely based on it.

In the 1980s and 1990s, the United States was the world leader in computer manufacturing. At the beginning of the 21st century, however, the high-tech manufacturing industry registered a decline. Employment in high-technology manufacturing fell by 415,000 jobs from January 2001 to December 2002, a decrease of 20%. Semiconductor manufacturing had been migrating out of the United States to East Asian countries, especially China, Taiwan, and Singapore, and research and development in that sector declined from 1999–2003. Certain long-established industries—especially clothing and steelmaking—have suffered from outmoded facilities that (coupled with high US labor costs) have forced the price of their products above the world market level. In 2002, the United States was the world's 3rd-leading steel producer (after China and Japan). Employment in the steel industry fell from 521,000 in 1974 to 190,000 in 1992. The steel industry at the end of 2002 was operating at less than 65% of capacity, the lowest level in 14 years, and 50,300 steelmaking jobs had been lost from 1997–2002. Automobile manufacturing was an ailing industry in the 1980s, but rebounded in the 1990s. The "Big Three" US automakers—General Motors, Ford, and Daimler-Chrysler—manufactured over 60% of the passenger cars sold in the United States in 1995. Passenger car production, which had fallen from 7.1 million units in 1987 to 5.4 million in 1991, rose to 6.3 million by 1995 and to 8.3 million in 1999. In 2001, over 11.4 million automobiles were produced, an 11% decrease from the 12.8 million produced in 2000.

The United States has a total of 153 oil refineries, with a production capacity in 2002 of 16,785,000 barrels per day. Crude oil and refined petroleum products are crucial imports, however.

30COMMERCE

Total retail sales in 2001 were estimated at $3.2 trillion with California, Texas, Florida, and New York leading in volume. Retail sales were estimated at $772.2 billion in the first quarter of 2003. Total e-commerce sales during that period were $11.9 billion, an increase of 25.9% from the first quarter of 2002. In 2001, sales by automotive dealers totaled $840.5 billion. Sales by retailers of grocery stores totaled $434.4 billion and by department stores totaled $234.3 billion.

The growth of great chains of retail stores, particularly in the form of the supermarket, was one of the most conspicuous developments in retail trade following the end of World War II. Nearly 100,000 single-unit grocery stores went out of business between 1948 and 1958; the independent grocer's share of the food market dropped from 50% to 30% of the total in the same period. With the great suburban expansion of the 1960s emerged the planned shopping center, usually designed by a single development organization and intended to provide different kinds of stores in order to meet all the shopping needs of the particular area. Between 1974 and 2000, the square footage occupied by shopping centers in the United States grew at a far greater rate than the nation's population.

Sales in 2001 by Wal-Mart, the top discount department store chain, totaled $202 billion; other leading retail chains in 2001, were Home Depot ($53.5 billion); Kroger ($50 billion); Target ($39.2 billion); and Sears ($37.3 billion). Kmart, previously the 2nd-largest retail chain in the United States after Wal-Mart, filed for bankruptcy in January 2002.

Installment credit is a major support for consumer purchases in the United States. Most US families own and use credit cards, and their frequency of use has grown significantly in the 1990s and 2000s with aggressive marketing by credit card companies which have made cards available to households that didn't qualify in the past. The number of cards per household in 2002 was 16.7, including bank credit cards, retail credit cards, and debit cards. The number of credit cards in circulation in 2003 was 1.3 billion. The average household credit card debt in the United States in 2002 was approximately $8,000, and the total credit card debt in the United States at the end of the first quarter 2002 was approximately $660 billion.

The US advertising industry is the world's most highly developed. Particularly with the expansion of television audiences, spending for advertising has increased almost annually to successive record levels. Advertising expenditures in 2002 reached an estimated $117.3 billion, up from $66.58 billion in 1982 and $11.96 billion in 1960. Of the 2002 total, $60.9 billion was spent in broadcast media (radio and television); $48.2 billion was spent on print media (newspapers and magazines), of which $2.8 billion was devoted to national newspapers; and internet advertising amounted to $5.7 billion.

In 2002 wholesale trade had combined total sales of $2.75 trillion.

The foreign trade position of the United States deteriorated in the 1980s as the United States became a debtor nation with a trade deficit that ballooned from $24 billion to over $100 billion by the end of the 1980s; by 1998, the trade deficit had reached an estimated $249 billion. In 2001 exports, consisting of automobiles, industrial supplies and raw materials, consumer goods, and agricultural products, were $998 billion, up from $393.6 billion in 1990. General imports for 2001 were valued at $1.36 trillion, a record high. California led the nation in value of exports originating in the state, followed by Texas and New York.

The United States' imports and exports for 2001 (in millions of US dollars) are distributed among the following categories:

ITEM (1)	EXPORTS	IMPORTS
Manufactured goods (3)	536,725	821,018
Agricultural commodities (3)	46,821	46,965
Mineral fuels (3)	12,865	122,875
Selected commodities (3)		
ADP equipment; office mach	49,403	75,861
Airplanes and spacecraft	44,689	21,091
Alcoholic bev., distilled	1,291	7,752
Aluminum	3,329	6,404
Animal feeds	4,478	621
Artwork/antiques	4,070	5,460
Cereal meal and preparations	1,993	2,057
Chemicals - cosmetics	3,369	2,546
Chemicals - dyeing and painting	3,870	2,480
Chemicals - fertilizers	2,247	1,950
Chemicals - inorganic	5,730	6,192
Chemicals - medicinal	15,421	18,624
Chemicals - n.e.s.	12,784	5,927
Chemicals - organic	16,948	29,626
Chemicals - polymers	19,283	10,379
Cigarettes	2,750	527
Clothing	7,013	63,861
Coal	1,955	1,023
Coffee	366	1,680
Copper	1,130	4,106
Cork, wood, lumber	3,629	7,970
Corn	4,765	135
Cotton, raw and linters	2,220	29
Crude oil	248	75,263
Electrical machinery	92,186	84,711
Fish and preparations	3,207	9,750
Footwear	806	15,235
Furniture and bedding	4,720	18,612
General industrial mach	33,748	33,259
Glass	2,526	2,201
Glassware	961	1,741
Gold, non-monetary	4,881	2,078
Hides and skins	1,998	162
Iron and steel mill products	5,970	13,857
Jewelry	2,596	6,265
Lighting, plumbing	1,120	4,584
Liquefied propane/butane	340	1,879
Live animals	898	2,239
Meat and preparations	7,379	4,253
Metal manufactures, n.e.s.	7,313	22,233
Metal ores; scrap	3,484	3,237
Metalworking machinery	5,297	6,589
Mineral fuels, other	3,721	2,681
Natural gas	538	16,303
Nickel	541	1,080
Oils/fats, vegetable	801	995
Optical goods	3,231	3,453
Paper and paperboard	11,231	14,819
Pearls, precious stones	4,475	11,577
Photographic equipment	3,739	5,577
Pottery	124	1,642
Power generating mach.	36,182	36,127
Printed matter	5,061	3,723
Pulp and waste paper	3,769	2,631
Rice	717	168

ITEM (1)	EXPORTS	IMPORTS
Selected commodities (continued)		
Rubber articles, n.e.s.	1,669	1,980
Rubber tires and tubes	2,402	5,020
Scientific instruments	31,274	21,399
Ships, boats	1,899	1,206
Silver and platinum	1,801	5,760
Specialized ind. mach.	27,491	12,064
Sugar	733	1,621
Television, VCR, radio, etc.	3,531	24,884
Textile yarn, fabric	10,472	14,613
Tobacco, unmanufactured	1,290	710
Toys/games/sporting goods	3,898	20,909
Travel goods	414	4,301
Vegetables and fruits	8,111	9,523
Motor vehicles and parts	58,140	158,565
Watches/clocks/parts	449	3,048
Wheat	3,382	282
Wood manufactures	1,652	7,000
Re-exports	50,969	(X)
Agricultural commodities	1,314	(X)
Manufactured goods	49,011	(X)
Mineral fuels	132	(X)

(-) Represents zero or less than one half unit of measurement shown. (X) Not applicable.
(1) Detailed data are presented on a census basis. The information needed to convert to a BOP basis is not available.
(2) Total exports (Domestic and Foreign)
(3) Domestic exports

The following 21 nations account for approximately 77% of US imports, and 79% of US goods exports: Argentina, Australia, Belgium, Canada, China (including Hong Kong), Egypt, Germany, France, Italy, Japan, Republic of Korea, Malaysia, Mexico, Netherlands, Saudi Arabia, Singapore, Spain, Switzerland, United Arab Emirates, United Kingdom, and Venezuela.

Principal trading partners in 2000 (in millions of US dollars) were as follows:

COUNTRY	EXPORTS	IMPORTS	BALANCE
Canada	164,841	232,678	-67,837
Mexico	104,909	137,448	-32,539
Japan	62,927	150,632	-87,705
United Kingdom	39,532	44,531	-4,999
China (inc. Hong Kong)	29,272	119,588	-90,316
Germany	28,174	60,161	-31,986
Korea	27,090	41,724	-14,634
France	19,606	30,482	10,876
Singapore	16,758	19,557	-2,799
Malaysia	10,392	26,394	-16,002

Since 1950, the United States has generally recorded deficits in its overall payments with the rest of the world, despite the fact that it had an unbroken record of annual surpluses up to 1970 on current-account goods, services, and remittances transactions. The balance of trade, in the red since 1975, reached a record deficit of $249 billion in 1998. The nation's stock of gold declined from a value of $22.9 billion at the start of 1958 to $10.5 billion as of 31 July 1971, only two weeks before President Nixon announced that the United States would no longer exchange dollars for gold. From 1990–98, the value of the gold stock was stable at $11 billion.

On 12 February 1973, pressures on the US dollar compelled the government to announce a 10% devaluation against nearly all of the world's major currencies. US international gold reserves thereupon rose from $14.4 billion in 1973 to $15.9 billion at the end of 1974; as of 1999, US gold reserves stood at $75 billion, down from $102 billion in 1990

Despite the decline in the value of the dollar in 2003, the current account was forecast to remain in substantial deficit for 2003/04. The volume of US imports and exports surpasses that of

Exports, Imports and Trade Balance by Country and Area: 2002 Annual Totals

In millions of dollars. Details may not equal totals due to rounding. (X) Not applicable. (-) Represents zero or less than one-half of value shown.
January–December, Cumulative

COUNTRY	TRADE BALANCE	RANK	EXPORTS F.A.S.	RANK	IMPORTS CUSTOMS	RANK
Total, BOP Basis	-482,871.8	(X)	681,874.0	(X)	1,164,745.8	(X)
Net Adjustments	-14,609.0	(X)	-11,229.2	(X)	3,379.8	(X)
Total, Census Basis	-468,262.8	(X)	693,103.2	(X)	1,161,366.0	(X)
Afghanistan	76.7	195	80.0	114	3.3	178
Albania	9.0	151	14.8	176	5.8	167
Algeria	-1,375.8	41	984.4	55	2,360.2	49
Andorra	10.2	154	11.0	183	0.8	201
Angola	-2,748.6	26	374.0	74	3,122.7	44
Anguilla	18.9	163	19.9	167	1.0	197
Antigua and Barbuda	77.8	196	81.4	113	3.5	177
Argentina	-1,601.9	35	1,585.4	44	3,187.3	42
Armenia	81.2	198	111.8	103	30.7	137
Aruba	-309.2	61	464.6	68	773.7	66
Australia	6,606.2	229	13,085.0	13	6,478.8	28
Austria	-1,387.5	40	2,427.4	38	3,814.9	35
Azerbaijan	35.3	183	69.6	121	34.4	136
Bahamas, The	525.6	220	975.3	56	449.7	72
Bahrain	24.4	169	419.3	71	394.9	76
Bangladesh	-1,865.1	30	269.1	81	2,134.2	53
Barbados	233.2	212	267.6	82	34.4	135
Belarus	-106.4	80	19.1	168	125.5	113
Belgium	3,519.0	228	13,325.8	12	9,806.8	22
Belize	60.0	190	137.7	98	77.7	121
Benin	34.5	180	35.2	143	0.7	203
Bermuda	392.2	219	415.1	72	22.9	143
Bhutan	0.1	119	1.0	212	0.8	200
Bolivia	31.7	178	192.1	93	160.4	107
Bosnia-Hercegovina	16.1	161	31.7	147	15.5	148
Botswana	2.4	138	31.7	146	29.3	138
Brazil	-3,404.6	25	12,376.0	15	15,780.6	13
British Indian Ocean Territory	0.1	118	0.4	218	0.4	210
British Virgin Islands	26.9	173	67.4	122	40.5	133
Brunei	-240.8	65	46.3	136	287.1	91
Bulgaria	-238.3	66	101.4	106	339.7	82
Burkina	15.9	160	18.8	169	2.9	180
Myanmar (Burma)	-346.2	58	10.1	186	356.4	81
Burundi	1.0	131	1.7	208	0.7	202
Cambodia	-1,041.7	44	29.2	152	1,071.0	64
Cameroon	-16.3	97	155.8	95	172.1	103
Canada	-48,164.9	3	160,922.6	1	209,087.6	1
Cape Verde	7.8	148	9.6	187	1.8	189
Cayman Islands	222.8	211	231.6	86	8.8	159
Central African Republic	4.4	142	6.4	191	2.0	187
Chad	121.6	206	127.3	101	5.7	168
Chile	-1,175.5	42	2,609.0	34	3,784.5	36
China	-103,064.7	1	22,127.8	7	125,192.5	3
Christmas Island	0.6	125	1.2	210	0.6	206
Cocos (Keeling) Island	0.7	128	1.0	211	0.2	216
Colombia	-2,021.9	27	3,582.5	29	5,604.3	32
Comoros	-5.2	106	0.1	225	5.3	169
Congo (ROC)	-129.7	76	52.4	132	182.1	102
Congo (DROC)	-175.9	70	28.1	155	204.1	98
Cook Islands	-0.3	111	0.8	215	1.1	196
Costa Rica	-25.3	93	3,116.5	31	3,141.8	43
Croatia	-67.5	87	78.1	117	145.6	111
Cuba	145.3	207	145.6	96	0.3	214
Cyprus	167.7	208	193.4	91	25.6	141
Czech Republic	-579.7	49	653.7	62	1,233.4	61
Denmark	-1,741.4	32	1,495.9	47	3,237.3	41
Djibouti	56.7	189	58.6	128	1.9	188
Dominica	40.3	186	45.0	137	4.7	172
Dominican Republic	81.2	199	4,250.1	26	4,168.9	33
East Timor	0.1	120	0.1	224	(-)	221

United States

Exports, Imports and Trade Balance by Country and Area: 2002 Annual Totals (Continued)

In millions of dollars. Details may not equal totals due to rounding. (X) Not applicable. (-) Represents zero or less than one-half of value shown.
January–December, Cumulative

COUNTRY	TRADE BALANCE	RANK	EXPORTS F.A.S.	RANK	IMPORTS CUSTOMS	RANK
Ecuador	-537.8	50	1,605.7	43	2,143.4	52
Egypt	1,512.5	225	2,868.4	33	1,356.0	60
El Salvador	-318.2	60	1,664.1	42	1,982.3	54
Equatorial Guinea	-393.2	56	108.7	104	501.9	70
Eritrea	28.4	176	28.8	153	0.4	211
Estonia	-82.1	85	81.5	112	163.6	104
Ethiopia	34.9	182	60.5	127	25.7	140
Falkland Islands	-5.6	105	0.4	219	6.0	166
Faroe Islands	-10.8	99	4.7	196	15.5	150
Federal Republic of Germany	-35,876.1	5	26,629.6	5	62,505.7	5
Fedrated States of Micronesia	12.0	156	27.2	158	15.2	152
Fiji	-139.4	74	16.9	174	156.3	109
Finland	-1,912.1	29	1,534.9	46	3,447.0	39
France	-9,223.9	13	19,016.2	8	28,240.1	9
French Guiana	242.3	213	249.7	84	7.5	162
French Polynesia	34.8	181	78.9	116	44.1	131
French Southern and Antarctic Lands	0.7	127	0.7	216	(-) 224	n.a.
Gabon	-1,521.9	37	65.5	124	1,587.5	59
Gambia, The	9.2	152	9.6	188	0.3	213
Gaza Strip Administered by Israel	-6.9	104	(-)	228	6.9	163
Georgia	81.4	200	98.8	108	17.5	146
Ghana	76.2	194	192.6	92	116.3	114
Gibraltar	24.6	170	25.7	159	1.1	194
Greece	605.6	221	1,151.8	51	546.2	69
Greenland	-18.6	94	4.0	199	22.6	144
Grenada	49.5	188	56.4	130	6.9	164
Guadeloupe	29.2	177	39.7	140	10.5	154
Guatemala	-751.9	47	2,044.4	40	2,796.4	45
Guinea	-8.7	100	62.9	125	71.6	124
Guinea-Bissau	2.5	139	2.6	203	(-)	220
Guyana	12.6	157	128.2	100	115.6	115
Haiti	318.2	216	573.2	65	255.0	94
Heard and McDonald Islands	0.1	117	0.1	226	(-)	227
Honduras	-690.3	48	2,571.1	35	3,261.3	40
Hong Kong	3,266.1	227	12,594.4	14	9,328.2	25
Hungary	-1,949.6	28	687.9	60	2,637.4	46
Iceland	-77.9	86	219.0	87	296.9	90
India	-7,717.3	15	4,101.1	27	11,818.3	19
Indonesia	-7,087.5	17	2,555.8	36	9,643.3	23
Iran	-124.5	77	31.8	145	156.3	108
Iraq	-3,516.6	24	31.6	148	3,548.2	37
Ireland	-15,692.6	6	6,745.1	21	22,437.7	12
Israel	-5,389.0	19	7,026.7	20	12,415.7	18
Italy	-14,163.5	7	10,056.8	17	24,220.3	10
Ivory Coast (Côte d'Ivoire)	-300.2	62	76.2	119	376.4	78
Jamaica	1,023.9	222	1,420.2	48	396.3	75
Japan	-69,979.4	2	51,449.3	3	121,428.7	4
Jordan	-7.9	103	404.4	73	412.3	73
Kazakhstan	270.0	215	604.6	63	334.6	83
Kenya	82.6	201	271.2	80	188.6	101
Kiribati	2.7	140	3.8	200	1.1	195
Korea (ROC)	-12,996.1	10	22,575.8	6	35,571.8	7
Kuwait	-925.7	45	1,014.7	54	1,940.4	55
Kyrgyzstan	26.3	172	31.1	149	4.8	171
Laos	1.6	135	4.2	197	2.6	185
Latvia	-106.2	81	90.8	111	197.0	99
Lebanon	255.8	214	317.4	77	61.7	126
Lesotho	-319.7	59	2.0	206	321.7	84
Liberia	-18.1	95	27.7	156	45.8	130
Libya	18.3	162	18.3	172	(-)	(X)
Liechtenstein	-223.2	67	14.5	177	237.7	96
Lithuania	-196.8	69	102.8	105	299.6	89
Luxembourg	180.2	210	480.1	67	300.0	88

Exports, Imports and Trade Balance by Country and Area: 2002 Annual Totals (Continued)

In millions of dollars. Details may not equal totals due to rounding. (X) Not applicable. (-) Represents zero or less than one-half of value shown.
January–December, Cumulative

COUNTRY	TRADE BALANCE	RANK	EXPORTS F.A.S.	RANK	IMPORTS CUSTOMS	RANK
Macao	-1,152.6	43	79.0	115	1,231.7	62
Macedonia (Skopje)	-54.5	89	18.6	170	73.2	123
Madagascar	-200.4	68	15.4	175	215.8	97
Malawi	-40.7	92	30.1	151	70.8	125
Malaysia	-13,665.3	9	10,343.7	16	24,008.9	11
Maldives	-109.5	78	4.1	198	113.6	117
Mali	8.6	149	11.2	181	2.6	184
Malta	-99.8	83	210.1	88	309.9	85
Marshall Islands	19.3	164	28.7	154	9.4	157
Martinique	23.1	167	23.7	163	0.7	204
Mauritania	21.9	166	22.9	165	0.9	198
Mauritius	-253.2	63	27.5	157	280.6	92
Mayott	(-)	114	(-)	229	(-)	226
Mexico	-37,145.5	4	97,470.3	2	134,615.8	2
Moldova	-8.5	101	30.7	150	39.1	134
Monaco	-3.7	107	11.4	180	15.1	153
Mongolia	-95.4	84	66.3	123	161.7	105
Montserrat	4.7	144	5.1	195	0.4	208
Morocco	173.0	209	565.4	66	392.4	77
Mozambique	86.1	202	94.6	109	8.5	160
Namibia	0.3	124	57.8	129	57.4	128
Nauru	2.4	137	2.9	202	0.5	207
Nepal	-132.4	75	20.0	166	152.4	110
Netherlands	8,462.2	230	18,310.7	10	9,848.5	21
Netherlands Antilles	379.7	217	741.4	58	361.7	80
New Caledonia	27.0	174	36.6	141	9.6	155
New Zealand	-468.5	51	1,813.1	41	2,281.6	51
Nicaragua	-242.6	64	437.0	69	679.6	68
Niger	40.0	185	40.9	138	0.9	199
Nigeria	-4,887.6	20	1,057.8	52	5,945.4	29
Niue	0.3	123	0.3	220	(-)	223
Norfolk Island	0.1	121	0.2	223	0.1	218
North Korea	24.9	171	25.0	161	0.1	219
Norway	-4,436.2	22	1,406.5	50	5,842.6	30
Oman	-44.6	91	356.0	76	400.6	74
Pakistan	-1,611.6	34	693.4	59	2,305.0	50
Palau	3.0	141	18.5	171	15.5	149
Panama	1,104.1	223	1,406.7	49	302.6	87
Papua New Guinea	-66.9	88	23.2	164	90.2	120
Paraguay	389.2	218	432.9	70	43.7	132
Peru	-376.9	57	1,562.5	45	1,939.3	56
Philippines	-3,703.9	23	7,276.0	19	10,979.9	20
Pitcairn Island	6.0	146	6.1	193	0.1	217
Poland	-422.2	54	686.3	61	1,108.5	63
Portugal	-811.3	46	861.3	57	1,672.6	58
Qatar	-170.7	72	313.9	78	484.7	71
Republic of Yemen	119.8	205	366.1	75	246.3	95
Reunion	-0.2	112	2.3	204	2.6	186
Romania	-446.9	52	248.2	85	695.1	67
Russia	-4,473.2	21	2,397.0	39	6,870.2	27
Rwanda	7.1	147	10.2	185	3.1	179
St. Helena	-2.0	109	2.1	205	4.1	173
St. Kitts and Nevis	0.8	129	49.5	133	48.6	129
St. Lucia	80.3	197	99.5	107	19.2	145
St. Pierre and Miquelon	-2.8	108	0.8	214	3.7	175
St. Vincent and the Grenadines	24.0	168	40.4	139	16.5	147
San Marino	4.6	143	5.8	194	1.2	192
São Tomé and Princípe	1.6	134	2.0	207	0.4	209
Saudi Arabia	-8,369.1	14	4,780.7	24	13,149.9	17
Senegal	71.1	193	74.6	120	3.6	176
Seychelles	-18.1	96	8.2	189	26.3	139
Sierra Leone	21.7	165	25.5	160	3.8	174
Singapore	1,415.7	224	16,217.9	11	14,802.2	15

United States

Exports, Imports and Trade Balance by Country and Area: 2002 Annual Totals (Continued)

In millions of dollars. Details may not equal totals due to rounding. (X) Not applicable. (-) Represents zero or less than one-half of value shown.
January–December, Cumulative

COUNTRY	TRADE BALANCE	RANK	EXPORTS F.A.S.	RANK	IMPORTS CUSTOMS	RANK
Slovakia	-167.6	73	92.7	110	260.3	93
Slovenia	-175.7	71	130.9	99	306.5	86
Solomon Islands	0.9	130	1.5	209	0.6	205
Somalia	5.8	145	6.2	192	0.3	212
South Africa	-1,508.6	38	2,525.5	37	4,034.1	34
Spain	-435.2	53	5,297.9	22	5,733.0	31
Sri Lanka	-1,638.5	33	171.9	94	1,810.4	57
Sudan	9.5	153	10.8	184	1.4	191
Suriname	-8.0	102	124.8	102	132.7	112
Svalbard, Jan Mayen Island	0.6	126	0.6	217	(-)	225
Swaziland	-103.0	82	11.5	179	114.5	116
Sweden	-6,063.3	18	3,153.0	30	9,216.3	26
Switzerland	-1,599.4	36	7,782.5	18	9,382.0	24
Syria	113.2	204	274.1	79	160.8	106
Taiwan	-13,766.1	8	18,381.8	9	32,147.9	8
Tajikistan	32.0	179	33.1	144	1.1	193
Tanzania	37.9	184	62.7	126	24.8	142
Thailand	-9,932.7	12	4,860.2	23	14,792.9	16
Togo	11.1	155	13.8	178	2.7	183
Tokelau	15.3	158	18.0	173	2.7	182
Tonga	1.9	136	11.0	182	9.1	158
Trinidad and Tobago	-1,420.1	39	1,020.2	53	2,440.3	47
Tunisia	101.6	203	194.8	90	93.2	119
Turkey	-403.0	55	3,113.0	32	3,516.0	38
Turkmenistan	-12.5	98	47.1	135	59.6	127
Turks and Caicos Islands	48.5	187	53.6	131	5.1	170
Tuvalu	0.1	116	0.1	227	(-)	228
Uganda	8.7	150	24.0	162	15.3	151
Ukraine	-107.6	79	254.8	83	362.4	79
United Arab Emirates	2,670.3	226	3,593.2	28	922.9	65
United Kingdom	-7,540.2	16	33,204.7	4	40,744.9	6
Uruguay	15.4	159	208.6	89	193.2	100
Uzbekistan	61.4	191	138.5	97	77.1	122
Vanuatu	-1.9	110	0.9	213	2.8	181
Vatican City	1.2	132	2.9	201	1.7	190
Venezuela	-10,663.8	11	4,429.7	25	15,093.5	14
Vietnam	-1,814.5	31	580.2	64	2,394.7	48
Wallis and Futuna	0.2	122	0.2	222	(-)	229
West Bank Administered by Israel	(-)	115	0.3	221	0.3	215
Western Sahara	(-)	113	(-)	230	(-)	222
Western Samoa	1.3	133	7.6	190	6.4	165
Yugoslavia	68.5	192	78.1	118	9.6	156
Zambia	27.9	175	35.7	142	7.9	161
Zimbabwe	-53.4	90	49.3	134	102.8	118
Unidentified	187.1	(X)	187.1	(X)	(-)	(X)
North America	-85,310.5	(X)	258,392.9	(X)	343,703.4	(X)
Western Europe	-88,938.2	(X)	157,029.8	(X)	245,968.0	(X)
Euro Area	-66,735.3	(X)	105,837.6	(X)	172,572.9	(X)
European Union (EU)	-82,080.2	(X)	143,691.3	(X)	225,771.4	(X)
European Free Trade Association	-6,336.7	(X)	9,422.5	(X)	15,759.2	(X)
Eastern Europe	-8,300.9	(X)	6,596.6	(X)	14,897.5	(X)
Former Soviet Republics	-4,505.8	(X)	4,111.5	(X)	8,617.3	(X)
Organization for Economic Cooperation & Development (OECD) in Europe	-88,818.3	(X)	156,244.7	(X)	245,063.0	(X)
Pacific Rim Countries	-214,903.6	(X)	178,569.1	(X)	393,472.7	(X)
Asia–Near East	-15,364.6	(X)	18,930.0	(X)	34,294.6	(X)
Asia–(NICS)	-22,080.2	(X)	69,769.9	(X)	91,850.1	(X)
Asia—South	-12,888.2	(X)	5,335.4	(X)	18,223.6	(X)
Assoc. of South East Asia Nations (ASEAN)	-34,256.1	(X)	41,329.1	(X)	75,585.2	(X)
APEC	-316,834.3	(X)	448,891.8	(X)	765,726.0	(X)
South/Central America	-17,952.2	(X)	51,551.1	(X)	69,503.3	(X)

Exports, Imports and Trade Balance by Country and Area: 2002 Annual Totals (Continued)

In millions of dollars. Details may not equal totals due to rounding. (X) Not applicable. (-) Represents zero or less than one-half of value shown.
January–December, Cumulative

COUNTRY	TRADE BALANCE	RANK	EXPORTS F.A.S.	RANK	IMPORTS CUSTOMS	RANK
Twenty Latin American Republics	-56,871.1	(X)	142,263.1	(X)	199,134.2	(X)
Central American Common Market	-2,028.3	(X)	9,833.1	(X)	11,861.4	(X)
Latin American Free Trade Association	-56,491.6	(X)	126,054.4	(X)	182,546.0	(X)
North Atlantic Treaty Organization (NATO) Allies	-133,683.6	(X)	313,205.0	(X)	446,888.5	(X)
Organization of Petroleum Exporting Countries (OPEC)	-34,432.7	(X)	18,811.9	(X)	53,244.6	(X)
Unidentified	187.1	(X)	187.1	(X)	(-)	(X)

(1) Detailed data are presented on a Census basis. The information needed to convert to a BOP basis is not available.

(2) Countries included in Euro Area are also included in European Union.

(3) Selected countries are included in more than one area grouping. Indonesia is included in both OPEC and Pacific Rim; Venezuela is included in both OPEC and South/Central America.

(4) The export totals reflect shipments of certain grains, oilseeds, and satellites that are not included in the country/area totals.

NOTE: For information on data sources, iron sampling errors and definitions, see the information section on page 26 of the FT-900, or at www.census.gov/foreign-trade/www/press.html or www.bea.gov/bea/rels.htm. **Source:** U.S. Census Bureau and the Bureau of Economic Analysis (BEA). "U.S. International Trade in Goods and Services: April 2003." Washington: United States Department of Commerce, 2003.

any other country, but exports of goods and services accounted for less than 11% of GDP in 2001.

The US Central Intelligence Agency (CIA) reports that in 2001 the purchasing power parity of the United States' exports was $723 billion while imports totaled $1.15 trillion resulting in a trade deficit of $425 billion.

The International Monetary Fund (IMF) reports that in 2001 the United States had exports of goods totaling $722 million and imports totaling $1.15 trillion. The services credit totaled $276 billion and debit $210 billion. The following table summarizes the United States' balance of payments as reported by the IMF for 2001 in billions of US dollars.

Current Account	-393
Balance on goods	-424
Balance on services	66
Balance on income	14
Current transfers	-49
Capital Account	1
Financial Account	387
Direct investment abroad	-128
Direct investment in the United States	131
Portfolio investment assets	-95
Portfolio investment liabilities	426
Other investment assets	-144
Other investment liabilities	196
Net Errors and Omissions	11
Reserves and Related Items	-5

From the end of World War II through 1952, US government transfers of capital abroad averaged about $5,470 million annually, while private investments averaged roughly $730 million. Portfolio investment represented less than $150 million a year, or only 2.5% of the annual aggregate.

After 1952, however, direct private investment began to increase and portfolio investment rose markedly. In the late 1950s, new private direct investment was increasing yearly by $2 billion or more, while private portfolio investment and official US government loans were climbing by a minimum annual amount of $1 billion each. During the 1960–73 period, the value of US-held assets abroad increased by nearly 12% annually. From the mid-1970s through the early 1980s, it rose most years by at least 15%, and doubled between 1980 and 1990. Direct investments abroad had a book value of $711.6 billion in 1995, over half of which was invested in Europe, with the single greatest concentration ($119.9 billion) in the United Kingdom. Asia and the Pacific Islands had the 2nd-largest regional total ($126 billion), with Japan ($39 billion) the leading country.

Foreign direct investment in the United States has risen rapidly, from $6.9 billion in 1960 to $27.7 billion in 1975 and $183 billion at the end of 1985. As of 1995 foreign direct investment in the United States was valued at $560 billion, of which $363.5 billion originated in Europe ($119.9 billion in the United Kingdom). Asia and the Pacific was the other major source of foreign direct investment, of which close to 90% ($108.6 billion) came from Japan. Total foreign assets in 1994 (current cost) were over $3.16 trillion. Over one-third of the investment volume was in manufacturing. In 1998 foreign direct investment reached $174.4 billion, up from $103.4 billion in 1997, and then increased to $283 billion in 1999. Foreign direct investment inflow into the United States peaked at a world record of $301 billion in 2000. In the global economic slowdown of 2001, foreign direct investment inflows dropped to $124.4 billion. The worldwide decline in foreign investment after the 11 September 2001 terrorist attacks was most dramatic in the United States. In 2002, estimated foreign direct investment inflow dropped more than 64% to an estimated $52.6 billion in 2002.

US outward foreign direct investment in 2002 totaled $109 billion, with the largest recipients being, in order, the United Kingdom, the Netherlands, and Canada.

31 CONSUMER PROTECTION

Consumer protection has become a major government enterprise during the 20th century. The Federal Trade commission (FTC), established in 1914, administers laws governing the granting and use of credit and the activities of credit bureaus; it also investigates unfair or deceptive trade practices, including price fixing and false advertising. The Securities and Exchange Commission, created in 1934, seeks to protect investors, while the Consumer Product Safety Commission, created in 1972, has the authority to establish product safety standards and to ban hazardous products. Overseeing the safety of air and highway transport is the National Transportation Safety Board, established in 1975. The Consumer Information Center Program of the General Services Administration (Pueblo, Colo.) and the Food Safety and Inspection Service and Food and Nutrition Service of the Department of Agriculture also serve consumer interests. Legislation that would have established a Department of Consumer

Affairs failed to win congressional approval several times during the 1970s, however.

Public interest groups have been exceptionally effective in promoting consumer issues. The Consumer Federation of America (CFA; founded in 1967), with 220 member organizations, is the largest US consumer advocacy body; its concerns include product pricing, credit, and the cost and quality of health care, education, and housing. The CFA also serves as a clearinghouse for consumer information. Consumers Union of the US, founded in 1936, publishes the widely read monthly Consumer Reports, which tests, grades, and comments on a variety of retail products. The National Consumers League, founded in 1899, was a pioneer in the consumer movement, focusing especially on labor laws and working conditions. Much of the growth of consumerism in the 1970s resulted from the public relations efforts of one man—Ralph Nader. Already a well-known consumer advocate concerned particularly with automobile safety, Nader founded Public Citizen in 1971 and an affiliated litigation group the following year. In 1994, Public Citizen claimed 100,000 supporters; its activities include research committees on tax reform, health care, work safety, and energy.

Other avenues open to consumers in most states include small claims courts, generally open to claims between $100 and $1,500 at modest legal cost. Complaints involving professional malpractice may be brought to state licensing or regulatory boards. Supported by the business community, the US Better Business Bureau provides general consumer information and arbitrate some customer-company disputes.

The US government publishes two helpful consumer guides. A listing of the publications is available from the government called, the "Consumer Information Catalog." This catalog is a free listing of about 200 of the best federal consumer publications. The federal publications range from planning a diet to financial planning. The publication, published quarterly by the Consumer Information Center of the US General Services Administration is available in most public libraries.

³²BANKING AND SECURITIES

The Federal Reserve Act of 1913 provided the United States with a central banking system. The Federal Reserve System dominates US banking, is a strong influence in the affairs of commercial banks, and exercises virtually unlimited control over the money supply. The Federal Reserve Bank system is an independent government organization, with important posts appointed by the President and approved by the Senate.

Each of the 12 federal reserve districts contains a federal reserve bank. A board of nine directors presides over each reserve bank. Six are elected by the member banks in the district: of this group, three may be bankers; the other three represent business, industry, or agriculture. The Board of Governors of the Federal Reserve System (usually known as the Federal Reserve Board) appoints the remaining three, who may not be officers, directors, stockholders, or employees of any bank and who are presumed therefore to represent the public.

The Federal Reserve Board regulates the money supply and the amount of credit available to the public by asserting its power to alter the rediscount rate, by buying and selling securities in the open market, by setting margin requirements for securities purchases by altering reserve requirements of member banks in the system, and by resorting to a specific number of selective controls at its disposal. The Federal Reserve Board's role in regulating the money supply is held by economists of the monetarist school to be the single most important factor in determining the nation's inflation rate.

Member banks increase their reserves or cash holdings by rediscounting commercial notes at the federal reserve bank at a rate of interest ultimately determined by the Board of Governors. A change in the discount rate, therefore, directly affects the capacity of the member banks to accommodate their customers with loans. Similarly, the purchase or sale of securities in the open market, as determined by the Federal Open Market Committee, is the most commonly used device whereby the amount of credit available to the public is expanded or contracted. The same effect is achieved in some measure by the power of the Board of Governors to raise or lower the reserves that member banks must keep against demand deposits. Credit tightening by federal authorities in early 1980 pushed the prime rate-the rate that commercial banks charge their most creditworthy customers-above 20% for the first time since the financial panics of 1837 and 1839, when rates reached 36%. As federal monetary policies eased, the prime rate dropped below 12% in late 1984; as of 2000 it was below 10%. In mid-2003 the federal funds rate was reduced to 1%, a 45-year low.

The financial sector is dominated by commercial banks, insurance companies, and mutual funds. There was little change in the nature of the sector between the 1930s, when it was rescued through the creation of regulatory bodies and deposit insurance, and the 1980s, when the market was deregulated. In the 1980s, the capital markets underwent extensive reforms. The markets became increasingly internationalized, as deregulation allowed foreign-owned banks to extend their operations. There was also extensive restructuring of domestic financial markets-interest-rate ceilings were abolished and competition between different financial institution intensified, facilitated by greater diversification.

Commercial and investment banking activities are separated in the United States by the Glass Steagall Act, which was passed in 1933 during the Great Depression. Fears that investment banking activities put deposits at risk led to a situation where commercial banks were unable to deal in non-bank financial instruments. This put them at severe commercial disadvantage, and the pressure for reform became so strong that the Federal Reserve Board has allowed the affiliates of commercial banks to enter a wide range of securities activities since 1986. Attempts to repeal the act were unsuccessful until November 1999, when the Gramm-Leach-Bliley Act (also known as the Financial Modernization Act) was passed by Congress. The Gramm-Leach-Bliley Act repeals Glass-Steagall and allows banks, insurance companies, and stock brokers and mutual fund companies to sell each other's products and services; these companies are also now free to merge or acquire one another.

The expansion and diversification in financial services was facilitated by information technology. Financial deregulation led to the collapse of many commercial banks and savings and loan associations in the second half of the 1980s. In the 1990s, change has continued in the form of a proliferation of bank mergers; with the passage in 1999 of Gramm-Leach-Bliley, further consolidation of the industry was predicted.

Prior to 1994 the banking system was highly fragmented; national banks were not allowed to establish branches at will, as they were subject to the banking laws of each state. Within states, local banks faced similar restraints on their branching activities. In 1988, only 22 states permitted statewide banking of national banks, while 18 allowed limited banking and ten permitted no branches. Consequently in 1988 over 60% of US commercial banks had assets of less the $150 million, while only 3% had assets valued at $500 million or more.

Such regulation rendered US banks vulnerable to merger and acquisition. Acquisitions have generally taken place through bank holding companies, which then fall under the jurisdiction of the Federal Reserve System. This has allowed banks to extend their business into non-bank activities such as insurance, financial planning, and mortgages, as well as opening up geographical markets. The number of such holding companies is estimated at 6,500. These companies are believed to control over 90% of total bank assets.

The Riegle-Neal Interstate Banking and Branching Efficiency Act of 1994 removed most of the barriers to interstate bank acquisitions and interstate banking. The new act allowed banks to merge with banks in other states although they must operate them as separate banks. In addition, banks are allowed to establish branches in neighboring states. Restrictions on branching activity were lifted as of June 1997. The legislation allowed banks to lessen their exposure to regional economic downturns. It also ensured a continuing stream of bank mergers. Liberalization has encouraged a proliferation of in-store banking at supermarkets. International Banking Technologies, Inc., reported that the number of supermarket bank branches rose to 7,100 in 1998, up from 2,191 in 1994. In the mid-1990s, the number of supermarket branch banks grew at an annual rate of around 30%, but growth from 1997 to 1998 slowed to just over 10%.

Under the provisions of the Banking Act of 1935, all members of the Federal Reserve System (and other banks that wish to do so) participate in a plan of deposit insurance (up to $100,000 for each individual account as of 2003) administered by the Federal Deposit Insurance Corporation (FDIC).

Savings and loan associations are insured by the Federal Savings and Loan Insurance Corporation (FSLIC). Individual accounts were insured up to a limit of $100,000. Savings and loans failed at an alarming rate in the 1980s. In 1989 the government signed legislation that created the Resolution Trust Corporation. The RTC's job is to handle the savings and loans bailout, expected to cost taxpayers $345 billion through 2029. Approximately 30 million members participated in thousands of credit unions chartered by a federal agency; state-chartered credit unions had over 20 million members.

The International Monetary Fund reports that in 2001, currency and demand deposits—an aggregate commonly known as M1—were equal to $1,595.5 billion. In that same year, M2—an aggregate equal to M1 plus savings deposits, small time deposits, and money market mutual funds—was $6,961.2 billion. The money market rate, the rate at which financial institutions lend to one another in the short term, was 3.89%. The discount rate, the interest rate at which the central bank lends to financial institutions in the short term, was 1.25%.

33INSURANCE

The number of life insurance companies has shrunk in recent years. Between 1985 and 1995 the number fell from 2,261 to 1,840; in 1998, there were 51 life insurance mergers and acquisitions. Life insurance premiums in 2001 totaled $375.1 billion, representing growth of 73% since 1992. Property and casualty premiums totaled 323.4 billion in 2001, a 42% change since 1992. Competition between financial institutions has been healthy and premium income has risen steadily. The overwhelming majority of US families have some life insurance with a legal reserve company, the Veterans Administration, or fraternal, assessment, burial, or savings bank organization. The passage in 1999 of the Gramm-Leach-Bliley Act allowed insurance companies, banks, and securities firms to sell each other's products and services; restrictions were also lifted on cross-industry mergers and acquisitions.

Hundreds of varieties of insurance may be purchased. Besides life, the more important coverages include accident, fire, hospital and medical expense, group accident and health, automobile liability, automobile damage, workers' compensation, ocean marine, and inland marine. Americans buy more life and health insurance than any other group except Canadians and Japanese. During the 1970s, many states enacted a "no fault" form of automobile insurance, under which damages may be awarded automatically, without recourse to a lawsuit.

34SECURITIES

When the New York Stock Exchange (NYSE) opened in 1817, its trading volume was 100 shares a day. In 1996, 51 million individuals and 10,000 institutional investors owned stocks or shares in mutual funds traded on the NYSE. The two other major stock markets in the United States are the American Stock Exchange (AMEX) and the NASDAQ (National Association of Securities Dealers). The NASD (National Association of Securities Dealers) is regulated by the SEC (Securities and Exchange Commission). On 17 December 1999, 1.35 billion shares were traded, the record high for shares traded in a single day. Record-setting trading volume occurred for 1999 as a whole, with 203.9 billion shares traded (a 20% increase over 1998) for a total value of $8.9 trillion, up from $7.3 trillion in 1998.

35PUBLIC FINANCE

Under the Budget and Accounting Act of 1921, the president is responsible for preparing the federal government budget. In fact, the budget is prepared by the Office of Management and Budget (established in 1970), based on requests from the heads of all federal departments and agencies and advice from the Board of Governors of the Federal Reserve System, the Council of Economic Advisers, and the Treasury Department. The president submits a budget message to Congress in January. Under the Congressional Budget Act of 1974, the Congress establishes, by concurrent resolution, targets for overall expenditures and broad functional categories, as well as targets for revenues, the budget deficit, and the public debt. The Congressional Budget Office monitors the actions of Congress on individual appropriations bills with reference to those targets. The president exercises fiscal control over executive agencies, which issue periodic reports subject to presidential perusal. Congress exercises control through the comptroller general, head of the General Accounting Office, who sees to it that all funds have been spent and accounted for according to legislative intent. The fiscal year runs from 1 October to 30 September.

The public debt, subject to a statutory debt limit, rose from $43 billion in 1939/40 to more than $3.3 trillion in 1993. In fiscal year 1991/92, the federal deficit reached $290 million, a record high. Pressured by Congressional Republicans, President Clinton introduced a taxing and spending plan to reduce the rate of growth of the federal deficit when he began his term in 1993. The Clinton Administration calculated the package of tax increases and spending would cut the deficit by $500 billion over a four year period; in fiscal year 1997/98, the budget experienced an estimated surplus of $69 billion. However, the tax cuts and extensive military spending of President George W. Bush in the first term of the new millenium erased the surplus and pushed the economy toward a record $455 billion deficit projected for the 2003 fiscal year ($475 billion projected for 2004). The total public debt as of 15 August 2003 was $6,770,542,657,467.

The table below gives estimated federal government receipts and expenditures in millions of dollars for 2003 as reported by the US Office of Management and Budget. In the table, the term off-budget refers to receipts and outlays that are excluded from budget totals and are not subject to Congressional budget control mechanisms, such as oversight and review. Social Security is the federally-owned entity that receives the highest level of off-budget protection.

		% OF TOTAL	% OF GDP
RECEIPTS BY SOURCE			
Individual Income Taxes	1,092,290	48.4	
Corporation Income Taxes (1)	227,293	10.1	
Social Insurance and Retirement Receipts			
Total	766,045	33.9	
(On-Budget)	205,233		
(Off-Budget)	560,812		
Excise Taxes	76,254	3.4	
Other	96,358	4.3	

		% OF TOTAL	% OF GDP
Total Receipts			
Total	2,258,240	100.0	
(On-Budget)	1,697,428		
(Off-Budget)	560,812		
OUTLAYS BY SUPERFUNCTION AND FUNCTION			
National defense	322,071	16.0	2.8
Human resources	1,364,518	67.7	11.9
Education, training, employment, and social services	81,304		
Health	224,390		
Medicare	242,114		
Income security	285,933		
Social security	477,137		
(On-budget)	14,479		
(Off-budget)	462,658		
Veterans benefits and services	53,640		
Physical resources	101,038	5.0	0.9
Energy	-112		
Natural resources and environment	27,670		
Commerce and housing credit	4,704		
(On-budget)	5,206		
(Off-budget)	-502		
Transportation	57,476		
Community and regional development	11,300		
Net interest	175,244	8.7	1.5
(On-budget)	260,665		
(Off-budget)	-85,421		
Other functions	113,734	5.6	1.0
International affairs	21,289		
General science, space and technology	21,377		
Agriculture	15,037		
Administration of justice	35,382		
General government	16,708		
Allowances	3,941		
Undistributed offsetting receipts	-60,379	-3.0	-0.5
(On-budget)	-51,218		
(Off-budget)	-9,161		
Total, Federal outlays	2,016,226	100.0	17.6
(On-budget)	1,648,652	81.8	14.4
(Off-budget)	367,574	18.2	3.2

(1) Includes trust fund receipts for the hazardous substance superfund.

36TAXATION

Measured as a proportion of the GDP, the total US tax burden is less than that in most industrialized countries. Federal, state, and local taxes are levied in a variety of forms. The greatest source of revenue for the federal government is the personal income tax, which is paid by citizens and resident aliens on their worldwide income. The main state-level taxes are sales taxes and state income taxes. The main local taxes are property taxes and local income taxes.

Generally, corporations are expected to prepay, through four installments, 100% of estimated tax liability. US corporate taxes are famous for their complexity, and it is estimated that amount spent trying to comply with, minimize and/or avoid business taxes is equal to half the tax yield. The Tax Reform Act of 1986 reduced the top corporate rate from 46% to 39%. The schedule has eight brackets with rates that begin with 15% (for taxable income up to $50,000), increase to 39% (for the increment of income between $100,000 and $335,000) and then applies rates of 34% to 38% on income increments above $335,000. Since 1969, an Alternative Minimum Tax (AMT) has been attached to each of the tax brackets except the lowest, 15%, bracket. The purpose of the AMT is to prevent what is considered an overuse of tax deductions. The corporation, therefore, pays the AMT if its calculated tax liability falls below the AMT. Including the AMT, therefore, the effective federal tax rates for each bracket in 2003 were as follows: $7,500 + 25% of excess between $50,000

and $75,000; $13,750 + 34% of excess between $75,000 and $100,000; $22,250 + 39% of excess between $100,000 and $335,000; $113,900 + 34% of excess between $335,000 and $10,000,000; $3,400,000 + 35% of excess between $10,000,000 and $15,000,000; $5,150,000 + 38% of excess between $15,000,000 and $18,333,333); and $6,416,667 + 35% of excess over $18,333.333). Personal service companies were taxed at a flat rate of 35%. Personal holding companies were subject to an additional tax on undistributed income of 15% in 2003, down from 38.6% in 2002. Accumulated taxable income in excess of $250,000 (for a corporation), or $150,000 (for a personal holding company) was subject to an additional 15% tax in 2003, down from $38.6% in 2002. The capital gains exclusion was eliminated in the 1986 reforms, and capital gains are taxed at the same rate as other corporate income. The reforms also reduced other deductions, and curtailed the number of tax shelters that could be used. Withholding tax on dividends is 15%, unless the investor being paid owns at least 10% of the company, in which case the withholding tax is 5%.

The Tax Reform Act of 1986 reduced the 14 graduated personal income tax brackets, ranging from 11% to 50%, to two brackets, 15% and 28%, but these were later expanded to five. In 2003 the five tax brackets ranged from 15% (up to $40,000 taxable income) to 39.6% (above $263,750). Inheritance and gift taxes ranged from 18% to 55%. Most states have individual income taxes, although, as of 2003, eight did not (including Florida and Texas). The lowest tax rates ranged from 0.743% in Ohio to 5.35% in Minnesota, and the highest rates ranged from Pennsylvania's flat rate of 2.8% to 11% on taxable income above $75,000 in Montana.

The United States has not adopted a national value-added tax (VAT) system. The main indirect taxes are state sales taxes. There is an importation duty of 0.7% on imported goods. Excise taxes are levied on certain motor vehicles, personal air transportation, some motor fuels (excluding gasohol), alcoholic beverages, tobacco products, tires and tubes, telephone charges, and gifts and estates.

In May 2003, President Bush signed into law the third tax cut in three years: a $1.35 trillion tax cut in 2001; a $96 billion stimulus package in 2002, and a $350 billion package in 2003. For 2003, Bush had asked for a $726 billion tax cut to stimulate an economy in which unemployment had risen from 4% in 2000 to 6.3% in 2003, with the loss of about 2.7 million jobs. Tax revenues had fallen below expectations in 2002 and the national budget deficit for fiscal 2003 was projected to be headed toward a record $459 billion.

Under the Trade Agreements Extension Act of 1951, the president is required to inform the US International Trade Commission (known until 1974 as the US Tariff Commission) of contemplated concessions in the tariff schedules. The commission then determines what the "peril point" is; that is, it informs the president how far the tariff may be lowered without injuring a domestic producer, or it indicates the amount of increase necessary to enable a domestic producer to avoid injury by foreign competition. Similarly, the act provides an "escape clause,"—in effect, a method for rescinding a tariff concession granted on a specific commodity if the effect of the concession, once granted, has caused or threatens to cause "serious injury" to a domestic producer. The Trade Expansion Act of 1962 grants the president the power to negotiate tariff reductions of up to 50% under the terms of GATT.

In 1974, The US Congress authorized the president to reduce tariffs still further, especially on goods from developing countries. As the cost of imported oil rose in the mid-1970s, however, Congress became increasingly concerned with reducing the trade imbalance by discouraging "dumping" of foreign goods on the US market. The International Trade Commission is required to impose a special duty on foreign goods offered for sale at what the commission determines is less than fair market value.

Most products are dutiable under most-favored nation (MFN) rates or general duty rates. The import tariff schedules contain over 10,000 classifications, most of which are subject to interpretation. Besides duties, the United States imposes a 17% "user fee" on all imports. Excise taxes and harsher maintenance fees are also imposed on certain imports. Under the terms of the North American Free Trade Agreement (NAFTA), which was approved by Congress in 1993, tariffs on goods qualifying as North American under the rules of origin will be phased out over a 15-year period.

37ECONOMIC DEVELOPMENT

By the end of the 19th century, regulation rather than subsidy had become the characteristic form of government intervention in US economic life. The abuses of the railroads with respect to rates and services gave rise to the Interstate Commerce Commission in 1887, which was subsequently strengthened by numerous acts that now stringently regulate all aspects of US railroad operations.

The growth of large-scale corporate enterprises, capable of exercising monopolistic or near-monopolistic control of given segments of the economy, resulted in federal legislation designed to control trusts. The Sherman Antitrust Act of 1890, reinforced by the Clayton Act of 1914 and subsequent acts, established the federal government as regulator of large-scale business. This tradition of government intervention in the economy was reinforced during the Great Depression of the 1930s, when the Securities and Exchange Commission and the National Labor Relations Board were established. The expansion of regulatory programs accelerated during the 1960s and early 1970s with the creation of the federal Environmental Protection Agency, Equal Employment Opportunity Commission, Occupational Safety and Health Administration, and Consumer Product Safety Commission, among other bodies. Subsidy programs were not entirely abandoned, however. Federal price supports and production subsidies remained a major force in stabilizing US agriculture. Moreover, the federal government stepped in to arrange for guaranteed loans for two large private firms—Lockheed in 1971 and Chrysler in 1980—where thousands of jobs would have been lost in the event of bankruptcy.

During this period, a general consensus emerged that, at least in some areas, government regulation was contributing to inefficiency and higher prices. The Carter administration moved to deregulate the airline, trucking, and communications industries; subsequently, the Reagan administration relaxed government regulation of bank savings accounts and automobile manufacture as it decontrolled oil and gas prices. The Reagan administration also sought to slow the growth of social-welfare spending and attempted, with only partial success, to transfer control over certain federal social programs to the states and to reduce or eliminate some programs entirely. Ironically, it was a Democrat, Bill Clinton, who, in 1996, signed legislation that replaced Aid to Families with Dependent Children with a system of block grants that would enable the states to design and run their own welfare programs.

Some areas of federal involvement in social welfare, however, seem safely entrenched. Old age and survivors' insurance, unemployment insurance, and other aspects of the Social Security program have been accepted areas of governmental responsibility for decades. With the start of the 21st century, the government faced the challenge of keeping the Medicare program solvent as the postwar baby-boomer generation reached retirement age. Federal responsibility has also been extended to insurance of bank deposits, to mortgage insurance, and to regulation of stock transactions. The government fulfills a supervisory and regulatory role in labor-management relations. Labor and management customarily disagree on what the role should be, but neither side advocates total removal of government from this field.

Since the Reciprocal Trade Agreement Act of 1934, government regulation of foreign trade has tended toward decreased levels of protection, a trend maintained by the 1945 Trade Agreements Extension Act, the 1962 Trade Expansion Act, and the 1974 Trade Act. The goals of free trade have also been furthered since World War II by US participation in the International Monetary Fund (IMF), the World Bank, and the General Agreement on Tariffs and Trade (GATT). With the formation in 1995 of the World Trade Organization (WTO), most-favored-nation policies were expanded to trade in services and other areas.

In 1993, Congress approved the North American Free Trade Agreement, which extended the Free Trade Agreement between Canada and the United States to include Mexico. NAFTA, by eliminating tariffs and other trade barriers, created a free trade zone with a combined market size of $6.5 trillion and 370 million consumers. The effect on employment was uncertain—estimates varied from a loss of 150,000 jobs over the next ten years to a net gain of 200,000. Labor intensive goods-producing industries, such as apparel and textiles, were expected to suffer, while it was predicted that capital goods industries would benefit. It was anticipated that US automakers would benefit in the short run by taking advantage of the low wages in Mexico and that US grain farmers and the US banking, financial, and telecommunications sectors would gain enormous new markets. As of 2003, the pros and cons of NAFTA were still being hotly debated. Spokespersons for organized labor claimed in 2000 that the agreement had resulted in a net loss of 420,000 jobs, while advocates of free trade insisted that 311,000 new jobs had been created to support record US exports to Canada and Mexico, with only 116,000 workers displaced—a net gain of 195,000 jobs.

In 2003, President George W. Bush introduced, and Congress passed a tax cut of $350 billion designed to stimulate the economy, which was in a period of slow growth. This came on the heels of a $1.35 trillion tax cut passed in 2001 and a $96 billion stimulus package in 2002. Democrats cited the loss of 2.7 million private sector jobs during the first three years of the Bush administration as evidence that the president did not have control over the economy. In 1998, for the first time since 1969, the federal budget closed the fiscal year with a surplus. In 2000, the government was running a surplus of $236 billion, or a projected $5.6 trillion over 10 years. By mid-2003, the federal budget had fallen into deficit; the deficit stood at $455 billion, which was 4.2% of gross domestic product (GDP). Congress was debating an overhaul of the Medicare program, to provide prescription drug coverage for the elderly and disabled.

38HEALTH

The US health care system is among the most advanced in the world. Escalating health care costs resulted in several proposals for a national health care program in the 1970s, early 1980s, and early 1990s. Most reform measures relied either on market-oriented approaches designed to widen insurance coverage through tax subsidies on a federally controlled single-payer plan, or on mandatory employer payments for insurance coverage. At the end of the 1990s, the health care industry was struggling with continued rising costs, as well as the financial burden of providing care to over 40 million people who were uninsured. As of 1998, 44.3 million people, or 16% of the population, were without health insurance coverage. The percentage among the nation's poor was much higher (32%).

In response to rising costs, the popularity of managed care grew rapidly in the latter half of the 1990s. By 2000, 59% of the population was insured by either an HMO (health maintenance organization) or PPO (preferred provider organization). In such organizations, medical treatment, laboratory tests, and other health services for each patient are subject to the approval of the insurer before they can be covered. From 1987 to 1996, enrollment in health maintenance organizations (HMOs) doubled. By the end of the decade, however, the quality of treatment under managed care organizations was coming under increased scrutiny.

Life expectancy for someone born in 2000 was 76.9 years. Males could expect to live 74.1 years, females 79.5 years. Projections for 2010 were an average of 78.5 years for both males and females (males, 75.6; females, 81.4). Infant mortality has fallen from 3,830 per 100,000 live births in 1945 to 848.7 in 1992. In 2000, infant mortality was 7 per 1,000 live births. The birth rate in 2002 was 14.1 per 1,000 people. In 1997, 1,328,000 abortions were performed in the United States. In 1999, 56.5% of US adults were overweight and 21.1% were obese. Although health indicators continued to improve overall in the 1990s, pronounced disparities between different segments of the population remained.

The overall death rate is comparable to that of most nations— an estimated 8.7 per 1,000 people as of 2002. Leading causes of death (total number/rate per 100,000 people) reported in 2000 were: heart disease (709,894/257.9); cancer (551,833/200.5); cerebrovascular diseases (166,028/60.3); chronic lower respiratory diseases (123,550/44.9); accidents (93,592/34); diabetes mellitus (68,662/24.9); pneumonia and influenza (67,024/24.3); Alzheimer's disease (49,044/ 17.8); suicide (28,332/10.3); and homicide (16,137/5.9).

Cigarette smoking has been linked to heart and lung disease; about 20% of all deaths in the United States were attributed to cigarette smoking in 1990. Smoking has decreased overall since the late 1980s. The overall trend in smoking mortality suggests a decrease in smoking among males since the 1960s, but an increase in mortality for female smokers. On 23 November 1998, the Master Settlement Agreement was signed, the result of a lawsuit brought by 46 states and the District of Columbia against tobacco companies for damages related to smoking. Payments from the settlement, totaling $206 billion, began in 1999.

The rate of HIV infection (resulting in acquired immune deficiency syndrome—AIDS), first identified in 1981, has risen in the intervening years. There were a cumulative total of 750,000 AIDS cases in the 1980s and 1990s, with 450,000 deaths from the disease. In the latter 1990s, both incidence and mortality decreased with the introduction of new drug combinations to combat the disease. The number of AIDS cases declined by 30% between 1996 and 1998 and deaths were cut in half. In 1999, the number of people living with HIV/AIDS was estimated at 850,000, with the number of deaths from AIDS that year estimated at 20,000 and the number of new HIV infections estimated at 40,000 annually. AIDS continued to affect racial and ethnic minorities disproportionately. In the same year, the breakdown of men reporting new HIV infections was 50% black, 20% Hispanic, 30% white. The breakdown for new cases among women was 64% black, 18% Hispanic, 18% white. As of 1999, 50% of new infections were in found in homeosexual men; 25% were in injecting drug users. HIV prevalence was 0.6 per 100 adults in 1999.

Medical facilities in the United States included 5,810 hospitals in 2000, with 984,000 beds (down from 6,965 hospitals and 1,365,000 beds in 1980). In the same year, there were 813,800 physicians. Of the total number of active classified physicians, the largest areas of activity were internal medicine, 88,700; general and family practice, 67,500; pediatrics, 42,200; obstetrics and gynecology, 31,700; and general surgery, 24,500. As of 2000, there were 2,697,000 registered nurses. Dentists numbered approximately 170,000. As of 1999, there were an estimated 2.7 physicians and 3.6 hospital beds per 1,000 people.

Per capita health care expenditures rose from $247 in 1967 to about $3,380 in 1993. National health care spending reached $1 trillion in 1996 and is projected to rise to $1.8 trillion by 2005. Hospital costs, amounting to over $371 billion in 1997, represented 34% of national health care spending in that year. In the late 1990s, total health care expenditures stabilized at around 13% of GDP, with most expenditures being made by the private sector.

Medicare payments have lagged behind escalating hospital costs; payments in 2000 totaled $215.9 billion. Meanwhile, the elderly population in the United States is projected to increase to 18% of the total population by 2020, thus exacerbating the conundrum of health care finance. As of June 1999, 39 states had adopted policies enabling Medicaid funds to be used to cover medical services for qualified individuals requiring services provided by assisted-living facilities.

39 SOCIAL WELFARE

Social welfare programs in the United States depend on both the federal government and the state governments for resources and administration. Old age, survivors', disability, and the Medicare (health) programs are administered by the federal government; unemployment insurance, dependent child care, and a variety of other public assistance programs are state administered, although the federal government contributes to all of them through grants to the states.

Between the early 1960s and 1993, the number of welfare (Aid to Families with Dependent Children) recipients rose to 4 million families in spite of efforts to get clients "off the welfare rolls and into the payrolls." In 1996, President Clinton signed into law a groundbreaking welfare reform act that turned nearly the entire responsibility for the welfare system over to the states in the form of block grants. It also set a two-year limit on continuous welfare payments and a five-year cap on all payments over the mother's lifetime. The new system has been successful in reducing the number of recipients and in encouraging them to make the transition from "welfare to work." However, critics attributed at least some of the program's success to the booming economy during this period.

The Food and Nutrition Service of the US Department of Agriculture oversees several food assistance programs. Eligible Americans take part in the food stamp program, and eligible pupils participate in the school lunch program. The federal government also expends money for school breakfasts, nutrition programs for the elderly, and in commodity aid for the needy. The present Social Security program differs greatly from that created by the Social Security Act of 1935, which provided that retirement benefits be paid to retired workers aged 65 or older. Since 1939, Congress has attached a series of amendments to the program, including provisions for workers who retire at age 62, for widows, for dependent children under 18 years of age, and for children who are disabled prior to age 18. Disabled workers between 50 and 65 years of age are also entitled to monthly benefits. Other measures increased the number of years a person may work; among these reforms was a 1977 law banning mandatory retirement in private industry before age 70. The actuarial basis for the Social Security system has also changed. In 1935 there were about nine US wage earners for each American aged 65 or more; by the mid–1990s, however, the ratio was closer to three to one.

In 1940, the first year benefits were payable, $35 million was paid out. By 1983, Social Security benefits totaled $268.1 billion, paid to more than 40.6 million beneficiaries. The average monthly benefit for a retired worker with no dependents in 1960 was $74; in 1983, the average benefit was $629.30. Under legislation enacted in the early 1970s, increases in monthly benefits were pegged to the inflation rate, as expressed through the Consumer Price Index. Employers, employees, and the self-employed are legally required to make contributions to the Social Security fund. Currently, 6.2% of employee earnings (12.4% of self-employed earnings) went toward old-age, disability, and survivor benefits. Wage and salary earners pay Social Security taxes under the Federal Insurance Contributions Act (FICA). As the amount of benefits and the number of beneficiaries have increased, so has the maximum FICA payment. In 1990, Social Security Taxes leveled off at 7.65% on earnings up to $51,300. Among workers with many dependents, the Social Security tax deduction can now exceed the federal income tax deduction.

In January 1974, the Social Security Administration assumed responsibility for assisting the aged, blind, and disabled under the Supplemental Security Income program. In 1998, the Social Security system paid out $375 billion in monthly and lump sum benefits, including $232.3 billion in monthly retirement benefits and $43.5 billion in disability benefits. Medicare, another program administered under the Social Security Act, provides hospital insurance and voluntary medical insurance for persons 65 and over, with reduced benefits available at age 62. Medicaid is a program that helps the needy meet the costs of medical, hospital, and nursing home care.

The laws governing unemployment compensation originate in the states. Therefore, the benefits provided vary from state to state in duration (generally from 26 to 39 weeks) and amount (about 50% of earnings); the average employer contribution to Workers' Compensation in 1995 was 2% of payroll; which covered all or most costs, depending on the state.

Private philanthropy plays a major role in the support of relief and health services. The private sector plays an especially important role in pension management.

The federal agency Corporation for National and Community Service, established in October 1993, absorbed most of the programs of ACTION, established in 1971. CNCS coordinates three principal US volunteer service efforts: AmeriCorps, which has 40,000 volunteers placed in programs such as Habitat for Humanity and Volunteers in Service to America (VISTA); Learn and Serve America; and the National Senior Service Corporation, enlisting senior Americans persons to work with children and others who have special physical, mental, or emotional needs.

40HOUSING

The housing resources of the United States far exceed those of any other country, with 115,904,641 housing units serving about 105,480 households, according to preliminary results of the 2000 census. About 66.2% of all units were owner-occupied. 3,578,718 units were considered to be seasonal or recreational housing. The average household had 2.9 people. The median home value was $119,600. The median payment for rent and utilities of rental properties was $602 per month. According to the National Coalition for the Homelessness, about 3.5 million people experience temporary or prolonged periods of homelessness each year.

The vast majority of housing units are single-unit structures. The majority of rental tenants are found in the large metropolitan areas. As of 1990, an estimated 94 million year-round households possessed and used electrical appliances. Of these, 90.3% had color television sets; 71.7% had washing machines; 64.7% had clothes dryers; 42.7% had electric dishwashers; 29.1% had room air conditioners; and 36.6% had central air conditioning. As of 1980, about 22% of all housing units in the United States had been built before 1940; 8% during 1940–49; 13% during 1950–59; 15% from 1960 to 1969; 23% during 1970–79; and 19% since 1980. The median construction year was 1964.

In 1993, the median age of US housing structures was 28 years. The median number of rooms per house that year was 5.3, with about 32% having two bedrooms, and 39% having three bedrooms. Nearly half of all housing units have one full bathroom. Houses being built in the 1990s were significantly larger than those built in the 1970s. The average area of single-family housing built in 1993 was 180.88 sq m (1,947 sq ft), compared to 139.35 sq m (1,500 sq ft) in 1970.

41EDUCATION

Education is compulsory in all states and a responsibility of each state and the local government. However, federal funds are available to help meet special needs at primary, secondary, or higher levels. Generally, formal schooling begins at the age of six and continues up to age 17. Each state specifies the age and circumstances for compulsory attendance. For 2001, federal government expenditure on education was estimated at $92.7 billion, or 4.7% of the total federal budget.

"Regular" schools, which educate a person toward a diploma or degree, include both public and private schools. Public schools are controlled and supported by the local authorities, as well as state or federal governmental agencies. Private schools are controlled and supported by religious or private organizations. Elementary schooling is from grade one through grade eight. High schools cover grades nine through 12. Colleges include junior or community colleges, offering two-year associate degrees; regular four-year colleges and universities; and graduate or professional schools. The school year begins in September and ends in June.

The enrollment rate of three- to five-year-olds in preprimary schools rose from 37% in 1970 to 64% in 2000. In 1999, 95% of primary-school-age children were enrolled in school, while 87% of those eligible attended secondary school. The percentage of persons 25 years old and over completing their college education was 11% in 1970 and 21% in 1992. By 1994, approximately 46.5% of the adult population had attended a post-secondary institution. In 2000, 15.8% of persons 25 years old and over had not finished high school; 33.1% completed high school, with no further education; 17.6% had attended college but not received a degree; 7.8% had an associate's degree; 17% had a bachelor's degree; and 8.6% had an advanced degree.

In 1999 total primary school enrollment (K-8) was 38,253,000 (33,488,000 public and 4,765,000 private). Total secondary enrollment (9–12) was 14,623,000 (13,369,000 public and 1,254,000 private); and total college enrollment was 14,791,000 (11,309,000 public and 3,482,000 private). In the same year there were a total of 3,304,000 elementary and secondary teachers at both public and private schools, for a total pupil-teacher ratio of 16 to 1. It was projected that by the year 2011, public schools would have 60.7 million students and private schools 10 million students. In 1994/1995, there were 3,688 higher education institutions, 1,473 of which were two-year and 2,215 were four-year colleges and universities. The literacy rate is estimated to be 98% (males 97% and females 98%).

42ARTS

The nation's arts centers are emblems of the importance of the performing arts in US life. New York City's Lincoln Center for the Performing Arts, whose first concert hall opened in 1962, is now the site of the Metropolitan Opera House, three halls for concerts and other musical performances, two theaters, the New York Public Library's Library and Museum of the Performing Arts, and the Juilliard School. The John F. Kennedy Center for the Performing Arts in Washington, D.C., opened in 1971; it comprises two main theaters, two smaller theaters, an opera house, and a concert hall.

The New York Philharmonic, founded in 1842, is the nation's oldest professional musical ensemble. Other leading orchestras include those of Boston, Chicago, Cleveland, Los Angeles, Philadelphia, Pittsburgh, and Washington, D.C. (the National Symphony). Particularly renowned for artistic excellence are the Lyric Opera of Chicago, San Francisco Opera, Opera Company of Boston, Santa Fe Opera, New York City Opera, and Metropolitan Opera.

The recording industry is an integral part of the music world. The US accounts for fully one-third of the global total of $40 billion in sales. Popular music (mostly rock), performed in halls and arenas in every major city and on college campuses throughout the US, dominates record sales. The Internet website Napster has challenged the recording industry's copyright rights by offering free downloads of popular music. The industry, threatened by the freedom that the Internet granted to those wishing to share music, succeeded in having Napster's operations suspended by an appeals judge in 2001.

Though still financially insecure, dance is winning an increasingly wide following. The American Ballet Theater, founded in 1940, is the nation's oldest dance company still active today; the New York City Ballet is equally acclaimed. Other important companies include those of Martha Graham, Merce Cunningham, Alvin Ailey, Paul Taylor, and Twyla Tharp, as well as the Feld Ballet, Joffrey Ballet, and Pilobolus.

Drama remains a principal performing art, not only in New York City's renowned theater district but also in regional, university, summer, and dinner theaters throughout the US. Television and the motion picture industry have made film the dominant modern medium.

The National Council on the Arts, established in 1964, advises the Chairman of the National Endowment for the Arts (NEA). Fourteen members of the Council, and six members of Congress serve in this function. As the largest single funder of the nonprofit arts sector in the United States, the NEA generated a total budget of $115.7 million in 2003. Grants are awarded to state, local, and regional organizations for projects in the following categories: creation and presentation, education and access, heritage and preservation, and planning and stabilization. Fellowship awards are made in the categories of Literature, American Jazz Masters, and National Heritage.

Since 1985, the NEA has assisted in the selection process for the National Medal of Arts, which is awarded by the president of the United States. Several winners are chosen each year, representing a variety of fields. Past medallists include: William "Smokey" Robinson (songwriter and musician, 2002); Al Hirschfeld (illustrator, 2002); Johnny Cash (singer, 2001); Yo-Yo Ma (cellist, 2001); Kirk Douglas (actor and producer, 2001); Mikhail Baryshnikov (dancer and director, 2000); Maya Angelou (poet and writer, 2000); Aretha Franklin (singer, 1999); Michael Graves (architect, 1999); Frank Gehry (architect, 1998); Edward Albee (playwright, 1997); Harry Callahan (photographer, 1996); Bob Hope (entertainer, 1995); Gene Kelly (dancer, 1994); Arthur Miller (playwright, 1993); and Frank Capra (film director, 1986), to name just a few. Organizations that have received medals include the Alvin Ailey Dance Foundation (2001), National Public Radio (2000), the Julliard School (1999), Steppenwolf Theater Company (1998), the Sarah Lee Corporation (corporate arts patron, 1998), and the Boys Choir of Harlem (1994).

The National Endowment for the Humanities (NEH) was created as an independent federal agency in 1965. It is the largest funder of humanities programs in the country. Grants are distributed to state and local programs in the following categories: Challenge Grants, Education Programs, Preservation and Access, Public Programs, and Research Programs. Besides offering support to outside organizations, the NEH sponsors touring exhibitions and programs through chapters in most states. The NEH budget request for the year 2004 was $152 million.

The NEH sponsors the Jefferson Lecture in the Humanities award, which was established in 1972 as the highest honor the federal government bestows for distinguished intellectual and public achievement in the humanities. Recipients have included Henry Louis Gates, Jr., (2002); Arthur Miller (2001); Toni

Morrison (1996); Gwendolyn Brooks (1994); Saul Bellow (1977); and Robert Penn Warren (1974). The National Humanities Medals, established in 1997, are awarded to individuals or groups whose work has had an impact on the understanding and preservation of the humanities. Medallists include the Iowa Writers' Workshop (2002); Donald Kagan (2002); Art Linkletter (2002); Richard Peck (2001); Ernest J. Gaines (2000); Garrison Keillor (1999); Jim Lehrer (1999); Steven Spielberg (1999); Stephen Ambrose (1998); Don Henley (1997); and Maxine Hong Kingston (1997).

Since 1950, the National Book Foundation, based in New York, has sponsored the National Book Awards, which have become the nation's preeminent literary prizes. The 2002 prizes went to Three Junes by Julia Glass (fiction), Master of the Senate: The Years of Lyndon Johnson by Robert A. Caro (non-fiction), In the Next Galaxy by Ruth Stone (poetry), and Philip Roth for Distinguished Contribution to American Letters. Notable past winners include: United States: Essays 1952-1992 by Gore Vidal (1993); Cold Mountain by Charles Frazier (1997); The White House by Henry A. Kissinger (1980); A Swiftly Tilting Planet by Madeleine L'Engle (1980); The Fall of America: Poems of these States, 1965-1971 by Allen Ginsberg (1974); Death at an Early Age by Jonathan Kozol (1968); The Centaur by John Updike (1964); The Invisible Man by Ralph Ellison (1953); Collected Poems by Marianne Moore (1952); and The Collected Stories of William Faulkner (1951).

43 LIBRARIES AND MUSEUMS

Of the 32,852 libraries in the United States in 2000, 9,837 were public, with 6,376 branches; 4,723 were academic; 1,874 were government; 1,906 were medical; and a number were religious, military, legal, and specialized independent collections. The country's vast public library system is administered by municipality. The largest of these is the New York Public Library system with a total of 33.6 million items, including 17.7 million bound volumes. Other major public library systems include the Miami-Dade Public Library System with 3.9 million volumes, the Los Angeles Public Library (5.8 million), the Chicago Public Library (6.5 million), and the Boston Public Library system (6.8 million).

The foremost library in the country is the Library of Congress, with holdings of more than 26 million books and pamphlets in 2000. Other great libraries are the public libraries of Philadelphia, Boston, Cleveland, and Baltimore, and the John Crerar and Newberry libraries in Chicago. Noted special collections are those of the Pierpont Morgan Library in New York; the Huntington Library in San Marino, Calif.; the Folger Shakespeare Library in Washington, D.C.; the Hoover Library at Stanford University; and the rare book divisions of Harvard, Yale, Indiana, Texas, and Virginia universities. Among the leading university libraries, as judged by the extent of their holdings in 2000, are those of Harvard (with 14 million volumes itself), Yale, Illinois (Urbana-Champaign), Michigan (Ann Arbor), California (Berkeley), Columbia, Stanford, Cornell, California (Los Angeles), Chicago, Wisconsin (Madison), and Washington (Seattle). In 1997, Cleveland, Chicago, and San Francisco all opened new, multimillion-dollar libraries.

There are about 5,000 nonprofit museums in the United States. The most numerous type is the historic building, followed in descending order by college and university museums, museums of science, public museums of history, and public museums of art. Eminent US museums include the American Museum of Natural History, the Metropolitan Museum of Art, the Museum of Modern Art, the Guggenheim Museum, the Whitney Collection of American Art, the Frick Collection, and the Brooklyn Museum, all in New York City; the National Gallery of Art and the Smithsonian Institution in Washington, D.C., which encompasses several important museums; the Boston Museum of

Fine Arts; the Art Institute of Chicago and the Chicago Museum of Natural History; the Franklin Institute and Philadelphia Museum of Art, both in Philadelphia; and the M. H. de Young Memorial Museum in San Francisco. Also of prominence are the Cleveland Museum of Art, the St. Louis Museum of Art, and the Baltimore Museum of Art. In 2000 the Hayden Planetarium at the American Museum of Natural History reopened after a six-year, $210 million renovation.

44COMMUNICATIONS

All major electric communications systems are privately owned but regulated by the Federal Communications Commission. The United States uses wire and radio services for communications more extensively than any other country in the world. In 2000 over 98% of all US households had telephones, utilizing some 194 million main telephone lines (as of 1997). In 1998, there were 69 million cellular phones in use.

Radio serves a variety of purposes other than broadcasting. It is widely used by ships and aircraft for safety; it has become an important tool in the movement of buses, trucks, and taxicabs. Forest conservators, fire departments, and the police operate with radio as a necessary aid; it is used in logging operations, surveying, construction work, and dispatching of repair crews. In 1999, broadcasting stations on the air comprised over 10,000 radio stations (both AM and FM) and more than 1,500 television stations. Nearly 1,000 stations were affiliated with the five major networks. As of 1997 the United States had some 9,000 cable television systems. In 2000 there were 2,118 radios and 854 televisions for every 1,000 people. In 2000, there were about 585 personal computers in use for every 1,000 people. By 2001, about 7,800 Internet service providers were serving 166 million subscribers nationwide.

The Post Office Department of the United States was replaced on 1 July 1971 by the US Postal Service, a financially autonomous federal agency. In addition to mail delivery, the Postal Service provides registered, certified, insured, express and COD mail service, issues money orders, and operates a postal savings system. Since the 1970s, numerous privately owned overnight mail and package delivery services have been established.

45PRESS

In 2002 there were over 1,500 daily newspapers in the United States. Twenty large newspaper chains account for almost 60% of the total daily circulation. The US daily newspapers with the largest circulations as of 2002 were as follows:

	CIRCULATION
USA Today (national)	2,149,930
Wall Street Journal (national)	1,780,605
New York Times	1,109,370
Los Angeles Times (CA)	944,300
Washington Post (DC)	759,860
New York Daily News	734,473
Chicago Tribune (IL)	675,850
Long Island/New York Newsday	577,354
Houston Chronicle (TX)	551,854
New York Post	533,860
Dallas Morning News (TX)	494,890
Chicago Sun-Times (IL)	480,920
Boston Globe (MA)	471,200
San Francisco Chronicle (CA)	455,693
Arizona Republic	451,290
Star-Ledger (Newark, NJ)	410,547
Register (Orange County, CA)	378,930
Philadelphia Inquirer	365,150
Cleveland Plain Dealer (OH)	359,980
Union-Tribune (San Diego, CA)	351,760

Modern Maturity, published bimonthly by AARP (formerly known as American Association of Retired Persons), had a circulation of 20 million in 2000. The two general circulation magazines that appealed to the largest audiences were *Reader's Digest* (about 17 million), and *TV Guide* (about 15 million). *Time* and *Newsweek* were the leading news magazines, with a weekly circulation of 4,630,140 and 3,100,000 respectively.

The US book-publishing industry consists of the major book companies (mainly in the New York metro area), nonprofit university presses distributed throughout the United States, and numerous small publishing firms. In 1994, 51,863 book titles were published in the United States.

The US Constitution provides for freedom of speech and of the press in its Bill of Rights, and the government supports these rights. Citizens enjoy a wide range of opinions in all media, where debate, editorial opinion, and government opposition viewpoints are represented in some form or another. Nearly all media are privately owned.

46ORGANIZATIONS

A number of industrial and commercial organizations exercise considerable influence on economic policy. The National Association of Manufacturers (NAM) and the US Chamber of Commerce, with numerous local branches, are the two central bodies of business and commerce. Various industries have their own associations, concerned with cooperative research and questions of policy alike.

Practically every profession in the United States is represented by one or more professional organizations. Among the most powerful of these are the American Medical Association (AMA), comprising regional, state, and local medical societies; the American Bar Association (ABA), also comprising state and local associations; the American Hospital Association (AHA); and the National Education Association (NEA). The most prestigious scientific and technical institutions are the National Academy of Sciences (NAS—founded 1863) and the National Academy of Engineering (NAE—1964).

Many private organizations are dedicated to programs of political and social action. Prominent in this realm are the National Association for the Advancement of Colored People (NAACP), the Urban League, the American Civil Liberties Union (ACLU), Common Cause, and the Anti-Defamation League. The League of Women Voters (LWV), which provides the public with nonpartisan information about candidates and election issues, began sponsoring televised debates between the major presidential candidates in 1976. The National Organization for Women (NOW) and the National Rifle Association (NRA) have each mounted nationwide lobbying campaigns on issues affecting their members. There are thousands of political action committees (PACs) that disburse funds to candidates for the House and Senate and other elected offices.

The great privately endowed philanthropic foundations and trusts play an important part in encouraging the development of education, art, science, and social progress in the United States. Prominent foundations include the Carnegie Corporation and the Carnegie Endowment for International Peace, the Ford Foundation, the Guggenheim Foundation, the Mayo Association for the Advancement of Medical Research and Education, and the Rockefeller Foundation. Private philanthropy was responsible for the establishment of many of the nation's most eminent libraries, concert halls, museums, and university and medical facilities; private bequests were also responsible for the establishment of the Pulitzer Prizes. Merit awards offered by industry and professional groups include the "Oscars" of the Academy of Motion Picture Arts and Sciences, the "Emmys" of the National Academy of Television Arts and Sciences, and the "Grammys" of the National Academy of Recording Arts and Sciences.

Funds for a variety of community health and welfare services are funneled through United Way campaigns, which raise funds annually. The American Red Cross has over 3,000 chapters, which pay for services and activities ranging from disaster relief to blood donor programs. Private organizations supported by contributions from the general public lead the fight against specific diseases.

The Boy Scouts of America, the Girl Scouts of the USA, rural 4-H Clubs, and the Young Men's and the Young Women's Christian Associations are among the organizations devoted to recreation, sports, camping, and education.

The largest religious organization in the United States is the National Council of the Churches of Christ in the USA, which embraces 32 Protestant and Orthodox denominations, whose adherents total more than 42 million. Many organizations, such as the American Philosophical Society, the American Association for the Advancement of Science, and the National Geographic Society, are dedicated to the enlargement of various branches of human knowledge. National, state, and local historical societies abound, and there are numerous educational, sports, and hobbyist groups.

The larger veterans' organizations are the American Legion, the Veterans of Foreign Wars of the United States, the Catholic War Veterans, and the Jewish War Veterans. Fraternal organizations, in addition to such international organizations as the Masons, include indigenous groups such as the Benevolent and Protective Order of Elks, the Loyal Order of Moose, and the Woodmen of the World. Many, such as the Ancient Order of Hibernians in America, commemorate the national origin of their members. One of the largest fraternal organizations is the Roman Catholic Knights of Columbus.

47TOURISM, TRAVEL, AND RECREATION

Among the most striking scenic attractions in the United States are: the Grand Canyon in Arizona; Carlsbad Caverns in New Mexico; Yosemite National Park in California; Yellowstone National Park in Idaho, Montana, and Wyoming; Niagara Falls, partly in New York; and the Everglades in Florida. The United States has a total of 49 national parks. Popular coastal resorts include those of Florida, California, and Cape Code in Massachusetts. Historical attractions include the Liberty Bell and Constitution Hall in Philadelphia; the Statue of Liberty in New York City; the White House, the Capitol, and the monuments to Washington, Jefferson, and Lincoln in the District of Columbia; the Williamsburg historical restoration in Virginia; various Revolutionary and Civil War battlefields and monuments in the East and South; the Alamo in San Antonio; and Mt. Rushmore in South Dakota. Among many other popular tourist attractions are the movie and television studios in Los Angeles; the cable cars in San Francisco; casino gambling in Las Vegas and in Atlantic City, N.J.; thoroughbred horse racing in Kentucky; the Grand Ole Opry in Nashville, Tenn.; the many jazz clubs of New Orleans; and such amusement parks as Disneyland (Anaheim, Calif.) and Walt Disney World (near Orlando, Fla.). For abundance and diversity of entertainment—theater, movies, music, dance, and sports—New York City has few rivals. In April 1993, Amtrak began the country's first regularly scheduled transcontinental passenger service, from Los Angeles to Miami.

Americans' recreational activities range from the major spectator sports—professional baseball, football, basketball, ice hockey, and soccer, horse racing, and collegiate football and basketball—to home gardening. Participant sports are a favorite form of recreation, including jogging, aerobics, tennis, and golf. Skiing is a popular recreation in New England and the western mountain ranges, while sailing, power boating, rafting, and canoeing are popular water sports.

Foreign visitors to the United States numbered 50,890,701 in 2000. Of these visitors, 28% came from Canada, 20% from

Mexico, and 10% from Japan. Travelers to the United States from all foreign countries spent US$85,1 billion in 2000. With a few exceptions, such as Canadians entering from the Western Hemisphere, all visitors to the United States are required to have passports and visas.

The cost of traveling in the United States varies from city to city. According to 1999 UN estimates, daily expenses were approximately $263 in Chicago, $275 in New York, $235 in Washington, and $213 in Miami. Costs are lower in smaller cities and rural areas.

48SPORTS

Baseball, long honored as the national pastime, is the nation's leading professional team sport, with two major leagues having 30 teams (2 in Canada). In the 1998 season, two teams were added to Major League Baseball—the Arizona Diamondbacks, playing in the National League West, and the Tampa Bay Devil Rays, playing in the American League East. During the 1997 regular season, over 63 million fans attended Major League Baseball games. In 1992, the Toronto Blue Jays became the first non-US team to win the World Series. In addition, there is an extensive network of minor league baseball teams, each of them related to a major league franchise. The National Basketball Association, created in 1946, included 29 teams in 2000. A labor dispute resulted in a lockout of the players for nearly half the 1999–2000 NBA season. The Women's National Basketball Association (WNBA), founded in 1997, included 14 teams as of 2003. During the WNBA's third season (1999), 1,959,733 fans attended regular season games, establishing an attendance record for women's professional sports. In 2003, the National Football League included 32 teams; Houston, Texas, was awarded a franchise in 2002 to establish the 32nd team. The National Hockey League (NHL) expanded to 30 teams in 2000, when teams in St. Paul, Minnesota (Minnesota Wild), and Columbus, Ohio (Columbus Blue Jackets), played their inaugural seasons. Prior expansion occurred in the 1998–99 season, with the Nashville Predators, and in 1999–2000, with the Atlanta Thrashers. In 1997, 15.7 million fans attended regular NHL season games, and 1.4 million attended NHL playoff games. The North American Soccer League (NASL), which appeared to be growing popular in the late 1970s, discontinued outdoor play in 1985. Indoor soccer continued, however, with the Major Indoor Soccer League. In 1994, however, soccer's World Cup games were played in nine US cities, with the final match held in Los Angeles. As of 2003, Major League Soccer fielded 10 teams in two divisions. Radio and television contracts are integral to the popular and financial success of all professional team sports. In 1994, a strike by baseball players caused the World Series to be canceled for the first time since 1904; hockey players also held strikes in 1992 and 1994.

Several other professional sports are popular nationwide. Thoroughbred racing is among the nation's most popular spectator sports, with an estimated 12 million fans visiting horse-racing tracks annually. Annual highlights of thoroughbred racing are the three jewels of the Triple Crown—the Kentucky Derby, the Preakness, and the Belmont Stakes—most recently won by Seattle Slew in 1977 and by Affirmed in 1978. In 2000, jockey Julie Krone became the first woman jockey to be inducted into the Horse Racing Hall of Fame. Harness racing is also popular; attracting millions of spectators annually and involving over $1.5 billion in wagering. In 1997, over 14.3 million fans watched greyhound racing. The prize money that Henry Ford won on a 1901 auto race helped him start his now-famous car company two years later; since then, automobile manufacturers have backed sports car, stock car, and motorcycle racing at tracks throughout the US. From John L. Sullivan to Muhammad Ali, the personality and power of the great boxing champions have drawn millions of spectators ringside. Glamor and top prizes also draw national followings for tennis and golf, two professional sports in which women are nationally prominent. Other professional sports include bowling and rodeo.

Football has been part of US college life since the game was born on 6 November 1869 with a New Jersey match between Rutgers and Princeton. The National Collegiate Athletic Association (NCAA) and National Association of Intercollegiate Athletics (NAIA) coordinate collegiate football and basketball. Colleges recruit top athletes with sports scholarships in order to win media attention, and to keep the loyalty of the alumni, thereby boosting fund-raising. Baseball, hockey, swimming, gymnastics, crew, lacrosse, track and field, and a variety of other sports also fill the intercollegiate competitive program

The Amateur Athletic Union (AAU), a national nonprofit organization founded in 1888, conducts the AAU/USA Junior Olympics, offering competition in 22 sports in order to help identify candidates for international Olympic competition. St. Louis hosted the 1904 summer Olympics; Los Angeles was home to the games in 1932 and 1984. The winter Olympic games were held in Squaw Valley, Calif., in 1960, and at Lake Placid, New York, in 1932 and 1980. Atlanta hosted the summer Olympic games in 1996. Salt Lake City, Utah, was the site of the 2002 winter Olympic games.

49 FAMOUS AMERICANS

Printer, publisher, inventor, scientist, statesman, and diplomat, Benjamin Franklin (1706–90) was America's outstanding figure of the colonial period. George Washington (1732–99), leader of the colonial army in the American Revolution, became first president of the United States and is known as the "father of his country." Chief author of the Declaration of Independence, founder of the US political party system, and third president was Thomas Jefferson (1743–1826). His leading political opponents were John Adams (1735–1826), second president, and Alexander Hamilton (b.West Indies, 1755–1804), first secretary of the treasury, who secured the new nation's credit. James Madison (1751–1836), a leading figure in drawing up the US Constitution, served as fourth president. John Quincy Adams (1767–1848), sixth president, was an outstanding diplomat and secretary of state.

Andrew Jackson (1767–1845), seventh president, was an ardent champion of the common people and opponent of vested interests. Outstanding senators during the Jackson era were John Caldwell Calhoun (1782–1850), spokesman of the southern planter aristocracy and leading exponent of the supremacy of states' rights over federal powers; Henry Clay (1777–1852), the great compromiser, who sought to reconcile the conflicting views of the North and the South; and Daniel Webster (1782–1852), statesman and orator, who championed the preservation of the Union against sectional interests and division. Abraham Lincoln (1809–65) led the United States through its most difficult period, the Civil War, in the course of which he issued the Emancipation Proclamation. Jefferson Davis (1808–89) served as the only president of the short-lived Confederacy. Stephen Grover Cleveland (1837–1908), a conservative reformer, was the strongest president in the latter part of the 19th century. Among the foremost presidents of the 20th century have been Nobel Peace Prize winner Theodore Roosevelt (1858–1919); Woodrow Wilson (1856–1924), who led the nation during World War I and helped establish the League of Nations; and Franklin Delano Roosevelt (1882–1945), elected to four terms spanning the Great Depression and World War II. The presidents during the 1961–88 period have been John Fitzgerald Kennedy (1917–63), Lyndon Baines Johnson (1908–73), Richard Milhous Nixon (1913–94), Gerald Rudolph Ford (Leslie Lynch King, Jr., b.1913), Jimmy Carter (James Earl Carter, Jr., b.1924), and Ronald Wilson Reagan (b.1911).

Of the outstanding US military leaders, four were produced by the Civil War: Union generals Ulysses Simpson Grant (1822–85), who later served as the eighteenth president, and William Tecumseh Sherman (1820–91); and Confederate generals Robert Edward Lee (1807–70) and Thomas Jonathan "Stonewall" Jackson (1824–63). George Catlett Marshall (1880–1959), army chief of staff during World War II, in his later capacity as secretary of state under President Harry S Truman (1884–1972), formulated the Marshall Plan, which did much to revitalize Western Europe. Douglas MacArthur (1880–1964) commanded the US forces in Asia during World War II, oversaw the postwar occupation and reorganization of Japan, and directed UN forces in the first year of the Korean conflict. Dwight D. Eisenhower (1890–1969) served as supreme Allied commander during World War II, later becoming the thirty-fourth president.

John Marshall (1755–1835), chief justice of the United States from 1801 to 1835, established the power of the Supreme Court through the principle of judicial review. Other important chief justices were Edward Douglass White (1845–1921), former president William Howard Taft (1857–1930), and Earl Warren (1891–1974), whose tenure as chief justice from 1953 to 1969 saw important decisions on desegregation, reapportionment, and civil liberties. The justice who enjoyed the longest tenure on the court was William O. Douglas (1898–1980), who served from 1939 to 1975; other prominent associate justices were Oliver Wendell Holmes (1841–1935), Louis Dembitz Brandeis (1856–1941), and Hugo Lafayette Black (1886–1971).

Indian chiefs renowned for their resistance to white encroachment were Pontiac (1729?–69), Black Hawk (1767–1838), Tecumseh (1768–1813), Osceola (1804?–38), Cochise (1812?–74), Geronimo (1829?–1909), Sitting Bull (1831?–90), Chief Joseph (1840?–1904), and Crazy Horse (1849?–77). Other significant Indian chiefs were Hiawatha (fl. 1500), Squanto (d.1622), and Sequoya (1770?–1843). Historical figures who have become part of American folklore include pioneer Daniel Boone (1734–1820); silversmith, engraver, and patriot Paul Revere (1735–1818); frontiersman David "Davy" Crockett (1786–1836); scout and Indian agent Christopher "Kit" Carson (1809–68); James Butler "Wild Bill" Hickok (1837–76); William Frederick "Buffalo Bill" Cody (1846–1917); and the outlaws Jesse Woodson James (1847–82) and Billy the Kid (William H. Bonney, 1859–81).

Inventors and Scientists

Outstanding inventors were Robert Fulton (1765–1815), who developed the steamboat; Eli Whitney (1765–1825), inventor of the cotton gin and mass production techniques; Samuel Finley Breese Morse (1791–1872), who invented the telegraph; and Elias Howe (1819–67), who invented the sewing machine. Alexander Graham Bell (b.Scotland, 1847–1922) gave the world the telephone. Thomas Alva Edison (1847–1931) was responsible for hundreds of inventions, among them the long-burning incandescent electric lamp, the phonograph, automatic telegraph devices, a motion picture camera and projector, the microphone, and the mimeograph. Lee De Forest (1873–1961), the "father of the radio," developed the vacuum tube and many other inventions. Vladimir Kosma Zworykin (b.Russia, 1889–1982) was principally responsible for the invention of television. Two brothers, Wilbur Wright (1867–1912) and Orville Wright (1871–1948), designed, built, and flew the first successful motor-powered airplane. Amelia Earhart (1898–1937) and Charles Lindbergh (1902–74) were aviation pioneers. Pioneers in the space program include John Glenn (b.1921), the first US astronaut to orbit the earth, and Neil Armstrong (b.1930), the first man to set foot on the moon.

Benjamin Thompson, Count Rumford (1753–1814), developed devices for measuring light and heat, and the physicist Joseph Henry (1797–1878) did important work in magnetism

Presidents of the United States

	NAME	BORN	DIED	OTHER MAJOR OFFICES HELD	RESIDENCE AT ELECTION
1	George Washington	Westmoreland County, Va., 22 February 1732	Mt. Vernon, Va., 14 December 1799	Commander in Chief, Continental Army (1775–83)	Mt. Vernon, Va.
2	John Adams	Braintree (later Quincy), Mass., 30 October 1735	Quincy, Mass., 4 July 1826	Representative, Continental Congress (1774–77); US vice president (1797–97)	Quincy, Mass.
3	Thomas Jefferson	Goochland (now Albemarle) County, Va., 13 April 1743	Monticello, Va., 4 July 1826	Representative, Continental Congress (1775–76); governor of Virginia (1779–81); secretary of state (1790–93); US vice president (1797–1801)	Monticello, Va.
4	James Madison	Port Conway, Va., 16 March 1751	Montpelier, Va., 28 June 1836	Representative, Continental Congress (1780–83; 1786–88); US representative (1789–97); secretary of state (1801–9)	Montpelier, Va.
5	James Monroe	Westmoreland County, Va. 28 April 1758	New York, N.Y., 4 July 1831	US senator (1790–94); governor of Virginia (1799–1802); secretary of state (1811–17); secretary of war (1814–15)	Leesburg, Va.
6	John Quincy Adams	Braintree (later Quincy), Mass., 11 July 1767	Washington, D.C., 23 February 1848	US senator (1803–8); secretary of state (1817–25); US representative (1831–48)	Quincy, Mass.
7	Andrew Jackson	Waxhaw, Carolina frontier, 15 March 1767	The Hermitage, Tenn., 8 June 1845	US representative (1796–97); US senator (1797–98)	The Hermitage, Tenn.
8	Martin Van Buren	Kinderhook, N.Y., 5 December 1782	Kinderhook, N.Y., 24 July 1862	US senator (1821–28); governor of New York (1829); secretary of state (1829–31); US vice president (1833–37)	New York
9	William Henry Harrison	Charles City County, Va., 9 February 1773	Washington, D.C., 4 April 1841	Governor of Indiana Territory (1801–13); US representative (1816–19); US senator (1825–28)	North Bend, Ohio
10	John Tyler	Charles City County, Va., 29 March 1790	Richmond, Va., 18 January 1862	US representative (1816–21); governor of Virginia (1825–27); US senator (1827–36); US vice president (1841)	Richmond, Va.
11	James K. Polk	Mecklenburg County, N.C., 2 November 1795	Nashville, Tenn., 15 June 1849	US representative (1825–39); governor of Tennessee (1839–41)	Nashville, Tenn.
12	Zachary Taylor	Orange County, Va., 24 November 1784	Washington, D.C., 9 July 1850	—	Louisiana
13	Millard Fillmore	Cayuga County, N.Y., 7 January 1800	Buffalo, N.Y., 8 March 1874	US representative (1833–35; 1837–43); US vice president (1849–50)	Buffalo, N.Y.
14	Franklin Pierce	Hillsboro, N.H., 23 November 1804	Concord, N.H., 8 October 1869	US representative, (1833–37); US senator (1837–43)	Concord, N.H.
15	James Buchanan	Mercersburg, Pa., 23 April 1791	Lancaster, Pa., 1 June 1868	US representative (1821–31); US senator (1834–45); secretary of state (1845–49)	Lancaster, Pa.
16	Abraham Lincoln	Hodgenville, Ky., 12 February 1809	Washington, D.C., 15 April 1865	US representative (1847–49)	Springfield, Ill.
17	Andrew Johnson	Raleigh, N.C., 29 December 1808	Carter Station, Tenn., 31 July 1875	US representative (1843–53); governor of Tennessee (1853–57; 1862–65); US senator (1857–62); US vice president (1865)	Greeneville, Tenn.
18	Ulysses S. Grant	Point Pleasant, Ohio, 27 April 1822	Mount McGregor, N.Y., 23 July 1885	Commander, Union Army (1864–65); secretary of war (1867–68)	Galena, Ill.
19	Rutherford B. Hayes	Delaware, Ohio, 4 October 1822	Fremont, Ohio, 17 January 1893	US representative (1865–67); governor of Ohio (1868–72; 1876–77)	Fremont, Ohio
20	James A. Garfield	Orange, Ohio, 19 November 1831	Elberon, N.J., 19 September 1881	US representative (1863–80)	Mentor, Ohio
21	Chester A. Arthur	Fairfield, Vt., 5 October 1829	New York, N.Y., 18 November 1886	US vice president (1881)	New York, N.Y.
22	Grover Cleveland	Caldwell, N.J., 18 March 1837	Princeton, N.J., 24 June 1908	Governor of New York (1882–84)	Albany, N.Y.
23	Benjamin Harrison	North Bend, Ohio, 20 August 1833	Indianapolis, Ind., 13 March 1901	US senator (1881–87)	Indianapolis, Ind.

PARTY	% OF POPULAR VOTE	% OF ELECTORAL VOTE[1,2]	TERMS IN OFFICE[5]	VICE PRESIDENTS	NOTABLE EVENTS	
Federalist	—	50.0	30 April 1789–4 March 1793	John Adams	Federal government organized; Bill of Rights enacted (1791); Whiskey Rebellion suppressed (1794); North Carolina, Rhode Island, Vermont, Kentucky, Tennessee enter Union.	1
Federalist	—	25.7	4 March 1797–4 March 1801	Thomas Jefferson	Alien and Sedition Acts passed (1798); Washington, D.C., becomes US capital (1800).	2
Dem.–Rep.	—	26.4[3] 92.0	4 March 1801–4 March 1805	Aaron Burr George Clinton	Louisiana Purchase (1803); Lewis and Clark Expedition (1803–6); Ohio enters Union.	3
Dem.–Rep.	—	69.7 58.9	4 March 1809–4 March 1818 4 March 1813–4 March 1817	George Clinton Elbridge Gerry	War of 1812 (1812–14); protective tariffs passed (1816); Louisiana, Indiana enter Union.	4
Dem.–Rep.	—	84.3	4 March 1817–4 March 1821 4 March 1821–4 March 1825	Daniel D. Tompkins Daniel D. Tompkins	Florida purchased from Spain (1819–21); Missouri Compromise (1820); Monroe Doctrine (1823); Mississippi, Illinois, Alabama, Maine, Missouri enter Union.	5
National Republican	30.9	38.0[4]	4 March 1825–4 March 1829	John C. Calhoun	Period of political antagonisms, producing little legislation; road and canal construction supported; Erie Canal opens (1825).	6
Democrat	56.0 54.2	68.2 76.6	4 March 1829–4 March 1833	John C. Calhoun Martin Van Buren	Introduction of spoils system; Texas Republic established (1836); Arkansas, Michigan enter Union.	7
Democrat	50.8	57.8	4 March 1837–4 March 1841	Richard M. Johnson	Financial panic (1837) and subsequent depression.	8
Whig	52.9	79.6	4 March 1841–4 April 1841	John Tyler	Died of pneumonia one month after taking office.	9
Whig	—	—	4 April 1841–4 March 1845	—	Monroe Doctrine extended to Hawaiian Islands (1842); Second Seminole War in Florida ends (1842).	10
Democrat	49.5	61.8	4 March 1845–4 March 1849	George M. Dallas	Boundary between US and Canada set at 49th parallel (1846); Mexican War (1846–48), ending with Treaty of Guadalupe Hidalgo (1848); California gold rush begins (1848); Florida, Texas, Iowa, Wisconsin enter Union.	11
Whig	47.3	56.2	4 March 1849–9 July 1850	Millard Fillmore	Died after 16 months in office.	12
Whig	—	—	9 July 1850–4 March 1853	—	Fugitive Slave Law (1850); California enters Union.	13
Democrat	50.8	85.8	4 March 1853–4 March 1857	William R. King	Gadsden Purchase (1853); Kansas–Nebraska Act (1854); trade opened with Japan (1854).	14
Democrat	45.3	58.8	4 March 1857–4 March 1861	John C. Breckinridge	John Brown's raid at Harpers Ferry, Va. (now W. Va.; 1859); South Carolina secedes (1860); Minnesota, Oregon, Kansas enter Union.	15
Republican	39.8 55.0	59.4 91.0	4 March 1861–4 March 1865 4 March 1865–15 April 1865	Hannibal Hamlin Andrew Johnson	Confederacy established, Civil War begins (1851); Emancipation Proclamation (1863); Confederacy defeated (1865); Lincoln assassinated (1865); West Virginia, Nevada attain statehood.	16
Republican	—	—	15 April 1865–4 March 1869	—	Reconstruction Acts (1867); Alaska purchased from Russia (1867); Johnson impeached but acquitted (1868); Nebraska enters Union.	17
Republican	52.7 55.6	72.8 78.1	4 March 1869–4 March 1873 4 March 1873–4 March 1877	Schuyler Colfax Henry Wilson	Numerous government scandals; financial panic (1873); Colorado enters Union.	18
Republican	48.0	50.1	4 March 1877–4 March 1881	William A. Wheeler	Federal troops withdrawn from South (1877); civil service reform begun.	19
Republican	48.3	58.0	4 March 1881–19 Sept. 1881	Chester A. Arthur	Shot after 4 months in office, dead 2½ months later.	20
Republican	—	—	19 Sept. 1881–4 March 1885	—	Chinese immigration banned despite presidential veto (1882); Civil Service Commission established by Pendleton Act (1883).	21
Democrat	48.5	54.6	4 March 1885–4 March 1889	Thomas A. Hendricks	Interstate Commerce Act (1887)	22
Republican	47.8	58.1	4 March 1889–4 March 1893	Levi P. Morton	Sherman Silver Purchase Act (1890); North Dakota, South Dakota, Montana, Washington, Idaho, Wyoming enter Union.	23

Presidents of the United States (continued)

	NAME	BORN	DIED	OTHER MAJOR OFFICES HELD	RESIDENCE AT ELECTION
24	Grover Cleveland	Caldwell, N.J., 18 March 1837	Princeton, N.J., 24 June 1908	Governor of New York (1882–84)	New York, N.Y.
25	William McKinley	Niles, Ohio, 29 January 1843	Buffalo, N.Y., 14 September 1901	US representative (1877–83; 1885–91); governor of Ohio (1892–96)	Canton, Ohio
26	Theodore Roosevelt	New York, N.Y., 27 October 1858	Oyster Bay, N.Y., 6 January 1919	Governor of New York (1899–1900); US vice president (1901)	Oyster Bay, N.Y.
27	William H. Taft	Cincinnati, Ohio, 15 September 1857	Washington, D.C., 8 March 1930	Governor of Philippines (1901–4); secretary of war (1904–8); chief justice of the US (1921–30)	Washington, D.C.
28	Woodrow Wilson	Staunton, Va., 28 December 1856	Washington, D.C., 3 February 1924	Governor of New Jersey (1911–13)	Trenton, N.J.
29	Warren G. Harding	Blooming Grove, Ohio, 2 November 1865	San Francisco, Calif., 2 August 1923	US senator (1915–21)	Marion, Ohio
30	Calvin Coolidge	Plymouth Notch, Vt., 4 July 1872	Northampton, Mass., 5 January 1933	Governor of Massachusetts (1919–20); US vice president (1921–23)	Boston, Mass.
31	Herbert Hoover	West Branch, Iowa, 10 August 1874	New York, N.Y., 20 October 1964	Secretary of commerce (1921–29)	Stanford, Calif.
32	Franklin D. Roosevelt	Hyde Park, N.Y., 30 January 1882	Warm Springs, Ga., 12 April 1945	Governor of New York (1929–1933)	Hyde Park, N.Y.
33	Harry S Truman	Lamar, Mo., 8 May 1884	Kansas City, Mo., 26 December 1972	US senator (1935–45); US vice president (1945)	Independence, Mo.
34	Dwight D. Eisenhower	Denison, Tex., 14 October 1890	Washington, D.C., 28 March 1969	Supreme allied commander in Europe (1943–44); Army chief of staff (1945–48)	New York
35	John F. Kennedy	Brookline, Mass., 29 May 1917	Dallas, Tex., 22 November 1963	US representative (1947–52); US senator (1953–60)	Massachusetts
36	Lyndon B. Johnson	Stonewall, Tex., 27 August 1908	Johnson City, Tex., 22 January 1973	US representative (1937–48); US senator (1949–60); US vice president (1961–63)	Johnson City, Tex.
37	Richard M. Nixon	Yorba Linda, Calif., 9 January 1913	New York, N.Y., 22 April 1994	US representative (1947–51); US senator (1951–53); US vice president (1953–61)	New York, N.Y.
38	Gerald R. Ford	Omaha, Neb., 14 July 1913	—	US representative (1949–73); US vice president (1973–74)	Grand Rapids, Mich.
39	James E. Carter	Plains, Ga., 1 October 1924	—	Governor of Georgia (1951–75)	Plains, Ga.
40	Ronald W. Reagan	Tampico, Ill., 6 February 1911	—	Governor of California (1967–76)	Los Angeles, Calif.
41	George H. W. Bush	Milton, Mass., 12 June 1924	—	US representative (1967–71) Vice president (1980–88)	Houston, Texas
42	William J. Clinton	Hope, Arkansas, 19 August 1946	—	Attorney general of Arkansas (1977–79) Governor of Arkansas (1979–81; 1983–92)	Little Rock, Arkansas
43	George W. Bush	New Haven, Conn. 6 July 1946	—	Governor of Texas (1994–2000)	Midland, Texas

[1]Percentage of electors actually voting.

[2]In the elections of 1789, 1792, 1796, and 1800, each elector voted for two candidates for president. The candidate receiving the highest number of votes was elected president; the next highest, vice president. Percentages in table are of total vote cast. From 1804 onward, electors were required to designate which vote was for president and which for vice president, and an electoral majority was required.

PARTY	% OF POPULAR VOTE	% OF ELECTORAL VOTE[1,2]	TERMS IN OFFICE[5]	VICE PRESIDENTS	NOTABLE EVENTS	
Democrat	46.1	62.4	4 March 1893–4 March 1897	Adlai E. Stevenson	Financial panic (1893); Sherman Silver Purchase Act repealed (1893); Utah enters Union.	24
Republican	51.0	60.6	4 March 1897–4 March 1901	Garret A. Hobart Theodore Roosevelt	Spanish–American War (1898); Puerto Rico, Guam, Philippines ceded by Spain; independent Republic of Hawaii annexed; US troops sent to China to suppress Boxer Rebellion (1900); McKinley assassinated.	25
Republican	56.4	70.6	14 Sept. 1901–4 March 1905 4 March 1905–4 March 1909	Charles W. Fairbanks	Antitrust and conservation policies emphasized; Roosevelt awarded Nobel Peace Prize (1906) for mediating settlement of Russo–Japanese War; Panama Canal construction begun (1907); Oklahoma enters Union.	26
Republican	51.6	66.5	4 March 1909–4 March 1913	James S. Sherman	Federal income tax ratified (1913); New Mexico, Arizona enter Union.	27
Democrat	41.8 49.2	81.9 52.2	4 March 1913–4 March 1917 4 March 1917–4 March 1921	Thomas R. Marshall Thomas R. Marshall	Clayton Antitrust Act (1914); US Virgin Islands purchased from Denmark (1917); US enters World War I (1917); Treaty of Versailles signed (1919) but not ratified by US; constitutional amendments enforce prohibition (1919), enfranchise women (1920).	28
Republican	60.3	76.1	4 March 1921–2 Aug. 1923	Calvin Coolidge	Teapot Dome scandal (1923–24).	29
Republican	54.1	71.9	3 Aug. 1923–4 March 1925 4 March 1925–4 March 1929	Charles G. Dawes	Kellogg–Briand Pact (1928).	30
Republican	58.2	83.6	4 March 1929–4 March 1933	Charles Curtis	Stock market crash (1929) inaugurates Great Depression.	31
Democrat	57.4 60.8 54.7 53.4	88.9 98.5 84.6 81.4	4 March 1933–20 Jan. 1937 20 Jan. 1937–20 Jan. 1941 20 Jan. 1941–20 Jan. 1945 20 Jan. 1945–12 April 1945	John N. Garner John N. Garner Henry A. Wallace Harry S Truman	New Deal social reforms; prohibition repealed (1933); US enters World War II (1941)	32
Democrat	—	—	12 April 1945–20 Jan. 1949 20 Jan. 1949–20 Jan. 1953	Alben W. Barkley	United Nations founded (1945); US nuclear bombs dropped on Japan (1945); World War II ends (1945); Philippines granted independence (1946); Marshall Plan (1945); Korean conflict begins (1950); era of McCarthyism.	33
Republican	55.1 57.4	83.2 86.1	20 Jan. 1953–20 Jan. 1957 20 Jan. 1957–20 Jan. 1961	Richard M. Nixon Richard M. Nixon	Korean conflict ended (1953); Supreme Court orders school desegregation (1954); Alaska, Hawaii enter Union.	34
Democrat	49.7	56.4	20 Jan. 1961–22 Nov. 1963	Lyndon B. Johnson	Conflicts with Cuba (1961–62); aboveground nuclear test ban treaty (1963); Kennedy assassinated.	35
Democrat	61.1	90.3	22 Nov. 1963–20 Jan. 1965 20 Jan. 1965–20 Jan. 1969	Hubert H. Humphrey	Great Society programs; Voting Rights Act (1965); escalation of US military role in Indochina; race riots, political assassinations.	36
Republican	43.4 60.7	55.9 96.7	20 Jan. 1969–20 Jan. 1973	Spiro T. Agnew Spiro T. Agnew Gerald R. Ford	First lunar landing (1969); arms limitation treaty with Soviet Union (1972); US withdraws from Viet–Nam (1973); Agnew resigns in tax scandal (1973); Nixon resigns at height of Watergate scandal (1974).	37
Republican	—	—	9 Aug. 1974–20 Jan. 1977	Nelson A. Rockefeller	First combination of unelected president and vice president; Nixon pardoned (1974).	38
Democrat	50.1	55.2	20 Jan. 1977–20 Jan. 1981	Walter F. Mondale	Carter mediates Israel-Egypt peace accord (1978); Panama Canal treaties ratified (1979); tensions with Iran (1979–81).	39
Republican	50.8 58.8	90.9 97.6	20 Jan. 1981–20 Jan. 1985 20 Jan. 1985–20 Jan. 1989	George H. W. Bush George H. W. Bush	Defense buildup; social spending cuts; rising trade and budget deficits; tensions with Nicaragua.	40
Republican	54.0	79.2	20 Jan. 1989–20 Jan. 1993	J. Danforth Quayle	Multi-national force repelled Iraqi invaders from Kuwait; savings and loan crisis; 1991 recession.	41
Democrat	43.0 49.2	69.7 70.4	20 Jan. 1993–20 Jan. 1997 20 Jan. 1997–20 Jan. 2001	Albert Gore, Jr.	Passed North American Free Trade Agreement; enacted crime bill banning assault weapons; sent troops to Haiti to restore first democratically elected Haitian president to power after military coup.	42
Republican	47.87	50.37	20 Jan. 2001–	Richard B. Cheney	Lowered taxes. Engaged in war in Afghanistan and Iraq after terrorist attacks on Washington and New York. Created the Department of Homeland Security. Substantially increased the federal deficit.	43

[3]Electoral vote tied between Jefferson and Aaron Burr; elections decided in House of Representatives.
[4]No candidate received a majority; election decided in House.
[5]In the event of a president's death or removal from office, his duties are assumed to devolve immediately upon his successor, even if he does not immediately take the oath of office.

and electricity. Outstanding botanists and naturalists were John Bartram (1699–1777); his son William Bartram (1739–1832); Louis Agassiz (b.Switzerland, 1807–73); Asa Gray (1810–88); Luther Burbank (1849–1926), developer of a vast number of new and improved varieties of fruits, vegetables, and flowers; and George Washington Carver (1864–1943), known especially for his work on industrial applications for peanuts. John James Audubon (1785–1851) won fame as an ornithologist and artist.

Distinguished physical scientists include Samuel Pierpont Langley (1834–1906), astronomer and aviation pioneer; Josiah Willard Gibbs (1839–1903), mathematical physicist, whose work laid the basis for physical chemistry; Henry Augustus Rowland (1848–1901), who did important research in magnetism and optics; and Albert Abraham Michelson (b.Germany, 1852–1931), who measured the speed of light and became the first of a long line of US Nobel Prize winners. The chemists Gilbert Newton Lewis (1875–1946) and Irving Langmuir (1881–1957) developed a theory of atomic structure.

The theory of relativity was conceived by Albert Einstein (b.Germany, 1879–1955), generally considered the greatest mind in the physical sciences since Newton. Percy Williams Bridgman (1882–1961) was the father of operationalism and studied the effect of high pressures on materials. Arthur Holly Compton (1892–1962) made discoveries in the field of X rays and cosmic rays. The physical chemist Harold Clayton Urey (1893–1981) discovered heavy hydrogen. Isidor Isaac Rabi (b.Austria, 1898–1988), nuclear physicist, did important work in magnetism, quantum mechanics, and radiation. Enrico Fermi (b.Italy, 1901–54) created the first nuclear chain reaction, in Chicago in 1942, and contributed to the development of the atomic and hydrogen bombs. Also prominent in the splitting of the atom were Leo Szilard (b.Hungary, 1898–1964), J. Robert Oppenheimer (1904–67), and Edward Teller (b.Hungary, 1908). Ernest Orlando Lawrence (1901–58) developed the cyclotron. Carl David Anderson (1905–91) discovered the positron. Mathematician Norbert Wiener (1894–1964) developed the science of cybernetics.

Outstanding figures in the biological sciences include Theobald Smith (1859–1934), who developed immunization theory and practical immunization techniques for animals; the geneticist Thomas Hunt Morgan (1866–1945), who discovered the heredity functions of chromosomes; and neurosurgeon Harvey William Cushing (1869–1939). Selman Abraham Waksman (b.Russia, 1888–1973), a microbiologist specializing in antibiotics, was codiscoverer of streptomycin. Edwin Joseph Cohn (1892–1953) is noted for his work in the protein fractionalization of blood, particularly the isolation of serum albumin. Philip Showalter Hench (1896–1965) isolated and synthesized cortisone. Wendell Meredith Stanley (1904–71) was the first to isolate and crystallize a virus. Jonas Edward Salk (1914–95) developed an effective killed-virus poliomyelitis vaccine, and Albert Bruce Sabin (1906–93) contributed oral, attenuated live-virus polio vaccines.

Adolf Meyer (b.Switzerland, 1866–1950) developed the concepts of mental hygiene and dementia praecox and the theory of psychobiology; Harry Stack Sullivan (1892–1949) created the interpersonal theory of psychiatry. Social psychologist George Herbert Mead (1863–1931) and behaviorist Burrhus Frederic Skinner (1904–90) have been influential in the 20th century.

A pioneer in psychology who was also an influential philosopher was William James (1842–1910). Other leading US philosophers are Charles Sanders Peirce (1839–1914); Josiah Royce (1855–1916); John Dewey (1859–1952), also famous for his theories of education; George Santayana (b.Spain, 1863–1952); Rudolf Carnap (b.Germany, 1891–1970); and Willard Van Orman Quine (b.1908). Educators of note include Horace Mann (1796–1859), Henry Barnard (1811–1900), and Charles William Eliot (1834–1926). Noah Webster (1758–1843) was the outstanding US lexicographer, and Melvil Dewey (1851–1931)

was a leader in the development of library science. Thorstein Bunde Veblen (1857–1929) wrote books that have strongly influenced economic and social thinking. Also important in the social sciences have been sociologists Talcott Parsons (1902–79) and William Graham Sumner (1840–1910) and anthropologist Margaret Mead (1901–78).

Social Reformers

Social reformers of note include Dorothea Lynde Dix (1802–87), who led movements for the reform of prisons and insane asylums; William Lloyd Garrison (1805–79) and Frederick Douglass (Frederick Augustus Washington Bailey, 1817–95), prominent abolitionists; Elizabeth Cady Stanton (1815–1902) and Susan Brownell Anthony (1820–1906), leaders in the women's suffrage movement; Clara Barton (1821–1912), founder of the American Red Cross; economist Henry George (1839–97), advocate of the single-tax theory; Eugene Victor Debs (1855–1926), labor leader and an outstanding organizer of the Socialist movement in the United States; Jane Addams (1860–1935), who pioneered in settlement house work; Robert Marion La Follette (1855–1925), a leader for progressive political reform in Wisconsin and in the US Senate; Margaret Higgins Sanger (1883–1966), pioneer in birth control; Norman Thomas (1884–1968), Socialist Party leader; and Martin Luther King, Jr. (1929–68), a central figure in the black civil rights movement and winner of the Nobel Peace Prize in 1964.

Religious leaders include Roger Williams (1603–83), an early advocate of religious tolerance in the United States; Jonathan Edwards (1703–58), New England preacher and theologian; Elizabeth Ann Seton (1774–1821), the first American canonized in the Roman Catholic Church; William Ellery Channing (1780–1842), a founder of American Unitarianism; Joseph Smith (1805–44), founder of the Church of Jesus Christ of Latter-day Saints (Mormon) and his chief associate, Brigham Young (1801–77); and Mary Baker Eddy (1821–1910), founder of the Christian Science Church. Paul Tillich (b.Germany, 1886–1965) and Reinhold Niebuhr (1892–1971) were outstanding Protestant theologians of international influence.

Famous US businessmen include Éleùthere Irénée du Pont de Nemours (b.France, 1771–1834), John Jacob Astor (Johann Jakob Ashdour, b.Germany, 1763–1848), Cornelius Vanderbilt (1794–1877), Andrew Carnegie (b.Scotland, 1835–1919), John Pierpont Morgan (1837–1913), John Davison Rockefeller (1839–1937), Andrew William Mellon (1855–1937), Henry Ford (1863–1947), and Thomas John Watson (1874–1956).

Literary Figures

The first US author to be widely read outside the United States was Washington Irving (1783–1859). James Fenimore Cooper (1789–1851) was the first popular US novelist. Three noted historians were William Hickling Prescott (1796–1859), John Lothrop Motley (1814–77), and Francis Parkman (1823–93). The writings of two men of Concord, Mass.—Ralph Waldo Emerson (1803–82) and Henry David Thoreau (1817–62)— influenced philosophers, political leaders, and ordinary men and women in many parts of the world. The novels and short stories of Nathaniel Hawthorne (1804–64) explore New England's Puritan heritage. Herman Melville (1819–91) wrote the powerful novel *Moby-Dick*, a symbolic work about a whale hunt that has become an American classic. Mark Twain (Samuel Langhorne Clemens, 1835–1910) is the best-known US humorist. Other leading novelists of the later 19th and early 20th centuries were William Dean Howells (1837–1920), Henry James (1843–1916), Edith Wharton (1862–1937), Stephen Crane (1871–1900), Theodore Dreiser (1871–1945), Willa Cather (1873–1947), and Sinclair Lewis (1885–1951), first US winner of the Nobel Prize for literature (1930). Later Nobel Prize–winning US novelists include Pearl Sydenstricker Buck (1892–1973), in 1938; William

Chief Justices of the United States, 1789–2003

	NAME	BORN	DIED	APPOINTED	SUPREME COURT TERM	MAJOR COURT DEVELOPMENTS
1	John Jay	New York City 12 December 1745	Bedford, N.Y., 17 May 1829	Washington	October 1789 June 1795	Organized court, established procedures.
2	John Rutledge	September 1739	Charleston, S.C., 18 July 1800	Washington		Presided for one term in 1795, but Senate refused to confirm his appointment.
3	Oliver Ellsworth	Windsor, Conn., 29 April 1745	Windsor, Conn. 26 Nov. 1807	Washington	March 1796 December 1800	
4	John Marshall	Fauquier County, Va., 24 September 1755	Philadelphia, Pa. 6 July 1835	Adams	February 1801 July 1835	Established principle of judicial review (*Marbury v. Madison*, 1803); formulated concept of implied powers (*McCulloch v. Maryland*, 1819).
5	Roger Brooke Taney	Calvert County, Md., 17 March 1777	Washington, D.C., 12 October 1864	Jackson	March 1836 October 1864	Held that slaves could not become citizens, ruled Missouri Compromise illegal (*Dred Scott v. Sanford*, 1857).
6	Salmon Portland Chase	Cornish, N.H., 13 January 1808	New York, N.Y. 7 May 1873	Lincoln	December 1864 May 1873	Ruled military trials of civilians illegal (*Ex parte Milligan*, 1866); Chase presided at A. Johnson's impeachment trial.
7	Morrison Remick Waite	Old Lynne, Conn., 29 November 1816	Washington, D.C., 23 March 1888	Grant	March 1874 March 1888	Held that businesses affecting the "public interest" are subject to state regulation (*Munn v. Illinois*, 1877).
8	Melville Weston Fuller	Augusta, Me., 11 February 1833	Sorvento, Me., 4 July 1910	Cleveland	October 1888 July 1910	Issued first opinions on cases under the Sherman Antitrust Act. (*US v. E.C. Knight Co.*, 1895; *Northern Securities Co. v. US*, 1904); held the income tax unconstitutional (*Pollock v. Farmers' Loan*, 1895).
9	Edward Douglass White	Lafourche Parish, La., 3 November 1845	Washington, D.C., 19 May 1921	Taft	December 1910 May 1921	Further qualified the Sherman Antitrust Act (*Standard Oil Co. v. US*, 1911) by applying the "rule of reason."
10	William Howard Taft	Cincinnati, Ohio 15 September 1857	Washington, D.C., 8 March 1930	Harding	July 1921 February 1930	Held against congressional use of taxes for social reform (*Bailey v. Drexel Furniture*, 1922).
11	Charles Evans Hughes	Glens Falls, N.Y., 11 April 1862	Osterville, Mass., 27 August 1948	Hoover	February 1930 June 1941	Upheld constitutionality of National Labor Relations Act, Social Security Act, invalidated National Industrial Recovery Act (*Schechter v. US*, 1935); F. Roosevelt's attempt to pack Court opposed.
12	Harlan Fiske Stone	Chesterfield, N.H., 11 October 1872	Washington, D.C., 22 April 1946	F Roosevelt	July 1941 April 1946	Upheld Court's power to invalidate state laws (*Southern Pacific Co. v. Arizona*, 1945).
13	Frederick Moore Vinson	Louisa, Ky., 22 January 1890	Washington, D.C., 8 September 1953	Truman	June 1946 September 1953	Overturned federal seizure of steel mills (*Youngstown Sheet and Tube Co. v. Sawyer*, 1952), Vinson dissenting.
14	Earl Warren	Los Angeles, Calif., 19 March 1891	Washington, D.C., 9 July 1974	Eisenhower	October 1953 June 1969	Mandated public school desegregation (*Brown v. Topeka, Kans., Board of Education*, 1954) and reapportionment of state legislatures (*Baker v. Carr*, 1962); upheld rights of suspects in police custody (*Miranda v. Arizona*, 1966).
15	Warren Earl Burger	St. Paul, Minn., 17 September 1907	Washington, D.C., 25 June 1995	Nixon	June 1969 August 1986	Legalized abortion (*Roe v. Wade*, 1973); rejected claim of executive privilege in a criminal case (*US v. Nixon*, 1974); first female justice (1981).
16	William Hubbs Rehnquist	Shorewood Village, Wis., 1 October 1924		Nixon	September 1986	Applied constitutional prohibition against taking of property without compensation to invalidate government regulation of property. (*Nollan v. California Coastal Commission*, 1987). Strengthened states' rights although invalidated Florida election procedures (*Bush v. Gore*, 2000) on equal protection grounds. Limited enforcement of school desegregation. Narrowed the scope of affirmative action.

Faulkner (1897–1962), in 1949; Ernest Hemingway (1899–1961), in 1954; John Steinbeck (1902–68), in 1962; Saul Bellow (b.Canada, 1915), in 1976; and Isaac Bashevis Singer (b.Poland, 1904–91), in 1978. Among other noteworthy writers are James Thurber (1894–1961), Francis Scott Key Fitzgerald (1896–1940), Thomas Wolfe (1900–1938), Richard Wright (1908–60), Eudora Welty (1909–2001), John Cheever (1912–82), Norman Mailer (b.1923), James Baldwin (1924–87), John Updike (b.1932), and Philip Roth (b.1933).

Noted US poets include Henry Wadsworth Longfellow (1807–82), Edgar Allan Poe (1809–49), Walt Whitman (1819–92), Emily Dickinson (1830–86), Edwin Arlington Robinson (1869–1935), Robert Frost (1874–1963), Wallace Stevens (1879–1955), William Carlos Williams (1883–1963), Marianne Moore (1887–1972), Edward Estlin Cummings (1894–1962), Hart Crane (1899–1932), and Langston Hughes (1902–67). Ezra Pound (1885–1972) and Nobel laureate Thomas Stearns Eliot (1888–1965) lived and worked abroad for most of their careers. Wystan Hugh Auden (b.England, 1907–73), who became an American citizen in 1946, published poetry and criticism. Elizabeth Bishop (1911–79), Robert Lowell (1917–77), Allen Ginsberg (1926–97), and Sylvia Plath (1932–63) are among the best-known poets since World War II. Robert Penn Warren (1905–89) won the Pulitzer Prize for both fiction and poetry and became the first US poet laureate. Carl Sandburg (1878–1967) was a noted poet, historian, novelist, and folklorist. The foremost US dramatists are Eugene (Gladstone) O'Neill (1888–1953), who won the Nobel Prize for literature in 1936; Tennessee Williams (Thomas Lanier Williams, 1911–83); Arthur Miller (b.1915); and Edward Albee (b.1928). Neil Simon (b.1927) is among the nation's most popular playwrights and screenwriters.

Artists

Two renowned painters of the early period were John Singleton Copley (1738–1815) and Gilbert Stuart (1755–1828). Outstanding 19th-century painters were James Abbott McNeill Whistler (1834–1903), Winslow Homer (1836–1910), Thomas Eakins (1844–1916), Mary Cassatt (1845–1926), Albert Pinkham Ryder (1847–1917), John Singer Sargent (b.Italy, 1856–1925), and Frederic Remington (1861–1909). More recently, Edward Hopper (1882–1967), Georgia O'Keeffe (1887–1986), Thomas Hart Benton (1889–1975), Charles Burchfield (1893–1967), Norman Rockwell (1894–1978), Ben Shahn (1898–1969), Mark Rothko (b.Russia, 1903–70), Jackson Pollock (1912–56), Andrew Wyeth (b.1917), Robert Rauschenberg (b.1925), and Jasper Johns (b.1930) have achieved international recognition.

Sculptors of note include Augustus Saint-Gaudens (1848–1907), Gaston Lachaise (1882–1935), Jo Davidson (1883–1952), Daniel Chester French (1850–1931), Alexander Calder (1898–1976), Louise Nevelson (b.Russia, 1899–1988), and Isamu Noguchi (1904–88). Henry Hobson Richardson (1838–86), Louis Henry Sullivan (1856–1924), Frank Lloyd Wright (1869–1959), Louis I. Kahn (b.Estonia, 1901–74), and Eero Saarinen (1910–61) were outstanding architects. Contemporary architects of note include Richard Buckminster Fuller (1895–1983), Edward Durrell Stone (1902–78), Philip Cortelyou Johnson (b.1906), and Ieoh Ming Pei (b.China, 1917). The United States has produced many fine photographers, notably Mathew B. Brady (1823?–96), Alfred Stieglitz (1864–1946), Edward Steichen (1879–1973), Edward Weston (1886–1958), Ansel Adams (1902–84), and Margaret Bourke-White (1904–71).

Entertainment Figures

Outstanding figures in the motion picture industry are D. W. (David Lewelyn Wark) Griffith (1875–1948), Sir Charles Spencer "Charlie" Chaplin (b.England, 1889–1978), Walter Elias "Walt" Disney (1906–66), and George Orson Welles (1915–85). John Ford (1895–1973), Howard Winchester Hawks (1896–1977),

Frank Capra (b.Italy, 1897–1991), Sir Alfred Hitchcock (b.England, 1899–1980), and John Huston (1906–87) were influential motion picture directors; Mel Brooks (Kaminsky, b.1926), George Lucas (b.1944), and Steven Spielberg (b.1947) have achieved remarkable popular success. Woody Allen (Allen Konigsberg, b.1935) has written, directed, and starred in comedies on stage and screen. World-famous American actors and actresses include the Barrymores, Ethel (1879–1959) and her brothers Lionel (1878–1954) and John (1882–1942); Humphrey Bogart (1899–1957); James Cagney (1899–1986); Spencer Tracy (1900–1967); Helen Hayes Brown (1900–93); Clark Gable (1901–60); Joan Crawford (Lucille Fay LeSueur, 1904–77); Cary Grant (Alexander Archibald Leach, b.England, 1904–86); Greta Garbo (Greta Louisa Gustafsson, b.Sweden, 1905–90); Henry Fonda (1905–82) and his daughter, Jane (b.1937); John Wayne (Marion Michael Morrison, 1907–79); Bette (Ruth Elizabeth) Davis (1908–89); Katharine Hepburn (1909–2003); Judy Garland (Frances Gumm, 1922–69); Marlon Brando (b.1924); Marilyn Monroe (Norma Jean Mortenson, 1926–62); and Dustin Hoffman (b.1937). Among other great entertainers are W. C. Fields (William Claude Dukenfield, 1880–1946), Al Jolson (Asa Yoelson, b.Russia, 1886–1950), Jack Benny (Benjamin Kubelsky, 1894–1974), Fred Astaire (Fred Austerlitz, 1899–1987), Bob (Leslie Townes) Hope (b.England, 1903–2003), Bing (Harry Lillis) Crosby (1904–78), Frank (Francis Albert) Sinatra (1915–98), Elvis Aaron Presley (1935–77), and Barbra (Barbara Joan) Streisand (b.1942). The first great US "showman" was Phineas Taylor Barnum (1810–91).

Composers and Musicians

The foremost composers are Edward MacDowell (1861–1908), Charles Ives (1874–1954), Ernest Bloch (b.Switzerland, 1880–1959), Virgil Thomson (1896–89), Roger Sessions (1896–1985), Roy Harris (1898–1979), Aaron Copland (1900–90), Elliott Carter (b.1908), Samuel Barber (1910–81), John Cage (1912–92), and Leonard Bernstein (1918–90). George Rochberg (b.1918), George Crumb (b.1929), Steve Reich (b.1936), and Philip Glass (b.1937) have won more recent followings. The songs of Stephen Collins Foster (1826–64) have achieved folk-song status. Leading composers of popular music are John Philip Sousa (1854–1932), George Michael Cohan (1878–1942), Jerome Kern (1885–1945), Irving Berlin (Israel Baline, b.Russia, 1888–1989), Cole Porter (1893–1964), George Gershwin (1898–1937), Richard Rodgers (1902–79), Woody Guthrie (1912–67), Stephen Joshua Sondheim (b.1930), Paul Simon (b.1941), and Bob Dylan (Robert Zimmerman, b.1941). Preeminent in the blues traditions are Leadbelly (Huddie Ledbetter, 1888–1949), Bessie Smith (1898?–1937), and Muddy Waters (McKinley Morganfield, 1915–83). Leading jazz figures include the composers Scott Joplin (1868–1917), James Hubert "Eubie" Blake (1883–1983), Edward Kennedy "Duke" Ellington (1899–1974), and William "Count" Basie (1904–84), and performers Louis Armstrong (1900–1971), Billie Holiday (Eleanora Fagan, 1915–59), John Birks "Dizzy" Gillespie (1917–93), Charlie "Bird" Parker (1920–55), John Coltrane (1926–67), and Miles Davis (1926–91).

Many foreign-born musicians have enjoyed personal and professional freedom in the United States; principal among them were pianists Artur Schnabel (b.Austria, 1882–1951), Arthur Rubinstein (b.Poland, 1887–1982), Rudolf Serkin (b.Bohemia, 1903–91), Vladimir Horowitz (b.Russia, 1904–89), and violinists Jascha Heifetz (b.Russia, 1901–87) and Isaac Stern (b.USSR, 1920). Among distinguished instrumentalists born in the United States are Benny Goodman (1909–86), a classical as well as jazz clarinetist, and concert pianist Van Cliburn (Harvey Lavan, Jr., b.1934). Singers Paul Robeson (1898–1976), Marian Anderson (1897–1993), Maria Callas (Maria Kalogeropoulos, 1923–77), Leontyne Price (b.1927), and Beverly Sills (Belle Silverman, b.1929) have achieved international acclaim. Isadora Duncan (1878–1927) was one of the first US dancers to win fame abroad. Martha Graham (1893–91) pioneered in modern dance. George Balanchine (b.Russia, 1904–83), Agnes De Mille (1905–93), Jerome Robbins (1918–98), Paul Taylor (b.1930), and Twyla Tharp (b.1941) are leading choreographers; Martha Graham (1893–1991) pioneered in modern dance.

Sports Figures

Among the many noteworthy sports stars are baseball's Tyrus Raymond "Ty" Cobb (1886–1961) and George Herman "Babe" Ruth (1895–1948); football's Samuel Adrian "Sammy" Baugh (b.1914), Jim Brown (b.1936), Francis A. "Fran" Tarkenton (b.1940), and Orenthal James Simpson (b.1947); and golf's Robert Tyre "Bobby" Jones (1902–71) and Mildred "Babe" Didrikson Zaharias (1914–56). William Tatum "Bill" Tilden (1893–1953) and Billie Jean (Moffitt) King (b.1943) have starred in tennis; Joe Louis (Joseph Louis Barrow, 1914–81) and Muhammad Ali (Cassius Marcellus Clay, b.1942) in boxing; William Felton "Bill" Russell (b.1934) and Wilton Norman "Wilt" Chamberlain (1936–99) in basketball; Mark Spitz (b.1950) in swimming; Eric Heiden (b.1958) in speed skating; and Jesse Owens (1913–80) in track and field.

⁵⁰BIBLIOGRAPHY

Ambrose, Stephen E. *To America: Personal Reflections of an Historian.* New York: Simon & Schuster, 2002.

America's Century: Year by Year from 1900–2000. London: Dorling Kindersley, 2000.

Ayres, Stephen M. *Health Care in the Unites States: The Facts and the Choices.* Chicago: American Library Association, 1996.

Bacchi, Carol Lee. *The Politics of Affirmative Action: 'Women', Equality, and Category Politics.* London: Sage, 1996.

Bailey, Richard. *Nineteenth Century English.* Ann Arbor, Mich.: University of Michigan Press, 1996.

Barone, Michael. *The Almanac of American Politics.* Washington, D.C.: National Journal, 1992.

Becker, Carl Lotus. *The Declaration of Independence: A Study in the History of Political Ideas.* New York: Knopf, 1960.

Bennett, Lerone. *Before the Mayflower: A History of Black America.* 6th ed. New York: Penguin, 1993.

Brown, Richard Maxwell. *No Duty to Retreat: Violence and Values in American History and Society.* New York: Oxford University Press, 1991.

Buckley, Susan. *Journeys in Time: A New Atlas of American History.* Boston: Houghton Mifflin, 2001.

Carnes, Mark C. *The American Nation: A History of the United States.* New York: Longman, 2003.

Chambers, S. Allen. *National Landmarks, America's Treasures: the National Park Foundation's Complete Guide to National Historic Landmarks.* New York: J. Wiley and Sons, 2000.

Commager, Henry Steele (ed.). *Documents of American History.* Englewood Cliffs, N.J.: Prentice-Hall, 1988.

Davies, Philip John. (ed.) *An American Quarter Century: US Politics from Vietnam to Clinton.* New York: Manchester University Press, 1995.

Donaldson, Gary. *America at War since 1945: Politics and Diplomacy in Korea, Vietnam, and the Gulf War.* Westport, Conn.: Praeger, 1996.

Earle, Carville. *The American Way: A Geographical History of Crisis and Recovery.* Lanham, Md.: Rowman & Littlefield, 2003.

Hart, James David (ed.). *Oxford Companion to American Literature.* 6th ed. New York: Oxford University Press, 1995.

Harvard Encyclopedia of American Ethnic Groups. Cambridge: Harvard University Press, 1980.

Health in the Americas, 2002 edition. Washington, D.C.: Pan American Health Organization, Pan American Sanitary Bureau, Regional Office of the World Health Organization, 2002.

Heidler, David Stephen. *Manifest Destiny.* Westport, Conn.: Greenwood, 2003.

Hummel, Jeffrey Rogers. *Emancipating Slaves, Enslaving Free Men: A History of the Civil War.* Chicago: Open Court, 1996.

Kammen, Michale (ed.). *The Origins of the American Constitution: A Documentary History.* New York: Penguin, 1986.

Kaplan, Edward S. *American Trade Policy, 1923–1995.* Westport, Conn.: Praeger, 1996.

Kennedy, David M. *Freedom from Fear: The American People in Depression and War.* New York: Oxford University Press, 2001.

Kennedy, Roger G. *Mr. Jefferson's Lost Cause: Land, Farmers, Slavery, and the Louisiana Purchase.* New York: Oxford University Press, 2003.

Martis, Kenneth C. *The Historical Atlas of Political Parties in the United States Congress 1789–1989.* New York: Macmillan, 1989.

McElrath, Karen (ed.). *HIV and AIDS: A Global View.* Westport, Conn.: Greenwood Press, 2002.

McNickle, D'Arcy. *Native American Tribalism: Indian Survivals and Renewals.* New York: Oxford University Press, 1993.

Morison, Samuel Eliot. *The Oxford History of the American People.* New York: New American Library, 1972.

Nevins, Allan. *Ordeal of the Union.* New York: Collier Books, 1992.

Newell, Clayton R. *United States Army, a Historical Dictionary.* Lanham, Md.: Scarecrow Press, 2002.

Reed, Carroll E. *Dialects of American English.* Amherst: University of Massachusetts Press, 1977.

Rein, Meiling, Nancy R. Jacobs, Maek S. Siegel (eds.). *Immigration and Illegal Aliens: Burden or Blessing?* Wylie, Tex.: Information Plus, 1999.

Robinson, Cedric J. *Black Movements in America.* New York: Routledge, 1997.

Sinclair, Andrew. *A Concise History of the United States.* Rev. ed. Stroud: Sutton, 1999.

Summers, Randal W., and Allan M. Hoffman (ed.). *Domestic Violence: A Global View.* Westport, Conn.: Greenwood Press, 2002.

Tocqueville, Alexis de. *Democracy in America.* New York: Knopf, 1994.

US Bureau of the Census. *Historical Statistics of the United States, Colonial Times to 1970.* Washington, D.C.: US Government Printing Office, 1879–date.

Who's Who in America: A Biographical Dictionary of Notable Living Men and Women. Chicago: Marquis, 1899—.

GLOSSARY

ANTEBELLUM: before the US Civil War.

BLUE LAWS: laws forbidding certain practices (e.g., conducting business, gaming, drinking liquor), especially on Sundays.

CAPITAL BUDGET: a financial plan for acquiring and improving buildings or land, paid for by the sale of bonds.

CAPITAL PUNISHMENT: punishment by death.

CIVILIAN LABOR FORCE: all persons 16 years of age or older who are not in the armed forces and who are now holding a job, have been temporarily laid off, are waiting to be reassigned to a new position, or are unemployed but actively looking for work.

CLASS I RAILROAD: a railroad having gross annual revenues of $83.5 million or more in 1983.

COMMERCIAL BANK: a bank that offers businesses and individuals a variety of banking services, including the right of withdrawal by check.

COMPACT: a formal agreement, covenant, or understanding between two or more parties.

CONSOLIDATED BUDGET: a financial plan that includes the general budget, federal funds, and all special funds.

CONSTANT DOLLARS: money values calculated so as to eliminate the effect of inflation on prices and income.

CONTINENTAL CLIMATE: the climate typical of the US interior, having distinct seasons, a wide range of daily and annual temperatures, and dry, sunny summers.

COUNCIL-MANAGER SYSTEM: a system of local government under which a professional administrator is hired by an elected council to carry out its laws and policies.

CREDIT UNION: a cooperative body that raises funds from its members by the sale of shares and makes loans to its members at relatively low interest rates.

CURRENT DOLLARS: money values that reflect prevailing prices, without excluding the effects of inflation.

DEMAND DEPOSIT: a bank deposit that can be withdrawn by the depositor with no advance notice to the bank.

ELECTORAL VOTES: the votes that a state may cast for president, equal to the combined total of its US senators and representatives and nearly always cast entirely on behalf of the candidate who won the most votes in that state on Election Day.

ENDANGERED SPECIES: a type of plant or animal threatened with extinction in all or part of its natural range.

FEDERAL POVERTY LEVEL: a level of money income below which a person or family qualifies for US government aid.

FISCAL YEAR: a 12-month period for accounting purposes.

FOOD STAMPS: coupons issued by the government to low-income persons for food purchases at local stores.

GENERAL BUDGET: a financial plan based on a government's normal revenues and operating expenses, excluding special funds.

GENERAL COASTLINE: a measurement of the general outline of the US seacoast. *See also* TIDAL SHORELINE.

GREAT AWAKENING: during the mid–18th century, a Protestant religious revival in North America, especially New England.

GROSS STATE PRODUCT: the total value of goods and services produced in the state.

GROWING SEASON: the period between the last 32°F (0°C) temperature in spring and the first 32°F (0°C) temperature in autumn.

HOME-RULE CHARTER: a document stating how and in what respects a city, town, or county may govern itself.

INSTALLED CAPACITY: the maximum possible output of electric power at any given time.

MAYOR-COUNCIL SYSTEM: a system of local government under which an elected council serves as a legislature and an elected mayor is the chief administrator.

MEDICAID: a federal-state program that helps defray the hospital and medical costs of needy persons.

MEDICARE: a program of hospital and medical insurance for the elderly, administered by the federal government.

METROPOLITAN AREA: in most cases, a city and its surrounding suburbs.

NO-FAULT INSURANCE: an automobile insurance plan that allows an accident victim to receive payment from an insurance company without having to prove who was responsible for the accident.

NORTHERN, NORTH MIDLAND: major US dialect regions.

OMBUDSMAN: a public official empowered to hear and investigate complaints by private citizens about government agencies.

PER CAPITA: per person.

POCKET VETO: a method by which a state governor (or the US president) may kill a bill by taking no action on it before the legislature adjourns.

PROVED RESERVES: the quantity of a recoverable mineral resource (such as oil or natural gas) that is still in the ground.

PUBLIC DEBT: the amount owed by a government.

RELIGIOUS ADHERENTS: the followers of a religious group, including (but not confined to) the full, confirmed, or communicant members of that group.

RETAIL TRADE: the sale of goods directly to the consumer.

REVENUE SHARING: the distribution of federal tax receipts to state and local governments.

RIGHT-TO-WORK LAW: a measure outlawing any attempt to require union membership as a condition of employment.

SAVINGS AND LOAN ASSOCIATION: a bank that invests the savings of depositors primarily in home mortgage loans.

SERVICE INDUSTRIES: industries that provide services (e.g., health, legal, automotive repair) for individuals, businesses, and others.

SOCIAL SECURITY: as commonly understood, the federal system of old age, survivors, and disability insurance.

SOUTHERN, SOUTH MIDLAND: major US dialect regions.

STOLPORT: an airfield for short-takeoff-and-landing (STOL) aircraft, which require runways shorter than those used by conventional aircraft.

SUNBELT: the southernmost states of the United States, extending from Florida to California.

SUPPLEMENTAL SECURITY INCOME: a federally administered program of aid to the aged, blind, and disabled.

TIDAL SHORELINE: a detailed measurement of the US seacoast that includes sounds, bays, other outlets, and offshore islands.

TIME DEPOSIT: a bank deposit that may be withdrawn only at the end of a specified time period or upon advance notice to the bank.

VALUE ADDED BY MANUFACTURE: the difference, measured in dollars, between the value of finished goods and the cost of the materials needed to produce them.

WHOLESALE TRADE: the sale of goods, usually in large quantities, for ultimate resale to consumers.

ABBREVIATIONS AND ACRONYMS

AD—Anno Domini
AFDC—Aid to Families with Dependent
  Children
AFL–CIO—American Federation of
  Labor–Congress of Industrial
  Organizations
AM—before noon
AM—amplitude modulation
American Ind.—American Independent
  Party
Amtrak—National Railroad Passenger
  Corp.
b.—born
BC—Before Christ
Btu—British thermal unit(s)
bu—bushel(s)
c.—circa (about)
C—Celsius (Centigrade)
CIA—Central Intelligence Agency
cm—centimeter(s)
Co.—company
comp.—compiler
Conrail—Consolidated Rail Corp.
Corp.—corporation
Cr.—creek
CST—Central Standard Time
cu—cubic
cwt—hundredweight(s)
d.—died
D—Democrat
e—evening
E—east
ed.—edition, editor
e.g.—exempli gratia (for example)
EPA—Environmental Protection Agency
est.—estimated
EST—Eastern Standard Time

et al.—et alii (and others)
etc.—et cetera (and so on)
F—Fahrenheit
FBI—Federal Bureau of Investigation
FCC—Federal Communications
  Commission
FM—frequency modulation
For.—forest
Ft.—fort
ft—foot, feet
GDP—gross domestic product
gm—gram
GMT—Greenwich Mean Time
GNP—gross national product
GRT—gross registered tons
Hist.—historic
I—interstate (highway)
i.e.—id est (that is)
in—inch(es)
Inc.—incorporated
Ind. Res.—Indian Reservation
Is.—isle, island
Jct.—junction
K—kindergarten
kg—kilogram(s)
km—kilometer(s)
km/hr—kilometers per hour
kw—kilowatt(s)
kwh—kilowatt-hour(s)
lb—pound(s)
m—meter(s); morning
m^3—cubic meter(s)
Mem.—memorial
mi—mile(s)
Mil. Res.—military reservation
Mon.—monument
mph—miles per hour

MST—Mountain Standard Time
Mt.—mount
Mtn.—mountain
mw—megawatt(s)
N—north
NA—not available
Natl.—National
Natl. Mon.—national monument
NATO—North Atlantic Treaty
  Organization
NCAA—National Collegiate Athletic
  Association
n.d.—no date
N.F.—national forest
N.P.—national park
N.W.R.—national wildlife refuge
oz—ounce(s)
PM—after noon
PST—Pacific Standard Time
r.—reigned
R—Republican
Ra.—range
Res.—reservoir, reservation
rev. ed.—revised edition
s—south
S—Sunday
Soc.—Socialist
S.P.—senic point
sq—square
St.—saint, state
UN—United Nations
US—United States
USIA—United States Information Agency
w—west
W.M.A.—wildlife management area

NAMES OF STATES AND OTHER SELECTED AREAS

	STANDARD ABBREVIATION(S)	POSTAL ABBREVIATION		STANDARD ABBREVIATION(S)	POSTAL ABBREVIATION
Alabama	Ala.	AL	Nebraska	Nebr. (Neb.)	NE
Alaska	*	AK	Nevada	Nev.	NV
Arizona	Ariz.	AZ	New Hampshire	N.H.	NH
Arkansas	Ark.	AR	New Jersey	N.J.	NJ
California	Calif.	CA	New Mexico	N.Mex. (N.M.)	NM
Colorado	Colo.	CO	New York	N.Y.	NY
Connecticut	Conn.	CN	North Carolina	N.C.	NC
Delaware	Del.	DE	North Dakota	N.Dak. (N.D.)	ND
District of Columbia	D.C.	DC	Ohio	*	OH
Florida	Fla.	FL	Oklahoma	Okla.	OK
Georgia	Ga.	GA	Oregon	Oreg. (Ore.)	OR
Hawaii	*	HI	Pennsylvania	Pa.	PA
Idaho	*	ID	Puerto Rico	P.R.	PR
Illinois	Ill.	IL	Rhode Island	R.I.	RI
Indiana	Ind.	IN	South Carolina	S.C.	SC
Iowa	*	IA	South Dakota	S.Dak. (S.D.)	SD
Kansas	Kans. (Kan.)	KS	Tennessee	Tenn.	TN
Kentucky	Ky.	KY	Texas	Tex.	TX
Louisiana	La.	LA	Utah	*	UT
Maine	Me.	ME	Vermont	Vt.	VT
Maryland	Md.	MD	Virginia	Va.	VA
Massachusetts	Mass.	MA	Virgin Islands	V.I.	VI
Michigan	Mich.	MI	Washington	Wash.	WA
Minnesota	Minn.	MN	West Virginia	W.Va.	WV
Mississippi	Miss.	MS	Wisconsin	Wis.	WI
Missouri	Mo.	MO	Wyoming	Wyo.	WI
Montana	Mont.	MT			

*No standard abbreviation

DATE DUE

GAYLORD			PRINTED IN U.S.A.

ISBN 0-7876-7338-2

90000

9 780787 673383

Alabama	Alaska	Arizona	Arkansas	California
Hawaii	Idaho	Illinois	Indiana	Iowa
Massachusetts	Michigan	Minnesota	Mississippi	Missouri
New Mexico	New York	North Carolina	North Dakota	Ohio
South Dakota	Tennessee	Texas	Utah	Vermont